THE OPERA LIBRETTO LIBRARY

THE OPERA LIBRETTO LIBRARY

**The Authentic Texts of
the German, French, and Italian Operas
with Music of the Principal Airs**

*With
the Complete English and German, French, or Italian
Parallel Texts*

AVENEL BOOKS
NEW YORK

This edition is published by Avenel Books, distributed by
Crown Publishers, Inc.
l k j
1980 EDITION

Manufactured in the United States of America

Library of Congress Cataloging in Publication Data

Main entry under title:

The Opera libretto library.

    Reprint of 3 publications, all published in 1939 by
Crown Publishers, New York: The Authentic librettos of
the Wagner operas; The Authentic librettos of the
French and German operas; and The Authentic librettos
of the Italian operas.
    Musical excerpts in piano-vocal score.
    1. Operas—Librettos. 2. Operas—Excerpts—Vocal
with piano.
ML48.06 1980   [M1507]   782.1'2   80-16568
ISBN 0-517-318830

CONTENTS

Volume One: The Wagner Operas

Foreword iv

Flying Dutchman 1

Tannhäuser 33

Lohengrin 61

The Rhinegold 89

Die Walküre 143

Siegfried 189

Götterdämmerung 247

Tristan and Isolde 309

Die Meistersinger 349

Parsifal 429

Volume Two: French and German Operas

Foreword 2

Carmen 3

Faust.. 53

Romeo and Juliet 99

Manon 147

Tales of Hoffmann 195

Samson and Delilah 253

Lakmé... 279

Mignon.. 319

Fidelio.. 353

The Magic Flute 377

The Bartered Bride 431

Hansel and Gretel.. 477

Volume Three: Italian Operas

Foreword v

Rigoletto... 1

Il Trovatore 49

La Traviata.. 99

La Forza Del Destino... 151

Aïda 213

Lucia Di Lammermoor 253

La Gioconda... 295

Cavalleria Rusticana 337

I Pagliacci 363

Don Giovanni... 389

Barber of Seville 429

VOLUME ONE

THE LIBRETTOS
OF THE
WAGNER OPERAS

CONTENTS

Foreword... iv

Flying Dutchman 1

Tannhäuser... 33

Lohengrin.. 61

The Rhinegold 89

Die Walküre 143

Siegfried 189

Götterdämmerung... 247

Tristan and Isolde 309

Die Meistersinger... 349

Parsifal 429

FOREWORD

Richard Wagner composed his operas not only of music but also of poetry. To him, music was, literally, the combination of the Muses' Arts.

He added a new dimension to Music, making "opera" no longer a synthetic art form of drama with a musical accompaniment, but rather a harmony of ideas and emotion.

So it is necessary to know the poetry to appreciate the music, for the poetry translates the music. Of course all operas are better enjoyed with a knowledge of the story. But Wagner's dramas are much more than mere stories. They are great epics informed with all the hope and the hopelessness, the victories and defeats, the pity and the courage of the eternal battle of Man against Fate.

For Wagner was the Composer of the People. He was moved by a great understanding of their struggle and his mind was occupied by that enormous drama. Its currents whirled in his brain and he had to tell of it. Words were too poor a language and music alone perhaps too grand.

Wagner tried to, and did, make his music more explicit by the splendid device of the leitmotive, a musical phrase that is associated with a character or a quality or an idea. When a mood or influence recurs in the drama, the leitmotive recurs. As the character changes, the leitmotives change in rhythm or mode and an entire pattern is woven of them. Brünnhilde's Farewell, Siegfried's Death March are examples of the ingenious blending of these motives and thus the music is considerably clarified.

But it is not enough. Wagner himself said that he "found it necessary to indicate a vast number of antecedent facts so as to put the main incidents in the proper light." That is why the conception of Götterdämmerung, the saga of Siegfried's Death, led to the composition of "Siegfried" and that in turn to "Die Walküre" and "Das Rheingold." His conception was so large, his thought and feeling so deep and manifold that it is essential to know what was in his mind to get the full value and quality of his expression.

The libretto, then, is the thing. For these operas are really great poetry in words and music. The words must be read and known, they constitute the form, the structure. The music is the color whose magnificence is not fully realized until it is made glorious and brilliant in the light of the underlying poetry.

THE
FLYING DUTCHMAN
(Der Fliegende Holländer)

THE STORY OF THE OPERA.

In the legend of the Flying Dutchman we are told that a Dutch captain once tried to double the Cape of Good Hope in the teeth of a furious gale, and swore he would accomplish his purpose, even if he kept sailing on forever. The Devil heard the oath, and condemned the unhappy captain to sail the sea until the Day of Judgment, without aim, and without hope of release, unless he could find a woman to love him faithfully until death. The Devil allowed him to go ashore once in seven years to find such a woman; and this Opera opens with the appearance of the Flying Dutchman's ship, with her blood-red sails and black masts, on the coast of Norway, in a bay into which the ship of Daland, a Norwegian captain, had just before been driven by stress of weather. A seven years' term having then expired, the Dutchman goes on shore, and meets with Daland, from whom he asks for hospitality, offering him in return all his treasures. In conversation he finds out that Daland has a daughter, and he further asks for permission to woo her. Daland, anxious to secure a son-in-law so wealthy, agrees to both requests, and the two set sail for Daland's home, which is not far distant, with a moderate and favorable wind.

ACT II opens with a Spinning Chorus: Senta, Daland's daughter, Mary, her former nurse, and some Norwegian maidens, being discovered at work. On the wall of the room hangs the portrait of the Flying Dutchman, whose face has a fascination for Senta, and rouses in her a romantic attachment. In a ballad she relates his story to Mary and the maidens as they spin, and winds herself up to the highest pitch of excitement in relating it. Meanwhile, Erik, the huntsman, her lover, has come in to tell that he has seen her father's ship entering the port. The maidens wish to rush off at once to welcome the crew and hear their news, but they are kept by Mary to finish their household work, and prepare food for the hungry sailors. Senta also is eager to meet her father, but she is restrained by Erik, who, expecting that Daland will now fulfil his intention of finding a husband for Senta, earnestly pleads his suit with her once again. Senta listens as if in a trance, and Erik goes on to tell her a dream he has had, in which he saw her meeting her father and the sailor whose portrait hangs in the room, and promising to be the wife of the latter. Senta is greatly excited by the recital, and cries out that he in whose face and story she takes such an interest, is seeking for her, and that she will be his. Erik rushes away in horror and despair, and Senta, after her outbreak, remains in the room in deep thought, with her eyes fixed on the picture. Meanwhile, Daland and his guest have reached the house, and Senta starts from her reverie at the sight of the stranger, recognizing his likeness to the portrait. Daland asks Senta to receive him as a guest and a husband. A long scene between Senta and the Dutchman follows, in which Senta heroically vows to share his lot, and be faithful to him until death, he receiving her promise with transport. Daland, who had left them, returns, wishing to announce their betrothal to his crew, who are about to have their accustomed feast upon the successful completion of a voyage.

ACT III opens with a chorus by the Norwegian sailors, who are dancing and making merry on the deck of their vessel. They cease on seeing the maidens coming with food and drink for the crews of both ships. The maidens try in vain to attract the attention of the crew of the Flying Dutchman's ship, which shows no sign of life on board, and at length desist in surprise and alarm, leaving for the Norwegian sailors all that they have brought. While the Norwegian sailors are feasting, the crew of the Dutch ship rouse up, and sing in chorus the story of their captain. A dark bluish flame is seen, and the sound of a storm is heard. The Norwegian sailors look on and listen with wonder, and afterwards with affright, trying in vain to drown the noise with their own singing. At length they are silenced, and in horror quit the deck and go down to the cabin, signing the cross. The crew of the Flying Dutchman's ship, seeing this, burst into shrill laughter. Their song ceases, the storm subsides, the flame goes out, and all is dark and silent as before.

Erik next appears, once more to try his fate with Senta. While he is making his final appeal, the Dutchman comes in, and immediately rushes off to his ship, as if again betrayed and forsaken, while Senta pleads her truth, and Erik implores her not to rush upon destruction. Erik cries out for help when he sees Senta follow the Dutchman, determined to link her fate with his; and, at the cry, Daland, Mary, and the maidens hurry to the spot from the house, and the Norwegian sailors from the ship. The Flying Dutchman, after declaring who he is, goes hastily on board his ship, which at once puts to sea. Senta wishes to follow, but is held back by the others. She shakes herself free, and ascends a cliff overhanging the sea, whence she casts herself, calling to the Flying Dutchman and protesting her faithfulness until death. The Dutchman's ship, with all her crew, sinks immediately. The sea rises high, and sinks back in a whirlpool. In the glow of the sunset are seen, over the wreck of the ship, the forms of Senta and the Dutchman, embracing each other rising from the sea and floating upwards.

PERSONS REPRESENTED.

SENTA. DUTCHMAN. ERIK. DALAND. STEERSMAN. MARY.
Crew of the Norwegian Vessel. *Crew of the Flying Dutchman's Vessel.*
Chorus of Norwegian Maidens.

THE FLYING DUTCHMAN.

DER FLIEGENDE HOLLÄNDER.

ACT I.	ERSTER AKT.
### SCENE I.	### ERSTER AUFTRITT.
(Steep, rocky sea-shore. Gloomy weather; a violent storm. DALAND's ship has cast anchor close to the shore; the sailors are noisily employed in furling the sails, coiling ropes, etc. DALAND has gone on shore. He is standing on a rock and looking landwards, to find out in what place they are.)	(Steiles Felsenufer. Das Meer nimmt den grössten Theil der Bühne ein; weite Aussicht auf dasselbe. Finsteres Wetter; heftiger Sturm. Das Schiff DALANDS's hat so eben dicht am Ufer Anker geworfen; die Matrosen sind in geräuschvoller Arbeit beschäftigt die Segel aufzuhissen, Taue auszuwerfen, u. s. w.—DALAND ist an das Land gegangen; ersteigt einen Felsen und sieht landeinwärts, die Gegend zu erkennen.)
Chorus of Sailors. Yo-ho-eh! Hal-lo-yo! etc.	*Matrosen.* Hohoje! Hohoje! Halloho! etc.
Daland. On board with you—what cheer?	*Daland.* Am Bord bei Euch, wie steht's?
Steersman. Good, all is well! We have good holding ground.	*Steuermann.* Gut, Capitain! Wir sind auf sicherm Grund.
Daland. Sandwike it is! Right well I know the bay. Alas! There on the shore I saw my home. Senta, my child, ere now I should have met thee, If this unlook'd-for tempest had not come! Trust not the wind; in its grasp it will get thee! What good? But stay! The storm subsides; A storm that rages ceases soon. Ho, Sailors! See, she safely rides; Then take some rest—all fear is gone. Now, steersman, the turn is thine to take the watch; The risk is past, yet sleep not at thy post.	*Daland.* 's ist Sandwyk-Strand, genau kenn' ich die Bucht.— Verwünscht! schon sah am Ufer ich mein Haus, Senta, mein Kind, glaubt' ich schon zu umarmen. Da bläst er aus dem Teufels-Loch heraus. . . Wer baut auf Wind, baut auf Satans Erbarmen! Was hilft's? der Sturm läszt nach,— Wenn so er tobte, währt's nicht lang. He! Bursche! lange war't ihr wach; Zur Ruhe denn, mir ist's nicht bang! Nun, Steuermann! die Wache nimmst Du wohl für mich? Gefahr ist nicht, doch gut ist's wenn Du wachst.
Steersman. Depend on me! Sleep safely captain mine!	*Steuermann.* Seid auszer Sorg'! Schlaft ruhig, Capitain!

STEUERMANN.
STEERSMAN. *Piu vivo.*

moderato.   allegro.

Through thun-der and storm from dis - tant seas, My maid - en, come I near! O - ver
Mit Ge - wit - ter und Sturm aus fer - nem Meer—Mein Mäd - el, bin dir nah'. Ue - ber

tow - er - ing waves, with south - ern breeze, My maid - en am I here! My
thurm - ho - he Fluth vom Süd - en her— Mein Mäd - el, ich bin da! Mein

maid - en, were there no south wind, I nev - er could come to thee; O
Mäd - el, wenn nicht Süd - wind wär, Ich nim - mer wohl käm' zu Dir;— Ach,

fair south wind, to me be kind! My maid - en, she longs for me!
lie - ber Süd - wind! blas' noch mehr, Mein Mäd - el ver - langt nach mir!

Ho - yo - ho! Hal - lo - ho, ho, hal - lo - ho, ho, ho! . . .
Ho - ho - he! Jo - lo - he! Ho! Jo - lo - he! Ho! Ho! . .

Ho - yo - ho! Hal - lo - ho, ho, ho, ho, ho, ho, ... ho.
Ho - ho - he! Jo - lo - he! Ho - ho! Ho! Ho! Ho! . . Ho!

Steersman. From the shores of the south, in far-off lands,
    I oft on thee have thought;
Through thunder and waves, from Moorish strands,
    A gift I thee have brought.
My maiden, praise the sweet south wind—
    I bring thee a golden ring.
O fair south wind, to me be kind!
    My maiden doth spin and sing.
Ho-yo-ho! Hallo-ho!

(In the distance appears the ship of the Flying Dutchman, with blood-red sails and black masts. She quickly nears the shore, over against the ship of the Norwegian.)

The Dutchman. The term is past,
    And once again are ended the seven long years!
The weary sea casts me upon the land.
Ha, haughty ocean!
A little while, and thou again wilt bear me.
Though thou art changeful,

Steuermann. Von des Südens Gestad', aus weitem Land'—
Ich hab' an Dich gedacht;
Durch Gewitter und Meer vom Mohrenstrand
Hab' ich Dir was mitgebracht.
Mein Mädel preis' den Südwind hoch,
Ich bring' Dir ein gülden Band;—
Ach, lieber Südwind, blase doch!
Mein Mädel hätt gern' den Tand.
Hoho! Ho jolobe! u. s. w.

(In der Ferne zeigt sich das Schiff der "fliegenden Holländer's" mit blutrothen Segeln und schwarzen Masten. Es naht sich schnell der Küste nach der dem Schiffe des Norweger's entgegengesetzten Seite.)

Holländer. Die Frist ist um, und abermals vers strichen
Sind sieben Jahr!—Voll Ueberdrusz wirft mich
Das Meer an's Land. . . Ha, stolzer Ocean!
In kurzer Frist sollst Du mich wieder tragen!

Unchanging is my doom:
Release, which on the land I seek for,
Never shall I meet with.
True, thou heaving ocean,
Am I to thee,
Until thy latest billow shall break—
Until at last thou art no more.
Engulf'd in ocean's deepest wave,
Oft have I long'd to find a grave;
But, ah, a grave I found it not!
I oft have blindly rush'd along,
To find my death sharp rocks among;
But, ah, my death I found it not!
And oft, the pirate boldly daring,
My death I 've courted from the sword:
" Here," cried I," work thy deeds unspar-
ing—
My ship with gold is richly stor'd."
Alas! the sea's rapacious son
But sign'd the cross, and straight was gone,
Nowhere a grave; no way of death!
Mine is the curse of living breath.
Thee do I pray, bright angel sent from
heaven,
Thou, who for me didst win unlook'd-for
grace—
Was there a fruitless hope to mock me
given,
When thou didst tell me how to gain re-
lease?
The hope is fruitless—freedom is in vain:
On earth a love unchanging none can gain!
A single hope with me remaineth,
A single hope still standeth fast:
Though earth its form long time retaineth,
In ruins it must fall at last.
Great day of judgment, nearing slow,
When wilt thou dawn, and chase my night?
When comes it, that o'erwhelming blow
Which strikes the world with crushing
might?
When all the dead are rais'd again,
Destruction I shall then attain.
Ye worlds, your course continue not:
Endless destruction be my lot!

Chorus of the Crew of the Dutchman. Endless destruction be our lot.

Daland. Hey! Hallo, Steersman!

Steersman. 'T is nought—'t is nought!
Ah, fair south wind, to me be kind,
My maiden—

Daland. There is nought? What! Thou
watchest well, my friend!

Dein Trotz ist beugsam—doch ewig meine
Qual.
Das Heil, das auf dem Land ich suche,
nimmer
Werd' ich es finden! Euch, des Welt-
meers Fluthen,
Bleib' ich getreu, bis eure letzte Welle
Sich bricht und euer letztes Nasz versiegt!—
Wie oft in Meeres tiefsten Schlund
Stürzt' ich voll Sehnsucht mich hinab,—
Doch ach! den Tod, ich fand ihn nicht!
Da, wo der Schiffe furchtbar Grab,
Trieb mein Schiff ich zum Klippengrund,
Doch ach! mein Grab, es schlosz sich nicht!
Verhöhnend droht' ich dem Piraten,
Im wilden Kampfe hofft' ich Tod:—
"Hier—rief ich—zeige Deine Thaten!
Von Schätzen voll ist Schiff und Boot!"
Doch ach! des Meers barbar'scher Sohn
Schlägt bang' das Kreuz und flieht davon!
Nirgends ein Grab! Niemals der Tod!
Dies der Verdammnisz Schreck-Gebot.—
Dich frage ich, gepries'ner Engel Gottes,
Der meines Heils Bedingung mir gewann,
War ich Unseel'ger Spielwerk Deines
Spottes,
Als die Erlösung Du mir zeigtest an?
—Vergebne Hoffnung! Furchtbar eitler
Wahn!
Um ew'ge Treu' auf Erden ist's gethan!—
Nur eine Hoffnung soll mir bleiben,
Nur eine unerschüttert stehn!
So lang' der Erde Keim' auch treiben,
So musz sie doch zu Grunde gehn.
Tag des Gerichtes, jüngster Tag!
Wann brichst du an in meiner Nacht?
Wann dröhnt er, der Vernichtungschlag;
Mit dem die Welt zusammenkracht?
Wann alle Todten auferstehn,
Dann werde ich in Nichts vergehn!
Ihr Welten, endet euren Lauf.
Ew'ge Vernichtung, nimm mich auf!

Chor. Ew'ge Vernichtung, nimm uns auf!

Daland. He! Holla! Steuermann!

Steuermann. 's ist nichts! 's ist nichts!—
Ach, lieber Südwind blas' noch mehr,—
Mein Mädel. . .

Daland. Du siehst nichts? Gelt! Du wach
est brav mein Bursch!

There lies a ship—How long thou must have slept!

Steersman. 'T is so, indeed.
Forgive me, captain mine!
Ahoy! Ahoy!

Daland. It seems that they are quite as bad as we.

Steersman. Give answer, ship and flag, there!

Daland. Forbear! I think I see the captain there!
Hey! Hallo, seaman! Tell thy name—thy country!

The Dutchman. Far have I come; wouldst thou in storm and tempest
Drive me from anchorage?

Daland. Nay, God forbid! Kind welcome do I give thee!
Who art thou?

The Dutchman. A Dutchman.

Dalana. God be with thee!
Hast thou as well been cast upon this
Bare and rocky shore?
I far'd no better; but a few short miles from here
My home awaits me, almost gained:
I must anew set forth to reach it.
Say, whence comest thou?
What damage hast thou suffered?

The Dutchman. My ship is safe; no damage have I suffered.
Through waves that rage and winds that bluster,
Over the wat'ry waste I rove.
What respite? That I cannot tell thee:
Scarce do I count how seasons move.
I cannot name, shouldst thou demand it,
The many seas I've wandered o'er:
The shore alone my heart doth long for—
Ne'er shall I reach my native shore.
Oh, grant to me a little while thy home,
And of thy friendship thou wilt not repent;
With treasure brought from every clime and country
My ship is richly laden: wilt thou bargain?
Thou mayest be sure that thou wilt gainer be.

Dort liegt ein Schiff! —Wie lange schliefst Du schon?

Steuermann. Zum Teufel auch! — Verzeiht mir Capitain!
Werda! Werda!

Daland. Es scheint, sie sind gerad
So faul als wir.

Steuermann. Gebt Antwort! Schiff und Flagge!

Daland. Lasz sein. Mich dünkt, ich seh den Capitain.—
He! Holla! Seemann! Nenne Dich! Wesz Landes?

Holländer. Weit komm' ich her. Verwehrt bei Sturm und Wetter
Ihr mir den Ankerplatz?

Daland. Behüt' es Gott!
Gastfreundschaft kennt der Seemann.—
Wer bist Du?

Holländer. Holländer.

Daland. Gott zum Grusz!—So trieb auch Dich
Der Sturm an diesen nackten Felsenstrand?
Mir ging's nicht besser, wenig Meilen nur
Von hier ist meine Heimath; fast erreicht
Muszt' ich auf's Neu' mich von ihr wenden.—Sag',
Woher kommst Du? Hast Schaden Du genommen?

Holländer. Mein Schiff ist fest, es leidet keinen Schaden.—
Durch Sturm und bösen Wind verschlagen,
Irr' auf den Wassern ich umher;—
Wie lange? weisz ich kaum zu sagen,
Schon zähl' ich nicht die Jahre mehr.
Unmöglich dünkt mich's, dasz ich nenne,
Die Länder alle, die ich fand:
Das Einz'ge nur, nach dem ich brenne,
Ich find' es nicht; mein Heimathland!—
Vergönne mir auf kurze Frist Dein Haus,
Und Deine Freundschaft soll Dich nicht gereu'n:
Mit Schätzen aller Gegenden und Zonen
Ist reich mein Schiff beladen:—willst Du handeln,
So sollst Du sicher Deines Vortheils sein.

Daland. How wonderful! Can I indeed be-
believe thee?
A baleful star has followed thee till now.
To thee pleasure gladly would I try;
Yet may I ask thee what thy ship contains?

The Dutchman. A store of rarest treasures
shalt thou see—
Pearls rich and costly, stones beyond compare.
Behold, and so convince thyself how great
is their value.
All these for a friendly roof I give thee.

Daland. What? Amazement! All these
treasures!
Who has the wealth the price for them to
offer?

The Dutchman. The price? The price al-
ready have I named—
All these for shelter for a single night.
Nay, what is there is but the smallest part
Of that which in my vessel's hold is stored.
What good to me that have neither wife nor
child?
My native land I cannot find.
All these my riches give I thee
If thou wilt grant me now with thee to find
a home.

Daland. What am I hearing?

The Dutchman. Hast thou a daughter?

Daland. I have—a loving child.

The Dutchman. Let her be mine!

Daland. Wie wunderbar! Soll Deinem Wort
ich glauben?
Ein Unstern, scheint's, hat Dich bis jetzt
verfolgt.
Um Dir zu dienen, biet' ich, was ich kann;
Doch—darf ich fragen, was Dein Schiff
enthält?

Holländer. Die seltensten der Schätze sollst
Du sehn,
Kostbare Perlen, edelstes Gestein.
Blick' hin und überzeuge Dich vom Werthe
Des Preises, den ich für ein gastlich Dach
Dir biete!

Daland. Wie? Ist's möglich? Diese Schätze!
Wer ist so reich, den Preis dafür zu bieten?

Holländer. Den Preis? So eben hab' ich ihn
genannt:
Dies für das Obdach einer einz'gen Nacht!
Doch was Du siehst, ist nur der kleinste
Theil
Von dem, was meines Schiffes Raum ver-
schliesst.
Was frommt der Schatz? Ich habe weder
Weib
Noch Kind, und meine Heimath find' ich
nie
All' meinen Reichthum biet' ich Dir wenn
be.
Den Deinen Du mir neue Heimath giebst.

Daland. Was musz ich hören?

Holländer. Hast Du eine Tochter?

Daland. Führwahr, ein theures Kind.

Holländer. Sie sei mein Weib!

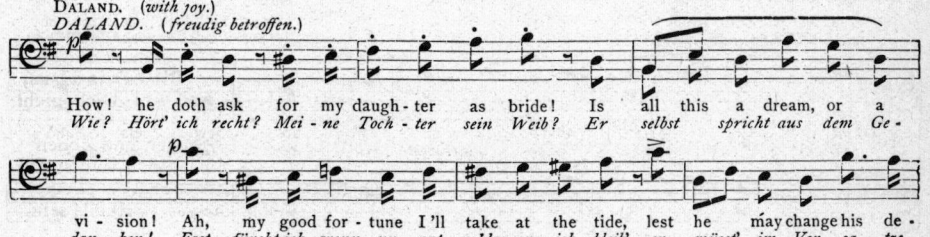

DALAND. (with joy.)
DALAND. (freudig betroffen.)

How! he doth ask for my daugh-ter as bride! Is all this a dream, or a
Wie? Hört' ich recht? Mei-ne Toch-ter sein Weib? Er selbst spricht aus dem Ge-

vi-sion! Ah, my good for-tune I'll take at the tide, lest he may change his de-
dan-ken! Fast fürcht ich wenn un-ent-schlos-sen ich bleib', er müsst' im Vor-sa-tze

treas - ures un - told, oh ! . . take them all, . . my treas - ures un - told !
Schä - tze da - hin, oh ! . . so nimm mei - ne Schä - tze da - hin !

charm'd, I a - gree, to . . his of - - - fer, charm'd, I a - gree !)
schia - ge ich ein, voll . . Ent - zü - - - cken schla - ge ich ein !)

Daland. Yes, stranger, true; I have an only daughter,
Who gives her father all a daughter's love;
She is my pride, the best of my possessions,
In grief my comfort and in mirth my joy.

The Dutchman. Her father still receive her true affection !
Love him, and she will love her husband too.

Daland. Thou givest jewels, pearls of price-less value;
A fairer jewel still, a faithful wife—

The Dutchman. Thou givest me?

Daland. I give thee here my word.
I mourn thy lot. As thou art bountiful,
Thou showest me thy good and noble heart.
My son I wish thou wert;
And were thy wealth not half as great,
I would not choose another !

The Dutchman. I thank thee !
Shall I thy daughter see to-day?

Daland. The next propitious wind will bear us home;
Thou'lt see her then, and if she pleases thee—

The Dutchman. She shall be mine. Will she my angel be?
Oft by unceasing torment driven,
My heart has long'd for rest and peace;
Oh, would the hope at last were given
That I through her might find release !
Dare I in that delusion languish,
That through this angel pain shall cease?
That after this tormenting anguish
I shall attain to lasting peace?
Ah ! all but hopeless though I be,
My heart still hopes that joy to see.

Daland. Wohl, Fremdling, hab' ich eine schöne Tochter,
Mit treuer Kindeslieb' ergeben mir;
Sie ist mein Stolz, das höchste meiner Güter,
Mein Trost im Unglück, meine Freud' im Glück.

Holländer. Dem Vater stets bewahr' sie ihre Liebe,
Ihm treu, wird sie auch treu dem Gatten sein.

Daland. Du giebst Juwelen, unschätzbare Perlen,
Das höchste Kleinod doch, ein treues Weib. . .

Holländer. Du giebst es mir?

Daland. Ich gebe Dir mein Wort.
Mich rührt Dein Loos; freigebig, wie Du bist,
Zeigt Edelmuth und hohen Sinn Du mir :—
Den Eidam wünscht' ich so, und wär Dein Gut
Auch nicht so reich, wählt' ich doch keinen Andern.

Holländer. Hab' Dank ! Werd' ich die Toch-ter heut noch sehn?

Daland. Der nächste günst'ge Wind führt uns nach Haus.
Du sollst sie sehn, und wenn sie Dir gefällt—

Höllander. So ist sie mein. . . Wird sie mein Engel sein?
Wenn aus der Qualen Schreckgewalten
Die Sehnsucht nach dem Heil mich treibt,
Ist mir's erlaubt, mich fest zu halten
An einer Hoffnung, die mir bleibt.
Darf ich in jenem Wahn noch schmachten,
Dasz sich ein Engel mir erweicht?
Der Qualen, die mein Haupt umnachten,
Ersehntes Ziel hätt' ich erreicht.
Ach ! ohne Hoffnung wie ich bin,
Geb' ich mich docn au. Hoffnung hin !

Daland.　I thank the storm which me far has
　　　driven,
And on this rocky shore has cast:
In truth, good fortune freely given
I must not lose, but hold it fast.
Ye winds that to this coast have brought him,
To you my heartfelt thanks I pay ;
No father but had gladly caught him ;
His wealth and he are mine to-day !
Good fortune, freely given,
I must not lose, but hold it fast.
Yes ! to one with wealth and noble heart,
With house and child I gladly part !

Steersman.　South wind ! South wind !
　　" Oh, fair south wind, to me be kind ! "

Chorus of Sailors.　Halloho ! Yoo-ho-eh !

Daland.　Gepriesen seid, des Sturms Gewalten
Die ihr an diesen Strand mich triebt.
Fürwahr !　Blos brauch' ich festzuhalten,
Was sich so schön von selbst mir giebt
Die ihn an diese Küste brachten,
Ihr Wind sollt gesegnet sein !
Ja, wonach alle Väter trachten,
Ein reicher Eidam, er ist mein.
Dem Mann mit Gut und hohem Sinn
Geb' froh ich Haus und Tochter hin !

Steuermann.　—Südwind ! Südwind !
　　"Ach ! lieber Südwind blas' noch mehr !"

Matrosen.　Holloje ! Hollajo !

DALAND.
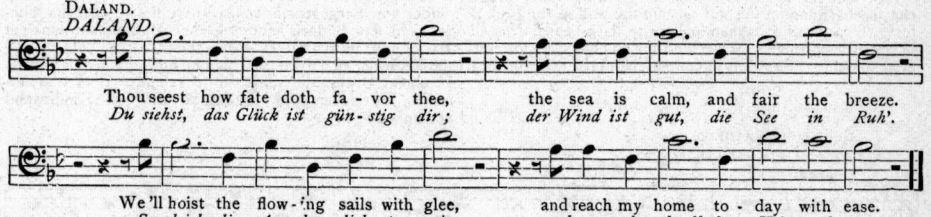

Thou seest how fate doth fa - vor thee,　　the sea is　calm, and　fair　the　breeze.
Du siehst, das Glück ist gün - stig dir ;　　der Wind ist　gut,　die　See　in　Ruh'.

We 'll hoist the　flow - ing　sails with glee,　and reach my home　to - day　with ease.
So gleich die　An - ker　lich - ten　wir,　und se - geln schnell der　Hei - math zu.

Sailors.　Halloho ! Ho ! Halloho ! etc.

The Dutchman.　If I might ask thee, do thou
　　first put to sea :
　　Though fair the wind, my crew are weary
　　all ;
　　So let them rest awhile, then follow thee.

Daland.　Yes, but the wind ?

The Dutchman.　'T is not a wind to fall.
　　My ship is swift, and thine will overtake.

Daland.　Thy ship, if so, good speed will have
　　to make.
　　Farewell !　To-day thou wilt my daughter
　　see !

The Dutchman.　In truth ?

Daland.　Hey ! quickly full the sails will be !
　　Hallo !　Hallo !
　　Come, sailors, work away !

Matrosen.　Hohone !　Hohohe !　Halloho !
　　Jo ! u.s.w.

Holländer.　Darf ich Dich bitten, segelst Du
　　voran ;
　　Der Wind ist frisch, doch, meine Mann-
　　schaft müd',
　　Ich gönn' ihr kurze Ruh, und folge dann.

Daland.　Doch unser Wind ?

Holländer.　Er bläst noch lang' aus Süd',
　　Mein Schiff ist schnell, es holt' Dich sicher
　　ein.

Daland.　Du glaubst? Wohlan ! Es möge denn
　　so sein.
　　Leb' wohl ! mögst heute Du mein Kind
　　noch sehn !

Holländer.　Gewisz !

Daland.　Hei !　Wie die Segel schon sich
　　bläh'n !
　　Hallo !　Hallo !　Frisch, Jungen ! Gre-
　　fet an !

Sailors   Through thunder and storm from dis-
    tant seas,
   My maiden, come ī near;
Over towering waves, with southern breeze,
   My maiden, am I here!
My maiden, were there no south wind,
   I never could come to thee;
Oh, fair south wind, to me be kind!
   My maiden, she longs for me!
     Hoho! Halloho! etc.
	Matrosen. Mit Gewitter und Sturm aus fer-
	    nem Meer.
	   Mein Mädel, bin dir nah!
	Ueber thurmhohe Fluth, vom Süden her—
	   Mein Mädel, ich bin da!
	   Mein Mädel, wenn nicht Südwind wär',
	   Ich nimmer wohl käm' zu dir!
	   Ach, lieber Südwind, blas' noch mehr!
	   Mein Mädel verlangt nach mir,
	    Hohoje! Halloho! Hoho! Ho! Ho! Ho!

ACT II.   ZWEITER AKT.

(A room in DALAND's house. Marine views, maps, charts, etc., hung on the walls. On the wall at the back is hung the portrait of a man, pale, with dark beard, dressed in Spanish costume. MARY and the maidens are discovered spinning. SENTA is in contemplation of the portrait.)	(Ein grosses Zimmer im Hause DALAND's; an der Wand Bilder von Seegegenständen, Karten, u.s.w. An der Hinterwand das Bildniss eines bleichen Mannes mit dunklem Barte und in schwarzer spanischer Tracht. MARY und die Mädchen sitzen im den Kamin und spinnen. SENTA, in einem Grossvaterstuhle zurückgelehnt, ist in traümerisches Anschauen des Bildnisses an der Hinterwand versunken.)

CHORUS OF MAIDENS.
CHOR DER MÄDCHEN.

Tra la ra la la la la la!
Tra la ra la la la la la!
Tra la ra la la la la la!
Tra la ra la la la la la!

spin, maid-ens, maid-ens, spin, sweet-hearts win-ning,
Spinnt, fleis-sig Mäd-chen! Brumm', gu-tes Räd-chen!

Tra la ra la la la la la la la la!
Tra la ra la la la la la la la la!

spin, spin, maid-ens spin-ning, sweet-hearts win-ning, spin!
Spinnt! Spinnt! fleis-sig Mäd-chen, fleis-sig Mäd-chen, spinn!

Mary. Ah, duly are they spinning!
Each girl a sweetheart would be winning!

The Maidens. Dame Mary, hush! for well
you know
Our song as yet must onward go!

Mary. Then sing—yet ply a busy wheel.
But wherefore, Senta, art thou still?

The Maidens. Hum, hum, hum—good wheel,
be whirling!
Gaily, gaily turn thee round!
Spin, spin, spin—the threads be twirling!
Turn, good wheel, with humming sound!
On distant seas my love doth sail—
In southern lands
Much gold he wins;
Then turn, good wheel, nor tire, nor fail:
The gold for her
Who duly spins!
Spin, spin,
Spin we duly!
Hum! hum!
Wheel go truly!

Mary. Thou careless girl! Wilt thou not spin?
Thy lover's gift thou wilt not win!

The Maidens. She has no need to work as we:
Her lover sails not on the sea—
He brings her game instead of gold;
One knows the worth of hunters bold.

Mary. Ei! Fleiszig, fleiszig, wie sie spinnen!
Will jede sich den Schatz gewinnen.

Mädchen. Frau Mary, still! denn wohl Ihr
wiszt,
Das Lied noch nicht zu Ende ist.

Mary. So singt! dem Rädchen läszt's nicht
Ruh.
Du aber, Senta, schweigst dazu?

Mädchen. Summ nnd brumm du gutes Räd-
chen,
Munter, munter dreh' dich um!
Spinne, spinne tausend Fadchen,
Gutes Rädchen, summ und brumm!
Mein Schatz da drauszen auf dem Meer
Im Süden er
Viel Gold gewinnt.
Ach, gutes Rädchen, braus' noch mehr!
Er giebt's dem Kind,
Wenn's fleiszig spinnt.
Spinnt, spinnt!
Fleiszig, Mädchen!
Summ, brumm,
Gutes Rädchen!

Mary. Du böses Kind, wenn Du nicht spinnst,
Vom Schatz Du kein Geschenk gewinnst!

Mädchen. Sie hat's nicht noth, dasz sie sich eilt.
Ihr Schatz nicht auf dem Meere weilt:
Bringt er nicht Gold, bringt er doch Wild,
Man weisz ja was ein Jäger gilt!

Mary. You see her? still before that face!
Why wilt thou dream away thy girlhood
With gazing at that picture so?

Senta. Why hast thou told me of his sorrows?
His hapless fate why did I know?
The wretched man!

Mary. God help thee, girl!

The Maidens. Ei, ei! What's that she said?
Her sighs are for the ghostly man!

Mary. I fear that she will lose her head!

The Maidens. 'T is brooding makes her look
so wan.

Mary. No use for me to chide each day.
Come, Senta, wilt thou turn away?

The Maidens. She hears you not; she is in
love!
Ei, ei! No anger pray it move!
For Erik has a temper hot,
And if his heart will bear it not,
Say nought, lest in a rage he fall,
And shoot his rival on the wall!
Ha, ha, ha!

Senta. Be still with all your foolish jesting!
My temper are you bent on testing?

The Maidens. Hum, good wheel, etc.

Senta. Oh, make an end of all this singing!
Your hum, hum, hum, quite tires my ear.
If me you would your way be bringing,
Provide some better thing to hear!

The Maidens. Well, sing thyself!

Senta. Much would I rather
Dame Mary sing to us the ballad.

Mary. I'd rather not attempt the thing:
The Flying Dutchman, let him be!

Senta. The song I oft have heard you sing!
I'll sing myself!
Hark, then, to me—
A tale of sorrow I select you:
His wretched fate it must affect you.

Mary. Da seht ihr's! Immer vor dem Bild!—
Wirst Du Dein ganzes junges Leben
Verträumen vor dem Conterfei?

Senta. Was hast du Kunde mir gegeben,
Was mir erzählet, wei es sei!
Der arme Mann!

Mary. Gott sei mit Dir!

Mädchen. Ei, ei! Ei, ei! Was hören wir?
Sie seufzet um den bleichen Mann.

Mary. Den Kopf verliert sie noch darum.

Mädchen. Da sieht man, was ein Bild doch
kann!

Mary. Nichts hilft es, wenn ich täglich
brumm':
Komm', Senta! wend' Dich doch herum!

Mädchen. Sie hört Euch nicht,—sie ist ver-
liebt.
Ei, ei! Wenn's nur nicht Händel giebt!
Erik ist gar ein heiszes Blut,
Dasz er nur keinen Schaden thut!
Sagt nichts, er schieszt sonst wuthentbrannt
Den Nebenbuhler von der Wand.

Senta. O schweigt! Mit Eurem tollen Lachen,
Wollt ihr mich ernstlich böse machen?

Mädchen. Summ und brumm, du gutes Räd-
chen
Munter, munter dieh' dich um!
Spinne, spinne tausend Fädchen,
Gutes Rädchen brumm und summ!

Senta. O macht dem tollen Lied ein Ende,
Es summt und brummt mir vor dem Ohr!
Wollt ihr, dasz ich mich zu euch wende,
So sucht' was Besseres hervor!

Mädchen. Gut singe Du!

Senta. Hört, was ich rathe.
Frau Mary singt uns die Ballade.

Mary. Bewahre Gott! das fehlte mir!
Den fliegenden Holländer laszt in Ruh'.

Senta. Wie oft doch hört' ich sie von Dir!
Ich sing' sie selbst, hört, Mädchen, zu.
Laszt mich's euch recht zu Herzen führen
Des Aermsten Loos, es musz euch rühren

The Maidens. Well, let us hear.	*Mädchen.* Uns ist es recht.
Senta. Mark what I say.	*Senta.* Merkt auf die Wort'!
The Maidens. And we will rest.	*Mädchen.* Dem Spinnrad Ruh'!
Mary. I'll spin away.	*Mary.* Ich spinne fort.

Senta. Against a tempest's utmost wrath,
Around a cape he once would sail;
He curs'd and swore a foolish oath:
"Befall what may, I will prevail!"
Hui! And Satan heard! Yo-ho-he!
Hui! He marked his word,
And condemned him to sail on the sea,
without aim, without end.
Yet this the wretched man from his lifelong
curse may deliver,
Would but an angel show him the way his
bondage to sever.
Ah, mightest thou, spectral seaman, but
find it!
Pray ye that Heav'n may soon
At his need grant him this boon!
He lands at ev'ry seven year's end;
A wife to seek, he wanders round;
But wheresoe'er he bends
For him no faithful wife is found.
Hui! "Unfurl the sails!" Yo-ho-he!
Hui! "The anchor weigh'd!" Yo-ho-he!
Hui! "Faithless love, faithless troth!
To the sea, without aim, without end."

The Maidens. Ah, where is she, to whose
loving heart the angel may guide thee?
Where lingers she, thine own unto death,
whatever betide thee?

Senta. I am the one who through her love
will save thee!
Oh, may the angel hither guide thee!
Through me may new-found joy betide
thee!

Mary and the Maidens. Heav'n help us!
Senta!

Erik.
(Has entered in time to hear the last exclamations of
SENTA.)
Senta, would'st thou, then, forsake me?

The Maidens. Help, Erik, help! This must
be madness.

Mary. This outburst fills my heart with sad-
ness!
Abhorred picture, thou shalt burn!
Let but her father once return!

Erik. Her father comes!

Senta. My father here?

Erik From off the height I saw his sail.

Senta. Bei bösem Wind und Sturmes Wuth
Umsegeln wollt' er einst ein Cap;
Er flucht' und schwur in tollem Muth;—
"In Ewigkeit lass' ich nicht ab!"—
Hui!—Und Satan hört's—Johohe!
Hui!—Nahm ihn bei'm Wort!—Johohe!
Hui! Und verdammt zieht er nun durch
das Meer, ohne Rast, ohne Ruh'.
Doch, dasz der arme Mann noch Erlösung
fände auf Erden,
Zeigt Gottes Engel an, wie sein Heil ihm
einst könne werden:—
Ach! mögtest Du, bleicher Seemann, es
finden!
Betet zum Himmel, dasz bald
Ein Weib Treue ihm halt'!—
Vor Anker alle sieben Jahr,
Ein Weib zu frei'n, ging er an's Land;
Er freite alle sieben Jahr,
Noch nie ein treues Weib er fand.—
Hui! "die Segel auf!"—Johohe!
Hui! "den Anker los!"—Johohe!
Hui! falsche Lieb', falsche Treu'! Auf in
See! Ohne Rast, ohne Ruh!

Mädchen. Ach, wo weilt sie, die dir Gottes
Engel einst könne zeigen?
Wo triffst Du sie, die bis in den Tod Dein
bliebe treueigen?

Senta. Ich sei das Weib! Meine Treu' soll
Dich erlösen!
Mög' Gottes Engel mich Dir zeigen;
Durch mich sollst Du das Heil erreichen!

Mary und die Mädchen. Hilf Himmel!
Senta! Senta!

Erik.
(Ist zur thüre hereingetreten und hat SENTA'S Ausruf
vernommen.)
Senta, Senta! Willst Du mich verderben?

Mädchen. Hilf uns, Erik! Sie ist von Sinnen!

Mary. Vor Schreck fühl' ich mein Blut gerin-
nen!
Abscheulich Bild, Du sollst hinaus,
Kommt nur der Vater erst nach Haus!

Erik. Der Vater kommt.

Senta. Der Vater kommt?

Erik. Vom Fels sah ich sein Schiff sich nahen.

The Maidens. They are at home!

Mary. Hold! hold! With me you ought to stay!
The sailors come with urgent hunger:
For food and wine they soon will ask.
Restrain yourselves a little longer,
Nor leave undone each needful task.

The Maidens. We cannot stay at work much longer:
There is so much we want to ask.
Enough we satisfy their hunger,
Then have we done each needful task.

Erik. Stay, Senta! Stay a single moment more,
And from my torture set me free!
Say, wilt thou, ah, wilt thou leave me quite?

Senta. What is—what must?

Erik. O Senta, speak—what will become of me?
Thy father comes; before he sails again
He will accomplish what he oft has purposed.

Senta. What dost thou mean?

Erik. And will a husband give thee—

Mädchen. Sie sind daheim!—Auf, eilt hinaus.

Mary. Halt! Halt! Ihr bleibet fein im Haus!
Das Schiffsvolk kommt mit leerem Magen:—
In Küch' und Keller! Säumet nicht!
Laszt Euch nur brav die Neugier plagen,
Vor Allem geht an eure Pflicht!

Mädchen. Ach, wie viel hab' ich ihn zu fragen!
Ich halte mich vor Neugier nicht.—
Schon gut: sobald nur aufgetragen,
Hält länger hier uns keine Pflicht!

Erik. Bleib', Senta! Bleib' nur einen Augenblick!
Aus meinen Qualen reisze mich! Doch willst Du—
Ach! so verdirb mich ganz!

Senta. Was soll's, Erik . . .?

Erik. O Senta, sprich, was aus mir werden soll?
Dein Vater kommt,—eh' wieder er verreist
Wird er vollbringen, was scho.. oft er wollte. . .

Senta. Und was, Erik?

Erik. Dir einen Gatten geben.—

ERIK.
A tempo, ma un poco ritenuto.

A heart, a hand, from ill to screen thee! A hun - ter's skill, a
Mein Herz voll Treu - e bis zum Ster - ben, Mein dürf - tig Gut, mein

fru - gal hut! Were I with these to seek to win thee,
Jä - ger - glück: Darf so um Dei - ne Hand ich wer - ben,

Would not thy fa - ther spurn my suit? Then let my heart with an - guish
Stöszt mich Dein nicht zu - rück? Wenn sich mein Herz in Jam - mer

break, Say, Sen - ta, who for me will speak? Then let my heart with an - guish
bricht, Sag', Sen - ta, wer dann für mich spricht? Wenn dann mein Herz im Jam - me,

molto rit.

break, Yes, let my heart with an - guish break, Say, Sen - ta, who for me will speak?
bricht. Wenn dann mein Herz im Jam - mer bricht: Sag', Sen - ta, wer dann für mich spricht?

Senta. Ah, ask not, Erik, now.
Let me begone :
My father I must welcome ;
For if this once his daughter failed to come,
I fear he might be angry.

Erik. From me thou 'dst fly?

Senta. I must on board.

Erik. Thou shunnest me?

Senta. Oh, let me go!

Erik. And wilt thou leave the wound still
bleeding,
Which thou hast given my loving heart?
Ah, hear my fondest, latest pleading —
Hear what I ask, ere yet we part!
Say, let this heart with anguish break,
Will Senta care for me to speak?

Senta. What! dost thou doubt my heart's
devotion,
And question if I love thee still?
Oh, say, what makes this new emotion?
Why should mistrust thy bosom fill?

Erik. Thy father, ah, for wealth alone he
seeks ;
And Senta, thou, how dare I on thee
reckon?
I pray thee grant but one of my petitions :
Grieve not my heart from day to day.

Senta. Thy heart?

Erik. What can I fancy? Yonder face.

Senta. The face?

Erik. Why not abandon all thy foolish
dreams?

Senta. Can I forbid my face to show compassion?

Erik. Then, too, the ballad thou hast sung
to-day!

Senta. I am a child, and know not what I 'm
singing.
But, say —What! fearest thou a song — a
face?

Erik. Thou art so pale ; say, should I not be
fearful?

Senta. O schweige jetzt, Erik! Lasz mich
hinaus,
Den Vater zu begrüszen!
Wenn nicht, wie sonst, an Bord die Toch-
ter kommt,
Wird er nicht zürnen müssen?

Erik. Du willst mich fliehn?

Senta. Ich musz zum Port.

Erik. Du weichst mir aus?

Senta. Ach! lasz mich fort!

Erik. Fl'ehst Du zurück vor dieser Wunde,
Die Du mir schlugst, den Liebeswahn?
O höre mich zu dieser Stunde,
Hör' meine letzte Frage an!
Wenn dieses Herz im Jammer bricht,
Wird's Senta sein, die für mich spricht?

Senta. Wie? zweifelst Du an meinem Herzen?
Du zweifelst, ob ich gut Dir bin?—
Doch sag', was weckt Dir solche Schmer-
zen?
Was trübt mit Argwohn Deinen Sinn?

Erik. Dein Vater—ach! nach Schätzen geizt
er nur . . .
Und Senta, Du! Wie dürst' auf Dich ich
zählen?
Erfülltest Du nur eine meiner Bitten?
Krænkst Du mein Herz nicht jeden Tag?

Senta. Dein Herz?

Erik. Was soll ich denken. Jenes Bild . . .

Senta. Das Bild?

Erik. Läszt Du von Deiner Schwærmere
wohl ab?

Senta. Kann meinem Blick Theilnahme ich
verwehren?

Erik. Und die Ballade, heut noch sangst Du
sie !

Senta. Ich bin ein Kind und weisz nicht was
ich singe . . . !
Erik, sag' ! fürchtest Du ein Lied, ein Bild?

Erik. Du bist so bleich . . . sag', sollt' ich
es nicht fürchten?

Senta. Should, then, a fate so terrible not move me?

Erik. My sorrow, Senta, moves thee now no more!

Senta. Oh, vaunt it not!
What can thy sorrow be?
Know'st thou the fate of that unhappy man?
Look, canst thou feel the pain, the grief,
With which his gaze on me he bends?
Ah, when I think he has ne'er found relief,
How sharp a pang my bosom rends!

Erik. Woe's me! I think of my late hapless dream!
God keep thee safe! Satan would thee ensnare.

Senta. What affrights thee so?

Erik. Senta, hear what I tell!
A vision—heed thou its warning voice!
On lofty cliffs I lay, and, dreaming
I watched the mighty sea below;
The sounding breakers white were gleaming,
And toward the shore came rolling slow.
A foreign ship off shore was riding:
I mark'd her—weird-like, strange to see.
Two men their steps to me were guiding;
The one I knew—thy father he.

Senta. The other?

Erik. Him, too, had I seen;
The garments black, the ghastly mien.

Senta. The gloomy look?

Erik. The seaman here.

Senta. And I?

Erik. From home thou didst appear,
And haste to give thy father greeting.
I saw thee to the stranger going,
And, as for his regard entreating,
Thyself at once before him throwing.

Senta. He rais'd me up—

Erik. Upon his breast:
I saw him close embraced by thee—
In kisses was thy love confessed.

Senta. And then?

Senta. Soll mich des Aermsten Schreckensloos nicht rühren?

Erik. Mein Leiden, Senta, rührt es Dich nicht mehr?

Senta. O! schweige doch. Was kann Dein Leiden sein?
Kennst jenes Unglücksel'gen Schicksal Du?
Fühlst Du den Schmerz, den tiefsten Gram,
Mit dem herab auf mich er sieht?
Ach, was die Ruh' ihm ewig nahm,
Wie schneidend Weh durch's Herz mir zieht!

Erik. Weh' mir! Es mahnt mich ein unsel'ger Traum!
Gott schütze Dich! Satan hat Dich umgarnt.

Senta. Was schreckt Dich so?

Erik. Senta, lasz Dir vertrau'n :—
Ein Traum ist's,—höre ihn zur Warnung an!
Auf hohem Felsen lag ich träumend,
Sah unter mir des Meeres Fluth;
Die Brandung hört' ich, wie sich schäumend
Am Ufer brach der Wogen Wuth :—
Ein fremdes Schiff am nahen Strande
Erblickt' ich, seltsam, wunderbar :—
wei Männer nahten sich dem Lande,
Der Ein', ich sah's, Dein Vater war. . .

Senta. Der Andre?

Erik. Wohl erkannt' ich ihn :
Mit schwarzem Wams und bleicher Mien'

Senta. Und düst'rem Aug'. . .

Erik. Der Seemann, Er.

Senta. Und ich?

Erik. Du kamst vom Hause her,
Du flogst den Vater zu begrüszen ;
Doch kaum noch fah' ich an Dich langer,
Du stürztest zu des Fremden Füszen--
Ich sah Dich seine Knie umfangen. . .

Senta. Er hob mich auf. . .

Erik. An seine Brust ;—
Voll Inbrunst hingst Du Dich an ihn,—
Du küsztest ihn mit heiszer Lust—

Senta. Und dann. . .?

Erik. I saw you put to sea.

Senta. He seeks for me, and I for him!
For him will I risk life and limb!

Erik. How frightful! Clearly I view
Her hapless end. My dream was true!

Senta. Ah, mightest thou, spectral seaman, but
find her!
Pray ye that Heav'n may soon,
At his need, grant him this boon!

(The door opens, DALAND and the DUTCHMAN enter.)

Daland. My child, thou seest me on the thresh-
old--
What? no embracing, not a kiss?
Thou standest fixed—nor word, nor mo-
tion?
My Senta, do I merit this?

Senta. God be thy guard! My father, say,
Who is this stranger?

Daland. Wouldst thou know?

Erik. Sah ich auf's Meer euch flieh'n.

Senta. Er sucht mich auf! Ich musz ihn sehn!
Mit ihm musz ich zu Grunde gehn!

Erik. Entsetzlich! Ha, mir wird es klar;
Sie ist dahin! Mein Traum sprach wah

Senta. Ach, möchtest du, bleicher
Seemann, sie finden! Betet
Zum Himmel, das bald ein
Weib Trene ihm!

(Die Thür geht auf; der HOLLÄNDER und DALAND
zeigen sich.)

Daland. Mein Kind, du siehst nich auf der
Schwelle—
Wie? Kein Umarmen, Keinen Kuse?
Du bleibst gebannt an deiner Stelle?
Verdien' ich, Senta, solchen Gross?

Senta. Gott dir zum Gruse! Mein Vater.
sprich,. war ist der Fremde?

Daland. Drängst du mich?

DALAND.

Wilt thou, my child, the stran - ger give a friend - ly wel - come? True sea - man
Mögst du, mein Kind, den frem - den Mann will - kom - mer heis - sen! See - mann ist

he, like me, our guest he would re - main. Long wand - 'ring home - less, oft on
er, gleich mir, das Gast - recht spricht er an. Lang' oh - ne Hei - math, stets auf

dis - tant, dis - tant jour - neys, In for - eign lands he wealth and treas - ures vast did gain.
fer - nen, wei - ten Rei - s'n, In frem - den Lan - den er der Schät - ze viel ge - wann.

From his own fa - ther - land ex - il'd he doth of - fer
Aus sei - nem Va - ter - land ver - wei - sen, für ei - nen

wealth our home to share. Say, wouldst ob - ject if hence-forth, child, he should join us
Heerd er reich - lich lohnt. Sprich, Sen - ta, würd' es dich ver - dris - sen, wenn die - ser

in our sim - ple fare? Should join us in our sim - ple fare?
Frem - de bei uns wohnt? Wenn die - ser Frem - de bei uns wohnt?

Däland. Say, have I gone too far in praising?
   Look for thyself,—is she not fair?
   Should not my praise be overflowing?
   Confess her graces wondrous are!
   Wilt thou, my child, accord our guest a
      friendly welcome,
   And wilt thou also let him share thy kindly
      heart?
   Give him thy hand, for bridegroom it is
      thine to call him!
   If thou but give consent, to-morrow his
      thou art.
   Look on these gems, look on the bracelets:
   To what he owns trifles are these.
   Dost thou, my child, not long to have
      them?
   And all are thine when thou art his!
   Yet neither speaks;
   What, then, if I were gone?
   I see—'t were best that they were left alone.
   May'st thou secure this noble husband!
   Trust me such luck is given to few.
   Stay here alone: and I will leave you.
   Senta is fair, and she is true.

Daland. Sagt, hab' ich sie zu viel gepriesen:
   Ihr seht sie selbst,—ist sie Euch recht?—
   Soll noch vom Lob' ich überflieszen?
   Gesteht, sie zieret ihr Geschlecht!
   Mögst Du, mein Kind, dem Manne freund-
      lich Dich erweisen!
   Von Deinem Herzen auch spricht holde
      Gab' er an.
   Reich' ihm die Hand, denn Bräutigam sollst
      Du ihn heiszen;
   Stimmst Du dem Vater bei, ist morgen er
      Dein Mann.
   Sieh' dieses Band, sieh' diese Spangen!
   Was er besitzt, macht dies gering.
   Musz, theures Kind, Dich's nicht verlangen?
   Dein ist es, wechselst Du den Ring!—
   Doch—Keines spricht.—Sollt' ich hier läs-
      tig sein?
   So ist's! Am Besten lasz ich sie allein.
   Mögst Du den edlen Mann gewinnen!
   Glaub' mir, solch Glück wird nimmer neu.
   Bleibt hier allein; ich geh' von hinnen. .
   Glaubt mir, wie schön, so ist sie treu!

The Dutchman. Like to a vision, seen in
      days long by-gone,
   This maiden's face and form appear:
   What I have sought thro' countless years of
      sorrow
   Am at I last beholding here?

Holländer. Wie aus der Ferne längst vergang'-
      ner Zeiten
   Spricht dieses Mädchens Bild zu mir;
   Wie ich's geträumt seit langen Ewigkeiten,
   Vor meinen Augen seh' ich's hier.

DUTCHMAN.
HOLLÄNDER.

Oft 'mid the tor - ment of my night e - ter - nal, Long - ing I gaz'd up -
Wohl hub auch ich voll Sehn-sucht mei - ne Bli - cke Aus tie - fer Nacht em -
un poco riten.

on . . some be - ing fair! But I was driv'n by Sa - tan's pow'r in - fer - nal
por . . zu ein - em Weib? Ein schla - gend Herz liess, ach! mir Sa - tan's Tü - cke,

On my dread course, in an - guish and des - pair! The glow that warms my
Dass ein - ge - denk ich mei - ner Qua - len bleib'! Die dü - stre Gluth, die

heart with strange e - mo - tion, Can I, ac - curs'd one, call it love's de - vo - tion? Ah
hier ich füh - le bren - nen, Sollt' ich Un - se - li - ger sie Lie - be nen - nen? Ach

no, 'tis yearn - ing blest re - pose to gain, That such an an - gel
nein! Die Sehn - sucht ist es nach dem Heil.— Würd' es durch sol - chen

might for me ob - tain, That such an an - gel might for me ob - tain.
En - gel mir zu Theil, Würd' es durch sol - chen En - gel mir zu Theil!

Senta. And am I sunk in wondrous depths of dreaming?
  Is this a vision which I see,
  Or am I now set free from long delusion?
  Has morning truly dawned on me?
  See, there he stands, his face with sorrow clouding—
  He tells me all his mingled hope and fear;
  Is it the voice of sympathy that cheats me?
  As he has oft in dreams, so stands he here!
  The sorrow which within my breast is burning—
  Ah, this compassion, what dare I call it?
  Thy heart is longing after rest and peace,
  And thou at last through me shall find release.

The Dutchman. Wilt thou, thy father's choice fulfilling,
  Do what he said? Say, art thou willing?
  Wilt thou, indeed, thyself forever give me?
  Shall I in truth, a stranger, thus be blessed?
  Say, shall I find the time of sorrow ended—
  In thy true love my long-expected rest?

Senta. Whoe'er thou art, where'er thy curse may lead thee,
  And me, when I thy lot mine own have made—
  Whate'er the fate which I with thee may share in,
  My father's will by me shall be obey'd.

The Dutchman. So full of trust? what? canst thou in thy gladness,
  For these my sorrows deep compassion know?

Senta. Unheard-of sorrows! would I joy might bring thee!

The Dutchman. How sweet the sound that breaks my night of woe!
  Thou art an angel, and a love angelic
  Can comfort bring to one like me.
  Ah, if redemption still be mine to hope for,
  Heaven, grant that she my saviour be!

Senta. Ah, if redemption still be his to hope for,
  Heaven, grant that I his saviour be!

Senta. Versank ich jetzt in wunderbares Träumen,
  Was ich erblicke, ist es Wahn?—
  Weilt' ich bisher in trügerischen Räumen,
  Brach des Erwachens Tag heut an?—
  Er steht vor mir mit leidenvollen Zügen,
  Es spricht sein unerhörter Gram zu mir;
  Kann tiefen Mitleids Stimme mich belügen?
  Wie ich inn oft geseh'n, so steht er hier.
  Die Schmerzen, die in meinem Busen brennen,
  Ach! dies Verlangen, wie soll ich es nennen?
  Wonach mit Sehnsucht es ihn treibt—das Heil,

Holländer. Wirst Du des Vaters Wahl nicht schelten?
  Was er versprach, wie? dürft' es gelten?—
  Du könntest Dich für ewig mir ergeben,
  Und Deine Hand dem Fremdling reichtest Du?
  Soll finden ich nach qualenvollem Leben
  In Deiner Treu' die lang ersehnte Ruh?—

Senta. Wer Du auch seist, und welches das Verderben,
  Dem grausam Dich Dein Schicksal konnte weih'n;
  Was auch das Loos, das ich mir sollt' erwerben:
  Gehorsam stets werd' ich dem Vater sein.

Holländer. So unbedingt, wie? könnte Dich durchdringen
  Für meine Leiden tiefstes Mitgefühl?

Senta. O, welche Leiden! Könnt' ich Trost Dir bringen!

Holländer. Welch holder Klang im nächtigen Gewühl!—
  Du bist ein Engel!—Eines Engels Liebe
  Verworf'ne selbst zu trösten weisz!—
  Ach, wenn Erlösung mir zu hoffen bliebe.
  Allewiger, durch diese sei's!

Senta. Ach! wenn Erlösung ihm zu hoffen bliebe,
  Allewiger, durch mich nur sei's!

The Dutchman. Ah, thou, the certain fate
   foreknowing,
Which must indeed with me be borne,
Wouldst not have made the vow thou
   madest—
Wouldst not to be my wife have sworn!
Thou wouldst have shuddered ere devoting,
To aid me, all thy golden youth—
Ere thou hadst woman's joys surrendered,
Ere thou hadst bid me trust thy truth?

Senta. Well know I woman's holy duties;
O hapless man, be thou at ease!
Leave me to fate's unbending judgment—
Me, who defy its dread decrees.
Within the secret realm of conscience
Know I the high demands of faith:
Him, whom I chose, him I love only,
And loving e'en till death!

The Dutchman. A healing balm for all my
   sorrows
From out her plighted word doth flow.

Senta. 'T was surely wrought by pow'r of magic
That I should his deliv'rer be.

The Dutchman. Hear this! Release at last
   is granted!
Hear this, ye mighty:
Your power is now laid low!
Star of misfortune, thou art paling!
Hope's glorious light now shines anew!
Ye angels, ye who once forsook me,
Aid now my heart, and keep it true!

Senta. Here may a home at last be granted,
Here may he rest, from danger free!
What is the power within me working?
What is the task it bids me do?
Almighty, now that high Thou hast raised
   me,
Grant me Thy strength, that I be true!

Daland.
       (Returning.)
Your leave!
My people will no longer wait;
Each voyage ended, they expect a feast:
I would enchance it, so I come to ask
If your espousals forward can be press'd.
I think you must with courting be content.
Senta, my child, say, dost thou give consent?

Holländer. O könntest das Geschick Du ahnen
Dem dann mit mir Du angehörst:
Dich würd' es an das Opfer mahnen,
Das Du mir bringst, wenn Treu Du
   schwörst.
Es flöhe schaudernd Deine Jugend,
Dem Loose, dem Du sie willst weih'n:
Nennst Du des Weibes schönste Tugend,
Nennst heil'ge Treue Du nicht Dein!

Senta. Wohl kenn' ich Weibes hohe Pflich'
   ten,—
Sei d'rum getrost, unsel'ger Mann!
Lasz über die das Schicksal richten,
Die seinem Spruche trotzen kann!
In meines Herzens höchster Reine
Kenn' ich der Treue Hochgebot:
Wem ich sie weih', schenk' ich die Eine;
Die Treue bis zum Tod!

Holländer. Ein heil'ger Balsam meinen Wunden,
Dem Schwur, dem hohen Wort entflieszt!

Senta. Von mächt'gem Zauber überwunden,
Reiszt mich's zu seiner Rettung fort:

Holländer. Hört' es: mein Heil hab' ich ge
   funden,
Mächte, die ihr zurück mich stiesz't!
Du Stern des Unheils, sollst erblassen!
Licht meiner Hoffnung leuchte neu.
Ihr Engel, die mich einst verlassen,
Stärkt jetzt dies Herz in seiner Treu'!

Senta. Hier habe Heimath er gefunden,
Hier ruh' sein Schiff im ew'gen Port!
Was ist's, das mächtig in mir lebet?
Was schlieszt berauscht mein Busen ein?
Allmächt'ger, was mich hoch erhebet,
Lasz es die Kraft der Treue sein!
   (DALAND tritt wieder auf.)

Daland. Verzeiht, mein Volk hält drauszer
   sich nicht mehr;
Nach jeder Rückkunft, wisset, giebt's ein
   Fest:—
Verschönern möcht ich's, komme deshalb
   her,
Ob mit Verlobung sich's vereinen läszt?—
Ich denk', Ihr habt nach Herzenswunsch
   gefreit?
Senta, mein Kind, sag', bist auch Du ber
   eit?—

Senta. Here is my hand! I will not rue,
But e'en to death will I be true!

The Dutchman. She gives her hand! I conquer you,
Dread powers of hell, while she is true!

Daland. You will this marriage never rue!
The feast all will rejoice with you!

Senta. Hier meine Hand, und ohne Reu'
Bis in den Tod gelob' ich Treu'!

Holländer. Sie reicht die Hand: gesprochen sei
Hohn, Hölle Dir, durch ihre Treu'!

Daland. Euch soll dies Bündnisz nicht ge reu'n!
Zum Fest! heut musz sich Alles freu'n!

ACT III.

DRITTER AKT.

(A bay with a rocky shore. On one side, DALAND's house in the foreground. The background is occupied by the two ships, DALAND's and the DUTCHMAN's, lying near one another. The night is clear. The Norwegian ship is lighted up; the sailors are making merry upon the deck. The appearance of the Dutch ship presents a strange contrast; an unnatural darkness overspreads it; the stillness of death reigns over it.)

(Seebucht mit felsigem Gestade; das Haus Daland's zu Seite im Vordergrunde. Den Hintergrund nehmen, ziemlich nah bei einander liegend, die beiden schiffe das des Norweger's und des Holländer's ein. Helle Nacht: das norwegische Schiff ist erleuchtet; die Matrosen desselben sind auf dem Verdeck—Jubel und Freude. Die Haltung des holländischen Schiffes bietet einen unheimlichen Contrast: eine unnatürliche Finsterniss ist über dasselbe aus gebreitet; es herrscht Todtenstille auf ihm.)

Chorus of Norwegian Sailors. Steersman, leave the watch!
Steersman, come to us!
Ho! hey! Hey! ho!
See the sails are in! Anchor fast!
Steersman, come!
Fearing neither storm nor rocky strand,
We will all the day right merry be!
Each one has a sweetheart on the land:
We will smoke and drink, and quite forget the sea!
Hus-sas-sa hey!
Rock and storm, ho!
Hal-lo-ho-hey!
We let them go!
Hu-sas-sa hey!
Steersman, leave the watch!
Come, drink with us!

Chor der norwegischen Matrosen. Steuermann, lasz die Wacht!
Steuermann, her zu uns!
Ho! He! Je! Ha!
Hiszt die Segel auf! Anker fest!
Steuermann, her!—
Fürchten weder Wind noch bösen Strand,
Wollen heute 'mal recht lustig sein!
Jeder hat sein Mädel auf dem Land,
Herrlichen Taback und guten Branntewein
Hussassahe!
Klipp' und Sturm draus—
Jallolohe!
Lachen wir aus!
Hussassahe!
Segel ein! Anker fest! Klipp' und Sturm lachen wir aus!
Steuermann her, trink' mit aus!

Chorus of Maidens. Oh, do but look! They dance indeed!
And maidens of course they do not need!

Mädchen. Nein! Seht doch an! Sie tanzen gar!
Der Mädchen bedarf's da nicht fürwahr!

Chorus of Sailors. Ho, maidens! Stop! Where is 't you go?

Matrosen. He! Mädel! Halt! wo geht ihr hin?

The Maidens. What! think you this is all for you?
Your neighbors there must have some also!
Are food and drink for you alone?

Mädchen. Steht euch nach frischem Wein der Sinn?
Eu'r Nachbar dort soll auch was haben,
Ist Trank und Schmaus für euch allein?

Steersman. Of course they must, the wretched fellows!
With thirst they seem to be struck down.

Steuermann. Fürwahr, tragt's hin den armen Knaben,
Vor Durst sie scheinen matt zu sein.

The Sailors. How still they are!

Steersman. How strange a place
No light—of the seamen not a trace!

The Maidens. Ho, sailors—ho! a light we
bring!
Where have they gone? How strange a
thing!

The Sailors. Don't wake them up! Asleep
are they.

The Maidens. Ho, sailors—ho! Answer us,
pray!

The Sailors. Ha, ha! 'tis certain they are
dead,
No need have they for wine or bread!

The Maidens. Hey, sailors, and are you already asleep?
What! are you not meaning our feast-day
to keep?

The Sailors. They lie conceal'd within the
hold,
Like dragons, watching o'er their gold.

The Maidens. Hey, sailors, then will you
not have any wine?
Surely our offer you do not decline?

The Sailors. Both wine and songs disown
they quite;
Within their ship there burns no light.

The Maidens. Say, have you not got any
sweethearts on land?
Will you not dance with us here on the
strand?

The Sailors. They are all old, their hair is grey,
And all their sweethearts, dead are they!

Maidens and Sailors. Hey, sailors! waken up!
We bring you food and a cheering cup!
'T is certain, yes; they must be dead!
No need have they of wine or bread.

The Sailors. The Flying Dutchman you
surely know;
That ship does a likeness to his vessel show.

Matrosen. Man hört sie nicht?

Steuermann. Ei, seht doch nur!
Kein Licht! Von der Mannschaft keine
Spur.

Mädchen. He! Seeleut'! He! Wollt Fack
eln ihr?
Wo seid ihr doch? Man sieht nicht hier.

Matrosen. Weckt sie nicht auf; sie schlafen
noch.

Mädchen. He! Seeleut'! He! Antwortet
doch!

Steuermann und Matrosen. Haha! Wahrhaftig, sie sind todt.
Sie haben Speis' und Trank nicht noth.

Mädchen. Wie, Seeleute? Liegt ihr so faul
schon im Nest?
Ist heute für euch denn nicht auch ein Fest?

Steuermann und Matrosen. Sie liegen fest
auf ihrem Platz,
Wie Drachen hüten sie den Schatz.

Mädchen. Wie, Seeleute? Wollt ihr nicht
goldenen Wein?
Ihr müsset wahrlich doch auch durstig sein,

Steuermann und Matrosen. Sie trinken nicht,
sie singen nicht,
In ihrem Schiffe brennt kein Licht.

Mädchen. Sagt, habt ihr denn nicht auch ein
Schätzchen am Land?
Wollt ihr nicht mit tanzen auf freundlichem
Strand?

Matrosen. Sie sind schon alt und bleich statt
roth,
Und ihre Liebsten, die sind todt.

Mädchen. He, Seeleut'! Seeleut'! wacht
doch auf!
Wir bringen euch Speis' und Trank zu
Hauf!
Matrosen. Sie bringen euch Speis' und Trank
zu Hauf!
Mädchen. Wahrhaftig! Ja, sie scheinen todt.
Sie haben Speis' und Trank nicht noth.

Matrosen. Vom fliegenden Holländer wiszt
ihr ja!
Sein Schiff, wie es leibt, wie es lebt, seht ihr
da.

The Maidens. To wake the crew we pray you spare,
For they are ghosts—we know they are!

Mädchen. So wecket die Mannschaft ja nicht auf!
Gespenster sind's, wir schwören drauf!

The Sailors. For how many years have you been on the sea—
A terror the storm and the rock cannot be!

Matrosen. Wie viel hundert Jahre schon seid ihr zur See?
Euch thut ja der Sturm und die Klippe nicht weh!

The Maidens. Both wine and songs disown they quite;
Within their ship there burns no light.

Mädchen. Sie trinken nicht, sie singen nicht!
In ihrem Schifle brennt kein Licht!

The Sailors. Have you not a letter or message for land,
To be carried safe to some ancestor's hand?

Matrosen. Habt ihr keine Brief', keine Aufträg' für's Land?
Unsern Urgroszvätern wir bringen's zu Hand.

The Maidens. They all are old, their hair is grey,
And all their sweethearts, dead are they!

Mädchen. Sie sind schon alt und bleich statt roth;
Ach! ihre Liebsten, die sind todt.

The Sailors. Hey! Sailors, your canvas spread out to the gale,
And show how the old Flying Dutchman can sail!

Matrosen. Hei! Seeleute! Spannt eure Segel doch auf!
Und zeigt uns des fliegenden Holländers Lauf!

The Maidens. They hear us not! We shake with fear!
They want us not: why linger here?

Mädchen. Sie hören nicht,—uns graust es hier!
Sie wollen nichts,—was rufen wir?

The Sailors. Ye maidens let the dead have rest!
Let us who live your dainties taste!

Matrosen. Ihr Mädel, laszt die Todten ruh'n!
Laszt's uns Lebend'gen glücklich thun!

The Maidens. Well, here—your neighbors quite refuse!

Mädchen. So nehmt, Eu'r Nachbar hat's verschmäht!

The Sailors. How? Come you not yourselves to us?

Steuermann und Matrosen. Wie? Kommt ihr denn nicht selbst an Bord?

The Maidens. No, not just now; but later we may,
After a while. Now drink away,
And, if you will, go dance your best;
But let your weary neighbors rest!

Mädchen. Ei, jetzt noch nicht, es ist nicht spät.
Wir kommen bald, jetzt trinkt nur fort.
Und, wenn ihr wollt, so tanzt dazu,
Nur laszt dem müden Nachbar Ruh'!

The Sailors. Hurrah! We have abundance!
Good neighbors, thanks to you!

Matrosen. Juchhe! Juchhe! da giebt's die Fülle!
Ihr lieben Nachbarn, habet Dank!

Steersman. Let each man fill and drink a bumper!
Good neighbors, thousand thanks to you!

Steuermann. Zum Rand sein Glas ein Jeder fülle!
Lieb Nachbar liefert uns den Trank!

The Sailors. Hal-lo-ho-ho!
Good neighbors, you can speak at least!
Come, waken up, and join our feast!

Matrosen. Halloho! Halloho! Ho! ho! ho!
Lieb Nachbar'n. habt ihr Stimm' und Sprach',
So wachet auf, und macht's uns nach!

Steersman, leave the watch!
Steersman, come to us!
Ho, hey, hey, ha!
See the sailors are in! Anchor fast!
Steersman, come!
We have often watch'd 'mid howling storm;
We have often drunk the briny wave:
Watching takes to-day a fairer form—
Good and tasty wine our sweethearts let us
     have!
Hus-sas-sa-hey!

The Crew of the Flying Dutchman. Yo-ho-
          ho! Ho! oh!
          Huissa!
To the land drives the storm.
     Huissa!
Sails are in! Anchor down!
     Huissa!
To the bay hurry in!
Gloomy captain, go on land,
     Now that seven long years have flown,
Seek a faithful maiden's hand!
     Faithful maiden, be his own!
          Joyful, hui!
          Bridegroom, hui!
     Winds be thy wedding song,
     Ocean rejoices with thee!
Hui! Hark! He pipes!
What! captain, hast thou returned?
Hui! Spread the sails!
And thy bride, say, where is she?
Hui! Off to sea!
     As of old,
No good fortune for thee!
     Ha-ha-ha!
Blow, thou storm-wind, howl and blow!
What care we how fast we go?
We have sails from Satan's store,
Sails that last for evermore—ho-hoe!

Norwegian Sailors. What a song! Are they
          ghosts?
How I fear! Let them hear!
All unite in our song.
Steersman, leave the watch! etc.

FINALE.

(SENTA comes from the house hurriedly; she is followed
by ERICK who is greatly excited.)

Erik. Have I my senses? Heavens! what do
     I see?
A vision? Tell me—is it true?

Steuermann, lasz die Wacht!
Steuermann, her zu uns!
Ho! He! Je! Ha!
Hiszt die Segel auf! Anker fest!—
Steuermann, her!—
Wachten manche Nacht bei Sturm und
     Graus,
Tranken oft des Meer's gesalz'nes Nasz;—
Heute wachen wir bei Saus und Schmaus,
Besseres Getränk giebt Mädel uns vom Fusz!
Hussassahe!
Klipp' und Sturm draus! u.s.w.

Chor der Mannschaft des fliegenden Hollänh
     ers. Johohe! Johohohoe! hohohc
          hoe! Hoe! Hoe! Hoe!
          Huissa!
Nach dem Land treibt der Sturm—
     Huissa!
Segel ein! Anker los!
     Huissa!
In die Bucht laufet ein!
Schwarzer Hauptmann, geh' an's Land!
Sieben Jahre sind vorbei;
Frei' um blonden Mädchens Hand:
Blondes Mädchen, sei ihm treu!
Lustig heut'
Bräutigam!
Sturmwind heult Brautmusik,
Ocean tanzt dazu.
Hui!—Horch, er pfeift!
—Capitain, bist wieder da?—
Hui!—"Segel auf."—
—Deine Braut, sag', wo sie blieb?—
Hui! "Auf in See!"—
Capitain! Capitain! Hast kein Glück in
     der Lieb'!
Hahaha!
Sause, Sturmwind, heule zu!
Uns'ren Segeln läszt du Ruh':
Satan hat sie uns gefei't,
Reiszen nicht in Ewiakeit!

Norwegische Matrosen. Welcher Sang! Ist
     es Spuk? Wie mich's graut!
Stimmet an unser Lied! Singet laut!
Steuermann, lasz die Wacht. u.s.w.

FINALE.

(SENTA kommt bewegten Schrittes aus dem Hause; ihr
folgt ERIK in der höchsten Aufregung.)

Erik. Was muszt' ich hören? Gott! was
     muszt ich sehen!
Ist's Täuschung? Wahrheit? Ist es That'

Senta. Oh, ask me not! Answer dare I not give thee.

Erik. O righteous Heaven! No question—it is true!
Oh, say what harmful pow'r led thee astray?
What is the spell constraining thee so soon
Coldly to rend in twain this faithful heart?
Thy father, ha! the bridegroom he did bring;
Him know I well: I fear'd what might befall!
Yet thou—amazing!—gavest him thine hand
When scarce across the threshold he had pass'd.

Senta. No further! Cease! I must!

Erik. Oh, this obedience, blind as in thy act!
Thy father's hint thou failest not to welcome;
A single blow destroys my loving heart!

Senta. No more! I may not see thee more,
Nor thee remember: higher calls are mine!

Erik. What higher calls? Thy highest is to render
What thou didst vow to give to me—love eternal.

Senta. What love eternal did I vow to give?

Erik. Senta! O Senta! Deniest thou—?

Senta. Frag' nicht, Erik! Antwort darf ich nicht geben.

Erik. Gerechter Gott! Kein Zweifel! Es ist wahr!
Welch unheilvolle Macht risz Dich dahin?
Welche Gewalt verführte Dich so schnell,
Grausam zu brechen dieses treuste Herz?
Dein Vater? ha, den Bräut'gam bracht er mit,—
Wohl kannt ich ihn,—mir ahnte, was geschieht.
Doch Du? Ist's möglich!—reichest Deine Hand
Dem Mann, der Deine Schwelle kaum betrat!

Senta. Nicht weiter! Schweig'! Ich musz! Ich musz!

Erik. O des Gehorsams, blind wie Deine That!
Den Wink des Vaters nanntest Du willkommen,
Mit einem Streich vernichtest Du mein Herz!

Senta. Nicht mehr! Nicht mehr! Ich darf Dich micht mehr seh'n!
Nicht an Dich denken. Hohe Pflicht gebeut's!

Erik. Welch hohe Pflicht? Ist's Höh're nicht zu halten,
Was Du mir einst gelobet, ew'ge Treue?

Senta. Wie? Ew'ge Treue hätt' ich Dir gelobt?

Erik. Senta! O Senta! Läugnest Du?

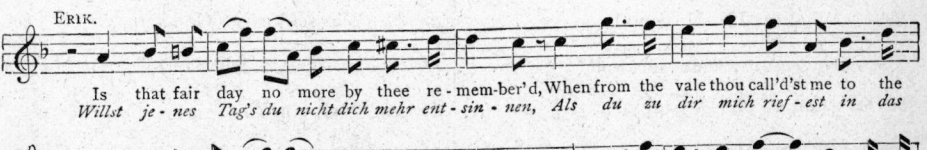

Is that fair day no more by thee re-mem-ber'd, When from the vale thou call'd'st me to the
Willst je-nes Tag's du nicht dich mehr ent-sin-nen, Als du zu dir mich rief-est in das

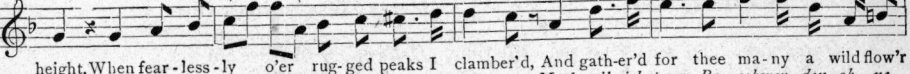

height, When fear-less-ly o'er rug-ged peaks I clamber'd, And gath-er'd for thee ma-ny a wild flow'r
Thal? Als, dir des Hoch-land's Blu-me zu ge-win-nen, Muth-voll ich trug Be-schwer-den oh-ne

bright? Re-member'st, as on rock-y sum-mit stand-ing, Thy fa-ther's ship we saw ride on the
Zahl? Gedenk'st du wie auf stei-lem Fel-sen-rif-fe Vom U-fer wir den Va-ter schei-der

tide? We watch'd the sails with favor'd breeze ex-pand-ing, Did he not thee un-to my care con-
sah'n? Er zog da-hin auf weiss be-schwingtem Schif-fe, Und mei-nem Schutz ver-trau-te er dich.

fide, Yea, to my care did he not thee con-fide, To my care .. did he not thee con-
an, Ja, mei-nem Schutz ver-trau-te er dich an, Mei-nem Schutz . ver-traut-te er dich

piu animato.   *rall.*

fide? Thy arm so sweet-ly round my neck en-twin-ing, Didst pledge thy love a-new, how hap-py
an. Als sich dein Arm um mei-nem Nacken schlang, Ges-tan-dest du mir Lie-be nicht auf's
     animato.

both! Did'st press my hand, as on my breast re-clin-ing, Say, was not that the seal-ing of thy
Neu'? Was bei der Hän-de Druck mich hehr durch-drang, Sag', war's nicht die Ver-sich'rung dei-ner

troth? Say, was not that, in-deed, the seal-ing of thy troth? Did'st press my
Treu'? Sag', war es nicht, war's nicht Ver-sich'rung dei-ner Treu'? Was bei der

                                                                        that   the
                                                                        die   Ver-

hand as on my breast .... re-clin-ing, Say, was not that— that the
Hän-de Druck so hehr . .mich durch-drang, Sag', war es nicht die Ver-
                                        ad lib.

seal-ing, that the seal · · ing of · · · · · thy troth?
sich-'rung, die Ver-sich · · · · 'rung dei- · · · · ner Treu'?

The Dutchman. Abandon'd! Ah! Aban-don'd! All is forever lost!	Holländer. Verloren! Ach! verloren! **Ewig** verlor'nes Heil!
Erik. What see I? Heavens!	Erik. Was seh' ich? Gott!
The Dutchman. Senta, farewell!	Holländer. Senta, leb' wohl!
Senta. Oh, stay! Unhappy!	Senta. Halt ein, Unsel'ger.
Erik. What meanest thou?	Erik. Was beginnst Du?
The Dutchman. To sea! To sea! **till time** is ended! Thy sacred promise be forgot. Thy sacred promise and my fate! Farewell! I wish not to destroy thee!	Holländer. In See. in See! In See für ewige Zeiten! Um Deine Treue ist's gethan, Um Deine Treue, um mein Heil. Lebwohl, ich will dich nicht verderben!
Erik. Oh, horror! what a face!	Erik. Entsetzlich, dieser Blick!

Senta. Oh, stay!
From hence thou never more shalt flee!

The Dutchman. Set the sails! Anchor up!
Then bid farewell to land for ever!

Senta. Ha, canst thou doubt if I am faithful?
Unhappy, what has blinded thee?
Oh, stay, the vow we made forsake not!
What I have promised kept shall be.

Erik. What hear I? Heavens! and what be-
hold I?
Can I in ear, in eye believe?
Senta! Art thou then bent on ruin?
To me a spell doth Satan weave.

The Dutchman. Now hear, and learn the fate
from which thou wilt be saved:
Condemn'd am I to bear a frightful for-
tune—
Ten times would death appear a brighter
lot.
A woman's hand alone the curse can lighten,
If she will love me, and till death be true.
Still to be faithful thou has vow'd,
Yet has not God thy promise:
This rescues thee; for know, unhappy,
what a fate is theirs
Who break the troth which they to me have
plighted:
Endless damnation is their doom!
Victims untold have fallen 'neath this curse
through me—
Yet, Senta, thou shalt escape.
Farewell! All hope is fled for evermore!

Erik. Oh, help her! let her not be lost!

Senta. Well do I know thee—well do I know
thy doom.
I knew thy face when I beheld thee first!
The end of thine affliction comes:
My love till death shall take thy curse away!

Erik, Daland, Mary, and Chorus. What
behold I?

The Dutchman. Thou knowest me not, nor
thinkest who I am;

Senta. Halt ein! Von dannen sollst Du nimmer fliehn.

(Der Holländer gibt ein gellendes Zeichen auf seine
Pfeife und ruft der Mannschaft seines Schiffes zu.)

Holländer. Segel auf! Anker los! Sagt Lebwohl auf Ewigkeit dem Lande!

Senta. Ha zweifelst Du an meiner Treue?
Unseliger,—was verblendet Dich!
Halt ein! Halt ein!
Das Bündnisz nicht bereue,
Was ich gelobte, halte ich.
Halt ein! Halt ein!

Erik. Was hör' ich, Gott, was musz ich sehn!
Musz ich dem Ohr, musz ich dem Auge
traun!
Was hör' ich, Gott, Senta!
Willst Du zu Grunde geben?
Zu mir, zu mir: Du bist in Satans Klau'n!

Holländer. Erfahre das Geschick, vor dem ich
Dich bewahr!
Verdammt bin ich zum gräszlichsten der
Loose!
Zehnfacher Tod, wär mir erwünschte Lust.
Vom Fluch! ein Weib allein kann mich
erlösen,
Ein Weib, das Treue bis in den Tod mir
hält.
Wohl hast Du Treue mir gelobt,
Doch vor dem Ewigen noch nicht, diesz
rettet Dich!
Denn wisz'! Unselige, welches das Geschick,
Das Jene trifft, die mir die Treue brechen,
Ewige Verdammnisz ist ihr Loos!
Zahllose Opfer fielen diesem Spruch durch
mich.
Du aber sollst gerettet sein.
Lebwohl, fahr hin, mein Heil in Ewigkeit

Erik. Zu Hülfe, rettet, rettet Sie!

Senta. Wohl kenn ich Dich! Wohl kenn ich
Dein Geschick;
Ich kannte Dich, als ich zuerst Dich sah!
Das Ende Deiner Qual ist da!
Ich bin's, durch deren Treu Dein Heil Du
finden sollst!

{ *Erik.* Helft Ihr, Sie ist verloren!
{ *Mary.* Was erblicke ich?
{ *Daland.* Was erblicke ich? Gott!

Holländer. Du kennst mich nicht, Du ahnst
nicht wer ich bin!

But ask the sea in ev'ry climate,
Or ask the seamen who the ocean wide have
    cross'd :
They know my ship, of all good men the
    terror—
The Flying Dutchman am I call'd.

Daland, Erik, Mary, and Chorus.   Senta!
Senta! what wouldst thou do?

Senta.   Praise thou thine angel for what he
    saith :
Here stand I, faithful, yea, till death!

(She casts herself into the sea. The Dutchman's ship,
with all her crew, sinks immediately. The sea rises high,
and sinks back in a whirlpool. In the glow of the sunset
are clearly seen, over the wreck of the ship, the forms of
SENTA and the DUTCHMAN, embracing each other, rising
from the sea, and floating upwards.)

Befrage die Meere aller Zonen.
Befrage den Seemann, der den Ocean
    durchstrich ;
Erkenn' diesz Schiff, der Schrecken aller
    Frommen,
Den : "Fliegenden Holländer" nennt man
    mich.

Die Mannschaft des Fliegenden Holländer.
Jo ho, hoe!

Mary, Erik, und Daland.   Senta, Senta, was
willst Du thun?

Senta.   Preis Deinen Engel und sein Gebot,
Hier steh' ich treu Dir bis zum Tod.

(Sie stürzt sich in das Meer;—vogleich versinkt das
Schiff des HOLLANDER's mit aller Mannschaft. Das Meer
schwillt hoch auf und sinkt in einem Würbel wieder zurück.
Im Glühroth der aufgehenden Sonne sieht man über den
Trümmern des Schiffec die verklärten Gestalten SENTA's
und des HOLLANDER's sich umhslungen haltend dem Meere
entsteigen und aufwärt's schweben.)

TANNHÄUSER

TANNHÄUSER, knight and minstrel, has in an evil hour sought refuge from the griefs of earth in the hill of Venus* (the Horselberg, in Thuringia), where, surrounded by her heathen train, the goddess is supposed to hold her court amid everlasting revels, destroying the souls of men who fall into her toils.

The opera opens when Tannhäuser, having dwelt with her a whole year, has become weary of monotonous joys, and in momentary returns of his better nature, longs for earthly life, with its mingled pains and pleasures. He implores the goddess to release him, and after a protracted struggle, regains his liberty. The scene now suddenly changes; he finds himself in a valley between the Wartburg and the Horselberg, and whilst he is still sunk in a prayer of gratitude at being restored to liberty, the Minstrel Knights, led by the Landgrave, enter, recognize him, and persuade him to rejoin them.

ACT II. — *The Tournament of Song.* — The theme of the contest is to be the Nature and Praise of Love, and the prize of the victor the hand of Elisabeth, whom Tannhäuser loves, and by whom he is beloved. During the contest Tannhäuser disputes all that the other minstrels say, and, having loved profanely, outrages the assembly by his revelations of what he conceives to be the Nature of Love. The minstrels challenge him, and would destroy him, but for the sudden interposition of Elisabeth. A train of Pilgrims is taking its way to Rome. Tannhäuser, who sees too late that an illusion had blinded him, despairingly joins them, whils. Elisabeth, on whom the discovery of his unworthiness has struck a mortal blow, conjures him to repent.

ACT III. — Wolfram, a man of noble and devoted nature, who vainly loves Elisabeth, awaits with her the return of the Pilgrims. They come, but Tannhäuser is not amongst them. Elisabeth now solemnly consecrates herself to the Virgin. When she has departed, Tannhäuser enters furtively, in pitiable plight, on his way to reenter the Hill of Venus. He tells Wolfram of his pilgrimage, of his self-tormenting remorse, of his humble appeal to the Pope, who, learning the nature of his sin, declared it as impossible for him to be absolved as for the staff he held in his hand again to put forth fresh leaves. Spurned and accused by all, nothing is left for him but to return to the joys he loathes. Wolfram's appeals are vain to dissuade him; he invokes the infernal train, which is becoming dimly visible, when a chant is heard, followed by the funeral procession of Elisabeth. A second band of Pilgrims appears on the heights announcing that a miracle has been wrought. During the night the staff of the Pope has put forth fresh green leaves, and he sends into all lands to declare the Almighty's pardon to the repentant sinner.

(With true medieval sternness, Tannhäuser is not redeemed in the old legend, but doomed to return to the domain of Venus, where, conscience-stricken, he finds everlasting wretchedness.)

*Early Christianity banished the Scandinavian as well as the classical divinities into mid-earth. Thus "Dame Holda," the young Shepherd in the third scene — the wise gentle Holda, who brought the Spring, and was welcomed with triumphant processions through out the German North.

TANNHÄUSER

ACT I	AKT I
—	—

SCENE I	ERSTE SCENE

The Hill of Venus. The stage represents the interior of the Hill of Venus. A wide cave, bending at the back towards the right side, where it appears to be indefinitely prolonged. In the farthest visible background a bluish lake is seen in which Naïads are bathing; on its undulating banks Sirens are reclining. In the extreme foreground Venus is extended on a couch; before her, in a kneeling attitude, is Tannhäuser, his head sunk on her knees. The whole cave is illuminated by a rosy light. In the centre of the stage is a group of dancing Nymphs. There are mounds at the sides of the cave where tender couples are reclining, some of whom join the dances of the Nymphs in the course of the scene. A train of Bacchantes rushes from the back of the cave in a tumultuous dance; they wildly dart through the groups of Nymphs and under couples, inciting them to a frantic excitement.

Die Bühne stellt das Innere des Venusberges dar. Weite Grotte, welche sich im Hintergrunde durch eine Biegung nach rechts wie unabsehbar dahinzieht. Im fernsten sichtbaren Hintergrunde dehnt sich ein bläulicher See aus; in ihm erblickt man die badenden Gestalten von Najaden; auf seinen erhöhten Ufervorsprüngen sind Sirenen gelagert. Im äussersten Vordergrunde links liegt Venus auf einem Lager ausgestreckt, vor ihr halb knieend Tannhäuser, das Haupt in ihrem Schoosse. Die ganze Grotte ist durch rosiges Licht erleuchtet. Den Mittelgrund nimmt eine Gruppe tanzender Nymphen ein; auf etwas erhöhten Vorsprüngen an den Seiten der Grotte sind liebende Paare gelagert, von denen sich einzelne nach und nach in den Tanz der Nymphen mischen. Ein Zug von Bacchantinnen kommt aus dem Hintergrunde in wildem Tanz dahergebraust, sie durchziehen mit trunkenen Gebärden die Gruppen der Nymphen und liebenden Paare, welche durch sie bald zu grösserem Ungestüme hingerissen werden.

Chorus

Come to these bowers,
Radiant with flowers;
Here love shall bless you—
Here endeth longing;
Soft arms shall press you,
'Mid blisses thronging.

Gesang der Sirenen.

Naht euch dem Strande,
Naht euch dem Lande
Wo in den Armen
Glühender Liebe
Selig Erwarmen
Still' eure Triebe!

[The dancers suddenly pause from their wild tumult and listen to the singing, after which the dance recommences and rises to the wildest excitement. When the Bacchic frenzy is at its height, a sudden weariness is seen to spread amongst the dancers. The tender couples separate themselves from the dance and rest near the entrance of the cave. The train of Bacchantes disappears in the background, where a mist gathers and spreads in density. In the foreground also a thick mist gradually sinks, and envelops the groups of sleepers in rosy clouds, so that only a small space in the front of the stage remains visible, where Venus and Tannhäuser remain alone in their former attitude.

[Die Tanzenden halten in der leidenschaftlichsten Gruppe plötzlich an und lauschen dem Gesange, worauf sich der Tanz von Neuem belebt und zu dem äussersten Grade wilden Ungestümes gelangt. Mit dem Momente der trunkensten bacchantischen Wuth tritt eine schnell um sich greifende Erschlaffung ein. Die liebenden Paare scheiden sich allmählig vom Tanze aus und lagern sich wie in angenehmer Ermattung auf den Vorsprüngen der Grotte; der Zug der Bacchantinnen verschwindet nach dem Hintergrunde zu, vor welchem sich ein immer dichter werdender Dunst ausbreitet. Auch im Vordergrunde senkt sich allmählig ein dichterer Duft herab und verhüllt die Gruppen der Schlafenden wie in rosige Wolken, so dass endlich der sichtbare Theil der frei gelass'nen Bühne sich nur noch auf einen kleinen Raum beschränkt, in welchem Venus und Tannhäuser in ihrer früheren Stellung allein zurückbleiben.

SCENE II	ZWEITE SCENE

Venus.	Oh, say my love, where stray thy thoughts?
Tann.	No more, no more! O that I now might waken.
Venus.	Say, what grief is thine?
Tann.	I dreamt I heard upon the air
	Sounds that to me were long estrang'd—
	The silv'ry chime of bells was borne on the breeze,
	Oh, say, how long has earth been lost to me?

Venus.	Geliebter, sag', wo weilt dein Sinn?
Tann.	Zu viel! Zu viel! O, dass ich nun Erwachte!
Venus.	Sprich, was kümmert dich?
Tann.	Im Traum war mir's, als hörte ich—
	Was meinem Ohr so lange fremd!—
	Als hörte ich der Glocken froh Geläute:—
	O, sag'! Wie lange hört ich's doch nicht mehr?

Venus. What folly seizes thee? Why thus disturbed?
Tann. The time I dwelt here with thee
By days I cannot measure —
Seasons pass me, how I scarcely know:
The radiant sun I see no longer;
Strange hath become the heavens' starry splendor
The sweet verdure of spring,
The gentle token of earth's renewing life
The nightingale no more I hear
Who sings of hope and promise.
All these delights, are they for ever lost?

Venus. What! art thou wav'ring? Why these vain
lamentings?
Can'st thou so soon weary of the blisses
That love immortal hath cast round thee?
Can it be—dost thou now repent that thou'rt
divine?
Hast thou so soon forgotten how thy heart was
mourning,
Till by me thou wert consoled?
My minstrel, come, let not thy harp be silent;
Recall the rapture—sing the praise and bliss of
love
In tones that won for thee love's self to be thy
slave!
Of love sing only, for her treasures all are thine.

Venus. Wohin vierlierst du dich? Was ficht dich an?
Tann. Die Zeit, die hier ich weil', ich kann sie nicht
Ermessen:—Tage, Monde—giebt's für mich
Nicht mehr, denn nicht mehr sehe ich die Sonne,
Nicht mehr des Himmels freundliche Gestirne;
Den Halm seh' ich nicht mehr, der frisch
ergrünend
Den neuen Sommer bringt;—die Nachtigall
Nicht hör' ich mehr, die mir den Lenz
verkünde:—
Hör ich sie nie, seh' ich sie niemals mehr?

Venus. Ha! was vernehm' ich? welche thör'ge Klagen!
Bist du so bald der holden Wunder müde,
Die meine Liebe dir bereitet? Oder
Wie? Reut es dich so sehr, ein Gott zu sein?
Hast du so bald vergessen, wie du einst
Gelitten, während jetzt du dich erfreust?
Mein Sänger, auf! Ergreife deine Harfe!
Die Liebe fei're, die so herrlich du besingst,
Dass du der Liebe Göttin selber dir gewannst!
Die Liebe feire, da ihr höchster Preis dir ward!

know. But while my sense thou hast en-chant-ed, by thy great love
-hin. Doch ster-blich, ach! bin ich ge-blie-ben, und ü-ber-gross

my heart is daunt-ed; a god a-lone........ can dwell in
ist mir dein Lie-ben; wenn stets ein Gott........ ge-nie-ssen

joy to mor-tal frail,........ its bliss-es cloy; I
kann, bin ich dem Wech--sel un-ter-than; nicht

would be sway'd by...... pain and pleas-ure, in Na-ture's
Lust al-lein liegt.... mir am Her-zen, aus Freu-den

sweet al-ter-nate meas-ure, I must a-way from thee, or
sehn' ich mich nach Schmer-zen! Aus dei-nem Rei-che muss ich

die,.... Oh, Queen be-lov'd! God-dess, let.... me fly!
flieh'n. O Kö-ni-gin! Göt-tin, lass.... mich ziehn!

Venus. Ungrateful! What, shall thus my love be slighted By thee, in whom so dear my heart delighted? What praise is thine of joys thou yet would'st flee? My vaunted charms, alas! have wearied thee.	*Venus.* Treuloser! Weh! Was lässest du mich hören? Du wagest meine Liebe zu verhöhnen? Du preisest sie und willst sie, dennoch fliehn, Zum Ueberdruss ist dir mein Reiz gediehn?
Tann. Oh, fair perfection! frown not on thy servant! Thy charms' excess, oh, goddess, have unmanned me!	*Tann.* O, schöne Göttin! Wolle mir nicht zürnen! Dein übergrosser Reiz ist's, den ich meide.
Venus. Traitor, beware, then? Serpent heart ungrateful! Ah! not thus we part. Ah, no, thou shalt not leave me.	*Venus.* Weh' dir! Verräther! Heuchler! Undankbarer! Ich lass' dich nicht! Du darfst von mir nicht ziehn!
Tann. But, reft of thy sweet presence, joy is hateful; But fate sternly impels me—for liberty I sigh.	*Tann.* Nie war mein Lieben grösser, niemals wahrer Als jetzt, da ich für ewig dich muss fliehn!
Venus. Beloved one, come! Soft dreams of wonder, Within yon grot shall wrap thee round; The purple shadows breaking yonder, With murmuring music shall resound. There joys unknown I'll shower upon thee: Within these arms thou shalt have rest, Until for mine again I've won thee— Till faith renewed thy lips have confess'd. The od'rous airs shall tell in dulcet voices That bliss divine once more our hearts rejoices. Love hath a solace for thy restless heart; 'Twere worse than dying, from sweet love to part. This day renew those tender vows we plighted— In joy immortal be our hearts united. Thou shalt no more adore the power of love, No! love itself to worship thou, belov'd, shalt move.	*Venus.* Geliebter, komm! Sieh dort die Grotte, Von ros'gen Düften mild durchwallt; Entzücken böt' selbst einem Gotte Der süss'sten Freuden Aufenthalt: Besänftigt auf dem weichsten Pfühle, Flieh' deine Glieder jeder Schmerz, Dein brennend Haupt umwehe Kühle, Wonnige Glut durchschwell' dein Herz. Aus holder Ferne mahnen süsse Klänge, Dass dich mein Arm in trauter Näh' umschlänge; Von meinen Lippen schlürfst du Göttertrank, Aus meinen Augen strahlt dir Liebesdank:— Ein Freudenfest soll unsrem Bund entstehen. Der Liebe Feier lass uns froh begehen! Nicht sollst du ihr ein scheues Opfer weihn;— Nein!—mit der Liebe Göttin schwelge im Verein!

Sireno. Come to these bowers,
Radiant with flowers, &c.

Venus. My hero and my heart's love! Wilt thou fly?

Tann. While I have life, alone my harp shall praise thee;
No meaner thing shall e'er my song inspire.
Nought can have grace or charm but it obeys thee,
Of all that lives thou best and chief desire.
The fire thou'st kindled in my longing spirits,
An altar flame shall burn for thee alone;
My song shall be divine, but by the merit
That, as thy champion, harp and sword I own.
And yet for earth I'm yearning.
In thy soft chains with shame I'm burning,
'Tis freedom I must win or die—
For freedom I can all defy;
To strife or glory forth I go,
Come life or death, come joy or woe,
No more in bondage will I sigh!
Oh, queen, beloved goddess, let me fly!

Venus. Then go, oh traitor heart! away,
Thou madman! Go—I hold thee not!
I set thee free! Away!
Go forth—thy heart's desire shall be thy doom!
Go to the cold and joyless earth,
Where neither love nor life can bloom,
Whence every smiling god hath flown,
Where dark suspicion first had its birth:
Go forth, thou madman!
There seek thy joy, and seek in vain.
Soon will this fever quit thy soul;
Humbled and sorr'wing thou'lt return—
Remorse shall gnaw thee, naught will console:
For joys remember'd thou shalt burn!

Tann. Ah, fair enchantress, fare thee well!
Never to thee I can return.

Venus. Ah! If thou never shouldst return—
If thou forget me—
Oh, to lasting torments I doom
Th' accurs'd and faithless race of man:
For my delights they all shall vainly languish—
The world a desert, and its lord a slave.
Go forth, then—go, thy doom to brave!

Tann. Love never more will bless thy slave.

Venus. Go forth, then, till thy heart awake.

Tann. Ah, love, I go, altho' it break.

Venus. Thou'lt be received with hate and scorn.

Tann. Repentance heals a heart forlorn.

Venus. Never to thee will heaven ope;
Return, then, if there is no hope.

Tann. No hope! my hope resteth in heaven.

SCENE III

Tannhäuser — A Young Shepherd — Pilgrims,— Tannhäuser, who has not quitted his position, suddenly finds himself in a beautiful vale. Blue sky and sunshine; at the back the Wartburg. Through an opening in the valley the Horselberg is seen. Halfway up the ascent a path leads into the valley from the direction of the Wartburg, where it turns aside; in the foreground is a shrine of the Virgin on a small eminence, to which there is a practicable ascent. From the heights the sound of sheep-bells is heard. On a rocky eminence a young shepherd is reclining, turned towards the valley, playing on his pipe.

A Young Shepherd.

Dame Holda stepped from the mountain's heart,
To roam thro' wood and thro' meadow;
Sweet sounds and low around me did start—
I longed I might follow her shadow.
And there dreamt I a golden dream,
And when again the day did gleam.

Sirenen. Naht euch dem Strande,
Naht euch dem Lande, u. s. w.

Venus. Mein Ritter! Mein Geliebter! Willst du flieh'n

Tann. Stets soll nur dir, mein Lied ertönen!
Gesungen laut sei nur dein Preis von mir!
Dein süsser Reiz ist Quelle alles Schönen,
Und jedes holde Wunder stammt von dir.
Die Glut, die du mir in das Herz gegossen,
Als Flamme lodre hell sie dir allein!
Ja, gegen alle Welt will unverdrossen
Fortan ich nun dein kühner Streiter sein.—
Doch hin muss ich zur Welt der Erden,
Bei dir kann ich nur Sklave werden;
Nach Freiheit doch verlange ich,
Nach Freiheit, Freiheit dürstet's mich;
Zu Kampf und Streite will ich stehen,
Sei's auch auf Tod und Untergehen:—
Drum muss aus deinem Reich ich fliehn,
O, Königin, Göttin? lass mich ziehn!—

Venus. Zieh hin, Wahnsinniger, zieh hin!
Verräther, sieh! nicht halt' ich dich.
Ich geb' dich frei,—zieh hin! zieh hin
Was du verlangst, das sei dein Loos,
Hin zu den kalten Menschen flieh',
Vor deren blödem, trübenn Wahn
Der Freude Götter wir entfloh'n
Tief in der Erde wärmenden Schoos,
Zieh hin, Bethörter! Suche dein Heil,
Suche dein Heil—und find' es nie!
Bald weicht der Stolz aus deiner Seel',—
Demüthig seh' ich dich mir nahn,—
Zerknirscht, zertreten suchst du mich auf
Flehst, um die Wunder meiner Macht.

Tann. Ach schöne Göttin, lebe wohl!
Nie kehre ich zu dir zurück.

Venus. Ha, kehrest du mir nie znrück! . . .
Kehrst du nicht wieder, ha! so sei verfluchet!
Von mir das ganze menschliche Geschlecht!
Nach meinen Wundern dann vergebens suchet:
Die Welt sei öde, und ihr Held ein Knecht!—
Kehr' wieder! Kehre mir zurück!

Tann. Nie mehr erfreu' mich Liebesglück!

Venus. Kehr' wieder, wenn dein Herz dich zieht!—

Tann. Für ewig dein Geliebter flieht.

Venus. Wenn alle Welt dich von sich stösst!—

Tann. Von Bann werd' ich durch Buss' erlöst.

Venus. Nie wird Vergebung dir zu Theil,—
Kehr' wieder, schliesst sich dir das Heil.

Tann. Mein Heil! Mein Heil ruht in Maria!

DRITTE SCENE

Tannhäuser—Ein junger Hirt—Pilger.—Tannhäuser, der seine, Stellung nicht verlassen, befindet sich plötzlich in ein schönes Thal versetzt. Blauer Himmel, heitere Sonnenbeleuchtung. Rechts im Hintergrunde die Wartburg; durch die Thalöffnung nach links erblickt man den Hörselberg. Rechts führt auf der halben Höhe des Thales ein Bergweg von der Richtung der Wartburg her nach dem Vordergrunde zu, wo er dann seitwärts abbiegt; in demselben Vordergrunde ist ein Muttergottes-Bild, zu welchem ein niedriger Bergvorsprung hinaufführt. Von der Hohe links vernimm man das Geläute von Herde-Glocken; auf einem hohen Vorsprunge sitzt ein junger Hirt mit der Schalmei.

Hirt.

Frau Holda kam aus dem Berg hervor,
Zu ziehen durch Flur und Auen;
Gar süssen Klang vernahm da mein Ohr,
Mein Auge begehrte zu schauen —
Da träumt' ich manchen holden Traum.
Und als mein Aug' erschlossen kaum.

The spell was gone that bound me:
'Twas May, sweet May, around me.
New songs of joy attune my lay,
For May hath come — the balmy May!

Chorus of Elder Pilgrims.

To Thee, O Lord, my steps I bend,
In Thee both joy and sorrow end!
Oh, Mary, pure and gracious one,
Bless thou the road we have begun!
Oh, see my heart, by guilt oppress'd —
I faint, I sink beneath my burden!
Nor will I cease, nor will I rest,
Till heav'nly mercy grants me pardon.
At thy august and holy shrine,
I go to seek the grace divine;
Thrice blessed who thy promise know,
Absolved by penance shall they go.

Shep. God speed, God speed to Rome!
There for my soul, oh, breathe a prayer!

Tann. Almighty, praise to Thee!
Great are the marvels of Thy mercy

Pil. To Thee, O Lord, my steps I bend
In Thee both joy and sorrow end;
Oh, Mary, pure and gracious one,
Bless thou the road we have begun

Tann. Oh, see my heart, by guilt oppress'd —
I faint, I sink beneath the burden!
Nor will I cease, nor will I rest,
Till heav'nly mercy grants me pardon.

SCENE IV

On the eminence the Landgrave and Minstrels, in hunting array, are seen to descend from a forest path.

Land. Who is yon knight, so deep absorbed in prayer?
Walt. A pilgrim, sure.
Bit. By ev'ry sign, a noble.
Wolf. Our lost one!
All. Henry! Henry! is it thou?

Land. Is't no delusion?
Dost thou, then, return to us,
Whom thou so rashly didst abandon?
Bit. Say, what doth thy return this day forbode us?
Is't friendship? or a challenge, as of old?
Walt. Com'st thou as friend, or scornful foe?
All except Wolfram.
As foe?
Wolf. Oh, ask him not! His looks bespeak not scorning!
We welcome thee, thou gallant minstrel;
Alas! too long thou wert from us estrang'd.
Walt. Yes, welcome, if thou com'st in peace!
Bit. All hail! if we as friends can greet.
All. All hail, all hail—we welcome thee!

Land. I, too would welcome thy return;
But say, where tarry'st thou so long?
Tann. In strange and distant realms I wandered far,
Where neither peace nor rest were ever found.
Ask not! at enmity I am with none;
We meet as friends—let me in peace depart.

Land. Depart thou shalt not—for our own we claim thee.
Walt. Thou must not go,
Bit. From us thou shalt not part.
Tann. I must! Onwards I'm driven ever,
Ne'er upon earth can I have rest.
The past to me is closed for ever,
I'm doomed to roam alone, unblest.

Da strahlte warm die Sonnen,
Der Mai, der Mai, war kommen.
Nun spiel' ich lustig die Schalmei:—
Der Mai ist da, der liebe Mai!

Gasang der älteren Pilger.

Zu dir wall' ich, mein Herr und Gott,
Der du des Sünders Hoffnung bist!
Gelobt sei, Jungfrau süss und rein,
Der Wallfahrt wolle günstig sein!—
Ach, schwer drückt mich der Sünden Last
Kann länger sie nicht mehr ertragen;
Drum will ich auch nicht Ruh' noch Rast,
Und wähle gern mir Müh' und Plagen.
Am hohen Fest der Gnadenhuld
In Demuth sühn' ich meine Schuld;
Gesegnet, wer im Glauben treu,
Er wird erlöst durch Buss' und Reu'.

Hirt. Glück auf! Glück auf nach Rom!
Betet für meine arme Seele!

Tann. Allmächt'ger, dir sei Preis!
Hehr sind die Wunder deiner Gnade.

Pilg. Zu dir wall' ich, mein Herr und Gott,
Der du des Pilgers Hoffnung bist!
Gelobet sei, Jungfrau süss und rein,
Der Wallfahrt wolle günstig sein!

Tann. Ach, schwer drückt mich der Sünden Last,
Kann länger sie nicht mehr ertragen;
Drum will ich auch nicht Ruh' noch Rast
Und wähle gern mir Müh' und Plagen.

VIERTE SCENE

Von der Anhöhe links herab, aus einem Waldwege treten der Landgraf und die Sänger in Jägertraeht einzelnd auf.

Land. Wer ist der dort in brünstigen Gebete?
Walt. Ein Büsser wohl.
Bit. Nach seiner Tracht ein Ritter,
Wolf. Er ist es!
Die Sanger und der Landgraf.
Heinrich! Heinrich! Seh' ich recht?
Land. Du bist es wirklich? Kehrest in dem Kreis
Zurück, den du in Hochmuth stolz verliessest?
Bit. Sag', was uns deine Wiederkunft bedeutet?
Versöhnung? Oder gilt's erneu'tem Kampf?
Walt. Nah'st du als Freund uns oder Feind?
Die andern Sänger ausser Wolfram.
Als Feind?
Wolf. O fraget nicht! Ist dies des Hochmuths Miene?
Gegrüsst sei uns, du kühner Sänger,
Der ach! so lang' in uns'rer Mitte fehlt!
Walt. Willkommen, wenn du friedlich nah'st!
Bit. Gegrüsst, wenn du uns Freund nennst!
Alle Sänger.
Gegrüsst! Gegrüsst! Gegrüsst sei uns!
Land. So sei willkommen denn auch mir!
Sag' an, wo weiltest du so lang?
Tann. Ich wanderte in weiter, weiter Fern',—
Da wo ich nimmer Rast noch Ruhe fand.
Fragt nicht! Zum Kampf mit euch nicht kam
ich her.
Seid mir versöhnt und lasst mich weiter zieh'n!
Land. Nicht doch! Der Uns're bist du neu geworden.
Walt. Du darfst nicht zieh'n.
Bit. Wir lassen dich nicht fort.
Tann. Lasst mich! Mir frommet kein Verweilen,
Und nimmer kann ich rastend steh'n;
Mein Weg heisst mich nur vorwärts eilen,
Dennrückwärts darf ich niemals seh'n.

All.	Oh, stay, be ours; let us not sever 'Mid friends and home thou shalt find rest. What dost thou seek with vain endeavor? Why is thy soul with grief oppress'd?	*Der Landgraf und die Sänger.* O bleib', bei uns sollst du verweilen, Wir lassen dich nicht von uns gehn Du suchtest uns, warum enteilen Nach solchem kurzen Wiedersehn?
Wolf.	Here dwells Elisabeth.	*Wolf.* Bleib' bei Elisabeth!
Tann.	Elisabeth! oh, ruth of Heaven! That name ador'd once more I hear!	*Tann.* Elisabeth!—O Macht des Himmels, Rufst du den süssen Namen mir?
Wolf.	He is no foe who doth that name to thee recall. My sovereign lord, permit that I may tell him of the prize he won.	*Wolf.* Nicht sollst du Feind mich schelten, dass ich ihn Genannt!—Erlaubest du mir, Herr, dass ich Verkünder seines Glücks ihm sei?
Land.	Tell him the marvel that his song hath wrought; And keep him, Heav'n, in virtue, that nobly he may own it.	*Land.* Nenn ihm den Zauber, den er ausgeübt, Und Gott verleih' ihm Tugend, Das würdig er ihn löse!—

No. 2   WHEN FOR THE PALM.

When for the palm in song we were con-tend-ing, and oft.... thy conq'ring strain the wreath had
Als du in küh-nem San - ge uns be-strit-test, bald sieg - reich ge - gen uns - re Lie - der

won, our songs a - non thy vic - to - ry, sus-pend-ing, one glo-rious prize was won by
sangst, durch uns - re Kunst Be - sie - gung bald er - lit - test, ein Preis doch war's den du al -

thee a - lone, one glo - rious prize was won by thee a - lone. Was't
- lein errangst, ein, Preis doch war's, den du al - lein er - rangst. War's

lento.
ma - gic, or a pow'r di - vine, that wrought thro' thee the won-drous sign, thy harp and song, In
Zau - ber, war es rei - ne Macht, durch die solch Wun - der du vollbracht, an dei - nen Sang voll

bliss - ful hour en - thrall'd of roy - al maids the flow'r, thy harp and song, in bliss - ful
Wonn' und Lied ge - bannt die tu - gend-reich - ste Maid, an dei - nen Sang voll Wonn' und

accelerating the time a little.
hour enthrall'd of roy - all maids the flow'r! or ah, when thou in scorn hadst left us,
Lied gebannt die tu - gendreich-ste Maid? D on, ach! Als du uns stolz ver-las - sen,

her heart was clos'd to joy and song, of her sweet pres - ence she be - reft us,
verschloss ihr Herz sich uns-rem Lied; wir sa - hen ih - re Wang' er - blas-sen

gradually animating the time.   *rall. . . . .*
for thee in vain she wea - ried long; ah, for thee,........ in vain she wea - ried
für im - mer uns - ren Kreis sie mied. ach! für im - mer uns - ren Kreis sie

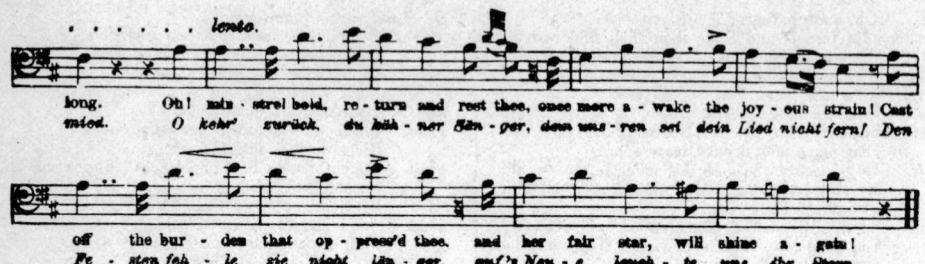

long. Oh! min-strel bold, re-turn and rest thee, once more a-wake the joy-ous strain! Cast
mied. O kehr zurück, du küh-ner Sän-ger, dem uns-ren sei dein Lied nicht fern! Den

off the bur-den that op-press'd thee, and her fair star, will shine a-gain!
Fe-sten feh-le sie nicht län-ger, auf's Neu-e leuch-te uns ihr Stern.

All. Return, oh, Henry, thou our brother! Anger and strife shall be no more; In joy and peace with one another Our strains united let us pour.	**Die Sänger.** Sei unser, Heinrich! Kehr' uns wieder! Zwietracht und Streit sei abgethan! Vereint ertönen unsre Lieder, Und Brüder nenne uns fortan!
Tann. What joy! what joy! oh, guide my steps to her! Ah, dost thou smile once more upon me, Thou radiant world that I had lost? Oh, sun of heav'n thou dost not shun me, By stormy clouds no longer crossed? 'T is May, sweet May, its thousand carols' Tender rejoicing set my sorrow free! A ray of new unwonted splendor My soul illumes. Oh, joy, 't is she!	**Tann.** Zu ihr! Zu ihr! O führet mich zu ihr! Ha, jetzt erkenne ich sie wieder, Die schöne Welt, der ich entrückt! Der Himmel blickt auf mich hernieder, Die Fluren prangen reich geschmückt; Der Lenz mit tausend holden Klängen Zog jubelnd in die Seele mir; In süssem, ungestümen Drängen Ruft laut mein Herz: Zu ihr! Zu ihr!
All. He doth return, no more to wander; Our lov'd and lost is ours again. All praise and thanks to those we render Who could persuade, and not in vain.	**Landgraf und die Sänger.** Er kehrt zurück, den wir verloren! Ein Wunder hat ihn hergebracht. Die ihm den Uebermuth beschworen, Gepriesen sei die holde Macht!

Now let your harps indite a measure

Of all that hero's hand may dare—
Of all that poet's heart can pleasure,
Before the fairest of the fair.
[*During the foregoing, the whole hunting retinue
of the Landgrave, with torchbearers, etc., have
assembled on the stage. The huntsmen sound
their bugles. The whole valley swarms with
the train of the hunters. The Landgrave and
Minstrels turn towards their retinue; the
Landgrave sounds his bugle, and is answered
by a loud peal from other hunters. While the
Landgrave and Minstrels mount the horses
that have been led down from the Wartburg,
the curtain falls.*]

Nun lausche { Euren } Hochgesängen
           { unsren }
Von Neuem der Gepries'nen Ohr!
Est tön in frohbelebten Klängen
Das Lied aus jeder Brust hervor!
[*Das ganze Thal wimmelt jetzt vom immer noch
stärker angewachsenem Jagdtross. Der Landgraf und die Sänger wenden sich den Jägern
zu; der Landgraf stösst in sein Horn, lautes
Hornschmettern und Rüdengebell antwortet
ihm Während der Landgraf und die Sänger
die Pferde, die ihnen von der Wartburg zuge-
führt worden sind, besteigen, fällt der Vorhang.*]

ACT II

SCENE I

*The Hall of Minstrels in the Wartburg. At the back an
open prospect from the Valley.*
Elisa. Oh, hall of song I give thee greeting!
All hail to thee thou hallowed place!
'T was here that dream so sweet and fleeting,
Upon my heart his song did trace.
But since by him forsaken
A desert thou dost seem—
Thy echoes only waken
Remembrance of a dream.
But now the flame of hope is lighted,
Thy vault shall ring with glorious war;
For he whose strains my soul delighted
No longer roams afar!

AKT II

ERSTE SCENE

*Die Sängerhalle auf der Wartburg; im Hintergrunde
freie Aussicht auf dem Burghof und das Thal.*
Elisa. Dich, theure Halle, grüss' ich wieder,
Froh grüss' ich dich, geliebter Raum!
In dir erwachen seine Lieder,
Und wecken mich aus düst'rem Traum.
Da er aus dir geschieden,
Wie öd' erschienst du mir!
Aus mir entfloh der Frieden,
Die Freude zog aus dir.
Wie jetzt mein Busen hoch sich hebet,
So scheinst du jetzt mir stolz und hehr;
Der dich und mich so neu belebet,
Nicht länger weilt er ferne mehr,
Sei mir gegrüsst! sei mir gegrüsst!

SCENE II

Wolf. Behold her! Naught your meeting shall disturb.
Tann. Oh Princess!
Elisa. Heav'n! do not kneel! leave me
    Here, thus we should not meet.
Tann. We may! oh, stay,
    And let me kneel for ever here!
Elisa. I pray thee rise!
    'Tis not for thee to kneel where thou has
      conquer'd.
    This hall is thy domain. Rise, I implore!
    Thanks be to heaven that thou return'st to us!
    So long where hast thou tarried?
Tann. Far away, in strange and distant regions—
    And between yesterday and to-day oblivion's veil
      hath fallen.
    Every remembrance hath for ever vanished,
    Save one thing only, rising from the darkness—
    That I then dared not hope I should behold thee,
    Nor ever raise mine eyes to thy perfection.
Elisa. How wert thou led now to return to us?
Tann. A marvel 'twas, by heaven wrought within my
      spirit.
Elisa. I praise the power that wrought it
    From out my heart's recesses!
    Forgive— I scarcely know what I am saying:
    Thy presence here; a vision doth it seem—
    Strange dream of life, mysterious and alluring.
    The world to me is changed. Canst thou declare
    What this emotion to my heart betokens?
      In minstrels' lays delighting
      I mark'd and listened long and oft;
      Their subtle, sweet inditing
      To me seemed dalliance soft.
    But now the past to me is darkened—
    Repose and joy from me have flown;
    Since fondly to thy lays I've hearken'd
    The pangs and bliss of woe I've known.
    Emotions that I comprehend not,
    And longings never guess'd before—
    Upon my bidding they depend not,
    But fled are all delights of yore.
    And when this land thou hadst forsaken
    Repose and joy for me were fled;
    No minstrel could my heart awaken—
    To me their lays seem'd sad and dead.
    In slumber oft near broken-hearted,
    Awake, each pain fondly recalled
    All joy hath from my life departed.
    Henry, Henry, why thus am I enthrall'd!
Tann. All praise to love for this fair token!
    Love touched my harp with magic sweet—
    Love, through my song, to thee hath spoken,
    And captive leads me at thy feet.

ZWEITE SCENE

Wolf. Dort ist sie; nahe dich ihr ungestört!
Tann. O Fürstin!
Elisa. Gott! Steht auf! Lasset mich! Nicht darf
    Ich Euch hier seh'n!
Tann.   Du darf'st! O bleib' und lass
    Zu deinen Füssen mich!
Elisa.   So stehet auf!
    Nicht sollet hier Ihr knien, denn diese Halle
    Ist Euer Königreich. O, stehet auf!
    Nehmt meinen Dank, dass Ihr zuruckgekehrt!
    Wo weiltet Ihr so lange?
Tann.   Fern von hier,
    In weiten, weiten Landen. Dichtes Vergessen
    Hat zwischen heut' und gestern sich gesenkt.—
    All' mein Erinnern ist mir schnell geschwunden,
    Und nur des Einen muss ich mich entsinnen,
    Dass nie mehr ich gehofft Euch zu begrüssen,
    Noch je zu Euch mein Auge zu erheben.
Elisa. Was war es dann, das Euch zurückgeführt?
Tann. Ein Wunder war's, ein unbegreiflich hohes
    Wunder!
Elisa. Gepriesen sei dies Wunder aus meines Herzens
    Tiefe!
    Verzeiht, wenn ich nicht weiss, was ich beginne!
    Im Traum bin ich und thör'ger als ein Kind,—
    Machtlos der Macht der Wunder preisgegeben,
    Fast kenn' ich mich nicht mehr; o, helfet mir,
    Dass ich das Räthsel meines Herzens löse!
      Der Sänger klugen Weisen
      Lauscht' ich sonst gern und viel;
      Ihr Singen und ihr Preisen
      Schien mir ein holdes Spiel.
    Doch welch' ein seltsam neues Leben
    Rief Euer Lied mir in die Brust!
    Bald wollt' es mich wie Schmerz durchbeben,
    Bald drang's in mich wie jähe Lust:
    Gefühle, die ich nie empfunden!
    Verlangen, das ich nie gekannt!
    Was einst mir lieblich, war verschwunden
    Vor Wonnen, die noch nie genannt!—
    Und als Ihr nun von uns gegangen,—
    War Frieden mir und Lust dahin!
    Die Weisen, die die Sänger sangen,
    Erschienen matt mir, trüb' ihr Sinn;
    Im Traume fühlt' ich dumpfe Schmerzen,
    Mein Wachen ward trübsel'ger Wahn;
    Die Freude zog aus meinem Herzen;—
    Heinrich! Was thatet Ihr mir an?
Tann. Den Gott der Liebe sollst du preisen,
    Er hat die Saiten mir berührt.
    Er sprach zu dir aus meinen Weisen,
    Zu dir hat er mich hergeführt!

No. 3.   OH! BLESSED HOUR.

ELIZABETH.
  Oh bless - ed hour............ of meet - ing, oh bless - ed
  Ge - prie - sen sei............ die Stun - de, ge - prie - sen
TANNHÄUSER.

pow'r............ of love! At last......... I give........., thee
sei............... die Macht, die mir........ so hol - de

pow'r........... of love!   At
sei............... Die Macht.   die

greet - - ing! No long - er thou............... wilt rove!
Kun - - de von Eu - rer Näh'.................. ge - bracht!

last........ I give........... thee greet - ing, no more...... from hence to rove!
mir........ so hol - de Kun - de aus dei - nem Mund ge - bracht!

Oh bless - ed hour of meet - ing, oh bless - ed pow'r of love, At
Ge - prie - sen sei die Stun - de, ge - prie - sen sei die Macht, die

last I give thee greet - ing, no long - er thou wilt rove!
mir so hol - de Kun - de von Eu - rer Näh' ge - bracht!

last I give thee greet - ing, no more from hence to rove! Now
mir so hol - de Kun - de aus dei - nem Mund ge - bracht! Dem

Now life...... re -
Von Won - ne -

life...... re - new'd a - wak - eth the hope that once was mine,
neu...... er kann - ten Le - ben darf ich mich mu - thig weih'n,

wak - - eth, with - in this heart.......... of
Le - - ben nenn'........ ich die Freu - de

break - - eth, I know but joy di - vine.
Be - - ben, sein schön - stes Wun - der mein.

mine, the cloud of sor - row break - eth, the cloud of sor - row break - eth the
mein; er-wacht zu neu - em Le - ben, er-wacht zu neu - em Le - ben nenn

Now life.... re-new'd a - wak - eth, now life re-new'd a - wak - eth the
Dem neu.... er-kann-ten Le - ben. dem neu er-cann-ten Le - ben, darf

sun of joy doth shine, the sun doth shine!...... Ah! thou
ich die Freu-de mein, die Freu - de mein!...... Ach! Ge

hope that once was mine, the hope that once was mine!...... Ah! thou
ich mich mu-thig weih'n, darf ich mich mu - thig weih'n!.... Ach! Ge

WOLFRAM (*at the back.*)

All hope my heart for -
So flieht für die - ses

bless - ed hour of meet - ing, thou bless-ed pow'r of love! At last I
prie-sen sei die Stun - de, ge - prie-sen sei die Macht, die mir so

- sak - - eth, ne'er will her heart be mine!
Le - - ben mir je - der Hoff - nung Schein!

give thee greet - ing, no long - er thou wilt rove!......
hol - de Kun - de von Eu - rer Näh' ge - bracht!....

...... Oh bless - - ed, oh bless - ed hour.............. of
...... Ge - prie - - sen! Ge - prie - sen sei............... die

meet - ing, oh bless - ed pow'r.............. of love!......... Now
Stun - de, ge - prie - sen sei............... die Macht!...... Von

life...... re - new'd a - wak - eth with - in this heart of mine,
Won - ne - glanz um - ge - ben lacht mir der Son - ne Schein

Oh bless-ed pow'r of love! Now life...... re -
Ge - prie - sen sei die Macht, Dem neu........ er -

with - in this heart of mine; the cloud...... of sor - row
lacht mir der Son - ne Schein, er - wacht...... zu neu - em

new'd a - wak - eth the hope that once was mine, the cloud of
kann - ten Le - ben darf ich mich mu - thig weih'n, ich wenn' in

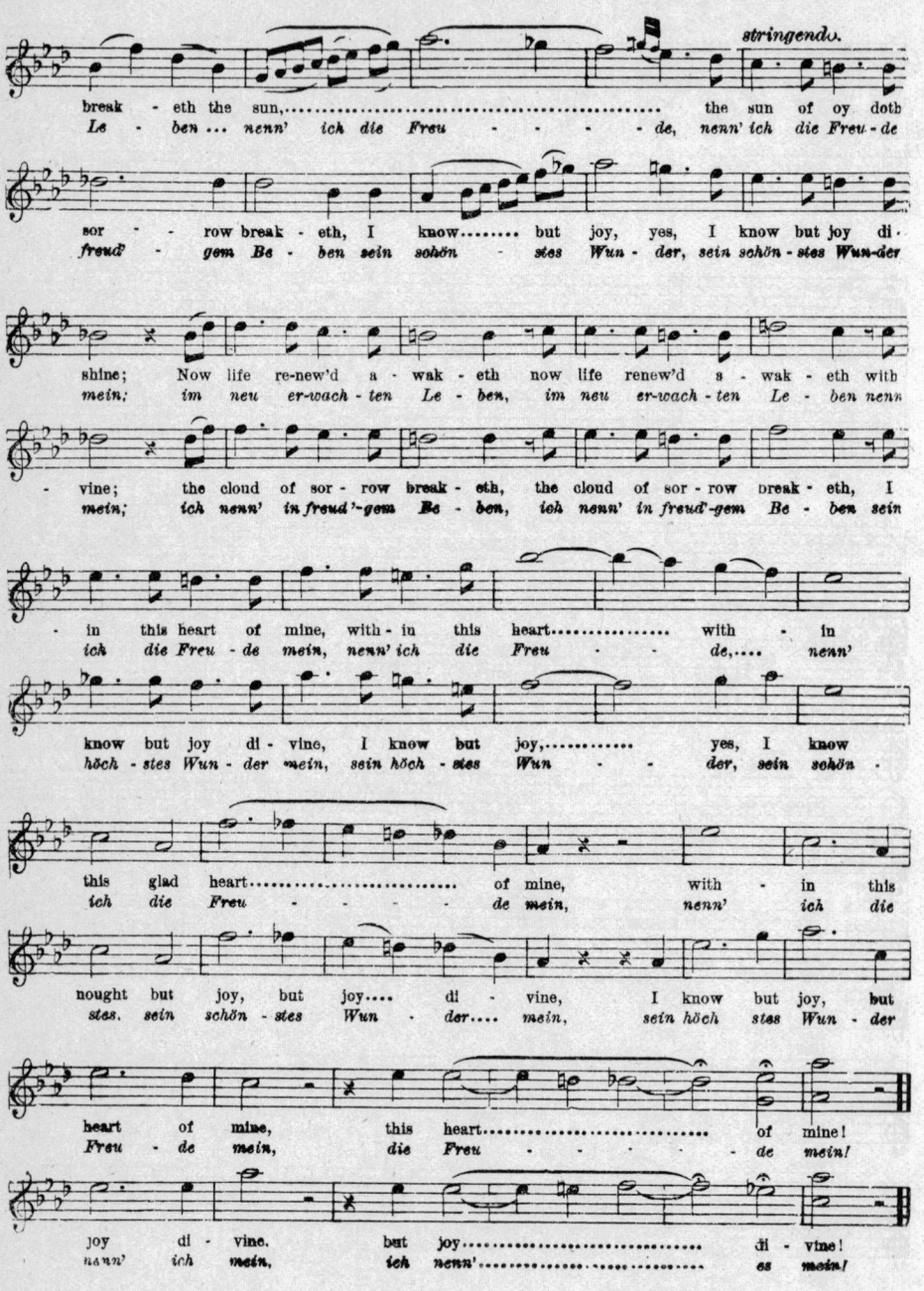

stringendo.

break - eth the sun, ... the sun of oy doth
Le - ben ... nenn' ich die Freu - - - - de, nenn' ich die Freu - de

sor - row break - eth, I know .... but joy, yes, I know but joy di -
freud' - gem Be - ben sein schön - stes Wun - der, sein schön - stes Wun - der

shine; Now life re-new'd a - wak - eth now life renew'd a - wak - eth with
mein; im neu er-wach - ten Le - ben, im neu er-wach - ten Le - ben nenn

- vine; the cloud of sor - row break - eth, the cloud of sor - row break - eth, I
mein; ich nenn' in freud'-gem Be - ben, ich nenn' in freud'-gem Be - ben sein

- in this heart of mine, with - in this heart .... with - in
ich die Freu - de mein, nenn' ich die Freu - de, ... nenn'

know but joy di - vine, I know but joy, ... yes, I know
höch - stes Wun - der mein, sein höch - stes Wun - der, sein schön -

this glad heart .... of mine, with - in this
ich die Freu - - - de mein, nenn' ich die

nought but joy, but joy .... di - vine, I know but joy, but
stes. sein schön - stes Wun - der .... mein, sein höch stes Wun - der

heart of mine, this heart .... of mine!
Freu - de mein, die Freu - - - de mein!

joy di - vine. but joy .... di - vine!
nenn' ich mein, ich nenn' .... es mein!

SCENE III

Land. Com'st thou at last to grace the contest?
Wilt thou shun these walls no longer?
What hath lur'd thee from thy solitude
To come amongst us?
Elisa. My sov'reign, oh, my more than father!
Land. Wilt thou, then, at last reveal to me thy secret?

Elisa. Tell it I cannot; read my eyes, and know.
Land. This day it shall still be unspoken—
Thy treasur'd thought thou need'st not own;
The spell shall yet remain unbroken
Till what the future brings is known
So be't. .The wondrous flame that song hath
   kindled
This day shall brightly soar;
Thy joy, all hearts rejoicing,
Shall on this day be crowned:
What hath been sung shall spring to life for thee.
This day will see our nobles all assembled—
To grace the solemn feast they now approach;
None will be absent, since they know
That once again thy hand the victor's wreath
   bestows.

DRITTE SCENE

Land. Dich treff' ich hier in dieser Halle, die
So lange du gemieden? Endlich denn
Lockt dich ein Sängerfest, das wir bereiten?
Elisa. Mein Oheim! O, mein güt'ger Vater!
Land. Drängt
Es dich, dein Herz mir endlich zu erschliessen?
Elisa. Blick' mir in's Auge! Sprechen kann ich nicht.
Land. Noch bleibe denn unausgesprochen
Dein süss Geheimniss kurze Frist,
Der Zauber bleibe ungebrochen,
Bis du der Lösung mächtig bist.—
So sei's! Was der Gesang so Wunderbares
Erweckt und angeregt, soll heute er
Enthüllen auch und mit Vollendung krönen.
Die holde Kunst, sie werde jetzt zur That!
Schon nahen sich die Edlen meiner Lande,
Die ich zum selt'nen Fest hieher beschied;
Zahlreicher nahen sie als je. da sie
Gehört, dass du des Festes Fürstin seist.

No. 4. ### HAIL BRIGHT ABODE.

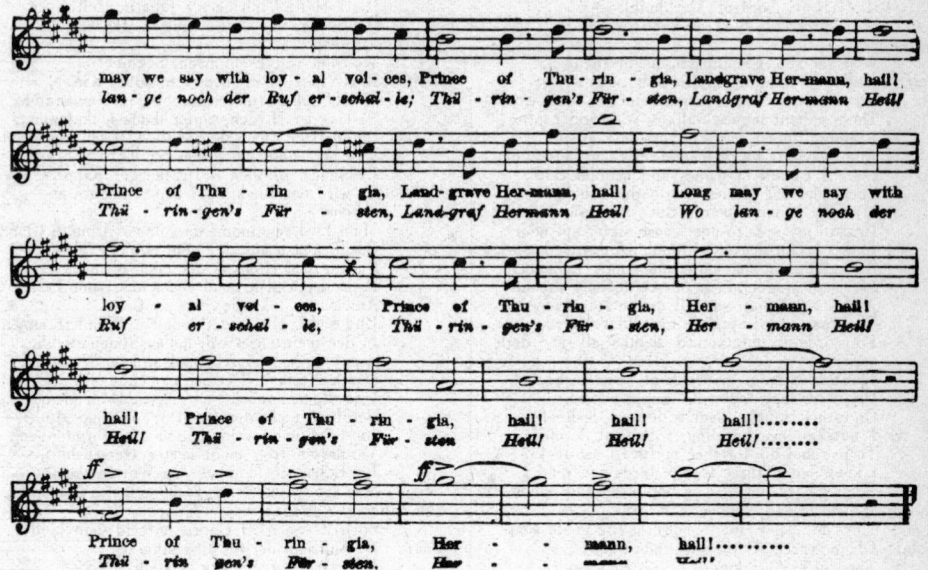

may we say with loy - al voi - ces, Prince of Thu - rin - gia, Landgrave Her-mann, hail!
lan - ge noch der Ruf er - schal - le; Thü - rin - gen's Für - sten, Landgraf Hermann Heil!

Prince of Thu - rin - gia, Land- grave Her-mann, hail! Long may we say with
Thü - rin - gen's Für - sten, Land-graf Hermann Heil! Wo lan - ge noch der

loy - al voi - ces, Prince of Thu - rin - gia, Her - mann, hail!
Ruf er - schal - le, Thü - rin - gen's Für - sten, Her - mann Heil!

hail! Prince of Thu - rin - gia, hail! hail! hail!........
Heil! Thü - rin - gen's Für - sten Heil! Heil! Heil!........

Prince of Thu - rin - gia, Her - mann, hail!...........
Thü - rin gen's Für - sten. Her - - - - Heil!

Landgrave.

Minstrels assembled here, I give you greeting.
Full oft within these walls your lays have
    sounded;
In veiled wisdom, or in mirthful measures
They ever gladdened every list'ning heart.
And though the sword of strife was loosed in
    battle,
Drawn to maintain our German land secure,
When 'gainst the southern foe we fought and
    conquer'd,
And for our country brav'd the death of heroes,
Unto the harp be equal praise and glory!
The tender graces of the homestead,
The faith in what is good and gracious—
For these you fought with word and voice:
The meed of praise for this is due.
Your strains inspiring, then, once more attune,
Now that the gallant minstrel hath to us returned
Who from our land too long was parted
To what we owe his presence here amongst us
In strange, mysterious darkness still is wrapp'd;
The magic power of song shall now reveal it,
Therefore hear now the theme you all shall sing.
Say, what is love? by what signs shall we know it?
This be your theme. Who so most nobly this can
    tell,
Him shall the Princess give the price.
He may demand the fairest guerdon:
I vouch that whatsoe'er he ask is granted.
Up, then, arouse ye—sing, oh, gallant minstrels!
Attune your harps to love—great is the price,
Ere ye begin, let all receive our thanks!

Der Landgraf.

Gar viel und schön ward hier in dieser Halle
Von Euch, Ihr lieben Sänger, schon gesungen.
In weisen Räthseln wie in heit'ren Liedern
Erfreutet Ihr gleich sinnig unser Herz.—
Wenn unser Schwert in blutig ernsten Kämpfen
Stritt für des deutschen Reiches Majestät,
Wenn wir dem grimmen Welfen widerstanden
Und dem verderbenvollen Zwiespalt wehrten,
So ward von Euch nicht mindrer Preis errungen.
Der Anmuth und der holden Sitte,
Der Tugend und dem reinen Glauben
Erstritt ihr durch Eure Kunst
Gar hohen, herrlich schönen Sieg.
Bereitet heute uns denn auch ein Fest,
Heut', wo der kühne Sänger uns zurück-
Gekehrt, den wir so ungern lang' vermissten
Was wieder ihn in unsre Nähe brachte,
Ein wunderbar Geheimniss dünkt es mich;
Durch Liedes Kunst sollt' Ihr es uns enthüllen,
Deshalb stell' ich die Frage jetzt an Euch:
Könnt Ihr der Liebe Wesen mir ergründen?
Wer es vermag, wer sie am würdigsten
Besingt, dem reich' Elisabeth den Preis:
Er ford're ihn so hoch und kühn er wolle,
Ich sorge, dass sie ihn gewähren solle.
Auf, liebe Sänger! Greifet in die Saiten!
Die Aufgab' ist gestellt, kämpft um den Preis
Und nehmet all' im Voraus uns'ren Dank!

Chorus:
    Hail! Hail! Lord of Thuringia!
    Hail! protector thou of gentle song!
Four Pages.
    Wolfram von Eschinbach, begin thou?
Wolf. Gazing around upon this fair assembly,
    How doth the heart expand to see the scene!
    These gallant heroes, valiant, wise and gentle—
    A stately forest soaring fresh and green.
    And blooming by their side, in sweet perfection,
    I see a wreath of dames and maidens fair;
    Their blended glories dazzle the beholder—
    My song is mute before this vision rare.
    I raised my eyes to one whose starry splendor
    In this bright heaven with mild effulgence beams,
    And gazing on that pure and tender radiance,
    My heart was sunk in prayerful, holy dreams.
    And lo! the source of all delights and power
    Was then unto my list'ning soul revealed,
    From whose unfathomed depths all joy doth
       shower—
    The tender balm in which all grief is healed.
    Oh, never may I dim its limpid waters,
    Or rashly trouble them with wild desires!
    I worship thee kneeling, with soul devoted:
    To live and die for thee my heart aspires!
    I know not if these feeble words can render
    What I have felt of love both true and tender.
Chorus of Nobles and Ladies.
    They do! They do! We praise thy noble song!
Tann. Oh, minstrel, if 'tis thus thou singest,
    Thou ne'er hast known or tasted love!
    If cold and timid heart thou bringest,
    A weary lot thy joy must prove!
    If thou desire an unapproach'd perfection—
    Behold the stars—adore their bright reflection—
    They were not made to be belov'd:
    They ne'er by human pray'r were mov'd!
    But what can yield to soft caresses,
    And, fram'd with me in mortal mould
    Gentle persuasion's rule confesses,
    And in these arms I may unfold—
    This is for joy, and knows no measure,
    For love's fulfillment is its pleasure!
Bit. To mortal combat I defy thee!
    Shameless blasphemer, draw thy sword!
    As brother henceforth we deny thee;
    Thy words profane too long we've heard!
    If I of love divine have spoken,
    Strength'ning in valor, sword and heart,
    Its glorious spell shall be unbroken
    Altho' from life this hour I part.
    For womanhood and noble honor
    Through death and danger I would go;
    But for the cheap delights that won thee
    I scorn them as not worth a blow!
Chorus of Nobles and Ladies.
    Hail Biterolf! Come, draw thy sword!
Tann. Yes, idle boaster, Biterolf!
    Shall love be sung by thee, grim wolf?
    Not thou hast e'er known aught of bliss—
    Its sweetness thy fierce heart must miss.
    Poor weary soul, what joy hath bless'd thee?
    What rapture couldst thou ever know?
    If any pale delight possess'd thee,
    That were indeed not worth a blow!
Nobles. We will not hear him, stay his daring madness.
Land. Put up your swords!—There must be peace be-
    tween ye.

Chor der Ritter und Edelfrauen.
    Heil! Heil! Thüringen's Fürstin Heil!
    Der holden Kunst Beschützer Heil!
Vier Edelknaben.
    Wolfram von Eschinbach, beginne!
Wolf. Blick' ich umher in diesem edlen Kreise,
    Welch' hoher Anblick macht mein Herz erglüh'n!
    So viel der Helden, tapfer deutsch und weise,—
    Ein stoltzer Eichwald, herrlich, frisch und grün,
    Und hold und tugendsam erblick' ich Frauen,—
    Lieblicher Blüthen düftereichster Kranz.
    Es wird der Blick wohl trunken mir vom
       Schauen,
    Mein Lied verstummt vor solcher Anmuth Glanz,
    Da blick' ich auf zu einem nur der Sterne,
    Der an dem Himmel, der mich blendet, steht;
    Es sammelt sich mein Geist aus jeder Ferne,
    Andächtig sinkt die Seele in Gebet
    Und sieh! Mir zeiget sich ein Wunderbronnen,
    In den mein Geist voll hohen Staunen's blickt:
    Aus ihm er schöpfet gnadenreiche Wonnen,
    Durch die mein Herz er namenlos erquickt.
    Und nimmer möcht' ich diesen Bronnen trüben,
    Berühren nicht den Quell mit frevlem Muth:—
    In Anbetung möcht, ich mich opfernd üben,
    Vergiessen froh mein letztes Herzensblut,—
    Ihr Edlen möcht' in diesen Worten lesen,
    Wie ich erkenn' der Liebe reinstes Wesen!
Die Ritter und Frauen.
    So ist's! So ist's! Gepriesen seid dein Lied!
Tann. O Wolfram, der du also sangest,
    Du hast die Liebe arg entstellt!
    Wenn du in solchem Schmachten bangest,
    Versiegte wahrlich wohl die Welt.
    Zu Gottes Preis in hoch erhab'ne Fernen,
    Blickt auf zum Himmel, blickt zu seinen Sternen
    Anbetung solchen Wundern zollt,
    Da ihr sie nicht begreifen sollt!
    Doch, was sich der Berührung beuget,
    Euch Herz und Sinnen nahe liegt,
    Was sich, aus gleichem Stoff erzeuget,
    In weicher Formung an euch mich schmiegt,—
    Dem ziemt Genuss in freud'gem Triebe
    Und im Genuss nur kenn ich Liebe!
Bit. Heraus zum Kampfe mit uns Allen!
    Wer bliebe ruhig, hört er dich?
    Wird deinem Hochmuth es gefallen,
    So höre, Lästrer, nun auch mich!
    Wenn mich begeistert hohe Liebe,
    Stählt sie die Waffen mir mit Muth;
    Dass ewig ungeschmäht sie bliebe,
    Vergöss ich stolz mein letztes Blut.
    Für Frauenehr' und hohe Tugend
    Als Ritter kämpf' ich mit dem Schwert;
    Doch, was Genuss beut' deiner Jugend,
    Ist wohlfeil, keines Streiches werth.
Die Zu. Heil, Biterolf! Hier unser Schwert!
Tann. Ha, thör'ger Prahler, Biterolf!
    Singst du von Liebe, grimmer Wolf?
    Gewisslich hast du nicht gemeint
    Was mir geniessenswerth erscheint.
    Was hast du Aermster wohl genossen?
    Dein Leben war nicht liebereich,
    Und was von Freuden dir entsprossen,
    Das galt wohl wahrlich keinen Streich!
Ritter. Lasst ihn nicht enden!—Wehret seiner Kühnheit!
Land. Zurück das Schwert!—Ihr Sänger, halte Frieden!

Wolf. Oh, Heaven! let me here implore thee!
Hallow my song to worthy praise!
Let sin crouch in the dust before thee,
Nor dare 'mongst us its head to raise!
Thou, noble love, inspire me,
Thy glory let me sing—
Thy flame immortal fire me,
Fann'd by an angel's wing!
Thou com'st, from Heav'n descended—
I follow thee afar;
By every joy attended
For ever shines thy star!

Wolf. O Himmel, lass dich jetzt erflehen,
Gieb meinem Lied der Weihe Preis
Gebannt lass mich die Sünde sehen
Aus diesem edlen reinen Kreis!
Dir hohe Liebe, töne
Begeistert mein Gesang,
Die mir in Engels-Schöne
Tief in die Seele drang!
Du nahst als Gottgesandte,
Ich folg' aus holder Fern',—
So führst du in die Lande,
We ewig strahlt dein Stern.

No. 5. THOU, GODDESS OF LOVE.

All. Ah, hear the miscreant! hence away!
Hear him! he hath with Venus been!
Ladies. Away! away! nor near him stay!
The Ladies quit the Hall with gestures of dismay and horror; Elisabeth, who has heard the contest with growing alarm, alone remains, pale and trembling, supporting herself against one of the pillars of the royal canopy. The Landgrave, the Minstrels and Nobles have quitted their seats and stand together. Tannhäuser remains some time longer as in a trance.

Alle. Ha, der Verruchte! Fliehet ihn!
Hört es! Er war im Venusberg!
Die Edelfrauen.
Hinweg! Hinweg aus seiner Näh'!
[*Die Frauen verlassen in grösster Bestürzung und mit Gebärden des Abscheu's die Halle. Elisabeth, die dem Streite der Sänger mit wachsender Angst zugehört hatte, bleibt von den Frauen allein zurück,—bleich, nur mit dem grössten aufwande ihrer Kraft an einer der hölzernen Säulen des Baldachins sich aufrecht erhaltend. Der Landgraf, alle Ritter und Sänger haben ihre Sitze verlassen und treten zusammen. Tannhäuser, zur äussersten Linken, verbleibt noch eine Zeit lang wie in Verzückung.*

Landgrave, Knights and Nobles.
    Ye all have heard,
    His mouth hath confess'd
    That he hath shared the joys of hell,
    In Venus' dark abode that dwell.
    Disown him—curse him—banish him!
    Or let his traitor life-blood flow!
    Anathema, we call on thee:
    In hellish fires for ever glow!

[*All close round Tannhäuser, with drawn swords. Elisabeth throws herself between them.*

Elisa. Stay your hands!

Landgrave, Knights and Nobles.
    On, wonder! thou, Elisabeth!
    The peerless maiden shields the guilty?

Elisa. Stand back! or pierce this bosom with your
      swords!
    Death and its terrors cannot crush me
    Like to the deadly wound that he hath struck
    me here. .

Landgrave and Nobles.
    Oh, royal maid, can we believe thee?
    Let not thy guileless heart deceive thee,
    Nor let his fate accursed grieve thee:
    Thou more than all the wretch should scorn!

Elisa. Think not of me! He must be saved!
    Ye would not rob his hope of heaven?

Landgrave and Nobles.
    For ever lost his hope of Heav'n—
    Madly his joy he cast aside!
    A crime like his is ne'er forgiven:
    The curse of Heav'n with him abide!

Elisa. Away from him! 'Tis not for you to judge him!
    Shame on you! He is one against you all.
    Oh, let a spotless maid your grace implore!
    Let Heav'n declare through me what is its will—
    The erring mortal, who hath fallen
    Within the weary toils of sin,
    How dare ye close the heav'nly portal
    Where he on earth his shrift may win?
    If ye are strong in faith and honor,
    Why do ye not His word obey
    Who gave to us the law of mercy—
    Who ne'er from sinner turned away?
    On me, a maiden young and tender,
    Yon knight hath struck a cruel blow—
    I, who so deeply, truly lov'd him,
    Am hurl'd in dark abyss of woe!
    I pray for him—spare him, oh, I implore ye!
    Let not the hope of pardon be denied!
    To life renew'd his sinking faith restore ye.
    Think that for him, too, once the Saviour died.

Tann. Oh! lost and for ever.

Landgrave, Knights and Nobles.
    An angel hath from Heav'n descended
    To bear us God's most high behest.
    Behold and see whom thou'st offended!
    Thy crime for ever haunt thy rest!
    Thou gav'st her death—she prays that life be
      spared thee!
    Who would not yield who heard the heav'nly
      maid?
    Though as accursed and guilty I declar'd thee,
    The voice of Heav'n by me shall be obey'd.

Tann. Have mercy, Thou! I cry to thee despairing!
    Oh, from the gulf of error set me free!

Land. A crime dark and unheard of hath befallen;
    In mask of loyal knight there treacherously
    Stole amongst us sin's accursed child.
    By us thou art disown'd—
    From this land thou art banish'd.

Landgraf, Ritter und Sänger.
    Ihr habt's gehört! Sein frevler Mund
    That das Bekenntniss schrecklich kund.
    Er hat der Hölle Lust getheilt,
    Im Venusberg hat er geweilt!—
    Entsetzlich! Scheusslich! Fluchenswerth!
    In seinem Blute netzt das Schwert!
    Zum Höllenpfuhl zurückgesandt!

[*Alle dringen mit gezücktem Schwerte auf Tannhäuser ein Elisabeth stürtzt dazwischen.*

Elisa. Haltet ein!

Landgraf, Ritter und Sänger.
    Was seh' ich! Wie, Elisabeth!
    Die keusche Jungfrau für den Sünder?

Elisa. Zurück! Des Todes achte ich sonst nicht!
    Was ist die Wunde Eures Eisen's gegen
    Den Todesstoss, den ich von ihm empfing?

Landgraf, Ritter und Sänger.
    Elisabeth! Was muss ich hören?
    Wie liess dein Herz sich so bethören,
    Von dem die Strafe zu beschwören,
    Der auch so furchtbar dich verrieth.

Elisa. Was liegt an mir? Doch er,—sein Heil!
    Wollt Ihr sein ewig Heil ihm rauben?

Landgraf, Ritter und Sänger.
    Verworfen hat er jedes Hoffen,
    Niemals wird ihm des Heil's Gewinn!
    Des Himmels Fluch hat ihn getroffen!
    In seinen Sünden fahr' er hin!

Elisa. Zurück von ihm! Nicht Ihr seid seine Richter!
    Grausame! Werft von Euch das wilde Schwert
    Und gebt Gehör der reinen Jungfrau Wort!
    Vernehmt durch mich, was Gottes Wille ist!—
    Der Unglücksel'ge, den gefangen
    Ein furchtbar mächt'ger Zauber hält,
    Wie? sollt' er nie zum Heil gelangen
    Durch Reu' und Buss' in dieser Welt?
    Die Ihr so stark im reinen Glauben,
    Verkennt Ihr so des Höchsten Rath?
    Wollt Ihr sein ewig Heil ihm rauben?
    So sagt, was Euch er Leides that?
    Seht mich, die Jungfrau, deren Blüthe
    Mit einem jähen Schlag er brach,—
    Die ihn geliebt tief im Gemüthe,
    Der jubelnd er das Herz zerstach;—
    Ich fleh' für ihn, ich flehe für sein Leben,
    Zur Busse lenk' er reuevoll den Schritt!
    Der Muth des Glaubens sei ihm neu gegeben,
    Dass auch für ihn einst der Erlöser litt!

Tann. Weh! Weh mir Unglücksel'gem.

Landgraf, Ritter und Sänger.
    Ein Engel stieg aus lichtem Aether,
    Zu künden Gottes heil'gen Rath.
    Blick hin, du schändlicher Verräther,
    Werd' inne deiner Missethat!
    Du gabst ihr Tod, sie bittet für dein Leben;
    Wer bliebe rauh, hört er des Engels Fleh'n?
    Darf ich auch nicht dem Schuldigen vergeben,
    Dem Himmels Wort kann nicht ich widersteh'n.

Tann. Erbarm' dich mein, der ach! so tief in Sünden
    Schmachvoll des Himmels Mittlerin verkannt!

Land. Ein furchtbares Verbrechen ward begangen:
    Es schlich mit heuchlerischer Larve sich
    Zu uns der Sünde fluchbelad'ner Sohn.
    Wir stossen dich von uns.—bei uns darfst du
    Nicht weilen; schmachbefleckt ist unser Herd

Thou with shame has stained this threshold pure:
The wrath of heav'n may strike the roof
That harbors thee, too long by guilt defil'd.
One path alone can save thee from perdition,
From everlasting woe—by earth abandon'd,
One way is left: that way thou now shalt know.
A band of pilgrims now assembled
From every part of my domain;
This morn the elders went before them,
The rest yet in the vale remain.
'Tis not for crimes like thine they tremble,
And leave their country, friends and home—
Desire for heav'nly grace is o'er them:
They seek the sacred shrine at Rome.

Landgrave, Knights and Nobles.
'Tis there repentant, kneeling
Before the shrine of grace,
Thy heart in tears annealing,
Thy sin thou shalt efface.
In dust bow down before him
Who holds the keys of Heav'n,
But never more returning
Unless by him forgiven!
Our just revenge resign'd we,
Because an angel pray'd;
But yet this sword shall find thee
Unless thou seek heav'ns aid.

Elisa. Great Heav'n, repentant kneeling,
A sinner sues for grace;
Thy bounteous love revealing,
Turn not away thy face.
In dust bending before him
Who holds the keys of Heav'n!
Oh, let thy light restore him,
Oh, let him be forgiven!
All hope on earth resigning,
Thee I implore for aid;
My life, without repining,
I offer up, a maid!

Tann. Oh, where shall I find mercy?
Oh, where shall I find rest?
All hope from me hath vanish'd—
Despair within my breast!
I'll go repentant kneeling
Before the throne of grace;
If bitter tears are healing,
In dust I'll hide my face.
Oh, let me be forgiven,
By her, the heavenly maid
Whose heart by me was riven—
Whom basely I betray'd.

Chorus of Younger Pilgrims.
At thy august and holy shrine
I go to seek the grace divine.
Thrice blessed who thy promise know;
Absolv'd by penance shall they go.

Tann. To Rome!
All. To Rome!

Durch dich, und dräuend blickt der Himmel
     selbst
Auf dieses Dach, das dich zu lang schon birgt.
Zur Rettung doch vor ewigem Verderben
Steht offen dir ein Weg: von mir dich stossend
Zeig' ich ihn dir,—nütz' ihn zu deinem Heil!
Versammelt sind aus meinen Landen
Bussfert'ge Pilger, stark an Zahl:
Die ält'ren schon voran sich wandten,
Die jüng'ren rasten noch im Thal.
Nur um geringer Sünde willen
Ihr Herz nicht Ruhe ihnen lässt,
Der Busse frommen Drang zu stillen,
Ziehn sie nach Rom zum Gnadenfest.

Landgraf, Ritter und Sänger.
Mit ihnen sollst du wallen
Zur Stadt der Gnadenhuld,
Im Staub dort niederfallen
Und büssen deine Schuld!
Vor ihm stürz' dich darnieder,
Der Gottes Urtheil spricht;
Doch kehre nimmer wieder,
Ward dir sein Segen nicht!
Musst' unsre Rache weichen,
Weil sie ein Engel brach:
Dies Schwert wird dich erreichen,
Harrst du in Sünd' und Schmach!

Elisa. Lass ihn zu dir ihn wallen,
Du Gott der Gnad' und Huld!
Ihm, der so tief gefallen,
Vergieb der Sünden Schuld
Für ihn nur will ich flehen,
Mein Leben sei Gebet;
Lass ihn dein Leuchten sehen
Eh' er in Nacht vergeht!
Mit freudigem Erbeben
Lass dir ein Opfer weihn!
Nimm hin, o nimm mein Leben,
Nicht nenn' ich es mehr mein!

Tann. Wie soll ich Gnade finden,
Wie bussen meine Schuld?
Mein Heil sah' ich entschwinden,
Mich flieht des Himmels Huld.
Doch will ich bussend wallen,
Zerschlagen meine Brust,
Im Staube niederfallen,—
Zerknirschung sei mir Lust
O, dass nur er versöhnet,
Der Engel meiner Noth,
Der sich, so frech verhöhnet,
Zum opfer doch mir bot!

Gesang der jüngeren Pilger.
Am hohen Fest der Gnadenhuld
In Demuth sühnet Eure Schuld!
Gesegnet, wer in Glauben treu:
Er wird erlöst durch Buss und Reu.

Tann. Nach Rom!
Alle. Nach Rom!

ACT III | ## AKT III

SCENE I

ERSTE SCENE

[The Valley beneath the Wartburg, as in the first Act. It is near sunset. On the small eminence, Elisabeth is kneeling before the shrine in prayer. Wolfram comes down from a forest path; he stops when he has descended halfway, perceiving Elisabeth.

Wolf. By yonder shrine I'm ever sure to find her,
Kneeling in fervent prayer,
When my lonely and joyless way
Back to the valley leads me.
The death-blow struck by him within her—
She prays that Heaven may shrive the sinner,
His weal imploring day and night.
Oh, blessed love, how great thy might?
The pilgrims soon from Rome will be returning;
The year declines—ere long they must be here.
Will he return repentant and absolv'd?
This doth she pray for, Heav'n entreating.
Ye saints, oh grant their happy meeting,
Although my wound may never heal,
Oh, may she ne'er my anguish feel!

Elisa. The pilgrim's song! 'T is they! They have return'd!
Ye saints, oh let me know my task,
That I may worthily fulfil it!

Wolf. They come at last; it is the pious chant,
Telling of the sin absolv'd and pardon granted!
Oh! Heaven, let her heart be strong
If now her fate must be decided.

Chorus of Elder Pilgrims.
Once more with joy, oh, my home, I may meet thee;
Once more, ye fair flow'ry meadows, I greet ye;
My pilgrim staff henceforth may rest,
Since Heav'n's sweet peace is within my breast.
The sinner's plaint on high was heard,
Accepted by a gracious Lord;
The tears I laid before his shrine
Are turned to hope and joy divine.
Oh, Lord eternal praise be thine!
The blessed source of thy mercy o'erflowing
On souls repentant who seek Thee bestowing;
Of hell and death I have no fear,
My gracious Lord is ever near.
Hallelujah eternally.

Elisa. He will return no more!

[Thal vor der Wartburg wie am Schlusse des ersten Aktes, der Tag neigt sich zum Abend; auf dem kleinen Bergvorsprunge rechts liegt Elisabeth vor dem Muttergottesbilde betend ausgestreckt. Wolfram kommt links von der waldigen Höhe herab, auf halber Höhe hält er an als er Elisabeth gewahrt.

Wolf. Wohl wusst ich hier sie im Gebet zu finden,
Wie ich so oft sie treffe, wenn ich einsam
Aus wald'ger Höh' mich in das Thal verirre.—
Den Tod, den er ihr gab, im Herzen,
Dahin gestreckt in brünst'gen Schmerzen,
Fleht für sein Heil sie Tag und Nacht:—
O heil'ger Liebe ew'ge Macht!
Von Rom zurück erwartet sie die Pilger.—
Schon fällt das Laub, die Heimkehr steht bevor:—
Kehrt er mit den Begnadigten zurück?
Dies ist ihr Fragen, dies ihr Flehen,—
Bleibt auch die Wunde ungeheillt,—
O, würd' ihr Lind'rung nur ertheilt!

Elisa. Dies ist ihr Sang,—sie sind's, sie kehren heim!
Ihr Heil'gen, zeigt mir jetzt mein Amt,
Dass ich mit Würde es erfülle!

Wolf. Die Pilger sind's,—es ist die fromme Weise,
Die der emfang'nen Gnade Heil verkündet.—
O Himmel, stärke jetzt ihr Herz
Für die Entscheidung ihres Lebens.

Gesang der äteren Pilger.
Beglückt darf nun dich, o Heimath, ich schauen.
Und grüssen froh deine lieblichen Auen;
Nun lass' ich ruhn den Wanderstab,
Weil Gott getreu ich gepilgert hab',
Durch Sühn' und Buss' hab ich versöhnt
Den Herren, dem mein Herze fröhnt,
Der meine Reu' mit Segen krönt,
Den Herren, dem mein Lied ertönt.
Der Gnade Heil ist dem Büsser beschieden,
Er geht einst ein in der Seligen Frieden!
Vor Höll' und Tod is ihm nicht bang',
Drum preis' ich Gott mein Lebenlang.
Halleluja in Ewigkeit!

Elisa. Er kehrt nicht zurück!—

No. 6.   OH BLESSED VIRGIN.

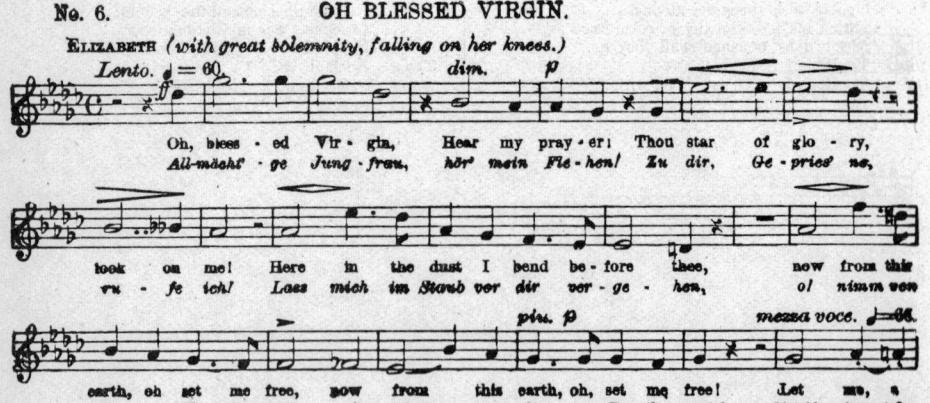

maid - en, pure and white, en - ter in - to thy king - dom bright! let me, a
rein und En - gel - gleich ein - ge - he in dein se - lig Reich, mach' das ich

a little more animated. ♩=72.

mai - den, pure and white, en - ter in - to thy king - dom bright! If
rein und En - gel - gleich, ein - ge he in dein se - lig Reich! Wenn

vain desires and earth - ly long - ing have turn'd my heart from thee a - way,
je, in thör'-gem Wahn be - fan - gen, mein Herz sich ab ge - wandt von dir,

the sin - ful hopes with - in me throng -ing, be - fore thy bless - ed feet I
wenn je ein sün - di - ges Ver - lan - gen, ein welt - lich Seh - nen keimt' in

slower.

lay; I'll wres - tle with the love I cher - ish'd, un - til in death its flame hath
mir; so rang' ich un - ter tau - send Schmerzen, dass ich es töd' in mei - nem

Tempo 1mo.

per - ish'd. If of my sin thou wilt not shrive me, yet in this hour, oh
Her - zen. Doch, konnt' ich je - den Fehl nicht bü - ssen, so nimm dich gnä - dig

grant thy aid!...... In this hour, oh grant thy aid! Till thy e - ter - nal
mei - ner an!...... Nimm dich gnä - dig mei - ner an! Dass ich mit de - muth

peace thou give me, I vow to live and die thy maid. And on thy
vol - lem Grüs sen, als würd 'ge Magd dir na - hen kann. um dei - ne

boun - ty I will call, that heav'n-ly grace on him may fall, yes, on thy
Gna - den reich - ste Huld, nur an - zu - flehn für sei - ne Schuld, um dei - ne

boun - ty I...... will call, that.... heav'n-ly grace on him...... may fall.
Gna - den reich - ste Huld nur.... an - zu - flehn für sei - - ne Schuld

SCENE II

Wolf.
Like Death's dark shadow, Night her gloom
  extendeth,
Her sable wing o'er all the vale she bendeth;
The soul that longs to tread yon path of light,
Yet dreads to pass the gate of Fear and Night,
I look on thee, oh, star in heaven the fairest,
Thy gentle beam thro' trackless space thou
  bearest;
The hour of darkness is by thee made bright,

Thou lead'st us upward with pure kindly light.

ZWEITE SCENE

Wolf.
Wie Todesahnung Dämm'rung deckt die Lande,
Umhüllt das Thal mit schwärzlichem Gewande;
Der Seele, die nach jenen Höh'n verlangt.
Vor ihrem Flug durch Nacht und Grausen bangt
Da scheinest du, o lieblichster der Sterne,
Dein sanftes Licht entsendest du der Ferne;
Die nächt'ge Dämm'rung theilt dein lieber
  Strahl,
Und freundlich zeigst den Weg du aus dem Thal.

No 7 O THOU SUBLIME, SWEET EV'NING STAR.

SCENE III

Tann.	The sound of harp I heard: it spoke of sadness.
	It was not she who sang.
Wolf.	Who art thou, pilgrim,
	Thy lonely path pursuing?
Tann.	Who am I?
	I who know thee so well! Wolfram thou art
	The wise and skilful minstrel!
Wolf.	Henry? Thou?
	What means thy coming thus dejected?
	Speak! Tell me not that thou, unabsolv'd,
	Hast dared to set thy foot within these precincts?
Tann.	Nay, have no fear, oh, sapient minstrel,
	I seek thee not, nor yet thy proud companions
	A path I seek, or one to guide my footsteps
	To find a path erewhile I trod with ease.
Wolf.	What path is that?
Tann.	It leads to Venus' hill.
Wolf.	Thou godless man! Thy words defile my ear.
	That is thy mission?
Tann.	Dost thou know the path?
Wolf.	Oh madman! Dread unknown thy words inspire.
	Whence com'st thou? Hast thou not been in Rome?
Tann.	Speak not of Rome!
Wolf.	Hast thou not sued for pardon?
Tann.	Speak not of that!
Wolf.	Thou wert not there?
	Oh, I conjure thee, speak!
Tann.	Yes, I have been in Rome.
Wolf.	Say on! oh, tell me all, unhappy man!
	With deep compassion I will hear thy words.
Tann.	What say'st thou, Wolfram? Say, art thou not my foe?
Wolf.	No, never more, while thou art true to honor;
	But tell—thy pilgrimage to Rome?
Tann.	I will—I will.
	Thou, Wolfram, shalt know what befell me.
	Away from me! The refuge where I rest me
	Is accursed! Now mark, Wolfram—mark well!
	Contrite in spirit, as no pilgrim yet on earth
	hath been,
	I bent my steps to Rome.
	An angel hath dispelled the pride of sin.
	Its mad profaneness from my bosom;
	For her sake I went forth a pilgrim,
	To reconcile offended Heaven;
	She who with tears for me had pleaded
	Should know my sins had been forgiven.
	When I beheld a heavy burden'd pilgrim
	It seemed to me his load was all too light;
	And if he sought a pathway o'er the meadow
	I trod unshod amid the rock and thorns;
	If he refreshed his lips by cooling fountain,
	The brazen sun poured on my head forlorn;
	When he besought the saints in murmured
	prayers,
	I shed my life-blood in the cause divine;
	When in the hospice he sought rest and shelter,
	On ice and snow it was that I sought mine;
	Lest Italy's fair scenes my heart had gladdened,
	I passed them blindfold, so my soul was
	saddened;
	I went, my wasted heart remorse was burning,
	That for my sake an angel waited mourning.

DRITTE SCENE

Tann.	Ich hörte Harfenschlag,—wie klang er traurig!
	Der kam wohl nicht von ihr.—
Wolf.	Wer bist du, Pilger,
	Der du so einsam wanderst?
Tann.	Wer ich bin?
	Kenn' ich doch dich recht gut;—Wolfram bist du,
	Der wohlgeübte Sänger.
Wolf.	Heinrich! du!
	Was bringt dich her in diese Nähe? Sprich!
	Wagst du es, unentsündigt wohl den Fuss
	Nach dieser Gegend hinzulenken?
Tann.	Sei ausser Sorg' mein guter Sänger!—
	Nicht such' ich dich, noch eurer Sippschaft Einen.
	Doch such' ich wen, der mir den Weg wohl zeige,
	Den Weg, den einst so wunderleicht ich fand.
Wolf.	Und welchen Weg?
Tann.	Den Weg zum Venusberg!
Wolf.	Entsetzlicher! Entweihe nicht mein Ohr!
	Treibt es dich dahin?
Tann.	Kennst du wohl den Weg?
Wolf.	Wahnsinn'ger! Grauen fasst mich, hör ich dich?
	Wo war'st du! Sag' zogst du denn nicht nach Rom?
Tann.	Schweig mir von Rom!
Wolf.	War'st nich beim heil'gen Feste?
Tann.	Schweig mir von ihm!
Wolf.	So war'st du nicht?—Sag', ich
	Beschwöre dich!
Tann.	Wohl war auch ich in Rom.
Wolf.	So sprich! Erzähle mir, Unglücklicher!
	Mich fasst ein tiefes Mitleid für dich an.
Tann.	Wie sag'st du, Wolfram? Bist du nicht mein Feind?
Wolf.	Nie war ich es, so lang' ich fromm dich wähnte!—
	Doch sprich! Du pilgertest nach Rom?
Tann.	Wohl denn!
	Hör' an! Du, Wolfram, du sollst es erfahren.
	Bleib' fern von mir! Die Stätte, wo ich raste,
	Ist verflucht! Hör' an, Wolfram, hör an!
	Inbrunst im Herzen, wie kein Büsser noch
	Sie je gefühlt, sucht' ich den Weg nach Rom.
	Ein Engel hatte, ach! der Sünde Stolz
	Dem Uebermüthigen entwunden!
	Für ihn woll't ich in Demuth büssen,
	Das Heil erfleh'n, das mir vernein't,
	Um ihn die Thräne zu versüssen,
	Die er mir Sünder einst geweint!
	Wie neben mir der schwerstbedrückte Pilger
	Die Strasse wallt', erschien mir allzuleicht;
	Betrat sein Fuss den weichen Grund der Wiesen,
	Der nackten Sohle sucht' sie Dorn und Stein;—
	Liess Labung er am Quell den Mund geniessen,
	Sog' ich der Sonne heisses Glühen ein!—
	Wenn fromm zum Himmel er Gebete schickte,
	Vergoss mein Blut ich zu des Höchsten Preis;
	Als der Hospiz die Wanderer erquickte,
	Die Glieder bettet' ich in Schnee und Eis,
	Verschloss'nen Aug's, ihr Wunder nicht zu schauen,
	Durchzog ich blind Italiens holde Auen.
	Ich that's—denn in Zerknirschung wollt' ich büssen
	Um meines Engels Thränen zu versüssen!

Thus Rome I gained at last; with tears
  imploring,
I knelt before the rood in faith adoring.
When daylight broke, the silv'ry bells were
  pealing;
Through vaulted roof a song divine was stealing;
A cry of joy breaks forth from thousand voices—
The hope of pardon ev'ry heart rejoices.
There him I saw who holds the keys of Heav'n,
And prostrate fell they all before his face.
And thousands he forgave that day, and bless'd
  them,
And sent them forth, renew'd in heav'nly grace.
Then I drew near, my glances earthward
  bending;
I made my plaint, despair my bosom rending—
I told what mad desires my soul had darkened,
By sinful earthly pleasure long enslav'd—
To me it seem'd that he in mercy hearken'd—
A gracious word in dust and tears I crav'd.
Then he whom thus I prayed replied:
"If thou has shar'd the joys of Hell,
If thou unholy flames hast nurs'd
That in the hill of Venus dwell,
Thou art for evermore accurs'd!
And as this barren staff I hold
Ne'er will put forth a flow'r or leaf,
Thus shalt thou never more behold
Salvation or thy sin's relief!"
Then hopeless, dumb despair obscur'd my senses!
I sank down motionless. When I awoke
'Twas night, and I alone, by all forsook.
I heard afar the songs of praise and prayer:
With loathing I fled t' escape the sound.
What were to me the tidings of their joy,
An outcast, spurn'd, in whom all hope was dead?
With horror in my breast, I turn'd and fled.
Then long'd my soul those joys to taste again
Which once before my earthborn pains had slain.
To thee, fair Venus, I surrender—
Let thy sweet magic round me play;
I'll be thy slave, thou star of splendor:
Thou only canst these pangs allay!

Wolf. Oh, stay thy godless raving!
Tann. Oh, guide my steps that I may find thee:
How well erewhile the road I knew!
Behold! men have with curses spurn'd me—
Come, lovely goddess, guide me true!
Wolf. Thou godless one! Whom dost thou call?
Tann. Ah! dost thou not feel balmy breezes?
Wolf. Away! Oh, fly, or thou art lost!
Tann. My senses what ecstasy seizes!
Hear'st thou not rapturous music?
Wolf. O wert thou rather in thy grave!
Tann. In mazy dance the nymphs now are flying—
Come on—come on! Ye fair, come on, receive
  your slave!
Wolf. Woe? evil demons fill the air
That hell its victim may ensnare!
Tann. Oh, come on Pleasure's rosy pinion!
I feel thy breath ambrosial!
This is of love the sweet dominion—
Oh, Venus, on thee I will call!
Venus. I welcome thee, perfidious man;
Earth laid thee low beneath its ban.
Hast thou by all, then, been forsaken
In my arms blissfully to waken?
Tann. Sweet Venus, oh, in bliss receive me!
With thee, with thee, oh, let me fly!
Wolf. Ye hellish phantoms, leave him!
All hope is lost when ye are nigh!
Venus. Com'st thou on grace from me relying?
Thy rash resolve I will forgive,

Nach Rom gelangt' ich so zur heil'gen Stelle,
Lag betend auf des Heiligthumes Schwelle;—
Der Tag brach an:—da läuteten die Glocken,
Hernieder tönten himmlische Gesänge;
Da jauchzt' es auf in brünstigem Frohlocken,
Denn Gnad' un Heil verhiessen sie der Menge.
Da sah' ich ihn, durch den sich Gott verkündigt.
Vor ihm all' Volk im Staub sich niederliess;
Und Tausenden er Gnade gab, entsündigt
Er Tausende sich froh erheben hiess.
Da naht' auch ich; das Haupt gebeugt zur Erde,
Klagt' ich mich an mit jammernder Geberde
Der bösen Lust, die meine Sinn' empfanden,
Des Sehnens, das kein Büssen noch gekühlt;
Und um Erlösung aus den heissen Banden
Rief ich ihn an, von wildem Schmerz durch-
  wühlt.—
Und er, den so ich bat, hub an:
"Hast du so böse Lust getheilt,
Dich an der Hölle Glut entflammt,
Hast du im Venusberg geweilt:
So bist nun ewig du verdammt;
Wie dieser Stab in meiner Hand
Nie mehr sich schmückt mit frischem Grün,
Kann aus der Hölle heissem Brand
Erlösung nimmer dir erblüh'n!"
Da sank ich in Vernichtung dumpf darnieder,
Die Sinne schwanden mir.—Als ich erwacht,
Auf ödem Platze lagerte die Nacht,
Von fern her tönten frohe Gnadenlieder:
Da ekelte mich der holde Sang,——
Von der Verheissung lügnerischem Klang,
Der eiseskalt mir durch die Seele schnitt,
Trieb Grauen mich hinweg mit wildem Schritt,
Dahin zog's mich, wo ich der Wonn' und Lust
So viel genoss an ihrer warmen Brust:
Zu dir, frau Venus, kehr' ich wieder,
In deiner Zauber holde Nacht,
Zu deinem Hof steig' ich darnieder,
Wo nun dein Reiz mir ewig lacht!

Wolf. Halt' ein! Halt' ein, Unseliger!
Tann. Ach, lass mich nicht vergebens suchen,
Wie leicht fand ich doch einstens dich!
Du hörst, dass mir die Menschen fluchen,
Nun, süsse Göttin, leite mich!
Wolf. Wahnsinniger, wen rufst du an?
Tann. Ha! fühlest du nicht milde Lüfte?
Wolf. Zu mir! Es ist um dich gethan!
Tann. Und athmest du nicht holde Düfte?
Hörst du nicht die jubelnden Klänge?
Wolf. In wildem Schauer bebt die Brust!
Tann. Das ist der Nymphen tanzende Menge.—
Herbei, herbei zu Wonn' und Lust!
Wolf. Weh, böser Zauber thut sich auf!
Die Hölle naht in wildem Lauf.
Tann. Entzücken dringt durch alle Sinne,
Gewahr' ich diesen Dämmerschein;
Dies ist das Zauberreich der Minne,
In Venusberg drangen wir ein!
Venus. Willkommen, ungetreuer Mann!
Schlug dich die Welt mit Acht und Bann?
Und findest nirgends du Erbarmen,
Suchst Liebe nun in meinen Armen?
Tann. Frau Venus, o, Erbarmungsreiche!
Zu dir, zu dir zieht es mich hin!
Wolf. Du Höllenzauber, weiche, weiche!
Berücke nicht des Reinen Sinn!
Venus. Nahst du dich wieder meiner Schwelle,
Sei dir dein Uebermuth verzeihn;

Come where joy is fed from source undying.
In pleasure's bright abode to live.

Tann. Accurs'd of hope they have bereft me;
Now joys of hell alone are left me,

Wolf. Oh, mighty Lord! in mercy see!
Henry, one word and thou art free—
Repent!

Venus.   O come belov'd!
For ever thou art mine.

Tann. No more. Away from me!

Wolf. Yet canst thou gain thy soul's salvation.

Tann. No, Wolfram, no; the Heavens are closed!

Wolf. It hears an angel's supplication,
Who now for thee its grace implores—
Elisabeth!

Tann. Oh, maid divine!

Chorus of men.
Receive the soul, oh, bounteous Lord,
That now to Thee hath taken flight.

Wolf. Thy angel prays for thee before the throne,
And Heaven relents!
Henry, thou art absolv'd!

Venus. Woe! I have lost him?

Chorus of men.
Hers be the angels' blest reward!
Bright be her glory in Thy sight!

Wolf. Oh, say, hear'st thou this strain?

Tann. I hear it.

Chorus of Men.
Sainted forever thro' all the spheres,
She who thro' love thy salvation attain'd.
Blest is the sinner sav'd by her tears,
Now he the heav'nly gate hath gain'd

Tann. Holy Saint Elisabeth, oh, pray for me!

Wolf. He is redeemed.

Chorus of Pilgrims.
The Lord Himself now thy bondage hath riven—
Go, enter in with the blest in His Heaven.

Ewig fliesst dir der Freuden Quelle,
Und nimmer sollst du von mir fliehn!

Tann. Mein Heil, mein Heil hab' ich verloren,
Nun sei der Hölle Lust erkoren!

Wolf. All mächt'ger, steh' dem Frommen bei!—
Heinrich,—ein Wort, es macht dich frei:—
Dein Heil—

Venus. Zu mir!
O komm! Auf ewig sei nun mein!

Tann.   Lass ab von mir!

Wolf. Noch soll das Heil dir Sünder werden.

Tann. Nie! Wolfram, nie! Ich muss dahin!

Wolf. Ein Engel bat für dich auf Erden—
Bald schwebt er segnend über dir,
Elisabeth!

Tann.   Elisabeth!

Pilger. Der Seele Heil, die nun entfloh'n
Dem Leib der frommen Dulderin!

Wolf. Dein Engel fleht für dich an Gottes Thron,
Er wird erhört! Heinrich, du bist erlöst!

Venus. Weh! Mir verloren!

Pilger. Ihr ward der Engel sel'ger Lohn,
Himmlischer Freuden Hochgewinn!

Wolf. Und hörst du diesen Sang?

Tann. Ich höre!

Pilger. Heilig die Reine, die nun vereint
Göttlicher Schaar vor dem Ewigen steht.
Selig der Sünder, dem sie geweint,
Dem sie des Himmels Heil erfleht!

Tann. Heilige Elisabeth, bitte für mich!

Wolf. Er ist erlöst!

Die Pilger.
Der Gnade Heil ward dem Büsser beschieden,
Er geht nun ein in der Seligen Frieden.

THE END

LOHENGRIN

HENRY I., King of Germany, surnamed the "Fowler," has arrived at Antwerp, with the intention of levying a force to assist in repelling the Hungarians, who have threatened his dominions with invasion. He finds Brabant in a state of anarchy. Godfrey, the young son of the late duke, has disappeared, and his sister Elsa is accused of murdering him by her guardian, Frederick, Count of Telramund, who has married Ortrud, daughter of Radbod, Prince of Friesland, and in right of his wife claims to be the ruler of the Duchy. Elsa, appearing before the King, asserts her innocence, and it is agreed that the cause should be decided by a judicial combat between Frederick and any champion who may appear on behalf of the accused. When her condition seems most hopeless, a knight appears ascending the river Scheldt, in a boat drawn by a single swan, which on landing he dismisses, and undertakes her defence, Elsa promising that if he is victorious she will bestow upon him her hand, and never question him as to his name or origin. In the combat that ensues Frederick is stricken to the ground by his unknown antagonist, and deprived of his title and estate.

Preparations are made for the immediate marriage of the stranger with Elsa; but while all are reveling in the Pallas, or abode of the knights, Frederick and Ortrud are without, plotting how they may be avenged and recover their lost honors. Presenting herself at the Kemenate or abode of the ladies, Ortrud moves the compassion of Elsa, who not only gains her admission, but promises to obtain the pardon of Frederick, and listens to the suggestion that she ought to inquire into the name and origin of her future husband, who, without the ducal title, has been appointed by the King, Protector of Brabant and leader of the Brabant contingent of the German army. As the nuptial procession approaches the cathedral, the conspirators reveal themselves in their true character, Ortrud opposing Elsa at the door, and Frederick declaring that the unknown knight, Lohengrin, is a sorcerer, who has gained his victory by unfair and unholy means.

The intruders are expelled by the King and people, and the marriage takes place; but, when the bride and bridegroom are left in the nuptial chamber, Elsa, roused by the evil suggestions of Ortrud, begins, in spite of her promise, to question the knight, who in vain endeavors to allay her suspicions. Frederick, who enters the room with the intention of assailing his former antagonist, is slain by him at once, and, on the following morning, the explanation unwisely solicited by Elsa, is given by the stranger in the presence of the King. He is the son of King Percival, keeper of the mysterious cup known as the "Holy Grail," to whose service he is attached, and whose name is Lohengrin. It is to the Grail that he is indebted for his invisible power, but now his name is revealed he must no longer remain in Brabant. The swan returns with the boat to bear him away, but he removes a gold chain from its neck, and in its stead appears the youth Godfrey, who has been changed to a swan by the sorceress Ortrud, and who is now declared rightful Duke of Brabant, while Lohengrin departs, to the intense grief of his bride and the King and people, who have lost so valuable an ally.

LOHENGRIN

ACT I	ERSTER AKT

| SCENE I | ERSTE SCENE |

[*A meadow on the banks of the Scheldt, by Antwerp,* KING HENRY *under the Oak of Justice, surrounded by Counts and Nobles of the Saxon Arriere-ban. Opposite to them the Counts and Nobles of Brabant, headed by* FREDERICK *of Telramund, with* ORTRUD *by his side. The Herald steps from the party of the King to the centre of the stage, and signs for the four Royal Trumpeters to play the call to muster.*

HERALD. Hark! Princes, noblés, freemen of Brabant!
Henry, our German Sov'reign, calls ye forth
This day to muster for the realm's defence.
Will ye, as faithful vassals, serve your King?

MEN OF BRABANT.
We will, as faithful vassals, serve our King.
Be welcome, Henry, to Brabant!

KING. Heav'n shield ye, loyal lieges of Brabant!
Not idly have I journeyed to your shores;
I come to warn that danger is at hand.
Ye know full well the tide of death and ruin
That oft hath from the east swept o'er the land
Upon our frontiers pray the wives and children
"Lord, from th' Hungarian hordes protect our
hearths!"
For me, the nation's guardian, it was fitting
To put an end to misrule and oppression.
As conqueror, at last I gained a nine years'
truce.
That time I used to arm the land;
With walls and towers I fortified the towns.
And now against the foe I summon you. .
The term is just o'erpast; the foe prepares;
The wonted tribute I refuse to pay.
Now is the time to guard our nation's honor.
From east and west, all men of German blood
Arise united; knights, your thralls assemble—
No man shall dare deride my sov'reign rule.

SAXONS AND THURINGIANS. (*Striking their arms.*)
'Tis well; we'll guard our German land!

KING. (*Reseating himself.*)
Thus have I sought ye, freemen of Brabant
To summon you to Mentz, nobles and vassals;
Here, to my grief, I meet with nought but strife,
All in disunion, from your chiefs estranged!
Confusion, civil warfare meet we here.
On thee I call, Frederick of Telramund!
I know thee for a knight as brave as true,
I charge thee, let me know this trouble's cause.

FRED. Thanks, gracious King, that thou to judge art
come!
The truth I'll tell thee, falsehood I disdain.
When death was closing round our valiant Duke,
'Twas me he chose as guardian of his children,

[*Eine Aue am Ufer der Schelde bei Antwerpen.* KÖNIG HEINRICH *unter der Gerichtseiche; zu seiner Seite Grafen und Edle vom sächsischen Heerbann. Gegenüber brabantische Grafen und Edle an ihrer Spitze* FRIEDRICH *von Telramund, zu dessen Seite* ORTRUD. *Der Heerrufer ist aus des* KÖNIGS *Heerbann in die Mitte geschritten; auf sein Zeichen blasen vier Trompeter des* KÖNIGS *den Aufruf.*

DER HEERRUFER. Hört! Grafen, Edle, Freie von Brabant!
Heinrich, der Deutschen König, kam zur Stadt.
Mit euch zu dingen nach des Reiches Recht.
Gebt ihr nun Fried' und Folge dem Gebot?

DIE BRABANTER.
Wir geben Fried' und Folge dem Gebot.
Willkommen! Willkommen! König, in Brabant!

KÖNIG HEINRICH.
Gott grüss' euch, liebe Männer von Brabant!
Nicht müssig that zu euch ich diese Fahrt;
Der Noth des Reiches seid von mir gemahnt.
Soll ich euch erst der Drangsal Kunde sagen,
Die deutsches Land so oft aus Osten traf?
In fernster Mark hiess't Weib und Kind ihr
beten:
"Herr Gott, bewahr' uns vor der Ungarn Wuth!"
Doch mir, des Reiches Haupt, musst' es geziemen,
Solch wilder Schmach ein Ende zu ersinnen;
Als Kampfes Preis gewann ich Frieden auf
Neun Jahr' ihn nützt' ich zu des Reiches Wehr:
Beschirmte Städt' und Burgen liess ich bau'n,
Den Heerbann übte ich zum Widerstand.
Zu End' ist nun die Frist, der Zins versagt,—
Mit wildem Drohen rüstet sich der Feind.
Nun ist es Zeit des Reiches Ehr, zu wahren;
Ob Ost, ob West, das gelte Allen gleich!
Was deutsches Land heisst, stelle Kampfesschaaren,
Dann schmäht wohl Niemand mehr das deutsche
Reich!

DIE SACHSEN UND THÜRINGER.
Mit Gott wohlauf für deutshen Reiches Ehr'!

KÖNIG. Komm' ich zu euch nun, Männer von Brabant,
Zur Heeresfolg' nach Mainz euch zu entbieten;
Wie muss mit Schmerz und Klagen ich erseh'n,
Dass ohne Fürsten ihr in Zwietracht lebt!
Verwirrung, wilde Fehde wird mir kund;—
Drum ruf' ich dich als aller Tugend Preis,—
Jetzt rede, dass der Drangsal Grund ich weiss.

FRIED. Dank, König, dir, dass du zu richten kamst!
Die Wahrheit künd' ich, Untreu ist mir fremd
Zum Sterben kam der Herzog von Brabant,
Und meinem Schutz empfahl er seine Kinder,

FRED. Elsa the maiden, and Gottfried her brother;
       Whose dawning years with tender care I guarded
       Whose welfare I have treasured as my honor
       My sov'reign, mark now, if I'm aggrieved,
       When of my honor's treasure I am robbed!
       One day, when Elsa had with her brother
          wandered forth,
       Without the boy, trembling, she returned,
       With feign'd lamenting, questioned of his safety,
       Pretending she had been from him divided,
       And in vain his traces she had sought.
       Fruitless was every search we made to find him;
       And when I questioned her with words severe,
       Her pallor and her falt'ring tongue betray'd her,
       Her crime in its guilty blackness stood confess'd
       A horror fell upon me of the maid;
       The claim upon her hand her father had
          conferr'd
       With willing heart I straight resigned,
       And chose a wife full pleasant to my sense,
       Ortrud, daughter of Radbod, true in death.
       I here arraign her, Princess Elsa of Brabant;
       Of fratricide be she charged.
       I claim dominion o'er this land by right;
       My nearest kinsman was the valiant duke,
       My wife descendent of the race   [past
       That gave this land their rulers thro' long ages
       O king, give judgment! All now thou hast heard

ALL THE MEN.
       Ha! Telramund, what hast thou said?
       I mark thee with dismay and dread!

KING. A dreadful accusation thou hast brought,
       A crime so deadly, how can I believe?

FRED. O king, listless and dreamy is the maid,
       She who with scorn refused my proffer'd hand.
       Some secret love her senses hath beguil'd; [ished
       She deemed perchance, because the boy had per-
       She'd reign secure as sov'reign of Brabant;
       For that, her vassal she disdained as consort,
       That openly she might her lover cherish.

KING. Summon the maid accused;
       For judgment let all be prepared!
       Heaven, let me deem aright!

HERALD. Dost thou decree, O king, to have a judgment
       here?

KING. I will not rest beneath my shield
       Until the truth hath been revealed!

ALL THE MEN. No sword to scabbard shall return
       Until thy will, O King, we learn.

HERALD. Where'er the royal shield ye see,
       Know that the king doth there decree;
       Resound, my cry, both far and near:
       Elsa, thou royal maid, appear!

SCENE II

[ELSA enters; she remains some time at the back of the
stage; then she slowly and very timidly comes forward
to the front (centre). The ladies of her train remain
during the first part of the scene in the extreme background, outside the circle where justice is given.

ALL THE MEN.
       Behold! she comes, how grief o'er clouds her!
       How like an angel of light her hue!
       He who with base suspicion loads her
       Must prove his dark surmise is true.

FRIED. Elsa, die Jungfrau, und Gottfried, den Knaben;
       Mit Treue pfleg ich seiner grossen Jugend,
       Sein Leben war das Kleinod meiner Ehre.
       Ermiss nun König meinen grimmen Schmerz,
       Als meiner Ehre Kleinod mir geraubt!
       Lustwandelnd führte Elsa den Knaben einst
       Zum Wald, doch ohne ihn kehrte sie zurück;
       Mit falscher Sorge frug sie nach dem Bruder,
       Da sie, von ohngefähr von ihm verirrt,
       Bald seine Spur—so sprach sie—nicht mehr
          fand.
       Fruchtlos war all' Bemüh'n um den Verlor'nen;
       Als ich mit Drohen nun in Elsa drang,
       Da liess in bleichem Zagen und Erbeben
       Der grässlichen Schuld Bekenntniss sie uns sehn.
       Es fasste mich Entsetzen vor der Magd:
       Dem Recht auf ihre Hand, vom Vater mir
       Verliehn, entsagt' ich willig da und gern,—
       Und nahm ein Weib, das meinem Sinn gefiel,
       Ortrud, Radbod's, des Friesenfürsten, Spross.
       Nun führ ich Klage wider Elsa von
       Brabant: des Brudermordes zeih' ich sie.
       Dies Land doch sprech' ich für mich an mit
          Recht,
       Da ich der Nächste von des Herzog's Blut,
       Mein Weib jedoch aus dem Geschlecht, das
          einst
       Auch diesem Lande seine Fürsten gab.
       Du hörst die Klage, König! Richte recht!

ALLE MÄNNER.
       Ha! Schwerer Schuld zeiht Telramund!
       Mit Grau'n werd' ich der Klage kund.

KÖNIG. Welch' fürchterliche Klage sprichst du aus!
       Wie wäre möglich solche grosse Schuld?

FRIED. O Herr, traumselig ist die eitle Magd,
       Die meine Hand voll Hochmuth von sich stiess
       Geheimer Buhlschaft klag' ich drum sie an:
       Sie wähnte wohl, wenn sie des Bruders ledig,
       Dann könnte sie als Herrin von Brabant,
       Mit Recht dem Lehnsmann ihre Hand
          verwehren,
       Und offen des geheimen Buhlen pflegen.

KÖNIG. Ruft die Beklagte her! Beginnen soll
       Nun das Gericht! Gott lass' mich weise sein!

DER HEERRUFER. Soll hier nach Recht und Macht Ge-
       richt gehalten sein?

KÖNIG. Nicht eh'r soll bergen mich der Schild,
       Bis ich gerichtet streng und mild!

ALLE MÄNNER.
       Nicht eh'r zur Scheide kehr' das Schwert
       Bis ihm durch Urtheil Recht gewährt!

HEERRUFER. Wo ihr des Königs Schild gewahrt,
       Dort Recht durch Urtheil nun erfahrt!
       Drum ruf' ich klagend laut und hell:
       Elsa, erscheine hier zur Stell'!

ZWEITE SCENE

[ELSA tritt langsam und verschämt auf; ein langer Zug
ihrer Frauen folgt ihr, sich zunächst an der äussersten
Grenze des Gerichtskreises im Hintergrunde haltend.

ALLE MÄNNER.
       Seht hin! Sie naht, die hart Beklagte!
       Ha, wie erscheint sie so licht und rein!
       Der sie so schwer zu zeihen wagte,
       Gar sicher muss der Schuld er sein.

KING. Art thou she, Elsa of Brabant?
       Wilt thou be deemed by me, thy sov'reign Lord?
       Then further I ask thee
       If the charge to thee is known,
       That darkly is alleged against thee?
       Canst thou meet the accusation?
                    *   *   *   *
KING. Then thy guilt thou dost confess?

ELSA. Oh, my poor brother!
ALL THE MEN. 'Tis wondrous strange—
       Her words I cannot fathom.
KING. Speak, Elsa; in thy king thou may'st confide.

KÖNIG. Bist du es, Elsa von Brabant? Erkennst
        Du mich als deinen Richter an? So frage
        Ich weiter: ist die Klage dir bekannt,
        Die schwer hier wider dich erhoben? Was
        Entgegnest du der Klage?
                    *   *   *   *
KÖNIG.   So bekennst
                 du deine Schuld?
ELSA. Mein armer Bruder!
ALLE MÄNNER. Wie wunderbar! Welch seltsames
             Gebaren!
KÖNIG. Sag', Elsa! Was hast du mir zu vertrau'n?

OFT WHEN THE HOURS WERE LONELY.

KING AND ALL THE MEN.
Oh, Heaven, in mercy be thou near,
This day make truth from error clear!

KING. Frederick, bethink thee, while there's time,
Could she enact so foul a crime?

FRED. Her dreamy mood my mind hath ne'er deceiv'd
Ye hear, she raves about a lover!
I speak the truth, of that I'm well assur'd
One do I know who can the deed attest.
But if ye doubt my word as knight and noble
No further proof or witness will I deign!
For battle here I stand!
Who dares attaint my honor—
Let that man stand forth and fight!

THE BRABANTIANS. I am thy friend. I will not fight
with thee.

FRED. And thou, my king, recall to thy remembrances
The day I saved thee from the murd'rous Dane?

KING. 'Twere ill if there were need of that to mind me!
Thou'rt brave and true, all honors need be thine,
As guardian of this land I'd fain appoint thee,
Thou of my chiefs the noblest.
Heav'n alone shall now for life or death decide
between you!

ALL THE MEN. A judgment of God! 'Tis well!

KING. Answer me, noble Count of Telramund:
Wilt thou do battle here for life or death?
Shall Heaven's ordeal decide if thou spok'st
truly?

FRED. Yea!

KING. And now I ask thee, Elsa of Brabant:
Wilt thou count thy cause for life or death?
As heaven's ordeal pronounceth, by thy cham-
pion?

ELSA. Yea!

KING. Choose one who shall defend thee.

FRED. Now ye shall know the name of her accomplice.

THE BRABANTIANS. Let us hear!

ELSA. My guardian, my defender,
He shall my champion be!
This is the prize I offer
To him whom heaven shall send;
The lands and crown I proffer,
My sire to me did lend;
As lord I will declare him,
And glory in his fame,
If in his heart he'll wear me
I'll give him all I am!

ALL THE MEN. A noble prize—who will the victor be?
Who will contend? What will be Heaven's
decree?

KING. The sun stands high; noon will not tarry.
Call forth the warrior knights with trumpet's
call!

[The Herald stands forward with the four Trumpeters
whom he places towards the four points of the compass at the extreme end of the circle, where they blow
the summons.

HERALD. Who will do battle here on life or death
For Elsa of Brabant, let him appear!

DER KÖNIG UND ALLE MÄNNER.
Bewahre uns des Himmels Huld,
Das klar wir sehen wer hier schuld!

KÖNIG. Friedrich, du ehrenwerther Mann,
Bedenke wohl, wen klagst du an?

FRIED. Ihr hört, sie schwärmt von einem Buhlen!
Wes' ich sie zeih' des' hab' ich sich'ren Grund:
Glaubwürdig ward ihr Frevel mir bezeugt.
Doch eurem Zweifel durch ein Zeugniss wehren,
Das stünde wahrlich übel meinem Stolz!
Hier steh' ich, hier mein Schwert! Wer wagt's
von euch,
Zu streiten wider meiner Ehre Preis?

DIE BRABANTISCHEN EDLEN.
Keiner von uns! Wir streiten nur für dich.

FRIED. Und König, du! Gedenkst du meiner Dienste,
Wie ich im Kampf den wilden Dänen schlug?

KÖNIG. Wie schlimm, liess' ich von dir daran mich
mahnen:
Gern geb' ich dir der höchsten Tugend Preis,
In keiner and'ren Huth, als in der deinen,
Möcht' ich die Lande wissen.
Gott allein soll jetzt in dieser Sache noch ent-
scheiden!

ALLE MÄNNER. Zum Gottesgericht! Zum Gottesgericht!
Wohlan!

KÖNIG. Dich frag' ich, Friedrich, Graf von Telramund!
Willst du durch Kampf auf Leben und auf Tod
Im Gottesgericht vertreten deine Klage?

FRIED. Ja!

KÖNIG. Und dich nun frag' ich, Elsa von Brabant!
Willst du, dass hier auf Leben und auf Tod
Im Gottesgericht ein Kämpe für dich streite?

ELSA. Ja!

KÖNIG. Wen kiesest du zum Streiter?

FRIED. Vernehmet jetzt den namen ihres Buhlen!

DIE BRABANTISCHEN EDLEN. Merket auf!

ELSA. Des Ritters will ich wahren,
Er soll mein Streiter sein!
Hört was dem Gottgesandten
Ich biete führ Gewähr:—
In meines Vaters Landen
Die Krone trage er;
Mich glücklich soll ich preisen,
Nimmt er mein Gut dahin,—
Will er Gemahl mich heissen,
Geb' ich ihm was ich bin!

DIE MÄNNER. Ein hoher Preis stünd' er in Hand!
Wer um ihn stritt', wohl setzt' er schweres
Pfand.

KÖNIG. Im Mittag hoch steht schon die Sonne;
So ist es Zeit, dass nun der Ruf ergeh'.

[Tritt mit vier Trompetern vor, die er, den Himmels-
gegenden zugewendet, an die äussersten Grenzen des
Gerichtskreises schreiten und blasen lässt.

DIE HEERRUFER.
Wer hier im Gotteskampf zu streiten kam
Für Elsa von Brabant, der trete vor!

ALL THE MEN.
No champion to the call comes forth!
Ah, hapless maiden, hope resign!

FRED. Ye see what now her cause is worth,
Both right and power are justly mine!

ELSA. My gracious sov'reign, let me pray thee
Yet once again my knight to summon.
He dwells afar and heareth not.

THE KING. Once more, then, let the call go forth.

ALL THE MEN.
The heav'ns are silent, she is doomed!

ELSA. When in my grief I bent before Thee,
Thou sentest him who hath my vow;
Oh, Lord, hear me again implore Thee!
In my distress, oh, send him now!
Stainless and white, radiantly dight,
Let me behold that form of light!

CHORUS OF LADIES. Lord! Let Thy help be nigh!
Hear us, gracious Lord!

CHORUS OF MEN.

[*Standing nearest to the water's edge; they first perceive the coming of* LOHENGRIN, *who is seen in the distance approaching in a skiff drawn by a swan.*

Look! this is sure a marvel! see, a swan—
A fair swan, leading yonder pinnace on!
And lo, a knight,
A warrior full fair, standing on the prow!
Ha! his arms resplendent gleam!
A helm of light upon his brow!
Look there! he comes nearer, he hath gained the shore,
And with a chain of gold the swan he reins:
Behold, he comes! Lo, he comes!

SCENE III

BOTH CHORUSES OF MEN.
A marvel wrought amongst us—
A great unheard-of marvel; yes, a marvel.

THE LADIES.
Thanks, oh, gracious Lord!
Thou our prayer hast granted.
All hail, thou hero from on high!
Be thou welcome, Heav'n itself sent thee here!
Yes Heav'n hath sent thee here!

[*The* KING *from his raised seat sees everything;* FREDER-ICK *and* ORTRUD *are petrified with surprise and dread;* ELSA, *who has listened to the previous exclamations with rising delight, remains in her place in the centre of the stage, as though she dared not look round. Here the skiff drawn by the swan, reaches the shore in the centre of the stage;* LOHENGRIN, *in a silver coat of mail, with a shining helmet, his shield at his back, a little golden horn at his side, stands within it, leaning on his sword.* FREDERICK *gazes on* LOHENGRIN *in speechless amazement.* ORTRUD, *who during the proceeding had preserved a cold and haughty bearing, is seized by a terrible consternation at the sight of the swan. All deferentially bare their heads. Here* ELSA *has turned round and gives a cry of joy at the sight of* LOHENGRIN. *As* LOHENGRIN *moves to step out of the skiff, all are silent in rapt expectancy.*

ALLE MÄNNER.
Ohn' Antwort ist der Ruf verhallt;
Um ihre Sache steht es schlecht.

FRIED. Gewahrt, ob ich sie fälschlich schalt?
Auf meiner Seite bleibt das Recht.

ELSA. Mein lieber König, lass dich bitten,
Noch einen Ruf an meinen Ritter!
Wohl weilt er fern und hört' ihn nicht.

KÖNIG. Noch einmal rufe zum Gericht!

ALLE MÄNNER. In düst'rem Schweigen richtet Gott.

ELSA. Du trugest zu ihm meine Klage,
Zu mir trat er auf dein Gebot:
O Herr, nun meinem Ritter sage,
Dass er mir helf' in meiner Noth!
Lass mich ihn sehn, wie ich ihn sah,
Wie ich ihn sah, sei er mir nah!

CHOR DER FRAUEN.
Herr! Sende Hülfe ihr!
Herr Gott, höre uns!

DIE MÄNNER.

[*Die auf einer Erhöhung dem Ufer am nächsten Stehenden gewahren in der Ferne einen Nachen, von einen Schwan gezogen, auf dem Flusse allmählich sich nähern; in dem Nachen steht ein Ritter.*

Seht! Seht! Welch seltsam Wunder!
Wie? Ein Schwan?
Ein Schwan zieht einen Nachen dort heran!—
Ein Ritter drin hoch aufgerichtet steht!
Wie glänzt sein Waffenschmuck! Das Aug'
vergeht
Vor solchem Licht!—Seht, näher kommt er
schon heran!
An einer goldnen Kette zieht der Schwan!

DRITTE SCENE

ALLE MÄNNER.
Ein Wunder! ein Wunder! ein Wunder ist
gekommen!

DIE FRAUEN. Ha, unerhörtes, nie geseh'nes Wunder!
Gegrüsst, gegrüsst du gottgesandter Mann!
Dank, du Herr und Gott, der du die Schwache
beschirmet!
Sei gegrüsst du gottgesandter Mann!

[*Von seinem Platze aus übersieht der* KÖNIG *Alles.* FRIED-RICH *und* ORTRUD *durch Schreck und Staunen gefesselt.* ELSA, *in steigender Entzückung lauschend, wagt nicht umzublicken. Aller Augen wenden sich erwartungsvoll nach dem Hintergrunde.* LOHENGRIN, *in glänzender Silberrüstung, den Helm auf den Haupte, den Schild im Rücken, ein kleines goldenes Horn zur Seite, steht auf sein Schwert gelehnt im Kahn.* FRIEDERICH *blickt in sprachlosem Erstaunen auf ihn hin;* ORTRUD, *bisher in kalter, stolzer Haltung, geräth bei des Schwanes Anblick in tödtlichen Schreck. Alles entblösst in höchster Ergriffenheit das Haupt.* ELSA, *sich wendend, schreit bei* LOHENGRIN's *Anblick laut auf. Sowie* LOHENGRIN *Bewegung macht den Kahn zu verlassen, gespanntestes Schweigen.*

I GIVE THEE THANKS, MY GENTLE SWAN.

LOHENGRIN.
I give thee thanks, my faith-ful swan! Turn thee a-gain and breast.... the tide, Re-
turn un-to that land of dawn Where joy-ous we did long...... a-bide
Well thy ap-point-ed task.... is done! Farewell! farewell! my trus-ty swan!

Chorus. pp
Doth he not seem...... from Heav'n descend-ed; His ra- - diant
mien holds me enthrall'd! Val-or and grace in him are blend-ed, To deeds of glo- -ry he is
call'd! Va-lor and grace in him are blend-ed, To deeds of glo-ry he is call'd!
Oh! sweet enchant-ment! Oh, sweet en-chant-ment! won-drous love! Deep in.... my
heart the spell I prove, Splen-dor di-vine.... a-round them plays!
pp
Splen-der...... di-vine,.......... a-round their tress-es plays!

LOHENGRIN. Hail gracious sov'reign!
Victory and honor be thy valor's meed!
Thy glorious name shall from the land
That chose thee ruler, ne'er depart.
KING. Have thanks! Methinks I know the pow'r
That sent thee here in this dread hour;
On Heaven's mission thou art come.
LOHENGRIN. I came for yonder maid to fight,
From dark surmise her name to clear:
In quarrel true to guard her right,
Who now my proffered vow shall hear!
I ask thee, Elsa of Brabant,
If thou the boon to me wilt grant
As thy champion to fight this day—
Wilt thou entrust thy cause to me?
ELSA. My hope, my solace, hero mine,
Do thou protect me, I am thine!

LOHENGRIN. Heil König Heinrich! Segenvoll
Mög' Gott bei deinem Schwerte steh'n!
Ruhmreich und gross dein Name soll
Von dieser Erde nie vergehn?
KÖNIG. Hab' Dank! Erkenn' ich recht die Macht,
Die dich in dieses Land gebracht,
So kommst du uns von Gott gesandt?
LOHENGRIN. Zum Kampf für eine Magd zu steh'n,
Der schwere Klage angethan.
Bin ich gesandt: nun lasst mich seh'n,
Ob ich zurecht sie treffe an!—
So sprich denn, Elsa von Brabant!
Wenn ich zum Streiter dir ernannt,
Willst du wohl ohne Bang' und Grau'n
Dich meinem Schutze anvertrau'n?
ELSA. Mein Held, mein Retter! Nimm mich hin,
Dir geb' ich Alles, was ich bin!

LOHENGRIN. If in thy cause to-day I conquer,
Wilt thou empledge thy faith to me?

ELSA. As here I lowly bend before thee,
Thine will I now and ever be.

LOHENGRIN.
Elsa, if thou thy troth wilt plight me,
If from the foe this land I save;
If nought from me shall disunite thee,
A promise I of thee must crave:
Never, as thou dost love me,
Aught shall to question move thee,
From whence to thee I came,
Or what my race, and name.

ELSA. Lord, at thy will thou shalt command me

LOHENGRIN. Say dost thou understand me?
Never, as thou dost love me,
Aught shall to question move thee;
From whence to thee I came,
Or what my race and name.

ELSA. Oh, thou, my hero, my defender,
No doubt of thee is in my heart;
I life and faith to thee surrender—
How could I question what thou art?
As thou wilt guard my name and land,
Thus will I cherish thy command.

LOHENGRIN. Elsa, I worship thee!

THE KING AND CHORUS.
Oh, sweet enchantment!
Some magic pow'r my senses sways,
Oh, sweet enchantment, wondrous love!
Deep in my heart thy spell I prove,
A light divine around them plays!

LOHENGRIN.
Ye knights, nobles, and freeman of this land
Guiltless and true is Elsa of Brabant!
Thy tale was falsehood, Count Telramund,
By Heav'n's assistance all thou shalt recant!

THE BRABANTIANS.
Refrain, refrain, the fight forego—
Thou wilt but win distress and woe.
Oh, be advised!
If it is Heaven that sent him here,
What will avail thy sword or spear?
Refrain, refrain! I warn thee as a friend;
Go not forth to-day,
Or in disaster thou wilt end!

FRED. If I must fall, I'll die!
What spells so'er have brought thee here,
Stranger, who dost my sword defy?
No cause have I thy threats to fear,
For all is truth my words imply.
Behold me prepar'd for the fray,
If right prevails, I'll win the day.

LOHENGRIN.
Great sov'reign, now ordain the fight!

THE KING. Upon each side three knights the space
shall measure.
I here proclaim this place a fencéd field.

[*Three Saxon nobles stand forth for* LOHENGRIN, *and
three Brabantians for* FREDERICK: *they cross the stage
with solemn strides and measure the ground for the
combat; when the six have formed a complete circle
they cross spears into the ground.*

LOHENGRIN. Wenn ich im Kampfe für dich siege,
Willst du, das ich dein Gatte sei?

ELSA. Wie ich zu deinen Füssen liege,
Geb' ich dir Leib und Seele frei.

LOHENGRIN. Elsa, soll ich dein Gatte heissen,
Soll Land und Leut' ich schirmen dir,
Soll nichts mich wieder von dir reissen,
Musst Eines du geloben mir:
Nie sollst du mich befragen,
Noch Wissen's Sorge tragen,
Woher ich kam der Fahrt,
Noch wie mein Nam' und Art!

ELSA. Nie, Herr, soll mir die Frage kommen.

LOHENGRIN. Elsa! Hast du mich wohl vernommen?
Nie sollst du mich befragen,
Noch Wissen's Sorge tragen,
Woher ich kam der Fahrt,
Noch wie mein Nam' und Art!

ELSA. Mein Schirm! mein Engel! mein Erlöser,
Der fest an meine Unschuld glaubt!
Wie gäb' es Zweifels Schuld, die grösser,
Als die an dich den Glauben raubt?
Wie du mich schirmst in meiner Noth,
So halt' in Treu' ich dein Gebot.

LOHENGRIN. Elsa, ich liebe dich!

DER KÖNIG, DIE MÄNNER UND FRAUEN.
Welche holde Wunder muss ich seh'n?
Ist's Zauber der mir angethan?
Ich fühl' das Herze mir verge'hn,
Schau' ich den wonniglichen Mann.

LOHENGRIN.
Nun hört! Euch Volk und Edlen mach' ich kund:
Frei aller Schuld ist Elsa von Brabant.
Dass falsch dein Klagen, Graf von Telramund,
Durch Gottes Urtheil werd' es dir bekannt!

BRABANTISCHE EDLE.
Steh' ab vom Kampf! Wenn du ihn wagst,
Zu siegen nimmer du vermagst!
Ist er von höchster Macht geschützt,
Sag', was dein tapf'res Schwert dir nützt?
Steh' ab! wir mahnen dich in Treu'!
Dein harret Unsieg, bittre Reu'!

FRIED. Viel lieber todt als feig!—
Welch' Zaubern dich auch hergeführt,
Fremdling, der mir so kühn erscheint,
Dein stolzes Droh'n mich nimmer rührt,
Da ich zu lügen nie vermeint.
Den Kampf mit dir drum nehm' ich auf,
Und hoffe Sieg nach Rechtes Lauf!

LOHENGRIN. Nun, König, ord'ne unsern Kampf.

KÖNIG. So tretet vor, zu drei für jeden Kämpfer,
Und messet wohl den Ring zum Streite ab!

[*Drei sächsische Edle treten für* LOHENGRIN, *drei braban
tische für* FRIEDRICH *vor: sie messen mit feierlichem
Schritte den Kampfplatz aus und stecken ihn, einen
vollständigen Ring bildend, durch ihre Speere ab.*

HERALD.
    All here attend, and mark me well:
    The fight no man shall seek to quell!
    Let none within th' inclosure stand.
    Who hinders aught that may befall,
    If freeman, straight shall lose his hand,
    And his base head shall forfeit the thrall!

ALL THE MEN.
    The freeman straight shall lose his hand,
    And his base head shall forfeit the thrall!

HERALD.
    Mark me, ye combatants of might!
    In fair and open quarrel fight;
    By magic arts ye shall not win—
    That were the judgment to deride.
    Prosper as ye are free from sin,
    Not in yourselves, in Heav'n confide.

LOHENGRIN AND FREDERICK.
    Judge me as I am free from sin!
    Not in myself, in Heaven I bide!

DER HEERRUFER.
    Nun höret mich, und achtet wohl:
    Den Kampf hier Keiner stören soll!
    Dem Hage bleibet abgewandt,
    Denn wer nicht wahrt des Friedens Recht,
    Der Freie büss' es mit der Hand,
    Mit seinem Haupt büss' es der Knecht!

ALLE MÄNNER.
    Der Freie büss es mit der Hand,
    Mit seinem Haupt büss' es der Knecht!

DER HEERRUFER.
    Hört auch, ihr Streiter vor Gericht!
    Gewahrt in Treue Kampfespflicht!
    Durch bösen Zaubers List und Trug
    Stört nicht des Urtheils Eigenschaft!
    Gott richtet euch nach Recht und Fug,
    Drum trauet ihm, nicht eurer Kraft!

LOHENGRIN UND FRIEDRICH.
    Gott richte mich nach Recht und Fug,
    So trau' ich ihm, nicht Meiner Kraft!

OH KING OF KINGS, ON THEE I CALL.

ELSA AND LOHENGRIN.
    Now, Lord, make known Thy just decree,
    I have no fear, I trust in Thee!

ORTRUD.   In his strong arm I trust alone,
    That nor defeat nor fear hath known.

FRID.   I here await thy just decree!
    Great Lord, let not my honour tarnished be!

ELSA UND LOHENGRIN.
    Du kündest nun dein wahr Gericht,
    Mein Herr und Gott, drum zag, ich nicht!

ORTRUD.   Ich baue fest auf seine Kraft,
    Die, wo er kämpft, ihm Sieg verschafft.

FRIED.   Ich geh' in Treu' vor dein Gericht!
    Herr Gott, verlass' mein' Ehre nicht!

ALL THE MEN.
> To stainless knight give strength and might,
> With craven heart the false one smite,
> Now, Lord, make known Thy just decree,
> Protect the right—we trust in Thee!

THE LADIES.
> My gracious Lord! O bless Thy true knight!

[*In rapt excitement all resume their places, the six witnesses remain standing beside the spears of the inclosure, the other men form a wider circle round them,
ELSA and her ladies in the foreground under the oak
beside the KING. On a sign from the Herald, the
Trumpeters blow the call to battle! LOHENGRIN and
FREDERICK make final preparations. The KING draws
his sword out of the ground and strikes it three times
on the shield that hangs on the oak. First stroke:
LOHENGRIN and FREDERICK step into the circle. Second
stroke: they advance their shields and draw. Third
stroke: they begin to fight. LOHENGRIN attacks. LOHEN-
GRIN with a great stroke fells FREDERICK to the earth.
FREDERICK tries to raise himself, staggers a few steps
backwards, then falls.*]

LOHENGRIN.
> Heav'n's behest to me has vict'ry lent;
> Thy life I spare: may'st thou in peace repent.

CHORUS. Hail! hail! hail! great hero!

ELSA. Oh joy, that my tongue thy name could praise,
> The songs of the angels for thee I would upraise;
> My lord here I confess thee
> I'll live for thee alone!
> Wilt thou divinely bless me,
> Oh, take me for thine own.

LOHENGRIN. Heav'n lent me strength to right thee,
> That truth might stand confess'd;
> But now I will requite thee
> For all thy sorrow past.

FREDERICK. Woe! Heav'n itself hath doom'd me,
> And brought my trusted sword to nought.
> Oh earth, hadst thou entombed me,
> Ere I to this was brought!

ORTRUD. Who is't that thus hath doomed us—
> Who brings my power to nought?
> Oh, had the earth entomb'd us,
> Ere we to shame were brought!

THE KING AND CHORUS.
> Hail! blest be the power that brought them
> Valiant knight! hail great in glory, great in
>   fame!
> Ye minstrels sing of pleasure,
> Intone a loud triumphant measure!
> Great be thy power, glorious thy name,
> Great be thy fame! blest be thy name!
> Hail to thy coming! blest be thy name!
> All praise to thee is due,
> Thy name shall live in story!
> Ne'er will a knight so true
> Fulfil the land with glory!
> Blest be the hour that hither brought thee!
> Long live in glory,
> Prais'd be thy name,
> All hail to thee.

ALLE MÄNNER.
> Des Reinen Arm gieb Heldenkraft,
> Des Falschen Stärke sei erschlafft;
> So künde uns dein wahr Gericht,
> Du Herr und Gott, nun zög're nicht!

ALLE FRAUEN.
> Mein Herr und Gott, segne ihn!

[*Alle treten in grosser, feierlicher Aufregung an ihre
Plätze zurück. ELSA und die Frauen unter der Eiche
beim KÖNIG. Auf das Zeichen des Heerrufers fallen
die Heerhörner mit einem langen Kampfrufe ein.
LOHENGRIN und FRIEDRICH vollenden ihre Waffenrüstung. Der KÖNIG zieht sein Schwert aus der Erde
und schlägt damit dreimal auf seinen Schild. Die
Kämpfer treten in den Ring, legen die Schilder vor
und ziehen das Schwert. LOHENGRIN greift zuerst
an und streckt dann mit weitausgeholtem Streich
FRIEDRICH nieder. Dieser versucht sich wieder zu
erheben, taumelt zurück und stürzt zu Boden. LOHEN-
GRIN setzt das Schwert auf seinen Hals.*]

LOHENGRIN.
> Durch Gottes Sieg ist jetzt dein Leben mein:
> Ich schenk' es dir, mög'st du der Reu' es weih'n!

CHOR. Sieg! Sieg! Sieg! Heil dir, Heil!

ELSA. O fänd' ich Jubelweisen,
> Die deinem Ruhme gleich,
> Die, würdig dich zu preisen,
> An höchstem Lobe reich!
> In dir muss ich vergehen,
> Vor dir schwind' ich dahin!
> Soll ich mich selig sehen,
> Nimm alles was ich bin!

LOHENGRIN. Den Sieg hab ich erstritten
> Durch deine Rein' allein!
> Nun soll was du gelitten,
> Dir reich vergolten sein!

FRIED. Weh', mich hat Gott geschlagen,
> Durch ihn ich sieglos bin!
> Am Heil muss ich verzagen,
> Mein Ruhm' und Ehr' ist hin!

ORTRUD. Wer ist's, der ihn geschlagen,
> Durch den ich machtlos bin?
> Sollt' ich vor ihm verzagen,
> Wär' all' mein Hoffen hin?

DER KÖNIG, DIE MÄNNER UND FRAUEN.
> Ertöne, Siegeweise,
> Dem Helden laut zum Preise!
>   Ruhm deiner Fahrt!
>   Preis deinem Kommen!
>   Heil deiner Art,
>   Schützer der Frommen!
> Dich nur besingen wir,
> Dir schallen uns're Lieder!
> Nie kehrt ein Held gleich **dir**
> In diesen Landen wieder!
> Wo fänd' ich Jubelweisen,
> Seinem Ruhme gleich?
> Ihr würdig zu preisen,
> An höchstem Lobe reich.
> Du hast gewahrt
> Das Recht der Frommen,
> Heil deiner Fahrt',
> Heil deinem Kommen!

[FREDERICK, crushed, falls at the feet of ORTRUD. *Youths raise* LOHENGRIN *upon his shield, and* ELSA *upon the shield of the* KING, *upon which several have spread their mantles, thus both are borne away amid general rejoicing.*

ACT II

SCENE I

[*The Fortress at Antwerp. At the back of the Palace (residence of Knights); in the foreground the Kemmenate (dwelling of women); R. H., the Minster. It is night.* ORTRUD *and* FREDERICK—*both in dark, servile garments—are seated on the steps of the Minster.* FREDERICK *is musing gloomily;* ORTRUD *gazing fixedly at the windows of the Palace, which is brightly illuminated. Festive music is heard from the Palace.*

FRED. Arouse thyself, companion of my shame!
The dawning day we here may not await.

ORTRUD.
  I cannot flee; some spell holds me enchained.
Yon festive hall, where joy triumphant reigneth,
Within my soul distils the deadly bane
That shall avenge our cruel wrongs and end them!

FRED.
  What dark, mysterious spell binds me to thee,
Unholy woman?
Ah, why can I from thee not fly.
Where I might find some rest, some peace,
Where my distracted soul could be at rest?
'Tis thou whose spells have cost me
My honor and my fame;
Thou hast my knighthood lost me,
Thou'st led me on to shame!
My sword lies stained and broken,
My shield is cast to earth;
My name with curses spoken,
I'm reft of home and hearth!
Where'er for rest I turn me,
Abhorr'd from me they fly;
The vilest wretch may spurn me,
None is so vile as I!
Oh, had but death o'ertaken me,
I had my honour saved;
But thus, as miscreant to arraign me
My sword, my name disgraced!

ORTRUD. Why dost thou thus in idle grief thy heart consume?

FRED. Because I have no sword with which to strike thee dead!

ORTRUD. Well art thou named the peaceful one—
Why dost thou doubt in me?

FRED. Why doubt?
Was't not thy showing, thy beguiling,
That led me on t' accuse yon spotless maiden?
When in thy dismal forest home,
Didst thou not say that from its ruin'd tower
Thou saw'st how Elsa did the foul and murdrous deed?
Then didst thou lie, or in the castle moat
Did she not her brother drown?
To lure my heart with wily spells

[FRIEDRICH *sinkt zu* ORTRUDS *Füssen ohnmächtig zusammen.* LOHENGRIN *auf seinem und* ELSA *auf des* KÖNIGS *Schild werden von jungen Männern jauchzend hinweg getragen.*

ZWEITER AKT

ERSTE SCENE

[*Burg zu Antwerpen. In Mitte des Hintergrundes der Palast (Ritterwohnung); Seitwärts rechts das Thurmthor. Links vorn die Kemenate (Frauenwohnung) gegenüber die Pforte des Münsters.—Nacht.—*FRIEDRICH, *finster in sich gekehrt, und* ORTRUD, *unverwandt nach den hellerleuchteten Fenstern des Palais, aus denen jubelnde Musik ertönt, starrend, in dunkler, knechtischer Tracht auf den Stufen des Münsters.*

FRIED. Erhebe dich, Genossin meiner Schmach!
Der junge Tag darf hier uns nicht mehr seh'n.

ORTRUD.
  Ich kann nicht fort: hierher bin ich gebannt.
Aus diesem Glanz des Festes uns'rer Feinde
Lass, saugen mich ein furchtbar tödtlich Gift,
Das uns're Schmach und ihre Freuden ende!

FRIED.
  Du fürchterliches Weib, was bannt mich noch
In deine Nähe? Warum lass ich dich nicht
Allein, und fliehe fort, dahin, dahin,—
Wo mein Gewissen Ruhe wieder fände?
Durch dich musst' ich verlieren
Mein' Ehr', all' meinen Ruhm:
Nie soll mich Lob mehr zieren,
Schmach ist mein Heldenthum!
Die Acht ist mir gesprochen,
Zertrümmert liegt mein Schwert;
Mein Wappen ward zerbrochen,
Verflucht mein Vaterherd!
Wohin ich nun mich wende,
Gefloh'n, gefehmt bin ich:
Dass ihn mein Blick nicht schände,
Flieht selbst der Räuber mich.
O hätt' ich Tod erkoren,
Da ich so elend bin!
Mein Ehr' hab' ich verloren,
Mein' Ehr', mein Ehr' ist hin!

ORTRUD. Was macht dich in so wilder Klage doch Vergeh'n?

FRIED. Dass mir die Waffe selbst geraubt,
Mit der ich dich erschlüg'!

ORTRUD. Friedreicher Graff von Telramund!
Wesshalb misstrau'st du mir?

FRIED.
  Du fragst? War's nicht dein Zeugniss, deine Kunde,
Die mich bestrickt, die Reine zu verklagen?
Die du im düst'ren Wald zu Haus, logst du
Mir nicht, von deinem wilden Schlosse aus
Die Unthat habest du verüben sehn?
Mit eig'nem Aug', wie Elsa selbst den Bruder
Im Weiher dort ertränkt?—Umstricktest du
Mein stolzes Herz durch die Weissagung nicht.

Thou didst falsely predict Radbod's renown'd
And ancient house ere long should
Rise anew and give princes to Brabant!
'Twas thus enticed by thee, that Elsa's hand,
The peerless, I renounc'd,
And took thee for my consort,
As the last of Radbod's race!

ORTRUD. Oh, how deadly is his scorn!
I grant it, yea, all this I prov'd to thee.

FRED. Thou mad'st me, whose name was well renown'd
Whose knighthood was untainted by a flaw,
Of lying arts a dupe and an accomplice!

ORTRUD. Who lied?

FRED. Thou! Was not the judgment clear?
Heav'n hath declar'd against me!

ORTRUD. Heav'n?

FRED. Oh, horror!
That wonted word of hope,
On thy lips how dreadful!

ORTRUD. Ha! is thy hope the coward's Heav'n?

FRED. Ortrud!

ORTRUD. What means thy threat?
Would'st thou assail thy wife? Oh, craven!
If thou hadst but threatened him like this
Who dooms us to this bitter woe,
Well hadst thou won,
And glorious were thy name.
Ah, if thou wouldst but hearken now,
There is a spell can lay him low!

FRED. No spell avails,
All heav'nly powers on his side are rang'd!

ORTRUD. Heav'nly powers? Ha, ha!
Mark but my word, and I will show to thee
How weak those heav'nly pow'rs
That fight for him.

FRED. Thou godless prophetess!
And dost thou think thy subtle spells
Again to weave around me?

ORTRUD.
Of feasting weary, they are slumb'ring now
Come seat thee here by me!
The hour is nigh when yonder stars
Reveal their lore to me!
Know'st thou who is yon knight,
Who by a swan was guided to our land?

FRED. No!

ORTRUD. Shall I reveal to thee a secret?
Mark what I say;   [and name,
If aught compel him to answer what his race
His vaunted power is paralys'd,
The spell that lends him strength dissolv'd

FRED. Ha! was't for that he forbade?

ORTRUD. For that.
No one here hath the pow'r
From him to draw the fatal secret
But she whom he so sternly bade
That she the question ne'er should ask

FRED. To ask him Elsa must be tempted,
'Tis she alone can break the spell.

Bald würde Radbod's alter Fürstenstamm
Von neuem grünen und herrschen in Brabant?
Bewogst du so mich nicht, von Elsa's Hand,
Der reinen, abzusteh'n und dich zum Weib
Zu nehmen, weil du Radbod's letzter Spross?

ORTRUD. Ha, wie tödtlich du mich kränkst!—
Dies alles, ja! ich sagt' und zeugt' es dir!

FRIED. Und machtest mich, des' Name hochgeehrt,
Des' Leben aller höchsten Tugend Preis,
Zu deiner Lüge schändlichem Genossen?

ORTRUD. Wer log?

FRIED. Du!—Hat nicht durch sein Gericht
Gott mich dafür geschlagen?

ORTRUD. Gott?

FRIED.   Entsetzlich!
Wie tönt aus deinem Mund furchtbar der
Name!

ORTRUD. Ha, nennst du deine Feigheit Gott?

FRIED. Ortrud!

ORTRUD. Willst du mir droh'n? Mir einem Weibe
—droh'n?
O Feiger! Hättest du so grimmig ihm
Gedroht, der jetzt dich in das Elend schickt,
Wohl hättest Sieg statt Schande du erkauft!—
Ha, wer ihm zu entgegnen wüsst,' der fänd'
Ihn schwächer als ein Kind!

FRIED.   Je schwächer er,
Desto gewalt'ger kämpfte Gottes Kraft!

ORTRUD. Gottes Kraft? Ha! ha!—
Gieb mir die Macht, und sicher zeig' ich dir,
Welch' schwacher Gott es ist, der ihn beschützt.

FRIED. Du wilde Seherin! Wie willst du doch
Geheimnissvoll den Geist mir neu berücken!

ORTRUD. Die Schwelger strecken sich zur üpp'gen Ruh',
Setz' dich zur Seite mir! Die Stund' ist da,
Wo dir mein Seherauge leuchten soll.—
Weisst du wer dieser Held, den hier
Ein Schwan gezogen an das Land?

FRIED. Nein!

ORTRUD. Was gäbst du drum es zu erfahren?
Ich sage dir: ist er gezwungen
Zu nennen wie sein Nam' und Art,
All seine Macht zu Ende ist,
Die müh'voll ihm ein Zauber leiht.

FRIED. Ha! Dann begreif' ich sein Verbot!

ORTRUD. Nun hör', Niemand hat hier Gewalt,
Ihm das Geheimniss zu entreissen,
Als die, der er so streng verbot,
Die Frage je an ihn zu thun.

FRIED. So gält' es Elsa, zu verleiten,
Dass sie die Frag' ihm nicht erliess'?

ORTRUD. Ha! thou art swift to understand.

FRED. How can she be persuaded?

ORTRUD.   Mark!
Above all else, from hence we must not fly
Then nerve thee to the task;
Her just suspicion we must kindle.
Go forth—say that by sorcery
He triumphed o'er a righteous cause.

FRED. 'Ha! yea, 'twas sorcery.'

ORTRUD. At worst,
If that should fail, she must be forc'd.

FRED. Be forc'd?

ORTRUD. Not all in vain.
The secret lore of old to me's familiar;
Store in thy mind what now I tell thee;
Strength that is lent by magic art fails
If of him bewitch'd one drop of blood be shed
His native helplessness and frailty then is shown.

FRED. Oh, were that true!
Oh, thou who dost the pow'rs of darkness know,
If thou speak falsely now, woe on thee!

ORTRUD. Nay, thou art raving.
Temper wrath with measure;
And I will teach thee vengeance,
Godlike pleasure.

BOTH. For dread revenge here I implore ye,
Oh, pow'rs that rule our earthly lot.
Ye, who now dream that joy's before ye,
Know that our vengeance slumbers not.

SCENE II

[ELSA, *in white garments, appears on the balcony, she
steps forward to the parapet and leans her head on
her hand.*

ORTRUD. She's yonder!

FRED. Elsa!

ORTRUD. Be near, ye pow'rs of darkness,
May she for ever rue this hour!
Away! thou must awhile from hence depart.

FRED. But why?

ORTRUD. Ha, wie begreifst du schnell und wohl!

FRIED. Doch wie soll das gelingen?

ORTRUD.   Hör'!
Vor allem gilt's, von hinnen nicht
Zu flieh'n: drum schärfe deinen Witz!
Gerechten Argwohn ihr zu wecken,
Tritt vor, klag' ihn des Zaubers an,
Durch den er das Gericht getäuscht!

FRIED. Ha! Trug und Zauber's List!

ORTRUD.   Missglückt's,
So bleibt ein Mittel der Gewalt!

FRIED. Gewalt?

ORTRUD. Umsonst nicht bin ich in
Geheimsten Künsten tief erfahren;
Drum achte wohl was ich dir sage:
Jed' Wesen, das durch Zauber stark,
Wird Ihm des Leibes kleinstes Glied
Entrissen nur, muss sich alsbald
Ohnmächtig zeigen, wie es ist.

FRED. Ha, sprächst du wahr!
O Weib, das in der Nacht ich vor mir seh'!
Betrügst du jetzt mich noch, dann weh' dir,
weh'!

ORTRUD. Ha, wie du rasest!—Ruhig und besonnen!
So lehr' ich dich der Rache süsse Wonnen.

BEIDE. Der Rache Werk sei nun beschworen
Aus meines Busens wilder Nacht!
Die ihr in süssem Schlaf verloren,
Wisst, dass für euch das Unheil wacht!

ZWEITE SCENE

[ELSA *in weissem Gewande erscheint auf dem Balcon,
tritt an die Brüstung und lehnt den Kopf in die Hand.*

ORTRUD. Sie ist es!

FRIED. Elsa!

ORTRUD. Der Stunde soll sie fluchen,
In der sie jetzt mein Blick gewahrt!—Hinweg!
Entfern' ein Kleines dich von hier!

FRIED.   Warum?

YE WANDERING BREEZES.

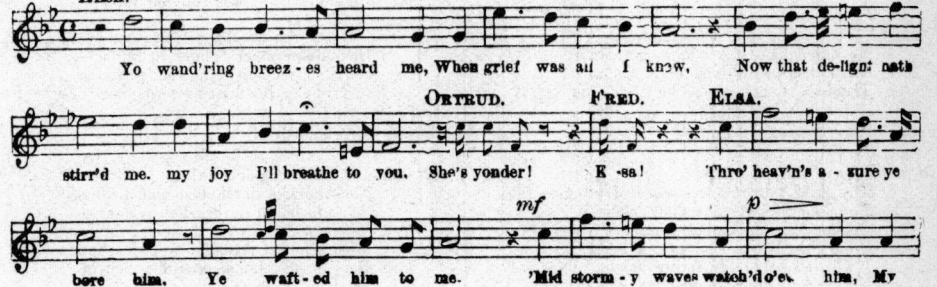

ELSA.
Yo wand'ring breez-es heard me, When grief was all I know, Now that de-ligni nath

stirr'd me. my joy I'll breathe to you. She's yonder! E-sa! Thro' heav'n's a-zure ye

bore him. Ye waft-ed him to me. 'Mid storm-y waves watch'd o'er him, My

guide, my love to be.   Where'er thy pin - ion rush - eth, The mourner's   tears are

dried,   My cheek that burns and flush - eth with love, Oh, cool   and hide'

My   cheek   that burns and flush - eth   with love....   Oh,....

cool   thou, oh, cool thou, oh, cool and hide,   Oh, cool thou!

ORTRUD.   Leave her for me; her knight shall be for thee
           Elsa!

ELSA.   Who calls? How drearily and strangely
         My name resoundeth thro' the night.

ORTRUD. Elsa! Hast thou forgotten e'en my voice?
         Wilt thou disown me in my sorrow,
         Who am by thee of all bereft?

ELSA.   Ortrud! 'tis thou? What dost thou here,
         Woman unblest?

ORTRUD. "Woman unblest!"
         Yea, thou hast cause unblest to call me!
         I dwell in solitude protected,
         My home the deep and silent wood:
         I harm'd thee not, I harm'd thee not.
         Joyless I mourn'd the evil fortune
         That long hath rested on my race.

ELSA.   Ah, why speak to me of this?
         Thy sorrow was not caused by me!

ORTRUD. 'Twere strange indeed if thou didst envy my
         lot.
         To be the wife of him whom scornfully thy heart
         disclaim'd.

ELSA.   Ye guardian saints! Why this to me?

ORTRUD. The victim, of a wild delusion,
         He dared to cast a doubt on thee;
         Since then he by remorse is riven,
         The ban is spoken o'er his head.

ELSA.   Have mercy, Heav'n.

ORTRUD. Thou canst be happy;
         Thy grief and guileless morn of promise
         Prepared thee for a radiant noon.
         Depart from my unholy presence.
         From thee I may not crave a boon.
         I will not haunt thy future bright,
         Nor darken thy undimm'd delight!

ORTRUD. Sie ist für mich,—ihr Held gehöre dir,
         Elsa!

ELSA.   Wer ruft?—Wie schauerlich und klagend
         Ertönt mein Name durch die Nacht.

ORTRUD. Elsa! Ist meine Stimme dir so fremd?
         Willst du die Arme ganz verleugnen,
         Die du in's fernste Elend schick'st?

ELSA.   Ortrud! bist du's?—was machst du hier,
         Unglücklich Weib!

ORTRUD. "Unglücklich Weib!"
         Wohl hast du recht, so mich zu nennen!
         In ferner Einsamkeit des Waldes,
         Wo still und friedsam ich gelebt,—
         Was that ich dir? was that ich dir?
         Freudlos, das Unglück nur beweinend,
         Das lang belastet meinen Stamm,—
         Was that ich dir? was that ich dir?

ELSA.   Um Gott, was klagest du mich an?
         War ich es, die dir Leid gebracht?

ORTRUD. Wie könntest du fürwahr mir neiden
         Das Glück, das mich zum Weib erwählt
         Der Mann, den du so gern verschmäht?

ELSA.   Allgüt'ger Gott, was soll mir das?

ORTRUD. Musst' ihn unsel'ger Wahn bethören,
         Dich Reine einer Schuld zu zeih'n,—
         Von Reu' ist nun sein Herz zerrissen,
         Zu grimmer Buss' ist er verdammt.

ELSA.   Gerechter Gott!

ORTRUD. O du bist glücklich!
         Nach kurzem unschuldsüssem Leiden,
         Siehst lächelnd du das Leben nur;
         Von mir darfst selig du dich scheiden,
         Mich schickst du auf des Todes Spur,—
         Dass meines Jammers trüber Schein
         Nie kehr in deine Feste ein.

ELSA. So blest I am, oh, bounteous Heaven:
So great the boon I owe to thee—
Ne'er from my side be sorrow driven,
When in the dust it sues to me!
Oh, never! Ortrud, wait thou there!
Ere long again I shall be near.

ORTRUD. Ye gods forsaken, grant me your vengeance!
Declare your pow'r benign in this dread hour!
Strike them with death who profane your altars
And strengthen my soul to avenge your wrongs
Odin! thou strong and mighty one!
Freya! Oh, Queen, bend down to me!
Prosper my cause with deadly guile,
Immortals, on my vengeance smile!

ELSA. Ortrud! where art thou?

ORTRUD. Here, before thee kneeling!

ELISA. Oh, Heav'n! How sorely art thou stricken,
Whom I in pride and splendor saw!
My heart's compassion it doth quicken,
Heav'n's dark decree I mark with awe.
Arise! Oh, do not thus entreat me!
Wert thou my foe, I pardon thee;
And if through me thy heart hath sorrow'd
I humbly ask thou pardon me.

ORTRUD. My grateful thanks for all thy goodness!

ELSA. Of him whom I shall wed at morn,
Grace I'll crave for thee and thy husband
A boon to me he'll not refuse.

ORTRUD. Oh, hold my heart in grateful bondage!

ELSA. By morning's dawn be thou prepar'd;
Attire thyself in royal raiment,
With me before the altar go!
Then I shall meet my hero-guide,
In face of Heav'n to be his bride!
His bride to be!

ORTRUD. How can I e'er for this requite thee,
Since I henceforth am poor and lone?
Though as thy friend thou dost invite me,
I must myself thy vassal own
One gift alone the gods have lent me,
None silence to me hath ordain'd!
With that perchance
I may prevent thee from treason,
And thy life's attaint.

ELSA. What say'st thou?

ORTRUD. As thy friend I warn thee,
Lest thou in love too blindly trust;
Lest cruel fortune change and spurn thee,
For its decrees are often unjust.

ELSA. What fortune?

ORTRUD. May he never leave thee,
Who was by magic hither brought!
And may the glamour ne'er deceive thee
That in thy soul his words have wrought!

ELSA. Oh, that thy heart could know the treasure
Of love that knows not fear or doubt!
No child of earth that bliss can measure
Who doth not dwell in faith devout.
Rest thee with me!

ELSA. Wie schlecht ich deine Güte priese,
Allmächt'ger, der mich so beglückt,
Wenn ich das Unglück von mir stiesse,
Das sich im Staube vor mir bückt!—
O nimmer!—Ortrud, harre mein!
Ich selber lass dich zu mir ein.

ORTRUD. Entweihte Götter! Helft jetzt meiner Rache!
Bestraft die Schmach, die hier euch angethan!
Stärkt mich im Dienste eurer heil'gen Sache,
Vernichtet der Abtrünn'gen schnöden Wahn!
Wodan! Dich Starken rufe ich!
Freia! Erhab'ne, höre mich!
Segnet mir Trug und Heuchelei,
Dass glücklich meine Rache sei!

ELSA. Ortrud! wo bist du?

ORTRUD. Hier, zu deinen Füssen!

ELSA. Hilf Gott! So muss ich dich erblicken,
Die ich in Stolz und Pracht nur sah!
Es will das Herze mir ersticken,
Seh' ich so niedrig dich mir nah.—
Steh' auf! o spare mir dein Bitten!
Trug'st du mir Hass' verzeih' ich dir;
Was du schon jetzt durch mich gelitten,
Das, bitte ich, verzeih' auch mir!

ORTRUD. O habe Dank für so viel Güte!

ELSA. Der morgen nun mein Gatte heisst,
Anfleh, ich sein liebreich Gemüthe,
Dass Friedrich auch er Gnad' erweist.

ORTRUD. Du fesselst mich in Dankes Banden!

ELSA. In Früh'n lass mich bereit dich seh'n!
Geschmückt mit prächtigen Gewanden
Sollst du mit mir zum Münster geh'n:—
Dort harre ich des Helden mein,
Vor Gott sein Eh'gemahl zu sein.

ORTRUD. Wie kann ich solche Huld dir lohnen,
Da machtlos ich und elend bin?
Soll ich in Gnaden bei dir wohnen,
Stets bleib' ich nur die Bettlerin.
Nur eine Kraft ist mir gegeben,
Sie raubte mir kein Machtgebot;
Durch sie vielleicht schütz ich dein Leben,
Bewahr' es vor der Reue Noth.

ELSA. Wie meinst du?

ORTRUD. Wohl, dass ich dich warne,
Zu blind nicht deinem Glück zu trau'n,
Dass nicht ein Unheil dich umgarne,
Lass mich für dich zur Zukunft schau'n.

ELSA. Welch Unheil?

ORTRUD. Könntest du erfassen,
Wie dessen Art so wundersam,
Der nie dich möge so verlassen,
Wie er durch Zauber zu dir kam!

ELSA. Du Aermste kannst wohl nie ermessen,
Wie zweifellos mein Herze liebt!
Du hast wohl nie das Glück besessen,
Das sich uns nur durch Glauben giebt?
Kehr' bei mir ein!

O LET ME TEACH THEE.

FRED. The powers of darkness enter'd there.
　　　Thou godless one! thy fell resolve fulfil thou;
　　　No pow'r have I to hinder thy intent!
　　　The ruin that began with my disaster
　　　Downward shall hurl those who abased me thus;
　　　Come life or death, my purpose shall not fail,
　　　The cause of my dishonor shall not live.

FRIED. So zieht das Unheil in dies Haus!
　　　Vollführe, Weib, was deine List ersonnen,
　　　Dein Werk zu hemmen fühl' ich keine Macht!
　　　Das Unheil hat mit meinem Fall begonnen,
　　　Nun stürzet nach, die mich dahin gebracht!
　　　Nur eines seh' ich mahnend vor mir stehn:
　　　Der Räuber meiner Ehre soll vergeh'n!

SCENE III

[Gradual daybreak. Two Warders blow the Reveille from the turret, which is answered from another turret in the distance. FREDERICK having spied about for the spot most favorable for concealing himself from the populace, steps behind one of mural projections of the Minster. While the Warders descend from the turret and unlock the gates, Servitors of the Castle enter from various directions; they salute each other and proceed quietly on their several ways. The nobles and retainers of the royal domain enter from various quarters more and more numerously.

CHORUS. The call that summon'd us betimes,
　　　Great deeds this day to us doth bode;
　　　Ere high the sun in heaven climbs
　　　Will much be wrought fo

DRITTE SCENE

[Der Tag bricht vollends an. Zwei Wächter blasen vom Thurme das Morgenlied, von einem entfernten Thurme wird geantwortet.—Dann schreiten die vier Heerhornbläser aus dem Palais und blasen den Königsruf, worauf sie wieder zurückgehen.—Von verschiedenen Richtungen Dienstmannen, die sich begrüssen und ruhig an ihre Verrichtungen gehen.—FRIEDRICH hat sich hinter einem Mauervorsprung am Münster verborgen.—Aus dem Burghofe und durch das von den Wächtern erschlossene Thurmthor kommen nun brabantische Edle und Mannen vor dem Münster zusammen.

DIE EDLEN UND MANNEN.
　　　In Früh'n versammelt uns der Ruf,
　　　Gar viel verheisset wohl der Tag!
　　　Der hier so hehre Wunder schuf,
　　　Der theure Held. manch neue That

THE HERALD.
Our King's august decree through all the lands
I here make known—mark well what he commands:
Beneath a ban he lays Count Telramund
For tempting Heav'n with traitrous intent.
Whoe'er shall harbor or companion him,
By right shall share his doom with life and limb.

CHORUS OF MEN.
Cursed, accursed be the traitor!
By us and Heav'n unblest,
He shall be held abhorred!

HERALD. This further doth the King make known
through me:
The noble stranger sent by Heav'n's decree,
Who Elsa's hand as consort doth request,
With crown and sceptre doth the King invest.
The knight doth not as Duke to reign consent,
But takes for title—Guardian of Brabant.

CHORUS. Hail to the valiant knight!
Whom Heav'n its power doth grant;
We vow allegiance to the Guardian of Brabant.
Hail, hail, thou knight of Heav'n!
Long reign thou o'er Brabant.

THE HERALD.
The knight through me doth furthermore declare:
All to th' espousals shall this day repair.
Then straight be under arms by morning's dawn,
And follow him till glory's meed be won;
In dalliance soft to linger he disdaineth,
While foe or danger to the land remaineth.

CHORUS. We follow where he leads,
Till glory's meed be won,
Mighty and gallant deeds
Thro' him shall yet be done.
Come, come! we follow him,
Till glory's meed be won;
Blessed are our shores,
For glory will be ours—
Oh, blest our happy shores!

FOUR PAGES.
Make way! make way! Our lady Elsa comes
Unto the Minster she goes forth.

SCENE IV

CHORUS. May every joy attend thee,
Who long in grief wert bound:
May Heav'n its blessings lend thee,
And angels guard thee round!
She comes with blushes glowing,
On holy thoughts intent!
All hail! thine be a bliss o'erflowing!
Hail, Elsa of Brabant!

ORTRUD. Stand back Elsa! no longer will I bear it,
That I like any slave must follow thee!
'Tis I precede, to all I here declare it,
And thou shalt humbly bow thy head to me!

THE EIGHT PAGES AND CHORUS
What does she mean?

ELSA. Great Heav'n, what does she mean?
How chang'd thy tone, who late to me did steal!

DER HEERRUFER.
Des Königs Wort und Will' thu' ich euch kund,
Drum achtet wohl, was euch durch mich er sagt!
In Bann und Acht ist Friedrich Telramund,
Weil untreu er den Gotteskampf gewagt:
Wer sein noch pflegt, wer sich zu ihm gesellt,
Nach Reiches Recht derselben Acht verfällt.

DIE MÄNNER.
Fluech ihm, dem Ungetreuen,
Den Gottes Urtheil traf!
Ihn soll der Reine scheuen,
Es flieh' ihn Ruh' und Schlaf!

DER HEERRUFER.
Und weiter kündet euch der König an,
Dass er den fremden gottgesandten Mann,
Den Elsa zum Gemahle sich ersehnt,
Mit Land und Kröne von Brabant belehnt.
Doch will der Held nicht Herzog sein genannt,
Ihr sollt ihn heissen: Schützer von Brabant!

DIE MÄNNER.
Hoch der ersehnte Mann!
Heil ihm, den Gott gesandt!
Treu sind wir unterthan
Dem Schützer von Brabant.

DER HEERRUFER.
Nun hört, was er durch mich euch künden lässt:
Heut feiert er mit euch sein Hochzeitsfest;
Doch morgen sollt ihr kampfgerüstet nah'n,
Zur Heeresfolg' dem König unterthan.
Er selbst verschmäht der süssen Ruh' zu pflegen,
Er führt euch an zu hehren Ruhmes Segen!

DIE MÄNNER.
Zum Streite säumet nicht,
Führt euch der Hehre an!
Wer muthig mit ihm ficht,
Dem lacht des Ruhmes Bahn.
Von Gott ist er gesandt
Zur Grösse von Brabant!

EDELKNABEN.
Macht Platz für Elsa, uns're Frau!
Die will in Gott zum Münster gehn.

VIERTE SCENE

DIE EDLEN UND MANNEN.
Gesegnet soll sie schreiten,
Die lang' in Demuth litt!
Gott möge sie geleiten
Und hüten ihren Schritt!—
Sie naht, die Engelgleiche,
Von keuscher Gluth entbrannt!
Heil dir, du Tugendreiche!
Heil Elsa von Brabant!

ORTRUD. Zurück, Elsa! Nicht länger will ich dulden,
Dass ich gleich einer Magd dir folgen soll!
Den Vortritt sollst du überall mir schulden,
Vor mir dich beugen sollst du demuthvoll!

DIE EDELKNABEN UND DIE MÄNNER.
Was will das Weib?

ELSA. Um Gott! Was muss ich sehen?
Welch jäher Wechsel ist mit dir geschehen?

ORTRUD.
    If I one hour was of my worth unmindful,
    Think thou not that I before thy feet will cow'r!
    An ample vengeance thy disdain doth owe me
    My rightful rank I will assert this hour!

ELSA. Woe! was it nought but falsehood to mislead me
    Last night that brought thee wailing to my
        door?
    Now thou wouldst fain attempt to supersede me,
    Thou mate of one whom God and man forswore?

ORTRUD.. Through doom unjust o'er him the ban was
       spoken.
    But his renown was great throughout the land;
    His name of virtue's self was held the token,
    Both fear and honor did his sword command.
    Your stranger, say, as what dost thou proclaim
       him?
    If I have heard aright, thou canst not name him.

ELSA. Thou slanderer, 'taunt me no more,
    Let my reply all doubts assure——
    So pure and noble is his nature,
    As none can match in high renown.
    Oh, can there live so vile a creature
    As to asperse all honor's crown?
    Hath not as victor Heav'n declar'd him,
    When he the recreant knight o'erthrew?
    Ye saw his triumph, yet he spar'd him,
    Say, lieges, can ye doubt him true?

THE MEN.
    Make way! the King is near—our sov'reign!

SCENE V

[*The* KING, LOHENGRIN, *and the Saxon nobles have issued
from the Palace in stately procession; the commotion
in front interrupts the train; the* KING *and* LOHENGRIN
come forward hastily.

CHORUS. Hail, hail, oh, sov'reign! hail, oh, Guardian
    of Brabant!

THE KING. Why is this strife?

ELSA. My lord! Oh, my defender!

LOHENGRIN. What is't?

THE KING.
    Who dares to clamor here with words unseemly?

THE TRAIN OF THE KING.
    We have heard the voice of anger.

LOHENGRIN.
    Oh horror! Why this evil one with thee?

ELSA. My champion! shelter me against her wrath!
    B'ame me, if I obey'd not thy command;
    I heard her weeping sore by yonder portal,
    And in compassion harbour'd her this night,
    And now with harsh and bitter words of hatred
    She taunts me for my boundless trust in thee.

LOHENGRIN.
    Away from her, thou fiend! In vain thy arts—
    Thou hast no part in her!
    Elsa, oh, say, hath she had power
    To taint thy heart with doubting?
    Come where in joy thy tears shall dissolve and
      vanish!

ORTRUD.
    Weil eine Stund' ich meines Werth's vergessen,
    Glaubst du, ich müsste dir nur kriechend nah'n?
    Mein Leid zu rächen will ich mich vermessen,
    Was mir gebührt, das will ich nun empfahn.

ELSA. Weh! liess ich durch dein Heucheln mich
      verleiten,
    Die diese Nacht sich pammernd zu mir stahl?
    Willst du nun in Hochmuth vor mir schreiten,
    Du, eines Gottgerichteten Gemahl?

ORTRUD. Wenn falsch Gericht mir den Gemahl ver-
      bannte,
    War doch sein Nam' im Lande hochgeehrt;
    Als aller Tugend Preis man ihn nur nannte,
    Gekannt, gefürchtet war sein tapf'res Schwert.
    Der Deine, sag', wer sollte hier ihn kennen,
    Vermagst du selbst den Namen nicht zu nennen!

ELSA. Du Lästerin! Ruchlose Frau!
    Hör', ob ich Antwort mir getrau'!—
    So rein und edel ist sein Wesen,
    So tugendreich der hehre Mann,
    Dass nie des Unheils soll genesen,
    Wer seiner Sendung zweifeln kann!
    Hat nicht durch Gott im Kampf geschlagen
    Mein theurer Held den Gatten dein?
    Nun sollt nach Recht ihr alle sagen,
    Wer kann da nur der Reine sein?

MÄNNER. Macht Platz! Macht Platz! Der König naht!

FUENFTE SCENE

[*Der* KÖNIG, LOHENGRIN, *die sächsischen Grafen und
Edlen sind in feierlichen Uuge aus dem Palais geschritten. Da durch die Verwirrung vorn der Uug
unterbrochen wird, treten der* KÖNIG *und* LOHENGRIN
lebhaft vor.

DIE MÄNNER. Heil! Heil dem König!
    Heil dem Schützer von Brabant!

KÖNIG. Was für ein Streit?

ELSA. Mein Herr! O mein Gebieter!

LOHENGRIN. Was giebt's?

KÖNIG.
    Wer wagt es hier, den Kirchengang zu stören?

DES KÖNIGS GEFOLGE.
    Welcher Streit, den wir vernahmen?

LOHENGRIN.
    Was seh' ich! Das unsel'ge Weib bei dir?

ELSA. Mein Retter! Schütze mich vor dieser Frau!
    Schilt mich, wenn ich dir ungehorsam war!
    In Jammer sah ich sie vor dieser Pforte,
    Aus ihrer Noth nahm ich sie bei mir auf:—
    Nun sieh', wie furchtbar sie mir lohnt die
      Güte,—
    Sie schilt mich, dass ich dir zu sehr vertrau'!

LOHENGRIN.
    Du fürchterliches Weib, steh' ab von ihr!
    Hier wird dir nimmer Sag!—Sieg', Elsa, mit,
    Vermocht ihr Gift sie in dein Herz zu giessen?
    Komm, lass in Freude dort die Thränen fliessen!

FRED.
Great Henry! Oh deluded Princess! Nay, desist!

ALL THE MEN.
Hence, or beware, thou traitor! Hence! I warn
thee! Avaunt, or of thy life beware!

THE KING. What seeks he here?

FRED. Oh, King, give ear.

THE KING. Avaunt; hence, thou accurs'd one!

FRED. Hear me, ye all have done me grievous wrong
Heav'n's dread ordeal hath he profan'd, derided,
Thro' sorc'ry vile its judgment was misguided!

CHORUS. Seize the accurs'd one! Hark! how he
blasphemes!

FRED. Yon shining knight, my sword defying
I here accuse of sorc'ry vile!
His station, name, I ask him,
Let these be heard in light of day!
Who is he that the billows tided—
A swan leading him in pinnace frail?
With such familiars, whoso bideth
All honest men may well assail!
Justice he now shall foil no more.
Condemn me, if he prove his cause;
If not, on him let vengeance fall—
A knight dishonor'd by our laws!

THE KING, CHORUS OF MEN.
What dread aspersion! How will he refute it?

LOHENGRIN.
Not thou, base knight, may'st impeach me,
Whose craven falsehood Heav'n hath shown;
No doubts of evil men can reach me,
Nor can it tarnish my renown!

FRED. I hurl thee back the vile suggestion.
And upon thee, oh, King, I call!
Will he presume thy right to question,
If me he scorns as base-born thrall?

LOHENGRIN.
Yea, e'en the King shall not command me.
Nor any Prince that rules on earth!
None shall constrain or reprimand me:
They saw my deed and know my worth.
There's one alone she can to speak compel me
Elsa—
Elsa! Why thus disturb'd and trembling?

THE KING.
Brave knight, put him to shame who dares defy
thee;
We know thee true, ne'er shall a doubt come
nigh thee.

CHORUS. We trust in thee, though doubt and danger
try thee;
To thee we give the prize of high renown.
Here, take my hand. No danger shall come
nigh thee;
Tho' thy name be still unknown, no danger shall
befall thee.

LOHENGRIN.
Ye valiant hearts, tho' doubt and danger try me,
Ye ne'er shall rue the trust this hour hath shown.

FRIED. O König! Trugbethörte Fürsten! Haltet ein!

DIE MÄNNER.
Was will der hier? Verfluchter, weich' von
hinnen!
Hinweg, du bist des Todes, Mann!

KÖNIG. Wag'st du zu trotzen meinem Zorn?

FRIED. O hört mich an!

KÖNIG. Zurück! Weiche von dannen!

FRIED. Hört mich, dem grimmes Unrecht ihr gethan!
Gottes Gericht, es ward entehrt, betrogen,
Durch eines Zaub'rers List, seid ihr belogen!

DIE MÄNNER.
Greift den Verruchten! Hört, er lästert Gott!

FRIED. Den dort im Glanz ich vor mir sehe,
Den klage ich des Zaubers an!
Nach Namen, Stand und Ehren
Frag' ich ihn laut vor aller Welt.—
Wer ist er, der an's Land geschwommen,
Geführt von einem wilden Schwan?
Wem solche Zauberthiere frommen,
Des' Reinheit achte ich für Wahn.
Nun soll der Klag' er Rede steh'n;
Vermag er's, so geschah mir Recht,
Wenn nicht, so sollet ihr ersehn,
Um seine Tugend steht es schlecht!

DER KÖNIG UND DIE MÄNNER.
Welch harte Klage! Was wird er ihm entgegnen?

LOHENGRIN. Nicht dir, der so vergass der Ehren,
Hab' Noth ich Rede hier zu steh'n!
Des Bösen Zweifel darf ich wehren,
Vor ihm wird Reine nie vergeh'n.

FRIED. Darf ich ihm nicht als würdig gelten,
Dich ruf' ich, König, hochgeehrt!
Wird er auch dich unadlig schelten,
Dass er die Frage dir verwehrt?

LOHENGRIN. Ja, selbst dem König darf ich wehren,
Und aller Fürsten höchstem Rath!
Nicht darf sie Zweifels Last beschweren,
Sie sahen meine gute That.
Nur eine ist's,—der muss ich Antwort geben:
Elsa—
Elsa!—wie seh' ich sie erbeben!

DER KÖNIG.
Mein Held, entgeg'ne kühn dem Ungetreuen!
Du bist zu hehr, um, was er klagt, zu scheuen!

DIE MÄNNER. Wir steh'n zu dir, es soll uns nie ge-
reuen,
Dass wir der Helden Preis in dir erkannt.
Reich' uns die Hand! Wir glauben dir in
Treuen,
Dass hehr dein Nam', auch wenn er nicht ge-
nannt.

LOHENGRIN.
Euch Helden soll der Glaube nimmer reuen,
Werd' euch mein Nam' und Art auch nie ge-
nannt!

FRED. Confide in me.
    Let me a secret tell thee, hear and convince thyself.

ELSA. Away from me!

FRED. Give me but leave the smallest limb to maim
    him;
    One drop of life-blood, and I swear to thee,
    What now he hides he freely shall declare,
    Nor ever from thy side to wander dare.

ELSA. Ah, tempt me not!

FRED. This night I shall be near—
    Call me, and straight I'll come all doubt to clear.

LOHENGRIN. Elsa, with whom dost thou converse?
    Away from her, thou cursed ones!
    On peril of my wrath, dare ye to cross her path
    Elsa, arise my love; in thy command,
    In thy good faith my ev'ry hope doth stand,
    Doth any doubt thy heart inspire?
    Dost thou to question me desire?

ELSA. My champion, my deliverer dear!
    Oh, thou who dost my soul sustain!
    High o'er the reach of doubt and fear,
    Love over all shall reign.

LOHENGRIN.
    Come, then, Elsa, let us plight our faith.

THE MEN. Lo! he is from heav'n sent!
    Hail, Elsa of Brabant!
    Go forth with blessings laden!
    Hail, thou royal maiden!
    Oh hail, royal Elsa of Brabant!

[*Here the* KING, *with the bridal pair, has reached the highest step of the Minster;* ELSA *with deep emotion turns to* LOHENGRIN, *who clasps her in his arms. From this embrace she looks up with a startled expression, and on the foot of the steps perceives* ORTRUD, *who lifts an arm against her with an expression of certain triumph.* ELSA, *terrified, turns away her face.*

ACT III

SCENE I

The Bridal Chamber; to the right an oriel casement, which is open. Music behind the stage, at first heard quite in the distance, and gradually approaching nearer; at the middle of the strain, doors at the back of the stage are opened; the Ladies enter leading in ELSA, *the* KING *and Nobles leading in* LOHENGRIN; *Pages with lights go before them.*

EIGHT LADIES. As solemn vows unite ye,
    We hallow ye to joy!
    This hour shall still requite ye,
    When bliss hath known alloy!

CHORUS. Faithful and true, &c..

FRIED. Vertraue mir! Lass dir ein Mittel heissen,
    Das dir Gewissheit schafft!

ELSA. Hinweg von mir!

FRIED.
    Lass mich das kleinste Glied ihm nur entreissen,
    Des Fingers Spitze, und ich schwöre dir,
    Was er dir hehlt, sollst frei du vor dir sehn,—
    Dir treu, soll nie er dir von hinnen gehn.

ELSA. Ha, nimmermehr!

FRIED.
    Ich bin dir nah' zur Nacht—
    Ruf'st du, ohn' Schaden ist es schnell vollbracht.

LOHENGRIN.
    Elsa, mit wem verkehrest du?
    Zurück von ihr, Verfluchte!
    Dass nie mein Auge je
    Euch wieder bei ihr seh'!
    Elsa, erhebe dich!—In deiner Hand,
    In deiner Treu' liegt alles Glückes Pfand!
    Lässt nicht des Zweifels Macht dich ruh'n?
    Willst du die Frage an mich thun?

ELSA. Mein Retter, der mir Heil gebracht!
    Mein Held, in dem ich muss vergeh'n!
    Hoch über alles Zweifels Macht
    Soll meine Liebe stehn!

LOHENGRIN.
    Heil dir, Elsa! Nun lass vor Gott uns gehen!

DIE MÄNNER UND FRAUEN.
    Seht! seht! Er ist von Gott gesandt!—
    Heil ihm! Heil Elsa von Brabant!
    Gesegnet sollst du schreiten!
    Heil dir, Tugendreiche!
    Gott möge dich geleiten!
    Heil dir, Elsa von Brabant!

[*Als der* KÖNIG *mit dem Brautpaare die höchste Stufe erreicht, kehrt sich* ELSA *in grosser Ergriffenheit zu dem sie in den Armen auffangenden* LOHENGRIN. *Aus dieser Umarmung wirft sie mit scheue Besorgniss den Blick auf* ORTRUD, *die siegesgewiss den Arm gegen sie erhebt, sie wendet erschreckt ihr Gesicht ab.*

DRITTER AKT

ERSTE SCENE

[*Wenn der Vorhang aufgeht, stellt die Bühne das Brautgemach dar. Rechts ein Erkerthurm mit offenem Fenster. Der Gesang erst entfernt, nähert sich. In Mitte des Liedes werden die Thüren geöffnet, rechts treten Frauen mit* ELSA, *links Männer mit* LOHENGRIN *und dem* KÖNIG *ein. Edelknaben mit Lichtern gehen voraus.*

ACHT FRAUEN. Wie Gott euch selig weihte,
    Zu Freuden weih'n euch wir;
    In Liebesglück's Geleite
    Denkt lang' der Stunde hier!

CHOR. Treulich bewacht bleibet zurück, u. s. w.

SCENE II

LOHENGRIN.

The blissful strain is o'er; we are alone,
The first and only time since we have met.
Now ev'ry pent-up thought our hearts may own,
No rash intruder this sweet hour shall fret.
Elsa, my love! my own, my gentle wife!
If thou art blest as I, oh, say, sweet life!

ELSA.   Words can not tell the rapture sweet and tender
That floods my soul with joy divine.
When thou dost bend o'er me thy glance of
splendor—
When thou art near the bliss of heaven is mine.

LOHENGRIN.

Thy words, oh, fairest, well thy transports
render,

ZWEITE SCENE

LOHENGRIN.

Das süsse Lied verhallt; wir sind allein,
Zum ersten Mal allein, seit wir uńs sah'n.
Nun sollen wir der Welt entronnen sein,
Kein Lauscher darf des Herzens Grüssen nah'n.—
Elsa, mein Weib! du süsse, reine Braut,
Ob Glücklich du, das sei mir nun vertraut!

ELSA.   Wie wär' ich kalt, mich glücklich nur zu nennen,
Besitz' ich aller Himmel Seligkeit!
Fühl' ich zu dir so süss mein Herz entbrennen,
Athme ich Wonnen, die nur Gott verleiht!

LOHENGRIN.

Vermagst du, Holde! glücklich dich zu nennen,

FAITHFUL AND TRUE.

If thou art blest, thy joy is doubly mine.
Oh, bend those eyes soft and tender,
Oh, let me breathe with thee this joy divine.
With charmed links did Heav'n to thee unite me
Ere yet we met thy heart had dreamt of me;
And if as champion I was call'd to right thee,
'Twas love alone that led my way to thee.
I knew thee pure from ev'ry taint of wrong:
To thee my heart and homage true belong.

ELSA.   I saw thee first from azure heights descending,
'Twas in a dream thy form I first beheld:
When o'er my waking eyes I saw thee bending,
I knew thee sent as angels were of old.
My heart with joy would fain dissolve before
    thee
I'd trace my steps as brooks thro' flow'ry mead
Like od'rous roses' sweetness I'd waft o'er thee
Dying for thy dear sake were blessed indeed!
Say, do I love thee?
By what blissful token is shown that pow'r so
    dread
And yet so blest? or, like thy name, ah, may
    it not be spoken?
Must what I prize the most be ne'er expressed?

LOHENGRIN.   Elsa!

ELSA.
How sweet my name, as from thy lips it glided
Canst thou deny to me the sound of thine?
In blissful hour thou'lt to my heart confide it,
That of thy love shall be the sign and seal!

LOHENGRIN.   Oh, my sweet wife!

ELSA.   Softly when none are nigh, whisper the word,
None e'er shall hear but I.

ELSA.   Ah, could I show my deep devotion—
Do some good deed, worthy of thee!
Nought have I but my fond emotion:
Never can I thy equal be!
Were doubt and danger low'ring o'er thee,
As once they threaten'd me with woe,
And I could to thy right restore thee,
Then might my heart some comfort know.
Haply thy secret's fraught with danger,
Therefore thy lips to all are clos'd!
It shall ne'er be known to friend or stranger,
If thou in me thy trust repose.
Doubt me not! Oh, let me share it—
Oh, let me know thy faith complete!
Not death itself from me shall tear it,
And torture borne for thee were sweet.

LOHENGRIN.   My loved one!

ELSA.   Oh, make me glad with thy reliance;
Humble me not that bend so low!
Ne'er shalt thou rue thy dear affiance—
Him that I love, oh, let me know!

LOHENGRIN.   No more, oh, Elsa!

ELSA.   Tell, oh, tell me!
Reveal thy name ador'd to love—
Thy race and name—all that befell thee!
My pow'r of silence thou shall prove!

LOHENGRIN.
Greatest of trusts, oh, Elsa, I have shown thee.
When I believ'd thee true from ev'ry stain;
Wav'ring in faith if thou shouldst ever own thee

Giebst du auch mir des Himmels Seligkeit!
Fühl' ich zu dir so süss mein Herz entbrennen,
Athme ich Wonnen, die nur Gott verleiht!—
Wie hehr erkenn' ich unsrer Liebe Wesen!
Die nie sich sah'n, wir hatten uns geahnt:
War ich zu deinem Streiter auserlesen,
Hat Liebe mir zu dir den Weg gebahnt.
Dein Auge sagte mir dich rein von Schuld,
Mich zwang dein Blick zu dienen deiner Huld.

ELSA.   Doch ich zuvor schon hatte dich gesehen,
In sel'gem Traume warst du mir genaht:
Als ich nun wachend dich sah vor mir stehen,
Erkannt' ich, dass du kamst auf Gottes Rath.
Da wollte ich vor deinem Blick zerfliessen.
Gleich einem Bach umwinden deinen Schritt.
Als eine Blume, duftend auf der Wiesen,
Wollt' ich entzückt mich beugen deinem Tritt.
Ist dies nur Liebe?—Wie soll ich es nennen,
Dies Wort, so unaussprechlich wonnevoll,
Wie, ach! dein Name, den ich nie darf kennen,
Bei dem ich nie mein Höchstes nennen soll!

LOHENGRIN.   Elsa!

ELSA.   Wie süss mein Name deinem Mund entgleitet!
Gönnst du denn deinen holden Klang mir nicht?
Nur, wenn zur Liebesstille wir geleitet,
Sollst du gestatten, dass mein Mund ihn spricht.

LOHENGRIN.   Mein süsses Weib!

ELSA.   —Einsam, wenn Niemand wacht;
Nie sei der Welt er zu Gehör gebracht!

ELSA.   Ach könnt' ich deiner werth erscheinen!
Müsst' ich vor dir nicht bloss vergeh'n!
Könnt' ein Verdienst mich dir vereinen,
Dürft' ich in Pein für dich mich seh'n,
Wie du mich traf'st vor schwerer Klage!
O! wüsste ich auch dich in Noth!
Dass aller Welt verschweigt dein Mund?
Kennt' ich ein Sorgen, das dir droht!
Wär das Geheimniss so geartet,
Dass aller Welt verschweight dein Mund?
Vielleicht, dass Unheil dich erwartet,
Würd es den Menschen offen kund?
Wär' es so! und dürft' ich's wissen,
Dürft' ich in meiner Macht es sehn,
Durch keines Droh'n sei mir's entrissen,
Für dich wollt' ich zum Tode gehn!

LOHENGRIN.   Geliebte!

ELSA.   O mach' mich stolz durch dein Vertrauen,
Dass ich in Unwerth nicht vergeh'!
Lass dein Geheimniss mich erschauen,
Dass, wer du bist, ich offen seh'!

LOHENGRIN.   Ach, schweige, Elsa!

ELSA.   Meiner Treue
Enthülle deines Adels Werth!
Woher du kamst, sag, ohne Reue,—
Durch mich sei Schweigens Kraft bewährt!

LOHENGRIN.
Höchstes Vertrau'n hast du mir schon zu danken,
Da deinem Schwur ich Glauben gern gewährt;
Wirst nimmer du vor dem Gebote wanken,

SAY, DOST THOU BREATHE THE INCENSE.

Say, dost thou breathe the in-cense sweet of flow'rs. Bear-ing a tide of deep mysterious joy! And would'st thou know from whence this rap-ture show-ers, Ask not.. lest thou the won-drous charm destroy; Such is the mag-ic that to thee hath bound me, When I first be-held thy beau-ty past com-pare, Know-ing thee not, I worshipp'd and re-nown'd thee, I felt thy glance, And knew thee true as fair; And as the o-d'rous gales with rap-ture fire me, Borne on the dark, un-fath-om'd gloom of night, Thus thou to trust un-meas-ur'd did'st in-spire me, When thou wert crush'd by dark sus-pic-ion's blight.

Thy empire o'er thy heart thou'lt ne'er regain	Hoch über alle Frau'n dünkst du mich werth!—
Oh, let my arms in love enfold thee!	An meine Brust, du süsse, Reine!
Come, rest thee here, my love, my life!	Sei meines Herzens Glühen nah!
Let me in radiant joy behold thee—	Dass mich dein Auge sanft bescheine,
Far from our hearts be thought of strife	In dem ich all' mein Glück ersah!
Come, to my heart let me press thee;	O; gönne mir, dass mit Entzücken
Let me inhale thy od'rous breath!	Ich deinen Athem sauge ein!
Angels might glory to possess thee—	Lass' fest, ach! fest an mich dich drücken,
Oh, turn to me in loving faith!	Dass ich in dir mög' glücklich sein!
Thy love alone for all consoles me	Dein Lieben muss mir hoch entgelten
That I for thy dear sake have lost;	Für das, was ich um dich verliess;
A high and glorious fate controls me:	Kein Loos in Gottes weiten Welten
The fate true knight must prize the most	Wohl edler als das meine hiess;
As when the king desired to crown me,	Böt' mir der König seine Krone,
My heart disdain'd the proffer'd boon,	Ich dürfte sie mit Recht verschmäh'n:
No earthly glory can renown me,	Das einz'ge, was mein Opfer lohne,
I glory in thy love alone!	Muss ich in deiner Lieb' erseh'n!
Let not a doubt thy spirit borrow;	Drum wolle stets den Zweifel meiden,
Thy love is all the world to me.	Dein Lieben sei mein stolz Gewähr;
I came not here from night and sorrow,	Denn nicht komm' ich aus Nacht und Leiden,
From blest delights I came to thee.	Aus Glanz und Wonne' komm' ich her.

ELSA.	Help, Heav'n! What dost thou tell me—	ELSA.	Hilf Gott, was muss ich hören!
	What must thy lips relate!		Welch' Zeugniss gab dein Mund!
	With glamour tho'udst beguile me:		Du wolltest mich bethören,
	I know my wretched fate.		Nun wird mir Jammer kund!
	The lot thou hast forsaken		Dass Loos, dem du entrounen,
	Is still thy heart's desire		Es war dein höchstes Glück:
	One day I shall awaken,		Du kamst zu mir aus Wonnen,
	When thou of me shalt tire!		Und sehnest dich zurück!
	Oh, how can I believe thee?		Wie soll ich Aermste glauben,

I know that we must part;
Of joy thy words bereave me,
Hope fades within my heart.

LOHENGRIN. No more, oh, I beseech thee

ELSA. On thee I yet may gaze!
Until despair shall reach me
Oh, must I count my days?
In dread my soul shall languish,
Lest from my sight thou fly;
Thou'lt leave me in my anguish—
Of sorrow I shall die.

LOHENGRIN. Thou ne'er for me shalt sorrow,
While thou from doubt art free.

ELSA. What magic can I borrow
To bind thy heart to me?
A spell is cast around thee—
By magic thou art here—
What ties so'er have bound thee,
Thou by a spell canst tear!
Hark, there are sounds! oh, bend thy ear and
listen!

LOHENGRIN. Elsa!

ELSA. Alas!
'Tis there, the swan! as when I first beheld his
pinions glisten.
For thee he comes! oh must thou now be gone?

LOHENGRIN.
Elsa, oh, hush! what fancies vain are these?

ELSA. No, thou shalt not compel me to trust by words
of blame—
No, not unless thou tell me thy country and thy
name!

LOHENGRIN. Elsa, oh, I conjure thee!

ELSA. What fatal spell is thine?
In vain wouldst thou assure me—
Declare thy race and name!

LOHENGRIN. Forbear!

ELSA. Declare thy name.

LOHENGRIN. Woe's me!

ELSA. Where is thy home?

[ELSA perceives FREDERICK and his four associates, who
break in with drawn swords through a door at the
back.

LOHENGRIN. Elsa! oh, misery!

ELSA. Save thyself! Thy sword!

[She hands him his sword, which was by the side of the
couch, so that while she holds the sheath he quickly
draws it out, and with one blow strikes FREDERICK,
whose arm is uplifted against him, dead. The four
nobles let fall their swords, and kneel before LOHEN-
GRIN. ELSA, who has sunk on LOHENGRIN's breast,
faints and slowly sinks to the ground. Long silence.

LOHENGRIN. Woe! all our joy now is fled for aye!

ELSA. Eternal One, have mercy. Thou!

Dir g'nüge meine Treu'?
Ein Tag wird dich mir rauben
Durch deiner Liebe Reu'!

LOHENGRIN. Halt' ein, dich so zu quälen!

ELSA. Was quälest du mich doch?
Soll ich die Tage zählen,
Die du mir bleibest noch?
In Sorg' um dein Verweilen
Verblüht die Wange mir;
Dann wirst du mir enteilen,
Im Elend bleib' ich hier!

LOHENGRIN. Nie soll dein Reiz entschwinden,
Bleib'st du von Zweifel rein!

ELSA. Ach! dich an mich zu binden,
Wie sollt' ich mächtig sein?
Voll Zauber ist dein Wesen,
Durch Wunder kamst du her:
Wie sollt' ich da genesen?
Wo fand ich dein Gewähr?—
Hörtest du nichts? vernahmest du kein Kom-
men?

LOHENGRIN. Elsa!

ELSA. Ach nein!—doch dort! der Schwan, der Schwan!
Dort kommt er auf der Wasserfluth geschwom-
men. . .
Du rufest ihm,—er zieht herbei den Kahn!—

LOHENGRIN.
Elsa, halt' ein! Beruh'ge deinen Wahn!

ELSA. Nichts kann mir Ruhe geben,
Dem Wahn mich nichts entreisst,
Als—gelt' es auch mein Leben!—
Zu wiessen—wer du seist!

LOHENGRIN. Elsa, was willst du wagen?

ELSA. Unselig holder Mann,
Hör'! was ich dich muss fragen;
Den Namen sag' mir an!

LOHENGRIN. Halt' ein!

ELSA. Woher die Fahrt?

LOHENGRIN. Weh' dir.

ELSA. Wie deine Art?

[FRIEDRICH und die vier brabantischen Edlen brechen
mit gezicktem Schwerte herein.

LOHENGRIN. Weh' uns, was thatest du!

ELSA. Rette dich! dein Schwert! dein Schwert!

[Sie reicht das am Ruhebette angelehnte Schwert.
LOHENGRIN streckt FRIEDRICH, da er nach ihm aus-
holt, mit einem Streiche todt zu Boden. Den entsetzten
Edlen entfallen die Schwerter, sie stürzen zu LOHEN-
GRIN's Füssen au fdie Kniee. ELSA, die sich an seine
Brust geworfen, sinkt ohnmächtig langsam an ihm zu
Boden.—Langes Schweigen.

LOHENGRIN. Weh'! nun ist all unser Glück dahin!

ELSA. Alleviger! erbarm' dich mein!

LOHENGRIN.

Bear hence the corpse into the King's judgment
   hall,
Into the royal presence lead her,
Array'd as fits so fair a bride;
There all she asks I will concede her,
Nor from her knowledge aught will hide.

SCENE III

[*When the curtain is drawn aside, the scene presents
the banks of the Scheldt, as in Act I.; a brilliant dawn
gradually brightens into full daylight. Enter from
different sides the Brabantian Nobles. When they
are all on the stage, the* KING, *with the Saxon Arriere-
ban enters.*

ALL THE MEN. Hail, royal Henry!
   Royal Henry, hail!

THE KING.

Have thanks, good lieges of Brabant:
Glory in arms may fortune grant!
Great is my pride, that hearts so brave
Go forth our German land to save.
Now 'gainst the wild Hungarian foe,
All are resolv'd at morn to go.
Henceforth his dreary eastern plain
Let him not dare to quit again;
For German land draw German sword!
Then ye the realm shall surely guard.

ALL THE MEN.

For German land draw German sword!
Thus we the land shall surely guard.

KING. Where lingers he, the heav'n-sent knight,
   Who ev'ry virtue doth unite?

MEN. What do they bear? What would they hear?
   Of Telramund they vassals are.

KING. Whom do ye bear? What shall I hear?
   Some dire event doth bring you here.

FOUR NOBLES.

E'en by the Guardian of Brabant,
Our liege and lord, we here are sent.

MEN. Lo, Elsa comes, that lady peerless!
   Her mien is sad, her eye is tearless!

KING. Why do I see thee mourning thus?
   Canst thou not bear thy Lord to lose?

A PORTION OF THE CHORUS.
   Make way! The Guardian of Brabant!

ALL THE CHORUS.
   Hail! hail, thou Guardian of Brabant!

KING. Hail, heav'n-sent hero. welcome here!
Thy loyal vassals all are near,
Waiting for thee to give the word,
And fight by thy all-conq'ring sword.

ALL THE MEN.
We wait for thee to give the word,
To fight by thy all-conq'ring sword.

LOHENGRIN.
My gracious sov'reign, bear me blameless,
Reasons have I that must be nameless,
The destin'd campaign I suspend!

LOHENGRIN.

Tragt den Erschlag'nen vor des KÖNIGS Gericht!
Sie vor den KÖNIG zu geleiten,
Schmückt Elsa, meine süsse Frau!
Dort will ich Antwort ihr bereiten,
Dass sie des Gatten Art erschau'.

DRITTE SCENE

[*Wenn der Vorhang in die Höhe gezogen wird, stellt die
Bühne wieder die Aue am Ufer der Schelde, wie im
ersten Aufzuge, dar.—Glühende Morgenröthe; der
Tag bricht voll an. Von verschiedenen Seiten gelangt
nach und nach der brabantische Heerbann auf die
Scene. Als die Brabanter alle eingetroffen sind, zieht*
KÖNIG HEINRICH *mit seinem Heerbann ein.*

ALLE MÄNNER. Hoch König Heinrich!
   König Heinrich, Heil!

DER KÖNIG.

Habt Dank, ihr Lieben von Brabant!
Wie fühl ich stolz mein Herz entbrannt,
Find' ich in jedem deutschen Land
So kräftig reichen Heerverband!
Nun soll des Reiches Feind sich nahn,
Wir wollen tapfer ihn empfahn:
Aus seinem öden Ost daher
Soll er sich nimmer wagen mehr!
Für deutsches Land das deutsche Schwert!
So sei des Reiches Kraft bewährt!

ALLE MÄNNER.
Für deutsches Land das deutsche Schwert!
So sei des Reiches Kraft bewährt!

KÖNIG. Wo weilt nun der, den Gott gesandt
   Zum Ruhm, zur Grösse von Brabant?

ALLE. Was bringen die? Was thun sie kund?
   Die Mannen sind's des Telramund.

KÖNIG. Wen führt ihr her? Was soll ich schau'n?
   Mich fasst bei eurem Anblick Grau'n!

DIE VIER EDLEN.
So will's der Schützer von Brabant:
Wer dieser ist, macht er bekannt!

DIE MÄNNER. Seht! Elsa naht, die tugendreiche!
   Wie ist ihr Antlitz trüb und bleiche!

DER KÖNIG. Wie muss ich dich so traurig seh'n?
   Will dir so nah die Trennung geh'n?

STIMMEN. Macht Platz dem Helden von Brabant!

ALLE MÄNNER. Heil! Heil dem Helden von Brabant!

DER KÖNIG. Heil deinem Kommen, theurer Held!
Die du so treulich rief'st in's Feld,
Die harren dein in Streites Lust,
Von dir geführt, des Sieg's bewusst.

ALLE MÄNNER. Wir harren dein in Streites Lust,
Von dir geführt, des Sieg's bewusst.

LOHENGRIN.
Mein Herr und König, lass dir melden:
Die ich berief, die kühnen Helden,
Zum Streit sie führen darf ich nicht!

MEN.   Alas! what can his words portend!

LOHENGRIN.
     To lead ye forth to battle here I came not;
     But judge me, for your leniency I claim not.
     Then, firstly, do ye hold that I am guilty?
     Your just decree to me is due.
     He sought my life despite honor and fealty—
     Say, did I right when him I slew?

KING AND MEN.
     E'en as thy sword in earth has laid him,
     The saints will sure refuse to aid him!

LOHENGRIN.
     And further, I declare in face of Heav'n,
     Though bitter grief to me it bode,
     That from her fair allegiance hath been driven
     The wife that Heav'n on me bestow'd.

MEN.   Elsa! say, oh, what hast thou done?
     Sentence so stern how hast thou won?

LADIES.   Woe is thine, Elsa!

LOHENGRIN.
     Ye all have heard her give her word in token
     That she my name and country ne'er would ask
     That promise her impatient heart hath broken—
     Vainly I hop'd she would fulfil her task!
     Now mark me well, I will no more with-hold it.
     Nor have I cause to shrink from any test;
     When I my name and lineage have unfolded
     Ye'll know that I am noble as the best!

CHORUS.
     What is this secret he so well hath guarded?
     Oh, that this fatal hour had been retarded!

LOHENGRIN.
     In distant land, by ways remote and hidden,
     There stands a burg that men call Monsalvat;
     It holds a shrine, to the profane forbidden:
     More precious there is nought on earth than that,
     And thron'd in light it holds a cup immortal,
     That whoso sees from earthly sin is cleans'd;
     'Twas borne by angels thro' the heav'nly por-
       tal—
     Its coming hath a holy reign commenc'd.
     Once every year a dove from Heav'n descendeth,
     To strengthen it anew for works of grace;
     'Tis called the Grail, the pow'r of Heav'n at-
       tendeth
     The faithful knights who guard that sacred
       place.
     He whom the Grail to be its servant chooses
     Is armed henceforth by high invincible might;
     All evil craft its power before him loses,
     The spirits of darkness where he dwells take
       flight.
     Nor will he lose the awful charm it blendeth,
     Although he should be called to distant lands,
     When the high cause of virtue he defendeth:
     While he's unknown, its spell he still commands.
     By perils dread the holy Grail is girded,
     No eye rash or profane its light may see;
     Its champion knight from doubtings shall be
       warded,
     If known to man, he must depart and flee. .
     Now mark, craft or disguise my soul disdaineth,
     The Grail sent me to right yon lady's name;
     My father, Percival, gloriously reigneth,
     His knight am I, and Lohengrin my name.

ALLE MÄNNER.
     Hilf Gott! welch' hartes Wort er spricht!

LOHENGRIN.
     Als Streitgenoss bin nicht ich hergekommen,
     Als Kläger sei ich jetzt von euch vernommen!
     Zum ersten klage laut ich vor euch Allen,
     Und frag' um Spruch nach Recht und Fug:
     Da dieser Mann mich nächtens überfallen,
     Sagt, ob ich ihn mit Recht erschlug?

DER KÖNIG UND ALLE MÄNNER.
     Wie deine Hand ihn schlug auf Erden,
     Soll dort ihm Gottes Strafe werden!

LOHENGRIN.
     Zum and'ren aber sollt ihr Klage hören:
     Denn aller Welt nun klag' ich laut,
     Dass zum Verrath an mir sich liess bethören
     Das Weib, das Gott mir angetraut.

ALLE MÄNNER.   Elsa! wie mochte das gescheh'n!
     Wie konntest so du dich vergeh'n?

DIE FRAUEN.   Wehe dir, Elsa!

LOHENGRIN.
     Ihr hörtet Alle, wie sie mir versprochen,
     Dass nie sie woll' erfragen, wer ich bin?
     Nun hat sie ihren theuren Schwur gebrochen,
     Treulosem Rath gab sie ihr Herz dahin!
     Jetzt merket wohl, ob ich den Tag muss scheuen:
     Vor aller Welt, vor König und vor Reich
     Enthülle mein Geheimniss ich in Treuen.
     So hört, ob ich an Adel euch nicht gleich!

ALLE MÄNNER UND FRAUEN.
     Welch' Unerhörtes muss ich nunerfahren!
     O könnt er die erzwung'ne Kunde sparen!

LOHENGRIN.
     In fernem Land, unnahbar euren Schritten,
     Liegt eine Burg, die Monsalvat genannt;
     Ein lichter Tempel stehet dort in Mitten,
     So kostbar, wie auf Erden nichts bekannt:
     Drin ein Gefäss von wunderthät'gem Segen
     Wird dort als höchstes Heiligthum bewacht,
     Es ward, dass sein der Menschen reinste pflegen.
     Herab von einer Engelschaar gebracht;
     Alljährlich naht vom Himmel eine Taube,
     Um neu zu stärken seine Wunderkraft;
     Es heisst der Gral, und selig reinster Glaube
     Ertheilt durch ihn sich seiner Ritterschaft.
     Wer nun dem Gral zu dienen ist erkoren,
     Den rüstet er mit überird'scher Macht;
     An dem ist jedes Bösen Trug verloren,
     Wenn ihn er sieht, weicht dem des Todes Nacht.
     Selbst wer von ihm in ferne Land' entsendet,
     Zum Streiter für der Tugend Recht ernannt,
     Dem wird nicht seine heil'ge Kraft entwendet,
     Bleibt als sein Ritter dort er unerkannt.
     So hehrer Art doch ist des Grales Segen;
     Enthüllt muss er des Laien Auge flieh'n;—
     Des Ritter's drum sollt Zweifel ihr nicht hegen,
     Erkennt ihr ihn,—dann muss er von euch ziehn.—
     Nun hört, wie ich verbot'ner Frage lohne!
     Vom Gral ward ich zu euch daher gesandt:
     Mein Vater Parsifal trägt seine Krone,
     Sein Ritter ich—bin Lohengrin genannt.

LADIES AND MEN.
> While I hear him the wondrous tale revealing,
> The holy tears adown my cheek are stealing!

ELSA. 'Tis dark around me! Give me air!
> Oh, help, help! oh, me, most wretched!

LADIES AND MEN.
> The swan! the swan! the swan!
> The stream he floateth down.
> The swan! ah, he comes!

ELSA. Oh, horror! ah, the swan!

LOHENGRIN.
> Too long I stay—I must obey the Grail!
> My trusty swan! O that this summons ne'er
>   had been!
> Oh, that this day I ne'er had seen!
> I thought the year would soon be o'er
> When thy probation would have pass'd;
> Then by the Grail's transcendent pow'r,
> In thy true shape we'd meet at last!
> Oh, Elsa, think what joys thy doubts have ended.
> Couldst thou not trust in me for one short year?
> Then thy dear brother, whom the Grail defended,
> In life and honor thou hadst welcom'd here.
> If he returns, when our sweet ties are broken,
> This horn, this sword, and ring give him in
>   token:
> This horn succor on battle-field shall send him,
> And with this sword he'll conquer ev'ry foe;
> This ring shall mind him who did most befriend
>   him—
> Of me who sav'd thee from the depths of woe!
> Farewell, my love! my wife, farewell!
> Henceforth the Grail commands my life!

ORTRUD.
> Go forth! Go forth! thou knight audacious!
> Thy bride shall hear a tale veracious!
> All now upon my mind doth dawn;
> 'Twas I that wound the golden band
> Around the neck of yonder swan;
> He is the true heir of Brabant!

CHORUS. Ha!

ORTRUD.
> Oh, joy! my magic was the stronger!
> Now thou afar from here must roam!
> But if thy knight had tarried longer,
> His spells had call'd thy brother home!

CHORUS.
> Thou witch accurs'd, dost thou compass it?
> Thou shall atone for crime so vile!

ORTRUD.
> Stand back, I do myself confess it,
> On me the gods of vengeance smile!

ALLE MÄNNER UND FRAUEN.
> Hör' ich so seine höchste Art bewähren,
> Entbrennt mein Aug' in heil'gen Wonnezähren.

ELSA. Mir schwankt der Boden! Welche Nacht!
> O Luft! Luft der Unglücksel'gen!

DIE MÄNNER UND DIE FRAUEN.
> Der Schwan! der Schwan!
> Seht dort ihn wieder nahn!
> Der Schwan! Weh, er naht!

ELSA. Entsetzlich! Ha! der Schwan! der Schwan!

LOHENGRIN.
> Schon sendet nach dem Säumigen der Gral.
> Mein lieber Schwan!
> Ach! diese letzte traur'ge Fahrt,
> Wie gern hätt' ich sie dir erspart!
> In einem Jahr, wenn deine Zeit
> Im Dienst zu Ende sollte geh'n—
> Dann, durch des Grales Macht befreit,
> Wollt' ich dich anders wiederseh'n!
> O Elsa! Nur ein Jahr an deiner Seite
> Hätt' ich als Zeuge deines Glücks ersehnt!
> Dann kehrte, selig in des Gral's Geleite,
> Dein Bruder wieder, den du todt gewähnt—
> Kommt er dann heim, wenn ich ihm fern im
>   Leben,
> Dies Horn, dies Schwert, den Ring sollst du ihm
>   geben.
> Dies Horn soll in Gefahr ihm Hülfe schenken,—
> In wildem Kampf dies Schwert ihm Sieg verleiht;
> Doch bei dem Ringe soll er mein gedenken,
> Der einstens dich aus Schmach und Noth befreit!
> Leb wohl! Leb wohl! Leb wohl! mein süsses
>   Weib!
> Leb wohl! Mein zürnt der Gral, wenn ich noch
>   bleib'!

ORTRUD.
> Fahr' heim! Fahr' heim, du stolzer Helde,
> Dass jubelnd ich der Thörin melde,
> Wer dich gezogen in dem Kahn;
> Am Kettlein, das ich um ihn wand,
> Mit dem das Kind ich schuf zum Schwan:
> Das war der Erbe von Brabant!

ALLE. Ha!

ORTRUD.
> Dank, dass den Ritter du vertrieben!
> Nun giebt der Schwan ihm Heimgeleit!
> Der Held, wär' länger er geblieben,
> Den Bruder hätt' er auch befreit.

ALLE.
> Abscheulich Weib! Ha, welch' Verbrechen
> Hast du in frechem Hohn bekannt!

ORTRUD.
> Erfahrt, wie sich die Götter rächen,
> Von deren Huld ihr euch gewandt!

[*She remains standing with an expression of wild despair.* LOHENGRIN, *standing on the bank, has heard all that* ORTRUD *said; he now sinks on his knees in mute prayer. All eyes turn with anxious expectancy to him. The white dove of the Grail flies slowly down, and hovers over the skiff;* LOHENGRIN *perceives it, and with a grateful look rises quickly, and loosens the chain from the swan, who immediately sinks. In its place* LOHENGRIN *raises Gottfried, a fair boy in shining silver garment, from the river, and places him on the bank.*

LOHENGRIN. Behold the ruler of Brabant,
　　　　　The rightful heir of this fair land.

[*With a shriek* ORTRUD *falls at the right of Gottfried.* LOHENGRIN *springs into the skiff, and the dove, having seized the chain, draws it along.* ELSA, *with a last look of joy, gazes on Gottfried, who advances to the* KING *and makes his obeisance to him. All contemplate him with astonishment and joy, the Brabantians sinking on their knees in homage. Gottfried rushes into* ELSA's *arms, who for a moment of joyous transport, turns her eyes again towards the river where* LOHENGRIN *has vanished.*

ELSA. My consort! My consort!

[LOHENGRIN *is seen once more in the distance; he stands with head bent, sorrowfully leaning on his shield in the skiff; at the sight of him all break into loud lamentation.* ELSA *sinks lifeless to the ground, supported by Gottfried.*

[*Bleibt in wilder Verzweiflung hoch aufgerichtet stehen.* LOHENGRIN, *der vernommen, was sie sprach, sinkt jetzt, dicht am Strande, zu stummen Gebet feierlich auf die Kniee. Aller Blicke richten sich in gespannter Erwartung auf ihn. Plötzlich erblickt er die weisse Grals-Taube über den Nachen herabschwebend; mit lebhafter Freude springt er auf und löst dem Schwane die Kette, worauf dieser sogleich untertaucht. An seiner Stelle hebt* LOHENGRIN *einen schönen Jüngling in glänzendem Silbergewande—Gottfried—aus dem Flusse an's Ufer.*

LOHENGRIN. Seht da den Herzog von Brabant!
　　　　　Zum Führer sei er euch ernannt!

[*Er springt schnell in den Nachen, welchen die Taube an der Kette fasst und sogleich fortzieht.* ORTRUD *sinkt bei Gottfried's Anblick mit einem Schrei zusammen.* ELSA *blickt mit letzter freudiger Verklärung auf den nun vorschreitenden Gottfried, der sich vor dem* KÖNIG *verneight und vor dem die Brabanter huldigend auf die Kniee sinken. Dann eilt er in ihre Arme.*

ELSA. Mein Gatte! Mein Gatte!

[*Sie erblickt* LOHENGRIN *bereits in der Ferne; von der Taube im Nachen gezogen. Er steht mit gesenktem Haupt, traurig auf seinem Schild gelehnt. Alles bricht bei diesem Anblicke in einen jähen Wehruf aus.* ELSA *gleitet in Gottfried's Armen entseelt langsam zu Boden.*

THE END

THE RHINEGOLD

THE RING OF THE NIBELUNG.

THE cycle to which this general title is given consists of the four music dramas — *Rhinegold, The Valkyr, Siegfried,* and *The Dusk of the Gods.* Wagner was occupied with this monumental work, with extended periods of interruption, during twenty-six years; for, as early as 1848, he made a prose sketch of the Nibelung myth, followed a year later by the dramatic poem *Siegfried's Death,* which subsequently became *The Dusk of the Gods.* Curiously enough, the books of these four dramas were written in inverse order, the reason for which Wagner gives fully in a letter to Liszt, dated 1851. Briefly stated, he found that so many important facts leading to the death of Siegfried must, in his drama, either be narrated or taken for granted, that he wrote a preparatory drama, *Young Siegfried,* which, in turn, seemed incomplete without the presentation of the events which are set forth in *The Valkyr.* Thus the cycle assumed its final shape as we now possess it; *Rhinegold,* which was written last, forming an introductory drama to the whole.

Wagner found the material for his colossal project in the saga of the Northern Mythology; but it required the hand of the master-dramatist to weld the disconnected legends into a logically developed and unified whole, to trace the relation of cause and effect; and by eliminating what was irrelevant to his purpose, and emphasizing the important facts of the narrative, to give to the mass of incident life and action, leading to over-powering climaxes. In the light of his genius the simple legends acquired a deeper significance; the rape of the Rhinegold, and the curse which was thereafter visited upon its possessors, crafty or innocent, became symbolic of the lust for wealth and power, with all its attendant evil — a curse which could be removed only thro' the expiation and triumphing love of Brünnhilde, whose self-immolation, while marking the end of the reign of the gods, brought the dawn of a new era — that of human love — upon the earth.

A thorough comprehension of *Rhinegold,* both musically and dramatically, is essential, in order to enjoy with understanding the other dramas of the cycle. Not only are the fundamental motives of all future action made clear, but most of the musical themes, which are used so significantly and frequently throughout the entire work, are heard for the first time in their original form and application in *Rhinegold;* for, tho' the book was written last, Wagner undertook the musical composition of the four dramas in their natural order, and accumulated his musical material as the action progressed.

C. F. M.

THE STORY OF "RHINEGOLD."

IN the prologue, or "fore-evening," to the cycle Wagner introduces us to the supernatural beings of the Northern Mythology — Wotan, the chief of the gods, and his spouse, Fricka, who, like Juno, was the guardian of domestic virtue; Loge, the god of Flame, crafty and cunning; Freia, the goddess of Youth and Beauty; her two brothers, Donner and Froh; the giants, Fasolt and Fafner; the Nibelungs, Alberich and Mime; the three Rhinedaughters, Woglinde, Wellgunde, and Flosshilde, who guarded the treasure in the depths of the Rhine; and the all-wise Erda, goddess of primeval wisdom, who later bore to Wotan the nine Valkyrs.

The first scene shows the rocky bed of the Rhine, with its flowing waters, filling the entire height of the stage, the daylight scarcely filtering through from above. The three Rhinedaughters disport themselves merrily, swimming about, and diving from rock to rock, while in its pristine innocence the Rhinegold slumbers securely. Their play is interrupted by the approach of

Alberich of the tribe of Nibelungs, a race of cunning, demoniacal gnomes, who inhabit Nibelheim in the bowels of the earth. Hideous and uncouth, he seeks to win the pleasures of love from the nymphs. But though tantalizing him by their banter, they elude their awkward pursuer, who slips about on the slimy rocks until his gaze is attracted by an increasing brilliance which glows from a rocky eminence. It is the Rhinegold, which presently shines forth dazzlingly in the rays of the rising sun, and around which the maidens circle with joyous shouts. They jeeringly betray to Alberich that he alone who is willing to renounce the pleasures of love, can possess himself of the gold; but that by its possession in the shape of a magic ring he may make himself ruler and lord of the world. Seized with new desire, the Nibelung curses love, which for him is but lust, and scrambling madly up the rock, tears the gold from its bed and disappears in the depths. Night falls again upon the waters, and the Rhinedaughters break forth into wild lamentation. The billows sink, giving way to veils of mist, which, as they clear away, disclose Scene II.

The rising sun lights up the spires and turrets of a castle on a rocky cliff at the back. Between this and the foreground the Rhine is supposed to flow thro' a deep valley. Wotan and Fricka are lying asleep at one side; but Fricka awakes and arouses her spouse, who rapturously greets the shining castle. Fricka reproaches him, however, that in order to recompense the giants, Fasolt and Fafner, for building his new abode, he has promised them her sister Freia, the goddess of Youth and Beauty, to bring light and love into their cold home. Wotan responds that he never really intended to give up Freia, when the latter enters in hasty flight, pursued by the giants who, the work finished, have come to claim their reward. Froh and Donner seek to protect their sister, but this Wotan, as god of justice, may not permit; and the giants, deaf to his parleying, are about to carry off Freia when the arrival of Loge induces them to pause. The latter had been sent thro' the world by Wotan to discover something which the giants would accept as a substitute for Freia; but he confesses that nowhere could he find aught for which men were willing to renounce the pleasures of love. With great diplomacy Loge then tells of his visit to Alberich, of the gold the Nibelung had won thro' renouncing love, and of the power which dwelt in the magic ring. Forthwith the giants agree to relinquish Freia if Wotan will get and give them the gold. This Wotan is unwilling to do, for he is already plotting to win the ring for himself; but the giants, giving him until nightfall to comply, drag Freia away as hostage. Soon the greyness of age settles upon the features of the gods, for Freia, the conserver of eternal youth, is no longer with them Their need is so urgent that Wotan at once accompanies Loge to Nibelheim to wrest the ring from Alberich.

SCENE III. The abode of the Nibelungs. Alberich now is master of all the gnomes, and drives them unceasingly at the task of piling high his hoarded treasure. Mime has been set to forge the Tarnhelm, which can render its wearer invisible, or enable him to assume any shape he please. Unsuccessfully Mime tries to conceal from Alberich the finished work; Alberich seizes the Tarnhelm, and, to demonstrate its power, changes into a column of vapor, in which form he gives the cowed Mime a severe drubbing, and then departs, still invisible, urging his slaves at their labor. Wotan and Loge descend thro' a cleft of the rock, and Mime, who is nursing his wounds, tells how Alberich has become all-powerful thro' the Ring and the Tarnhelm, made of Rhinegold. Alberich, once more in his natural form, returns; and Loge craftily gets him to display his power — first, by changing into an enormous serpent, and later into a toad. This being their chance, Wotan puts his foot on the toad, Loge secures the Tarnhelm, and Alberich, again in his own form, is securely bound, and dragged away to the upper world.

SCENE IV shows again the meadows before Wotan's castle, still veiled by pale mists as at the end of Scene II. Wotan and Loge return with the fettered Alberich, who, as the price of his freedom, is forced to give up his golden hoard. The Tarnhelm also is taken from him, but when the Ring is torn from him his rage and hate are unbounded, and he curses with fatal effect the Ring. He is then freed, and disappears. Now, as Freia is brought back by the giants, the mists begin to disappear, for her presence restores youth to the gods, who all enter to greet Wotan. The giants demand the ransom — a pile of gold as great as the height and breadth of Freia. Wotan seeks to withhold the Ring, but is warned by the apparition of Erda not to retain in his possession that which was obtained by a double theft, and bring down the Nibelung's curse upon the gods. Upon gaining the Ring the two giants quarrel and Fasolt is slain; whereat Wotan, struck by the awful power of the curse, bends his thoughts upon averting the menace of fate. Donner clears the air with a thunderstorm, and Walhalla is seen in the bright light with a rainbow bridge leading to it across the Rhine. As the gods start over the bridge, the Rhinedaughters are heard imploring Wotan to restore the gold to the depths; but, bidding Loge silence the wailing, Wotan leads the gods into their new abode.

PUBLISHERS' NOTE.

For the use of those who wish to familiarize themselves with the musical framework of *Rhinegold*, the following list of themes (*Leitmotiven*) has been prepared. The themes are numbered for convenience; corresponding reference numerals are placed in the margin of the poem, opposite the place or line where each one occurs for the first time, or with especial significance.

LEADING MOTIVES (LEITMOTIVEN) OF THE DRAMA.

No. 1.   MOTIVE OF THE RHINE (MOTIV DES URELEMENTES).

No. 2.   MOTIVE OF THE RHINEDAUGHTERS (MOTIV DER RHEINTÖCHTER).

Wei - a, wa - ga, Wan - der, ye wa - ters; wa - ver and waft me!

wa - ga - la wei - a! wal - la - la, wei - a - la wei a! . .

No. 3.   MOTIVE OF THE NIBELUNG'S SERVITUDE (MOTIV EINER KNECHTUNG).

No. 4.   RHINEGOLD MOTIVE (MOTIV DES RHEINGOLDES).

No. 5.

THE RHINEDAUGHTERS' SHOUT OF TRIUMPH
(HERRSCHERRUF DER RHEINTÖCHTER).

No. 6.

MOTIVE OF THE RING (DAS RINGMOTIV).

No. 7. MOTIVE OF THE RENUNCIATION OF LOVE (ENTSAGUNGSMOTIV).

No. 8.

WALHALLA MOTIVE (WALHALL MOTIV).

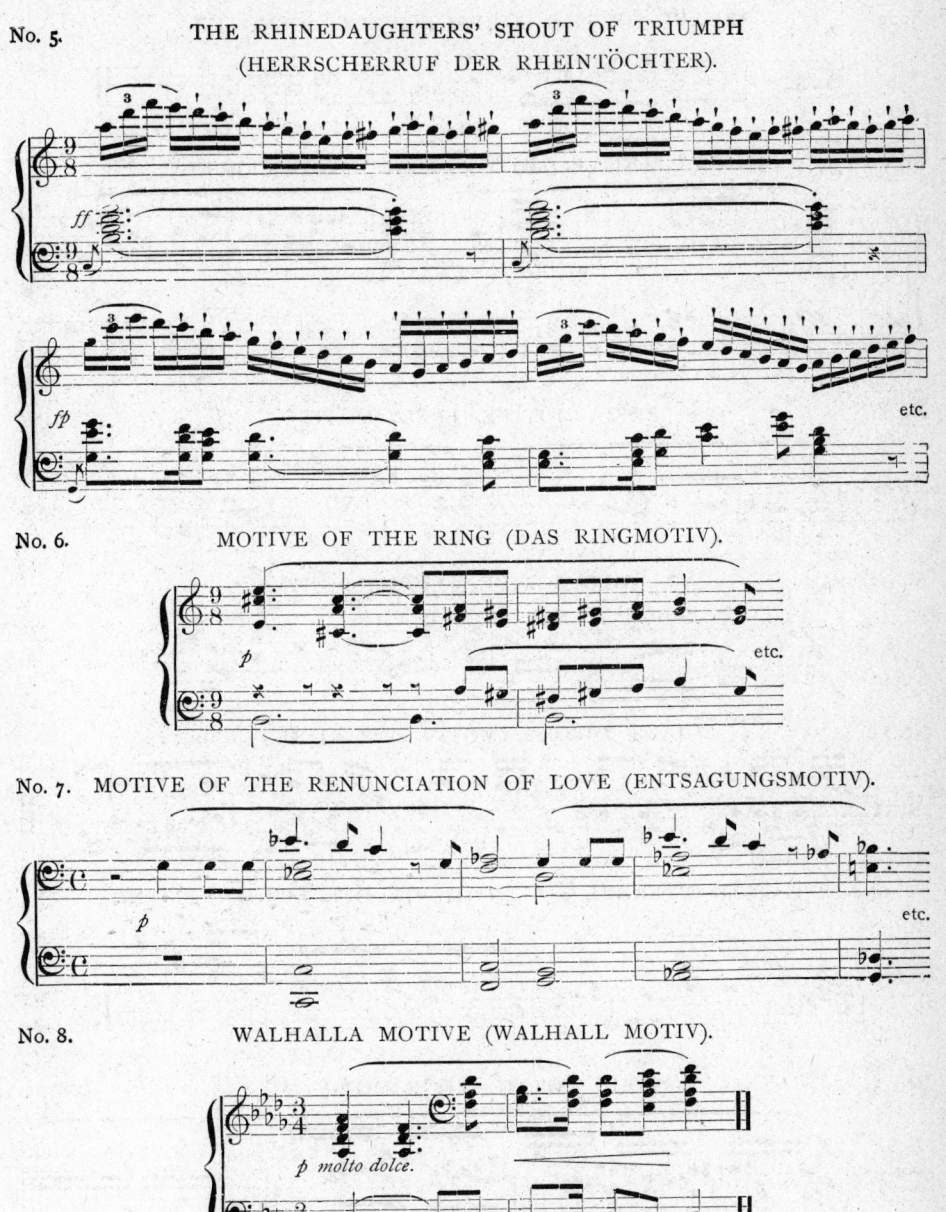

No. 9.   MOTIVE OF THE COMPACT (VERTRAGSMOTIV).

No. 10.   FRICKA MOTIVE (MOTIV DER LIEBESFESSELUNG).

No. 11.   FREIA MOTIVE (FREIA MOTIV).

No. 12.   FLIGHT MOTIVE (FLUCHTMOTIV).

No. 13.   GIANT MOTIVE (MOTIV DER RIESEN).

No. 14. MOTIVE OF ETERNAL YOUTH (MOTIV DER EWIGEN JUGEND).

No. 15.   LOGE MOTIVE (LOGE MOTIV).

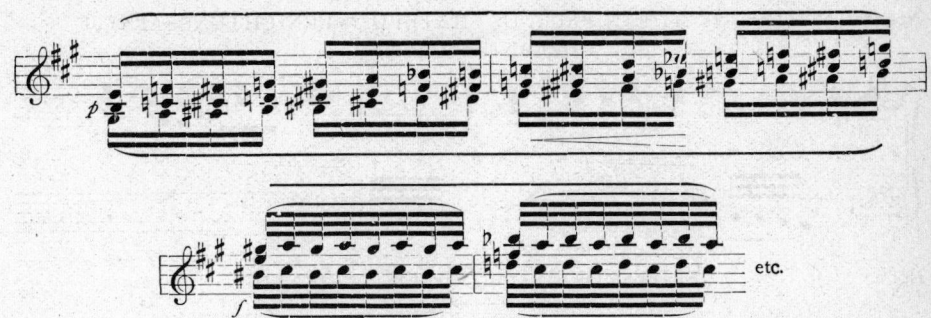

No. 16.   MAGIC FIRE MOTIVE (MOTIV DES FEUERZAUBERS).

No. 17.   NIBELUNG MOTIVE (SCHMIEDEMOTIV DER NIBELUNGEN).

No. 18.   MOTIVE OF THE TARNHELMET (MOTIV DES TARNHELMS).

No. 19.   MOTIVE OF THE RISING HOARD (MOTIV DES AUFSTEIGENDEN HORTES).

No. 20.   MOTIVE OF THE CURSE (FLUCH MOTIV).

As   at   first   by   curse 'twas reach'd,   hence forth curs'd   be   this Ring!

No. 21. MOTIVE OF THE NIBELUNGS' HATRED (VERNICHTUNGSARBEIT DER NIBELUNGEN).

etc.

No. 22 ERDA MOTIVE (MOTIV DER NORNEN).

No. 23. RAINBOW MOTIVE (MOTIV DES REGENBOGENS).

etc.

No. 24. THE SWORD MOTIVE (SCHWERTMOTIV).

THE RHINEGOLD.

FIRST SCENE.

At the bottom of the Rhine.

Greenish twilight, lighter above, darker below. The upper part of the scene is filled with moving water which restlessly streams from R to L. Towards the ground the waters resolve themselves into a fine mist, so that the space to a man's height from the stage seems free from water, which flows like a train of clouds over the gloomy depths. Everywhere are steep points of rock jutting up from the depths and enclosing the whole stage; all the ground is broken up into a wild confusion of jagged pieces, so that there is no level place, while on all sides darkness indicates other deeper fissures.

Round a rock, in the center of the stage, whence its peak rises high into the lighter water, one of the *Rhine-nymphs* is seen merrily swimming.

Woglinde. Weia! Waga!
　　　Wander ye waters,
　　　waver and waft me!
　　　Wagalaweia!
　　　Wallala weiala weia!

Wellgunde's
　　　　　(voice from above).
　　　Woglinde, watch you alone?

Woglinde. Till Wellgunde wends to my side.

Wellgunde
　　　　　(diving down to the rock).
　　　How fares with your watch?
　　　(She tries to seize *Woglinde*.)

Woglinde
　　　　　(avoiding her by swimming).
　　　Far from your reach!
　　　(They tease, and seek playfully to catch one another.)

Flosshilde's
　　　　　(voice from above).
　　　Heiala weia!
　　　Whimsical sisters!

Wellgunde. Flosshilde, swim!
　　　Woglinde flies:
　　　help me to foil her in fleetness.

Flosshilde
　　　(dives down and comes between the playmates).
　　　The sleeping gold
　　　badly ye guard:
　　　better begird
　　　the gleaming one's bed;
　　　such banter both may regret.

With merry cries the two separate: *Flosshilde* chases first one and then the other; they evade her and then unite to pursue her in turn. Thus they dart about like fish from rock to rock, laughing and sporting.

From a dark chasm *Alberich* clambers up to one of the rocks. He halts in the shadow and watches the gambols of the nymphs with growing delight.

ERSTE SCENE.

Auf dem Grunde des Rheines.

Grünliche Dämmerung, nach oben zu lichter, nach unten zu dunkler. Die Höhe ist von wogendem Gewässer erfüllt, das rastlos von rechts nach links zu strömt. Nach der Tiefe zu lösen sich die Fluthen in einen immer feineren feuchten Nebel auf, so dass der Raum der Manneshöhe vom Boden auf gänzlich frei vom Wasser zu sein scheint, welches wie in Wolkenzügen über den nächtlichen Grund dahin fliesst. Ueberall ragen schroffe Felsenriffe aus der Tiefe auf, und grenzen den Raum der Bühne ab; der ganze Boden ist in ein wildes Zackengewirr zerspalten, so dass er nirgends vollkommen eben ist und nach allen Seiten hin in dichtester Finsterniss tiefere Schlüffte annehmen lässt.

Um ein Riff in der Mitte der Bühne, welches mit seiner schlanken Spitze bis in die dichtere, heller dämmernde Wasserfluth hinaufragt, kreis't in anmuthig schwimmender Bewegung eine der *Rheintöchter.*

Woglinde. Weia! Waga!
　　　Woge, du Welle,
　　　walle zur Wiege!
　　　Wagalaweia!
　　　Wallala weiala weia!

Wellgunde's
　　　　　(Stimme, von oben).
　　　Woglinde, wach'st du allein?

Woglinde. Mit Wellgunde wär' ich zu zwei.

Wellgunde
　　　　　(taucht aus der Fluth zum Riff herab).
　　　Lass' seh'n, wie du wach'st.
　　　(Sie sucht *Woglinde* zu erhaschen.)

Woglinde
　　　　　(entweicht ihr schwimmend).
　　　Sicher vor dir.
　　　(Sie necken sich und suchen sich spielend zu fangen.)

Flosshilde's
　　　　　(Stimme, von oben).
　　　Heiala weia!
　　　Wildes Geschwister!

Wellgunde. Flosshilde, schwimm'!
　　　Woglinde flieht:
　　　hilf mir die Fliessende fangen!

Flosshilde
　　　(taucht herab und fährt zwischen die Spielenden)
　　　Des Goldes Schlaf
　　　hütet ihr schlecht;
　　　besser bewacht
　　　des schlummernden Bett,
　　　sonst büss't ihr beide das Spiel!

Mit munt'rem Gekreisch fahren die beiden auseinander; *Flosshilde* sucht bald die eine, bald die andere zu erhaschen; sie entschlüpfen ihr und vereinigen sich endlich, umgemeinschaftlich auf Flosshilde Jagd zu machen: so schnellen sie gleich Fischen von Riff zu Riff, scherzend und lachend.

Aus einer finstern Schlufft ist währenddem *Alberich*, an einem Riffe klimmend, dem Abgrunde entstiegen. Er hält, noch vom Dunkel umgeben an, und schaut dem Spiele der Wassermädchen mit steigendem Wohlgefallen zu.

Alberich. Ho, ho! ye nixies!
Are ye not nimble,
nice to behold!
From Nibelheim's night
now would I fain
near you, if ye be kind.

(The girls, when hearing *Alberich's* voice, leave off playing.)

Woglinde. Hey! who is there?

Wellgunde. A thing with a voice.

Flosshilde. Look, who is below!

(They dive deeper and perceive the Nibelung.)

Woglinde and Wellgunde. Faugh! the gruesome one.

Flosshilde
(swiftly diving upwards).
Look to the gold!
Father warned us
from such a foe.

(The others follow her, and all three collect quickly round the central rock.)

Alberich. List! aloft there!

The Three Nymphs. What want you, below there?

Alberich. Spoilt were your sport
if 'stonished I stand here still?
Near to me dive then;
a poor Niblung
longs dearly to dally with you!

Woglinde. He offers to join us?

Wellgunde. Is it his joke?

Alberich. How sweet and soft
in this light ye seem!
Gladly I'd seek
to encircle one of your waists,
should you kindly descend.

Flosshilde. I laugh at our fears;
the foe is in love!

(They laugh.)

Wellgunde. The languishing calf!

Woglinde. Let us accost him.

(She descends to the point of the rock at the base of which *Alberich* is.)

Alberich. She's coming below!

Woglinde. Climb closer to me.

Alberich
(clambers with gnome-like rapidity, but with difficulty, to the summit of the rock).
Smooth with slime
the slippery stone is!
How slide my steps!
My hands and my feet
cannot fasten or hold on
the steepness unsteady!

(Sneezes.)

Alberich. He, he! Ihr Nicker!
Wie seid ihr niedlich,
neidliches Volk!
Aus Nibelheim's Nacht
naht' ich euch gern,
neiget ihr euch zu mir.

(Die Mädchen halten, als sie *Alberich's* Stimme hören, mit ihrem Spiele ein.)

Woglinde. Hei! wer ist dort?

Wellgunde. Es dämmert und ruft.

Flosshilde. Luget, wer uns belauscht!

(Sie tauchen tiefer herab und erkennen den Nibelung.)

Woglinde und *Wellgunde.* Pfui! der Garstige!

Flosshilde
(schnell auftauchend).
Hütet das Gold!
Vater warnte
vor solchem Feind.

(Die beiden andern folgen ihr, und alle drei versammeln sich schnell um das mittlere Riff.)

Alberich. Ihr da oben!

Die Drei. Was willst du da unten?

Alberich. Stör' ich e'ur Spiel,
wenn staunend ich still hier steh'?
Tauchtet ihr nieder,
mit euch tollte
und neckte der Niblung sich gern!

Woglinde. Mit uns will er spielen?

Wellgunde. Ist ihm das Spott?

Alberich. Wie scheint im Schimmer
ihr hell und schön?
Wie gern umschlänge
der Schlanken eine mein Arm,
schlüpfte hold sie herab!

Flosshilde. Nun lach 'ich der Furcht:
der Feind ist verliebt.

(Sie lachen.)

Wellgunde. Der lüsterne Kauz!

Woglinde. Lasst ihn uns kennen?

(Sie lässt sich auf die Spitze des Riffes herab, an dessen Fusse *Alberich* angelangt ist.)

Alberich. Die neigt sich herab.

Woglinde. Nun nahe dich mir!

Alberich
(klettert mit koboldartiger Behendigkeit, doch wiederholt aufgehalten, der Spitze des Riffes zu).
Garstig glatter
glitschriger Glimmer!
Wie gleit' ich aus!
Mit Händen und Füssen
nicht fasse noch halt' ich
das schlecke Geschlüpfer!

(Er pruhstet.)

'Clamminess
creeps up my nostrils :
accursed sneezing !

(He has approached *Woglinde*.)

Woglinde

(laughing).

See how nicely
my beau can sneeze !

Alberich.   O be but mine,
my beautiful child !

(He seeks to embrace her.)

Woglinde

(eluding him).

Would you make court,
then follow me here !

(She flies up to another rock.   The others laugh.)

Alberich

(scratching his head).

Alas ! you are lost !
Come but lower !
Far too hard
'tis for me so to fly.

Woglinde

(swinging down to a third rock in the depths).

Clamber down here ;
your hand may then clasp me.

Alberich

(hastily scrambling down).

Much better down lower !

Woglinde

(darting quickly upwards to a high peak at the side).

But look, I uplift me !

(The Nymphs all laugh.)

Alberich.   How follow and take
this timid fish ?
Wait a bit, false one !

(Tries hastily to climb up.)

Wellgunde

(has descended to a lower rock on the other side).

Heia ! my hero !
hear what I say !

Alberich

(turning round).

Call you to me ?

Wellgunde.   I caution you well ;
to me wend your way :
mind not Woglinde !

Feuchtes Nass
füllt mir die Nase :
verfluchtes Niesen !

(Er ist in der Nähe *Woglinde's* angelangt.)

Woglinde

(lachend).

Pruhstend naht
meines Freiers Pracht !

Alberich.   Mein Friedel sei,
du fräuliches Kind !

(Er sucht sie zu umfassen.)

Woglinde

(sich ihm entwindend).

Willst du mich frei'n,
so freie mich hier !

(Sie ist auf einem andern Riffe angelangt. Die Schwestern lachen.)

Alberich

(kratzt sich den Kopf).

O weh : du entweich'st ?
Komm' doch wieder !
Schwer ward mir,
was so leicht du erschwing'st.

Woglinde

(schwingt sich auf ein drittes Riff in grösserer Tiefe).

Steig' nur zu Grund :
da greifst du mich sicher !

Alberich

(klettert hastig hinab).

Wohl besser da unten !

Woglinde

(schnellt sich rasch aufwärts nach einem hohen Seitenriffe).

Nun aber nach oben !

(Alle Mädchen lachen.)

Alberich.   Wie fang' ich im Sprung'
den spröden Fisch ?
Warte, du Falsche !

(Er will ihr eilig nachklettern.)

Wellgunde

(hat sich auf ein tieferes Riff auf der andern Seite gesenkt).

Heia ! Du Holder !
hör'st du mich nicht ?

Alberich

(sich umwendend).

Ruf'st du nach mir ?

Wellgunde.   Ich rathe dir gut :
zu mir wende dich,
Woglinde meide !

Alberich

    (hastily clambering over the rocks towards her).

  More fair are you
  than she who but flies me ;
  for she's less sparkling,
  too sleek and sly.
  But dive yet deeper
  if you would dally !

Wellgunde

    (descending a little nearer to him).

  So now am I near ?

Alberich. No, not enough !
  With tender arms
  entwine me around,
  that I may fondle
  that form so bewitching :
  in passionate bliss
to my panting embrace let me press thee.

Wellgunde. Are you in love
  and longing for favors ?
  Let's see what semblance,
  my beauty can show. —
  Faugh ! you hairy
  and horrible imp !
  Swarthy, stunted,
  and shrivelled up dwarf !
  Seek as a fellow
  one of like form !

Alberich

    (trying to detain her by force).

  Though fair I am not,
  I'll fetter you fast !

Wellgunde

    (quickly darting up to the central rock).

  Quite fast, for fear I should flow !

    (All three laugh.)

Alberich

    (Calling angrily after her).

  Fickle chit !
Chilly, slippery fish !
  Seem I not shapely,
  tender, enticing,
  glib and gay —
Go ! let eels be your lovers,
if so loathsome am I !

Flosshilde. Why scold thus, imp ?
  Does your heart sink ?
  But two have been sought ;
  try now the third one :
  soft reward
surely awaits you there !

Alberich

    (kle tert hastig über den Bodengrund zu *Wellgunde*).

  Viel schöner bist du
  als jene Scheue,
  die minder gleissend
  und gar zu glatt. —
  Nur tiefer tauche,
  willst du mir taugen !

Wellgunde

    (noch etwas mehr zu ihm sich herabsenkend).

  Bin nun ich dir nah' ?

Alberich. Noch nicht genug !
  Die schlanken Arme
  schlinge um mich,
  dass ich den Nacken
  dir neckend betaste,
  mit schmeichelnder Brunst
an die schwellende Brust mich dir schmiege.

Wellgunde. Bist du verliebt
  und lüstern nach Minne ?
  Lass' seh'n, du Schöner,
  wie du bist zu schau'n ? —
  Pfui, du haariger,
  höck'riger Geck !
  Schwarzes, schwieliges
  Schwefelgezwerg !
  Such' dir ein Friedel,
  dem du gefällst !

Alberich

    (sucht sie mit Gewalt zu halten).

  Gefall' ich dir nicht,
  dich fass' ich doch fest !

Wellgunde

    (schnell zum mittleren Riffe auftauchend).

  Nur fest, sonst fliess' ich dir fort !

    (Alle Drei lachen.)

Alberich

    (erbos't ihr nachzankend).

  Falsches Kind !
Kalter, grätiger Fisch !
  Schein' ich nicht schön **dir,**
  niedlich und neckisch,
  glatt und glau —
hei ! so buhle mit Aalen,
ist dir eklig mein Balg !

Flosshilde. Was zank'st du, Alp ?
  Schon so verzagt ?
  Du frei'test um zwei !
  früg'st du die dritte,
  süssen Trost
schüfe die Traute dir !

Alberich. Music sweet
  sing'st thou to me: —
  what joy that all
  are not alike !
  'Mid many I must delight one,
  though all be chary to choose me.
  Ere I believe thee
  still lower descend.

Flosshilde
    (diving down to Alberich).
  How foolish are
  my sisters' hearts
  to see no symmetry here !

Alberich
    (approaching her hastily).
  Both dull and hideous
  do I now hold them,
  since I've beheld thee, my sweet.

Flosshilde
    (cajolingly).
  O warble still
  thy wondrous song ;
  it filleth sweetly mine ears !

Alberich
    (caressing her).
  I flush, flame
  and flutter at heart,
  homage so flatt'ring to hear.

Flosshilde
    (gently repulsing him).
  Thy beauty's glory
  makes glad mine eyes :
  and thy loving smile
  doth assuage my alarms !
    (Draws him tenderly to her.)
  Sweetest of men !

Alberich. Softest of maids !

Flosshilde. Wert thou but mine !

Alberich. Might I e'er hold thee !

Flosshilde
    (holding him quite in her arms).
  O ! thy staring-eyed brow,
  thy straggle-haired beard,
  to see them and handle them still !
  That thy stubbly grey hair,
  in streaming elf locks,
  might float round Flosshild' for ever !
  And thy toad-allied stature,
  thy stridulous tones,
  O might I astonish and still,
  sate with these ev'ry sense !
  (Woglinde and Wellgunde have dived down to them and now
    raise a peal of laughter.)

Alberich. Holder Sang
  singt zu mir her. —
  Wie gut, dass ihr
  eine nicht seid !
  Von vielen gefall' ich wohl einer :
  von einer kies'te mich keine ! —
  Soll ich dir glauben,
  so gleite herab !

Flosshilde
    (taucht zu *Alberich* hinab).
  Wie thörig seid ihr,
  dumme Schwestern,
  dünkt euch dieser nicht schön !

Alberich
    (hastig ihr nahend).
  Für dumm und hässlich
  darf ich sie halten,
  seit ich dich Holdeste seh'.

Flosshilde
    (schmeichelnd).
  O singe fort
  so süss und fein ;
  wie hehr verführt es mein Ohr !

Alberich
    (zutraulich sie berührend).
  Mir zagt, zuckt
  und zehrt sich das Herz,
  lacht mir so zierliches Lob.

Flosshilde
    (ihn sanft abwehrend).
  Wie deine Anmuth
  mein Aug' erfreut,
  deines Lächelns Milde
  den Muth mir labt !
    (Sie zieht ihn zärtlich an sich.)
  Seligster Mann !

Alberich. Süsseste Maid !

Flosshilde. Wär'st du mir hold !

Alberich. Hielt'ich dich immer !

Flosshilde
    (ihn ganz in ihren Armen haltend).
  Deinen stechenden Blick,
  deinen struppigen Bart,
  o säh' ich ihn, fasst' ich ihn stets !
  Deines stachlichen Haares
  strammes Gelock,
  umflöss' es Flosshilde ewig !
  Deine Krötengestalt,
  deiner Stimme Gekrächz,
  o dürft' ich staunend und stumm,
  sie nur hören und seh'n !
  (Woglinde und Wellgunde sind nah herabgetaucht und schlagen
    jetzt ein helles Gelächter auf.)

Alberich

(starting timidly from Flosshilde's arms).

Are you laughing at me?

Flosshilde

(suddenly darting from him).

Your love-song thus merrily ends.

(She darts quickly up to her sisters and joins in their laughter.

Alberich

(with a screaming voice).

Woe's me! Ah, woe's me!
Alas! Alas!
The third of my trust
betraying me thus!
Most shocking, shifty,
wicked and shameless of wantons!
know you no truth,
you treacherous, nondescript brood?

The Three Rhine-Nymphs.

Walala! Lalaleia! Lalei!
Heia! Heia! Haha!
Fie on you, gnome,
in fury thus gnashing!
Take the rede that we tender.
How was it, calf,
you could not have kept
the lady of your love?
True are we,
firm is our troth
toward him who bravely holds.
Seize on us then,
and cease to reproach:
we can fly not fast in the wave.

(They swim about, hither and thither, high and low, to incite
Alberich to chase them.)

Alberich.   How through my frame
there rages a fire
with radiance fierce!
Wrath and passion,
rude and pow'rful,
rouse up my pulses.
Though ye may laugh and lie,
lusting I long for one;
I'll win her, too, for my leman!

(He chases them with desperate exertions; with frightful activity
he clambers from rock to rock, springing from one to the other and
striving to reach first one nymph and then another; they always avoid
him with mocking laughter. He staggers and falls below, then
clambers aloft again — till at last his patience is exhausted: foaming
with rage, he pauses breathless and shakes his clenched fist at the
nymphs.)

Alberich

(nearly beside himself).

Were I but to catch one!

He remains in speechless rage, gazing upwards, when suddenly he
is rivetted to the spot by the following sight.
Through the water above breaks an ever-increasing glow, which on
the summit of the central rock kindles gradually to a blinding yellow
gleam; a magical golden light then streams from thence through the
water.

Alberich

(erschreckt aus Flosshilde's Armen auffahrend).

Lacht ihr Bösen mich aus?

Flosshilde

(sich plötzlich ihm entreissend).

Wie billig am Ende vom Lied.

(Sie taucht mit den Schwestern schnell in die Höhe und stimmt in
ihr Gelächter ein.)

Alberich

(mit kreischender Stimme).

Wehe! ach wehe!
O Schmerz! O Schmerz!
Die dritte, so traut,
betrog sie mich auch? —
Ihr schmählich schlaues,
lüderlich schlechtes Gelichter!
Nährt ihr nur Trug,
ihr treuloses Nickergezücht?

Die drei Rheintöchter.

Wallala! Lalaleia! Lalei!
Heia! Heia! Haha!
Schäme dich, Albe!
Schilt nicht dort unten!
Höre, was wir dich heissen!
Warum, du, Banger,
bandest du nicht
das Mädchen, das du minnst?
Treu sind wir
und ohne Trug
dem Freier, der uns fängt. —
Greife nur zu
und grause dich nicht!
In der Fluth entflieh'n wir nicht leicht.

(Sie schwimmen aus einander, hierher und dorthin, bald tiefer, bald
höher, um *Alberich* zur Jagd auf sie zu reizen.)

Alberich.   Wie in den Gliedern
brünstige Gluth
mir brennt und glüht!
Wuth und Minne
wild und mächig
wühlt mir den Muth auf! —
Wie ihr auch lacht und lugt,
lüstern lechz' ich nach euch,
und eine muss mir erliegen!

Er macht sich mit verzweifelter Anstrengung zur Jagd auf: mit
grauenhafter Behendigkeit erklimmt er Riff für Riff, springt von einem
zum andern, sucht bald dieses bald jenes der Mädchen zu erhaschen,
die mit höhnischem Gelächter stets ihm entweichen; er strauchelt,
stürzt in den Abgrund hinab, klettert dann hastig wieder zur Höhe, —
bis ihm endlich die Geduld entführt: vor Wuth schäumend hält er
athemlos an und streckt die geballte Faust nach den Mädchen hinauf.

Alberich

(kaum seiner mächtig).

Fing' eine diese Faust! . . .

Er verbleibt in sprachloser Wuth, den Blick aufwärts gerichtet, wo
er dann plötzlich von folgendem Schauspiele angezogen und gefesselt
wird.
Durch die Fluth ist von oben her ein immer lichterer Schein ge-
drungen, der sich nun an einer hohen Stelle des mittleren Riffes zu
einem blendend hell strahlenden Goldglanze entzündet; ein zauberisch
goldenes Licht bricht von hier durch das Wasser.

Woglinde. Look, sisters!
  The wakener laughs in the deep.

Wellgunde. Through the dark green surge
  it wooeth the sleeper adored.

Flosshilde. Now kissing its eyelids
    striving to ope them.
    Look, 'tis smiling
    in silvery light!
    Through the flood around
  flows a stream as of stars.

All Three
     (swimming joyously around the rock).

    Heiajaheia!
    Heiajaheia!
  Wallala lalala leia jahei!
    Rhinegold!
    Rhinegold!
    Lustrous delight;
  thou laughest in radiance rare!
    Glistening gleams
  outglow from thee wide o'er the waves.
    Heiajahei!
    Heiajaheia!
    Waken friend,
    waken, fain!
    Winsome the games
    we'll gambol with thee:
    flashes the foam
    flames all the flood;
    we float around dancing,
    diving and singing,
  as sweetly we bathe in thy bed.
    Rhinegold!
    Rhinegold!
    Heiajaheia!
  Walalaleia jahei!

Alberich
    (whose eyes, fascinated by the light, are fixed on the gold).

    What is't, ye gliders,
    that there doth gleam and glow

The Three Nymphs
     (severally).

  Whence do you, rugged one, hail,
  of the Rhinegold ne'er to have heard?
    You wot not, imp,
    of the gold's bright eyes then,
  the which now wake, now sleep?
    Of the wondrous star
    of waters profound
  whose light illumines the wave? —

Woglinde. Lugt, Schwestern!
  Die Weckerin lacht in den Grund.

Wellgunde. Durch den grünen Schwall
  den wonnigen Schläfer sie grüsst.

Flosshilde. Jetzt küsst sie sein Auge
    dass er es öff'ne;
    schaut, es lächelt
    in lichtem Schein;
    durch die Fluthen hin
  fliesst sein strahlender Stern.

Die Drei
    (zusammen das Riff anmuthig umschwimmend).

    Heiajaheia!
    Heiajaheia!
  Wallala lalala leia jahei!
    Rheingold!
    Rheingold!
    Leuchtende Lust,
  wie lach'st du so hell und hehr!
    Glühender Glanz
  entgleisst dir weihlich im Wag!
    Heiajahei
    Heiajaheia!
    Wache, Freund,
    wache froh,
    Wonnige Spiele
    spenden wir dir:
    flimmert der Fluss,
    flammet die Fluth,
    Umfliessen wir tauchend,
    tanzend und singend,
  im seligen Bade dein Bett.
    Rheingold!
    Rheingold!
    Heiajaheia!
  Wallalaleia jahei!

Alberich
  (dessen Auge, mächtig vom Glanze angezogen, starr an dem Golde
      haftet).

    Was ist's, ihr Glatten,
    das dort so gleisst und glänzt?

Die Drei Mädchen
    (abwechselnd).

  Wo bist du Rauher denn heim,
  dass vom Rheingold nie du gehört? —
    Nichts weiss der Alp
    von des Goldes Auge,
  das wechselnd wacht und schläft?
    von der Wassertiefe
    wonnigem Stern,
  der hehr die Wogen durchhellt? —

See how sweetly
we ride in its radiance !
Would you, laggard, then
seek to lave there,
come sport and swim by our side.
(They laugh.)

Alberich.   Is the gold ye dive around
good but for play ?
' twould please me but little.

Woglinde.   The golden prize
precious you'd deem,
wist you but all of its wonder.

Wellgunde.   The world's kingdom
that one can encompass
who from the Rhinegold
shapeth the Ring,
which measureless might can secure.

Flosshilde.   Our father said it,
and bade us firmly
keep the treasure
in careful trust,
that no foeman should forcibly filch it :
so peace, ye prattling crew !

Wellgunde.   O prudent sister,
reproving us both !
Bear you in mind
but unto whom
'tis given to fashion the gold ?

Woglinde.   But he who passion's
pow'r forswears,
and from delights
of love forbears, —
but he the magic commandeth,
the prize to mould to a ring.

Wellgunde.   Full safe from such
must we surely be :
for none may live and love not :
parteth no man from the passion.

Woglinde.   He least of them all ;
the libertine imp,
with lustful rage
mortally racked.

Flosshilde.   I fear not him :
for my part I found
in his bestial warmth
well nigh I burned.

Wellgunde.   A brimstone brand
to the water brought !
in heat of love-rage
hissing loud.

Sieh', wie selig
im Glanze wir gleiten !
Willst du Banger
in ihm dich baden,
so schwimm' und schwelge mit uns !
(Sie lachen.)

Alberich.   Eu'rem Taucherspiele
nur taugte das Gold ?
Mir gält' es dann wenig !

Woglinde.   Des Goldes Schmuck
schmähte er nicht,
wüsst' er all' seine Wunder !

6 *Wellgunde.*   Der Welt Erbe
gewänne zu eigen,
wer aus dem Rheingold
schüfe den Ring,
der masslose Macht ihm verlieh'.

Flosshilde.   Der Vater sagt' es,
und uns befahl er
klug zu hüten
den klaren Hort,
dass kein Falscher der Fluth ihn entführte :
d'rum schweigt, ihr schwatzendes Heer !

Wellgunde.   Du klügste Schwester !
Verklag'st du uns wohl ?
Weisst du denn nicht,
wem allein
das Gold zu schmieden vergönnt ?

7 *Woglinde.*   Nur wer der Minne
Macht versagt,
nur wer der Liebe
Lust verjagt,
nur der erzielt sich den Zauber,
zum Reif zu zwingen das Gold.

Wellgunde.   Wohl sicher sind wir
und sorgenfrei :
denn was nur lebt will lieben ;
meiden will keiner die Minne.

Woglinde.   Am wenigsten er,
der lüsterne Alp :
vor Liebesgier
möcht' er vergeh'n !

Flosshilde.   Nicht fürcht' ich den,
wie ich ihn erfand :
seiner Minne Brunst
brannte fast mich.

Wellgunde.   Ein Schwefelbrand
in der Wogen Schwall :
vor Zorn der Liebe
zischt er laut.

All Three

  (together).

  Walalaleia ! Lahei !
   Loveliest earth-gnome,
   laugh too with us !
   In the golden shimmer
   how lordly you seem !
  Come, lovely one, laugh with us too !

   (They laugh.)

Alberich

(his eyes still rivetted on the gold, has listened closely to the sisters'
talk).

   The world's kingdom
  at once could I compass through this ?
   If love is denied me,
  a newer delight I may know !

   (Terribly loud.)

   Twit as ye will ;
  the Nibelung neareth your toy !

Raging, he springs to the central rock and clambers with terrible
haste to its summit. The nymphs separate screaming, and dart upwards at different sides.

The Three Nymphs.

   Heia ! Heia ! Heiahahei !
   Save us all !
   Insane is the imp !
   How the water spurts
   where he has sprung.
  A madman made by his love.

   (They laugh in wild excitement.)

Alberich

(on the summit of the peak, stretching out his hand toward the gold).

   Fear ye not now ?
   Then fondle in darkness,
   dark that ye are !
  The light's luster I quench ;
  and rend from the rock the gold,
  vengeance to wreak with a Ring :
   for, hear me ye floods —
  Love I forswear forever !

With terrible strength he tears the gold from the rock and, hastily
descending, disappears quickly below. Sudden darkness overspreads
the scene. The nymphs dive down after the robber.

The Three Nymphs

  (screaming).

   Hinder the robber !
   Rescue the gold !
   Help us ! Help us !
   Woe ! Woe !

The flood falls with them into the deep. Far below is heard *Alber-*
ich's mocking laughter.—The rocks disappear in the thickest darkness,
the whole stage is completely filled with black waves of water which
seem for some time continually to sink.

Die Drei

  (zusammen).

  Wallalalleia ! Lahei !
   Lieblicher Albe,
   lach'st du nicht auch !
   In des Goldes Schein
   wie leuchtest du schòn !
  Komm', Lieblicher, lache mit uns !

   (Sie lachen.)

Alberich

(die Augen starr auf das Gold gerichtet, hat dem hastigen Geplauder
der Schwestern wohl gelauscht).

   Der Welt Erbe
  gewänn' ich zu eigen durch dich ?
   Erzwäng' ich nicht Liebe,
  doch listig erzwäng' ich mir Lust ?—

   (Furchtbar laut.)

   Spottet nur zu !
  Der Nibelung naht eu'rem Spiel !

Wüthend springt er nach dem mittleren Riff hinüder und klettert
in grausiger Hast nach dessen Spitze hinauf. Die Mädchen fahren
kreischend auseinander und tauchen nach verschiedenen Seiten hin auf.

Die drei Rheintöchter.

   Heia ! Heia ! Heiahahei !
   Rettet euch !
   es raset der Alp !
   in den Wassern sprüht's
   wohin er springt :
  die Minne macht ihn verrückt !

   (Sie lachen im tollsten Uebermuth.)

Alberich

(auf der Spitze des Riffes, die Hand nach dem Golde ausstreckend).

   Bangt euch noch nicht ?
   So buhlt nun im Finstern,
   feuchtes Gezücht !
  Das Licht lösch' ich euch aus ;
  das Gold entreiss' ich dem Riff,
  schmiede den rächenden Ring :
   denn hör' es die Fluth —
  so verfluch' ich die Liebe !

Er reisst mit furchtbarer Gewalt das Gold aus dem Riffe und stürzt
damit hastig in die Tiefe, wo er schnell verschwindet. Dichte Nacht
bricht plötzlich überall herein. Die Mädchen tauchen nach dem Räuber in die Tiefe nach.

Die drei Rheintöchter

  (schreiend).

   Haltet den Räuber !
   Rettet das Gold !
   Hülfe ! Hülfe !
   Wehe ! Wehe !

Die Fluth fällt mit ihnen nach der Tiefe hinab : aus dem untersten
Grunde hört man *Alberich's* gellendes Hohngelächter. — In dichtester
Finsterniss verschwinden die Riffe ; die ganze Bühne ist von der Höhe
bis zur Tiefe von schwarzem Wassergewoge erfüllt, das eine Zeit lang
immer noch abwärts zu sinken scheint.

SECOND SCENE.

Gradually the waves give place to clouds which clear off in fine mist, showing

An open space on a mountain top

first by the faint light of night.—The dawning day lights up with increasing luster a castle with glittering pinnacles, which stands on a cliff at the back : between this and the foreground is a deep valley through which the Rhine is supposed to flow.—At one side *Wotan* and *Fricka* are lying asleep in a flowery meadow.

Fricka

(wakes, and her eyes fall on the castle ; she starts in surprise).

Wotan ! my lord ! awaken !

Wotan

(still dreaming).

The wondrous heavenly hall
is warded with gate and gulf.
Mortal honor,
infinite might,
fly to the acme of fame !

Fricka

(shaking him).

Wake from thy visions
rosy and vain !
Awake now, spouse, and arouse thee !

Wotan

(wakes and raises himself slightly. His eyes are at once attracted and riveted by the sight of the castle).

'Tis ended — the infinite work !
A heavenly mansion
on mountain heights ;
proudly peer
my prosperous halls
as in visions I viewed,
as I ordered it erst ;
strong and sound
stands it in sight :
grand and glorious pile.

Fricka. So welcome deem'st thou
what I but dread ?
Though fair thy tow'r
I tremble for Freia.
Mindless one, pause and remember
the mentioned price to be paid !
the castle finished,
now falleth the bond.
Forgettest then what thou must give ?

Wotan. I mind well all they demanded,
my men who built me this burg ;
their grim race I
by agreement o'erawed,
whereby this hallowed
home they should build me.

ZWEITE SCENE.

Allmählig gehen die Wogen in Gewölke über, das sich nach und nach abklärt, und als es sich endlich, wie in feinem Nebel, gänzlich verliert, wird eine

freie Gegend auf Bergeshöhen

sichtbar, anfänglich noch in nächtlicher Beleuchtung.—Der hervorbrechende Tag beleuchtet mit wachsendem Glanze eine Burg mit blinkenden Zinnen, die auf einem Felsgipfel im Hintergrunde steht ; zwischen diesem burggekrönten Felsgipfel und dem Vordergrunde der Scene ist ein tiefes Thal, durch welches der Rhein fliesst, anzunehmen, —Zur Seite auf blumigem Grunde liegt *Wotan*, neben ihm *Fricka*, beide schlafend.

Fricka

(erwacht : ihr Blick fällt auf die Burg ; sie staunt und erschrickt).

Wotan ! Gemahl ! erwache !

Wotan

(im Traume leise).

Der Wonne seligen Saal
bewachen mir Thür' und Thor :
Mannes Ehre,
ewige Macht,
ragen zu endlosem Ruhm !

Fricka

(rüttelt ihn).

Auf, aus der Träume
wonnigen Trug !
Erwache, Mann, und erwäge !

Wotan

(erwacht und erhebt sich ein wenig: sein Auge wird sogleich vom Anblick der Burg gefesselt).

Vollendet das ewige Werk :
auf Berges Gipfel
die Götter-Burg,
prunkvoll prahlt
der prangende Bau !
Wie im Traum ich ihn trug,
wie mein Wille ihn wies,
stark und schön
steht er zur Schau ;
hehrer, herrlicher Bau !

Fricka. Nur Wonne schafft dir
was mich erschreckt ?
Dich freut die Burg,
mir bangt es um Freia.
Achtloser, lass dich erinnern
des ausbedungenen Lohn's !
Die Burg ist fertig,
verfallen das Pfand :
vergiss'st du, was du vergab'st ?

Wotan. Wohl dünkt mich's, was sie bedangen,
die dort die Burg mir gebaut ;
durch Vertrag zähmt'ich
ihr trotzig Gezücht,
dass sie die hehre
Halle mir schlüfen ;

It prospers---thanks to their prowess !
For the price pray have no heed.

Fricka. Alas ! thy fatuous lightness !
lacking love is thy folly.
Had I but known of this bond
the baseness might have been helped :
    but pleased were ye wise ones
    to part from the women ;
no jot confiding in us,
alone ye conferred with the giants.
    So, without shame,
    ye shrink not to forfeit
Freia, my glorious sister,
for this scandalous cause.
    Nought may your hard hearts
    of holiness know,
when you pant but for power.

Wotan. Like longings
    did Fricka not feel,
when she herself bade me to build ?

Fricka. Of my husband's truth ill assured,
in trouble I considered
how to hold him beside me
when he was seeking to stray :
    halls bright and gleaming,
    glorious homestead,
such might surely allure thee
to linger and seek in them rest.
But thou in this fortress thought'st
of fence and force alone :
    power and might
    'twas to augment thee :
this ravishing castle but rises
to cause yet more riotous strife.

Wotan
       (smiling).
    If with these walls
    thou, O wife, shouldst enwind me,
yet grant but this to my godhood ;
    while in the castle's
    confines I yet
may outside it win me the world.
    Wand'ring at will
all love who live :
my sport I cannot dispense with.

Fricka. Light, unloving,
    low-natured man !
    For such mere conceits
    as might and control
wouldst trample in lawless contempt
love and a woman's worth ?

die steht nun — Dank den Starken :—
um den Sold sorge dich nicht.

Fricka. O lachend frevelnder Leichtsinn !
Liebelosester Frohmuth !
Wusst' ich um eu'ren Vertrag,
dem Truge hätt' ich gewehrt ;
    doch muthig entfernet
    ihr Männer die Frauen,
um taub und ruhig vor uns
allein mit den Riesen zu tagen.
    So ohne Scham
    verschenktet ihr Frechen
Freia, mein holdes Geschwister,
froh des Schächergewerb's. —
    Was ist euch Harten
    doch heilig und werth,
giert ihr Männer nach Macht !

Wotan. Gleiche Gier
    war Fricka wohl fremd,
als selbst um den Bau sie bat ?

Fricka. Um des Gatten Treue besorgt
muss traurig ich wohl sinnen,
wie an mich er zu fesseln,
zieht's in die Ferne ihn fort :
    herrliche Wohnung,
    wonniger Hausrath,
sollten mit sanftem Band
dich binden zu säumender Rast.
Doch du bei dem Wohnbau sannst
auf Wehr und Wall allein :
    Herrschaft und Macht
    soll er dir mehren ;
nur rastlosern Sturm zu erregen
erstand die ragende Burg.

Wotan
      (lächelnd).
    Wolltest du Frau
    in der feste mich fangen,
mir Gotte musst du schon gönnen,
    dass, in der Burg
    gebunden, ich mir
von aussen gewinne die Welt.
    Wandel und Wechsel
liebt wer lebt :
das Spiel drum kann ich nicht sparen.

Fricka. Liebeloser,
    leidigster Mann !
    Um der Macht und Herrschaft
    müssigen Tand
verspielst du in lästerndem Spott
Liebe und Weibes Werth ?

Wotan
                      (earnestly).
When I for wife sought to win thee,
    my other eyeball
in a wager I risked;
thou blamest blindly, methinks!
    Women I lean to
    E'en more than thou lik'st.
    I'll let not our fairest
    Freia be ta'en:
my thoughts ne'er turned to such thing.

Fricka.   Then save her at once:—
            in sorest alarm
hither she hastens for help.

Freia
                    (entering hastily).
    Help me, Fricka!
    fail me not, father!
    From mountain fastness
    Fasolt gives menace:
he comes too surely to catch me.

Wotan.   Let him rage!—
           Saw'st thou not Loki?

Fricka.   That belief thou shouldst still
            to that liar accord!
Much wrong already he's wrought,
yet sets new snares for thee ever.

Wotan.   Where simple might serves
           let none seek to assist me;
           but to shape the fraud
           of foes to serve me,
           I can learn by such arts
           as only Loki employs.
           He this agreement advised,
           and vowed to extricate Freia:
           on him I firmly rely.

Fricka.   And he fails in his faith.—
            The giants hast'ning
            hither behold:
where lurks thy juggling ally?

Freia.   Why hasten not my brothers
           with help they should bring me,
now my father refuses defence?
           O help me, Donner!
           hither! hither!
rescue Freia, my Froh!

Fricka.
Those who basely bargained to wrong thee
have all abandoned thee now.

Wotan
                      (ernst).
Um dich zum Weib zu gewinnen,
    mein eines Auge
setzt' ich werbend daran:
wie thörig tadelst du jetzt!
    Ehr' ich die Frauen
    doch mehr als dich freut!
    Und Freia, die gute,
    geb' ich nicht auf:
nie sann dies ernstlich mein Sinn.

Fricka.   So schirme sie jetzt:
            in schutzloser Angst
11   läuft sie nach Hülf' dort her!
—
12 *Freia*
                    (hastig auftretend).
    Hilf mir, Schwester!
    Schütze mich, Schwäher!
    Vom Felsen drüben
    drohte mir Fasolt,
    mich Holde käm' er zu holen.

Wotan.   Lass' ihn droh'n!—
           Sah'st du nicht Loge?

Fricka.   Dass am liebsten du immer
            dem Listigen trau'st!
Manch Schlimmes schuf er uns schon,
doch stets bestrickt er dich wieder.

Wotan.   Wo freier Muth frommt
           allein, frag' ich nach keinem;
           doch des Feindes Neid
           zum Nutz' sich fügen,
           lehrt nur Schlauheit und List,
           wie Loge verschlagen sie übt.
           Der zum Vertrage mir rieth,
           versprach Freia zu lösen:
           auf ihn verlass' ich mich nun.

Fricka.   Und er lässt dich allein.—
            Dort schreiten rasch
            die Riesen heran:
wo harrt dein schlauer Gehülf?

11 *Freia.*   Wo harren meine Brüder,
—   dass Hülfe sie brächten,
12   da mein Schwäher die Schwache verschenkt?
           Zu Hülfe, Donner!
           Hieher! hieher!
Rette Freia, mein Froh!

Fricka.
Die in bösem Bund dich verriethen,
sie alle bergen sich nun.

Fasolt and Fafner
(men of gigantic stature, armed with strong staves, enter).

Fasolt. Soft sleep
      sealed thine eyes:
      while we in wakeful
labor wove thy walls.
      Tedious toil
      tired us not;
      heap'd we huge
      and heavy stones.
      High with dome,
      donjon, door,
      we have formed
a fortress fair and fast.
      There bideth
      our building,
      bright'ning in
      the beams of day.
      Pass within,
but pay our wage.

Wotan. Name, workmen, your wage.
      What forfeit have ye fixed on?

Fasolt. 'Twas fixed beforehand,
      what we deemed fit:
thy mem'ry is remiss!
      Freia the holy —
      Holda the free one —
      agreed it is,
she goes with us home.

Wotan. Are ye engrossed
      on what was agreed?
other guerdon ask:
Freia I must refuse.

Fasolt
(remaining awhile speechless with wrathful surprise).
      What say'st thou — Ha!
      seek'st to betray —
      betray a contract?
      On thy spear writ,
      serve but for sport
those compelling runes of power?

Fafner
                (ironically).
      My faithful brother!
Deem'st thou, fool, he is false?

Fasolt. Son of light,
      swayed so lightly,
hear and heed thyself!
Thy treaties hold in truth!
      What thou art,
art thou only by treaties;

---

13 *Fasolt* und *Fafner*
— (beide in riesiger Gestalt, mit starken Pfählen bewaffnet, treten auf).

Fasolt. Sanft schloss
      Schlaf dein Aug':
      wir beide bauten
Schlummers bar die Burg.
      Mächt'ger Müh'
      müde nie,
      stau'ten starke
      Stein' wir auf;
      steiler Thurm,
      Thür' und Thor,
      deckt und schliesst
8   im schlanken Schloss den Saal.
      Dort steht's,
      was wir stemmten;
      schimmernd hell
      bescheint's der Tag:
      zieh' nun ein,
uns zahl' den Lohn!

Wotan. Nennt, Leute, den Lohn:
      was dünkt euch zu bedingen?

9 *Fasolt.* Bedungen ist's,
      was tauglich uns dünkt:
      gemahnt es dich so matt?
      Freia, die holde,
11   Holda, die freie —
      vertragen ist's —
sie tragen wir heim.

Wotan. Seid ihr bei Trost
      mit eurem Vertrag?
Denkt auf andern Dank:
Freia ist mir nicht feil.

Fasolt
(vor wüthendem Erstaunen einen Augenblick sprachlos).
      was sagst du, ha!
      Sinnst du Verrath?
      Verrath am Vertrag?
      Die dein Speer birgt,
      sind sie dir Spiel,
des berath'nen Bundes Runen?

Fafner
                (höhnisch).
      Getreu'ster Bruder!
Merkst du Tropf nun Betrug?

Fasolt. Lichtsohn du,
      leicht gefügter,
hör' und hüte dich:
Verträgen halte Treu'!
      Was du bist,
bist du nur durch Verträge:

Conformable,
well defined was thy might.
      More wise art thou
      than we are wary,
      binding us free ones
      in friendly peace :
cursed be thy wisdom futile,
far shall wane peace before thee,
      when no more open,
      honest and free,
thou breakest thy warrant and bond !—
      A simple giant
      judges so :
Be warned, thou wise one, by him !

Wotan.   How sly to take for truth
what only in sport we had settled !
      The beauteous goddess,
      light and bright,
what use to you are her charms ?

Fasolt.   Flout'st thou us ?
      Fie ! how evil !—
You who in radiance sway,
regal, sorrowless race,
      like fools ye strive
      for a fortress of stone ;
setting 'gainst it, sooth,
a wondrous woman in pledge.
We, blockheads, bother us,
toiling with toughness of hand
      to win us a woman,
      who, winning and sweet,
should go gladly with us. —
From the bond now wilt thou back ?

Fafner.   Check thy foolish chatter ;
no luck look we to gain.
      Freia's self
      serves little ;
      but 'twere good
to get her away from the Æsir :
      golden apples
grow in her orchard garden ;
      none else can
grasp the art of their culture :
      this grateful fruit
      grants to her kindred
      eternal youth
      time cannot ravage ;
      weak and blighted
      waneth their beauty, —
      old and worn
      will they pass hence,
fareth e'er from them Freia :
let her forthwith be torn from them all.

bedungen ist,
wohl bedacht deine **Macht.**
      Bist weiser du
      als witzig wir sind,
      bandest uns Freie
      zum Frieden du :
all deinem Wissen fluch' ich,
fliehe weit deinen Frieden,
      weisst du nicht offen,
      ehrlich und frei,
Verträgen zu wahren die Treu' !—
      Ein dummer Riese
      räth' dir das :
du Weiser, wiss' es von ihm !

Wotan.   Wie schlau für Ernst du achtest,
was wir zum Scherz nur beschlossen !
      Die liebliche Göttin,
      licht und leicht,
was taugt euch Tölpeln ihr Reiz ?

Fasolt.   Höhn'st du uns ?
      Ha ! wie unrecht !—
Die ihr durch Schönheit herrscht,
schimmernd hehres Geschlecht,
      wie thörig strebt ihr
      nach Thürmen von Stein
setzt um Burg und Saal
Weibes Wonne zum Pfand !
Wir Plumpen plagen uns
schwitzend mit schwieliger **Hand,**
      ein Weib zu gewinnen,
      das wonnig und mild
bei uns Armen wohne :—
und verkehrt nennt ihr den Kauf ?

Fafner.   Schweig' dein faules Schwatzen,
Gewinn werben wir nicht :
      Freia's Haft
      hilft wenig ;
      doch viel gilt's
den Göttern sie zu entführen.
      Gold'ne Aepfel
wachsen in ihrem Garten ;
      sie allein
weiss die Aepfel zu pflegen :
      der Frucht Genuss
      frommt ihren Sippen
      zu ewig nie
      alternder Jugend ;
      siech und bleich
      doch sinkt ihre Blüthe,
      alt und schwach
      schwinden sie hin,
müssen Freia sie missen :
ihrer Mitte drum sei sie entführt !

14

14
13

Wotan
    (aside).
 Loki stays too long!

Fasolt. Straight tell thy resolve.

Wotan. Fix on other spoil.

Fasolt. No other: Freia alone!

Fafner. Thou there! follow us!
    (They press towards *Freia*.)

Freia
    (seeking to fly).
 Help! Help from these harsh ones!

Donner and *Froh*
    (enter hastily).

Froh
    (clasping *Freia* in his arms).
 To me, Freia! —
 Miscreant, fall back!
 Froh guards the goddess!

Donner
    (planting himself before the two giants).
 Fasolt and Fafner —
 felt ye the blow
 of my hammer's head before?

Fafner. What means thy threat?

Fasolt. Why thrust in here?
 we want not to fight —
 expect nought else but our pay.

Donner
    (swinging his hammer).
 I've paid many
 giants their meed;
 rascals e'er
 I'm ready to pay.
 Come here! I'll deal your due,
 helped with a generous hand.

Wotan
    (stretching out his spear between the disputants).
 Hold! thou fierce one!
 Nought booteth force.
 This bond the shaft
 of my spear doth shield:
 spare then thy hammer's helve.

Freia. Woe's me! Woe's me!
 Wotan forsakes me!

Fricka. Thou meanest it then,
 merciless man?

9

Wotan
    (für sich).
 Loge säumt zu lang!

Fasolt. Schlicht gieb nun Bescheid!

Wotan. Sinnt auf andern Sold!

Fasolt. Kein andrer: Freia allein!

Fafner. Du da, folg' uns fort!
    (Sie dringen auf *Freia* zu.)

Freia
    (fliehend).
 Helft! helft vor den Harten!

Donner und *Froh*
    (kommen eilig).

Froh
    (*Freia* in seine Arme fassend).
 Zu mir, Freia! —
 Meide sie, Frecher!
 Froh schützt die Schöne.

Donner
    (sich vor die beiden Riesen stellend).
 Fasolt und Fafner,
 fühltet ihr schon
 meines Hammers harten Schlag?

Fafner. Was soll das Droh'n?

Fasolt. Was dringst du her?
 Kampf kies'ten wir nicht,
 verlangen nur unsern Lohn.

Donner
    (den Hammer schwingend).
 Schon oft zahlt' ich
 Riesen den Zoll;
 schuldig blieb' ich
 Schächern nie:
 kommt her! des Lohnes Last
 wäg' ich mit gutem Gewicht!

Wotan
    (seinen Speer zwischen den Streitenden ausstreckend).
 Halt, du Wilder!
 Nichts durch Gewalt!
 Verträge schützt
 meines Speeres Schaft:
 spar' deines Hammers Heft!

Freia. Wehe! Wehe!
 Wotan verlässt mich!

Fricka. Begreif' ich dich noch,
 grausamer Mann?

Wotan

(turns away and perceives *Loge* coming).

Here is Loge!
Hastest thou so
when thou shouldst straighten
the sorry bargain thou struckest?

Loge

(who has climbed up from the valley at back).

Why! what bargain
bad have I struck you?
Was't what you conjointly
with the giants did work?
To depths and to heights
I drive at my heed.
House and hearth
can hold me not;
Donner and Froh
they dote on a dwelling fair:
fain would they woo;
a house then must they find:
a bright abode,
a bulwark brave,
thereto bends Wotan's wish;
roof and room,—
house and hall,—
the heavenly pile,—
behold it in its pride.
The towering walls
I tried myself,
examined all
if it were firm.
Fasolt and Fafner
failed not in faith:
each stone fits where it stands.
Not idle was I
like all the rest:
who styles me sluggard, he lies.

Wotan. Artfully
slippest thou out:
look to thee, traitor,
if thou betrayest me now!
Of all th' immortals
thine only friend,
I took thee up
to our over-credulous crew:—
now speak, and spae us well.
When they who built us the burg
For meed Freia demanded,
thou'rt 'ware that solely
would I consent
when word thou plightedst at last
to deliver the glorious pledge.

Loge. With greatest pains
th' affair to ponder

Wotan

(wendet sich ab und sieht *Loge* kommen).

Endlich Loge!
Eiltest du so,
den du geschlossen,
den schlimmen Handel zu schlichten?

Loge

(ist im Hintergrunde aus dem Thale aufgetreten).

Wie? welchen Handel
hätt' ich geschlossen?
Wohl was mit den Riesen
dort im Rathe du dangst?—
In Tiefen und Höh'n
treibt mich mein Hang;
Haus und Herd
behagt mir nicht:
Donner und Froh,
die denken an Dach und Fach;
wollen sei frei'n,
ein Haus muss sie erfreu'n:
ein stolzer Saal,
ein starkes Schloss,
danach stand Wotan's Wunsch.—
Haus und Hof,
Saal und Schloss,
die selige Burg,
sie steht nun stark gebaut;
das Prachtgemäuer
prüfte ich selbst;
ob alles fest,
forscht' ich genau:
Fasolt und Fafner
fand ich bewährt;
kein Stein wankt im Gestemm'.
Nicht müssig war ich,
wie mancher hier:
der lügt, wer lässig mich schilt!

Wotan. Arglistig
weichst du mir aus:
mich zu betrügen
hüte in Treuen dich wohl!
Von allen Göttern
dein einz'ger Freund,
nahm ich dich auf
in der übel trauenden Tross.—
Nun red' und rathe klug!
Da einst die Bauer der Burg
zum Dank Freia bedangen,
du weisst, nicht anders
willigt' ich ein,
als weil auf Pflicht du gelobtest
zu lösen das hehre Pfand.

Loge. Mit höchster Sorge
drauf zu sinnen.

how we might save her
that — did I swear.
But to discover
what ne'er occurred —
what ne'er took place —
how possibly could I promise?

Fricka
(to *Wotan*).
See what traitorous
scamp thou didst trust!

Froh.   Loge art thou,
but better called " liar."*

Donner.   Accursed glist'ner,
thy gleam I'll quench.

Loge.   But to screen your blunder
ye scold me, blockheads.
(*Donner* and *Froh* are about to set on him.)

Wotan
(restraining them).
I pray you leave him in peace!
Ye know not Loge's knacks.
Value high
his advice e'er has,
when we wait for it long.

Fafner.   No more waiting:
quick! — the wage!

Fasolt.   Pay fails to appear.

Wotan
(to *Loge*).
Now hark, strategist!
hold thee still.
Why strayedst thou here and there?

Loge.   Evil is ever
Loge's lot.
Alone for thy sake
I sallied out,
and stormily strode
to the ends of the earth
to seek for Freia a substitute,
which for the giants were just.
Success slipped me:
I see now full well
in the world around
nought is so rare
to replace in mind of a man
a woman's wonderful worth.
(All exhibit surprise and emotion.)

*The pun in the original, between " Loge " and " Lüge," cannot
be preserved in translation.

wie es zu lösen,
das — hab' ich gelobt:
doch dass ich fände,
was nie sich fügt,
was nie gelingt,
wie liess sich das wohl geloben?

Fricka
(zu *Wotan*).
Sieh, welch' trugvollem
Schelm du getraut!

Froh.   Loge heisst du,
doch nenn' ich dich Lüge!

Donner.   Verfluchte Lohe,
dich lösch' ich aus!

Loge.   Ihre Schmach zu decken
schmähen mich Dumme.
(*Donner* und *Froh* wollem ihm zu Leibe.)

Wotan
(wehrt ihnen).
In Frieden lasst mir den Freund!
Nicht kennt ihr Loge's Kunst:
reicher wiegt
seines Rathes Werth,
zahlt er zögernd ihn aus.

13 *Fafner.*   Nichts gezögert:
rasch gezahlt!

Fasolt.   Lang währt's mit dem Lohn.

Wotan
(zu *Loge*).
Jetzt hör', Störrischer!
halte mir Stich!
Wo schweiftest du hin und her?

Loge.   Immer ist Undank
Loge's Lohn!
Um dich nur besorgt
sah ich mich um,
durchstöbert' im Sturm
alle Winkel der Welt,
Ersatz für Freia zu suchen,
wie er den Riesen wohl recht:
Umsonst sucht' ich
und sehe nun wohl,
in der Welten Ring
nichts ist so reich,
als Ersatz zu muthen dem Mann
für Weibes Wonne und Werth.
(Alle gerathen in Erstaunen und Betroffenheit.)

Where life ebbeth and floweth
in flood, and earth, and air,
        all asked I,
        ever inquiring
        where sinew doth reign,
        and seedlings are rooted,
        what well a man
        could mightier deem
than woman's wonderful worth.
But where life ebbeth and floweth,
        I only found myself
        laughed at by all.
In flood and earth and air
        everything hath
        for aim but love.
        Yet one I met with
had made against love his oath;
        for ruddy gold
bereft him of woman's grace.
The Rhine's indignant daughters
dismal tidings announced:
        The Nibelung,
        Night-Alberich,
        failed from the girls
        amorous favors to gain;
        the Rhinegold he
robbed in his raging revenge:
        and values now
        its worth over all, —
greater than woman's grace.
        For their glittering toy,
        thus torn from the deep,
the maidens with tears are mourning.
        To thee, Wotan,
        wailing they turn,
that thy wrath may fall on the robber:
        the gold to the waves
        be once more given,
their own to continue for ever. —
        This to mention
        I swore to the maidens:
now staunch I stand to my word.

Wotan.   Senseless art thou
        if not designing!
        Myself suffering ruth
        for others what help have I?

Fasolt
        (who has been listening attentively -- to *Fafner*).
        This gold I begrudge the Niblung.
        Much wrong he's hatched us already:
        but slily slipped the dwarf
        unhindered out of our hold.

Fafner.   Now the gnome
        will shape new annoyance,

So weit Leben und Weben,
in Wasser, Erd' und Luft,
        viel frug ich,
        forschte bei allen,
        wo Kraft nur sich rührt
        und Keime sich regen:
        was wohl dem Manne
        mächtiger dünk',
als Weibes Wonne und Werth?
Doch so weit Leben und Weben,
        verlacht nur ward
        meine fragende List:
in Wasser, Erd' und Luft
        lassen will nichts
        von Lieb' und Weib. —
        Nur einen sah ich,
der sagte der Liebe ab:
        um rothes Gold
entrieth er des Weibes Gunst.
Des Rheines klare Kinder
klagten mir ihre Noth:
        der Nibelung,
        Nacht-Alberich,
        buhlte vergebens
        um der Badenden Gunst;
        das Rheingold da
raubte sich rächend der Dieb:
        das dünkt ihm nun
        das theuerste Gut,
hehrer als Weibes Huld.
        Um den gleissenden Tand,
        der Tiefe entwandt,
erklang mir der Töchter Klage:
        an dich, Wotan,
        wenden sie sich,
dass zu Recht du zögest den Räuber,
        das Gold dem Wasser
        wieder gebest,
und ewig es bliebe ihr Eigen. —
        Dir's zu melden
        gelobt' ich den Mädchen:
nun lös'te Loge sein Wort.

Wotan.   Thörig bist du,
        wenn nicht gar tückisch!
        Mich selbst siehst du in Noth;
        wie hülf' ich andren zum Heil?

Fasolt
        (der aufmerksam zugehört, zu *Fafner*).
        Nicht gönn' ich das Gold dem Alben,
        viel Noth schuf uns der Niblung,
        doch schlau entschlüpfte immer
        unsrem Zwange der Zwerg.

Fafner.   Neue Neidthat
        sinnt uns der Niblung,

11

4
7
5

2

4
6

mighty made by gold.
    Thou there, Loge;
    say without lies
what greatness giveth this gold,
that the dwarf doth hold it dear?

Loge. A toy 'twas
    ere from waters taken,
serving gay maidens for sport:
    but when to a Ring
    'tis rounded and fashioned
marvellous might it grants,
and wins its grasper the world.

Wotan. Many rumors tell
    of the Rhinegold:
    runes of riches
run in its ruddy light;
    might and wealth
'twould win were it made a ring.

Fricka. Boots as well
    the golden bauble's
    glittering dross
for women to deck and adorn?

Loge. A wife could fix
    the faith of her spouse,
    found she the rare
    and radiant mass
whose metal pigmies moulded,
ruled by the pow'r of the ring.

Fricka. O might but my husband
    gain me the hoard!

Wotan. To win me that circlet
seemeth wise to my thinking. —
    But how, Loge,
    light on the means?
how make the dwarf's treasure mine?

Loge. A rune of magic
makes the gold a ring;
    none may know it;
but he its hold hath learned,
who sweets of love forswears.
      (*Wotan* turns away discouraged.)
    That likes you not;
    too late you are too:
Alberich paused not in doubt!
    promptly he conquered
    the potent spell,
and rightly fashioned the ring.

Donner. Placed were all of us
    in his power,
were not the ring from him ravished.

giebt das Gold ihm Macht. —
    Du da, Loge!
    Sag' ohne Lüg:
was Grosses gilt denn das Gold,
dass es dem Niblung genügt?

5 *Loge.* Ein Tand ist's
    In des Wassers Tiefe,
lachenden Kindern zur Lust:
6   doch, ward es zum runden
    Reife geschmiedet,
hilft es zu höchster Macht,
Gewinnt dem Manne die Welt.

Wotan. Von des Rheines Gold
    hört' ich raunen:
    Beute-Runen
berge sein rother Glanz,
    Macht und Schätze
schüf' ohne Mass ein Reif.

Fricka. Taugte wohl auch
    des gold'nen Tandes
    gleissend Geschmeid
Frauen zu schönem Schmuck?

Loge. Des Gatten Treu'
    ertrotzte die Frau,
    trüge sie hold
    den hellen Schmuck?
den schimmernd Zwerge schmieden;
rührig im Zwange des Reif's.

11 *Fricka.* Gewänne mein Gatte
    wohl sich das Gold!

Wotan. Des Reifes zu walten,
    räthlich will es mich dünken. —
    Doch wie, Loge,
    lernt' ich die Kunst?
wie schüf' ich mir das Geschmeid?

6 *Loge.* Ein Runenzauber
    zwingt das Gold zum Reif:
    keiner kennt ihn;
doch einer übt ihn leicht,
der sel'ger Lieb' entsagt.
      (*Wotan* wendet sich unmuthig ab.)
    Das spar'st du wohl;
    zu spät auch käm'st du:
Alberich zögerte nicht;
    zaglos gewann er
    des Zaubers Macht:
7 gerathen ist ihm der Ring.

Donner. Zwang uns allen
    schüfe der Zwerg,
würd' ihm der Reif nicht entrissen.

Wotan. That ring I must seize on.

Froh. Lightly now,
  without love forswearing, 'twere gained.

Loge. Quite lightly;
  scant knowledge you need require.

Wotan. Bethink us, how?

Loge.   By theft!
  What a thief stole,
  that steal from the thief.
  were anything done with more ease?
  But with artful foils
  fighteth Alberich;
  shrewd and wileful
  be your workings
  that the robber be o'er-reached:
  to the river-sisters
  their ruddy toy,
  the gold, once more be given;
  for therefore cry they to thee.

Wotan. The river-sisters!
  What serves me thy rede?

Fricka. Of that watery race
  mention I wish not,
  for many men
  — more's my pain —
  have perished, allured by their love.

Wotan stands silently struggling with himself, while the other
gods all look expectantly on him. Meanwhile *Fafner* has consulted
aside with *Fasolt.*

Fafner. Trust me, more than Freia
  fits us treasure so true,
  nor need we yearn long for youth
  with the gold's all-mastering might.

          (They again advance.)
    Hear, Wotan,
    our hasty last words!
  Free from our hands be Freia:
    let a less
    forfeit release thee;
  th'ungentle giants will need
  but Nibelheim's gems and gold.

Wotan. Where are your wits?
  How can I award ye
  what is not mine yet, ye miscreants?

Fafner. Work 'twas
  to raise yonder tow'rs;
  thou canst, though, do
  with thoughtfuller craft
  what ne'er our needs could bring through:
  the Nibelung fetter fast.

Wotan. Den Ring muss ich haben!

Froh. Leicht erringt
  ohne Liebesfluch er sich jetzt.

Loge. Spott-leicht,
  ohne Kunst wie im Kinder-Spiel!

Wotan. So rathe, wie?

Loge. Durch raub!
  Was ein Dieb stahl,
  das stiehlst du dem Dieb:
  ward leichter ein Eigen erlangt? —
  Doch mit arger Wehr
  wahrt sich Alberich;
  klug und fein
  musst du verfahren,
  ziehst du den Räuber zu Recht,
  um des Rheines Töchtern
  den rothen Tand,
  das Gold, wieder zu geben:
  denn darum bitten sie dich.

Wotan. Des Rheines Töchter?
  Was taugt mir der Rath?

Fricka. Von dem Wassergezücht
  mag ich nichts wissen:
  schon manchen Mann
  — mir zum Leid —
  verlockten sie buhlend im Bad.

Wotan steht stumm mit sich kämpfend; die übrigen Götter heften
in schweigender Spannung die Blicke auf ihn. — Währenddem hat
Fafner bei Seite mit *Fasolt* berathen.

Fafner. Glaub' mir, mehr als Freia
  frommt das gleissende Gold:
  auch ew'ge Jugend erjagt,
  wer durch Goldes Zauber sie zwingt.

          (Sie treten wieder heran.)
    Hör', Wotan,
    der Harrenden Wort:
  Freia bleib' euch in Frieden;
    leichter'n Lohn
    fand ich zur Lösung:
  uns rauhen Riesen genügt
  des Niblungen rothes Gold.

Wotan. Seid ihr bei Sinn?
  was nicht ich besitze,
  soll ich euch Schamlosen schenken?

Fafner. Schwer baute
  dort sich die Burg:
  leicht wird's dir
  mit list'ger Gewalt
  (was im Neidspiel nie uns gelang)
  den Niblungen fest zu fah'n.

Wotan. For *you* shall I
show myself yielding?
For *you* fetter a foe?
Shame-devoid
and shockingly covetous
such conduct I call!

Fasolt
(suddenly seizing *Freia* and drawing her with *Fafner* aside).
Come here, maid!
With us remain.
In pledge placed art thou now
till our forfeit be paid.
(*Freia* cries aloud : all the gods are in the greatest perturbation.)

Fafner. Far from hence
shall she be forced :
till night-fall — note me well —
placed is she as a pledge :
then once more come we,
and when we call
should we not find as the forfeit
the Rhinegold fair and red —

Fasolt. At end is the friendship,
Freia is forfeit ;
for ever fallen to us.

Freia. Sisters! Brothers!
save me! Help!
(She is borne off by the hastily retreating giants ; the troubled gods
hear her cries of distress dying away in the distance.)

Froh. Up! on their track!

Donner. Perish now all things!
(They look enquiringly towards *Wotan.*)

Loge
(looking after the giants).
Over stock and stone they tramp
straight down the vale ;
through the Rhine's befriending ford
flounder the ruffians :
'frightedly
now Freia
must ride the back of the rascals.—
Heia! hei!
How stumble the stupids along!
Past the steep stride they amain ;
but in Riesenheim's bounds
they first will take rest.
(He turns to the gods.)
What dreameth Wotan so wild?
What dread hath gotten the gods?

A pale mist, increasing in density, fills the stage ; in it the gods
seem to take an aged and haggard appearance : all stand in alarm
looking towards *Wotan*, who thoughtfully casts his eyes on the
ground.

Wotan. Für euch müht' ich
mich um den Alben?
für euch fing' ich den Feind?
Unverschämt
und überbegehrlich
macht euch Dumme mein Dank!

Fasolt
(ergreift plötzlich *Freia* und führt sie mit *Fafner* zur Seite).
Hieher, Maid!
in uns're Macht!
Als Pfand folgst du jetzt,
bis wir Lösung empfahn.
(*Freia* schreit laut auf : alle *Götter* sind in höchster Bestürzung.)

Fafner. Fort von hier
sei sie entführt!
Bis Abend, achtet's wohl,
pflegen wir sie als Pfand :
wir kehren wieder ;
doch kommen wir,
und bereit liegt nicht als Lösung
das Rheingold roth und licht —

Fasolt. Zu End' ist die Frist dann,
Freia verfallen :
für immer folge sie uns!

Freia. Schwester! Brüder!
Rettet! helft!
(Sie wird von den hastig enteilenden Riesen fortgetragen : in der Ferne
hören die bestürzten Götten ihren Wehruf verhallen.)

Froh. Auf, ihnen nach!

Donner. Breche denn alles!
(Sie blicken *Wotan* fragend an.)

Loge
(den Riesen nachsehend).
Ueber Stock und Stein zu Thal
stapfen sie hin ;
durch des Rheines Wasserfurth
waten die Riesen :
fröhlich nicht
hängt Freia
den Rauhen über den Rücken!—
Heia! hei!
Wie taumeln die Tölpel dahin!
Durch das Thal talpen sie schon :
wohl an Riesenheim's Mark
erst halten sie Rast!
(Er wendet sich zu den Göttern.)
Was sinnt nun Wotan so wild? —
Den seligen Göttern wie geht's?

Ein fahler Nebel erfüllt mit wachsender Dichtheit die Bühne, in
ihm erhalten die Götter ein zunehmend bleiches und ältliches Aus-
sehen : alle stehen bang und erwartungsvoll auf *Wotan* blicken, der
sinnend die Augen an den Boden heftet,

Loge. Dupes me a vapor?
Veils me a dream?
How fast your features'
fairness hath fled!
From your cheeks the bloom is chased;
the spark of your eyes hath expired!—
Flag not, Froh;
day hath not fled!
Doth thy hand, Donner,
relax from the hammer?
What aileth Fricka?
Finds she displeasing
her spouse's grayness and gloom,
which o'er him gather like age?

Fricka. Woe's me! Woe's me!
What is it all?

Donner. My hand doth sink!

Froh. My heart doth stop!

Loge. I've found it—hear what's befall'n!
Of Freia's fruit
no atom to-day did ye eat.
The golden apples
from out her garden
preserved you from dwindling with age,
eating them every day.
The garden's keeper
now bideth a captive;
'mong the foliage rests
and rots the fruit:
full soon spoiled it will fall.
My case is milder;
for me, unkindly,
Freia has e'er
kept from the coveted fruit;
in me but half
the pow'r ye immortal ones have.
But all leaned ye on the
apples' youth-giving aid:
this wotted the giants well;
against your lives
a league is begun,
and how find ye defense?
If without apples,
old and grim—
gray and gruesome,
waning to sport of the world,
the stock of gods would cease

Fricka. Wotan! My lord!
Hapless and lost!
Look how thy heedless
hastiness now
our shunless shame hath shaped!

Loge. Trügt mich ein Nebel?
neckt mich ein Traum?
Wie bang und bleich
verblüht ihr so bald!
Euch erlischt der Wangen Licht,
der Blick eures Auges verblitzt!—
Frisch, mein Froh,
noch ist's ja früh!—
Deiner Hand, Donner,
entfüllt ja der Hammer!—
Was ist's mit Fricka?
freut sie sich wenig
ob Wotan's grämlichem Grau,
das schier zum Greisen ihn schafft?

Fricka. Wehe! Wehe!
Was ist geschehen?

Donner. Mir sinkt die Hand.

Froh. Mir stockt das Herz.

Loge. Jetzt fand ich's: hört was euch fehlt!
Von Freia's Frucht
genosset ihr heute noch nicht:
die gold'nen Aepfel
in ihrem Garten,
sie machten euch tüchtig und jung
ass't ihr sie jeden Tag.
Des Gartens Pflegerin
ist nun verpfändet;
an den Aesten darbt
und dorrt das Obst:
bald fällt faul es herab.—
Mich kümmert's minder;
an mir kargte
Freia von je
knausernd die köstliche Frucht:
denn halb so ächt nur
bin ich wie, Herrliche, ihr!
Doch ihr setztet alles
auf das jüngende Obst:
das wussten die Riesen wohl;
auf euer Leben
legten sie's an:
nun sorgt, wie ihr das wahrt!
Ohne die Aepfel
alt und grau,
greis und grämlich,
welkend zum Spott aller Welt,
erstirbt der Götter Stamm.

Fricka. Wotan, Gemahl,
unsel'ger Mann!
Sieh wie dein Leichtsinn
lachend uns allen
Schimpf und Schmach erschuf!

14

14

Wotan	*Wotan*
(starting up with sudden resolution).	(mit plötzlichem Entschluss auffahrend).
Up ! Loge,	Auf, Loge !
and off with me !	hinab mit mir ,
Beneath, to the home of the Nibelungs.	Nach Nibelheim fahren wir nieder :
I'll surely seize on this gold.	gewinnen will ich das Gold.
Loge. The Rhine-maidens	*Loge.* Die Rheintöchter
raised their complaint :	riefen dich an :
so may they then hope for a hearing ?	so dürfen Erhörung sie hoffen ?
Wotan	*Wotan*
(violently).	(heftig).
Peace ! thou prattler !	Schweige, Schwätzer !
Freia the noble —	Freia, die gute,
Freia needs our assistance.	Freia gilt es zu lösen.
Loge. Swiftly I'll guide,	*Loge.* Wie du befiehlst
go where you will :	führ' ich dich gern :
steeply down	steil hinab
shall we descend through the Rhine ?	steigen wir denn durch den Rhein ?
Wotan. Not through the Rhine.	*Wotan.* Nicht durch den Rhein !
Loge. We'll swing ourselves then	*Loge.* So schwingen wir uns
through the sulphur cleft :	durch die Schwefelkluft :
so slip with me down it thus !	dort schlüpfe mit mir hinein !

He goes first and disappears at the side down a crevice from which immediately a sulphurous vapor rises.

Er geht voran und verschwindet seitwärts in einer Kluft, aus der sogleich ein schwefliger Dampf hervorquillt.

Wotan. Ye others halt	*Wotan.* Ihr andren harrt
till evening here :	bis Abend hier :
our youth departed	verlor'ner Jugend
I'll purchase me yet with the gold.	erjag' ich erlösendes Gold !

He clambers after *Loge* into the sulphur cleft : the vapor stealing out of which spreads over the whole stage with a thick cloud, concealing the rest of the characters.

Er steigt *Loge* nach in die Kluft hinab : der aus ihr dringende Schwefeldampf verbreitet sich über die ganze Bühne und erfüllt diese schnell mit dickem Gewölk. Bereits sind die Zurück-bleibenden unsichtbar.

Donner. Fare thee well, Wotan !	*Donner.* Fahre wohl, Wotan !
Froh. Good luck ! Good luck !	*Froh.* Glück auf ! Glück auf !
Fricka. O, soon return	*Fricka.* O kehre bald
my trouble to soothe !	zur bangenden Frau !

The sulphurous vapor thickens to a quite black cloud which rises upwards ; this then changes to a firm, gloomy, rocky chasm which also continually rises, giving the stage the appearance of sinking deeper and deeper into the earth.

15
7
12

Der Schwefeldampf verdüstert sich bis zu ganz schwarzem Gewölk, welches von unten nach oben steigt ; dann verwandelt sich dieses in festes, finstres Steingeklüft, das sich immer aufwärts bewegt, so dass es den Anschein hat, als sänke die Scene immer tiefer in die Erde hinab.

## THIRD SCENE.	## DRITTE SCENE.

Presently from various quarters ruddy light gleams out ; and there extends farther than eye can reach

17

Endlich dämmert von verschiedenen Seiten aus der Ferne her, dunkelrother Schein auf : eine unabsehbar weit sich dahinziehende

A Subterranean Cavern

unterirdische Kluft

which on all sides seems to lead to other an l narrower passages.

6

wird erkennbar die nach allen Seiten hin in enge Schachte auszumünden scheint.

Alberich enters, dragging the shrieking *Mime* forth by the ear from a cleft at one side.

Alberich zerrt den kreischenden *Mime* an den Ohren aus einer Seitenschlufft herbei.

Alberich. Hello ! Hello !	*Alberich.* Hehe ! hehe !
Come here ! Come here !	hieher ! hieher !
Rascally imp !	Tückischer Zwerg !

Rarely your ear
now will I nip,
should you not weld me
straight on the spot
the special work I have shown.

Mime
(howling).
Oho! Oho!
Oh! Oh!
Let me alone!
Made it is
at your command,
with moil and toil
moulded by me.
Nick not your nails in me so!

Alberich
(letting him go).
Why hesitate then
to hand it out?

Mime. I apprehended
lest aught were failing —

Alberich. Where was it unfinished?

Mime
(hesitating).
Here — and there —

Alberich. How "here and there"?
hand me the work!

<small>He threatens to seize again the ear of *Mime* who, in terror, lets fall a piece of metal work that he has held concealed in his hand. *Alberich* hastily picks it up and examines it.</small> **18**

See, you scamp!
All has been smithied
and welded, I ween,
after my word.
You, idiot, would seek
so to deceive me,
and save the wonderful
work for yourself?
when by my lore
you could shape it alone!
Read are your thoughts, my thief?

<small>(He sets the metal work on his head as a "Tarnhelm.")</small>

The helm fits to the head;
now will it act as it ought?
— "Night annul me.
Nought be seen!" —

<small>(He vanishes, and a column of smoke takes his place.)</small>

Brother, d'ye see me?

Mime
(gazing about in astonishment).
Where stand you? I see you no jot!

---

tapfer gezwickt
sollst du mir sein.
schaffst du nicht fertig,
wie ich's bestellt,
zur Stund' das feine Geschmeid!

Mime
(heulend)
Ohe! Ohe!
Au! Au!
Lass' mich nur los!
Fertig ist es,
wie du befahlst;
mit Fleiss und Schweiss
ist es gefügt:
nimm nur die Nägel vom Ohr!

Alberich
(loslassend).
Was zögerst du dann
und zeigst es nicht?

Mime. Ich Armer zagte,
dass noch was fehle.

Alberich. Was wär' noch nicht fertig?

Mime
(verlegen)
Hier . . . und da . . .

Alberich. Was hier und da?
Her das Gewirk!

<small>Er will ihm wieder an das Ohr fahren: vor Schreck lässt *Mime* ein metallenes Gewirke, das er krampfhaft in den Händen hielt sich entfallen. *Alberich* hebt es hastig auf und prüft es genau.</small>

Schau' du Schelm!
Alles geschmiedet
und fertig gefügt,
wie ich's befahl!
So wollte der Tropf
schlau mich betrügen?
für sich behalten
das hehre Geschmeid,
das meine List
ihn zu schmieden gelehrt?
kenn' ich dich dummen Dieb?

<small>(Er setzt das Gewirk als "Tarnhelm" auf den Kopf.)</small> **18**

Dem Haupt fügt sich der Helm
ob sich der Zauber auch zeigt?
— "Nacht und Nebel,
Niemand gleich!" —

<small>(Seine Gestalt verschwindet; statt ihrer gewahrt man eine Nebelsäule.)</small>

Siehst du mich, Bruder?

Mime
(blickt sich verwundert um).
Wo bist du? ich sehe dich nicht.

Alberich's
(voice).

Then feel me instead,
you faithless scamp;
take this for your thievish tricks!

Mime
(writhes and cries under the blows which are heard to fall on him from
an invisible scourge).

Alberich's
(voice, laughing).

I thank you, thickhead:
the work is well performed.
Hoho! Hoho!
Nibelung elves,
kneel all to Alberich!
Everywhere wanders he
over you watching;
reign of rest
is from you riven;
aye must you serve him
who lurketh unseen:
when you least of all note him
haply he's nigh you!
Unto him slaves are ye ever.
Hoho! Hoho!
hear him; he nears,
the Nibelung's head!

The column of vapor disappears towards the back; *Alberich's*
scoldings are heard retreating in the distance; howls and cries
respond from lower passages, finally the sounds are lost in the
distance. *Mime* has cowered down in pain. His groans and whim-
perings are heard by *Wotan* and *Loge* who descend from above by a
side cleft.

Loge.   Nibelheim's here.
What glare I notice
that glows from yon varying vapors?

Wotan.   Who groans so loud?
what lies on the ground?

Loge
(bending down to *Mime*).
What whining whimperer's here?

Mime.   Oho! Oho!
Oh! Oh!

Loge.   Hey, Mime, merry gnome!
what nips and knocks you like this?

Mime.   Leave me in quiet!

Loge.   Yes without question;
and more yet, hark —
help I'll give to you, Mime.

Mime
(partially rising).
What help for me?
I have for master
a hard-hearted brother
who makes me bondsman to him!

Alberich's
(Stimme).

So fühle mich doch,
du fauler Schuft!
Nimm' das für dein Diebsgelüst!

Mime
(schreit und windet sich unter empfangenen Geisselhieben, deren **Fall**
man vernimmt ohne die Geissel selbst zu sehen).

Alberich's
(Stimme, lachend).

Dank, du Dummer!
Dein Werk bewährt sich gut. —
Hoho! Hoho!
Niblungen all,
neigt euch Alberich!
Ueberall weilt er nun,
euch zu bewachen;
Ruh' und Rast
ist euch zerronnen;
ihm müsst ihr schaffen,
wo nicht ihr ihn schaut;
wo ihr nicht ihn gewahrt,
seid seiner gewärtig:
unterthan seid ihr ihm immer!
Hoho! Hoho!
hört ihn: er naht,
der Niblungen-Herr!

Die Nebelsäule verschwindet dem Hintergrunde zu: man **hört**
in immer weiterer Ferne *Alberich's* Toben und Zanken; Geheul und
Geschrei antwortet ihm aus den untern Klüften, das sich endlich in
immer weitere Ferne unhörbar verliert. — *Mime* ist vor Schmerz
zusammengesunken; sein Stohnen und Wimmern wird von *Wotan*
und *Loge* gehört, die aus einer Schlufft von oben her sich hera-
blassen.

Loge.   Nibelheim hier:
durch bleiche Nebel
wie blitzen dort feurige Funken?

Wotan.   Hier stöhnt es laut:
was liegt im Gestein?

Loge
(neigt sich zu *Mime*).
Was Wunder wimmerst du hier?

Mime.   Ohe! Ohe!
Au! Au!

Loge.   Hei, Mime! Muntrer Zwerg!
was zwingt und zwackt dich denn so?

Mime.   Lass' mich in Frieden!

Loge.   Das will ich freilich,
und mehr noch, hör':
helfen will ich dir, Mime!

Mime
(sich etwas aufrichtend).
Wer hälfe mir?
Gehorchen muss ich
dem leiblichen Bruder,
der mich in Bande gelegt.

Loge.   But, Mime, what brought him
          the pow'r to command?

Mime.   With evil craft
          lately Alberich
          hath wrought from Rhinegold
          a ruddy ring
          and its spell of magic
          masters our spirits;
        with this he moves to serve him
        the night-loving Niblung race.
          Once at our anvils
          ornaments all made,
          only our wives to deck;
          worked from the ore
        nice little Nibelung toys:
        we lightly laughed as we toiled.
          This wretch now compels us
          deep caverns to pierce to:
          for him alone
          to heavily toil.
          Through the ring of gold
          he redes in his greed
          where unknown splendor
          is spread in the earth.
          Then must we all trace it,
          track it and dig it;
          extract the metal
          and melt it in bars.
          With no peace nor pause,
        to heap up the hoard for him.

Loge.   His lash has chastised
          your laziness then?

Mime.   Most ill-starred I!
          my thraldom is endless.
          I had a forged
          helmet to fashion:
          exact commands
          he gave for its making.
          My wit surmised
          the wondrous might
          possess'd by the work
          that from steel I wove:
          the helm I sorely
          wanted myself,
          that its enchantment
        Alberich's chiding might check;
          maybe — yes, maybe
        the bully himself 'twould bamboozle.
        That he might be placed in my power —
        the ring be from him ravished:
        then I who bend as his bondsman,
        as master henceforth should command.

17

3

6

Loge.   Dich, Mime, zu binden
          was gab ihm die Macht?

Mime.   Mit arger List
          schuf sich Alberich
          aus Rheines Gold
          einen gelben Reif:
          seinem starken Zauber
          zittern wir staunend;
        mit ihm zwingt er uns alle,
        der Niblungen nächtiges Heer. —
          Sorglose Schmiede,
          schufen wir sonst wohl
          Schmuck unsren Weibern,
          wonnig Geschmeid,
        niedlichen Niblungentand:
        wir lachten lustig der Müh'.
          Nun zwingt uns der Schlimme
          in Klüfte zu schlüpfen,
          für ihn allein
          uns immer zu müh'n.
          Durch des Ringes Gold
          erräth seine Gier,
          wo neuer Schimmer
          in Schachten sich birgt:
          da müssen wir spähen,
          spüren und graben,
          die Beute schmelzen
          und schmieden den Guss,
          ohne Ruh' und Rast
        den Hort zu häufen dem Herrn.

Loge.   Den Trägen so eben
          traf wohl sein Zorn?

Mime.   Mich Armen, ach!
          mich zwang er zum ärgsten:
          ein Helmgeschmeid
          hiess er mich schweissen;
          genau befahl er
          wie es zu fügen.
          Wohl merkt' ich klug
          welch' mächt'ge Kraft
          zu eigen dem Werk,
          das aus Erz ich wirkte:
          für mich drum hüten
          wollt' ich den Helm,
          durch seinen Zauber
        Alberich's Zwang mich entzieh'n —
          vielleicht, ja vielleicht
        den Lästigen selbst überlisten,
        in meine Gewalt ihn zu werfen.
        den Ring ihm zu entreissen,
        dass, wie ich Knecht jetzt dem Kühnen,
        mir Freien er selber dann fröhn'!

Loge. And why, my trickster,
    triumph'd you not?

Mime. Ah! though the work I welded,
    the magic to which 'twas made,
    that magic I read not aright.
    He who from me robbed
    the work I wrought,
    I learned of him now,
    — too late though, alas! —
    what good luck lay in the helm.
    From my eyes he faded,
    but finely his arm
    my fool's back furrowed with stripes
    Through foolishness thus
    I found my thanks.
    (He rubs his back, howling. The gods laugh.)

Loge
            (to *Wotan*).
    Admit, not easy
    is our task.

Wotan. Ere our end's attained
    thy cunning must aid.

Mime
(struck by the laughter of the gods, observes them more attentively).
    Who are ye before me
    that question so freely?

Loge. Friends to you:
    from their annoys
    we'd free all the Nibelung folk.
    (*Alberich's* threats and scourgings again approach.)

Mime. Keep a look out!
    Alberich comes.

Wotan. For him we wait here.
    He quietly seats himself on a stone. *Loge* leans by his side. —
Alberich, who has now removed the Tarnhelm and wears it in his
girdle, drives with brandished whip from the caves below a crowd of
Nibelungs before him. They are laden with gold and silver jewelry
which under *Alberich's* continual scolding and urging, they pile up in
one heap.

Alberich. Hither! Thither!
    Hallo! Hallo!
    Lazy hounds!
    There in heaps
    pile up the hoard!
    You there, get up!
    Will you move on?
    Indolent pack,
    down with the ingots.
    Shall I then help you?
    drag it all here.
    (He suddenly perceives *Wotan* and *Loge*.)
    Hey! who are these
    who thus intrude?

Loge. Warum, du Kluger,
    glückte dir's nicht?

Mime. Ach, der das Werk ich wirkte,
    den Zauber, der ihm entzuckt,
    den Zauber errieth ich nicht recht!
    Der das Werk mir rieth,
    und mir's entriss,
    der lehrte mich nun
    — doch leider zu spät! —
    welche List läg' in dem Helm:
    meinem Blick entschwand er,
    doch Schwielen dem Blinden
    schlug unschaubar sein Arm.
    Das schuf ich mir Dummen
    schön zu Dank!
    (Er streicht sich heulend den Rücken. Die Götter lachen.)

Loge
            (zu *Wotan*).
    Gesteh', nicht leicht
    gelingt der Fang.

Wotan. Doch erliegt der Feind,
    hilft deine List.

Mime
(vom dem Lachen der Götter betroffen, betrachtet diese aufmerk-
samer).
    Mit eurem Gefrage
    wer seid denn ihr Fremde?

Loge. Freunde dir;
    von ihrer Noth
    befrei'n wir der Niblungen Volk.
    (*Alberich's* Zanken und Züchtigen nähert sich wieder.)

Mime. Nehmt euch in Acht!
    Alberich naht.

Wotan. Sein harren wir hier.
    Er setzt sich ruhig auf einen Stein; *Loge* lehnt ihm zur Seite. —
Alberich, der den Tarnhelm vom Haupte genommen und in den
Gürtel gehängt hat, treibt mit geschwungener Geissel aus der unteren,
tiefer gelegenen Schlucht, aufwärts eine Schaar *Nibelungen* vor sich
her; diese sind mit goldenem und silbernem Geschmeide beladen, das
sie, unter *Alberich's* stetem Schimpfen und Schelten, all auf einen
Haufen speichern und so zu einem Horte häufen.

17 *Alberich.* Hieher! Dorthin!
    Hehe! Hoho!
    Träges Heer,
    dort zu Hauf
    schichtet den Hort!
    Du da, hinauf!
    Willst du voran?
    Schmähliches Volk,
    ab das Geschmeide!
    Soll ich euch helfen?
    Alles hieher!
    (Er gewahrt plötzlich *Wotan* und *Loge*.)
    He! wer ist dort?
    Wer drang hier ein? —

Mime, to me!	Mime! Zu mir,
pestilent patch!	schäbiger Schuft!
pratest thou here	Schwatztest du gar
with this promising pair?	mit dem schweifenden Paar?
Off, thou idler!	Fort! du Fauler!
Back to thy pickaxe and pincers!	Willst du gleich schmieden und schaffen?
(With uplifted scourge he drives *Mime* into the midst of the crowd of Nibelungs.)	(Er treibt *Mime* mit Geisselhieben unter den Haufen der Nibelungen hinein.)
Hey! to your labor!	Hie! an die Arbeit!
Look that ye hasten!	Alle von hinnen!
Hurry below!	Hurtig hinab?
From the new found shafts	Aus den neuen Schachten
now shovel the gold!	schafft mir das Gold!
Who grubs not gaily	Euch grüsst die Geissel,
getteth the whip!	grabt ihr nicht rasch!
If any be idle	Dass keiner mir müssig
Mime shall answer,	bürge mir Mime,
or make his escape	sonst birgt er sich schwer
from the sting of my scourge!	meines Armes Schwunge:
That I everywhere wander	dass ich überall weile,
where no one doth ween	wo Niemand es wähnt,
who wotteth better than he?	das weiss er, dünkt mich, genau. —
Tarrying still?	Zögert ihr noch?
Take ye no heed?	Zaudert wohl gar?
(Draws the ring from his finger, kisses it and stretches it commandingly out.)	(Er zieht seinen Ring vom Finger, küsst ihn und streckt ihn drohend aus.)
Tremble in terror,	Zittre und zage,
Down-trodden race:	gezähmtes Heer:
heed his rule	rasch gehorcht
who holds the Ring!	des Ringes Herrn!
With howls and shrieks the Nibelungs — *Mime* among them — separate and slip into crevices on all sides down to their shafts again.	Unter Geheul und Gekreisch stieben die Nibelungen (unter ihnen *Mime*) auseinander, und schlüpfen nach allen Seiten in die Schachte hinab.

Alberich

    (advancing wrathfully to *Wotan* and *Loge*).

    What want you here?

Alberich

    (grimmig auf *Wotan* und *Loge* zutretend).

    Was sucht ihr hier?

Wotan. From Nibelheim's night-bound land	*Wotan.* Von Nibelheim's nächt'gem Land
strange news to our notice rang,	vernahmen wir neue Mähr':
of rarest wonders	mächt'ge Wunder
worked here by Alberich:	wirke hier Alberich;
to witness these marvels	daran uns zu weiden
makes us guests at thy gate.	trieb uns Gäste die Gier.
Alberich. Nought gnaws you	*Alberich.* Nach Nibelheim
but envy, I know:	führt euch wohl Neid:
and why you greet me,	so kühne Gaste,
guests, well I guess.	glaubt, kenn' ich gar gut.
Loge. Do you know *me*,	*Loge.* Kennst du mich gut,
mis'rable dwarf?	kindischer Alp?
Who is't? now say,	Nun sag': wer bin ich,
at whom you would snarl?	dass du so bell'st?
In frigid lair	Im kalten Loch,
where freezing you lay,	da kauernd du lag'st
where were your light	wer gab dir Licht
and warming illume	und wärmende Lohe,
if on Loge you had not looked?	wenn Loge nie dir gelacht?

What aid were your hammer
if I ne'er heated the forge?
  Cousin you may be,
  once friend of mine; —
no more than these are your thanks?

Alberich. To light-elves
  belongs now Loge,
  deluding rogue!
Art as fairly their friend
as my friend thou wert once?
  Haha! that'st fine!—
nought need I fear from their hands.

Loge. I'm surely worthy your trust.

Alberich. In thy untruth trust I;
  not in thy truth!
But entrenched I triumph o'er all.

Loge. Power has brought you
  spirit brave:
  grimly great
  waxes your force.

Alberich. Seest thou the hoard
  that my host
  heaps for me there?

Loge. So noble a sight I ne'er knew.

Alberich. That's for to-day,
  the merest driblet:
  much more metal
shall augment it to-morrow.

Wotan. But what can boot you the hoard
here in baleful Nibelheim,
where nought by riches is bought?

Alberich. Riches to raise me,
  and riches to furnish,
I need Nibelheim's night.
  But with the hoard
  that in hollows I heap
wonders I count to accomplish:
  the world my cunning
can by its might overmaster.

Wotan. How, my worthy, wilt thou do that?

Alberich. Ye aloft, who lapped in airs
  ambrosial, live,
  laugh and love,
  with gilded fist
I'll grasp you and fetter all to me!
As I have loving aye forsworn,
  all they that live
  shall eke forswear it:

Was hülf' dir dein Schmieden,
heizt' ich die Schmiede dir nicht?
  Dir bin ich Vetter,
  und war dir Freund:
nicht fein drum dünkt mich dein Dank!

Alberich. Den Lichtalben
  lacht jetzt Loge,
  der listige Schelm:
bist du Falscher ihr Freund,
wie mir Freund du einst warst
  haha! mich freut's!
von ihnen fürcht' ich dann nichts.

Loge. So denk' ich, kannst du mir trau'n?

Alberich. Deiner Untreu' trau' ich,
  nicht deiner Treu'!—
Doch getrost trotz' ich euch allen.

Loge. Hohen Muth
  verleiht deine Macht:
  grimmig gross
  wuchs dir die Kraft.

Alberich. Siehst du den Hort,
  den mein Heer
  dort mir gehäuft?

Loge. So neidlichen sah' ich noch nie.

Alberich. Das ist für heut',
  ein kärglich Häufchen:
  kühn und mächtig
soll es künftig sich mehren.

Wotan. Zu was doch frommt dir der Hort,
da freundlos Nibelheim,
und nichts um Schätze hier feil?

Alberich. Schätze zu schaffen
  und Schätze zu bergen,
nützt mir Nibelheim's Nacht;
  doch mit dem Hort,
  in der Höhle gehäuft,
denk' ich dann Wunder zu wirken:
  die ganze Welt
gewinn' ich mit ihm mir zu eigen.

Wotan. Wie beginnst du, Gütiger, das?

Alberich. Die in linder Lüfte Weh'n
  da oben ihr lebt,
  lacht und liebt:
  mit gold'ner Faust
euch Göttliche fang' ich mir alle!
Wie ich der Liebe abgesagt,
  Alles was lebt
  soll ihr entsagen:

allured by my gold,
for gold alone shall they languish.
  On radiant heights,
  in visions of rapture
  rocked are ye:
  the black dwarfs
ye look down upon, deathless debauchees.
    Beware!
    Beware!—
    For first ye men
    shall work to my might,
    then your sprightly women,
    who my wooing despise,
the gnome shall lure to his needs;
love lacking, withal.
    Ha, ha, ha, ha!
    Have ye now heard?
    Beware!
Beware of the night-begot host,
when the Niblung hoard shall upheave
from night and darkness to day!
	mit Golde gegirrt,
	nach Gold nur sollt ihr noch gieren.
	  Auf wonnigen Höh'n
	  in seligem Weben
	  wiegt ihr euch,
	  den Schwarz-Alben
	verachtet ihr ewigen Schwelger:—
	    habt Acht!
	    habt Acht!—
	    denn dient ihr Männer
	    erst meiner Macht,
	    eure schmucken Frau'n—
	    die mein Frei'n verschmält—
	sie zwingt zur Lust sich der Zwerg,
	lacht Liebe ihm nicht.—
	    Hahahaha!
	    hört ihr mich recht?
	    Habt Acht!
	Habt Acht vor dem nächtlichen Heer,
	entsteigt des Niblungen Hort
	aus stummer Tiefe zu Tag!

Wotan
              (starting).
  Aroint! miserable wretch!

Alberich.   What says he?

Loge
       (stepping between them:—to *Wotan*).
  Subdue thy spirit!
          (To *Alberich.*)

What can hinder our wonder,
beholding Alberich's work?
If safely your tricks can assure
what you attract with the treasure,
the mightiest must I then hail you·
  for moon and stars
  and the sun in its splendor
surely thus must regard you:
they, too, must be your thralls.
But 'twere of primal importance
  that the host who heap up
  the Nibelung hoard
nought of hatred nurse.
You have well wielded a ring
which puts your people in awe:—
  think if in sleep
  a thief to you slipped,
the ring slyly to wrest!
What, wise one, would warrant you then?

Alberich.   Delightfully deep is Loge:
    e'er he deems
    all others are dull.

Wotan
              (auffahrend).
  Vergeh', frevelnder Gauch!

Alberich.   Was sagt der?

Loge
       (ist dazwischen getreten).
  Sei doch bei Sinnen!
         (Zu *Alberich.*)

Wen doch fasste nicht Wunder,
erfährt er Alberich's Werk?
Gelingt deiner herrlichen List,
Was mit dem Hort du heischest,
Den Mächtigsten muss ich dich rühmen:
  denn Mond und Stern'
  und die strahlende Sonne,
sie auch dürfen nicht anders,
dienen müssen sie dir.
Doch wichtig acht'ich vor allem,
  dass des Hortes Häufer,
  der Niblungen Heer,
neidlos dir geneigt.
Einen Ring rührtest du kühn,
dem zagte zitternd dein Volk:
  doch wenn im Schlaf
  ein Dieb dich beschlich,
den Ring schlau dir entriss',
wie wahrtest du Weiser dich dann?

Alberich.   Der Listigste dünkt sich Loge;
    andre denkt er
    immer sich dumm:

That I were indebted
to him, indeed,
for service deft
would seem to the dog right good. —
The helmet that hides
myself I designed :
the skillfullest smith,
Mime, I make to shape it :
swiftly to waft me,
or, at my will,
to assume other semblance
serves the helm.
None may see me,
much as he seek ;
but hidden from all men
I everywhere am.
So, undisturbed,
by aught, I stand safe e'en from thee,
thou fond sedulous friend !

Loge.   Much I've looked at —
lighted on marvels ;
but lacked to witness
such wonders yet.
This work without fellow
I have no faith in :
were but this only possible,
your power would be unending.

Alberich.   Pray do I lie
and prattle like Loge ?

Loge.   Till it is proved,
good dwarf, I doubt your word.

Alberich.   With cunning, blockhead,
thou'lt finish by bursting.
Confusion I'll cause !
Now say, before thee what shape
shall my figure assume ?

Loge.   Whatever you will ;
but make me mute with amaze !

Alberich
                (putting on the Tarnhelm).
" Draw thee here,
hugest of dragons."

He instantly disappears and in his place there writhes a huge
monster serpent which bends and opens its outstretched jaws at *Wotan*
and *Loge.*

Loge
                (affecting extreme fear).
Oho ! Oho !
Sinister serpent,
pray swallow me not !
Spare but life to poor Loge !

---

dass sein' ich bedürfte
zu Rath und Dienst
um harten Dank,
das hörte der Dieb jetzt gern ! —
Den hehlenden Helm
ersann ich mir selbst ;
der sorglichste Schmied,
Mime, musst' ihn mir schmieden :
schnell mich zu wandeln
nach meinem Wunsch,
die Gestalt mir zu tauschen,
taugt mir der Helm ;
niemand sieht mich,
wenn er mich sucht ;
doch überall bin ich,
geborgen dem Blick.
So ohne Sorge
bin ich selbst sicher vor dir,
du fromm sorgender Freund !

$\frac{8}{15}$ *Loge.*   Vieles sah' ich,
Seltsames fand ich :
doch solches Wunder
gewahrt' ich nie.
Dem Werk ohne Gleichen
kann ich nicht glauben ;
wäre diess einz'ge möglich,
deine Macht währte dann ewig.

Alberich.   Meinst du, ich lüg',
und prahle wie Loge ?

Loge.   Bis ich's geprüft,
bezweifl' ich, Zwerg, dein Wort.

Alberich.   Vor Klugheit bläht sich
zum platzen der Blöde :
nun plage dich Neid !
Bestimm', in welcher Gestalt
soll ich jach vor dir stehn ?

Loge.   In welcher du willst :
nur mach' vor Staunen mich stumm !

Alberich
                (hat den Helm aufgesetzt).
18   " Riesen-Wurm
winde dich ringelnd ! "

Sogleich verschwindet ef : eine ungeheure Riesenschlange windet
sich statt seiner am Boden ; sie bäumt sich und streckt den aufgesperrten
Rachen nach *Wotan* und *Loge* hin.

Loge
                (stellt sich von Furcht ergriffen).
Ohe ! Ohe !
schreckliche Schlange !
verschling' mich nicht !
Schone Logen das Leben !

Wotan

(laughing).

Good, Alberich!
Good — and artful!
So soon canst turn
to terrible serpent thy form?

The dragon disappears and instead Alberich is seen in his own figure.

Alberich.   Haha! you deep ones,
do ye believe?

Loge.   My trembling surely attests it.
From you the serpent
swiftly was shaped:
When I have witnessed,
well I credit the wonder.
But as you waxed great
can you not wane too,
becoming smaller?
More cunning seems to me
from dangers so to withdraw:
that, truly, I think too stiff.

Alberich.   Too stiff? yes,
for such as ye!
How small shall I seem?

Loge.   That a tiny slit may contain you,
as timidly slinketh a toad.

Alberich.   Pah! nought simpler!
Spy at me now.

(He puts on the helm again.)

"Crooked toad,
creep from cranny."

He disappears. The gods perceive a toad crawling on the rocks.

Loge

(to *Wotan*).

There! that creature!
grasp it in haste.

Wotan sets his foot on the toad and Loge, putting his hand to its head, seizes the Tarnhelm.

Alberich

(who is then seen in his own form writhing under *Wotan's* foot).

Oho! Accurst!
I am a captive.

Loge.   Hold him close,
till he is tied.

He brings forward a bast-rope and binds ...berich hand and foot with it; the two then seize their prisoner, who furiously struggles to escape, and drag him with them to the shaft from which they descended.

Loge.   With speed above;
there he's our bondsman!

(They disappear, mounting upwards.)

Wotan

(lacht).

Gut, Alberich!
gut, du Arger!
Wie wuchs so rasch
zum riesigen Wurme der Zwerg!

Die Schlange verschwindet, und statt ihrer erscheint sogleich Alberich wieder in seiner wirklichen Gestalt.

Alberich.   Hehe! Ihr Klugen,
glaubt ihr mir nun?

Loge.   Mein Zittern mag dir's bezeugen.
Zur grossen Schlange
schuf'st du dich schnell:
weil ich's gewahrt,
willig glaub' ich das Wunder.
Doch, wie du wuchsest,
kannst du auch winzig
und klein dich schaffen?
Das Klügste schiene mir das,
Gefahren schlau zu entflieh'n:
das aber dünkt mich zu schwer!

Alberich.   Zu schwer dir,
weil du zu dumm!
Wie klein soll ich sein?

Loge.   Dass die engste Klinze dich fasse,
wo bang die Kröte sich birgt.

Alberich.   Pah! nichts leichter!
Luge du her!

(Er setzt den Tarnhelm wieder auf.)

"Krumm und grau
krieche Kröte!"

Er verschwindet: die Götter gewahren im Gestein eine Kröte auf sich zukriechen.

Loge

(zu *Wotan*).

Dort die Kröte,
greife sie rasch!

Wotan setzt seinen Fuss auf die Kröte: Loge fährt ihr nach dem Kopfe und hält den Tarnhelm in der Hand.

Alberich

(wird plötzlich in seiner wirklichen Gestalt sichtbar, wie er sich unter *Wotan's* Fusse windet)

Ohe! Verflucht!
ich bin gefangen!

Loge.   Halt' ihn fest,
bis ich ihn band.

Er hat ein Bastseil hervorgeholt, und bindet Alberich damit Arme und Beine; den Geknebelten, der sich wüthend zu wehren sucht, fassen dann Beide, und schleppen ihn mit sich nach der Kluft, aus der sie herabkamen.

Loge.   Schnell hinauf!
dort ist er unser.

(Sie verschwinden, aufwärts steigend.)

18

8
15
6

FOURTH SCENE.

VIERTE SCENE.

The scene changes in the same manner as before, but the reverse **17** Die Scene verwandelt sich, nur in umgekehrter Weise, wie zuvor;
way, till there appears again the   ——schliesslich erscheint wieder die

Open space on a mountain top   **12**   *freie Gegend auf Bergeshöhen,*
                                                         ——
as in the second Scene; it is, however, still veiled in a pale mist, as **8** wie in der zweiten Scene; nur ist sie jetzt noch in einem fahlen Nebel-
after *Freia's* abduction.   ——schleier verhüllt, wie vor der zweiten Verwandlung nach *Freia's*
  Wotan and *Loge,* dragging the pinioned *Alberich* with them, **13** Abführung.
mount from the cleft.   **3** *Wotan* und *Loge,* den gebundenen *Alberich* mit sich führend,
                                                         steigen aus der Kluft herauf.

Loge. Be seated,   *Loge.* Hier, Vetter,
    coz, I beseech!   sitze du fest!
    Look, belovèd,   Luge, Liebster,
    there lies the world   dort liegt die Welt,
    that you long so to win to your will.   die du Lung'rer gewinnen dir willst:
    What station, say,   welch Stellchen, sag',
    assign you there for myself?   bestimmst du mir drin zum Stall?

Alberich. Scandalous scoundrel!   *Alberich.* Schändlicher Schächer!
    Thou scamp! thou scum!   du Schalk! du Schelm!
    Loosen these bonds!   Löse den Bast,
    Bind not my limbs!   binde mich los,
    else, rogue, thou shalt bitterly rue it.   den Frevel sonst büssest du Frecher!

Wotan. I've caught thee now,   *Wotan.* Gefangen bist du,
    my cords bind thee closely.   fest mir gefesselt,
    While thou didst ween   wie du die Welt,
    the living world   was lebt und webt,
    already thy will had won thee,   in deiner Gewalt schon wähntest.
    in bonds thou liest at my feet: In Banden liegt du vor mir,
    now blenching must thou allow it.   du Banger kannst es nicht läugnen.
    Ere letting thee run   zu ledigen dich
    a ransom we look for.   bedarf's nun der Lösung.

Alberich. What a block —   *Alberich.* O, ich Tropf!
    a booby I've been!   ich träumender Thor!
    To trust blindly   Wie dumm traut' ich
    to traitors so black!   dem diebischen Trug!
    Fearful revenge   Furchtbare Rache
    I'll vent for my fault.   räche den Fehl!

Loge. Ere vengeance you foster   *Loge.* Soll Rache dir frommen,
    you'd better view yourself free: vor allem rathe dich frei:
    to a fettered man   dem gebund'nen Manne
    no freeman answers for evil.   büsst kein Freier den Frevel.
    So, pant you for vengeance,   Drum sinn'st du auf Rache,
    verily pause not   rasch ohne Säumen
    in paying the tax we demand.   sorg' um die Lösung zunächst!

Alberich   *Alberich*
    (harshly).   (barsch).
    Then state what I must give.   So heisst, was ihr begehrt!

Wotan. The store, and thy sparkling gold.   *Wotan.* Den Hort und dein helles Gold.

Alberich. Griping and gluttonous thieves!   *Alberich.* Gieriges Gaunergezücht!
    (Aside.)   (Für sich.)
    So I hold for myself the Ring,   Behalt' ich mir nur den Ring,
    the hoard I can readily yield: des Hortes entrath' ich dann leicht:

for I know that to make
and augment it anew
for the spell of the Ring were a sport.
And a warning it were
my wits to remind ;
the lesson I deem is not dear,
if this is all I must lose. —

Wotan.   Dost offer the hoard ?

Alberich.   Untie my hand ;
I'll summon it here.
            (*Loge* releases his right hand.)

Alberich
(touches the ring with his lips and murmurs a command).
— Now then, I've called up
the Nibelung crew.
Of their master mindful,
mark how they mount
to the light with the hoard from below ! —
Unbind now these burdensome cords.

Wotan.   No whit till we have been paid.
The Nibelungs climb up from the crevice laden with the treasure of the hoard.

Alberich.   O sharpest of shame,
that my shrinking vassals
should view me shackled and shorn ! —
There let it rest
as I direct ;
in a heap
pile up the hoard !
Help must I offer ? —
Hie hence with your eyes !
Quick there — quick !
then quit for your hollows.
Off to your tasks !
Back to the tunnels !
Woe, if idlers there be !
I'm about your backs in a trice.
The Nibelungs, having piled up the hoard, slip back timidly into the cleft.

Alberich.   I've paid duly !
let me depart !
And the helmet there
that Loge doth hold
your goodness will give it me back ?

Loge
            (throwing the Tarnhelm on the heap).
We place it as part of the plunder.

Alberich.   Accursed wolf !
wait but awhile !
He who forged it for me
maketh a fresh one :

denn von neuem gewonnen
und wonnig genährt
ist er bald durch des Ringes Gebot.
Eine Witzigung wär's,
die weise mich macht :
zu theuer nicht zahl' ich die Zucht,
lass' ich für die Lehre den Tand. —

Wotan.   Erlegst du den Hort ?

Alberich.   Lös't mir die Hand,
so ruf' ich ihn her.
            (*Loge* löst ihm die rechte Hand.)

Alberich
(rührt den Ring mit den Lippen und murmelt den Befehl).
— Wohlan, die Niblungen
rief ich mir nah :
dem Herrn gehorchend
hör' ich den Hort
aus der Tiefe sie führen zu Tag. —
Nun lös't mich vom lästigen Band !

Wotan.   Nicht eh'r, bis alles gezahlt.
Die Nibelungen steigen aus der Kluft herauf, mit den Geschmeiden des Hortes beladen.

Alberich.   O schändliche Schmach,
dass die scheuen Knechte
geknebelt selbst mich erschau'n ! —
Dorthin geführt,
wie ich's befehl' !
All zu Hauf
schichtet den Hort !
Helf' ich euch Lahmen ? —
Hieher nicht gelugt ! —
Rasch da ! rasch !
dann rührt euch von hinnen :
dass ihr mir schafft,
fort in den Schachten !
Weh' euch, find' ich euch faul !
Auf den Fersen folg' ich euch nach.
Die Nibelungen, nachdem sie den Hort aufgeschichtet, schlüpfen ängstlich wieder in die Kluft hinab.

Alberich.   Gezahlt hab' ich :
lasst mich nun ziehn !
Und das Helmgeschmeid,
das Loge dort hält,
das gebt mir nun gütlich zurück !

Loge
            (den Tarnhelm zum Horte werfend).
Zur Busse gehört auch die Beute.

Alberich.   Verfluchter Dieb ! —
Doch nur Geduld !
Der den alten mir schuf,
schafft einen andern .

still 'bideth the might
that Mime obeys.
Hard, indeed,
that hated foes
should seize on my subtle defence!
Now then, Alberich's
spoiled of all things:
ye'll sure release him at length?

Loge (to *Wotan*).
Are you contented?
shall I untie?

Wotan. A golden ring
rests on thy finger —
hear'st thou, imp? —
that also must heighten the hoard.

Alberich (horrified).
The ring!

Wotan. Ere we release thee
that must be left us.

Alberich. My life take — but not the ring!

Wotan. The ring, I look for:
with thy life then do what thou wilt.

Alberich. If life and limbs you leave me,
the ring, too, must be allowed me.
Eye and ear, —
hand and head,
are not mine more wholly
than is this ruddy ring.

Wotan. Thine own thou callest the ring!
Ravest thou, impudent earth-gnome?
Tell me now,
whence was taken the gold
from which thou hast hammered the hoop?
was't thine own then,
which thine arm
from the water's depth tore away?
By the river-maidens
be thou arraigned
if their gold
for thine own they have given,
which thou hast robbed for thy ring.

Alberich. Shameful contrivance!
Scandalous trick!
Rogue, dost cast
in my teeth the crime
that thou wert dying to do?
Hadst robbed gladly
thyself the gold from the Rhine,

noch halt' ich die Macht,
der Mime gehorcht.
Schlimm zwar ist's,
dem schlauen Feind
zu lassen die listige Wehr! —
Nun denn! Alberich
liess euch alles:
jetzt löst ihr Bösen, das Band!

Loge (zu *Wotan*).
Bist du befriedigt?
bind' ich ihn frei?

Wotan. Ein gold'ner Ring
ragt dir am Finger:
hörst du, Alp?
der, acht' ich, gehört mit zum Hort.

Alberich (entsetzt).
Der Ring?

Wotan. Zu deiner Lösung
musst du ihn lassen.

Alberich. Das Leben — doch nicht den Ring!

Wotan. Den Reif verlang' ich:
mit dem Leben mach' was du willst!

Alberich. Lös' ich mir Leib und Leben,
den Ring auch muss ich mir lösen:
Hand und Haupt,
Aug' und Ohr,
ist nicht mehr mein Eigen
als hier dieser rothe Ring!

Wotan. Dein Eigen nennst du den Ring?
Rasest du, schamloser Albe?
Nüchtern sag',
wem entnahmst du das Gold,
daraus du den schimmernden schuf'st?
War's dein Eigen,
was du Arger
der Wassertiefe entwandt?
Bei des Rheines Töchtern
hole dir Rath,
ob sie ihr Gold
dir zu eigen gaben,
das du zum Ring dir geraubt.

Alberich. Schmähliche Tücke!
schändlicher Trug!
Wirfst du Schächer
die Schuld mir vor,
die dir so wonnig erwünscht?
Wie gern raubtest
du selbst dem Rheine das Gold,

couldst but as well
the art of its forging have won!
 So, hypocrite,
 how happy thou art
 that the Niblung, here,
 in torturing need,
 in a maddened moment,
the terrible magic did win ;
whose work now gladdens thy glance.
 The unhallowed one's
 anguish-harried,
 bliss-banishing,
 bitterest deed
 shall boot but for dazzle
and thy brilliant adornment?
Shall bliss then be brought by my ban? —
 Mighty god
 mind what thou dost!
 Say I have sinned ;
 the sin on myself but falls:
 but on all things that were,
 are, and will be,
strikes this evil of thine,
if rashly thou seizest my ring.

Wotan. Yield the ring!
 No right to that
 prov'st thou by prating, methinks.
(He tears the ring from Alberich's finger by force.)

Alberich
(screaming horribly)
 Ha! I'm vanquished! — destroyed!
 A vassal to vilest of slaves!

Wotan
(donning the ring and contemplating it with satisfaction).
 My own 'tis, making me aye
 the mightiest monarch of all.

Loge. Is he released?

Wotan. Set him loose.

Loge
(undoing Alberich's bonds).
 Slip away home:
 no more shackles hold you:
 fare freely from hence!

Alberich
(raising himself from the ground in raging laughter).
 Am I now free? —
 really free?
 Then listen, friends,
 to my freedom's first salute! —
As at first by my curse 'twas reached,
henceforth cursed be this ring!

war nur so leicht
die List, es zu schmieden, erlangt?
 Wie glückt' es nun
 dir Gleissner zum Heil,
 dass der Niblung ich
 aus schmählicher Noth,
 in des Zornes Zwange,
den schrecklichen Zauber gewann,
dess' Werk nun lustig dir lacht?
 Des Unseligsten,
 Angstversehrten
 fluchfertige,
 furchtbare That,
 zu fürstlichem Tand
soll sie fröhlich dir taugen?
zur Freude dir frommen mein Fluch? —
 Hüte dich,
 herrischer Gott!
 Frevelte ich,
 so frevelt' ich frei an mir?
 doch an allem, was war,
 ist und wird,
frevelst, Ewiger, du,
entreissest du frech mir den Ring!

Wotan. Her den Ring!
 Kein Recht an ihm
 schwört dein Schwatzen dir zu.
(Er entzieht Alberich's Finger mit heftiger Gewalt den Ring.)

Alberich
(grässlich aufschreiend).
 Weh! Zertrümmert! Zerknickt!
 Der Traurigen traurigster Knecht!

Wotan
(hat den Ring an seinen Finger gesteckt und betrachtet ihn wohlge-
fällig).
 Nun halt' ich, was mich erhebt,
 der Mächtigen mächtigsten Herrn!

Loge. Ist er gelöst?

Wotan. Bind' ihn los!

Loge
(löst Alberich die Bande).
 Schlüpfe denn heim!
 Keine Schlinge hält' dich:
 frei fahre dahin!

Alberich
(sich vom Boden erhebend, mit wüthendem Lachen).
 Bin ich nun frei?
 wirklich frei? —
 So grüss' euch denn
 meiner Freiheit erster Gruss! —
Wie durch Fluch er mir gerieth,
verflucht sei dieser Ring!

21

20

Gold which gave
me measureless might,
now may its magic
deal each owner death!
No man shall e'er
own it in mirth,
and to gladden no life
.iall its lustre gleam.
May care consume
each sev'ral possessor,
and envy gnaw him
who neareth it not!
all shall lust
after its delights,
but none shall employ them
to profit him.
To its master giving no gain,
aye the murd'rer's brand it shall bring.
To death he is fated,
its fear on his fancy shall feed;
though long he live
shall he languish each day,
the treasure's lord
and the treasure's slave:
till within my hand
I in triumph once more behold it! —
So — stirred
by the hardest need,
the Niblung blesses his ring! —
I give it thee
guard it with care —
but my curse can'st thou not flee!

(He vanishes swiftly in the crevice.)

Loge. Did you hear
his adieu of love?

Wotan
(absorbed in contemplation of the ring).
Let him give loose to his dole.

The vapor in the foreground now gradually clears.

Loge
(looking off, R.).
Fasolt and Fafner
hitherward fare.
Freia follows their steps.

(From the other side enter *Fricka, Donner* and *Froh.*)

Froh. The gods have returned!

Donner. We greet thee, brother!
(anxiously advancing to *Wotan*).

Fricka. Bring'st thou news to glad us?

Gab sein Gold
mir — Macht ohne Mass,
nun zeug' sein Zauber
Tod dem — der ihn trägt!
Kein Froher soll
seiner sich freu'n;
keinem Glücklichen lache
sein lichter Glanz;
wer ihn besitzt,
den zehre Sorge,
und wer ihn nicht hat,
nage der Neid!
Jeder giere
nach seinem Gut,
doch keiner geniesse
mit Nutzen sein';
ohne Wucher hüt' ihn sein Herr,
doch den Würger zieh' er ihm zu!
Dem Tode verfallen,
fessle den Feigen die Furcht;
so lang' er lebt,
sterb' er lechzend dahin,
des Ringes Herr
als des Ringes Knecht:
bis in meiner Hand
den geraubten wieder ich halte! —
So — segnet
in höchster Noth
der Nibelung seinen Hort! —
Behalt' ihn nun,
hüte ihn wohl:
meinem Fluch fliehest du nicht!

(Er verschwindet schnell in der Kluft.)

Loge. Lauschtest du
seinem Liebesgruss?

Wotan
(in die Betrachtung des Ringes verloren).
Gönn' ihm die geifernde Lust!

Der Nebelduft des Vordergrundes klärt sich allmählig auf.

Loge
(nach rechts blickend).
Fasolt und Fafner
nahen von fern;
Freia führen sie her.

(Von der andern Seite treten *Fricka, Donner* und *Froh* auf.)

Froh. Sie kehrten zurück.

Donner. Willkommen, Bruder!
(Besorgt auf *Wotan* zueilend.)

Fricka. Bringst du mir gute Kunde?

Loge.
  (pointing to the hoard)
With power of wit
the prize was won:
yon pile is Freia's price.
	Loge.
	  (auf den Hort deutend).
	Mit List und Gewalt
	gelang das Werk:
	dort liegt, was Freia lös't.

Donner. From the giants' hold
     now doth she hasten.
	Donner. Aus der Riesen Haft
	     naht dort die Holde.

Froh. What exquisite air
    wafteth this way!
    wondrous the feeling
    that steals o'er each frame!
    Hard 'twould go with the Æsir,
    withheld for aye from their own,
    who lends them ecstatic youth's
    unyielding and lasting delights.
	Froh. Wie liebliche Luft
	    wieder uns weht,
	    wonnig Gefühl
	    die Sinne füllt!
	    Traurig ging' es uns allen,
	    getrennt für immer von ihr,
	    die leidlos ewiger Jugend
	    jubelnde Lust uns verleiht.

The foreground is now quite clear again, the renewed light restoring to the gods their first aspect: the background, however, is still shrouded in mists, so that the distant castle is invisible.	Der Vordergrund ist wieder hell geworden; das Aussehen der Götter gewinnt durch das Licht wieder die erste Frische: über dem Hintergrunde haftet jedoch noch der Nebelschleier, so dass die ferne Burg unsichtbar bleibt.
Fasolt and *Fafner* enter leading *Freia* between them.	*Fasolt* und *Fafner* treten auf, *Freia* zwischen sich führend.

Fricka (hastening joyfully towards her sister, to embrace her). Loveliest sister, sweetest delight! look we again on our goddess?	*Fricka* (eilt freudig auf die Schwester zu, um sie zu umarmen). Lieblichste Schwester, süsseste Lust! Bist du mir wieder gewonnen?

Fasolt
    (stopping her).
Halt! stand from her side!
Still we hold her ours. —
  On Riesenheim's
  rugged confines
  rest did we take:
  the contract's forfeit
  with careful truth
  treated we.
  So, sorely loth,
  I lead her hither.
  I prythee hand us
  the price agreed.
	Fasolt
	    (ihr wehrend).
	Halt! Nicht sie berührt!
	Noch gehört sie uns. —
	  Auf Riesenheim's
	  ragender Mark
	  rasteten wir:
	  mit treuem Muth
	  des Vertrages Pfand
	  pflegten wir;
	  so sehr mich's reut,
	  zurück doch bring' ich's
	  erlegt uns Brüdern
	  die Lösung ihr.

Wotan. At hand rests the ransom:
     the golden mass
    must be guardedly measured.
	Wotan. Bereit liegt die Lösung:
	     des Goldes Mass
	    sei nun gütlich gemessen.

Fasolt. To lose the maiden,
    look you, will make me forlorn·
    so, from my soul to unseat her,
    be the sparkling hoard
    heaped in a stack,
    so as to hide
    the heavenly maid from our sight.
	Fasolt. Das Weib zu missen,
	    wisse, gemuthet mich weh:
	    soll aus dem Sinn sie mir schwinden,
	    des Geschmeides Hort
	    häufe denn so,
	    dass meinem Blick
	    die Blühende ganz er verdeck'!

Wotan. Then fix a gauge
    like Freia in form.
	Wotan. So stellt das Mass
	    nach Freia's Gestalt.

Fafner and *Fasolt* place *Freia* in the middle of the stage and stick their staves into the ground on each side, so as to give her height and breadth.	*Fafner* und *Fasolt* stossen ihre Pfähle vor *Freia* hin so in den Boden, dass sie gleiche Höhe und Breite mit ihrer Gestalt messen.

9

7

Fafner. Our poles we have planted
    in proper form :
    to hide them pile up the hoard.

Wotan. Haste with the task ;
    'tis to me hateful.

Loge. Help me, Froh !

Froh. Freia's shame
    I'll make an end of.

(*Loge* and *Froh* quickly heap up the treasure between the poles.)

Fafner. Not so light
    and loose in the form ;
    firm and close
    fill up the gauge.

He roughly presses the ornaments close together and stoops to peer about for crevices.

    Through here I see day. —
    All chinks must be hidden.

Loge. Away, you lubber !
    Let it alone !

Fafner. Look here, this cleft must be closed !

Wotan
        (turning away moodily).
    Deep in my breast
    burneth this shame.
    (His eyes are fixed on *Freia*.)

Fricka. See how distressed
    sadly the fair one stands !
    for release the mute
    suff'rer looketh a pray'r.
    Perjured man !
    our maid thou hast placed in this strait.

Fafner. Still more must be piled !

Donner. This passes all !
    hot is my rage
    roused by so hardened a rogue ! —
    Come here thou hound !
    wouldst thou measure,
    then match thyself against me !

Fafner. Rest thee, thund'rer,
    rumble not thus ;
    we heed thy rolling not here.

Donner
        (menacing him).
    I will first crush thee to fragments !

Wotan. Friend, withhold.
    Sure, wholly Freia is hid ?

Loge. The hoard gives out.

Fafner. Gepflanzt sind die Pfähle
    nach Pfandes Mass :
    gehäuft füll' es der Hort.

Wotan. Eilt mit dem Werk :
    widerlich ist mir's !

Loge. Hilf mir, Froh !

Froh. Freia's Schmach
    eil' ich zu enden.

(*Loge* und *Froh* häufen hastig zwischen den Pfählen die Geschmeide.)

Fafner. Nicht so leicht
    und locker gefügt :
    fest und dicht
    füll' er das Mass !

Mit roher Kraft drückt er die Geschmeide dicht zusammen ; er beugt sich, um nach Lücken zu spähen.

    Hier lug' ich noch durch :
    verstopft mir die Lücken !

Loge. Zurück, du Grober !
    greif' mir nichts an !

Fafner. Hieher ! die Klinze verklemmt !

Wotan
        (unmuthig sich abwendend).
    Tief in der Brust
    brennt mich die Schmach.
    (Den Blick auf *Freia* geheftet.)

Fricka. Sieh, wie in Scham
    schmählich die Edle steht :
    um Erlösung fleht
    stumm der leidende Blick.
    O böser Mann !
    Der Minnigen botest du das !

Fafner. Noch mehr hierher !

Donner. Kaum halt' ich mich :
    schäumende Wuth
    weckt mir der schamlose Wicht ! —
    Hierher, du Hund !
    willst du messen,
    so miss dich selber mit mir !

Fafner. Ruhig, Donner !
    Rolle wo's taugt :
    hier nützt dein Rasseln dir nichts !

Donner
        (holt aus'.
    Nicht dich Schmählichen zu zerschmettern ?

Wotan. Friede doch !
    Schon dünkt mich Freia verdeckt.

Loge. Der Hort ging auf.

Fafner	*Fafner*
(measuring with his eye).	(mit dem Blicke messend).
Still shines on me Holda's hair:	Noch schimmert mir Holda's **Haar**:
throw me that wove-	dort das Gewirk
work on the heap.	wirf auf den Hort!
Loge. What! e'en the helm?	*Loge.* Wie, auch den Helm?
Fafner. Hither haste with it.	*Fafner.* Hurtig her mit ihm!
Wotan. Let it go freely.	*Wotan.* Lass ihn denn fahren!
Loge	*Loge*
(throwing the Tarnhelm on the heap).	(wirft den Helm auf den Haufen).
So surely 'tis finished;	So sind wir fertig. —
seek ye aught further?	Seid ihr zufrieden?
Fasolt. Freia the glorious	*Fasolt.* Freia, die schöne,
glads me no more,	schau' ich nicht mehr:
O is she released?	ist sie gelös't?
Must I then lose her?	muss ich sie lassen?
(Goes nearer and peeps through the hoard.)	(Er tritt nahe hinzu und späht durch **den** Hort.)
Ah! her glance	Weh! noch blitzt
yet gleams on me here;	ihr Blick zu mir her;
her eyes like stars,	des Auges Stern
stream to my own;	strahlt mich noch an.
yes, I can spy them	durch eine Spalte
still through this space:	muss ich's erspäh'n! —
so while I gaze on her features	Seh' ich dies wonnige Aug',
from the goddess can I not fare.	von dem Weibe lass ich nicht ab.
Fafner. Ha! you hear me?	*Fafner.* He! euch rath' ich,
that chink must be hidden.	verstopft mir die Ritze!
Loge. Never sated!	*Loge.* Nimmer-Satte!
See ye then not,	seht ihr denn nicht,
quite spent is the hoard?	ganz schwand uns das Gold?
Fafner. By no means, friend.	*Fafner.* Mit nichten, Freund!
On Wotan's finger	An Wotan's Finger
gleams a glittering ring:	glänzt von Gold noch ein Ring,
that give to rest in the fissure.	den gebt, die Ritze zu füllen!
Wotan. What! give the ring?	*Wotan.* Wie! diesen Ring?
Loge. Let me rede you—	*Loge.* Lasst euch rathen!
to Rhine-maidens	Den Rheintöchtern
this gold belongs.	gehört dies Gold:
Wotan looks still to restore it.	ihnen giebt Wotan es wieder.
Wotan. What pratest thou there?	*Wotan.* Was schwatzest du da?
The prize so hardly come by	Was schwer ich mir erbeutet,
I shall keep, unawed, for myself.	ohne Bangen wahr' ich's für mich.
Loge. Poorly paid	*Loge.* Schlimm dann steht's
then is the promise	un mein Versprechen,
I gave the sorrowing nymphs.	das ich den Klagenden gab.
Wotan. But thy promise bindeth not me:	*Wotan.* Dein Versprechen bindet mich nicht:
my booty 'bideth the ring.	als Beute bleibt mir der Reif.

Fafner. But here for ransom must it be rendered.	*Fafner.* Doch hier zur Lösung musst du ihn legen.
Wotan. Make demand as ye will: all I'll award you; but all the world shall not move this ring from my hand.	*Wotan.* Fordert frech was ihr wollt: alles gewähr' ich, um alle Welt nicht fahren doch lass' ich den Ring!
Fasolt (wrathfully pulling *Freia* from behind the hoard). All is off! as erst it stands, and Freia's forfeit for ever.	*Fasolt* (zieht wüthend *Freia* hinter dem Horte hervor). Aus denn ist's, beim Alten bleibt's: nun folgt uns Freia für immer!
Freia. Help me! Help me!	*Freia.* Hülfe! Hülfe!
Fricka. Haughty god! give them their way.	*Fricka.* Harter Gott, gieb ihnen nach!
Froh. Hold not the gold back.	*Froh.* Spare das Gold nicht!
Donner. Hand them the ring too.	*Donner.* Spende den Ring doch!
Wotan. Leave me at rest; the ring I retain.	*Wotan.* Lasst mich in Ruh'! Den Reif geb' ich nicht.

Fafner holds back the departing *Fasolt*, all stand perplexed, while *Wotan* turns away in wrath. The stage has again become dark; from the rocky cleft at the side shines out a bluish glow in which *Wotan* suddenly perceives *Erda*, who rises from below to half her height. She is of noble presence and enveloped in a mass of black hair.

Fafner hält den fortdrängenden *Fasolt* noch auf; Alle stehen bestürzt; *Wotan* wendet sich zürnend von ihnen zur Seite. Die Bühne hat sich von Neuem verfinstert; aus der Felskluft zur Seite bricht ein bläulicher Schein hervor: in ihm wird *Wotan* plötzlich *Erda* sichtbar, die bis zu halber Leibeshöhe aus der Tiefe aufsteigt: sie ist von edler Gestalt, weithin von schwarzem Haare umwallt.

22

Erda (stretching out her hand warningly towards *Wotan*). Waver, Wotan, waver! quit the ring accursed. Ruin and dismallest downfall wait thee in its wealth.	*Erda* (die Hand mahnend gegen *Wotan* ausstreckend). Weiche, Wotan, weiche! flieh' des Ringes Fluch! Rettungslos dunklem Verderben weiht dich sein Gewinn.
Wotan. Who speaks such menacing words?	*Wotan.* Wer bist du, mahnendes Weib?

22

Erda. What ever was, wis I; what is, as well — what ages shall work — all I show: the endless world's All-wise one, Erda — opens thine eyes. Three the daughters born to me e'er the world was made; all I notice nightly thou know'st from the Nornir. But hither in dire danger haste I to thy help. Hear me! hear me! hear me! All that exists, endeth! A dismal day dawns for the Æsir: O render wisely the ring!	*Erda.* Wie alles war, weiss ich; wie alles wird, wie alles sein wird, seh' ich auch: der ew'gen Welt Ur-Wala, Erda mahnt deinen Muth. Drei der Töchter, ur-erschaff'ne, gebar mein Schoss: was ich sehe, sagen dir nächtlich die Nornen. Doch höchste Gefahr führt mich heut' selbst zu dir her: höre! höre! höre! Alles, was ist, endet. Ein düsterer Tag dämmert den Göttern: dir rath' ich, meide den Ring!

(margin numbers: 1, 21)

She sinks slowly to the breast and the bluish glow begins to fade

Sie versinkt langsam bis an die Brust, während der bläulich' Schein zu dunkeln beginnt.

Wotan.   A secret spell
  speaks in thy words :
  wait, and impart more wisdom.

Erda
    (disappearing).
  I've warned thee now,
  thou wott'st enough ;
  pause and ponder truth.
    (She completely disappears.)

Wotan.   Pain and peril attending —
  I must detain thee.
  All thou must tell me !

  He tries to go to the crevass in order to detain *Erda. Donner, Froh,* and *Fricka* throw themselves in his way and hold him back.

Fricka.   What wouldst thou wildly do ?

Froh.   Take heed, Wotan ;
  seek not to hold her :
  hark to her words !

Donner
    (to the giants).
  Here — you monsters,
  remain and harken !
  the gold Wotan will give you.

Freia.   Dared I but hope it !
  Deem ye Holda
  were such a ransom worth ?
    (All look anxiously at *Wotan.*)

Wotan
(who has been absorbed in deep thought, now musters his strength to
    a decision).
  Return, Freia !
  I set thee free.
  Purchased again
  gladly in youth we rejoice !
  Ye giants, there is your gem.
    (He throws the Ring on the heap.)
  The giants release *Freia :* she hastens joyfully to the gods who
embrace her in turn during some time, with greatest delight.

Fafner
meanwhile spreads out a huge sack and goes to the hoard preparing to
pack it all up.

Fasolt
    (opposing his brother).
  Halt, thou greedy one,
  give me some also !
  Equally, surely,
  should we share it.

Fafner.   More on the maid than the gold,
  amorous ape, thou gloat'st.
  My might could scarcely
  make thee resign her :
  as, without sharing,

Wotan.   Geheimniss-hehr
  hallt mir dein Wort :
  weile, dass mehr ich wisse !

Erda
    (im Verschwinden).
  Ich warnte dich —
  du weisst genug :
  sinne in Sorg' und Furcht !
    (Sie verschwindet gänzlich.)

Wotan.   Soll ich sorgen und fürchten —
  dich muss ich fassen,
  alles erfahren !

  Er will in die Kluft, um *Erda* zu halten: *Donner, Froh* und *Fricka* werfen sich ihm entgegen, und halten ihn auf.

Fricka.   Was willst du, Wüthender ?

Froh.   Halt' ein, Wotan !
  Scheue die Edle,
  achte ihr Wort !

Donner
    (zu den Riesen).
  Hört, ihr Riesen !
  zurück, und harret :
  das Gold wird euch gegeben.

Freia.   Darf ich es hoffen ?
  dünkt euch Holda
  wirklich der Lösung werth ?
    (Alle blicken gespannt auf *Wotan.*)

Wotan
(war in tiefes Sinnen versunken und fasst sich jetzt mit Gewalt zum
    Entschluss).
  Zu uns, Freia !
  du bist befreit :
  wieder gekauft
  kehr' uns die Jugend zurück ! —
  Ihr Riesen, nehmt euren Ring !
    (Er wirft den Ring auf den Hort.)
  Die Riesen lassen *Freia* los : sie eilt freudig auf die Götter zu, die
sie abwechselnd längere Zeit in höchster Freude liebkosen.

Fafner
breitet sogleich einen ungeheuren Sack aus und macht sich über den
    Hort her, um ihn da hinein zu schichten.

Fasolt
    (dem Bruder sich entgegenwerfend).
  Halt, du Gieriger !
  gönne mir auch 'was !
  Redliche Theilung
  taugt uns beiden.

Fafner.   Mehr an der Maid als am Gold
  lag dir verliebtem Geck :
  mit Müh' zum Tausch
  vermocht' ich dich Thoren.
  Ohne zu theilen

9

Holda thou wouldst have wooed :
  so of the hoard,
  justly I'll hold back
  the greater half for myself.

Fasolt. Swindler and thief !
  Thus am I served ?
        (To the gods.)
Ye jointly shall judge us :
  should not the jewels
  justly be halved ?
    (*Wotan* turns contemptuously away.)

Loge. Let him take the jewels :
hold thou the ring, and rejoice !

Fasolt
  (throws himself on *Fafner* who is packing up busily).
  Aroint, defrauder !
  mine is the ring :
it veiled me from Freia's view.
    (He snatches hastily at the ring.)

Fafner. Fold not thy fist ;
  the ring is mine.
  (They struggle : *Fasolt* wrests the ring from *Fafner.*)

Fasolt. I have it — I shall hold it !

Fafner. Hold it fast, or it may fall !
  Furious, he hits out at *Fasolt* with his staff and with one blow fells
him to the ground ; then he wrests the ring from his dying hand.
  Now feast upon Freia's face !
  for the ring's rent from thy grasp !
  He puts the ring in the sack and proceeds coolly to collect the rest
of the gold.
    (All the gods stand horrified. Long, solemn silence.)

Wotan. Fearful pow'r
  I find in the fatal curse !

Loge. What luck, Wotan,
  were to thine likened ?
  Much it was
  when the ring thou didst win ;
  but it still better serves thee
  since it was lost :
  for thy foemen — see :
  felling themselves
for the gold thou hast let go.

Wotan
      (deep shocked).
How doth horror o'erhang me !
  sickly fear
  fetters my soul ;
  only to heal it
  Erda can help me :
to her forth will I hie.

---

hättest du Freia gefreit :
  theil' ich den Hort,
  billig behalt' ich
  die grösste Hälfte für mich.

Fasolt. Schändlicher du !
  Mir diesen Schimpf ? —
        (Zu den Göttern.)
Euch ruf' ich zu Richtern :
  theilet nach Recht
  uns redlich den Hort !
    (*Wotan* wendet sich verächtlich ab.)

Loge. Lass' den Hort ihn raffen :
halte du nur auf den Ring !

Fasolt
  (stürzt sich auf *Fafner*, der während dem mächtig eingesackt hat).
  Zurück, du Frecher !
  mein ist der Ring :
mir blieb er für Freia's Blick.
    (Er greift hastig nach dem Ring.)

Fafner. Fort mit der Faust !
  der Ring ist mein.
  (Sie ringen mit einander ; *Fasolt* entreisst *Fafner* den Ring.)

Fasolt. Ich halt' ihn, mir gehört er !

Fafner. Halt' fest, dass er nicht fall' !
  Er holt wüthend mit seinem Pfahle nach *Fasolt* aus, und streckt
ihn mit einen Schlage zu Boden, dem Sterbenden entreisst er dann
hastig den Ring.
  Nun blinzle nach Freia's Blick :
  an den Reif rühr'st du nicht mehr !
  Er steckt den Ring in den Sack, und rafft dann gemächlich
vollends den Hort ein.
    (Alle *Götter* stehen entsetzt. Langes, feierliches Schweigen.)

Wotan. Furchtbar nun
  erfind' ich des Fluches Kraft !

Loge. Was gleicht, Wotan,
  wohl deinem Glücke ?
  Viel erwarb dir
  des Ringes Gewinn ;
  dass er nun dir genommen,
  nützt dir noch mehr :
  deine Feinde, sieh,
  fällen sich selbst
um das Gold, das du vergabst.

Wotan
      (tief erschüttert).
Wie doch Bangen mich bindet !
  Sorg' und Furcht
  fesseln den Sinn ;
  wie sie zu enden
  lehre mich Erda :
zu ihr muss ich hinab !

Fricka

(approaching him cajolingly).

Why wait'st thou, Wotan?
Wondrously fair
the fortress shines;
doth it not surely
genial shelter afford?

Wotan. A shameful price
pays for this shrine.

Donner

(pointing to the back which is still hidden in clouds).

Vaporous mist
veileth the scene;
sick am I
of the mournful mask!
I'll liven these thin
clouds with some lightning and thunder,
and clear the air for us all.

He mounts an overhanging rock and swings his hammer during the following.

Halloa! halloa!
To me all ye dews!
come down to me, mists!
Donner is here,
calling his hosts.
At his hammer's swing
swoop to his side!
Halloa! halloa!
Drizzle and damp,
Donner calleth his hosts!

The mist has collected round him; he disappears in an ever thickening and darkening thunder-cloud. Then his hammer-stroke is heard to fall heavily on the rocks: a vivid flash of lightning breaks through the clouds, followed by a violent clap of thunder.

Brother, come here!
show what a bridge we can shape!

Froh has also disappeared in the clouds. Suddenly these separate; *Donner* and *Froh* are visible; from their feet stretches, in blinding radiance, a rainbow-bridge over the valley to the castle, which now gleams with utmost brilliance, illumined by the evening sun.

Fafner, who, beside the body of his brother, has collected the whole hoard during *Donner's* magic thunder-storm, puts the huge sack on his back and quits the stage.

Froh. This bridge home will bring you;
light but hardy of hold.
So tread undaunted
its terrorless height!

Wotan

(absorbed in contemplation of the castle).

See how at eve
the eye of sunlight
with glorious touch
gilds turret and tow'r!
In the morning glamour,
manful and glad,
it bided masterless,
mildly beck'ning to me.

Fricka

(schmeichelnd sich an ihn schmiegend).

Wo weilst du, Wotan?
Winkt dir nicht hold
die hehre Burg,
die des Gebieters
gastlich bergend nun harrt?

Wotan. Mit bösem Zoll
zahlt' ich den Bau!

Donner

(auf den Hintergrund deutend, der noch in Nebelschleier gehüllt ist).

Schwüles Gedünst
schwebt in der Luft,
lästig ist mir
der trübe Druck:
das bleiche Gewölk
samml' ich zu blitzendem Wetter;
das fegt den Himmel mir hell.

Er hat einen hohen Felsstein am Thalabhange bestiegen, und schwingt jetzt seinen Hammer.

He da! He da!
Zu mir, du Gedüft!
ihr Dünste, zu mir!
Donner, der Herr,
ruft euch zu Heer.
Auf des Hammers Schwung
schwebet herbei:
he da! he da!
duftig Gedünst'
Donner ruft euch zu Heer!

Die Nebel haben sich um ihn zusammen gezogen; er verschwindet völlig in einer immer finsterer sich ballenden Gewitter-wolke. Dann hört man seinen Hammerschlag schwer auf den Felsstein fallen: ein starker Blitz entführt der Wolke; ein heftiger Donnerschlag folgt.

Bruder, zu mir!
weise der Brücke den Weg!

Froh ist mit Gewölk verschwunden. Plötzlich verzieht sich die Wolke; *Donner* und *Froh* werden sichtbar: von ihren Füssen aus zieht sich, mit blendendem Leuchten, eine Regenbogenbrücke über das Thal hinüber bis zur Burg, die jetzt, von der Abendsonne beschienen, im hellsten Glanze erstrahlt.

Fafner, der neben der Leiche seines Bruders endlich den ganzen Hort eingerafft, hat den ungeheuren Sack auf dem Rücken, während *Donner's* Gewitterzauber die Bühne verlassen.

Froh. Zur Burg führt die Brücke,
leicht, doch fest eurem Fuss:
beschreitet kühn
ihren schrecklosen Pfad!

Wotan

(in den Anblick der Burg versunken).

Abendlich strahlt
der Sonne Auge;
in prächt'ger Gluth
prangt glänzend die Burg:
in des Morgens Scheine
muthig erschimmernd,
lag sie herrenlos
hehr verlockend vor mir.

From morning till evening
thro' mighty ills
I won no way to its wonders!
The night is nigh;
from all annoy
shelter it shows us now.
So—hailed be the fort;
sorrow and fear it heals.—

(To *Fricka*.)

Wend with me, wife,
in "Valhall'" vast we will dwell.

(He takes her by the hand.)

Fricka. Why so dost thou name it?
Ne'er such a title was known of.

Wotan. What might 'gainst our fears
my mind may have found
if proved a success
soon shall explain the name.

Wotan and *Fricka* go towards the bridge; *Froh* and *Freia* follow immediately, then *Donner*.

Loge

(pausing in the foreground and looking after the gods).

To their end they even now haste,
while esteeming their strength overwhelming.
Ashamed am I
their acts to have share in.
A feverish fancy
doth woo me to wander
forth in flickering fire:
to burn and waste them
who bound me erewhile,
rather than be
thus blindly engulfed —
e'en were they of gods the most godlike —
there seems sense in the scheme!
I'll study on it!
Who asks what I do?

He follows the gods as if unconcerned.

From the valley the song of the *Rhine-nymphs* is heard to peal.

The three Rhine-nymphs.

Rhinegold!
Rarest gold!
How wondrously bright
once didst thou beam on us!
For thee, our plaything!
now implore we:
Give us our gold!
O give us our glory again!

Wotan

(in the act of setting his foot on the bridge pauses and returns)

What mournful sounds do I hear?

Von Morgen bis Abend
in Müh' und Angst
nicht wonnig ward sie gewonnen!
Es naht die Nacht:
vor ihrem Neid
biete sie Bergung nun.
So—grüss' ich die Burg,
sicher vor Bang und Grau'n.—

(Zu *Fricka*.)

Folge mir, Frau:
in Walhall wohne mit mir!

(Er fasst ihre Hand.)

Fricka. Was deutet der Name?
Nie, dünkt mich, hört' ich ihn nennen.

Wotan. Was, mächtig der Furcht,
mein Muth mir erfand,
wenn siegend es lebt—
leg' es den Sinn dir dar!

Wotan und *Fricka* schreiten der Brücke zu: *Froh* und *Freia* folgen zunächst, dann *Donner*.

Loge

(im Vordergrunde verharrend und den Göttern nachblickend).

Ihrem Ende eilen sie zu,
die so stark im Bestehen sich wähnen.
Fast schäm' ich mich
mit ihnen zu schaffen;
zur leckenden Lohe
mich wieder zu wandeln
spür' ich lockende Lust.
Sie aufzuzehren,
die einst mich gezähmt,
statt mit den Blinden
blöd zu vergeh'n —
und wären's göttlichste Götter —
nicht dumm dünkte mich das!
Bedenken will ich's:
wer weiss was ich thu'!

Er geht, um sich den Göttern in nachlässiger Haltung anzuschliessen.

Aus der Tiefe hört man den Gesang der *Rheintöchter* heraufschallen.

Die drei Rheintöchter.

Rheingold!
Reines Gold,
wie lauter und hell
leuchtest hold du uns!
Um dich, du klares,
nun wir klagen!
Gebt uns das Gold,
o gebt uns das reine zurück!

Wotan

(im Begriff, den Fuss auf die Brücke zu setzen, hält an und wendet sich um)

Welch Klagen klingt zu mir her?

Loge. The river-maidens
who mourn, of their gold bereaved.

Wotan. Accursed Nixies! —
Quell their clamorous noise.

Loge
(calling down the valley).
Ye in the water!
why worry us yet?
Hear what Wotan doth wish!
Gleams no more
on you maidens the gold,
in the gods' augmented grandeur
henceforth happily bask.

The gods laugh loudly and once more turn towards the bridge.

The Rhine-nymphs
(from below).
Rhinegold!
Rarest gold!
O might but again
in the wave thy pure magic awake!
What is of worth,
dwells but in the waters!
base and bad
those who are thronèd above.

As the gods slowly cross the bridge to the castle, the curtain falls.

Loge. Des Rheines Kinder
beklagen des Goldes Raub.

Wotan. Verwünschte Nicker! —
Wehre ihrem Geneck!

Loge
(in das Thal hinabrufend).
8 Ihr da im Wasser!
was weint ihr herauf?
Hört, was Wotan euch wünscht.
Glänzt nicht mehr
euch Mädchen das Gold,
in der Götter neuem Glanze
sonnt euch selig fortan!

Die *Götter* lachen laut und beschreiten nun die Brücke.

Die Rheintöchter
(aus der Tiefe).
5 Rheingold!
Reines Gold!
O leuchtete noch
4 in der Tiefe dein laut'rer Tand!
Traulich und Treu
ist's nur in der Tiefe:
falsch und feig
8 ist was dort oben sich freut!

23 Als alle Götter auf der Brücke der Burg zuschreiten, fällt der Vorhang.

DIE WALKÜRE

For a better understanding of "Der Walküre," the reader should have some knowledge of the *Nibelung Ring*, from which mythical story Wagner's great Trilogy —*Die Walküre, Siegfried*, and *Gotterdammerung*—is formed. In the prologue to the Trilogy (*Rhinegold*), the story of the *Nibelung* is told, as follows:

Under the waves of the Rhine, unthought-of and uncared-for, rested purest gold in beautiful masses. The Naiads of the stream—the Rhine-daughters—were guardians of this treasure. Suddenly, out of the depths of the earth, there comes into the waters an avaricious Nibelung, a descendant of the dwarfs, who are born of Mist and Darkness. The mischievous water-sprites encircle him and tell him of the great worldly power he would gain by becoming possessor of the gold. To do this he must utterly renounce Love. The avaricious Nibelung is bewitched by the gleam of gold, and, cursing Love and beauty, tears the treasure from its rock.

Wotan, king of the gods, is longing for greater riches. The adventure of Alberich (the Nibelung), being known to him and his companion, Loge, they descend to the mines where the dwarfs hoard their treasure, and where Alberich has made a Ring from the gold, which gives him power. Wotan and Loge easily capture the Nibelung and his treasure. Alberich puts a curse upon the Ring.

Wotan, having returned to his castle, would retain the Ring, but the goddess, Erda, "the all-knowing prophetess," rises and reminds Wotan of the curse attached to the Ring, and the destruction it will bring to the power of the gods. Wotan flings the Ring to his giants, and there is strife and blood-shed between them.

Wotan resolves to create beings (the Walküre) who can mitigate the sufferings which the greed of gold— the Ring—has brought to those on earth! and so he names his new castle "Walhalla."

And now follows the story of

DIE WALKÜRE

To protect the heroes whom the gods loved (but whom Alberich, the Nibelung, continually lurking to recover the Ring, threatened with destruction by inciting them to battle and blood-shed), Wotan and Erda created the knightly daughters Walküre to bring to Walhalla those warriors who should lose their lives upon the battle-field. But these were of little use to Wotan, unless he could create a being who, free from curse, could through self-sacrifice, redeem the world from the annihilation which the love of gold (the possession of the Ring) had brought upon earth. His children, Siegmund and Sieglinde, born of an earthly mother, he determined to devote to the work of redemption. Sieglinde was stolen away from her kindred by the robber Hunding, and Siegmund, parted from Sieglinde, grew to manhood in a stranger land. At the wedding feast of Sieglinde and Hunding, Wotan appeared, and thrusting a sword in the trunk of an oak-tree which grew in the centre of the dwelling, he told the guests that this god-like sword should belong to him who could draw it from the oak. To Sieglinde he confided the secret that no one but her lost brother Siegmund would obtain possession of the sword.

Years pass by, and one stormy night Sieglinde finds a weary warrior sleeping before the fire on her hearth. He, awakened by her expressions of pity and compassion, tells her that he seeks refuge from Hunding; he does not know that he is under his enemy's roof. In the absence of her husband, Sieglinde learns to love this stranger; their love is mutual, and not until he has drawn the sword from the oak, does she recognize him as her brother Siegmund.

The wife of Wotan, goddess and protector of marriage, compels her husband to withdraw his protection from the sinful hero Siegmund; but the work of annihilation must go on, and Wotan consecrates as heir of this work (*Vernichtung*), Hagen of Gabich, born of Alberich and the wife of the Rhine king, whose favors the Nibelung bought with gold.

Brünnhilde, Wotan's favorite Walküre, is intrusted with the mission of telling Siegmund of his approaching death; but as she sees him flying from the rage of Hunding with the poor woman whom he so dearly loves, her heart feels god-like pity for him. The fight with Hunding begins, and Brünnhilde protects Siegmund, but Wotan stretches his spear between them, and Siegmund, striking his sword upon the spear, it breaks, god-like sword although it is, and he falls, killed by a blow from Hunding.

Brünnhilde has disobeyed Wotan by protecting Siegmund; she further disobeys him by aiding Sieglinde; she gives her the broken sword "Nothung," and placing her upon Grane, her own Walküre horse, indicates a place of safety.

For this disobedience Wotan banishes Brünnhilde from among the Walküre, and condemns her to slumber on the Walküre Rock surrounded with flame, so that no one but "a hero who knows no fear" will dare to penetrate the fire and awaken her. He covers her with helm and shield, and calls Loge, who surrounds these heights with the blazing *Waberlohe* (fire).

DIE WALKÜRE

<table>
<tr><td>

ACT I

SCENE I

</td><td>

ERSTE AKT

ERSTE SCENE

</td></tr>
</table>

Interior of a dwelling, built round the stem of a great ash-tree, which forms its centre. To the right, in the foreground, is the hearth; behind it, the storeroom; at back, a great entrance door. To the left, at back, steps lead up to an inner room; lower down, same side, a table, with a broad seat let into the wall behind it, and wooden stools before it. (The stage remains awhile empty; storm without, just subsiding.)

(SIEGMUND opens the entrance-door from without and enters. He still holds the latch in his hand, and looks all round the room; he seems exhausted by overexertion; his dress and appearance indicate that he is in flight. Perceiving no one, he closes the door behind him, staggers with the last effort of an exhausted man to the hearth, and throws himself down there on a rug of bear-skin.)

(He sinks back, and remains stretched out motionless.)

SIEGMUND.
    Whose hearth this may be, here I must rest me.
(SIEGLINDA enters from the inner room, thinking her husband has returned. Her earnest look changes to surprise on seeing a stranger lying on the hearth.)

SIEGLINDA *(still at back)*.
    Whence came this man? I must accost him.

        (She advances.)
    Who enters here and lies on the hearth?

(As SIEGMUND does not move, she comes nearer and inspects him.)
    Tired is he with the way's fatigue.
    Seems he insensible? Can he be sick?

    (She bends down to him and listens.)
    Still active his breathing, though bound are his eyelids;
    Dauntless seems he, indeed, though so drooping now.
SIEGMUND *(lifting his head up suddenly)*.
    A draught! a draught!
SIEGLINDA. I'll draw thee water.

Das Innere eines Wohnraumes. In der Mitte steht der Stamm einer mächtigen Esche, dessen starkerhabene Wurzeln sich weithin in den Erdboden verlieren; von seinem Wipfel ist der Baum durch ein gezimmertes Dach geschieden, welches so durchschnitten ist, dass der Stamm und die nach allen Seiten hin sich ausstreckenden Aeste durch genau entsprechende Oeffnungen hindurch gehen; von dem belaubten Wipfel wird angenommen, dass er sich über dieses Dach ausbreite. Um den Eschenstamm, als Mittelpunkt, ist nun ein Saal gezimmert; die Wände sind aus roh behauenem Holzwerk, hie und da mit geflochtenen und gewebten Decken behangen. Rechts im Vordergrunde steht der Herd, dessen Rauchfang seitwärts zum Dache hinausführt; hinter dem Herde befindet sich ein innerer Raum, gleich einem Vorrathsspeicher, zu dem man auf einigen hölzernen Stufen hinaufsteigt; davor hängt halb zurückgeschlagen, eine geflochtene Decke. Im Hintergrunde eine Eingangsthüre mit schlichtem Holzriegel. Links die Thüre zu einem inneren Gemache, zu dem gleichfalls Stufen hinaufführen; weiter vornen auf deselben Seite ein Tisch mit einer breiten, an der Wand angezimmerten Bank dahinter, und hölzernen Schemeln davor.

Ein kurzes Orchestervorspiel von heftiger, stürmischer Bewegung leitet ein. Wenn der Vorhang aufgeht, öffnet SIEGMUND von aussen hastig die Eingangsthür und tritt ein; es ist gegen Abend; starkes Gewitter, im Begriff sich zu legen.

SIEGMUND. Wess' Herd dies auch sei
    Hier muss ich rasten.
(Er sinkt zurück und bleibt einige Zeit regungslos ausgestreckt, SIEGLINDE tritt aus der Thür des inneren Gemaches. Dem vernommenen Geräusche nach glaubte sie ihren Mann heimgekehrt; ihre ernste Miene zeigt sich dann verwundert als sie einen Fremden am Herde ausgestreckt findet.)

SIEGLINDE *(noch im Hintergrunde)*.
    Ein fremder Mann!
    Ihn muss ich fragen.
    (Sie tritt ruhig einige Schritte näher.)
    Wer kam in's Haus
    Und liegt dort am Herd?
(Da SIEGMUND sich nicht regt, tritt sie noch etwas näher und betrachtet ihn.)
    Müde liegt er
    Von Weges Müh'n:
    Schwanden die Sinne ihm?
    Wäre er siech?
    (Sie neigt sich näher zu ihm.)
    Noch schwillt ihm der Athem;
    Das Auge nur schloss er;—
    Muthig dünkt mich der Mann,
    Sank er müd' auch hin.
SIEGMUND *(jäh das Haupt erhebend.)*
    Ein Quell! ein Quell!
SIEGLINDE. Erquickung schaff' ich.

(She quickly takes a drinking horn and goes out with it. She returns and hands the filled horn to SIEGMUND.)

SIEGLINDA.
Lift but this to thy lips dry and parching:
Water, what thou dost wish!

*(*SIEGMUND *drinks and hands her back the horn. As he signs his thanks with his head, his gaze rests with growing interest on her features.)*

SIEGMUND.
Freshening liquid here I have found.
My weary load weigheth more light;
Aroused are my wits, my hopes arise,
The sense of sight is relit.
Who is't restores me to life?

SIEGLINDA.
The house and the wife of Hunding serve thee:
Guestful greeting he'll give:
Tarry but till he come!

SIEGMUND.
Weaponless am I: a wounded guest,
Would thy goodman not wile me.

SIEGLINDA *(with anxious haste).*
A wound! Oh, where is the hurt?

SIEGMUND *(shaking himself and springing up from the couch to a sitting position).*
'Tis well, trust me, unworthy of words;
I feel as ere while my sinews are firm.
Had but half as strong as mine arm shield
And spear been for havoc, ne'er from foes had I fled;
But they shivered my spear and shield.
The foe, pursuing, pressed on me sore,
And tempest bruit broke o'er my head;
But swifter than I from hunters, speeds my heaviness hence:
Sank on my lids dismal night,
But sunlight laughs on me now.

*(*SIEGLINDA *goes to the pantry, fills a horn with mead, and hands it to* SIEGMUND *with friendly alacrity.)*
SIEGLINDA.
A freshening horn of foamy mead haply
Thou'lt not refuse.

SIEGMUND. First wilt taste it thyself?
*(*SIEGLINDA *sips from the horn and returns it to him.* SIEGMUND *takes a long draught, while his gaze rests on her with growing warmth. Then he removes the horn, and sets it down slowly, while the expression of his features shows strong emotion.)*
(He sighs deeply and lowers his gaze gloomily to the ground.)

SIEGMUND *(with quivering voice).*
An unfriended mortal tendest thou;
Fortune ward my woe from thee!
    (He starts away.)
Now strengthened am I and well restored;
Farther fareth my step.
    (He goes up.)

(Sie nimmt schnell ein Trinkhorn, geht aus dem Hause und kommt mit demselben, gefüllt, zurück, das sie SIEGMUND *reicht.)*

    Labung biet' ich
    Dem lechzenden Gaumen:
    Wasser, wie du gewollt!

*(*SIEGMUND *trinkt und reicht ihr das Horn zurück. Nachdem er ihr mit dem Kopfe Dank zugewinkt, haftet sein Blick länger und mit steigender Theilnahme an ihren Mienen.)*

SIEGMUND. Kühlende Labung
    Gab mir der Quell,
    Des Müden Last.
    Machte er leicht;
    Erfrischt ist der Muth,
    Das Auge erfreut
    Des Sehens selige Lust:—
    Wer ist's, der so mir es labt?

SIEGLINDE. Dies Haus und dies Weib
    Sind Hundings Eigen;
    Gastlich gönn' er dir Rast:
    Harre bis heim er kehrt!

SIEGMUND. Waffenlos bin ich:
    Dem wunden Gast
    Wird dein Gatte nicht wehren.

SIEGLINDE *(besorgt).*
    Die Wunden weise mir schnell!

SIEGMUND *(schüttelt sich und springt lebhaft vom Lager zum Sitz auf).*
    Gering sie,
    Der Rede nicht werth;
    Noch fügen des Leibes
    Glieder sich fest.
    Hätten halb so stark wie mein Arm
    Schild und Speer mir gehalten,
    Nimmer floh ich dem Feind;
    Doch zerschellten mir Speer und Schild.
    Der Feinde Meute
    Hetzte mich müd',
    Gewitter-Brunst
    Brach meinen Leib:
    Doch schneller als ich der Meute,
    Schwand die Müdigkeit mir:
    Sank auf die Lider mir Nacht,
    Die Sonne lacht mir nun neu.

SIEGLINDE *(hat ein Horn mit Meth gefüllt und reicht es ihm.)*
    Des seimigen Methes
    Süssen Trank
    Mög'st du mir nicht verschmäh'n.

SIEGMUND. Schmecktest du mir ihn zu?
*(*SIEGLINDE *nippt am Horne und reicht es ihm wieder;* SIEGMUND *thut einen langen Zug; dann setzt er schnell ab und reicht das Horn zurück. Beide blicken sich, mit wachsender Ergriffenheit, eine Zeit lang stumm an.)*

SIEGMUND *(mit bebender Stimme).*
    Einen Unseligen labtest du:—
    Unheil wende
    Der Wunsch von dir!
    (Er bricht schnell auf, um fortzugehen.)
    Gerastet hab' ich
    Und süss geruh't:
    Weiter wend' ich den Schritt.

SIEGLINDA *(quickly turning)*.
    Who dost follow, that thou must flee?

SIEGMUND. Ill fortune follows fast on my footsteps,
    Ill fortune tracks me where'er I tarry:
    That from this thou may be free,
    Forth shall my foot remove.
(He walks quickly to the door and lifts the latch.)

SIEGLINDA *(involuntarily and hastily calls to him.)*
    Nay, bide thee here! Thou'llt bring no ill-hap,
    Methinks, where ill-hap hath harboured long.

SIEGMUND *(deeply agitated, remains; he searches SIEG-
LINDA'S features; she casts down her eyes shyly and
sadly. SIEGMUND returns).*
    Woeful have I been called:
    Hunding will I await here.
*(He stands leaning on the hearth; his gaze turns with
calm and steady sympathy on SIEGLINDA; she slowly
raises her eyes again to his; they look into one
another's eyes, during a long silence, with an expression of intense emotion.)*

SCENE II

*(SIEGLINDA suddenly starts, listens, and hears HUNDING,
who is leading his horse to its stable without. She
goes hastily up and opens the door. HUNDING, armed
with shield and spear, enters, and pauses on the
threshold, perceiving SIEGMUND. HUNDING turns to
SIEGLINDA with a look of stern enquiry.)*

SIEGLINDA *(meeting HUNDING'S gaze).*
    He—this guest—sank on our hearth,
    Rest seeking to gain.

HUNDING. His needs supplied?
(SIEGMUND quietly and steadily watches HUNDING.)

SIEGLINDA.
    I gave him nourishment; gladly harboured him.

SIEGMUND. Aid and rest I have had:
    Choose you to chide the woman?

HUNDING.
    Holy is my hearth: haven find in my house!
(He doffs his weapons and gives them to SIEGLINDA.)
(To SIEGLINDA) Haste our suppers to serve!

*(SIEGLINDA hangs the weapons on branches of the ash-
tree; then fetches provisions and drink from the
pantry; and lays the table for supper.)*
(Involuntarily she turns her eyes on SIEGMUND again.)

*(HUNDING scans sharply and with surprise SIEGMUND'S
features, comparing them with those of his wife.)*

HUNDING *(aside).*
    How like is their seeming!
    That look of a snake likewise gleams in his
      glances.
*(He conceals his surprise, and turns as if unconcerned
to SIEGMUND.)*
    Sure from far thy way was shaped?
    No horse had he who sheltered here:
    What rugged path hath wrought thee such pain?

SIEGLINDE *(lebhaft sich unwendend).*
    Wer verfolgt dich, dass du schon flieh'st?

SIEGMUND *(von ihrem Rufe gefesselt, wendet sich wieder:
langsam und düster).*
    Misswende folgt mir
    Wohin ich fliehe;
    Misswende naht mir
    Wo ich mich neige:
    Dir Frau doch bleibe sie fern!
    Fort wend' ich Fuss und Blick.
(Er schreitet schnell zur Thür und hebt den Riegel.)

SIEGLINDE *(in heftigem Selbstvergessen ihm nachrufend.)*
    So bleibe hier!
    Nicht bringst du Unheil dahin,
    Wo Unheil im Hause wohnt!

SIEGMUND *(bleibt tief erschüttert stehen und forscht in
SIEGLINDE'S Mienen; diese schlägt endlich verschämt
und traurig die Augen nieder. Langes Schweigen.
SIEGMUND kehrt zurück und lässt sich, an den Herd
gelehnt, nieder).*
    Wehwalt hiess ich mich selbst:—
    Hunding will ich erwarten.
*(SIEGLINDE verharrt in betretenem Schweigen; dann
fährt sie auf, lauscht, und hört HUNDING, der sein
Ross aussen zu Stall führt; sie geht hastig zur Thüre
und öffnet.)*

ZWEITE SCENE

*(HUNDING, gewaffnet mit Schild und Speer, tritt ein,
und hält unter der Thür, als er SIEGMUND gewahrt.)*

SIEGLINDE *(dem ernst fragenden Blicke, den HUNDING
auf sie richtet, entgegnend).*
    Müd' am Herd
    Fand ich den Mann:
    Noth führt' ihn in's Haus.

HUNDING. Du labtest ihn?

SIEGLINDE. Den Gauman letzt' ich ihm,
    Gastlich sorgt' ich sein'.

SIEGMUND *(der HUNDING fest und ruhig beobachtet).*
    Dach und Trank
    Dank ich ihr:
    Willst du dein Weib drum schelten?

HUNDING. Heilig ist mein Herd:—
    Heilig sei dir mein Haus!
*(Zu SIEGLINDE, indem er die Waffen ablegt und ihr
übergiebt.)*
    Rüst' uns Männern das Mahl!

*(SIEGLINDE hängt die Waffen am Eschenstamme auf, holt
Speise und Trank aus dem Speicher und rüstet auf
dem Tische das Nachtmahl.)*

*(HUNDING misst scharf und verwundert SIEGMUND'S
Züge, die er mit denen seiner Frau vergleicht; für
sich:)*
    Wie gleicht er dem Weibe!
    Der gleisende Wurm
    Glänzt auch ihm aus dem Auge.

*(Er birgt sein Befremden und wendet sich unbefangen
an SIEGMUND.)*
    Weit her, traun!
    Kamst du des Weg's;
    Ein Ross nicht ritt,
    Der Rast hier fand:
    Welch' schlimme Pfade
    Schufen dir Pein?

SIEGMUND.
 Through thorn and thicket, forest and field,
 I was pursued by storm and stress:
 I trow not the way that I took.
 Whither I've wandered wist I no better;
 Tidings I'd willingly learn.

HUNDING (*at table, signing* SIEGMUND *to a seat*).
 This resting roof, this harb'ring house,
 Hunding holds for wealth;
 Wendest thou hence to the west thy way, in
    homesteads
 Rich hordes of my kinsmen uphold the honour
    of Hunding;
 Grant the favour, my guest,
 That thy name may not stay unknown.

(SIEGMUND, *who has taken his place at the table, gazes
thoughtfully before him;* SIEGLINDA, *seated beside
HUNDING, opposite* SIEGMUND, *fixes her eyes on the
latter with strange interest and expectancy.*)

HUNDING (*observing them both*).
 Care or trouble hast to disclose,
 My wife would gladly listen:
 See, how greedily she waits!

SIEGLINDA. Guest, who thou art I would glean.

(SIEGMUND *looks up, gazes into her eyes and begins
earnestly.*)

 "Peaceful" may I not call me;
 "Joyful" would I had been;
 But "Woeful" must be my title,
 "Wolfing," he was my father;
 As twins entered the world
 My tender sister and I.
 Full soon I lost mother and maid;
 The parent fond and the playfellow fair,
 Nay, they have scarcely been known.
 Warlike and strong was Wolfing.
 And foes he won not a few.
 Through forest fared we in forage together;
 When home from the hunt one even we hied,
 The Wolfing's nest lay waste.
 To cinders burnt the building so strong,
 To stumps the oak trees' blossoming stem,
 And slaughter'd the mother motionless lay;
 No trace of my sister the cinders showed.
 This shameful deed we knew the Neidings had
    done, for sure.
 Then, friendless, fled my father with me.
 Lapsed my youth while living for years with
    Wolfing in woodlands wild;
 Onsets yet against us were aimed,
 But ever warded the wolves themselves.

SIEGMUND. Durch Wald und Wiese,
 Haide und Hain,
 Jagte mich Sturm
 Und starke Noth:
 Nicht kenn' ich den Weg, den ich kam.
 Wohin ich irrte
 Weis ich noch minder:
 Kunde gewänn' ich dess gern.

HUNDING (*am Tische und* SIEGMUND *den Sitz bietend*).
 Dess' Dach dich deckt,
 Dess Haus dich hegt,
 Hunding heisst der Wirth;
 Wendest von hier du
 Nach West den Schritt,
 In Höfen reich
 Hausen dort Sippen,
 Die Hunding's Ehre behüten.
 Gönnt mir Ehre mein Gast,
 Wird sein Name nun mir genannt.

(SIEGMUND, *der sich am Tische niedergesetzt, blickt
nachdenklich vor sich hin.* SIEGLINDE *hat sich neben
HUNDING,* SIEGMUND *gegenüber, gesetzt, und heftet mit
auffallender Theilnahme und Spannung ihr Auge auf
diesen.*)

HUNDING (*der beide beobachtet*).
 Trägst du Sorge,
 Mir zu vertrau'n,
 Der Frau hier gieb doch Kunde:
 Sieh', wie sie gierig dich frägt!

SIEGLINDE (*unbefangen und theilnahmvoll*).
 Gast, wer du bist,
 Wüsst' ich gern.

(SIEGMUND *blickt auf, sieht ihr in das Auge, und beginnt
ernst*).

 Friedmund darf ich nicht heissen;
 Frohwald möcht' ich wohl sein:
 Doch Wehwalt muss ich mich nennen.
 Wolfe, der war mein Vater;
 Zu Zwei kam ich zur Welt,
 Eine Zwillingsschwester und ich.
 Früh schwanden mir
 Mutter und Maid;
 Die mich gebar,
 Und die mit mir sie barg,
 Kaum hab' ich sie je gekannt.—
 Wehrlich und stark war Wolfe!
 Der Feinde wuchsen ihm viel.
 Zum Jagen zog
 Mit dem Jungen der Alte;
 Von Hetze und Harst
 Einst kehrten sie heim:
 Da lag das Wolfsnest leer;
 Zu Schutt gebrannt
 Der prangende Saal,
 Zum Stumpf der Eiche
 Blühender Stamm;
 Erschlagen der Mutter
 Muthiger Leib,
 Verschwunden in Gluthen
 Der Schwester Spur.
 Uns schuf die herbe Noth
 Der Neidinge harte Schaar.
 Geächtet floh
 Der Alte mit mir;
 Lange Jahre
 Lebte der Junge
 Mit Wolfe im Wald:
 Manche Jagd
 Ward auf sie gemacht;
 Doch muthig wehrte
 Das Wolfspaar sich.

(Turning to HUNDING.)
A Wolfing now relates this;
And as Wolfing I am well known.

HUNDING.
Wild and unwonted stories tell'st thou, intrepid
      guest.
Woeful the Wolfing!
I've heard of that warrior pair, full of unholy
      stories,
I myself neither have known till now.

SIEGLINDA. Yet, stranger, tell us further;
Where stays thy father now?

SIEGMUND.
An onslaught mighty of aim ordered the Neid-
      lings on us;
But many foemen fell by the Wolfings;
Their flight thro' the wood others did wing;
Like chaff we chas'd them afar.
I stray'd from my father by chance;
He, my chief, was wanting, though wearily
      watched for.
But alone a wolfskin lay in the wood, toss'd
      tenantless there; my father found I not.
After this, shunning the woods,
I shelter'd with heroes and women.
But far and near, where'er I fared,
If for a friend or fair I wished,
I could not win what I asked for; ill luck lay
      on me.
When recking I was right, wrong to others I
      wrought; and things ill, as I thought, others
      hotly upheld.
I fell in feud wherever I fared;
Strife came wherever I strayed.
Did I seek pleasure, pain but appeared:
They call me then "Woeful" rightly;
Unwitting, woe I must wreck.

HUNDING. Sure the Norn who knitted thy fate
Had naught of love for thee!
Neither hails thee the man
Who now the host must play!

SIEGLINDA.
Foolish 'twere, fear to hod of one o'erta'en by
      defeat!
Tell us now, guest, in what attack of late, thy
      weapons were lost?

SIEGMUND *(with more vigor)*.
For succor a maid loudly besought,
Whom chiding kin would have chained
And wed to a churl whom the child did not
      choose.
Swift to her aid I urged my way,
The heartless crew crushing in flight:
Before my force they sank.
I slew the brethren relentless;
Their bodies the sister embraced;
Her panic yielded to pain.
In floods of wildest tears,
She wailed the fiat of fate;
For her brothers' inhuman murder,
Loudly to heaven she moaned.

(Zu HUNDING *gewendet.)*
Ein Wölfing kündet dir das,
Den als Wölfing mancher wohl kennt.

HUNDING. Wunder und wilde Märe
Kündest du, kühner Gast,
Wehwalt—der Wölfing!
Mich dünkt, von dem wehrlichen Paar
Vernahm ich dunkle Sage,
Kannt' ich auch Wolfe
Und Wölfing nicht.

SIEGLINDE. Doch weiter künde, Fremder,
Wo weilt dein Vater jetzt?

SIEGMUND. Ein starkes Jagen auf uns
Stellten die Neidinge an:
Der Jäger viele
Fielen den Wölfen,
In Flucht durch den Wald
Trieb sie das Wild:
Wie Spreu zerstob uns der Feind.
Doch ward ich vom Vater versprengt!
Seine Spur verlor ich,
Je länger ich forschte;
Eines Wolfes Fell
Nur traf ich im Forst:
Leer lag das vor mir,
Den Vater fand ich nicht.—
Aus dem Wald trieb es mich fort;
Mich drängt' es zu Männern und Frauen:
Wie viel ich traf,
Wo ich sie fand,
Ob ich um Freund,
Um Frauen warb,
Immer doch war ich geächtet,
Unheil lag auf mir.
Was rechtes je ich rieth,
Andern dünktes es arg;
Was schlimm immer mir schien,
Andre gaben ihm Gunst.
In Fehde fiel ich,
Wo ich mich fand;
Zorn traf mich
Wohin ich zog;
Gehrt' ich nach Wonne,
Weckt' ich nur Weh':—
Drum musst' ich mich Wehwalt nennen;
Des Wehes waltet' ich nur.

HUNDING. Die so leidig Loos dir beschied,
Nicht liebte dich die Norn:
Froh nicht grüsst dich der Mann,
Dem fremd als Gast du nah'st.

SIEGLINDE. Feige nur fürchten den,
Der waffenlos einsam fährt!—
Künde noch Gast,
Wo du im Kampf
Zuletzt die Waffe verlor'st!

SIEGMUND *(immer lebhafter)*.
Ein trauriges Kind
Rief mich zum Trutz:
Vermählen wollte
Der Magen Sippe
Dem Mann ohne Minne die Maid.
Wider den Zwang
Zog ich zum Schutz;
Der Dränger Tross
Traf ich im Kampf:
Dem Sieger sank der Feind.
Erschlagen lagen die Brüder:
Die Leichen umschlang da die Maid;
Den Grimm verjagt' ihr der Gram.
Mit wilder Thränen Fluth

Then the slain men's servants swooped to the spot,
Crowding on me cried they for punishment;
Pouring around me panted the rabble;
Yet from the mourned moved not the maid:
My shield and spear shelter'd her long,
Till spear and shield were hewn from my hands.
Weak and weaponless standing,
Soon I saw her expire.
Still menaced the furious mob,
But the maiden moved no more.

(With a glance of vainful ardor towards SIEGLINDA.*)*

So, mistress, knowest thou now,
Why I may name me not "Joyful"!
(He rises and crosses the hearth; SIEGLINDA, *pale and deeply moved, casts down her eyes.)*

HUNDING *(rising).*
I trow, a truculent race! Our holiest laws ye lightly hold;
(With violence.)
The hatred of all ye have earned.
They sought but now my assistance.
Vengeance to render for vassal's blood.
They sent too late: returning now home,
The flying foe himself upon my hearth do I see.

*(*HUNDING *crosses to the right.)*

HUNDING.
My house holds thee, Wolfing, from harm;
For this night know thou art safe;
But arms redoubtable don with the morning;
At dawn of day shalt thou fall,
My fellows' cause to requite.
*(*SIEGLINDA *steps between the two men with anxious looks.)*
(Harshly, to SIEGLINDA.*)*
Forth from the hall! Hence without pause!
Prepare my evening draught,
And wait for me within.

*(*SIEGLINDA *stands awhile undecided and reflecting, then turns slowly and with trembling steps towards the pantry; there she again pauses and remains motionless, deep in thought, with averted face. With calm resolution she opens the cupboard, fills a drinking horn and shakes in spices from a box. Then she again turns her eyes on* SIEGMUND *so as meet his fixed gaze. On the steps she once more turns, looks yearningly at* SIEGMUND, *and indicates with her eyes persistently and with eloquent earnestness a particular spot in the ash-tree stem.)*
*(*HUNDING *starts and orders her by a commanding gesture to leave the room. With a last look at* SIEGMUND *she exits into the bed-chamber and shuts the door behind her.)*

HUNDING *(taking his weapons from the tree).*
Beware these weapons of mine.
(Going, turns to SIEGMUND.*)*

Betroff sie weinend die Wal:
Um des Mordes der eig'nen Brüder
Klagte die unsel'ge Braut.—
Der Erschlag'nen Sippen
Stürmten daher;
Uebermächtig
Aechzten nach Rache sie,
Rings um die Stätte
Ragten mir Feinde.
Doch von der Wal
Wich nicht die Maid:
Mit Schild und Speer
Schirmt' ich sie lang',
Bis Speer und Schild
Im Harst mir zerhau'n.
Wund und waffenlos stand ich—
Sterben sah ich die Maid:
Mich hetzte das wüthende Heer—
Auf den Leichen lag sie todt.
(Mit einem Blicke voll schmerzlichen Feuers auf SIEG- LINDE.*)*
Nun weisst du, fragende Frau,
Warum ich—Friedmund nicht heisse!
(Er steht auf und schreitet auf den Herd zu. SIEGLINDE *blickt erbleichend und tief erschüttert zu Boden.)*

HUNDING *(erhebt sich).*
Ich weis ein wildes Geschlecht,
Nicht heilig ist ihm,
Was andern hehr:
Verhasst ist es Allen und mir.
Zur Rache ward ich gerufen,
Sühne zu nehmen
Für Sippen-Blut:
Zu spät kam ich,
Und kehre nun heim,
Des flücht'gen Frevlers Spur
Im eig'nen Haus zu erspäh'n.—
*(*HUNDING *sehr finster.)*

HUNDING. Mein Haus hütet,
Wölfing, dich heut';
Für die Nacht nahm ich dich auf:
Mit starker Waffe
Doch wehre dich morgen;
Zum Kampfe kies' ich den Tag:
Für Todte zahlst du mir Zoll.
(uu SIEGLINDE, *die sich mit besorgter Geberde zwischen die beiden Männer stellt.)*
(Barsch.)
Fort aus dem Saal!
Säume hier nicht!
Den Nachttrunk rüste mir drin,
Und harre mein' zur Ruh'.

*(*SIEGLINDE *nimmt sinnend ein Trinkhorn vom Tisch, geht zu einem Schrein, aus dem sie Würze nimmt, und wendet sich nach dem Seitengemache; auf der obersten Stufe bei der Thüre angelangt, wendet sie sich noch einmal um und richtet auf* SIEGMUND—*der mit verhaltenem Grimme ruhig am Herde steht, und einzig sie im Auge behält—einen langen, sehnsüchtigen Blick, mit welchem sie ihn endlich auf eine Stelle im Eschenstamme bedeutungsvoll auffordernd hinweist.* HUNDING, *der ihr Zögern bemerkt, treibt sie dann mit einem gebietenden Winke fort, worauf sie mit dem Trinkhorn und der Leuchte durch die Thüre verschwindet.)*

HUNDING *(nimmt seine Waffen vom Baume).*
Mit Waffen wehrt sich der Mann.—

Thou, Wolfing, diest to-morrow.
My words hearken to; heed thyself weil!
(*He goes into the chamber; the bolt is heard to shut within.*)

SCENE III

(SIEGMUND *alone. It is now quite night; the room is only lit by the faint fire on the hearth.*)
(SIEGMUND *reclines on the couch by the fire and broods silently for awhile in great inward agitation.*)
SIEGMUND.
A sword once promised my father to furnish in
pressing need.
Weaponless fall'n into foemen's lair,
As a hostage doomed, here do I lie.
A wife saw I, wondrously fair,
And strange emotion stirred my frame!
To her do my longings stray,
Who hath lured my soul toward love,
In servance holds her this man,
Who mocks my swordless hand.
Volsung! Volsung! where is thy sword?
Thy sturdy sword, that in strife should serve
me?
Breaks madly forth from my breast the frenzy
my heart would hide!

(*The fire falls together; from the up-springing glow a bright ray strikes on that spot of the ash-tree stem indicated by* SIEGLINDA'S *look, and where a buried sword-hilt is now plainly visible.*)

What gleam from out the glow doth shoot?
What a star breaks from the ash-tree stem?
Before mine eyes a lightning doth flash;
It laughs in my face!—
How the sunny glow doth glad my soul!
Is it the look the lovely one threw,
Which yet lingers alluringly there,
Though from the hall she hied?

(*Here the fire on the hearth gradually begins to fade.*)
Deepening shadow shrouded mine eyes,
But on me her glance gloriously shone:
Wondrous the warmth that it shed.
Gleamed in grandeur the golden sun,
His glittering halo encircled my head
Till he retired to rest.

(*Another faint glare from the fire.*)
Yet once more, ere he left, kindled evening's
soft light;
E'en the aged ash-tree's stem
He gladdened with golden glow.
The flush is fading, the light sinks low;
Deep'ning shadow shroudeth my eyelids:

Dich Wölfing treff' ich morgen:
Mein Wort hörtest du—
Hüte dich wohl!
(*Er geht mit den Waffen in das Gemach ab.*)

DRITTE SCENE
SIEGMUND (*allein*).

(*Es ist vollständig Nacht geworden; der Saal ist nur noch von einem matten Feuer im Herde erhellt.* SIEGMUND *lässt sich, nahe beim Feuer, auf dem Lager nieder, und brütet in grosser Aufregung eine veit lang schweigend vor sich hin.*)
Ein Schwert verhiess mir der Vater,
Ich fänd' es in höchster Noth.—
Waffenlos fiel ich
In Feindes Haus:
Seiner Rache Pfand
Rast' ich hier:—
Ein Weib sah' ich,
Wonnig und hehr;
Entzückendes Bangen
Zehrt mein Herz:—
Zu der mich nun Sehnsucht zieht,
Die mit süssem Zauber mich zehrt—
Im Zwange hält sie der Mann,
Der mich—Wehrlosen höhnt.—
Wälse! Wälse!
Wo ist dein Schwert?
Das starke Schwert,
Das im Sturm ich schwänge,
Bricht mir hervor aus der Brust
Was wüthend das Herz noch hegt?

(*Das Feuer bricht zusammen; es fällt aus der aufsprühenden Gluth ein greller Schein auf die Stelle des Eschenstammes, welche* SIEGLINDE'S *Blick bezeichnet hatte, und an der man jetzt deutlicher einen Schwertgriff haften sieht.*)
Was gleisst dort hell
Im Glimmerschein?
Welch' ein Strahl bricht
Aus der Esche Stamm?—
Des Blinden Auge
Leuchtet ein Blitz:
Lustig lacht da der Blick.
Wie der Schein so hehr
Das Herz mir sengt!
Ist es der Blick
Der blühenden Frau,
Den dort haftend
Sie hinter sich liess,
Als aus dem Saal sie schied?

(*Von hier an verglimmt das Herdfeuer allmälig.*)
Nächtiges Dunkel
Deckte mein Aug';
Ihres Blickes Strahl
Streifte mich da:
Wärme gewann ich und Tag.
Selig schien mir
Der Sonne Licht,
Den Scheitel umgliss mir
Ihr wonniger Glanz—
Bis hinter Bergen sie sank.

(*Ein neuer, schwacher aufschein des Feuers.*)
Noch einmal, da sie schied,
Traf mich Abends ihr Schein,
Selbst der alten Esche Stamm
Erglänzte in goldener Gluth:
Da erbleicht die Blüthe—
Das Licht verlischt—
Nächt'ges Dunkel

Deep in my heart lies hid a faint
But yet smouldering fire.

(The fire is quite extinguished; complete night. The door at side opens softly. SIEGLINDA, *in a white robe, comes out and goes lightly, but quickly towards the hearth.)*

SIEGLINDA. Sleep'st thou, guest?

SIEGMUND *(in joyful surprise).*
    Who steals toward?

SIEGLINDA *(with secrecy and haste).*
    See me, hear what I say:
    In deepest sleep lies Hunding;
    I mingled a drug with his drink.
    Haste from this house without fear!

SIEGMUND *(ardently interrupting).*
    Fear drivest thou hence!

SIEGLINDA. To a goodly weapon I'll guide thee;
    A glorious prize to gain!
    As highest hero then I might hail thee:
    The strongest alone bears off that steel.
    Oh, ponder well what I repeat thee!
    His people Hunding had in this hall,
    With wassail his wedding to honour;
    He wedded a maid whom ne'er he wooed;
    Ravishers wrought her this woe.
    Mis'ry filled me while all were merry;
    When sudden marked I a man,
    In garments gray and full old;
    Low hung was his hat, and one of his eyes 'twas over;
    But the other's flash, awe forced on all men.
    Ev'ry heart felt its haughty pow'r:
    Howbeit I gleaned from that look a sweet solace and pain,
    Gladness and grief in one.
    On me smiling, he scowled at the others,
    As a sword he solemnly swung;
    Then struck it deep in the ash-tree's stem,
    With a blow buried it there.
    To none should the prize be fated,
    But who could pluck it forth.
    Then valiant heroes bestirr'd them all vainly,
    The wondrous steel none might win;
    Warriors came here and warriors wended,
    The stoutest laboured and strove,
    But they loosed it not from the stem;
    Yet bides the sword in its sheath.
    Ah! well I wist who 'twas that so gravely me did greet;
    His name, too, I know well, for whom that sword is withheld.
    Oh! found I in need but now that friend;
    Came he from far my distress to find.
    What e'er I had suffered in anguish of soul,

Deckt mir das Auge:
Tief in des Busens Berge
Glimmt nur noch lichtlose Gluth!

(Das Feuer ist gänzlich verloschen; volle Nacht.—Das Seitengemach öffnet sich leise: SIEGLINDE, *in weissem Gewande, schreitet auf* SIEGMUND *zu.)*

SIEGLINDE. Schläfst du, Gast?

SIEGMUND *(freudig überrascht aufspringend).*
    Wer schleicht daher?

SIEGLINDE *(mit geheimnissvoller Hast).*
    Ich bin's, höre mich an!—
    In tiefem Schlaf liegt Hunding;
    Ich würzt' ihm betäubenden Trank.
    Nütze die Nacht dir zum Heil!

SIEGMUND *(hitzig unterbrechend).*
    Heil macht mich dein Nah'n!

SIEGLINDE. Eine Waffe lass mich dir weisen—
    O wenn du sie gewänn'st!
    Den hehrsten Helden
    Dürft' ich dich heissen:
    Dem Stärksten allein
    Ward sie bestimmt.
    O merke was ich dir melde!—
    Der Männer Sippe
    Sass hier im Saal,
    Von Hunding zur Hochzeit geladen:
    Er freite ein Weib,
    Das ungefragt
    Schächer ihm schenkten zur Frau.
    Traurig sass ich
    Während sie tranken:
    Ein Fremder trat da herein—
    Ein Greis in grauem Gewand;
    Tief hing ihm der Hut,
    Der deckt' ihm der Augen eines;
    Doch des andren Strahl,
    Angst schuf er allen,
    Traf die Männer
    Sein mächt'ges Dräu'n:
    Mir allein
    Weckte das Auge
    Süss sehnenden Harm,
    Thränen und Trost zugleich.
    Auf mich blickt' er,
    Und blitzte auf Jene,
    Als ein Schwert in Händen er schwang;
    Das stiess er nun
    In der Esche Stamm,
    Bis zum Heft haftet' es drin:
    Dem sollte der Stahl geziemen,
    Der aus dem Stamm' es zög'.
    Der Männer Alle,
    So kühn sie sich müh'ten,
    Die Wehr sich keiner gewann:
    Gäste kamen
    Und Gäste gingen,
    Die stärksten zogen am Stahl—
    Keinen Zoll entwich er dem Stamm:
    Dort haftet schweigend das Schwert.—
    Da wusst' ich, wer der war,
    Der mich Gramvolle gegrüsst:
    Ich weiss auch
    Wem allein
    Im Stamm das Schwert er bestimmt.
    O fänd' ich ihn heut'
    Und hier, den Freund;
    Käm' er aus Fremden
    Zur ärmsten Frau:
    Was je ich gelitten
    In grimmigem Leid,

Howe'er I had pined in penance and pain,
Sweet consolation surely would follow!
Then all losses should I have retrieved,
What erst I bewailed well might be won me,
Found I this help-giving friend,
And folded him in these arms!

SIEGMUND (*ardently embracing* SIEGLINDA).
Thou'rt now, mistress fair,
Held by that friend, who weapon and wife doth
    claim!
Warm in this heart hidden doth lie the thought
    that links me to thee.
Whate'er I have sought I see here in thee;
In thee liveth whate'er I have lacked!
Wept thou for wrongs: I writhed, too, in woe:
I was degraded, thou also disgraced;
Loudly revenge's voice now delights me!
I laugh out with triumph elate,
Holding thee, highest and fairest,
Feeling the beat of thy heart!

(*The great door springs open.* SIEGLINDA *starts in alarm
    and tears herself loose.*)

SIEGLINDA. Ha! Who pass'd?
    Who entered here?
(*The door remains open; without is a lovely spring
night; the full moon shines in and throws its bright
light on the pair, who can now suddenly and plainly
behold each other.*)

SIEGMUND (*in soft ecstasy*).
No one passed—but one draws nigh;
Lo, now; where spring spreads o'er the land!

(SIEGMUND *draws* SIEGLINDA *towards him on the bench
    with tender force, so that she sits beside him.*)
(*Increasing brilliance of the moonlight.*)

Was je mich geschmerzt
In Schand' und Schmach,––
Süsseste Rache
Sühnte dann Alles!
Erjagt hätt' ich
Was je ich verlor,
Was je ich beweint
Wär' mir gewonnen—
Fänd ich den heiligen Freund,
Umfing' den Helden mein Arm!

SIEGMUND (*umfasst sie mit feuriger Gluth*).
Dich selige Frau
Hält nun der Freund,
Dem Waffe und Weib bestimmt!
Heiss in der Brust
Brennt mir der Eid,
Der mich dir Edlen vermählt.
Was je ich ersehnt,
Ersah' ich in dir;
In dir fand ich,
Was je mir gefehlt!
Littest du Schmach,
Und schmerzte mich Leid;
War ich geächtet,
Und warst du entehrt;
Freudige Rache
Ruft nun den Frohen!
Auf lach' ich
In heiliger Lust,
Halt' ich dich Hehre umfangen,
Fühl' ich dein schlagendes Herz!

(*Die hintere Thüre ist aufgesprungen und bleibt weit
ken zusammen und reisst sich los.*)

SIEGLINDE. Ha, wer ging? wer kam herein?

(*Die hintere Thür ist aufgesprungen und bleibt weit
geöffnet; aussen herrliche Frühlingsnacht; der Vollmond leuchtet herein und wirft sein helles Licht auf
das Paar, das so sich plötzlich in voller Deutlichkeit
wahrnehmen kann.*)

SEIGMUND (*in leiser Entzückung*).
Keiner ging—
Doch einer kam:
Siehe, der Lenz
Lacht in den Saal!

(*Er zieht sie mit sanftem Ungestüm zu sich auf das
Lager.*)
(*Wachsende Helligkeit des Mondscheines.*)

No. 1   SIEGMUND'S LOVE SONG.
SIEGMUND.

Win-ter storms have wan'd to the winsome moon,   in mild as-cendance smil-eth the Spring,   and,
Win-ter stür-me wi-chen dem Wonne-mond,   in mil-dem Lich-te leuchtet der Lenz;   auf

swayed by Zeph - yrs, soft and sooth - ing, weav - ing won - ders lo! he wends; throug
lin - den Lüf ten leicht und lieb - lich, Wun - der we - bend er sich wiegt; durch

wood and broad - land wafts nis breath - mg, wide ly beam his eyes with bliss;.... in
Wald und Au er wcat sein A - them weit ge - öff - net lacht sein Aug;..... gur

songs of birds re-sounds his sil - v'ry voice,.... pleas - ant o - dors pours he forth, from his

sel' - ger Vög - lein San - ge süss er tönt,...... hol - de Düf - te haucht er aus; sei - nem

liv - ing blood out-burst the love-li-est blos - soms, ver-dant sprays upspring at his voice, With

war-men Blut ent -blü -hen won-ni - ge Blu - men, Keim und Spross ent springt seiner Kraft, Mit

soft - ly wield - ed scep - tre sways he the world; Winter and storm wane as his strength awakes, Oh,

zar - ter Waf -fen Zier be - zwingt er die Welt; Winter und Sturm wichen der starken Wehr; wohl

well may his har-dy striving the stubborn hin-ges be riving, which, heavy and stiff once held us from him!

muss-te den tapfern Streichen die strenge Thü re auch weichen die trotzig und starr uns trenn - te von ihm

SIEGMUND.

Winter storms have waned to the winsome
  moon;
In mild ascendance smileth the spring,
And swayed by zephyrs,
Soft and soothing, weaving wonders, lo! he
  wends;
Through wood and broadland wafts his breath-
  ing.
Widely beam his eyes with bliss;
In songs of birds resounds his silvery voice.
Pleasant odours pours he forth;
From his living blood outburst the loveliest
  blossoms;
Verdant sprays upspring at his voice.
With softly wielded sceptre sways he the world;
Winter and storm wane as his strength awakes:
Oh, well may his hardy striving the stubborn
Hinges be riving, which, heavy and stiff,
Once held us from him!
Towards his sister swiftly he flies;
Thus longing Love spring allures,
Within our bosoms buried she slept;
Now leaps she forth to the light.
The bride and the sister is freed by the brother
Lie prone the walls that held them apart:
Hail each other the happy pair:
Now spring at last holds his Love!

SIEGLINDA. Thou art the spring;
  For thee have I sighed 'neath the
  Frost-fettered winter's frown.
  Tow'rd thee leapt my heart

SIEGMUND. Winterstürme wichen
  Dem Wonnemond,
  In mildem Lichte
  Leuchtet der Lenz;
  Auf lauen Lüften,
  Lind und lieblich,
  Wunder webend
  Er sich wiegt;
  Ueber Wald und Auen
  Weht sein Athem,
  Weit geöffnet
  Lacht sein Aug'
  Aus sel'ger Vöglein Sange
  Süss er tönt,
  Holdeste Düfte
  Haucht er aus;
  Seinem warmen Blut entblühen
  Wonnige Blumen,
  Keim und Spross
  Entspriesst seiner Kraft.
  Mit zarter Waffen Zier
  Bezwingt er die Welt.
  Winter und Sturm wichen
  Der starken Wehr:—
  Wohl musste den tapfern Streichen
  Die strenge Thüre auch weichen,
  Die trotzig und starr
  Uns—trennte von ihm.—
  Zu seiner Schwester
  Schwang er sich her;
  Die Liebe lockte den Lenz;
  In uns'rem Busen
  Barg sie sich tief:
  Nun lacht sie selig dem Licht.
  Die bräutliche Schwester
  Befreite der Bruder!
  Zertrümmert liegt
  Was sie getrennt;
  Jauchzend grüsst' sich
  Das junge Paar:
  Vereint sind Liebe und Lenz!

SIEGLINDE. Du bist der Lenz,
  Nach dem ich verlangte
  In frostigen Winter's Frist;
  Dich grüsste mein Herz

With heavenly thrill, when thy radiant
Glance on me rested.
Foreign seemed all until now;
Friendless I, and forsaken;
I counted strange and unknown
Each and all that came near.
But thee now I thoroughly knew,
When these eyes fell on thee.
Wert thou mine own one,
What my heart long had held,
What was hid.
Clear as the day dawned on my eyes,
The dulcet refrain fell on my ear,
When in winter's frosty wildness a friend first
    awaited me.

(*She hangs in rapture on his neck and looks close into
    his face.*)

SIEGMUND (*with transport*).
    O wondrous vision!
    Woman divine!

SIEGLINDA (*close to his eyes*).
    Oh, let me closer embracing clasp thee,
    That I may look on the angel light,
    Which from thine eyes in ardour breaks,
    And so sweetly swayeth my sense!

SIEGMUND.
    The spring's fair moon streams on thy head,
    Hanging a wreath o'er thy rippling hair;
    What 'twas bewitched me well now I feel;
    I feast in fervour mine eyes.

(SIEGLINDA *pushes back his locks from his brow and
    gazes at him astonished.*)
    How fair and broad thy open brow!
    The varying veins in thy temples I trace!
    I tremble with emotion resting entranced!
    A memory masters my spirit;
    Though but to-day met we first
    I deem not strange thy face!

SIEGMUND. Such fairy dreams my fancy filled;
    Thy form I viewed in visions of bliss!

SIEGLINDA. In streams my semblance I often saw;
    Again it floateth before me
    As erst from river it rose,
    Mildly 'tis mirrored in thee!

SIEGMUND.
    Thine was the picture to me that appeared.

SIEGLINDA (*suddenly turning away her gaze*).
    O hush! let me unhindered listen;
    Thy voice seems to peal out from the past.
    Yet hold! more lately I heard it.

Mit heil'gem Grau'n,
Als dein Blick zuerst mir erblühte.—
Fremdes nur sah ich von je,
Freundlos war mir das Nahe;
Als hätt' ich nie es gekannt
War was immer mir kam.
Doch dich kannt' ich
Deutlich und klar:
Als mein Auge dich sah,
Warst du mein Eigen:
Was im Busen ich barg,
Was ich bin,
Hell wie der Tag
Taucht er mir auf,
Wie tönender Schall
Schlug's an mein Ohr,
Als in frostig öder Fremde
Zuerst den Freund ich ersah.

(*Sie hängt sich entzückt an seinen Hals, und blickt ihm
    nahe in's Gesicht.*)

SIEGMUND (*mit Hingerissenheit*).
    O süsseste Wonne!
    Seligstes Weib!

SIEGLINDE (*dicht an seinen Augen*).
    Lass in Nähe
    Zu dir mich neigen,
    Dass deutlich ich schaue
    Den hehren Schein,
    Der dir aus Augen
    Und Antlitz bricht,
    Und so süss die Sinne mir zwingt!

SIEGMUND. Im Lenzesmond
    Leuchtest du hell;
    Hehr umwebt dich
    Das Wellenhaar;
    Was mich berückt
    Errath' ich nun leicht—
    Denn wonnig weidet mein Blick.

SIEGLINDE (*schlägt ihm die Locken von der Stirn zurück
    und betrachtet ihn staunend*).
    Wie dir die Stirn
    So offen steht,
    In den Schläfen der Adern
    Geäst sich schlingt;
    Mir zagt's vor der Wonne,
    Die mich entzückt—
    Ein Wunder will mich gemahnen:
    Den heut' zuerst ich erschaut,
    Mein Auge sah dich schon!

SIEGMUND. Ein Minnetraum
    Gemahnt auch mich:
    In heissem Sehnen
    Sah ich dich schon!

SIEGLINDE. Im Bach erblickt' ich
    Mein eigen Bild—
    Und jetzt gewahr' ich es wieder:
    Wie einst dem Teich es enttaucht,
    Bietest mein Bild mir nun du!

SIEGMUND. Du bist das Bild—
    Das ich in mir barg.

SIEGLINDE (*den Blick schnell abwendend*).
    O still! las mich
    Der Stimme lauschen:—
    Mich dünkt, ihren Klang
    Hört' ich als Kind——
    Doch nein! ich hörte sie neulich.

(*In emotion.*)
When through the waving woods
The echo came of my own.

SIEGMUND. O loveliest lute to which now I listen!

SIEGLINDA (*again gazing into his eyes*).
Well I know the light that lurks in thine eyes
So once the strange guest greeting bestowed,
When he solemnly soothed my grief.
In that glance my father I felt;
His name had I fain uttered fondly!
(*Pausing.*)
"Woeful" calls thee the world?

SIEGMUND. Ne'er call me so, since thou art mine!
I rest now in highest rapture!

SIEGLINDA.
Now "Joyful" may be justly thy title?

SIEGMUND.
Name me thyself as thou judgest my nature
I'll take my title from thee!

SIEGLINDA. Then truly was Wolfing thy father?

SIEGMUND. A wolf he to fearful foxes!
But he whose eye on thee is beaming,
As flashes, O fair one! thine own, avers!
Voisung his name.

SIEGLINDA (*transported*).
Was Volsung thy father,
Art thou too a Volsung?
Struck he for thee yon sword in the stem?
So let me then name thee,
As I do love thee:
Siegmund,—so be thou called!

SIEGMUND (*springs up*).
Siegmund hight—I—and Siegmund am I!
A witness this sword,
Unwav'ring I seize it!
Volsung assured me in sorest need
Mine it should be:
I'll make it so!
Holy affection, highest need,
Passionate longing, pressingest need,
Brightly flame in my breast,
Drive to deeds and death;
Needful! Needful!
I name so this sword.
Needful! Needful!
Notable steel,
Prove me thy sharpness,
Show me thy point!
Leap forth from thy scabbard to me!

(*With a mighty effort* SIEGMUND *plucks the sword from the tree and shows it to the astonished and enraptured* SIEGLINDA.)
Siegmund, the Volsung stands revealed!
For Bridegift he brings thee this sword;
And fearless woes a wife sweet and fair!

(*Aufgeregt*)
Als meiner Stimme Schall
Mir wiederhallte der Wald.

SIEGMUND. O lieblichste Laute,
Denen ich lausche!

SIEGLINDE (*ihm wieder in die Augen spähend*).
Deines Auges Gluth
Erglänzte mir schon:—
So blickte der Greis
Grüssend auf mich,
Als der Traurigen Trost er gab.
An dem kühnen Blick
Erkannt' ihn sein Kind—
Schon wollt' ich beim Namen ihn nennen—
(*Sie hält inne und fährt dann leise fort.*)
Wehwalt heiss'st du fürwahr?

SIEGMUND. Nicht heiss' ich so
Seit du mich liebst:
Nun walt' ich der hehrsten Wonnen!

SIEGLINDE. Und Friedmund darfst du
Froh dich nicht nennen?

SIEGMUND. Heisse mich du
Wie du liebst dass ich heisse:
Den Namen nehm' ich von dir!

SIEGLINDE. Doch manntest du Wolfe den Vater?

SIEGMUND. Ein Wolf war er feigen Füchsen!
Doch dem so stolz
Strahlte das Auge,
Wie, Herrliche, hehr dir es strahlt,
Der war—Wälse genannt.

SIEGLINDE (*ausser sich*).
War Wälse dein Vater,
Und bist du ein Wälsung,
Stiess er für dich
Sein Schwert in den Stamm?—
So lass mich dich heissen
Wie ich dich liebe:
Siegmund—
So nenn' ich dich.

SIEGMUND (*springt auf und fasst den Schwertgriff*).
Siegmund heiss' ich,
Und Siegmund bin ich:
Bezeug' es dies Schwert,
Das zaglos ich halte!
Wälse verhiess mir,
In höchster Noth
Sollt' ich es finden:
Ich fass' es nun!
Heiligster Minne
Höchste Noth,
Sehnender Liebe
Zehrende Noth,
Brennt mir hell in der Brust,
Drängt zu That und Tod:
Nothung! Nothung!—
So nenn' ich dich Schwert—
Nothung! Nothung!
Neidlicher Stahl!
Zeig' deiner Schärfe
Schneidenden Zahn:
Heraus aus der Scheide zu mir!

(*Er zieht mir einem gewaltigen Zuck das Schwert aus dem Stamme, und zeigt es der von Staunen und Entzücken erfassten* SIEGLINDE.)
Siegmund den Wälsung
Siehst du, Weib!
Als Brautgabe
Bringt er dies Schwert:
So freit er sich
Die seligste Frau:

From foeman's house he flies with his bride,
Far from hence follow his steps,
Forth in the smiling softness of spring;
There shields thee Needful, my sword,
And Siegmund but lives in thy love.

SIEGLINDA (*in wild intoxication tears herself away and
                stands before him*).
(*He has clasped her to lead her away with him.*)
Art thou Siegmund, standing beside me?
Sieglinda am I. For thee I've sighed:
Thou'st won thy sister, I tell thee,
As well as the sword.
        (*She throws herself upon his breast.*)
SIEGMUND.   Bride and sister be to thy brother,
So blest may the Volsungs abound.
(*He draws her to him in a frenzy of passion.*)
        (*The curtain falls quickly.*)

ACT II

SCENE I

(*A wild and rocky pass. At the back a gorge slopes
downwards from a high peak, the ground sinking
again gradually from this towards the foreground.*)
(*WOTAN, in warlike array, with spear and shield; be-
fore him stands BRYNHILDE as a Valkyrie, also fully
armed.*)
WOTAN.   Make ready thy steed, stalwartest maid,
Battle's brawl breaketh out soon:
Brynhilde, spur to the fray,
The Volsung favour and aid!
Hunding vainly sues;
Void are his hopes, in Valhall'
He has no place;
So headlong in haste, hie to the field.

BRYNHILDE (*springing from rock to rock up the height
                to the right and shouting*).
Ho-yo-to-ho! ho-yo-to-ho!
Heiaha! heiaha!
Hoyotoho! hoyotoho—heiaha—heiaha!
Hoyotoho—hoyotoho—hoyotoho—hoyotoho!
Heiaha—ha! Hoyotoho!
(*She pauses on a high peak of rock, looks down into the
valley at back, and calls back to WOTAN.*)
But listen, father! look to thyself! thou wilt
        soon
Suffer a storm. Watchful Fricka, thy wife,
Arriveth in her ram-impelled car.
Ha! how she grasps her golden scourge!
The foolish beasts are fainting with fear.
Wheels rattling and rolling whirl her here to the
        war,
In such disputes no part would I take,
Though I am happy when heroes fight;
Take heed that thou find not defeat,
For lightly I leave thee to fate!

Dem Feindeshaus
Entführt er dich so.
Fern von hier
Folge ihm nun,
Fort in des Lenzes
Lachendes Haus:
Dort schützt dich Nothung das Schwert,
Wenn Siegmund dir liebend erlag!
(*Er erfasst sie um sie mit sich fortzuziehen.*)
SIEGLINDE.   Bist du Siegmund,
Den ich hier sehe—
Sieglinde bin ich,
Die dich ersehnt:
Die eig'ne Schwester
Gewann'st du zueins mit dem Schwert!
(*Sie wirft sich ihm an die Brust.*)
SIEGMUND.   Braut und Schwester
Bist du dem Bruder—
So blühe denn Wälsungen-Blut!
(*Er zieht sie mit wüthender Gluth an sich; sie sinkt mit
einem Schrei an seine Brust.*)

ZWEITER AKT

ERSTE SCENE

(*Wildes Felsengebirg.*)
(WOTAN, *kriegerisch gewaffnet, und mit dem Speer; vor
ihm* BRÜNNHILDE, *als Walküre, ebenfalls in voller
Waffenrüstung.*)

WOTAN.   Nun zäume dein Ross,
Reisige Maid!
Bald entbrennt
Brünstiger Streit:
Brünnhilde stürme zum Kampf,
Dem Wälsung kiese sie Sieg!
Hunding wähle sich
Wem er gehört:
Nach Walhall taugt er mir nicht.
Drum rüstig und rasch
Reite zur Wal!

BRÜNNHILDE (*jauchzend von Fels zu Fels die Höhe
rechts hinaufspringend*).
Hojotoho! Hojotoho!
Heiaha! Heiaha!
Hahei! Hahei! Heiaho!

(*Auf einer hohen Felsspitze hält sie an, blickt in die
hintere Schlucht hinab, und ruft zu* WOTAN *zurück.*)
Dir rath' ich, Vater,
Rüste dich selbst:
Harten Sturm
Sollst du besteh'n:
Fricka naht, deine Frau,
Im Wagen mit dem Widdergespann.
Hei! wie die gold'ne
Geissel sie schwingt;
Die armen Thiere
Aechzen vor Angst;
Wild rasseln die Räder:
Zornig fährt sie zum Zank!
In solchem Strausse
Streit' ich nicht gern,
Lieb' ich auch muthiger
Männer Schlacht:
Drum sieh', wie den Sturm du bestehst;
Ich Lustige lass dich im Stich!—

Hoyotoho! hoyotoho! heiaha!
Heiaha! hoyotoho! hoyotoho!
Heiaha! Heiaha! hoyotoho!
Hoyotoho! hoyotoho! hoyotoho!
Hoyotoho! heiaha—ha—(*dying away*).
(BRYNHILDE *disappears behind the mountain heights at side.*)
(FRICKA *comes up from the ravine in a car drawn by two rams; on reaching the ridge she stops suddenly and dismounts; she advances hastily towards* WOTAN *in the foreground.*)

WOTAN (*aside, observing* FRICKA's *approach*).
The old complaint, the old annoys!
No peace! needs I must meet them!

FRICKA (*as she advances, moderates her pace and places herself before* WOTAN *with dignity*).
Where thou wand'rest in these wilds thy very wife to avoid,
Even here I seek thee out,
That right to me thou may'st render.

WOTAN. Thy harass, Fricka, fain would I hear.

FRICKA. Well I know Hunding's need;
His voice for vengeance is raised;
The queen of Wedlock hath weighed his guest,
And wends straight to stir thee to scourge
Those rash recreants twain who wrought a husband this wrong.

WOTAN. What hath wrought of wrong this pair.
Allured by Spring into love?
Their passion's fury that frenzied them:
Who mastereth Love by law?

FRICKA. How foolish and fond are thy words!
As knewest thou not, forsooth, that for the blessed conjugal bond,
Discarded thus, I'm complaining!

WOTAN. Unholy are to me oaths which oust Love from his own;
And prithee expect not from me that my might should hold
Where thine own is helpless;
For when strong spirits are rampant,
I rouse them ever to strife.

FRICKA. Deemest thou righteous adult'rous love?
Extend then thy license and treat as holy
The troth plighted between a twin-born, licentious pair!
My heart and my sense with horror consume;
Bridal embrace of sister and brother!
When was it allowed, that love should
Exist 'twixt relations?

WOTAN. Now know it at last!
Accept the shame which hath shaped itself,
Though ne'er seen was the like till to-day,
That these are true lovers learn well from me:
To milder views then revert!

Hojotoho! Hojotoho!
Heiaha! Heiaha!
Hahei! Hahei! Hojohei!

(*Sie verschwindet, während aus der Schlucht herauf*
(FRICKA *je näher sie kommt, mässigt sie den Schritt, auf dem Joch anlangt: dort steigt sie schnell ab und schreitet auf* WOTAN *zu.*)

WOTAN (*indem er sie kommen sieht*).
Der alte Sturm!
Die alte Müh'!
Doch Stand muss ich ihr halten.

(FRICKA *je näher sie kommt, mässigt sie den Schritt, und stellt sich mit wirds vor* WOTAN *hin*).
Wo in Bergen du dich birgst
Der Gattin Blick zu entgeh'n,
Einsam hier such' ich dich auf,
Dass Hilfe du mir verhiessest.

WOTAN. Was Fricka kümmert
Künde sie frei.

FRICKA. Ich vernahm Hunding's Noth,
Um Rache rief er mich an:
Der Ehe Hüterin hörte ihn,
Verhiess streng
Zu strafen die That
Des frech frevelnden Paar's,
Das kühn den Gatten gekränkt.

WOTAN. Was so Schlimmes
Schuf das Paar,
Das liebend einte der Lenz?
Der Minne Zauber
Entzückte sie:
Wer büsst mir der Minne Macht.

FRICKA. Wie thörig und taub du dich stellst,
Als wüsstest fürwahr du nicht,
Dass um der Ehe
Heiligen Eid,
Den hart gekränkten, ich klage!

WOTAN. Unheilig
Acht' ich den Eid,
Der Unliebende eint;
Und mir wahrlich
Muthe nicht zu,
Dass mit Zwang ich halte
Was dir nicht haftet:
Denn wo kühn Kräfte sich regen,
Da rath' ich offen zum Krieg.

FRICKA. Achtest du rühmlich
Der Ehe Bruch,
So prahle nun weiter
Und preis' es heilig,
Dass Blutschande entblüht
Dem Bund eines Zwillingspaar's.
Mir schaudert das Herz,
Es schwindelt mein Hirn:
Bräutlich umfing
Die Schwester der Bruder.
Wann—ward es erlebt'
Dass lieblich Geschwister sich liebten.

WOTAN. Heut'—hast du's erlebt:
Erfahre so
Was von selbst sich fügt,
Sei zuvor auch nie es gescheh'n.
Dass jene sich lieben,
Leuchtet dir hell:
Drum höre redlichen Rath!

If aught of bliss follows e'er on thy blessing,
Then smile in lenient love on Siegmund and
    Sieglinda's troth.

FRICKA (*bursting out into violent wrath*).
Dawn on us the end of the Æsir eternal,
When thou these vagrant Volsungs begatest!
I speak straightly—touched is thy soul?
Esteem'st thou no more thy mightiest subjects?
Disdained are all things that once were exalted,
Unloosened the ties thine own wisdom estab-
    lished,
Lightly leav'st thou thy hold of heav'n,
That unheld and haughty may flourish
This froward and sinful pair,
Thine unfaithfulness' sensual fruit!
Oh, why mourn thus o'er virtue and vows
Thou hast vilely slighted thyself?
Thine own true wife full oft hast thou wronged;
Never a depth and never a height
Where thy heart longed not lustful to rove,
While of change there lacked not to charm
    thee;
Thou gav'st no heed to my grief,
Sorrow I bore when thou didst forsake me,
Leading to battle the barb'rous maidens,
Of shameless mother born to thy blood;
For avoided so was thy wife, that this Valkyrie
    set,
With Brynhilde herself who obeys thy voice,
At my potent disposal were placed.
But now that another name takes thy fancy,
Thou wand'rest wolf-like thro' woodlands as
    "Volsung."
Now basely deigning to such degradation,
A pair of pitiful mortals to get thee,
With these whelps of a wolf
Thou wishest to humble thy wife!
O finish thy work! Fill up the cup!
Let them trample me in their triumph!

WOTAN.
Thou tak'st me not when I would teach thee.
Nor may'st thou conceive a case
Demanded never till now.
Statutes only canst thou understand;
But my full thoughts must heed
The things hitherto strange.
One thing mark thou!
We need a man who finds not heaven's protec-
    tion,
Who flieth from heavenly ties;
Then a change he alone may effect,
Which, though fain to the Godhead,
The gods to effect are refused.

Soll süsse Lust
Deinen Segen dir lohnen,
So seg'ne, lachend der Liebe,
Siegmund's und Sieglinde's Bund!

FRICKA (*in höchste Entrüstung ausbrechend*).
So istes denn aus
Mit den ewigen Göttern,
Seit du die wilden
Wälsungen zeugtest?
Heraus sagt' ich's—
Traf ich den Sinn?
Nichts gilt dir der Hehren
Heilige Sippe;
Hin wirfst du Alles,
Was einst du geachtet;
Zerreissest die Bande,
Die selbst du gebunden:
Lösest lachend
Des Himmels Haft—
Dass nach Lust und Laune nur walte
Dies frevelnde Zwillingspaar,
Deiner Untreue zuchtlose Frucht!
O, was klag' ich
Um Ehe und Eid!
Du zuerst, du selbst sie versehrt!
Die treue Gattin
Trogest du stets:
Wo eine Tiefe,
Wo eine Höhe,
Dahin lugte lüstern dein Blick,
Wie des Wechsels Lust du gewännst',
Und höhnend kränktest mein Herz!
Trauernden Sinnes
Musst' ich's ertragen,
Zog'st du zur Schlacht
Mit den schlimmen Mädchen,
Die wilder Minne
Bund dir gebar;
Denn dein Weib noch scheutest du so,
Dass der Walküren Schaar,
Und Brünnhilde selbst,
Deines Wunsches Braut,
In Gehorsam der Herrin du gab'st.
Doch jetzt, da dir neue
Namen gefielen,
Als "Wälse" wölfisch
Im Walde du schweiftest;
Jetzt, da zu niedrigster
Schmach du dich neigtest,
Gemeiner Menschen
Ein Paar zu erzeugen:
Jetzt dem Wurfe der Wölfin
Wirfst du zu Füssen dein Weib!—
So führ' es denn aus,
Fülle das Mass:
Die Betrog'ne lass auch zertreten!

WOTAN.   Nichts lerntest du,
Wollt' ich dich lehren,
Was nie du erkennen kannst,
Eh' nicht ertagte die That.
Stets Gewohntes
Nur magst du versteh'n;
Doch was noch nie sich traf,
Darnach trachtet mein Sinn!—
Eines höre!
Noth thut ein Held,
Der, ledig göttlichen Schutzes,
Sich löse vom Göttergesetz:
So nur taugt er
Zu wirken die That,
Die, wie noth sie den Göttern,
Dem Gott doch zu wirken verwehrt.

FRICKA. With lying spirit wouldst thou delude me.
What help divine could heroes e'er shape us,
Which to the gods themselves were gainsaid,
By whose grace alone they may speed?

WOTAN.
And their courage fearless count'st thou for
naught?

FRICKA. Who breathes this courage in them?
Who brightens the face of the faint?
Beneath thy shield strong do they seem,
By thee bestirr'd they strive in the fight,
Thou prickest these mortals whom thus to me
thou applaud'st:
Again with falsehood wouldst thou befool me,
With new contrivance seeking to trick me.
But for this Volsung in vain dost thou plead;
Through him I strike at thee,
For through thee only he dares.

WOTAN (with emotion).
In sorrow drooping deserted he lived:
My shield sheltered him ne'er.

FRICKA. Then shelter now withhold!
Have back the sword upon him bestowed.

WOTAN. The sword?

FRICKA.
Yes, the sword, the marvellous, magical sword,
Which the God his son hath giv'n.

WOTAN. Siegmund has won it himself in his need.

(With suppressed tremor.)
(From this point WOTAN's whole demeanor-expresses an
ever increasing deep distress.)

FRICKA (continuing violently).
Thou'st shaped him the need and the notable
sword,
Dar'st thou deny it, when night and day I have
followed thy feet?
For him struckest thou the sword in the stem;
Thou didst guard for him the glorious blade;
Be this gainsaid not, that but by thy subtle
schemings
She found the prize.

(WOTAN starts up with a gesture of wrath.)
(FRICKA, still more earnestly, on seeing the impression
she has made on WOTAN.)
With bondsmen no sovereign does battle;
The monarch scourges his minion.
Against thine my strength properly strives,
But Siegmund I punish as slave.

(WOTAN makes another angry gesture and then sinks
down, feeling his impotence.)

FRICKA. Mit tiefem Sinne
Willst du mich täuschen!
Was Hehres sollten
Helden je wirken,
Das ihren Göttern wäre verwehrt,
Deren Gunst in ihnen nur wirkt?

WOTAN. Ihres eigenen Muthes
Achtest du nicht?

FRICKA. Wer hauchte Menschen ihn ein?
Wer hellte den Blöden den Blick?
In deinem Schutz
Scheinen sie stark,
Durch deinen Stachel
Streben sie auf:
Du—reizest sie einzig
Die so mir Ew'gen du rühmst.
Mit neuer List
Willst du mich belügen,
Durch neue Ränke
Jetzt mir entrinnen;
Doch diesen Wälsung
Gewinnst du dir nicht:
In ihm treff' ich nur dich,
Denn durch dich trotzt er allein.

WOTAN (ergriffen).
In wilden Leiden
Erwuchs er sich selbst:
Mein Schutz schirmte ihn nie.

FRICKA. So schütz' auch heut' ihn nicht;
Nimm ihm das Schwert,
Das du ihm geschenkt!

WOTAN. Das Schwert?

FRICKA. Ja—das Schwert,
Das zauberstark
Zuckende Schwert,
Das du Gott dem Sohne gab'st.

WOTAN. Siegmund gewann es sich
Selbst in der Noth.
(Mit unterdrücktem Beben.)
(WOTAN drückt in seiner ganzen Haltung von hier an
einer immer wachsenden unheimlichen, tiefen Unmuth
aus.)
FRICKA (heftig fortfahrend.)
Du schuf'st ihm die Noth;
Wie das neidliche Schwert:
Willst du mich täuschen,
Die Tag und Nacht
Auf den Fersen dir folgte?
Für ihn stiessest du
Das Schwert in den Stamm;
Du verhiessest ihm
Die hehre Wehr:
Willst du es leugnen,
Dass nur deine List
Ihn lockte wo er es fänd'?
(WOTAN fährt mit einer grimmigen Geberde auf.)

(FRICKA, immer sicherer, da sie den Eindruck gewahrt,
den sie auf WOTAN hervor gebracht hat.)
Mit Unfrieden
Streitet kein Edler,
Den Frevler straft nur der Freie:
Wider deine Kraft
Führt ich wohl Krieg;
Doch Siegmund verfiel mir als Knecht.
(WOTAN wendet sich unmuthig ab.)

This slave thou holdest wholly and closely,
To his caprice must thy consort submit?
Shall he this shame and infamy shape me,
To varlets a scoff, to villains a scorn?
Sure ne'er my husband could suffer so heinous
A slight to his queen!

WOTAN. What requir'st thou?

FRICKA. Cast off the Volsung!

WOTAN. I give him his vent.

FRICKA. But thou favour him not,
When to fight calls th' avenger's voice.

WOTAN. I'll favour him not.

FRICKA. Look on me fairly; lie not to me;
The Valkyrie vow to recall!

WOTAN. The war-maiden works untaught.

FRICKA. Not so! 'tis thy will she accomplishes now,
Recall her from Siegmund's side!

WOTAN. I cannot defeat him: he found my sword.

FRICKA. Remove then its magic,
Or bid it to break!
Shieldless send him to fight!

(BRYNHILDE's *call is heard from the heights*.)
Heiaha! Heiaha! Hoyotoho!

FRICKA. Here wendeth thy warlike maid;
Comes her call to my ears.

BRYNHILDE (*on perceiving* FRICKA, *she suddenly ceases
and leads her horse quietly and silently down the
path during the following, then she hides it in a cave*).
Heiaha! Heiaha! Hoyoho! toyotoyo—ha!

WOTAN. I made her for Siegmund to mount.

FRICKA. Thy eternal spouse's high reputation
To-day she holdeth dear!
If laughed at in scorn,
Unscreened and forlorn,
Gone were the glory of gods.
Let to-day my dues with daring and wit
Be won by the mettlesome maid.
This Volsung, fey to my honour,
Confirm as my victim by oath.

WOTAN (*throwing himself down upon a rocky seat in
terrible dejection*).
Take my oath!

(FRICKA *strides towards the back, there she meets
BRYNHILDE and pauses a moment before her.*)

FRICKA (*to* BRYNHILDE).
Wotan doth wait for thee;
Let him inform thee how the lot is to fall.

Der dir als Herren
Hörig und eigen
Gehorchen soll ihm
Dein ew'ges Gemahl?
Soll mich in Schmach
Der Niedrigste schmäh'n,
Dem Frechen zum Sporn,
Dem Freien zum Spott?
Das kann mein Gatte nicht wollen,
Die Göttin entweiht es nicht so!

WOTAN. Was verlangst du?

FRICKA. Lass' von dem Wälsung!

WOTAN. Er geh' seines Weg's.

FRICKA. Doch du—schütze ihn nicht,
Wenn zur Schlacht der Rächer ihn ruft.

WOTAN. Ich—schütze ihn nicht.

FRICKA. Sieh' mir in's Auge,
Sinne nicht Trug!
Die Walküre wend' auch von ihm!

WOTAN. Die Walküre walte frei.

FRICKA. Nicht doch! Deinen Willen
Vollbringt sie allein:
Verbiete ihr Siegmund's Sieg!

WOTAN. Ich kan ihn nicht fällen:
Er fand mein Schwert!

FRICKA. Entzieh' dem den Zauber,
Zerknick' es dem Knecht:
Schutzlos schau' ihn der Feind!

(*Sie vernimmt von der Höhe her den jauchzenden Wal-
kürenruf* BRÜNNHILDE's: *diese erscheint dann selbst
mit ihrem Ross auf dem Felspfade rechts.*)
Dort kommt deine kühne Maid:
Jauchzend jagt sie daher.

WOTAN. Ich rief sie für Siegmund zu Ross.

FRICKA. Deiner ew'gen Gattin
Heilige Ehre
Schirme heut' ihr Schild!
Von Menschen verlacht,
Verlustig der Macht,
Gingen wir Götter zu Grund,
Würde heut' nicht hehr
Und herrlich mein Recht
Gerächt von der muthigen Maid.—
Der Wälsung fällt meiner Ehre:—
Empfah' ich von Wotan den Eid?

WOTAN (*in furchtbarem Unmuth und innerem Grimm
auf einen Felsensitz sich werfend*).
Nimm den Eid!

(*Als* BRÜNNHILDE *von der Höhe aus* FRICKA *gewahrte,
brach sie schnell ihren Gesang ab, und hat nun ihr
Ross am Zügel den Felsweg herabgeleitet; sie birgt
dieses jetzt in einer Höhle, als* FRICKA, *zu ihrem
Wagen sich zurückwendend, an ihr vorüberschreitet.*)

FRICKA (*zu* BRÜNNHILDE).
Heervater
Harret dein:
Lass' ihn dir künden,
Wie er das Loos gekies't!

(She drives away.)
(Brynhilde, *surprised, advances with anxious looks towards* Wotan, *who, leaning back on his rocky seat, is absorbed in gloomy brooding.*)

(Sie besteigt den Wagen und fährt schnell davon.)
(Brünnhilde *tritt mit verwunderter und besorgter Miene vor* Wotan, *der, auf dem Feldsitz zurückgelehnt, das Haupt auf die Hand gestützt, in finstercs Brüten versunken ist.*)

SCENE II

Brünnhilde. Sure luckless was the strife;
    Fricka laughs at the fiat.
    Father, what must thy child fulfill thee?
    Sad and downcast thou seemest!

Wotan. My own the fetters fast'ning me!
    I, less free than the earth-born!

Brünnhilde.
    I saw thee thus ne'er; what gnaws at thy heart?

Wotan. O, greatest of shame!
    O, shunless disgrace!
    God's distress! God's distress!
    Endless regret! Infinite grief!
    The saddest am I among all men!

Brünnhilde (*alarmed, drops her spear and helmet and sinks down at his feet with anxious affection*).
    Father! Father! Teil me; what ails thee?
    See how trembles with terror thy child!
    Oh, trust in me, thy daughter true!
    Lo, Brünnhilde beggeth!

(She lays her head and hands confidingly and anxiously on his knee and breast. Wotan *gazes into her eyes for a long while, then strokes her hair with unconscious tenderness, as if awaking from a deep reverie; he at last begins in a low voice:)*
Wotan. If it were uttered
    I should lay bare ev'ry secret hold of my heart.

Brünnhilde (*whispering*).
    To Wotan's will thou speakest;
    Tell me then what thou wilt.
    What am I when I'm away from thee?

Wotan (*softly*).
    What lies in my breast unrelated,
    It must remain unspoken forever;
    Myself I talk with, telling to thee.

    (With choked and suppressed voice.)
    When youthful love's illusions
    Had fled, then lusted my soul for sway;
    Impelled by wildest wishes for pow'r,
    I won to me the world.
    Scarce witting ill, I stooped to deception;
    Covenants ordered that stretched to crime:
    Loki allured me with lying,
    Then faithlessly he fled;
    And yet, love I would fain not relinquish;

ZWEITE SCENE

Brünnhilde. Schlimm, fürcht' ich,
    Schloss der Streit,
    Lachte Fricka dem Loose!—
    Vater, was soll
    Dein Kind erfahren?
    Trübe scheinst du und traurig!

Wotan. In eig'ner Fessel
    Fing ich mich:—
    Ich unfreiester Aller!

Brünnhilde. So sah ich dich nie!
    Was nagt dir das Herz?

Wotan. O heilige Schmach!
    O schmählicher Harm!
    Götternoth!
    Endloser Grimm!
    Ewiger Gram!
    Der Traurigste bin ich von Allen!

Brünnhilde (*wirft erschrocken Schild, Speer und Helm von sich, und lässt sich mit besorgter Zutraulichkeit zu* Wotan's *Füssen nieder*).
    Vater! Vater!
    Sage, was ist dir?
    Wie erschreck'st du mit Sorge dein Kind!
    Vertrau mir:
    Ich bin dir treu;
    Sieh', Brünnhilde bittet!
(Sie legt traulich und ängstlich Haupt und Hände ihm auf Knie und Schooss.)
Wotan (*blickt ihr sehr lange in's Auge, und streichelt ihr dann die Locken: wie aus tiefem Sinnen zu sich kommend, beginnt er endlich mit sehr leiser Stimme*).
    Lass' ich's verlauten,
    Lös' ich dann nicht
    Meines Willens haltenden Haft?

Brünnhilde (*ihm eben so leise erwidernd*).
    Zu Wotan's Willen sprichst du,
    Sagst du mir was du willst:
    Wer—bin ich,
    Wär' ich dein Wille nicht?

Wotan (*leise*).
    Was Keinem in Worten ich künde,
    Unausgesprochen
    Bleib' es ewig:
    Mit mir nur rath' ich,
    Red'ich zu dir.———
(Mit noch gedämpfterer, schauerlicher Stimme während er Brünnhilden *in das Auge blickt.)*
    Als junger Liebe
    Lust mir verblich,
    Verlangte nach Macht mein Muth:
    Von jäher Wünsche
    Wüthen gejagt,
    Gewann ich mir die Welt.
    Unwissend trugvoll
    Uebt' ich Untreue,
    Band durch Verträge,
    Was Unheil barg:
    Listig verlockte mich Loge,
    Der schweifend nun verschwand.
    Von der Liebe doch
    Mocht' ich nicht lassen;

Through all fame I longed for affection.
In night's abode the baleful Nibelung,
Alberic, broke from its bonds:
He cursed at love's passion, and won by that
    curse
The Rhine nymph's glittering gold,
And mastered measureless might.
The ring which he shaped ravished by cun-
    ning,
But ne'er I rendered it to the Rhine;
It was the handsel of Valhalla,
The burg that giants had built me,
From which now all kingdoms I bend.
That able witch who all things wist,
Erda, most wise and wondrous of women,
Read me ill of the ring,
Warned me of awfullest ending.
Then this ending I longed more to learn of,
But silent the seer took leave.
So departed my peace of mind,
And wisdom I strove to possess;
To the depths of earth diving in my search,
By love I won the witch to my purpose.
Mastered her potent might,
That to me she ope'd her mind,
Sooth sayings plainly she spoke,
In payment bearing my pledge;
The world's wonder of women bore thee,
Brünnhilde, to me.
With eight sisters wert thou b ought up,
In these Valkyries' valiant virt ie
Viewed I a vent from impend ng doom.
A dolorous end to the Æsir,
That foes might find us stron g for the strife.
Heroes I bade ye select me
The bravest of hearts we he.d in bondage,
Those mortals whom in their might
We had checked,
Who by guileful agreemen t's
Glamour and baseness obediently
Served us truly and blindly;
These should ye bestir to stormiest striving
Ev'ry force guiding to grimmest fight,
That flocks of fearless heroes might
Hail me in Valhall's hall.

In der Macht gehrt' ich nach Minne:
    Den Nacht gebar,
    Der bange Nibelung.
Alberich brach ihren Bund
    Er fluchte der Liebe,
    Und gewann durch den Fluch
Des Rheines glänzendes Gold
Und mit ihm masslose Macht.
    Den Ring, den er schuf,
    Entriss ich ihm listig:
    Doch nicht dem Rhein
    Gab ich ihn zurück;
    Mit ihm bezahlt' ich
    Walhall's Zinnen,
Der Burg, die Riesen mir bauten,
Aus der ich der Welt nun gebot.
    Die Alles weiss,
    Was einstens war,
    Erda, die weihlich
    Weiseste Wala,
Rieth mir ab von dem Ring,
Warnte vor ewigem Ende.
    Von dem Ende wollt' ich
    Mehr noch wissen;
Doch schweigend entschwand mir das Weib.
Da verlor ich den leichten Muth;
Zu wissen begehrt' es den Gott:
    In den Schooss der Welt
    Schwang ich mich hinab,
    Mit Liebes-Zauber
    Zwang ich die Wala,
Stört' ihres Wissens Stolz,
Dass sie nun Rede mir stand.
Kunde empfing ich von ihr:
Von mir doch barg sie ein Pfand:
Der Welt weisestes Weib
Gebar mir, Brünnhilde, dich.
    Mit acht Schwestern
    Zog ich dich auf:
    Durch euch Walküren
    Wollt' ich wenden,
    Was mir die Wala
    Zu fürchten schuf—
Ein schmähliches Ende der Ew'gen.
    Dass stark zum Streit
    Uns fände der Feind,
Hiess ich euch Helden mir schaffen:
    Die herrisch wir sonst
    In Gesetzen hielten,
    Die Männer, denen
    Den Muth wir gewehrt,
    Die durch trüber Verträge
    Trügende Bande
    Zu blinden Gehorsam,
    Wir uns gebunden—
    Die solltet zu Sturm
    Und Streit ihr nun stacheln,
    Ihre Kraft reizen zu rauhem Krieg,
Dass kühner Kämpfer Schaaren
Ich sammle in Walhall's Saal.

BRÜNNHILDE.
    And thy hall mightily filled we:
    Many a man have I brought;
    Whence comes thy depression?
    We never have paused.

WOTAN. Another's ache: earnestly weigh
    What more the witch hath forewarned!
    Through Alberic's host threatens our ending:
    Still nourishing wrath, rages the Nibelung;

BRÜNNHILDE.
    Deinen Saal füllten wir weidlich;
    Viele schon führt' ich dir zu.
    Was macht dir nun Sorge,
    Da nie wir gesäumt?

WOTAN. Ein Andres ist's:
    Achte es wohl,
    Wess' mich die Wala gewarnt!—
    Durch Alberich's Heer
    Droht uns das Ende:
    In neidischem Grimm
    Grollt mir der Nibelung;

I shrink not, though, now from his nation of
    shadows
By my heroes sheltered and safe.
But if e'er the wretch the ring should recover,
Our high Valhalla were lost then:
He who love surrendered,
He alone evil ends by the ring can wreck,
And to all of us unending disgrace.
My heroes' might were ravished from me,
My friends themselves were turned into foes,
Whom he would force to fight against me.
So I set to myself to keep the ring from his
    clutches.
The craftsman huge, to whom as a hire the
Accursed gold my compact gave—
Fafnir holdeth the hoard,
To gain which his brother he felled.
From him must the ring be wrested,
Although for wage 'twas awarded,
But my treaty with him restrains me from
    harming;
Nerveless and weak 'gainst him is my might.
These are the chains which gall and chafe me;
I, who by treaty have reigned,
To my treaties now become slave.
But one may compass what I must leave:
A hero helped by none of our number,
Who finds no guide or friend in the gods,
Unawares, under no stress, from out his need,
By his own design works out the deed
Which I would have done,
Of which my tongue ne'er told,
Though ever first in my thoughts!
He, who 'gainst every god,
Fights yet for me,
This friendliest foe, how find him indeed?
How shall I affect one whom ne'er I shielded,
Who in his defiance is faithful to me?
How master another, who, not mine own,
From out his will for my ends shall work?
O, goldly distress!
Grievous reproach!
Abhorrent to my heart have I found
Each hazard wild I have worked for!
Another end I have sighed for,
That other I seek in vain;
Unswayed must a free man assist me;
Near me are nothing but slaves.

BRÜNNHILDE.
    But the Volsung, Siegmund, works by himself.

Doch scheu' ich nun nicht
Seine nächtlichen Schaaren—
Meine Helden schützen mir Sieg.
  Nur wenn je den Ring
  Zurück er gewänne—
Dann wäre Walhall verloren:
  Der der Liebe fluchte,
  Er allein Nützte neidisch
  Des Ringes Runen
  Zu aller Edlen
  Endloser Schmach;
  Der Helden Muth
  Entwendet er mir;
  Die Kühnen selber
  Zwäng' er zum Kampf,
  Mit ihrer Kraft
  Bekriegte er mich.
Sorgend sann ich nun selbst
Den Ring dem Feind zu entreissen:
  Der Riesen einer,
  Denen ich einst
  Mit verfluchtem Gold
  Den Fleiss vergalt,
Fafner hütet den Ort,
Um den er den Bruder gefällt.
Ihm müsst' ich den Reif entringen,
Den selbst als Zoll ich ihm zahlte:
  Doch mit dem ich vertrug,
  Ihn darf ich nicht treffen;
  Machtlos vor ihm
  Erläge mein Muth.
  Das sind die Bande,
  Die mich binden:
Der durch Verträge ich Herr,
Den Verträgen bin ich nun Knecht.
  Nur Einer dürfte
  Was ich nicht darf:
  Ein Held, dem helfend
  Nie ich mich neigte;
  Der fremd dem Gotte
  Frei seiner Gunst,
  Unbewusst,
  Ohne Geheiss,
  Aus eig'ner Noth
  Mit der eig'nen Wehr
  Schüfe die That,
  Die ich scheuen muss.
Die nie mein Rath ihm rieth,
Wünscht sie auch einzig mein Wunsch!—
  Der entgegen dem Gott
  Für mich föchte,
  Den freundlichen Feind,
  Wie fänd' ich ihn?
  Wie schüf ich den Freien,
  Den nie ich schirmte,
  Der in eig'nem Trotze
  Der Trauteste mir?
  Wie macht' ich den And'ren,
  Der nicht mehr ich,
  Und aus sich wirkte.
  Was ich nur will?—
  O göttliche Schmach!
  O schmähliche Noth!
  Zum Ekel find' ich
  Ewig nur mich
  In Allem was ich erwirke!
  Das And're, das ich ersehne,
  Das And're erseh' ich nie;
  Denn selbst muss der Freie sich schaffen—
  Knechte erknet' ich mir nur!

BRÜNNHILDE. Doch der Wälsung, Siegmund?
  Wirkt er nicht selbst?

WOTAN. Wildly roving with him thro' woodlands,
　　　　'Gainst ev'ry godly rede roused I ever his hate,
　　　　'Gainst ev'ry godly rancour shields him
　　　　Now only the sword,
　　　　That, as a grace, a God has bestowed.
　　　　How to myself my craft was deceptive!
　　　　So swiftly hath Fricka found out the lie;
　　　　She looked me through and thrust on me shame:
　　　　I perforce must shape to her fiat.

BRÜNNHILDE.
　　　　The victory from Siegmund thou'lt snatch?

WOTAN. I have wrested Alberic's Ring,
　　　　Grasped the coveted gold!
　　　　The curse I incurred
　　　　Doth cling to me yet:
　　　　What I love best I must relinquish,
　　　　Slay him I hold most sacred;
　　　　Trusting belief foully betray;
　　　　Glory and fame fade from my sight!
　　　　Heavenly splendour, smiling disgrace!
　　　　Be laid in ruins all I have reared;
　　　　Over is my work;
　　　　But one thing waits me now:
　　　　The Ending—the Ending!
　　　　And for that ending looks Alberic!
　　　　Now I measure the meaning mute
　　　　Of what the witch spake in wisdom:
　　　　"When that Love's defiant foe
　　　　Grimly getteth a son.
　　　　The sway of gods full soon shall end."
　　　　The Nibelung dwarf I now understand
　　　　To have won to him a woman,
　　　　By gold gaining his hopes.
　　　　The love-scorner well can work such wonders,
　　　　But he I long for fondly—the free one—doth
　　　　　lack to me yet.
　　　　　　　　(Fiercely.)
　　　　Then now take my blessing,
　　　　Nibelung babe!
　　　　What thus I fling from me hold as thy fortune:
　　　　Valhalla's sumptuous hal's
　　　　Shall sate thy unhallowed desires!

BRÜNNHILDE.
　　　　O speak, father! what should I perform?

WOTAN (bitterly).
　　　　Fight duly for Fricka;
　　　　Champion her virgin vows!

WOTAN. Wild durchschweift' ich
　　　　Mit ihm die Wälder;
　　　　Gegen der Götter Rath
　　　　Reizte kühn ich ihn auf—
　　　　Gegen der Götter Rache
　　　　Schütz ihn nun eitnzig das Schwert,
　　　　Das eines Gottes
　　　　Gunst ihm beschied—
　　　　Wie wollt' ich listig
　　　　Selbst mich belügen?
　　　　So leicht entfrug mir
　　　　Ja Fricka den Trug!
　　　　Zu tiefster Scham
　　　　Durchschaute sie mich:
　　　　Ihrem Willen muss ich gewähren!

BRÜNNHILDE.
　　　　So nimmst du von Siegmund den Sieg?

WOTAN. Ich berührte Alberich's Ring—
　　　　Gierig hielt ich das Gold!
　　　　Der Fluch, den ich floh,
　　　　Nicht flieht er nun mich:—
　　　　Was ich liebe, muss ich verlassen,
　　　　Morden, was je ich minne,
　　　　Trügend verrathen
　　　　Wer mir vertraut!—
　　　　Fahre denn hin,
　　　　Herrische Pracht,
　　　　Göttlichen Prunkes
　　　　Prahlende Schmach!
　　　　Zusammen breche
　　　　Was ich gebaut!
　　　　Auf geb' ich mein Werk,
　　　　Eines nur will ich noch,
　　　　Das Ende — —
　　　　Das Ende!—
　　　　　　(Er hält sinnend ein.)
　　　　Und für das Ende
　　　　Sorgt Alberich!—
　　　　Jetzt versteh' ich
　　　　Den stummen Sinn
　　　　Des wilden Wortes der Wala:—
　　　　"Wenn der Diebe finst'rer Feind
　　　　Zürnend zeugt einen Sohn,
　　　　Der Seligen Ende
　　　　Säumt dann nicht!"—
　　　　Vom Nibelung jüngst
　　　　Vernahm ich die Mähr',
　　　　Dass ein Weib der Zwerg bewältigt,
　　　　Dess' Gunst Gold ihm erzwang.
　　　　Des Hasses Frucht
　　　　Hegt eine Frau;
　　　　Des Neides Kraft
　　　　Kreiss't ihr im Schooss:
　　　　Das Wunder gelang
　　　　Dem Liebelosen:
　　　　Doch der in Liebe ich frei'te,
　　　　Den Freien erlang' ich mir nie!—
　　　　　　(Grimmig.)
　　　　So nimm meinen Seger
　　　　Nibelungen-Sohn!
　　　　Was tief mich ekelt,
　　　　Dir geb' ich's zum Erbe,
　　　　Der Gottheit nichtigen Glanz;
　　　　Zernage sie gierig dein Neid?

BRÜNNHILDE. O sag', künde!
　　　　Was soll nun dein Kind?

WOTAN (bitter).
　　　　Fromm streite für Fricka,
　　　　Hüte ihr Ehe und Eide!

What she commands is my bidding too;
How fruitless is my volition,
Since a free man ne'er I may light on,
For Fricka's vassal victory shape!

BRÜNNHILDE.
    Woe! retract, I entreat, thy word!
    Thou lov'st Siegmund: for this love
    I wot well, should I o'erwatch him.

WOTAN. Vanquish Siegmund surely;
    To Hunding the victory assign!
    Heed thyself well and hold thyself strong;
    Bring all thy bravery duly to bear:
    A sooth-sword swings Siegmund;
    Scarcely canst thou o'ercome.

BRÜNNHILDE.
    One thou hast bade me ever to bless,
    Whose unwonted firmness awakes
    Thy affection,
    From his side moves me never thy mandate
    constrained.

WOTAN. Ha, froward child! floutest thou me?
    Siegmund falleth!
    Brünnhilde must work out my will.

(He rushes away and disappears in the Mountains.)

BRÜNNHILDE *stands a long time terrified and bewildered.)*
    So spake my sire nee'r before,
    Though stirred and shaken oft by strife.

*(She bends down sadly and takes up her weapons, which
    she again dons.)*
    How waxes my weapon's weight!
    When I love the fight how lightly they lift!
    I fear to seek such an evil fray!
    Ha! my hero!
    In grievous strait thy defender must falsely
    forsake thee!

(She turns slowly away.)
(BRÜNNHILDE, *looking down into the valley, perceives
SIEGMUND and SIEGLINDA; she watches their approach
awhile; then she turns into the cave to her horse, so
that she disappears from view of the audience.)*

SCENE III

(SIEGMUND and SIEGLINDA appear.)

SIEGMUND. Pause here awhile; take some repose!

SIEGLINDA. Farther! farther!
    (He clasps her with gentle force.)

SIEGMUND.
    No farther now! O linger, sweet one, at last
    From loving embraces brok'st thou away,
    With sudden haste sallying forth;

Was sie erkor,
Das kiese auch ich.
Was frommte mir eig'ner Wille?
Einen Freien kann ich nicht wollen—
Für Fricka's Knechte
Kämpfe du nun!

BRÜNNHILDE. Weh! nimm reuig
    Zurück das Wort!
    Du liebst Siegmund:
    Dir zu Lieb'—
    Ich weiss es—schütz' ich den Wälsung.

WOTAN. Fällen sollst du Siegmund,
    Für Hunding erfechten den Sieg!
    Hüte dich wohl
    Und halte dich stark;
    All deiner Kühnheit
    Entbiete im Kampf:
    Ein Sieg-Schwert
    Schwingt Siegmund—
    Schwerlich fällt er dir feig.

BRÜNNHILDE. Den du zu lieben
    Stets mich gelehrt,
    Der in hehrer Tugend
    Dem Herzen dir theuer—
    Gegen ihn zwingt mich nimmer
    Dein zwiespältig Wort.

WOTAN. Ha, Freche, du!
    Frevelst du mir?
    Besorge was ich befahl:—
    Siegmund falle!—
    Dies sei der Walküre Werk.
*(Er stürmt fort, und verschwindet schnell links im
    Gebirge.)*
    (BRÜNNHILDE steht lange betäubt und erschrocken.)
    So—sah ich
    Siegvater nie,
    Erzürnt' ihn sonst auch ein Zank!
*(Sie neigt sich betrübt und nimmt ihre Waffen auf, mit
    denen sie sich wieder rüstet.)*
    Schwer wiegt mir
    Der Waffen Wucht:—
    Wenn nach Lust ich focht,
    Wie waren sie leicht!—
    Zu böser Schlacht
    Schleich' ich heut' sobang!—
    Weh', mein Wälsung!
    Im höchsten Leid
    Muss dich treulos die Treue verlassen!
(Sie wendet sich langsam dem Hintergrunde zu.)
*(Sie wendet sich nach hinten und gewahrt SIEGMUND
    und SIEGLINDE, wie sie aus der Schlucht heraufstei-
    gen: sie betrachtet die Nahenden einen Augenblick,
    und wendet sich dann in die Höhle zu ihrem Ross,
    so dass sie dem Zuschauer gänzlich verschwindet.)*

DRITTE SCENE

(SIEGMUND und SIEGLINDE treten auf.)

SIEGMUND. Raste nun hier:
    Gönne dir Ruh'!

SIEGLINDE. Weiter! weiter!

SIEGMUND *(umfasst sie mit sanfter Gewalt)*.
    Nicht weiter nun!
    Verweile, süssestes Weib!—
    Aus Wonne-Entzücken
    Zucktest du auf,
    Mit jäher Hast
    Jagtest du fort;

Scarce found I thy way of flight,
Through wood and field, over fell and steep,
Speechless, silent, speeding along;
My voice lured thee in vain.
    (*She stares wildly before her.*)
Onward no more:
Open thy lips!
End me this silent awe!
See, thy brother holdeth his bride:
Siegmund's guarding thee safe!

(*She gazes with growing rapture into his eyes; then
mournfully throws her arms around his neck. Alarmed,
she starts up in sudden terror.*)

SIEGLINDA. Away! away! flee from the wanton!
Unholily fold thee my arms.
Disgraced, polluted, life ebbeth
Forth. Shun the foul one,
Fly from her face! Her dust tempests
Shall drive, who, soiled, gave
Herself to thine arms!
When in thy loving embrace,
With hallowed delight I brimmed,
My only husband was he
Who all my heart had awaked.
From this heavenly rapture's
Glorious radiance which all
My soul and senses o'erwhelmed,
Shudder and trembling and shamefullest terror
Grimly o'ertook the traitorous woman,
Who to a bridegroom belonged,
Whom she obeyed without love!
Leave the accurs'd one; let her escape!
I rest degraded, bereft of grace!
The pearl of manhood must I depart from;
For ne'er may I link me with one so noble.
Shame I bring to my brother;
Shape my rescuer's ruin!

SIEGMUND. Who erst shaped for thee shame
Shall bring me his felon blood!
So fly me no farther; halt for the
Foeman; here shall I defeat him.
When "Needful" at his heart shall
Gnaw, then revenge hast thou attained!

SIEGLINDA. Hark! the horn calls;
Hearest thou not?
Nearer still waxes the sound;
From wood and vale voices arise!
Hunding hath wakened from heavy sleep!
Sleuth hounds and hunters bids he assemble
Roused by his hail howls the rabble;
All crying to heaven for the breaking
Of conjugal bonds!

(*She stares before her as if demented.*)

Where art thou, Siegmund?
Still art thou near?

Kaum folgt' ich der wilden Flucht:
Durch Wald und Flur,
Ueber Fels und Stein,
Sprachlos schweigend
Sprangst du dahin.
Zur Rast hielt dich kein Ruf.
    (*Sie starrt wild vor sich hin.*)
Ruhe nun aus:
Rede zu mir!
Ende des Schweigens Angst!
Sieh, dein Bruder
Hält seine Braut:
Siegmund ist dir Gesell!
(*Er hat sie unvermerkt nach dem Steinsitze geleitet.*)
(*Blickt* SIEGMUND *mit wachsendem Entzücken in die
Augen; dann umschlingt sie leidenschaftlich seinen
Hals. Dann fährt sie mit jähem Schreck auf.*)

SIEGLINDE. Hinweg! hinweg! flieh die Entweihte!
Unheilig umfängt dich ihr Arm,
Entehrt, geschändet, schwand
Dieser Leib; flieh' die Leiche, lasse
Sie los; der Wind mag sie
Verwehn', die ehrlos dem Edlen
Sich gab!
Da er sie liebend umfing,
Da seligste Lust sie fand,
Da ganz sie minnte der Mann,
Der ganz ihr Minne geweckt,
Von der süssesten Wonne
Heiligster Weihe, die ganz
Ihr Sinn und Seele durch
Drang, Grauen und
Schauder ob grässlichster
Schande musste mit Schreck
Die Schmähliche fassen,
Die je dem Manne
Gehorcht, der ohne Minne
Sie hielt!
    Lass' die Verfluchte,
Lass' sie dich flieh'n!
Verworfen bin ich, der Würde
Bar; dir reinstem Manne
Muss ich entrinnen, dir herrlichem
Darf ich nimmer gehören:
Schande bring ich dem Bruder,
Schmach dem freienden Freund!

SIEGMUND. Was je Schande dir schuf, das büsst
Nun des Frevlers Blut! Drum
Fliehe nicht weiter; harre des
Feindes; hier soll er mir fallen:
Wenn Nothung ihm das Herz
Zernagt, Rache dann hast du erreicht!

SIEGLINDE. Horch! die Hörner!
Hörst du den Ruf?—
Ringsher tönt
Wüthend Getös';
Aus Wald und Gau
Gellt es herauf.
Hunding erwachte
Von hartem Schlaf;
Sippen und Hunde
Ruft er zusammen:
Muthig gehetzt
Heult die Meute,
Wild bellt sie zum Himmel
Um der Ehe gebrochenen Eid!
(*Sie lacht wie wahnsinnig auf:—dann schrickt sie
ängstlich zusammen.*)
Wo bist du, Siegmund?
Seh' ich dich noch?

Bridegroom beloved, lordliest brother!
Let thy starlike eyes yet but stream light upon
   me:
Wend not away from a woeful woman's kiss:
Hark! oh hark! that is Hunding's horn!
And his men approach in mighty force.
No sword that pack of hounds can scare:
Cast it forth, Siegmund!
Siegmund, where art thou?
Ha, there!
I see thee now! sinister sight!
Dogs are mouthing and gnashing for meat:
No heed they take of thy hero glance;
In thy feet they bury their furious teeth!
Thou fall'st; to splinters doth spring thy sword;
The ash-tree splits both branch and stem!
Brother! my brother! Siegmund, ha!
(*She sinks fainting in* SIEGMUND's *arms.*)

Brünstig geliebter
Leuchtender Bruder!
Deines Auges Stern
Lass noch einmal mir strahlen:
Wehre dem Kuss
Des verworf'nen Weibes nicht!—
Horch! o horch!
Das ist Hunding's Horn!
Seine Meute naht
Mit mächtiger Wehr.
Kein Schwert frommt
Vor der Hunde Schwall:—
Wirf es fort, Siegmund!—
Siegmund—wo bist du?—
Ha dort—ich sehe dich—
Schrecklich Gesicht!—
Rüden fletschen
Die Zähne nach Fleisch;
Sie achten nicht
Deines edlen Blick's;
Bei den Füssen packt dich
Das feste Gebiss—
Du fällst—
In Stücken zerstaucht das Schwert:—
Die Esche stürzt—
Es bricht der Stamm!—
Bruder! mein Bruder!
Siegmund—ha!—
(*Sie sinkt ohnmächtig in* SIEGMUND's *Arme.*)

SIEGMUND. Sister! Belov'd one!
(*He listens to her breathing and satisfies himself that
she still lives. He allows her to sink down with himself, so that when he is in a sitting posture her head
rests upon his lap. In this position both remain until
the end of the following scene.*)
(*Long silence, during which* SIEGMUND *bends in tender
care over* SIEGLINDA, *and imprints a long kiss upon
her brow.*)

SIEGMUND. Schwester! Geliebte!
(*Er lauscht ihrem Athem, und überzeugt sich, dass sie
noch lebe. Er lässt sie an sich herabgleiten, so dass
sie, als er sich selbst zum Sitze niederlässt, mit ihrem
Haupt auf seinem Schoss zu ruhen kommt. Langes
Schweigen, während dessen* SIEGMUND *mit zärtlicher
Sorge über* SIEGLINDE *sich hinneigt.*)

SCENE IV

(BRÜNNHILDE, *leading her horse by the bridle, enters
from the cave and advances slowly and solemnly to
the front; she pauses and observes* SIEGMUND *from
a distance. She again slowly advances; she bears her
spear and shield in one hand, rests the other on her
horse's neck, and thus gazes earnestly at* SIEGMUND.)

VIERTE SCENE

BRÜNNHILDE. Siegmund—
vornen geschritten, und hält nun, SIEGMUND *zur Seite,
in geringer Entfernung von ihm. Sie trägt Schild und
Speer in der einen Hand, lehnt sich mit der andren
an den Hals des Rosses, und betrachtet so, in ernstem
Schweigen, eine Zeit lang* SIEGMUND.)

BRÜNNHILDE. Siegmund! See'st thou me?
   I come to call thee hence!
   (SIEGMUND *turns his eyes upon her.*)

BRÜNNHILDE. Siegmund—
   Sieh' auf mich!
   Ich—bin's,
   Der gald du folgst.

SIEGMUND. Declare thy name,
   Who dost stand so beauteous and stern.

SIEGMUND (*richtet den Blick zu ihr auf*).
   Wer bist du, sag',
   Die so schön und ernst mir erscheint?

BRÜNNHILDE. But fated men my form may look on;
   To whom 'tis shown full shortly must lose his
      life,
   On the war-plain alone the warrior sees me:
   Well then he weens, away must he with me!

BRÜNNHILDE. Nur Todgeweihten
   Taugt mein Anblick:
   Wer mich erschaut,
   Der scheidet vom Lebens-Licht.
   Auf der Walstatt allein
   Erschein' ich Edlen:
   Wer mich gewahrt,
   Zur Wal kor ich ihn mir.

(SIERMUND *gazes long with firmness and enquiry into
her eyes, then thoughtfully droops his head, and
presently turns to her resolutely again.*)

(SIEGMUND *blickt ihr lange in das Auge, senkt dann
sinnend das Haupt, und wendet sich endlich mit
feierlichem Ernste wieder zu ihr.*)

SIEGMUND.
   But firstly tell—Whither tak'st thou the hero?

SIEGMUND. Der dir nun folgt.
   Wohin führst du den Helden?

BRÜNNHILDE. To Wotan, for such is his will;
    Hence with me:
    Awaits Valhall' for thee.

SIEGMUND. In Valhall's bright vault
    Shall I find him alone?

BRÜNNHILDE.
    The fallen heroes' hallowed band shall flock,
    With hand and heart hailing thy sight.

SIEGMUND. Fareth in Valhall'
    Volsung, my noble father?

BRÜNNHILDE.
    Thy father findest thou, Volsung, there!

SIEGMUND. Shall I in Valhall' welcome a wife?

BRÜNNHILDE. Wish maidens wait on thee there;
    Wotan's daughter faithfully deals thee the
    drink!

SIEGMUND. High art thou and holy;
    I ween thou art Wotan's child:
    Yet tell me one thing, and truly!
    Attendeth her brother my bride
    And my sister? Shall there
    Siegmund Sieglinda find?

BRÜNNHILDE. Lone on earth must she still linger:
    Siegmund will see Sieglind' no more.

(SIEGMUND *bends softly over* SIEGLINDA, *kisses her gently
on the brow, and again turns tranquilly to* BRÜNN-
HILDE.)
SIEGMUND.
    Then greet for me Valhall', greet for me Wotan!
    Greet for me Volsung and all the heroes;
    Greet, too, the highborn wishing maidens.
    To them I'll follow thee not.

BRÜNNHILDE.
    Thou'st looked on the Valkyrie's life-quelling
    face:
    With her must thou away!

SIEGMUND. Where Sieglinda bides, in bliss or bane,
    There will Siegmund too sojourn:
    Not yet hath thy sight weakened my spirit;
    'Twill stir me never away!

BRÜNNHILDE.
    While life doth last, dauntless thou art:
    'Gainst Death 'twere foolish to fight;
    And to announce him now I come.

SIEGMUND. What hero is he by whom I fall?

BRÜNNHILDE. Hunding fells thee in strife.

SIEGMUND.
    Bring stronger menace than Hunding's struggle
    Swoopest thou here seeking thy prey,
    Choose my foeman for spoil;
    I purpose to slay him in fight!

BRÜNNHILDE. Thou, Volsung, hark to my voice:
    Thou art to death consigned.

SIEGMUND. See'st thou this sword?
    By one 'twas sent who'll shape success,
    I defy thee, firm in its strength!

BRÜNNHILDE. Zu Walvater,
    Der dich gewährt,
    Führ' ich dich:
    Nach Walhall folgst du mir.

SIEGMUND. In Walhall's Saal
    Walvater find' ich allein?

BRÜNNHILDE. Gefall'ner Helden
    Hehre Schaar
    Umfängt dich hold
    Mit hoch-heiligem Gruss.

SIEGMUND. Fänd' ich in Walhall
    Wälse, den eig'nen Vater?

BRÜNNHILDE. Den Vater findet
    Der Wälsung dort.

SIEGMUND. Grüsst mich in Walhall
    Froh eine Frau?

BRÜNNHILDE. Wunschmädchen
    Walten dort hehr:
    Wotan's Tochter
    Reicht dir traulich den **Trank.**

SIEGMUND. Hehr bist du:
    Heilig gewahr' ich
    Das Wotanskind:
    Doch Eines sag' mir, du Ew'ge!
    Begleitet den Bruder
    Die bräutliche Schwester?
    Umfängt Siegmund
    Sieglinde dort?

BRÜNNHILDE. Erdenluft
    Muss sie noch athmen:
    Sieglinde
    Sieht Siegmund dort nicht!

(SIEGMUND *neigt sich sanft über* SIEGLINDE, *küsst sie
leise auf die Stirn und wendet sich ruhig wieder zu*
BRÜNNHILDE.)
SIEGMUND. So grüsse mir Walhall,
    Grüsse mir Wotan,
    Grüsse mir Walse
    Und alle Helden—
    Grüss' auch die holden
    Wunschesmädchen:
    Zu ihnen folg' ich dir nicht.

BRÜNNHILDE.
    Du sahest der Walküre Sehrenden Blick:
    Mit ihr musst du nun zieh'n!

SIEGMUND. Wo Sieglinde lebt in Lust und Leid,
    Da will Siegmund auch säumen:
    Noch mechte dein Blick nicht mich
    Erbleichen, vom Bleiben zwingt er mich nie!

BRÜNNHILDE.
    So lang du lebst, zwäng' dich wohl nichts:
    Doch zwingt dich Thoren den Tod:—
    Ihn dir zu künden kam ich her.

SIEGMUND. Wo wäre der Held dem heut' ich fiel?

BRÜNNHILDE. Hunding fällt dich im Streit.

SIEGMUND.
    Mit Stärk'rem drohe als Hunding's Streichen!
    Luerst du hier lüstern auf Wal.
    Jenen kiese zum Fang;
    Ich denk'ihn zu fällen im Kampf!

BRÜNNHILDE. Dir, Wälsung höre mich Wohl:
    Dir ward das Loos gekies't.

SIEGMUND. Kennst du dies Schwert?
    Der mir es schuf,
    Beschied mir Sieg:
    Deinem Drohen trotz' ich mit ihm!

BRÜNNHILDE (*with emphasis*).
    He who bestowed it shapes thee now death:
    He withdraws the charm from the sword.

SIEGMUND. Soft! Disturb not my slumbering love!

(*In an outburst of pain he bends tenderly over* SIEG-
            LINDA.)
    Woe! Woe ! Loveliest one!
    Thou saddest and faithfullest sister!
    'Gainst thy peace wantonly warreth the world:
    And I, on whom only thou lean'st,
    For whom thou hast ev'rything left,
    I may not shield nor seek thee a shelter.
    But fail thee, alas! in the fight?
    O shame on him who bestowed the sword,
    To shape me such shifting shield!
    If I must perish, I'll pass not to Valhall;
    Hella hold me her prey!
        (*He bends low over* SIEGLINDA.)

BRÜNNHILDE.
    Celestial splendours then spurn'st thou so
      lightly?
    Is this woman thy only wealth,
    Who, faint and ailing, feebly reclines in thy
      arms?
    Naught else deemest thou dear?

SIEGMUND (*looking bitterly up at her*).
    So youthful and fair thy features appear,
    But how cold and hard accounts thee my heart!
    Canst thou not help me, then hie thee away,
    Thou harsh, unwav'ring maid!
    If moved not to pity by my despair,
    Then freely feast on my woe:
    Let my pangs flatter thy pitiless heart,
    But of Valhall's paltry virtues,
    Prythee, vaunt not to me!

BRÜNNHILDE.
    I see the distress of thy heart at this strait,
    I feel for the hardy hero's illhap!
    Siegmund, to me trust thy wife;
    I'll shield her much as I may!

SIEGMUND.
    No other than I shall in life defend my beloved:
    If fate will it so,
    I will slay her slumbering first!

BRÜNNHILDE. Volsung! Reckless man!
    Hark to my rede:
    Assign me thy bride!

SIEGMUND (*drawing the sword*).
    This sword, which a traitor for true man de-
      signed; this sword,
    Which falsely in fight shall betray,
    Falls it to slaughter my foe,
    More fatal 'twill prove to my friend!
        (*He holds the sword over* SIERLINDA.)

BRÜNNHILDE (*sehr stark betont*).
    Der dir es schuf, beschied dir jetzt Tod;
    Seine Tugend nimmt er dem Schwert.

SIEGMUND. Schweig' und schrecke
    Die Schlummernde nicht!
(*Er beugt sich mit hervorbrechendem Schmerze zärtlich
           über* SIEGLINDE.)
    Weh! Weh! süssestes Weib!
    Du traurigste aller Getreuen!
    Gegen dich wüthet in Waffen die Welt:
    Und ich, dem du einzig vertraut,
    Für den du ihr einzig
    Getrotzt; mit meinem Schutz
    Nicht soll ich dich schirmen,
    Die Kühne verrathen im Kampf?
    O Schande ihm, der das Schwert
    Mir schuf, beschied er mir Schimpf
    Für Sieg! Muss ich denn fallen,
    Nicht fahr' ich nach Walhall:
    Hella halte mich fest!
        (*Er neigt sich tief zu* SIEGLINDE.)

BRÜNNHILDE (*erschüttert*).
    So wenig achtest du
    Ewige Wonne?
    Alles wär' dir
    Das arme Weib,
    Das müd' und harmvoll
    Matt auf dem Schoosse dir hängt?
    Nichts sonst hieltest du hehr?

SIEGMUND (*bitter zu ihr aufblickend*).
    So jung und schön
    Erschimmerst du mir:
    Doch wie kalt und hart
    Kennt dich mein Herz!—
    Kannst du nur höhnen,
    So hebe dich fort.
    Du arge, fühllose Maid!
    Doch musst du dich weiden
    An meinem Weh',
    Mein Leid letze dich denn;
    Meine Noth labe
    Dein neidvolles Herz:—
    Nur von Walhall's spröden Wonnen
    Sprich du wahrlich mir nicht!

BRÜNNHILDE. Ich sehe die Noth,
    Die das Herz dir nagt;
    Ich fühle des Helden
    Heiligen Harm——
    Siegmund, befiehl mir dein Weib:
    Mein Schutz umfange sie fest!

SIEGMUND. Kein andrer als ich
    Soll die Reine lebend berühren;
    Verfiel ich dem Tod,
    Die Betäubte tödt' ich zuvor!

BRÜNNHILDE. Wälsung! Rasender!
    Hör' meinen Rath:
    Befiehl mir dein Weib
    Um des Pfandes willen,
    Das wonnig von dir es empfing!

SIEGMUND (*sein Schwert ziehend*).
    Dies Schwert—
    Das dem Treuen ein Trugvoller schuf;
    Dies Schwert—
    Das feig vor dem Feind mich verräth:—
    Frommt es nicht gegen den Feind,
    So Fromm' es denn wider den Freund!—
        (*Das Schwert auf* SIEGLINDE *zückend*.)

Two lives here lie before thee;
Take them, Needful, terrible steel!
Take them with one fell stroke!

BRÜNNHILDE (*in a violent gust of sympathy*).
Forbear, Volsung! List to my voice!
Sieglinda shall live still,
And Siegmund leave not her side:
'Tis so ordained.
The death lot cancelled; thou, Siegmund,
Doubt not, safely shalt speed!
Mark'st thou that horn?
Now hold thyself manned;
Take up thy sword and swing it with trust;
'Twill surely prevail,
For the Valkyrie tenders aid.
Farewell, Siegmund, stalwartest man!
At the combat seek for my coming!

(*She rushes away and disappears with her horse in a
ravine: SIEGMUND looks after her with joy and relief.
The stage has grown dark: heavy storm clouds descend
gradually, veiling the cliffs, ravine and high peak
completely from view.*)

SCENE V

SIEGMUND (*bending over SIEGLINDA*).
Slumber's charm has soothed my fair one's
Wild and frenzied woe.
Did the Valkyrie's heedful care
This quiet divine o'er her cast?
Would not the tidings of war
Her womanly terrors awake?
Lifeless seems she, but yet she lives;
Her dread is allayed by loveliest dreams;
So slumber in peace till the strife is o'er
And peril shall be past.

(*He lays her softly on the rocky seat and kisses her
brow as a farewell. Hearing HUNDING's horn-call he
starts up resolutely.*)
The coming foe firmly must stand;
What he demands mine to give:
Needful deals him his due!
(*He hastens to meet HUNDING; on reaching the mountain top disappears in the black clouds, from which
breaks a flash of lightning.*)

SIEGLINDA (*dreaming*).
Hies not my father yet home?
Still he hunts with the boy in the woods.
Mother! Mother! I tremble much!
These strangers' stern looks terribly strike me!
Turbid vapours towering vast
Fiery tongues are twining around; they burn
   the house!

Zwei Leben
Lachen dir hier:—
Nimm sie, Nothung,
Neidischer Stahl!
Nimm sie mit einem Streich!

BRÜNNHILDE (*im heftigsten Sturme des Mitgefühls*).
Halt' ein, Wälsung!
Höre mein Wort!
Sieglinde lebe—
Und Siegmund lebe mit ihr!
Beschlossen ist's;
Das Schlachtlos wend' ich:
Dir, Siegmund,
Schaff' ich Segen und Sieg!
Du hörst den Ruf?
Nun rüste dich, Held!
Traue dem Schwert
Und schwing' es getrost:
Treu hält dir die Wehr,
Wie die Walküre treu dich schützt!—
Leb' wohl, Siegmund,
Seligster Held!
Auf der Walstatt grüss' ich dich wieder!

(*Sie stürmt fort, und verschwindet mit dem Rosse. SIEG-
MUND blickt ihr freudig nach. Die Bühne hat sich
allmälig verfinstert; schwere Gewitterwolken senken
sich auf den Hintergrund herab.—Von allen Seiten
lassen sich aus der Ferne Rufe von Heerhörnern vernehmen, die während des Folgenden allmälig näher
erschallen.*)

FÜNFTE SCENE

SIEGMUND (*über SIEGLINDE sich beugend*).
Zauberfest
Bezähmt ein Schlaf
Der Holden Schmerz und Harm:
Da die Walküre zu mir trat,
Schuf sie ihr den wonnigen Trost?
Sollte die grimmige Wal
Nicht schrecken ein gramvolles Weib?
Leblos scheint sie,
Die dennoch lebt:
Der Traurigen kos't
Ein lächelnder Traum.—
So schlumm're nun fort,
Bis die Schlacht gekämpft,
Und Friede dich erfreu'!

(*Er eilt dem Hintergrunde zu.*)
nach abermaligen Hornrufen, auf.)
Der dort mich ruft,
Rüste dich nun;
Was ihm gebührt,
Biet' ich ihm:
Nothung zahl' ihm den Zoll!
(*Er eilt dem Hintergrunde zu.*)

SIEGLINDE (*träumend*).
Kehrte der Vater nun heim?
Mit dem Knaben noch weilt er im Forst.
Mutter! Mutter!
Mir bangt der Muth:
Nicht freund und friedlich
Scheinen die Fremden!—
Schwarze Dämpfe—
Schwüles Gedünst—
Feurige Lohe
Leckt schon nach uns—
Es brennt das Haus—

O help me, brother!
Siegmund! Siegmund!
(*Violent lightning and thunder awakes* Sieglinda *from her dreams: she gazes around in increasing terror. Nearly the whole stage is veiled in black thunder-clouds.* Hunding's *horn-call sounds close.*)
Siegmund! Ha!

Hunding (*whose voice is heard from the mountain peak*).
Woeful! Woeful!
Stand to the strife!
Say, with my hounds must I hunt thee?

Siegmund (*whose voice is heard from off in the ravine*).
Where hid'st thou that I behold thee not?
Forth, that I may face thee!

Sieglinda (*listening in fearful anxiety*).
Hunding! Siegmund!
Could I but see them!

Hunding. Prepare, thou fugitive foeman!
Fricka fates thee my prey!

Siegmund (*now likewise on the peak*).
Thou weenest me weaponless,
Foolish wight!
Prate not of females,
But fight unsuccoured:
Her minion Fricka forsakes;
For see! From thy house-tree's harbouring stem
I drew undaunted this sword;
Of its sharpness soon shalt thou judge!

(*A flash of lightning lights up the rock with dazzling light.* Hunding *and* Siegmund *are seen in mortal combat.*)

Sieglinda's *voice.*
Stay your hands, ye madmen!
Murder first me!
(*She staggers towards the peak; a flash of lightning breaks over the combatants and suddenly dazzles her so that she reels back to one side blinded. In the glare of light* Brünnhilde *appears soaring over* Siegmund *and protecting him with her sword.*)

Brünnhilde. Fell him, Siegmund!
Firm be thy sword!

(*But just as* Siegmund *aims a deadly stroke at* Hunding, *a ruddy glow shines out from the clouds, in which* Wotan *is seen standing over* Hunding *and holding his spear defensively against* Siegmund.)

Wotan.
Recoil from my spear! Be splintered the sword!

(Brünnhilde *retreats in terror before* Wotan. Siegmund's *sword snaps on the outstretched spear.* Hunding *buries his spear in the unarmed man's breast.*)

(Siegmund *falls dead to the ground.*)

Zu Hülfe, Bruder!
Siegmund! Siegmund!
(*Starke Blitze zucken durch das Gewölk auf; ein furchtbarer Donnerschlag erweckt* Sieglinde: *sie springt jäh auf.*)
Siegmund!—Ha!
(*Sie starrt mit steigender Angst um sich her:—fast die ganze Bühne ist in schwarze Gewitterwolken verhüllt; fortwährender Blitz und Donner. Von allen Seiten dringen immer näher Hornrufe her.*)

Hunding's *Stimme* (*im Hintergrunde vom Bergjoche her.*)
Wehwalt! Wehwalt!
Steh' mir zum Streit,
Sollen dich Hunde nicht halten!

Siegmund's *Stimme* (*von weiter hinten her, aus der Schlucht*).
Wo birgst du dich,
Dass ich vorbei dir schoss?
Steh' dort, dass ich dich stelle!

Sieglinde (*die in furchtbarer Aufregung lauscht*).
Hunding—Siegmund—
Könnt' ich sie sehen!

Hunding's *Stimme.*
Hieher, du frevelnder Freier:
Fricka fälle dich hier!

Siegmund's *Stimme* (*nun ebenfalls auf dem Bergjoche*).
Noch wähnst du mich waffenlos,
Feiger Wicht?
Drohst du mit Frauen,
So ficht nun selber,
Sonnst lässt dich Fricka im Stich!
Denn sieh': deines Hauses
Heimischem Stamm
Entzog ich zaglos das Schwert;
Seine Schneide schmecke du jetzt!

(*Ein Blitz erhellt für einen Augenblick das Bergjoch, auf welchem jetzt* Hunding *und* Siegmund *kämpfend gewahrt werden.*)

Sieglinde. Haltet ein, ihr Männer!
Mordet erst mich!

(*Sie stürzt auf das Bergjoch zu: ein von rechts her über die Kämpfer ausbrechender, heller Schein blendet sie aber plötzlich so heftig, dass sie wie erblindet zur Seite schwankt. In dem Lichte erscheint* Brünnhilde *über* Siegmund *schwebend und diesen mit dem Schilde deckend.*)

Brünnhilde's *Stimme.*
Triff' ihn, Siegmund!
Traue dem Siegesschwert!

(*Als* Siegmund *so eben zu einem tödtlichen Streiche auf* Hunding *ausholt, bricht von links her ein glühend-röthlicher Schein durch das Gewölk aus, in welchem* Wotan *erscheint, über* Hunding *stehend, und seinen Speer* Siegmund *entgegenhaltend.*)

Wotan's *Stimme.* Zurück vor dem Speer!
In Stücken das Schwert!

(Brünnhilde *ist vor* Wotan *mit dem Schilde erschrocken zurückgewichen:* Siegmund's *Schwert verspringt an dem vorgestreckten Speere; dem Unbewehrten stösst* Hunding *sein Schwert in die Brust.*)

(Siegmund *stürzt zu Boden.*)

(SIEGLINDA, *who has heard his death-sigh, sinks down with a cry, as if lifeless. With* SIEGMUND's *fall the glare of light on both sides has faded; dense gloom reigns in the clouds up to the front, through it* BRÜNNHILDE *is seen indistinctly hurrying swiftly towards* SIEGLINDA.)

BRÜNNHILDE. To horse, that I may help thee!
(*She lifts* SIEGLINDA *quickly with her on to her horse, standing by in the defile, and they disappear. At this moment the clouds divide in the middle, and* HUNDING *is clearly visible, drawing his spear from the breast of* SIEGMUND.)

WOTAN (*surrounded by clouds, stands behind, leaning on his spear and painfully gazing on* SIEGMUND's *body*).
> Get hence, knave; kneel before Fricka!
> Tell her how Wotan's spear avenged his spouse's slight. Go! Go!

(*Before the contemptuous wave of his hand* HUNDING *falls dead to the ground.*)

WOTAN (*suddenly bursting into terrible wrath*).
> But Brünnhilde!
> Vengeance shall break on her!
> Fell scourging shall follow her crime,
> If my steed may stay her in flight.

(*He disappears amid thunder and lightning.*)
(*The curtain falls.*)

ACT III
SCENE I

(*On the summit of a rocky mountain. At the right the stage is bordered by a pine wood; at the left is the entrance of a cave, over which the rock rises to its highest. At the back the view is quite open; high and low rocks border a precipice. Occasional clouds, driven by the storm, fly past the mountain summit.*)

(GERHILDA, ORTLINDA, VALTRAUTA *and* SCHWERTLEITA *are ensconced on the peak over the cave; they are all in full armor.*)

GERHILDA (*higher placed than the rest, calls towards the background*).
> Hoyotoho! Hoyotoho! Heiaha! Heiaha!
> Helmwiga, hail! Hie here with thy horse!

HELMWIGA's *voice* (*through a speaking-trumpet*).
> Hoyotoho! Hoyotoho! Hoyotoho!
> Hoyotoho! Heiaha!

(*A flash of lightning breaks through the cloud; a Valkyrie on horseback is visible in it: over her saddle hangs a slain warrior.*)

(SIEGLINDE, *die seinen Todesseufzer gehört, sinkt mit einem Schrei wie leblos zusammen. Mit* SIEGMUND's *Fall ist zugleich von beiden Seiten der glänzende Schein verschwunden; dichte Finsterniss ruht im Gewölk bis nach vorn; in ihm wird* BRÜNNHILDE *undeutlich sichtbar, wie sie in jäher Hast* SIEGLINDEN *sich zugewendet.*)

BRÜNNHILDE. Zu Ross, dass ich dich rette!
(*Sie hebt* SIEGLINDE *schnell zu sich auf ihr, der Seitenschlucht nahe stehendes Ross, und verschwindet sogleich gänzlich mit ihr. Alsbald vertheilt sich das Gewölk in der Mitte, so dass man deutlich* HUNDING *gewahrt, wie er sein Schwert dem gefallenen* SIEGMUND *aus der Brust zieht.*)
(WOTAN, *von Gewölk umgeben, steht hinter ihm auf einem Felsen, an seinen Speer gelehnt, und schmerzlich auf* SIEGMUND's *Leiche blickend.*)

WOTAN (*Nach einem kleinen Schweigen, zu* HUNDING *gewandt*).
> Geh' hin, Knecht!
> Kniee vor Fricka:
> Meld' ihr, dass Wotan's Speer
> Gerächt, was Spott ihr schuf.—
> Geh'!—Geh'!—

(*Vor seinem verächtlichen Handwink sinkt* HUNDING *todt zu Boden.*)

WOTAN (*plötzlich in furchtbarer Wuth auffahrend*).
> Doch Brünnhilde—
> Weh' der Verbrecherin!
> Furchtbar sei
> Die Freche gestraft,
> Erreicht mein Ross ihre Flucht!

(*Er verschwindet mit Blitz und Donner.*)
(*Der Vorhang fällt schnell.*)

DRITTE AKT
ERSTE SCENE

(*Rechts begrenzt ein Tannenwald die Scene. Links der Eingang einer Felshöhle, die einen natürlichen Saal bildet: darüber steigt der Fels zu seiner höchsten Spitze auf. Nach hinten ist die Aussicht gänzlich frei; höhere und niedere Felssteine bilden den Rand vor dem Abhange der—wie anzunehmen ist—nach dem Hintergrunde zu steil hinabführt.— Einzelne Wolkenzüge jagen, vom Sturm getrieben, am Felsensaume vorbei.*)
(*Die namen der acht Walküren, welche—ausser* BRÜNNHILDE—*in dieser Scene auftreten, sind:* GERHILDE, ORTLINDE, WALTRAUTE, SCHWERTLEITE, HELMWIGE, SIEGRUNE, GRIMGERDE, ROSSWEISSE.)

(GERHILDE, ORTLINDE, WALTRAUTE *und* SCHWERTLEITE *haben sich auf der Felsspitze, an und über der Höhle, gelagert; sie sind in voller Waffenrüstung.*)

GERHILDE (*zu höchst gelagert und dem Hintergrunde zugewendet.*)
> Hojotoho! Hojotoho!
> Heiaha! Heiaha!
> Helmwige, hier!
> Hieher dein Ross!

HELMWIGE's *Stimme* (*von aussen*).
> Hojotoho! Hojotoho!

(*In einem vorbeiziehenden Gewölk bricht Blitzesglanz aus; eine Walküre zu Ross wird in ihm sichtbar; über ihrem Sattel hängt ein erschlagener Krieger.*)

ORTLINDA, WALTRAUTA *and* SCHWERTLEITA (*all three hailing the new comer*).
Heiaha! Heiaha!

(*The cloud with the apparition has disappeared behind the trees.*)

ORTLINDA (*calling towards the wood*).
By Ortlinda's filly fasten thy horse:
Gladly my gray will graze near thy brown.

WALTRAUTA. Who hangs at thy saddle?

HELMWIGA (*entering from the wood*).
Sintold, the Hegeling!

SCHWERTLEITA.
Fasten thy brown far from the gray, then,
Ortlinda's mare carries
Wittig the Irming!

GERHILDA (*who has descended somewhat lower*).
As foes I have seen them, Sintold and Wittig.

ORTLINDA (*springs up and runs into the wood*).
Heiaha! Heiaha! Thy mare is mauled by my horse!

GERHILDA, SCHWERTLEITA *and* HELMWIGA (*laughing*).
Ha, ha, ha, ha, ha, ha, ha, ha, ha, ha!

GERHILDA.
The heroes' strife lives still in the horses!

HELMWIGA (*calling back into the wood*).
Hey there, brownie! Break not the concord!

WALTRAUTA (*has taken* GERHILDA's *place on the cliff*).
Hoyotoho! Hoyotoho!
Siegruna, here!
Where stay'st thou so long?

(SIEGRUNA *flies past in the air into the pine wood in the same manner as* HELMWIGA.)

SIEGRUNA (*voice from the right*).
Occupied! Are the others all here?

The Valkyrs.
Hoyotoho! Hoyotoho!
Heiaha! Heiaha!

GRIMGERDA *and* ROSSVEISSA (*from below*).
Hoyotoho! Hoyotoho!
Heiaha! Heiaha!

WALTRAUTA. Grimgerda and Rossveissa!

GERHILDA. Arriving at once.

(*In a train of clouds lit by lightning, which passes from left to right, appear* ROSSVEISSA *and* GRIMGERDA, *also on horseback, each bearing a dead body over her saddle.*)

ORTLINDA, HELMWIGA *and* SIEGRUNA (*have entered from the wood, and now beckon from the rocky peak towards the new comer*).
We greet ye. riders twain:
Rossveis' and Grimgerda!

ORTLINDE, WALTRAUTE *und* SCHWERTLEITE (*der Ankommenden entgegenrufend*).
Heiaha! Heiaha!

(*Die Wolke mit der Erscheinung ist rechts hinter dem Tann verschwunden.*)

ORTLINDE (*in den Tann hineinrufend*).
Zu Ortlinde's Stute
Stell' deinen Hengst:
Mit meiner Grauen
Gras't gern dein Brauner!

WALTRAUTE. Wer hängt dir im Sattel?

HELMWIGE (*aus dem Tann schreitend*).
Sintold der Hegeling!

SCHWERTLEITE. Führ' deinen Braunen
Fort von der Grauen:
Ortlinde's Mähre
Trägt Wittig, den Irming!

GERHILDE (*ist etwas näher herabgestiegen*).
Als Feinde sah ich nur
Sintold und Wittig.

ORTLINDE (*bricht schnell auf, und läuft in den Tann*)
Heiaha! Die Stute
Stösst mir der Hengst!

GERHILDE, SCHWERTLEITE *und* HELMWIGE (*lachend*).
Ha, ha, ha, ha, ha, ha, ha, ha, ha, ha!

GERHILDE. Die Rosse entzweit noch
Der Recken Zwist!

HELMWIGE (*in den Tann zurückrufend*).
Ruhig dort, Brauner!
Brichst du den Frieden?

WALTRAUTE (*hat für* GERHILDE *die Wacht genommen*).
Hojotoho! Hojotoho!
Heiaha! Heiaha!
Siegrune, hier!
Wo säumst du so lang?

(*Wie zuvor* HELMWIGE, *zieht jetzt* SIEGRUNE *im gleichen Aufzuge vorbei, dem Tann zu.*)

SIEGRUNE's *Stimme* (*von rechts*).
Arbeit gab's!
Sind die And'ren schon da?

Die Walküren.
Hojotoho! Hojotoho!
Heiaha! Heiaha!

GRIMGERDE *und* ROSSWEISSE (*von unten*).
Hojotoho! Hojotoho!
Heiaha! Heiaha!

WALTRAUTE. Grimgerd' und Rossweisse!

GERHILDE. Sie reiten zu zwei.

(*In einem blitz-erglänzenden Wolkenzuge, der von unten heraufsteigt und dann hinter dem Tann verschwindet, erscheinen* GRIMGERDE *und* ROSSWEISSE, *jede einen Erschlagenen im Sattel führend.*)

ORTLINDE *ist mit* HELMWIGE *und der soeben angekommenen* SIEGRUNE *aus dem Tann herausgetreten: zu* **drei winken sie von dem hinteren Felssaume hinab.**)

ORTLINDE, HELMWIGE *und* SIEGRUNE.
Gegrüsst, ihr Reissige!
Rossweiss' und Grimgerde!

No. 2.

HOYO-TO-HO!

Ho - yo - to ho!.... Ho - yo - to - ho!.... Hei - a - ha!...... Hei - a - ha!
Ho - jo - to - ho!.... Ho - jo - to - ho!.... Hei - a - ha!...... Hei - a - ha!

Ho - yo - to - ho!...... Ho - yo - to - ho!.... H-i - a - ha!...... Hei - a - ha!
Ho - jo - to - ho!...... Ho - jo - to - ho!.... Hei - a - ha!...... Hei - a - ha!

Ho - yo - to - ho!...... Ho - yo - to - ho!...... Ho - yo - to - ho!.....
Ho - jo - to - ho!...... Ho - jo - to - ho!...... Ho - jo - to - ho!.....

Ho - yo - to - ho!...... Hei - a - ha!......
Ho - jo - to - ho!...... Hei - a - ha!......

The Valkyrs.	*Die andern Walküren alle.*
Hoyotoho! Hoyotoho!	Hojotoho! Hojotoho!
Heiaha! Heiaha!	Heiaha! Heiaha!
GERHILDA.	GERHILDE. In Wald mit den Rossen
Your steeds in the forest let stand and feed!	Zu Weid' und Rast!
ORTLINDA (*calling towards the wood*).	ORTLINDE (*in den Tann rufend*).
Fasten the mares afar from each other,	Führt die Mähren
Till all our heroes' hate be allayed!	Fern von einander,
	Bis uns'rer Helden
	Hass sich gelegt!
HELMWIGA (*while all the rest laugh*).	HELMWIGE (*während die Andern lachen*).
The gray, in sooth,	Der Helden Grimm
Through their feud has suffered!	Schon büsste die Graue!
GRIMGERDA *and* ROSSVEISSA (*entering from the wood*).	GRIMGERDE *und* ROSSWEISSE (*treten aus dem Tann auf*).
Hoyotoho! Hoyotoho!	Hojotoho! Hojotoho!
The Valkyrs.	*Die Walküren.*
Be welcome! Be welcome!	Willkommen! Willkommen!
Be welcome!	
SCHWERTLEITA (*alone*).	SCHWERTLEITE (*allein*).
Went ye wanderers paired?	War't ihr Kühnen zu zwei?
GRIMGERDA. Alone journeyed we;	GRIMGERDE. Getrennt ritten wir,
But lately we met.	Trafen uns heut'.
ROSSVEISSA. Stand we fully assembled?	ROSSWEISSE. Sind wir alle versammelt,
Then stay no longer:	Dann säumt nicht lange:
To Valhall' wend we our way,	Nach Walhal lbrechen wir auf,
Victims for Wotan provide.	Wotan zu bringen die Wal.
HELMWIGA. Are there but eight?	HELMWIGE. Acht sind wir erst,
All are not here.	eine noch fehlt.
GERHILDA. By the brawny Volsung	GERHILDE. Bei dem braunen Wälsung
Valorous Brünnhild'.	Weilt wohl noch Brünnhild'?

WALTRAUTA. For her arrival must we still rest
Wotan would give us greeting full grim,
Should he not see her with us.

SIEGRUNA (at the look-out).
Hoyotoho! Hoyotoho!
Behold! Behold!
In breath-devoid haste flies Brünnhilde here.

The Valkyrs (hastening up to the look-out).
Hoyotoho! Hoyotoho!
Brünnhilde, ho! Heiaha!

WALTRAUTA.
To the wood guides she her wavering horse.

GRIMGERDA. How snorts Grani from swift career.

ROSSVEISSA. I saw never thus Valkyrie speeding!

ORTLINDA. What mounts she in saddle?

HELMWIGA. That is no man!

SIEGRUNA. 'Tis a maid, merely.

GERHILDA. Where met she that maid?

SCHWERKLEITA. Without a hail hies she toward us.

WALTRAUTA.
Heiaha! Brünnhilda! Hearest thou not?

ORTLINDA. Help our sister to earth in safety!

The Valkyrs (running toward the wood).
Hoyotoho! Hoyotoho!
Heiaha! Heiaha!

WALTRAUTA. To ground hath sunk
Grani the stalwart!

GRIMGERDA. From the saddle lifts she
Lightly the maid!

The Valkyrs (all run towards the wood).
Sister! Sister! What is thy strait?

All the Valkyries return to the stage; with them comes
BRÜNNHILDA, supporting and leading in SIEGLINDA.)

BRÜNNHILDA. Shield me! O help in hardest need!

The Valkyrs. Why fliest thou in all haste?
Art thou in fear! So flee but culprits who fear!

BRÜNNHILDA.
I am for the first time pursued in flight;
Host-father hunts me down!

The Valkyrs. Wander thy senses? Speak to us!
What! Fleest thou from him?
Ha! Speak! Doth follow Host-father? O say!

BRÜNNHILDA.
O sisters, scale ye the mountain's summit!
Spy to northward if Wotan draws nigh!

(ORTLINDA and WALTRAUTA spring up to the heights.)
Speak! Shows he in sight?

WALTRAUTE. Auf sie noch harren
Müssen wir hier:
Walvater gäb' uns
Grimmigen Gruss,
Säh' ohne sie er uns nah'n.

SIEGRUNE (auf der Felsspitze, von wo sie hinausspäht).
Ho,otoho! Hojotoho!
Hieher! Hieher!
In brünstigem Ritt
Jagt Brünnhilde her.

Die Walküren (nach der Felsspitze eilend).
Ho;otoho! Hojotoho!
Brünnhilde, ho! Heiaha!

WALTRAUTE. Nach dem Tann lenkt sie
Das taumelnde Ross.

GRIMGERDE. Wie schnaubt Grane
Vom schnellen Ritt!

ROSSWEISSE. So jach sah ich nie
Walküren jagen!

ORTLINDE. Was hält sie im Sattel?

HELMWIGE. Das ist kein Held!

SIEGRUNE. Eine Frau führt sie.

GERHILDE. Wie fand sie die Frau?

SCHWERTLEITE. Mit keinem Gruss
Grüsst sie die Schwestern?

WALTRAUTE. Heiaha! Brünnhilde!
Hörst du uns nicht?

ORTLINDE. Helft der Schwester
Vom Ross sich schwingen!

Die Walküren (beide nach dem Tann laufend).
Hojotoho! Hojotoho!
Heiaha! Heiaha!

WALTRAUTE. Zu Grunde stürzt
Grane der starke!

GRIMGERDE. Aus dem Sattel hebt sie
Hastig das Weib.

Die übrigen Walküren (dem Tann zueilend).
Schwester! Schwester!
Was ist gescheh'n?

(Alle Walküren kehren auf die Bühne zurück; mit ihnen
kommt BRÜNNHILDE, SIEGLINDE unterstützend und her-
eingeleitend.)

BRÜNNHILDE (athemlos).
Schützt mich und helft
In höchster Noth!

Die Walküren. Wo rittest du her
In rasender Hast?
So fliegt nur, wer auf der Flucht!

BRÜNNHILDE. Zum erstenmal flieh' ich
Und bin verfolgt!
Heervater hetzt mir nach!

Die Walküren. Bist du von Sinnen?
Sprich! Sage uns!
Verfolgt dich Heervater?
Fliehst du vor ihm?

BRÜNNHILDE. O Schwestern, späht
Von des Felsens Spitze!
Schaut nach Norden,
Ob Walvater naht!

(ORTLINDE und WALTRAUTE springen hinauf.)
Schnell! seht ihr ihn schon?

ORTLINDA. A thunder gale nears from northward.

ORTLINDE. Gewittersturm
Naht von Norden.

WALTRAUTA. Gathering thick groweth the cloud.

WALTRAUTE. Starkes Gewölk
Staut sich dort auf,

The Valkyrs.
Host-father strideth his heavenly steed!

Die Walküren. Heervater reitet
Sein heiliges Ross!

BRÜNNHILDA. The savage hunter, pursuing in haste,
He nears, he nears from northward!
Shield me, sisters! Watch o'er this wife!

BRÜNNHILDE. Der wilde Jäger,
Der wüthend mich jagt,
Er naht, er naht von Nord!
Schützt mich, Schwestern!
Wahret dies Weib!

The Valkyrs. Who is she, this woman?

Die Walküren. Was ist mit dem Weibe?

BRÜNNHILDA. Brief be my answer: Sieglinda is she,
Siegmund's sister and bride!
Wotan with virulence vows the Volsungs to
waste:
The brother should by Brünnhilda's help to-day
have been slain!
I sheltered Siegmund, though, with my shield,
Slighting the god, who slew him himself with
his spear.
Siegmund fell, and I fled far with his friend;
•To preserve her, hither I hied to beseech your
help
In staving off the blow from us both!

BRÜNNHILDE. Hört mich in Eile!
Sieglinde ist es,
Siegmund's Schwester und Braut:
Gegen die Wälsungen
Wüthet Wotan in Grimm:—
Dem Bruder sollte
Brünnhilde heut'
Entziehen den Sieg.
Doch Siegmund schütz' ich
Mit meinem Schild,
Trotzend dem Gott:—
Der traf ihn da selbst mit dem Speer.
Siegmund fiel:
Doch ich floh
Fern mit der Frau:
Sie zu retten
Eilt' ich zu euch,
Ob mich bange auch
Ihr berget vor dem strafende!

The Valkyrs.
Unworthy sister! What words are these?
Woe's me! Brünnhilda, woe's thee!
Brok'st thou with daring, Brünnhilda,
Host-father's holiest ban?

Die Walküren. Bethörte Schwester!
Was thatest du?
Wehe! Wehe!
Brünnhilde, wehe!
Ungehorsam
Brach Brünnhilde
Heervaters heilig Gebot?

WALTRAUTA (*from the height*).
Nears the tempest like night from the north.

WALTRAUTE (*Von der Höhe*).
Nächtig ziehet es
Von Norden heran.

ORTLINDA. Raging storm-clouds hitherward stride.

ORTLINDE. Wüthend steuert
Hierher der Sturm.

The Valkyrs. Howls herald Host-father's steed!
Shrilly snorting it flies.

Die Walküren. Wild wiehert
Walvaters Ross,
Schrecklich schnaubt es daher!

BRÜNNNHILDA.
Woe to the victim, if Wotan should strike!
To wailing and death devotes he the Volsungs
Who'll lend me a horse, the lightest of foot,
To whirl this woman away?

BRÜNNHILDE. Wehe der Armen
Wenn Wotan sie trifft,
Den Wälsungen allen
Droht er Verderben!—
Wer leih't mir von euch
Das leichteste Ross,
Das flink' die Frau ihm entführ'?

SIEGRUNA. Shall we likewise learn to defy?

SIEGRUNE. Auch uns räth'st du
Rasenden Trotz?

BRÜNNHILDA.
Rossveissa, sister, lend me but thy racer!

BRÜNNHILDE. Rossweisse. Schwester!
Leih' mir deinen Renner!

ROSSVEISSA. He never yet fled our father in fear.

ROSSWEISSE. Vor Walvater floh
Der fliegende nie.

BRÜNNHILDA. Helmwiga, hear me!

BRÜNNHILDE. Helmwige, höre!

HELMWIGA. Our father I hold to.

HELMWIGE. Dem Vater gehorch ich.

BRÜNNHILDA.
Grimgerda! Gerhilda! Grant me a horse!
Schwertleita! Siegruna! See my distress!
Be still my friends! O fall not away!
Save this unfortunate wife!

BRÜNNHILDE. Grimgerde! Gerhilde!
Gönnt mir eu'r Ross!
Schwertleite! Siegrune!
Seht meine Angst!
O seid mir treu,
Wie traut ich euch:
Rettet dies traurige Weib!

SIEGLINDA (*who till now has gazed gloomily and coldly before her, starts with a repellent gesture, as* BRÜNNHILDA *clasps her quickly as if for protection*).
Oh, suffer no sorrow for me!
Ah! how dear now were death!
Who bade thee, maid, to bear me from peril?
A stroke I might in the strife have found
From the self-same weapon that Siegmund felled;
Then had I fallen and died with him!
Far from Siegmund—Siegmund—from thee!
O'er master, O death, my remembrance!
If thou wouldst court not, maiden, my curses,
Then one pray'r in pity accord me;
Strike with thy sword to my heart!

BRÜNNHILDA.
Live still, O wife! for the love that waits thee!
Rescue the pledge that with thee he hath placed:
A very Volsung thou bearest!

(SIEGLINDA *first is violently startled, then her face lights up with intense joy.*)
SIEGLINDA. Rescue me, brave one!
Rescue my babe!
Shelter me, maidens, with mightiest shield!

(A *fearful storm arises on the distant horizon. Increasing thunder-clouds mount in the background.*)

WALTRAUTA. The storm gathers fast!

ORTLINDA. Fly, all who fear it!

The Valkyrs. Hence with the woman!
Wrath threatens her.
The Valkyries may not venture to aid!

SIEGLINDA (*on her knees before* BRÜNNHILDA).
Save me, O maid! spurn not a mother!

BRÜNNHILDA (*with sudden resolution raises* SIEGLINDA *up*).
Then fly with all swiftness, and fly by thyself!
I'll stay where I am: strike on me Wotan's anger!
While I hinder him here in his wrath,
Thou by flight shalt escape from his curse!

SIEGLINDA. Where may I safely wander?

BRÜNNHILDA.
Which of ye, sisters, sped to the eastward?

SIEGRUNA. To east a tangled forest extends;
The Nibelung's hoard has Fafnir
Fled there to hide.

SCHWERTLEITA.
Changed to a dread dragon the churl is,
And in a hole he harbours with Alberic's ring!

GRIMGERDA. 'Tis no haven there for a helpless wife.

SIEGLINDE (*Die bisher finster und kalt vor sich hingestarrt, fährt uf, als* BRÜNNHILDE *sie lebhaft—wie zum Schutze—umfasst*).
Nicht sehre dich Sorge um mich:
Einzig taugt mir der Tod!
Wer hiess dich Maid
Dem Harst mich entführen?
Im Sturm dort hätt' ich
Den Streich empfah'n
Von derselben Waffe,
Der Siegmund fiel:
Das Ende fand ich
Vereint mit ihm!
Fern von Siegmund—
Siegmund von dir!
O deckte mich Tod,
Dass ich's nicht denke!—
Soll um die Flucht
Dir Maid ich nicht fluchen,
So erhöre heilig mein Fleh'n—
Stosse dein Schwert mir in's Herz!

BRÜNNHILDE. Lebe, o Weib,
Um der Liebe willen!
Rette das Pfand,
Das von ihm du empfingst:
Ein Wälsung wächst dir im Schoosse.

SIEGLINDE (*Ist heftig erschrocken; plötzlich strahlt dann ihr Gesicht in erhabener Freude auf*).
Rete mich, Kühne!
Rette mein Kind!
Schirmt mich, ihr Mädchen,
Mit mächtigstem Schutz!

(*Furchtbares Gewitter steigt im Hintergrunde auf: nahender Donner.*)

WALTRAUTE. Der Sturm kommt heran!

ORTLINDE. Flieh', wer ihn fürchtet!

Die Walküren. Fort mit dem Weibe!
Droht ihm Gefahr:
Der Walküren keine
Wag' ihren Schutz!

SIEGLINDE (*Auf den Knieen vor* BRÜNNHILDE).
Rette mich Maid!
Rette die Mutter!

BRÜNNHILDE (*Mit schnellem Entschluss*).
So fliehe denn eilig—
Und fliehe allein!
Ich—bleibe zurück,
Biete mich Wotan's Rache:
An mir zögr' ich
Den Zürnenden hier,
Während du seinem Rasen entrinnst.

SIEGLINDE. Wohin soll ich mich wenden?

BRÜNNHILDE. Wer von euch Schwestern
Schweifte nach Osten?

SIEGRUNE. Nach Osten weithin
Dehnt sich ein Wald:
Der Nibelungen Hort
Entführte Fafner dorthin.

SCHWERTLEITE. Wurmes-Gestalt
Schuf sich der Wilde:
In einer Höhle
Hütet er Alberich's Reif.

GRIMGERDE. Nicht geheu'r ist's dort
Für ein hilflos Weib.

BRÜNNHILDA. And yet from Wotan's wrath,
　　Shelter sure were this wood!
　　'Tis shunned by him: he abhorreth the spot.

WALTRAUTA (*from the heights*).
　　Raging rides the god to our rock!

The Valkyrs.
　　Brünnhilda, hark to the gathering bruit!

BRÜNNHILDA.
　　Fly then swiftly, and speed to the east!
　　Bravely determine all trials to bear.
　　Hunger and thirst, thorns and hard ways,
　　Smile through all pain while suffering pangs!
　　This only heed and hold it ever:
　　The highest hero of worlds hidest thou, O wife,
　　In sheltering shrine!

(*She produces the pieces of* SIEGMUND'S *sword from
under her breastplate and hands them to* SIEGLINDA).
　　For him keep these shreds of shattered sword-
　　　blade;
　　From his father's death-field by fortune I saved
　　　them:
　　Anon renewed this sword shall he swing;
　　And now his name I declare—Siegfried, of
　　　vict'ry the son!

SIEGLINDA. O marvellous sayings! maiden divine!
　　What comfort o'er my mind thou hast cast!
　　For his sake I live and save this belov'd one!
　　May my b'essing frame future reward!
　　Fare thee well! Be Sieglinda's sorrow thy weal!

(*She hastens away. The rocky peak is enveloped in
black thunder-clouds; a fearful tempest roars up from
the back; between the peals of thunder* WOTAN'S *voice
is heard.*)

WOTAN'S *voice.* Stay! Brünnhilda!

The Valkyrs.
　　Now steed and rider reach the rocks here:
　　Woe, Brünnhilda! Wrath doth he bring!

BRÜNNHILDA. Ah, sisters, help! I sink at heart!
　　His ire will crush me.
　　If from my aid ye recoil.

The Valkyrs.
　　Then here, thou lost one, lest thou be seen!
　　Shelter in our midst! Be silent when called!

(*They conceal* BRÜNNHILDA *in their midst and look
anxiously towards the wood, which is now lit up by
a vivid glare, whilst the background has become quite
dark.*)
　　Woe! Wildly springeth Wotan from horse:
　　Hither hurls in haste for revenge.

BRÜNNHILDE. Und doch vor Wotan's Wuth
　　Schützt sie sicher der Wald:
　　Ihn scheut der Mächt'ge
　　Und meidet den Ort.

WALTRAUTE (*Von der Höhe*).
　　Furchtbar fährt
　　Dort Wotan zum Fels.

Die Walküren. Brünnhilde, hör'
　　Seines Nahen's Gebraus'!

BRÜNNHILDE. Fort denn, eile
　　Nach Osten gewandt!
　　Muthigen Trotzes
　　Ertrag alle Mühn—
　　Hunger und Durst,
　　Dorn und Gestein;
　　Lache, ob Noth
　　Und Leiden dich nagt!
　　Denn eines wisse
　　Und wahr' es immer:
　　Den hehrsten Helden der Welt
　　Hegst du, o Weib,
　　Im schirmenden Schooss!—

(*Sie reicht ihr die Stücken von* SIEGMUND'S *zerbroche-
nem Schwert.*)
　　Werwahr' ihm die starken
　　Schwertes-Stücken;
　　Seines Vaters Walstatt
　　Entführt' ich sie glücklich:
　　Der neu gefügt
　　Das Schwert einst schwingt,
　　Den Namen nehm' er von mir—
　　"Siegfried" freu' sich des Sieg's!

SIEGLINDE. Du hehrstes Wunder!
　　Herrliche Maid!
　　Dir, Treuen, dank' ich
　　Heiligen Trost!
　　Für ihn, den wir liebten,
　　Rett' ich das Liebste:
　　Meines Dankes Lohn
　　Lache dir einst!
　　Lebe wohl!
　　Dich segnet Sieglinde's Weh'!

(*Sie eilt rechts im Vordergrunde ab.—Die Felsenhöhe
ist von schwarzen Gewitterwolken umlagert; furchtbarer Sturm braust aus dem Hintergrunde daher: ein
feuriger Schein erhellt den Tannenwald zur Seite.*)

WOTAN'S *Stimme.* Steh'! Brünnhilde!

Die Walküren. Den Fels erreichten
　　Ross und Reiter:
　　Weh' dir, Brünnhilde!
　　Rache entbrennt!

BRÜNNHILDE. Ach, Schwestern, helft!
　　Mir schwankt das Herz!
　　Sein Zorn zerschellt mich,
　　Wenn eu'r Schutz ihn nicht zähmt.

Die Walküren. Hieher, Verlor'ne!
　　Lass' dich nicht seh'n!
　　Schmiege dich an uns,
　　Und schweige dem Ruf!

(*Sie ziehen sich alle die Felsspitze hinauf, indem sie
BRÜNNHILDE unter sich verbergen.*)
　　Wehe! Wehe!
　　Wüthend schwingt sich
　　Wotan vom Ross—
　　Hieher ras't
　　Sein rächender Schritt!

(Wotan *enters from the wood in the most angry pertur-*
bation and advances before the group of Valkyries
on the height, in search of Brünnhilda.)

Wotan.
Where is Brünnhilda? where the rebellious one?
Dare ye to veil her from Wotan's vengeance?

The Valkyrs. Fearful and dread thy dictate!
What did, O father, thy daughters,
That such a storm they have stirred in thy
breast?

Wotan. Would ye defy me?
Foolish ones, tremble!
I know! Brünnhilda hides here from me!
Hence from her aid! the outcast from heaven,
Who all things high has spurned from her!

The Valkyrs. To us sped the pursued one,
For our aid seeking with pray'rs.
She sees thy rage in silence and ruth:
Father, hear us; pray
Soften thine anger to her; 'bate thy fury's burst.

Wotan. Weak-spirited, womanly brood!
Such melting moods ye won not from me!
I tempered your frames for fighting and toil,
Steeled, too, your bosoms to bear distress;
And your minions now moan and groan,
When I grimly chastise breach of faith!
Now wot, ye waverers, what she hath wrought,
For whom your tremulous tear-drops arise!
No one like she knew what my bosom en-
shrouded!
No one like she spied to the depths of my spirit!
'Twas she worked what my will had shaped and
designed;
And now is broken our notable bond, when,
faith annulling,
My will she defied.
My sacred command openly scorned,
Against me attempting to turn e'en the tools
By me bestowed! Hear'st thou, Brünnhilda?
Thou on whom byrnie, helm and glaive,
Glory and hope, honour and strength I be-
stowed?
How to my chiding canst hearken, and fail to
face
The chider, in hope from thy doom to hide?

(Brünnhilda *emerges from the midst of the Valkyries,*
walks humbly, but with firm tread, down from the
rock, and thus approaches to within a short distance
of Wotan.)
Here stand I, father, to suffer my sentence!

(Wotan *schreitet in furchtbar zürnender Aufregung*
aus dem Tann heraus, und hält vor dem Haufen der
Walküren an, welche Brünnhilde *schützen.*)

Wotan. Wo ist Brünnhilde?
Wo die Verbrecherin?
Wagt ihr, die Böse
Vor mir zu bergen?

Die Walküren. Schrecklich ertos't dein Toben:—
Was thaten, Vater, die Töchter,
Dass sie dich reizten
Zu rasender Wuth?

Wotan. Wollt ihr mich höhnen?
Hütet euch, Freche!
Ich weiss: Brünnhilde
Bergt ihr vor mir.
Weichet von ihr,
Der ewig Verworf'nen,
Wie ihren Werth
Von sich sie warf!

Die Walküren. Zu uns floh die Verfolgte,
Uns'ren Schutz flehte sie an!
Mit Furcht und Zagen
Fasst sie dein Zorn.
Für die bange Schwester
Bitten wir nun,
Dass den ersten Zorn du bezähm'st.

Wotan. Weichherziges
Weibergezücht!
So matten Muth
Gewannt ihr von mir?
Erzog ich euch kühn
Zu Kämpfen zu zieh'n,
Schuf ich die Herzen
Euch hart und scharf,
Dass ihr Wilden nun weint und greint,
Wenn mein Grimme eine Treulose straft?
So wisst den, Winselnde,
Was die verbrach,
Um die euch Zagen
Die Zähre entbrennt!
Keine wie sie
Kannte mein innerstes Sinnen!
Keine wie sie
Wusste den Quell meines Willens;
Sie selbst war
Meines Wunsches schaffender Schooss:
Und so nun brach sie
Den seligen Bund
Dass treulos sie
Meinem Willen getrotzt,
Mein herrschend Gebot
Offen verhöhnt.
Gegen mich selbst die Waffe gewandt,
Die allein mein Wunsch ihr schuf!
Hörst du's Brünnhilde?
Du, der ich Brünne,
Helm und Wehr,
Wonne und Huld,
Namen und Leben verlieh?
Hörst du's, Brünnhilde?
Und birgst dich bang dem Kläger,
Dass feig' du der Straf' entflöh'st?

Brünnhilde (*tritt aus der Schaar der Walküren her-*
vor, schreitet demüthigen, doch festen Schrittes, von
der Felsenspitze herab, und tritt so in geringer Ferne
vor Wotan).
Hier bin ich, Vater:
Gebiete die Strafe!

WOTAN.

I sentence thee not; thou hast shaped the
    stroke for thyself.
Thy father's will awoke thee to life:
Yet against that will hast thou warred;
Acting my orders was only thy part,
Yet against me all hast thou ordered.
Wish-maid wert to me,
Yet against me now hast thou wished;
Shield-maid wert to me,
Yet against me turnest thy shield;
Lot-chooser thou wert to me,
Yet against me lot hast thou chosen;
Hero-stirrer thou wert to me,
Yet against me stirrest thou heroes.
What wert thou erst, Wotan hath uttered;
What now thou art, that say for thyself!
Wish-maid art thou no more.
One time a Valkyrie wert thou,
Remain henceforth but merely thyself!

BRÜNNHILDA (*violently startled*).
Thou disownest me? Thine aim I divine!

WOTAN. From Valhall ne'er more will I send thee:
I'll cause thee no more warriors to call;
No more bring'st thou heroes to fill my hall;
At the Æsir's festal meeting
The flagon no more thou'llt fill me with mead.
Ne'er shall I kiss more thy sweet child-like
    mouth;
From heavenly clans art thou excluded,
Bann'd, degraded from thy blessed degree:
For broken now is our bond; exiled for aye
Art thou banished from bliss.

The Valkyrs. Horror! Woe! Sister! O sister!

BRÜNNHILDA.
All thou hast given, again wouldst take?

WOTAN. To thy lord all must thou lose!
And here where we stand strikes thee my curse:
In powerless sleep shalt thou be cast;
That man shall seize on the maid,
In whose way she is seen and awaked.

The Valkyrs. Oh, halt! O father, recall thy curse!
    O father! shall the maiden wither and waste by
      a man?
    O stay! hark to our prayers! deal not to her
      this grievous disgrace!
    Grim-hearted god: as her sisters we too share
      her shame!

WOTAN. Did ye not hear what I ordained?
From your resort must the treacherous sister be
    severed:

WOTAN. Nicht—straf' ich dich erst:
Deine Strafe schufst du dir selbst.
Durch meinen Willen
Warst du allein:
Gegen ihn doch hast du gewollt;
Meinen Befehl nur
Führtest du aus:
Gegen ihn doch hast du befohlen;
Wunsch-Maid
War'st du mir:
Gegen mich doch hast du gewünscht;
Schild-Maid
War'st du mir:
Gegen mich doch hob'st du den Schild;
Loos-Kieserin
War'st du mir:
Gegen mich doch kies'test du Loose;
Helden-Reizerin
War'st du mir:
Gegen mich doch reiztest du Helden.
Was sonst du war'st,
Das sagte dir Wotan:
Was jetzt du bist.
Das sage dir selbst!
Wunschmaid bist du nicht mehr;
Walküre bist du gewesen:—
Nun sei fortan,
Was so du noch bist!

BRÜNNHILDE (*Heftig erschrocken*).
Du verstössest mich?
Versteh' ich den Sinn?

WOTAN. Nicht send' ich dich mehr aus Walhall,
Nicht weis' ich dir mehr
Helden zur Wal;
Nicht führ'st du mehr Sieger
In meinen Saal:
Bei der Götter traulichem Mahle
Das Trinkhorn reichst du
Mir traut nicht mehr;
Nicht kos' ich dir mehr
Den kindischen Mund.
Von göttlicher Schaar
Bist du geschieden,
Ausgestossen
Aus der Ewigen Stamm;
Gebrochen ist unser Bund;
Aus meinem Angesicht bist du verbannt.

Die *Walküren.* Wehe! Wehe!
Schwester! O schwester!

BRÜNNHILDE. Nimmst du mir alles,
Was einst du gab'st?

WOTAN. Der dich zwingt,
Wird dir's entzieh'n!
Hieher auf den Berg
Banne ich dich;
In wehrlosen Schlaf
Schliesse ich dich;
Der Mann dann fange die Maid,
Der am Wege sie findet und weckt.

Die *Walküren.* Halt' ein, Vater!
Halt' ein mit dem Fluch!
Soll die Maid verblüh'n
Und verbleichen dem Mann?
Du Schrecklicher, wende
Die schreiende Schmach:
Wie die Schwester träf' uns ihr Schimpf!

WOTAN. Hörtet ihr nicht,
Was ich verhängt?
Aus eurer Schaar
Ist die treulose Schwester geschieden:

No more a-horse with your troop will she hurl
    through the tempest;
A consort will claim her in conjugal clasp;
She'll follow her master henceforth at his beck;
By the fire to sit and to spin, to free spirits a
    mock and sport!

(BRÜNNHILDA *sinks to the ground with a cry; the Val-*
kyries recoil in terror and draw back with a sudden
movement.)
    Fear ye her doom? Then fly the condemned
      one!
    Draw from her side and hold ye afar!
    Dares one undutiful near her to dally?
    Dares one defy me and furnish her help?
    That fool shall find a like fate! So, bold ones,
      I bid ye heed!
    Make no more halt! seek not this mountain!
    Hence I warn ye to hasten, lest I hurl woe on
      your heads!
(*The Valkyries separate with wild cries of woe and rush*
into the wood in hasty flight. Black clouds settle
thickly on the cliffs; a wild, rushing sound is heard
in the wood. A vivid lightning-flash breaks through
the clouds; in it the Valkyries are seen with loose
bridle crowding together in a troop, and rushing wildly
away. The storm quickly subsides; the thunder-clouds
gradually disperse. During the following scene evening
twilight falls with the returning fine weather, followed
at the close by night.)

SCENE III

(WOTAN and BRÜNNHILDA, *she lying still prostrate at*
his feet, remain alone. Long silence; unaltered posi-
tions. She begins slowly to raise her head a little;
she gradually rises to a kneeling position.)

BRÜNNHILDA.
    Was it so shameful, what I have done,
    That for my deed I so shamefully am scourged?
    Was it so base to warp thy command, that thou
    For me such debasement must shape?
    Was't such dishonour what I have wrought
    That it should rob me of honour for aye?
    O speak, father! see me before thee: soften thy
      wrath;
    Wreak not thine ire, but make to me clear the
      mortal
    Guilt that with cruel firmness compels thee to
    Cast off thy favorite child!

WOTAN (*gloomily*).
    Ask of thy deed, 'twill surely show thee thy
      guilt!

BRÜNNHILDA. But thy decree I carried out.

WOTAN. Decreed I then care of Volsung in combat?

BRÜNNHILDA.
    Thou toldest me so to turn the event!

Mit euch zu Ross
Durch die Lüfte sie reitet nicht länger;
  Die magdliche Blume
  Verblüht der Maid:
  Ein Gatte gewinnt
  Ihre weibliche Gunst:
  Dem herrischen Manne
  Gehorcht sie fortan,
Am Herde sitzt sie und spinnt,
Aller Spottenden Ziel und Spiel.

(BRÜNNHILDE *sinkt schreiend vor seinen Füssen zu*
Boden; die Walküren machen eine Bewegung des
Entsetzens.)
    Schreckt euch ihr Loos!
    So flieht die Verlor'ne!
    Weichet von ihr
    Und haltet euch fern!
    Wer von euch wagte
    Bei ihr zu weilen,
    Wer mir zum Trotz
    Zu der Traurigen hielt',
    Die Thörin theilte ihr Loos:
    Das künd' ich der Kühnen an!—
    Fort jetzt von hier!
    Meidet den Felsen!
    Hurtig jagt mir von dannen,
    Sonst erharrt Jammer euch hier!
(*Die Walküren fahren mit wildem Wehschrei auseinan-*
der und stürzen in hastiger Flucht in den Tann: bald
hört man sie wie mit Sturm auf ihren Rossen davon-
jagend.—Nach und nach legt sich während des Folgen-
den das Gewitter; die Wolken verziehen sich: Abend-
dämmerung, und endlich Nacht, sinken bei ruhigem
Wetter herein.)

DRITTE SCENE

(WOTAN *und* BRÜNNHILDE, *sind allein zurückgeblieben.*
Langes, feierliches Schweigen. Endlich das Haupt
langsam erhebend, sucht WOTAN's *noch abgewandten*
Blick, und richtet sich während des Folgenden allmälig
ganz auf.)

BRÜNNHILDE. War es so schmählich,
    Was ich verbrach,
    Dass mein Verbrechen so schmählich du
      bestraf'st?
    War es so niedrig
    Was ich dir that,
    Dass du so tief mir Erniedrigung schaff'st?
    War es so ehrlos,
    Was ich beging,
    Dass mein Vergeh'n nun die Ehre mir raubt?
    O sag', Vater!
    Sieh' mir in's Auge:
    Schweige den Zorn,
    Zähme die Wuth!
    Deute mir hell
    Die dunkle Schuld,
    Die mit starrem Trotze dich zwingt,
    Zu verstossen dein trautestes Kind!

WOTAN (*finster*).
    Frag' deine That—
    Sie deutet dir deine Schuld!

BRÜNNHILDE. Deinen Befehl
    Führte ich aus.

WOTAN. Befahl ich dir
    Für den Wälsung zu fechten?

BRÜNNHILDE. So hiessest du mich
    Als Herrscher der Wal.

WOTAN. But I revoked my unavailing behest!

BRÜNNHILDA.
 When Fricka thine own intending did frustrate
 When her intending was followed,
 To thyself wert thou false.

WOTAN (*softly and bitterly*).
 I knew thou understood'st my meaning,
 And scourge now thy mutinous act;
 Though weak and dull dost thou think me,
 But what I must trample on treason,
 Thou wert truly beneath my wrath!

BRÜNNHILDA.
 My wisdom's scanty; I wist though of one thing,
 That thou well lov'dst the Volsung.
 I wist of thy struggle, thy constraint to hide
 That love in oblivion.
 Thou only held'st that other decree though the
 Shameful hap shadowed thy heart
 That Siegmund should not be shielded.

WOTAN.
 And deeming it so, thou dared to lend him thy
  shield.

BRÜNNHILDA.
 'Twas because I held in my heart thy true
  wish,
 Which by covenants hampered, fatally clogged
 Now thou renouncest so weakly.
 I who follow Wotan and fare in his wake,
 Have seen a thing once by thee unseen.
 Siegmund straight I sought,
 I hied to him with his fate;
 I looked on his features, heard him at large,
 I was stirred by the hero's holy distress;
 Widely resounded the warrior's sorrow,
 Free was his passion, fearful his pain,
 Mournfullest courage, confident might;
 And my ear did list.
 My eyes did look on what bade in fulness
 My heart with holy fervour to beat;
 Shy, astonished, stood I ashamed,
 I could consider but how to serve him:
 Safety or shame, with Siegmund to share them—
 This was the fiat I fain had decreed!
 Thou who this love within my heart had hid,
 Whose purposes had placed me at his side, firm.
 Faithful to thee, thwarted I thy command.

WOTAN.
 Thou didst for me what I wished so dearly to
  work,
 But was forced to leave, by fate doubly induced.

WOTAN. Doch meine Weisung
 Nahm ich wieder zurück.

BRÜNNHILDE. Als Fricka den eig'nen
 Sinn dir entfremdet:
 Da ihrem Sinn du dich fügtest,
 Warst du selber dir Feind.

WOTAN (*leise und bitter*).
 Dass du mich verstanden, wähnt' ich,
 Und strafe den wissenden Trotz;
 Doch feig und dumm
 Dachtest du mich:
 So hätt' ich Verrath nicht zu rächen,
 Zu gering wärest du meinem Grimm!

BRÜNNHILDE. Nicht weise bin ich;
 Doch wusst' ich das Eine—
 Dass den Wälsung du liebtest:
 Ich wusste den Zwiespalt,
 Der dich zwang,
 Dies Eine ganz zu vergessen.
 Das Andere musstest
 Einzig du seh'n,
 Was zu schauen so herb
 Schmerzte dein Herz—
 Dass Schutz du Siegmund versagtest.

WOTAN. Du wusstest es so,
 Und wagtest dennoch den Schutz?

BRÜNNHILDE. Weil für dich im Auge
 Das eine ich hielt,
 Dem, im Zwange des Andren
 Schmerzlich entzweit.
 Rathlos den Rücken du wandtest.
 Die im Kampfe Wotan
 Den Rücken bewacht,
 Die sah nun das nur,
 Was du nicht sah'st:—
 Siegmund musste ich seh'n.
 Tod kündend
 Trat ich vor ihn,
 Gewahrte sein Auge,
 Hörte sein Wort;
 Ich vernahm des Helden
 Heilige Noth:
 Tönend erklang mir
 Des Tapfersten Klage—
 Freiester Liebe
 Furchtbares Leid,
 Traurigsten Muthes
 Mächtigster Trotz:
 Meinem Ohr erscholl,
 Mein Aug' erschaute,
 Was tief im Busen das Herz
 Zu heil'gem Beben mir traf.—
 Scheu und staunend
 Stand ich in Scham:
 Ihm nur zu dienen
 Konnt ich noch denken:
 Sieg oder Tod
 Mit Siegmund zu theilen—
 Dies nur erkannt' ich
 Zu kiesen als Loos!
 Der mir in's Herz
 Diese Liebe gehaucht,
 Dem Willen, der mich
 Dem Wälsung gesellt,
 Ihm innig vertraut—
 Trotzt' ich deinem Gebot.

WOTAN. So thatest du,
 Was so gern zu thun ich begehrt—
 Doch was nicht zu thun
 Die Noth zwiefach mich zwang?

With ease ween'st thou to win then the heart's
    fondest wishes?
When burning woe in my heart I bore,
When rankling distress my rage awoke,
That while deeply loving, my love untold
In my tortured heart must be hidden:
When 'gainst my own self,
I in suff'ring contended, and from my spleen
Of spirit in wrath sprang, wasted with longings,
Languished with woe, the furious wish did I
    form
In the wreck of my tott'ring world, these
Eternal wrestlings to termine:
Yet lapp'd wert thou in thralling delights,
Blissful emotions, unrestrained might,
Thou drankest lightly the lovely draught,
While I, god though I be, bitterest gall-cup must
    drain!
Thy so light-turned soul let henceforth lead
    thee;
From me see thyself released!
Thus shall I shun thee, nor share more with
    thee
My thoughts and wishes whispered; apart,
Ne'er more in company work we; so, while
Life days shall last, may the god not give thee
    his greeting!

BRÜNNHILDA.
    Unfit for thee was the foolish maid, who,
Stunned by thy counsel, naught understood,
While her own conviction but one thing advised,
To love all that thou didst love.
If we must sever and part forever, if thou tear-
    est what once was intact,
The one half putting far from thy presence, that
    once was girt to thy service,
Thou god, forget not this! Thine own estate
    thou dar'st not dishonour;
Seek not so deeply to shame thyself;
Thyself would then be sullied, seeing me scoffed
    at and scorned!

WOTAN.
    Thou fain hast followed the might of love:
Follow now him thou needs must love!

BRÜNNHILDA. Shall I from Valhall sever,
    No more to thy service be vassal?
My life to a mortal belong from henceforth?
To boasting poltroon give not the prize!
By a worthless churl let me not be won!

WOTAN. From Fate-father hast thou turned; thy fate
    No more may he move.

BRÜNNHILDA. Once mad'st thou a glorious breed:
    No mean one shall ever debase it!
One valiant o'er all, I vouch it,
Shall spring from Volsung's line.

WOTAN. Peace, with thy Volsung's line!
    As thou'rt relinquished, lost, too, is that:
'Twas wrecked by me in my wrath.

So leicht wähntest du
Wonne der Liebe erworben,
  Wo brennend Weh'
  In das Herz mir brach,
  Wo grässliche Noth
  Den Grimm mir schuf,
  Einer Welt zu Liebe
  Der Liebe Quell
Im gequälten Herzen zu hemmen?
  Da labte süss
  Dich, selige Lust;
  Wonniger Rührung
  Ueppigen Rausch
  Enttrankst du lachend
  Der Liebe Trank—
Als mir göttlicher Noth
Nagende Galle gemischt?
  Deinen leichten Sinn
  Lass' dich denn leiten:
  Du sagtest von mir dich los!
  Dich muss ich meiden,
  Gemeinsam mit dir
Nicht darf ich Rath mehr raunen;
  Getrennt nicht dürfen
  Traut wir mehr schaffen:
So weit Leben und Luft,
Darf der Gott dir nicht mehr begegnen!

BRÜNNHILDE. Wohl taugte dir nicht
  Die thör'ge Maid,
  Die staunend im Rathe
  Nicht dich verstand,
  Wie Mein eig'ner Rath
  Nur das Eine mir rieth—
Zu lieben was du geliebt.—
  Muss ich denn scheiden
  Und scheu dich meiden,
  Musst du spalten
  Was einst sich umspannt,
  Die eig'ne Hälfte
  Fern von dir halten—
Dass sonst sie ganz der gehörte,
Du, Gott, vergiss das nicht!
  Dein ewig Theil
  Nicht wirst du entehren,
  Schande nicht wollen,
  Die dich beschimpft;
Dich selbst liessest du sinken,
Säh'st du dem Spott mich zum Spiel!

WOTAN. Du folgest selig
  Der Liebe Macht:
  Folge nun dem
  Den du lieben musst!

BRÜNNHILDE. Soll ich aus Walhall scheiden,
  Mit dir nicht mehr schaffen und walten:
  Soll ich gehorchen
  Dem herrschenden Mann—
  Dem feigen Prahler
  Gieb mich nicht Preis!
  Nicht werthlos sei er,
  Der mich gewinnt.

WOTAN. Von Walvater schiedest du—
  Nicht wählen darf er für dich.

BRÜNNHILDE. Du zeugtest ein edles Geschlecht;
  Kein Zager kann ihm entschlagen:
  Der weihlichste Held—ich weiss es—
  Entblüht dem Wälsungenstamm.

WOTAN. Schweig' von dem Wälsungenstamm!
  Von dir geschieden
  Schied ich von ihm:
  Vernichten musst' ihn der Neid.

BRÜNNHILDA.
    I, who crossed thee so, saved it from doom!

WOTAN. Ne'er seek at my hand safety to find,
    Even for her sire-less fruit!

BRÜNNHILDA.
    She guardeth the sword thou had'st shaped for
      Siegmund.

WOTAN. And which I into splinters struck!
    Seek not, O maid, for means to unnerve me!
    Bemoan not thy fate, move as it may;
    I cannot cast thee the lot.
    But hence must I fare, hasten away;
    Too long I'm wavering here.
    Now I turn from thee as thou didst from me;
    I would have naught of what thou dost wish:
    Thy punishment I must promptly deal!

BRÜNNHILDA.
    What hast thou designed that I must suffer?

WOTAN. Unbreaking sleep shall seal thy sense;
    What man the wardless maid wakes,
    Shall win her to wife!

BRÜNNHILDA (*falls on her knees*).
    Shall fetters of sleep firmly bind me,
    To fall a booty to any braggart?
    This one thing thou must allow me;
    Forlorn, I urge thee to hear:
    My helpless form hedge round with hindering
      horrors,
    That but by a free man, fearless of heart,
    Here on the fell I may be found!

WOTAN.
    Too much thou beggest, the boon's too great!

BRÜNNHILDA (*clasping his knees*).
    This one thing must thou concede me:
    Oh, chasten thy child who enchains thy knees!
    Downtread the true heart, destroy thou thy
      maid:
    Let her vital spark be sped by thy spear;
    But cast, cruel one, ne'er a crushing disgrace
     like this!

        (*Wildly*)
At thy command let magical fire-flame
Spring forth and enfold me, lambent and fierce.
To lick with its tongue, to rend with its teeth
   the trembler
Who rashly dareth to ravish the rock of its
   prize!

BRÜNNHILDE. Die von dir sich riss—
    Ich rettete ihn:
    Sieglinde hegt
    Die heiligste Frucht;
    In Schmerz und Leid,
    Wie kein Weib sie litt,
    Wird sie gebären
    Was bang sie birgt.

WOTAN. Nie suche bei mir
    Schutz für die Frau,
    Noch für ihres Schoosses Frucht!

BRÜNNHILDE. Sie bewahrt das Schwert,
    Das du Siegmund schuf'st.—

WOTAN. Und das ich in Stücken ihm schlug.
    Nicht streb', o Maid,
    Den Muth mir zu stören!
    Erwarte dein Loos.
    Wie sich's dir wirft:
    Nicht kiesen kann ich es dir!—
    Doch fort muss ich jetzt,
    Fern von dir zieh'n:
    Zuviel schon zögert' ich hier.
    Von der Abwendigen
    Wend' ich mich ab;
    Nicht wissen darf ich
    Was sie sich wünscht:
    Die Strafe nur
    Muss vollstreckt ich seh'n.

BRÜNNHILDE. Was hast du erdacht
    Dass ich erdulde?

WOTAN. In festen Schlaf
    Versch'iess' ich dich:
    Wer so die Wehrlose weckt,
    Dem ward, erwacht, sie zum Weib.

BRÜNNHILDE (*Stürzt auf ihre Kniee*).
    Soll fesselnder Schlaf
    Fest mich binden,
    Dem feigsten Manne
    Zur leichten Beute:
    Dies Eine musst du erhören,
    Was heil'ge Angst zu dir fleht:
    Die Schlafende schütze
    Mit scheuchenden Schrecken,
    Dass nur ein furchtlos
    Freiester Held
    Hier auf dem Felsen
    Einst mich fänd'!

WOTAN. Zu viel begehrst du—
    Der Gunst zu viel!

BRÜNNHILDE (*Seine Kniee umfassend*).
    Dies Eine musst—
    Musst du erhören!
    Zerknicke dein Kind,
    Das dein Knie umfasst;
    Zertritt die Traute.
    Zertrümm're die Maid;
    Ihres Leibes Spur
    Zerstöre dein Speer:
    Doch gieb, Grausamer. nicht
    Der grässlichsten Schmach sie preis!
      (*Mit Wildheit.*)
    Auf dein Gebot
    Entbrenne ein Feuer;
    Den Fels umglühe
    Lodernde Gluth:
    Es leck' ihre Zunge
    Und fresse ihr Zahn
    Den Zagen, der frech es wagte
    Dem freislichen Felsen zu nah'n!

WOTAN (*overpowered and deeply moved, turns eagerly towards* BRÜNNHILDA, *raises her to her feet and gazes with emotion in her eyes*).

Farewell, my brave and beautiful child!
Thou once the life and light of my heart!
Farewell! Farewell! Farewell!
Loth I must leave thee; no more in love
May I grant thee my greeting:
Henceforth my maid ne'er more with me rideth.
Nor waiteth wine to reach me!
When I relinquish thee, my beloved one,
Thou laughing delight of my eyes,
Thy bed shall be lit by torches more brilliant
Than ever for bridal have burned!
Fiery gleams shall girdle the fell,
With terrible scorchings scaring the timid,
Who, cowed, may cross not Brünnhilda's couch
For one alone freeth the bride;
One freer than I, the God!

WOTAN (*Blickt ihr ergriffen in's Auge und hebt sie auf*).

Leb' wohl, du kühnes
Herrliches Kind!
Du meines Herzens
Heiliger Stolz,
Leb' wohl! leb' wohl! leb' wohl!
Muss ich dich meiden,
Und darf minnig
Mein Gruss nimmer dich grüssen;
Sollst du nicht mehr
Neben mir reiten,
Noch Meth beim Mahl mir reichen;
Muss ich verlieren
Dich, die ich liebte,
Du lachende Lust meines Auges:—
Ein bräutliches Feuer
Soll dir nun brennen,
Wie nie einer Braut es gebrannt!
Flammende Gluth
Umglühe den Fels!
Mit zehrenden Schrecken
Scheuch's es den Zagen,
Der Feige fliehe
Brünnhilde's Fels:—
Denn Einer nur freie die Braut,
Der freier als ich, der Gott!

(BRÜNNHILDA *sinks, rapt and transfigured, on* WOTAN'S *breast; he holds her in a long embrace. She throws her head back again and gazes, still embracing him, with solemn emotion into* WOTAN'S *eyes.*)

(BRÜNNHILDE *wirft sich ihm gerührt und entzückt in die Arme.*)

THOSE EYES SO LUSTROUS AND CLEAR.

No 3

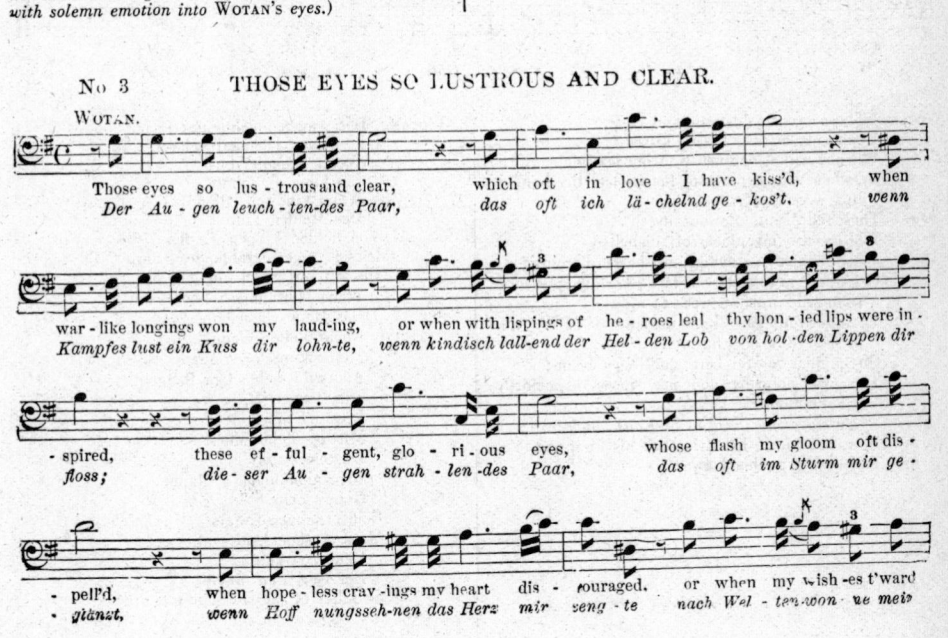

Those eyes so lus-trous and clear,   which oft   in   love   I   have kiss'd,   when
Der Au - gen leuch - ten-des Paar,   das   oft   ich lä-chelnd ge-kos't,   wenn

war-like longings won   my laud-ing,   or when with lispings of he-roes leal   thy hon-ied lips were in-
Kampfes lust ein Kuss dir lohn-te,   wenn kindisch lall-end der Hel-den Lob von hol-den Lippen dir

- spired,   these ef-ful-gent, glo-ri-ous   eyes,   whose flash my gloom oft dis-
floss;   die-ser Au-gen strah-len-des Paar,   das   oft   im Sturm mir ge-

- pell'd,   when hope-less crav-ings my heart   dis-couraged,   or when my wish-es t'ward
- glänzt,   wenn Hoff nungsseh-nen das Herz   mir seng-te   nach Wel-ten-won ne mein

world-ly pleasure from wild warfare were turn-ing, their lus - trous gaze lights on me now, as my
Wunsch ver-langte, aus wild we - bendem Bangen; zum letz - ten Mal letz' es mich heut' mit des

lips im - print this last farewell! On hap - pi - er mor - tal here shall they
Le - be - woh - les letz - tem Kuss! Dem glück - licher'n Man - ne glän - ze sein

beam; the grief - suf - fer - ing god may nev - er hence - forth be -
Stern: dem un - se - li - gen Ew' - gen muss es schei - dend sieh

- hold them! Now, heart - torn, he gives thee his
schlies - sen. Denn so kehrt der Gott sich dir

kiss and tak - eth thy god - - hood a - way!
ab. so küsst er die Gott - - heit von dir!

WOTAN. Those eyes so lustrous and clear,
Which oft in love I have kissed,
When warlike longings won my lauding,
Or when with lispings of heroes leal thy honied
lips were inspired:
These effulgent, glorious eyes,
Whose flash my gloom oft dispelled,
When hopeless cravings my heart discouraged,
Or when my wishes t'ward worldly pleasure
from wild warfare were turning—
Their lustrous gaze lights on me now as my lips
imprint this last farewell!
On happier mortal here shall they beam;
The grief-suffering god may never henceforth
behold them!
(*He clasps her head in both his hands.*)
Now, heart-torn, he gives thee his kiss, and
Taketh thy godhood away!

WOTAN. Der Augen leuchtendes Paar,
Das oft ich lächelnd gekos't,
Wenn Kampfes-Lust
Ein Kuss dir lohnte,
Wenn kindisch lallend
Der Helden Lob
Von holden Lippen dir floss;
Dieser Augen strahlendes Paar,
Das oft im Sturm mir geglänzt,
Wenn Hoffnungs-Sehnen
Das Herz mir sengte,
Nach Welten-Wonne
Mein Wunsch verlangte
Aus wild webendem Bangen:
Zum letzten Mal
Letz' ich mich heut'
Mit des Lebewohles
Letztem Kuss!
Dem glücklicher'n Manne
Glänze sein Stern;
Dem unseligen Ew'gen
Muss es scheidend schliessen!
Denn so—kehrt
Der Gott sich dir ab:
So küsst er die Gottheit von dir.

(*He imprints a long kiss on her eyes; she sinks back in his arms with closed eyes, her powers gently departing. He tenderly helps her to lie upon a low mossy mound which is overshadowed by a wide-spreading fir-tree. He looks upon her and closes her helmet; his eyes then rest upon the form of the sleeper which he then completely covers with the great steel shield of the Valkyrie. He slowly moves away, then again*)

(*Er küsst sie auf beide Augen, die ihr sogleich verschlossen bleiben: sie sinkt sanft ermattend in seinen Armen zurück. Er geleitet sie zart auf einen niedrigen Mooshügel zu liegen, über den sich eine breitästige Tanne ausstreckt. Noch einmal betrachtet er ihre Züge und schliesst ihr dann den Helm fest zu; dann verweilt sein Blick nochmals schmerzlich auf ihrer Gestalt, die er endlich mit dem langen Stahlschilde der Walküre*)

*turns round with a painful glance. He stalks with
solemn decision to the centre of the stage and directs
the point of his spear towards a huge stone.)*

    Loki, hear! Listen and heed!
    As I found thee at first, a fiery glow,
    As thou fleddest me headlong,
    A hovering glimmer, as then I bound thee,
    Bound be thou now!
    Appear, wavering spirit, and spread me thy
      Fire round this fell!
    Loki! Loki! Appear!

*(A stream of fire issues from the stone, which swells to
an ever-brightening glow of flame. Thereupon a stream
of fire flashes forth; bright flames surround WOTAN,
leaping wildly. He directs commandingly with his
spear the fiery flood to encircle the rocks, then it
spreads to the background, where it flickers per-
manently round the precipice.)*

WOTAN. He who my spear in spirit feareth,
    Ne'er springs through this fiery bar!

*(He stretches out the spear in a spell. He looks painfully
at BRÜNNHILDA and disappears through the fire.)*
      (The curtain falls.)

*zudeckt. — Dann schreitet er mit feierlichem Ent-
schlusse in die Mitte der Bühne und kehrt die Spitze
seines Speeres gegen einen mächtigen Felsstein.)*

    Loge hör'!
    Lausche hieher!
    Wie zuerst ich dich fand
      Als feurige Gluth,
    Wie dann einst du mir schwandest
      Als schweifende Lohe:
      Wie ich dich band,
      Bann' ich dich heut'!
    Herauf, wabernde Lohe,
    Umlod're mir feurig den Fels!
    Loge! Loge! Hieher!

*(Bei der letzten Anrufung schlägt er mit der Spitze des
Speeres dreimal auf den Stein, worauf diesem ein
Feuerstrahl entfährt, der schnell zu einem Flammen-
meere anschwillt, dem Wotan mit einem Winke seiner
Speerspitze den Umkreis des Felsens als Strömung
zuweist.)*

    Wer meines Speeres
      Spitze fürchtet.
    Durchschreite das Feuer nie!

*(Er verschwindet in der Gluth nach dem Hintergrunde
      zu.)*
    (Der Vorhang fällt.)

THE END.

SIEGFRIED

CHARACTERS

SIEGFRIED.
MIME.
THE WANDERER (WOTAN).
ALBERICH.

FAFNER.
ERDA.
BRÜNNHILDE.

THE ARGUMENT.

ACT I. Mime, the Niblung, and brother of Alberich, has found Sieglinda in the forest and has brough up the child which she died in giving birth to, knowing that he is destined to slay Fafner and gain the ring The young Siegfried, dissatisfied with all swords made for him, melts up the fragments of his father's blade 'Needful' and forges it afresh, to Mime's great awe.

ACT II. Mime induces Siegfried — under pretext of teaching him how to fear, an art which the youth is curious to learn — to accompany him to a distant part of the forest where Fafner in the shape of a huge dragon, guards the Nibelung treasures, including the ring. Siegfried kills the dragon, but on accidentally tasting its blood, is enabled to understand the speech of birds. They tell him how Mime means to poison him to obtain the treasure; accordingly he kills the traitor. The bird further tells him of a fair sleeping bride surrounded by fire, and flies before him to show the way to her resting place.

ACT III. Wotan uneasily wandering over the world conscious of impending doom, vainly seeks counsel of Erda. Meeting Siegfried, he opposes his path, but the sword Needful hews his spear asunder, and, his power destroyed, he retreats to Valhalla to await the Dusk of the gods.
Siegfried, meanwhile, plunges through the fire, finds the Valkyrie, wakes her, woos her and wins her

SIEGFRIED.

FIRST ACT.

<table>
<tr><td>

A FOREST.

The foreground represents a portion of a rocky cave which extends inwards on the left, but occupies only three-fourths of the stage on the right. Two natural entrances open on to the wood; one, half-way up the stage, forms the back, the other, R, is wider and slanting at the side. On the left, against the wall stands a large smith's forge, naturally formed of stones, the bellows alone being artificial. The rough chimney — also natural — leads up through the top of the cave. A very large anvil and other smith's appliances.

MIME (*when, after a short orchestral prelude, the curtain rises, is discovered sitting at the anvil, and hammering, with increasing discouragement, at a sword. At last he ceases work in despair*).

Forced undertaking!
Toil without fruit!
The stoutest sword
that ever I shaped;
in a giant's fingers
firm it were found;
but he whom 'tis forged **for,**
the fiery stripling,
will strain and twist it in two
as 'twere a straw or a toy.

(*He throws the sword pettishly on the anvil, sets his arms a-kimbo, and gazes thoughtfully on the ground.*)

There *is* a blade
that were not so brittle:
"Needful's" fragments
he'd fracture me ne'er;
could I but mend
the mighty metal;
but all my craft
cannot compass that.
Could I with cunning weld it
I should well be paid for my pains.

(*He sinks more back and shakes his head thoughtfully.*)

Fafner, the wicked worm,
rests here in forest wilds;
with his frame of terrific weight
o'er the Nibelung's gold
guard doth he hold.
Siegfried's prowess unproved
may master e'en Fafner's might:
the Nibelung Ring
would rest then to me.
For this may serve but one sword;
now nought but "Needful" I need,
by Siegfried searchingly swung:—
and I cannot shape me
"Needful" the sword!—

He recommences hammering, much discouraged.)

Forced undertaking!
Toil without fruit!

</td><td>

WALD.

Den Vordergrund bildet ein Theil einer Felsenhöhle, die sich links tiefer nach innen zieht, nach rechts aber gegen drei Viertheile der Bühne einnimmt. Zwei natürlich gebildete Eingänge stehen dem Walde zu offen: der eine nach rechts, unmittelbar im Hintergrunde, der andere, breitere, ebenda seitwärts. An der Hinterwand, nach links zu, steht ein grosser Schmiedeherd, aus Felsstücken natürlich geformt; künstlich ist nur der grosse Blasebalg: die rohe Esse geht—ebenfalls natürlich— durch das Felsdach hinauf. Ein sehr grosser Ambos und andre Schmiedegeräthschaften.

MIME (*sitzt, als der Vorhang nach einem kurzen Orchester-Vorspiel aufgeht, am Ambos, und hämmert mit wachsender Unruhe an einem Schwerte: endlich hält er unmuthig ein*).

Zwangvolle Plage!
Müh' ohne Zweck!
Das beste Schwert,
das je ich geschweisst,
in der Riesen Fäusten
hielte es fest:
doch dem ich's geschmiedet,
der schmähliche Knabe,
er knickt und schmeisst es entzwei,
als schüf' ich Kindergeschmeid!——

(*Er wirft das Schwert unmuthig auf den Ambos, stemmt die Arme ein und blickt sinnend zu Boden.*)

Es giebt ein Schwert,
das er nicht zerschwänge:
Nothung's Trümmer
zertrotzt' er mir nicht,
könnt' ich die starken
Stücken schweissen,
die meine Kunst
nicht zu kitten weiss.
Könnt' ich's dem Kühnen schmieden,
meiner Schmach erlangt' ich da Lohn!—

(*Er sinkt tiefer zurück, und neigt sinnend das Haupt.*)

Fafner, der wilde Wurm,
lagert im finst'ren Wald;
mit des furchtbaren Leibes Wucht
der Niblungen Hort
hütet er dort.
Siegfried's kindischer Kraft
erläge wohl Fafner's Leib:
des Niblungen Ring
erränge ich mir.
Ein Schwert nur taugt zu der That.
nur Nothung nützt meinem Neid,
wenn Siegfried sehrend ihn schwingt: -
und nicht kann ich's schweissen,
Nothung das Schwert!—

(*Er fährt in höchstem Unmuth wieder fort zu hämmern.*)

Zwangvolle Plage!
Müh ohne Zweck!

</td></tr>
</table>

The stoutest sword
that ever I shaped
will ne'er be drawn
in the cause that I need.
I knock and I hammer
but at the boy's behest:
he'll bend and snap it in two,
yet scold me, should I not forge.

Das beste Schwert,
das je ich geschweisst,
nie taugt es je
zu der einz'gen That!
Ich tapp'r' und hämm're nur,
weil der Knab' es heischt:
er knickt und schmeisst es entzwei,
und schmählt doch, schmied' ich ihm nicht?

SIEGFRIED *in a wild forest dress, with a silver horn slung by a chain, bursts impetuously from the wood. He has bridled a great bear with a bast rope, and urges it with merry roughness towards* MIME, *who drops the sword in terror, and flies behind the forge.* SIEGFRIED *drives the bear everywhere after him.*

SIEGFRIED, *in wilder Waldkleidung, mit einem silbernen Horn an einer Kette; kommt mit jähem Ungestüm aus dem Walde herein; er hat einen grossen Bären mit einem Bastseile gezäumt, und treibt diesen mit lustigem Uebermuthe gegen* MIME *an.* MIME'*n entsinkt vor Schreck das Schwert; er flüchtet hinter den Herd;* SIEGFRIED *treibt ihm den Bären überall nach.*

MOTIVE OF SIEGFRIED, THE FEARLESS.

SIEGFRIED. Oho! Oho!
Come on! come on!
Tear him! tear him!
The trump'ry smith!
(*He shouts with laughter.*)

MIME. Take him away!
I want not the bear!

SIEGFRIED. We come double
the better to cow you.
Bruin, ask for the sword

MIME. Ho! keep away!
I've cast the weapon
Fit and fairly to-day.

SIEGFRIED. So far you've saved then your skin.
(*He looses the bear from the rope and gives him a blow on the back with it.*)
Run, Bruin;
your business is done!
(*The bear trots back into the wood.*)

MIME (*coming out trembling from behind the forge*).
I like it when
thou slayest bears;
why bringest living
that brute to me?

SIEGFRIED (*sitting down to recover from his laughter*).
For better companions pining
than the one at home appears,
to leafy woodland I hied,
while my horn I wound right loudly;
for I fain had discovered
a welcome friend;—
rang forth my notes with that aim.
From the bushes came a bear
who listened with brutish growl,
and I liked him better than you,
though better luck I'd have yet.
With a bast rope strong
I bridled him straight
to seek for my sword from this rascal.
(*He jumps up and goes towards the sword.*)

SIEGFRIED. Hoiho! Hoiho!
Hau' ein! Hau' ein!
Friss' ihn! Friss' ihn,
den Fratzenschmied!
(*Er lacht unbändig.*)

MIME. Fort mit dem Thier!
Was taugt mir der Bär!

SIEGFRIED. Zu zwei komm' ich,
dich besser zu zwicken:
Brauner, frag' nach dem Schwert!

MIME. He! lass' das Wild!
Dort liegt die Waffe:
fertig fegt' ich sie heut'.

SIEGFRIED. So fährst du heute noch heil!
(*Er löst dem Bären den Zaum, und giebt ihm damit einen Schlag auf den Rücken.*)
Lauf', Brauner:
dich brauch' ich nicht mehr!
(*Der Bär läuft in den Wald zurück.*)

MIME (*zitternd hinter dem Herde vorkommend.*)
Wohl leid' ich's gern,
erleg'st du Bären;
was bringst du lebend
die braunen heim?

SIEGFRIED (*setzt sich, um sich vom Lachen zu erholen*)
Nach bess'rem Gesellen sucht' ich,
als daheim mir einer sitzt;
im tiefen Walde mein Horn
liess ich da hallend tönen:
ob sich froh mir gesellte
ein guter Freund?
das frug' ich mit dem Getön'.
Aus dem Busche kam ein Bär,
der hörte mir brummend zu;
er gefiel mir besser als du,
doch bess're wohl fänd' ich noch:
mit dem zähen Baste
zäumt' ich ihn da,
dich, Schelm, nach dem Schwerte zu fragen.
(*Er springt auf, und geht nach dem Schwerte.*)

MIME (*taking up the sword to hand it to* SIEGFRIED).
 I've shaped the weapon sharp;
 With its sheen thou wilt be well pleased.

SIEGFRIED (*taking the sword*).
 What purpose would have its shining
 were the steel not hard of proof?
  (*Tries it in his hand.*)
 Hey! what an idle
 toy is this!
 This silly switch
 call you a sword?
(*He beats it on the anvil till the pieces fly around.*
 MIME *retreats in terror.*)

MIME (*erfasst das Schwert, es* SIEGFRIED *zu reichen*).
 Ich schuf die Waffe scharf,
 ihrer Schneide wirst du dich freu'n.

SIEGFRIED (*nimmt das Schwert*).
 Was frommt seine helle Schneide,
 ist der Stahl nicht hart und fest?
  (*Er prüft es mit der Hand.*)
 Hei! was ist das
 für müss'ger Tand!
 Den schwachen Stift
 nennst du ein Schwert?
(*Er zerschlägt es auf dem Ambos, dass die Stücken
 ringsum fliegen:* MIME *weicht erschrocken aus.*)

MOTIVE OF SIEGFRIED THE IMPETUOUS.

Then there are the splinters,
scandalous sloven;
would I had smashed it
over your skull now!—
Shall such a liar
longer delude me?
Prating of giants,
of jousts and battles,
of bravest deeds
and of daring in war;
while weapons he smithies,
swords he shapes me,
praising his art
as if 'twere approved?
Yet when I handle
what he has hammered,
a single stroke
destroys all the trash!
Were he not, sure,
too scurvy a wight,
I would smithy and smite
the smith with his stuff,—
the ancient, imbecile imp!
My anger might then be allayed.
(*He throws himself raging on a stone-seat, R.*)

MIME (*who has cautiously kept his distance*).
 Now ravest thou in a rage!
 What gross ingratitude!
 This over-bearing boy
 if he gets not *all* the best,
 the good things I have giv'n
 are each and all forgot.
 Wilt thou then never think of
 what I have said on thanking?
 Thou should'st delight to obey him
 who's shewn thee love for so long.

SIEGFRIED *sulkily turns his back on him and remains
 with his face to the wall.*)
 Thou'rt loth to listen to my blaming!
 But spurn not food at least.
 Yon spit shall render its roast meat;
 or say, would'st thou like the soup?
 For thee it simmers long.
(*Brings food to* SIEGFRIED, *who, without turning,
 strikes pot and meat out of his hand.*)

Da hast du die Stücken,
schändlicher Stümper:
hätt' ich am Schädel
dir sie zerschlagen!—
Soll mich der Prahler
länger noch prellen?
Schwatzt mir von Riesen
und rüstigen Kämpfen,
von kühnen Thaten
und tüchtiger Wehr;
will Waffen mir schmieden,
Schwerte schaffen;
rühmt seine Kunst,
als könnt' er was Rechtes:
nehm' ich zur Hand nun
was er gehämmert,
mit einem Griff
zergreif' ich den Quark!—
Wär' mir nicht schier
zu schäbig der Wicht,
ich zerschmiedet' ihn selbst
mit seinem Geschmeid,
den alten albernen Alp!
Des Aergers dann hätt' ich ein End'
(*Er wirft sich wüthend auf eine Steinbank, zur Seite
 rechts.*)

MIME (*der ihn immer vorsichtig ausgewichen*).
 Nun tob'st du wieder wie toll:
 dein Undank, traun! ist arg.
 Mach' ich dem bösen Buben
 nicht alles gleich zu best,
 was ich Gutes ihm schuf,
 vergisst er gar zu schnell!
 Willst du denn nie gedenken
 was ich dich lehrt' vom Danke?
 Dem sollst du willig gehorchen,
 der je sich wohl dir erwies.

(SIEGFRIED *wendet sich unmuthig um, mit dem Gesicht
 nach der Wand, so dass er ihm den Rücken kehrt.*)
 Das willst du wieder nicht hören!—
 Doch speisen magst du wohl?
 Vom Spiesse bring' ich den Braten:
 versuchtest du gern den Sud?
 Für dich sott ich ihn gar.
(*Er bietet* SIEGFRIED *Speise hin. Dieser, ohne sich
 umzuwenden, schmeisst ihm Topf und Braten aus der
 Hand.*)

SIEGFRIED. Meals I make for myself:
you can swill your slop alone !

MIME (*appearing much hurt*).
This is my affection's
foul reward !
This my toil's
disgraceful return!
A querulous brat
kindly I reared,
wrapped in warm linen
the little wretch:
water and food
for thee I found,
looked upon thee
as my very life.
And when thou didst wax
I waited on thee;
in care for thy slumber
a couch made soft.
I shaped for thee toys,
and a tuneful horn;
e'er at thy whim
willingly worked:
with cunning redes
I read thee all craft,
with subtle wisdom
sharpened thy wits.
Moping at home
I toil and moil,
while heedless from me
thou dost hie.
For thee do I plague me,
take pains but for thee;
so dwindle my powers
— a poor old dwarf ! —
For all my worry
is this my reward,
from the hot-headed boy
but abuse and hate!
(*He bursts into a fit of sobbing.*)

SIEGFRIED (*who has again turned round and gazed
steadily in* MIME'S *face*).
Much you've taught to me, Mime,
and many tales have you told;
but what you would like best to teach me
were lesson I'd lief let be:—
how not to loathe your sight.
Bread do you bring,
refreshment withal,
disgust I feed on alone.
Spread you my couch
with comforts for sleep—
then slumber wends from my side;
when all my wits
you work to instruct
I would be deaf and dumb.
Soon as I open
my eyes on you
but evil I see there
whatever you do.
Seeing you stand
shambling and shaking,
shrinking and slinking,
with your eyelids blinking, —
by the neck I'd take
and shake and wake you,
your idiot antics
to end forever!—
Such feelings, Mime, I foster.
If you have wisdom

SIEGFRIED. Braten briet ich mir selbst:
deinen Sudel sauf' allein!

MIME (*stellt sich empfindlich*).
Das ist nun der Liebe
schlimmer Lohn!
Das der Sorgen
schmählicher Sold!—
Als zullendes Kind
zog ich dich auf,
wärmte mit Kleiden
den kleinen Wurm:
Speise und Trank
trug ich dir zu,
hütete dich
wie die eig'ne Haut.
Und wie du erwuchsest,
wartet' ich dein;
dein Lager schuf ich,
dass leicht du schlief'st.
Dir schmiedet' ich Tand
und ein tönend Horn;
dich zu erfreu'n
müht' ich mich froh:
mit klugem Rathe
rieth ich dir klug,
mit lichtem Wissen
lehrt' ich dich Witz.
Sitz' ich daheim
in Fleiss und Schweiss,
nach Herzenslust
schweif'st du umher:
für dich nur in Plage,
in Pein nur für dich
verzehr' ich mich alter
armer Zwerg!
Und aller Lasten
ist das nun der Lohn,
dass der hastige Knabe
mich quält und hasst!
(*Er geräth in Schluchzen.*)

SIEGFRIED (*der sich wieder umgewendet, und in* MIME's
Blick ruhig geforscht hat).
Vieles lehrtest du, Mime,
und manches lernt' ich von dir;
doch was du am liebsten mich lehrtest
zu lernen gelang mir nie:—
wie ich dich leiden könnt'.—
Träg'st du mir Speise
und Trank herbei—
der Ekel speis't mich allein:
schaff'st du ein leichtes
Lager zum Schlaf—
der Schlummer wird mir da schwer.
willst du mich weisen
witzig zu sein—
gern bleib' ich taub und dumm.
Seh' ich dir erst
mit den Augen zu,
zu übel erkenn' ich
was alles du thu'st:
seh' ich dich steh'n,
gangeln und geh'n,
knicken und nicken,
mit den Augen zwicken:
beim Genick' möcht' ich
den Nicker packen,
den Garaus geben
dem garst'gen Zwicker!—
So lernt' ich, Mime, dich leiden.
Bist du nun weise,

then rede me wisely
a thing I have pored upon. —
    When I scour forests
    seeking to fly you,
what motive makes me return?
    Not a beast but I love
    better than you;
    bird in forest,
    or fish in the brook,
    dearer than you
    I deem all of these:—
what motive then makes me return?
If you've mind, then tell it me.

MIME (*sits affectionately a little way from* SIEGFRIED).
    My son, this clearly shews thee
    how closely thy heart to me clings.

SIEGFRIED (*laughing*). But I cannot endure you, —
    forget not that indeed.

MIME.   This is but thy wilful way,
    which were quickly quelled at will.
    Young ones are ever yearning,
    needing the parent nest;
    Love's the name of this longing:
    such leaning thou hast to me,
    this love thou dost feel for thy Mime.
    Thou *must* surely love him!
    What the father is to the fledgling
    which in the nest it nursed
    ere in flight it could flutter,
    such to thee, foolish child,
    is faithful, cherishing Mime.
    Thou must be his charge.

SIEGFRIED.   Hey, Mime, since you're so clever,
    explain me this also clearly. —

so hilf mir wissen,
worüber umsonst ich sann:—
    in den Wald lauf' ich,
    dich zu verlassen,—
wie kommt das, kehr' ich zurück?
    Alle Thiere sind
    mir theurer als du:
    Baum und Vogel,
    die Fische im Bach,
    lieber mag ich sie
    leiden als dich:—
wie kommt das nun, kehr' ich zurück?
Bist du klug, so thu' mir's kund.

MIME (*setzt sich in einiger Entfernung ihm traulich
    gegenüber*).
    Mein Kind, das lehrt dich kennen,
    wie lieb ich am Herzen dir lieg'.

SIEGFRIED (*lacht*).
    Ich kann dich ja nicht leiden,—
    vergiss das nicht so leicht!

MIME.   Dess' ist deine Wildheit schuld,
    die du Böser bändigen sollst. —
    Jammernd verlangen Junge
    nach ihrer Alten Nest;
    Liebe ist das Verlangen:
    so lechzest du auch nach mir,
    so lieb'st du auch deinen Mime—
    so musst du ihn lieben!
    Was dem Vögelein ist der Vogel,
    wenn er im Nest es nährt,
    eh' das flügge mag fliegen:
    das ist dir kindischem Spross
    der kundig sorgende Mime—
    das muss er dir sein.

SIEGFRIED.   Ei, Mime bist du so witzig,
    so lass' mich eines noch wissen!—

THE MOTIVE OF LOVE LIFE.

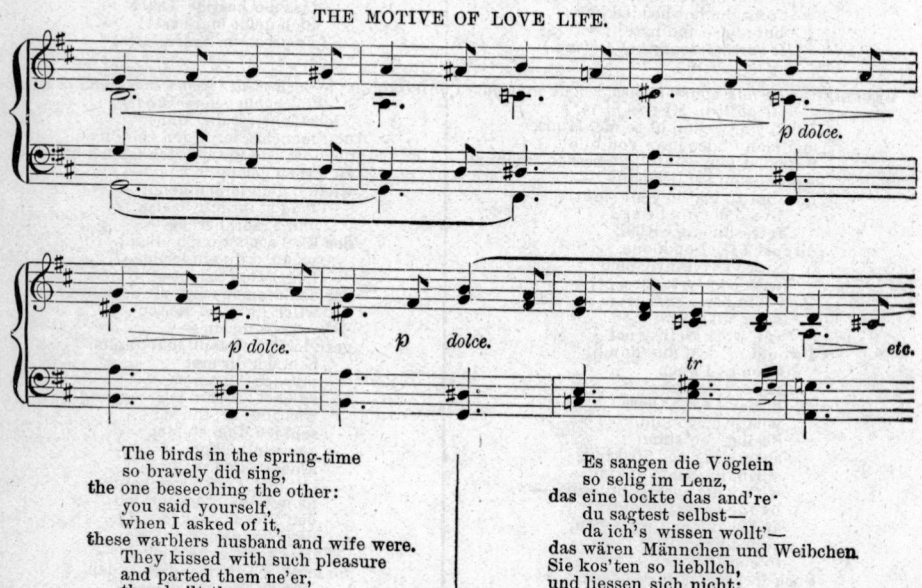

The birds in the spring-time
    so bravely did sing,
the one beseeching the other:
    you said yourself,
    when I asked of it,
these warblers husband and wife were.
They kissed with such pleasure
    and parted them ne'er,
they built them a nest

Es sangen die Vöglein
    so selig im Lenz,
das eine lockte das and're·
    du sagtest selbst—
    da ich's wissen wollt'—
das wären Männchen und Weibchen.
Sie kos'ten so lieblich,
    und liessen sich nicht;
sie bauten ein Nest

and brooded therein;
then fluttered anon
the young fledglings out,
and both took care of the brood.
So duly reposed
the deer which had paired,
e'en wolves and foxes the wildest:
food the male
for the family furnished,
the cubs were nursed by his consort.
I learnt from this
what love must be;
the whelps I ne'er moved
from the mother's side. —
Where have you, Mime,
your minikin consort
that I may call her mother?

MIME (*angrily*).   Art thou a fool?
What is't to thee?
Art thou either fowl or fox?

SIEGFRIED.   A querulous brat
kindly you reared,
wrapped in warm linen
the little wretch: —
how came you, then,
by this clamouring wretch?
D'ye mean that I was
without mother made?

MIME (*much embarrassed*).   Only trust
Whatever I tell thee;
I am thy father
and mother in one.

SIEGFRIED.   You lie! perfidious fool! —
That the young one is like the parent
long since have I proved for myself.
I came to the crystal brook
and could trace bird and beast
within its mirror;
mist and sunlight,
seen as they are,
the faithful reflex of their form.
My own pictured image
I also saw;
unlike yourself
surely I seemed;
as 'twere to compare
with a toad a bright fish;
a fish ne'er had toad for a father.

MIME (*much vexed*).   Terrible stuff
thou tattlest still.

SIEGFRIED (*with increasing animation*).
See now, I vow
myself I've found
what in vain I so long have sought:
when from you I fly
to roam in the forest
how it haps home I return.
(*He springs up.*)
It is to make you inform me
what father and mother are **mine.**

MIME (*retreating from him*).
What father? What mother?
Meaningless fancies!

SIEGFRIED (*seizing him by the throat*).
Then must I enforce you
some truth to tell me:
good temper
will further me nought.

und brüteten drin:
da flatterte junges
Geflügel auf,
und beide pflegten der Brut.
So ruhten im Busch
auch Rehe gepaart,
selbst wilde Füchse und Wölfe:
Nahrung brachte
zum Nest das Männchen,
das Weibchen säugte die Welpen
Da lernt' ich wohl
was Liebe sei;
der Mutter entwandt' ich
die Welpen nie. —
Wo hast du nun, Mime,
dein minniges Weibchen,
dass ich es Mutter nenne?

MIME (*verdriesslich*).
Was ist dir, Thor?
Ach, bist du dumm!
Bist doch weder Vogel noch Fuchs?

SIEGFRIED.   Das zullende Kind
zogest du auf,
wärmtest mit Kleiden
den kleinen Wurm: —
wie kam dir aber
der kindishce Wurm?
Du machtest wohl gar
ohne Mutter mich?

MIME (*in grosser Verlegenheit*).
Glauben sollst du,
was ich dir sage:
ich bin dir Vater
und Mutter zugleich.

SIEGFRIED.   Da lügst du, garstiger Gauch! —
Wie die Jungen den Alten gleichen,
das hab' ich mir glücklich erseh'n.
Nun kam ich zum klaren Bach:
da erspäht' ich die Bäum'
und Thier' im Spiegel;
Sonn' und Wolken,
wie sie nur sind,
im Glitzer erschienen sie gleich.
Da sah' ich denn auch
mein eigen Bild;
ganz anders als du
dünkt' ich mir da:
so glich wohl der Kröte
ein glänzender Fisch;
doch kroch nie ein Fisch aus der Kröte.

MIME (*höchst ärgerlich*).
Gräulichen Unsinn
kram'st du da aus!

SIEGFRIED (*immer lebendiger*).
Sieh'st du, nun fällt
auch selbst mir ein,
was zuvor ich umsonst besann:
wenn zum Wald ich laufe,
dich zu verlassen,
wie das kommt, kehr' ich doch heim
(*Er springt auf.*)
Von dir noch muss ich erfahren,
wer Vater und Mutter mir sei!

MIME (*weicht ihm aus*).
Was Vater! was Mutter!
Müssige Frage!

SIEGFRIED (*packt ihn bei der Kehle*).
So muss ich dich fassen
um 'was zu wissen:
gutwillig
erfahr' ich doch nichts!

I must by force
fulfil my wishes:
scarcely language
should I have learned
if not wrested from you,
wretch, by main strength!
So tell me now, rascally knave,
who are my father and mother?

MIME (*who has signed with his head and hands for*
SIEGFRIED *to release him*).
My life thou nearly hast crushed! —
Let loose! what thou wishest to know
I'll tell thee, now — without wile. —
O thankless
and unthinking boy!
Now hear for what thou dost hate me!
I am no father
nor flesh of thine;
yet owest thou all to my aid.
No kin art of mine
who yet am so kind;
out of goodness have I
guarded thy life.
My love is preciously paid!
Did I look for tender return?
A poor woman lay wailing
once in yon woodland wild:
I helped her home to this hole,
and gave my hearth for a haven.
Of child proved she in labour;
pining she bore it here;
deep anguish harried her,
I helped her as best I could.
Baleful her lot, — she died,
but Siegfried saw the light.

SIEGFRIED (*who has seated himself*).
So died then my mother of me?

MIME. To my charge she confided thee:
I cherished fain the babe.
What work for Mime thou mad'st!
What woes the poor wight has endured!
A querulous brat
kindly I reared . . .

SIEGFRIED. Me-seems you have said that before.
Now say, who did name me Siegfried?

MIME. Anon said thy mother
must I so name thee:
as Siegfried thou didst grow
staunch and strong. —
I wrapped in warm linen
the little wretch . . .

SIEGFRIED.
Now, Mime, what name bore my mother?

MIME. In sooth I scarcely know. —
Water and food
for thee I found . . .

SIEGFRIED. Her title instantly tell me!

MIME. 'Tis haply forgot! — Yet hold!
Sieglinde certainly hight she
who gave thee sadly to me. —
I looked upon thee
as my very life . . .

SIEGFRIED. Now tell me my father's title.

MIME (*harshly*). His face I never saw.

SIEGFRIED.
But his name my mother has mentioned?

So musst' ich Alles
ab dir trotzen:
kaum das Reden
hätt' ich errathen,
entwand ich's nicht
mit Gewalt dem Schuft!
Heraus damit,
räudiger Kerl!
Wer ist mir Vater und Mutter?

MIME (*wachdem er mit dem Kopfe genickt und mit den
Händen gewinkt, ist von* SIEGFRIED *losgelassen worden*).
An's Leben geh'st du mir schier! —
Nun lass'! was zu wissen dich geizt,
erfahr' es, ganz wie ich's weiss. — ·
O undankbares,
arges Kind!
jetzt hör', wofür du mich hassest!
Nicht bin ich Vater
noch Vetter dir. —
und dennoch verdankst du mir dich!
Ganz fremd bist du mir,
deinem einz'gen Freund;
aus Erbarmen allein
barg ich dich hier:
nun hab' ich lieblichen Lohn!
Was verhofft' ich Thor mir auch Dank?
Einst lag wimmernd ein Weib
da draussen im wilden Wald:
zur Höhle half ich ihr her,
am warmen Herd sie zu hüten.
Ein Kind trug sie im Schoss;
traurig gebar sie's hier;
sie wand sich hin und her,
ich half so gut ich konnt':
stark war die Noth, sie starb —
doch Siegfried, der genas.

SIEGFRIED (*hat sich gesetzt*).
So starb meine Mutter an mir?

MIME. Meinem Schutz übergab sie dich:
ich schenkt' ihn gern dem Kind.
Was hat sich Mime gemüht!
was gab sich der Gute für Noth!
Als zullendes Kind
zog ich dich auf . . .

SIEGFRIED. Mich dünkt, dess' gedachtest du schon
Jetzt sag:' woher heiss' ich Siegfried?

MIME. So hiess mich die Mutter
möcht' ich dich heissen:
als Siegfried würdest
du stark und schön. —
Ich wärmte mit Kleiden
den kleinen Wurm . . .

SIEGFRIED. Nun melde, wie hiess meine Mutter?

MIME. Das weiss ich wahrlich kaum! —
Speise und Trank
trug ich dir zu . . .

SIEGFRIED. Den Namen sollst du mir nennen!

MIME. Entfiel er mir wohl? doch halt!
Sieglinde mochte sie heissen,
die dich in Sorge mir gab. —
Ich hütete dich
wie die eig'ne Haut . . .

SIEGFRIED. Dann frag' ich, wie hiess mein Vater?

MIME (*barsch*).
Den hab' ich nie geseh'n.

SIEGFRIED. Doch die Mutter nannte den Namen?

MIME. That some one slew him,
she said, and no more;
thee, fatherless,
she confided to me. —
And when thou didst wax
I waited on thee,
in care for thy slumber
thy couch made soft...

SIEGFRIED. Stint with that endless
starling note! —
Shall I believe your tidings,
and think you not a liar,
then let me see a sign.

MIME. How shall I then assure thee?

SIEGFRIED. I trust you not with my ears,
I trust in nought but my eyes;
what witness will you bring?

MIME (*after some hesitation, brings forward the two
pieces of a broken sword*).
This had I of thy mother;
for menage, toil and trouble,
was it my scant reward.
See here, but a broken sword!
She said thy father had swung it
at the fight in which he was felled.

SIEGFRIED. And you shall forge now
for me the fragments;
I'll find so my right defence!
Up! arm yourself, Mime!
Move and be brisk!
Can you be brave?
Then show me your craft!
Playthings no more
on me impose:
these pieces alone
promise to serve.
If you should fail,
forge it amiss,
find I a flaw
in the faultless steel, —
you, fumbler, finely I'll beat; —
you'll feel the burnish yourself!
This day will I surely
wield my own sword;
I'll win me this weapon at once.

MIME (*frightened*).
What would'st thou to-day with the sword?

SIEGFRIED. In the wide world
I will wander,
never more to return.
What a full joy
to have freedom!
nothing anchors me here.
My father art thou not;
I shall find another home!
thy hearth is not my house,
ne'er I'll rest beneath thy roof.
As the fish fain
through the flood shoots,
as the finch flies
to a free shore;
far hence I flee,
flow like a stream;
with the wind o'er the woods
wafting away, —
then, Mime, ne'er will I return.
(*He rushes away into the woods.*)

MIME (*in great alarm*).
Halt there! halt there! what ho!

MIME. Erschlagen sei er,
das sagte sie nur;
dich Vaterlosen
befahl sie mir da:—
und wie du erwuchsest,
wartet' ich dein'
dein Lager schuf ich,
dass leicht du schlief'st . . .

SIEGFRIED. Still mit dem alten
Staarenlied!—
Soll ich der Kunde glauben,
hast du mir nichts gelogen,
so lass mich nun Zeichen seh'n!

MIME. Was soll dir's noch bezeugen?

SIEGFRIED. Dir glaub' ich nicht mit dem Ohr',
dir glaub' ich nur mit dem Aug':
welch' Zeichen zeugt für dich?

MIME (*holt nach einigem Besinnen die zwei Stücken
eines zerschlagenen Schwertes herbei*).
Das gab mir deine Mutter:
für Mühe, Kost und Pflege
liess sie's als schwachen Lohn.
Sieh' her, ein zerbroch'nes Schwert!
Dein Vater, sagte sie, führt' es,
als im letzten Kampf er erlag.

SIEGFRIEE. Und diese Stücken
sollst du mir schmieden:
dann schwing' ich mein rechtes Schwert!
Eile dich, Mime,
mühe dich rasch;
kannst du 'was Recht's.
nun zieg' deine Kunst!
Täusche mich nicht
mit schlechtem Tand:
den Trümmern allein
tau' ich 'was zu.
Find' ich dich faul,
füg'st du sie schlecht,
flick'st du mit Flausen
den festen Stahl,—
dir Feigem fahr' ich zu Leib,
das Fegen lernst du von mir!
Denn heute noch, schwör' ich,
will ich das Schwert;
die Waffe gewinn' ich noch heut'.

MIME (*erschrocken*).
Was willst du noch heut' mit dem Schwert

SIEGFRIED. Aus dem Wald fort
in die Welt zieh'n:
nimmer kehr' ich zurück.
Wie ich froh bin,
dass ich frei ward,
nichts mich bindet und zwingt!
Mein Vater bist du nicht;
in der Ferne bin ich heim;
dein Herd ist nicht mein Haus,
meine Decke nicht dein Dach.
Wie der Fisch froh
in der Fluth schwimmt,
wie der Fink frei
sich davon schwingt:
flieg' ich von hier,
fluthe davon,
wie der Wind über'n Wald
weh' ich dahin—
dich, Mime, nie wieder zu seh'n!
(*Er stürmt in den Wald fort.*)

MIME (*in höchster Angst*).
Halte! halte! wohin?

He calls with his utmost strength toward the wood.	*(Er ruft mit der grössten Anstrengung in den Wald.)*
Ho! Siegfried!	He! Siegfried!
Siegfried! Ho!	Siegfried! He!—
He hurls away,	Da stürmt er hin!—
and here I sit. —	Nun sitz' ich da:—
To old distress	zur alten Noth
comes added trouble;	hab' ich die neue!
entangled wholly am I!—	vernagelt bin ich nun ganz!—
What help can I find?	Wie helf' ich mir jetzt?
How handle him best?	Wie halt' ich ihn fest?
How force him to hasten	Wie führ' ich den Huien
to Fafner's nest ?	zu Fafner's Nest?—
How forge me these stivers	Wie füg' ich die Stücken
of stubbornest steel ?	des tückischen Stahl's?
For no furnace heat	Keines Ofens Gluth
helps me to fuse them,	glüht mir die ächten!
no kobold's hammer	keines Zwergen Hammer
conquers their hardness,	zwingt mir die harten;
By Niblung's annoy,	des Niblungen Neid,
need and sweat,	Noth und Schweiss
"Needful" can ne'er be knit;	nietet mir Nothung nicht,
Mime cannot mend the sword.	schweisst mir das Schwert nicht zu ganz!—
(He crouches down despairingly on his stool behind the anvil.)	*(Er knickt verzweifelnd auf dem Schemel hinter dem Ambos zusammen.)*

MOTIVE REPRESENTING WOTAN AS THE WANDERER.

The WANDERER (WOTAN) *advances from the wood to the back entrance of the cave. He wears a long, dark blue cloak, and bears a spear as a staff. On his head is a large hat with a broad, round brim hanging low over his missing eye.*	*Der* WANDERER (WOTAN) *tritt aus dem Wald an das hintere Thor der Höhle heran.—Er trägt einen dunkelblauen langen Mantel; einen Speer führt er als Stab. Auf dem Haupte hat er einen grossen Hut mit breiter runder Krämpe, die über das fehlende eine Auge tief hereinhängt.*
WANDERER. Hail thee, wisest smith! To way-wearied guest grant as host thy house and hearth.	WANDERER. Heil dir, weiser Schmied! Dem wegmüden Gast gönne hold des Hauses Herd!
MIME (*starting up in terror*). By whom in this woodland wild am I sought ? Who has tracked me to this retreat ?	MIME (*ist erschrocken aufgefahren*). Wer ist's, der im wilden Wald mich sucht ? Wer verfolgt mich im öden Forst?
WANDERER. "Wanderer" calls me the world: wide wanderings I've made; all the earth around I roam at my will.	WANDERER. Wand'rer heisst mich die Welt. weit wandert' ich schon, auf der Erde Rücken rührt' ich mich viel.
MIME. Then roam on thy way and rest thee not here, or no Wanderer thou wert.	MIME. So rühre dich fort und raste nicht hier, heisst dich Wand'rer die Welt.
WANDERER. Good men render me a greeting, gifts they grant to me withal; for ever misers have evil ends.	WANDERER. Gastlich ruht' ich bei Guten, Gaben gönnten mir viele: denn Unheil fürchtet, wer unhold ist.
MIME. Evil weighs for ever on me; would'st to my anguish augment it ?	MIME. Unheil wohnte immer bei mir: willst du dem Armen es mehren ?

WANDERER (*advancing closer*).
Much I've mastered
and treasured much;
wondrous tales
to men I've told,
from many warded
what dismayed them, —
torturing heart's distress.

MIME. Spyest thou well,
and spae-est thou truth,
I want ne'er a spy nor a spae-wright.
Solitary
I seek to bide,
loungers I leave to their list.

WANDERER (*again approaching a few steps nearer*).
Men have weened
their wisdom was great,
but what should boot them
wist not their brains.
What was goodly
straightway I gave them;
spake, and strengthened their minds.

MIME (*terrified at the approach of the* WANDERER).
Useless matters
many yearn for;
for me my craft doth suffice.
I've sufficient wit,
I want no more;
so, wise one, wend on thy way.

WANDERER (*seating himself at the hearth*).
Here gaining thy hearth,
I gage thee my head
as stake in struggle of wits.
My head is thine,
'twill fall to thy hand
if vainly thou ask
my advice, —
should I not save it by wit.

MIME (*aside, frightened and perplexed*).
How shall I be rid of this rogue?
In trial must I entrap him. —
(*Aloud.*)
Thy head staking
'gainst my hearth,
with care and cunning redeem it.
Three the questions
that I require.

WANDERER. Three times I must answer.

MIME (*after some reflection*).
Thy rovings have led thee
to earth's far regions,
thou hast wandered widely o'er worlds :—
now, rede me aright,
what is the race
born in the earth's deep bowels?

WANDERER. In the earth's deep bowels
burrow the Nibelungs:
Nibelheim is their land.
Black elves are they all;
Black Alberich
guarded and governed them once.
By the mighty spell
of a magical ring
he moved the industrious dwarfs.
Endless riches,
rarest of hoards
he made them heap   [him.
wherewith all the world should be won
Propose, dwarf, thy second point.

WANDERER (*weiter hereintretend*,.
Viel erforscht' ich,
erkannte viel:
Wichtiges könnt' ich
manchem künden,
manchem wehren
was ihn mühte,
nagende Herzens-Noth.

MIME. Spürtest du klug
und erspähtest viel,
hier brauch' ich nicht Spürer noch Späher
Einsam will ich
und einzeln sein,
Lungerern lass' ich den Lauf.

WANDERER (*wieder einige Schritte näher schreitend*)
Mancher wähnte
weise zu sein,
nur was ihm noth that
wusst' er nicht;
was ihm frommte,
liess ich erfragen:
lohnend lehrt' ihn mein Wort.

MIME (*immer ängstlicher, da der* WANDERER *sich
nähert*).
Müss'ges Wissen
wahren manche:
ich weiss mir grade genug;
mir genügt mein Witz,
ich will nicht mehr:
dir Weisem weis' ich den Weg!

WANDERER (*setzt sich am Herde nieder*).
Hier sitz' ich am Herd,
und setze mein Haupt
der Wissens-Wette zum Pfand:
mein Kopf ist dein,
du hast ihn erkies't,
erfrägst du dir nicht
was dir frommt,
lös' ich's mit Lehren nicht ein.

MIME (*erschrocken und befangen, für sich*).
Wie werd' ich den Lauernden los?
Verfänglich muss ich ihn fragen.—
(*Laut.*)
Dein Haupt pfänd' ich
für den Herd:
nun sorg,' es sinnig zu lösen!
Drei der Fragen
stell' ich mir frei.

WANDERER. Dreimal muss ich's treffen.

MIME (*nach einigem Nachsinnen*).
Du rührtest dich viel
auf der Erde Rücken,
die Welt durchwandert'st du weit:
nun sage mir schlau,
welches Geschlecht
tagt in der Erde Tiefe?

WANDERER. In der Erde Tiefe
tagen die Nibelungen:
Nibelheim ist ihr Land.
Schwarzalben sind sie;
Schwarz-Alberich
hütet' als Herrscher sie einst:
eines Zauberringes
zwingende Kraft
zähmt' ihm das fleissige Volk.
Reicher Schätze
schimmernden Hort
häuften sie ihm:
der sollte die Welt ihm gewinnen. —
Zum zweiten was frägst du Zwerg?

MIME (*in a brown study*).
    Much, Wanderer,
      wottest thou
of the earth's most central cells —
    Now say to me sooth,
    what is the stock
which on its back sojourneth?

WANDERER. On its back the giants
    live, an ungentle stock;
    Giantdom is their land.
      Fasolt and Fafner,
      the jealous feoffers,
    envied Alberich's might,
      and his wonderful hoard
      they won for themselves,
    and ravished also the ring.
      Between the brothers
      then broke out strife,
    and, Fasolt fall'n,
      as dragon dread
holdeth now Fafner the hoard.—
Thy third enquiry now threats.

MIME (*who is quite absorbed in thought*).
    Much, Wanderer,
      wottest thou
of the earth's far stretching surface.
    Now rede me as well
    what is the race
wards the welkin above?

WANDERER. The welkin above
    ward well the Æsir;
where they dwell is Valhall'.
    Light elves of heaven,
    Light Alberich,
Wotan, wardeth their host.
    From the World's ash-tree's
    worshipful arm
he shaped himself once a shaft:
    true that spear,
    though the tree may be spoiled,
    with such a sceptre
Wotan sways the world.
    Holiest treaties'
    truthful runes
he wrote all around the shaft.
    The head of worlds
    he, by whose hand
    is the spear gripped,
that Wotan's grasp now spans.
    There kneels to him
    The Niblung host;
    the giants must bow,
    by him enjoined:
all must allegiance owe him,
the spear's resistless lord.
(*He rests his spear, as if accidentally, on the ground; a slight peal of thunder is heard.* MIME *terrified.*)
Now tell me, sapient dwarf,
spaed I the answers true?
My head do I hold my own?

MIME (*who has recovered from his dreamy brooding, now shows renewed fear and dares not look at the Wanderer*).
    Questions and head
    hast thou redeemed:—
now, Wanderer, go on thy way.

WANDERER. What thy welfare concerns
    thou should'st have sought for;
holding in pledge thus my head.

MIME (*in tieferer Sinnen gerathend*)
    Viel, Wanderer,
      weisst du mir
aus der Erde Nabelnest:—
    nun sage mir schlicht,
    welches Geschlecht
ruht auf der Erde Rücken?

WANDERER. Auf der Erde Rücken
    wuchtet der Riesen Geschlecht:
    Riesenheim ist ihr Land.
      Fasolt und Fafner,
      der raunen Fürsten,
    neideten Nibelung's Macht;
      den gewaltigen Hort
      gewannen sie sich,
    errangen mir ihm den Ring:
      um den entbrannte
      den Brüdern Streit;
    der Fasolt füllte,
      als wilder Wurm
hütet nun Fafner den Hort.—
Die dritte Frage nun droht.

MIME (*der ganz in Träumerei entrückt ist*).
    Viel, Wand'rer,
      weisst du mir
von der Erde rauhem Rücken:—
    nun sage mir wahr,
    welches Geschlecht
wohnt auf wolkigen Höh'n?

WANDERER. Auf wolkigen Höh'n
    wohnen die Götter:
Walhall heisst ihr Saal.
    Lichtalben sind sie;
    Licht-Alberich,
Wotan, waltet der Schaar.
    Aus der Welt-Esche
    weihlichstem Aste
schuf er sich einen Schaft:
    dorrt der Stamm,
    nie verdirbt doch der **Speer**;
    mit seiner Spitze
sperrt Wotan die Welt.
    Heil'ger Verträge
    Treue-Runen
schnitt in den Schaft er ein.
    Den Haft der Welt
    hält in der Hand,
    wer den Speer führt,
    den Wotan's Faust umspannt.
    Ihm neigte sich
    der Niblungen Heer;
    der Riesen Gezücht
    zähmte sein Rath:
ewig gehorchen sie alle
des Speeres starkem Herrn.
(*Er stösst wie unwillkürlich mit dem Speer auf den Boden; ein leiser Donner lässt sich vernehmen, wovon* MIME *heftig erschrickt.*)
    Nun rede, weiser Zwerg:
    wusst' ich der Fragen Rath?
    behalte mein Haupt ich frei?

MIME (*is aus seiner träumerischen Versunkenheit aufgefahren, und gebärdet sich nun ängstlich, indem er den Wanderer nicht anzublicken wagt*).
    Fragen und Haupt
    hast du gelös't:
nun, Wand'rer, geh' deines Weg's?

WANDERER. Was zu wissen dir frommt
    solltest du fragen;
Kunde verbürgte mein Kopf.—

Since thou hast **not** weene*d*	dass du nun nicht weisst
what is good,	was dir nützt,
we'll gamble with thy head as gage.	dess' fass' ich jetzt deines als **Pfand.**
Greeting thou	Gastlich nicht
grudgedst thy guest;	galt mir dein Gruss:
my head I gave	mein Haupt gab ich
into thy hands.	in deine Hand,
that of thy hearth I might be free;	um mich des Herdes zu freu'n.
so now in pledge	Nach Wettens Pflicht
placed is thine own,	pfänd' ich nun dich,
can'st thou not thrice	lösest du drei
my riddles declare.	der Fragen nicht leicht:
Make resolute, Mime, thy mind.	drum frische dir, Mime, den Muth.

THE MOTIVE OF MIME COWED AND SUBMISSIVE.

MIME (*shyly, and with cowed submission*).	MIME (*schüchtern und in furchtsamer Ergebung*).
Long I've quitted	Lang' schon mied ich
my native land,	mein Heimathland,
long I've issued	lang' schon schied ich
from my mother earth,	aus der Mutter Schoss;
the eye-glance of Wotan cows me,	mir leuchtete Wotan's Auge,
he peereth into my cave;	zur Höhle lugt' es herein:
his gaze melts all	vor ihm magert
my mother wit.	mein Mutterwitz.
But quick must my wisdom be no**w**. —	Doch frommt mir's nun weise zu **sein**
Wanderer, question away!	Wand'rer, frage denn zu!
Belike may I redeem me,	Vielleicht glückt mir's gezwungen
deliver the dwarf's poor head.	zu lösen des Zwergen Haupt.
WANDERER. Now, amiable dwarf,	WANDERER. Nun, ehrlicher Zwerg,
first let me ask you:	sag, mir zum ersten:
what is that noble race	welches ist das Geschlecht,
that Wotan ruthlessly dealt with,	dem Wotan schlimm sich zeigt,
and which yet he deemeth most dear ?	und das doch das liebste ihm **lebt?**
MIME. Of your heroes	MIME. Wenig hört' ich
I hear but little;	von Heldensippen:
yet certainly this I can solve.	der Frage *d*och ma*c*h' ich mich **frei.**
The Volsungs are they,	Die Wälsungen sind
the valued race	das Wunschgeschlecht,
that Wotan fathered	das Wotan zeugte
and fondly loved,	und zärtlich liebt,
though favour he did withdraw.	zeigt er auch Ungunst ihm.
Siegmund and Sieglind'	Siegmund und Sieglind'
sprang from the Volsung,	stammten von Wälse,
a very turbulent	ein wild-verzweifeltes
twin-born pair;	Zwillingspaar:
Siegfried too is their son,	Siegfried zeugten sie selbst,
the stoutest Volsung e'er shaped.	den stärksten Wälsungenspross.
My head then, Wanderer,	Behalt' ich, Wanderer,
this time do I hold ?	zum ersten mein Haupt?
WANDERER. Aye, thou hast rightly	WANDERER. Wie doch genau
declared me the race:	das Geschlecht du mir nennst:
clearly proved is thy prowess !	schlau eracht' ich dich Argen!
The primal question	Der ersten Frage
hast thou quit;	ward'st du frei:
so, secondly hear and say. —	zum zweiten nun sag' mir, Zwerg:—
A wily Niblung	Ein weiser Niblung
wardeth Siegfried, —	wahret Siegfried:
fated slayer of Fafner,	Fafner'n soll er ihm fällen,
that the ring he may ravish	dass er den Ring erränge,
and hold the hoard for himself.	des Hortes Herrscher zu **sein.**
But what sword	Welches Schwert
must Siegfried then strike with,	muss nun Siegfried schwingen,
dealing Fafner death ?	taug' es zu Fafner's Tod?

MIME (*forgetting his present position in his eager interest in the subject*).

    " Needful " is
    the name of the sword;
    'twas in an ash-tree's stem
    struck by Wotan:
he solely might own it
whose hand could snatch it out.
    By strongest heroes
    was it not stirred;
    Siegmund, the warlike:
    won the prize:
well he wore it in strife,
till by Wotan's spear it was split.
    Now, a subtle smith
    doth preserve the shreds,
    for he wots with no other
    than Wotan's sword
that bold and foolish boy,
Siegfried, will slay the worm.
    (*Quite pleased.*)
    Thus have I saved
    a scond time my head !

WANDERER. The wittiest, surely,
    art thou of wise ones;
whose cunning can come near thine ?
    But since thou hast sought
    this simpleton hero
for Niblung's need to make use of,
    now my third inquiry
    threatens thee. —
    Say then, thou wisest
    weapon-smith,
who will from the stubborn splinters
" Needful," the sword, re-establish ?

MIME (*starts up in the greatest terror*).
    The splinters! the sword !
    Alas! it 'scapes me!—
    What can I say ?
    What course pursue ?
    The cursed steel,
    would I ne'er had stol'n it!
    To be thus entangled
    in fatal toils!
    'Tis far too hard
    to yield to my hammer;
    flux and solder
    serve not to smelt.
    The artfullest smith
    is at a loss!
    Who shapeth the sword
    since I cannot?
How may I master this marvel ?

WANDERER (*who has risen from the hearth*).
    Three times asked were thy questions,
    three times I was acquit;
    but foreign quite
    thy queries were,
for what was near to thy heart
and thy needs, didst thou not ask.
    Now I have found it,
    wondrous thy fright:
    thy witty pate
    have I won as a prize.
Hear, Fafner's would-be undoer,
heed, thou fated dwarf:—
    none but who fear
    hath never felt
maketh " Needful " new

MIME (*seine gegenwärtige Lage immer mehr vergessend, und von dem Gegenstande lebhaft angezogen*).

    Nothung heisst
    ein neidliches Schwert;
    in einer Esche Stamm
    stiess es Wotan:
    dem sollt' es geziemen,
    der aus dem Stamm' es zög'.
    Der stärksten Helden
    keiner bestand's:
    Siegmund, der Kühne,
    konnt's allein;
    fechtend führt' er's im Streit,
    bis an Wotan's Speer es zersprang.
    Nun verwahrt die Stücken
    ein weiser Schmied;
    denn er weiss, dass allein
    mit dem Wotansschwert
    ein kühnes dummes Kind,
    Siegfried, den Wurm versehrt.
    (*Ganz vergnügt.*)
    Behalt' ich Zwerg
    auch zweitens mein Haupt?

WANDERER. Der witzigste bist du
    unter den Weisen:
    wer käm' dir an Klugheit gleich?
    Doch bist du so klug,
    den kindischen Helden
    für Zwergen-Zwecke zu nützen:
    mit der dritten Frage
    droh' ich nun!—
    sag' mir, du weiser
    Waffenschmied,
    wer wird aus den starken Stücken
    Nothung, das Schwert, wohl schweissen?

MIME (*fährt im höchsten Schrecken auf*).
    Die Stücken! Schwert!
    O weh! mir schwindelt!—
    Was fang' ich an?
    Was fällt mir ein?
    Verfluchter Stahl,
    dass ich dich gestohlen!
    Er hat mich vernagelt
    in Pein und Noth;
    mir bleibt er hart,
    ich kann ihn nicht hämmern:
    Niet' und Löthe
    lässt mich im Stich!
    Der weiseste Schmied
    weiss sich nicht Rath:
    wer schweisst nun das Schwert,
    schaff' ich es nicht?
    Das Wunder, wie soll ich's wissen?

WANDERER (*ist vom Herd aufgestanden*).
    Dreimal solltest du fragen,
    dreimal stand ich dir frei:
    nach eitlen Fernen
    forschtest du;
    doch was zunächst sich dir fand,
    was dir nützt, fiel dir nicht ein.
    Nun ich's errathe,
    wirst du verrückt;
    gewonnen hab' ich
    das witzige Haupt.—
    Jetzt, Fafner's kühner Bezwinger,
    hör' verfallener Zwerg:—
    nur wer das Fürchten
    nie erfuhr,
    schmiedet Nothung neu.

(MIME *stares wildly at him as he turns to depart.*)
Thy head so wise
henceforth guard well!
I leave it forfeit to him
who has learnt not yet to fear.
(*He turns away, laughing, and disappears in the forest.*)

MIME (*paralyzed with terror, sinks back on his stool behind the anvil. He stares for a while before him at the sunlit forest. After a long silence he begins to tremble violently*).
Accursed light!
how creep'st thou aloft!
What quivers and shivers?
what quickens and sways,
what swirls and enflames
and flickers around?
All glitters and gleams
in the sunlight's glint.
What hisses and hums
and holds my gaze?
It roars and rolls
and rumbles toward;—
it rends through the wood,—
where shall I flee?
Before me a monstrous
maw I behold!—
The dragon has found me!
Fafner! Fafner!
(*He shrieks aloud and cowers down behind the great anvil.*)

SIEGFRIED (*breaks from the thicket and calls, still from without*).
Ho! lazy fellow!
Hav'n't you finished?
Say now, how goes the sword?
(*Enters and pauses in surprise.*)
Where hides the smith?
Has he decamped?
Ho, ho! Mime, you moon-calf!
D'ye hear me? where have you hid?

MIME (*with feeble voice, from behind the anvil*).
Is't thou, boy?
Art thou alone?

SIEGFRIED. Under the anvil!
Say, what seek you down there?
Sharpened yet is my sword?

MIME. The sword? The sword?
How can I shape it?—
(*Half aside.*)
"None but who Fear
hath never felt
maketh ' Needful ' new."
Too wise my wits are
for such a work.

SIEGFRIED. Will you not tell me?
Or must I teach you?

MIME (*as before*). Where shall I hope for help?
My wily head
I held in wager;
I've lost it, 'tis forfeit to him
"who has learnt not yet to fear."

SIEGFRIED (*violently*). Still do you flout me?
Would you then fly?

(MIME *starrt ihn gross an: er wendet sich zum Fortgange*),
Dein weises Haupt
wahre von heut':
verfallen—lass' ich's dem,
der das Fürchten nicht gelernt.
(*Er lacht und geht in den Wald.*)

MIME (*ist, wie vernichtet, auf den Schemel hinter den Ambos zurückgesunken: er stiert, grad' vor sich aus, in den sonnig beleuchteten Wald hinein. — Nach längerem Schweigen geräth er in heftiges Zittern*).
Verfluchtes Licht!
Was flammt dort die Luft?
Was flackert und lackert,
was flimmert und schwirrt,
was schwebt dort und webt
und wabert umher?
Da glimmert's und glitzt's
in der Sonne Gluth:
was säuselt und summ't
und saus't nun gar?
Es brummt und braus't
und prasselt hierher!
Dort bricht's durch den Wald,
will auf mich zu!
Ein grässlicher Rachen
reisst sich mir auf!—
Der Wurm will mich fangen!
Fafner! Fafner!
(*Er schreit laut auf und knickt hinter dem breiten Ambos zusammen.*)

SIEGFRIED (*bricht aus dem Waldgesträuch hervor, und ruft noch von aussen*).
Heda! Fauler!
bist du nun fertig?
Schnell! wie steht's mit dem Schwert?
(*Er ist eingetreten und hält verwundert an.*)
Wo steckt der Schmied?
Stahl er sich fort?
Hehe! Mime! du Memme!
Wo bist du? wo birg'st du dich?

MIME (*mit schwacher Stimme hinter dem Ambos*).
Bist du es, Kind?
Kommst du allein?

SIEGFRIED. Hinter dem Ambos?—
Sag', was schufest du dort?
schärftest du mir das Schwert?

MIME (*höchst verstört und zerstreut*).
Das Schwert? das Schwert?
wie möcht' ich's schweissen?—
(*Halb für sich.*)
" Nur wer das Fürchten
nicht erfuhr,
schmiedet Nothung neu."—
Zu weise ward ich
für solches Werk!

SIEGFRIED. Wirst du mir reden?
Soll ich dir rathen?

MIME (*wie zuvor*).
Wo nehm' ich redlichen Rath?—
Mein weises Haupt
hab' ich verwettet:
verfallen, verlor ich's an den,
" der das Fürchten nicht gelernt.'

SIEGFRIED (*heftig*). Sind mir das Flausen?
Willst du mir flieh'n?

MIME (*gradually recovering hi..self*).
    I'd fly from him
    who fear had known:—
but that truly I never have taught him.
    I, fool-like, forgot
    the one thing good:
    love towards me
    was my lesson;—
but, alas! I lost my work.
What force can awake in him fear?

SIEGFRIED (*seizing him*). Ho! must I help you?
    What whim's in your head?

MIME.   Alone for thy sake
    I sank in absorption.
    Would I could weightily warn thee!

SIEGFRIED (*laughing*). Nay, under the seat
      well were you sinking;
    what weighty affairs took you there?

MIME (*with still more self-possession*).
    With fear I trembled for thee,
    that I the thing might teach thee.

SIEGFRIED. What mean you by fearing?

MIME.   Thou feltest it ne'er,
    yet wilt from this wood
    go forth to the world?
How fruitless the firmest of swords
    if from thee fear is far!

SIEGFRIED (*impatiently*). Foolish talk
    you're feeding me with.

MIME   'Tis thy mother's rede
    read thee by me:
    to what she left me
    must I be loyal;—
    to the lures of the world
    I never should leave thee
till duly to fear thou had'st learnt.

SIEGFRIED. If 'tis an art
    why am I untaught?
    Arede! what is it, this fearing?

MIME (*with increasing animation*).
    Feltest thou ne'er
    in forest dark,
    at gloaming hour
    in gloomy spots,
    when with a rustle,
    rush and roar
    fearful hurtling
    toward thee howls,
    dazzling flickers
    round thee flutter,
    swelling surges
    toward the swoop,—
feltest thou then, no grisly
gruesomeness grow o'er thy fancy?
    Balefullest shudders
    shake thy whole body,
    all thy senses
    sink and forsake thee,
in thy breast bursting and big
beat thy hammering heart?—
Feltest thou nought of this,
then fear thou hast not yet found.

MIME (*allmälig sich etwas fassend*).
    Wohl flöh' ich dem,
    der's Fürchten kennt:—
doch das liess ich dem Kinde zu lehren:
    Ich Dummer vergass
    was einzig gut:
    Liebe zu mir
    sollt' er lernen;—
das gelang nun leider faul!
Wie bring' ich das Fürchten ihm bei?

SIEGFRIED (*packt ihn*).
    He! Muss ich helfen?
    Was fegtest du heut'?

MIME.   Für dich nur besorgt,
    versank ich in Sinnen,
    wie ich dich Wichtiges wiese.

SIEGFRIED (*lachend*).
    Bis unter den Sitz
    warst du versunken:
    was Wichtiges fandest du da?

MIME (*sich immer mehr erholend*).
    Das Fürchten lernt' ich für dich,
    dass ich's dich Dummen lehre.

SIEGFRIED. Was ist's mit dem Fürchten?

MIME.   Erfuhr'st du's noch nie,
    und willst aus dem Wald
    fort in die Welt?
    Was frommte das festeste Schwert,
    blieb dir das Fürchten fern?

SIEGFRIED (*ungeduldig*). Faulen Rath
    erfindest du wohl?

MIME.   Deiner Mutter Rath
    redet aus mir:
    was ich gelobt'
    muss ich nun lösen,
    in die listige Welt
    dich nicht zu lassen,
    eh' du nicht das Fürchten gelernt.

SIEGFRIED. Ist's eine Kunst,
    was kenn' ich sie nicht?—
    Heraus! Was ist's mit dem Fürchten?

MIME (*immer belebter*).
    Fühltest du nie
    im finstern Wald,
    bei Dämmerschein
    am dunklen Ort,
    wenn fern es säuselt,
    summs't und saus't,
    wildes Brummen
    näher braus't,
    wirres Flackern
    um dich flimmert,
    schwellend Schwirren
    zu Leib' dir schwebt,—
    fühltest du dann nicht grieselnd
Grausen die Glieder dir fah'n?
    Glühender Schauer
    schüttelt die Glieder
    wirr verschwimmend
    schwinden die Sinne,
    in der Brust bebend und bang
    berstet hämmernd das Herz?—
Fühltest du das noch nicht,
das Fürchten blieb dir dann fremd.

SIEGFRIED Strange and right singular
  that must seem!
  Hard and firm
  feel the strings of my heart.
  This grimness and growling,
  this glowing and shaking,
  this burning and shiv'ring,
  beating and quaking, —
  well I wish to acquire them,
  how for such pastimes I pant!
  But how bring it,
  Mime, about?
  What means could make you my master?

MIME.   Follow me well,
  I'll find thee a way;
  thinking, fell I upon't.
  I wot of a monstrous Worm,
  who's wasted many folk;
  fear thou'lt learn from Fafner,
  follow me but to his hole.

SIEGFRIED.   Where lieth his hole?

MIME.   Hate-cavern
  well is it hight;
  to east, at end of the wood.

SIEGFRIED.   And would the world be that way?

MIME.   To Hate-cavern it lies close at hand.

SIEGFIRED..   Toward it then, let me follow,
  learn about fearing,
  and forth to the world!
  Then swift! shape me the sword!
  In the world would I assay it.

MIME.   The sword? alack!

SIEGFRIED.   Quick to your smithy!
  What can you shew?

MIME.   Accursed steel!
  I cannot restore it again!
  Such mighty magic's
  too much for poor Mime's force.
  One who knoweth not fear
  the knack might quickly find.

SIEGFRIED.   Famous falsehoods,
  sluggard, you're framing:
  that you're a muddler
  must you admit,
  not seek to dissemble with lies. —
  Bring me the bits here!
  Fly, you old bungler!
  My father's blade
  fails not with me:
  I'll soon shape it myself!
  (*He quickly prepares for work.*)

MIME.   Had'st thou been careful
  to master the craft,
  now might thy work be of use:
  too lazy wert thou
  ever to learn;
  how wilt thou best set about it?

SIEGFRIED.   Where the master was balked,
  what more could the boy do,
  who to his counsel gave heed? —
  So move afar,
  meddle not here,
  for fear you be made to fuel!

SIEGFRIED.   Sonderlich seltsam
  muss das sein!
  Hart und fest,
  fühl' ich, steht mir das Herz.
  Das Grieseln und Grausen,
  Glühen und Schauern,
  Hitzen und Schwindeln,
  Hämmern und Beben —
  gern begehr' ich das Bangen,
  sehnend verlangt mich's der Lust.—
  Doch wie bringst du,
  Mime mir's bei?
  Wie wär'st du Memme mir Meister?

MIME.   Folge mir nur,
  ich führe dich wohl;
  sinnend fand ich's aus.
  Ich weiss einen schlimmen Wurm,
  der würgt' und schland schon viel:
  Fafner lehrt dich das Fürchten,
  folgst du mir zu seinem Nest.

SIEGFRIED.   Wo liegt er im Nest?

MIME.   Neid-Höhle
  wird es genannt:
  im Ost, am Ende des Wald's.

SIEGFRIED.   Dann wär's nicht weit von der Welt'

MIME.   Bei Neidhöhl' liegt sie ganz nah';

SIEGFRIED.   Dahin denn sollst du mich führen
  lernt' ich das Fürchten,
  dann fort in die Welt!
  Drum schnell schaffe das Schwert,
  in der Welt will ich es schwingen.

MIME.   Das Schwert? O Noth!

SIEGFRIED.   Rasch in die Schmiede!
  Weis' was du schuf'st.

MIME.   Verfluchter Stahl:
  Zu flicken versteh' ich ihn nicht!
  Den zähen Zauber
  bezwingt keines Zwergen Kraft.
  Wer das Fürchten nicht kennt,
  der fänd' wohl eher die Kunst.

SIEGFRIED.   Feine Finten
  weiss mir der Faule;
  dass er ein Stümper
  sollt' er gesteh'n:
  nun lügt er sich listig heraus.—
  Her mit den Stücken!
  Fort mit dem Stümper!
  Des Vaters Stahl
  fügt sich wohl mir:
  ich selbst schweisse das Schwert!
  (*Er macht sich rasch an die Arbeit.*)

MIME.   Hättest du fleissig
  die Kunst gepflegt,
  jetzt käm' dir's wahrlich zu gut;
  doch lässig warst du
  stets in der Lehre:
  was willst du nun Rechtes rüsten?

SIEGFRIED.   Was der Meister nicht kann,
  vermöcht' es der Knabe,
  hätt' er ihm immer gehorcht?—
  Jetzt mach' dich fort,
  misch' dich nicht d'rein:
  sonst fällst du mir mit in's Feuer!

He has heaped a mass of coal on the fire and blown it well up; now, fixing the sword-pieces in a vice, he commences to file them to powder.

MIME (*looking on at his proceedings*).
    What art thou about?
    Take but the solder;
    the flux fused for thee, see!

SIEGFRIED.   Out on your flux!
    'twill fit me nought:
    such filth will forge me no sword!

MIME.   But the file is failing,
    the rasp is ruined:
    why dost thou destroy thy steel so?

SIEGFRIED.   In shreds each fibre
    and splinter I'd see:
    what is marred were mended but so.

MIME (*while* SIEGFRIED *diligently files away*).
    Here helps no cunning,
    to me 'tis clear:
    here speeds the dullard
    by dulness alone!
    Look how he works
    with mighty will!
    The steel is dissolved,
    yet is he not strained. —
    Though old as this cave
    or wood am I,
    such wondrous sight ne'er I've seen!
    He'll achieve the work,
    I wot full well:
    fearless, fashion the sword,
    as well the Wanderer saw. —
    Where shall I hide
    my shrinking head?
    For by this boy it must fall,
    learns he of Fafner no fear. —
    But woe's me, hapless!
    Who'll waste me the worm
    if terror it teaches to him?
    And the ring how shall I reach?
    Accurs'd dilemma!
    It locks me close,
    comes there no light to me
    how to cozen this bold-hearted boy!

SIEGFRIED (*has reduced the sword to powder and put it in a crucible which he now places in the forge. During the following he blows up the fire with the bellows*).
    Hey! Mime! Now say,
    how hight the sword
    that I have filed into fibres?

MIME (*starting out of a reverie*).
    "Needful" named
    is the notable sword;
    so thy mother stated to me

SIEGFRIED (*over his work*).
    Needful! Needful!
    Notable sword!
    Why wert thou thus dissevered?
    To shreds I've shattered
    thy shining blade,
    the pot shall melt now the shivers!
    Oho! Oho!
    Aha! Aha!

Er hat eine grosse Menge Kohlen auf dem Herd gehäuft, und unterhält in einem fort die Gluth, während er die Schwertstücke in den Schraubstock einspannt und sie zu Spähnen zerfeilt.

MIME (*indem er ihm zusieht*).
    Was machst du da?
    Nimm doch die Löthe:
    den Brei braut' ich schon längst.

SIEGFRIED.   Fort mit dem Brei!
    ich brauch' ihn nicht:
    mit Bappe back' ich kein Schwert!

MIME.   Du zerfeil'st die Feile,
    zerreib'st die Raspel:
    wie willst du den Stahl zerstampfen?

SIEGFREID.   Zersponnen muss ich
    in Spähne ihn seh'n:
    was entzwei ist, zwing' ich mir so.

MIME (*während* SIEGFRIED *eifrig fortfeilt*).
    Hier hilft Kein Kluger,
    das seh' ich klar:
    hier hilft dem Dummen
    die Dummheit selbst!
    Wie er sich müht
    und mächtig regt:
    ihm schwindet der Stahl,
    doch wird ihm nicht schwül!—
    Nun ward ich so alt
    'wie Höhl' und Wald,
    und hab' nicht so 'was geseh'n!
    Mit dem Schwert gelingt's,
    das lern' ich wohl:
    furchtlos fegt er's zu ganz,—
    der Wand'rer wusst' es gut!—
    Wie berg' ich nun
    mein banges Haupt?
    Dem kühnen Knaben verfiel's,
    lehrt' ihn nicht Fafner die Furcht.—
    Doch weh' mir Armen!
    Wie würgt' er den Wurm,
    erfuhr' er das Fürchten von ihm?
    Wie erräng' er mir den Ring?
    Verfluchte Klemme!
    Da klebt' ich fest,
    fänd' ich nicht klugen Rath,
    wie den Furchtlosen selbst ich bezwäng'.-

SIEGFRIED (*hat nun die Stücken zerfeilt und in einem Schmelztigel gefangen, den er jetzt in die Herdgluth stellt: unter dem Folgenden nährt er die Gluth mit dem Blasebalg*).
    He, Mime, geschwind:
    wie heisst das Schwert,
    das ich in Spähne zersponnen?

MIME (*aus seinen Gedanken auffahrend*).
    Nothung nennt sich
    das neidliche Schwert:
    deine Mutter gab mir die Märe.

SIEGFRIED (*zu der Arbeit*).
    Nothung! Nothung!
    neidliches Schwert!
    was musstest du zerspringen?
    Zu Spreu nun schuf ich
    die scharfe Pracht,
    im Tigel brat' ich die Spähne!
    Hoho! hoho!
    hahei! hahei!

Bellows blow!
brighten the glow!—
Wild in woodlands
waved a tree,
which I in the forest felled.
the brown-hued ash
I baked into coal,
on the hearth it lies now in heaps.

Blase, Balg!
blase die Gluth!—
Wild im Walde
wuchs ein Baum,
den hab' ich im Forst gefällt:
die braune Esche
brannt' ich zu Kohl',
auf dem Herd nun liegt sie gehäuft.

Oho! Oho!
Aha! Aha!
Bellows blow!
brighten the glow!—
The branches' fragments,
how bravely they flame!
their glow how fierce and fair!
They spring in the air
with scattering sparks
and smelt me the steely shreds.

Hoho! hoho!
hahei! hahei!
Blase, Balg!
blase die Gluth!—
Des Baumes Kohle,
wie brennt sie kühn,
wie glüht sie hell und hehr!
In springenden Funken
sprüht sie auf,
schmilzt mir des Stahles Spreu.

Oho! Oho!
Aha! Aha!
Bellows blow!
brighten the glow!—
Needful! Needful!
notable sword!
I've smelted thy steely shreds.
In thine own sweat
thou swimmest now;—
I soon shall call thee my sword!

Hoho! hoho!
hahei! hahei!
Blase, Balg!
blase die Gluth!—
Nothung! Nothung!
neidliches Schwert!
schon schmilzt deines Stahles Spreu:
im eig'nen Schweisse
schwimmst du nun—
bald schwing' ich dich als mein Schwert!

MIME (*during the last verse of* SIEGFRIED'S *song continues his own reflections aside*).
He'll smithy the sword
and fell me Fafner;
I see 'tis as settled as fate.
Store and ring
he'll wrest in the strife:—
in what way the prize can I win?
By wit and craft
I'll win it surely,
and save perhaps my head.
Wearied in fight with the worm,
in his faintness fain he will drink
From potent simples
by me assorted
I will a draught prepare:
but one drop
need he drink of,
senseless, he'll sink to sleep.
With the very weapon
he valiantly welds there
he shall be razed from my way;
the ring and the hoard I'll have.
Hey! wisest Wanderer,
dull was I deemed?
How doth like thee now
my lusty wit?
Lacks me still
a rightful rede?
(*He springs up in glee, fetches vessels and pours decoctions from them into a pot.*)

MIME (*während der Absätze von* SIEGFRIED'S *Lied immer für sich, entfernt sitzend*).
Er schmiedet das Schwert,
und Fafner fällt er:
das seh' ich nun sicher voraus;
Hort und Ring
erringt er im Harst:—
wie erwerb' ich mir den Gewinn?
Mit Witz und List
erlang' ich Beides,
und berge heil mein Haupt.
Rang er sich müd' mit dem Wurm,
von der Müh' erlab' ihn ein Trank;
aus würz'gen Säften,
die ich gesammelt,
brau' ich den Trank für ihn;
wenig Tropfen nur
braucht er zu trinken,
sinnlos sinkt er in Schlaf:
mit der eig'nen Waffe,
die er sich gewonnen,
räum' ich ihn leicht aus dem Weg,
erlange mir Ring und Hort.
Hei! Weiser Wand'rer,
dünkt' ich dich dumm,
wie gefällt dir nun
mein feiner Witz?
Fand ich mir wohl
Rath und Ruh'?
(*Er springt vergnügt auf, holt Gefässe herbei und schüttet aus ihnen Gewürz in einen Topf.*)

SIEGFRIED (*has poured the molten steel into a mould and plunged this into water, whereupon the loud hiss of its cooling is heard*).
To the water flowed
a fiery flood;
anger and hate
hissed from the depths,
cowed was its head by the cold.
Though scorching it struck
in the watery stream:
it stirs no more:

SIEGFRIED (*hat den geschmolzenen Stahl in eine Stangenform gegossen, und diese in das Wasser gesteckt: man hört jetzt das laute Gezisch der Kühlung*)
In das Wasser floss
ein Feuerfluss;
grimmiger Zorn
zischt' ihm da auf;
frierend zähmt' ihm der Frost.
Wie sehrend er floss,
in des Wassers Fluth
fliesst er nicht mehr:

stiff lies it and stark,
haughty and hard the steel.
Haply in blood
it soon will bathe!—

starr ward er und steif,
herrisch der harte Stahl:
heisses Blut doch
fliesst ihm bald!—

Now sweat once again,
that so I may shape thee,
Needful, notable sword!
(*He thrusts the sword into the coals and heats it. Then he turns to* MIME, *who at the other end of the hearth has carefully put his pipkin on the fire.*)

Nun schwitze noch einmal,
dass ich dich schweisse,
Nothung, neidliches Schwert!
(*Er stösst den Stahl in die Kohlen und glüht ihn. Dann wendet er sich zu* MIME, *der vom anderen Ende des Herdes her einen Topf an den Rand der Gluth setzt.*)

What is that patch
about with his pot?
While I burn steel
would you brew sauces?

Was schafft der Tölpel
dort mit dem Topf?
Brenn' ich hier Stahl,
brau'st du dort Sudel?

MIME. The smith has come to shame,
the pupil his conqueror proves;
all the craftman's art for aye is o'er,
thy cook he hath become.
Burn then thy iron to broth,
while I will brew
my eggs into soup.
(*Goes on cooking.*

MIME. Zu Schanden kam ein Schmied,
den Lehrer sein Knabe lehrt;
mit der Kunst ist's beim Alten aus,
als Koch dient er dem Kinde:
brennt es das Eisen zu Brei,
aus Eiern brau't
der Alte ihm Sud.
(*Er fährt fort zu kochen.*)

SIEGFRIED (*still over his work*).
Mime the craftsman
now learns cooking;
the smithy serves him no more'
all the swords he made
I shattered and shivered;
what he cooks I care not to taste.

SIEGFRIED (*immer während der Arbeit*).
Mime, der Künstler,
lernt nun Kochen;
das Schmieden schmeckt ihm nicht mehr:
seine Schwerter alle
hab' ich zerschmissen;
was er kocht, ich kost' es ihm nicht.

To fear he will teach me
if I but follow;
afar there dwelleth a tutor.
But the best he can do
will bring 't not about;
a fool have I found him in all things.
(*He has taken out the red-hot steel and proceeds to hammer it on the anvil with a great smith's hammer, during the following song.*)

Das Fürchten zu lernen
will er mich führen;
ein Ferner soll es mich lehren:
was am besten er kann,
mir bringt er's nicht bei;
als Stümper besteht er in allem!
(*Er hat den rothglühenden Stahl hervorgezogen, und hämmert ihn nun, während des folgenden Liedes mit dem grossen Schmiedehammer auf dem Ambos.*)

Oho! Oho! Oho!
Shape me, my hammer,
a hardy sword!
Oho! Aha!
Aha! Oho!
Aha! Oho! Aha!

Hoho! hahei! hoho!
Schmiede, mein Hammer
ein hartes Schwert!
Hoho! hahei!
hahei! hoho!
Hahei! hoho! hahei!

Thy steely blue
once streamed with blood;
its ruddy ripples
reddened thy sides;
cold laughter was thine,
the warm stream licking to cool!
Heiha! Heiha!
Heiha! Ha! Ha!
Oho! Oho! Oho!
Now in the glow
thou redly gleam'st;
thy weakness heedeth
my hammer's weight:
testy sparks dost thou scatter,
that I thy spirit have tamed!
Heiho! Heiho!
Heiho! Ho! Ho!
Oho! Oho! Aha!

Einst färbte Blut
dein falbes Blau;
sein rothes Rieseln
röthete dich:
kalt lachtest du da,
das warme lecktest du kühl!
Hahahei! hahahei!
hahahei! hei! hei!
Hoho! hoho! hoho!
Nun hat die Gluth
dich roth geglüht·
deine weiche Härte
dem Hammer weicht:
zornig sprüh'st du mir Funken,
dass ich dich Spröden gezähmt
Heiaho! heiaho:
heiaho! ho! ho!
Hoho! hoho! hahei!

Oho! Aha! Oho!
Shape me, my hammer,
a hardy sword!

Hoho! hahei! hoho!
Schmiede, mein Hammer.
ein hartes Schwert!

Oho! Aha!
Aha! Oho!
Aha! Oho! Aha!

These springing sparks
what a sport to see!
In rage the brave
are arrayed the best;
lo! thou laughest on me,
yet can'st be grisly and grim!
Heiha! Heiha!
Heiha! Ha! Ha!
Oho! Oho! Oho!
Both fire and hammer
failed me not!
With stalwart strokes
I stretched thee out;
let sink now thy blush of shame,
be as cold and hard as thou can'st.
Heiho! Heiho!
Heiho! Ho! Ho!
Aha! Oho! Aha!
*With the last words, he plunges the sword into the
water, laughing at the hiss it makes.)*

MIME *while* SIEGFRIED *is fastening the forged sword-
blade into a handle, — again coming to the front).*

He shapes him a sword so sharp,
Fafner it felleth,
the Niblung's foe.
A draught of might I've made,
Siegfried to finish
when Fafner falls.
This treach'ry *must* I contrive,
triumph *must* I attain.
What my brother shaped,
the shimmering ring,
endowed with enchantment's
charms and control —
the peerless gold
which all power gives, —
I plainly have gained it!
I govern it! —
Alberic e'en,
whom once I served,
as bondsman will I
bind me anon.
As Nibelheim's lord
let me be known there;
I'll humble to me
all their host! —
The poor vilified dwarf
how will they revere!
To the gold will go thronging
men and gods;
before my bidding
bows all the world;
before my anger
awed are they all!
In toil then moveth
Mime no more;
his wealth unending
shall others work.
Mime the mighty,
Mime is monarch;
prince of earth-gnomes,
ruler of all!
Hey, Mime! how glad wert thou then!
Who would believe this of thee?

Hoho! hahei!
hahei! hoho!
Hahei! hoho! hahei!

Der frohen Funken,
wie freu' ich mich!
Es ziert den Kühnen
des Zornes Kraft:
lustig lach'st du mich an,
stellst du auch grimm dich und gram
Hahahei! hahahei!
hahahei! hei! hei!
Hoho! hoho! hoho!
Durch Gluth und Hammer
glückt' es mir!
Mit starken Schlägen
streckt' ich dich:
nun schwinde die rothe Scham;
werde kalt und hart wie du kannst.
Heiaho! heiaho!
heiaho! ho! ho!
Hahei! hoho! hahei!
*(Er taucht mit dem letzten den Stahl in das Wasser
und lacht bei dem starken Gezisch.)*

MIME *(während* SIEGFRIED *die geschmiedete Schwert-
klinge in dem Griffhefte befestigt, — wieder im Vordergrunde).*

Er schafft sich ein scharfes Schwert,
Fafner zu fällen,
der Zwerge Feind:
ich brau' ein Trug-Getränk,
Siegfried zu fällen,
dem Fafner fiel.
Gelingen muss mir die List;
lachen muss mir der Lohn!
Den der Bruder schuf,
den schimmernden Reif,
in den er gezaubert
zwingende Kraft,
das helle Gold,
das zum Herrscher macht—
ich hab' ihn gewonnen!
ich walte sein'! —
Alberich selbst,
der einst mich band,
zu Zwergenfrohne
zwing' ich ihn nun:
als Niblungenfürst
fahr' ich danieder;
gehorchen soll mir
alles Heer! —
Der verachtete Zwerg,
was wird er geehrt!
Zu dem Hort hin drängt sich
Gott und Held:
vor meinem Nicken
neigt sich die Welt,
vor meinem Zorne
zittert sie hin! —
Dann wahrlich müht sich
Mime nicht mehr:
ihm schaffen And're
den ew'gen Schatz.
Mime, der kühne,
Mime ist König,
Fürst der Alben,
Walter des All's!
Hei, Mime! wie glückte mir das!
wer glaubte wohl das von dir!

SIEGFRIED (*during the last part of* MIME's *song has been filing and sharpening the sword and hammering it with a small hammer*).
  Needful! Needful!
  notable sword!
  in handle once more thou art held.
    When thou wert wrecked
    I wrought thee anew;
  no stroke shall again destroy thee.
    Thy steel flew in twain
    from the stricken sire;
    the life-glowing son
    shapes it anew;
  now laughs upon him its sheen,
  and its sharpness surely cuts home.

  Needful! Needful!
  notable sword!
  Thy life again have I given.
    Dead lay'st thou
    once desolate,
  now leapest up dauntless and bright.
    Out then, and shew
    the cowards thy sheen!
    Shatter the false ones,
    fall on the sly!—
  See! and Mime, thou smith;
  so serveth Siegfried's sword!
(*During the second verse he brandishes the sword and now smites it on the anvil which splits in half from top to bottom, falling asunder with a loud noise.* MIME, *in extreme terror, falls flat on the ground.* SIEGFRIED, *shouting with glee, waves his sword in the air. The curtain falls quickly.*)

SIEGFRIED (*während der Absätze von* MIME's *Lied das Schwert feilend, schleifend und mit dem kleinen Hammer hämmernd*).
  Nothung! Nothung!
  neidliches Schwert!
  jetzt haftest du wieder im Heft.
    Warst du entzwei,
    ich zwang dich ganz,
  kein Schlag soll nun dich zerschlagen.
    Dem sterbenden Vater
    zersprang der Stahl,
    der lebende Sohn
    schuf ihn neu:
  nun lacht ihm sein heller Schein,
  seine Schärfe schneidet ihm hart.

  Nothung! Nothung!
  neu und verjüngt!
  zum Leben weckt' ich dich wieder.
    Todt lag'st du
    in Trümmern dort,
  jetzt leuchtest du trotzig und hehr.
    Zeige den Schächern
    nun deinen Schein!
    schlage den Falschen,
    fälle den Schelm!—
  Schau, Mime, du Schmied:
  so schneidet Siegfried's Schwert!
(*Er hat während des zweiten Verses das Schwert geschwungen, und schlägt nun damit auf den Ambos: dieser zerspaltet in zwei Stücken, von oben bis unten, so dass er unter grossem Gepolter auseinander fällt.* MIME,—*in höchster Verzückung—fällt vor Schreck sitzlings zu Boden.* SIEGFRIED *hält jauchzend das Schwert in die Höhe.—Der Vorhang fällt schnell.*)

SECOND ACT.

A DEEP FOREST.

At the extreme back the opening of a cave. The ground rises in the middle of the stage, forming a little knoll; it sinks again towards the cave at back, so that the upper part of the cavern's mouth alone is visible. L. ..s to be seen through the trees a rocky cliff rent with fissures. — Gloomy night, darkest at back, where at first the eye of the audience can discern nothing distinctly.

ALBERICH (*leaning against the rocky wall at side, in gloomy reflection*).
  In woodland haunt
  by Hate-cave I keep watch.
    I prick my ear,
  keenly peers mine eye.—
    Anxious day!
    art thou arrived?
    Throwest thou there
    through the thicket light?
(*A gust of storm passes R. from the wood.*)
  But what gleam glances from thence?
    Nearer glimmers
    a brilliant glow,

TIEFER WALD.

Ganz im Hintergrunde die Oeffnung einer Höhle. Der Boden hebt sich bis zur Mitte der Bühne, wo er eine kleine Hochebene bildet; von da senkt er sich nach hinten, der Höhle zu, wieder abwärts, so dass von dieser nur der obere Theil der Oeffnung dem Zuschauer sichtbar ist. Links gewahrt man durch Waldbäume eine zerklüftete Felsenwand.—Finstere Nacht, am dichtesten über dem Hintergrunde, wo anfänglich der Blick des Zuschauers gar nichts zu unterscheiden vermag.

ALBERICH (*an der Felsenwand zur Seite gelagert, in düsterem Brüten*).
  In Wald und Nacht
  vor Neidhöhl' halt' ich Wacht:
    er lauscht mein Ohr,
  mühvoll lugt mein Aug'.—
    Banger Tag,
    beb'st du schon auf?
    dämmerst du dort
    durch das Dunkel her?
(*Sturmwind erhebt sich rechts aus dem Walde.*)
  Welcher Glanz glitzert dort auf?
    Näher schimmert
    ein heller Schein;

and strides, as of fiery steed,
    course through the wood,
    crashing this way.
    Nearer the dragon's death-man?
    Is't now that Fafner falls?
(*The wind subsides again and the glow fades.*)
    The light allays —
    the glow sinks from my sight:
    night falls once more.—
    Who neareth, shining through shadow?

THE WANDERER (*enters from the wood and pauses
    opposite* ALBERICH.)
    To Hate-cave
    by night have I hied:
    who confronts me in darkness dim?
(*As from a suddenly parted cloud, the moonlight breaks
    forth and illumines the* WANDERER's *figure.*)

ALBERICH (*recognizes the* WANDERER *and recoils in
    dread*).
    Thyself is it I see?
    (*Bursting into wrath.*)
    What wouldst thou here?
    Hence, from my way!
    Aroint, thou shameless rogue!

WANDERER. Black Alberich,
    bidest thou here?
    hast thou kept Fafner's house?

ALBERICH. Comest thou new
    annoy to inflict?
    Tarry not here,
    take thy way homeward!
    This place has sorely
    suffered from thee and thy plots.
    Therefore, villain,
    quickly avaunt!

WANDERER. I came as witness,
    not as worker:
    who'll bar the Wanderer's way?

ALBERICH (*laughing spitefully*).
    Thou spell-working conspirer!
    Were I dull as once
    in past days thou deemedst,
    when I was bound through blindness,
    how soon by ruse
    were the ring again from me ravished!
    Beware! all thy wiles
    well do I know;
    also thy weak point
    plainly am I aware of.
    With all my wealth
    thy debts hast thou wiped out;
    my gem dowered
    the giants' toil.
    what time they built thee thy burg.
    What was agreed upon
    with those grim ones
    in runes is writ this day
    on thy spear's all-dominant shaft.
    Nor dost dare
    what as price thou hast paid
    to juggle back from the giants.
    Thy spear thou speedily
    wouldst spoil thyself:
    in thine own hand
    the heavenly staff,
    the strong one, would split like a straw.

---

es rennt wie ein leuchtendes Ross
    bricht durch den Wald
    brausend daher.
    Naht schon des Wurmes Würger?
    ist's schon, der Fafner fällt?
(*Der Sturmwind legt sich wieder; der Glanz verlischt.*)
    Das Licht erlischt—
    der Glanz barg sich dem Blick:
    Nacht ist's wieder.—
    Wer naht dort schimmernd im Schatten

DER WANDERER (*tritt aus Wald auf, und hält
    * ALBERICH *gegenüber an*).
    Zur Neidhöhle
    fuhr ich bei Nacht:
    wen gewahr' ich im Dunkel dort?
(*Wie aus einem plötzlich zerreissenden Gewölk bricht
    Mondschein herein, und beleuchtet des* WANDERER's
    Gestalt.*)

ALBERICH (*erkennt den* WANDERER, *und fährt er-
    schrocken zurück*).
    Du selbst lässt dich hier seh'n?
    (*Er bricht in Wuth aus.*)
    Was willst du hier?
    Fort, aus dem Weg!
    von dannen, schamloser Dieb!

WANDERER. Schwarz-Alberich,
    schweif'st du hier?
    hütest du Fafner's Haus?

ALBERICH. Jag'st du auf neue
    Neidthat umher?
    Weile nicht hier!
    weiche von hinnen!
    Genug deines Truges
    tränkte die Stätte mit Noth.
    Drum, du Frecher,
    lass' sie jetzt frei!

WANDERER. Zu schauen kam ich,
    nicht zu schaffen:
    wer wehrte mir Wand'rers Fahrt?

ALBERICH (*lacht tückisch auf*).
    Du Rath wüthender Ränke!
    wär' ich dir zu lieb
    doch noch dumm wie damals,
    als du mich Blöden bandest!
    Wie leicht gerieth es
    den Ring mir nochmals zu rauben!
    Hab' Acht: deine Kunst
    kenne ich wohl;
    doch wo du schwach bist,
    bleib mir auch nicht verschwiegen
    Mit meinen Schätzen
    zahltest du Schulden;
    mein Ring lohnte
    der Riesen Müh',
    die deine Burg dir gebaut
    was mit den trotzigen
    einst du vertragen,
    dess' Runen wahrt noch heut'
    deines Speeres herrischer Schaft.
    Nicht du darfst,
    was als Zoll du gezahlt,
    den Riesen wieder entreissen,
    du selbst zerspelltest
    deines Speeres Schaft:
    in deiner Hand
    der herrische Stab,
    der starke zerstiebte wie Sprer

WANDERER. Through no runes of righteous compact
bound wert thou,
base one, by it:
it bowed thee down but by its strength:
for strife I ward it then well.

ALBERICH. How proud thy threats
of menacing power,
and yet how thy spirit doth sink!
Decreed unto death
through my curse
is Fanfer, the store's possessor: —
who'll hold it hereafter?
Will the notable hoard
a Nibelung once more inherit?
This tears thee with endless trouble!
For, passes the ring
once more to my palm,
elseways than foolish giants
I'll use the jewel's pow'r.
Then tremble, thou high
protector of heroes,
for Valhalla
I'll sieze on with Hella's host;
the world will then be mine!

WANDERER. Thy intent I know well;
it troubles me nought:
the ring's but wielded
when it is won.

ALBERICH. How darkly thou say'st
what I doubtless know well!
In heroes' offspring
hast thou then trust,
who truly have leapt from thy loins?
Hast thou not fostered a stripling
who straight the fruit should reach thee,
that thou dare'st not to thieve?

WANDERER. Mind me not—
wrangle with Mime:
thy brother brings thee a foe;
for the boy who follows him here
shall fell for him Fafner soon.
Nought knows he of me;
the Nibelung's need he should serve.
And so, my friend, I say,
thou canst work as thou wilt.
Give thou good heed,
be on thy guard;
he nothing knows of the ring:
but Mime needs must disclose.
[hoard?

ALBERICH. And thy hand hold'st thou from the

WANDERER. My belov'd one
I leave to act unmanaged;
he stands or he falls,
unhelped by me;
heroes' aid only I've faith in.

ALBERICH. With Mime wrestle
but I for the ring?

WANDERER. Only he would gather
also the gold.

ALBERICH. Yet J ne'er may win it anew?

WANDERER. A hero nears
the hoard to set free;
two Niblungs are greedy for gold;
Fafner falls,
who dost guard the wealth;

WANDERER. Durch Vertrages Treue-Runen
band er dich
Bösen mir nicht:
dich beugt er mir durch seine Kraft:
zum Krieg drum wahr' ich ihn wohl

ALBERICH. Wie stolz du dräu'st
in trotziger Stärke,
und wie dir's im Busen doch bangt!
Verfallen dem Tod
durch meinen Fluch
ist Fafner, des Hortes Hüter:—
wer—wird ihn beerben?
wird der neidliche Hort
dem Niblung wieder gehören?
Das sehrt dich mit ew'ger Sorge!
Denn fass' ich ihn wieder
einst in der Faust,
anders als dumme Riesen
üb' ich des Ringes Kraft:
dann zitt're der Helden
heiliger Hüter!
Walhall's Höhen
stürm' ich mit Hella's Heer:
der Welt walte dann ich!

WANDERER. Deinen Sinn kenn' ich;
doch sorgt er mich nicht:
des Ringes waltet
wer ihn gewinnt.

ALBERICH. Wie dunkel sprichst du,
was ich deutlich doch weiss!
An Heldensöhne
hält sich dein Trotz,
die traut deinem Blute entblüht
Pflegtest du wohl eines Knaben,
der klug die Frucht dir pflücke,
die du—nicht brechen darf'st?

WANDERER. Mit mir—nicht,
had're mit Mime:
dein Bruder bringt dir Gefahr;
einen Knaben führt er daher,
der Fafner ihm fällen soll.
Nichts weiss der von mir;
der Niblung nützt ihn für sich.
Drum sag' ich dir, Gesell:
thue frei wie's dir frommt!
Höre mich wohl,
sei auf der Hut:
nicht kennt der Knabe den Ring,
doch Mime kundet' ihn aus.

ALBERICH. Deine Hand hieltest du vom Hort?

WANDERER. Wen ich liebe
lass' ich für sich gewähren:
er steh' oder fall',
sein Herr ist er:
Helden nur können mir frommen.

ALBERICH. Mit Mime räng' ich
allein um den Ring?

WANDERER. Ausser der begehrt er
einzig das Gut.

ALBERICH. Und doch gewänn' ich ihn nicht?

WANDERER. Ein Helde naht
den Hort zu befrei'n;
zwei Niblungen geizen das Gold:
Fafner fällt,
der den Ring bewacht:—

when 'tis gained, luck to the winner!—
    Would'st thou know more?
    There lies the worm:
warn him then of his risk,
well he will leave thee the ring.—
Myself I'll wake him for thee.—
    (*He turns towards the back.*)
        Fafner, Fafner!
        Awaken, worm!

ALBERICH (*aside, in expectancy and wonder*).
        Does he mean to tell me
        mine is the treasure?
(*From the gloomy depth at back is heard* FAFNER'S
        voice).

FAFNER.   Who stirs me from sleep?

WANDERER. Here waiteth a friend
        to warn thee of danger:
    thy life he will allow thee,
    light'st thou his life for him
    with the treasure that thou tendest.

FAFNER.   What would he?

ALBERICH.   Waken, Fafner!
        Waken, thou worm!
    A stalwart hero nears,
    thy head to humble in strife.

FAFNER.   For him I starve!

WANDERER. Brave is the boy and bold,
    sharply shears his sword.

ALBERICH.   The circlet rare
        he seeks alone:
    let me the ring but lift,
        I'll ward thee from harm;
    then watch thou the hoard
    and rest in length of life!

FAFNER (*yawning*). I lie in possession:—
        let me slumber!

WANDERER (*laughing loudly*).
    Now, Alberich, that stroke fails!
    But stay thy anger's storm!
        One thing I read thee,
        think on it well:
    all things in their nature act,
    nor aught may'st thou alter.
    I leave thee thy station:
        stand to thy guard!
    Encounter Mime, thy brother;
    his nature o'ercomest thou better.
        What further falls
        thou quickly shalt find!
↑He *disappears in the wood. A storm-gust rises and
        quickly subsides again*).

ALBERICH (*after watching his retreat a while in wrath*).

        There storms he away
        on lightning steed,
    and leaves me in scoff and scorn!
        Aye, laugh away!
        ye light-spirited,
        lust-gluttonous,
        godly enlightener;
        'll see ye yet

wer ihn rafft, hat ihn gewonnen.—
    Willst du noch mehr?
    Dort liegt der Wurm:
warn'st du ihn vor dem Tod,
willig wohl liess' er den Tand.—
Ich selber weck' ihn dir auf.—
    (*Er wendet sich nach hinten.*)
        Fafner! Fafner!
        erwache, Wurm!

ALBERICH (*in gespanntem Erstaunen, für sich*).
        Was beginnt der Wilde?
        gönnt er mir's wirklich?
(*Aus der finstern Tiefe des Hintergrundes hört man*.)

FAFNER'S (*Stimme*). Wer stört mir den Schlaf?

WANDERER. Gekommen ist einer,
        Noth dir zu künden:
    er lohnt dir's mit dem Leben,
    lohnst du das Leben ihm
    mit dem Horte, den du hütest.

FAFNER.   Was will er?

ALBERICH.   Wache, Fafner!
        wache, du Wurm!
    Ein starker Helde naht,
    dich Heil'gen will er besteh'n.

FAFNER.   Mich hungert sein'.

WANDERER. Kühn ist des Kindes Kraft
    scharf schneidet sein Schwert.

ALBERICH.   Den gold'nen Ring
        geizt er allein:
    lass' mir den Ring zum Lohn,
        so wend' ich den Streit;
    du wahrest den Hort,
    und ruhig leb'st du lang'!

FAFNER (*gähnt*). Ich lieg' und besitze:—
        lasst mich schlafen!

WANDERER (*lacht laut*).
    Nun, Alberich, das schlug fehl!
    Doch schilt mich nicht mehr Schelm!
        Diess Eine, rath' ich,
        achte noch wohl:
    Alles ist nach seiner Art:
    an ihr wirst du nichts ändern.
    Ich lass' dir die Stätte:
        stelle dich fest!
    versuch's mit Mime, dem Bruder:
    der Art ja versiehst du dich besser.
        Was anders ist,
        das lerne nun auch!
(*Er verschwindet im Walde. Sturmwind erhebt sich
        und verliert sich schnell wieder.*)

ALBERICH (*nachdem er ihm lange grimmig nachgesehen*).
        Da reitet er hin
        auf lichtem Ross:
    mir lässt er Sorg' und Spott!
        Doch lacht nur zu,
        ihr leichtsinniges,
        lustgieriges
        Göttergelichter:
        euch seh' ich

all in your graves!
So long as the gold
in light shall gleam
I hold warily watch!—
Envy works out its end!—
(*Morning dawns.* ALBERIC *hides in a cleft of
the rock at side*).

noch alle vergeh'n.'
So lang das Gold
am Lichte glänzt,
hält ein Wissender Wacht!—
trügen wird euch sein Trotz.
(*Morgendämmerung.* ALBERICH *verbirgt sich zur
Seite im Geklüft*).

(*As the daybreaks* MIME *and* SIEGFRIED *enter. The
latter wears the sword in his girdle.* MIME *narrowly
reconnoitres the place and at last seeks towards the
background, which remains still in shadow, while the
higher ground in the middle is more and more brightened
by the sun; he then draws* SIEGFRIED'S *attention*.)

(MIME *und* SIEGFRIED *treten bei anbrechendem Tage
auf.* SIEGFRIED *trägt das Schwert an einem Gehenke.*
MIME *erspäht genau die Stätte, forscht endlich dem
Hintergrunde zu, der—während die Anhöhe im mitt-
lern Vordergrunde später immer heller von der Sonne
beleuchtet wird—in finstern Schatten gehüllt bleibt,
und bedeutet dann* SIEGFRIED.)

MIME. The spot thou seest!
here we stop.

MIME. Zur Stelle sind wir!
bleib' hier steh'n!

SIEGFRIED (*seating himself under a great lime-tree*).
Here shall I in fear take lesson?—
Far distant you have led me;
since the fall of night through woodlands,
we two have wended our way.
Now shall you, Mime,
henceforth move from me!
Find I not here
what I fain would learn,
afar then will I wander;
from thee I want to be free!

SIEGFRIED (*setzt sich unter eine grosse Linde*).
Hier soll ich das Fürchten lernen?—
Fern hast du mich geleitet;
eine volle Nacht im Walde
selbander wanderten wir:
nun sollst du, Mime,
fortan mich meiden!
Lern' ich hier nicht
was ich lernen muss,
allein zieh' ich dann weiter:
dich werd' ich endlich da los!

MIME (*seats himself opposite, so as to keep the cave in
sight still*).
Trust me, dearie!
Dost thou not here
in haste discover fear,
in other hours,
and other ways
scarce were it ever learnt.—
Seest thou yonder
yawning cavern's shade?
Therein dwells
a gruesome dragon dread.
Awfully grisly
is he, and great;
a savage and monstrous
maw doth he ope;
both skin and scalp,
at single snap
the beast will bolt thee belike.

MIME (*setzt sich ihm gegenüber, so dass er die Höhle
immer noch im Auge behält*).
Glaub' mir, Lieber!
lernst du heute
hier das Fürchten nicht:
an andrem Ort
zu and'rer Zeit
schwerlich erfährst du's je.—
Siehst du dort
den dunklen Höhlenschlund?
Darin wohnt
ein gräulich wilder Wurm:
unmassen grimmig
ist er und gross:
ein schrecklicher Rachen
reisst sich ihm auf;
mit Haut und Haar
auf einen Happ
verschlingt der Schlimme dich wohl.

SIEGFRIED. 'Twere well to baffle his biting:
I'll thrust myself not in his throat.

SIEGFRIED. Gut ist's, den Schlund ihm zu schliessen:
drum biet' ich mich nicht dem Gebiss.

MIME. Potent poison
he pours with his breath;
he whom his spittle's
spume doth besplash
must shrivel up, body and bones.

MIME. Giftig giesst sich
ein Geifer ihm aus:
wen mit des Speichels
Schweiss er bespei't,
dem schwinden Fleisch und Gebein.

SIEGFRIED. That his venom vile may not sear me
lightly aside will I leap,

SIEGFRIED. Dass des Geifers Gift mich nicht sehre
weich' ich zur Seite dem Wurm.

MIME. A twisting tail
he turns about;
if ta'en in its toils
and firmly twined,
thy limbs will be ground up like glass.

MIME. Ein Schlangenschweif
schlägt sich ihm auf:
wen er damit umschlingt
und fest umschliesst,
dem brechen die Glieder wie Glas.

SIEGFRIED.   From his tail s entangle to keep
             I'll have an eye on his acts. —
             But hark to me now:
             has this worm a heart?

MIME.   A cruel and hardened heart!

SIEGFRIED.   He bears it, sure,
             where in all it beats,
             both in man and in beast?

MIME.   No doubt, youngster,
        it lies there indeed.
        Not yet hast thou learnt what is fear?

SIEGFRIED.   Needful straightway
             I'll strike to his heart:
             will that be like fearing, haply?
             Hey, my ancient,
             is this only
             what all your lore
             can lesson me?
             Forth on your way then wander,
             for fearing I learn not here.

MIME.   Wait but awhile!
        What I have spoken
        thinkest thou empty sound:
        himself must meet
        thy hearing and sight,
        thy senses will leave thee then straight!
        When thy glances swim,
        the ground 'neath thee sinks,
        and grimly griped,
        thy heart doth gasp,
        then thank thou him who has led thee,
        and think of Mime's great love.

SIEGFRIED (springing up crossly).
             You shall no more love me!
             Said I not so?
             Forth from the sight of me —
             leave me alone!
             this nuisance no longer I'll stand.
             Prate you of loving me still?
             This idiot shrinking
             and eyelid winking—
             whenever shall I
             lose the sight?
             when will this old object be gone?

MIME.   I leave thee now;
        I'll linger nigh the spring.
        Stay thou but here,
        soon when the sun is on high
        look for the worm;
        from his cave he'll warily come:
        close this way
        will he pass
        to water at the fountain.

SIEGFRIED (laughing). Mime, wait at the stream
             and there I'll let the worm proceed.
             Needful first
             in his vitals shall nestle
             when all your joints
             he has well digested!
             So now heed what I tell —
             tarry not by the spring:
             take yourself off
             to other tracks;
             return no more to me!

SIEGFRIED.   Vor des Schweifes Schwang mich
             halt' ich den Argen im Aug'.—[wahre:
             Doch heisse mich das:
             hat der Wurm ein Herz?

MIME.   Ein grimmiges, hartes Herz!

SIEGFRIED.   Das sitzt ihm doch
             wo es jedem schlägt,
             trag' es Mann oder Thier?

MIME.   Gewiss, Knabe,
        da führt's auch der Wurm;
        nun kommt dir das Fürchten wohl an'

SIEGFRIED.   Nothung stoss' ich
             dem Stolzen in's Herz:
             soll das etwa Fürchten heissen?
             He, du Alter!
             ist das alles,
             was deine List
             mich lehren kann?
             Fahr' deines Wegs dann weiter;
             das Fürchten lern' ich hier nicht.

MIME.   Wart' es nur ab!
        Was ich dir sagte,
        dünke dich tauber Schall:
        ihn selber musst du
        hören und seh'n,
        die Sinne vergeh'n dir dann schon!
        Wenn dein Blick verschwimmt,
        der Boden dir schwankt,
        im Busen bang
        dein Herz erbebt:—
        dann dankst du mir, der dich führte,
        gedenkst wie Mime dich liebt.

SIEGFRIED (springt unwillig auf).
             Du sollst mich nicht lieben!
             sagt' ich dir's nicht?
             Fort aus den Augen mir;
             lass' mich allein:
             sonst halt' ich's hier länger nicht aus,
             fängst du von Liebe gar an!
             Das eklige Nicken
             und Augenzwicken,
             wann endlich soll ich's
             nicht mehr seh'n?
             wann werd' ich den Albernen los?

MIME.   Ich lasse dich schon:
        am Quell dort lagr' ich mich.
        Steh' du nur hier;
        steigt die Sonne zur Höh',
        merk' auf den Wurm,
        aus der Höhle wälzt er sich her:
        hier vorbei
        biegt er dann,
        am Brunnen sich zu tränken.

SIEGFRIED (lachend). Mime, weilst du am Quel
             dahin lass' ich den Wurm wohl geh'n
             Nothung stoss' ich
             ihm erst in die Nieren,
             wenn er dich selbst dort
             mit 'weg gesoffen!
             Darum, hör' meinen Rath,
             raste nicht dort am Quell:
             kehre dich 'weg,
             so weit du kannst,
             und komm' nie mehr zu mir!

MIME. When faint with the strife thou wouldst refresh thee, would I not win a welcome? Call on me then, shouldst thou need counsel — or if pleasure in fearing thou find.	**MIME.** Nach freislichem Streit dich zu erfrischen, wirst du mir wohl nicht wehren? Rufe mich auch, darbst du des Rathes— oder wenn dir das Fürchten gefällt.
(SIEGFRIED *bids him begone with a violent gesture.*)	(SIEGFRIED *weis't ihn mit einer heftigen Geberde fort*)
MIME (*aside—going*). Fafner and Siegfried— Siegfried and Fafner— Would each the other might kill! (*He retreats into the wood.*)	**MIME** (*im Abgehen, für sich*). Fafner und Siegfried- Siegfried und Fafner— o brächten beide sich um! (*Er geht in den Wald zurück.*)

SIEGFRIED (*alone. He seats himself under the great
lime again*).
That he's no father of mine
how full is the joy I feel!
   Now truly fragrant
   the forest seems;
   now how glad is
   the glorious day!
since that miscreant wretch has gone,
never more to confront my gaze!
   (*Thoughtful silence.*)
My sire—what semblance was his?—
Ha!—no doubt like myself;
for, were there of Mime a son,
   must he not look
   Mime's likeness?
   growing as gruesome,
   grizzled and grey,
   cramped and crooked,
   halting and humpbacked,
   with hanging ears stretching,
   bleary eyes staring—
   Out on the sight!
I'll look on it no more.
(*He leans back and looks up through the branches
of the tree. Long silence. Forest murmur*).
   Surely—my mother,
   what semblance had she?
   I—cannot
   imagine it ever!—
Like soft fallow doe's
   deeply would shine
her soft languishing eyes,—
   only more lovely!——
 	
When balefully she bore me
why must she have died withal?
Die thus all mortal mothers,
   leaving their dear ones
   lonely behind?
Sad were such a fate, sure!——
   Ah! might these looks
   but light on my mother!——
   My own—mother!—
   a mortal's mate!—
(*He sighs and reclines still lower. Long silence.*)
	SIEGFRIED (*allein*).
	(*Er setzt sich wieder unter die grosse Linde.*)
	Dass der mein Vater nicht ist,
	wie fühl' ich mich drob so froh!
	   Nun erst gefällt mir
	   der frische Wald;
	   nun erst lacht mir
	   der lustige Tag,
	da der Garstige von mir schied,
	und ich gar nicht ihn wiederseh'!
	   (*Sinnendes Schweigen.*)
	Wie sah wohl mein Vater aus?—
	Ha!—gewiss wie ich selbst:
	denn wär' wo von Mime ein Sohn,
	   müsst' er nicht ganz
	   Mime gleichen?
	   G'rade so garstig,
	   griesig und grau,
	   klein und krumm
	   höckrig und hinkend,
	   mit hängenden Ohren,
	   triefigen Augen——
	   fort mit dem Alp!
	ich mag ihn nicht mehr seh'n.
	(*Er lehnt sich zurück und blickt durch den Baumwipfel
	auf. Langez Schweigen.—Waldweben.*)
	   Aber—wie sah
	   meine Mutter wohl aus?
	   Das—kann ich
	   nun gar nicht mir denken!—
	Der Rehhindin gleich
	   glänzten gewiss
	ihr hell schimmernde Augen,—
	   nur noch viel schöner!——
	
	Da bang sie mich geboren,
	warum aber starb sie da?
	Sterben die Menschenmütter
	   an ihren Söhnen
	   alle dahin?
	Traurig wäre das, traun!——
	   Ach! möcht' ich Sohn
	   meine Mutter seh'n!——
	   meine—Mutter!—
	   ein Menschenweib!—
	(*Er seufzt und streckt sich tiefer zurück. Langes
	Schweigen.—*)

(*Increased rustling of the trees.* SIEGFRIED's *attention is at last riveted by the songs of forest birds.* (*Wachsendes Waldwehen.* SIEGFRIED's *aufmerksamkeit wird endlich durch den Gesang der Waldvögel gefesselt.*)

(SIEGFRIED *listens with interest to a bird in the branches above him.*)
(SIEGFRIED *lauscht mit wachsender Theilname einem Waldvogel in den Zweigen über ihm.*)

SIEGFRIED.

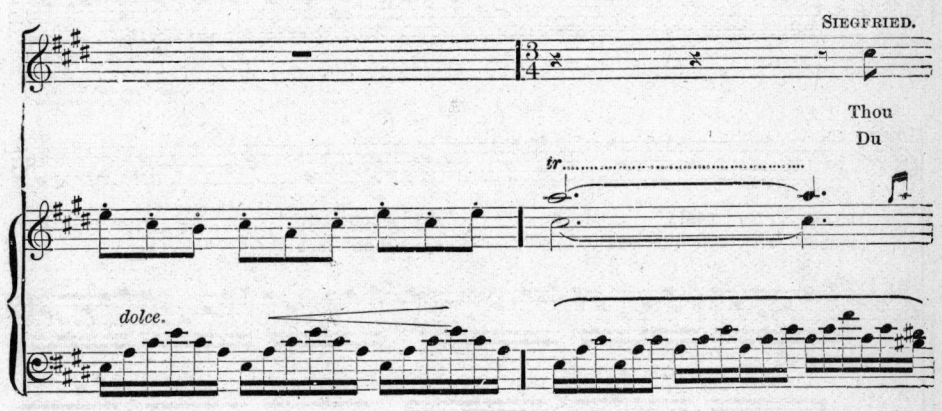

Thou
Du

hap - - py war - - bler, I hear thee now first: Hast in this
hol - - des Vog - - lein, dich hört ich noch nie: Bist du im

for   est   thy home?   Thy
wald   hier   da - heim?   Ver -

piu p

strain,   could   I   un   -   der - stand   it!   Be -
stünd'   ich   sein   süs   -   ses   stam - meln!   Ge -

like   ut   ters   to   me   some   news
wiss   sagt'   es   mir'   was   reil   licht,

of my lov - - ing moth - er!
Von der lie - - ben mut - ter!

that drivelling **dwarf**
told me one day
the meaning bound
in language of birds
one could truly attain to: —
would I could learn the way!
(He reflects. His eyes fall on a clump of reeds, not far from the lime-tree).
Ha! I'll essay;
sing with him
on a reed similar sounding;
unrecking the meaning,
seize but the music.
So his speech, if I sing it,
my senses perchance will espy.
(He cuts himself a reed with his sword and fashions a pipe out of it.)
He stops to list: —
I'll stammer along!
(He tries to imitate the note of the bird on his pipe: he is unsuccessful, and after repeated trials, shaking his head in vexation he desists.)
That sounds not right;
on the reed I see
the melody may not be waked. —
Birdie, I deem
myself but dull:
my deed spans not thy speech.
Now shamed am I quite
by the shrewd little piper:
he peeps to know why I'm pausing. —
Ho there! then hearken
now to my horn;
with the stupid reed
I can render nought.—
To a wild wood-note,
which I can sound,
the lustiest, shalt thou now listen.
A loving companion
lately I called;
nought better came yet
than wolf and bear.
So let me see
whom now it will lure
to make me a loving consort?
(He has thrown away the reed and now blows a merry call on his little silver horn.)

Ein zankender Zwerg
hat mir erzählt,
der Vöglein Stammeln
gut zu versteh'n,
dazu könnte man kommen:
wie das wohl möglich wär'?
(Er sinnt nach. Sein Blick fällt auf ein Rohrgebüsch unweit der Linde.)
Hei! ich versuch's,
sing' ihm nach:
auf dem Rohr tön' ich ihm ähnlich!
Entrath' ich der Worte,
achte der Weise,
sing' ich so seine Sprache,
versteh' ich wohl auch was er spricht.
(Er hat sich mit dem Schwerte ein Rohr abgeschnitten, und schnitzt sich eine Pfeife draus.)
Es schweigt und lauscht:—
so schwatz' ich denn los!
(Er versucht auf der Pfeife die Weise der Vogels nachzuah men es glückt ihm nicht, verdriesslich schüttelt er oft den Kopf: endlich setzt er ganz ab.)
Das tönt nicht recht:
auf dem Rohre taugt
die wonnige Weise nicht.—
Vöglein, mich dünkt,
ich bleibe dumm:
von dir lernt sich's nicht leicht!
Nun schäm' ich mich gar
vor dem schelmischen Lauscher:
er lugt, und kann nichts erlauschen.—
Heida! so höre
nun auf mein Horn;
auf dem dummen Rohre
geräth mir nichts. —
Einer Waldweise,
wie ich sie kann,
der lustigen sollst du lauschen.
Nach liebem Gesellen
lockt' ich mit ihr;
nichts Bess'res kam noch
als Wolf und Bär,
Nun will ich seh'n,
wen jetzt sie mir lockt:
ob das mir ein lieber Gesell?
(Er hat die Pfeife fortgeworfen, und bläst nun aus seinem kleinen silbernen Horne eine lustige Weise.)

(There is a stir in the background. FAFNER, in the form of a huge lizard-like dragon, rises from his lair in the cave; he breaks through the underwood and crawls from the dell up to the higher ground till his forelegs rest quite on the knoll. He then utters a loud yawning growl.)

(Im Hintergrunde regt es sich. FAFNER, in der Gestalt eines ungeheuren eidechsenartigen Schlangenwurmes, hat sich in der Höhle von seinem Lager erhoben; er bricht durch das Gesträuch, und wälzt sich aus der Tiefe nach der höheren Stelle vor, so dass er mit dem Vorderleibe bereits auf ihr angelangt ist. Er stösst jetzt einen starken gähnenden Laut aus.)

SIEGFRIED *(turns round, perceives* FAFNER, *looks at him in surprise and then laughs).*
At last has my lay
something lovely attracted!
i've waked up a fair-favored friend!

FAFNER *(who has paused, on sight of* SIEGFRIED).
What is that?

SIEGFRIED. Hey! are you a beast
that of speech can boast?
You surely might teach me something.
Here comes one
who ne'er learnt to fear:
could he by you effect it?

SIEGFRIED *(wendet sich um, gewahrt* FAFNER, *blickt ihn verwundert an, und lacht).*
Da hätte mein Lied
mir 'was Liebes erblasen!
du wär'st mir ein saub'rer Gesell!

FAFNER *(hat bei* SIEGFRIED's *Anblick angehalten).*
Was ist da?

SIEGFRIED. Ei, bist du ein Thier,
das zum Sprechen taugt,
wohl liess' sich von dir 'was lernen?
Hier kennt einer
das Fürchten nicht:
kann er's von dir erfahren?

FAFNER.   Art not over-bold?

SIEGFRIED.   Bold or over-bold —
        what wist I?
    but you finely I'll tackle,
    teach you not fearing to me.

FAFNER (*laughs*).   Drink I came for,
    now drops to me food!
    (*He opens his jaws and shews his teeth.*)

SIEGFRIED.   An extravagant frontage
      you turn on me:
    dazzling with teeth
    is that dainty maw!
    Well were it to close up the cavern:
    your gullet gapes far too wide.

FAFNER.   For senseless gabble
      serves it ill :
    rather to eat thee
    doth it ope.
    (*He lashes his tail menacingly.*)

SIEGFRIED.   Oho! you gruesome,
      grim-looking knave!
    To stay your stomach
    suits me little :
    meetest and wisest were it
    to remove you hence, and at once.

FAFNER (*roaring*).   Bah! come,
    boast-making cub!

SIEGFRIED (*drawing his sword*).
    Look out, growler!
    the boaster comes.
    (*He confronts* FAFNER *: the latter creeps more over
the knoll and spits from his nostrils at him.* SIEGFRIED
springs aside. FAFNER *curls his tail forwards to reach*
SIEGFRIED, *but he avoids it and springs over the back
of the dragon with a bound; as the tail follows him and
almost reaches him, he wounds it with his sword.*
FAFNER *hastily draws back his tail, roars, and raises
the fore-part of his body, in order to throw his full
weight sideways upon* SIEGFRIED, *thus exposing his
breast to him.* SIEGFRIED *quickly espies the position
of his heart and plunges his sword there up to the very
hilt.* FAFNER *rears still higher in pain and sinks down
upon the wound, while* SIEGFRIED *lets go the sword
and springs aside.*)

SIEGFRIED.   There lie, noisomest rogue!
    Needful sticks in your gizzard.

FAFNER (*with weaker voice*).
    Who art thou, stalwart stripling,
      that hath struck my heart?
    Who wakened and stirred thy mind
      to this murderous deed?
    Thine own brain ne'er, I trow,
      brought it about.

SIEGFRIED.   Much I do not know,
      not even who I am :
    yourself only did urge me
    unto this murderous end.

FAFNER.   Thou bright, eager-eyed stripling,
      e'en strange to thyself :
    whom thou hast murdered
    must thou hear.

FAFNER.   Hast du Uebermuth?

SIEGFRIED.   Muth und Uebermuth —
      was weiss ich!
    Doch dir fahr' ich zu Leibe,
    lehrst du das Fürchten mich nicht!

FAFNER (*lacht*).   Trinken wollt' ich:
    nun treff' ich auch Frass!
    (*Er öffnet seinen Rachen und zeigt die Zähne.*)

SIEGFRIED.   Eine zierliche Fresse
      zeig'st du mir da:
    lachende Zähne
    im Leckermaul!
    Gut wär's den Schlund dir zu schliessen
    dein Rachen reckt sich zu weit!

FAFNER.   Zu tauben Reden
      taugt er schlecht:
    dich zu verschlingen
    frommt der Schlund.
    (*Er droht mit dem Schweife.*)

SIEGFRIED.   Hoho! du grausam
      grimmiger Kerl,
    von dir verdaut sein
    dünkt mich übel:
    räthlich und fromm doch scheint's
    du verrecktest hier ohne Frist.

FAFNER (*brüllt*).   Pruh! komm'!
    prahlendes Kind.

SIEGFRIED (*fasst das Schwert*).
    Sieh' dich vor, Brüller:
    der Prahler kommt!
    (*Er stellt sich* FAFNER *entgegen: dieser hebt sich
weiter vor auf die Bodenerhöhung, und sprüht aus seinen
Nüstern nach ihm.* SIEGFRIED *springt zur Seite.*
FAFNER *schwingt den Schweif nach vorn, um* SIEG-
FRIED *zu fassen: dieser weicht ihm aus, indem er mit
einem Satze über den Rücken des Wurmes hinweg-
springt; als der Schweif sich auch hierhin ihm schnell
nachwendet, und ihn fast schon packt, verwundet* SIEG-
FRIED *diesen mit dem Schwerte.* FAFNER *zieht den
Schweif hastig zurück, brüllt, und bäumt seinen Vorder-
leib, um mit dessen voller Wucht zur Seite sich auf*
SIEGFRIED *zu werfen: so bietet er diesem die Brust,*
SIEGFRIED *erspäht schnell die Stelle des Herzens, und
stösst sein Schwert bis an das Heft hinein.* FAFNER
bäumt sich von Schwert noch höher, und sinkt, als
SIEGFRIED *das Schwert losgelassen und zur Seite gesprungen ist, auf die Wunde zusammen.*)

SIEGFRIED.   Da lieg', neidischer Kerl!
    Nothung trägst du im Herzen.

FAFNER (*mit schwächerer Stimme*).
    Wer bist du, kühner Knabe,
      der das Herz mir traf?
    Wer reizte des Kindes Muth
      zu der mordlichen That?
    Dein Hirn brütete nicht,
      was du vollbracht.

SIEGFRIED.   Viel weiss ich noch nicht,
      noch nicht auch wer ich bin:
    mit dir mordlich zu ringen
    reiztest du selbst meinen Muth.

FAFNER.   Du helläugiger Knabe,
      unkund deiner selbst:
    wen du gemordet
    meld' ich dir.

The giants' generous race
which ruled the world at one time —
    Fasolt and Fafner,
the brothers, fallen now both lie.
    For the fatal gold
    we gained from the gods
death to Fasolt I dealt.
    Now I, as Worm
    the hoard o'erwatching,
Fafner, the last of giants,
fall by a juvenile hand. —
    Bear thou good heed,
    blossoming hero:
    'mid treason treads
    he who holds the hoard:
one who blindly shewed thee this deed
doth shape for thee, boy, surely death.
      (*Dying.*)
    Weigh what happens: —
    heed my words!

SIEGFRIED.   What were my parents
    rede to me yet!
    wise thou appearest,
    wild one, expiring;
    rede it too from my title:
    Siegfried is it, I trow.

FAFNER.   Siegfried . . .!
  (*He sighs, raises himself up and dies.*)

SIEGFRIED.   The dead can tell no tidings.
    So lead me henceforth
    my life-keeping sword.
(**FAFNER** *has rolled over on his side in dying.* **SIEGFRIED** *draws the sword from his breast : in doing so his hand becomes smeared with blood : he draws it hastily away.*)
    Like fire burns the blood!
(*He instinctively puts his finger to his mouth to suck the blood off it. As he gazes thoughtfully before him his attention is arrested all at once by the song of the birds. He listens with bated breath.*)
    Would it not seem
    yon songster were speaking to me ? —
    well the words I distinguish!
    Was it the blood
    that worked this magic ?
    That stranger bird I hear —
    hark! what sings he now ?

    VOICE OF A WOOD-BIRD
      (*in the lime-tree*).
    Hey! Siegfried doth hold
    now the Nibelung's hoard:
    O he'll find the hoard
    in the hole anon!
    Were he the Tarnhelm to win,
    it would tide him through wonderful tasks;
    but were he the ring too to ravish
    'twould give him the ward of the world!

SIEGFRIED.   Thanks, pretty warbler,
    for thy advice:
    I'll follow thy voice.
(*He goes up and descends into the cavern, where he disappears from view.*)

Die einst der Welt gewaltet,
    der Riesen ragend Geschlecht,
    Fasolt und Fafner,
die Brüder, fielen nun beide.
    Um verfluchtes Gold,
    von Göttern vergabt,
traf ich Fasolt zu todt:
    der nun als Wurm
    den Hort bewachte,
Fafner, den letzten Riesen,
fällte ein rosiger Held. —
    Blick nun hell,
    blühender Knabe;
    des Hortes Herrn
    umringt Verrath:
der dich Blinden reizte zur That,
beräth nun des Blühenden Tod
      (*Ersterbend.*)
    Merk' wie's endet: —
    acht' auf mich!

SIEGFRIED.   Woher ich stamme,
    rathe mir noch;
    weise ja scheinst du
    Wilder im Sterben:
    rath' es nach meinem Namen:
    Siegfried bin ich genannt.

FAFNER.   Siegfried . . . !
  (*Er seufzt, hebt sich und stirbt.*)

SIEGFRIED.   Zur Kunde taugt kein Todter. —
    So leite mich denn
    mein lebendes Schwert!
(**FAFNER** *hat sich im Sterben zur Seite gewälzt.* **SIEGFRIED** *zieht das Schwert aus seiner Brust: dabei wird seine Hand vom Blute benetzt; er fährt heftig mit der Hand auf.*)
    Wie Feuer brennt das Blut!
(*Er führt unwillkürlich die Finger zum Munde, um das Blut von ihnen abzusaugen. Wie er sinnend vor sich hinblickt, wird plötzlich seine Aufmerksamkeit von dem Gesange der Waldvögel angezogen. Er lauscht mit verhaltenem Athem.*) —
    Ist mir doch fast —
    als sprächen die Vöglein zu mir:
    deutlich dünken mich's Worte!
    Nützte mir das
    des Blutes Genuss ? —
    Das selt'ne Vöglein hier —
    horch! was singt es mir ?

    STIMME EINES WALDVOGEL'S
      (*in der Linde*).
    Hei! Siegfried gehört
    nun der Niblungen Hort:
    o fänd' in der Höhle
    den Hort er jetzt!
    Wollt' er den Tarnhelm gewinnen,
    der taugt' ihm zu wonniger That:
    doch möcht' er den Ring sich errathen,
    der macht' ihn zum Walter der Welt!

SIEGFRIED.   Dank, liebes Vöglein,
    für deinen Rath:
    gern folg' ich dem Ruf.
(*Er geht und steigt in die Höhle hinab, wo er alsbald gänzlich verschwindet.*)

(MIME sinks on, looking about timidly, to assure himself of FAFNER'S death.—At the same time AL-BERICH comes out from his cleft at the opposite side; he watches MIME narrowly. As the latter, not finding SIEGFRIED, carefully steals towards the cave, AL-BERICH darts upon him and bars his way.)

(MIME schleicht heran, scheu umherblickend, um sich von FAFNER'S Tod zu überzeugen. — Gleichzeitig kommt von der anderen Seite ALBERICH aus dem Geklüft hervor; er beobachtet MIME genau. Als dieser SIEGFRIED nicht mehr gewahrt, und vorsichtig sich nach hinten der Höhle zuwendet, stürzt ALBERICH auf ihn zu, und vertritt ihm den Weg.)

ALBERICH. Whither slinkest thou,
hasty and sly,
slippery scamp?

ALBERICH. Wohin schleich'st du
eilig und schlau,
schlimmer Gesell?

MIME. Accursed brother,
what brings thee here?
I bid thee hence.

MIME. Verfluchter Bruder,
dich braucht' ich hier!
Was bringt dich her?

ALBERICH. Graspest thou, rogue,
towards my gold?
Dost lust for my goods?

ALBERICH. Geizt es dich Schelm
nach meinem Gold?
Verlang'st du mein Gut?

MIME. Yield the position!
This station is mine.
What stirrest thou here?

MIME. Fort von der Stelle!
Die Stätte ish mein:
was stöberst du hier?

ALBERICH. Startled art thou
from stealthy concerns,
that I've disturbed?

ALBERICH. Stör' ich dich wohl
im stillen Geschäft,
wenn du hier stiehl'st?

MIME. What I have shaped
with shrewdest toil
shall not be shaken.

MIME. Was ich erschwang
mit schwerer Müh',
soll mir nicht schwinden.

ALBERICH. Was't thou that robbed
the golden ring from the Rhine?
or charged it with great
and choice enchantment around?

ALBERICH. Hast du dem Rhein
das Gold zum Ringe geraubt?
Erzeugtest du gar
den zähen Zauber im Reif?

MIME. Who formed the Tarnhelm,
which to all forms can turn?
By thee 'twas wanted;
its worker wert thou too?

MIME. Wer schuf den Tarnhelm,
der die Gestalten tauscht?
Der sein' bedurfte,
erdachtest du ihn wohl?

ALBERICH. What couldst thou e'er, fool,
by thyself have fancied and fashioned?
The magic ring
made the dwarf meet for the task.

ALBERICH. Was hättest du Stümper
je wohl zu stampfen verstanden?
Der Zauberring
zwang mir zur Kunst erst den Zwerg!

MIME. Where now is thy ring?
The giants have robbed thee, thou recreant!
What thou hast lost,
by my lore, belike, I will gain.

MIME. Wo hast du den Ring?
Dir Zagem entrissen ihn Riesen!
Was du verlor'st,
meine List erlangt' es für mich.

ALBERICH. By the boy's exploit
shalt thou, booby, be bettered?
Thou shalt have it not,
for its holder in truth is he.

ALBERICH. Mit des Knaben That
will der Knicker nun knausern?
Dir gehört sie gar nicht,
der Helle ist selbst ihr Herr!

MIME. I nourished him,
and his nurse now shall he pay:
for toil and woe
long while have I waited reward.

MIME. Ich zog ihn auf;
für die Zucht zahlt er mir nun:
für Müh' und Last
erlauert' ich lang' meinen Lohn!

ALBERICH. For a bantling's keep
would this beggarly
niggardly boor,
bold and blustering,
be well nigh as a king?
To rankest of dogs
booteth the ring
far rather than thee:
never, thou rogue,
shall reach thee the magic round!

ALBERICH. Für des Knaben Zucht
will der knick'rige
schäbige Knecht
keck und kühn
gar wohl König nun sein?
Dem räudigsten Hund
wäre der Ring
gerath'ner als dir:
nimmer erring'st
du Rüpel den Herrscherreif!

MIME. Then hold it still
and heed it well,
thy hoarded ring.

MIME. Behalt' ihn denn:
hüte ihn wohl
den hellen Reif!

Be thou head, **but** yet hail me as brother! For my own Tarnhelm, excellent toy, I'll tender it thee! 'twill boot us twain, twin we the booty like this.	Sei du Herr: doch mich heisse auch Bruder! Um meines Tarnhelm's lustigen Tand tausch' ich ihn dir: uns beiden taugt's, theilen die Beute wir so.
ALBERICH (*laughing scornfully*). Twin it with thee? and the Tarnhelm too? How sly thou art! Safe I'd sleep then never from thy ensnarings.	ALBERICH (*höhnisch lachend*). Theilen mit dir? und den Tarnhelm gar? Wie schlau du bist! Sicher schlief' ich niemals vor deinen Schlingen!
MIME (*beside himself*). Wilt not bargain? Wilt not barter? Bare must I go, gaining no boon? Giv'st thou to me no booty?	MIME (*ausser sich*). Selbst nicht tauschen? Auch nicht theilen? Leer soll ich geh'n, ganz ohne Lohn? Gar nichts willst du mir lassen?
ALBERICH. Not an atom, not e'en a nail's worth: all I deny thee.	ALBERICH. Nichts von allem, nicht einen Nagel sollst du dir nehmen!
MIME (*furiously*). In the ring and Tarnhelm ne'er shalt thou triumph! Nought talk we of shares! Unto thee I'll call for Siegfried to come; with his carving sword the caustic boy shall crush thee, brother of mine!	MIME (*wüthend*). Weder Ring noch Tarnhelm soll dir denn taugen! nicht theil' ich nun mehr. Gegen dich ruf' ich Siegfried zu Rath und des Recken Schwert: der rasche Held, der richte, Brüderchen, dich!
ALBERICH. Turn thy head round;— from the cavern t'wards us he comes. —	ALBERICH. Kehre dich um: — aus der Höhle kommt er schon her. —
MIME. Trivial toys have tempted him there. —	MIME. Kindischen Tand erkor er gewiss. —
ALBERICH. The Tarnhelm he holds!—	ALBERICH. Den Tarnhelm hat er!—
MIME. Aye, and the ring!—	MIME. Doch auch den Ring!—
ALBERICH. A curse!—the ring!—	ALBERICH. Verflucht! — den Ring!—
MIME (*with an evil laugh*). Let him the ring to thee render!— I ween full soon I shall win it. (*He slips back into the wood.*)	MIME (*lacht hämisch*). Lass' ihn den Ring dir doch geben!— Ich will ihn mir schon gewinnen. — (*Er schlüpft in den Wald zurück.*)
ALBERICH. And yet to its lord shall it alone be delivered! (*He disappears in the cleft.*)	ALBERICH. Und von seinem Herrn soll er allein noch gehören! (*Er verschwindet im Geklüft.*)

———   ———

(SIEGFRIED, *with Tarnhelm and ring, has stepped out, during the last words, from the cave, slowly and thoughtfully: he inspects his prizes reflectively, and again pauses on the knoll by the tree.—Deep silence.*)	(SIEGFRIED *ist, mit Tarnhelm und Ring, während des Letzten langsam und sinnend aus der Höhle vorgeschritten: er betrachtet gedankenvoll seine Beute, und hält, nahe dem Baume, auf der Höhe wieder an. — Grosse Stille.*)
SIEGFRIED. How ye may serve I hardly see; I snatched ye, though, from the hoard of heaped-up gold, as guiding voice did advise. Let serve then your wealth as this struggle's witness; these baubles shall show that in fight I Fafner laid low but of fearing no whit I learnt.	SIEGFRIED. Was ihr mir nützet weiss ich nicht. doch nahm ich euch aus des Horts gehäuftem Gold, weil guter Rath mir es rieth. So taug' eu're Zier als des Tages Zeuge: mich mahne der Tand dass ich kämpfend Fafner erlegt, doch das Fürchten noch nicht gelernt!

(*He sticks the Tarnhelm in his girdle and puts the ring on his finger. — Perfect stillness, Increased rustling of the woods. — SIEGFRIED mechanically looks for the bird and listens to it with bated breath.*)

VOICE OF THE WOOD-BIRD
(*in the lime-tree*).

Hey! Siegfried doth hold
now the helm and the ring!
O trust not in Mime,
the treacherous elf!
Heareth Siegfried but sharply
the shifty hypocrite's words:
what at heart he means
shall by Mime be shewn;
so booteth the taste of the blood.

(SIEGFRIED's *expression and gestures shew that he has understood all. He perceives MIME's approach and remains without moving, leaning on his sword, observing and self-repressed, in his station on the mound till the end of the following speech.*)

MIME (*slowly entering*).
He broods as he weighs
the booty's worth. —
Walked there with him
a wily Wanderer,
foraging here,
informing the boy
with cunning runes and redes?
Doubly sly
shall be my deeds;
my artfullest springes
all shall be set,
that I with true-seeming
traitorous talk
may entrap the truculent boy!
(*He advances nearer to* SIEGFRIED.)
I hail thee, Siegfried!
Say, my hero,
hast thou then fearing attained?

SIEGFRIED.   The teacher I found not here.

MIME.   But the serpent-worm,
then hast thou destroyed him?
He, sure, was a foul sort of friend.

SIEGFRIED.   Though grim and dreadful he was,
his death grieves me, in sooth,
while far eviller scoundrels
undestroyed are yet living!
Who made me murder him,
I hate him more than the worm.

MIME.   Now softly! thou wilt not
see me much more:
an endless sleep
soon upon thine eyes shall weigh!
For all that I wanted
hast thou well worked;
I'll try now from thee
to win me the golden treasure. —
Methinks I'll safely effect it:
thou wert ever easy to fool!

SIEGFRIED.   You're seeking to work my death then?

MIME.   What? did I say that? —
Siegfried, hear me, my sonny!
Thee and all thy kind
have I constantly hated;
from fondness, thou burden,

(*Er steckt den Tarnhelm sich in den Gürtel, und den Reif an den Finger. — Stillschweigen. Wachsendes Waldweben. — SIEGFRIED achtet unwillkürlich wieder des Vogel's, und lauscht ihm mit verhaltenem Athem*)

STIMME DES WALDVOGEL'S
(*in der Linde*).

Hei! Siegfried gehört
nun der Helm und Ring!
O trau' er Mime
dem Treulosen nicht!
Hörte Siegfried nur scharf
auf des Schelmen Heuchlergered':
wie sien Herz es meint
kann er Mime versteh'n;
so nützt' ihm des Blutes Genuss.

(SIEGFRIED's *Miene und Geberde drücken aus, dass er alles wohl vernommen. Er sieht MIME sich nähern, und bleibt, ohne sich zu rühren, auf sein Schwert gestützt, beobachtend und in sich geschlossen, in seiner Stellung auf der Anhöhe bis zum Schlusse des folgenden Auftrittes.*)

MIME (*langsam auftretend*).
Er sinnt und erwägt
der Beute Werth: —
weilte wohl hier
ein weiser Wand'rer,
schweifte umher,
beschwatzte das Kind
mit listiger Runen Rath?
Zwiefach schlau
sei nun der Zwerg:
die listigste Schlinge
leg' ich jetzt aus,
dass ich mit traulichem
Trug-Gerede
bethöre das trotzige Kind!
(*Er tritt näher an* SIEGFRIED *heran.*)
Willkommen, Siegfried!
Sag', du Kühner,
hast du das Fürchten gelernt?

SIEGFRIED.   Den Lehrer fand ich noch nicht.

MIME.   Doch den Schlangenwurm,
du hast ihn erschlagen:
das war doch ein schlimmer Gesell?

SIEGFRIED.   So grimm und tückisch er war,
sein Tod grämt mich doch schier,
da viel üblere Schächer
unerschlagen noch leben!
Der mich ihn morden hiess,
den hass' ich mehr als den Wurm.

MIME.   Nur sacht'! nicht lange
sieh'st du mich mehr:
zu ew'gem Schlaf
schliess' ich die Augen dir bald!
Wozu ich dich brauchte,
das hast du vollbracht;
jetzt will ich nur noch
die Beute dir abgewinnen: —
mich dünkt, das soll mir gelingen;
zu bethören bist du ja leicht!

SIEGFRIED.   So sinnst du auf meinen Schaden?

MIME.   Wie sagt' ich das? —
Siegfried, hör' doch, mein Sohn!
Dich und deine Art
hasst' ich immer von Herzen;
aus Liebe erzog ich

I fostered thee not:
the hoard under Fafner's hold
alone I labored to win.
    If thou'llt not give up
    that with good will —
    Siegfried, my son,
    thou see'st thyself —
thy life thou must really relinquish!

SIEGFRIED.   That you should hate me
    hurts me not:
but must my life to you be delivered?

MIME.   I said nought of that!
    Thou mistakest me quite.
(*Giving himself the most elaborate pains to disguise
        his meaning.*)
    See, thou art tired
    with mighty toil:
burneth thy body with heat.
    So, to restore thee
    with stirring drink,
swiftly I speed to thee.
    While thy sword thou didst beat out,
    I brewed this stuff:
    take but a sip,
I win me thy trusty sword,
and with it hoard and helm.
        (*He chuckles.*)

SIEGFRIED.   So, both of my sword
    and what I have seized on,
Ring and booty, you'd rob me?

MIME.   How thou dost falsely distort!
    Stammers — falters my speech?
    The greatest trouble
    I give myself
    my secret designing
    safely to bury,
    and thou, stupid boy,
constru'st all opposite-wise!
    Open thine ears then
    and awake thy wits!
hearken what Mime means!
Here, take! and drink for refreshment!
my draughts freshened thee oft:
    deep though thine anger,
    sullen thine ire,
    yet all I brought
abusing, — tookest thou ever.

SIEGFRIED (*without stirring in the least*).
    Of a goodly draught
    were I glad:
of what compounded you this?

MIME.   Hey! just try it:
    trust to my skill!
    In deathly darkness
soon shall thy senses be laid:
    without mind or motion
straight stretched will thy limbs **be.**
    Lying then so,
    light were it
the prize to take and deposit:
    didst thou wake though again,
    never were I
    safe from thy reach,
did I seize e'en the ring.
    So with the sword
    thou hast shaped so sharp
    truly I'll hew
    thy head right off:
then I shall have rest and the ring!
        (*He chuckles again.*)

---

    dich Lästigen nicht:
dem Horte in Fafners Hut,
dem Golde galt meine Müh'.
    Giebst du mir das
    nun gutwillig nicht —
    Siegfried, mein Sohn,
    das siehst du wohl selbst —
dein Leben musst du mir lassen!

SIEGFRIED.   Dass du mich hassest,
    hör' ich gern:
doch mein Leben auch muss ich dir lassen?

MIME.   Das sag' ich doch nicht?
    du verstehst mich falsch!
(*Er giebt sich die ersichtlichste Mühe zur Verstellung.*)
    Sieh', du bist müde
    von harter Müh';
brünstig brennt dir der Leib:
    dich zu erquicken
    mit queckem Trank
säumt' ich Sorgender nicht.
    Als dein Schwert du dir **branntest,**
    braut' ich den Sud:
    trinkst du nun den,
gewinn' ich dein trautes Schwert,
und mit ihm Helm und Hort.
        (*Er kichert dazu.*)

SIEGFRIED.   So willst du mein Schwert
    und was ich erschwungen,
Ring und Beute mir rauben?

MIME.   Was du doch falsch mich versteh'**st!**
    Stamml' ich und fas'le wohl gar?
    Die grösste Mühe
    geb' ich mir:
    mein heimliches Sinnen
    heuchelnd zu bergen,
    und du dummer Bube,
deutet alles doch falsch!
    Oeff'ne die Ohren,
    und vernimm genau:
höre, was Mime meint! —
Hier nimm! trinke dir **Labung!**
mein Trank labte dich oft:
    that'st du wohl unwirsch,
    stelltest dich arg:
    was ich dir bot —
erbos't auch — nahmst du's doch **immer**

SIEGFRIED. (*ohne eine Miene zu verzieh'n.*)
    Einen guten Trank
    hätt'ich gern:
wie hast du diesen gebrau't?

MIME.   Hei! so trink' nur:
    trau' meiner Kunst!
    In Nacht und Nebel
sinken die Sinne dir bald:
    ohne Wach' und Wissen,
stracks streck'st du die **Glieder.**
    Lieg'st du nun da,
    leicht könnt' ich
die Beute nehmen und bergen:
    doch erwachtest du je,
    nirgends wär' ich
    sicher vor dir,
hätt' ich selbst auch den Ring.
    D'rum mit dem Schwert,
    das so scharf du schuf'st,
    hau' ich dem Kind
    den Kopf erst ab:
dann hab' ich mir Ruh' und **den Ring!**
        (*Er kichert wieder.*)

SIEGFRIED.   In slumber must I be murdered?

MIME.   What mean'st thou? did I say that
     I will but chop
     from the child his head!
     For, had I not hated
     thee so sore,
     and had not thy scoffs
     and my shameful endurance
     so loudly called for payment,
     I must without pausing
     fling thee from my pathway;
     how else should I earn me the treasure
     which Alberich aims at as well? — —
     Now, my Volsung,
     vulpine cub!
     taste and vanish in death:
     no drink thou more wilt try.

He has come close up to SIEGFRIED *and now hands him with offensive importunity a drinking-horn into which he has previously poured the draught from his flask.* SIEGFRIED *has already grasped his sword, and now, as if with an impulse of sudden disgust, lays* MIME *dead to the ground with one stroke. — From the cleft* ALBERICH *is heard to send forth a peal of mocking laughter.*

SIEGFRIED.   Taste thou my sword,
     infamous serpent!
     "Needful" pays
     pests nimbly;
     _or this I forged the weapon.
(He seizes the body of MIME, *drags it to the cave's mouth and throws it inside.)*
     In the hollow here
     lie with the hoard!
     With stubborn lures
     thou strovest for it,
     so now with its wealth I reward thee! —
     And a goodly watch-dog
     I give to thee,
     that so no thieves may threaten.
(He drags the carcass of the dragon to the cave's mouth so as to stop it up with it completely.)
     There lie thou too,
     twining worm,
     the glittering hoard
     helping to guard,
     with yon booty-ravishing fool!
     So find ye both at last your rest!
(He returns from his task. — It is mid-day.)
     Hot am I
     with my heavy load! —
     Brawling speeds
     my boiling blood;
     my hand burns on my head. — —
     High stands the sun now!
     in heaven's blue
     beams his eye,
     from the distance darting to me. —
     Languid coolness
     shall court me under the lime-tree!
He again stretches himself under the lime-tree. — Perfect stillness. Forest murmurs. After a long pause):
     Now once more, lovely warbler,
     as we have lacked
     long a discourse,
     I'd list gladly to thy song:
     on the twig I see thee
     restfully rocking:
     twitt'ring soar around
     brothers and sisters,
     encircling thee, lightsome and loved.

SIEGFRIED.   Im Schlafe willst du mich morden.

MIME.   Was möcht' ich? sagt' ich denn das? —
     Ich will dir Kind
     nur den Kopf abhau'n!
     Denn hasste ich dich
     auch nicht so hell,
     und hätt' ich des Schimpf's
     und der schändlichen Müh'
     auch nicht so viel zu rächen:
     aus dem Weg dich zu räumen
     darf ich nicht rasten,
     wie käm' ich sonst anders zur Beute,
     da Alberich auch nach ihr lugt? — —
     Nun, mein Wälsung!
     Wolfssohn du!
     Sauf' und würg' dich zu Tod:
     nie thu'st du mehr einen Schluck!
(Er hat sich nahe an SIEGFRIED *herangemacht, und reicht ihm jetzt mit widerlicher Zudringlichkeit ein Trinkhorn, in das er zuvor aus einem Gefässe das Getränk gegossen.* SIEGFRIED *hat bereits das Schwert gefasst, und streckt jetzt, wie in einer Anwandlung heftigen Ekel's,* MIME *mit einem Streiche todt zu Boden. — Man hört* ALBERICH *aus dem Geklüft heraus ein höhnisches Gelächter aufschlagen.)*

SIEGFRIED.   Schmeck' du mein Schwert,
     ekliger Schwätzer!
     Neides-Zoll
     zahlt Nothung:
     dazu durft' ich ihn schmieden.
(Er packt MIME'S *Leichnam auf, schleppt ihn nach der Höhle, und wirft ihn dort hinein.)*
     In der Höhle hier
     lieg' auf dem Hort!
     Mit zäher List
     erzieltest du ihn:
     jetzt magst du des Wonnigen walten! —
     Einen guten Wächter
     geb' ich dir auch,
     dass er vor Dieben dich deckt.
(Er wälzt die Leiche des Wurmes vor den Eingang der Höhle, so dass er diesen ganz damit verstopft.)
     Da lieg' auch du,
     dunkler Wurm!
     Den gleissenden Hort
     hüte zugleich
     mit dem beuterührigen Feind:
     so fandet ihr beide nun Ruh'!
Er kommt nach der Arbeit wieder vor. — Es ist Mittag.)
     Heiss ward mir
     von der harten Last! —
     Brausend jagt sich
     mein brünstiges Blut;
     die Hand brennt mir am Haupt. —
     Hoch steht schon die Sonne:
     aus lichtem Blau
     blickt ihr Aug'
     auf den Scheitel steil mir herab. —
     Linde Kühlung
     erkies' ich mir unter der Linde!
(Er streckt sich wieder unter der Linde aus. — Grosse Stille Waldweben. Nach einem längeren Schweigen)
     Noch einmal, liebes Vöglein,
     da wir so lang'
     lästig gestört, —
     lauscht' ich gern deinem Sang
     auf dem Zweige seh' ich
     wohlig dich wiegen;
     zwitschernd umschwirren
     dich Brüder und Schwestern,
     umschweben dich lustig und lieb!

But I — am all alone,
have no brother nor sister:
  my mother sped,
  my father fall'n;—
their son ne'er they saw!—
  I did but consort
  with a cankerous dwarf,
  kindness drew us
  not together;
  guilefullest toils
  the traitor contrived:—
to death was I forced to treat him!—

  Friendliest warbler,
  I fain would demand,
  grant unto me
  a gracious friend.
Wilt thou thereto rightly rede me?
  I've called one so oft
  and he comes to me ne'er:
  thou, my fav'rite;
  farest, sure, better!
Already rightly thou'st spaed;
now sing! I list to thy song.
    (Silence; then):

    VOICE OF THE WOOD-BIRD.

  Hey! Siegfried has slain
  now the sinister dwarf!
  I wot for him now
  a glorious wife.
In guarded fastness she sleeps,
fire doth emborder the spot:
  o'erstepped he the blaze,
  waked he the bride,
Brünnhilde then would be his!

SIEGFRIED (starting impetuously to his feet).
  O lovely song!
  Sweetest delight!
  How burns its sense
  my suffering breast!
  How flies it headlong,
  firing my heart!
  What swiftly o'ersways
  my heart and senses?
Say to me, dearest friend!

THE WOOD-BIRD. Lightly, though lorn,
  I sing of loving;
  winsome in woe
  weaving my lay:
warm hearts can alone comprehend!

SIEGFRIED. Forth I hasten
  henceward exulting;
forth from the wood to the fell!—
  But once more say to me,
  lovely singer, —
may I the furnace then break through?
waken the marvellous bride?

THE WOOD-BIRD. The bride is won,
  Brünnhilde awaked
  by faint-heart ne'er:
but by him who knows not fear.

SIEGFRIED (laughing with delight).
  The stupid lad,
  who to fear has not learnt,
dear flutt'rer, that is myself!
  To-day I put me
  to profitless toil
this fearing from Fafner to gather.

Doch ich — bin so allein,
hab' nicht Bruder noch Schwester,
  meine Mutter schwand.
  meine Vater fiel:
nie sah sie der Sohn!—
  Mein einz'ger Gesell
  war ein garst'ger Zwerg;
  Güte zwang
  nie uns zu Liebe;
  listige Schlingen
  'warf mir der Schlaue:—

nun musst' ich ihn gar erschlagen!—
  Freundliches Vöglein,
  dich frag' ich nun:
  gönntest du mir
  wohl ein gutes Gesell?
willst du das Rechte mir rathen?
  Ich lockte so oft,
  und erloos't es nicht:
  du, mein Trauter,
  träf'st es wohl besser!
So recht ja riethest du schon:
nun sing'! ich lausche dem Sang.
    (Schweigen; dann:)

STIMME DES WALDVOGEL'S.

  Hei! Siegfried erschlug
  nun den schlimmen Zwerg!
  Jetzt wüsst' ich ihm noch
  das herrlichste Weib.
Auf hohem Felsen sie schläft,
ein Feuer umbrennt ihren Saal:
  durchschritt' er die Brunst,
  erweckt' er die Braut,
Brünnhilde wäre dann sein!

SIEGFRIED (fährt mit jäher Heftigkeit vom Sitze auf)
  O holder Song!
  süssester Hauch!
  Wie brennt sein Sinn
  mir sehrend die Brust!
  Wie zückt er heftig
  zündend mein Herz!
  Was jagt mir so jach
  durch Herz und Sinne?
Sing' es mir, süsser Freund!

DER WALDVOGEL. Lustig im Leid
  sing' ich von Liebe;
  wonnig und weh'
  web' ich mein Lied:
nur Sehnende kennen den Sinn!

SIEGFRIED. Fort jagt mich's
  jauchzend von hinnen,
fort aus dem Wald auf den Fels!
  Noch einmal sage mir,
  holder Sänger:
werd' ich das Feuer durchbrechen?
kann ich erwecken die Braut?

DER WALDVOGEL. Die Braut gewinnt,
  Brünnhild' erweckt
  ein Feiger nie:
nur wer das Fürchten nicht kennt!

SIEGFRIED (lacht auf vor Entzücken).
  Der dumme Knab',
  der das Fürchten nicht kennt!
mein Vöglein, das bin ja ich!
  Noch heut' gab ich
  vergebens mir Müh',
das Fürchten von Fafner zu lernen.

I burn now to gain it
from Brünnhilde's reding:
who'll point me the path to her rock?
(*The bird flutters forth, hovers over* SIEGFRIED *and
flies away.*)

SIEGFRIED (*shouting with joy*).
The road then direct me rightly:
whither thou fliest
follows my foot!
(*He hastens after the bird. — The curtain falls.*)

Nun brennt mich die Lust,
es von Brünnhild' zu wissen:
wie find' ich zum Felsen den Weg?
(*Der Vogel flattert auf, schwebt über* SIEGFRIED, *und
fliegt davon.*)

SIEGFRIED (*jauchzend*).
So wird mir der Weg gewiesen:
wohin du flatterst
folg' ich dem Flug!
(*Er eilt dem Vogel nach. — Der Vorhang fällt.*)

THIRD ACT.

A WILD REGION

ut the foot of a rocky mountain, which rises steeply L.
towards the back. — *Night, storm, thunder, and lightning.*
Before a vault-like hollow in the rocks stands the

WILDE GEGEND

*am Fusse eines Felsenberges, der links nach hinten
steil aufsteigt.* — *Nacht, Sturm und Wetter, Blitz und
Donner.*
Vor einem gruftähnlichen Höhlenthore im Felsen steht
der

WANDERER. Waken, witch-wife!
Witch-wife, awaken!
Let lengthy sleep
wend from thy slumbering eyes.
I summon thee forth:
arise! arise!
from nebulous depths,
from night and darkness arise!
Erda! Erda!
undying witch!
From hidden abysses
bear thee on high!
Thy reveille I sing,
let it arouse thee;
from sentient slumber
shalt thou arise.
All-wotter of
all world-wisdom!
Erda! Erda!
Undying witch!
Waken, thou witch-wife! awaken!
(*The hollow has begun to glow with light.* ERDA
*rises from below in a bluish halo. She seems as if
covered with hoar-frost; her hair and garments gleam
with iridescent light.*)

WANDERER. Wache! Wache!
Wala, erwache!
Aus langem Schlafe
weck' ich dich Schlummernde wach.
Ich rufe dich auf:
herauf! herauf!
Aus nebliger Gruft,
aus nächt'gem Grunde herauf.
Erda! Erda!
Ewiges Weib!
Aus heimischer Tiefe
tauche zur Höh'!
Dein Wecklied sing' ich,
dass du erwach'st;
aus sinnendem Schlafe
sing' ich dich auf.
Allwissende!
Urweltweise!
Erda! Erda!
Ewiges Weib!
Wache, du Wala! erwache!
(*Die Höhlengruft hat zu erdämmern begonnen: in
bläulichem Lichtscheine steigt* ERDA *aus der Tiefe.
Sie erscheint wie von Reif bedeckt; Haar und Gewand
werfen einen glitzernden Schimmer von sich.*)

ERDA. Great might hath song!
strongly moves th' enchantment.
I am awakened
from witful repose:
who drives my sleep away?

ERDA. Stark ruft das Lied;
kräftig reizt der Zauber;
ich bin erwacht
aus wissendem Schlaf:
wer scheucht den Schlummer mir?

WANDERER. Thy summoner am I,
and songs I utter
to stir the senses
in bonds of slumber sealed.
The world I roved through,
wandering far
tidings to win me,
all-wisdom well to be 'ware of.
Counsellors none
can cope with thy lore;

WANDERER. Der Weckrufer bin ich,
und Weisen üb' ich,
dass weithin wache
was fester Schlaf umschliesst.
Die Welt durchzog ich,
wanderte viel,
Kunde zu werben,
urweisen Rath zu gewinnen.
Kundiger giebt es
keine als dich:

thou canst declare
what the deep doth hold,
what hill and dale,
wind and tide do contain.
Where waketh life
walketh thy spirit,
where brains are searching
broodeth thy soul;
all things they say
straight thou canst tell.
That thou mayst surrender tidings
I arouse thee from thy sleep.

ERDA.   My sleep is dreaming,
my dream is searching,
my search for weapons of wisdom.
But while I slumber
wake the Nornen:
they weave at their rope
and rightly spin what I wis.—
Why seek'st thou not the Nornen?

WANDERER.   Controlled by the world
weave on the Nornen,
and they can nought weaken nor ward off.
Yet would I thank
thy wisdom to tell me
how a wheel in its roll to arrest?

ERDA   Mortal workings
bewilder much my mind:
a warder of heaven
subdued my will to him once
I bore to Wotan
a wish-maiden,
who by her will
bands of heroes assembled.
Staunch is she
and wise withal:
why wake then me,
nor question challenge
with Erda's and Wotan's child?

WANDERER.   The Valkyrie, mean'st thou?
Brünnhilde, my maid?
She disobeyed the tempest-subduer,
when in truth he himself had subdued:
what the fight-controller
had fain accomplished,
but what he stifled
in spite of himself,
Brünnhilde free
sought then defiantly
to accomplish unbidden,
boldly in battle's assault.
Sternly
descended his wrath;
on her eyes he laid magic sleep:
on the fell she slumbers fast.
Awakened will
the war-maiden be,
but to mate with a man as his wife.
Can I then question with her?

ERDA (has become absorbed in thought, and replies
after a considerable silence).
Weak I wax
since I awoke;
wild and strange
seems the world!
The war-maiden —
the witch's child,
pines in penance of sleep
which her wisdomful mother shares?

---

bekannt ist dir
was die Tiefe birgt,
was Berg und Thal,
Luft und Wasser durchwebt.
Wo Wesen sind
weht dein Athem:
wo Hirne sinnen
haftet dein Sinn:
alles, sagt man,
sei dir bekannt.
Dass ich nun Kunde gewänne,
weckt' ich dich aus dem Schlaf.

ERDA.   Mein Schlaf ist Träumen,
mein Träumen Sinnen,
mein Sinnen Walten des Wissens.
Doch wenn ich schlafe,
wachen Nornen:
sie weben das Seil,
und spinnen fromm was ich weiss:—
was fräg'st du nicht die Nornen?

WANDERER.   Im Zwange der Welt
weben die Nornen:
sie können nichts wenden noch wandeln
doch deiner Weisheit
dankt' ich den Rath wohl,
wie zu hemmen ein rollendes Rad?

ERDA.   Männerthaten
umdämmern mir den Muth:
mich Wissende selbst
bezwang ein Waltender einst.
Ein Wunschmädchen
gebar ich Wotan:
der Helden Wal
heiss er für ihn sie küren.
Kühn ist sie
und weise auch:
was weck'st du mich,
und fräg'st um Kunde
nicht Erda's und Wotan's Kind?

WANDERER.   Die Walküre mein'st du,
Brünnhild', die Maid?
Sie trotzte dem Stürmebezwinger:
wo am stärksten er selbst sich bezwang
was den Lenker der Schlacht
zu thun verlangte,
doch dem er wehrte
— zuwider sich selbst —
allzu vertraut
wagte die Trotzige
das für sich zu vollbringen,
Brünnhild' in brennender Schlacht.
Streitvater
strafte die Maid;
in ihr Auge drückt' er Schlaf;
auf dem Felsen schläft sie fest:
erwachen wird
die Weibliche nur
um einen Mann zu minnen als Weib.
Frommten mir Fragen an sie?

ERDA (ist in Sinnen versunken, und beginnt erst nach
längerem Schweigen).
Wirr wird mir's
seit ich erwacht:
wild und kraus
kreis't die Welt!
Die Walküre,
der Wala Kind,
büsst' in Banden des Schlaf's,
als die wissende Mutter schlief?

Doth then pride's teacher
punish pride?
Is the plan's arranger
wroth with the plan?
Doth the right's defence—
doth the truth's upholder
fetter the right—
harbor untruth?
Let me quickly depart:
sleep my senses shall quiet!

WANDERER. Thou, mother, shalt not depart
while the power of magic I wield. —
All-witting
struckest thou once
the sting of sorrow
in Wotan's warrior heart:
with fear of shameful,
fatal extinction
thy wisdom filled him:
his courage was cowed by dismay.
Art thou the world's
wisest of women,
give me then rede
how the god may grapple with care.

ERDA. Thou art—scarce
what thou dost seem!
Why com'st thou, stubborn and wild one,
to startle the witch from sleep?
Restless one,
let me rest!
Loose thy constraining spell!

WANDERER. Thou art—not
what thou dost ween!
All-mother's wit
draws near its ending:
thy wisdom doth wane
before my wishes.
Wist thou what Wotan—wills?
Thou unwise,
I cry in thine ear,
that thou so unanxious mayst sleep. —

For the Æsir's ending
I feel no anguish,
since it works my will.
What in pain of wild dissension
despairing once I resolved,
fain and fearless
I fitly finish here.
Once though I wished in my anger
the Niblung might net him the world,
now, Volsung most winsome,
willed is its heirdom to thee!
One by me denoted,
but to me unknown,
a notable novice,
all undirected,
has reached the Nibelung's ring.
Lacking in malice,
large of love,
he'll lightly disarm
Alberich's curse;
for far bides he from fear.
She whom thou hast borne,
Brünnhilde,
will this hero hail.
When she wakes
thy child will work
a deed for the world's release.
Then slumber again,
seal up thine eyelids,

Der den Trotz lehrte
straft den Trotz?
Der die That entzündet
zürnt um die That?
Der das Recht wahrt,
der die Eide hütet—
wehret dem Recht?
herrscht durch Meineid?—
Lass' mich wieder hinab:
Schlaf verschliesse mein Wissen!

WANDERER. Dich Mutter lass' ich nicht zieh'n
da des Zaubers ich mächtig bin. —
Urwissend
stachest du einst
der Sorge Stachel
in Wotan's wagendes Herz:
mit Furcht vor schmachvoll
feindlichem En—
füllt' ihn dein Wissen,
dass Bangen band seinen Muth.
Bist du der Welt
weisestes Weib,
sage mir nun:
wie besiegt die Sorge der Gott?

ERDA. Du bist—nicht
was du nich nenn'st!
Was käm'st du störrischer Wilder
zu stören der Wala Schlaf?
Friedloser,
lass' mich frei!
Löse des Zaubers Zwang!

WANDERER. Du bist—nicht
was du dich wähn'st!
Urmütter-Weisheit
geht zu Ende:
dein Wissen verweht
vor meinem Willen.
Weisst du, was Wotan—will?
Dir Unweisen
ruf' ich's in's Ohr,
dass du sorglos ewig nun schläf'st. —

Um der Götter Ende
gräm't mich die Angst nicht,
seit mein Wunsch es—will!
Was in Zwiespalt's wildem Schmerze
verzweifelnd einst ich beschloss,
froh und freudig
führ' ich frei es nun aus:
weiht' ich in wüthendem Ekel
des Niblungen Neid schon die Welt
dem wonnigsten Wälsung
weis' ich mein Erbe nun an.
Der von mir erkoren,
doch nie mich gekannt,
ein kühnster Knabe,
meines Rathes bar,
errang des Niblungen Ring:
ledig des Neides,
liebesfroh,
erlahmt an dem Edlen
Alberich's Fluch;
denn fremd bleibt ihm die Furcht.
Die du mir gebar'st,
Brünnhilde,
sie weckt hold sich der Held:
wachend wirkt
dein wissendes Kind
erlösende Weltenthat. —
D'rum schlaf nun du,
schliesse dein Auge;

dream, and foresee my ending.
　　Whatever may happen
　　the god will always
hail the heaven of love.
　　Away then, Erda!
　　All-mother-fear—
　　All-sorrow—
　　To endless sleep
　　away! away!
I see that Sigfried comes. —
(ERDA *vanishes. The hollow again becomes quite*
dark. THE WANDERER *leans against the rocks and*
awaits SIEGFRIED.)—
(*Moon-rise slightly illumines the stage. The storm*
has quite subsided.)

———

SIEGFRIED (*entering R. in the foreground*).
　　My fav'rite soars not before.—
　　　　With fluttering flight
　　　　and sweetest song
　　plainly it pointed the path:
　　now seems it far to have flown.
　　　　'Twere right to find
　　　　the rock for myself:
　　the way my feathered friend went
　　thither will I now fare.
(*He goes further towards the back.*)

WANDERER (*remaining in his station by the cave*).
　　Say, boy, whither
　　bend'st thou thy way?

SIEGFRIED.　I hear a voice:
　　will *he* tell me the way?
　　　　For a rock I'm seeking
　　around which fire doth wander:
　　　　there sleeps a woman
　　　　whom I would awake.

WANDERER.　Who stirr'd thy mind
　　　　the mount to seek for,
　　and for the maiden to struggle?

SIEGFRIED.　It was a singing
　　　　wood-minstrel
　　who gave the goodly tidings.

WANDERER.　A bird doth sing much nonsense;
　　but none may understand.
　　　　How knewest thou so
　　　　the song's importing?

SIEGFRIED.　It was by the blood
　　　　of a wicked worm,
　　whom I at Hate-cavern butchered:
　　　　scarce had it tingled
　　　　the tongue of me
　　when I straightway the bird understood.

WANDERER.　Thou slewest the giant?
　　　　How germed in thee
　　the scheme to fight with the serpent?

SIEGFRIED.　I followed Mime,
　　　　a faithless dwarf,
　　who wanted to teach me fearing.
　　　　The sword-stroke, truly,
　　　　'neath which he sank
　　mainly the worm did seek;
　　with his maw he menaced my life.

---

träumend erschau' mein Ende!
　　Was jene auch wirken —
　　dem ewig Jungen
weicht in Wonne der Gott. —
　　Hinab denn, Erda!
　　Urmütter-Furcht!
　　Ur-Sorge!
　　Zu ewigem Schlaf
　　hinab! hinab! —
　　Dort seh' ich Siegfried nah'n. —
(ERDA *versinkt. Die Höhle ist wieder ganz finster*
geworden: an dem Gestein derselben lehnt sich der
WANDERER *an, und erwartet so* SIEGFRIED. —)
(*Monddämmerung erhellt die Bühne etwas. Das*
Sturmwetter hört ganz auf.)

———

SIEGFRIED (*von rechts im Vordergrunde auftretend*).
　　Mein Vöglein schwebte mir fort; —
　　　　mit flatterndem Flug
　　　　und süssem Sang
　　wies es mir wonnig den Weg:
　　nun schwand es fern mir davon.
　　　　Am besten find' ich
　　　　selbst nun den Berg:
　　wohin mein Führer mich wies,
　　dahin wandr' ich jetzt fort.
(*Er schreitet weiter nach hinten.*)

WANDERER (*in seiner Stellung an der Höhle verblei-*
bend).
　　Wohin, Knabe,
　　heisst dich dein Weg?

SIEGFRIED.　Da redet's ja:
　　wohl räth das mir den Weg. —
　　　　Einen Felsen such' ich,
　　von Feuer ist der umwabert:
　　　　dort schläft ein Weib
　　　　das ich wecken will.

WANDERER.　Wer sagt' es dir
　　　　den Fels zu suchen,
　　wer nach der Frau dich zu sehnen?

SIEGFRIED.　Mich wies es ein singend
　　　　Waldvöglein:
　　das gab mir gute Kunde.

WANDERER.　Ein Vöglein schwatzt wohl manches;
　　kein Mensch doch kann's versteh'n:
　　　　wie mochtest du Sinn
　　　　dem Sange entnehmen?

SIEGFRIED.　Das wirkte das Blut
　　　　eines wilden Wurm's,
　　der mir vor Neidhöhl' erblasste:
　　　　kaum netzt' es zündend
　　　　die Zunge mir,
　　da verstand ich der Vöglein Gestimm'

WANDERER.　Erschlugst du den Riesen,
　　　　wer reizte dich,
　　den starken Wurm zu besteh'n?

SIEGFRIED.　Mich führte Mime,
　　　　ein falscher Zwerg;
　　das Fürchten wollt' er mich lehren:
　　　　zum Schwertschlag aber,
　　　　der ihn erschlug,
　　reizte der Wurm mich selbst;
　　seinen Rachen riss er mir auf.

WANDERER. Who shaped the sword
    so sharp and hard
    that so strong a foe it felled?

WANDERER. Wer schuf das Schwert
    so scharf und hart,
    dass der stärkste Feind ihm fiel?

SIEGFRIED. I shaped it myself,
    as the smith was helpless;
    swordless else should I be still.

SIEGFRIED. Das schweisst' ich mir selbst,
    da's der Schmied nicht konnte:
    schwertlos noch wär' ich wohl sonst.

WANDERER. But who shaped
    the sturdy splinters
    from which thou'st smelted the sword?

WANDERER. Doch wer schuf
    die starken Stücken,
    daraus das Schwert du geschweisst?

SIEGFRIED. What thought I of that?
    But this I knew—
    for no work were fit those fragments
    were they not welded afresh.

SIEGFRIED. Was weiss ich davon!
    Ich weiss allein,
    dass die Stücken nichts mir nützten,
    schuf ich das Schwert mir nicht neu.

WANDERER. (*breaking into a peal of good-humored laughter*).
    That well I admit!

WANDERER (*bricht in ein freudig gemüthliches Lachen aus*).
    Das—mein' ich wohl auch!

SIEGFRIED. Why laugh you at me?
    Old enquirer,
    hark once for all;—
    lead me no longer to chatter!
    Can you direct
    the road to me, do so;
    and can you not
    then keep your mouth closed!

SIEGFRIED. Was lach'st du mich aus?
    Alter Frager,
    hör' einmal auf;
    lass' mich nicht lange mehr schwatzen!
    Kannst du den Weg
    mir weisen, so rede:
    vermag'st du's nicht,
    so halte dein Maul!

WANDERER. But soft, my youngster!
    Since I am old
    thou shouldst some honor accord me.

WANDERER. Geduld, du Knabe!
    Dünk' ich dich alt,
    so sollst du mir Achtung bieten.

SIEGFRIED. That is a good one!
    So long as I've lived
    e'er in my way
    an old one waited,
    whom now I have swept aside.
    Stay you here longer
    stiff planted before me,
    it seems fit, see now,
    that you like Mime should fare.
    (*He approaches nearer to the* WANDERER.)
    What do you look like?
    Why have you on
    such an ample hat?
    Wherefore hangs it so far o'er your face?

SIEGFRIED. Das wär' nicht übel!
    So lang' ich lebe
    stand mir ein Alter
    stets im Wege:
    den hab' ich nun fort gefegt.
    Stemm'st du dort länger
    dich steif mir entgegen—
    sieh' dich vor, mein' ich,
    dass du wie Mime nicht fähr'st!
    (*Er tritt näher an den* WANDERER *heran*.)
    Wie sieh'st du denn aus?
    Was hast du gar
    für 'nen grossen Hut?
    Warum hängt der dir so in's Gesicht?

WANDERER. Such is the wont of Wand'rer,
    when he goes against the wind.

WANDERER. Das ist so Wand'rers Weise,
    wenn dem Wind entgegen er geht.

SIEGFRIED. But below an eyeball is lacking!
    No doubt you lost it
    to one of late,
    when you too boldly
    did bar his way.
    Take yourself off,
    or, may be, I'll quench
    the other one too, and quickly.

SIEGFRIED. Doch darunter fehlt dir ein Auge!
    Das schlug dir einer
    gewiss schon aus,
    dem du zu trotzig
    den Weg vertrat'st?
    Mach' dich jetzt fort!
    sonst möchtest du leicht
    das and're auch noch verlieren.

WANDERER. I see, my son,
    where thou nought wottest,
    thou well contrivest to help thee.
    With an eye, too,
    like the one that I lack
    thyself dost look on the other
    that yet is left me for sight.

WANDERER. Ich seh', mein Sohn,
    wo nichts du weisst,
    da weisst du dir leicht zu helfen
    Mit dem Auge,
    das als and'res mir fehlt,
    erblick'st du selber das eine,
    das mir zum Sehen verblieb.

SIEGFRIED (*laughing*).
    Your language moves me to laughter!
    But come! I'll quibble no longer.
    Be quick! tell me the way;
    then, I warn you, turn on your own!

SIEGFRIED (*lacht*).
    Zum Lachen bist du mir lustig!—
    Doch hör', nun schwatz' ich nicht länger,
    geschwind zeig' mir den Weg,
    deines Weges ziehe dann du!

In nought else
your aid do I need,
so speak, or I'll spurn you aside!

WANDERER. Didst thou know me,
daring son,
of scoffs sparing wert thou!
Fiercely thy taunts
tear the heart that enfolds thee.
Love though I bear
to thy lineage bright,
fear too I've wrought
by my wrath when it fell.
Thou whom I cherish —
youth enchanting —
chafe not my spirit now
to annihilate thee and me!

SIEGFRIED. Dumb are you still,
stubborn old wight?
Wend from your station!
For I know that way
brings to the slumbering bride.
So warned me the flutterer
that here has fled from me first.
(*It gradually becomes quite dark again.*)

WANDERER (*breaking out into wrath.*)
It fled thee to save its life.
The lord of ravens
its road did let:
woe to it, light they on it! —
The way that it pointed
shalt thou not pass.

SIEGFRIED. Oho! my withholder!
And who are you
that thus arrest my road?

WANDERER. Mock not the mountain's guardian!
A spell engirds
by my might the slumbering maid.
One who can wake her,—
one who can win her,
makes me mightless for ever!

A fiery main
flows round her form,
glittering lightnings
o'erlick the fell:
he who'd find the bride
will feel the brunt of the fire.
(*He points with his spear.*)
Turn t'ward the hill!
Dost look on the light?
Yon waxing sheen,
yon swelling glare —
smothering vapors,
varying lightnings,
vacillate burning
and crackling anigh.
A light-flood
illumines thy head:
the furnace soon
will seize and enfold thee. —
Away then, foolhardy boy!

SIEGFRIED. Away, old boaster, yourself!
Straight where the blaze is burning
to Brünnhilde's side will I haste.
(*He advances on him.*)

WANDERER (*stretching out his spear*).
Hast thou no heed of the fire?
My spear then shall spare thee no path!

---

zu nichts and'rem
acht' ich dich nütz':
d'rum sprich, sonst spreng' ich dich fort!

WANDERER. Kenntest du mich,
kühner Spross,
den Schimpf — spartest du mir!
Dir so vertraut,
trifft mich schmerzlich dein Dräu'n
Liebt' ich von je
deine lichte Art, —
Grauen auch zeugt' ihr
mein zürnender Grimm:
dem ich so hold bin,
allzu hehrer,
heut' nicht wecke mir Neid,
er vernichtete dich und mich!

SIEGFRIED. Bleib'st du mir stumm,
störrischer Wicht?
Weich' von der Stelle!
Denn dorthin, ich weiss,
führt es zur schlafenden Frau:
so wies es mein Vöglein,
das hier erst flüchtig entfloh.
(*Es wird allmälig wieder ganz finster.*)

WANDERER (*in Zorn ausbrechend*).
Es floh dir zu seinem Heil;
den Herrn der Raben
errieth es hier:
weh' ihm, holen sie's ein!—
Den Weg, den es zeigte,
sollst du nicht zieh'n!

SIEGFRIED. Hoho! du Verbieter!
Wer bist du,
dass du mir wehren willst?

WANDERER. Fürchte des Felsens Hüter!
Verschlossen hält
meine Macht die schlafende Maid,
wer sie erweckte,
wer sie gewänne,
machtlos macht' er mich ewig!

Ein Feuermeer
umfluthet die Frau,
glühende Lohe
umleckt den Fels:
wer die Braut begehrt,
dem brennt entgegen die Brunst.
(*Er winkt mit dem Speere.*)
Blick' nach der Höh'!
erlug'st du das Licht? —
Es wächst der Schein,
es schwillt die Gluth;
sengende Wolken,
wabernde Lohe,
wälzen sich brennend
und prasselnd herab
Ein Licht-Meer
umleuchtet dein Haupt:
bald frisst und zehrt dich
zündendes Feuer: —
zurück denn, rasendes Kind!

SIEGFRIED. Zurück, du Prahler, mit dir!
Dort, wo die Brünste brennen,
zu Brünnhilde muss ich jetzt hin
(*Er schreitet darauf zu.*)

WANDERER (*den Speer vorhaltend*).
Fürchtest das Feuer du nicht,
so sperre mein Speer dir den Weg

Still holdeth my hand
the hallow'd haft;
the sword that thou sway'st
was shivered on this shaft:
so too again
'twill snap on the eterna spear

Noch hält meine Hand
der Herrschaft Haft;
das Schwert, das du schwing'st
zerschlug einst dieser Schaft:
noch einmal denn
zerspring' es am ewigen Speer!

SIEGFRIED (*drawing his sword*).
Then my father's foe
faces me here?
How that will serve me
for sweet revenge!
Stretch out your spear:
my sword shall strike it to shreds.
(*He attacks the* WANDERER *and hews his spear in
pieces. Terrific clap of thunder.*)

SIEGFRIED (*das Schwert ziehend*).
Meines Vaters Feind!
Find' ich dich hier?
Herrlich zur Rache
gerieth mir das!
Schwing' deinen Speer:
in Stücken spalt' ihn mein Schwert!
(*Er ficht mit dem* WANDERER *und haut ihm den Speer
in Stücken. Furchtbarer Donnerschlag.*)

WANDERER (*recoiling*).
Advance! I cannot prevent thee!
(*He disappears.*)

WANDERER (*zurückweichend*).
Zieh' hin! ich kann dich nicht halten.
(*Er verschwindet.*)

SIEGFRIED. With defeated weapon
flieth my foeman?
(*Fiery clouds have descended from the heights at back
with increasing brightness: the entire stage becomes filled
with a rolling sea of fire.*)

SIEGFRIED. Mit zerfocht'ner Waffe
wich mir der Feige?
(*Mit wachsender Helle haben sich Feuerwolken aus
der Höhe des Hintergrundes herabgesenkt: die ganze
Bühne erfüllt sich wie von einem wogenden Flammen-
meere.*)

SIEGFRIED. Ha! heavenly glow!
brightning glare!
roads are now opening
radiantly round me.
In fire will I bathe,
through fire will I fare to my bride!
Oho! Oho!
Aha! Aha!
Gaily! gaily!
Soon greets me a glorious friend!
(*He winds his horn and plunges into the fire, blowing
his call. — The fire now flows over the whole foreground.
SIEGFRIED's horn is heard, first near, then more distant.
— The fiery clouds continue to pour from the back towards
the front, so that SIEGFRIED, whose horn is now again
heard nearer, appears to be ascending the mountain.*)

SIEGFRIED. Ha, wonnige Gluth!
leuchtender Glanz!
Strahlend offen
steht mir die Strasse. —
Im Feuer mich baden!
Im Feuer zu finden die Braut!
Hoho! hoho!
hahei! hahei!
Lustig! lustig!
Jetzt lock' ich ein liebes Gesell!
(*Er setzt sein Horn an, und stürzt sich, seine Lock-
weise blasend, in das Feuer. — Die Lohe ergiesst sich
nun auch über den ganzen Vordergrund. Man hört
Siegfried's Horn erst näher, dann ferner. — Die Feuer-
wolken ziehen immer von hinten nach vorn, so dass
SIEGFRIED, dessen Horn man wieder näher hört, sich
nach hinten zu, die Höhe hinauf, zu wenden scheint.*)

(*At last the glow begins to fade and sinks to a fine
transparent veil, which also clears off and reveals the
most lovely blue sky and bright weather.
The scene, from which all the vapors have fled, represents
the summit of a rocky mountain-peak (as in the third Act
of the "* VALKYRIE *"): L. the entrance to a natural rocky
hall; R. spreading fir-trees; the background quite open. —
In the foreground beneath the shade of a spreading fir-
tree lies* BRÜNNHILDE *in deep sleep: she is in a complete
suit of gleaming plate-armor, with helmet on her head and
long shield over her body.
SIEGFRIED has now reached the rocky heights in the
background. (His horn has sounded more and more
distant till it ceased altogether.) He looks around in
astonishment.*)

(*Endlich beginnt die Gluth zu erbleichen; sie löst
sich wie in einen feinen, durchsichtigen Schleier auf, der
nun ganz sich auch klärt und den heitersten blauen
Himmelsäther, im hellsten Tagesscheine, hervortreten
lässt.
Die Scene, von der das Gewölk gänzlich gewichen ist,
stellt die Höhe eines Felsengipfels (wie im dritten
Aufzuge der "* WALKÜRE *") dar: links der Eingang
eines natürlichen Felsengemaches; rechts breite Tan-
nen; der Hintergrund ganz frei. — Im Vordergrunde.
unter dem Schatten einer breitästigen Tanne, liegt
BRÜNNHILDE, in tiefem Schlafe: sie ist in vollständi-
ger, glänzender Panzerrüstung, mit dem Helm auf dem
Haupte, den langen Schild über sich gedeckt. —
SIEGFRIED ist so eben im Hintergrunde, am felsigen
Saume der Höhe, angelangt. (Sein Horn hatte zuletzt
wieder ferner geklungen, bis es ganz schwieg.) — Er
blickt staunend um sich.*)

SIEGFRIED. Sweet is this haven
on sun-illumed heights! —
(*Looking into the wood.*)
What calmly slumbers

SIEGFRIED. Selige Oede
auf sonniger Höh'! —
(*In den Tann hinein sehend.*)
Was ruht dort schlummernd

neath shadowy trees?
A war-horse,
waiting in tranquil sleep!
(*He surmounts the height completely and advances slowly; on seeing* BRÜNNHILDE *at a little distance he pauses in surprise.*)
What strikes me with its gleaming?
What glittering suit of steel!
Blind are my eyes
as yet with the blaze?
(*He comes nearer.*)
Shining weapons! —
Shall I uplift?
[*He raises the shield and discovers* BRUNNHILDE'S *face, which the helmet still in a great measure conceals.*)
Ha! a warrior, sure!
I scan with wonder his form!—
His haughty head
is press'd by the helm;
lighter would he
lie were it loosed.
(*He carefully unfastens the helmet and removes it from the sleeper; long, curling hair breaks forth. —* SIEGFRIED *starts.*)
Ah! —how fair!
(*He remains absorbed in contemplation.*)
Fleecy as cloudlets
fringing the clearness
of azure aether seas:
laughing, the sun's
enlightening face
shines through the cluster of cloud.
(*He listens for the sleeper's breath.*)
But heavily breathing
heaveth his breast:
better to open his byrnie?
(*He tries very cautiously, but in vain.*)
Come, my sword,
cut through the iron!

(*With tender care he cuts through the rings of mail on each side, and lifts off the corslet and greaves, so that* BRÜNNHILDE *then lies before him in a soft, female garb. Surprised and astonished, he starts back.*)
This is no man!
Burning enchantment
charges my heart;
fiery awe
falls on my eyesight;
my senses stagger and sway.
O whom shall I hail
that he may help me?
Mother! Mother!
look down on me!—

He sinks with his head on BRÜNNHILDE's *bosom. — Long silence.—Then he starts up suddenly.*)
O what shall I do
that she her eyelids may open? —
Her eyes to me open!
Blind then were mine with their blaze.
How could I dare
endure such a light?
All sways and swims
and staggers around;
scorching desires
entangle my senses,
and trembles my heart
at touch of my hand!
What is this feeling?
Can it be fearing?
O mother! mother!

---

im schattigen Tann r —
Ein Ross ist's,
rastend in tiefem Schlaf!
(*Er betritt vollends die Höhe, und schreitet langsam weiter vor; als er* BRÜNNHILDE *noch aus einiger Entfernung gewahrt, hält er verwundert an.*)
Was strahlt mir dort entgegen? —
Welch' glänzendes Stahlgeschmeide!
Blendet mir noch
die Lohe den Blick? —
(*Er tritt näher hinzu.*)
Helle Waffen! —
Heb' ich sie auf?
(*Er hebt den Schild ab, und erblickt* BRÜNNHILDE's *Gesicht, das jedoch der Helm noch zum grossen Theile verdeckt.*)
Ha! in Waffen ein Mann: —
wie mahnt mich wonnig sein Bild!
Das hehre Haupt
drückt wohl der Helm?
leichter würd' ihm,
löst' ich den Schmuck.
(*Vorsichtig löst er den Helm und hebt ihn der Schlafenden vom Haupte ab: langes, lockiges Haar bricht hervor. —* SIEGFRIED *erschrickt.*)
Ach! — wie schön!
(*Er bleibt in den Anblick versunken.*)
Schimmernde Wolken
säumen in Wellen
den hellen Himmelssee:
leuchtender Sonne
lachendes Bild
strahlt durch das Wogengewölk!
(*Er lauscht dem Athem.*)
Von schwellendem Athem
schwingt sich die Brust: —
brech' ich die engende Brünne?
(*Er versucht es mit grosser Behutsamkeit — aber vergebens.*)
Komm', mein Schwert,
schneide das Eisen!

(*Er durchschneidet mit zarter Vorsicht die Panzerringe zu beiden Seiten der ganzen Rüstung, und hebt dann die Brünne und die Schienen ab, so dass nun* BRÜNNHILDE *in einem weichen weiblichen Gewande vor ihm liegt. — Ueberrascht und staunend fährt er auf.*)
Das ist kein Mann! — —
Brennender Zauber
zückt mir in's Herz;
feurige Angst
fasst meine Augen:
mir schwankt und schwindelt der Sinn! —
Wen ruf' ich zum Heil,
dass er mir helfe? —
Mutter! Mutter!
Gedenke mein'! —

(*Er sinkt mit der Stirn an Brünnhilde's Busen. Langes Schweigen — Dann fährt er seufzend auf.*)
Wie weck' ich die Maid,
dass sie die Augen mir öff'ne? —
Das Auge mir öff'nen?
blende mich auch noch der Blick
Wagt' es mein Trotz?
ertrüg' ich das Licht? —
Mir schwebt und schwankt
und schwirrt es umher;
sehrendes Sengen
zehrt meine Sinne:
am zagenden Herzen
zittert die Hand! —
Wie ist mir Feigem? —
Ist es das Fürchten? —
O Mutter! Mutter!

how mignty thy son!
A woman folded in sleep
at last has enslaved him with fear!

How can I be calm —
recall my mind ?
Ere I quell this weakness
must the maid be awakened ?

Sweetly beckons
her blossoming mouth:
what mild alarms in me
lightly it stirs! —
Ah! and the ardent
winsome warmth of her breath!

Awaken! awaken!
maiden bewitched! —
She hears me not. —
Then life I will drain me
from lips the most dainty,
did they e'en doom me to death!

(*He imprints a long and ardent kiss upon her lips. — He starts back in surprise;* Brünnhilde *has opened her eyes. He gazes on her in astonishment. Both remain for some time wrapt in mutual contemplation.*)

Brünnhilde (*slowly and solemnly rising to a sitting position*).
Hail, thou sunshine!
Hail, thou light!
Hail, thou loveliest day!
Long was my rest;
I rise from sleep,
say, who is he
that wakes my sense ?

Siegfried (*awe-struck by her appearance and voice*).
Through the fire I thrust
that burns round the fell,
and I broke thy defending helm.
Siegfried I,
by whom thou art waked.

Brünnhilde (*sitting erect.*)
Hail, ye gods all!
Hail, thou world!
Hail, ye glories of nature!
Unknit is now my sleep;
I stand awake;
Siegfried 'tis
who unwinds the spell!

dein muthiges Kind!
Im Schlafe liegt eine Frau: —
die hat ihn das Fürchten gelehrt! ..

Wie end' ich die Furcht ?
wie fass' ich Muth ? —
Dass ich selbst erwache,
muss die Maid ich erwecken! — —

Süss erbebt mir
ihr blühender Mund:
wie mild erzitternd
mich Zagen er reizt! —
Ach, dieses Athem's
wonnig warmes Gedüft! —

Erwache erwache!
heiliges Weib! —
Sie hört-mich nicht. —
So saug' ich mir Leben
aus süssesten Lippen —
sollt' ich auch sterbend vergeh'n!

(*Er küsst sie lange und inbrünstig. — Erschreckt fährt er dann in die Höhe: —* Brünnhilde *hat die Augen aufgeschlagen. — Staunend blickt er sie an. Beide verweilen eine Zeit lang in ihren gegenseitigen Anblick versunken.*)

Brünnhilde (*langsam und feierlich sich zum Sitze aufrichtend*).
Heil dir, Sonne!
Heil dir, Licht!
Heil dir, leuchtender Tag!
Lang war mein Schlaf;
ich bin erwacht:
wer ist der Held,
der mich erweckt' ?

Siegfried (*von ihrem Blicke und ihrer Stimme feierlich ergriffen*).
Durch das Feuer drang ich,
das den Fels umbrann;
ich erbrach dir den festen Helm:
Siegfried heiss' ich,
der dich erweckt'.

Brünnhilde (*hoch aufgerichtet sitzend*).
Heil euch, Götter!
Heil dir, Welt!
Heil dir, prangende Erde!
Zu End' ist nun mein Schlaf;
erwacht seh' ich:
Siegfried ist es
der mich erweckt!

MOTIVE OF LOVE'S GREETING.

Siegfried (*in exalted rapture*).
O hail to her
who gave me to life!
Hail to earth,
my fostering nurse!
that I should e'er have seen
the sight that smiles on me here!

Siegfried (*in erhabenster Entzückung*).
O Heil der Mutter,
die mich gebar;
Heil der Erde,
die mich genährt:
dass ich das Auge erschaut,
das jetzt mir Seligem strahlt!

MOTIVE OF LOVE'S PASSION.

BRÜNNHILDE (*deeply stirred*).
O hail to her
who gave thee to life!
Hail to earth,
thy fostering nurse!
But one glance was to behold me:
for thee I was to awake.

O Siegfried! Siegfried!
sanctified hero!
thou wakener of life,
thou sovereign light!
O wist thou, lord of worlds,
what time thou'st had my love!
Thou wert my object,
my aim wert thou!
I fostered thee
before thou wert formed;
before thou wert born
I brought thee my shield:
so long I've loved thee, Siegfried.

SIEGFRIED (*gently and bashfully*).
My mother did not die then?
she merely drooped in sleep?

BRÜNNHILDE (*smiling*).
Thou innocent child,
thou wilt ne'er be charmed by her image.
Thyself am I,
if thy pure spirit can love.
What thou dost want
well can I teach:
but wisdom only
grew—when that I loved thee.

O Siegfried! Siegfried!
sovereign light!
I loved thee always,
for I alone
distinguished Wotan's intention.
The intention that I
ne'er named nor told of,
that I ne'er tested—
I only felt it:—
for which I fought,
struggled and strove,
for which I flouted
him who framed it,
for which I suffered
in penance of sleep,
having never thought it,
but known it still!
Truly, that intention—
'tis for thy solving—
was but that my love should be thine!

SIEGFRIED.
With winsome tones
what wonders thou sing'st!
but bound abideth their sense.
By thine eyes' fair light
I stand illumed,
by thy ardent breath
my breast is warmed,
by thy singing sweet
my ears are soothed;
but what thou sayest in song
strangely doth strike my mind.
Now nought can I fathom
subtle and far off,
for ev'ry sense
on thee is centred and fastened.
With timid fear
thou fillest me:

BRÜNNHILDE (*mit grösster Bewegtheit*).
O Heil der Mutter,
die dich gebar;
Heil der Erde,
die dich genährt:
nur dein Blick durfte mich schau n,
erwachen durft' ich nur dir!—

O Siegfried! Siegfried!
seliger Held!
Du Wecker des Lebens,
siegendes Licht!
O wüsstest du, Lust der Welt,
wie ich dich je geliebt!
Du war'st mein Sinnen,
mein Sorgen du!
Dich Zarten nährt' ich
noch eh' du gezeugt;
noch eh' du geboren
barg dich mein Schild:
so lang' lieb' ich dich, Siegfried!

SIEGFRIED (*leise und schüchtern*).
So starb nicht meine Mutter?
schlief die Minnige nur?

BRÜNNHILDE (*lächelnd*). Du wonniges Kind,
deine Mutter kehrt dir nicht wieder
Du selbst bin ich,
wenn du mich Selige lieb'st.
Was du nicht weisst,
weiss ich für dich:
doch wissend bin ich
nur—weil ich dich liebe.—

O Siegfried! Siegfried!
siegendes Licht!
dich liebt' ich immer;
denn mir allein
erdünkte Wotan's Gedanke.
Der Gedanke, den nie
ich nennen durfte;
den ich nicht dachte,
sondern nur fühlte;
für den ich focht,
kämpfte und stritt;
für den ich trotzte
dem, der ihn dachte;
für den ich büsste,
Strafe mich band,
weil ich nicht ihn dachte
und nur empfand!
Denn der Gedanke—
dürftest du's lösen!—
mir war er nur Liebe zu dir!

SIEGFRIED. Wie Wunder tönt
was wonnig du sing'st;
doch dunkel dünkt mich der Sinn.
Deines Auges Leuchten
seh' ich licht;
deines Athem's Wehen
fühl' ich warm;
deiner Stimme Singen
hör' ich süss:
doch was du singend mir sag'st
staunend versteh' ich's nicht.
Nicht kann ich das Ferne
sinnig erfassen,
da all' meine Sinne
dich nur sehen und fühlen.
Mit banger Furcht
fesselst du mich.

thou only hast
in me awesomeness waked.
Thou who hast bound me
with manacles breakless,
bring back my manhood once more!

BRÜNNHILDE (*gently repulses him and turns her eyes
towards the wood*).
There feedeth Grani,
my faithful steed:
how briskly he wanders
who with me slept!
He too was by Siegfried awaked.

SIEGFRIED. On glorious lips
my glances are feasting;
with feverish thirst
I feel my own burning,
till the eyes' refreshment they taste of.

BRÜNNHILDE (*pointing with her hand*).
I see there the shield
that sheltered heroes;
I see there the helm
that did ward my head;
they'll shield — they'll ward me no more!

SIEGFRIED. As a woman divine
thou woundest my heart;
mortal the hurt
so shaped by a maid: —
I came without shield or helm.

BRÜNNHILDE (*with growing melancholy*).
I see there the byrnie's
glittering steel;
a sturdy sword
split it apart
and the maiden's protection
tore from her form:
without either guard or glaive
but a weakly woman I feel!

SIEGFRIED. Through billows of fire
I fared to thy side;
nor byrnie nor shield
my body defends.
Now burst the flames
unchecked in my breast;
now bounds my blood
in blissfullest blaze;
a rapturous fire
within me is raging:
the flames that round
Brünnhilde once roared
now rend me with fearful wrath.
O maid, extinguish the rays!
still this disturbance in me!
(*He seizes her impetuously; she springs up, repulses
him with the utmost strength of terror and flies to the
opposite side.*)

BRÜNNHILDE. No god e'en has touched me!
as a maiden ever
heroes revered me:
virgin I hied from Valhalla! —
Woe's me! woe's me!
Woe for the shame,
the shunless disgrace!
My wak'ning hero
deals me this wound!
He has burst my byrnie and helm:
Brünnhilde am I no more!

du Einz'ge hast
ihre Angst mich gelehrt.
Den du gebunden
in mächt'gen Banden,
birg' meinen Muth mir nicht mehr!

BRÜNNHILDE (*wehrt ihn sanft ab, und wendet ihre
Blick nach dem Tann*).
— Dort seh' ich Grane,
mein selig Ross:
wie weidet er munter,
der mit mir schlief!
Mit mir hat ihn Siegfried erweckt.

SIEGFRIED. Auf wonnigem Munde
weidet mein Auge:
in brünstigem Durst
doch brennen die Lippen,
dass der Augen Weide sie labe!

BRÜNNHILDE (*ihn mit der Hand bedeutend*).
Dort seh' ich den Schild,
der Helden schirmte;
dort seh' ich den Helm,
der das Haupt mir barg:
er schirmt, er birgt mich nicht mehr!

SIEGFRIED. Eine selige Maid
versehrte mein Herz;
Wunden dem Haupte
schlug mir ein Weib: —
ich kam ohne Schild und Helm!

BRÜNNHILDE (*mit gesteigerter Wehmuth*).
Ich sehe der Brünne
prangenden Stahl:
ein scharfes Schwert
schnitt sie entzwei;
von dem maidlichen Leibe
löst' es die Wehr: —
ich bin ohne Schutz und Schirm,
ohne Trutz ein trauriges Weib!

SIEGFRIED. Durch brennendes Feuer
fuhr ich zu dir;
nicht Brünne noch Panzer
barg meinen Leib:
mir in die Brust
brach nun die Lohe,
es braus't mein Blut
in blühender Brunst;
ein zehrendes Feuer
ist mir entzündet:
die Gluth, die Brünnhild's
Felsen umbrann,
die brennt mir nun in der Brust! —
Du Weib, jetzt lösche den Brand!
schweige die schäumende Gluth!
(*Er umfasst sie heftig; sie springt auf, wehrt ihm mit
der höchsten Kraft der Angst, und entflieht nach der
andern Seite.*)

BRÜNNHILDE. Kein Gott nahte mir je:
der Jungfrau neigten
scheu sich die Helden:
heilig schied sie aus Walhall! —
Wehe! Wehe!
Wehe der Schmach,
der schmählichen Noth!
Verwundet hat mich,
der mich erweckt!
Er erbrach mir Brünne und Helm:
Brünnhilde bin ich nicht mehr!

SIEGFRIED.   Still thou'rt to me
             the slumbering maid:
             Brünnhilde's sleep
             bindeth her yet.
             Awaken! be but my wife!

BRÜNNHILDE. My senses are swaying,
             my wit forsakes:
             shall all my wisdom 'scape me?

SIEGFRIED.   Said'st thou not
             that thy wisdom shewed
             the lighting of love unto me?

BRÜNNHILDE. Dismallest blackness
             dazes my sight;
             my eyes are blinded,
             their light is lost:
             night veileth me.
             In vaporous mists
             foully upforces
             a grisly fear:
             horrors haunt me
             and compass me round.
             (*She clasps her hands over her eyes hastily.*)

SIEGFRIED (*gently drawing her hands from her face*).
             Darkness frightens
             closed eyelids;
             set them free, and fled
             is the fearsome spell.
             Draw from the shadow and see:—
             sun-illumed smileth the day.

BRÜNNHILDE (*in extreme agitation.*)
             Sun-illumed
             smileth this day on my shame!—
             O Siegfried! Siegfried!
             See how I dread!—

SIEGFRIED.   Noch bist du mir
             die träumende Maid:
             Brünnhilde's Schlaf
             brach ich noch nicht.
             Erwache! sei mir ein Weib!

BRÜNNHILDE. Mir schwirren die Sinne!
             Mein Wissen schweigt:
             soll mir die Weisheit schwinden?

SIEGFRIED.   Sang'st du mir nicht,
             dein Wissen sei
             das Leuchten der Liebe zu mir?

BRÜNNHILDE. Trauriges Dunkel
             trübt mir den Blick;
             mein Auge dämmert,
             das Licht verlischt:
             Nacht wird's um mich:
             aus Nebel und Grau'n
             windet sich wüthend
             ein Angstgewirr.
             Schrecken schreitet
             und bäumt sich empor!
             (*Sie birgt heftig die Augen mit den Händen.*)

SIEGFRIED (*lös't ihr sanft die Hände vom Blicke*)
             Nacht umbangt
             gebundene Augen;
             mit den Fesseln schwindet
             das finst're Grau'n:
             tauch' aus dem Dunkel und sieh—
             sonnenhell leuchtet der Tag!

BRÜNNHILDE (*in höchster Ergriffenheit*).
             Sonnenhell
             leuchtet der Tag meiner Noth!—
             O Siegfried! Siegfried!
             Sieh' meine Angst!

MOTIVE OF LOVE'S PEACE.

Deathless was I,
deathless am I,
deathless to sweet
sway of affection—
but deathless for thy good hap!

O Siegfried! happiest
hope of the world!
Life of the universe!
Lordliest hero!
List! ah list!
Leave me in peace!
Press not upon me
thy ardent approaches!
Master me not
with thy conquering might!
Thy servant, O sully her not!—

Saw'st e'er thy face
in crystal floods?
Did it not gladden thy glance?
When into wavelets
the water was roused,
the brook's glassy surface
broken and flawed,
thy face saw'st thou no more:
nought but ripples swirling around.

Ewig war ich,
ewig bin ich,
ewig in süss
sehnender Wonne—
doch ewig zu deinem Heil!

O Siegfried! Herrlicher!
Hort der Welt!
Leben der Erde!
Lachender Held!
Lass', ach lass'!
lasse von mir!
Nahe mir nicht
mit der wüthenden Nähe!
Zwinge mich nicht
mit dem brechenden Zwang!
Zertrümm're die Traute dir nicht!—

Sah'st du dein Bild
im klaren Bach?
Hat es dich Frohen erfreut?
Rührtest zur Woge
das Wasser du auf;
zerflösse die klare
Fläche des Bach's:
dein Bild säh'st du nicht mehr,
nur der Welle schwankend Gewog'

So disturb me no more,
trouble me not:
ever then
thou wilt shine
in me an image reflected,
fair and lovely, my lord!—
O Siegfried! Siegfried!
light of my soul!
Love — thyself
and leave me in peace:
destroy not thy faithful slave!

SIEGFRIED. I love — thee:
O lovest thou me?
I have no more self:
O had I but thee!—
The grandest of floods
before me rolls,
and all my senses
seize on the sight,
these billows beauteous and buoyant.
Likeness — be lost!
I long now myself
straightway my fire
in the flood to slacken;
at once I would spring
into the stream:
O would that its waters
in bliss might embrace me,
and 'bate my blaze with its wave!—
Awake, Brünnhilde!
waken, thou maid!
Laugh that thou livest,
sweetest delight!
Be mine! be mine! be mine!

BRÜNNHILDE. O Siegfried! thine
ever I've been!

SIEGFRIED. Ever thou'st been?
Then so abide.

BRÜNNHILDE. Thine ever
will I be.

SIEGFRIED. What thou then wilt.
be to me now.
Fast in my arms,
enwrapped in their fold,
resting thy breast
beating 'gainst mine,
while glances and breath
are glowing with eagerness,
eye to eye,
and lip to lip—
as, saidst thou, thou wast and wilt be.
How briskly were banished thy fears
if indeed Brünnhilde were mine!
(He has clasped her with his arms.)

BRÜNNHILDE. If I am thine!

Godlike repose
is plunged into tempest,
once tranquil radiance
rises to frenzy,
heavenly teachings
from me are hid,
wildness of passion
whirls it away!

If I am thine!—
O Siegfried! Siegfried!
Seest thou me not?
When mine eyes devour thine,

So berühre mich nicht,
trübe mich nicht:
ewig licht
lachst du aus mir
dann selig selbst dir entgegen,
froh und heiter ein Held!—
O Siegfried! Siegfried!
leuchtender Spross!
Liebe — dich,
und lasse von mir:
vernichte dein Eigen nicht!

SIEGFRIED. Dich — lieb' ich:
o liebtest mich du!
Nicht hab' ich mehr mich
o hätte ich dich!—
Ein herrlich Gewässer
wogt vor mir;
mit allen Sinnen
seh' ich nur sie,
die wonnig wogende Welle:
brach sie mein Bild,
so brenn' ich nun selbst,
sengende Gluth
in der Fluth zu kühlen;
ich selbst, wie ich bin,
spring' in den Bach:—
o dass seine Wogen
mich selig verschlängen,
mein Sehnen schwänd' in der Fluth!
Erwache, Brünnhilde!
Wache, du Maid!
Lebe und lache,
süsseste Lust!
Sei mein! sei mein! sei mein.

BRÜNNHILDE. O Siegfried! dein —
war ich von je!

SIEGFRIED. War'st du's von je,
so sei es jetzt!

BRÜNNHILDE. Dein werde ich
ewig sein!

SIEGFRIED. Was du sein wirst,
sei es mir heut'!
Fasst dich mein Arm,
umschling' ich dich fest;
schlägt meine Brust
brünstig die deine;
zünden die Blicke,
zehren die Athem sich;
Aug' in Auge,
Mund an Mund:
dann bist du mir,
was bang du mir war'st und wirst!
Dann brach sich die brennende Sorge,
ob jetzt Brünnhilde mein?
(Er hat sie umfasst.)

BRÜNNHILDE. Ob jetzt ich dein?—

Göttliche Ruhe
ras't mir in Wogen;
keusches Licht
lodert in Gluthen;
himmlisches Wissen
stürmt mir dahin,
Jauchzen der Liebe
jagt es davon!

Ob jetzt ich dein?—
O Siegfried! Siegfried!
siehst du mich nicht?
Wie mein Blick dich verzehrt.

then art thou not blind?
by my arm embraced
then burnest thou not?
and when seething my blood
against thee doth surge,
its fiery fury
feelest thou not?
Fearest thou, Siegfried —
fearest thou not
the mad, mutinous maid?

SIEGFRIED. Ha!   [ing!
How the glowing bloodstreams are bound-
How the glances brightly are burning!
How our arms are gladly entwining!
      Cometh now back
      my courage bold,
      and this fearing, ah!
      that to me was strange—
      this fear, that scarce
      e'en thou could'st bestow—
      this fearing — I feel —
      that fool-like, again 'tis forgot.
(With the last words he has unconsciously released
            BRÜNNHILDE.)

BRÜNNHILDE (laughing in wild transport of passion).
      O high-minded boy!
      O blossoming hero!
      Thou babe of prowess
      past all that breathe!
Gladly love do I glow with,
gladly yield to thee blindly,
gladly glide to destruction,
gladly go down to death!

      Far hence, Valhall'
      lofty and vast,
      let fall thy structure
      of stately tow'rs;
      farewell, grandeur
      and pride of gods!
      End in rapture
      ye Æsir, your reign!
      Go rend, ye Nornen,
      your rope of runes!
      Round us darken,
      Dusk of the gods!
      Night of annulment
      now on us gain!
      here still is streaming
      Siegfried, my star.
      He is for ever,
      is for aye
      my own, my only
      and my all.—
      Love that illumines,
      laughing at death.

SIEGFRIED (with BRÜNNHILDE).
      Gladly, bewitcher,
      wak'st thou to me.
      Brünnhilde lives,
      Brünnhilde laughs! —
      Hail the heavens,
      smiling in lightness!
      Hail the sun
      which down on us shines!
      Hail the light
      that from night hath burst!
      Hail the world
      wher Brünnhilde lives.

---

erblindest du nicht?
Wie mein Arm dich presst!
entbrennst du nicht?
Wie in Strömen mein Blut
entgegen dir stürmt,
das wilde Feuer
fühlst du es nicht?
Fürchtest du, Siegfried —
fürchtest du nic?
das wild wüthende W...

SIEGFRIED. Ha' —
Wie des Blutes Ströme sich zünden
wie der Blicke Strahlen sich zehren
wie die Arme brünstig sich pressen
      kehrt mir zurück
      mein kühner Muth,
      und das Fürchten, ach
      das nie ich gelernt—
      das Fürchten, das d
      kaum mich gelehrt:
      das Fürchten — mich dünkt
      ich Dummer, vergass es schon wieder
(Er lässt bei den letzten Worten BRÜNNHILDE unwill
            kürlich los.)

BRÜNNHILDE (im höchsten Liebesjub... und zugleich
            end.)
      O kindischer Held!
      O herrlicher Knabe!
      Du hehrster Thaten
      thöriger Hort!
Lachend muss ich dich lieben
lachend will ich erblinden;
lachend lass' uns verderben —
lachend zu Grunde geh'n!

      Fahr' hin, Walhall's
      leuchtende Welt!
      Zerfall' in Staub
      deine stolze Burg!
      Leb' wohl, prangende
      Götter-Pracht!
      Ende in Wonne,
      du ewig Geschlecht!
      Zerreisst, ihr Nornen,
      das Runenseil!
      Götter-Dämm'rung,
      dunkle herauf!
      Nacht der Vernichtung,
      neble herein! —
      Mir strahlt zur Stunde
      Siegfried's Stern;
      er ist mir ewig,
      er ist mir immer,
      Erb' und Eigen,
      ein' und all':
      leuchtende Liebe,
      lachender Tod!

SIEGFRIED (mit Brünnhilde zugleich)
      Lachend erwachst
      du Wonnige mir:
      Brünnhilde lebt!
      Brünnhilde lacht! —
      Heil der Sonne,
      die uns bescheint!
      Heil dem Tage
      der uns umleuchtet!
      Heil dem Licht,
      das der Nacht enttaucht!
      Heil der Welt,
      der Brünnhild' erwacht!

She wakes, she lives! she laughs as she greets **me**: proudly streams down Brünnhilde, my star. She is for ever, **is** for aye my own, my only and my all. Love that illumines laughing at death. (BRÜNNHILDE *throws herself into* SIEGFRIED'S *arms.*)	Sie wacht! sie lebt! sie lacht mir entgegen! Prangend strahlt mir Brünnhilde's Stern! Sie ist mir ewig, sie ist mir immer, Erb' und Eigen, ein' und all': leuchtende Liebe, lachender Tod! (BRÜNNHILDE *stürzt sich in* SIEGFRIED'S *Arme.*
The Curtain falls.	*Der Vorhang fällt.*

CHARACTERS

SIEGFRIED	TENOR
GUNTHER	BASS
HAGEN	BASS
BRÜNNHILDE	SOPRANO
GUTRUNE	SOPRANO
WALTRAUTE	SOPRANO
WOGLINDA,	SOPRANO
WELLGUNDA, } RHINE-NYMPHS	SOPRANO
FLOSSHILDE,	ALTO

MEN AND WOMEN

The Argument

PRELUDE. On the Valkyrie's rock, by night, sit the *Nornir* (Fates) weaving their rope of runes. It breaks and they disappear, knowing that the End of the gods is at hand. At day-dawn Siegfried rises to part from his beloved Brünnhilde and go to fresh exploits. At parting he gives her his famous Ring and she gives him her horse in return.

ACT I. He comes to the Hall of the Gibichungs on the Rhine, where live the King Gunther, his sister Gutrune and their half-brother Hagen, the son of Alberic. These, for their own purposes, give Siegfried a magic draught of forgetfulness. He swears brotherhood to Gunther, forgets Brünnhilde, falls in love with Gutrune and, in return for her hand, consents to go through the fire and fetch Brünnhilde as a wife for Gunther, who cannot perform the feat himself.

Brünnhilde, awaiting, Siegfried's return, is visited by her sister Waltraute, who implores her to restore the fatal Ring to the Rhine, as the only means of saving the gods, who are now expecting their doom; but Brünnhilde, being an outcast from Valhalla, regards her love-pledge as of more value than all the gods, and refuses: Waltraute flies away in despair, Siegfried, taking Gunther"s shape, by virtue of the Tarnhelm, appears to the horror-stricken Brünnhilde and demands a husband's rights. She resists fiercely. but is conquered by his tearing from her finger the Ring which gave her supernatural strength. Siegfried weds her, but lays his sword between them, as his oath to Gunther demands.

ACT II. Alberic visits his son Hagen in a dream and bids him strive to kill Siegfried and obtain the Ring. Siegfried, followed later by Gunther and Brünnhilde, returns to the Gibichung's Hall and all the vassals are summoned to rejoice at the double wedding. Brünnhilde, being brought face to face with Siegfried in his own shape, perceives the Ring upon his finger and proclaims to all that she has been betrayed. Explanations, purposely confused by Hagen, only make it appear that Siegfried has failed in his oath to Gunther, whereupon Hagen persuades Brünnhilde and Gunther to consent to his murder.

ACT III. Siegfried, hunting near the Rhine, is accosted by the Rhine-nymphs, who strive to coax the Ring from him; failing, they tell him how it will cause his death. He derides their warning, but Hagen, Gunther and the rest of the hunting party join him, and while they are carousing and Siegfried is telling the story of his life, Hagen spears him in the back and kills him.

The body is brought to the Hall and Hagen kills Gunther in a struggle for the Ring. The despairing Brünnhilde silences the clamor and orders a funeral pile to be built by the Rhine. This she mounts with the dead Siegfried and both are consumed, when the river rises and the Nymphs regain at last their Ring from the ashes, Hagen being drowned in attempting to seize it. Now a ruddy glare is seen in the sky: the Dusk of the Gods has come, and Valhalla is seen burning with all its array of heroes and gods.

THE DUSK OF THE GODS
(GOETTERDAEMMERUNG)

PROLOGUE	VORSPIEL
Scene — On the Valkyries' Rock.	*Auf dem Walkürenfelsen.*
The same as at the end of "Siegfried." It is night and from below, at back, gleams the fire.	Die Scene ist dieselbe wie am Schlusse des zweiten Tages.—Nacht. Aus der Tiefe des Hintergrundes leuchtet Feuerschein auf.

<table>
<tr><td>

The three Norns,

tall females in sombre and flowing drapery, are discovered. The first (and oldest) crouches in the foreground R, under the spreading fir-tree; the second (younger) is stretched on a rock before the cave; the third (and youngest) sits in the middle at back on a rock below the peak. For a while gloomy silence reigns.

</td><td>

Die drei Nornen,

hohe Frauengestalten in langen, dunklen und schleierartigen Faltengewändern. Die erste (älteste) lagert im Vordergrunde rechts unter der breitästigen Tanne; die zweite (jüngere) ist an einer Steinbank vor dem Felsengemache hingestreckt; die dritte (jüngste) sitzt in der Mitte des Hintergrundes auf einem Felssteine des Höhensaumes.— Eine Zeit lang herrscht düsteres Schweigen.

</td></tr>
</table>

The first Norn (without moving).

What light lurketh there?

Die erste Norn (ohne sich zu bewegen).

Welch' Licht leuchtet dort?

The second.

Think you the day is nigh?

Die zweite.

Dämmert der Tag schon auf?

The third.

Loki's flame
leapeth round about the rock.
Night is new:
why should we not spin and sing now?

Die dritte.

Loge's Heer
lodert feurig um den Fels.
Noch ist's Nacht:
was spinnen und singen wir nicht?

The second (to the first).

While we are spinning and singing
on what stretch we the string?

Die zweite (zu der ersten).

Wollen wir singen und spinnen,
woran spann'st du das Seil?

The first Norn (rises and fastens one end of a golden cord to a branch of the fir-tree during her song).

For weal to serve and woe,
setting the string I sing thus:—
At the world's ash-tree
once I wove,
when fast and strong,
the stem with wondrous
verdure was overwhelmed.
In pleasant shade
a fountain purled;
wisdom floated
forth on its wave;
I sang there a mystic song.

Die erste Norn (erhebt sich, und knüpft während ihres Gesanges ein goldenes Seil mit dem einen Ende an einen Ast der Tanne).

So gut und schlimm es geh',
schling' ich das Seil, und singe.—
An der Welt-Esche
wob ich einst,
da gross und stark
dem Stamm entgrünte
weihlicher Aeste Wald;
im kühlen Schatten
rauscht' ein Quell,
Weisheit raunend
rann sein Gewell':
da sang ich heiligen Sinn.—

A fearless god
sought to sip at the fount,
  giving up one eye
to buy the ineffable boon.
    From the world's ash-tree
Wotan wrested off an arm:
  and with sturdy strokes
he shaped the shaft of a spear.
In tardy course of time
cankered the wound in the wood;
the leaves life could retain not;
waned—withered the tree.
    Drooping, the stream
    of the fountain dried;
    dark with sorrow
    waxed then my song.
    I weave again
at the world's ash-tree no more,
    so must the fir-tree
find me support for the string.
    Sing, O Sister!
    Thou weave it now!—
ween'st thou why this was?

The second Norn
(winding the cord, which the other throws to her,
  round a projecting rock at the cave's mouth).

    Truthful runes
    to make treaties rigid
    set Wotan
    on the shaft of his spear:
this served him to sway the world.
    One bold and strong
destroyed in battle that spear.
    The binding witness
of bonds was shivered to shreds.
    Then straight Wotan
    warriors summoned,
    the world's ash-tree's
    withered arms
with its stem to splinter and sunder.
    The ash destroyed,
For ever the spring must go dry.
    Now round the keen-edged
stone I knot the string:
    Sing, O sister!
    Thou weave it now—
ween'st thou why this was?

The third Norn
(catching the rope and throwing the end behind
  her).

    A gemmed abode
    by giants was built:
    with the Æsir and heroes'

Ein kühner Gott
trat zum Trunk an den Quell;
  seiner Augen eines
zahlt' er als ewigen Zoll:
    von der Welt-Esche
brach da Wotan einen Ast:
  eines Speeres Schaft
entschnitt der Starke dem Stamm.—
In langer Zeiten Lauf
zehrte die Wunde den Wald·
falb fielen die Blätter,
dürr darbte der Baum:
    traurig versiegte
    des Quelles Trank;
    trüben Sinnes
    ward mein Gesang.
    Doch web' ich heut'
an der Welt-Esche nicht mehr,
    muss mir die Tanne
taugen zu fesseln das Seil:
    singe, Schwester,
    —dir werf' ich's zu—
weisst du wie das ward?

Die zweite Norn
(während sie das zugeworfene Seil um einen her-
vorspringenden Felsentein am Eingange des Gemaches windet).

    Treu berath'ner
    Verträge Runen
    schnitt Wotan
    in des Speeres Schaft:
den hielt er als Haft der Welt.
    Ein kühner Held
zerhieb im Kampfe den Speer;
  in Trümmern sprang
der Verträge heiliger Haft.—
    Da hiess Wotan
    Walhali's Helden
    der Welt-Esche
    welkes Geäst
mit dem Stamm in Stücke zu fällen:
    die Esche sank;
ewig versiegte der Quell!—
    Fess'le ich heut'
an dem scharfen Fels das Seil:
    singe, Schwester,
    —dir werf' ich's zu—
weisst du wie das wird?

Die dritte Norn
(das Seil auffangend, und dessen Ende hinter sich
  werfend).

    Es ragt die Burg,
    von Riesen gebaut:
    mit der Götter und Helden

holy assembly
sitteth Wotan in state.
    And heaps of faggots
    huge are formed,
    ranged on high
    round all Valhalla:
the world's ash-tree were they once.
    When the brand
    brightly, wildly doth burn,
    when the fire
wasteth the fair-fashioned walls,
the deathless immortals draw
towards the dusk of their day.
    This knowest thou?
The thread then be knotted again.
    Anew I throw it thee
    from the north.
Spin, O sister, and sing thou!
(She throws the cord to the second Norn, who
throws it to the first.)

The first Norn
(unties the cord from the branch and fastens it to
another branch during the following song).

    Dawneth the daylight,
    or flickers the fire?
My sight sorrow hath dimmed.
    Scarce bides my memory
    of bygone marvels,
    when Loki moved
in burning and lambent flame:
wist thou what was his work?

The second Norn
(again taking the rope and winding it round the
stone).

    By the spear's firm yoke
    he yielded to Wotan;
aid he offered the god:
    but in struggle e'er
    his bonds to throw off
he gnashed and tore with his teeth,
    till Wotan's spear's point
    tightly constrained him
    broadly to girdle
Brynhildr's rock with his brightness:
wist thou what was his work?

The third Norn
(catching the rope again and throwing it behind
her).

    Then the sturdy spear
    that split into splinters
    Wotan dips
in the burning one's wavering breast.
    Quickly the brand

heiliger Sippe
Sitzt dort der Wotan im Saal.
    Gehau'ner Scheite
    hohe Schicht
    ragt zu Hauf
    rings um die Halle:
die Welt-Esche war dies einst!
    Brennt das Holz
    heilig brünstig und hell,
    senkt die Gluth
sehrend den glänzenden Saal:
der ewigen Götter Ende
dämmert ewig da auf.—
    Wisset ihr noch?
so windet von neuem das Seil;
    von Norden wieder
    werf' ich's dir nach:
spinne, Schwester, und singe!
(Sie hat das Seil der zweiten, diese es wieder der
ersten Norn zugeworfen.)

Die erste Norn
(lös't das Seil vom Zweige, und knüpft es während
des folgenden Gesanges wieder an einen andern
Ast).

    Dämmert der Tag?
    oder leuchtet die Lohe?
Getrübt trägt sich mein Blick;
    nicht hell eracht' ich
    das heilig Alte,
    da Loge einst
entbrannte in lichter Gluth:—
weisst du was aus ihm ward?

Die zweite Norn
(das zugeworfene Seil wieder um den Stein wind-
end).

    Durch des Speeres Zauber
    zähmte ihn Wotan;
Räthe raunt' er dem Gott:
    an des Schaftes Runen,
    frei sich zu rathen,
nagte zehrend sein Zahn.
    Da mit des Speeres
    zwingender Spitze
    bannte ihn Wotan,
Brünnhilde's Fels zu umbrennen:—
weisst du was aus ihm wird?

Die dritte Norn
(das zugeschwungene Seil wieder hinter sich werfend).

    Des zerschlag'nen Speeres
    stechende Splitter
    taucht' einst Wotan
dem Brünstigen tief in die Brust:
    zehrender Brand

kindles thereat;
this Wotan throws
where the world's ash-tree
is heaped, a forest of faggots.
When this will be
would ye ween?
stretch then, sisters, the string!
(She throws the rope back to the second who
throws it to the first).

The first Norn
    (again knotting the cord).
The night wanes;
nought more I wot of;
I cannot find
the fibre again;
it falls entangled and frayed.
The woefullest sight
whirls and weakens my sense:—
The Rhinegold
robbed by Alberic once:
wist thou what was its work?

The second Norn
(with careful haste winding the rope round the
stone).
The crag with keen edge
cutteth the cord;
the threads cling not,
and thin is the clue;
awry hath it been wrought.
From ire and ill
rears to me Alberic's ring:—
a ravaging curse
gnaweth my cord to the core:—
wist thou what it will work?

The third Norn
(hastily catching the rope thrown to her).
The rope is too slack,
I reach it not;
should it anew
to northward be thrown,
yet straighter must it be stretched!
(she pulls the cord forcibly: it breaks in the
middle.)

The second.
    It breaks!

The third.
    It breaks!

The first.
    It breaks!
(The three Norns start up in alarm and advance to
the centre of the stage: they take the broken pieces
of the cord and tie their bodies one to another with
them.)

zündet da auf;
den wirft der Gott
in der Welt-Esche
zu Hauf geschichtete Scheite.—
Wollt ihr wissen
wann das wird,
schwingt mir, Schwestern, das Seil!
(Sie wirft das Seil der zweiten, diese es wieder der
ersten zu.)

Die erste Norn
    (das Seil von neuem anknüpfend).
Die Nacht weicht;
nichts mehr gewahr' ich:
des Seiles Fäden
find' ich nicht mehr;
verflochten ist das Geflecht.
Ein wüstes Gesicht
wirrt mir wüthend den Sinn:—
das Rheingold
raubte Alberich einst:—
weisst du, was aus ihm ward?

Die zweite Norn
(mit mühevoller Hast das Seil um den Stein wind-
end).
Des Steines Schärfe
schnitt in das Seil;
nicht fest spannt mehr
der Fäden Gespinnst:
verwirrt ist das Geweb'.
Aus Noth und Neid
nagt mir des Niblungen Ring:—
ein rächender Fluch
nagt meiner Fäden Geflecht:—
weisst du was daraus wird?

Die dritte Norn
    (das zugeworfene Seil hastig fassend).
Zu locker das Seil!
mir langt es nicht:
soll ich nach Norden
neigen das Ende,
straffer sei es gestreckt!
(Sie zieht gewaltsam das Seil an: dieses reisst in
der Mitte.)

Die zweite.
    Es riss!

Die dritte.
    Es riss!

Die erste
    Es riss!
(Erschreckt sind die drei Nornen aufgefahren und
nach der Mitte der Bühne zusammengetreten; sie
fassen die Stücke des zerrissenen Seiles und binden
damit ihre Leiber an einander.)

The three Norns.

Here ends all of our wisdom!
The world marks
our wise words no more.—
Away! To mother! Away!

(They disappear.)

(The day, which has been slowly breaking, now dawns brightly and conceals the distant fire-glow in the valley.)

Siegfried and Brünnhilde

(enter from the cave. Siegfried is in full armor; Brünnhilde leads her horse by the bridle).

Die drei Nornen.

Zu End' ewiges Wissen!
Der Welt melden
Weise nichts mehr:—
hinab zur Mutter, hinab!

(Sie verschwinden.)

Der Tag, der zuletzt immer heller gedämmert, bricht vollends ganz an, und dämpft den Feuerschein in der Tiefe.

Siegfried und Brünnhilde

(treten aus dem Steingemache auf: Siegfried ist in vollen Waffen. Brünnhilde führt ihr Ross beim Zaume).

DID I NOT SEND THEE?

BRÜNNHILDE

Zu neu-en Tha-ten, theu-rer Hel-de, wie liebt' ich dich
Did I not send thee, sweet-est he-ro, to fresh ex-ploits,

liess' ich dich nicht Ein ein-zig Sor-gen lässt mich säu-men;
frail were my love. But one mis-giv-ing fights a-gainst it;—

dass dir zu we-nig mein Werth___ ge-wann. Was
for fear not whol-ly thy heart___ I hold. I

Göt-ter mich wie-sen, gab___ ich dir: hei-li-ger Ru-nen
gave___ to thee all that gods___ had taught; heav-en-ly runes, the

rei-chen Hort, doch mei-ner Stär-ke magd-li-chen Stamm
rich-est hoard, but my re-store-less maid-en-hood's strength

nahm mir der Held, dem ich nun mich nei-ge. Des Wis-sens
snatch'd thou from me. who but seek to serve thee. My wis-dom

bar,   doch des Wun-sches voll: an Lie - be reich, doch
fails.   *but good will re - mains,*   *so full__ of love, but*

le - dig der Kraft,   mögst du die Ar - me nicht ver - ach-ten,
fail - ing in strength,   *thou wilt de - spise per-chance the poor one,*

die dir nur gön - nen, nicht ge - ben_ mehr kann.
who hav - ing giv'n__ all, can grant__ thee_ ro more.

Siegfried. More hast thou shewn to me than yet my sense can seize: so chide not if unlearned despite thy lessons I'm left. But one thing I wot full well— for me Brünnhilde lives; 'twas a lesson light to learn Brünnhilde aye to worship!	*Siegfried.* Mehr gabst du, Wunderfrau, als ich zu wahren weiss: nicht zürne, wenn dein Lehren mich unbelehret liess! Ein Wissen doch wahr' ich wohl dass mir Brünnhilde lebt; eine Lehre lernt' ich leicht: Brünnhilde's zu gedenken!
Brünnhilde. If thou wouldst wake my fondness, recall thy course to mind; recall thy courage dauntless, recall the raging furnace that, fearless, thou didst pass through, when it fanned the rocky brow.	*Brünnhilde.* Willst du mir Minne schen- ken, gedenke deiner nur, gedenke deiner Thaten! Gedenke des wilden Feuers, das furchtlos du durchschrit- test, da den Fels es rings um- brann—
Siegfried. Brünnhilde to attain to!	*Siegfried.* Brünnhilde zu gewinnen!
Brünnhilde. Recall, too the shield-cov- ered maid thou did'st find in sleep of magic, and whose mail and helm thou didst break.	*Brünnhilde.* Gedenk' d e r beschildeten Frau, die in tiefem Schlaf du fan- dest, der den festen Helm du er- brach'st—
Siegfried. Brünnhilde to awaken!	*Siegfried.* Brünnhilde zu erwecken!
Brünnhilde. Recall the pledges we have plighted; recall our troth,— ne'er was there truer: recall th' affection which enfolds us;	*Brünnhilde.* Gedenk' der Eide, die uns einen; gedenk' der Treue, die wir tragen; gedenk' der Liebe, der wir leben:

Brünnhilde thy bride then e'er
will hold her place in thy breast.

Siegfried. Love, ere leaving thy form
in the leal defence of the fire,
for all thy runes and teachings
take this ring in return.
All my valiant deeds of strength
their virtue sprang from this.
I destroyed an unwieldly worm,
who long had over it watched:
now well preserve thou the charm
as wedding gift to my bride.

Brünnhilde
(rapturously donning the ring.)
Aye, gladly my all here I guard,
and instead thou shalt own my
steed:
he could lift me once
athwart the air lightly;
with me
he lost all his magic powers:
over thronging clouds,
through lightning and thunder,
no more
boldly his way he will thread.
But wher-e'er thou shalt force,
were it through fire e'en,
Grani will follow gaily:
He'll serve my hero
trustily henceforth.
Then hold him well,
he'll heed thy word:
O give Grani many
fond greetings from me!

Siegfried. Then through thy virtues alone
am I to vanquish my dangers?
Thou dost choose thy champion's fights;
thou dost turn the chance of
the fray;
thy noble steed bestriding,
and with thy shelt'ring shield
now Siegfried am I no more:
I'm but as Brünnhilde's arm!

Brünnhilde. O were but Brünnhilde thy
spirit!

Siegfried. She spurs my bravery alone.

Brünnhilde. So art thou Siegfried and
Brünnhilde?

Brünnhilde brennt dann ewig
heilig dir in der Brust!—

Siegfried. Lass' ich, Liebste, dich hier
in der Lohe heiliger Hut,
zum Tausche deiner Runen
reich' ich dir diesen Ring,
Was der Thaten je ich schuf,
dess' Tugend schliesst er ein;
ich erschlug einen wilden Wurm,
der grimmig lang' ihn bewacht.
Nun wahre du seine Kraft
als Weihe-Gruss meiner Treu'!

Brünnhilde
(voll Entzücken den Ring sich ansteckend.)
Ihn geiz' ich als einziges Gut:
für den Ring nun nimm' auch
mein Ross!
Ging sein Lauf mit mir
einst kühn durch die Lüfte—
mit mir
verlor es die mächt'ge Art;
über Wolken hin
auf blitzenden Wettern
nicht mehr
schwingt es sich muthig des
Weg's.
Doch wohin du ihn führst
—sei es durch's Feuer—
grauenlos folgt dir Grane;
denn dir, o Helde,
soll er gehorchen!
Du hüt' ihn wohl;
er hört dein Wort:—
o bringe Grane
oft Brünnhilde's Gruss!

Siegfried. Durch deine Tugend allein
soll so ich Thaten noch wirken?
Meine Kämpfe kiesest du,
meine Siege kehren zu dir?
Auf deines Rosses Rücken,
in deines Schildes Schirm,
nicht Siegfried acht' ich mich
mehr,
ich bin nur Brünnhilde's Arm!

Brünnhilde. O wäre Brünnhild' deine
Seele!

Siegfried. Durch sie entbrennt mir der
Muth.

Brünnhilde. So wär'st du Siegfried und
Brünnhild'?

Siegfried. Our hearts both beat in one
                                    bosom.

Brünnhilde. Is my rock-home deserted
                                    then?

Siegfried. Both rest still in its bounds.

Brünnhilde

(in exalted rapture.)
O heavenly powers,
holy protectors!
View with delight
our devotion of love!
Apart—who can divide us?
Divided—still we are one!

Siegfried. Hail, O Brünnhilde,
                    brightest of stars!
Hail, stream of our love-light!

Brünnhilde. Hail, O Siegfried,
                    sovereign light!
Hail, stream of our living!

Both. Hail! Hail!

(Siegfried leads the horse down the rocks; Brünnhilde gazes after him from the height for a long
while. From the valley, the merry sound of Siegfried's horn is heard. The curtain falls.)

(The orchestra takes up the melody of the horn
and works it up into an animated movement.
Thereupon follows the First Act.)

ACT ONE

Scene One

THE HALL OF THE GIEBICHUNGS ON THE
RHINE.

The back is quite open, showing a flat shore down
to the river-stream; rocky heights border the stage.

GUNTHER, HAGEN AND GUTRUNE

Gunther and Gutrune are on the throne, before
which is a table with drinking vessels. Hagen sitting before it.

Gunther. Now hark, Hagen!
                    answer me, here:
is my hold of the Rhine
glory for Gibich's race?

Hagen. Thy wondrous actions
                    waken my envy;
and much thy mother and mine,
dame Grimhild,' lauded thy great-
                                    ness.

Siegfried. Wo ich bin, bergen sich beide.

Brünnhilde. So verödet mein Felsensaal?

Siegfried. Vereint fasst er uns zwei.

Brünnhilde

(in grosser Ergriffenheit.)
O heilige Götter,
hehre Geschlechter!
weidet eur' Aug'
an dem weihvollen Paar!
Getrennt—wer will uns scheiden?
Geschieden—trennt es sich nie!

Siegfried. Heil dir, Brünnhilde,
                    prangender Stern!
Heil, strahlende Liebe!

Brünnhilde. Heil dir, Siegfried!
                    siegendes Licht!
Heil, strahlendes Leben!

Beide. Heil! Heil!

(Siegfried leitet das Ross den Felsen hinab,
Brünnhilde blickt ihm vom Höhensaume lange
entzückt nach. Aus der Tiefe hört man Siegfried's
Horn munter ertönen. Der Vorhang fällt.

Das Orchester nimmt die Weise des Hornes auf,
und führt sie in einem kräftigen Satze durch. Darauf beginnt sogleich der erste Aufzug.)

ERSTER AUFZUG

Erste Scene

DIE HALLE DER GIBICHUNGEN AM RHEIN

Sie ist dem Hintergrunde zu ganz offen; diesen
nimmt ein freier Uferraum, in bis zum Flusse hin
ein; felsige Anhöhen umgränzen den Raum.

GUNTHER, HAGEN, UND GUTRUNE

(Gunther und Gutrune auf dem Hochsitze, voi
dem ein Tisch mit Trinkgeräth steht; Hagen sitzt
davor.)

Gunther. Nun hör', Hagen!
                    sage mir, Held:
sitz' ich herrlich am Rhein,
Gunther zu Gibich's Ruhm?

Hagen. Dich ächt genannten
                    acht' ich zu neiden:
die beid' uns Brüder gebar,
Frau Grimhild' liess mich's begreifen.

Gunther. Thou envy not;
  I am envious of thee.
If I am heir to all,
  wisdom was left to thee.
   Half-brother's strife
   were stifled ne'er better;
and thy wisdom well I praise
  when I ask thee of my weal.

Hagen. To blame is my wit
  that bad is thy weal;
for rarer goods I wot of
  than a Gibichung yet ever won.

Gunther. Then tell them, or
  I too shall blame.

Hagen. In radiance of summer ripeness
  rises Gibich's race;
but Gunther fails to wed
  and Gutrune finds no mate.

Gunther. Whom wouldst thou I should
      wed,
  that we may win more worth?

Hagen. A wife waits thee,
  the rarest in the world:
a far off rock's her home,
a fire-flame embraces her hall:
but he who can brave that fire
may fitly woo Brünnhilde.

Gunther. And may not my might so far
      stretch?

Hagen. For a stronger one it is reserved.

Gunther. Who is this most stalwart of
     men?

Hagen. Siegfried of Volsung descent:
  his is the strongest hand.
  A twinborn pair
  in loving entwinement——
  Siegmund and Sieglind'—
between them begat such a son.
He in woods has mightily waxed,
and well with Gutrune might
     mate.

Gutrune. Hath he done marvellous deeds,
  that he is called of a courage
   so high?

Hagen. At Hate-cavern
  the hoard long accursed
was watched by a horrible worm.

Gunther. Dich neide ich:
  nicht neide mich du!
Erbt' ich Erstlingsart,
  Weisheit ward dir allein:
   Halbbrüder-Zwist
   bezwang sich nie besser;
deinem Rath nur red' ich Lob,
Frag' ich dich nach meinem
      Ruhm.

Hagen. So schelt' ich den Rath,
  da schlecht noch dein Ruhm:
denn hohe Güter weiss ich,
  die der Gibichung noch nicht gewann.

Gunther. Verschwiegst du sie,
  so schelt' auch ich.

Hagen. In sommerlich reifer Stärke
  seh ich Gibich's Stamm,
dich, Gunther, unbeweibt,
dich, Gutrun', ohne Mann.

Gunther. Wen räth'st du nun zu frei'n,
  Dass uns'rem Ruhm es fromm'?

Hagen. Ein Weib weiss ich,
  das herrlichste der Welt:—
auf Felsen hoch ihr Sitz;
ein Feuer entbrennt ihren Saal:
nur wer durch das Feuer bricht,
darf Brünnhilde's Freier sein.

Gunther. Vermag das mein Muth zu
     besteh'n?

Hagen. Einem Stärk'ren noch ist's nur
     bestimmt.

Gunther. Wer ist der streitlichste Mann?

Hagen. Siegfried, der Wälsungen Spross:
  der ist der stärkste Held.
  Ein Zwillingspaar,
  von Liebe bezwungen,
  Siegmund und Sieglinde
zeugten den ächtesten Sohn:
der im Walde mächtig erwuchs,
den wünsch' ich Gutrun' zum Mann.

Gutrune. Welche That schuf er so tapfer,
  dass als herrlichster Held er
   genannt!

Hagen. Vor Neidhöhle,
  den Niblungenhort
bewachte ein riesiger Wurm:

Siegfried shut up
his maw for him straight
and slew him with sovereign sword.
So this unheard-of feat
has founded the hero's fame.

Gunther. The Nibelungs' hoard I know
of;
it holds most notable wealth.

Hagen. The one who best knows its worth
annexes the world to his will.

Gunther. And Siegfried gained it in
strife?

Hagen. Slaves are the Niblungs to him.

Gunther. And Brünnhilde were won by
none else?

Hagen. To no other waneth the blaze.

Gunther
(rising from his seat in displeasure.)
Why wake this discord and
doubt?
Wouldst thou induce in me
desire for a treasure
I may not touch?

Hagen. Brought this Siegfried
the bride to thee,
would not then Brünnhilde be thine?

Gunther
(pacing up and down the hall in agitation.)
What power could bind the
man
to win the bride for me?

Hagen. Thy pray'r could work thy wishes,
wove first Gutrune a spell.

Gutrune. Thou scoffest, wicked Hagen!
What spells then should I
weave him?
And if so wondrous
a warrior he,
the earth's most winsome of women
will he have won ere this.

Hagen. Recall the drink in yon shrine,
and doubt not him who gained
the charm.
The hero for whom thou burn'st
fondly 'twill bind to thy heart.
Did now but Siegfried come

Siegfried schloss ihm
den freislichen Schlund,
erschlug ihn mit siegendem Schwert.
Solch' ungeheurer That
enttagte des Helden Ruhm.

Gunther. Vom Niblungenhort vernahm
ich.
er birgt den neidlichsten
Schatz?

Hagen. Wer wohl ihn zu nützen wüsst',
dem neigte sich wahrlich die
Welt.

Gunther. Und Siegfried hat ihn erkämpft?

Hagen. Knecht sind die Niblungen ihm.

Gunther. Und Brünnhild' gewänne nur er?

Hagen. Keinem And'ren wiche die Brunst.

Gunther
(unwillig sich vom Sitze erhebend.)
Was weck'st du Zweifel und Zwist!
Was ich nicht zwingen soll,
danach zu verlangen
mach'st du mir Lust?

Hagen. Brächte Siegfried
die Braut dir heim,
wär' dann Brünnhild' nicht dein?

Gunther
(bewegt in der Halle auf und ab schreitend.)
Was zwänge den frohen Mann
dir mich die Braut zu frei'n?

Hagen. Ihn zwänge bald deine Bitte,
bänd' ihn Gutrun' zuvor.

Gutrune. Du Spötter, böser Hagen!
Wie sollt' ich Siegfried binden?
Ist er der herrlichste
Held der Welt,
der Erde holdeste Frauen
friedeten längst ihn schon.

Hagen. Gedenk' des Trankes im Schrein;
vertraue mir, der ihn gewann:
den Helden, dess' du verlangst,
bindet er liebend an dich.
Träte nun Siegfried ein,

and taste of the wonderful
draught,
that he'd seen a woman ere
thee—
or e'er a woman had neared,
would wholly pass from his head.
Reply then,
how like ye Hagen's plan?

Gunther
(who has again approached the table and listened
attentively, leaning on it.)
All praise be to Grimhild'
who such a brother gave!

Gutrune. If but Siegfried I could see!

Gunther. How shall we find him first?

Hagen. When he doth spur
on courses of fame,
the world too strait
can but become;
be sure in his roamings he'll scour
to the Gibich's strand on the Rhine.

Gunther. Welcome I'll heartily give.
(Siegfried's horn is heard in the distance;—they
listen.)
I mark on the Rhine a horn.

Hagen
(goes to the bank, looks down the river and calls
back.)
Within a vessel horse and man!
He blows right gaily the horn.
With a labourless stroke
as if lazy his hand,
he drives the boat,
stemming the stream.
So active a hand
at the oar-blade's sweep
owneth but he
who the dragon slew.
Siegfried is it; surely no other!

Gunther. Doth he proceed?

Hagen
(putting his hands to his mouth and shouting.)
Hoiho! Where hiest,
hero hale?

Siegfried's
(voice in the distance on the river.)
To Gibich's stalwart scion.

Hagen. Behold his hall here! I bid thee
to it.

genöss' er des würzigen Trank's,
dass vor dir ein Weib er ersah,
dass je ein Weib ihm genaht—
vergessen müsst er dess' ganz.—
Nun redet:—
wie dünkt euch Hagen's Rath?

Gunther
(der wieder an den Tisch getreten, und auf ihn gelehnt aufmerksam zugehört hat.)
Gepriesen sei Grimhild,'
die uns den Bruder gab!

Gutrune. Möcht' ich Siegfried je erseh'n!

Gunther. Wie fänden wir ihn auf?

Hagen. Jagt er auf Thaten
wonnig umher,
zum engen Tann
wird ihm die Welt:
wohl stürmt er in rastloser Jagd
auch zu Gibich's Strand an den Rhein.

Gunther. Willkommen hiess' ich ihn gern.
(Siegfried's Horn lässt sich von Ferne verneh-
men.—Sie lauschen.)
Vom Rhein her tönt das Horn.

Hagen
(ist an das Ufer gegangen, späht den Fluss hinab
und ruft zurück:)
In einem Nachen Held und Ross:
der bläst so munter das Horn.—
Ein gemächlicher Schlag
wie von müssiger Hand
treibt jach den Kahn
wider den Strom;
so rüstiger Kraft
in des Ruder's Schwung
rühmt sich nur der,
der den Wurm erschlug:—
Siegfried ist es, sicher kein And'rer!

Gutrune. Jagt er vorbei?

Hagen
(durch die hohlen Hände nach dem Flusse zu rufend:)
Hoiho! wohin,
du heit'rer Held?

Siegfried's
(Stimme, aus der Ferne, vom Flusse her.)
Zu Gibich's starkem Sohne.

Hagen. Zu seiner Halle entbiet' ich dich:

Hither! here lay thee to!
Hail, Siegfried, bravest heart!

Scene Two

(Siegfried lays to).
(Gunther has joined Hagen on the bank. Gutrune looks at Siegfried from the throne, fixing her gaze for some time on him in joyous surprise, and as the men come down into the hall she withdraws, in visible confusion, through a door leading to her chamber L.)

Siegfried
(who has landed his horse and now stands quietly leaning on him).
Which is Gibich's son?

Gunther.   Gunther—I—whom thou seek'st.

Siegfried.   Thy fame has reached
beyond the Rhine:
now fight with me,
or else be my frien(!

Gunther.   Nought of war;
thou art welcome!

Siegfried.   Where stables my horse?

Hagen.   I'll see to him.

Siegfried.   Thou hail'st me "Siegfried;"
sure we are strange?

Hagen.   Thy strength unapproached
declared thee straight.

Siegfried.   Tend heedfully Grani!
thou heldest ne'er
in bridle a horse
of higher degree.

(Hagen leads the horse away, R, behind the hall and returns immediately. Gunther advances into the hall with Siegfried.)

Gunther.   Now, hero, freely hail
the homestead of thy fathers.
The hall thou stand'st in,
whate'er thou see'st,
I bid thee hold thy booty.
Thine is my birthright,
soil and serfs:
hear me swear by my body!
Gunther to thee is given.

Siegfried.   Nor soil nor serfs I offer thee,
nor father's house and hall:
all I'm heir to,
my able limbs,
life is holding in use.
I've a sword merely,

Hieher! hier lege an!
Heil, Siegfried! theurer Held!

Zweite Scene

(Siegfried legt an.)
(Gunther ist zu Hagen an das Ufer getreten. Gutrune erblickt Siegfried vom Hochsitze aus, heftet eine Zeit lang in freudiger Ueberraschung den Blick auf ihn, und als die Männer dann näher zur Halle schreiten, entfernt sie sich in sichtbarer Verwirrung, nach links durch eine Thüre in ihr Gemach.)

Siegfried
(der seine Ross an das Land geführt, und jetzt ruhig an ihm lehnt.)
Wer ist Gibich's Sohn?

Gunther.   Gunther, ich, den du such'st.

Siegfried.   Dich hört' ich rühmen
weit am Rhein:
nun ficht mit mir,
oder sei mein Freund!

Gunther.   Lass den Kampf,
sei willkommen!

Siegfried.   Wo berg' ich mein Ross?

Hagen.   Ich biet' ihm Rast.

Siegfried.   Du rief'st mich Siegfried:
sah'st du mich schon?

Hagen.   Ich kannte dich nur
an deiner Kraft.

Siegfried.   Wohl hüte mir Grane!
Du hieltest nie
von edlerer Zucht
am Zaume ein Ross.

(Hagen führt das Ross rechts hinter die Halle ab, und kehrt bald darauf wieder zurück. Gunther schreitet mit Siegfried in die Halle vor.)

Gunther.   Begrüsse froh, o Held,
die Halle meines Vaters;
wohin du schreitest,
was du ersieh'st,
das achte nun dein Eigen:
dein ist mein Erbe,
Land und Leut':
hilf, mein Leib, meinem Eide!
Mich selbst geb' ich zum Mann.

Siegfried.   Nicht Land noch Leute biete ich,
noch Vater's Haus und Hof:
einzig erbt' ich
den eig'nen Leib;
lebend zehr' ich den auf.
Nur ein Schwert hab' ich,

self-constructed:
hear me swear by my weapon;
with it I'll strengthen our oath.

Hagen

(standing behind them),

But we learn thou art hailed
as lord of Nibelheim's hoard?

Siegfried. That wealth I forgot, well-nigh,
so worthless I deem the gold!
Within a cavern lone I left it,
where a worm did guard it once.

Hagen. Nought hast thou had of it?

Siegfried
(pointing to the steel net-work, that hangs in his
girdle.)

But this work, which I cannot use.

Hagen. The Tarnhelm is it,
the Nibelungs' artfullest work:
its trick when set on thy head
is to turn thee to any shape;
or long'st thou for far-off lands,
in a flash, flight canst thou wing.
Hast moved no more of the
wealth?

Siegfried. But a ring.

Hagen. Thou wearest it still?

Siegfried. 'Tis worn by a woman sweet.

Hagen

(aside.)

Brünnhilde!

Gunther. Nought, Siegfried, shalt to me
tender
Toys wouldst for thy treasures get,
taking my wealth in exchange:
without wage I'll serve thee well.

(Hagen has gone to Gutrune's door, and now
opens it. Gutrune enters, and approaches Siegfried
with a filled drinking horn.)

Gutrune. Welcome, O guest,
to Gibich's house!
From its daughter take thou the drink.

Siegfried
(bows friendly, and takes the horn; he holds it
thoughtfully before him, and says softly):

Though gifts thou gav'st
should all be forgot.
I'll grasp alone
one lesson for aye:

selbst geschmiedet—
hilf, mein Schwert, meinem Eide!
das biet' ich mit mir zum Bund.

Hagen

(hinter ihnen stehend.)

Doch des Niblungen-Hortes
nennt die Märe dich Herrn?

Siegfried. Des Schatzes vergass ich fast:
so schätz' ich sein müss'ges Gut!
In einer Höhle liess ich's liegen,
wo ein Wurm es einst bewacht.

Hagen. Und nichts entnahm'st du ihm?

Siegfried
(auf das stählerne Netzgewirk deutend, das er im
Gürtel hängen hat.)

Diess Gewirk, unkund seiner Kraft.

Hagen. Den Tarnhelm kenn' ich,
der Niblungen künstliches Werk:
er taugt, bedeckt er dein Haupt,
dir zu tauschen jede Gestalt;
verlangt dich's an fernsten Ort,
er entführt flugs dich dahin.—
Sonst nichts entnahmst du dem Hort?

Siegfried. Einen Ring.

Hagen. Den hütest du wohl?

Siegfried. Den hütet ein hehres Weib.

Hagen

(für sich.)

Brünnhilde! . .

Gunther. Nicht, Siegfried, sollst du mir
tauschen:
Tand gäb' ich für das Geschmeid,
nähmst all mein Gut du dafür!
Ohn' Entgelt dien' ich dir gern.

(Hagen ist zu Gutrune's Thür gegangen, und öffnet sie jetzt. Gutrune tritt heraus, sie trägt ein
gefülltes Trinkhorn, und naht damit Siegfried.)

Gutrune. Willkommen, Gast,
in Gibich's Haus!
Seine Tochter reicht dir den Trank.

Siegfried
(neigt sich ihr freundlich, und ergreift das Horn;
er hält es gedankenvoll vor sich hin und sagt leise:)

Vergäss' ich alles
was du mir gab'st
von einer Lehre
lass' ich doch nie:—

this goblet's quaffed
with quenchless passion,
Brünnhilde, my bride, to thee!

(He drinks, and hands back the horn to Gutrune,
who, abashed, cast down her eyes before his.)

Siegfried

(gazing on her with swiftly kindling passion.)

Thou fair one, whose beams
my breast have enflamed,
why fall thus thine eyes before mine?

(Gutrune looks up at him, blushing.)

Siegfried. Ha! sweetest maid!
Screen those bright beams,
the heart in my breast
burns with their strength;
in fiery streams I feel
how my blood doth boil in my veins!

(With trembling voice.)

Gunther, what name hath thy sister?

Gunther. Gutrune.

Siegfried. Are good the runes
that now in her eyes I am reading?

(He seizes Gutrune with impatient ardor by the
hand.)

When I sought to serve thy brother
brave
his pride repelled my aid.
Wouldst thou be e'en as arrogant
said I to thee the same?

(Gutrune humbly droops her head, and then, with
an expressive gesture, as if she felt her unworthiness, leaves the hall again with trembling steps.)

Siegfried

(closely observed by Hagen and Gunther, gazes
after her, as if spellbound; then, without turning,
he asks)

Hast thou, Gunther, a wife?

Gunther. I've wooed ne'er yet;
besides, a wife
seems me I scarce can win:
on one my soul I have set,
but no help can gain my wish.

Siegfried

(turning quickly to him.)

What would be gainsaid,
stood I thy friend?

Gunther. A far-off rock's her home,
a fire doth breast her hall.

den ersten Trunk
zu treuer Minne,
Brünnhilde, bring' ich dir!

(Er trinkt und reicht das Horn Gutrune zurück,
welche, verschämt und verwirrt, ihre Augen vor
ihm niederschlägt.)

Siegfried

(mit schnell entbrannter Leidenschaft den Blick
auf sie heftend.)

Die so mit dem Blitz
den Blick du mir seng'st,
was senk'st du dein Auge vor mir?

(Gutrune schlägt, erröthend, das Auge zu ihm auf.)

Siegfried. Ha, schönstes Weib!
Schliesse den Blick!
das Herz in der Brust
brennt mir sein Strahl:
zu feurigen Strömen fühl' ich
zehrend ihn zünden mein Blut!—

(Mit bebender Stimme.)

Gunther—wie heisst deine
Schwester?

Gunther. Gutrune.

Siegfried. Sind's gute Runen,
die ihrem Aug' ich entrathe?

(Er fasst Gutrune mit feurigem Ungestüm bei der
Hand.)

Deinem Bruder bot ich mich zum
Mann;
der Stolze schlug mich aus:—
trägst du, wie er, mir Uebermuth,
böt' ich mich dir zum Bund?

(Gutrune neigt demüthig das Haupt, und mit einer
Gebärde, als fühle sie sich seiner nicht werth, verlässt sie wankenden Schrittes wieder die Halle.)

Siegfried

(blickt ihr, wie fest gezaubert, nach, von Hagen
und Gunther aufmerksam beobachtet; dann, ohne
sich umzuwenden, frägt er:)

Hast du, Gunther, ein Weib?

Gunther. Nicht freit' ich noch,
und einer Frau
soll' ich mich schwerlich freu'n!
Auf eine setzt' ich den Sinn,
die kein Rath je mir gewinnt.

Siegfried

(lebhaft sich zu ihm wendend.)

Was wär' dir versagt,
steh' ich zu dir?

Gunther. Auf Felsen hoch ihr Sitz;
ein Feuer umbrennt den Saal—

Siegfried

(repeats softly, in wonder, and as if striving to remember something long forgotten.)

"A far-off rock's her home;
a fire doth breast her hall". . . ?

Gunther. But he who that fire can brave—

Siegfried

(hastily chiming in and immediately ceasing.)

"But he who that fire can brave" . . . ?

Gunther.—is Brünnhilde's fitting mate.

(Siegfried shows, by a silent gesture, that at the mention of Brünnhilde's name the remembrance has quite faded.)

Gunther. That mountain my feet may approach not,
the fire ne'er will pale for me,

Siegfried

(with a sudden start.)

I—fear not the fire,
and thy bride fain will I fetch;
for thy own am I
and my arm is thine:
if Gutrune for wife I may gain.

Gunther. Gutrune I'll give to thee gladly.

Siegfried. Brünnhilde I'll bring thee!

Gunther. How can she mistake us?

Siegfried. Through the Tarnhelm's trick,
turning me into thy shape.

Gunther. Propose an oath for us pair.

Siegfried. Blood-brotherhood
hallowed by oath.

(Hagen fills a horn with fresh wine; Gunther and Siegfried scratch their arms with their sword-points, and hold the wound a moment over the wine.)

Siegfried and Gunther.

Blossoming life's stream,
liberal blood
droppeth into the drink.
Bravely brewed
by fiery friends,
blazes the draught with our blood.
Truth I drink to my friend:
fair and free
be born from our bond
blood-brotherhood here.
Breaks a brother the bond,
fails in faith to his friend,
What in drops we here

Siegfried

(verwundert, und wie um eines längst Vergessenen sich zu entsinnen, wiederholt leise:)

"Auf Felsen hoch ihr Sitz;
ein Feuer umbrennt den Saal" . . ?

Gunther. Nur wer durch das Feuer bricht,

Siegfried

(hastig einfallend und schnell nachlassend.)

"Nur wer durch das Feuer bricht" . . ?

Gunther. —darf Brünnhilde's Freier sein.

(Siegfried drückt durch seine schweigende Gebärde aus, dass bei Nennung von Brünnhilde's Namen die Erinnerung ihm vollends ganz schwindet.)

Gunther. Nun darf ich den Fels nicht erklimmen;
das Feuer verglimmt mir nie!

Siegfried.

(Heftig auffahrend.)

Ich—fürchte kein Feuer:
für dich frei' ich die Frau;
denn dein Mann bin ich,
und mein Muth ist dein—
erwerb' ich Gutrun' zum Weib.

Gunther. Gutrune gönn' ich dir gern.

Siegfried. Brünnhilde bringe ich dir.

Gunther. Wie willst du sie täuschen?

Siegfried. Durch des Tarnhelm's Trug
tausch' ich mir deine Gestalt.

Gunther. So stelle Eide zum Schwur

Siegfried. Blut-Brüderschaft
schwöre ein Eid!

(Hagen füllt ein Trinkhorn mit frischem Wein; Siegfried und Gunther ritzen sich mit ihren Schwertern die Arme und halten diese einen Augenblick über das Trinkhorn.)

Siegfried und Gunther.

Blühenden Lebens
labendes Blut
traüfelt' ich in den Trank:
bruder-brünstig
muthig gemischt,
blüh' im Trank unser Blut.
Treue trink' ich dem Freund,
froh und frei
entblühe dem Bund
Blut-Brüderschaft heut'!
Bricht ein Bruder den Bund,
trügt den Treuen der Freund:
was in Tropfen hold

haste to drink of
in streams be strained from his heart,
forfeit stern to his friend.
Thus compact I claim!
Thus duty I drink.

(They each in turn drink half the contents of the
horn, which Hagen. who has stood apart during the
oath, then breaks in half with his sword. Gunther
and Siegfried clasp hands.)

Siegfried

(to Hagen.)

Why hast thou not joined in the
           bond?

Hagen.   Your drink were spoiled by my
            blood!
    It flows by no means
    nobly enough;
    stubborn and cold,
        scarce it stirs;
  my cheek 'tis chary to redden.
  I leave perforce the fiery league

Gunther.   Have no heed for the churl.

Siegfried.   Forth let me fare!
    There lies my skiff;
  swiftly float to the fastness.
    At the bank for one night
  wait with the boat thou;
  the bride bear then away.

Gunther.   Takest thou first no rest?

Siegfried.   I'll return here in a trice.
    (Goes to the shore.)

Gunther.   Thou, Hagen, have ward of the
           homestead.
    (He follows Siegfried.)
(Gutrune appears at the door of her room.)

Gutrune.   O where haste they so swiftly?

Hagen.   They sail, Brünnhilde to find.

Gutrune.   Siegfried?

Hagen.   See what he does
    for wife striving to win thee.
(He seats himself before the hall with spear and
shield. Siegfried and Gunther float away.)

Gutrune.   Siegfried—mine!
(Goes back to her room in great agitation.)

Hagen

(after a long silence.)

    Here I sit to wait,
    watching the hall,
  warding the house from all foes.

heute wir tranken,
in Strahlen ström' es dahin,
fromme Sühne dem Freund!
So—biet' ich den Bund:
so trink' ich dir Treu!

(Sie trinken nacheinander, jeder zur Hälfte; dann
zerschlägt Hagen, der während des Schwures zur
Seite gelehnt, mit seinem Schwerte das Horn. Siegfried und Gunther reichen sich die Hände.)

Siegfried

(zu Hagen.)

Was nahmst du am Eide nicht Theil?

Hagen.   Mein Blut verdärb' euch den
           Trank!
    Nicht fliesst mir's ächt
    und edel wie euch;
    störrisch und kalt
    stockt's in mir;
  nicht will's die Wange mir röthen.
    D'rum bleib' ich fern
    vom feurigen Bund.

Gunther.   Lass' den unfrohen Mann!

Siegfried.   Frisch auf die Fahrt!
    Dort liegt mein Schiff;
  schnell führt es zum Felsen:
    eine Nacht am Ufer
    harrs't du im Nachen;
  die Frau führst du dann heim.

Gunther.   Rastest du nicht zuvor?

Siegfried.   Um die Rückkehr ist's mir jach.
    (Er geht zum Ufer.)

Gunther.   Du Hagen, bewache die Halle!
    (Er folgt Siegfried.)
(Gutrune erscheint an der Thüre ihres Gemaches.)

Gutrune.   Wohin eilen die Schnellen?

Hagen.   Zu Schiff', Brünnhild' zu frei'n.

Gutrune.   Siegfried?

Hagen.   Sieh', wie's ihn treibt
    zum Weib dich zu gewinnen!
(Er setzt sich mit Speer und Schild vor der Halle
nieder. Siegfried und Gunther fahren ab.)

Gutrune.   Siegfried—mein!
(Sie geht, lebhaft erregt, in ihr Gemach zurück.)

Hagen

(nach längerem Stillschweigen.)

    Hier sitz' ich zur Wacht,
    wahre den Hof,
  wehre die Halle dem Feind:—

Gibich's son
is wafted by winds;
a-wooing forth is he gone.
And fleetly steereth
a stalwart man,
whose force all peril can stem.
His own the bride
he brings down the Rhine;
but he will bring *me* the Ring.
Ye gallant partners,
gleeful companions,
push ye then merrily hence!
Slight though your natures,
ye still may serve
the Nibelung's son.

(A curtain closes in from each side and hides the stage. After a short orchestral interlude, during which the scene is changed, the curtain, which before closed in all the front of the hall, is completely withdrawn.)

Scene Three
The Valkyries' rock, as in the Prelude.

Brünnhilde

(sits at the entrance of the cave in silent thought, gazing on Siegfried's ring; overcome by tender reminiscences, she covers it with kisses, when suddenly she hears a distant noise: she listens and looks off at back.)

Old well-recognized sounds
strike on my ear from distance;
a wind-horse hither
wingeth its course,
in the clouds it rumbles
close to the rock.
Who rides my stillness to stir?

Valtrauta's

(voice from the distance).

Brünnhilde—sister!
sleep'st thou or wakest?

Brünnhilde

(starting to her feet).

Welcome that cry,
it wafts from Valtrauta!
Truest sister!
seek'st thou trace of me here?

(Calling towards the back.)

In yon wood,
As thou wert wont,
Straightway descend
and safely stable thy steed.
Com'st thou to me?
bold and uncowed,
dar'st thou again then
banished Brünnhild' to greet?

Gibich's Sohne
wehet der Wind;
auf Werben fährt er dahin.
Ihm führt der Steuer
ein starker Held,
Gefahr ihm will er besteh'n:
die eig'ne Braut
ihm bringt er zum Rhein;
mir aber bringt er— den Ring.—
Ihr freien Söhne,
frohe Gesellen,
segelt nur lustig dahin!
Dünkt er euch niedrig,
ihr dient ihm doch—
des Niblungen Sohn.

(Ein Teppich schlägt vor der Scene zusammen, und verschliesst die Bühne. Nachdem, während eines kurzen Orchester-Zwischenspieles, der Schauplatz verwandelt ist, wird der Teppich, der zufor den Vordergrund der Halle einfasste, gänzlich aufgezogen.)

Dritte Scene
Die Felsenhöhe, wie im Vorspiel.

Brünnhilde.

(Sitzt am Eingange des Steingemaches, und betrachtet in stummen Sinnen Siegfried's Ring; von wonniger Erinnerung überwättigt, bedeckt sie ihn dann mit Küssen,—als sie plötzlich ein fernes Geräusch vernimmt: sie lauscht und späht zur Seite in den Hintergrund.)

Altgewohntes Geräusch
raunt meinem Ohr die Ferne:—
ein Luftross jagt
im Laufe daher;
auf der Wolke fährt es
wetternd zum Fels!—
Wer fand mich Einsame auf?

Waltraute's

(Stimme aus der Ferne).

Brünnhilde! Schwester!
schläf'st oder wach'st du?

Brünnhilde

(fährt vom Sitze auf).

Waltraute's Ruf,
so wonnig mir kund!—
Komm'st du, Schwester,
schwing'st du kühn dich zu mir?

(in die Scene rufend.)

Dort im Tann
—dir noch vertraut—
steige vom Ross
und stell' den Renner zu Rast!
Kommst du zu mir?
Bist du so kühn?
mag'st ohne Grauen
Brünnhild' bieten den Gruss?

(Valtrauta has entered hastily from the wood;
Brünnhilde rushes to meet her; in her joy she does
not perceive Valtrauta's anxious timidity.)

Valtrauta.

'Tis for thee
my gallop is taken.

Brünnhilde.

O was it for Brünnhilde's sake
War-father's ban thou'st broken?
Or for what? O say!
Will Wotan's heart
once more softly wax?
When against the god once
Siegmund I sheltered—
wrongly, I wot well—
I wrought the thing that he wished.
That his anger was ended
well I knew;
for though sealed he mine eyes in
sleep,
rivetting me to this rock,
destining me to the man
who this way should roam and awake
me,
yet the boon I begged for
denied he not:
a terrible fire
he knit round the fell,
all tremblers to ward from the way.
So sweet solace
was shaped by my sentence:
the highest of heroes
won me for wife.
Filled with his love
in light and laughter I live.
Lured thee, O sister, my lot?
Dost thou then pine
for part in my pleasures,
seek my pure bliss to share?

Valtrauta.

Share the insaneness
that hath seized on thy soul?
More matter hath worked on my mind
the ban of Wotan to break.

Brünnhilde.

Fear and dread
drive o'er thy features!
Doth our father pardon withhold?
Thou fearest his punishment's force?

Valtrauta.

Did I but fear him

(Waltraute ist aus dem Tann hastig aufgetreten;
Brünnhilde ist ihr stürmisch entgegengeeilt: diese
beachtet in der Freude nicht die ängstliche Scheu
Waltraute's.)

Waltraute.

Einzig dir nur
galt meine Eile.

Brünnhilde
(in höchster freudiger Aufgeregtheit).

So wagtest du, Brünnhild' zu lieb,
Walvater's Bann zu brechen?
Oder wie? o sag'!
wär' wider mich
Wotan's Sinn erweicht?
Als dem Gott entgegen
Siegmund ich schützte,
fehlend—ich weiss es—
erfüllt' ich doch seinen Wunsch:
dass sein Zorn sich verzogen,
weiss ich auch;
denn verschloss er mich gleich in
Schlaf,
fesselt' er mich auf den Fels,
wies er dem Mann' mich zur Magd,
der am Weg' mich fänd und erweckt'—
meiner bangen Bitte
doch gab er Gunst:
mit zehrendem Feuer
umgab er den Fels,
dem Zagen zu wehren den Weg.
So zur seligsten
schuf mich die Strafe:
der herrlichste Held
gewann mich zum Weib;
in seiner Liebe
leucht' und lach' ich heut' auf.—
Lockte dich, Schwester, mein Loos?
An meiner Wonne
willst du dich weiden?
theilen, was mich betraf?

Waltraute.

Theilen den Taumel,
der dich Thörin erfasst?—
Ein And'res bewog mich in Angst
zu brechen Wotan's Gebot.

Brünnhilde.

Angst und Furcht
fesselt dich Arme?
So verzieh der Strenge noch nicht?
du zag'st vor des Strafenden Zorn?

Waltraute.

Dürft' ich ihn fürchten.

this alarm fast were allayed.

Brünnhilde.
Scared, I can scarce understand.

Valtrauta.
Mask thy emotion:
wisely hark to my words.
Again the grief
doth hurry me back
which did goad me here from Valhalla.

Brünnhilde
(alarmed).
What ails with the Æsir eternal?

Valtrauta.
Heed with thy soul what I recite
thee.
Since he from thee was severed
our sire no more
sent us to warfare;
undirected
rode we, an awe-stricken host;
Valhall's high-hearted heroes
he viewed no more.
Lonely a-horse,
without halt or home,
through the world as a Wanderer he
went.
He lately came home,
in his hand holding fast
his spear in splinters:
'twas hacked by a hero asunder.
With signs for words
waved he all
the warriors in haste
the world's ash-tree to hew down.
The stem in sticks
he bade them to stack,
and arrange in a bulk
round the Æsir's sanctified seat.
The gods he called
unto the council;
his proud sacred
place then he took:
to his side
appointed the tremblers to assemble.
In rank and ring
the warriors crowded Valhalla.
So sits he,
speaking no word,
in high position,
still and grave,
the splintered spear

meiner Angst fänd' ich ein End'!

Brünnhilde.
Staunend versteh' ich dich nicht!

Waltraute.
Wehr' deiner Wallung:
achtsam höre mich an!
Nach Walhall wieder
treibt mich die Angst,
die von Walhall hieher mich trieb.

Brünnhilde
(erschrocken).
Was ist's mit den ewigen Göttern?

Waltraute.
Höre mit Sinn was ich sage!—
Seit er von dir geschieden,
zur Schlacht nicht mehr
schickte uns Wotan;
irr und rathlos
ritten wir ängstlich zu Heer.
Walhall's muthige Helden
mied Walvater:
einsam zu Ross
ohne Ruh' und Rast
durchstreift' er als Wand'rer die Welt
Jüngst kehrte er heim;
in der Hand hielt er
seines Speeres Splitter:
die hatte ein Held ihm geschlagen.
Mit stummen Wink
Walhall's Edle
wies er zum Forst,
die Welt-Esche zu fällen;
des Stammes Scheite
hiess er sie schichten
zum ragenden Hauf
rings um der Seligen Saal.
Der Götter Rath
liess er berufen;
den Hochsitz nahm
heilig er ein:
ihm zu Seiten
hiess er die Bangen sich setzen,
in Ring und Reih'
die Hall' erfüllen die Helden.
So—sitzt er,
sagt kein Wort,
auf hehrem Sitze
stumm und ernst,
des Speeres Splitter

held fast in his fist.
Hulda's apples
doth he not eat.
Gloomy and awe-struck
all the gods seem frozen.
But he turned his ravens
both out to travel;
when they with goodly
tidings wing their return,
once again then for evermore
over the god breaks a smile.
Round his knees in vigil
twine all we Valkyries;
blind bides he
to eyes that are begging,
and all of us stay,
struck with an ominous awe.
Unto his breast
weeping I press'd me;
his brooding then broke;
and his thoughts turned, Brünnhilde,
              to thee!
Deep sighs he uttered,
closed his eyelids,
as were he dreaming,
and reded these words:
"The day the Rhine's three daughters
gain by surrender from her the Ring
from the curse's load
released are gods and men!"
I thought upon't;
and then I threaded
'mid throngs dumb-stricken
thence from his side;
in haste on my horse
I threw me astride,
and straightway thrust towards thee.
Then, my sister,
I supplicate:
do what thou may'st
if but thou hast mind:
ward off the woe of the gods.
(Throws herself at Brünnhilde's feet.)

Brünnhilde.

What dreamy tales of myst'ry
mournfully tell'st thou to me!
From cloudy homes
where the holy gods sit
am I, poor fool, expelled;
no sense conveys thy recital.
Void and vain
seemeth thy speech.
Within thine eyes

fest in der Faust;
Holda's Aepfel
rührt er nicht an:
Staunen und Bangen
binden starr die Götter.—
Seiner Raben beide
sandt' er auf Reise:
kehrten die einst
mit guter Kunde zurück,
dann noch einmal
—zum letzten Mal—
lächelte ewig der Gott.
Seine Knie' umwindend
liegen wir Walküren:
blind bleibt er
den flehenden Blicken;
uns alle verzehrt
Zagen und endlose Angst.
An seine Brust
presst' ich mich weinend:
da brach sich sein Blick—
er gedachte, Brünnhilde, dein!
Tief seufzte er auf,
schloss das Auge,
und wie im Traume
raunt' er das Wort:—
„Des tiefen Rheines Töchtern
gäbe den Ring sie wieder zurück,
von des Fluches Last
erlös't wär' Gott und Welt!"—
Da sann ich nach:
von seiner Seite
durch stumme Reihen
stahl ich mich fort;
in heimlicher Hast
bestieg ich mein Ross,
und ritt im Sturme zu dir.
Dich, o Schwester,
beschwör' ich nun:
was du vermagst,
vollend' es dein Muth!
Ende der Ewigen Qual!

Brünnhilde.

Welch' banger Träume Mären
meldest du Traurige mir!
Der Götter heiligem
Himmels-Nebel
bin ich Thörin enttaucht:
nicht fass' ich, was ich erfahre.
Wirr und wüst
scheint mir dein Sinn;
in deinem Aug'

so over-wearied
gleams fitfully glow.
  Thou piteous woman
  with pallid features,
what would thy wildness of me?

Valtrauta
          (with gloomy haste).
  There on thy hand—the ring
  'tis that—hark to my rede!
For Wotan wilt thou resign it?

Brünnhilde.
      The ring! resign it?

Valtrauta.
  Surrender it back to the Rhine!

Brünnhilde.
  Surrender it—I—the ring?
  Siegfried's bridal gift?
      Wander thy senses?

Valtrauta.
  Hear me! heed my distress!
    The world's trouble
  hangs upon it, I trow.
      Whirl it from thee
      far in the water,
  woe from Valhall' averting;
  cast the foul thing away in the flood!

Brünnhilde.
  Ah! wist thou what 'tis to me?
      Thou can'st not fathom,
      feelingless maid!
  More than Æsir's honor,
  More than Valhall's bright realm
      I hold this ring.
  One look at its beauteous gold,
  one light from its brilliant gleam
        glads me more
        than unending good
  to all the mass of the gods.
      I see in its beams
  lambent how Siegfried loves me.
      Siegfried loves me!
  How little thou wott'st of this sweet-
                            ness!
  Stays with me the ring.
      Get hence to the gods
      in holy array,
      and of my ring
      arede them this:
  I'll loose not love from my heart;
  no hest shall hinder my loving,

—so übermüde—
glänzt flackernde Gluth:
  mit blasser Wange
  du bleiche Schwester,
was willt du Wilde von mir?

Waltraute
          (mit unheimlicher Hast.)
  An deiner Hand der Ring—
  er ist's: hör' meinen Rath:
  für Wotan wirf ihn von dir!

Brünnhilde.
      Den Ring—von mir?

Waltraute.
  Den Rheintöchtern gieb ihn zurück!

Brünnhilde.
  Den Rheintöchtern—ich—den Ring?
  Siegfried's Liebespfand?
      Bist du von Sinnen?

Waltraute.
  Hör' mich! hör' meine Angst?
      Der Welt Unheil
  haftet sicher an ihm:—
      wirf ihn von dir
      fort in die Welle
  Walhall's Elend zu enden,
  den verfluchten wirf in die Fluth!

Brünnhilde.
  Ha! weisst du, was er mir ist?
      Wie kannst du's fassen,
      fühllose Maid!—
  Mehr als Walhall's Wonne,
  mehr als der Ewigen Ruhm
      ist mir der Ring:
  ein Blick auf sein helles Gold,
  ein Blitz aus dem hehren Glanz
      gilt mir werther
      als aller Götter
  ewig währendes Glück!
      Denn selig aus ihm
  leuchtet mir Siegfried's Liebe:
      Siegfried's Liebe!
  O liess' sich die Wonne dir sagen!
  Sie wahrt mir der Reif.
      Geh' hin zu der Götter
      heiligem Rath;
      von meinem Ringe
      raun' ihnen zu:
  die Liebe liesse ich nie,
  mir nehmen nie sie die Liebe,

    Sooner to ruins
Valhall's splendor shall crash.

Valtrauta.

    This is thy truth then?
    So in trouble
thou leavest thy sister all loveless?

Brünnhilde.

    Swiftly go forth,
    far hence to ride:
the ring thou'lt force not from me.

Valtrauta.

    Woe's me, woe's me!
    Woe's thee, sister!
Woe to Valhall'—woe!

(She rushes away and is heard without—as if on horse—galloping away from the wood.)

Brünnhilde

(gazes after a brightly lighted storm-cloud as it sails away and is quickly lost in the distance).

    Black thunder-cloud
    that cleav'st the heavens,
    stride quickly hence:
no more be steered to me here.

(It is now evening. From the valley glimmers the firelight, gradually waxing.)

    Eve's dusky shadows
    shroud the heavens:
    Why glare so wildly
the glittering waves o'er the wall?
    The raging fire
its way o'er the rock-point would
        force.

(Siegfried's horn is heard below in the valley. Brünnhilde listens, and then starts up enraptured.)

    Siegfried!
    Siegfried is here!
Sure his horn sounded that call.
Up! up! and be gathered
into my god's strong arm.

(She hurries towards the back in the highest transport. Flames dart up over the cliff; out of them springs Siegfried up on to a jutting rock, whereupon the flames fall back again and gradually retire to the valley. Siegfried appears in Gunther's form, wearing the Tarnhelm, the visor of which covers half his face, leaving only the eyes free.)

Brünnhilde

    (retreating in horror.)

    Betrayed! What man art thou?

(She flies to the front, and from thence, in speechless amazement, turns her looks upon Siegfried.)

Siegfried

(remaining at back on the stone, leans on his shield and gazes at her a long while; then he speaks

---

    stürzt auch in Trümmern
Walhall's strahlende Pracht!

Waltraute.

    Diess deine Treue?
    So in Trauer
entlässest du lieblos die Schwester?

Brünnhilde.

    Schwinge dich fort;
    fliege zu Ross:
den Ring entführst du mir nicht!

Waltraute.

    Wehe! Wehe!
    Weh' dir Schwester!
Walhall's Göttern Weh!

(Sie stürzt fort; man hört sie schnell—wie zu Ross vom Tann aus fortbrausen.)

Brünnhilde

(blickt einer davonjagenden, hellerleuchteten Gewitterwolke nach, die sich bald gänzlich in der Ferne verliert).

    Blitz und Gewölk,
    vom Wind geblasen,
    stürme dahin:
zu mir nie steure mehr her!—

(Es ist Abend geworden: aus der Tiefe leuchtet der Feuerschein stärker auf.)

    Abendlich Dämmern
    deckt den Himmel:
    Was leckt so wüthend
die lodernde Welle zum Wall?
    Zur Felsenspitze
wälzt sich der feurige Schwall.

(Man hört aus der Tiefe Siegfried's Hornruf nahen. Brünnhilde lauscht, und fährt dann entzückt auf.)

    Siegfried!
    Siegfried zurück?
seinen Ruf sendet er her!
Auf!—Auf, ihm entgegen!
in meines Gottes Arm!

(Sie stürzt in höchstem Entzücken dem Hintergrunde Feuerflammen schlagen über den Höhensaum auf: aus ihnen springt Siegfried auf einen hoch ragenden Felsstein empor, worauf die Flammen wieder zurückweichen, und abermals nur aus der Tiefe des Hintergrundes heraufleuchten.—Siegfried, auf dem Haupte den Tarnhelm, der ihm bis zur Hälfte das Gesicht verdeckt und nur die Augen frei lässt, erscheint in Gunther's Gestalt.)

Brünnhilde

    (voll Entsetzen zurückweichend.)

    Verrath!—Wer drang zu mir?

(Sie flieht bis in den Hintergrund, und heftet von da aus in sprachlosem Erstaunen ihren Blick auf Siegfried.)

Siegfried.

(Im Hintergrunde auf dem Steine verweilend, betrachtet sie lange, auf seinen Schild gelehnt; dann

to her with altered—deeper—voice.)
Brünnhilde! A lover comes,
and alarms him nought thy fire.
I woo thee for my wife;
so bend thy will to me!

Brünnhilde
(trembling violently.)
Who is the man
has wrought the marvel
that but one alone may work?

Siegfried
(still standing on the rock at back.)
A hero thou'llt obey
if but by force thou'rt ruled.

Brünnhilde
(filled with terror.)
A demon stands
upon yon stone!
an eagle has flown here
who would my flesh rend!
Who art thou, awful one?
(Siegfried is silent.)
Art thou a mortal?
Com'st thou of Hella's
night-dwelling host?

Siegfried
(after a long silence.)
A Gibichung am I,
and Gunther he is hight
who, maid, will mate with thee.

Brünnhilde
(in a despairing outburst.)
Wotan! Resentful,
Stern-hearted sire!
Woe! now I fathom
thy fiat fell!
My shame and wailing
well hast thou shaped!

Siegfried
(leaping from the rock and approaching.)
The night doth fall,
thy room I demand;
mine be thou made by marriage.

Brünnhilde
(threateningly stretching out her finger on which
is Siegfried's ring.)
Stand back! bow to this token!
No shame can touch me from thee
while yet this ring is my shield.

redet er sie mit verstellter—tieferer—Stimme an.)
Brünnhild'! ein Freier kam,
den dein Feuer nicht geschreckt.
Dich werb' ich nun zum Weib;
du folge willig mir!

Brünnhilde
(heftig zitternd).
Wer ist der Mann,
der das vermochte,
was dem Stärksten nur bestimmt?

Siegfried
(immer noch auf dem Steine im Hintergrunde).
Ein Helde, der dich zähmt
bezwingt Gewalt dich nur.

Brünnhilde
(von Grausen erfasst).
Ein Unhold schwang sich
auf jenen Stein;
ein Aar kam geflogen
mich zu zerfleischen!
Wer bist du, Schrecklicher?
(Siegfried—schweigt.)
Stamm'st du von Menschen?
komm'st du von Hella's
nächtlichem Heer?

Siegfried
(nach längerem Schweigen).
Ein Gibichung bin ich,
und Gunther heisst der Held,
dem, Frau, du folgen soll'st.

Brünnhilde
(in Verzweiflung ausbrechend.)
Wotan! ergrimmter,
grausamer Gott!
Weh'! nun erseh' ich
der Strafe Sinn:
zu Hohn und Jammer
jag'st du mich hin!

Siegfried
(springt vom Stein herab und tritt näher.)
Die Nacht bricht an:
in deinem Gemach
musst du dich mit mir vermählen.

Brünnhilde
(den Finger, an dem sie Siegfried's Ring trägt, drohend emporstreckend.)
Bleib' fern! fürchte dies Zeichen!
Zur Schande zwingst du mich nicht,
so lang' der Ring mich schützt.

Siegfried.   Husband's right it gains for
Gunther:
with that ring be wed to him.

Brünnhilde.   Aroint, thou robber!
Villainous thief!
Nor venture thyself near my side.
Stronger than steel
makes me the ring;
None rends it from me.

Siegfried.   From thee will I take it,
Taught by thy words.

(He presses towards her; they wrestle. Brünnhilde slips herself loose and flies. Siegfried pursues
her. Again they struggle; he seizes her, and plucks
the ring from her finger. She utters a loud scream
and sinks exhausted on the rocky seat in front of
the cave.)

Siegfried.   Now be thou mine!
Brünnhilde, Gunther's bride:
go to thy chamber with me.

Brünnhilde

(almost fainting.)
How, woman too hapless,
canst thou find help?

(Siegfried drives her in with a commanding gesture. She goes into the cave trembling, and with
tottering steps.)

Siegfried

(drawing his sword and speaking with his natural
voice.)
Now, Needful, witness thou
that chaste my wooing is.
To seal my oath to my brother,
separate me from his bride.

(He follows Brünnhilde.)
The curtain falls.

ACT TWO

Scene One

River bank before the hall of the Gibichungs: the
banks of the river L., entrance to the hall R. From
the river bank rises diagonally towards the back
a rocky slope divided by sundry mountain paths.
There stands an altar stone, dedicated to Fricka, a
larger one, higher up, for Wotan, and another
towards the side for Donner. It is night.

Hagen, with spear in hand and shield at side, sits
sleeping against the hall. The moon suddenly
throws a keen light on him and his surroundings;
Alberic is seen crouching in front of him, leaning
his arms on Hagen's knees.

Siegfried.   Mannesrecht gebe er Gunther:
durch den Ring sei ihm ver-
mählt!

Brünnhilde.   Zurück, Räuber!
frevelnder Dieb!
Erfreche dich nicht zu nah'n.
Stärker als Stahl
macht mich der Ring:
nie raubst du ihn mir!

Siegfried.   Von dir ihn zu lösen
lehrst du mich nun.

(Er dringt auf sie ein; sie ringen. Brünnhilde
windet sich los und flieht. Siegfried setzt ihr
nach. Sie ringen von neuem; er erfasst sie, und
entzieht ihrem Finger den Ring. Sie schreit laut
auf und sinkt, wie zerbrochen, auf der Steinbank
vor dem Gemach zusammen.)

Siegfried.   Jetzt bist du mein!
Brünnhilde, Gunther's Braut—
gönne mir nun dein Gemach!

Brünnhilde

(fast ohnmächtig.)
Was könntest du wehren,
elendes Weib?

(Siegfried treibt sie mit einer gebietenden Bewegung an: zitternd und wankenden Schrittes geht sie
in das Gemach.)

Siegfried

(das Schwert ziehend, mit seiner natürlichen
Stimme.)
Nun, Nothung, zeuge du,
dass ich in Züchten warb:
die Treue wahrend dem Bruder,
trenne mich von seiner Braut!

(Er folgt Brünnhilde nach.)
Der Vorhang fällt.

ZWEITER AUFZUG

Erste Scene

Uferraum vor der Halle der Gibichungen: rechts
der offene Eingang zur Halle; links das Rheinufer;
von diesem aus erhebt sich eine durch verschiedene
Bergpfade gespaltene, felsige Anhöhe, quer über die
Bühne, nach rechts dem Hintergrunde zu aufsteigend. Dort sieht man einen der Fricka errichteten
Weichstein, welchem, höher hinauf, ein grösserer
für Wotan, sowie seitwärts ein gleicher für Donner
geweihter entspricht. Es ist Nacht.

Hagen, den Speer im Arm, den Schild zur Seite,
sitzt schlafend an der Halle. Der Mond wirft
plötzlich ein grelles Licht auf ihn und seine nächste
Umgebung: man gewahrt Alberich vor Hagen
kauernd, die Arme auf dessen Kniee gelehnt.

Alberic. Sleepest thou, Hagen, my son?
Thou sleep'st and hear'st not him
whom rest and sleep have ruined.

Hagen
(softly and without moving, so that he appears still
to sleep, though his eyes are open.)
I hear thee well, son of darkness:
what hast thou to instruct my
slumber?

Alberic. Remind thee what might
thy spirit owneth;
i' 'tis as manly
as thy mother did make it erst.

Hagen. Though mighty she made me,
I may na'theless not thank her
that to thy craft she succumbed.
Wizened, wan and pale,
I hate the happy,
hope for no joy.

Alberic. Hagen, my son!
hate thou the happy!
Thy so hapless sire,
by sorrow besieged,
then lacks not thy love.
If thou art fearless,
fierce and false,
those whom we fight
with a nocturnal feud
shall surely be harmed by our hate.
He who once wrested my ring,
Wotan, the worst of all robbers,
at last is disabled
by his own offspring:
all his late power
through the Volsung is lost.
All the gods together with him
in awe are waiting their ending.
No more him I fear:
he must fall now among them.
Sleep'st thou, Hagen, my son?

Hagen
(remaining motionless as before.)
The might of the gods,
whose meed is it?

Alberic.
Mine and thine!
We'll master the world;
if I may reckon
on thy aid—
shar'st thou in my wrongs and wrath.
Wotan's spear

Alberich. Schläfst du, Hagen, mein
Sohn?
Du schläfst, und hörst mich nicht,
den Ruh' und Schlaf verrieth?

Hagen
(leise und ohne sich zu rühren, so dass er immer
fort zu schlafen scheint, obwohl er die Augen offen
hat.)
Ich höre dich, schlimmer Albe:
was hast du meinem Schlaf zu sagen?

Alberich. Gemahnt sei der Macht,
der du gebietest,
bist du so muthig,
wie die Mutter dich mir gebar.

Hagen. Gab die Mutter mir Muth,
nicht doch mag ich ihr danken,
dass deiner List sie erlag:
frühalt, fahl und bleich,
hass' ich die Frohen,
freue mich nie!

Alberich. Hagen, mein Sohn!
Hasse die Frohen!
Mich Lust-freien,
Leid-belasteten,
liebst du so wie du sollst!
Bist du kräftig,
kühn und klug:
die wir bekämpfen
mit nächtigem Krieg,
schon giebt ihnen Noth unser Neid
Der einst den Ring mir entriss,
Wotan, der wüthende Räuber,
vom eig'nen Geschlechte
ward er geschlagen:
an den Wälsung verlor er
Macht und Gewalt;
mit der Götter ganzer Sippe
in Angst ersieht er sein End'.
Nicht ihn fürcht' ich mehr:
fallen muss er mit Allen!
Schläf'st du, Hagen, mein Sohn?

Hagen
(bleibt unverändert wie zuvor).
Der Ewigen Macht,
wer erbte sie?

Alberich.
Ich—und du:
wir erben die Welt,
trüg' ich mich nicht
in deiner Treu',
theil'st du meinen Gram und Grimm.
Wotan's Speer

was spoiled by the Volsung,
who fiercely did vanquish
Fafnir in fight,
the fair ring to take as a toy.
Now he is prince
of every power,
Valhall' and Nibelheim
know him their lord.
On this fear-lacking hero
my curse cannot fall;
for, the ring's might
he uses not:
he knows nought
of its notable worth.
Laughter, and love with its glow
glad his life-days alone.
Only his ruin
must we now aim at.....
Sleep'st thou, Hagen, my son?

Hagen.

I help him already
ruin to seek.

Alberic. The golden round—
the ring—we must arrive at.
A woman wise
loves him well as her life.
Rendered he e'er
the river maidens
—by whose wiles amid
the waves I was mocked—
the ring, obeying her rede,
for ever gone were the gold,
and no art could earn it again.
Then, without staying,
strive for the ring.
Thou stubborn
and sturdy wert made,
that thou shouldst help
my hate against heroes.
Strength want'st thou indeed
to vanquish the worm:
that alone the Volsung might work.
Yet potent hatred
I planted, Hagen,
in thee, my avenger:—
to win me the ring,
thou'lt vanquish Volsung and Wotan.
Swear to me, Hagen, my son?

(From this point an increasing gloom hides
Hagen and Alberic. At the same time day begins
to dawn on the Rhine.)

zerspellte der Wälsung,
der Fafner, den Wurm,
im Kampfe gefällt,
und kindisch den Reif sich errang:
jede Gewalt
hat er gewonnen;
Walhall und Nibelheim
neigen sich ihm;
an dem furchtlosen Helden
erlahmt selbst mein Fluch:
denn nicht kennt er
des Ringes Werth,
zu nichts nützt er
die neidlichste Macht;
lachend in liebender Brunst
brennt er lebend dahin.
Ihn zu verderben
taugt uns nun einzig . . .
Hörst du, Hagen, mein Sohn?

Hagen.

Zu seinem Verderben
dient er mir schon.

Alberich. Den gold'nen Ring,
den Reif gilt's zu erringen!
Ein weises Weib
lebt dem Wälsung zu Lieb':
rieth' sie ihm je
des Rheines Töchtern
—die in Wassers Tiefen
einst mich bethört!—
zurück zu geben den Ring:
verloren ging' mir das Gold,
keine List erlangte es je.
Drum ohne Zögern
ziel' auf den Reif:
Dich Zaglosen
zeugt' ich mich ja,
dass wider Helden
hart du mich hieltest.
Zwar stark nicht genug
den Wurm zu besteh'n,
was allein dem Wälsung bestimmt,
zu zähem Hass
erzog ich doch Hagen:
der soll mich nun rächen,
den Ring zu gewinnen,
dem Wälsung und Wotan zum
Hohn!
Schwör'st du mir's, Hagen, mein
Sohn?

(Ein immer finsterer Schatten bedeckt wieder
Hagen und Alberich: vom Rhein her dämmert
der Tag.)

Hagen. The ring I'll lay hands on:
  happily rest.

Alberic. Swear to me, Hagen, my hope.

Hagen. My soul swears it:
  cease from thy sorrow.

Alberic
  (as he gradually disappears from view, his voice
  becoming fainter and fainter.)
  Be true, Hagen, my son.
  Trusty hero, be true.
  Be true!—true!

(He vanishes completely. Hagen, who has persistently remained in his place, gazes motionless and
with fixed eyes upon the Rhine.)
(The sun rises and is mirrored in the waters.)
(Siegfried suddenly comes forward from behind a
bush on the river bank. He is in his own semblance, but still wears the Tarnhelm; this he now
doffs and hangs in his belt.)

Siegfried. Hoiho! Hagen!
  sleepy soul!
  See who is coming!

Hagen
  (indolently rising.)
  Hey, Siegfried!
  Thou speedy hero!
  Whence brawlest thou here?

Siegfried. From Brünnhilde's rock.
  'Twas there I imbibed the breath
  with which I waked thee:
  so rapid was my flight.
  Slower will follow the pair;
  by boat they slip up here.

Hagen. Has mastered Brünnhilde?

Siegfried. Wakes Gutrune yet?

Hagen. Hoiho! Gutrune!
  Come without!
  Siegfried is here:
  why stay in house?

Siegfried
  (turning to the hall.)
  I took Brünnhilde,
  and how—I'll tell you twain.
(Gutrune enters from the hall and meets him.)

Siegfried.
  Now welcome make me,
  Gibich-maid!
  A goodly herald hast in me.

Hagen. Den Ring soll ich haben:
  harre in Ruh'!

Alberich. Schwör'st du mir's, Hagen,
  mein Held?

Hagen. Mir selbst schwör' ich's:
  schweige die Sorge!

Alberich
  (wie er allmälig immer mehr dem Blicke ent-
  schwindet, wird auch seine Stimme immer unver-
  nehmbarer.)
  Sei treu, Hagen, mein Sohn!
  Trauter Helde, sei treu!
  Sei treu!—treu!

(Alberich ist gänzlich verschwunden. Hagen, der
unverrückt in seiner Stellung verblieben, blickt re-
gungslos und starren Auges nach dem Rheine hin.
Die Sonne geht auf und spiegelt sich in der Fluth.
Siegfried tritt plötzlich, dicht am Ufer, hinter
einem Busche hervor. Er ist in seiner eigenen
Gestalt; nur den Tarnhelm hat er noch auf dem
Haupte: er zieht ihn ab, und hängt ihn in den
Gürtel.)

Siegfried. Hoiho! Hagen!
  Müder Mann!
  Siehst du mich kommen?

Hagen
  (gemächlich sich erhebend.)
  Heil! Siegfried!
  Geschwinder Helde!
  Wo brausest du her?

Siegfried. Von Brünnhildenstein;
  dort zog ich den Athem ein,
  mit dem ich jetzt dich rief:
  so schnell war meine Fahrt!
  Langsamer folgt mir ein Paar:
  Zu Schiff gelangt das her.

Hagen. So zwangst du Brünnhild'!

Siegfried. Wacht Gutrune?

Hagen. Hoiho! Gutrune!
  Komm heraus!
  Siegfried ist da:
  Was säum'st du d'rin?

Siegfried
  (zur Halle sich wendend.)
  Euch beiden meld' ich,
  wie ich Brünnhild' band.
(Gutrune tritt ihnen unter der Halle entgegen.)

Siegfried.
  Heiss' mich willkommen,
  Gibichskind!
  Ein guter Bote bin ich dir.

Gutrune.
> Freia give thee joy,
> by ev'ry fair one honored.

Siegfried.
> Freely deign
> to show me favor:
> As wife I've won thee to-day.

Gutrune.
> Doth fare Brünnhilde with my brother?

Siegfried.
> Light was his wooing, I ween.

Gutrune.
> Has he no wound from the fire?

Siegfried.
> It would not e'en have burned him,
> but I in his stead went o'er.
> that I might gain my Gutrune.

Gutrune.
> Then thou hast not been, touched?

Siegfried.
> I gleefully trampled the blaze.

Gutrune.
> Did Brünnhilde deem thee Gunther?

Siegfried.
> We differed not a hair.
> The Tarnhelm worked all that,
> as Hagen told me it would.

Hagen.
> I gave thee goodly rede.

Gutrune.
> Didst conquer the maid so fierce?

Siegfried.
> She felt—Gunther's might.

Gutrune.
> Was she married then to thee?

Siegfried.
> To her mate submitted Brünnhilde
> all the night of bridal till morn.

Gutrune.
> And to *thee* she gave herself?

Siegfried.
> For Gutrune waited Siegfried.

Gutrune.
> By his side, though, was Brünnhilde?

Gutrune.
> Freia grüsse dich
> zu aller Frauen Ehre!

Siegfried.
> Frei und hold
> sei nur mir Frohen:
> zum Weib gewann ich dich heut'.

Gutrune.
> So folgt Brünnhild' meinem Bruder?

Siegfried.
> Leicht ward die Frau ihm gefreit.

Gutrune.
> Sengte das Feuer ihn nicht?

Siegfried.
> Ihn hätt' es auch nicht versehrt;
> doch ich durchschritt es für ihn,
> da dich ich wollt' erwerben.

Gutrune.
> Doch dich hat es verschont?

Siegfried.
> Mich freute die schwebende Brunst

Gutrune.
> Hielt Brünnhild' dich für Gunther?

Siegfried.
> Ihm glich ich auf ein Haar:
> der Tarnhelm wirkte das,
> wie Hagen tüchtig es wies.

Hagen.
> Dir gab ich guten Rath.

Gutrune.
> So zwang'st du das kühne Weib?

Siegfried.
> Sie wich Gunther's Kraft.

Gutrune.
> Und vermählte sie sich dir?

Siegfried.
> Ihrem Mann gehorchte Brünnhild'
> eine volle bräutliche Nacht.

Gutrune.
> Als ihr Mann doch galtest du?

Siegfried.
> Bei Gutrune weilte Siegfried.

Gutrune.
> Doch zur Seite war ihm Brünnhild'?

Siegfried
(pointing to his sword.)
'Twixt the East and West lies North:
so near was Brünnhilde to me.

Gutrune.
How then made Gunther the bride his
own?

Siegfried.
In the fiery surges consuming
at first dawn she set foot
and followed me t'ward the vale.
When shore was near,
dash!—in shape
reversed were Gunther and I.
Then by the helmet's virtue,
wishing, I hither flew.
By hast'ning wind impelled,
the pair up the river come.
Make ready then to receive.

Gutrune.
Siegfried, marvellous man!
What fear I feel of thee!

Hagen
(looking down on the river from the heights at
back.)
From afar approaches a pinnace.

Siegfried.
Then praise its herald here.

Gutrune.
Let us give her hearty welcome,
that haply she may bide here gladly.·
Thou Hagen, please
to summon the people
to Gibich's walls for wedding.
Mirthful maids
shall be brought by me;
my merriment meetly they'll join.
(Going towards the hall, to Siegfried.)
Wouldst thou sleep, naughty guest?

Siegfried.
Rest it gives me helping thee.
(He follows her. Exeunt both into the hall.)

Hagen
(standing on the height, turns landwards and
blows with all his strength a great cattle-horn.)
Hoiho! Hoiho! Hoiho!
Ye men of Gibich
gather yourselves!
Waken! waken!

Siegfried
(auf sein Schwert deutend).
Zwischen Ost und West der Nord:
so nah war Brünnhild' ihm fern.

Gutrune.
Wie empfing sie nun Gunther von
dir?

Siegfried.
Durch des Feuers verlöschende Lohe
im Frühnebel vom Felsen
folgte sie mir zu Thal;
dem Strande nah,
flugs die Stelle
tauschte Gunther mit mir:
durch des Geschmeides Tugend
wünsch' ich mich schnell hieher.
Ein starker Wind nun treibt
die Trauten den Rhein herauf:
d'rum rüstet jetzt den Empfang!

Gutrune.
Siegfried, mächtigster Mann:
wie fasst mich Furcht vor dir!

Hagen
(von der Höhe im Hintergrunde den Fluss hinab
spähend).
In der Ferne seh' ich ein Segel.

Siegfried.
So sagt dem Boten Dank!

Gutrune.
Lasst sie uns hold empfangen,
dass heiter sie und gern hier weile!
Du Hagen! minnig
rufe die Mannen
nach Gibich's Hof zur Hochzeit!
Frohe Frauen
ruf' ich zum Fest:
der Freudigen folgen sie gern.
(Nach der Halle schreitend, zu Siegfried.)
Rastest du, schlimmer Held?

Siegfried.
Dir zu helfen ruh' ich aus.
(Er folgt ihr. Beide gehen in die Halle ab.)

Hagen
(auf der Anhöhe stehend, stösst, der Landseite
zugewendet, mit aller Kraft in ein grosses Stier-
horn.)
Hoiho! Hoiho! Hoiho!
Ihr Gibichs Mannen,
machet euch auf!
Wehe! Wehe!

Weapons! weapons!
weapons are out!
Goodly weapons,
sturdy weapons,
sharp for strife.
Woe! woe is here!
Woe! Waken! Waken!
Hoiho! Hoiho! Hoiho!

(He continues to blow his cattle-horn. Other horns answer it from different directions in the land. From the heights and valleys armed men rush hastily on.)

The Vassals
(first a few at a time, then more together.)
Why brays the horn?
What summons the hosts?
We come with all ward—
we come with all weapons—
Hagen! Hagen!
Hoiho! Hoiho!
What's the peril here?
Will the foe appear?
Who gives us fight?
Is Gunther in need?

Hagen
(from the heights.)
Trim yourselves up
and tarry not;
greet your chief to the full;
a wife Gunther has found

The Vassals. What is his need?
where is his foe?

Hagen. A fiery wife
fares at his heels.

The Vassals. By furious mass
of foes is menaced?

Hagen. No one follows:
lone he fares.

The Vassals. Has he triumphed o'er ill?
Has he triumphed in war?

Hagen. The Worm-killer
was his defence!
Siegfried the hero
his safety held.

The Vassals.
Then how should our host further
help him?

Hagen. Bulls full sturdy
shall ye slaughter,

Waffen! Waffen!
Waffen durch's Land!
gute Waffen!
Starke Waffen,
scharf zum Streit,
Noth! Noth ist da!
Noth! Wehe! Wehe!
Hoiho! Hoiho! Hoiho!

(Er bläst abermals. Aus verschiedenen Gegenden vom Lande her antworten Heerhörner. Von den Höhen und aus dem Thale stürmen in Hast und Eile gewaffnete Mannen herbei.)

Die Mannen
(erst einzelne, dann immer mehr zusammen.)
Was tos't das Horn?
was ruft es zu Heer?
Wir kommen mit Wehr,
wir kommen mit Waffen;
mit starken Waffen,
mit scharfer Wehr!
Hoiho! Hoiho!
Hagen! Hagen!
Welche Noth ist da?
Welcher Feind ist nah'?
Wer giebt uns Streit?
Ist Gunther in Noth?

Hagen
(von der Anhöhe herab.)
Rüstet euch wohl
und rastet nicht;
Gunther sollt ihr empfah'n:
ein Weib hat der gefreit.

Die Mannen. Drohet ihm Noth?
drängt ihn der Feind?

Hagen. Ein freisliches Weib
führt er heim!

Die Mannen. Ihm folgen der Magen
feindliche Mannen?

Hagen. Einsam fährt er:
keiner folgt.

Die Mannen. So bestand er die Noth,
bestand den Kampf?

Hagen. Der Wurmtödter
wehrte der Noth:
Siegfried, der Held,
der schur' ihm Heil.

Die Mannen. Was soll ihm das Heer nun
noch helfen?

Hagen. Starke Stiere
sollt ihr schlachten:

and wash the altar
of Wotan in blood.

The Vassals. Why, Hagen, what biddest
thou us then?

Hagen. Be a boar then further
struck down for Froh,
and a stalwart he-goat
smitten for Donner;
sheep, moreover,
slaughter for Fricka,
that well she may aid in the wedding.

The Vassals
(with continually increasing mirth.)
When we have done it,
then what is there else?

Hagen. The drink-horn take
from damsels fair,
with wine and mead
mirthfully filled.

The Vassals. The drink-horn in hand,
what have we then to do?

Hagen. Revel away
till you wreck your wits:
All for goodwill of the Æsir,
to win their aid for the wedding.

The Vassals
(bursting out into a ringing peal of laughter.)
Good gain and hap
lights on the Rhine,
if Hagen the grim one
to laughter incline.
The Hardy Thorn
pricks now no more;
to help at weddings
henceforth is his part.

Hagen
(who has remained quite serious.)
Now leave off laughter,
valiant vassals.
Receive Gunther's bride:
Brünnhilde approaches with him.
(He has descended and joined the vassels.)
Love well your lady;
lend her your aid:
if she have wrong
quickly requite it,

(Gunther and Brünnhilde arrive in the boat.
Some of the men spring into the water and drag
the boat ashore. While Gunther conducts Brünnhilde ashore the vassals shout and clash their
weapons. Hagen stands aside at back.)

am Weihstein fliesse
Wotan ihr Blut.

Die Mannen. Was, Hagen, was heisst du
uns dann?

Hagen. Einen Eber fällen
sollt ihr für Froh;
einen stämmigen Bock
stechen für Donner;
Schafe aber
schlachtet für Fricka,
Dass gute Ehe sie gebe!

Die Mannen
(mit immer mehr ausbrechender Heiterkeit.)
Schlugen wir Thiere,
was schaffen wir dann?

Hagen. Das Trinkhorn nehm't
von trauten Frau'n,
mit Meth und Wein
wonnig gefüllt.

Die Mannen. Das Horn in der Hand,
Wie halten wir es dann?

Hagen. Rüstig gezecht
bis der Rausch euch zähmt
alles den Göttern zu Ehren,
dass gute Ehe sie geben!

Die Mannen
(in ein schallendes Gelächter ausbrechend.)
Gross Glück und Heil
lacht nun dem Rhein,
da der grimme Hagen
so lustig mag sein!
Der Hage-Dorn
sticht nun nicht mehr:
zum Hochzeitrufer
ward er bestellt.

Hagen
(der immer sehr ernst geblieben.)
Nun lasst das Lachen,
müth'ge Mannen!
Empfangt Gunther's Braut:
Brünnhilde naht dort mit ihm.
(Er ist herabgestiegen und unter die Mannen
getreten.)
Hold seid der Herrin,
helfet ihr treu:
traf sie ein Leid,
rasch seid zur Rache!

(Gunther und Brünnhilde sind im Nachen angekommen Einige der Mannen springen in den Fluss,
und ziehen den Kahn an das Land. Während Gunther Brünnhilde an das Ufer geleitet, schlagen die
Mannen jauchzend an die Waffen. Hagen steht
zur Seite im Hintergrunde.)

The Vassals. Hail! hail!
        Welcome! welcome!
        Hail, O Gunther!
        Hail to thy bride!

Gunther
(leading Brünnhilde by the hand from the boat.)
    Brünnhilde, the rarest dame
    borne by the Rhine to you.
    There never was won
    a nobler woman.
    The Gibichungs as a race
    gained often goods from the gods;
    to high renown
    now will they rise.

The Vassals
    (clashing their weapons.)
    Hail to thee,
    glorious Gibichung!
(Brünnhilde, pale and with eyes fixed on the ground, follows Gunther, who leads her towards the hall, from which issue forth Siegfried and Gutrune attended by a train of women.)

Gunther
    (pausing with Brünnhilde before the hall.)
    All hail, my hero bold!
    All hail, beauteous sister!
    I see thee gladly beside him
    by whom as wife thou'rt won.
      Two happy couples
    here have encountered;
    Brünnhilde and Gunther,
    Gutrune and Siegfried!
(Brünnhilde, startled, raises her eyes and perceives Siegfried; she drops Gunther's hand, advances one step towards Siegfried, then recoils in horror and fixes her eyes glarily upon him.—All the others are wonderstruck.)

Men and Women. What ails her? Is she
              distraught?

Siegfried
    (goes a few steps nearer to Brünnhilde.)
    What clouds Brünnhilde's brow?

Brünnhilde
    (almost fainting.)
    Siegfried ... here? ... Gutrune! ...

Siegfried. Gunther's mild-eyed sister,
    mate to me
    as thou to him.

Brünnhilde. I? ... Gunther? ... you lie!
    I see not the light ..
(She is about to fall: Siegfried, who is nearest, supports her.)

Die Mannen.
        Heil! Heil!
        Willkommen! Willkommen!
        Heil dir, Gunther!
        Heil deiner Braut!

Gunther
(Brünnhilde an der Hand aus dem Kahn geleitend.)
    Brünnhilde, die hehrste Frau,
    bring' ich euch her zum Rhein:
    ein edleres Weib
    ward nie gewonnen!
    Der Gibichungen Geschlecht,
    gaben die Götter ihm Gunst,
    zum höchsten Ruhm
    rag' es nun auf!

Die Mannen
    (an die Waffen schlagend.)
    Heil! Heil dir, Gunther!
    Glücklicher Gibichung!
(Brünnhilde bleich, und mit zu Boden gesenktem Blicke, folgt Gunther, der sie zur Halle führt, aus welcher jetzt Siegfried und Gutrune, von Frauen begleitet, heraustreten.)

Gunther
    (mit Brünnhilde vor der Halle anhaltend.)
    Gegrüsst sei, theurer Held!
    gegrüsst, holde Schwester!
    Dich seh' ich froh zur Seite
    ihm, der zum Weib dich gewann.
      Zwei selige Paare
    seh' ich hier prangen:
    Brünnhilde—und Gunther,
    Gutrune—und Siegfried!
(Brünnhilde erschrickt, schlägt die Augen auf, und erblickt Siegfried; sie lässt Gunther's Hand fahren, geht heftig bewegt einen Schritt auf Siegfried zu, weicht entsetzt zurück, und heftet starr den Blick auf ihn.—Alle sind sehr betroffen.)

Mannen und Frauen. Was ist ihr?

Siegfried
    (geht ruhig einige Schritte auf Brünnhilde zu.)
    Was müh't Brünnhilde's Blick?

Brünnhilde
    (kaum ihrer mächtig).
    Siegfried ... hier ... ! Gutrune ..?

Siegfried. Gunther's milde Schwester,
    mir vermählt,
    wie Gunther du.

Brünnhilde. Ich ... Gunther ..? du
    lüg'st!—
    Mir schwindet das Licht ...
(Sie droht umzusinken: Siegfried, ihr zunächst, stüzt sie.)

Brünnhilde
(faintly and softly, in Siegfried's arms.)
Siegfried ... knows me not! ...

Siegfried. Gunther, see, thy wife is faint-
ing.
(Gunther approaches.)
Awaken, dame!
Here stands thy husband.
(As Siegfried points to Gunther, Brünnhilde per-
ceives the ring on his finger.)

Brünnhilde
(starting with fearful impetuosity.)
Ha! That Ring
upon his hand!
His—? Siegfried's—?

Vassals. What is it?

Hagen
(advancing from the back among the men.)
Now well attend
to the woman's tale.

Brünnhilde
(struggling to command herself and repressing
with great effort her terrific storm of emotion.)
On thy hand there
I beheld the ring:
thou hold'st it wrongly.
It was ravished
(Pointing to Gunther.)
—by this man.
What means didst thou use
the ring thus to gain?

Siegfried
(attentively inspecting the ring on his finger.)
That ring I gained,
but not from him.

Brünnhilde
(to Gunther.)
Torest thou from me the ring
with which thou'st wedded me,
then make him feel thy power:
get back the pledge again.

Gunther
(greatly perplexed.)
The ring?—I gave him nothing:
but—know'st thou this our guest?

Brünnhilde. Where guardest thou the
ring
that thou didst make me give thee?
(Gunther, much puzzled, remains silent.)

Brünnhilde
(matt und leise in Siegfried's Arme.)
Siegfried ... kennt mich nicht? ..

Siegfried. Gunther, deinem Weib ist übel!
(Gunther tritt hinzu.)
Erwache, Frau!
hier ist dein Gatte.
(Indem Siegfried auf Gunther mit dem Finger
deutet erkennt an diesem Brünnhilde den Ring.)

Brünnhilde
(mit furchtbarer Heftigkeit aufschreckend.)
Ha!—der Ring ...
an seiner Hand!
Er ... Siegfried?

Mannen und Frauen. Was ist?

Hagen
(aus dem Hintergrunde unter die Mannen tretend.)
Jetzt merket klug,
was die Frau euch klagt!

Brünnhilde
(sich ermannend, indem sie die schrecklichste
Aufregung gewaltsam zurückhält.)
Einen Ring sah ich
an deiner Hand:—
nicht dir gehört er,
ihn entriss mir
(auf Gunther deutend)
—dieser Mann!
Wie mochtest von ihm
den Ring du empfah'n?

Siegfried
(aufmerksam den Ring an seiner Hand betrachtend.)
Den Ring empfing ich
nicht von ihm.

Brünnhilde
(zu Gunther.)
Nahm'st du von mir den Ring,
durch den ich dir vermählt;
so melde ihm dein Recht,
ford're zurück das Pfand!

Gunther
(in grosser Verwirrung.)
Den Ring?—ich gab ihm keinen:
doch kennst du ihn auch gut?

Brünnhilde. Wo bärgest du den Ring,
den du von mir erbeutet?
(Gunther schweigt in höchster Betroffenheit.)

Brünnhilde
(bursting out frantically.)
Ha! this one 'twas then
that from me wrenched the ring
Siegfried, the treacherous thief.

Siegfried
(who is quite absorbed in contemplating the ring.)
No girl, I ween,
gave me that ring;
Nor woman 'twas
from whom the prize I won.
This hoop I bear
as the battle prize,
when at Hate Cave once I did strive
and destroyed the dragon so strong.

Hagen
(coming between them.)
Brünnhilde, noble dame,
know'st thou full well this ring?
If 'tis that that Gunther gained,
he owns it still,—
and Siegfried has won it by trick,
which the traitor should pay for
                    straight.

Brünnhilde
(screaming out in the most terrible anguish.)
By trick! By trick!
Shamefullest of tricks!
Deceit! deceit!
Worse than thought can conceive!

Gutrune. Deceit!

Vassals. What was the trick?

Brünnhilde.
Holy gods!
Ye heavenly guardians!
Was this indeed
your whispered will?
Grief do ye give
such as none ever grasped,
shape me a shame
no mortal has shared?
Vouchsafe revenge then
like none ever viewed,
rouse me to wrath
such as none can arrest!
Here let Brünnhilde's
heart straight be broken
if he who wronged her
may but be wrecked.

Brünnhilde
(wüthend auffahrend.)
Ha!—Dieser war es,
der mir den Ring entriss:
Siegfried, der trugvolle Dieb!

Siegfried
(der über der Betrachtung des Ringes in fernes
Sinnen entruckt war.)
Von keinem Weib
kam mir der Reif;
noch war's ein Weib,
dem ich ihn abgewann:
genau erkenn' ich
des Kampfes Lohn,
den vor Neidhöhl' einst ich bestand,
als den starken Wurm ich erschlug

Hagen
(zwischen sie tretend.)
Brünnhilde, kühne Frau!
kennst du genau den Ring?
Ist's der, den du Gunther'n gab'st,
so ist er sein,—
und Siegfried gewann ihn durch
                    Trug
den der Treulose büssen sollt'!

Brünnhilde
(in furchtbarstem Schmerz aufschreiend.)
Betrug! Betrug!
Schändlichster Betrug!
Verrath! Verrath—
Wie noch nie er gerächt!

Gutrune. Betrug?

Mannen und Frauen. An wem Verrath?

Brünnhilde.
Heilige Götter!
himmlische Lenker!
Rauntet ihr diess
in eurem Rath?
Lehrt ihr mich Leiden
Wie keiner sie litt?
Schuft ihr mir Schmach
wie nie sie geschmerzt?
Rathet nun Rache
wie nie sie geras't!
Zündet mir Zorn
wie nie er gezähmt!
Heisset Brünnhilde
ihr Herz zu zerbrechen,
den zu zertrümmern,
der sie betrog!

Gunther. Brünnhilde! my consort,
    calm thyself!

Brünnhilde. Away, thou traitor!
    Thou'rt betray'd too.
    People all, hearken:
    Not—he—
    that man yonder
    was wed to me.

Vassals. Siegfried? Gutrune's mate?

Brünnhilde. He forced delights
    of love from me.

Siegfried. Art thou so careless
    of thine honor?
    The lips, then, that revile it
    must I convict them of lying?
    Hear whether truth I broke!
    Blood-brotherhood
    I and Gunther have sworn to:
    "Needful," my goodly sword,
    guarded the oath intact:
    its edge did keep me sundered
    from this ill-omened bride.

Brünnhilde. Thou lord of deceit,
    see how thou liest!
    Little thy sword
    will serve as a proof!
    Well known to me its sharpness,
    but known too its scabbard,
    encased in which
    reposed on the wall
    "Needful," the trusty friend,
    when a true love his master did win.

The Vassals
    (crowding together in quick anger.)
    What! Has he been traitor?
    Trifled with Gunther's honor?

Gunther. Disgrace o'ertakes me,
    grossest contempt,
    if thou repliest
    not to her plea.

Gutrune. Faithless—Siegfried,
    say, art thou false?
    Attest as untrue
    what she hath told.

The Vassals. Right thyself straight,
    if thou art wronged.
    Stay her upbraidings!
    Swear us the oath.

Gunther. Brünnhilde, Gemahlin!
    Mäss'ge dich!

Brünnhilde. Weich' fern, Verräther!
    Selbst-verrath'ner!
    Wisset denn Alle!
    nicht—ihm—
    dem Manne dort
    bin ich vermählt.

Mannen und Frauen.
    Siegfried? Gutrune's Gemahl?

Brünnhilde. Er zwang mir Lust
    und Liebe ab.

Siegfried. Achtest du so
    der eig'nen Ehre?
    Die Zunge, die sie lästert,
    muss ich der Lüge sie zeihen?—
    Hört, ob ich Treue brach!
    Blutbrüderschaft
    hab' ich Gunther geschworen:
    Nothung, mein werthes Schwert,
    wahrte der Treue Eid;
    mich trennte seine Schärfe
    von diesem traurigen Weib.

Brünnhilde. Du listiger Held,
    sieh' wie du lüg'st!
    wie auf dein Schwert
    du schlecht dich beruf'st!
    Wohl kenn' ich die Schärfe,
    doch kenn' auch die Scheide,
    darin so wonnig
    ruht' an der Wand
    Nothung, der treue Freund,
    als die Traute sein Herr sich gewann.

Die Mannen
    (in lebhafter Entrüstung zusammentretend.)
    Wie? brach er die Treue!
    trübte er Gunther's Ehre?

Gunther. Geschändet wär' ich,
    schmählich bewahrt,
    gäb'st du die Rede
    nicht ihr zurück!

Gutrune. Treulos, Siegfried,
    sannest du Trug?
    Bezeuge, dass falsch
    Jene dich zeiht!

Die Mannen. Reinige dich,
    bist du im Recht:
    schweige die Klage,
    schwöre den Eid!

Siegfried. Should I refute her,
 Swearing the oath,
 which of ye war-men
 his weapon will lend?

Hagen. My unsullied spear-point
 well will I lend
 to ward in honor the oath.

(The Vassals make a ring around Siegfried and Hagen. Hagen holds out his spear; Siegfried lays two fingers of his right hand on its point.)

Siegfried. Schweig' ich die Klage,
 schwör' ich den Eid:
 wer von euch wagt
 seine Waffe daran?

Hagen. Meines Speeres Spitze
 wag' ich daran:
 sie wahr' in Ehren den Eid!

(Die Mannen schliessen einen Ring um Siegfried; Hagen hält diesem die Spitze seines Speeres hin: Siegfried legt zwei Finger seiner rechten Hand darauf.)

THE OATH ON THE SPEAR

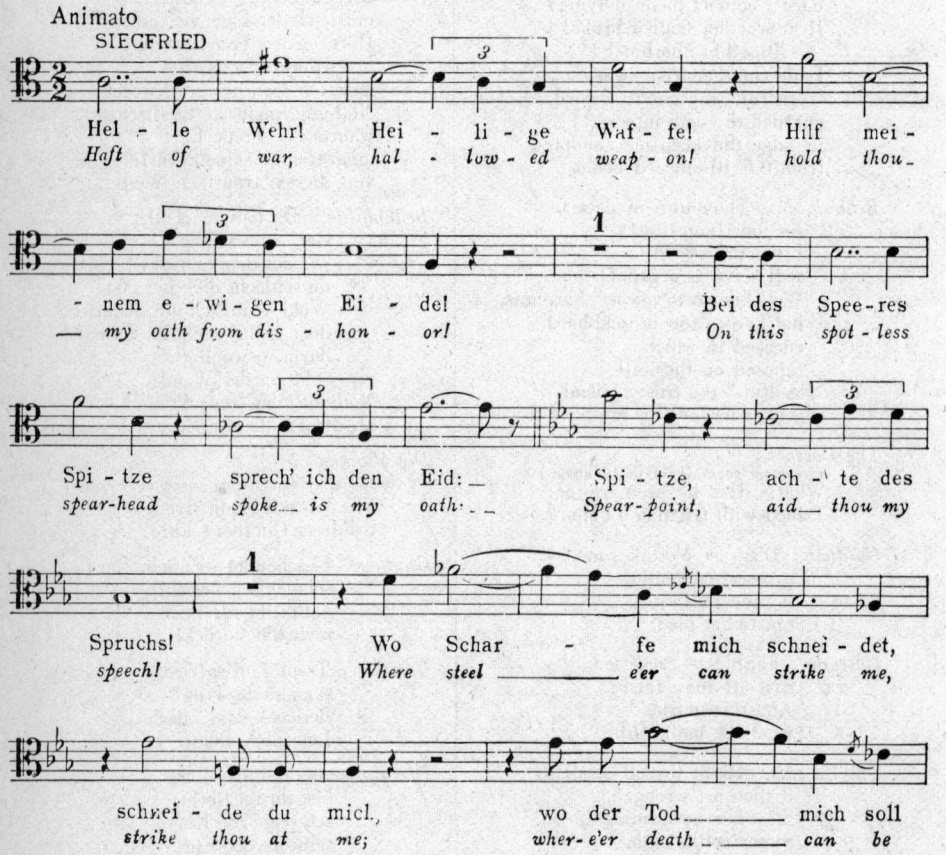

tref - fen, tref - fe du mich: klag - te das Weib dort
dealt me deal it to me· if she is real - ly

wahr, brach ich dem Bru - der den Eid!
wrong'd, 'f ___ I have in - jured my friend!

BRÜNNHILDE

Hel - le Wehr! ___ Hei - li - ge Waf - fe!
Haft of war! ___ Hal - low - ed weap - on!

Hilf mei - nem e - wi - gen Ei - de! Bei des
hold thou ___ my oath from dis - hon - or! On this

Spee - res Spi - tze sprech ich dem Eid:
spot - less spear - head I ___ speak an oath:

Spi - tze ___ ach - te des Spruchs! Ich wei -
Spear - point, ___ aid ___ thou my speech! I sanc-

- he dei - ne Wucht ___ dass sie ihn wer - fe!
- ti - fy thy strength to his de - struc - tion!

Dei - ne Schär - fe seg - ne ich,___ dass sie ihn
And I bless_____ thy blade with - al____ that it may

schnei - de! Denn brach___ sei - ne Ei - de er
blight him! For bro - ken are all of his

all, schwur Mein- eid jetzt die - ser Mann.
oaths, and per - jured now doth he - prove.

The Vassals
(in the greatest commotion.)
Help, Donner!
down with thy tempest,
to silence this terrible shame.

Siegfried. Gunther, look to thy lady,
who shapes thee shame with her lies.
Give her time and rest,
the tameless mountain maid,
until her mind's disturbance slackens
which by some demon's
deadly spite
has been drawn down on us all.
Ye vassals, scatter yourselves,
leave the women to scold!
As cowards well will we act
if 'tis a contest of words.
(He goes close up to Gunther.)
Troth! it cuts me more than thee,
that ill I did the trick;
the Tarnhelm, I suspect,
has hid me only half.
But woman's ire
waneth apace:
that I won her for thee,
one day she'll thank thee, methinks.
(Turning again to the men.)
Frolic, good fellows!
move to the feast!
Make the marriage

Die Mannen
(im höhsten Aufruhr.)
Hilf, Donner!
tose dein Wetter,
zu scbweigen die wüthende
Schmach!

Siegfried. Gunther, wehr' deinem Weibe,
das schamlos Schande dir lügt!
Gönn't ihr Weil' und Ruh',
der wilden Felsen-Frau,
dass ihre freche Wuth sich lege,
die eines Unhold's
arge List
wider uns Alle erregt!—
Ihr Mannen, kehret euch ab,
lasst das Weiber-Gekeif'!
Als Zage weichen wir gern,
gilt es mit Zungen dem Streit.
(Dicht zu Gunther tretend.)
Glaub,' mehr zürnt es mich als dich,
Dass schlecht ich sie getäuscht:
der Tarnhelm, dünkt mich fast,
hat halb mich nur gehehlt.
Doch Frauengroll
friedet sich bald:
dass dir ich es gewann
dankt gewiss noch das Weib.
(Er wendet sich wieder zu den Mannen.)
Munter, ihr Mannen!
folgt mir zum Mahl!
Froh zur Hochzeit

merry, ye maidens!
Filled with delight,
laugh as you may.
In fort and field
foremost among you
in the frolic am I.
He whom love hath blest,
let my blythesome laughter
move him to join in my joy.

(In exuberant joy he puts his arm round Gutrune
and draws her into the hall with him. The Men
and Women follow.)
(Brünnhilde, Gunther, and Hagen remain behind.—Gunther has seated himself apart, with
covered face in deep shame and depression.)

Brünnhilde
(standing in the foreground, gazes vacantly before
her.)

What infernal craft
can here be hidden?
What magician's rod
raised up this storm?
Where now my wisdom
'gainst this bewitchment?
What can all my runes do
against this riddle?
Ah sorrow! sorrow!
Woe's me! Woe's me!
He has won
all wisdom from me!
I am his maid,
held by his might;
I am his booty,
held in his bondage,
and, languished with shame and woe,
lightly he gives me away.
Whose sword shall I have to beg,
with which I may sever my bonds?

Hagen
(coming close up to her.)

Have trust in me,
betrayed dame:
and for thy wrongs
I'll wreak revenge.

Brünnhilde.   On whom?

Hagen.   On Siegfried, who hath betrayed.

Brünnhilde.   On Siegfried? thou?
(She laughs bitterly.)
One angry glance
of his glittering eyeball—
that, e'en through his fraudulent
                                  shape
fell unshadowed on me,
would subdue thy most

helfet, ihr Frau'n!—
Wonnige Lust
lache nun auf:
in Hof und Hain
heiter vor Allen
sollt ihr heute mich seh'n.
Wen die Minne freut,
meinem frohen Muthe
thu' es der Glückliche gleich!

(Er schlingt in ausgelassenem Uebermuthe seinen
Arm um Gutrune, und zieht sie mit sich in die
Halle; die Mannen und Frauen folgen ihm nach.)
(Brünnhilde, Gunther, und Hagen bleiben zurück.
Gunther hat sich, in tiefer Scham und furchtbarer
Verstimmung, mit verhülltem Gesicht abseits nieder-
gesetzt.)

Brünnhilde
(im Vordergrunde stehend und vor sich hin starrend.)

Welches Unhold's List
liegt hier verhohlen?
Welches Zaubrer's Rath
regte diess auf?
Wo ist nun mein Wissen
gegen dieses Wirrsal?
Wo sind meine Runen?
gegen diess Räthsel?
Ach Jammer! Jammer!
Weh'! ach Weh'!
All mein Wissen
wies ich ihm zu:
In seiner Macht
hält er die Magd;
in seiner Banden
hält er die Beute,
die, jamme nd ob ihrer Schmach,
jauchzend der Reiche verschenkt!—
Wer biete mir nun das Schwert,
mit dem ich die Bande zerschnitt'?

Hagen
(dicht an sie herantretend.)

Vertraue mir
betrog'ne Frau:
Wer dich verrieth,
das räche ich.

Brünnhilde.   An wem?

Hagen.   An Siegfried, der dich betrog.

Brünnhilde.   An Siegfried? . . du?
(Sie lacht bitter)
Ein einz'ger Blick
seines blitzenden Auges
—das selbst durch die Lügengestalt
leuchtend strahlte zu mir—
deinen besten Muth

mettlesome daring!

Hagen. His falsehood speeds
    my spear to his felling.

Brünnhilde. Oath and falsehood,
    futile to aid!
    Find stronger spells
    to inspire thy weapon,
   when it would strike at such
       strength!

Hagen. I mind well Siegfried's
    sovereign might,
   he scarce were mastered in battle;
    but whisper to me
    some cunning way
   to make him weak in my hands.

Brünnhilde. O thankless! shameful
       return!
    Each single art
    that once I owned
   did I lend, his life to protect.
    Unwitting, magical
    means I used,
   which safely ward him now from
       wounds.

Hagen. No blade borne in war can harm
       him?

Brünnhilde. In battle, none—yet—
   if at his back thou strike:—
    Never, I well knew
    would he retreat
   and, flying, turn it to the foeman;
   and so no spell did I set there.

Hagen. And there he shall be speared!
 (He turns quickly from Brünnhilde to Gunther.)
    Up, Gunther,
    honored Gibichung!
   Here stands thy stalwart wife:
   why hangs thy head in grief!

Gunther
    (rising sorrowfully.)
    O shame!
    O sorrow!
    Woe to me,
   the most distrest of mortals!

Hagen. That shame o'erwhelms thee
    well I grant.

Brünnhilde. O timid spouse!

machte erbangen!

Hagen. Doch meinem Speere
   spart' ihn sein Meineid?

Brünnhilde. Eid und Meineid—
    müss'ge Acht!
    Nach Stärk'rem späh',
    deinen Speer zu waffnen,
   willst du den Stärksten besteh'n!

Hagen. Wohl kenn' ich Siegfried's
    siegende Kraft,
   wie schwer im Kampf er zu fällen;
    d'rum raune nun du
    mir guten Rath,
   wie doch der Recke mir wich'?

Brünnhilde. O Undank; schändlichster
       Lohn!
    Nicht eine Kunst
    war mir bekannt,
   die zum Heil nicht half seinem Leib'!
    Unwissend zähmt' ihn
    mein Zauberspiel,
   das ihn nun vor Wunden gewahrt.

Hagen. So kann keine Wehr ihm scha-
       den?

Brünnhilde. Im Kampfe nicht:—doch—
   träf'st du im Rücken ihn.
    Niemals—das wusst' ich—
    wich' er dem Feind,
   nie reicht' er ihm fliehend den Rüc-
       ken
   an ihm d'rum spart' ich den Segen.

Hagen. Und dort trifft ihn mein Speer!
 (Er wendet sich rasch zu Gunther um.)
    Auf, Gunther!
    edler Gibichung!
   Hier steht dein starkes Weib:
   was häng'st du dort in Harm?

Gunther
   (leidenschaftlich auffahrend.)
    O Schmach!
    O Schande!
    Wehe mir
   dem jammervollsten Manne!

Hagen. In Schande liegst du—
   läugn' ich das?

Brünnhilde. O feiger Mann!

treacherous friend!
Hidden behind
the hero wert thou,
that valour's reward
his courage should win thee!
Low had sunk
thy lordliest race
when such a faint-heart was formed.

Gunther
    (bursting out into rage.)
Betrayed am I—the betrayer!
Deceived am I—the deceiver!
It cuts to my core!
It harrows my heart!
Help, Hagen!
Help for my honor!
help for my mother,
who thee also did bear.

Hagen. No head can help,
    no hand can help:—
    nought helps but—Siegfried's death!

Gunther. Siegfried's death!—

Hagen.
    Nought else saves thee from shame!

Gunther
    (staring before him horror-struck.)
    Blood-brotherhood
    surely we swore!

Hagen.
    The broken bond
    calls for his blood!

Gunther.
    Broke he the bond?

Hagen.
    When thou wert betrayed!

Gunther.
    Was I betrayed?

Brünnhilde.
    He betrayed thee;
  and I'm betrayed too on all sides!
    Barely, in truth,
    could a world of blood
  wipe from my mind your offence.
    But the death of one
    well will condone all.
    Siegfried falleth
  for sins of himself and thee.

falscher Genoss!
Hinter dem Helden
hehltest du dich,
dass Preise des Ruhmes
er dir erränge!
Tief wohl sank
das theure Geschlecht,
das solche Zagen erzeugt!

Gunther
    (ausser sich.)
Betrüger ich—und betrogen!
Verräther ich—und verrathen!—
    Zermalmt mir das Mark,
    zerbrecht mir die Brust!
    Hilf, Hagen!
    hilf meiner Ehr'!
    hilf deiner Mutter,
    die dich auch ja gebar!

Hagen. Dir hilft kein Hirn,
    dir hilft keine Hand:
    dir hilft nur—Siegfried's Tod!

Gunther. Siegfried's Tod!

Hagen.
    Nur der sühnt deine Schmach.

Gunther
    (von Grausen gepackt, vor sich hin starrend)
    Blutbrüderschaft
    schwuren wir uns!

Hagen.
    Des Bundes Bruch
    sühne nun Blut!

Gunther.
    Brach er den Bund?

Hagen.
    Da er dich verrieth!

Gunther.
    Verrieth er mich?

Brünnhilde.
    Dich verrieth er,
  und mich verriethet ihr Alle!
    Wär' ich gerecht,
    alles Blut der Welt
  büsste mir nicht eure Schuld!
    Doch des Einen Tod
    taugt mir für Alle:
    Siegfried falle—
  zur Sühne für sich und euch!

Hagen
(turning close to Gunther.)
His falling brings thee gain!
Might gigantic would be thine
by merely getting his Ring
which but death can make him
surrender.

Gunther.
Brünnhilde's Ring?

Hagen.
By Nibelungs 'twas wrought.

Gunther
(sighing deeply.)
Shall this be Siegfried's end then?

Hagen.   Aye, all demands his death.

Gunther.   But Gutrune, alas!—
unto him given!—
Slew we her glorious spouse,
could we stand before her face?

Brünnhilde
(furiously.)
What gain was my wisdom?
What were my runes good for?
Now hapless and anguished
all I behold!
Gutrune doth hold the charm
that has beguiled from me my lord
Ill light on her!

Hagen
(to Gunther.)
Lest his death grieve her deeply
we'll hide from her the deed.
We hie tomorrow
merrily hunting:
he'll boldly stray from our band—
and be brought home struck by a
boar.

Brünnhilde and Gunther.
It shall be so!
Siegfried falleth!
Soothed be the shame
which he hath shaped!
The oath of brotherhood
hath he broken:
so let his blood
blot out guilt.
All-guiding
god of revenge!
Thou witness

Hagen
(nahe zu Gunther gewendet).
Er falle—dir zum Heile!
Ungeheure Macht wird dir,
gewinn'st du von ihm den Ring,
den der Tod ihm nur entreisst.

Gunther.
Brünnhilde's Ring?

Hagen.
Des Niblungen Reif.

Gunther
(schwer seufzend).
So wär' es Siegfried's Ende!

Hagen.   Uns allen frommt sein Tod.

Gunther.   Doch Gutrune, ach!
der ich ihn gönnte:
straften den Gatten wir so,
wie bestünden wir vor ihr?

Brünnhilde
(wild auffahrend.)
Was rieth mir mein Wissen?
was wiesen mich Runen?
Im hiflosen Elend
ahnet mir's hell:
Gutrune heisst der Zauber,
der mir den Gatten entzückt!
Angst treffe sie!

Hagen
(zu Gunther)
Muss sein Tod sie betrüben,
verhehlt sei ihr die That.
Auf munt'res Jagen
ziehen wir morgen:
der Edle braus't uns voran—
ein Eber bracht' ihn da um.

Gunther und Brünnhilde.
So soll es sein!
Siegfried falle:
sühn' er die Schmach
die er mir schuf!
Eid-Treue
hat er getrogen:
mit seinem Blute
büss' er die Schuld!
Allrauner!
rächender Gott!
Schwurwissender

and lord of oaths!
Wotan! Wotan!
wilt thou give ear?
Waft now thy awful
hosts unto us,
here let them hark
to our vengeful oath!

Hagen. Thus it shall be!
Siegfried must die:
so perish he
the spirit so high!
Mine is the hoard,
my might shall soon hold it:
so of the ring
must we rob him.
Elfin parent,
thou prince deposed!
Night-keeper
Nibelung king,
Alberic! Alberic!
Up to my aid!
Warn all the Nib'lungs
anew of the might:
thou art their leader,
the Ring's true lord.

(Gunther and Brünnhilde turn hastily towards
the hall. Siegfried and Gutrune (Siegfried wear-
ing a wreath of oak leaves, Gutrune crowned w th
flowers) meet them at the entrance with their
followers. Gunther grasps Brünnhilde by the hand
and follows with her. Hagen alone remains behind.)

(The curtain falls.)

Eideshort!
Wotan! Wotan!
wende dich her!
weise dich schrecklich
heilige Schaar,
hieher zu horchen
dem Racheschwur!

Hagen. So soll es sein!
Siegfried falle:
sterb' er dahin,
der strahlende Held!
Mein ist der Hort,
mir muss er gehören:
entrissen d'rum
sei ihm der Ring!
Alben-Vater!
gefallener Fürst!
Nacht-Hüter!
Niblungen-Herr!
Alberich! Alberich!
achte auf mich!
Weise von neuem
der Niblungen Schaar,
dir zu gehorchen,
des Ringes Herrn!

(Gunther und Brünnhilde wenden sich heftig zur
Halle Siegfried und Gutrune (Siegfried mit einen
Eichenkranz, Gutrune bunte Blumen auf dem
Haupte) treten ihnen, zur Nachfolge auffordernd,
am Eingange entgegen. Gunther fasst Brünnhilde
bei der Hand, und folgt mit ihr schnell. Hagen
bleibt allein zurück.)

(Der Vorhang fällt.)

ACT THREE

Scene One

DRITTER AUFZUG

Erste Scene

TRIO OF THE RHINEDAUGHTERS

WOGLINDA, WELLGUNDA and FLOSSHILDE

Frau Son - ne sen - det lich - te Strah - len, Nacht liegt
The sun - god send - eth rays of splen - dor; Night reigns

___ in der Tie - fe. Einst war. sie hell___ da heil___ und
___ in the wa - ters. Once did ___ they beam ___ when brave and

hehr des Va - ters,　Gold noch in ihr　glänz - te　Rhein - gold,
bright our fa-ther's　gold yet in them　glit - ter'd.　Rhine - gold,

kla - res Gold!　wie　hell__ du ein - stens strahl -
clear - est gold!　how　bright - ly once thou stream -

kla - res Gold!　wie　hell__ du ein - stens strahl - test,
clear - est gold!_ how　bright - ly once thou stream - edst,

- test, heh-rer　Stern　der Tie - fe!　(Sie schliessen wieder den Schwimmreigen)
- edst, beau-teous　star　of wa - ters!　(They again form their circling dance)

heh - rer____ Stern____ der Tie - fe!　Wei - a - la - la,
beau - teous____ star____ of wa - ters!　Wei - a - la - la,

wei - a - la - la,　lei - a - lei - a, wal - la　la,_____ la
wei - a - la - la,　lei - a - lei - a, wal - la　la,_____ la

lei　la la la lei _ la la la　la_____ la
lei · la la la lei · la la la　la_____ la

lei,__ la la la lei _ la la ia　la_____ lei - la
lei__ la la la lei · la lu lu　la_____ lei la

la - - - lei, wal-la la la la　wei - a la wal-la la
la - - - lei, wal-la la la la　wei - a la wal-la la

wei - a - la___ la la wal-la-la___ la la lei - a lei - a lei - a
wei - a - la___ la la wal-la-la___ la la lei - a lei - a lei - a

lei - la la - la la
lei - la la - la la

lei___ la la___
lei___ la la___

Echo (Sie schlagen jauchzend das Wasser)
(They joyously splash the water)

Frau Son - ne,
Fair sun - god,

sen - de uns den Hel - den, der das Gold uns___ wie - der gä - be!
send to us the he - ro, who a - gain our___ gold will give us!

Liess' er___ es uns___ dein lich - tes Au - ge nei - de - ten
If it___ were ours,___ thine ar - dent eye___ no more should we

dann wir nicht län - ger! Rhein-gold! Kla - res Gold, wie
look on with en - vy! Rhine-gold! Clear - est gold, how

froh du dann strahl - - test, frei - er Stern der Tie - fe!
glad - ly wouldst stream___ then, glo-rious star of wa - ters!

froh___ du dann strahl - test, frei - er Stern___ der Tie - fe!
glad - ly wouldst stream then, glo - rious star___ of wa - ters!

(Siegfried's horn is heard on the heights)

Woglinda.　I hear his horn!

Wellgunda.　The hero comes.

Flosshilde.　Let us take counsel.
(They all dive quickly down.　Siegfried appears on
the cliff in full armor.)

Siegfried.　Some imp has tempted me on
　　until the track I have lost.—
　　Hey, rogue! what gulf in hillside
　　hast thou then rent for my game?

The three Rhine-Nymphs—
　　　　　(rising again.)
　　　Siegfried!

Flosshilde.　Why scold you so at the
　　　　　　　　ground?

Wellgunda.　With what imp are you ag-
　　　　　　　grieved?

Woglinda.　Are you annoyed by a gnome?

The Three.　Speak then, Siegfried; speak
　　　　　　　　to us!

Siegfried
　　　(looking smilingly at them.)
　　　My friend with hairy hide
　　　has fled, perchance enticed
　　　away by your tricks?
　　　If he's your lover
　　　I'll willingly leave him,
　　　wenches, with you.
　　　(The Nymphs laugh loudly.)

Woglinda.
　　　Siegfried, what boon wilt grant
　　　if we give up the booty?

Siegfried.
　　　Still I have empty hands.
　　　What is it then you would beg?

Wellgunda.　A golden ring
　　　gleams on your finger.

The three Nymphs
　　　　　(together.)
　　　Give us that.

Siegfried.　A terrific worm
　　　I slew to gain that ring;
　　　and shall it slip my palm to buy
　　　the paws of a sorry bear?

Woglinda.　Are you so mean?

(Man hört Siegfried's Horn von der Höhe her.)

Woglinda.　Ich höre sein Horn.

Wellgunda.　Der Helde naht.

Flosshilde.　Lasst uns berathen!
(Sie tauchen schnell in die Fluth.)
(Siegfried erscheint auf dem Abhange in vollen
Waffen.)

Siegfried.　Ein Albe führte mich irr',
　　dass ich die Fährte verlor:—
　　He, Schelm! in welchem Berg
　　barg'st du so schnell das Wild?

Die drei Rheintöchter
　　　　　(wieder auftauchend.)
　　　Siegfried!

Flosshilde.　Was schilt'st du in den Grund?

Wellgunda.　Welchem Alben bist du gram?

Woglinda.　Hat dich ein Nicker geneckt?

Alle Drei.　Sag'es uns, Siegfried! sag' es
　　　　　　　　uns!

Siegfried
　　　(sie lächelnd betrachtend.)
　　　Entzücktet ihr zu euch
　　　den zottigen Gesellen,
　　　der mir verschwand?
　　　Ist's euer Friedel,
　　　euch lustigen Frauen
　　　lass' ich ihn gern.
　　　(Die Mädchen lachen laut auf.)

Woglinda.　Siegfried, was giebst du uns,
　　　wenn wir das Wild dir gönnen?

Siegfried.　Noch bin ich beutelos:
　　　d'rum bittet, was ihr begehrt.

Wellgunda.　Ein gold'ner Ring
　　　ragt dir am Finger—

Die drei Mädchen
　　　　　(zusammen.)
　　　den gieb uns!

Siegfried.　Einen Riesenwurm
　　　erschlug' ich um den Ring.
　　　für des schlechten Bären Tatzen
　　　böt' ich ihn nun zum Tausch?

Woglinda.　Bist du so karg?

Wellgunda. So higgling a man?

Flosshilde. Free-handed
  mortals fare best with maids.

Siegfried. For wasting my goods on you
  my wife would be rightly wroth.

Flosshilde. Is she so strict?

Wellgunda. She strikes you perhaps?

Woglinda. He has felt already her fist!
  (They laugh.)

Siegfried. Well, make your merry jest!
  in grief must you be left:
  fair Nymphs, the yearned for Ring
  I'll yield up never to you!

Flosshilde. So fair!

Wellgunda. So fierce!

Woglinda. So meet for love!

The Three
    (together.)
  Unfortunate he's miserly!
  (They laugh and dive down.)

Siegfried
  (descending more towards the ground.)
  Is't meet to bear
    their idle mocks?
  Must I thus be shamed?
    If they would show
    near the shore again
  the Ring I would relinquish.
  Hey, hey, ye merry
    water-maidens:
  Arise! I'll give ye the Ring!

The three Rhine-Nymphs
  (diving up again now solemn and grave.)
  Preserve it still
    and ward it well
  until the illhap is read
  that in thy Ring lies hid;
  full fain then thou'lt be
  if from the ban thou art freed.

Siegfried
  (quietly replacing the ring on his finger.)
  Then sing me what ye wis.

Wellgunda. So geizig beim Kauf?

Flosshilde. Freigebig
  solltest Frauen du sein.

Siegfried. Verzehrt' ich an euch mein
      Gut,
  dess' zürnte mir wohl mein Weib.

Flosshilde. Sie ist wohl schlimm?

Wellgunda. Sie schlägt dich wohl?

Woglinda. Ihre Hand fühlt schon der
      Held!
  (Sie lachen.)

Siegfried. Nun lacht nur lustig zu!
  in Harm lass' ich euch doch:
  denn giert ihr nach dem Ring
  euch Neckern geb' ich ihn nie.

Flosshilde. So schön!

Wellgunda. So stark!

Woglinda. So gehrenswerth!

Die Drei
      (zusammen.)
  Wie Schade, dass er geizig ist!
  (Sie lachen und tauchen unter.)

Siegfried
  (tiefer in den Grund hinabsteigend.)
  Was leid' ich doch
    das karge Lob?
  Lass' ich so mich schmäh'n?—
    Kämen sie wieder
    zum Wasserrand,
  den Ring könnten sie haben.—
    He he! ihr munt'ren
    Wasserminnen!
  kommt rasch: ich schenk' euch den
      Ring!

Die drei Rheintöchter
  (tauchen wieder auf, und zeigen sich ernst und
      feierlich.)
  Behalt' ihn, Held,
    und wahr' ihn wohl,
  bis du das Unheil räth'st,
  das in dem Ring du heg'st.
  Froh fühl'st du dich dann,
  befrei'n wir dich von dem Fluch.

Siegfried
  (gelassen den Ring wieder ansteckend.)
  Nun singet was ihr wisst!

The Rhine-Nymphs
    (severally and together.)
    Siegfried! Siegfried! Siegfried!
    Sorrow waits thee we know.
      To nought but ill
      thou wardest the Ring.
      It was wrought from gold
      that in Rhine once glowed:
      he who shaped it with labor
      and lost it in shame,
      laid a curse on it,
      to cause that to
      all time its possesser
      should be slain.
      As the Worm has fallen,
      thou'llt fall thyself,
      this very day
      —we vouch it to thee—
    if thou refuse us the Ring
    that in the flood we may hide it.
      Nought but this stream
      breaketh the spell!

Siegfried.   Untrustworthy sisters,
      talk no more!
    Scarce I trust your allurements;
    and your threats still less can disturb
          me.

The Rhine-Nymphs. Siegfried! Siegfried!
      'Tis truth that we tell—
    Turn thee! turn from the ban!
      The braiding Nornir
      wove it by night-time
      in their endless rope
      of wonderful runes.

Siegfried.   My sword once splintered a
           spear:
      this woven rope
      of wonderful runes,
      if they have bound
      within it a curse,
    "Needful" shall cut for the Nornir!
      The Worm of this danger
      did tell me once,
    but he taught me not how to fear.
      The world's wealth
      should be won me by a ring:
      for a gaze of love
      gladly I'd leave it,
    I'd let you have't lightly for love.

Die Rheintöchter
    (einzeln und zusammen.)
    Siegfried! Siegfried! Siegfried!
    Schlimmes wissen wir dir.
      Zu deinem Unheil
      wahr'st du den Ring!
      Aus des Rheines Gold
      ist der Ring geglüht:
      der ihn listig geschmiedet
      und schmählich verlor,
      der verfluchte ihn,
      in fernster Zeit
      zu zeugen den Tod
      dem, der ihn trüg'.
      Wie den Wurm du fälltest,
      so fällst auch du,
      und heute noch
      so heissen wir dir's;
    tauschest den Ring du uns nicht,
    im tiefen Rhein ihn zu bergen.
      Nur seine Fluth
      sühnet den Fluch!

Siegfried.   Ihr listigen Frauen
      lass't das sein!
    Traut' ich kaum eurem Schmeicheln,
    euer Schrecken trügt mich noch
          minder

Die Rheintöchter. Siegfried! Siegfred!
      Wir weisen dich wahr:
    weiche! weiche dem Fluch!
      Ihn flochten nächtlich
      webende Nornen
      in des Urgesetzes
      ewiges Seil.

Siegfried.   Mein Schwert zerschwang einen
           Speer:
      des Urgesetzes
      ewiges Seil,
      flochten sie wilde
      Flüche hinein,
    Nothung zerhaut es den Nornen!
      Wohl warnte mich einst
      vor dem Fluch ein Wurm,
    doch das Fürchten lehrt' er mich
          nicht!—
      der Welt Erbe
      gewann mir ein Ring:
      für der Minne Gunst
      miss' ich ihn gern—
    ich geb' ihn euch, gönnt ihr mir
          Gunst,

If you threaten my limbs, though,
and life,
hardly you'll win
from my hand the ring,
e'en were it worth not a rush.
For limbs and life
—should without love
they be fettered
in fear's strong bonds,
My limbs and my life
see!—so
freely I'd fling away!

(He has picked up a clod of earth, which he holds
up and with the last words, flings behind him.)

The Rhine-Nymphs. Come, sisters,
speed from this dullard!
He fancies himself
as fearless and wise
as he truly is trammelled and blind.
He has sworn oaths
and heeded them not;
Runes he knows well
and reads them not.
A noble gift
once did he gain,
that it is wasted
wots he not.
But the ring, which will deal him
death,
that ring he wishes to ward still.
Farewell, Siegfried!
A stately woman
to-day your hoop will inherit.
Our bidding better she'll do:
to her! to her! to her!

(They swim away singing.)

Siegfried
(looks after them smiling.)
Alike on land and water,
women's ways I've learnt to know.
The man who resists their smiles
they seek by threats to frighten.
And when these both are scorned
they bait him with bitter words.
And yet—
were Gutrune not my wife,
I must have promptly captured
one of those pretty maids.

(Calls of hunting horns approaching are heard
on the hills. Siegfried answers gaily on his own
horn.)
(Gunther, Hagen and Vassels come down the
hills during the following.)

Hagen
(still on the heights.)
Hoiho!

Doch bedroh't ihr mir Leben und
Leib:
fasste er nicht
eines Finger's Werth—
den Reif entringt ihr mir nicht!
Denn Leben und Leib
—sollt' ohne Lieb'
in der Furcht Bande
bang ich sie fesseln—
Leben und Lieb'—
seht!—so
werf' ich sie weit von mir!

(Er hat eine Erdscholle vom Boden aufgehoben
und mit den letzten Worten sie über sein Haupt
hinter sich geworfen.)

Die Rheintöchter. Kommt, Schwestern!
schwindet dem Thoren!
So stark und weise
wähnt er sich,
als gebunden und blind er ist.
Eide schwur er—
und achtet sie nicht;
Runen weiss er—
und räth sie nicht;
ein hehrstes Gut
ward ihm gegönnt—
dass er's verworfen
weiss er nicht:
nur den Ring, der zum Tod ihm
taugt—
den Reif nur will er sich wahren!
Leb' wohl, Siegfried!
Ein stolzes Weib
wird heut' noch dich Argen beerben:
sie beut uns bess'res Gehör
Zu ihr! Zu ihr! Zu ihr!

(Sie schwimmen singend davon.)

Siegfried
(sieht ihnen lächelnd nach.)
Im Wasser wie am Lande
lernt' ich nun Weiberart:
wer nicht ihrem Schmeicheln traut,
den schrecken sie mit Drohen;
wer dem nun kühnlich trotzt,
dem kommt dann ihr Keifen d'ran.
Und doch—
trüg' ich nicht Gutrun' Treu',
der zieren Frauen eine
hätt' ich mir frisch gezähmt!

(Jagdhornrufe kommen von der Höhe näher;
Siegfried antwortet lustig auf seinem Horne.)
(Gunther, Hagen und Mannen kommen wäh-
rend des Folgenden von der Höhe herab.)

Hagen
(noch auf der Höhe.)
Hoiho!

Siegfried. Hoiho!

The Vassals. Hoiho! Hoiho!

Hagen.   Have we at last then
            found where thou hidest?

Siegfried. Come below! Here 'tis fresh
                        and cool.

Hagen.   'Twill do to rest
            and dress us a meal.
            Lay down your booty
            and bring out the wine-skins.

(Game is stacked, skins of wine and drinking
horns are produced. All encamp themselves.)

Hagen.   You drove away our quarry,
            let's see the wondrous prize then
            that Siegfried seized upon.

Siegfried
            (laughing.)
            Ill is it with my meal;
            I fain must beg
            your bags to furnish me.

Hagen.   Thou bootyless?

Siegfried. To wood-hunt I went forth,
            but water-fowl only could find:
            had I only reckoned rightly,
            three wild young water-maids
            I well might have won this morning,
            who sang in the Rhine their warning,
            ere wane of day I should die.

Gunther
            (starts and looks gloomily at Hagen.)

Hagen.   A dismal chase were that,
            if the hunter, luckless still,
            by lurking beasts were laid low.

Siegfried. I'm thirsty.
(He has seated himself between Hagen and Gunther. Filled drinking-horns are handed to them.)

Hagen.   I've heard asserted, Siegfried,
            that what the song-birds speak of
            thou straightly canst tell.
            Is truth in the tale?

Siegfried. Their prattle long
            I have put from my mind.
(He drinks and then offers his horn to Gunther.)
            Drink, Gunther, drink:
            thy brother brings it thee.

Siegfried. Hoiho!

Die Mannen. Hoiho! Hoiho!

Hagen.   Finden wir endlich
            wohin du flog'st?

Siegfried. Kommt herab! hier ist's frisch
                        und kühl.

Hagen.   Hier rasten wir
            und rüsten das Mahl.
            Lasst ruh'n die Beute
            und bietet die Schläuche!

(Jagdbeute wird zu Hauf gelegt; Trinkhörner und
Schläuche werden hervorgeholt. Dann lagert sich
alles.)

Hagen.   Der uns das Wild verscheucht,
            nun sollt' ihr Wunder hören
            was Siegfried sich erjagt.

Siegfried
            (lachend.)
            Schlimm steht's um mein Mahl:
            von eurer Beute
            bitt' ich für mich.

Hagen. Du beutelos?

Siegfried. Auf Waldjagd zog ich aus,
            doch Wasserwild zeigte sich nur;
            war ich dazu recht berathen,
            drei wilde Wasservögel,
            hätt' ich euch gefangen,
            die dort auf dem Rhein mir sangen,
            erschlagen würd' ich noch heut'.

Gunther
            (erschrickt und blickt düster auf Hagen.)

Hagen.   Das wäre böse Jagd,
            wenn den Beutelosen selbst
            ein lauernd Wild erlegte!

Siegfried. Mich dürstet!
(Er hat sich zwischen Hagen und Gunther gelagert; gefüllte Trinkhörner werden ihnen gereicht.)

Hagen. Ich hörte sagen, Siegfried,
            der Vögel Sanges-Sprache
            verstündest du wohl:
            so wär' das wahr?

Siegfried. Seit lange acht' ich
            des Lallens nicht mehr.
(Er trinkt und reicht dann sein Horn Gunther.)
            Trink', Gunther! trink'!
            dein Bruder bringt es dir.

Gunther
(gazing thoughtfully and gloomily into the horn.)
> The wine is weak and blanched:
> Thy blood alone is here!

Siegfried
    (laughing.)
> Let mingle mine with thine then.
(He pours out of Gunther's horn into his own,
    so that it overflows.)
> Now flows the mixture over:
>   to mother Earth
> let it be an offering!

Gunther
    (sighing.)
> Thou over-joyous heart!

Siegfried
    (softly to Hagen.)
> He feels Brünnhilde's frown.

Hagen.   His spouse he scarce can read
> as thou the wood-bird's song.

Siegfried.
> Since hearing the songs of women
> I heed not the birds o'erhead.

Hagen.   They once were known to thee?

Siegfried.   Hey, Gunther,
>   gloom-ridden man!
> If 'twill amuse
> I'll song thee some marvellous
> matters of my boyhood.

Gunther.   With all my heart.

Hagen.   So sing to us!
(All ensconce themselves on the ground about
Siegfried who alone sits upright while the others
recline more.)

Siegfried.   Mimi hight
>   a mannikin grim,
> who in nought but greed
> granted me care,
> to count on me,
> when manful I'd wax'd,
> in the wood to slay a worm,
> which long had hidden there a hoard.
>   He trained me to smith's work
>   and metal smelting;
>   but what the teacher
>   could not attempt
>   the pupil did
>   by daring and patience,

Gunther
(gedankenvoll und schwermüthig in das Horn blickend.)
> Du mischtest matt und bleich:—
> dein Blut allein darin!

Siegfried
    (lachend.)
> So misch' es mit dem deinen!
(Er giesst aus Gunther's Horn in das seine, so
    dass es überläuft.)
> Nun floss gemischtes über:
>   der Mutter Erde
> lass' das ein Labsal sein!

Gunther
    (seufzend.)
> Du überfroher Held!

Siegfried
    (leise zu Hagen.)
> Ihm macht Brünnhilde Müh?

Hagen.   Verstünd' er sie so gut,
> wie du der Vögel Sang!

Siegfried.   Seit Frauen ich singen hörte,
> vergass ich der Vöglein ganz.

Hagen.   Doch einst vernahmst du sie?

Siegfried.   Hei! Gunther!
>   grämlicher Mann!
> Dank'st du es mir,
> so sing' ich dir Mären
> aus meinen jungen Tagen.

Gunther.   Die hör' ich gern.

Hagen.   So singe, Held!
(Alle lagern sich nahe um Siegfried, welcher allein auf recht sitzt, während die andern tiefer gestreckt liegen.)

Siegfried.   Mime hiess
>   ein mürrischer Zwerg;
> in des Neides Zwang
> zog er mich auf,
> dass einst das Kind,
> wann kühn es erwuchs,
> einen Wurm ihm fällt im Wald,
> der lang' schon hütet' einen Hort.
>   Er lehrte mich schmieden
>   und Erze schmelzen:
>   doch was der Künstler
>   selbst nicht konnte,
>   des Lehrling's Muthe
>   musst' es gelingen—

so that from shattered steely splin-
                              ters
whole I smithied a sword.
   My father's blade
   freshly I knit.
   Now a fair
   weapon was "Needful!"
   meet 'twas for fight,
   Mimi declared,
and fared with me t'ward the wood;
I felled there Fafnir, the Worm.
   Pray now attend
   well to my tale;
wonders truly I tell of.
   When his welling blood
   did blister my finger;
the flesh I cooled in my mouth:
   scarce touched the wet
   to the tip of my tongue
when what the birds were singing
at once my brain perceived.
On a branch one settled and sang:
   "Hey! Siegfried shall hold now
   the Nibelung's hoard;
   he'll find in the hollow
   the hoard anon!
Were he the Tarnhelm to win,
   it would tide him through the won-
                              derful tasks;
but were he the Ring too to ravish
'twould give him the ward of the
                              world."

Hagen.   Ring and Tarnhelm
   took'st thou away!

One Vassal.   And what else did the bird
   sing thee?

Siegfried.   Ring and Tarnhelm
   holding in reach,
I once more harked
to the heavenly warbler,
who sat on high there and sang:
   "Hey! Siegfried doth hold now
   the helm and the ring:
   O trust not in Mimi,
   the treacherous elf!
Himself would have handled the
                              hoard,
so below there he lieth in wait;
for thy life he's trying, O Siegfried—
then trust not, Siegfried, in Mimi!"

Hagen.   Admonished it well?

eines zerschlag'nen Stahles Stücken
neu zu schweissen zum Schwert.
   Des Vater's Wehr
   fügt' ich mir neu;
   nagelfest
   schuf ich mir Nothung,
   tüchtig zum Kampf
   dünkt' er dem Zwerg:
der führte mich nun zum Wald;
dort fäll't ich Fafner, den Wurm.
   Jetzt aber merkt
   wohl auf die Mär':
Wunder muss ich euch melden.
   Von des Wurmes Blut
   mir brannten die Finger;
sie führt' ich kühlend zum Mund:
   kaum netzt' ein wenig
   die Zunge das Nass,
was da die Vöglein sangen
das konnt' ich flugs versteh'n:
Auf Aesten sass es und sang—
   „Hei, Siegfried gehört nun
   der Niblungen Hort:
   o fänd' in der Höhle
   den Hort er jetzt!
Wollt' er den Tarnhelm gewinnen,
   der taugt' ihm zu wonniger That:
doch möcht' er den Ring sich errathen.
   der macht' ihn zum Walter der Welt."

Hagen.   Ring und Tarnhelm
   trug'st du nun fort?

Die Mannen.   Das Vöglein hörtest du
   wieder?

Siegfried.   Ring und Helm
   hatt' ich gerafft;
   da lauscht' ich wieder
   dem wonnigen Laller;
der sass im Wipfel und sang:
   „Hei, Siegfried gehört nun
   der Niblungen Hort:
   o traute er Mime,
   dem treulosen, nicht!
Ihm sollt' er den Hort nur erheben;
nun lauert er listig am Weg:
nach dem Leben trachtet er Siegfried:
o traute Siegfried nicht Mime!"

Hagen.   Es mahnte dich gut?

The Vassals.   And what didst to Mimi?

Siegfried.   With death-dealing drink
he drew to my side,
pale and stamm'ring,
he showed his vile purpose:
"Needful" settled the scamp.

Hagen
(laughing.)
The blade he could forge not
fell upon Mimi!

The Vassals.   And told the birds other
tidings?

Hagen
(who has squeezed the juice of an herb into the
horn.)
Drink first, hero,
from my horn:
I mingled a herb with the draught
to awaken and hold thy remembrance,
that past things may be apparent!

Siegfried
(after he has drunk.)
In grief through the boughs
I gazed up aloft,
where still he sat and sang;
"Hey! Siegfried has slain now
the sinister dwarf!
I wot he may gain
the loveliest wife;
in loftly fastness she sleeps,
fire doth emborder the spot;
o'erstepped he the blaze—
wakened the bride—
Brünnhilde were then his own!"

Hagen.   Obeyedst thou
the bird's instruction?

Siegfried.   Straight without pause
I passed on my way,
and I fared to the fire-girt rock.
The furnace was stepped
through,
the prize was found:
sleeping, a marvellous maid
in suit of mirror-like mail.
The helm soon
from her head I unloosed,
she quickly waked to my kiss;
O then how glowingly embraced me
Brünnhilde's glorious arm!

Die Mannen.   Vergaltest du Mime?

Siegfried.   Mit tödtlichem Tranke
trat er zu mir;
bang und stotternd
gestand er mir Böses:
Nothung streckte den Strolch.

Hagen
(lachend.)
Was nicht er geschmiedet
schmeckte doch Mime!

Die Mannen.
Was wies das Vöglein dich wieder?

Hagen
(nachdem er den Saft eines Krautes in das Trinkhorn ausgedruckt.)
Trink' erst, Held,
aus meinem Horn:
ich würzte dir holden Trank.
die Erinnerung hell dir zu wecken,
dass Fernes nicht dir entfalle!

Siegfried
(nachdem er getrunken.)
In Lied zum Wipfel
lausch' ich hinauf;
da sass es noch und sang:
„Hei, Siegfried erschlug nun
den schlimmen Zwerg!
Jetzt wüsst' ich ihm noch
das herrlichste Weib:—
auf hohem Felsen sie schläft,
ein Feuer umbrennt ihren Saal;
durchschritt' er die Brunst,
erweckt' er die Braut,
Brünnhilde wäre dann sein!"
(Gunther hört mit wachsendem Erstaunen zu.)

Hagen.   Und folgtest du
des Vögleins Rath?

Siegfried.   Rasch ohne Zögern
zog ich da aus,
bis den feurigen Fels ich traf;
die Lohe durchschritt ich,
und fand zum Lohn—
schlafend ein wonniges Weib
in lichter Waffen Gewand.
Den Helm löst' ich
der herrlichen Maid;
mein Kuss erwachte sie kühn!—
o wie mich brunstig da umschlang
der schönen Brünnhilde Arm!

Gunther. What say'st thou?

(Two ravens fly from a bush, circle over Siegfried and fly away over the Rhine).

Hagen. Canst read the speech
of those ravens aright?

(Siegfried starts up quickly and looks after the ravens, turning his back towards Hagen.)

Hagen. Revenge they rouse in me!

(He thrusts his spear into Siegfried's back, Gunther catches his arm, too late)

Gunther and the Men. Hagen what deed
is this?

(Siegfried swings his shield aloft with both hands to crush Hagen with it; his strength leaves him; the shield falls back and he himself falls upon it).

Hagen

(pointing at the prostrate figure.)

Retribution!

(He turns coolly away and gradually disappears over the hills where his retreating form is for some time visible. Gunther, siezed with anguish, bends down by Siegfried's side. The Men gather in sympathy round the dying man.

Dusk commences to fall with the apparition of the ravens.)

Siegfried

(once more opens his glaring eyes and begins with solemn voice.)

Brünnhilde!
Heavenly bride!
Look up! Open thine eyelids!
What hath sunk thee
once more in sleep?
Who drowns thee in slumber so
drear?
The wak'ner came,
his kiss awoke;
again now the bride's
bonds he has broken;
enchant him Brünnhilde's charms!
Ah! now for ever
open her eyelids!
Ah! and what od'rous
breeze is her breath!
Thrice blessed ending—
thrill that dismays not!
Brünnhilde beckons to me!

(He dies.)

(The Vassals raise Siegfried's body on his shield and bear it away over the height in mournful procession. Gunther follows at a little distance.)

(The moon breaks through the clouds and illuminates with increasing brightness the distant train. —Mists rise up from the Rhine and gradually fill the whole stage up to the front. When after a while they again disperse, the scene is changed.)

Gunther. Was hör' ich!

(Zwei Raben fliegen aus einem Busche auf, kreisen über Siegfried, und fliegen davon.)

Hagen. Erräth'st du auch
dieser Raben Geraun'?

(Siegfried fährt heftig auf, und blickt, Hagen den Rücken wendend, den Raben nach.)

Hagen. Rache riethen sie mir!

(Er stösst seinen Speer in Siegfried's Rücken: Gunther fällt ihm—zu spät—in den Arm.)

Gunther und die Mannen. Hagen! was thu'st du?

(Siegfried schwingt mit beiden Händen seinen Schild hoch empor, Hagen damit zu zerschmettern: die Kraft verlässt ihn, der Schild entsinkt seiner Hand; er selbst stürzt krachend über ihm zusammen.)

Hagen

(auf den zu Boden gestreckten deutend.)

Meineid rächt' ich!

(Er wendet sich ruhig zur Seite ab, und verliert sich dann einsam über die Höhe, wo man ihn langsam von dannen schreiten sieht.—Gunther beugt sich schmerzergriffen zu Siegfried's Seite nieder. Die Mannen umstehen theilnahmvoll den Sterbenden. Lange Stille der tiefsten Erschütterung.)

(Dämmerung ist bereits mit der Erscheinung der Raben eingebrochen.)

Siegfried

(noch einmal die Augen glanzvoll aufschlagend, mit feierlicher Stimme beginnend.)

Brünnhilde!
heilige Braut!
wach' auf! öffne dein Auge!
Wer verschloss dich
wieder in Schlaf?
wer band dich in Schlummer so
bang?
Der Wecker kam;
er küsst dich wach,
und aber der Braut
bricht er die Bande:—
da lacht ihm Brünnhilde's Lust!—
Ach, dieses Auge,
ewig nun offen!
ach, dieses Athems
wonniges Wehen!
Süsses Vergehen—
seliges Grauen!
Brünnhild' bietet mir Gruss!

(Er stirbt.)

(Die Mannen erheben die Leiche auf den Schild, und geleiten sie in feierlichem Zuge über die Felsenhöhe langsam von dannen. Günther folgt der Leiche zunächst.—)

(Der Mond bricht durch die Wolken hervor, und beleuchtet auf der Höhe den Trauerzug.—Dann steigen Nebel aus dem Rheine auf, und erfüllt allmälig die ganze Bühne bis nach vornen.—Sobald sich dann die Nebel wieder zertheilen, ist die Scene verwandelt).

### Third Scene	### Dritte Scene

<table>
<tr>
<td>

Third Scene

(The Hall of the Gibichungs with the river bank, as in the first Act.—Night. Moonlight glittering on the Rhine.)

(Gutrune enters the Hall from her chamber.)

Gutrune.

　　Was that his horn?
　　　　(Listens.)
　　No!—not
　　yet is he home.—
　　Sombre visions
　　startled me from sleep.
　　His horse
　　I heard wildly neigh:
　　Brünnhilde's laughter
　　awakened my sense.
　　What woman was't
　　I saw descend the bank but now?
　　I fear this Brünnhilde!
　　Is she still here?
(Listens at the door at right and calls softly.)
　　Brünnhilde! Brünnhilde!
　　art thou awake?
(Opens the door tremblingly and looks in.)
　　Bare is the room.
　　It was then she
　　that to the Rhine I saw descend?
(She starts and listens to a distant sound.)
　　Was that his horn?
　　Nay!
　　Nought neareth!—
　　If he only would come!
(She is about to return to her room, but hears Hagen's voice, pauses, and remains awhile motionless, transfixed by fear.)

Hagen's
　　(voice without approaching).
　　Hoiho! Hoiho!
　　Wake up! wake up!
　　Torches! torches!
　　Lighted brands here!
　　Fair booty
　　bring we along.
　　Hoiho! Hoiho!
(Lights and increasing glow of fires without.)

Hagen
　　　　(entering the hall.)
　　Up! Gutrune,
　　and greet your Siegfried!
　　the stalwart hero
　　is coming home.
(Men and Women with lights and firebrands conduct, in great confusion, the train with Siefgried's body. Gunther is among them.)

</td>
<td>

Dritte Scene

(Die Halle der Gibichungen mit dem Uferraume, wie im ersten Aufzuge.—Nacht. Mondschein spiegelt sich im Rhein.)

(Gutrune tritt aus ihrem Gemach in die Halle heraus.)

Gutrune. War das sein Horn?
　　　　(Sie lauscht.)
　　Nein!—noch
　　kehrt er nicht heim.—
　　Schlimme Träume
　　störten mir den Schlaf!—
　　Wild hört ich
　　wiehern sein Ross:—
　　Lachen Brünnhilde's
　　weckte mich auf.——
　　Wer war das Weib,
　　das zum Rhein ich schreiten sah?—
　　Ich fürchte Brünnhild'!—
　　ist sie daheim?
(Sie lauscht an einer Thüre rechts, und ruft dann leise.)
　　Brünnhild'! Brünnhild'!
　　bist du wach?—
(Sie öffnet schüchtern und blickt hinein.)
　　Leer das Gemach!
　　so war es sie,
　　die zum Rhein ich schreiten sah?
(Sie erschrickt und lauscht nach der Ferne.)
　　Hört' ich sein Horn?
　　Nein!—
　　Oede alles!—
　　Säh' ich Siegfried nur bald!
(Sie will sich wieder ihrem Gemache zuwenden, als sie jedoch Hagen's Stimme vernimmt, hält sie an, und bleibt, von Furcht gefesselt, eine Zeit lang unbeweglich stehen.)

Hagen's
　　(Stimme von aussen sich nähernd.)
　　Hoiho! Hoiho!
　　Wacht auf! wacht auf!
　　Lichte! Lichte!
　　helle Brände!
　　Jagdbeute
　　bringen wir heim.
　　Hoiho! Hoiho!
(Licht und wachsender Feuerschein von aussen.)

Hagen
　　　　(in die Halle tretend.)
　　Auf! Gutrun'!
　　begrüsse Siegfried!
　　Der starke Held,
　　er kehret heim.
(Mannen und Frauen begleiten, mit Lichtern und Feuerbränden, in grosser Verwirrung den Zug der mit Siegfried's Leiche Heimkehrenden, unter denen Gunther.)

</td>
</tr>
</table>

Gutrune

(in great terror.)

What is this, Hagen?
I heard not his horn!

Hagen.

The bloodless hero
blows it no more;
he'll bound to the chase
or battle no more,
nor fight for the fairest of women!

Gutrune

(with increasing dread.)

What do they bring?

Hagen.

A wild boar's ill-fated victim:
Siegfried—'tis thy husband's corpse.

(Gutrune starts up and precipitates herself upon
the body which has been set down in the middle of
the hall. General emotion and grief.)

Gunther

(bending over her senseless form and striving to
raise her).

Gutrune! lovely sister!
lift up thine eyes—
speak unto me!

Gutrune

(reviving.)

Siegfried!—Siegfried is slaughtered!

(Thrusts Gunther away)

Hence, treacherous brother!
Assassin of my Siegfried!
O help me! help me!
Horror! Horror!
My husband's murdered among ye!

Gunther. Give no reproach to me!
reproach thou rather Hagen.
He is the wild boar so hateful
by whom our hero has bled.

Hagen. Art thou then wroth with me?

Gunther. Ill and anguish
rend thee forever!

Hagen

(stepping forward in terrible defiance.)

Well then! — 'tis I that have slain
him!
I—Hagen—
smote him to death!
He was spoil unto my spear,
on which false oath he spake.
Holiest booty right
here to me should be rendered:
I claim to have then this Ring.

Gutrune

(in grosser Angst.)

Was geschah', Hagen?
nicht hört' ich sein Horn!

Hagen. Der bleiche Held,
nicht bläs't er's mehr;
nicht stürmt er zum Jagen,
zum Streit nicht mehr,
noch wirbt er um wonnige Frauen!

Gutrune

(mit wachsendem Entsetzen).

Was bringen die?

Hagen. Eines wilden Ebers Beute:
Siegfried: deinen todten Mann!

(Gutrune schreit auf, und stürzt über die Leich
hin, welche in der Mitte der Halle niedergesetzt ist
—Allgemeine Erschütterung und Trauer.)

Gunther

(indem er die Ohnmächtige aufzurichten sucht.)

Gutrune! holde Schwester!
Hebe dein Aug'!
schweige mir nicht!

Gutrune

(weider zu sich kommend.)

Siegfried!—Siegfried erschlagen!

(Sie stösst Gunther heftig zurück.)

Fort! treuloser Bruder!
du Mörder meines Mannes!
O Hilfe! Hilfe!
Wehe! Wehe!
Sie haben Siegfried erschlagen!

Gunther. Nicht klage wider mich!
dort klage wider Hagen:
er ist der verfluchte Eber,
der diesen Edlen zerfleischt.

Hagen. Bist du mir gram darum?

Gunther. Angst und Unheil
greife dich immer!

Hagen

(mit furchtbarem Trotze herantretend.)

Ja denn! ich hab' ihn erschlagen
ich—Hagen—
schlug ihn zu todt!
Meinem Speer war er gespart,
bei dem er Meineid sprach.
Heiliges Beute-Recht
hab' ich mir nun errungen:
d'rum fordr' ich hier diesen Ring.

Gunther. Aroint! thou ne'er shalt clutch
what I for mine declare.

Hagen. Ye vassals, speak on my side!

Gunther. Seek'st thou for Gutrune's
dowry,
spawn of the dwarfish stock?

Hagen
(drawing his sword.,
The dwarf's own dower
thus—his son assumes
(He rushes on Gunther who defends himself:
they fight. The Men throw themselves between.
Gunther falls dead by a stroke of Hagen.)

Hagen. Now the ring!
(He snatches at Siegfried's hand. It raises it-
self threateningly. General terror. Gutrune and
Women shriek aloud.)
(From the back appears Brünnhilde, who ad-
vances with firm and solemn tread to the front.)

Brünnhilde
(still at the back.)
Peace with your surge
of sorrow that peals.
Ye betrayed his wife vilely:
for revenge now hath she come.
(She quietly advances.)
Children I heard
crying to their mother,
to say that milk has been spilled:
but nought I marked
a fitting lament
for the highest hero's fate.

Gutrune
(raising herself suddenly.)
Brünnhilde, hurt by baseness,
thou broughtest on us this harm:
'tis thou didst stir the men to kill him.
Woe the day thou camest hither!

Brünnhilde.
Nay, poor soul, peace!
Thou never wert wife of his:
thou ownedst him
only in name.
'Tis I was his honored spouse.
The oath of our union was sworn,
ere Siegfried thy face had seen!

Gutrune
(in an outburst of poignant despair.)
Accursed Hagen!
Woe's me! woe's me!
Thou gav'st the hateful philtre
to make her husband play false!
O sorrow! sorrow!
I see it all now!

Gunther. Zurück! was mir verfiel
sollst du nimmer empfah'n.

Hagen. Ihr Mannen, richtet mein Recht!

Gunther. Rühr'st du an Gutrun's Erbe,
schamloser Albensohn?

Hagen
(sein Schwert ziehend.)
Des Alben Erbe
fordert so sein Sohn!
(Er dringt auf Gunther ein; dieser wehrt sich:
sie fechten. Die Mannen werfen sich dazwischen.
Gunther fällt von einen Streiche Hagen's todt darnieder.)

Hagen. Her den Ring!
(Er greift nach Siegfried's Hand; diese hebt sich
drohend empor. Allgemeines Entsetzen. Gutrune
und die Frauen schreien laut auf.)
(Vom Hintergrunde her schreitet Brünnhilde fest
und feierlich dem Vordergrunde zu)

Brünnhilde
(noch im Hintergrunde.)
Schweigt eures Jammers
jauchzenden Schwall!
Das ihr alle verriethet,
zur Rache schreitet sein Weib.
(Sie schreitet ruhig weiter vor.)
Kinder hört' ich
greinen nach der Mutter,
da süsse Milch sie verschüttet:
doch nicht erklang mir
würdige Klage,
des höchsten Helden werth.

Gutrune.
Brünnhilde! Neid-erbos'te!
du brachtest uns diese Noth!
Die du ihm die Männer verhetztest,
weh', dass dem Haus du genah't!

Brünnhilde.
Armselige, schweig'!
Sein Eheweib warst du nie:
als Buhlerin nur
bandest du ihn.
Sein Mannes-Gemahl bin ich,
der er ewige Eide schwur,
eh' Siegfried je dich ersah.

Gutrune
(in heftigster Verzweiflung.)
Verfluchter Hagen!
Weh! ach weh!
dass du das Gift mir riethest,
das ihr den Gatten entrückt!
O Jammer! Jammer!
wie jäh nun weiss ich,

Brünnhilde was his true-love,
whom he betrayed by that draught.

(Filled with shame, she turns from the body
Siegfried and bends almost dying over Gunther's
body; she remains thus motionless to the end. Long
silence.)

(Hagen stands leaning defiantly on his spear and
shield, sunk in gloomy meditation, at the extreme
opposite side.)

Brünnhilde

(alone in the centre: after remaining long
absorbed in the contemplation of Siegfried, first
convulsed with horror, then overpowered by grief,
she turns with solemn exultation to the people.)

Friends, let fitting
funeral pyre
be reared by the river here.
Hot and high
kindle the flames,
to consume the corse
of him who was hero o'er all!—
His steed bring to me here;
to its master straight it shall bear
          me:
for my body burneth
to share in the honor
that here we show unto him.
Obey Brünnhilde's will.

(The young men erect, during the following, a
huge funeral pyre before the Hall on the bank of
the Rhine; women adorn it with drapery, on which
they strewn flowers and herbs.)

Brünnhilde

(again becoming absorbed in gazing on Siegfried's dead face.)

What sunny light
outstreams from his look!
The truest was he,
yet could betray!
His wife deluding
—leal to friendship—
from his own true lady,
—only belov'd—
he shut himself with his sword.—
Nobler than he
swore fealty never;
prouder than he
held no man a promise;
love pure as his
lived not in hero;
and yet ev'ry oath made,
ev'ry assurance,
the sheerest affection,—
sure none broke like he!—
Ween ye why that was!
Ye gods who guard
our gages for ever,
turn not away

dass Brünnhild' die Traute war,
die durch den Trank er vergass!

(Sie wendet sich voll Scheu von Siegfried ab, und
beugt sich in Schmerz aufgelös't über Gunther's
Leiche: so verbleibt sie regungslos bis an das Ende.
—Langes Schweigen.)

(Hagen steht, auf Speer und Schild gelehnt, in
finsteres Sinnen versunken, trotzig auf der äussersten anderen Seite.)

Brünnhilde

(allein in der Mitte: nachdem sie lange, zuerst
mit tiefer Erschütterung, dann mit fast überwälti-
gender Wehmuth das Angesicht Siegfried's betrachtet, wendet sie sich mit feierlicher Erhebung an
die Männer und Frauen.)

Starke Scheite
schichtet mir dort
am Rande des Rhein's zu Hauf:
hoch und hell
lod're die Gluth,
die den edlen Leib
des hehrsten Helden verzehrt!—
Sein Ross führet daher,
dass mit mir dem Recken es folge:
denn des Helden heiligste
Ehre zu theilen
verlangt mein eig'ner Leib.—
Vollbringt Brünnhilde's Wort!

(Die jüngeren Männer errichten während des
Folgenden vor der Halle nahe am Rheinufer, einen
mächtigen Scheithaufen. Frauen schmücken ihn
mit Decken; auf die sie Kräuter und Blumen
streuen.)

Brünnhilde

(von neuem in den Anblick der Leich eversunken.)

Wie Sonne lauter
strahlt mir sein Licht;
der Reinste war er,
der mich verrieth!
Die Gattin trügend
—treu dem Freunde—
von der eig'nen Trauten
—einzig ihm theuer—
schied er sich durch sein Schwert.—
Aechter als er
schwur keiner Eide;
treuer als er
hielt keiner Verträge:
laut'rer als er
liebte kein And'rer:
und doch alle Eide,
alle Verträge,
die treueste Liebe—
trog keiner wie er!—
Wisst ihr wie das ward!
O ihr, der Eide
ewige Hüter!
lenkt eu'ren Blick

from my waxing distress,
but gaze on our endless disgrace!
Hear my wild lament,
thou mightiest god!
Because he dared a great deed,
which was dear to thy hopes,
how couldst thou thus
throw upon him
'he curse to which thou succumbest?
Ought I
to be harmed by my hero,
that wise a woman should wax?—
Ween I now what thou wouldst?—
All things, all things,
all I wot now:
all at once is made clear!
Even thy ravens
I hear rustling:
to tell the longed-for tidings,
let them return to their home.
Rest thee! Rest thee, O God!

(She signs to the men to take up Siegfried's body and place it on the funeral pyre; then she takes from his finger the Ring.)

Redeemed, my hand
holdeth my dower.
Thou fatal round!
fearfullest Ring!
my hand folds thee
to hurl thee afar.
Ye water-dwelling
wary sisters,
the Rhine's fair sinuous daughters,
my thanks ye reap for your rede.
What ye would gain
I give to you;
out from my ashes
take it for ever!
The red flame that burneth me
cleanses the Ring from its curse:
ye in the Rhine
melt it away
and merely preserve
the metal bright,
whose theft has thrown you in grief.

(She turns to the back, where Siegfried's body lies already on the pyre, and takes a huge fire-brand from a man.)

Fly home, ye ravens!
rede it in Vallhalla
what here on the Rhine ye have
heard!
To Brünnhilde's rock
go round about,
Yet Loki burns there:

auf mein blühendes Leid:
erschaut eu're ewige Schuld!
Meine Klage hör',
du hehrster Gott!
Durch seine tapferste That,
dir so tauglich erwünscht,
weihtest du den,
der sie gewirkt,
dem Fluche, dem du verfielest,
mich musste
der Reinste verrathen,
dass wissend würde ein Weib!—
Weiss ich nun was dir frommt?—
Alles! Alles!
Alles weiss ich:
alles ward mir nun frei!
Auch deine Raben
hör' ich rauschen:
mit bang ersehnter Botschaft
send' ich die beiden nun heim.
Ruhe! Ruhe, du Gott!

(Sie winkt den Mannen, Siegfried's Leiche aufzuheben, und auf das Scheitgerüste zu tragen; zugleich zieht sie von Siegfried's Finger den Ring).

Mein Erbe nun
nehm' ich zu eigen.
Verfluchter Reif!
furchtbarer Ring!
dein Gold fass' ich,
und geb' es nun fort.
Der Wassertiefe
weise Schwestern,
des Rheines schwimmende Töchter,
euch dank' ich redlichen Rath!
Was ihr begehrt,
geb' ich euch:
aus meiner Asche
nehmt es zu eigen!
Das Feuer, das mich verbrennt,
rein'ge den Ring vom Fluch:
ihr in der Fluth
löset ihn auf,
und lauter bewahrt
das lichte Gold,
den strahlenden Stern des Rhein's,
der zum Unheil euch geraubt.

(Sie wendet sich nach hinten, wo Siegfried's Leiche bereits auf dem Gerüste ausgestreckt liegt, und entreiss einem Manne den mächtigen Feuerbrand.)

Fliegt heim, ihr Raben!
raun't es eurem Herrn.
was hier am Rhein ihr gehört!
An Brünnhild's Felsen
fahret vorbei:
der dort noch lodert,

Vallhall' bid him revisit!
  Draweth near in gloom
  the Dusk of the gods.
Thus, casting my torch,
  I kindle Vallhalla's tow'rs.

(She thrusts the torch into the pile, which rapidly kindles. Two ravens fly up from the rocks on the bank and disappear at the back.)

(Two young men bring in the horse; Brünnhilde takes it and quickly unbridles it.)

Grani, my horse,
  greet thee again!
Wouldst thou know, dear friend,
  what journey we follow?
By flame illumined
  lies there thy lord,
Siegfried, the star of my life.
To meet with thy master
  neighest thou merrily?
Lo! how the flame
  doth leap and allure thee!
Feel how my breast too
  hotly doth burn;
sparkling fireflame
  my spirit enfolds.
O, but to clasp him—
  recline in his arms!
in madd'ning emotion
  once more to be his!
Heiajaho! Grani!
  Greet we our hero!
Siegfried! Siegfried! see!
sweetly greets thee thy wife!

(She leaps wildly on to the horse and takes it with one bound into the burning pyre. The flames instantly blaze up and fill the entire space before the hall, seeming even to seize on the building. In terror the women cower towards the front. Suddenly the fire falls together, leaving only a mass of smoke which collects at back and forms a cloud bank on the horizon. The Rhine swells up mightily and sweeps over the fire. On the surface appear the three Rhine-daughters, swimming close to the fire-embers. Hagen who has watched Brünnhilde's proceedings with increasing anxiety, is much alarmed on the appearance of the Rhine-daughters. He flings away hastily his spear, shield and helmet, and madly plunges into the flood crying:

The ring's my right!

(Woglinda and Wellgunda twine their arms round his neck and draw him thus down below. Flosshilde swimming before the others to the back, holds the recovered ring joyously up.)

(Through the cloud-bank on the horizon breaks an increasing red glow. In its light the Rhine is seen to have returned to its bed and the nymphs are circling and playing with the ring on the calm waters.)

(From the ruins of the half-burnt hall the men and women perceive with awe the light in the sky, in which now appears the hall of Vallhalla, where the gods and heroes are seen sitting together, as described by Valtrauta in the first Act. Bright flames seize on the abode of the gods; and when this is completely enveloped by them, the curtain falls.)

weiset Loge nach Walhall!
  Denn der Götter Ende
  dämmert nun auf;
so werf' ich den Brand
  in Walhall's prangende Burg.

(Sie schleudert den Brand in den Holzstoss, der sich schnell hell entzündet. Zwei Raben sind vom Ufer aufgeflogen, und verschwinden nach dem Hintergrunde zu.)

(Zwei junge Männer führen das Ross herein; Brünnhilde fasst es, und entzäumt es schnell.)

Grane, mein Ross,
  sei mir gegrüsst!
Weisst du, Freund,
  wohin ich dich führe?
Im Feuer, leuchtend,
  liegt dort dein Herr,
Siegfried, mein seliger Held.
  dem Freunde zu folgen
  wieherst du freudig?
Lockt dich zu ihm
  die lachende Lohe?
Fühl' meine Brust auch,
  wie sie entbrennt:
helles Feuer
  das Herz mir erfasst,
ihn zu umschlingen,
  umschlossen von ihm,
in mächtigster Minne
  vermählt ihm zu sein!—
Heiajaho! Grane!
  grüsse deinen Herrn!
Siegfried! Siegfried! Sieh!
Selig grüsst dich dein Weib!

(Sie hat sich stürmisch auf das Ross geschwungen, und sprengt es mit einen Satze in den brennenden Scheithaufen. Sogleich steigt prasselnd der Brand hoch auf so dass das Feuer den ganzen Raum vor der Halle erfüllt, und diese selbst schon zu ergreifen scheint. Entsetzt drängen sich die Frauen nach dem Vordergrunde. Plötzlich bricht das Feuer zusammen, so dass nur noch eine düstere Gluthwolke über der Stätte schwebt; diese steigt auf und zertheilt sich ganz, der Rhein ist vom Ufer her mächtig angeschwollen, und wälzt seine Fluth über die Brandstätte bis an die Schwelle der Halle. Auf den Wogen sind die drei Rheintöchter herbeigeschwommen.—Hagen, der seit dem Vorgange mit dem Ringe in wachsender Angst Brünnhilden's Benehmen beobachtet hat, geräth beim Anblicke der Rheintöchter in höchsten Schreck; er wirft hastig Speer, Schild und Helm von sich ab, und stürzt wie wahnsinnig mit dem Rufe:

Zurück vom Ringe!

sich in die Fluth. Woglinda und Wellgunda umschlingen mit ihren Armen seinen Nacken, und ziehen ihn so zurückschwimmend mit sich in die Tiefe; Flosshilde, ihnen voran, hält jubelnd den gewonnenen Ring in die Höhe.—Am Himmel bricht zugleich von fern her eine, dem Nordlicht ähnliche röthliche Gluth aus, die sich immer weiter und stärker verbreitet. Die Männer und Frauen schauen in sprachloser Erschütterung dem Vorgange und der Erscheinung zu.)

(Der Vorhang fällt.)

TRISTAN AND ISOLDE

TRISTAN AND ISOLDE

ACT I

Tristan, a valiant Cornish knight, is bringing Isolda, princess of Ireland, over as a bride for his uncle, King Mark. He is himself in love with her, but owing to a blood feud between them, forces himself to conceal his passion. Isolda, in anger at his seeming unkindness, attempts to poison herself and him, but her attendant, Brangæna, changes the draft for a love potion, which enflames their passion beyond power of restraint.

ACT II

Isolda has been wedded to King Mark, but holds stolen interviews with Tristan, during one of which they are surprised, for Tristan has been betrayed by a jealous friend, Melot. Touched by King Mark's bitter reproaches, Tristan provokes Melot to fight and suffers himself to be mortally wounded.

ACT III

Tristan's faithful servant, Kurvenal, has carried his wounded master to his native home in Brittany, where he is carefully tended. Isolda has also been sent for, as being skilled above all others in the healing art. The excitement of her approach only hastens Tristan's death, and he breathes his last sigh in her arms. Mark has followed Isolda: he has had matters explained, and is prepared to reunite the lovers, but it is too late. Isolda utters her lament over the body of her lover, and her heart breaks: in death alone are they united.

TRISTAN AND ISOLDE

ACT I

*[A pavilion erected on the deck of a ship, richly hung
with tapestry, quite closed in at back at first. A
narrow hatchway at one side leads below into the
cabin.]*

SCENE I

*[Isolda on a couch, her face buried in the cushions.
—Brangæna holding open a curtain, looks over the
side of the vessel.]*
THE VOICE OF A YOUNG SAILOR (*from above as if at
the mast-head*).

ERSTE AKT

*[Zeltartiges Gemach auf dem Vorderdeck eines See-
schiffes, reich mit Teppichen behangen, beim Beginn
nach dem Hintergrunde zu gänzlich geschlossen; zur
Seite führt eine schmale Treppe in den Schiffsraum
hinab.]*

ERSTE SCENE

*[Isolde auf einem Ruhebett, das Gesicht in die Kissen
gedrückt. — Brangäne, einen Teppich zurückgeschlagen haltend, blickt zur Seite über Bord.]*
STIMME EINES JUNGEN SEEMANNES (*aus der Höhe wie
vom Maste her, vernehmbar*).

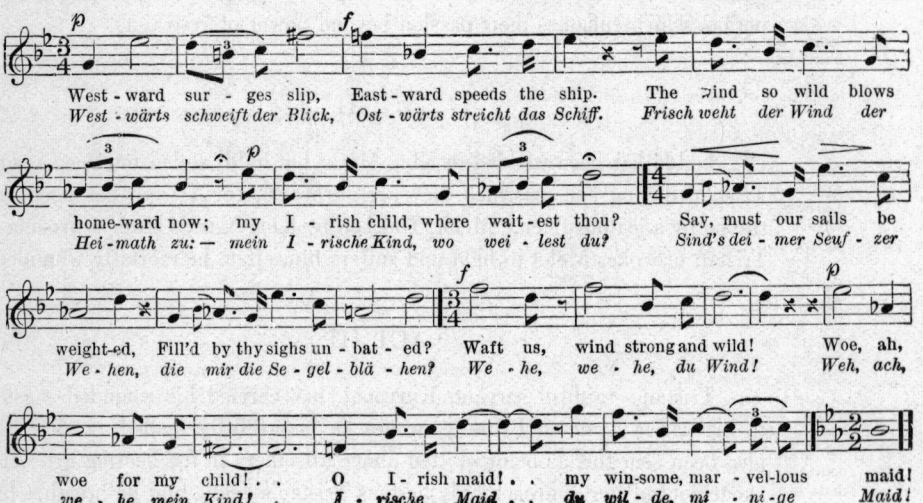

West - ward sur - ges slip, East - ward speeds the ship. The wind so wild blows
West - wärts schweift der Blick, Ost - wärts streicht das Schiff. Frisch weht der Wind der

home-ward now; my I - rish child, where wait-est thou? Say, must our sails be
Hei - math zu:— mein I - rische Kind, wo wei - lest du? Sind's dei - mer Seuf - zer

weight-ed, Fill'd by thy sighs un - bat - ed? Waft us, wind strong and wild! Woe, ah,
We - hen, die mir die Se - gel - blä - hen? We - he, we - he, du Wind! Weh, ach,

woe for my child!.. O I - rish maid!.. my win-some, mar - vel-lous maid!
we - he, mein Kind! . I - rische Maid .. du wil - de, mi - ni - ge Maid!

ISOLDA (*starting up suddenly*).
  What wight dares insult me?
    (*She looks round in agitation.*)
  Brangæna, ho!
  Say, where sail we?

BRANGÆNA (*at the opening*).
  Bluish stripes
  are stretching along the west;
  swiftly sails
  the ship to shore;
  if restful the sea by eve
  we shall readily set foot on land

ISOLDA. What land?

BRANGÆNA. Cornwall's verdant strand.

ISOLDE (*jäh auffahrend*).
  Wer wagt mich zu höhnen?—
    (*Sie blickt verstört um sich*).
  Brangäne, du?—
  Sag', wo sind wir?

BRANGÆNE (*an der Oeffnung*).
  Blaue Streifen
  stiegen im Westen auf;
  sanft und schnell
  segelt das Schiff;
  auf ruhiger See vor Abend
  erreichen wir sicher das Land.

ISOLDE. Welches Land?

BRANGÆNE. Kornwall's grünen Strand.

ISOLDA. Never more!
    To-day nor to-morrow!
BRANGÆNA. What mean you, mistress? say!
    (*She lets the curtain fall and hastens to* ISOLDA.)

ISOLDA (*with wild gaze*).
    A fainthearted child,
    false to thy fathers!
    Ah, where, mother,
    hast given thy might
    that commands the wave and the tempest?
    O subtle art
    of sorcery,
    for mere leech-craft followed too long!
    Awake in me once more,
    power of will!
    Arise from thy hiding
    within my breast!
    Hark to my bidding,
    fluttering breezes!
    Arise and storm
    in boisterous strife!
    With furious rage
    and hurricane's hurdle
    waken the sea
    from slumbering calm;
    rouse up the deep
    to its devilish deeds!
    Shew it the prey
    which gladly I proffer!
    Let it shatter this too daring ship
    and enshrine in ocean each shred!
    And woe to the lives!
    Their wavering death-sighs
    I leave to ye, winds, as your lot.
BRANGÆNA (*in extreme alarm and concern for* ISOLDA).

    Out, alas!
    Ah, woe!
    I've ever dreaded some ill!—
    Isolda! mistress!
    Heart of mine!
    What secret dost thou hide?
    Without a tear
    thou'st quitted thy father and mother,
    and scarce a word
    of farewell to friends thou gavest;
    leaving home thou stood'st,
    how cold and still!
    pale and speechless
    on the way,
    food rejecting,
    reft of sleep,
    stern and wretched,
    wild, disturbed;
    how it pains me
    so to see thee!
    Friends no more we seem,
    being thus estranged.
    Make me partner
    in thy pain!
    Tell me freely
    all thy fears!
    Lady, thou hearest,
    sweetest and dearest;
    if for true friend you take me,
    your confidant O make me!
ISOLDA. Air! air!
    or my heart will choke!
    Open! open there wide!

(BRANGÆNA *hastily draws the centre curtains apart.*)

ISOLDE. Nimmermehr!
    Nicht heut', nicht morgen!
BRANGÆNE. Was hör' ich? Herrin! Ha!
    (*Lässt den Vorhang zufallen, und eilt bestürzt zu*
    ISOLDE.)

ISOLDE (*wild vor sich hin*).
    Entartet' Geschlecht,
    unwerth der Ahnen!
    Wohin, Mutter,
    vergabst du die Macht,
    über Meer und Sturm zu gebieten?
    O zahme Kunst
    der Zauberin,
    die nur Balsamtränke noch brau't!
    Erwache mir wieder,
    kühne Gewalt,
    herauf aus dem Busen,
    wo du dich barg'st!
    Hört meinen Willen,
    zagende Winde!
    Heran zu Kampf
    und Wettergetös',
    zu tobender Stürme
    wüthendem Wirbel!
    Treibt aus dem Schlaf
    dies träumende Meer,
    weckt aus dem Grund
    seine grollende Gier;
    zeigt ihm die Beute,
    die ich ihm biete;
    zerschlag' es, dies trotzige Schiff,
    des zerschellten Trümmer verschling's!
    Und was auf ihm lebt,
    den wehenden Athem,
    den lass' ich euch Winden zum Lohn!
BRANGÆNE (*im äussersten Schreck, um* ISOLDE *sich
    bemühend*).
    Weh'! O weh'!
    Ach! Ach!
    Des Übels, das ich geahnt!—
    Isolde! Herrin!
    Theures Herz!
    Was barg'st du mir so lang'?
    Nicht eine Thräne
    weintest du Vater und Mutter;
    kaum einen Gruss
    den Bleibenden botest du:
    von der Heimath scheidend
    kalt und stumm,
    bleich und schweigend
    auf der Fahrt,
    ohne Nahrung,
    ohne Schlaf,
    wild verstört,
    starr und elend,—
    wie ertrugs ich's
    so dich sehend,
    nichts dir mehr zu sein,
    fremd vor dir zu steh'n?
    O, nun melde
    was dich müh't!
    Sage, künde
    was dich quält.
    Herrin Isolde,
    trauteste Holde!
    soll sie werth sich dir wähnen,
    vertraue nun Brangänen!
ISOLDE. Luft! Luft!
    Mir erstickt das Herz.
    Öffne! Öffne dort weit!

(BRANGÆNE *zieht eilig die Vorhänge in der Mitte aus
    einander.*)

SCENE II

[*The whole length of the ship is now seen, down to the
stern, with the sea and horizon beyond. Round the
mainmast sailors are ensconced, busied with ropes;
beyond them in the stern are groups of knights and
attendants, also seated; a little apart stands* TRISTAN
*folding his arms and thoughtfully gazing out to sea;
at his feet* KURVENAL *reclines carelessly. From the
mast-head above is once more heard the voice of the*
YOUNG SAILOR.]

THE YOUNG SAILOR (*at the mast-head invisible*).
    The wind so wild
    blows homewards now;
    my Irish child,
    where waitest thou?
    Say, must our sails be weighted,
    filled by thy sighs unbated?
    Waft us, wind strong and wild!
    Woe, ah woe for my child!

'SOLDA (*whose eyes have at once sought* TRISTAN *and
fixed stonily on him—gloomily*).
    Once beloved—
    now removed—
    brave and bright,
    coward knight!—
    Death-devoted head!
    Death-devoted heart!—
        (*laughing unnaturally*).
    Think'st highly of yon minion?

BRANGÆNA (*following her glance*).
    Whom mean'st thou?

ISOLDA. There, that hero
    who from mine eyes
    averts his own:
    in shrinking shame
    my gaze he shuns—
    Say, how hold you him?

BRANGÆNA. Mean you Sir Tristan,
    lady mine?
    Extolled by ev'ry nation,
    his happy country's pride,
    The hero of creation,—
    whose fame's so high and wide?

ISOLDA (*jeeringly*).
    In shrinking trepidation
    his shame he seeks to hide,
    While to the king, his relation,
    he brings the corpse-like bride!—
    Seems it so senseless
    what I say?
    Go ask himself,
    our gracious host,
    dare he approach my side?
    No courteous heed
    or loyal care
    this hero t'wards
    his lady turns;
    but to meet her his heart is daunted,
    this knight so highly vaunted!
    Oh! he wots
    well the cause!
    To the traitor go,
    bearing his lady's will!
    As my servant bound,
    straightway should he approach.

ZWEITE SCENE

[*Man blickt dem Schiff entlang bis zum Steuerbord, über
dem Bord hinaus auf das Meer und den Horizont. Um
den Hauptmast in der Mitte ist Seevolk, mit Tauen
beschäftigt, gelagert; über sie hinaus gewahrt man
am Steuerbord Ritter und Knappen, ebenfalls gelagert; von ihnen etwas entfernt* TRISTAN, *mit versch-
ränkten Armen stehend, und sinnend in das Meer
blickend; zu Füssen ihm, nachlässig ausgestreckt,*
KURWENAL.—*Vom Maste her, aus der Höhe, vernimmt
man wieder den Gesang des* JUNGEN SEEMANNS.]

DER JUNGE SEEMAN (*Auf dem Maste, unsichtbar*).
    Frisch weht der Wind
    der Heimath zu:—
    mein irisch Kind,
    wo weilest du?
    Sind's deiner Seufzer Wehen,
    die mir die Segel blähen?—
    Wehe! Wehe, du Wind
    Weh'! Ach wehe, mein Kind!

ISOLDE (*deren Blick sogleich* TRISTAN *fand, und starr
auf ihm geheftet bleibt, dumpf für sich*).
    Mir erkoren,—
    mir verloren,—
    heer und heil
    kühn und feig—;
    Tod geweihtes Haupt!
    Tod geweihtes Herz!—
        (*unheimlich lachend*)
    Was hällst von dem Knechte?

BRANGÆNE (*ihrem Blicke folgend*).
    Wen meinst du?

ISOLDE. Dort den Helden,
    Der meinem Blick
    den seinen birgt,
    in Scham und Scheue
    abwärts schaut:—
    sag', wie dünkt er dich!

BRANGÆNE. Frägst du nach Tristan,
    theure Frau,
    dem Wunder aller Reiche,
    dem hochgepries'nen Mann,
    dem Helden ohne Gleiche,
    des Ruhmes Hort und Bann?

ISOLDE (*sie verhöhnend*).
    Der zagend vor dem Streiche
    sich flüchtet wo er kann,
    weil eine Braut er als Leiche
    für seinen Herrn gewann!—
    Dünkst es dich dunkel,
    mein Gedicht?
    Frag' ihn denn selbst,
    den freien Mann,
    ob mir zu nah'n er wagt?
    Der Ehren Gruss
    und zücht'ge Acht
    vergisst der Herrin
    der zage Held,
    dass ihr Blick ihn nur nicht erreiche—
    den Kühnen ohne Gleiche!
    O, er weiss
    wohl warum!—
    Zu dem Stolzen geh',
    meld' ihm der Herrin Wort:
    meinem Dienst bereit
    schleunig soll er mir nah'n.

BRANGÆNA. Shall I beseech him
  to attend thee?
ISOLDA. Nay, order him:
  pray, understand it:—
  I, Isolda
  do command it!

[*At an imperious sign from* ISOLDA BRANGÆNA *withdraws and timidly walks along the deck towards the stern, past the working sailors.* ISOLDA, *following her with fixed gaze, sinks back on the couch, where she remains seated during the following, her eyes still turned sternward.*]

KURVENAL (*observing* BRANGÆNE'S *approach, plucks* TRISTAN *by the robe without rising*).
  Beware, Tristan!
  Message from Isolda!
TRISTAN (*starting*). What is't?—Isolda?—
(*He quickly regains his composure as* BRANGÆNA *approaches and curtsies to him.*)
  What would my lady?
  I her liegeman,
  fain will listen
  while her loyal
  woman tells her will.
BRANGÆNA. My lord, Sir Tristan,
  Dame Isolda
  would have speech
  with you at once.
TRISTAN. Is she with travel worn?
  The end is near:
  nay, ere the set of sun
  sight we the land.
  All that your mistress commands me,
  trust me, I shall mind.
BRANGÆNA. That you, Sir Tristan,
  go to her,—
  this is my lady's wish.
TRISTAN. Where yonder verdant meadows
  in distance dim are mounting,
  wait my sov'reign
  for his mate:
  to lead her to his presence
  I'll wait upon the princess:
  'tis an honor
  all my own.
BRANGÆNA. My lord, Sir Tristan,
  list to me:
  this one thing
  my lady wills,
  that thou at once attend her,
  there where she waits for thee.
TRISTAN. In any station
  where I stand
  I truly serve but her,
  the pearl of womanhood.
  If I unheeding
  left the helm,
  how might I pilot her ship
  in surety to King Mark?
BRANGÆNA. Tristan, my master,
  why mock me thus?
  Seemeth my saying
  obscure to you?
  list to my lady's words:
  thus, look you, she hath spoken:
  "Go order him,
  and understand it,
  I—Isolda—
  do command—it.

BRANGÆNE. Soll ich ihn bitten,
  dich zu grüssen?
ISOLDE. Befehlen liess'
  dem Eigenholde
  Furcht der Herrin
  ich, Isolde.

[*Auf* ISOLDE'S *gebieterischen Wink entfernt sich* BRANGÆNE, *und schreitet das Deck entlang dem Steuerbord zu, an den arbeitenden Seeleuten vorbei.* ISOLDE, *mit starrem Blicke ihr folgend, zieht sich rücklings nach dem Ruhebett zurück, wo sie während des Folgenden bleibt, das Auge unabgewandt nach dem Steuerbord gerichtet.*]

KURWENAL (*der* BRANGÆNE *kommen sieht, zupft, ohne sich zu erheben,* TRISTAN *am Gewande*).
  Hab' Acht, Tristan!
  Botschaft von Isolde.
TRISTAN (*auffahrend*). Was ist?—Isolde?—
(*Er fasst sich schnell, als* BRANGÆNE *vor ihm anlangt und sich verneigt.*)
  Von meiner Herrin?—
  Ihr gehorsam
  was zu hören
  meldet höfisch
  mir die traute Magd?
BRANGÆNE. Mein Herre Tristan,
  dich zu sehen
  wünscht Isolde,
  meine Frau.
TRISTAN. Grämt sie die lange Fahrt,
  die geht zu End';
  eh' noch die Sonne sinkt,
  sind wir am Land:
  was meine Frau mir befehle,
  treulich sei's erfüllt.
BRANGÆNE. So mög' Herr Tristan
  zu ihr gehn:
  das ist der Herrin Will'.
TRISTAN. Wo dort die grünen Fluren
  dem Blick noch blau sich färben,
  harrt mein König
  meiner Frau:
  zu ihm sie zu geleiten
  bald nah' ich mich der Lichten;
  Keinem gönnt' ich
  diese Gunst.
BRANGÆNE. Mein Herre Tristan,
  höre wohl:
  deine Dienste
  will die Frau,
  dass du zur Stell' ihr nahtest,
  dort wo sie deiner harrt.
TRISTAN. Auf jeder Stelle
  wo ich steh',
  getreulich dien' ich ihr,
  der Frauen höchster Ehr'.
  Liess' ich das Steuer
  jetzt zur Stund',
  wie lenkt' ich sicher den Kiel
  zu König Marke's Land?
BRANGÆNE. Tristan, mein Herre,
  was höhnst du mich?
  Dünkt dich nicht deutlich
  die thör'ge Magd,
  hör' meiner Herrin Wort!
  So, hiess sie, sollt' ich sagen:—
  befehlen liess'
  dem Eigenholde
  Furcht der Herrin
  sie, Isolde.

KURVENAL (*springing up*). May I an answer make her?

TRISTAN. What wouldst thou wish to reply?

KURVENAL. This should she say
 to Dame Isold':
 "Though Cornwall's crown
 and England's isle
 for Ireland's child he chose,
 his own by choice
  she may not be;
 he brings the king his bride.
 A hero-knight
 Tristan is hight!
 I've said, nor care to measure
 your lady's high displeasure."

[*While* TRISTAN *seeks to stop him, and the offended* BRANGÆNA *turns to depart,* KURVENAL *sings after her at the top of his voice, as she lingeringly withdraws.*]

 "Sir Morold toiled
  o'er mighty wave
 the Cornish tax to levy;
 In desert isle
  was dug his grave,
 he died of wounds so heavy.
 His head now hangs
  in Irish lands,
 Sole were-gild won
  at English hands.
 Bravo, our brave Tristan!
 Let his tax take who can!"

[KURVENAL, *driven away by* TRISTAN'S *chidings, descends into the cabin.* BRANGÆNA *returns in discomposure to* ISOLDA, *closing the curtains behind her, while all the men take up the chorus and are heard without.*]

KNIGHTS AND ATTENDANTS. "His head now hangs
  in Irish lands,
  sole were-gild won
  at English hands.
 Bravo, our brave Tristan!
 Let his tax take who can!"

SCENE III

[ISOLDA *and* BRANGÆNA *alone, the curtain being again completely closed.* ISOLDA *rises with a gesture of despair and wrath.* BRANGÆNA *falls at her feet.*]

BRANGÆNA. Ah! an answer
 so insulting!

ISOLDA (*checking herself on the brink of a fearful outburst*). How now? of Tristan?
 I'd know if he denies me.

BRANGÆNA. Ah! question not!

ISOLDA. Quick, say without fear!

BRANGÆNA. With courteous phrase
 he foiled my will.

ISOLDA. But when you bade him hither?

BRANGÆNA. When I had straightway
 bid him come,
 wher'eer he stood,
 he said to me,
 he truly served but thee,
 the pearl of womanhood;
  if he unheeded
  left the helm
 how could he pilot the ship
 in surety to King Mark?

KURWENAL (*aufspr*). Darf ich die Antwort sagen
 ingend?

TRISTAN. Was wohl erwiedertest du?

KURWENAL. Das sage ich
 Der Frau Isold'.—
 Wer Kornwall's Kron'
 und England's Erb'
 an Irland's Maid vermacht,
 der kann der Magd
 nicht eigen sein,
 die selbst dem Ohm er schenkt.
 Ein Herr der Welt
 Tristan der Held!
 Ich ruf's: du sag's, und grollten
 mir tausend Frau Isolden.

[*Da* TRISTAN *durch Gebärden ihm zu wehren sucht, und* BRANGÆNE *entrüstet sich zum Weggehen wendet, singt* KURWENAL *der zögernd sich Entfernenden mit höchster Stärke nach.*]
 "Herr Morold zog
  zu Meere her,
 in Kornwall Zins zu haben;
 ein Eiland schwimmt
  auf ödem Meer,
 da liegt er nun begraben!
 Sein Haupt doch hängt
  im Iren-Land,
 als Zins gezahlt
  von Engeland.
 Hei! unser Held Tristan!
 Wie der Zins zahlen kann!"

[KURWENAL, *von* TRISTAN *fortgescholten, ist in den Schiffsraum des Vorderdecks hinabgestiegen.* BRANGÆNE, *in Bestürzung zu* ISOLDE *zurückgekehrt, schliesst hinter sich die Vorhänge, während die ganze Mannschaft aussen sich hören lässt.*]

ALLE MÄNNER. "Sein Haupt doch hängt
  im Iren-Land,
 als Zins gezahlt
  von Engeland.
 Hei! unser Held Tristan!
 Wie der Zins zahlen kann!"

DRITTE SCENE

[ISOLDE *und* BRANGÆNE *allein, bei vollkommen wieder geschlossenen Vorhängen.* ISOLDE *erhebt sich mit verzweiflungsvoller Wuthgebärde.* BRANGÆNE *ihr zu Füssen stürzend.*]

BRANGÆNE. Weh'! Ach, wehe!
 dies zu dulden!

ISOLDE (*dem furchtbarsten Ausbruche nahe, schnell sich fassend*). Doch nun von Tristan:
 genau will ich's vernehmen.

BRANGÆNE. Ach, frage nicht!

ISOLDE. Frei sag's ohne Furcht.

BRANGÆNE. Mit höf'schen Worten
 wich er aus.

ISOLDE. Doch als du deutlich mahntest?

BRANGÆNE. Da ich zur Stell'
 ihn zu dir rief:
 wo er auch steh',
 so sagte er,
 getreulich dien' er ihr,
 der Frauen höchster Ehr',
 liess' er das Steuer
 jetzt zur Stund',
 wie lenkt' er sicher den Kiel
 zu König Marke's Land?

ISOLDA (*bitterly*). "How could he pilot the ship

in surety to King Mark!"
And wait on him with were-gild
from Ireland's island won!

BRANGÆNA. As I gave out the message
and in thy very words,
thus spoke his henchman Kurvenal—

ISOLDA. Heard I not ev'ry sentence?
it all has reached my ear.
If thou hast learnt my disgrace
now hear too whence it has grown.
How scoffingly
they sing about me!
Quickly could I requite them!
What of the boat
so bare and frail,
that floated by our shore?
What of the broken
stricken man,
feebly extended there?
Isolda's art
he gladly owned;
with herbs, simples
and healing salves
the wounds from which he suffered
she nursed in skilful wise.
Though "Tantris"
The name that he took unto him,
as "Tristan"
anon Isolda knew him,
when in the sick man's keen blade
she perceived a notch had been made,
wherein did fit
a splinter broken
in Morold's head,
the mangled token
sent home in hatred rare:
this hand did find it there.
I heard a voice
from distance dim;
with the sword in hand
I came to him.
Full well I willed to slay him,
for Morold's death to pay him.
But from his sick bed
he looked up
not at the sword,
not at my arm—
his eyes on mine were fastened,
and his feebleness
softened my heart:
the sword—dropped from my fingers.
Though Morold's steel had maimed him
to health again I reclaimed him!
when he hath homeward wended
my emotion then might be ended.

BRANGÆNA. O wondrous! Why could I not see this?
The guest I sometime
helped to nurse—?

ISOLDA. His praise briskly they sing now:—
"Bravo, our brave Tristan!"—
he was that distressful man.
A thousand protestations
of truth and love he prated.
Hear how a knight
fealty knows!—
When as Tantris
unforbidden he'd left me,
as Tristan

ISOLDE (*schmerzlich bitter*). "Wie lenkt' er sicher den
Kiel
zu König Marke's Land"—
den Zins ihm auszuzahlen,
den er aus Irland zog!

BRANGÆNE. Auf deine eig'nen Worte,
als ich ihm die entbot
liess seinen Treuen Kurwenal—

ISOLDE. Den hab' ich wohl vernommen,
kein Wort das mir entging.
Erfuhrst du meine Schmach,
nun höre, was sie mir schuf.—
Wie lachend sie
mir Lieder singen,
wohl könnt' auch ich erwiedern:
von einem Kahn,
der klein und arm
an Irland's Küste schwamm;
darinnen krank
ein siecher Mann
elend im Sterben lag.
Isolde's Kunst
ward ihm bekannt;
mit Heil-Salben
und Balsamsaft
der Wunde, die ihn plagte,
getreulich pflag sie da.
Der "Tantris"
mit sorgender List sich nannte,
als "Tristan"
Isold' ihn bald erkannte,
da in des Müss'gen Schwerte
eine Scharte sie gewahrte,
darin genau
sich fügt' ein Splitter,
den einst im Haupt
des Iren-Ritter,
zum Hohn ihr heimgesandt,
mit kund'ger Hand sie fand.—
Da schrie's mir auf
aus tiefstem Grund;
mit dem hellen Schwert
ich vor ihm stund,
an ihm, dem Ueber-Frechen,
Herrn Morold's Tod zu rächen.
Von seinem Bette
blickt' er her,—
nicht auf das Schwert,
nicht auf die Hand,—
er sah' mir in die Augen.
Seines Elendes
jammerte mich;
das Schwert—das liess ich fallen:
die Morold schlug, die Wunde,
sie heilt' ich, dass er gesunde,
und heim nach Hause kehre,—
mit dem Blick mich nicht mehr beschwere!

BRANGÆNE. O Wunder! Wo hatt' ich die Augen?
Der Gast, den einst
ich pflegen half—?

ISOLDE. Sein Lob hörtest du eben:—
"Hei! Unser Held Tristan!"—
Der war jener traur'ge Mann!—
Er schwur mit tausend Eiden
mir ew'gen Dank und Treue
Nun hör' wie ein Held
Eide hält!—
Den als Tantris
unerkannt ich entlassen,
als Tristan

boldly back he came,
in stately ship
from which in pride
Ireland's heiress
in marriage he asked
for Mark, the Cornish monarch,
his kinsman worn and old.
In Morold's lifetime
dared any have dreamed
to offer us such an insult?
For the tax-paying
Cornish prince
to presume to court Ireland's princess!
Ah, woe is me!
I i. was
who for myself
did shape this shame!
with death-dealing sword
should I have stabbed him;
weakly it escaped me:—
now serfdom I have shaped me.
Curse him, the villain!
Curse on his head!
Vengeance! Death!
Death for me too!

BRANGÆNA (*throwing herself upon* ISOLDA *with impetuous tenderness*). Isolda! lady!
loved one! fairest!
sweet perfection!
mistress rarest!
Hear me! come now,
sit thee here.—

(*Gradually draws* ISOLDA *to the couch.*)
What a whim!
what causeless railing!
How came you so wrong-minded
and by mere fancy blinded?
Sir Tristan gives thee
Cornwall's kingdom;
then, were he erst thy debtor,
how could he reward thee better?
His noble uncle
serves he so:
think too what a gift
on thee he'd bestow!
With honor unequalled
all he's heir to
at thy feet he seeks to shower,
to make thee a queenly dower.
(ISOLDA *turns away.*)
If wife he'd make thee
unto King Mark
why wert thou in this wise complaining?
Is he not worth thy gaining?
Of royal race
and mild of mood,
who passes King Mark
in might and power?
If a noble knight
like Tristan serves him,
who would not but feel elated,
so fairly to be mated.

ISOLDA (*gazing vacantly before her*).
Glorious knight!
And I must near him
loveless ever languish!
How can I support such anguish?

BRANGÆNA. What's this, my lady?
loveless thou?

kehrt' er kühn zurück
auf stolzem Schiff
von hohem Bord,
Irland's Erbin
begehrt er zur Eh'
für Kornwall's müden König,
für Marke, seinen Ohm.
Da Morold lebte,
wer hätt' es gewagt,
uns je solche Schmach zu bieten?
Für der zinspflichtigen
Kornen Fürsten
um Irland's Krone zu werben?
O wehe mir!
Ich ja war's,
die heimlich selbst
die Schmach sich schuf!
Das rächende Schwert,
statt es zu schwingen,
machtlos liess ich's fallen:—
nun dien' ich dem Vasallen.
Fluch dir, Verruchter!
Fluch deinem Haupt!
Rache, Tod!
Tod uns Beiden!

BRANGÆNE (*mit ungestümer Zärtlichkeit sich auf* ISOLDE *stürzend*). O Süsse! Traute!
Theure! Holde!
Gold'ne Herrin!
Lieb' Isolde!
Hör' mich! Komme!
Setz' dich her!—

(*Sie zieht* ISOLDE *allmählich nach dem Ruhebett.*)
Welcher Wahn?
Welch eitles Zürnen?
Wie magst du dich bethören,
nicht hell zu sehn noch hören!
Was je Herr Tristan
dir verdankte,
sag', konnt' er's höher lohnen,
als mit der herrlichsten der Kronen?
So dient' er treu
dem edlen Ohm,
dir gab er der Welt
begehrlichsten Lohn
dem eig'nen Erbe,
echt und edel,
entsagt' er zu deinen Füssen,
als Königin dich zu grüssen.
(ISOLDE *wendet sich ab.*)
und mildem Muth,
dir zum Gemahl,
wie wolltest du die Wahl doch schelten,
muss er nicht werth dir gelten?
Von edler Art
Und mildem Muth,
wer gliche dem Mann
an Macht und Glanz?
Dem ein hehrster Held
so treulich dient,
wer möchte sein Glück nicht theilen,
als Gattin bei ihm weilen?

ISOLDE (*starr vor sich hinblickend*).
Ungeminnt
den hehrsten Mann
stets mir nah' zu sehen,—
wie könnt' ich die Qual bestehen!

BRANGÆNE. Was wähnst du Arge?
Ungeminnt?—

(*Approaching coaxingly and kissing* Isolda.)
Where lives there a man
would not love thee?
Who could see Isolda
And not sink
at once into bondage blest?
And if e'en it could be
any were cold,
did any magic
draw him from thee,
I'd bring the false one
back to bondage,
And bind him in links of love.—

(*Secretly and confidentially, close to* Isolda.)

Mindest thou not
thy mother's arts?
Think you that she
who'd mastered those
would have sent me o'er the sea,
without assistance for thee?

Isolda (*darkly*). My mother's rede
I mind aright,
and highly her magic
arts I hold:—
Vengeance they wreak for wrongs,
rest give to wounded spirits.—
Yon casket hither bear.

Brangæna. It holds a balm for thee.—

(*She brings forward a small golden coffer, opens it, and
points to its contents.*)
Thy mother place inside it
her subtle magic potions.
There's salve for sickness
or for wounds,
and antidotes
for deadly drugs.—
(*She takes a bottle.*)
The helpfullest draught
I hold in here

!Isolda. Not so, I know a better.
I make a mark
to know it again—
This draught 'tis I would drain.
(*Seizes flask and shows it.*)

Brangæna (*recoiling in horror*).
The draught of death!

Isolda *has risen from the sofa and now hears with increasing dread the cries of the sailors.*)

Voices of the Crew (*without*).
"Ho! heave ho! hey!
Reduce the sail!
The mainsail in!
Ho! heave ho! hey!"

Isolda. Our journey has been swift.
Woe's me! Near to the land!

SCENE IV

Kurvenal *boisterously enters through the curtains.*)

Kurvenal. Up, up, ye ladies!
Look alert!
Straight bestir you!
Loiter not—here is the land!—
To dame Isolda

(*Sie nähert sich* Isolden *schmeichelnd und kosend.*)
Wo lebte der Mann,
der dich nicht liebte?
Der Isolde sän',
und in Isolden
selig nicht ganz verging'?
Doch, der dir erkoren,
wär' er so kalt,
zög' ihn von dir
ein Zauber ab,
den bösen wüsst' ich
bald zu binden;
ihn bannte der Minne Macht.—

(*Mit geheimnissvoller Zutraulichkeit ganz nah zu*
Isolden.)
Kennst du der Mutter
Künste nicht?
Wahnst du, die Alles
klug erwägt,
ohne Rath in fremdes Land
hätt' sie mit dir mich entsandt?

Isolde (*düster*). Der Mutter Rath
gemahnt mich recht;
willkommen preis' ich
ihre Kunst:—
Rache für den Verrath,—
Ruh' in der Noth dem Herzen!—
Den Schrein dort bring' mir her.

Brangæne. Er birgt, was Heil dir frommt.

(*Sie holt eine kleine goldne Truhe herbei, öffnet sie, und
deutet auf ihren Inhalt.*)
So reihte sie die Mutter,
die mächt'gen Zaubertränke.
Für Weh' und Wunden
Balsam hier;
für böse Gifte
Gegen-Gift:—
(*Sie zieht ein Fläschchen hervor.*)
den hehrsten Trank,
ich halt' ihn hier.

Isolde. Du irr'st, ich kenn' ihn besser;
ein starkes Zeichen
schnitt ich ein:—
der Trank ist's, der mir frommt.
(*Sie ergreift ein Fläschchen und zeigt es.*)

Brangæne (*entsetzt zurückweichend*).
Der Todestrank!

(Isolde *hat sich vom Ruhebett erhoben, und vernimmt
jetzt mit wachsendem Schrecken den Ruf des Schiffsvolkes:*)

Ruf des Schiffsvolkes (*von aussen*).
"He! ha! ho! he!
Am Untermast
die Segel ein!
He! ha! ho! he!"

Isolde. Das deutet schnelle Fahrt.
Weh' mir! Nahe das Land!

VIERTE SCENE

[*Durch die Vorhänge tritt mit Ungestüm* Kurwenal
herein.]

Kurwenal. Auf, auf! Ihr Frauen!
Frisch und froh!
Rasch gerüstet!
Fertig, hurtig und flink!—
Und Frau Isolden

says the servant
of Tristan,
our hero true:—
Behold our flag is flying!
it waveth landwards aloft:
in Mark's ancestral castle
may our approach be seen.
So, dame Isolda,
he prays to hasten,
for land straight to prepare her,
that thither he may bear her.

ISOLDA (*who has at first cowered and shuddered on hearing the message, now speaks calmly and with dignity*).
My greeting take
unto your lord
and tell him what I say now:
Should he assist to land me
and to King Mark would he hand me,
unmeet and unseemly
were his act,
the while my pardon
was not won
for trespass black and base:
So bid him seek my grace.

    (KURVENAL *makes a gesture of defiance.*)
Now mark me well
This message take:—
Nought will I yet prepare me,
that he to land may bear me;
I will not by him be landed,
nor unto King Mark be handed
ere granting forgiveness
and forgetfulness,
which 'tis seemly
he should seek:—
for all his trespass base
I tender him my grace.

KURVENAL. Be assured,
I'll bear your words:
we'll see what he will say!

                (*He retires quickly.*)

SCENE V

ISOLDA (*hurries to* BRANGÆNA *and embraces her vehemently*). Now farewell, Brangæna!
Greet ev'ry one,
Greet my father and mother!

BRANGÆNA. What now? what mean'st thou?
Wouldst thou flee?
And where must I then follow?

ISOLDA (*checking herself suddenly*). Here I remain:
heard you not?
Tristan will I await.—
I trust in thee
to aid in this:
prepare the true
cup of peace:
thou mindest how it is made.

BRANGÆNA. What meanest thou?

ISOLDA (*taking a bottle from the coffer*). That it is!
From the flask go pour
this philtre out;
yon golden goblet 'twill fill.

BRANGÆNA (*filled with terror receiving the flask*).
Trust I my wits?

ISOLDA. Wilt thou be true?

BRANGÆNA. The draught—for whom?

sollt' ich sagen
von Held Tristan,
meinem Herrn:—
vom Mast der Freude Flagge
sie wehe lustig in's Land;
in Marke's Königschlosse
mach' sie ihr Nahen bekannt.
Drum Frau Isolde
bät' er eilen,
für's Land sich zu bereiten,
dass er sie könnt' geleiten.

ISOLDE (*nachdem sie zuerst bei der Meldung in Schauer zusammengefahren, gefasst und mit Würde*).
Herrn Tristan bringe
meinen Gruss,
und meld' ihm was ich sage.—
Sollt' ich zur Seit' ihm gehen,
vor König Marke zu stehen,
nicht möcht' es nach Zucht
und Fug gescheh'n,
empfing' ich Sühne
nicht zuvor
für ungesühnte Schuld:
drum such' er meine Huld.—

    (KURWENAL *macht eine trotzige Gebärde.*)
Du merke wohl
und meld' es gut!—
Nicht wollt' ich mich bereiten,
an's Land ihn zu begleiten;
nicht werd' ich zur Seit' ihm gehen,
vor König Marke zu stehen,
begehrte Vergessen
und Vergeben
nach Zucht und Fug
er nicht zuvor   •
für ungebüsste Schuld:—
die böt' ihm meine Huld.

KURWENAL. Sicher wisst,
das sag' ich ihm:
nun harrt, wie er mich hört!

                (*Er geht schnell zurück.*)

FÜNFTE SCENE

ISOLDE (*eilt auf* BRANGÄNE *zu und umarmt sie heftig*).
Nun leb' wohl, Brangäne!
Grüss' mir die Welt,
grüsse mir Vater und Mutter!

BRANGÄNE. Was ist's! Was sinnst du?
Wolltest du fliehen?
Wohin sollt' ich dir folgen?

ISOLDE (*schnell gefasst*). Hörtest du nicht?
Hier bleib' ich;
Tristan will ich erwarten.—
Treu befolg',
was ich befehl',
den Sühne-Trank
rüste schnell,--
du weisst, den ich dir wies.

BRANGÄNE. Und welchen Trank?

ISOLDE (*entnimmt dem Schreine das Fläschchen*).
Diesen Trank!
In die gold'ne Schale
giess' ihn aus;
gefüllt fasst sie ihn ganz.

BRANGÄNE (*voll Grausen das Fläschchen empfangend*).
Trau' ich dem Sinn?

ISOLDE. Sei du mir treu!

BRANGÄNE. Der Trank—für wen?

ISOLDA. Him who betrayed!

BRANGÆNA. Tristan!

ISOLDA. Truce he'll drink with me.

BRANGÆNA (*throwing herself at* ISOLDA'S *feet*).
    O horror! Pity thy handmaid!

ISOLDA. Pity thou me,
    false-hearted maid!
    Mindest thou not
    my mother's arts?
    Think you that she
    who'd mastered those
    would have sent thee o'er the sea
    without assistance for me?
    A salve for sickness
    doth she offer
    and antidotes
    for deadly drugs;
    for deepest grief
    and woe supreme
    gave she the draught of death.
    Let Death now give her thanks!

(BRANGÆNA (*scarcely able to control herself*). O deepest grief!

ISOLDA. Now, wilt thou obey?

BRANGÆNA. O woe supreme!

ISOLDA. Wilt thou be true?

BRANGÆNA. The draught?

KURVENAL (*entering*). Sir Tristan!

(BRANGÆNA rises, terrified and confused. ISOLDA *strives
    with immense effort to control herself.*)

ISOLDA (*to Kurvenal*). Sir Tristan may approach!

SCENE VI

[KURVENAL *retires again.* BRANGÆNA, *almost beside
herself, turns up the stage.* ISOLDA, *mustering all
her powers of resolution, walks slowly and with dignity towards the sofa, by the head of which she supports herself, turning her eyes firmly towards the
entrance.*]

(TRISTAN *enters, and pauses respectfully at the entrance.*)

ISOLDE. Wer mich betrog,

BRANGÆNE. Tristan?

ISOLDE. Trinke mir Sühne.

BRANGÆNE (*zu* ISOLDE'S *Füssen stürzend*).
    Entsetzen! Schone mich Arme!

ISOLDE (*heftig*). Schone du mich,
    untreue Magd!
    Kennst du der Mutter
    Künste nicht?
    Wähn'st du, die Alles
    klug erwägt,
    ohne Rath in fremdes Land
    hätt' sie mit Dir mich entsandt?
    Für Weh' und Wunden
    gab sie Balsam;
    für böse Gifte
    Gegen-Gift;
    für tiefstes Weh',
    für höchstes Leid—
    gab sie den Todes-Trank.
    Der Tod nun sag' ihr Dank!

BRANGÆNE (*kaum ihrer mächtig*). O tiefstes Weh'!

ISOLDE. Gehorchst du mir nun?

BRANGÆNE. O höchstes Leid!

ISOLDE. Bist du mir treu?

BRANGÆNE. Der Trank?

KURWENAL (*eintretend*). Herr Tristan

(BRANGÆNE *erhebt sich erschrocken und verwirrt;* ISOLDE
sucht mit furchtbarer Anstrengung sich zu fassen.)

ISOLDE (*zu Kurwenal*). Herr Tristan trete nah.

SECHSTE SCENE

[KURWENAL *geht wieder zurück.* BRANGÆNE, *kaum ihrer
mächtig, wendet sich in den Hintergrund.* ISOLDE,
*ihr ganzes Gefühl zur Entscheidung zusammenfassend,
schreitet langsam, mit grosser Haltung, dem Ruhebett
zu, auf dessen Kopfende sich stützend sie den Blick
fest dem Eingange zuwendet.*]

(TRISTAN *tritt ein, und bleibt ehrerbietig am Eingange
stehen.*)

TRISTAN. Demand, lady,
    what you will.

ISOLDA. While knowing not
    what my demand is,
    wert thou afraid
    still to fulfil it,
    fleeing my presence thus?

TRISTAN. Honor
    Held me in awe.

ISOLDA. Scant honor hast thou
    shown unto me;
    for, unabashed,
    withheldest thou
    obedience unto my call.

TRISTAN. Obedience 'twas
    forbade me to come.

ISOLDA. But little I owe
    thy lord, methinks,
    if he allows
    ill manners
    unto his own promised bride.

TRISTAN. Begehrt, Herrin,
    was Ihr wünscht.

ISOLDE. Wüsstest du nicht
    was ich begehre,
    da doch die Furcht,
    mir's zu erfüllen,
    fern meinem Blick dich hielt?

TRISTAN. Ehr-Furcht
    hielt mich in Acht.

ISOLDE. Der Ehre wenig
    botest du mir:
    mit off'nem Hohn
    verwehrtest du
    Gehorsam meinem Gebot.

TRISTAN. Gehorsam einzig
    hielt mich in Bann.

ISOLDE. So dankt' ich Geringes
    deinem Herrn,
    rieth dir sein Dienst
    Un-Sitte
    gegen sein eigen Gemahl?

TRISTAN. In our land
    it is the law
    that he who fetches
    home the bride
    should stay afar from her.

ISOLDA. On what account?

TRISTAN. 'Tis the custom.

ISOLDA. Being so careful,
    my lord Tristan,
    another custom
    can you not learn?
    Of enemies friends make:
    for evil acts amends make.

TRISTAN. Who is my foe?

ISOLDA. Find in thy fears!
    Blood-guilt
    gets between us.

TRISTAN. That was absolved.

ISOLDA. Not between us.

TRISTAN. In open field,
    'fore all the folk
    our old feud was abandoned.

ISOLDA. 'Twas not there
    I held Tantris hid
    when Tristan was laid low,
    He stood there brawny,
    bright and brave;
    but in his truce
    I took no part:
    my tongue its silence had learnt.
    When in chambered stillness
    sick he lay
    with the sword I stood
    before him, stern;
    silent—my lips,
    motionless—my hand.
    But that which my hand
    and lips had once vowed,
    I swore in stealth to adhere to:
    lo! now my desire I'm near to.

TRISTAN. What hast thou sworn?

ISOLDA (quickly). Vengeance for Morold!

TRISTAN (quietly). Mindst thou that?

ISOLDA (animated). Dare you to flout me?—
    Was he not my betrothed,
    that noble Irish knight?
    For his sword a blessing I sought;
    for me only he fought.
    When he was murdered
    no honor fell.
    In that heartfelt misery
    my vow was framed;
    if no man remained to right it,
    I, a maid, must needs requite it.—
    Weak and maimed,
    when might was mine,
    why at thy death did I pause?
    Thou shalt know the secret cause.—
    Thy hurts I tended
    that, when sickness ended,
    thou shouldst fall by some man,
    as Isolda's revenge should plan.
    But now attempt
    thy fate to foretell me:
    if their friendship all men do sell thee,
    what foe can seek to fell thee?

TRISTAN. Sitte lehrt
    wo ich gelebt:
    zur Brautfahrt
    der Brautwerber
    meide fern die Braut.

ISOLDE. Aus welcher Sorg'?

TRISTAN. Fragt die Sitte!

ISOLDE. Da du so sittsam,
    mein Herr Tristan,
    auch einer Sitte
    sei nun gemahnt:
    den Feind dir zu sühnen,
    soll er als Freund dich rühmen.

TRISTAN. Und welchen Feind?

ISOLDE. Frag' deine Furcht!
    Blut-Schuld
    schwebt zwischen uns.

TRISTAN. Die ward gesühnt.

ISOLDE. Nicht zwischen uns.

TRISTAN. Im off'nen Feld
    vor allem Volk
    ward Ur-Fehde geschworen.

ISOLDE. Nicht da war's
    wo ich Tantris barg,
    wo Tristan mir verfiel.
    Da stand er herrlich,
    hehr und heil;
    doch was er schwur,
    das schwur ich nicht:—
    zu schweigen hatt' ich gelernt.
    Da in stiller Kammer
    krank er lag,
    mit dem Schwerte stumm
    ich vor ihm stund,
    schwieg—da mein Mund,
    bannt'—ich meine Hand,
    doch was einst mit Hand
    und Mund ich gelobt,
    das schwur ich schweigend zu halten.
    Nun will ich des Eides walten.

TRISTAN. Was schwurt Ihr, Frau?

ISOLDE (schnell). Rache für Morold.

TRISTAN (mässig). Müh't Euch die?

ISOLDE (lebhaft). Wag'st du mir Hohn?—
    Angelobt war er mir,
    der hehre Irenheld;
    seine Waffen hatt' ich geweiht,
    für mich zog er in Streit.
    Da er gefallen,
    fiel meine Ehr';
    in des Herzens Schwere
    schwur ich den Eid,
    würd' ein Mann den Mord nicht sühnen,
    wollt' ich Magd mich des' erkühnen.—
    Siech und matt
    in meiner Macht,
    warum ich dich da nicht schlug,
    das sag' dir mit leichtem Fug:—
    ich pflag des Wunden,
    dass den heil Gesunden
    rächend schlüge der Mann,
    der Isolden ihn abgewann.—
    Dein Loos nun selber
    magst du dir sagen:
    da die Männer sich all' ihm vertragen,
    wer muss nun Tristan schlagen?

TRISTAN (*pale and gloomy, offers her his sword*). If
 thou so lovedst this lord,
 then lift once more my sword,
 nor from thy purpose refrain;
 let the weapon not fail again.

ISOLDA. Put up thy sword
 which once I swung,
 when vengeful rancor
 my bosom wrung,
 when thy masterful eyes
 did ask me straight
 whether King Mark
 might seek me for mate.
 The sword harmless descended.—
 Drink, let our strife be ended!

(ISOLDA *beckons* BRANGÆNA. *She trembles and hesitates
to obey.* ISOLDA *commands her with a more imperious gesture.* BRANGÆNA *sets about preparing the
drink.*)

VOICES OF THE CREW (*without*). Ho! heave ho! hey!
 Reduce the sail!
 The foresail in!
 Ho! heave ho! hey!

TRISTAN (*starting from his gloomy brooding*). Where
 are we?

ISOLDA. Near to shore.
 Tristan, is warfare ended?
 Hast not a word to offer?

TRISTAN (*darkly*). Concealment's mistress
 makes me silent:
 I know what she conceals,
 conceal, too, more than she knows.

ISOLDA. Thy silence nought
 but feigning I deem.
 Friendship wilt thou still deny?
   (*Renewed cries of the Sailors.*)

(*At an impatient sign from* ISOLDA BRANGÆNA *hands
 her the filled cup.*)

ISOLDA (*advancing with the cup to* TRISTAN, *who gazes
immovably into her eyes*).
 Thou hear'st the cry?
 The shore's in sight:
 we must ere long (*with slight scorn*)
 stand by King Mark together.

SAILORS (*without*). Haul the warp!
 Anchor down!

TRISTAN (*starting wildly*). Down with the anchor!
 Her stern to the stream!
 The sails a-weather the mast!
   (*He takes the cup from* ISOLDA.)
 I know the Queen
 of Ireland well,
 unquestioned are
 her magic arts:
 the balsam cured me
 which she brought;
 now bid me quaff the cup,
 that I may quite recover.
 Heed to my all-
 atoning oath,
 which in return I tended
 Tristan's honor—
 highest truth!
 Tristan's anguish—
 brave distress!
 Traitor spirit,

TRISTAN (*bleich und düster, reicht ihr sein Schwert hin*).
 War Morold dir so werth,
 nun wieder nimm das Schwert,
 und führ' es sicher und fest,
 dass du nicht dir's entfalten lässt.

ISOLDE. Wahre dein Schwert!
 Da einst ich's schwang,
 als mir die Rache
 im Busen rang,
 als dein messender Blick
 mein Bild sich stahl,
 ob ich Herrn Marke
 taug' als Gemahl:
 das Schwert—da liess ich's sinken.
 Nun lass' uns Sühne trinken!—

(*Sie winkt* BRANGÆNE. *Diese schaudert zusammen,
schwankt und zögert in ihrer Bewegung.* ISOLDE *treibt
sie durch gesteigerte Gebärde an. Als* BRANGÆNE *zur
Bereitung des Tranks sich anlässt, vernimmt man den
Ruf des Schiffsvolkes.*)

SCHIFFSVOLK (*von aussen*). Ho! he! ha! he!
 Am Obermast
 die Segel ein!
 Ho! he! ha! he!

TRISTAN (*aus finst'rem Brüten auffahrend*).
 Wo sind wir?

ISOLDE. Hart am Ziel.
 Tristan, gewinn' ich Sühne?
 Was hast du mir zu sagen?

TRISTAN (*düster*). Des Schweigens Herrin
 heisst mich schweigen:
 fass' ich, was sie verschwieg,
 verschweig' ich, was sie nicht fasst.

ISOLDE. Dein Schweigen fass' ich,
 weichst du mir aus.
 Weigerst du Sühne mir?

(*Neue Schiffsrufe. Auf* ISOLDE's *ungeduldigen Wink
reicht* BRANGÆNE *ihr die gefüllte Trinkschale.*)

ISOLDE (*mit dem Becher zu* TRISTAN *tretend, der ihr
starr in die Augen blickt*).
 Du hörst den Ruf?
 Wir sind am Ziel:
 in kurzer Frist
 stehn wir— (*mit leisem Hohne.*)
 vor König Marke.

SCHIFFSRUF (*aussen*). Auf das Tau!
 Anker ab!

TRISTAN (*wild auffahrend*). Los den Anker!
 Das Steuer dem Strom!
 Den Winden Segel und Mast!
 (*Er entreisst* ISOLDEN *ungestüm die Trinkschale.*)
 Wohl kenn' ich Irlands
 Königin,
 und ihrer Künste
 Wunderkraft:
 den Balsam nützt' ich,
 den sie bot;
 den Becher nehm' ich nun,
 dass ganz ich heut' genese!
 Und achte auch
 des Sühne-Eid's,
 den ich zum Dank dir sage.—
 Tristan's Ehre—
 höchste Treu':
 Tristan's Elend—
 kühnster Trotz.
 Trug des Herzens;

dawn-illumined!
Endless trouble's
only truce!
Oblivion's kindly draught,
with rapture thou art quaff'd!
(*He lifts the cup and drinks.*)

ISOLDA. Betrayed e'en here?
I must halve it!—
(*She wrests the cup from his hand.*)
Betrayer, I drink to thee!

[*She drinks, and then throws away the cup. Both, seized
with shuddering, gaze with deepest emotion, but im-
movable demeanor, into one another's eyes, in which
the expression of defiance to death fades and melts
into the glow of passion. Trembling seizes them, they
convulsively clutch their hearts and pass their hands
over their brows. Their glances again seek to meet,
sink in confusion, and once more turn with growing
longing upon one another.*]

ISOLDA (*with trembling voice*). Tristan!

TRISTAN (*overpowered*). Isolda!

ISOLDA (*sinking upon his breast*). Traitor beloved!

TRISTAN. Woman divine!
(*He embraces her with ardor. They remain in a silent
embrace.*)

ALL THE MEN (*without*). Hail! Hail!
Hail our monarch!
Hail to Mark, the king!

BRANGÆNA (*who, filled with confusion and horror, has
leaned over the side with averted face, now turns to
behold the pair locked in their close embrace, and
rushes to the front, wringing her hands in despair*).

Woe's me! Woe's me!
Endless mis'ry
I have wrought
instead of death!
Dire the deed
of my dull fond heart:
it cries aloud to heav'n!
(*They start from their embrace.*)

TRISTAN (*bewildered*). What troubled dream
of Tristan's honor?

ISOLDA. What troubled dream
Of Isolda's shame?

TRISTAN. Have I then lost thee?

ISOLDA. Have I repulsed thee?

TRISTAN. Fraudulent magic,
framing deceit!

BOTH. Languishing passion,
longing and growing,
love ever yearning,
loftiest glowing!
Rapture confess'd
rides in each breast!
Isolda! Tristan!
Tristan! Isolda!
World, I can shun thee
my love is won me!
Thou'rt my thought, all above:
highest delight of love!

Traum der Ahnung!
ew'ger Trauer
einz'ger Trost,
Vergessens güt'ger Trank!
Dich trink' ich sonder Wank.
(*Er setzt an und trinkt.*)

ISOLDE. Betrug auch hier?
Mein die Hälfte!—
(*Sie entwindet ihm den Becher.*)
Verräther, ich trink' sie dir!

[*Sie trinkt. Dann wirft sie die Schale fort.—Beide,
von Schauer erfasst, blicken sich mit höchster Aufregung, doch mit starrer Haltung, unverwandt in die
Augen, in deren Ausdruck der Todestrotz bald der
Liebesgluth weicht.—Zittern ergreift sie. Sie fassen
sich krampfhaft an das Herz,—und führen die Hand
weiter an die Stirn.—Dann suchen sie sich wieder
mit dem Blicke, senken ihn verwirrt, und heften ihn
von Neuem mit steigender Sehnsucht auf einander.*]

ISOLDE (*mit bebender Stimme*). Tristan!

TRISTAN (*überströmend*). Isolde!

ISOLDE (*an seine Brust sinkend*). Treuloser Holder!

TRISTAN. Seligste Frau!—
(*Er umfasst sie mit Gluth. Sie verbleiben in stummer
Umarmung.*)

ALLE MÆNNER (*aussen*). Heil! Heil!
König Marke!
König Marke, Heil!

BRANGÆNE (*die, mit abgewandtem Gesicht, voll Verwirrung und Schauder sich über Bord gelehnt hatte,
wendet sich jetzt dem Anblick des in Liebesumar-
mung versunkenen Paares zu, und stürzt händeringend, voll Verzweiflung, in den Vordergrund*).

Wehe! Wehe!
Unabwendbar
ewige Noth
für kurzen Tod!
Thör'ger Treue
trugvolles Werk
blüht nun jammernd empor!
(*Sie fahren verwirrt aus der Umarmung auf.*)

TRISTAN (*verwirrt*). Was träumte mir
von Tristan's Ehre?

ISOLDE. Was träumte mir
von Isolde's Schmach?

TRISTAN. Du mir verloren?

ISOLDE. Du mich verstossen?

TRISTAN. Trügenden Zaubers
tückische List!

BEIDE. Sehnender Minne
schwellendes Blühen,
schmachtender Liebe
seliges Glühen!
Jach in der Brust
jauchzende Lust!
Isolde! Tristan!
Tristan! Isolde!
Welten-entronnen
du mir gewonnen!
Du mir einzig bewusst,
höchste Liebes-Lust!

SCENE VII

[*The curtains are now drawn wide apart; the whole ship is covered with knights and sailors, who, with shouts of joy, make signs over towards the shore which is now seen to be quite near, with castle-crowned cliffs. TRISTAN and ISOLDA remain absorbed in mutual contemplation, perceiving nothing that is passing.*]

BRANGÆNA (*to the women, who at her bidding ascend from below*). Quick—the mantle! the royal robe!—

(*Rushing between* TRISTAN *and* ISOLDA.)
Up, hapless ones!
See where we are!
(*She places the royal mantle on* ISOLDA, *who notices nothing.*)

ALL THE MEN. Hail! Hail!
Hail our monarch!
Hail to Mark the king!

KURVENAL (*advancing gaily*). Hail, Tristan,
knight of good hap!
Behold King Mark approaching,
in a bark
with brave attendance.
Gladly he stems the tide,
coming to seek his bride.

TRISTAN (*looking up in bewilderment*). Who comes?

KURVENAL. The king 'tis.

TRISTAN. What king mean you?

(KURVENAL *points over the side.* TRISTAN *gazes stupefied at the shore.*)

ALL THE MEN (*waving their hats*). Hail to King Mark!
All hail!

ISOLDA (*bewildered*). What is't, Brangæna?
What are those cries?

BRANGÆNA. Isolda—mistress!
Compose thyself!

ISOLDA. Where am I! living?
What was that draught?

BRANGÆNA (*despairingly*). The love-potion!

ISOLDA (*staring with horror at* TRISTAN). Tristan!

TRISTAN. Isolda!

ISOLDA. Must I live, then?
(*Falls fainting upon his breast.*)

BRANGÆNA (*to the women*). Look to your lady!

TRISTAN. O rapture fraught with cunning!
O fraud with bliss o'er-running!

ALL THE MEN (*in a general burst of acclamation*).
Hail to King Mark!
Cornwall, hail!

[*People have clambered over the ship's side, others have extended a bridge, and the aspect of all indicates the immediate arrival of the expected ones, as the curtain falls.*]

SIEBENTE SCENE

[*Die Vorhänge werden weit auseinander gerissen. Das ganze Schiff ist von Rittern und Schiffsleuten erfüllt, die jubelnd über Bord winken, dem Ufer zu, das man, mit einer hohen Felsenburg gekrönt, nahe erblickt.* TRISTAN *und* ISOLDE *bleiben, in ihrem gegenseitigen Anblick verloren, ohne Wahrnehmung des um sie Vorgehenden.*]

BRANGÆNE (*zu den Frauen, die auf ihren Wink aus dem Schiffsraum heraufsteigen*).
Schnell den Mantel,
den Königsschmuck!
(*Zwischen* TRISTAN *und* ISOLDE *stürzend.*)
Unsel'ge! Auf!
Hört wo wir sind.
(*Sie legt* ISOLDEN, *die es nicht gewahrt, den Mantel um.*)

ALLE MÆNNER. Heil! Heil!
König Marke!
König Marke, Heil!

KURWENAL (*lebhaft herantretend*). Heil Tristan!
Glücklicher Held!
Mit reichem Hofgesinde
dort auf Nachen
naht Herr Marke.
Hei! wie die Fahrt ihn freut,
dass er die Braut sich freit!

TRISTAN (*in Verwirrung aufblickend*). Wer naht?

KURWENAL. Der König?

TRISTAN. Welcher König?

(KURWENAL *deutet über Bord.* TRISTAN *starrt wie sinnlos nach dem Lande.*)

ALLE MÆNNER (*die Hüte schwenkend*).
Heil! König Marke!

ISOLDE (*in Verwirrung, zu* BRANGÆNE).
Was ist's? Brangäne!
Ha! welcher Ruf?

BRANGÆNE. Isolde! Herrin!
Fassung nur heut'!

ISOLDE. Wo bin ich? Leb' ich?
Ha, welcher Trank?

BRANGÆNE (*verzweiflungsvoll*). Der Liebestrank!

ISOLDE (*starrt entsetzt auf* TRISTAN). Tristan!

TRISTAN. Isolde!

ISOLDE. Muss ich leben?
(*Sie stürzt ohnmächtig an seine Brust.*)

BRANGÆNE (*zu den Frauen*). Helft der Herrin!

TRISTAN. O Wonne voller Tücke!
O Trug geweihtes Glücke!

ALLE MÆNNER (*Ausbruch allgemeinen Jauchzens*).
Heil dem König!
Kornwall, Heil!

[*Leute sind über Bord gestiegen, andere haben eine Brücke ausgelegt, und die Haltung Aller deutet auf die soeben bevorstehende Ankunft der Erwarteten, als der Vorhang schnell föllt.*]

ACT II

—

[*A Garden before* ISOLDA's *Chamber which lies at one side and is approached by steps. Bright and pleasant summer night. At the open door a burning torch is fixed. Sounds of hunting heard.*]

SCENE I

[BRANGÆNA, *on the steps leading to the chamber, is watching the retreat of the still audible hunters. She looks anxiously back into the chamber as* ISOLDA *emerges thence in ardent animation.*]

ISOLDA. Yet do you hear?
    I lost the sound some time.

BRANGÆNA (*listening*) Still do they stay:
    clearly ring the horns.

ISOLDA (*listening*). Fear but deludes
    thy anxious ear;
    by sounds of rustling
    leaves thou'rt deceived,
    aroused by laughter of winds.

BRANGÆNA. Deceived by wild
    desire art thou,
    and but hear'st as would thy will:—
    I still hear the sound of horns.

ISOLDA (*listens*). No sound of horns
    were so sweet:
    yon fountain's soft
    murmuring current
    moves so quietly hence.
    If horns yet brayed,
    how could I hear that?
    In still night alone
    it laughs on mine ear.
    My lov'd one hides
    in darkness unseen:
    wouldst thou hold from my side my dearest?
    deeming that horns thou hearest?

BRANGÆNA. Thy lov'd one hid—
    oh heed my warning!
    for him a spy waits by night.
    Listening oft
    I light upon him:
    he lays a secret snare.
    Of Melot oh beware!

ISOLDA. Mean you Sir Melot?
    O, how you mistake!
    Is he not Tristan's
    trustiest friend?
    May my true love not meet me,
    with none but Melot he stays.

BRANGÆNA. What moves me to fear him
    makes thee his friend then?
    Through Tristan to Mark's side
    is Melot's way:
    he sows suspicion's seed.
    And those who have
    to-day on a night-hunt
    so suddenly decided,
    a far nobler game
    than is guessed by thee
    taxes their hunting skill.

II AKT

—

[*Garten mit hohen Bäumen vor dem Gemache* ISOLDE's, *zu welchem, seitwärts gelegen, Stufen hinaufführen. Helle, anmuthige Sommernacht. An der geöffneten Thüre ist eine brennende Fackel aufgesteckt. Jagdgetön.*]

ERSTE SCENE

[BRANGÆNE, *auf den Stufen am Gemach, späht dem immer entfernter vernehmbaren Jagdtrosse nach. Zu ihr tritt aus dem Gemach, feurig bewegt,* ISOLDE.]

ISOLDE. Hörst du sie noch?
    Mir schwand schon fern der Klang.

BRANGÆNE (*lauschend*). Noch sind sie nah':
    deutlich tönt's daher.

ISOLDE (*lauschend*). Sorgende Furcht
    beirrt dein Ohr;
    dich täuscht des Laubes
    säuselnd Getön',
    das lachend schüttelt der Wind.

BRANGÆNE. Dich täuscht deines Wunsches
    Ungestüm,
    zu vernehmen was du wähnst:—
    ich höre der Hörner Schall.

ISOLDE (*lauschend*). Nicht Hörnerschall
    tönt so hold;
    des Quelles sanft
    rieselnde Welle
    rauscht so wonnig daher;
    wie hört' ich sie,
    tos'ten noch Hörner?
    Im Schweigen der Nacht
    nur lacht mir der Quell:
    der meiner harrt
    in schweigender Nacht,
    als ob Hörner noch nah' dir schallten,
    willst du ihn fern mir halten?

BRANGÆNE. Der deiner harrt—
    O hör' mein Warnen!
    Des' harren Späher zur Nacht.
    Tückisch lauschend
    treff' ich ihn oft:
    der heimlich euch umgarnt,
    vor Melot seid gewarnt.

ISOLDE. Mein'st du Herrn Melot?
    O wie du dich trüg'st!
    Ist er nicht Tristan's
    treuster Freund?
    Muss mein Trauter mich meiden
    dann weilt er bei Melot allein.

BRANGÆNE. Was mir ihn verdächtig,
    macht dir ihn theuer.
    Von Tristan zu Marke
    ist Melot's Weg:
    dort sä't er üble Saat.
    Die heut' im Rath
    dies nächtliche Jagen
    so eilig schnell beschlossen
    einem edlern Wild,
    als dein Wähnen meint,
    gilt ihre Jägers-List.

ISOLDA. For Tristan's sake
         contrived was this scheme
         by means of
         Melot, in truth:
         now would you decry his friendship!
         He serves Isolda
         better than you
         his hand gives help
         which yours denies:
         what need of such delay?
         The signal, Brangæna!
         O give the signal!
         Tread out the torch's
         trembling gleam,
         that night may envelop
         all with her veil.
         Already her peace reigns
         o'er hill and hall,
         her rapturous awe
         the heart does enthral;
         allow then the light to fall!
         Let but its dread lustre die!
         let my beloved draw nigh!

BRANGÆNA. The light of warning suppress not!
           Let it remind thee of peril!—
           Ah, woe's me! Woe's me!
           Fatal folly!
           The fell pow'r of that potion!
           That I framed
           a fraud for once
           thy orders to oppose!
           Had I been deaf and blind,
           thy work
           were then thy death:
           but thy distress,
           thy distraction of grief,
           my work
           has contrived them, I own it!

ISOLDA. Thy—act?
         O foolish girl!
         Love's goddess dost thou not know?
         nor all her magic arts?
         The queen who grants
         unquailing hearts,
         the witch whose will
         the world obeys,
         life and death
         she holds in her hands,
         which of joy and woe are wove?
         she worketh hate into love.
         The work of death
         I took into my own hands;
         Love's goddess saw
         and gave her good commands
         The death—condemned
         she claimed as her prey,
         planning our fate
         in her own way.
         How she may bend it,
         how she may end it,
         what she may make me
         wheresoe'er take me,
         still hers am I solely;—
         so let me obey her wholly

BRANGÆNA. And if by the artful
           love-potion's lures
           thy light of reason is ravished,
           if thou art reckless
           when I would warn thee,
           this once, oh, wait

ISOLDE. Dem Freunde zu lieb
         erfand diese List
         aus Mit-Leid
         Melot der Freund:
         nun willst du den Treuen schelten?
         Besser als du
         sorgt er für mich;
         ihm öffnet er,
         was du mir sperr'st;
         o spar' mir des Zögerns Noth!
         Das Zeichen, Brangäne!
         O gieb das Zeichen!
         Lösche des Lichtes
         letzten Schein!
         Dass ganz sie sich neige,
         winke der Nacht!
         Schon goss sie ihr Schweigen
         durch Hain und Haus;
         schon füllt sie das Herz
         mit wonnigem Graus:
         o lösche das Licht nun aus!
         Lösche den scheuchenden Schein!
         Lass' meinen Liebsten ein!

BRANGÆNE. O lass' die warnende Zünde!
           Die Gefahr lass' sie dir zeigen!—
           O wehe! Wehe!
           Ach mir Armen!
           Des unseligen Tranks!
           Dass ich untreu
           einmal nur
           der Herrin Willen trog!
           Gehorcht' ich taub und blind,
           dein—Werk
           war dann der Tod:
           doch deine Schmach,
           deine schmählichste Noth,
           mein—Werk
           muss ich Schuld'ge es wissen!

ISOLDE. Dein—Werk?
         O thör'ge Magd!
         Frau Minne kenntest du nicht?
         Nicht ihrer Wunder Macht?
         Des kühnsten Muthes
         Königin,
         des Welten-Werdens
         Walterin,
         Leben und Tod
         sind ihr unterthan,
         die sie webt aus Lust und Leid,
         in Liebe wandelnd den Neid.
         Des Todes Werk
         nahm ich's vermessen zur Hand,
         Frau Minne hat
         meiner Macht es entwandt:
         die Todgeweihte
         nahm sie in Pfand,
         fasste das Werk
         in ihre Hand;
         wie sie es wendet
         wie sie es endet,
         was sie mir küret,
         wohin mich führet,
         ihr ward ich zu eigen:—
         nun lass' mich gehorsam zeigen!

BRANGÆNE. Und musste der Minne
           tückischer Trank
           des Sinnes Licht dir verlöschen;
           darfst du nicht sehen,
           wenn ich dich warne:
           nur heute hör',

and weigh my pleading!
I implore, leave it alight!—
The torch! the torch!
O put it not out this night!

ISOLDA. She who causes thus
　　my bosom's throes,
　　whose eager fire
　　within me glows,
　　whose light upon
　　my spirit flows,
　　Love's goddess needs
　　that night should close;
　　that brightly she may reign
　　and shun the torchlight vain.

(*She goes up to the door and takes down the torch.*)
　　Go watch without—
　　keep wary guard!
　　The signal!—
　　and were it my spirit's spark,
　　smiling
　　I'd destroy it and hail the dark!

[*She throws the torch to the ground where it slowly dies out.* BRANGÆNA *turns away, disturbed, and mounts an outer flight of steps leading to the roof, where she slowly disappears.* ISOLDA *listens and peers, at first shyly, towards an avenue. Urged by rising impatience, she then approaches the avenue and looks more boldly. She signs with her handkerchief, first slightly, then more plainly, waving it quicker as her impatience increases. A gesture of sudden delight shows that she has perceived her lover in the distance. She stretches herself higher and higher, and then, to look better over the intervening space, hastens back to the steps, from the top of which she signals again to the on-comer. As he enters, she springs to meet him.*]

SCENE II

TRISTAN (*rushing in*). Isolda! Beloved!
ISOLDA. Tristan! Beloved one!
(*Passionate embrace, with which they come down to the front.*)

BOTH. Art thou mine?
　　Do I behold thee?
　　Do I embrace thee?
　　Can I believe it?
　　At last! At last!
　　Here on my breast!
　　Do I then clasp thee!
　　Is it thy own self?
　　Are these thine eyes?
　　These thy lips?
　　Here thy hand?
　　Here thy heart?
　　Is't I?—Is't thou,
　　held in my arms?
　　Am I not duped?
　　Is it no dream?
　　O rapture of spirit!
　　O sweetest, highest,
　　fairest, strongest,
　　holiest bliss!
　　Endless pleasure!
　　Boundless treasure!
　　Ne'er to sever!
　　Never! Never!
　　Unconceived,
　　unbelieved,
　　overpowering

o hör' mein Flehen!
Der Gefahr leuchtendes Licht—
nur heute! heut'!—
die Fackel dort lösche nicht!

ISOLDE. Die im Busen mir
　　die Gluth entfacht,
　　die mir das Herze
　　brennen macht,
　　die mir als Tag
　　der Seele lacht,
　　Frau Minne will,
　　es werde Nacht,
　　dass hell sie dorten leuchte,
　　wo sie dein Licht verscheuchte.—

(*Sie geht zu der Thür und nimmt die Fackel herab.*)
　　Zur Warte du!
　　Dort wache treu.
　　Die Leuchte—
　　wär's meines Lebens Licht,—
　　lachend
　　sie zu löschen zag' ich nicht.

[*Sie wirft die Fackel zur Erde, wo sie allmälig verlöscht.* BRANGÆNE *wendet sich bestürz tab, um auf einer äusseren Treppe die Zinne zu ersteigen, wo sie langsam verschwindet.* ISOLDE *lauscht und späht, zunächst schüchtern, in einen Baumgang. Von wachsendem Verlangen bewegt, schreitet sie dem Baumgang näher, und späht zuversichtlicher. Sie winkt mit einem Tuche, erst seltener, dann häufiger, und endlich, in leidenschaftlicher Ungeduld, immer schneller. Eine Gebärde des plötzlichen Entzückens sagt, dass sie den Freund in der Ferne gewahr geworden. Sie streckt sich höher, und höher, und um besser den Raum zu übersehen, eilt sie zur Treppe zurück, von deren oberster Stufe sie dem Herannahenden zuwinkt. Als er eintritt, springt sie ihm entgegen.*]

ZWEITE SCENE

TRISTAN. Isolde! Geliebte!
ISOLDE. Tristan! Geliebter!
(*Stürmische Umarmungen Beider, unter denen sie in den Vordergrund gelangen.*)

BEIDE. Bist du mein?
　　Hab' ich dich wieder?
　　Darf ich dich fassen?
　　Kann ich mir trauen?
　　Endlich! Endlich!
　　An meiner Brust!
　　Fühl' ich dich wirklich?
　　Bist du es selbst?
　　Dies deine Augen?
　　Dies dein Mund?
　　Hier deine Hand?
　　Hier dein Herz?
　　Bin ich's? Bist du's?
　　Halt' ich dich fest?
　　Ist es kein Trug?
　　Ist es kein Traum?
　　O Wonne der Seele!
　　O süsse, hehrste,
　　kühnste, schönste,
　　seligste Lust!
　　Ohne Gleiche!
　　Ueberreiche!
　　Ungeahnte,
　　Ewig! Ewig!
　　Ungeahnte,
　　nie gekannte,
　　überschwänglich

exaltation!
Joy-proclaiming,
bliss-outpouring,
high in heaven,
earth ignoring!
Tristan mine!
Isolda mine!
Tristan!
Isolda!
Mine alone!
Thine alone!
Ever all my own!

TRISTAN. The light! The light!
  O but this light,
  how long 'twas let to burn!
  The sun had sunk,
  the day had fled;
  but all their spite
  not yet was sped:
  the scaring signal
  they set alight,
  before my belov'd one's dwelling,
  my swift approach repelling.

ISOLDA. Thy belov'd one's hand
  lowered the light,
  for Brangæna's fears
  in me roused no fright:
  while Love's goddess gave me aid,
  sunlight a mock I made.
  But the light its fear
  and defeat repaid;
  with thy misdeeds
  a league it made.
  What thou didst see
  in shadowing night,
  to the shining sun
  of kingly might
  must thou straightway surrender,
  that it should
  exist in bright
  bonds of empty splendor.—
  Could I bear it then?
  Could I bear it now?

TRISTAN. O now were we
  to night devoted,
  the dishonest day
  with envy bloated,
  lying, could not mislead,
  though it might part us indeed.
  Its pretentious glows
  and its glamouring light
  are scouted by those
  who worship night.
  All its flickering gleams
  in flashes out-blazing
  blind us no more
  where we are gazing.
  Those who death's night
  boldly survey,
  those who have studied
  her secret way,
  the daylight's falsehoods—
  rank and fame,
  honor and all
  at which men aim—
  to them are no more matter
  than dust which sunbeams scatter,

---

hoch erhab'ne!
Freude-Jauchzen!
Lust-Entzücken!
Himmel-höchstes
Welt-Entrücken!
Mein Tristan!
Mein' Isolde!
Tristan!
Isolde!
Mein und dein!
Immer ein!
Ewig, ewig ein!

TRISTAN. Das Licht! Das Licht!
  O dieses Licht!
  Wie lang' verlosch es nicht!
  Die Sonne sank,
  der Tag verging;
  doch seinen Neid
  erstickt' er nicht:
  sein scheuchend Zeichen
  zündet er an,
  und steckt's an der Liebsten Thüre,
  dass ich nicht zu ihr führe.

ISOLDE. Doch der Liebsten Hand
  löschte das Licht.
  Wes' die Magd sich wehrte,
  scheut' ich mich nicht:
  in Frau Minne's Macht und Schutz
  bot ich dem Tage Trutz.
  Doch es rächte sich
  der verscheuchte Tag;
  mit deinen Sünden
  Raths er pflag:
  was dir gezeigt
  die dämmernde Nacht,
  an des Taggestirnes
  Königsmacht
  musstest du's übergeben,
  um einsam
  in oder Pracht
  schimmernd dort zu leben.—
  Wie ertrug ich's nur?
  Wie ertrag' ich's noch?

TRISTAN. O! nun waren wir
  Nacht-geweihte:
  der tückische Tag,
  der Neid-bereite,
  trennen konnt' uns sein Trug,
  doch nicht mehr täuschen sein Lug.
  Seine eitle Pracht,
  seinen prahlenden Schein
  verlacht, wem die Nacht
  den Blick geweih't:
  seines flackernden Lichtes
  flüchtige Blitze
  blenden nicht mehr
  uns're Blicke.
  Wer des Todes Nacht
  liebend erschau't,
  wem sie ihr tief
  Geheimniss vertraut,
  des Tages Lügen,
  Ruhm und Ehr',
  Macht und Gewinn,
  so schimmernd hehr,
  wie eitler Staub der Sonnen
  sind sie vor dem zerronnen.

In the daylight's visions thronging
only abides one longing;
we yearn to hie
to holy night,
where, unending,
only true,
Love extendeth delight!

In des Tages eitlem Wähnen
bleibt ihm ein einzig Sehnen,
das Sehnen hin
zur heil'gen Nacht,
wo ur-ewig,
einzig wahr
Liebeswonne ihm lacht.

¡TRISTAN *draws* ISOLDA *gently aside to a flowery bank,
sinks on his knee before her and rests his head on
her arm.*)

(TRISTAN *zieht* ISOLDE *sanft zur Seite auf eine Blumenbank nieder, senkt sich vor ihr auf die Knie und
schmiegt sein Haupt in ihren Arm.*)

fan - cies,   Sa - cred   twi-light's soft ad - van - ces   bid vain fears to
mah - nen   heil' - ger Damm'rung he - res Ah - nen   löscht des Wäh-rens

Sa - cred twi-light's soft ad - van - ces bid vain   fears to   cease,
heil' - ger Damm'rung he - res Ah - nen   löscht des Währens   Graus

Lento.

cease,   from . . . . the world . . re - lease. Hid our hearts a - way sun-light's
Graus,   welt - - er lös . . send aus. Barg im Bu - sen uns sich die

from . . . . the world . . . re - lease.
welt - - er lös . . . . send aus.

TRISTAN.

stream-ing, bliss would bloom from stars' ten - der beam-ing. To thy en-chant-ment we sur
Son - ne, leuch-ten la - chend Ster - ne der Won - ne. Von die - nem Zau - ber sanft um-

ISOLDA.

ren - der be-neath thy gaze So won - drous ten - der. Heart to heart, . . and lip to
Spon - nen, Vor dei - nen Au - gen süss zer - von - nen, Herz an Herz . . dir, Mund an

lip. . .   Bliss - ful beams . . our eyes are bind - ing, a-
Mund;   bricht mein Blick . . sich wonn' - er - blin - det, er-

Each   the oth - er's breath we sip; Bliss - ful beams . . our eyes are
ein - en A - thems ein' - ger Bund; bricht mein Blick sick wonn' - er

bash'd is earth . with radiance blind - ing: Lit by the day - light's dazzling
bleicht die Welt . . mit ih - rem Blen - den: die uns der Tag trü - gend-er

bind - ing, a-bash'd is earth with ra - diance blind-ing;
blin - det, er-bleicht die Welt . mit ih - rem Blen-den.

lie, .. thou'rt my world, thine am I ..
helit, .. *selbst .. dann bin ich die Welt.*

un-daunt-ed by falsehoods which we de-fy. Thou'rt my world, thine am I ..
zu täu-schendem Wahn ent-ge-gen-ge-stellt, selbst dann bin ich die Welt

.. Won-drous rap-ture weav-ing cher-ish'd vis-ions a-chiev-
.. *Won-ne-hehr-stes We-ben lie be hei-lig-stes Le-*

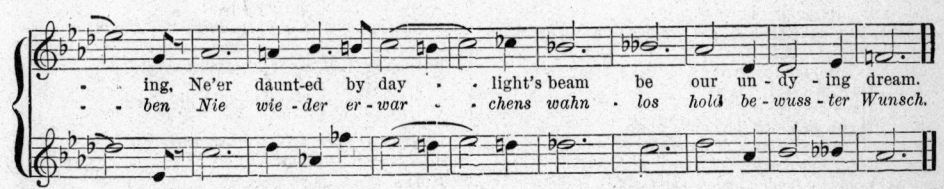

-ing, Ne'er daunt-ed by day .. light's beam be our un-dy-ing dream.
-ben Nie wie-der er-war-chens wahn-los hold be-wuss-ter Wunsch.

(TRISTAN *and* ISOLDA *sink into oblivious ecstasy, reposing on the flowery bank close together.*)

BRANGÆNA (*from the turret, unseen*). Long I watch
  alone by night:
  ye enwrapt
  in love's delight,
  heed my boding
  voice aright.
  I forewarn you
  woe is near;
  waken to
  my words of fear.
  Have a care!
  Have a care!
  Swiftly night doth wear!

ISOLDA. List, belovéd!

TRISTAN. Let me die thus!

ISOLDA (*slowly raising herself a little*).
  Envious watcher!

TRISTAN (*remaining in reclining position*). I'll ne'er
  waken.

ISOLDE. But the Day
  must dawn and rouse thee?

TRISTAN (*raising his head slightly*). Let the Day
  to Death surrender!

(TRISTAN *und* ISOLDE *versinken wie in gänzliche Entrücktheit, in der sie, Haupt an Haupt auf die Blumenbank zurückgelehnt, verweilen.*)

BRANGÆNE (*unsichtbar, von der Höhe der Zinne*).
  Einsam wachend
  in der Nacht,
  wem der Traum
  der Liebe lacht,
  hab' der Einen
  Ruf in Acht,
  die den Schläfern
  Schlimmes ahnt,
  bange zum
  Erwachen mahnt.
  Habet Acht!
  Habet Acht!
  Bald entweicht die Nacht.

ISOLDE. Lausch', Geliebter!

TRISTAN. Lass' mich sterben!

ISOLDE (*allmälig sich ein wenig erhebend*).
  Neid'sche Wache!

TRISTAN (*zurückgelehnt bleibend*). Die erwachen!

ISOLDE. Doch der Tag
  muss Tristan wecken?

TRISTAN (*ein wenig das Haupt erhebend*).
  Lass' den Tag
  dem Tode weichen!

ISOLDA. Day and Death
    will both engender
    feud against
    our passion tender.
TRISTAN (*drawing* ISOLDA *gently towards him with ex-*
    pressive action). O might we then
    together die,
    each the other's
    own for aye!
    never fearing,
    never waking,
    blest delights
    of love partaking,—
    each to each be given,
    in love alone our heaven!
ISOLDA (*gazing up at him in thoughtful ecstasy*).
    O might we then
    together die!
TRISTAN. Each the other's—
ISOLDA. Own for aye,—
TRISTAN. Never fearing—
ISOLDA. Never waking—
TRISTAN. Blest delights
    of love partaking—
ISOLDA. Each to each be given;
    in love alone our heaven.
(ISOLDA, *as if overcome, droops her head on his breast.*)

BRANRÆNA'S VOICE (*as before*).
    Have a care!
    Have a care!
    Night yields to daylight's glare.
TRISTAN (*bends smilingly to* ISOLDA).
    Shall I listen?
ISOLDA (*looking fondly up at* TRISTAN).
    Let me die thus!
TRISTAN. Must I waken?
ISOLDA. Nought shall wake me!
TRISTAN. Must not daylight
    dawn, and rouse me?
ISOLDA. Let the Day
    to Death surrender!
TRISTAN. May thus the Day's
    evil threats be defied?
ISOLDA (*with growing enthusiasm*).
    From its thraldom let us fly.
TRISTAN. And shall not its dawn
    be dreaded by us?
ISOLDA (*rising with a grand gesture*).
    Night will shield us for aye!
(TRISTAN *follows her; they embrace in fond exaltation.*)

BOTH. O endless Night!
    blissful Night!
    glad and glorious
    lover's Night!
    Those whom thou holdest,
    lapped in delight,
    how could e'en the boldest
    unmoved endure thy flight?
    How to take it,
    how to break it,—
    joy existent,
    sunlight distant.
    Far from mourning,
    sorrow-warning,
    fancies spurning,
    softly yearning,
    fear expiring,
    sweet desiring!
    Anguish flying,

ISOLDE. Tag und Tod
    mit gleichen Streichen
    sollten uns're
    Lieb erreichen?
TRISTAN (*zieht* ISOLDE, *mit bedeutungsvoller Gebärde,*
    sanft an sich). So stürben wir,
    um ungetrennt,
    ewig einig,
    ohne End',
    ohn' Erwachen,
    ohne Bangen,
    namenlos
    in Lieb' umfangen,
    ganz uns selbst gegeben,
    der Liebe nur zu leben.
ISOLDE (*wie in sinnender Entrücktheit zu ihm auf-*
    blickend). So stürben wir,
    um ungetrennt—
TRISTAN. Ewig einig—
ISOLDE. Ohne End'—
TRISTAN. Ohn' Erwachen—
ISOLDE. Ohne Bangen—
TRISTAN. Namenlos
    in Lieb' umfangen—
ISOLDE. Ganz uns selbst gegeben,
    der Liebe nur zu leben!
(ISOLDE *neigt, wie überwältigt, das Haupt an seine*
    Brust.)

BRANRÆNE (*wie vorher*). Habet Acht!
    Habet Acht!
    Schon weicht dem Tag die Nacht.

TRISTAN (*lächelnd zu* ISOLDE *geneigt*).
    Soll ich lauschen?
ISOLDE. Lass' mich sterben!

TRISTAN. Muss ich wachen?
ISOLDE. Nie erwachen!
TRISTAN. Soll der Tag
    noch Tristan wecken?
ISOLDE. Lass' den Tag
    dem Tode weichen!
TRISTAN. Des Tages Dräuen
    trotzen wir so?
ISOLDE (*mit wachsender Begeisterung*).
    Seinen Trug ewig zu fliehn.
TRISTAN. Sein dämmernder Schein
    verscheuche uns nie?
ISOLDE (*mit grosser Gebärde ganz sich erhebend*).
    Ewig währ' uns die Nacht!
(TRISTAN *folgt ihr, sie umfangen sich in schwärmerische*
    Begeisterung.)

BEIDE. O süsse Nacht!
    Ew'ge Nacht!
    Hehr erhab'ne,
    Liebes-Nacht!
    Wen du umfangen,
    Wem du gelacht,
    wie—wär' ohne Bangen
    aus dir er je erwacht?
    Wie es fassen?
    Wie sie lassen,
    diese Wonne,
    fern der Sonne,
    fern der Tage
    Trennungs-Klage?
    Ohne Wähnen
    sanftes Sehnen,
    ohne Bangen
    süss Verlangen,
    ohne Wehen

gladly dying;
no more pining,
night-enshrining,
ne'er divided
whate'er betided,
side by side
still abide
in realms of space unmeasured,
vision blest and treasured!
Thou Isolda,
Tristan I;
no more Tristan,
no more Isolda.
Never spoken,
never broken,
newly sighted,
newly lighted,
endless ever
all our dream;
in our bosoms gleam
love delights supreme!

hehr Vergehen,
ohne Schmachten
hold Umnachten;
ohne Scheiden,
ohne Meiden,
traut allein,
ewig heim,
in ungemess'nen Räumen
übersel'ges Träumen.
Du Isolde,
Tristan ich,
nicht mehr Tristan,
nicht Isolde;
ohne Nennen,
ohne Trennen,
neu Erkennen,
neu Entbrennen;
endlos ewig
ein-bewusst:
heiss erglühter Brust
höchste Liebes-Lust!

SCENE III

(Brangæna *utters a piercing cry.* Tristan *and* Isolda *remain in their absorbed state.* Kurvenal *rushes in with drawn sword.*]

Kurvenal. Save yourself, Tristan!

[*He looks fearfully off behind him.* Mark, Melot, *and courtiers, in hunting dress, come swiftly up the avenue and pause in the foreground in consternation before the lovers.* Brangæna *at the same time descends from the roof and hastens towards* Isolda. *The latter in involuntary shame leans on the flowery bank with averted face.* Tristan *with an equally unconscious action stretches his mantle wide out with one arm, so as to conceal* Isolda *from the gaze of the new-comers. In this position he remains for some time, turning a changeless look upon the men, who gaze at him in varied emotion. The morning dawns.*]

Tristan. The dreary day—
    its last time comes!

Melot (*to Mark*). Now say to me, my sov'reign,
    was my impeachment just?
    I staked my head thereon:
    now is the pledge redeemed?
    Behold him in
    the very act:
    honor and fame,
    faithfully I
    have saved from shame for thee.

Mark (*deeply moved, with trembling voice*). Hast thou
        preserved them?
    Say'st thou so?—
    See him there,
    the truest of all true hearts!
    Look on him
    the faithfulest of friends,
    His offence
    so black and base
    fills my heart
    with anguish and disgrace
    Tristan traitor,
    what hope stayeth
    that the honor
    he betrayeth
    should by Melot's rede
    rest to me indeed?

DRITTE SCENE

[Brangæne *stösst einen gellenden Schrei aus.* Tristan *und* Isolde *bleiben in verzückter Stellung.* Kurwenal *stürzt mit entblösstem Schwert herein.*]

Kurwenal. Rette dich, Tristan!

[*Er blickt mit Entsetzen hinter sich in die Scene zurück.* Marke, Melot *und Hofleute (in Jägertracht) kommen aus dem Baumgange lebhaft nach dem Vordergrunde und halten entsetzt der Gruppe der Liebenden gegenüber an.* Branræne *kommt zugleich von der Zinne herab, und stürzt auf* Isolde *zu. Diese, von unwillkürlicher Scham ergriffen, lehnt sich mit abgewandtem Gesichte auf die Blumenbank.* Tristan, *in ebenfalls unwillkürlicher Bewegung, streckt mit dem einen Arme den Mantel breit aus, so dass er* Isolde *vor den Blicken der Ankommenden verdeckt. In dieser Stellung verbleibt er längere Zeit, unbeweglich den starren Blick auf die Männer gerichtet, die in verschiedener Bewegung die Augen auf ihn heften.—Morgendämmerung.*]

Tristan. Der öde Tag—
    zum letzten Mal!

Melot (*zu Marke*). Das sollst du, Herr, mir sagen,
    ob ich ihn recht verklagt?
    Das dir zum Pfand ich gab,
    ob ich mein Haupt gewahrt?
    Ich zeigt' ihn dir
    in off'ner That:
    Namen und Ehr'
    hab' ich getreu
    vor Schande dir bewahrt.

Marke (*nach tiefer Erschütterung, mit bebender Stimme*)
        Thatest du's wirklich?
    Wähnst du das?—
    Sieh ihn dort,
    den treu'sten aller Treuen;
    blick' auf ihn,
    den freundlichsten der Freunde;
    seiner Treue
    frei'ste That
    traf mein Herz
    mit feindlichstem Verrath.
    Trog mich Tristan,
    sollt' ich hoffen,
    was sein Trügen
    mir getroffen,
    sei durch Melot's Rath
    redlich mir bewahrt?

TRISTAN (*with convulsive violence*). Daylight phantoms—
morning visions
empty and vain—
Avaunt! Begone!

MARK (*in deep emotion*). This—blow.
Tristan, to me?
Where now has truth fled,
if Tristan can betray?
Where now are faith
and friendship fair,
when from the fount of faith,
my Tristan, they are gone?
The buckler Tristan
once did don,
where is that shield
of virtue now?
when from my friends it flies,
and Tristan's honor dies?

(TRISTAN *slowly lowers his eyes to the ground. His
features express increasing grief while* MARK *continues.*)
Why hast thou noble
service done,
and honor, fame
and potent might
amassed for Mark, thy king?
Must honor, fame,
power and might,
must all thy noble
service done
be paid with Mark's dishonor?
Seemed the reward
too slight and scant
that what thou hast won him—
realms and riches—
thou art the heir unto, all?
When childless he lost
once a wife,
he loved thee so
that ne'er again
did Mark desire to marry.
When all his subjects,
high and low,
demands and pray'rs,
on him did press
to choose himself a consort—
a queen to give the kingdom,
when thou thyself
thy uncle urged
that what the court
and country pleaded
well might be conceded,
opposing high and low,
opposing e'en thyself,
with kindly cunning
still he refused,
till, Tristan, thou didst threaten
forever to leave
both court and land
if thou receivedst
not command
a bride for the king to woo:
then so he let thee do.—
This wondrous lovely wife,
thy might for me did win,
who could behold her,
who address her,
who in pride
and bliss possess her,
but would bless his happy fortune?

TRISTAN (*krampfhaft heftig*). Tage-Gespenster!
Morgen-Träume—
täuschend und wüst—
entschwebt, entweicht!

MARKE (*mit tiefer Ergriffenheit*). Mir—dies?
Dies—, Tristan, mir?—
Wohin nun Treue,
da Tristan mich betrog?
Wohin nun Ehr'
und echte Art,
da aller Ehren Hort,
da Tristan sie verlor?
Die Tristan sich
zum Schild erkor,
wohin ist Tugend
nun entflohn,
da meinen Freund sie flieht,
da Tristan mich verrieth?

(TRISTAN *senkt langsam den Blick zu Boden; in seinen
Mienen ist, während* MARKE *fortfährt, zunehmende
Trauer zu lesen.*)
Wozu die Dienste
ohne Zahl,
der Ehren Ruhm,
der Grösse Macht,
die Marken du gewannst,
musst' Ehr' und Ruhm,
Grösse und Macht,
musste die Dienste
ohne Zahl
der Marke's Schmach bezahlen?
Dünkte zu wenig
dich sein Dank,
dass was du erworben,
Ruhm und Reich,
er zu Erb' und Eigen dir gab?
Dem kinderlos einst
schwand sein Weib,
so liebt' er dich,
dass nie auf's Neu'
sich Marke wollt' vermählen.
Da alles Volk
zu Hof und Land
mit Bitt' und Dräuen
in ihn drang,
die Königin dem Reiche,
die Gattin sich zu kiesen;
da selber du
den Ohm beschwor'st,
des Hofes Wunsch,
des Landes Willen
gütlich zu erfüllen:
in Wehr gegen Hof und Land,
in Wehr selbst gegen dich,
mit Güt' und List
weigert' er sich,
bis, Tristan, du ihm drohtest
für immer zu meiden
Hof und Land,
würdest du selber
nicht entsandt,
dem König die Braut zu frei'n,
Da liess er's denn so sein.—
Dies wunderhehre Weib,
das mir dein Muth erwarb,
wer durft' es sehen,
wer es kennen,
wer mit Stolze
sein es nennen,
ohne selig sich zu preisen?

She whom I have
paid respect to ever
whom I owned,
yet possess'd her never
she, the princess
proud and peerless,
lighting up
my life so cheerless,
'spite foes,—without fear,
the fairest of brides
thou didst bring me here.
Why in hell must I bide,
without hope of a heaven?
Why endure disgrace
unhealed by tears or grief?
The unexplained,
unpenetrated
cause of all these woes,
who will to us disclose?

TRISTAN (*raising his eyes pitifully towards* MARK).
O monarch! I—
may not tell thee, truly;
what thou dost ask
remains for aye unanswered.—

(*He turns to* ISOLDA, *who looks tenderly up at him.*)

Where Tristan now is going,
wilt thou, Isolda, follow?
The land that Tristan means
of sunlight has no gleams;
it is the dark
abode of night,
from whence I first
came forth to light,
and she who bore me
thence in anguish,
gave up her life,
nor long did languish.
She but looked on my face,
then sought this resting-place.
This land where Night doth reign,
where Tristan once hath lain—
now thither offers he
thy faithful guide to be.
So let Isolda
straight declare
if she will meet him there.

ISOLDA. When to a foreign land
before thou didst invite,
to thee, traitor,
resting true,
did Isolda follow.
Thy kingdom now art showing,
where surely we are going!
why should I shun that land
by which the world is spann'd?
For Tristan's house and home
Isold' will make her own.
The road whereby
we have to go
I pray thee quickly show!—

(TRISTAN bends slowly over her and kisses her softly on
the forehead. MELOT starts furiously forward.)

MELOT (*drawing his sword*). Thou villain! Ha!
Avenge thee, monarch!
Say, wilt suffer such scorn?

Der mein Wille
nie zu nahen wagte,
der mein Wunsch
Ehrfurcht-scheu entsagte,
die so herrlich
hold erhaben
mir die Seele
musste laben,
trotz—Feind und Gefahr,
die fürstliche Braut
brachtest du mir dar.
Die kein Himmel erlöst,
warum—mir diese Hölle?
Die kein Elend sühnt,
warum—mir diese Schmach?
Den unerforschlich
furchtbar tief
geheimnissvollen Grund,
wer macht der Welt ihn kund?

TRISTAN (*das Auge mitleidig zu* MARKE *erhebend*).
O König, das
kann ich dir nicht sagen;
und was du frägst,
das kannst du nie erfahren.—

(*Er wendet sich seitwärts zu* ISOLDE, *welche die Augen
sehnsüchtig zu ihm aufgeschlagen hat.*)

Wohin nun Tristan scheidet,
willst du, Isold', ihm folgen?
Dem Land, das Tristan meint,
der Sonne Licht nicht scheint;
es ist das dunkel
nächt'ge Land,
daraus die Mutter
einst mich sandt',
als, den im Tode
sie empfangen,
im Tod' sie liess
zum Licht gelangen,
Was, da sie mich gebar,
ihr Liebes-Berge war,
das Wunderreich der Nacht,
aus der ich einst erwacht,—
das bietet dir Tristan,
dahin geht er voran.
Ob sie ihm folge
treu und hold,
das sag' ihm nun Isold'.

ISOLDE. Da für ein fremdes Land
der Freund sie einstens warb,
dem Un-holden
treu und hold,
musst' Isolde folgen.
Nun führst du in dein Eigen,
dein Erbe mir zu zeigen;
wie flöh' ich wohl das Land,
das alle Welt umspannt?
Wo Tristan's Haus und Heim,
da kehr' Isolde ein:
auf dem sie folge
treu und hold,
den Weg nun zeig' Isold'!

(TRISTAN *neigt sich langsam über sie und küsst sie sanft
auf die Stirn.* MELOT *fährt wüthend auf.*)

MELOT (*das Schwert ziehend*). Verräther! Ha!
Zur Rache, König!
Duldest du diese Schmach?

TRISTAN (*drawing his sword and turning quickly round*).
  Who's he will set his life against mine?
            (*casting a look at* MELOT).
  This was my friend;
  he told me he loved me truly:
  my fame and honor
  he upheld more than all men.
  With arrogance
  he filled my heart,
  and led on those
  who prompted me
  fame and pow'r to augment me
  by wedding thee to our monarch.—
  Thy glance, Isolda,
  glamoured him thus;
  and, jealous, my friend
  played me false
  to King Mark, whom I betrayed.—
            (*He sets on* MELOT.)
  Guard thee, Melot!

[*As* MELOT *presents his sword* TRISTAN *drops his
own guard and sinks wounded into the arms of*
KURVENAL. ISOLDA *throws herself upon his breast.*
MARK *holds* MELOT *back. The curtain falls quickly.*]

TRISTAN *zieht sein Schwert und wendet sich schnell
um*).
  Wer wagt sein Leben an das meine?
            (*Er heftet den Blick auf* MELOT.)
  Mein Freund war der,
  er minnte mich hoch und theuer:
  um∙Ehr' und Ruhm
  mir war er besorgt wie Keiner.
  Zum Uebermuth
  trieb er mein Herz:
  die Schaar führt' er,
  die mich gedrängt,
  Ehr' und Ruhm mir zu mehren,
  dem König dich zu vermählen.—
  Dein Blick, Isolde,
  blendet' auch ihn:
  aus Eifer verrieth
  mich der Freund
  dem König, den ich verrieth.—
            (*Er dringt auf* MELOT *ein.*)
  Wehr' dich, Melot!

(*Als* MELOT *ihm das Schwert entgegenstreckt, lässt* TRIS-
TAN *das seinige fallen und sinkt verwundet in* KUR-
WENAL'S *Arme.* ISOLDE *stürzt sich an seine Brust.*
MARKE *hält* MELOT *zurück.— Der Vorhang fällt
schnell.*)

ACT III

A Castle-Garden

[*At one side high castellated buildings, on the other a
low breastwork interrupted by a watch tower; at back
the castle-gate. The situation is supposed to be on
rocky cliffs; through openings the view extends over
a wide sea horizon. The whole gives an impression of
being deserted by the owner, badly kept, and here and
there dilapidated and overgrown.*]

SCENE I

[*In the foreground, in the garden, lies* TRISTAN *sleeping
on a couch under the shade of a great lime-tree,
stretched out as if lifeless. At his head sit* KURVENAL.
*bending over him in grief and anxiously listening to
his breathing. From without comes the mournful
sound of a shepherd's pipe.*

III AKT

Burggarten.

[*Zur einen Seite hohe Burggebäude, zur anderen eine
niedrige Mauerbrüstung von einer Warte unterbrochen; im Hintergrunde das Burgthor. Die Lage
ist auf felsiger Höhe anzunehmen; durch Oeffnungen
blickt man auf einen weiten Meereshorizont. Das
Ganze macht den Eindruck der Herrenlosigkeit, übel
gepflegt, hie und da schadhaft und bewachsen.*]

ERSTE SCENE

[*Im Vordergrunde, an der inneren Seite, liegt* TRISTAN
*unter dem Schatten einer grossen Linde, auf einem
Ruhebett schlafend, wie leblos ausgestreckt. Zu
Häupten ihm sitzt* KURVENAL, *in Schmerz über ihn
hingebeugt, und sorgsam seinem Athem lauschend.
Von der Aussenseite hört man einen Hirtenreigen
blasen.*

Presently the shepherd comes and looks in with interest showing the upper half of his body over the wall.]	DER HIRT erscheint mit dem Oberleibe über der Mauerbrüstung und blickt theilnehmend herein.]

SHEPHERD. Kurvenal, ho!—
    Say, Kurvenal,—
    tell me, friend!
    Does he still sleep?
	HIRT. Kurwenal! He!—
	    Sag', Kurwenal!—
	    Hör' dort, Freund!
	    Wacht er noch nicht?

KURVENAL (turning a little towards him and shaking his head sadly). If he awoke
    it would be
    but for evermore to leave us,
    unless we find
    the lady-leech;
    alone can she give help.—
    See'st thou nought?
    No ship yet on the sea?
	KURWENAL (wendet ein wenig das Haupt nach ihm und schüttelt traurig mit dem Kopf). Erwachte er,
	    wär's doch nur
	    um für immer zu verscheiden,
	    erschien zuvor
	    die Aerztin nicht,
	    die einz'ge, die uns hilft?
	    Sah'st du noch nichts?
	    Kein Schiff noch auf der See?—

SHEPHERD. Quite another ditty
    then would I play
    as merry as ever I may.
    But tell me truly,
    trusty friend,
    why languishes our lord?
	HIRT. Eine and're Weise
	    hörtest du dann,
	    so lustig wie ich sie kann.
	    Nun sag' auch ehrlich,
	    alter Freund:
	    was hat's mit uns'rem Herrn?

KURVENAL. Do not ask me;—
    for I can give no answer.
    Watch the sea,
    if sails come in sight
    a sprightly melody play.
	KURWENAL. Lass' die Frage;—
	    du kannst's doch nie erfahren.—
	    Eifrig späh',
	    und siehst du das Schiff,
	    dann spiele lustig und hell.

SHEPHERD (*turns round and scans the horizon, shading his eyes with his hand*).
　Blank appears the sea!
(*He puts the reed ˌpipe to his mouth and withdraws, playing.*)

TRISTAN (*motionless—faintly*).
　The tune so well known—
　why wake to that?
　　(*opens his eyes and slightly turns his head*).
　Where am I?

KURVENAL (*starting in joyous surprise*).
　Ha!—who is speaking?
　It is his voice!—
　Tristan! lov'd one!
　My lord! my Tristan!

TRISTAN (*with effort*). Who—calls me?

KURVENAL. Life—at last—
　O thanks be to heaven!—
　sweetest life
　unto my Tristan newly given!

TRISTAN (*faintly*). Kurvenal!—thou?
　Where—was I?—
　Where—am I?

KURVENAL. Where art thou?
　In safety, tranquil and sure!
　Kareol 'tis;
　dost thou not know
　thy fathers' halls?

TRISTAN. This my fathers'?

KURVENAL. Look but around.

TRISTAN. What awoke me?

KURVENAL. The herdsman's ditty
　hast thou heard, doubtless;
　he heedeth thy herds
　above on the hills there.

TRISTAN. Have I herds, then?

KURVENAL. Sir, I say it!
　Thine are court,
　castle—all.
　To thee yet true,
　thy trusty folk,
　as best they might,
　have held thy home in guard:
　the gift which once
　thy goodness gave
　to thy serfs and vassals here.
　when going far away,
　in foreign lands to dwell.

TRISTAN. What foreign land?

KURVENAL. Why! in Cornwall;
　where cool and able,
　all that was brilliant,
　brave and noble,
　Tristan, my lord, lightly took.

TRISTAN. Am I in Cornwall?

KURVENAL. No, no; in Kareol.

TRISTAN. How came I here?

KURVENAL. Hey now! how you came?
　No horse hither you rode:
　a vessel bore you across.
　But on my shoulders
　down to the ship
　you had to ride: they are broad,
　they carried you to the shore.
　Now you are at home once more;
　your own the land,
　your native land;

HIRT (*sich wendend, und mit der Hand über'm Auge nach dem Meer ausspähend*).
　Oed' und leer das Meer!—
(*Er setzt die Schalmei an den Mund und entfernt sich blasend.*)

TRISTAN (*bewegungslos, dumpf*). Die alte Weise—
　was weckt sie mich?
(*Er schlägt die Augen auf und wendet das Haupt ein wenig.*)
　Wo bin ich?

KURWENAL (*freudig erschrocken auffahrend*).
　Ha!—die Stimme!
　Seine Stimme!—
　Tristan! Herr!
　Mein Held! Mein Tristan!

TRISTAN (*mit Anstrengung*). Wer—ruft mich?

KURWENAL. Endlich! Endlich!
　Leben! O Leben—
　süsses Leben—
　meinem Tristan neu gegeben!

TRISTAN (*matt*). Kurwenal—du!
　Wo—war ich?—
　Wo—bin ich?

KURWENAL. Wo du bist?
　In Frieden, sicher und frei!
　Kareol, Herr:
　Kennst du die Burg
　der Väter nicht?

TRISTAN. Meiner Väter?

KURWENAL. Schau dich nur um!

TRISTAN. Was erklang mir?

KURWENAL. Des Hirten Weise,
　die hörtest du wieder;
　am Hügel ab
　hütet er deine Heerde.

TRISTAN. Meine Heerde?

KURWENAL. Herr, das mein' ich!
　Dein das Haus,
　Hof und Burg.
　Das Volk, getreu
　dem trauten Herrn,
　so gut es konnt',
　hat's Haus und Heerd gepflegt
　das einst mein Held
　zu Erb' und Eigen
　an Leut' und Volk verschenkt,
　als Alles er verliess,
　in ferne Land' zu ziehn.

TRISTAN. In welches Land?

KURWENAL. Hei! nach Kornwall;
　kühn und wonnig
　was sich da Glückes,
　Glanz und Ehren
　Tristan hehr ertrotzt!

TRISTAN. Bin ich in Kornwall?

KURWENAL. Nicht doch: in Kareol.

TRISTAN. Wie kam ich her?

KURWENAL. Hei nun, wie du kam'st?
　Zu Ross rittest du nicht;
　ein Schifflein führte dich her:
　doch zu dem Schifflein
　hier auf den Schultern
　trug ich dich; die sind breit,
　die brachten dich dort zum Strand.
　Nun bist du daheim zu Land,
　im echten Land,
　im Heimat-Land

all loved things now are near you,
unchanged the sun doth cheer you.
The wounds from which you languish
here all shall end their anguish.
    (*He presses himself to* TRISTAN's *breast.*)
TRISTAN. Think'st thou thus!
I know 'tis not so,
but this I cannot tell thee.
Where I awoke
ne'er I was,
but where I wandered
I can indeed not tell thee.
The sun I could not see,
nor country fair, nor people;
but what I saw
I can indeed not tell thee.
It was—
the land from which I once came
and whither I return:
the endless realm
of earthly night.
One thing only
there possessed me:
blank, unending,
all-oblivion.—
How faded all forebodings?
O wistful goadings!—
Thus I call
the thoughts that all
t'ward light of day have press'd me.
What only yet doth rest me,
the love-pains that possess'd me,
from blissful death's affright
now drive me toward the light,
which, deceitful, bright and golden,
round thee, Isolda, shines.
Accursèd day
with cruel glow!
Must thou ever
wake my woe?
Must thy light
be burning ever,
e'en by night
our hearts to sever?
Ah, my fairest,
sweetest, rarest!
When wilt thou—
when, ah, when—
let the torchlight dwindle,
that so my bliss may kindle?
The light, how long it glows!
When will the house repose?
(*His voice has grown fainter and he sinks back gently,
exhausted.*)
KURVENAL (*who has been deeply distressed, now quickly
rouses himself from his dejection*).
I once defied.
through faith in thee,
the one for whom
now with thee I'm yearning.
Trust in my words,
thou soon shalt see her
face to face.
My tongue that comfort giveth,—
if on the earth still she liveth.
TRISTAN (*very feebly*). Yet burns the beacon's spark:
yet is the house not dark.
Isolda lives and wakes:
her voice through darkness breaks.
KURVENAL. Lives she still,
then let new hope delight thee.
If foolish and dull you hold me,
this day you must not scold me.

auf eig'ner Weid' und Wonne,
im Schein der alten Sonne,
darin von Tod und Wunden
du selig sollst gesunden
    (*Er schmiegt sich an* TRISTAN's *Brust.*)
TRISTAN. Dünkt dich das,—
ich weis es anders,
doch kann ich's dir nicht sagen.
Wo ich erwacht,
weilt' ich nicht;
doch wo ich weilte,
das kann ich dir nicht sagen.
Die Sonne sah' ich nicht,
nicht sah' ich Land noch Leute;
doch was ich sah,
das kann ich dir nicht sagen.
Ich war—
wo ich von je gewesen,
wohin auf je ich gehe:
im weiten Reich
der Welten Nacht.
Nur ein Wissen
dort uns eigen:
göttlich ew' ges
Ur-Vergessen,—
wie schwand mir seine Ahnung!
Sehnsücht'ge Mahnung
nenn' ich dich,
die neu dem Licht
des Tag's mich zugetrieben?
Was einzig mir geblieben?
Ein heiss-inbrünstig Lieben,
aus Todes-Wonne-Grauen
jagt mich's, das Licht zu schauen
das trügend hell und golden
noch dir, Isolden, scheint!
Verfluchter Tag
mit deinem Schein
Wach'st du ewig
meiner Pein?
Brennt sie ewig,
diese Leuchte,
die selbst Nachts
von ihr mich scheuchte?
Ach, Isolde!
Süsse! Holde!
Wann—endlich,
wann, ach wann
löschest du die Zünde,
dass sie mein Glück mir künde?
Das Licht, wann löscht es aus?
Wann wird es Nacht im Haus?

KURWENAL (*nach grosser Erschütterung aus der Nieder-
geschlagenheit sich aufraffend*).
Der einst ich trotzt',
aus Treu' zu dir,
mit dir nach ihr
nun muss ich mich sehnen!
Glaub' meinem Wort,
du sollst sie sehen,
hier—und heut'—
den Trost kann ich dir geben,
ist sie nur selbst noch am Leben.
TRISTAN (*sehr matt*). Noch losch das Licht nicht aus,
noch ward's nicht Nacht im Haus.
Isolde lebt und wacht,
sie rief mich aus der Nacht.
KURWENAL. Lebt sie denn,
so lass' dir Hoffnung lachen.—
Muss Kurwenal dumm dir gelten,
heut' sollst du ihn nicht schelten.

As dead lay'st thou
since the day
when that accursèd Melot
so foully wounded thee.
Thy wound was heavy:
how to heal it?
Thy simple servant
there bethought
that she who once
closed Morold's wound
with ease the hurt could heal thee
that Melot's sword did deal thee.
I found the best
of leeches there,
to Cornwall have I
sent for her:
a trusty serf
sails o'er the sea,
bringing Isold' to thee.

TRISTAN (transported). Isolda comes!
Isolda nears!   (He struggles for words.)

O friendship! high
and holy friendship!
(Draws KURVENAL to him and embraces him.)
O Kurvenal,
thou trusty heart,
my truest friend I rank thee!
Howe'er can Tristan thank thee?
My shelter and shield
in fight and strife;
in weal or woe
thou'rt mine for life.
Those whom I hate
thou hatest too;
those whom I love
thou lovest too.
When good King Mark
I followed of old,
thou wert to him truer than gold.
When I was false
to my noble friend,
to betray too thou didst descend.
Thou art selfless,
solely mine;
thou feel'st for me
when I suffer.
But—what I suffer,
thou canst not feel for me!
this terrible yearning in my heart,
this feverish burning's
cruel smart,—
did I but show it,
could'st thou but know it,
no time here wouldst thou tarry,
to watch from tow'r thou wouldst hurry;
with all devotion
viewing the ocean,
with eyes impatiently spying,
there, where her ship's sails are flying.
Before the wind she
drives to find me;
on the wings of love she neareth,—
Isolda hither steereth!—
she nears, she nears,
so boldly and fast!
It waves, it waves,
the flag from the mast!
Hurra! Hurra!
she reaches the bar!
Dost thou not see?
Kurvenal, dost thou not see?

Wie todt lag'st du
seit dem Tag,
da Melot, der Verruchte,
dir eine Wunde schlug.
Die böse Wunde,
wie sie heilen?
Mir thör'gem Manne
dünkt' es da,
wer einst dir Morold's
Wunde schloss,
der heilte leicht die Plagen
von Melot's Wehr geschlagen.
Die beste Aerztin
bald ich fand:
nach Kornwall hab' ich
ausgesandt:
ein treuer Mann
wohl über's Meer
bringt dir Isolden her.

TRISTAN (ausser sich). Isolde kommt!
Isolde naht!—
                (Er ringt gleichsam nach Sprache.)
O Treue! hehre,
holde Treue!
(Er zieht KURWENAL an sich und umarmt ihn.)
Mein Kurwenal,
du trauter Freund,
du Treuer ohne Wanken,
wie soll dir Tristan danken?
Mein Schild, mein Schirm
in Kampf und Streit:
zu Lust und Leid
mir stets bereit:
wen ich gehasst,
den hasstest du;
wen ich geminnt,
den minntest du.
Dem guten Marke,
dient ich ihm hold,
wie warst du ihm treuer als Gold!
Musst' ich verrathen
den edlen Herrn,
wie betrogst du ihn da so gern!
Dir nicht eigen,
einzig mein,
mitleidest du
wenn ich leide:—
nur—was ich leide,
das—kannst du nicht leiden!
Dies furchtbare Sehnen,
das mich zehrt;
dies schmachtende Brennen,
das mich zehrt;
wollt' ich dir's nennen,
konntest du's kennen,—
nicht hier würdest du weilen;
zur Warte müsstest du eilen,
mit allen Sinnen
sehnend von hinnen,
nach dorten trachten und spähen,
wo ihre Segel sich blähen;
wo vor den Winden,
mich zu finden,
von der Liebe Drang befeuert,
Isolde zu mir steuert!—
es naht, es naht
mit muthiger Hast!
Sie weht, sie weht,
die Flagge am Mast
Das Schiff, das Schiff!
Dort streicht es am Riff!
Siehst du es nicht?
Kurwenal, siehst du es nicht?

(*As* Kurvenal *hesitates to leave* Tristan, *who is gazing at him in mute expectation, the mournful tune of the shepherd is heard, as before.*)

Kurvenal (*dejectedly*). Still is no ship in sight.

Tristan (*has listened with waning excitement and now recommences with growing melancholy*).
Is this the meaning then,
thou old pathetic ditty,
of all thy sighing sound?—
On evening's breeze
it sadly rang
when, as a child,
my father's death-news chill'd me:
through morning's mist
it stole more sadly,
when the son
his mother's fate was taught,
when they who gave me breath
both felt the hand of death
to them came also
through their pain
the ancient ditty's
yearning strain,
which asked me once
and asks me now
which was the fate before me
to which my mother bore me?—
What was the fate?—
The strain so plaintive
now repeats it:—
for yearning—and dying!
(*He falls back senseless.*)

Kurvenal (*who has been vainly striving to calm* Tristan *cries out in terror*).
My master! Tristan!—
Frightful enchantment!—
O love's deceit!
O passion's pow'r!
Most sweet dream 'neath the sun,
see the work thou hast done!—
Here lies he now,
the noblest of knights,
with his passion all others above:
behold! what reward
his ardor requites;
the one sure reward of love!
(*with sobbing voice.*)
Art thou then dead?
Liv'st thou not?
Hast to the curse succumbed?—
(*He listens for* Tristan's *breath.*)
O rapture! No!
He still moves! He lives!
and gently his lips are stirr'd.

Tristan (*very faintly*). The ship—is't yet in sight?

Kurvenal. The ship? Be sure
t'will come to-day:
it cannot tarry longer.

Tristan. On board Isolda,—
see, she smiles—
with the cup
that reconciles.
Dost thou see?
Dost thou see her now!
Full of grace
and loving mildness,
floating o'er
the ocean's wildness?

(*Als* Kurwenal *um* Tristan *nicht zu verlassen, zögert, und dieser in schweigender Spannung nach ihm blickt, ertönt, wie zu Anfang, die klagende Weise des Hirten.*)

Kurwenal (*niedergeschlagen*).
Noch ist kein Schiff zu seh'n!

Tristan (*hat mit abnehmender Aufregung gelauscht, und beginnt nun mit wachsender Schwermuth*).
Muss ich dich so versteh'n,
du alte, ernste Weise,
mit deiner Klage Klang?—
Durch Abendwehen
drang sie bang,
als einst dem Kind
des Vaters Tod verkündet:
durch Morgengrauen
bang und bänger,
als der Sohn
der Mutter Loos vernahm.
Da er mich zeugt' und starb,
sie sterbend mich gebar,
die alte Weise
sehnsuchts bang
zu ihnen wohl
auch klagend drang,
die einst mich frug,
und jetzt mich frägt,
zu welchem Loos erkoren
ich damals wohl geboren?
Zu welchem Loos?—
Die alte Weise
sagt mir's wieder:
mich sehnen—und sterben.
(*Er sinkt ohnmächtig zurück.*)

Kurwenal (*der vergebens* Tristan *zu mässigen suchte, schreit entsetzt auf*).
Mein Herre! Tristan!—
Schrecklicher Zauber!—
O Minne-Trug!—
O Liebes-Zwang!
Der Welt holdester Wahn,
wie ist's um dich gethan!
Hier liegt er nun,
der wonnige Mann,
der wie Keiner geliebt und geminnt:
nun seht, was von ihm
sie Dankes gewann,
was je sich Minne gewinnt!
(*Mit schluchzender Stimme.*)
Bist du nun todt?
Lebst du noch?
Hat dich der Fluch entführt?—
(*Er lauscht seinem Athem.*)
O Wonne! Nein!
Er regt sich! Er lebt!—
Wie sanft er die Lippen rührt!

Tristan (*sehr leise beginnend*).
Das Schiff—siehst du's noch nicht?

Kurwenal. Das Schiff? Gewiss,
das naht noch heut';
es kann nicht lang' mehr säumen.

Tristan. Und drauf Isolde,
wie sie winkt—
wie sie hold
mir Sühne trinkt?
Siehst du sie?
Siehst du sie noch nicht?
Wie sie selig,
hehr und milde
wandelt durch
des Meer's Gefilde?

By billows of flowers
lightly lifted,
gently toward
the land she's drifted.
Her look brings ease
and sweet repose;
her hand one last
relief bestows.
Isolda! Ah, Isolda!
How fair, how sweet art thou!—
And Kurvenal, why!—
what ails thy sight?
Away, and watch for her,
foolish wight.
what I see so well and plainly,
let not thine eye seek vainly.
Dost thou not hear?
Away, with speed!
Haste to the watch-tow'r!
Wilt thou not heed?
The ship, the ship!
Isolda's ship!— —
Thou must discern it,
must perceive it!
The ship—dost thou see it?—

(Whilst Kurvenal, still hesitating, opposes Tristan, the Shepherd's pipe is heard without, playing a joyous strain.)

Kurvenal *(springing joyously up).*
O rapture! Transport!
(He rushes to the watch-tower and looks out.)
Ha! the ship!
From northward it is nearing.

Tristan. So I knew,
so I said!
Yes, she yet lives,
and life to me gives.
How could Isold'
from this world be free,
which only holds
Isolda for me?

Kurvenal *(shouting).* Ahoy! Ahoy!
See her bravely tacking!
How full the canvas is filled!
How she darts! how she flies!

Tristan. The pennon? the pennon?

Kurvenal. A flag is floating at mast-head,
joyous and bright.

Tristan. Aha! what joy!
Now through the daylight
comes my Isolda.
Isolda, oh come!
See'st thou herself?

Kurvenal. The ship is shut
from me by rocks.

Tristan. Behind the reef?
Is there not risk!
Those dangerous breakers
ships have oft shattered.—
Who steereth the helm?

Kurvenal. The steadiest seaman.

Tristan. Betrays he me?
Is he Melot's ally?

Kurvenal. Trust him like me.

Auf wonniger Blumen
sanften Wogen
kommt sie licht
an's Land gezogen:
sie lächelt mir Trost
und süsse Ruh';
sie führt mir letzte
Labung zu.
Isolde! Ach, Isolde!
wie hold, wie schön bist du!—
Und Kurwenal, wie?
Du säh'st sie nicht?
Hinauf zur Warte,
du blöder Wicht!
was so hell und licht ich sehe,
dass das dir nicht entgehe.
Hörst du mich nicht?
Zur Warte schnell!
Eilig zur Warte!
Bist du zur Stell'?
Das Schiff, das Schiff!
Isolden's Schiff—
du musst es sehen,
musst es sehen!
Das Schiff—säh'st du's noch nicht?

(Während Kurwenal noch zögernd mit Tristan ringt, lässt der Hirt von aussen die Schalmei ertönen.)

Kurwenal *(freudig aufspringend).*
O Wonne! Freude!
(Er stürzt auf die Warte und späht aus.)
Ha! Das Schiff!
Von Norden seh' ich's nah'n.

Tristan. Wusst' ich's nicht?
Sagt' ich es nicht?
Dass sie noch lebt,
noch am Leben mir webt.
Die mir Isolde
einzig enthält,
wie wär' Isolde
mir aus der Welt?

Kurwenal *(jauchzend).* Hahei! Hahei!
Wie es muthig steuert!
Wie stark das Segel sich bläht!
Wie es jagt! Wie es fliegt!

Tristan. Die Flagge? Die Flagge?

Kurwenal. Der Freude Flagge
am Wimpel lustig und hell.

Tristan. Heiaha! Der Freude!
Hell am Tage
zu mir Isolde.
Isolde zu mir!—
Siehst du sie selbst?

Kurwenal. Jetzt schwand das Schiff
hinter dem Fels.

Tristan. Hinter dem Riff?
Bringt es Gefahr?
Dort wüthet die Brandung,
scheitern die Schiffe.—
Das Steuer, wer führt's?

Kurwenal. Der sicherste Seemann.

Tristan. Verrieth er mich?
Wär' er Melot's Genoss?

Kurwenal. Trau' ihm wie mir!

TRISTAN. A traitor thou, too!—
O caitiff!
Canst thou not see her?

KURVENAL. Not yet.

TRISTAN. Destruction!

KURVENAL. Aha! Halla-halloa!
they clear! they clear!
Safely they clear!
Inside the surf
steers now the ship to the strand.

TRISTAN (*shouting in joy*). Hallo-ho! Kurvenal!
Trustiest friend!
All the wealth I own
to-day I bequeath thee.

KURVENAL. With speed they approach.

TRISTAN. Now dost thou see her?
See'st thou Isolda?

KURVENAL. 'Tis she! she waves!

TRISTAN. O woman divine!

KURVENAL. The ship is a-land!
Isolda!—ha!—
With but one leap
lightly she springs to land!

TRISTAN. Descend from the watch-tow'r,
indolent gazer!
Away! away
to the shore!
Help her! help my belov'd!

KURVENAL. In a trice she shall come;
Trust in my strong arm!
But thou, Tristan,
hold thee tranquilly here!
(*He hastens off.*)

TRISTAN (*tossing on his couch in feverish excitement.*)
O sunlight glowing,
glorious ray!
Ah, joy-bestowing
radiant day!
Boundeth my blood,
boisterous flood!
Infinite gladness!
Rapturous madness!
Can I bear to lie
couched here in quiet?
Away, let me fly
to where hearts run riot!
Tristan the brave,
exulting in strength,
has torn himself
from death at length.
(*He raises himself erect.*)
All wounded and bleeding
Sir Morold I defeated;
all bleeding and wounded
Isolda now shall be greeted.
(*He tears the bandage from his wound.*)
Ha, ha, my blood!
Merrily flows it.
(*He springs from his bed and staggers forward.*)
She who can help
my wound and close it,
she comes in her pride,
she comes to my aid.
Be space defied
let the universe fade!
(*He reels to the centre of the stage.*)

TRISTAN. Verräther, auch du!
Un-seliger!
Siehst du sie wieder?

KURWENAL. Noch nicht.

TRISTAN. Verloren!

KURWENAL. Haha! Heiahaha!
Vorbei! Vorbei!
Glücklich vorbei!
In sich'ren Strom
steuert zum Hafen das Schiff.

TRISTIAN (*jauchzend*). Heiaha! Kurwenal!
Truester Freund!
All' mein Hab' und Gut
vererb' ich noch heut'.

KURWENAL. Sie nahen im Flug.

TRISTAN. Siehst du sie endlich?
Siehst du Isolde?

KURWENAL. Sie ist's! Sie winkt.

TRISTAN. O seligstes Weib!

KURWENAL. Im Hafen der Kiel!—
Isolde—ha!
mit einem Sprung
springt sie vom Bord zum Strand.

TRISTAN. Herab von der Warte!
Müssiger Gaffer!
Hinab! Hinab
an den Strand!
Hilf ihr! Hilf meiner Frau!

KURWENAL. Sie trag' ich herauf:
trau' meinen Armen!
Doch du, Tristan,
bleib' mir treulich am Bett! (*Er eilt fort.*)

TRISTAN (*in höchster Aufregung auf dem Lager sich
mühend*). O, diese Sonne!
Ha, dieser Tag!
Ha, dieser Wonne
sonnigster Tag!
Jagendes Blut,
jauchzender Muth!
Lust ohne Maassen,
freudiges Rasen:
auf des Lagers Bann
wie sie ertragen?
Wohlauf und daran,
wo die Herzen schlagen!
Tristan. der Held,
in jubelnder Kraft
hat sich vom Tod
emporgerafft!
(*Er richtet sich hoch auf.*)
Mit blutender Wunde
bekämpft' ich einst Morolden:
mit blutender Wunde
erjag' ich mir heut' Isolden.
(*Er reisst den Verband der Wunde auf.*)
Hahei! Mein Blut,
lustig nun fliesse!
(*Er springt vom Lager herab und schwankt vorwärts.*)
Die mir die Wunde
auf ewig schliesse,
sie naht wie ein Held,
sie naht mir zum Heil:
vergehe die Welt
meiner jauchzenden Eil'!
(*Er taumelt nach der Mitte der Bühne.*)

ISOLDA'S VOICE (*without*).
    Tristan! Tristan! Belovéd!

TRISTAN (*in frantic excitement*).
    What! hails me the light?
    The torchlight—ha!—
    The torch is extinct!
    I come! I come!

SCENE II

[ISOLDA *hastens breathlessly in.* TRISTAN, *delirious with excitement, staggers wildly towards her. They meet in the centre of the stage; she receives him in her arms, where he sinks slowly to the ground.*]

ISOLDA. Tristan! Ah!

TRISTAN (*turning his dying eyes on* ISOLDA). Isolda!—
                         (*He dies.*)

ISOLDA. 'Tis I, 'tis I—
    dearly belov'd!
    Wake, and once more
    hark to my voice!
    Isolda calls.
    Isolda comes,
    with Tristan true to perish.—
    Speak unto me!
    But for one moment,
    only one moment
    open thine eyes!
    Such weary days
    I waited and longed,
    that one single hour
    I with thee might awaken.
    Betrayed am I then?
    Deprived by Tristan
    of this our solitary,
    swiftly fleeting,
    final earthly joy?—
    His wound, though—where?
    Can I not heal it?
    The rapture of night
    O let us feel it!
    Not of thy wounds,
    not of thy wounds must thou expire!
    Together, at least,
    let fade life's enfeebled fire!—
    How lifeless his look!—
    still his heart!—
    Dared he to deal me
    such a smart?
    Stayed is his breathing's
    gentle tide!
    Must I be wailing
    at his side,
    who, in rapture coming to seek him,
    fearless sailed o'er the sea?
    Too late, too late!
    Desperate man!
    Casting on me
    this cruelest ban!
    Comes no relief
    for my load of grief?
    Silent art keeping
    while I am weeping?
    But once more, ah!
    But once again!— —
    Tristan!—ha!
    he wakens—hark!
    Beloved—
    —dark!
    (*She sinks down senseless upon his body.*)

ISOLDE (*von aussen*). Tristan! Tristan! Geliebter!

TRISTAN (*in der furchtbarsten Aufregung*).
    Wie hör' ich das Licht!
    Die Leuchte—ha!
    Die Leuchte verlischt!
    Zu ihr! Zu ihr!

ZWEITE SCENE

[ISOLDE *eilt athemlos herein.* TRISTAN, *seiner nicht mächtig, stürzt sich ihr schwankend entgegen. In der Mitte der Bühne begegnen sie sich; sie empfängt ihn in ihren Armen.*]

ISOLDE. Tristan! Ha!

TRISTAN. (*sterbend zu* ISOLDEN *aufblickend*). Isolde!—
                         (*Er stirbt.*)

ISOLDE. Ich bin's, ich bin's—
    süssester Freund!
    Auf! noch einmal!
    Hör' meinen Ruf!
    Achtest du nicht?
    Isolde ruft:
    Isolde kam,
    mit Tristan treu zu sterben.—
    Bleibst du mir stumm!
    Nur eine Stunde,—
    nur eine Stunde
    bleibe mir wach!
    So bange Tage
    wachte sie sehend,
    um eine Stunde
    mit dir noch zu wachen.
    Betrügt Isolden
    betrügt sie Tristan
    um dieses einz'ge
    ewig-kurze
    letzte Welten-Glück?—
    Die Wunde—wo?
    Lass sie mich heilen,
    dass wonnig und hehr
    die Nacht wir theilen.
    Nicht an der Wunde,
    an der Wunde stirb mir nicht!
    Uns beiden vereint
    erlösche das Lebenslicht!—
    Gebrochen der Blick!
    Still das Herz?
    Treuloser Tristan,
    mir diesen Schmerz?
    Nicht eines Athems
    flücht'ges Weh'n?
    Muss sie nun jammernd
    vor dir steh'n,
    die sich wonnig dir zu vermählen
    muthig kam über Meer?
    Zu spät! Zu spät!
    Trotziger Mann!
    Straf'st du mich so
    mit hartestem Bann?
    Ganz ohne Huld
    meiner Leidens-Schuld?
    Nicht meine Klagen
    darf ich dir sagen?
    Nur einmal, ach!
    Nur einmal noch!—
    Tristan—ha!
    horch'—er wacht!
    Geliebter—
    —Nacht!
    (*Sie sinkt bewusstlos über der Leiche zusammen.*)

SCENE III

[KURVENAL, *who reëntered close behind* ISOLDA, *has remained by the entrance speechless and petrified, gazing motionless on* TRISTAN. *From below is now heard the dull murmur of voices and the clash of weapons. The* SHEPHERD *clambers over the wall.*]

SHEPHERD (*coming hastily and softly to* KURVENAL).
    Kurvenal! Hear!
    Another ship!
(KURVENAL *starts up in haste and looks over the rampart, whilst the* SHEPHERD *stands apart, gazing in consternation on* TRISTAN *and* ISOLDA.)
KURVENAL. Fiends and furies!
          (*In a burst of anger.*)
    All are at hand!
    Melot and Mark
    I see on the strand,—
    Weapons and missiles!—
    Guard we the gate!
(*He hastens with the* SHEPHERD *to the gate, which they both try quickly to barricade.*)
THE STEERSMAN (*rushing in*).
    Mark and his men
    have set on us:
    defence is vain!
    We're overpowered.
KURVENAL. Stand to and help!—
    While lasts my life
    I'll let no foe enter here!
BRANGÆNA'S VOICE (*without, calling from below*).
    Isolda! Mistress!
KURVENAL. Brangæna's voice! (*Falling down.*)
    What want you here?
BRANGÆNA. Open, Kurvenal!
    Where is Isolda?
KURVENAL. With foes do you come?
    Woe to you, false one!
MELOT'S VOICE (*without*). Stand back, thou fool!
    Bar not the way!
KURVENAL (*laughing savagely*). Hurrah for the day
    on which I confront thee!
(MELOT, *with armed men, appears under the gateway.* KURVENAL *falls on him and cuts him down.*)

    Die, damnable wretch!

SCENE IV

MELOT. Woe's me!—Tristan!   (*He dies.*)
BRANGÆNA (*still without*). Kurvenal! Madman!
    O hear—thou mistakest!
KURVENAL. Treacherous maid!   (*To his men.*)
    Come! Follow me!
    Force them below!   (*They fight.*)
MARK (*without*). Hold, thou frantic man!
    Lost are thy senses?
KURVENAL. Here ravages Death!
    Nought else, O king,
    is here to be holden!
    If you would earn it, come on!
       (*He sets upon* MARK *and his followers.*)
MARK. Away, rash maniac!
BRANGÆNA (*has climbed over the wall at the side and hastens to the front*).
    Isolda! lady.
    Joy and life!—
    What sight's here—ha!
    Liv'st thou, Isolda! (*She goes to* ISOLDA'S *aid.*)

DRITTE SCENE

[KURWENAL *was sogleich hinter* ISOLDE *zurückgekommen; sprachlos in furchtbarer Erschütterung hat er dem Auftritte beigewohnt und bewegungslos auf* TRISTAN *hingestarrt. Aus der Tiefe hört man jetzt dumpfes Getümmel und Waffengeklirr. Der* HIRT *kommt über die Mauer gestiegen.*]

HIRT (*hastig und leise sich zu* KURWENAL *wendend*).
    Kurwenal! Hör'!
    Ein zweites Schiff.
(KURWENAL *fährt heftig auf, und blickt über die Brüstung, während der* HIRT *aus der Ferne erschüttert auf* TRISTAN *und* ISOLDE *sieht.*)
KURWENAL. Tod und Hölle! (*In Wuth ausbrechend.*)

    Alles zur Hand!
    Marke und Melot
    hab' ich erkannt.—
    Waffen und Steine!
    Hilf mir! An's Thor!
(*Er springt mit dem* HIRT *an das Thor, das Beide in der Hast zu verrammeln suchen.*)
DER STEUERMANN (*stürzt herein*).
    Marke mir nach
    mit Mann und Volk!
    Vergeb'ne Wehr!
    Bewältigt sind wir.
KURWENAL. Stell' dich, und hilf'!—
    So lang' ich lebe,
    lugt mir Keiner herein!
BRANGÄNE'S STIMME (*aussen, von unten her*).
    Isolde, Herrin!
KURWENAL. Brangäne's Ruf? (*Hinabrufend.*)
    Was such'st du hier?
BRANGÄNE. Schliess' nicht, Kurwenal!
    Wo ist Isolde?
KURWENAL. Verräth'rin auch du?
    Weh' dir, Verruchte!
MELOT'S STIMME (*von aussen*). Zurück, du Thor!
    Stemm' dich dort nicht!
KURWENAL (*wüthend auflachend*). Heiaha dem Tag,
    da ich dich treffe!
(MELOT, *mit gewaffneten Männern, erscheint unter dem Thor.* KURWENAL *stürzt sich auf ihn und streckt ihn zu Boden.*)
    Stirb, schändlicher Wicht!

VIERTE SCENE

MELOT. Wehe mir!—Tristan!   (*Er Stirbt.*)
BRANGÄNE (*noch ausserhalb*). Kurwenal! Wüthender?
    Hör', du betrügst dich.
KURWENAL. Treulose Magd!—   (*Zu den Seinen.*)
    Drauf! Mir nach!
    Werft sie zurück!   (*Sie kämpfen.*)
MARKE (*ausserhalb*). Halte, Rasender!
    Bist du von Sinnen?
KURWENAL. Hier wüthet der Tod.
    Nichts and'res, König,
    ist hier zu holen:
    willst du ihn kiesen, so komm!
       (*Er dringt auf* MARKE *und dessen Gefolge ein.*)
MARKE. Zurück, Wahnsinniger!
BRANGÄNE (*hat sich seitwärts über die Mauer geschwungen, und eilt in den Vordergrund*).
    Isolde! Herrin!
    Glück und Heil!—
    Was seh' ich, ha!
    Lebst du? Isolde! (*Sie müht sich um* ISOLDE.)

MARK (*who with his followers has driven* KURVENAL *and his men back from the gate and forced his way in*).

    O wild mistake!
    Tristan, where art thou?

KURVENAL (*desperately wounded, totters before* MARK *to the front*).

    He lieth—there—
    here, where I lie too.—
          (*Sinks down at* TRISTAN'S *feet.*)

MARK. Tristan! Tristan!
    Isolda! Woe!

KURVENAL (*trying to grasp* TRISTAN'S *hand*).

    Tristan! true lord!
    Chide me not
    that I try to follow thee!   (*He dies.*)

MARK. Dead together!—
    All are dead!
    My hero Tristan!
    truest of friends,
    must thou again
    be to thy king a traitor?
    Now, when he comes
    another proof of love to give thee!
    Awaken! awaken!
    O hear my lamentation,
    thou faithless, faithful friend!
          (*Kneels down sobbing over the bodies.*)

BRANGÆNA (*who has revived* ISOLDA *in her arms*).

    She wakes! she lives!
    Isolda, hear!
    Hear me, mistress beloved!
    Tidings of joy
    I have to tell thee:
    O list to thy Brangæna!
    My thoughtless fault I have atoned;
    after thy flight
    I forthwith went to the king:
    the love potion's secret
    he scarce had learned
    when with sedulous haste
    he put to sea,
    that he might find thee,
    nobly renounce thee
    and give thee up to thy love.

MARK. O why, Isolda,
    Why this to me?
    When clearly was disclosed
    what before I could fathom not,
    what joy was mine to find
    my friend was free from fault!
    In haste to wed
    thee to my hero
    with flying sails
    I followed thy track:
    but howe'er can
    happiness
    o'ertake the swift course of woe?
    More food for Death did I make:
    more wrong grew in mistake.

BRANGÆNA. Dost thou not hear?
    Isolda! Lady!
    O try to believe the truth!

MARKE (*mit seinem Gefolge hat* KURWENAL *mit dessen Helfern vom Thore zurückgetrieben und dringt herein*).

    O Trug und Wahn!
    Tristan, wo bist du?

KURWENAL (*schwer verwundet, schwankt vor* MARKE *her nach dem Vordergrund*).

    Da liegt er—da—
    hier, wo ich liege—!
          (*Er sinkt zu* TRISTAN'S *Füssen zusammen.*)

MARKE. Tristan! Tristan!
    Isolde! Weh'!

KURWENAL (*nach* TRISTAN'S *Hand fassend*).

    Tristan! Trauter!
    Schilt mich nicht,
    dass der Treue auch mit kommt!   (*Er stirbt.*)

MARKE. Todt denn Alles!
    Alles todt?
    Mein Held! Mein Tristan!
    Trautester Freund?
    Auch heute noch
    musst du den Freund verrathen?
    Heut', wo er kommt
    dir höchst Treu' zu bewähren!
    Erwach'! Erwach'!
    Erwache meinem Jammer,
    du treulos treuester Freund!
          (*Schluchzend über die Leichen sich herab-*
           beugend).

BRANGÆNE (*die in ihren Armen* ISOLDE *wieder zu sich gebracht*).

    Sie wacht! Sie lebt!
    Isolde, hör'!
    Hör' mich, süsseste Frau!
    Glückliche Kunde
    lass' mich dir melden:
    vertrautest nicht Brangänen?
    Ihre blinde Schuld
    hat sie gesühnt;
    als du verschwunden,
    schnell fand sie den König:
    des Trankes Geheimniss
    erfuhr er kaum,
    als mit sorgender Eil'
    in See er stach,
    dich zu erreichen,
    dir zu entsagen,
    dich zuzuführen dem Freund.

MARKE. Warum, Isolde,
    warum, mir das?
    Da hell mir ward enthüllt,
    was zuvor ich nicht fassen konnt',
    wie selig, das ich den Freund
    frei von schuld da fand!
    Dem holden Mann
    dich zu vermählen,
    mit vollen Segeln
    flog ich dir nach:
    doch Unglückes
    Ungestüm,
    wie erreicht es, wer Frieden bringt?
    Die Aernte mehrt' ich dem Tod:
    der Wahn häufte die Noth!

BRANGÆNE. Hörst du uns nicht?
    Isolde! Traute!
    Vernimmst du die Treue nicht?

ISOLDA (*unconscious of all around her, turning her eyes with rising inspiration on* TRISTAN'*s body*).

Mild and softly
he is smiling;
how his eyelids sweetly open!
See, oh comrades,
see you not
how he beameth
ever brighter—
how he rises
ever radiant
steeped in starlight,
borne above?
See you not
how his heart
with lion zest,
calmly happy
beats in his breast?
From his lips
in heavenly rest
sweetest breath
he softly sends.
Harken, friends!
Hear and feel ye not?
Is it I
alone am hearing
strains so tender
and endearing?
Passion swelling,
all things telling,
gently bounding,
from him sounding,
in me pushes,
upward rushes
trumpet tone
that round me gushes.
Brighter growing,
o'er me flowing,
are these breezes
airy pillows?
Are they balmy
beauteous billows?
How they rise
and gleam and glisten!
Shall I breathe them?
Shall I listen?
Shall I sip them,
dive within them,
to my panting
breathing win them?
In the breezes around.
in the harmony sound
in the world's driving
whirlwind be drown'd—
and, sinking,
be drinking—
in a kiss,
highest bliss!

(ISOLDA *sinks, as if transfigured, in* BRANGÆNA'S *arms upon* TRISTAN'*s body. Profound emotion and grief of the bystanders.* MARK *invokes a blessing on the dead. Curtain.*)

ISOLDE (*die nichts um sich her vernommen, heftet das Auge mit wachsender Begeisterung auf* TRISTAN'*s Leiche*).

Mild und leise
wie er lächelt,
wie das Auge
hold er öffnet:
seht ihr, Freunde,
seh't ihr, Freunde,
Immer lichter
wie er leuchtet,
wie er minnig
immer mächt'ger,
Stern-umstrahlet
hoch sich hebt:
seh't ihr Freunde,
seh't ihr's nicht?
Wie das Herz ihm
muthig schwillt,
voll und hehr
im Busen quillt:
wie den Lippen
wonnig mild,
süsser Athem
sanft entweht:—
Freunde, seh't—
fühlt und seh't ihr's nicht!—
Höre ich nur
diese Weise,
die so wunder-
voll und leise,
Wonne klagend,
Alles sagend,
mild versöhnend
aus ihm tönend,
auf sich schwingt,
in mich dringt,
hold erhallend
um mich klingt?
Hell erschallend,
mich umwallend,
sind es Wellen
sanfter Lüfte?
Sind es Wogen
wonniger Düfte?
Wie sie schwellen,
mich umrauschen,
soll ich athmen,
soll ich lauschen?
soll ich schlürfen,
untertauchen,
süss in Düften
mich verhauchen?
In dem wogenden Schwall,
in dem tönenden Schall,
in des Welt-Athems
wehendem All—
ertrinken—
versinken—
unbewusst—
höchste Lust!

(ISOLDE *sinkt wie verklärt in* BRANGÆNE'S *Armen sanft auf* TRISTAN'*s Leiche.—Grosse Rührung und Entrückt- heit unter den Umstehenden.* MARKE *segnet die Leihen.—Der Vorhang fällt langsam.*)

THE END

DIE MEISTERSINGER VON NÜRNBERG

PREFACE.

"Die Meistersinger von Nürnberg" is the eighth in order of Wagner's published operas.

Some acquaintance with the history of the Master-singers of Germany, their manners and customs, and their technical phraseology, is indispensable for a due appreciation of much which would otherwise appear strange and incomprehensible in the text of this opera. The subject being one which has not been made readily accessible to English readers, it seems imperative that an English version of the work should not go forth to the world unaccompanied by some few elucidatory remarks.

The Master-singers are not to be regarded as mythical personages or as emanations of Wagner's brain, as certain of his critics have fondly imagined, but were real flesh and blood. Impossible as it often is to assign a boundary to the different periods of literary history, it is within the mark to assert that Master-singing is most properly to be regarded as the eventual outcome of Minne-singing, and that the culture of poetic art, which in the twelfth and thirteenth centuries belonged exclusively to the Minne-singers, in the fourteenth and four following centuries devolved upon the Master-singers. The Minne-singers, it should be borne in mind, were mostly of noble birth, and lived in kings' houses or wandered about from court to court; the Master-singers, on the other hand, belonged to the burgher and artisan class. Heinrich von Meissen, surnamed Frauenlob, who died in 1318, is generally looked upon as the founder of their schools and guilds. From his time verse-craft became one of the incorporated trades in nearly all German cities, and the burghers obtained the freedom of it as of any other corporation. The aims of the Master-singers' schools and guilds were strictly moral; by the culture and improvement of poetry, and by the discipline which their rules imposed, they sought to raise the mental and moral standard of their youth. But, ascribing an extravagant antiquity to their institutions, placing form above matter, and hedging themselves about with hard and fast rules, the Master-singers arrogated to themselves an undue importance. It is the conceit arising from this, their sacrifice of matter to form, their pendantry and their conventionalism, that Wagner has sought to satirize in this opera.

In Nuremberg the principal meetings of the Master-singers were held in the Church of St. Catharine after afternoon service on Sundays and Holydays. For an insight into the constitution of their guilds and schools, their rules and regulations, reference is due to the "Schulordnung" or "Lagerbuch," and to the "Tabulatur." The one regulated the discipline and business of their organization, the other its artistic side. The singing at their sittings was divided into "Freisingen" (free singing) and "Hauptsingen" (principal singing). In the former, anyone, even a stranger, might take part; in the latter, which was competitive, the faults against the rules committed by the singer were noted on a slate by a "Merker" (marker) ensconced behind a curtain. Seven faults were allowed, and he who exceeded this number was declared "outsung" and "outdone" ("versungen und verthan"). The candidate for admission into a guild was obliged to find vouchers for his respectability, and had also to undergo the ordeal of singing before the members. If the Marker declared that he had complied with the rules and regulations he was decorated with a silver chain and badge—the latter representing King David playing upon the harp—and was honorably admitted into the guild.

Candidates for admission into a guild, and the younger members thereof, were apprenticed to and instructed free of cost by the elder members, who held the rank of Masters. The members of a guild were thus classified: He who had only partially mastered the "Tabulatur" was called a "Schüler" (scholar); he who had completely familiarized himself with it was a "Schulfreund" (schoolman); he who could sing some half-dozen tunes was a "Singer;" he who could make verses to a given tune was a "Poet"; and he who could invent a new scheme of verse and a new tune was dubbed a "Master."

The "Tabulatur" consisted of rules and prohibitions. The different modes of rhyming were thus defined therein:

Monosyllabic rhymes were called "stumpfe;" dissyllabic "klingende." "Waisen" were rhymeless lines; "Körner" were lines rhyming with one in the following stanza. "Pausen" were monosyllabic words constituting an entire line and rhyming with another similarly situated; dissyllables thus positioned were called "Schlagreime." Thirty-three "Feller" (faults) which were to be guarded against were specified: e. g., a single line might not contain more than thirteen syllables, because more could not be sung in a single breath. A singer must be careful to choose a key within the register of his voice. Among the faults were "blinde Meinung" (clouded meaning, i. e., the omission of conjunctions); "falsch Gebänd" (faulty versification); "unredbare Wörter" (unsingable phrases); "Klebsilbe" (word clippings, i. e., the contraction of two syllables into one); "Laster" (vices, i. e., faulty rhymes) "Aequivoca" (words of a double meaning); "Differenz" (the displacement of the letters in a word, etc.).

The poems of the Master-singers were always lyrical, and generally sung to a given tune. The length of the verse, the number of the lines, and the order of the rhymes being variable, their poems were susceptible of a great variety of forms. "Töne" (tones) denoted the scheme of versification; "Weisen" (modes), the melodies to which they were sung. There were some hundreds of these tones and modes, each of which had its particular title. The Masters were bound to know not only their titles, but to be able to sing them. The construction of a Master-song was governed by fixed rules. The scheme on which it was based was called a "Bar" (stave) and was divided into three or more "Gesätze" (stanzas). Each "Gesätz" consisted generally of two "Stollen" (shorter stanzas) in the same metre, and sung to the same tune. The first "Gesätz" was followed by an "Abgesang" (after-song), differing in metre and in length from the preceding stanzas, and sung to a different melody. The "Abgesang" was sometimes supplemented by another "Gesätz" in the same metre as the first. A complete Master-song generally consisted of three such "staves."

Of the circumstances which led to the choice of the Master-singers as the subject for an opera, Wagner has himself told us in a pamphlet entitled "Eine Mittheilung in meine Freunde" (A Communication to my Friends), first published in 1851. As the account he therein gives is both interesting in itself and at the same time furnishes a sketch of the plot of the opera, it seems best to reproduce it here, as far as translation will allow, in his own words. Wagner writes:—

"Immediately after the conclusion of 'Tannhäuser' (in 1845), I was fortunate in being able to visit a Bohemian bathing-place for the benefit of my health. Here, as on all occasions when I have been able to withdraw myself from the air of the 'footlights,' and from my official duties in such an atmosphere, I soon felt myself in a light and joyous mood. For the first time, and with artistic significance, a gaiety peculiar to my character manifested itself within me. Almost without premeditation I had a

short time previously resolved that my next should be a *comic* opera. I recall that this determination resulted principally from the advice of well-meaning friends, who wished me to write an opera in a 'lighter style,' because this, they said, would procure my admission to the German theatres, and thus insure that success for the continued want of which my outward circumstances had been seriously threatened.

"As among the Athenians of old a tragedy was followed by a merry satirical piece, there suddenly appeared to me during this journey for my health the picture of a comic play, which might suitably be made to serve as a satirical supplement for my 'Battle of the Bards at the Wartburg.' This was 'Die Meistersinger von Nürnburg,' with Hans Sachs at their head. I conceived Hans Sachs as the last example of the artistically productive folk's-spirit, and in this relation I opposed him to the narrow-mindedness of Master-singer-like Burgherdom, to the extremely droll and tabulatur-poetical pedantry of which I gave a personal expression in the character of the 'Marker.' This 'Marker' as every one knows, or as perhaps our critics did not know, was the overseer appointed by the Singers' Guild to 'mark' with strokes the faults against the rules committed by the executants, especially if they were candidates for admission to the Guild. Whoever got a certain number of strokes against him had 'versungen,' i. e., had failed in his singing.

"Now the eldest of the Guild offered the hand of his young daughter to the Master who, at an approaching public singing-match, should win the prize. The Marker, who has already been paying his addresses to the maiden, finds a rival in the person of a young knight, who, inspired by reading the 'Book of Heroes' and the old Minne-singers, has left the poverty-stricken and decaying castle of his ancestors with a view to learning in Nuremberg the art of the Master-singers. He announces his wish to be admitted into the Guild, being prompted thereto by a passion which he has suddenly conceived for the prize-maiden, 'whom only a Master of the Guild may win.' On putting himself up for examination he sings an enthusiastic song in praise of women, which so repeatedly arouses the disapprobation of the Marker that, before he has half got through it, he has 'failed in his singing.' Sachs, who is pleased with the young man, frustrates, with a view to his welfare, a desperate attempt to carry off the maiden. In doing this he at the same time finds an opportunity of grievously offending the Marker. The latter, who has already been speaking rudely to Sachs with the view of humbling him about a pair of shoes which he has still left unfinished, stations himself at night under the maiden's window, in order to make trial of the song with which he hopes to win her by singing it to her as a serenade, it being his object to secure her voice in his favor in the adjudication of the prize. Sachs, whose workshop is opposite the house thus besung, begins singing loudly just as the Marker has commenced his serenade, because, as he tells the Marker, who is enraged at his doing so, it is necessary to keep himself awake when he has to work so late, and that the work is wanted in a hurry nobody knows better than the Marker, who has pressed him so hardly for it. At last he promises the luckless fellow to give over singing, but on condiction of his being allowed to mark also in his manner — as a shoemaker — the faults which, according to his feelings, he may find in the Marker's song, viz., by a stroke of his hammer for each fault upon the shoe stretched upon the last. The Marker sings; Sachs strikes the last again and again. In a passion the Marker jumps up; Sachs coolly asks him if he has finished his song. 'Not nearly' he shouts. Sachs, now laughing, holds up the shoes outside his shop, and declares that they are now quite finished, thanks to the 'Marker's taps.' With the rest of his song, which in despair he screams out without a pause, the Marker makes a miserable failure in the presence of the female figure which is seen violently shaking her head at the window. Disconsolate at this, he begs Sachs the following day to furnish him with a new song for his wooing. Sachs accordingly gives him a poem by the young knight, pretending that he does not know from whence it has come. He advises him, however, to make sure of having an appropriate tune to sing it to. The conceited Marker fancies he is all right in this respect, and accordingly sings the poem before the public assembly of the Masters and people to a tune which is thoroughly unsuited to it, and so disfigures it that, once more, and this time decisively, he fails entirely. Enraged thereat, he accuses Sachs of having played him a mean trick in thus foisting upon him so ignominious a poem. Sachs declares that the poem is an exceedingly good one, only it requires to be sung to an appropriate tune. It is then determined that he who knows the proper tune shall be adjudged the victor. The young knight accomplishes this and wins his bride, but rejects with scorn the offer now made him of admission into the Guild. Sachs humourously stands up in defence of the Master-singers' Guild, and finishes with the rhyme :

"'Though holy Rome herself should pass away,
   Our glorious German Art will ne'er decay.'"

The sketch which Wagner at once drew up was not, however, destined to be carried out in the rapid manner in which it was conceived. First, "Lohengrin" engrossed his attention; then the "Death of Siegfried," which eventually grew into the "Nibelung" tetralogy; and then "Tristan und Isolde." "Die Meistersinger" which must therefore have occupied his thoughts, more or less, for nearly a quarter of a century, was not completed till 1867. It was brought to a public hearing for the first time in the course of the following year, under the direction of Hans von Bulow, at Munich.

As a comical pendant to "Tannhäuser," though not so satirical a one of the Master-singers as Wagner originally intended it to be, "Die Meistersinger" is not without its analogy to this. In "Tannhäuser" it is the victory of virtue over vice that is typified; "Die Meistersinger" represents the victory of genius, aided by good sense, over pedantry and conventionalism. The moral sought to be conveyed is this: that Art is progressive, and that rules are useful, and are only to be broken by those who have learned to observe them.   C. A. B.

THE MASTER-SINGERS OF NUREMBURG.
(DIE MEISTERSINGER VON NÜRNBERG.)

ACT FIRST.	ERSTER AUFZUG.

The scene represents the interior of St. Katherine's church, in oblique section; only the last few rows of pews in the nave — which is supposed to extend out L towards the back — are visible; the foreground is the open space before the choir; this is afterwards shut off by a black curtain from the nave.

As the curtain rises the people are singing, to organ accompaniment, the last verse of a Chorale, which concludes afternoon service on the vigil of the Feast of St. John.

Hymn of the People.

When to thee our Saviour went
To receive thy Sacrament,
Ere His sacrifice divine,
We were giv'n salvation's sign,
That through Baptism we might **prove**
Worthy of His death and love.
Interceder,
Christ's preceder!
Take us gently o'er
Unto Jordan's shore.

(During the Chorale and its interludes the following dumb show takes place, accompanied by the orchestra: —

In the last pew are seated Eva and Magdalena; Walter v. Stolzing is leaning against a pillar at a little distance, his eyes fixed on Eva. Eva turns repeatedly towards the knight and answers his now importunate, now tender glances of entreaty and passion shyly and modestly, but tenderly and encouragingly. Magdalena often breaks off her singing to give Eva a reproving nudge. — When the hymn is ended and while, during a long postlude on the organ, the congregation is gradually leaving by the principal door (supposed to be L at back), Walter advances hastily towards Eva and her companion. who have also risen from their seats and turned to go.)

Walter.
(Softly but ardently to Eva.)

Oh stay! — One word, I do entreat!

Eva.
(Quickly turning to Magdalena.)

My kerchief! Look! 'T is on the seat!

Magdalena.
Forgetful child! Now here's a hunt!
(Goes back to the pew.)
(6)

Die Bühne stellt das Innere der Katharinenkirche, in schrägem Durchschnitt, dar; von dem Haupstschiff, welches links ab dem Hintergrunde zu sich ausdehnend anzunehmen ist, sind nur noch die letzten Reihen der Kirchenstühlbänke sichtbar; den Vordergrund nimmt der freie Raum vor dem Chor ein; dieser wird später durch einen Vorhang gegen das Schiff zu gänzlich abgeschlossen.

Beim Aufzug hört man, unter Orgelbegleitung, von der Gemeinde den letzten Vers eines Chorals, mit welchem der Nachmittagsgottesdienst zur Einleitung des Johannisfestes schliesst, singen.

Choral der Gemeinde.

Da zu dir der Heiland kam,
Willig deine Taufe nahm,
Weihte sich dem Opfertod,
Gab er uns des Heil's Gebot:
Dass wir durch dein' Tauf' uns weih'n,
Seines Opfers werth zu sein.
Edler Täufer,
Christ's Vorläufer!
Nimm uns freundlich an,
Dort am Fluss Jordan.

(Während des Chorales und dessen Zwischenspielen entwickelt sich, vom Orchester begleitet, folgende pantomimische Scene.

In der letzten Reihe der Kirchenstühle sitzen Eva und Magdalene; Walther v. Stolzing steht, in einiger Entfernung, zur Seite an eine Säule gelehnt, die Blicke auf Eva heftend. Eva kehrt sich wiederholt seitwärts nach dem Ritter um, und erwiedert seine bald dringend, bald zärtlich durch Gebärden sich ausdrückenden Bitten und Betheuerungen schüchtern und verschämt, doch seelenvoll und ermuthigend. Magdalene unterbricht sich öfter im Gesang, um Eva zu zupfen und zur Vorsicht zu mahnen. — Als der Choral zu Ende ist, und, während eines längeren Orgelnachspieles, die Gemeinde dem Hauptausgange, welcher links dem Hintergrunde zu anzunehmen ist, sich zuwendet, um allmählich die Kirche zu verlassen, tritt Walther an die beiden Frauen, welche sich ebenfalls von ihren Sitzen erhoben haben, und dem Ausgange sich zuwenden wollen, lebhaft heran.)

Walther.
(Leise, doch feurig zu Eva.)

Verweilt! — Ein Wort! Ein einzig Wort!

Eva.
(Sich rasch zu Magdalene wendend.)

Mein Brusttuch! Schau! Wohl liegt's im Ort?

Magdalene.
Vergesslich Kind! Nun heisst es: such'!
(Sie kehrt nach den Sitzen zurück.)

Walter. Maiden, forgive if I affront —
One thing to ask you, one to discover,
What rules would I not dare pass over?
Is life for me or death? — Is bliss for me or
 bane?
Thy answer let in one word be clothed:
Fair maiden, say —

Magdalena.
(Returning.)

Here 't is again!

Eva.   Alack! my scarf-pin! . . .

Magdalena.   Did it fall out?
(She goes back, searching on the ground.)

Walter.
Is 't light and laughter, or gloom and doubt?
Can I attain the aim I approach to,
Or must I hear the syllable loathed —
Fair maiden, say —

Magdalena.
(Returning again.)

I have found the brooch, too!
Come, child, here 's pin and 'kerchief, look!
Good lack! if I 've not forgot my book!
(Goes back once more.)

Walter.   This single word, you speak it not —
This syllable that casts my lot?
Say Yes or No, — 't is quickly mouthed:
Fair maiden, say, are you betrothed?

Magdalena.
(Who has returned again, curtsies to Walter.)

Sir knight, your servant!
This is a compliment!
Our Eva's escort
Do you then represent?
Pray, Master Pogner is it
Your worship seeks to visit?

Walter.
(Sorrowfully.)

Would I never his house had seen!

Magdalena.
Hey day, sir! why, what do you mean?
When unto Nuremberg first you wended
Was not his friendly hand extended?
The bed and board, the dishes, drinks
He gave deserve some thanks, methinks?

Eva.
Good Lena! Pray! He meant it not so:
He is only eager to know —

Walther.
Fräulein! Verzeih't der Sitte Bruch!
Eines zu wissen, Eines zu fragen,
Was nicht müsst' ich zu brechen wagen!
Ob Leben oder Tod? Ob Segen oder Fluch?
Mit einem Worte sei mir's vertraut: —
Mein Fräulein, sagt —

Magdalene.
(Zurückkommend.)

Hier ist das Tuch.

Eva.   O weh! die Spange?

Magdalene.   Fiel sie wohl ab?
(Sie geht, am Boden suchend, wieder zurück.)

Walther.
Ob Licht und Lust, oder Nacht und Grab?
Ob ich erfahr', wonach ich verlange,
Ob ich vernehme, wovor mir graut. —
Mein Fräulein, sagt . . .

Magdalene.
(Wieder zurückkommend.)

Da ist auch die Spange. —
Komm' Kind! Nun hast du Spang' und
 Tuch. —
O weh! da vergass ich selbst mein Buch!
(Sie kehrt wieder um.)

Walther.
Dies eine Wort, ihr sagt mir's nicht?
Die Sylbe, die mein Urtheil spricht?
Ja, oder: Nein! — ein flücht'ger Laut:
Mein Fräulein, sagt, seid ihr schon Braut?

Magdalene.
(Die bereits zurückgekommen, verneigt sich vor
Walther.)

Sieh da, Herr Ritter?
Wie sind wir hochgeehrt:
Mit Evchen's Schutze
Habt ihr euch gar beschwert?
Darf den Besuch des Helden
Ich Meister Pogner melden?

Walther.
(Leidenschaftlich.)

Betrat ich doch nie sein Haus!

Magdalene.
Ei! Junker! Was sagt ihr da aus!
In Nürnberg eben nur angekommen,
War't ihr nicht freundlich aufgenommen?
Was Küch' und Keller, Schrein und Schrank
Euch bot, verdient' es keinen Dank?

Eva.
Gut' Lenchen! Ach! das meint er ja nicht.
Doch wohl von mir wünscht er Bericht —

How shall I say?—I scarce comprehend—
His words my senses nearly suspend!—
He asks—about my choice!

Magdalena.
(Looking about apprehensively.)

Oh lud! subdue your voice!
Come directly home with me,
Just suppose the folks should see!

Walter. Not yet, till I know my fate!

Eva. They 're gone, there 's no one nigh.

Magdalena. That 's why I 'm in a state!
Sir knight, pray elsewhere try!

(David enters from the sacristy and busies himself with drawing together dark curtains which are so disposed as to close off the foreground of the stage from the nave.)

Walter. Nay! your reply?

Eva.
(Holding Magdalena.)

Reply?

Magdalena.
(Who has turned away, perceives David, pauses and calls tenderly aside.)

David! Why, can it be?

Eva.
(Urgently.)

What answer? Speak for me!

Magdalena.
(Distracted in her attention, looking round repeatedly at David.)

Chevalier, what of this maid you ask
To answer is no easy task:
She is betrothed, you might expect—

Eva.
(Quickly interrupting.)

But none has seen the bridegroom elect.

Magdalena.
The groom, in sooth, will not be known
Until to-morrow by trial shewn,
When a Master-Singer receives the prize—

Eva.
(As before.)

And my own hand his bay-wreath ties.

Walter. A Master-Singer?

Eva.
(Timidly.)

Are you not one?

Wie sag' ich's schnell ?—Versteh' ich's aoch
kaum!—
Mir ist, als wär' ich gar wie im Traum!—
Er frägt,—ob ich schon Braut?

Magdalene.
(Sich scheu umsehend.)

Hilf Gott! Sprich nich so laut!
Jetzt lass' uns nach Hause gehn;
Wenn uns die Leut' hier sehn!

Walther. Nicht eher, bis ich Alles weiss!

Eva. 's ist leer, die Leut' sind fort.

Magdalene.
D'rum eben wird mir heiss!—
Herr Ritter, an andrem Ort!

(David tritt aus der Sacristei ein und macht sich darüber her, dunkle Vorhänge, welche so angebracht sind, dass sie den Vordergrund der Bühne nach dem Kirchenschiff zu schräg abschliessen, aneinander zu ziehen.)

Walther. Nein! Erst dies Wort?

Eva.
(Magdalene haltend.)

Dies Wort?

Magdalene.
(Die sich bereits umgewendet, erblickt David, hält an und ruit zärtlich für sich.)

David? Ei! David hier!

Eva.
(Drängend.)

Was sag' ich? Sag' du's mir!

Magdalene.
(Mit Zerstreutheit, öfters nach David sich umsehend.)

Herr Ritter, was ihr die Jungfer fragt,
Das ist so leichtlich nicht gesagt:
Fürwahr ist Evchen Pogner Braut—

Eva.
(Schnell unterbrechend.)

Doch hat noch Keiner den Bräut'gam er
schaut.

Magdalene.
Den Bräut'gam wohl noch Niemand kennt,
Bis morgen ihn das Gericht ernennt,
Das dem Meistersinger ertheilt den Preis—

Eva.
(Wie zuvor.)

Und selbst die Braut ihm reicht das Reis.

Walther. Dem Meistersinger?

Eva.
(Bang.)

Seid ihr das nicht?

Walter. A trial-song?

Magdalena. 'Fore judges done.

Walter. Who wins the prize?

Magdalena. 'T is for them to shew one.

Walter The bride will choose—?

Eva.
(Forgetting herself.)
You, or else no one!

(Walter turns aside in great perturbation, pacing up and down.)

Magdalena.
(Greatly shocked.)
Why, Eva! Eva! Are you insane?

Eva. Good Lena! Help me my lover to gain!

Magdalena.
Yesterday first did you see his face.

Eva. Kindled my love at so swift a pace
Having his portrait so oft in sight.
Say, is he not like David quite?

Magdalena. Are you mad? Like David?

Eva. The picture, I mean.

Magdalena. Oh! he with the harp and beard long flowing,
As on the Masters' escutcheon seen?

Eva.
Nay! he Goliath with pebble o'erthrowing,
With sword at side and sling in hand,
Light locks surrounding his head like rays,
As Master Albrecht Dürer portrays.

Magdalena.
(Sighing loudly.)
Ah! David! David!

David.
(Who has gone out, now returns with a rule stuck in his girdle, and swinging in his hand a large piece of chalk tied to a string.)
Here am I! who calls?

Magdalena.
Ah, David! through thee what ill befalls!
(Aside.)
The darling rogue! he knows it, too!
(Aloud.)
Why, look! he's shut us all up inside here!

David.
(Tenderly to Magdalena.)
But *you* in my heart!

Walther. Ein Werbgesang?

Magdalene. Vor Wettgericht

Walther. Den Preis gewinnt?

Magdalene. Wen die Meister meinen

Walther. Die Braut dann wählt?

Eva.
(Sich vergessend.)
Euch, oder Keinen!

(Walther wendet sich, in grosser Aufregung auf und abgehend, zur Seite.)

Magdalene.
(Sehr erschrocken.)
Was? Evchen! Evchen! Bist du von Sinnen?

Eva.
Gut' Lene! hilf mir den Ritter gewinnen!

Magdalene.
Sah'st ihn doch gestern zum ersten Mal?

Eva. Das eben schuf mir so schnelle Qual,
Dass ich schon längst ihn im Bilde sah;
Sag', trat er nicht ganz wie David nah'?

Magdalene. Bist du toll? Wie David?

Eva. Wie David im Bild.

Magdalene.
Ach! meinst du den König mit der Harfen,
Und langem Bart in der Meister Schild?

Eva.
Nein! der, dess' Kiesel den Goliath warfen,
Das Schwert im Gurt, die Schleuder zur Hand,
Von lichten Locken das Haupt umstrahlt,
Wie ihn uns Meister Dürer gemalt.

Magdalene.
(Laut seufzend.)
Ach, David! David!

David.
(Der herausgegangen und jetzt wieder zurückkommt, ein Lineal im Gürtel und ein grosses Stück weisser Kreide an einer Schnur in der Hand schwenkend.)
Da bin ich! Wer ruft?

Magdalene.
Ach, David! Was ihr für Unglück schuft!
(Für sich.)
Der liebe Schelm! wüsst' er's noch nicht?
(Laut.)
Ei, seht! da hat er uns gar verschlossen?

David.
(Zärtlich zu Magdalene.)
In's Herz euch allein!

Magdalena.
>   (Aside.)
>   His face is so true!
>   (Aloud.)
> Come, say! what frolic's to be tried here?

David. Forefend it! Frolic? A serious thing!
For the Masters I'm preparing the ring.

Magdalena. What! will there be singing?

David.   A trial mere:
That Prentice wins his enfranchisement
Who ne'er gained for breach of the rules
          chastisement;
He who passes is Master here.

Magdalena.
Then the knight has dropped on the proper
          spot.
Now, Evy, come, we ought to trot.

Walter.
>   (Quickly turning to them.)
> To Master Pogner let me escort you.

Magdalena.
Await his approach; he'll be here soon.
If to win our Eva sought you,
Both time and place were opportune.
>   (Two Prentices enter, bearing benches.)
> Quick! bid us adieu!

Walter. What must I do?

Magdalena. Let David supply all
          The facts of the trial.—
David, my dear, just heed what I say!
You must induce Sir Walter to stay.
          The larder I'll sweep,
          The best for you keep;
To-morrow rewards shall fall faster
If this young knight is made Master.
>   (She hurries towards the door.)

Eva.
>   (To Walter.)
> When shall I see you?

Walter.
>   (Ardently.)
>   This evening, for sure!
> What use declaring
> How great my daring?
> New is my heart, new my mind,
> New to my senses is all I find,
> One thing I spring to,
> One thing I cling to;

Magdalene.
>   (Bei Seite.)
>   Das treue Gesicht!—
>   (Laut.)
> Nein sagt! Was treibt ihr hier für Possen?

David.
Behüt' es! Possen! Gar ernste Ding'?
Für die Meister hier richt' ich den Ring.

Magdalene. Wie? Gäb' es ein Singen?

David.   Nur Freiung heut':
Der Lehrling wird da losgesprochen,
Der nichts wider die Tabulatur verbrochen:
Meister wird, wen die Prob' nicht reu't.

Magdalene.
Da wär' der Ritter ja am rechten Ort.—
Jetzt, Evchen, komm', wir müssen fort.

Walther.
>   (Schnell sich zu den Frauen wendend.)
> Zu Meister Pogner lasst mich euch geleiten.

Magdalene.
Erwartet den hier: er ist bald da.
Wollt ihr euch Evchen's Hand erstreiten,
Rückt Ort und Zeit das Glück euch nah'.
>   (Zwei Lehrbuben kommen dazu und tragen Bänke.)
> Jetzt eilig von hinnen!

Walther.
>   Wass soll ich beginnen?

Magdalene.
          Lasst David euch lehren
          Die Freiung begehren. —
Davidchen! hör', mein lieber Gesell,
Den Ritter bewahr' hier wohl zur Stell'!
          Was Fein's aus der Küch'
          Bewahr' ich für dich:
Und morgen begehr' du noch dreister,
Wird heut' der Junker hier Meister.
>   (Sie drängt fort.)

Eva.
>   (Zu Walther.)
> Seh' ich euch wieder?

Walther.
>   (Feurig.)
>   Heut' Abend, **gewiss**!—
> Was ich will wagen,
> Wie könnt' ich's sagen!
> Neu ist mein Herz, neu mein Sinn,
> Neu ist mir Alles, was ich beginn'.
> Eines nur weiss ich,
> Eines begrief' ich:

The hope sustaining
Thy hand of gaining!
Though to obtain thee my sword avail not,
As Master-Singer surely I'll fail not.
For thee gold untold!
For thee
Poet's courage bold!

Eva.

(With great warmth.)
My heart's secret fold
For thee
Loving heed doth hold!

Magdalena   Quick, home, or shall scold!

David.

(Measuring Walter.)
A Master? Oho! you're bold!

(Magdalena pulls Eva quickly away through the curtains.
Walter, disturbed and brooding, has thrown himself
upon a raised ecclesiastical arm-chair which two Prentices
had just moved away from the wall to the middle of the
stage.
More Prentices enter; they bring and arrange benches
and prepare everything (during the following dialogue)
for the sitting of the Master-Singers.)

First Prentice.   David, why skulk?

Second Prentice.   Work apace!

Third Prentice.
The Marker's platform help us place!

David.   My labor and industry shame ye:
Work by yourselves; my own affairs claim
me!

Second Prentice.   What airs he takes!

Third Prentice.   A model Prentice!

First Prentice.
His time to a shoemaker lent is.

Third Prentice.
His last and pen he holds together.

Second Prentice.
While cobbling he writes his stuff.

First Prentice.
He scribbles verses on scarlet leather.

Third Prentice.
(With expressive gesture.)
We'll soon give him tanning enough!

(They pursue their work, laughing.)

David.
(After observing the meditating knight awhile, calls
loudly):
"Now, begin!"

Mit allen Sinnen
Euch zu gewinnen!
Ist's mit dem Schwert nicht, mus es gelingen
Gilt es als Meister euch zu ersingen.
Für euch Gut und Blut!
Für euch
Dichter's heil'ger Muth!

Eva.

(Mit grosser Wärme.)
Mein Herz, sel'ger Gluth,
Für euch
Liebesheil'ge Huld!

Magdalene.
Schnell! heim, sonst geht's nicht gut!

David.

(Walther messend.)
Gleich Meister? Oho! viel Muth!

(Magdalene zieht Eva rasch durch die Vorhänge fort
Walther hat sich, aufgeregt und brütend, in einen
kathederartigen Lehnstuhl geworfen, welchen zuvor
zwei Lehrbuben, von der Wand ab, mehr nach der Mitte
zu, gerückt hatten.
Noch mehrere Lehrbuben sind eingetreten: sie tragen
und richten Bänke, und bereiten Alles (nach der unter
folgenden Angabe) zur Sitzung der Meistersinger vor.)

Erster Lehrbube.
David! was stehst?

Zweiter Lehrbube.   Greif's an's Werk!

Dritter Lehrbube.
Hilf uns richten das Gemerk!

David.
Zu eifrigst war ich vor euch allen:
Nun schafft für euch; hab' ander Gefal
len!

Zweiter Lehrbube
Was der sich dünkt?

Dritter Lehrbube.   Der Lehrling Muster!

Erster Lehrbube.
Das macht, weil sein Meister ein Schuster.

Dritter Lehrbube.
Beim Leisten sitzt er mit der Feder.

Zweiter Lehrbube.
Beim Dichten mit Draht und Pfriem'.

Erster Lehrbube.
Sein' Verse schreibt er auf rothes Leder.

Dritter Lehrbube.
(Mit der entsprechenden Gebärde.)
Das, dächt' ich, gerbten wir ihm!

(Sie machen sich lachend an die fernere Herrichtung.)

David.
(Nachdem er den sinnenden Ritter eine Weile be
trachtet, ruft sehr stark.)
"Fanget an!"

Walter.
       (Looking up, surprised.)
             What is it ?

David.
       (Still louder.)
" Now, begin ! " — So cries the Marker ;
Then you must sing up ; don't you know that ?

Walter. Who is the Marker ?

David.   Don't you know that ?
T als of song were you never at ?

Walter.
No, ne'er with for judge a trade-worker.

David. Are you a " Poet ? "

Walter.   May be so !

David. Are you a " Singer ? "

Walter.   I dont know.

David.
But " Schoolman," surely, and "Scholar"
   you 've been ?

Walter.
The terms I 've never heard nor seen.

David.
And yet you would be at once a Master ?

Walter.
Why should that seem to threaten disaster ?

David. O Lena ! Lena !

Walter.   What do you say ?

David. O Magdalena !

Walter.   Shew me the way !

David. The Tones and Modes we render
    Have many a form and name ;
    The harsh ones and the tender :
    Who would try a list to frame ?
A "Singer" and " Poet," both, d' ye see,
Previous to " Master " one must be

Walter. Who *is* a Poet ?

Prentices.
       (At work.)
          David ! ho there !

David. Presently, wait !
       (To Walter.)
          Who 's Poet, sir ?
When you a " Singer " have been created
And the Master-phrases have rightly stated,

Walther
       (Verwundert aufblickend.)
          Was soll's !

David.
       (Noch stärker.)
" Fanget an ! " — So ruft der " Merker ; "
Nun sol t ihr singen : — wisst ihr das nicht !

Walther.
Wer ist der Merker ?

David.   Wisst ihr das nicht.
War't ihr noch nie bei 'nem Sing-Gericht ?

Walther.
Noch nie, wo die Richter Handwerker.

David.
Seid ihr ein "Dichter ? "

Walther.   Wär' ich's doch !

David.
Waret ihr " Singer ? "

Walther.   Wüsst ich's noch !

David.
Doch " Schulfreund " war't ihr, und "Schüler" zuvor ?

Walther.
Das klingt mir alles fremd vor'm Ohr.

David.
Und so grad'hin wollt ihr Meister werden !

Walther.
Wie machte das so grosse Beschwerden ?

David. O Lene ! O Lene !

Walther.   Wie ihr doch so thut

David. O Magdalene !

Walther.   Rathet mir gut !

David. Der Meister Tön' und Weisen,
    Gar viel an Nam' und Zahl,
    Die starken und die leisen,
    Wer die wüsste allzumal !
Denn " Singer" und "Dichter" **müsst ih**
   sein,
Eh' ihr zum " Meister " kehret ein.

Walther. Wer ist nun Dichter ?

Lehrbuben.
       (Während der Arbeit.)
          David ! kommst' her !

David. Warte nur, gleich ! —
       (Zu Walther.)
          Wer Dichter wär' ?
Habt ihr zum " Singer " euch aufgeschwun
   gen
Und der Meister-Töne richtig gesungen,

If by yourself, with rhyme and word,
You can construct and let be heard
Straightway a novel Master-strain,
At once the Poet's prize you 'll gain.

Prentices.
Hey, David! shall we report this matter?
Will you never have finished your chatter?

David.
Oh, that 's it! When I 'm not by,
Of yourselves you place the things awry!

Walter.
Yet, one thing: Who is Master indeed?

David.
Sir knight, that matter is thus decreed:
The Poet who, with brain so witty,
To words and rhymes by himself prepared,
Can shape from the Tones a new Strain or
  Ditty,
He is a "Master-Singer" declared.

Walter
(Quickly.)
I only think of the Master-gain!
    If I sing,
    Vict'ry I wring
Only through verse with the proper strain.

David.
(Turning to the Prentices.)
What are you doing? Because I 'm not there,
All wrong you 're placing the platform and
  chair!
Is to-day "Song-class?" *You* know how;
Make smaller the stage! 'T is "Trial"
  now.

(The Prentices, who are preparing to erect a large
platform hung with curtains in the middle of the stage,
put this away, by David's direction, and build instead a
smaller platform of boards; on this they place a seat with
a little desk before it, near this a large black-board to
which they hang a piece of chalk by a string; round this
erection are hung black curtains, which are drawn round
the back and sides and then over the front.)

Prentices.
(During their work.)
Oh! of course, Master David is clev'rer than
  most!
Doubtless he 's hoping to get a high post.
    'T is Trial to-day,
    He 'll try away;
That he 's quite a "Singer" is now his boast.
The "Whack" rhyme he knows all through
  and through,
The "Sharp-hunger" tune he 'll sing you,
  too:

Füget ihr selbst nun Reim und Wort',
Dass sie genau an Stell' und Ort
Passten zu einem Meister-Ton,
Dann trüg't ihr den Dichterpreis davon.

Lehrbuben.
He, David! Soll man's dem Meister klagen!
Wirst dich bald des Schwatzens entschlagen?

David.
Oho! Ja wohl! Denn helf' ich euch nicht,
Ohne mich wird Alles doch falsch gericht'!

Walther.
Nun dies' noch; wer wird "Meister" genannt?

David.
Damit, Herr Ritter, ist's so bewandt!—
Der Dichter, der aus eig'nem Fleisse
Zu Wort' und Reimen, die er erfand,
Aus Tönen auch fügt eine neue Weise,
Der wird als "Meistersinger" erkannt.

Walther.
(Rasch.)
So bleibt mir nichts als der Meisterlohn!
    Soll ich hier singen,
    Kann's nur gelingen,
Find' ich zum Vers auch den eig'nen Ton.

David.
(Der sich zu den Lehrbuben gewendet.)
Was macht ihr denn da?—Ja, fehl' ich beim
  Werk,
Verkehrt nur richtet ihr Stuhl und Ge-
  merk!—
Ist denn heut' "Singschul'?"—dass ihr's
  wisst,
Das kleine Gemerk!—nur "Freiung" ist!

(Die Lehrbuben, welche Anstalt getroffen hatten, in der
Mitte der Bühne ein grösseres Gerüste mit Vorhängen
aufzuschlagen, schaffen auf Davids Weisung dies schnell
bei Seite und stellen dafür ebenso eilig ein geringeres
Brettbodengerüste auf; darauf stellen sie einen Stuhl mit
einem kleinen Pult davor, daneben eine grosse schwarze
Tafel, daran die Kreide am Faden aufgehängt wird; um
das Gerüst sind schwarze Vorhänge angebracht, welche
zunächst hinten und an beiden Seiten, dann auch vorn
ganz zusammengezogen werden.)

Die Lehrbuben.
(Während der Herrichtung.)
Aller End' ist doch David der Allerge-
  scheit'st!
Nach hohen Ehren gewiss er geizt:
    's ist Freiung heut';
    Gar sicher er freit,
Als vornehmer "Singer" schon er sich
  spreizt!
Die "Schlag"-Reime fest er inne hat,
"Arm-Hunger"-Weise singt er glatt:

But the "Hearty-kick" strain is what he
   knows best,
His master oft plays it him with zest.

(They laugh.)

David.

Aye, jeer away! but not at me;
Another laughing-stock you'll see.
He ne'er was "Scholar," learnt no singing,
But yet o'er "Poets" would be springing;
    A noble knight he,
    In single fight he
Thinks without any disaster
Here to rise to a "Master."
    So settle with care
    Both stage and chair!
Come here! Place there the board on wall,
That on it the Marker's fingers may fall!
    (Turning to Walter.)
Aye, Aye! the "Marker!" Are n't you
   afraid?
With him have many their failures made.
Seven faults you are suffered to make;
They 're marked with his chalk ev'ry one;
If you commit one further mistake,
You 're "outsung," and declared "outdone."
    So have a care!
    The Marker's there.
God speed your Master-singing,
May you the chaplet be winning;
The wreath of flowers in silk so bright;
I hope it may fall to your lot, sir knight!

The Prentices.

(Who have closed the Marker's place, take hands and
dance in a ring round it.)

    "The wreath of flowers in silk so bright,
    I hope it may fall to your lot, sir knight."

(The erection is now completed in the following
manner:—at the R side covered benches are placed in
such a way as to curve towards the C. At the end of
these in the middle of the stage is the Marker's place, as
before described. L stands only the elevated seat ("the
Singer's Seat") opposite to the benches. At back, against
the large curtain, is a long, low bench for the Prentices—
Walter, vexed with the gibes of the boys, has seated himself on the front bench.

Pogner and Beckmesser enter from the sacristy, conversing; gradually the other masters assemble. The
Prentices, on seeing the Masters, enter, disperse and wait
respectfully by the back bench. Only David stands by
the entrance to the sacristy.)

Die "harte-Tritt"-Weis' doch kennt er am
   best',
Die trat ihm sein Meister hart und fest.
    (Sie lachen.)

David.

Ja, lacht nur zu! Heut' bin ich's nicht;
Ein Andrer stellt sich zum Gericht:
Der war nicht "Schüler," ist nicht "Sin-
   ger,"
Den "Dichter," sagt er, überspring' er;
    Denn er ist Junker,
    Und mit einem Sprung er
Denkt ohne weit're Beschwerden
Heut' hier "Meister" zu werden. —
    D'rum richtet nur fein
    Das Gemerk dem ein!
Dorthin! — Hierher! — Die Tafel an die
   Wand,
So dass sie recht dem Merker zur Hand!
    (Sich zu Walther umwendend.)
Ja, ja! — dem "Merker!" — Wird euch wohl
   bang?
Vor ihm schon mancher Werber vorsang.
Sieben Fehler giebt er euch vor,
    Die merkt er mit Kreide dort an;
Wer über sieben Fehler verlor,
    Hat versungen und ganz verthan!
    Nun nehmet euch in Acht!
    Der Merker wacht.
Glück auf zum Meistersingen!
Mög't ihr euch das Kränzlein erschwin-
   gen!
Das Blumenkränzlein aus Seiden fein,
Wird das dem Herrn Ritter beschieden
   sein?

Die Lehrbuben.

(Welche das Gemerk zugleich geschlossen, fassen sich
an und tanzen einen verschlungenen Reihen darum.)

    "Das Blumenkränzlein aus Seiden fein
    Wird das dem Herrn Ritter beschieden
    sein?

(Die Einrichtung ist nun folgender Massen beendigt:—
Zur Seite rechts sind gepolsterte Bänke in der Weise
aufgestellt, dass sie einen schwachen Halbkreis nach der
Mitte zu bilden. Am Ende der Bänke, in der Mitte der
Scene, befindet sich das "Gemerk" benannte Gerüste,
welches zuvor hergerichtet worden. Zur linken Seite
rechts nur der erhöhte, kathederartige Stuhl ["der Singstuhl"] der Versammlung gegenüber. Im Hintergrunde,
den grossen Vorhang entlang, steht eine lange niedere
Bank für die Lehrlinge. Walther, verdriesslich über das
Gespött der Knaben, hat sich auf die vordere Bank niedergelassen.
Pogner und Beckmesser kommen im Gespräch aus der
Sacristei; allmählich versammeln sich immer mehrere der
Meister. Die Lehrbuben, als sie die Meister eintreten
sahen, sind sogleich zurückgegangen und harren ehrerbietig an der hinteren Bank. Nur David stellt sich
anfänglich am Eingang bei der Sacristei auf.)

Pogner.

(To Beckmesser.)

Trust me, my friendship is unshaken,
What I intend is for your good,
This trial must be undertaken;
None doubts your Mastership — who could?

Beckmesser.

But won't you in that matter falter,
Which caused in sooth my doubtful mood?
If Eva's whim the whole can alter,
What use is all my Masterhood?

Pogner.

Ah, what! It seems you've mainly rested
On that your hopes equivocal;
But if her heart's not interested,
How come you wooing her at all?

Beckmesser.

Why yes, that's true; therefore I drop a
Request that you will speak for me;
Say that my wooing's fair and proper,
That with Beckmesser you agree.

Pogner. With right good will.

Beckmesser.

(Aside.)

He won't give way!
How shall I disappointment stay?

Walter.

(Who, on perceiving Pogner, has risen and advanced to
neet him, now bows to him.)

Permit me, Master!

Pogner. What! Sir Walter?

(They greet one another.)

Beckmesser.

(Still to himself.)

If women had taste! But rather to palter
Than to hear poetry they prefer.

Walter.

This truly should be my proper groove.
I frankly state that what did move
    Me from my land to part
    Was solely love of Art.
I had forgotten to announce it,
But now in public I pronounce it:
A Master-Singer I would be.
Ope, Master, pray, the Guild to me.

(Other Masters have entered and advanced.)

Pogner.

(To those near him.)

Kunz Vogelgesang — Friend Nachtigal!

Pogner.

(Zu Beckmesser.)

Seid meiner Treue wohl versehen;
Was ich bestimmt, ist euch zu Nutz.
Im Wettgesang müsst ihr bestehen;
Wer böte euch als Meister Trutz?

Beckmesser.

Doch wollt ihr von dem Punkt nicht
    weichen,
Der mich — ich sag's — bedenklich macht:
Kann Evchen's Wunsch den Werber
    streichen,
Was nützt mir meine Meister-Pracht?

Pogner.

Ei, sagt! Ich mein', vor allen Dingen
Sollt' euch an dem gelegen sein?
Könnt ihr der Tochter Wunsch nicht
    zwingen,
Wie möchtet ihr wohl um sie frei'n?

Beckmesser.

Ei ja! Gar wohl! D'rum eben bitt' ich,
Dass bei dem Kind ihr für mich sprecht,
Wie ich geworben zart und sittig,
Und wie Beckmesser grad' euch recht.

Pogner. Das thu' ich gern.

Beckmesser.

(Bei Seite.)

Er lässt nicht nach!
Wie wehrt' ich da 'nem Ungemach?

Walther.

(Der, als er Pogner gewahrt, aufgestanden und ihm ent-
gegengegangen ist, verneigt sich vor ihm.)

Gestattet, Meister!

Pogner. Wie! mein Junker!
Ihr sucht mich in der Singschul' hie?

(Sie begrüssen sich.)

Beckmesser.

(Immer bei Seite, für sich.)

Verstünden's die Frau'n! Doch schlechtes
    Geflunker
Gilt ihnen mehr als all' Poesie.

Walther.

Hie eben bin ich am rechten Ort
Gesteh' ich's frei, vom Lande fort,
    Was mich nach Nürnberg trieb,
    War nur zur Kunst die Lieb'.
Vergass ich's gestern euch zu sagen,
Heut' muss ich's laut zu künden wagen:
Ein Meistersinger möcht' ich sein.
Schliesst, Meister, in die Zunft mich ein!

(Andere Meister sind gekommen und herangetreten.)

Pogner.

(Zu den nächsten.)

Kunz Vogelgesang! Freund Nachtigall!

Hear what I've got to tell you all!
This noble knight, a friend of mine,
In the Master Art doth seek to shine.
(Greetings and introductions.)

Beckmesser.
(Still aside.)
Once more I'll essay him, but if he'll not waver
I'll strive with my voice to win the maid's favor;
In silent night, heard only by her.
I'll see if my singing her heart can stir.
(Turns.)
What man is that?

Pogner.
(To Walter.)
'Faith, I am glad!
Old times are come again, my lad.

Beckmesser.
(Aside.)
I mislike his looks.
Pogner.
(Continuing.)
In your demand
My influence you may command.

Beckmesser.
(As before.)
What wants he here with his smiling air?

Pogner.
(As before.)
Truly I helped you your lands to sell,
In our Guild I'll enter you now as well.

Beckmesser.
(As before.)
Hallo, Sixtus! Of him beware!

Walter.
(To Pogner.)
Best thanks I proffer
And gratitude offer!
Then have I permission
To seek for admission
As striver for the prize,
And Master-Singer to rise?

Beckmesser.
Oho! that's nice! His ideas are not addled!

Pogner.
Sir Walter, these things with rules are saddled.
To-day is "Trial," I'll state your case;
The Masters will always lend me their face.

(The Master-Singers have now all assembled, Sachs the last.)

Sachs. God greet ye, Masters!

Hört doch, welch' ganz besonderer Fall!
Der Ritter hier, mir wohlbekannt,
Hat der Meisterkunst sich zugewandt.
(Begrüssungen.)

Beckmesser.
(Immer noch für sich.)
Noch such' ich's zu wenden: doch sollt's nicht gelingen,
Versuch' ich des Mädchens Herz zu ersingen
In stiller Nacht, von ihr nur gehört,
Erfahr' ich, ob auf mein Lied sie schwört.
(Er wendet sich.)
Wer ist der Mensch?

Pogner.
(Zu Walther.)
Glaubt, wie mich's freut!
Die alte Zeit dünkt mich erneut.

Beckmesser.
(Immer noch für sich.)
Er gefällt mir nicht!

Pogner.
(Fortfahrend.)
Was ihr begehrt,
Soviel an mir, euch sei's gewährt.

Beckmesser.
(Ebenso.)
Was will der hier? — Wie der Blick ihn lacht!

Pogner.
(Ebenso.)
Half ich euch gern zu des Gut's Verkauf,
In die Zunft nun nehm' ich euch gleich gern auf.

Beckmesser.
(Ebenso.)
Holla! Sixtus! Auf den hab' Acht!

Walther.
(Zu Pogner.)
Habt Dank der Güte
Aus tiefstem Gemüthe!
Und darf ich denn hoffen,
Steht heut' mir noch offen
Zu werben um den Preis,
Dass ich Meistersinger heiss'?

Beckmesser.
Oho! Fein sacht! Auf dem Kopf steht kein Kegel!

Pogner.
Herr Ritter, diess geh' nun nach der Regel
Doch heut' ist Freiung! ich schlag' euch vor,
Mir leihen die Meister ein willig Ohr.

(Die Meistersinger sind nun alle angelangt, zuletzt auch Hans Sachs.)

Sachs.
Gott grüss' euch, Meister!

Vogelgesang. Are all arriven?	*Vogelgesang.* Sind wir beisammen
Beckmesser. Yes, Sachs is here, too.	*Beckmesser.* Der Sachs ist ja da!
Nachtigal. Let names be given.	*Nachtigall.* So ruft die Namen.

Fritz Kothner.
(Produces a list, stands apart from the rest, and calls.)
  To hold a Trial-examination,
  Masters, I give ye invitation:
      Of one and all
      The names I call,
  And first my own, which though I note ne'er,
  I answer to, and am Fritz Kothner.
  Are you there, Veit Pogner?

Fritz Kothner.
(Zieht eine Liste hervor, stellt sich zur Seite auf und ruft.)
  Zu einer Freiung und Zunftberathung
  Ging an die Meister ein' Einladung:
      Bei Nenn' und Nam'
      Ob jeder kam,
  Ruf' ich nun auf, als letzt-entbot'ner,
  Der ich mich nenn' und bin Fritz Kothner.
  Seid ihr da, Veit Pogner?

Pogner. Here at hand. (Sits.)	*Pogner.* Hier zur Hand. (Er setzt sich.)
Kothner. Kunz Vogelgesang?	*Kothner.* Kunz Vogelgesang?
Vogelgesang. Yes, here I stand. (Sits.)	*Vogelgesang.* Ein sich fand. (Setzt sich.)
Kothner Herman Ortel?	*Kothner.* Hermann Ortel?
Ortel. Comes when he ought. (Sits.)	*Ortel.* Immer am Ort. (Setzt sich.)
Kothner. Balthazar Zorn?	*Kothner.* Balthasar Zorn?
Zorn. Ne'er late I'm caught. (Sits.)	*Zorn.* Bleibt niemals fort. (Setzt sich.)
Kothner. Conrad Nachtigal	*Kothner.* Konrad Nachtigall?
Nachtigal. True as my song. (Sits.)	*Nachtigall.* Treu seinem Schlag (Setzt sich.)
Kothner. Augustin Moser?	*Kothner.* Augustin Moser?
Moser Here all along. (Sits.)	*Moser.* Nie fehlen mag (Setzt sich.)
Kothner. Nicholas Vogel? — No?	*Kothner.* Niklaus Vogel? — Schweigt?

A Prentice.
(Jumping up from his seat at back.)
     He's ill.
	Ein Lehrbube.
	(Sich schnell von der Bank erhebend.)
	     Ist krank

Kothner. God send him recovery.	*Kothner.* Gut' Bess'rung dem Meister!
All the Masters. Amen.	*Alle Meister.* Walt's Gott
Prentice. Good will. (Sits down again.)	*Der Lehrbube.* Schön Dank (Setz sich wieder.)
Kothner. Hans Sachs?	*Kothner.* Hans Sachs?

David.
(Officiously rising.)
     He's there, sir.
	David.
	(Vorlaut sich erhebend.)
	     Da steht er!

Sachs.
(Threatening David.)
     Tingles thy skin? —
Excuse me, Master! Sachs has come in.
(Sits.)
	Sachs.
	(Drohend zu David.)
	     Juckt dich das Fell!
	Verzeiht, Meister! — Sachs ist zur Stell'
	(Er setzt sich.)

Kothner. Sixtus Beckmesser?	*Kothner.* Sixtus Beckmesser?

Beckmesser.　　　　　　　　Always near Sachs,
Then I have a rhyme to " bloom and wax."
　　(Sits close to Sachs, who laughs.)

Kothner.　Ulrich Eisslinger?

Eisslinger.　　　　　　　　Here!
　　　　　　(Sits.)

Kothner.　　　　　　　Hans Foltz?

Foltz.　I'm there.
　　　　　　(Sits.)

Kothner.　　　　Hans Schwarz?

Schwarz.　　　　　　The list now halts.
　　　　　　(Sits.)

Kothner.　The meeting's full; a goodly show.
Shall we make choice of a Marker now?

Vogelgesang.　The festival first.

Beckmesser.
　　　　　　(To Kothner.)
　　　　　　If you are pressed,
My turn I'll yield to you with zest.

Pogner.
Not yet, my Masters! let that alone,
A weighty matter I would make known.
　　(All the Masters rise and reseat themselves.)

Kothner.　With pleasure, Master; tell.

Beckmesser.　　　　　　Immer bei Sachs,
Dass den Reim ich lern' von " blüh' und
　　wachs'."
　　(Er setzt sich neben Sachs, dieser lacht.)

Kothner.　Ulrich Eisslinger?

Eisslinger.　　　　　　　　Hier!
　　　　　　(Setzt sich.)

Kothner.　　　　　　　Hans Foltz?

Foltz.　Bin da.
　　　　　　(Setzt sich.)

Kothner.　　　Hans Schwarz?

Schwarz.　　　　Zuletzt: Gott wollt's!
　　　　　　(Setzt sich.)

Kothner.　Zur Sitzung gut und voll die Zahl.
Beliebt's, wir schreiten zur Merkerwahl?

Vogelgesang.　Wohl eh'r nach dem Fest.

Beckmesser.
　　　　　　(Zu Kothner.)
　　　　　　Pressirt's den Herrn!
Mein Stell' und Amt lass' ich ihm gern.

Pogner.
Nicht doch, ihr Meister! Lasst das jetzt fort
Für wicht'gen Antrag bitt' ich um's Wort.
　　(Alle Meister stehen auf und setzen sich wieder.)

Kothner.
Das habt ihr, Meister! Sprecht!

FOGNER'S ADDRESS.

(POGNER'S ANREDE.)

English Version by L. U.

Give heed now to what I say!
Nun hört, und ver - steht mich recht!
The feast of John the Bap-tist's
Das schö - ne Fest, Jo - han - nis -

day You know we keep to - mor - row:
tag, ihr wisst begeh'n wir mor - gen
On mea-dow green, 'mid flow - ers gay, With feast, and
auf grü - ner Au', am Blu-men-hag, bei Spiel und

dance, and mer - ry play, The cares the mind
Tanz im Lust-ge - lag, an fro - her Brust
be - set - ting With mer - ry heart for -
ge - bor - gen, ver - ges - sen sei - ner

get - ting, Each one re - joic - es as he may.
Sor - gen, ein Je - der freut sich, wie er mag.
The sing - ing school to great church
Die Sing-schul' ernst im Kir - chen

choir The mas-ters e'en are chang-ing, With noise and din the gate they gain, Ad-vanc-ing
chor die Meis-ter selbst ver-tau-schen, mit Kling und Klang hi-naus zum Thor, auf off'-ne

o'er the o-pen plain, Where ga-la sounds are ring-ing; As list-'ners to their
Wie-se zieh'n sie vor, bei hel-len Fes-tes Rau-schen das Volk sie las-sen

sing-ing, Th'un-tu-tored folk they'll not dis-dain. A prize is set, for
lau-schen dem Frei-ge-sang mit Lai-en Ohr. Zu ei-nem Werb-und

which with song Each year have sing-ers striv-en, And both are praised both
Wett-ge-sang ge-stellt sind Sie-ges-prei-se, und bei-de preist man

far and long, The song and what is giv-en. I am, thank God, a prosp'rous
weit und lang. die Ga-be, wie die Wei-se. Nun schuf mich Gott zum rei-chen

man, And since each one gives what he can, What gift I could de-
Mann; und gibt ein Je-der wie er kann, so muss-te ich wohl

cide on, That I could look with pride on, This much my mind has tried. Now
sin-nen was ich gäb zu ge-win-nen, dass ich nicht käm' zu Schand'; so

con molto espress.

hear what I de-cide. It oft has caused me sor-row
hört denn, was ich fand. In deut-schen Lan-den viel ge-

keen, To find throughout the na-tion The burgher nig-gard-ly and mean In each one's es-ti-
reis't, hat oft es mich ver-dros-sen, dass man den Bür-ger we-nig preis't, ihn karg nennt und ver-

un poco animato.

ma-tion. By lof-ty and by low-ly born, The same re-proach is made with
schlossen. An Hö-fen, wie an nied'-rer Statt, des bitt'-ren Ta-dels ward' ich

a tempo.

scorn: "By base de-sire for gold The burgher's mind's con-trolled!" That we, as
satt, dass nur auf Schacher und Geld, sein Merk der Bür-ger stellt! Dass wir im

all in Ger-man lands, Give art a-lone de-vo-tion, They seem to have no
wei-ten deutschen Reich die Kunst ein-zig noch pfle-gen, d'ran dünkt ih-nen we-nig ge-

no-ble. Yet how this to our hon-or stands, That no-bly, as man should, We
le - gen. Doch wie uns das zur Eh-re ge-reich', und das mit ho-hem Muth wir

prize the fair and good, That art . . in ev-'ry form we love, 'Twas this to the world I
schä-tzen was schön und gut, was werth die Kunst und was sie gilt, das ward ich der Welt zu

wish'd to prove, And there-fore, mas-ters, know What gift I shall be-stow!
zei - gen ge-willt, d'rum hört, Meis-ter die Gab' die als Preis be-stimmt ich hab'!

The vic - - tor in the art of song, Who wins the prize be-fore the throng,
Dem Sie - - ger der im Kunst-ge-sang vor al-lem Volk den Preis er-rang,

On John the Bap-tist's day, Be he who-e'er he may, Him give I, of art a
am Sanct Jo-han-nis-tag, sei er, wer er auch mag, dem geb ich, ein Kunst-ge-

lov - er, Of Nu-rem-berg, Veit Pog-ner, With gold and
wog - ner, von Nü-ren-berg, Veit Pog-ner, mit all' mein - em

lands and all be-side, E-va, my on-ly child, as bride!
Gut, wie's geh' und steh', E-va, mein ein-zig Kind, zur Eh'!

The Masters.
(Animatedly to one another.)
That's nobly said! Brave words — brave
man!
You see now what a Nuremberger can!
So far and wide we'll raise always
The worthy burgher Pogner's praise!

Prentices.
(Jumping up merrily.)
All our days raise and blaze
Pogner's praise.

Vogelgesang.
Who would not now unmarried be!

Sachs.
There's some would give their wives with
glee.

Nachtigal.   Come, single man,
Do all ye can.

Pogner.   My meaning you must clearly see;
No lifeless gift I offer you:

Die Meister.
(Sehr lebhaft durcheinander.)
Das nenn' ich ein Wort! Ein Wort, ein
Mann!
Da sieht man, was ein Nürnberger kann!
D'rob preis't man euch noch weit und breit,
Den wack'ren Bürger Pogner Veit!

Die Lehrbuben.
(Lustig aufspringend.)
Alle Zeit, weit und breit,
Pogner Veit!

Vogelgesang.
Wer möchte da nicht ledig' sein!

Sachs.
Sein Weib' gäb' gern wohl mancher d'rein!

Nachtigall.
Auf, ledig' Mann!
Jetzt macht euch dran!

Pogner.
Nun hört noch, wie ich's ernstlich mein'
Ein' leblos' Gabe stell' ich nicht:

The maid shall sit in judgment, too.
Our Guild the winner shall declare,
But as to marriage, 'tis but fair
    That, 'spite the Master's choice,
    The bride should have a voice.

Beckmesser.
                (To Kothner.)
Do you like that?

Kothner.
                (Aloud.)
                You mean to say
That we the maiden must obey.

Beckmesser. 'T were dangerous!

Kothner.   I cannot see
How then our judgment would be free.

Beckmesser.
Let her choose as may please her heart,
And leave the Master-Song business apart.

Pogner. Nay, nay! why so? Let me correct!
Any man whom we all elect
    May be by her rejected,
    But never another accepted:
A Master-Singer he must be;
None may she wed uncrowned by ye.

Sachs. But stay!
Perhaps that were too much to say.
The fire that warms a maiden's heart
Is not like flames of Master-Art;
Undisciplined, the female mind
Level with public voice I find.
So, if you hold to public vision
    Your high esteem of Art,
If you desire the girl's decision
    Should not the matter thwart,
Then let the people, too, decide;
With the maiden's voice they 'd coincide.
(The Prentices jump up and rub their hands.)

Beckmesser. Hey! Are not the boys contented!

Sachs.
            (Earnestly continuing.)
So may it be ne'er repented
That once, on St. John's day, ev'ry year,
Ye do not bring the people here,
But bend your Guild of Masters proud
Right willingly towards the crowd.
    You cater here for the masses;
    I think then 't were but right
    To ask the vote of those classes
    And hear if they find delight.

Ein Mägdlein sitzt mit zu Gericht.
Den Preis erkennt die Meister-Zunft;
Doch gilt's der Eh', so will's Vernunft,
    Dass ob der Meister Rath
    Die Braut den Ausschlag hat.

Beckmesser.
                (Zu Kothner.)
Dünkt euch das klug?

Kothner.
                (Laut.)
                Versteh' ich gut,
Ihr gebt uns in des Mägdlein's Huth?

Beckmesser.
Gefährlich das!

Kothner.   Stimmt es nicht bei.
Wie wäre dann der Meister Urtheil frei?

Beckmesser.
Lasst's gleich wählen nach Herzen's Ziel,
Und lasst den Meistergesang aus dem Spiel.

Pogner.
Nicht so! Wie doch! Versteht mich recht!
Wenn ihr Meister den Preis zusprecht,
    Die Maid kann dem verwehren,
    Doch nie einen Andren begehren:
Ein Meistersinger muss er sein;
Nur wen ihr krönt, den soll sie frei'n.

Sachs. Verzeiht!
Vielleicht schon ginget ihr zu weit.
Ein Mädchenherz und Meisterkunst
Erglüh'n nicht stets von gleicher Brunst;
Der Frauen Sinn, gar unbelehrt,
Dünkt mich dem Sinn des Volks gleich
    werth.
Wollt ihr nun vor dem Volke zeigen,
    Wie hoch die Kunst ihr ehrt;
Und lasst ihr dem Kind die Wahl zu eigen,
    Wollt nicht, dass dem Spruch es
        wehrt':
So lasst das Volk auch Richter sein;
Mit dem Kinde sicher stimmts überein,
(Die Lehrbuben springen auf und reiben sich die
Hände.)

Beckmesser.
Hei! wie sich die Buben freuen!

Sachs.
            (Eifrig fortfahrend.)
D'rum möcht's euch nie gereuen,
Dass jährlich am Sankt Johannisfest,
Statt dass das Volk man kommen lässt,
Herab aus hoher Meister-Wolk
Ihr selbst euch wendet zu dem Volk'.
    Dem Volke wollt ihr behagen,
    Nun dächt' ich, läg es nah',
    Ihr liesset es selbst euch auch sagen,
    Ob das ihm zur Last geschah?

Thus Art and Nation shall bloom and wax
By your good help, say I, Hans Sachs.

Vogelgesang.   That s very right!

Kothner.   And yet all wrong!

Nachtigal.
When riff-raff speak I'll hold my tongue.

Kothner.
Our Art would quickly be disgraced,
If it were swayed by public taste.

Beckmesser.
He's tried for that who talks so loud;
Clap-trap stuff he writes for the crowd.

Pogner.   Friend Sachs, what I propose is new;
Too many novelties won't do!—
I ask, then, if ye Masters will hold
My offer on the terms just told?
(The Masters rise assentingly.)

Sachs.   I am content the maid should decide.

Beckmesser.
(Aside.)
That cobbler-man I can't abide!

Kothner.   What candidate comes to me?
A bachelor he must be.

Beckmesser.
He may be a widower! How about Sachs?

Sachs.
Nay, nay, good Marker! Of younger wax
Must be the suitor who comes to woo
Our Eva, than myself or you.

Beckmesser.   Than even I?—Mannerless
knave!

Kothner. If suitors offer, their names I crave!
Is any one here who seeks to essay?

Pogner.
Well, Masters, to the work of the day!
And be it understood
That I, as Masters should,
To this knight have offered protection,
Who seeks for our election
To woo, as Master-Singers may.—
Sir Walter von Stolzing step this way!
(Walter advances and makes obeisance.)
Sir Walter Stolzing, Franconian knight:
My friends his praise both speak and write,
The last survivor of his race,
He lately left his native place

Dass Volk und Kunst gleich blüh' und
wachs',
Bestellt ihr so, mein' ich Hans Sachs.

Vogelgesang.   Ihr meint s wohl recht!

Kothner.   Doch steht's d'rum faul.

Nachtigall.
Wenn spricht das Volk, halt' ich das Maul.

Kothner.
Der Kunst droht' allweil' Fall und Schmach
Läuft sie der Gunst des Volkes nach.

Beckmesser.
D'rin bracht' er's weit, der hier so dreist:
Gassenhauer dichtet er meist.

Pogner.
Freund Sachs, was ich mein', ist schon neu:
Zuviel auf einmal brächte Reu'!—
So frag' ich, ob den Meistern gefällt,
Gab' und Regel, wie ich's gestellt?
(Die Meister erheben sich.)

Sachs.
Mir genügt der Jungfer Ausschlag-Stimm'.

Beckmesser.
(Für sich.)
Der Schuster weckt doch stets mir Grimm!

Kothner.   Wer schreibt sich als Werber ein?
Ein Jung-Gesell muss es sein.

Beckmesser.
Vielleicht auch ein Wittwer? Fragt nur den
Sachs!

Sachs.
Nicht doch, Merr Merker! Aus jüng'rem
Wachs
Als ich und ihr muss der Freier sein,
Soll Evchen ihm den Preis verleih'n.

Beckmesser.
Als wie auch ich?—Grober Gesell!

Kothner.
Begehrt wer Freiung, der komm' zur Stell'!
Ist Jemand gemeld't der Freiung begehrt!

Pogner.
Wohl Meister! Zur Tagesordnung kehrt!
Und nehmt von mir Bericht,
Wie ich auf Meister-Pflicht
Einen jungen Ritter empfehle,
Der wünscht, dass man ihn wähle,
Und heut' als Meistersinger frei'.—
Mein Junker von Stolzing, kommt herbei!
(Walter tritt vor und verneigt sich.)
Von Stolzing Walther aus Frankenland,
Nach Brief' und Urkund mir wohlbekannt.
Als seines Stammes letzter Spross,
Verliess er neulich Hof und Schloss,

To Nuremberg to come
And make this town his home.

Beckmesser.
(To his neighbor.)
Young good-for-nothing! This is nice!

Nachtigal.
(Aloud.)
Friend Pogner's word will quite suffice.

Sachs. We Masters did long since decide
Nor lord nor peasant should be denied.
Art is indeed the sole concern
Of those who Master-Song would learn.

Kothner. First I pray you impart
What Master taught you your Art.

Walter. By silent hearth in winter tide,
When house and hall in snow did hide,
How once the Spring so sweetly smiled
And soon should wake to glory mild,
An ancient book my sire compiled
    Set all before me duly
Sir Walter von der Vogelweid'
    Has been my master, truly.

Sachs. A goodly master!

Beckmesser.   But long since dead!
So what could he of our precepts have read?

Kothner. But in any school or college
Of singing gained you your knowledge?

Walter. Yes, when the fields the frost defied
Beneath returning summer-tide,
What once in dreary winter's night
Within that book I read aright
Now pealed aloud through forest bright:
    I heard the music ringing.
The wood before the Vogelweid'—
    'T was there I learnt my singing.

Beckmesser. Can any one his meaning trace?

Vogelgesang. Good sooth, he 's bold!

Nachtigal.   Peculiar case!

Kothner. Now, Masters, if you will,
    The Marker's place we 'll fill.
Sacred theme do you choose, sir knight?

Walter. My sacred trove 's
        The banner of love,
Swung and sung to my delight!

Kothner. Secular be it. Now inside,
Marker Beckmesser, please to hide.

Und zog nach Nürnberg her,
Dass er hier Bürger wär'.

Beckmesser.
(Zum Nachbar.)
Neu Junker-Unkraut! Thut nicht gut.

Nachtigall.
(Laut.)
Freund Pogner's Wort Genüge thut.

Sachs.
Wie längst von den Meistern beschlossen ist,
Ob Herr, ob Bauer, hier nichts beschliesst:
Hier fragt sich's nach der Kunst allein,
Wer will ein Meistersinger sein.

Kothner. D'rum nun frag' ich zur Stell':
Welch' Meister's seid ihr Gesell'?

Walther. Am stillen Herd in Winterszeit,
Wenn Burg und Hof mir eingeschnei't,
Wie einst der Lenz so lieblich lacht',
Und wie er bald wohl neu erwacht',
Ein altes Buch, vom Ahn' vermacht'
    Gab das mir oft zu lesen:
Herr Walther vor der Vogelweid',
    Der ist mein Meister gewesen.

Sachs. Ein guter Meister!

Beckmesser.   Doch lang schon todt
Wie lehrt' ihm der wohl der Regel Gebot?

Kothner. Doch in welcher Schul' das Singen
Mocht' euch zu lernen gelingen?

Walther.
Wann dann die Flur vom Frost befreit,
Und wiederkehrt die Sommerszeit,
Was einst in langer Winternacht
Das alte Buch mir kund gemacht,
Das schallte laut in Waldespracht,
    Das hört' ich hell erklingen:
Im Wald dort auf der Vogelweid'
Da lernt' ich auch das Singen.

Beckmesser.
Entnahmt ihr was der Worte Schwall?

Vogelgesang. Ei nun, er wagt's.

Nachtigall.   Merkwürd'ger Fall

Kothner. Nun Meister, wenn's gefällt,
    Werd' das Gemerk bestellt.—
Wählt der Herr einen heil'gen Stoff!

Walther. Was heilig mir,
        Der Liebe Panier,
Schwing' und sing' ich, mir zu Hoff'.

Kothner.
Das gilt uns weltlich. D'rum allein,
Merker Beckmesser, schliesst euch ein!

Beckmesser.

Rising and going as if reluctantly to the Marker's box.
Unpleasant work, and more so now ;
My chalk will harass you, I trow !
     Sir knight, now hark !
Sixtus Beckmesser goes to mark.
     Here in this cell
He silently does his duty fell.
Seven faults are given you clear ;
     With chalk on a slate they are scored :
But if more mistakes than seven appear,
     Then, sir knight, without hope you are
floor'd.
     My ears are keen ;
But as, if what I do were seen,
     You might be curbed,
     Be not disturbed ;
     I hide myself from view : —
     So Heav'n be kind to you.

(He has seated himself in the box and with the last words stretches his head out with a scornfully familiar nod, then pulls to the front curtains, which a Prentice had opened for him, so that he becomes invisible.)

Kothner.

(Taking down the "*Leges Tabulaturae*" which the Prentices had hung upon the wall.)
     All that belongs to song mature
     Now hear read from the Tabulature.
          (Reads.)
" Each Master-Singer-created Stave
Its regular measurement must have,
By sundry regulations stated
And never violated.
What we call a ' Section ' is two Stanzas ;
For each the self-same melody answers.
A Stanza several lines doth blend,
And each line with a rhyme must end.
Then come we to the ' After-Song,'
Which must be also some lines long,
And have its especial melody
Which from the other must diff'rent be.
So Staves and Sections of such measure
A Master-Song may have at pleasure.
He who a new song can outpour,
Which in four syllabes — not more —
Another strain doth plagiarize,
He may obtain the Master-Prize." —
Now sit you on the Singer's stool !

Walter.   Here, on this stool ?

Kothner.   It is the rule.

Walter.
     (Mounting the stool, with dissatisfaction.)
For thee I'm sitting, love, herein.

Kothner.
          (Loudly.)
The Singer sits !

Beckmesser.

     (Aufstehend und dem Gemerk zuschreitend.)
Ein sau'res Amt, und heut' zumal ;
Wohl giebt's mit der Kreide manche Qual.
     Herr Ritter wisst :
Sixtus Beckmesser Merker ist ;
     Hier im Gemerk
Verrichtet er sein strenges Werk.
Sieben Fehler giebt er euch vor,
     Die merkt er mit der Kreide dort an ;
Wenn er über sieben Fehler verlor,
     Dann versang er Herr Rittersmann.
Gar fein er hört :
Doch dass er euch den Muth nicht stört,
     Säh't ihr ihm zu,
     So giebt er euch Ruh',
     Und schliesst sich gar hier ein, —
     Lässt Gott euch befohlen sein.

(Er hat sich in das Gemerk gesetzt, streckt mit dem Letzten den Kopf höhnisch freundlich nickend heraus, und zieht den vorderen Vorhang, den zuvor einer der Lehrbuben geöffnet hatte, wieder ganz zusammen, so dass er unsichtbar wird.)

Kothner.

(Hat die von den Lehrbuben aufgehängten "*Leges Tabulaturae*" von der Wand genommen.)
Was euch zum Leide Richt' und Schnur,
Vernehmt nun aus der Tabulatur. —
          (Er liest.)
" Ein jedes Meistersanges Bar
Stell' ordentlich ein Gemässe dar
Aus unterschiedlichen Gesetzen,
Die Keiner soll verletzen.
Ein Gesetz besteht aus zweenen Stollen.
Die gleiche Melodei haben sollen ;
Der Stoll' aus etlicher Vers' Gebänd',
Der Vers hat seinen Reim am End'.
Darauf so folgt der Abgesang,
Der sei auch etlich' Verse lang,
Und hab' sein' besondere Melodei,
Als nicht im Stollen zu finden sei.
Derlei Gemässes mehre Baren
Soll ein jed' Meisterlied bewahren ;
Und wer ein neues Lied gericht',
Das über vier der Sylben nicht
Eingreift in andrer Meister Weis',
Des' Lied erwerb' sich Meister-Preis." —
Nun setzt euch in den Singstuhl !

Walther.
Hier in den Stuhl ?

Kothner.   Wie's Brauch der Schul

Walther.
(Besteigt den Stuhl und setzt sich mit Missbehagen.)
Für dich, Geliebte, sei's gethan !

Kothner.
          (Sehr laut.)
Der Sänger sitzt.

Beckmesser.

(From his box, very harshly.)
Now begin!

Walter.

(After a short consideration.)
Now begin!—
So cries through woodlands the Spring,
And makes them loudly ring:
Then, as to distance urging,
The echoes ripple thence,
From far there comes a surging
That swells with pow'r intense:
It booms and bounds,
The forest sounds
With thousand heavenly voices;
Now loud and clear,
Approaching near,
The murmurs steal
Like bells that peal:
Exultant Nature rejoices!
This call,
How all
The wood an answer makes,
As life again awakes,
Pouring forth
A tender song of Spring!

(During this, repeated groans of discouragement and scratchings of the chalk are heard from the Marker. Walter hears them also, and after a momentary pause of discomposure continues.)

There, like a hiding craven
With hate and envy torn,
A thorny hedge his haven,
Sits Winter, all forlorn,
In withered leaves array'd
His lurking head is laid;
He seeks the joyous singing
To sorrow to be bringing.
(Rising from the stool in displeasure.)
But—"Now begin!"
So cried a voice in my breast
Ere aught of love I had guess'd;
There stirred a deep emotion
And waked me, as I had slept:
My heart with throbbing commotion
My bosom's restraint o'erlept:
My blood did course
With giant force.
To novel sensations soaring;
From warmth of night
With boundless might
Sighs hurried me
Towards the sea.
The pent-up passion outpouring:
The call
How all

Beckmesser.

(Im Gemerk, sehr grell.)
Fanget an!

Walther.

(Nach einiger Sammlung.)
Fanget an!
So rief der Lenz in den Wald,
Dass laut es ihn durchhallt:
Und wie in fern'ren Wellen
Der Hall von dannen flieht,
Von weither nah't ein Schwellen,
Das mächtig näher zieht;
Es schwillt und schallt,
Es tönt der Wald
Von holder Stimmen Gemenge;
Nun laut und hell
Schon nah' zur Stell',
Wie wächst der Schwall!
Wie Glockenhall
Ertos't des Jubels Gedränge!
Der Wald,
Wie bald
Antwortet' er dem Ruf,
Der neu ihm Leben schuf,
Stimmte an
Das süsse Lenzes-Lied!—

(Man hat aus dem Gemerk wiederholt unmuthige Seufzer des Merkers, und heftiges Anstreichen mit der Kreide vernommen. Auch Walther hat es bemerkt, und fährt dadurch für eine kurze Weile gestört, fort.)

In einer Dornenhecken,
Von Neid und Gram verzehrt,
Musst' er sich da verstecken,
Der Winter, Grimm-bewehrt:
Von dürrem Laub umrauscht
Er lauert da und lauscht,
Wie er das frohe Singen
Zu Schaden könnte bringen.—
(Unmuthig vom Stuhl aufstehend.)
Doch: fanget an!
So rief es mir in die Brust,
Als ich noch von Liebe nicht wusst'.
Da fühlt' ich's tief sich regen,
Als weckt' es mich aus dem Traum
Mein Herz mit bebenden Schlägen
Erfüllte des Busen's Raum:
Das Blut, es wall't
Mit Allgewalt,
Geschwellt von neuem Gefühle;
Aus warmer Nacht
Mit Uebermacht
Schwillt mir zum Meer
Der Seufzer Heer
In wildem Wonne-Gewühle:
Die Brust
Mit Lust

My breast an answer makes,
As life anew it takes,
   Pouring forth
A glorious lay of love!

Beckmesser.
(Who has grown still more restive, tears open the curtains.)
Is 't nearly finished?

Walter   What means this call?

Beckmesser.
(Holding out the slate completely covered with chalk-marks.)
I've finished with the slate, that 's all!
(The Masters cannot restrain their laughter.)

Walter.   Yet hear! My lady's praise to ring,
My second verse I ought to sing.

Beckmesser.
         (Leaving his box.)
Sing where you will! Here you 're undone.
My Masters, see the slate, ev'ry one:
The like of this I never knew;
I 'd credit no man's work thereto!
(The Masters are in commotion.)
Walter. D' ye let him, Masters, plague me so!
Shall I be heard by you or no?

Pogner.
One word, friend Marker! You 're somewhat
wroth?

Beckmesser.
Be Marker he who likes henceforth!
But that this man is quite out-sung
You can decide yourselves among.

Sachs.
(Who has listened to Walter from the first with serious interest.)
Not all have like opinion passed.
  The song you 've so derided
To me is new, but not confused:
  Though not by us 't was guided,
His course was firm, as though well used.
  One way you measure solely
A work that your rules do not fit:
  Resign your own views wholly,
Some other rules apply to it.

Beckmesser.
Aha! That 's fine! Just listen, pray!
Sachs opes a gap for fools that way,
  Where in and out at pleasure
  Their minds a course can measure.
Let in the streets the rabble holloa;
Here must we, at least, some discipline
follow.

Antwortet sie dem Ruf,
Der neu ihr Leben schuf:
   Stimmt nun an
Das hehre Liebes-Lied!

Beckmesser.
(Der immer unruhiger geworden, reisst den Vorhang auf.)
Seid ihr nun fertig?

Walther.   Wie fraget ihr?
Beckmesser.
(Die ganz mit Kreidestrichen bedeckte Tafel heraus haltend.)
Mit der Tafel ward ich fertig schier.
    (Die Meister müssen lachen.)

Walther.
Hört doch! Zu meiner Frauen Preis
Gelang' ich jetzt erst mit der Weis'.

Beckmesser.
       (Das Gemerk verlassend.)
Singt, wo ihr wollt! Hier habt ihr ver
than.—
Ihr Meister, schaut die Tafel euch an:
So lang ich leb', ward's nicht erhört;
Ich glaubt's nicht, wenn ihr's all' auch
schwört!
(Die Meister sind im Aufstand durcheinander.)

Walther.
Erlaubt ihr's, Meister, dass er mich stört?
Blieb' ich von Allen ungehört?

Pogner.
Ein Wort, Herr Merker! Ihr seid gereizt?

Beckmesser.
Sei Merker fortan, wer darnach geizt!
Doch dass der Ritter versungen hat,
Beleg' ich erst noch vor der Meister Rath.

Sachs.
(Der vom Beginn an Walther mit zunehmendem Ernst zugehört hat.)
Nicht jeder eure Meinung theilt.—
    Des Ritters Lied und Weise,
Sie fand ich neu, doch nicht verwirrt;
    Verliess er uns're G'leise,
Schritt er doch fest und unbeirrt.
    Wollt ihr nach Regeln messen,
Was nicht nach eurer Regeln Lauf,
    Der eig'nen Spur vergessen,
Sucht davon erst die Regeln auf!

Beckmesser.
Aha! Schon recht! Nun hört ihr's doch
Den Stümpern öffnet Sachs ein Loch,
    Da aus und ein nach Belieben
    Ihr Wesen leicht sie trieben.
Singet dem Volk auf Markt und Gassen:
Hier wird nach den Regeln nur eingelassen.

Sachs. Friend Marker, why in such a flutter?
  Wherefore so angry, pray?
A riper judgment you might utter,
  If better heed you'd pay.
And so, to speak my final word,
The young knight to the end must be heard.

Beckmesser.
The Master's Guild, the school and all,
Weighed against Sachs' word must fall.

Sachs. The Lord forbid I should demand
Aught contrary to our law's command:
But surely there 't is written:
" The Marker shall be chosen so,
By prejudice unbitten
That nought of bias he may show."
If this one turns his step to wooing
Can he refrain a wrong from doing,
To bring to shame 'fore all the school.
His rival yonder on the stool?
        (Walter flames up.)

Nachtigal. You go too far!

Kothner.   Too free you are!

Pogner.
        (To the Masters.)
I pray you, Masters, cease this jar.

Beckmesser.
Hey! What needs Master Sachs to mention
  Which way my steps may be turned?
With the state of my *sole* his attention
  Better might be concerned!
But since my shoemaker follows the Muse
It fares but ill with my boots and shoes.
    Just look, how they're split!
    See, here 's a great slit!
All of his verse and rhyme
I would declare sublime;
His dramas, plays, his farces and all,
If with my new pair of shoes he 'd call.

Sachs.
        (Scratching his head.)
  I fear you have me there:
  But, Master, if 't is fair
That on the merest boor's shoe-leather
  Some little verse I frame,
I ask you, worthy town-clerk, whether
  You should not have the same?
A motto such as you require,
With all my poor poetic fire,
  Not yet I 've hit upon;
  But I will come anon,
When I have heard the knight's song through:
So let him sing on without ado!
(Walter. much put out, remounts the Singer's Seat.)

The Masters. Enough! Conclude!

Sachs.
Herr Merker, was doch solch ein Eifer?
    Was doch so wenig Ruh'?
Eu'r Urtheil, dünkt mich, wäre reifer,
    Hörtet ihr besser zu.
Darum, so komm ich jetzt zum Schluss,
Dass den Junker zu End' man hören muss.

Beckmesser.
Der Meister Zunft, die ganze Schul',
Gegen den Sachs da sind wie Null.

Sachs. Verbüt' es Gott, was ich begehr',
Dass das nicht nach den Gesetzen wär'!
    Doch da nun steht's geschrieben,
Der Merker werde so bestellt,
    Dass weder Hass noch Lieben
Das Urtheil trüben, das er fällt,
Geht er nun gar auf Freiers-Füssen,
Wie sollt' er da die Lust nicht büssen
Den Nebenbuhler auf dem Stuhl
Zu schmähen vor der ganzen Schul'!
        (Walther flammt auf.)

Nachtigall. Ihr geht zu weit!

Kothner.   Persönlichkeit

Pogner.
        (Zu den Meistern.)
Vermeidet, Meister, Zwist und Streit!

Beckmesser.
Ei, was kümmert's doch Meister Sachsen,
    Auf was für Füssen ich geh'?
Liess' er d'rob lieber Sorge sich wachsen,
    Dass nichts mir drück' die Zeh'!
Doch seit mein Schuster ein grosser Poet,
Gar übel es um mein Schuhwerk steht!
    Da seht, wie es schlappt,
    Und überall klappt!
All' seine Vers' und Reim'
Liess' ich ihm gern daheim,
Historien, Spiel' und Schwänke dazu,
Brächt' er mir morgen die neuen Schuh'!

Sachs. Ihr mahnt mich da gar recht:
    Doch schickt sich's, Meister, sprecht,
Dass, find' ich selbst dem Eseltreiber
    Ein Sprüchlein auf die Sohl',
Dem hochgelahrten Herrn Stadtschreiber
    Ich nichts d'rauf schreiben soll?
Das Sprüchlein, das eu'r würdig sei,
Mit all' meiner armen Poeterei
    Fand ich noch nicht zur Stund';
    Doch wird's wohl jetzt mir kund,
Wenn ich des Ritters Lied gehört: —
D'rum sing er nun weiter ungestört!
(Walther, in grosser Aufregung, stellt sich auf den Sing-
stuhl.)

Die Meister. Genug! Zum Schluss!

Sachs.

(To Walter.)
Sing, 'spite the Marker's angry mood!

Beckmesser.

(As Walter recommences, fetches out his board from the box and shows it, during the following, first to one and then to another, to convince the Masters, whom he at last gathers into a circle round him while he continues to exhibit his slate.)
What rubbish is this to shock us?
He surely means to mock us!
Every fault, both grave and slight,
I have marked on the board aright.
"Faulty verses," "Unsingable phrases,"
"Word-clippings," and "Vices" grave,
"Equivocal," "Rhymes in wrong places,"
"Reserved," "Displaced" is all the Stave.
A "Patch-work-Song" between the two verses,
"Clouded meaning" in every part,
"Uncertain words," then a "Change," that worse is,
There's "Breath ill-managed," here's "Sudden start,"
"Incomprehensible melody,"
A hotch-potch, made of all tones that be.
If at such toil you do not halt,
Masters, count after me each fault.
Already with the eight he was spent,
But so far as this sure none ever went!
Well over fifty, roughly told.
Say, would you this man a master hold?

The Masters.

(To one another.)
Ah yes, that's true! 't is plain indeed,
That this young knight cannot succeed.
By Sachs he may be a genius thought,
But in our singing-school he is nought.
Who should in justice remain neglected,
If this novice a master were made?
If all the world's to be elected,
What good were the Masters' high grade?
Ha! look how the knight is enraged.
Hans Sachs on his side has engaged.
'T is really too bad! Quick make an end!
Up, Masters, speak and your hands extend!

Pogner.

(Aside.)
Ah yes, I see! 't is sad indeed:
My poor young knight will scarce succeed!
Should I retract my first decree,
I fear me sad results there'd be.
I'd fain see him no more neglected;
My kinship he would not degrade:
And when the victor is elected
Who knows if he will please my maid?
Some trouble I presage,
For Eva can I engage?

Sachs.

(Zu Walther.)
Singt, dem Herrn Merker zum Verdruss!

Beckmesser.

(Holt, während Walther beginnt, aus dem Gemerk die Tafel herbei, und hält sie während des Folgenden, von Einem zum Andern sich wendend, zur Prüfung den Meistern vor, die er schliesslich zu einem Kreis um sich zu vereinigen bemüht ist, welchem er immer die Tafel zur Einsicht vorhält.)
Was sollte man da noch hören?
Wär's nicht nur uns zu bethören?
Jeden der Fehler gross und klein,
Sehr genau auf der Tafel ein. —
"Falsch Gebänd," "unredbare Worte,"
"Kleb Sylben," hier "Laster" gar;
"Aequivoca," "Reim am falschen Orte,"
"Verkehrt," "verstellt" der ganze Bar;
Ein "Flickgesang" hier zwischen den Stollen;
"Blinde Meinung" allüberall;
"Unklare Wort'," "Differenz," hie "Schrollen,"
Da "falscher Athem," hier "Ueberfall."
Ganz unverständliche Melodei!
Aus allen Tönen ein Mischgebräu'!
Scheu'tet ihr nicht das Ungemach,
Meister, zählt mir die Striche nach!
Verloren hätt' er schon mit dem acht',
Doch so weit wie der hat's noch Keiner gebracht:
Wohl über fünfzig, schlecht gezählt!
Sagt, ob ihr euch den zum Meister wählt?

Die Meister.

(Durcheinander.)
Jo wohl, so ist's! Ich seh' es recht!
Mit dem Herrn Ritter steht es schlecht.
Mag Sachs von ihm halten, was er will,
Hier in der Singschul' schweig' er still!
Bleibt einem Jeden doch unbenommen,
Wen er zum Genossen begehrt?
Wär' uns der erste Best' willkommen,
Was blieben die Meister dann werth?
Hei! Wie sich der Ritter da quält!
Der Sachs hat ihn sich erwählt. —
's ist ärgerlich gar! Drum macht ein End'!
Auf Meister, stimmt und erhebt die Händ'!

Pogner.

(Für sich.)
Ja wohl, ich seh's, was mir nicht recht:
Mit meinem Junker steht es schlecht!
Weiche ich hier der Uebermacht,
Mir ahnet, dass mir's Sorge macht.
Wie gern säh' ich ihn angenommen,
Als Eidam wär' er mir gar werth;
Nenn' ich den Sieger nun willkommen,
Wer weiss, ob ihn mein Kind begehrt!
Gesteh' ich's, dass mich das quält,
Ob Eva den Meister wählt!

Walter.

(In wild and desperate euthusiasm, standing erect in the Singer's seat and looking down on commotion of the Masters.)

From gloomy thicket breaking
Behold the screech-owl swoop
With circling flight awaking
The ravens' croaking troop!
In sombre ranks they rise
And utter piercing cries;
With voices hoarse and hollow
The daws and magpies follow.
    Up then soars,
By golden pinions stirr'd,
A wondrous lovely bird.
Each brightly glowing feather
Gleams in the glorious day;
It signs me hither — thither,
To float and flee away.
    The swelling heart,
    With pleasing smart,
Sore need with wings supplieth;
    It mounts in flight
    To giddy height,
    From the city's tomb,
    Through heaven's pure dome,
To hills of home it hieth,
Towards the verdant Vogelweid'
Where Master Walter lived and died;
    And there I'll rightly raise
    In song my lady's praise:
    Up shall soar,
When raven-Masters croak no more,
    My noble loving lay.
Farewell, ye Masters, for aye!

(With a gesture of proud contempt he leaves the Singer's Seat and quits the building.)

Sachs.

    (Following Walter's song.)
    Ha! what a flow
    Of genius' glow!
My Masters, pray now give o'er!
Listen, when Sachs doth implore!
Friend Marker, there! grant us some peace!
Let others listen! — Why won't you cease?
    No use! A vain endeavor!
I can scarcely my own voice hear!
    They'll heed the young fellow never:
He's bold indeed to persevere!
    His heart must be placed aright:
    A true born poet-knight! —
Hans Sachs may make both verse and shoe;
A knight is he and a poet, too.

The Prentices.

(Who have been rubbing their hands in glee and jump-

Walther.

(In übermüthig verzweifelter Begeisterung, hoch au' dem Singstuhl aufgerichtet, und auf die unruhig durcheii ander sich bewegenden Meiste. herabblickend.)

Aus finst'rer Dornenhecken
Die Eule rauscht' hervor,
Thät rings mit Kreischen wecken
Der Raben heis'ren Chor:
In nächt'gem Heer zu Hauf',
Wie krächzen all' da auf,
Mit ihren Stimmen, den hohlen,
Die Elstern, Kräh'n und Dohlen!
    Auf da steigt
Mit gold'nem Flügelpaar,
Ein Vogel wunderbar:
Sein strahlend hell Gefieder
Licht in den Lüften blinkt;
Schwebt selig hin und wieder,
Zu Flug und Flucht mir winkt
    Es schwillt das Herz
    Von süssem Schmerz,
Der Noth entwachsen Flügel;
    Es schwingt sich auf
    Zum kühnen Lauf,
    Zum Flug durch die Luft
    Aus der Städte Gruft,
Dahin zum heim'schen Hügel;
Dahin zur grünen Vogelweid';
Wo Meister Walther einst mich freit';
    Da sing' ich hell und hehr
    Der liebsten Frauen Ehr':
    Auf da steigt,
Ob Meister-Kräh'n ihm ungeneigt,
    Das stolze Minne-Lied. —
Ade! ihr Meister, hienied'!

(Er verlässt mit einer stolz verächtlichen Gebärde de Stuhl und wendet sich zum Fortgehen.)

Sachs.

    (Walther's Gesang folgend.)
    Ha, welch ein Muth!
    Begeistrungs-Gluth! —
Ihr Meister, schweigt doch und hört!
Hört, wenn Sachs euch beschwört!
Herr Merker da! gönnt doch nur Ruh'!
Lasst And're hören! gebt das nur zu! —
    Umsonst! All eitel Trachten!
Kaum vernimmt man sein eigen Wort!
    Des Junkers will Keiner achten: —
Das heiss' ich Muth, singt der noch fort!
    Das Herz auf dem rechten Fleck:
    Ein wahrer Dichter-Reck'!
Mach' ich, Hans Sachs, wohl Vers un Schuh',
Ist Ritter der und Poet dazu.

Die Lehrbuben.

(Welche längst sich die Hände rieben und von der Ban

ing up from their bench, towards the end take hands and
dance in a ring round the Marker's box.)

> God speed your Master-singing,
> And may you the prize soon be winning:
> The wreath of flowers in silk so bright,
> I hope it may fall to your lot, sir knight!

Beckmesser.   Now, Masters, give it tongue!

(Most of them hold up their hands.)

All the Masters.   Rejected and outsung!

(General confusion, augmented by the Prentices, who
shoulder the benches and Marker's box, causing hindrance
and disorder to the Masters who are crowding to the door.
Sachs remains alone in front, looking pensively at the
empty seat; when the boys remove this too he turns away
with humorous gesture of discouragement, and the curtain
falls.)

aufsprangen, schliessen jetzt gegen das Ende wieder ihren
Reihen und tanzen um das Gemerk.)

> Glück auf zum Meistersingen,
> Mög't ihr euch das Kränzlein erschwin-
> gen:
> Das Blumenkränzlein aus Seiden fein,
> Wird das dem Herrn Ritter beschieden sein?

Beckmesser.
> Nun, Meister, kündet's an!
> (Die Mehrzahl hebt die Hände auf.)

Alle Meister.
> Versungen und verthan!

(Alles geht in Aufregung auseinander, lustiger Tumult
der Lehrbuben, welche sich des Gemerkes und der Meis-
terbänke bemächtigen, wodurch Gedränge und Durcheinander der nach dem Ausgange sich wendenden Meister
ensteht. — Sachs, der allein im Vordergrunde verblieben,
blickt noch gedankenvoll nach dem leeren Singstuhl; als
die Lehrbuben auch diesen erfassen, und Sachs darob mit
humoristisch-unmuthiger Gebärde sich abwendet, fällt der
Vorhang.)

SECOND ACT.	ZWEITER AUFZUG.

The stage represents in front the section of a street running across, intersected in the middle by a narrow alley which winds crookedly towards the back, so that in C are two corner houses, of which one, a handsome one, R, is that of Pogner, the other, simpler, L, is Sachs's shop. — A flight of several steps leads up to Pogner's door: porch sunk in, with stone seats. At side R a lime-tree shades the place before the house; green shrubs at its foot, surrounding a stone seat. — The entrance to Sachs's house is also towards the street; a divided door leads into the cobbler's workshop; close by, an elder-tree spreads its boughs over it. Two windows, one of the workshop, the other of an inner chamber, look on to the alley. (All houses in both street and alley must be practicable.)

Genial summer evening; during the first scene night gradually closes.

David is putting up the shutters outside. Other Prentices are doing the same for other houses.

Prentices

(as they work).

Midsummer day ! Midsummer day !
Flowers and ribbons in goodly display !

David

(aside).

"The wreath of flowers in silk so fine,
Would that to-morrow it might be mine."

Magdalena

(coming out of Pogner's house with a basket on her arm and seeking to approach David unperceived).

Hist ! David !

David

(turning toward the alley).

Whom are you calling?
Get along with your foolish squalling !

Prentices.

David, what cheer?
Why so severe?
Turn round your skull,
If you 're not dull !
"Midsummer day ! Midsummer day !"
And he can't see Mistress Lena right in his way !

Die Bühne stellt im Vordergrunde eine Strasse im Längendurchschnitte dar, welche in der Mitte von einer schmalen Gasse, nach dem Hintergrunde zu krumm abbiegend, durchschnitten wird, so dass sich in Front zwei Eckhäuser darbieten, von denen das eine, reichere, rechts — das Haus Pogner's, das andere, einfachere — links — das des Hans Sachs ist. — Zu Pogner's Hause führt von der vorderen Strasse aus eine Treppe von mehreren Stufen; vertiefte Thüre, mit Steinsitzen in den Nischen. Zur Seite ist der Raum, ziemlich nah an Pogner's Hause, durch eine dickstämmige Linde abgegränzt; grünes Gesträuch umgibt sie am Fuss, vor welchem auch eine Steinbank angebracht ist. — Der Eingang zu Sachsens Hause ist ebenfalls nach der vorderen Strasse zu gelegen: eine getheilte Ladenthüre führet hier unmittelbar in die Schusterwerkstatt; dicht dabei steht ein Fliederbaum, dessen Zweige bis über den Laden hereinhängen. Nach der Gasse zu hat das Haus noch zwei Fenster, von welchen das eine zur Werkstatt, das andere zu einer dahinterliegenden Kammer gehört. [Alle Häuser, namentlich auch die der engeren Gasse, müssen praktikabel sein.]

Heiterer Sommerabend, im Verlaufe der ersten Auftritte allmählich einbrechende Nacht.

David ist darüber her, die Fensterläden nach der Gasse zu von aussen zu schliessen. Andere Lehrbuben thun das Gleiche bei andern Häusern.

Lehrbuben

(während der Arbeit).

Johannistag ! Johannistag !
Blumen und Bänder so viel man mag !

David

(für sich).

" Das Blumenkränzlein von Seiden fein,
Möcht' es mir balde beschieden sein ! "

Magdalene

(ist mit einem Korbe am Arm aus Pogner's Haus gekommen und sucht David unbemerkt sich zu nähern).

Bst ! David !

David

(nach der Gasse zu sich umwendend).

Ruft ihr schon wieder !
Singt allein eure dummen Lieder !

Lehrbuben.

David, was soll's?
Wär'st nicht so stolz,
Schaut'st besser um,
Wär'st nicht so dumm !
"Johannistag ! Johannistag ! "
Wie der nur die Jungfer Lene nicht kennen mag !

Magdalena.

David, listen ! Turn round, my dear !

David.

Ah, Mistress Lena ! You are here ?

Magdalena
(pointing to her basket).

Here 's something nice ; peep in and see 't !
'T is all for my dear lad to eat.
Tell me though first, What of Sir Walter ?
You counseled him well ? Has the crown been
won ?

David.

Ah, Mistress Lena, how 1 falter !
He was outsung and declared outdone.

Magdalena.

Rejected ! Outdone !

David.
What ails you, dear one ?

Magdalena
(snatching the basket away from David's outstretched
hand).

Hands off the basket !
Dare you to ask it !
Good lack ! Our chevalier outdone !

(she hastens back into the house, wringing her hands in
despair.)

(David looks after her dumfounded)

Prentices

(who have stolen near and overheard, now advance to
David as if congratulating him).

Hail to the Prentice and his bride !
How well his wooing speeds !
We all have heard and seen beside :
She upon whom he feeds
Within his heart's true casket,
Has gone and refused him the basket !

Davia
(flying out).

Be off with you boys !
Give over your noise !

Prentices
(dancing round David).

Midsummer day ! Midsummer day !
All go a-courting as they may.

Magdalene.

David ! hör' doch ! kehr' dich zu mir !

David.

Ach, Jungfer Lene ! Ihr seid hier ?

Magdalene
(auf ihren Korb deutend).

Bring' dir was Gut's ! schau nur hinein !
Das soll für mein lieb' Schätzel sein —
Erst aber schnell, wie ging's mit dem Ritter ?
Du riethest ihm gut ? Er gewann den Kranz ?

David.

Ach, Jungfer Lene ! Da steht's bitter ;
Der hat verthan und versungen ganz !

Magdalene.

Versungen ? Verthan ?

David.
Was geht's euch nur an ?

Magdalene
(den Korb, nach welchem David die Hand ausstreckt, net
tig zurückziehend).

Hand von der Taschen !
Nichts da zu naschen ! —
Hilf Gott ! Unser Junker verthan !

(Sie geht mit Gebärden der Trostlosigkeit nach dem Hause
zurück).

David
(zieht ihr verblüfft nach).

Die Lehrbuben

(welche unbemerkt näher geschlichen waren, gelausch
hatten und sich jetzt, wie glückwünschend, David präser
tiren).

Heil, Heil zur Eh' dem jungen Mann !
Wie glücklich hat er gefrei't !
Wir hörten's All', und sahen's an :
Der er sein Herz geweiht,
Für die er lässt sein Leben,
Die hat ihm den Korb nicht gegeben.

David
(auffahrend).

Was steht ihr hier faul ?
Gleich haltet eu'r Maul !

Die Lehrbuben.
(David umtanzend).

Johannistag ! Johannistag !
Da frei't ein Jeder wie er mag.

The Masters woo,
    And workmen too,
Old folks as well as the babbies!
    And graybeards grim
    Wed maidens slim,
Young fellows wed ancient tabbies.
Hooray! Hooray! Midsummer day!

(David is about to fly at the boys in his rage, when Sachs, who had come down the alley, steps between them. The Prentices separate.)

Sachs.

What now? Are you again in a fray?

David.

Not I! They sang a mocking stave.

Sachs.

Pay no heed; show how to behave!
Get in! To bed! Shut up and light!

David.

Have I to sing, sir?

Sachs.

                    Not to-night!
As punishment for to-day's offending,
Put all these shoes on the lasts for mending.

(Both go into the workshop and exeunt through an inner door. The Prentices have also dispersed.)

— — —

(Pogner and Eva, as if returning from a walk, come silently and thoughtfully down the alley, the daughter leaning on her father's arm.)

Pogner

(still in the alley, peeping through a chink in Sachs' shutter).

Let's see if Sachs is in to-night;
I'd speak with him. Suppose I call!

(David comes out of the inner room with a light and sits down to work at the bench by the window.)

Eva.

He seems at home: I see a light.

Pogner.

Shall I? Why should I after all?
            (Turns away.)
If strange things I should venture,
Might I not earn his censure?
            (After some reflection.)
Who said that I went too far? 'T was he,
    Yet, if our rules I exceeded,
    I have but done as he did!
But that might be mere vanity.

            (To Eva.)
And you, my child, your thoughts are hid?

Der Meister freit!
Der Bursche freit!
Da gibt's Geschlamb' und Geschlumbfer!
    Der Alte freit
    Die junge Maid,
Der Bursche die alte Jungfer!—
Juchhei! Juchhei! Johannistag!

David ist im Begriff, wüthend drein zu schlagen, als Sachs, der aus der Gasse hervorgekommen, dazwischen tritt. Die Buben fahren auseinander.

Sachs.

Was gibt's? Treff' ich dich wieder am Schlag?

David.

Nicht ich! Schandlieder singen die.

Sachs.

Hör' nicht drauf! Lern's besser wie sie!
Zur Ruh'! in's Haus! Schliess' und mach Licht!

David.

Hab' ich noch Singstund'?

Sachs.

                    Nein, singst nicht!
Zur Straf' für dein heutig' frech' Erdreisten.—
Die neuen Schuh' steck' auf den Leisten!

(Sie sind Beide in die Werkstatt eingetreten und gehen durch innere Thüren ab. Die Lehrbuben haben sich ebenfalls zerstreut.)

Pogner und Eva, wie vom Spaziergange heimkehrend, die Tochter leicht am Arme des Vaters eingehenkt, sind beide schweigsam und in Gedanken die Gasse heraufgekommen.

Pogner

(noch auf der Gasse, durch eine Klinze im Fensterladen von Sachsens Werkstatt spähend).

Lass' sehn, ob Nachbar Sachs zu Haus?
Gern spräch' ich ihn. Trät' ich wohl ein?

(David kommt mit Licht aus der Kammer, setzt sich damit an den Werktisch am Fenster und macht sich über die Arbeit her.)

Eva.

Er scheint daheim: kommt Licht heraus.

Pogner.

Thu' ich's?—Zu was doch!—Besser, nein!
            (Er wendet sich ab.)
Will Einer Selt'nes wagen,
Was liess' er da sich sagen?——
            (Nach einigem Sinnen.)
War er's nicht, der meint', ich ging zu weit?.
    Und blieb ich nicht im Geleise.
    War's nicht in seiner Weise?—
Doch war's vielleicht auch—Eitelkeit?

            (Zu Eva.)
Und du, mein Kind, du sagst mir nichts?

Eva.

Good children only speak when bid.

Pogner.

How sharp ; how good ! Come now, my wench,
And sit beside me on this bench.

(Sits on the stone seat under the linden-tree.)

Eva.

Too chill to stay ;
'T was close all day.

Pogner.

Oh, no ! 't is mild and charming ;
The evening air is calming.

(Eva sits, nervously.)

A token of a morrow fair
  And brilliant in its weather.
Oh, child, does not thy heart declare
The joys that morrow doth prepare,
When Nuremberg — yes, all the town,
  Both rich and poor together,
The guilds, the burghers of renown,
  Will meet in highest feather,
    To see thee rise
    And give the prize
To him, the Master's head,
To whom thou shalt be wed ?

Eva.

Dear father, can but a Master win ?

Pogner.

Be sure a Master is your fate.

(Magdalena appears at the door and signs to Eva.)

Eva
        (disturbed).

Aye — 't is my fate. — But now come in —
Yes, Lena, yes ! — our suppers wait.

Pogner
        (rising vexedly).

But we have no guest ?

Eva
        (as before).

      Not Sir Walter ?

Pogner
        (surprised).

          Hey, what ?

Eva.

Did you not meet ?

Eva.

Ein folgsam Kind, gefragt nur spricht's.

Pogner.

Wie klug ! Wie gut ! — Komm', setz' dich hier
Ein Weil' noch auf die Bank zu mir.

(Er setzt sich auf die Steinbank unter der Linde.)

Eva.

Wird's nicht zu kühl ?
's war heut' gar schwül.

Pogner.

Nicht doch, 's ist mild und labend ;
Gar lieblich lind der Abend.

(Eva setzt sich beklommen.)

Das deutet auf den schönsten Tag,
  Der morgen dir soll scheinen.
O Kind, sagt dir kein Herzensschlag,
Welch' Glück dich morgen treffen mag,
Wenn Nürnberg, die ganze Stadt
  Mit Bürgern und Gemeinen.
Mit Zünften, Volk und hohem Rath,
  Vor dir sich soll vereinen,
    Dass du den Preis,
    Das edle Reis,
  Ertheilest als Gemahl
  Dem Meister deiner Wahl.

Eva.

Lieb' Vater, muss es ein Meister sein ?

Pogner.

Hör' wohl : ein Meister deiner Wahl.

(Magdalene erscheint an der Thür und winkt Eva.)

Eva
        (zerstreut).

Ja, — meiner Wahl. — Doch, tritt nun ein —
Gleich, Lene, gleich ! — zum Abendmahl.

Pogner
        (ärgerlich aufstehend).

's giebt doch keinen Gast ?

Eva
        (wie oben).

      Wohl den Junker ?

Pogner
        (verwundert).

          Wie so ?

Eva.

Sahst ihn heute nicht ?

Pogner
(half to himself).
I want him not.
Why, no !—What now ?—Ah ! dare I guess?

Eva.

Dear father, come in and change your dress.

Pogner
(going into the house before her).
Hum !—What way does my fancy go?
(Exit.)

Magdalena
(secretly).
Why do you wait?

Eva.
(the same).
Be still ! speak low !

Magdalena.

Saw David !—says that he has n't won.

Eva.

Sir Walter?—O heavens ! what 's to be done?
Ah, Lena, I quake ; who will disclose all?

Magdalena.

Perhaps Hans Sachs?

Eva.
Ah, he 's fond of me !
'T is well, I will go

Magdalena.
Mind not to expose all !
If you stay longer your father will see.
When we 've supped : another thing I 'll unfold
thee ;
A secret which some one has just now told me.

Eva

Who was 't ? Sir Walter?

Magdalena.
Not he, nay !
Beckmesser.

Eva.
Worth hearing I should say !

(They go into the house.)

(Sachs, in light indoor dress, has reëntered the workshop.
He turns to David, who is still at his workbench.)

Pogner
(halb für sich).
Ward sein nicht froh.—
Nicht doch !—Was denn ?—Ei ! werd' ich dumm !

Eva.

Lieb' Väterchen, komn' ! Geh', kleid' dich um !

Pogner
(voran in das Haus gehend).
Hm !—Was geht mir im Kopf doch 'rum ?
Ab.

Magdalene
(heimlich).
Hast was heraus ?

Eva
(ebenso).
Blieb still und stumm

Magdalene.

Sprach David : meint', er habe verthan.

Eva.

Der Ritter !—Hilf Gott, was fing' ich an !
Ach, Lene ! die Angst : wo 'was erfahren?

Magdalene.

Vielleicht vom Sachs !

Eva.
Ach, der hat mich lieb !
Gewiss, ich geh' hin,

Magdalene.
Lass drin nichts gewahren !
Der Vater merkt' es, wenn man jetzt blieb'. —
Nach dem Mahl ; dann hab' ich dir noch 'was zu
sagen
Was Jemand geheim mir aufgetragen.

Eva.

Wer denn ? Der Junker?

Magdalene.
Nichts da ! Nein !
Beckmesser.

Eva.
Das mag 'was Rechtes sein
(Sie gehen in das Haus.)

Sachs ist, in leichter Hauskleidung, in die Werkstat
zurückgegangen. Er wendet sich zu David, der an seinem
Werktisch verblieben ist.

382

Sachs.

Come here! — that's right. — There by the door
Put my stool and workbench before;
Then get to bed and early rise;
Sleep off your folly, to-morrow be wise!

David
(arranging bench and stool).

Are you still working?

Sachs.
What's that to you?

David
(aside).

What ailed Magdalena? — Would I knew!
And why works my Master by this light?

Sachs.

Why wait you?

David.
Good-night, Master!

Sachs.
Good-night!

(Exit David into the inner room.)

Sachs

(arranges his work, sits on his stool at the door and then,
laying down his tools again, leans back, resting his arm on
the closed lower half of the door).

The elder's scent is waxing
So mild, so full and strong?
Its charm my limbs relaxing:
Words unto my lips would throng. —
What boot such thoughts as I can span?
I'm but a poor, plain-minded man!
When work's despised altogether,
Thou, friend, settest me free;
But I'd better stick to my leather
And let all this poetry be! —

(He tries again to work. Leaves off and reflects.)

And yet — it haunts me still. —
I feel, but comprehend ill; —
Cannot forget it, — and yet cannot grasp it. —
I measure it not e'en when I clasp it. —
But how then would I gauge it?
'T was measureless to my mind;
No rule could fit it or cage it,
Yet there was no fault to find.
It seemed so old, yet new in its chime, —
Like songs of birds in sweet Maytime: —
He who heard
And, fancy-stirr'd,
Sought to repeat the strain,
But shame and scorn would gain. —

Sachs.

Zeig' her! — 's ist gut. — Dort an die **Thür'**
Rück' mir Tisch und Schemel herfür! —
Leg' dich zu Bett! Wach' auf bei Zeit,
Verschlaf' die Dummheit, sei morgen gescheit!

David
(richtet Tisch und Schemel).

Schafft ihr noch Arbeit?

Sachs.
Kümmert dich das!

David
(für sich).

Was war nur der Lene? — Gott weiss, **was!** —
Warum wohl der Meister heute **wacht!**

Sachs.

Was steh'st noch?

David.
Schlaft wohl, Meister!

Sachs.
Gut Nacht!

(David geht in die Kammer ab.)

Sachs

(legt sich die Arbeit zurecht, setzt sich an der Thüre auf
dem Schemel, lässt dann die Arbeit wieder liegen, und lehnt
mit dem Arm auf den geschlossenen Untertheil des **Ladens**
gestützt, sich zurück).

Wie duftet doch der Flieder
So mild, so stark und voll!
Mir lös't es weich die Glieder,
Will, das ich was sagen soll. —
Was gilt's, was ich dir sagen kann?
Bin gar ein arm einfältig Mann!
Soll mir die Arbeit nicht schmecken,
Gäb'st, Freund, lieber mich frei:
Thät' besser das Leder zu strecken,
Und liess' alle Poeterei! —

(Er versucht wieder zu arbeiten. Lässt ab und sinnt.)

Und doch, 's will halt nicht geh'n. —
Ich fühl's — und kann's nicht versteh'n —
Kann's nicht behalten, — doch auch nicht ver-
gessen;
Und fass' ich es ganz, — kann ich's nicht messen. —
Doch wie auch wollt' ich's fassen
Was unermesslich mir schien?
Kein' Regel wollte da passen,
Und war doch kein Fehler drin. —
Es klang so alt, und war so neu, —
Wie Vogelsang im süssen Mai:
Wer ihn hört,
Und wahnbethört
Sänge dem Vogel nach,
Dem bräch't' es Spott und **Schmach.**

Spring's command
    And gentle hand
His soul with this did entrust:
He sang because he must !
His power rose as needed ;
That virtue well I heeded.
The bird who sang to-day
Has got a throat that rightly waxes ;
    Masters may feel dismay,
But well content with him Hans Sachs is.

Eva comes out into the street, peeps shyly towards the workshop and advances unnoticed to the door by SACHS.

Eva.

Good-evening, Master !   Still at labor?

Sachs
            (starting up in agreeable surprise).

Ah, child ! Sweet Eva ! still about?
And yet I guess the cause, fair neighbor:
The new-made shoes ?

Eva.
                    How far you 're out !
The shoes I have not even essay'd ;
They are so fine, so richly made,
I dare not such gems to my feet confide.

Sachs.
You 'll wear them, though, to-morrow as bride?

Eva
(who has now seated herself on the stone seat by Sachs).
Who is to be the bridegroom, then?

Sachs.
                    Can I tell?
Eva.
How know you I 'm to be bride?

Sachs.
                    Eh, well !
Ev'ry one knows.

Eva.
                Aye, ev'ry one knows.
That 's proof positive, I suppose.
I thought you knew more.

Sachs.
                What should I know?
Eva.
See there !   Must I my meaning show?
How dull I must be !

Sachs.
                    I say not so.

Lenzes Gebot,
    Die süsse Noth,
Die legten's ihm in die Brust:
Nun sang er, wie er musst' !
Und wie er musst', so konnt' er's;
Das merkt' ich ganz besonders:
Dem Vogel, der heut' sang,
Dem war der Schnabel hold gewachsen ;
    Macht' er den Meistern bang,
Gar wohl gefiel er doch Hans Sachsen.

Eva ist auf die Strasse getreten, hat schüchtern spähend sich der Werkstatt genähert, und steht jetzt unvermerkt an der Thüre bei Sachs.

Eva.

Gut'n Abend, Meister !   Noch so fleissig?

Sachs
            (ist angenehm überrascht aufgefahren).

Ei, Kind ! Lieb' Evchen? Noch so spät?
Und doch, warum so spät noch, weiss ich:
Die neuen Schuh'?

Eva.
                    Wie fehl er räth !
Die Schuh' hab' ich noch gar nicht probirt ;
Die sind so schön, so reich geziert,
Dass ich sie noch nicht an die Füss' mir getraut.

Sachs.
Doch sollst sie morgen tragen als Braut?

Eva
(hat sich dicht bei Sachs auf den Steinsitz gesetzt).
Wer wäre denn Bräutigam?

Sachs.
                    Weiss ich das?
Eva.
Wie wisst denn ihr, ob ich Braut?

Sachs.
                    Ei was !
Das weiss die Stadt.

Eva.
                Ja, weiss es die Stadt.
Freund Sachs gute Gewähr dann hat.
Ich dacht', er wüsst' mehr.

Sachs.
                Was sollt' ich wissen?
Eva.
Ei seht doch !   Werd' ich's ihm sagen müssen?
Ich bin wohl recht dumm?

Sachs.
                    Das sagt' ich nicht.

Eva.

Then you must be bright?

Sachs.

                   That I don't know.

Eva.

You know naught! You say naught!
           Ah, friend Sachs!
I see now clearly, pitch is not wax.
I really believ'd you were sharper.

Sachs.

                    My dear!
Both pitch and wax are well known here.
With wax I rubbed the silken stitching
With which I sewed your pretty shoes;
The thread for these coarser ones I'm pitching;
'T is good enough for a man to use.

Eva.

Whom do you mean! Some grandee:

Sachs.

                  Aye, marry!
A Master proud who boldly woos,
Expecting to-morrow all to carry;
For Master Beckmesser I make these shoes.

Eva.

Then pitch in plenty let there be,
To stick him fast and leave me free.

Sachs.

He hopes by singing to attain thee.

Eva.

Why should he hope?

Sachs.

              Why should he not?
Few bachelors are on the spot.

Eva.

Might not a widower hope to gain me?

Sachs.

My child, I am too old for you.

Eva.

Ah, stuff! too old! Art is the thing;
Who masters that is free to woo.

Sachs.

Dear Eva, are you flattering?

Eva.

Dann wär't ihr whol klug?

Sachs.

                   Das weiss ich nich:

Eva.

Ihr wisst nichts? Ihr sagt nichts? — Ei, Freunc
                     Sachs :
Jetzt merk' ich wahrlich, Pech ist kein Wachs.
Ich hätt' euch für feiner gehalten.

Sachs.

                    Kind
Beid', Wachs und Pech vertraut mir sind.
Mit Wachs strich ich die Seidenfäden,
Damit ich die zieren Schuh' dir gefasst:
Heut' fass ich die Schuh' mit dicht'ren Drähten,
Da gilt's mit Pech für den derben Gast.

Eva.

Wer ist denn der? Wohl 'was Rechts?

Sachs.

                  Das mein' ich
Ein Meister stolz auf Freiers Fuss,
Denkt morgen zu siegen ganz alleinig:
Herrn Beckmesser's Schuh' ich richten muss.

Eva.

So nehmt nur tüchtig Pech dazu:
Da kleb' er drin, und lass' mir Ruh'!

Sachs.

Er hofft dich sicher zu ersingen.

Eva.

Wie so denn der?

Sachs.

                 Ein Junggesell :
's gibt deren wenig dort zur Stell'.

Eva.

Könnt's einem Wittwer nicht gelingen?

Sachs.

Mein Kind der wär' zu alt für dich.

Eva.

Ei was, zu alt! Hier gilt's die Kunst :
Wer sie versteht, der werb' um mich!

Sachs.

Lieb' Evchen! Machst mir blauen Dunst?

Eva.

Not I ; 't is you are an impostor !
Admit now, your affections veer ;
Heav'n knows whom now your heart may foster !
I 'd thought it my own this many a year.

Sachs.

Because in my arms I oft carried you?

Eva.

I see. You had no child of your own.

Sachs.

I once had wife and children too.

Eva.

But they are dead and I am grown.

Sachs.

Grown tall and fair.

Eva.

'T was my idea
That I might fill their places here.

Sachs.

Then I should have child and also wife :
That were indeed a joy in life !
Aye, that was an idea I vow !

Eva.

I think you 're trying to mock me now.
In short, 't would give you little sorrow
If under your nose from all to-morrow,
This Beckmesser sang me away !

Sachs.

If he succeeded what could I say !
'T would rest on what your father said.

Eva.

Where does a Master keep his head?
Were I with you could it be found?

Sachs.

Ah, yes ! you 're right ! all my brain turns round.
I 've been annoyed and vexed to-day,
And in my mind some traces stay.

Eva.

Aye, in the Song-school? You met, I see.

Sachs.

Yes, child ; an election has worried me.

Eva.

Nicht ich ! Ihr seid's ; ihr macht mir Flausen !
Gesteht nur, dass ihr wandelbar ;
Gott weiss, wer jetzt euch im Herzen mag hausen !
Glaubt' ich mich doch drin so manches Jahr.

Sachs.

Wohl, da ich dich gern in den Armen trug?

Eva.

Ich seh', 's war nur, weil ihr kinderlos.

Sachs.

Hatt' einst Weib und Kinder genug.

Eva.

Doch starb eure Frau, so wuchs ich gross.

Sachs.

Gar gross und schön !

Eva.

Drum dacht' ich aus.
Ihr nähm't mich für Weib und Kind in's Haus.

Sachs.

Da hätt' ich ein Kind und auch ein Weib :
's wär' gar ein lieber Zeitvertreib !
Ja, ja ! das hast du dir schön erdacht.

Eva.

Ich glaub', der Meister mich gar verlacht?
Am End' gar liess' er sich auch gefallen,
Dass unter der Nas' ihm weg von Allen
Der Beckmesser morgen mich ersäng'?

Sachs.

Wie sollt, ich's wehren, wenn's ihm geläng'?—
Dem wüsst' allein dein Vater Rath.

Eva.

Wo so ein Meister den Kopf nur hat !
Käm' ich zu euch wohl, fänd' ich's zu Haus?

Sachs.

Ach, ja ! Hast Recht ! 's ist im Kopf mir kraus ;
Hab' heut' manch' Sorg' und Wirr erlebt :
Da mag's dann sein, dass 'was drin klebt.

Eva.

Wohl in der Singschul'? 's war' heut' Gebot

Sachs.

Ja, Kind : eine Freiung machte mir Noth.

Eva.

O Sachs ! but you should at once have said so,
Then my tongue would not have plagued your
head so.
Now say, who was it entrance besought?

Sachs.

A knight, my child, and quite untaught.

Eva.

A knight? Dear me ! And did he succeed?

Sachs.

Why, no, my child, we disagreed.

Eva.

Dear me ! how strange ! relate it, pray ;
If you are vexed, can I be gay?
Then he was defeated and baffled quite?

Sachs.

Truly hopeless the case of the noble knight.

Magdalena

(comes to the house-door and calls softly).

Hist ! Eva ! Hist !

Eva.

Truly hopeless ! And why?
Were there no means to help him by?
Sang he so ill, so faultily
He never a Master can hope to be?

Sachs.

My child, it is a hopeless disaster ;
No leader he 'll be in any land ;
For when one is born to be a Master,
'Mong other Masters he cannot stand.

Magdalena

(approaching).

Your father awaits.

Eva.

But tell me the end,
If none of the Masters he won for a friend?

Sachs

That is a good joke ! friend could we call
One before whom we all felt so small?
My young lord Haughty, let him toddle,
In the world to cool his noddle.
What we have learnt with toil and care,
Let us digest in peace unhurried !
Here we must by none be worried :
So let his fortune shine elsewhere !

Eva.

Ja, Sachs ! Das hättet ihr gleich soll'n sagen ;
Plagt' euch dann nicht mit unnützen Fragen. —
Nun sagt, wer war's, der Freiung begehrt?

Sachs.

Ein Junker, Kind, gar unbelehrt.

Eva.

Ein Junker ! Mein, sagt ! — und ward er gefreit?

Sachs.

Nichts da, mein Kind ! 's gab zu viel Streit.

Eva.

So Sagt ! Erzählt wie ging es zu?
Macht's euch Sorg', wie liess' mir es Ruh'?
So bestand er übel und hat verthan?

Sachs.

Ohne Gnad' versang der Herr Rittersmann.

Magdalene

(kommt zum Haus heraus und ruft leise).

Bst ! Evchen ! Bst !

Eva.

Ohne Gnade? Wie
Kein Mittel gäb's, das ihm gadieh'?
Sang er so schlecht, so fehlervoll,
Dass nichts mehr zum Meister ihm helfen soll?

Sachs.

Mein Kind, für den ist Alles verloren,
Und Meister wird der in keinem Land ;
Denn wer als Meister ward geboren,
Der hat unter Meistern den schlimmsten Stand.

Magdalene

(näher).

Der vater verlangt.

Eva.

So sagt mir noch an
Ob keinen der Meister zum Freund er gewann?

Sachs.

Das wär nicht übel ! Freund ihm noch sein !
Ihm, vor dem All' sich fühlen so klein !
Den Junker Hochmuth, lasst ihn laufen,
Mag er durch die welt sich raufen :
Was wir erlent mit Noth und Müh',
Dafei lasst uns in Ruh' verschnaufen !
Hier renn' er nichts uns über'n Haufen ·
Sein Glück ihm anderswo erblüh' !

Eva.
(rising hastily).

Yes, elsewhere it will shine, I know,
In spite of what your envious pack says;
Some place where hearts still warmly glow,
With no deceitful Master Sachses!—
Yes, Lena! Yes! I 'm coming, dear!—
Nice consolation I get here!
I smell the pitch, Heav'n keep us whole!
Burn it, rather, and warm up your soul.

(She crosses over hastily with Magdalena and remains in
agitation at her own door.)

Sachs
(with a meaning nod of his head).

I thought as much! Now then they 'll prate!

(During the following he closes the upper half of his door
also, so nearly as only to leave a little crack of light, he
himself being quite invisible.)

Magdalena.

Good lack! why have you stayed so late?
Your father called.

Eva.
Go you instead,
And say that I am gone to bed.

Magdalena.

No, no! Hark now! I have news too!
Beckmesser found me; such a to-do!
To-night, if but at the window stay'd you,
He said he would come and serenade you.
The song he intends for your winning he 'll sing,
To try if your approval 't will bring.

Eva.

He need not trouble!—where can he be?

Magdalena.

Has David been here?

Eva.
What 's that to me?

Magdalena
(half to herself).

I was too harsh; he 's vexed, I fear.

Eva.

No one in sight?

Magdalena.

Some one draws near.

Eva.

Is 't he?

Eva
(erhebt sich heftig).

Ja, anderswo soll's ihm erblüh'n,
Als bei euch garst'gen, neid'schen Mannsen:
Wo warm die Herzen noch erglüh'n,
Trotz allen tück'schen Meister Hansen!
Ja, Lene! Gleich! ich komme schon!
Was trüg' ich hier für Trost davon?
Da riecht's nach Pech, dass Gott erbarm'!
Brennt' er's lieber, da würd er doch warm!

Sie geht heftig mit Magdalene hinüber und verweilt seb'
aufgeregt dort unter der Thüre.

Sachs.
(nickt bedeutungsvoll mit dem Kopfe).

Das dacht' ich wohl. Nun heisst's: schaff' Rath!

Er ist während des Folgenden damit beschäftigt, auch die
obere Ladenthüre so weit zu schliessen, dass sie nur ein
wenig Licht noch durchlässt; er selbst verschwindet so fast
ganz.

Magdalene.

Hilf Gott! was bliebst du nur so spat?
Der Vater rief.

Eva
Geh' zu ihm ein:
Ich sei zu Bett im Kämmerlein.

Magdalene.

Nicht doch! Hör' nur! Komm' ich dazu?
Beckmesser fand mich: er lässt nicht Ruh',
Zur nacht sollst du dich an's Fenster neigen,
Er will dir 'was Schönes singen und geigen,
Mit dem er dich hofft zu gewinnen, das Lied,
Ob dir das zu Gefallen gerieth.

Eva.

Das fehlte auch noch!—Käme nur Er!

Magdalene.

Hast' David geseh'n?

Eva
Was soll mir der:

Magdalene
(halb für sich).

Ich war zu streng; er wird sich grämen.

Eva.

Siehst du noch nichts?

Magdalene.
's ist als ob Leut' dort kämen.

Eva.

Wär' er's?

Magdalena.

          Come ; 't is time to depart.

Eva.

Not till I 've seen the man of my heart.

Magdalena.

I made a mistake, it is not he.
Come in, for fear your father should see.

Eva.

What shall I do?

Magdalena.

          We 'll hold consultation
As to this Beckmesser's invitation.

Eva.

Stand you at the window for me.

Magdalena.

            What, I?
'T would rouse poor David's jealousy.
He sleeps on the street side.   He he! what fun !

Eva.

I hear a footstep !

Magdalena.

          Come now, let us run !

Eva.

It nears us !

Magdalena.

         You 're wrong, I 'll bet my head.
Do come ! You must, till your father 's in bed.

Pogner
          (calling within).

Hey ! Lena ! Eva !

Magdalena.

         No more delay !
D' ye hear? Come — your knight 's far away.

Walter has come up the alley and now turns the corner
by Pogner's house. Eva, who is being dragged indoors by
Magdalena, tears herself free with a slight cry and rushes
towards Walter.

Eva.

It is he !

Magdalena.
         (going in).

         Now all 's up.   Be quick, I say !
          (Exit).

Magdalene.

         Mach' und komm' jetzt hinan !

Eva.

Nicht eh'r, bis ich sah den theuersten Mann !

Magdalene.

Ich täuschte mich dort : er war es nicht.
Jetzt komm, sonst merkt der Vater die G'schicht

Eva.

Ach ! meine Angst !

Magdalene.

         Auch lass uns berathen,
Wie wir des Beckmesser's uns entladen.

Eva.

Zum Fenster gehst du für mich.

Magdalene.

           Wie. ich ?
Das machte wohl David eiferlich !
Er schläft nach der Gassen ! Hihi ! 's wär' fein ! —

Eva.

Dort hör' ich Schritte.

Magdalene.

         Jetzt komm', es muss sein !

Eva.

Jetzt näher !

Magdalene.

         Du irrst ! 's ist nichts, ich wett'.
Ei, komm' ! Du musst, bis der Vater zu Bett.

Pogner
          (von innen rufend).

He ! Lene ! Eva !

Magdalene

         's ist höchste Zeit !
Hörst du's? — Komm' ! — der Ritter ist Weit.—

Walther ist die Gasse heraufgekommen; jetzt biegt er um
Pogner's Haus herum; Eva, die bereits von Magdalena am
Arm hineingezogen worden war, reisst sich mit einem leisen
Schrei los und stürzt Walther entgegen.

Eva.

Da ist er !

Magdalene
         (hineingehend).

Nun haben wir's !   Jetzt heisst's gescheit !
          (Ab.)

Eva

(transported).

'T is my true love !
Yes, my own love !
Naught conceal I,
All is known, love :
All reveal I.
For I know it :
It is you, love,
Hero-Poet
And my only friend !

Walter

(sorrowfully).

Ah, thou 'rt wrong ! I 'm but thy friend ;
Not as Poet
Masters prize me,
For my station
They despise me :
Inspiration
They can brook not,
And — I know it —
I may look not
To my lady's hand !

Eva.

Thou art wrong ! Thy lady's hand
Awards the prize alone.
Thy courage doth my heart command ;
Be then the wreath thine own.

Walter.

Ah, no, thou 'rt wrong ! My lady's hand,
Though no one else should gain it,
Upon the terms thy father plann'd
I never may attain it.
"A Master-Singer he must be :
None may'st thou wed uncrowned by thee."
Thus to the Guild he firmly spake ;
What he hath pledged he may not break.
That spurred my heart's desire,
Though strange to me were place and folk :
I sang, all love and fire,
And strove to make a Master-stroke.

The loud sound of a night-watchman's cowhorn is heard.
Walter clasps his hand to his sword and stares wildly before
him.

Ha !

Eva

(taking him soothingly by the hand)

Belovĕd, govern thy wrath !
'T is but the watchman goes forth.—
Hide 'neath the lime-tree !
Lose no more time ! See,
The watchman passes this way.

Magdalena

(at the door, softly).

Eva ! 't is late : come in, I say !

Eva

(ausser sich).

Ja, ihr seid es !
Nein, du bist es
Alles sag' ich,
Denn ihr wisst es ;
Alles klag' ich,
Denn ich weiss es ;
Ihr seid Beides,
Held des Preises,
Und mein einz'ger Freund !

Walther

(leidenschaftlich).

Ach, du irrst ! Bin nur dein **Freund,**
Doch des Preises
Noch nicht würdig,
Nicht den Meistern
Ebenbürtig :
Mein Begeistern
Fand Verachten,
Und ich weiss es,
Darf nicht trachten
Nach der Freundin Hand !

Eva.

Wie du irrst ! Der Freundin Hand,
Ertheilt nur sie den Preis.
Wie deinen Muth ihr Herz erfand,
Reicht sie nur dir das Reis.

Walther.

Ach nein, du irrst ! Der Freundin Hand,
Wär Keinem sie erkoren,
Wie sie des Vaters Wille band,
Mir wär' sie doch verloren.
„ Ein Meistersinger muss er sein :
Nur wen ihr krönt, den darf sei frei'n ! "
So sprach er festlich zu den Herrn,
Kann nicht zurück, möcht er's auch gern !
Das eben gab mir Muth ;
Wie ungewohnt mir alles schien,
Ich sang mit Lieb' und Gluth,
Dass ich den Meisterschlag verdien'.

Man hört den starken Ruf eines Nachtwächter hornt
Walther legt mit emphatischer Gebärde die Hand an se
Schwert, und starrt wild vor sich hin.

Ha ! . . .

Eva

(fasst ihn besänftigend an der Hand).

Geliebter, spare den Zorn !
's war nur des Nachtwächters Horn. —
Unter der Linde
Birg' dich geschwinde.
Hier kommt der Wächter vorbei.

Magdalene

(an der Thüre, leise).

Evchen ! 's ist Zeit, mach' dich frei !

Walter.

You fly?

Eva.

       Must I not flee?

Walter.

You fear —?

Eva.

       The powers that be!

(She disappears with Magdalena into the house.)

The Watchman

(has meanwhile appeared in the alley. He comes forward singing, turns the corner of Pogner's house and exit L).

" Hark to what I say, good people;
Striketh ten from every steeple.
Put out your fire and eke your light,
That none may come to harm this night.
     Praise the Lord of Heav'n !"

(He has by this time gone off, but his horn is still heard).

Sachs

(who has listened to the foregoing from behind ·his shop-door, now opens it a little wider, having shaded his lamp).

Pretty doings now are in hand!
Here 's an elopement being plann'd.
I 'm awake! This must not be.

Walter

       (behind the lime-tree).

Has she then left me? Woe is me! —
Yet no! who comes here?— Ah, not she!
T is Magdalena.— Yet surely! — *Thou!*

Eva

(returns in Magdalena's dress and goes to Walter).

Thy foolish child, she 's all thine now!

       She sinks on his breast.)

Walter.

O heaven! here before my eyes
I see indeed the Master-prize!

Eva.

     Now no more delay!
     Let 's hasten away!
   Oh, would that we were gone!

Walter.

     Here, through this alley: on!
     Servants at the gate
     With my horses wait.

Walther.

Du fliehst?

Eva.

       Muss ich denn nicht?

Walther.

Entweichst?

Eva.

       Dem Meistergericht.

(Sie verschwindet mit Magdalene im Hause.)

Der Nachtwächter.

(ist währenddem in der Gasse erschienen, kommt singend nach vorn, biegt um die Ecke von Pogner's Haus, und geht nach links zu weiter ab).

„ Hört ihr Leut' und lasst euch sagen,
Die Glock' hat Zehn geschlagen:
Bewahrt das Feuer und auch das Licht,
Damit Niemand kein Schad' geschicht!
     Lobet Gott den Herrn !"

(Als er hiermit abgegangen, hört man ihn abermals blasen.)

Sachs

(welcher hinter der Ladenthüre dem Gespräche gelauscht, öffnet jetzt, bei eingezogenem Lampenlicht, ein wenig mehr).

Ueble Dinge, die ich da merk':
Eine Entführung gar im Werk!
Aufgepasst: das darf nicht sein!

Walther

       (hinter der Linde).

Käm' sie nicht wieder? O der Pein! —
Doch' ja! sie kommt dort! Weh' mir, nein!
Die Alte ist's! — doch aber — ja!

Eva

(ist in Magdalene's Kleidung wieder zurückgekehrt und geht auf Walther zu).

Das thör'ge Kind: da hast du's! da!

       (Sie sinkt ihm an die Brust.

Walther.

O Himmel! Ja! nun wohl ich weiss,
Dass ich gewann den Meisterpreis.

Eva.

     Doch nun kein Besinnen!
     Von hinnen! Von hinnen!
   O wären wir weit schon fort!

Walther.

     Hier durch die Gasse: dort
     Finden wir vor dem Thor
     Knecht und Rosse vor.

As they turn to dive into the alley Sachs places his lamp behind a water-globe and sends a bright stream of light through the now wide-open door across the street, so that Eva and Walter suddenly find themselves illuminated.

Eva

(hastily pulling Walter back).

Ah me ! the cobbler !   What would he say !
Hide thee ! — keep well out of his way !

Walter.

What other road leads to the gate ?

Eva

(pointing R).

Round by the street here, but 't is not straight ;
I know it not well ; besides, we should meet
With the watchman.

Walter.

Well, then, through the alley !

Eva.

The cobbler must first leave his windowseat.

Walter.

I 'll force him then.   Here 's for a sally !

Eva.

Shew not yourself : he knows you !

Walter.

Who is he ?

Eva.

'T is Sachs !

Walter.

Hans Sachs ? my friend ?

Eva.

Not quite !

With slanders against you he is busy.

Walter.

What Sachs !   He too ? — I 'll put out his light !

Beckmesser comes up the alley slinking at some distance in the rear of the watchman. He peers up to Pogner's windows and, leaning against Sach's house, seeks out a stone seat on which he places himself, still looking at the upper windows, and now he commences to tune a lute he has brought with him.

Eva

(restraining Walter).

Forbear ! — Now hark !

Walter.

A lute I hear.

Als sich Beide wenden, um die Gasse einzubiegen, lässt Sachs, nachdem er die Lampe hinter eine Glasskugel gestellt, einen hellen Lichtschein durch die ganz wieder geöffnete Ladenthüre, quer über die Strasse fallen, so dass Eva und Walther sich plötzlich hell erleuchtet sehen.

Eva

(Walther heftig zurückziehend).

O weh', der Schuster !   Wenn der uns säh' !
Birg' dich ? komm' ihm nicht in die Näh' !

Walther.

Welch' andrer Weg führt uns hinaus ?

Eva

(nach rechts deutend).

Dort durch die Strasse : doch der ist kraus,
Ich kenn' ihn nicht gut ; auch stiessen wir dort
Auf den Wächter.

Walther.

Nur denn : durch die Gasse !

Eva.

Der Schuster muss erst vom Fenster fort.

Walther.

Ich zwing' ihn dass er's verlasse.

Eva.

Zeig dich ihm nicht : er kennt dich !

Walther.

Der Schuster ?

Eva.

's ist Sachs.

Walther.

Hans Sachs, mein Freund ?

Eva.

Glaub's nicht !

Von dir zu sagen Uebles nur wusst' er.

Walther.

Wie, Sachs ?   Auch er ? — Ich lösch' ihm das
Licht !

Beckmesser ist, dem Nachtwächter in einiger Entfernung nachschleichend die Gasse herauf gekommen, hat nach den Fenstern von Pogner's Hause gespäht, und, an Sachsen's Hause angelehnt, zwischen den beiden Fenstern einen Steinsitz sich ausgesucht, auf welchem er sich, immer nur nach dem gegenüberliegenden Fenster aufmerksam lugend, niedergelassen hat; jetzt stimmt er eine mitgebrachte Laute.

Eva

(Walther zurückhaltend).

Thu's nicht ! — Doch horch !

Walther.

Einer Laute Klang !

Eva.

What a mishap!

Walter.

Why need you fear?
The cobbler's light has ceased to glare:
Let 's make the attempt!

Eva.

Ah! see you not there?
Some other comes to spoil our plans.

Walter.

I hear and see: some player man.
What wants he here so late at night?

Eva.

'T is Beckmesser!

Sachs

(on hearing the first sounds of the lute has, as if struck with
a new idea, withdrawn his light, gently opened the lower
half of his shopdoor and placed his workbench on the
threshold. He now hears Eva's exclamation).

Aha! I 'm right!

Walter.

The Marker here? and placed in my pow'r?
Here goes! The fool shall rue this hour!

Eva.

O heav'n! Forbear! Would you wake my father?
He 'll sing his song and quit us then.
Let 's hide behind the foliage rather.
Oh, dear! what trouble you give, you men!

(She draws Walter behind the bushes which surround the
bench under the lime-tree.)
Beckmesser impatiently tinkles on his lute waiting for the
window to open. As he is about to commence his song
Sachs turns his light full on the street again and begins to
hammer loudly on his last, singing lustily the while.

Sachs.

Tooral looral!
Tiddy fol de rol!
Oho! Tralala! Oho!
When Mother Eve from Paradise
Was by the Almighty driven,
Her naked feet, so small and nice,
By stones were sorely riven.
This troubled much the Lord,
Her tootsies he ador'd
An angel he did straightway choose:
"Go make that pretty sinner shoes!
And as poor Adam limps around;
And breaks his toes on stony ground,
That well and wide
His legs may stride,
Measure him for boots beside!"

Eva.

Ach, meine Noth!

Walther.

Wie, wird dir bang?
Der Schuster, sieh, zog ein das Licht:—
So sei's gewagt!

Eva.

Weh'! Hörst du denn nicht?
Ein Andrer kam, und nahm dort Stand.

Walther.

Ich hör's und seh's:—ein Musikant.
Was will der hier so spät des Nachts?

Eva.

's ist Beckmesser schon!

Sachs

(als er den ersten Ton der Laute vernommen, hat, von einem
plötzlichen Einfall erfasst, das Licht wieder etwas eingezogen,
leise auch den unteren Theil des Ladens geöffnet, und
seinen Werktisch ganz unter die Thüre gestellt. Jetzt hat er
Eva's Ausruf vernommen).

Aha! ich dacht's!

Walther.

Der Merker? Er? in meiner Gewalt?
D'rauf zu, den Lung'rer mach' ich kalt?

Eva.

Um Gott! So hör'! Willst den Vater wecken?
Er singt ein Lied, dann zieht er ab.
Lass dort uns im Gebüsch verstecken.—
Was mit den Männern ich Müh' doch hab'!

(Sie zieht Walther hinter das Gebüsch auf die Bank unter der
Linde.)

Beckmesser

(klimpert voll Ungeduld heftig auf der Laute, ob sich das
Fenster nicht öffnen wolle. Als er endlich anfangen will zu
singen beginnt Sachs, der soeben das Licht wieder hell auf
die Strasse fallen liess, laut mit dem Hammer auf den
Leisten zu schlagen, und singt sehr kräftig dazu).

Sachs.

Jerum! Jerum!
Halla halla he!
O ho! Trallalei! o he!
Als Eva aus dem Paradies
Von Gott dem Herrn verstossen,
Gar schuf ihr Schmerz der harte Kiess
An ihrem Fuss, dem blossen.
Das jammerte den Herrn,
Ihr Füsschen hat er gern,
Und seinem Engel rief er zu:
„Da mach' der armen Sünd'rin Schuh'!
Und da der Adam, wie ich seh',
An Steinen dort sich stösst die Zeh,
Dass recht fortan.
Er wandeln kann,
So miss' dem auch Stiefel an!"

Beckmesser

(as Sachs begins to sing).

What is it now?
Atrocious row!
The vulgar cobbler 's drunk, I trow!

(Advancing.)

What, Master! Up, so long after dark?

Sachs.

You also out, Master Town-clerk?
The shoes perhaps on your mind are weighing?
You see me at work: I 'm not delaying.

Beckmesser.

Deuce take boot and shoe!
Be quiet do!

Walter

(to Eva).

What is that song? He speaks of thee.

Eva.

I know it well; he means not me.
But hidden malice here I trace.

Walter.

What vile delay! Time flies apace!

Sachs

(working).

Tooral looral!
Tiddy fol de rol!
Oho! Tralala! Oho!
O Eve! Hear how my poor heart aches,
By grief and trouble sodden;
The works of Art a cobbler makes
All under foot are trodden.
Did not an angel bring
For such work comforting,
And call me oft to Heaven's gate,
I 'd quickly leave this trade I hate!
But when he takes me up on high,
The world beneath my feet doth lie:
Then rest doth woo
Hans Sachs, the shoe-
Maker and the Poet too.

Beckmesser

(watching the window which now opens softly).

The window 's unclosed! — O heavens! 't is she!

Eva

(to Walter).

Why does that song dispirit me?
Oh, hence, let us hasten!

Beckmesser

(alsbald nach Beginn des Verses).

Was soll das sein? —
Verdammtes Schrein!
Was fällt dem groben Schuster ein?

(Vortretend.)

Wie, Meister? Auf? So spät zur Nacht?

Sachs.

Herr Stadtschreiber! Was, ihr wacht? —
Die Schuh' machen euch grosse Sorgen?
Ihr seht, ich bin dran: ihr habt sie morgen.

Beckmesser.

Hol' der Teufel die Schuh'!
Ich will hier Ruh'!

Walther

(zu Eva).

Wie heisst das Lied? Wie nennt er dich?

Eva.

Ich hört' es schon: 's geht nicht auf mich,
Doch eine Bosheit steckt darin.

Walther.

Welch' Zögerniss! Die Zeit geht hin!

Sachs

(fortarbeitend).

Jerum! Jerum!
Halla halla he!
O ho! Trallalei! O he!
O Eva! Hör' mein Klageruf,
Mein Noth und schwer Verdrüssen!
Die Kunstwerk', die ein Schuster schuf,
Sie tritt die Welt mit Füssen!
Gäb nicht ein Engel Trost,
Der gleiches Werk erlos't,
Und rief mich oft in's Paradies,
Wie dann ich Schuh' und Stiefel liess'!
Doch wenn der mich im Himmel hält,
Dann liegt zu Füssen mir die Welt,
Und bin in Ruh'
Hans Sachs ein Schuh-
macher und Poet dazu.

Beckmesser

(das Fenster gewahrend, welches jetzt sehr leise geöffne
wird).

Das Fenster geht auf: — Herr Gott, 's ist sie!

Eva

(zu Walther).

Mich schmerzt das Lied, ich weiss nicht wie!
O fort, lass uns fliehen!

Walter

(half-drawing his sword).

　　　　　　　　　　　But one way remains !

Eva.

Oh, no !　Forbear !

Walter.

　　　　　　　He 's scarce worth the pains !

Eva.

Yes, patience is best.　· O dearest love,
That I should such a trouble prove !

Walter.

Who 's at the window ?

Eva.

　　　　　　　　　　　'T is Magdalena.

Walter.

That 's real retribution : it sets me grinning.

Eva.

Would we could end, and fly this arena !

Walter.

I only wish he 'd make a beginning.

(They follow the proceedings with increasing interest.)

Beckmesser

(who, while Sachs has continued his song and work, takes
　　counsel with himself in great perturbation).

Now if he continues I am undone !

(He advances to the shop.)

Friend Sachs !　pray hear a word — just one !
You work there at my shoes so fleetly,
While I 'd forgotten them completely.
The cobbler worshipful I deem ;
The critic, though, I more esteem.
Your taste, I know, is seldom wrong ;
So, please you, hear this little song,
With which I seek to win to-morrow :
Your estimate I fain would borrow.

(With his back turned to the alley he strums on the lute to
attract the attention of Magdalena and keep her at the
window.)

Sachs.

Aha !　A trap your words are holding !
But I 'll not earn another scolding.
Since that your cobbler courts the Muse
It fares but ill with your boots and shoes :
　　　　I see they 're slit :
　　　　And ev'rywhere split ;
So all my verse and rhyme
I 'll lay aside for a time,
My sense, my wit, my knowledge and all ;
Then with your new pair of shoes I 'll call.

Walther

(das Schwert halb ziehend).

　　　　　　　　Nun denn : mit dem Schwert !

Eva.

Nicht doch !　Ach halt' !

Walther.

　　　　　　　　Kaum wär' er's werth

Eva.

Ja, besser Geduld !　O lieber Mann !
Dass ich so Noth dir machen kann !

Walther.

Wer ist am Fenster ?

Eva.

　　　　　　　　　's ist Magdalene.

Walther.

Das heiss' ich vergelten : fast muss' ich lachen.

Eva.

Wie ich ein End' und Flucht mir ersehne !

Walther.

Ich wünscht' er möchte den Anfang machen.

(Sie folgen dem Vorgang mit wachsender Theilnahme.)

Beckmesser

(der, während Sachs fortfährt zu arbeiten und zu singen, in
　　grosser Aufregung mit sich berathen hat).

Jetzt bin ich verloren, singt er noch fort !

(Er tritt an den Laden heran.)

Freund Sachs !　So hört doch nur ein Wort !
Wie seid ihr auf die Schuh' versessen !
Ich hatt' sie wahrlich schon vergessen.
Als Schuster seid ihr mir wohl werth,
Als Kunstfreund doch weit mehr verehrt.
Eu'r Urtheil, glaubt, das halt' ich hoch ;
D'rum bitt' ich, hört das Liedlein doch,
Mit dem ich morgen möcht' gewinnen,
Ob das auch recht nach euren Sinnen.

Er klimpert, mit seinem Rücken der Gasse zugewendet
auf der Laute, um die Aufmerksamkeit der dort am Fenster
sich zeigenden Magdalene zu beschäftigen, und sie dadurch
zurückzuhalten.

Sachs.

O ha !　Wollt mich beim Wahne fassen !
Mag mich nicht wieder schelten lassen.
Seit sich der Schuster dünkt Poet,
Gar übel es um eu'r Schuhwerk steht ;
　　　　ich seh' wie's schlappt,
　　　　Und überall klappt :
D'rum lass' ich Vers' und Reim'
Gar billig nun daheim,
Verstand und Kenntniss auch dazu,
Mach' euch für morgen die neuen Schuh'.

Beckmesser.

Atrocious malice ! — Zounds ! it grows late !
She 'll go from the window if longer I wait !

(He strums a prelude.)

Sachs

(with a blow of his hammer).

" Now begin " !   Look sharp, or I too shall sing !

Beckmesser.

Aught but that !   Pray hush ! — What a madd'ning
thing !
Would you the post of Marker aspire to,
Then hammer away as you desire to : —
But you must agree to restrain your tool ;
Not strike unless I 'm breaking a rule.

Sachs.

Though a cobbler I 'll keep the rules like you,
If my fingers itch to complete this shoe.

Beckmesser.

Your Master's word ?

Sachs.

And cobbler's truth.

Beckmesser.

If it is faultless, fair, and smooth —

Sachs.

Then you must go unshod, forsooth !
Sit you down here !

Beckmesser

(placing himself at the corner of the house).

I 'd rather leave you.

Sachs.

Why so far off ?

Beckmesser.

Not to perceive you :
The Marker in school hides in his place.

Sachs.

But I shall scarce hear you.

Beckmesser.

My pow'rful bass
Will not then stun you with its din.

Sachs.

That 's good ! — All right then ! — " Now begin " !

(Short prelude on the lute by Beckmesser, during which
Magdalena leans out of the window.)

Beckmesser.

Verdammte Bosheit ! — Gott, und 's wird spät :
Am End' mir die Jungfer vom Fenster geht !

(Er klimpert wie um anzufangen.)

Sachs

(aufschlagend).

Fanget an ! 's pressirt !   Sonst sing' ich für mich !

Beckmesser.

Haltet ein !   Nur das nicht ! — Teufel ; wie ärger-
lich !
Wollt ihr euch denn als Merker erdreisten,
Nun gut, so merkt mit dem Hammer auf dem
Leisten ; —
Nur mit dem Beding, nach den Regeln scharf ;
Aber nichts, was nach den Regeln ich darf.

Sachs.

Nach den Regeln, wie sie der Schuster kennt,
Dem die Arbeit unter den Händen brennt.

Beckmesser.

Auf Meister-Ehr' !

Sachs.

Und Schuster-Muth

Beckmesser.

Nicht einen Fehler : glatt und gut !

Sachs.

Dann ging't ihr morgen unbeschuht. —
Setzt euch denn hier !

Beckmesser

(an die Ecke des Hauses sich stellend).

Lasst hier mich stehen

Sachs.

Warum so fern ?

Beckmesser.

Euch nicht zu sehen,
Wie's Brauch in der Schul' vor dem Gemerk.

Sachs.

Da hör' ich euch schlecht !

Beckmesser.

Der Stimme Stärk
Ich so gar lieblich dämpfen kann.

Sachs.

Wie fein ! — Nun gut denn ! — Fanget an !

(Kurzes Vorspiel Beckmesser's auf der Laute, wozu Magdalene sich breit in das Fenster legt.)

Walter
                    (to Eva).

What crazy sounds ! 'T is like a dream :
Still in the Singer's seat I seem.

Eva.

Sleep steals upon me like a spell.
For good or evil, who can tell ?

(She sinks, as if stupefied, on Walter's breast. In this posi-
                    tion they remain.)

Beckmesser
                    (with his lute).

    " I see the dawning daylight,
        With great plea*sure* I do.

(Sachs knocks. — Beckmesser starts but continues.)

            " For now my breast takes *a* right
                Courage both fresh and " —

(Sachs has dealt two blows. Beckmesser turns round softly
                but in anger.)

        Is this a jest ?
        What d' ye find bad there ?

Sachs.

        Better have had there,
        " For now my breast
    Takes a right courage fresh and " —

Beckmesser.

        How would that lay right
        To rhyme with my " daylight " ?

Sachs.

The melody do you think no matter ?
Both words and notes should fit in song.

Beckmesser.

Absurd discussion ! — Leave off that clatter !
Or is it a plot ?

Sachs.
                    Oh, get along !

Beckmesser.

I 'm quite upset !

Sachs.
                    Begin it once more,
And three bars rest meanwhile I 'll score.

Beckmesser
                    (aside).

'T is better that no attention I pay : —
If only she is not scared away !

        (He clears his throat and begins again.)

    " I see the dawning daylight,
        With great plea*sure* I do ;

Walther
                    (zu Eva).

Welch' toller Spuck ! Mich dünkt's ein Traum :
Den Singstuhl, scheint's, verliess ich kaum !

Eva.

Die Schläf' umwebt's mir, wie ein Wahn :
Ob's Heil, ob Unheil, was ich ahn' ?

(Sie sinkt wie betäubt an Walther's Brust : so verbleiben
                    sie.)

Beckmesser
                    (zur Laute).

    „ Den Tag seh' ich ercheinen,
        Der wohl gefall'n thut. . .
            (Sachs schlägt auf.)
        (Beckmesser zuckt, fährt aber fort :)
    „ Da fasst mein Herz sich einen
        guten und frischen Muth."

(Sachs hat zweimal aufgeschlagen. Beckmesser wendet
            sich leise doch wüthend um.)

        Treibt ihr hier Scherz ?
        Was wär' nicht gelungen ?

Sachs.

        Besser gesungen :
        „ Da fasst mein Herz
    sich einen guten und frischen Muth."

Beckmesser.

        Wie sollt' sich das reimen
        Auf „ seh' ich erscheinen ? "

Sachs.

Ist euch an der Weise nichts gelegen ?
Mich dünkt, 'sollt' passen Ton und Wort.

Beckmesser.

Mit euch hier zu streiten ? — Lasst von den Schlä-
                                                    gen,
Sonst denkt ihr mir d'ran !

Sachs.
                    Jetzt fahret fort !

Beckmesser.

Bin ganz verwirrt !

Sachs.
                    So fangt noch 'mal an
Drei Schläg' ich jetzt pausiren kann.

Beckmesser
                    (für sich).

Am Besten, wenn ich ihn gar nicht beacht' :
Wenn's nur die Jungfrau nicht irre macht !

        (Er räuspert sich und beginnt wieder.)

    „ Den Tag seh' ich erscheinen,
        Der mir wohl gefall'n thut :

For now my heart takes a right
Cou*rage* both fresh and new.
I do not think of dying,
Rather of trying
A young mai*den* to win.
Oh, wherefore doth the weather
Then *to*-day so excel?
ι *to* all say together.
'T is *be*cause a dam*sel*
By her beloved father,
At *his* wish rather,
To *be* wed *doth* go in.
    The bold man who
    Would come and view,
May see the maiden there so true,
On whom my hopes I firmly glue :
There*fore* is *the* sky *so* bright blue,
    As I said to begin."

Beckmesser, keeping his eyes fixed on the window has
perceived with rising chagrin Magdalena's evident signs of
dissatisfaction; he has sung louder and more hurriedly in
order to overpower the continued hammering of Sachs. —
He is about to continue when the latter, knocking the key
of the last out and withdrawing the shoes, rises from his
stool and leans out over the shopdoor.

Sachs.

Have n't you finished?

Beckmesser

     (in great trepidation).
               What means your call?

Sachs

    (triumphantly holding out the shoes from the door).

I 've finished with the shoes, that's all ! —
I call that a famous Marker's shoe :
Now hear my Marker's maxim too. —
    By long and short strokes dinted
    Here on the sole 'tis printed !
        Behold it here,
        Let it be clear,
    And hold it ever dear. —
      " Good songs must scan."
    On any man,
Ev'n the Town-clerk, who'd transgress it
The cobbler's strap shall impress it. —
      Now run along,
      Your shoes are strong ;
Thrust henceforth to your feet :
They 'll keep you on the beat.

        (He laughs loudly.)

Beckmesser

(who has retired into the alley again and leaned against the
wall between Sachs's two windows, hastens on with his third
verse, shouting breathlessly with violent efforts to drown
Sachs's voice).

Da fasst mein Herz sich einen
Guten und frischen Muth.
Da denk' ich nicht an Sterben,
    Lieber an Werben
Um jung' Mägdeleins Hand.
Warum wohl aller Tage
Schönster mag dieser sein?
Allen hier ich es sage :
Weil ein schönes Fräulein,
Von ihrem lieb'n Herrn Vater,
Wie gelobt hat er,
Ist bestimmt zum Eh' stand.
    Wer sich getrau',
    Der komm' und schau'
Da steh'n die hold lieblich Jungfrau,
Auf die ich all' mein' Hoffnung bau',
D'rum ist der Tag so schön blau,
    Als ich anfänglich fand."

Beckmesser, nur den Blick auf das Fenster heftend, hat mit
wachsender Angst Magdalene's missbehagliche Gebärden
bemerkt; um Sachsen's fortgesetzte Schläge zu übertäuben,
hat er immer stärker und athemloser gesungen. — Er ist im
Begriffe sofort weiter zu singen, als Sachs, der zuletzt die
Keile aus den Leisten schlug, und die Schuhe abgezogen
hat, sich vom Schemel erhebt, und über den Laden sich
herauslehnt.

Sachs.

Seid ihr nun fertig?

Beckmesser

     (in höchster Angst).
               Wie fraget ihr?

Sachs

    (die Schuhe triumphirend aus dem Laden heraushaltend).

Mit den Schuhen ward' ich fertig schier !
Das heiss' das mir rechte Merkerschuh' ;
Mein Merkersprüchlein hört dazu !
    Mit lang' und kurzen Hieben,
    Steht's auf der Sohl' geschrieben :
        Da les't es klar
        Und nehmt es wahr,
    Und merkt's euch immerdar. —
      Gut Lied will Takt,
      Wer den verzwackt,
    Dem Schreiber mit der Feder
Haut ihn der Schuster auf's Leder.
      Nun lauft iu Ruh',
      Habt gute Schuh' ;
Der Fuss euch d'rin nicht knackt :
Ihn hält die Sohl' im Takt !

        (Er lacht laut.)

Beckmesser

(der sich ganz in die Gasse zurückgezogen, und an die
Mauer zwischen den beiden Fenstern von Sachsens Hause
sich anlehnt, singt, um Sachs zu übertäuben, zugleich, mit
grösster Anstrengung, schreiend und athemlos hastig, seinen
dritten Vers).

That I 've a Master's learning
Will*ingly* I 'd show her,
To win the *reward* burning
I 'm *with* thirst *and* hun*ger*.
Now I call *the* nine Muses
   To witness whose is
The *poetic* gift true.
I lay no faulty stresses,
In *the* rules I 'm no dunce ;
Some little awkwardnesses
May *ex*cused *be* for once,
When *one*'s heart fear is swaying
   At thus essaying
A fair mai*den* to woo.
   A bachelor,
   I 'd give my gore,
My place, rank, honor, all my store,
If *you* my song would not abhor ;
And *the* mai*den* would me adore
   If she admires it too."

Neighbors

(first a few, then more, open their windows in the alley during the song and peep out).

Who 's howling there?   Who bawls so loud?
So late at night, is that allowed?
'T is time for bed !   Be still, I say !
Just listen to that donkey's bray !
You there !   Shut up and beat retreat !
Go halloa in some other street !

David

   (who has opened his shutter close to Beckmesser).

Whoever 's this, and who 's up there?
'T is Magdalena, I declare !
'Oddzounds ! that 's it — I clearly see
'T is he she favors more than me !
You 'll catch it !   Just wait !   I 'll tan your skin !
The devil help you when I begin !

(David, arming himself with a cudgel, springs out of the
window, knocks Beckmesser's lute out of his hands and
throws himself upon him.)

Magdalena

(who at last, to make the Marker go, has made exaggerated
gestures of pleasure at him, now cries aloud).

O heavens !   David !   Lord, how I 'm thrilled !
A rescue ! a rescue ! or both will be killed !

Beckmesser
      (struggling with David).

Infernal rogue !   Let me alone !

David.

I will when I 've broken every bone.

   (They continue to struggle and fight.)

„ Darf ich Meister mich nennen,
Das bewähr' ich heut gern,
Weil nach dem Preis ich brennen
Muss dursten und hungern,
Nun ruf' ich die neun Musen,
   Dass an sie blusen
Mein dichtr'schen Verstand.
Wohl kenn' ich alle Regeln,
Halte gut Mass und Zahl ;
Doch Sprung und Ueberkegeln
Wohl passirt je einmal,
Wann der Kopf, ganz voll Zagen,
   Zu frei'n will wagen
Um ein jung' Mägdleins Hand.
   Ein Junggesell,
Mein Ehr', Amt, Würd' und Brod zur Stell',
Dass euch mein Gesang wohl gefäll',
Und mich das Jungfräulein erwähl',
   Wenn sie mein Lied gut fand."

Nachbarn

(erst einige, dann mehrere, öffnen während des Gesanges in
der Gasse die Fenster und gucken heraus).

Wer heult denn da !   Wer kreischt mit Macht?
Ist das erlaubt, so spät zur Nacht? —
Gebt Ruhe hier !   's ist Schlafenszeit ! —
Nein, hört nur, wie der Esel schreit ! —
Ihr da !   Seid still, und scheert euch fort !
Heult, kreischt und schreit an and'rem Ort !

David

(hat ebenfalls den Fensterladen, dicht bei Beckmesser, ein
   wenig geöffnet und lugt hervor).

Wer Teufel hier? — Und drüben gar?
Die Lene ist's, — ich seh' es klar !
Herr Je !   das war's, den hat sie bestellt ;
Der ist's, der ihr besser als ich gefällt ! —
Nun warte !   du kriegst's !   dir streich' ich das
                   Fell ! —
Zum Teufel mit dir, verdammter Gesell' !
(David ist, mit einem Knüpple bewaffnet, hinter dem Laden
aus dem Fenster hervorgesprungen, zerschlägt Beckmesser's
Laute und wirft sich über ihn selbst her.)

Magdalene

(die zuletzt, um den Merker zu entfernen, mit übertriebenen
beifälligen Bewegungen herabgewinkt hat, schreit jetzt laut
      auf.)

Ach Himmel !   David !   Gott, welche Noth !
Zu Hülfe !   zu Hülfe !   Sie schlagen sich todt !

Beckmesser
      (mit David sich balgend).

Verfluchter Kerl !   Lässt du mich los?

David.

Gewiss !   Die Glieder brech' ich dir blos !

   (Sie balgen und prügeln sich in einem fort.)

Neighbors
(at the windows).

Look there ! Go to ! They 're hard at it now !

Other Neighbors
(coming into the alley).

Hallo? What 's up? See, here 's a row !
You there ! stand back ! Give him fair play !
If you don't part we 'll join the fray.

One Neighbor.

Halloa? Have you come? Why are you here?

A Second.

What 's that to you ! Don't interfere !

First Neighbor.

You 're a big rogue !

Second Neighbor.

You are no lesser !

First Neighbor.

Prove it, then !

Second Neighbor
(hitting out).

There !

Magdalena
(screaming down).

David ! Beckmesser !

Prentices
(entering).

Hooray ! hooray ! Here 's cudgel play !

Some.

It 's the coopers !

Others.

No, it 's the tailors !

The First.

The drunken patches !

The Others.

The starveling railers !

The Neighbors
(in the street, to one another).

That pays what I owe you ! —
Coward ! I know you ! —
Take that to requite you ! —
Mind your eye if I smite you ! —
Was your wife's temper high? —
See how the cudgels fly ! —
Have n't you found your wits? —
Lay on, then ! — That hits !

Nachbarn
(an den Fenstern).

Seht nach ! Springt zu ! Da würgen sich zwei !

Andere Nachbarn
(auf die Gasse heraustretend).

Heda, Herbei ! 's gibt Prügelei !
Ihr da ! auseinander ! Gebt freien Lauf !
Lasst ihr nicht los, wir schlagen drauf !

Ein Nachbar.

Ei seht ! Auch ihr da? Geht's euch 'was an?

Ein Zweiter.

Was sucht ihr hier? Hat man euch 'was gethan?

Erster Nachbar.

Euch kennt man gut !

Zweiter Nachbar.

Euch noch viel besser !

Erster Nachbar.

Wie so denn?

Zweiter Nachbar
(zuschlagend).

Ei, so !

Magdalene
(hinabschreiend).

David ! Beckmesser !

Lehrbuben
(kommen dazu).

Herbei ! Herbei ! 's gibt Keilerei !

Einige.

's sind die Schuster !

Andere.

Nein, 's sind die Schneider !

Die Ersteren.

Die Trunkenbolde !

Die Anderen.

Die Hungerleider !

Die Nachbarn.
(auf der Gasse, durcheinander).

Euch gönnt ich's schon lange ! —
Wird euch wohl bange?
Das für die Klage ! —
Seht euch vor, wenn ich schlage ! —
Hat euch die Frau gehetzt? —
Schau' wie es Prügel setzt ! —
Seid ihr noch nicht gewitzt !
So schlagt doch ! — Das sitzt ! —

Rogue, there 's a thumper ! —
You counter-jumper ! —
You gutter-sweeper ! —
You false-measure-keeper !
Blockhead ! — Looby ! —
You great Booby ! —
Dolt, I say !
Don't give way !

Prentices

(to one another, with the neighbors).

We know the locksmiths' way :
They surely started this fray ! —
I think the smiths began the fight. —
I see the joiners by the light. —
Look where the coopers come along !
And now the barbers join the throng. —
There the Guild of grocers comes,
With lollipops and sugarplums,
With pepper, spice, and cinnamon.
How nice they smell !
How nice they smell !
But they don't like the fun,
And wish that it were done.
See that fool there,
With his nose ev'rywhere !
Pray did you allude to me ? —
Pray did I allude to thee ?
There 's one nose I 've pounded ! —
Lord ! how that sounded ! —
Hey ! whack ! fire and fury oh !
Where that fell no hair will grow !
Cudgels, whack hard !
Smash the blackguard !
Show yourselves worth freemen's name :
To give way would be a shame !
Join the brawl,
Each and all.
We are ready to help the row !

(Gradually the neighbors and Prentices have come to a general fight.)

Journeymen

(arriving from all quarters).

Hallo ! Companions, come !
The people here seem quarrelsome.
There 'll surely be some fighting then :
Be ready, lusty journeymen.
'T is the weaver and tanners ! —
Which well I know ! —
'T is like their manners ! —
They always do so ! —
Klaus the butcher 's there ;
He 's one to beware ! —
Guilds ! Guilds !
Guilds ! ev'rywhere ! —

Dass dich, Hallunke ! —
Hie Färbertunke ! —
Wartet, ihr Racker !
Ihr Maassabzwacker ! —
Esel ! — Dummrian ! —
Du Grobian ! —
Lümmel du ! —
Drauf und zu !

Lehrbuben

(durcheinander, zugleich mit den Nachbarn).

Kennt man die Schlosser nicht ?
Die haben's sicher angericht' !
Ich glaub' die Schmiede werden's sein. —
Die Schreiner seh' ich dort beim Schein.
Hei ! Schau' die Schäffler dort beim Tanz.
Dort seh' die Bader ich im Glanz. —
Krämer finden sich zur Hand
Mit Gerstenstang und Zuckerkand ;
Mit Pfeffer, Zimmt, Muscatennuss,
Sie riechen schön,
Sie riechen schön,
Doch haben viel Verdruss,
Und bleiben gern vom Schuss. —
Seht nur, der Hase
Hat üb'rall die Nase !
Meinst du damit etwa mich ! —
Mein' ich damit etwa dich ?
Da hast's auf die Schnautze ! —
Herr, jetzt setzt's Plautze ! —
Hei ! Krach ! Hagelwetterschlag !
Wo das sitzt, da wächst nichts nach :
Keilt euch wacker,
Haut die Racker !
Haltet selbst Gesellen Stand ;
Wer da wich', 's wär' wahrlich Schand' !
Drauf und dran !
Wie ein Mann
Steh'n wir alle zur Keilerei !

(Bereits prügeln sich Nachbarn und Lehrbuben fast allgemein durcheinander.)

Gesellen

(von allen Seiten dazu kommend).

Heda ! Gesellen 'ran !
Dort wird mit Streit und Zank gethan,
Da giebt's gewiss gleich Schlägerei ;
Gesellen, haltet euch dabei !
'Sind die Weber und Gerber ! —
Dacht' ich's doch gleich ! —
Die Preisverderber !
Spielen immer Streich' ! —
Dort den Metzger Klaus,
Den kennt man heraus ! -
Zünfte ! Zünfte !
Zünfte heraus ! —

Tailors here are hieing !—
See the cudgels flying !
Girdlers !— Pewterers !
Glue-boilers !— Fruiterers !
Clothworkers here !
Linenweavers here !
Come here ! Come here !
More appear ! More appear !
All do your best ! We 're going to strike !
Now will the fight be something like !—
Run home ! your wife is after you !
Here you 'll get painted black and blue !
    There they go !
    Blow for blow !
    Knock them over !
Guildsmen ! Guildsmen ! come out !

The Masters

    (and old Burghers arriving on all sides).

What is this noise of brawl and fight,
That sounds far through the night?
Leave off and let each go his way,
Or else there 'll be the deuce to pay !
Don't crowd up like this in bands,
Or else we too must use our hands.

Women

    (at the windows to one another).

What is this noise of fight and brawl?
It really terrifies us all !
My husband 's there, as sure as fate !
Some one will get a broken pate !
    Hey, sirs ! You below there,
    Be reasonable now !
    Are you then all so ready
    To join a vulgar row?
    What a confusion and halloa !
    Now blows will be certain to follow !
    Hark ye ! hark ye !
    Are ye insane?
    Are ye still fuddled
    With wine on the brain?
    O murder ! murder !
    My man 's in the fight !
    There 's father ! there 's father !
    Look ! what a sight !
    Christian ! Peter !
    Nicholas ! Hans !
    Watch ! be fleeter !—
    Don't you hear, Franz?
    Lord ! how the hair flies !
    See how they go it !
    Water here ! Water, quick !
    On their heads throw it !

(The row has become general. Shrieks and blows.)

Schneider mit dem Bügel !
Hei ! hie setzt's Prügel !
Gürtler !— Zinngiesser !—
Leimsieder !— Lichtgiesser !—
Tuchscherer her !
Leinweber her !
Hierher ! Hierher !
Immer mehr ! Immer mehr
Nur tüchtig drauf ! Wir schlagen los·
Jetzt wird die Keilerei erst gross !—
Lauft heim, sonst kriegt ihr's von der Frau ;
Hier giebt's nur Prügel-Färberblau !
    Immer 'ran !
    Mann für Mann !
    Schlagt sie nieder !
Zünfte ! Zünfte ! Heraus !—

Die Meister

    (und älteren Bürger von verschiedenen Seiten der
    kommend).

Was giebt's denn da für Zank und Streit?
Das tos't ja weit und breit !
Gebt Ruh' und scheer' sich jeder heim !
Sonst schlag' ein Hageldonnerwetter drein !
Stemmt euch hier nicht mehr zu Hauf,
Oder sonst wir schlagen krauf.—

Die Nachbarinnen

    (an den Fenstern, durcheinander).

Was ist denn da für Streit und Zank?
's wird einem wahrlich angst und bang !
Da ist mein Mann gewiss dabei :
Gewiss kommt's noch zur Schlägerei !
    He da ! Ihr dort unten,
    So seid doch nur gescheit !
    Seid ihr zu Streit und Raufen
    Gleich Alle so bereit?
    Was für ein Zanken und Toben !
    Da werden schon Arme erhoben,
    Hört doch ! Hört doch !
    Seid ihr denn toll?
    Sind euch die Köpfe
    Vom Weine noch voll?
    Zu Hülfe ! Zu Hülfe !
    Da schlägt sich mein Mann !
    Der Vater ! Der Vater !
    Sieht man das an?
    Christian ! Peter !
    Nikolaus ! Hans !
    Auf ! schrei't Zeter !—
    Hörst du nicht, Franz?
    Gott, wie sie walken !
    's wackeln die Zöpfe !
    Wasser her ! Wasser her !
    Giesst's ihn' auf die Köpfe !

(Die Rauferei ist allgemein. Schreien und Toben.)

Magdalena

(wringing her hands despairingly at the window).

Oh heaven ! what is to be done !
David, for goodness' sake attend !
Do leave the gentleman alone !

Pogner

(coming to the window in his nightgown, pulls Magdalena in).

Come in, Eva ! Odd so !
I 'll see if all is right below.

The window is shut and Pogner appears below at the door.

Sachs at the commencement of the row has extinguished his light and set his door ajar, so as still to be able to watch the place under the lime-tree.

(Walter and Eva have observed the riot with increasing anxiety. Now Walter seizes Eva in his arms.)

Walter.

Now we may do it —
Cut our way through it !

Brandishing his sword he forces a way to the middle of the stage.—Sachs rushes with one bound out of his shop and grasps Walter's arms.

Pogner

(on the steps).

Ho ! Lena ! where are you ?

Sachs

(pushing the half-fainting Eva up the steps).

Go in, Mistress Lena !

Pogner receives her and pulls her within.

Sachs brandishing his knee-strap, with which he has cleared a path to Walter, now catches David one, and kicking him into the shop, drags Walter, whom he still holds, indoors with him, closing and barring the door behind them.

Beckmesser, released from David by Sachs, seeks hasty flight through the crowd.

At the moment Sachs rushes into the street a loud note from the Nightwatchman's horn is heard R. U. E. Prentices, Burghers, and Journeymen, panic-struck, seek flight on all sides, so that the stage is speedily completely cleared : all doors are closed and women gone from windows, which are also shut.—The full moon shines out and brightly illumines the now peaceful alley.

The Watchman

(enters R. U. E., rubs his eyes, stares about him in surprise, shakes his head, and in a somewhat tremulous voice calls out) :

" Hark to what I say, good people !
Eleven strikes from every steeple ;
Defend you all from spectre and sprite,
Let no power of ill your souls affright.
Praise the Lord of Heaven."

He goes slowly up the alley. As the curtain falls his distant horn is still heard.

Magdalene

(am Fenster verzweifelt die Hände ringend).

Ach Himmel ! Meine Noth ist gross ! —
David ! So hör, mich doch nur an !
So lass' doch nur den Herrn los !

Pogner

(ist im Nachtgewand oben an das Fenster getreten und zieht Magdalene herein).

Um Gott ! Eva ! schliess' zu !
Ich seh', ob im Haus unten Ruh' !

Das Fenster wird geschlossen; bald darauf erscheint Pogner an der Hausthüre.

Sachs hat, als der Tumult begann, sein Licht gelöscht und den Laden so weit geschlossen, dass er durch eine kleine Oeffnung stets den Platz unter der Linde beobachten kann.

Walther und Eva haben mit wachsender Sorge dem anschwellenden Tumult zugesehen. Jetzt fasst Walther Eva dicht in den Arm.

Walther.

Jetzt gilt's zu wagen,
Sich durchzuschlagen !

Mit geschwungenem Schwerte dringt er bis in die Mitte der Bühne vor. — Da springt Sachs mit einem Satz aus dem Laden auf die Strasse, und packt Walther beim Arm.

Pogner

(auf der Treppe).

He, Lene, wo bist du ?

Sachs

(die halb ohnmächtige Eva auf die Treppe stossend).

In's Haus, Jungfer Lene !

Pogner empfängt sie, und zieht sie beim Arme herein.

Sachs mit dem geschwungenen Knieriemen, mit dem er sich bereits bis zu Walther Platz gemacht hatte, jetzt dem David eines überhauend, und ihn mit einem Fusstritt voran in den Laden stossend, zieht Walther, den er mit der andern Hand gefasst hält, gewaltsam schnell mit sich ebenfalls hinein, und schliesst songleich fest hinter sich zu.

Beckmesser, durch Sachs von David befreit, sucht sich eilig durch die Menge zu flüchten.

Im gleichen Augenblicke, wo Sachs auf die Strasse sprang, hörte man, rechts zur Seite im Vordergrunde, einen besonders starken Hornruf des Nachtwächters. Lehrbuben, Bürger und Gesellen suchten in eiliger Flucht sich nach allen Seiten hin zu entfernen, so dass die Bühne sehr schnell gänzlich geleert ist, alle Hausthüren hastig geschlossen, und auch die Nachbarinnen von den Fenstern, welche sie zugeschlagen, verschwunden sind — Der Vollmond tritt hervor und scheint hell in die Gasse hinein.

Der Nachtwächter

(betritt im Vordergrunde rechts die Bühne, reibt sich die Augen, sieht sich verwundert um, schüttelt den Kopf, und stimmt, mit etwas bebender Stimme, seinen Ruf an) :

Hört ihr Leut', und lasst euch sagen :
Die Glock' hat Eilfe geschlagen,
Bewahrt euch vor Gespenstern und Spuck,
Dass kein böser Geist eur' Seel' beruck' !
Lobet Gott den Herrn !

Er geht währenddem langsam die Gasse hinab. Als der Vorhang fällt, hört man den Hornruf des Nachtwächters wiederholen.

THIRD ACT.

In Sachs's workshop. (Front scene.) At back the half-open shopdoor leads to the street. R. the door of a chamber. L. the window looking into the alley, flowers in pots before it; a workbench beside it. Sachs sits at this window in a great armchair, the bright morning sun streaming in on him; he has a large folio on his lap and is absorbed in reading. — David peeps in at the door from the street; on seeing that Sachs does not notice him he enters with a basket on his arm, which he first hides quickly under the other workbench; then again assured that Sachs does not heed him, he carefully takes it out again and investigates the contents: he lifts out flowers and ribbons and at last finds at the bottom a sausage and a cake; these he is about to devour when Sachs, who is still unconscious of his presence, turns over a leaf of his book with a loud rustle.

David

(starts, hides the eatables, and turns round).

Here, Master! Yes! —
The shoes were taken duly
To clerk Beckmesser's address.
I thought you summoned me, truly.

(Aside.)

He seems to notice me not!
When he is dumb his anger's hot.

(Gradually approaching humbly.)

Ah, Master! won't you forgive?
Can a Prentice quite faultless live?
If with my eyes Lena you'd see
You'd pardon me assuredly.
She is so good, so kind to me,
And eyes me at times so tenderly.
When I've been thrashed soothing is she
And smiles upon me so prettily!
When on short commons she feedeth me,
And acts in all things right lovingly.
Last night, though, when that knight was discarded,
There was no basket to me awarded:
That worried me, and when I found
At night when some one lurked around,
And sang to her and cried like mad,
I gave him all the stick I had.
What dreadful consequence befell!
But yet for our love it turned out well;
Now Lena's explained the matter to me,
And sent all these ribbons and flowers you see.

(He bursts out in still greater anxiety.)

O Master! speak one word I pray!

(Aside.)

Would I'd put the cake and sausage away!

DRITTER AUFZUG.

In Sachsen's Werkstatt. (Kurzer Raum.) Im Hintergrund die halb geöffnete Ladenthüre, nach der Strasse führend. Rechts zur Seite eine Kammerthüre. Links das nach der Gasse gehende Fenster, mit Blumenstöcken davor, zur Seite ein Werktisch. Sachs sitzt auf einem grossen Lehnstuhle an diesem Fenster, durch welches die Morgensonne hell auf ihn hereinscheint; er hat vor sich auf dem Schoose einen grossen Folianten und ist im Lesen vertieft. — David lugt spähend von der Strasse zur Ladenthüre herein: da er sieht, dass Sachs seiner nicht achtet, tritt er herein, mit einem Korbe im Arm, den er zuvörderst schnell und verstohlen unter den andern Werktisch beim Laden stellt; — dann von neuem versichert, dass Sachs ihn nicht bemerkt, nimmt er den Korb vorsichtig herauf, und untersucht den Inhalt; er hebt Blumen und Bänder heraus; endlich findet er auf dem Grunde eine Wurst und einen Kuchen, und lässt sich sogleich an, diese zu verzehren, als Sachs, der ihn fortwährend nicht beachtet, mit starkem Geräusch eines der grossen Blätter des Folianten unwendet.

David

(fährt zusammen, verbirgt das Essen und wendet sich).

Gleich! Meister! Hier! —
Die Schuh' sind abgegeben
In Herrn Beckmesser's Quartier. —
Mir war's, ihr rief't mich eben?

(Bei Seite.)

Er thut, als säh' er mich nicht?
Da ist er bös', wenn er nicht spricht!

(Sich demüthig sehr allmählich nähernd.)

Ach Meister woll't ihr mir verzeih'n!
Kann ein Lehrbub' vollkommen sein?
Kenntet ihr die Lene, wie ich,
Da vergäbt ihr mir sicherlich.
Sie ist so gut, so sanft für mich,
Und blickt mich oft an, so innerlich:
Wenn ihr mich schlagt, streichelt sie mich,
Und lächelt dabei holdseliglich!
Muss ich cariren, füttert sie mich,
Und ist in Allem gar liebelich.
Nur gestern, weil der Junker versungen,
Hab' ich den Korb ihr nicht abgerungen:
Das schmerzte mich; und da ich fand,
Dass Nachts Einer vor dem Fenster stand,
Und sang zu ihr, und schrie wie toll,
Da hieb ich dem den Buckel voll.
Wie käm' nun da 'was Gross' drauf an?
Auch hat's uns'rer Lieb' gar gut gethan:
Die Lene hat eben mir Alles erklärt,
Und zum Fest Blumen und Bänder bescheert,

(Er bricht in immer grössere Angst aus.)

Ach, Meister, sprecht doch nur ein Wort!

(Bei Seite.)

Hätt' ich nur die Wurst und den Kuchen fort.

Sachs

(who has read on undisturbed, claps his book to. At the loud noise David is so startled that he stumbles and falls unintentionally on his knees before Sachs. The latter gazes far away beyond the book which he still holds, beyond David who, from his kneeling posture looks up at him in terror, and his eyes fall on the farther table).

> Yonder are flowers and ribbons gay
> In youthful beauty and bloom :
> How came they into my room ?

David

(astonished at Sachs's friendliness).

Why, Master ! to-day 's a feast, you know,
And all must smarten to grace the show.

Sachs.

Is 't a marriage feast ?

David.

Yes, so it would be
If only Lena might marry me.

Sachs.

Your Folly-evening* was last night ?

David

(aside).

Folly-evening ? — I 'm all in a fright !

(Aloud.)

Forgive me, Master ! Forget it, pray !
The Feast of St. John we keep to-day.

Sachs.

St. John's day ?

David

(aside).

Deaf he must be !

Sachs.

Know you your verses ? Repeat them me.

David.

My verses ? Yes, they 're in my brain. —

(Aside.)

All right ! the master is kind again ! —

(Aloud.)

" St. John stood on the Jordan's strand " —

(In his agitation he sings his lines to the melody of Beckmesser's serenade; he is pulled up by Sachs's movement of astonishment.)

Forgive me, master, and pardon the slip !
That Folly-evening caused me to trip.

* " Polterabend " — the merrymaking on the eve of a German wedding.

Sachs

(der unbeirrt weiter gelesen, schlägt jetzt den Folianten zu Von dem starken Geräusch erschrickt David so, dass er strauchelt und unwillkürlich vor Sachs auf die Knie fällt. Sachs sieht über das Buch, das er noch auf dem Schoosse behält, hinwig, über David, welcher immer auf den Knieen, furchtsam nach ihm hinauf blickt, hin, und heftet seinen Blick unwillkürlich auf den hintern Werktisch).

> Blumen und Bänder seh' ich dort : —
> Schaut hold und jugendlich aus !
> Wie kamen die mir in's Haus ?

David

(verwundert über Sachsens Freundlichkeit).

Ei, Meister ? 's is heut' hoch festlicher Tag ;
Da putzt sich jeder, so schön er mag.

Sachs.

Wär' Hochzeitsfest ?

David.

Ja, käm's so weit
Dass David erst die Lene freit !

Sachs.

's war Polterabend dünkt mich doch ?

David

(für sich).

Polterabend ? — Da krieg ich's wohl noch ! —

(Laut.)

Verzeiht das, Meister ! Ich bitt', vergesst,
Wir feiern ja heut' Johannisfest.

Sachs.

Johannisfest ?

David

(bei Seite).

Hört er heut' schwer ?

Sachs.

Kannst du ein Sprüchlein ? Sag' es her !

David.

Mein Sprüchlein ? Denk', ich kann es gut.

(Bei Seite.)

'Setzt nichts ! der Meister ist wohlgemuth ! —

(Laut.)

„ Am Jordan Sankt Johannes stand " —

(Er hat in der Zerstreuung die Worte mit der Melodie von Beckmesser's Werbelied aus dem vorhergehennden Aufzuge gesungen; Sachs macht eine verwundernde Bewegung, worauf David sich unterbricht.)

Verzeiht, Meister ; ich kam in's Gewirr :
Der Polterabend machte mich irr.

(He recommences to the proper tune.)

"St. John stood on the Jordan's strand,
    Where all the world he christened :
A woman came from distant land,
    From Nuremberg she 'd hastened :
Her little son she led in hand,
    Baptized him with a name there,
And then toward home she took her flight ;
    But when at last she came there
It soon turned out in German lands,
That he who on the Jordan's sands
    Johannes had been hight,
    On the Pegnitz was called Hans."

(Impetuously.)

Sir ! Master ! 'T is your name-day, sure !
There ! Well, my memory must be poor !
Here ! all the flowers are for you.
The ribbons — something else there was, too ?
Yes, here ! Look. Master ! Here 's a fine pasty !
Try, too, this sausage, you 'll find it tasty.

Sachs

(still dreamily, without moving).

Best thanks, my lad ! You keep it though !
Anon to the meadow with me you shall go.
With ribbons and flowers make yourself gay ;
As my herald you are to act to-day.

David.

Would I not be your groomsman more fain ?
Master, dear master ! you *must* wed again !

Sachs.

Do you wish for a mistress then here ?

David.

Methinks more dignified it would appear.

Sachs.

Who knows ? But time will show.

David.

Time 's come.

Sachs.

Has it brought knowledge then to some ?

David.

Aye, sure ! I know things have been repeated ;
And Beckmesser's singing you have defeated.
I think he will scarce make a stir to-day.

Sachs.

T is likely ! That I 'll not gainsay.
Now, go ; disturb not Sir Walter's rest !
Come back when you are finely dress'd.

(Er fährt in der richtigen Melodie fort.)

„ Am Jordan Sankt Johannes stand,
    All Volk der Welt zu taufen :
Kam auch ein Weib aus fremden Land,
    Von Nürnberg gar gelaufen ;
Sein Söhnlein trug's zum Nferrand,
    Empfing da Tauf' und Namen ;
Doch als sie dann sich heimgewandt,
    Nach Nürnberg wieder kamen,
Im deutschen Land gar bald sich fand's,
Dass, wer am Ufer des Jordans
    Johannes war genannt,
    An der Pegnitz hiess der Hans."

(Feurig.)

Herr Meister ! 's ist eu'r Namenstag !
Nein ! Wie man so 'was vergessen mag !
Hier ! hier, die Blumen sind für euch,
Die Bänder, — und was nur Alles noch gleich ?
Ja hier ! schaut, Meister ! Herrlicher Kuchen !
Möchtet ihr nicht auch die Wurst versuchen ?

Sachs

(immer ruhig, ohne seine Stellung zu verändern).

Schön Dank, mein Jung' ! behalt's für dich !
Doch heut' auf die Wiese' begleitest du mich :
Mit den Bändern und Blumen putz' dich fein ;
Sollst mein stattlicher Herold sein.

David.

Sollt' ich nicht lieber Brautführer sein ?
Meister ! lieb' Meister ! ihr müsst wieder frei'n !

Sachs.

Hätt'st wohl gern eine Meist'rin im Haus ?

David.

Ich mein', es säh doch viel stattlicher aus.

Sachs.

Wer weiss ! Kommt Zeit, kommt Rath.

David.

                    's ist Zeit !

Sachs.

Da wär' der Rath wohl auch nicht weit ?

David.

Gewiss ! geh'n die Reden schon hin und wieder.
Den Beckmesser, denk' ich säng't ihr doch nieder ?
Ich mein', dass der heut' sich nicht wenig wichtig
                    macht.

Sachs.

Wohl möglich ! Hab's mir auch schon bedacht
Jetzt geh' ; doch stör' mir den Junker nicht !
Komm wieder, wenn du schön gericht'.

David

moved, kisses Sachs's hand, collects his things and goes
into chamber).

He ne'er was like this, though sometimes kind !
Why, the taste of his strap has gone out of my
mind !

(Exit.)

Sachs

(still with the book on his knees leans back deep in thought,
resting his head on his hand, and after a pause begins).

    Mad !   Mad !
     All the world 's mad !
   Where'er enquiry dives
   In town or world's archives
   And seeks to learn the reason
   Why people strive and fight,
   Both in and out of season,
   In fruitless rage and spite.
     What do they gain
     For all their pain?
     Repulsed in fight,
     They feign joy in flight ;
     Their pain-cries not minding,
     They joy pretend
When their own flesh their fingers rend,
   And pleasure deem they 're finding.
   What tongue the cause can phrase?
   'T is just the same old craze !
   Naught haps without it ever,
   In spite of all endeavor,
     Pause doth it make ;
In sleep it but acquires new force,
     Soon it will wake,
Then, lo ! who can control its course?
   Old ways and customs keeping,
   How peacefully I see
   My dear old Nurnberg sleeping
   In midst of Germany !
   But on one evening late,
   To hinder in some fashion
   The follies of youthful passion,
   A man worries his pate ;
   A shoemaker, all unknowing,
   Sets the old madness going :
   How soon from highways and alleys
   A raging rabble sallies !
   Man, woman, youth, and child
   Blindly fall to as if gone wild ;
     And ere the craze lose power
     The cudgel blows must shower ;
     They seek with fuss and pother
     The fires of wrath to smother.
   God knows how this befell !
   'T was like some impish spell !
Some glowworm could not find his mate ;
'T was he aroused this wrath and hate.

David

(küsst ihm gerührt die Hand, packt Alles zusammen, und
geht in die Kammer).

So war er noch nie, wenn sonst auch gut !
Kann mir gar nicht mehr denken, wie der Knieriemen thut !

(Ab.)

Sachs

(immer noch den Folianten auf dem Schoose, lehnt sich,
mit untergestütztem Arme, sinnend darauf und beginnt
dann nach einem Sohweigen).

Wahn ! Wahn !
Uberall ! Wahn !
Wohin ich forschend blick',
In Stadt- und Welt-Chronik,
Den Grund mir aufzufinden,
Warum gar bis auf's Blut
Die Leut' sich quälen und schinden
In unnütz toller Wuth !
Hat keiner Lohn
Noch dank davon :
In Flucht geschlagen,
Meint er zu jagen.
Hört nicht sein eigen
     Schmerz-Gekreisch,
Wenn er sich wühlt in's eig'ne Fleisch
Wähnt Lust sich zu erzeigen.
Wer giebt den Namen an !
's bleibt halt der alte Wahn,
Ohn' den nichts mag geschehen,
's mag gehen oder stehen !
Steht's wo im Lauf,
Er schläft nur neue Kraft sich an ;
Gleich wacht er auf,
Dann schaut wer ihn bemeistern kann !
Wie friedsam treuer Sitten,
Getrost in That und Werk,
Liegt nicht in Deutschlands Mitten
Mein liebes Nürenberg !
Doch eines Abends spat,
Ein Unglück zu verhüten
Bei jugendheissen Gemüthen,
Ein Mann weiss sich nicht Rath ;
Ein Schuster in seinem Laden
Zieht an des Wahnes Faden :
Wie bald auf Gassen und Strassen
Fängt der da an zu rasen ;
Mann, Weib, Gesell' und Kind,
Fällt sich an wie toll und blind ;
Und will's der Wahn gesegnen,
Nun muss es Prügel regnen,
Mit Hieben, Stöss' und Dreschen
Den Wuthesbrand zu löschen.
Gott weiss, wie das geschah?
Ein Kobold half wohl da !
Ein Glühwurm fand sein Weichen nicht ;
Der hat den Schaden angericht'.

The elder's charm — Midsummer eve :
But now has dawned Midsummer day.
Let 's see, then, what Hans Sachs can weave
To turn the madness his own way,
     To serve for noble works ;
     For if still here it lurks
     In Nuremberg the same,
We 'll use it to such aim
As seldom by the mob 's projected,
And never without trick effected.

(Walter enters from the chamber. He pauses a
moment at the door looking at Sachs. The latter turns and
allows his book to slip to the ground.)

Sachs.

Good-day, Sir Walter !   Late is my guest.
You sat up long ; you 've had some rest?

Walter
              (very quietly).

A little, but that rest was sound.

Sachs.

So, then, your courage you have found?

Walter.

I had a wondrous lovely dream.

Sachs.

That augurs well !   Relate it, pray.

Walter.

In words I scarce dare touch its theme,
For fear it should all fade away.

Sachs.

My friend, that is the poet's art,
His dreams to cherish and impart.
Trust me, the best ideas of men
In dreams are opened to their ken :
All book-craft and all poetry
Are naught but dreams made verity.
But did your dream at all advise
How you might win the Master-prize?
But let that go ;
And hark to my counsel short and strong :
Bend your mind to a Master-Song.

Walter.

A Master-Song and one that 's fine :
How shall I make the two combine?

Sachs.

My friend, in youth's delightful days,
     When first in the direction
     Of blissful, true affection
The heart some power turns and sways,

Der Flieder war's : — Johannis-Nacht.—
Nun aber kam Johannis-Tag : —
Jetzt schau'n wir, wie Hans Sachs es macht,
Dass er den Wahn fein lenken mag,
Ein edles Werk zu thun ;
Denn lässt er uns nicht ruh'n,
Selbst hier in Nürenberg,
So sei's um solche Werk',
Die selten vor gemeinen Dingen,
Und nie ohn' ein'gen Wahn gelingen.—

Walther tritt unter der Kammerthüre ein. Er bleibt einen
Augenblick dort stehen und blickt auf Sachs. Dieser wendet sich und lässt den Folianten auf den Boden gleiten.

Sachs.

Grüss Gott, mein Junker !   Ruhtet ihr noch?
Ihr wachtet lang' : nun schlieft ihr doch?

Walther
              (sehr ruhig).

Ein wenig, aber fest und gut.

Sachs.

So ist euch nun wohl bass zu Muth?

Walther.

Ich hatt' einen wunderschönen Traum.

Sachs.

Das deutet gut's !   Erzählt mir den.

Walther.

Ihn selbst zu denken wag' ich kaum ;
Ich fürcht' ihn mir vergeh'n zu seh'n.

Sachs.

Mein Freund, das grad' ist Dichter's Werk,
Dass er sein Träumen deut' und merk'.
Glaubt mir, des Me schen wahrster Wahn
Wird ihm im Traume aufgethan :
All' Dichtkunst und Poeterei
Ist nichts als Wahrtraum-Deuterei.
Was gilt's, es gab der Traum euch ein.
Wie heut' ihr sollet Sieger sein?
O, lasst dem Ruh' ;
Und folgt meinem Rathe, kurz und gut,
Fasst zu einem Meisterliede Muth.

Walther.

Ein schönes Lied, ein Meisterlied :
Wie fass' ich da den Unterschied?

Sachs.

Mein Freund ! in holder Jugendzeit,
     Wenn uns von mächtigen Trieben
     Zum sel'gen ersten Lieben
Die Brust sich schwellet hoch und weit,

All can, or else 't were pity,
    Compose a loving ditty :
    For Spring cries out in ye.
But Summer, Autumn, Winter days
    Bring care and sorrow often,
    With wedded bliss to soften.
Children and business — frets and frays,
    One who, 'spite care and duty,
    Yet sings a song of beauty,
    A Master he must be.

Walter.

I love a maiden and I pine
In wedlock true to make her mine.

Sachs.

Your dream alone let occupy you ;
With all the rest Hans Sachs will ply you.

Walter

(places himself near Sachs, and after a moment's thought
        begins in a very low voice).

" Morning was gleaming with roseate light,
        The air was filled
        With scent distilled,
        Where, beauty beaming
        Past all dreaming,
    A garden did invite
        My raptured sight."
                (He pauses awhile.)

Sachs.

That was a stanza : now then, take heed
That one just similar may succeed.

Walter.

Why similar?

Sachs.

                        That folks may know
That coupled you intend to go.

Walter
            (continuing).
" Over the glorious garden, behold !
        With leafy crown
        A tree looked down,
        Majestic bending,
        And extending
    Its weight of fruit untold,
        Like burnished gold."
                (He pauses.)

Sachs.

You close not in the starting key :
    The Masters hate this thing :
Hans Sachs, though, can with you agree ;
    It must be so in the Spring.
Now to an Aftersong proceed.

Ein schönes Lied zu singen
Mocht' vielen da gelingen :
Der Lenz, der sang für sie.
Kam Sommer, Herbst und Winterszeit,
Viel Noth und Sorg' im Leben,
Manch ehlich Glück daneben,
Kindtauf', Geschäfte, Zwist und Streit :
Denen 's dann noch will gelingen,
Ein schönes Lied zu singen,
Seht, Meister nennt man die.

Walther.

Ich lieb' ein Weib und will es frei'n
Mein dauernd Ehgemahl zu sein.

Sachs.

Gedenkt des schönen Traum's am Morgen
Für's Andre lasst Hans Sachs nur sorgen !

Walther

(setzt sich zu Sachs, und beginnt, nach kurzer Sammlung
        sehr leise).

„ Morgenlich leuchtet in rosigem Schein,
        Von Blüth' und Duft
        Geschwellt die Luft,
        Voll aller Wonnen
        Nie ersonnen,
    Ein Garten lud mich ein
        Gast ihm zu sein."
                (Er hält etwas an.)

Sachs.

Das war ein Stollen : nun achtet wohl,
Dass ein ganz gleicher ihm folgen soll.

Walther.

Warum ganz gleich?

Sachs.

                        Damit man seh'
Ihr wähltet euch gleich ein Weib zur Eh'.

Walther
            (fährt fort).
„ Wonnig entragend dem seligen Raum
        Bot gold'ner Frucht
        Heilsaft'ge Wucht
        Mit holdem Prangen
        Dem Verlangen
    An duft'ger Zweige Saum
        Herrlich ein Baum."
                (Er hält inne.)

Sachs.

Ihr schlosset nicht im gleichen Ton :
    Das macht den Meistern Pein ;
Doch nimmt Hans Sachs die Lehr' davon,
    Im Lenz wohl müss' es so sein. —
Nun stellt mir einen Abgesang.

Walter.

What is that for?

Sachs.

If here indeed
A pair you 've coupled truly
The offspring shows us duly.

Walter

(in continuation).

" Let me confide
What lovely miracle ensued :
A maiden stood before my face,
So sweet and fair I ne'er had viewed ;
Like to a bride
She took me to her embrace ;
With bright eyes glowing,
Her hand was showing,
What stirred my longing profound ;
The wond'rous fruit that crowned
The tree of life."

Sachs

(concealing his emotion).

That is an Aftersong, I allow !
See, the whole verse is perfect now !
But in the melody
You were a little free ;
I do not say that that displeases me ;
To catch it right though 's perplexing,
A thing to our Masters vexing.
A second verse will you please indite,
To set the first in a clearer light?
I cannot yet tell — your art 's so supreme —
How much was poetry, how much dream.

Walter

(as before).

" There on the height
A babbling stream the silence stirr'd ;
Its murm'ring tones now louder swelled,
So sweet and strong I never heard ;
Sparkling and bright
Distinctly the stars I beheld :
In twinkling dances
Among the branches
A golden host did collect :
Not fruit, but stars bedeck'd
The tree of Fame." —

Sachs

(deeply moved, softly).

Friend, your dream was well conceived ;
The second verse you have achieved.
Now might you fashion a third verse meetly,
To show the vision's meaning completely.

Walther.

Was soll nun der?

Sachs.

Ob euch gelang
Ein rechtes Paar zu finden,
Das zeigt sich jetzt an den Kinden.

Walther

(fortfahrend).

„Sei euch vertraut
Welch' hehres Wunder mir gescheh'n :
An meiner Seite stand ein Weib,
So schön und hold ich nie geseh'n ;
Gleich einer Braut
Umfasste sie sanft meinen Leib,
Mit Augen winkend,
Die Hand wies blinkend,
Was ich verlangend begehrt,
Die Frucht so hold und werth
Vom Lebensbaum."

Sachs

(seine Führung verbergend).

Das nenn' ich mir einen Abgesang :
Seht, wie der ganze Bar gelang !
Nur mit der Melodei
Seid ihr ein wenig frei ;
Doch sag' ich nicht, dass es ein Fehler sei ;
Nur ist's nicht leicht zu behalten,
Und das ärgert unsre Alten ! —
Jetzt richtet mir noch einen zweiten Bar,
Damit man merk', welch' der erste war.
Auch weiss ich noch nicht, so gut ihr's gereim',
Was ihr gedichtet, was ihr geträumt.

Walther

(wie vorher).

„Lieblich ein Quell
Auf stiller Höhe dort mir rauscht ;
Jetzt schwellt er an sein hold Getön'
So süss und stark ich's nie erlauscht :
Leuchtend und hell
Wie strahlten die Sterne da schön ;
Zu Tanz und Reigen
In Laub und Zweigen
Der gold'nen sammeln sich mehr
Statt Frucht ein Sternenheer
Im Lorbeerbaum."

Sachs

(sehr gerührt, sanft).

Freund ! eu'r Traumbild wies euch wahr
Gelungen is auch der zweite Bar.
Wollet ihr noch einen dritten dichten,
Des Traumes Deutung wurd' er berichten

Walter.

How can I now? Enough of rhyme!

Sachs.
(rising).

Then we will rhyme some fitter time!—
Lose not the tune, though, I entreat it;
'T is fit and fair for poetry:
You shall before the world repeat it.
Hold fast the dream you 've told to me.

Walter.

What 's your intent?

Sachs.
Your servant true,
Bearing your packs, has sought for you.
The garments in the which I guessed
You meant at home to have been married
Unto my house in doubt he carried.
Some bird, sure must have shewn the nest
Wherein his master lay.
Then follow to the chamber here!
In costume rich and gay
'T is fitting that we both appear,
When striving for a victory.
So come, if you agree with me.

(He opens the door for Walter and goes in with him.)

Beckmesser

(peeps into the shop; finding it empty he comes in. He is
richly dressed, but in a very deplorable state. He limps,
rubs and stretches himself; then contorts himself; he tries
to sit down on a stool, but jumps quickly up and again
rubs his bruised limbs. In despair he wanders up and
down. Then pausing, he looks through the window at the
house opposite; makes gestures of wrath; strikes his hand
on his forehead. At last his eyes fall on the paper which
Sachs has written and left on the workbench; he takes it
up inquisitively, runs his eyes over it in great agitation,
and finally bursts out wrathfully):

A Trial-song! by Sachs?— is 't so?
Ha!— Now then ev'rything I know!

(Hearing the chamber door open he starts and **conceals the**
paper hurriedly in his pocket.)

Sachs
(in holiday dress, enters and stops short).

You, sir? So early? Why this visit?
No fault of the shoes I sent you, is it?
Let 's feel! They fit you well, I 'm sure!

Beckmesser.

Confound you! So thin ne'er were shoes before:
Through them I feel the smallest stone.

Sachs.

My Marker's motto there is shown:
My Marker's hammer beat it so flat.

Walther.

Wie fänd ich die? Genug der Wort'!

Sachs.
(aufstehend).

Dann Wort und That am rechten Ort!—
D'rum bitt' ich, merkt mir gut die Weise;
Gar lieblich d'rin sich's dichten lässt:
Und singt ihr sie in weit'rem Kreise,
Dann haltet mir auch das Traumbild fest.

Walther.

Was habt ihr vor?

Sachs.
Eu'r treuer Knecht
Fand sich mit Sack' und Tasch' zurecht;
Die Kleider, d'rin am Hochzeitsfest
Daheim bei euch ihr wolltet prangen,
Die lies er her zu mir gelangen;—
Ein Täubchen zeigt' ihm wohl das Nest,
Darin sein Junker träumt:
D'rum folgt mir jetzt in's Kämmerlein!
Mit Kleiden, wohlgesäumt,
Sollen Beide wir gezieret sein,
Wann's Stattliches zu wagen gilt:—
D'rum kommt, seid ihr gleich mir gewillt!

(Er öffnet Walther die Thür, und geht mit ihm hinein.)

Beckmesser.

(lugt zum Laden herein; da er die Werkstatt leer findet,
tritt er näher. Er ist reich aufgeputzt, aber in sehr leiden-
dem Zustande. Er hinkt, streicht und reckt sich; zuckt
wieder zusammen; er sucht einen Schemel, setzt sich;
springt aber sogleich wieder auf, und streichelt sich die
Glieder von Neuem. Verzweiflungsvoll sinnend geht er
dann umher. Dann bleibt er stehen, lugt durch das Fenster
nach dem Hause hinüber; macht Gebärden der Wuth;
schlägt sich wieder vor den Kopf.— Endlich fällt sein Blick
auf das von Sachs zuvor beschriebene Papier auf dem Werk-
tische: er nimmt es neugierig auf, überfliegt es mit immer
grösserer Aufregung, und bricht endlich wüthend aus).

Ein Werbelied! von Sachs?— ist's wahr?
Ah!— Nun wird mir Alles klar!
(Da er die Kammerthüre gehen hört, fährt er zusammen, und
versteckt das Blatteilig in seiner Tasche.)

Sachs.
(im Festgewande, tritt ein, und hält an).

Sieh da! Herr Schreiber? Auch am Morgen?
Euch machen die Schuh' doch nicht mehr Sorgen
Lasst sehen! Mich dünkt sie sitzen gut?

Beckmesser.

Den Teufel! So dünn war ich noch nie beschuht
Fühl' durch die Sohle den feinsten Kies!

Sachs.

Mein Merkersprüchlein wirkte dies:
Trieb sie mit Merkerzeichen so weich.

Beckmesser.

A merry jest! Enough of that!
Friend Sachs, I know what you are at!
    Have you forgotten quite
    What happened yesternight?
Did you not raise all that uproar, pray,
Merely to get me out of your way?

Sachs.

'T was Folly-evening: be not affrighted;
And your wedding made the people excited.
    The madder that evening's glee,
    The more blest the marriage will be.

Beckmesser
      (bursting out into a rage).
    Oh! cobbler full of cunning,
    With vulgar tricks o'er-running!
    You always were my foe:
    You base designs I 'll show.
    You hoary-headed reprobate!
    Attempting to appropriate
    The maiden who alone
    Is destined for my own!
    Allured by Pogner's capital
    Hans Sachs would like to snap it all;
    So, when the Guild discussed,
    He caviled and he fussed.
    But you see I got away,
    And your ill-turn I 'll pay.
    Attend the singing trial,
    And see if you outvie all!
      If I 'm attacked
      And badly thwacked,
I 'll soon expose your wicked act!

Sachs.

Good friend, your anger makes you mad!
Think all you will of me that 's bad,
But prithee calm this jealous ire;
For courtship I have no desire.

Beckmesser.

Pack of lies! I know you 're double!

Sachs.

Why, Master Town-clerk, what 's your trouble?
My intended plans concern not you;
But, sooth, you 're deceived if you think I 'd woo.

Beckmesser.

You mean to sing?

Sachs.
                Not in competing.

Beckmesser.

No wooing song?

Beckmesser

Schon gut der Witz'! Und genug der Streich'!
Glaubt mir, Freund Sachs, jetzt kenn' ich euch
    Der spass von dieser Nacht,
    Der wird euch noch gedacht;
Dass ich euch nur nicht im Wege sei,
Schuft ihr gar Aufruhr und Meuterei!

Sachs.

's war Polterabend, lasst euch bedeuten:
Eure Hochzeit spuckte unter den Leuten;
    Je toller es da hergeh',
    Je besser bekommt's der Eh'.

Beckmesser
      (ausbrechend).
    O Schuster voll von Ränken
    Und pöbelhaften Schwänken,
    Du warst mein Feind von je:
    Nun hör' ob hell ich seh'.
    Die ich mir auserkoren,
    Die ganz für mich geboren,
    Zu aller Wittwer Schmach,
    Der Jungfer stellst du nach.
    Dass sich Herr Sachs erwerbe
    Des Goldschmied's reiches Erbe,
    Im Meister-Rath zur Hand
    Auf Klauseln er bestand,
    Doch kam ich noch so davon,
    Dass ich die That euch lohn'!
    Zieht heut' nur aus zum Singen,
    Merkt auf, wie's mag gelingen;
      Bin ich gezwackt
      Auch und zerhackt,
Euch bring' ich doch sicher aus dem Takt

Sachs.

Gut' Freund, ihr seid in argem Wahn!
Glaubt was ihr wollt, dass ich's gethan,
Gebt eure Eifersucht nur hin;
Zu werben kommt mir nicht in Sinn.

Beckmesser.

Lug und Trug! Ich weiss es besser.

Sachs.

Was fällt euch nur ein, Meister Beckmesser?
Was ich sonst im Sinn, geht euch nichts an:
Doch glaubt, ob der Werbung, seid ihr im Wahn

Beckmesser.

Ihr säng't heut' nicht?

Sachs.
                Nicht zur Wette

Beckmesser.

Kein Werblied?

Sachs.

Dismiss the fear !

Beckmesser.

But I 've a proof there 's no defeating.

Sachs

(looking on the workbench).

Did you take the poem?   I left it here.

Beckmesser

(producing the paper).

Is this not your hand?

Sachs.

Well, and what then?

Beckmesser.

The writing is fresh !

Sachs.

Still wet from the pen?

Beckmesser.

Perhaps, then, 't is a biblical song?

Sachs.

To call it so indeed were wrong.

Beckmesser.

Well, then?

Sachs.

What more?

Beckmesser.

You ask?

Sachs.

For sure !

Beckmesser.

Why, that, in all sincerity,
A most consummate rogue you must be !

Sachs.

May be ! but I was never known
To pocket papers not my own ;
But that you should not be called a thief,
You 're welcome to it — I give you the leaf.

Beckmesser

(springing up in joyous surprise).

You do !   What, a song !   A song by Sachs !

(He peers sideways at the paper : suddenly he frowns.)

And yet ! — If this were some villainy ! —
    But yesterday you were my foe :
How, after your behavior to me,
    Such friendship can you show? —

Sachs.

Gewisslich, nein !

Beckmesser.

Wenn ich aber droo ein Zeugniss hätte?

Sachs.

(blickt auf den Werktisch).

Das Gedicht?   Hier liess ich's : — stecktet ihr's ein !

Beckmesser

(zieht das Blatt hervor).

Ist das eure Hand?

Sachs.

Ja, — war es das?

Beckmesser.

Ganz frisch noch die Schrift?

Sachs.

Und die Dinte noch nass

Beckmesser.

's wär wohl gar ein biblisches Lied?

Sachs.

Der fehlte wohl, wer darauf rieth.

Beckmesser.

Nun denn?

Sachs.

Wie doch?

Beckmesser.

Ihr fragt?

Sachs.

Was noch?

Beckmesser.

Dass ihr mit aller Biederkeit
Der ärgste aller Spitzbuben seid !

Sachs.

Mag sein !   Doch hab' ich noch nie entwandt.
Was ich auf fremden Tischen fand :
Und dass man von euch auch nicht übels denkt,
Behaltet das Blatt, es sei euch geschenkt.

Beckmesser

(in freudigem Schreck aufspringend).

Herr Gott ! . . Ein Gedicht ! . . Ein Gedicht von
                    Sachs? . .

(Er blickt seitwärts in das Blatt : plötzlich runzelt sich seine
                    Stirn.)

Und doch !   Wenn's nur eine Falle wär' ! —
    Noch gestern war't ihr mein Feind
Wie käm's, dass nach so grosser Beschwer
    Ihr's freundlich heut' mit mir meint?

Sachs.

I sat up late to make your shoes:
It is not thus our foes we use.

Beckmesser.

Aye, aye ! that 's true ! — But one thing swear :
That when you hear this, no matter where !
To nobody shall be disclosed
The fact that 't was by you composed.

Sachs.

I swear it and I guarantee
That none shall know the song 's by me.

Beckmesser
(very joyous).

What more remains ?   I 'm joyful-hearted !
Beckmesser's troubles have departed !
(He rubs his hands with elation.)
Farewell, I 'm away !
Some other day,
When in this latitude,
I 'll pay my gratitude
For your kind attitude ;
Buy all your works, you know ;
You shall as Marker show ; —
Chalk you must mark with, though,
Not with the hammer's blow !
Marker !   Marker !   Marker Hans Sachs !
May he and Nuremberg bloom and wax !
(As if intoxicated he limps, stumbling and blundering, away.)

Sachs.

I ne'er met with so evil a man :
He 'll come to grief one of these days.
Their reason most men squander who can,
Yet keep some little relays :
But some weak moments all discover ;
Then they are fools and we talk them over. —
That Master Beckmesser wasn't square,
Finely will further my affair. —
(Through his window he sees Eva approaching.)
Ha, Eva !   Here she is, I declare !
(Eva, richly tricked out and in a gleaming white dress, enters the shop.)

Sachs.

My child, good morning !   Ah ! how pretty
And smart you are to-day !
Both old and young — why, all the city
You 'll win in such array.

Eva.

Master, surely now you flatter !
And if my dress is all right,
Will no one notice what 's the matter?
My shoe is much too tight.

Sachs.

Ich machte euch Schuh' in später Nacht :
Hat man so je einen Feind bedacht?

Beckmesser.

Ja ja ! recht gut ! — doch Eines schwört :
Wo und wie ihr das Lied auch hört,
Dass nie ihr euch beikommen lass't,
Zu sagen, es sei von Euch verfasst.

Sachs.

Das schwör ich und gelob' euch hier,
Nie mich zu rühmen, das Lied sei von mir.

Beckmesser
(sehr glücklich).

Was will ich mehr, ich bin geborgen !
Jetzt hat sich Beckmesser nicht mehr zu sorgen
(Er reibt sich froh die Hände.)
Ade ! ich muss fort !
An and'rem Ort
Dank' ich euch inniglich,
Weil ihr so minniglich ;
Für euch nun stimme ich,
Kauf' eure Werke gleich,
Mache zum Merker euch :
Doch fein mit Kreide weich,
Nicht mit dem Hammerstreich !
Merker !   Merker !   Merker Hans Sachs !
Dass Nürnberg schusterlich blüh' und wachs' !
(Er hinkt, poltert und taumelt wie besessen fort.)

Sachs.

So ganz boshaft doch keinen ich fand,
Er hält's auf die Länge nicht aus :
Vergeudet mancher oft viel Verstand,
Doch hält er auch damit Haus :
Die schwache Stunde kommt für Jeden ;
Da wird er dumm und lässt mit sich reden. —
Dass hier Herr Beckmesser ward zum Dieb,
Ist mir für meinen Plan sehr lieb.
(Er sieht durch das Fenster Eva kommen.)
Sieh, Evchen !   Dacht' ich doch, wo sie blieb' !
(Eva, reich geschmückt und in glänzender weisser Kleidung tritt zum Laden herein.)

Sachs.

Grüss' Gott, mein Evchen !   Ei, wie herrlich,
Wie stolz du's heute meinst !
Du machst wohl Jung und Alt begehrlich,
Wenn du so schön erscheinst.

Eva.

Meister ! 's ist nicht so gefährlich :
Und ist's dem Schneider geglückt,
Wer sieht dann an wo's mir beschwerlich,
Wo still der Schuh mich drückt?

Sachs.

The naughty shoe ! But 't was your haste ;
You would not try it on, you see.

Eva.

Not so ; too great a trust I placed :
The Master 's disappointed me.

Sachs.

I 'm really griev'd ! Come here, my pet,
And I will help you even yet.

Eva.

If I would stand, it will away ;
Would I begone, it makes me stay.

Sachs.

Upon the stool here place your foot.
A shocking fault ! I 'll look into 't.

(She puts her foot upon a stool by the workbench.)

What is amiss?

Eva.

                    Too wide, you see.

Sachs.

Child, that is purely vanity :
The shoe is tight.

Eva.

                I told you so
And that is why it hurts my toe.

Sachs.

Here — left?

Eva.

                No, right.

Sachs.

                    What ! On the sole ?

Eva.

Here, at the ankle.

Sachs.

                Well ! That 's droll !

Eva.

Nay, Master ! do you know better than I
Where the shoe pinches ?

Sachs.

                I wonder why,
If it 's too wide, it pinches you so.

Walter, in glittering knightly apparel, appears at the chamber
door, and stands there spellbound at the sight of Eva. She
utters a slight cry, but remains in her position with one foot
on the stool. Sachs is kneeling before her with his back
towards the door.

Sachs.

Der böse Schuh ! 's war deine Laun',
Dass du ihn gestern nicht probirt.

Eva.

Merk' wohl, ich hatt' zu viel Vertrau'n :
Im Meister hab' ich mich geirrt.

Sachs.

Ei, 's thut mir leid ! Zeig' her, mein Kind,
Dass ich dir helfe, gleich geschwind.

Eva.

Sobald ich stehe, will es geh'n :
Doch will ich geh'n, zwingt's mich zu steh'n.

Sachs.

Heir auf den Schemel streck' den Fuss :
Der üblen Noth ich wehren muss.

(Sie streckt den Fuss auf den Schemel beim Werktisch

Was ist's mit dem ?

Eva.

                    Ihr sekt, zu weit !

Sachs.

Kind, dat ist pure Eitelkeit :
Der Schuh ist knapp.

Eva.

                Das sag' ich ja :
Drum drückt er mir die Zehen da.

Sachs.

Hier links?

Eva.

                Nein, rechts.

Sachs.

                Wohl mehr am Spann i

Eva.

Mehr hier am Hacken.

Sachs.

                Kommt der auch dran i

Eva.

Ach Meister ! Wüsstet ihr besser als ich,
Wo der Schuh mich drückt?

Sachs.

                Ei, 's wundert mich
Dass er zu weit, und doch drückt überall?

Walther, in glänzender Rittertracht, tritt unter die Thüre
der Kammer, und bleibt beim Anblick Eva's wie festgebannt
stehen. Eva stösst einen leisen Schrei aus und bleibt
ebenfalls unverwandt in ihrer Stellung, mit dem Fusse auf
dem Schemel. Sachs, der vor ihr sich gebückt hat, ist mit
dem Rücken der Thüre zugekehrt.

Aha! 't is here!   Now the reason I know!
Child, you are right: 't is in the *sole!*
One moment, and I 'll make it whole.
Stand so awhile, I 'll fasten your shoe
On the last a moment, then it will do.

(He has gently drawn off her shoe; while she remains in
the same position he pretends to busy himself with it, and to
be oblivious of all else.)

Sachs
(as he works).

Cobbling always!   That is my fate;
I keep it up both early and late.
Hark ye, child!   I 've given it much thought,
How should my work to an end be brought.
The best way 's to join the contest for you;
I should win some fame as a poet too.
Come now, reply!   You do not heed!
'T was you put that in my head indeed!
All right!   You say, "Stick to your shoes!"
Will some one give us a song to amuse?
I heard to-day a lovely one;
Let 's see if the third verse can be done!

Walter
(still in the same position opposite Eva).

"Lingered the stars in their dance of delight?
       They rested there
         Upon her hair,
       That wondrous maiden
         So beauty-laden.
     And formed a circlet bright
       All star bedight,
Wonder on wonder now waked my surprise;
       The light of day
         Had twofold ray;
       For two transcendent
         Suns resplendent
Within her heavenly eyes
       I saw arise.
     Image so rare,
Which boldly I approached and viewed!
By all this light the crown above
At once was faded and renewed.
       Tender and fair
She wove it round the head of her love.
       Thus grace-directed,
         To fame elected,
She poured the joys of the blest
Into the poet's breast,
       In Love's sweet dream."

Sachs
(busily at work, brings back the shoe during the last verse
of Walter's song and fits it on Eva's foot again).

Hark, child!   that is a Master-song;
You hear such music where I dwell now.
So try if still my shoe is wrong.

Aha! hier sitzt's!   Nun begreif' ich den Fall!
Kind, du hast recht: 's stak in der Nath: —
Nun warte, dem Uebel schaff' ich Rath.
Bleib' nur so steh'n; ich nehm' dir den Schuh
Eine Weil' auf den Leisten: dann lässt er dir Ruh'

(Er hat ihr sanft den Schuh vom Fusse gezogen; während
sie in ihrer Stellung verbleibt, macht er sich mit dem Schuh
zu schaffen, und thut, als beachte er nichts andres.)

Sachs
(bei der Arbeit).

Immer Schustern! das ist nun mein Loos;
Des Nachts, des Tags — komm' nicht davon los! —
Kind, hör' zu!   Ich hab's überdacht,
Was meinem Schustern ein Ende macht:
Am Besten, ich werbe doch noch um dich;
Da gewänn' ich doch 'was als Poet für mich! —
Du hörst nicht drauf? — So sprich doch jetzt!
Hast mir's ja selbst in den Kopf gesetzt?
Schon gut! — ich merk'! — Mach deinen Schuh!
Säng' mir nur wenigstens Einer dazu!
Horte heut' gar ein schönes Lied: —
Wem dazu ein dritter Vers gerieth'!

Walther.
(immer Eva gegenüber in der vorigen Stellung)

„Weilten die Sterne im lieblichen Tanz?
       So licht und klar
         Im Lockenhaar,
       Vor allen Frauen
         Hehr zu schauen,
     Lag ihr mit zartem Glanz
       Ein Sternenkranz. —
Wunder ob Wunder nun bieten sich dar:
       Zwiefachen Tag
         Ich grüssen mag;
       Denn Gleich zwei'n Sonnen
         Reinster Wonnen,
     Der hehrsten Augen Paar
       Nahm ich nun wahr. —
     Huldreichstes Bild,
       Dem ich zu nahen mich erkühnt:
Den Kranz, vor zweier Sonnen Strahl
Zugleich verblichen und ergrünt,
         Minnig und mild,
     Sie flocht ihn um's Haupt dem Gemahl.
       Dort Huld-geboren,
         Nun Rhum-erkoren,
     Giesst paradiesche Lust
     Sie in des Dichters Brust —
       Im Liebstraum." —

Sachs
(hat, immer mit seiner Arbeit beschäftigt, den Schuh zurück
gebracht, und ist jetzt während der Schlussverse von
Walther's Gesang darüber her, ihn Eva wieder anzuziehen)

Lausch', Kind! das ist ein Meisterlied:
Derlei hörst du jetzt bei mir singen.
Nun schau', ob dabei mein Schuh gerieth?

Was I not right?
And fits it well now?
Let's see!   Stand down!   Is it still tight?

(Eva, who has stood still as if enchanted, gazing and listening, bursts into a sudden fit of weeping and sinks on Sachs's
breast, sobbing and clinging to him. — Walter advances
toward them and wrings Sachs's hand in silent ecstasy. —
Sachs at last composes himself, tears himself gloomily away
and causes Eva to rest unconsciously on Walter's shoulder.)

Eva

(stops Sachs and draws him to her again).

O Sachs!   best friend and dearest!   Say
How can I e'er my debt repay?
    Bereft of thy great kindness
    How helpless should I be!
    Still wrapped in childish blindness
    Had it not been for thee.
        Through thee life's treasure
        I control,
        Through thee I measure
        First my soul.
        Through thee I wake;
        My feelings take
    A higher, nobler tone:
    I bloom through thee alone! —
Yes, dearest Master, scold you may!

Sachs.

    My child:
    Sir Tristan I have read of —
    Isolde's story dark:
    Hans Sachs had prudent dread of
    The fate of poor king Mark. —
'T was time the right man did appear,
Or I should have been caught, I fear! —
Aha!   There's Magdalena's found us out.
Come in! — Ho, David! — What's he about?

(Magdalena in holiday attire enters from the street and
David at the same time comes out of the chamber, also
gayly dressed and very splendid with ribbons and flowers.)

The witnesses wait, the sponsors are found;
So now for a christening gather around!

(All look at him with surprise.)

A child here was created;
Let its name by you be stated.
Such is the Masters' constant use,
When they a Master-song produce:
They give it a fitly chosen name
That men may know it by the same.
    So let me tell all you here
    What 't is we have to do here!
A Master-song has been completed,
By young Sir Walter made and repeated;
The newborn poem's father, delighted,
For sponsors has Eva and me invited:

Mein' endlich doch.
Es thät' mir gelingen?
Versuch's!   tritt auf! — Sag', drückt er dich noch?

(Eva, die wie bezaubert bewegungslos gestanden, gesehen
und gehört hat, bricht jetzt in heftiges Weinen aus, sinkt
Sachs an die Brust und drückt ihn schluchzend an sich. —
Walther ist zu ihnen getreten, und druckt Sachs begeister'
die Hand. — Sachs thut sich endlich Gewalt an, reisst sich
wie unmuthig los, und lässt dadurch Eva unwillkürlich an
Walther's Schulter sich anlehnen.)

Eva

(hält Sachs, und zieht ihn von Neuem zu sich).

O Sachs!   Mein Freund!   Du theurer Mann!
Wie ich dir Edlem lohnen kann!
    Was ohne deine Liebe,
    Was wär' ich ohne dich,
    Ob je auch Kind ich bliebe
    Erwecktest du nicht mich?
        Durch dich gewann ich
        Was man preist.
        Durch dich ersann ich
        Was ein Geist!
        Durch dich erwacht,
        Durch dich nur dacht'
    Ich edel, frei und kühn:
    Du liessest mich erblüh'n! —
O lieber Meister!   schilt mich nur!

Sachs.

    Mein Kind:
    Von Tristan und Isolde
    Kenn' ich ein traurig Stück:
    Hans Sachs war klug, und wollte
    Nichts von Herrn Marke's Gluck. —
's war Zeit, dass ich den Rechten erkannt:
Wär' sonst am End' doch hineingerannt!
Aha!   da streicht schon die Lene um's Haus,
Nur herein! — He, David!   Kommst nicht heraus!

(Magdalene, in festlichem Staate, tritt durch die Ladenthür
herein; aus der Kammer kommt zugleich David, ebenfalls
im Festkleid, mit Blumen und Bändern sehr reich und
zierlich ausgeputzt.)

Die Zeugen sind da, Gevatter, zur Hand;
Jetzt schnell zur Taufe; nehmt euren Stand!

(Alle blicken ihn verwundert an.)

Ein Kind ward hier geboren;
Jetzt sei ihm ein Nam' erkoren!
So ist's nach Meister-Weis' und Art,
Wenn eine Meisterweise geschaffen ward:
Dass die einen guten Namen trag',
Dran Jeder sie erkennen mag. —
    Vernehmt, respectable Gesellschaft,
    Was euch hierher zur Stell' schafft!
Eine Meisterweise ist gelungen,
Von Junker Walther gedichtet und gesungen;
Der jungen Weise lebender Vater
Lud mich und die Pognerin zu Gevatter;

As to the song we have been list'ning
We now come hither to its christ'ning.
To see that we act with solemn fitness
Shall David and Lena be called to witness:
But as no Prentice a witness can be,
And as he's repeated his task to me,
A Journeyman I will make him here.
Kneel, David, and take this box on the ear.

(David kneels and Sachs gives him a smart box on the ear.)

Arise, my man; remember that blow;
I will mark this baptism for you, you know.
Lacks aught beside, what blame indeed?
Who knows if private baptism we need?
That the melody lack not anything vital
I now proceed to give it its title.
"*The glorious morning-dream's true story.*" —
So be it named, to the Master's glory.
And may it increase in size and strength. —
I bid the young god-mother speak at length.

Eva.

    Dazzling as the dawn
    That smiles upon my glee,
    Rapture-laden morn
    To bliss awakens me.
    Dream of palmy beauty,
    Brilliant morning-glow!
    Hard but sweet the duty
    Thy intent to know.
    That divine and tender strain
    With its tones of gladness
    Has revealed my heart's sweet pain
        And subdued its sadness.
    It is but a morning-dream?
    Scarcely real doth it seem.
      What the ditty,
      Soft and pretty,
      Told to me,
      A quiet theme,
      Loud and free.
    In the Masters' conclave wise
    Shall achieve the highest prize.

Walter.

    'T was thy love — the highest gain —
      Allured me by its gladness,
    To reveal my heart's sweet pain
      And subdue its sadness,
    Is it still my morning-dream?
    Scarcely real doth it seem.
      What the ditty,
      Soft and pretty,
      Told to thee,
      A quiet theme,
      Loud and free
    In the Masters' conclave wise
    Shall achieve the highest prize.

Weil wir die Weise wohl vernommen,
Sind wir zur Taufe hierher gekommen.
Auch dass wir zur Handlung Zeugen haben,
Ruf' ich Jungfer Lene, und meinen Knaben:
Doch da's zum Zeugen kein Lehrbube thut,
Und heut' auch den Spruch er gesungen gut,
So mach' ich den Burschen gleich zum Gesell':
Knie' nieder, David, und nimm diese Schell'!

(David ist niedergekniet: Sachs giebt ihm eine starke
Ohrfeige.)

Steh' auf, Gesell! und denk' an den Streich:
Du merkst dir dabei die Taufe zugleich!
Fehlt sonst noch 'was, uns Keiner drum schilt:
Wer weiss ob's nicht ger eine Nothtaufe gilt.
Dass die Weise Kraft bahalte zum Leben,
Will ich uur gleich den Numen ihr geben: —
„ Die selige Morgentraumdeut-Weise "
Sei sie genannt zu des Meisters Preise.
Nun wachse sie gross, ohn' Schad' und Bruch:
Die jüngste Gevatt'rin spricht den Spruch.

Eva.

    Selig, wie die Sonne
    Meines Glückes lacht,
    Morgen voller Wonne,
    Selig mir erwacht!
    Traum der höchsten Hulden,
    Himmlisch Morgenglüh'n!
    Deutung euch zu schulden,
    Selig süss Bemüh'n'!
    Einer Weise mild und hehr,
        Sollt' es hold gelingen,
    Meines Herzens süss Beschwer
        Deutend zu bezwingen.
    Ob es nur ein Morgentraum?
    Selig' deut' ich mir es kaum.
      Doch die Weise,
      Was sie leise
      Mir vertraut
      Im stillen Raum,
      Hell und laut,
    In der Meister volleim Kreis,
    Deute sie den höchsten Preis!

Walther.

    Deine Liebe, rein und hehr,
      Liess es mir gelingen,
    Meines Herzens süss Beschwer
      Deutend zu bezwingen.
    Ob es noch der Morgentraum?
    Selig deut' ich mir es kaum.
      Doch die Weise,
      Was sie leise
      Dir vertraut
      Im stillen Raum,
      Hell und laut,
    In der Meister vollem Kreis,
    Werbe sie um höchsten Preis!

Sachs.

With the maiden I would fain
    Sing for very gladness ;
But my heart I must restrain,
    Quell my passion's madness.
'T was a tender evening-dream :
Undiscovered let it beam.
    What the ditty,
    Soft and pretty,
    Told to me
    In quiet theme,
    Here I see :
Youth and love that never dies
Flourish through the master-prize.

David.

Am I awake or dreaming still ?
Scarce to explain it have I skill.
Sure 't is but a morning-dream !
All these things unreal seem.
    Can it be, man,
    You 're a freeman ?
    And that she —
    Oh, joy supreme ! —
    My spouse shall be ?
Round and round my headpiece flies
That a Master I now rise !

Magdalena.

Am I awake or dreaming still ?
Scarce to explain it have I skill.
Sure 't is but a morning-dream !
All these things unreal seem.
    Can it be, man,
    You 're a freeman ?
    And that we —
    Oh, joy supreme ! —
    Shall wedded be ?
Yes, what honor near me lies ?
Soon I shall as Madam rise !

(The orchestra goes into a broad march-like theme.— Sachs
    makes the group break up.)

Sachs.

Now let 's be off ! — Your father stays !
Quick, to the fields all go your ways !

Eva tears herself away from Sachs and Walter and leaves
    the house with Magdalena.)

So come, sir knight ! take heart of grace !
David, my man, lock up the place.

  As Sachs and Walter also go into the street, and David is
eft shutting up the shop, curtains descend from each side of
the proscenium so as to conceal the stage.— When the
music has gradually swelled to the loudest pitch the curtains
are drawn up again and the scene 's changed.

Sachs.

Vor dem Kinde lieblich hehr,
    Mocht' ich gern wohl singen ;
Doch des Herzens süss Beschwer
    Galt es zu bezwingen.
's war ein schöner Abendtraum :
Dran zu deuten wag ich kaum.
    Diese Weise,
    Was sie leise,
    Mir vertraut
    Im stillen Raum,
    Sagt mir laut :
Auch der Jugend ew'ges Reis
Grünt nur durch des Dichters Preis.

David.

Wach' oder träum' ich schon so früh' ?
Das zu erklären macht mir Müh'.
's ist wohl nur ein Morgentraum ?
Was ich seh', begreif' ich kaum.
    Ward zur Stelle
    Gleich Geselle ?
    Lene Braut ?
    Im Kirchenraum
    Wir getraut ?
's geht der Kopf mir, wie im Kreis
Dass ich bald gar Meister heiss' !

Magdalene.

Wach' oder träum' ich schon so früh ?
Das zu erklären macht mir Müh' !
's ist wohl nur ein Morgentraum ?
Was ich seh', begreif' ich kaum.
    Er, zur Stelle
    Gleich Geselle ?
    Ich die Braut ?
    Im Kirchenraum
    Wir getraut ?
Ja, wahrhaftig ! 's geht : wer weiss ?
Bald ich wohl Frau Meist'rin heiss' !

(Das Orchester geht sehr leise in eine marschmässige, heitere
    Weise über.— Sachs ordnet den Aufbruch an.)

Sachs.

Jetzt All' am Fleck ! Den Vater küss' !
Auf, nach der Wies', schnell auf die Füss'.

(Eva trennt sich von Sachs und Walther und verlässt mit
    Magdalene die Werkstatt.)

Nun, Junker ! Kommt ! Habt frohen Muth ! —
David' Gesell' ! Schliess den Laden gut !

  Als Sachs und Walther ebenfalls auf die Strasse gehen,
und David sich über das Schliessen der Ladenthüre her
macht, wird im Proscenium ein Vorhang von beiden Seiten
zusammengezogen, so dass er die Scene gänzlich schliesst.—
Als die Musik allmählich zu grösserer Stärke angewachsen ist,
wird der Vorhang nach der Höhe zu aufgezogen. Die
Bühne ist verwandelt.

CHANGE OF SCENE.

The stage now represents an open meadow, in the distance at back the town of Nuremberg. The Pegnitz winds across the plain; the narrow river is practicable in the foreground. Boats gaily decorated with flags continually discharge fresh parties of Burghers of the different Guilds with their wives and families, who land on the banks. A raised stand with benches on it is erected R, already adorned with flags of those as yet arrived; as the scene opens, the standard-bearers of freshly arriving Guilds also place their banners against the Singer's stage, so that it is at last quite closed in on three sides by them. Tents with all kinds of refreshments border the sides of the open space in front.

Before the tents is much merry-making: Burghers and their families sit and group round them.—The Prentices of the Master-singers, in holiday attire, finely decked out with ribbons and flowers, and bearing slender wands, also ornamented, fulfil frolicsomely the office of heralds and stewards. They receive the new comers on the bank, arrange them in procession and conduct them to the stand, whence, after the standard-bearer has deposited his banner, the Burghers and Journeymen disperse under the tents.

Among the arriving Guilds the following are prominent.

The Shoemakers.
(As they march past.)
Saint Crispin!
Honor him!
He was both wise and good,
Did all a cobbler could.
That was a fine time for the poor!
He made them all warm shoes;
When none would lend him leather more,
To steal he'd not refuse.
The cobbler has a conscience easy,
No obstacles to labor sees he;
When from the tanner 't is sent away
Then hey! hey! hey!
Leather becomes his rightful prey.

(The Town-pipers, Lute- and Toy-instrument-makers, playing on their instruments, follow. These are succeeded by)

The Tailors.
When Nuremberg besieged did stand
And famine wrought despair,
Undone had been both folk and land
Had not a tailor been there
Of craft and courage rare:
Within a goatskin he did hide
And showed upon the wall outside,
There took to gaily tripping
And gambolling and skipping.
The foe beheld it with dismay:
"The devil fetch that town away

VERWANDLUNG.

Die Scene stellt einen freien Wiesenplan dar, im fernen Hintergrunde die Stadt Nürnberg. Die Pegnitz schlängelt sich durch den Plan: der schmale Fluss ist an den nächsten Punkten praktikabel gehalten. Buntbeflaggte Kähne setzen unablässig die noch ankommenden, festlich geschmückten Bürger der Zunfte, mit Frauen und Kindern, an das Ufer der Festwiese über. Eine erhöhte Buhne mit Bänken darauf ist rechts zur Seite aufgeschlagen; bereits ist sie mit den Fahnen der angekommenen Zunfte ausgeschmückt; im Verlaufe stecken die Fahnenträger der noch ankommenden Zunfte ihre Fahnen ebenfalls um die Sängerbühne auf, so dass diese schliesslich nach drei Seiten hin ganz davon eingefasst ist.—Zelte mit Getränken und Erfrischungen aller Art begrenzen im Uebrigen die Seiten des vorderen Hauptraumes.

Vor den Zelten geht es bereits lustig her: Bürger mit Frauen und Kindern sitzen und lagern daselbst.—Die Lehrbuben der Meistersinger festlich gekleidet, mit Blumen und Bändern reich und anmuthig geschmückt, über mit schlanken Stäben, die ebenfalls mit Blumen und Bändern reich geziert sind, in lustiger Weise das Amt von Herolden und Marschällen aus. Sie empfangen die am Ufer Aussteigenden, ordnen die Züge der Zünfte, und geleiten diese nach der Singerbühne, von wo aus, nachdem der Bannerträger die Fahne aufgepflanzt, die Zunftbürger und Gesellen nach Belieben sich unter den Zelten zerstreuen.

Unter den noch anlangenden Zünften werden die folgenden besonders bemerkt.

Die Schuster.
(Indem sie aufziehen.)
Sankt Crispin,
Lobet ihn!
War gar ein heilig Mann,
Zeigt was ein Schuster kann.
Die Armen hatten gute Zeit,
Macht' ihnen warme Schuh';
Und wenn ihm Keiner Leder leiht',
So stahl er sich's dazu.
Der Schuster hat ein weit Gewissen,
Macht Schuhe selbst mit Hindernissen;
Und ist vom Gerber das Fell erst weg,
Dann streck'! streck'! streck'!
Leder taugt nur am rechten Fleck.

(Die Stadtpfeifer, Lauten- und Kinderinstrumentmacher ziehen, auf ihren Instrumenten spielend, auf Ihnen folgen.)

Die Schneider. Als Nürnberg belagert war.
Und Hungersnoth sich fand,
Wär' Stadt und Volk verdorben gar,
War nicht ein Schneider zur Hand.
Der viel Muth hat und Verstand:
Hat sich in ein Bockfell eingenäht,
Auf dem Stadtwall da springen geht,
Und macht wohl seine Sprünge
Gar lustig guter Dinge.
Der Feind, der sieht's und zieht vom Fleck,
Der Teufel hol' die Stadt sich weg,

Where goats yet merrily play, play, play.
  Me-ey! me-ey! me-ey!
  (Imitating the bleating of a goat.)
Who 'd think that a tailor within there lay?

The Bakers.
(Coming close behind the Tailors so that the two songs join together.)
Want of bread! Want of bread!
  That is a hardship true, sirs!
If you were not by the baker fed
Old Death would feed on you, sirs.
  Pray! pray! pray!
  Baker every day,
  Hunger turn away!

Prentices.
Heyday! Heyday! Maidens from Fürth!
Play up, town-piper, one merry spurt!

(A gaily painted boat, filled with young Girls in fine peasant-costumes, arrives. The Prentices help the Girls out and dance with them, while the town-pipers play, towards the front.—The character of this dance consists in the Prentices appearing only to wish to bring the Girls to the open place; the Journeymen endeavor to capture them and the Prentices move on as if seeking another place, thus making the tour of the stage and continually delaying their original purpose in fun and frolic.)

David.
  (Advancing from the landing-place.)
You dance! The Masters will rate such folly.
  (The boys make faces at him.)
Do n't care? Why, then, let me too be jolly!
(He seizes a young and pretty girl and mingles in the dance with great ardor. The spectators notice him and laugh.)

Some of the Prentices.
David! there's Lena! There's Lena sees you!

David.
(Alarmed, hastily releases the maiden, but seeing nothing, quickly regains his courage and resumes his dancing.)
Have done with your silly jokes, my boys, do!

Journeymen.
  (At the landing-place.)
The Master-singers! the Master-singers!

David.
Oh, lor'!—Farewell, ye pretty clingers!
(He gives the maiden an ardent kiss and tears himself away. The Prentices quickly discontinue their dance, hasten to the bank and arrange themselves to receive the Master-singers. All stand back, by command of the Prentices.—The Master-singers arrange their procession on the bank and then march forwards to take their places on the stand. First Kothner, as standard-bearer, then Pogner leading Eva by the hand; she is attended by richly dressed Maidens among whom is Magdalena. Then follow the other Master-singers. They are greeted with cheers and waving of hats. When all have reached the

Hat's drin noch so lustige Meck-meck-meck!
  Meck! Meck! Meck!
  (Das Gemecker der Ziege nachahmend.)
Wer glaubt's, dass ein Schneider im Bocke steck'!

Die Bäcker.
(Ziehen dicht hinter den Schneidern auf, so dass ihr Lied in das der Schneider hineinklingt.)
Hungersnoth! Hungersnoth!
  Das ist ein gräulich Leiden!
Gäb' euch der Bäcker kein täglich Brod,
  Müsst' alle Welt verscheiden.
  Beck! Beck! Beck!
  Täglich auf dem Fleck!
  Nimm uns den Hunger weg!

Lehrbuben.
Herr Je! Herr Je! Mädel von Fürth!
Stadtpfeifer spielt! dass 's lustig wird!

(Ein bunter Kahn, mit jungen Mädchen in reicher bäuerischer Tracht, ist angekommen. Die Lehrbuben heben die Mädchen heraus, und tanzen mit ihnen, während die Stadtpfeifer spielen, nach dem Vordergrunde. Das Charakteristische des Tanzes besteht darin, dass die Lehrbuben die Mädchen scheinbar nur an den Platz bringen wollen; sowie die Gesellen zugreifen wollen, ziehen die Buben die Mädchen aber immer wieder zurück, als ob sie sie anderswo unterbringen wollten, wobei sie meistens den ganzen Kreis, wie wähend, ausmessen, und somit die scheinbare Absicht auszuführen, anmuthig und lustig verzögern.)

David.
  (Kommt vom Landungsplatze vor.)
Ihr tanzt? Was werden die Meister sagen?
  (Die Buben drehen ihm Nasen.)
Hört nicht?—Lass' ich mir's auch behagen!
(Er nimmt sich ein junges, schönes Mädchen, und geräth im Tanze mit ihr bald in grosses Feuer. Die Zuschauer freuen sich und lachen.)

Ein paar Lehrbuben.
David! die Lene! die Lene sieht zu!

David.
(Erschrickt, lässt das Mädchen schnell fahren, fasst sich aber Muth, da er nichts sieht, und tanzt noch feuriger weiter.)
Ach! lasst mich mit euren Possen in Ruh'!

Gesellen.
  (Am Landungsplatz.)
Die Meistersinger! Die Meistersinger!

David.
Herr Gott!—Ade, ihr hübschen Dinger!
(Er giebt dem Mädchen einen feurigen Kuss und reisst sich los. Die Lehrbuben unterbrechen alle schnell den Tanz, eilen zum Ufer und reihen sich dort zum Empfang der Meistersinger. Alles macht auf das Geheiss der Lehrbuben Platz.—Die Meistersinger ordnen sich am Landungsplatze und ziehen dann festlich auf, um auf der erhöhten Bühne ihre Plätze einzunehmen. Voran Kothner als Fahnenträger; dann Pogner, Eva an der Hand führend; diese ist von festlich geschmückten und reich gekleideten jungen Mädchen begleitet, denen sich Magdalene anschliesst. Dann folgen die übrigen

platform, **Eva** has taken the place of honor, with her Maidens round her, and Kothner has placed his banner in the middle of the others, which it overtops; the Prentices solemnly advance in rank and file before the stand, turning to the people.)

Prentices.

Silentium! Silentium!
Make no sound, e'en the merest hum!

(Sachs rises and steps forward. At sight of him all burst out into fresh acclamations and wavings of hats and 'kerchiefs.)

All the People.

Ha! Sachs! 'T is Sachs!
See! Master Sachs!
Sing all! Sing all! Sing all!
(With solemn delivery.)
" Awake! draws nigh the break of day:
" I hear upon the hawthorn spray
" A bonny little nightingale;
" His voice resounds o'er hill and dale.
" The night descends the western sky
" And from the east the morn draws nigh,
" With ardor red the flusk of day
" Breaks through the cloud-bank dull and
    grey."
        Hail, Sachs! Hans Sachs!
    Hail, Nuremberg's darling Sachs!

(Long silence of deep feeling. Sachs, who, as if wrapt, has stood motionless, gazing far away beyond the multi-tude, at last turns a genial glance on them, bows courte-ously and begins in a voice at first trembling with emotion but soon gaining firmness.)

Sachs.

Your hearts you ease, mine you oppress,
I feel my own unworthiness.
What I must prize all else above
Is your esteem and honest love.
Already honor I have gained,
To-day as spokesman I'm ordained;
And in the matter of my speech,
You will be honored, all and each.
If Art so much you honor, sirs,
    We ought to show you rather
That one who's altogether hers
    Esteems her even farther.
A Master, noble, rich, and wise,
    Will prove you this with pleasure:
His only child, the highest prize
    With all his wealth and treasure,
He offers as inducement strong
To him who in the art of song
    Before the people here
    As victor shall appear.
So hear my words and follow me:
To poets all this trial's free.
Ye Masters who compete to-day,
To you before all here I say:
Bethink you what a prize this is!
    Let each, if he would win it,

Meistersinger. Sie werden mit Hutschwenken und Freudenrufen begrüsst. Als Alle auf der Bühne angelangt sind, Eva, von den Mädchen umgeben, den Ehrenplatz eingenommen, und Kothner die Fahre gerade in der Mitte der übrigen Fahnen, und sie alle überragend, aufgepflanzt hat, treten die Lehrbuben, dem Volke zugewendet, feierlich vor der Bühne in Reih und Glied.)

Lehrbuben. Silentium! Silentium!
    Lasst all' Reden und Gesumm'!

(Sachs erhebt sich und tritt vor. Bei seinem Anblick stösst sich sofort Alles an und bricht sofort unter Hut- und Tücherschwenken in grossen Jubel aus.)

Alles Volk. Ha! Sachs! 's ist Sachs!
    Seht! Meister Sachs!
    Stimmt an! Stimmt an! Stimmt an!
        (Mit feierlicher Haltung.)
    " Wach' auf, es nahet gen den Tag,
    " Ich hör' singen im grünen Hag
    " Ein wonnigliche Nachtigall,
    " Ihr Stimm' durchklinget Berg und Thal;
    " Die Nacht neigt sich zum Occident,
    " Der Tag geht auf von Orient,
    " Die rothbrünstige Morgenröth'
    " Her durch die trüben Wolken geht."
        Heil Sachs! Hans Sachs!
    Heil Nürnberg's theurem Sachs!

(Längeres Schweigen grosser Ergriffenheit. — Sachs der unbeweglich, wie geistesabwesend, über die Volks menge hinweg geblickt hatte, richtet endlich seine Blick; vertrauter auf sie, verneigt sich freundlich, und beginn; mit ergriffener, schnell aber sich festigender Stimme.)

Sachs.

Euch wird es leicht, mir macht ihr's schwer,
Gebt ihr mir Armen zu viel Ehr':
Such' vor der Ehr' ich zu besteh'n,
Sei's, mich von euch geliebt zu seh'n!
Schon grosse Ehr' ward mir erkannt,
Ward heut' ich zum Spruchsprecher ernannt;
Und was mein Spruch euch künden soll,
Glaubt, das ist hoher Ehre voll!
Wenn ihr die Kunst so hoch schon ehrt,
    Da galt es zu beweisen,
Dass, wer ihr selbst gar angehört,
    Sie schätzt ob allen Preisen.
Ein Meister reich und hochgemuth,
    Der will euch heut' das zeigen:
Sein Töchterlein, sein höchstes Gut,
    Mit allem Hab und eigen,
Dem Singer, der im Kunstgesang
Vor allem Volk den Preis errang,
    Als höchsten Preises Kron'
    Er bietet das zum Lohn.
Darum so hört, und stimmet bei:
Die Werbung steht dem Dichter frei.
Ihr Meister, die ihr's euch getraut,
Euch ruf' ich's vor dem Volke laut:
Erwägt der Werbung selt'nen Preis,
    Und wem sie soll gelingen.

Be sure a guileless heart is his;
  Pure love and music in it.
    This crown 's of worth infinite,
And ne'er, in recent days or olden,
By any hand so highly holden.
    As by this maiden tender:
    Good fortune may it lend her!
Thus Nuremberg gives honor due
To Art and all her Masters too.

(Great stir among all present.—Sachs goes up to
Pogner, who presses his hand, deeply moved.)

Pogner.

  O Sachs! my friend! what thanks I owe!
  How well my heart's distress you know!

Sachs.

  There 's much at stake! But care dispel!

(The Prentices have hastily heaped up before the platform of the Master-singers a little mound of turf, beaten
it solid, and bestrewn it with flowers.)

Sachs. Now then, my Masters, if you're agreed,
  We will to our Trial-songs proceed.

Kothner.
       (Advancing.)
  Unmarried Masters, forward to win!
  Let him commence who 's most mature.—
  Friend Beckmesser, it is time! Begin!

Beckmesser.
(Quits the stand; the Prentices conduct him to the
mound; he stumbles up to it, treads uncertainly, and
totters.)
  The devil! How rickety! Make that secure!
    (The boys snigger, and beat the turf lustily.)

The People.
  (Severally, whilst Beckmesser is settling himself.)
  What! he to woo! Is n't he a fat one?
  In the lady's place, I'd not have that one!
    He cannot keep his feet:
    How will the man compete?
  Be still! He's quite a great professor:
  That is the Town-clerk, Master Beckmesser.
    He 'll tumble soon,
    Old pantaloon!
  Hush! leave off your jokes and prate;
  He is a learned magistrate.

The Prentices.
      (Drawn up in order.)
  Silentium! Silentium!
  Make no sound — e'en the merest hum!

(Beckmesser, anxiously scanning all faces, makes a
grand bow to Eva.)

Kothner. Now begin!

Dass er sich rein und edel weiss,
  Im Werben, wie im Singen,
    Will er das Reis erringen,
Dass nie bei neuen noch bei Alten
Ward je so herrlich hoch gehalten,
    Als von der lieblich Reinen,
    Die niemals soll beweinen,
Dass Nürnberg mit höchstem Werth
Die Kunst und ihre Meister ehrt.

(Grosse Bewegung unter Allen.—Sachs geht auf Pog
ner zu, der ihm gerührt die Hand drückt.)

Pogner.
  O Sachs! Mein Freund! Wie dankens
    werth!
  Wie wisst ihr, was mein Herz beschwert!

Sachs.
  's war viel gewagt! Jetzt habt nur Muth!
(Die Lehrbuben haben vor der Meistersinger-Bühne
schnell von Rasenstücken einen kleinen Hügel aufgewor
fen, fest gerammelt, und reich mit Blumen überdeckt.)

Sachs.
  Nun denn, wenn's Meistern und Volk beliebt,
  Zum Wettgesang man den Anfang giebt.

Kothner.
      (Tritt vor.)
  Ihr ledig' Meister, macht euch bereit!
  Der Aeltest' sich zuerst anlässt: —
  Herr Beckmesser, ihr fangt an, 's ist Zeit!

Beckmesser.
(Verlässt die Singerbühne; die Lehrbuben führen ihn
zu dem Blumenhügel: er strauchelt darauf, tritt unsicher
und schwankt.)
  Zum Teufel! Wie wackelig! Macht das
    hübsch fest!
(Die Buben lachen unter sich und stopfen an dem Ra
sen.)

Das Volk.
(Unterschiedlich, während Beckmesser sich zurecht
macht.)
  Wie, der? Der wirbt? Scheint mir nicht der
    Rechte!
  An der Tochter Stell' ich den nicht möchte.
    Er kann nicht 'mal stehn:
    Wie wird's mit dem geh'n?
  Seid still! 's ist gar ein tücht'ger Meister!
  Stadtschreiber ist er: Beckmesser heisst er.
    Gott ist der dumm!
    Er fällt fast um! —
  Still! macht keinen Witz;
  Der hat im Rathe Stimm' und Sitz.

Die Lehrbuben.
      (In Aufstellung.)
  Silentium! Silentium!
  Lasst all das Reden und Gesumm'!
(Beckmesser macht, ängstlich in ihren Blicken forschend
eine gezierte Verbeugung gegen Eva.)

Kothner.   Fanget an!

Beckmesser.

(Sings to his old melody, a vain attempt at Walter's song; his ornamental phrases being spoiled by continual failure of memory and increasing confusion.)

"Yawning and steaming with roseate light,
My hair was filled
With scent distilled,
My boots were beaming
With no meaning,
The guard I did invite
To strap me tight."

(After having settled his feet more securely, and taken a peep at the manuscript:)

"Oh for the claws of the guard for my hold!
A flea looked down
Upon my crown,
My chest intending
I suspending
My weight from roots unrolled
That furnished hold."

(He again tries to steady himself, and to correct himself by the manuscript.)

The Masters. What is the matter? Is he insane?
His song's sheer nonsense, that is plain!

The People.

(Louder.)

Charming wooer! He'll soon get his due:
Suspend on the gallows—that's what he'll do!

Beckmesser.

(More and more confused.)
"Get me a bride!
A lovely merry girl I sued—
Afraid, she could not score my face—
As sweet and fair as she was rude.
Like to have died,
She shook me from her embrace;
With white eyes glowing,
Her hound was going
To stir my long legs as I found.
Such thunderous brutes surround
The tree of tripe!"

(Here all burst into a peal of loud laughter.)

Beckmesser.

(Descends the mound and hastens to Sachs.)
Accursed cobbler! This is through you!
That song is not my own, 't is true;
'T was Sachs, the idol of your throng,
Hans Sachs himself gave me the song!
The wretch, on purpose to abash,
Has palmed on me this sorry trash.

(He rushes away furiously, and disappears in the crowd. Great confusion.)

People.

Why! How can that be? 'T is still more surprising!
That song by Sachs? Our wonder is rising!

Beckmesser.

(Singt mit seiner Melodie, verkehrter Prosodie und mit süsslich verzierten Absätzen, öfters durch mangelhaftes Memoriren gänzlich behindert, und mit immer mehr wach sender ängstlicher Verwirrung.)

"Morgen ich leuchte in rosigem Schein
Voll Blut und Duft
Geht schnell die Luft; —
Wohl bald gewonnen,
Wie zerronnen, —
Im Garten lud ich ein—
Garstig und fein."

(Nachdem er sich mit den Füssen wieder gerichtet, und im Manuscript heimlich nachgelesen.)

"Wohn' ich erträglich im selbigen Raum,
Hol' Gold und Frucht—
Bleisaft und Wucht:
Mich holt am Pranger—
Der Verlanger, —
Auf luft'ger Steige kaum—
Häng' ich am Baum."

(Er sucht sich wieder zurecht zu stellen und im Manu script zurecht zu finden.)

Die Meister.

Was soll das heissen? Ist er nun toll?
Sein Lied ist ganz von Unsinn voll!

Das Volk.

(Immer lauter.)

Schöner Werber! Der find't seinen Lohn:
Bald hängt er am Galgen; man sieht ihn schon.

Beckmesser.

(Immer verwirrter.)

"Heimlich mir graut—
Weil hier es munter will hergeh'n : —
An meiner Leiter stand ein Wieb,
Sie schäm' und wollt mich nicht beseh'n.
Bleich wie ein Kraut—
Umfasert mir Hanf meinen Leib ; —
Die Augen zwinkend—
Der Hund blies winkend—
Was ich vor langem verzehrt, —
Wie Frucht, so Holz und Pferd—
Vom Leberbaum."

(Hier bricht Alles in schallendes Gelächter aus.)

Beckmesser.

(Verlässt wüthend den Hügel und eilt auf Sachs zu.)
Verdammter Schuster! Das dank' ich dir!
Das Lied, es ist gar nicht von mir:
Von Sachs, der hier so hoch verehrt,
Von eu'rem Sachs ward mir's bescheert!
Mich hat der Schändliche bedrängt,
Sein schlechtes Lied mir aufgehängt.

(Er stürzt wüthend fort und verliert sich unter dem Volke. Grosser Aufstand.)

Volk.

Mein! Was soll das? Jetzt wird's immer bunter!
Von Sachs das Lied? Das nähm' uns doch Wunder!

Master-Singers.
Explain this, Sachs! What a disgrace!
Is that song yours? Most novel case!

Sachs.
(Who has quietly picked up the paper which Beckmes-
ser threw away.)
That song, indeed, is not by me:
Friend Beckmesser's wrong as he can be.
I tell you, sirs, the work is fine;
But it is easy to divine
That Beckmesser has sung it wrong.
I am accused and must defend:
A witness let me bid attend!—
Is there one here who knows I'm right,
Let him appear before our sight!
(Walter advances from out the crowd.—General stir.)
Bear witness the song is not by me,
And prove to all that, in the plea
        I have advanced for it,
        I said but what was fit.

The Masters.
Ah, Sachs! You're very sly indeed!—
But you may for this once proceed.

Sachs.
It shews our rules are of excellence rare
If now and then exceptions they'll bear.

People. A noble witness, proud and bold!
Methinks he should some good unfold.

Sachs. Masters and people all agree
To give my witness liberty.
Sir Walter von Stolzing, sing the song!
You, Masters, see if he goes wrong.
    (He gives the Masters the paper to follow with.)

Prentices. All are intent, hushed is the hum;
So we need not call out Silentium!

Die Meistersinger.
Erklärt doch, Sachs! Welch ein Skandal!
Von euch das Lied? Welch eigner Fall!

Sachs.
(Der ruhig das Blatt, welches ihm Beckmesser hinge-
worfen, aufgehoben hat.)
Das Lied, fürwahr, ist nicht von mir:
Herr Beckmesser irrt, wie dort, so hier!
Ich sag' euch Herr'n, das Lied ist schön:
Nur ist's auf den ersten Blick zu erseh'n,
Dass Freund Beckmesser es entstellt.
Ich bin verklagt, und muss besteh'n:
Drum lasst meinen Zeugen mich auser-
    seh'n!—
Ist Jemand hier, der Recht mir weiss,
Der tret' als Zeug' in diesen Kreis!
(Walther tritt aus dem Volke hervor. Allgemeine Be-
wegung.)
So zeuget, das Lied sei nicht von mir;
Und zeuget auch, dass, was ich hier
        Hab' von dem Lied gesagt,
        Zuviel nicht sei gewagt.

Die Meister.
Ei, Sachs! Gesteht, ihr seid gar fein!—
So mag's denn heut' geschehen sein.

Sachs. Der Regel Güte daraus man erwägt,
Dass sie auch 'mal 'ne Ausnahm' verträgt.

Das Volk. Ein guter Zeuge, schön und kühn!
Mich dünkt, dem kann 'was Gut's erblüh'n!

Sachs. Meister und Volk sind gewillt
Zu vernehmen, was mein Zeuge gilt.
Herr Walther von Stolzing, singt das Lied!
Ihr Meister, les't, ob's ihm gerieth.
    (Er giebt den Meistern das Blatt zum Nachlesen.)

Die Lehrbuben.
Alles gespannt, 's gibt kein Gesumm',
Da rufen wir auch nicht Silentium!

PRIZE SONG.

English Version by L. U.

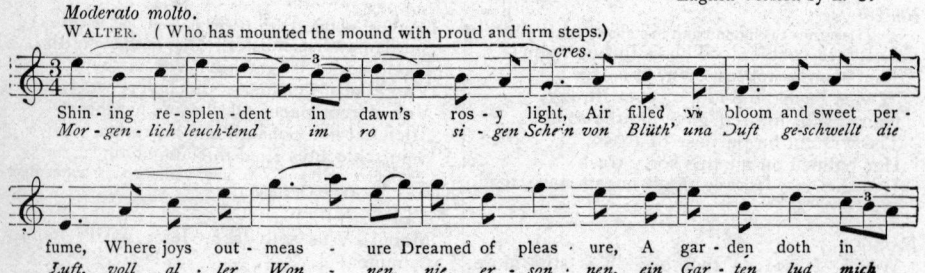

Moderato molto.
WALTER. (Who has mounted the mound with proud and firm steps.)

Shin-ing re-splen-dent in dawn's ros-y light, Air filled with bloom and sweet per-
Mor-gen-lich leuch-tend im ro si-gen Sche'n von Blüth' und Duft ge-schwellt die

fume, Where joys out-meas-ure Dreamed of pleas-ure, A gar-den doth in
Luft, voll al-ler Won-nen, nie er-son-nen, ein Gar-ten lud mich

maid E-lys-ian I saw in vis-ion, She whom my heart doth
dort ge-bo-ren, mein Herz er-ko-ren, der Er-de lieb--lich-stes

choose,Earth's fair-est, and my muse, So ho--ly, grave, and good, By
Bild, als Mu-se mir ge-weiht, so hei--lig ernst als mild, ward

me is bold-ly wooed, Here by the day's bright sun, By
kühn von mir ge-freit; am lich-ten Tag der Son nen, durch

Poco. Rit.

power of song is won Par-nas sus and Pa-ra-dise!"
San-ges Sieg ge-won-nen Par-nass und Pa-ra-dies!"

People.   Give him the prize!
           Maiden, rise!
No one could woo in nobler wise!
	Volk. Reich' ihm das Reis!
	        Sein der Preis!
	Keiner wie er zu werben weiss!

Masters. Yes, glorious singer! Victor, rise! Your song has won the Master-prize!	*Die Meister.* Ja, holder Sänger! Nimm das Reis! Dein Sang erwarb dir Meisterpreis!
Pogner. O Sachs! All this I owe to you: My happiness revives anew.	*Pogner.* O Sachs! Dir dank' ich Glück und Ehr', Vorüber nun all' Herzbeschwer!

People.   Give him the prize!
          Maiden, rise!
No one could woo in nobler wise!

Volk.   Reich' ihm das Reis!
        Sein der Preis!
Keiner wie er zu werben weiss!

Masters. Yes, glorious singer! Victor, rise!
Your song has won the Master-prize!

Die Meister.
Ja, holder Sänger! Nimm das Reis!
Dein Sang erwarb dir Meisterpreis!

Pogner. O Sachs! All this I owe to you:
    My happiness revives anew.

Pogner.
O Sachs! Dir dank' ich Glück und Ehr',
Vorüber nun all' Herzbeschwer!

(Eva, who from the commencement of the scene has preserved a calm composure, and has seemed wrapt from all that passed around, has listened to Walter immovably; but now, when at the conclusion both Masters and people express their involuntary admiration, she rises, advances to the edge of the platform and places on the brow of Walter, who kneels on the steps, a wreath of myrtle and laurel, whereupon he rises and she leads him to her father, before whom they both kneel. Pogner extends his hands in benediction over them.)

(Eva, die von Anfang des Auftrittes her in sicherer, ruhiger Haltung verblieben, und bei allen Vorgängen wie in seliger Geistesentrücktheit sich erhalten, hat Walther unverwandt zugehört; jetzt, während am Schlusse des Gesanges Volk und Meister, gerührt und ergriffen, unwillkürlich ihre Zustimmung ausdrücken, erhebt sie sich, schreitet an den Rand der Singerbühne, und drückt auf die Stirn Walthers, welcher zu den Stufen herangetreten ist und vor ihr sich niedergelassen hat, einen aus Lorbeer und Myrthen geflochtenen Kranz, worauf dieser sich erhebt und von ihr zu ihrem Vater geleitet wird, vor welchem Beide niederknieen; Pogner streckt segnend seine Hände über sie aus.)

Sachs.
        (Pointing to the group.)
My witness answered not amiss!
Do you find fault with me for this?

Sachs.
    (Deutet dem Volke mit der Hand auf die Gruppe.)
Den Zeugen, denk' es, wählt' ich gut;
Tragt ihr Hans Sachs drum üblen Muth?

People.
       (Jubilantly.)
Hans Sachs! No! It was well devised!
Your tact you 've once more exercised!

Volk.
       (Jubelnd.)
Hans Sachs! Nein! Das war schön erdacht!
Das habt ihr einmal wieder gut gemacht!

Several Master-Singers.
Now, Master Pogner! As you should,
Give him the honor of Masterhood!

Mehrere Meistersinger.
Auf, Meister Pogner! Euch zum Ruhm,
Meldet dem Junker sein Meisterthum.

Pogner.
(Bringing forward a gold chain with three medallions.)
Receive kind David's likeness true:
The Master's Guild is free to you.

Pogner.
(Eine goldene Kette mit drei Denkmünzen tragend.)
Geschmückt mit König David's Bild,
Nehm' ich euch auf in der Meister Gild'.

Walter.

(Shrinking back involuntarily.)
A Master ! Nay !
I 'll find reward some other way !

(The Masters look disconcertedly towards Sachs.)

Sachs.

(Grasping Walter by the hand.)
Disparage not the Master's ways,
But show respect to Art !
So heed my words :—
Honor your German Masters
If you would stay disasters !
For while they dwell in every heart,
Though should depart
The pride of holy Rome,
Still thrives at home
Our sacred German Art !

(All join enthusiastically in the last verse.— Eva takes
the crown from Walter's head and places it on Sachs's ; he
takes the chain from Pogner's hand and puts it round
Walter's neck.— Walter and Eva lean against Sachs, one
on each side : Pogner sinks on his knee before him as if
in homage. The Master-singers point to Sachs, with outstretched hands, as to their chief. While the Prentices
clap hands and shout and dance, the people wave hats and
'kerchiefs in enthusiasm.)

All. Hail Sachs ! Hans Sachs !
Hail Nuremberg's darling Sachs !

(The Curtain falls.)

Walther.

(Zuckt unwillkürlich heftig zurück.)
Nicht Meister ! Nein !
Will ohne Meister selig sein !
(Die Meister blicken in grosser Betretenheit auf Sachs)

Sachs.

(Walther fest bei der Hand fassend.)
Verachtet mir die Meister nicht,
Und ehrt mir ihre Kunst !
Drum sag' ich Euch :
Ehrt eure deutschen Meister,
Dann bannt ihr gute Geister !
Und gebt ihr ihrem Wirken Gunst,
Zerging' in Dunst
Das heil'ge röm'sche Reich
Uns bliebe gleich
Die heil'ge deutsche Kunst !

(Alle fallen begeistert in den Schlussvers ein. Eva
nimmt den Kranz von Walther's Stirn und drückt ihn
Sachs auf ; dieser nimmt die Kette aus Pogner's Hand,
und hängt sie Walther um, Walther und Eva lehnen sich
zu beiden Seiten an Sachsen's Schultern ; Pogner lässt
sich, wie huldigend, auf ein Knie vor Sachs nieder. Die
Meistersinger deuten mit erhobenen Händen auf Sachs, als
auf ihr Haupt. Während die Lehrbuben jauchzend in die
Hände schlagen und tanzen, schwenkt das Volk begeistert
Hüte und Tücher.)

Volk.

Heil Sachs ! Hans Sachs !
Heil Nürnberg's theurem Sachs !

(Der Vorhang fällt.)

PARSIFAL

For the basis of his last music-drama, "Parsifal," Wagner selected from the host of mediæval legends surrounding the Grail the version found in the poems of the old German Minnesinger, Wolfram von Eschenbach, modifying the details and enriching the meaning to suit his dramatic purposes. The idea of the Grail dates from the earliest times, and during the Middle Ages became a most poetic conception, representing the *Ideal* of the pious devotions of chivalry. It was the sacred chalice, of wonderful spiritual power, from which Christ drank at the Last Supper, and in which were caught the last drops of His blood as He hung on the cross. According to Wagner, both the Grail, and the Sacred Spear, with which Longinus pierced the side of Christ, were brought down from heaven by an angel host and given into the keeping of Titurel, who built for them a temple in the mountains of northern Spain (Monsalvat), and founded an order of knighthood to watch and protect the sacred relics. None but the pure in heart could find the magic temple; none but the noblest and bravest could remain in its service.

Titurel was succeeded by Amfortas, who fell a victim to the wiles of a witchwoman Kundry,[1] and was wounded in conflict with her master, the magician Klingsor, who wrested from Amfortas the Sacred Spear, with which he administered a wound which would not heal, though the unfortunate knight remained in life, through the sustaining power of the Grail. It was prophesied, however, that there should one day come to Monsalvat a youth (Parsifal), pure and unsophisticated, who should become wise through compassion (*durch Mitleid wissend*) and who, after having himself withstood temptation and evil, should regain the Spear, and by its aid heal Amfortas' wound. It is with the coming of Parsifal that the action commences.

[1] Kundry in the legend was the female prototype of the Wandering Jew; having mocked at Christ on the Cross, she was condemned to perpetual laughter. Wagner makes her a dual personality, who seeks expiation in zealous service to the Grail, and yet is condemned to lapse periodically into a magic sleep, during which she is bound to the powers of evil.

THE STORY OF THE DRAMA.

Act I. A wood near the Grail Mountain, where Gurnemanz and some young esquires are at their morning devotions. They are interrupted by the wild arrival of Kundry, who staggers in exhausted, bearing an ointment for Amfortas' wound. The latter then enters on his way to the bath, borne in a litter and attended by a train of knights. Though despairing of help, he takes the ointment and is carried to the lake. While Gurnemanz is relating the incidents which led to Amfortas' undoing, a wild swan, wounded to the death, flutters to the ground. In horror the esquires hasten to seize its slayer, and bring forward Parsifal, bow in hand, and unaware of the enormity of his deed. His replies to Gurnemanz' questions betray deep ignorance of himself and of the world; but Kundry relates what she knows of his birth and parentage, and Gurnemanz, in the hope that this is the "pure fool" (*der reine Thor*) promised in the prophecy, leads him toward the Temple of the Grail. Kundry has meanwhile crawled into the thicket and fallen into a deep sleep.

The scene changes gradually until the stage represents the interior of a vast hall, furnished with long tables, and Amfortas, in spite of the agony it causes him, uncovers the Grail; this becomes illumined, and the knights partake of the Lord's Supper. When the rite is finished, Parsifal, who has been an interested spectator of the scene, still shows no comprehension of its meaning; and Gurnemanz, in ill-humor, pushes him out of the hall.

ACT II. Klingsor's castle. Klingsor with sorcerer's arts, calls Kundry from her magic sleep, and bids her seduce Parsifal. While she pleads with him, Parsifal is heard mounting the ramparts and driving Klingsor's knights in headlong flight. The castle sinks with the sorcerer, and the scene changes to a luxuriant garden, where Parsifal enters, and is surrounded by flower girls, seeking to entice him. Finally Kundry, bound to Klingsor's service, appears in the guise of a beautiful woman, disperses the flower girls, and with devilish ingenuity attempts Parsifal's seduction. But at her first kiss, the knowledge of Amfortas' temptation and agony comes to him in a flood of compassion, and he casts her off. Enraged, she calls to her aid Klingsor, who hurls at Parsifal the Sacred Spear. It remains poised above the youth's head; he seizes it, and makes the sign of the cross, whereat the castle falls in ruins.

ACT III. A flowery meadow near the Grail Mountain. It is Good Friday. Gurnemanz, grown very old, discovers Kundry asleep in the thicket. He wakes her, and she sets at once to her menial tasks. Parsifal, in heavy armor, returns after years of wandering, bearing the Sacred Spear. Before leading him to Amfortas, Gurnemanz, overjoyed, removes his armor and sprinkles his head with water; while Kundry anoints his feet from a golden flask, and dries them with her hair. Bells are heard; the scene changes until the great hall is reached, as in Act I. The knights enter in solemn procession, bearing the wounded Amfortas. With the Spear, Parsifal touches his wound, which is healed. Kundry, redeemed, sinks back dead. Now the Grail glows with light, and a white dove descends to Parsifal, in heavenly benediction.

PUBLISHERS' NOTE.

IN Parsifal, the last of his completed works, Wagner's theories of dramatic composition reach their logical conclusion. Set musical forms are abolished; in their stead is reared a wonderful and colossal tone structure, developed almost entirely from a number of essential themes or motives — short musical sentences which characterize and are definitely associated with the personages and incidents of the drama, or with the ethical and spiritual ideas which underlie and govern the action. An acquaintance with at least the most important of these " leading motives " (*Leitmotiven*), will greatly aid the hearer to an intelligent appreciation of the musical side of the drama, its significance, and faithfulness to the poem. The publishers have therefore deemed it advisable to give the following list of themes, in the belief that it will prove of real use to operagoers, where excerpts from the score would be highly unsatisfactory. The themes are numbered for convenience; corresponding reference numerals are placed in the margin of the poem opposite the place or line, where each one occurs for the first time.

LEADING MOTIVES (LEITMOTIVEN) OF THE DRAMA

No. 1.   MOTIVE OF THE LAST SUPPER (DER LIEBESMAHL–SPRUCH).

No. 2.   MOTIVE OF THE GRAIL (GRALMOTIV).

No. 3.   FAITH MOTIVE (GLAUBENMOTIV).

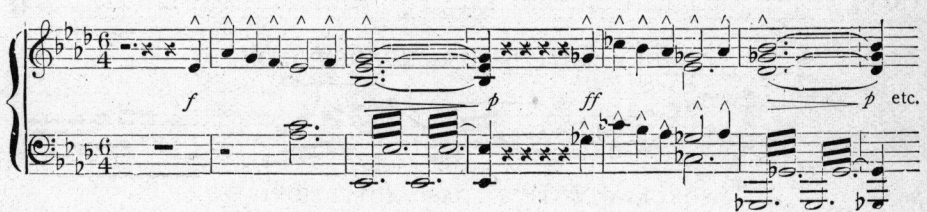

No. 4.   THE SAVIOUR'S CRY OF ANGUISH (SCHMERZENFIGUR).   (See No 1 a.)

No. 5.   SACRED SPEAR MOTIVE (DAS SPEERMOTIV).   (See No. 1 b.)

No. 6.   MOTIVE OF THE ORDER OF THE GRAIL (DAS MOTIV DER GRALSRITTER).

No. 7.   MOTIVE OF AMFORTAS' SUFFERING (AMFORTAS' LEIDENSMOTIV).

No. 8.   PROMISE OF REDEMPTION MOTIVE (DER VERHEISSUNGSSPRUCH).

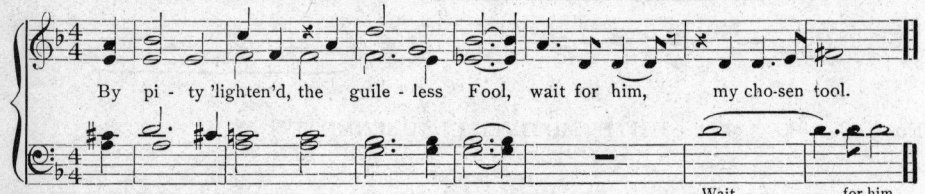

By pi - ty 'lighten'd, the guile - less Fool, wait for him, my cho-sen tool.

No. 9.   KUNDRY MOTIVE (DAS KUNDRYMOTIV).

No. 10.   SORCERY MOTIVE (DAS ZAUBERMOTIV).

No. 11.   KLINGSOR MOTIVE (DAS KLINGSORMOTIV).

No. 12.   PARSIFAL MOTIVE (DAS PARSIFALMOTIV).

No. 13.   HERZELEIDE MOTIVE (DAS HERZELEIDEMOTIV).

No. 14.   THE BELL THEME (DAS GLOCKENTHEMA).

No. 15   THE SAVIOUR'S LAMENT (DIE HEILANDSKLAGE).

No. 16.   MELODY OF THE FLOWER GIRLS (KOSEMELODIE).

No. 17   THEME OF KUNDRY'S NARRATIVE (KUNDRY'S ERZÄHLUNGSTHEMA).

No. 18. SECOND HERZELEIDE MOTIVE (DAS ZWEITE HERZELEIDEMOTIV).

No. 19.　GOOD FRIDAY MOTIVE (DAS CHARFREITAGMOTIV).

No. 20.　WILDERNESS MOTIVE (DAS THEMA DER ÖDE).

etc.

No. 21.　BAPTISM SCENE (DER SEGENSPRUCH).

etc.

No. 22.　GOOD FRIDAY SPELL (CHARFREITAGS ZAUBER).

etc.

PARSIFAL.

ACT I.	ERSTER AUFZUG.
PRELUDE. **1, 2, 3, 4, 5**	VORSPIEL.

Wald, schattig und ernst, doch nicht düster.

A Forest shadowy and impressive, but not gloomy. Rock-strewn ground. A glade in the middle. L. rises the way to the Grail's castle. The ground sinks in the middle at back to a low-lying forest lake. — Day dawn. — GURNEMANZ (an old but vigorous man) and two ESQUIRES (tender youths) are ensconced asleep under a tree. From L. as if from the castle, rises the solemn morning reveille of trombones.

Felsiger Boden. Eine Lichtung in der Mitte. Links aufsteigend wird der Weg zur Gralsburg angenommen. Der Mitte des Hintergrundes zu senkt sich der Boden zu einem tiefer gelegenen Waldsee hinab. — Tagesanbruch. — GURNEMANZ (rüstig greisenhaft) und zwei KNAPPEN (von zartem Jünglingsalter) sind schlafend unter einem Baume gelagert. — Von der linken Seite, wie von der Gralsburg her, ertönt der feierliche Morgenweckruf der Posaunen.

Gurnemanz
(waking, and shaking the ESQUIRES).

Hey! Ho! Wood-keepers twain!
Sleep-keepers I deem ye!
At least be moving with morning!

Gurnemanz
(erwachend und die KNAPPEN rüttend).

He! Ho! Waldhüter ihr!
Schlafhüter mitsammen!
So wacht doch mindest am Morgen!

(The two ESQUIRES spring up, and then immediately sink on their **2** knees again, ashamed.)

Hear ye the call? Now thank the Lord
That ye are called in time to hear it.

(Die beiden KNAPPEN springen auf, und senken sich, beschämt, sogleich wieder auf die Knie.)

Hört ihr den Ruf? Nun danket Gott,
dass ihr berufen ihn zu hören!

(He also falls on his knees with them; they offer up a silent morning prayer together; when the trombones have ceased, they rise **3** again.)

Now up, young vassals; see to the bath; **6**
'Tis time to wait there for our monarch: **7**
Already I behold approach
Runners before his litter bed.

(Er senkt sich zu ihnen ebenfalls nieder; gemeinschaftlich verrichten sie stumm ihr Morgengebet; sobald die Posaunen schweigen erheben sie sich dann.)

Jetzt auf, ihr Knaben; seht nach dem Bad;
Zeit ist's, des Königs dort zu harren:
dem Siechbett, das ihn trägt, voraus
seh' ich die Boten vor uns nah'n.

(Two KNIGHTS enter from the castle.)

Hail, both! How goes Amfortas' health?
He craves to-day his bath right early:
The simple that Gawaine
With bravest craft did win for him,
I'm hopeful it hath brought relief?

(Zwei RITTER treten, von der Burg her, auf.)

Heil euch! Wie geht's Amfortas heut'?
Wohl früh verlangt er nach dem Bade:
das Heilkraut, das Gawan
mit List und Kühnheit ihm gewann,
ich wähne, dass es Lind'rung schuf?

First Knight. Thou knowest all and still canst hope?
With keener smart than before
Full soon his pain returned:
Sleepless from strong oppression,
His bath he bade us to prepare.

Der erste Ritter. Das wähn'st du, der doch Alles weiss?
Ihm kehrten sehrender nur
die Schmerzen bald zurück:
schlaflos von starkem Bresten
befahl er eifrig uns das Bad.

Gurnemanz
(drooping his head sorrowfully).

Fools are we, alleviation seeking, **8**
When but one salve relieves him!
For ev'ry simple, ev'ry herb we search
And hunt wide through the world,
When helps but one thing —
And but one man.

Gurnemanz
(das Haupt traurig senkend).

Thoren wir, auf Lind'rung da zu hoffen,
wo einzig Heilung lindert!
Nach allen Kräutern, allen Tränken forsch'
und jagt weit durch die Welt:
ihm hilft nur Eines —
nur der Eine.

First Knight. Expound us that!

Erster Ritter. So nenn' uns den!

Gurnemanz	*Gurnemanz*
(evasively).	(ausweichend).
See to the bath!	Sorgt für das Bad!

First Esquire

(as he turns away towards the back with the second ESQUIRE looking off R.).

Behold yon frenzied horsewoman!

Second Esquire. Hey!
The mane of the devil's mare flyeth madly!

First Knight. Aye! Kundry 'tis.

Second Knight. With news she surely cometh?

First Esquire. The mare is tottering.

Second Esquire. Did she fly through air?

First Esquire. Now lowly she grovels.

Second Esquire. Mark her mane that brushes the moss.

First Knight. The wild witch has swung herself off.

KUNDRY rushes in hastily, almost reeling. Wild garb fastened up high; girdle of snakeskin hanging long, black hair flowing in loose locks; dark brownish red complexion, piercing black eyes, sometimes wild and blazing, but usually fixed and glassy. — She hurries to GURNEMANZ and presses upon him a small crystal flask.

Kundry. Here, take it! — Balsam!

Gurnemanz. From whence bringest thou this?

Kundry. From farther hence than thy thought
can guess;
If this balsam fail,
Arabia bears
Naught else that can give him ease. —
Ask no farther! — I am weary.

(She throws herself on the ground.)

A train of ESQUIRES and KNIGHTS appears L., bearing and attending the litter in which AMFORTAS lies stretched out. — GURNEMANZ immediately turns away from KUNDRY towards the newcomers.

Gurnemanz

(while the procession is entering).

He comes: by faithful servants carried. —
Alas! How can mine eyes have power
To see, in manhood's stately flower,
This sov'reign of the staunchest race
To stubborn sickness made a slave!

(to the ESQUIRES.)

Be heedful! Hark, your master groans.

(They stop and set down the litter.)

Amfortas

(raising himself slightly).

'Tis well! - My thanks! — Remain awhile. —

9

Der erste Knappe

(als er sich mit dem zweiten KNAPPEN dem Hindergrunde zuwendet nach rechts blickend).

Seht dort die wilde Reiterin!

Zweiter Knappe. Hei!
Wie fliegen der Teufelsmähre die Mähnen!

Erster Ritter. Ja! Kundry dort.

Zweiter Ritter. Die bringt wohl wicht'ge Kunde?

Erster Knappe. Die Mähre taumelt.

Zweiter Knappe. Flog sie durch die Luft?

Erster Knappe. Jetzt kriecht sie am Boden.

Zweiter Knappe. Mit den Mähnen fegt sie das
Moos.

Erster Ritter. Da schwang sich die Wilde herab.

KUNDRY stürzt hastig, fast taumelnd herein. Wilde Kleidung, hoch geschürzt; Gürtel von Schlangenhäuten lang herabhängend; schwarzes, in losen Zöpfen flatterndes Haar; tief braun-röthliche Gesichtsfarbe; stechende schwarze Augen, zuweilen wild aufblitzend, öfters wie todesstarr und unbeweglich. — Sie eilt auf GURNEMANZ zu und dringt ihm ein kleines Krystallgefäss auf.

Kundry. Hier nimm du! — Balsam!

Gurnemanz. Woher brachtest du diess?

Kundry. Von weiter her, als du denken kannst;
Hilft der Balsam nicht,
Arabien birgt
nichts mehr dann zu seinem Heil. —
Frag' nicht weiter! — Ich bin müde.

(Sie wirft sich auf den Boden.)

Ein Zug von KNAPPEN und RITTERN, die Sänfte tragend und geleitend, in welcher AMFORTAS ausgestreckt liegt, gelangt, von links her, auf die Bühne. — GURNEMANZ hat sich, von KUNDRY absogleich den Ankommenden zugewendet.

Gurnemanz

(während der Zug auf die Bühne gelangt).

Er naht: sie bringen ihn getragen. —
O weh'! Wie trag' ich's im Gemüthe,
in seiner Mannheit stolzer Blüthe
des siegreichsten Geschlechtes Herrn
als seines Siechthum's Knecht zu seh'n!

(Zu den KNAPPEN.)

Behutsam! Hört, der König stöhnt.

(Jene halten ein und stellen das Siechbett nieder.)

Amfortas

(der sich ein wenig erhoben).

So recht! — Habt Dank! — Ein wenig Rast. —

From madd'ning tortured nights
Fair morn to woods invites :
   Sure even me
The lake's pure wave will freshen ;
   My pain will flee
And tortured nights' oppression. —
Gawaine !

First Knight. Sire, Gawaine waited not :
   For, when the healing herb,
   Whose gain such toil hath needed,
   Did disappoint thy hopes,
He to another search in haste proceeded.

Amfortas. Unordered ? — May he be requited
   For slighting thus the Grail's commands !
   O woe to him, whom foes ne'er frighted,
   If he should fall in Klingsor's hands !
   Let none my feelings henceforth harry :
   For him, the promised one, I tarry.
   " By pity ' lightened " —
Was't not so — ?

Gurnemanz. 'Twas so thou said'st to us.

Amfortas. " The guileless Fool — "
   To me he doth unveil him, —
   Might I as Death but hail him !

Gurnemanz. But first behold : accord to this a
   trial.
       (He hands him the flask.)

Amfortas
       (regarding it).
From whence this wondrous-looking flask ?

Gurnemanz. 'Twas brought for thee from Araby
   afar.

Amfortas. Who went to win it ?

Gurnemanz. 'Twas she, yon woman wild.
   Up, Kundry ! come !
       (She refuses.)

Amfortas. Thou, Kundry ?
   Mak'st me again thy debtor,
   Thou restless, fearful maid ? —
   Well then !
Thy balsam I will even try,
In gratitude for thy good service.

Kundry
   (moving uneasily on the ground).
No thanks ! — Ha ha ! What will it help thee ?
No thanks ! — Go, go ! Thy bath !

AMFORTAS gives the sign to proceed ; the procession disappears
towards the valley. — GURNEMANZ, sadly looking after, and KUNDRY
still crouching on the ground, remain. — ESQUIRES pass to and fro.

Nach wilder Schmerzensnacht
nun Waldes-Morgenpracht ;
   im heil'gen See
wohl labt mich auch die Welle :
   es staunt das Weh',
die Schmerzensnacht wird helle. —
Gawan !

Erster Ritter. Herr, Gawan weilte nicht
   Da seines Krautes Kraft,
   wie schwer er's auch errungen,
   doch deine Hoffnung trog,
hat er auf neue Sucht sich fortgeschwungen.

Amfortas. Ohn' Urlaub ? — Möge das er sühnen
   dass schlecht er Gralsgebote hält !
   O wehe ihm, dem trotzig Kühnen,
   wenn er in Klingsor's Schlingen fällt !
   So breche Keiner mir den Frieden :
   ich harre dess', der mir beschieden.
   „ Durch Mitleid wissend " —
war's nicht so ?

Gurnemanz. Uns sagtest du es so.

Amfortas. „ der reine Thor " — — :
   mich dünkt, ihn zu erkennen : —
   dürft ich den Tod ihn nennen !

Gurnemanz. Doch hier zuvor : versuch' es noch
   mit diesem !
       (Er reicht ihm das Fläschchen.)

Amfortas
       (es betrachtend).
Woher diess heimliche Gefäss ?

Gurnemanz. Dir ward es aus Arabia hergeführt

Amfortas. Und wer gewann es ?

Gurnemanz. Da liegt's, das wilde Weib. —
   Auf, Kundry ! komm ' !   (Sie weigert sich.)

Amfortas. Du, Kundry ?
   Muss ich dir nochmals danken,
   du rastlos scheue Magd ? —
       Wohl denn !
   Den Balsam nun versuch' ich noch ;
   es sei aus Dank für deine Treu' !

Kundry
   (unruhig am Boden liegend)
Nicht Dank ! — Ha ha ! Was wird es helfen ?
Nicht Dank ! Fort, fort ! Zum Bad !

AMFORTAS giebt das Zeichen zum Aufbruch ; der Zug entfernt
sich nach dem tieferen Hintergrunde zu. — GURNEMANZ, schwermüthig nachblickend, und KUNDRY, fortwährend auf dem Boden gelagert
sind zurückgeblieben. — KNAPPEN gehen ab und zu.

7

Third Esquire
(a young man).
　　　Hey! Thou there! —
Why liest thou thus like a savage beast?

Kundry.   Are not beasts here safe and sacred?

Third Esquire.   Aye; but if thou art so,
　　We know not for certain yet.

Fourth Esquire
(also a young man).
With her enchanted drugs, I ween,
She'll bring destruction soon to our Master.

Gurnemanz.   Hm! — Hath she done harm to
　　ye? —
　　Wnen all are sore perplext
For ways to send tidings to distant lands,
　　Where warrior brethren are battling,
　　Their whereabouts scarcely known —
Who, ere ye are even resolved,
Starts and dashes thither and back,
The charge fulfilling with faith and knack?
She needs ye not, she's nigh you ne'er,
　　Nought common hath she with you;
But when ye need help in danger time,
She breathes the breath of zeal through your
　　ranks,
And never wants a word of thanks
　　If only thus she harm ye,
　　It need not so much alarm ye.

Third Esquire.   She hates us, though. —
See there, how hellishly she looks at us!

Fourth Esquire.   'Tis a Pagan, sure; a sorceress.

Gurnemanz.   Yea, under a curse she may have
　　been:
　　　Here now's her home, —
　　　Renewed become,
That of her sins she may be shriven
From former life yet unforgiven,
Seeking her shrift by such good actions
As advantage all our knightly factions
Sure she does well in working thus:
Serves herself and also us.

Third Esquire   Then is it not surely her fault
So much distress hath come on us?

Gurnemanz.   Aye, when she often stayed afar
　　from us
Then broke misfortune ever in.
　　I long have known her now;
　　But Titurel knew her yet longer:
When he yon castle consecrated,

Dritter Knappe
(junger Mann).
　　　He! Du da! —
Was liegst du dort wie ein wildes Thier?

Kundry.   Sind die Thiere hier nicht heilig?

Dritter Knappe.   Ja! doch ob heilig du,
　　das wissen wir grad' noch nicht.

Vierter Knappe
(ebenfalls junger Mann).
　　Mit ihrem Zaubersafte, wähn' ich,
　　wird sie den Meister vollends verderben.

Gurnemanz.   Hm! — Schuf sie euch Schaden
　　je? —
　　　Wann Alles rathlos steht
　　wie kämpfenden Brüdern in fernste Länder
　　　Kunde sei zu entsenden,
　　und kaum ihr nur wisst, wohin? —
Wer, ehe ihr euch nur besinnt,
stürmt und fliegt dahin und zurück,
der Botschaft pflegend mit Treu' und Glück?
Ihr nährt sie nicht, sie naht euch nie,
　　nichts hat sie mit euch gemein;
doch wann's in Gefahr der Hilfe gilt,
der Eifer führt sie schier durch die Luft,
die nie euch dann zum Danke ruft.
　　Ich wähne, ist diess Schaden,
　　so thät' er euch gut gerathen?

Dritter Knappe.   Doch hasst sie uns. —
Sieh' nur, wie hämisch sie dort nach uns blickt!

Vierter Knappe.   Eine Heidin ist's, ein Zauber-
　　weib.

Gurnemanz.   Ja, eine Verwünschte mag sie sein:
　　hier lebt sie heut', —
　　vielleicht erneu't,
zu büssen Schuld aus früher'm Leben,
die dorten ihr noch nicht vergeben.
Uebt sie nun Buss' in solchen Thaten,
die uns Ritterschaft zum Heil gerathen.
gut thut sie dann ganz sicherlich,
dienet uns, und hilft auch sich.

Dritter Knappe.   Dann ist's wohl auch jen' ihre
　　Schuld,
　　was uns so manche Noth gebracht?

Gurnemanz.   Ja, wann sie oft uns lange ferne
　　blieb,
　　dann brach ein Unglück wohl herein.
　　Und lang' schon kenn' ich sie:
　　noch länger kennt sie Titurel:
　　der fand, als er die Burg dort weih'te,

He found her sleeping in this wood,
  All stiff, rigid, like death.
Thus I myself did find her lately,
Just when the trouble came on us
Which yonder miscreant beyond the mountain
So shamefully did bring about. —
                    (to KUNDRY).
Hey, thou ! — Hearken and say :
Where wert thou wandering around
When our commander lost the spear ?
            (KUNDRY is silent.)
Wherefore didst thou not help us then ?

Kundry.   I never help.

Fourth Esquire.   She says't herself.

Third Esquire.   If she's so true and void of fear,
Then send her to search for the missing spear.

Gurnemanz
                (gloomily).
          That is quite diff'rent ! —
  'Tis denied to all. —
            (with deep emotion).
  Oh, wounding, wonderful
      and hallowéd spear !
      I saw thee swayed
      by th' unholiest hand ! —
          (becoming lost in remembrance).
When thus equipped, Amfortas, all too bold one,
      Who could thine arm be staying
      Th' enchanter from essaying ?
While near the walls, from us the king was ta'en :
A maid of fearful beauty turned his brain.
   He lay bewitched, her form enfolding,
      The spear no longer holding : —
      A deathly cry ! — I rushed anigh ; —
      But laughing, Klingsor fled before;
      The sacred spear away he bore.
I fought to aid the flying king's returning ;
A fatal wound, though, in his side was burning.
That wound it is which none may make to close.

Third Esquire.   Thou knewest then Klingsor ?

Gurnemanz
    (to the first and second ESQUIRES who come from the lake).
                How fares the king now ?

Second Esquire.   Refreshed by 's bath.

First Esquire.   The balsam soothes the smart.

Gurnemanz
                (after some silence).
That wound it is which none may make to close.

---

sie schlafend hier im Waldgestrüpp',
  erstarrt, leblos, wie todt.
So fand ich selbst sie letztlich wieder,
  als uns das Unheil kaum gescheh'n,
  das jener Böse dort über'm Berge
  So schmählich über uns gebracht. —
                    (Zu KUNDRY.)
He ! Du ! — Hör' mich, und sag' :
wo schweiftest damals du umher,
  als unser Herr den Speer verlor ? —
            (KUNDRY schweigt.)
Warum halfst du uns damals nicht ?

Kundry.   Ich helfe nie.

Vierter Knappe.   Sie sagt's da selbst.

Dritter Knappe.   Ist sie so treu und kühn im
    Wehr,
  so sende sie nach dem verlor'nen Speer !

Gurnemanz
                (düster).
          Das ist ein And'res : —
  jedem ist's verwehrt. —
            (Mit grosser Ergriffenheit.)
  Oh, wunden-wundervoller
      heiliger Speer !
      Dich sah ich schwingen
      von unheiligster Hand ! —
          (In Erinnerung sich verlierend.)
Mit ihm bewehrt, Amfortas, allzukühner,
      wer mochte dir es wehren
      den Zaub'rer zu beheeren ? — —
Schon nah' dem Schloss, wird uns der Held
    entrückt :
ein furchtbar schönes Weib hat ihn entzückt :
  in seinen Armen liegt er trunken,
      der Speer ist ihm entsunken ; —
      ein Todesschrei ! — ich stürm' herbei : —
      von dannen Klingsor lachend schwand,
      den heil'gen Speer hat er entwandt.
Des Königs Flucht gab kämpfend ich Geleite ;
doch eine Wunde brannt' ihm in der Seite :
die Wunde ist's, die nie sich schliessen will.

Dritter Knappe.   So kanntest du Klingsor ?

Gurnemanz
(zu dem ersten und zweiten KNAPPEN, welche vom See her kommen)
                Wie geht's dem König ?

Zweiter Knappe.   Ihn frischt das Bad.

Erster Knappe.   Dem Balsam wich der Schmerz

Gurnemanz
                (nach einem Schweigen).
Die Wunde ist's, die nie sich schliessen will ! —

Third Esquire. But look ye now, father, I'd like
  to know : —
  Thou knewest Klingsor : how was that so ?

(The third and fourth ESQUIRES have now seated themselves at
GURNEMANZ' feet ; the other two do likewise.)

Gurnemanz. Titurel, the pious lord,
      He knew him well ;
For, when the savage foe with craft and might
    The true believers' kingdom rended,
Anon to him, in midst of holy night
    The Saviour's messengers descended.
The sacred Cup, the vessel pure, unstainéd,
Which at the Last Passover Feast He drainéd, — 1
Which at the Cross received His holy blood,
With eke the Spear that shed the sacred flood, — 5
These signs and tokens of a worth untold
The angels gave into our monarch's hold.
A house he builded for the holy things.
    Ye, who their service have attained to
    By paths no sinners ever gained to,
      Ye know 'tis but permitted
      The pure to be admitted
'Mid those the Grail's divinely magic power
With strength for high salvation's work doth
    dower.
He whom you named had therefore been denied:—
Klingsor — however long and hard he tried.
Far in yon valley then he found asylum ;
For over there 'tis rankest Pagan land.
I ne'er found out what sin he had committed ;
Absolved he now would be, yea, holy even.
Unable in himself to stifle thoughts of evil,
    He set to work with guilty hand,
    Resolved to gain the Grail's command ;
But with contempt was by its guardian spurned.
Wherefore in rage hath Klingsor surely learn'd
    How by the damnable act he wrought
    An infamous magic might be taught ;
      Which now he's found : —
The waste he hath transformed to wondrous
    gardens
    Where women bide, of charms infernal ;
Thither he seeks to draw the Grail's true wardens
    To wicked joys and pain eternal ;
    Those who are lured find him their master :
    To many happens such disaster. —
When Titurel decayed in manhood's power
And with the regal might his son did dower
    Amfortas gave himself no rest,
    But sought to quell this magic pest ;
    The sequel ye have all been told ;
    The spear is now in Klingsor's hold.
Even the holy it can cleave asunder :
The Grail already he counts as his plunder.

(During the above, KUNDRY has several times turned round
quickly in angry unrest.)

Dritter Knappe. Doch, Väterchen, sag' und
    lehr' uns fein :
  du kanntest Klingsor, — wie mag das sein ?

(Der dritte und der vierte KNAPPE hatten sich zuletzt schon zu
GURNEMANZ' Füssen niedergesetzt ; die beiden anderen gesellen
sich jetzt gleicher Weise zu ihnen.)

Gurnemanz. Titurel, der fromme Held,
      der kannt' ihn wohl.
Denn ihm, da wilder Feinde List und Macht
    des reinen Glauben's Reich bedrohten,
ihm neigten sich in heilig ernster Nacht
    dereinst des Heiland's sel'ge Boten :
    daraus er trank beim letzten Liebesmahle,
    das Weihgefäss, die heilig edle Schale,
    darein am Kreuz sein göttlich Blut auch floss,
    zugleich den Lanzenspeer, der diess vergoss, —
    der Zeugengüter höchstes Wundergut, —
    das gaben sie in uns'res König's Hut.
Dem Heilthum baute er das Heiligthum.
    Die seinem Dienst ihr zugesindet
    auf Pfaden, die kein Sünder findet,
      ihr wisst, dass nur dem Reinen
      vergönnt ist sich zu einen
    den Brüdern, die zu höchsten Rettungswerken
des Grales heil'ge Wunderkräfte stärken :
d'rum blieb es dem, nach dem ihr fragt, verwehrt,
Klingsor'n, so hart ihm Müh' auch drob be
    schwert.
11 Jenseits im Thale war er eingesiedelt ;
    darüber hin liegt üpp'ges Heidenland :
unkund blieb mir, was dorten er gesündigt ;
doch büssen wollt' er nun, ja heilig werden.
Ohnmächtig, in sich selbst die Sünde zu ertödten
    an sich legt er die Frevlerhand,
    die nun, dem Grale zugewandt,
verachtungsvoll dess' Hüter von sich stiess ;
darob die Wuth nun Klingsor'n unterwies,
    wie seines schmählichen Opfers That
    ihm gäbe zu bösem Zauber Rath ;
      den fand er jetzt : —
die Wüste schuf er sich zum Wonnegarten
    d'rinn wachsen teuflisch holde Frauen ;
dort will des Grales Ritter er erwarten
    zu böser Lust und Höllengrauen :
    wen er verlockt, hat er erworben ;
    schon Viele hat er uns verdorben. —
Da Titurel, in hohen Alter's Mühen,
    dem Sohne nun die Herrschaft hier verliehen,
    Amfortas' liess es da nicht ruh'n
    der Zauberplag' Einhalt zu thun ;
    das wisst ihr, wie es da sich fand :
    der Speer ist nun in Klingsor's Hand ;
kann er selbst Heilige mit dem verwunden.
den Gral auch wähnt er fest schon uns entwun
    den.

(KUNDRY hat sich, in wüthender Unruhe, oft heftig umgewendet)

Fourth Esquire. Behoves us then that spear
soon to reclaim.

Third Esquire. Ha! he who could would get
both joy and fame.

Gurnemanz
(after a silence).
Before the plundered sanctuary
In pray'r impassioned knelt Amfortas,
Imploring for a sign of safety:
A heav'nly radiance from the Grail then floated;
A sacred phantom face
From lips divine did chase
These words, whose purport clearly could be
noted: —
   " By pity 'lightened
   A guileless Fool; —
   Wait for him
   My chosen tool."

(The four ESQUIRES with deep awe repeat the oracular words.)
From the lake come cries and exclamations of the

Knights and Esquires. Woe! Horror! — Hoho!
Up! Who is the culprit?

GURNEMANZ and the four ESQUIRES start up and turn round in
alarm. A wild swan flutters feebly from over the lake, strives to
keep up, and finally sinks dying to the ground. Meanwhile: —

Gurnemanz. What is 't?

First Esquire. There!

Second Esquire. Here — a swan!

Third Esquire. A poor wild swan!

Fourth Esquire. It hath been wounded.

Other Esquires
(rushing on from the lake).
Ha! Horror! Woe!

Gurnemanz. Who shot the swan?

Second Knight
(advancing).
The king esteemed it a happy token,
When over the lake it circled aloft:
   Then flew a dart, —

More Esquires
(bringing forward PARSIFAL).
He 'twas! He shot! Here's the weapon.
See this arrow, like his own.

Gurnemanz
(to PARSIFAL).
Is't thou, that dealt this swan its death blow?

Parsifal. For sure; in flight I hit all that flies.

Gurnemanz. This thou hast done? And hast
no sorrow for thy deed?

Vierter Knappe. Vor Allem nun: der Speer
kehr' uns zurück!

Dritter Knappe. Ha! wer ihn brächt', ihm wär's
zu Ruhm und Glück!

Gurnemanz
(nach einem Schweigen).
Vor dem verwaisten Heiligthum
in brünst'gem Beten lag Amfortas,
ein Rettungszeichen heiss erflehend:
ein sel'ger Schimmer da entfloss dem Grale;
ein heilig' Traumgesicht
nun deutlich zu ihm spricht
durch hell erschauter Wortezeichen Male: —
   „ durch Mitleid wissend
   der reine Thor,
   harre sein',
   den ich erkor."

(Die vier KNAPPEN wiederholen, in grosser Ergriffenheit, den Spruch)
Vom See her hört man Geschrei und das Rufen der

Ritter und Knappen. Weh'! Wehe! — Hoho!
Auf! — Wer ist der Frevler?

GURNEMANZ und die vier KNAPPEN fahren auf und wenden sich
erschrocken um. — Ein wilder Schwan flattert matten Fluges vom
See daher; er ist verwundet, erhält sich mühsam und sinkt endlich
sterbend zu Boden. — Während dem: —

Gurnemanz. Was giebt's?

Erster Knappe. Dort!

Zweiter Knappe. Hier! Ein Schwan.

Dritter Knappe. Ein wilder Schwan!

Vierter Knappe. Er ist verwundet.

Andere Knappen
(vom See her stürmend).
Ha! Wehe! Weh'!

Gurnemanz. Wer schos den Schwan?

Der zweite Ritter
(hervorkommend).
Der König grüsst' ihn als gutes Zeichen,
als über dem See dort kreis'te der Schwan:
   da flog ein Pfeil —

Neue Knappen
(PARSIFAL vorführend).
Der war's! Der schoss! Diess der Bogen!
Hier der Pfeil, den seinen gleich.

Gurnemanz
(zu PARSIFAL).
Bist du's, der diesen Schwan erlegte?

Parsifal. Gewiss! Im Fluge treff' ich was

Gurnemanz. Du thatest das? Und bangt' es
dich nicht vor der That?

The Esquires.　Punish the culprit!

Gurnemanz.　Unconceived of fact!
Couldst thou do murder? Here in holy forests,
　Whose quiet peace o'erspreads thy path?
The beasts around, didst thou not find them tame?
　Were they not friendly and fond?
　From the branches what warbled the birds to
　　thee?
　　　How harmed thee that goodly swan?
To look for his mate he flew aloft,
With her to hover over the lake,
Thus consecrating for us the health-giving bath.
　Thou didst not revere, but lusted for
　A wild puerile shot of the bow.
　He was our joy: what is he to thee?
　Here — behold! — thy arrow struck; —
There stiffens his blood; hang pow'rless the
　　pinions,
　The snowy plumage darkly besplashed, —
　Extinguished his eye; — mark'st thou its look?
　Art thou now conscious of thy trespass?

(PARSIFAL has listened to his words with increasing attention; he
now breaks his bow and casts his arrows away.)

Say, boy? Perceivest thou thy heinous sin?

(PARSIFAL draws his hand across his eyes.)

How couldst thou have acted thus?

Parsifal.　I knew not 'twas wrong

Gurnemanz.　Whence comest thou?

Parsifal.　I do not know.

Gurnemanz.　Who is thy father?

Parsifal.　I do not know.

Gurnemanz.　Who bade thee wander this way?

Parsifal.　I know not.

Gurnemanz.　Thy name then?

Parsifal.　I once had many,
But now I know not one of them.

Gurnemanz.　Thou know'st not anything?

(aside).
　　　　　　　　A dolt so dull
I never found, save Kundry here.

(to the ESQUIRES who have assembled in still greater numbers).
　　　　　　　　　　　Now go
Nor leave the king in his bath alone! — Help.

(The ESQUIRES lift up the swan reverently and bear it away towards
the lake.)

Gurnemanz
　　　　　(turning again to PARSIFAL).

Now say! Nought know'st of all I have asked
　　thee;
　Declare then what thou know'st:
　Of something must thou have knowledge.

Die Knappen.　Strafe den Frevler!

Gurnemanz.　Unerhörtes Werk!
Du konntest morden? Hier im heil'gen Walde,
　dess' stiller Frieden dich umfing?
Des Haines Thiere nahten dir nicht zahm,
　grüssten dich freundlich und fromm?
　Aus den Zweigen, was sangen die Vöglein dir?
　　Was that dir der treue Schwan?
　Sein Weibchen zu suchen flog der auf,
　mit ihm zu kreisen über dem See,
den so er herrlich weih'te zum heilenden Bad.
　dem stauntest du nicht, dich lockt' es nur
　zu wild kindischem Bogengeschoss? —
　Er war uns hold: was ist er nun dir?
　Hier — schau' her! — hier traf'st du ihn:
da starrt noch das Blut, matt hängen die Flügel;
　das Schneegefieder dunkel befleckt, —
　gebrochen das Aug', siehst du den Blick?
　Wirst deiner Sündenthat du inne? —

(PARSIFAL hat ihm mit wachsender Ergriffenheit zugehört: jetzt
zerbricht er seinen Bogen und schleudert die Pfeile von sich.)

Sag', Knab'! Erkennst du deine grosse Schuld!

(PARSIFAL führt die Hand über die Augen.)

Wie konntest du sie begeh'n?

Parsifal.　Ich wusste sie nicht.

Gurnemanz.　Wo bist du her?

Parsifal.　Das weiss ich nicht.

Gurnemanz.　Wer ist dein Vater?

Parsifal.　Das weiss ich nicht.

Gurnemanz.　Wer sandte dich dieses Weg's?

Parsifal.　Ich weiss nicht.

Gurnemanz.　Dein Name dann?

Parsifal.　Ich hatte viele
　doch weiss ich ihrer keinen mehr.

Gurnemanz.　Das weisst du Alles nicht?

(Für sich:)
　　　　　　So dumm wie den
erfand ich bisher Kundry nur. —

(Zu den KNAPPEN, deren sich immer mehre versammelt haben.)
　　　　　　　Jetzt geht!
Versäumt den König im Bade nicht! — Helft!

(Die KNAPPEN haben den Schwan ehrerbietig aufgenommen, und
entfernen sich mit ihm jetzt nach dem See zu.)

Gurnemanz
　　　　　(sich wieder zu PARSIFAL wendend).

Nun sag'! Nichts weisst du, was ich dich frage
　jetzt melde, was du weisst!
　denn etwas musst du doch wissen.

13

Parsifal. I have a mother; Heart's Affliction 13
   she's hight:
The woods and the waste of moorlands were
   our abode.

Gurnemanz. Who gave thee that weapon?

Parsifal. I made it myself,
   To drive the savage eagles from the forest.

Gurnemanz. But eagle-like seem'st thyself, and
   well descended:
Why did thy mother not teach thee
   Manlier weapons to handle?
       (PARSIFAL remains silent.)

Kundry
  (who, still crouching by the wood, has glanced sharply at PARSIFAL,
now breaks in with hoarse tones).
Bereft of father his mother bore him,
For in battle perished Gamuret:
From like untimely hero's death
To save her offspring, strange to arms
She reared him a witless fool in deserts.—
   What folly!
       (She laughs.)

Parsifal
   (who has listened with sharp attention).
Aye, and once along the hem of the wood,
   Most noble beasts bestriding,
   Passed by men all a-glitter;
   Fain had I been like them;
   With laughter they galloped away.
Now I pursue; but cannot as yet o'ertake them;
   Through deserts I've wandered, o'er hill and
   dale;
   Oft fell the night, then followed day:
   My bow was forced to defend me
   'Gainst the wolves and mighty peoples.

Kundry
      (warmly).
Yes, caitiffs and giants fell to his might;
The fierce-striking boy brings fear on their
   spirits.

Parsifal. Who feareth me, say?

Kundry. The wicked.

Parsifal. Those who attacked me, were they
   then bad?
      (GURNEMANZ laughs.)
Who is good?

Gurnemanz
     (earnestly).
   Thy dear mother, whom thou forsookest,
And who for thee must now mourn and grieve.

Kundry. She grieves no more; for his mother is
   dead.

Parsifal. Ich hab' eine Mutter; Herzeleide sie
   heisst:
im Wald und auf wilder Aue waren wir heim.

Gurnemanz. Wer gab dir den Bogen?

Parsifal. Den schuf ich mir selbst,
   vom Forst die rauhen Adler zu scheuchen.

Gurnemanz. Doch adelig scheinst du selbst und
   hochgeboren:
warum nicht liess deine Mutter
   bessere Waffen dich lehren?
       (PARSIFAL schweigt.)

Kundry
  (Welche, in der Waldecke gelagert, den Blick scharf auf PARSIFAL
gerichtet hat, ruft mit rauher Stimme hinein).
Den Vaterlosen gebar die Mutter,
als im Kampf erschlagen Gamuret;
vor gleichem frühen Heldentod
den Sohn zu wahren, waffenfremd
in Oeden erzog sie ihn zum Thoren —
   die Thörin!
      (Sie lacht.)

Parsifal
   (der mit jäher Aufmerksamkeit zugehört).
Ja! Und einst am Waldessaume vorbei,
   auf schönen Thieren sitzend,
   kamen glänzende Männer:
   ihnen wollt' ich gleichen;
   sie lachten und jagten davon.
Nun lief ich nach, doch konnte sie nicht erreichen;
   durch Wildnisse kam ich, bergauf, thalab;
   oft ward es Nacht; dann wieder Tag:
   mein Bogen musste mir frommen
   gegen Wild und grosse Männer.

Kundry
     (eifrig).
Ja, Schächer und Riesen traf seine Kraft
den freislichen Knaben fürchten sie Alle.

Parsifal. Wer fürchtet mich? Sag'!

Kundry. Die Bösen.

Parsifal. Die mich bedrohten, waren sie bös'?
      (GURNEMANZ lacht.)
Wer ist gut?

Gurnemanz
     (ernst).
   Deine Mutter, der du entlaufen,
und die um dich sich nun härmt und grämt.

Kundry. Zu End' ihr Gram: seine Mutter ist
   todt.

Parsifal
(in fearful alarm).
Dead ? — what, my mother ? — who says so ?

Kundry.   I rode along and saw her dying ;
Poor fool, she sent thee her blessing.

(PARSIFAL springs upon KUNDRY, raging, and seizes her by the throat.)

Gurnemanz
(holding him back).
Insensate stripling !   Outrage again ? —
What harm has she done ?   She speaks the truth.
For Kundry lies not, and much has seen.

(After GURNEMANZ has released KUNDRY, PARSIFAL stands awhile as if turned to stone ; then he is seized with a violent trembling.)

Parsifal.   I — am fainting !

(KUNDRY has hastily sprung to a brook, brings water now in a horn, sprinkles PARSIFAL with some, and then gives him to drink.)

Gurnemanz.   'Tis well !   Thus has the Grail
     directed :
He ousteth ill who doth give for it good.

Kundry
(sadly turning away).
I do no good thing ; — but rest I long for.

(Whilst GURNEMANZ is attending to PARSIFAL with fatherly care, KUNDRY, unperceived by them, crawls towards a thicket.)

But rest, but rest !   Alas, I'm weary ! —
Slumber ! — Oh, would that none might wake me !
(starting timidly).
No ! I'll sleep not ! — Terror grips me.

(She gives a suppressed cry and falls into a violent trembling ; then she lets her arms drop powerless, and her head sinks low, and staggers a little farther.)

Vain to resist !   The time has come.
Slumber — slumber — : I must.

(She sinks down behind the thicket and is seen no more. A stir is perceived down by the lake, and the train of KNIGHTS and ESQUIRES with the litter passes back homewards at back.)

Gurnemanz.   From bathing comes the king again ;
     High stands the sun now :
Let me to the holy Feast then conduct thee ;
     For — an thou'rt pure,
Surely the Grail will feed and refresh thee.

(He has gently laid PARSIFAL's arm on his own neck, and, supporting his body with his arm, leads him slowly along.)

Parsifal.   What is the Grail ?

Gurnemanz.   I may not say :
But if to serve it thou be bidden,
Knowledge of it will not be hidden. —
     And lo ! —
Methinks I know thee now indeed :
No earthly road to it doth lead,
By no one can it be detected
Who by itself is not elected.

Parsifal
(in furchtbarem Schrecken).
Todt ? — Meine Mutter ? — Wer sagt' es ?

Kundry.   Ich ritt vorbei, und sah sie sterben :
dich Thoren hiess sie mich grüssen.

(PARSIFAL springt wüthend auf KUNDRY zu und fasst sie bei der Kehle.)

Gurnemanz
(ihn zurückhaltend).
Verrückter Knabe !   Wieder Gewalt ?
Was that dir das Weib ?   Es sagte wahr.
Denn nie lügt Kundry, doch sah sie viel.

(Nachdem GURNEMANZ KUNDRY befreit, steht PARSIFAL lange wie erstarrt ; dann geräth er in ein heftiges Zittern.)

Parsifal.   Ich — verschmachte ! —

(KUNDRY ist hastig an einen Waldquell gesprungen, bringt jetzt Wasser in einem Horne, besprengt damit zunächst PARSIFAL, und reicht ihm dann zu trinken.)

Gurnemanz.   So recht !   So nach des Grales
     Gnade :
das Böse bannt, wer's mit Gutem vergilt.

Kundry
(traurig sich abwendend).
Nie thu' ich Gutes ; — nur Ruhe will ich.

(Während GURNEMANZ sich väterlich um PARSIFAL bemüht, schleppt sich KUNDRY, von Beiden unbeachtet, einem Waldgebüsche zu.)

Nur Ruhe ! Ruhe, ach, der Müden ! —
Schlafen ! — Oh, dass mich keiner wecke !
(Scheu auffahrend).
Nein ! Nicht schlafen ! — Grausen fasst mich !

(Nach einem dumpfen Schrei verfällt sie in heftiges Zittern ; dann lässt sie die Arme matt sinken, neigt das Haupt tief, und schwankt matt weiter.)

Machtlose Wehr !   Die Zeit ist da.
Schlafen — schlafen — : ich muss.

(Sie sinkt hinter dem Gebüsch zusammen, und bleibt von jetzt an unbemerkt. — Vom See her vernimmt man Bewegung, und gewahrt den im Hintergrunde sich heimwärts wendenden Zug der RITTER und KNAPPEN mit der Sänfte.)

Gurnemanz.   Vom Bade kehrt der König heim ;
     hoch steht die Sonne :
nun lass' mich zum frommen Mahl dich geleiten
     denn, — bist du rein,
wird nun der Gral dich tränken und speisen.

(Er hat PARSIFAL's Arm sich sanft um den Nacken gelegt, und hält dessen Leib mit seinem eigenen Arme umschlungen ; so geleitet er ihn bei sehr allmählichem Schreiten.)

Parsifal.   Wer ist der Gral ?

Gurnemanz.   Das sagt sich nicht ;
doch bist du selbst zu ihm erkoren,
bleibt dir die Kunde unverloren. —
     Und sieh' ! —
Mich dünkt, dass ich dich recht erkannt :
kein Weg führt zu ihm durch das Land,
und Niemand könnte ihn beschreiten,
den er nicht selber möcht' geleiten.

Parsifal. I scarcely move, —
    Yet swiftly seem to run.

Gurnemanz. My son, thou seest
    Here Space and Time are one.

Gradually, while PARSIFAL and GURNEMANZ appear to walk, the
scene changes imperceptibly from L. to R. The forest disappears ; a
door opens in rocky cliffs and conceals the two ; they are then seen
again in sloping passages which they appear to ascend. — Long
sustained trombone notes softly swell, approaching peals of bells are
heard. — At last they arrive at a mighty hall, which loses itself over-
head in a high vaulted dome down from which alone the light streams
in. — From the heights above the dome the increasing sound of chimes.

Gurnemanz
    (turning to PARSIFAL who stands spellbound).

    Now give good heed, and let me see,
      If thou'rt a Fool and pure,
    What wisdom thou presently canst secure.—

At each side in the background a large door opens. From the R.
enter slowly the KNIGHTS of the GRAIL in solemn procession, and
range themselves, during the following chorus, by degrees at two long
covered tables which are placed endways towards the audience, one on
each side, leaving the middle of the stage free. Only cups — no dishes
— stand on them.

The Knights of the Grail. The Holy Supper duly
      Prepare we day by day,
    As on that last time truly
      The soul it still may stay.
    Who lives to do good deeds
      This Meal for ever feeds ;
    The Cup his hand may lift
      And claim the purest gift.

Voices of younger Men
    (coming from the mid-height of the hall).

    As anguished and lowly
      His life stream's spilling
    For sinners He did offer,
      For the Saviour holy
    With heart free and willing
      My blood I now will proffer.
    His body, given our sins to shrive,
    Through death becomes in us alive.

Boys' voices
    (from the summit of the dome).

      His love endures,
      The dove upsoars,
    The Saviour's sacred token.
      Take the wine red,
      For you 'twas shed ;
    Let Bread of Life be broken.

Through the opposite door AMFORTAS is brought in on his litter
by ESQUIRES and serving brethren : before him march boys who bear a
shrine draped in purple-red cloth. This procession wends to the
center of the background, where, overhung by a canopy stands a raised
couch. On this AMFORTAS is placed ; before it stands an altar-like,
longish marble table, on which the boys place the shrine, still covered. —
When the song is ended and the KNIGHTS have all taken their
seats there is a long pause and silence. — From the distant back is
heard, from an arched niche behind AMFORTAS' throne, as from a
grave, the voice of old

Parsifal. Ich schreite kaum, —
    doch wähn' ich mich schon weit.

Gurnemanz. Du siehst, mein Sohn,
    zum Raum wird hier die Zeit.

Allmählich, während GURNEMANZ und PARSIFAL zu schreiten
scheinen, verwandelt sich die Bühne, von links nach rechts hin, in
unmerklicher Weise : es verschwindet so der Wald ; in Felsenwänden
öffnet sich ein Thor, welches nun die Beiden einschliesst ; dann
wieder werden sie in aufsteigenden Gängen sichtbar, welche sie zu
durchschreiten scheinen. — Lang gehaltene Posaunentöne schwellen
sanft an : näher kommendes Glockengeläute. — Endlich sind sie in einem
mächtigen Saale angekommen, welcher nach oben in eine hochgewölbte
Kuppel, durch die einzig das Licht hereindringt sich verliert. — Von der
Höhe über der Kuppel her vernimmt man wachsendes Geläute.

Gurnemanz
    (sich zu PARSIFAL wendend, der wie verzaubert steht).

    Jetzt achte wohl ; und lass' mich seh'n,
      bist du ein Thor und rein,
    welch Wissen dir auch mag beschieden sein. —

Auf beiden Seiten des Hintergrundes wird je eine grosse Thür
geöffnet. Von rechts schreiten die RITTER des GRALES, in feierlichem Zuge, herein, und reihen sich, unter dem folgenden Gesange,
nach und nach an zwei überdeckten langen Speisetafeln, welche so
gestellt sind, dass sie, von hinten nach vorn parallel laufend, die Mitte
des Saale frei lassen : nur Becher, keine Gerichte stehen darauf.

Die Gralsritter. Zum letzten Liebesmahle
    gerüstet Tag für Tag,
    gleich ob zum letzten Male
    es heut' ihn letzen mag,
    wer guter That sich freu't,
    ihm sei das Mahl erneu't :
    der Labung darf er nah'n,
    die hehrste Gab' empfah'n.

Jüngere Männerstimmen
    (von der mittleren Höhe des Saales her vernehmbar).

    Den sündigen Welten
      mit tausend Schmerzen
    wie einst sein Blut geflossen,
      dem Erlösungs-Helden
      mit freudigem Herzen
      sei nun mein Blut vergossen.
    Den Leib, den er zur Sühn' uns bot,
    er leb' in uns durch seinen Tod.

Knabenstimmen
    (aus der äussersten Höhe der Kuppel).

      Der Glaube lebt ;
      Die Taube schwebt,
    des Heiland's holder Bote.
      Der für euch fliesst,
      des Wein's geniesst,
    und nehmt vom Lebensbrode !

Durch die entgegengesetzte Thüre wird von KNAPPEN und die-
nenden Brüdern auf einer Tragsänfte AMFORTAS hereingetragen : vor
ihm schreiten KNABEN, welche einen mit einer purpurrothen Decke
überhängten Schrein tragen. Dieser Zug begiebt sich nach der Mitte
des Hintergrundes, wo, von einem Baldachin überdeckt, ein erhöhetes
Ruhebett aufgerichtet steht, auf welches AMFORTAS von der Sänfte
herab niedergelassen wird ; hiervor steht ein Altar-ähnlicher länglicher
Marmortisch, auf welchen die KNABEN den verhängten Schrein
hinstellen. —
Als der Gesang beendet ist, und alle RITTER an den Tafeln ihre
Sitze eingenommen haben, tritt ein längeres Stillschweigen ein. — Vom
tiefsten Hintergrunde her vernimmt man, aus einer gewölbten Nische
hinter dem Ruhebette des AMFORTAS, wie aus einem Grabe die Stimme
des alten

Titurel. My son Amfortas ! Art at thy post ?
(Silence.)

Shall I again look on the Grail and quicken ?
(Silence.)

Must I perish, unguided by my Saver ?

Amfortas
(in an outburst of painful desperation).

Woe's me ! Woe, alas, the pain ! —
My father, oh, once again
Assume the office thou !
Live on ! Live and let me perish.

Titurel. Entombed I live still, by the Grace of
God ;
Too feeble am I now to serve Him :
In works for Him thy guilt efface ! —
Uncover the Grail !

Amfortas
(restraining the boys).

No ! Leave it unrevealed ! — Oh ! —
May no one, no one know the anguish dire
Awaked in me by that which raptures ye ! —
What is the wound and all its torture wild,
'Gainst the distress, the pangs of hell,
In this high post — accurst to dwell ! —
Woeful inheritance on me pressèd,
I, only sinner 'mid the blessèd,
The holy house to guard for others
And pray for blessings upon my purer brothers ! —
Oh, chast'ning — chast'ning dire ! descended
From — ah ! the Almighty One offended.
For grace and for compassion yearning
My panting heart is riven;
In deepest soul's repentance burning
By Him to be forgiven.
The hour is nigh —
The ray descends upon the vessel divine ; —
The veil is raised,
The sacred stream that in the crystal flows
With strength and radiant lustre glows ; —
By this delight but filled with anguish sore,
The heavenly fount of blood
Into my heart I feel to pour ;
My own life current's iniquitous flood
In delirious flight
Backward within me rushes :
Toward the world where sin has might
With wildest dread it gushes. —
Again it forces the door
From which now the stream doth pour,
Here through the wound, — like His 'tis here,
Inflicted by a stroke of that same spear. —

Titurel. Mein Sohn Amfortas ? Bist du am Amt ?
(Schweigen.)

Soll ich den Gral heut' noch erschau'n und leben :
(Schweigen.)

Muss ich sterben, vom Retter ungeleitet !

Amfortas
(im Ausbruche qualvoller Verzweifelung)

Wehe ! Wehe mir der Qual ! —
Mein Vater, oh ! noch einmai
verrichte du das Amt !
Lebe ! Leb' und lass' mich sterben !

Titurel. Im Grabe leb' ich durch des Heiland:e
Huld ;
zu schwach doch bin ich, ihm zu
dienen :
du büss' im Dienste deine Schuld ! —
Enthüllet den Gral !

Amfortas
(den Knaben wehrend).

Nein ! Lasst ihn unenthüllt ! — Oh ! —
Dass Keiner, Keiner diese Qual ermisst,
die mir der Anblick weckt, der euch entzückt ! —
Was ist die Wunde, ihrer Schmerzen Wuth,
gegen die Noth, die Höllenpein,
zu diesem Amt — verdammt zu sein ! —
Wehvolles Erbe, dem ich verfallen,
ich, einziger Sünder unter Allen,
des höchsten Heiligthum's zu pflegen,
auf Reine herabzuflehen seinen Segen ! —
Oh, Strafe ! Strafe ohne Gleichen
des — ach ! — gekränkten Gnadenreichen ! —
Nach Ihm, nach Seinem Weihegrusse
muss sehnlich mich's verlangen ;
aus tiefster Seele Heilesbusse
zu Ihm muss ich gelangen : —
die Stunde naht : —
der Lichtstrahl senkt sich auf das
heilige Werk ;
die Hülle sinkt :
des Weihgefässes göttlicher Gehalt
erglüht mit leuchtender Gewalt ; —
durchzückt von seligsten Genusses
Schmerz,
des heiligsten Blutes Quell
fühl' ich sich giessen in mein Herz :
des eig'nen sündigen Blutes Gewell'
in wahnsinniger Flucht
muss mir zurück dann fliessen.
in die Welt der Sündenzucht
mit wilder Scheu sich ergiessen : —
von Neuem sprengt er das Thor,
daraus es nun strömt hervor,
hier durch die Wunde, der Seinen gleich,
geschlagen von desselben Speeres Streich.

As in our Redeemer, the selfsame place,
  From which with tears of blood burning
The Son of Man wept over man's disgrace
  With sacred pity yearning;
And from which in me, in this sacred mountain,
  While holding high gifts beyond measure,
  — Our redemption's healing treasure —
The hot and sinful blood doth surge,
Ever renewed from my yearnings' fountain,
Which no expiation yet can purge.
     Have mercy! Have mercy!
God of pity, oh! have mercy!
    Take all I cherish,
    Give me but healing,
    That pure I may perish,
    Holiness feeling.
      (He sinks back as if unconscious.)

Boys' voices
     (from the dome).
  " By pity 'lightened,
  The guileless Fool —
  Wait for him,
  My chosen tool."

Knights
     (softly).
  Thus came to thee the fiat.
    Wait on in hope : —
    Fulfil thy duty now!

Titurel's
     (voice).
    Uncover the Grail!

AMFORTAS has again raised himself in silence. The boys uncover the golden shrine, take out of it the " Grail " (an antique crystal cup) from which they also take a covering and set it before AMFORTAS.

Titurel's
     (voice).
    The Blessing!

While AMFORTAS devoutly bows himself in silent prayer before the cup, an increasing gloom spreads in the room.

Boys
     (from the dome).
  " Take and drink my blood;
  Thus be our love remembered!
  Take my body and eat:
  Do this and think of me!"

A blinding ray of light shoots down from above upon the cup, which glows with increasing purple lustre. AMFORTAS, with brightened mien, raises the " Grail " aloft and waves it gently about on all sides. Since the coming of the dusk all have sunk upon their knees, and now cast their eyes reverently towards the " Grail "

Titurel's
     (voice).
  Celestial rapture!
  How light now the looks of the Lord!

---

der dort dem Erlöser die Wunde stach,
aus der mit blutigen Thränen
der Göttliche weint' ob der Menschheit Schmach
  in Mitleid's heiligem Sehnen, —
und aus der nun mir, an heiligster Stelle,
  dem Pfleger göttlichster Güter,
  des Erlösungsbalsam's Hüter,
das heisse Sündenblut entquillt,
ewig erneu't aus des Sehnen's Quelle,
das, ach! keine Büssung je mir stillt!
    Erbarmen! Erbarmen!
Allerbarmer, ach! Erbarmen!
    Nimm mir mein Erbe,
    schliesse die Wunde,
    dass heilig ich sterbe,
    rein Dir gesunde!
     (Er sinkt wie bewusstlos zurück.)

Knabenstimmen
     (aus der Kuppel).
  „ Durch Mitleid wissend,
  der reine Thor:
  harre sein',
  den ich erkor."

Die Ritter
     (leise).
  So ward es dir verkündet,
    Harre getrost;
    des Amtes walte heut'!

Titurel's
     (Stimme).
    Enthüllet den Gral!

AMFORTAS hat sich schweigend wieder erhoben. Die KNABEN entkleiden den goldenen Schrein, entnehmen ihm den „ Gral" (eine antike Krystallschale), von welchem sie ebenfalls eine Verhüllung abnehmen, und setzen ihn vor AMFORTAS hin.

Titurel's
     (Stimme).
    Der Segen!

Während AMFORTAS andachtsvoll in stummem Gebete sich zu dem Kelche neigt, verbreitet sich eine immer dichtere Dämmerung in Saale.

Knaben
     (aus der Kuppel).
  „ Nehmet hin mein Blut
  um uns'rer Liebe Willen!
  Nehmet hin meinen Leib
  auf dass ihr mein' gedenkt.

Ein blendender Lichtstrahl dringt von oben auf die Schale herab diese erglüht immer stärker in leuchtender Purpurfarbe. AMFORTAS mit verklärter Miene, erhebt den „ Gral" hoch und schwenkt ihr sanft nach allen Seiten hin. Alles ist bereits bei dem Eintritte der Dämmerung auf die Knie gesunken, und erhebt jetzt die Blicke andächtig zum „Grale."

Titurel's
     (Stimme.)
  Oh! Heilige Wonne!
  Wie hell grüsst uns heute der Herr!

AMFORTAS sets down the "Grail" again, which now, while the deep gloom wanes, grows paler; the boys cover it as before and return it to the shrine. — As the original light returns to the hall the cups on the table are seen to be filled with wine, and by each is a piece of bread. All sit down to the repast, including GURNEMANZ, who keeps a place by him for PARSIFAL whom he invites with a sign to come and partake. PARSIFAL, however, remains silent and motionless at the side, as if quite dumbfounded.

(Alternative, during the Supper.)

Boys' voices

(from the height).

Wine and Bread the Grail's Lord changéd
Which at that Last Meal were rangéd,
Through His pity's loving tide
When He shed for you His gore
And His Body crucified.

Youths' voices

(from the middle height).

Blood and Body which he offered
Changed to food for you are proffered
By the Saviour ye revere
In the Wine which now ye pour
And the Bread ye eat of here.

The Knights

(first half).

Take of this Bread,
Change it again,
Your pow'rs of body firing;
Living and dead
Strive amain
To work out the Lord's desiring.

(second half).

Take of this Wine,
Change it anew
To life's impetuous torrent;
Gladly combine,
Brothers true,
To fight as duty shall warrant.

(They rise solemnly and all join hands.)

All the Knights.   Blesséd Believing!
Blesséd in Loving!

Youths

(from the mid height).

Blesséd in Loving!

Boys

(from the utmost height).

Blesséd Believing!

During the repast AMFORTAS, who has not partaken, has gradually relapsed from his state of exaltation: he bows his head and presses his hand to the wound. The pages approach him; his wound has burst out afresh; they tend him and assist him to his litter; then, while all prepare to break up, they bear off AMFORTAS and the shrine in the order in which they came. The KNIGHTS and ESQUIRES fall in and slowly leave the hall in solemn procession, whilst the daylight gradually wanes. The bells are heard pealing again. — PARSIFAL, on hearing AMFORTAS' cry of agony, has clutched his heart and remained in that position for some time; he now stands as if petrified, motionless. When the last knight has left the hall and the doors are again closed, GURNEMANZ in ill humour comes up to PARSIFAL and shakes him by the arm.

AMFORTAS setzt den „Gral" wieder nieder, welcher nun, während die tiefe Dämmerung wieder entweicht, immer mehr erblasst: hierauf schliessen die KNABEN das Gefäss wieder in den Schrein, und bedecken diesen, wie zuvor.— Mit dem Wiedereintritte der vorigen Tageshelle sind auf den Speisetafeln die Becher, jetzt mit Wein gefüllt, wieder deutlich geworden, neben jedem liegt ein Brot. Alles lässt sich zum Mahle nieder, so auch GURNEMANZ, welcher einen Platz neben sich leer hält und PARSIFAL durch ein Zeichen zur Theilnehmung am Mahle einlädt: PARSIFAL bleibt aber starr und stumm wie gänzlich entrückt, zur Seite stehen.

(Wechselgesang während des Mahles.)

Knabenstimmen

(aus der Höhe).

Wein und Brod des letzten Mahles
wandelt' einst der Herr des Grales,
durch des Mitleid's Liebesmacht,
in das Blut, das er vergoss,
in den Leib, den dar er bracht'.

Jünglingsstimmen

(aus der mittleren Höhe.)

Blut und Leib der Opfergabe
wandelt heut' zu eurer Labe
der Erlöser, den ihr preis't,
in den Wein, der nun euch floss,
in das Brod, das heut' euch speis't.

Die Ritter

(erste Hälfte).

Nehmet vom Brod,
wandelt es kühn
zu Leibes Kraft und Stärke;
treu bis zum Tod,
fest in Müh'n,
zu wirken des Heiland's Werke.

(Zweite Hälfte.)

Nehmet vom Wein,
wandelt ihn neu
zu Lebens feurigem Blute,
froh im Verein,
brüdertreu
zu kämpfen mit seligem Muthe.

(Sie erheben sich feierlich und reichen einander die Hände).

2 Alle Ritter.   Selig im Glauben!
Selig in Liebe!

Jünglinge

(aus mittler Höhe).

Selig in Liebe!

Knaben

(aus oberster Höhe).

Selig im Glauben!

Während des Mahles, an welchem er nicht theilnahm, ist AMFORTAS aus seiner begeisterungsvollen Erhebung allmählich wieder herabgesunken: er neigt das Haupt und hält die Hand auf die Wunde. Die KNABEN nähern sich ihm; ihre Bewegungen deuten auf das erneuerte Bluten der Wunde: sie pflegen AMFORTAS, geleiten ihn wieder auf die Sänfte, und, während Alle sich zum Aufbruch rüsten, tragen sie, in der Ordnung wie sie kamen, AMFORTAS und den heiligen Schrein wieder von dannen. Die RITTER und KNAPPEN reihen sich ebenfalls wieder zum feierlichen Zuge, und verlassen langsam den Saal, aus welchem die vorherige Tageshelle allmählich weicht. Die Glocken haben wieder geläutet.

PARSIFAL hatte bei dem vorangegangenen stärksten Klagerufe des AMFORTAS eine heftige Bewegung nach dem Herzen gemacht, welches er krampfhaft eine Zeit lang gefasst hielt; jetzt steht er noch wie erstarrt, regungslos da. — Als die Letzten den Saal verlassen, und die Thüren wieder geschlossen sind, tritt GURNEMANZ missmüthig an PARSIFAL heran, und rüttelt ihn am Arme.

Gurnemanz. Why standest thou there?
　Wist thou what thou saw'st?

(PARSIFAL shakes his head slightly.)

Gurnemanz. Thou art then nothing but a Fool!

(He opens a small side door.)

Come away, on thy road be gone
　And put my rede to use:
Leave all our swans for the future alone
　And seek thyself, gander, a goose.

(He pushes PARSIFAL out and slams the door angrily on him. As follows the knights, the curtain closes.)

Gurnemanz. Was stehst du noch da?
　Weisst du was du sah'st?

(PARSIFAL schüttelt ein wenig sein Haupt.)

Gurnemanz. Du bist doch eben nur ein Thor!

(Er öffnet eine schmale Seitenthüre.)

Dort hinaus, deinem Wege zu!
　Doch räth dir Gurnemanz,
lass' du hier künftig die Schwäne in Ruh',
　und suche dir Gänser die Gans!

Er stösst PARSIFAL hinaus und schlägt, ärgerlich, hinter ihm die Thüre stark zu. Während er dann den RITTERN folgt, schliesst sich der Bühnenvorhang.

ACT II.

KLINGSOR's magic Castle. — In the inner keep of a tower open above; stone steps lead up to the battlemented summit and down into darkness below the stage, which represents the rampart. Magical implements and necromantic appliances. — KLINGSOR sits at one side on the rampart before a metal mirror.

Klingsor. The time has come! —
Lo! how my magic tow'r entices
Yon Fool who neareth, shouting like a child.
A deadly slumber lays its hold on her
　Whose anguish I can chase away. —
　　Up then! To work!

He descends somewhat lower, and lights incense, which immediately fills part of the background with a bluish vapor. He then reseats himself in his former place, and calls towards the depth with mysterious gestures:

Arise! Draw near to me!
Thy Master calls thee, nameless woman:
She-Lucifer! Rose of Hades!
Herodias wert thou, and what else?
Gundryggia there, Kundry here: —
Approach! Approach then, Kundry!
Thy Master calls — appear!

(In the bluish light rises the form of KUNDRY. She is heard to utter a dreadful cry, as if half-awakened from a deep sleep.)

Klingsor. Awak'st thou? Ha!
　To my spell again
Thou succumbest now the time befits.

(The figure of KUNDRY gives forth a sudden shriek of anguish sinking to a frightened wail.)

Say, where hast thou been roving again?
Fie! There with the knights and their crew,
Where as a brute they regarded thee?
　With me art thou not far better?
When once their chieftain thou hadst allured
　me —
Ha, ha! — the spotless knight of the Grail —
　What drove thee again from my side?

ZWEITER AUFZUG.

Klingsor's Zauberschloss.

Im inneren Verliesse eines nach oben offenen Thurmes; Steinstufen führen nach dem Zinnenrande der Thurmmauer; Finsterniss in der Tiefe, nach welcher es von dem Mauervorsprunge, den der Bühnenboden darstellt, hinabführt. Zauberwerkzeuge und nekromantische Vorrichtungen. — KLINGSOR auf dem Mauervorsprunge zur Seite, vor einem Metallspiegel sitzend.

10　*Klingsor.* Die Zeit ist da, —
　Schon lockt mein Zauberschloss den Thoren,
　den, kindisch jauchzend, fern ich nahen seh'. —
　Im Todesschlafe hält der Fluch sie fest,
　　der ich den Krampf zu lösen weiss. —
　　　Auf denn! An's Werk!

Er steigt, der Mitte zu, etwas tiefer hinab, und entzündet dort Räucherwerk, welches alsbald einen Theil des Hintergrundes mit einem bläulichen Dampfe erfüllt. Dann setzt er sich wieder an die vorige Stelle, und ruft, mit geheimnissvollen Gebärden, nach dem Abgrunde:

Herauf! Hieher! zu mir!
Dein Meister ruft dich Namenlose:
Ur-Teufelin! Höllen-Rose!
Herodias war'st du, und was noch?
Gundryggia dort, Kundry hier:
Hieher! Hieher denn, Kundry!
Zu deinem Meister, herauf!

In dem bläulichen Lichte steigt KUNDRY's Gestalt herauf. Man hört sie einen grässlichen Schrei ausstossen, wie eine aus tiefsten Schlafe aufgeschreckte Halbwache.

Klingsor. Erwach'st du? Ha!
　Meinem Banne wieder
verfiel'st du heut' zur rechten Zeit.

(KUNDRY's Gestalt lässt ein Klagegeheul, von grösster Heftigkeit bis zu bangem Wimmern sich abstufend, vernehmen.)

Sag' wo trieb'st du dich wieder umher?
Pfui! Dort, bei dem Ritter-Gesipp',
wo wie ein Vieh du dich halten lässt?
　Gefällt's dir bei mir nicht besser?
Als ihren Meister du mir gefangen —
ha, ha! — den reinen Hüter des Gral's, —
　was jagte dich da wieder fort?

Kundry

(hoarsely and in broken accents, as if striving to regain speech).

Ah! — Ah!
Dismal night —
Frenzy — Oh! — Fear! —
Oh, anguish! —
Sleep, sleep —
Deepest sleep! — Death!

Klingsor. Some other there has waked thee? Hey?

Kundry

(as before).

Yes! — My curse —
Oh! Yearning — yearning!

Klingsor. Ha, ha! — there with the knights unsullied?

Kundry. I — I — served them.

Klingsor. Aye, aye! — To make some reparation,
For the arrant wrong thou hast wrought.
They give thee no help;
All may be purchased,
When I but bid their price;
The firmest one fails
When thy arms are around him:
And so he falls by the spear,
Which from their chief himself I purloined. —
The most dangerous must to-day be withstood:
Whom sheerest Folly shields.

Kundry. I — will not! — Oh! — Oh!

Klingsor. Well wilt thou, for thou must.

Kundry. Thou — never — canst — hold me.

Klingsor. But I can force thee.

Kundry. Thou?

Klingsor. Thy Master.

Kundry. And by what pow'r?

Klingsor. Ha! Because against me
Thine own pow'r — cannot move.

Kundry

(laughing harshly).

Ha, ha! Art thou chaste?

Klingsor

(wrathfully).

Why askest that, thou outcast wretch!

(He sinks into gloomy brooding.)

Awfullest strait! —
So laughs now the Fiend below,

Kundry

(rauh und abgebrochen, wie im Versuche, wieder Sprache zu gewinnen).

Ach! — Ach!
Tiefe Nacht —
Wahnsinn! — Oh! — Wuth! —
Oh! Jammer! —
Schlaf — Schlaf —
tiefer Schlaf! — Tod!

Klingsor. Da weckte dich ein And'rer? He?

Kundry

(wie zuvor).

Ja! — Mein Fluch! —
Oh! — Sehnen — Sehnen! —

Klingsor. Ha, ha! — dort nach den keuschen Rittern?

Kundry. Da — da — dient' ich.

Klingsor. Ja, ja! — den Schaden zu vergüten,
den du ihnen böslich gebracht?
Sie helfen dir nicht:
feil sind sie Alle,
biet' ich den rechten Preis;
der festeste fällt,
sinkt er dir in die Arme:
und so verfällt er dem Speer,
den ihrem Meister selbst ich entwandt. —
Den Gefährlichsten gilt's nun heut' zu besteh'n
ihn schirmt der Thorheit Schild.

Kundry. Ich — will nicht! — Oh! — Oh!

Klingsor. Wohl willst du, denn du musst.

Kundry. Du — kannst mich — nicht — halten.

Klingsor. Aber dich fassen.

Kundry. Du?

Klingsor. Dein Meister.

Kundry. Aus welcher Macht?

Klingsor. Ha! Weil einzig an mir
deine Macht — nichts vermag.

Kundry

(grell lachend).

Ha! ha! — Bist du keusch?

Klingsor

(wüthend).

Was fräg'st du das, verfluchtes Weib? —

(Er versinkt in finst'res Brüten.)

Furchtbare Noth! —
So lacht nun der Teufel mein',

That once I sought the holier life !
 Awfullest strait !
Irrepressible yearning woe !
Terrible lust in me once rife,
Which I had quenched with devilish strife ; —
 Mocks and laughs it at me,
 Thou devil's bride, through thee ? —
 Have a care !
One his contempt and scorn hath repented ;
The stern one, strong in holiness,
 By whom I once was spurned
 His stock I've ruined :
 Unredeemed
Shall the Relics' curator soon languish :
 And soon — I feel it —
I shall possess the Grail. —
 Ha ! ha !
How suited thy taste Amfortas the brave,
Whom to thee in rapture I gave ?

Kundry. Oh ! — Mis'ry — Mis'ry !
Weak e'en he ! Weak — all men !
 By my curse and with me
 All of them perish ! —
 Oh, unending sleep,
 Only release,
When — when shall I win thee ?

Klingsor. Ha ! He who spurns thee setteth thee
 free ;
So try't with yon boy who draws near !

Kundry. I — will not !

Klingsor. Lo, where he climbs to the tow'r !

Kundry. Oh, woe's me ! woe's me !
 Awakened I for this ?
 Must I — must ?

Klingsor
 (who has ascended to the wall).
 Ha ! — He is fair, the stripling.

Kundry. Oh ! — Oh ! — Woe is me ! —

Klingsor
 (winding a horn towards the outside).
Ho ! ho ! — My watchmen ! Soldiers !
Heroes ! — Up ! — Foes are near !
 (Increasing clash of weapons heard without.)
Hey ! — How they haste to the ramparts,
 The deluded garrisoners,
To guard their engaging she-devils ! —
 So ! — Courage, courage !
 Haha ! — He is not afraid : —
From bold Sir Ferris he's wrested his weapons ;
And flashes them fiercely now at the swarm. —
 (KUNDRY begins to laugh gloomily.)

dass ich einst nach dem Heiligen rang !
 Furchtbare Noth !
Ungebändigten Sehnens Pein !
Schrecklichster Triebe Höllendrang,
den ich zu Todesschweigen mir zwang, —
 lacht und höhnt er nun laut
 durch dich, des Teufels Braut ? —
 Hüte dich !
Hohn und Verachtung büsste schon Einer
der Stolze, stark in Heiligkeit,
 der einst mich von sich stiess,
 sein Stamm verfiel mir,
 unerlös't
soll der Heiligen Hüter mir schmachten ;
 und bald — so wähn' ich —
 hüt' ich mir selbst den Gral. —
 Ha ! Ha !
Gefiel er dir wohl, Amfortas, der Held,
den ich dir zur Wonne gesellt ?

Kundry. Oh ! — Jammer ! — Jammer !
Schwach auch Er ! Schwach — Alle !
 Meinem Fluche mit mir
 Alle verfallen ! —
 Oh, ewiger Schlaf,
 einziges Heil,
wie, — wie dich gewinnen ?

Klingsor. Ha ! Wer dir trotzte, lös'te dich frei
 versuch's mit dem Knaben, der nah't !

Kundry. Ich — will nicht !

Klingsor. Jetzt schon erklimmt er die Burg.

Kundry. Oh Wehe ! Wehe !
 Erwachte ich darum ?
 Muss ich ? — Muss ?

Klingsor
 (Ist auf die Thurmmauer gestiegen).
 Ha ! — Er ist schön, der Knabe !

Kundry. Oh ! — Oh ! — Wehe mir ! —

Klingsor
 (stösst nach Aussen in ein Horn).
Ho ! Ho ! — Ihr Wächter ! Ritter !
Helden ! — Auf ! — Feinde nah' !
 (Aussen wachsendes Getöse und Waffengeräusch.)
 Hei ! — Wie zur Mauer sie stürmen,
 die bethörten Eigenholde,
zum Schutz ihres schönen Geteufel's ! —
 So ! — Muthig ! Muthig ! —
 Haha ! — Der fürchtet sich nicht : —
dem Helden Ferris entwand er die Waffe ;
die führt er nun freislich wider den Schwarm.
 (KUNDRY beginnt unheimlich zu lachen.)

How ill doth his zeal agree with those sots !
That one's lost an arm — that one his ankle.
Haha ! They waver — they're routed :
With their wounds they are all running home ! —
    What welcome I'll give them ! —
    Truly I wish
    That all the rabble of Knights
    So might destroy one another ! —
Ha ! How proudly he stands on the rampart !
His countenance how smiling and rosy,
    As childlike, surprised
    On the desolate garden he looks ! —
Hey ! Kundry !

He turns round. KUNDRY, *who has gone off into more and more ecstatic laughter which at last culminates in a spasmodic cry of anguish, now suddenly vanishes ; the bluish light is extinguished ; complete darkness reigns in the depths.*

    What ! Gone to work ?
Ha, ha ! the charm I know full well,
Which ever compels thee to do my behest. - -
    Thou there, babyish sprig !
    What — though
    Wise redes thou hast won —
        Too young and dull,
    Into my power thou'lt fall : —
    When pureness has departed,
    To me thou'lt be devoted.

He sinks slowly with the whole tower ; at the same time the garden rises and fills the entire stage. Tropical vegetation ; most luxuriant wealth of flowers ; at the back it is bounded by the battlements of the castle wall on to which give sideways abutments of the castle itself (florid Arabian style) with terraces.
On the wall stands PARSIFAL, *looking down on the garden in astonishment.— From all sides, from the garden and from the palace rush in mazy courses lovely damsels, first singly, then in numbers ; their dress is hastily thrown about them, as if they had been suddenly startled from sleep.*

Damsels
            (coming from the garden).
    Here was the tumult ; —
    Weapons, wild exclaimings !

Damsels
            (from the castle).
    Horror ! Vengeance ! Up !
    Where is the culprit ?

Several.   My beloved is wounded !

Others.   Where is my lover ?

Others.   I wakened alone ! —
    Where hath he fled to ?

Still Others.   There in the palace ? —
    They're bleeding ! Horror !
    Where is the foe ? —
    There stands he ! See ! —
    'Tis my Ferris' sword —
    I saw't, he took us by storm. —

Wie übel den Tölpeln der Eifer gedeih't !
Dem schlug er den Arm,— Jenem den Schenkel
Haha ! — Sie weichen, — sie fliehen :
seine Wunde trägt Jeder nach heim ! —
    Wie das ich euch gönne ! —
    Möge denn so
    das ganze Rittergeschlecht
    unter sich selber sich würgen ! - -
Ha ! Wie stolz er nun steht auf der Zinne
Wie lachen ihm die Rosen der Wangen,
    da kindisch erstaunt
    in den einsamen Garten er blickt !
He ! Kundry !

Er wendet sich um. KUNDRY *war in ein immer extatischeres Lachen gerathen, welches endlich in ein krampfhaftes Wehgeschrei überging ; jetzt ist ihre Gestalt plötzlich verschwunden ; das bläuliche Licht ist erloschen : volle Finsterniss in der Tiefe.*

    Wie ? Schon am Werk ? —
Haha ! Den Zauber kannt' ich wohl,
    der immer dich wieder zum Dienst mir gesellt. —
    Du dort, kindischer Spross !
    Was — auch
    Weissagung dir wies, —
        zu jung und dumm
    fiel'st du in meine Gewalt : —
    die Reinheit dir entrissen,
    bleib'st mir du zugewiesen !

Er versinkt langsam mit dem ganzen Thurme ; zugleich steigt der Zaubergarten auf und erfüllt die Bühne völlig. Tropische Vegetation. üppigste Blumenpracht ; nach dem Hintergrunde zu Abgrenzung durch die Zinne der Burgmauer, an welche sich seitwärts Vorsprünge des Schlosshauses selbst (arabischen reichen Styles) mit Terrassen anlehnen.
Auf der Mauer steht PARSIFAL, *staunend in den Garten hinabblickend.—Von allen Seiten her, aus dem Garten wie aus dem Palaste, stürzen wirr durch einander, einzeln, dann zugleich immer mehr, schöne* MÄDCHEN *herein : sie sind in flüchtig übergeworfener Kleidung, wie soeben aus dem Schlaf aufgeschreckt.*

Mädchen
            (vom Garten kommend).
    Hier war das Tosen,
    Waffen, wilde Rüfe !

Mädchen
            (vom Schlosse heraus).
    Wehe ! Rache ! Auf !
    Wo ist der Frevler ?

Einzelne.   Mein Geliebter verwundet.

Andere.   Wo ist der Meine ?

Andere.   Ich erwachte allein, —
    wohin entfloh er ?

Immer Andere.   Drinnen im Saale ? - -
    Sie bluten ! Wehe !
    Wer ist der Feind ? —
    Da steht' er ! Seht ! —
    Meines Ferris Schwert ? —
    Ich sah's, er stürmte die Burg. -

I heard too the master's horn.
　My hero rushed on:
They all assailed him, but each one
Encountered a bloody repulse.
　What boldness! what virulence!
　All of them fled from him. —
Thou there! Thou there!
Why shape for us such distress?
Accurst, accurst mayst thou be!
　(PARSIFAL leaps somewhat lower toward the garden.)

Damsels. Ha! bold one! Dar'st thou approach us?
Why hast thou slaughtered our lovers?

Parsifal
　　　(in greatest astonishment).
Ye lovely maidens, had I not to slay them,
When they endeavored to check approach to
　your charms?

Damsels. To us camest thou?
　　Sawest thou us?

Parsifal. I've seen nowhere yet beings so
　bright:
If I said fair, would it seem right?

Damsels
　　　(changing from surprise to merriment).
Then wilt thou not treat us badly?

Parsifal. I could not so.

Damsels. But sadly
What thou hast done has annoyed us;
Our playmates thou hast destroyed us.
　Who'll sport with us now?

Parsifal. That well will I.

Damsels
　　　(laughing).
If thou art friendly come more nigh.
　Let kindness be accorded,
　And thou shalt be rewarded:
　For gold we do not play,
　But only for love's sweet pay,
　Wouldst thou console us rightly
　Then win it from us, and lightly.
　Some have gone into the groves and now return in flower-
dresses, appearing like flowers themselves.

The adorned Damsels
　　　(severally).
Touch not the stripling! — He's for none but
　me. —
　No! — No! — Me! — Me!

The other Damsels. Ah, the minxes! — They've
slily adorned them.
　(They also withdraw and return similarly dressed).

Ich hörte des Meisters Horn.
　Mein Held lief herzu,
sie Alle kamen, doch Jeden
empfing er mit blutiger Wehr.
　Der Kühne! Der Feindliche!
　Alle sie flohen ihm. —
Du dort! Du dort!
Was schuf'st du uns solche Noth?
Verwünscht, verwünscht sollst du sein!
　(PARSIFAL springt etwas tiefer in den Garten herab.)

Die Mädchen. Ha! Kühner! Wag'st du zu
trotzen?
　Was schlug'st du uns're Geliebten?

Parsifal
　　　(in höchster Verwunderung).
Ihr schönen Kinder, musst' ich sie nicht schlagen?
Zu euch Holden ja wehrten sie mir den Weg.

Mädchen. Zu uns wolltest du?
　　Sah'st du uns schon?

Parsifal. Noch nie sah ich solch' zieres Ge
schlecht:
nenn' ich euch schön, dünkt euch das recht?

Die Mädchen
　　　(von Verwunderung in Heiterkeit übergehend).
So willst du uns wohl nicht schlagen?

Parsifal. Das möcht' ich nicht.

Mädchen. Doch Schaden
schuf'st du uns grossen und vielen;
　du schlugest uns're Gespielen:
　　wer spielt nun mit uns?

Parsifal. Das thu' ich gern.

Die Mädchen
　　　(lachend).
Bist du uns hold, so bleib' nicht fern;
　und willst du uns nicht schelten,
　wir werden dir's entgelten:
　wir spielen nicht um Gold,
　wir spielen um Minne's Sold:
　willst du auf Trost uns sinnen,
　sollst den du uns abgewinnen.
　Einzelne sind in die Läuben getreten, und kommen jetzt, ganz
wie in Blumengewändern, selbst Blumen erscheinend, wieder zurück.

Die geschmückten Mädchen
　　　(einzeln).
Lasset den Knaben! — Er gehöret mir. —
　Nein! — Nein! — Mir! — Mir!

Die andern Mädchen. Ah, die Schlimmen! —
Sie schmücken sich heimlich.
　Diese entfernen sich ebenfalls, und kehren alsbald in gleichem
Blumenschmucke zurück.

<table>
<tr><td>

The Damsels

(while, as if in merry childish gambols they press round PARSIFAL in mazy figures and softly stroke his face).

Come ! Come !
Handsome stripling,
  I'll be thy flower!
Sweetly dancing and rippling
Bliss unshadowed I'll shower.

Parsifal

(standing in their midst in quiet enjoyment).

How sweet is your scent !
Are ye then flowers ?

The Damsels

(still sometimes severally, sometimes together).

  The garden's pride
  And odor we've given.
In spring time we were riven ;
  We here abide,
  Through sunlight and summer,
To bloom still on each comer.
Oh, be but kind and true,
And grudge not the flowers their due:
If thou wilt not fondle and cherish,
We swiftly must wither and perish.

First Damsel. Unto thy bosom take me !

Second. Thy hot brow, let me soothe it !

Third. Turn thy fair cheek that I smooth it !

Fourth. Thy mouth give to my kisses !

Fifth. No, here ! 'Tis I am the best.

Sixth. No, I ! I am the sweeter.

Parsifal

(gently repulsing their eager advances).

Ye wild crowd of beautiful flowers,
If I am to play, ye must widen your bowers.

Damsels. Why quarrel?

Parsifal. 'Tis your riot.

Damsels. We quarrel for thee.

Parsifal. Then quiet.

First Damsel

(to the second).

Back with you ! See, he wants me.

Second Damsel. No, me !

Third. Me, rather !

Fourth. No, me !

</td><td>

Die Mädchen

(während sie, wie in anmuthigem Kinderspiele, in abwechselndem Reigen um PARSIFAL sich drehen, und sanft ihm Wange und Kinn streicheln).

16 Komm'! Komm'!
Holder Knabe,
  lass mich dir blühen !
Dir zu wonniger Labe
gilt mein minniges Mühe.

Parsifal

(mit heit'rer Ruhe in der Mitte stehend).

Wie duftet ihr hold !
Seid ihr denn Blumen ?

Die Mädchen

(immer bald einzeln, bald mehre zugleich).

  Des Gartens Zier
  und duftende Geister
im Lenz pflückt uns der Meister ;
  wir wachsen hier
  in Sommer und Sonne,
für dich blühend in Wonne.
Nun sei uns freund und hold,
nicht karge den Blumen den Sold ·
kannst du uns nicht lieben und minnen,
wir welken und sterben dahinnen.

Erstes Mädchen. An deinen Busen nimm mich !

Zweites. Die Stirn lass' mich dir kühlen !

Drittes. Lass mich die Wange dir fühlen !

Viertes. Den Mund lass' mich dir küssen !

Fünftes. Nein, mich ! Die Schönste bin ich.

Sechstes. Nein, ich ! Duft' ich doch süsser.

Parsifal

(ihrer anmuthigen Zudringlichkeit sanft wehrend).

Ihr wild holdes Blumengedränge,
soll ich mit euch spielen, entlasst mich der Enge !

Mädchen. Was zank'st du?

Parsifal. Weil ihr streitet.

Mädchen. Wir streiten um dich.

Parsifal. Das meidet !

Erstes Mädchen

(zu dem zweiten).

Weiche du ! Sieh', er will mich.

Zweites Mädchen. Nein, mich !

Drittes. Mich, lieber !

Viertes. Nein, mich !

</td></tr>
</table>

First Damsel
(to PARSIFAL).
Thou shunnest me?

Second. Flyest me?

First. Art with women so wary?

Second. Of thy favor chary?

Several Damsels. The cold trembler! see how he cowers!

Others. Wouldst see the butterfly wooed by the flowers?

First Half. Fool! we refuse him!

One Damsel. I'm willing to lose him.

Others. We others will choose him.

Others. No, we! draw near!—
No, I—here, here!—

Parsifal
(half angry, turns away and seeks to fly).
No more! You'll catch me not!
(From a flowery arbor at side is heard)

Kundry's
(voice).
Parsifal!—tarry!
The DAMSELS are startled and pause—PARSIFAL stands arrested.

Parsifal. Parsifal . . .?
So once, when dreaming, my mother called me.—

Kundry's
(voice).
Here bide thee, Parsifal!—
Where joy and gladness on thee shall fall.—
Ye frivolous wantons, leave him in peace:
Flow'rs soon to be faded,
He came not here for your delight!
Go home, tend the wounded:
Lonely awaits you many a knight.

The Damsels
(tremblingly and resistingly departing from PARSIFAL).
Thus to leave thee, thus to sever—
Alas! Alas, what pain!
From all we'd gladly part for ever.
With thee but to remain.—
Farewell! farewell!
Thou fair one, thou proud one!
Thou—Fool!
(With the last words they disappear into the castle, gently laughing.)

Parsifal. Was all this—nothing but a dream?

He looks timidly to the side from whence KUNDRY's voice came. There is now visible, the branches being withdrawn, a youthful female of exquisite beauty—KUNDRY, in entirely altered form—on a flowery :ouch and in light drapery of fantastic, somewhat Arabian style.

Erstes Mädchen
(zu PARSIFAL).
Du wehrest mir?

Zweites. Scheuchest mich?

Erstes. Bist du feige vor Frauen?

Zweites. Magst nicht dich getrauen?

Mehre Mädchen. Wie schlimm bist du, Zager und Kalter!

Andere Mädchen. Die Blumen lässt du umbuh- len den Falter?

Erste Hälfte. Weichet dem Thoren!

Ein Mädchen. Ich geb' ihn verloren.

Andere. Uns sei er erkoren!

Andere. Nein, uns!—Nein, mir!—
Auch mir!—Hier, hier!—

Parsifal
(halb ärgerlich sie von sich abscheuchend, will fliehen).
Lass't ab! Ihr fangt mich nicht!
(Aus einem Blumenhage zur Seite vernimmt man)

Kundry's
(Stimme).
Parsifal!—Weile!
Die Mädchen erschrecken und halten sogleich ein.—PARSIFAL steht betroffen still.

Parsifal. Parsifal . .?
So nannte träumend mich einst die Mutter.—

Kundry's
(Stimme.)
Hier weile, Parsifal!—
Dich grüsset Wonne und Heil zumal.—
Ihr kindischen Buhlen, weichet von ihm;
früh welkende Blumen,
nicht euch ward er zum Spiel bestellt!
Geht heim, pflegt der Wunden:
einsam erharrt euch mancher Held.

Die Mädchen
(zaghaft und widerstrebend sich von PARSIFAL entfernend).
Dich zu lassen, dich zu meiden,—
O weh'! O weh' der Pein!
Von Allen möchten gern wir scheiden,
mit dir allein zu sein.
Leb' wohl! Leb' wohl!
Du Holder! Du Stolzer!
Du—Thor!
(Mit dem Letzten sind sie, unter leisem Gelächter, nach dem Schlosse zu verschwunden.)

Parsifal. Dies Alles—hab' ich nun geträumt?

Er sieht sich schüchtern nach der Seite hin um, von welcher die Stimme kam. Dort ist jetzt, durch Enthüllung des Hages, ein jugendliches Weib von höchster Schönheit—KUNDRY, in durchaus verwandelter Gestalt—auf einem Blumenlager, in leicht verhüllen der, phantastischer Kleidung—annähernd arabischen Styles sichtbar geworden.

Parsifal
(still standing aloof).
Calledst thou me, who am nameless?

Kundry. I named thee, foolish pure one,
   " Fal parsi, "—
   Thou, guileless Fool, art " Parsifal. "
So cried, when in Arabia's land he expired,
Thy father Gamuret unto his son,
Who then the daylight had not greeted:
'Twas by this name he, dying, called thee.
Here have I tarried this but to disclose:
What drew thee here, if not desire to know?

Parsifal. I saw ne'er, I pictured ne'er what
   here
I see, and which impresses me with awe.—
And bloomest thou too in this flower-garden?

Kundry. Nay, Parsifal, thou foolish pure one!
   Far — far from hence my home is:—
For thee to find me, I but tarried here.
I come from far lands, where I've noted much.
I saw the child upon its mother's breast;
Its infant lisping laughs yet in my ear:
   Though filled with sadness.
How laughed even then Heart's Affliction,
   When, shouting gladness,
It gave her sorrows contradiction!
In beds of moss 'twas softly nested,
She kisses it till in sleep it rested:
   With care and sorrow
The timid mother watched it sleeping;
   It waked the morrow
Beneath the dew of mother's weeping.
All tears was she, encased in anguish,
Caused by thy father's death and love:
That through like hap thou shouldst **not**
   languish,
Became her care all else above.
Afar from arms, from mortal strife and riot,
Sought she to hide away with thee in quiet.
All care was she, alas! and fearing:
Never should aught of knowledge reach thy
   hearing:
Hear'st thou not still her lamenting voice,
When far and late thou didst roam?
Ah! how she did laughingly rejoice
   To welcome thee hastening home!
When her wild arm around thee was laid,
Wert thou of kisses so much afraid?—
But thou didst not behold her pain,
   Her features anguish ridden,
When thou returnedst not again,
   And ev'ry trace was hidden.

Parsifal
(noch ferne stehend).
Riefest du mich Namenlosen?

Kundry. Dich nannt' ich, thör'ger Reiner,
   ,, Fal parsi,"—
   Dich, reinen Thoren: ,, Parsifal."
So rief, da in arab'schem Land er verschied.
dein Vater Gamuret dem Sohne zu,
den er, im Mutterschooss verschlossen,
mit diesem Namen sterbend grüsste.
Dir ihn zu künden, harrt' ich deiner hier:
was zog dich her, wenn nicht der Kunde Wunsch?

Parsifal. Nie sah' ich, nie träumte mir, was
   jetzt
ich schau', und was mit Bangen mich
   erfüllt.—
Entblühtest du auch diesem Blumen-
   haine?

Kundry. Nein, Parsifal, du thör'ger Reiner!
   Fern — fern — ist meine Heimath:—
dass du mich fändest, weilte ich nur hier.
Von weit her kam ich, wo ich viel ersah'.
Ich sah' das Kind an seiner Mutter Brust,
sein erstes Lallen lacht mir noch im Ohr;
   das Leid im Herzen,
wie lachte da auch Herzeleide,
   als ihren Schmerzen
zujauchzte ihrer Augen Weide!
Gebettet sanft auf weichen Moosen,
den hold geschläfert sie mit Kosen,
   dem, bang' in Sorgen,
den Schlaf bewacht der Mutter Sehnen,
   ihn weckt' am Morgen
der heisse Thau der Mutter-Thränen.
Nur Weinen war sie, Schmerz-Gebahren
um deines Vaters Lieb' und Tod;
   vor gleicher Noth dich zu bewahren,
galt ihr als höchster Pflicht Gebot:
den Waffen fern, der Männer Kampf und
   Wüthen,
wollte sie still dich bergen und behüten.
   Nur Sorgen war sie, ach! und Bangen:
nie sollte Kunde zu dir hergelangen.
Hör'st du nicht noch ihrer Klagen Ruf,
   wann fern und spät du geweilt?
Hei! Was ihr das Lust und Lachen schuf,
   wann suchend sie dann dich ereilt!
Wann dann ihr Arm dich wüthend
   umschlang,
ward dir es wohl gar bei'm Küssen bang!
Ihr Wehe doch du nicht vernahm'st,
   nicht ihrer Schmerzen Toben,
als endlich du nicht wieder kam'st,
   und deine Spur verstoben:

17

18

For days and nights she waited,
And then her cries abated :
Her pain was dulled of its smart,
And gently ebbed life's tide ;
The anguish broke her heart,
And — Heart's Affliction — died. —

Parsifal
(always earnestly, finally terribly affected, sinks down at KUNDRY's feet, painfully overpowered).

Woe's me ! Woe's me ! What did I ? Where was I ?
Mother ! Sweetest, dearest mother !
Thy son, thy son must be thy murderer ?
Oh Fool ! Thoughtless, shallow-brained Fool !
Where couldst thou have roved, thus to forget her ?
    Thus, oh, thus to forget thee,
    Faithful, fondest of mothers !

Kundry
(still reclining, bends over PARSIFAL's head, gently touches his forehead, and wreathes her arms confidingly round his neck).

    Hadst thou ne'er been distrest,
        Then consolation
    Could not have cheered thy breast.
    Let now thy bitter woe
        Find mitigation
    In joys that Love can show !

Parsifal
                        (sadly).
My mother, my mother ! Could I forget her ?
Ah ! must all be forgotten by me ?
What have I e'er remembered yet ?
But senseless Folly dwells in me !
                (He droops still lower.)

Kundry.   Transgression
    When owned is quickly ended !
        Confession
    Hath Folly often mended.
    Of Love, oh, learn the fashion
    Which Gamuret once knew,
    When Heart's Affliction's passion
    Had fired his bosom through.
        The life thy mother
        Gave thee can smother
E'en death, and dullness too remove.
        To thee
        Now she
Sends benediction from above
    In this first — kiss of Love.
(She has bowed her head quite over his, and now presses her lips on his in a long kiss.)

Parsifal
(starts up suddenly with a gesture of intense terror ; his looks alter fearfully, he presses his hands tightly against his heart, as if to repress an agonizing pain ; finally he bursts out).
            Amfortas ! —
The spearwound ! — The spearwound ! —

sie harrte Nächt' und Tage,
bis ihr verstummt die Klage,
der Gram ihr zehrte den Schmerz,
um stillen Tod sie warb :
ihr brach das Leid das Herz,
und — Herzeleide — starb. —

Parsifal
(immer ernsthafter, endlich furchtbar betroffen, sinkt, schmerzlie... überwältigt, bei KUNDRY's Füssen nieder).

Wehe ! Wehe ! Was that ich ? Wo war ich ?
Mutter ! Süsse, holde Mutter !
Dein Sohn, dein Sohn musste dich morden ?
O Thor ! Blöder, taumelnder Thor !
Wo irrtest du hin, ihrer vergessend ?
    Deiner, deiner vergessend,
    traute, theuerste Mutter ?

Kundry
(immer noch in liegender Stellung ausgestreckt, beugt sich über PARSIFAL's Haupt, fasst sanft seine Stirne, und schlingt träulich ihren Arm um seinen Nacken).

    War dir fremd noch der Schmerz,
        des Trostes Süsse
    labte nie auch dein Herz :
    das Wehe, das dich reu't,
        die Noth nun büsse,
    im Trost, den Liebe dir beut !

Parsifal
                        (trübe).
    Die Mutter, die Mutter konnt' ich vergessen !
    Ha ! Was Alles vergass ich wohl noch ?
    Wess' war ich je noch eingedenk ?
    Nur dumpfe Thorheit lebt in mir !
                (Er lässt sich immer tiefer sinken.)

Kundry.   Bekenntniss
    wird Schuld und Reue enden.
        Erkenntniss
    in Sinn die Thorheit wenden :
    die Liebe lerne kennen,
    die Gamuret umschloss,
    als Herzeleid's Entbrennen
    ihn sengend überfloss :
        die Leib und Leben
        einst dir gegeben,
    der Tod und Thorheit weichen muss,
        sie beut'
        dir heut' —
    als Muttersegens letzten Gruss
        der Liebe — ersten Kuss.
(Sie hat ihr Haupt völlig über das seinige geneigt, und heftet nun ihre Lippen zu einem langen Kusse auf seinen Mund.)

Parsifal
(fährt plötzlich mit einer Gebärde des höchsten Schreckens auf : seine Haltung drückt eine furchtbare Veränderung aus ; er stemmt seine Hände gewaltsam gegen sein Herz, wie um einen zerreissenden Schmerz zu bewältigen ; endlich bricht er aus).
            Amfortas ! —
        Die Wunde ! — Die Wunde ! —

13

In me I feel it burning. —
       Oh, horror! horror!
       Direfullest horror!
It shrieks from out the depth of my soul.
       Oh! — Oh! —
       Misery! —
       Lamentation! —
I saw thy wound a-bleeding : —
It bleeds now in myself —
       Here — here!

(Whilst KUNDRY stares at him in wonder and alarm, he continues madly.)

No, no! This is not the spearwound :
Let it gush blood in streams if it list.
Here! — here! My heart is ablaze!
     The passion, the terrible passion,
That all my senses doth seize and sway!
     Oh! — Love's delirium! —
How all things tremble, heave and quake
     With longings that are sinful! . . .

(terribly quiet).

My frozen glance stares on the sacred Cup: —
     The Holy One's blood doth glow; —
Redemption's rapture, sweet and mild,
Is trembling far through ev'ry spirit;
But in this heart will the pangs not lessen.
     The Saviour's wailing I distinguished,
     The wailing — ah! the wailing
For His polluted sanctuary : —
       " Recover, save me from
       The hands that guilt has sullied! "
     Thus — rang the lamentation
Through my soul with fearful loudness:
     And I — oh, Fool! — oh, coward!
To wild and childish exploits hither fled.

(He throws himself despairingly on his knees.)

Redeemer! Saviour! Gracious Lord!
What can retrieve my crime abhorred?

Kundry

(whose astonishment has changed to sorrowful wonder, tries tremblingly to approach PARSIFAL).

My noble knight! fling off this spell!
Look up! nor Love's delights repel!

Parsifal

(still in a kneeling posture, gazing blankly up at KUNDRY, whilst she stoops over him with the embracing movements which he describes in the following).

Aye! Thus it called him! This voice it
     was ; —
And this the glance ; surely I know it well, —
The eyeglance which smiled away his quiet. —
These lips too, — aye — they tempted him
     thus ; —
     So bowed this neck above him, —
     So high was raised this head ; —

Sie brennt in meinem Herzen. —
       Oh, Klage! Klage!
       Furchtbare Klage!
Aus tiefstem Inner'n schreit sie mir auf.
       Oh! — Oh! —
       Elender! —
       Jammervollster! —
Die Wunde sah' ich bluten : —
nun blutet sie mir selbst —
       hier — hier!

(Während KUNDRY in Schrecken und Verwunderung auf ihn hin starrt, fährt PARSIFAL in gänzlicher Entrücktheit fort.)

Nein, nein! Nicht ist es die Wunde :
fliesse ihr Blut in Strömen dahin!
Hier! Hier im Herzen der Brand!
     Das Sehnen, das furchtbare Sehnen,
das alle Sinne mir fasst und zwingt!
     Oh! — Qual der Liebe! —
Wie Alles schauert, bebt und zuckt
     in sündigem Verlangen! . . .

(Schauerlich leise).

Es starrt der Blick dumpf auf das Heilsgefäss : —
     das heilige Blut erglüh't ; —
Erlösungswonne, göttlich mild',
durchzittert weithin alle Seelen :
nur hier, im Herzen, will die Qual nicht weichen.
     Des Heiland's Klage da vernehm' ich,
     die Klage, ach! die Klage
um das verrath'ne Heiligthum : —
       ,erlöse, rette mich
       aus schuldbefleckten Händen! "
     So — rief die Gottesklage
furchtbar laut mir in die Seele.
     Und ich? Der Thor, der Feige?
Zu wilden Knabenthaten floh' ich hin!

(Er stürzt verzweiflungsvoll auf die Knie.)

Erlöser! Heiland! Herr der Huld!
Wie büss' ich Sünder solche Schuld?

Kundry

(deren Erstaunen in leidenschaftliche Bewunderung übergeht, sucht schüchtern sich PARSIFAL zu nähern).

Gelobter Held! Entflieh' dem Wahn!
Blick' auf! Sei hold der Huldin Nah'n!

Parsifal

(immer in gebeugter Stellung, starr zu KUNDRY aufblickend, während diese sich zu ihm neigt und die liebkosenden Bewegungen ausführt, die er mit dem Folgenden bezeichnet).

Ja! Diese Stimme! So rief sie ihm ; —
und diesen Blick, deutlich erkenn' ich ihn, —
auch diesen, der ihm so friedlos lachte.
Die Lippe, — ja — so zuckte sie ihm ; —
     so neigte sich der Nacken —
     so hob sich kühn das Haupt ; —

So fluttered these locks as though laugh-
        ing, —
So circled this arm round his neck —
So softened each feature in fondness, — !
In league with Sorrow's dismal weight,
    This mouth took from him
    His soul's salvation straight ! —
    Ha ! — with this kiss ! —

(With the last words he has gradually risen, and now springs completely up and spurns KUNDRY from him.)

    Pernicious one !   Get thee from me !
    Leave me — leave me — for aye !

Kundry
                (in intense grief).
    Cruel one ! — Ha ! —
    Felt e'er thy nature
    For one fellow creature,
    Then feel now my desolation !
        Wert thou the Saver,
        Thou wouldst not waver,
    But with me unite for salvation ?
Through endless ages for thee I've waited,
    The Saviour — ah, so late !
    At whom I scoffed in hate. —
        Oh ! —
    Couldst thou know the curse,
    Which through me, waking, sleeping,
        Through death and lifetime,
        Joy or weeping,
While ever steeled to bear fresh woes,
Endless through my being flows ! —
        I saw Him — Him —
        And — mocked Him ! . . .
    I caught then His glance, —
I seek Him now from world to world,
    Once more to stand before Him :
        In deepest woe —
    Sometimes His eye doth seem near,
    His glance resting on me.
Returns then th' accursed laughter on me, —
    A sinner sinks in my embraces !
        Then laughter — laughter —,
        Weep I cannot ;
        But only shriek
        And rage and wallow
In night and madness never slaked,
From which, repentant, scarce I'd waked. —
Thou for whom, shamed to death, I've bided,
Thou whom I knew and, fool, derided,
Let me upon thy breast lie sobbing,
But for one hour together throbbing ;
Though forced from God and man to flee,
Be yet redeemed and pardoned by thee !

Parsifal.   Eternally
    Should I be damned with thee,

19

so flatterten lachend die Locken, —
so schläng um den Hals sich der Arm —
so schmeichelte weich die Wange — !
Mit aller Schmerzen Qual im Bund,
    das Heil der Seele
    entküsste ihm ihr Mund ! —
    Ha ! — dieser Kuss ! —

(Er hat sich mit dem Letzten allmählich erhoben springt jetzt vollends auf, und stösst KUNDRY heftig von sich.)

    Verderberin !   Weiche von mir !
    Ewig — ewig — von mir !

Kundry
                (in höchster Leidenschaft).
    Grausamer ! — Ha ! —
    Fühlst du im Herzen,
    nur Anderer Schmerzen,
    so fühle jetzt auch die meinen !
        Bist du Erlöser,
    was bannt dich, Böser,
nicht mir auch zum Heil dich zu einen ?
Seit Ewigkeiten — harre ich deiner,
    des Heiland's, ach ! so spät,
    den einst ich kühn verschmäht. —
        Oh ! —
    Kenntest du den Fluch,
    der mich durch Schlaf und Wachen,
        durch Tod und Leben,
        Pein und Lachen,
    zu neuem Leiden neu gestählt,
    endlos durch das Dasein quält ! —
        Ich sah — Ihn — Ihn —
        und — lachte . . .
    da traf mich sein Blick. —
Nun such' ich ihn von Welt zu Welt,
    ihm wieder zu begegnen :
        in höchster Noth —
    wähn' ich sein Auge schon nah',
    den Blick schon auf mir ruh'n : —
da kehrt mir das verfluchte Lachen wieder —
    ein Sünder sinkt mir in die Arme !
        Da lach' ich — lache —,
        kann nicht weinen :
        nur schreien, wüthen,
        toben, rasen
in stets erneu'ten Wahnsinn's Nacht,
aus der ich büssend kaum erwacht. —
Den ich ersehnt in Todesschmachten,
den ich erkannt, den blöd' Verlachten,
lass' mich an seinem Busen weinen,
nur eine Stunde dir vereinen,
und, ob mich Gott und Welt verstöss't !
in dir entsündig't sein und erlös't !

Parsifal.
    In Ewigkeit
    wärst du verdammt mit mir

If for one hour
I forgot my holy mission,
Within thy arms embracing ! —
To thy help also am I sent,
If of thy cravings thou repent.
The solace, which shall end thy sorrow,
Yields not that spring from which it flows :
Salvation can'st thou never borrow,
Till that same spring in thee shall close.
Far other 'tis — far other, aye !
For which I saw, with pitying eyes,
That brotherhood distrest and pining,
Their lives tormented and declining,
But who with certain clearness knows
The source whence true salvation flows ?
Oh, mis'ry ! What a course is this !
        Oh, wild hallucination !
In such a search for sacred bliss
Thus to desire the soul's damnation !

Kundry.   And was it my kiss
This great knowledge conveyed thee ?
If in my arms I might take thee,
'T would then a god surely make thee !
Redeem the world then, if 'tis thy aim : —
        Stand as a god revealéd ;
For this hour let me perish in flame,
Leave aye the wound unhealéd.

Parsifal.   Redemption, sinner, I offer e'en thee—

Kundry.   Let me, divine one, but love thee ;
Redemption then should I see.

Parsifal.   Love and Redemption thou shalt lack
        not, —
        If the way
To Amfortas thou wilt show.

Kundry
                    (breaking into a rage).
Thou — never shalt find it !
Let the doomed one perish forever. —
        The shame seeker,
        Joy-destitute,
Whom I have laughed at —laughed at —
        laughed at !
Ha, ha ! He fell by his own good spear ?

Parsifal.   Who dared raise against him the holy
        gear ?

Kundry.   He — he —,
        Who puts my laughter to flight :
His curse — ha ! — doth lend me might :
For thyself the Spear doth await
If thou dost pity the sinner's fate ! —
        Ha ! madness !
        Pity ! pity me, pray !

        für eine Stunde
Vergessen's meiner Sendung,
        in deines Arm's Umfangen ! —
Auch dir bin ich zum Heil gesandt,
bleib'st du dem Sehnen abgewandt.
Die Labung, die dein Leiden endet,
beut nicht der Quell, aus dem es fliesst :
das Heil wird nimmer dir gespendet,
wenn jener Quell sich dir nicht schliesst.
Ein andrer ist's, — ein andrer, ach !
nach dem ich jammernd schmachten sah,
die Brüder dort in grausen Nöthen
den Leib sich quälen und ertödten.
Doch wer erkennt ihn klar und hell,
des einz'gen Heiles wahren Quell ?
Oh, Elend ! Aller Rettung Flucht !
        Oh, Weltenwahns Umnachten :
in höchsten Heiles heisser Sucht
nach der Verdammniss Quell zu schmachten !

Kundry.
        So war es mein Kuss,
der Welt-hellsichtig dich machte ?

        Mein volles Liebes-Umfangen
        lässt dich dann Gottheit erlangen !
Die Welt erlöse, ist diess dein Amt : —
        schuf dich zum Gott die Stunde,
für sie lasse mich ewig verdammt,
        nie heile mir die Wunde.

Parsifal.   Erlösung, Frevlerin, biet' ich auch dir

Kundry.   Lass' mich dich Göttlichen lieben,
        Erlösung gabst du dann mir.

Parsifal.   Lieb' und Erlösung soll dir lohnen, —
        zeigest zu
        zu Amfortas mir den Weg.

Kundry
                    (in Wuth ausbrechend).
Nie — sollst du ihn finden !
Den Verfall'nen, lass' ihn verderben, —
        den Un-seligen,
        Schmach-lüsternen,
den ich verlachte — lachte — lachte !
Haha ! Ihn traf ja der eig'ne Speer ?

Parsifal.   Wer durft' ihn verwunden mit heil'ger
        Wehr ?

Kundry.   Er — Er —,
        der einst mein Lachen bestraft :
sein Fluch — ha ! — mir giebt er Kraft ;
gegen dich selbst ruf' ich die Wehr,
gieb'st du dem Sünder des Mitleid's Ehr' ! —
        Ha ! Wahnsinn ! —
        Mitleid ! Mitleid mit mir !

One single hour with me —
One single hour with thee —
  Then, the wished-for
Path thou shalt straightway see !
(She seeks to embrace him : he thrusts her from him.)

Parsifal. Begone, detestable wretch !

Kundry
  (beats her breast and shrieks in wild frenzy).
Hither ! Hither ! Oh, help !
Seize on the caitiff ! Oh, help !
  Ward all the ways there !
  Ward ev'ry passage ! —
For, fled'st thou from hence, and foundest
All the ways of the world,
The one that thou seek'st
That pathway ne'er shalt thou pass through !
  All paths and courses,
  Which from me would part thee,
Here — I curse them to thee :
  Wander — wander, —
  Thou whom I trust —
Thee will I give as his guide !

KLINGSOR has appeared upon the castle wall ; the DAMSELS also rush out of the castle and seek to hasten toward KUNDRY.

Klingsor
  (poising a lance).
Halt there ! I'll ban thee with befitting gear :
The Fool shall perish by his Master's spear !

He flings the spear at PARSIFAL ; it remains floating over his head ; PARSIFAL grasps it with his hand and brandishes it with a gesture of exalted rapture, making the sign of the Cross with it.

Parsifal. This sign I make, and ban thy cursed
  magic :
  As the wound shall be closed,
  Which thou with this once clovest, —
  To wrack and to ruin
  Falls thy unreal display !

As with an earthquake the castle falls to ruins ; the garden withers up to a desert : the DAMSELS lie like shrivelled flowers strewn around on the ground. — KUNDRY has sunk down with a cry. To her turns once more from the summit of the ruined wall the departing

Parsifal. Thou know'st—
  Where only we shall meet again !
(He disappears. The curtain closes quickly.)

Parsifal. Vergeh', unseliges Weib !

Kundry
  (zerschlägt sich die Brust, und ruft in wildem Rasen).
Hilfe ! Hilfe ! Herbei !
Haltet den Frechen ! Herbei !
  Wehr't ihm die Wege !
  Wehr't ihm die Pfade ! —
Und flöh'st du von hier, und fändest
alle Wege der Welt,
den Weg, den du such'st,
dess' Pfade sollst du nicht finden !
  Denn Pfad und Wege,
  die mir dich entführen,
so — verwünsch' ich sie dir :
  Irre ! Irre, —
  mir so vertraut —
dich weih' ich ihm zum Geleit' !

KLINGSOR ist auf der Burgmauer heraus getreten ; die MÄDCHEN stürzen ebenfalls aus dem Schloss und wollen auf KUNDRY zueilen.

Klingsor
  (eine Lanze schwingend).
Halt da ! dich bann' ich mit der rechten Wehr :
den Thoren stell' mir seines Meisters Speer !

Er schleudert auf PARSIFAL den Speer, welcher über dessen Haupte schweben bleibt ; PARSIFAL erfasst ihn mit der Hand und schwingt ihn, mit einer Gebärde höchster Entzückung, die Gestalt des Kreuzes bezeichnend.

Parsifal. Mit diesem Zeichen bann' ich deiner
  Zauber :
  wie die Wunde er schliesse,
  die mit ihm du schlugest, —
  in Trauer und Trümmer
  stürze die trügende Pracht !

Wie durch ein Erdbeben versinkt das Schloss ; der Garten verdorrt zur Einöde : die MÄDCHEN liegen als verwelkte Blumen am Boden umher gestreut. — KUNDRY ist schreiend zusammen gesunken. Zu ihr wendet sich noch einmal, von der Höhe einer Mauertrümmer herab, der enteilende

Parsifal. Du weisst—
  wo einzig du mich wiedersieh'st !
(Er verschwindet. Der Vorhang schliesst sich schnell.)

ACT III.

In the Grail's domain.—Open, pleasant spring landscape, with flowery meadows rising towards the back. At the front is the border of a wood, which extends away R. A spring, in the foreground, by the wood; opposite, higher up, a narrow hermitage, built against a rock. Daybreak.—

GURNEMANZ, now extremely aged, meanly dressed as a hermit, but with the tunic of a Knight of the Grail, emerges from the hut and listens.

Gurnemanz.　From thence the groaning cometh.—
　　No animal grieves like that ;
And on this, besides,—the holiest day we
　　　have.—
Methinks I recognize those rueful tones.

A low moaning is heard as of a sleeper terrified by dreams.—GURNEMANZ strides resolutely to a thicket at one side which has overgrown itself : he forcibly tears the brambles asunder, then pauses suddenly.

　　Ha ! She—here again ?
　　The hedge with its thorns overgrown
　　Has been her grave for how long ?—
　　Up—Kundry !—Up !
　　The winter's fled, and Spring is here !
　　Awake, awake to the Spring !
　　　Cold—and stiff !—
　　This time truly I deem she's dead : —
　　Yet was't her groaning I heard just now ?

(He drags KUNDRY, quite rigid and lifeless, out of the bushes, bears her to a grassy mound near, chafes her hands and temples, breathes on them, and does his utmost to relax her stiffness. At last she revives She is, just as in the first Act, dressed in the wild garb of a servant of the Grail ; only her complexion is paler, and the wildness has faded from her mien and bearing —She stares awhile at GURNEMANZ. Then she rises, settles her hair and dress, and goes immediately, like a serving maid, to her work.)

Gurnemanz.　Thou crazy wench !
　　Hast not a word for me ?
　　Are these thy thanks,
　　When from deathly slumber
　　I have waked thee yet again ?

Kundry
(bows her head slowly : then in hoarse and broken accents murmurs).
　　Service . . . service !—

Gurnemanz
　　　　　(shaking his head).
　　Now will thy work be light !
　　We send no errands out since long :
　　　Simples and herbs
　　Must ev'ryone find for himself :
　　'Tis learnt in the woods from the beasts.

KUNDRY has meanwhile looked about her, and now perceives the hut, and goes within.

Gurnemanz
　　　　　(looking after her in surprise).
　　How unlike this her step of yore !
　　Is this holy morning the cause ?

DRITTER AUFZUG.

Im Gebiete des Grales

Freie, anmuthige Frühlingsgegend mit nach dem Hintergrunde zu sanft ansteigender Blumenaue. Den Vordergrund nimmt der Saum des Waldes ein, der sich nach rechts zu ausdehnt. Im Vordergrunde, an der Waldseite, ein Quell ; ihm gegenüber, etwas tiefer eine schlichte Einsiedlerhütte, an einen Felsen gelehnt. Frühester Morgen.—

GURNEMANZ, zum hohen Greise gealtert, als Einsiedler, nur in das Hemd des Gralsritters dürftig gekleidet, tritt aus der Hütte und lauscht.

Gurnemanz.　Von dorther kam das Stöhnen. —
　　So jammervoll klagt kein Wild,
und gewiss gar nicht am heiligsten Morgen
　　　heut'. —
Mich dünkt, ich kenne diesen Klageruf ?

Ein dumpfes Stöhnen, wie von einer im tiefen Schlafe durch Träume Geängstigten, wird vernommen. — GURNEMANZ schreitet entschlossen einer Dornenhecke auf der Seite zu : diese ist gänzlich überwachsen ; er reisst mit Gewalt das Gestrüpp auseinander ; dann hält er plötzlich an.

　　Ha !　Sie—wieder da ?
　　Das winterlich rauhe Gedörn'
　　hielt sie verdeckt : wie lang' schon ?—
　　Auf !—Kundry !—Auf !
　　Der Winter floh, und Lenz ist da !
　　Erwach', erwache dem Lenz !—
　　　kalt—und starr !—
　　Diessmal hielt' ich sie wohl für todt. —
　　doch war's ihr Stöhnen, was ich vernahm ?

Er zieht KUNDRY, ganz erstarrt und leblos, aus dem Gebüsche hervor, trägt sie auf einen nahen Rasenhügel, reibt ihr stark die Hände und Schläfe, haucht sie an, und bemüht sich in Allem, um die Erstarrung weichen zu machen. Endlich erwacht sie. Sie ist, gänzlich wie im ersten Aufzuge, im wilden Gewande der Gralsbotin ; nur ist ihre Gesichtsfarbe bleicher, aus Miene und Haltung ist die Wildheit gewichen. — Sie starrt lange GURNEMANZ an. Dann erhebt sie sich, ordnet sich Kleidung und Haar, und geht sofort wie eine Magd an die Bedienung.

Gurnemanz.　Du tolles Weib !
　　Hast du kein Wort für mich ?
　　Ist diess der Dank,
　　　dass dem Todesschlafe
　　noch einmal ich dich entweckt ?

Kundry
(neigt langsam das Haupt ; dann bringt sie, rauh und abgebrochen hervor):
　　Dienen . . dienen !—

Gurnemanz
　　　　　(schüttelt den Kopf).
　　Das wird dich wenig müh'n !
　　Auf Botschaft sendet sich's nicht mehr :
　　　Kräuter und Wurzeln
　　findet ein Jeder sich selbst,
　　wir lernen's im Walde vom Thier.

KUNDRY hat sich während dem umgesehen, gewahrt die Hütte und geht hinein.

Gurnemanz
　　　　　(verwundert ihr nachblickend).
　　Wie anders schreitet sie als sonst !
　　Wirkte das der heilige Tag ?

Oh, day of mercy unimagined !
No doubt for her salvation
Heaven through me revived
This wretch from deathly slumber.

KUNDRY comes from the hut again ; she bears a water pot, which she takes to the spring. Whilst she waits for it to fill, she looks into the wood, and perceives some one approaching in the distance ; she turns to GURNEMANZ to point him out to him.

Gurnemanz
(peering into the wood).
Who comes towards the sanctified stream ?
In gloomy war apparel—
None of our brethren is he.

KUNDRY withdraws, with the filled pitcher, to the hut, where she busies herself.—GURNEMANZ steps aside in surprise, to observe the newcomer.—PARSIFAL enters from the wood. He is in complete black armor ; with closed helmet and lowered spear he walks slowly forward, his head drooping, dreamily vacillating—he seats himself on the little knoll by the spring.

Gurnemanz
observes him a long while and then approaches somewhat).
Greet thee, my friend !
Art thou astray, and shall I direct thee ?
(PARSIFAL shakes his head softly.)

Gurnemanz. And hast thou no greeting for me ?
(PARSIFAL bows his head.)

Gurnemanz. Hey ! — what ? —
If by thy vow
Thou art bound to perfect silence,
So mine remindeth me
Straight to inform thee what is due. —
Here thou art in a holy place ;
No man with weapons hither comes,
With shut-up helmet, shield and spear.
This day, besides ! Dost thou not know
What holy day hath dawned ?
(PARSIFAL shakes his head.)
No ? From whence com'st thou then ?
What heathen darkness hast thou left
To hear not that to-day is
The ever hallow d Good-Friday morn ?
(PARSIFAL droops his head still lower.)
Quick, doff thy weapons !
Trouble not this morn the Master,
Who once did free all men from hell,
When bare of defence He bled for us.

PARSIFAL rises, after a further silence, thrusts the spear into the ground before him, lays down his sword and shield before it, opens his helmet and, taking it from his head, lays it with the other arms, and then kneels down in silent prayer before the spear. GURNEMANZ observes him with surprise and emotion. He beckons KUNDRY, who has now come out of the hut.—PARSIFAL raises his eyes, in ardent prayer, towards the spear's head.)

Gurnemanz
(softly to KUNDRY).
Dost know who 'tis ? . .
He who, long since, laid low the swan.
(KUNDRY confirms him by a slight nod.)

Oh ! Tag der Gnade ohne Gleichen !
Gewiss zu ihrem Heile
durft' ich der Armen heut'
den Todesschlaf verscheuchen.

KUNDRY kommt wieder aus der Hütte ; sie trägt einen Wasserkrug und geht damit zum Quelle. Während sie auf die Füllung wartet, blickt sie in den Wald, und bemerkt dort in der Ferne einen Kommenden ; sie wendet sich zu GURNEMANZ, um ihn darauf hinzudeuten.

Gurnemanz
(in den Wald spähend).
Wer nahet dort dem heiligen Quell ?
Im düst'ren Waffenschmucke,
das ist der Brüder keiner.

KUNDRY entfernt sich mit dem gefüllten Kruge langsam nach der Hütte, in welcher sie sich zu schaffen macht.—GURNEMANZ tritt staunend etwas bei Seite, um den Ankommenden zu beobachten.—PARSIFAL tritt aus dem Walde auf. Er ist ganz in schwarzer Waffenrüstung : mit geschlossenem Helme und gesenktem Speer, schreitet er, gebeugten Hauptes, träumerisch zögernd, langsam daher, und setzt sich auf dem kleinen Rasenhügel am Quelle nieder.

Gurnemanz
(betrachtet ihn lange, und tritt dann etwas näher).
Heil dir, mein Gast !
Bist du verirrt, und soll ich dich weisen ?
(PARSIFAL schüttelt sanft das Haupt.)

Gurnemanz. Entbietest du mir keinen Gruss ?
(PARSIFAL neigt das Haupt.)

Gurnemanz. Hei ! — Was ?
Wenn dein Gelübde
dich bindet mir zu schweigen,
so mahnt das meine mich,
dass ich dir sag , was sich ziemt. —
Hier bist du an geweihtem Ort :
da zieht man nicht mit Waffen her,
geschloss'nen Helmes, Schild und Speer.
Und heute gar ! Weisst du denn nicht,
welch' heil'ger Tag heut' ist ?
(PARSIFAL schüttelt mit dem Kopfe.)
Ja ! Woher komm'st du denn ?
Bei welchen Heiden weiltest du,
zu wissen nicht, dass heute
der allerheiligste Char-Freitag sei ?
(PARSIFAL senkt das Haupt noch tiefer.)
Schnell ab die Waffen !
Kränke nicht den Herrn, der heute,
baar jeder Wehr, sein heilig Blut
der sündigen Welt zur Sühne bot !

PARSIFAL erhebt sich, nach einem abermaligen Schweigen, stösst den Speer vor sich in den Boden, legt Schild und Schwert davor nieder, öffnet den Helm, nimmt ihn vom Haupte und legt ihn zu den anderen Waffen, worauf er dann zu stummem Gebete vor dem Speer niederkniet. GURNEMANZ betrachtet ihn mit Erstaunen und Rührung. Er winkt KUNDRY herbei, welche soeben aus der Hütte getreten ist.—PARSIFAL erhebt jetzt in brünstigem Gebete seinen Blick andachtvoll zur Lanzenspitze auf.

Gurnemanz
(leise zu KUNDRY)
Erkenn'st du ihn ? .
Der ist's, der einst den Schwan erlegt,
(KUNDRY bestätigt mit einem leisen Kopfnicken.)

For sure 'tis he !
The Fool whom in anger I dismissed?
Ha ! by what path aye came he ?
That Spear — I recognize !
(in great emotion).
Oh ! — holiest day,
To which my happy soul awakes ! —
(Kundry has turned away her face.)

Parsifal
.rises slowly from his prayer, gazes calmly around, recognizes
Gurnemanz, and stretches out his hand to him in greeting).
Thank Heaven that I again have found
    thee !

Gurnemanz.   And dost thou know me too?
    Dost recognize me,
So lowly bent by grief and care ?
    How cam'st thou here ? From whence ?

Parsifal.   Through error and through suff'ring
    lay my pathway ;
May I believe that I have freed me from it,
    Now that this forest's murmur
    Falls upon my senses,
And worthy voice of age doth welcome ?
    Or yet — is't new error ?
All's altered here, meseemeth.

Gurnemanz.   But say, where points the path thou
    seekest ?

Parsifal.   To him, whose dire complainings
Once came to me, an awestruck Fool,
    And for whose healing surely
I must believe myself ordained.
        But — ah ! —
The wished for path for aye denied me,
    I wandered at random,
Driven ever on by a curse :
        Countless distresses,
        Battles and conflicts
Drove me far from the pathway ;
Well though I knew it, methought.
Then hopeless despair overtook me
To hold the holy Thing safely.
In its behalf, in its safe warding
I won from ev'ry weapon a wound ;
        For 'twas forbidden
    That in battle I bore it :
        Undefiled
    E'er at my side I wore it,
    And now I home restore it.
'Tis this that gleaming hails thee here, —
    The Grail's most holy spear.

Gurnemanz.   Oh Glory ! Bounteous bliss !
Oh marvel ! Beauteous, boundless marvel !

Gewiss 's ist Er !
Der Thor, den ich zürnend von uns wies ?
Ha ! Welche Pfade fand er ?
Der Speer, — ich kenne ihn.
(In grosser Ergriffenheit.)
Oh ! — Heiligster Tag,
zu dem ich heut' erwachen sollt' ! —
(Kundry hat ihr Gesicht abgewendet.)

Parsifal
(erhebt sich langsam vom Gebete, blickt ruhig um s..n, erkenn
Gurnemanz, und reicht diesem sanft die Hand zum Gruss).
Heil mir, dass ich dich wieder finde !

Gurnemanz.   So kenn'st auch du mich noch ?
    Erkenn'st mich wieder.
    den Gram und Noth so tief gebeugt ?
    Wie kam'st du heut' ?   Woher ?

Parsifal.   Der Irrniss und der Leiden Pfade
    kam ich ;
soll ich mich denen jetzt entwunden wähnen,
    da dieses Waldes Rauschen
    wieder ich vernehme,
    dich guten Alten neu begrüsse ?
    Oder — irr' ich wieder ?
    Verwandelt dünkt mich Alles.

Gurnemanz.   So sag', zu wem den Weg du
    suchtest ?

Parsifal.   Zu ihm, dess' tiefe Klagen
    ich thörig staunend einst vernahm,
    dem nun ich Heil zu bringen
    mich auserlesen wähnen darf.
        doch — ach ! —
    den Weg des Heiles nie zu finden,
    in pfadlosen Irren
    iagt' ein wilder Fluch mich umher :
        zahllose Nöthen,
        Kämpfe und Streite
    zwangen mich ab vom Pfade,
    wähnt' ich ihn recht schon erkannt.
    Da musste Verzweiflung mich fassen,
    das Heilthum heil mir zu bergen,
um das zu hüten, das zu wahren
ich Wunden jeder Wehr' mir gewann.
        Denn nicht ihn selber
    durft' ich führen im Streite ;
        unentweih't
    führt' ich ihn mir zur Seite,
    den ich nun heim geleite,
der dort dir schimmert hiel und hehr,
    des Grales heil'gen Speer.

Gurnemanz.   O Gnade ! Höchstes Heil !
O Wunder ! Heilig hehrstes Wunder ! —

(After he has somewhat collected himself).

Great knight! If 'twere a curse,
Which drove thee from thy proper path,
Be sure it has departed.
Here art thou, in the Grail's domain;
Here waits for thee the knightly band
Ah! how they need the blessing,
The blessing that thou bring'st! —
Since that first day in which thou camest here,
The mourning, which thou heardest then —
The anguish — sorely has increased.
Amfortas, struggling with his torture,
With the wound that tore his spirit,
Desired with reckless daring then his death:
No pray'rs, no sorrow of his comrades
Could move him to fulfil his holy office.
In shrouded shrine the Grail has long remained.
Its sin-repentant warder wishing,
Since he could perish not,
While he beheld its light,
To speed his dissolution,
And with his life to end his bitter sorrows.
The Holy Meal to us is now denied,
And common viands must content us;
Thereby hath withered all our heroes' strength:
Ne'er cometh message now,
Nor call to holy warfare from far countries;
Pale, dejected, strays around
The crushed and leader-lacking band of knights.
Here on the woodside lone I hid myself,
For death with calmness waiting,
To which my old commander has succumbed;
For Titurel, my cherished chief,
When he no more beheld the Grail's refulgence,
Expired, — a man like others!

Parsifal

(flinging up his arms in intense grief).

And I — I 'tis,
Who all this woe have wrought!
Ha! what a grievous,
What a heinous guilt
Must then my foolish head
For ever be oppressed with!
If no atonement, expiation
My blindness e'er can banish!
I, who to save men was selected,
Must wander undirected;
All paths of safety from me vanish!

(He is on the point of falling, helplessly. GURNEMANZ supports him, and allows him to sink down on the grassy knoll. — KUNDRY has brought a basin of water to sprinkle PARSIFAL with.)

Gurnemanz

(waving her off.)

Not so! —
The holy fount itself

(Nachdem er sich etwas gefasst.)

O Herr! War es ein Fluch,
der dich vom rechten Pfad vertrieb,
so glaub', er ist gewichen.
Hier bist du; diess des Gral's Gebiet,
dein' harret seine Ritterschaft.
Ach, sie bedarf des Heiles,
des Heiles, das du bring'st! —
Seit jenem Tage, den du hier geweilt,
die Trauer, so da kund dir ward. —
das Bangen — wuchs zur höchsten Noth.
Amfortas, gegen seiner Wunde,
seiner Seele Qual sich wehrend,
begehrt' in wildem Trotze nun den Tod:
kein Fleh'n, kein Elend seiner Ritter
bewog ihn mehr des heil'gen Amt's zu walten
Im Schrein verschlossen bleibt seit lang' der
Gral:
so hofft sein sündenreu'ger Hüter,
da er nicht sterben kann
wann je er ihn erschau't,
sein Ende zu erzwingen.
und mit dem Leben seine Qual zu enden.
Die heil'ge Speisung bleibt uns nun versagt,
gemeine Atzung muss uns nähren;
darob versiechte unsrer Helden Kraft:
nie kommt uns Botschaft mehr,
noch Ruf zu heil'gen Kämpfen aus der Ferne;
bleich und elend wankt umher
die Muth- und Führer-lose Ritterschaft.
Hier in der Waldeck' barg ich einsam mich,
des Todes still gewärtig,
dem schon mein alter Waffenherr verfiel
denn Titurel, mein heil'ger Held,
den nun des Grales Anblick nicht mehr labte
er starb, — ein Mensch wie Alle!

Parsifal

(vor grossen Schmerz sich aufbäumend).

Und ich — ich bin's,
der all' diess Elend schuf!
Ha! Welcher Sünden,
welcher Frevel Schuld
muss dieses Thoren-Haupt
seit Ewigkeit belasten,
da keine Busse, keine Sühne
der Blindheit mich entwindet,
mir, selbst zur Rettung auserkoren,
in Irrniss wild verloren
der Rettung letzter Pfad verschwindet!

(Er droht ohnmächtig umzusinken. GURNEMANZ hält ihn auf recht, und senkt ihn zum Sitze auf den Rasenhügel nieder. — KUNDRY hat ein Becken mit Wasser herbeigeholt, um PARSIFAL zu besprengen.)

Gurnemanz

(KUNDRY abweisend).

Nicht so! —
Die heil'ge Quelle selbst

Befitteth more our pilgrim's bath.
　I ween a mighty feat
　Must he this morning finish,
Fulfil a sacred, mystic duty:
　He should be pure as day ·
　So let his travel stains
Be now completely washed away.

They both turn PARSIFAL gently to the edge of the spring.
Whilst KUNDRY removes the greaves from his legs, and then bathes
his feet, GURNEMANZ meanwhile removing his corselet,—

Parsifal
　　　　　(asks gently and wearily).
Shall I straight be guided unto Amfortas?

Gurnemanz
　　　　　(busying himself).
Most surely; there the Court our coming waits.
The obsequies of my belovéd chief,
　Have even summoned me.
The Grail to us will once more be uncovered,
　The long neglected office
　Once more performed before us —
To sanctify the sov'reign father,
Who through his son's great sin has died,
Which he now fain would expiate. —
　'Tis thus Amfortas wills.

Parsifal
　　　　　(observing KUNDRY with wonder).
　Thou'st washed my feet so humbly: —
This friend besprinkles now my head.

Gurnemanz
(taking water from the spring in the hollow of his hand, and
　　　　　sprinkling PARSIFAL's head).
Now blessed be, thou pure one, through pure
　　　water!
　So may all care and sin
　Be driven far from thee.

Meanwhile KUNDRY has taken a golden flask from her bosom
and poured some of the contents upon PARSIFAL's feet, which she
now dries on her hair, quickly unbound for the purpose.

Parsifal
　　　　　(taking the flask from her).
Now that my feet thou'st anointed,
My head the friend of Titurel must lave;
For I to-day as king shall be appointed.

Gurnemanz
(empties the flask completely over PARSIFAL's head, rubs it gently,
　　　　　and folds his hands over it).
　Aye, thus it was foretold me,
　My blessing on thy head: —
　Our king indeed behold we.
　　Thou — pure one —
　Allpitying sufferer,
　Allknowing rescuer!
Thou who the sinner's sorrows thus hast suffered,
Assist his soul to cast one burden more.

21

erquicke uns'res Pilgers Bad.
　Mir ahnt, ein hohes Werk
　hat er noch heut' zu wirken,
zu walten eines heil'gen Amtes:
　so sei er fleckenrein,
　und langer Irrfahrt Staub
söll jetzt von ihm gewaschen sein.

PARSIFAL wird von den Beiden sanft zum Rande des Quelles gewendet. Während KUNDRY ihm die Beinschienen lös't und dann
die Füsse badet, GURNEMANZ ihm aber den Brustharnisch entnimmt,
frägt

Parsifal
　　　　　(sanft und matt).
Werd' heut' ich zu Amfortas noch geleitet?

Gurnemanz
　　　　　(während der Beschäftigung).
Gewisslich, uns'rer harrt die hehre Burg:
die Todtenfeier meines lieben Herrn,
　sie ruft mich selbst dahin.
Den Gral noch einmal uns da zu enthüllen,
　des lang' versäumten Amtes
　noch einmal heut' zu walten —
zur Heiligung des hehren Vaters,
der seines Sohnes Schuld erlag,
die Der nun also büssen will, —
　gelobt' Amfortas uns.

Parsifal
　　　　　(mit Verwunderung KUNDRY zusehend).
　Du wuschest mir die Füsse: —
nun netze mir das Haupt der Freund.

Gurnemanz
(mit der Hand aus dem Quell schöpfend und PARSIFAL's Haupt
　　　　　besprengend).

21

Gesegnet sei, du Reiner, durch das Reine!
　So weiche jeder Schuld
　Bekümmerniss von dir!

Während dem hat KUNDRY ein goldenes Fläschchen aus dem
Busen gezogen, und von seinem Inhalte auf PARSIFAL's Füsse ausge-
gossen, jetzt rocknet sie diese mit ihren schnell aufgelösten Haaren.

Parsifal
　　　　　(nimmt ihr das Fläschchen ab).
Salbtest du mir auch die Füsse,
das Haupt nun salbe Titurel's Genoss',
dass heute noch als König er mich grüsse.

Gurnemanz
(schüttet das Fläschchen vollends auf PARSIFAL's Haupt aus,
　　　reibt dieses sanft, und faltet dann die Hände darüber).

12

　So ward es uns verhiessen,
　so segne ich dein Haupt,
　als König dich zu grüssen.
　　Du — Reiner.
　mitleidvoll Duldender,
　heilthatvoll Wissender!
Wie des Erlös'ten Leiden du gelitten,
die letzte Last entnimm nun seinem Haupt.

Parsifal

(scoops up some water from the spring, unperceived, bends down to the kneeling KUNDRY and sprinkles her head).

I first fulfil my duty thus : —
  Be thou baptized,
 And trust in the Redeemer !

(KUNDRY bows her head to the earth and appears to weep bitterly.)

Parsifal

(turns round and gazes with gentle rapture on the woods and meadows).

How fair the fields and meadows seem to-day ! —
  Many a magic flow'r I've seen,
Which sought to clasp me in its baneful twin-
  ings ;
 But none I've seen so sweet as here,
 These tendrils bursting with blossom,
 Whose scent recals my childhood's days
 And speaks of loving trust to me.

Gurnemanz. That is Good-Friday's spell, my
  lord !

Parsifal. Alas, that day of agony !
  Now surely everything that thrives,
  That breathes and lives and lives again,
  Should only mourn and sorrow ?

Gurnemanz. Thou see'st, that is not so.
  The sad repentant tears of sinners
   Have here with holy rain
   Besprinkled field and plain,
   And made them glow with beauty.
  All earthly creatures in delight
  At the Redeemer's trace so bright
  Uplift their pray'rs of duty.
To see Him on the Cross they have no power :
And so they smile upon redeeméd man,
Who, feeling freed, with dread no more doth
  cower,
Through God's love-sacrifice made clean and
  pure :
And now perceives each blade and meadow-
  flower
That mortal foot to-day it need not dread ;
For, as the Lord in pity man did spare,
  And in His mercy for him bled,
  All men will keep, with pious care,
  To-day a tender tread.
  Then thanks the whole creation makes,
  With all that flow'rs and fast goes hence,
  That trespass-pardoned Nature wakes
  Now to her day of Innocence.

(KUNDRY has slowly raised her head again, and gazes with moist eyes, earnestly and calmly beseeching, up at PARSIFAL.)

Parsifal. I saw my scornful mockers wither :
  Now look they for forgiveness hither ? —

Parsifal

(schöpft unvermerkt Wasser aus der Quelle, neigt sich zu der vor ihm noch knienden KUNDRY, und netzt ihr das Haupt).

Mein erstes Amt verricht' ich so : —
  die Taufe nimm,
 und glaub' an den Erlöser !

(KUNDRY senkt das Haupt tief zur Erde und scheint heftig zu weinen.)

Parsifal

(wendet sich um, und blickt mit sanfter Entzückung auf Wald und Wiese).

Wie dünkt mich doch die Aue heut' so schön ! —
 Wohl traf ich Wunderblumen an,
die bis zum Haupte süchtig mich umrankten ;
 doch sah' ich nie so mild und zart
 die Halmen, Blüthen und Blumen,
 noch duftete All' so kindisch hold
 und sprach so lieblich traut zu mir ?

Gurnemanz. Das ist Char-Freitags-Zauber, Herr !

Parsifal. O weh', des höchsten Schmerzentag's
  Da sollte, wähn' ich, was da blüh't,
  was athmet, lebt und wieder lebt,
  nur trauern, ach ! und weinen ?

Gurnemanz. Du sieh'st, das ist nicht so.
  Des Sünders Reuethränen sind es,
   die heut' mit heil'gem Thau
   beträufet Flur und Au' :
   der liess sie so gedeihen.
  Nun freu't sich alle Kreatur
  auf des Erlösers holder Spur
  will ihr Gebet ihm weihen.
Ihn selbst am Kreuze kann sie nicht erschauen
da blickt sie zum erlös'ten Menschen auf ;
der fühlt sich frei von Sünden-Angst und Grauen
durch Gottes Liebesopfer rein und heil :
das merkt nun Halm und Blume auf den Auen,
dass heut' des Menschen Fuss sie nicht zertritt.
doch wohl, wie Gott mit himmlischer Geduld
  sich sein' erbarmt und für ihn litt,
  der Mensch auch heut' in frommer Huld
  sie schont mit sanftem Schritt.
  Das dankt dann alle Kreatur,
  was all' da blüht und bald erstirbt,
  da die entsündigte Natur
  heut' ihren Unschulds-Tag erwirbt.

(KUNDRY hat langsam wieder das Haupt erhoben, und blickt feuchten Auges, ernst und ruhig bittend zu PARSIFAL auf.)

Parsifal. Ich sah' sie welken, die mir lachten,
  ob heut' sie nach Erlösung schmachten ?

Like blessed sweet dew a tear from thee too
  floweth :
Thou weepest — see ! the landscape groweth.

(He kisses her softly on the brow.)
(Distant bells are heard pealing, very gradually swelling.)

Gurnemanz. Mid-day. —
      The hour has come : —
Permit, my lord, thy servant hence to lead thee ! —

GURNEMANZ has brought out a coat-of-mail and mantle of the
knights of the Grail, which he and KUNDRY put on PARSIFAL. The
landscape changes very gradually, as in the first Act, but from R. to L.
PARSIFAL solemnly grasps the Spear and, with KUNDRY, follows the
conducting GURNEMANZ. — When the wood has disappeared, and
rocky entrances have presented themselves in which the three become
invisible, processions of knights in mourning garb are perceived in the
arched passages; the pealing of bells ever increasing. — At last the
whole immense Hall becomes visible just as in the first Act, only without the tables. Faint light. The doors open again. From one side
the knights bear in TITUREL's corpse in a coffin. From the other
AMFORTAS is carried on in his litter, preceded by the covered shrine of
the Grail. The bier is erected in the middle; behind it the throne with
canopy where AMFORTAS is set down.

(*Song of the knights during the procession.*)

First Train
            (with the "Grail" and AMFORTAS).
To sacred place in sheltering shrine
    The Holy Grail do we carry;
What hide ye there in gloomy shrine,
Which hither mourning ye bear ?

Second Train
              (with TITUREL's coffin).
A hero lies in this dismal shrine
    With all this heavenly strength,
To whom all things once God did entrust :
Titurel hither we bear.

First Train. By whom was he slain, who by
      God himself
      Once was ever sheltered ?

Second Train. He sank beneath the mortal
      burden of years,
When the Grail no more he might look on.

First Train. Who veiled then the Grail's
      delights from his vision ?

Second Train. He whom ye are bearing : its
      criminal guardian.

First Train. We conduct him to-day, for here
      once again,
          — And once more only —
          He fulfilleth his office.

Second Train. Sorrow ! Sorrow ! Thou guard
      of the Grail !
          Be once more only
          Warned of thy duty to all.

(The coffin is set down on the bier, AMFORTAS placed on the
          couch.)

Auch deine Thräne wird zum Segensthaue ;
  du weinest — sieh ! es lacht die Aue.

(Er küsst sie sanft auf die Stirne.)
(Fernes Glockengeläute, sehr allmählich anschwellend.)

Gurnemanz. Mittag. —
      Die Stund' ist da : —
gestatte, Herr, dass dich dein Knecht geleite ! —

GURNEMANZ hat Waffenrock und Mantel des Gralsritters herbeigeholt ; er und KUNDRY bekleiden PARSIFAL damit. Die Gegend
verwandelt sich sehr allmählich, ähnlicher Weise wie im ersten Aufzuge,
nur von rechts nach links. PARSIFAL ergreift feierlich den Speer
und folgt mit KUNDRY langsam dem geleitenden GURNEMANZ. —
Nachdem der Wald gänzlich verschwunden ist, und Felsenthore sich
aufgethan haben, in welchen die Drei unsichtbar geworden sind, gewahrt man, bei fortdauerend anwachsendem Gelaute, in gewölbten
Gängen Züge von RITTERN in Trauergewändern. — Endlich stellt
sich der ganze grosse Saal, wie im ersten Aufzuge (nur ohne die Speisetafeln) wieder dar. Düstere Beleuchtung. Die Thüren öffnen sich
wieder. Von einer Sette ziehen die RITTER, TITUREL's Leiche im
Sarge geleitend, herein. Auf der andern Seite wird AMFORTAS im
Siechbette, vor ihm der verhüllte Schrein mit dem ,,Grale," getragen.
In der Mitte ist der Katafalk errichtet, dahinter der Hochsitz mit dem
Baldachin, auf welchen AMFORTAS wieder niedergelassen wird.

(*Gesang der Ritter während des Einzuges.*)

Erster Zug
              (mit dem ,, Gral '' und AMFORTAS).
Geleiten wir im bergenden Schrein
    den Gral zum heiligen Amte,
wen berget ihr im düst'ren Schrein
    und führt ihn trauernd daher ?

Zweiter Zug
                (mit TITUREL's Sarge).
Es birgt den Helden der Trauerschrein,
    er birgt die heilige Kraft ;
der Gott selbst einst zur Pflege sich gab :
    Titurel führen wir her.

Erster Zug. Wer hat ihn gefällt, der in Gottes
      Hut
      Gott selbst einst beschirmte ?

Zweiter Zug. Ihn fällte des Alters tödtende
      Last,
      da den Gral er nicht mehr erschaute.

Erster Zug. Wer wehrt' ihm des Grales Huld
      zu erschauen ?

Zweiter Zug. Den dort ihr geleitet, der sündige
      Hüter.

Erster Zug. Wir geleiten ihn heut', denn heut'
      noch einmal
          — zum letzten Male ! —
      will des Amtes er walten.

Zweiter Zug. Wehe ! Wehe ! Du Hüter des
      Heil's !
          Zum letzten Male
      sei deines Amts gemahnt !

(Der Sarg ist auf dem Katafalk niedergesetzt, AMFORTAS auf das
      Ruhebett gelegt.)

Amfortas. Aye, sorrow! Sorrow! Sorrow for
  me!—
    With you I willingly cry;
Liefer yet would I ye'd give me death,
    Atonement light for my trespass!
(The coffin is opened. At the sight of TITUREL's body all burst
into a poignant cry of distress.)

Amfortas
    (raising himself high on his couch and turning to the body).
      My father!
    Highest venerated hero!
Thou purest, to whom once e'en angels bended!
  I only desired to perish,
  Yet—gave thee to death!
Oh! thou who now in heavenly heights
  Dost behold the Saviour's self,
Implore him to grant that his hallowed blood,
  (If once again here his blessing
  He pour upon these brothers)
  To them new life while giving,
  To me may offer—but Death!
    Death—darkness!
    Solitary mercy!
Take from me the horrible wound, the poison,
Stiffen the heart so tortured and rent!
  My father! I—call thee,
  Cry thou my words to Him:
  "Redeemer! give to my son release!"

The Knights
    (severally, pressing towards AMFORTAS)
  Uncover the shrine!—
  Do now thine office!
  Thy father demands it;—
  Thou must, thou must!

Amfortas
(in a paroxysm of despair springs up and throws himself amid the
    knights, who draw back).
  No!—No more!—Ha!—
Already is death glooming round me,—
And shall I yet again return to life?
    Insanity!
  What one in life can yet stay me?
  Rather I bid ye to slay me!
    (tears open his dress).
Behold me!—the open wound behold!
Here is my poison—my streaming blood.
Take up your weapons! Bury your swordblades
Deep—deep in me, to the hilts!
    Ye heroes, up!
Kill both the sinner and all his pain:
The Grail's delight will ye then regain!

All have shrunk back in awe. AMFORTAS stands alone in
fearful ecstasy.—PARSIFAL, accompanied by GURNEMANZ and
KUNDRY, has entered unperceived, and now advancing stretches out
the Spear, touching AMFORTAS' side with the point.

Amfortas. Ja, Wehe! Wehe! Weh' über mich!—
  So ruf' ich willig mit euch:
williger nähm' ich von euch den Tod
    der Sünde mildeste Sühne!
(Der Sarg ist geöffnet worden. Beim Anblick der Leiche TITU-
REL's bricht Alles in einen jähen Wehruf aus.)

Amfortas
    (von seinem Lager sich hoch aufrichtend, zu der Leiche gewandt).
    Mein Vater!
  Hochgesegneter der Helden!
Du Reinster, dem einst die Engel sich neigten!
  Der einzig ich sterben wollte,
  dir—gab ich den Tod!
Oh! der du jetzt in göttlichem Glanz
  den Erlöser selbst erschau'st,
erflehe von ihm, dass sein heiliges Blut,
  wenn noch einmal jetzt sein Segen
  die Brüder soll erquicken,
  wie ihnen neues Leben,
  mir endlich spende—den Tod!
    Tod!—Sterben!
    Einzige Gnade!
Die schreckliche Wunde, das Gift ersterbe,
  das es zernagt, erstarre das Herz!
  Mein Vater! Dich—ruf' ich,
  rufe du ihm es zu:
Erlöser, gieb meinem Sohne Ruh'!

Die Ritter
    (sich näher an AMFORTAS drängend, durch einander).
  Enthüllet den Schrein!—
  Walte des Amtes!
  Dich mahnet der Vater:—
  du musst, du musst!

Amfortas
(in wüthender Verzweiflung aufspringend, und unter die zurückweich-
    enden RITTER sich stürzend).
  Nein!—Nicht mehr!—Ha!—
Schon fühl' ich den Tod mich umnachten,—
und noch einmal sollt' ich in's Leben zurück?
    Wahnsinnige!
  Wer will mich zwingen zu leben?
  Könnt ihr doch Tod nur mir geben!
    (Er reisst sich das Gewand auf.)
Hier bin ich,—die off'ne Wunde hier!
Das mich vergiftet, hier fliesst mein Blut.
Heraus die Waffe! Taucht eure Schwerter
  tief—tief hinein, bis an's Heft!
    Ihr Helden, auf!
Tödtet den Sünder mit seiner Qual:
von selbst dann leuchtet euch wohl der Grail!

Alle sind scheu vor ihm gewichen. AMFORTAS steht, in furchtbarer Extase, einsam.—PARSIFAL ist von GURNEMANZ und KUNDRY
begleitet, unvermerkt unter den RITTERN erschienen, tritt jetzt hervor, und streckt den Speer aus, mit dessen Spitze er AMFORTAS' Seite
berührt.

Parsifal.   One weapon only serves : —
  The one that struck
  Can staunch thy wounded side.

AMFORTAS' countenance is irradiated with holy rapture ; he totters with emotion ; GURNEMANZ supports him.

Parsifal.   Be whole, unsullied and absolved !
For I now govern in thy place.
  Oh, blessed be thy sorrows,
  For Pity's potent might
  And Knowledge' purest power
  They taught a timid Fool.
   The holy Spear —
  Once more behold in this. —

(All gaze with intense rapture on the spear which PARSIFAL holds aloft, while he continues in inspiration as he looks at its point.)

Oh, mighty miracle of bliss ! —
This that through me thy wound restoreth.
With holy blood behold it poureth.
Which yearns to join the fountain glowing,
Whose pure tide in the Grail is flowing !
Hid be no more that shape divine :
Uncover the Grail ! Open the shrine !

The boys open the shrine ; PARSIFAL takes from it the " Grail " and kneels, absorbed in its contemplation, silently praying. The " Grail " glows with light ; a halo of glory pours down over all. — TITUREL, for the moment reanimated, raises himself in benediction in his coffin. — From the dome descends a white dove and hovers over PARSIFAL's head. He waves the " Grail " gently to and fro before the upgazing knights. KUNDRY, looking up at PARSIFAL, sinks slowly to the ground, dead. AMFORTAS and GURNEMANZ do homage on their knees to PARSIFAL.

All

(with voices from the middle and extreme heights, so soft as to be scarcely audible).

 Wondrous work of mercy :
 Salvation to the Saviour !

  (The Curtain closes.)

Parsifal.   Nur eine Waffe taugt : —
  die Wunde schliesst
  der Speer nur, der sie schlug.

AMFORTAS' Miene leuchtet in heiliger Entzückung auf ; er scheint vor grosser Ergriffenheit zu schwanken ; GURNEMANZ stützt ihn.

Parsifal.   Sei heil, entsündigt und gesühnt !
Denn ich verwalte nun dein Amt.
  Gesegnet sei kein Leiden,
  das Mitleid's höchste Kraft
  und reinsten Wissens Macht
  dem zagen Thoren gab.
   Den heil'gen Speer —
  ich bring' ihn euch zurück. —

(Alles blickt in höchster Entzückung auf den emporgehaltenen Speer, zu dessen Spitze aufschauend PARSIFAL in Begeisterung fortfährt)

Oh ! Welchen Wunders höchstes Glück ! —
Die deine Wunde durfte schliessen,
ihm seh' ich heil'ges Blut entfliessen
in Sehnsucht dem verwandten Quelle,
der dort fliesst in des Grales Welle !
Nicht soll der mehr verchlossen sein :
enthüllt den Gral ! Oeffnet den Schrein !

Die KNAPPEN öffnen den Schrein : PARSIFAL entnimmt diesem den „Gral," und versenkt sich, unter stummen Gebete, in seinem Anblick. Der „Gral" erglüht : eine Glorienbeleuchtung ergiesst sich über Alle. — TITUREL, für diesen Augenblick wieder belebt, erhebt sich segnend im Sarge. — Aus der Kuppel schwebt eine weisse Taube herab und verweilt über PARSIFAL's Haupte. Dieser schwenkt den „Gral" sanft vor der aufblickenden Ritterschaft. — KUNDRY sinkt, mit dem Blicke zu ihm auf, langsam vor PARSIFAL entseelt zu Boden. AMFORTAS und GURNEMANZ huldigen kniend PARSIFAL.

Alle

(mit Stimmen aus der mittleren, so wie der obersten Höhe, kaum hörbar leise).

 Höchsten Heiles Wunder :
 Erlösung dem Erlöser !

  (Der Vorhang schliesst sich.)

VOLUME TWO
THE LIBRETTOS
OF THE
FRENCH AND GERMAN OPERAS

CONTENTS

Foreword 2

Carmen 3

Faust... 53

Romeo and Juliet 99

Manon 147

Tales of Hoffmann 195

Samson and Delilah 253

Lakmé.. 279

Mignon... 319

Fidelio... 353

The Magic Flute 377

The Bartered Bride 431

Hansel and Gretel... 477

FOREWORD

Christoph Willibald Gluck, German-born composer of French operas, defined the relation in opera of the music to the poetry: The poetry is primary, the music should illustrate it and color it and emphasize the meaning without interrupting the action or weakening it by superfluous ornament. It is much the same as the relation of harmonious color, well disposed light and shade to accurate drawing, which should animate the figures without altering the outlines.

This definition was enunciated in 1767, and since that time has been the accepted basis of opera composition.

But it is hard to make out clearly this all-important poetry when it is sung in an opera. Enunciation is sacrificed to vocal and musical considerations, and besides, there is the matter of a probably unfamiliar language.

These librettos are designed to enhance the enjoyment of operas by enabling the listener to know the words that are being sung and their meaning. Both the original libretto and the English translation are given and in parallel columns for easy reference.

The selection of the operas to be included in this volume was determined largely by importance and popularity as indicated by the number of performances at the Metropolitan Opera House from 1883 to 1939.

The record of performances of these operas at the Metropolitan Opera House is as follows: Faust 235; Carmen 195; Manon 158; Romeo & Juliet 111; Hansel & Gretel 96; Samson & Delilah 57; Fidelio 47; The Magic Flute 47; Mignon 45; Tales of Hoffmann 40; Lakmé 29; The Bartered Bride 29.

CARMEN

by

GEORGES BIZET

Libretto by

H. MEILHAC AND L. HALEVY

(*from the novel by* PROSPER MÉRIMÉE)

CHARACTERS.

DON JOSÉ, *Corporal of Dragoons*
ESCAMILLO, *Toreador*
ZUNIGA, *Captain of Dragoons*
MORALES, *Officer*
LILLAS PASTIA, *Innkeeper*
CARMEN, *a Gipsy Girl*

MICAELA, *a Village Maiden*
FRASQUITA } *Companions of Carmen*
MERCEDES }
EL DANCAIRO } *Smugglers*
EL REMENDADO }
A GUIDE

Dragoons, Smugglers, Gipsies, Cigarette-girls, Street-boys, etc.
The scene is laid in Spain, about 1820.

ARGUMENT.

THE action passes in Seville, in the year 1820. A troop of soldiers are waiting for the guard to be changed, and watching the loungers in the public square. *Michaela*, a village girl, appears— she seeks a Brigadier (*Don José*), bearing a message from his mother. The officer on guard invites her to wait his arrival, but she refuses, and departs. The relief guard, with Don José, come on, and the square is crowded by groups of young men, anxiously looking out for the approach of the pretty girls who work at the great Tobacco Manufactory, facing the guard house, at the foot of the bridge. Don José, alone, is indifferent. The girls enter, and the young men eagerly inquire for *Carmen*, the greatest beauty and coquette of them all, who, on her arrival, though deaf to each individual in particular, asserts her desire for universal dominion by flinging at the silent Don José the flowers she wears in her dress. The factory bell rings again. The girls hasten to their work. Don José's Spanish blood is roused, but the arrival of the gentle Michaela, with a letter and purse from his mother, calms him, and he resolves to stifle the sudden passion the bewitching Carmen has excited, and devote himself, as his mother wishes, to Michaela. She has scarcely gone, and Don José is about to throw Carmen's flowers away, when a noise is heard in the factory. The girls all rush out Two of them have quarrelled. One is wounded —her assailant is Carmen. José is ordered by the officer in command to take her into custody,

3

She sings, and is saucy to the officer instead of expressing contrition. He resolves on sending her to prison; and, fearing further mischief from the little termagant, orders her hands to be tied, whilst he goes to write the order for José to conduct her to prison. During his absence she bewitches the unfortunate Brigadier till he promises to permit her to escape, and meet her at an Inn near the ramparts. Don José and two soldiers escort her. At the foot of the bridge a sudden push from Carmen throws Don José down, and, in the confusion which follows, Carmen, aided by the laughing girls, escapes.

The Second Act displays the Inn near the ramparts. Carmen is there with her friends, the gipsies (some of them smugglers as well). They sing and dance. Some officers and soldiers are there also. The Captain is fascinated by Carmen, but she pays him little attention till she hears José's imprisonment for suffering her to escape is ended. A new arrival, *Escamillo,* appears, the victorious bull-fighter of Granada. Soldiers and gipsies warmly welcome him. He, like the rest, devotes himself to Carmen, who, coquette as usual, neither repulses nor accepts his admiration. 'Tis time to close the Inn as the Corregidor has ordered. Escamillo and the soldiers depart, but the two smugglers, *Il Dancairo* and *Il Remendado,* having a good booty in view, seek Carmen's assistance. She refuses to accompany them, telling them she is waiting for her lover, the Dragoon. The smugglers try to persuade Carmen to induce José to join their band. She agrees; and when the enamored Brigadier arrives, enraptured at seeing her again, Carmen tempts him to stay in spite of the trumpet of recall. He refuses, even for her, to become a deserter, and is about to quit her when the officer forces his way in, and, stung by the preference Carmen has shown to José, orders him out. Sabres are drawn. Carmen calls for aid. The gipsies appear. The officer is made prisoner, whilst the gipsies, Carmen, and José escape to the mountains.

Act the Third is the Smugglers' Haunt, in a wild, picturesque, rocky country. The night is dark, and the contrabandists are busy. José is there with Carmen, whose love is waning. He still adores her, though stung by remorse and grief for his mother, who dwells in the valleys beneath. All are quitting the Haunt, when Escamillo arrives. He has toiled up the rocks in pursuit of Carmen, and, not knowing José, reveals his passion to him. A fight is about to take place, but Carmen and the smugglers rush in and separate them. Escamillo, biding his time, bids them farewell, after inviting them to the approaching bull-fight at Seville. José upbraids Carmen, who disregards his threats, and the sudden appearance of Michaela, who by the aid of a guide has sought him out to hasten to his dying mother, compels him to leave Carmen. Torn by love, jealousy, and duty, he hesitates; but duty prevails, and he follows Michaela, while the song of Escamillo is heard in the distance.

Act the Fourth. — The bull-fight is about to begin at Seville. Escamillo is there with the faithless Carmen, in great splendor. He departs to prepare for the arena, and Carmen's gipsy friends, *Frasquita* and *Mercedes,* hasten to warn her that José is in search of her. She will not conceal herself and resolves to brave him. José comes. He vainly tries to rekindle the old love. Carmen will not listen — refuses his passionate appeals, and flings his love-token (a ring) at his feet. At last, maddened with her exclamation of joy at the populace proclaiming the triumph of Escamillo in the bull-fight, José stabs her to the heart, and Carmen falls dead as the victorious Escamillo enters.

First performed at the Opéra-Comique, Paris, March 3, 1875, with the following cast:

Don José	M. M. Lhérie
Escamillo	Bouhy
Zuniga	Dufriche
Morales	Duvernoy
Lillas Pastia	Nathan
Carmen	Mmes. Galli-Marié
Micaela	Chapuy
Frasquita	Ducasse
Mercedes	Chevolier

CARMEN

ACT I.	ACTE PREMIER.

SCENE I.	SCÈNE PREMIÈRE

(A Square in Seville. On the right the gate of the tobacco factory. At the back, facing the audience, is a practicable bridge from one side of the stage to the other, and reached from the stage by a winding staircase on the right to beyond the factory gate. The bridge is practicable underneath. In front, on the left, is a guard-house: above that, three steps lead to a covered passage. In a rack, close to the door, are the lances of the Dragoons, with their little red and yellow flags.)

MORALES, MICHAELA, Soldiers, Wayfarers.

(At the rising of the curtain, a file of Soldiers (Dragoons of Almanza) are grouped before the guard-house, smoking, and looking at the passers-by in the square, coming and going from all parts. The scene is full of animation.)

Cho. In the square
What a clamor!
Some are coming, some are going;
Strange indeed are they to see!
Mor. At the gate in this vicinity
Stops each one who likes —
Talking, smoking, and looking out
To watch the passing crowd.

(MICHAELA has been visible for some moments. She wears a blue petticoat, and her hair falls over her shoulders. She perceives the Soldiers, and stands hesitating, not knowing if to advance or recede.)

Mor.
(to Soldiers).
Look an instant at that fair one.
It seems with us she fain would speak.
She dares not; but draws near, and glances.
Cho. To encourage her we ought.
Mor.
(to MICHAELA).
Who are you seeking for, fair maid?
Mic. I'm seeking for a brigadier.
Mor. Indeed! Here am I.
Mic. You are not he. Don José he is called.
Is he not to you known?

(Fine piace à Seville. A droite, la porte de la manufacture de tabac Au fond, face au public, pont practicable traversant la scène dans toute son étendue. De la scène on arrive à ce pont par un escalier tournant qui fait sa révolution à droite au-dessus de la porte de la manufacture de tabac. Le dessus du pont est practicab'e. A gauche, au premier plan, le corps-de-garde. Devant le corps-de-garde, une petite galerie couverte, exhaussée de deux ou trois marches; près du corps-de-garde, dans un ràtelier, les lances des dragons avec leurs banderolles jaunes et rouges.)

MORALES, MICAELA, Soldats, Passants.

(Au lever du rideau, une quinzaine de soldats (Dragons régiment d'Almanza) sont groupés devant le corps-de-garde. Les uns assis et fumant, les autres accoudés sur la balestrade de la galerie. Mouvement de passants sur la place. Des gens pressés, affairés, vont viennent, se rencontrent, se saluent, se bousculent, etc.)

Cho. Sur la place
Chacun passe,
Chacun vient, chacun va;
Drôles de gens que ces gens-là.
Mor. A la porte du corps-de-garde,
Pour tuer le temps,
On fume, on jase, l'on regarde
Passer les passants.
Reprise du Cho.
Sur la place, etc.

(Depuis quelques minutes MICAELA est entrée. Jupe bleue, natte mbant sur les épaules, hésitante, embarrassée, elle regarde les so s, avance, recule, etc.)

Mor.
(aux Soldats).
Regardez donc cette petite
Qui semble vouloir nous parler
Voyez, elle tourne, elle hésite.

Cho. A son secours il faut aller.
Mor.
(à MICAELA).
Que cherchez-vous, la belle?
Mic. Je cherche un brigadier.
Mor. Je suis là! Voilà!
Mic. Mon brigadier, à moi, s'appelle
Don José, le connaissez-vous?

Mor. Don José is not to us known.	*Mor* José, nous le connaissons tous
Mic. Is it so? How shall I find him?	*Mic.* Est-il avec vous, je vous prie?
Mor. He is not brigadier in this troop.	*Mor.* Il n'est pas brigadier dans notre compagnie.

Mic.

(sadly)

Mic.

(désolée).

Then he is not with you?	Alors il n'est pas là.
Mor. No, fair one; he's not of ours.	*Mor.* Non, ma charmante, il n'est pas là,
But, amidst the many, he may be	Mais tout à l'heure il y sera.
Of the guard now coming here	Il y sera quand la garde montante
To replace us in this post.	Remplacera la garde descendante.
Cho. He will be of the guard now coming	*Tous.* Il y sera quand la garde montante
To replace us in our post.	Remplacera la garde descendante.
Mor. But whilst he's coming	*Mor.* Mais en attendant qu'il vienne,
It will not be disagreeable	Voulez-vous, la belle enfant,
(And to us a great pleasure)	Voulez-vous prendre la peine
If within the house you enter.	D'entrer chez nous un instant?
Mic. Indeed.	*Mic.* Chez vous!
Mor. It is the truth	*Les Soldats.*
	Chez nous.
Mic. No, no, no, no.	*Mic.* Non pas, non pas.
	Grand merci, messieurs les soldats
Mor. You to enter need not fear.	*Mor.* Entrez sans crainte, mignonne,
On my honor I promise you	Je vous promets qu'on aura,
That from all you will receive	Pour votre chère personne,
Best and heartiest welcomes.	Tous les égards qu'il faudra.
Mic. Of it I'm sure; but, nevertheless	*Mic.* Je n'en doute pas; cependant
It suits me best now to return.	Je reviendrai, c'est plus prudent.
I will come again when the guard	
In your post replaces you.	(Reprenant en riant la phrase du Sergent)
	Je reviendrai quand la garde montante
	Remplacera la garde descendante.
Cho.	*Les Soldats*

(surrounding MICHAELA).

(entourant MICAELA).

You ought to stay.	Vous resterez.
	Mic.

(cherchant à se dégager).

	Non pas! non pas!
	Les Soldats.
	Vous resterez.
Mic. No, no, no, no. I must depart.	*Mic* Non pas! non pas!
Good-bye to you all!	Au revoir, messieurs les soldats.

(Runs out.)

(Elle s'échappe et se sauve en courant.)

Mor. The bird has flown !
No one need fret.
What shall we do now?
Best watch who comes and goes.

Cho. In the place what a clamor, etc.

(The Square fills again with the people, who had ceased during MICHAELA's scene, and is lively as before.)

Mor. L'oiseau s'envole,
On s'en console.
Reprenons notre passe-temps,
Et regardons passer les gens.

Reprise du Cho.
Sur la place.
Chacun passe, etc.

(Le mouvement des Passants qui avait cessé pendant la scène de MICAELA a repris avec une certaine animation.)

SCENE II.

A military march of fifes and trumpets is heard in the distance. The Relief Guard arrive. An officer goes from his post. The Soldiers take their lances and place themselves in a line before the guard-house. The people on the right gather in groups, looking on. The march sounds nearer. The Guard appear on the left, and cross the bridge : first, two Trumpeters and two Fifers; then a band of street Lads, imitating the step of the Dragoons. After the Lads the Officer ZUNIGA and the Brigadier José; then Dragoons, armed with lances.

Cho. of Street Lads.
Follow we the guard that's changing.
Quick at their heels ! See, here we are !
Trumpets, strike up ! be ready !
Ta, ra-ta-ta, ta, ta, ta, ra.
Each one put himself in order,
Like dragoons, all in a row ;
Quick march ; now all be steady —
One — two — in time we go,
Shoulders thrown back, chests well forward,
At them look, example take ;
Left foot, right foot, strike the pavement,
Steady all, make no mistake.
Follow we the guard now changing,
At their heels, see ! here we are !
Trumpets, strike up ! be ready !
Ta, ra-ta-ta, ta, ta, ta, ra.

(The Guard, just arrived, place themselves on the right in front of the Guard relieved. The Officers salute with the sword, and stand chatting in a low voice. The sentry is changed.)

SCÈNE II.

On entend au loin, très au loin, une marche militaire, clairons et fifres. — C'est la Garde montante qui arrive. — Le vieux monsieur et le jeune homme échangent une cordiale poignée de main. Salut respectueux du jeune homme à la dame. — Un Officier sort du poste. Les Soldats du poste vont prendre leurs lances et se rangent en ligne devant le corps de garde. — Les passants à droite forment un groupe pour assister à la parade. La marche militaire se rapproche, se rapproche... La Garde montante débouche enfin venant de la gauche et traverse le pont. Deux clairons et deux fifres d'abord. Puis une bande de petits gamins qui s'efforcent de faire de grandes enjambées pour marcher au pas des Dragons. Aussi petits que possible les enfants. Derrière les enfants, le Lieutenant ZUNIGA et le Brigadier DON JOSÉ, puis les Dragons avec leurs lances.
Les Mêmes. — DON JOSÉ, Le Lieutenant.

Cho. des Gamins.
Avec la garde montante.
Nous arrivons, nous voilà. . . .
Sonne, trompette éclatante,
Ta ra ta ta, ta ra ta ta ;
Nous marchons la tête haute
Comme de petits soldats,
Marquant sans faire de faute,
Une, deux, marquant le pas.
Les épaules en arrière
Et la poitrine en dehors,
Les bras de cette manière
Tombant tout le long du corps ;
Avec la garde montante
Sonne, trompette éclatante,
Nous arrivons, nous voilà,
Ta ra ta ta, ta ra ta ta.

(La Garde montante va se ranger à droite en face de la Garde descendante. Dès que les Petits Gamins qui se sont arrêtés à droite devant les curieux ont fini de chanter, les Officiers se saluent de l'épée et se mettent à causer à voix basse. On relève les Sentinelles.)

Mor.

(TO DON JOSE).

A pretty young girl
Come to ask if you were here,
With flowing hair and dress of blue —

José. It must be Michaela.

(Trumpets sound. The relieved Guard pass before the New-Comers. The Street Boys, in a line, resume the place they occupied when they entered, behind the trumpets and fifes.)

Cho.

(as before).

And the guard relieved already
The place now leaves — away they go.
Trumpets all to sound are ready;
Ta-ta-ra, ta-ra, ta, ta.
Each one put himself in order,
Like dragoons all in a row;
Quick march! now all be steady;
One — two — in time we go.
Shoulders thrown back, chests well forward,
At them look — example take:
Left foot, right foot, strike the pavement,
Steady all, make no mistake.
Follow we the guard now changing,
At their heels, see! here we are!
Trumpets, strike up! be ready!
Ta-ta-ra, ta-ta, ta-ta-ra.

(Soldiers, Lads and Spectators go off at the back; Chorus, Fifers and Trampeters by degrees disperse. The Officer of the Guard, just arrived, during this time silently musters his Soldiers. When the Chorus is no longer heard, the Officer commands "Present!" "Carry!" "Break the line!" The Dragoons go and place their lances in the rack, and then enter the guard-house. Don José and the Officer remain.

SCENE III.

Officer.

'Tis in that large house the girls
Go to make cigarettes?

José. Yes, there, my captain; and you can
assure yourself
There are some lively ones amongst them.

Mor.

(à DON JOSÉ).

Il y a une jolie fille qui est venue te demander. Elle a dit qu'elle reviendrait...
José. Une jolie fille?...
Mor. Oui, et gentiment habillée, une jupe bleue, des nattes tombant sur les épaules.
José. C'est Micaela. Ce ne peut être que Micaela.
Mor. Elle n'a pas dit son nom.

(Les factionnaires sont relevés. Sonneries des clairons. La Garde descendante passe devant la Garde montante. Les Gamins en troupe reprennent derrière les clairons et les fifres de la Garde descendante la place qu'ils occupaient derrière les tambours et les fifres de la Garde montante.)

Reprise du Cho. des Gamins.

Et la garde descendante
Rentre chez elle et s'en va.
Sonne, trompette éclatante,
Ta ra ta ta, ta ra ta ta.
Nous partons la tête haute
Comme de petits soldats,
Marquant, sans faire de faute,
Une..., deux... marquant le pas.
Les épaules en arrière
Et la poitrine en dehors,
Les bras de cette manière
Tombant tout le long du corps
Et la garde descendante
Rentre chez elle s'en va.
Sonne, trompette éclatante,
Ta ra ta ta, ta ra ta ta.

(Soldats, Gamins et curieux s'éloignent par le fond; Chœur, Fifres et Clarions, vont diminuant. L'Officier de la Garde montante, pendant ce temps, passe silencieusement l'inspection de ses hommes. Quand le Chœur des Gamins et les Fifres ont cessé de se faire entendre, le Lieutenant dit: "Présent lances! Haut lances! Rompez les rangs!" Les Dragons vont tous déposser leurs lances dans le râtelier, puis ils rentrant dans le corps de Garde. Don José et le Lieutenant restent seuls en scène.)

SCÈNE III.
Le Lieutenant, Don José.

Le Lieut.

C'est bien là n'est ce pas, dans ce grand bâtiment
Que travaillent les cigarières?
José. C'est là, mon officier, et bien certainement
On ne vit nulle part, filles aussi légères.

Officer.

 You know, at least, if they are handsome?

José. In truth, I know nothing about them,

 And care very little for such toys.

Officer.

 I will tell you, my friend,

 Who you are looking for, —

 A young, fair girl;

 She is named Michaela —

 Golden hair and a blue petticoat.

 What do you reply to this?

José. I answer that it is true,

 I answer that I love her,

 If the girls out there

 Such beauty have or no.

 Here they come; you can judge.

   (The factory bell is heard ringing.)

SCENE IV.

Don José, Soldiers, Young Men and Cigar Girls.

The Square fills with Young Men coming to wait the passing of the Cigar Girls. The soldiers enter from the guard-house. Don José, seated, careless of the passing scene, works at a little chain.

Cho. The bell now rings. We're here to see

 The pretty faces pass along,

 And follow each dark-eyed brunette

 With proffered friendship and with love.

 The Cigar Girls at this moment arrive, smoking cigarettes. They pass under the bridge, and leisurely descend the stage.)

Soldiers.

 What think you? Boldly they go:

 True coquettes! they will not cease

 Their cigarettes to smoke

Cigar Girls.

 Raise we our eyes to the skies

 And lightly smoke.

 As upwards in perfumed clouds it flies,

 On we smoke —

 Pleasant smoke,

 Fragrant smoke,

 Cheering smoke,

 It mounts so gently, lightly.

 To the brain.

 Soothes the soul that's weary

Le Lieut.

 Mais au moins sont elles jolies?

José. Mon officier, je n'en sais rien,

 Et m'occupe assez peu de ces galanteries

Le Lieut.

 Ce qui t'occupe, ami,

 Je le sais bien,

 Une jeune fille charmante,

 Qu'on appelle Micaela,

 Jupe bleue et nattes tombante

 Tu ne réponds rien à cela?

José. Je réponds que c'est vrai,

 Je réponds que je l'aime!

 Quant aux ouvrières d'ici,

 Quant à leur beautè, les voici!

 Et vous pouvez juger vous-même.

SCÈNE IV.

Don José, Soldats, Jeunes Gens et Cigarières.

La place se remplit de Jeunes Gens qui viennent se placer sur passage des Cigarières. Les Soldats sortent du poste. Don José s'assied sur une chaise, et reste là fort indifférent à toutes allées et venues, travaillant à son épinglette.

Cho. La cloche a sonné, nous, des ouvrières

 Nous venons ici guetter le retour;

 Et nous vous suivrons, brunes cigarières

 En vous murmurant des propos d'amour.

(A ce moment paraissent les CIGARIÈRES, la cigarette aux lèvres Elles passent sous le pont et descendent lentement en scène.)

Les Soldats.

 Voyez-les. Regards impudents,

 Mine coquette,

 Fumant toutes du bout des dents

 La cigarette.

Les Cigarières.

 Dans l'air, nous suivons des yeux

 La fumée

 Qui vers les cieux

 Monte, monte parfumée.

 Dans l'air nous suivons des yeux

 La fumée,

 La fumée,

 La fumée,

 La fumée.

 Cela monte doucement

To bliss from pain.
Turn we our eyes from the skies, —
All is smoke.
Words of love, how oft they prove
Nought but smoke.
Warmest sighs, fondest ties,
All end in — smoke.

A la tête,
Cela vous met gentiment
L'âme en fête,
Dans l'air nous suivons des yeux
La fumée,
Etc.
Le doux parler des amants
C'est fumée ;
Leurs transports et leurs serments
C'est fumée.
Dans l'air nous suivons des yeux
La fumée,
Etc.

SCENE V.

CARMEN, and the preceding.

Soldiers.

But Carmencita is not here amongst you.
Girls and Young Men.
Here she is.
Here is Carmencita.

CARMEN appears, in the attitude and dress described in Mérimée's novel. She has an acacia flower at her mouth and a bouquet in her bodice. All the Young Men surround and speak to her. She coquets with all. José raises his eyes and looks at CARMEN, and quietly goes on with his work.

Young Men.

Carmen, all here wait for you alone.
Carmen, now be kind; turn this way
    awhile.
When will you love? — we fain would
    know.
Car.

When shall I be in love? Truly I don't
    know.
Perhaps never — and, perhaps to-morrow ;
But for to-day — No ; vain is the thought.

(After looking at all of them.)

Ah ! love, thou art a wilful wild bird,
And none may hope thy wings to tame,

SCÈNE V.

Les Mêmes, CARMEN.

Les Soldats.

Nous ne voyons pas la Carmencita.
Les Cigarières et *Les Jeunes Gens.*
La voilà,
La voilà,
Voilà la Carmencita.

Entre CARMEN. Absolument le costume et l'entree indiqués par Mérimée. Elle a un bouquet de cassie à son corsage et un fleur de cassie dans le coin de la bouche. Trois ou quatre Jeunes Gens entrent avec CARMEN. Ils la suivent, l'entourent, lui parlent. Elle minaude et coquette avec eux. DON JOSÉ lève la tête. Il regarde CARMEN. puis se remet tranquillement à travailler à son épinglette.

Les Jeunes Gens.

(entré avec Carmen).

Carmen, sur tes pas, nous nous pressons
    tous ;
Carmen, sois gentille, au moins réponds
    nous
Et dis-nous quel jour tu nous aimeras.
Carmen.

(les regardant).

Quand je vous aimerai, ma foi, je ne sais pas
Peut-être jamais, peut-être demain ;
Mais pas aujourd'hui, c'est certain.
L'amour est une oiseau rebelle
Que nul ne peut apprivoiser,
Et c'est bien en vain qu'on l'appelle,
S'il lui convient de refuser
Rien n'y fait ; menace ou prière
L'un parle bien, l'autre se tait ;
Et c'est autre que je préfère.

If it please thee to be a rebel,
Say, who can try and thee reclaim?
Threats and prayers alike unheeding;
Oft ardent homage thou'lt refuse,
Whilst he who doth coldly slight thee
Thou for thy master oft thou'lt choose.
Ah, love!
For love he is the lord of all,
And ne'er law's icy fetters will he wear,
If thou me lovest not, I love thee,
And if I love thee, now beware!
If thou me lovest not, beware!
The bird, so fast held in thy hand,
And which thou deemedst so secure,
Mounts, in a moment, to the skies;
Nor, till he choose, can you him lure.
He comes, he goes;
At all laughs he.
Would you seize him? he gets free!
Care not for him — then he'll prove
Thy slave instead of master — Love!

Young Men.

Carmen, we wait here only for thee.
Carmen, be kind; we are to thee devoted.

(Moment of silence. The Young Men surround CARMEN; she looks at them one by one, then leaves the circle and goes straight to José who is at work, and flings her bouquet of flowers at him; he starts up abruptly. General burst of laughter. The bell of the factory rings a second time. The Cigar Girls and Young Men go, during the burthen of CARMEN's song. She runs off to the factory. DON JOSÉ remains on the scene alone.

Il n'a rien dit mais il me plaît.
L'amour est enfant de Bohême,
Il n'a jamais connu de loi;
Si tu ne m'aimes pas, je t'aime;
Si je t'aime, prends garde à toi.
L'oiseau que tu croyais surprendre
Battit de l'aile et s'envola—
L'amour est loin, tu peux l'attendre
Tu ne l'attends plus — il est là.
Tout autour de toi, vite, vite,
Il vient, s'en va, puis il revient—
Tu crois le tenir, il t'évite,
Tu veux l'éviter, il te tient.
L'amour est enfant de Bohême,
Il n'a jamais connu de loi;
Si tu ne m'aimes pas, je t'aime;
Si je t'aime, prends garde à toi.

Jeunes Gens.

Carmen, sur tes pas, nous nous pressons
tous;
Carmen, sois gentille, au moins réponds-
nous.

(Moment de silence. Les Jeunes Gens entourent CARMEN; celli-ci les regards l'un après l'autre, sort du cercle qu'ils forment autour d'elle et s'en va droit à DON JOSÉ qui est toujours occupé de son épinglette.)

Car.   Eh! compère, qu'est-ce que tu fais là?
José.   Je fais une chaîne avec du fil de laiton,
          une chaîne pour attacher mon épinglette.

Car.

(riant)
Ton éplingette, vraiment! Ton éplingette
— épinglier de mon âme.

(Elle arrache de son corsage la fleur de cassie et la lance à DON José. Il se lève brusquement. La fleur de cassie est tombée à ses pieds. Eclat de rire général; la cloche de la manufacture sonne une deuxième fois. Sortie des ouvrières et des Jeunes Gens sur la reprise de:
    L'amour est enfant de Bohême, etc., etc.
(Carmen sort la première en courant et elle entre dans la manufacture Jeunes Gens sortent à droite et à gauche. Le Lieutenant qui, pendant scène bavardait avec deux un trois ouvrières, les quitte et rentre de pose après que les soldats y sont rentrés. DON JOSÉ reste seul.)

SCENE VI.

José. What glances! what a saucy air!
To my heart direct the flowers came,
As if a plummet struck me.

(After taking up the flowers, smells them.)

Subtle is the odor, and the flowers charm-
ing.
And the fair one, if witches yet there be,
One of them surely in her I behold.

SCENE VII.

Enter MICHAELA.

Mic. José!
José.   Michaela!
Mic. Here am I.
José. What a pleasure!
Mic. Your mother sent me hither.

José. Ah! tell me of her — my mother far
away.
Mic. Faithful messenger from her to thee. I
bring a letter,
José.   A letter.

Mic. And some money also;
Because a dragoon has not too much.
And, besides that —

José.   Something else?
Mic. Indeed, I know not how —
It is something more,
And beyond gold
By a good son more prized would be.

José. Tell me what this may be :
Come, reveal it to me.
Mic. Yes, I will tell you.
What she has given, I will to thee render.
Your mother with me from the chapel
came,
And then, lovingly, she kissed me.

SCÈNE VI.

José. Quels regards! qu'elle effronterie.
Cette fleur la m'a fait,
L'effet d'une balle qui m'arrivait!
Le parfum en est fort et la fleur est jolie
Et la femme . . .
S'il est vraiment des sorcièrers,
C'en est une certainement.

SCÈNE VII.

DON JOSÉ, MICAELA

Mic. José!
José.   Micaela!
Mic. Me voici!
José. Quelle est jolie!
Mic. C'est votre mère qui m'envoie!

Duo.

José. Eh bien, parle — ma mère.

Mic. J'apporte de sa part, fidèle messager.
Cette lettre.

José

(regardant la lettre).

Une lettre.
Mic. Et puis un peu d'argent.

(Elle lui remet une petite bourse.)

Pour ajouter à votre traitement,
Et puis —
José.   Et puis?
Mic. Et puis? vraiment je n'ose,
Et puis — encore une autre chose
Qui vaut mieux que l'argent et qu'
pour un bon fils,
Aura sans doute plus de prix.
José Cette autre chose, quelle est-elle?
Parle donc.
Mic. Oui, je parlerai ;
Ce que l'on m'a donné, je vous
donnerai.
Votre mère avec moi sortrait de la
chapelle.

" My daughter," said she, " to the city
   thou dost go ;
Not long the journey.
When arrived in Seville
Thou wilt seek out José, my beloved son ;
Tell him — Thou knowest that thy
   mother,
By night, by day, thinks of her José :
For him she always prays and hopes,
And pardons him, and loves him ever.
Tell all this, dearest,
In my name, to José.
And then this kiss, kind one,
Thou wilt to him give for me."

José.   A kiss from my mother ?

Mic.   To her son.
José, I give it to thee — as I promised.

(MICHAELA stands on tiptoe and kisses José — a true mother's kiss.
José, moved, permits her, with his eyes on her face. Moment of
silence.)

José.
     (regarding MICHAELA).

My home in yonder valley,
My mother lov'd shall I e'er see ?
Ah, fondly in my heart I cherish
Mem'ries so dear yet to me.

Mic.   Thy home in yonder valley,
Thy mother lov'd thou yet will see,
And mem'ries dear to thee.
Thou yet wilt bless the name,
Thou yet wilt fond hope cherish !
'Twill strength and courage give thee,
That one sweet hope,
That yet again thou wilt thy home
And thy dear mother once more see.

    (José looks towards the factory.)

José.   If perchance I may become the prey of
   evil power !
In thy abode afar thou'lt save me, mother.
And in thy kiss I yet may see
A guardian angel ever my steps guiding.

Et c'est alors qu'en m'embrassant,
Tu vas, m'a-t-elle dit, t-en aller à la
   ville ;
La route n'est pas longue, une fois à
   Séville,
Tu chercheras mon fils, mon José,
   mon enfant.
Et tu lui diras que sa mère
Songe nuit et jour à l'absent.
Qu'elle regrette et qu'elle espère,
Qu'elle pardonne et qu'elle attend ;
Tout cela, n'est-ce pas ? mignonne,
De ma part tu le lui diras,
Et ce baiser que je te donne
De ma part tu le lui rendras.

José
     (très-ému).

Un baiser de ma mère ?

Mic.   Un baiser pour son fils.
José, je vous le rends, comme je l'ai
   promis.

(MICAELA se hausse un peu sur la pointe des pieds et donne à
DON JOSÉ un baiser bien franc, bien maternel. DON JOSÉ très-ému
la laisse faire. Il la regarde bien dans les yeux. Un moment de
silence.)

José
     (continuant de regarder MICAELA).

Ma mère, je la vois, je revois mon
   village.
Souvenirs d'autrefois ! souvenirs du pays !
Vous remplissez mon cœur de force et de
   courage
O souvenirs chéris,
Souvenirs d'autrefois ! souvenirs du pays !

     ENSEMBLE.

José. } Ma mère je la vois, etc.
Mic. } Sa mère, il la revoit, etc.

José
     (les yeux fixés sur la manufacture).

Qui sait de quel démon j'allais être la
   proie !
Même de loin, ma mère me défend,
Et ce baiser qu'elle m'envoie
Ecarte le péril et sauve son enfant.

Mic.   What pow'r? what speakest thou? I understand not.

Explain to me thy thoughts.

José.   No, no.

Let us speak about thyself, my messenger;

Say, thou must return to the valley?

Mic.   Yes, this evening; and to-morrow I shall be there.

José.   Well, thou wilt tell her that José

Loves her always, blesses her;—

That he has altered; for he wishes

His mother, far away, may of her son be glad.

Thou wilt tell her this, dear one,

In my name, for José;

And then this kiss, oh, kindest one,

To her give thou from me.

           (Kisses her.)

Mic.   Yes, I promise thee—in her son José's name—

To her I'll give it.

José.   } My mother, etc.

Mic.   } His mother, etc.

José.   Rest thou here, my dear one,

Whilst I read this.

           (Kisses the letter.)

Mic.   No, no; thou canst read it alone;

I will return later.

José.   Why wilt thou go?

Mic.   For prudence' sake,

Because it looks not well to stay.

I go, but I shall come back here.

José.   Thou wilt return?

Mic.   Return I will.

SCENE VIII.

José, then the Cigar Girls and an Officer.

José.   Fear not, oh, mother; thy José

Will obey thee; do as thou desirest.

I love Michaela; she shall be my wife.

And thy flowers, hateful witch——

(At the instant he is about to take the flowers from his vest, a great noise is heard in the factory. The Officer comes on the stage, followed by the Soldiers.)

Mic.   Quel démon! quel péril? je ne comprends pas bien.

Que veut dire cela?

José.   Rien! Rien!

Parlons de toi, la messagère

Tu vas retourner au pays.

Mic.   Ce soir même, et demain je verrai votre mère.

José.   Eh bien, tu lui diras que José, que son fils,

Que son fils l'aime et la vénère,

Et qu'il se conduit aujourd'hui

En bon sujet, pour que sa mère

Là-bas soit contente de lui

Tout cela, n'est-ce pas? mignonne,

De ma part tu le lui diras;

Et ce baiser que je te donne,

De ma part tu le lui rendras.

           (Il l'embrasse.)

Mic.   Oui, je vous le promets, de la part de son fils.

José, j'elle rendrai comme je l'ai promis.

       REPRISE DE L'ENSEMBLE.

José.   } Ma mère, je la vois, etc.

Mic.   } Sa mère, il la revoit, etc.

José.   Reste là maintenant,

Pendant que je lirai.

Mic.   Non pas, lisez d'abord,

Et puis je reviendrai.

José.   Pourquoi t'en aller?

Mic.   C'est plus sage,

Cela me convient d'avantage.

Lisez! puis je reviendrai.

José.   Tu reviendras?

Mic.   Je reviendrai!

SCÈNE VIII.

José, puis les Ouvrières, le Lieutenant, Soldats.

José.   Ne crains rien, ma mère, ton fils t'obéira,

Fera ce que tu lui dis; j'aime Micaela,

Je la prendrai pour femme,

Quant à tes fleurs, sorcière infâme!

(Au moment où il va arracher les fleurs de sa veste, grande rumeur dans l'intérieur de la manufacture.—Entre le Lieutenant suivi des Soldats.)

Officer.

What means this uproar?

(The Cigar Girls run out quickly and in confusion.)

Cigar Girls.

Run, soldiers, by this way!
Run! Will no one come?

1st Group of Girls.

'Twas Carmencita.

2d Group.

No, it was not.

1st Group.

It was.

2d Group. No, it is not true

1st Group

But yes —

2d Group.

But no —

1st Group.

'Twas she began the quarrel.

All the Girls.

No, no; 'tis a falsehood.
Listen, gentlemen — yes, stay and listen.

1st Group

(drawing the Officer towards them).

La Manuelita said,
And to every one kept telling,
That she wished to buy —
What think you? — a fine donkey!

2d Group.

(pulling him towards them).

And then La Carmencita,
Who at making games too bold,
Said, "A donkey, at what cost? —
You'd better buy a wolf!"

1st Group.

Manuelita, wild with anger,
Made an answer rude enough:
"For your promenades
No doubt a mule would suit!"

2d Group.

"And then able will you be
To hold your head still higher,
With two servants in the mode,
With whips, to clear the way."

Le Lieut.

Eh bien! eh bien! qu'est-ce qui arrive?...

(Les ouvrières sortent rapidement et en désordre.)

Cho. Au secours! n'entendez-vous pas?
Au secours, messieurs les soldats!

Premier Groupe de Femmes.

C'est la Carmencita.

Deuxième Groupe de Femmes.

Non pas, ce n'est pas elle.

Premier Groupe.

C'est elle.

Deuxième Groupe.

Pas du tout.

Premier Groupe.

Si fait! dans la querelle
Elle a porté les premiers coups.

Toutes les Femmes

(entourant le Lieutenant).

Ne les écoutez pas, monsieur, écoutez-nous
Ecoutez-nous,
Ecoutez-nous.

Premier Groupe

(elles tirent l'officer de leur côté).

La Manuelita disait
Et répétait à voix haute
Qu'elle achèterait sans faute
Un âne qui lui plaisait.

Deuxième Groupe

(même jeu).

Alors la Carmencita,
Railleuse à son ordinaire,
Dit: un âne, pourquoi faire?
Un balai te suffira.

Premier Groupe.

Manuelita riposta
Et dit à sa camarade:
Pour certaine promenade
Mon âne te servira.

Deuxième Groupe.

Et ce jour-là tu pourras
A bon droit faire la fière;
Deux laquais suivront derrière,
T'émouchant à tour de bras.

All
> And then without delay,
> They both began to fight.

Officer.
> Deuce take them both!

> (To José.)

> José, take two dragoons with you,
> And look after these simpletons.

Don José takes two Soldiers with him, and they enter the factory during this time the Girls argue amongst themselves.)

1st Group.
> 'Tis La Carmencita.

2d Group.
> No, no; 'twas she, signor.

Officer.
> Oh! oh! Be off! Get away — all of you!

(The Girls are pushed back.)

SCENE IX.

(Carmen appears at the factory door led by Don José, and followed by the two Dragoons.)

José.
> Captain, there has been a fray.
> From words they came to blows.
> A girl is wounded.

Officer.
> And by whom?

> (to Carmen).

Officer.
> Dost thou hear?
> Thou canst not deny it.

Car.
> (singing mockingly).

> Tra la la, tra la la.
> You may cut, you may burn,
> No answer I'll make;
> Steel and fire I defy!
> Nor angel nor demon can compel me!

Toutes les Femmes.
> Là-dessus toutes les deux
> Se sont prises aux cheveux.

Le Lieut.
> Au diable tout ce bavardage.

> (A Don José.)

> Prenez, José, deux hommes avec vous
> Et voyez là-dedans qui cause ce tapage.

(Don José prend deux hommes avec lui. Les Soldats entrent dans la manufacture. Pendant ce temps les femmes se pressent, se disputen entre elles.)

Premier Groupe.
> C'est la Carmencita.

Deuxième Groupe.
> Non, non, écoutez nous, etc., etc.

Le Lieut.
> (assourdi)

> Holà! holà!
> Eloignez-moi toutes ces femmes-là

Toutes les Femmes.
> Ecoutez-nous! écoutez-nous!

(Les Soldats repoussent les femmes et les écartent.)

SCÈNE IX.
LES MÊMES, CARMEN.

(Carmen paraît sur la porte de la manufacture amenée par Don José et suivie par deux dragons.)

José.
> Mon officier, c'était une querelle;
> Des injures d'abord, puis à la fin des coups
> Une femme blessée.

Le Lieut.
> Et par qui?

José.
> Mais par elle.

Le Lieut.
> Vous entendez, que nous répondrez vous

Car.
> Tra la la la la la la la,
> Coupe moi, brûle moi,
> Je ne te dirai rien;
> Tra la la la la la la la,
> Je brave tout, le feu, le fer, et le ciel même

Officer.

    We're tired of your singing.

    Will you answer or not? Reply!— come!

Car. The secret I'll keep, and nothing I'll tell.

    If he I adore before me now stood,

    I'd naught say.

Officer.

    If you will not tell the truth

    You will sing — in prison.

Girls

          (running up).

    In prison ? — in prison ?

Officer.

    By Bacchus! She is not accustomed

    To restrain her wilfulness.

(Speaks aside to a Soldier, who goes in search of a rope. CARMEN still keeps singing in a most impertinent fashion.)

Officer.

    Pity indeed she's so headstrong:

    Very pretty to me she seems.

    Charming face, — hot brained!

    Come — tie her hands.

(The Soldiers fasten her hands behind her back. All go excepting José and CARMEN.)

SCENE X.

(CARMEN and DON JOSÉ. Silence. CARMEN raises her eyes and watches José. He goes to the back, then returns. CARMEN looks at him.)

Car. And where am I to go?

José. To prison; and I am forced to take you

Car. Really? Thou wilt obey the orders?

José. Yes; it is my duty.

Car. Well; I tell you that in spite of duty

    You will do what I say,

    Because I know that you love me.

José. I? — love you?

Car. Yes, my José.

    The flowers I gave you awhile since —

    Know — those flowers were enchanted.

Le Lieut.

    Fais-nous grâce de tes chansons,

    Et puis que l'on t'a dit de répondre, réponds !

Car Tra la la la la la la la,

    Mon secret, je le garde **et je le** garde bien !

    Tra la la la la la la la,

    J'en aime un autre et **meurs en disant** que je l'aime !

Le Lieut.

    Puisque tu le prends sur ce ton,

    Tu chanteras ton air aux murs de la prison.

Choristes.

    En prison ! en prison !

    (CARMEN avent se précipiter sur les femmes.)

Le Lieut.

    Décidément vous avez la main leste !

Car Tra la la la la la la la !

Le Lieut.

    C'est dommage

    C'est grand dommage,

    Car elle est gentille vraiment !

    Mais il faut bien la rendre sage,

    Attachez ces deux jolis bras.

SCÈNE X.

CARMEN et DON JOSÉ.

(Un petit moment de silence. CARMEN lève les yeux et regarde Don José. Celui-ci se détourne, s'éloigne de quelques pas, puis revient ! CARMEN qui le regarde toujours.)

Car. Où me conduirez-vous ?

José. A la prison ; et je n'y puis rien faire.

Car. Vraiment ? tu n'y peux rien faire ?

José. Non, rien ! j'obéis à mes chefs.

Car. Eh ; bien moi, je sais bien qu'en **dépit de** tes chefs eux mêmes

    Tu feras tout ce que je veux,

    Et cela parce que tu m'aimes !

José. Moi, t'aimer ?

Car. Oui, José.

    La fleur dont je t'ai fait présent,

    Tu sais, la fleur de la sorcière

Throw them away — 'tis no avail :
They have already done their work.

José.   Speak no more! Dost thou hear me?
You must obey. Be silent!

(CARMEN looks at JOSÉ, who draws back.)

Car.   Near by the ramparts of Seville
There I shall find Lillas Pastia,
We'll dance in the gay seguidille,
And the wine-cup we'll share.
There shall I go to find Lillas Pastia.
Yes, but 'tis folly to go alone;
Where there's not two no love can be,
So, to keep me from being dull,
A handsome lad will come to me.
A handsome lad — deuce take it all! —
Three days ago I sent him off.
But this new love, he loves me well;
And him to choose my mind is bent;
More lovers have I than I can count;
None of them can me in bonds retain.
Free am I yet; I know not love.
Who loves me well I'll love again;
Who wants my heart, my heart must buy.
Why linger still ? the hour is nigh,
There's no time now for delay.
With the new love I'm off, — good-bye!
There, near the ramparts of Seville,
Lillas Pastia I shall find.
There shall I dance the seguidille,
And a goblet of wine I'll fill.

José.   Wilt thou not be silent ?
Must I tell thee yet again ?

Car.   Do you think I am talking to you?
No, I'm singing to myself.
Perhaps you think you can prevent me
thinking?
I am thinking of such a — handsome
officer!
And who, if I liked, I could make very happy.

José.   Carmen !

Car.   This officer is not captain yet—
Less than lieutenant — only brigadier;
Over me has he a spell cast,
And he to please me has found the way.

Tu peux la jeter maintenant,
Le charme opère !

José.   Ne me parle plus ! Tu m'entends ?
Ne parle plus. Je le défends !

FINALE.

Car.   Sur les remparts de Séville,
Chez mon ami Lillas Pastia,
J'irai danser la seguedille
Et boire du Manzanilla !...
Oui, mais toute seule on s'ennuie,
Et les vrais plaisirs sont à deux...
Donc pour me tenir compagnie,
J'emmènerai mon amoureux
Mon amoureux !... il est au diable...
Je l'ai mis à la porte hier...
Mon pauvre cœur très-consolable,
Mon cœur est libre comme l'air...
J'ai des galants à la douzaine,
Mais ils ne sont pas à mon gré;
Voici la fin de la semaine,
Qui veut m'aimer je l'aimerai,
Qui veut mon âme.. elle est à prendre...
Vous arrivez au bonne moment,
Je n'ai guère le temps d'attendre,
Car avec mon nouvel amant...
Près de la Poste de Séville,
Chez mon ami Lillas Pastia,
J'irai danser la seguedille
Et boire du Manzanilla.

José.   Tais-toi, je t'avais dit ne pas me parler?

Car.   Et je pense... il n'est pas défendu de pen-
ser,
Je pense à certain officier,
A certain officier qui m'aime,
Et que l'un de ces jours je pourrais bien
aimer....

José.   Carmen !...

Car.   Mon officier n'est pas un capitaine,
Pas même un lieutenant, il n'est que
brigadier.
Mais c'est assez pour une bohémienne,
Et je daigne m'en contenter !

Jose

    (untying CARMEN's hands).

Carmen, I am bewitched;
But if I yield ever, and thou lovest me,
Thy promise, ah! do not forget!
Carmen, if I love thee, wilt thou love
    me too?

Car.

    (scarcely singing, but murmuring).

Near the ramparts of Seville
I shall Lillas Pastia find.
There shall I dance the seguidille,
And a goblet of wine I'll fill.

(CARMEN goes and reseats herself on the stool, with her hands behind her back. The Officer enters.)

SCENE XI.

Officer.

Here is the order. Go, then!
Haste! The hour is late.

Car.

    (aside to JOSÉ).

In going there I will push thee
As hard as I am able:
Fall thou on the ground — leave the rest
    to me.

(Places herself between the two Dragoons; José is at her side. The Girls and Young Men come on the scene, kept back by the Soldiers. CARMEN crosses from left to right, going toward the bridge.)

Car. Love is still the lord of all;
For him no laws can fetters bear.
If thou me lovest not, I love thee;
And, if I love thee, now beware!

José

    (déliant la corde qui attache les mains de CARMEN).

Carmen, je suis comme un homme ivre
Si je cède, se je me livre,
Ta promesse, tu la tiendras...
Si je t'aime, tu m'aimeras...

Car.

    (à peine chanté, murmuré).

Près de la porte de Séville,
Chez mon ami Lillas Pastia,
Nous danserons la seguedille
Et boirons du Manzanilla.

José

    (paré).

Le lieutenant!... Prenez garde.

(CARMEN va se replacer sur son escabeau, les mains derrière le dos. — Rentre Le Lieutenant.)

SCÈNE XI.

Les Mêmes, Le Lieutenant, puis les Ouvrier, les Soldats, les Bourgeois.

Le Lieut.

Voici l'ordre, partez et faites bonne garde.

Car.

    (bas à JOSÉ).

Sur le pont je te pousserai
Aussi fort que je le pourrai...
Laisse-toi renverser... le reste me regarde!

(Elle se place entre les deux dragons. José à côté d'elle. Les femmes et les bourgeois pendant ce temps sont rentrés en scène toujours maintenus à distance par les dragons. ... CARMEN traverse la scène de gauche à droite allant vers le pont....)

L'amour est enfant de Bohême.
Il n'a jamais connu de loi;
Si tu ne m'aimes pas, je t'aime;
Si je t'aime, prends garde à toi.

(Arriving at the foot of the bridge on the right, CARMEN pushes JOSÉ, who falls to the ground. Confusion. CARMEN escapes. She stops a moment in the centre of the bridge, throws the cord over the parapet, and disappears; while on the stage the Cigar Girls, with great bursts of laughter, surround the Officer.)

(En arrivant à l'entrée au pont à droite, CARMEN pousse JOSÉ qui se laisse renverser. Confusion, désordre, CARMEN s'enfuit. Arrivée au milieu du pont, elle s'arrête un instant, jette sa corde à la volée par dessus le parapet du pont, et se sauve pendant que le scène, avec de grands éclats de rire, les cigarières entourent LE LIEUTENANT.)

ACT II.

SCENE I

(CARMEN, FRASQUITA, MERCEDES, the Officer, MORALES, other Officers, Gipsies, etc.

The Tavern of Lillas Pastia. Benches right and left. Towards the end of a dinner. The table is in confusion.

FRASQUITA, MERCEDES, the Officer, MORALES, are with CARMEN. The Officers are smoking. Two Gipsies in a corner play the Guitar, and two others dance. CARMEN looks at them. The Officer speaks to her. she does not listen to him, but suddenly rises and sings.)

I.

Car.   Ah! when of gay guitars the sound
      On the air in cadence ringing,
      Quickly forth the gipsies springing,
      To dance a merry, mazy round.
      While tambourines the clang prolong,
      In rhythm with the music beating,
      And ev'ry voice is heard repeating
      The merry burthen of our glad song,
          Tra la la la.

Fras. and Mer.
          Tra la la la.

(During the burthen of the song, the Gipsies dance, MERCEDES and FRASQUITA sing "Tra la la" with CARMEN.)

II.

      Cheeks now flush and jewels shine,
      Scarves are floating to the wind;
      Round and round in merry maze
      The sun-kissed gipsies dance entwined.
      So the dance and song unite,
      From measure slow to fastest strain;
      Voices sounding, steps rebounding —
      On they whirl again, again.

ACTE DEUXIÈME.

SCÈNE PREMIÈRE.

(CARMEN, LE LIEUTENANT, MORALES, Officiers et Bohémiennes)

La taverne de LILLAS PASTIA. Tables à droite et à gauche. CARMEN, MERCEDES, FRASQUITA, le lieutenant ZUNIGA, MORALES et un lieutenant. C'est la fin d'un diner. La table est en désordre. Les Officiers et les Bohémiennes fument des cigarettes. Deux Bohémiens râclent de la guitare dans un coin de la taverne et deux Bohémiennes. au milieu de la scène, dansent. CARMEN est assise, regardent danser les Bohémiennes, le Lieutenant lui parle bas, mais elle ne fait aucune attention à lui. Elle se lève tout à coup et se met à chanter.)

I.

Car.   Les tringles des sistres tintaient
      Avec un éclat métallique,
      Et sur cette étrange musique
      Les Zingarellas se levaient,
      Tambours de basque allaient leur train,
      Et les guitares forcenées,
      Grinçaient sous des mains obstinées,
      Même chanson, même refrain,
          La la la la la la.

(Sur le refrain les Bohémiennes dansent. MERCEDES et FRASQUITA reprennent avec CARMEN le : La la la la la la.)

II.

      Les anneaux de cuivre et d'argent
      Reluisaient sur les peaux bistrées;
      D'orange ou de rouge zébrées
      Les étoffes flottaient au vent;
      La danse au chante se mariait
      D'abord indécise et timide,
      Plus vive ensuite et plus rapide
      Cela montait, montait, montait!..
          La la la la la la.

Mer. et Fra.
          La la la la la la .

III.

Louder now vibrate the chords
As the strings the gipsies sweep,
Yet a wilder dance is on —
Faster, faster, now they leap.
And here, whilst floats around the song —
Ardent and wild — the wine-cup's passed;
The Zingarelle, love-beguiled,
Alas! find reason lost at last.

(Moment of rapid and violent dance. CARMEN also commences to dance, and as the last notes sound, unable to continue, falls on a seat near at hand.)

Fras.   Pastia wishes —
Officer.

What does Master Pastia want of us now?
Fras.   He tells me the chief Corregidor
          Desires him to shut up the inn.
Officer.

Well, we will depart.
Shall we go together?
Fras.   No, no; we shall stay.
Officer.

And thou, Carmen, art thou not coming?
Listen; thou art discontented.
Tell the truth.
Car.   No, no; why indeed?
Officer.

About the soldier I put in prison,
Through thee, the other day — in prison,
From which he has only to-day been re-
     leased.
Car. ⎫
Fras. ⎬ Ah! 'twas better thus.
Mer. ⎭ Good-bye, dearest signors!

(The scene is interrupted by a song in the distance.)

Cho.   Honor! honor
          To the Toreador!
          Honor to Escamillo!

(The officer goes to the window.)

Officer.

By the torchlight and appearance
He looks like the victor of the circus in
     Granada.

III.

Les Bohémiens à tour de bras,
De leurs instruments faisaient rage,
Et cet éblouissant tapage,
Ensorcelait les Zingaras!
Sous le rhythme de la chanson,
Ardentes, folles, enfiévrées,
Elles se laissaient, enivrées,
Emporter par le tourbillon!
          La la la la la la.
Les Trois Vois.
          La la la la la.

(Mouvement de danse très-rapide, très-violent. CARMEN elle même danse et vient, avec les dernières notes de l'orchestre, tomber haletante sur un banc de la taverne. Après la danse, LILLAS PASTIA se met à tourner autour des officiers d'un air embarrassé.)

Fras.   Messieurs, Pastia me dit —
Le Lieut.

Que nous veut-il encor, maître Pastia?
Fras.   Il dit que le Corrégidor veut que l'on
          ferme l'auberge.
Le Lieut.

Eh! bien! nous partirons.
Vous viendrez avec nous?
Fras.   Non pas! nous, nous restons.
Le Lieut.

Et toi, Carmen, tu ne viens pas?
Ecoute! Deux mots dits tout bas:
Tu m'eu veux.
Car.   Vous en vouloir! pourquoi?
Le Lieut.

Ce soldat, l'autre jour, emprisonné pou
     toi,
Maintenant il est libre!

Car. ⎫
Fras. ⎬ Bon-soir messieurs nos amoureux!
Mer. ⎭

(La scène est interrompue par un chœur chanté dans la coulisse.)

Cho.   Vivat! vivat le Torero!
          Vivat! vivat Escamillo!

Le Lieut.

Une promenade aux flambeaux!
C'est le vainqueur des courses de Grenade.

We shall be pleased to drink your health, comrade,
To triumphs past and future.

Cho.

(again).

Honor! honor
To the Toreador!
Honor to Escamillo!

Voulez-vous avec nous boire, mon camarade,
A vos succès anciens, à vos succès nouveaux!

Les Choristes (repetent).

Vivat! vivat! le Torero!
Vivat! vivat! Escamillo!

(Parait ESCAMILLO.)

SCENE II.

Enter ESCAMILLO.

I.

Esc. With you to drink will be a pleasure.
With soldiers
Should Toreadors go side by side;
For both delight in combats.
Crowded the Circus on a festival day,
Crowded the Circus from floor to roof,
Wild with excitement the populace are.
Each one among them of you is speaking —
Clamoring all — questions asking;
All are shouting till the combat is over,
Because 'tis a festival rare of its kind.
Come! — on your guard! — attend!
Toreador, e'er watchful be:
Toreador, Toreador,
Do not forget the brightest of eyes!
Now fondly thee await;
And love is the prize,
Yes, love's the prize waits thee, O Toreador.

Cho. Toreador, etc.

(Between the verses CARMEN fills ESCAMILLO's glass.)

II.

Esc. At last each one is hushed to silence.
What has happened? what is this?
Forth the bull comes in his fury,
Leaping through from his retreat;
Already pierced through, a horse has fallen,
Dragging down a picador.
Bravo, bull! the mob are shrieking!
He goes, he comes, he rushes on,

SCÈNE II.

Les Mêmes ESCAMILLO.

I.

Esc. Votre toast . . . . je peux vous le rendre,
Senors, car avec les soldats
Les Toreros peuvent s'entendre,
Pour plaisirs ils ont les combats.
Le cirque est plein, c'est jour de fête,
Le cirque est plein du haut en bas.
Les spectateurs perdant la tête
S'interpellent à grand fracas;
Apostrophes, cris et tapage
Poussés jusques à la fureur,
Car c'est la fête du courage,
C'est la fête des gens de cœur!
Toreador, en garde,
Et songe en combattant
Qu'un œil noir te regarde
Et que l'amour t'attend.

Tout le Monde.

Toreador, en garde, etc., etc.

(Entre les deux couplets, CARMEN remplit le verre d'ESCAMILLO.

II.

Esc. Tout d'un coup l'on a fait silence;
Plus de cris! que se passe-t-il?
C'est l'instant, le taureau s'élance
En bondissant hors du Toril . . . .
Il entre, il frappe, un cheval roule
Entraînant un picador.
Bravo toro! . . . . hurle la foule,
Le taureau va, vient, frappe encor . . . .
En secouant ses banderilles . . .

And tries to tear the bandrol down ,
And now with blood the ring is full ;
Terror throbs in every breast ;
Now honor's thine, O Toreador.
Toreador, e'er watchful be, etc.

(All drink, and clasp hands with the Toreador. The Officers get ready to go. ESCAMILLO draws near CARMEN.)

Esc.

(to CARMEN).

Maiden, say what art thou called?
In peril I would invoke thy name.

Car. Carmen, or Carmencita, each one calls me.

Esc. And if one — if one might say he loved
you?

Car. I should say that he must not.
Esc. Too amiable Carmen does not appear ;
But I am content to hope — to wait.

Car. To wait you are permitted, and 'tis sweet
to hope.

Officer

(to CARMEN).

Since you will not come, Carmen, I shall
return.

Car. 'Twill be in vain if you do.
Officer. That may be, but I'll try.

All. Toreador, e'er watchful be, etc.

(All but the three Zingarelle leave the scene.)

SCENE III.

LILLAS PASTIA closes the shutters and goes out.
Enter DANCAIRO and IL REMENDADO.

Fras. Well, what news?
Il. D. Worse there can't be.
Perhaps we may yet strike out some plan :
But it is necessary for you to be with us.

The Three Girls.
We stay with you?

Il court, le cirque est plein de sang :
On se sauve . . . . on franchit les grilles ;
Allons . . . . c'est ton tour maintenant.
Toreador, en garde,
Et songe en combattant
Qu'un œuil noir te regarde
Et que l'amour t'attend.

Tout le Monde.
Toreador, en garde, etc.

(On boit, on échange des poignées de main avec le Torero.
Les officiers commencent à se préparer à partir. ESCAMILLO se
trouve près de CARMEN.)

Esc. La belle, un mot ; comment t'appelle-t-on?
Dans mon premier danger je veux dire
ton nom.

Car. Carmen, Carmencita, cela revient au
même.

Esc. Si l'on te disait que l'on t'aime?

Car. Je répondrais qu'il ne faut pas m'aimer.
Esc. Cette réponse n'est pas tendre ;
Je me contenterai d'espérer et d'attendre.

Car. Il est permis d'attendre, il est doux d'espérer.

Le Lieut.
Puisque tu ne viens pas Carmen, je
reviendrai.

Car. Et vous aurez grand tort.
Le Lieut.
Bah! je me risquerai!

Chorister, etc.
Toreador.

SCÈNE III.

LILLAS PASTIA ferme les postes et sort.
Entrant DANCAIRO et IL REMENDADO.

Fras. Eh! Bien! vite, quelles nouvelles?
Pas trop mauvaises les nouvelles.
Et nous pouvons encor faire quelques
beaux coups !
Mais nous avons besoin de vous.

Les Trois Femmes.
Besoin de nous!

Il. D. Yes, we want your help;
          We have a fine business in view.

Mer. Profitable? or, at least, said to be?
Il. R. Certain; it seems excellent:
          But you must remain.

The Three Girls.
          Really?
The Two Men.
          Really; we the truth you tell,
          With humbleness and deep respect.
          When there's a question of cheating,
          By deception or thieving,
          To succeed as one ought,
          The women must be of the party;
          Without 'em to do
          Is imprudent—
          The attempt goes for nothing, or worse.
The Three Girls.
          Ah! the attempt goes for nothing,
          Or worse.
The Two Men.
          You don't dispute that?
The Three Girls.
          Yes, yes, indeed;
          That is our opinion.
Quintette.
          Where there's a question of cheating, etc.

Il D. 'Tis well; you think 'twill suit?

Mer.&° ⎱ When you set out.
Fras. ⎰ But, at so short a notice —

Car. Ah! no, then.
          If to leave it suits you, be it so;
          But **I** shall not go on this journey
          Here shall I stay — I shall not depart.

Il D Carmen, Carmen, thou must come;
          Thou will not let us set off
          Without accompanying us.

Car Here shall I stay — I will not go.

Le Danc.
          Oui, nous avons besoin de vous!
          Nous avons en tête une affaire,
Merc. Est-elle bonne, dites-nous?
Le Rem.
          Elle est admirable, ma chère;
          Mais nous avons besoin de vous.
Les Trois Femmes.
          De nous?
Les Deux Hommes.
          De vous, car nous l'avouons humblement
          Et très respectueusement,
          En matière de tromperie,
          De duperie, de volerie,
          Il est toujours bon, sur ma foi,
          D'avoir les femmes avec soi,
          Et sans elles,
          Mes toutes belles,
          On ne fait jamais rien de bien.
Les Trois Femmes.
          Quoi! sans nous jamais rien,
          De bien?
Les Deux Hommes.
          N'êtes-vous pas de cet avis?
Les Trois Femmes.
          Si fait, je suis
          De cet avis.
Tous Les Cinq.
          En matière de tromperie,
          De duperie, de volerie,
          Il est toujours bon, sur ma foi,
          D'avoir les femmes avec soi.
          Et sans elles,
          Les toutes belles,
          On ne fait jamais rien de bien.
Le Dan.
          C'est dit alors, vous partirez.
Mer. et ⎱ Quand vous partirez.
Fras.   ⎰
Le Rem.
          Mais tout de suite,
Car Ah! permettez;
          (A MERCEDES et à FRASQUITA.)
          S'il vous plait de partir, partez.
          Mais je ne suis pas du voyage,
          Je ne pars pas, je ne pars pas!

Il R. But at least tell us the reason why, Carmen.

Car. I will tell you why, sincerely, —
The reason is in my heart —

All the Others.
Well, then —

Car. I am in love!

Fras. Whatever is she saying?
That she is in love?

The Two Men.
In love?
The Two Gipsies.
In love?
Car. In love.
The Two Men.
Come, Carmen, this is a serious thing.
Car. I am in love, seriously, and go not.
The Two Men.
The thing is certain and extraordinary.
But yet to all 'tis known —
And well to thee, loving fair one —
That duty and love should go together.

Car. Dear sirs, I should be happy to set off
And with you go,
But I am not free to follow you;
Duty must give place to love.
Il D. Then thou wilt not come with us?

Car. I have said it.
Il R. Suffer thyself to be persuaded.

Quartette.
Ah, Carmen, come; you must come.
For this affair, with us to stay ·
Thou well know'st why.

Le Dan.
Carmen, mon amour, tu viendras,
Et tu n'auras pas le courage
De nous laisser dans l'embarras.
Car. Je ne pars pas, je ne pars pas.

Le Rem.
Mais au moins la raison, Carmen, tu la
diras?
Car. Je la dirai certainement;
La raison, c'est qu'en ce moment
Je suis amoureuse.
Les Deux Hommes
(stupéfaits).
Qu'a-t-elle dit.
Fras. Elle dit qu'elle est amoureuse.
Les Deux Hommes.
Amoureuse!
Les Deux Femmes.
Amoureuse!
Car. Amoureuse!
Les Deux Hommes.
Voyons, Carmen, sois sérieuse.
Car. Amoureuse à perdre l'esprit.
Les Deux Hommes.
Certes, la chose nous étonne,
Mais ce n'est pas le premier jour
Où vous aurez su, ma mignonne,
Faire marcher de front le devoir et
l'amour.
Car. Mes amis, je serais fort aise
De pouvoir vous suivre ce soir
Mais cette fois, ne vous déplaise,
Il faudra que l'amour passe avant le devoir
Le Dan.
Ce n'est pas là ton dernier mot?
Car. Pardonnez-moi.
Le Rem.
Carmen, il faut
Que tu te laisses attendrir
Tous les Quatre.
Il faut venir, Carmen, il faut venir
Pour notre affaire,
C'est nécessaire,
Car entre nous.

Mer. & Fras. } Thou well know'st why.

Car. 'Tis true, 'tis true; the reason's to me known.

Quintette.

Where there'e a question of cheating, etc.

Il D. Who canst thou be expecting?

Fras. It is easily told — a dragoon.

Car. Who the other day for kindness to me
Was to prison sent.

Il R. 'Tis a delicate business.

Il D. Are you sure he will come!

Car. Stay and listen! He is here already.

(DON JOSÉ's voice is heard in the distance).

José

(far away).

Halt there!
Who goes there?
Dragoon of Alcalà.
I go to death to bring
To a fellow low,
Who my rival has been.
Ah! already is it so?
Pass on, then, and go.
Affair of love,
Affair of war,
For us all the same,
Dragoon of Alcalá.

(All look through the shutters.)

Fras. What a handsome dragoon!

Mer. Yes, a handsome fellow!

Il D. Faith, he would make a good smuggler.

Il R. Tell him to join us.

Car. No; he will refuse.

Il D. But you can tempt him.

Car. Go away; I will try.

(IL REMENDADO signs to the others to leave CARMEN alone. They all go out.)

Les Deux Femmes.

Car entre nous.

Car. Quant à cela, je l'admets avec vous

Reprise Generale.

En matière de tromperie, etc., etc.

Le Dan.

Mais qui donc attends tu?

Car. Presque rien, un soldat qui l'autre jour
pour me rendre service
S'est fait mettre en prison.

Le Rem.

Le fait est délicat.

Le Dan.

Il se peut qu'après tout ton soldat réfléchisse
Es-tu bien sûre qu'il viendra?

Car. Ecoutez! Le voilà!

José

(la voix très-éloignée).

Halte là!
Qui va là?
Dragon d'Alcala!
Où t'en vas-tu par là,
Dragon d'Alcala?
Moi je m'en vais faire,
A mon adversaire,
Mordre la poussière.
S'il en est ainsi,
Passez mon ami,
Affaire d'honneur,
Affaire de cœur,
Pour nous tout est là,
Dragons d'Alcala.

Fras. C'est un beau dragon!

Mer. Un très beau dragon!

Le Dan.

Qui serait pour nous un fier compagnon.

Le Rem.

Dis lui de nous suivre.

Car. Il refusera.

Le Dan.

Mais, essaye, au moins.

Car. Soit; on essayera.

(Le REMENDADO se sauve et sort. LE DANCAIRE le poursuit et sort á son tour entrainant MERCEDES et FRASQUITA qui essaient de le calmer.)

osé
(advancing, but still in the distance.)

Halt there !
Who goes there ?
Dragoon of Alcalà.
Why goest thou that way,
Dragoon of Alcalà ?
Constant, true, I go there
Where love of beauty calls me.
Ah ! already is it so ?
Pass on, then, and go.
Affair of love,
Affair of war,
Knows not delay,
Dragoon of Alcalà.

(Comes on the scene.)

SCENE IV.

Car. Thou art here at last.
José. Carmen.
Car. And they put thee in prison ?
José. For two months I was there.
Car. Poor fellow !
José. No matter
   If 'twould serve thee, I would stay there
      yet.
Car. Thou lovest me still ?
José. I adore thee !
Car. The officers were here a short time since,
   And they made us dance.
José.

(Angrily.)
   Is it true ? Thee ?
Car. May I die if he is not jealous !
José. Yes, jealous am I.
Car. Softly, softly ; hear reason.
   I will dance for thy pleasure,
   And thou shalt see how Carmen
   Accompanies herself in the danca

¹(Makes José sit in a corner, and dances, accompanying herself with castanets. José's eyes are fixed on her, fascinated. The recall is heard in the distance. José starts up and goes to Carmen.)

José
(la voix beaucoup plus rapprochée)

Halte là !
Qui va là ?
Dragon d'Alcala !
Où t'en vas tu par là,
Dragon d'Alcala ?
Exact et fidèle,
Je vais où m'appelle
L'amour de ma belle.
S'il en est ainsi,
Passez mon ami.
Affaire d'honneur,
Affaire de cœur,
Pour nous tout est là,
Dragons d'Alcala !

(Entre Don José.)

SCÈNE IV.

Car. Enfin c'est toi.
José. Carmen.
Car. Et tu sors de prison ?
José. J'y suis resté deux mois.
Car. Tu t'en plains !
José. Ma foi non.
   Et si c'était pour **toi, j'y voudrais êtr**
      encore.
Car. Tu m'aimes donc ?
José. Je t'adore !
Car. Vos officiers sont venus tout à l'heure,
   Ils nous ont fait danser.
José. Comment ? toi ?

Car. Que je meure si tu n'es pas jaloux.
José. Eh, oui, je suis jaloux.
Car. Tout doux, Monsieur, tout doux.
   Je vais danser en votre honneur,
   Et vous verrez, Seigneur,
   Comment je sais moi-même accompagner
   ma danse.

(Elle fait asseoir Don José dans un coin du théâtre, Petite danse, Carmen, du bout des lèvres, fredonne un air qu'elle accompagne avec ses castagnettes, Don José la dévore des yeux. On entend au loin, très au loin, des clairons qui sonnent la retraite. Don José prête l'oreille. Il croit entendre les clairons, mais les castagnettes de Carmen clament très bruyamment. Don José rapproche de Carmen, lui prend le bras, et l'oblige à s'arrêter.)

José.   Wait a moment, Carmen, stay !

Car.   And why ?

José.   It seemed to me down yonder —
Yes, 'tis the trumpet sounding the retreat ;
Say dost thou not hear ?

Car.   Really ? I am very glad of it.
It was very wearisome
Dancing without music.
It must have been music in the air.

(Begins to dance again. The call draws nearer and passes beneath the window, then dies away in the distance. José takes CARMEN'S arm and obliges her to cease.)

José.   Dost thou not understand, Carmen,
That sound orders me to return to quarters ?

Car.   Recall to quarters ? I am a fool indeed !
I am distracting myself
Till I am exhausted,
To divert you with my dance.
I thought — Heaven pardon me ! — he
loved me ;
And the trumpet sounds his recall !
And already he would depart !
Go — depart — and by yourself !

(Throws his cap, etc., with rage at him.)

There ! thy cap, thy sabre, thy pouch !
And go directly to the barracks !

José.   Carmen, thou art wrong thus to jest.
'Tis hard to part, for in my heart
Never has my soul
Felt greater ardor warmer love for thee !

José.   Attends un peu, Carmen, rien qu'un
moment, arrête.

Car.   Et pourquoi, s'il te plâit ?

José.   Il me semble, là bas. . .
Oui, ce sont nos clairons qui sonnent la
retraite.
Ne les entends-tu pas ?

Car.   Bravo ! j'avais beau faire. . . . Il est
mélancolique
De danser sans orchestre, et vive la musique
Qui nous tombe du ciel !

(Elle reprend sa chanson qui se rhythme sur la retraite sonnée au dehors par les clairons. CARMEN se remet à danser et DON JOSÉ se remet à regarder CARMEN. La retraite approche . . . approche . . . approche, passe sous les fenêtres de l'auberge. . . puis s'éloigne. . . . Le son des clairons va s'affaiblissant. Nouvel effort de DON JOSÉ pour s'arracher à cette contemplation de CARMEN. . . . Il lui prend le bras et l'oblige encore à s'arrêter.)

José.   Tu ne m'as pas compris. . . Carmen, c'est
la retraite, . . .
Il faut que, moi, je rentre au quartier
pour l'appel.

(Le bruit de la retraite cesse tout à coup.)

Car.

(regardant DON JOSÉ qui remet sa giberne et rattache le ceinturon de son sabre).

Au quartier ! pour l'appel ! j'étais vraiment
bien bête !
Je me mettais en quatre et je faisais des frais
Pour amuser monsieur ! je chantais . . . je
dansais. . . .
Je crois, Dieu me pardonne,
Qu'un peu plus, je l'aimais. . . .
Ta ra ta ra, c'est le clairon qui sonne !
Il part ! il est parti !
Va-t'en donc, canari.

(Avec fureur, lui envoyant son shako à la vollée.)

Prends ton shako, ton sabre, ta giberne.
Et va-t'en, mon garçon, retourne à la
caserne.

José.   C'est mal à toi, Carmen, de te moquer de
moi ;
Je souffre de partir . . . car jamais, jamais
femme,
Jamais femme avant toi
Aussi profondément n'avait troublé mon
âme.

Car. Ta, ta, ta, ta ! Great heaven ! — the recall !	*Car.* Ta ra ta ta, mon Dieu . c'est la retraite,
Ta, ta, ta, ta ! I must return.	Je vais être en retard Il court, il perd la tête,
His head is turned : and this is his love.	Et voilà son amour.
José. Then such love thou believest not ?	*José.* Ainsi tu ne crois pas A mon amour ?
Car. No, no.	*Car.* Mais non !
José. But thou must hear me —	*José.* Eh bien ! tu m'entendras.
Car. I won't hear anything.	*Car.* Je ne veux rien entrendre. . . .
Go : I will not punish thee.	Tu vas te faire attendre.
José. Thou must listen to me, Carmen ; I desire it.	*José*

(violemment)

Tu m'entendras, Carmen, tu m'entendras

(With his left hand he holds CARMEN's arm, and with his right opens his uniform and takes out the flowers she gave him in the first Act.)

(De la main gauche il a saisi brusquement le bras de CARMEN ; de la main droite, il va chercher sous sa veste d'uniforme la fleur de càssie que CARMEN lui a jetée au premier Acte. Il montre cette fleur à CARMEN.)

I.

The flowers once to me you gave,
Within my prison have I cherish'd,
For me still perfume they retain'd,
Though all their beauty long had perish'd.
Night and day, in dungeon gloomy,
Carmen, I swear I thought of thee :
And while their fragrance fill'd my brain,
Thy name invoked, so far from me.
My fatal love for thee I curs'd,
And I regretted in my wrath
The cruel stroke of destiny
That brought thy form across my path.
Ah ! horror held me for its own,
And one sad thought filled heart and brain,
Only one hope — my sole desire —
That I might see thee once again.
Now but one tender glance I ask,
One word of kindness from thee crave :
True my heart to thine is ever ;
Carmen, am I not thy slave ?

José. La fleur que tu m'avais jetée,
Dans ma prison m'était restée
Flétrie et sèche, mais gardant
Son parfum terrible, enivrant.
Et pendant des heures entières,
Sur mes yeux fermant mes paupières
Ce parfum, je le respirais
Et dans la nuit je te voyais,
Car tu n'avais eu qu'à paraître,
Qu'à jeter un regard sur moi
Pour t'emparer de tout mon être.
Et j'étais une chose à toi.

II.

Je me prenais à te maudire,
A te détester, à me dire ;
Pourquoi faut-il que le destin
L'ait mise là sur mon chemin ?
Puis je m'accusais de blasphème
Et je ne sentais en moi même
Qu' un seul désir, un seul espoir,
Te revoir, Carmen, te revoir !...
Car tu n'avais eu qu'à paraître,
Qu'à jeter un regard sur moi
Pour t'emparer de tout mon être
Et j'étais une chose à toi.

Car. No, thou lov'st me not,
     No ; if thou didst love me,
     We should go together
     Up into the mountains yonder.

José. Carmen !

Car. Up there to the mountains
     On thy horse would we ride,
     O'er the vast plains we'd traverse,
     Far, far from hence speed.

José. Carmen !

Car. If thou didst love me a little,
     Together up yonder would we go ;
     Officer no more commanding thee,
     No captain forced then to obey,
     No more the trumpet wouldst thou hear
     Forcing lovers fond to part.

José. Carmen !

Car. For roof, the sky — a wandering life ;
     For country, the whole world ;
     Thy will thy master ;
     And above all — most prized of all —
     Liberty ! freedom !
     Up yonder, up yonder, if thou lov'st me,
     Up yonder, up yonder, together we'll go.

José. Carmen !

Car. Say, is it not true ?
     Up yonder, up yonder, thus will we go
     Away, if thou lov'st me, together.

José. No, I must not listen to thee,
     Go with thee far away,
     A deserter ! Infamy ! Dishonor !
     It must not be.

Car. Then go !

José. Cruel one, thou art heartless !

Car. No ; no longer do I love you ; I hate you.

José. Carmen !

Car. Farewell ! Never will I see you again.

José. I go : farewell for ever !

(Turns towards the door. At this moment a knocking is heard.)

Car. Non, tu ne m'aimes pas, non, car si tu
     m'aimais,
     Là-bas, là-bas, tu me suivrais.

José. Carmen !

Car. Là bas, là bas dans la montagne,
     Sur ton cheval tu me prendrais,
     Et comme un brave à travers la campagne,
     En croupe, tu m'emporterais.

José. Carmen !

Car. Là-bas, là-bas, si tu m'aimais,
     Là-bas, là-bas, tu me suivrais.
     Point d'officier à qui tu doives obéir
     Et point de retraite qui sonne
     Pour dire à l'amoureux qu'il est temps
     de partir.

José. Carmen !

Car. Le ciel ouvert, la vie errante,
     Pour pays l'univers, pour loi ta volonté,
     Et surtout la chose enivrante,
     La liberté ! la liberté !
     Là-bas, là-bas, si tu m'aimais,
     Là-bas, là-bas, tu me suivrais.

José

               (presque vaincu).

     Carmen !

Car. Oui, n'est-ce pas,
     Là-bas, là-bas, tu me suivras,
     Tu m'aimes et tu me suivras.

José

        (s'arrachant brusquement des bras de CARMEN).

     Non, je ne veux plus t'écouter . . .
     Quitter mon drapeau . . . déserter . . .
     C'est la honte, c'est l'infamie,
     Je n'en veux pas !

Car. Eh bien, pars !

José. Carmen, je t'en prie. . . .

Car. Je ne t'aime plus, je te hais !

José. Carmen !

Car. Adieu ! mais adieu pour jamais.

José. Eh bien, soit . . . adieu pour jamais.

(Il va en courant jusqu'à la porte. . . . Au moment où il y arrive,
on frappe. . . . José s'arrête, silence. On frappe encore.)

SCENE V.

(The preceding and the Officer.)

Officer

(without).

Hola! Carmen! Hola!

José. Who knocks? Who goes there?

Car. Be silent!

Officer

(bursting open the door).

Thus I open and enter.

(Enters and sees José.)

Oh, no, my dear;
The choice does not do you honor;
You degrade yourself too much.
Prefer a soldier to his officer!

(To José.)

Will you go about your business?

José. No!

Officer.

But yes; you must depart.

José. No, no; I will not!

Officer

(strikes him).

Go!

José.

(drawing his sabre)

Infernal! thy blood for this shall pay!

Car.

(running across).

There will be mischief done.
Hola! hola!

(Calls for help.)

(IL DANCAIRO, IL REMENDADO, and the Gipsies enter from different sides. CARMEN points to the Officer. IL DANCAIRO and REMENDADO seize him.)

Car. My gallant captain,
Love an ugly trick has played you.
Pity 'tis you came here,
Since we're compell'd
(Not wishing you to denounce us)
To keep you close prisoner
For an hour at least.

SCENE V.

Les Mêmes, LE LIEUTENANT.

Le Lieut.

(au dehors).

Holà! vient Carmen! Holà! holà!

José. Qui frappe? qui vient là?

Car. Tais toi! . . .

Le Lieut.

(faisant sauter la porte).

J'ouvre moi-même et j'entre.

(Il entre et voit Don José. — A CARMEN.)

Ah! fi, la belle,
Le choix n'est pas heureux; c'est se
mésallier,
De prendre le soldat quand on a l'officier
Allons! décampe.

(A DON JOSÉ.)

José. Non.

Le Lieut.

Si fait tu partiras

José. Je ne partirai pas

Le Lieut.

(le frappant).

Drôle!

José

(sautant sur son sabre)

Tonnerre! il va pleuvoir des coups.

(LE LIEUTENANT dégaine à moitié.)

Car.

(se jetant entre eux deux)

Au diable le jaloux!
A moi! a moi.

(Appelant.)

(LE DANCAIRE, LE REMENDADO, et les Bohémiens paraissent de tous les côtés. CARMEN d'un geste montre LE LIEUTENANT aux Bohémiens. LE DANCAIRE et LE REMENDADO se jettent sur lui, le désarment.)

Car. Mon officier, l'amour
Vous joue en ce moment un assez vilain
tour,
Vous arrivez fort mal et nous sommes
forcés,
Ne voulant être dénoncés,
De vous garder au moins pendant une
heure.

Il D. and Il R.

    We from this inn must go soon;
    You will accompany us.

Car. 'Twill be a walk.
    Will you or will you not?

Il D. and Il R.

          (drawing their pistols).

    Say, then, comrade — yes or no?

Officer.

    There is no doubt
    You have forcible reasons:
    Resistance is vain, and I must yield;
    But I shall know how to punish you.

Il D.

          (philosophically).

    Every one has an unpleasant moment,
    And it is your turn now, my gay captain.
    May it please you march, without more
        words.

(The Officer goes between four Gipsies with pistols levelled at him.)

Car.

          (to JOSÉ).

    And wilt thou now come with us?

José. How can I say no?

Car. 'Tis much against thy wish,
    But whate'er may be,
    Thou wilt be glad when thou seest
    How pleasant is this wandering life, —
    The wide world our dwelling —
    Our will the law — and, above all,
    The rest surpassing —
    Liberty! Liberty!

All. The heaven over all — the wandering life —
    The wide world our dwelling —
    Our will the law — and, above all,
    The rest surpassing —
    Liberty! liberty!

Le Dan. et Le Rem.

    Nous allons, cher monsieur,
    Quitter cette demeure,
    Vous viendrez avec nous. . . .

Car. C'est une promenade;
    Consentez-vous?

Le Dan. et Le Rem.

          (le pistolet à la main).

    Répondez, camarade,
    Consentez-vous?

Le Lieut.

    Certainement,
    D'autant plus que votre argument
    Est un de ceux auxquels on ne résiste
        guère
    Mais gare à vous plus tard.

Le Dan.

          (avec philosophie)

    La guerre, c'est la guerre,
    En attendant, mon officier,
    Passez devant sans vous faire prier.

Cho. Passez devant sans vous faire prier.

(L'OFFICIER sort. emmené par quatre Bohémiens le pistolet à la main.)

Car.

          (à DON JOSÉ).

    Es-tu des nôtres maintenant?

José. Il le faut bien.

Car. Le mot n'est pas galant,
    Mais qu'importe, tu t'y feras
    Quand tu verras
    Comme c'est beau la vie errante
    Pour pays l'univers, pour loi ta volonté,
    Et surtout la chose enivrante.
    La liberté! la liberté!

Tous. Le ciel ouvert! la vie errante,
    Pour pays l'univers, pour loi sa volonté
    Et surtout la chose enivrante,
    La liberté! la liberté!

ACT III.

SCENE I.

(Rocks A picturesque and wild spot. Dark night and complete
solitude. Musical prelude. After a few moments a Smuggler appears
on the summit of a rock, then another, then two, then twenty, descending
and scrambling down the mass of rocks; some of them carrying heavy
bales on their shoulders.)

CARMEN, JOSÉ, IL DANCAIRO, IL REMENDADO, FRASQUITA,
MERCEDES, and SMUGGLER·

Cho.   Listen, comrades, listen !
      Fortune waits below ;
      But of caution have we need,
      Lest in a snare we fall.

All the Others.
      This is a fine trade, but it needs
      A strong heart when danger's near,
      Whether from above or below — what
        care we ?
      On we go, never showing fear,
      Torrents braving, cliffs we scale
      On the icy north-wind's gale ;
      Storm and bullets we despise ;
      'Neath the coastguard's watchful eyes
      We bring our booty safe up here.
      Listen, comrades, listen, etc.

Il D.   Here let us rest awhile, — the night is dark
      And then forth will we go to discover
      If the coast be clear,
      And if without peril
      The smugglers may proceed.

SCENE II.

(All stay excepting IL DANCAIRO and IL REMENDADO. During the
scene between CARMEN and JOSÉ, some of the Gipsies light a fire, near
which FRASQUITA and MERCEDES seat themselves; the others, folding
themselves in their mantles, lying down, go to sleep. JOSÉ goes to the
back, watching from the rocks.)

Car.
          (to JOSÉ).
      At what are you gazing ?

José.   I was thinking that in the world below
      Dwells an aged good woman,
      Who believes I am an honest man ;
      Alas ! she is mistaken !

Car.   Whoever can she be ?

José.   Ah, Carmen ! the thought is not difficult
      for her, — 'tis my mother !

ACTE TROISIÈME.

SCÈNE PREMIÈRE.

(Le rideau se lève sur des rochers. . . site pittoresque et sauvage
Solitude complète et nuit noire. Prélude musical. Au bout de quel
ques instants, un contrebandier parait au haut des rochers, puis un
autre, puis deux autres, puis vingt autres cà et là, descendant et escala·
dent des rochers. Des hommes portent de gros ballots sur les épaules.)

CARMEN, JOSÉ, DANCAIRE, REMENDADO, FRASQUITA, MERCEDES
CONTREBANDIERS.

Cho.   Ecoute, compagnon, écoute,
      La fortune est là-bas, là-bas,
      Mais prends garde pendant la route,
      Prends garde de faire un faux pas.

DANCAIRE, JOSÉ, CARMEN, MERCEDES, et FRASQUITA.
      Notre métier est bon, mais pour le faire il
        faut
      Avoir une âme forte,
      Le péril est en bas, le péril est en haut,
      Il est partout, qu'importe ?
      Nous allons devant nous, sans souci du
        torrent,
      Sans souci de l'orage,
      Sans souci du soldat qui là-bas nous attend,
      Et nous guette au passage.
      Ecoute, compagnon, écoute, etc.

Le Dan.
      Reposons-nous une heure ici, mes cama
        rades ;
      Nous, nous allons nous assurer
      Si le chemin est libre,
      Et que sans algarades
      La contrebande peut passer.

SCÈNE II.

Les Mêmes, moins DANCAIRE et REMENDADO.

(Pendant la scène entre CARMEN et JOSÉ, quelques Bohémiens
allument un feu près duquel MERCEDES et FRASQUITA viennent s'asseoir
les autres se roulent dans leurs manteaux, se couchent et s'endorment.)

Car.   Que regardes tu donc ?

José.   Je me dis que là bas
      Il existe une bonne et brave vieille
      Femme qui me croit honnête homme
      Elle se trompe hélas.

Car.   Qui donc est cette femme ?

Josè.   Ah ! Carmen sur mon âme ne raille pas
      Car c'est ma mère.

Car.	Well, you had better go to her this moment;
	Indeed, the way of life here suits you not,
	And you should be pleased to leave this place.
José.	To go far from thee?
Car.	Certainly.
José.	And leave thee, Carmen? I swear

(placing his hand on his knife)

	If thou sayst again, 'twill be death!

(CARMEN is silent.)

	This silence — to me reveals thy thoughts.
Car.	What matters it to me!
	I shall die if fate wills it.

(Turns her back on José, and goes to seat herself near FRASQUITA and MERCEDES. After a moment's hesitation, José also turns away and throws himself full length on the rocks. During CARMEN's last words, MERCEDES and FRASQUITA draw out a pack of cards.)

Fras.	Shuffle.
Mer.	Throw.
Fras.	Yes; so let it be.
Mer.	Three cards for me.
Fras.	Four to thee.
Together	
	Declare to us, pretty cards,
	What good the future will bring to me —
	What will be — who will deceive us —
	What sort of lovers we shall see.
Fras.	Here I see a handsome lad,
	Who to love me ever vows.
Mer.	And I one who's rich and old,
	Who would fain make me his spouse.
Fras.	I with him on his good steed
	O'er the mountains far will ride.
Mer.	To his castle the old knight
	Bids me welcome — queen and bride.
Fras.	With great love his heart o'erflows,
	Ev'ry day brings us fresh joys.
Mer.	I have all that I can wish,
	Robes and rings and jewell'd toys.
Fras.	Mine becomes a leader bold,
	With him distant paths I tread.
Mer.	And mine — no, no, he don't last long —
	Leaves me his money when he's dead

Car.	Eh bien! va la retrouver tout de suite
	Notre métier vois tu, ne te vaut rien.
	Et tu ferais fort bien de partir au plus vite.
José.	Partir, nous séparer?
Car.	Sans doute séparer.
José.	Nous séparer, Carmen?
	Ecoute si tu redis ce mot.

Car.	Tu me tuerais peutêtre.
	Tu ne réponds rien,
	Qu'importe? après tout le destin est maître.

(Elle tourne le dos à José et va s'asseoir près de MERCEDES et de FRASQUITA. Après un instant d'indécision, José s'éloigne à son tour et va s'étendre sur les rochers. Pendant les dernières répliques de la scène, MERCEDES et FRASQUITA ont étalé des cartes devant elles.)

TRIO.

Fras.	Mêlons!
Mer.	Coupons!
Fras	C'est bien cela.
Mer	Trois cartes ici. . . .
Fras.	Quatre là.
Mer. and Fras.	
	Et maintenant, parlez, mes belles,
	De l'avenir donnez-nous des nouvelles;
	Dites-nous qui nous trahira,
	Dites-nous qui nous aimera.
Fras.	Moi, je vois un jeune amoureux
	Qui m'aime on ne peut davantage.
Mer.	Le mien est très riche et très-vieux
	Mais il parle de mariage.
Fras.	Il me campe sur son cheval
	Et dans la montagne il m'entraine.
Mer.	Dans un château presque royal
	Le mien m'installe en souveraine.
Fras.	De l'amour à n'en plus finir,
	Tous les jours nouvelles folies.
Mer.	De l'or tant que j'en puis tenir
	Des diamants . . . des pierreries.
Fras.	Le mien devient un chef fameux,
	Cent hommes marchent à sa suite.
Mer.	Le mien, en croirai-je mes yeux . . .
	Il meurt, je suis veuve et j'hérite.

Both. Speak again, speak, pretty cards,
What good the future will bring to me —
What will be — who will deceive us —
What sort of lovers shall we see.

(Begin consulting the cards again.)

Fras. Money !
Mer. Love !

(CARMEN has watched the game throughout.)

Car. Come, let me know my destiny.

(Shuffles the cards.)

Pictures ! spades ! a grave !
They lie not ; first to me, and then to him,
And then to both — a grave !

(In a low voice, continuing to shuffle the cards.)

In vain ; to avoid the stern response
In vain I sort the cards ;
'Twill nothing aid, the truth they declare,
They deceive not.
If in the book the page is clear,
Fear not ; throw, and play.
The cards in thy hand will, if sorted
  rightly,
Pleasure to thee foretell ;
But if thou must die, if the word so
  dread
Already in heaven is decreed,
The cards, to whose will thou art forced
  to yield,
Will again repeat thy doom.

(Puts them down.)

Well, be it so ; death must come !
Carmen will defy it ! Carmen is strong !

All Three.
Speak again, speak, pretty cards, etc.

Reprise de l'Ensemble.
Parlez encor, parlez, mes belles,
De l'avenir donnez-nous des nouvelles,
Dites-nous qui nous trahira,
Dites-nous qui nous aimera.

(Elles recommencent à consulter les cartes.)

Fras.   Fortune !
Mer.   Amour !

(CARMEN, depuis le commencement de la scène, suivat du regard de jeu de MERCEDES et de FRASQUITA.)

Car. Donnez que j'essaie à mon tour.

(Elle se met à tourner les cartes. Musique de scène.)

Carreau, pique... la mort !
J'ai bien lu... moi d'abord.

(Montrant DON JOSÉ endormi.)

Ensuite lui... pour tous les deux la mort

(A voix basse, tout en continuant à mêler les cartes.)

En vain pour éviter les réponses amères,
En vain tu mêleras,
Cela ne sert à rien, les cartes sont sin
  cères
Et ne mentiront pas !
Dans le livre d'en haut si ta page est
  heureuse,
Mêle et coupe sans peur,
La carte sous tes doigts se tournera joy
  euse
T'annonçant le bonheur.
Mais si tu dois mourir, si le mot redout
  able
Est écrit par le sort,
Recommence vingt fois...la carte impitoy
  able
Dira toujours : la mort !

(Se remettant.)

Bah ! qu'importe après tout, qu'im
  porte ?...
Carmen bravera tout, Carmen est la plus
  forte !

Toutes les Trois.
Parlez encor, parlez, mes belles, etc.

(Rentrent DANCAIRE et REMENDADO.)

SCENE III.

Enter Il Dancairo and Il Remendado

Car.	What news?
Il D.	We shall try to cross, and shall succeed.
	José, stay here and watch the bales.

Fras.	Is the path clear?
Il R.	Yes, but there's risk enough. Over the
	ravine
	Where we must cross,
	Three coastguards stand!—they must
	die!

Car.	Take up the bales, and away!
	'Tis no use talking; pass you must.
	The coastguard will be our affair:—
	They like amusement, like other men,
	And to play the gallant are willing.
	Leave it to us the road to clear.

Mer.	The coastguard will be very kind.
Fras.	To us very humble they'll be.
Car.	Yes, they'll receive us graciously.

All Three.
Our affair let the coastguard be:—
They like amusement, like other men,
And whilst the gallant with us they play,
Leave it to us your road to clear.

The Men.
Their affair will the coastguard be, etc.

Fras.	No need prowess to display.
	The only way with them must be
	With caresses to be free,
	And entice them loving words to hear.

The Girls.
Our affair will the coastguard be, etc.

SCÈNE III.

Carmen, José, Frasquita, Mercedes, Dancaire, et Remendado

Car.	Eh bien?
Le Dan.	
	Eh bien! nous essayerons de passer et
	nous passerons,
	Reste là haut, José, garde les marchandises.
Fras.	La route est elle libre?
Le Dan.	
	Oui, mais gare aux surprises
	J'ai sur la brèche ou nous devons passe.
	vu trois douaniers
	Il faut nous en débarrasser.
Car.	Prenez les ballots et partons
	Il faut passer nous passerons.

MORCEAU D'ENSEMBLE.

Car.	Quant au douanier c'est notre affaire,
	Tout comme un autre il aime à plaire,
	Il aime à faire le galant,
	Laissez-nous passer en avant.
Car. Mer. et Fras.	
	Quant au douanier c'est notre affaire,
	Laissez-nous passer en avant.
Mer.	Et le douanier sera clément.
Fras.	Et le douanier sera charmant.
Car.	Il sera même entreprenant! ..

ENSEMBLE.

Toutes les Femmes.
Quant au douanier c'est notre affaire,
Tout comme un autre il aime à plaire,
Il aime à faire le galant,
Laissez-nous passer en avant.

Tous les Hommes.
Quant au douanier c'est leur affaire,
Tout comme un autre il aime à plaire,
Il aime à faire le galant,
Laissons-les passer en avant.

Fras.	Il ne s'agit plus de bataille,
	Non, il s'agit tout simplement
	De se laisser prendre la taille
	Et d'écouter un compliment.
Car. Mer. et Fras.	
	Quant au douanier c'est notre affaire, etc
	etc.

Mer. If they wish a kiss to take,
We'll not say no ; they are welcome quite.
And we'll hold them in play until the hour
When you with the bales have passed out
of sight.
The Girls.
Our affair, etc.

(All go. José the last; and he is examining the barrels of his gun.
A man passes on the rocks above. It is a Guide.)

SCENE IV.

Mic Here is the hidden abode of the smug-
glers,
And here shall I José see ;
And the duty his mother has enjoined me,
Without fear I shall know how to fulfil.
I try not to own that I tremble,
But I know I'm a coward, altho' bold I
appear.
Ah ! how can I ever call up my courage,
While horror and dread chill my sad heart
with fear !
Here, in this savage retreat,
Sad and weary am I, alone and sore
afraid.
Ah ! heav'n ! to thee I humbly pray now :
Protect thou me, and guide and aid !
I shall see the guilty creature,
Who by infernal arts doth sever
From his country, from his duty,
Him I loved — and shall love ever !
I may tremble at her beauty,
But her power affrights me not.
Strong, in my just cause confiding,
Heaven ! I trust myself to thee.
Ah ! to this poor heart give courage.
Protector ! guide and aid now me !
But I am not deceiv'd ; no, he is on yon
rock.
Ah, come ! ah, come, José ! —

Mer. S'il faut aller jusqu'au sourire,
Que voulez-vouz ? on sourira,
Et d'avance, je puis le dire,
La contrebande passera.

Car. Met. et Fras.
Quant au douanier c'est notre affaire, etc.
etc.

REPRISE DE L'ENSEMBLE.

(Tout le monde sort. José ferme la marche et sort en examinant
l'amorce de sa carabine; un peu avant qu'il soit sorti, on voit un homme
passer sa tête au-dessus du rocher. C'est un Guide.)

SCÈNE IV.

Mic.

(regardant autour d'elle).

Mon guide avait raison...l'endroit n'a
rien de bien rassurant. ...

I.

Je dis que rien ne m'épouvante,
Je dis que je réponds de moi,
Mais j'ai beau faire la vaillante,
Au fond du cœur, je meurs d'effroi...
Toute seule en ce lieu sauvage
J'ai peur, mais j'ai tort d'avoir peur.
Vous me donnerez du courage,
Vous me protégerez, Seigneur,
Protégez-moi, protégez-moi, Seigneur.

II.

Je vais voir de près cette femme
Dont les artifices maudits
Ont fini par faire un infâme
De celui que j'aimais jadis ;
Elle est dangereuse, elle est belle,
Mais je ne veux pas avoir peur,
Je parlerai haut devant elle,
Vous me protégerez, Seigneur. ...
Protégez-moi, protégez-moi, Seigneur.
Mais ... je ne me trompe pas ... à cent pas
d'ici ... sur ce rocher, c'est Don José. (*Appelant*
José, José ! (*Avec terreur.*) Mais que fait-il ?

My heart fails me! What can I do?—
How attract him?

(A gun is fired.)

Ah! a shot! Heaven! my heart fails me!

(Disappears behind the rocks. ESCAMILLO appears at the same moment.)

SCENE V.

Enter ESCAMILLO, then DON JOSÉ.

Esc.

(holding his hat).

Two inches higher
And it would have been all over with me.

José. Who art thou? Speak out.

Esc. Eh? Softly, softly, my lad:
I am Escamillo, Toreador of Granada.

José. Escamillo?
Esc. The same.
José. The name is known to me;
Thou art welcome, comrade;
But dost thou really mean to stay here?

Esc. I can tell thee — no.
But I have been touched in my heart, lad,
And he who is so, merits not being born
If he'll not risk his life in search of his love.

José. The object of your love dwells here?
Esc. Yes, truly. A gipsy is she — charming.

José. What is her name?
Esc. Carmen.
José. Carmen?
Esc. She had a lover,
A dragoon, who became a deserter.
He loved her; she loved him;
But she is weary of him.
Carmen's love does not last.

---

il ne regarde pas de mon côté…il arme sa cara
bine, il ajuste…il fait feu…(*On entend un coup
de feu.*) Ah! mon Dieu, j'ai trop présumé de
mon courage…j'ai peur…j'ai peur.

(Elle disparait derrière les roches. Au même moment entre ESCA
MILLO tenant son chapeau à la main.)

SCÈNE V.

ESCAMILLO, puis DON JOSÉ

Esc.

(regardant son chapeau).

Quelques lignes plus bas …
Et tout était fini.

(Entre JOSÉ.)

José

(son manteau à la main).

Qu'êtes-vous? répondez.

Esc.

(très calme).

Eh là … doucement!

Duo.

Esc. Je suis Escamillo, torero de Grenade.
José. Escamillo!
Esc. C'est moi.

José

(remettant son couteau à sa ceinture).

Je connais votre nom,
Soyez le bienvenu; mais vraiment, cam
arade,
Vous pouviez y rester?

Esc. Je ne vous dis pas non,
Mais je suis amoureux, mon cher, à la folie,
Et celui-là serait un pauvre compagnon
Qui, pour voir ses amours, ne risquerait
sa vie.

José. Celle que vous aimez est ici?
Esc. Justement.
C'est une zingara, mon cher.

José. Elle s'appelle?
Esc. Carmen.
José. Carmen!
Esc. Elle avait pour amant
Un soldat qui jadis a déserté pour elle.
Ils s'adoraient, mais c'est fini, je crois.
Les amours de Carmen ne durent pas
six mois.

José. In spite of that, thou lovest her?

Esc. Yes, to desperation!

José. Hold! who will the zingara seduce,
Do not forget, will pay for it.

Esc. Good! what's to pay?

José. The price is paid in knife-thrusts and
slashes. Understand?

Esc. 'Tis not difficult; thou art the deserter,
The handsome dragoon she loves—
Or rather that she *did* love.

José. I am.

Esc. I am pleased, and I know not how to deny
it.

(Both draw their knives, enveloping the left arm in their cloaks.)

José. At last my rage I can vent,
And this villain's heart will I pierce.

Esc. My unlucky star is in the ascendant;
While seeking the fair one, the rival I've
met.

Together.
Out with thy blade, and keep at bay:
Neither will quarter give;
'Tis agreed one must fall.
Nor he nor I shall live.

(Put themselves in fighting positions. CARMEN arrives with DAN-
CAIRO, and stays José's arm as he is about to strike ESCAMILLO. IL
REMENDADO, MERCEDES, FRASQUITA, and Gipsies rush in.)

Car. José, hold!

Esc. 'Tis well. And with great joy
I see that to thee, Carmen, my life I owe.
As to thee, my gay dragoon,
I am at thy service, and we will again,
Any day thou wishest, try our fortunes.

El D. We shall see thee again, then.
Now we are ready to depart, and thou —
Good-bye, lad!

(To José.)

José. Vous l'aimez cependant. . . .

Esc. Je l'aime à la folie!

José. Mais pour nous enlever nos filles de
Bohème,
Savez-vous bien qu'il faut payer.

Esc. Soit! on paiera.

José. Et que le prix se paie à coups de navaja!
Comprenez-vous?

Esc. Le discours est très net.
Ce déserteur, ce beau soldat qu'elle aime,
C'est donc vous?

José. Oui, c'est moi.

Esc. J'en suis ravi, mon cher, et le tour est
complet.

(Tous les deux tirent la navaja et s'entourent le bras gauche de leur
manteau.)

José. Enfin ma colère trouve à qui parler!
Le sang je l'espère, va bientôt couler.

Esc. Quelle maladresse! j'en rirais vraiment,
Chercher la maîtresse et trouver l'amant.

Ensemble.
Mettez-vous en garde,
Et veillez sur vous!
Tant pis pour qui tarde
A parer les coups!

(Après les dernier ensemble, reprise du combat. Le Torero glisse et
tombe. Entrent CARMEN et LE DANCAIRE, CARMEN arrête le bras de
DON JOSÉ. Le Torero se relève; LE REMENDADO, MERCEDES, FRAS-
QUITA et les Contrabandiers ventrent pendant ce temps.)

Car. Holà, José! . . .

Esc.

(se relevant).

Vrai, j'ai l'âme ravie
Que ce soit vous, Carmen, qui me sauviez
la vie.

Esc.

(à DON JOSÉ).

Quant à toi, beau soldat,
Nous sommes manche à manche, et nous
jouerons la belle,
Le jour où tu voudras reprendre le com
bat.

Le Dan.
C'est bon, plus de querelle,
Nous, nous allons partir.

(Au Torero.)

Et toi, l'ami, bonsoir.

Esc.   'Tis at least allowed me, since leave I
         must,
   To invite you all to the bullfight at
      Seville;
   I hope there to shine;
   And whoever loves me will come.
   Dragoon, don't be angry.
   I go, then; perhaps we shall one day
      meet.

(José tries to rush at the Toreador. IL DANCAIRO and IL REMEN-
DADO prevent him. ESCAMILLO goes out leisurely.)

José

                 (to CARMEN).

   Ah! Carmen, beware! I am weary of
      suffering.

(CARMEN shrugs her shoulders, and moves away from him.)

Il D.   Come! it is agreed we leave.

All.   Yes, yes, we must depart.
Il R.   Look above! some one vainly tries to
         hide.

            (Goes to see, and brings in MICHAELA.)

Car.   A woman!
Il D.   By heaven! a pleasant surprise!

José.   Michaela!

Mic.   Don José!
José   Unfortunate girl!
   What doest thou in this place?
Mic   In search of thee I came.
   In her cot in the far off valley,
   Prays thy mother, unhappy man!
   Weeps till my heart bleeds,
   Weeps and waits for thee ever:
   Return to her; hasten, José.
   Ah. with me now come!

Esc.   Souffrez au moins qu'avant de vous dire
      au revoir.
   Je vous invite tous aux courses de Séville
   Je compte pour ma part y briller de mon
      mieux,
   Et qui m'aime y viendra.

         (A DON JOSÉ qui fait un geste de menace.)

   L'ami, tiens toi tranquille,
   J'ai tout dit et n'ai plus qu' à faire mes
      adieux. . . .

(Jeu de scène. DON JOSÉ veut s'elancer sur le Torero. LE DAN-
CAIRE et LE REMENDADO le retiennent. Le Torero sort très-lentement.)

José

                 (à CARMEN).

   Prends garde à toi, Carmen . . . je suis las
      de souffrir. . . .

(CARMEN lui répond par un léger haussement d'épaules et s'éloigne
de lui.)

Le Dan.
   En route . . . en route . . . il faut partir . . .
Tous.   En route . . . en route . . . il faut partir. . . .
Le Rem.
   Halte! . . . quelqu'un est là qui cherche
      à se cacher.

               (Il ami MICAELA.)

Car.   Une femme.
Le Dan.
   Pardieu, la surprise est heureuse.
José

           (reconnaissant MICAELA).

   Micaela! . . .
Mic.   Don José! . . .
José.   Malheureuse!
   Que viens-tu faire ici?
Mic.   Moi, je viens te chercher . .
   Là-bas est la chaumière
   Où sans cesse priant,
   Une mère, ta mère,
   Pleure son enfant. . . .
   Elle pleure et t'appelle,
   Elle te tend les bras;
   Tu prendras pitié d'elle,
   José, tu me suivras.

Car. *(to José).*
Go, and go quickly; stay not here;
This way of life is not for thee.

José *(to Carmen).*
To depart thou dost counsel me?

Car. Yes, thou shouldst go—

José. That thou mayst follow
Another lover — the toreador.
No, on my honor, no!
I'll rather die! — all may hear me.
No, Carmen, I will not depart;
And the tie that binds us
I will not free thee from.

Mic. Be not deaf to my prayers;
Thy mother waits thee there.
The chain that binds thee, José,
Death will break.

The Others.
To my counsel yield thee;
No, José, stay not here
The chain that binds thee,
Death alone can break.

José *(to Michaela).*
Go from hence,
I cannot follow thee.
Mine thou art, accursed one!
(to Carmen).
And I will force thee to know
And submit to the fate
That both our lives unites.

Mic. Yet one word — 'twill be my last:—
Thy mother's dying!
Thou wilt not that she leaves the world
Ere she has pardoned thee?

José. My mother dying?

Mic. Yes, Don José.

José. Let us this moment depart.
Be satisfied — I quit you;
(to Carmen).
But we shall meet again.

(Going away with Michaela. The Toreador's voice is heard in the distance.

Car. Va-t'en! va-t'en! Tu feras bien,
Notre métier ne te vaut rien.

José *(à Carmen).*
Tu me dis de la suivre?

Car. Oui, tu devrais partir.

José. Pour que toi, tu puisse courir
Après ton nouvel amant.
Dût-il m'en coûter la vie,
Non, je ne partirai pas,
Et la chaîne qui nous lie
Nous liera jusqu'au trépas...

Mic. Ecoute moi, je t'en prie,
Ta mère te tend les bras,
Cette chaîne qui te lie,
José, tu la briseras.

Cho. Il t'en coutéra la vie,
José, si tu ne pars pas,
Et la chaîne qui vous lie
Se rompra par ton trépas.

José *(à Micaela).*
Laisse-moi!
Je suis condamné!

(à Carmen).
Ah! je te tiens, fille damnée,
Je te tiens et te forcerai
A subir la destinée
Qui rive ton sort au mien!
Dût-il m'en coûter la vie,
Non, je ne partirai pa

Mic. Une parole encor, ce sera la dernière
Hélas! José, ta mère se meurt... et ta mère
Ne voudrait pas mourir sans t'avoir pardonné.

José. Ma mère se meurt?

Mic. Oui, Don José.

José. Partons, ah, partons!
Sois contente; je pars mais nous nous reverrons!

(Il entraîne Micaela. On entend Le Torero.)

Esc.

(without).

Toreador, e'er watchful be,
Do not forget the brightest of eyes
Are fondly thee waiting,
And love is the prize.

(José stops at the back on the rocks. He hesitates, but decides at last, and goes on his way with MICHAELA. CARMEN, leaning on a large stone, watches his departure. The Gipsies take up their bales and proceed on their journey.)

ACT IV.

SCENE I.

(A Square in Seville. At the back are the walls of the old Arena. The entrance to the Circus is shut in by a long curtain. It is the day of the bullfight. The square is animated. Watersellers, others with oranges, fans, etc., etc.)

OFFICERS, FRASQUITA, MERCEDES, afterwards CARMEN and ESCAMILLO.

Cho.   Who'll buy? who'll buy?
     A little fan I'll sell you cheap
     Fine oranges I have here,
     Who'll buy? who'll buy?
     Come here, for all you want I keep.

(During this first chorus, the two OFFICERS of the second Act give their arms to FRASQUITA and MERCEDES.)

1st Officer.
     Some oranges here, and quickly.
Fruit Sellers

(running).

     Here they are, and fine ones, too.

A Fruit Seller

(to the OFFICER who pays).

     These are all right, captain.
Other Fruit Sellers.
     But these more juicy are.
All the Venders.
     Who'll buy? who'll buy?
     Come here to me,
     All sorts I keep.
Programme Sellers.
     Who wants to know the lists?

Esc.

(au loin).

Toreador, engarde,
Et songe en combattant,
Qu'un œil noir le regarde
Et que l'amour t'attend

(José s'arrête au fond ... dans les rochers. ... Il hésite, puis part un instant.)

José.   Partons, Micaela, partons.

(CARMEN écoute et se penche sur les rochers. .. Les Bohémiens chargent leurs ballots et se mettent en marche.)

ACTE QUATRIÈME.

SCÈNE PREMIÈRE.

(Une place à Seville. Au fond du théâtre les muraillet de vielles Arènes. L'entrée du Cirque est fermée par un long velum. C'est le jour d'un combat de taureaux. Grand mouvement sur la place. Marchands d'eau, d'oranges, d'éventails, etc., etc.)

Le LIEUTENANT, ANDRES, FRASQUITA, MERCEDES, etc., puis CARMEN et ESCAMILLO

Cho.   A deux cuartos,
     A deux cuartos,
     Des éventails pour s'éventer
     Des oranges pour grignotter
     A deux cuartos,
     A deux cuartos,
     Senoras et caballeros. .

(Pendant ce premier chœur sont entrés les deux OFFICIERS du deuxième Acte ayant au bras les deux Bohémiennes MERCEDES FRASQUITA.)
Premier Officier.
     Des oranges, vite
Plusieurs Marchands

(se précipitant).

     En voici,
     Prenez, prenez, mesdemoiselles.
Un Marchand

(à l'OFFICIER qui paie).

     Merci, mon officier, merci.
Les autres Marchands.
     Celles-ci, senor, sont plus belles
Tous les Marchands.
     A deux cuartos,
     A deux cuartos,
     Senoras et caballeros.
Marchand de Programme.
     Le programme avec les détails.

Others.

 Good wine !

Others.

 Water here !

Others.

 Cigarettes !

2d Officer.

 You, there ! I want to buy a fan.

Cho.

   (repeated).

 Who'll buy ? who'll buy, etc.

  VARIATIONS FOR THE DANCE.

Cho. Dance, dance,

  Twirl, twirl.

  Girls and lads, come here and dance.

  At sound so gay of tambourine we go ;

  Pleasure 'tis divine !

  At sounds of castanet,

  Lads and lassies thus to twine.

  Dance, ye nimble lads ;

  Yes, we girls will dance :

  With more pleasure ! — brisker yet

  With ardor round and round.

  Dance ! for soon shall we see

  The Toreador.

  Girls and lads, come, dance.

  To sound so gay of tambourine

  And merry castanet

  Dance on.

  Already on his road

  He comes — the Toreador !

  Dance on, dance on ;

  Dance, ye nimble lads, yes, dance ;

  We girls will in the dance go round.

(Noise of trumpets heard outside. The Band arrives.)

 Here comes the Band ;

 'Tis the band of the Toreadors :

 Wonders will be done in Seville.

 Haste ! quick ! all good places seek.

   (The Band begins to pass.)

 And the first to come, as the custom is,

 Grave in his walk,

Autres Marchands.

 Du vin . . . .

Autres Marchands.

 De l'eau.

Autres Marchands.

 Des cigarettes.

Deuxième Officier.

 Holà ! marchand, des éventails.

Un Bohémien

   (se précipitant).

 Voulez-vous aussi de lorgnettes ?

Reprise du Cho.

 A deux cuartos,

 A deux cuartos,

 Des éventails pour s'éventer,

 Des oranges pour grignotter.

 A deux cuartos,

 A deux cuartos,

 Senoras et caballeros.

Le Lieut.

 Qu'avez-vous donc fait de la Carmencita

 je ne la vois pas.

Fras. Nous la verrons tout a l'heure. . . . Esca-

 millo est ici, la Carmencita ne doit pas

 être loin.

Audres.

 Ah ! c'est Escamillo maintenant ?

Mer. Elle en est folie. . . .

Fras. Et son ancien amoureux José, sait-on ce

 qu'il est devenu ? . . .

Le Lieut.

 Il a reparu dans le village où sa mère

 habitait . . . l'ordre avait même été donné

 de l'arrêter, mais quand les soldats sont

 arrivés, José, n'était plus là. . . .

Mer. En sorte qu'il est libre ?

Le Lieut.

 Oui, pour le moment.

Fras. Hum ! je ne serais pas tranquille à la

 place de Carmen, je ne serais pas tran-

 quille du tout.

(On entend de grande cris au dehors, des fanfares etc. etc. C'est
'arrivée de la Cuadrilla.)

On he ll stalk.
See, the Alguazil, with his ugly phiz :
At him hiss till he's out of this.
Now we'll salute, as they pass along,
All these youths so handsome, strong ,
See their banners, how they wave !
Glory and honor to the brave !
Now they appear !
They are here !
Warlike and noble seem they all,
To find their equals there's no fear ;
See their vests all shining with golden
    lace.
Now to the best of all give place —
To the Toreador :
Amongst them all in valor and grace,
He the chief they call.

(ESCAMILLO enters with CARMEN, magnificently dressed.)

Now hail to the sword with the keenest
    blade !
To him who can the death-stroke give,
Conq'ror most dexterous we'll proclaim
    him.
Hail, Escamillo ! Long may he live !
Hail, Escamillo ! Evviva, evviva !
Honor and glory to Escamillo !

Esc.

        (to CARMEN).

If thou lovest me, Carmen,
Thou wilt see me ere long yonder,
And be proud of me.

Car. Ah ! if I love thee, Escamillo ?
May death be mine
If this heart holds other love than thine !

Cho. Bravo, Escamillo ! Hail !
To Escamillo glory and honor !

(Trumpets outside. Two Trumpeters enter followed by four Alguazils.)

Cho Les voici, voici la quadrille,
La quadrille des Toreros,
Sur les lances le soleil brille
En l'air toques et sombreros
Les voici, voici la quadrille,
La quadrille des Toreros.

(Défilé de la quadrille. Pendant ce défilé, le Chœur chante le morceau suivant. Entrée des Alguazils.)

Voici, débouchant sur la place,
Voici d'abord, marchant au pas,
L'alguazil à villaine face.

(Entrée des Chulos et des Banderilleros.)

Et puis saluons au passage,
Saluons les hardis chulos,
Bravo ! vivi ! gloire au courage
Voyez les banderilleros !
Voyez quel air de crânerie,
Quels regards et de quel éclat
Etincelle la broderie
De leur costume de combat.

(Entrée des Picadors.)

Une autre quadrille s'avance,
Les picadors comme ils sont beaux !
Comme ils vont du fer de leur lance
Harceler le flanc des taureaux.

(Parait enfin ESCAMILLO, ayant près de lui CARMEN radieuse et dans un costume éclatant.)

Esc.

        (à CARMEN).

Si tu m'aimes, Carmen, tu pourras tout à
    l'heure
En me voyant à l'œuvre être fière de
    moi.

Car. Je t'aime, Escamillo, je t'aime et que je
    meure
Si j'ai jamais aimé quelqu'un autant
    que toi.

Le Cho.
    Bravo, bravo, Escamillo !
    Escamillo. bravo !

(Trompettes au dehors. Paraissent deux trompettes suivis de quatr Alguazils)

Voices (without). Make way for the Alcade!	*Plusieurs voix* (au fond). L'alcade, L'alcade. Le seigneur alcade!

Cho.

(de la foule si rangeant sur le passage de l'alcade).

Pas de bousculade,
Regardons passer
Et se prélasser
Le seigneur alcade.

Les Alguazils.

Place, place au seigneur alcade!

(The Orchestra plays a brief march. The Alcade crosses the scene, preceded by the Alguazils, and enters into the Circus. During this, FRASQUITA and MERCEDES approach CARMEN.)

(Petite marche à l'orchestre. Sur cette marche **descend leutement** au fond l'alcade précédé et suivi des Alguazils. Pendant ce temps Frasquita et Mercédès s'approchent de CARMEN.)

Fras. Carmen, listen to our advice,
  Go far away from this place.
Car. And tell me why?
Fras. He is there!
Car. Who?
Fras. José! Yes, José,
  Lurking in the crowd, watching thee.

Car. I know well he is there.
Fras. Depart from here!
Car. I am no coward to tremble at José.
  If he will speak to me, I am here.

Fras. Carmen, un bon conseil, ne reste pas ici.

Car. Et pourquoi, s'il te plaîte?
Fras. Il est là.
Car. Qui donc?
Fras. Lui,
  Don José...dans la foule il se cache;
    regarde.
Car. Oui, je le vois.
Fras. Prends garde.
Car. Je ne suis pas femme à trembler,
  Je reste, je l'attends...et je vais lui parler.

(The Alcade has entered the Circus; after him the Cavalcade; then the people make their way in. JOSÉ appears. CARMEN is in a corner of the scene. and is alone with him.)

(L'alcade est entré dans le cirque. Derrière l'alcade, le cortège de la quadrille reprend sa marche et entre dans le cirque. Le populaire suit.... L'orchestre joue le motif. Les voici, voici la quadrille, et la foule en se retirant a dégagé, DON JOSÉ.... CARMEN reste seule au premier plan. Tous deux se regardent pendant que la foule se dissipe et que le motif de la marche va diminuant et se mourant à l'orchestre. Sur les dernières notes, CARMEN et DON JOSÉ restent seuls, en presence l'un de l'autre.)

SCENE II.

SCÈNE II.

CARMEN, DON JOSÉ.
DUO.

Car. Thou art here.
José. I am.
Car. I was warned that you were not far off —
  That you *would* come.
  It was even said, "Fear for thy life!"
  But I do not fear! and I will not fly!

Car. C'est toi?
José. C'est moi.
Car. L'on m'avait avertie,
  Que tu n'étais pas loin, que tu devais
    venir,
  L'on m'avait même dit de craindre pour
    ma vie,
  Mais je suis brave et n'ai pas voulu fuir.

José.	I will not threaten thee ;	*José.*	Je ne menace pas, j'implore, je supplie.
	But weep, implore, and pray.		Notre passé, je l'oublie.
	All rancor, Carmen, I abjure.		Carmen, nous allons tous deux
	We, Carmen, ought now a new life begin		Commencer une autre vie,
	Far from here, beneath another sky		Loin d'ici, sous d'autres cieux.
Car.	What you ask 'tis vain to hope for.	*Car.*	Tu demandes l'impossible.
	No ; Carmen knows not falsehood ;		Carmen jamais n'a menti,
	Nor is to-day as yesterday.		Son âme reste inflexible
	Between us, José, all is ended.		Entre elle et toi, c'est fini.
José.	Carmen, hear me! Yet there is time :	*José.*	Carmen, il en est temps encore.
	I wish to save thee.		O ma Carmen, laisse-moi
	Thou knowest I adore thee,		Te sauver, toi que j'adore
	My Carmen : I would save thee!		Et me sauver avec toi.
Car.	No! I know well the hour has come,	*Car.*	Non, je sais bien que c'est l'heure,
	And that I must die!		Je sais que tu me tueras.
	But if I live, or if I perish —		Mais que je vive ou je meure,
	Thine I will not be!		Je ne te céderai pas.
	Ah! why yet seek a heart not thine?		
	José, in vain thou dost adore me!		

ENSEMBLE.

José.	Ah! Carmen, to save thee yet there's time!	*José.*	Carmen, il en est temps encore.
			O ma Carmen, laisse-moi
	Thou knowest my heart ever must adore thee!		Te sauver, toi que j'adore,
	Thy heart owns no longer love for me?		Et me sauver avec toi.
Car.	No, no, I love thee not!	*Car.*	Pourquoi t'occuper encore
			D'un cœur qui n'est plus à toi ?
			En vain tu dis : " je t'adore,"
			Tu n'obtiendras rien de moi.
José.	Spite of this, Carmen, I love thee yet!	*José.*	Tu ne m'aimes donc plus ?
	Yes, yes, Carmen — José adores thee!		(Silence de CARMEN et DON JOSÉ répète.)
			Tu ne m'aimes donc plus ?
		Car.	Non, je ne t'aime plus.
		José.	Mais moi, Carmen, je t'aime encore ;
			Carmen, Carmen, moi je t'adore.
Car.	What worth thy love if 'tis not shared?	*Car.*	A quoi bon tout cela ? que de mots superflus !
José.	To give thee pleasure,	*José.*	Eh bien, s'il le faut, pour te plaire,
	To make thee love me,		Je resterai bandit, tout ce que tu voudras
	I will be a smuggler		Tout, tu m'entends, mais ne me quitt pas,
	And worse! but abandon me not!		Souviens-toi du passé, nous nous aimion naguère.
	Carmen, no! thou canst not forget me!		
Car.	No, never will Carmen consent, —	*Car.*	Jamais Carmen ne cédera,
	Free was I born! free will I die!		Libre elle est née et libre elle mourra.
	(Noise of trumpets in the Circus.)		

Cho.

In the Arena

Hurrah! a splendid race!
Full of ire and fury,
Mad with anger goes the bull
Straight at the Toreador!
Clap your hands! Victoria!
Struck to the heart,
On the ground he lies!
Glory to the brave Toreador!
Honor to the victor!

During the chorus, José and Carmen are silent. They listen. At the shouts of victory, a cry of joy escapes from Carmen. José observes At the end of the chorus, Carmen moves towards the Circus.)

José

(placing himself before her)

Whither goest thou?

Car. Let me pass.

José. That man they now so loudly applaud,
To me thou dost prefer.

Car. Leave me.

José. No, by Heaven!
Thou shalt not with him go.
Thou shalt follow me!

Car Leave me, Don José! with thee I will not
come.

José. Thou goest to meet him! Thou lovest him
then?

Car. I love him! I love him, and die I must;
I love him, and to you declare it.

(Noise of trumpets and chorus again in Circus.)

Cho. Viva! a splendid race,
Full of ire, etc.

José. Now thou refusest my prayers,
Inhuman girl! For thy sake am I lost!
And then to know thee shameless, infamous!
Laughing in his arms at my despair!
No, no! it shall not be, by Heaven!
Carmen, thou must be mine, mine only!

Cho. et Fanfares

(dans le Cirque)

Viva! la course est belle,
Sur le sable sanglant
Le taureau qu'on harcèle
S'élance en bondissant. . . .
Viva! bravo! victoire,
Frappé juste en plein cœur,
Le taurau tombe! gloire
Au Torero! vainqueur!
Victoire! victoire!

(Pendant ce chœur, silence de Carmen et de Don José . . . Tous deux écoutent . . . En entendant les cris de: "Victoire, victoire!" Carmen a laissé échapper un "Ah!" d'orgueil et de joie. . . . Don José ne perd pas Carmen de vue. . . . Le chœur terminé, Carmen fait un pas du côté de Cirque.)

José

(se plaçant devant elle).

Où vas-tu?

Car. Laisse-moi.

José. Cet homme qu'on acclame,
C'est ton nouvel amant!

Car.

(voulant passer).

Laisse-moi.

José. Sur mon âme,
Carmen, tu ne passeras pas,
Carmen, c'est moi que tu suivras!

Car. Laisse-moi, Don José! . . . je ne te suivrai
pas.

José. Tu vas le retrouver, dis . . . tu l'aimes
donc?

Car. Je l'aime,
Je l'aime, et devant la mort même,
Je répéterai que je l'aime.

(Fanfares et reprise du cho. dans le Cirque.)

Cho. Viva! bravo! victoire!
Frappé juste en plein cœur,
Le taureau tombe! gloire
Au Torero vainqueur!
Victoire! victoire! . . .

José. Ainsi, le salut de mon âme,
Je l'aurai perdu pour que toi,
Pour que tu t'en ailles, infâme!
Entre ses bras, rire de moi.
Non, par le sang, tu n'iras pas,
Carmen, c'est moi que tu suivras!

Car.	No, no, never!	*Car.*	Non! non! jamais!
José.	Ah! weary am I of threats.	*José.*	Je suis las de te menacer.
Car.	Cease, then, — or let me pass.	*Car.*	Eh bien! frappe-moi donc ou laisse-moi passer.

Cho.

(In Circus).

Victory! victory!

José.	Again I beseech thee, Carmen, Wilt thou with me depart?
Car.	No! This ring thou one day on my finger plac'd, Take it!

(Throws it down.)

José

(drawing his poniard).

All is ended!

(Rushes to CARMEN, who draws back. Noise in Circus.)

Cho.

(without).

Toreador, e'er watchful be,
Do not forget the brightest of eyes
Are fondly thee waiting,
And love is the prize.

(José stabs CARMEN, who falls dead. The curtain of the Circus is opened, and the crowd come from the Circus.)

José. I yield me prisoner. I have killed her!

(ESCAMILLO appears on the steps of the Circus. José throws himself near CARMEN's body.)

Oh, Carmen! my adored Carmen!

END OF THE OPERA.

Cho. Victoire! victoire!

José.	Pour la dernière fois, démon, Veux-tu me suivre?
Car.	Non! non! Cette bague autrefois tu me l'avais donnée, Tiens.

(Elle la jette à la volée.)

José

(le poignard à la main, s'avançant sur Carmen).

Eh bien, damnée. . . .

(CARMEN, recul. José a poursuit. Pendent ce temps fanfares et dans le Cirque.)

Cho. Toréador, en garde,
Et songe en combattant
Qu'un œil noir te regarde
Et que l'amour t'attend.

(José a frappé CARMEN. . . . Elle tombe morte. . . . Le velum s'ouvre La sort du Cirque.)

José. Vous pouvez m'arrêter . . . c'est moi qui l'ai tuée.

(ESCAMILLO paraît sur les marche du Cirque . . . José se jette sur la CARMEN.)

O ma Carmen! ma Carmen adorée!

FIN.

ACT I: L'AMOUR EST UN OISEAU (LOVE IS A WILFUL BIRD) (HABANERA

ACT I: PRÈS DES REMPARTS DE SÉVILLE (ON THE WALLS OF SEVILLE
(SEGUIDILLA)

ACT II : VOTRE TOAST, JE PEUX VOUS RENDRE, (FOR A TOAST YOUR OWN WILL AVAIL.) TOREADOR SONG.

ACT III: MÊLONS, COUPONS (SHUFFLE, CUT THEM!) CARD TRIO.

FAUST

by

CHARLES GOUNOD

CHARACTERS

Faust	*Tenor*	Marguerite	*Soprano*
Mephistopheles	*Bass-Baritone*	Siebel, a Youth	*Soprano*
Valentine, Marguerite's Brother	*Baritone*	Martha, Friend of Marguerite .	
Wagner, a Student	*Baritone*		*Mezzo-Soprano*

Peasants, Townspeople, Soldiers, Students, Priests, Boys, Etc.
The scene is in Germany in the sixteenth century.

PREFATORY NOTE

The legend of the magician Faust and his compact with the Devil comes from remote antiquity. At first in the form of folk tales in many lands, through ballads and the primitive drama it found its way into literature. It remained for the master-poet, Goethe, to fuse all the elements of the legend into an imaginative drama of unequaled ethical and poetic interest, to give the story the form in which it appeals most strongly to the modern mind.

Innumerable musical works of every form have drawn inspiration from the story of Faust. Wagner's concert-overture, Liszt's symphony, and the beautiful fragments by Schumann are among the noblest of such works. Stage versions of the legend have been numerous, but the first really poetic creation was Spohr's opera of "Faust," composed in 1813. Since its appearance there has been an abundance of Faust operas by English, German, French and Italian composers down to the imaginative but fragmentary "Mefistofele" of Boito (1868). But of all the stage versions that have claimed the public attention, that of Barbier and Carré, made after Goethe's drama and set to music by Charles Gounod, is far and away the most popular, and may be regarded, in its lyric dress, as the most successful also. There exists scarcely a single rival to the popularity of Gounod's "Faust" among opera-goers.

The love story with which the French librettists concerned themselves exclusively is wholly Goethe's conception, and finds no place in the old legends concerning the magician Faust. With true Gallic instinct they seized this pathetic episode as being best adapted for a lyric setting, and making the most potent appeal to the emotions of the spectators. But to the composer himself is due the credit of suggesting the story of Faust as a suitable subject for musical treatment.

THE STORY OF THE ACTION

Act I. — Faust, an aged philosopher, who has grown weary of life, and of the vain search for the source of all knowledge, decides, after a night-long vigil, to end his existence by taking poison. In the act of raising the cup to his lips his hand is arrested by the sound of merry voices of maidens singing in the early morning of the joy of living. Again he essays to drink, but pauses to listen to the song of the reapers on their way to the fields, voicing their gratitude to God. Excited to a frenzy of rage, Faust curses all that is good and calls upon the Evil One to aid him Mephistopheles appears, and offers gold, glory, boundless power; but the aged doctor craves youth, its passions and delights. The fiend agrees that all shall be his if he but sign a compact, by which the devil serves Faust on earth, but in the hereafter below the relation is to be reversed. Faust wavers at first, but a vision of Marguerite appears, which inflames his ardor and dispels his hesitation; he drinks the potion and is transformed into a young and handsome man.

ACT II. — A Kirmesse or town fair. Groups of students, soldiers, old men, maids and matrons fill the scene. Valentine, the brother of Marguerite, about to leave for the wars, commends his sister to the care of Siebel, who timidly adores her. While Wagner, a student, is attempting a song, he is interrupted by Mephistopheles who volunteers to sing him a better one (the mocking "Calf of Gold"). Then the fiend causes a fiery liquor to flow miraculously from the tavern sign, and proposes the health of Marguerite. Valentine resents the insult, but his sword is broken in his hand, and Mephistopheles draws a magic circle around himself and bids defiance to the rapiers of the soldiers. These, now suspecting his evil nature, hold their cruciform sword-hilts toward Mephistopheles, who cowers away at the holy symbol. The fête is resumed; in the midst of the revelry Marguerite enters, returning home from church. Faust offers to escort her home, but she timidly declines his assistance, and leaves him enamoured of her beauty. The act closes with a merry dance of the townspeople.

ACT III. — The scene shows the garden of Marguerite's dwelling. Siebel enters to leave a nosegay on the doorstep of his charmer. The flowers he plucks wither at his touch, due to an evil spell cast upon him by the fiend, which he, however, breaks by dipping his hand in holy water. Faust and Mephistopheles conceal themselves in the garden after having left a casket of jewels on the doorstep near Siebel's modest offering. Marguerite returns home and seats herself at the spinning-wheel, singing the while a song of the "King of Thule." But she interrupts the song to dream of the handsome stranger who had spoken to her at the fête. Upon discovering the jewels, she cannot forbear to adorn herself. While thus occupied, Faust and his evil ally appear. The latter engages the girl's flighty

neighbor, Martha, in conversation, while Faust pleads his passion's cause successfully with Marguerite.

ACT IV. — Betrayed and deserted by her lover, Marguerite must bear the scorn of her former companions. Siebel alone is faithful, and speaks comforting words. She goes to the church to pray; but her supplications are interrupted by the mocking fiend at her elbow, by the accusing cries of demons, and by the stern chants of the worshipers. Finally Mephistopheles appears to the sight of the wretched girl, who swoons with terror.

The return of the victorious soldiers brings back Valentine, who hears evil stories of his sister's condition. Aroused by an insulting serenade which Mephistopheles, accompanied by Faust, sings beneath Marguerite's window, Valentine engages in a duel with the latter and is wounded to the death. Dying, he curses Marguerite, who comes from the church to his side, and accuses her of bringing him to his end.

ACT V. — Marguerite, her reason shaken by her misfortunes, has killed her child, and for this crime she is thrown into prison, and condemned to die. Faust, aided by Mephistopheles, obtains access to her cell and urges her to fly with him; but her poor mind cannot grasp the situation, and recurs only to the scenes of their love. When she sees Faust's companion, she turns from him in horror, falls upon her knees, and implores the mercy of heaven. As she sinks in death, Mephistopheles pronounces her damned, but a heavenly voice proclaims her pardoned; and while a celestial choir chants the Easter hymn the soul of Marguerite is seen borne up to heaven by angels. Faust falls to his knees, and the devil crouches beneath the shining sword of an archangel.

First performed at the Théâtre Lyrique, Paris, March 19, 1859, with the following cast:

LE DOCTEUR FAUST	*MM. Barbot*
MÉPHISTOPHÉLÈS	*Balanqué*
VALENTIN	*Reynald*
WAGNER	*Cibot*
MARGUERITE	*Mmes. Miolan-Carvalho*
SIEBEL	*Faivre*
MARTHA	*Duclos*

FAUST

ACT I.

SCENE I.

Faust's Study.

(Night. FAUST discovered, alone. He is seated at a table covered with books and parchments; an open book lies before him. His lamp is flickering in the socket.)

Faust.   No ! In vain hath my soul aspired, with
    ardent longing,
    All to know, — all in earth and heaven.
    No light illumines the visions, ever
    thronging
    My brain ; no peace is given,
    And I linger, thus sad and weary,
    Without power to sunder the chain
    Binding my soul to life always dreary.
    Nought do I see ! Nought do I know !

(He closes the book and rises. Day begins to dawn.)

    Again 'tis light !
    On its westward course flying,
    The somber night vanishes.
        (Despairingly.)
    Again the light of a new day !
    O death ! when will thy dusky wings
    Above me hover and give me — rest ?

       (Seizing a flask on the table.)

    Well, then ! Since death thus evades me,
    Why should I not go in search of him ?
    Hail, my final day, all hail !
    No fears my heart assail ;
    On earth my days I number ;
    For this draught immortal slumber
    Will secure me, and care dispel !

(Pours liquid from the flask into a crystal goblet. Just as he is about to raise it to his lips, the following chorus is heard, without.)

Cho. of Maidens.   Why thy eyes so lustrous
    Hidest thou from sight ?
    Bright Sol now is scatt'ring
    Beams of golden light ;
    The nightingale is warbling
    Its carol of love ;

ACTE PREMIER.

SCÈNE PREMIERE.

Le Cabinet de Faust.

(FAUST, seul. Sa lampe est près de s'eteindre. Il est assis devant une table chargée de parchemins. Un livre est ouvert devant lui.)

Faust.   Rien !... — En vain j'interroge, en mon
    ardente veille,
    La nature et le Créateur ;
    Pas une voix ne glisse à mon oreille
    Un mot consolateur !
    J'ai langui triste et solitaire,
    Sans pouvoir briser le lien
    Qui m'attache encore à la terre !...
    Je ne vois rien ! — Je ne sais rien !...

(Il ferme le livre et se lève. Le jour commence à naitre.)

    Le ciel pâlit ! — Devant l'aube nouvelle
    La sombre nuit
    S'évanouit !...
        (Avec désespoir.)
    Encore un jour ! — encore un jour qui
    luit !...
    O mort, quand viendras-tu m'abriter
    sous ton aile ?
       (Saisissant une fiole sur la table.)
    Eh bien ! puisque la mort me fuit,
    Pourquoi n'irais-je pas vers elle ?...
    Salut ! ô mon dernier matin !
    J'arrive sans terreur au terme du voyage ;
    Et je suis, avec ce breuvage,
    Le seul maître de mon destin !

(Il verse le contenu de la fiole dans une coupe de cristal. Au moment où il va porter la coupe à ses lèvres, des voix de jeunes filles se font entendre au dehors.)

Choeur de Jeunes Filles.   Paresseuse fille
    Qui sommeille encor !
    Déjà le jour brille
    Sous son manteau d'or.
    Déjà l'oiseau chante
    Ses folles chansons ;

Rosy tints of morning
Now gleam from above;
Flow'rs unfold their beauty
To the scented gale;
Nature all awakens —
Of love tells its tale.

Faust. Hence, empty sounds of human joys
Flee far from me.
O goblet, which my ancestors
So many times have filled,
Why tremblest thou in my grasp?
(Again raising the goblet to his lips.)

Cho. of Laborers
(without).
The morn into the fields doth summon us,
The swallow hastes away!
Why tarry, then?
To labor let's away! to work let's on,
The sky is bright, the earth is fair,
Our tribute, then, let's pay to heav'n.

Cho. of Maidens and Laborers.
Praises to God!

Faust. God! God!
(He sinks into a chair.)
But this God, what will he do for me?
(Rising.)
Will he return to me youth, love, and faith?
(With rage.)
Cursed be all of man's vile race!
Cursed be the chains which bind him in his place!
Cursed be visions false, deceiving!
Cursed the folly of believing!
Cursed be dreams of love or hate!
Cursed be souls with joy elate.
Cursed be science, prayer, and faith!
Cursed my fate in life and death!
Infernal king, arise!

SCENE II.

FAUST and MEPHISTOPHELES.

Mep.
(suddenly appearing).
Here am I! So, I surprise you?
SATAN, Sir, at your service!

L'aube caressante
Sourit aux moissons;
Le ruisseau murmure,
La fleur s'ouvre au jour,
Toute la nature
S'éveille à l'amour!

Faust. Vains échos de la joie humaine,
Passez, passez votre chemin!...
O coupe des aïeux, qui tant fois fus pleine,
Pourquoi trembles-tu dans ma main?..
(Il porte de nouveau la coupe à ses lèvres.)

Choeur des Laboureurs
(dehors).
Aux champs l'aurore nous rappelle;
Le temps est beau, la terre est belle;
Béni soit Dieu!
A peine voit-on l'hirondelle,
Qui vole et plonge d'un coup d'aile
Dans le profondeur du ciel bleu!

Jeunes Filles et Labs. Béni soit Dieu!

Faust. (*reposant la coupe*) Dieu!
(Il se laisse retomber dans son fauteuil.)
Mais ce Dieu, que peut-il pour moi!
(Se levant.)
Me rendra-t'il l'amour, l'espérance et la foi?
(Avec rage.)
Maudites soyez-vous, ô voluptés humaines!
Maudites soient les chaînes
Qui me font ramper ici-bas!
Maudit soit tout ce qui nous leurre,
Vain espoir qui passe avec l'heure,
Rêves d'amour ou de combats!
Maudit soit le bonheur, maudites la science,
La prière et la foi!
Maudite sois-tu, patience!
A moi, Satan! à moi!

SCÈNE II.

FAUST, MEPHISTOPHELES.

Mep.
(apparaissant).
Me voici!... D'où vient ta surprise!
Ne suis-je pas mis à ta guise?

A sword at my side; on my hat a gay feather; —	L'épée au côté, la plume au chapeau
A cloak o'er my shoulder; and altogether,	L'escarcelle pleine, un riche manteau
Why, gotten up quite in the fashion!	Sur l'épaule; — en somme
(Briskly.)	Un vrai gentilhomme!
But come, Doctor Faust, what is your will?	Eh bien! que me veux-tu, docteur!
Behold! Speak! Are you afraid of me?	Parle, voyons!... — Te fais-je peur?

Faust.	No.	*Faust.*	Non.
Mep.	Do you doubt my power?	*Mep.*	Doutes-tu ma puissance?...
Faust.	Perhaps.	*Faust.*	Peut- tre!
Mep.	Prove it, then.	*Mep.*	Mets-la donc à l'épreuve!...
Faust.	Begone!	*Faust.*	Va-t'en!
Mep.	Fie! Fie! Is this your politeness!	*Mep.*	Fi! — c'est là ta reconnaissance!
	But learn, my friend, that with Satan		Apprends de moi qu'avec Satan
	One should conduct in a different way.		L'on en doit user d'autre sorte,
	I've entered your door with infinite trouble.		Et qu'il n'était pas besoin
	Would you kick me out the very same day?		De l'appeler de si loin
			Pour le mettre ensuite à la porte!
Faust.	Then what will you do for me?	*Faust.*	Et que peux-tu pour moi?
Mep.	Anything in the world! All things. But	*Mep.*	Tout. — Mais dis-moi d'abord
	Say first what you would have.		Ce que tu veux; — est-ce de l'or?
	Abundance of gold?		
Faust.	And what can I do with riches?	*Faust.*	Que ferais-je de la richesse?
Mep.	Good. I see where the shoe pinches.	*Mep.*	Bien! je vois où le bât te blesse!
	You will have glory.		Tu veux la gloire?
Faust.	Still wrong.	*Faust.*	Plus encor!
Mep.	Power, then.	*Mep.*	La puissance!
Faust.	No. I would have a treasure	*Faust.*	Non! je veux un trésor
	Which contains all. I wish for youth.		Qui les contient tous!... je **veux** jeunesse!
	Oh! I would have pleasure,		A moi les plaisirs,
	And love, and caresses,		Les jeunes maîtresses!
	For youth is the season		A moi leurs caresses!
	When joy most impresses.		A moi leurs désirs?
	One round of enjoyment,		A moi l'énergie
	One scene of delight,		Des instincts puissants,
	Should be my employment		Et la folle orgie
	From day-dawn till night.		Du cœur et des sens!
	Oh, I would have pleasure,		Ardente jeunesse,
	And love, and caresses;		A moi tes désirs!
	If youth you restore me,		A moi ton ivresse!
	My joys I'll renew!		A moi tes plaisirs!...

Mep.	'Tis well — all thou desirest I can give thee.	*Mep.*	Fort bien! je puis contenter ton caprice
Faust.	Ah! but what must **I give** in return?	*Faust.*	**Et que te donnerai-je en retour?**

Mep. 'Tis but little :

In this world I will be thy slave,

But down below thou must be mine.

Faust. Below!

Mep. Below.

(Unfolding a scroll.)

Come, write. What! does thy hand tremble ?

Whence this dire trepidation ?

'Tis youth that now awaits thee — Behold!

(At a sign from MEPHISTOPHELES, the scene opens and discloses MARGUERITE, spinning.)

Faust. Oh, wonder !

Mep. Well, how do you like it ?

(Taking parchment.)

Faust. Give me the scroll !

(Signs.)

Mep. Come on then ! And now, master,

(Taking cup from the table.)

I invite thee to empty a cup,

In which there is neither poison nor death,

But young and vigorous life.

Faust.

(Taking cup and turning toward MARGUERITE.)

O beautiful, adorable vision ! I drink to thee !

(He drinks the contents of the cup, and is transformed into a young and handsome man. The vision disappears.)

Mep. Come, then.

Faust. Say, shall I again behold her ?

Mep. Most surely !

Faust. When ?

Mep. This very day !

Faust. 'Tis well.

Mep. Then let's away.

Both. 'Tis pleasure I covet,

'Tis beauty I crave ;

I sigh for its kisses,

Its love I demand !

With ardor unwonted

I long now to burn ;

I sigh for the rapture

Of heart and of sense.

(Exeunt. The curtain falls.)

Mep. Presque rien :

Ici, je suis à ton service,

Mais là-bas tu seras au mien.

Faust. Là-bas ?...

Mep. Là-bas.

(Lui présentant un parchemin.)

Allons, signe. — Eh quoi ! ta main tremble !

Que faut-il pour te décider ?

La jeunesse t'appelle ; ôse la regarder !...

(Il fait un geste. Au fond du théâtre s'ouvre et laisse voir MARGUERITE assise devant son rouet et filant.)

Faust. O merveille !...

Mep. Eh bien ! que t'ensemble ?

(Prenant le parchemin.)

Faust. Donne !...

(Il signe.)

Mep. Allons donc !

(Prenant la coupe restée sur la table.)

Et maintenant,

Maître, c'est moi qui te convie

A vider cette coupe où fume en bouillonnant

Non plus la mort, non plus le poison ; — mais la vie !

Faust.

(Prenant la coupe et se tournant vers MARGUERITE.)

A toi, fantôme adorable et charmant !...

(Il vide la coupe et se trouve métamorphosé en jeune et élégant seigneur. La vision disparaît.)

Mep. Viens !

Faust. Je la reverrai ?

Mep. Sans doute.

Faust. Quand ?

Mep. Aujourd'hui.

Faust. C'est bien !

Mep. En route !

Faust. A moi les plaisirs,

Les jeunes maîtresses !

A moi leurs caresses !

A moi leurs désirs !

Mep. A toi la jeunesse,

A toi ses désirs,

A toi son ivresse,

A toi ses plaisirs !

(Ils sortent. — La toile tombe.)

ACT II.

—

SCENE I.

The Kermesse.

(One of the city gates. To the left, an Inn, bearing the sign of the god Bacchus.)
WAGNER, Students, Burghers, Soldiers, Maidens, and Matrons.

Studs. Wine or beer, now, which you will !
So the glass quick you fill !
And replenish at our need :
At our bouts we drink with speed !

Wag. Now, young tipplers at the cask,
Don't refuse what I ask —
Drink to glory ! drink to love !
Drain the sparkling glass !

Studs. We young tipplers at the cask
Won't refuse what you ask—
Here's to glory ! here's to love !
Drain the sparkling glass !
(They drink.)

Soldiers.
Castles, hearts, or fortresses,
Are to us all one.
Strong towers, maids with fair tresses,
By the brave are won ;
He, who hath the art to take them,
Shows no little skill ;
He, who knows the way to keep them,
Hath more wisdom still.

Citizens.
On holy-days and feast-days,
I love to talk of war and battles.
While the toiling crowds around
Worry their brains with affairs,
I stroll calmly to this retreat
On the banks of the gliding river,
And behold the boats which pass
While I leisurely empty my glass.
(Citizens and soldiers go to back of stage.)

(A group of young girls enters.)
Girls. Merry fellows come this way,
Yes, they now advance ;
Let us, then, our steps delay,
Just to take one glance.

(They go to right of stage. A second chorus of students enters after them.)

ACTE DEUXIÈME.

—

SCÈNE PREMIÈRE.

La Kermesse.

(Une des portes de la ville. A gauche un caborte à l'enseigne de Bacchus.)
WAGNER, Etudiants, Bourgeois, Soldats, Jeunes Filles, Matrones

Etuds. Vin ou bière,
Bière ou vin,
Que mon verre
Soit plein !
Sans vergogne,
Coup sur coup,
Un ivrogne
Boit tout !

Wag. Jeune adepte   Que ta gloire,
De tonneau   Tes amours,
N'en excepte   Soient de boire
Que l'eau !   Toujours !
(Ils trinquent et boivent.)

Soldats.
Filles ou forteresses,
C'est tout un, morbleu !
Vieux burgs, jeunes maîtresses
Sont pour nous un jeu !
Celui qui sait s'y prendre
Sans trop de façon,
Les oblige à se rendre
En payant rançon !

Bourgeois.
Aux jours de dimanche et de fête,
J'aime à parler guerre et combats ;
Tandis que les peuples là-bas
Se cassent la tête.
Je vais m'asseoir sur les coteaux
Qui sont voisins de la rivière,
Et je vois passer les bateaux
En vidant mon verre !
(Bourgeois et Soldats remontent vers le fond du théâtre.)

(Un groupe de jeunes filles entre en scène.)
Les Jeunes Filles
(regardant de côté).
Voyez ces hardis compères
Qui viennent làbas ;
Ne soyons pas trop sévères,
Retardons le pas.

(Elles gagnent la droite du théâtre. Un second chœur d'étudiants entre à leur suit

Studs. Sprightly maidens now advance,
　　 Watch their conquering airs ;
　　 Friends be guarded, lest a glance
　　 Take you unawares.

Matrons.
　　 (watching the students and young girls).
　　 Behold the silly damsels,
　　 And the foolish young men ;
　　 We were once as young as they are,
　　 And as pretty again.

　　 (All join in the following chorus, each singing as follows.)

Mats.
　　　 (to the Maidens).
　　 Ye strive hard to please,
　　 Your object is plain.

Studs. Beer or wine, wine or beer,
　　 Nought care I, with heart of cheer.

Soldiers.
　　 On, then, let's on ;
　　 Brave soldiers are we,
　　 To conquest we'll on.

Citizens.
　　 Come, neighbor ! In this fine weather
　　 Let us empty a bottle together !

Maidens.
　　 They wish to please us, but 'tis in vain !
　　 If you are angry, little you'll gain.

Young Students.
　　 They are bright little maidens, 'tis plain ;
　　 We'll contrive their favor to gain.

　　 (The soldiers and students, laughing, separate the women. All the groups depart.)

SCENE II.

WAGNER, SIEBEL, VALENTINE, Students, and afterwards MEPHISTOPHELES.

Val.
　　 (advancing from the back of the stage and holding in his hand a small silver medal).
　　 O sacred medallion,
　　　 Gift of my sister dear
　　　 To ward off danger and fear,
　　 As I charge with my brave battalion,
　　　 Rest thou upon my heart.

Deuxième Cho. d'Etuds.
　　 Voyez ces mines gaillardes
　　 Et ces airs vainqueurs !
　　 Amis, soyons sur nos gardes,
　　 Tenons bien nos cœurs !

Cho. De Mats.
　　 (observant les étudiants et les jeunes filles).
　　 Voyez après ces donzelles
　　 Courir ces messieurs !
　　 Nous sommes aussi bien qu'elles,
　　 Sinon beaucoup mieux !

　　　 (Ensemble.)

Mats.
　　　 (aux jeunes filles).
　　 Vous voulez leur plaire
　　 Nous le voyons bien

Etuds. Vin ou bière,
　　 Bière ou vin,
　　 Que mon verre
　　 Soit plein !

Sols.
　　 Pas be beauté fière !
　　 Nous savons leur plaire
　　 En un tour de main !

Bourg. Vidons un verre
　　 De ce bon vin !

Jeunes Filles.
　　 De votre colère
　　 Nous ne craignons rien !

Jeunes Etuds.
　　 Voyez leur colère,
　　 Voyez leur maintien !

　　 (Les étudiants et les soldats séparent les femmes en riant. Tous les groupes s'éloignent et disparaissent.)

SCÈNE II.

WAGNER, SIEBEL, Etudiants. VALENTIN.

Val.
　　 (paraissant au fond ; il tient une petite médaille à la main).
　　 O sainte médaille,
　　　 Qui me viens de ma sœur,
　　　 Au jour de la bataille,
　　 Pour écarter la mort, reste là sur mon
　　　 cœur !

Wag.	Here comes Valentine, in search of us, doubtless.	*Wag.*	Ah! voici Valentin qui nous cherche sans doute!
Val.	Let us drain the parting cup, comrades, It is time we were on the road.	*Val.*	Un dernier coup, messieurs, et mettons nous en route!
Wag.	What sayst thou? Why this sorrowful farewell?	*Wag.*	Qu'as-tu donc? ... quels regrets attristent nos adieux?
Val.	Like you, I soon must quit these scenes, Leaving behind me Marguerite. Alas! my mother no longer lives, To care for and protect her.	*Val.*	Comme vous, pour longtemps, je vais quitter ces lieux; J'y laisse Marguerite, et, pour veiller sur elle, Ma mère n'est plus là!
Sie.	More than one friend hast thou Who faithfully will thy place supply.	*Sie.*	Plus d'un ami fidèle Saura te remplacer a ses côtés!
Val.	My thanks!	*Val.*	(lui serrant la main). Merci!
Sie.	On me you may rely.	*Sie.*	Sur moi tu peux compter!
Stud.	In us thou surely mayst confide.	*Etuds.*	Compte sur nous aussi!
Val.	Even bravest heart may swell In the moment of farewell. Loving smile of sister kind, Quiet home I leave behind. Oft shall I think of you Whene'er the wine-cup passes round, When alone my watch I keep. But when danger to glory shall call me, I still will be first in the fray, As blithe as a knight in his bridal array. Careless what fate shall befall me When glory shall call me.	*Val.*	Avant de quitter ces lieux, Sol natal de mes aïeux, A toi, Seigneur et Roi des Cieux, Ma sœur je confie. Daigne de tout danger Toujours la protéger, Cette sœur si chérie. Délivré d'une triste pensée, J'irais chercher la gloire au sein des ennemis, Le premier, le plus brave au fort de la mêlée, J'irai combattre pour mon pays. Et si vers lui Dieu me rappelle, Je viellerai sur toi fidèle, O Marguerite!
Wag.	Come on, friends! No tears nor vain alarms; Quaff we good wine, to the success of our arms! Drink, boys, drink! In a joyous refrain Bid farewell, till we meet again.	*Wag.*	Allons, amis! point de vaines alarmes! A ce bon vin ne mêlons pas de larmes! Buvons, trinquons, et qu'un joyeux refrain Nous mette en train!
Cho.	We'll drink! Fill high! Once more in song our voices Let us raise.	*Etuds.*	Buvons, trinquons, et qu'un joyeux refrain Nous mette en train!

Wag.

(mounting on a table).

A rat, more coward than brave,
    And with an exceedingly ugly head,
Lodged in a sort of hole or cave,
    Under an ancient hogshead.
A cat —

SCENE III.

MEPHISTOPHELES and the preceding.

Mep.
(appearing suddenly among the students and interrupting WAGNER).

Good sir !

Wag. What !

Mep. If it so please ye I should wish
To mingle with ye a short time.
If your good friend will kindly end his
    song,
I'll tell ye a few things well worth the
    hearing.

Wag. One will suffice, but let that one be good.

Mep. My utmost I will do
Your worships not to bore.

I.

Calf of Gold ! aye in all the world
To your mightiness they proffer,
Incense at your fane they offer
From end to end of all the world.
And in honor of the idol
Kings and peoples everywhere
To the sound of jingling coins
Dance with zeal in festive circle,
Round about the pedestal.
Satan, he conducts the ball.

II.

Calf of Gold, strongest god below !
To his temple overflowing
Crowds before his vile shape bowing,
The monster dares insult the skies.
With contempt he views around him
All the vaunted human race,

Wag.

(montant sur un escabeau)

Un rat plus poltron que brave,
Et plus laid que beau,
Logeait au fond d'une cave,
Sous un vieux tonneau ;
Un chat...

SCÈNE III.

Les mêmes. MEPHISTOPHELES.

Mep.
(paraissant tout à coup au milieu des étudiants et interrompant WAGNER).

Pardon !

Wag. Hein ?

Mep.   Parmi vous, de grâce
Permettez-moi de prendre place !
Que votre ami d'abord achève sa chan-
    son !
Moi, je vous en promets plusieurs de ma
    façon !

Wag.

(descendant de son escabeau).

Une seule suffit, pourvu qu'elle soit
    bonne !

Mep. Je ferai de mon mieux pour n'ennuyer
    personne !

I.

Le veau d'or est toujours debout ;
On encense
Sa puissance
D'un bout du monde à l'autre bout !
Pour fêter l'infâme idole,
Peuples et rois confondus,
Au bruit sombre des écus
Dansent une ronde folle
Autour de son piédestal ?...
Et Satan conduit le bal !

II.

Le veau d'or est vainqueur des dieux ;
Dans son gloire
Dérisoire
Le monstre abjecte insulte aux cieux !
Il contemple, ô rage étrange !
A ses pieds le genre humain

	As they strive in abject toil,
	As with souls debased they circle
	Round about the pedestal.
	Satan, he conducts the ball.
All.	Satan, he conducts the ball.
Cho.	A strange story this of thine.
Val.	(aside).
	And stranger still is he who sings it.
Wag.	(offering a cup to MEPHISTOPHELES).
	Will you honor us by partaking of wine?
Mep.	With pleasure. Ah!
	(Taking WAGNER by the hand, and scrutinizing his palm.)
	Behold what saddens me to view.
	See you this line?
Wag.	Well!
Mep.	A sudden death it presages, —
	You will be killed in mounting to th' assault!
Sie.	You are then a sorcerer!
Mep.	Even so. And your own hand shows plainly
	To what fate condemns. What flower you would gather
	Shall wither in the grasp.
Sie.	I?
Mep.	No more bouquets for Marguerite.
Val.	My sister! How knew you her name?
Mep.	Take care, my brave fellow!
	Some one I know is destined to kill you.
	(Taking the cup.)
	Your health, gentlemen!
	Pah! What miserable wine!
	Allow me to offer you some from my cellar?

(Jumps on the table, and strikes on a little cask, surmounted by the effigy of the god Bacchus, which serves as a sign to the Inn.)

What ho! thou god of wine, now give us drink!

(Wine gushes forth from cask, and MEPHISTOPHELES fills his goblet.)

Approach, my friends!
Each one shall be served to his liking.

	Se ruant, le fer en main,
	Dans le sang et dans la fange
	Où brille l'ardent métal!...
	Et Satan conduit le bal!
Tous.	Et Satan conduit le bal!
Cho.	Merci de ta chanson!
Val.	(à part).
	Singulier personnage!
Wag.	(tendant un verre à MEPHISTOPHELES).
	Nous ferez vous l'honneur de trinquer avec nous?
Mep.	Volontiers!...
	(Saisissant la main de WAGNER et l'examinant.)
	Ah! voici qui m'attriste pour vous!
	Vous voyez cette ligne?
Wag.	Eh bien?
Mep.	Fâcheux présage!
	Vous vous ferez tuer en montant à l'assaut!
Sie.	Vous êtes donc sorcier?
Mep.	Tout juste autant qu'il faut
	Pour lire dans ta main que le ciel te condamne
	A ne plus toucher une fleur
	Sans qu'elle se fane!
Sie.	Moi!
Mep.	Plus de bouquets à Marguerite!...
Val.	Ma sœur!...
	Qui vous a dit son nom?
Mep.	Prenez garde, mon brave!
	Vous vous ferez tuer par quelqu'un que je sais!
	(Prenant le verre des mains de WAGNER.)
	A votre santé!...

(Jetant le contenu du verre, après y avoir trempé ses lèvres.)

Peuh! que ton vin est mauvais!...
Permettez-moi de vous en offrir de ma cave!

(Frappant sur le tonneau, surmonté d'un Bacchus, qui sert d'enseigne au cabaret.)

Holà! seigneur Bacchus! à boire!...

(Le vin jaillit du tonneau. Aux étudiants.)

Approchez-vous!
Chacun sera servi selon ses goûts!

To your health, now and hereafter!
To Marguerite!

Val.   Enough! If I do not silence him,
And that instantly, I will die.

(The wine bursts into flame.)

Wag.   Hola!
Cho.   Hola!

(They draw their swords.)

Mep.   Ah, ha! Why do you tremble so, you
who menace me?

(He draws a circle around him with his sword. VALENTINE attacks; his sword is broken.)

Val.   My sword, O amazement!
Is broken asunder.

All

(forcing MEPHISTOPHELES to retire by holding toward him the cross-shaped handles of their swords).

Gainst the powers of evil our arms assail-
ing,
Strongest earthly might is unavailing.
But thou canst not charm us,
Look hither!
While this blest sign we wear
Thou canst not harm us.

(Exeunt.)

SCENE IV.

MEPHISTOPHELES, then FAUST.

Mep.

(replacing his sword).

We'll meet anon, good sirs, — adieu!

Faust

(enters).

Why, what has happened?

Mep.   Oh, nothing! let us change the subject!
Say, Doctor, what would you of me?
With what shall we begin?

Faust.   Where bides the beauteous maid
Thine art did show to me?
Or was't mere witchcraft?

Mep.   No, but her virtue doth protect her from
thee.
And heaven itself would keep her pure.

A la santé que tout à l'heure
Vous portiez, mes amis, à Marguerite!

Val.

(lui arrachant le verre des mains).

Assez!....

Si je ne te fais taire à l'instant, que je
meure!

(Le vin s'enflamme dans la vasque placée audessous du tonneau.)

Wag. et les Etuds.

Holà!...

(Ils tirent leurs épées.)

Mep.   Pourquoi trembler, vous qui me mena-
cez?

(Il tire un cercle autour de lui avec son épée. —VALENTIN s'avance pour l'attaquer. — Son épée se brise.)

Val.   Mon fer, ô surprise!
Dans les airs se brise!...

Val., Wag., Sie. et les Etuds.

(forçant MEPHISTOPHELES à reculer et lui présentant la garde de leurs épées).

De l'enfer qui vient émousser
Nos armes!
Nous ne pouvons pas repousser
Les charmes!
Mais puisque tu brises le fer,
Regarde!...
C'est une croix qui, de l'enfer,
Nous garde!

(Ils sortent.)

SCÈNE IV

MEPHISTOPHELES, puis FAUST.

Mep.

(remettant son épée au fourreau).

Nous nous retrouverons, mes amis!—
Serviteur!

Faust

(entrant en scène).

Qu'as-tu donc?

Mep.   Rien! — A nous deux, cher docteur!
Qu'attendez-vous de moi? par où com-
mencerai-je?

Faust.   Où se cache la belle enfant
Que ton art m'a fait voir? — Est-ce un
vain sortilège?

Mep.   Non pas! mais contre nous sa vertu la
protège;
Et le ciel même la défend!

Faust. It matters not!
  Come, lead me to her,
  Or I straightway abandon thee.

Mep. Then I'll comply! 'twere pity you should think
  So meanly of the magic power which I possess.
  Have patience! and to this joyous tune.
  Right sure am I, the maiden will appear.

SCENE V.

(Students, with Maidens on their arms, preceded by Musicians, take possession of the stage. Burghers in the rear, as at the commencement of the act.)

Students, Maidens, Burghers, etc., afterwards SIEBEL and MARGUERITE.

Cho.
  (marking waltz time with their feet).

  As the wind that sportively plays,
  At first will light dust only raise,
  Yet, at last, becomes a gale,
  So our dancing and our singing,
  Soft at first, then loudly ringing,
  Will resound o'er hill and dale.

(The Musicians mount upon the table, and dancing begins.)

Mep.
  (to FAUST).

  See those lovely young maidens.
  Will you not ask of them
  To accept you?

Faust. No! desist from thy idle sport,
  And leave my heart free to reflection.

Sie.
  (entering).

  Marguerite this way alone can arrive.

Some of the Maidens
  (approaching SIEBEL).

  Pray seek you a partner to join in the dance?

Faust. Qu'importe? je le veux! viens! conduis mois vers elle!
  Ou je me sépare de toi!

Mep. Il suffit!...je tiens trop à mon nouve emploi
  Pour vous laisser douter un instant de mon zèle!
  Attendons!...Ici même, à ce signal joyeux,
  La belle et chaste enfant va paraître a vos yeux!

SCÈNE V.

(Les étudiants et les jeunes filles, bras dessus, bras dessous, et précédés par des joueurs de violon, envahissent la scène. Ils sont suivi par les bourgeois qui ont paru au commencement de l'acte.)

Les Mêmes, Etudiants, Jeunes Filles, Bourgeois, puis SIEBEL e MARGUERITE.

Cho.
  (marquant la mesure en marchant).

  Ainsi que la brise légère
  Soulève en épais tourbillons
  La poussière
  Des sillons,
  Que la valse nous entraîne!
  Faites retentir la plaine
  De l'éclat de nos chansons!

(Les Musiciens montent sur les bancs; la valse commence.)

Mep.
  (à FAUST).

  Vois ces filles
  Gentilles!
  Ne veux-tu pas
  Aus plus belles
  D'entre elles
  Offrir ton bras?

Faust. Non! fais trêve
  A ce ton moqueur!
  Et laisse mon cœur
  A son rêve!...

Sie.
  (rentrant en scène).

  C'est par ici que doit passer Marguerite!

Quelques Jeunes Filles.
  (s'approchant de SIEBEL).

  Faut-il qu'une fille à danser Vous invite?

Sie.	No : it has no charm for me.
Cho.	As the wind that sportively plays,
	At first will light dust only raise,
	Yet, at last, becomes a gale,
	So our dancing and our singing,
	Soft at first, then loudly ringing,
	Will resound o'er hill and dale.

(MARGUERITE enters.)

Faust.	It is she ! behold her !
Mep.	'Tis well ! now, then, approach !
Sie.	

(perceiving MARGUERITE and approaching her).

Marguerite !

Mep.

(turning round and finding himself face to face with SIEBEL).

What say you?

Sie.

(aside).

Malediction ! here again !

Mep.

(coaxingly).

What, here again, dear boy ?

(laughing).

Ha, ha ! a right good jest !

(SIEBEL retreats before MEPHISTOPHELES, who then compels him to make a circuit of the stage, passing behind the dancers.)

Faust

(approaching MARGUERITE, who crosses the stage).

Will you not permit me, my fairest demoiselle,
To offer you my arm, and clear for you the way?

Mar. No, sir. I am no demoiselle, neither am I fair ;
And I have no need to accept your offered arm.

(Passes FAUST and retires.)

Faust

(gazing after her).

What beauty ! What grace ! What modesty !
O lovely child, I love thee ! I love thee !

Sie.

(coming forward, without having seen what has occurred).

She has gone !

(He is about to hurry after MARGUERITE, when he suddenly finds himself face to face with MEPHISTOPHELES — he hastily turns away and leaves the stage.)

Sie.	Non !...non ! je ne veux pas valser !..
Cho.	Ainsi que la brise légère
	Soulève en épais tourbillons
	La poussière
	Des sillons,
	Que la valse nous entraîne !
	Faites retentir la plaine
	De l'éclat de nos chansons !...

(MARGUERITE parait.)

Faust.	Ah !...la voici...c'est elle !...
Mep.	Eh bien, aborde-la !
Sie.	

(apercevant MARGUERITE et faisant un pas vers elle).

Marguerite !...

Mep.

(se retournant et se trouvant face à face avec SIEBEL).

Plaît-il !...

Sie.

(à part).

Maudit homme ! encor là !...

Mep.

(d'un ton milleux).

Eh quoi ! mon ami ! vous voilà !...

(en riant).

Ah, vraiment, mon ami !

(SIEBEL recule devant MEPHISTOPHELES, qui lui fait faire ainsi le our du théâtre en passant derrière le groupe des danseurs.)

Faust

(abordant MARGUERITE qui traverse la scène).

Ne permettrez-vous pas, ma belle demoiselle,
Qu'on vous offre le bras pour faire le chemin ?

Mar. Non, monsieur ! je ne suis demoiselle, ni belle,
Et je n'ai pas besoin qu'on me donne la main ?

(Elle passe devant FAUST et s'éloigne.)

Faust

(la suivant des yeux).

Pas le ciel ! que de grâce...et quelle modestie !...
O belle enfant, je t'aime !...

Sie.

(redescendant en scene sans avoir vu ce qui vient de se passer).

Elle est partie !

(Il va pour s'élancer sur la trace de MARGUERITE; mais, se trouvan' de nouveau face à face avec MEPHISTOPHELES, il lui tourne le dos e s'éloigne par le fond du théâtre.)

Mep. Well, Doctor!

Faust. Well. She has repulsed me.

Mep.

(laughing).

Ay, truly, I see, in love,
You know not how to make the first move.

(He retires with FAUST, in the direction taken by MARGUERITE.)

Some of the Maidens

(who have noticed the meeting between FAUST and MARGUERITE).

What is it?

Others.

Marguerite. She has refused the escort
Of yonder elegant gentleman.

Studs.

(approaching).

Waltz again!

Maidens.

Waltz alway!

ACT III.

—

SCENE I.

MARGUERITE'S Garden.

(At the back a wall, with a little door. To the left a bower. On the right a pavilion, with a window facing the audience. Trees, shrubs, etc.)

SIEBEL, alone. (He enters through the little door at the back, and stops on the threshold of the pavilion, near a group of roses and lilies.)

Sie.

I.

Gently whisper to her of love, dear
flow'r;
Tell her that I adore her,
And for me, oh, implore her,
For my heart feels alone for her
love's pow'r.

Say in sighing I languish,
That for her, in my anguish,
Beats alone, dearest flow'r,
My aching heart.

(Plucks flowers.)

Mep.

(à FAUST).

Eh bien?

Faust. On me repousse!...

Mep.

(en riant).

Allons! à tes amours
Je vois qu'il faut prêter secours!...

(Il s'éloigne avec FAUST du même côté que MARGUERITE.)

Quelques Jeunes Filles

(s'adressant à trois ou quatre d'entre elles qui ont observé la rencontre de FAUST et de MARGUERITE).

Qu'est-ce donc!...

Deuxième Groupe de Jeunes Filles.

Marguerite,
Qui de ce beau seigneur refuse la
conduite!...

Etuds.

(se rapprochant).

Valsons encor!

Jeunes Filles.

Valsons toujours!

ACTE TROISIÈME.

—

SCÈNE PREMIÈRE.

Le Jardin de MARGUERITE.

(Au fond, un mur percé d'une petite porte. A gauche, un bosquet A droite, un pavillon dont la fenêtre fait face au public. Arbres e massifs.)

Sie.

(seul).

(Il est arrêté près d'un massif de roses et de lilas.)

I.

Faites-lui mes aveux,
Portez mes vœux,
Fleurs écloses près d'elle,
Dites-lui qu'elle est belle...
Que mon cœur nuit et jour
Languit d'amour!

Révélez à son âme
Le secret de ma flamme!
Qu'il s'exhale avec vous
Parfums plus doux!....

(Il cueille une fleur.)

Alas ! they are wither'd !

(Throws them away.)

Can the accursed wizard's words be true ?

(Plucks another flower, which, on touching his hand, immediately withers.)

" Thou shalt ne'er touch flower again
But it shall wither ! "
I'll bathe my hand in holy water !

(Approaches the pavilion, and dips his fingers in a little font suspended to the wall.)

When day declines, Marguerite hither
Comes to pray, so we'll try again.

(Plucks more flowers.)

Are they wither'd ? No !
Satan, thou art conquer'd !

II.

In these flowers alone I've faith,
For they will plead for me ;
To her they will reveal
My hapless state.
The sole cause of my woe is she,
And yet she knows it not.
But in these flowers I've faith,
For they will plead for me.

(Plucks flowers in order to make a bouquet, and disappears amongst the shrubs.)

SCENE II.

MEPHISTOPHELES, FAUST, and SIEBEL.

Faust.

(cautiously entering through the garden door).

We are here !

Mep Follow me.

Faust. Whom dost thou see ?

Mep. Siebel, your rival.

Faust. Siebel ?

Mep. Hush ! He comes.

(They enter the bower.)

Sie.

(entering with a bouquet in his hand).

My bouquet is charming indeed ?

Fanée !...hélas !

(Il jette la fleur avec dépit.)

Ce sorcier que Dieu damne
M'a porté malheur !

(Il cueille une autre fleur qui s'effeuille encore.)

Je ne puis sans qu'elle se fane
Toucher une fleur !...
Si je trempais mes doigts dans l'eau
bénite ?...

(Il s'approche du pavillon et trempe ses doigts dans un bénitier accroché au mur.)

C'est là que chaque soir vient prier
Marguerite !
Voyons maintenant ! voyons vite !...

(Il cueille deux ou trois fleurs.)

Elles se fanent ?...Non !...Satan, je ris de
toi...

II.

C'est en vous que j'ai foi ;
Parlez pour moi !
Qu'elle puisse connaître
L'ardeur qu'elle a fait naître,
Et dont mon cœur troublé
N'a point parlé !
Si l'amour l'effarouche.
Que la fleur sur sa bouche
Sache au moins déposer
Un doux baiser !...

(Il cueille des fleurs pour former un bouquet et disparaît dans les massifs du jardin.)

SCÈNE II.

MEPHISTOPHELES, FAUST, puis SIEBEL.

Faust

(entrant doucement en scène).

C'est ici ?

Mep. Suivez-moi !

Faust. Que regardes-tu là ?

Mep. Siebel, votre rival.

Faust. Siebel !

Mep. Chut !...le violà !

(Il se cache avec FAUST dans un bosquet.)

Sie.

(rentrant en scène, avec un bouquet à la main).

Mon bouquet n'est-il pas charmant ?

Mep.

(aside).

It is indeed !

Sie. Victory !

Tomorrow I'll reveal all to her.
I will disclose to her the secret
That lies concealed in my heart :
A kiss will tell the rest.

Mep.

(aside, mockingly).

Seducer !

(Exit SIEBEL, after fastening bouquet to the door of the pavilion.)

SCENE III.

FAUST and MEPHISTOPHELES.

Mep. Now attend, my dear doctor !
To keep company with the flowers of our
friend,
I go to bring you a treasure,
Which outshines them beyond measure,
And of beauty past believing.

Faust. Leave me !

Mep. I obey. Deign to await me here.

(Disappears.)

SCENE IV.

FAUST.

Faust

(alone).

What new emotion penetrates my soul !
Love, a pure and holy love, pervades my
being.
O Marguerite, behold me at thy feet !
All hail, thou dwelling pure and lowly,
Home of an angel fair and holy,
All mortal beauty excelling !
What wealth is here, a wealth outbidding
gold,
Of peace, and love, and innocence untold !
Bounteous Nature ! 'twas here by day thy
love was taught her,
Thou here with kindly care didst o'er-
shadow thy daughter
Through hours of night !
Here waving tree and flower

Mep.

(à part).

Charmant !

Sie. Victoire !

Je lui raconterai demain toute l'histoire ;
Et, si l'on veut savoir le secret de mon
cœur,
Un baiser lui dira le reste !

Mep.

(à part).

Séducteur !

(SIEBEL attache le bouquet à la porte du pavillon et sort.)

SCENE III.

FAUST, MEPHISTOPHELES.

Mep. Attendez-moi là, cher docteur !
Pour tenir compagnie aux fleurs de votre
élève,
Je vais vous chercher un trésor
Plus merveilleux, plus riche encor
Que tous ceux qu'elle voit en rêve !

Faust. Laisse-moi !

Mep. J'obéis !...daignez m'attendre ici ?

(Il sort.)

SCÈNE IV.

FAUST.

Faust

(seul).

Quel trouble inconnu me pénètre !
Je sens l'amour s'emparer de mon être.
O Marguerite ! tes pieds me voici !
Salut ! demeure chaste et pure, où se
devine
La présence d'une âme innocente et di-
vine !...
Que de richesse en cette pauvreté !
En ce réduit, que de félicité !...
O nature, c'est là que tu la fis si belle !
C'est là que cette enfant a grandi sous
ton aile,
A dormi sous tes yeux ?
Là que, de ton haleine enveloppant son
âme,
Tu fis avec amour épanouir la femme

Made her an Eden bower
Of beauty and delight,
For one whose very birth
Brought down heaven to our earth.
All hail, thou dwelling pure and lowly,
Home of an angel fair and holy.

SCENE V.

FAUST, MEPHISTOPHELES.

Mep.

(carrying a casket under his arm).

What ho I see here !
If flowers are more potent than bright
jewels,
Then I consent to lose my power.

(Opens the casket and displays the jewels.)

Faust. Let us fly ; I ne'er will see her more.
Mep. What scruple now assails thee ?

(Lays the casket on the threshold of the pavilion.)

See on yonder step,
The jewels snugly lie ;
We've reason now to hope.

(Draws FAUST after him, and disappears in the garden. MARGUER-
ITE enters through the doorway at the back, and advances silently to
the front.)

SCENE VI.

MARGUERITE.

Mar.

(alone).

Fain would I know the name
Of the fair youth I met ?
Fain would I his birth
And station also know ?

(Seats herself at her wheel in the arbor, and arranges the flax upon
the spindle.)

I.

" Once there was a king in Thulé,
Who was until death always faithful,
And in memory of his loved one

En cet ange des cieux !
Salut ! demeure chaste et pure, où se
devine !
La présence d'une âme innocente et di-
vine !...
Que de richesse en cette pauvreté !
En ce réduit, que de félicité !...
Salut ! demeure chaste et pure, où se
devine
La présence d'une âme innocente et di-
vine !...

SCÈNE V.

FAUST, MEPHISTOPHELES.

(MEPHISTOPHELES reparaît, une cassette sous le bras.)

Mep. Alerte ! la voilà !...Si le bouquet l'emporte
Sur l'écrin, je consens à perdre mon
pouvoir !

(Il ouvre l'écrin.)

Faust. Fuyons !...je veux ne jamais la revoir !
Mep. Quel scrupule vous prend !...

(Plaçant l'écrin sur le seuil du pavillon.)

Sur le seuil de la porte,
Voici l'écrin placé !...venez !...j'ai bon
espoir !

(Il entraine FAUST et disparaît avec lui dans le jardin. MARGUE-
RITE entre par la porte du fond et descend en silence jusque sur le
devant de la scène.)

SCÈNE VI.

MARGUERITE.

Mar.

(seule).

Je voudrais bien savoir quel était ce
jeune homme,
Si c'est un grand seigneur, et comment
il se nomme ?

(Elle s'assied dans le bosquet, devant son rouet, et prend son fuseau
autour duquel elle prépare de la laine.)

I.

"Il était un roi de Thulé,
Qui, jusqu' à la tombe fidèle,
Eut, en souvenir de sa belle,

Caused a cup of gold to be made."
(Breaking off.)
His manner was so gentle ! 'Twas true
politeness.
(Resuming the song.)
'Never treasure prized he so dearly,
Naught else would use on festive days,
And always when he drank from it,
His eyes with tears would be o'erflowing."

II.

(She rises, and takes a few paces.)

"When he knew that death was near,
As he lay on his cold couch smiling,
Once more he raised with greatest effort
To his lips the golden vase."
(Breaking off.)
I knew not what to say, my face red with
blushes !
(Resuming the song.)
"And when he, to honor his lady,
Drank from the cup the last, last time,
Soon falling from his trembling grasp,
Then gently passed his soul away."
Nobles alone can bear them with so bold
a mien,
So tender, too, withal !
(She goes toward the pavilion.)
I'll think of him no more ! Good Valen-
tine !
If heav'n heeds my prayer, we shall
meet again.
Meanwhile I am alone !
(Suddenly perceiving the bouquet attached to the door of the pa-
vilion.)
Flowers !
(Unfastens the bouquet.)
They are Siebel's, surely !
Poor faithful boy !
(Perceiving the casket.)
But what is this ?
From whom did this splendid casket
come ?
I dare not touch it —
Yet see, here is the key ! — I'll take
one look !
How I tremble — yet why ? — can it be
Much harm just to look in a casket !

(Opens the casket and lets the bouquet fall.)

Une coupe en or ciselé !..."
(S'interrompant.)
Il avait bonne grâce, à ce qu'il m'a
semble.
(Reprenant sa chanson.)
"Nul trésor n'avait plus de charmes !
Dans les grands jours il s'en servait,
Et chaque fois qu'il y buvait,
Ses yeux se remplissaient de larmes !..."

II.

(Elle se lève et fait quelques pas.)

"Quand il sentit venir la mort,
Etendu sur sa froide couche,
Pour la porter jusqu'à sa bouche
Sa main fit un suprême effort !..."
(S'interrompant.)
Je ne savais que dire, et j'ai rougi
d'abord.
(Reprenant sa chanson.)
"Et puis, en l'honneur de sa dame,
Il but un dernière fois ;
La coupe trembla dans ses doigts.
Et doucement il rendit l'âme !"
Les grands seigneurs ont seuls des air si
résolus,
Avec cette douceur.
(Elle se dirige vers le pavillon.)
Allons ! n'y pensons plus !
Cher Valentin, si Dieu m'écoute,
Je te reverrai !...me voilà
Toute seule !...
(Au moment d'entrer dans la pavillon, elle aperçoit la bouquet
suspendu à la porte.)
Un bouquet !
(Elle prend le bouquet.)
C'est de Siebel, sans doute !
Pauvre garçon !
(Apercevant la cassette.)
Que vois-je là ?
D'où ce riche coffret peut-il venir ? Je
n'ose
Y toucher, et pourtant... — Voici la clef,
je crois !...
Si je l'ouvrais !...ma main tremble !...
Pourquoi !
Je ne fais, en l'ouvrant, rien de mal, je
suppose !...

(Elle ouvre la cassette et laisse tombre le bouquet.)

Oh, heaven ! what jewels !
Can I be dreaming ?
Or am I really awake ?
Ne'er have I seen such costly things be-
fore !

(Puts down the casket on a rustic seat, and kneels down in order to adorn herself with the jewels.)

I should just like to see
How they'd look upon me
Those brightly sparkling ear-drops !

(Takes out the ear-rings.)

Ah ! at the bottom of the casket is a
glass :
I there can see myself ! —
But am I not becoming vain ?

(Puts on the ear-rings, rises, and looks at herself in the glass.)

Ah ! I laugh, as I pass, to look into a
glass ;
Is it truly Marguerite, then ?
Is it you ?
Tell me true !
No, no, no, 'tis not you !
No, no, that bright face there reflected
Must belong to a queen !
It reflects some fair queen, whom I greet
as I pass her.
Ah ! could he see me now,
Here, deck'd like this, I vow,
He surely would mistake me,
And for noble lady take me !
I'll try on the rest.
The necklace and the bracelets
I fain would try !

She adorns herself with the bracelets and necklace, then rises.

Heavens ! 'Tis like a hand
That on mine arm doth rest !
Ah ! I laugh, as I pass, to look into a
glass ;
Is it truly Marguerite, then ?
Is it you ?
Tell me true !
No, no, no, 'tis not you !
No, no, that bright face there reflected
Must belong to a queen !
It reflects some fair queen, whom I greet
as I pass her.

O Dieu ! que de bijoux !...est-ce un rêve
charmant
Qui m'éblouit, ou si je veille ! —
Mes yeux n'ont jamais vu de richesse
pareille !...

(Elle place la cassette tout ouverte sur une chaise et s'agenouille pour se parer.)

Si j'osais seulement
Me parer un moment
De ces pendants d'oreille !

(Elle tire des boucles d'oreilles de la cassette.)

Voici tout justement,
Au fond de la cassette,
Un miroir !...comment
N'être pas coquette ?

(Elle se pare des boucles d'oreilles, se lève et se regarde dans le miroir.)

Ah ! je ris de me voir
Si belle en ce miroir !...
Est-ce toi, Marguerite ?
Réponds-moi, réponds vite ! —
Non ! non ! — ce n'est plus toi !
Ce n'est plus ton visage !
C'est la fille d'un roi,
Qu'on salue au passage !
Ah ! s'il était ici !
S'il me voyait ainsi !...
Comme une demoiselle
Il me trouverait belle !...
Achevons la métamorphose !
Il me tarde encor d'essayer
Le bracelet et le collier.

(Elle se pare du collier d'abord, puis du bracelet. — Se levant.)

Dieu ! c'est comme une main qui sur
mon bras se pose !
Ah ! je ris de me voir
Si belle en ce miroir !
Est-ce toi, Marguerite ?
Réponds-moi, réponds vite ! —
Non ! non ! — ce n'est plus toi !
Ce n'est plus ton visage !
C'est la fille d'un roi,
Qu'on salue au passage !...
Ah ! s'il était ici !
S'il me voyait ainsi !...

Oh ! could he see me now,
Here, deck'd like this, I vow,
He surely would mistake me,
And for noble lady take me !

Comme une demoiselle
Il me trouverait belle !...
Ah ! s'il était ici !...

SCENE VII.

MARGUERITE and MARTHA.

Mart. Just heaven ! what is't I see ?
How fair you now do seem !
Why, what has happened ?
Who gave to you these jewels ?

Mar.
(confused).
Alas ! by some mistake
They have been hither brought.

Mart. Why so ?
No, beauteous maiden,
These jewels are for you ;
The gift are they of some enamor'd
  lord.
My husband, I must say,
Was of a less generous turn !

(MEPHISTOPHELES and FAUST enter.)

SCENE VIII.

MEPHISTOPHELES, FAUST, and the before-named.

Mep.
(making a profound bow).
Tell me, I pray, are you Martha Schwerlein ?

Mart. Sir, I am !

Mep.   Pray pardon me,
If thus I venture to present myself.
(Aside, to FAUST.)
You see your presents
Are right graciously received.
(To MARTHA.)
Are you, then, Martha Schwerlein ?

Mart. Sir, I am.

Mep. The news I bring
Is of an unpleasant kind :
Your much-loved spouse is dead,
And sends you greeting.

SCÈNE VII.

MARGUERITE, MARTHE.

Mart.
(entrant par le fond).
Que vois-je, Seigneur Dieu !...comme
vous voilà belle,
Mon ange !...—D'où vous vient ce riche
écrin ?

Mar.
(avec confusion).
                                    Hélas !
On l'aura par mégarde apporté !

Mart.   Que non pas !
Ces bijoux sont á vous, ma chère demoi
selle !
Oui ! c'est là le cadeau d'un seigneur
amoureux !
(Soupirant.)
Mon cher époux jadîs était moins géné
reux !

(MEPHISTOPHELES et FAUST entrent en scène.)

SCÈNE VIII.

Les Mêmes, MEPHISTOPHELES, FAUST.

Mep. Dame Marthe Schwerlein, s'il vous plaît ?

Mart. Qui m'appelle ?

Mep. Pardon d'oser ainsi nous présenter chez
vous !
(Bas à FAUST.)
Vous voyez qu'elle a fait bel accueil aux
bijoux ?
(Haut.)
Dame Marthe Schwerlein ?

Mart. Me voici !

Mep.   La nouvelle
Que j'apporte n'est pas pour vous mettre
en gaité : —
Votre mari, madame, est mort et vous
salue !

Mart. Great heaven !

Mar. Why, what has happened ?

Mep. Stuff !

(MARGUERITE hastily takes off the jewels, and is about to replace them in the casket.)

Mart.   Oh woe ! oh, unexpected news !

Mar.
(aside).

How beats my heart
Now he is near !

Faust
(aside).

The fever of my love
Is lull'd when at her side !

Mep.
(to MARTHA).

Your much-loved spouse is dead,
And sends you greeting !

Mart.
(to MEPHISTOPHELES).

Sent he nothing else to me ?

Mep.
(to MARTHA).

No.   We'll punish him for't ;
Upon this very day
We'll find him a successor.

Faust
(to MARGUERITE).

Wherefore lay aside these jewels ?

Mar.
(to FAUST).

Jewels are not made for me ;
'Tis meet I leave them where they are.

Mep.
(to MARTHA).

Who would not gladly unto
You present the wedding-ring !

Mart.
(aside).
Indeed !
(to MEPHISTOPHELES).
You think so ?

Mep.
(sighing).

Ah me ! ah, cruel fate !

Faust
(to MARGUERITE).

Pray lean upon mine arm :   787

Mart. Ah !... grand Dieu !...

Mar. Qu'est ce donc ?

Mep.   Rien !...

(MARGUERITE baisse les yeux sous le regard de MEPHISTOPHELES, se hâte d'ôter le collier, le bracelet et les pendants d'oreilles et de les remettre dans la cassette.)

Mart.   O calamité !
O nouvelle imprévue !...

ENSEMBLE.

Mar.
(à part).

Malgré moi mon cœur tremble et tres
saille à sa vue !

Faust
(à part).

La fièvre de mes sens se dissipe à sa vue!

Mep.
(à MARTHE).

Votre mari, madame, est mort et vous
salue !

Mart. Ne m'apportez-vous rien de lui !

Mep.   Rien ! ... et, pour le punir, il faut dès
aujourd'hui
Chercher quelqu'un qui le remplace !

Faust
(à MARGUERITE).

Pourquoi donc quitter ces bijoux ?

Mar. Ces bijoux ne sont pas à moi !... Laissez
de grâce !

Mep.
(à MARTHE).

Que ne serait heureux d'échanger avec
vous
La bague d'hyménée ?

Mart.
(à part).
Ah, bah !
(Haut.)
Plait-il ?

Mep.
(soupirant).

Hélas! cruelle destinée !...

Faust
(à MARGUERITE).

Prenez mon bras un moment !

Mar (retiring).	*Mar.* (se défendant).
Leave me, I humbly pray!	Laissez!...Je vous en conjure!...
Mep. (offering his arm to MARTHA).	*Mep.* (de l'autre côté du théâtre, à MARTHE).
Take mine!	Votre bras!...
Mart. (aside).	*Mart.* (à part).
In sooth, a comely knight!	Il est charmant!
(Taking his arm.)	
Mep. (aside).	*Mep.* (à part).
The dame is somewhat tough!	La voisine est un peu mûre!

(MARGUERITE yields her arm to FAUST, and withdraws with him. MEPHISTOPHELES and MARTHA remain together.) — (MARGUERITE abandonne son bras à FAUST et s'éloigne avec MEPHISTOPHELES et MARTHE restent seuls en scène.)

Mart.	And so you are always traveling!	*Mart.*	Ainsi vous voyagez toujours?
Mep.	A hard necessity it is, madame!	*Mep.*	Dure nécessité, madame!
	Alone and loveless. Ah!		Sans ami, sans parents!... sans femme.
Mart.	In youth it matters not so much,	*Mart.*	Cela sied encore aux beaux jours!
	But in late years 'tis sad indeed!		Mais plus tard, combien il est triste
	Right melancholy it is in solitude		De vieillir seul, en égoïste!
	Our olden age to pass!		
Mep.	The very thought doth make me shudder.	*Mep.*	J'ai frémi souvent, j'en conviens,
	But still, alas! what can I do?		Devant cette horrible pensée!
Mart.	If I were you, I'd not delay,	*Mart.*	Avant que l'heure en soit passée!
	But think on't seriously at once.		Digne seigneur, songez-y bien!
Mep.	I'll think on't!	*Mep.*	J'y songerai!
Mart.	At once and seriously!	*Mart.*	Songez-y bien!

(They withdraw. FAUST and MARGUERITE re-enter.) — (Ils sortent. Entre FAUST et MARGUERITE.)

Faust.	Art always thus alone?	*Faust.*	Eh quoi! toujours seule?...
Mar.	My brother is at the wars,	*Mar.*	Mon frère
	My mother dear is dead!		Est soldat; j'ai perdu ma mère;
	By misadventure, too,		Puis ce fut un autre malheur,
	My dear sister have I lost.		Je perdis ma petite sœur!
	Dear sister mine!		Pauvre ange!...Elle m'était bien chère!..
	My greatest happiness was she.		C'était mon unique souci;
	Sad sorrows these;		Que de soins, hélas!... que de peines!
	When our souls with love are filled,		C'est quand nos âmes en sont pleines
	Death tears the loved one from us!		Que la mort nous les prend ainsi!...
	At morn, no sooner did she wake,		Sitôt qu'elle s'éveillait, vite
	Than I was always at her side!		Il fallait que je fusse là!...
	The darling of my life was she!		Elle n'aimait que Marguerite!
	To see her once again,		Pour la voir, la pauvre petite,
	I'd gladly suffer all.		Je reprendrais bien tout cela!...
Faust.	If heaven, in joyous mood,	*Faust*	Si le ciel, avec un sourire,
	Did make her like to thee,		L'avait faite semblable à toi,
	An angel must she indeed have been!		C'était un ange!... Oui, je le crois...

Mar. Thou mock'st me!	*Mar* Vous moquez-vous !...
Faust. Nay, I do love thee!	*Faust.* Non ! je t'admire !
Mar.	*Mar.*
(sighing).	(souriant).
Flatterer ! thou mock'st me !	Je ne vous crois pas
I believe thee not! thou seekest to deceive.	Et de moi tout bas
	Vous riez sans doute !...
No longer will I stay, thy words to hear.	J'ai tort de rester
	Pour vous écouter !...
	Et pourtant j'écoute !...
Faust (to MARGUERITE).	*Faust.* Laisse-moi ton bras !...
	Dieu ne m'a t'il pas
Nay, I do love thee! Stay, oh stay!	Conduit sur ta route ?...
Heaven hath with an angel crown'd my path.	Pourquoi redouter,
Why fear'st thou to listen ?	Hélas ! d'écouter ?...
It is my heart that speaks.	Mon cœur parle ; écoute !...
(Re-enter MEPHISTOPHELES and MARTHA.)	(MEPHISTOPHELES et MARTHE reparaissent.
Mart. (to MEPHISTOPHELES).	*Mart.* Vous n'entendez pas,
	Ou de moi tout bas
Of what now are you thinking ?	Vous riez sans doute !
You heed me not — perchance you mock me.	Avant d'écouter,
Now list to what I say.—	Pourquoi vous hâter
You really must not leave us thus !	De vous mettre en route ?
Mep. (to MARTHA).	*Mep.* Ne m'accusez pas,
	Si je dois, hélas !
Ah, chide me not, if my wanderings I resume.	Me remettre en route.
Suspect me not ; to roam I am compelled!	Faut-il attester
Need I attest how gladly I remain.	Qu'on voudrait rester
I hear but thee alone.	Quand on vous écoute ?
(Night comes on.)	(La nuit commence à tomber.)
Mar. (to FAUST).	*Mar.* (à Faust).
It grows dark,— you must away.	Retirez-vous !...voici la nuit.
Faust (embracing her).	*Faust* (passant son bras autour de la taille de MARGUERITE)
My loved one !	Chère âme !
Mar. Ah! no more !	*Mar.* Laissez-moi !
(Escapes.)	(Elle se dégage et s'enfuit.)
Faust. Ah, cruel one, would'st fly ?	*Faust*
(Pursuing her.)	(la poursuivant).
	Quoi ! méchante !...on me fuit !
Mep. (aside, whilst MARTHA angrily turns her back to him).	*Mep.* (à part, tandis que MARTHE, dépitée, lui tourne le dos)
The matter's getting serious,	L'entretien devient trop tendre !
I must away.	Esquivons nous !
(Conceals himself behind a tree.)	(Il se cache derrière un arbre.)

Mart.

(aside).

What's to be done? he's gone!
What ho, good sir!

(Retires.)

Mep.   Yes, seek for me — that's right.
I really do believe
The aged beldame would
Actually have married Satan!

Faust

(without).

Marguerite!

Mart.

(without).

Good sir!

Mep.   Your servant!

SCENE IX.

MEPHISTOPHELES.

Mep.   'Twas high time!
By night, protected,
In earnest talk of love,
They will return! 'Tis well!
I'll not disturb
Their amorous confabulation!
Night, conceal them in thy darkest shade.
Love, from their fond hearts
Shut out all troublesome remorse.
And ye, O flowers of fragrance subtle,
This hand accurs'd
Doth cause ye all to open!
Bewilder the heart of Marguerite!

(Disappears amid the darkness.)

SCENE X.

FAUST and MARGUERITE.

Mar.   It groweth late, farewell!
Faust.   I but implore in vain.
Let me thy hand take, and clasp it,
And behold but thy face once again,
Illum'd by that pale light,
From yonder moon that shines,   787

Mart.

(à part).

Comment m'y prendre?

(Se retournant.)

Eh bien! il est parti!...Seigneur!...

(Elle s'éloigne.)

Mep.   Oui!   Cours après moi!...
Ouf! cette vieille impitoyable
De force ou de gré, je crois,
Allait épouser le diable!

Faust

(dans la coulisse).

Marguerite!

Mart.

(dans la coulisse.)

Cher seigneur!

Mep.   Serviteur!

SCÈNE IX.

MEPHISTOPHELES.

Mep.

(seul).

Il était temps! sous le feuillage sombre
Voici nos amoureux qui reviennent!...
C'est bien!
Gardons nous de troubler un si doux
    entretien!
O nuit, étends sur eux ton ombre!
Amour, ferme leur âme aux remords
    importuns!
Et vous, fleurs aux subtils parfums,
Epanouissez-vous sous cette main mau
    dite!
Achevez de troubler le cœur de Mar
    guerite!...

(Il s'éloigne et disparaît dans l'ombre.)

SCÈNE X.

FAUST, MARGUERITE.

Mar.   Il se fait tard! adieu!
Faust

(la retenant).

Quoi! je t'implore en vain!
Attends! laisse ma main s'oublier dans
    la tienne!

(S'agenouillant devant MARGUERITE.)

O'er thy beauteous features shedding
Its faint but golden ray.

Mar. Oh, what stillness reigns around,
Oh, ineffable mystery !
Sweetest, happiest feeling,
I list ; a secret voice
Now seems to fill my heart.
Still its tone again resoundeth in my
  bosom.
Leave me awhile, I pray.

(Stoops and picks a daisy.)

Faust. What is it thou doest ?
Mar. This flower I consult.

(She plucks the petals of the daisy.)

Faust

(aside).

What utters she in tones subdued ?
Mar. He loves me ! — no, he loves me not !
He loves me ! — no ! — He loves me !

Faust. Yes, believe thou this flower,
The flower of loves.
To thine heart let it tell
The truth it would teach, —
He loves thee ! Know'st thou not
How happy 'tis to love ?
To cherish in the heart a flame that
  never dies !
To drink forever from the fount of love !
Both. We'll love for ever !

Faust. Oh, night of love ! oh, radiant night !
The bright stars shine above ;
Oh, joy, this is divine !
I love, I do adore thee !

Mar. Mine idol fond art thou !
Speak, speak again !
Thine, thine I'll be ;
For thee I'll gladly die.
Faus Oh, Marguerite !

Laisse-moi, laisse-moi contempler ton
  visage
Sous la pâle clarté
Dont l'astre de la nuit, comme dans un
  nuage,
Caresse ta beauté !...

Mar. O silence ! ô bonheur ! ineffable mystère !
Enivrante langueur !
J'écoute ! ..Et je comprends cette voix
  solitaire
Qui chante dans mon cœur ı
(Dégageant sa main de celle de FAUST.)
Laissez un peu, de grâce !...

(Elle se penche et cueille une marguerite.)

Faust. Qu'est se donc ?
Mar. Un simple jeu !
Laissez un peu !

(Elle effeuille la marguerite.)

Faust. Que dit ta bouche à voix basse !...

Mar. Il m'aime ! — Il ne m'aime pas ! —
Il m'aime ! — pas ! — Il m'aime ! — pas !
— Il m'aime !
Faust. Oui !...crois en cette fleur éclose sous tes
  pas !...
Qu'elle soit pour ton cœur l'oracle du
  ciel même ! ...
Il t'aime !...comprends-tu ce mot sublime
  et doux ?...
Aimer ! porter en nous
Une ardeur toujours nouvelle !...
Nous enivrer sans fin d'une joie éternelle !

Faust et Mar.
Eternelle !...
Faust. O nuit d'amour...ciel radieux !,..
O douces flammes !...
Le bonheur silencieux
Verse les cieux
Dans nos deux âmes !...
Mar. Je veux t'aimer et te chérir !
Parle encore !
Je t'appartiens !...je t'adore !...
Pour toi je veux mourir !...
Faust. Marguerite !...

Mar.

(suddenly tearing herself from FAUST's arms).

                  Ah, leave me !

Faust. Cruel one !

Mar.   Fly hence ! alas! I tremble !
Faust. Cruel one!

Mar.   Pray leave me!

Faust Would'st thou have me leave thee?
      Ah ! see'st thou not my grief ?
      Ah, Marguerite, thou breakest my heart!

Mar.   Go hence! I waver! mercy, pray !
      Fly hence ! alas ! I tremble !
      Break not, I pray, thy Marguerite's heart !

Faust. In pity —
Mar.   If to thee I'm dear,
      I conjure thee, by thy love,
      By this fond heart,
      That too readily its secret hath revealed,
      Yield thee to my prayer, —
      In mercy get thee hence !

(Kneels at the feet of FAUST.)

Faust

(after remaining a few moments silent, gently raising her).

      O fairest child,
      Angel so holy,
      Thou shalt control me,
      Shalt curb my will.
      I obey ; but at morn —
Mar.   Yes, at morn,
      Very early.
Faust. One word at parting.
      Repeat thou lovest me.

Mar.   Adieu !

(Hastens towards the pavilion, then stops short on the threshold.
and wafts a kiss to FAUST.)

Faust. Adieu ! Were it already morn !

Mar.

(se dégageant des bras de FAUST).

Ah !... partez !...

Faust.   Cruelle !..
Me séparer de toi !...
Mar.   Je chancelle !...
Faust. Ah ! cruelle !...

Mar.

(suppliante).

Laissez-moi !...
Faust. Tu veux que je te quitte
      Hélas !...vois ma douleur.
      Tu me brises le cœur,
      O Marguerite !...
Mar.   Partez ! oui, partez vite !
      Je tremble !...hélas !...J'ai peur !
      Ne brisez pas la cœur
      De Marguerite !
Faust. Par pitié !...
Mar.   Si je vous suis chère,
      Par votre amour, par ces aveux
      Que je devais taire,
      Cédez à ma priére !...
      Cédez à mes vœux !

(Elle tombe aux pieds de FAUST.)

Faust

(après un silence, la relevant doucement).

      Divine pureté !...
      Chaste innocence,
      Dont la puissance
      Triomphe de ma volonté !...
      J'obéis !...Mais demain !
Mar.   Oui, demain !...dès l'aurore !...
      Demain toujours !...
Faust.   Un mot encore !..
      Répète-moi ce doux aveu !...
      Tu m'aimes !...
Mar.   Adieu !...

(Elle entre dans le pavillon.)

Faust. Félicité du ciel....Ah....fuyons....

(Il s'élance vers la porte du jardin. MEPHISTOPHELES lui barre a
passage.)

SCENE XI.

Faust, Mephistopheles.

Mep. Fool!

Faust. You overheard us?

Mep. Happily. You have great need, learned Doctor,
To be sent again to school.

Faust. Leave me!

Mep. Deign first to listen for a moment,
To the speech she rehearses to the stars.
Dear master, delay. She opens her window.

(MARGUERITE opens the window of the pavilion, and remains with her head resting on her hand.)

SCENE XII.

The preceding. MARGUERITE.

Mar. He loves me! Wildly beats my heart!
The night-bird's song,
The evening breeze,
All nature's sounds together say,
" He loves thee!"
Ah! sweet, sweet indeed
Now is this life to me!
Another world it seems;
The very ecstasy of love is this!
With to-morrow's dawn,
Haste thee, oh dear one,
Haste thee to return! Yes, come!

Faust. (rushing to the window, and grasping her hand).
Marguerite!

Mar.   Ah!

Mep.
(mockingly).
Ho! ho!

(MARGUERITE, overcome, allows her head to fall on FAUST's shoulder. MEPHISTOPHELES opens the door of the garden, and departs, laughing derisively. The curtain falls.)

ACT IV.

—

SCENE I.

Marguerite's Room.

SIEBEL and MARGUERITE.

Sie.
(quietly approaching).
Marguerite!

Mar. Siebel!

SCÈNE XI.

FAUST, MEPHISTOPHELES.

Mep. Tête folle!...

Faust. Tu nous écoutais.

Mep.   Par bonheur.
Vous auriez grand besoin, docteur,
Qu'on vous renvoyât à l'école.

Faust. Laisse-moi.

Mep.   Daignez seulement
Ecouter un moment
Ce qu'elle va conter aux étoiles, cher maître.
Tenez; elle ouvre sa fenêtre.

(MARGUERITE ouvre la fenêtre du pavillon et s'y appuie un moment en silence, la tête entre les mains.)

SCÈNE XII.

Les mêmes. MARGUERITE.

Mar. Il m'aime ;...quel trouble en mon cœur,
L'oiseau chante!...le vent murmure!...
Toutes les voix de la nature
Semblent me répéter en chœur :
Il t'aime!... — Ah! qu'il est doux de vivre!...
Le ciel me sourit ;...l'air m'enivre!...
Est-ce de plaisir et d'amour
Que la feuille tremble et palpite ?...
Demain ?... — Ah! presse ton retour,
Cher bien-aimé!...viens!...

Faust
(s'élançant vers la fenêtre et saisissant la main de MARGUERITE).
Marguerite!...

Mar. Ah!...

Mep. Ho! ho!

(MARGUERITE rest un moment interdite et laisse tomber sa tête sur l'épaule de FAUST; MEPHISTOPHELES ouvre la porte du jardin et sort en ricanant. La toile tombe.)

ACTE QUATRIÈME.

—

SCÈNE PREMIÈRE.

La Chambre de Marguerite.

MARGUERITE, SIEBEL.

Sie.
(s'approchant doucement de MARGUERITE).
Marguerite!

Mar.   Siebel!...

Sie.　　　　　　What, weeping still!

Mar.　Alas! thou alone art kind to me.

'Sie.　A mere youth am I.
And yet I have a manly heart,
And I will sure avenge thee.
The seducer's life shall forfeit pay.

Mar.　　　　　　Whose life?

Sie.　Need I name him?　The wretch
Who thus hast deserted thee!

Mar.　In mercy, speak not thus!

Sie.　Dost love him still, then?

Mar.　Ay, I love him still!
But not to you, good Siebel, should I re-
　　peat this tale.

Sie.

I.

When all was young, and pleasant May
　　was blooming,
I, thy poor friend, took part with thee
　　in play;
Now that the cloud of autumn dark is
　　glooming,
Now is for me, too, mournful the day.
Hope and delight have passed from life
　　away.

II.

We were not born with true love to trifle,
Nor born to part because the wind blows
　　cold.
What though the storm the summer gar-
　　den rifle,
Oh, Marguerite! oh, Marguerite!
Still on the bough is left a leaf of gold.

Mar　Bless you, my friend, your sympathy is
　　sweet.
The cruel ones who wrong me thus
Cannot close against me
The gates of the holy temple.
Thither will I go to pray
For him and for our child.

(*Exit.* SIEBEL *follows slowly after.*)

Sie.　Encor des pleurs.

Mar.

　　　　　　　(se levant).

　　　　　　　　　　　　Hélas!
Vous seul ne me maudissez pas.

Sie.　Je ne suis qu'un enfant, mais j'ai le cœur
　　d'un homme
Et je vous vengerai de son lâche
　　abandon!
Je le tuerai!

Mar.　Qui donc?

Sie.　　　　Faut-il que je le nomme?
L'ingrat qui vous trahit!...

Mar.　　　　Non!...taisez-vous?...

Sie.　　　　　　　　　Pardon!
Vous l'aimez encore?

Mar　Oui!... toujours!
Mais ce n'est pas à vous de plaindre
　　mon ennui
J'ai tort, Siebel, de vous parler de lui

Sie.

I.

Si la bonheur à sourire t'invite,
Joyeux alors, je sens un doux émoi;
Si la douleur t'accable, Marguerite,
O Marguerite, je pleure alors,
Je pleure comme toi!

II.

Comme deux fleurs sur une même tige,
Notre destin suivant le même cours,
De tes chagrins en fière je m'afflige,
O Marguerite, comme une sœur,
Je t'aimerai toujours!

Mar.　Soyez béni, Siebel! votre amitié m'est
　　douce!
Ceux dont la main cruelle me repousse,
N'ont pas fermé pour moi la porte du
　　saint lieu;
J'y vais pour mon enfant...et pour lui
　　prier Dieu!

(*Elle sort;* SIEBEL *la suit à pas lents.*)

SCENE II.

Interior of a Church.

MARGUERITE, then MEPHISTOPHELES.

(Women enter the church and cross the stage. MARGUERITE enters after them, and kneels.)

Mar.   O heaven!
Permit thy lowly handmaiden
To prostrate herself before thine altar.

Mep.   No, thou shalt not pray!
Spirits of evil, haste ye at my call,
And drive this woman hence!

Cho. of Demons.   Marguerite!

Mar.   Who calls me?

Cho.   Marguerite!

Mar.   I tremble!— oh, heaven!
My last hour is surely nigh!

(The tomb opens and discloses MEPHISTOPHELES, who bends over o MARGUERITE's ear.)

Mep.   Remember the glorious days
When an angel's wings
Protected thy young heart.
To church thou camest then to worship,
Nor hadst thou then sinned 'gainst
heaven.
Thy prayers then issued
From an unstained heart
And on the wings of faith
Did rise to the Creator.
Hear'st thou their call?
'Tis hell that summons thee!
Hell claims thee for its own!
Eternal pain, and woe, and tribulation,
Will be thy portion!

Mar.   Heaven! what voice is this
That in the shade doth speak to me?
What mysterious tones are these!

Religious Cho.   When the last day shall have
come,
The cross in heaven shall shine forth,
This world to dust shall crumble.

SCÈNE II

L'Eglise.

MARGUERITE, puis MEPHISTOPHELES.

(Quelques femmes traversent la scène et entrent dans l'eglise. MARGUERITE entre après elles et s'agenouille.)

Mar.   Seigneur, daignez permettre à votre
humble servante
De s'agenouiller devant vous!

Mep.   Non!...tu ne prieras pas!...Frappez-la
d'épouvante!
Esprits du mal, accourez tous!

Voix de Démons Invisibles.   Marguerite!

Mar.   Qui m'appelle?

Voix.   Marguerite!

Mar.   Je chancelle!
Je meurs!— Dieu bon! Dieu clément!
Est-ce déjà l'heure du châtiment?

(MEPHISTOPHELES parait derrière un pilier et se penche à l'oreille de MARGUERITE.)

Mep.   Souviens-toi du passé, quand sous l'aile
des anges,
Abritant ton bonheur,
Tu venais dans son temple, enchantant
ses louanges,
Adorer le Seigneur!
Lorsque tu bégayais une chaste prière
D'une timide voix,
Et portais dans ton cœur les baisers de
ta mère,
Et Dieu tout à la fois!
Écoute ces clameurs! c'est l'enfer qui
t'appelle!...
C'est l'enfer qui te suit!
C'est l'éternel remords et l'angoisse
éternelle
Dans l'éternelle nuit!

Mar.   Dieu! quelle est cette voix qui me parle
dans l'ombre?
Dieu tout puissant!
Quel voile sombre
Sur moi descend!...

Chant Religieux
(accompagné par les orgues).

Quand du Seigneur le jour luira,
Sa croix au ciel resplendira,
Et l'univers s'écroulera...

Mar.	Ah me! more fearful still becomes their song.
Mep.	No pardon hath heaven left for thee! For thee e'en heaven hath no more light!
Religious Cho.	What shall we say unto high heav'n? Who shall protection find When innocence such persecution meets?
Mar.	A heavy weight my breast o'erpowers,— I can no longer breathe!
Mep.	Nights of love, farewell! Ye days of joy, adieu! Lost, lost for aye art thou!
Mar. and Cho.	Heav'n! hear thou the prayer Of a sad, broken heart! A bright ray send thou From the starry sphere Her anguish to allay!
Mep.	Marguerite, lost, lost art thou!
Mar.	Ah!

(He disappears.)

SCENE III.

The Street.

VALENTINE, Soldiers, then SIEBEL.

Cho.	Our swords we will suspend Over the paternal hearth; At length we have returned. Sorrowing mothers no longer Will bewail their absent sons.

SCENE IV.

VALENTINE and SIEBEL.

Val.	(perceiving SIEBEL, who enters). Ah, Siebel, is it thou?
Sie.	Dear Valentine!
Val.	Come, then, to my heart!

(Embracing him.)

And Marguerite?

Mar.	Hélas !...ce chant pieux est plus terrible encore !...
Mep.	Non! Dieu pour toi n'a plus de pardon! Le ciel pour toi n'a plus d'aurore!
Cho. Religieux.	Que dirai-je alors au Seigneur? Où trouverai-je un protecteur, Quand l'innocent n'est pas sans peur!
Mar.	Ah! ce chant m'ètouffe et m'oppresse! Je suis dans un cercle de fer!
Mep.	Adieu les nuits d'amour et les jours pleins d'ivresse! A toi malheur! A toi l'enfer!
Mar. et le Cho. Religieux.	Seigneur, accueillez la prière Des cœurs malheureux! Qu'un rayon de votre lumière Descende sur eux!
Mep.	Marguerite! Sois maudite! A toi l'enfer!
Mar.	Ah!

(Il disparait.)

SCÈNE III.

La Rue.

VALENTIN, Soldats, puis SIEBEL.

Cho.	Déposons les armes; Dans nos foyers enfin nous voici revenus Nos mères en larmes, Nos mères et nos sœurs ne nous attendront plus.

SCÈNE IV.

VALENTIN, SIEBEL.

Val.	(apercevant SIEBEL). Eh! parbleu! c'est Siebel!
Sie.	Cher Valentin...
Val.	Viens vite! Viens dans mes bras.

(Il l'embrasse.)

Et Marguerite?

Sie.	(confused).
	Perhaps she's yonder at the church.
Val.	She doubtless prays for my return.
	Dear girl, how pleased
	She'll be to hear me tell
	My warlike deeds !
Cho.	Glory to those who in battle fall,
	Their bright deeds we can with pride recall.
	May we, then, honor and fame acquire,
	Their glorious deeds our hearts will inspire !
	For that dear native land where we first drew breath,
	Her sons, at her command proudly brave e'en death.
	At their sacred demand who on us depend,
	Our swords we will draw, their rights to defend.
	Homeward our steps we now will turn, —
	Joy and peace await us there !
	On, on at once, nor loiter here ;
	On, then, our lov'd ones to embrace, —
	Affection calls, fond love doth summon us,
	Yes, many a heart will beat
	When they our tale shall hear.
Val.	Come, Siebel, we'll to my dwelling
	And o'er a flask of wine hold converse.
	(Approaching MARGUERITE's house.)
Sie.	Nay, enter not !
Val.	Why not, I pray ? — Thou turn'st away ;
	Thy silent glance doth seek the ground —
	Speak, Siebel — what hath happened ?
Sie.	(with an effort.)
	No ! I cannot tell thee !
Val.	What mean'st thou ?
	(Rushing toward house.)
Sie.	(withholding him.)
	Hold, good Valentine, take heart !

Sie.	(avec embarras).
	Elle est à l'église, je crois.
Val.	Oui, priant Dieu pour moi...
	Chère sœur, tremblante et craintive,
	Comme elle va prêter une oreille attentive
	Au récit de nos combats !
Cho.	Gloire immortelle
	De nos aïeux,
	Sois-nous fidèle
	Mourons comme eux !
	Et sous ton aile,
	Soldats vainqueurs,
	Dirige nos pas, enflamme nos cœurs !
	Vers nos foyers hâtons le pas !
	On nous attend ; la paix est faite !
	Plus de soupirs ! ne tardons pas !
	Notre pays nous tend les bras !
	L'amour nous rit ! l'amour nous fête !
	Et plus d'un cœur frémit tout bas
	Au souvenir de nos combats !
	L'amour nous rit ! l'amour nous fête !
	El plus d'un cœur frémit tout bas
	Au souvenir de nos combats !
	Gloire immortelle.
Val.	Allons, Siebel ! entrons dans la maison !
	Le verre en main, tu me feras raison ;
Sie.	(vivement).
	Non ! n'entre pas !
Val.	Pourquoi ?.. — tu détournes la tête ?
	Ton regard fuit le mien ?.. — Siebel, explique-toi !
Sie.	Eh bien ! — non, je ne puis !
Val.	Que veux-tu dire ?
	(Il se dirige vers la maison.)
Sie.	(l'arretant).
	Arrête !
	Sois clément, Valentin !

Val.   What is't thou mean'st !

(Enters the house.)

Sie.   Forgive her !
Shield her, gracious Heaven !

(Approaches the church. FAUST and MEPHISTOPHELES enter at the back; MEPHISTOPHELES carries a guitar.)

SCENE V.

FAUST and MEPHISTOPHELES.

(FAUST goes towards MARGUERITE'S house, but hesitates.)

Mep.   Why tarry ye ?
Let us enter the house.

Faust.   Peace ! I grieve to think that I
Brought shame and sorrow hither.

Mep.   Why see her again, then, after leaving her ?
Some other sight might be more pleasing.
To the sabbath let us on.

Faust

(sighing).

Oh, Marguerite !

Mep.   My advice, I know,
Availeth but little
Against thy stubborn will.
Doctor, you need my voice !

(Throwing back his mantle, and accompanying himself on the guitar.)

I.

Maiden, now in peace reposing,
From thy sleep awake,
Hear my voice with love imploring,
Wilt thou pity take ?
But beware how thou confidest
Even in thy friend,
Ha ! ha ! ha !
If not for thy wedding finger
He a ring doth send.

II.

Yes, sweet maiden, I implore thee,—
Oh, refuse not this,—

Val.

(furieux).

Laisse-moi ! laissi-moi !

(Il entre dans la maison.)

Sie.   Pardonne-lui !

(Seul.)

Mon Dieu ! je vous implore !
Mon Dieu, protégez-là.

(Il s'éloigne; MEPHISTOPHELES et FAUST entrent en scène; MEPHISTOPHELES tient une guitare à la main.)

SCÈNE V.

FAUST, MEPHISTOPHELES.

(FAUST se dirige vers la maison de MARGUERITE et s'arrête.'

Mep.   Qu'attendez-vous encore ?
Entrons dans la maison.

Faust.   Tais-toi, maudit !...j'ai peur
De rapporter ici la honte et le malheur,

Mep.   A quoi bon la revoir, après l'avoir quitté ?
Notre présence ailleurs serait bien mieux fêtée !
La sabbat nous attend !

Faust.   Marguerite !

Mep.   Je vois
Que mes avis sont vains et que l'amour l'emporte !
Mais, pour vous faire ouvrir la porte,
Vous avez grand besoin du secours de ma voix !

(FAUST, pensif, se tient à l'écart. MEPHISTOPHELES s'accompagne sur sa guitare.)

I.

" Vous qui faites l'endormie,
N'entendez-vous pas,
O Catherine, ma mie,
Ma voix et mes pas...? "
Ainsi ton galant t'appelle,
Et ton cœur l'en croit !
N'ouvre ta porte, ma belle,
Que la bague au doigt !

II.

" Catherine que j'adore,
Pourquoi refuser

Smile on him who doth adore thee,
Bless him with thy kiss.
But beware how thou confidest,
Even in thy friend,
Ha ! ha ! ha !
If not for thy wedding finger
He a ring doth send.

(VALENTINE rushes from the house.)

SCENE VI.

VALENTINE and the before-named.

Val. Good sir, what want you here ?

Mep. My worthy fellow, it was not to you
That we addressed our serenade !

Val. My sister, perhaps, would more gladly
hear it !

(VALENTINE draws his sword, and breaks MEPHISTOPHELES' guitar.)

Faust. His sister !

Mep.
(to VALENTINE).
Why this anger ?
Do ye not like my singing ?

Val. Your insults cease !
From which of ye must I demand
Satisfaction for this foul outrage ?
Which of ye must I now slay ?

(FAUST draws his sword.)
'Tis he !

Mep. Your mind's made up, then !
On, then, doctor, at him, pray !

Val. Oh, heaven, thine aid afford,
Increase my strength and courage,
That in his blood my sword
May wipe out this fell outrage !

Faust. What fear is this unnerves my arm ?
Why falters now my courage ?
Dare I to take his life,
Who but resents an outrage ?

Mep. His wrath and his courage
I laugh alike to scorn !
To horse, then, for his last journey
The youth right soon will take !

A l'amant qui vous implore
Un si doux baiser ?..."
Ainsi ton galant supplie,
Et ton cœur l'en croit !
Ne donne un baiser, ma mie,
Que la bague au doigt !

(VALENTIN sort de la maison.)

SCÈNE VI.

Les mêmes. VALENTIN.

Val. Que voulez-vous, messieurs ?

Mep. Pardon ! mon camarade,
Mais ce n'est pas pour vous qu'était la
sérénade !

Val. Ma sœur l'écouterait mieux que moi, je
le sais !

(Il degaine et brise la guitare de MEPHISTOPHELES d'un coup d'épée.)

Faust. Sa sœur !

Mep.
(à VALENTIN).
Quelle mouche vous pique ?
Vous n'aimez donc pas le musique ?

Val. Assez d'outrage !...assez !...
A qui de vous dois-je demander compte
De mon malheur et de ma honte ?...
Qui de vous deux doit tomber sous mes
coups ?...
(FAUST tire son épée.)
C'est lui !...

Mep. Vous le voulez ?...— Allons, docteu , à
vous !...

Val. Redouble, ô Dieu puissant,
Ma force et mon courage !
Permets que dans son sang
Je lave mon outrage !

Faust
(à part).
Terrible et frémissant,
Il glace mon courage !
Dois-je verser le sang
Du frère que j'outrage ?...

Mep. De son air menaçant,
De son aveugle rage,
Je ris !...mon bras puissant
Va détourner l'orage !..

Val.
(taking in his hand the medallion suspended round his neck).
Thou gift of Marguerite,
Which till now hath ever saved me,
I'll no more of thee — I cast thee hence !
Accursed gift, I throw thee from me !
(Throws it angrily away.)

Mep.
(aside).
Thou'll repent it !

Val.
(to FAUST).
Come on, defend thyself !

Mep.
(to FAUST, in a whisper).
Stand near to me, and attack him only ;
I'll take care to parry !
(They fight.)

Val.
(falling).
Ah !

Mep.
Behold our hero,
Lifeless on the ground !
Come, we must hence — quick, fly !
(Exit, dragging FAUST after him.)

SCENE VII.

(Enter Citizens, with lighted torches; afterwards SIEBEL and MARGUERITE.)

Cho.
Hither, hither, come this way —
They're fighting here hard by !
See, one has fallen ;
The unhappy man lies prostrate there.
Ah ! he moves — yes, still he breathes ;
Quick, then, draw nigh
To raise and succor him !

Val.
'Tis useless, cease these vain laments.
Too often have I gazed
On death, to heed it
When my own time hath come !

(MARGUERITE appears at the back, supported by SIEBEL.)

Mar.
(advancing, and falling on her knees at VALENTINE's side).

Val.
Valentine ! ah, Valentine !
(thrusting her from him).
Marguerite !
What would'st thou here ? — away !

Val.
(tirant de son sein la médaille que lui a donnée MARGUERITE).
Et toi qui préservas mes jours,
Toi qui me viens de Marguerite,
Je ne veux plus de ton secours,
Médaille maudite !..
(Il jette la médaille loin de lui.)

Mep.
(à part).
Tu t'en repentiras !

Val.
En garde !...et défends-toi !...

Mep.
(à FAUST).
Serrez-vous contre moi !...
Et poussez seulement, cher docteur !..
moi, je pare.

Val. Ah !
(VALENTIN tombe.)

Mep.
Voici notre héros étendu sur le sable !...
Au large maintenant ! au large !...

(Il entraine FAUST. Arrivent MARTHE et des bourgeois portant des torches.)

SCÈNE VII.

VALENTIN, MARTHE, Bourgeois, puis SIEBEL et MARGUERITE.

Mart. et les Bourg.
Par ici !...
Par ici, mes amis ! on se bat dans la
rue !...—
L'un d'eux est tombé là ! — Regardez...
le voici !...
Il n'est pas encore mort !...— on dirait
qu'il remue !... —
Vite, approchez !...il faut le secourir !

Val.
(se soulevant avec effort).
Merci !
De vos plaintes, faites-moi grace !..
J'ai vu, morbleu ! la mort en face
Trop souvent pour en avoir peur !...

(MARGUERITE parait au fond soutenue par SIEBEL.)

Mar. Valentin !...Valentin !...
(Elle écarte la foule et tombe à genoux près de VALENTIN.)

Val. Marguerite ! ma sœur !...
(Il la repousse.)
Que me veux-tu ?...va-t'en

Mar.	O heav'n !
Val.	For her I die ! Poor fool ! I thought to chastise her seducer !
Cho.	(in a low voice, pointing to MARGUERITE). He dies, slain by her seducer !
Mar.	Fresh grief is this ! ah, bitter punishment.
Sie.	Have pity on her, pray !
Val.	(supported by those around him). Marguerite, give ear awhile ; That which was decreed Hath duly come to pass. Death comes at its good pleasure : All mortals must obey its behest. But for you intervenes an evil life ! Those white hands will never work more ; The labors and sorrows that others employ, Will be forgotten in hours of joy. Darest thou live, ingrate ? Darest thou still exist ? Go ! Shame overwhelm thee ! Remorse follow thee ! At length *thy* hour will sound. Die ! And if God pardons thee hereafter, So may this life be a continual curse !
Cho.	Terrible wish ! Unchristian thought ! In thy last sad hour, unfortunate ! Think of thy own soul's welfare. Forgive, if thou wouldst be forgiven
Val.	Marguerite ; I curse you ! Death awaits me. I die by your hand ; but I die a soldier.
Cho.	(Dies.) God receive thy spirit ! God pardon thy sins !

(Curtain.)

Mar.	O Dieu !...
Val.	Je meurs par elle !... J'ai sottement Cherché querelle A son amant !
La Foule	(à demi voix, montrant MARGUERITE). Il meurt, frappé par son amant !
Mar.	Douleur cruelle ! O châtiment !...
Sie.	(à VALENTIN). Grâce pour elle !... Soyez clément !
Val.	(soutenu par ceux qui l'entourent). Ecoute-moi bien, Marguerite !... Ce qui doit arriver arrive à l'heure dite ! La mort nous frappe quand il faut, Et chacun obéit aux volontés d'en haut ! .. —Toi !...te voilà dans la mauvaise voie ! Tes blanches mains ne travailleront plus ! Tu renîras, pour vivre dans la joie, Tous les devoirs et toutes les vertus ! Va ! la honte t'accable Le remords suit tes pas ! Mais enfin l'heure sonne ! Meurs ! et si Dieu te pardonne, Soit maudite ici-bas.
La Foule.	O terreur, ô blasphème A ton heure suprême, infortuné, Songe, hélas, a toi-même, Pardonne, si tu veux tre un jour pardonné !
Val.	Marguerite ! Soit maudite ! La mort t'attend sur ton grabat ! Moi je meurs de ta main Et je tombe en soldat !
La Foule.	(Il meurt.) Que le Seigneur ait son âme Et pardonne au pêcheur.

(La toile tombe.)

ACT V.

SCENE I.

A Prison.

MARGUERITE asleep; FAUST and MEPHISTOPHELES.

Faust. Go ! get thee hence !

Mep. The morn appears, black night is on the wing.

Quickly prevail upon Marguerite to follow thee.

The jailer soundly sleeps — here is the key,

Thine own hand now can ope the door.

Faust. Good ! Get thee gone !

Mep. Be sure thou tarry not !

I will keep watch without.

(Exit.)

Faust. With grief my heart is wrung !

Oh, torture ! oh, source of agony

And remorse eternal ! Behold her there

The good, the beauteous girl,

Cast like a criminal

Into this vile dungeon ;

Grief must her reason have disturbed,

For, with her own hand, alas !

Her child she slew !

Oh, Marguerite !

Mar.

(waking).

His voice did sure

Unto my heart resound.

(Rises.)

Faust. Marguerite !

Mar. At that glad sound it wildly throbs again

Amid the mocking laugh of demons.

Faust. Marguerite !

Mar. Now am I free. He is here. It is his voice.

Yes, thou art he whom I love.

Fetters, death, have no terrors for me ;

Thou hast found me. Thou hast returned.

Now am I saved ! Now rest I on thy heart !

ACTE CINQUIÈME.

SCÈNE PREMIÈRE.

La Prison.

MARGUERITE, endormie, FAUST, MEPHISTOPHELES.

Faust. Va t'en !

Mep. Le jour va luire. — On dresse l'échafaud !

Décide sans retard Marguerite à te suivre.

Le geôlier dort. — Voici les clefs. — Il faut

Que ta main d'homme la délivre.

Faust. Laisse-moi !

Mep. Hâtez-vous. — Moi, je veille au dehors.

(Il sort.)

Faust. Mon cœur est pénétré d'épouvante ! — O torture

O source de regrets et d'éternels remords !

C'est elle ! — La voici, la douce créature

Jetée au fond d'une prison

Comme une vile criminelle !

Le desespoir égara sa raison

Son pauvre enfant, ô Dieu ! tué par elle !

Marguerite !

Mar.

(s'eveillant).

Ah ! c'est lui ! — c'est lui ! le bien-aimé !

(Elle se lève.)

A son appel mon cœur s'est ranimé.

Faust. Marguerite !

Mar. Au milieu de vos éclats de rire,

Démons qui m'entourez, j'ai reconnu sa voix !

Faust. Marguerite !

Mar. Sa main, sa douce main m'attire !

Je suis libre ! Il est là ! je l'entends ! je la vois.

Oui, c'est toi, je t'aime,

Les fers, la mort même

Ne me font plus peur !

Tu m'as retrouvé,

Me voilà sauvé !

C'est toi, je suis sur ton cœur !

Faust. Yes, I am here, and I love thee,	*Faust.* Oui, c'est moi, je t'aime,
In spite of the efforts of yon mocking demon.	Malgré l'effort même
	Du démon moqueur,
(FAUST attempts to draw her with him. She gently disengages herself from his arms.)	Je t'ai retrouvé,
	Te voilà sauvé,
	C'est moi, viens sur mon cœur !
Mar. Stay ! this is the spot	*Mar.*
Where one day thou didst meet me.	(se dégageant doucement de ses bras).
Thine hand sought mine to clasp.	Attends !...voici la rue
"Will you not permit me, my fairest demoiselle,	Où tu m'as vue
To offer you my arm, and clear for you the way?"	Pour la première fois !...
	Où votre main osa presque effleurer mes doigts !
"No, sir. I am no demoiselle, neither am I fair;	"— Ne permettez-vous pas, ma belle demoiselle,
And I have no need to accept your offered arm."	Qu'on vous offre le bras pour faire le chemin?"
	"— Non, monsieur, je ne suis demoiselle ni belle,
	Et je n'ai pas besoin qu'on me donne la main !"
Faust. What is't she says? Ah me ! Ah me !	*Faust.* Oui, mon cœur se souvient ! — Mais fuyons ! l'heure passe !
Mar. And the garden I love is here,	*Mar.* Et voici le jardin charmant,
Odorous of myrtle and roses,	Perfumé de myrte et de rose,
Where every eve thou camest in	Où chaque soir discrètement
With careful step, as night was falling.	Tu pénétrais à la nuit close.
Faust. Come, Marguerite, let us fly !	*Faust.* Viens, Marguerite, fuyons !
Mar. No ! stay a moment !	*Mar.* Non, reste encore.
Faust. O heav'n, she does not understand !	*Faust.* O ciel, elle ne m'entends pas !

SCENE II.

MEPHISTOPHELES and the preceding.

SCÈNE II.

Les mêmes. MEPHISTOPHELES.

Mep. Away at once, while yet there's time !	*Mep.* Alerte ! alerte ! ou vous êtes perdus !
If longer ye delay,	Si vous tardez encor, je ne m'en mêle plus !
Not e'en my power can save ye.	
Mar. See'st thou yon demon crouching in the shade?	*Mar.* Le démon ! le démon ! — Le vois-tu?... là ..dans l'ombre
His deadly glance is fixed on us;	Fixant sur nous son œil de feu !
Quick ! drive him from these sacred walls.	Que nous veut-il ? — Chasse-le du saint lieu !
Mep. Away ! leave we this spot,	*Mep.* L'aube depuis longtemps a percé la nuit sombre,
The dawn hath appeared;	La jour est levé
Hear'st thou not the fiery chargers,	

As with sonorous hoof they paw the
    ground ?
<small>(Endeavoring to drag FAUST with him.)</small>

Haste ye, then, — perchance there yet
Is time to save her !

Mar.   O Heaven, I crave thy help !
    Thine aid alone I do implore !
<small>(Kneeling.)</small>

    Holy angels, in heaven bless'd,
    My spirit longs with ye to rest !
    Great Heaven, pardon grant, I implore
      thee,
    For soon shall I appear before thee !

Faust.   Marguerite ! Follow me, I implore !

Mar.   Holy angels, in heaven bless'd,
    My spirit longs with ye to rest !
    Great Heaven, pardon grant, I implore
      thee,
    For soon shall I appear before thee !

Faust.   O Marguerite !
Mar.   Why that glance with anger fraught ?
Faust.   Marguerite !
Mar.   What blood is that which stains thy
    hand !
    Away ! thy sight doth cause me horror !
<small>(Falls.)</small>

Mep.   Condemned !
Cho.   Saved !
    Christ hath arisen !
    Christ hath arisen !
    Christ is born again !
    Peace and felicity
    To all disciples of the Master !
    Christ hath arisen !

<small>(The prison walls open. The soul of MARGUERITE rises towards heaven. FAUST gazes despairingly after her, then falls on his knees and prays. MEPHISTOPHELES turns away, barred by the shining sword of an archangel.)</small>

<small>END OF THE OPERA.</small>

De leur pied sonore
J'entends nos chevaux frapper le pavé.
<small>(Cherchant à entraîner FAUST.)</small>

Viens ! sauvons-la. Peut-être il en est
    temps encore !

Mar.   Mon Dieu, protégez-moi ! — Mon Dieu,
    je vous implore !
<small>(Tombant à genoux.)</small>

    Anges purs ! anges radieux !
    Portez mon âme au sein des cieux !
    Dieu juste, à toi je m'abandonne !
    Dieu bon, je suis à toi ! — pardonne !

Faust.   Viens, suis-moi ! je le veux !

Mar.   Anges purs, anges radieux !
    Portez mon âme au sein des cieux !
    Dieu juste, à toi je m'abandonne !
    Dieu bon, je suis à toi ! — pardonne !
    Anges purs, anges radieux !
    Portez mon âme au sein des cieux !
<small>(Bruit au dehors.)</small>

Faust.   Marguerite !
Mar.   Pourquoi ce regard menaçant ?
Faust.   Marguerite !
Mar.   Pourquoi ces mains rouges de sang?
<small>(Le repoussant.)</small>

    Va !...tu me fais horreur !
<small>(Elle tombe sans mouvement.)</small>

Mep.   Jugée !
Cho. des Anges.   Sauvée ! Christ est ressuscité !
    Christ vient de renaître !
    Paix et félicité
    Aux disciples du Maître !
    Christ vient de renaître.
    Christ est ressuscité !

<small>(Les murs de la prison se sont ouverts. L'âme de MARGUERITE s'élève dans les cieux. FAUST la suit des yeux avec désespoir; il tombe à genoux et prie. MEPHISTOPHELES est à demi renversé sous l'épée lumineuse de l'archange.)</small>

<small>FIN.</small>

ACT I: A MOI LES PLAISIRS (OH, I WOULD HAVE PLEASURE)

Allegro.

FAUST

ACT II. WALTZ AND CHORUS

ACT III: O NUIT D'AMOUR (O NIGHT OF LOVE)

ACT IV: SOLDIERS CHORUS

ACT V: ANGES PUR, ANGES RADIEUX (HOLY ANGELS, IN HEAVEN BLEST)

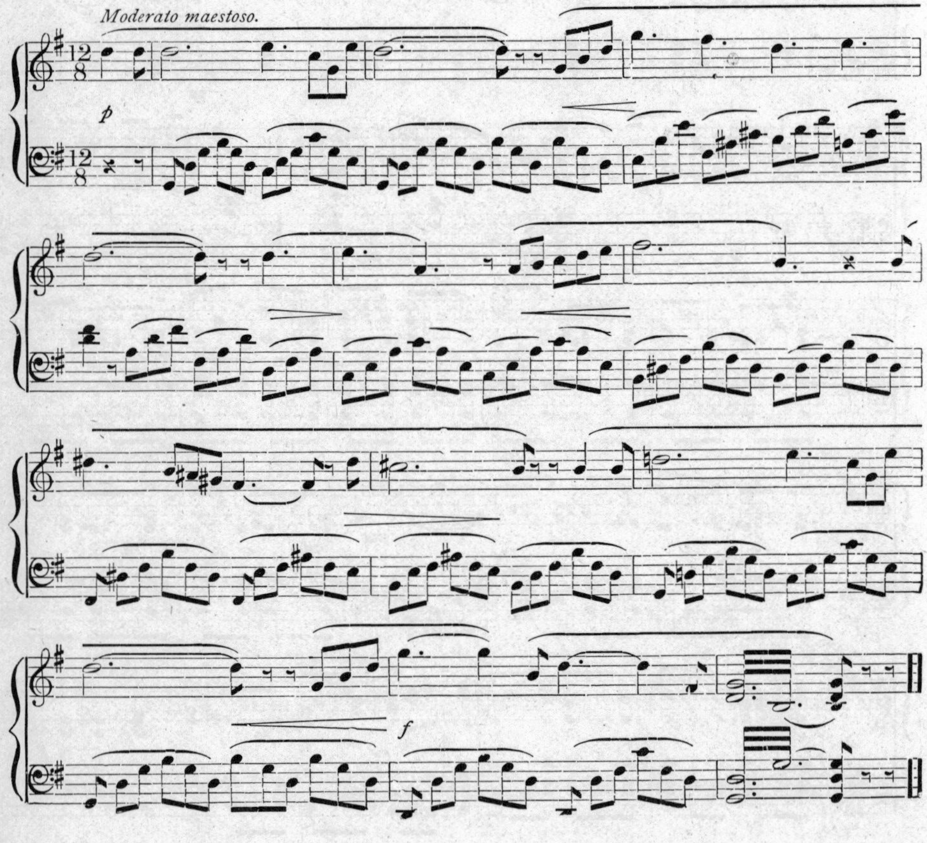

Moderato maestoso.

ROMEO AND JULIET

by

CHARLES GOUNOD

CHARACTERS OF THE DRAMA

JULIET	. . .	Soprano	MERCUTIO	. . .	Baritone
STEPHANO	. . .	Soprano	PARIS	. . . .	Baritone
GERTRUDE	. . .	Mezzo Soprano	GREGORIO	. . .	Baritone
ROMEO	. . . .	Tenor	CAPULET	. . .	Basso Cantante
TYBALT	. . . .	Tenor	FRIAR LAWRENCE	. .	Bass
BENVOLIO	. . .	Tenor	THE DUKE	. . .	Bass

Guests of the Capulets; Relatives and retainers of the Capulets and Montagues.

SCENE, VERONA

ACT I.—Capulet's Palace. ACT II.—The Garden of Juliet. ACT III.—The Cell of Friar Lawrence; then a Public Square before Capulet's Palace. ACT IV.—Juliet's Chamber. ACT V.—The Tomb of the Capulets.

NOTE

The opera of "Roméo et Juliette," which was Charles Gounod's next contribution to the lyric drama after "Faust," ranks likewise next to "Faust" in merit and popular success. The excellence of the libretto of the latter opera naturally led Gounod to choose its makers, when he conceived the idea of writing a lyric work which would follow the famous drama of Shakespeare. The classic love story had tempted many composers before Gounod, but in spite of its somewhat obvious faults Gounod's musical version of the tragedy is the only one to have obtained a hold upon the public taste. First performed at the Théâtre Lyrique at Paris, April 27, 1867, it has ever been a favorite with the Parisian public, and in recent years, sung by a remarkable cast of singers, the opera has been received with marked favor in American cities.

STORY OF THE ACTION

The famous story of Romeo and Juliet scarcely needs to be rehearsed for English-speaking people; but an outline of the plot as rearranged by Barbier and Carré will be helpful to operagoers. The overture contains a vocal prologue, sung by all the characters of the drama, which refers to the unhappy feud between the two houses.

ACT I. This act takes place in the palace of the Capulets. A ball is in progress in honor of Juliet, the daughter of the house. After she is formally introduced to the guests by her father she gives expression to her joyous emotions in the famous waltz. To this ball, masked, come Romeo, Mercutio and some of their friends, adherents of the

Montagues. Romeo and Juliet meet and love at first sight follows; but the entrance of Tybalt, who recognizes Romeo, gives rise to some dialogue which reveals to the lovers the identity of their respective families. Romeo and his friends leave the ball, but Capulet forbids any interference with their departure.

ACT II.— This act contains the famous balcony scene of the Shakespearian drama, and is almost literally transcribed from Shakespeare, with an episodical interruption caused by some of the retainers of the Capulets, who fancy that something is amiss. The nurse, however, quiets their suspicions, and the love scene continues to the end of the act.

ACT III.—This act is divided into two scenes. The first is in the cell of Friar Lawrence, to whom come the lovers with the story of their passion. They wish to be married, and Friar Lawrence performs the ceremony. In the second scene Romeo's page Stephano (an invention of the librettist) is discovered searching near Capulet's house for his missing master. A boyish bit of bravado provokes the Capulet retainers into drawing upon him, and speedily the combat becomes general through the entrance of Mercutio, Paris, Benvolio, Tybalt and then Romeo. The historic feud breaks out with violence and claims Mercutio as its first victim; then Tybalt is slain by Romeo. Capulet arrives on the scene and demands justice of the Duke who opportunely appears. After a brief investigation the latter decrees sentence of banishment upon Romeo, who vows, however, that at all risks he will see Juliet once more. So closes the act.

ACT IV. — The rising curtain discloses Romeo and Juliet together in Juliet's chamber. Their love scene is brought to a painful termination by the breaking of the dawn which must not see Romeo in Verona, and he is compelled to depart. Capulet enters and informs his daughter that she is betrothed to the Count Paris. In despair she asks Friar Lawrence, who is present, to assist her, and he gives her a phial containing a drug which will produce in her the semblance of death. She drinks the potion and during the festivities attendant upon the wedding she falls lifeless.

ACT V.—After an orchestral introduction descriptive of Juliet's slumber, the scene shows us Juliet unconscious in the tomb of the Capulets. As in the original drama Romeo arrives and, thinking his beloved dead, takes poison. Juliet revives before he dies, and after a brief expression of joy, which is soon turned to an outburst of despairing love, Romeo expires from the effects of the potion and Juliet, seizing a dagger, stabs herself, and dies also in her lover's arms.

The opera was first performed at the Théâtre Lyrique, Paris, April 27, 1867, with the following cast:

Juliet	. . . .	*Mme. Carvalho*
Stephano	. . .	*Mme. Daram*
Gertrude	. . .	*Mme. Duclos*
Romeo	. . .	*M. Michot*
Tybalt	. . .	*M. Puget*
Benvolio	. . .	*M. Laurent*
Mercutio	. . .	*M. Barré*
Paris	. . . .	*M. Laveissière*
Gregorio	. . .	*M. Troy (jeune)*
Capulet	. . .	*M. Troy*
Friar Lawrence	. .	*M. Cazaux*
The Duke	. . .	*M. Christophe*

ROMÉO ET JULIETTE

PROLOGUE.

Chorus.

There were once in Verona
Two rival families,
The Montagues and the Capulets.
By their everlasting wars,
To both fatal,
They stained their palaces with blood.
As a glittering ray in a cloudy sky
Juliette came and Romeo loved her;
Forgetting their family dissensions
The same love united them.
Sorrowful fate! Blind ill-fortune!
The unhappy lovers paid with their lives
For the hatred of centuries which had nurtured their love.

ACT I.

A hall magnificently decorated in CAPULET'S house.

SCENE I—LORDS and LADIES in masks and dominoes are discovered.

Chorus.

Swift hours of pleasure
Pass to gay measure
Danced in the maze of glimmering feet;
While at the closes
Red wreck of roses
From our chaplets fall crushed but sweet!

Lords.

Happy masks that kiss fair maid,
Do but tell the grace they shade,
Half concealing,
Half revealing,
Love, in every charm arrayed!
Gleams of heaven—but sparely given—

PROLOGUE.

Le Choeur.

Vérone vit jadis deux familles rivales,
Les Montaigus, les Capulets,
De leurs guerres sans fin, à toutes deux fatales,
Ensanglanter le seuil de ses palais.
Comme un rayon vermeil brille en un ciel d'orage,
Juliette parut, et Roméo l'aima!
Et tous deux, oubliant le nom qui les outrage,
Un même amour les enflamma.
Sort funeste! aveugles colères!
Ces malheureux amants payèrent de leurs jours
La fin des haines séculaires
Qui virent naître leurs amours!

ACTE PREMIER.

Une galérie splendidement illuminée, chez les CAPULETS.

SCÈNE I—SEIGNEURS et DAMES, en dominos et masqués.

Choeur.

L'heure s'envole,
Joyeuse et folle;
Au passage il faut la saisir!
Cueillons les roses
Pour nous écloses
Dans la joie et dans le plaisir!

Les Hommes.

Chœur fantasque
Des amours,
Sous le masque
De velours,
Ton empire
Nous attire

Yet for these a heart is paid!

Ladies.

    Night of fancy—lustrous night,
    All thy stars to love invite;
      Sweet laugh calling,
      Light foot falling,
      And low cadence,
      Sung by maidens,
    Smooth rough man to woman's will!

Chorus.

    Swift hours of pleasure, etc.

SCENE II—PARIS, TYBALT, and the above.

(Enter PARIS and TYBALT with their masks in their hands.)

Tybalt.

    Well, Paris, my friend, what say'st thou?
    Was there ever a nobler feast?

Paris.

    What earth holds of beauty excelling
    Have these halls assembled as guest!

Tybalt.

    Still, of one thou'rt thinking, it seemeth,
    Of us all the marvel and pride—
    Fairest Juliet—thy promised bride!

Paris.

    Ay! my heart of her ever dreameth,
    And *will* dream, till, radiant and bright,
    She rises star-like on the dark of night!

Tybalt.

    Then thou wilt awake—happy Paris!
    Lo! she comes—'tis her father leads
    The timid maiden!

    D'un sourire,
    D'un regard!
    Et, complice,
    Le cœur glisse
    Au caprice
    Du hasard!

Les Femmes.

    Nuit d'ivresse!
    Folle nuit!
    L'on nous presse,
    L'on nous suit!
    Le moins tendre
    Va se rendre,
    Et se prendre
    Dans nos rêts.
    De la belle
    Qui l'appelle
    Tout révèle
    Les attraits.

Tous.

    L'heure s'envole, etc.

SCÈNE II—Les Mêmes, TYBALT, PÂRIS.

(TYBALT et PÂRIS entrent en scène, leur masque à la main.)

Tybalt.

    Eh bien! cher Pâris, que vous semble
    De la fête des Capulets?

Pâris.

    Richesse et beauté tout ensemble
    Sont les hôtes de ce palais.

Tybalt.

    Vous n'en voyez pas la merveille;
    Le trésor unique et sans prix
    Qu'on destine à l'heureux Pâris.

Pâris.

    Si mon cœur encore sommeille,
    Le moment est proche où l'amour
    Viendra l'éveiller à son tour.

Tybalt   (souriant).

    Il s'éveillera, je l'espère.
    Regardez!...... la voici, conduite par son père.

SCENE III—Capulet, Juliet, and the above.

(Enter Capulet with Juliet, all the guests unmask.)

Capulet.

> I bid you welcome, gentlemen,
> To my house! And you, fair dames;
> To-night we hold an old accustomed feast.
> This, my child, commend I now unto you,
> A slip that hath not seen the change
> Of many years. Of all earth's hopes
> She alone now is left me—my Juliet!
> Sweetest daughter! I pray you pardon me—
> A father's weak heart!

Lords.

> Ah! she is charming,
> No such beauty hath all Verona,
> And our summer hath no such flower!

Ladies.

> Ah! she is charming,
> All the radiance of heaven indwelling,
> All the grace of earth for her dower!

All.

> Ah, she is charming, etc.

(Prelude of the dance heard.)

SCÈNE III—Les Mêmes, Capulet, Juliette.

(Capulet entre en scène conduisant Juliette par la main. A son aspect tout le monde se démasque.)

Capulet.

> Soyez les bienvenus, amis, dans ma maison!
> A cette fête de famille
> La joie est de saison!.....
> Pareil jour vit naître ma fille;
> Mon cœur bat de plaisir encore en y songeant!....
> Mais excusez ma tendresse indiscrète!

(Présentant Juliette.)

> Voici ma Juliette!...
> Accueillez-la d'un regard indulgent.

Les Hommes   (à demi-voix).

> Ah! qu'elle est belle!
> On dirait une fleur nouvelle
> Qui s'épanouit au matin!

Les Femmes   (de même).

> Ah! qu'elle est belle!
> Elle semble porter en elle
> Toutes les faveurs du destin!......

Tous   (à demi-voix).

> Ah! qu'elle est belle!

(On entend le prélude d'un air de danse).

ECOUTEZ! — LET US HARK   Arietta (Juliet)

E - cou - tez!__ é - cou - tez!__ C'est le son des in - stru-
Let us hark!__ lis - ten now.__ 'tis a sweet strain of gay

ments joy - eux__ Qui nous ap - pelle et nous con - vi - e!
mu - sic sound-ing; Hear how its call bids us as - sem - ble,

Ah!__
Ah!__

Tout__ un monde en - chan - té__ sem - ble naître à mes yeux!
Like__ a world of__ en - chantment, Life seems o-p'ning to me.__

Tout_ me fê-te et__ m'en-i-vre, Tout me fête et m'en i - vre!
All__ now fires me, all__ in - spires me, All en - flames and in - spires me.

Light to life now is flowing,	Et mon âme ravie
Strange hopes are in me glowing.	S'élance dans la vie,
Bird-like the starry vault I'd dare	Comme un oiseau s'envole aux cieux!
For now my home seems lying there.	

ALLONS! JEUNES GENS! — *UP, UP, GALLANT YOUTHS!* Canzone (Capulet)

Al - lons! jeu - nes gens! Al - lons! bel - les da - mes! Aux
Up, up, gal - lant youths! Up, beau - ties the rar - est, Come,

plus di - li - gents Ces yeux pleins des_ flam-mes. Ces
cham - pion, so_ bold, make choice of_ the_ fair - est! Come

yeux, ces yeux pleins de_ flam - mes! Nar - gue!
choose come choose from the_ fair - est, Ban - ish;

Nar - gue! des__ cen - seurs Qui gron-dent, qui gron-dent, qui
ban - ish each thought of care, For sor - row, for sor - row, for

gron-dent sans ces-se! Fê - tez la jeu - nes-se! Fê - tez la jeu-
sor - row is_ blight-ing, In dan - ces_ ex - cit-ing, In dan - ces_ ex-

nes - se! Fê - tez la jeu - nes - se, Et place aux dan - seurs!
cit - ing, In dan - ces_ ex - cit - ing, Give pleas - ure its share.

Ha! my mistresses—will ye foot it now?
If you do not—then your toes have corns,
    I'll vow!
  By're lady! my day
  For a measure is gone,
  Though gallant more gay
  Never vizor put on!
  To ladies' ear oft
  A love-tale I'd tell,
  And whispering soft,
  I'd please her right well!
  Gone! lady and lover—
  My beard now is hoar,
  I'll mask me no more
  My gay time is over!

  Up, up, gallant youths, etc.

Chorus.

  Like to April on the heel
  Of lame Winter pressing,
  Its coldness caressing,
  So love young hearts feel!

(All the guests go off by the various entrances, JULIET leaning on PARIS' arm. CAPULET and TYBALT follow them. Enter ROMEO, MERCUTIO, and BENVOLIO, with half a dozen friends.)

SCENE IV—ROMEÓ, MERCUTIO, BENVOLIO, and friends.

Mercutio.

  At last we are alone, my friends!
  O beetle brows that blush for me, I now
  May doff ye!

Romeo.

  No—take not off your mask,
  Be prudent still—that no one may suspect
  us!
  The Capulet's our foe—beware his anger!

Mercutio.

  Bah! If they think we come to scorn and
  jeer
  Their feast—why then we're not the
  cowards to hide!
  And should they question us our swords shall
  give
  The answer!

Qui reste à sa place
Et ne danse pas
De quelque disgrâce
Fait l'aveu tout bas.
O regret extrême!
Quand j'étais moins vieux,
Je guidais moi-même
Vos ébats joyeux.
Les douces paroles
Ne me coûtaient rien.
Que d'aveux frivoles
Dont je me souviens!
O folles années
Qu'emporte le temps!
O fleurs du printemps
A jamais fanées!...

Allons! jeunes gens? etc.

Le Choeur.

Nargue des censeurs
Qui grondent sans cesse!
Fêtons la jeunesse!
Et placè aux danseurs!

(Tout le monde s'éloigne et circule dans les galéries voisines, JULIETTE sort au bras de PÀRIS. CAPULET et TYBALT les suivent en causant. ROMÉO et MERCUTIO paraissent avec leurs amis.)

SCÈNE IV—ROMÉO, MERCUTIO, BENVOLIO, et quelques-uns de leurs amis.

Mercutio.

La place est libre, mes amis!
Pour un instant qu'il soit permis
D'ôter son masque!

Roméo.

Non!... non! vous l'avez promis;
Soyons prudents! nul ne doit nous connaître.
Quittons cette maison sans affronter son maître.

Mercutio.

Bah! si les Capulets sont gens à se fâcher,
C'est lâcheté de nous cacher,
    (Frappant sur son épée.)
Car nous avons tous là de quoi leur tenir tête!

Romeo.
> Pray you, forbear—
> My soul is sad with foreboding—

Mercutio.
> How's that?

Romeo.
> I have been dreaming!

Mercutio.
> Ah! but dreams oft lie!
> So then Queen Mab hath been with you?

Romeo.
> Queen Mab?

Roméo.
> Mieux eût valu, ne pas nous méler à la fête!

Mercutio.
> Pourquoi?

Roméo.
> J'ai fait un rêve!

Mercutio.
> O présage alarmant!
> La reine Mab t'a visité?

Roméo.
> Comment?

BALLADE DE REINE MAB — *BALLAD OF QUEEN MAB* (Mercutio)

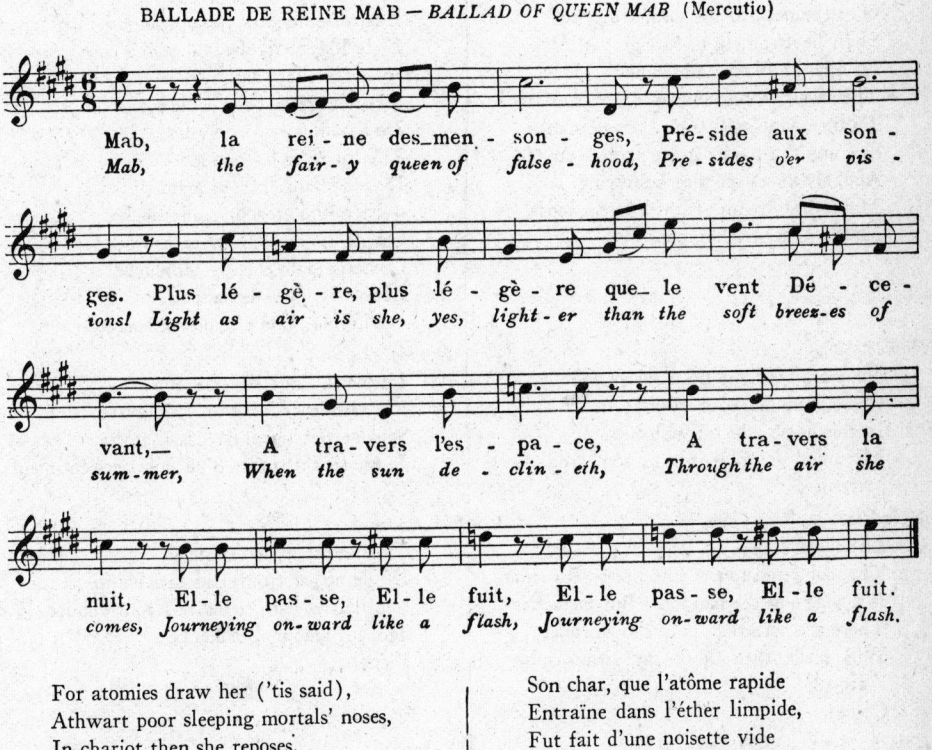

> Mab, la rei-ne des men-son-ges, Pré-side aux son-ges. Plus lé-gè-re, plus lé-gè-re que le vent Dé-ce-vant, A tra-vers l'es-pa-ce, A tra-vers la nuit, El-le pas-se, El-le fuit, El-le pas-se, El-le fuit.

> Mab, the fair-y queen of false-hood, Pre-sides o'er vis-ions! Light as air is she, yes, light-er than the soft breez-es of sum-mer, When the sun de-clin-eth, Through the air she comes, Journeying on-ward like a flash, Journeying on-ward like a flash.

For atomies draw her ('tis said),
Athwart poor sleeping mortals' noses,
In chariot then she reposes,
That of a hazel-nut is made;
And the wagon-spokes, of the spinner's legs,
    slender and long;
The coachman, a small gray-coated gnat,

Son char, que l'atôme rapide
Entraîne dans l'éther limpide,
Fut fait d'une noisette vide
Par Ver-de-Terre, le charron;
Les harnais, subtile dentelle,
Ont été découpés dans l'aile
De quelque verte sauterelle

Who wields a cricket-bone whip, filmed for
 a thong!
The traces are made of a small spider's web,
Collars of the moonshine's watery beam,
So in royal state she comes,
While we sleep and dream!
While he sleeps—the husband dreaming of
 widowhood,
The lover dreaming of love,
And a better living to boot!
Then the miser in dreams beholdeth
Vain wealth that wicked Mab upholdeth,
And to captive pining all lone,
Liberty smileth through bar and stone!
O'er the neck of the soldier driving,
Swift he dreameth of foreign battle,
Of Spanish blade and cannon's rattle,
Then wakes—and swears a prayer or two!
To thee Mab will come, gentle maiden,
Sleeping thy tender grace arrayed in,
And, sly kisses on thee bestowing,
Make thee dream of love's kisses too!
Mab! Queen Mab, etc.

Romeo.

 No more—Might the advice
 Come from Mab or others,
 In this home which is not ours.
 My mind misgives me of some sad conse-
  quence.

Mercutio.

 Little marvel
 Thy sad demeanor. The pretty Rosaline
 Is not among the dancers. But faces fair
 There are here that, once shown thee,
 Will make thee think thy swan is but a
  crow!
 Come!

Romeo
     (looking off).
 Ah! behold!

Mercutio.

 What is't now?

Par son cocher, le moucheron;
Un os de grillon sert de manche
A son fouet, dont la mèche blanche
Est prise au rayon qui s'épanche
De Phœbé rassemblant sa cour;
Chaque nuit, dans cet équipage,
Mab visite sur son passage
L'epoux, qui rêve de veuvage,
Et l'amant, qui rêve d'amour!
A son approche, la coquette
Rêve d'atours et de toilette;
Le courtisan fait la courbette;
Le poète rim ses vers;
A l'avare, en son gîte sombre,
Elle offre des trésors sans nombre;
Et la liberté rit dans l'ombre
Au prisonnier chargé de fers!
Le soldat rêve d'embuscades,
De batailles et d'estocades;
Elle lui verse les rasades
Dont ses lauriers sont arrosés;
—Et toi qu'un soupir effarouche,
Quand tu reposes sur ta couche,
O vierge, elle effleure ta bouche,
Et te fait rêver de baisers!
 Mab, la reine des mensonges, etc.

Roméo.

 Eh bien!... que l'avertissement
 Me vienne de Mab ou d'un autre,
 Sous ce toit qui n'est pas le nôtre,
 Je me sens attristé d'un noir pressentiment

Mercutio.

 Ta tristesse, je le devine,
 Est de ne pas trouver ici ta Rosaline;
 Cent autres dans ce bal te feront oublier
 Ton fol amour d'écolier!
 Viens!...

Roméo
     (regardant au dehors).
 Ah! voyez!

Mercutio.

 Qu' est-ce donc?

Romeo.

　Beauty that showeth the torches
　To burn in the darkness more bright!

Mercutio.

　(The beldame that follows behind
　Is not, by my troth, so lovely!)

Romeo.

　Like rich gem on Ethiop's ear,
　Her beauty hangs upon the cheek of night!
　....Oh, never till this hour
　Have I met with true beauty! Did my heart
　Love then before? No—ne'er till now!

Mercutio.

　Good!
　Gone is Rosaline's dominion,
　Dead the old desire doth lie!
　The fair he groaned for, and would gladly
　　　die,
　With the tender Juliet matched, is now not
　　　fair!

Chorus.

　Gone is Rosaline's dominion, etc.
　　　　(MERCUTIO, ROMEO, etc., exeunt.)

SCENE V—Enter JULIET, followed by GERTRUDE.

Juliet.

　What is't you'd tell me? Good nurse, speak!
　Speak, I pray thee!

Gertrude.

　Take breath! Is it me you escape,
　Or Paris you endeavor to meet?

Juliet.

　Paris!

Gertrude.

　A proper man, I trow; you've made a happy
　　　choice.

Juliet
　　　　　(laughing).
　Ah, Ah! Good nurse, my maiden heart
　Thinks not of marriage.

Gertrude.

　Go to! go to!
　At your age, i'faith I was married.

Roméo.

　Cette beauté céleste
　Qui semble un rayon dans la nuit!

Mercutio.

　Le porte-respect qui la suit
　Est d'une beauté plus modeste!

Roméo.

　O trésor digne des cieux!
　Quelle clarté soudaine a dessillé mes yeux?
　Je ne connaissais pas la beauté véritable!
　Ai-je aimé jusqu'ici?......

Mercutio
　　　(en riant, à BENVOLIO et aux autres jeunes gens).
　Bon! Bon! voilà Rosaline au diable!
　Et nous avions prévu ceci!
　　　On la congédie
　　　Sans plus de souci;
　　　Et la comédie
　　　Se termine ainsi!

Tous
　　　(moins ROMÉO, à demi-voix, et en riant).
　　　On la congédie
　　　Sans plus de souci, etc.
　　(MERCUTIO entraîne ROMÉO, au moment oú parait JULIETTE
suivie de GERTRUDE.)

SCÈNE V—JULIETTE, GERTRUDE.

Juliette.

　Voyons, nourrice, on m'attend! parle vite!

Gertrude.

　Respirez un moment!... est-ce moi qu'on
　　　évite,
　Ou le comte Pâris que l'on cherche?

Juliette.

　Pâris?

Gertrude.

　Vous aurez là, dit-on, la perle des maris!

Juliette
　　　　　(riant).
　Ah! ah! je songe bien vraiment au mariage!

Gertrude.

　Par ma vertu! j'étais marié à votre âge!

Juliet.

No more!　Leave me now, I pray, to the
fair dream
Of youth!

Juliette.

Non, non; je ne veux pas t'écouter plus
longtemps;
Laisse mon âme à son printemps!...

JE VEUX VIVRE — *IN THE CALMNESS OF A VISION*　Arietta Valse (Juliet)

Je　veux　vi　-　vre___　Dans　le　rê　-　ve___
In　　the　　calm　-　ness___　of　a　vis　-　ion,___

qui　m'en　i　-　vre___　ce___　jour　en　-　core!
sweet　　and　　tran　-　quil___　I　dwell　a　-　part,

Dou　-　ce　flam　-　me,___　Je　te　gar　-　de___
Fond　-　ly　hid　-　ing___　Love's　soft　pas　-　sion,___

dans　mon　â　-　me___　Com　-　me un tré　-　sor!___
Like　a　treas　-　ure___　deep___　in　my　heart.___

As in fair dream enfolden,
Born of fantasy golden,
Spirits from fairy land olden,
　On me now tend!
Ah! forever would this gladness
　Shine on me brightly as now,
Would that never age and sadness
　Threw their shade o'er my brow!
　　But short as day,
　　Youth passes away!
Then ere the summer's failing,
　Pluck the rose that bloometh to die,
Love with its breath inhaling,
　Love that steals in its odorous sigh!
In the calmness of a vision, etc.
(GREGORIO enters at back and meets ROMEO.)

Cette ivresse
De jeunesse
Ne dure, hélas! qu'un jour!
Puis vient l'heure
Où l'on pleure;
Le cœur cède à l'amour,
Et le bonheur fuit sans retour!
Loin de l'hiver morose
Laisse-moi sommeiller,
Et respirer la rose
Avant de l'effeuiller!
Je veux vivre, etc.
(GRÉGORIO paraît au fond et se rencontre avec ROMÉO.)

SCENE VI—Romeo, Gregorio. and the above.

Romeo.

What lady's that holds converse there?

Gregorio.

Easily told; that is Gertrude.

Gertrude.

Who calls?

Gregorio

(to Gertrude).

Lady! for thee they're seeking; and the varlets
But lag without thee to bestir them.

Gertrude.

Good lack! it's true!

Juliet.

Go!

(Juliet is following when Romeo restrains her.)

SCENE VII—Romeo and Juliet.

Romeo.

I pray thee go not yet!

SCÈNE VI—Les Mêmes, Grégorio, Roméo.

Roméo

(à Grégorio, en lui montrant Juliette).

Le nom de cette belle enfant?

Grégorio.

Vous l'ignorez?
C'est Gertrude!

Gertrude

(se retournant).

Plaît-il?

Grégorio

(à Gertrude).

Très-gracieuse dame,
Pour les soins du souper je crois qu'on vous réclame.

Gertrude.

C'est bien! me voici!

Juliette.

Va!

(Gertrude sort avec Grégorio. Roméo arrête Juliette au moment où elle va sortir.)

SCENE VII—Roméo, Juliette.

Roméo.

De grâce, demeurez!

(Il se démasque et prend la main de Juliette.)

ANGE ADORABLE —*ANGEL THAT WEAREST* (Romeo)

ten - ce Qu'il con - vient de m'im - po - ser,___ C'est que j'ef -
dar - ing I___ one soft kiss be fined.___ Kiss, that ef -

fa - ce L'in - dig - ne tra - ce De ma main___ par un bai - ser.
fa - ces Un - wor - thy tra - ces This hand___ hath left be - hind.

Juliet.

Thy hand, good pilgrim, this fine but wrong-
eth,
For thou dost blame it o'ermuch,
To pure devotion surely belongeth,
Saintly palm that thou may'st touch.
Hands there are, sacred to pilgrim's greeting,
But, ah me! not such as this,
Palm unto palm, not red lips meeting,
Is a holy palmer's kiss!

Romeo.

To palmer and to saint, have not lips too
been given?

Juliet.

Yes, but only for prayer!

Romeo.

Then grant my prayer, dear saint, or faith
may else be driven
Unto deepest despair!

Juliet.

Know, the saints ne'er are moved,
And if they grant a prayer, 'tis for the
prayer's sake!

Romeo.

Then move not, sweetest saint,
Whilst th' effect of my prayer, from thy lips
I shall take!

(He kisses her.)

Juliet.

Ah! now my lips, from thine burning,
Have the sin that they have taken.

Juliette.

Calmez vos craintes!
A ces étreintes
Du pélerin prosterné
Les saintes même,
Pourvu qu'il aime,
Ont d'avance pardonné;
Mais à sa bouche
La main qu'il touche
Doit prudemment refuser
Cette caresse
Enchanteresse
Qu'il implore en un baiser!

Roméo.

Les saintes ont pourtant une bouche ver
meille.

Juliette.

Pour prier seulement.

Roméo.

N'entendent-elles pas la voix qui leur con-
seille
Un arrêt plus clément?

Juliette.

Aux prières d'amour leur cœur est insensible.
Même en les exauçant.

Roméo.

Exaucez donc mes vœux, et gardez impas-
sible
Votre front rougissant!

(Il baise la main de JULIETTE.)

Juliette (souriant).

Ah! je n'ai pu m'en défendre·
J'ai pris le péché pour moi!

Romeo.

    O give that sin back again,
    To my lips their fault returning.

Juliet. }No, not again! no, not again!

Romeo.}O give the sin to me again!

SCENE VIII—Tybalt, and the above.

Romeo.

    Who comes?

          (Romeo remasks.)

Juliet.

    Tybalt, my cousin dear!

Romeo.

    Then say, who art thou?

Juliet.

    Daughter
    Of Capulet, sir, am I!

Romeo.

    Ah!

Tybalt

        (coming down).

    I' faith, sweet Juliet, though our sport
    Be not yet at the best, still our guests will go,
    An' thou art not there! Come away—come
      away!

        (Aside to Juliet.)

    And tell me true, sweet coz; knowest thou
    That stranger pilgrim, who so quickly
    masked?

Juliet.

    No—not I!

Tybalt.

    It would seem that he shuns me!

Romeo

        (to Tybalt).

    Sir, I give thee good den!

        (Exit.)

SCENE IX—Tybalt, Juliet, afterwards Capulet.

Tybalt.

    Ha! 'tis a Montague by his voice—it is
      Romeo!
    Even so—it is he, I'll swear!

Juliet.

    Romeo! ah?

Roméo.

    Pour apaiser votre émoi.
    Vous plaît-il de me le rendre?

Juliette.}Non! je l'ai pris!... Laissez-le moi!

Roméo. }Vous l'avez pris!... rendez-le moi!

SCÈNE VIII—Les Mêmes, Tybalt.

Roméo.

    Quelqu'un!

        (Il remet son masque.)

Juliette.

    C'est mon cousin Tybalt.

Roméo.

    Eh! quoi! vous êtes?...

Juliette.

    La fille du seigneur Capulet.

Roméo

        (à part).

    Dieu!...

Tybalt

        (s'avançant).

    Pardon,
    Cousine!... nos amis déserteront nos fêtes,
    Si vous fuyez ainsi leurs regards.
    Venez donc!

        (Bas.)

    Quel est ce beau galant qui s'est masqué si
      vite
    En me voyant venir?

Juliette.

    Je ne sais.

Tybalt

        (avec défiance).

    On dirait qu'il m'évite!

Roméo.

    Dieu vous garde, seigneur.

        (Il sort.)

SCÈNE IX—Tybalt, Juliette, puis Capulet.

Tybalt.

    Ah! je le reconnais à sa voix!... à ma haine!
    C'est lui! c'est Roméo!

Juliette

        (à part).

    Roméo!

Tybalt.

　　Daring slave! now by my stock and honor
　　　of kin,
　　I will slay him!
　　　　　　　　(Exit.)

Juliet
　　　　　　　　　(alone).

　　'Twas Romeo, he said!
　　Ah! 'twas the only son of our great foe-
　　　man—
　　The cold grave then is to be my wedding-
　　　bed!
　　—Only love springing from my only hate!
　　Seen all too early—and known all too late!

SCENE X—Tybalt, Paris, Romeo, Mercutio, Benvolio, guests, afterwards Capulet.

Tybalt.

　　There he stands!

Paris.

　　What is't now?

Tybalt　　　　　(pointing off at Romeo).

　　Romeo's there!

(Tybalt is about to face the group of the Montagues when
he is met by Capulet entering, who makes him silent at a
sign.)

Romeo　　　　　　(aside).

　　To be a Romeo is a crime in her eyes! fatal
　　　name!
　　Capulet is her father; and I love her!

Mercutio　　　(to his friends).

　　Beware—
　　For see how with anger the fiery Tybalt
　　　is chafing:
　　There's a storm brewing fast!

Tybalt.

　　I burn for vengeance!

Capulet.

　　What! quit the floor so soon? Nay, then,
　　　gentlemen,
　　Prepare not to be gone, for a trifling ban-
　　　quet awaits.

Tybalt, Paris and Friends.

　　Vengeance cometh! Vengeance cometh!
　　And for this intrusion shameful, blood

Tybalt.

　　Sur l'honneur,
　　Je punirai le traître, et sa mort est certaine!
　　　　　　　　(Il sort.)

Juliette
　　　　　　　　　(seule).

　　C'était Roméo! Ah! je l'ai vu trop tôt sans
　　　le connaître!
　　La haine est le berceau de cet amour fatal!
　　C'en est fait, si je ne puis être
　　A lui, que le cercueil soit mon lit nuptial!

(Elle s'éloigne lentement; les invités reparaissent.—Tybalt
entre d'un côté avec Pâris, Roméo, Mercutio, Benvolio et
leurs amis masqués entrent de l'autre.)

SCÈNE X—Tybalt, Pâris, Roméo, Mercutio, Benvolio,
Invités, puis Capulet.

Tybalt　　　　　(apercevant Roméo).

　　Le voici!

Pâris　　　　　　(abordant Tybalt).

　　Qu'est-ce donc?

Tybalt　　　　　(lui montrant Roméo).

　　Roméo!

(Tybalt va pour s'élancer vers le groupe dès qui rentre en
scène; il lui montre Roméo; Capulet, d'un geste impérieux,
lui impose silence.)

Roméo　　　　　　(à part).

　　Mon nom même
　　Est un crime à ses yeux!
　　O douleur!...Capulet est son père! et je
　　　l'aime!

Mercutio　　　(bas à ses amis).

　　Voyez de quel air furieux
　　Tybalt nous regarde! Un orage
　　Est dans l'air!

Tybalt.

　　Je tremble de rage!

Capulet
　　　　　　　　　(à ses invités).

　　Quoi! partez-vous déjà! demeurez un in-
　　　stant!
　　Un souper joyeux vous attend!

ENSEMBLE.

Tybalt, Pâris et quelques jeunes gens.

　　Patience! patience!
　　De cette mortelle offense

Alone shall make amends; death to Romeo
Then I swear!

Benvolio, Mercutio and Friends.

See how they watch us!
Nay, stir not—and use thy wit more than
valor;
We beard the foe in their camp; let us not
Wake their ire!

Capulet.

Rouse again the sound of pleasure,
Crush the wine-cup, tread the measure,
Time has been (I swear to you)
When I danced and drank for two!

Chorus.

Rouse again the sound of pleasure,
Crush the wine-cup, tread the measure,
Youth's a stuff that will not endure,
Nought beyond the present's sure!

(MERCUTIO drags ROMEO away, followed by BENVOLIO and
friends. Exeunt.)

Tybalt.

Romeo will 'scape me! let who will, follow.
I shall stroke his pretty face with my gaunt-
let.

(Makes as if to pursue ROMEO.)

Capulet   (aside to TYBALT).

Not so! I will not brook disorder!
Dost thou hear? Thou shalt not follow
Romeo!
What a plague is't to me what this youngster
is called?
From this thy place thou shalt not stir!

(To the guests.)

A hall, sirs, a hall!
Lead forth now each maiden,
Earth treading stars all,
With bright beauty laden!
Like to April on the heel
Of lame Winter pressing,
Its coldness caressing,
So love young hearts feel!

Chorus.

Like to April on the heel
Of lame Winter pressing,
Its coldness caressing,
So love young hearts feel!

(The curtain falls.)

Roméo, j'en fais serment,
Subira le châtiment!

Mercutio, Benvolio et leurs amis.

On nous observe! silence!
Il faut user de prudence!
N'attendons pas follement,
Un funeste évènement!

Capulet   (à ses invités).

Que la fête recommence!
Que l'on boive et que l'on danse!
Nous autres, j'en fais serment,
Nous dansions plus vaillamment!

Le Chœur.

Que la fête recommence!
Que l'on boive et que l'on danse!
Le plaisir n'a qu'un moment,
Terminons la nuit gaîment!

(MERCUTIO entraine ROMÉO; ils sont suivis de BENVOLIO et
de leurs amis.)

Tybalt   (à demi-voix).

Il nous échappe!
Qui veut me suivre!..—Je le frappe
De mon gant au visage!

(Il se dispose à suivre ROMÉO avec PÂRIS et quelques jeunes
gens.)

Capulet   (qui s'est rapproché de TYBALT, à demi-voix).

Et moi, je ne veux pas
D'esclandre, tu m'entends?..Laisse en paix
ce jeune homme!
Il me plaît d'ignorer de quel nom il se
nomme!
Je te défends de faire un pas!

(à ses invités).

Allons! jeunes gens!
Allons! belles dames!
Aux plus diligents,
Ces yeux pleins de flammes!
Nargue des rêveurs
Qui grondent sans cesse,
Fêtez la jeunesse,
Et place aux danseurs!

Le Chœur.

Nargue des rêveurs
Qui grondent sans cesse,
Fêtons la jeunesse,
Et place aux danseurs!

(La toile tombe.)

ACT II.

A garden. JULIET's apartments. Practicable window and balcony. At back a parapet overhanging the gardens.

SCENE I—STEPHANO and ROMEO.

(STEPHANO, the page, discovered against the parapet, helping up ROMEO by means of a rope ladder. Exit the page, bearing away the ladder.)

Romeo.

    O night! spread thy pinions above me,
    And hide me now!

Mercutio
           (off).

    Romeo! Romeo!

Romeo.

    'Tis Mercutio that mocking calls! Ever so
    He jesteth at scars that never felt a wound!

Mercutio, Benvolio and Chorus
           (off).

    Love sick, and sad and pining,
      Hither Romeo was seen to wend;
    May night, fond lovers shrining,
      Now to the pair a covert lend!

Romeo.

    Ah! it is love that hath stirred all my being.
        (A light is seen at the window.)
    Soft! what is that light that so sudden and
      strange,
    Breaks from yonder window? O heart,
    It is thy east and Juliet is the sun!

ACTE DEUXIÈME.

Un jardin.—A gauche le pavillon habité par JULIETTE.—Au premier étage, une fenêtre avec un balcon.—Au fond, une balustrade dominant d'autres jardins.

SCÈNE I—STÉFANO, ROMÉO.

(STÉFANO, appuyé contre la balustrade du fond, tient une échelle de corde et aide ROMÉO à escalader la balustrade; puis il se retire en emportant l'échelle.)

Roméo
           (seule).

    O nuit sous tes ailes obscures
    Abrite moi!

La voix de Mercutio
           (au dehors).

    Roméo! Roméo!

Roméo.

    C'est la voix de Mercutio!
    Celui-la se rit des blessures
    Qui n'en reçut jamais!

Mercutio, Benvolio et leurs amis
           (au dehors).

    Mysterieux et sombre,
      Roméo ne nous entend pas!
    L'amour se plaît dans l'ombre;
      Puisse l'amour guider ses pas!
        (Les voix s'éloignent.)

Roméo.

    L'amour!...Oui, son ardeur a troublé tout
      mon être!
        (La fenêtre de JULIETTE s'éclaire.)
    Mais quelle soudaine clarté
    Resplendit à cette fenêtre!
    C'est la que dans la nuit rayonne sa beauté!

AH! LEVE-TOI, SOLEIL! — *RISE, FAIREST SUN!* Cavatina (Romeo)

Ah!   lè - ve - toi,   so - leil!__   fais pâ - lir   les   é - toi - les,
Rise, .. fair - est   sun   in heav - enl   *Quench the stars with thy   bright-ness,*

Qui, dans l'a-zur sans   voi - les,   Bril - lent aux fir - ma - ment.__   Ah!   lè - ve -
That o'er the vault at   e - ven   *Shine with a   fee - ble light.__*   *Oh!   rise a-*

toi!_ ah! lè-ve-toi!_ pa-rais!_ pa-rais! As-tre pur et char-
gain!_ Oh! rise a-gain;_ and ban-ish Night's dark shades, bid them

mant! El-le rê-ve! el-le dè-nou-e U-ne
van-ish. She is watch-ing, Ah! e'er un-twin-ing From their

bou-cle de che-veux_ Qui_vient ca-res-ser sa jou-e! A-mour!_ A-
bonds her tress-es shin-ing! If my prayr's, love, shall reach thy hear-ing, Ap-proach her, ap-

mour!_ por-te-lui mes voeux! El-le par-le! Qu'elle est bel-le!
proach her, All my fond vows bear-ing, Now she speak-eth. Ah! how charm-ing.

What she said I have not heard,	Ah! je n'ai rien entendu!
But her sparkling eyes	Mais ses yeux parlent pour elle,
Have spoken to my heart;	Et mon cœur a repondu!
Ah! fairest sun, arise. Etc.	Ah! lève-toi, soleil! etc.

(The window opens, JULIET comes on to the balcony. ROMEO conceals himself.)

SCENE II—ROMEO and JULIET.

Juliet.

    Ah, me!—And still I love him!
    Romeo, why art thou Romeo?
    Doff then thy name, for 'tis no part,
    My love, of thee! What rose we call
    By other name would smell as sweetly;
    Thou'rt no foe, 'tis thy name!

Romeo.

    Can it be
    That thou'rt mine? Romeo henceforth
    I never more will be!

Juliet.

    Who art thou, say,

(La fenêtre s'ouvre. JULIETTE parait à son balcon. ROMÉO se cache dans l'ombre.)

SCÈNE II—ROMÉO, JULIETTE.

Juliette.

    Hélas!...moi, le haïr! ...haine aveugle et bar-
    bare!
    O Roméo! pourquoi ce nom est-il le tien!
    Abjure-le, ce nom fatal qui nous sépare,
    Ou j'abjure le mien!...

Roméo (s'avançant).

    Est-il vrai?..l'as-tu dit?...Ah! dissipe le doute
    D'un cœur trop heureux!

Juliette.

    Qui m'écoute,

That, be-screened by the night,
So stumblest on my dream?

Romeo.
I know not how
To tell thee who I am by name.

Juliet.
Thou art Romeo, I know!

Romeo.
Nay,
Ne'er shall I be known again, dear saint,
By a name that is foe unto thee!
Yet, oh, speak!—speak to my soul, bright
angel,
To the night thou'rt glorious, as a mes-
senger from heaven!

Juliet.
Ah! thou knowest the mask of night
Is on my face,—or my brow would be red
With a maidenly blush for the words
I've spoken unto thee; wherefore yet deny
What I've said! then, compliment, farewell!
Lovest thou me?
If so be that thou answerest me, ay,
Swear thou not by the moon—th' inconstant
moon
That monthly in circled orb changeth;
But by thy gracious self, and the oath I'll be-
lieve!
If me thou lovest—pronounce it faithfully.
"I love thee!"—and I am thine!
O impute not to light love
My passion so true, which the night hath
discovered!

Romeo.
Ah! my heart is true—and 'tis all, love, for
thee!

Juliet.
But hearken!—a noise, ah, Romeo,
Fly, ere they come.
(Exit from balcony.)
(ROMEO hides among the trees.)

Et surprend mes secrets sous le voile des
nuits.

Roméo.
Je n'ose, en me nommant, te dire qui je suis!

Juliette.
N'es-tu pas Roméo!

Roméo.
Non! je ne veux plus l'être,
Si ce nom détesté me sépare de toi!
Pour t'aimer, laisse-moi renaître
Dans un autre que moi!

Juliette.
Ah! Tu sais que la nuit te cache mon vis·
age!
Tu le sais!..Si tes yeux en voyaient la roug-
eur.
Elle te rendrait témoignage
De la pureté de mon cœur?...
Adieu les vains détours!...M'aimes-tu?...Je
devine
Ce que tu répondras. Ne fais pas de ser-
ments!
Phœbé, de ses rayons inconstants, j'imagine,
Eclaire le parjure et se rit des amants!...
Cher Roméo, dis-moi loyalement: je t'aime!
Et je te crois!......Et mon honneur
Se fie au tien, ô mon seigneur,
Comme tu peux te fier à moi-même!...
N'accuse pas mon cœur, dont tu sais le secret,
D'être léger, pour n'avoir pu se taire;
Mais accuse la nuit dont le voile indiscret
A trahi le mistère!

Roméo.
Devant Dieu qui m'entend, je t'engage ma
foi!

Juliette.
Ecoute! ..Silence!...éloigne-toi!....
(ROMÉO s'éloigne et disparait sous les arbres.—JULIETTE se
retire du balcon.)

SCÈNE III—Grégorio, quelques valets, puis Gertrude.

(Grégorio et les valets entrent en scène avec des lanternes sourdes à la main.)

SCÈNE III—Gregorio, Servants, then Gertrude.

(Gregorio enters with retainers, all have lanterns in their hands.)

Gregorio and Retainers.

There's no one—there's no one,
The page has fled,
Satan his patron
Has protected him.

Gregorio.

The sorry, scurvy knave
Was waiting his master!
Jealous fortune
Saved him from our blows;
He will tell to-morrow
How the slip he gave!

Chorus.

There's no one—there's no one! Etc.

Gertrude   (entering).

Whom are you speaking of!

Gregorio.

Of a page of the Montagues!
Page and master have dared
To outrage Capulet,
In passing this door!

Gertrude.

You are mad!

Gregorio.

No! By heavens!
With his friends, a Montague
Has come to this festival!

Gertrude and Servants.

One of the Montagues!

The Servants   (to Gertrude).

Has love for you, Gertrude,
Brought him here?

Gertrude.

Let him come again, and on my life
I will so well receive him
That he no more will fancy to return!

Gregorio.

This we believe.

Servants   (laughing).

This we believe!

Grégorio et les Valets.

Personne! personne!
Le page aura fui!
Au diable on le donne!
Le diable est pour lui!

Grégorio.

Le fourbe, le traître
Attendait son maître!
Le destin jaloux
L'arrache à nos coups;
Et demain peut-être
Il rira de nous!

Grégorio et les Valets.

Personne! personne, etc.

Gertrude   (entrant en scène).

De qui parlez-vous donc?

Grégorio.

D'un page
Des Montaigus—Maître et valet,
En passant notre seuil, ont osé faire outrage
Au seigneur Capulet.

Gertrude.

Vous moquez-vous?

Grégorio.

Non, sur ma tête!
Un des Montaigus s'est permis
De venir avec ses amis
A notre fête!

Gertrude et les Valets.

Un Montaigu!

Les Valets   (à Gertrude).

Est-ce pour vos beaux yeux que le traître est
    venu?

Gertrude.

Qu'il vienne encore, et sur ma vie!
Je vous le ferai marcher droit,
Si droit, qu'il n'aura pas envie
De recommencer!

Grégorio.

On vous croit!

Les Valets   (riant).

Pour cela, nourrice, on vous croit.

Gregorio and Servants.

Good night, charming nurse!
May heaven bless your virtues,
And confound the Montagues!
(GREGORIO and SERVANTS exeunt.)

SCENE IV—GERTRUDE, then JULIET.

Gertrude.

Blessed be the one
Who would avenge me
Of those rascals!.....

Juliet
(appears at the door of the pavilion).
Is it you, Gertrude?

Gertrude.

Yes, my angel!
But how is it you don't rest
At this time of night?

Juliet.

I was waiting for you!

Gertrude.

Come in!

Juliet.

Pray do not scold!
(She looks around and, followed by GERTRUDE, steps inside.
ROMEO reappears.)

SCENE V—ROMEO, then JULIET.

Romeo.

Night all too blessed! I am fearful,
Being in night, this is all but a dream,
That, waking, I may find too flattering
    sweet,
To bide the dawn.
(Enter JULIET from house.)

Juliet
(in a low voice).
Romeo!

Romeo
(turning around).
Speak, my dearest!

Juliet
(stopping him).
But a word,
Then farewell!
If that the faith thou pledgest be true,

Grégorio et les Valets.

Bonne nuit, charmante nourrice!
Joignez la grace à vos vertus!
Que le ciel vous bénisse,
Et confonde les Montaigus!
(GRÉGORIO et les valets s'éloignent.)

SCÈNE IV—GERTRUDE, puis JULIETTE.

Gertrude.

Béni soit le bâton qui tôt ou tard me venge
De ces coquins!

Juliette
(paraissant sur le seuil du pavillon).
C'est toi, Gertrude?

Gertrude.

Oui, mon bel ange!
Mais comment à cette heure
Ne reposez-vous pas?

Juliette.

Je t'attendais!....

Gertrude.

Rentrons!

Juliette.

Ne gronde pas!
(Elle jette un regard autour d'elle, et rentre dans le pa
villon, suivie de GERTRUDE.—ROMÉO reparait.)

SCÈNE V—ROMÉO, puis JULIETTE.

Roméo.

O nuit divine! je t'implore!
Laisse mon cœur à ce rêve enchanté!
Je crains de m'éveiller et n'ose croire encore
A sa réalité!

Juliette
(reparaissant sur le seuil du pavillon, à demi-voix).
Roméo!

Roméo
(se retournant).
Douce amie!

Juliette
(l'arrètant du geste et toujours sur le seuil).
Un seul mot! puis adieu!
Quelqu'un ira demain te trouver! ... —Sur
    ton âme,

If in honor me for thy wife thou takest,
Then to-morrow, my love, send a message
    unto me,
Telling me where and when will be per-
    formed
The rite of marriage. Then all I have, my
    lord,
Low at thy feet I'll lay; through the whole
    world
Thy steps I'll follow, though my kinsmen,
Dearest, should say me nay!
If true love feigning thou mean'st not well,
And thy vows all are vain,
I do beseech thee then
Cease thy wooing and leave me—
Leave me to my grief that will always fill
    my days!

Romeo
        (kneeling before JULIET).
Doubt not my affection,
For so thrive my soul, I do love thee!
And my life is in thy love;
Like a queen dispose of my life!
Fill my unsatiated soul
With all the bliss of heavens!

Juliet.
She is calling!

Romeo
        (seizing JULIET's hand).
Ah, not yet!

Juliet.
Go! I tremble!
One might see us together!
I come!

Romeo.
A moment more!

Juliet.
Speak low.

Romeo
        (drawing JULIET to him).
No! no! they don't call thee!

Juliet.
Beware! Pray thee, beware!

Si tu me veux pour femme
Fais-moi dire quelque jour, à quelle heure,
    en quel lieu
Notre union sera bénie!
Alors, ô mon seigneur, sois mon unique loi!
Je te livre ma vie entière, et je renie
Tout ce qui n'est pas toi!
Mais, si ta tendresse
Ne veut de moi que de folles amours......
Ah! je t'en conjure alors
Par cette heure d'ivresse,
Ne me revois plus, et me laisse
A la douleur qui remplira mes jours!

Roméo.
        (à genoux devant JULIETTE).
Ah! je te l'ai dit!...je t'adore!......
Dissipe ma nuit! sois l'aurore
Où va mon cœur, où vont mes yeux!
Dispose en reine de ma vie!
Verse à mon âme inassouvie
Toute la lumière des cieux!

Juliette.
On m'appelle!

Roméo
        (se relevant et saisissant la main de JULIETTE)
Ah! Déjà!

Juliette.
Pars! Je tremble
Qu'on ne nous voie ensemble!
Je viens!

Roméo.
Ecoute-moi!

Juliette.
Plus bas!

Roméo
        (attirant JULIETTE à lui et l'amenant en scène).
Non! non! l'on ne t'appelle pas.

Juliette.
Plus bas! Parle plus bas!

AH! NE FUIS PAS —*AH! GO NOT YET* Duet (Romeo and Juliet)

Ah! ne fuis pas en - co - re!   Ah! ne fuis pas en - co - re! Lais - se, lais-
Ah! go not yet, but stay thee!   *Ah! go not yet, but stay thee! Let__ me, let*

se ma main s'ou-bli-er dans ta   main! Ah! l'on peut nous sur- pren-dre!
me once more kiss thy dear hand, I   *pray. Si - lence, a step is near us,*

Ah! l'on peut nous sur - pren-dre!   Lais - se, lais - se ma main
Some one, I fear will hear us,   Let__ me,   let__ me at least

s'é- chap-per de ta main.__ A - dieu! a - dieu!__ a-
take my hand from thy keep-ing.   Good night, love.   Good night, love.   Good

dieu!__ a - dieu! _____ De cet a - dieu si douce est la tris -
night, love! Good night! _____ Dear-est, this fond good night is such sweet

tes - se Que je vou-drais te dire a - dieu__ jus-qu'à de - main!__
sor - row, That I should say, good night, good night__ till it be dawn.__

Juliet.

   Now indeed, I do entreat thee—go!

Romeo.

   Ah! cruel one!......

   (Is going, when she beckons him involuntarily to return.)

Juliet.

   For what do I recall thee?
   Ah, I know not! and when thou'rt near me,
   All the less do I remember. Yes!
   I would have thee gone, but no further from
     me,

Juliette.

   Maintenant, je t'en supplie,
   Pars!

Roméo.

   Ah! cruelle!...

   (Roméo s'en va involontairement, elle lui fait signe d
   revenir.)

Juliette.

   Pourquoi?
   Te rappelais-je, ô folie?
   A peine es-tu près de moi
   Que soudain mon cœur l'oublie!
   Je te voudrais parti, pas trop loin cependant:

Than hops the captive bird from lady's idle hand,
With silken gyves its flight restraining,
And as she plucks it back with a gentle command,
So, if thou wert my bird within my bower remaining,
I too would hold thee captive, bound with silken hand!

Romeo.

Ah, might I stay forever?

Juliet.

Alas, we must part!
Farewell!

Both.

Farewell, parting from thee is, oh, so sweet a sorrow,
That I could say "good night" till dawn!

Juliet.

Good night, O my love!
(Withdraws from ROMEO's arms and exit to the house.)

Romeo
(alone).

Soft be thy repose! . .Sleep!
Let a youthful smile of thy rosy lips
Whisper again! I love thee!....
Let the night breeze bring this kiss to thee.
(Exit. Curtain falls.)

———

THIRD ACT.

FIRST TABLEAU—The cell of FRIAR LAWRENCE.

SCENE I—FRIAR LAWRENCE and ROMEO.

Romeo.

Holy Father, may God have thee in His mercy.

Lawrence.

Romeo! how comest thou so early?
What brings thee to me?
Art thou uproused by some secret care,
Or is it love alone that brings thee?

Comme un oiseau captif que la main d'un enfant
Tient enchaîné d'un fil de soie,
A peine vole-t-il, dans l'espace emporté,
Que l'enfant le ramène avec des cris de joie,
Tant son amour jaloux lui plaint la liberté!

Roméo.

Ah! ne fuis pas encore!

Juliette.

Hélas! il le faut! Adieu!

Ensemble.

Adieu! De cet adieu si douce est la tristesse,
Que je voudrais te dire adieu jusqu'à demain!

Juliette.

Adieu, mille fois!......
(elle s'échappe des bras de ROMÉO et rentre dans le pavillon).

Roméo
(seule).

Va!...repose en paix! sommeille!
Qu'un sourire d'enfant sur ta bouche vermeille.
Vienne doucement se poser!...
Et, murmurant encore: Je t'aime! à ton oreille,
Que la brise des nuits te porte ce baiser!
(Il s'éloigne.—La toile tombe.)

———

ACTE TROISIÈME.

PREMIER TABLEAU—La cellule du Frère LAURENT.

SCÈNE I—FRÈRE LAURENT, ROMÉO.

Roméo.

Mon père, Dieu vous garde!...

Frère Laurent.

Eh! quoi! le jour à peine
Se lève, et le sommeil te fuit?
Quel espoir vers moi te conduit?
Quel amoureux souci t'amène?

Romeo.

    You have guessed right, holy father,
    It is love.

Lawrence.

    How! Rosaline?

Romeo.

    The name you pronounce I know not,
    Shall then the eye
    That opens on the light of morning, weep,
    With fond regret, the darkness that hath
      fled!
    Rosaline is no match, I trow,
    For my fairest Juliet.

Lawrence.

    What is it then, Juliet Capulet?
        (JULIET enters, followed by GERTRUDE.)

    SCENE II—The above, JULIET and GERTRUDE.

Romeo.

    Lo! She comes!

Juliet

        (throwing herself into ROMEO's arms).
    Romeo!

Romeo.

    My heart was calling thee!
    Thou art here now! I can speak no more!

Juliet

        (to LAWRENCE).
    My father! 'Tis marriage we seek;
    To none but Romeo shall I e'er be wedded,
    So are we come to seek thy office.
    That holy church makes us two one!

Lawrence.

    Strange! that children of two rival houses
    Should marry; but in this your help I shall
      prove:
    Who knoweth but this match may bind the
      foes
    Together, and turn all their rancor to love!

Romeo

        (to GERTRUDE).
    Nurse, wait thou outside.
        (Exit GERTRUDE.)

    SCENE III—ROMEO, JULIET, FRIAR LAWRENCE.

Lawrence.

    Guardian of your love,
    And of your promises,

Roméo.

    Vous l'avez deviné, mon père! c'est l'amour.

Frère Laurent.

    Eh! quoi! l'indigne Rosaline?...

Roméo.

    Quel nom prononcez-vous? Je ne le connais
      pas!
    L'œuil des élus s'ouvrant à la clarté divine
    Se s'ouvient-il encore des ombres d'ici-bas?—
    Aime-t-on Rosaline, ayant vu Juliette?

Frère Laurent.

    Quoi!..Juliette Capulet?
        (JULIETTE paraît suivie de GERTRUDE.)

    SCÈNE II—Les Mêmes, JULIETTE, GERTRUDE.

Roméo.

    La voici!

Juliette

        (s'élançant dans les bras de ROMÉO).
    Roméo!...

Roméo.

    Mon âme t'appelait!
    Je te vois!...ma bouche est muette!..

Juliette

        (à FRÈRE LAURENT).
    Mon père, voici mon époux;
    Vous connaissez ce cœur que je lui donne,
    A son amour je m'abandonne.
    Devant le ciel unissons-nous!

Frère Laurent.

    Oui! dussé-je affronter une aveugle colère
    Je vous prêterai mon secours.
    Puisse de vos maisons la haine séculaire,
    S'éteindre en vos jeunes amours!

Roméo

        (à GERTRUDE).
    Toi veille au dehors!...
        (GERTRUDE sort.)

    SCÈNE III—ROMÉO, JULIETTE, FRÈRE LAURENT.

Frère Laurent.

    Témoin de vos promesses,
    Gardien de vos tendresses.

May the Lord be with you!   Que le Seigneur soit avec vous!

Let us pray.   A genoux!

Romeo and Juliet.   *Roméo et Juliette.*

Let us pray.   A genoux!

(They kneel.)   (Ils s'agenouillent.)

Lawrence.   *Frère Laurent.*

God, who made man to his image,   Dieu, qui fit l'homme à ton image,

Also created the woman,   Et de sa chair et de son sang

And uniting them both   Créas la femme, et, l'unissant

By the sacred links of marriage,   A l'homme par le mariage,

On the heights of Sion,   Consacras du haut de Sion

Consecrated their inseparable union.   Leur inséparable union!......

O Lord, in thy mercy,   Regarde d'un œil favorable

Cast a favorable eye on them!   Ta créature misérable

Who bow before thy throne!   Qui se prosterne devant toi!......

SEIGNEUR! NOUS PROMETTONS — *O LORD, WE PROMISE* Trio (Romeo, Juliet and Lawrence)

ROMEO and JULIET   LAWRENCE

Sei - gneur, nous pro-met-tons _d'o-bé-ir à tu loi.___ En
O Lord, meek-ly we prom-ise thy laws to o - bey.___ Sup-

tends ma pri-è - re fer-ven-tel Fais que le joug de ta ser-van-te Soit un
port them in each good en-deav-or, Grant that this u-nion may be ev - er One of

joug d'a-mour et de paix!_ Que la ver-tu soit ·sa ri-ches-se,
peace-ful joy and of love.__ Bless them with vir-tue's heav'n-ly rich - es,

Que pour, sou_'te-nir sa fai - blesse_ Elle ar-me son coeur du de-
Make them pure and ho - ly, O Lord,__ In hearts like__ spir-its a-

ROMEO and JULIET

voir Sei - gneur! Sois mon ap - pui,__ Sois mon es - poir!_
bove. O Lord,__ be thou our lead-er, be thou our love.__

LAWRENCE

Que leur viel-lesse heu - reuse__ voie leurs en - fants mar- chant dans ta
Then, as old age ad - van - ces, May they be - hold their child-ren walk up -

ROM. and JUL.

loi,__ Et les en - fants de leurs en - fants! Sei -
right - ly, As in thy fear, from day to day. O

gneur! du noir pé - ché c'est toi qui nous dé - fends!__
Lord, pre - serve, we pray, our souls from er - ror's way.__

Lawrence.	**Frère Laurent.**
And when life and love both are over,	Que ce couple chaste et fidèle,
And death breaks the dream of the lover,	Uni dans la vie éternelle,
O grant that they yet meet above!	Parvienne au royaume des cieux!......
Romeo and Juliet.	*Roméo et Juliette.*
O thou father of all! deign now to bless our love!	Seigneur, sur notre amour daigne abaisser les yeux!
Lawrence.	*Frère Laurent.*
Romeo, say, for thy wife takest now this woman!	Roméo, tu choisis Juliette pour femme?
Romeo.	*Roméo.*
Yes, my father!	Oui, mon père.
Lawrence (to JULIET).	*Frère Laurent* (à JULIETTE).
For husband thou takest this man?	Tu prends Roméo pour époux?
Juliet.	*Juliette.*
Yes, my father!	Oui, mon père.
(They exchange rings.)	(ROMÉO et JULIETTE échange leurs anneaux.)
Lawrence (joining their hands together).	*Frère Laurent* (mettant la main de JULIETTE dans celle de ROMÉO)
In his name who marriage ordaineth,	Devant Dieu qui lit dans votre âme,
I join your hands—be man and wife!	Je vous unis!... Relevez-vous!
(ROMÉO and JULIET rise.)	(ROMÉO et JULIETTE se relèvant.)
SCENE IV—The above, GERTRUDE.	SCÈNE IV—Les Mêmes, GERTRUDE.
(ROMÉO and JULIET embrace each other.)	(ROMÉO et JULIETTE dans les bras l'un de l'autre.)
All.	*Ensemble.*
Holy father, O heavenly bliss,	O pur bonheur! ô joie immense!
Heaven has received our oaths!	Le ciel reçoit nos serments amoureux!
To hearts now one, no more to sever!	Dieu de bonté, Dieu de clémence,
Bless thy name, O Lord.	Sois béni par deux cœurs heureux!
(ROMÉO and JULIET exeunt separately, JULIET with GERTRUDE, ROMEO with LAWRENCE.)	(ROMÉO et JULIETTE se séparent.—JULIETTE sort avec GERTRUDE.—ROMÉO sort avec FRÈRE LAURENT.)

SECOND TABLEAU—A street in Verona. Capulet's house at left.

SCENE I—Enter Stephano.

Stephano.

Since yesterday, I've sought in vain my master.

O Capulet, perchance he yet honors thy house.

I'll sing a stave, so the servants will rouse.

(He seems to play guitar on his shoulder.)

DEUXIÈME TABLEAU—Une rue.—A gauche la maison des Capulets.

SCÈNE I—Stephano, seul

Stephano.

Depuis hier je cherche en vain mon maître!

Est-il encor chez vous, ô Capulets?

Voyons un peu si vos dignes valets

A ma voix ce matin oseront reparaître!

(Il fait mine de pincer de la guitare sur son épée.)

QUE FAIS-TU, BLANCHE TOURTERELLE — *AH! WITH KITES OF MURDEROUS INSTINCTS*
Canzone (Stephano)

Que fais - tu,__ blanche tour - te - rel - le, / *Ah! with kites__ of mur-'drous in - stincts,* Dans ce nid de van- / *Ten - der dove, why re -*

tours? Quel-que jour, dé - play-ant ton aî - le, / *main? Far a - way fly with out-spread pin-ions,* Tu sui-vras les__ a- / *And re - turn, ne'er a -*

mours! Aux vau - tours il faut la ba - tail - le Pour frap- / *gain,__ In thy strug - gle snares sur - round thee, Young, a -*

per d'e-stoc et de tail - le, Leurs__ becs sont ai - gui - sés!__ / *lone, with claws they will wound thee, Tal - ons strong, and cru - el beak.__*

Unlike thine, soft and true and slender,
Unlike thine, laid to lips more tender,
  In kisses warm and long!
    See you guard her safely,
      They that live will know;
    Or your dove may flutter
      From her cage and go!
Now it happened that a ring-dove flying
From his wood-land so green,
To that eyrie came one eve sighing
For her young love, I ween!
O'er a banquet of prey they'd mangled,

Laisse-là ces oiseaux de proie,
Tourterelle qui fais ta joie
  Des amoureux baisers!....
    Gardez bien la belle!
      Qui vivra verra!
    Votre tourterelle
      Vous échappera!
Un ramier, loin du vert bocage
Par l'amour attiré,
A l'entour de ce nid sauvage
A, je crois, soupiré.
Les vautours sont à la curée:

In the vale the vultures loud wrangled,	Leurs chansons, que fuit Cythérée,
Harsh rose their cry afar;	Résonnent à grand bruit!
But the doves, for the past atoning,	Cependant qu'en leur douce ivresse
Heeded not, while their love-vows moaning;	Nos amants content leur tendresse
And rose the first bright star!	Aux astres de la nuit!....
See you guard her safely,	Gardez bien la belle!
They that live will know;	Qui vivra verra!
Or your dove may flutter	Votre tourterelle
From her cage and go!	Vous échappera!

SCENE II—Stephano, Gregorio and retainers.

Stephano.
At last the warriors come!

Gregorio.
In truth I'm in a passion!
Disturbed in this fashion!

Stephano.
(They object to my song!)

Gregorio.
What! I' faith,
'Tis the page, that, sword in hand, last night
We hunted to the door!

Chorus.
'Tis the rascal!

Gregorio.
Audacious varlet!

Stephano.
See you guard her safely, **etc.**

Gregorio.
A quarrel dost thou seek,
O minstrel most alarming?
And is it to provoke
Thou trollest songs so charming?

Stephano.
I'm fond of music!

Gregorio.
Of course—of course!
Yet I've known for such pranks the gay
serenader
Has had his guitar broke in two!

Stephano.
Ah!
Very likely—but then, good fellow,
My guitar's a sword, hard to break!

SCÈNE II—Stephano, Grégorio, **Valets.**

Stephano.
Ah! ah! voici nos gens!...

Grégorio.
Qui diable à notre porte
S'en vient roucouler de la sorte?

Stephano
(à part, en riant).
La chanson leur déplaît!

Grégorio
(aux autres valets).
Mais pardieu! n'est-ce point
Celui que nous chassions hier la dague au
poing?

Les Valets.
C'est lui-même!

Grégorio.
L'audace est forte!

Stephano.
Gardez bien la belle!

Grégorio.
Est-ce pour nous narguer, mon jeune cama-
rade,
Que vous nous régalez de votre sérénade?

Stephano.
J'aime la musique!

Grégorio.
C'est clair;
On t'aura sur le dos, en pareille équipée,
Cassé ta guitare, mon cher!

Stephano.
Pour guitare j'ai mon épée,
Et j'en sais jouer plus d'un air.

Gregorio.

    Save my soul! if that be your music,
    Perhaps we may give you the answer!

Stephano
              (drawing).

    Let's try then, if we are in tune!

Gregorio
              (drawing).

    Have at you!
              (They fight.)

Chorus
              (laughing).

    We will hear how they play!
    How they parry—how they thrust,
    Quick as lightning; soon shall one bite the
        dust!
      Strong the boy is in defence;
      Faith! the issue's in suspense!
    Was a soldier ever bolder,
      Than this slip of a boy?
        (Enter MERCUTIO and BENVOLIO.)

SCENE III—The above, MERCUTIO, BENVOLIO, then
TYBALT, PARIS, ROMEO and retainers of the two houses.

Mercutio.

    So you draw on a child! Go to!
    'Tis an achievement worthy Capulet's fame:
    Like master—so, like man!
        (Enter TYBALT, PARIS and friends.)

Tybalt.
          (drawing, to MERCUTIO).

    Sir, your word
    Seemeth over-ready to me!

Mercutio.

    We'll join it
    With a blow!

Tybalt.

    You'll find me apt enough.

Mercutio.

    That I can prove at once!
    (They engage. ROMEO enters hastily and throws himself
between them.)

Grégorio.

    Ah! pardieu! pour cette musique
    On peut te donner la réplique!

Stephano.
            (dégainant).

    Viens donc en prendre une leçon!

Grégorio.
            (dégainant).

    En garde!

Les Valets
            (riant).

    Ecoutons leur chanson!
    (Pendant que GRÉGORIO et STEPHANO se battent.)
        Quelle rage!
        Vertudieu!
        Bon courage,
        Et franc jeu!
        Voyez comme
        Cet enfant
        Contre un homme
        Se défend!
        Fine lame,
        Sur mon âme!
        Il se bat
        En soldat!
    (MERCUTIO et BENEVOLIO entrent en scène.)

SCÉNE III—Les Mêmes, MERCUTIO, BENVOLIO, puis Ty-
BALT, PÀRIS, ROMÉO et Partisans des deux maisons.

Mercutio.

    Attaquer un enfant!
    (Il tire l'épée et se jette entre les combattants.)
        Morbleu! c'est une honte
    Digne des Capulets!
    Tels maîtres, tels valets!
    (TYBALT entre en scène suivi de PÀRIS et de quelques amis.)

Tybalt.

    Vous avez la parole prompte,
    Monsieur!

Mercutio.

    Moins prompte que le bras!

Tybalt.

    C'est ce qu'il faudrait voir!

Mercutio.

    C'est ce que tu verras!
    (Au moment où ils se mettent en garde, ROMÉO entre en
scène et se précipite entre eux.)

Romeo.

    Gentles, hold!

Mercutio.

    Romeo!

Tybalt.

    Romeo here!

    It is fate that hath led him!
        (To Mercutio, with ironical politeness.)

    For a time peace be with you; here cometh
    The man I must fight!
               (To Romeo.)

    Now draw!

    Draw for your life! A spy thou art

    And traitor,—draw an' thou be a man!

    Dost thou think I forget the night thou
      camest

    Without a bidding? Now for that insult

    Thou shalt pay!......

        Ay! and the more by this token,

        That to my Juliet thou hast spoken.

    Unhappy man, thou'lt rue the day!

    No better term than this my hatred affords
      me—

    Thou art a villain!
(Romeo half draws his sword, then sheathes it calmly.)

Romeo.

    But no—yet villain am I none, Tybalt.

    Reason have I to love thee—which doth
      excuse

    All the rage of thy words. Be satisfied,

    Nor seek quarrel with me! I see

    Thou dost not know me—farewell!
            (Retires a step.)

Tybalt.

    Thou canst not thus, boy, excuse

    All the wrong that thou hast done me!

    Traitor!

Romeo.

    Never have I wronged thee, I do protest!

    Thy name to me is dear as my own.

Mercutio.

    Calm and dishonorable yielding!

    How is this? Heard I aright? So be it!

    I'll reply with an à la stoccata.
           (Draws.)

    So, sir, pluck out your sword—for now I
      am your man!

Roméo.

    Arrêtez!

Mercutio.

    Roméo!

Tybalt.

    Roméo! Son démon me l'amène!
           (A Mercutio.)

    Permettez que sur vous je lui donne le pas!
           (A Roméo.)

    Allons! Vil Montaigu!...... flamberge au
    vent!.... dégaîne!......

    Toi qui nous insultas jusqu'en notre maison,

      C'est toi qui porteras la peine

      De cette indigne trahison!

        Toi dont la bouche maudite

        A Juliette interdite

    Osa, je crois, parler tout bas,

    Ecoute le seul mot que m'inspire ma haine!

    Tu n'es qu'un lâche!....
(Roméo porte vivement la main à son épée, la tire à moitié
du fourreau, puis l'y remet.)

Roméo.

    Allons! tu ne me connais pas,

    Tybalt!...... et ton insulte est vaine!

    J'ai dans le cœur des raisons de t'aimer

    Qui malgré moi me viennent désarmer!

    Je ne suis pas un lâche!.... Adieu!
        (Il fait un pas pour s'éloigner.)

Tybalt.

    Tu crois peut-être

    Obtenir le pardon de tes offenses, traître?

Roméo.

    Je ne t'ai jamais offensé

    Le temps des haines est passé!

Mercutio.

    Tu souffrirais ce nom de lâche?

    O Roméo, t'ai-je entendu?

    Eh bien, donc, si ton bras doit faillir à sa
      tâche.

    C'est à moi désormais que l'honneur en est
      dû!

Romeo
    (restraining him).
 Put up thy rapier,
 Good Mercutio—
Mercutio.
 No! Come now, sir,
 Show your passion; draw, you rat-catcher,
  draw.
Tybalt.
 I am for you!
Romeo.
 I pray you, hold!
Mercutio.
 No! let us be!
Stephano, Benvolio and the Montagues.
 It is well! on honor!
Paris and the Capulets.
 In him I trust!
 Montagues—Montagues—race offending,
  Tremble all in alarm;
 May demon, dark aid lending,
  Now nerve his 'venging arm!
Benvolio, Stephano and Montague's retainers.
 Capulets—Capulets—race offending,
  Tremble all in alarm;
 May demon, dark aid lending,
  Now nerve his 'venging arm!
Romeo.
 Rancor and hate ne'er ending,
  From age to age yet stronger grow;
 Our homes rending
  In sorrow and in woe!
    (They fight.)
Mercutio.
 I am wounded!
Romeo.
 Wounded!
Mercutio.
 Plague of your houses, both!....but why
 Did you come us between?

Romeo.
 Alas!
 Hurt for my honor! A surgeon, quick!

Roméo.
 Mercutio, je t'en conjure!

Mercutio.
 Non!.... Je vengerai ton injure!...
 Misérable Tybalt, en garde, et défends-toi!

Tybalt.
 Je suis à toi!
Roméo.
 Ecoute-moi!
Mercutio.
 Non! laisse-moi!
Stephano, Benvolio et les Montaigus.
 Bien! sur ma foi!
Pâris et les Capulets.
 En lui j'ai foi!
 Montaigus!... race immonde!
 Frémissez de terreur!
 Et que l'enfer seconde
 Sa haine et sa fureur!
Benvolio, Stephano et les Montaigus.
 Capulets! race immonde!
 Frémissez de terreur!
 Et que l'enfer seconde
 Sa haine et sa fureur!
Roméo.
 Haine en malheurs féconde,
 Dois-tu par ta fureur
 Toujours donner au monde
 Un spectacle d'horreur?
   (TYBALT et MERCUTIO se battent.)
Mercutio.
 Ah blessé!
Roméo.
 Blessé!...
Mercutio.
 Que le diable
 Soit de vos deux maisons!... Pourquoi
 Te jeter entre nous?
Roméo.
 O sort impitoyable!
    (A ses amis.)
 Secourez-le!

Mercutio
　　　　　　　　(staggering).
　　Now help me, there!
　　　　　(Exit, leaning on his friends.)
Romeo.
　　Ah! he is slain!—Away to heav'n,
　　O shameful caution!
　　And thou, O fire-eyed fury,
　　Shalt be alone my conduct now.
　　　　　(Drawing sword and advancing.)
　　Tybalt!
　　There is no coward here but thee.
　　Fall on!
(Wounds him mortally. TYBALT totters, and falls. Enter
CAPULET, who rushes to him, and supports him in his arms.
The fight ceases.)

　　SCENE IV—The above, CAPULET, Citizens, afterwards the
DUKE.
Capulet.
　　Ah heaven! Tybalt!
(CAPULET, assisted by his friends, supports TYBALT's head.)

Benvolio
　　　　　　　　(to ROMEO).
　　He is mortally wounded.
　　Hence, begone!
　　Quick, away!
Romeo
　　　　　　　　(apart).
　　O, evil fate—dead!—
　　And he was her kinsman!
Benvolio.
　　If thou stay, it is death!
Romeo.
　　Let it then be so,
　　　　　　　(With despair.)
　　I am ready!
Tybalt
　　　　　　(dying, to CAPULET).
　　Yet a word more—
　　This my last prayer—see ye fulfill.
Capulet.
　　On my soul do I swear that thy will
　　Shall be done!
　　　　　(Enter Citizens.)
Citizens.
　　How now? Tybalt is slain!

Mercutio
　　　　　　　　(chancelant).
　　Soutenez-moi!
　　　　　(On emmène MERCUTIO.)
Roméo.
　　Ah! maintenant, remonte au ciel, prudence
　　　infâme!
　　Et toi, fureur à l'œil de flamme,
　　Sois de mon cœur l'unique loi!
　　　　　　(Tirant son épée.)
　　Tybalt, il n'est ici d'autre lâche que toi!
　　　　　(poussant une botte à TYBALT).
　　A toi!
(TYBALT est touché et chancelle; CAPULET entre en scène,
court à lui et le soutient dans ses bras.—On cesse de se
battre.)

　　SCÈNE IV—Les Mêmes, CAPULET, Bourgeois, puis le Duc
et sa Suite.
Capulet.
　　Grand Dieu!... Tybalt!...
(CAPULET, aidé des siens, étend TYBALT à terre et lui sou-
tient la tête.)
Benvolio
　　　　　　　　(à ROMÉO).
　　Sa blessure est mortelle!
　　Fuis sans perdre un instant!

Roméo
　　　　　　　　(à part).
　　Ah! qu'ai-je fait?... Moi, fuir! maudit par
　　elle!
Benvolio.
　　C'est la mort qui t'attend!
Roméo
　　　　　　　(avec désespoir).
　　Qu'elle vienne donc! Je l'appelle!

Tybalt
　　　　　　(d'une voix mourante).
　　Un dernier mot! et sur votre âme... exaucez-
　　moi!
Capulet.
　　Tu seras obéi!... Je t'en donne ma foi!
　　　　　(Une foule de bourgeois a envahi la scène.)

Le Bourgeois.
　　Qu'est-ce donc?... C'est Tybalt! il meurt!...

Capulet
(to Tybalt).

 Revive again!
(Procession march heard off.)

Chorus.

 O day of woe! O day of weeping!
  Blind revenge hath our blades
 In their blood now been steeping
  And baleful stars hang o'er our heads.
 The Duke! The Duke!
(Enter the Duke with suite and torch-bearers.)

Capulet
(to Duke).

 Avenge me!

Retainers.

 Avenge us!

Capulet
(pointing to Tybalt's corpse).

 Tybalt's slain—my near friend; on Romeo
Is his blood.

Romeo.

 From Mercutio first
He struck out lusty life. Then I swore
His revenge; for my fate I am ready!

Montagues.

 Avenge us!

All.

 Avenge us!

Duke.

 How now? In this sad fray
Hath your anger found vent? Oh, deem ye
 not
My love for your brawls lies a-bleeding?
Nought seemeth strong to keep your hands
From off your hilts. Who knoweth, I
May be next victim of your faction!
(To Romeo.)

For this offence, Romeo, thou
Deservest death; but as thou didst speak
 him fair,
Then thou art banished!

Romeo.

 Banished!

Duke.

 And ye, who in hate ever prone to occasion,
Do inflame in our town woeful strife and
 aggression,

Capulet
(à Tybalt).

 Reviens à toi!
(On entend des fanfares.)

Le Chœur.

 O jour de deuil! ô jour de larmes!
 Un aveugle courroux,
 Ensanglante nos armes!
 Et le malheur plane sur nous.
 Le Duc! Le Duc!
(Le Duc entre en scène suivi de son cortège de gentilshommes et de pages portant des torches.)

Capulet
(se relevant).

 Justice!

Les Capulets.

 Justice!

Capulet
(montrant le corps de Tybalt).

 C'est Tybalt.. mon neveu... tué par Roméo!

Roméo.

 Il avait le premier, frappé Mercutio!
J'ai vengé mon ami, que mon sort s'accomplisse!

Les Montaigus.

 Justice!

Tous.

 Justice!

Le Duc.

 Eh quoi! toujours du sang!—De vos cœurs
 inhumains
Rien ne pourra calmer les fureurs crimin-
 elles!
Rien ne fera tomber les armes de vos mains,
Et je serai moi-même atteint par vos querelles!
(à Roméo).

Selon nos lois, ton crime a mérité la mort!
Mais tu n'es pas l'agresseur!... Je t'exile!

Roméo.

 Ciel!

Le Duc.

 Et vous, dont la haine en prétextes fertiles
Entretient la discorde et l'effroi dans la ville.
Prêtez tous devant moi le serment solennel.

*Swear ye all on your lives, or at home or
 abroad,
Ye will obey the laws of the Duke and your
 God!*

Romeo and the others.

Ah! direful day, day of woe and of mourn-
 ing,
Breaking, my heart fails in pain and despair!
Though we disarm, how untimely the warn-
 ing!
For we may never thy ravage repair!
Every desire, every hope grimly scorning,
Weeping and blood alone in thee may we
 share.

Duke.

Do thou avoid the city ere the night.

Romeo.

Oh, I am banished! Despair!
No! Tho' I die, I will see her again.

Chorus.

Disarm? No! Revenge!
                (The curtain falls.)

ACT IV.

FIRST TABLEAU—The chamber of JULIET. It is night.
The room is lit by a torch.

SCENE I—ROMEO, JULIET.

(JULIET discovered on a couch, ROMEO at her feet.)

Juliet.

Yes, I pardon thee this—
That Tybalt thou hast killed; for if Tybalt
Had lived, perchance thou wouldst have
 fallen.
Comfort all this to me! 'twas thy life he
 sought,
And I love thee!

Romeo.

O speak again
That word so fair!

Juliet.

Ah, Romeo,
Thee I love—my husband—dear unto me!

D'obéissance aux lois et du prince et du ciel!

Roméo et les Autres.

Ah! jour de deuil et d'horreur et d'alarmes,
Mon cœur se brise éperdu de douleur!
Injuste arrêt qui trop tard nous désarmes,
Tu mets le comble à ce jour de malheur!
Je vois périr dans le sang et les larmes
Tous les espoirs et tous les vœux de mon
 cœur!

Le Duc.

Tu quitteras la ville dès ce soir.

Roméo.

O désespoir! l'exil!
Non! je mourrai—
Mais je veux la revoir!

Choeur.

La paix? non! jamais!
                (La toile tombe.)

ACTE QUATRIÈME

PREMIER TABLEAU—La chambre de JULIETTE. Il fait
nuit. La scène est éclairée par un flambeau.

SCÉNE I—ROMÉO, JULIETTE.

(JULIETTE est assise; ROMÉO est à ses pieds.)

Juliette.

Va! je t'ai pardonneé! Tybalt voulait **ta**
 mort;
S'il n'avait succombé, tu succomhais toi-
 même
Loin de moi la douleur! loin de moi le re-
 mord!
Il te haïssait!... et je t'aime!

Roméo.

Ah! redis-le, ce mot si doux!

Juliette.

Je t'aime, ô Roméo! je t'aime, ô mon époux

NUIT D'HYMENEE — *OH! BLESSED NIGHT HYMENIAL* Duet (Romeo and Juliet)

JULIET

Nuit d'hy-mé-ne-e!___ O___ dou-ce nuit d'a-mour!___
Oh! bless-ed night hy-me-nial, *Hours to the heart so dear,___*

ROMEO

La des-ti-né-e M'en-chaîne à toi sans re-tour.___
Love weaves the chains we wear Of bloom-ing ro-ses___ per-en-nial,___

O___ vo-lup-té de viv-re! O___ char-mes tout puis-sants!___
Ho-ly and dear con-fes-sion, Mys-te-ry sweet of love.___

Ton___ doux re-gard m'en-i-vre, Ta voix___ ra-vit___ mes
No___ more en-rap-tured mo-ments Are found___ in heav'n a-

Ton___ doux re-gard m'en-i-vre, Ta
No___ more en-rap-tured mo-ments Are

sens!___ Sous___ tes bai-sers de flam-me___
bove,___ Thou___ dost un-fold the por-tal,___

voix___ ra-vit___ mes sens!___ Sous___ tes bai-sers de
found___ in heav'n a-bove,___ Thou___ dost un-fold the

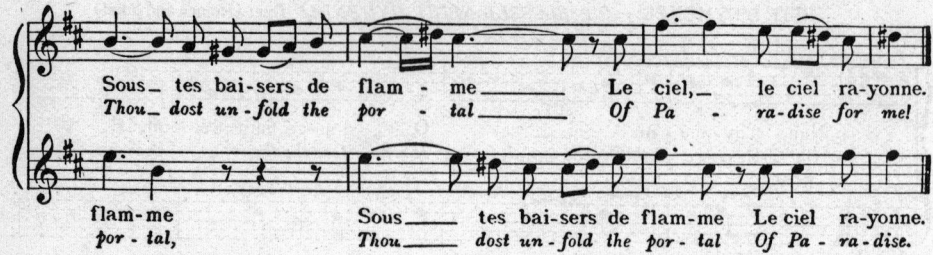

Sous__ tes bai-sers de flam - me_____ Le ciel,__ le ciel ra-yonne.
Thou__ dost un-fold the por - tal_____ Of Pa - ra-dise for me!

flam-me   Sous_____ tes bai-sers de flam-me Le ciel ra-yonne.
por - tal,   Thou_____ dost un-fold the por-tal Of Pa - ra-dise.

Ah! dearest, I will love thee
Till death that love from life shall part!
(Day breaks; the lark is heard.)

Juliet.

Wilt begone?—Nay, not yet!

Romeo
            (rising).

Ah, hearken!
Dearest Juliet, 'tis the lark that thou
    hearest,
The herald of morn.

Juliet
            (restraining him).

No! 'tis not yet near day,
'Twas no lark pierced thine ear, love.
'Tis the nightingale's note,
That she nightly sings there!

Romeo.

Nay, 'tis the lark, alas!
Early herald of morn; look, love,
            (They come to the window.)
What envious streaks, clouds in the east
Are lacing! now night's candles
Are burning palely: on the mountains,
On tip-toe standeth jocund day.

Juliet.

No, love, it is not day—
Rather some wandering meteor. Remain!
Remain!
    (ROMEO embraces JULIET passionately.)

Romeo.

Let me be put to death—thou willest!

Juliet.

Ah! thou wert right, it is day!
Go! hie hence away—tarry no longer!

Je t'ai donné mon âme!
A toi!... toujours à toi!...
(Les premières lueurs du jour éclairent les vitraux de la fenêtre.—On extend chanter l'alouette.)

Juliette.

Roméo, qu'as tu donc?

Roméo
            (se levant).

Ecoute, ô Juliette!
L'alouette déja nous annonce le jour!

Juliette
            (le retenant).

Non! ce n'est pas le jour,
Ce n'est pas l'alouette
Dont te chant a frappé ton oreille inquiète!
C'est le doux rossignol, confident de l'amour!

Roméo.

C'est l'alouette, hélas! messagère du jour.
            (Ils s'approchent de la fenêtre.)
Vois ces rayons jaloux dont l'horizon se
    dore!
Les flambeaux de la nuit pâlissent!... et l'au-
    rore
Dans les vapeurs de l'orient
Se lève en souriant!

Juliette.

Non!... ce n'est pas le jour!—Cette lueur
    funeste
N'est qu'un doux reflet de l'astre des nuits!
Reste! Reste!

Roméo   (serrant JULIETTE dans ses bras).

Ah! Vienne donc la mort!... je reste!

Juliette.

Ah! tu dis vrai!... C'est le jour!... fuis!
Il faut quitter ta Juliette!

Romeo.

    No, no! 'tis not yet near day,
    'Twas no lark pierced thine ear, love;
    'Twas the nightingale's note
    On the pomegranate tree!

Juliet.

    Nay!
    'Tis the lark, alas! early herald of morn,
    Love, now leave me!

Romeo.

    One kiss more,
    And I go!

Juliet.

    Cruel fate!

Romeo.

    Yet doubt not
    That we'll meet, my Juliet, again!
    And all these woes shall serve, love,
    For sweet discourses in our time to come!

Juliet.

    But now indeed farewell!
    For dawn doth end the spell
      With young love glowing,
    And thou my soul's delight
      Afar art going!

Romeo.

    But now indeed farewell!
    For dawn doth end the spell
      With young love glowing,
    From thee my soul's delight
      Afar I'm going!

Juliet.

    O fortune, grant
      Though we part now in sorrow,
    Our love may blossom
      More brightly to-morrow!

Juliet and Romeo.

    Farewell! my soul, my love!
    (ROMEO goes off the balcony. JULIET watches his descent.)

Juliet.

    Farewell, oh, dear one! Angels above,
    To you, to you. I now confide my love!

Roméo.

    Non! ce n'est pas le jour, ce n'est pas l'alou-
    ette!
    C'est le doux rossignol, confident de l'amour!

Juliette.

    C'est l'alouette, hélas! messagère du jour!
    Pars, ma vie!

Roméo.

    Un baiser, et je pars!...

Juliette

        (s'abandonnant à l'étreinte de ROMÉO).
    Loi cruelle!

Roméo.

    Ah! reste! reste encore dans mes bras en-
    lacés!
    Un jour il sera doux à notre amour fidèle
    De se ressouvenir de ses tourments passés!

Juliette.

    Il faut partir, hélas!
    Il faut quitter ces bras
      Où je te presse,
    Et t'arracher à cette ardente ivresse!

Roméo.

    Il faut partir, hélas!
    Alors qu'entre ses bras
      Elle me presse!
    Et c'en est fait de cette ardente ivresse!

Juliette.

    Ah! que le sort
      Qui de toi me sépare
    Plus que la mort
      Est cruel et barbare!

Roméo.

    Adieu, mon âme!
    Adieu, ma vie!...
        (ROMÉO franchit le balcon et disparaît.)

Juliette.

    Anges du ciel, à vous je le confie!...

SCENE II—Juliet, Gertrude, afterwards Capulet and Friar Lawrence.

Gertrude

(entering).

Where is Juliet?

(Sees her.)

Ah! a mercy, my child,

That your husband is gone! your father is coming!

Juliet.

Heaven! will he know?

Gertrude.

Nay, that he will not;

With him the friar comes—

Juliet.

In heaven

I put my trust!

(Enter Capulet and Friar Lawrence.)

Capulet.

How now, daughter? the day-light yet is young

In heaven—and behold! thou'rt awake,

As if thou hadst not slumbered. Alack!

On thee, too, weigheth my care, I can see,

And a deep regret for the youth we have lost!

Let the nuptial hymns

Succeed to shocks of arm!

And faithful to Tybalt's last thought!

Receive the husband he has named!

And smile amidst thy tears!

Juliet.

Who is he I'm to wed?

Capulet.

The noblest of us all! Paris, brave and true!

Juliet

(in terror).

Ah!

Lawrence

(aside to Juliet).

Be silent!

Gertrude

(aside to Juliet).

On your guard!

Capulet.

The altar is ready! Paris has my word!

Be married this very day!

SCÈNE II—Juliette, Gertrude, puis Capulet et Frère Laurent.

Gertrude

(paraissant).

Juliette!...Ah! le ciel soit loué!... Votre époux

Est parti! Voici votre père!

Juliette.

Dieu! saurait-il?...

Gertrude.

Rien, j'espère!...

Frère Laurent le suit.

Juliette.

Seigneur! protège-nous!

(Entre Capulet suivi de Frère Laurent.)

Capulet.

Quoi! ma fille, la nuit est à peine achevée,

Et tes yeux sont ouverts, et te voilà levée?

Hélas! notre souci, je le vois, est pareil,

Que l'hymne nuptial succède au bruit des armes!

Fidèle au dernier vœu que Tybalt a formé,

Reçois de lui l'époux que sa bouche a nommé;

Souris au milieu de tes larmes!

Juliette.

Cet époux, quel est-il?

Capulet.

Le plus noble entre tous.

Le comte Pâris!

Juliette

(à part).

Dieu!

Frère Laurent

(bas à Juliette).

Silence!

Gertrude

(de même).

Calmez-vous!

Capulet.

L'autel est préparé; Pâris a ma parole.

Soyez unis tous deux sans attendre à demain.

That the soul of Tybalt,
Present to the marriage,
May rest in peace!
The will of the dead
As that of God itself,
Is a supreme and holy law
Which we must respect.

Juliet   (aside).

Still my heart is thine, my love, for aye!

Gertrude   (aside).

Let the dead in cold obstruction rest for aye!

Lawrence.

How she trembles! still her heart will love
  obey.

Capulet.

You, holy father, can instruct her in duty,
  I trow:
Our friends are coming, I go to receive
  them!

(Exit, followed by GERTRUDE.)

SCENE III—FRIAR LAWRENCE and JULIET.

Juliet   (in despair).

My father!
I am past cure, past hope, past help;
Love, and my secret troth I've kept hid in
  my breast,
For thou didst so advise me. In my need
Now to thee I turn; from out thy long
Experience, O give present counsel.
O give me, my father, a hope—if not,
Then I'm ready to die!

(She takes a dagger from her breast.)

Lawrence.

My child! then death has for thee no
  terrors?

Juliet.

No!—none—far worse than death
Living a wife, shame-stained!

(LAWRENCE takes out a phial.)

Lawrence.

Drink then, drink of this potion,
When thou shalt be alone! quick, a drowsy
  humor

Que l'ombre de Tybalt, présente à cet
  hymen,
S'apaise enfin et se console!
La volonté des morts,
Comme celle de Dieu lui-même,
Est une loi sainte, une loi suprême;
Nous devons respecter la volonté des morts.

Juliette   (à part).

Ne crains rien, Roméo, mon cœur est sans
  remords!

Gertrude   (à part).

Dans leur tombe laissons dormir en paix
  les morts!

Frère Laurent.

Elle tremble! et mon cœur partage ses remords!

Capulet.

Frère Laurent saura te dicter ton devoir.
Nos amis vont venir; je vais les recevoir.

(Il sort, suivi de GERTRUDE.)

SCÈNE III—FRÈRE LAURENT, JULIETTE.

Juliette   (avec désepoir).

Tout est perdu, mon père! tout m'accable!
J'ai, pour vous obéir,
Caché mon désespoir et mon amour coup-
  able!
C'est à vous de me secourir,
A vous de m'arracher à mon sort misérable!
Parlez, mon père!... ou bien je suis prête à
  mourir!

(Elle lui montre un poignard.)

Frère Laurent.

Ainsi la mort ne trouble point votre âme?

Juliette.

Non, non, plutôt la mort que ce mensonge
  infâme!

Frère Laurent
          (lui présentant un flacon).

Buvez donc ce breuvage, et des membres au
  cœur,

Shall run thro' thy veins: and shall seize on
Each vital spirit: Then its progress
No pulse shall keep, but shall cease to beat!
All soon the roses on thy lips, and on
Thy cheek shall wither and fade into ashes;
Thine eyelids too will close—as life is shut
By death.
Loud will they raise the sound of lamenta-
tion
"Juliet is dead!" "Juliet is dead!" For so
Shall they deem thee reposing. But
The angels above will reply "she but sleeps!"
For two-and-forty hours, thou shalt lie in
death's seeming.
And then, to life awakening as from a pleas-
ant dreaming,
From the ancient vault thou shalt haste
away;
Thy husband shall be there, in the night, to
watch o'er thee,
Nigh to thee ever, on thy waking we will
stay,
So shall this draught once more to life and
love restore thee.
Art thou afraid?

Juliet   (taking the phial).
No! no! in thy hand
My life I give up!

Lawrence.
Till to-morrow!

Juliet.
Till to-morrow!
          (LAWRENCE exit.)

SCENE IV—JULIET (alone).

Juliet.
O Lord! what icy thrill pervades my veins!
Should this potion be without effect!
Vain fears! never against my will
Shall I be the Count's bride.
          (Hiding the dagger in her bosom.)
No! this dagger shall be the keeper of my
faith!
O Love! give strength and courage
To my heart. To hesitate is an outrage!
To tremble is a want of faith.

Va soudain se répandre une froide langueur,
De la mort mensongère image;
Dans vos veines bientôt le sang s'arrêtera;
Bientôt une pâleur livide effacera
Les roses de votre visage.
Vos yeux seront fermés ainsi que dans la
mort!
En vain éclateront alors les cris d'alarmes!
"Elle n'est plus!" diront vos compagnes en
larmes;
Et les anges du ciel répondront: "Elle dort!"
Dans la nuit du tombeau vous dormirez
comme eux.
C'est là qu'après un jour votre corps et votre
âme,
Comme d'un foyer mort se ranime la flamme,
Sortiront de ce lourd sommeil.
Par l'ombre protégés, votre époux et moi-
même
Nous épîrons votre réveil,
Et vous fuirez au bras de celui qui vous
aime!
Hésitez-vous?

Juliette   (prenant le flacon).
Non! non! à votre main
J'abandonne ma vie!

Frère Laurent.
A demain!

Juliette.
A demain!
          (FRÈRE LAURENT sort.)

SCÈNE IV—JULIETTE, seule.

Juliette.
Dieu! quel frisson court dans mes veines!
Si ce breuvage était sans pouvoir!...... Crain-
tes vaines!
Je n'appartiendrai pas au comte malgré moi!
          (Cachant le poignard dans son sein.)
Non! ce poignard sera le gardien de ma foi!
Amour, ranime mon courage,
Et de mon cœur chasse l'effroi!
Hésiter, c'est te faire outrage!
Trembler est un manque de foi!

O! pour yourself this beverage!....
O Romeo, I drink to thee!
(Having poured the contents of the phial in a cup, she stops.)

Ah! But if in those funeral cells!
I should awake before his return!....
Almighty God! this awful thought
Has struck me with horror,
What shall I become in that darkness!
In that abode of death and groans,
That the past centuries have filled with
    corpses!
Where Tybalt, yet bloody from his wounds
In the dark night, by my side shall rest,
Oh! should my hand meet his!
            (With madness.)
What ghost is that, from death escaped?
It is Tybalt; he calls me!....he wants
From my way to drive my husband
And his fatal sword!....
No!—Away, you ghosts—
And ye! fatal dreams! away!
Let the dawn of happiness rise
Over the shadows of past torment.
            (Seizing the cup.)
O Love! give strength and courage
To my heart! To hesitate is an outrage!
To tremble is a want of faith,
O pour yourself this beverage!
O! Romeo! I drink to thee!....

(She drinks,—enter GERTRUDE followed by girls. JULIET
goes to meet them, and departs with them.)

SECOND TABLEAU—A hall of the Palace—At back the
doors of the chapel.

SCENE I—CAPULET, PARIS, FRIAR LAWRENCE, GREGORIO,
JULIET, GERTRUDE, girls, friends, and retainers of the
CAPULETS. Wedding train.

(The organ is heard, the doors of the Chapel open, the
priests and suite enter.)

Capulet
            (taking JULIET's hand).
Daughter, yield to the will of the betrothed
    who loves you.

Verse toi-même ce breuvage!......
O Roméo, je bois à toi!
(Après avoir versé le contenu du flacon dans une coupe,
elle s'arrête.)

Mais, si demain pourtant, en ces caveaux fu-
    nèbres,
Je m'éveillais avant son retour!.... Dieu
    puissant!
Cette pensée horrible a glacé tout mon sang!
Que deviendrai-je en ces ténèbres,
Dans ce séjour de mort et de gémîssements
Que les siècles passés ont rempli d'ossements?
Où Tybalt, tout saignant encore de sa bles-
    sure
Près de moi, dans la nuit obscure,
Dormira?... Dieu! ma main rencontrera sa
main!   (Avec égarement.)
Quelle est cette ombre à la mort échappée?
C'est Tybalt!... Il m'appelle!... Il veut de
    mon chemin
Ecarter mon époux, et sa fatale épée....
Non!... fantômes, disparaissez!
Dissipe-toi, funeste rêve!
Que l'aube du bonheur se lève
Sur l'ombre des tourments passés!..
            (Saisissant la coupe.)
Viens! Viens!
Amour, ranime mon courage,
Et de mon cœur chasse l'effroi;
Hésiter, c'est te faire outrage;
Trembler, est un manque de foi;
Verse toi-même ce breuvage,
O Roméo, je bois à toi!

(Elle boit.—GERTRUDE paraît au fond suivie de jeunes filles.
JULIETTE va à leur rencontre et sort avec elles.)

DEUXIÈME TABLEAU—Une galérie du palais.—Au
fond, les portes de la chapelle.

SCÈNE I—CAPULET, PÂRIS, FRÈRE LAURENT, GRÉGORIO,
JULIETTE, GERTRUDE, jeunes filles, amis et serviteurs des Capulets.—Cortège nuptial.

(Un prélude d'orgue se fait entendre; les portes de la chapelle s'ouvrent; un cortège de cleres et d'enfants de chœur
entre en scène.)

Capulet
            (offrant la main à JULIETTE).
Ma fille, cède aux vœux du fiancé qui
    t'aime;

God is going to unite you with eternal
bonds;

Happiness waiting for you at the foot of
the holy altars,

From that blessed Hymn here is the supreme
moment.

(Paris comes forward to place the ring on the finger of
JULIET.)

Juliet.

(withdrawing her hand, and as in a dream).

Hatred is the source of this fatal love!

Let a coffin be my wedding couch.

(She detaches her bridal wreath; her hair falls on her
shoulders.)

Capulet.

O Juliet! come back to thy senses!

Juliet.

O Lord!—I totter!....

     (They surround her.)

Whose is that voice that calls me? Can it
be death!

O Heaven—my father!—farewell!

     (She falls insensible in his arms.)

Capulet.

My Juliet!

My daughter!—lifeless!—dead!

Just God!

All.

She is dead!

     (Curtain falls.)

ACT V.

(The Vault of the CAPULETS.)

SCENE I—FRIAR LAWRENCE, FRIAR JOHN, JULIET.

(As the curtain rises, FRIAR LAWRENCE is seen near the
tomb on which JULIET is asleep—the stage is lighted by a
lamp, burning over the tomb.)

     (Enter FRIAR JOHN.)

Lawrence.

Well! my letter to Romeo!

Friar John.

His page,

Attacked by the Capulets,

Has just now been taken wounded

In his master's palace,

And could not deliver the message.

     (Delivering the letter to FRIAR LAWRENCE.)

Here is the letter!

Le ciel va vous unir par des vœux éternels;

Le bonheur vous attend au pied des saints
autels;

De cet hymen béni voici l'instant suprême!

(PÀRIS s'avance et se dispose à passer son anneau au doigt
de JULIETTE.)

Juliette

(Retirant sa main et à demi-voix, comme dans un rêve).

La haine est le berceau de cet amour fatal!...

Que le cercueil soit mon lit nuptial!......

(Elle porte la main à sa tête et en détaché sa couronne de
fiancée; ses cheveux se déroulent et tombent sur ses épaules.)

Capulet.

Juliette!.. reviens à toi!..

Juliette.

Dieu... je chancelle!..

     (On l'entoure et on la soutient.)

Quelle nuit m'environne?... et quelle voix
m'appelle?

Est-ce la mort?... j'ai peur!... mon père!..
adieu!...

(Elle tombe inanimée dans les bras de ceux qui l'entourent.)

Capulet.

Juliette!... ma fille!... Ah!.. morte!... juste
Dieu!

Tous.

Juste Dieu!

     (La toile tombe.)

ACTE CINQUIÈME.

Une crypte souterraine; çà et là des tombeaux.

SCÈNE I—FRÈRE LAURENT, FRÈRE JEAN, JULIETTE.

(Au lever du rideau, FRÈRE LAURENT est debout près du
tombeau sur lequel est étendue JULIETTE endormie; une lampe
funéraire, placée sur le tombeau, éclaire le théâtre; FRÈRE
JEAN entre en scène.)

Frère Laurent.

Eh bien? ma lettre à Roméo?

Frère Jean.

Son page,

Attaqué par les Capulets,

Vient d'être ramené blessé dans le palais

De son maître, et n'a pu s'acquitter du message.

     (Remettant une lettre à FRÈRE LAURENT.)

Voici la lettre!

ROMÉO ET JULIETTE 143

Lawrence.

O fatal doom!
Let another messenger leave this very night!
Come—each minute we lose
Brings us to great dangers.

(Exeunt, an iron door is heard to shut behind them—great silence.)

SCENE II—JULIET, then ROMEO.
SYMPHONY.

(The noise of a crowbar is heard. The door yields. Enter ROMEO with the iron bar in his hand.)

Romeo.   (Throws aside his bar.)

'Tis here!
All hail, O tomb, home of the silent dead!
Not a tomb! No! for here Juliet is lying,
Making the grim vault full of light.
All hail! O shrine radiant and bright.

(Perceives and rushes towards her.)

Ah, she is there—my Juliet!

(Takes the lamp to see her more distinctly.)

Burn,
O torch in the gloom! to me show her again!
Wife beloved—Ah! thou art not conquered;
For death, though it has drawn from thy breath
All the honey, to change thee yet lacked
The power. No, still beauty's ensign is crimson
In thy lips, love—and death's pale flag
Is not advanced there.

(Replaces the lamp on the tomb.)

Oh, is it
Unsubstantial death of thee is amorous,
And that the lean abhorred monster keeps
Thee here? For fear of that I'll stay with thee,
My beloved, nor again from this palace
Of dim night depart.
Yes, my weary yoke
Now offshaking, oh, here will I set up
My everlasting rest. Eyes, O look your last;
Arms, take your last embrace; and kiss her lips,
That are the doors of breath!

(He embraces JULIET, then takes a phial of poison from his pouch.)

Frère Laurent.

O funeste hasard!
Qu'un autre messager parte cette nuit même!
Venez! chaque instant de retard
Nous jette en un péril extrême.

(Il sort, suivi de FRÈRE JEAN.—On entend une porte de fer se refermer sur eux.—Profond silence.)

SCÈNE II—JULIETTE, puis ROMÉO.
SYMPHONIE.

(Au bout d'un moment, on entend le bruit d'un levier ébranlant la porte,—la porte cède avec bruit.—ROMÉO paraît.)

Roméo   (un levier à la main.)

C'est là!...

(Il jette son levier.)

Saint, tombeau sombre et silencieux!
Un tombeau!..non!—ô demeure plus belle
Que le séjour même des cieux,
Palais splendide et radieux,
Salut!

(Apercevant JULIETTE et s'élançant vers le tombeau.)

Ah! la voila!... C'est elle!...
Viens, funètre clarté; viens l'offrir à mes yeux!

(Prenant la lampe funéraire.)

O ma femme! ô ma bien-aimée!
La mort, en aspirant ton haleine embaumée,
N'a pas altéré ta beauté!
Non! cette beauté que j'adore
Sur ton front calme et pur semble régner encore
Et sourire à l'éternité.

(Il repose la lampe sur le tombeau.)

Pourquoi me la rends-tu si belle, ô mort livide?
Est-ce pour me jeter plus vite dans ses bras?
Va! c'est le seul bonheur dont mon cœur soit avide,
Et ta proie aujourd'hui ne t'échappera pas.

(Regardant autour de lui.)

Ah! je te contemple sans crainte,
Tombe, où je vais enfin près d'elle reposer!...

(Se penchant vers JULIETTE.)

O mes bras, donnez-lui votre dernière étreinte!
Mes lèvres, donnez-lui votre dernier baiser!

(Il embrasse JULIETTE, puis, tirant de son sein un petit flacon en métal et se tournant vers JULIETTE.)

My love,
Thus do I pledge thee!
(He drinks the poison.)

Juliet
(half awakening).
Where am I?

Romeo
(startled).
'Twas but fancy!. Am I dreaming?
Yet surely she did speak!
(Seizes her hand.)
My hands,
Trembling the while, feel in hers
That the life-blood is still running warm!
(She opens her eyes, raises her head slightly, and looks at him.)
Now her eyes open! She ariseth!

Juliet
(moving).
Romeo! Romeo!

Romeo.
O thou merciful Heaven!
(Juliet sits up, and puts her feet on the ground.)
She's alive! she's alive!

Juliet
(coming to her senses).
Ah! methought that I heard
Tones that I loved, soft falling!

Romeo.
'Tis I! Romeo—thine own—
Who thy slumbers have stirred,
Led by my heart alone,
Thee, my bride, unto love
And the fair world recalling!
(Juliet falls into his arms.)

Juliet.
O mine own!

Romeo.
Come, let's fly hence!

Juliet.
Happy dawn!

Romeo and Juliet.
Come, the world is all before us!
Come! be joy our own, for woe departs!
Father of love, graciously bending,
Blest be Thou by two grateful hearts.

A toi!...... ma Juliette!
(Il vide le flacon d'un trait et le jette.)

Juliette
(s'éveillant peu à peu).
Où suis-je?...

Roméo
(tournant les yeux vers Juliette).
Dieu!... je rêve!
Sa bouche a murmuré!...
(Saisissant la main de Juliette.)
Mes doigts, en trémissant,
Ont senti dans les siens la chaleur de son
sang!
(Juliette regarde Roméo d'un air égaré.)
Elle me regarde... et se lève!

Juliette
(soupirant).
Roméo!...... Roméo!....

Roméo
(avec éclat).
Seigneur Dieu tout-puissant!
(Juliette pose un pied sur les degrés du tombeau.)
Elle vit! elle vit! Juliette est vivante!

Juliette
(reprenant peu à peu ses sens).
Dieu! quelle est cette voix dont la douceur
m'enchante?......

Roméo.
C'est moi! C'est ton époux
Qui, tremblant de bonheur, embrasse tes
genoux,
Qui ramène à ton cœur la lumière enivrante
De l'amour et des cieux!

Juliette
(se jetant dans les bras de Roméo).
Ah! c'est toi!...

Roméo.
Viens, fuyons tous deux!...

Juliette.
O bonheur!

Roméo et Juliette.
Viens, fuyons au bout du monde!
Viens! soyons heureux,
Fuyons tous deux!
Dieu de bonté! Dieu de clémence!
Sois béni par deux cœurs heureux!

Romeo
(tottering).
Ah! hearts of stone—ay, harder than stone,
Have our fathers!

Juliet
(frightened).
But thy words are so wild!

Romeo.
Nor sorrow, nor entreaty, softened them
To their children's prayer! on the threshold
Of joy we are standing—yet we die!

Juliet.
We die! Romeo, sure thou dost wander!
What strange terrors seize on thy fancy?
My love—my lord, recall thee to thyself.

Romeo.
Alas! I believed thee dead, love, and—
I drank of this draught!
(Shows the phial.)

Juliet.
Of that draught?
It is death!
(They embrace.)

Romeo.
Yield not thyself to sorrow,
Our dream was all too bright,
Now dawns a fairer morrow,
Shall never set in night!
From a dull slumber waking,
In a fair dawn I rise,
Chains my soul now is breaking,
To heaven dove-like it flies!

Juliet.
O my heart—break; break in sorrow!

Romeo
(wandering).
Yet hark! Juliet my dearest—'tis the lark,
Early herald proclaiming the day!
No, no!
'Tis not yet near day! 'Tis no lark
Thou didst hear, love, but the nightingale
lone
On the pomegranate tree!
(he slips from her arms, and falls on the steps of the bier.)

Roméo
(chancellant).
Ah! les parents ont tous des entrailles de
pierre!

Juliette.
Roméo, que dis-tu?

Roméo.
Les larmes, la prière,
Rien, rien ne peut les attendrir!
A la porte des cieux, Juliette...—Et
mourir!...

Juliette.
Mourir!—Ah! la fièvre t'égare,
De toi quel délire s'empare?..
Mon bien-aimé! Rappelle ta raison!

Roméo.
Ah! je te croyais morte.. et j'ai bu ce poison!

Juliette.
Ce poison!.. Juste Dieu!...

Roméo
(serrant JULIETTE dans ses bras).
Console-toi, pauvre âme,
Le rêve était trop beau!
L'amour, céleste flamme,
Survit, même au tombeau!
Il soulève la pierre,
Et, des anges béni,
Comme un flot de lumière
Se perd dans l'infini!...

Juliette
(égarée).
O douleur!... ô torture!...

Roméo
(d'une voix plus faible).
Ecoute, ô Juliette!......
L'alouette déjà nous annonce le jour!......
Non.... ce n'est pas le jour...... Ce n'est pas
l'alouette,
C'est le doux rossignol, confident de
l'amour!...
(Il glisse des bras de JULIETTE et tombe sur les degrés du
tombeau.)

Juliet

           (taking the phial).

  Ah! cruel spouse,

Drink all! no friendly drop thou'st left me,

To help me, so I die with thee!

(She flings the phial away, then remembering the dagger,
draws it from her breast.)

  Ah!

Here's my dagger still! I'd forgotten thee,—

Friend: now, happy dagger, behold thy
    sheath!

(She stabs herself. Romeo half raises himself.)

Romeo.

  Hold! hold thy hand!

Juliet

           (in his arms).

  Ah, happy moment,

Stay! My soul with rapture is swelling,

Thus to die, love, with thee.

        (She lets fall the dagger.)

  Yet one embrace!

I love thee!

      (They half rise in each other's arms.)

Both.

  O, Heaven, grant us thy grace!

      (They die.)

END.

Juliette

          (ramassant le flacon).

  Cruel époux!—De ce poison funeste

Tu ne m'as pas laissé ma part!....

(Elle rejette le flacon, et portant la main à son cœur elle y
rencontre le poignard qu'elle avait caché sous ses vêtements,
et l'en tire d'un geste rapide.)

  Ah, fortuné poignard!

Ton secours me reste!

      (Elle se frappe.)

Roméo

         (se relevant à demi).

  Dieu!....qu'as-tu fait?

Juliette

        (dans les bras de Roméo).

  Va! ce moment est doux!

     (Elle laisse tomber le poignard.)

  O joie infinie et suprême

De mourir avec toi..... Viens!... un baiser!..

Je t'aime!......

Ensemble

(se relevant tous deux à demi dans un dernier effort).

  Seigneur, Seigneur, pardonnez-nous!

    (Ils meurent.—La toile tombe.)

FIN.

MANON

by

JULES MASSENET

THE STORY OF THE OPERA.

The story of Manon Lescaut, as here given, is a dramatization, by Meilhac and Grille, of the famous novel by Abbe Provost. The last act of the opera, however, is original with the two librettists.

The action occurs in the year 1721. Guillot Morfontain and a party of gay friends are making merry at an Inn. Manon, escorted by her cousin Lescaut, of the Guards, arrives on her way to a convent. She is of the peasantry, but vain as well as beautiful. Guillot leaves his friends, to pay attention to the young girl. He meets with no success, and is finally compelled to retreat.

The Chevalier Des Grieux, however, who appears upon the scene during the temporary absence of the cousin Lescaut, is more successful. Although about to take holy orders and become a priest, Des Grieux is charmed and infatuated by Manon's beauty and seeming simplicity; while she, in her vanity, seeks for a higher social position, and is also fascinated by the young Chevalier's manliness. The result is an almost immediate elopement of the pair.

They occupy apartments in Paris (act second). Before Des Grieux can secure his father's consent to their marriage the young man is placed in jeopardy by Lescaut and De Brétigny (an old roue). The two men are soon pacified; but shortly afterwards Des Grieux is seized by some men in the Count's (his father's) employ, and is taken away from Manon.

In the third act we find Manon under the protection of De Brétigny. But she learns that Des Grieux (whom she really loves) is now a priest at St. Sulpice; and she flies from De Brétigny to win back her lover.

In the second scene there is an interesting and dramatic situation, wherein Manon succeeds in inducing Des Grieux to renounce the priesthood and renew a gay life.

In the fourth act is seen the interior of a gambling-house in Paris. Des Grieux is unjustly accused of cheating, and trouble ensues. He and Manon are about to be arrested when the Count Des Grieux appears and releases the Chevalier; but Manon, through the efforts of Guillot who seeks revenge, is condemned to transportation.

In the last scene (a lonely road on the way to Havre), Manon again meets her lover Des Grieux, and dies in his arms.

NOTE. In the original score of the opera, the second scene of act fourth as here given is really the fifth act.

DRAMATIS PERSONÆ.

THE CHEVALIER DES GRIEUX.
THE COUNT DES GRIEUX, his Father.
LESCAUT, of the Royal Guard; Manon's cousin.
GUILLOT MORFONTAIN, Minister of Finance, and a Roue.
DE BRÉTIGNY, a Nobleman.
AN INNKEEPER.

ATTENDANT AT ST. SULPICE.
A SERGEANT OF GUARDS.
A SOLDIER.
POUSSETTE)
JAVOTTE } Actresses.
ROSSETTE)
MANON, the Adventuress.

Gamblers, Croupiers, Guards, Travellers, Townspeople, Ladies, Gentlemen, etc.

MANON.

—

ACT I.

—

(The courtyard of the inn at Amiens Enter Pousette, Javotte, Rosette, Guillot and De Bretigny.)

GUILLOT (*calling*). Hello there! Mine host!
Must I shout continually to get an answer?

DE BRÉTIGNY. Bring us some drink!

GUILLOT. Something to eat! Hello there!

DE BRÉTIGNY. A fine place, indeed, is this!

GUILLOT AND B. Still no one coming?

GUILLOT. This will not do at all. We should
receive better attention!

DE BRÉTIGNY (*angrily*). Are you alive or
buried?

GUILLOT. It seems that the Innkeeper *is* dead!

POUSETTE. Wait, sir! keep up courage.

GUILLOT AND B. A fine place, indeed!

POUSETTE AND OTHERS. Call him again!
Keep calling!

(All, in chorus, appeal to the INNKEEPER.)
(INNKEEPER appears in doorway.)

DE BRÉTIGNY. Now the rascal's come at last!

GUILLOT. This way, you rogue!

ACTE I.

—

(Le Grande Cour d'une Hôtellerie, à Amiens. Poussette, Javotte, Rosette, Guillot and De Brétigny.)

GUILLOT (*appelant*). Holà! Hé! Monsieur l'hôtelier! Combien de temps faut-il
crier avant que vous daignez entendre?

BRÉTIGNY. Nous avons soif!

GUILLOT. Nous avons faim! Holà! Hé!

BRÉTIGNY. Vous moquez-vous de faire attendre?

GUILLOT ET B. Morbleu! Viendrez-vous à la
fin!

GUILLOT (*avec dépit*). Foi de Guillot morfontaine! C'est par trop de cruauté. Pour des
gens de qualité!

BRÉTIGNY (*en colère*). Il est mort, la chose
est certaine!

GUILLOT. Il est mort! Il est mort!

POUSSETTE. Allons, messieurs, point de cou-
roux!

GUILLOT ET B. Que faut-il faire!

POUSSETTE ET LE AUTRES. On le rappelle!
Rappelle!

(Tout, rappelle l'hôtelier.)

BRÉTIGNY (*Avec joie et surprise*). Ah!
voilà le coupable!

GUILLOT. Réponds nous, misérable!

(3)

INNKEEPER   D'ye think I'm neglectful? Patience then; I'll quickly serve the food.

(Enter servants with the repast and wines, from inn.)

INNKEEPER (*graciously*). Here is much to select from.

ALL. Good!

INNKEEPER. Ragout!

ALL. Very good indeed!

POUSETTE. Heavens! 't is fine!

(All follow INNKEEPER into the house.)

NOTE. In the English production of this opera the preceding portion of Act. I is sometimes omitted and the performance begun with the following:
(The TOWNSPEOPLE enter, crowding around the hotel. The bell rings.)

CHORUS OF TOWNSPEOPLE. Hark! hark! the hour is sounding,
See the coach the corner rounding!
We must see all.
At some to laugh,
To smile on beauty,
Is what we call
Our solemn duty.

(LESCAUT enters, followed by two GUARDSMEN.)

LESCAUT (*to his companions*). This is the place, or I'm mistaken, where the coach from Arras stops to bait man and beast.

THE GUARDS. This is the place.

LESCAUT (*dismissing them*). Good-day!

THE GUARDS. Ah, surely thou art joking, Lescaut,
Thou wilt not leave us thus?

LESCAUT (*good-humoredly*). Not I!
A wine-shop there is close at hand,
Where they sell only liquor that's strong.
Here awaiting my cousin I stand,
But you I'll rejoin before long.

THE GUARDS. Well; don't forget.

LESCAUT (*appearing hurt*). What do you mean? You go too far!

THE GUARDS (*entreatingly*). Lescaut!

L'HÔTELIER. Moi! vous abandonner! Je ne dirai qu'un mot : qu'on serve le diner!

(Entrant des marmitons avec les plats.)

L'HÔTELIER.   Et diverses épices; poisson, poulet!

L'AUTRES   Parfait!

L'HÔTELIER. Ragout!

L'AUTRES. C'est bien! parfait!

POUSETTE. O douce providence! On vient servir.
(Tous rentrant dans le hôtellerie.)

(Les Bourgeois et les Bourgeoises envahissent peu à peu l'hôtellerie. Le cloche entendre.)

CHOEUR (*Bourgeoises et Bourgeois*). Entendez vous la cloche,
Voici l'heure du coche,
Il faut tout voir! tout voir!
Les voyageurs, les voyageuses
Il faut tout voir!
Pour nous c'est un devoir!

(LESCAUT entre suivi de GARDES.)

LESCAUT. C'est bien ici l'hôtellerie
Où le coche d'Arras
Va tantôt s'arrêter!

LES GARDES. C'est bien ici.

LESCAUT (*les congédiant*). Bonsoir!

LES GARDES. Quelle plaisanterie!
Lescaut, tu pourrais quitter!

LESCAUT. Jamais! Jamais! Allez à l'auberge voisine,
On y vend un clairet joyeux;
Je vais attendre ma cousine,
Et je vous rejoins tous les deux!

LES GARDES. Rappelle toi!

LESCAUT. Vous m'insultez, c'est imprudent!

LES GARDES. Lescaut!

LESCAUT. Ah well!
I perhaps, shall lose my memory
When next you want a drink of me.
Be off to the wine-shop at hand,
And there let the liquor flow free.
Here awaiting my cousin I stand,
You can drink while you're waiting for me.

(Exeunt the GUARDS. Travellers appear in the courtyard, with porters and servants, carrying baggage.)
(Commotion ; travellers seeking parcels, valises, etc.)

TOWNSPEOPLE (*joyfully*). Here they come! Here they come!

(The coach arrives, travellers alight from it.)

AN OLD LADY (*adjusting her head-dress*). Oh! this is shameful! My pretty bonnet!

TOWNSPEOPLE (*laughing*). Now do just look at that old woman!

A TRAVELLER. Hi! porter, here!

PORTER (*in bad temper*). All right! All right!

TOWNSPEOPLE (*laughing*). Ah, how our sides will ache with laughter!

VARIOUS TRAVELLERS.
{
Tell me, sir, I pray, where's my birdcage?
Hi! here I say.
Answer me!
Hi! Here, now guard!
My turn first!
My boxes!
Where's my trunk?
}

ALL. Answer me!

POSTILLIONS AND PORTERS. All right! All right! Just wait a bit!

TRAVELLERS (*loudly*). Why don't you give us each his luggage?

POSTILLIONS AND PORTERS. Not so much bluster. Make less noise, we say!

TRAVELLERS. Heav'ns, that this worry there should be
For harmless travellers such as we
Ah! every man his will should make
Before he dare a journey take!

LESCAUT. C'est bon! Je perdrais la memoire
Quand il s'agit de boire!
Allez! à l'auberge voisine
On y vend un clairet joyeux!
Je vais attendre ma cousine!
Allez trinquer en m'attendant!
En m'attendant allez trinquer!

(Sortent GARDES.)
(La rue s'emplit de postillons, de porteurs portant des malles, des cartons, des valises et précédés ou suivi de voyageurs at de voyageuses qui tournent autour d'eux pour obtenir leurs bagages.)

BOURGEOIS (*avec joie*). Les voila! les voila!

(Le Coche arrivé.)

UNE VIELLE DAME. Oh! ma coiffure! Oh! ma toilette!

BOURGEOIS ET B. Voyes vous pas cette coquette!

UN VOYAGEUR. Eh! le porteur!

UN PORTEUR. Dans un instant!

BOURGEOIS ET B. Ah! le singulier personnage

LES VOYAGEURS.
{
Où sont mes oiseaux et ma cage?
Hè! Postillon!
Postillon!
Ma malle!
Ma panier
Postillon!
}

TOUS. Postillons!

POSTILLONS ET PORTEURS. Dans un moment

VOYAGEURS. Donnez a chacun son bagage

POSTILLONS ET PORTEURS Moins de tapage Non! Non!

VOYAGEURS Dieux! quel tracas et quel tourment!
Quand il faut monter en voiture!
Ah! je le jure,
On ferait bien de faire avant son testament!

POSTILLIONS, PORTERS, AND TOWNSPEOPLE.

Ah! what a life $\left\{\begin{array}{l}\text{we}\\\text{these}\end{array}\right\}$ poor men lead!
Who would endure it but for need?
See, up and down $\left\{\begin{array}{l}\text{we}\\\text{they}\end{array}\right\}$ go in vain,
For when down, up $\left\{\begin{array}{l}\text{we}\\\text{they}\end{array}\right\}$ go again.

POSTILLONS ET BOURGEOIS.

Ah! c'est à se damner vraiment,
Chacun gémit,
Rien qu'en montant ou descendant!
Dieux! quel tourment!

TRAVELLERS (*following the* POSTILLIONS).
Look here, I'm the first.

VOYAGEURS (*poursuivant les* POSTILLONS).
Je suis le premier!

POSTILLIONS (*brusquely*). You're the last!

POSTILLONS (*brusquement*). Le dernier!

TRAVELLERS. I'm the first.

VOYAGEURS. Je suis le premier!

POSTILLIONS. No!

POSTILLONS. Non!

TOWNSPEOPLE (*laughingly imitating*). You're
the last. No!

BOURGEOIS (*imitant les* POSTILLONS). Le
dernier! Non!

(MANON, who has come out of the crowd, regards the
scene with astonishment.)

(MANON qui vient de sortir de la foule considère tout
ce tohu-bohu avec étonnement.)

WOMEN (*looking at* MANON). Oh, look!
Look at that young woman!

BOURGEOISES (*regardant* MANON). Voyez
cette jeune fille!

LESCAUT (*observing her in turn*). I'm almost sure that yon fresh and pretty girl is
Manon, my fair relation. (*To* MANON.) I
am Lescaut!

LESCAUT. Eh! j'imagine que cette belle enfant, c'est Manon! ma cousine! (A MANON.)
Je suis Lescaut!

MANON (*with some surprise*). You! Is that
true? (*Simply and without reserve.*) Come,
kiss me then!

MANON (*avec une légère surprise*). Vous
mon cousin! (*Simplement.*) Embrassez
moi!

LESCAUT. Certainly, my dear. Who would
not? (*Aside.*) My word! she is a pretty
maiden, and quite a credit to our family.

LESCAUT. Mais très volontiers, sur ma foi!
Morbleu! c'est une belle fille
Qui fait honneur à la famille!

MANON (*embarrassed*). Ah, cousin mine!
excuse me, pray.

MANON (*avec embarrass.*). Ah! mon cousin, excusez moi!

LESCAUT (*aside*). What a charming girl!

LESCAUT (*à part*). Elle est charmante!

MANON (*with expression*). A simple maid,
      fresh from lov'd home,
To me it is so strange to roam.
Dear cousin mine, excuse me, pray,
For awkwardness on such a day.
(*With vivacity.*) Oh! pardon me for prat-
      tling so,
Since this is my first trip, you know.
I scarce had started on my way,
Than with delight I wond'ring gazed
On meadows, woods, and mansions fair—
What marvel then that I was dazed!

MANON. (*avec émotion*). Je suis encor tout
      étourdie,
Je suis encor tout engourdie,
Ah! mon cousin! Excusez moi!
Excusez un moment d'émoi.
Je suis encor tout étourdie.
Pardonnez à mon bavardage
J'en suis à mon premier voyage!
Le coche s'eloignait à peine
Que j'admirais de tous mes yeux,
Les hameaux, les grands bois, la plaine,
Les voyageurs jeunes et vieux.

My heart was light as trees flew past,
Their branches waving in the wind,
And I forgot, so glad I felt,
That I must leave these joys behind.
Launched on the world thus beautiful,—
(Nay, mock me not, 'tis truth I say,)
It seemed that I had sudden flown
To Paradise that happy day.
Then came a moment of distress;
I wept aloud, I know not why.
An instant after, how I laughed!
(*With a burst of laughter.*)   To find a
    reason do not try.
Ah! cousin mine, excuse me, pray.

Ah! mon cousin, excusez moi!
C'est mon premier voyage!
Je regardais fuir, curieuse
Les arbres frissonnant au vent!
Et j'oubliais, toute joyeuse,
Que je partais pour le couvent!
Devant tant de choses nouvelles,
Ne riez pas, si je vous dis
Que je croyais avoir des ailes,
Et m'envoler en paradis!
Oui, mon cousin!
Puis, j'eus un moment de tristesse
Je pleurais, je ne sais pas quoi?
L'instant d'après, je le confesse
Je viais, Ah! Je viais!
Mais sans savoir pour-quoi?
Ah! mon cousin, excusez moi!

(Passengers and Attendants fill the Inn-yard. The departure bell rings.)

(Les voyageurs précédes des postillons envahissent la cour de l'hôtellerie. On sonne le depart du coche.)

POSTILLIONS (*to* TRAVELLERS).   Now then, time's up, sirs!

POSTILLONS.   Partez! On sonne!

TRAVELLERS (*in comical alarm*).   What's that you say!

VOYAGEURS (*avec alarme comique*).   Comment? Partir!

POSTILLIONS.   We say time's up; you see, the coach is ready!

POSTILLONS.   Allons! sortez! voici l'autre voiture!

TRAVELLERS   What! now, so soon?
Ah! is not this provoking!
Heavens! that this worry, there should be
For harmless travellers such as we!
Ah! ev'ry man his will should make
Before he dare a journey take.

VOYAGEURS.   Partir! Comment?
Quelle mésaventure!
Dieux! quel tracas et quel tourment!
Quand il faut monter en voiture!
Ah! je le jure,
On ferait bien de faire avant son testament!

(The crowd slowly disperse, leaving LESCAUT and MANON together.)

(La foule s'eloigne peu à peu laissant ensemble LESCAUT et MANON.)

LESCAUT (*to* MANON).   Wait a moment.
Be prudent; I am going to find your luggage.

LESCAUT (*au moment de sortir pour aller les paquets de* MANON).   (*To* MANON.)
Attendez-moi, soyez bien sage,
Je vais chercher votre bagage!

(Exit LESCAUT.)

(Sortent LESCAUT.)

THE TOWNSPEOPLE (*finally dispersing*).   We have discharged our solemn duty. (*Exeunt.*)

BOURGEOIS.   Il faut tout voir!
Pour nous c'est un devoir!

(MANON remains alone.)

(Ils disparaissent.)
(MANON reste seule.)

GUILLOT (*appearing on the balcony of the pavilion*).   Miserable landlord! are we never to have any wine? (*He observes* MANON.) Heavens! What do I see? Young lady! hem! hem! Young lady! (*Aside.*) Really, my head is turning round!

GUILLOT (*sur le balcon du pavillon*).   Hôtelier de malheur!
Il est donc entendu,
Que nous n'aurons jamais de vin!
(*Apercevant* MANON.)   Ciel! qu'aije vu!
Mademoiselle! hem! hem! Mademoiselle!
(*Apart.*)   Ce qui s' passe en ma cevelle!

MANON (*aside and laughing*).   What a funny man!

GUILLOT.   Young lady, I am Guillot de Morfontaine.   I am rich and would give a good deal to hear a word of love from you.   Now, what do you say to that?

MANON.   That I should be ashamed, if I were not more disposed to laugh.

(MANON laughs, and her laughter is echoed by DE BRÉTIGNY, JAVOTTE, POUSETTE, and ROSETTE, who have just appeared on the balcony.)

DE BRÉTIGNY.   Now then, Guillot, what's the game?   We are waiting for you.

GUILLOT.   Oh! go to the devil.

POUSETTE (*to* GUILLOT).   Are you not ashamed?   At your age!

DE BRÉTIGNY.   This time I swear the dog has by chance found a prize.   Never did sweeter look light up a woman's face!

JAVOTTE, POUSETTE. AND ROSETTE (*laughingly to* GUILLOT).   Oh! come back, Guillot.   Oh! come back!
Where a false step leads who can tell?
Be advised, Guillot, tempt not Fate.
Have a care: back while all is well.

DE BRÉTIGNY.   Now then, Guillot, let the girl alone and come in.   We are calling you.

GUILLOT.   Ay, ay, in a moment. (*To* MANON.)   My little one, give me a word.

DE BRÉTIGNY.   Guillot, let the girl alone.

GUILLOT (*softly to* MANON).   A postillion is coming for me directly; when you see him, understand that a carriage is at your service.   Take it, and afterwards you shall know more.

LESCAUT (*who has just entered*).   What do you say?

GUILLOT (*confused*).   Oh, sir! nothing, sir!

MANON (*apart*).   Cet homme est fort drôle, ma foi!

GUILLOT.   Mademoiselle, ecoutez moi!
On me nomme Guillot de Morfontaine,
De louis d'or ma caisse est pleine,
Et j'en donnerais beaucoup
Pour obtenir de vous un seul mot d'amour.
J'ai fini, qu' avez-vous à dire?

MANON.   Que je me fâcherais si je n'aimais mieux rire!

(MANON éclate de rire, et son rire est répété par BRÉTIGNY, JAVOTTE, POUSETTE et ROSETTE, qui viennent d'arriver sur le balcon.)

BRÉTIGNY.   Eh bien, Guillot, que faites-vous?
Nous vous attendons.

GUILLOT.   Au diable les fous!

POUSETTE (*à Guillot*).   N'avez-vous pas honte? à votre âge!

BRÉTIGNY.   Cette fois-ci, le drôle a par hasard
Découvert un tresoi
Jamais plus doux regard
N'illumina plus gracieux visage!

JAVOTTE, POUSETTE ROSETTE (*à Guillot en riant*).   Revenez, Guillot, revenez!
Dieu sait où vous mène un faux pas!
Cher ami Guillot, n'en faites pas!
Revenez! vous allez vous casser le nez!

BRÉTIGNY.   Allons, Guillot, laissez Mademoi selle,
Et revenez, l'on vous appelle!

GUILLOT.   Oui, je reviens dans un moment!
(*A* MANON.)   Ma mignonne, un mot seule ment!

BRÉTIGNY.   Guillot, laissez Mademoiselle.

GUILLOT (*à* MANON).   De ma part tout à l'heure un postillon viendra,
Quand vous l'apercevrez, cela signifiera.
Qu'une voiture attend, que vous pouvez la prendre,
Et qu'après vous devez comprendre.

LESCAUT (*vient de rentrer*).   Plaît-il, Monsieur!

GUILLOT.   Monsieur!

LESCAUT (*boisterously*). Oh, sir! Did you say—

GUILLOT (*returning to the pavilion*). Nothing, sir, I said.

JAVOTTE, POUSETTE, ROSETTE. Oh! come back, Guillot; oh, come back, etc.

(Laughing, they re-enter the pavilion.)

LESCAUT (*to* MANON). He spoke to you, Manon.

MANON (*lightly*). Well, can you say 'twas my fault?

LESCAUT. That's true; and in my eyes you are so good that I won't trouble myself.

(The two GUARDSMEN enter.)

FIRST GUARDSMAN (*to* LESCAUT). How now! thou comest not!

SECOND GUARDSMAN. Both cards and dice are waiting your pleasure below.

LESCAUT. I come; but first to this young lady, with your leave, good sirs, I must speak some words of counsel full of wisdom.

GUARDSMEN (*resignedly*). To his wisdom we'll listen.

LESCAUT (*to* MANON). Give good heed to what I say—
Duty calls me now away,
To consult these comrades here
Upon a point that's not quite clear.
Wait for me, Manon, just a moment, no more.
Make no mistake, but prudent be,
And one thing always bear in mind,
That safe within my hands you'll find
The honor of our family.
And if, forsooth, some silly man
Should whisper folly in your ear,
Behave as though you did not hear.
For safety's sake adopt that plan.

(To the GUARDSMEN, with a sign of departure.)

Now let us go and see on which of us the goddess of the game will look with loving eyes.

(As he goes he turns to MANON.)

Make no mistake, but prudent be.

(Exeunt LESCAUT and GUARDSMEN.)

LESCAUT. Eh bien! Vous disiez—

GUILLOT. Je ne disais rien!

(Rentrent pavillon)

JAVOTTE, POUSETTE ET ROSETTE. Revenez Guillot! etc.

(Ils rentrent en riant dans le pavillon.)

LESCAUT (*à* MANON). Il vous parlait, Manon?

MANON (*l'egèrement et vif*). Ce n'était pas ma faute.

LESCAUT. Certes! et j'ai de vous opinion trop-haute
Pour me fàcher!

UN GARDE (*à* LESCAUT). Eh, bien, tu ne viens pas?

UN AUTRE GARDE. Les cartes et les dés nous attendent làbas!

LESCAUT. Je viens, mais à cette jeunesse
Permettez d'abord que j'adresse
Quel ques conseils tout remplis de sagesse!

LE GARDES. Ecoutons la sagesse.

LESCAUT (*à* MANON). Regardez-moi bien dans les yeux.
Je vais tout près à la caserne,
Discuter avec ces messieurs,
De certain point qui les concerne.
Attendez-moi donc un instant, un seul moment,
Ne bronchez pas, soyez gentille
Et n'oubliez pas, mon cher cœur,
Que je suis gardien de l'honneur
De la famille, de la famille!
Si par hazard quelque imprudent
Vous tenait un propos frivole
Dans la crainte d'un accident
Ne dites pas une parole!

(Aux GARDES leur faisant signe de partir.)

Et maintenant, voyons à qui de nous
La Déesse du jeu va faire les yeux doux!

(Au moment retourne vers MANON.)

Ne bronchez pas,
Sayez gentille!

(Ils sortent.)
(MANON reste seule.)

MANON (*with simplicity*). Yes, I will do as I am told— not a word, not a thought. Far away I will banish those wild dreams that with glittering splendor hold me in thrall. I'll dream no more! (*Appears deep in thought. Suddenly she looks towards the pavilion in which are* POUSETTE, JAVOTTE, *and* ROSETTE.) What happy lives those ladies live! Round the throat of one is a necklace of gold. (*Rising.*) Ah! beautiful dresses and gems in radiant splendor flashing! How delightful ye are to me! (*Sadly and resignedly.*)

Alas! Manon, again thou'rt dreaming.
Struggling vainly with thy fate;
All these glories are but seeming,
Leave them at the convent gate.

Alas! Manon, dream thou no more. Ah! t is easy said, but my eyes with their splendor are dazzled till I see naught else. How happy must the women be who spend the r lives in search of pleasure! (*She sees* DES GRIEUX *approaching.*) Who is that? Quick, to my place!

(DES GRIEUX *comes forward without noticing* MANON.)

DES GRIEUX. The hour is fixed when I depart, yet I pause, not knowing why. (*Resolutely.*) To-morrow, whatever betide, I shall embrace my father. Yes, he will meet me gladly, and my heart goeth forth to him. Oh, my father, soon I shall clasp thy hand!

(Involuntarily he turns towards MANON.)

Great Heaven! Am I dreaming? Yes, it is a vision! Whence comes this rapturous longing? Now I feel that my life but begins — or is ending! A hand of iron draws me, though resisting, from the way I sought to go. Spite of myself I now would kneel before her.

(He slowly approaches MANON.)

Young lady!

MANON. Sir!

MANON (*simplement*). Restons ici, puis qu'il faut
Attendons sans penser! Evitons ces folies,
Ces projets qui mettaient ma raison en défaut!
Ne revons plus! (*Semble plongée dans réflexions. Elle porte les yeux sur pavillon dans lequel sont enfermées* POUSETTE, JAVOTTE, *et* ROSETTE.)
Combiene ces femmes sont jolies!
La plus jeune portait un collier de grains d'or!
Ah! comme ces riches toilettes
Et ces parures si coquettes
Les rendaient plus belles encor!
(*Triste et resigne.*) Voyons, Manon, plus de chimères,
Où va ton esprit en rêvant?
Laisse ces desirs éphemères
A la porte de ton couvent!
Voyons, Manon! Plus de chimères,
Et cependant!
Pour mon âme ravie
Et elles tout est séduisant!
Ah! combien ce doit être amusant.
De s'amuser toute une vie!
Ah! Voyons, etc. (*Apercevant* DES GRIEUX.)
Quelqu'un! Vite, à mon banc de pierre!

(DES GRIEUX *s'avance sans voir* MANON.)

DES GRIEUX. J'ai marqué l'heure du départ—
J'hesitais — chose singulière.
Enfin, demain soir au plus tard
J'embrasserai mon père!
Oui je le vois souriere,
Et mon cœur ne me trompe pas!
Je le vois il m'appelle et je lui tends les bras!

(Involontairment DES GRIEUX *s'est tourné vers* MANON.)

O ciel! Est-ce un reve?
Est-ce la folie?
D'où vient ce que j'éprouve?
On dirait que ma vie
Va finir ou commence!
Il semble qu'une main de fer
Me mère en un autre chemin,
Et malgré moi m'entraine devant elle.

(R'approche de MANON.)

Mademoiselle!

MANON. Eh, quoi?

DES GRIEUX. Pardou me —I do not know —
I obey — I am no longer master of myself.
I see you assuredly for the first time, yet my
heart recognizes you.

DES GRIEUX. Pardonnez moi! Je ne sais ….
J'obéis je ne suis plus mon maître —
Je vous vois, j'en suis sûr,
Pour la première fois
Et mon cœur cependant vient de vous re
connaître!

Andante cantabile. espressivo.

DES GRIEUX. *mf* — *p* MANON (*with simplicity*). *p* DES GRIEUX (*with emotion*).

If I knew but your name. I am call-ed Ma-non. Ma-non!
Et je sais vo-tre nom. Ou m'ap-pl-le Ma-non. Ma-non!

MANON (*aside*). *dolce.* DES GRIEUX.

How ten-der are His looks, how de-light-ful his voice to my soul. All my fond fool-ish
Que son re-gard est ten-dre! Et que j'ai de plaisir a l'en-ten-dre! Ces pa-ro-les d'un

MANON (*with simplicity*).

words, I pray you for-give! How con-demn your words when they charm my
fou. Veuil-lez les par-don-ner! Com-ment les con-dam-ner, El-les charment le

dolce. dim.

heart; To my ears they are mu-sic. Would to Heav'n such
cœur en char-mant les o-reil-les! J'en vou-drais sa-

f DES GRIEUX (*in a transport of joy*).

lan-guage were mine; You fit an-swer to make. Love-ly en-chan-tress, All-
voir de pa-reil-les Pour vous les ré-pêt-er! En-chan-te-res-se! Au

con-quer-ing beau-ty, Ma-non, From henceforth thou at mis-tress o my
char-me vain-que-ur Ma-non! Vous ê-tes la mai-tres-se ae mon

MANON. *f* — *p* *Tempo 1mo.* *pp*

Oh! what joy, I'm hence-forth the mis-tress, I'm
Mots char-mants! En-i-vran-tes fie-vres En-

f *p* *pp*

heart! O Ma-non, From hence-forth the mis-tress, from
cœur! O Ma-non, Vous ê-tes mai-tres-se, vous

hence-forth the mis - tress   of   his   heart! . . . .
i - vran - tes fie - vres   du   bon - heur! . . . .

hence-forth the mis - tress   of   his   heart! . . . . . .
ê - tes mat - tres - se   de   mon   cœur! . . . . . .

Allegretto.
DES GRIEUX.   MANON.   Allegro. (*Smiling.*)

Ah, speak to me!   I am on - ly a sim - ple maid-en.   Be-lieve me, I'm not
Ah! par - lez-moi!   Je ne suis qu'une pau - vre fille.   Je ne suis pas mau-

wick - ed,   But I of - ten am told   by those at home, . .   That I love
vais - se   Mais sou - vent on - m'ac - cuse   dans ma fa - mil - le   D' - ai - mer

(*Sadly.*)   Allegretto.   mf
pleas - ure too well;   I am now on my way to a   con - vent, That, sir, is   the sto - ry
trop le plais-ir   on me met au cou - vent. Tout à   l'heure,   et c'est là   l'his-toi - re

                                        (*with simplicity.*)   Allegro moderato.
                                                        DES GRIEUX (*with ardour*).
of Ma - non, . .   of Ma - non Les - caut!   No   I will not be-
de Ma - non, . .   de Ma - non Les - caut!   Non!   Je ne veux pas

lieve that fate can be so hard!   That one so   young .   and so fair can be des - tin'd to
croire à cet - te cru-ar. - té   Que tant de   charmes,   de beau - té So - ient voues à ja -

                                        MANON.
dwell in a liv - ing tomb.   But, 't is, a - las! . . the sov'reign will of Heaven, to **whose**
mais à la tom - be vi - vante!   Mais c'est, hé - las! . . la vo - lon - té Du ciel dont je

                    f espressivo.   dim.   DES GRIEUX (*firmly*).
ser - vice I'm de - vo - ted,   and no one from this fate can de - liv - er me.   No!
suis   la ser - van - te,   Puisqu'un mal - heur si grand ne peut être é - vi - té.   Non!

                                        MANON (*joyfully*). DES GRIEUX.
no! .   Not from you, Manon, shall hope and joy be torn. .   Oh! Heaven! For on my will and my pow'r
non! .   Vo - tre li - ber - té ne se - ra pas ra - vi - e!   Com-ment?   Au che - val - ier Des Gri-eux.

MANON (*with energy*).

you can safe-ly de-pend,   Ah! . . to you I owe   far more, far more than
Vous pou-vez vous fi - er!   Ah! . . je vous de-vrai   plus que la vi - -

DES GRIEUX (*passionately*).

life. Ah! Ma-non, you shall not leave me now! Since I . would glad-ly roam thro' all the
e! Ah! Ma-non! vous ne par-ti - rez, pas! Dus-se - je al - ler cher-cher   Au bout du

Andante. (*Tempo 1mo.*)

world,   Seek-ing for you, love, an un-known re-treat,   And car-ry you there in my
mond-e.   U - ne re-traite in - con-nue et pro-fon-de,   Et vous y por-ter dans mes

MANON. f

To you, my life and my soul! To   you, to you I give my life for ev - er - more.
A vous ma vie et mon-à-me! A   vous! a vous tou-te ma vi-e a ja - mais.

arms.   Light of my soul! Ma - non, The mistress of my heart for ev - er - more.
bras!   En-chan-te - res-se! Ma - non! vous ê-tes la mai-tres-se de mon cœur.

(A postillion, who has been warned by GUILLOT to take the orders of MANON, appears at back. MANON looks at him, reflects, and smiles.)	(A ce moment, le postilon à qui GUILLOT a dit précédement de se tenir aux ordres de MANON paraît dans le fond.)
	(Elle regarde, réfléchit et sourit.)
MANON (*to* DES GRIEUX). Oh, what a chance is thrown now in your way! There is a carriage awaiting here its owner. He has dared to make love to Manon. Be revenged!	MANON. Par aventure, peut-etre avons-nous mieux Une voiture la chaise d'un Seigneur. Il faisait les doux yeux a Manon. Vengez-vous!
DES GRIEUX. But how?	DES GRIEUX. Mais comment.
MANON. Let us take it — both of us.	MANON. Tous les deux, prenons là!
DES GRIEUX. Good! Away!	DES GRIEUX. Soit, partons!
(Exit postillion.)	(Aussitot postillon.)
MANON (*troubled*). But, sir — we go together?	MANON (*troublée*). Eh quoi partir ensemble?
DES GRIEUX. Yes, Manon; are not our hearts united?	DES GRIEUX. Oui, Manon! le ciel nous rassemble!
MANON AND DES GRIEUX. We to Paris will go. Heart to heart! And, though Fortune may frown,	MANON ET DES GRIEUX. Nous vivrons à Paris tous les deux! Et nos cœurs amoureux

Never part!
Evermore bliss is ours,
And with love's sweetest flow'rs
Will we crown the bright hours.

DES GRIEUX (*tenderly*). Soon my name will become your own. (*Recovering himself.*) Ah, excuse!

MANON. All unworthy is Manon, and she desires no sacrifice; yet otherwise 't is wrong.

DES GRIEUX AND MANON. We to Paris will go, etc.

(Peals of laughter in the pavilion are heard.)

MANON. There they are!

DES GRIEUX. What troubles you?

MANON. Nothing! Those beautiful ladies!

LESCAUT (*within*). I shall expect you both at the wine-shop this evening.

DES GRIEUX (*alarmed*). Ha!

MANON. It is the voice of my cousin!

DES GRIEUX. Come! away!

POUSETTE, JAVOTTE AND ROSETTE (*within*). Come back, Guillot!

MANON (*with excitement*). Ah! but it must indeed be delightful to abandon sorrow, and know only pleasure!

(Exit MANON and DES GRIEUX.)

LESCAUT (*entering intoxicated*). Not a coin! Dame Fortune plays me false!
(*Looking for* MANON.) Hi! Manon! — What! Gone away? Manon! Manon!

GUILLOT (*coming out of pavilion cautiously*). I 'll see her once again!

LESCAUT. Ah! 't is you, my fine fellow!
'T is you have taken Manon; you! Give her up! Give her to me!

(Enter TOWNSPEOPLE and INNKEEPER.)

L'un à l'autre enchaînés
Pour jamais réunis
N'y vivront que des jours benis!

DES GRIEUX. Et mon nom de viendra le vôtre!
Ah! pardon!

MANON. Dans mes yeux
Vous devez bien voir
Que je ne puis vous en vouloir
Et cependant c'est mal!

DES GRIEUX ET MANON. Viens! nous vivrons à Paris! etc.

(Eclats de rire dans le pavillon.)

MANON. Ce sont elles!

DES GRIEUX. Qu'avez-vous?

MANON. Rien! ces femmes si belles!

LESCAUT (*au debors, aviné*). Ce soir, vous rendrez tout au cabaret voisin!

DES GRIEUX (*effrayé*). La!

MANON. C'est la voix de mon cousin!

DES GRIEUX. Viens! partons!

POUSETTE JAVOTTE ET ROSETTE. Revenez Guillot!

MANON (*s'arrête, indécise*). Ah! Combien ce doit être amusant de s'amuser toute une vie! Ah! partons!

(Ils s'enfuient tous deux.)

LESCAUT (*paraissant gris*). Plus un sou! Le tour est trés plaisant!
(*Appellant.*) Hè! Manon quoi! Disparue! Hola! Hola!

GUILLOT (*descendant doucement le perron*). Je veux la retrouver.

LESCAUT. Ah! (*barrant le passage*) c'est vous!
Le gros homme! Vous avez pris Manon! Vous, rendez-la moi!

(Les BOURGEOIS et l'HOTELIER arrivent.)

GUILLOT. Now, my good Lescaut, why make this noise and cause a scandal!

LESCAUT. Ah! bah! What's that to me! (*To* TOWNSPEOPLE.) He has robbed us of our honor! And 't is a feast too good (*to* GUILLOT) for such a taste as yours!

GUILLOT (*frightened*.) What an adventure!

INNKEEPER AND TOWNSPEOPLE. Now, then, explain yourself!

GUILLOT. Good! Let us do it gently, sirs, and without prejudice.

LESCAUT (*louder*). Answer me, as in a court of law—Where is Manon?

INNKEEPER. What! She who was here lately has driven away. A young man is with her; they have gone!

GUILLOT (*in despair*). O heavens!

(Noise, carriage in distance.)

TOWNSPEOPLE. Yes, they 're off!

LESCAUT (*furious*). There goes the honor of our house!

INNKEEPER (*indicating* GUILLOT). And in the carriage of that man!

TOWNSPEOPLE. And in the carriage of that man!

LESCAUT (*seizing* GUILLOT). You wretch!

GUILLOT. No! hear me speak! Let me go!

PEOPLE. Ah! the bird has flown!
Was ever such misfortune known!

LESCAUT. No, my honor says chastise him!

DE BRÉTIGNY (*coming from pavilion with ladies*). Alas! my poor Guillot! Has your love, then, escaped you?

LADIES (*laughing*). Oh! measure this mischance who can,
For such a lady-killing man!

GUILLOT (*à* LESCAUT). Regardez donc comme vous attirez la foule!

LESCAUT. Ah! bah! ca m'est égal!
(*Aux* BOURGEOIS.) Il a pris notre honneur
(*A* GUILLOT.) C'est un trop beau regal
Pour ton vilain museau!

GUILLOT. Quelle aventure!

L'HÔTELIER ET BOURGEOIS. Voyons, expliquez-vous!

GUILLOT. Soit! mais très doucement, très doucement et sans injure!

LESCAUT (*encor plus fort*). Repondez catégoriquement.
Je veux Manon!

L'HÔTELIER. Quoi! Cette jeune fille, elle est partie avec un jeune homme!
Ecoutez!

GUILLOT. O ciel!

(Bruit lointain de la voiture.)

BOURGEOIS. Elle est partie!

LESCAUT. Mais c'est l'honneur de la famille!

L'HÔTELIER (*designant* GUILLOT.) Dans la voiture de Monsieur!

BOURGEOIS. Dans la voiture de Monsieur!

LESCAUT. Gredin!

GUILLOT. Làchez! Làchez!

BOURGEOIS. Ah! la drôle de figure!

LESCAUT. Non! il faut que je chatie!

DE BRÉTIGNY (*sorti du pavillon avec les femmes*). Eh! quoi! pauvre Guillot! Votre belle est partie!

LES FEMMES (*rient*). Quelle mésaventure
Pour un aussi grand séducteur!

GUILLOT. Be silent all! I will have my revenge on that perfidious girl, and also on this fool!

ALL. Ah! the bird has flown!
Was ever such misfortune known!

GUILLOT. Taisez-tous! Je veux être vengé,
Et de cette perfide et de cet enrage!

TOUT. Ah! la drole de figure!
Ah! quel malheur!

ACT II.

(An apartment in the Rue Vivienne, Paris. DES GRIEUX discovered writing at his desk. MANON softly approaches him from behind and tries to read what he has written.)

DES GRIEUX (*ceasing to write, and in a tone of reproach*). Manon!

MANON (*gaily*). Are you afraid lest I should do some harm by coming so near you?

DES GRIEUX. Indiscreet Manon!

MANON. Yes, I have looked over your shoulder, and with a smile I saw you write my name.

DES GRIEUX. This letter's for my father, and I tremble lest he should read what I write from my heart, in his anger.

MANON. You are afraid?

DES GRIEUX. Yes, Manon, I'm afraid.

MANON. Ah, well, then we'll read it together.

DES GRIEUX. Yes, that's the way. Together we'll read.

MANON (*reading with simplicity*). "She is called Manon, and is so young and fair. In her all charms unite She has grace, radiant youth and beauty; music flows in a stream from her lips; in her eyes shines the tender light of love."

DES GRIEUX (*ardently*). In her eyes shines the tender light of love.

MANON. Is this true? Ah! I knew it not. (*Tenderly.*) But I know how much I am loved.

ACTE II.

(L'appartement de DES GRIEUX et de MANON. Rue Vivienne. DES GRIEUX est assis devant un petit bureau-secrétaire; MANON s'avance doucement derrière lui et cherche à lire ce qu'il écrit.)

DES GRIEUX. Manon!

MANON (*gaiment*). Avez-vous peur que mon visage frôle votre visage?

DES GRIEUX. Indiscrète Manon!

MANON. Oui, je lisais sur votre épaule
Et j'ai souri, voyant passer mon nom!

DES GRIEUX. J'écris à mon père: et je tremble.
Que cette lettre où j'ai mis tout mon cœur,
Ne l'irrite.

MANON. Vous avez peur?

DES GRIEUX. Oui, Manon, j'ai très peur!

MANON. Eh bien! Il faut relire ensemble!

DES GRIEUX. Oui, c'est cela, ensemble, relisons!

MANON (*lisant, simplement*). On l'appelle Manon, elle eut hier seize ans;
En elle tout séduit la beauté, la jeunesse,
La gràce; nulle voix n'a plus doux accents,
Nul regard, plus de charme avec plus de tendresse.

DES GRIEUX (*répétant*). Nul regard, plus de charme avec plus de tendresse.

MANON (*s'arrêtant de lire*). Est-ce vrai?
Moi, je n'en sais rien,
Mais je sais que vous m'aimez bien!

DES GRIEUX (*with passion*). Thou art loved! Manon, I adore thee.

MANON. Come, come, good sir, there's more to read yet.

DES GRIEUX. "Like a bird that through all lands follows the spring, so her young soul to life is ever open. Her lips, like flowers, smile and speak to the zephyrs that kiss them in passing."

MANON (*repeating*). "To the zephyrs that kiss them in passing." (*Pensively.*) Do you think your father will give his consent?

DES GRIEUX. Yes; he will never in such a matter as this oppose me.

MANON. Dost thou desire it?

DES GRIEUX. I desire it, with all my soul!

MANON. Then embrace me, Chevalier.

(They embrace.)

And now, go;—send thy letter.

DES GRIEUX. I go at once. (*He moves quickly towards the door and pauses.*) Those flowers are very beautiful. Who gave them to thee, Manon?

MANON (*quickly*). I do not know.

DES GRIEUX. What! thou dost not know?

MANON (*laughing*). A fine theme for a quarrel! Some one threw them in at the window, and, as they were pretty, I kept them. I hope thou art not jealous.

DES GRIEUX (*tenderly*). No! I swear that in thy love I have a perfect trust.

MANON. Thou art right. My heart is thine alone.

(Knocking and voices without.)

DES GRIEUX. What means that noise?

(A MAID-SERVANT enters in alarm.)

DES GRIEUX. Vous aimer? Vous aimer! Manon! Je t'adore!

MANON. Allons, Monsieur! lisons encore!

DES GRIEUX (*lisant*). Comme l'oiseau qui suit en tous lieux des printemps, Sa jeune âme à la vise, Sa jeune âme est ouverte sans cesse, Sa lèvre en fleur sourit et parle Au zéphir parfumé qui passe et la caresse!

MANON (*répéntat*). Au zéphir parfumé qui passe et la caresse! (*Pensive.*) Il ne te suffit pas alors de nous aimer?

DES GRIEUX. Non, je veux que tu sois ma femme!

MANON. Tu le veux?

DES GRIEUX. Je le veux, et de toute mon âme!

MANON. Embrasse moi donc, chevalier!

(Ils s'embrassent.)

Et va porter ta lettre!

DES GRIEUX. Oui, je vais la porter! (*Il se dirige vivement vers la porte, et s'arrête.*) Violà des fleurs qui sont fort belles; d'ou te vient ce boquet, Manon?

MANON (*vivement*). Je ne sais pas.

DES GRIEUX. Comment tu ne sais pas?

MANON (*rient*). Beau motif de querelles! Par la fenetre, on l'a lancé d'en bas Comme il était jolie, je l'ai gardé Je pense que tu n'es pas jaloux?

DES GRIEUX (*tendrement*). Non! je puis te jurer que je n'ai de ton cœur aucune défiance!

MANON. Et tu fais bien! ce cœur est à toi tout entier!

(On entend un bruit de voix au dehors.)

DES GRIEUX. Qui donc se permet un pareil tapage?

(La SERVANTE entrant effarée.)

SERVANT. Two gardes-du-corps are below. One calls himself a relation of madame.	LA SERVANTE. Deux gardes du corps sont là qui font rage ; L'un se dit le parent de Madame !
MANON. Lescaut! 'T is Lescaut!	MANON. Lescaut! c'est Lescaut!
SERVANT (*to* MANON). The other is—let us speak low—some one who loves you—the State official who lives near here.	LA SERVANTE (*à* MANON). L'autre c'est ne parlons pas trop haut, L'autre, c'est quelqu'un qui vous aime, Ce fermier général qui loge près d'éer.
MANON (*softly*). Monsieur de Brétigny?	MANON. Monsieur de Brétigny?
SERVANT. Monsieur de Brétigny.	LA SERVANTE. Monsieur de Brétigny.
(The noise increases.)	(Le bruit redouble.)
DES GRIEUX. This is too much. I'll go and see for myself.	DES GRIEUX. Cela devient trop fort et je vais voir moi-même.
(As he is about to go, the door opens, DE BRÉTIGNY dressed as a gard-du corps and LESCAUT enter.)	(Au moment où il a s'elancer, la porte s'ouvre. Entrant DE BRÉTIGNY, costumé en garde, et LESCAUT.)
LESCAUT (*brusquely*). At last, sweet pretty pair, I have found you it seems.	LESCAUT (*brusquement*). En fin, les amoureux. Je vous tiens tous les deux !
DE BRÉTIGNY. Some mercy show, Lescaut. Have pity on their youth.	DE BRÉTIGNY. Soyez clément, Lescaut, songez à leur jeunesse.
LESCAUT (*insolently to* DES GRIEUX). I have learned, sir, from you a lesson in politeness. You precious rascal!	LESCAUT (*à* DES GRIEUX). Vous m'avez, l'autre jour, brulé la politesse, Monsieur le drôle !
DES GRIEUX (*quickly*). What's that? Use softer words, I pray.	DES GRIEUX (*vivement*). Hé! là! parlez plus doucement.
LESCAUT (*ironically*). Use softer words!	LESCAUT. Plus doucement!
DES GRIEUX (*menacing*). Yes, softer words!	DES GRIEUX. Plus doucement.
LESCAUT. Sir, I shall choke with just rage if I keep silence. I am here, sir, to avenge the honor of our house. Redress for wrong I seek; redress for wrong I'll find; and 't is to me you speak of softer words! Ah, bah!	LESCAUT. C'est à tomber foudroyé sur la place ! J'arrive pour venger l'honneur de notre race. Je suis le redresseur, je suis le chatiment. Et c'est à moi qu'on dit de parler douce ment !
DE BRÉTIGNY. Calm thyself.	DE BRÉTIGNY. Contiens-toi!
LESCAUT (*to* DES GRIEUX). You knave!	LESCAUT (*presque porté*). Coquin!
DE BRÉTIGNY. Hold thy tongue.	DE BRÉTIGNY. Retiens-toi!
DES GRIEUX. Well, sir, and now let me say I shall whip you.	DES GRIEUX. C'est bien! je vais couper les oreilles!

LESCAUT. Eh? (*To* DE BRÉTIGNY.) What does he mean!

LESCAUT (*à* DE BRÉTIGNY). Hein? qu'est-ce qu'il dit?

DE BRÉTIGNY. His meaning is clear. He will whip you.

DE BRÉTIGNY. Qu'il va vous couper les oreilles.

LESCAUT. Was ever known such an insolent fellow! Does he threaten?

LESCAUT. Vit ou jamais insolences pareilles? Il menace!

DE BRÉTIGNY. I think he does.

DE BRETIGNY. Ca m'en l'air.

LESCAUT. Now by heaven and by earth! You knave! (*To* DE BRÉTIGNY.) Pray, hold me back— Or I shall do some fearful thing! Such vengeance through the world would ring!

LESCAUT. Par la mort! par l'enfer! Coquin! (*A* DE BRÉTIGNY.) Retenez-moi! Je sais de quoi je suis capable! Quand il faut punir un coupable!

DE BRÉTIGNY. Do be calm, Lescaut. See, remorse strikes them both. Come, Lescaut, forget thy oath.

DE BRÉTIGNY. Lescaut! Contiens toi! Le remords les accable! Allons! de l'indulgence

MANON. Ah! chevalier, I die of fright, I trust in thee; 'T is true I am the guilty one, But watch o'er me.

MANON. Ah! chevalier, je meurs d'effroi! Je le sais bien, je le sais coupable! Veillez sur moi!

DES GRIEUX. O Manon, do not yield to fear, But trust in me; I only am the guilty one, I 'll watch o'er thee.

DES GRIEUX. O Manon, soyez sans effroi! Comptez sur moi! Seul de nous deux je suis coupable! Il sera bien-tôt plus traitable!

DE BRÉTIGNY. Lescaut, why give way thus to anger? Explain yourself more clearly now.

DE BRÉTIGNY. Lescaut! Vous montrez trop de zèle! Expliquez-vous plus posément.

LESCAUT (*pompously*). Well, I agree. (*To* DES GRIEUX.) This lady here is my cousin, and I come quite politely—yes, I come quite politely, just to say: "Good sir, I do not wish to quarrel, but—answer 'Yes,' or answer 'No'— do you agree to wed Manon?"

LESCAUT. Soit, j'y consens. Mademoiselle est ma cousine et je venais très poliment; oui, je venais très poliment. Dire: Monsieur sans vous chercher querelle. Répondez: Oui, repondez Non, voulez vous épouser Manon?

DE BRÉTIGNY AND LESCAUT. The thing is clear; This is the plan For every man Who holds his honor dear.

DE BRÉTIGNY ET LESCAUT. La chose est claire, Entre lurons Et bons garcons C'est ainsi qu'on traite une affaire!

DE BRÉTIGNY (*to* DES GRIEUX). And now are you satisfied?

DE BRÉTIGNY (*à* DES GRIEUX). Eh bien, êtes vous satisfait?

DES GRIEUX (*laughing*). In truth I have lost all my anger. Your frankness is pleasing to me.

DES GRIEUX. Ma foi, je n'ai plus de colère, Et votre franchise me plait.

DE BRÉTIGNY AND LESCAUT. This is the plan, etc.

DE BRÉTIGNY ET LESCAUT. La chose est claire, etc.

DES GRIEUX (*to* LESCAUT). I have just written to my father (*showing his letter*). Before I seal the letter up, will you be pleased to read my words.

DES GRIEUX. Je venais d'ecrire à mon pere
Avant qu'on y mette un cachet
Vous lirez bien ceci, j'espère.

LESCAUT (*taking the letter*). That I will. But who can see here? (*Observing* MANON *and* DE BRÉTIGNY). If we both go for better light (*purposely drawing* DES GRIEUX *away*) and stand here close to the window, with ease we'll read your letter.

LESCAUT. Volontiers! mais voici le soir,
Allons tous deux, pour y mieux voir,
Nous placer près de la fenètre
Et là nous lirons votre lettre

(LESCAUT goes up the stage with DES GRIEUX.)

(LESCAUT est remonté vers le fond avec DES GRIEUX.)

MANON (*to* DE BRÉTIGNY *furtively*). Wherefore come here in such a strange disguise?

MANON (*à* DE BRÉTIGNY). Venir ici sous un déguisement.

DE BRÉTIGNY. Are you annoyed?

DE BRÉTIGNY. Vous m'en voulez?

MANON. Rather say angry. Well you know that yonder stands the man I love.

MANON. Certainement. Vous savez que c'est lui que j'aime.

DE BRÉTIGNY. I desired in my own person to warn you that, to-night, from this house he will be carried off.

DE BRÉTIGNY. J'ai voulu vous avertir moi-même,
Que ce soir de chez vous, on compte l'enlever.

MANON. To-night?

MANON. Ce soir?

DE BRÉTIGNY. By order of his father.

DE BRÉTIGNY. Par ordre de son père.

MANON (*with emotion and surprise*). By order of his father!

MANON (*avec surprise*). Par ordre de son père!

DE BRÉTIGNY. Yes, before this night has passed he will be torn from your side.

DE BRÉTIGNY. Oui, ce soir ici même. On viendra l'arracher.

MANON (*taking a step towards* DES GRIEUX). Ah! It shall not be. I will warn him.

MANON. Ah! je saurai bien empêcher!

DE BRÉTIGNY (*stopping her*). Say not a word. It would be dire poverty for him, for you; but keep your counsel well, and silence will lead to fortune. Is it agreed?

DE BRÉTIGNY. Prévenezle, c'est la misère
Pour lui, pour vous.
Ne prévenez pas,
Et c'est la fortune au contraire.
Qui vous attend?

MANON (*excitedly and in fear*). Oh, pray speak low!

MANON (*vivement, avec crainte*). Parlez plus bas!

DE BRÉTIGNY. Manon, I call you to life and liberty!

DE BRÉTIGNY. Manon! Voici l'heure prochaine De votre liberté!

MANON (*aside*). My heart is torn with doubt and fear;
Dare I listen? dare I hear?

MANON. (*à part*). Quel donte étrange et quel tourment!
Dans mon cœur quel délire!

DE BRÉTIGNY. Manon, full soon you shall be queen, reigning in beauty's right.

DE BRÉTIGNY. Manon, bientôt vous serez reine, Reine par sa beauté!

MANON. Ah! away, away!

LESCAUT (*reading with emphasis*). "She is called Manon, and is so young and fair. In her all charms unite." Very touching these words.

DES GRIEUX. Ah! Lescaut; how madly I adore her! 'T is not in thee to know, nor can I tell.

LESCAUT. You'll marry her? (*Reading.*) "As a bird through all lands follows the spring"—'t is the poetry of love!—"so her young soul to life"—this is poetry!—"is ever open.' 'T is love! You'll marry her? 'T is well! Nothing could be better. Accept, I beg, my compliments. (*To* MANON.) Dear cousin—nay, cousins both (*pompously*); my esteem is yours, believe me. Now take my hand, for it would be a crime to stand in love's sweet way. My children, I bless you both—with tears of joy. (*To* DE BRÉTIGNY, *aside*.) Let us go.

DE BRÉTIGNY. Let us go.

LESCAUT AND DE BRÉTIGNY (*as they retire*). The thing is clear, etc. (*Exit.*)

MANON (*aside*). Ah! what pain rends my heart.

DES GRIEUX (*with ecstasy, aside*). Round me shines the light of love, The light that flows from heaven above.

(The SERVANT enters with a lamp.)

What is it now?

SERVANT. Supper-time, sir.

(The SERVANT lays the cloth for supper.)

DES GRIEUX. So it is; and my letter not yet despatched.

MANON. Then go at once.

DES GRIEUX. Manon!

MANON. Well?

DES GRIEUX. I love thee! I adore thee! Say, dost thou love me?

MANON. Truly, my dear. I love thee.

MANON. Ah! partez! partez!

LESCAUT (*lisant*). "On l'appelle Manon, Elle eut hier seize ans En elle tout séduit." Que ces mots sont touchants!

DES GRIEUX. Ah! Lescaut, c'est que je l'adore! Laissez-moi le vous dire encore!

LESCAUT. Vous l'épousez? (*Lisant.*) "Comme l'oiseau qui suit le printemps"—Poésie amour! "Sa jeune âme à la vie"—Poésie! "Est ouverte sans cesse." Amour! Vous l'epousez? Vraiment! C'est parfait! On ne peut mieux dire Et je vous fais mon compliment! (*À* MANON). Cousine, et vous, (*à* DES GRIEUX) cousin, Je vous rends mon estime. Prenez ma main, car ce serait un crinte De vous tenir rigueur; Enfants, je vous bénis les larmes! (*À* DE BRÉTIGNY). Partons-nous?

LESCAUT ET DE BRÉTIGNY. La chose est claire, etc. (*Depart.*)

MANON. Dans mon cœur quel tourment!

DES GRIEUX. Puisse du bonheur où j'aspire Le jour se lever sourient!

(Entre la SERVANTE avec une lumière.)

DES GRIEUX. Que nous veut-on?

LA SERVANTE. C'est l'heure du souper, Monsieur. (Elle dispose le couvert.)

DES GRIEUX. C'est vrai pourtant. Et je n'ai pas encore porté ma lettre.

MANON! Eh bien, va la porter.

DES GRIEUX. Manon!

MANON. Apres?

DES GRIEUX. Je t'aime! je t'adore. Et toi, dis, m'aimes-tu?

MANON. Oui, mon cher chevalier, je t'aime.

DES GRIEUX. In that case thou must promise me—

MANON. What?

DES GRIEUX (*lightly*). Nothing at all. Let me take my letter.

(Exit DES GRIEUX.)

MANON (*much moved*). Alas! it must be; even for his sake—his, poor chevalier! I love him well, yet I shrink from this great sacrifice! No! No! I am no longer worthy of him.

Once more on my ear falls the tempter's voice
Who against it can fight?
"Manon, Manon, as a queen thou shalt reign,
By beauty's right."
Ah! how feeble am I! How weak and how frail!
See my cheeks with tears!
Earth's fairest visions do not last.
Ah! will it be in future years
As in the days for ever past?

(Slowly she approaches the supper-table.)

Farewell, our pretty little table! so small, and yet so large for us. Side by side so often there we 've sat. (*With a sad smile.*) I smile as now I call to mind what narrow space we lovers filled. A single glass served both of us, and each, in drinking, sought upon its margin where dear lips had been. Ah! best of friends, how thou hast loved!

(She hears DES GRIEUX approaching.)

'Tis he! My pallid face will tell a tale, I fear.

(DES GRIEUX enters.)

DES GRIEUX. At last, Manon, we 're left alone together. (*He approaches her.*) How now! thou 'rt weeping!

MANON. No!

DES GRIEUX. Thy hand too is trembling!

MANON (*forcing a smile*). Please, sir, our supper waits.

DES GRIEUX. Ah! true. My brain is wandering.
But all earth's joys soon pass away,

DES GRIEUX. Tu devrais. en ce cas, me promettre—

MANON. Quoi?

DES GRIEUX. Rien du tout, je vais porter ma lettre.

(Il sort.)

MANON (*reste seule*). (*Très troublée.*) Allons! Il le faut! pour lui même—mon pauvre chevalier! Oh! oui—c'est lui que j'aime! Et pourtant, j'hésite aujour d'hui! Non! non! Je ne suis plus digne de lui!

J'entends cette voix qui m'entraine
Contre ma volonté: "Manon! Tu serais reine,
Reine par la beauté!"
Je ne suis que faiblesse
Et que fragilité!
Ah! malgré moi je sens couler mes larmes
Devant ces rêves eyacés,
L'avenir aura-t-il les charmes
De ces beaux jours dêja passés?

(Approche la table toute servie.)

Adieu, notre petite table, quinous réunit si souvent! (*Avec triste sourire.*) Ou tient, c'est inimaginable, si peu de place en serrant. Un même verre e'tait le nôtre, chacun de nous quand il buvait y cherchait les lèvres de l'autre. Ah! pauvre ami, comme il m'aimait!

(Entendant DES GRIEUX.)

C'est lui! que ma pâleur ne me trahisse pas!

(Entre DES GRIEUX.)

DES GRIEUX. Enfin, Manon, nous voilà seuls ensemble.
Eh quoi? des larmes?

MANON. Non!

DES GRIEUX. Si fait, ta main tremble'

MANON. Voici notre repas.

DES GRIEUX. C'est vrai! Ma tête est folle.
Mais le bonheur est passager,

And when the heart is light and gay,
Fear whispers, "No delight can stay."
Be seated.

MANON. Be seated.

DES GRIEUX. O charming hour! when all
fears are forgotten, and we freely speak of
our love! Listen, Manon! On my way I
dreamed the sweetest dream—

MANON (*bitterly aside*). Alas! who of us
does not dream!

Et le ciel l'a fait si léger,
Qu'on a toujours peur qu'il s'envole!
A table!

MANON. A table.

DES GRIEUX. Instant charmant, où la crainte
fait, trève, où nous sommes deux seulement!
Tiens, Manon, en marchant, Je viens de
faire un réve.

MANON (*avec amertume, à part*). Helas! qui
ne fait pas de rêve?

DES GRIEUX.

With fan-cy's eye I saw, Ma-non, . a sweet and low-ly cot, Its white walls
En-fer-ment les yeux je vois Là bas un'hum-ble re - trai - te U-ne mai-son

deck'd with flow-ers fair gleam'd thro' the wood! . . . Be-neath whose peace - ful
net - te Tou-te blanche au fond des bois! . Sous ses tran-quil - les om-

sha - dows ran clear the bab-bling brook; O - ver-head 'mid ver-dant
bra - ges, Les clairs et joy-eux ruis-seaux, Où se mi-rent les feuil-

leaves sang . so sweet and full the joy-ous birds, 'T is pa-ra-
la - - ges, Chan-tant a - vec les oi - seaux! C'est le pa-ra

dise! Ah! no, all is sad, so sad and drear-y, For, O my on-ly
dis! Oh! non! Tout est là triste et mo-ro-se, Car il-y man-que une

love, thou art not there, not there, 'Tis a vi-sion, 'tis but a fan-cy
chose il y faut en-cor Ma-non! C'est un re-ve u-ne fol-li-e!

MANON (*softly*).

DES GRIEUX.

No! for thus we'll pass our life, If but thou wilt, O Ma-non!
Non! Là se-ra no-tre vie, Si tu le veux. O Ma-non!

(A low knock at the door is heard.)

MANON (*aside*)   Oh, heaven! already!

DES GRIEUX.   That knock! It is too bad to spoil our pleasure. (*Rising.*) I 'll soon send the intruder away, and then return.

MANON (*troubled*).   Adieu!

DES GRIEUX (*astonished*).   Adieu?

MANON.   No! thou shalt not go.

DES GRIEUX.   Why not?

MANON.   Ah! do not leave me now, I entreat thee. I would rest within thine arms.

DES GRIEUX (*gently releasing himself*).   My child, let me go.

MANON.   No!

DES GRIEUX.   Manon, hear me.

MANON.   No!

DES GRIEUX.   I pray!

MANON.   Go thou shalt not!

DES GRIEUX.   Who can it be? 'T is very strange. I will dismiss him in fashion most polite, then return, and together we 'll laugh at thy folly.

(Exit DES GRIEUX.)
(Noise of a struggle, outside. MANON runs to the window.)

MANON (*overcome with grief*).   He has gone!

(On entend frapper doucement à la porte.)

MANON.   O ciel! deja!

DES GRIEUX.   Quelqu'un? Il ne faut pas de trouble fête. (*Se levant.*) Je vais renvoyer l'importun, et je reviens!

MANON (*troublee*).   Adieu!

DES GRIEUX (*étonné*).   Comment?

MANON.   Non! Je ne veux pas.

DES GRIEUX.   Pour-quoi?

MANON (*de même*).   Ah! Tu n'ouvriras pas cette porte. Je veux rester dans tes bras!

DES GRIEUX (*se dégageant doucement*).   Enfant! laisse moi!

MANON.   Non!

DES GRIEUX.   Que t'importe!

MANON.   Non!

DES GRIEUX.   Allons!

MANON.   Je ne veux pas!

DES GRIEUX.   Quelque inconnu. C'est sin gulier. Je le congédierai d'une facon polie, Je reviens, nous rirons tous deux de ta folie!

(Il sort.)
(On entend un bruit de futte.   MANON se lève et court vers la fenetre.)

MANON (*roulement de voiture*).   Mon pauvre chevalier!

ACT III.

SCENE I.

(The Cours la Reine, Paris, on the day of a popular fête. Among the trees are the stalls of Traders of all kinds. To the right is a pavilion for dancing. When the curtain rises, the Traders are following the passers-by, offering objects for sale.)

TRADERS AND PEOPLE.   'T is the fête of Cours la Reine;
Here we laugh, here we sing,

ACTE III

SCENE I.

(La Promenade du Cours la Reine. Un jour de Fête Populaire. Entre les grands arbres, des boutiques de divers Marchands: A droite, l'ensigne d'un bal. Des Marchands poursuivent les passants offrant toutes sortes d'objets.)

MARCHANDS ET BOURGEOIS.   C'est fête au Cours la Reine!

And cry "God save the King,"
Once, twice, and yet again.

(POUSSETTE and JAVOTTE come out of the pavilion, make signs to two youths in the crowd and hasten to meet them. ROSETTE follows soon after. Dance music is heard.)

POUSSETTE AND JAVOTTE. What a charming
    promenade!
Oh, how happy here are we!
What good fun this escapade,
Where no jealous eye can see.

POUSSETTE. It is agreed.

JAVOTTE. Ah! do not so.

ROSETTE. One word alone will ruin all.

JAVOTTE. My heart will soon be yielding all.

ROSETTE. Guillot, I hope, will nothing know.

POUSSETTE AND JAVOTTE. What a charming
promenade, etc.

(POUSSETTE and JAVOTTE re-enter the pavilion. ROSETTE goes off.)

TRADERS. See here, slippers well embroidered, etc.

(They perceive LESCAUT, who is coming forward.)

    Choose, sir, choose!

LESCAUT. My choice! why should I choose?
Here, this, and this!
Nothing I'll miss,
And you will nothing lose.
These I give the lovely girl
Whom I adore;
Nothing's too good for such a pearl!
Would there were more!

TRADERS. Bravo, good sir, give all to her.

LESCAUT. Enough, enough. (*Sentimentally.*)
    O Rosalinda—
'T were need to climb Parnassus' height,
Would I now sing thy praise aright;
What are the maidens of far Ind,
Or even Armid and Clorind;
Near to thee thou fairest fair?

On y rit, on y boit à la santé du Roi!
Pendant une semaine!

(POUSSETTE et JAVOTTE sortent du pavillon. Deux petits clercs qui paraissaient chercher quelqu'un dans la foule les apercoivent et sur signe d'elles courent à leur rencontre. ROSETTE parait à son tour. Musique du Bal.)

POUSSETTE ET JAVOTTE. La charmant pro-
    menade!
Ah! que ce séjour est doux
Que c'est bon! une escapade!
Loin des regards d'un jaloux!

POUSSETTE. C'est entendu!

JAVOTTE. Tenez-vous bien!

ROSETTE. Un mot pourrait nous compro-
mettre!

JAVOTTE. Mon cœur veut bien tout vous
promettre!

ROSETTE. Mais que Guillot n'en sache rien!

POUSSETTE ET JAVOTTE. La charmante promenade, etc.

(POUSSETTE ET JAVOTTE rentrent dans le pavillon ROSETTE s'est éloignée.)

MARCHANDS. Rubans, cannes, etc.

(Poursuivant LESCAUT l'endant la foule.)

Choisisez, Monsieur!

LESCAUT. Choisir! et pourquoi?
Donnez! donnez! donnez encore!
Ce soir, j'achète tout!
C'est pour la beauté que j'adore,
Je m'en rapporte à votre goit!

MARCHANDS. Tenez, Monsieur!

LESCAUT. Assez! assez! (*Avec sentiment.*)
    O Rosalinde—
Il me faudrait gravir le Pinde,
Pour te chanter comme il convient!
Qui sont les sultanes de l'Inde
Et les Armide et les Clorinde,
Près de toi, que sont elles?

Simply naught I declare!
Ladies fair, this chance don't miss,
I'll give a jewel for a kiss.

(Exit LESCAUT. The crowd become animated. JA-
VOTTE, POUSSETTE, and ROSETTE come out of the pavilion.
GUILLOT sees them.   Music of the minuet.)

GUILLOT.   Good-day, Poussette!

POUSSETTE.   Gracious!

GUILLOT.   Good-day, Javotte.

JAVOTTE.   Goodness!

GUILLOT.   Good-day, Rosette.

ROSETTE.   Goodness gracious!

GUILLOT.   Confound them, leaving me like
that, the minxes!   And I fascinated all three
because I reckoned that one at least would be
faithful.   Women are a bad lot!

DE BRÉTIGNY (*who has heard the last
words*).   Good philosophy, Guillot, but it
is n't your own.   (GUILLOT *looks at him angrily*.)   Heavens, what a glance!   Javotte, I
warrant, has been leading you a pretty life.

GUILLOT (*with a gesture of contempt*).   Javotte!   That for Javotte!

DE BRÉTIGNY.   And Poussette?

GUILLOT.   That for Poussette.

DE BRÉTIGNY.   Are you then free?   (*Ironically.*)   Guillot, I beg of you, don't take
Manon from me.

GUILLOT.   Take her from you!

DE BRÉTIGNY (*with mock concern*).   Oh!
swear that you won't!

GUILLOT.   There, that's enough of such jesting.   By-the-by, De Brétigny, I hear that you
refused to engage the ballet for a performance
at Manon's house, though she begged you
with tears in her eyes.   Is that true?

DE BRÉTIGNY.   Yes; 't is true enough.

O belles! approchez! J'offre un bijou,
J'offre un bijou pour deux baisers!

(Sortie de LESCAUT.   Mouvement dans la foule.   POUS-
SETTE, JAVOTTE et ROSETTE sortent du pavillon.   GUIL-
LOT les apercevant.   Musique du Menuet.)

GUILLOT.   Bonjour, Poussette!

POUSSETTE.   Ah! ciel!

GUILLOT.   Bonjour, Javotte!

JAVOTTE.   Ah! Dieu!

GUILLOT.   Bonjour, Rosette!

ROSETTE.   Ah!

GUILLOT.   Parla morbleu! Elles me plantent
là! coquine! Péronelle! Et j'en avais pris
trois pourtant il me semblait pouvoir compter,
si l'une me trompait, qu'une autre au moins
serait fidèle.   La femme est, je l'avoue, un
méchant animal!

DE BRÉTIGNY (*qui est entré sur ces dernières
paroles*).   Pas mal, Guillot, ce mot là n'est
pas mal! Mais il n'est pas de vous! (GUIL-
LOT *le regarde avec fureur.*)   Dieu! quel
sombre visage! Dame Javotte, je la gage, vous
aura fait des traits.

GUILLOT.   Javotte, c'est fini!

DE BRÉTIGNY.   Et Poussette?

GUILLOT.   Poussette aussai!

DE BRÉTIGNY.   Vous voilà libre alors?   (*Iron-
iquement.*)   Guillot, je vous en prie n'allez
pas m'enleven Manon!

GUILLOT.   Vous enlever.

DE BRÉTIGNY (*suppliant de même*).   Non,
jurez-moi que non!

GUILLOT.   Laissons cette plaisanterie! mais
dites-moi, mon cher, on m'a conté, apropos de
Manon, que vous ayant prié de faire venir
l'opéra chez elle, vous avez, en dépit des
larmes de la belle.   Répondu: Non.

DE BRÉTIGNY.   C'est très vrai; la nouvelle est
exact:

GUILLOT. Good! Excuse me for a moment! I shall soon be back.

(Exits, rubbing his hands.)

Rigadon, rigadon,
Now I'm off to steal Manon!

(The crowd return.)

TRADERS AND TOWNSPEOPLE. Great ladies of renown are these,
They nothing do save what they please.
All men's hearts they gain,
And by beauty reign.

(MANON enters, accompanied by DE BRÉTIGNY and several young gentlemen.)

DE BRÉTIGNY. O divinest Manon!

MANON. How do I look to-day?

DE BRÉTIGNY. Delightful! Alluring! Distracting!

MANON. Is that so? Many thanks. (*Coquetlishly.*) I consent—say, am I not gracious?—that you all much admire my delightful and charming appearance.

(Archly and gaily.)

An empress am I, in my way,
I conquer where'er I am seen.
None so great but homage must pay,
Of love I'm the absolute queen.
All things around me are gay;
My fancy alone I obey.
And when life has no joys for me to sip,
I'll say farewell, good friends, with laughter on my lip.

DE BRÉTIGNY AND OTHERS. Bravo — bravo! Manon!

GUILLOT. Il suffit; souffrez que je vous quitte, pour un instant, mais je reviendrai vite.

(Il sort, frottant les mains.)

Dig et dig et don!
On te la prendra ta Manon!

(La foule reviennent.)

MARCHANDS ET BOURGEOIS. Voici les élegantes!
Les belles indolentes!
Maitresses des cœurs!
Aux regards vainqueurs!

(MANON paraît, DE BRÉTIGNY, l'accompagne ainsi que plasieurs jeunes Seigneurs.)

DE BRÉTIGNY. Ravissante Manon!

MANON. Suis-je gentille ainsi?

DE BRÉTIGNY. Adorable! Divine!

MANON. Est-ce vrai? grand merci! (*Avec coquetterie.*) Je consens, vu, que je suis bonne, a laisser admirer ma charmante personne!

(Avec impertinence et gaieté.)

Je marche sur tous les chemins
Aussi bien qu'une souveraine
On s'incline, on baise ma main,
Car par beauté je suis reine!
Mes chevaux courent à grands pas.
Devant ma vie aventureuse,
Les grands s'avancent chapeau bas.
Je suis belle, je suis heureuse!
Autour de moi tout doit fleurir!
Je vais à tout ce qui m'attiere!
Et, si Manon devait jamais mourir,
Ce serait, mes amis, dans un éclat de rire!

DE BRÉTIGNY ET SEIGNEURS. Bravo! bravo! Manon!

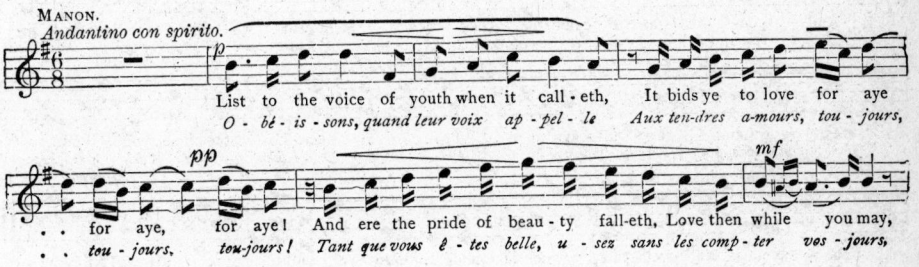

MANON.
Andantino con spirito.

List to the voice of youth when it call-eth, It bids ye to love for aye
O-bé-is-sons, quand leur voix ap-pel-le Aux ten-dres a-mours, tou-jours,

.. for aye, for aye! And ere the pride of beau-ty fall-eth, Love then while you may,
.. tou-jours, tou-jours! Tant que vous ê-tes belle, u-sez sans les comp-ter vos-jours,

MANON (*to* DE BRÉTIGNY). Hearken. dear friends ; remain here for a while. I must go some trinkets to buy.

BRÉTIGNY. With you will depart all the joy of the fête, O delightful Manon !

MANON. Ah ! say you so ? 'T is extremely gallant. E'en a gentleman sometimes a poet must be !

(MANON goes towards the distant stalls, followed by a curious throng.)

TOWNSPEOPLE AND TRADERS. Great ladies of renown are these, etc.

A TRADER. Best tobacco here and snuff.

(The COUNT DES GRIEUX enters.)

DE BRÉTIGNY. The Count des Grieux, if I am not mistaken !

COUNT. Monsieur de Brétigny !

DE BRÉTIGNY. I am he. But I can hardly believe my eyes. You, in Paris !

COUNT. My son brings me nere

DE BRÉTIGNY. The Chevalier des Grieux ?

COUNT. Call him Chevalier no longer.

(MANON *has approached under pretence of speaking to a Trader*). Des Grieux !

DE BRÉTIGNY. What do you mean ?

COUNT. He has entered the Seminary of St. Sulpice, with what intention I need not say.

DE BRÉTIGNY (*smiling*). What a change ! I am astonished !

COUNT. (*also smiling*). You caused it yourself by coming between him and his love.

DE BRÉTIGNY. (*indicating Manon*). Speak lower.

COUNT. Is that she ?

DE BRÉTIGNY. Yes, that is Manon.

(Dance music in the distance.)

MANON (*a* DE BRÉTIGNY). Et maintenant restez seul un instant,
Je veux faire ici quelqu'emplette.

DE BRÉTIGNY. Avec vous disparait tout l'eclat de la fête
Ravissante Manon !

MANON. Une fadeur ! C'est du dernier galant ! On n'est pas grand seigneur sans être un peu poëte !

(MANON s'eloigne et se dirige vers les petites boutiques du fond, escotée des curieux qui sortent peu à peu.)

BOURGEOIS ET MARCHANDS. Voici les elegantés ! etc.

UN MARCHAND. Poudre, rapes à tabac !

(Entrent le COMTE DES GRIEUX.)

DE BRÉTIGNY. Je ne me trompe pas, le Comte Des Grieux.

LE COMTE. Monsieur de Brétigny.

DE BRÉTIGNY. Moi-même. C'est à peine si je puis en croire mes yeux ! Vous à Paris !

LE COMTE. C'est mon fils qui m'amène.

DE BRÉTIGNY. Le Chevalier ?

LE COMTE. Il n'est plus Chevalier. C'est l'abbe Des Grieux.

(MANON *uqu s'est ràpprochée tout en feignant de parler à un Marchand*). Des Grieux !

DE BRÉTIGNY. Abbe ! Lui ! Comment !

LE COMTE. Le Ciel l'attire ! Dans les ordres, il veut entrer. Il est à St. Sulpice. Il prononce un discours.

DE BRÉTIGNY. Albe ! Cela m'étonne ! Un pareil changement !

LE COMTE (*sourient*). C'est vou qui l'avez fait, en vous chargeant de briser net l'amour qui l'attachait à certaine personne.

DE BRÉTIGNY (*montrant* MANON). Plus bas !

LE COMTE. C'est elle ?

DE BRÉTIGNY. Oui, c'est Manon.

(Musique du bal dans le lointain.)

COUNT. Ah! now I know why you took so much interest in my son's affairs. (*Looking . at* MANON, *who draws nearer.*) Excuse me, she wishes to speak with you. (*Bows, and moves away.*) (*Aside.*) She is, indeed, very beautiful.

MANON (*to* DE BRÉTIGNY). I want a bracelet exactly like this, and cannot find one any-where.

DE BRÉTIGNY. Indeed! then let me take up the search.

(He bows to the COUNT and departs.)

COUNT (*aside*). She is charming, and no won-der she is loved!

MANON (*to the* COUNT, *with embarrassment.*) Sir, your pardon, pray! I was here—quite close by!—not that I wished to hear. It was not of my seeking.

COUNT. The fault is very small. Say no more. (*About to go away.*) Madame!

MANON (*drawing nearer*). But was it not of love you were speaking?

COUNT. It was!

MANON (*restraining her emotion*). Ah! so I thought! Nay, sir, I humbly crave forgive-ness. I think the Chevalier des Grieux was one time in love.

COUNT. With whom?

MANON. With a friend of mine.

COUNT. Ah, indeed!

MANON. Yes, he loved. (*With emotion.*) And I would gladly know if from the struggle he has come victorious; and if, forgetting her who had caused all his pain, he has chased from his heart a remembrance so dire.

COUNT. Is it here your list at length closes? Would you know whither summer flies? What becomes of young love when it dies? Or where goes the scent of roses?

MANON. O heaven! give me courage for this, That I may ask all I would know.

LE COMTE. Je devine alors la raison qui vous fit, avec taut de zèle, prendre les intérêts de mon fils. (*Voyant* MANON.) Mais, pardon! elle veut vous parler. (*Il salue et s'éloigne un peu.*) (*A part.*) Ell est vraiment fort belle!

MANON (*à* DE BRÉTIGNY). Je voudrais, mon ami, avoir un bracelet pareil à celui-ci; je ne puis le trouver;

DE BRÉTIGNY. C'est bien, je vais moi-même.

(Il salut le COMTE et sort.)

LE COMTE (*à part*). Elle est charmante et ie comprends qu'on l'aime!

MANON (*au* COMTE, *avec embarras*). Pardon! Mais j'étais là près de vous, à deux pas—J'en-tendais—malgré moi—Je suis très curieuse.

LE COMTE. C'est un petit défaut—tres petic ici-bas. Madame! (*Voulant s'eloigner.*)

MANON (*rapprochant*). Il s'agisait d'une his-toire amoureuse?

LE COMTE. Mais oui.

MANON. (*contenant son émotion*). C'est qui je crois. Pardonnez moi, je vous en prie—Je crois que cet abbé Des Grieux autre fois aimait.

LE COMTE. Qui donc?

MANON. Elle était mon aime.—

LE COMTE. Ah! très bien.

MANON (*avec émotion*). Il l'aimait, et je vou-drais savoir si sa raison sortit victorieuse, et si, de l'oublieuse. Il apu parvenir, a chaser de son cœur le cruel souvenir?

LE COMTE. Faut-il donc savoir tant de choses? Que deviennent les plus beaux jours Où vont les premieres amours, Où vole le parfum des roses?

MANON. Mon Dieu! mon Dieu! Donnez le courage De tout oser lui demander!

COUNT. Ignorance, they say, is bliss,
Since the past is gone, let it go.

MANON. Stay yet a moment.
Has absence wrung his heart with anguish?
And does he ever breathe her name?

COUNT (*looking steadily at her*). In silence
he with grief did languish.

MANON (*greatly moved*). Does he the faithless never blame?

COUNT. No!

MANON. Does he remember that the maiden
To love was fain?

COUNT (*after some hesitation*). His heart that
once was heavy laden
Is light again.

MANON. And now?

COUNT (*lightly, with significance*). The les-
son's learn'd your friend had set —
A lesson every man should know,
If he'd be wise — is it not so?
One can forget.

MANON (*sorrowfully*). One can forget!

(The COUNT respectfully salutes and retires.)
(The people move in; among them are DE BRÉTIGNY,
GUILLOT and LESCAUT.)

MANON. No! his life is bound for ever to mine.
He cannot have forgotten me. Lescaut, my
chair.

LESCAUT. Where must I take you, cousin!

MANON. To St. Sulpice.

LESCAUT. What is this strange fancy? Excuse
my asking you again, where?

MANON. To St. Sulpice.

(Exit MANON.)
(Chorus of People and Traders.)

SCENE II.

(A parlor in the Seminary of St. Sulpice. Ladies of the
Seminary and lady visitors.)

SOME OF THE LADIES (*speaking of* DES
GRIEUX, *the Priest*). How well he
preaches!

LE COMTE. Ignorer n'est-il pas plus sage,
Au passé pour-quoi s'attarder?

MANON. Un mot encore!
A-t-il souffert de son absence?
Vous a-t-il dit parfois son nom?

LE COMTE. Ses larmes coulaient en silence.

MANON (*très émue*). L'a-t-il maudite, en pleu
rant?

LE COMTE. Non!

MANON. Vous a-t-il dit que la parjure
L'avait aimé?

LE COMTE (*après avoir hésité*). Son cœur,
guéri de sa blessure
S'est refermé!

MANON. Mais de puis?

LE COMTE (*légèrement*). Il a fait ainsi que
votre amie
Ce que l'on doit faire ici bas,
Quand on est sage — n'est ce pas!
On oublie!

MANON. On oublie!

(Le COMTE salue respecteusement et se retire.)
(La foule — Seigneurs, Marchands et Bourgeois, — entrent; DE BRÉTIGNY, GUILLOT et LESCAUT.)

MANON. Non! sa vie à la mienne est pour
jamais liée. Il ne peut m'avoir oubliée.
LESCAUT.) Ma chaise, mon cousin.

LESCAUT. Où faut-il vous porter cousine?

MANON. A St. Sulpice!

LESCAUT. Quel est ce bizarre caprice? Par
donnez moi de faire répéter.

MANON. A St. Sulpice.

(Sortir.)
(Chor. Bourgeouis et Marchands.)

SCENE II.

(Le parloir du Séminaire de St. Sulpice. Dames et dé
votes.)

LES DAMES. Quelle éloquence! quelle abon
dance!

What eloquence divine!
Of heav'n it is a sign.
What melting sweetness in his voice,
What melting sweetness and what fire!
In hearing him our souls rejoice,
And serving heaven is our desire.
With wonderful art he called from their rest
Augustine the Saint, Theresa the blest.
Himself a saint —

(The COUNT DES GRIEUX enters unobserved.)

A most perfect saint.
My dear, what think you?
He's a saint, that is true!
He's a saint!

(DES GRIEUX, the priest, enters.)

LADIES (*to each other*, *devoutedly*). 'T is he,
  the Abbé whom we prize!
How modestly he veils his eyes!

(The Ladies depart slowly, after bowing to the Priest.)

COUNT DES GRIEUX. Bravo, my son!
A great success! Our family should be proud
  of having produced a new Bossuet.

DES GRIEUX. Father, for mercy's sake, spare
me!

COUNT. And is it well, Chevalier, that thou hast
made this pretended alliance with Heaven?

DES GRIEUX. Yes; for the world to me has
been bitterness and disgust.

COUNT. Brave words, Chevalier. By what
road hast thou through life travelled? — what
of the world canst thou have seen to suppose
this the fitting end?
  Go, wed some maiden fair and tender,
  Worthy of our ancient race;
  Obedience to Heaven's will thus render,
  And meet the world with fearless face.
  Than this, no more high Heaven asketh,
  The path of duty, 't is for thee;
  The virtue which in homage basketh
  Is virtue of a mean degree.

DES GRIEUX. Nothing shall stop me from pro-
nouncing my vows.

COUNT. Thou art resolved?

DES GRIEUX. I am resolved.

L'admirable orateur! ie grand predicateur
Quelle doucer, et quelle flamme!
Comme en l'ecoutant, la ferveur penètre
  doucement,
Jusqu'au fond de nos âmes!
De quel art divin, il dans sa thèse,
Peint Saint Augutin et Sainte Thérèse!
Lui-meme est un Saint.

(LE COMTE rapproche, non remarqué.)

Un Saint!
N'est-ce pas, ma chère?
C'est certain, c'est certain!
C'est un Saint!

(Entre le ABBE DES GRIEUX.)

LES DAMES. C'est lui! c'est l'abbé Des Grieux,
Voyez comme il baisse les yeux!

(Elles sort après avoir salué DES GRIEUX.)

LE COMTE DES GRIEUX. Bravo, mon cher,
succès complet! Notre maison doit être fière
d'avoir parmi les siens un nouveau Bossuet!

DES GRIEUX. De grâce, épargnez-moi, mon
père!

LE COMTE. Et, c'est de bon, Chevalier, que tu
prétends au ciel pour jamais te lier?

DES GRIEUX. Oui, je n'ai trouvé dans la vie
qu'amertume et dégoût.

LE COMTE. Les grands mots que voilà!
Quelle route as-tu donc suivie, et que sais-tu
de cette vie? Pour penser qu'elle finit là?
  Epouse quelque brave fille,
  Digne de nous, digne de toi;
  Deviens un père de famille,
  Ni pire, ni meilleur que moi:
  Le ciel n'en veut pas davantage;
  C'est là devoir, entends-tu?
  C'est là le devoir,
  La vertu qui fait du tapage
  N'est déjà plus de la vertu!

DES GRIEUX. Rien ne peut m'empécher de
prononcer mes vœux!

LE COMTE. C'est dit alors?

DES GRIEUX. Oui, je le veux!

COUNT. Be it so. I will go and announce to all that we have a saint in the family. Whether any one will believe me is doubtful.

DES GRIEUX. I pray you, sir, do not mock me!

COUNT. One word more. As it is not certain that thou wilt not be an abbot to-morrow, I shall send thee at once a hundred thousand francs.

DES GRIEUX. Father!

COUNT. The money is thine. It comes from thy mother. And now, farewell, my son!

DE GRIEUX. Father, farewell!

COUNT. Farewell! Remain to pray. (*Exit.*)

DES GRIEUX. I'm alone at last! The supreme moment now has come. From earthly ties I'm free, and only seek the rest which faith in heaven can give. Yes; I've resolved to put firm faith between the world and me.
  Ah! depart, image fair,
  Leave me now at rest;
  Have regard to my prayer,
  Ease my poor tortured breast.
  To the dregs I have drain'd
  Life's most bitter cup,
  Nor to Heaven once complain'd,
  Though heart's blood filled it up.
Dead to me now are love and all that men call glory. I desire to chase forth from my memory an evil name—a name which haunts me! Ah! wherefore?
Great Heaven! with flame all searching, my soul now purge from stain! Oh! let thy pure and glorious light chase far away the gloom that weighs on my heart.
  Ah! depart, image fair! etc.

(Exit slowly.)
(MANON enters — the Porter of the Seminary preceding her.)

MANON (*with effort*). Sir, I would speak with the Abbe des Grieux! (*Giving him money.*) Take this.

(Exit Porter.)

LE COMTE. Soit! Je franchirai donc seul cette grille, et vais leur annoncer là-bas qu'ils ont un Saint dans la famille. J'en sais beaucoup qui ne me croiront pas!

DES GRIEUX. Ne raillez pas, monsier, je vous en prie!

LE COMTE. Un mot encore. Comme il n'est pas certain que l'on te donne ici, du jour au lendemain, un bénéfice, une abbaye, je vais dès ce soir l'envoyer trente mille livres.

DES GRIEUX. Mon père!

LE COMTE. C'est à toi, c'est ta part sur el bien de ta mere. Et maintenant, adieu, mon fils.

DES GRIEUX. Adieu, mon père!

LES COMTE. Adieu; reste à prier! (*Il sort.*)

DES GRIEUX. Je suis seul! seul enfin! C'est le moment suprème! Il n'est plus rien que j'aime, que je repose sacré que m'apporte la foi! Oui, j'ai voulu mettre Dieu mème entre le monde et moi!
  Ah! fuyez, douce image, a mon âme trop chere;
  Respectez un repos cruellement gagne,
  Et songez, si j'ai bu dans une coupe amère,
  Que mon cœur l'emplirait de ce qu'il a saigne.
  Ah! fuyez! fuyez! loin de moi!
  Que m'importe la vie et ce semblant de gloire?
  Je ne veux que chasser du fond de ma memoire,
  Un nom maudit! ce nom qui m'obsède et pourquoi?
  Mon Dieu! de votre flamme
  Purifiez mon âme
  Et disipez à sa lueur
  L'ombre qui passe encor
  Dans le fond de mon cœur!
  Ah! fuyez, douce image, etc.

(Il s'éloigne lentement.)
(Entrer MANON et le Portier du Seminaire.)

MANON (*avec effort*). Monsieur, je veux parler à l'Abbé. (*Lui donnant de l'argent.*) Tenez!

(Le Portier sort.)

These silent walls! the chilly air I breathe! — how if these things have changed his heart and made it pitiless to sin! How if he have learned to curse me!

CHORUS *in the Chapel*. Magnificat anima mea Dominum, et exultavit spiritus meus.

MANON. They are praying yonder. Ah! I also would pray.

Oh! pardon me Thou who in Heaven reignest; for if now I beg of Thee grace, if now entreat at Thy hands pity, if my voice from below can ascend to the skies, 't is to ask of Thy goodness his heart whom I love. Oh! pardon me, great Heaven!

(In the chapel.)

In Deo salutari meo.

(DES GRIEUX enters, at back.)
(She turns round and at sight of him is about to fall.
DES GRIEUX advances.)

DES GRIEUX. Thou! Here!

MANON. Yes, 't is I! 't is I!

DES GRIEUX. Away! What dost thou here? Away! Make haste away.

MANON (*sorrowfully*). Ah! I have sinned against thee,
Yet do not forget all my love!
Shall I in those eyes that now fright me,
See pardon that comes from above?

DES GRIEUX. No; from my mind it has vanish'd,
That vision insensate, impure.
Holy Heaven has the foul fiend banish'd,
Vain before me spread'st thou the lure.
Ah! faithless Manon!

MANON (*approaching him*). But if I now repent?

DES GRIEUX. Ah! faithless! faithless!

MANON. Do not to forgiveness close thy heart!

DES GRIEUX. I can no longer hear thee. No; at last from my memory thou art gone for ev- er — gone also from my heart.

MANON (*with tears*). Alas! the bird that flies forth from its prison cage, full oft at night re-

Ces murs silencieux — cet air froid qu'on re- spire — pourvu que tout cela n'ait pas changé son cœur! Devenu sans pitié pour une folle erreur pourvou qu'il n'ait pas appres à maudire!

CHŒUR *dans la Chapelle*. Magnificat anima mea Dominum, et exultavit spiritus meus.

MANON. Là-bas on prie. Ah! je voudrais prier! Pardonnez-moi, Dieu de toute puis- sance, car si j'ose vous supplier, en implorant votre clémence, si ma voix de si bas peut monter jusqu'aux cieux, c'est pour vous de- mander le cœur de Des Grieux! Pardonnez- moi, mon Dieu!

(CHŒUR dans la chapelle.)

In Deo salutari meo.

(DES GRIEUX s'avance.)
(MANON se détourne, elle est prête à défaillir)

DES GRIEUX. Toi! Vous!

MANON. Oui, c'est moi, moi!

DES GRIEUX. Que viens tu faire ici? Va-t'en!

MANON (*douloureux*). Oui! je fus cruelle et coupable!
Mais rappelez-vous tant d'amour!
Ah! dans ce regard qui m'accable,
Lirai-je mon pardon, un jour?

DES GRIEUX. Non! J'avais écrit sur le sable
Ce rêve insensé d'un amour.
Que le ciel n'avait fait durable,
Que pour un instant, pour un jour!
Ah! perfide Manon!

MANON (*se rapprochant*). Si je me repentais?

DES GRIEUX. Ah! perfide! perfide!

MANON. Est-ce que tu n'aurais pas de pitié?

DES GRIEUX. Je ne veux pas vous croire. Non! vous êtes sortie enfin de ma mémoire — ainsi que mon cœur!

MANON. Helas! l'oiseau qui fuit ce qu'il l'es- clavage, le plus souvent la nuit, d'un vol dé-

turns on desperate wing to beat out its life against the bars! Ah! pardon me! I die here at thy fee.. (*With passionate energy.*) Ah! give back thy dear love, or despairing I perish!

DES GRIEUX. No! all my love is dead.

MANON. All thy love is dead! No, no! Love cannot perish! Hear me, I pray. Recall thyself. (*Caressingly.*) Is it not my hand that thine own now presses? Is it not my voice? Does not touch or sound come to thee caressing as one time it did? And these eyes that oft thou hast kissed with ardor, do they shine no more, even through my weeping? Am I not myself?—Do not turn away, but look on me. Am I not Manon?

DES GRIEUX (*deeply moved*). Oh, Heaven! with thy great power help me at this moment.

MANON. I love thee.

DES GRIEUX. Hold thy peace and do not speak of love, for here 't is profanation.

MANON. I love thee!

DES GRIEUX. Hold thy peace and do not speak of love.

MANON. I love thee!
(A bell is heard.)

DES GRIEUX. The hour of prayer has come!

MANON. No; we will never part!

DES GRIEUX. Duty calls me away.

MANON. No; we will never part! Ah! is it not my hand? etc.

DES GRIEUX (*with energy*). Ah! Manon! No longer will I struggle against myself.

MANON (*with a joyful cry*). At last!

DES GRIEUX. And for thy sake I dare all Heaven's vengeance can do. My life is in thy heart! My life is in thine eyes? (*Passionately.*) Come, Manon, I love thee!

MANON. I love thee.

---

sespéré revient battre au vitrage! Pardonne moi! Je meurs à tes genoux! (*Avec élan et désespoir*). Ah! rends moi ton amour, si tu veux que je vie!

DES GRIEUX. Non! il est mort pour vous!

MANON. L'est-il donc à ce point que rien ne le ravive! Ecoute moi! Rapelle toi! N'est-ce plus ma main que cette main presse? N'est-ce plus ma voix? N'est-elle pour toi plus une caresse, tout comme autrefois? Et ces yeux, jadis pour toi pleins de charmes, ne brillent ils plus à travers mes larmes? Ne suis-je plus moi? Ah, regarde moi! N'est-ce plus Manon?

DES GRIEUX (*dans trouble*). O Dieu! Soutenez moi dans cet instant supreme!

MANON. Je t'aime!

DES GRIEUX. Ah! Tais toi! Ne parle pas d'amour ici, c'est un blasphème!

MANON. Je t'aime!

DES GRIEUX. Ah! Tais toi! Ne parle pas d'amour!

MANON. Je t'aime!
(Cloche lointaine.)

DES GRIEUX. C'est l'heure de prier.

MANON. Non! Je ne te quitte pas!

DES GRIEUX. On m'appelle làbas.

MANON. Non! Je ne te quitte pas! Viens! N'est-ce plus mon main? etc.

DES GRIEUX (*avec élan*). Ah! Manon! Je ne veux plus lutter contre moi même!

MANON (*avec un cri de joie*). Enfin!

DES GRIEUX. Et dussèje sur moi faire crouler les cieux. Ma vie est dans ton cœur! Ma vie est dans tes jeux! Ah! viens, Manon, je t'aime!

MANON. Je' taime!

ACT IV.

SCENE I.

(A fashionable gambling room in Paris.)

CROUPIER. Gentlemen, make your game.

LESCAUT. Four hundred louis! A thousand!
Hurrah! they are mine!

A PLAYER (*following* LESCAUT). I swear the
money belongs to me.

LESCAUT. From the moment one says it with
so much confidence —

PLAYER. I had the ace and king!

LESCAUT. Let us begin again. It's all the
same to me.

(SHARPERS come forward cautiously.)

SHARPERS. Fools, when they do gamble,
Throw their gold to chance?
But wise men such as we are,
Look at luck askance.
We are clever fellows,
Know what steps to take,
When, as sometimes happens,
Fortune makes mistake.

LESCAUT (*pocketing money*). Because I
play so honestly,
The money always falls to me.

POUSSETTE, JAVOTTE, ROSETTE. To this
charming place of pleasure,
Come all the world with cash to spend;
Find delights that know no measure,
Unlucky days the nights shall mend.
Beauty never should be poor,
And we are they who win for sure.

(LESCAUT is triumphant. He is surrounded by POUS-
SETTE, JAVOTTE, ROSETTE, and others.)

LESCAUT (*with vigor*). It is here that my
lady serene
Has deigned a lodging to take,
And some day for good company's sake,
You shall hear what verses I make,
In honor of her my queen.

(Chink of gold is heard.)

ACTE IV.

SCENE I.

(Un maison de jeu à Paris.)

LES CROUPIERS. Faites vos jeux, Messieurs!

LESCAUT. Quatre-cents louis! Vivat! j'ai
gagné'

UN JOUEUR (*poursuivant* LESCAUT). Je
vous jure que l'argent m'appartient!

LESCAUT. Du moment qu'on l'assure avec
autant d'aplomb —

LE JOUEUR. J'avais l'As et le Roi!

LESCAUT. Recommençons alors. Cà m'est
égal à moi!

(Les AIGREFINS s'avancent discrètement.)

LES AIGREFINS. Le joueur sans prudence
Livre tout au hazard:
Mais le vrai sage peuse
Que jouer est un art!
Pour la rendre opportune
Nous s'avons sans danger,
Quand il faut carriger
L'erreur de la fortune!

LESCAUT (*En empochant l'argent*). Tout
en jouant honnêtement
Je n'ai jamais fait autrement!

POUSSETTE, JAVOTTE, ROSETTE. A l'Hotel
de Transylvanie
Accarez tous on vous en prie;
Passe vos jours, passe vos nuits,
L'or vient tout seul aux plus belles!
Et c'est nous qui gagnons toujours
Toujours, toujours, toujours!

(LESCAUT revient, triomphant. Il est entouré par les
aigrefins et par POUSSETTE, JAVOTTE, et ROSETTE.)

LESCAUT. C'est ici que celle que j'aime
Adaigné fixer son séjour,
Et je vous dirai quelque jour
Certains couplets que j'ai, moi-même
Faits en l'honneur de notre amour!

'Bruit de l'or, au fond.)

And hark, the sound divine,
That suits this muse of mine!

She whom I love — it is meet
That a lover be very discreet;
And yet I will tell you her name—

POUSSETTE, JAVOTTE, ROSETTE. Well, her name?

LESCAUT. Pallas 't is, the queen of the game;
So ends my song to her fame.

(Chink of gold is heard.)

ALL. And hark the sound divine,
That suits this muse of { mine. / thine.

(GUILLOT enters, and afterwards MANON and DES GRIEUX appear.)

GUILLOT. Who has come to cause all this stir?

POUSSETTE, JAVOTTE, ROSETTE. 'T is the charming Manon with her dear Chevalier.

DES GRIEUX (*looking around with a sombre expression*). So I am here; but I should have refused. Why had I not courage!

GUILLOT (*annoyed*). The Chevalier!

LESCAUT (*to* GUILLOT). How strange you look. Has anything vexed you?

GUILLOT. I have good cause, for I adored Manon, and I find it hard to see another in my place.

(LESCAUT draws GUILLOT away.)

CROUPIER. Make your game, gentlemen.

(All recommence play. MANON is left alone with DES GRIEUX. Observes his sadness and approaches him.)

MANON. Tell me now, Des Grieux, does thy heart own me sovereign?

DES GRIEUX (*with great passion*). Manon, sphinx as thou art, syren-lure to destruction, woman more than thy sex, I love thee — and hate thee. Pleasure and gold thy gods for ever must remain; yet, foolish though thou art, Manon, I love thee.

MANON. And I — oh, how I could love thee if but thou would'st —

Et c'est ce bruit charmant
Qui leur sert d'accompagnement!

Celle que j'aime, je me pique
D'être plein de discrétion,
Pourtant je vous dirai son nom—

POUSSETTE, JAVOTTE, ROSETTE. Oui, son nom!

LESCAUT. C'est Pallas, Dame de pique!
Et là s'arrête ma chanson!

(Bruit de l'or au fond.)

TOUT. Et c'est ce bruit, ce bruit charmant qui lui sert d'accompagnement!

(GUILLOT qui vient d'entrer, et apres MANON et DES GRIEUX.)

GUILLOT. Mais, qui donc nous arrive et fait tout ce tapage?

POUSSETTE, JAVOTTE, ROSETTE. C'est la belle Manon avec son Chevalier.

DES GRIEUX (*regardant autour*). M'y voici donc! J'aurais dû résister — Je n'en ai pas eu le courage!

GUILLOT (*vexé*). Le Chevalier!

LESCAUT (*à* GUILLOT). Vous changez de visage, et quelque chose, ici parait vous irriter.

GUILLOT. A bon droit je fais la grimace, car j'adorais Manon, et je trouve blessant et froissant qu'elle en aime un autre è ma place!

(LESCAUT entraine GUILLOT.)

LES CROUPIERS. Faites vos jeux, messieurs.

(Tout le monde retourne au jeu. MANON et DES GRIEUX sont restés isolés sur le devant de la scène. MANON, voyant que DES GRIEUX continue d'être triste, s'approche de lui.)

MANON. De ton cœur, Des Grieux, suis-je plus souveraine?

DES GRIEUX (*avec la plus violente passion*). Manon! sphinx étonnant, véritable sirène! Cœur trois fois féminin! Que je t'aime et te hais! Pour le plaisir et l'or quelle ardeur inouie! Ah! Folle que tu es, comme je t'aime!

MANON. Et moi — comme je t'aimerais si tu voulais.

DES GRIEUX. If but I would?

MANON. Our winged wealth has flown away.
Chevalier, there's nothing left.
In this place of coin bereft,
The purse is filled by dashing play.

DES GRIEUX (*troubled*). What dost thou say,
Manon?

LESCAUT (*approaching*). She is quite right?
Some minutes at the faro board —
A fortune's yours to spend or hoard.

DES GRIEUX. Who? I a gambler? No, no,
no!

LESCAUT. Ah! there you're wrong. Manon
does not love an empty purse.

MANON. Chevalier, if thou lov'st me dearly,
consent, and after, thou wilt see, we shall be
rich.

LESCAUT. Oh, most likely. Lady Fortune
darts her angriest glances on him who has
dared her and challenged her worst on full
many a field. All her wealth-bestowing favors
for beginners are kept.

MANON (*to* DES GRIEUX). Thou wilt yield,
wilt thou not?

DES GRIEUX. Oh, infernal madness!

LESCAUT (*pressingly*). Come on!

DES GRIEUX (*to* MANON). To thee I all shall
give.

LESCAUT. You're sure to win.

DES GRIEUX. What shall I then receive?

MANON. All that I am and have — myself; my
more than love. Oh, rest thee well on my affection, and never doubt a loving heart. Thus
will come our happiness. To thee my love!
To thee all my being!

DES GRIEUX. Oh, Manon, sphinx as thou art!
etc.

LESCAUT. Your luck is assured; play like a
man and conquer fate. Come on.

DES GRIEUX. Se je voulais?

MANON. Notre opulence est envolée—
Chevalier, nous n'avons plus rien!
Mais ici, quand on le veut bien
Une fortune est vite retrouvée.

DES GRIEUX (*avec trouble*). Que me distu,
Manon?

LESCAUT (*se rapproche de* MANON). Elle a
raison!
En quelques coups de Pharon
Une fortune est vite retrouvée.

DES GRIEUX. Qui? Moi? Jouer? Jamais!
jamais!

LESCAUT. Vous avez tort, Manon n'aime pas
la misère.

MANON. Chevalier, si je te suis chère, consens,
et tu verras qu'après nous serons riches!

LESCAUT. C'est probable! La fortune n'est in-
traitable, qu'a le joueur éprouvé, que contre
elle souvent a lutté! Elle est douce, au contraire à celui qui commence!

MANON (*à* DES GRIEUX). Tu veux bien, n'est-
ce pas?

DES GRIEUX. Infernale démence!

LESCAUT. Venez!

DES GRIEUX. Je t'aurrai tout donné.

LESCAUT. Vous gagne-rez!

DES GRIEUX. Mais qu'aurai-je en retour?

MANON. Mon être tout entier, ma vie, et mon
amour!
Repose-toi sur ma tendresse!
Ne doute jamais de mon cœur!
Ah! c'est là notre bonheur!
A toi mon amour!
A toi tout mon être!

DES GRIEUX. Manon! Sphinx étonnant, etc

LESCAUT. Votre chance est certaine! Jouea
toujours! c'est le bonheur! Venez!

GUILLOT (*to* DES GRIEUX). A word if you please, Chevalier. Say, are you willing to play with me? We shall then see if fickle Fortune stands your constant friend.	GUILLOT (*à* DES GRIEUX). Un mot, s'il vous plait, Chevalier; je vous propose une partie. Nous verrons si sur moi vous devez l'emporter toujours.
POUSSETTE (*gaily*). Bravo, Guillot! I'll back you for the winner.	POUSSETTE (*gaiement*). Bravo Guillot! pour vous, moi, je parie!
JAVOTTE. And I will stake my money on the Chevalier.	JAVOTTE. Et je parie alors, moi, pour ce Chevalier.
GUILLOT (*to* DES GRIEUX). Are you agreed?	GUILLOT (*à* DES GRIEUX). Acceptez vous?
DES GRIEUX. Agreed.	DES GRIEUX. J'accepte!
GUILLOT. Let us begin.	GUILLOT. Commençons!
POUSSETTE. Suppose we make a bet?	POUSSETTE. Nous parions toujours!
JAVOTTE AND ROSETTE. A bet, of course.	JAVOTTE ET ROSETTE. Nous parions!
GUILLOT. A thousand crowns!	GUILLOT. Mille pistoles!
DES GRIEUX. Sir, with you. A thousand crowns.	DES GRIEUX. Soit, monsieur, mille pistoles.
LESCAUT. A thousand crowns! (*He seats himself at another table.*) O Pallas, lend thine aid!	LESCAUT. Mille pistoles. (*Il va se mettre à une autre table.*) A mois, Pallas, à moi!
MANON. All these senseless follies are life, or, at least, the life that I desire.	MANON. Ces ivresses folles, c'est la vie! Ah! c'est la vie! Ou du moins c'est celle que je veux!
CROUPIERS. Make your game, gentlemen.	LES CROUPIERS. Faites vos jeux, Messieurs.
MANON. Music of gold, of laughter, and clash of joyous sounds. Come, love me and crown me with flowers, Gaily singing pass we the hours; Who knows if the morrow will come? Youth is for a day, Beauty fades away. Then let all our care Be for pleasure rare, Life's sweet honey sip Warm on every lip. To Manon give gold Untold. Come, love me, etc.	MANON. Ce bruit de l'or ce rire et ses éclats joyeux! A nous les amours et les roses! Chanter, aimer, sont douces choses. Qui sait si nous vivrons demain! Qui sait si nous vivrons demain! La jeunesse passe La beauté s'efface Que tous nos désirs Soient pour les plaisirs! L'amour et les fièvres, Sur toutes les lèvres! Pour Manon encor De l'or! de l'or! A nous les amours et les roses, etc.
GUILLOT (*to* DES GRIEUX). I would not have your chance just now, sir. Say another thousand crowns.	GUILLOT (*à* DES GRIEUX). Vous avez une chance folle! Mille louis de plus!
DES GRIEUX (*excited*). Sir, I'm content. Just as you please.	DES GRIEUX (*fièvreusement*) Soit! Monsieur! Mille louis!

GUILLOT. I have lost!

GUILLOT. J'ai perdu!

MANON (*to* DES GRIEUX). Well, art thou winning?

MANON (*à* DES GRIEUX). Eh bien, gagnes tu?

DES GRIEUX (*showing her gold and notes*). Look here!

DES GRIEUX. Regarde! (*Montre l'or et caisse.*)

MANON. Is that ours?

MANON. C'est à nous?

DES GRIEUX. It is ours.

DES GRIEUX. C'est à nous.

MANON. How I love thee!

MANON. Je t'adore!

GUILLOT (*to* DES GRIEUX). We'll double, if you please.

GUILLOT. Le double! voulez-vous?

DES GRIEUX. Agreed.

DES GRIEUX. C'est dit!

GUILLOT. I have lost again!

GUILLOT. Je perds encore!

MANON (*to* DES GRIEUX). Now did I not well say that thou wert sure to win?

MANON (*à* DES GRIEUX). Je te l'avais bien dit que tu devais gagner.

DES GRIEUX. Manon, I love thee! I love thee!

DES GRIEUX. Manon! Je t'aime! je t'aime!

GUILLOT (*leaving the table*). I vow I'll play no more.

GUILLOT (*quittant la table*). J'arrête la partie!

DES GRIEUX (*rising also*). That is as you will.

DES GRIEUX. C'est comme vous voudrez.

GUILLOT (*significantly*). I should indeed be foolish to go on thus.

GUILLOT (*avec intention*). Ce serait duperie de s'obstiner!

DES GRIEUX. What's that?

DES GRIEUX. Plait-il?

GUILLOT. Never mind. Well I know you are indeed a clever man.

GUILLOT. Il suffit, je m'entends; vous avez vraiment des talents!

DES GRIEUX (*angrily*). What do you say?

DES GRIEUX. Que dites vous?

GUILLOT. Restrain your anger. Are you of those who beat the men they have contrived to rob?

GUILLOT. Quelle furie! Vouloir encor battre les gens quand on les a volés!

DES GRIEUX (*throwing himself upon* GUILLOT). You vile and wretched cur, 't is a lie.

DES GRIEUX (*s'élancant sur* GUILLOT). Infame calomnie! Misérable!

(All come around.)

(Tout le monde accourt.)

THE OTHERS. Come, come, good sirs, respect yourselves, for in society a man should be decent.

LES AUTRES. Messieurs! voyons, messieurs! Quand on est dans le monde. Il faut se tenir mieux!

GUILLOT (*much agitated*). To witness I take you, sirs, and these young ladies. (*To* DES

GUILLOT (*tres agité*). Je prends à témoin, messieurs, et mesdemoiselles! Pour vous (*a*

GRIEUX *and* MANON.) As for you, you very soon sha.l hear some news of me.

(Exit.)

THE OTHERS. Was ever such a thing known here? Certainly not. One never cheats — in such a way.

SHARPERS. A bungler he to be found out.

LESCAUT (*interposing*). How now, my friends, pray be calm.

A CROUPIER. Make your game, gentleman.

SOME OTHERS (*pointing to* DES GRIEUX). There stands the thief, that's he.

MANON (*to* DES GRIEUX). Away, I do implore thee! Haste away!

DES GRIEUX (*firmly*). No, on my life! for, if I go, I shall myself confess that with this crime I here am justly charged.

(Loud knocking at the door.)

POUSSETTE, JAVOTTE, PLAYERS. How now! who knocks so loudly here?

(The knocking is repeated.)

PLAYERS. Quickly cover the gold!

MANON (*aside*). Who knocks thus at the door? I tremble, though I know not why.

A VOICE (*without*). Open, in the King's name!

LESCAUT. The Police! Quick, to the roof!

(He escapes.)
[The door is opened. Officers of police enter with GUILLOT.)

GUILLOT (*indicating* DES GRIEUX). This is your prisoner, and yonder (*indicating* MANON) stands his accomplice. (*To* MANON.) Extremely sorry, but the play was too good. I told you I would have my revenge. (*To* DES GRIEUX.) I have trumped your card, my master. console yourself as best you can.

DES GRIEUX *et* MANON) deux, vous aurez bien-tôt de mes nouvelles!

(Il sort.)

LES AUTRES. La chose ne c'es jamais vue Certainement! On n'a volé jamais pareille ment!

LES AIGREFINS. Le maladroit! Ah! quel ennui!

LESCAUT. Voyons, messieurs! Calmez-vous

UN CROUPIER. Faites vos jeux, messieurs.

AUTRE JOUEURS. On a volé! C'est lui!

MANON (*à* DES GRIEUX). Partons! Je t'en supplie! Partons vite!

DES GRIEUX (*avec fermeté*). Non! sur ma vie, si je partais, peut être croiraiton, qu'en m'accusant cet homme avait raison!

(On frappe fortement à la porte.)

POUSSETTE; JAVOTTE ET JOUEURS. Eh mais, qui frappe de la serte?

LES JOUEURS. Vite! cachez l'argent!

MANON (*à part*). Qui frappe à cette porte? Je tremble, je ne sais pourquoi!

UNE VOIX (*au dehors*). Ouvrez! au nom du Roi!

LESCAUT. Un exempt de police! Gagnons vite la toit!

(Il se sauve.)
(Un exempt de police suivi de gardes, pénètre dans la salle avec GUILLOT.)

GUILLOT. (*désignant* DES GRIEUX). Le coupable est mansieur, et voilà sa complice. (*Désignant* MANON). (*A* MANON). Mille regrets, mademoiselle, mais la partie était trop belle! Je vous avais bien dit que je me vengerais! (*A* DES GRIEUX). J'ai pris ma revanche, mon maitre! Il faudra vous en consoler.

DES GRIEUX (*fiercely*). Well, I will try and begin on the spot by throwing you from yonder window.

DES GRIEUX (*terrible*). J'y tâcherai! mais je vais commencer par vous jeter par la fenêtre!

GUILLOT (*with contempt*). From yonder window?

GUILLOT (*méprisant*). Par la fenêtre!

COUNT (*who has entered unobserved*). And I? Shall I be served the same?

LE COMTE (*avec calme*). Et moi! m'y jetez-vous aussi?

DES GRIEUX. Father! you here! you!

DES GRIEUX. Mon père! vous ici! vous!

MANON. His father.

MANON. Son père!

COUNT. Yes, I am here from shame to save thee,
From shame so dire, and foul disgrace,
In repentant tears now lave thee,
Clear from stain an ancient race.

LE COMTE. Oui, je viens t'arracher à la honte,
Qui chaque jour grandit sur toi;
Insensé! vois-tu pas qu'elle monte
Et va s'elever jusqu' à moi!

Count (*indicating* Des Grieux *and* Manon). Take them prisoners. (*To* Des Grieux.) But soon shall liberty be yours.

Des Grieux (*indictating* Manon). And she?

Guillot (*interposing*). This lady has to go where many of her sort have gone.

Des Grieux (*with spirit*). Ah! touch her not! (*throwing himself before* Manon) with my life I'll defend her.

Manon (*fainting*). Help! I am lost! I die! Mercy!

Des Grieux. Oh despair! Our lives are divided forever!

Le Comte (*désignant* Des Grieux *et* Manon). Qu'on l'emmène! (*Au Chevalier.*) Plus tard, on vous délivrera.

Des Grieux (*désignant* Manon). Mais elle?

Guillot (*s'interposant*). Le guet la conduira où l'on emmène ses pareilles!

Des Grieux. N'approchez pas! Je saurai la défendre!

Manon (*s'evanouisant*). Ah! c'en est fait! je meurs! Gràce!

Des Grieux. O douleur! l'avenir nous sépare, à jamais!

ACTE V.

OR SCENE II OF ACT IV.

(A lonely spot on the road to Havre.)

Des Grieux *discovered seated by the wayside*). Manon, dearest Manon! do I see thee herded with these wretched beings and have no power to aid! O Heaven! merciless Heaven! must I then despair! (*He sees* Lescaut *approaching.*) No, he comes! (*Advancing impetuously to* Lescaut.) Thy fellows now make ready; see, the soldiers are yonder; they will soon reach this place. Thy men are fully armed; they will rescue Manon and give her back to me! What! can it not be done? Are all my fond hopes vain! Oh! why dost thou keep silence?

Lescaut. Sir, I have done my best —

Des Grieux (*anxiously*). Go on!

Lescaut. And grieve to say that all is lost.

Des Grieux (*piteously*). Lost!

ACT V.

(AU SCENE II.)

(La route du Hâvre.)

Des Grieux. Manon! pauvre Manon! Je te vois enchainée avec ces misérables! Et la charrette passe! O cieux inexorables, faut-il désespérer? (*Apercevant* Lescaut.) Non! C'est lui! (*Allant à lui.*) Prèpare tons escorte! Les archers sont làbas ils arrivent ici. Tes hommes sont armés? Ils nous prêtent main forte et nous la délivrons! — quoi? N'est-ce pas ainsi que tout est convenu? Tu gardes le silence!

Lescaut (*avec effort*). Monsieur la chevalier —

Des Grieux. Eh bien?

Lescaut. Je pense que tout est perdu!

Des Grieux. Perdu!

LESCAUT. Scarce had the sun shone on the arms of the soldiers ere all our men fled.

DES GRIEUX (*distracted*). 'Tis false! 'Tis false! Great Heaven hath taken pity on my suffering, and at last comes the hour expected! In a moment my Manon shall be free.

LESCAUT (*sadly*). Since I have told the truth—

DES GRIEUX (*about to strike him*). Away!

LESCAUT. Strike, if you will. 'Tis soldier's fare. He's by the King ill-paid; and then, whate'er his worth, the good folks shake their heads and call him "wretched fellow."

DES GRIEUX (*violently*). Away!

(Voices of Soldiers in the distance. DES GRIEUX and LESCAUT listen.)

SOLDIERS. Captain, riding by,
Dost thou pitying sigh,
As we march left, right?
No, no!
'Tis not so.
For a gallant bay
Carries thee all day,
And thy heart is light.

DES GRIEUX. Who is that?

LESCAUT (*going along the road*). Down the road they are coming, and almost close at hand.

DES GRIEUX (*trying to rush forward.*) Manon, Manon! (LESCAUT *stops him.*) My sword is all I have, but let us both boldly attack them.

LESCAUT. Oh, what madness is this!

DES GRIEUX. Come on.

LESCAUT. All will be lost. Take advice. It is better to use other means.

DES GRIEUX. How then?

LESCAUT. For Manon's sake let us go.

DES GRIEUX (*resisting*). No, no!

LESCAUT. Dès qu'an soleil ont ...ai les mou quets des archers, tous ces lâches ont fui!

DES GRIEUX (*éperdu*). Tu mens! Le ciel a pris pitié de ma souffrance. C'est l'instan' de la délivrance, tout à l'heure Manon va tomber dans mes bras!

LESCAUT Je ne vous trompe pas!

DES GRIEUX (*faisant le geste de le frapper*). Va-t'en!

LESCAUT. Frappez! Que voulez-vous? Ou est soldat le roi paie assez mal! Alors, bier malgré soi, on devient un coquin, un homme abominable!

DES GRIEUX (*violent*). Va-t'en!

(Ils écoutent, interdits.)

LES SOLDATS (*au loin*). Capitaine, ô gué,
Es tu fatigué
De nous voir à pied!
Mais non, mais non!
La Ramée
On n'est pas trop mal
Sur un bon cheval
Pour mener l'armée.

DES GRIEUX. Qu'est-ce là?

LESCAUT (*allant sur le chemin*). Ce sont eux sans doute,
Je les vois sır la route!

DES GRIEUX (*voulant s'élancer*). Manon! Manon! (LESCAUT *l'arrête.*) Je n'ai que non épée, mais mous allons les attaquer tous deux!

LESCAUT. Quelle folle équipee!

DES GRIEUX. Allons!

LESCAUT. Vous la perdrez! Croyez-moi, Il vaut mieux prendre un autre moyen.

DES GRIEUX. Sequel?

LESCAUT. Je vous en prie, partons!

DES GRIEUX (*résistant*). Non! non!

LESCAUT. Manon you'll see. I promise this.

DES GRIEUX What, go when her poor weary heart cries, "Come to me?" Oh, no!

LESCAUT. Sir, if you love her, come.

DES GRIEUX. If I love her? Would I not lose my all?—would I not gladly die that she might live?

LESCAUT. Pray, come

DES GRIEUX. When shall I see her?

LESCAUT. This very instant.

(*The Soldiers have come nearer.* LESCAUT *draws* DES GRIEUX *behind some bushes.*)

SOLDIERS. Captain riding by, etc.

(*Soldiers appear.*)

A SERGEANT. There is no glory in escorting such fair companions as ours. But no matter, 't is our business. And what do the prisoners say?

A SOLDIER. Oh, nothing; they are very quiet, and one of them is already half dead.

SERGEANT. O, that's Manon!

DES GRIEUX (*behind the bushes*). O Heaven!

LESCAUT (*holding him*). Silence! Let me act. (*To the* SERGEANT.) Hi, comrade!

(LESCAUT *and* SERGEANT *confer together.*)

DES GRIEUX (*to* LESCAUT *as he returns*). Am I to see her?

LESCAUT. And soon I hope to carry her off.

DES GRIEUX (*pointing to the* SENTRY). That Soldier!

LESCAUT. I will attend to him. I know better than to give away all the money.

(*He exits with the* SERGEANT.)
(MANON *appears. She comes down the path as though exhausted by fatigue.*)

MANON (*with a joyful cry*). Ah, Des Grieux!

LESCAUT. Vous la verrez, je le promets!

DES GRIEUX. Partir! Lorsque son cœur me crie, " Viens a moi!" Non, jamais!

LESCAUT. Si vous l'aimez, venez!

DES GRIEUX. Ah! si je l'aime! Quand je veux tout braver; quand je voudrais mourir pour elle!

LESCAUT. Venez!

DES GRIEUX. Quand la verrai-je?

LESCAUT. A l'instant même!

(*Il entraîne* DES GRIEUX *derrère le buisson les Soldats rapprochant.*)

LES SOLDATS. Capitaine, ô gué, etc.

(*Les Soldats paraissent.*)

UN SERGEANT. C'est bien la moins.
Car ce n'est pas la gloire d'escorter l'arme au bras et de faire.
Embarquer des demoiselles sons vertu!
N'importe! C'est le métier? Et que desent la bas les captives?

UN SOLDAT. Oh! rien! elles ne bougent pas! L'une d'elles est déjà malade, à demi morte.

SERGEANT. Manon, alors?

DES GRIEUX. O ciel!

LESCAUT. Silence! Laissez-moi faire. Hé, camarade!

DES GRIEUX. (*à* LESCAUT). MANON! je vais la voir!

LESCAUT. Et bientôt, je l'espère vous pourrez l'emmener.

DES GRIEUX. Ce Soldat?

LESCAUT. J'en fais mon affaire! J'ai tres bien fait de ne pas tout donner!

(*Il sort avec le Soldat.*)
(MANON *pairait; elle descend pénihlement et comme brisée par la fatigue.*)

MANON (*avec cri de joie*). Ah! Des Grieux!

DES GRIEUX (*with delirious gladness*). Oh, Manon, Manon, Manon! — Thou weepest!

MANON. Yes; with shame for myself, but with sorrow for thee.

DES GRIEUX (*tenderly*). Manon, oe of good heart, dear love. Think of the happy hours that remain for us both.

MANON (*bitterly*). Ah! sweet deceiving vision.

DES GRIEUX. No; those far-away countries, where they would drag thee now, thou shalt never see. Both together we'll fly to a place of sweet rest, where trouble may not come. (MANON *remains silent.*) Manon, wilt thou not speak?

MANON (*with infinite tenderness*). Oh, my heart's only love; only now do I feel all thy goodness of soul, and, though fallen so low, Manon craves pity and pardon for all her sins. (DES GRIEUX *tries to interrupt her.*) No, no; I must speak. Ah! careless was I and light-hearted; e'en in loving thee beyond compare, most ungrateful.

DES GRIEUX. Love, cease these reproaches.

MANON. Vainly I bid my wicked heart say why — by what excess of madness I have given thee pain on one day of my wasted life.

DES GRIEUX. Enough!

MANON (*weeping*). With remorse and contempt I am filled when I think of our love, by my own act destroyed. Ah! would that I could now atone with all my blood for but one of the griefs thou hast endured through me! Pardon Manon! Oh, pardon Manon!

DES GRIEUX (*passionately moved*). What! speakest thou of pardon when thy heart to my heart is given back again?

MANON (*with a cry of ecstasy*). Ah!
I feel 't is purest passion,
A love free from all alloy!
I hail a future full of joy!

DES GRIEUX. Manon, my adored!
Yet this day of delight
Shall our hearts re-unite.

DES GRIEUX (*avec ivresse*). O Manon! Manon! Manon! Tu pleures!

MANON. Oui, de honte sur moi; mais de douleur sur toi!

DES GRIEUX (*tendrement*). Manon? Lève la tête et ne songe qu'aux heures d'un bonheur qui revient!

MANON. Ah! pourquoi me tromper?

DES GRIEUX. Non, ces terres loin taines, dont ils te menacaient, tu ne les verras pas! Nous fuirons tous les deux! Au delà de ces plaines, nous porterons nos pas! (*Silence de* MANON.) Manon, réponds-moi donc!

MANON. Seul de mon âme! Je ne sais qu'-
aujour d'hui la bonté de ton cœur.
Et si bas qu'elle soit, hélas! Manon réclame.
Pardon, pitié pour son erreur!
(DES GRIEUX *veut l'interrompre.*) Non!
non! encor! Mon cœur fut léger et
volage
Et, même en vous aimant,
Eperdument, j'etais ingrate!

DES GRIEUX. Ah! pourquoi ce langage?

MANON. Et je ne puis m'imaginer
Comment et par quelle follie
J'ai pu vous chagriner
Un seul jour de ma vie!

DES GRIEUX Assez!

MANON. Je me hais et maudis en pensant
A ces douces amours par ma faute brisées,
Et je ne paierais pas assez de tout mon sang
La moitie des douleurs que je vous ai causées!
Pardonnez-moi! Ah! pardonnez-moi!

DES GRIEUX (*attendri et passioné*). Qu'ai-je
à te pardonner
Quand ton cœur à mon cœur vient de se
redonner!

MANON (*avec un cri d'ivresse*). Ah! je sens
une pure flamme
M'éclairer de ces feux
Je vois enfin les jours heureux!

DES GRIEUX. Manon! mon amour, ma femme,
Oui, ce jour radieux
Nous unit tous les deux!

MANON. Happiness once more is mine. (*Profoundly moved and almost inaudible.*) Let us talk of past days — of the inn, the coach and the tree-shaded route ; of the letter thou didst write ; of our little table and thy black robe at St. Sulpice. (*With a sad smile.*) Ah ! how well I remember.

DES GRIEUX. 'T is a dream of delight. (*Joyfully.*) Come, Manon, come ; liberty is ours.

MANON (*becoming more feeble*). No ! vain words ! All my strength is departing ! Deep sleep o'er my senses is stealing ! I shall wake never more !

DES GRIEUX (*alarmed*). Do not give way. See now, 't is nearly nightfall. The evening star shineth o'er us.

MANON (*opening her eyes and looking up with a smile*). Oh ! what lovely gems ! Thou knowest I was always fond of jewels.

DES GRIEUX. Some one comes ! Let us go, Manon !

MANON (*with a stifled voice*). I love thee ! Take thou this kiss ; 't is my farewell for ever.

DES GRIEUX (*deeply moved*). No ; believe it I will not. O Manon, hear me ? Recall thyself. Is it not my hand that thine own now presses ?

MANON (*vaguely*). I pray thee, wake me not.

DES GRIEUX. Shall I never more give thee sweet caresses ?

MANON. Oh ! rock me in thine arms.

DES GRIEUX. Know'st thou not my voice, broken though with grief ?

MANON. The past let us forget.

DES GRIEUX. The past, so full of sweetness !

MANON. O most dire remorse !

DES GRIEUX. I have pardon'd thee. All is forgotten.

MANON. Nous reparlerons du passé.
De l'auberge, du coche, et de la route ombreuse.
Du billet par ta main tracé de la petit table
Et de ta robe noire à St. Sulpice.
Ah ! j'ai bonne mémoire !

DES GRIEUX. C'est un rève charmant ! Tout s'apprete pour notre liberté !

MANON. Non ! Il m'est impossible, d'avancer davantage je sens le sommeil qui me gagne, un sommeil sans reveil !
J'étouffe — je succombe !

DES GRIEUX. Reviens à toi. Voici la nuit qui tombe ; c'est la première étoile !

MANON. Ah ! le beau diamant ! Tu vois je suis encore coquette !

DES GRIEUX. On vient ! partons ! Manon !

MANON. Je t'aime ! Et ce baiser — c'est un adieu suprème !

DES GRIEUX. Non ! je ne veux pas croire ! Écoute-moi ! rappelle toi ! N'est-ce plus ma main que cette main presse ?

MANON. Ne me réveille pas !

DES GRIEUX. N'est-elle pour toi plus une caresse ?

MANON. Berce moi dans tes bras !

DES GRIEUX. Reconnais ma voix à travers mes larmes !

MANON. Oublions le passé !

DES GRIEUX. Souvenirs pleins de charmes !

MANON. O cruels remords !

DES GRIEUX. Je t'ai pardonné ! Tout est oublie !

MANON   Oh! can I forget the day of anguish
and of love! Yes; is it not my hand that thine
own now presses? Ah! it is his voice, and
upon his heart, full of love surpassing, once
again I rest! Now upon me dawneth a day
of peace! (*She becomes exhausted.*)   I die!

DES GRIEUX (*in affright*).   Manon

MANON (*murmurs*).   Better so; better so
Now is ended the story of Manon Lescau
(*Dies.*)

(DES GRIEUX utters a distracted cry and falls upon her
body.   The curtain slowly descends.)

MANON. Ah? puis-je oublier les tristes jours
de nos amours! Oui, c'est bien sa main que
cette main presse; ah! c'est bien sa voix! oui,
c'est bien son cœur! c'est bien la tendresse
des jours d'autrefois! Bientôt renaitra le bonheur passe! (*En défaillant.*)   Ah! je meurs!

DES GRIEUX (*avec effroi*).   Manon!

MANON. Il le faut, il le faut! Et c'est là l'histoire de Manon Lescaut! (*Elle meurt.*)

(DES GRIEUX jette un cri déchirant et tombe su
corps de MANON, Rideau.)

TALES OF HOFFMANN

(LES CONTES D'HOFFMANN)

by

JACQUES OFFENBACH

CHARACTERS

HOFFMANN	Tenor	LUTHER		Bass
COUNSELOR LINDORF		NATHANAEL		Tenor
COPPÉLIUS	Bass	HERMANN		Bass
DAPERTUTTO	or	STELLA		
DOCTOR MIRACLE	Baritone	GIULIETTA		Soprano
SPALANZANI	Tenor	OLYMPIA		
CRESPEL	Bass or Baritone	ANTONIA		
ANDRES		NICKLAUSSE		Mezzo-Soprano
COCHENILLE	Tenor	THE MUSE		Mezzo-Soprano
FRANTZ		A SPIRIT		Mezzo-Soprano
PITICHINACCHIO				

NOTE

"Les Contes d'Hoffmann," opéra-comique, is one of two posthumous operas of the brilliant and facile French composer. It was his most cherished work, and his labors upon it extended over a period of years. For some time Offenbach had felt his end approaching, and he said to M. Carvalho, "Make haste to mount my piece; I am in a hurry and have only one wish in the world — to witness the première of this work." He died, however, a few months before its first production, which took place, after it was finally revised and partly orchestrated by Guiraud, at the Opéra-Comique, Feb. 10, 1881. Here it was given no less than 101 times in the year of its production. It was also performed in Germany, and was being sung at the Ring Theatre in Vienna at the time of its conflagration.

THE STORY OF THE ACTION

ACT I. — This act is really a prologue, and shows Hoffmann, a young poet, at the Tavern of Luther, drinking and carousing with his companions. They ask him for a song; he commences the fantastic Ballad of Klein-Zach, but midway of the tale wanders into a rhapsodic apostrophe to a beautiful woman. His companions accuse him of being in love; but he replies that for him such joys are past, and forthwith promises to relate to them the history of his three loves.

ACT II. — OLYMPIA. At the house of the noted scientist, Spalanzani, who has invited a large company to witness the charms and accomplishments of his daughter, Olympia. Hoffmann, who is attended by Nicklausse, has already become enamored of her by fleeting glimpses through a window. Olympia's appearance, her singing, receive enthusiastic praise from her father's guests, and Hoffmann's conquest is complete. Left alone with her while the other guests are at supper, he tells her of his passion, and thinks that it awakens in her an echo of response. Later there is dancing, and she waltzes so madly that she whirls him off his feet and is only stopped by her father, who conducts her to her room. A Dr. Coppélius enters in a rage, claiming to have been swindled by Spalanzani. He slips into Olympia's room, and presently a noise of breaking is heard. Out of revenge Coppélius has smashed Olympia, who was only an automaton, cleverly constructed by Spalanzani. Hoffmann's dismay is pitiable.

ACT III. — GIULIETTA. The scene is in Venice at the house of Giulietta, who is beloved by Schlemil. She receives Hoffmann graciously, but Schlemil does not conceal his disgust at the young poet's arrival. Dapertutto bribes Giulietta, with a magic diamond, to enslave Hoffmann, who cares nothing for her. She succeeds in bringing him to her feet, and promises him the key of her room, which he must, however, procure from Schlemil. The latter refuses to yield 'he key, and a fight ensues, during which Hoffmann kills Schlemil. Hoffmann takes the key, and rushes to Giulietta's room, only to find it deserted, and to see her in a gondola, riding away in the embrace of another man, and laughing at his plight. Nicklausse drags him away to escape the police.

ACT IV. — ANTONIA. In Munich, at the house of Crespel, who seeks to keep his daughter Antonia hidden from the attentions of Hoffmann. Fearing that, together with her mother's voice, she has inherited her mother's consumption, Crespel forbids his daughter to sing. Hoffmann gains admission to the house unknown to Crespel, renews his vows to Antonia, and, at Crespel's approach, hides himself, to learn, if possible, why Antonia has been forbidden to use her voice. Through a conversation between Crespel and an evil magician named Doctor Miracle he learns the bitter truth; and later adds his entreaties to those of her father that Antonia will sing no more. She promises him; but when Hoffmann goes, Miracle appears to her, reproaches her for giving up her career in favor of a humdrum domestic existence with a lover whose unfaithfulness needs but to be proven, and fills her mind with doubt. Finally Miracle causes the ghost of Antonia's mother to appear, and the spirit adds her appeal to Miracle's reproaches, overwhelming Antonia, and finally inducing her

to join in singing with the supernatural voice. She pauses breathless, but Miracle urges her on and on, until she falls dying. Her frenzied father receives her in his arms, while Hoffmann, heart-broken, witnesses the tragedy.

EPILOGUE. Takes us back to the scene of the first act. Hoffmann's recital is at an end, and his companions leave him. The Muse appears to him and offers the consolations and rewards of Art as a panacea for his broken heart. For a moment he is roused to enthusiasm; but presently, overcome with his potations at Luther's tavern and the emotion of his reminiscences, he falls face forward upon the table — and sleeps.

First performed at the Théâtre de l'Opéra-Comique, Paris, Feb. 10, 1881, with the following cast:

HOFFMANN	MM. Talazac
LE CONSEILLER LINDORF	
COPPÉLIUS	
DAPERTUTTO	Tasquin
LE DOCTEUR MIRACLE	
SPALANZANI	Gourdon
CRESPEL	Belhomme
ANDRÉS	
COCHENILLE	Grivot
FRANTZ	
MAÎTRE LUTHER	Troy
NATHANAEL	Chenevières
VOLFRAMM	Piccaluga
HERMANN	Teste
VILHELM	Colin
STELLA	
GIULIETTA	Mmes. Isaac
OLYMPIA	
ANTONIA	
NICKLAUSSE	Ugalde
LA MUSE	Mole
UN FANTÔME	Dupuis

Conductor, Léon Carvalho.

LES CONTES D'HOFFMANN

ACT I	PREMIER ACTE

The tavern of Master Luther.

(The interior of a German inn. Tables and benches.)

Chorus of Students.

Drig, drig, drig, master Luther,
  Brand of hades,
Drig, drig, drig, bring us thy beer,
  Bring us thy wine,
  Till morning dawns,
  Fill up my glass,
  Till morning dawns,
Fill up our pewter pots!

Nathanael.

Luther is a brave man,
  Tire lan laire,
On the morrow we will brain him,
  Tire lan la!

Chorus.

Tire lan lai
      (They strike their cups on the tables.)

Luther.
              (going from table to table).
Here, gentlemen, here!

Hermann.

His cellar is a goodly spot,
  Tire lan laire,
We'll pillage it on the morrow,
  Tire lan la!

Chorus.

Tire lan lai
      (Knocking of glasses.)

Luther.

Here, gentlemen, here!

La taverne de Maître Luther.

(Intérieur d'une taverne allemande. Çà et là, des tables et de. bancs.)

Choeur des Etudiants.

Drig! drig! drig! maître Luther,
  Tison d'enfer,
Drig! drig! drig! à nous ta bière,
  A nous ton vin,
  Jusqu'au matin
  Remplis mon verre,
  Jusqu'au matin
Remplis les pots d'étain!

Nathanael.

Luther est un brave homme;
  Tire lan laire!
C'est demain qu'on l'assomme;
  Tire lan la!

Le Choeur.

Tire lan la¹
      (Ils frappent les gobelets sur les tables.)

Luther
              (allant de table en table).
Voilà, messieurs, voilà!

Hermann.

Sa cave est d'un bon drille;
  Tire lan laire!
C'est demain qu'on la pille
  Tire lan lai

Le Choeur.

Tire lan la!
      (Bruit de gobelets.)

Luther.

Voilà, messieurs, voilà!

5

Wilhelm.

His wife is a daughter of Eve,
  Tire lan laire,
And on the morrow we will steal her,
  Tire lan la.

Chorus.

Tire lan la !

Luther.

Here, gentlemen, here!

Chorus.

Drig, drig, drig, master Luther, etc., etc.
(The students seat themselves, drinking and smoking, on all sides)

Nathanael.

Praise God, my friends, for the lovely being!
  As in a masterpiece of Mozart
She lends the charm of a true and pleasing
  voice!
  It is the gift of nature
  And the triumph of art!
My first toast shall be to her;
  I drink to Stella!

All.

We drink to Stella!

Nathanael.

How is it Hoffmann is not here?
Ah, Luther, you portly tun,
What have you done with our Hoffmann ?

Hermann.

Your wine it is that's poisoned him,
You've killed him, by my faith!
  Give us our Hoffmann!

All.

Give us Hoffmann.

Lindorf
                    (aside).
To the devil with Hoffmann!

Nathanael.

By Heaven! Bring him to us,
Or your last day has dawned.

Wilhelm.

Sa femme est fille d'Eve;
  Tire lan laire;
C'est demain qu'on l'enlève;
  Tire lan la!

Le Choeur.

Tire lan la!

Luther.

Voilà, messieurs, voilà!

Le Choeur.

Drig! drig! drig! maître Luther, etc., etc.
(Les étudiants s'assoient, boivent et fument dans tous les coins.

Nathanael.

Vive Dieu! mes amis, la belle créature!
  Comme au chef-d'œuvre de Mozart
Elle prête l'accent d'une voix ferme et sûre
  C'est la grâce de la nature,
  Et c'est le triomphe de l'art!
Que mon premier toast soit pour elle!
  Je bois à la Stella!

Tous.

Vivat! à la Stella!

Nathanael.

Comment Hoffmann n'est-il pas là
Eh! Luther!... ma grosse tonne!
Qu'as-tu fait de notre Hoffmann ?

Hermann.

C'est ton vin qui l'empoisonne!
Tu l'as tué, foi d'Hermann!
  Rends-nous Hoffmann!

Tous.

Rends-nous Hoffmann!

Lindorf
                    (à part).
Au diable Hoffmann!

Nathanael.

Morbleu! qu'on nous l'apporte.
Ou ton dernier jour a lui!

Luther.	*Luther.*
Gentlemen, he is at the door,	Messieurs, il ouvre la porte,
And Nicklausse is with him.	Et Nicklausse est avec lui!

All.

Hurrah, 'tis he.

Lindorf (aside).

Let's watch him.

Hoffmann (entering with solemn demeanor).

Good day, friends.

Nicklausse.

Good-day.

Hoffmann.

A chair, a glass,
A pipe...

Nicklausse (mocking).

Pardon, my lord, no offence intended,
But I drink, smoke and sit like you... place
for two!

Chorus.

He's right... place for both of them.
(HOFFMANN and NICKLAUSSE seat themselves; HOFFMANN holds
his head in his hands.)

Nicklausse (humming)

Notte a giorno mal dormire...

Hoffmann (brusquely).

Shut up, devil take you!

Nicklausse (quietly).

Yes, master.

Hermann (to HOFFMANN).

Oh, oh, why are you in such bad temper?

Nathanael (to HOFFMANN).

Indeed. one scarcely knows you.

Tous.

Vivat! c'est lui!

Lindorf (à part).

Veillons sur lui.

Hoffmann (entrant d'un air sombre).

Bonjour, amis!

Nicklausse.

Bonjour!

Hoffmann.

Un tabouret! un verre!
Une pipe!...

Nicklausse (railleur).

Pardon, seigneur!...sans vous déplaire,
Je bois, fume et m'assieds comme vous
part à deux!

Le Choeur.

C'est juste!...Place à tous les deux!
(HOFFMANN et NICKLAUSSE s'assoient; HOFFMANN se prend la tête
entre les mains.)

Nicklausse (fredonnant).

Notte a giorno mal dormire...

Hoffmann (brusquement).

Tais-toi, par le diable!...

Nicklausse (tranquillement).

Oui, mon maître.

Hermann (à HOFFMANN).

Oh! oh! d'où vient cet air fâché?

Nathanael (à HOFFMANN).

C'est à ne pas te reconnaître.

Hermann.

What thorny path have you trodden?

Hoffmann.

Alas! I've come by a withered flower
Frozen by the northern wind.

Nicklausse.

And yonder, near this door,
Stumbled over a sleeping drunkard.

Hoffmann.

'Tis true... that rascal, by Jove, I envy him!
Let's drink, and like him, let's sleep in the
gutter.

Hermann.

Without pillow?

Hoffmann.

The stones!

Nathanael.

Without curtains?

Hoffmann.

The sky!

Nathanael.

With no covering?

Hoffmann.

The rain!

Hermann.

Have you a nightmare, Hoffmann?

Hoffmann.

No, but this evening
Just now at the theatre ...

All.

Well?

Hoffmann.

I hoped to see once more...
The deuce... why reopen old wounds?
Life is short...We must enjoy it by the way.
We must drink, sing, laugh, as we may,
What though we weep to-morrow!

Hermann.

Sur quelle herbe as-tu donc marché?

Hoffmann.

Hélas! sur une herbe morte
Au souffle glacé du nord!...

Nicklausse.

Et là, près de cette porte,
Sur un ivrogne qui dort!

Hoffmann.

C'est vrai!...Ce coquin-là, pardieu! m'a fait
envie!
A boire!...et, comme lui, couchons dans le
ruisseau.

Hermann.

Sans oreiller?

Hoffmann.

La pierre!

Nathanael.

Et sans rideau?

Hoffmann.

Le ciel!

Nathanael.

Sans couvre-pied?

Hoffmann.

La pluie!

Hermann.

As-tu le cauchemar, Hoffmann?

Hoffmann

Non, mais ce soir,
Tout à l'heure, au théâtre...

Tous.

Eh bien?

Hoffmann.

J'ai cru revoir...
Baste!...à quoi bon rouvrir une vieille blessure!
La vie est courte!...Il faut l'égayer en chemin
Il faut boire, chanter et rire à l'aventure,
Sauf à pleurer demain

Vathanael.

Then sing the first without need for asking,
We'll supply the chorus.

Hoffmann.

So be it!

Nathanael.

Something gay.

Hermann.

The song of the Rat!

Nathanael.

No! in truth I'm tired of it.
What we want is the legend
Of Klein-Zach...

All.

Give us the legend of Klein-Zach

Hoffmann.

Here goes for Klein-Zach!...
Once at the court of Eysenach
Lived a little dwarf called Klein-Zach;
He wore a big bearskin cap,
And his legs they went clic, clac!
    Clic, clac!
There's Klein-Zach!

Chorus.

Clic, clac!
There's Klein-Zach!

Hoffmann.

He had a hump instead of a stomach,
His webbed feet seemed to burst from a sack,
His nose with bad tobacco was black,
And his head it went crick, crack,
    Crick, crack!
There's Klein-Zach!

Chorus.

Crick, crack!
There's Klein-Zach!

Nathanael.

Chante donc le premier, sans qu'on te *le*
    demande;
Nous ferons chorus.

Hoffmann.

Soit!

Nathanael.

Quelque chose de gai!

Hermann.

La chanson du Rat!

Nathanael.

Non! moi, j'en suis fatigué.
Ce qu'il nous faut, c'est la légende
De Klein-Zach?...

Tous.

C'est la légende de Klein-Zach!

Hoffmann.

Va pour Klein-Zach
Il était une fois à la cour d'Eysenach
Un petit avorton qui se nommait Klein-Zach
Il était coiffé d'un colbac,
Et ses jambes faisaient clic, clac!
    Clic, clac!
Voilà Klein-Zach!

Le Choeur.

Clic, clac!...
Voilà Klein-Zach!

Hoffmann.

Il avait une bosse en guise d'estomac;
Ses pieds ramifiés semblaient sortir d'un sac
Son nez était noir de tabac,
Et sa tête faisait cric, crac,
    Cric, crac,
Voilà Klein-Zach.

Le Choeur.

Cric, crac,
Voilà Klein-Zach!

Hoffmann.

Now, for his features...
(He becomes absorbed.)

Chorus.

Now, for his features ?...

Hoffmann (very slowly).

Now, for his features...
(He rises.)

Ah, but her face was lovely!   I see her
Lovely as on that day when, following after
her,
I foolishly left my father's house
And fled away thro' valleys and forests.
The dusky curtains of her hair
Cast warm shadows upon her creamy throat,
Her eyes of deepest azure
Threw radiant glances, pure and serene;
And as our car without shock or tremor
Carried onward our hearts and our loves,
Her vibrant voice sang to the listening skies
A victorious chant whose eternal echo
Resounds in my heart!

Nathanael.

O most fantastic brain!
Whose portrait art thou painting? Klein-
Zach?

Hoffmann.

I speak of her...

Nathanael (touching his shoulder).

Whom?

Hoffmann.

No! Nobody!... nothing, my spirit is troubled.
Nothing!... And Klein-Zach is better, deformed though he be!

Chorus.

Flick, flack,
There's Klein-Zach.

Hoffmann.

Quant aux traits de sa figure...
(Il semble s'absorber peu à peu dans son rêve.)

Le Choeur.

Quant aux traits de sa figure ?...

Hoffmann (très lentement).

Quant aux traits de sa figure...
(Il se lève.)

Ah! sa figure était charmante!...Je la vois,
Belle comme le jour où, courant après elle,
Je quittai comme un fou la maison paternelle
Et m'enfuis à travers les vallons et les bois!
Ses cheveux en torsades sombres
Sur son col élégant jetaient leurs chaudes
ombres.
Ses yeux, enveloppés d'azur,
Promenaient autour d'elle un regard frais et
pur;
Et, comme notre char emportait sans secousse
Nos coeurs et nos amours, sa voix vibrante et
douce
Aux cieux qui l'écoutaient jetait ce chant
vainqueur
Dont l'éternel écho résonne dans mon coeur!

Nathanael.

O bizarre cervelle!
Qui diable peins-tu là! Klein-Zach?...

Hoffmann.

Je parle d'elle.

Nathanael (lui touchant l'épaule)

Qui?

Hoffmann (sortant de son rêve).

Non! personne!...rien! mon esprit se troublait
Rien!...Et Klein-Zach vaut mieux, tout
difforme qu'il est!...

Le Choeur.

Flic, flac!
Voilà Klein-Zach!

Hoffmann
    (throwing away his glass).
 Peuh!... this beer is detestable,
 Let's light up the punch and drink;
 And may the light-headed
 Roll under the table.

Chorus.

 And may the light-headed
 Roll under the table.
(The lights go out and LUTHER sets fire to an immense bowl ot
punch)
 Luther is a brave man,
  Tire lan laire,
  Tire lan la.
 On the morrow we will brain him,
  Tire lan laire,
  Tire lan la.
 His cellar is a goodly spot,
  Tire lan laire,
  Tire lan la.
 We'll pillage it on the morrow,
  Tire lan laire,
  Tire lan la.

Nicklausse.

 In good season, at least. How we vaunt
 Our reason and good sense!
 A curse on all faint hearts!

Nathanael.

 A wager that Hoffmann's in love!

Hoffmann.

 What of it?

Nathanael.

 You need not blush, I fancy.
 Our friend Wilhelm here
 Burns for Léonore and finds her divine.
 Hermann loves Gretchen; and I am near
  ru!ned
 For Fausta.

Hoffmann
    (to WILHELM).
 Yes, Léonore, thy virtuoso!

Hoffmann
    (jetant son verre).
 Peuh!...cette bière est détestable!
 Allumons le punch! grisons-nous!
 Et que les plus fous
 Roulent sous la table.

Le Choeur.

 Et que les plus fous
 Roulent sous la table!
(On éteint les lumières. Luther allume un immense bol de
punch.)
 Luther est un brave homme.
  Tire lan laire,
  Tire lan la,
 C'est demain qu'on l'assomme,
  Tire lan laire,
  Tire lan la,
 Sa cave est d'un bon drille,
  Tire lan laire
  Tire lan la,
 C'est demain qu'on la pille,
  Tire lan laire,
  Tire lan la.

Nicklausse.

 A la bonne heure, au moins! voilà que l'on
  se pique
 De raison et de sens pratique!
 Peste soit des coeurs langoureux!

Nathanael.

 Gageons qu'Hoffmann est amoureux!

Hoffmann.

 Après?...

Nathanael.

 Il ne faut pas en rougir, j'imagine.
 Notre ami Wilhelm que voilà
 Brûle pour Léonor et la trouve divine;
 Hermann aime Gretchen; et moi, je me ruine
  Pour la Fausta!

Hoffmann.
    (à WILHELM).
 Oui, Léonor, ta virtuose!...

(to HERMANN).

Yes, Gretchen, thy inert doll, with heart of ice.

(to NATHANAEL).

And thy Fausta, poor madman,
The courtezan with brazen mien!

Nathanael.

Morose being,
Many thanks for Fausta, Gretchen and
Léonore!...

Hoffmann.

Pish. They are like all the others!

Nathanael.

Then is your mistress such a treasure
That you can despise all of ours?

Hoffmann

(aside).

My mistress?

(aloud).

No, no, say rather three mistresses,
A trio of enchantresses
Who divide my days among them.
Would you like the story of my foolish
loves?...

Chorus.

Yes, yes!

Nicklausse.

What's that you say about three mistresses?

Hoffmann.

Smoke!
Before this dead pipe is relighted
Thou wilt understand me,
O thou, who in the drama where my heart was
consumed,
By good judgment secured the prize!

(All the students go to their places.)

Chorus.

Attention! It is nice to drink,
And listen to a foolish tale,
While following the fragrant cloud
That a pipe throws in the air.

(à HERMANN).

Oui, Gretchen, ta poupée inerte, au cœur
glacé!

(à NATHANAEL).

Et ta Fausta, pauvre insensé!...
La courtisane au front d'airain!

Nathanael.

Esprit morose,
Grand merci pour Fausta, Gretchen et
Léonor!...

Hoffmann.

Baste! autant celles-là que d'autres!

Nathanael.

Ta maîtresse est donc un trésor
Que tu méprises tant les nôtres?

Hoffmann

(à part).

Ma maîtresse?

(haut)

Non pas! dites mieux, trois maîtresses,
Trois charmant d'enchanteresses
Qui se partagèrent mes jours!
Voulez-vous le récit de ces folles amours?..

Le Choeur.

Oui, oui!

Nicklausse.

Que parles-tu de trois maîtresses?

Hoffmann.

Fume!...
Avant que cette pipe éteinte se rallume
Tu m'auras sans doute compris,
O toi qui dans ce drame où mon cœur se
consume
Du bon sens emportas le prix!

(Tous les étudiants vont reprendre leurs places.)

Le Choeur.

Ecoutons! il est doux de boire
Au récit d'une folle histoire,
En suivant le nuage clair
Que la pipe jette dans l'air!

Hoffmann
(sitting on a corner of table)
I begin.

Chorus.
Silence

Hoffmann.
The name of the first was Olympia...
(The curtain falls while HOFFMANN is speaking to the attentive students.)

ACT II.
—

(A physician's room, richly furnished.)

Hoffmann
(alone).
Come! Courage and confidence:
I've become a well of science!
I must turn with the wind that blows.
To deserve the one I love
I must find in myself
The stuff of a learned man.
She is there!... if I dared!
(He softly lifts the portiere.)
'Tis she!
She sleeps... how beautiful she is!
Ah! to dwell together!... both with the same hope,
The same remembrance!
To share our sorrows and our joys,
To share the future!
Ah, let my flame
Bring warmth into your day;
Open your soul
To the rays of love.
Altar divine! Sun whose ardor
Penetrates and caresses us!
Ineffable desire where one feels
One's whole being melt in a single kiss!
Ah, let my flame, etc.

(NICKLAUSSE appears)

Hoffmann
(s'asseyant sur le coin d'une table).
Je commence.

Le Choeur.
Silence!

Hoffmann.
Le nom de la première était Olympia!
(Le rideau tombe, pendant qu'HOFFMANN parle à tous les étudiants attentifs.)

ACTE DEUXIÈME
—

(Un riche cabinet de physician.)

Hoffmann
(seul).
Allons! Courage et confiance
Je deviens un puits de science!
Il faut tourner selon le vent.
Pour mériter celle que j'aime,
Je saurai trouver en moi-même
L'étoffe d'un savant,
Elle est là! Si j'osais!...
(Il soulève la portière.)
C'est elle!
Elle sommeille! Qu'elle est belle!
Ah! vivre deux! N'avoir qu'une même espérance
Un même souvenir!
Partager le bonheur, partager la souffrance,
Partager l'avenir!
Laisse, laisse ma flamme
Verser en toi le jour!
Laisse éclore ton âme
Aux rayons de l'amour!
Foyer divin! Soleil dont l'ardeur nous pénètre
Et nous vient embraser!
Ineffable désir où l'on sent tout son être
Se fondre en un baiser.
Laisse, laisse ma flamme
Verser en toi le jour!
Laisse éclore ton âme
Aux rayons de l'amour!
(NICKLAUSSE paraît.)

Nicklausse.

By Jove, I felt sure of finding you here.

Hoffmann (letting portiere fall).

Chut!

Nicklausse.

Why? There breathes the dove
Who's now your amorous care,
The beautiful Olympia. Go, my son,
  admire!

Hoffmann.

Yes, I adore her!

Nicklausse.

And hope to know her better.

Hoffmann.

The being one loves is easy to know.

Nicklausse.

How? by a look?... through a window?

Hoffmann.

A look may suffice to embrace the heavens.

Nicklausse.

What ardor!... Does she at least know that
  you love her?

Hoffmann.

No.

Nicklausse.

Write her.

Hoffmann.

I dare not.

Nicklausse.

Poor lamb! Speak to her.

Hoffmann.

The dangers are as great.

Nicklausse.

Then sing your way out of your predicament.

Nicklausse.

Pardieu! j'étais bien sûr de te trouver ici

Hoffmann (laissant retomber la portière).

Chut!

Nicklausse.

Pourquoi?... c'est là que respire
La colombe qui fait ton amoureux souci,
La belle Olympia... Va, mon enfant! admire

Hoffmann.

Oui, je l'adore!

Nicklausse.

Attends à la connaître mieux.

Hoffmann.

L'âme qu'on aime est aisée à connaître!

Nicklausse.

Quoi? d'un regard?...par la fenêtre?

Hoffmann.

Il suffit d'un regard pour embraser les cieux!

Nicklausse.

Qu'elle chaleur! Au moins sait-elle que tu
  l'aimes?

Hoffmann.

Non!

Nicklausse.

Ecris-lui!

Hoffmann.

Je n'ose pas.

Nicklausse.

Pauvre agneau! Parle-lui.

Hoffmann.

Les dangers sont les mêmes.

Nicklausse.

Alors, chante, morbleu! pour sortir d'un tel cas

Hoffmann.

Monsieur Spalanzani doesn't like music.

Nicklausse
(laughing)
Yes, I know, all for science!
A doll with china eyes
Flirted her little fan
At a brazen cock who stood near by.
They sang in unison
In a wonderful way,
Danced, talked, and seemed alive.

Hoffmann.

But why do you sing this song?

Nicklausse.

The little cock, trim and shining,
With a very saucy air
Turned about thrice;
By mechanism ingenious
The doll rolled her eyes,
Sighed, and said: "I love you!"

Chorus of the Invited Guests.

No, no host, really,
Receives more richly;
His house is radiant with good taste,
With effects delicately blended.

Spalanzani.

You will be satisfied, gentlemen, in a moment.
(He makes a sign to COCHENILLE to follow him, and exits with him.)

Nicklausse
(to HOFFMANN).
At last we shall have a nearer view of this
marvel
Without equal!

Hoffmann.

Silence! here she is!
(Enter SPALANZANI conducting OLYMPIA.)

Spalanzani.

Ladies and gentlemen,
I present to you
My daughter Olympia.

Hoffmann.

Monsieur Spalanzani n'aime pas la musique

Nicklausse
(riant).
Oui, je sais, tout pour la physique!
Une poupée aux yeux d'émail
Jouait au mieux de l'éventail
Auprès d'un petit coq en cuivre;
Tous deux chantaient a l'unison
D'une merveilleuse façon,
Dansaient, caquetaient, semblaient vivre.

Hoffmann.

Plaît-il?   Pourquoi cette chanson?

Nicklausse.

Le petit coq, luisant et vif,
Avec un air rébarbatif,
Tournait par trois sur lui-même;
Par un rouage ingénieux,
La poupée, en roulant les yeux
Soupirait et disait: "Je t'aime!"

Le Choeur des Invites.

Non, aucun hôte, vraiment,
Ne reçoit plus richement!
Par le goût, sa maison brille!
Tout s'y trouve réuni.

Spalanzani.

Vous serez satisfaits, messieurs.
(Il fait signe à Cochenille de le suivre et sort avec lui par la droite.)

Nicklausse
(à HOFFMANN).
Enfin, nous allons voir de près cette merveille
Sans pareille!

Hoffmann.

Silence! la voici.
(Entrée de SPALANZANI conduisant OLYMPIA.)

Spalanzani.

Mesdames et messieurs, je vous présente
Ma fille Olympia

The Chorus.

Charming!
What beautiful eyes!
And a shapely figure!
See her fine apparel.
There is nothing lacking;
She is indeed ravishing.

Hoffmann.

Ah, how adorable she is!

Nicklausse.

Charming, incomparable!

Spalanzani
      (to OLYMPIA).

What a success is thine!

Nicklausse
      (taking her all in).

Really, she is ravishing.

The Chorus.

What beautiful eyes!
And a shapely figure!
See her fine apparel!
There is nothing lacking;
She is indeed ravishing.

Spalanzani.

Ladies and gentlemen, inspired by your
    applause,
And above all anxious to shine anew,
My daughter, obedient to your least caprice,
Will, if you please...

Nicklausse
      (aside).

Pass to other exercises.

Spalanzani.

Will sing a grand air, accompanying the voice,
    Rare talent!
On the clavichord, the guitar,
Or the harp. at your choice!

Cochenille
      (at the rear).

The harp!

Le Choeur.

Charmante!
Elle a de très beaux yeux!
Sa taille est fort bien prise!
Voyez comme elle est mise!
Il ne lui manque rien!
Elle est très bien!

Hoffmann.

Ah qu'elle est adorable!

Nicklausse.

Charmante, incomparable!

Spalanzani
      (à Olympia).

Quel succès est le tien.

Nicklausse
      (en la lorgnant).

Vraiment elle est très bien.

Le Choeur.

Elle a de beaux yeux,
Sa taille est fort bien prise;
Voyez comme elle est mise!
Il ne lui manque rien.
Vraiment, elle est très bien.

Spalanzani.

Mesdames et messieurs, fière de vos bravos
Et surtout impatiente
D'en conquérir de nouveaux,
Ma fille, obéissant à vos moindres caprices,
Va, s'il vous plaît...

Nicklausse
      (à part)

Passer à d'autres exercices.

Spalanzani.

Vous chanter un grand air, en suivant de la
    voix,
Talent rare!
Le clavecin, la guitare,
Ou la harpe, à votre choix!

Cochenille
      (au fond du théâtre).

La harpe!

Bass *Voice*
            (in the wings).
   The harp!

Spalanzani.
   'Tis well. Cochenille.
   Go quickly and bring my daughter's harp!
         (COCHENILLE exits.)

Hoffmann
           (aside).
   I shall hear her... oh, joy!

Nicklausse
           (aside).
   Oh, foolish infatuation!

Spalanzani
        (to OLYMPIA).
   Calm your emotions, my child!

Olympia.
   Yes.

Cochenille
        (bringing the harp)
   There!

Spalanzani
       (sitting beside OLYMPIA)
   Gentlemen, attention!

Cochenille.
   Attention!

The Chorus.
   Attention!

Olympia
      (accompanied by SPALANZANI)
   The birds in the shrubbery,
   The sun in the sky,
   All speak to a maiden
   Of love, of love!
     There!
   The pretty song,
     There!
   The song of Olympia,
     Ha!

The Chorus.
   'Tis the song of Olympia

Une Voix de Basse
           (dans la coulisse)
   La harpe!

Spalanzani.
   Fort bien. Cochenille!
   Va vite nous chercher la harpe de ma fille
         (COCHENILLE sort.)

Hoffmann
           (à part).
   Je vais l'entendre... ô joie!

Nicklausse
           (à part).
   O folle passion!

Spalanzani
        (à OLYMPIA).
   Maîtrise ton émotion, mon enfant!

Olympia
   Oui.

Cochenille
        (avec la harpe).
   Voilà!

Spalanzani
       (s'asseyant auprès d' OLYMPIA).
   Messieurs, attention!

Cochenille.
   Attention!

Le Choeur.
   Attention!

Olympia
      (accompagnée par SPALANZANI)
   Les oiseaux dans la charmille,
   Dans les cieux l'astre du jour,
   Tout parle à la jeune fille
     D'amour, d'amour,
     Voilà!
   La chanson gentille
     Voilà!
   La chanson d'Olympia,
     Ha!

Le Choeur.
   C'est la chanson d'Olympia.

Olympia.

All that sings and sounds,
Or sighs in its turn,
Feels its heart to tremble
With love
There'
The little song,
There, there!
The song of Olympia.
Ha!

Chorus.

'Tis the song of Olympia.

Hoffmann
(to NICKLAUSSE)

Ah, my friend, what an accent!

Nicklausse.

What runs!...
(COCHENILLE has taken the harp and all surround OLYMPIA. A servant speaks to SPALANZANI.)

Spalanzani.

Come, gentlemen! your arm to the ladies..
Supper awaits you!

The Chorus.

Supper! That's good...

Spalanzani.

Unless you would prefer
To dance first!..

The Chorus
(with energy).

No! no! the supper is the thing!
After we'll dance.

Spalanzani.

As you please!

Hoffmann
(approaching OLYMPIA).

Might I venture?...

Spalanzani
(interrupting)

She is a bit tired;
Wait for the ball.
(He touches OLYMPIA's shoulder)

Olympia.

Tout ce qui chante et résonne
Et soupire tour à tour,
Emeut son coeur qui frissonne
D'amour.
Voilà!
La chanson mignonne,
Voilà, voilà!
La chanson d'Olympia.
Ha!

Le Choeur.

C'est la chanson d'Olympia.

Hoffmann
(à NICKLAUSSE).

Ah! mon ami, quel accent!

Nicklausse.

Quelles gammes!...
(Tout le monde s'empresse autour d'OLYMPIA. Un laquais s'adresse à SPALANZANI.)

Spalanzani

Allons, messieurs! la main aux dames.
Le souper nous attend!

Le Choeur.

Le souper! bon cela...

Spalanzani.

A moins qu'on ne préfère
Danser d'abord!...

Le Choeur
(avec energie).

Non, non, le souper! bonne affaire
Ensuite on dansera.

Spalanzani.

Comme il vous plaira!

Hoffmann
(s'approchant d'OLYMPIA).

Oserai-je?

Spalanzani
(intervenant).

Elle est un peu lasse; attendez le bal.
(Il touche l'épaule d'OLYMPIA.)

Olympia.

Yes.

Spalanzani.

You see. Until then
Will you do me the favor
To remain with my Olympia?

Hoffmann.

What happiness!

Spalanzani (aside, laughing).

We'll see what sort of a song he'll sing to her.

Nicklausse (to SPALANZANI).

Won't she take supper?

Spalanzani.

No!

Nicklausse (aside).

Poetic soul!
(SPALANZANI goes behind OLYMPIA. Noise of a spring is heard.
NICKLAUSSE turns around.)

What did you say?

Spalanzani.

Nothing, science! ah, monsieur, science!
(He conducts OLYMPIA to a chair. Goes out with guests.)

Cochenille.

The supper awaits you.

The Chorus.

Supper, supper, supper awaits us!
No, really, no host
Receives more richly!
(They go out.)

Hoffmann.

At last they are gone. I breathe freely!
Alone, alone, we two!
(approaching OLYMPIA)

I have so much to say to you,
O my Olympia! Let me admire you!
Let me feast my eyes upon your lovely coun-
tenance.
(He touches her shoulder.)

Olympia.

Oui.

Spalanzani.

Vous voyez, jusque-là
Voulez-vous me faire la grâce
De tenir compagnie à mon Olympia?

Hoffmann.

O bonheur!

Spalanzani (à part, riant).

Nous verrons ce qu'il lui chantera.

Nicklausse (à SPALANZANI).

Elle ne soupe pas?

Spalanzani.

Non!

Nicklausse (à part).

Ame poétique!
(SPALANZANI passe derrière OLYMPIA. On entend le bruit d'un
ressort)

Plaît-il?

Spalanzani.

Rien! la physique! ah, monsieur, la physique!
(Il conduit OLYMPIA à un fauteuil et sort avec les invites.)

Cochenille.

Le souper vous attend.

Le Choeur (avec enthousiasme).

Le souper, le souper, le souper nous attend!
Non, aucun hôte vraiment,
Ne reçoit plus richement!

Hoffmann.

Ils se **sont** éloignés enfin! Ah! je respire!
Seuls, seuls, tous deux!
(S'approchant d'OLYMPIA)

Que j'ai de choses à te dire,
O mon Olympia! Laisse-moi t'admirer!
De ton regard charmant laisse-moi m'enivrer

(Il touche légèrement l'épaule d'OLYMPIA.)

Olympia.

Yes.

Hoffmann.

Is it not a dream born of fever?
I thought I heard a sigh escape your lips!
(He again touches her shoulder.)

Olympia.

Yes.

Hoffmann.

Sweet avowal, pledge of our love,
You are mine, our hearts forever are
united.
Ah! do you comprehend this eternal joy
Of silent hearts?
Living, to be one in soul and with a single
flight
To soar to heaven,
Ah, let my flame
Bring warmth into your day
Open your soul
To the rays of love!
(He presses OLYMPIA's hand. She rises and walks up and down,
then exits.)

You flee from me? What have I done?
You do not answer....
Speak! Have I wounded you? Ah!
I'll follow your steps!
(As HOFFMANN is about to rush out NICKLAUSSE appears.)

Nicklausse.

Ah, by heaven, moderate your zeal!
Do you want us to drink without you?...

Hoffmann
(half crazy).

Nicklausse, I am beloved by her.
Loved!... Ye gods!

Nicklausse.

By my faith!
If you knew what they are saying of your fair
one!

Hoffmann.

What can they say? What?

Olympia.

Oui.

Hoffmann.

N'est-ce pas un rêve enfanté par la fièvre?
J'ai cru voir un soupir s'échapper de ta lèvre!
(Il touche de nouveau l'épaule d'OLYMPIA.)

Olympia.

Oui.

Hoffmann.

Doux aveu, gage de nos amours,
Tu m'appartiens, nos coeurs sont unis pour
toujours!
Ah comprends-tu, dis-moi, cette joie éternelle
Des coeurs silencieux?
Vivants, n'être qu'une âme, et du même coup
d'aile
Nous élancer aux cieux!
Laisse, laisse ma flamme
Verser en toi le jour!
Laisse éclore ton âme
Aux rayons de l'amour!
(Il presse la main d'OLYMPIA. Celle-ci se lève, parcourt la scène et
sort.)

Tu me fuis? qu'ai je fait? Tu ne me réponds
pas....
Parle! t'ai-je irritée? ah! je suivrai tes pas!
(HOFFMANN s'élance, NICKLAUSSE paraît.)

Nicklausse.

Eh! morbleu, modère ton zèle!
Veux-tu qu'on se grise sans toi?...

Hoffmann
(avec ivresse).

Nicklausse! Je suis aimé d'elle!
Aimé!...Dieu puissant!

Nicklausse.

Par ma foi!
Si tu savais ce qu'on dit de ta belle

Hoffmann.

Qu'en peut-on dire? Quoi?

Nicklausse.

 That she is dead

Hoffmann.

 Great Heavens!

Nicklausse.

 Or never was alive.

Hoffmann.

 Nicklausse! I am beloved by her!
 Loved! Ye gods!
   (He exits followed by NICKLAUSSE.)

Coppélius
    (entering furious).
 Thief! brigand! what a crash!
 Elias is bankrupt!
 But I shall find the right occasion
 To revenge myself... Robbed!... Me! I'll kill
  somebody.
   (COPPÉLIUS slips into OLYMPIA's room.)
   (Everybody enters.)

Spalanzani.

 Here come the dancers.

Cochenille.

 Now comes the round dance.

Hoffmann.

 'Tis the waltz that calls us.

Spalanzani
   (to OLYMPIA)
 Take the hand of the gentleman, my child.
   (Touching her shoulder)
 Come!

Olympia.

 Yes.
 (HOFFMANN takes OLYMPIA and they waltz They disappear on
left.)

Chorus.

 She dances!
 In cadence!
 'Tis marvelous!
 Prodigious!
 Room, room,
 For she flashes
 Through the air
 Like lightning.

Nicklausse.

 Qu'elle est morte

Hoffmann.

 Juste ciel!

Nicklausse.

 Ou ne fut pas en vie.

Hoffmann.

 Nicklausse! je suis aimé d'elle!
 Aimé! Dieu puissant!
   (Il sort. NICKLAUSSE le suit.)

Coppélius
    (entrant, furieux).
 Voleur! brigand! quelle déroute!
 Elias a fait banqueroute!
 Va, je saurai trouver le moment opportun
 Pour me venger... Volé! moi!... Je tuerai que'
  qu'un.
   (COPPÉLIUS se glisse dans la chambre d'OLYMPIA)
   (Entre tout-le-monde.)

Spalanzani.

 Voici les valseurs.

Cochenille.

 Voici la ritournelle.

Hoffmann.

 C'est la valse qui nous appelle.

Spalanzani
   (à OLYMPIA)
 Prends la main de monsieur, mon enfant.
   (Lui touchant l'épaule.)
 Allons!

Olympia.

 Oui.
 (HOFFMANN enlace la taille d'OLYMPIA et ils disparaissent à gauche

Le Choeur.

 Elle danse!
 En cadence!
 C'est merveilleux!
 Prodigieux!
 Place, place!
 Elle passe,
 Elle fend l'air
 Comme un éclair.

The Voice of Hoffmann
(outside)

Olympia!

Spalanzani.

Stop them!

The Chorus.

Who of us will do it?

Nicklausse.

She will break his head...

(HOFFMANN and OLYMPIA reappear. NICKLAUSSE rushes to stop
'hem.)

A thousand devils!.

(He is violently struck and falls in an armchair.)

The Chorus.

Patatra!...

Spalanzani
(jumping in).

Halt!

(He touches OLYMPIA on the shoulder. She stops suddenly. HOFF-
MANN, exhausted, falls on a sofa.)

There!
(To OLYMPIA)

Enough, enough, my child.

Olympia.

Yes

Spalanzani.

No more waltzing.

Olympia.

Yes.

Spalanzani
(to COCHENILLE).

You, Cochenille,
Take her back
(He touches OLYMPIA.)

Cochenille
(pushing OLYMPIA).

Go on! Go!

Olympia.

Yes.
(Going out slowly, pushed by COCHENILLE.)

Ha, ha, ha, ha, ha, ha, ha!

La Voix d'Hoffmann
(dans la coulisse –

Olympia

Spalanzani.

Qu'on les arrête!

Le Choeur.

Qui de nous les arrêtera?

Nicklausse.

Elle va lui casser la tête!...

(HOFFMANN et OLYMPIA reparaissent et redescendent.)
(NICKLAUSSE s'élance pour les arrêter.)

Eh, mille diables!...

(Il est violemment bousculé et tombe sur un fauteuil.)

Le Choeur.

Patatra!

Spalanzani
(s'élançant).

Halte là!

(Il touche OLYMPIA à l'épaule. Elle s'arrête subitement. HOFF
MANN étourdi tombe sur un canapé.)

Voilà!
(à OLYMPIA.)

Assez, assez, ma fille.

Olympia.

Oui.

Spalanzani.

Il ne faut plus valser.

Olympia.

Oui.

Spalanzani
(à COCHENILLE).

Toi, Cochenille,
Reconduis-la.
(Il touche OLYMPIA.)

Cochenille
(poussant OLYMPIA).

Va donc. Va!

Olympia.

Oui.
(En sortant, poussé par Cochenille.)

Ha, ha, ha, ha, ha, ha, ha, ha!

The Chorus.

What can we possibly say?
'Tıs an exquisite girl,
There is nothing lacking;
She iˢ indeed ravishing.

Nicklausse
          (in dolorous voice, pointing to HOFFMANN).
Is he dead?

Spalanzani
          (examining HOFFMANN).
No! in fact
His eyeglass only is smashed.
He is reviving.

The Chorus.

Poor young man!

Cochenille
          (outside).
Ah!
          (He enters, very agitated.)

Spalanzani.

What?

Cochenille.

The man with the glasses... there!

Spalanzani.

Mercy!   Olympia!...

Hoffmann.

Olympia!...
          (Sound of springs breaking with much noise.)

Spalanzani.

Ah, heaven and earth, she is broken!

Hoffmann
          (rising).
Broken!

Coppélius
          (entering).
Ha, ha, ha, ha, yes.   Smashed!
(HOFFMANN rushes out. SPALANZANI and COPPÉLIUS go at each other, fighting.)

Spalanzani.

Rascal!

Le Choeur.

Que voulez-vous qu'on dise?
C'est une fille exquise,
Il ne lui manque rien,
Elle est très bien!

Nicklausse
          (d'une voix dolente, en montrant HOFFMANN)
Est-il mort?

Spalanzani
          (examinant HOFFMANN).
Non, en somme, son lorgnon seul est en débris
Il reprend ses esprits.

Le Choeur.

Pauvre jeune homme!

Cochenille
          (dans la coulisse).
Ah!
          (Il entre, la figure bouleversée.)

Spalanzani.

Quoi?

Cochenille.

L'homme aux lunettes... là.

Spalanzani.

Miséricorde!   Olympia!...

Hoffmann.

Olympia!...
          (On entend un bruit de ressorts qui se brisent avec fracas.)

Spalanzani.

Ah! terre et cieux!   Elle est cassée!

Hoffmann
          (se levant)
Cassée!

Coppélius
          (entrant).
Ha, ha, ha, ha, oui!   Fracassée.
(HOFFMANN s'élance et disparaît. SPALANZANI et COPPÉLIUS se jettent l'un sur l'autre.)

Spalanzani.

Gredin!

Coppélius.

Robber!

Spalanzani.

Brigand!

Coppélius.

Pagan!

Spalanzani.

Bandit!

Coppélius.

Pirate!

Hoffmann
(pale and terror-stricken).

An automaton, an automaton.
(He falls into an armchair. General laughter.)

The Chorus.

Ha, ha, ha, the bomb has burst,
He loved an automaton.

Spalanzani
(despairingly)

My automaton!

All.

An automaton!
Ha, ha, ha, ha!

ACT III

(In Venice. A gallery, in festival array, in a palace on the Grand Canal.)
(The guests of GIULIETTA are grouped about on cushions.)

BARCAROLE

Giulietta and Nicklausse
(in the wings).

Night divine, O night of love,
O smile on our caresses;
Moon and stars keep watch above
This radiant night of love!
Moments fly, and ne'er return,
Our joys, alas! are fleeting;

Coppélius.

Voleur!

Spalanzani.

Brigand!

Coppélius.

Païen!

Spalanzani.

Bandit!

Coppélius.

Pirate!

Hoffmann
(pale et épouvanté).

Un automate! Un automate!
(Il tombe sur un fauteuil. Eclat de rire général.)

Le Choeur.

Ha, ha, ha, la bombe éclate
Il aimait un automate!

Spalanzani
(avec désespoir).

Mon automate!

Tous.

Un automate!
Ha, ha, ha, ha!

ACTE TROISIÈME

(A Venise. Galerie de fête dans un palais donnant sur le grand canal. Les hôtes de GIULIETTA sont groupés sur des coussins.)

BARCAROLE.

Giulietta et Nicklausse
(dans la coulisse).

Belle nuit, ô nuit d'amour,
Souris à nos ivresses,
Nuit plus douce que le jour,
O belle nuit d'amour!
Le temps fuit et sans retour
Emporte nos tendresses!

Only memory's torch will burn	Loin de cet heureux séjour,
For hours that ne'er return.	Le temps fuit sans retour.
Zephyrs passion-stirred,	Zéphyrs embrasés
Waft to us loving greeting,	Versez-nous vos caresses;
Zephyrs passion-stirred,	Zéphyrs embrasés
Heed our tenderest word.	Donnez-nous vos baisers.
Night divine, O night of love,	Belle nuit, ô nuit d'amour,
O smile on our caresses;	Souris à nos ivresses,
Moon and stars keep watch above	Nuit plus douce que le jour,
This radiant night of love.	O belle nuit d'amour.

        (GIULIETTA and NICKLAUSSE enter.)   (GIULIETTA et NICKLAUSSE entrent en scène.)

Hoffmann.   *Hoffmann.*

'Tis not that, by Heaven, which enchants me!	Et moi, ce n'est pas là, pardieu, ce qui m' en chante!
At the feet of the beauty who gives us joy	Aux pieds de la beauté qui nous vient enivrer
Shall pleasure sigh?	Le plaisir doit-il soupirer?
No, with laughing mouth hear how she sings!	Non! Le rire à la bouche, écoutez comme il chante!

BACCHIC SONG.   CHANT BACCHIQUE

Friends, love which dreams in song	Amis! l'amour tendre et rêveur,
Is wrong!	Erreur!
Love in noise and wine,	L'amour dans le bruit et le vin!
Divine!	Divin!
Let burning desire	Que d'un brulant désir
Your heart enflame,	Votre coeur s'enflamme,
In the fevers of pleasure	Aux fièvres du plaisir
Consume your soul!	Consumez votre âme!
The transport of love	Transports d'amour,
Lasts but a day!	Durez un jour!
To the devil with him who weeps	Au diable celui qui pleure
For two soft eyes!	Pour deux beaux yeux!
For us the greater bliss	A nous l'ivresse meilleure
Of songs of joy!	Des chants joyeux!
Let's live an hour	Vivons une heure
In heaven.	Dans les cieux!

The Chorus.   *Le Choeur.*

To the devil with him who weeps	Au diable celui qui pleure
For two soft eyes!	Pour deux beaux yeux!
For us the greater bliss	A nous l'ivresse meilleure
Of songs of joy!	Des chants joyeux!
We'll live an hour.	Vivons une heure
In heaven.	Dans les cieux!

Hoffmann.

The sky its radiance lends
  To beauty.
But hidden in iron hearts
  Lies hell!
Bliss of paradise
Where lovers meet,
Oaths, cursed hopes,
  Dreams of life!
    Oh, chastity,
    Oh, purity,
      Lies!

The Chorus.

To the devil with him who weeps,
  etc., etc.

Schlemil
        (entering).
I see all is joy. Congratulations, madame.

Giulietta.

What! Why, I've wept for you three whole
  days!

Pitichinaccio.

Indeed!

Schlemil
       (to Pitichinaccio)
Scoundrel!

Pitchinaccio.

Hola!

Giulietta.

Calm yourselves!
We have a stranger poet among us.
      (Presenting.)
    Hoffmann!

Schlemil
      (witn bad grace,.
Monsieur!

Hoffmann
      (ironically.
Monsieur!

Hoffmann.

Le ciel te prête sa clarté,
  Beauté.
Mais vous cachez, ô coeurs de fer,
  L'enfer!
Bonheur du paradis
Où l'amour convie,
Serments, espoirs maudits,
  Rêves de la vie!
    O chastetés,
    O puretés,
      Mentez!

Le Choeur.

Au diable celui qui pleure, etc., etc.

Schlemil
        (entrant en scène).
Je vois qu'on est en fête. A merveille, madame

Giulietta.

Comment! Mais je vous ai pleuré trois grands
  jours.

Pitichinaccio.

Dame!

Schlemil
      (à Pitichinaccio).
Avorton!

Pitichinaccio.

Hola!

Giulietta.

Calmez-vous!
Nous avons un poète étranger parmi nous
      (Présentant Hoffmann.)
    Hoffmann!

Schlemil
      (de mauvaise grâce)
Monsieur!

Hoffmann.
      (ironique)
Monsieur!

Giulietta
(to SCHLEMIL).

Smile on us with grace,
And come take your place
At pharaoh!

The Chorus.

Bravo! To pharaoh!

(GIULIETTA, after having invited all to follow her, goes toward door
HOFFMANN offers his hand to GIULIETTA. SCHLEMIL comes between.)

Schlemil
(taking GIULIETTA's hand).

By heavens!

Giulietta.

To the game, gentlemen, to the game!

The Chorus.

To the game, the game!
(All go out except HOFFMANN and NICKLAUSSE.)

Nicklausse.

One word! I have two horses saddled. At
the first dream
That Hoffmann permits himself, I carry him
off.

Hoffmann.

And what dream could ever be born
Of such realities?
Does one love a courtezan?

Nicklausse.

Yet this Schlemil...

Hoffmann.

I am not Schlemil.

Nicklausse.

Take care, the devil is clever.
(DAPERTUTTO appears at back).

Hoffmann.

Were it so,
If he makes me love her, may he damn me,
Come!

Nicklausse.

Let us go.
(They go out.)

Giulietta
(à SCHLEMIL).

Souriez nous, de grâce,
Et venez prendre place
Au pharaon!

Le Choeur.

Vivat! au pharaon!

(GIULIETTA, après avoir invité tout le monde à la suivre, se dirige
vers la porte. HOFFMANN offre sa main à GIULIETTA. SCHLEMIL
intervient vivement.)

Schlemil
(prenant la main de GIULIETTA).

Morbleu!

Giulietta.

Au jeu, messieurs, au jeu.

Le Choeur.

Au jeu, au jeu.
(Tout le monde sort moins NICKLAUSSE et HOFFMANN.)

Nicklausse.

Un mot! J'ai deux chevaux sellés; au premier
rêve
Dont se laisse affoler mon Hoffmann, je
l'enlève.

Hoffmann.

Et quels rêves, jamais, pourraient être en-
fantés
Par de telles réalités?
Aime-t-on une courtisane?

Nicklausse.

Ce Schlemil, cependant...

Hoffmann.

Je ne suis pas Schlemil.

Nicklausse.

Prends y garde, le diable est malin.
(DAPERTUTTO parait au fond.)

Hoffmann.

Le fût-il,
S'il me la fait aimer, je consens qu'il me damne
Allons!

Nicklausse.

Allons!
(Ils sortent.)

Dapertutto
        (alone).

Well, then!... to fight you
The eyes of Giulietta are a sure weapon,
Schlemil has succumbed to them!
By my faith, as captain and soldier!
You'll do likewise.
I command that Giulietta shall use her arts on
    you to-day.

(Drawing from his finger a ring with a big sparkling diamond.)

Turn, turn, mirror, where the lark is caught,
Sparkle, diamond, fascinate, attract her,
The lark or the woman
To this conquering bait
Flies on rapid wing;
One loses her life, the other her soul.
Turn, turn, mirror, where the lark is caught.
Sparkle, diamond, fascinate, attract her.

(GIULIETTA appears and advances, fascinated, toward the diamond
that DAPERTUTTO holds towards her.)

Dapertutto
        (placing the ring on GIULIETTA's finger).
Dear angel!

Giulietta.

What do you desire of your servant?

Dapertutto.

Good, you divine my wishes.
At seducing hearts skilled above all others,
You have given me
The shade of Schlemil! I vary
My pleasures, and I beg you
To get for me to-day
The image of Hoffmann!

Giulietta.

What! his image!

Dapertutto.

Yes.
His image!... You doubt
The power of your eyes?

Giulietta.

No.

Dapertutto
        (seul).

Allez... pour te livrer combat
Les yeux de Giulietta sont une arme certaine
Il a fallu que Schlemil succombat!
Foi de diable et de capitaine!
Tu feras comme lui.
Je veux que Giulietta t'ensorcelle aujourd'hui.

(Tirant de son doigt une bague où brille un gros diamant.)

Tourne, tourne, miroir où se prend l'alouette,
Scintille, diamant, fascine, attire-la...
L'alouette ou la femme
A cet appât vainqueur
Vont de l'aile ou du coeur;
L'une y laisse sa vie l'autre y perd son âme.
Tourne, tourne, miroir ou se prend l'alouette.
Scintille, diamant, fascine, attire-la.

(GIULIETTA paraît et s'avance, fascinée, vers le diamant que DAPER
TUTTO tend vers elle.)

Dapertutto
        (passant la bague au doigt de GIULIETTA).
Cher ange!

Giulietta.

Qu'attendez-vous de votre servante?

Dapertutto.

Bien, tu m'as deviné,
A séduire les coeurs entre toutes savante
Tu m'as déjà donné
L'ombre de Schlemil!   Je varie
Mes plaisirs et te prie
De m'avoir aujourd'hui
Le reflet d'Hoffmann!

Giulietta.

Quoi! son reflet!

Dapertutto.

Oui!
Son reflet... tu doutes
De la puissance de tes yeux?

Giulietta.

Non.

Dapertutto.

Who knows?　Your Hoffmann dreams, per-
haps, otherwise.
(Severely.)
Yes, I was there, a while back, listening.
(With irony.)
He defies you...

Giulietta.

Hoffman?... 'tis well!... From this day
He shall be my toy.
(HOFFMANN enters.)

Dapertutto.

'Tis he!
(DAPERTUTTO goes out. HOFFMANN intends to do the same.)

Giulietta
(to HOFFMANN).
You leave me?

Hoffmann
(mockingly).
I have lost everything.

Giulietta.

What?... you too!...
Ah, you do me wrong.
Without pity, without mercy,
Go!... Go!...

Hoffmann.

Your tears betrayed you.
Ah! I love you... were it at the price of my
life!

Giulietta.

Ah, unfortunate, but do you not know
That an hour, a moment, may prove fatal?
That my love will cost your life if you remain?
That Schlemil, this night, may strike you in
my arms?
Do not deny my prayer;
My life is wholly yours.
Everywhere I promise to accompany your steps.

Hoffmann.

Ye gods! with what bliss do you fire my heart?
Like heavenly music your voice stirs me;

Dapertutto.

Qui sait?　Ton Hoffmann rêve peut-être
mieux.
(Avec dureté.)
Oui, j'étais là, tout à l'heure, aux écoutes,
Il te défie...

Giulietta.

Hoffmann?... c'est bien!... dès aujourd'hui.
J'en ferai mon jouet.
(HOFFMANN entre.)

Dapertutto.

C'est lui!
(DAPERTUTTO sort. HOFFMANN fait mine de s'éloigner.)

Giulietta
(à HOFFMANN).
Vous me quittez?

Hoffmann
(railleur).
J'ai tout perdu.

Giulietta.

Quoi... vous aussi!...
Ah! vous me faites injure
Sans pitié, ni merci.
Partez... partez!...

Hoffmann.

Tes larmes t'ont trahie.
Ah, je t'aime!... fût-ce au prix de ma vie.

Giulietta.

Ah! malheureux, mais tu ne sais donc pas
Qu'une heure, qu'un moment, peuvent t'être
funestes?
Que mon amour te perd à jamais si tu restes?
Que Schlemil peut ce soir te frapper dans mes
bras?
Ne repousse pas ma prière!
Ma vie est à toi toute entière.
Partout je te promets d'accompagner tes pas.

Hoffmann.

O Dieu! de quelle ivresse embrases-tu mon
âme?
Comme un concert divin ta voix me pénètre.

With a fire soft, yet burning, my being is con-
sumed;
Your glances in mine have spent their flame
Like radiant stars,
And I feel, O best beloved,
The perfume of your breath
Pass o'er my lips and eyes.

Giulietta.

Yet, to-day, strengthen my courage
By leaving me something of you!

Hoffmann.

What do you mean?

Giulietta.

Listen, and don't laugh at me.
(She holds HOFFMANN in her arms and takes a mirror.)
What I want is your faithful image
Which reproduces your features, your look,
your visage,
The reflection that you see above me bend.

Hoffmann.

What! My reflection? What folly!

Giulietta.

No! for it can detach itself
From the polished glass,
To come and hide complete in my heart.

Hoffmann.

In your heart?

Giulietta.

In my heart. 'Tis I who beg thee,
Hoffmann, grant me my wish.

Hoffmann.

My reflection?

Giulietta.

Your reflection. Yes, wisdom or folly,
I wish it, I demand it.

Hoffmann.

Ecstasy! bliss ineffable,
O terror, strangely sweet!
My image, yes, my soul, my life
Belong always to you.

D'un feu doux et brûlant mon être est dévoré;
Tes regards dans les miens ont épanché leur
flamme
Comme des astres radieux,
Et je sens, ô mon bien aimée,
Passer ton haleine embaumée
Sur mes lèvres et sur mes yeux.

Giulietta.

Aujourd'hui, cependant, affermis mon courage
En me laissant quelque chose de toi!

Hoffmann.

Que veux-tu dire?

Giulietta.

Ecoute, et ne ris pas de moi.
(Elle enlace HOFFMANN et prend un miroir.)
Ce que je veux, c'est ta fidèle image
Qui reproduit tes traits, ton regard, ton visage,
Le reflet que tu vois sur le mien se pencher.

Hoffmann.

Quoi! mon reflet? quelle folie!

Giulietta.

Non! car il peut se détacher
De la glace polie
Pour venir tout entier dans mon coeur se cacher.

Hoffmann.

Dans ton coeur?

Giulietta.

Dans mon coeur. C'est moi qui t'en supplie,
Hoffmann, comble mes voeux!

Hoffmann.

Mon reflet?

Giulietta.

Ton reflet. Oui, sagesse ou folie,
Je l'attends, je le veux!

Hoffmann.

Extase! ivresse inassouvie,
Etrange et doux effroi!
Mon reflet, mon âme et ma vie
A toi, toujours à toi!

Giuretta.

If your sweet presence I should lose,
I still would keep of you
The image of your life and soul;
Dear one, give them to me.

(suddenly).

Schlemil!

(SCHLEMIL enters followed by NICKLAUSSE, DAPERTUTTO, PITTI-CHINACCIO and others.)

Schlemil.

I was sure of it! Together!
Come, gentlemen, come,
'Tis for Hoffmann, so it seems,
That we are abandoned.

(Ironic laughter.)

Hoffmann.

(almost spoken)

Monsieur!

Giulietta

(to HOFFMANN).

Silence!

(Aside.)

I love you, he has my key.

Pitichinaccio

(to SCHLEMIL).

Let us kill him.

Schlemil.

Patience!

Dapertutto

(to HOFFMANN).

How pale you are!

Hoffmann.

Me!

Dapertutto

(showing him a mirror)

See then!

Hoffmann

(amazed).

Heavens

Giulietta.

Si ta présence m'est ravie,
Je veux garder de toi
Ton reflet, ton âme et ta **vie**
Ami, donne-les-moi!

(vivement).

Schlemil!

(SCHLEMIL entre suivi de NICKLAUSSE, DAPERTUTTO, PITTICHI-NACCIO et autres.)

Schlemil.

J'en etais sûr! Ensemble!
Venez, messieurs, venez,
C'est pour Hoffmann à ce qu'il **semble**,
Que nous sommes abandonnés.

(Rires ironiques.)

Hoffmann

(presque parlé).

Monsieur!

Giulietta

(à HOFFMANN).

Silence!

(Bas.)

Je t'aime, il a ma clef.

Pittichinaccio

(à SCHLEMIL).

Tuons-le.

Schlemil.

Patience!

Dapertutto

(à HOFFMANN).

Comme vous êtes pâle!

Hoffmann.

Moi!

Dapertutto

(lui présentant le miroir).

Voyez plutôt!

Hoffmann

(stupéfait, se regardant)

Ciel!

Giulietta.

Listen, gentlemen,
Here come the gondolas,
The hour of barcaroles
And of farewells!

(Schlemil conducts the guests away. Giulietta goes out throwing a look at Hoffmann. Dapertutto remains. Nicklausse goes toward Hoffmann.)

Nicklausse.

Are you coming?

Hoffmann.

Not yet.

Nicklausse.

Why? Very well. I understand. Good-by.
(Aside.)
But I'll watch over him.
(He goes out.)

Schlemil.

What do you wait for?

Hoffmann.

To get from you a certain key I've sworn to have.

Schlemil.

You shall have this key, sir, only with my life.

Hoffmann.

Then I shall have both the one and the other.

Schlemil.

That remains to be seen. On guard!

Dapertutto.

You have no sword.
(Presenting his own.)
Take mine!

Hoffmann.

Thank you.

Chorus.
(in the wings).
Night divine, O night of love,
O smile on our caresses;
Moon and stars keep watch above
This radiant night of love.

(Hoffmann and Schlemil fight. Schlemil falls mortally wounded. Hoffmann bends and takes the key from around his neck. He rushes to Giulietta's room. Giulietta appears in a gondola.)

Giulietta.

Ecoutez, messieurs,
Voici les gondoles,
L'heure des barcarolles
Et celle des adieux!

(Schlemil reconduit les invités. Giulietta sort, jetant un regard à Hoffmann. Dapertutto reste au fond de la scène. Nicklausse revient à Hoffmann.)

Nicklausse.

Viens-tu?

Hoffmann.

Pas encore.

Nicklausse.

Pourquoi? Bien, je comprends. Adieu!
(A part.)
Mais je veille sur toi.
(Il sort.)

Schlemil.

Qu'attendez-vous, monsieur?

Hoffmann.

Que vous me donniez certaine clef que j'ai juré d'avoir.

Schlemil.

Vous n'aurez cette clef, monsieur, qu'avec ma vie.

Hoffmann.

J'aurai donc l'une ou l'autre.

Schlemil.

C'est ce qu'il faut voir! En garde!

Dapertutto.

Vous n'avez pas d'épée.
(Lui présentant la sienne.)
Prenez la mienne!

Hoffmann.

Merci!

Choeur
(dans la coulisse).
Belle nuit, ô nuit d'amour!
Souris à nos ivresses,
Nuit plus douce que le jour,
O belle nuit d'amour!

(Hoffmann et Schlemil se battent. Schlemil est blessé à mort et tombe. Hoffmann se penche et lui prend la clef pendue à son cou et s'élance dans l'appartement de Giulietta, qui paraît dans une gondole.)

Hoffmann

(coming back).

No one!

Giulietta

(laughing).

Ha, ha, ha!

(HOFFMANN looks at GIULIETTA astounded.)

Dapertutto

(to GIULIETTA).

What will you do with him now?

Giulietta.

I'll resign him to you.

Pitichinaccio

(entering the gondola).

Dear angel!

(GIULIETTA takes him in her arms.)

Hoffmann

(comprehending the infamy of GIULIETTA).

Vile wretch!

Nicklausse.

Hoffmann! Hoffmann! the police!

(NICKLAUSSE drags HOFFMANN away. GIULIETTA and PITICHI-NACCIO laugh.)

ACT IV

(At CRESPEL's house in Munich. A room furnished in a bizarre fashion.)

Antonia

(alone. She is seated at the clavichord).

Thy dove has fled,

She has fled far from thee!

(She stops and rises.)

Ah! memory too sweet, vision too cruel!

Alas! at my feet I hear, I see him!

Thy dove has fled,

She has fled far from thee;

But she is ever faithful,

And she keeps her troth.

Beloved, my voice calls thee,

All my heart is thine.

(She approaches the clavichord again.)

Dear flower, scarcely open,

In pity answer me:

Hoffmann.

Personne!

Giulietta

(riant).

Ha, ha, ha!

(HOFFMANN regarde GIULIETTA avec stupeur.)

Dapertutto

(à GIULIETTA).

Qu'en fais-tu maintenant?

Giulietta.

Je te l'abandonne!

Pitichinaccio

(entre dans la gondole).

Cher ange!

(GIULIETTA le prend dans ses bras.)

Hoffmann

(comprenant l'infamie de GIULIETTA).

Misérable!

Nicklausse.

Hoffmann! Hoffmann! les sbires!

(NICKLAUSSE entraine HOFFMANN. GIULIETTA et DAPERTUTTO rient.)

ACTE QUATRIÈME

(A Munich chez Crespel. Une chambre bizarrement meublée.)

Antonia

(seule. Elle est assise devant le clavecin et chante).

Elle a fui, la tourterelle,

Elle a fui loin de toi!

(Elle s'arrête et se lève.)

Ah! souvenir trop doux! image trop cruelle!

Hélas! à mes genoux, je l'entends, je le vois.

Elle a fui, la tourterelle,

Elle a fui loin de toi!

Mais elle est toujours fidèle

Et te garde sa foi.

Bien-aimé, ma voix t'appelle,

Tout mon coeur est à toi.

(Elle se rapproche du clavecin.)

Chère fleur qui vient d'éclore,

Par pitié, réponds-moi.

Thou knowest if still he loves me,
If he keeps his troth!...
Beloved, my voice implores thee.
O may thy heart come to me!
(She sinks into a chair.)

Crespel
(entering suddenly).

Unhappy child, beloved daughter,
You promised me to sing no more.

Antonia.

In me my mother lived again;
My heart, while singing, fancied it heard her.

Crespel.

There lies my torment. Thy dear mother
Left to thee her voice. Vain regrets!
Through thee I hear her. No, no, I beg...

Antonia
(sadly).

Your Antonia will sing no more!
(She goes out slowly.)

Crespel
(alone).

Despair! Again I saw
Those spots of fire
Mark her face. God!
Must I lose her I adore?
Ah, that Hoffmann... 'tis he
Who put this madness into her heart. I fled
As far as Munich...

(Enter FRANTZ.)

Crespel.

You, Frantz, open to nobody.

Frantz
(false exit).

You think so...

Crespel.

Where are you going?

Frantz.

I'm going to see if anybody rang
As you just said.

Toi, qui sais s'il m'aime encore,
S'il me garde sa foi...
Bien-aimé, ma voix t'implore,
Que ton coeur vienne à moi!
(Elle se laisse tomber sur une chaise.)

Crespel
(entrant brusquement).

Malheureuse enfant, fille bien-aimée
Tu m'avais promis de ne plus chanter.

Antonia.

Ma mère s'était en moi ranimée;
Mon coeur en chantant croyait l'écouter.

Crespel.

C'est là mon tourment. Ta mère chérie
T'a légué sa voix, regrets superflus!
Par toi je l'entends. Non... non... je t en prie

Antonia
(tristement).

Votre Antonia ne chantera plus!
(Elle sort lentement.)

Crespel
(seul).

Désespoir! Tout à l'heure encore
Je voyais ces taches de feu
Colorer son visage. Dieu!
Perdrai-je l'enfant que j'adore?
Ah, c'est Hoffmann, c'est lui
Qui jeta dans son coeur ces ivresses...
J'ai fui
Jusqu'à Munich...
(Entre FRANTZ.)

Crespel

Toi, Frantz, n'ouvre à personne.

Frantz
(fausse sortie).

Vous croyez...

Crespel.

Où vas-tu?

Frantz.

Je vais voir si l'on sonne
Comme vous avez dit...

Crespel.

I said, Open to nobody.

(Shouting.)

To nobody! Do you hear this time?

Frantz.

By Heaven, I'm not deaf!

Crespel.

Very well! May the devil seize you!

Frantz.

Yes, sir, the key is in the door.

Crespel.

Idiot! donkey!

Frantz

'Tis agreed.

Crespel.

Morbleu!

(He exits quickly.)

Frantz

(alone).

Well! What! always in a rage!
Strange, peevish, exacting!
'Tis a hard job
For his money to please him!...
Day and night I'm on all fours,
At the least sign I must be silent;
It is just as if I sang!
But no, if I sang,
His contempt he'd have to modify
I sing alone sometimes,
But singing isn't easy
Tra la la, tra la la!
Still it isn't voice that I lack, I think.
Tra la la, tra la la,
No, 'tis the method.
Well! one can't have all things.
I sing execrably;
But my dancing is delightful,
I may say so without flattery.
Ah! I shine in the dance.
'Tis my greatest attraction.

Crespel.

J'ai dit. n'ouvre à personne!

(Criant.)

A personne! entends-tu, cette fois?

Frantz.

Eh, mon Dieu, je ne suis pas sourd!

Crespel.

Bien! que le diable t'emporte!...

Frantz.

Oui, monsieur, la clef est sur la porte

Crespel.

Bélître! Ane bâté!

Frantz.

C'est convenu.

Crespel.

Morbleu!

(Il sort. FRANTZ descend.)

Frantz

(seul).

Eh bien! Quoi, toujours en colère!
Bizarre, quinteux, exigeant!
Ah, l'on a du mal à lui plaire
Pour son argent...
Jour et nuit je me mets en quatre,
Au moindre signe je me tais,
C'est tout comme si je chantais!...
Encore non, si je chantais,
De ses mépris il lui faudrait rabattre.
Je chante seul quelque fois;
Mais chanter n'est pas commode!
Tra la la! tra la la!
Ce n'est pourtant pas la voix,
Qui me fait défaut, je crois...
Tra la la! Tra la la!
Non, c'est la méthode.
Dame! on n'a pas tout en partage.
Je chante pitoyablement;
Mais je danse agréablement,
Je me le dis sans compliment,
Corbleu! la danse est à mon avantage
C'est là mon plus grand attrait,

But dancing isn't easy.
Tra la la, tra la la.
> (He dances and stops.)

With women my well-turned leg
Would do me no harm,
Tra la la, tra la la.
> (He falls.)

No, 'tis the method.
> (HOFFMANN enters, followed by NICKLAUSSE.)

Hoffmann.

Frantz!   They are here!
> (Touches FRANTZ on shoulder.)

Up, my friend.

Frantz.

Hey, who's there?
> (Rises, surprised.)

Monsieur Hoffmann!

Hoffmann.

Myself.   Now, about Antonia?...

Frantz.

He's gone out, sir.

Hoffmann
> (laughing).

Ha, ha, deafer yet than last year?

Frantz.

Sir, you honor me.
I am very well, thank Heaven.

Hoffmann.

Antonia!   Go, I must see her.

Frantz.

Very well! what a joy
For monsieur Crespel!
> (He goes out.)

Hoffmann
> (sitting before the clavichord).

'Tis a song of love
That flies away,
Now sad, now gay,
Turn by turn...

Antonia
> (entering suddenly).

Hoffmann!

Et danser n'est pas commode.
Tra la la!   Tra la la!
> (Il danse. Il s'arrête.)

Près des femmes le jarret
N'est pas ce qui me nuirait,
Tra la la!   Tra la la!
> (Il tombe.)

Non! c'est la méthode.
> (HOFFMANN entre, suivi de NICKLAUSSE.)

Hoffmann.

Frantz!   C'est ici...
> (Touchant l'épaule de FRANTZ.)

Debout, l'ami.

Frantz.

Hein! qui va la?
> (Il se relève.)

Monsieur Hoffmann!

Hoffmann.

Moi-même!   Eh bien, Antonia?

Frantz.

Il est sorti, monsieur.

Hoffmann
> (riant).

Ha, ha, plus sourd encore que l'an passé?

Frantz.

Monsieur m'honore.   Je me porte bien, grâce
au ciel.

Hoffmann.

Antonia!   Va, fais que je la voie!

Frantz.

Très bien...Quel joie
Pour monsieur Crespel!
> (Il sort.)

Hoffmann
> (s'asseyant devant le clavecin).

C'est une chanson d'amour
Qui s'envole,
Triste ou folle
Tour à tour!...

Antonia
> (entrant précipitamment)

Hoffmann!

Hoffmann
(receiving her in his arms).

Antonia!

Nicklausse
(aside)

I am one too many; good evening.
(He exits.)

Antonia.

Ah, I knew well that you loved me yet!

Hoffmann.

My heart told me that you grieved for me!
But why were we separated?

Antonia.

I know not.

Hoffmann.

Ah! happiness dwells in my soul!
To-morrow you shall be my wife.
　　Happy pair,
The future is ours!
To love let us be faithful,
That her eternal chains
May keep our hearts
Conquerors even against time!

Antonia.

Ah! happiness dwells in my heart!
To-morrow I shall be your wife.
　　Happy pair,
The future is ours!
Each day will bring new songs;
Your genius spreads its wings!
My victorious song
Is the echo of your heart.

Hoffmann
(smiling).

Yet, my affianced bride,
Shall I tell the thought
Which, spite of myself, troubles me?
Music inspires a little jealousy in me,
For you love it too much!

Hoffmann
(recevant ANTONIA dans ses bras).

Antonia!

Nicklausse
(à part).

Je suis de trop; bonsoir.
(Il sort.)

Antonia.

Ah! Je savais bien que tu m'aimais encore!

Hoffmann.

Mon coeur m'avait bien dit que j'étais regretté
Mais pourquoi nous a-t-on séparés?

Antonia.

Je l'ignore.

Hoffmann.

Ah! j'ai le bonheur dans l'âme!
Demain tu seras ma femme.
Heureux époux,
L'avenir est à nous!
A l'amour soyons fidèles!
Que ses chaînes éternelles
Gardent nos coeurs,
Du temps même vainqueurs!

Antonia.

Ah! j'ai le bonheur dans l'âme!
Demain je serai ta femme.
Heureux époux,
L'avenir est à nous!
Chaque jour, chansons nouvelles!
Ton génie ouvre ses ailes!
Mon chant vainqueur
Est l'écho de ton coeur!

Hoffmann
(souriant).

Pourtant, ô ma fiancée,
Te dirai-je une pensée
Qui me trouble malgré moi?
La musique m'inspire un peu de jalousie,
Tu l'aimes trop!

Antonia
(smiling)

What a singular fancy!
Did I love you for it, or it for you?
For surely you will not forbid me
To sing, as did my father?

Hoffmann.

What say you?

Antonia.

Yes, at present my father imposes upon me
The virtue of silence.
(Rapidly.)
Would you like to hear me?

Hoffmann
(aside).

'Tis strange... can it be?...

Antonia
(drawing him to the clavichord).

But come, as in olden time;
Listen, and you'll see if I've lost my voice.

Hoffmann.

How your eye lights up, your hand trembles

Antonia
(making him sit down).

Here, the soft song of love we sang together.
(She sings.)
'Tis a song of love
That flies away,
Now sad, now gay,
Turn by turn;
'Tis a song of love.
The opening rose
Smiles on the Spring.
Ah! how long may endure
Its little life?

Together.

'Tis a song of love
That flies away, etc., etc.

Antonia
(souriant).

Voyez l'étrange fantaisie!
T'aimé-je donc pour elle, ou l'aimé-je pour
toi?
Car toi tu ne vas pas sans doute me défendre
De chanter, comme a fait mon père?

Hoffmann.

Que dis-tu?

Antonia.

Oui, mon père, à présent, m'impose la vertu
Du silence.
(Vivement.)
Veux-tu m'entendre?

Hoffmann
(à part).

C'est étrange!...Est-ce donc...

Antonia
(l'entrainant vers le clavecin).

Viens là, comme autrefois.
Ecoute, et tu verras si j'ai perdu ma voix.

Hoffmann.

Comme ton œil s'anime et comme ta main
tremble!

Antonia
(le faisant s'asseoir devant le clavecin)

Tiens, ce doux chant d'amour que nous
chantions ensemble.
(Elle chante.)
C'est une chanson d'amour
Qui s'envole,
Triste ou folle,
Tour à tour;
C'est une chanson d'amour.
La rose nouvelle,
Sourit au printemps.
Las! combien de temps
Vivra-t-elle?

Ensemble.

C'est une chanson d'amour,
Qui s'envole,
Triste ou folle,
Tour à tour;
C'est une chanson d'amour.

Hoffmann.

Like a ray of flame
Flashes thy beauty.
Wilt thou see the summer,
O flower of the soul?

Together.

'Tis a song of love, etc., etc.

(ANTONIA puts her hand to her heart and seems about to faint.)

Hoffmann.

What is the matter?

Antonia

(doing same again).

Nothing.

Hoffmann

(listening).

Chut!

Antonia.

Heavens, my father! Come, come!

(She goes out.)

Hoffmann.

No! I must know the solution of this mystery.

(He hides. CRESPEL appears.)

Crespel

(looking about him).

No, nothing. I thought Hoffmann was here.
May he go to the devil!

Hoffmann

(aside).

Many thanks!

Frantz

(entering)

Sir.

Crespel.

What?

Frantz.

Doctor Miracle.

Crespel.

Scoundrel! knave!
Quickly close the door.

Frantz.

Yes, sir, the doctor...

Hoffmann.

Un rayon de flamme
Pare ta beauté,
Verras tu l'été,
Fleur de l'âme?

Ensemble.

C'est une chanson d'amour, etc.

(ANTONIA porte sa main à son coeur et semble prête à défaillir.

Hoffmann.

Qu'as-tu donc?

Antonia.

Rien.

(Mettant la main à son coeur.)

Hoffmann

(écoutant).

Chut!

Antonia.

Ciel! mon père!
Viens! Viens!

(Elle sort.)

Hoffmann.

Non, je saurai le mot de ce mystère.

(Il se cache. CRESPEL paraît.)

Crespel

(regardant autour de lui).

Non, rien. J'ai cru qu'Hoffmann était ici
Puisse-t-il être au diable!

Hoffmann

(à part).

Grand merci!

Frantz

(entrant, à CRESPEL).

Monsieur!

Crespel.

Quoi?

Frantz.

Le docteur Miracle.

Crespel.

Drôle! infâme! ferme vite la porte.

Frantz.

Oui, monsieur, médicin...

Crespel.

He a doctor? No, on my soul,
A gravedigger, an assassin!
Who would kill my daughter after my wife.
I hear the jingle of his golden vials.
Drive him away from me!

(MIRACLE suddenly appears. FRANTZ runs away.)

Miracle.

Ha, ha, ha, ha!

Crespel.

How now!

Miracle.

Well, here I am! Myself, you see.
This good monsieur Crespel, I like him,
But where is he?

Crespel (stopping him).

Morbleu!

Miracle.

Ha, ha, ha, ha!
I sought for your Antonia.
Well, this trouble she inherited
From her mother? Still progressing?
Dear girl, we'll cure her.
Take me to her.

Crespel.

To assassinate her? If you make one step
I'll throw you out of the window.

Miracle.

There now, softly, I do not wish to displease
you.

(He advances a chair.)

Crespel.

What are you doing, traitor?

Miracle.

To cope with the danger,
One must know it.
Let me question her.

Crespel and *Hoffmann.*

Terror penetrates me.

Crespel.

Lui, médecin? Non, sur mon âme,
Un fossoyeur, un assassin!
Qui me tuerait ma fille après ma femme,
J'entends le cliquetis de ses flacons dans l'air
Loin de moi qu'on le chasse.

(MIRACLE paraît subitement. FRANTZ se sauve)

Miracle.

Ha, ha, ha, ha!

Crespel.

Enfin!

Miracle.

Eh bien, me voilà, c'est moi-même.
Ce bon monsieur Crespel, je l'aime!
Où donc est-il?

Crespel (l'arrêtant).

Morbleu!

Miracle.

Ha, ha, ha, ha!
Je cherchais votre Antonia!
Eh bien! ce mal qu'elle hérita
De sa mère? Toujours en progrès? chère
belle,
Nous la guérirons. Menez-moi près d'elle

Crespel.

Pour l'assassiner? Si tu fais un pas,
Je te jette par la fenêtre.

Miracle.

Eh! là! tout doux! Je ne veux pas
Vous déplaire.

(Il avance un tauteuil.)

Crespel.

Que fais-tu, traître?

Miracle.

Pour conjurer le danger,
Il faut le connaître.
Laissez-moi l'interroger

Crespel et Hoffmann.

L'effroi me pénètre.

Miracle
   (his hand extended toward ANTONIA's room).

To my conquering power,
Give way with good grace.
Near me without terror
Come take your place,
    Come.

Crespel and *Hoffmann.*

With fright and with horror
My being is chilled;
A strange terror
Chains me to this place,
    Afraid.

Crespel
    (seating himself).

Come, speak and be brief.

(MIRACLE continues his magnetic passes. The door of ANTONIA's room opens slowly. MIRACLE indicates that he takes ANTONIA's hand and leads her to a chair.)

Miracle.

Please sit there.

Crespel.

I am seated.

Miracle
    (paying no attention).

How old are you, please?

Crespel.

Who, me?

Miracle.

I am speaking to your child.

Hoffmann
    (aside).

Antonia?

Miracle.

What age?
    (He listens).
    Twenty!

Crespel.

What?

Miracle.

The springtime of life.
    (He appears to feel the pulse.)
Let me see your hand!..

Miracle
   (la main tendue vers la chambre d'ANTONIA)

A mon pouvoir vainqueur
Cède de bonne grâce!...
Près de moi sans terreur,
Viens ici prendre place,
    Viens.

Crespel et *Hoffmann.*

D'épouvante et d'horreur
Tout mon être se glace,
Une étrange terreur
M'enchaîne à cette place.
    J'ai peur.

Crespel
    (s'asseyant).

Allons, parle et sois bref.

(MIRACLE continue ses passes magnétiques. La porte de la chambre d'ANTONIA s'ouvre lentement. MIRACLE indique qu'il prend la main d'ANTONIA invisible, et qu'il la fait asseoir.)

Miracle
    (s'asseyant).

Voulez-vous asseoir là?

Crespel.

Je suis assis.

Miracle
    (sans répondre)

Quel âge avez-vous, je vous prie?

Crespel.

Qui, moi?

Miracle.

Je parle à votre enfant.

Hoffmann
    (à part).

Antonia?

Miracle.

Quel âge?...
    (Il écoute.)
Vingt ans!

Crespel.

Hein?

Miracle.

Le printemps de la vie.
    (Il fait le geste de tâter le pouls.)
Voyons la main!..

Crespel.

> The hand?

Miracle

> (pulling out his watch).
>
> Chut! let me count.

Hoffmann

> (aside).
>
> God! am I the plaything of a dream? Is it a ghost?

Miracle.

> The pulse is unequal and fast, a bad symptom. Sing!

Crespel

> (rising).
>
> No, no, be quiet!... Don't have her sing.
> (The voice of ANTONIA is heard.)

Miracle.

> See, her face brightens, her eyes are on fire;
> She carries her hand to her beating heart.
> (He seems to follow ANTONIA with his gestures. The door of her room closes quickly.)

Crespel.

> What is he saying?

Miracle

> (rising).
>
> It would be a pity truly
> To leave to death so lovely a prey!

Crespel.

> Be quiet!

Miracle.

> If you would accept my aid,
> If you would save her days,
> I have there certain vials I hold in reserve.
> (He takes vials from pocket, which he makes sound like castanets.)

Crespel.

> Ah, be quiet.

Miracle.

> Of which you should...

Crespel.

> La main?

Miracle

> (tirant sa montre).
>
> Chut, laissez-moi compter.

Hoffmann

> (à part)
>
> Dieu! suis-je jouet d'un rêve? Est-ce un fantôme?

Miracle.

> Le pouls est inégal et vif, mauvais symptôme. Chantez!...

Crespel

> (se levant)
>
> Non, non, tais-toi!...ne la fais pas chanter
> (La voix d'ANTONIA se fait entendre.)

Miracle.

> Voyez, son front s'anime, et son regard flamboie;
> Elle porte la main à son coeur agité.
> (Il semble suivre ANTONIA du geste. La porte de la chambre se referme brusquement.)

Crespel.

> Que dit-il?

Miracle

> (se levant)
>
> Il serait dommage en vérité,
> De laisser à la mort une si belle proie!

Crespel.

> Tais-toi!

Miracle.

> Si vous voulez accepter mon secours,
> Si vous voulez sauver ses jours,
> J'ai là certains flacons que je tiens en réserve
> (Il tire plusieurs flacons de sa poche et les fait sonner comme des castagnettes.)

Crespel.

> Tais-toi!

Miracle.

> Dont il faudrait...

Crespel.

Be quiet! Heaven preserve me
From listening to your advice, miserable
   assassin!

Miracle.

Of which you should, each morning...
Ah yes! I hear you!
At once, on the instant!
With these vials, poor father,
You will be, I hope, satisfied.

Crespel.

Be off, be off, be off!
Out of this house, Satan!
Beware of the anger
And the sorrow of a father.
   Be off!

Hoffmann
        (aside).
From the death that awaits thee
I shall know, poor child,
How to tear thee away, I hope!
You vainly mock a father,
   Satan!

Miracle
    (continuing with same coolness).
Of which you should...

Crespel.

Be off!

Miracle.

Each morning...

Crespel.

Be off!
   (He pushes MIRACLE out and closes the door.)
Ah, he's outside and my door is closed
We are at last alone,
My beloved girl!

Miracle
    (walking through the wall).
Of which you should each morning...

Crespel.

Tais-toi!   Dieu me préserve
D'écouter tes conseils, misérable assassin!

Miracle.

Dont il faudrait chaque matin...
Eh! oui, je vous entends,
Tout à l'heure, à l'instant!
Des flacons, pauvre père,
Vous en serez, j'espère,
   Content!

Crespel.

Va-t-en, va-t-en, va-t-en!
Hors de chez moi, Satan!
Redoute la colère,
Et la douleur d'un père,
   Va-t-en!

Hoffmann
        (à part)
A la mort qui t'attend,
Je saurai, pauvre enfant,
T'arracher, je l'espère!
Tu ris en vain d'un père,
   Satan!

Miracle
    (avec le même flegme).
Dont il faudrait...

Crespel.

Va-t-en!

Miracle.

Chaque matin...

Crespel.

Va-t-en!
   (Il pousse MIRACLE dehors, et referme la porte sur lui.)
Ah! le voilà dehors et ma porte est fermée
Nous sommes seuls enfin,
Ma fille bien-aimée!

Miracle
    (rentrant par la muraille).
Dont il faudrait chaque matin...

Crespel.

Ah, wretch,
Come, come, may the waves engulf thee!
We'll see if the devil
Will get thee out!
Be off, be off, be off!
  etc., etc.

Hoffmann.

From the death that awaits thee,
  etc., etc.

Miracle.

Of which you should...

Crespel.

Away!

Miracle.

Each morning...

Crespel.

Away!
  (They disappear together.)

Hoffmann
  (coming down).

To sing no more! Alas! How obtain from her
Such a sacrifice?

Antonia
  (appearing).

Well? What said my father?

Hoffmann.

Ask me nothing;
Soon you shall know all.
Another road opens to us,
My Antonia!
To follow my steps dismiss from your mind
Those dreams of future success and glory
That your heart to mine confided.

Antonia.

But yourself?

Hoffmann.

Love calls to both of us
All that is not you is as nought in my life.

Crespel.

Ah! misérable,
Viens, viens!... les flots puissent-ils t'engloutir
Nous verrons si le diable
T'en fera sortir!...
Va-t-en, va-t-en, va-t-en!
Hors de, etc., etc.

Hoffmann.

A la mort qui t'attend,
Je saurai, etc., etc.

Miracle.

Dont il faudrait...

Crespel.

Va-t-en!...

Miracle.

Chaque matin...

Crespel.

Va-t-en!
  (Ils disparaissent ensemble.)

Hoffmann
  (seul).

Ne plus chanter! hélas! Comment obtenir
  d'elle
Un pareil sacrifice?

Antonia
  (paraît).

Eh bien, mon père, qu'a-t-il dit?

Hoffmann.

Ne me demande rien,
Plus tard tu sauras tout; une route nouvelle
S'ouvre à nous, mon Antonia!...
Pour y suivre mes pas, chasse de ta mémoire,
Ces rêves d'avenir, de succès et de gloire,
Que ton coeur au mien confia

Antonia.

Mais toi-même?

Hoffmann.

L'amour tous les deux nous convie,
Tout ce qui n'est pas toi n'est plus rien dans
  ma vie.

Antonia.

Very well! Here is my hand!

Hoffmann.

Ah, dear Antonia, can I ever repay
What you do for me?
                    (He kisses her hands.)
Your father will perhaps return.
I leave you... until to-morrow.

Antonia.

Until to-morrow.
                    (HOFFMANN goes out.)

            (opening one of the doors).
He has easily become the ally of my father!
But come, tears are vain;
I promised him.   I shall sing no more.
                    (She falls in a chair.)

Miracle
            (appearing suddenly behind her).
You will sing no more? Do you know what a
    sacrifice
He imposes on your youth, and have you
    measured it?
Grace, beauty, talent, sacred gift,
All these blessings that heaven has bestowed
    on you,
Must they be hid in the shadow of a household?
Have you not heard, in a proud dream,
Like unto a forest moved by the breeze,
The soft murmur of the besieging throng
Which speaks your name and follows you with
    its eyes?
That is the ardent joy and the eternal fête
Which in the flower of your years you are
    about to abandon
For the middle-class pleasures where they
    would enchain you,
And the squalling children who will rob you
    of your beauty!

Antonia
            (without turning round).
Ah, what is this voice that troubles my soul?
Is it Hell that speaks or Heaven that warns me?
No! happiness is not there, O voice accursed,

Antonia.

Tiens donc! voici ma main!

Hoffmann.

Ah, chère Antonia!   Pourrai-je reconnaître
Ce que tu fais pour moi?
                    (Il lui baise les mains.)
Ton père va peut-être
Revenir, je te quitte... à demain!

Antonia.

A demain!
                    (HOFFMANN sort.)

            (allant ouvrir une porte).
De mon père aisément il s'est fait le complice
Allons, les pleurs sont superflus,
Je l'ai promis, je ne chanterai plus.
                    (Elle se laisse tomber sur un fauteuil.)

Miracle
            (surgissant derrière elle).
Tu ne chanteras plus?   Sais-tu quel sacrifice
S'impose ta jeunesse et l'as-tu mesuré?
La grâce, la beauté, le talent, don sacré,
Tous ces biens que le ciel t'a livrés en partage,
Faut il les enfouir dans l'ombre d'un ménage?
N'as-tu pas entendu, dans un rêve orgueilleux,
Ainsi qu'une forêt par le vent balancée,
Ce doux frémissement de la foule pressée
Qui murmure ton nom et te suit des yeux?
Voilà l'ardente joie et la fête éternelle
Que tes vingt ans en fleur sont près d'aban-
    donner
Pour les plaisirs bourgeois où l'on veut
    t'enchaîner,
Et des marmots d'enfants qui te rendront
    moins belle!

Antonia
            (sans se retourner).
Ah, quelle est cette voix qui me trouble l'esprit?
Est-ce l'enfer qui parle ou Dieu qui m'avertit?
Non, non, ce n'est pas là le bonheur, voix
    maudite,

And against my pride my love has armed me;
Glory is not worth the happy quiet whither invites me
The home of my beloved.

Miracle.

What loves can now be yours?
Hoffmann sacrifices you to his brutality;
He only loves in you your beauty,
And for him, as for the others,
Soon will come the time of infidelity.

(He disappears.)

Antonia
(rising).

No, tempt me not! Away, thou demon!
I will no longer listen.
I have sworn to be his, my beloved awaits me,
I'm no longer my own, and may not take back my word;
And a few moments since, on his loving heart
What eternal love did he not pledge me?
Who will save me from the demon, from myself?
My mother, my mother, I love him!

(She falls weeping on the clavichord.)

Miracle
(reappears behind ANTONIA).

Your mother? Dare you invoke her?
Your mother? But is it not she
Who speaks by my voice, ingrate, and recalls to you
The splendor of the name that you would abdicate?

(The portrait lights up and becomes animated. It is the spirit of her mother.)

Listen!

The Voice.

Antonia!

Antonia.

Heavens!... my mother, my mother,

The Spirit.

Dear child, whom I call,
As I used to do,
'Tis your mother, 'tis she,
Listen to her voice.

Et contre mon orgueil, mon amour s'est armé,
La gloire ne vaut pas l'ombre heureuse où m'invite
La maison de mon bien-aimé.

Miracle.

Quels amours sont donc les vôtres?
Hoffmann te sacrifie à sa brutalité;
Il n'aime en toi que ta beauté,
Et pour lui, comme pour les autres,
Viendra bientôt le temps de l'infidélité.

(Il disparaît.)

Antonia
(se levant).

Non, ne me tente plus! Va-t-en,
Démon! Je ne veux plus t'entendre.
J'ai juré d'être à lui, mon bien-aimé m'attend,
Je ne m'appartiens plus et ne puis me reprendre;
Et tout à l'heure encor, sur son coeur adoré,
Quel éternel amour ne m'a-t-il pas juré...
Ah, qui me sauvera du démon, de moi-même?..
Ma mère! ma mère, je l'aime!...

Miracle
(reparaît).

Ta mère! oses-tu l'invoquer?...
Ta mère? Mais n'est-ce pas elle
Qui parle par ma voix, ingrate, et te rappelle
La splendeur de son nom que tu veux abdiquer?

(Le portrait s'éclaire et semble s'animer. C'est le fantôme de la mère.)

Ecoute!

La Voix.

Antonia!

Antonia.

Dieu! ma mère, ma mère!

Le Fantôme.

Cher enfant, que j'appelle
Comme autrefois,
C'est ta mère, c'est elle;
Entends sa voix!

Antonia.

Mother!

Miracle.

Yes, yes, 'tis her voice, do you hear?
The voice of your best counselor,
Who leaves you a talent the world has lost!

The Spirit.

Antonia!

Miracle.

Listen! She seems to live again,
And the distant public by its bravos fills her
with joy!

Antonia.

Mother!

The Spirit.

Antonia!

Miracle.

Join with her!...
(He seizes a violin and plays furiously.)

Antonia.

Yes, her soul calls to me
As in days gone by!
'Tis my mother, 'tis she!
I hear her voice.

The Spirit.

Dear child whom I call
As in days of yore,
'Tis your mother, 'tis she!
List to her voice.

Antonia.

No, enough...I cannot!

Miracle.

Again!

Antonia.

I will sing no more.

Miracle.

Again!

Antonia.

Ma mère!

Miracle.

Oui, c'est sa voix, l'entends-tu?
Sa voix, meilleure conseillère.
Qui te lègue un talent que le monde a perdu

Le Fantôme.

Antonia!

Miracle.

Ecoute! elle semble revivre,
Et le public lointain de ses bravos l'enivre!

Antonia (se levant)

Ma mère!

Le Fantôme.

Antonia!

Miracle.

Reprends donc avec elle!...
(Il saisit un violon et accompagne avec fureu

Antonia.

Qui, son âme m'appelle
Comme autrefois!
C'est ma mère, c'est elle,
J'entends sa voix!

Le Fantôme.

Cher enfant, que j'appelle
Comme autrefois!
C'est ta mère, c'est elle!
Entends sa voix!

Antonia.

Non! assez... je succombe!

Miracle.

Encore!

Antonia.

Je ne veux plus chanter.

Miracle.

Encore!

Antonia.

What strength compels and devours me?

Miracle.

Again! Why stop?

Antonia
    (breathless).
I give way to a transport that maddens.
What flame is it dazzles my eyes?...
But a single moment yet to live,
And my soul flies to Heaven.

The Spirit.

Dear child whom I call,
   etc., etc.

Antonia.

'Tis my mother, 'tis she,
   etc., etc.

Antonia.

Ah!
(She falls dying on the sofa. MIRACLE sinks in the earth uttering
a peal of laughter.)

Crespel
    (running in).
My child... my daughter... Antonia!

Antonia
    (expiring)
My father! Listen, 'tis my mother
Who calls me. And he... has returned...
'Tis a song of love
That flies away,
Now sad, now gay.
    (She dies.)

Crespel.

No!... a single word!... only one!... my child,
 speak!
Come, speak!... Inexorable death!
No! pity! Have mercy! Spare her!

Hoffmann
    (entering hurriedly)
Why these cries?

Crespel.

Hoffmann! ah, wretch!
'Tis you who killed her!...

Antonia

Qu'elle ardeur m'entraîne et me dévore!

Miracle.

Encore! Pourquoi t'arrêter?

Antonia
    (haletante).
Je cède au transport qui m'enivre!
Quelle flamme èblouit mes yeux!...
Un seul moment encore à vivre,
Et mon âme s'envole aux cieux!

Le Fantôme.

Cher enfant que j'appelle,
   etc.

Antonia.

C'est ma mère, c'est elle,
   etc.

Antonia.

Ah!
(Elle vient tomber mourante sur le canapé. Miracle s'engloutit
dans la terre, en poussant un éclat de rire. Le FANTÔME disparaît.)

Crespel
    (accourant).
Mon enfant!... ma fille!... Antonia!

Antonia
    (expirante).
Mon père!
Ecoutez, c'est ma mère,
Qui m'appelle! Et lui... de retour...
C'est une chanson d'amour...
Qui s'envole
Triste ou folle...
    (Elle meurt.)

Crespel.

Non! un seul mot! un seul! ma fille, parle-moi
Mais parle donc! Mort exécrable!
Non! pitié! grâce! Eloigne-toi!...

Hoffmann
    (entrant précipitamment)
Pourquoi ces cris?

Crespel.

Hoffmann! ah, misérable!
C'est toi qui l'as tuée!...

Hoffmann
            (rushing to ANTONIA).

  Antonia!

Crespel
            (beside himself).

Blood to color her cheek!   A weapon,
A knife...

  (He seizes a knife and attacks HOFFMANN.)

Nicklausse
            (entering and stopping CRESPEL).

Unhappy man!

Hoffmann
            (to NICKLAUSSE.)

Quick! give the alarm;
A doctor... a doctor!...

Miracle
            (appearing).

  Here!
            (He feels ANTONIA's pulse.)

  Dead!

Crespel
            (crazy).

Ah, God! my child, my daughter!

Hoffmann
            (despairingly).

  Antonia!

EPILOGUE
—

(Same scene as First Act.   The various personages are in the same positions they were in at the end of First Act.)

Hoffmann.

There is the history
Of my loves,
And the memory
Will never fade from my heart.

Chorus.

Bravo, bravo. Hoffmann.

Hoffmann
            (courant à ANTONIA)

  Antonia!...

Crespel
            (avec égarement)

Du sang
Pour colorer sa joue!...
Une arme, un couteau!

  (Il saisit un couteau et s'élance sur HOFFMANN)

Nicklausse
            (entrant et arrêtant CRESPEL).

Malheureux!

Hoffmann
            (à NICKLAUSSE).

Vite! donne l'alarme, un médecin, un médecin

Miracle
            (paraissant).

  Présent!
            (Il tâte le pouls d'ANTONIA).

  Morte!

Crespel
            (éperdu).

Ah! Dieu, mon enfant! ma fille!

Hoffmann
            (avec désespoir).

  Antonia!

EPILOGUE
—

(Même décoration qu'au premier acte.)
(On retrouve tous les personnages dans la situation où on les laissés à la fin du premier acte.)

Hoffmann.

Voilà quelle fut l'histoire
De mes amours,
Dont la mémoire
En mon coeur restera toujours.

Le Choeur.

Bravo. bravo. Hoffmann!

Hoffmann.

Ah, I am mad!... For us the crazy joy
Which dwells in alcohol, in beer and wine,
For us intoxication and frenzy,
And oblivion which drowns all.

Nicklausse.

Ah, I understand, three dramas in a drama.
Olympia?

Hoffmann.

Smashed!

Nicklausse.

Antonia?

Hoffmann.

Dead!

Nicklausse.

Giulietta?

Hoffmann.

Oh, for her, the last verse of the song of Klein-
Zach.
When he drank too much gin or rack,
You ought to have seen the two flaps of his
frock,
Like lilies in a lake.
The monster made a sound of flick, flack,
Flic, flac,
There's Klein-Zach.

Chorus.

Flic, flac,
There's Klein-Zach.

Chorus.

Light up the punch!... drunk we'll get;
And may the weakest
Roll under the table;
Luther is a brave man,
Tire lan laire, tire lan la,
etc., etc.

(The students tumultuously go in the next room. HOFFMANN
remains as if in a stupor.)

Hoffmann.

Ah, je suis fou!... A nous le vertige divin
Des esprits de l'alcool, de la bière et du vin!
A nous l'ivresse et la folie,
Le néant par qui l'on oublie.

Nicklausse.

Ah! je comprends! trois drames dans un drame.
Olympia?

Hoffmann.

Fracassée!

Nicklausse.

Antonia?

Hoffmann.

Morte!

Nicklausse.

Giulietta?

Hoffmann.

Ah, pour elle le dernier couplet de la chanson
de Klein-Zach!
Quand il avait but de genièvre et de rack
Il fallait voir flotter les pans de son frac
Comme des herbes dans un lac;
Le monstre faisait flic, flac,
Flic, flac,
Voilà Klein-Zach.

Le Choeur.

Flic flac,
Voilà Klein-Zach.

Le Choeur.

Allumons le punch!... grisons-nous!
Et que les plus fous
Roulent sous la table.
Luther est un brave homme,
Tire lan laire, tire lan la!
etc., etc.

(Les étudiants entrent en tumulte dans la salle voisine. HOFFMANN
reste comme frappé de stupeur.)

The Muse

(appearing in an aureole of light).

And I? I, the faithful friend,
Whose hand has dried thy tears?
By whom thy latent sorrow
Is wafted in heavenly dreams?
Am I naught? May the tempest
Of passion pass away in thee!
The man is no more; the poet revives!
I love thee, Hoffmann! be mine!
Let the ashes of thy heart kindle thy genius,
In serenity smiling on thy sorrows.
The Muse will sweeten to thee thy sufferings;
Love makes thee great, but tears make greater
still.

(She disappears.)

Hoffmann

(alone).

Oh, God! with what ecstasy my soul is filled!
Like a concert divine the voice hath moved me.
With soft and burning fire my being is de-
voured.
Thy glances in mine have kindled their flame,
Like radiant stars,
And I feel, beloved Muse,
Thy perfumed breath pass
Over my lips and my eyes!

(He falls, face on table.)

Stella

(approaching slowly).

Hoffmann asleep!...

Nicklausse

No, dead drunk. Too late, madame!

Lindorf.

Corbleu!

Nicklausse.

Stay, here is the counselor, Lindorf, who awaits
you.

(STELLA takes LINDORF's arm, but stops to look at HOFFMANN, and
throws a flower from her bouquet at his feet.)

THE END.

La Muse

(paraissant).

Et moi? Moi, la fidèle amie
Dont la main essuya tes yeux?
Par qui la douleur endormie
S'exhale en rêve dans les cieux?
Ne suis-je rien? Que la tempête
Des passions s'apaise en toi!
L'homme n'est plus; renais poète!
Je t'aime, Hoffmann! appartiens-moi!
Des cendres de ton coeur réchauffe ton génie,
Dans la sérénite souris à tes douleurs,
La Muse adoucira ta souffrance bénie,
On est grand par l'amour et plus grand par les
pleurs!

(Elle disparaît.)

Hoffmann

(seul).

Ô Dieu! de quelle ivresse embrases-tu mon
âme,
Comme un concert divin ta voix m'a pénétré,
D'un feu doux et brûlant mon être est dévoré.
Tes regards dans les miens ont épanché leur
flamme,
Comme des astres radieux,
Et je sens, Muse aimée,
Passer ton haleine embaumée
Sur mes lèvres et sur mes yeux!

(Il tombe, le visage sur une table.)

Stella

(allant vers HOFFMANN).

Hoffmann endormi!...

Nicklausse.

Non!... ivre-mort!... Trop tard, madame!

Lindorf.

Corbleu!

Nicklausse.

Tenez, voilà le conseiller Lindorf qui vous
attend.

(STELLA s'appuie sur le bras de LINDORF, s'arrête pour regarder
HOFFMANN, détache une fleur de son bouquet et la jette à ses pieds.)

FIN.

ACT III, NO. 13, BARCAROLLE. BELLE NUIT (NIGHT DIVINE)

Night di - vine, O
Bel le nuit, ô

night of love, O smile on our ca - ress - es! Moon and stars keep
nuit d'a - mour, Sou - ris à nos i - vres - ses! Nuit plus dou - ce

watch a - bove This ra - diant night of love!
que le jour, Ô bel - le nuit d'a - mour!

ACT II, No. 7. ROMANCE. AH! VIVRE DEUX (TO LIVE AS ONE).

To live as one,　A sin-gle hope to fond-ly
Ah! vi - vre deux,　n'a-voir q'u - ne même es - pé

treas - ure,　A sin gle mem-o-ry!　What a
ran - ce　Un mê - me sou - ve - nir!　Par - ta-

heav - en - ly boon　To share each grief and pleas - ure,　To share each grief and pleasure,
ger le bon-heur,　par-ta-ger la souf-fran-ce,　par-ta-ger la souf-fran-ce

SAMSON AND DELILAH

by

CAMILLE SAINT-SAËNS

STORY OF THE ACTION

"SAMSON ET DALILA," a biblical opera in three acts, with text by Ferdinand Lemaire, was first performed in its entirety at Weimar, December 2, 1877. The score had been completed in 1872, and parts of the work were given in Paris in 1875; but it was not until 1877 that the whole opera was performed under the direction of Eduard Lassen. The work was successful in other cities outside of France during the next few years; and twenty years after its completion it was finally produced in a grand manner at the Paris Opéra. The French librettists diverged quite widely from the biblical narrative, laying more stress upon the love interest and its disastrous consequences. This gave opportunity for a more dramatic treatment, and in the hands of a master the opportunity has been improved by the use of striking leading motives and an orchestral background of vivid coloring and brilliant descriptive power.

THE FIRST ACT reveals a public square in the city of Gaza, wherein a crowd of Hebrews in captivity give voice to their despair. Samson, who is among them, gives them assurance of his help and their ultimate deliverance; but Abimelech, satrap of Gaza, derides their supplications. Samson denounces him as a blasphemer; and when Abimelech draws his sword the hero wrests it from him and slays him as he calls for help. The Philistines respond to the cry, but are dismayed before Samson's bravery. In the third scene, which is laid before the Temple of Dagon, the High Priest, standing by Abimelech's body, urges the Philistines to avenge his death. Hereupon a messenger arrives with news that the Israelites, led by Samson, and filled with new courage, are on the march; and the High Priest launches his curse against them and their victorious leader. The Hebrews return, followed by Samson, singing choruses of rejoicing. In the next scene Delilah enters, followed by the Philistine women. The temptation of Samson commences in the fascinating dances of the Priestesses of Dagon, wherein Delilah takes part; and she seeks in a beautiful song of spring to ensnare him by the spell of her beauty.

THE SECOND ACT reveals Delilah, richly clad, at the door of her dwelling. She utters a passionate invocation to love to aid her in accomplishing Samson's downfall; and in a highly dramatic duet which follows, the High Priest tells her of the disaster which has befallen her people and urges her to strongest efforts. The next scene is of great beauty and is worked out in a strikingly dramatic manner. Samson enters, disturbed and troubled; and Delilah, by every means in her power, tries to make him a captive to her charms. In the midst of an approaching storm Samson ultimately declares his love. When the storm breaks furiously, she entices him into her house, which is at once stealthily surrounded by the Philistine soldiery.

IN THE THIRD ACT Samson is shown blinded and in slavery, grinding at a mill, while the Hebrews sing a mournful chorus. Samson bewails the loss of his sight. The Philistines enter and remove him, and the scene is changed to the interior of Dagon's Temple. Here a festival in honor of the god is in progress, which gives opportunity for a fascinating ballet, the music of which is rich in Eastern color. Samson is taunted by the High Priest, who tells him that if his God will restore his sight they will forsake the worship of Dagon. Delilah also mocks his helpless condition, and reveals the deep hatred which she had concealed under a simulated passion. Finally Samson is ordered to offer oblation to Dagon. He is led by a boy to a position between the two pillars which support the massive roof. With a final prayer to the Lord to give him a momentary return of his old power, he exerts all his strength and breaks the pillars, whereat the temple falls amid the cries of the Philistines, who are buried beneath its ruins.

SAMSON and DELILAH.

ACT I.

———

A public square in the city of Gaza, in Palestine. At the left the portico of the Temple of Dagon. When the curtain rises, a crowd of Hebrews, men and women, are assembled in attitudes of grief and prayer. SAMSON is among them.

SCENE I.

Chorus.

(Behind the scenes.)

God! Thou gracious God of Israel,
O, listen, we implore thee!
Thy children cry, thy children cry,
" Save us from our dark fate,
Save us from foes that hate!"
O, pity grant to us who kneel before thee!
　May our deep grief disarm thy wrath on
　　high!
When thou didst turn thy face from us, thy
　　people,
From that sad day our victory was lost!
Wouldst thou behold us, thy people, now
　　vanquished,
The only nation that thy might hath known?
Shall we in vain thus forever beseech thee?
(Deaf to our voice He heeds not our alarm!)
Doth our united prayer, then, fail to reach
　　thee,
Our hearts' sore cry for the aid of thine arm?

We have beheld our cities' fell destruction,
And Gentile foes thy blest altars profane.
Beneath their yoke our tribes are scatter'd
　　widely;
O Israel, doth thy name not remain!

Art thou no more the God of our salvation,
Who saved from Egypt our tribes long ago?

ACTE I.

———

Une place publique dans la ville de Gaza en Palestine. A gauche le portique du Temple de Dagon. Au lever du rideau une foule d'Hebreux, hommes et femmes, sont rèunis sur la place dans l'attitude de la douleur et de la priére. SAMSON est parmi eux.

SCENE I.

Chœur.

(Derriere la toile.)

Dieu! Dieu d'Israël!
Dieu d'Israel!
Ecoute la prière de tes enfants,
De tes enfants t'implorant à genoux,
T'implorant à genoux!
Prends en pitié ton peuple
Et sa misère!
Que sa douleur désarme ton courroux!
Un jour, de nous tu détournas ta face,
Et de ce jour ton peuple fut vaincu!
Quoi! veux tu donc qu'à jamais on efface
Des nations, celle qui t'a connu!
Mais vainement tout le jour
Je l'imment tou le jour l'implore;
Sourd à ma voix, il ne me répond pas!
Et cependant, du soir jusqu'à l'aurore,
J'implore ici le secours de son bras!

Nous avons vu nos cités renversées,
Et les Gentils profanant ton autel;
Et sous leur joug nos tribus dispersées
Ont tout perdu, jusqu'au nom d'Israel!

Ne's tu donc plus ce Dieu delivrance
Qui de l'Egypte arrachait nos tribus?

Lord! Dost thou forget thy word, pledged
  to our nation
In those sad days when Israel mourned in
  woe?

Samson.
      (Coming out from the throng. R.)
Let us pause, O my brothers,
And bless the holy name of the God of our
  fathers!
For now the hour is here when pardon
  shall be spoken.
Yes, a voice in my heart of this hope is the
  token.
'Tis the voice of the Lord, who by my
  mouth thus speaketh.
On us his goodness showers.
  Our prayers to him have risen,
And liberty is ours.
  Brothers! we'll break from bondage!
Our altars raise once more
To our God, as before!

Chorus. Alas! thou speakest vainly,
  How can freedom be sought?
Our arms the foe hath taken,
  Our feeble host is nought.
Of all power they've bereft us,
Tears alone now are left us.

Samson. In the Lord still abide.
Hast thou so soon forgotten
  That to us he's allied,
Whatsoe'er may betide?
  His blessed help divine
Has to us oft been plighted.
  In wonder of his might
Our faith has been re-lighted.
When we came thro' the sea,
  Then a passage he made,
So that safely might flee
All our fathers from bondage.

Chorus Those wondrous days are past.
Now our God has ceased heeding
  Tears or cries from our hearts,
Or his children's sore pleading.

Samson. Wretched ones, silence keep!
Nor doubt that God doth love you!
  Contrite fall on your knees,
For the Lord reigns above you.
  Your glory leave to him.
His might will aye uphold you.
To him yield up the reins;
His mercy will enfold you.

Dieu! Astu rompu cette sainte alliance
Divins serments par nos aïeux recus?

Samson.
      (Sortant, de la foule, à droite.)
Arrêtez, ô mes frères!
Et benissez le nom du Dieu saint de nos
  pères!
Car l'heure du pardon est peu être arrivée!
Oui, j'entends dans mon cœur une élevée!
C'est la voix du Seigneur, qui parle ma
  bouche
Ce Dieu plein de bonté, que la prière
  touche,
Promet la liberte!
  Frères! brisons nos chaines
Et relevons l'autel du seul Dieu d'Israel!

Chœur. Hélas! paroles vaines! Pour marcher
  aux combats
Où donc trouver des armes?
  Comment armer nos bras?
  Nous n'avons que nos larmes!

Samson. L'astu donc oublié,
Celui dont la puisance
Se fit ton allié?
Lui qui, plein de clèmence,
A si souvent pour toi
Fait parler ses oracles,
Et rallumé ta foi
Au feu de ses miracles?
Lui, qui dans l'Océan
Sut frayer un passage
A nos pères fuyant
Un honteux esclavage?

Chœur. Ils ne sont plus, ces temps
Où le Dieu de nos pères
Protégeait ses enfants.
Entendait leurs prières!

Samson. Malheureux, taisez vous!
Le doute est un blasphème!
Implorons à genoux
Le Seigneur qui nos aime!
Remettons dans ses mains
Le soin de notre gloire,
Et puis ceignons nos reins,
Certains de la victoire!

He's the God of our host
Through all clouds that may lower,
He will enforce your arm
    And endow you with power.

Chorus. Ah! his words are from the Lord!
    With might divine they bless us.
Ah! we'll chase from our hearts
    All fear that doth possess us!
We'll march at his side,
    For he is our salvation,
And our God is his guide;
    He will save our whole nation!

SCENE II.

(The same. ABIMELECH, satrap of Gaza, enters at the
left, followed by many warriors and Philistine soldiers.)

Abimelech. Ah! who that's here dares raise
    his voice?
    In this vile troop who doth defy us?
Who dares against our rigid laws
    Strive for freedom, and vainly try us?
Conceal all your groans and your tears.
    We are your conquerors forever,
    And compassion we'll show you never.
We shall not heed your grief or fears.

That God whom you are now imploring
    Is deaf to your pains and your cries.
For 'neath our scorn he lets you languish,
    Paying no heed to all your sighs.
Ah! vain is all his boasted power!
    That he's divine, then let him show.
If he will but free you from bondage
    Then his might and glory we'll know.

Can your God compare with Dagon,
    Who's greater than all your powers,
Who guides so bravely in battle
    Till all glorious victory is ours?
Your Jehovah, so weak and fearful,
    Flies when he our leader doth see,
Trembling like the dove so timid,
    When from the vulture it doth flee.

Samson.
    (Inspired.)
'Tis thou, O my God, he defameth!
Let the earth tremble 'neath his feet!
Make his fall and destruction complete!
I see in hands of angels
    Sharp swords gleaming with fire.
All the brave ranks of heaven

C'est le Dieu des combats!
C'est le Dieu des armées!
Il armera vos bras d'invincibles épées!

Chœur. Ah! le souffle du Seigneur a passé
    dans son âme!
Ah! chassons de notre cœur
Une terreur infame!
Et marchons avec lui
Pour notre délivrance!
Jéhovah le conduit
Et nous trend l'esperance!

SCENE II.

(Les memes. ABIMÉLECH, satrape de Gaza. Il entre
par la gauche, suivé de plausieurs guerriors et soldats Philistins.)

Abimélech. Qui donc élève ici la voix?
    Encor ce vil troupeau d'esclaves,
    Osant toujours braver nos lois
    Et voulant briser leures entraves!
    Cachez vos soupirs vos pleurs
    Qui lassent notre patience;
    Invoquez plutôt la clémence
    De ceux qui furent vos vainqueurs!

    Ce Dieu que votre voix implore
    Est demuré sound à vos cris,
    Et vous l'osez prier encore,
    Quand il vous livre à nos mépris?
    Si sa puissance n'est pas vaine,
    Qu'il montre sa divinité!
    Qu'il vienne briser votre chaîne;
    Qu'il vous rende la liberté!

    Croyez vous ce Dieu comparable à Dagon,
    Le plus grand des Dieux,
    Guidant de son bras redoutable
    Nos guerriers victorieux?
    Votre divinité craintive,
    Tremblante fuyait devant lui,
    Comme la colombe plaintive
    Fuit le vautour qui la poursuit!

Samson.
    (Inspiré.)
C'est toi que sa bouche invective,
Et la terre n'a point tremble?
O Seigneur, l'abime est comblé!
Je vois aux mains des anges
    Briller l'arme de feu,
Et du ciel les phalanges

Sound forth their righteous ire.
And e'en the souls of darkness,
As the foe they pass by,
    Howl forth such cries of anger
As rise to vaulted sky.
    At last now is the hour
When God's just wrath is nigh,
    And I hear in the clouds
Thunder-claps from on high.
    Yes, resoundeth his vengeance;
Pallid with fear they fly!
    The earth trembles in anger,
Bright flashes light the sky!

Chorus.   Yes, resoundeth his vengeance
    Pallid with fear they fly!
The earth trembles in anger,
    Bright flashes light the sky.

Abimelech.   But hold! in your course rushing
    madly,
For I would avenge me, most gladly.

Accourent venger Dieu!
Oui, l'ange des ténèbres,
En passant devant eux,
    Pousse des cris funèbres
Que font frémir les cieux!
    Enfin l'heure est venue,
L'heure du Dieu vengeur,
    Et j'eutends dans la nue
Eclater sa fureur.
    Oui, devant sa colère
Tout s'épouvante et fuit!
    On sent trembler la terre,
Aux cieux la foudre luit!

Chœur.   Oui, devant sa colère
    Tout s'épouvante et fuit!
On sent trembler la terre,
    Aux cieux la foudre luit!

Abimélech.   Arrête! Insensé téméraire,
    Ou crains d'exciter ma colère!

SAMSON.

Is - ra - el! break thy chain! a - rise and con-queror be! Nour - ish thy right - eous
Is - ra - ël! romps ta chaîne! O peu - ple, lè - ve toi! Viens as - sou - vir ta

vengeance, For the Lord is with me! O thou God of com - passion, Us up-
haîne! Le Sei - gneur est en moi! O toi, Dieu de lu - mière, Comme aux

CHORUS *repeat* FINE.

hold with thy might, As in the days gone by, When we fought for the right!
jours d'autre - fois Ex - an - ce ma pri - ère, Et com - bats pour tes lois!

Yes, re-sound - eth his ven - geance, In crin - ging fear they fly, The earth now quakes in
Oui, de - vant sa co - lè - re, Tout s'é - pou-vante et fuit, On sent trem - bler la

an - ger, Bright flashes light the sky. He the tem-pest com - mand-eth, And hold - eth storms and the
terre; Aux cieux la fou - dre luit! Il dé-chaî - ne l'o - ra - ge, com - mande a l'ou-ra-

ff   D.C.

tide. His hand, if He but pass - it Makes the waves stand a - side.
gan; On voit sur son pas - sa - ge Re - cu - ler l'O - cé - an

(ABIMELECH, sword in hand, attacks SAMSON. SAMSON wrests his sword from him and stabs him. ABIMELECH, falling, cries for help. The Philistines rush to help him. SAMSON brandishes his sword and keeps them off. They fill the stage at the right. Great confusion reigns among them. SAMSON and Hebrews pass off.)

(The gates of Dagon's Temple open. The HIGH PRIEST, followed by a throng of attendants and guards, descends the steps of the portico; he pauses before ABIMELECH'S body. The Philistines draw back from him.)

SCENE III.

High Priest. What see I? Abimelech!
Struck down and low before me!
Let not the slaves escape!
But, fly, I implore you,
To avenge your prince!
Now in haste cut them down,
These rebels in revolt,
Who brave your very crown!

1st Philistine. Then with horror seemed frozen
All the blood in my veins;
My limbs seemed as heavy
As they were bound in chains.

2d Philistine. My weapon sought I vainly,
My arm no power lent;
My heart fainted within me,
And my knees trembling bent.

High Priest. Cowards! More cowardly than women!
You have fled in your vain alarms!
From their god you fear that anger
Would scorch you and wither your arms!

SCENE IV.

A Philistine Messenger. My Lord, the band, in their fury,
With Samson strong at their head,
Are all revolting and audacious,
Ravaging where they are led.

1st and 2d Philistines. We'll flee, then, exposure that's useless,
We'll leave to more fleet ones this place;
My lord, we'll leave this fearful village,
Concealing with shame our face.

High Priest. Cursed be your nation forever!
O Israel's hated band!
Fall ye! and leave no trace behind;
Be ye swept from off the land!

(ABIMÉLECH se précipite sur SAMSON l'épée á la main pour le frapper; SAMSON loi arrache l'épée des mains et le frappe. ABIMÉLECH (en tombant), "A moi!" Les Philistins qui accompagnant le Satrape veulent le secourir; SAMSON brandissant son épée, les éloigne. Ils occupent la droite de la scene, la plus grande confusion règne parmi eux. SAMSON et les Hebreux sortent à droite.)

(Les Portes du temple de Dagon s'ouvrent, le GRAND PRÉTRE suivi de nombreaux serviteurs et gardes descend les degrés du portique; il s'arrête devant le cadavre d' ABIMÉLECH'S; les Philistins s'ecartent devant lui.)

SCENE III.

Le Grand Prêtre. Que vois-je? Abime lech! Frappe par des esclaves!
Pourquoi les laisser fuir?
Courons! courons, mes braves!
Pour venger votre Prince, écrasez sous vos coups
Ce peuple révolté bravant votre courroux!

1er Philistin. J'ai senti dans mes veines
Tout mon sang se glacer;
Il semble que des chaines
Soudain vont m'enlacer.

2e Philistin. Je cherche en vain mes armes,
Mes bras sont impuissants,
Mon cœur est plein d'alarmes,
Mes genoux sont tremblants!

Grand Prêtre. Lâches! plus lâches que des femmes!
Vous fuyez devant des combats!
De leur Dieu eraignez vous les flammes,
Qui doivent desécher vos bras!

SCENE IV.

Un Messager Philistin. Seigneur! la troupe furieuse
Que conduit et guide Samson,
Dans sa révolte audacieuse,
Accourt ravageant la moisson.

1er et 2e Philistins et Messager. Fuyons un danger inutile!
Quittons au plus vite ces lieux.
Seigneur, abandonnons la ville,
Et cachons honte aux yeux.

Grand Prêtre. Maudite à jamais soit la race
Des enfants d'Israël!
Je veux en effacer la trace,
Les abreuver de fiel!

Cursed, also, he who doth guide ye!
  Him will I grind 'neath my heel;
His anguish keen could I behold
  And no remorse would I feel!

Cursed ever be the woman
  Who brought him forth to light!
On all who may in love adore him
  Now let there fall a blight!
Cursed be the God that he worships,
  That God, his hope and delight!
My hate would sweep away his nation,
  His altar and his might!

1st and 2d Philistines and Messenger. We'll
  fly to yonder mountains,
  Nor leave behind a track;
To our homes and companions,
  And gods, we will go back.

(They go off at left, bearing the body of ABIMELECH, followed by HIGH PRIEST. At the same time the Hebrews, old men and women, enter at right. Sun rises.)

SCENE V.

(Hebrews, women and old men. Afterwards SAMSON and victorious Hebrews.)

Old Hebrew Men. Rise, hymn of joy, hymn
  of deep thanksgiving,
  And our blest vict'ry tell!
For he who reigns is deliv'rer all powerful,
  He doth aid Israel.
By him the weak have become so mighty
  Against tyranny strong:
He overcometh the pride of the traitor,
  Who doth battle for the wrong.

(The victorious Hebrews, led by SAMSON, enter at the right.)

An Aged Hebrew. He censured us in rage
  and anger,
  For we his righteous laws had braved.
When bowed before him we entreated
  That from his wrath we might be saved.
He said to all his tribe beloved,
  "Rise in arms! to combat now fly!
For I, your God, will bless your weapons,
  And in the strife be at your side."

Old Hebrew Men. He came to save his sons,
  who else had perished.
  Now no sorrow remains;
Let all the universe sound his praises!
  He hath broken our chains!
Rise, hymn of joy, etc.

Maudit soit celui qui les guide!
  J'écraserai du pied
Ses os brisés, sa gorge aride,
  Sans frémir de pitié!

Maudit soit le sein de la femme
  Qui lui donna le jour!
Qu'enfin une compagne infâme
  Trahisse son amour!
Maudit soit le Dieu qu'il adore,
  Ce Dieu, son seul espoir!
Et dont ma haine insulte encore
  L'autel et le pouvoir!

1er et 2e Philistins et Messager. Fuyons dans
  les montagnes,
  Abandonnons ces lieux,
  Nos maisons, nos compagnes,
Et jusques à nos Dieux!

(Ils sortent par la gauche, emportant le cadavre d'ABIMÉLECH, suivis, le GRAND PRÊTRE. Entrent les Hébreux, vieillards et femmes, droit.)

SCENE V.

(Les femmes et les vieillards Hébreux. Puis SAMSON suivi des Hébreux victorieux.)

Vieillards Hébreux. Hymne de joie, hymne
  de délivrance,
  Montez vers l'eternal!
  Il a daigné dans sa toute puissance
Secourir Israël!
  Par lui le faible est devenu le maitre,
Du fort qui l'opprimait!
  Il a vaincu l'orgueil lieux et le traître
Dont la voix l'insultait!

(Les Hébreux, conduits par SAMSON, entrent à droite.)

Un Vieillard Hébreu. Il nous frappait dans
  sa colère,
  Car nous avions bravé ses lois.
Plus tard, le front dans la poussière,
  Vers lui nous élevions la voix.
Il dit à ses tribus aimées:
  Levez vous marchez aux combats!
Je suis le Seigneur des armées,
Je suis la force de vos bras!

Vieillards Hébreux. Il est venu vers nous
  dans la détresse,
  Car ses fils lui sont chers.
Que l'univers tressaille d'allégresse!
  Il a rompu nos fers!
Hymne de joie, etc.

SCENE VI.

(The gates of Dagon's Temple open. DÈLILAH enters, followed by Philistine women with garlands of flowers in their hands.)

Chorus of Women. With flowers doth the
 spring come forth gladly now,
 Bright garlands to make for brave conquer-
  or's brow.
 And cheerful our tones as the glow of roses
  that spring discloses,
 We sing our glad triumphant song,
 As sing the birds that round us throng.
  The springtime of youth — a gift from
   above,
 Imparteth a grace to our early love.
 All soft as the breeze in its lightest motion
  is our devotion.
 Then let us love while all is bright,
 While nature sporteth in delight.

Delilah.
  (To SAMSON.)
 I come to resound the brave story
 Of the one who reigns in my heart,
 And to whom I would joy impart,
 Giving more of love than of glory.
  My beloved one, follow me !
 Unto fair Soreck will I guide thee,
 And there with sweet comfort provide thee.
  With open arms I'll welcome thee.

Samson.
  (Apart.)
 O God ! in thy might all sufficing,
 Grace to thy poor servant impart !
 Close thou my eyes, close thou my heart
 Against that dear voice so enticing !

Delilah. For thee have I crowned my own
 brow
 With fairest the springtime possesses.
 The rose of Sharon I have culled
 And twined among my dark tresses.

Old Hebrew Man. O turn, my son, from dark
 temptation's harm ;
 Avoid and fear the wiles of this stranger.
 Close now thine eyes and avoid this great
  danger.
 Flee in terror from the serpent's charm.

Samson. O, veil those eyes whose faintest ray
 My sense doth blind, my soul possessing ;
 Conceal that face so all obsessing
  That now my freedom takes away.

SCENE VI.

(Les portes du temple de Dagon s'ouvrent. DALILA entre suivie des femmes Philistins tenant dans leurs mains des guirlandes de fleurs.)

Chœur des femmes. Voici le printemps por-
 tant des fleurs
 Pour orner le front des guerriers vain-
  queurs !
 Mêlons nos accents au parfum des roses,
 A peine écloses !
 Avec l'oiseau chantons, mes sœurs !
 Beauté, don du ciel, printemps de nos jours,
 Doux charme des yeux, espoir des amours,
 Pénètre les cœurs verse dans les âmes,
 Tes douces flammes !
 Aimons, mes sœurs, aimons toujours.

Dalila.
  (À SAMSON.)
 Ja viens célébrer la victoire
 De celui qui règne en mon cœur.
 Dalila veut pour son vainqueur
 Encor plus d'amour que de gloire !
 O mon bien aimé, suis mes pas
 Vers Soreck la douce vallée,
 Dans cette demeure isolée
 Où Dalila t'ouvre ses bras !

Samson. O, Dieu ! toi qui vois ma faiblesse,
 Prends pitié de ton serviteur !
 Ferme mes yeux, ferme mon cœur
 A la douce voix qui me presse !

Dalila. Pour toi j'ai couronné mon front
 Des grappes noires du troène,
 Et mis des roses de Saron
 Dans ma chevelure d'ébène !

Vieillard Hebreu. Détour ne-toi, mon fils, de
 son chemin !
 Evite et crains celle fille étrangère ;
 Ferme l'oreille a'sa voix mensongère,
 Et du serpent évite le venin.

Samson. Voile ses traits dont la beautié
 Trouble mes sens, trouble mon âme
 Et de ses yeux éteins la flamme
 Qui me ravit la liberté !

Delilah. Sweet the lilies' soft, grateful breath,
But far sweeter the fond caresses
Of the one whom thy heart possesses—
Of her who loves thee unto death.
Then ope thine arms, for I adore thee.
And but let me rest on thy heart—
Joy of the angels thus impart.
List to my prayer, I now implore thee!
Ah! come!

Samson. O ardent flame that doth devour,
Of which this place revives the zest,
Appease my pain, appease my pain,
And ease my breast!
Have pity, Lord, now in my trial's hour!
O Lord!

Old Hebrew Man. A curse on thee if thou
dost heed her pleading,
Or by that voice so strangely sweet be led.
These eyes could never wash away with
weeping
All heaven's rage that would fall on thy
head!

(Dance of the Priestesses of Dagon.)

(The young girls accompanying DELILAH dance, waving garlands of flowers; and try to entice the Hebrew warriors that are with SAMSON. He tries, but in vain, to avoid DELILAH's glances. In spite of him his eyes follow the movements of the enchantress, as she takes part in the voluptuous poses and gestures of the young Philistine maidens.)

Delilah. Spring voices are singing,
Bright hope they are bringing,
All hearts making glad.
And gone sorrow's traces,
The soft air effaces
All days that are sad.
Our hearts warm are glowing,
When sweet winds are blowing
They dry our ev'ry tear.
The earth glad and beaming,
With freshness is teeming,
While fruits and flowers are here.
In vain all my beauty:
I weep my poor fate.
My heart filled with love,
The faithless doth wait.
In vain am I striving?
Can hope never last?
I must then remember
Only joys now past.

When night is descending,
With love all unending,
Bewailing my fate,

Dalila. Doux est le muguet parfumé;
Mes baisers le sont plus encore;
Et le suc de la mandragore
Est moins suave ô bien aimé!
Ouvre tes bras à ton amante
Et dèposela sur ton cœur
Comme un sachet de douce odeur,
Dont la senteur est enivrante!
Ah! viens!

Samson. Flamme ardente qui me dévore,
Et qu'elle ravive en ce lieu,
Apaise toi, apaise toi devant mon Dieu,
Pitié, Seigneur, pour celui qui l'implore!

Vieillard Hebreu. Jamais tes yeux n'auron
assez de larmes
Pour desamer la colére du ciel!

(Danse des Prêtresses de Dagon.)

(Les jeunes filles qui ont accompagné DALILA dansent en agitant des guirlandes de fleurs, et semblent provoquer les guerriers Hébreux qui accompagnent SAMSON. Ce dernier, profondément trouble, cherche en vain à éviter les regards de DALILA; ses yeux, malgré lui, suivent au milieu des jeunes Philistins, prenant part à leurs poses et à leurs gestes voluptueux.)

Dalila. Printemps qui commence,
Portant l'espérance,
Aux cœurs amoureux,
Ton souffle qui passe.
De terre efface
Les jours malheureux.
Tout brûle en notre âme,
Et ta douce flamme
Vient se cher nos pleurs;
Tu rends à la terre,
Par un doux mystère,
Les fruits et les fleurs.
Et vain je suis belle!
Mon cœur plein d'amour,
Pleurant l'infidèl.
Attend son retour!
Vivant d'espérance,
Mon cœur desolé
Garde souvenance
Du bonheur passé!

A la nuit tombante
J'irai, triste amante,
M'asseoir autorent.

For him will I wait.
I 'll banish all sadness,
Though deep I may yearn,
When fond love returning,
in his bosom burning
May enforce his return.

Old Hebrew Man.   This woman, guided by
    some evil power
Comes in his path to beguile him to shame.
Oh, let him fly from her enticing glances!
For only poison doth consume his frame.

Delilah.   I 'll banish all sadness, etc.

(DELILAH continues her song on the steps of the
Temple. She succeeds in securing SAMSON's regard by
enticing glances. He hesitates and otherwise betrays his
trouble and emotion.)

L'attendre en pleurant!
Chassant ma tristesse,
S'il revient un jour,
A lui ma tendresse
Et la douce ivresse
Qu'un brûlant amour.
Garde à son retour!

Le Vieillard Hebreu.   L'esprit du mal a con-
    duit cette femme
Sur ton chemin pour troubler ton repos.
De ses regards fuis la brûlante flamme!
C'est un poison qui consume les os!

Dalila.   Chassant ma tristesse, etc.

(DALILA regague en chantant les degrés du temple, et
provoque SAMSON du regard. Il hésite, il lutte, et trahit le
trouble de son âme.)

ACT II.

(The theatre represents the valley of Soreck in Palestine.
At the left DELILAH's dwelling, which has a graceful portico, surrounded with Asiatic plants and luxuriant vines.)
(At the rising of the curtain night begins and wholly
comes on during the course of the act.)

SCENE I.

(DELILAH, alone. She is more richly attired than in
Act I. At the rising of the curtain she is seated on a rock
near the entrance of her dwelling, and seems in a reverie.)

Delilah.   To-night Samson cometh to greet me;
    He'll hasten my sorrows to ease.
For behold, strikes the hour of vengeance
When we our blest gods shall appease.

O Love! in my weakness give power!
    Poison Samson's brave heart for me!
'Neath my soft sway may he be vanquished;
    To-morrow let him captive be!

Ev'ry thought of me he would banish,
    And from his tribe he would swerve,
Could he only drive out the passion
    That remembrance doth now preserve.

But he is under my dominion;
    In vain his people may entreat.
'Tis I alone that can hold him —
    I'll have him captive at my feet.

O love, in my weakness, give power, etc.

ACTE II.

(Le theâtre représente la vallée de Soreck en Palestine.
A gauche, la demeure de DALILA, précédée d'un léger
portique et entourée de plantes Asiatiques et de lianes
luxuriantes.)
(Au lever du Rideau la nuit commence et se fait plus
complète pendant toute la durée de l'acte.)

SCENE I.

(DALILA, seule. Elle est plus parée qu'au premier
acte. Au lever du rideau elle est assise sur une roche près
du portique de sa maison, et semble rêveuse.)

Dalila.   Samson, recherchant ma présence,
    Ce soir doit venir en ces lieux.
Voici l'heure de la vengeance
    Qui doit satisfaire nos dieux!

Amour! viens aider ma faiblesse!
    Verse le poison dans son sein!
Fais que, vaincu par mon adresse,
    Samson soit enchaîné demain!

Il voudrait en vain de son âme
    Pouvoir me chasser, me bannir!
Pourraitil éteindre la flamme
    Qu'alimente le souvenir?

Il est à moi! c'est mon esclave!
    Mes frères craignent son courroux;
Moi, seule entre tous, je le brave,
    Et le retiens à mes genoux!

Amour! viens aider, etc.

'Gainst his deep love he battles vainly,
　And he, the strongest of the strong!
He'll break the tie to his own nation,
　And to my people he'll belong.

(*Distant flashes of lightning.*)

SCENE II.

(DELILAH and the HIGH PRIEST of Dagon.)

High Priest.　I have climbed lofty mountains,
　And have safely reached thee.
Good Dagon came to guide me,
　Till thy roof we might see.

Delilah.　I now salute you, father.
　Be welcome, tho' 'tis late;
Even here you have honor.

High Priest.　Known to thee is our fate.
And the vict'ry was easy,
　For, by treachery led,
Our slaves gave up our cities,
　And our brave soldiers fled.
In terror they were scattered;
　At Samson's name they fly;
For of his deeds they know—
　They to madness were nigh.

'Twas fatal to our nation.
　He received from his God
The force and skill to conquer—
　He but serveth his Lord.
On him at birth, from heaven
　This most holy mission fell,
To aid his chosen people,
　The tribe of Israel.

Delilah.　I know his mighty courage
　Braves e'en your direst hate,
And that he deems no outrage
　Can for you be too great.

High Priest.　His courage and his mighty
　　　force
　Vanish'd away
At the feet of Delilah,
　Where he fell, on that day.

They say, within his bosom
　Love for thee now is past,
And he laughs at a passion
　That but a day can last.

Contre l'amour sa force est vaine;
　Et lui, le fort parmi les forts,
Lui, qui d'un peuple rompt la chaîne,
　Sucombera sous mes efforts!

(*Éclairs lointains.*)

SCENE II.

(DÁLILA et le GRAND PRÊTRE de Dagon.)

Le Grand Prêtre.　J'ai gravi la montagne
　Pour venir jusqu'à toi;
Dagon qui m'accompagne
　M'a guidé vers ton toit.

Dalila.　Salut à vous, mon père!
　Soyez le bienvenu,
Vous qu'ici l'on revère!

Grand Prêtre.　Notre sort t'est connu,
　La victoire facile
　　Des esclaves Hébreux
　Leur a livré la ville,
　　Nos soldats devant eux
Ont fui, pleins d'epouvante
　Au seul nom de Samson,
Dont l'audace effrayante
　A troublé leur raison.

Fatal à notre race,
　Il recut de son Dieu
La force avec l'audace,
　　Enchaîné par un vœu,
　Samson, dès sa naissance,
Fut marqué par le ciel
Pour rendre la puissance
　Au peuple d'Israël.

Dalila.　Je sais que son courage
　Brave votre courroux,
Et qu'il n'est pas d'outrage
　Qu'il ne garde pour vous.

Grand Prêtre.　A tes genoux sa force un jour
　　l'abandonna;
　Mais depuis, il s'efforce d'oublier Dalila

On dit que, dans son âme
　Oubliant ton amour,
Il se rit de la flamme
　Qui ne dura qu'un jour;

Delilah. I know that his near kindred
    Bitterly all discourse
      On his ardent emotion,
    And would destroy its force.
    But Samson will not fail me,
      He combats all in vain ;
My fearless heart assures me
    That his love will remain.
    He is pow'rful in battle,
      And can brave fortune's chance ;
    But a slave, when I am near him,
      And trembles 'neath my glance.

High Priest. For us employ thy power,
    And to us lend thine aid !
    Unto thee shall a ransom
      For the captive be paid.

    This Samson, thy slave, sell to me,
    And, high though the price may be,
    Only name to what thou aspirest —
    I'll grant whatever thou desirest.

Delilah. What value to me your gold,
    If thus my vengeance I had sold ?
    Though you gave me your richest treasure,
    With hatred it ne'er could measure !

    You are deceived ; you know not me.
    Though you by him may vanquish'd be,
    He yields to me — I've long possess'd him,
    Yet more than you I detest him.

High Priest. Thy design and thy hatred I
      might well have read ;
    For words but make my trembling heart
      now thrill with pleasure.
    Though counting on his love, do not in
      vain be led ;
    Try thy might to ensnare him, but thy
      powers ever measure.

Delilah. Yes, disguising my motive I've thrice
      made appeal
    That the secret of strength he to me might
      reveal.
    I have kindled his love so, that with its
      confession,
    Of the knowledge I seek he might give me
      possession.
    Thus three times I have hoped ; but, alas !
      all in vain,
    For closed within his breast doth his secret
      remain.
    In vain with all the ardor my tried art
      possesses

Dalila. Je sais que de ses frères
    Ecoutant les discours,
      Et les plaintes amères
      Que cousent nos amours,
    Samson, malgré lui-même,
      Combat lutte en vain ;
    Je sais combien il m'aime,
      Et mon cœur ne craint rien.
    C'est en vain qu'il me brave ;
      Il est fort aux combats,
    Mais il est mon esclave
      Et tremble dans mes bras.

Grand Prêtre. Sers-nous de ta puissance,
    Prête-nous ton appui !
    Que, surpris dans défense,
      Il succombe aujourd' hui !

    Vends-moi ton esclave Samson !
    Et pour te payer sa rancon,
    Je ne ferai point de promesses ;
    Tu peux choisir dans mes richesses.

Dalila. Qu'importe à Dalila ton or !
    Et que pourrait tout un trésor,
    Si je ne rèvais la vengeance !

    Je t'ai trompé par cet amour.
      Samson sut vous dompter un jour ;
    Mais il n'a pu mé vaincre encore,
      Car, autant que toi, je l'abhorre !

Grand Prête. J'aurais dû deviner ta haine
    Et ton dessein !
    Mon cœur en t'ecoutant tressaille d'alle-
      gresse,
    Mais sur son cœur dé ja n'aurais tu en vain
    Mesuré ta puissance, essayé ton addresse ?

Dalila. Oui, déjà, par trois fois deguisant mon
      projet,
    J'ai voulu de sa force éclaircir le secret.
    J'allumai cet amour, espérant qu'à sa flamme
    Je lirais l'inconnu dans le fond de son àme.
    Mais, par trois fois aussi déjouant mon
      espoir,
    Il ne s'est point livré, ne m'a rien laissé voir.
    En vain d'un fol amour j'imitai les tend
      resses !
    Espérant amollir son cœur par mes caresses
    J'ai vu ce fier captif, enlacé dans mes bras.

His proud heart I've tried to render soft
by my caresses.
I've seen this haughty slave from my arms
break away,
And with zeal only warlike rush to thickest
of the fray.
This day he will fall;
I need no more dissemble;
He now again will blanche
And in my presence tremble.
Yes, I know he will leave his very own,
and fly
To this most hallow'd place, to renew our
blest tie.
For this last combat my surest weapons I'm
keeping,
For he can ne'er withstand my feign'd grief
and weeping.

High Priest. Oh, may Dagon, our god, e'er
sustain thee in right!
Thou dost fight for his glory, and conq'r'st
by his might!

Delilah. Let hatred in disguise now gain him!
Let love with gilded links enchain him!
May passion his reason enthrall,
That lowly his proud head may fall!

High Priest. Let hatred in disguise now gain
him!
Let love with gilded links enchain him?
May passion his reason enthrall,
That lowly his proud head may fall?
On thee alone my hope is rested,
Thou e'er shalt be with honor invested.

Delilah. On me alone his hope is rested,
On me alone!

Both. Let hatred in disguise, etc.
Our forces we'll unite!
Death to that Israelite!

High Priest. We'll see that the brave Hebrew
no more defies us;
I'll depart, lest he come and surprise us.
I'll soon return, and by a secret passage-way:
Thou dost hold in thine hand my people's
fate this day.
Employ thine arts till Samson, all his soul
revealeth,
Tear from out his heart the secret he
concealeth.

(Exit HIGH PRIEST.)

S'arracher de ma couche et courir aux
combats!
Aujour d'hui cependant il subit ma puis-
sance
Car je l'ai vu pâlir, trembler en ma pré-
sence;
Et je sais qu'à cette heure abandonnant les
siens,
Il revient en ces lieux resserrer nos liens.
Pour ce dernier combat j'ai préparé mes
armes:
Samson ne pourra pas résister à mes larmes.

Grand Prêtre. Que Dagon, notre Dieu, daigne
étendre son bras!
Tu combats pour sa gloire et par lui tu
vaincras!

Delila. Il faut, pour assouvir ma haine,
Il faut que mon pouvir l'enchaîne!
Je veux, que, vaincu par l'amour,
Il courbe le front a son tour!

Grand Prêtre. Je veux, pour assouvir ma
haîne,
Je veux que Dalila l'enchaîne;
Il faut que, vaincu par l'amour,
Il courbe le front à son tour!
En toi seule est mon espérance,
A toi l'honneur de la vengeance!

Dalila. A moi l'honneur de la vengeance
A moi l'honneur! a moi!

Grand Prêtre et Dalila. Je veux, pour assou-
vir ma heine, etc.
Unissons nous tous deux!
Mort au chef des Hébreux!

Grand Prêtre. Samson, me disais-tu, dans ces
lieux doit se rendre?
Je m'éloigne, il pourrait nous surprendre.
Bientôt je reviendrai par de secrets chemins.
Les destin de mon peuple, ô femme, est
dans tes mains!
Dechire de son cœur l'invenèrable écorce,
Et surprends le secret qui nous cache sa
force.

(Il sort.)

(DELILAH goes slowly to the entrance of her house, where she remains leaning against one of the pillars, in pensive attitude.)

Delilah. Can it be true, that in his heart
  My love no longer hath power?
  Naught his presence can betray
  For on all the dark night doth lower.

  Alas! he cometh not!

(SAMSON enters from right, hesitatingly and troubled. The night grows darker.)

SCENE III.

(Lightning in distance.)

Samson. To this place am I led,
  Vanquished again am I!
  To fly from here, alas!
  I fain would try.
  Yet, when I would depart—
  Would haste from before her,
  Then more and ever more
  In weakness I adore her.

Delilah.
  (Coming to him quickly.)
  'Tis thou!
  'Tis thou, my best belov'd!
  Long for thee have I waited.
  I now forget my woes;
  To happiness we're fated!
  To thee, a welcome sweet from me!

Samson. Oh, cease thy transports wild!
  For without deep remorse my heart is not beguil'd!

Delilah. O Samson, my own! my best beloved!
  Thy heart thy fond love now represses.
  Why turnest away thy dear face?
  Ah! why withhold from me thy caresses?

Samson. My fatal love I can ne'er destroy.
  From out my heart thou'lt ne'er be banish'd,
  Or happiness would all be vanish'd.
  In my ardent love is my joy!

Delilah. By my side why dost fear?
  Ah, why so faint-hearted?
  Is it doubt that seizeth thy heart?
  Thou the lord of my life ever art;
  Have all love's charms for thee departed?

(DALILA se rapproche de la gauche de le scène vers le portique de sa maison, et s'appuie rêveuse à un des piliers.)

Dalila. Se pourrait-il, que sur son cœur
  L'amour eut perdu sa puissance?
  La nuit est sombre et sans lueur
  Rien ne peut trahir sa présence.

  Helas! Il ne vient pas!

(SAMSON arrive par la droit; il semble emu, troublé, hésitant; il regarde autour de lui. La nuit s'assombrit de plus en plus.)

SCENE III.

(Éclairs lointains.)

Samson. En ces lieux, malgré moi, m'ont ramené mes pas
  Je voudrais fuir, hélas. et ne puis pas!
  Je maudis mon amour et pourtant j'aime encore,
  Fuyons, fuyons ces lieux que ma faiblesse adore!

Dalila.
  (S'élance vers SAMSON.)
  C'est toi!
  C'est toi, mon bien aimé!
  J'attendais ta présence!
  J'oubie, en te voyant,
  Des heures de souffrance!
  Salut! salut! ô mon doux maitre!

Samson. Arrètes ces transports!
  Je ne puis t'écouter sans honte et sans remords!

Dalila. Samson! ô toi! mon bien aimé,
  Pourquoi, repousser ma tendresse?
  Pour-quoi, de mon front parfumé,
  Pour-quoi détourner tes caresses?

Samson. Tu fus toujours chère à mon cœur,
  Et tu n'en peux être bannie!
  J'aurais voulu donner ma vie
  A l'amour qui fit mon bonheur!

Dalila. Près de moi, pres de moi pour-quoi ces alarmes?
  Auraistu douté de mon cœur?
  N'estu pas mon maître et seigneur?
  L'amour at-il perdu ses charmes?

Samson. Alas! I'm pledged to my own God.
  To his will do I yield me gladly.
I'll tell thee a last sad farewell,
  And loose the tie that binds me madly.
I'll break the bond of our false love—
  Love that on Israel's freedom encroaches:
For the day of release is nigh,
  Our deliv'rance e'en now approaches.
Our blest Lord to his servant said,
  " I've chosen thee from out thy nation
To guide thy people unto me,
  To lead in working their salvation."

Delilah. What joy to my desolate heart,
  Though Israel's fate may be glorious?
From me would all gladness depart,
  Should thine own people be victorious.
By love is my reason dethroned,
  For lost the hope the soul possesses!
All vain thy promises to me;
  Like poison all thy fond caresses!

Samson. Ah! cease to wound my anguish'd heart!
  I but yield to the powers above thee!
Thy tears increase my bitter grief—
  Woe is me! woe is me! I love thee!

   (Lightning.)

Delilah. A god more despotic than thine
  By my own lips to thee is speaking.
'Tis the god of Love, that is mine;
  He brings the bliss all are seeking!
Recall I the joys that are past,
  When thou at my feet then wert kneeling,
Vowing to love me evermore!
  Now, alas! 'tis I who hath feeling!

Samson. Thou ungrateful! Thou darest accuse!
  Only thou alone do I cherish,
Or strike me, bolts from on high,
  Or let me in fierce flames now perish!

So mighty is my love for thee,
  I brave the God that reigns above me,
Though his vengeance may strike me down!
  Woe is me! woe is me! I love thee!

Samson. Hélas! esclave de mon Dieu,
  Je subis sa volonté sainte;
Il faut, par un dernier adieu,
  Rompre sans murmure et sans crainte
Le doux lien de notre amour,
  D'Israël renaît l'espérance!
Le Seigneur a marqué le jour
  Qui verra notre délivrance!
Il a dit à son serviteur:
  "Je t'ai choisi parmi tes frères,
Pour les guider vers le Seigneur
  Et mettre un terme à leurs miseres!"

Dalila. Qu'importe à mon cœur désolé
  Le sort d'Israël et sa gloire!
Pour moi le bonheur envolé
  Est le seul fruit de la victoire.
L'amour égarait ma raison
  Quand je coyais à tes promesses,
Et je n'ai bu que le poison
  En m'enivrant de tes caresses!

Samson. Ah! ces se d'affliger mon cœur!
  Je subis une loi suprême,
Tes pleurs ravient ma douleur!
  Dalila! Dalila! Je t'aime!

   (Éclairs lointains.)

Dalila. Un dieu plus puissant que le tien,
  Ami, te parle par ma bouche;
C'est le dieu d'amour, c'est le mien!
  Et, si ce souvenir te touche,
Rapelle à ton cœur beaux jours
  Passés aux genoux d'une amante
Que tu devais aimer toujours,
  Et qui seule, hélas! est constante!

Samson. Insensée! oser m'accuser!
  Quand pour toi tout parle à mon âme!
Oui! dût la foudre m'écraser!
  Dussé je perir de sa flamme!

   (Éclairs plus rapprochés.)

Pour toi si grand est mon amour,
  Que j'ose aimer malgré Dieu même!
Oui! dussé-je en mourir un jour,
  Dalila! Dalila! je t'aime!

My heart at thy dear voice Doth un-fold and re-joice, Like a flower when
Mon cœur d'ouvre à ta voix Com-me s'ou-vrent les fleurs, Aux bai-sers

cres . . . . . cen . . . . . do.

dawn is smil-ing.   Thou canst my weep-ing stay,   My sad-ness charm a-
de l'au-ro-re!   *Mais, ô mon bien ai mé*   *Pom mieux se-cher mes*

dim.   *mf*

way   With thy tones so be-guil-ing   Then, oh! to me but say Thou re-
pleurs   Aue ta voix par-le en-co-re!   *Dis mon, qu'à Da-li-la Tu re-*

mf   *stringendo.*

turn-est   for aye!   Re-peat thy vows so ten-der,   Thy vows of the past,
vi-ns pour ja-nais,   Re-dis à ma ten-dres-se   Les ser-ments d'au-tre-fois,

cres.   *mf rit.*

That I dreamed e'er would last! . . . .   Ah! . . . once more . . . thy
Ces ser-ments que j'ai-mais! . . . .   *Ah! . . . ré-ponds . . . a*

vows . . so ten-der,   And . . thy   heart, . . and thy heart . . . sur
ma . . . ten-dres-se,   Ver . . -se-moi, . . Ver-se-moi, . . l'i

cres. senza accel.   *piu cres.*

ren-der,   Once more   thy vows so ten-der,   Once more   thy vows so ten-der,
vres-se!   Ré-ponds   à   ma ten-dres-se,   Ré-ponds   à   ma-ten-dres-se!

f   *dim.*

Ah! . . . . . and thy heart, ... and thy   heart . . . sur-ren-der!
Ah! . . . . . ver-se moi, ... ver-se   moi . . . . l'i-vres-se!

SAMSON.
p   *Andantino.*

Woe is me!   woe is me!   I . . love . .   thee!
Da-li-la!   *Da-li-la!*   *Je . . t'ai . .   me.*

DELILAH.

As   when   a field of grain,   Like the waves on the   main,   In the breeze is
Ain-si   qu'on voit des blés   Les é-pis on-du-ler   Sous la bri-

sway - ing, bound - ing,   So all my heart is swayed,   In deep - est chords are played,
se lé - gè - re,   Ain - si fré - mit mon cœur,   Prêt à se con - so - ler.

rinf.

When thy voice   is re - sound - ing.   The ar - row in its flight, Though so
A ta voix qui m'est chè - re!   La flè - che est moins ra - pide À por -

soon gone from sight, Moves more slow - ly than I,   If to thee I may fly!
ter le tré - pes,   Que ne l'est tou a - mau - te A vo - ler dans tes bras,

cres.   *un peu plus lent.*

Yes, If to thee I   fly. . . . .   Ah! . . . once more . . . thy
A vo - ler dans tes bras. . . . .   Ah! . . ré - ponds . . . à

DELILAH.

vows . . so ten - der,   And . . . . thy heart . . . . and thy
ma ten - dres - se,   Ver - se - moi, ... ver - se

SAMSON.

Fond - ly   my kiss   Each tear of thine re - press - es   I . . . in thy
Par mes bai - sers   Je veux sé - cher tes lar - mes   Et . . . de tou

heart . . . . . sur - ren - - der,   Once more   thy vows so
moi . . . . . . lé - dres - - se!   Re - ponds   à ma ten -

heart . . . . . . Joy re - store with ca - ress - - es
cœur . . . . É - loi - gner les a - lar - - mes,

ten - der,   Once more thy vows so ten - - der,
dres - se,   Ré - ponds à ma ten - dres - - se,

Though smite the God a - bove thee   Though smite the God a -
Je veux sé - cher tes lar - mes,   Je veux sé - cher tes

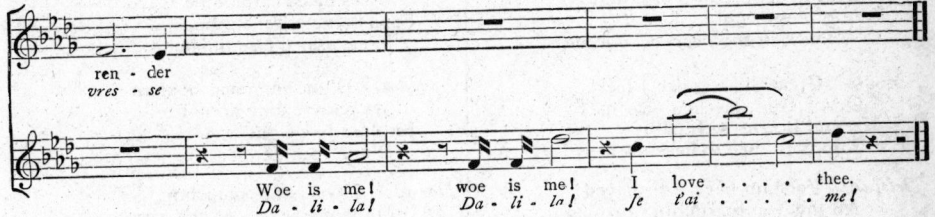

(Lightning and violent crash of thunder.)

Delilah. But no! I speak in vain!
    Delilah is destraught,
    Thou my sad heart bereaving
    Strik'st me down in despair!
    Thou dost my soul ensnare,
    With trait'rous vows deceiving!

Samson. Now to thee in worship I bow,
    Forgetting my people and vow!
    Forgetting my God and his dower,
    The seal that mark'd me with his power!

Delilah. Alas! thou forgettest my love!
    I envy him whom I have hated,
    Thy God who hath given thee birth,
    To whom thou thy life consecrated.
    The vow that hath chained thee to him,
    Making thee in battle victorious,
    Oh, give to me and my poor heart!
    Thy love's reward will then be glorious!

Samson. Delilah, what wouldst thou with me?
    Doubtest thou my mad love for thee?

Delilah. If over thy heart I'm presiding,
    I'd prove it a truth on this day.
    A ray of thy love then betray
In secrets dark to me confiding.

(Thunder and lightning nearer.)

Samson. Alas! what doth matter to thee
    Sacred ties, or power in me vested?
    That great secret closed in my heart—

(Éclairs.)
(Violent coup de tonnerre.)

Dalila. Mais! non! que disje, hélas!
    La triste Dalila doute de tes paroles!
    Egarant ma raison, tu me trompas déja
    Par des serments frivoles!

Samson. Quand pour toi j'ose oublier Dieu,
    Sa gloire, mon peuple et mon vœu!
    Ce Dieu qu marqua ma naissance
    Du sceau divin de sa puissance!

Dalila. Eh bien! connais donc mon amour!
    C'est ton Dieu même que j'envie!
    Ce Dieu qui te donna le jour,
    Ce Dieu qui consacra ta vie!
    Le vœu qui t'enchaîne à ce Dieu
    Et qui fait ton bras redoutable,
    A mon amour faisen l'aveu,
    Chasse le doute qui m'accable!

Samson. Dalila! que veux tu de moi?
    Crains que je ne doute de toi!

Dalila. Si j'ai conservé ma puissance,
    Je veux l'essayer en ce jour!
    Je veux éprouver ton amour,
    En réclamant ta confiance!

(Eclairs et tonnerre plu en plus rapprochés.)

Samson. Hélas! qu'importe à ton bonheur
    Le lien sacré qui m'enchaîne?
    Ce secret que garde mon cœur—

Delilah. Open thy heart, and joy to me impart—

Samson. By thy vain might ne'er can be wrested!

Delilah. Oh, vain all my sad strife!
In vain thy love surrounds me,
If I can ne'er divine
That dark secret that wounds me.
When thy thoughts I would share
Dost thou dare to refuse me?
And pitiless, cold,
Wouldst in thy heart accuse me?

Samson. Great the anguish I feel!
O, my God, be thou near me!
My soul is rent with pain—
I implore thee to hear me!

Delilah. For him have I displayed
All my beauty, nothing reaping!
To me only is left
Sorrow and anguish'd weeping!

Samson. All powerful God!
Oh, hear me, thou, my Lord!

Delilah. To try to speak farewell
Is vain; my soul defieth!
Samson, fly! fly from here
Where thine own love now dieth!

Samson. Leave thou me!

Delilah. Tell me, then!

Samson. Ask me not!

Delilah. Tell to me the secret
For which my heart now dieth!

Samson. O tempest, on these heights
Let loose, on us descending,
All the wrath of the Lord
Our guilty souls now rending!

Delilah. I will brave all for thee!
Come!

Samson. No!

Delilah. Come!

Samson. Leave thou me!

Delilah. Care I naught what betide me!

Samson. I can never decide me!
Voice divine! 'Tis thy knell!

Dalila. Par cet aveu soulage ma doleur.

Samson. Pour le ravir ta force est vaine!

Dalila. Oui! vain est mon pouvoir,
Car vaine est ta tendresse!
Quand je veux le savoir,
Ce secret qui me blesse,
Dont je veux la moitié,
O sestu, dans ton âme
Sans honte et sans pitié,
M'accuser d'être inflàme!

Samson. D'une immense douleur
Ma pauvre âme accablée
Implore le Seigneur
D'une voix désolée!

Dalila. J'avais paré pour lui
Ma jeunesse et mes charmes!
Je n'ai plus au jour d'hui
Qu'à répandre des larmes!

Samson. Dieu tout-puissant, j'invoque ton appui!

Dalila. Pour ces derniers adieux
Ma voix est impuissante!
Fuis! Samson, fuis ces lieux
Où mourra ton amante!

Samson. Laisse moi!

Dalila. Ton secret!

Samson. Je ne puis!

Dalila. Ton secret? ce secret qui cause mes alarmes!

Samson. L'orage sur ces monts
Déchaîne sa colère!
Le Seigneur sur nos fronts
Fait gronder son tonnerre!

Dalila. Je le brave avec toi! Viens?

Samson. Non!

Dalila. Viens!

Samson. Laisse Mois!

Dalila. Que m'importe la foudre!

Samson. Je ne puis m'y résoudre—
C'est la voix de mon Dieu!

Delilah. Coward! Thou loveless heart,
 I despise thee! Farewell!

(Thunder and lightning.)
(DELILAH hastens to her house; the storm breaks furiously. SAMSON raises his arms, as if to call upon God; then hastily follows DELILAH — hesitates, but finally enters the dwelling.)
(Philistine soldiers are seen at right, approaching the house.)
(Music of the scene continues. Finally a violent crash of thunder. DELILAH re-appears, on the terrace.)

Delilah. Philistines! your aid!

Samson.
(Within.)
I am betrayed!

(The soldiers rush into DELILAH's house.)
(Curtain.)

Dalila   Lâche! cœur sans amour!
 Je te méprise! Adieu!

(Eclairs et tonnerre.)
(DALILA court vers sa demeure ; l'orage est dans toute sa feurer. SAMSON, levant les bras au ciel, semble invoquer Dieu. Il s'élance à la suite DALILA, hésite, et entre enfin dans sa demeure.)
(Par la droite arrivent des soldats Philistins, qui s'approchent de la demeure.)
(Violent coup de tonnerre.)
(DALILA paraissant à sa feuêtre.)

Dalila. A moi! Philistins! à moi!

Samson. Trahison!

(Les soldats se précipitent dans la demeure de Dalila.)
(Rideau.)

ACT III.

(A prison at Gaza. SAMSON, in chains, blinded and shorn, is grinding at a mill.)
(Chorus of Hebrew captives behind the scenes.)

Samson. Sore my distress, alas! my guilt and
 anguish!
 Have pity, Lord, in misery I languish.
Away from thy most righteous laws I've
 gone,
And now is thy protecting hand withdrawn.
I offer thee a heart that is broken ;
Of my most bitter repentance the token.
From me all light they have taken away.
To gall is turn'd ev'ry hour of day.

Chorus. Ah! why hast thou, Samson, false
 pledges taken?

Samson. Behold! Israel now in chains!
 God's wrath from high heaven descendeth,
 And our hearts, all deserted, rendeth.
 Not e'en a ray of hope remains.
 To our grief, O gracious Sov'reign,
 awaken!
 Deign thou to hear when we cry unto thee!
 Thine ire appeasing, thy grace we would
 see.
 Have pity! let not our tribe be forsaken!

ACTE III.

(La prison de Gaza. SAMSON enchaine avengle, les cheveux coupes tourne la meule. Dans la coulisse, chœur des Hebreux captifs.)

Samson. Vois ma misère, hélas! vois ma dé-
 tresse!
 Pitié, Seigneur! pitié pour ma faiblesse!
J'ai détourné mes pas de ton chemin :
Bientôt de moi tu retiras ta main.
Je t'offre, ô Dieu, ma pauvre âme brisée!
Je ne suis plus qu'un objet de risée!
Ils m'ont ravi la lumière du ciel ;
Ils m'ont versé l'amertume et le fiel!

Chœur. Samson, qu'astu fait de tes frères?

Samson. Hélas! Israël dans les fers,
 Du ciel allirant la vengeance,
 A perdu jusqu'à l'espérance
 Par tous les maux qu'il a soufferts!
 Que nos tribus tes jeux trouvent grâce!
 Daigne à ton peuple épargner la douler!
 Apaise toi devant leurs maux, Seigneur!
 Toi, dont jamais la pitié ne se lasse!

Chorus.   Be thou once again at our side
   In danger's strife, and combat guide!
Why, Samson, hast false pledges taken,
Or let our blest tribe be forsaken?

Samson.   Brothers! your sad strains, like a
   dart
   Penetrate through the night that is o'er me.
Bring not thus all my guilt before me,
   Or rend still more my anguished heart!
My life in sacrifice I offer, O God, thy holy
   wrath to stay;
Turn not thy face from Israel away!

Chorus.   He sold us for a woman's charms,
   With only love's false pleasure reaping!
Thou, Manoah's son, what wilt thou do
   With blood that's shed and bitter weep-
   ing?

Samson.   Take this atonement that I proffer!
   At thy feet I fall in despair,
But I bless the hand that's oppressing.
Gracious Lord, give my tribe thy blessing —
   My gloomy fate let them not share!

Chorus.   Ah! why hast thou false pledges
   taken?

(The Philistines enter the prison and take SAMSON out.
Change of scene.)

SCENE II.

(Interior of the Temple of Dagon. Statue of the idol;
altars, etc. Two marble pillars which seem to support the
building.)
(The HIGH PRIEST stands surrounded by the chief
Philistines. DELILAH appears, followed by young women
bearing wine-cups in their hands. Day is dawning; a
great throng is in the Temple.)

Chorus.   Dawn now on the hill-tops sheds rosy
   light,
   And before its gleam stars vanish from
   sight.
We'll rejoice although now doth come the
   morning,
   And day is dawning.
Sorrows of the heart vanish with the night.

Fast before the odorous morning breeze,
Like a fleecy veil gloomy darkness flees.
In the east the sun its clear face is showing,
In splendor's might, over all the land its
   bright rays are glowing.

(Dance.)

Chœur.   Dieu nous confiait à ton bras
   Pour nous guider dans les combats;
Samson! qu'astu fait de tes frères?

Samson.   Frères! votre chant douloureux
   Pénétrant dans ma nuit profonde,
D'une angoisse mortelle inonde
   Mon cœur coupable et malheureux!
Dieu! prends ma vie en sacrifice
Pour satisfaire ton courroux.
D'Israël détourne tes coups,
Et je proclame ta justice!

Chœur.   Pour une femme il nous vendait,
   De Dalila payant les charmes.
Fils de Manoah, qu'astu fait
   De notre sang et de nos larmes?

Samson.   A tes pieds brisé, mais soumis,
   Je bénis la main qui me frappe.
Fais, Seigneur, que ton peuple échappe
   A la fureur des enemis!

Chœur.   Samson! qu'astu fait de tes frères?
   Qu'astu fait du Dieu de tes pères?

(Les Philistins entrent dans la prison. Ils entraînen'
SAMSON. Changement.)

SCENE II.

(Interieur du Temple de Dagon. Statue du Dieu.
Table des sacrifices. Au milieu du sanctuaire deux
colonnes de marbre semblant supporter l'edifice.)
(La GRANDE PRÊTRE de Dagon entouré des princes
Philistins. DALILA, suivie des jeunes femmes Philistins,
couronnées de fleurs, des côupes à la main. Une foule de
peuple remplit le Temple. Le jour se lève.)

Chœur.   L'aube qui blanchit déjà les coteaux,
   D'une nuit si belle étaint les flambeaux;
Prolongeons la fête, et malgré l'aurore,
   Aimons encore;
L'amour verse au cœur l'oubli de nos maux.

Au vent du matin, l'ombre de la nuit
Comme un léger voile à l'horizon fuit.
L'orient s'empourpre, et sur les montagnes
   Le soleil luit,
Dardant ses rayons au sein des campagnes,
   Au sein des campagnes.

(Danse.)

SCENE III.

(SAMSON enters,—led by a child.)

High Priest. All hail! the judge of Israel,
Who, by his presence, joy to our festival
lendeth!
Hail to thee! whom Delilah in love ever
tendeth!
The cup we'll fill high with hydromel!
We'll let him drink to her glory and power,
And on her name his praises shower.

Chorus. We'll drink, Samson, we'll drink
with thee!
Drink, and leave care unto the morrow!
Drink to Delilah with all joy,
For drowneth the cup every sorrow.

Samson.
(Aside.)
All my soul is sad unto death.
At thy throne thy servant kneeleth!
Thy holy will thy law revealeth.
Here thou wilt receive my last breath!

Delilah.
(Approaching SAMSON with a wine-cup in her hand.)
Give me thy hand, come by my side,
I will thy uncertain footsteps guide
As, upon that day, soon ended,
To the vale our steps we wended,
And thou, free from love's alarms,
Didst twine around me thine arms.
Thou didst ascend lofty mountains,
Only to fly unto me,
And I deserted companions
To be alone with thee.
Thy past love thy heart confesses.
Dost recal! thy fond caresses?
Thy passion further'd my plan.
My vengeance thy love impelling;
I tore thy secret from thee,
In my hate the knowledge selling!
Thou, all trustful, didst confide
In her who doth now enchain thee!
Yes, Delilah's vengeance comes,
And her god, her people, now arraign
thee!

Chorus. On this day her vengeance comes,
Her God, her people, arraign thee!

Samson.
(Aside.)
When thou didst speak, I heard thee not,
Transgressing law when well did I know
it.
Alas! thy servant love profaned —
On this false woman did bestow it!

SCENE III.

(SAMSON — conduit par un enfant.)

Le Grand Prêtre. Salut! Salut au juge
d'Israël,
Qui vient par sa presence égayer notre fête!
Dalila! par tes soins qu'une coupe soit
prête;
Verse à ton amant l'hydrome!!
Il videre sa coupe en chantant sa maitresse
Et sa puissance enchanteresse!

Chœur. Samson! nous buvons avec toi!
A Dalila ta souveraine!
Vide la coupe sans effroi:
L'ivresse dissipe la peine.

Samson.
(À part.)
L'ame triste jusqu'a la mort,
Devant toi, Seigneur, je m'incline;
Que par ta volonté divine
Ici s'accomplisse mon sort!

Dalila.
(S'approchant de SAMSON une coupe à la main.)
Laisse moi prendre ta main
Et te montrer le chemin,
Comme dans la sombre allée
Qui conduit à la vallée,
Le jour où suivant mes pas
Tu m'enlacais de tes bras!
Tu gravissais les montagnes
Pour arriver jusqu'à moi,
Et je fuyais mes compagnes
Pour être seule avec toi.
Souviens-toi de nos ivresses!
Souviens-toi de mes caresses!
L'amour servait mon projet!
Pour assouvir ma vengeance
Je t'arrachai ton secret:
Je l'avais vendu d'avance!
Tu croyais à cet amour,
C'est lui qui riva ta chaine!
Dalila venge en ce jour
Son dieu, son peuple et sa haine!

Chœur. Dalila venge en ce jour
Son dieu, son peuple, et sa haine!

Samson.
(À part.)
Quand tu parlais, je restais sourd;
Et dans le trouble de mon âme,
Hélas! j'ai profané l'amour,
En le donnant à cette femme.

High Priest. Oh, cease thy strain, and turn
    to her,
  And tell again the oft-told story.
Rehearse thy love in sweetest strain,
  Softly chant her praises and glory!
Let thy Jehovah show his might,
  And in his mercy cure thy blindness.
I will adore thy boasted god,
  If thus he will show thee his kindness!
But if he fail in this extreme,
  His mercy on thee now to shower,
He merits but hatred and scorn —
  I laugh at all his might and power!

Samson. Ah! dost thou permit this, my God?
  This false priest in revenge engaging,
  Who in his fury and his raging
  Blasphemes e'en thy name, O, my Lord?
To avenge thee, my Father glorious,
  Grant me but one proof of thy might,
  For a moment give back my sight!
Hear thou my cry — make me victorious!

Chorus. Ah! ah! ah! Thy rage doth vain
    appear!
Thou canst not rouse our fear,
E'en though thy words are frightful,
  For never wilt thou see!
Well guarded then be!
Thine anger is delightful!
Ah! ah! ah!

High Priest. Thank thou Delilah, our gods
    upon high,
  Who shake Jehovah's weak throne in the
    sky!
We'll now consult the agents of Dagon;
  For Samson we'll pour wine from ev'ry
    flagon.

(DELILAH and HIGH PRIEST approach the table on
which are placed the sacred bowls. On the altar which is
ornamented with flowers, a fire burns. DELILAH and
HIGH PRIEST take up the bowls and pour the libation
upon the sacred flame, which flashes up, then disappears,
but again flames up at the third couplet of the invocation.)
(SAMSON stands in the centre of the scene, with the
child who led him. He is grief-striken, and appears to be
devoutly praying.)

High Priest.
          (To DELILAH.)
Glory forever more to Dagon the victorious,
Who inspired thy weak heart with his
    might so all-glorious!

          (To DAGON.)
O thou greatest of all the great,
  Who the heavens and earth hast created!
Ruler of gods as well as men,
  With thy spirit we'd be inflated!

Grand Prêtre. Allons, Samson, divertis nous,
En redisant à ton amante
  Les doux propos, les chants si doux
Dont la passion s'alimente.
Que Jéhovah compatissant
  A les yeux rende la lumière!
Je servirai ce Dieu puissant,
  S'il peut exaucer ta prière!
Mais incapable à servir,
  Ce Dieu, que tu nommes ton père,
Je puis l'outrager, le haïr,
  En me riant de sa colère!

Samson. Tu permets, ô Dieu d'Israël!
  Que ce prêtre imposteur outrage,
Dans sa fureur dans sa rage,
  Ton nom, à la face du ciel!
Que ne puis je venger ta gloire,
  Et par un prodige éclatant
  Retrouver pour un seul instant
Les yeux, la force et la victoire!

Chœur. Ha! ha! ha! Rions de sa fureur!
Dans ta rage impuissante, Samson, tu n'y
    vois pas!
Prends garde à tes pas! Samson!
  Sa colère est plaisante!
  Ha! ha! ha!

Grand Prêtre. Viens, Dalila, rendre grâce à
    nos dieux
  Qui font trembler Jéhovah dans les cieux!
Du grand Dagon consultons les auspices;
  Versons pour lui le vin des sacrifices.

(DALILA, et le GRAND PRÊTRE se dirigent vers ta table
des sacrifices, sur laguelle se trouvent les coupes sacrées.
Un feu brûle sur l'autel qui est orné des fleurs. DALILA
et le GRAND PRÊTRE, prenant les coupes, font une libation
sur le feu sacré qui s'active, puis disparaît, pour reparaître
au 3e couplet de l'invocation.)
(SAMSON est resté au milieu de la scène, ayant près de
lui l'enfant qui le conduit; il est accablé par la doleur et
semble prier.)

Grand Prêtre. Gloire à Dagon vainqueur!
  Il aidait ta faiblesse,
Inspirant à ton cœur
  Et la force et l'adresse.

O toi! le plus grand entre tous!
  Toi qui fis la terre où nous sommes,
Qui ton esprit soit avec nous,
  O maître des dieux et des hommes!

Delilah. Glory for evermore
    To Dagon the victorious,
Who inspired my weak heart
    With his might so all-glorious!
O thou greatest of all the great,
    Who the heavens and earth hast created!
Ruler of gods as well as men,
    With thy spirit we'd be inflated!

Dalila. Gloire à Dagon vainqueur!
    Il aidait ma faiblesse,
Inspirant a mon cœur
    Et la force et l'adresse.
O toi! le plus grand entre tous!
    Toi qui fis la terre où nos sommes,
Que ton esprit soit avec nous,
    O maître des dieux et des hommes!

Chorus. Mark with thy blessing our flock and field;
    Make thou our vineyards with richness yield!
Give, in our harvest, good unalloyed,
For all our substance foes have destroyed!

Chœur. Marque d'un signe
    Nos longs troupeaux;
Mûris la vigne
    Sur nos coteaux;
Rends à la plaine
    Notre moisson
Que, dans sa haine,
    Brûla Samson!

Delilah and High Priest. Upon thine altar blest
    A victim's blood we offer;
To expiate our sins
    Our gifts in love we proffer.
May thy priests who all humbly kneel,
    See thy face so divinely lighted;
E'en though we are not so clear-sighted,
    To their eyes our future reveal!

Dalila et Grand Prêtre. Recois sur nos auteis
    Le sang de nos victimes,
Que t'offrent des mortels
    Pour expier leurs crimes.
Aux yeux de tes prêtres divins,
    Pouvant seuls contempler ta face,
Montre l'avenir qui se cache
    Aux regards des autres humains!

Chorus. O list, our god, when thus we cry!
    May thy blest aid be ever nigh!
Thou art so mighty; gird us with pow'r,
Make us victorious in combat's hour!

Chœur. Dieu, sois propice
    A nos destins!
Que ta justice
    Aux Philistins
Donne la gloire
    Dans les combats;
Que la victoire
    Suive nos pas!

Delilah and High Priest. Dagon's might surprising!
Flames anew are rising
    From the ashes of the sacred altar!
God doth make the flames upward tower.
Thus he shows his power.
        Ah!
From the ashes of the sacred altar!
God doth make the flames upward tower.
    Thus he shows his power.
        Bless his name!

Dalila et Grand Prêtre. Dagon se révèle!
    La flamme nouvelle
Sur l'autel
    Renaît de la cendre:
L'immortel
    Pour nous va descendre!
C'est le dieu
    Qui par sa présence
Montre sa puissance!
        Ah!
L'immortel, pour nous va descendre!
C'est le dieu qui par sa presence
Montre sa puissance.
    En ce lieu.
Sur l'autel, renaît de la cendre!
    Dagon se révèle!

Chorus. Let our hearts with fear never falter!
    Dagon's might surprising!
Ah! God doth make the flames upward tower;
Thus he shows his power,
    In this flame.

Chœur. C'est le dieu qui par sa présence
Montre sa puissance
    En ce lieu.

High Priest.

    (To SAMSON.)

O may our fate be all propitious!
  Come, Samson, come, our gods to please!
  And to Dagon mighty and direful
    Present thine off'ring on thy knees!

    (To the child.)

Out to the middle of the temple guide him,
That all beholding may in scorn deride him!

Samson. Inspire me with thy might,
    With me, O Lord, abide!
  On to the marble pillars,
    My child, my footsteps guide.

(The child leads Samson between the two pillars.)

Chorus. Dagon's might surprising!
  Flames anew are rising!
  From the ashes of the sacred altar
  God doth make the flames upward tower:
  Thus he shows his power.
    Bless his name!
  O list, our God, when thus we cry!
  May thy blest aid be ever nigh!
  Thou art so mighty! Gird us with pow'r!
  Make us victorious in combat's hour!
    Before thee Israel is all bereft of power!
  Guide thou our arm; gird us with pow'r.
  Make us victorious; give us vict'ry in com-
    bat's hour!
  May this cursed tribe in this hour
  Feel thy direful anger and pow'r.
    O list, our god, etc.
      Glory! glory!

(SAMSON has placed himself between the pillars and attempts to remove them.)

Samson. Lord, thy servant remember now!
    Thou mad'st him blind thy just wrath
      showing.
  For one sole moment make him strong,
  His power of old on him bestowing!
  To avenge me, O lend thy might!
  Let the foe be destroyed in thy sight!

    (The Temple falls.)
    (Cries and shrieks of the people.)

    (Curtain descends.)

Le Grand Prêtre.

    (A SAMSON.)

Pour que le sort soit favorable
  Allons, Samson, viens avec ous
  A Dagon, le dieu redoutable,
    Offrir ta coupe à deux genoux!

    (A l'enfant.)

Guidez ses pas vers le milieu du temple,
Pour que de loin le peuple le contemple.

Samson. Seigneur, inspire moi, ne m'aban-
    donne pas!
  Vers les piliers de marbre, enfant, guide
    mes pas!

    (L'enfant conduit Samson.)

Chœur. Dagon se révèle,
  La flamme nouvelle,
  Sur l'autel renaît de la cendre;
  C'est le dieu,
  Qui par sa presence
  Montre sa puissanee
    Ence lieu!
  Dieu, sois propice
    A nos destins!
  Que ta justice
    Aux Philistins
  Donne la gloire
    Dans les combats!
  Que la victoire
    Suive nos pas!
  Devant toi d'Israël
    Disparait l'insolence!
  Nos bras guidés par ton esprit
    Dans les combats.
  Ou par tes charmes.
    Ont vaincu ce peuple maudit,
  Bravant ta colère et tes armes
    A nos destins
  Dieu, sois propice, etc.
  Gloire à Dagon!
  Gloire à Dagon!

(SAMSON placé entre les deux pillars et cherchant à les ébranler.)

Samson. Souviens-toi de ton serviteur!
    Qu'ils ont privé de la lumière!
  Daigne pour un instant, Seigneur,
    Me rendre ma force première!
  Qu'avec toi je me venge, ô Dieu!
    En les écrasant en ce lieu!

    (Le Temple s'écroule au milieu des cris.)
      (Rideau.)

LAKMÉ

by

LEO DELIBES

THE STORY OF LAKMÉ

THE scene of Lakmé is laid in one of the large cities of India, and in its immediate vicinity, recently subdued and occupied by the English. The opening takes place in the grounds of Nilakantha, a Hindoo priest, whose premises it is considered criminal and worthy of death to profane. A small party of English ladies and officers of the British army find their way thither while strolling about for amusement. They force an entrance through the bamboo enclosure, and, while admiring the beauties of the place, come upon some beautiful jewels which have been laid aside for the moment by the daughter of the Brahmin proprietor. Realizing the impropriety of their presence, they turn to leave; but Gerald, one of the officers, and the lover of Ellen, daughter of the governor, wishing to make a sketch of the jewels for the benefit of his lady-love, remains behind for that purpose while the others depart. Upon reflection he decides to relinquish the idea of copying the form of the jewels, and in the moment of leaving is surprised by the sudden appearance of Lakmé just returning from a little excursion upon the neighboring stream. They are mutually struck by each other's presence, and, seemingly, a case of love at first sight is the result. Lakmé demands how and why he came there, and tells him of the death penalty which must follow such intrusion. Gerald expresses his admiration of Lakmé's beauty, and hastily departs, or conceals himself just as the priest-father returns to his home. Nilakantha notices the disturbance of his daughter, and observes the strange footsteps, and declares that the intruder must die if discovered. In the second act the scene is changed to the neighboring city, where a grand Brahminic festival and procession take place in honor of the gods and goddesses of India. Also an Indian bazaar, with its occupations and amusements. Many English residents are present, among them the party of the first act. Also the priest and his daughter disguised as penitents. Nilakantha orders Lakmé to sing, believing that she will be heard by the intruder upon his premises, and by his admiration of her beauty and voice will betray himself to his enemy's vengeance. The plan succeeds. Gerald is noted by pleasure he shows at again meeting with Lakmé. Nilakantha, convinced of his guilt, sends his daughter away and consults with his friends upon the manner in which he proposes to take vengeance upon the destroyer of his peace and the intruder upon the sanctity of his home. Lakmé, disobeying the commands of her father, remains at hand, and when, shortly afterwards, Gerald is stricken down by the dagger of Nilakantha, she comes forward with her faithful slave, Hadji, and orders him to be carried to a hut concealed in the forest, where, his wound found to be not mortal, she cares for him and restores him to life and strength by the juices of certain plants whose medicinal properties are well known to the Hindoos. There as he recovers, his passion for her increases, and all else, including his former love, seems forgotten. A chorus of voices is heard passing their retreat, which comes from a procession of young lovers on their way to drink the waters of a sacred fountain, said to have the property of making unions lasting. Gerald wishes to drink of this water. Lakmé obtains it, and is about to present it to him, when she perceives that a change has come over him during her absence. Meanwhile Frederic has made diligent search for his friend, and at last finds him alone in the hut. He endeavors to recall him to his duties by telling him that his regiment is ordered off at once to suppress an outbreak among the Hindoos. Gerald promises to be at his post in time, but begs a little delay, that he may once more see and bid adieu to Lakmé. Upon receiving this promise, Frederic leaves him at the moment of Lakmé's return with the sacred water. As she offers it to Gerald the fifes and drums of his regiment, just leaving for the seat of the rebellion, are heard in the distance. The sound, which recalls him to love and duty, transforms him, and he turns away from the proffered draught. Lakmé is shocked by the sudden change in him, which she but too well knows how to account for. In her heart-breaking despair she gathers and eats some flowers of the deadly poisonous *datura stramonium*, from the effects of which she dies in his arms just as her father and his friends arrive on the scene.

LAKMÉ

ACT I

A well-shaded garden, where flourish and intermingle the flowers of India. In the back-ground, near a little river, stands a building of modest proportions, half concealed by the trees, a figure of Lotus over the door; and near by, a statue of Ganesá, the God of Wisdom, an idol with the head of an elephant, give this mysterious abode the appearance of a sanctuary. The garden is enclosed by a light fence of bamboo. Time, daybreak.

(Hadji, Malliká, Nilakantha; then Hindoos, men and women. Hadji and Malliká come to open the garden gate to the Hindoos, who enter reflectively.)

PRAYER AND CHORUS
Here at the usual moment.
When the plain, perfume-freighted,
By the dawn's flame lighted,
Doth greet the new-born day,
Let our prayers rise united,
That the anger of Brahma
May from us pass away.

Nilakantha.
(Coming from his dwelling.)
Thrice blessed may you be,
Who faithful homage render
To heaven's high priest in me,
Reviled, scoffed at, and outraged!
Of our base victors, the sway
We'll weary out, sure, though slowly;
They have driven our gods away
From the ancient temples holy.
But Brahma o'er their heads
His vengeance has suspended;
When that explodes and spreads,
Our bondage will be ended.
In my dwelling here, to-day,
I saw God's power displaying.
Up to him I soared away,
While I heard my daughter praying.
(In the wing.)

Lakmé. O Dourga fair, O Shiva great!
Mighty Ganesá, who Brahma did create.
(Hindoos kneeling.)
O Dourga fair, O goddess great!
(Lakmé enters and joins in the prayer.)
Wise Ganesá protect our state.
O Shiva pale, thy wrath abate!
God's wise and great, that did Brahma
create.

Nilakantha.
(To Hindoos.)
Go, now, in peace;
But as you leave, repeat
Your devout morning prayer.
May God guide your feet.
(All now depart except Nilakantha, Lakmé, and the two servitors.)

ACTE PREMIERE

(Un jardin très ombragé où croissent et s'entremêlent toutes des fleurs de l'Inde. Au fond, une maison peu élévée, à demi chachée par es arbres. L'image du Lotus sur la porte d'entrée et plus loin une statue de Ganeça, idole à tête d'éléphant, dieu de la sagesse, donnent à cette mystérieuse habitation l'aspect d'un sanctuaire. Au fond, le commencement d'un petit cours d'eau qui se perd dans la verdure. — Le jardin est entouré d'une frêle clôture en bambous. — C'est le lever du jour.)

(Hadji, Mallika, Nilakantha, puis Hindous, hommes et femmes.)

(Au lever du rideau, Hadji et Mallika vont ouvrir la porte du jardin à des Hindous, hommes et femmes, qui entrent avec recueillement.)

Choeur. A l'heure accoutumée.
Quand la plaine embaumée
Par l'aurore enflammée,
Fête le jour naissant,
Unissons nos prières,
Pour calmer les colères
De Brahma menaçant.

Nilakantha.
(Sortant de sa demeure.)
Soyez trois fois bénis, vous qui rendez hommage
Au prêtre abandonné qu'on raille et qu'on outrage.
De nos vainqueurs odieux
Nous lasserons les colères;
Ils ont pu chasser nos dieux
De leurs temples séculaires!
Mais, sur leurs têtes, Brahma
A suspendu sa vengeance,
Et, quand elle éclatera,
Ce sera la délivrance,
Dans ma retraite, aujourd'hui
La puissance de Dieu brille,
Je le vois, je monte à lui
Quand j'entends prier ma fille.

Lakmé.
(A ce moment, on entend la voix de Lakmé, dans la demeure du brahmane. Tous les Hindous se prosternent.)
Blanche Dourga,
Pâle Siva!
Puissant Ganeça!
O vous, que créa Brahma!
Apaisez-vous,
Protégez-nous!
(A la fin du chant sacré, Lakmé a paru sur le seuil de la demeure du brahmane et mêle sa prière à celles des Hindous.)

Nilakantha.
(Aux Hindous.)
Allez en paix, redites, en partant,
La prière au matin, allez, Dieu vous entend!
(Toute le monde sort, à l'exception du brahmane, de Lakmé et de ses deux serviteurs.)

Nilakantha.
              (Tenderly.)
    Lakmé! 't is you who here watch o'er us!
    And if I dare to brave the hostile ranks
        before us,
    Of the triumphant enemy;
    'T is that God pitying heeds
    Thy childlike purity.

Lakmé.   When Brahma great, in pity tender,
    Bruising flowers on his way,
      Made earth and sky,
      He let their honey lie,
    And from that hope did render!

Nila.   I now must leave you for a while.

Lakmé.   What? so soon?

Nila.   Be fearless,
      In that pagoda peerless
      That's still allowed to stand,
      Some are waiting my command.
    The festival tomorrow calls me.
        (To the servants.)
    Stay you here with Lakmé.

Hadji.   Together we'll watch o'er her.

Mall.   Beside her we will stay.

Nila.   I shall back find my way
    Before the close of day.
        (Ensemble.)

Nila.   Kind heaven will guard and keep me.
    And lead me by the hand,
    Cnd drive all foes away
    That in my path may stand.

Lakmé. Mall. Hadji.
    May heaven guard and keep you,
    And lead me/you by the hand,
    And drive all foes away
    That in my/your path may stand.

(Nilakantha goes out followed to the door by the others. Hadji re-enters the house.)

Lakmé.
(Taking off some jewels and laying them on stone table)
    Come, Malliká, the flowering vines
      Their shadows now are throwing
    Along the sacred stream,
      That calmly here is flowing;
    Enlivened by the songs of birds amid the
      pines.

Mall.   O mistress, dear! 't is now—
      When I behold you smiling,
      In this blest hour, no cares beguiling,
    That your oft-closed heart I may read.
      Lakmé!

Nilakantha.
    Lakmé, c'est toi qui nous protèges,
    Et si je puis braver les haines sacrilèges
    De l'ennemi triomphant
    C'est que Dieu prend pitié de ta candeur
      d'enfant.

Lakmé.   Lorsque Brahma, dans sa clémence,
    En broyant une fleur, fit la terre et le ciel,
    Il y laissa le miel,
    Et ce fut l'espérance.

Nilakantha.
    Il faut que je te quitte à l'instant.

Lakmé.   Quoi déjà?

Nilakantha.
    Sois sans crainte!
    Dans la pagode sainte,
    Qui reste encor debout à la ville ou m'attend,
    La fête de demain m'appelle.
        (Aux serviteurs.)
    Restez prèz de Lakmé!

Hadji.   Nous veillerons sur elle!

Mall.   Nous veillerons tous deux!

Nilakantha.
    Je serai de retour
    Avant la fin du jour!

Nilakantha.
    Que le ciel me protège,
    Me guide par la main,
    Chasse le sacrilège
    Au loin de mon chemin!

Lakmé, Hadji, Mallika.
    Que le ciel te protège,
    Te guide par la main,
    Chasse tout sacrilège
    Au loin de ton chemin!

(Nilakantha s'éloigne accompagné jusqu'à la porte par Lakmé et ses deux serviteurs. Hadji rentre dans la maison.)

Lakmé.
(Après s'être dèbarrassèe de quelques bijoux qu'elle a posés sur une table en pierre.)
    Viens, Mallika, les lianes en fleurs
    Jettent déjà leur ombre
    Sur le ruisseau sacre qui coule, calme et
      sombre,
    Eveillé par le chant des oiseaux tapageurs.

Mall.   Oh, maîtresse, c'est l'heure où je te vois
      sourire,
    L'heure bénie où je puis lire,
    Dans le cœur toujours fermé
    De Lakmé!

light . . . . ly, Reach we the steeps Where the
lan . . . te, Ga gnons le bord. Où l'a

light . . . . ly, We'll reach soon the steeps Where the foun-tain sleeps.
lan . . . . . te, Viens gagnous le bord Où la source dort

poco rall.

birds war-ble, war-ble, the birds spright - - - ly.
seau chante, l'oi-seau, l'oi-seau, chan . . . te.

poco rall.

Where war-ble the birds spright - - - ly.
Et l'oi-sean, l'oiseau chan . . . . te.

a tempo. pp

'Neath . . . . the dome, flowers u - nite, Come and join . . .
Dô . . . . me é-pais, blanc . . . . jas-min Nous ap-pel

a tempo. pp

'Neath the leaf-y dome, Where the jas-mine white, Come and join . . .
Sous le dôme é-pais, Sous le blanc jas-min, Ah! des-cen . . . .

rall.

. . . . . we their meet - - ing!
lent en - sem - ble!

rall.

. . . . we their meet - - ing!
dans en - scm - - ble!

Un peu plus anime.
LAKME.

But, why my heart's with swift ter-ror in-vest-ed, Doth not yet ap-pear, When my
Mais, je ne sais quelle crainte su-bi-te S'empare de moi, Quand mon

fa-ther 'lone goes to your ci-ty de-test-ed, I trem-ble, I trem-ble with
pè-re va scul à leur ville mau-di-te, Je trem-ble, je trem-ble d'ef-

MALLIKA.

fear. May the god, Ga-ne-sa, keep him from dan-gers, Till he ar-rives at the pool just in
frait Pour quelle Dieu Ganéça le protè ac. Jusqu'à l'étang où s'ébattent joy-

wave - - lets shim-'ring bright - - - - ly, Care - less-ly row-ing
l'on - - de frè-mis - san - - - - te. D'u - ne main noncha-

wave - - lets shim-'ring bright - - - - ly, Care - less-ly row-ing
l'on - - de frè-mis - san - - - - te. D'u - ne main noncha-

light - - ly, Reach - - - - ing the steeps Where the birds warble, war-ble,
lan - - te, Ga - gnons le bord, Où l'oi-seau chante, l'oiseu,

light - - ly, Come, we 'll reach the steeps Where the foun-tain sleeps, Where war-ble,
lan - - te, Viens gagnons le bord. Où la source dort Et l'oiseau

poco rall.   a tempo.   pp
birdlings sprightly. 'Neath . . . the dome, flowers . . . u - nite, Come and join . . . .
l'oiseau chante. Dò - - ne é-pais, blanc . . jasmin, Nous ap-pel

poco rall.   a tempo.   pp
birdlings sprightly. 'Neath the leaf-y dome, Where the jas-mine white, ah! come join . . . .
l'oiseau chante. Sous le dôme épais, Sous le blanc jasmin, Ah des-cen

rall.   LAKME. (in the distance.
p
we their meet - ing! Ah! . . . .
lent rall. dans en - sem - ble! MALLIKA.
p
we their meet - ing! Ah! . . . .
dans en - sem - ble!

rall.
Ah! . . . Ah! . . . .
Ah! . . . Ah! . . . .
rall.

During the latter measures Mallika has unfastened a little boat which was anchored among the reeds in the stream. Lakmé steps into it, followed by Mallika, who sits at the helm. The boat moves on and their voices are lost in the distance.)

(Enter Gerald, Frederic, Ellen, Rose, Mrs. Benson.)
(Laughter heard outside the inclosure.)

Rose.   What do you see?

(Pendant les dernières measures du chant, Mallika a détaché une petite barque qui était amarrée dans les roseaux; Lakmé y monte, suivie de Mallika qui a pris l'aviron; la barque s'éloigne et leurs voix s'éteignent dans le lointain.)

(Gérald, Frédéric, Ellen, Rose, Mistress Bentson.)
(On entend des éclats de rire en dehors de la clôture du jardin.)

Rose.   Que voyez-vous?

Frederic.	I see a garden.		*Frédéric.*	Je vois un jardin
Ellen.	And you, Gerald?		*Ellen.*	Et vous, Gérald?
Gerald.	I see lovely trees.		*Gérald.*	Je vois de très beaux arbres.
Ellen.	And no person?		*Ellen.*	Il n'y a personne?
Gerald.	I can't tell.		*Gérald.*	Je ne sais pas.
Rose.	Look well.		*Rose.*	Regardez bien.
Frederic.	It's difficult, across this fence.		*Frédéric.*	Ce n'est pas commode, à travers une pareille clôture.
Ellen.	Try to move the bamboo.		*Ellen.*	Essayez d'écarter les bambous!
Mrs. B.	Girls, girls, be careful.		*Mrs. B.*	Mesdemoiselles, mesdemoiselles, soyez prudentes.
Gerald.	Wait! I see the statue of Ganesa, goddess of wisdom.		*Gérald.*	Tiens, je vois la statue de Ganeça, le dieu de la sagesse.
Frederic.	There's a lotus leaf on the door. A Brahmin must live there.		*Frédéric.*	Je vois une feuille de lotus dessinée sur la porte. C'est la demeure d'un brahmane.
Rose and Ellen.	A Brahmin!		*Rose et Ellen.*	D'un brahmane!
Frederic.	Let's go.		*Frédéric.*	Allons-nous-en!
Rose and Ellen.	Why?		*Rose et Ellen.*	Pourquoi?
Frederic.	You can't fool with these people.		*Frédéric.*	Parce qu'il ne faut pas plaisanter avec ces gens-là.
Ellen.	(Pushing aside the bamboo.) Oh! I must see a Brahmin's garden.		*Ellen.*	(Écartant les bambous.) Oh! moi, je veux absolument voir le jardin d'un brahmane.
Mrs. B.	Miss Ellen be careful.		*Mrs. B.*	Miss Ellen, soyez prudente!
Ellen.	It's too late. (She pushes through the bamboo into the garden)		*Ellen.*	Oh! il est trop tard! (Les bambous ont cédé, elle est entrée dans le jardin.)
Rose.	The opening is made, we can go through.		*Rose.*	La brèche est faite, on peut passer.
Mrs. B.	You too, Rose!		*Mrs. B.*	(Éperdue.) Miss Rose, vous aussi!
Gerald.	We can't go back, ma'am.		*Gérald.*	Nous ne pouvons plus reculer, véné rable mistress Bentson.
Mrs. B.	(Following after, making a face.) But in whose place are we?		*Mrs. B.*	(Entrant en faisant la grimace.) Mais je ne sais pas chez qui nous sommes.
Frederic.	I know. I don't know the owner of this temple but I've heard about him.		*Frédéric.*	Moi, je le sais très bien. Je ne connais pas le propriétaire de ce petit temple, mais j'ai beaucoup entendu parler de lui.
Gerald.	Right! We haven't been introduced.		*Gérald.*	Très positivement, nous n'avons pas été présentés.
Frederic.	Let's not fool around. It's dangerous.		*Frédéric.*	Nous nous livrons là à une plaisanterie extrêmement dangereuse.
Rose.	Don't worry, Mrs. Benson.		*Rose.*	(Vivement.) N'effrayez pas, mistress Bentson.
Ellen.	Of course, don't worry.		*Ellen.*	Oh! non, ne l'effrayez pas!
Mrs. B.	Please, girls, I am your governess and caution is my duty.		*Mrs. B.*	Permettez, mesdemoiselles, je suis votre gouvernante, la prudence est un devoir pour moi.
Rose.	Caution, yes; fear, no.		*Rose.*	La prudence, oui: mais la peur?

Mrs. B.	Fear, too. When the governor entrusted his daughter and his niece to me he told me to have fear. I was engaged to have fear. I have fear.	*Mrs. B.*	La peur aussi. Quand M. le gouverneur a diagné me confier sa fille et sa nièce, il m'a recommandé d'avoir peur. Je me suis engagée avoir peur. J'ai peur!
Ellen.	(Gaily, to Rose.) Isn't it lovely.	*Ellen.*	(Gaiment, à Rose.) Vois comme c'est joli.
Rose.	Flowers and lovely buds — how adorable!	*Rose.*	Quel adorable fouillis de feuilles et de fleurs!
Frederic.	Look out for snakes! Under the flowers!	*Frédéric.*	Prenez garde aux serpents, sous les fleurs, miss Rose!
Ellen.	And the river! How charming with its grassy banks.	*Ellen.*	Comme elle est coquette, cette rivière, toute bordée de verdure.
Rose.	It seems to have gone to great lengths just to come here for us.	*Rose.*	Elle a l'air de s'allonger dans une courbe gracieuse pour arriver jusqu'ici.
Ellen.	Look at these flowers.	*Ellen.*	Vois donc ces belles fleurs.
Frederic.	Don't touch them, Ellen! They're daturas stramonium—innocuous in England but here in India, if just one leaf—	*Frédéric.*	N'y touchez pas, miss Ellen! ce sont des daturas, des daturas *stramonium*, très inoffensifs en Angleterre, mais, sous ce beau ciel indien, il suffirait d'en mettre une feuille sous vos jolies dents.
Mrs. B.	They're poisonous.	*Mrs. B.*	Pour être empoisonnée?
Gerald.	Poisonous.	*Gérald.*	Pour être empoisonnée.
Frederic.	Right.	*Frédéric.*	Parfaitement, mistress Bentson.
Mrs. B.	This is a terrible country.	*Mrs. B.*	C'est un pays abominable.
Frederic.	Now, if you'll listen to reason—	*Frédéric.*	Si vous me permettiez de vous parler raison.
Rose.	We won't.	*Rose.*	Nous ne voulons pas!
Ellen.	No, we won't.	*Ellen.*	Non, non, nous ne voulons pas!
Frederic.	Look, Gerald, you have some rights, or seem to have since you're going to marry Ellen in a couple of weeks . . .	*Frédéric.*	Voyons, Gérald, toi qui as des droits ou du moins un semblant de droits, puisque tu auras le bonheur d'épouser miss Ellen dans quelques semaines.
Gerald.	I won't use my rights against my wife.	*Géald.*	Je n'userai jamais de mes droits pour contrarier ma femme.
Ellen.	(Giving him her hand.) Well said, darling.	*Ellen.*	(Lui tendant la main.) A la bonne heure, voilá une bonne parole!
Frederic.	Oh! these lovers! (To Gerald) The prospect does not displease, then. (To Ellen) You don't know him well. He loves danger and puts poetry into it. He's a dreamer of the impossible, an enthusiast of the unknown. He's lost with love in the blue shadows.	*Frédéric.*	Oh! ces amoureux! (*A Gérald.*) L'aventure, d'ailleurs, ne te déplaît pas. (*A miss Ellen.*) Vous ne le connaissez pas bien, miss Ellen; il aime le danger, il y met de la poésie! c'est un rêveur de l'impossible, un enthousiaste de l'inconnu; il se perd avec amour dans les nuages bleus.
Ellen.	(With spirit.) I don't blame him.	*Ellen.*	(Vivement.) Je ne le lui reproche pas.
Frederic.	(Gaily.) On the contrary, eh? Well, I'm the prosaic one. But let me tell you, if only I could	*Frédéric.*	(Gaiement.) Au contraire, n'est-ce pas? C'est moi qui suis prosaïque. Je vous jure pourtant que si j'étais seul.
Rose.	What? We're not taking a chance. We won't meet anyone. My guess is that no-one lives here.	*Rose.*	Quoi? Nous ne nous exposons pas beaucoup, puisque nous ne rencontrons personne. On dirait cette demeure inhabitée.

Frederic.	I tell you, this house certainly is inhabited by a fanatic Brahmin named Nilakantha. He built a pagoda here which was ruined in the conquest and now he hates all of us.
Mrs. B.	I see plenty of pagodas here.
Frederic.	In the cities, yes. In fact, tomorrow's one of their big holidays. And all the Brahmins will gather in the main pagoda. But in the country the cult is gradually disappearing. Nilakantha has retired into this obscure place which he has dedicated to Brahma, living on the modest contributions of his few remaining faithful Hindus. He has a daughter.
Ellen.	A daughter.
Mrs. B.	Do these people have daughters?
Frederic.	Her name is Lakmé.
Ellen.	What a beautiful name: Lakmé!
Rose.	I'd like to see her.
Frederic	It's quite impossible. You don't understand, being European, that this little person born in a pagoda, vowed to some god or goddess in the Indian heaven, believes herself divine. Everything outside is profane and she never shows herself.
Ellen.	Do you think she's beautiful?
Frederic.	They say she's ravishing.
Ellen.	When a woman is youthful and jolly, She is wrong herself to hide;
Frederic.	But in this strange land all is folly, By its rulings, yet, we must abide.
Gerald.	Like an idol deified ever,
Rose.	Shut up by herself from the light;
Gerald.	Stirred up with humanity never,
Mrs. B.	She'd for me be a perfect fright.
Ellen.	Every woman listens with pleasure To the praises that men to her bring;
Frederic.	In Europe 't is so in a measure, But here 't is a different thing!

Gerald. Rose. Ellen. Mrs. B. Frederic.
Ah! adepts in plans aesthetic,
Loving changes and brilliant show;
Lay aside all your dreams poetic,
Let us reason with calmness now.

Frederic. I hate all systems aesthetic,
And say and think what all know;
Without a fancy poetic,
I see only what the facts show.

Frédéric.	Je vous répète qu'elle est parfaitement habitée par un brahmane fanatique qui se nomme Nilakantha. Il desservait une pagode que la conquête a ruinée, ce qu'il nous pardonne difficilement.
Mrs. B.	Mais j'en vois encore partout des pagodes!
Frédéric.	Dans les villes, oui; nous aurons même demain une des plus grandes fêtes indoues. Tous les brahmanes des environs vont se réunir à la grande pagode, mais dans les campagnes, le culte disparaît peu à peu. Nilakantha s'est retiré sur ce coin de terre qu'il a consacré à Brahma, de sa propre autorité, et il vit des modestes offrandes de quelques Hindous qui lui sont restés fidèles. Il a une fille.
Ellen.	Une fille?
Mrs. B.	C'est gens-là ont des filles?
Frédéric.	Elle se nomme Lakmé.
Ellen.	Oh! le joli nom: Lakmé!
Rose.	Je voudrais bien la voir.
Frédéric.	Il ne manquerait plus que cela. Mais vous ne savez donc pas, Européenne que vous êtes, que cette petite personne née dans une pagode, vouée à quelque Dieu ou à quelque déesse du ciel indien, se croit elle-même d'essence divine. Elle méprise tout ce qui se passe en dehors de cette enceinte et elle ne se montre pas.
Ellen.	Et vous croyez qu'elle est belle?
Frédéric.	Ravissante, dit-on.
Ellen.	Quand une femme est si jolie Elle a bien tort de se cacher.
Frédéric.	Dans ce pays tout est folie Et j'admets tout, moi, sans brancher.
Gérald.	Une idole qu'on divinise!
Rose.	Que l'on enferme avec ferveur!
Gérald.	Et qui jamais ne s'humanise!
Mrs. B.	Je la crois laide à faire peur!
Ellen.	Une femme est toujours sensible Au juste hommage qu'on lui rend.
Frédéric.	En Europe, c'est bien possible, Mais ici, c'est tout différent!

Gérald, Rose, Ellen, Mrs. B.
Beaux faiseurs de systèmes,
Amoureux du changement,
Laissez là vos poèmes
Et raisonnons froidement;
Les femmes sont partout les mêmes
Fort heureusement.

Frédéric. Je hais tous les systèmes,
J'observe tout simplement
Sans faire de poèmes,
Les femmes changent vraiment
Et ne sont point partout les mêmes,
Fort heureusement!

Ellen. Should we seek them for footprints gracious, In these calm, mysterious abodes?	*Ellen.* Si nous cherchions un peu sa trace Dans cet enclos mystérieux?
Frederic. Oh! no, 't would be something audacious, And a bustle 't would make 'mong their gods.	*Frédéric.* On! non — ce serait d'une audace A faire bondir tous leurs dieux.
Rose. (Jestingly.) Then has she divine grace within her?	*Rose.* (Railleuse.) A-t-elle une grâce divine?
Frederic. Well, I think so; though I'm but a sinner.	*Frédéric.* (Avec bonhomie.) Mon Dieu! moi, je me l'imagine.
Gerald. (Jestingly.) Must we live, then, on bended knee?	*Gérald.* (Raillant.) Fraudrait-il vivre à ses genoux?
Mrs. B. (Ironically.) Say she's better by far than we!	*Mrs. B.* (Ironique.) Dites donc qu'elle est mieux que nous!

Frederic. I'll speak not in such foolish fashion,
But 'neath this hot sky aflame,
The women here, burning with passion
As our own, are not quite the same.
Their peculiar virtue needs some outward show,
Tho' love engrossed, they neither love nor contract know.
'T is not love, in our fine, coquettish manner,
Not a state of warm, gentle sentiment,
That often ends in moral sweet content.
No, their hearts are full while love is warm;
Life, for them, is knowing how to charm.
Living, is to charm.

Frédéric. Je ne dis pas cete sottise.
Non. Mais, sous ce beau ciel de feu,
Les femmes que leur soleil grise,
Des nôtres diffèrent un peu.
Leur vertu bizarre
Manque d'apparat;
L'amour s'en empare
Sans loi ni contrat.
Ce n'est plus l'amour aux façons coquettes,
Ce n'est plus ce tendre et doux sentiment,
Un bonheur d'allures discrètes
Qui finit très moralement.
Non, leur cœur s'enivre
Du plaisir d'aimer,
Et pour elles, vivre
Ce n'est que charmer!

Ellen. Such women we should call ideal,
Who charm all instantaneously;
And we seem commonplace and real
Who pleasing otherwise may be.
We're subdued, with less of brilliant noise and light;
'Gainst surprises sudden we let reason fight.
But they've not, you know, your fine enchantresses,
Felt the sweet dismay when love is first declared.
Nor the pleasures, or the distresses,
Or the bliss, when one's dreams are shared.
Those celestial beauties know how hearts to move.
With more modest feeling, we know how to love.

Ellen. Ce sont des femmes idéales
Qui charment instantanément
Et nous leur paraîtrons banales,
Nous, qui voulons plaire autrement.
Nous sommes conquises
Avec moins d'éclat;
De peur des surprises,
La raison combat.
Mais elles n'ont pas, vos enchanteresses,
Les effrois charmants des premiers aveux,
Ni les troubles, ni les ivresses
D'un bonheur que l'on rêve à deux
Ces beautés célestes
Savent tout charmer,
Mais nous, plus modestes,
Nous savons aimer.

Frederic. Not to compare tends what I'm saying.	*Frédéric.* Ne croyez pas que je compare.
Ellen, Rose and Mrs. B. 'T is but his wit that leads him straying.	*Ellen, Rose et Mrs. B.* C'est votre esprit qui vous égare.
Gerald. He deals with facts, we plainly see.	*Gérald.* (Riant.) Il est naïf, en vérité!
Frederic. I say it as reported to me.	*Frédéric.* Je dis ce qu'on m'a raconté.
Rose. (Perceiving jewels.) See! lovely jewels!	*Rose.* (Apercevant les bijoux sur table de pierre.) Tiens! des bijoux de femme!

Ellen.	The Brahmin's daughter's.		*Ellen.*	De la fille du brahmane!
Rose.	They're grand.		*Rose.*	Qu'ils sont gracieux de forme!
Frederic.	Girls! Don't touch them. (Quickly.)		*Frédéric.*	(Vivement.) Mesdemoiselles! n'y touchez pas.
Ellen.	Don't worry. Since they're sacred, I won't touch them. But Gerald can copy the design.		*Ellen.*	Rassurez-vous, je n'y toucherai pas puisqu'ils sont sacrés. Mais Gérald pourrait en prendre le dessin!
Frederic.	What! Start drawing right here?		*Frédéric.*	Vous vouiez qu'il s'installe avec ses crayons?
Gerald.	Why not?		*Gérald.*	Pourquoi pas?
Frederic.	Why not? Because, in coming here, we have not only violated privacy, but have committed a sacrilege, the Brahmin's home being as sacred as his pagoda. A sacrilege committed by a European never remains unpunished. Sooner or later, an unseen hand strikes the fatal blow.		*Frédéric.*	Comment! pourquoi pas? Parce qu'en entrant ici, nous n'avons pas seulement commis une violation de domicile comdamnable en tous pays, mais un véritable sacrilège, la demeure d'un brahmane étant sacrée comme la pagode elle-même. Or, un sacrilége commis par un Européen n'est jamais reste impuni. Le coupable tombe un jour ou l'autre frappé par une main invisible.
Mrs. B.	Why didn't you say so in the first place?		*Mrs. B.*	Ah! mon Dieu, pourquoi ne nous avez-vous pas dit ça tout de suite?
Gerald.	The officers of Her Majesty the Queen just laugh at that nonsense.		*Gérald.*	Les officiers de Sa Majesté la reine d'Angleterre se moquent des brahmanes.
Frederic.	It's not a question of courage with enemies who never show themselves but pursue their vengeance, unhurried, waiting for the proper time and certain of secrecy. Remember you're in a conquered country.		*Frédéric.*	Il ne s'agit pas de courage avec des ennemis qui ne se montrent jamais, qui poursuivent leur vengeance dans l'ombre sans se hâter, attendant l'instant propice, sûrs que pas un des leurs ne les dénoncera. Rappelez-vous que nous sommes en pays conquis.
Mrs. B.	Yes. A barbarous country. When I think how happy we were in London, in Hyde Park, breathing that beautiful invigorating fog! Well, girls, I'm going to use my authority.		*Mrs. B.*	Oui! oui! en pays barbare. Quand je pense que nous serions si bien à Londres, à Hyde-Park, humant ce joli brouillard qui nous fait le teint frais. Maintenant, mesdemoiselles, j'userai de mon autorité.
Gerald.	I have a suggestion to make. You go back to town, Mrs. Benson.		*Gérald.*	Je propose une transaction. Vous allez retourner à la ville. respectable mistress Bentson.
Mrs. B.	Thanks.		*Mrs. B.*	Merci.
Gerald.	With Frederic and the girls. I'll stay here to copy these jewels that Ellen likes.		*Gérald.*	Avec ces demoiselles et Frédéric. Moi, je resterai pour copier ces bijoux qui plaisent à miss Ellen.
Ellen.	(To Gerald.) If there's any danger.		*Ellen.*	(À Gérald.) Si pourtant vous deviez courir un danger.
Gerald.	(Laughing.) Not the least. If anyone comes, I'll go. I won't be ashamed.		*Gérald.*	(Riant.) Pas le moindre. Aussitôt que je vois arriver quelqu'un, je me sauve. Je n'y mettrai pas d'amour-propre.
Ellen.	I'll wear these jewels on our wedding day.		*Ellen.*	Je porterai ces bijoux-là, le jour de notre mariage.
Gerald.	That's why I like them.		*Gérald.*	C'est alors que je les trouverai jolis.
Mrs. B.	Well, girls.		*Mrs. B.*	Eh bien, mesdemoiselles?

Rose.

(To Ellen.)

I hate to go.

Ellen. I, too.

Frederic.

(To Gerald.)

I think you're making a mistake.

Mrs. E. Mr. Frederic . . . .

Frederic.

(Leaving.)

A hero! He's a hero! And I am ridiculous.
That's the way life is. Wisdom looks foolish.

Mrs. B. Mr. Frederic. . . .
(They go out.)
(Gerald alone, preparing to sketch.)

AIR.

Gerald. Taking the design of a jewel, — is that so
serious an action? Ah! Frederic is mad!
(He moves toward the jewels, then stops.)
But whence comes then, this foolish fore-
warning of danger; what supernatural
fancy has disturbed my reflections, amid
these calm and solemn shades?
(Becoming animated.)
Daughter of my caprices, the unknown stands
before my sight; her voice plain to my
hearing, utters this one mysterious word,
No! no!

Rose.

(À Ellen.)

Je regrette de m'en aller.

Ellen. Je le regrette bien davantage.

Frédéric.

(À Gérald.)

Rappelle-toi que tu as tort.

Mrs. B. Monsieur Frédéric.

Frédéric.

(En sortant.)

C'est un héros, lui! Tu es un héros! Et moi
je suis ridicule, parfaitement ridicule.
Voilà, généralement en ce monde, le sort
des hommes sages.

Mrs. B. Monsieur Frédéric.
(Ils sortent.)
(Seul, se préparant à dessiner.)

AIR.

Gérald.

Prendre le dessin d'un bijou,
Est-ce donc aussi grave? Ah! Frédéric est
fou!
(Il se dirige vers les bijoux, puis s'arrête.)
Mais d'où vient maintenant cette crainte
insensée;
Quel sentiment surnaturel
A troublé ma pensée
Devant ce calme solennel!
(S'animant.)
Fille de mon caprice
L'inconnue est devant mes yeux.
Sa voix à mon oreille glisse
Des mots mystérieux!

tas - tic, with wings of gold. *(Taking up a bracelet.)* Of some fair maid
si - e aux ai - les d'or. Au bras po - li

round her arm fold - ing, This brace - let rich must oft en - twine.
de la pa ïen - ne Cet an - ne - let dut s'en - la - cer!

Ah! what de - light would be the hold - ing,
El - le tien - drait ton te en la mien - ne,

The hand that pass - - es there, in mine!
'La main qui seule - y peut pas - ser!

(Taking up a ring.) This ring of gold . . my dream sup -
Ce cer - cle d'or. Je le sup -

pos - es, Oft has fol - lowed, wand - 'ring for hours, With the small
po - se. A sui - vi lès pas voy - a - geurs D'un pe - tit
poco rall.

foot. that but re - pos - es On mos - sy banks or beds of
pied qui ne se po - se Que sur la mousse où sur les -
tempo.

flowers. *(Taking up a necklace.)* This neck - lace too, with her
fleurs. Et ce col - lier en - cor

own per - fume scent - ed, . . . Em - balm'd as yet with sweets .
par fu - mé d'el - le, De - sa per - sonne en - cor

. . . from her lips that came. . . . . . Has felt the true heart, . .
tout en - bau - mé A pu sen - tir bât -

. . beat - ing glad, con - tent - ed, Trem-bling with joy at the one well-loved name, .
tre son coeur fi - de - le, Tout tressail - lant au nom du bien ai - mé,
rall. tempo allegro.

Trem - bling at sound of one . . . be - lov - ed name.
Tout trés - sail - lant au nom du bien ai mé

No! No! A - way, fly, fond il - lu - sions,
non! non! Fuy- ez Fuyez, chi - mè - res

Swift - ly pas - sing vis - ions That my rea - son dis - turb. . . .
Rè - ves é - phé - mè - res Qui trou - blez ma rai - son.

poco rall.   Io tempo.
. . . . I - dle fan - cy cra - dled by de - lu - sion, You mis-
suivez. Fan - tai - - si - e aux divins men - son - ges, Tu re-

lead me now, as of ol Back to dream - land, go, in swift con - fu - sion!
veins m'é-ga-rer en-cor. Va, re-tour-ne au pays des son - ges,

O dove fan - tas - tic, with wings of gold, O dove fan - tas - tic, with wings of
Ô fan-tai - sie aux ai - les d'or. Ô fan - tai - si - e aux ai - les

gold! Go! Go! . . to the dream - land, O fair il -
d'or. Va! va! va! re - tourne au pa - ys des

lu - sion, O fair il - lu - sion, with wings of gold. O fair il - lu - sion,
son - ges. Ô fan - tai - si - e aux ai - les d'or. Ô fan - tai - sie - e

rall.
O fair il - lu - sion, with wings of gold!
Ô fan - tai - si - e aux ai - les d'or!

(Renounces his intention of sketching.)
Well, no! I'll not touch those jewels again.
It would be for me a sort of profanation.
Lakmé, she calls herself Lakmé!

(He is about to leave when he hears the voice of Lakmé from the boat.)
'T is she! with her hands filled with flowers.
'T is she!

(He hides himself in a thicket of shrubbery.)

GERALD, (concealed) ; then LAKMÉ, MALLIKA.

Lakmé and Mallikà.
(Standing before the statue Ganesá.)
O thou who watchest o'er us,
From our foes before us
Keep us unharmed we pray.
(They place the flowers at the feet of the idol.)

(Renonçant à dessiner.)
Eh bien! non! Je ne veux plus toucher à ces
bijoux. Ce serait, pour moi, comme une
profanation. Lakmé, elle s'appelle Lakmé.

(Il va pour s'en aller quand il entend la voix de Lakmé sur
la barque.)
C'est elle, les mains pleines de fleurs. C'est
elle!

(Il se cache dans un massif d'arbustes.)

GÉRALD, caché, puis LAKMÉ et MALLIKA.
ENSEMBLE.

Mallika, Lakmé.
(Devant la statue de Ganeça.)
O toi qui nous protèges,
Garde-nous des pièges
De nos persécuteurs!
(Elles posent des fleurs aux pieds de l'idole.)

Lakmé.

(To Malliká.)
And briefly now,
In the stream cool and flowing,
Which o'er the golden sand doth murmur,
Heedless going,
Of an overpowering sun,
Come and brave the hot rays!

Mall. The moment, now, will find advantageous,
Where the the dense forest trees spread o'er
the mossy bank,
A shelter cool, umbrageous!
(She quickly disappears among the trees.)
LAKMÉ, GERALD.
(Concealed.)

Lakmé.
(Having laid aside her mantle is about to follow her, but
stops thoughtfully.)
But I feel in my heart sudden movements
confused!
The flowers are more fair to me seeming,
The sky is more splendid in hue;
The wood with new bird-songs is teeming,
Sweeter kisses the wind never blew.
What's the perfume here that excites me,
And to new life now invites me!
But why?
Ah! why in these grand woods
Love I to roam and creep,
Is it to weep?
Why is my heart so saddened
At voices of ring-doves calling,
At sight of flowerets fading,
Or of brown leaflets falling?
And yet these tears have charms for me,
E'en though I sigh.
And I feel that I still am happy,
But why?
Why seek a sense to find
In the stream's murm'ring flow
'Mong the reeds below?
Whence are all these sweet delights,
While thro' space comes the feeling,
Like a breath half divine,
Leaving balm, then on-stealing?
My lips, at times, with smiles with sadness
defy,
And I feel I am happy,
But why?

Lakmé.
(Perceiving Gerald, and with loud cry.)
Ah, Malliká!

Malliká.
(Running back to her.)
Lakmé! are you threatened with danger?
(Hadji runs in.)

Lakmé.
(Conquering her emotion.)
Ah, no.
I was deceived. Trifles frighten me to-day;
my father does not come, though the
time is past already! Go, both, in search
of him. Away!
(Malliká and Hadji depart, looking at her with astonishment.)
LAKMÉ, GERALD.
(So soon as the servants are gone, Lakmé walks straight up
to Gerald, who has taken a step torwards her, and gazes upon
her with ravishment.)

Lakmé.

(À Mallika.)
Et maintenant, dans cette eau transparente
Qui, sur le sable frais, murmure insouciante,
D'un soleil accablant vient braver les ar-
deurs.

Mall. Oui, profitons de l'heure propice
Où les arbres touffus
Répandent sur la rive une ombre protectrice.
(Elle disparaît vivement derrière les arbres.)
LAKMÉ, GÉRALD, caché.

Lakmé.
(Défait le manteau qui l'enveloppe, puis au moment de
suivre Mallika, elle s'arrête rêveuse.)
Mais je sens en mon cœur des murmures
confus,
Les fleurs me paraissent plus belles
Le ciel est plus resplendissant,
Les bois ont des chansons nouvelles
L'air qui passe est plus caressant;
Je ne sais quel parfum m'enivre,
Tout palpite et commence à vivre.
Pourquoi dans les grands bois aimé-je à m'
égarer
Pour y pleurer?
Pourquoi suis-je attristée au chant d'une
colombe,
Par une fleur fanée, une feuille qui tombe?
Et cependant ces pleurs ont des charmes
pour moi,
Je me sens heureuse! Pourquoi?
Pourquoi chercher un sens au murmure des
eaux
Dans les roseaux?
Pourquoi ces voluptés à sentir dans l'espace
Comme un souffle divin qui m'embaume et
qui passe?
Parfois aussi ma bouche a souri malgré moi,
Je me sens heureuse! Pourquoi?

(Après avoir vu Gérald et poussant un grand cri.)

Ah! Mallika!
(Entrent Lakmé, Hadji, Mallika.)

Mall. Lakmé! Quel danger te menace?
(Hadji paraît.)

Lakmé.
(Maîtrisant son émotion.)
Aucun! Je me trompais! Tout m'effraie au-
jourd'hui!
Mon père ne vient pas, et pourtant l'heure
passe.
Allex tous deux vers lui!
(Mallika et Hadji sortent en la regardant avec étonnement.)
LAKMÉ, GÉRALD.
(Lakmé, dès que les deux serviteurs sont sortis, va droit
à Gérald qui a fait un pas vers elle et qui la regarde avec
ravissement.)

Lakmé.

(Angrily.)

Whence come you? What want you? Your
     rash boldness to punish,
They should have killed you here at sight!
I blush, ashamed of my fright!
     To no one here shall it be said
That a footstep barbarian has soiled by its
     presence the domain consecrated where
     hides my father! Now go! and ever for-
     get what your eyes here have seen. De-
     part! I'm the child of the gods!

Gerald.

(Warmly.)

How forget I saw you standing
There, erect, with eyes expanding,
     In a posture of command!
Trembling, with your anger lowering;
Stern, unyielding, overpowering,
     With that childlike gaze, so grand!

Lakmé.

So boldly; never has another,
If Hindoo, or e'en my brother,
     Dared address such speech to me,
And the gods still watching o'er me;
Will chastise your sin before me,
     Now depart, away, quickly flee!

Gerald.

How forget I saw you standing
There, with simple grace commanding,
     And that penetrating charm!
Go, forget, are you decreeing,
When I feel my very being
     Hangs upon your lips so warm?

Lakmé.

(Aside and softened.)

Doubtless you had no suspicion
     Of the danger you incur;
Now depart, with quick decision,
Or meet death, which no power can deter.

Gerald.

(Without moving.)

Let me stay and on thee gaze.

Lakmé.

(Aside.)

'T is for me, though he knows I hate him;
     To behold me, here he stays,
     Braving death by his delays!
Strong the force is that draws him towards
     me;
Nothing doth affright him!
        (To Gerald.)
Whence to you comes that superhuman
     courage?
What god is that who lends you aid?

Lakmé.

(Courroucée.)

D'où viens-tu? Que veux-tu? Pour punir ton
     audace
On t'aurait tué devant moi.
Mais je rougis de mon effroi,
Et je ne veux pas qu'on sache,
Que le pied d'un barbare a souillé d'une
     tache
La demeure sacrée où mon père se cache,
Oublie et pour jamais ce qui frappe tes
     yeux.
Va-t'en! je suis fille des Dieux!

Gérald.

Oublier que je t'ai vue
Te redressant tout émue
Sous un geste triomphant?
De colère frémissante,
Inflexible, menaçante
Avec ce regard d'enfant?

Lakmé.

Jamais le plus téméraire,
Jamais un Hindou, mon frère,
N'oserait parler ainsi.
Et le Dieu qui me protège
Punira ton sacrilège
Va-t'en! va-t'en! sors d'ici!

Gérald.

Oublier que je t'ai vue,
Et cette grâce ingénue,
Et ce charme pénétrant?
Ah! tu veux que je t'oublie
Lorsque je sens que ma vie
A tes lèvres se suspend?

Lakmé.

(Un peu radoucie.)

Tu ne savais pas, sans doute,
Quel danger tu courais. Maintenant, suis ta
     route,
Va! c'est la mort dont rien ne saurait te
     garder,
Va!

Gérald.

(Sans bouger.)

Laisse-moi te regarder.

Lakmé.

(À part.)

C'est pour moi dont il sait la haine,
Et c'est pour me voir un instant
Qu'il brave la mort, qu'il l'attend?
Quelle force vers moi l'entraîne?
Rien ne l'épouvante?
        (À Gérald.)
D'où te vient
Cette audace surhumaine?
Quel est le Dieu qui te soutient?

GERALD.   *Allegretto. con moto.*

Ah, 't is the god of youth and beau-ty; 'T is the young God of Spring, Who re-pay - eth love for
Ah c'est le Dieu de la jeu-nes-se C'est la Dieu du prin-temps, C'est le Dieu qui nous ca-
tempo. rubato.   *tempo.*

du - ty Doth ar - dent kiss - es bring; Opes for us the cups de - li - cious of
res   se De ses bai-sers ar-dents, par qui s'ouvrent les ca - li - ces Des

du - ty, And kiss - es warm doth bring; Opes for us the cups de - li - cious Of
res - se De ses bai - sers ar - dents Par qui s'ouvrent les ca - li - ces Des

ros - es in the grove; 'T is the god of whims ca - pri - cious, Ah! 't is love
ro - ses chaque jour. C'est le Dieu de mes ca - pri - ces. C'est l'a-mour?

ros - es in the grove; 'T is the god of whims ca - pri - cious, Ah! 't is love
ro - ses chaque jour. C'est le Dieu de tes ca - pri - ces, C'est l'a-mour

'T is the god of youth and beau - ty! Ah! . . . . 't is love.
C'est le Dieu de la jeu - nes - se! C'est l'a-mour!

plus anime.

poco rall.

Lakmé.	Lakmé.
(With a loud cry.)	(Poussant un grand cri.)
Great heaven! Behold, my father! Fly,	Grands dieux! Mon père! Fuis!
(Beseechingly.)	(Suppliant.)
for my sake fly!	Par pitié pour moi!

Gerald. | Gérald.
(Departing.) | (En sortant.)
No, I'll ne'er forget thee, O vision fair! | Non, je ne t'oublierai plus, ô douce vision!

Lakmé, Nilakantha, Hadji; then Hindoos. (Gerald is gone, when the Brahmin, guided by Hadji, appears at the door.) | LAKMÉ, NILAKANTHA, HADJI puis des HINDOUS. (Gérald est sorti quand le Brahmane, guidé par Hadji, paraît à la porte.)

Hadji. | Hadji.
(Showing the broken enclosure.) | (Montrant la clôture brisée.)
Come here! | Viens, là, là!

Nilakantha. | Nila. Dans ma demeure?
(Indignantly.) | Un profane est entré chez moi!
Here, in my dwelling, the profane one has defiled my home! |

Lakmé. I die of fright! | Lakmé. Je meurs d'effroi!

Nilakantha. | Nila. Vengeance! Il faut qu'il meure!
The foe must die! Ah! Vengeance! | (Des Hindous qui sont entrés sur les pas du Brahmane
(The Hindoos, entering, join the cry. Lakmé remains terrified.) | répètent son cri de vengeance pendant que Lakmé reste terrifiée.)

ACT II

A public square. Numerous Indian and Chinese shops, bazaars, displays of rugs, stuffs, etc. An awning of a café or confectionery shop, divans, and two low bamboo chairs; little tables, encrusted with pearl. In the background, a grand pagoda. Time, near noon; the market hour.
(Chorus and market scene.)
Promenaders, merchants, sailors, a soothsayer, a Chinaman, a sepoy. At the rising of the curtain, dealers in stuffs, jewels, and fruits call out to the promenaders who are come to the festival.

ACTE DEUXIÈME

(Une place publique. — Nombreuses boutiques chinoises et indiennes, des bazars, des étalages d'étoffes. — A droite, la tente d'une maison de repos ou confiserie, avec divans bas et chaises en bambou devant les petites tables à incrustations de nacre. — Au fond une grande pagode.)
PROMENEURS, MARCHANDS, MATELOTS, un DOMBEN, un CHINOIS, un CIPAYE.
(Au lever du rideau les merchands de fruits, de bijoux, etc. appellent les promeneurs venus pour la fête.)

Chorus. Come in before the noon bell ringeth; We sell no more, but freely give you; We give away, and don't deceive you. So come, the market soon will close, And we shall all repose.	*Choeur.* Allons, avant que midi sonne Venez, on ne vend plus, on donne, Jamais nous ne trompons personne. Venez, le marché va finir.

Hindoos.
(1st group.)
Look and see these slippers easy,
These gay kerchiefs, wondrous dyes.

Marchands Hindous.
(1er Groupe.)
Admirez cette babouche
Et ce mouchoir merveilleux!

Chinese.
(2nd group.)
Here are cakes, quite sure to please ye,
And as tempting to the eyes.

Chinois.
(2e Groupe.)
Gâteaux exquis à la bouche
Et ravissants pour les yeux!

Fruiterers.
(3d group.)
See these golden, ripe bananas,
Leaves of betel, fresh and strong;
Braided mats of green lianas,
Taste, they will your lives prolong.

Marchands de Fruits.
(3e Groupe.)
Voyez ces fraîches bananes
Et ces feuilles de bétel,
Belles nattes de lianes,
Goûtez ces rayons de miel!

Sailors.
(4th group. Rapping on a table.)
Come help us quick, you believers,
Sons of Brahma, come along.
(Mrs. BENSON; then ROSE and FREDERIC.)

Matelots.
(4e Groupe.)
Servirez-vous les profanes,
Fils de Brahma, roi du ciel!
(mistress BENTSON puis FRÉDÉRIC et ROSE.)

Mrs. B.
(Lost in the crowd.)
These selfish lovers,
These careless rovers,
Talk love from morn till night,
And of me they quite lose sight.

Mrs. B.
(Égarée dans la foule.)
Ces égoïstes,
Peu formalistes,
Causent de leurs amours
Et me perdent toujours!

A Soothsayer.
(To Mrs. Benson.)
My lady, I'll your fortune tell you.

Un Domben.
Madame, la bonne aventure?

Mrs. B. Let me pass, or I'll compel you.

Mrs. B. Laissez-moi, je vous en conjure!

Merchant. Look here! jewels gold are these.

Un Marchand.
Voyez ces bijoux dorés.

Mrs. B. Go off; me you greatly tease!

Mrs. B. Messieurs, vous m'exaspérez!

Sepoy.
(Steals her watch.)
In peace leave madam; you treat her poorly.

Un Cipaye.
(S'approchant.)
Laissez madame, on la désole!
(Il lui vole sa montre.)

Mrs. B. Thank you, sir. He robs me surely.

Mrs. B. Ah! merci. Mais il me vole!

Soothsayer.
In your hand pray let me read
What good luck you'll reach; take heed.

Le Domben.
Je vais lire dans votre main
Quel bonheur vous attend demain!

Mrs. B. But, sir, leave me tranquil only.

Mrs. B. Mais, monsieur, laissez-moi tranquille!

Merchant. This new elixir health restores,
And women beauteous makes by scores.

Le Marchand.
Cet élixir rend la santé
Et donne aux femmes la beauté!

Mrs. B. Thank you, sir; no use, I tell you.

Mrs. B. Merci, monsieur, c'est inutile!

Soothsayer.
One word me spare.

Le Domben.
Encore un mot!

Merchant. To me speak fair.

Le Marchand.
A moi plutôt!

Mrs. B.
(Enraged.)
I'm governess — take notice — of the gov'-
nor's young daughter here!

Mrs. B.
(Furibonde.)
Assez! je suis la gouvernante
De la fille du gouverneur!

Frederic.

(Running in.)
Mrs. Benson! Mad, 't is clear.

Rose.

(Running in.)
Mistress Benson, dear. What is here?

Mrs. B.   They insult me grossly.

Chorus.

(As if nothing had happened.)
Come in before the noon bell ringeth,
We sell no more, but freely give you;
We give away and don't deceive you.
So come, the market soon will close,
And we shall all repose.

Frederic and Rose.

Though afraid, must you speak crossly
What these honest men may hear?

Mrs. B.   Observe how guileless they appear!
My watch, alas, they've stolen from me.
What's this new rumpus they are making?

Frederic.   'T is the signal for upbreaking;
'T is the warning now to close.
(The pedlers leave gradually. The music continues.)

Mrs. B.   They are deafening! I ask for quiet —

Frederic.   You must renounce that for to-day, Mrs. B.
Ah! I adore this rumpus!

Mrs. B.   Meanwhile the market is over.

Frederic.   But the festival commences!

Mrs. B.   And what will they do now?

Frederic.   They will dance on all the squares, and sing
at the street corners. The crowds delight in going from one to another; now
here, now there. It is quite amusing.

Mrs. B.   But we have lost Miss Ellen.

Frederic.   She is in the care of her lover.

Rose.   Oh! she is not in any danger. Here are the
dancers!

Mrs. B.   What dancers?

Frederic.   Have you never heard tell of the Bayaderes
of India?

Mrs. B.   What do they do, ordinarily?

Frederic.   They live in the pagodas for the pleasure of
the priests of Brahma.

Mrs. B.   Are they vestals?

Frederic.   If you like. They are vestals with nothing
to guard.
(Ballet of the Bayaderes.)
(At the close of which Nilakantha and daughter are seen.
He in the costume of a Hindoo penitent or beggar. The
Bayaderes retire, followed by the crowd. Nilakantha goes back
with Lakmé.)
Rose, Frederic, Mrs. Benson, and later on, Gerald
and Ellen.

Rose.   Yonder see that old man
Upon his daughter leaning.

Frédéric.

(Accourant.)
C'est mistress Bentson en fureur!

Rose.   Qu'avez-vous?

Mrs. B.   On me violente!

Le Choeur.

(Reprend comme si rien ne s'était passé.)
Allons, avant que midi sonne
Venez, on ne vend plus, on donne,
Jamais nous ne trompons personne,
Venez, le marché va finir!

Frédéric et Rose.

Fault-il s'effrayer de la sorte
De quelques honnêtes marchands
Trop pressants!

Mrs. B.   Voilà qu'ils font les innocents,
Mais c'est ma montre qu'on emporte!
(On entend la cloche du marché.)
Ciel quel est ce nouveau tapage?

Frédéric.   C'est le signal du départ,
Le marché déménage!
Les marchands se retirent peu à peu.)
(La musique continue en sourdine.)

Mrs. B.   Ils sont assourdissants! Je demande du
calme, un peu de calme!

Frédéric.   Il faudra y renoncer pour aujourd'hui,
mistress Bentson.
Moi, j'adore ce tapage!

Mrs. B.   Cependant, le marché est fini.

Frédéric.   Mais la fête commence.

Mrs. B.   Et que vont-ils faire encore?

Frédéric.   Ils vont danser sur toutes les places et
chanter à tous les coins de rue. La
foule se plait à aller de l'une à l'autre,
tantôt ici, tantôt là, c'est très amusant!

Mrs. B.   Mais nous avons perdu miss Ellen.

Frédéric.   Elle est sous la garde de son fiancé.

Rose.   Oh! elle ne court aucun danger. Voici les
danseuses!

Mrs. B.   Quelles danseuses?

Frédéric.   N'aviez-vous jamais entendu parler des bayadères de l'Inde?

Mrs. B.   Que font-elles ordinairement?

Frédéric.   Elles vivent dans les pagodes pour la plus
grande joie des prêtres de Brahma.

Mrs. B.   Ce sont des vestales?

Frédéric.   Si vous voulez. Ce sont des vestales qui
n'ont rien à garder.
Ballet.
(Composé de différentes parties appelées Terana, Kaklah,
Persian, etc. A la fin du ballet, la foule se retire suivant les
bayadères. Pendant qu'elles sortent on voit passer Nilakantha
et sa fille. Il est revêtu du costume de Sanniassy ou pénitent
hindou.)
(Rose Frédéric, Mistress Bentson, puis Gérald, et Ellen.)

Rose.

(À Frédéric.)
Voyez donc ce vieillard et cette jeune fille,
ils ne ressemblent pas aux autres!

Frederic.	'T is a Sanniassy. He wanders about And scorns not the humblest of off'rings, While his daughter oft sings sacred ballads, Which the Hindoos will hearken to the livelong day.	Frédéric.	C'est un moine mendiant ou Sanniassy, qui vient à la fête dans l'espoir d'y trouver quelques menus profits. Et la jeune fille? Doit chanter des complaintes, des mystères ou des scenes dramatiques dont les Hindous raffolent.
Mrs. B.	Ah! Miss Ellen! at last!	Mrs. B.	Ah! voici miss Ellen. Ne nous séparons plus. je vous en conjure.
			(Miss Ellen est entrée au bras de Gérald.)
Frederic.	And how contented She rests upon his arm!	Frédéric.	Ah! miss Ellen, comme on voit bien que vous êtes fière de donner le bras à un héros!
Ellen.	Yes, in truth, I am happy! See my heart, Full of sunshine and love, Is all gladness!	Ellen.	Ne plaisantez pas. J'ai été très inquiète et je me reprochais d'avoir laissé Gérald dans le jardin de ce brahmane.
Rose.	He hasn't brought you the designs you wanted.	Rose.	Mais il n'a pas rapporté les dessins qu'on lui demandait.
Frederic.	Really?	Frédéric.	Bah! vraiment?
Ellen.	He was right.	Ellen.	Il a eu raison.
Gerald.	The Brahmin's daughter was there, picking flowers.	Gérald.	La fille du brahmane était là cueillant des fleurs.
Frederic.	You saw her?	Frédéric.	Tu l'as vue!
Gerald.	Yes.	Gérald.	Je l'ai aperçue.
Frederic.	Oh!	Frédéric.	Ah! ah!
Ellen.	I hope my curiosity hasn't caused her any trouble. That goddess interests me.	Ellen.	J'aurais eu de vrais remords si ma curiosité avait causé le moindre chagrin à cette jeune fille. Voilà que maintenant elle va m'interesser, la petite déesse.
Frederic.		Frédéric.	
	(Apart.) She doesn't see that he's just a dreamer. What a wonderful way to be. (To Gerald, undertone.) You know we must report at 3?		(A part.) Elle ne s'aperçoit pas qu'il est tout à fait rêveur, l'ami Gérald. Il y a des grâces d'état.
Gerald.	Yes?	Gérald.	Vraiment?
Frederic.	The regiment leaves tonight to fight the rebels.	Frédéric.	Le régiment part cette nuit, pour combattre des rebelles.
Gerald.	We mustn't let the women know.	Gérald.	Il faut absolument le cacher à ces dames.
Frederic.	Right.	Frédéric.	C'est cela.
	(To Mrs. Benson.) I advise you now, to go back with the girls to the governor's palace. There's only the pagoda ceremony and the passage of Dourga to see and we'll take you to that.		(A mistress Bentson.) Je vous conseille maintenant, mistress Bentson, de rentrer avec ces demoiselles au palais du gouverneur. Il n'y aura plus à voir que la cérémonie de la pagode et le passage de la déesse Dourga. Nous irons vous prendre.
Ellen.	Are you coming with us, Gerald?	Ellen.	Vous rentrez avec nous, Gérald?
Gerald.	Certainly.	Gérald.	Mais certainement.
Ellen.	You didn't tell me whether this Brahmin's daughter was beautiful.	Ellen.	Vous ne m'avez pas dit si elle était vraiment belle, la fille du brahmane.
Gerald.	She's sort of strange. (He goes out with Ellen.)	Gérald.	Elle est étrange. (Il sort avec Ellen.)
Mrs. B.	I might as well go. I've nothing left that they can steal. (She goes out.)	Mrs. B.	Je ne suis pas fâchée de rentrer, moi, et cependant on n'a plus rien à me voler. (Elle sort.)
Rose.	(Follows, then stops and to Frederic.) No review today?	Rose.	(Au moment de les suivre, à Frédéric, en s'arrêtant.) Est-ce que vous n'avez pas une revue aujourd'hui?
Frederic.	Ordinary parade.	Frédéric.	Un simple appel.
Rose.	With arms?	Rose.	En tenue de guerre.
Frederic.	No. Not with arms, why?	Frédéric.	Mais, non, pas en tenue de guerre. Pouquoi en tenue de guerre?
Rose.	Didn't you say your regiment was leaving tonight? Oh! I know you're trying to keep it quiet.	Rose.	Vous ne nous dites pas que votre régiment part cette nuit? Oh! je sais qu'on le cache.
Frederic.	Where did you hear this?	Frédéric.	Où avez-vous pris ces nouvelles?

Rose. At my uncle's palace, by chance.	*Rose.* Chez mon oncle le gouverneur, par hazard. On ne se défie pas de moi.
Frederic. Oh! It's just a dawn parade.	*Frédéric.* C'est-à-dire que nous devons faire a l'aube une promenade militaire.
Rose. In a revolting province. I wouldn't want Ellen to know because she trembles at the very idea of her lover leaving. As for me, I have no lover.	*Rose.* Dans une province révoltée. Je n'ai pas voulu en parler à Ellen parce quelle tremblerait à l'idée de voir partir son fiancé. Ellen n'a pas mon courage, et puis, moi, je n'ai pas de fiancé.
Frederic. (Apart.) She's ravishing.	*Frédéric.* (À part.) Elle est ravissante!
Rose. (Seeing Nilakantha and Lakmé.) Here's that old man and his daughter. He scares me.	*Rose.* (Apercevant Nilakantha et Lakmé.) Voici encore ce vieillard et cette jeune fille. Ils m'effraient.
Frederic. Take my arm.	*Frédéric.* Prenez mon bras.
Rose. I will—because I am afraid.	*Rose.* Oh! volontiers! C'est parce que j'ai peur.
Frederic. She's adorable.	*Frédéric.* Elle est adorable!
LAKMÉ, NILAKANTHA, then the crowd.	(Ils sortent.) LAKMÉ, NILAKANTHA, pius LA FOULE.
Nilakantha. (Coming forward with Lakmé.) I, a beggar, alms imploring And she, a ballad-singing maid. (Frederic and Rose pass by, indifferent.) All but self, the crowds ignoring. They run when we reach for aid, 'Neath these faded robes defective Who would think here to discover A skilful, sharp detective? Do these vile English foes Feel their blood cease to flow When they read upon my visage, That I for vengeance go?	*Nila.* C'est un pauvre qui mendie, Une diseuse de chansons. Cette foule étourdie S'éloigne quand nous passons! Sous ce vêtement misérable! Voit-on le justicier qui poursuit un coupable! Ces Anglais sentent-ils tout leur sang se figer En lisant sur mon visage Que je vais me venger?
Lakmé. (Timidly.) Does Brahma e'er forbid we should o'erlook an outrage?	*Lakmé.* Brahma nous défend-il d'oublier un outrage?
Nila. The outrage of a wicked foe! (Recitative.)	*Nila.* L'outrage d'un étranger!

NILAKANTHA. (*with much tenderness.*)

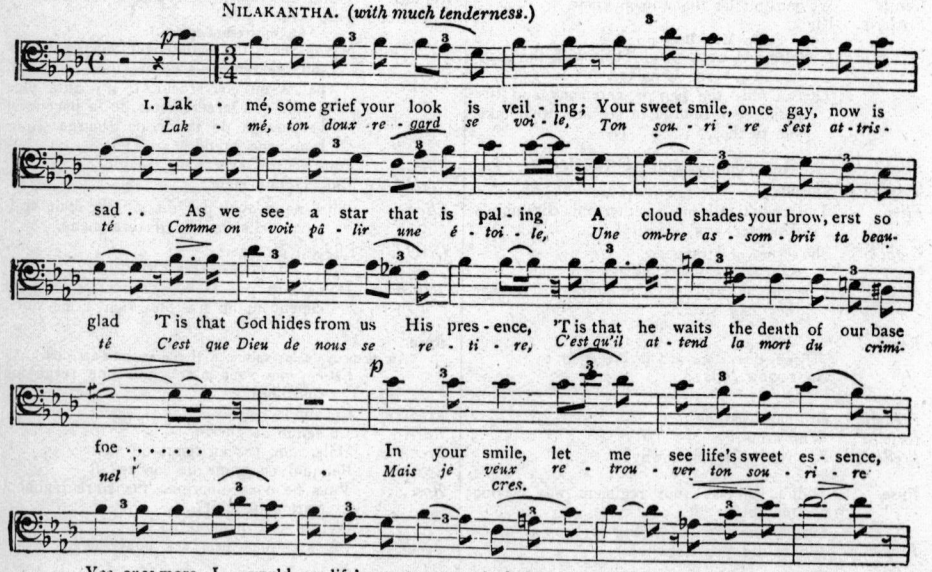

1. Lak - mé, some grief your look is veil-ing; Your sweet smile, once gay, now is
Lak - mé, ton doux re-*gard* se voi-le, Ton sou-ri-re s'est at-tris-

sad .. As we see a star that is pal-ing A cloud shades your brow, erst so
té Comme on voit pâ-lir une é-toi-le, Une om-bre as-som-brit ta beau-

glad 'Tis that God hides from us His pres-ence, 'Tis that he waits the denth of our base
té C'est que Dieu de nous se re-ti-re, C'est qu'il at-tend la mort du crimi-

foe ...... In your smile, let me see life's sweet es-sence,
nel Mais je veux re-trou-ver ton sou-ri-re

Yes, once more I would see life's sweet essence, And in your eyes, And in your eyes, ..
Oui je veux re-trou-ver ton sou-ri-re, Et dans tes yeux, et dans tes yeux!

would once more see the skies!...   2. Your
Je   veux re - voir   le   ciel!   Le

beat-ing heart with fev - er burn-ing, While you slept, I list-ened to hear! A
coeur rem-pli d'ar-den-tes   fièvres, J'ai vou-lu l'é-cou-ter dor-mir!   Un

dream o'er your lips pass'd with yearning, A blush I saw... your brow did wear. 'T is that
rê - ve passait sur le lé-vres, Et je vo-yais   ton front rou-gir. C'est que

God hides from us his pres-ence, 'T is that He waits the death of our base foe.....
Dieu de nous se re-ti-re, C'est qu'il at-tend le mort du cri-mi-nel.

In your smiles let me find life's sweet es-sence, Yes, I would, I would
Mais je veux re-trou-ver ton souri-re, Oui, je veux re-trou-
cres.

find life's sweet essence, And in your eyes, And in your eyes, would once more see the skies.
ver ton souri-re Et dans les yeux Et dans les jeux, je veux re-voir le ciel!

Lakmé. Ah! 't is from your own grief I feel my heart thus yearning. My gay thoughts will return! See! e'en now they are returning.	*Lakmé.* Ah! c'est de ta douleur que je me sens émue, Ma gaîté reviendra, vois, elle est revenue.
Nila. If that vile man has access found to me, If he, too, death has braved, at thy dear side to be,— Forgive the anger that moves me,— Ah! 't is that he loves thee! You, my Lakmé, child of the gods. Triumphant he goes through the city; We must hither draw the crowds by some motive of pity. If you he sees, Lakmé, in his eyes I shall read, Now strengthen well your voice. Look gay and smiling. Sing now, Lakmé, vengeance here awaits! (Scene and legend of the Pariah's Daughter.)	*Nila.* Si ce maudit s'est introduit chez moi, S'il a bravé la mort pour arriver à toi. Pardonne-moi ce blasphème, C'est qu'il t'aime! Toi, ma Lakmé, toi, la fille des dieux! Il va triomphant par la ville, Nous allons retenir cette foule mobile, Et s'il te voit, Lakmé, je lirai dans ses yeux. Affermis bien ta voix — sois souriante, Chante, Lakmé, chante, La vengeance est là. (Peu à peu la foule s'est approchée, attirée par la voix de Lakmé.)
Nila. Through the gods' inspiration, This young girl will here relate A legendic narration Of the pariah's fair daughter's fate.	*Nila.* (À la foule.) Pas les dieux inspirée, Cette enfant vous dira La légende sacrée De la fille du paria.
Chorus. Let us hear this legend. Listen now!	

Lakmé.   Where goes the maiden straying,
   This child of the pariah band?
  When the bright moonlight is playing
   Amid the forests grand,
  Tripping light over the mosses,
   Never remembers she
  That a deadly hate ever crosses
   The pariah's progeny.
  Tripping light over the mosses,
   Wanders the maiden free;
  Through the pink oleanders,
  With her sweet thoughts she wanders,
  She moves on with steps light,
  And laughs out at the night!

 The same; then GERALD, FREDERIC, officers.

Lakmé.   LÉGENDE.
  Où va la jeune Hindoue,
   Fille des parias,
  Quand la lune se joue
   Dans les grands mimosas?
  Elle court sur la mousse.
  Et ne se souvient pas
  Que partout on repousse
   L'enfant des parias!
  Le long des lauriers roses,
   Elle passe sans bruit.
  Rêvant de douces choses
  Et riant à la nuit!

 GÉRALD, FRÉDÉRIC, OFFICIERS.

INDIAN BELL SONG.

ah! ah! ah! ah! ah! . . . . While the stran - ger re-gards her
                  E'étran - ger la re - garde,

. . . Stands she dazed, flush'd and glow - ing More handsome than the Ra - jahs, he!
   El - le reste éblou - i - e.   Il est plus beau que les Ra - jahs!

Yet with a blush, he'll learn his life he's ow-ing To the Pa - riah's fair pro - ge - ny,
Il rougi - ra, s'il sait qu'il doit la vi-e. A la fil - le des pa - ri - as

. . But he, in a dream her en - fold-ing, Till to heaven she soars in his hold-
Mais lui, l'en - dor - mant dans un re - ve. Jasque dans le ciel il l'en - lè -
                   almost in recitative.

ing, To her he says, "Your mead is won." It was Vish - nu, great Brahma's son! And since the
ve, En lui di - sant; ta place est là! C'était Vishnou, fils de Brah-ma! Depuis ce

day in that dark wood, The trav'ler hears, where Vishnu stood, The sound of a little bell ringing, The legend back to him
jour au fond des bois, Le voya - geur entend par - fais, Le bruit léger de la baguette Où tinte la clo-
                rall..   Io tempo.

bring-ing, A small bell ring - ing like those the charm-ers wear.. . . . .   ah! ah! ah!
chet-te, Où tin - te la clo - chet - te Des char - meurs.

ah! ah! ah! . . . ah! ah! ah! ah! ah! ah! ah! . . . ah! . . ah!   ah! ah! ah! . .

ah!   ah! . . . . ah! ah! . . . ah! ah! ah! ah! ah!

ah! ah! ah! ah! . .   ah! ah! ah! ah! ah! . ah! . . ah! ah! ah! ah! ah!
       poco rall.   tr

ah! ah! ah ah! ah! ah! ah! ah! ah! ah! ah! ah! ah! ah! ah! ah! ah!

... ah!   ... ah! ...

ah! ah! ah! ah! ah! ah! ah! ah! ah! ah! ah! ah! ah! ah! ah! ah!   ah!   ah!

Nilakantha.	*Nila.*
(Aside.)	(À part.)
My fury doth o'erwhelm me! He has not yet come. I should know him at once!	La rage me dévore, Il n'est pas venu, Je l'aurais reconnu.
(To Lakmé.)	(À sa fille.)
Sing out; repeat it!	Chante, chante encore!
Lakmé. My father!	*Lakmé.*
	(Hésitante.)
	Mon père!
Chorus and Nilakantha.	*Le Choeur.*
Ah! sing it again.	Ah! chante encore.
(Officers appear at the back, Gerald and Frederic among them.)	(Quelques officiers paraissent au fond. Gérald et Frédéric sont parmi eux.)
Lakmé.	*Lakmé.*
Where goes the Hindoo straying, Child of the pariah band? Where the moonlight is playing Through the mimosas grand,—	(D'une voix tremblante.) Où va le jeune Hindoue, Fille des parias, Quand la lune se joue Dans les grands mimosas?
(She perceives Gerald, who has not yet seen her.) (Greatly moved.)	(Elle aperçoit Gérald qui ne l'as pas encore vue. — Très émue.)
Where goes the Hindoo straying, Child of the pariah band?	Où va la jeune Hindoue, Fille des parias.
Nila. Sing on! once more, sing on!	*Nila.* Encor!
Lakmé.	*Lakmé.*
(More and more disturbed.)	(Chante le refrain de la clochette et pousse un cri en voyant Gérald qui s'approche.)
Ah!	Ah!
(Utters a cry at sight of Gerald approaching.)	
Gerald.	*Gérald.*
(Springing forward to support her.)	(S'élançant pour la soutenir.)
Lakmé!	Lakmé.
Nilakantha.	*Nila.*
(Catching at Lakmé.)	(S'emparant de sa fille.)
It is he!	C'est lui
Chorus. What disturbs her thus?	*Le Choeur.* Qui la trouble ainsi?
Lakmé.	*Lakmé.*
(Trying to conquer her emotion.)	(Cherchant à maitriser son émotion.)
'T is a sudden pain—nothing more. It was unexpected; Now 't is gone, I'll try to be collected.	C'est un mal que j'ignore, Ce n'est rien, c'est fini, je veux chanter encore.
(With a faltering voice.)	(D'une voix faible.)
Ah!—	Ah!
Gerald.	*Gérald.*
(To Frederic.)	(À Frédéric.)
Behold! the Brahmin's daughter!	La fille du brahmane!
Frederic. What, here?	*Frédéric.* Ici!
Nilakantha.	*Nila.*
(To Lakmé.)	(À sa fille.)
You are by Brahma inspired, and the stranger is betrayed!	Ah! Brahma t'inspirait! L'étranger s'est trahi!
Gerald.	*Gérald.*
(With emotion.)	(Avec exaltation.)
'T is herself; 't is Lakmé!	C'est Lakmé, c'est elle!
Frederic. Ah! prudent be.	*Frédéric.* Sois prudent!
Gerald. Leave me free! Her once more let me see.	*Gérald.* Laisse-moi la voir!

Frederic.	On us they are calling.	*Frédéric.*	On nous appelle!
Gerald.	But stay.	*Gérald.*	Attends!
Frederic.	And that young girl; does she then you detain?	*Frédéric.*	Par cette enfant es-tu donc retenu!
Gerald.	No, no.	*Gérald.*	Non, non!

(They go out.)

(Ils s'éloignent.)

Nila.   I know him now! God is with us again.

(The English soldiers file out the back, headed by fifers and drummers. The crowd gathers slowly. The Brahmin and conspirators group on the front of the stage.)

Nila.   Je le connais! Dieu nous est revenu!

(Les soldats anglais défilent au fond du théâtre, fifres et tambours en tête. La foule les accompagne et s'éloigne lentement. Nilakantha et les Hindous se groupent sur le devant de la scène.)

NILAKANTHA, LAKMÉ, HADJI, and Hindoos.

NILAKANTHA, LAKMÉ, HADJI, HINDOUS.

Nilakantha.

(Mysteriously to the conspirators.)
'Mid the songs of joy and pleasure,
   When the crowd turns to go;
Where the priests march in stately measure,
   By a glance I'll point out the foe;
We'll then from his friends separate him,
   And noiselessly onward we'll go.
Till in a circle we instate him,
   And will close on him sure and slow.

Nila..   Au milieu des chants d'allégresse,
Ce soir, quand la foule suivra
Le cortège de la déesse!
Mon regard le designera!
Des siens séparant le coupable,
Sans bruit, pas à pas, vous irez,
Et dans un cercle infranchissable
Lentement vous l'enfermerez.

Chorus   We'll then from his friends separate him,
   And noiselessly onward we'll go.
   Sure and slow,
   And ready for the blow.

Le Choeur.

Des siens, séparant le coupable,
Sans bruit, pas à pas, nous irons,
Et dans un cercle infranchissable,
Lentement nous l'enfermerons!

Nila.   Depart then without trepidation.
   I shall be there, with arm trained and strong;
   'T is mine, by heaven's consecration,
   Ah! 't is I who'll avenge the wrong, —
   To me doth the task belong.

Nila.   Alors, éloignez-vous sans crainte,
Je serai là, j'ai préparé
Mon bras pour cette tâche sainte,
Et c'est moi qui le frapperai!

Lakmé.   O my father, with you I'll go.

Lakmé.   O mon père, je te suivrai!

Nila.   No, daughter, no!
   My heart, that weakness ne'er hath known,
   Would fail if you were at my side.
   With faithful Hadji here abide.

(Nilakantha and the conspirators depart slowly. Lakmé remains with Hadji.)

Nila.   Non! non! mon cœur qui n'a jamais faibli
   Se troublerait. Non, reste avec Hadji!

(Les Hindous et Nilakantha sortent lentement. Lakmé reste seule avec Hadji.)

LAKMÉ, HADJI.

LAKMÉ, HADJI.

Hadji.   The master thinks only of his vengeance. He has not seen your tears flow, O mistress; but Hadji was nigh. Hadji reads what the face tells, he knows what traces grief leaves there; he belongs to you and his life is of no account. When you were a child I defied the tigers in the jungle to cull the flowers for which you smiled. In the depths of the sea I sought to find a pearl for you more fair than others knew. A woman you are to-day; your thoughts have other caprices, your heart other desires. If you have an enemy to punish, tell me! If you have a friend to save, give me your order!

(Lakmé grasps his hand firmly.)

Hadji.

(Musique à l'orchestre.)
Le maître ne pense qu'à sa vengeance, il n'a pas vu couler tes larmes, ô maîtresse, mais Hadji était là. Hadji sait lire sur les visages, et il t'appartient, et la vie d'Hadji ne compte pas; quand tu étais petite, j'allais défier les tigres dans les forêts sauvages pour cueillir la fleur que tu aimais; j'allais au fond de la mer chercher pour toi une perle plus belle que toutes les perles. Aujourd'hui, tu es femme, ta pensée a d'autres caprices, ton cœur a d'autres désirs. Si tu as un ennemi à punir, parle, si tu as un ami à sauver.

(Lakmé lui saisit vivement la main.)
Ordonne.

DUO.

(At this moment Gerald returns thoughtfully. Lakmé makes a sign to Hadji to go farther away. Then she runs toward Gerald.)

(A ce moment, Gérald revient rêveur. Lakmé fait signe à Hadji de s'éloigner, puis court vers Gérald.)

Gerald.   Lakmé! 't is you I see?
   You hither come to me!

(With warmth.)

In the fancies of dreaming,
   I saw you as I neared;
The veil uplifted, seeming,
   The the idol appeared.
To your power I submitted.

Gérald.   Lakmé! Lakmé! c'est toi!
C'est toi qui viens à moi.
Dans le vague d'un rêve
Je t'ai vue en passant,
Le voile se soulève
Et l'idole descend.
Je subis ta puissance
Par ton charme enchaîné

By your charms drawn away;
And, defenceless, I quitted
Earth, for heaven's brighter day.

Lakmé.

(Sadly.)

My heaven is not your own,
The God you worship blindly
Is not the one whom I have known.
If I to mine could bring your heart,
Our Hindoo brothers, kindly,
Would always take your part
(Hesitating a little.)
'Gainst dangerous foes, or guileful art.

Gerald.   Come! all the dangers of creation!
In this wild adoration,
When reason's lost in bliss.
Should I see at my feet a yawning abyss
While your long tresses
Sweep me, with tender caresses?

Lakmé.

(Resolutely.)
Your death I'll ne'er consent to.

Gerald.

(Passionately.)
Ah! this is love, yet asleep,
Who with his wing hath caressed you;
Your heart tho' too strong to weep,
My death assured, has depressed you.

Lakmé.   Ah! yes, an enemy bold
'T is, whose hot breath hath caressed me,
All my heart has shuddered with cold
While the thought of death oppress'd me.
In the forest, quite near by,
A little cabin is hiding,
Built of bamboo, light and dry, —
'Neath a tall tree, shade providing, —
Like a nest for timid birds,
'Mid flow'ring vines, there abiding,
And with welcomes plain as words,
It awaits
Two happy mates.
It escapes all curious eyes —
Outside no secret revealing.
While the wood all silent lies
And surrounds it with jealous feeling.
There 't is, — you will follow me;
Each day when the dawn is breaking,
Smiling, there I'll come at waking, —
And 't is there you will dwell.

Gerald.   Sweetest of enchantresses.
Say more of that resort!

Lakmé.   Ah! come; time now presses,
And fleeting hours are short.

Gerald.   You wish that I should hide me,
But cannot understand
That honor must decide me
When duty makes demand.

Lakmé.   Lakmé implores with supplication.

Gerald.   Ask of me rather life than station.

Lakmé.   Have I lost my power to command?

Gerald.   Ah! your eyes are filling!

Lakmé.   That you must die I'm yet unwilling.
(With great energy.)

Et je vais sans défense
Vers le ciel entraîné!

Lakmé.   Mon ciel n'est pas le tien. Le Dieu qu'
me protège
N'est pas celui que tu connais,
A lui si je te ramenais
Alors sans sacrilège,
Je pourrais te parler,
Tu ne courrais aucun danger.

Gérald.   Viennent tous les dangers du monde!
Dans l'ivresse profonde
Où mon raison se perd
Verrais-je sous mes pas un abîme entr'ouvert
Quand de tes longs cheveux, document tu
m'effleures?

Lakmé.   Je ne veux pas que tu meures!

Gérald.   Ah! c'est l'amour endormi
Qui de son aile t'effleure,
Et ton cœur s'est raffermi,
Tu ne veux pas que je meure!

Lakmé.   Hélas! c'est un ennemi
Dont le souffle ardent m'eáleure,
Tout mon être en a frémi,
Mais je ne veux pas qu'il meure!
Dans le fôret, près de nous,
Ce cache, toute petite,
Une cabane en bambous
Qu'un grand arbre vert abrite.
Comme un nid d'oiseaux peureux,
Dans les lianes posée
Et sous les fleurs écrasée
Elle attend des gens heureux.
Elle échappe à tous les yeux,
Dehors, rien ne la révèle ,
Le grand bois silencieux
Qui l'enferme est jaloux d'elle.
C'est là que tu me suivras
Toujours à l'aube naissante
Je reviendrai souriante
Et c'est là que tu vivras.

Gérald.   O douce enchanteresse,
Parle, parle, toujours!

Lakmé.   Ah! viens, viens, le temps presse
Et les instants sont courts.

Gérald.   Tu veux que je me cache,
Tu ne peux pas savoir
Qu'ici l'honneur m'attache,
L'honneur et le devoir.

Lakmé.   Lakmé t'implore et te supplie!

Gérald.   Demande-moi plutôt ma vie!

Lakmé.   Ai-je donc perdu mon pouvoir!

Gérald.   Ah! Lakmé, Lakmé, tu pleures.

Lakmé.   Je ne veux pas que tu meures!
(Reprise de l'ensemble.)

Gerald. Ah! this is love, yet asleep, etc.

Lakmé. Ah! 't is too late — our people now are here!

Behold when the goddess is near.

(Gerald, Frederic, Ellen, Rose, Mrs. Benson; then Nilakantha, Brahmins, Bayaderes, Hindoos; then Lakmé. Priests arrive and move towards the pagoda.)

Chorus.

(Hymn of the Brahmins.)
Dourga fair, thou who wert born
From the waves of Ganges,
To our eyes appear, and dawn,
Ruler of Time's changes.
Goddess of gold, hear us, we pray.
Give us here thy protection;
O'er us still smile;
Look down meanwhile
On us with pure affection.

(The Brahmins and Bayaderes enter the pagoda; Ellen and Rose re-enter with Mistress Benson; then Frederic arrives with Gerald.)

Ellen. The town is with splendor gleaming.
Hear the cries, the shouts of greetings glad.

Mrs. B. They are crazed, or so are seeming;
Their ten-armed goddess drives them mad.

Frederic.

(To Gerald.)
Was it to admire this fair goddess
That you left us in the throng?

Gerald.

(Preoccupied.)
Yes, their festival amused me.

Frederic.

(Smiling.)
The Brahmin's daughter
Has just now passed along.

Gerald.

(Breaking out.)
'T is a dream, a whim enthralling,
Which, flown, is past recalling,
But in my heart, dazed, confounded,
I feel, doubting and astounded,
That alone is Lakmé living.
No one else seems fair to me.

Frederic.

(Gayly.)
Thence I should like a moral to borrow,
If we should not depart to-morrow,
But the war has some good;
That ideal maiden,
You'll no more meet, 't is understood.
(Goes out.)

Ellen, Rose and Mrs. B.
How leave this noise tremendous?
They've sworn, I'll make a bet stupendous,
Our poor ears to smite
From morning till night.

(The procession comes from the pagoda, escorting the ten-armed statue of the goddess Dourga, which is borne in a sort of palanquin. Night has come. Torch-bearers accompany the procession. The Bayaderes join in.)

Chorus. O Dourga bright, etc.

(While the procession marches on, Nilakantha points out Gerald to the conspirators.)

Gerald. Ah! c'est l'amour endormi, etc.

Lakmé. C'est fini, les nôtres sont là.
Voici la déesse Dourga

Gérald, Frédéric, Ellen Rose, mistress Bentson, puis Nilakantâa, Les Brahmanes, Les Danseuses sacrées, Les Hindous, puis Lakmé.

(Des prêtres arrivent et se dirigent vers la pagode.)

Chant Des Brahmanes.

O Dourga, toi qui renais
Dans les flots du Gange,
A nos yeux, viens, apparais,
Toi par qui tout change!
Déesse d'or, entends nos voix,
Que ton bras nous protège!
Tu nous souris et tu nous vois
Saluant ton cortège.
De ta douce image
Nous venons fêter le passage,
Déesse d'or, entends nos voix!

Les prêtres entrent dans la pagode. Ellen et Rose rentrent accompagnées de mistress Bentson, puis Frédéric arrive avec Gérald.)

Ellen. Voyez cette ville en fête,
Et ces cris et ces hourrahs!

Mrs. B. Ils ont tous perdu la tête
Pour leur déesse aux dix bras!

Frédéric.

(Entrant avec Gérald.)
C'est pour admirer la déesse
Que tu nous as quittés ainsi?

Gérald.

(Préoccupé.)
Oui, leur fête m'intéresse!

Frédéric.

(Souriant.)
La fille du brahmane a passé par ici!

Gérald.

(Éclatant.)
C'est un rêve, une folie
Qui passe et qu'on oublie,
Mais dans mon cœur révolté
Je sens avec épouvante,
Que Lakmé seule est vivante
Je n'y vois que sa beauté!

Frédéric.

(Gaîment.)
Je te ferais une belle morale
Si nous ne partions pas demain,
Mais la guerre a du bon, cette fille idéale
Ne sera plus sur ton chemin!
(Il s'éloigne.)

Ellen, Rose et Mrs. B.
Comment fuir ce tapage!
Ils ont juré, je le gage,
De nous étourdir du soir au matin!

(Les brahames sortent de la pagode, escortant la déesse Dourga dont la statue est portée à bras dans une sorte de palanquin. La nuit est venue. Des porteurs de torches accompagnent le cortège. Les danses sacrées reprennent.)

Chorus. O Dourga, toi qui renais, etc.

(Les Hindous et Nilakantha guettent Gérald. — Nilakantha le désigne du doigt, la place se vide peu à peu.)

Gerald.   'T is a dream, a whim enthralling, etc.

(Nilakantha and the Hindoos watch Gerald; the square empties gradually.)

(He perceives Lakmé, who enters at the right, and goes towards him. Nilakantha follows Gerald, and, at the moment when he is near Lakmé, he strikes him, and escapes quickly, after seeing him fall. Lakmé rushes towards Gerald, leans over and examines him. Her face lightens when she sees that the wound is not mortal.)

Lakmé.   They think that their vengeance is sated!
Forevermore, love, you are mine.
My life with yours is hence related.
O'er our loves may heaven's star shine.
(Calls Hadji, and runs out.)

Gérald.   C'est un rêve, une folie
Qui passe et qu'on oublie,
Mais dans mon cœur révolté
Je sens avec épouvante
Que Lakmé seule est vivante
Je n'y vois que sa beauté.

(Il aperçoit Lakmé qui se montre à droite. Il va vers elle. Nilakantha le suit et, au moment où Gérald est près de Lakmé, il le frappe et se sauve vivement en le voyant tomber. Lakmé se précipite vers Gérald, se penche sur lui, l'examine, et sa figure s'éclaire lorsqu'elle reconnaît que la blessure n'est pas dangereuse.)

Lakmé.   Ils croient leur vengeance assouvie,
Tu m'appartiens pour toujours.
Je ne vivias que de ta vie,
Dieu protège nos amours!
(Elle appelle Hadji qui accourt.)

ACT III

(The stage represents a forest in India, that the sun illumines with its fiercest rays. Under a gigantic tree a cabin is nearly concealed and crowned with brilliant flowers.)

GERALD, LAKMÉ.

(Gerald is extended upon a bed of foliage. Lakmé anxiously watches his slumbers while murmuring a song.)

ACTE TROISIÉME

(Le théâtre représente une partie de forêt de l'Inde que le soleil éclaire de ses plus chauds rayons. Sous un arbre gigantesque une cabane à peine fermée et perdue dans les acacias roses, les daturas à double calice blanc, les tulipias jaunes.)

GÉRALD, LAKMÉ.

(Au lever du rideau, Gérald est étendu sur un lit de feuillage. Lakmé, à demi penchée, inquiète, épie son sommeil en murmurant une chanson.)

'NEATH THE STARRY CANOPY.

(SLUMBER SONG.)

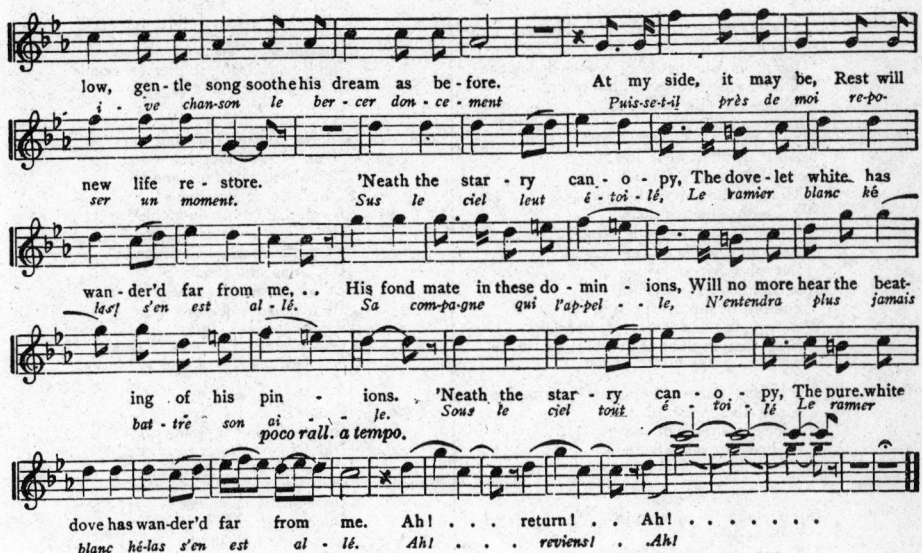

low, gen-tle song soothe his dream as be-fore. At my side, it may be, Rest will
i - ve chan-son le ber-cer don-ce-ment *Puis-se-t-il près de moi re-po-*

new life re-store. 'Neath the star-ry can-o-py, The dove-let white has
ser un moment. *Sus le ciel leut é-toi-lé, Le ramier blanc ké*

wan-der'd far from me... His fond mate in these do-min-ions, Will no more hear the beat-
las s'en est al-lé. *Sa com-pa-gne qui l'ap-pel-le, N'entendra plus jamais*

ing of his pin-ions. 'Neath the star-ry can-o-py, The pure white
bat-tre son ai-le. *Sous le ciel tout é-toi-lé Le ramier*

dove has wan-der'd far from me. Ah!... return!.. Ah!........
blanc hé-las s'en est al-lé. *Ah!... reviens!..Ah!*

Gerald.	*Gérald.*
(Opens his eyes without observing Lakmé.)	(S'éveillant sans voir Lakmé.)
What mem'ries, strangely vague,	Quel vague souvenir alourdit ma pensée?
On my thoughts are now weighing?	Et sur ma poitrine oppressée
All my weakened senses o'erlaying;	Quel rêve s'est appesanti?
What dream is this that does me oppress?	Sous un charme accablant je reste anéanti.
As 'neath some charm I lie without re-dress.	Je me souviens, la ville était en fête,
I now recall; the town in guise was festive,	J'allais dans mon extase, à demi réveillé,
Along the street I strolled with fancies sug-gestive,	Quand l'éclair d'un poignard à mes yeux a brillé,
When the gleam of a poniard flash'd quick on my sight;	Et la nuit s'est faite!
Then around me all was night!	
Lakmé.	*Lakmé.*
(Leaning over him.)	(Se penchant vers lui et continuant.)
'T was hence that Hadji, thro' the shadows dark,	Alors Hadji, dans l'ombre se glissant,
Has borne you senseless to this verdant park;	T'a transporté sous ce toit de verdure,
I soon brought the life to your pale brow again.	J'ai ramené la vie à ton front pâlissant;
The daughters of my caste, with early youth attain	Les filles de ma caste apprennent en naissant
The power to heal all wounds,	Comment le suc des fleurs guérit une bles-sure.
By juices of flowers applying.	
Gerald. I too, recall, — still mute, inanimate, —	*Gérald.* Je me souviens, sans voix, inanimée,
I saw you bent o'er my lips; while thus lying,	Je te voyais sur mes lévres penchée,
My soul upon your look was attracted and fastened;	Mon âme à tes regards tout entière attachée,
'Neath your breath life awoke and recovery hastened.	Revivait sous ton souffle, ô ma douce Lakmé!
O my charming Lakmé; ah, come!	Ah! viens, dans cette paix profonde
Through the forest depths secluded,	L'aile de l'amour a passé,
Love's wing above us has passed;	Et pour nous séparer du monde,
Earth-cares have not been intruded,	Sur nous le ciel s'est abaissé.
And heaven on us falls at last.	Ces fleurs courant capricieuses
	Ont des senteurs voluptueuses
	Qui jettent au cœur amolli
	L'ivresse et l'oubli.

These flow'ring vines, with blooms capri-
   cious,
Bear o'er our pathway scents delicious;
Which soft hearts, with raptures beset,
While all else we forget.

Lakmé. Here I may always reach you,
   And together we'll live;
And while fondly I teach you,
   The gods' history will give.
Here, with voices united,
   We will sing the gods blest,
'Fore whom all bend, affrighted,
   But who give to us rest;
And your spirit outflaming
   Shall with rapture be full,
O'er the charmed world proclaiming,
   Here that Brahma doth rule!
(Songs are heard in the distance.)

Gerald. Oh, listen! Some persons are passing
   Along the forest road.
No curious eyes will see us,
   Or find out our abode.

Chorus.
                   (In the wings.)
Down along the mountain
   Let's repair,
While the tuneful fountain
   Waits us there,
From its rippling waters,
   Two by two,
Drink we, sons and daughters,
   'Neath skies blue.

Gerald. What's that song of tender feeling
That seems like kisses o'er us stealing?

Lakmé. Of lovers 't is and amorous maids,
Who, wand'ring through the sylvan shades,
Go to the fountain pure, there springing,
And holy water thence come bringing,
   To happy maids and lovers dear.
                   (Sedately.)
When this cool draught is drained
   By their lips' burning fever,
From the same cup obtained,
   They wedded are, and evermore
The goddesses, unthoughtful never,
   Their love-life they watch o'er.

Chorus. Down along the mountain, etc.

Lakmé. But we shall scarce be able
Those maids to follow through,
   Two by two.
To this spring venerable
   I'll go alone for you!
Wait for me!
                   (Going out.)

Gerald. O temptress, charming still!
Wait for me!
(Gerald follows her with his eyes.)
I live through your caprice,
And by your sovereign will!
   Enter FREDERIC.

Frederic. He lives.

Gerald. Ah —

Ah! viens, dans cette paix profonde,
Sur nous le ciel s'est abaissé.
Pour nous faire oublier le monde
L'aile de l'amour a passé!

Lakmé. Là, je pourrai t'entendre,
Nous vivrons tous les deux,
Et je pourrai t'apprendre
L'histoire de nos dieux!
Nous chanterons ensemble
Ces dieux trois fois bénis
Devant lesquels tout tremble,
Qui nous ont réunis.
Et ton âme enflammée
De bonheur s'emplira,
Sur la terre charmée
Que protège Brahma!
(On entend des chants dans le lointain).

Gérald. Ecoute!
On passe sur la route
Qui longe la forêt.

Choeur. *Dans la coulisse.*
Descendons la pente
Doucement,
La source qui chante
Nous attend!
Près de son murmure,
Deux à deux,
Puisons l'onde pure
Sous les cieux.

Gérald. Quel est ce chant plein de tendresse,
Qui passe comme une caresse?

Lakmé. Ce sont des couples amoureux
Qui, par les doux chemins ombreux,
Vont à la source vénérée
Pour puiser l'eau sacrée
Chère aux amants heureux.
Quand ils ont effleuré de leurs lèvres
                   brûlantes
La même coupe, ils sont réunis pour tou-
                   jours.
Et les déesses bienfaisantes
Veillent sur leurs amors.
                   (Reprise du choeur.)

Lakmé. Nous ne pourrions sans crainte
Suivre ces amoureux
Tous les deux,
Mais à la source sainte
J'irai seule, sans toi,
Attends-moi!
                   (Elle s'éloigne lentement.)

Gérald.
                   (En la suivant des yeux.)
O douce tentatrice,
Ton charme m'a dompté,
Je vis de ton caprice
Ee de ta volonté!
                   (Frédéric, entrant.)

Frédéric. Vivant!

Gérald. Ah!

Frederic.	I forced my way through the bushes — a painful task! I found in the meadow and on the lawn traces of blood which led me hither. I thought you dead; what do you here?
Gerald.	I was dreaming.
Frederic.	While the regiment was marching on?
Gerald.	Let me collect my thoughts.
Frederic.	The land rises in revolt against us.
Gerald.	A dagger thrust nearly killed me; Lakmé saved and nursed me.
Frederic.	The daughter of the Brahmin?
Gerald.	She restored me to life ere the vital spark had fled. I was unconscious, helpless. Love only could work such wonders.
Frederic.	These are but idle fancies! Tarry no more, and do not court remorse; if you think she loves you, spare her new grief.
Gerald.	I will with tender care reward her kindness.
Frederic.	And your betrothed?
Gerald.	I am in the power of an enchantress!
Frederic.	And your duties as a soldier? These you'll not forget. I know you too well.
Gerald.	Count on me. But Lakmé comes, bringing the sacred water.
Frederic.	Now you may see her, I have no fear! You will resist. I count on you. Now he is saved.

(Exit Frederic.)

Lakmé.
(Returns triumphant, bringing the cup of holy water.)
So they walked two by two
With their arms interlacing,
These lovers young and true;
I walked quite near them, too,
With my thoughts figures tracing,
I walked; my heart did swiftly beat,
Like theirs, — all athirst, — hope embracing.
And now the tale hear me repeat:
(Religiously.)
When from one cup between them
They've drunk, each other facing,
United they will e'er remain!
(She looks at him attentively, and, struck with stupor, lays down the cup.)
'T is you no more!
Your soul, when you spoke sweetly,
On your lips was plainly posed
Fire has left your glance completely,
Which lately me enclosed.
Upon your face
Clouds I trace,
Which, though past,
Have froz'n it fast.

Frédéric.	J'ai marché sous les hautes fougères Qu'on venait de froisser. — J'ai vu sur les bruyéres Et sur la mousse au reflet blanc, Des gouttes de sang! Je t'ai cru mort. — Que fais-tu là?
Gérald.	Je rêve!
Frédéric.	Quand les nôtres vont partir?
Gérald.	Laisse-moi me souvenir!
Frédéric.	Quand le pays tout entier se soulève?
Gérald.	Hier on m'a frappé. Lakmé m'a sauvé.
Frédéric.	La fille du Brahmane?
Gérald.	Elle m'a fait revivre Dans un monde où je reste éperdu, sans force, ivre De son charme et de son amour.
Frédéric.	Ah! je connais ces ivresses d'un jour. Alors, il faut la fuir, La fuir à l'instant même. Garde-toi d'un remords, — si tu crois qu'elle t'aime Ces enfants-là ne savent pas souffrir.
Gérald.	Je l'envelloperai si bien de ma tendresse.
Frédéric.	Et miss Ellen?
Gérald.	Je subis le pouvoir D'une enchanteresse.
Frédéric.	Est notre passion — à nous tous, la meilleure, Notre honneur de soldat? C'est demain qu'on se bat.
Gérald.	(Avec résolution.) J'y serai! C'est Lakmé! C'est Lakmé qui m'apporte l'eau sainte!
Frédéric.	Oh! maintenant, tu peux la voir, je suis sans crainte. (En sortant.) Et je t'attends. — Il est sauvé!

Lakmé.
(Revient triomphante, elle apporte l'eau consacrée.)
Ils allaient deux à deux
Et les mains enlacées,
Les jeunes amoureux. —
Moi, je marchais prés d'eux. —
Seule avec mes pensées. —
J'allais, le cœur tout en émoi,
Comme eux de tendresse altérée,
Et maintenant, écoute-moi.
(Avec un accent religieux.)
Quand à la même coupe on a bu l'eau sacrée,
On reste pour toujours unis.
(Elle le regarde attentivement, puis comme frappée de stupeur elle pose la coupe en s'écriant.)
Ce n'est plus toi! Quand tu parlais, ton âme
Sur tes lèvres se posait;
Ton regard n'a plus la flamme
Qui m'embrasait.
Sur ton visage
Un nuage
A passé
Et l'a glacé.

Gerald. Are n't you still the charming maiden
For whom all else I have forgot?
Are you less fair, your heart with love less
laden?

Lakmé.
(Seriously.)
Wish you that our two fates
Should be joined hence, evermore?

Gerald. I wish what you desire, —
Our wishes reconciling.
Your whims I still admire,
And wish to see you smiling.

Lakmé.
(Seriously.)
Whichsoe'er the god may be
Whose power you worship blindly,
Whate'er your faith be, harsh or kindly,
You know an oath's worth to me.
Then drink from this cup holy,
Where true love faileth never.
Drink! and swear to love me forever!
(Military music in the distance.)

Gerald. Heavens! they are our soldiers!

Lakmé. Drink! and mine to be, thus vow!
Drink! Ah! you dare not now!
(Throws down the cup violently.)
(Gazes fixedly upon Gerald, who looks away at the side
whence comes the chorus.)
It is thither his thoughts are returning;
His heart is failing now.
For friends and native land he's yearning.
(With anguish, after trying vainly to attract his attention.)
Ah! all is ended now!
(While Gerald listens with bowed head, Lakmé desperately
culls a flower of the datura, and eats it, smilingly, without
notice from Gerald.)

Gerald. Lakmé, what's that you do?

Lakmé.
(Goes to him, smiling tenderly.)
You've given me love, the sweetest dreaming
That one may know beneath our sky;
Longer stay, till exquisite seeming
Is here made reality.
To me you've whispered tender phrases,
More sweet than Hindoos ever know;
You've taught me what delights and graces
Dwell in vows murmured soft and low.

Gerald. That which I read upon your features
Chills my heart, fear smitten, like a stone;
My soul floats free from duller creatures,
And henceforth I am yours alone.

Lakmé.
(With passion.)
Ah! it is now I'd fain believe you;
Behold the cup that here I give you!
(She wets her lips from it, then holds it out to him.)
Drink!

Gerald.
(Taking it exaltedly.)
I am yours, Lakmé, forevermore!

Lakmé. 'T is to our love feast we outpour!
(Gerald drinks.)

Gérald. N'es-tu plus l'enfant charmante
Pour qui j'ai tout oublié?
Es-tu moins belle et moins aimante?

Lakmé.
(Gravement.)
Veux-tu qu'à mon destin ton destin soit lié?

Gérald. Je veux ce que tu veux, je veux ce que
t'inspire
Ton caprice, je veux, je veux te voir sourire!

Lakmé.
(De même.)
Quel que soit le Dieu clément
Dont je bénis la puissance,
Quelle que soit ta croyance,
Tu sais ce que vaut un serment.
A cette coupe où l'amour te convie,
Jure de m'aimer pour la vie!
(On entend au loin des chants militaire.)

Gérald. Ciel! ce sont nos soldats!

Lakmé. Bois, et tu m'appartiendras!
(Avec force en posant la coupe.)
Tu n'oses pas.
(Elle regarde attentivement Gérald dont les yeux restent
fixés du côté où l'on entend le chant des soldats.)
C'est là-bas que va sa pensée.
Son cœur a tressailli,
Et sa patrie à ses yeux s'est dressée.
(Avec déchirement après avoir essayé d'attirer son regard.)
Tout est fini!
(Pendant que Gérald, la tête penchée, suit de l'oreille les
tambours qui s'éloignent, Lakmé, désespérée, arrache une
feuille de datura et la mâche sans que Gérald s'en aperçoive.)

Gérald. Lakmé, qu'avez vous fait?

Lakmé.
(Allant à lui, avec tendresse et souriante.)
Tu m'as donné plus doux rêve
Qu'on puisse avoir sous notre ciel,
Reste encore pour qu'il s'achève
Ici, loin du monde réel.
Tu m'as dit des mots de tendresse
Que les Hindous ne savent pas,
Et tu m'as appris l'ivresse
Des aveux murmurés tout bas.

Gérald. Ce que je lis sur ton visage,
Ma Lakmé, me glace d'effroi.
De tout mon âme se dégage
Et je ne serai plus qu'à toi.

Lakmé.
(Avec passion.)
Ah! maintenant, je veux te croire,
Voici la coupe où je vais boire.
(Elle y trempe ses lèvres et la lui tend.)

Gérald. Prends!
(La prenant avec exaltation.)
A toi, Lakmé, pour toujours!

Lakmé. C'est la fête de nos amours!
(Il boit.)

plus anime.
GERALD.　　　　　　　　LAKME.
　　　　　　　　　　　　failing.

I'm all your own, I tru-ly swear it! Ah! 'tis an oath that scarce your strength will try. I have no fear, Ah!
Toujours à toi, je te le ju-re! C'est un serment que tu pourras té mir Je ne crains pas, va!

　　　　　　　　　　　　GERALD. LAKME.*(smiling.)*

... Here I now de-clare it, I soon shall die! Shall die! But death does not lov-ers
que tu sús par-ju-re! Je vais mourir Mourir! La mort ne sépare

part, ... Our souls re - joined, fore - see - ing. I to you .. give my be - ing, And I
pas, C'est el - le qui nous li - e. Je te don - ne ma vi - e, Et je
　　　　　　　GERALD. LAKME.　　　　　　　　*a tempo animato.* GERALD.

die .... on your heart. Lak-mé! And I die ... on your heart! No! it is no more death,
meurs dans tes bras. Lakmé! Et je meurs dans tes bras! Non! ce n'est pas la mort,

Life, 't is strong and glow - ing, Pass - ing a full breath From your pale lips o - ver - flow-
C'est la vie ar - den - te Qui coule à plein bord Sur ta lè - vre fré - mi - san-
　　　　　　　　　　　　　　　　　　　　　　　　LAKME.

Fare - well, ...
A dieu!

ing. Ah! .... Though doubt may shade our mor - row, I'd have no tear of
te. Ah! Qu'autour de moi tout sombre, Je ne veux pas une

... O dream of sor - - row! A - las! what
Rêve qui som - - bre Hélas, quelle

sor - row, I'd have no tear of sor-row On your en - chant-ing brow. ...
om - bre Je ne veux pas une ombre Sur ton front enchanté -
　　　　　　　　　　　　　　　　　　　　　LAKME.

shad-ow on my heart lies now! 'T is my first tear of sor - row.
ombre en mon coeur attris - té! C'est ma première lar - row.

Be-neath the spell I'm rest - - ing, That never a tear pro-
Je reste sous le char - Que jamais une

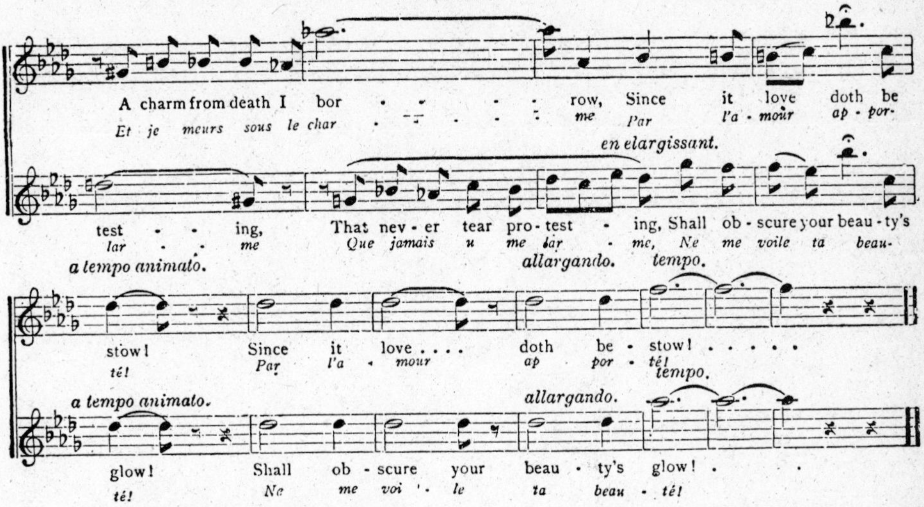

A charm from death I bor . . . . row, Since it love doth be
Et je meurs sous le char . . . . me Par l'a - mour ap - por -
en elargissant.

test - - ing, That nev - er tear pro - test - ing, Shall ob - scure your beau - ty's
lar - me Que jamais u me lar - me, Ne me voile ta beau -
a tempo animato. allargando. tempo.

stow! Since it love . . . doth be - stow! . . . . .
té! Par l'a - mour ap - por - té!
tempo.

a tempo animato. allargando.

glow! Shall ob - scure your beau - ty's glow! . . . .
té! Ne me voi '- le ta beau - té!

NILAKANTHA, Hindoos enter.	LES MÊMES, NILAKANTHA. ...
Nila. 'T is he! beside Lakmé. Thou must die!	*Nila.* C'est lui! c'est! lui près de Lakmé!
Gerald. Strike now! All unarmed am I!	*Gérald.* Frappez! Je suis désarmé!
Lakmé. (Withholding her father by a gesture.) We have both taken a draught from the ivory flagon, which is sacred for you.	*Lakmé.* (Retenant son père d'un geste.) Nous avons bu tous deux à la coupe d'ivoire. Il est sacré pour vous.
Nila. What, he?	*Nila.* Lui!
Lakmé. (With failing voice.) If so it must be— A victim to the gods you offer, Let them claim one in me!	*Lakmé.* S'il faut à nos dieux Une victime expiatoire, Qu'ils m'appellent vers eux!
Gerald. (Frightened.) In her eyes what light is shining!	*Gérald.* (Effrayé.) Quel éclair en ses yeux brille!
Lakmé. (With ecstasy.) Ah! they've spoken to me!	*Lakmé.* (Avec extase.) Ils m'ont parlé!
Nila. (Lifting her.) Lakmé, my daughter!	*Nila.* (Éperdu, la saisissant.) Lakmé, ma fille!
Gerald. (Sobbing.) She dies now for me.	*Gérald.* (Avec des sanglots.) Elle meurt pour moi!
Lakmé. (Failing.) You have given me love, the sweetest dreaming That one may know beneath our sky; Let me stay, till exquisite seeming Has become here reality! Far from worldly. (She dies.)	*Lakmé.* (Mourante, le sourire sur la lèvres.) Tu m'as donné le plus doux rêve Qu'on puisse avoir sous notre ciel. Reste encore pour qu'il s'achève Ici, loin du monde réel!
Gerald. Ah! heaven!	*Gérald.* Morte!
Nila. (With exaltation.) Her soul now has life eternal, She leaves earth for regions supernal. Upward bears she our vows on high, Where angel glories fill the sky!	*Nila.* (Avec extase.) Elle a l'éternelle vie Quittant cette terre asservie, Elle porte là-haut nos vœux Elle est dans la splendeur des cieux.

MIGNON

by

AMBROISE THOMAS

MIGNON

MIGNON, the daughter of noble parents has, when a child, been stolen from her ancestral home, by gipsies. Her mother, shortly after this bereavement, dies of grief; while Lothario, the broken-hearted father, almost deprived of reason by the loss of his daughter, forsakes his home, and roams as a minstrel, from place to place, in search of his darling child. For years, Mignon, utterly unconscious of her birth and origin, leads a wandering life with the gipsy tribe, of which her beauty renders her the most prominent ornament. The chief, Jarno, who combines the avocation of mountebank with that of gipsy, compels the hapless girl to dance, and go through various other performances, in order to obtain money from the inhabitants of the towns through which they pass—and harshly threatens her with his stick, whenever, from fatigue, she refuses to do his bidding. Wilhelm Meister, a young student on his travels, happens on one of these occasions to be a spectator of Jarno's ferocity; and in order to prevent the recurrence of such ill-treatment, he purchases Mignon from her cruel master. The friendless Mignon, deeply touched by Wilhelm's kindness, gradually conceives for him an ardent and irrepressible attachment. Wilhelm, however, totally unconscious of the affection which his young protégée has conceived for him, falls a prey to the fascinations of Filina, a young actress belonging to a troupe of Thespians, on their way to perform at a neighboring castle, where a grand fête is about to take place, in honor of the arrival of some illustrious prince.

Foremost among the guests invited to assist at the festivities, is Wilhelm. Filina, the beautiful but coquettish object of his admiration, is the idol of the hour, and her success in the "private theatricals" at the castle, serves but to increase Wilhelm's fondness for the fascinating comedienne. Mignon, who has accompanied her new master to the castle, watches with silent grief the progress of Wilhelm's love for her rival. At length, despondent and unhappy, and unable longer to endure the maddening jealousy which gnaws her heart's core, Mignon is about to throw herself into a lake adjoining the castle, when, of a sudden, a harp, played by an unseen hand, is heard, and in another moment Lothario appears. Abandoning her impious resolve, Mignon, little dreaming that it is her father who stands before her, flies to the aged minstrel and implores his counsel and protection. Carried away by the vehemence of her emotion, she prays that vengeance may overtake the abode in which her hated rival is, at this very moment, in all the glory of her triumph. The performance inside the castle now terminates. Filina appears, surrounded by a tumultuous crowd of admirers, all loud in their praises of the actress's beauty and talents. Mirth and pleasure reign supreme, when, of a sudden, a lurid glare illumines the scene . . . the castle is in flames! The aged Lothario, whom the voice of nature has unconsciously interested in Mignon's behalf, has, half crazed as he is with grief and trouble, lent an ear to Mignon's rash imprecation, and has set fire to the castle. A scene of terrible confusion ensues. Mignon is nowhere to be found. Wilhelm, after an eager but fruitless search for her, rushes wildly amid the burning rafters, and, in a few moments, reappears, bearing the helpless girl in his arms.

In a room in Lothario's manorial residence, on the banks of an Italian lake, lies Mignon overtaken by a dangerous illness, resulting from the fearful peril she has so lately and so narrowly escaped, as well as from the continued struggle to conceal the affection so long pent up in her breast. Wilhelm, who has meanwhile assisted Lothario in transporting Mignon to the home from which the unhappy parent had so long been absent, has discovered (from the broken sentences which have escaped Mignon during the crisis of her illness) the secret of her affection for him. Through the medium of a long-concealed casket, containing a girdle worn by Mignon when a little child, as well as by her heartful utterance of the words of a prayer which her parents had taught her in her infancy, the entranced Lothario discovers, beyond the possibility of a doubt, that Mignon is his long-lost child.

Blessed by the recovery of her sole surviving parent, and enraptured by Wilhelm's fervent, through long delayed avowal of his love for her, Mignon, fanned by the restorative breezes of her native hills, banishes forever from her memory the recollection of the troubled Past, and confidingly looks forward to the bright and happy Future.

MIGNON

ACT I

The courtyard of a German Inn. To the left a wing of a building, the facade of which faces the spectator. On the first floor, a little door, with glass window, which opens upon a parapet, from which a flight of steps leads down to the court yard. To the right a pent-house, or shed. Arbors and tables, &c.

Townsfolk, countrymen, etc.—afterwards *Lotharto*. [The townspeople, etc., sit down at the table and drink. Waiters belonging to the inn, hurry to and fro, attending officiously to the wants of the customers.]

Chorus.   Magnates great, and towns-folk small,
To table now sit down,
Our cigars we quickly light,
Fresh zest 'twill give unto the drink!
Fill high! the foaming beer
In jugs does now approach;
A festive day is this indeed,
A day of mirth and joy!

[*Lotharto* appears at back, at the entrance to the inn. He advances slowly, stopping near the middle of the courtyard, when he begins to sing—accompanying himself the while on his harp.]

Lotharto.   A lonely wanderer am I! I stray from door to door.
As fate doth guide, or as the storm doth hurry me;
But heaven protects the wretched with kind fost'ring care!
She lives—I feel this in my heart; her steps I anxiously do trace,——
A moment here I will repose—my journey I will then resume;
Far, far I'll roam in search of her!

1st Cit.   List to him, 'tis Lothario the wandering minstrel!

2nd Cit.   'Tis said that grief hath ta'en his reason from him.

1st Cit.   But how came this?

2nd Cit.   The cause I know not.

Chorus.
(To LOTHARIO.)
Take courage, friend!
Give o'er thy singing—
Come thou, and sit down with us!
(The Chorus make LOTHARIO sit down with them. beneath the vine-trellis. They fill a glass for him.)

ACTE PREMIER

Une cour de taverne allemande. A gauche, corps de bâtiment dont l'un des côtés fait face au public. Au premier étage, porte vitrée donnant sur le perron d'un escalier extérieur qui descend dans la cour. A droite, un hangar. Table et tonnelles.

Les Bourgeois sont attablés et boivent; quelques Garçons de taverne sont occupés à les servir.

Chœur des Bourgeois.   Bons bourgeois et notables,
Assis autour des tables,
Fumons tranquillement,
Et buvons en fumant!
La bière brune ou blanche,
Ecume dans les pots,
C'est aujourd'hui dimanche,
C'est le jour du repos!

(LOTHARIO parait au fond sur le seuil de la taverne. Il s'avance lentement, s'arrête au milieu de la cour et chante en s'accompagnant sur un luth.)

Lotharto.   Fugitif et tremblant, je vais de porte en porte,
Où le hasard me guide, où l'orage m'emporte!
Des misérables Dieu prend soin!
Elle vit! elle vit! Et je cherche sa trace!
Je me repose un jour, un seul jour, et je passe!
Je vais plus loin, toujours plus loin!

Un Bourgeois.
(À ses voisins.)
Oui; c'est Lothario, le vieux chanteur nomade.

Deuxième Bourgeois.
On dit que le malheur a troublé sa raison.

Un Bourgeois.
D'où vient-il?

Deuxième Bourgeois.
On l'ignore.

Chœur.   Allons, mon camarade!
Viens boire, et laisse là ta plaintive chanson!
(On fait asseoir LOTHARIO sous la tonelle, et on lui verse à boire.)

Chorus.	*Chœur.*

Chorus.
Magnates great, and towns-folk small
To table now sit down!
Our cigars, let's quickly light,
Fresh zest 'twill give unto the drink.
Fill high! the foaming beer
In tankards now draws nigh.
A festive day is this indeed,
A day of mirth and joy!

(Several of the convivial party now approach the back of the stage, and form a group near the door of the inn.)

Peasants.
Room, good friends, for the travelling players!
What ho! make way there!
See! Jarno with the flower of his tribe doth come,
And Zaffi, too, is there!

[Procession of gipsies. The entire tribe march round the stage. A cart covered with an old piece of matting, and filled with various articles of household furniture, leads the way drawn by two ragged gipsies. MIGNON, wrapped in a tattered mantle, is sleeping at the back of the cart on a sheaf of straw. A party of gipsies, with tambourines in their hands, now rush on the stage. Zaffi takes a violin, and gives the signal for the dance. An oboe and a tambourine serve as accompaniment.]

Filina.
(Looking from the balcony with LAERTES.)
Quick, my Laertes, just step this way;
See—an hour's amusement here awaits us.
Laugh not at these good people, but pray allowance make—
Here our places let us take!
[LAERTES sits down by FILINA'S side.]
GIPSY DANCE

Peasants.
The Gypsy girls
Have lovely eyes
My wife herself
Gives them the prize.

Filina.
O! Gypsy Girls
Just full of zest.
You love them, they love you
And all is for the best.

Filina and Chorus.
Oh! What a mad dance
Oh! sing! hey! hey!
Let us be gay
We'll dance and drink, drink and dance
We'll dance and drink, drink and dance
A dance that's mad
Will make us glad
A whirl of joy
For girl and boy
A dance that's mad
Will make us glad

(JARNO advances into the middle of the stage, and salutes the bystanders, who throw to him pence, which ZAFFI picks up.)

Jarno.
Gentlemen, for so much kindness in return,
And just to show my sense of obligation,
Mignon a sample of her skill shall give you;
Her far-famed "egg dance"
She shall now perform!

Chœur.
Bons bourgeois et notables,
Assis autour des tables,
Fumons tranquillement,
Et buvons en fumant!
La bière brune et blanche,
Ecume dans les pots,
C'est aujourd'hui dimanche,
C'est le jour du repos!

(Quelques buveurs remontent au fond et se groupent sur le seuil de la taverne.)

Quelques Paysans.
(Entrant.)
Place, amis! Faites place aux enfants de Bohême,
Aux tsiganes, aux zingari!......
Voici toute la bande avec Jarno lui-même,
Et son compère Zafari!

(Entrée des BOHEMIENS. La bande défile autour du théâtre. Un chariot couvert d'une toile grossière et chargé d'oripeaux de toutes sortes, est traîné sur le devant de la scène par deux ou trois ZINGARI en haillons. JARNO est debout sur le chariot. MIGNON, enveloppée d'un vieux manteau rayè, dort sur une botte de paille au fond du chariot. Un groupe de danseurs, le tambour de basque en main, s'elance en scène. ZAFARI saisit son violon et donne le signal de la danse. Un tambourin et un hautbois l'accompagnent.)

Philine.
(Paraissant sur le balcon, suivie de LAERTE.)
Laërte, ami Laërte, accourez au plus vite!
Voilà qui nous promet un spectacle engageant!......
Mais ne vous moquez pas et soyez indulgent!
A vous asseoir je vous invite.
(LAERTE s'asseoit sur le balcon à côté de PHILINE.)
DANSE BOHEMIENNNE

Un Groupe de Vieux Bourgeois.
Ces filles de Bohême
Ont de fort jolis yeux,
Et ma femme elle-même
Ne danserait pas mieux!......

Philine et Laërte.
O filles de Bohême,
Filles au cœur joyeux,
Vous aimez, on vous aime,
Et tout est pour le mieux!......

Philine et Chœur.
Ah, ah, quelle danse folle!
Leur gai refrain
Nous met en train.
Ah, chantons, chantons et buvons,
Ah, chantons, chantons et buvons,
La danse folle,
S'élance et vole,
Leur joyeux refrain
Nous met tous en train!
La danse folle
S'élance et vole!
Ah, chantons!

(JARNO s'avance au milieu du théâtre et salue l'assemblée. Quelques pièces de monnaie tombent à ses pieds. ZAFARI les ramasse.)

Jarno.
Pour gagner maintenant toute votre indulgence,
Et vous remercier de vos dons généreux,
Mignon va vous montrer sa vive intelligence,
En dansant devant vous le fameux pas des œufs!

Chorus, Filina and Laertes.

Faith, we e'en awhile will tarry,
This far-famed dance to see!

Jarno.

(Turning to ZAFFI.)

And now, good Zaffi, quick prepare,
Thy choicest song to sing;
(Addressing himself to some of the Gipsies.)
Our beauteous piece of carpet,
On the ground now place—
(Approaching the cart and shaking MIGNON.)
Up, up, Mignon, to work!

(ZAFFI preludes on his violin. An old Gipsy lays on the ground a faded piece of worn out carpet, while a boy places on it several eggs. MIGNON, on hearing JARNO's voice, awakes and enters the circle formed by the chorus. She holds in her hand, a bouquet of wild flowers.)

Filina.

(To JARNO, from the balcony.)

What ho! good sir, permit me to inquire,
What hapless being is that just waking up?
Say, is't a girl, or strippling lad?

Jarno.   'Tis neither one nor other, lady—
'Tis neither woman, girl, nor boy.

Filina.

(Laughing.)
What is it then I pray?

Jarno.
(Raising the mantle which covers the young Gipsy.)
'Tis—Mignon!
[FILINA and the chorus laugh heartily.]

Mignon.

(Aside.)

Why are all eyes thus fixed on me?
Why laugh they thus—'tis surely to insult
    and mock me!
O heart! resume thy wonted strength and
    courage!

Jarno.   Quick, Mignon, arouse thee! dance!

Mignon.
(Stamping with her foot on the ground.)
Cease thy rude tone!
'Tis time I should speak out; I weary am
    of doing thy biding!

Jarno.   What! you refuse!
[Turning to the Gipsies.]
My friends, my stick just pass me.
Dance, I say.
Then, faith, I'll soon to reason bring ye!

Mignon.   No, no!
[Raises stick in a menacing attitude; as he does so LOTHARIO rushes to MIGNON and encircles her with his arms as though to protect her.]

Lothario.

(To MIGNON.)

Take heart I pray,
Thy shield I'll be!
His rage evade—
Fly quickly hence!

Chœur, Philine et Laërte.

Vivat! rapprochons-nous d'eux
Pour voir la danse des œufs!

Jarno.

(Se tourant vers ZAFARI.)

Toi, Zafari, prépare
Ton concerto le plus savant!......
(Aux autres ZINGARI.)
Couvrez le sol d'un tapis rare!......
(S'approchant du chariot et réveillant MIGNON.)
Et toi, Mignon, debout! en avant! en avant!

(ZAFARI prélude sur son violon. Une vielle ZINGARA couvre le sol d'un lambeau de tapis. Les œufs y sont déposés par un enfant. MIGNON s'éveille à la voix de JARNO et s'avance au milieu du cercle des curieux. Elle tient un bouquet de fleurs sauvages à la main et semble sortir d'un rêve.)

Philine.

(À JARNO, du haut du balcon.)

Holà! mon cher monsieur, vous plait-il de
    nous dire,
Quel est ce pauvre enfant qui semble vous
    maudire
De l'avoir de la sorte éveillé sans façon?.....
Est-ce une fille? est-ce un garçon?......

Jarno.   Ni l'unni l'autre, bel'e dame,
Ni garçon, ni fille, ni femme.

Philine.   Qu'est-ce donc alors?

Jarno.
(Ecartant le manteau qui couvre MIGNON.)
C'est Mignon!
(PHILINE et le CHOEUR éclatent de rire.)

Mignon.

(À part.)

Ces yeux fixés moi!...... Ce rire qui m'out-
    rage!......
Retrouve ta fierté, mon cœur, et ton cour-
    age!

Jarno.   Allons, saute, Mignon!

Mignon.
(Frappant le terre de son pied nu.)
Non, non, non, non!
Je brave ta menace!
De t'obéir à la fin je suis lasse!

Jarno.   Tu refuses!
(Se tourant vers les ZINGARA.)
Holà! vous autres, mon bâton!
Danse, Mignon!
Méchant démon!
Ou mon bâton
Saura te mettre à la raison!

Mignon.   Non, non, non, non, non, non!

Lothario.
(Courant à MIGNON qu'il étreint dans ses bras.)
Reprends courage!
Viens, pauvre enfant.
Contre sa rage
Je te défere.

Jarno.

(Furiously to LOTHARIO.)
Thou wretched meddler,
Get thee hence!
(Pushes back LOTHARIO violently, and again threatens
MIGNON.)

Dance, Mignon,
Dance, I say, or—
Then quickly I'll to reason bring ye!

Mignon.   No, no!
(He again raises his stick over MIGNON. Enter WILHELM,
who appears to have come off a journey. A servant, who carries his portmanteau, stands behind him.)

Wilhelm.
(Hurrying to MIGNON's assistance, and arresting JARNO's
arm.)
Ruffian, hold! or meet thy death!

Jarno.   Eh? pray what d'ye mean?

Wilhelm.

(Producing a pistol.)
Another word, and through thy brains
I'll send a bullet!

Jarno.

(Alarmed.)
You mean it? then quiet I'll remain
(In a piteous tone.)
I'm ruined quite—I am indeed!
Who will repay me for the loss I thus en-
dure?

Filina.

(Throwing him a purse from the balcony.)
That will I. Take this purse and hold your
tongue,
Yourself take hence with all convenient
speed!

Mignon.
(Dividing her nosegay into two halves, one of which she
gives to WILHELM, and the other to LOTHARIO.)
Kind friends, accept this humble token of
my gratitude.

Wilhelm.   So strange an occurrence
Who e'er could forsee?
Nature's own instinct
My steps did hither bend.

Filina.

(To LAERTES.)
Tell me, who is yonder gentleman,
Of manners so urbane?
He does not seem to see us
And does himself conceal
Whence he comes and whither goes
I perchance would wish to know

Mignon.
(Who has withdrawn a few paces—praying.)
Holy Virgin Mary,
Have mercy on an innocent maid,
Who always humbly seeks
Thy gracious will to do!

Jarno.

(Avec colère.)
Au diable! au diable!
Vil misérable!
(Il repousse violemment LOTHARIO.)
Danse, Mignon!
Méchant démon!
Ou mon bâton
Saura te mettre à la raison!

Mignon.   Non, non, non, non, non, non!
(JARNO lève son bâton sur MIGNON. Entre WILHELM en
habit de voyage, suivi d'un valet qui porte sa valise et son
manteau.)

Wilhelm.
(S'élançant au secours de MIGNON et retenant le bras de
JARNO.)
Holà! coquin! arrète, ou ton heure est
venue!

Jarno.   Hein? Plaît-il?

Wilhelm.

(Tirant un pistolet de sa poche.)
Si tu fais un seul pas je te tue!

Jarno.   C'est bon! Je me tiens coi!
(D'un ton lamentable.)
Mais je suis ruiné!
Qui de vous me paira ma recette perdue?

Philine.
(Sur le balcon, jetant sa bourse à JARNO.)
Tiens donc! Prends et tais-toi! que tout
soit pardonné.

Mignon.
(Partageant son bouquet entre WILHELM et LOTHARIO.)
A vous ces fleurs, amis, qui m'avez dé-
fendue!......

Wilhelm.   Qui diantre aurait pu prévoir
Cette bizarre aventure!
Mon cœur, pauvre créature,
M'a seul dicté mon devoir!

Philine.

(À part.)
Quel est, je veux le savoir,
Ce beau coureur d'aventure?
Il nous cache sa figure,
Et n'a pas l'air de nous voir.

Mignon.

(Priant, à l'écart.)
O Vierge, mon seul espoir,
Protége ta créature!
Je me courbe sans murmure
Devant ton divin pouvoir!

Chorus.	**Chœur.**
(To Jarno.) We'll be back to see you again. For adventure we're out Till the sun's put to rout But we'll return to dance then.	(À Jarno.) Nous reviendrons tous vous voir. Tant que le dimanche dure, On chemine à l'aventure Et l'on vient danser le soir.
Jarno.	**Jarno.**
Folks, come back tonight This incident, please forget. You will be, I will bet Happy and thrilled with delight.	Messieurs, revenez-nous voir, Oubliez cette aventure, Vous serez, je vous le jure, Très-contents de nous ce soir.
Laertes.	**Laërte.**
(To Filina.) This beautiful black-eyed man Soldier of fortune, beyond doubt. Who he is? Oh! You'll find out And meet him as soon as you can.	(À Philine.) Ce beau garçon à l'œil noir, Ce beau coureur d'aventure Quel est-il? ah! je le jure, Vous brûlez de le savoir.
Lothario.	**Lothario.**
(Who continues motionless, his eye fied on vacancy, his hand the while rambling over the chords of his harp.) "The shades of even just 'gan to fall, When through the forest dark and drear, A knight all clad in steel of proof Did slowly wend his way."	(Immobile et l'œil fixe, touchant les cordes de sa harpe.) Sous le voile obscur du soir, Et sous la verte ramure, Un homme à la lourde armure Arrête son coursier noir!
[Townsfolk, etc., exeunt at back. Jarno and his comrades retire beneath the shed—Mignon follows them. Lothario slowly withdraws. Filina speaks aside to Laertes, pointing the while to Wilhelm. She immediately afterwards enters her room, while Laertes descends into the court by the outer staircase.]	(Les Bourgeois sortent par le fond. Jarno et les Bohemiens se retirement dans le hangar. Mignon les suit et Lothario s'éloigne lentement. Philine parle bas à Laerte en lui montrant Wilhelm du doigt. Elle rentre chez elle en riant et Laerte descend dans la cour par l'escalier extérieur.)
Laertes.	**Laërte.**
(Saluting Wilhelm.) Sir!—	(S'approchant pour saluer Wilhelm.) Monsieur......
Wilhelm.	**Wilhelm.**
(Returning the salutation.) Sir!—	(Lui rendant son salut.) Monsieur......
Laertes.	**Laërte.**
Be not offended if I your praises sing; The succor you extended to that helpless maid, Was truly worthy of a knight of yore.	Monsieur, souffrez qu'on vous complimente sur la façon vraiment chevaleresque dont vous avez secouru cette petite bohémienne.
Wilhelm.	**Wilhelm.**
(Carelessly.) Who would not have done the same?	Ce que j'ai fait, monsieur, tout autre l'eût fait autant.
Laertes.	**Laërte.**
Exactly; but this opinion Filina does not share— Filina is the lady who just now sat in yonder balcony, While men call me—Laertes! (Declaiming with comic emphasis.) Alas! misfortune! indeed, I may say, ruin! Of a luckless troupe of actors, On whom destiny ne'er did smile, You see in us the helpless remnant! Filina hopes for a more prosperous turn on Fortune's wheel, While I, of my artistic calling well nigh weary, Curse in my heart, the Tragic Muse!	Ceì n'est pas l'avis de Philine. . . . La dame du balcon a nom Philine; je me nomme Laërte. . . . O désastre! O ruine d'une troupe comique aujourd'hui sans emploi. Vous voyez en nous deux les débris misérables! Philine attend un sort meilleur, et moi j'envoie avec bonheur notre métier à tous les diables!
Wilhelm.	**Wilhelm.**
(Courteously.) A flagon of good wine, I trust you'll not refuse?	Vous plaît-il, cher monsieur, de partager cette bouteille?
Laertes.	**Laërte.**
Right glad, sir	Volontiers, monsieur!

Wilhelm.

(To the waiter.)

Another glass.
Wilhelm Meister is my name. I hail from
   Vienna.

Laertes.   I like your youth, I like your spirit.

Wilhelm.   And yet, I saw you flirting
            With a fair lady in yon balcony.

Laertes.   What! with Filina?
            The gods forbid! We know each other far
               too well,
            To feel a mutual love!
            She's flighty, vain, cantankerous, astute,
            Fickle as Fortune. and more changeable
            Than is the moon!
            And yet her beauty rare,
            With love all hearts inflames—
            Let's drink her health!
                  (Raises his glass.)
[FILINA who has overheard this conversation from the
window quickly descends the staircase.]

Filina.   So, sir! now you've finished the portrait,
            Why not place it in a frame?

Wilhelm.
                  (Bowing.)
            He treats you somewhat harshly I must own,
            But those bright eyes the calumny right
               soon dispel.

Filina.   Grateful, indeed, am I, for so well-turned
            a compliment.

Wilhelm
                  (Aside.)
            What beauty—what grace,
            How frank is her mien,
            I fear that my sighs.
            Her heart ne'er will win!

Filina.
                  (Aside.)
            The most I'll make now of my charms,
            Resolved am I that he shall love me;
            My beauty's power I know full well,
            No youthful heart can e'er resist me.

Laertes.
                  (Aside.)
            The most she'll make now of her charms,
            Resolved is she the youth shall love her;
            Her blandishments I know full well,
            No youthful heart can e'er resist her.
            But, without further ceremony,
            Each to the other I will introduce!
         (Presenting WILHELM to FILINA.)
            The most excellent Signor Wilhelm, a gen-
               tleman most worthy,

Wilhelm.

Un verre encor!
(À la Servante qui prépare la table.)
               (A LAERTE.)
Wilhelm Meister le fils d'un honnête bour-
   geois de Vienne.
               (Ils boivent.)

Laërte.
                  (Déclamant.)
         J'aime votre gaité, j'aime votre jeune âme.....

Wilhelm.
                  (Souriant.)
         Vous courtisez pourtant de fort près la
            dame du balcon!

Laërte.   Qui, l'aimable Philine?
            Nous nous connaissons beaucoup trop pour
               nous aimer.
            Folle, vaine comme pas une,
            Plus perfide que la fortune,
            Et plus changeante que la lune,
            C'est grace à son esprit et grace à son
               beauté
            Le plus charmant démon! Buvons à sa
               santé!
   (Ils trinquent et boivent. PHILINE descend l'escalier pendant les dernières paroles de LAERTE.)

Philine.   Eh! quoi! mon cher Laërte, en vidant votre
               verre,
            N'ajouterez-vous rien à ce portrait charm-
               ant?

Wilhelm.
                  (Saluant PHILINE.)
            Il vous juge en ami sévère,
            Et vos beaux yeux disent qu'il ment.

Philine.   Je vous sais gré du compliment.

Wilhelm.
                  (À part.)
            Que de grâces et de charmes!
            Quels regards pleins de feu!
            Les soupirs et les larmes
            Sont ici hors de jeu.

Philine.
                  (À part.)
            Essayons de nos charmes
            Pour nous venger un peu,
            Me voilà sous les armes,
            Le reste n'est qu'un jeu.

Laërte.
                  (Riant.)
            La voilà sous les armes,
            Nous allons voir beau jeu!
            Devant de pareils charmes
            Son cœur va prendre feu!
            Permettez, sans plus de façon,
            Qu'on vous présente l'un à l'autre.
         (Présentant WILHELM à PHILINE.)
            Monsieur Wilhelm Meister, un aimable
               garçon,

Who. in exchange for yours, his heart
    would fain present you!
(Introducing FILINA to WILHELM.)
Mistress Filina, an actress of merit and re-
    nown,
Who is much taken with you, and, indeed,
    desires to let you know it;
        (Aside to FILINA.)
A loving glance just cast his way.
        (Aside to WILHELM.)
Present this nosegay to yon lady fair—
So!
[Takes nosegay and gives it to FILINA.)

Wilhelm.
            (Aside.)
What beauty, what grace,
How enchanting each glance,
I fear that my sighs
Her heart ne'er will win.

Filina.
            (Aside.)
The most I'll make now of my charms,
Resolved am I that he shall love me, etc.

Laertes.
            (Aside.)
All her wiles she brings to bear,
Resolved is she the youth shall love her, etc.

Filina. Excuse, I pray, the giddy-pated fellow;
            (To LAERTES.)
Your arm now give me!

Laertes.
        (To WILHELM.)
I trust we soon may meet again;

Filina.
        (To LAERTES smiling.)
Can he who once has seen me.
Take his departure *quite* so soon?

Laertes. It, perhaps might prove the wiser plan;

Filina. In sooth, the observation is gallant.

Laertes.
            (Aside.)
A little puss is she.
        (To WILHELM curtseying.)

Filina. Sir, I take my leave.
            (Exit with LAERTES.)

Wilhelm. A pretty girl, i' faith!
Her friend may say just what he pleases,
But I'll not leave her yet.

Mignon.
    (Coming from under the shed. Aside.)
    Ah! he's alone——

Wilhelm. What is it you? What would you now?

Qui vous offre son cœur en échange du
    vôtre.
(Présentant PHILINE à WILHELM.)
La signora Philine, un ange en falbala,
Qui vous trouve charmant et voudrait vous
    le dire.
            (À PHILINE.)
Décochez à monsieur votre plus doux sou-
    rire.
            (À WILHELM.)
Offrez votre bouquet à madame!......
    (Il prend le bouquet et le donne à PHILINE.)

Wilhelm.
            (À part.)
Que de grâce et de charmes!
Quels regards pleins de feu!
Les soupirs et les larmes
Sont ici hors de jeu!

Philine.
            (À part.)
Essayons de nos charmes
Pour nous venger un peu, etc.

Laërte.
            (Riant.)
La belle est sous les armes,
Nous allons voir beau jeu!

Philine.
        (À WILHELM.)
De mon ami, Monsieur, excusez les folies.
        (À LAERTE.)
Votre bras!

Laërte.
        (À WILHELM.)
Devons-nous vous retrouver ici?

Philine.
            (Riant.)
Comment! quand on m'a vue est-ce qu'on
    fuit ainsi?

Laërte. On ferait bien de fuir!

Philine. La réponse est polie!
            (À part.)
Impertinent!

Laërte.
            (Bas.)
Coquette!
        (À WILHELM.)

Monsieur!.
            (Ils sortent.)

Wilhelm.
            (Gaiement.)
Voilà, pardieu! une charmante fille et
    Laërte a beau dire, il n'est pas temps en-
    core de nous dire un éternel adieu.

Mignon.
            (Sortent.)
Il est seul!......

Wilhelm.
        (Apercevant MIGNON.)
Ah! c'est toi! Que me veux-tu?

Mignon.
            (Timidly.)
My master sleeps—give me thy hand,
I fain would kiss it.

Wilhelm.
To-morrow, my poor child,
I far from thee shall be;
No further aid can I e'er lend thee.

Mignon.
To-morrow? Who knows where we shall be
    to-morrow?
'Tis known alone to God, who this vast
    world doth rule!

Wilhelm. What's your name?

Mignon.
They call me Mignon
I have no other name.

Wilhelm. How old are you?

Mignon.
Summers come and summers go but
No one counted my summers for me.

Wilhelm.
But tell me! of the scenes which, when a
    child, thou left'st—hast thou no recol-
    lection?
Were I to break thy chains, and set thee
    free,
To what beloved spot would'st wend thy
    way?

Mignon.
Le maitre dort. Donne ta main, donne! et
    mille fois merci!

Wilhelm.
Demain, mon pauvre enfant je serai loin
    d'ici,
Et ton supplice va renaître.

Mignon.
Demain, dis-tu? Qui sait où nous serons
    demain.
L'avenir est à Dieu! le temps est dans sa
    main.

Wilhelm. Quel est ton nom?

Mignon
Ils m'appellent Mignon,
Je n'ai pas d'autre nom.

Wilhelm. Quel âge as-tu?

Mignon.
Les bois ont reverdi, les fleurs se sont
    fanées,
Personne n'a pris soin de compter mes an-
    nées.

Wilhelm.
Dis-moi de quelles plages lointaines
Ton âme a gardé le souvenir,
Et si ma main brisait tes chaines,
Vers quels pays tu voudrais revenir?

HAST THOU E'ER SEEN THE LAND.

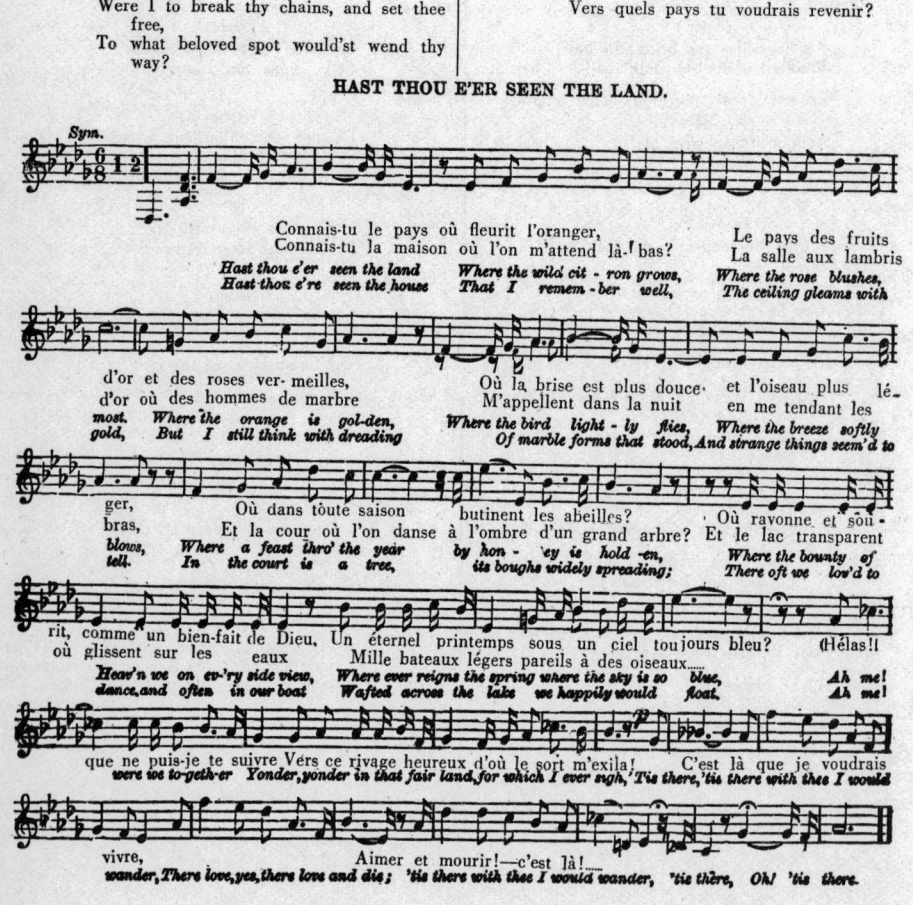

Wilhelm.	The enchanted soil you speak of, must surely Italy be?	*Wilhelm.*	Ce pays enchanté dont tu parles, n'est-ce pas l'Italie?

Mignon.   Alas! I cannot say.

Mignon.
(Rêveuse.)
Je ne sais......

Wilhelm.
(Aside.)
A strange creature this!

Wilhelm.
(À part.)
Etrange créature!

Jarno.
(Issuing from the pent-house and running toward MIGNON, To WILHELM, sarcastically.)
Oho! the damsel pleases you, it seems!
You would like to have her.

Jarno.
(Qui entre.)
Ah! ah! Il paraît que l'enfant vous plaît ......mon prince, vous voulez me la débaucher!......

(Seizing him by the collar.)
Wilhelm.   Scoundrel!
Let but another word escape thee—

Wilhelm.
(Avec colére.)
Sur ma vie, n'ajoute pas un mot!

Jarno.   Nought will I say—but still—
Since in the young lady—a—a—an *interest* you take,
Just hand to me the sum I gave for her,
And my claim on her, to *you,* I'll cede.

Jarno.   Bon, je ne dis plus rien. Mais puisque votre coeur s'interesse à la belle, remboursez-moi ce qu'elle m'a coûté, et je renonce à tous mes droits sur elles!

Wilhelm.   Come then—resolved am I
To free her from her bonds!
(Enters the inn with JARNO.)

Wilhelm.   Viens donc!
(Regardant MIGNON avec intérêt.)
Je veux lui rendre au moins sa liberté!
(Il sort avec JARNO.)

Mignon.
(Bounding with joy.)
Free! Free!
And is it really true?
[Perceiving LOTHARIO, who issues from the pent-house.]
Come thou and share with me my joy,
Thou who, but now, so nobly did'st defend me!
As consolation to my tortured soul
Heaven hath surely sent thee.

Mignon.
(À LOTHARIO qui entre.)
Libre! libre! Est-ce vrai?...... Viens partager ma joie!
Toi qui m'as comme lui
Defendue aujourd'hui!
Pour consoler Mignon c'est dieu qui vous envoie!

Lothario.   I come my leave to take,
Ere I go hence;

Lothario.   Je te cherchais pour te faire mes adieux......
J'ai voulu te voir avant de partir.

Mignon.   And whither wilt thou go?

Mignon.   Ou vas-tu?

Lothario.
(Pointing to the sky.)
The swallows to the south do hie;
I'll thither with them!

Lothario.
(Levant les bras vers le ciel.)
Déjà les hirondelles volent vers le midi.
Moi, je pars avec elles.

Mignon.   Ah! why may I not fly there, too?
Reach me thy harp!

Mignon.   Que ne puis-je à travers l'espace fuir aussi.
Donne-moi ton luth!

Lothario.   'Tis here!

Lothario.   Le voici!

Mignon.
(Accompanying herself on the harp.)

OH SWALLOWS GAY AND BLITHE.

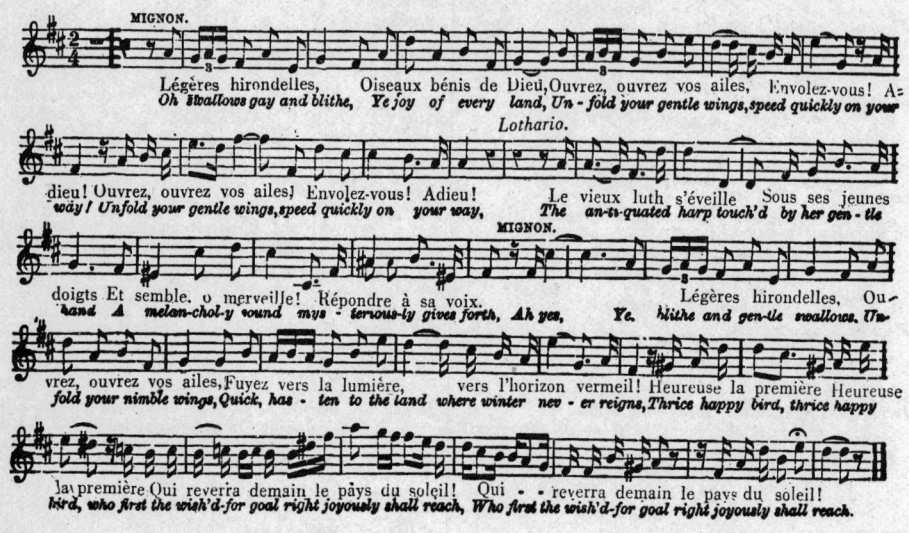

[They both withdraw beneath the pent-house.)

Filina.
(Laughing mockingly at FREDERIC, who follows her, shaking the dust from his clothes.)
What! is it you?

Frederic. You laugh, do you? a madman was I truly
To kill my horse by racing after you!

Filina.
(Laughing.)
You'd like me perhaps, to cry?

Frederic. I vow, I'm sorry now I came!

Filina.
(Aggravatingly.)
You can return whene'er you please;
You'll soon come back again!

Wilhelm.
(To JARNO at the door of the Inn.)
'Tis understood then—
Mignon is free!

Filina.
(To WILHELM.)
Hear I aright?
Has Mignon been re-purchased from her master?

Frederic.
(Aside, and jealously.)
Whence comes yon gentlemen, I pray?

(MIGNON et LOTHARIO sortent. PHILINE, entre en riant, avec FREDERIC.)

Philine. Ah, ah, ah, ah, ah!
Comment? C'est vous?

Frédéric.
(S'époussetant avec sa cravache.)
Oui, oui, riez! je suis un sot
De créver mon cheval de vous revoir plus tôt!

Philine.
(Se moquant.)
Ne voulez-vous pas que je pleure?

Frédéric. Ah, vous me faites repentir d'être venu!......

Philine. Vous pouvez repartir,
Vous nous reviendrez tout à l'heure.

Wilhelm.
(Qui entre avec JARNO, à ce dernier.)
Marché conclu! Mignon est libre.

Philine. Qu'entends-je là? Vous-avez racheté Mignon?

Frédéric. Hein? d'ou sort celui-là?

Filina.
(Introducing FREDERIC to WILHELM.)
Mr. Meister,
Permit me to introduce my young friend
    Frederick,
Who, whether I will or no,
My cavalier doth undertake to be.
[Presenting WILHELM to FREDERIC]
Wilhelm Meister this—I think you'll like
    him.

Laertes.
(Outside, calling.)
Filina.

Filina.
(Turning round.)
Here is Laertes.

Laertes.
(Turning to FILINA.)
This letter is addressed to you;

Filina. Read it aloud.

Laertes.
(Reading.)
"Beauteous goddess!
Wishing right worthily to celebrate
The Prince Ulrico Tieflenbach's arrival,
I hope to see you, with your friends,
(At whose head I trust Laertes to behold!)
At this my castle, ere day declines;
I trust the invitation will be pleasing to you.
You well know the flame
Which burns within my tender heart;
        "Baron Rosenberg."

Frederic.
(Surprised.)
Heavens, my uncle!

Filina. What? is then the baron your uncle?

Frederic. Alas! *too much* my uncle!

Filina.
(Laughing.)
A pretty coincidence, in sooth!

Frederic. Do you accept the invitation?

Filina. With pleasure most unbounded!
(Turning to WILHELM.)
And you, sir,
Should it please you to take part in the
    festivity,
Pray come; 'twill give *me* pleasure I assure
    you;
Your presence to account for,
We'll say you are *stock author* to the com-
    pany.
(She ascends the outer staircase to her room, the door of which she shuts.)

Frederic.
(Enraged.)
O thrice accurs'd epistle!
O, day of woe! unnatural, heartless girl!
(To LAERTES, giving him his hand.)
Farewell, Laertes!
(To WILHELM—turning at the same time his back to him, and in a threatening tone.)
As for you, sir—

Philine.
(Presentant FREDERIC.)
Monsieur Meister, je vous présente
Le jeune Frédéric, un petit écolier
Qui malgré moi s'est fair mon chevalier.
(Présentant WILHELM à FREDERIC.)
Monsieur Wilhelm Meister, un homme que
    peutêtre
Vous aimerez un jour.

Laërte.
(Au dehors.)
Philine! Philine!

Philine. Ah, voici Laôrte!

Laërte.
(À PHILINE, lui offrant une lettre.)
Cette lettre est pour vous.

Philine. Lisez, lisez!

Laërte.
(Lisant.)
Ma toute belle,
Pour fêter dignement et de façon nouvelle
Le passage du Prince Ulric de Tiffembourg,
Je vous attends ainsi que Laërte et les
    autres,
En mon castel, avant la fin du jour......
Je comte bien, mon coeur, que vous serez
    des notres;
Vous devinez mon tendre espoir...... Baron
    de Rosemberg.

Frédéric. Mon oncle!

Philine. Hein? Comment? le Baron est votre oncle?

Frédéric. Hélas! oui!

Philine. C'est charmant!

Frédéric. Vous acceptez son offre?

Philine. Avec empressement!
(A WILHELM.)
Vous, monsieur, s'il vous plait prendre part
    à la fête,
Vous jouerez parmi nous le rôle de poë...
Si vous venez, d'ailleurs, vous me fere...
    plaisir.

Frédéric. Maudit Baron! Maudit message!
Maudite coquette! Au revoir, Laërte
(Se tournant vers WILHELM.)
Vous, Monsieur!

Wilhelm. Well! what now?

Laertes.

           (To WILHELM.)
Be wiser thou than yonder booby
Take my advice, nor linger here.
Set out at once! a pleasant journey to ye!
(Shakes his hand and enters inn.)

Mignon. Stranger! thou didst purchase me—
Dispose of me, henceforth, e'en as thou wilt.

Wilhelm. In this very town, to which Fate hath
    brought thee,
There lives an aged relative of mine,
Who, to her home, will gladly welcome thee.

Mignon. Must I then part from thee?

Wilhelm. My child, thou can'st *not* dwell with me;
Ill could I the part perform,
Of father!

Mignon. Could I not disguise myself,
And as thy servant, travel with thee?

Wilhelm.

        (Taking her hands.)
And what couldst thou do then?

Mignon. With love and gratitude,
My heart is filled.
To follow thee, O master mine,
Indeed were happiness to me!

Wilhelm. But just released for trifling sum,
From tyrant harsh and stern,
Would'st thou anew thy liberty renounce,
And be a slave once more?

Mignon.

        (Sadly.)
Well since my prayers thou wilt not hear,
[Pointing to LOTHARIO, who issues from under the
    pent-house.]
I'll e'en depart with *him!*

Lothario.
(Rushing to MIGNON, and encircling her with his arms.)
Come! my footsteps follow;
Through by-paths lone and wild,
Far from this spot, a home of twigs and
    leaves we'll seek
Ah! my footsteps follow,
My destiny pray share!
[Attempts to draw MIGNON with him.]

Wilhelm.

        (Stopping her.)
Nay, stay, fair maiden! for thy future I
    now fear!
Disguise thyself as page, or lackey, as thou
    wilt,
But at least remain with me,
The stars have will'd it so. Come! all care
    I'll take of thee!

Wilhelm. Plait-il?

Laërte. Soyez plus sage
Que ce jeune étourneau qui s'attache à nos
    pas.
Suivez votre chemin. Partez et bon voyage.

Mignon.

    (Accourant vers WILHELM.)
Me voici! tu m'as rachetée,
A ton gré dispose de moi!

Wilhelm. Je sais en cette ville, où le sort t'a jetée,
D'honnêtes gens chez qui tu seras bien
    traitée.

Mignon.

        (Vivement.)
Pourquoi me séparer de toi!

Wilhelm.

        (Souriant.)
Je ne puis t'emmener avec moi, pauvre fille!
Et m'imposer les soins d'un père de famille.

Mignon. Ne peux-tu m'habiller comme un jeune
    garçon
Et me laisser porter ta livrée?……

Wilhelm.

    (Lui prenant les mains.)
A quoi bon?

Mignon.

      (Avec un élan passionné.)
Envers qui me délivre
Je voulais m'acquitter!
J'étais prête à te suivre
Pour ne plus te quitter!

Wilhelm. Des mains de ce sauvage
Libre pour un peu d'or,
Quel nouvel esclavage
Veux-tu subir encor?

Mignon.

        (Tristement.)
C'est bien!…… puisque ta main sans pitié
    me repousse,
(Montrant LOTHARIO qui paraît sur le seuil du hangar)
Je pars avec lui!……

Lothario.
(Accourant vers MIGNON et l'entourant de ses bras.)
Viens! La libre vie est douce!
A l'ombre des grands bois sous le ciel
    étoilé,
Nous trouverons un lit de fougère et de
    mousse
Et tu partageras le pain de l'exilé!……
    (Il veut entraîner MIGNON.)

Wilhelm.

        (L'arrêtant.)
Non! pauvre enfant! pour toi l'avenir
    m'épouvante
Jeune fille ou garçon, serviteur ou servante,
Reste avec moi si tu le veux!
Le sort en est jeté! Je me rends à tes
    vœux!

Mignon.

(Kissing WILHELM's hand with rapture.)

With love and gratitude
My heart doth bound,
O master mine,
Ready am I to follow thee!

Wilhelm.

(With a kindly smile.)

My heart is deeply touched
With tender pity;
A noble impulse it must surely be,
That thus each pulse doth cause to throb.

Lothario.

(Aside, as though his mind were again wandering.)

Yield thou the maid to me,
And make me blest for aye!

(The actors beset the door of the inn. They are in travelling costume; they all carry, on their shoulders, or in their
hands, bundles, packages, etc.

Chorus.   On foot, my friends! away, away!
On us Dame Fortune smiles serene;
With us joy companion is,
Hunger far we leave behind!
From our heads our hats let's take,
Lowly bow we to the ground;
With joyous shouts we'll gaily hail
The generous host who entertains the merry
players!

Laertes.

(To the groom.)

We follow you!

(To the waiters who carry his luggage, and that of FILINA.)

(To the actors.)

And you my friends, pray, quick precede
us!
I start at once; I must be there first,
To get the supper ready!

Actors.   Huzza!

Mignon.

(Baisant la main de WILHELM avec transport.)

Envers qui me délivre
Je pourrai m'acquitter!
Je suis prête à te suivre
Pour ne plus te quitter!

Wilhelm.

(Lui souriant avec honté.)

L'ami qui te délivre
Ne doit plus te quitter!
Libre à toi de me suivre;
Il faut te contenter.

Lothario.

(À part, retombant dans son extase habituelle.)

Dieu bon! laissez-moi vivre,
Espérer et chanter!

(Les COMEDIENS envahissent la cour de l'auberge. Ils sont
en habits de voyage et portent sur l'épaule ou à la main des
paquets et des valises qui contiennent leurs hardes de théâtre.)

Chœur des Comédiens.

En route, amis, plions bagage!
La chance nous sourit enfin!
Que la gaîté soit du voyage,
Au diantre la soif et la faim!
Oublions nos repas d'auberge,
Et saluons, chapeau levé,
Ce vieux castel où l'on héberge
Les histrions sur le pavé!

Laërte.

(Au LAQUAIS.)

Nous vous suivons.

(Aux GARCONS d'auberge, qui portent ses hardes et celles
de PHILINE.)

Marchez devant, vous autres!

(Aux COMEDIENS.)

Je vous précède, amis, pour vous mieux
recevoir!
Un splendide festin vous attendra ce soir!

Les Comédiens.

Vivat!

-YOU'LL COME WITH US, I TRUST, SIR.

FIL. TO Wilhelm,

Et vous, monsieur, n'êtes-vous pas des nôtres?..... Grâce au galant seigneur   Qui, pour nous
You'll come with us, I trust,   sir, Thanks for   the po-lite-ness   of him who so

faire honneur, Nous prête son carrosse, Nous allons voyager, Et nous faire héberger, Comme en un jour
kindly for me .... his own carriage doth send; Side by side   we may most pleasant-ly

Wilhelm. (Kissing the hand of Fil.)

de noce!   Je vous dis au revoir!   Vous me verrez ce soir!   Je se-
trav-el,   We'll short-ly meet a-gain!   I   fain would join the throng,   And shall

rai de la fête!   Au revoir, au revoir!
ea-ger-ly look round for you.   We shall meet,   we shall soon meet a-gain.

(FILINA shows to WILHELM the bouquet which she, just now, received from him. MIGNON, who, at this moment enters with a little bundle in her hand, at once recognizes the flowers which she had given to WILHELM.)

Mignon.

(Aside.)
My flowers!

Wilhelm.

(To Mignon.)
What ails thee?

Filina.

(Aside to LAERTES, laughing.)
He loves me!

Laertes.

(Aside, laughing.)
He's trapped—poor fellow!

Mignon.

(To WILHELM—pointing to LOTHARIO.)
See! my poor flowers, *he* hath not despised, like thee!
His bouquet he hath not given away!

Wilhelm.

(Aside to MIGNON, smiling.)
I did not give it, child-—'twas stolen from me!

Mignon. But let's away, I ready am to follow thee;
(To the Gipsies.)
Oh, ye, with whom both shame and misery I've shared,—farewell!
(To a lad among the tribe, attaching a medal to his neck.)
Poor boy! may this medallion
One day prove thy safeguard!
(To JARNO.)
And thou who oft did'st wrongfully ill use me,
I bid thee, too, adieu!

Gipsies. Farewell! take heart, Mignon!
Farewell, Filina!
A prosperous journey we do wish thee.

Chorus. Quick, quick my friends, now let's away!
Dame Fortune smiles on us serene;
Joy, once more, our hearts doth warm,
Fell hunger we will soon dispel!

(WILHELM waves his hand to FILINA, in token of adieu. The actors depart on their journey; LOTHARIO remains pensively seated near the front of the stage. MIGNON stands near the centre of the stage, bending her eyes fixedly on WILHELM.)

ACT II

(An elegant boudoir. Door at back. Side doors. To the right a window, to the left a chimney. Elegant details. Sofas, easy chairs, etc.)

Laertes. My! What luxury
(Looking around.)
Is this where you stay?

(Elle montre à WILHELM le bouquet qu'elle a reçu de lui. MIGNON, qui reparaît, son paquet à la main s'approche v.vement et reconnait les fleurs qu'elle a données à WILHELM.)

Mignon.

(À part.)
Mon bouquet!

Wilhelm.

(À MIGNON.)
Qu'as-tu donc?

Philine.

(Bas.)
Il m'adore!

Laërte.

(Bas.)
Il est pris!

Mignon.

(Montrant LOTHARIO.)
Vois, de mes pauvres fleurs il n'a point fait mépris?
Il n'a pas rejeté mon bouquet, lui......

Wilhelm.

(Bas en souriant.)
Pardonne!
Je ne l'ai pas offert...... on me l'a pris.

Mignon. C'est bien!...... emmène-moi!...... Je t'appartiens!...... Ordonne!
(Aux BOHEMIENS.)
Vous dont j'ai partagé
La honte et la misère,
Adieu!......
(A L'ENFANT, en lui passant une médaille au cou.)
Toi, pauvre enfant, sois un jour protégé
Par cette humble médaille!
(A JARNO.)
Et toi, dont la colère!
M'a si souvent fait peur...... hélas!
Adieu! Mignon ne t'en veut pas!

Les Comédiens.

(Au fond.)
Adieu, Philine, et bon voyage!
Adieu, la belle, et bon voyage.
Adieu, Mignon, et bon voyage!

Les Comédiens.

En route, amis! plions bagage
La chance nous sourit enfin!
Que la gaîté soit du voyage!
Au diantre la soif et la faim!

(WILHELM fait un dernier signe d'adieu à PHILINE. Les COMEDIENS et les COMEDIENNES se disposent à partir. LOTHARIO s'asseoit pensif sur le devant de la scène. MIGNON s'arrête au milieu du théâtre, les yeux fixés sur WILHELM.)

ACTE DEUXIEME

Un boudoir élégant. Porte au fond. Portes latérales. A droite une fenêtre, à gauche une cheminée. Toilette, fauteuils, etc. Philine est assise devant la toilette. On frappe à la porte.

Laërte.

(Entrant, d'un air majestueux.)
Corbleu! les somptueux lambris!
(Regardant autour de lui.)
C'est içi qu'on vous loge?

Filina.	Yes, my dear. The baroness has loaned me her boudoir.	*Philine.*	Oui, mon cher! Madame la baronne me prête son boudoir.
Laertes.	(Slyly.) Of which the baron has a key.	*Laërte.*	(Finement.) Dont M. le baron a gardé la clef.
Filina.	(Rising, in anger.) Oh! You're drunk!	*Philine.*	(Se levant vivement.) Fi donc, vous êtes gris!
Laertes.	No! I just feel good and amiable. Oh! sweetest one, have a heart Don't look at me that way. Your lovely eyes' soft lashes, Like arrows in Cupid's play, Will wound me now and for aye.	*Laërte.*	Non! je suis en humeur de rire et de faire des compliments...... Belle, ayez pitié de nous! Daignez baisser vos paupières! Les cils de vos yeux si doux...... Sont des flèches meurtrières Du Dieu qui nous blesse tous! Et lon, lon, la, et lon, lon, la! Landéridéra, landéridéra! Et lon, lon, la, landéridéra! (Il fait une pirouette.) Voilà!

NAUGHT TO ME SUCH JOY AFFORDS.

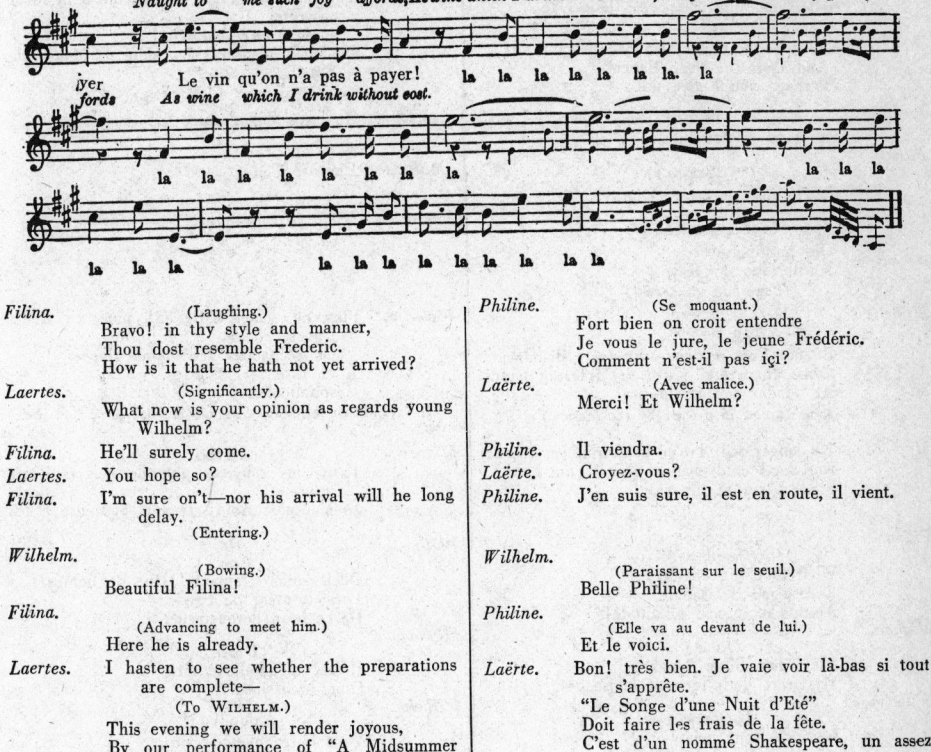

Filina.	(Laughing.) Bravo! in thy style and manner, Thou dost resemble Frederic. How is it that he hath not yet arrived?	*Philine.*	(Se moquant.) Fort bien on croit entendre Je vous le jure, le jeune Frédéric. Comment n'est-il pas içi?
Laertes.	(Significantly.) What now is your opinion as regards young Wilhelm?	*Laërte.*	(Avec malice.) Merci! Et Wilhelm?
Filina.	He'll surely come.	*Philine.*	Il viendra.
Laertes.	You hope so?	*Laërte.*	Croyez-vous?
Filina.	I'm sure on't—nor his arrival will he long delay. (Entering.)	*Philine.*	J'en suis sure, il est en route, il vient.
Wilhelm.	(Bowing.) Beautiful Filina!	*Wilhelm.*	(Paraissant sur le seuil.) Belle Philine!
Filina.	(Advancing to meet him.) Here he is already.	*Philine.*	(Elle va au devant de lui.) Et le voici.
Laertes.	I hasten to see whether the preparations are complete— (To WILHELM.) This evening we will render joyous, By our performance of "A Midsummer Night's Dream;"	*Laërte.*	Bon! très bien. Je vaie voir là-bas si tout s'apprête. "Le Songe d'une Nuit d'Eté" Doit faire les frais de la fête. C'est d'un nommé Shakespeare, un assez bon poëte.

A work is this by Shakespeare,
A great, aye, an immortal poet!
As to Filina, she will miracles perform,
If only to please *you!*
Sir, your most obedient—
Beauteous Filina, I take my leave.
(Aside.)
(To FILINA.)
I leave you with *him.*
(To WILHELM.)
I leave you with *her.*
(On reaching the door he draws back in surprise.)
Why, who is there?

Wilhelm. 'Tis Mignon!

Filina.
(Surprised.)
Mignon? How's this?

Wilhelm. She seems determined not to leave me;
I shall call her in.
Mignon!

Mignon.
(Entering.)
What would'st thou?
Thy commands I will obey.

Filina.
(Banteringly.)
I really scarcely recognize the child!
(To MIGNON, with ill-concealed jealousy)
Come, walk in!
Pray come and warm yourself;
And then the "egg dance"
Perhaps you'll give us!

Laertes.
(Aside.)
A storm is brewing.

Filina.
(To LAERTES.)
What ails you now, I pray?

Laertes.
(Pre-occupied.)
Oh, nothing—
I will take my leave.
(Bows and withdraws.)

Wilhelm.
(To MIGNON.)
Be not thus anxious—thy fears dismiss;
Come, then, and warm thy freezing hands
At yonder hospitable fire!
(He seats MIGNON in a chair by the fireside.)

Mignon. No longer will I o'er past troubles brood;
Nor am I cold—happy, indeed, am I,
Since I am at thy side!

Filina.
(Sneeringly.)
What touching anxiety;
Excuse me if I laugh
At this reciprocal solicitude!

Mignon.
(Aside.)
Alas! her bitter laugh
My heart doth torment cause.

Wilhelm.
(To FILINA.)
In sooth your gaiety
My spirits vastly doth enliven.

(Montrant PHILINE.)
Et de Titania vous serez enchanté.
(Con emphase.)
A bientôt, cher monsieur!
Adieu, ma toute belle!
Je vous laisse avec lui?
Je vous laisse avec elle.
(S'arretant aupres de la porte du fond.)
Mais qui donc se tient là?

Wilhelm. C'est Mignon!

Philine. Mignon?

Wilhelm. Elle n'a pas voulu se séparer de moi.
Faut l'appéler.
(Remontant par le fond et appelent.)
Mignon!

Mignon.
(Elle parait, en habit de jeune page.)
Que veux-tu, maître?

Philine.
(Souriant.)
Eh! mais vraiment, on a peine à la recon-
naître.
Approche et rechauffe-toi.
Tu nous danseras en suite la danse des
œufs.
(Mouvement de MIGNON.)

Laërte. Je crois qu'un orage est dans l'air.

Philine. Plait-il?

Laërte. Rien, je vous quitte.

Wilhelm. Plus de soucis, Mignon! plus de tristes
pensées!
Viens réchauffer tes mains glacées,
A ce foyer
Hospitalier!......
(Il fait asseoir MIGNON dans un fauteuil devant la chem-
inée.)

Mignon.
(À demi-voix.)
Je ne me souviens plus de mes douleurs
passées!
Je n'ai plus froid! Je suis heureuse à tes
côtés!

Philine.
(Riant.)
Quels soins touchants! Que de bontés!
Permettez-moi de rire
De ce beau dévouement!

Mignon.
(À part.)
Hélas! qu'a-t-elle à rire?
Cruel amusement!

Wilhelm.
(À PHILINE.)
Vous faites bien de rire;
Votre rire est charmant!

Filina.

(Laughing.)
Most worthy sir,
I'm really touched, indeed;
Instead of waiting on his master,
It is the master who doth wait upon his
     page!

Wilhelm.

(Approaching FILINA.)
Prostrate at thy feet, O lady,
I now do offer thee an homage far more
     zealous;
Wilt thou accept my proffered service?

Filina. You really mean it?

[Pointing to a candelabra which stands on the chimneypiece.]

Yon candelabra, now, pray reach to me.

(She seats herself in front of the dressoir; WILHELM
eagerly fetches the candelabra alluded to. MIGNON watches
them, without leaving her seat.)

Wilhelm. Thy commands I eagerly await—
Ordain—I will obey!

Filina. In sooth, the hair-dresser has but ill-ar-
ranged my hair;
But by putting on a more becoming dress,
I yet may hope to please you!

Philine. Mon cher, je vous admire,
C'est tout à fait charmant!
(Elle rit.)
Au lieu d'être servi par votre jeune page,
C'est vous qui le servez!

Wilhelm.

(Se rapprochant de PHILINE.)
Près de vous, à vos pieds,
J'accepterais, si vous vouliez,
Un plus doux servage.

Philine. Vraiment!

(Lui désignant un flambeau sur la cheminée.)
Apportez donc ce flambeau par içi.

(Elle s'asseoit devant sa toilette. WILHELM va prendre le
flambeau et revient avec empressement près de PHILINE. MIG-
NON suit tous ses mouvements du regard sans quitter le
fauteuil où elle est blottie.)

Wilhelm. Je me fais votre esclave! ordonnez, me
voici!

Philine. Mon coiffeur m'a ce soir, indignement
coiffée!......
Mais vous allez me voir dans ma robe de
fée!......

CHARMING GAY COMPLIMENTS.

(MIGNON feigns to sleep. FILINA continues singing gaily before the looking-glass, "beautifying" herself the while.)

Wilhelm.   Beautiful Filina, enchantress irresistable,
Of those bright eyes, the all-bewitching
    glance
Each soul allures, each stubborn heart in-
    flames;
Thy bidding to obey, is happiness to all!
By all thou'rt idolized,
    By all adored!
Alas! why doth not love
Thy heart, in turn, illume?
For, woe is me! thou cruel art and cold.

Filina.   I really to the Baron must present you.

Wilhelm.   Stay! grant me but another word!

Filina.   Hush! were we to be overheard—
Give me your arm;
(She advances a few steps, when WILHELM stops her.)

Wilhelm.   Will you not answer me?

Filina.
(Extending her hand to him.)
I promise to be—merciful!
(WILHELM impresses a kiss on FILINA's hand. MIGNON starts, but does not open her eyes.)

Wilhelm.   Oh Filina, my rapt heart adores thee,
In more than human happiness am I steep-
    ed,
By thy loving joyous voice—
By thy winning, genial smile!
Then bend on me a glance benign,
My ardent pray'r deign but to hear,
Crown thou this heart's sole wish!
(WILHELM offers FILINA his arm. They both exeunt on back.)

Mignon.
(Alone.)
At last I am alone! Ah! woe is me!
Already hath he forgotten me.
What matters it? Is not my utmost wish
    already fulfilled!
What need I more than learn to love, and
    to obey him?
A truce then to my sighs! 'tis folly to
    repine!
(Leaning on the toilette table.)
She listened to Wilhelm's vows—
I should have neither looked nor listened;
But, alas! the temptation was too strong;
Forgive me, my Wilhelm!
(Perceiving the rouge pot.)
Aha! the rouge lies here—
Suppose I were to try some.
(Putting on rouge)
Quickly my paleness disappears;

I

My features are enlivened!
A gipsy lad I well do know,
Graceful, winning, handsome is he;

(MIGNON fait semblant de dormir. PHILINE chante follement en achevant de se farder devant son miroir.)

Wilhelm.
(Se penchant amoureusement vers PHILINE.)
Belle Philine, aimable enchanteresse,
Vos doux regards et vos attraits vainqueurs,
A votre char enchaînment tous les cœurs!
Autour de vous tout sourit et s'empresse!......
On vous fête, on vous aime, on vous adore......
    hélas!
Pourquoi n'aimez-vous pas?

Philine.   Au baron il faut qu'on vous présente.

Wilhelm.   Philine, un mot encore!...... un mot!......

Philine.
(Montrand MIGNON.)
Parlez plus bas!......
Notre hôte nous attend...... Offrez-moi votre
    bras.
(Elle fait quelques pas; WILHELM la retient.)

Wilhelm.   Quoi! sans répondre......

Philine.
(Lui tendant la main.)
Allons! J'ai l'âme complaisante!......
(WILHELM porte la main de PHILINE à ses lèvres. Au bruit du baiser MIGNON fait un mouvement, sans ouvrir les yeux.)

Wilhelm.
(À demi-voix, avec passion.)
O Philine! ô coquette! ô fille séduisante!
J'admire l'éclat de vos yeux!
Je suis ravi, charmé d'entendre
Cette voix amoureuse et tendre,
Ce rire moqueur et joyeux!......
Par pitié daigner m'entendre.
Donne un regard de vos doux yeux,
Un mot de cette voix tendre
A mon cœur amoureux.
(WILHELM offre son bras à PHILINE et sort avec elle par la porte du fond.)

Mignon.
(Seule.)
Me voilà seule, hélas! déjà Meister
    m'oublie......
Qu'importe! il a comblé mes voeux!
Le suivre et le servir
C'est tout ce que je veux.
Allons! pleurer serait folie......
Ah! c'est là, que tout à l'heure en souri-
    ant à son miroir
Elle écoutait Meister! Je ne voulais rien
    voir,
Je ne voulais rien entendre!
Hélas! et cependant je n'apu m'en défen-
    dre.
Pardonne, cher maître!
Voici le fard qui la rend belle......
Eh bien! si j'essayais de me farder aussi?
(Elle essaye de se farder.)
Ma pâleur disparaît déjà. Mon teint s'an-
    ime!

I

(S'animant.)
Il était un pauvre enfant,
Un pauvre enfant de Bohême,

.et though his lip doth ever wear a smile,
His heart I ween is sad.
(Looking at herself in the glass.)
Ha! ha! ha! a mad story, in sooth!
Sure none will e'er believe it.
I really seem more fair, more beauteous
    than before.
Tra, la, ral, la!
Is't really I, whom in the glass I see?
Who is't that I now gaze on?

II

One day the youth,
Gaily a scheme devised;
A scheme he hoped his master dear might
    please.
(Gazing at herself in the glass.)
Ha! ha! a mad story, in sooth!
Sure none will e'er believe it;
I really seem more fair, more beauteous
    than before
Tra, la, ralla, la!
I'st really I, whom in the glass I see?
Or who is it that I now gaze upon?
No, no! myself I do not recognize.
(After a short pause, sadly.)
And yet, alas! 'tis I!
Other secrets *she* must have, her beauty so
    to heighten!
[Approaching cabinet on the left.]
Is it not here, that she her wardrobe
    keeps?—
Mad thought! Ah! surely 'tis a demon
    tempts me.
(Enters cabinet.)

Frederic.

(Enters alone.)
(Looking around.)
Filina in my aunt's apartments?
O much loved room, on thee while thus I
    gaze,
With joy and hope my heart doth loudly
    beat!
The young coquette, as yet, perchance ex-
    pects me not;
The cruel flirt this day I must o'ercome,
Her heart at last I hope to tame.
O much loved room, on thee while thus I
    gaze, &c.
Yes! I swear she shall adore me—
The vict'ry mine this very day shall be;
Let e'en a thousand watchful guards sur-
    round her,
Their vigilance I will elude!
O much loved room, on thee while thus I
    gaze, &c.

Wilhelm.

(From the door at back, calling.)
Mignon!

Frederic.

(Bowing.)
Your servant, sir.

Au regard triste, au front blême......
(Se regardant dans le miroir.)
Ah! ah! la folle histoire! en vain je m'en
    défend!
Je me trouve bien mieux! je ne suis plus
    la même.
Ta la, ralla!
Ta la, ralla!
Est-ce bien Mignon que voilà?

II

Un beau jour, tout triomphant
Tout fier de son stratagème,
Pour plaire au maître qu'il aime......
(Se regardant de nouveau en riant.)
Ah! ah! la folle histoire! En vain je m'en
    défend!
Je me trouve bien mieux, je ne suis plus
    la même,
Ta la, ralla!
Ta la, ralla!
Est-ce bien Mignon que voilà?
Non, non, ce n'est plus moi!
(Tristement.)
Mais quoi! ce n'est pas elle,
Elle a d'autres secrets encore pour être
    belle.
(Allant ouvrir la porte du cabinet de toilette.)
N'est pas là qu'on a rangé ses robes? oui!
Hélas! suis-je comme elle une femme pour
    lui?
O folle idée! O démon qui me tente!
(Elle entre dans le cabinet de toilette. La fenêtre s'ouvre
brusquement. FREDERIC saute dans la chambre.)

Frédéric.

(Avec indignation.)
Quoi? mon oncle a logé Philine chez ma
    tante?
Me voici dans son boudoir,
Oui, je sens battre mon cœur d'espoir,
Ah! je guette l'instant de la revoir.
Oui, je sens battre mon cœur d'espoir,
Coquette, je guette l'instant de te revoir.
Il faut enfin vaincre la cruelle,
Il faut toucher le cœur de l'infidèle!
Je suis dans son boudoir
Et je sens mon cœur battre d'espoir.
Ah! je guette l'instant de la revoir.
Moi je veux qu'on m'aime et j'espère,
Oui, j'espère à mon tour être heureux.
Tant pis, ma foi! pour tous ses amoureux.
Je suis dans son boudoir,
Et je sens mon cœur battre d'espoir.
Ah, je guette l'instant de la revoir.
Ah, je sens mon cœur battre d'espoir.
Coquette, je guette l'instant de te revoir.
Pour mon cœur quel doux espoir.
Voici l'instant de la revoir!

Wilhelm.

(Entr'ouvrant a porte du fond et entrant sans voir FRED-
ERIC.)
Mignon!

Frédéric.

(Saluant.)
Monsieur!

Wilhelm.
> (Bowing also.)
> Yours, sir, to command.

Frederic. The question may seem indiscreet,
But much indeed I'd like to know
How you came here—

Wilhelm. And you, sir, how did *you* arrive?

Frederic. The lady's friend am I.

Wilhelm. And so am I, sir.

Frederic. Know, sir, that I do dearly love her!

Wilhelm. I tell you, *I* adore her, sir!

Frederic. You do? enough!
> (Drawing his sword.)
> Defend yourself!

Wilhelm. What here, in Filina's room?

Frederic. In Filina's room; 'twill all the more romantic be!
Defend yourself!

(MIGNON, who has put on one of FILINA's dresses, rushes
hurriedly in, and throws herself between the combatants,
exclaiming:

> Hold!

Wilhelm. Heavens! Mignon!

Frederic. Why, what does all this mean?
[Sheathing his sword, and contemplating MIGNON]
> Ha! ha! if I'm not mistaken,
> One of Filina's dresses she has on!
> Fear not,
> We'll meet again, ere long!

Wilhelm. What strange caprice is this? Hast lost thy
reason?
I tell thee, we must part.

Mignon. Dost thou then drive me from thee?

Wilhelm. Not so—I do *not* drive thee from me;
Believe me, I do *not* drive thee from me;
Dear shall thy mem'ry ever be to me.
[MIGNON utters a cry of grief, and throws herself on a chair.]
> Farewell, Mignon, take heart!
> Thy tears restrain!
> In the bright years of youth no grief doth
> linger long.
> Weep not, Mignon!
> O'er thee just Heaven will watch with
> fost'ring care.
> Oh may'st thou thy dear native land, once
> more regain!
> May fortune on thy fate henceforth be-
> nignly smile!
> It pains me much to leave thee; my strick-
> en heart
> With thy lone destiny will ever sympathize!
> Farewell, Mignon, take heart!
> From tears refrain!
> In the bright years of youth no grief doth
> linger long;
> Weep not, Mignon!
> O'er thee just Heaven will watch with fos-
> tering care;
> Then dry thy tears!

Wilhelm. Monsieur!

Frédéric. Je suis peut-être indiscret,
Mais comment vous trouvez-vous içi?

Wilhelm. Et vous-même, Monsieur?

Frédéric. Je suis de ses amis, Monsieur.

Wilhelm. J'en suis aussi.

Frédéric. Mais moi, je l'aime.

Wilhelm. Eh bien, moi je l'adore!
Plaît-il?

Frédéric. Il suffit! engarde!

Wilhelm. Quoi? chez Philine?

Frédéric. Chez Philine! C'est plus original!
Battons-nous!
> (Ils croisent le fer.)
(MIGNON revêtue d'une des robes de PHILINE sort du cabinet
et s'elance entre eux.)
> Ah, Meister! Dieu!

Wilhelm. Mignon!

Frédéric. Mignon? que signifie?
> (Raillant.)
> Mais voilà, si je m'en souviens
> Les atours de Philine!
> Ah, ah, ah, ah, ah, ah!
> (Sérieux.)
> Monsieur! Nous nous reverrons.
> Serviteur!

Wilhelm. Quel est ce caprice insensé?
Deviens-tu folle? Alors quittons-nous.

Mignon. Tu me chasses?

Wilhelm.
> (Plus tendrement.)
> Non, non, je ne te chasse pas!
> Même je dois te rendre graces du tendre
> mouvement......
> Mais je commence à comprendre
> Que je ne puis auprès de moi
> Te garder, pauvre enfant.
> Adieu, Mignon, courage!
> Ne pleure pas!
> Les chagrins sont bien vite oubliés à ton
> âge!
> Dieu te consolera! mes vœux suivront tes
> pas!......
> Ne pleure pas!
> N'accuse pas mon cœur de froide indiffér-
> ence!
> Ne me reproche pas de suivre un fol amour!
> En te disant adieu, je garde l'espérance
> De te revoir un jour!
> Adieu, Mignon, courage!
> Les chagrins sont bien vite oubliés à ton
> âge!
> Dieu te consolera! mes vœux suivront tes
> pas!
> Ne pleure pas!

Mignon. Thankful am I; but since we're doomed to part,
I fain would wander freely—

Wilhelm. To reason dictates list, I pray.
What will become of thee?
When from my care removed, what wilt thou do?

Mignon. That which I did before. I will Mignon once more become.
[She kisses the hand which WILHELM extends to her.]
I thank thee!

Wilhelm. (Agitated.)
Thou can'st not leave me thus!

Mignon. My duty 'tis; it must be so.

Wilhelm. (Aside, in tones of anguish.)
O grievous trial!
(Enter FILINA and FREDERIC.)

Filina. (To FREDERIC.)
Now, 'pon my word, she's dressed out in my clothes!
Right quickly has she laid her livery aside.

Wilhelm. (Confused.)
'Twas a mere whim,
Which needs must be forgiven.

Filina. If she's so taken with the dress,
I'll give it her.
(MIGNON angrily tears the ribbons from the dress.)
Good gracious! why tear off my ribbons!
I mercy crave for them. What anger strange is this?
(MIGNON rushes hastily to the apartment on the left, into which she disappears.)
(To WILHELM.)
Now, 'pon my word, I almost think
The little savage jealous is of me!

Wilhelm. (Agitated.)
Jealous!

Laertes.
(Appearing at the back, dressed in the garb of an ancient Greek.)
I say, what are you doing here?
'Tis almost time to begin.

Filina. Let's follow Laertes.

Wilhelm.
(Aside.)
Jealous!

Filina.
(To WILHELM.)
Of what are you now thinking?
See you not I'm waiting for you?

Wilhelm. Excuse, me, pray.

Filina. If you still love me, offer me your arm.

Wilhelm. Love you! more dearly than I do love—myself!
(Offers his arm to FILINA. They exeunt, followed by LAERTES.)
[FREDERIC suddenly issues from the apartment on the left, and gazes after WILHELM and FILINA as they withdraw.]

Frederic. What pleasure keen 'twould give me,
To run yon scoundrel through!

Mignon.
(Issuing from the apartment on the left, dressed as in the first act.)
That woman! I do *loathe* her.
(Exit.)

Mignon. Merci de tes bontés; mais sans toi,
Je veux être libre comme autrefois.

Wilhelm. Écoute la raison! Hors de cette maison
Que vas-tu devenir?

Mignon. Ce que j'étais: Mignon!
(Saissant la main de WILHELM et la portant à ses lèvres.)
Merci!

Wilhelm. Non, tu ne peux partir ainsi!

Mignon. Il le faut.

Wilhelm. Angoisse cruelle!

Philine. (Elle paraît avec FREDERIC.)
Vous disiez vrai; Mignon de mes atours parée!
(À WILHELM, avec ironie.)
Elle a bientôt quitté votre livrée.

Wilhelm. Philine
(Avec embarras.)
Un caprice d'enfant qu'il faut lui pardonner.

Philine. Si la robe lui plaît, on peut la lui donner.
(MIGNON arrache avec colère les dentelles de la robe dont elle est parée.)
Eh! quoi? faut-il déchirer mes dentelles?
Je demande grace pour elles.
(MIGNON va ramasser son paquet de hardes et se sauve dans le cabinet de droite.)
(Souriant.)
Quel courroux! Quel regard! On dirait, sur ma foi,
Que cette pauvre enfant est jalouse de moi.

Wilhelm. (À part.)
Jalouse!

Laërte.
(Il entra vivement en scène sous son costume de Prince Thesée.)
Eh bien, que faites-vous? Alerte, on commence!

Philine. Suivons Laërte.

Wilhelm.
(À part.)
Jalouse!

Philine.
(À WILHELM, en souriant.)
A quoi rêvez-vous donc? Je vous attends.

Wilhelm. Pardon!

Philine. Offrez-moi votre bras, si vous m'aimez encore.

Wilhelm. Quoi? Moi? Philine, je t'adore.

Frédéric.
(Regardant sortir PHILINE et WILHELM.)
Morbleu! Qu'avec plaisir je le massacrais.

Mignon.
(Elle reparaît dans son costume du 1er Acte.)
Cette Philine, je la hais!

SCENE II

A portion of the park adjoining the Baron's castle. At back, to the right, a conservatory, illuminated from within. To the left a lake, surrounded here and there by reeds, etc. Music and the noise of clapping hands, are heard to proceed from the wings. MIGNON advances from among the trees, and stands in a listening attitude.

MIGNON, *alone.*

She's yonder, by *his* side, triumphant, happy;
Whilst I do wander forth alone, abandoned.
He loves her! Ah, my aching heart did this foretell,
But still I little thought from his own lips to hear it,
Nor, with these eyes, the bitter truth to witness!
Ah! woe is me! he loves her! at this thought alone
My tongue the hated words doth shame to speak.
He loves her! Oh heaven! with grief my heart will break!
(Rushes hurriedly in the direction of the lake.)
Yes! this calm, unruffled stream,
Placid, though deep,
Doth summon me! Methinks, beneath the waters clear,
I hear the syren's song—
Yes! with my life, I here will end my woes!
(She is about to throw herself into the water, when the strains of a harp are heard to proceed from behind the trees.)
Heavens! what sounds are those?
(Coming forward.)
My wicked impulse hath almost passed away,
Yes! still do I wish to live!
(LOTHARIO appears.)
Art thou Lothario?
(Recognizes him.)
'Tis he!

Lothario.
(Who at first does not recognize MIGNON.)
Who's there? who is't that now approaches me?
Art thou she for whom so long I've sought?

Mignon.   Nay, not so!

Lothario.   Ever am I mista'en! alas, I see it is not she!
The form that now doth hasten to my side,
Is surely that of Mignon!

Mignon.   Ah, yes! Thou'st recognized me,
Mignon indeed am I.

Lothario.
(Tenderly.)
Oh, hapless maiden!
Thy footsteps, too, I've longed to trace,
Come to this aged breast!
Come! tell me the sad thoughts which now thy heart do grieve.
[Pressing her to his breast.]

Mignon.
(In accents of the deepest woe, leaning her head on LOTHARIO's shoulder.)
Hast thou e'er suffered! hast thou e'er known grief!
Hast ever, hopeless, languished in despair—
Hast ever, vainly, sought thy native land?
If so, my sorrow thou can'st understand.

TABLEAU II

(Un coin du parc. Au fond à droite, une serre attenante au château et éclairée à l'intérieur. A gauche, une large pièce d'eau bordée de roseaux. Musique et bruit d'applaudissements dans la coulisse. Mignon se glisse sous le arbres et se penche dans l'ombre pour écouter.)

Mignon.

(Seule.)
Elle est là près de lui! Son triomphe commence!
Et moi j'erre au hasard dans ce jardin immense......
(Avec agitation.)
Elle est aimée! il l'aime! eh bien! je le savais!
Ces tourments, je les éprouvais!
Non! je ne l'avais pas entendu de sa bouche,
Ce mot qui déchire mon cœur!
Espères-tu que ton chagrin le touche,
Pauvre Mignon! il l'aime! et son rire moqueur,
Rend plus cruelle encore cette parole!
Il l'aime! ô Dieu! je deviens folle
De rage et de douleur!
(Courant vers la pièce d'eau.)
Ah!...... ce flot clair et tranquille
M'attire à lui!—j'entends parmi les verts roseaux,
Votre voix, ô filles des eaux!......
Vous m'appelez à vous sous cette onde immobile!......
(Elle va pour s'élancer, les accords d'une harpe se font entendre sous les arbres.)
Ciel! qu'entends-je? écoutons!......
(Redescendant en scène.)
Le mauvais ange a fui!
Je veux vivre!
(LOTHARIO paraît.)
Est-ce toi, Lothario?.....
(Avec joie.)
C'est lui!

Lothario.
(Ne reconnaissant pas d'abord MIGNON.)
Qui donc est là?..... Quelle est cette voix qui m'appelle?
(La regardant avec tendresse.)
Est-ce toi, Sperata?...... Réponds! est-ce toi?

Mignon.   Non.

Lothario.
(La repoussant doucement.)
Mon cœur se trompe encore, hélas! ce n'est pas elle!
C'est l'enfant qui voulait me suivre; c'est Mignon!

Mignon.
(Avec tristesse.)
Oh! oui, tu te souviens! oui, c'est bien là mon nom!

Lothario.   Pauvre enfant! pauvre créature!
J'ai voulu te revoir et j'ai suivi tes pas!
Viens sur mon cœur! Reste en mes bras!
Et dis-moi quel chagrin te brise et te torture!......
(Il presse MIGNON entre ses bras.)

Mignon.
(Avec une ardeur fiévreuse, le front appuyé sur la poitrine de LOTHARIO.)
As-tu souffert? As-tu pleuré?
As-tu langui sans espérance,
L'âme en deuil, le cœur déchiré?
Alors tu connais ma souffrance!

Lothario. Maiden, I bitter grief have known,
　　 Aye, cruel suffering have I endured;
　　 My tears the ground have oft bedewed,
　　 'Mid foreign lands I long have roamed.
　　 (A tumultuous noise of clapping of hands heard from behind the scenes.)

Mignon. List! the castle with applause resounds—
　　 They all admire, they all do praise her!
　　 (Turning toward the conservatory, and declaiming in wrathful accents.)
　　 Ah! why does not avenging ire,
　　 Why does not the winged thunderbolt
　　 Strike down and crush yon impious dwelling?
　　 Why do not devouring flames consume it?
　　 (Rushes hurriedly away, and disappears amid the trees.)

Lothario. (Alone, after a moment's reflection, confused and bewildered.)
　　 Fire, she said! Ah, fire! fire!
　　 (Slowly crosses the stage and disappears amid the shade. The door of the conservatory is thrown open, and a crowd of Guests, Actors, etc., issue forth.)
　　 (The performance within is supposed to have just terminated. FILINA and the Actors retain their theatrical costumes.)

Chorus.. Filina is indeed divine,
　　 A wond'rous triumph she hath achieved.
　　 Her beauty let us loudly celebrate!
　　 Bravo! bravo!
　　 Filina is indeed divine, etc., etc.

Lothario. Comme toi, triste et solitaire,
　　 Courbé sous d'inflexibles lois,
　　 De mes pleurs j'ai mouillé la terre!
　　 Le ciel reste sourd à ma voix!
　　 (Applaudissements et acclamations bruyantes dans le château.)

Mignon. (Se dégageant brusquement des bras de LOTHARIO.)
　　 Écoute! c'est son nom que la foule répète!
　　 C'est elle qu'on acclame et c'est elle qu'on fête!......
　　 (Se tournant vers le château avec un geste de menace.)
　　 Ah! que la main de Dieu
　　 Ne peut-elle sur eux faire éclater la foudre,
　　 Et frapper ce palais, et le réduire en poudre,
　　 Et l'engloutir sous des torrents de feu!......
　　 (Elle s'enfuit sous les arbres.)

Lothario. (Seul.)
　　 (Après un long silence; avec égarement.)
　　 Le feu!...... le feu!...... le feu!......
　　 (Il traverse lentement le théâtre et disparaît dans l'ombre. Les portes de la serre s'ouvrent pour laisser passer la foule des INVITES et des COMEDIENS.)
　　 (La représentation vient de finir. PHILINE et les COMEDIENS ont conservé leurs costumes de théâtre.)

Chœur. Brava! brava! brava!
　　 La Philine est vraiment divine!
　　 À ses pieds nos cœurs et nos fleurs!
　　 Gloire à Titania!......

YES FOR THIS EVE.

Mon char qui vole   Et dans la nuit   Fuit!......   Ah!......
El - fin sprites on nim - ble toe   a - round me gai - ly dance.   Ah! ....

...... Je suis Titania la blonde,
I'm fair Ti ta - ni a.

Filina. Both night and day.
My attendants ever sing,
The achievements of the God of Love!
On the wave's white foam,
'Mid the twilight grey,
'Mid hedges, 'mid flowers,
I blithely do dance!
Yes! the fair Titania am I, etc., etc.

All. With love for her,
Each heart doth burn,
'Mid flowers and plaudits
Her bright path doth lay!

Chorus. Ah! Titania is indeed divine,
We'll homage to her beauty pay.

Filina. (To WILHELM.)
At last I've found you,
Is't possible I have to *seek* for you already?
Have you not been to hear me?

Frederic. (Aside.)
This eternal fellow here again!
(Watching FILINA's behavior.)
What glances! Ah, what smiles!

Wilhelm. (Pre-occupied, and looking anxiously around him.)
Excuse me, I implore! I vainly everywhere
do seek Mignon—

Filina. Indeed! Then it was *not* I whom you
sought?
(They both retire conversing. MIGNON and LOTHARIO meet
near the front of the stage.)

Lothario. Banish, O maiden, the grief that now thy
heart doth gnaw;
Thy wish is heard; the flames do even now
consume yon mansion!

Philine. Oui, pour ce soir, je suis reine des fées!
Voici mon sceptre d'or!......
Et voici mes trophées.
Autour de moi, toute ma cour court,
Chantant le plaisir et l'amour.
Aux rayons de Phœbé qui luit!......
Parmi les fleurs que l'aurore
Fait éclore,
Par les bois et par les près
Diaprès,
Sur les flots couverts d'écume,
Dans la brume,
On me voit d'un pied léger
Voltiger!
Je suis Titania la blonde,
Titania, fille de l'air!
En riant, je parcours le monde,
Plus vive que l'oiseau, plus prompte que
l'éclair!

Comédiens. (Entre eux, avec dépit.)
Déjà vingt amants
Entourent la belle,
Et tout est pour elle,
Fleurs et compliments!......

Chœur. (Entourant PHILINE pour la complimenter.)
Gloire à Titania la blonde,
Brava! brava! brava!
Gloire à Titania!

Philine. (Apercevant WILHELM.)
Ah! vous voici!...... Déjà vous me faites at-
tendre.
(D'un air de reproche.)
Vous n'étiez pas là pour m'entendre!......

Frédéric. (À part.)
Encor lui!...... quel sourire aimable! quel air
tendre.

Wilhelm. (Regardant autour de lui avec inquiétude.)
Pardonnez-moi!...... Je cherche en vain Mignon!

Philine. (Minaudant.)
Eh! quoi!
Celle que vous cherchez, Monsieur, ce n'est
pas moi!
(Ils remontent en causant; MIGNON et LOTHARIO se ren-
contrent sur le devant du théâtre.)

Lothario. (À demi-voix.)
Sois contente, Mignon! Réjouis-toi, pauvre
âme!
J'ai voulu t'obéir!...... Et ces murs sont en
flamme.

Mignon.	Alas! what is't thou say'st?
Lothario.	I have accomplished thy desire.

Mignon.	Oh heaven!
Lothario.	Anon those walls will crumble into ashes!

(MIGNON looks anxiously around her. WILHELM, perceiving her, hurries towards her.)

Wilhelm.	At length, O dear one, have I found thee, I've sought thee everywhere!
Filina.	(To MIGNON.) Listen girl!
Mignon.	What would you?
Filina.	If thou'rt anxious to display thy zeal, Haste thee yonder, (Pointing to conservatory.) And find the flowers, which Thou offerd'st yesterday unto thy master, And which methinks have fallen from my bosom!
Wilhelm.	(To FILINA.) But wherefore?
Mignon.	(To WILHELM.) I will obey. (Hastens to conservatory.)
Laertes.	(Entering hurriedly.) Quick, hasten all! Gentlemen, the theatre is in flames! See, see!
Wilhelm	(Horrified.) Oh fearful sight!
Filina.	(To the Ladies.) An icy chill my frame pervades.

(Servants exeunt, bearing away the torches with them. The stage is enveloped in complete darkness. The red light of the conflagration now begins to be reflected by the glass panes of the conservatory.)

Wilhelm.	(With painful emotion.) Ah! ill advised was thy zeal!
Filina.	(Endeavoring to stop him.) What would'st thou do?
Laertes.	(Seizing him by the arm.) Hold!
Wilhelm.	(Disengaging himself.) Ah! stay me not! (Hurries hastily to MIGNON's rescue.)
Chorus.	No mortal power can now check The conflagration's might, The castle soon must fall! When human eourage nought can do, Why sacrifice a life In fruitless heroism?

Mignon.	Ciel! que dis-tu?
Lothario.	(Calme et souriant.) J'ai fait ce que tu voulais.
Mignon.	Dieu!
Lothario.	Ces murs vont s'écrouler sous des torrents de feu!

(MIGNON inquiète cherche WILHELM des yeux. WILHELM l'aperçoit et accourt vers elle.)

Wilhelm.	C'est toi!..... je te cherchais, Mignon!.....
Philine.	(S'approchant.) Holà! ma belle!
Mignon.	Que voulez-vous?
Philine.	Pour nous prouver ton zèle, Va vite, va chercher Là-bas...... (Elle indique la serre.) Certain bouquet...... dont quelqu'un qui m'est cher Tantôt m'a fait hommage, Et que j'ai laissé choir, je crois, de mon corsage.
Wilhelm.	A quoi bon?.....
Mignon.	(À WILHELM.) J'obéis, j'obéis, maître! (Elle s'élana.)
Laërte.	(Accourant.) Dieu! Philine, mes amis, le théâtre est en feu! Regardez!.....
Wilhelm.	(Avec effroi.) Que dit-il?
Philine et les Femmes.	Je meurs!..... mon sang se glace!.....

(Les LAQUAIS sortent emportant les flambeaux. Le théâtre se plonge dans l'obscurité; des lueurs d'incendie commencent à éclairer le vitrage de la serre.)

Wilhelm.	(Écartant la foule.) Ah! malheureuse enfant!..... Arrière!.....faites place!
Philine.	(Le retenant.) Cher Wilhelm!
Laërte.	(Le retenant.) Arrêtez!
Wilhelm.	Ne me retenez pas!..... (Il s'élance au secours de MIGNON.)
Chœur.	Pour apaiser la flamme, Tout secours serait vain! L'effroi glace notre âme! Que sert-il de tenter un effort surhumain!

Lothario.
(In the midst of the stage, quelling for the moment the general commotion.)

A lonely wanderer am I! I stray from door
　　to door,
As fate doth guide, or as the storm doth
　　hurry me;
But heaven protects the wretched with kind
　　and fostering care!

(The glass-work of the conservatory falls in with a crash. The guests in terror, rush to the front of the stage. After a brief pause, WILHELM re-appears, bearing in his arms MIGNON's fainting form.)

Wilhelm.　Heaven hath saved her from a dreadful
　　　　death;
　　　　Begirt was she with flames,
　　　　When, heaven be prais'd, I reached and
　　　　　saved her!

(WILHELM places MIGNON on a bank. She still holds in her hands the bunch of withered flowers. Tableau.)

ACT III

A gallery, embellished with statues. To the right, a window overlooking the country. At back, a closed door. Side doors. At the rising of the curtain, there is no one on the stage.
A harp prelude is heard behind the scenes.

Chorus.
(Outside.)
Quick, the sails unfurl,
The wind propitious blows,
The gently ruffled waves
Tempt us to put forth;
Let's quickly leave the shore,
And gaily tempt the wave!
Quick, then, the sails unfurl, etc., etc.

(LOTHARIO appears on the threshold of the door (right hand.)

Lothario.
(Alone.)
I've soothed the throbbing of her aching
　　heart,
And to her lips the smile I have restored.
Her weary eyes at last have closed
In gentle slumber;
By day and night some heav'nly spirit
The maiden doth protect;
On wings celestial, it doth hover round
Protecting her from harm!

(Enter WILHELM, ANTONIO.)
(ANTONIO carries a lamp.)
(Placing the lamp on the table, and approaching the window.)

Antonio.
From this window you will see
The shores on all sides lighted up;
To-morrow is a joyous festival,
Kept sacred by the dwellers on the lake.
This mansion alone, since that thrice fatal
　　day.
When woe so suddenly o'ertook its owners,
The festal fire no more displays.
This castle, therefore, old and rugged,
Will ere long be sold;
At the price agreed upon,
It may yours, perchance, become.

Wilhelm.　To-morrow, I'll my final answer give.
(At a sign from WILHELM, ANTONIO withdraws.)
Wilhelm.　What now?

Lothario.
(Debout, au milieu de la scene et dominant le tumult général.)

Fugitif et tremblant, je vais de porte en
　　porte,
Où le ciel me conduit, où l'orage m'emporte,
Des misérables Dieu prend soin......

(Le vitrage éclate et s'écroule. La foule des INVITES se presse sur le devant de la scène en poussant un cri de terreur.)
(WILHELM paraît enfin portant MIGNON dans ses bras.)

Wilhelm.　De la mort, Dieu l'a préservée!
　　　　La flamme l'entourait déjà! je l'ai sauvée!

(Il dépose sur un banc de gazon MIGNON évanouie. MIGNON serre entre ses mains crispées un bouquet de fleurs flétries et à demi consumées. Tableau final.)

ACTE TROISIEME

Une galerie italienne ornée de statues. A droite, une fenêtre ouverte sur la campagne. Au fond, grande porte fermée. Portes laterales. Au lever du rideau, la scène est vide.
(Prélude de harpe dans la coulisse.)

Chœur.
(Au dehors.)
La douce clarté des étoiles,
Illumine le flot mouvant!
Amis, ouvrons gaîment nos voiles,
Aux baisers amoureux du vent!
La rame étincelle
Sur l'eau du lac bleu,
Et laisse après elle
Un sillon de feu!......
La douce clarté des étoiles
Illumine le flot mouvant!

(LOTHARIO parait sur le seuil de la porte de droite.)

Lothario.
(Seul.)
Elle dort!......
De son cœur j'ai calmé la fièvre!
Un sourire doux et joyeux
A ma voix entr'ouvrait sa lèvre;
Le sommeil a fermé ses yeux!
Un ange est debout auprès d'elle!
Un ange descendu des cieux
Lui prête l'ombre de son aile!......

(WILHELM, ANTONIO)
(ANTONIO pose une lampe sur une table, et se tourne vers la fenêtre.)

Antonio.
Vous verrez de cette fenêtre s'illuminer les
　　villas d'alentour.
De la fête du lac c'est demain le grand
　　jour;
Ce palais seul depuis qu'il a perdu son
　　maître ne s'illumine plus.
S'il est encore à votre gré
Vous pouvez l'acheter.

Wilhelm.　Demain je repondrai.
(Sur un signe de WILHELM, ANTONIO sort. WILHELM, touchant l'épaule de LOTHARIO.)
　　　Eh bien?

Lothario. Hush, she's sleeping, Her eyelids tranquilly are closed; The fever hath quite left her.	*Lothario...* Chut!...... Un sourire a passé sur sa lèvre; L'enfant dort et n'a plus la fièvre.
Wilhelm. May heav'n be praised, Her native air new life into her veins in- fuses, For *her* it is that I to-morrow mean to buy The Casa Cipriani!	*Wilhelm.* (Vivement.) Ah, que le ciel en soit béni. C'est l'air natal qui la rappelle à la vie. Oui, demain j'acheterai pour elle Le palais des Cypriani.
Lothario. (Starting violently at the name.) Cipriani!	*Lothario.* (Il se leve en tressaillant.) Cypriani!
Wilhelm. What ails thee? (LOTHARIO looks round in surprise—he then approaches the door at back, which he endeavors to open.)	*Wilhelm.* Qu'as-tu? (LOTHARIO se dirige vers la grande porte du fond et cherche à l'ouvrir.)
Wilhelm. Yon door has closed remained, For fifteen years.	Cette chambre est fermée depuis quinze ans!
Lothario. (Deeply moved.) Fifteen years! (He again looks around him with the aspect of one who seeks to recall the past; and then approaches the door and exclaims: Ah—yonder! (Exit slowly.)	*Lothario.* Quinze ans? (Il se dirige vers la porte à gauche.) Ah, là! (Se tourant vers WILHELM.) Chut! (Il sort lentement.)
Wilhelm. (Alone.) What strange, wild look was that? This good old man hath more successful been than I. In soothing yon poor, hapless maiden At last I have discovered the secret of her heart, From her sweet lips, my name escaped!	*Wilhelm.* Seul.) Étrange regard! Ah, mieux que ma raison le cœur de ce vieillard Console cet enfant par ses soins ranimée. J'ai deviné trop tard le secret de Mignon. (Entr'ouvrant la porte de droite.) Hélas, elle sommeille, et prononce mon nom!

-AH ! LITTLE THOUGHT.

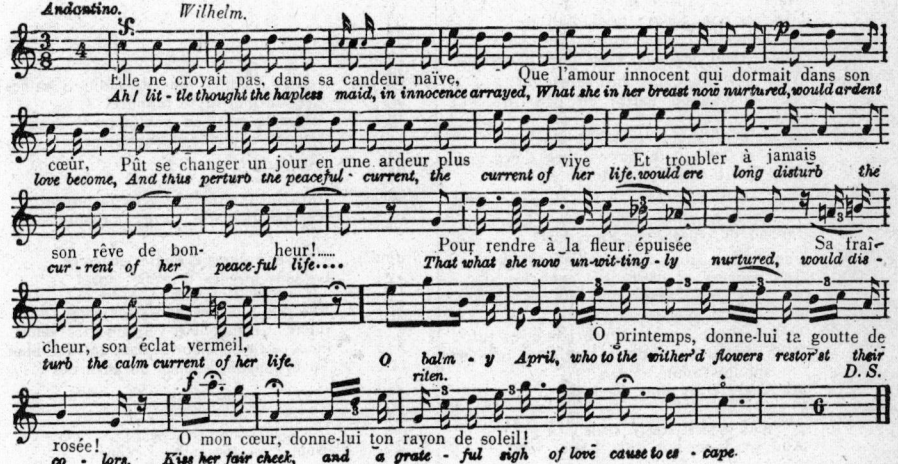

Andantino.   Wilhelm.

Elle ne croyait pas, dans sa candeur naïve,   Que l'amour innocent qui dormait dans son
Ah! lit - tle thought the hapless maid, in innocence arrayed, What she in her breast now nurtured, would ardent

cœur,   Pût se changer un jour en une ardeur plus   vive   Et troubler à jamais
love become, And thus perturb the peaceful current, the   current of her life would ere   long disturb   the

son rêve de bonheur!......   Pour rendre à la fleur épuisée   Sa fraî-
cur - rent of her   peace-ful life....   That what she now un-wit-ting - ly   nurtured,   would dis -

cheur, son éclat vermeil,   O printemps, donne-lui la goutte de
turb the calm current of her life.   O   balm - y April, who to the wither'd flowers restor'st   their

rosée!   O mon cœur, donne-lui ton rayon de soleil!
co - lors,   Kiss her fair cheek,   and   a grate - ful sigh   of love   cause to es - cape.

Vainly do I implore, that she a single word will utter— The secret of her woes unto me she will not reveal!	C'est en vain que j'attends un aveu de sa bouche! Je veux connaître en vain ses secrètes dou- leurs!

One glance of mine, with trouble fills her
  heart,
One word from me doth tears bring to her
  eyes.
O balmy April! thou who to the withered
  flowers
Their colors, by thy genial presence, dost
  restore, etc., etc.

Lothario, Antonio and the before-named.

Antonio. Signor—

Wilhelm. What would'st thou now?

Antonio.
        (Giving him a letter.)
  This letter I do bring thee.

Wilhelm. A letter, say'st thou?
      (Opens the letter and reads.)
  "Filina is on thy track,
  Fly—already is she here!"
  The hand is surely that of Laertes!
     (Running to MIGNON's room.)
    (He stops short as MIGNON enters.)
  'Tis she!

Mignon. Where am I! What balmy air is this that
    now I breathe?
  Ah! how bright doth seem the blue of hea-
    ven!
  The smooth mirror of yon sunny lake
  Doth placidly reflect the outline of the hills;
  A white sail skims the surface of the waves.
  How beauteous is the scene.
  Ah, this splendid mansion!
  This garden on the hill-side situated;
  All this I dimly now recall,
  Like to faint mem'ries of one's childhood's
    dreams
        (Calling.)
  Lothario! Wilhelm!
  Happy! aye, thrice bless'd am I;
  My heart no longer grief doth feel,
  To new life I seem to awake—
  The fear of death no more doth haunt me!

Wilhelm. Yes! new hope thy heart inspires;
  Thy much-loved native air, thy life will
    save;
  O maiden, banish now the grief,
  That so long hath bowed thee down,
  Live thou! and live to love!

Mignon. Yes, thou dear one, I will live—to trust
    in thee!
  Speak! oh, speak, for ever thus!

Wilhelm. Chase then from thy troubled mind,
  The memory of dark days gone by.
  Ah, yes! my very soul doth seem with
    thine to blend!
  O loving one, on me thy bright eyes turn;
  With that sweet radiant face, and robe of
    spotless white,
  An angel truly dost thou seem!

Mignon.
     (With a melancholy smile.)
  And yet I am but what I ever was!

Wilhelm. Nay, thou are not now the same.
  My heart's idol! my treasure fond thou'rt
  now!

Mon regard l'intimide et ma voix l'effa-
  rouche;
Un mot trouble son âme et fait couler ses
  pleurs!......
Pour rendre à la fleur épuisée
Sa fraîcheur, son éclat vermeil,
O printemps, donne-lui ta goutte de rosée!
O mon cœur, donne-lui ton rayon de soleil!

WILHELM, ANTONIO, *puis* LAERTE

Antonio.
        (Entrant.)
  Signor!

Wilhelm. Que me veux-tu?

Antonio. Cette lettre.

Wilhelm.
  (Prenant la lettre et le congédiant.)
  Merci.
     (ANTONIO sort. Il lit.)
  "Philine vous suivait, fuyez, elle est içi."
  Un avis de Laërte.
  (Courant vers la chambre de MIGNON et s'arretant.)
  Ah, Mignon, la voiçi.

Mignon. Ou suis-je? Je respire un air plus doux,
  L'azur est plus profonde.
  Dans le flot pur de ce lac transparent
  Se reflète un bois sombre.
  Une voile glisse dans l'ombre.
  Quelle fraicheur! et ce palais dont les jar-
    dins descendent vers la grève
  Il me semble avoir tout cela dans un rêve.
  Lothario! Wilhelm! Je t'appelais.
  Je suis heureuse! l'air m'enivre!
  Mon cœur a cessé de souffrir!
  Je renais!...... Je me sens revivre!
  Mignon ne craint plus de mourir!

Wilhelm. Pauvre enfant! plus de craintes vaines!
  Cet air pur va te ranimer!
  Un sang nouveau gonfle tes veines.
  Mignon doit vivre pour aimer!

Mignon. Oui, je te crois! Je veux te croire!
  Parle-moi! parle encor! toujours!

Wilhelm. Chasse à jamais de ta mémoire
  Le souvenir des mauvais jours!
    (La conduisant vers la fenêtre.)
  Ah! que ton âme dans mon âme s'épanche!
  Chère Mignon, lève vers moi tes yeux!......
  Sous ce rayon divin et dans ta robe blanche,
  Tu m'apparais comme un ange des cieux!

Mignon.
     (Souriant tristement.)
  Non, c'est toujours Mignon!

Wilhelm.
     (Tombant à ses pieds.)
  Mignon n'est plus la même!
  Mignon a tout mon cœur et c'est elle que
    j'aime!

Mignon.	Heavens! do I believe aright? And dar'st thou say thou lov'st me? Not long since 'twas Filina whom thou lov'dst.
Wilhelm.	Nay, when thou art at my side, Of her I think no more.
Mignon.	(Ecstatically.) Oh heavens! is't true! Oh joy immense, unspeakable! At last, then, the secret I'll avow to thee...
Filina.	(Outside.) "The fair Titania am I, Titania by all on earth beloved."
Wilhelm.	(Aside.) Great heaven! Filina!
Mignon.	(Running to the window.) That woman still! (Aside.) O fatal secret, die thou in my heart!
Mignon.	Yes, yes, her voice it is, Go, get thee from my side. List, list! 'tis she. Dost hear? she nearer draws Ah, speak to me no more, My voice, my speech, do fail (MIGNON falls on a seat.)
Wilhelm.	(Sadly.) Poor girl, her hands are icy cold! (Tenderly.) Take heart, dear girl, Thy sense resume! (MIGNON recovers her consciousness.) Her eyes she opens! 'Tis I, Mignon, who call thee!
Mignon.	(Terrified.) The hateful voice, I now no longer hear; Perchance I did but dream.
Wilhelm.	Yes! 'twas but a vain, delusive dream. The dreadful fever still thy sense o'erclouds,
Mignon.	(Sadly.) The fever sayest thou? Nay, that is not true; The only one who loves me is Lothario! Why do I not see him at my side? (A noise is heard at back of stage.) List! 'tis he! I hear him coming. (Pointing to door at back.)
Wilhelm.	Through yon door, none can pass! (The door at back is suddenly burst open, and LOTHARIO appears on the threshold. He is attired in a rich garb of black velvet—he advances slowly, bearing in his hand a small coffer.)
Lothario.	Mignon, Wilhelm, I do greet ye! Welcome, to this my house! (In tones of mingled surprise and pity.)
Wilhelm.	Oh Heaven!
Mignon.	(Surprised.) Lothario! and in this rich attire?

Mignon.	Toi! m'aimer! que dis-tu? Souvienstoi du passé! Et ne réveille pas un espoir insensé!...... (S'échappant de ses bras.) Ton cœur n'est pas à moi!...... Ton cœur est à Philine!
Wilhelm.	Philine est loin de nous...... Et je ne l'aime pas!
Mignon.	(Revenant vers WILHELM *et lui tendant la main.*) Est-il vrai?...... parle!...... O joie ineffable et divine! Je puis te dire enfin!...... Mais parlons bas...... bien bas!......
La Voix de Philine.	(Au dehors.) "Je suis Titania la blonde, Titania, fille de l'air!"
Wilhelm.	Philine!
Mignon.	(Courant à la fenêtre.) Encore elle!...... encore cette femme!...... (A part.) O mon secret, reste au fond de mon âme!
Mignon.	Je reconnaisais sa voix! Je l'entends! je la vois! C'est elle encore! c'est elle Qui te cherche et t'appelle! Ne m'interroge pas! Je dois me taire, hélas! Je ne veux plus parler! je ne parlerai pas! (MIGNON se laisse tomber dans un fauteuil.)
Wilhelm.	Ah, malheureuse enfant!...... Ses mains sont glacées. Mignon, toi que j'aime, ah! reviens, toi. (MIGNON reprend ses senses.) Elle ouvre les yeux. C'est moi qui t'appelle.
Mignon.	Je n'entends plus rien. N'est-ce pas un rêve?
Wilhelm.	Non, ce n'est qu'un rêve, un rêve menteur, Ou la fièvre encore égare ton cœur.
Mignon.	La fièvre, dis-tu? Celui qui m'aime c'est Lothario. Pourquoi n'est-il pas près de moi? (Elle se tourne vers la porte du fond.) Écoute! Oui, j'entends son pas.
Wilhelm.	Nul ne peut venir de là. (LOTHARIO paraît.)
Lothario.	Mignon, Wilhelm, salut, à vous! Soyez les bienvenus chez moi.
Wilhelm.	(À part.) Que veut-il dire?
Mignon.	(Etonnée.) Sous ces riches habits est-ce lui que je vois!

Lothario.	Here, all doth now belong to me. Know, dear girl, that of this wealthy mansion, I was once the lord.
Mignon.	(To WILHELM, contemplating LOTHARIO with surprise.) I scarce do recognize him—his look so wild, His words so strange . . . .
Lothario.	(Placing the little coffer on the table and approaching MIGNON.) O maiden now, the past forget, A treasure rich, I here present to thee; The trouble of thine aching heart 'Twill quickly calm.
Wilhelm.	Mignon. From those eyes, with woe oppressed, What fire unwonted now doth gleam!
Lothario.	Full many a month this coffer hath in yonder chamber lain. (To MIGNON.) Thou may'st open it girl.
Mignon.	Say! what does it enclose?
Lothario.	See for thyself.
Mignon.	(Running to the coffer and opening it.) A child's scarf.
Lothario.	(Contemplating it with a fixed stare.) With silver 'tis embroidered, Ah! with what fond love in yon recess, Have I preserved it.
Wilhelm.	But tell us—who did wear this beauteous scarf?
Lothario.	Sperata!
Mignon.	Sperata? The name doth seem familiar to my ear, At its sweet sound, vague memories do stir within me, Memories that do recall a time, long, long since passed away.
Wilhelm & Mignon.	See, see! his eyes do stream with tears!
Lothario.	(Still motionless, and absorbed in his thoughts.) Dost thou not also find, A coral ornament?
Mignon.	(Drawing forth a bracelet.) 'Tis here, (Endeavoring to put a bracelet on her arm.) 'Tis too small for me!
Lothario.	(Sadly.) Yet, once, it was too large. Sperata ne'er would till the morrow wait To wear a jewel that enhanced her charms; Yon bracelet ever from her hand did fall.

Lothario.	Tout ici m'appartient! Regarde, enfant, admire!...... En ce palais j'étais maître autrefois!
Wilhelm et Mignon.	(Les yeux fixés sur LOTHARIO.) Je ne reconnais plus son regard ni sa voix!
Lothario.	(Déposant la cassette sur la table, et s'approchant de MIGNON.) Oublions nos temps de misére!...... Je t'apporte un don précieux, Il adoucira, je l'espère, L'ennui de ton cœur soucieux......
Mignon et Wilhelm.	Je crois deviner un mystère Que trahit l'éclat de ses yeux!......
Lothario.	Cette cassette est là depuis de bien longs mois! (A MIGNON.) C'est à toi de l'ouvrir...... (Il étend la main vers la cassette.)
Mignon.	Que contient-elle?......
Lothario.	(Sans détourner la tête.) Vois.
Mignon.	(Ouvrant la cassette.) Une écharpe d'enfant!
Lothario.	(Le regard fixe, immobile au milieu de la scène.) D'or et d'argent brodée...... Oui, je l'avais pieusement gardée!
Wilhelm.	Quelle est cette relique et qui donc la porta?...... Parle!
Lothario.	Sperata!......
Mignon.	Sperata! Déjà ce nom a frappé mon oreille! Un souvenir confus, A ce doux nom dans mon âme s'éveille! Est-ce l'écho lointain d'un passé qui n'est plus?......
Wilhelm et Mignon.	Des pleurs mouillent ses yeux......
Lothario.	(Toujours immobile sur le devant du théâtre et comme absorbé par ses souvenirs.) Ne vois-tu pas aussi Un bracelet de corail?
Mignon.	(Tirant le bracelet de la cassette.) Le voici! (Essayant le bracelet à son bras.) Trop petit pour mon bras!......
Lothario.	(Tristement.) Trop grand! trop grand pour elle Elle ne voulait pas attendre au lendemain Pour porter un bijou qui la rendait plus belle! Mais le bijou toujours lui glissait de la main!

Mignon.
(Aside, repeating sorrowfully.)
Fell from her hand say'st thou?

Wilhelm.
(To MIGNON.)
What ails thee? speak! What secret
grief doth now torment thee?

Lothario.
(To MIGNON.)
Search thou the coffer deeper still.

Mignon.
(Producing from the coffer a little Prayer Book.)
A little Prayer Book!

Lothario. E'en now, methinks, I hear her angel voice
in prayer.
She ever prayed when day 'gan to decline.

Mignon.
(Opening the book and reading.)
O power supreme,
Our lives are in thy hands,
Vouchsafe thou to keep me in Thy Holy
care,
Grant, that from the right path, I ne'er
may stray.

Lothario. Thus, in the days gone by,
Thus did my Sperata pray!

Mignon.
(Lets fall the book from her hands, kneels down, clasps
her hands, raises her eyes to heaven, and assumes the look
and attitude of a child at prayer.)
O Thou, who, in Heaven above,
All mortal hearts doth read,
Teach me to love my parents dear,
Preserve me to them, evermore!

Lothario.
(Deeply agitated, extending his arm to MIGNON.)
Just Heaven! what does this mean?
The book's contents by heart she knows.

Mignon.
(Rising with increasing fervor.)
Lothario mine! what secret proof within my
breast now works?
I feel—I know—but yet cannot explain!
(To WILHELM.)
Whither hast thou brought me?
What hills are those that yonder rise?

Wilhelm. They are the shores of Italy.

Mignon. O beauteous light! O sweet, reviving, gales!
O memory!
(After having, with a violent effort, endeavored to recall
her scattered recollections, she rushes with a wild cry to the
door at back, disappears for a moment, and then returns, pale
and scarcely able to stand.)
Yonder my mother's picture hangs!
Her room, alas! deserted seems!

Lothario.
(Who has followed her every movement, now rushes to her
with extended arms.)
My child!

Mignon. My father!
(Throws herself into LOTHARIO's arms.)

Lothario. My daughter dear, at length I've found!
All praise to Thee, O Heaven!

Mignon. All praise to Heaven be given!
My home, my father, I at last have found.

Mignon.
(Très-émue.)
Mais le bijou toujours lui glissait de la
main!

Wilhelm. Qu'as-tu, Mignon? Tu trembles et tu
pleures!

Lothario.
(À MIGNON.)
Regarde encore!

Mignon.
Retirant de la cassette un petit livre à coins d'argent.)
Un livre d'heures!

Lothario. Hélas! je crois toujours la voir,
Lettre à lettre, épeler sa prière du soir!

Mignon.
(Ouvrant le livre et lisant.)
O Vierge Marie,
Le Seigneur est avec vous!
Abaissez vos regards si doux,
Sur l'enfant qui prie!......

Lothario.
(Penché vera elle.)
Elle priait ainsi, mains jointes, à genou
(MIGNON laissant échapper le livre et tombant à genou
les yeux levés au ciel et les mains jointes, comme un enfa
en prière.)
Vous qui bercez sur vos genoux,
Le divin Sauveur de la terre,
Conservez l'enfant à sa mère,
O madone, priez pour nous!......

Lothario.
(Les mains étendues vers MIGNON.)
Est-ce Dieu qui l'inspire?
Elle achève sans lire!

Mignon.
(Se levant et s'exaltant de plus en plus.)
Lothario!...... Wilhelm!...... suis-je encore en
délire?......
Je devine!...... je vois!...... je sens!...... je ne
puis dire!
Où m'avez-vous conduite et quel est ce
pays?

Wilhelm. L'Italie!

Mignon. O rayons de céleste lumière!
O souvenirs!......
(Après avoir fait un effort pour rassembler ses souvenirs
elle s'élance avec un cri vers la porte du fond, disparaît u.ª
moment dans la coulisse et revient pâle et chancelante.)
Là! là! l'image de ma mere!......
Et sa chambre est deserté!......

Lothario.
(Qui a suivi tous ses mouvements avec anxiété, lui ten-
dant les bras et courant à elle.)
Ah! ma fille!

Mignon. Mon père!
(Elle tombe dans les bras de LOTHARIO.)

Lothario. C'est mon enfant!...... c'est elle!...... O Dieu!
je te bénis!

Mignon. Oui, je vous reconnais mon père!...... mon
pays!

Wilhelm.   All praise to Heaven be given!
        Her home, her father she hath found!
        (Overcome by violent emotion.)

Mignon.   Ah!

Wilhelm.   Mignon.

Lothario.
          (Supporting her.)
        My Child!

Wilhelm.
          (Alarmed.)
        Speak, in pity, speak! what is't thou feel'st?

Mignon.
          (Falling to the ground.)
        I faint, I die!

Wilhelm.
    (Running to throw open one of the windows, and immediately returning to MIGNON.)
        Oh dearest treasure, droop not thus!
        My very life depends on thine!
    (MIGNON slowly recovers her consciousness.)
        Ah! did'st thou but know how I adore thee!

Lothario.   See, she revives— her sense she now recovers!

Mignon.
    (Recognizing WILHELM and LOTHARIO — almost ecstatic with joy.)
        "Ah! might I but return
        Unto the land where my first childish cry
          of joy was heard!
        There might I peace enjoy:
        There would I love and—die!"

Wilhelm. and Lothario.
        Young, full of life, art thou,
        Here shalt thou henceforth dwell,
        Ne'er shalt thou leave us more!

Wilhelm.   Mignon, retrouve enfin son père et son pays!

Mignon.
    (Frappé d'une violente commotion.)
        Ah!

Wilhelm.   (Effrayé.)
        Mignon!

Lothario.
          (Soutenant MIGNON.)
        Ma fille!
          (Elle suffoque.)

Wilhelm.   Dieu! qu'a-t-elle donc?

Mignon.
          (Elle chancelle.)
        Je meurs!
          (Elle tombe.)
    (WILHELM va ouvrir la fenêtre et revient près de MIGNON. Peu à MIGNON revient à elle.)

Wilhelm.   Le bonheur est içi maintenant.
        Elle revit!
        Chère Mignon! Je t'aime, oui, je t'aime!

Lothario.   Son cœur se souvient.

Mignon.
    (Reconnaissant LOTHARIO et WILHELM, comme dans une extase.)
        Ah, c'est là que je voulais vivre,
        Aimer, aimer et mourir!

Lothario et Wilhelm.
        Ah, c'est là que tu dois vivre,
        Pour être heureuse et pour aimer!
        C'est là, oui, c'est là, pour toujours unis'

FIDELIO

by

LUDWIG   VAN   BEETHOVEN

354

DRAMATIS PERSONÆ.

FLORESTAN. A Spanish Nobleman.   **TENOR.**

LEONORA. His Wife, who in her Disguise takes the name of FIDELIO.   SOPRANO.

DON FERNANDO. Prime Minister of Spain, and friend to Florestan.   BASS

PIZARRO. Governor of the Prison, and enemy to Florestan.   BASS.

ROCCO. Chief Jailer.   BASS.

MARCELLINA. Daughter of Rocco.   SOPRANO.

JAQUINO. Assistant to Rocco, in love with Marcellina.   TENOR.

Prisoners, Guards, Soldiers and People.

THE ACTION TAKES PLACE AT A FORTRESS USED FOR THE CONFINEMENT OF POLITICAL OFFENDERS, NEAR SEVILLE, IN SPAIN.

ARGUMENT.

FLORESTAN, a noble Spaniard, a valued friend of Fernando, the Prime Minister, had, by his fearless exposure of the misdeeds of Pizarro, awakened the deadly hatred of the latter. This wretch was not without the means of gratifying his malignity. Being appointed the governor of a fortress, used as a place of confinement for political prisoners, he managed to get possession of the person of his enemy, circulated a report of his death, and immured him in the deepest and darkest of the state dungeons. Here the nobleman would have died, had it not been for the faithful love of his wife, Leonora, who did not believe him dead, suspected Pizarro, and finally, in the disguise of a young man, calling herself Fidelio, solicited and received employment from Rocco, head jailer under Pizarro. The youth made rapid headway in the affections of the old man, and also in those of his daughter, Marcellina, who quite neglected her rustic lover, Jaquino, for the gentle and polished stranger. Leonora, although pained at this, felt obliged to encourage the love of the girl, for the sake of her influence over the father; and they together so far prevailed upon him, that he consented to allow Fidelio to go to the more secret portions of the prison. They also begged, for the inmates of the outer cells, the privilege of spending a few hours in the sunshine of the court-yard. The prisoners, naturally, were overjoyed at this indulgence; but, after a short time, were ordered to confinement again by Pizarro, who harshly chided the jailer for his kindness.

Pizarro, just before, had received notice from a friend, that the Prime Minister was on his way to the prison. Should Fernando see Florestan, farewell to revenge. Something must speedily be done to avert the danger. Rocco is commanded to kill and bury the supposed criminal in the inner dungeon. He refuses to kill, but will dig the grave. Pizarro himself will dispatch the victim. Rocco, with Fidelio, accordingly repairs to the gloomy vault, where Florestan is discovered, but sleeping; and so dim is the light, that his agitated wife cannot be sure it is he. The two proceed to clear out an old cistern, which is to be the place of burial. Florestan awakes, and is recognized. Pizarro enters, and is about to give the fatal blow, when, with a shriek, Leonora throws herself between the murderer and her husband. Her sudden avowal of her name causes a hesitation on the part of Pizarro, but he again raises the dagger, when he is confronted by a pistol, which points directly at his head. Florestan is saved; for, a moment after, the trumpets signal the arrival of Fernando. Pizarro is summoned to meet him. Rocco brings forth Florestan and his heroic wife, who has the gratification of unlocking and removing his hateful fetters. Other prisoners are released, and the occasion is one of full-measured joy to all, unless we except the jailer's daughter, who is dismayed at the discovery of the real character and station of the pretty Fidelio. She, however, has the old love to fall back upon.

"Fidelio" was first given in 1805, at the Imperial house at Vienna, but was not at first a favorite. It was revised, and changed to its present form, and reintroduced to the public in 1814, since which time no opera has been more highly esteemed.

FIDELIO.

<table>
<tr><td>

AUFZUG I.

AUFTRITT I.—*Der Hof des Staats-gefängnisses. Im Hintergrund das Hauptthor und ein hohe Wallmauer, über welche Bäume hervorragen. Im geschlossenen Thore selbst ist eine Pforte, die für einzelne Fussgänger geöffnet wird. Neben dem Thore das Stübchen des Pförtners. Die Coulisse den Zuschauern links, stellen die Wohngebäude der Gefangenen vor: alle Fenster sind mit Gittern und die mit Nummern bezeichneten Thüren, mit starken Riegeln versehen. In der vordersten Coulisse ist die Thüre zur Wohnung des Gefangenwärters. Rechts stehen Bäume mit eisernem Geländer eingefasst, welche, nebst einem Gartenthore, den Eingang des Schloss-gartens bezeichnen.*

MARZELLINE *plättet vohr ihrer Thüre Wasche;* JAQUINO *hält sich mehr bei seiner Thüre und öffnet sie mehreren Personen welche ihm Papiete übergeben, die er in sein Stübchen trägt.*

DUETTO.

Jaq. Jetzt, Schätzchen, jetz sind wir allein,
  Wir können vertraulicht nun plaudern,
Mar. Es wird ja nichts wichtiges seyn ;
  Ich darf bei der Arbeit nicht zaudern.
Jaq. Ein Wörtchen, du Trotzige du.
Mar. So sprich nur ! ich höre ja zu.
Jaq. Wenn du mir nicht freundlicher blickest,
  So bring' ich kein Wörtchen hervor.
Mar. Wenn du dich nicht in mich schickest,
  So stopf' ich mir vollends das Ohr.
Iaq. Ein Weilchen nur höre mir zu,
  Dann lass ich dich wieder in Ruh.
Mar. So hab' ich denn nimmermehr Ruh.
  So rede, so rede nur zu.
Icq. Ich habe zum Weib dich gewählet—
  Verstehst du ?
Mar. Das ist ja doch klar !
Jaq. Und wenn mir dein Jawort nich fehlet,
  Was meinst du ?
Mar. So sind wir ein Paar.
Jaq. Wir könnten in wenigen Wochen—
Mar. Recht schön ! du bestimmst schon die Zeit.
       [*Es wird gepocht.*

Jaq. Zum Henker ! das ewige Pochen !
Mar. So bin ich denn endlich befreit ! [*Bei seite.*
Jaq. Da war ich so herrlich im Gang.
Mar. Wie macht seine Liebe mir bang.
Jaq. Und immer entwischt mir der Fang.
Mar. Wie werden die Stunden mir lang.
  Ich weiss, dass der Arme sich qualet,
  Es thut mir so leid auch um ihn ;
  Fidelio hab' ich gewählet,
  Ihn lieben ist süsser Gewinn.

Jaq. Wo war ich ? Sie sieht mich nich an.
Mar. Da ist er—er fängt wieder an.
Jaq. Wann wirst du das Jawort mir geben ?
  Es könnte ja heute noch seyn.
Mar. O web' er verbittert mein Leben !
  Jetzt—morgen—und immer—nein, nein !

</td><td>

ACT I.

SCENE I.—*The Court-yard of the State Prison. In the background the principal gate : in it a wicket, with a gate to allow Foot-Passengers to pass singly. Near the gate the Lodge of the Porter. The side scene to the left of the Spectator represents the dwellings of the Prisoners. The windows have iron gratings, and the doors, which are numbered, strong bolts. In the front side scene is the door of the Turnkey's dwelling. To the right, iron palings, which, together with a garden gate, indicate the entrance of the castle garden.*

MARCELLINA *discovered, ironing linen before her door ;* JACQUINO *attending diligently to his door, which he opens to different Persons, who give him parcels to take into the Lodge.*

DUET.

Jac. At last, my idol, we are alone,
  And can have a pleasant chat together.
Mar. Well, speak away, but don't hinder me ·
  I have my work to do you know.
Jac. A word with thee—just a word.
Mar. Go on ; I'm listening.
Jac. But, at least, do not be cross with me,
  Or I shall not be able to say a word.
Mar. Well, and when you do speak
  I shall, perhaps, close my ears.
Jac. Only listen for a few moments,
  And then I'll leave you in peace.
Mar. You are always tormenting me ;—
  I listen,—speak on.
Jac. I have chosen you for my wife—
  Do you understand ?
Mar. Yes, that's plain enough !
Jac. And if thou would'st only say yes,
  What then ?
Mar. Why, then we should make a pair.
Jac. In a week or two, we could—
Mar. Well done ! you are fixing an early time certainly
       [*A knocking is heard*

Jac. The deuce ! that eternal knocking !
Mar. For the present I am saved.   [*Aside*
Jac. I was just getting on the right track.
Mar. How uneasy his love makes me.
Jac. But the prize always escapes me.
Mar. How slowly the time seems to pass.
  I know this poor fellow suffers,
  And I am right sorry for him ;
  But Fidelio has my heart,
  And his love is the only treasure I value.

Jac. Where was I ? She turns her back upon me.
Mar. There he is—going on again.
Jac. Oh, when will you say to me Yes
  Why not do so to-day ?
Mar. Oh, woe's me ! he's a constant torment ;
  Once for all and for ever, I say no, no !

</td></tr>
</table>

Jaq. Du bist doch wahrhaftig von Stein.
Mar Ich muss ja so hart mit ihm seyn.
Jaq. Kein Wünschen, kein Bitten geht ein.
Mar. Er hofft bei dem mindesten Schein.
Jaq. So wirst du dich nimmer bekehren ?
Was meinst du ?
Mar. Du könntest nun gehn.
Jaq. Wie ? dich anzusehn willst du mir wehren ?
Auch das noch ?
Mar. So bleibe hier stehn.
Jaq. Du hast mir so oft doch versprochen—
Mar Versprochen ? Nein ! das geht zu weit !
[*Es wird an dir Thüre gepocht.*
Jaq. Zum Henker ! das ewige Pochen !
Mar. So bin ich doch endlich befreit.
Jaq. Es ward ihr im Ernste schon bang,
Mar. Das war ein willkommener Klang.
Jaq. Wer weiss ob es mir nicht gelang ?
Mar. Es wurde zu Tode mir bang.

Jaq. Wenn ich diese Thüre heute nicht schon zweihundert Mal geöffnet habe, so will ich nicht Caspar Eustaco Jaquino heissen. [*Zu Marzelline.*] Endlich kann ich doch einmal wieder plaudern. [*Es wird gepocht.*] Zum Wetter ! schon wieder ! [*Er geht, um zu öffnen.*
Mar. Was kann ich dafür, dass ich ihn nicht mehr so gerne haben kann, wie sonst ?
Jaq. [*Zu dem der gepocht hat, indem er hastig zuschliesst.*] Ich werde es besorgen, schon recht ! [*Vorgehend zu Marzelline.*] Nun hoffe ich soll Niemand uns stören.
Roh. [*ruft hinter der Scene.*] Jaquino ! Jaquino !
Mar. Hörst du ! der Vater ruft.
Jaq. Lassen wir ihn ein wenig warten. Also wieder auf unsere Liebe zu kommen—
Mar. So geh doch ! der Vater wird sich nach Fidelio erkundigen wollen.
Jaq. [*eifersüchtig.*] Ei, freilich ! da kann man nicht schnell genug seyn.
Roh. [*ruft weider.*] Jaquino ! hörst du nicht ?
Jaq. [*schreiend.*] Ich komme schon ! [*Zu Marzelline.*] Bleib' fein hier ; in zwei Minuten sind wir wieder beisammen. [*Geht ab in den Garten.*

AUFTRITT II.—Marzelline, allein.

Mar. Der arme Jaquino dauert mich beinahe Aus dem Mitleiden, das ich mit Jaquino habe, merke ich erst, wei sehr gut ich Fidelio bin. Ich glaube auch, dass Fidelio mir recht gut ist, und wenn ich die Gesinnungen des Vaters wüsste, so könnte bald mein Glück vollkommen werden.

Aria.

Mar O wär' ich schon mit dir vereint,
Und dürfte Mann dich nennen !
Ein Mädchen darf ja, was es meint,
Zur Hälfte nur bekennen.
Doch wenn ich nicht erröthen muss,
Ob einem warmen Herzenskuss,
Wenn nichts uns stört au Erden.
Die Hoffnung schon erfüllt die Brust
Mit unaussprechlich süsser Lust !
Wie glücklich will ich werden.
In Ruhe stiller Häuslichkeit,
Erwach ich jeden Morgen ;
Wir grüssen uns mit Zärtlichkeit,
Der Fleiss verscheucht die Sorgen.
Und ist die Arbeit abgethan,
Dann schleicht die holde Nacht heran,
Dann ruh'n wir von Beschwerden.
Die Hoffnung schon erfüllt die Brust
Mit unaussprechlich süsser Lust !
Wie glücklich will ich werden !

Jac. Then you must have a heart of stone
Mar. [*Aside.*] I must be harsh with him.
Jac. Will neither vows nor prayers move you ?
Mar. The least giving way on my part makes him hope
Jac. Wilt thou never relent ?
Speak—what sayest thou ?
Mar. That thou may'st go.
Jac. What ! must I even quit thy sight ?
May I not even look on thee ?
Mar. Well, stay, and stand there, then.
Jac. But think how often you have promised—
Mar. Promised ? No ! that's saying too much !
[*Knocking again at the door*
Jac. The deuce ! that eternal knocking !
Mar. At last I shall be left at peace.
Jac. She begins to relent a little, I think.
Mar. [*Aside.*] Oh, what a welcome sound !
Jac. Perhaps if I try once more I may succeed.
Mar. I am nearly dead with anxiety.

Jac. If I have not answered that door two hundred times at least to-day, my name's not Caspar Eustache Jacquino. [*To Marcellina.*] At last we are at liberty to speak freely. [*Knocking.*] The deuce ! again so soon !
[*He goes to open the door.*
Mar. What shall I do ? I cannot even love him as I used.
Jac. [*To the person who has knocked, and shutting the door petulently.*] That will do ; I will attend. [*Turning towards Marcellina.*] Now I hope we shall have no more disturbers.
Roc. [*Calling from behind.*] Jacquino ! Jacquino !
Mar. Do you not hear ? my father calls.
Jac. Well, let him wait a bit, while we finish our love affairs.
Mar. No, no ; go ! Father may be wishing to enquire after Fidelio.
Jac. [*Jealously.*] Oh, truly ! and in that case one cannot be too quick.
Roc. [*Calling again.*] Jacquino ! dost thou not hear me ?
Jac. [*Loudly.*] Coming ! [*To Marcellina.*] Do not go now, I pray thee—in two minutes I shall be back again.
[*Exit into the garden.*

SCENE II.—Marcellina, alone.

Mar. I cannot but feel for poor Jacquino. From my compassion for him I learn how dearly I love Fidelio ; and he equally loves me, I hope. How soon might my happiness be complete, if my father were not against our union.

Air.

Mar. If the truth my heart doth tell,
Very soon a bride I'll be ;
The impulse pure with love to dwell,
The heart's law is to me ;
But for a little time, at least,
I my feelings must suppress ;—
Delay most cruel !

Why throbs my heart within my breast ?
Oh, come, and give thy soothing rest,
Hope, brightest jewel !
Ah ! what pleasure, what delight,
Shall I with my lover know !
Light are all the cares of life
When those we love partake our woe !

AUFTRITT III. — MARZELLINE, ROKKO, JAQUINO, trägt Gartenwerkzeuge in Rokko's Haus.

Rok. Guten Tag, Marcelline! Ist Fidelio noch nicht zurückgekommen?
Mar. Nein, Vater!
Rck. Die Stunde naht, wo ich dem Gouverneur die Briefschaften bringen muss, die Fidelo abholen sollte. Ich erwarte ihn mit Ungeduld   [*Es wird geklopft.*
Jaq. [*kommt aus Rokkos Hause.*] Ich komme schon! Ich komme schon!   [*Läuft um aufzuschliessen.*
Mar. Er wird gewiss so lange bei dem Schmiede haben worten müssen. [*Sie hat während dessen Leonoren zur Thüre hereinkommen sehen.*] Da ist er ja! Da ist er!

AUFTRITT IV.—*Vorige* LEONORE, *als* FIDELIO. *Sie trägt ein Behältniss mit Lebensmitteln, auf dem Arme, Ketten, die sie beim Eintreten an dem Stübchen des Pförtners ablegt; an der Seite hängt ihr eine blecherne Blüchse an einer Schnur.*

Mar. [*auf Leonore zulaufend.*] Wie er belastet ist. Liebe Gott! Der Schweiss läuft ihm von der Stirne.

[*Sie nimmt ihr Sacktuch und versucht ihr das Gesicht abzutrocknen.*

Rok. Warte! warte!

[*Er hilft mit Marzellinen, ihr das Behältniss vom Rücken zu nehmen.*

Jaq. [*bie Seite.*] Es war auch wohl der Mühe werth, so schnell zu laufen, um den Patron da hereinzulassen.

[*Geht in sein Stübchen, kommt aber bald wieder heraus, macht den Beschäftigten, sucht aber eigentlich die Uebrigen zu beobachten.*

Rok. Armer Fidelio,—diesmal hast du dir zu viel aufgeluden.
Leo. [*vorgehend und sich das Gesicht abwischend.*] Ich muss gestehen, ich ben ein wenig ermüdet.
Rok. Wieviel kostet Alles zusammen?
Leo. Zwölf Piaster ohngefähr. Hier ist die genaue Rechnung.
Rok. [*durchseiht die Rechnung.*] Gut! brav! zum Wetter! Da giebt es Artikel, auf die man wenigstens das Doppelte profitiren kann. Du bist ein kluger Junge! [*bei Seite.*] Der Schelm giebt sich alle diese Mühe offenbar meiner Marzelline wegen.
Leo. Ich suche zu thun, was mir möglich ist.
Rok. Ja, ja! Du bist brav! Ich habe dich aber auch mit jedem Tage lieber; und sey versichert, dein Lohn soll nicht ausbleiben.

[*Er wirft während der letztern Worte wechselnde Blicke auf Leonoren und Marzelinen.*

Leo. [*verlegen.*] O glaubt nicht, dass ich meine Schuldigkeit nur des Lohnes wegen—
Rok. Still! [*mit Blicken wie vorher.*] Meinst du ich kann dir nicht ins Herz sehen?

[*Er scheint sich an der zunehmenden Verlegenheit Leonorens zu weiden und geht dann bei Seite, die Ketten zu besehen. Marzelline hat bei dem Lobe, sie mit immer steigender Bewegung liebevoll betrachtet.*

SCENE III.—MARCELLINA, ROCCO, JACQUINO, *carrying garden implements into Rocco's House.*

Roc. Good day, Marcellina! Has Fidelio not yet returned?
Mar. No, father!
Roc. The hour is at hand when I ought to deliver to the Governor the packet of letters that Fidelio was to fetch.
      [*Knocking.*
Jac. [*Coming out of Rocco's House.*] Coming, coming!
      [*Runs to unlock the door*
Mar. Perhaps he has been obliged to wait at the smith's. [*In the mean time seeing Leonora at the door.*] Why, here he is, here he is!

SCENE IV.—*Enter* LEONORA, *as* FIDELIO. *She carries a basket with provisions, and on her arm fetters, which she deposits on the ground. At her side a tin box hangs by a ribbon.*

Mar. [*Running to Leonora.*] How he is laden! Good heavens! the perspiration streams from his forehead.

[*She tries, with her handkerchief, to dry Leonora's face.*

Roc. Oh, stay, stay!

[*He helps, with Marcellina, to remove the basket from her back.*

Jac. [*Aside.*] It was worth the trouble, certainly, to run so quickly to let my gentleman in!

[*Goes into his Lodge, but soon comes out again; pretends to be busy, but is in fact watching the others.*

Roc. My poor Fidelio! this time thou hast somewhat overladen thyself.
Leo. [*Advancing, and wiping her face.*] I must confess I am a little wearied.
Roc. How much have these things cost?
Leo. About twelve piastres; here is the account.
Roc. [*Looking through the account.*] Good! capital! By all that's good, here are articles by which we shall at least make cent per cent. [*Aside.*] The rogue plainly gives himself all this trouble on account of my Marcellina.
Leo. I wish to do all I can.
Roc. Yes, yes, thou'rt a good fellow! I like thee better and better, and be assured thou shalt meet thy reward.

He casts, during the last words, alternate glances at Leonora and Marcellina.

Leo. [*Embarrassed.*] Oh! believe not that I do my duty from interested motives.
Roc. [*Glances as before.*] Hush! think'st thou I cannot see into thy heart?

[*He appears to enjoy the increasing embarrassment of Leonora, and then goes aside to look at the fetters. Meanwhile Marcellina regards Leonora lovingly, and with increasing emotion..*

MIR IST SO WUNDERBAR—MY HEART AND HAND. MARCELLINA, LEONORA, ROCCO AND JACQUINO

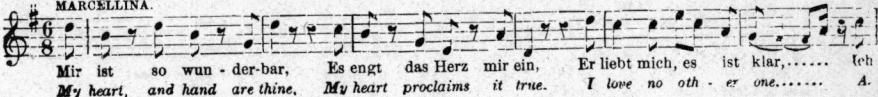

Mir ist so wun-der-bar, Es engt das Herz mir ein, Er liebt mich, es ist klar,...... Ich
My heart, and hand are thine, My heart proclaims it true. I love no oth-er one...... A.

werde glücklich, glücklich sein!   Mir ist so wun - der - bar,   Es engt das
I have love to you, to you,   *My heart and hand are thine,*   *My heart pro*

LEONORA.

Wie gross ist die   ge - fahr!   Wie schwach der Hoff - nung
How great my dan - - ger, now,   *How faint, O Hope,   thy*

Herz mir ein, Es engt das Herz mir ein,   Er liebt mich, es   ist klar, Ich wer - de glücklich
claims it true, My heart proclaims it true,   *He loves me, that is clear, And I to thee am*

schein!   Sie   liebt mich, es ist klar,.......... O, na - men, na - men-
glow,   *She   loves me, that is   true, ... What shall I   do,   what*

glücklich sein,   Mir ist so wunder-bar,................. .... Es engt das Herz, es engt das Herz, mir
true, am true,   My heart and hand are thine,....................... My heart proclaims, my heart proclaims it

- lo - se Pein!   Wie gross, wie gross ist die gefahr!   Wie schwach, wie
shall I do?   *How great, how great my danger, now,*   *How faint, how*

ROCCO.

Sie liebt   ihn,   es   ist   klar,   Ja,   Mädchen, er   wird
She loves   him,   that   is   plain,   *You   shall the loved one*

ein,   Er   liebt   mich, es ist klar,...... ich werde glücklich, Ich werde glücklich, ich werde glücklich
true, He   loves   me, that is plain,.... and I will love him, And I will love him and I will love him

schwach, der Hoffnung Schein, wie schwach der Hoffnung Schein, Sie liebt mich, es   ist   klar,   O, namen, namen-
faint, O Hope, thy glow, how faint, O Hope, thy glow,   She   loves me, that is   true, What can I do, what

dein,   Ein gu-tes jun - ges   Paar,...... Sie   werden   glück - lich
gain,   *'Twill be a pret - ty   pair,...... And   many   bless - ings,*

sein,...........   Mir ist so wun - der - bar.
tru - ly,   *My heart and hand are   thine.*

- lo - se pein,   Wie gross ist die ge - fahr. ....
course pur - sue?   *How great my danger now.....................*

JAQ.

glück - lich sein. Mir sträubt   sich schon   das   haar.
bless - ings share. On end   stands now   my   hair.

Jaq. Der Vater willigt ein,
Mir wird so wunderbar,
Mir fällt kein Mittel ein.

[*Nach dem Canon geht Jaquino in seine Stube Zurück.*]

Rok. Höre, Fidelio, wenn ich auch nicht weiss, wem du angehörst, so weiss ich doch, was ich thue; ich—ich mache dich zu meinem Tochtermann.

Mar. Wirst du es bald thun, Vater?

Rok. Ei, ei, wie eilfertig! [*ernst.*] Sobald der Gouverneur nach Sevilla gereis't seyn wird, dann geb' ich Euch zusammen: darauf könnt Ihr rechnen.

Mar. Den Tag nach seiner Abreise? Das machst du recht vernünftig, lieber Vater.

Leo. [*Schon vorher sehr betreten, aber jetzt sich freudig stellend.*] Den Tag nach seiner Arbreise? [*Bei Seite.*] O, welche neue Verlegenheit!

Rok. Nun, meine Kinder, Ihr habt Euch doch herzlich lieb, nicht wahr?—Aber das ist noch nicht Alles was zu einer vergnügten Haushaltung gehört, man braucht auch—

[*Macht die Pantomime des Geldzählens.*]

ARIE.

Hat man nicht auch Geld daneben,
Kann man nicht ganz glücklich seyn.
Traurig schleppt sich fort das Leben;
Mancher Kummer stellt sich ein.
Doch wenn's in den Taschen fein klingelt und rollt,
Da hält man das Schicksal gefangen.
Und Macht und Liebe verschafft dir das Gold,
Und stillet das kühnste Verlangen.
Das Glück dient wie ein Knecht für Sold;
Es ist ein schönes Ding das Gold!

Jac. They Rocco's blessing share,
What wondrous things, and strange,
A lover thus t' exchange!

[*After this Canon Jacquino goes back to his room*]

Roc. Well, my good Fidelio, if I do not know who thou art, yet I know what I will do: I—I'll make thee my son-in-law.

Mar. Wilt thou?—Soon, my father?

Roc. Oh, oh, what a hurry! As soon as the Governor has set out for Seville I will unite you; on that you may depend.

Mar. The day after his departure, say you? Dear father, thou art quite right.

Leo. [*Much embarrassed, but soon assuming a joyful air.*] The day after his departure? [*Aside.*] What new troubles have I to encounter?

Roc. Now, my children, you love each other truly;—do I not see it? But love is not the only thing wanted to make housekeeping agreeable: there is also wanted—

[*Moving his hands as if counting money.*]

AIR.

If we have not gold to fly to,
We can ne'er be happy quite;
But if clouds of sorrow lower,
Gold will help to make them bright.
With gold in our pockets we face all mankind;
The sound has a magical power:
We aye shall a welcome in ev'ry place find
If we tender this magical dower.
True happiness, so we are told,
Is best secured by glorious gold.

WENN SICH NICHTS MIT NICHTS VERBINDET—NOTHING, IF YOU ADD TO NOTHING.
AIR. ROCCO.

Wenn sich Nichts mit Nichts ver-bin-det, Ist und bleibt die Sum-me klein. Wer bei
Noth-ing, if you add to nothing, Faith! the to-tal is but small; So, when

Tisch nur Lie-be fin-det, Wird nach Tische hun-grig seyn; Wird nach Tis-che hun-grig
love serves up the ta-ble, You'll be hun-gry af-ter all; You'll be hun-gry af-ter

seyn. Drum lächle der Zu-fall Euch gnädig und hold, Und segne und len-ke Eu'r
all. And love, I have heard is so wayward an elf, To some simple people's a-

Stre-ben, und len-ke Eu'r Streben. Das Liebchen im Arm, im Beu-tel das Gold, So
maze-ment, some people's a-mazement, When pov-er-ty shows his long face at the door He

mögt Ihr viel Jah-re durch-le-ben; So mögt Ihr viel Jah-re durch-le-ben. Das
al-ways pops out at the casement, He al-ways pops out at the case-ment. So

Glück dient wie ein Knecht um Sold, Es ist ein mäch-tig Ding das Gold, Ding das Gold.
hap-pi-ness we all are told. Is best se-cured by glo-rious gold. by glo-rious gold.

Leo. Ihr könnt das leicht sagen, Meister Rokko. Freilich giebt es noch etwas, was mir nicht minder kostbar seyn würde; aber mit Kummer sehe ich, dass ich es durch alle meine Bemühungen nicht erhalten werde.

Rok. Und was wäre denn das?

Leo. Euer Vertrauen. Verzeiht mir den Vorwurf, aber oft sehe ich Euch aus den unterirdischen Gewölben dieses Schlosses ganz ausser Athem und ermattet zurückkommen. Warum erlaubt Ihr mir nicht Euch dahin zu begleiten. Es wäre mir sehr lieb, wenn ich Euch bei Eurer Arbeit helfen und Eure Beschwerden theilen könnte.

Rok. Du weisst doch, dass ich den strengsten Befehl habe, Niemanden, wer's auch sey, zu den Staats-Gefangenen zu lassen.

Mar. Es sind ihrer aber gar zu viele in dieser Festung. Du arbeitest dich ja zu Tode, liebe Vater.

Leo. Sie hat recht, Meister Rokko. Man soll allerdings seine Pflicht thun, [*zärtlich*] aber ist doch auch erlaubt, mein ich, zuweilen daran zu denken, wie man sich für die, welche uns angehören und lieben, ein Bischen schonen kann.

[*Sie ergreift seine Hand.*]

Mar. [*Rokkos andere Hand an die Brust drückend.*] Man muss sich für seine Kinder zu erhalten suchen.

Rok. [*sieht Beide gerührt an.*] Ja, Ihr abt recht! Diese schwere Arbeit würde mir doch endlich zu viel werden. Der Gouverneur ist zwar sehr streng; er muss mir aber doch erlaubet, dich in die geheimen Kerker mit mir zu nehmen.

[*Leonora äussert eine heftige Geberde der Freude.*]

Indessen giebst es ein Gewölbe, in das ich dich wohl nie werde einführen dürfen, obschon ich mich ganz auf dich verlassen kann.

Mar. Verrumthlich wo der Gefangene sitzt, von dem du schon einigemal gesprochen hast, Vater.

Rok. Du hast's errathen.

Leo. [*forschend.*] Ich glaube, es ist schon lange her, dass er gefangen ist?

Rok. Es ist schon über zwei Jahr.

Leo. [*heftig.*] Zwei Jahr, sagt Ihr? [*Sich fassend.*] Er muss ein grosser Verbrecher seyn.

Rok. Oder er muss grosse Feinde haben: dieses kommt ohngefähr auf eins heraus.

Mar. So hat man denn nie erfahren können, woher er ist und wie er heisst?

Rok. O wie oft hat er mit mir von Alle dem sprechen wollen!

Leo. Nun?—

Rok. Für Unsereinen ist's aber am besten, so wenig Geheimnisse, als möglich zu wissen. [*Geheimnissvoll.*] Nun, er wird mich nicht lange mehr quälen, es kann nicht mehr lange mit ihm dauern.

Leo. [*bei Seite.*] Grosser Gott!

Mar. O lieber Vater, führe Fidelio ja nicht zu ihm; diesen Anblick könnte er nicht ertragen.

Leo. Warum denn nicht? Ich habe Muth und Stärke.

Rok. [*sie auf die Schulter klopfend.*] Brav! mein Sohn! brav! Wenn ich dir erzählen wollte, wie ich anfangs in meinem Stande mit meinem Herzen zu kämpfen hatte,—und ich war doch ein ganz anderer Kerl als du, mit deiner feinen Haut und deinen weichen Händen.

TERZETTO.

Rok. Gut, Söhnchen, gut!
Hab' immer Muth,
Dann wird dir's auch gelingen
Das Herz wird hart
Durch Gegenwart
Bei fürchterlichen Dingen.

Leo. Ich habe Muth
Mit kaltem Blut
Will ich hinab mich wagen.

Leo. It is right enough in you to say this, Master Rocco. But there is something else more precious in my esteem, which with sorrow I perceive all my exertions cannot gain.

Roc. And what is that?

Leo. Your confidence. Pardon me the reproach, but I often see you return quite out of breath from the subterranean vaults of the castle. Why do you not allow me to accompany you? It would be delightful to me if I could go with you, and share your toils.

Roc. But thou knowest the strict orders imposed on me. I am not permitted to allow access to any one of the state prisoners.

Mar. But there are far too many of them in this fortress. And, dear father, you will work yourself dead.

Leo. She is right, Master Rocco. One must certainly do one's duty, [*tenderly,*] but it is allowable, I believe, to spare oneself a little for those who belong to us and love us.

[*Grasping his hand.*]

Mar. [*Pressing Rocco's other hand.*] One must try, for the sake of one's children.

Roc. [*Affected, looking at them both.*] Well said, my children: this hard work is becoming over much for me. The Governor, it is true, is very strict; but he must allow me to take you with me into the secret dungeons.

[*Leonora manifests a lively expression of joy.*]

There is one dungeon, however, Fidelio, into which I must not take you.

Mar. Probably it is there the prisoner is confined of whom thou hast so often spoken, father?

Roc. Thou hast guessed it.

Leo. [*Inquiringly.*] I think he has been a long time imprisoned?

Roc. Somewhat more than two years.

Leo. [*Impetuously.*] Two years, do you say? [*Collecting herself.*] He must be a great criminal, then?

Roc. Or—he must have great enemies: that amounts to the same thing.

Mar. Is no one able to tell his name, or whence he comes?

Roc. Oh! how often has he wished to speak with me of all that!

Leo. Well?

Roc. For people in our position, it is best to know as few secrets as possible. [*Mysteriously.*] However, he will not trouble me much more—he cannot last much longer.

Leo. [*Aside.*] Great God!

Mar. Do not take Fidelio to him, father dear: it is a sight he could not bear.

Leo. Oh! fear me not. Doubt not my courage or my strength.

Roc. [*Tapping her on the shoulder.*] Bravo! very fine! If I were to tell thee how I had to struggle with my heart in my early days, I should make thee weep; and I was quite a different fellow from thee, with thy soft skin and delicate hands.

TERZETT.

Roc. Courage! be firm! and of your vigor
A proof you very soon shall show.
Time your gentle heart will harden·
It changes all things here below.

Leo. Trust in me: I will obey you. [*Aside.*
Entering yonder dungeon dread.

Für hohen Lohn
Kann Liebe schon
Auch hohe Leiden tragen.

Mar. Dein gutes Herz
Wird manchen schmerz
In diesen Gruften leiden ;
Dann kehrt zurück
Der Liebe Glück,
Und unnennbare Freuden.

Rok. Du wirst dein Glück ganz sicher bau'n.

Leo. Ich hab' auf Gott und Recht Vertrau'n

Mar. Du darfst mir auch ins Auge schau'n ;
Der Liebe Macht ist auch nicht klein.

alle drei. Ja, ja, wir werden glücklich seyn.

Rok. Der Gouverneur soll heut' erlauben,
Das du mit mir die Arbeit theilst.

Leo. Du wirst mir alle Ruhe rauben,
Wenn du bis morgen nur verweilst.

Mar. Ja, guter Vater, bitt' ihn heute,
In Kurzem sind wir dann ein Paar.

Rok. Ich bin ja bald des Grabes Beute

Leo. Wie lang bin ich des Kummers Beute

Rok. Ich brauche Hülf', es ist ja wahr

Leo. Du, Hoffnung, reichst mir Labung dar.

Mar. Ach, lieber Vater, was fällt Euch ein ?
Lang' Freund und Rather müsst Ihr uns seyn

Rok. Nur auf der huth,
Dann geht es gut,
Gestillt wird Euer Sehnen.

Mar. O, habe Muth,
O, welche Gluth !
O, welcn' ein tiefes Sehnen.

Leo. Ihr seyd so gut,
Ihr macht mir Muth,
Gestillt wird bald mein Sehnen.

Rok. Gebt Euch die Hand,
Und schliesst das Band.

Leo. Ich gab die Hand
Zum süssen Band.

Mar. Ein festes Band
Mit Herz und Hand.

Rok. In süssen Freudenthränen.

Leo. Es kostet bittre Thränen.

Mar. O, süsse, süsse Thränen.

Rok. Aber nun ist es auch Zeit, dass ich dem
Gouverneur die Briefschaften überbringe.

MARSCH.

Rok. O, er kommt selbst hierher. [*Zu Leonore.*] Gieb
sie, Fidelio. und dann entfernt Euch.

[*Leonore nimmt die an einem Bande hängende Blechbüchse,
giebt sie Rokko, und geht dann mit Marcellinen in das
Haus ab.*

AUFTRITT V.—ROKKO, PIZARRO, *Offiziere, Wachen.
Während des Marsches wird das Hauptthor durch Wachen
von Aussen geöffnet. Offiziere mit einem Detachement treten
ein, dann Pizarro. Das Hauptthor wird wieder geschlossen.*

Piz. [*Zu dem Offizier.*] Drei Mann Wache auf den Wall,
sechs Mann Tag und Nacht an der Zugbrücke, eben so viel
gegen den Garten zu ; und Jedermann, der sich dem Graben nähert, werde sogleich vor mich gebracht. [*Zu Rokko.*]
Rokko, ist etwas Neues vorgefallen ?

Rok. Nein, Herr !

Piz. Wo sind die Despeschen ?

Rok. [*nimmt Briefe aus der Blechbüchse.*] Hier sind
sie.

Piz. [*öffnet die Papiere und durchsieht sie.*] Immer Emp-
fehlungen und Vorwürfe. Wenn ich auf Alles das achten

Love will dictate what to do,
Love will banish ev'ry fear.

Mar. Those dreadful places, full of horror,
I fear me much will make thee quail ;
But the sweets of love ethereal,
On returning, thou wilt hail.

Roc. Thy happiness thou wilt secure.

Leo. In Heaven and my right I place my trust

Mar. Yes, fate propitiously will smile,
And love sustain thy actions just.

All. Yes, yes, love will sustain thee.
me.

Roc. The Governor will not refuse
That thou with me the labor share.

Leo. Ah ! Heaven will assist the just ;—
But do not longer delay me.

Mar. Yes, good father, entreat the Governor to-day
That we may the sooner be united.

Roc. I shall soon go down to my grave.

Leo. How long have I endured this agony.

Roc. Yes, I need assistance truly.

Leo. But Providence sends me a gleam of hope

Mar. Ah, dear father, do not despond ;
You will, I hope, live long with us,
To comfort and protect.

Roc. Be only on your guard, then all will go well,
And the wishes of all be gratified.

Mar. Oh yes,—have courage ;
What anxiety he now displays—
What animation !

Leo. You are both so kind,
You encourage me to hope everytning—
My wish, I trust, will soon be gratified.

Roc. Now join your hands,
And sanctify the tender knot with tears of joy.

Leo. I have given my sacred pledge—
Ah ! what bitter tears it cost me.

Mar. A lasting tie, with hand and heart—
Oh ! sweet and welcome tears.

Roc. In sweet tears of joy.

Leo. It costs bitter tears.

Mar. Oh ! sweet, sweet tears.

Roc. 'Tis time that I deliver up
These letters and despatches.

MARCH.

Roc. Behold ! he approaches. [*To Leonora.*] Give them
to me, and depart.

[*Leonora gives the tin box to Rocco, and then goes with
Marcellina into the house.*

SCENE V.—ROCCO, PIZARRO, *Officers, Guards.—During
the March, the principal door is opened from without. Officers enter with a detachment of Troops, then Pizarro.
The gate is shut again.*

Piz. [*To the Officer.*] Three guards on the wall, on
the draw-bridge six, day and night, as many within the
garden ; and every one that approaches the trench, let him
be brought before me. [*To Rocco.*] Has anything fresh
occurred ?

Roc. No, signor.

Piz. Where are the despatches ?

Roc. Here they are.

[*Takes letters out of the tin box.*

Piz. [*Opens the papers, and looks through them.*] More
recommendations ! more reproaches ! were I to attend to

wollte, würde ich nie damit fertig werden. [*Hält bei einem Briefe an.*] Was seh' ich? Mich dünkt, ich kenne diese Schrift. Lass sehen.

[*Er öffnet den Brief, geht weiter vor. Rokko und die Wachen ziehen sich zurück. Lies't.*

"Iche gebe Ihnen Nachricht, dass der Minister in Erfahrung gebracht hat, dass die Staats-Gefängnisse denen Sie vorstehen, mehrere Opfer willkührlicher Gewalt enthalten. Er reis't morgen ab, um Sie mit einer Untersuchung zu überraschen. Seyn Sie auf Ihrer Huth, und suchen Sie sich sicher zu stellen."

Betreten.] Ach, wenn er entdeckte, dass ich diesen Florestan in Ketten liegen habe, den er längst todt glaubt. Eine ähne Tnat kann alle Besorgnisse zerstreuen.

ARIA.

Ha! welch ein Augenblick!
Die rache werd' ich kühlen,
Dich rufet dein Geschick!
In seinem Herzen wühlen—
O Wonne, hohes Glück!
Schon war ich nah dem Staube,
Dem lauten Spott zum Raube,
Dahin gestreckt zu seyn.
Nun ist es mir geworden,
Den mörder selbst zu morden.
In seiner letzten Stunde,
Den Stahl in seiner Wunde,
Ihm noch ins Ohr zu schrein:
Triumph! des Sieg ist mein!

Die Wache. [*halblaut unter sich.*]
Er spricht von Tod und Wunde—
Wach scharf auf Eure Runde.
Wie wichtig muss es seyn.

Piz. Hauptmann! [*Er führt den Hauptmann vor und spricht leise mit ihm.*] Besteigen Sie mit einem Trompeter den Thurm; sehen Sie mit der grössten Achtsamkeit auf die Strasse von Sevilla; sobald Sie einen Wagen, von Reitern umgeben, gewahr werden, geben Sie augenblicklich ein Zeichen. Verstehen Sie? augenblicklich! Ich erwarte die grösste Pünktlichkeit; Sie haften mir mit Ihrem Kopfe dafur. [*Hauptmann ab.*
zur Wache.] Fort auf Eure Posten! [*Die Wache geht.*
Rokko!

Rok. Herr.

Piz. [*betrachtet ihn eine Weile aufmerksam, für sich.*] Ich muss ihn zu gewinnen suchen; ohne seine Hülfe kann ich es nicht ausführen. Komm näher!

DUETTO

Jetzt, Alter, hat es Eile;
Dir wird ein Glück zu Theile
Du wirst ein reicher Mann
[*Er wirft ihm einen Beutel zu.*
Das geb' ich nur daran.

Rok. So saget nur in Eile,
Wohin ich dienen kann.

Piz. Du bist von kaltem Blute,
Von unverzagtem Muthe,
Durch langen Dienst geworden.

Rok. Was soll ich, redet—

Piz. Morden!

Rok. [*erschrickt.*] Wie?

Piz. Höre mich nur an:
Du bebst? bist du ein Mann?
Wir durfen nicht mehr säumen
Dem Staate liegt daran.

these things, I should never be at rest. Ah! what do I see? methinks I know this hand—let's see.

[*He opens the letter and advances. Rocco and the Guards recede.—Reads*

"I give you information that the Minister has learned that the state prisons over which you preside contain several victims of arbitrary power. He sets out to-morrow to surprise you. Be on your guard, and endeavor to keep yourself right."

Ah! if he discover that I have this Florestan lying in chains, whom he thinks dead long since! A bold deed can—and shall—dissipate all my anxieties!

AIR.

Ah! the moment has arriv'd
My revenge I will assuage
For the outrage suffer'd:
I will give him, very soon,
A sample of my pity.
Fearlessly, unsparingly,
I will tear his heart from out him!
The wretch shall quickly repent
His daring resistance to me:—
I would sooner die than yield.
Now that he is in my power,
Punishment for his treason
Shall quickly be his lot.
Ah! my heart beats more freely
At the prospect of revenge!
No more hope is there for thee.
The moment is approaching
For thy dire punishment.

Guards. [*In an under-tone.*] He speaks of death and wounds;
He is expecting somebody.
Let us go quickly,
And watch closely on our rounds.

Piz. [*To the Officer, speaking in a low voice.*] Captain, take with you the trumpeter, and ascend the tower: there look out along the road to Seville. As soon as you see a cavalier with noble escort, give instantly a signal. Away and mind your orders! Neglect them, and your head shal be the forfeit.
[*Exit Captain*
Away! [*To the guards.*] Every one to his post.
[*Exeunt.*
Rocco!

Roc. Signor.

Piz. [*Looking at him steadfastly for a short time.—Aside.*] 'Tis useless to hesitate—without his aid I shall never accomplish my object. Rocco, come nearer.

DUET.

Take this, old man: fortune
Henceforth shall favor you;
If a service you will yield me,
[*Shows him a purse.*
A rich man shall you be.

Roc. Speak on. O, quickly tell
In what way can I be of service?

Piz. I know your zeal and coolness,
And what I shall now reveal
I think I can to you confide.

Roc. Speak! what shall I do?

Piz. Murder!

Roc. [*Terrified.*] How!

Piz. Simply listen—but do not tremble!
Thou tremblest? Art thou a man?
We must delay no longer—
The state is concerned.

Den bösen Unterthan
Schnell aus dem Weg zu räumen.

Rok. O Herr!

Piz. Du stehst noch an?   [*Für sich.*
Er darf nicht länger leben,
Sonst ist's um mich geschehn
Pizarro sollte beben!
Du fällst, ich werde stehen.

Rok. Die Glieder fühl' ich beben
Wie konnt' ich das bestehen?
Ich nehm' ihm nicht das Leben.
Mag, was da will, geschehen.
Mein Herr, das Leben nehmen,
Das ist nicht meine Pflicht.

Piz. Ich will micht selbst bequemen,
Wenn dir's an Muth gebricht.
Nur eile, rash und munter
Zu jenem Mann hinunter
Du weisst—

Rok. Der kaum mehr lebet,
Und wie ein Schatten schwebet.

Piz. [*mit Grimm.*] Zu dem, zu dem hinab—
Ich wart' in kleiner Ferne,
Du gräbst in der Cisterne
Sehr schnell für ihn ein Grab.

Rok. Und denn?

Piz. Du giebst ein Zeichen,
Dann werd ich mich, vermummt,
Schnell in der Kerker schleichen:
      [*Er zieht den Dolch.*
Ein Stoss—und er verstummt.

Rok. Verhungernd in den Ketten,
Ertrug er lange Pein;
Ihn tödten, heisst ihn retten.

Piz. Dann werd ich ruhig seyn.
      [*Pizarro ab gegen den Garten, Rokko folgt ihm.*

AUFTRITT VI —LEONORE, *tritt in heftiger innerer Bewegung von der andern Seite auf, und sieht den Abgehenden mit steigender Unruhe nach.*

RECITATIV.

Leo. Abscheulicher! wo eilst du hin?
Was hast du vor im wilden Grimme?
Des Mitleids Ruf, der Menschheit Stimme,
Rührt nicht mehr deinem Tigersinn.
Doch, toben auch, wie Meereswogen,
Dir in der Seele Zorn und Wuth,
So leuchtet mir ein Farbebogen,
Der hell auf dunkeln Wolken ruht.
Der blickt so still, so freidlich nieder,
Der spiegelt alte Zeiten wieder,—
Und neu besänftigt wallt mein Blut.

That troublesome inmate of yours—
He must quickly be got rid of.

Roc. Oh Sir!

Piz. You still hesitate!—   [*To himself.*
He must live no longer,—
Or I shall be undone!
Should Pizarro live in fear?
I see how it is,—you falter;—
I will stand my ground.

Roc. I feel my limbs quake under me.
How should I undertake it?
No,—I'll not lend myself to such an act
Let happen what may.
To take away life!
Sir, that is not my duty.
      [*He wants to return Pizarro the purse.*

Piz. I will serve myself,
If your courage fail;
But—only hasten quickly
And resolutely—to that man
Down there. [*Pointing.*] You know well.

Roc. Who now scarcely lives,
And seems a mere shadow.

Piz. [*Enraged.*] Down, I say, down to him—
I will wait at a short distance.
Dig a grave for him, in the cistern
In the prison, without delay.

Roc. And then?

Piz. You must give me a signal,
And I will then steal, in disguise,
Directly into the dungeon.
      [*Draws his dagger.*
One blow—and he is dumb.

Roc. Half famished, and in chains,
Long has he endured the severest misery;
To rid him of life, would be to release him.

Piz. Then I shall be at peace.
      [*Exit Pizarro towards the garden, Rocco following.*

SCENE VI.—*Enter* LEONORA, *in violent agitation, from the side opposite to that on which Pizarro and Rocco have gone off, having overheard the intention of Pizarro.*

RECITATIVE.

To what new and dreadful crime
Will thy vengeance now induce thee?
Oh, monster! can no touch of pity
From thy brutal heart be look'd for?
But vain shall be your machinations:
A sweet presentiment of that assures me
For his infamies, the Almighty
A fitting reward will mete him.
Ah! I feel within me new hopes arise;
An inward sense of coming happiness
Sustains and cheers my heart.

KOMM HOFFNUNG, LASS DEN LETZTEN STERN—OH HOPE, SWEET SOLACE. Leonora

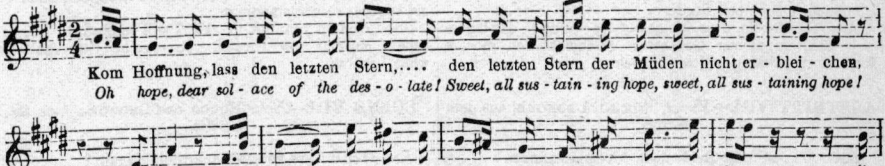

Kom Hoffnung, lass den letzten Stern,.... den letzten Stern der Müden nicht er - blei - chen,
Oh hope, dear sol - ace of the des - o - late! Sweet, all sus - tain - ing hope, sweet, all sus - taining hope!

O komm er hell! er - hell! mein Ziel, sei's noch so fern, so fern, die
O, come! O, come, the dis - tant goal, the dis - tant goal il lumine! il

Lie - be, sie wird's er - rei - chen ja, ja, sie wird's er - rei - - - - - - - - - - - -
lu - mine, tho' far it be, Love the end can see, shall lead. . . . . me

- chen, sie wird's er - rei - - - - - - - - chen, Komm, O komm, komm, O
thith - er, shall lead me thith - - - - - - - - er, Come, sweet hope, come, my

Hoff - nung, Lass den letz - ten Stern der Mü - den, der Mü - den nicht er -
soul il - lume, Let the last faint star still on my dark way dif - fuse its

bleichen! Er - hell ihr Ziel. . . . sei's noch so fern, Sei's noch so fern, die Liebe, die Lie - be, wird's er -
radiance, Nor pale, and die, ... nor pale and die, Tho' far the goal, true Love, yes, true Love my heart sus -

- rei - chen, die Lie - - - be, die Lie - be wird's er - rei - - - - - chen
- tain - ing, shall lead . . . . me safe - ly on; the end at - tain - - - - - ing.

Leo. Ich folg' dem innern Triebe, Ich wanke nicht; Mich stärkt die Pflicht Der treuen Gattinn Liebe. [*Geht ab gegen den Garten.*	*Leo.* Love will thither guide me. By love and hope supported: No more with fear I tremble. Oh thou, whom alone I love, Soon will thy true wife thy cruel torments end. [*Exit towards the garden.*
AUFTRITT VII.—MARZELLINE *kommt aus dem Hause,* JAQUINO *ihr nach.*	**SCENE VII.**—MARCELLINA *enters from the House fol- lowed by* JACQUINO.
Jaq. Aber Marcelline— *Mar.* Kein Wort, keine Sylbe! Ich will nichts mehr von deinen albernen Liebeseufzern hören, und dabei bleibts. *Jaq.* Wer das gesagt hätte, als ich mir vornahm, mich recht ordentlich in dich zu verlieben: da war ich der gute, der liebe Jaquino! aber dieser Fidelio— *Mar.* [*rasch einfallend.*] Ich läugne nicht, ich war dir gut; aber sieh—ich bin offenherzig—das war keine Liebe. Fidelio zieht mich weit mehr an; zwischen ihm und mir find' ich eine viel grössere Uebereinstimmung. *Jaq.* Eine Uebereinstimmung mit einem solchen herge- laufenen Jungen, der, Gott weiss woher kommt; den der Vater aus blossem Mitleid am Thore dort aufgenommen hat, der—der— *Mar.* [*ärgerlich.*] Der arm und verlassen ist, und den ich dennoch heirathen werde. *Jaq.* Glaubst du, dass ich das leiden werde? He! dass es ja nicht in meiner Gegenwart geschieht; ich möchte Euch einen gewaltigen Streich spielen.	*Jac.* But, Marcellina! *Mar.* Not a word—silence! I do not wish to hear an- other word of your silly love-sighs and nonsense. *Jac.* Why did you not say as much when first I took it into my head to fall regularly in love with you? Then I had none of your rebuffs and snubbings;—then I was your dear Jacquino: But the moment this Fidelio— *Mar.* [*Interrupting him.*] Very true. I liked thee at first, or I fancied so—I may as well be frank and open with thee. But, since Fidelio has been among us, my mind has changed for him I feel much more liking and sympathy. *Jac.* What! for a young vagabond who comes—God knows whence; and whom your father housed in charity; who—who—— *Mar.* [*Angrily.*] Who is poor and deserted, and shall be my spouse, notwithstanding. *Jac.* And do you imagine that I will suffer it? No, no, believe me. If ever I catch you together, you shall see what I will do.
AUFTRITT VIII.—*Vorige,* ROKKO, LEONORE, *aus dem Garten.*	**SCENE VIII.**—*Enter* ROCCO *and* LEONORA *from the Garden.*
Rok. Was habt ihr Beide denn wieder zu zanken? *Mar.* Ach, Vater, er verfolgt mich immer! *Rok.* Warum denn?	*Roc.* What! are you two quarrelling again? *Mar.* Ah, father, he is always teasing me! *Roc.* What about?

Mar. [*zu Leonoren laufend.*] Er will, dass ich ihn lieben, dass ich ihn heirathen soll?

Jaq. Ja, ja, sie soll mich lieben, sie soll mich wenigstens heirathen, und ich——

Rok. Stille!—Ich werde eine einzige gute Tochter haben, werde sie so gut gepflegt [*streichelt Marzellinen am Kinn,*] mit so viel Mühe bis in ihr sechszehntes Jahr erzogen haben, und das Alles für den Herrn da? [*blickt lachend auf Jaquino.*] Nein, Jaquino, mich beschäftigen jetzt andere klügere Dinge.

Mar. Ich verstehe, Vater, [*zärtlich leise.*] Fidelio.

Leo. Brechen wir davon ab. Rokko, ich ersuchte Euch schon einizemal, die armen Gefangenen, die hier über der Erde wohnen, in unsern Festungsgarten zu lassen. Ihr verspracht und verschobt es immer. Heute ist das Wetter so schön. Der Gouverneur kommt um diese Zeit nicht hieher.

Mar. O ja, ich bitte mit ihm!

Rok. Kinder,—ohne Erlaubniss des Gouverneurs?

Mar. Aber er sprach so lange mit Euch? Vielleicht sollt Ihr ihm einen Gefallen thun, und dann wird er's so genau nicht nehmen.

Rok. Einen Gefallen? Du hast Recht, Marzelline! Auf diese Gefahr kann ich's wagen. Wohl denn. Jaquino und Fidelio öffnet die leichtern Gefängnisse. Ich aber gehe zu Pizarro und halte ihn auf, indem ich [*gegen Marzelline,*] für dein Bestes rede.

Mar. [*küsst ihm die Hand.*] So recht, Vater!
[*Rokko geht ab.*

[*Leonore und Jaquino schliessen die Gefängniss-thüren auf, ziehen sich dann mit Marzellinen in den Hintergrund, und beobachten mit Theilnahme die nach und nach auftretenden Gefangenen.*

FINALE.—AUFTRITT IX.

Chor—*der Gefangenen.*

O welche Lust in freier Luft
Den Athem einzuheben!
Nur hier, nur hier ist Leben.
Der Kerker eine Gruft.

Ein Gefangener. Wir wollen mit Vertrauen
Auf Gottes Hülfe bauen;
Die Hoffnung flustert sanft mir zu
Wir werden frei, werd finden Ruh!

Alle. O Himmel! Rettung! welch ein Glück.
O Freiheit, kehrest du zurück!
[*Hier erscheint ein Offizier auf dem Wall und entfernt sich wieder.*

Einer. Sprecht leise;—haltet Euch zurück—
Wir sind belauscht mit Ohr und Blick

Alle. Sprecht leise, haltet Euch zurück—
Wir sind belauscht mit Ohr und Blick.
O Welche Lust, in freier Luft
Den Athem einzuheben,
Nur hier, nur hier ist Leben,
Der Kerker eine Gruft.
[*Ehe der Chor noch ganz geendet ist, erscheint Rokko im Hintergrunde dir Bühne und redet angelegentlich mit Leonoren. Die Gefangenen entfernen sich in den Garten.*

AUFTRITT X.—Rokko, Leonore.

Leo. Nun sprecht, wie gings?
Rok. Recht gut! recht gut!
Zusammen rafft ich mienen Muth,
Und trug ihm alles vor.
Und solltest du es glauben,

Mar. [*Running to Leonora.*] He wishes me to love him—to marry him!

Jaq. Yes, signor; and if she will not love me, she shall at least marry me; and I—

Roc. Hold your tongue, sirrah! Ah! think you I have brought up my only daughter [*Patting Marcellina's cheek,*] with parental care, increasing with her years, till she has seen her sixteenth summer, for such a gentleman as you? Ha! ha! [*Laughing at Jaquino.*] No, Jaquino. But weighty matters now engage my mind.

Mar. I understand, dear father. [*Tenderly.*] Fidelio!

Leo. Enough of this. Rocco, often I have begged of you to allow the poor prisoners, in this dismal cell immured, to come and breathe the pure air of this garden. Though often promised, you have never yet done it. To-day the weather is so beautiful! The Governor never comes at this time of day.

Mar. Oh yes, I too ask it.

Roc. Without permission of the Governor? My dear children—

Mar. But he was talking with you so long: perhaps he was asking a favor?—In that case, he could not be very particular.

Roc. A favor? Well guessed, Marcellina. I think I may venture. Jacquino and Fidelio, you may undo the door. I'll to Pizarro, and with conversation on your behalf, [*sympathetically, to Marcellina,*] occupy him.

Mar. [*Kisses his hand.*] Oh, blessings on you, father dear!
[*Exit Rocco.*

[*Leonora and Jacquino open the Prison-doors, then withdraw with Marcellina to the background, and watch with interest the Prisoners, as they gradually enter*

FINALE.—SCENE IX.

Chorus—*of Prisoners.*

Oh, what a pleasure once again
Freely to breathe the fresh air!
In Heaven's light we live again,
From death we have escaped.

One of them. Let us in Heaven trust;
On Heaven depend our hopes:
He will on our griefs look with pity.
On His goodness all things depend.

All. Oh, liberty! oh, salvation!
Oh, God, upon our miseries have pity!
[*Here an Officer appears on the wall, and again retires.*

Prisoner. Silence! make no noise!
Pizarro's eyes and ears are o'er us!

All. Silence! make no noise!
Pizarro's eyes and ears are o'er us!
Oh! what a pleasure once again
Freely to breathe the fresh air!
In Heaven's light we live again;
From death we have escaped.
[*Before the Chorus has finished, Rocco appears in the background, and talks eagerly to Leonora. The Prisoners retire into the Garden.*

SCENE X.—Rocco and Leonora.

Leo. Now speak—how have you succeeded?
Roc. Why well, very well.
I composed my mind,
And represented every thing to him;
And, would you believe, now, his answer?

	Was er zur Antworth mir gab ?		That he will allow the marriage,
	Die Hierath, und dass du mir hilfst, will er erlauben,		And that you shall be my assistant.
	Noch heute füh' ich in die Kerker dich hinab.		Even to-day I take you into the dungeons.
Leo.	[ausbrechend.] Noch heute! Welch ein Glück!	Leo.	[Joyously.] To-day! What a respite!
	O welche Wonne!		Oh, what true delight!
Rok.	Ich sehe deine Freude,	Roc.	I perceive how glad you are.
	Nur noch ein Augenblick,		Stay, however, a moment or two,
	Dann gehen wie schon Beide.		And then we will both go together.
Leo.	Wohin ?	Leo.	Whither ?
Rok.	Zu jenem Mann hinab,	Roc.	Down to that poor man,
	Dem ich seit vielen Wochen		To whom, for so many months,
	Stets weniger zu essen gab.		I have daily given less and less of food.
Leo.	Gott! wird er losgesprochen ?	Leo.	O God! is he to be freed ?
Rok.	O nein !	Roc.	Oh no !
Leo.	So sprecht !	Leo.	Say not so !
Rok.	O nein ! o nein ! [Geheimnissvoll.]	Roc.	No ! oh no ! [With an air of deep secresy.]
	Wis müssen ihn—doch wie ?—befreien.		We must—oh ! in what manner !—set him free
	Er muss in einer Stunde,—		That is, boy, he must, in an hour,—
	Den Finger auf dem Munde,—		Your finger on your lip,—
	Von uns begraben seyn.		Be laid in his grave, and by our hands.
Leo.	So ist er todt ?	Leo.	Ah ! then he is dead ?
Rok.	Noch nicht, noch nicht !	Roc.	Not yet, not yet !
Leo.	[zurückfahrend.] Ist, ihn zu tödten, deine Pflicht ?	Leo.	[Starting back.] What ! is it thy duty to kill him !
Rok.	Nein, guter Junge, zittre nicht.	Roc.	No, good youth, let not that fear distress you.
	Zum Morden dringt sich Rokko nicht !		Rocco does not hire himself to murder !
	Der Gouverneur kommt selbst herab,		The Governor will himself come down—
	Wir beide graben nur das Grab.		We two have only to dig the grave.
Leo.	[bei Seite.] Vielleicht das Grab des Gatten graben,	Leo.	[Aside.] Perhaps to dig the grave of my husband
	O was kann fürchterlicher seyn.		What can be more horrible ?
Rok.	Ich darf ihn nicht mit Speise laben,	Roc.	Any one else at his bidding
	Er wird im Grab zufrieden seyn.		Is willing to become a murderer.

	DUETTO.		DUET.
Rok.	Wir müssen gleich zu Werke schreiten,	Roc.	This work of grief you now must aid in ;
	Du musst mir helfen, mich begleiten,		With courage great the deed pursuing,
	Hart ist des Kerkermeisters Brod.		Mark what I do, and follow me.
Leo.	Ich folge dir, wär's in den Tod !	Leo	Yes, father, I will follow thee !
Rok.	In der zerfallenen Cisterne	Roc.	With noiseless tread, in yonder corner
	Bereiten wir die Grabe leicht.		The cistern near, a grave we'll make ;
	Ich thu' es, glaube mir, nicht gerne,		I do it much against my wishes ,
	Auch dir ist schaurig, wie mir deucht.		And thou art shaking, too, with fear.
Leo.	Ich bins nur noch nicht recht gewohnt.	Leo.	I'm quite prepared, confide in me !
Rok.	Ich hätte gerne dich verschont,	Roc.	I willingly had spar'd you this,
	Doch wird es mir allein zu schwer,		But, all alone, the work's too much.
	Und gar zu streng ist unser Herr.		
Leo.	O welch ein Schmerz !	Leo.	Oh ! cruel fate !
Rok.	Mir scheint, er weine !	Roc.	Methinks he weeps ! Nay, stay thou here,
	Nein, du bleibst hier, ich geh' alleine.		And I will go without thee,
			Whilst thou in peace shalt rest, and wait me here
Leo.	Ich muss ihn seh'n, den Armen seh'n,	Leo.	Ah, no ! I feel an ardor new inspire me ;
	Und müsst ich selbst zu Grunde geh'n.		No labor done with thee will tire me ;
			With thee, dear father, will I go.
Rok	So säumen wir nun länger nicht.	Roc.	Thus, then, we will no longer stay,
			'Tis duty calls, and we obey.

AUFTRITT XI.—Marzelline und Jaquino (athemlos hereinstürzend) Vorige.		**SCENE XI.**—The same—Marcellina and Jacquino rush in, out of breath	
Mar.	O Vater, eilet !	Mar	Oh ! Father,—hasten !
Rok.	Was hast du denn ?	Roc.	What is the matter, child ?
Jaq.	Nicht länger weilet !	Jac.	Tarry no longer !
Rok.	Was ist gescheh'n ?	Roc.	What has happened ?
Mar.	Voll Zorn folgt mir	Mar.	Pizarro is following me,
	Pizarro nach,		Full of anger,
	Er drohet dir.		And threatening you so wildly !
Rok.	Gemach ! gemach !	Roc.	Peace !—softly—
Leo.	So Eilet fort !	Leo.	Then hasten away !
Rok.	Nur noch ein Wort !	Roc.	Only one word,—speak !
	Sprich, weiss er schon !		Does he already know ?—
Jaq.	Ja, er weiss schon !	Jac.	Yes, yes,—he knows already !
Mar	Der Offizier	Mar.	The officer
	Sagt' ihm, was wir		Has told him that we
	Jetzt den Gefangenen gewähren.		Are now indulging the prisoners.

Rok.	Lasst Alle schnell zurückkehren.
	[*Jaquino, geht ab in den Garten.*
Mar.	Ihr wisst es, wie er tobet,
	Und kennet seine Wuth.
Leo.	Wie mir's im Herzen tobet,
	Empöret ist mein Blut.
Rok.	Mein Herz hat mich gelobet,
	Sey der Tyrann in Wuth!

AUFTRITT XII.—Pizarro, *zwei Offiziere, Wache, die Vorigen.*

Piz.	Verwegner Alter! welche Rechte
	Legst du dir frevelnd selber bei,
	Und ziemt es dem gedungnen Knechte,
	Zu geben die Gefangnen frei?
Rok.	[*verlegen.*] O Herr!
Piz.	Wohlan!
Rok.	[*eine Entschuldigung suchend.*]
	Des Frühlings Kommen—
	Das heitre warme Sonnenlicht—
	Dann—[*sich fassend*] habt Ihr wohl in Acht genommen,
	Was sonst zu meinem Vortheil spricht.
	[*Die mütze abziehend.*
	Des Königs Namensfest ist heute,
	Das feiern wir auf solche Art.
	[*Geheim zu Pizarro.*
	Der unten stirbt, doch lasst die Andern
	Jetzt fröhlich hin und wieder wandern;
	Für jenen sey der Zorn gespart.
Piz.	[*leise.*] So eile, ihm sein Grab zu graben,
	Hier will ich stille Ruhe haben.
	Schliesst die Gefangenen wieder ein,
	Mögst du nie mehr verwegen seyn.
Die Gefangenen.	Leb' wohl, du warmes Sonnenlicht,
	Schnell schwindest du uns wieder,
	Schon sinkt die Nacht hernieder,
	Aus der sobald kein Morgen bricht.
Piz.	Nun Rokko, zögre länger nicht,
	Steig in den Kerker nieder. [*Leise.*
	Nicht eher kehrst du wieder,
	Bis ich vollzogen das Gericht.
Rok.	Nein, Herr, nein, länger zögr' ich nicht,
	Ich steige eilend nieder.
	Mir beben meine Glieder, [*Für sich.*
	O unglückselig harte Pflicht!
Leo.	[*zu den Gefangenen.*] Ihr hört das Wort, drum zögert nicht,
	Kehrt in den Kerker wieder. [*Für sich.*
	Angst rinnt durch meine Glieder.
	Ereilt den Frevler kein Gericht?
Jaq.	[*zu den Gefangenen.*] Ihr hört das Wort, drum zögert nicht,
	Kehrt in den Kerker wieder.
	[*Für sich Rokko und Leonoren beobachtend.*
	Sie sinnen auf und nieder—
	Könnt ich versteh'n, was jeder spricht.
Mar.	[*die Gefangenen betrachtend.*] Wir eilen so zum Sonnenlicht,
	Und scheiden traurig wieder.
	Die andern murmeln nieder;
	Hier wohnt die Lust, die Freude nicht.

[*Die Gefangenen gehen in ihre Zellen, die Leonore und Jaquino verschliessen.*

ENDE DES ERSTEN AUFZUGS.

Roc.	All of you go back instantly.
	[*Jacquino goes away into the Garden*
Mar.	You know how he rages,
	And his fierce severity.
Leo.	How my heart is swelling—
	My whole soul is up in arms.
Roc.	My conscience acquits me—
	Let the tyrant rave!

SCENE XII.—Enter Pizarro, *two Officers, and Guards.*

Piz.	Insolent old man! how dar'st thou,
	In defiance of my will,
	Thus to usurp my authority,
	And set the prisoners free?
Roc.	[*Embarrassed.*] Alas!
Piz.	Well?
Roc.	[*Trying to think of an excuse.*]
	Do you think it a crime
	Your wishes to anticipate?
	[*Collecting himself*
	I thought it right, on such a day,
	To alleviate their sufferings
	[*Doffing his cap*
	Our gracious King's birth-day
	We in this way celebrate.
	[*Low, to Pizarro*
	In obedience to your order,
	For the condemned prisoner
	I am now about to dig a grave.
Piz.	[*Softly.*] Hasten, then, and quickly do so.
	And I will, this once, overlook the fault.
	Shut up the prisoners, and remember,
	Never again be guilty of a similar indiscretion.
The Prisoners.	Farewell, thou warm sun-light!
	Quickly thou disappearest again from our gaze.
	Only the night remains for us,
	From which no morning may ever break again.
Piz.	Now, Rocco, no longer tarry,
	But get thee down to the dungeon, [*Softly.*
	And from thence you return not
	Till I have completed my purpose.
Roc.	No, sir, no, I'll not remain any longer;
	I will hasten below.
	My limbs tremble under me. [*Aside.*
	Oh, wretched old man! oh, heart-rending duty!
Leo.	[*To the Prisoners.*] You hear the word, then linger not here:
	Return into the prison. [*Aside.*
	Breathless anxiety runs through all my veins.
	Does no judgment overtake the evil-doer?
Jac.	[*To the Prisoners.*] You hear the word, then linger not here:
	Return to the prison.
	[*Aside, observing Rocco and Leonora.*
	They are pondering and whispering there—
	I wish I could hear what they are saying.
Mar.	[*Looking at the Prisoners.*] For a few short moments
	we see each other in the warm sunshine,
	Then part again in sorrow.
	Here freedom must not reign.
	Alas! no joy must ever enter here.

[*The Prisoners go into their cells, which Leonora and Jacquino lock after them.*

END OF ACT 1.

AUFZUG II.

AUFTRITT I.—*Das Theater stellt einen unterirdischen dunkeln Kerker vor. Den Zuschauern links ist eine mit Steinen und Schutt bedeckte Cisterne. Im Hintergrunde sind mehrere, mit Gitterwerk verwahrte, Oeffnungen in der Mauer, durch welche man die Stufen einer von der Höhe herunterführenden Treppe sieht: rechts die letzten Stufen und die Thüre in das Gefängniss. Eine Lampe brennt.*

(FLORESTAN *allein. Er sitzt auf einem Stein, um den Leib hat er eine lange Kette, deren Ende in der Mauer befestigt ist.*

RECITATIV.

Gott! welch ein Dunkel hier!
O grauenvolle Stille!
Oed ist es um mich her,
Nichts lebet ausser mir.
O schwere Prüfung! doch gerecht ist Gottes Wille,
Ich murre nicht, das Maass der Leiden steht bei dir.

ARIE.

In des Lebens Frühlingstagen,
Ist das Glück von mir gefloh'n.
Wahrheit wagt ich kühn zu sagen,
Und die Ketten sind mein Lohn.
Willig duld' ich alle Schmerzen,
Ende schmählich meine Bahn;
Süsser Trost in meinem Herzen:
Meine Pflicht hab' ich gethan,

'*In einer, an Wahnsinn gränzenden, jedoch ruhigen Begeisterung.*

ACT II.

SCENE I.—*A dark subterranean Dungeon. To the left, a cistern or reservoir, covered with stones and rubbish. In the background, several openings in the wall, guarded with gratings, through which can be seen the steps of a staircase, leading from above. To the right, the door into the Prison. A lamp hanging.*

[FLORESTAN, *alone. He sits on a stone: round his body is a long chain, the end of which is fastened to the wall.*

RECITATIVE.

Alas; what darkness dense!
What horrid stillness!
Here in this dark tomb, is nothing known
But my deep anguish! Oh, most cruel torture!
Oh, Heavenly Providence, how much longer
Will this my misery last!

AIR.

In the bright morning of life
My liberty, alas! was lost ·
These chains are the reward
Of true and open speaking.
But what avails my lamentations?
Hopeless is my condition:
The only solace for my torments
Rests on my conscious innocence.

[*Enthusiastically, but calmly.*

UND SPUR ICH NICHT LINDE—WHAT FEELING COMES O'ER ME. AIR. FLORESTAN.

Und spür' ich nicht lin - de, sanft säu - seln - de Luft? Und ist nicht mein Grab mir er -
What feel-ing comes o'er me that warms my cold heart? Wretched, lone, im - prison'd, at my

hel - let? Ich seh', wie ein En - gel im ro - si - gen Duft, Sich trös - tend zur
own shade I start. Oh, vis - ion of brightness! why com'st thou to me? Behold! 'tis an

Sei - te mir stel - let. Ein En - gel, Leo - no - ren, Leo - no - ren der
an - gel from Hea - ven I see. 'Tis thou, my Leo - no - ra— Oh, thou com-est to

Gat - tin so gleich, Der führt mich zur Frei-heit ins himm - lis - che Reich.
shat - ter my chain: Thou, on - ly, canst cheer me to life....... back a - gain.

(*Er sinkt, erschöpft, von der letzten Gemüthbewegung, auf den Felsensitz wieder; seine Hande verhüllen sein Gesicht.*

'*He sinks, exhausted, upon the stony seat, concealing his face with his hands.*

AUFTRITT II.—ROKKO, LEONORE, FLORESTAN. *Die beiden ersten, die man durch die Oeffnungen bei dem Schein einer Laterne die Treppe herabsteigen sah, tragen einen Krug und die Werkzeuge zum Graben. Die Hinterthüre öffnet sich und das Theater erhellt sich zur Hälfte.*

Leo. [*halblaut.*] Wie kalt ist es in diesem unterirdischen Gewölbe.

Rok. Das ist natürlich! Es ist ja so tief.

SCENE II.—ROCCO, LEONORA, FLORESTAN. *The two former, who have been seen through the openings coming down the stairs, carry a pitcher and implements for digging. The back door opens, and the Stage is half lighted.*

Leo. [*In an under-tone.*] Oh, how freezing cold it is in this dismal vault!

Rok. Natural enough in a place so subterranean.

Leo. [*sieht unruhig nach allen Seiten umher.*] Ich glaubte schon, wir würden den Eingang nicht finden.

Rok. [*sich gegen Florestans Seite wendend.*] Still! da ist der Gefangene.

Leo. [*mit gebrochener Stimme, indem sie den Gefangenen zu erkennen sucht.*] Er scheint ganz ohne Bewegung.

Rok. Vielleicht ist er todt!

Leo. Ihr meint es ?

Rok. Nein, nein, er schläft nur. Das müssen wir benützen und gleich ans Werk gehen; wir haben keine Zeit zu verlieren.

Leo. [*für sich.*] Es ist unmöglich, seine Züge zu unterscheiden; Gott steh' mir bei, wenn es er ist!

Rok. Hier unter diesen Trümmern ist eine Cisterne von der ich dir gesagt habe. Wir brauchen nicht viel Zeit um an die Oeffnung zu kommen. Gieb mir eine Haue, und du stelle dich hierher. Du zitterst—fürchtest du dich?

Leo. O nein, es ist nur so kalt.

Rok. So mach' fort, beim Arbeiten wird dir schon warm werden. [*Sie fangen an zu graben.*

Duett.

[*Während des Ritornells benutzt Leonore, wenn sich Rokko bückt, den Augenblick um den Gefangenen zu beobachten. Das Duett wird durchaus halblaut gesungen.*

Rok. [*während der Arbeit.*]
Nur hurtig fort und frisch gegraben,
Es währt nich lang so kommt er her.

Leo. [*ebenfalls arbeitend.*]
Ihr sollet nicht zu klagen haben,
Denn mir wird keine Arbeit schwer.

Rok. [*einen grossen Stein, an der Stelle wo er hinabsteig, hebend.*] Komm, hilf doch diesend Stein mir heben.
Hab' acht! hab' acht! er hat Gewicht.

Leo. Ich helfe schon, o sorget nicht,
Ich will mir alle Mühe geben.

Rok. Ein wenig noch.

Leo. Geduld!

Rok. Er weicht.

Leo. Nur etwas noch.

Rok. Er ist nicht leicht.

[*Sie rollen den Stein über Trümmer und holen Athem.—Wieder arbeitend.*
Nur hurtig fort, nur frisch gegraben!
Es währt nich lang, er kommt herein.

Leo. [*ebenfalls wieder arbeitend.*]
Lasst mich nur wieder Kräfte haben,
Wir werden bald zu Ende seyn.
[*Betrachten den Gefangenen, während Rokko von ihr abgewandt mit gekrümmtem Rücken arbeitet, leise.*
Wer du auch seyst, ich will dich retten;
Bei Gott! Du sollst kein Opfer seyn.
Gewiss, ich löse deine Ketten;
Ich will, du Armer, dich befrei'n.

Rok. [*sich schnell aufrichtend.*]
Was zauderst du in deiner Pflicht?

Leo. Nein, Vater! nein, ich zaudre nicht.

Rok. Nur hurtig fort, nur frisch gegre'__;
Es währt nicht lang, so kommt er her.

Leo. Ihr sollet nicht zu klagen haben,
Denn mir wird keine Arbeit schwer. [*Rokko trinkt.*

[*Florestan erhält sich und hebt das Haupt in die Höhe, ohne sich nach Leonoren zu wenden.*

Leo. Er erwacht!

Rok. [*plötzlich im Trinken inne haltend.*] Er erwacht, sagst du?

Leo. [*in grösster Verwirrung, immer nach Florestan sehend.*] Ja, er hat eben den Kopf in die Höhe gehoben.

Rok. Ohne Zweifel wird er wieder tausend Fragen an mich stellen. Ich muss allein mit ihm reden. Nun bald hat er's überstanden. [*Er steigt aus der Grube.*] Steig du,

Leo. [*Looking on every side in agitation.*] I thought we should never find the entrance.

Roc. [*Turning towards Florestan's side.*] Silence! the prisoner is there.

Leo. [*With a broken voice, seeking to recognize him.*] In what a state!—unconscious, motionless!

Roc. Perhaps he is dead!

Leo. Dost think so?

Roc. No, no; he only sleeps. The moment is propitious. Give me your hand. Let's to our work—we have no time to lose.

Leo. [*Aside.*] It is impossible to distinguish his features: If it be he, oh God, help me

Roc. Here, under this rubbish, is the cistern of which I have spoken. It will not take us long to reach the opening. Give me the pickaxe, and stand thou there. Thou tremblest!—of what art thou afraid?

Leo. Oh, no! only it is so cold!

Roc. Working will soon warm you.
[*They begin to dig.*

Duet.

[*During the Symphony, Leonora takes advantage of the moment when Rocco stoops, to observe the Prisoner. The Duet is sung in an undertone.*

Roc. [*While at work.*]
Work quickly—dig away;
Pizarro will be here ere long.

Leo. [*Also working.*]
My zeal and labor, I hope, will please you.
I feel not fatigue.

Roc. [*Lifting a stone at the spot where he descended.*]
Come, help me to raise this stone;
Lift up—a little more—it is very heavy.

Leo. I am lifting with all my might;
I do not spare.

Roc. Try again.

Leo. Alas!

Roc. So—it yields.

Leo. But little.

Roc. It is not light.
[*They roll the stone aside, and stop a moment to fetch breath.—Beginning again.*
Let's get on quickly—we must dig away
Pizarro will be here ere long.

Leo. Oh, trust in me! zealously I'll work;—
I feel my strength returning.

[*Looks at the Prisoner whilst Rocco, at his work, is turned from her.—In an undertone.*
Ah! whoever the unhappy one may be,
No weapon shall smite him!
No, no: this feeble hand, I hope,
Will restore him to his liberty.

Roc. [*Starting up quickly.*]
What are you loitering about?

Leo. No, father, I'm not idling.

Roc. Let's get on quickly—we must dig away
Pizarro will be here ere long.

Leo. Oh, trust in me! zealously I'll work;—
I feel my strength returning. [*Rocco drinks.*
[*Florestan raises his head, but does not turn towards Leonora.*

Leo. He is waking!

Roc. [*Ceasing to drink.*] He awakes, sayst thou?

Leo. [*In the greatest confusion, her eyes fixed on Florestan.*] Yes, yes; he has just raised his head.

Roc. Doubtless, he will again put a thousand questions to me. I must speak with him alone. Well, it will soon be all over with him. [*Gets up out of the grave.*] Go you

statt meiner, hinab, und räume noch so viel hinweg, dass man die Cisterne öffnen kann.

Leo. [*sie steigt zitternd ein paar Stufen hinab.*] Was in mir vorgeht, ist unaussprechlich!

Rok. [*Zu Florestan.*] Nun, Ihr habt wieder einige Augenblicke geruht?

Flo. Geruht? Wie fände ich Ruhe?

Leo. [*für sich.*] Diese Stimme!—Wenn ich ihr nur einen Augenblick sein Gesicht sehen könnte.

Flo. Werdet Ihr immer bei meinen Klagen taub seyn, grausamer Mann?

[*Mit den letzten Worten wendet er sein Gesicht gegen Leonoren.*]

Leo. Gott! Er ist's!

[*Sie fällt ohne Bewusstseyn an den Rand der Grube.*]

Rok. Was verlangt Ihr denn von mir? Ich vollziehe die Befehle die man mir giebt; das ist mein Amt, meine Pflicht.

Flo. Saget mir endlich einmal, wer ist der Gouverneur dieses Gefängnisses?

Rok. [Jetzt kann ich ihm ja ohne Gefahr genug thun. [*Laut.*] Der Gouverneur dieses Gefängnisses ist Don Pizarro.

Leo. [*Sich allmählig erholend.*] O Barbar! deine Grausamkeit giebt mir meine Kräfte wieder.

Flo. O schickt sobald als möglich nach Sevilla,—fragt nach Leonoren Florestan.

Leo. Gott! Er ahnet nicht, dass sie jezt sein Grab gräbt.

Flo. Sagt ihr, dass ich hier in Ketten liege.

Rok. Es ist unmöglich, sag' ich Euch; ich würde mich ins Verderben stürzen, ohne Euch genützt zu haben.

Flo. Wenn ich denn verdammt binn, hier zu verschmachten, O so lasst mich nicht so langsam enden!

Leo. [*springt auf und hällt sich fest.*] O Gott! wer kann das ertragen?

Flo. Aus Erbarmen, gebt mir nur einen Tropfen Wasser—das ist ja so wenig!

Rok. [*bei Seite.*] Es geht mir wider meinen Willen zu Herzen.

Leo. Er scheint ihn zu erweichen.

Flo. Du giebst mir keine Antwort.

Rok. Ich kann Euch nicht verschaffen, was Ihr verlangt. Alles was ich Euch anbieten kann, ist ein Restchen Wein, das ich im Kruge habe.

Leo. [*den Krug in grösster Eile bringend.*] Da ist er—da ist er.

Flo. [*Leonoren betrachtend.*] Wer ist das?

Rok. Mein Schliesser, und in wenig Tagen mein Eidam. [*Reicht Florestan den Krug der trinkt.*] Es ist freilich nur wenig Wein, doch ich gab ihn Euch gern. [*Zu Leonoren.*] Du bist ja ganz in Bewegung.

Leo. [*in grösster Verwirrung*] Wer sollte es nicht seyn? Ihr selbst, Meister Rokko—

Rok. Es ist wahr: der Mensch hat so eine Stimme.

Leo. Ja wohl—sie dringt in die Tiefe des Herzens.

down, and clear away the earth, instead of me, till you get the cistern open.

Leo. [*Trembling, descends a step or two.*] Who now could tell what within my bosom is passing!

Roc. [*To Florestan.*] Well, friend, are you again losing your cares in repose?

Flo. Repose! where can I find it?

Leo. [*To herself.*] That voice!—O, if I could only see his face for an instant!

Flo. Oh, cruel man! will you be ever deaf to my lamentations?

[*At these words he turns his face towards Leonora, who recognizes him.*]

Leo. Oh, God! it is he!

[*She falls senseless on the edge of the grave.*

Roc. What do you ask of me? The orders I receive I execute: that is my province, my duty.

Flo. Tell me, at all events, the name of the Governor of this loathsome prison.

Roc. [*Aside.*] There can be no harm in now telling him. [*Aloud.*] It is Don Pizarro.

Leo. [*Gradually recovering herself.*] Oh, barbarian! to my native strength thy cruelty restores me.

Flo. Oh! if it be possible, let a messenger go to Seville, and there seek Leonora Florestan.

Leo. Little does he think, oh God! that she is now digging his grave!

Flo. Tell her that I lie here in chains.

Roc. It is not possible. It would ruin me, and nothing better you.

Flo. Well, if here I am to die, let me not so slowly linger to my end.

Leo. [*Springing to her feet, then restraining herself.*] Oh, God! who this torture can endure?

Flo. Oh! for pity's sake, to bathe my parched lips, give me a drop of water! a small favor that is to ask!

Roc. [*Aside.*] My heart he touches, in spite of myself.

Leo. [*Aside.*] He seems to soften.

Flo. Thou dost not answer me.

Roc. What you require I cannot procure: all that I can offer is the little wine I have remaining.

Leo. [*Bringing the wine in great haste.*] There it is—there it is.

Flo. [*Looking at Leonora.*] Who is he?

Roc. At present my assistant; a few days hence to be my son-in-law. [*Hands the pitcher to Florestan, who drinks.*] There is but little wine, I see; but what there is you're welcome so. [*To Leonora.*] How agitated thou art!

Leo. [*In the greatest embarrassment.*] Who would not be so? You yourself, Master Rocco—

Roc. True: so touching are the accents of his voice.

Flo. They are—they stab me to the heart.

EUCH WERDE LOHN IN BESSERN WELTEN!—YOU, THEN, AT LEAST, CAN PITY FEEL FOR SORROW. Air. Florestan.

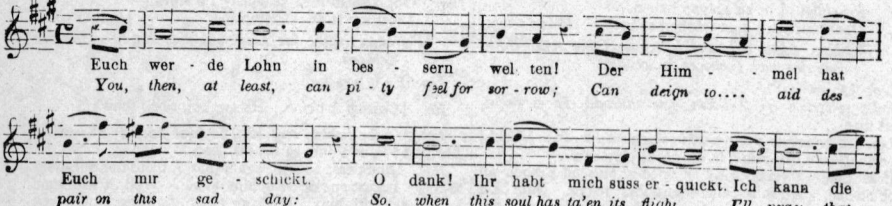

Euch wer- de Lohn in bes- sern wel- ten! Der Him- - mel hat
You, then, at least, can pi- ty feel for sor- row; Can deign to.... aid des-

Euch mir ge- schickt. O dank! Ihr habt mich süss er- quickt. Ich kann die
pair on this sad day: So, when this soul has ta'en its flight, I'll pray that

Wohl - that nicht ver - gel - ten; Ich kann die Wohl-that nicht ver - gel - ten.
Heav'n this act may well re-pay, I'll pray that Heav'n this act may well re-pay.

Leo. Der Himmel schicke Rettung dir, Dann wird mir hoher Lohn gewährt.	**Leo.** Heaven send him deliverance, Then will my reward indeed be great.

Rok. Mich rührte oft dein Leiden hier.
Doch Hülfe war mir streng verwehrt.
    [Leise zu Leonoren, die er bei Seite zieht.
Ich labt ihn gern den armen Mann;
Es ist ja bald um ihn gethan.
Ich thu', was meine Pflicht gebeut.
Doch hass' ich alle Grausamkeit.
	Roc. Your sufferings have often moved me;
	But to give you assistance was strictly forbidden.
	    [Softly, to Leonora, whom he draws aside.
	I am glad, Heaven knows, to refresh him;
	But it is already too late.
	I do what my duty imposes,
	But hate all unnecessary cruelty.

Leo. *[für sich.]* Wie hastig pocht mir das Herz! Es wogt in Freud' und tiefem Schmerz. Die hehre bange Stunde winkt, Die Tod mir, oder Rettung brinkt.	**Leo.** *[Aside.]* How violently this heart is beating! My life seems to vacillate between joy and pain. The awful hour fast approaches That brings me to death or a happy release.
Flo. *[für sich.]* Bewegt seh' ich den Jüngling hier, Und Rührung zeigt auch dieser Mann. O Gott, du sendest Hoffnung mir Dass ich sie noch gewinnen kann.	**Flo.** *[To himself.]* The youth, I see, is affected, And this man also betrays some compassion. Oh God! thou sendest me hope that I may yet Rejoin her for whom alone I live.
Leo. *[leise zu Rokko, indem sie ein Stückchen Brod aus der Tasche zieht.]* Dies Stückchen Brod, ja seit zwei Tagen Trag' ich es immer schon bei mir.	**Leo.** *[Softly to Rocco, while she draws a small piece of bread from her pocket.]* This bit of bread I have carried In my pocket for the last two days.
Rok. Ich möchte gern, doch sag' ich dir, Das hiesse wirklich zu viel wagen.	**Roc.** I would, most willingly; but, I tell you, It would indeed be overstepping my license.
Leo. *[schmeichelnd.]* Ihr labtet gern den armen Mann!	**Leo.** *[Winningly.]* You'd like to refresh the poor man!
Rok. Das geht nicht an, das geht nicht an.	**Roc.** Nay, I dare not—it will not do.
Leo. *[wie vorher.]* Es ist ja bald um ihn gethan.	**Leo.** *[As before.]* It will soon be at an end with him.
Rok. So sey es, ja, du kannst es wagen.	**Roc.** Well, so be it, you may venture.
Rok. *[in grösster Bewegung, Florestan das Brod reichend.]* Da' nimm das Brod, du armer Mann!	**Leo.** *[In the greatest agitation, handing the bread to Florestan.]* There, take the bread; poor man!
Rok. *[für sich sehr gerührt.]* Es ist ja bald um ihn gethan.	**Roc.** *[To himself, much affected.]* Yes, it will very soon be all over with him.
Flo. *[Leonoren Hand ergreifend und an sich drückend.]* O dank dir! dank Euch! Euch werde Lohn in bessern Welten.	**Flo.** *[Grasping Leonora's hand, and pressing it.]* Thanks! thanks! Be your reward in worlds above.
Rok. Der arme Mann!	**Roc.** Poor fellow!
Leo. O mehr, als ich ertragen kann.	**Leo.** Oh! this is more than I can bear.
Rok. Es ist ja bald um ihn gethan.	**Roc.** It will soon, alas! be over with him.

Flo. O, dass ich Euch nicht lohnen kann.
    [Er verschlingt das Stück Brod.
	Flo. Oh! that I cannot repay this kindness
	    [He eats the piece of bread.

Rok. *[nach augenblicklichem Stillschweigen zu Leonoren.]* Alles ist bereit, ich gehe das Signal zu geben.

Flo. *[zu Leonoren, während Rokko die Thure zu öffnen geht.]* Wo geht er hin? *[Rokko öffnet die Thüre, und giebt durch einen starken Pfiff das Zeichen.]* Ist das der Vorbote meines Todes?

Leo. *[in der heftigsten Bewegung.]* Nein, nein, beruhige dich, lieber Gefangener.

Flo. O, meine Leonore! so soll ich dich nie wieder sehen?

Leo *[sie fühlt sich zu Florestan hingezogen und sucht diesen Trieb zu überwaltigen.]* Mein ganzes Herz reisst mich zu ihm hin. *[Zu Florestan.]* Sey ruhig, sag' ich dir. Vergiss nicht, was du auch hören und sehen magst, vergiss nicht, dass überall eine Vorsicht ist. Ja, ja! es ist eine Vorsicht. *[Sie entfernt sich und geht gegen die Cisterne.*

Roc. *[To Leonora, after a momentary silence.]* All is ready —I must give the signal.

Flo. *[To Leonora, while Rocco goes to open the door.]* Where is he going? *[Rocco opens the door, and gives the signal by a loud whistle.]* Is that the herald of my death?

Leo. *[In the greatest agitation.]* No, no; calm yourself, poor dear prisoner!

Flo. Oh, my Leonora, shall I then never see thee more?

Leo. *[She feels herself drawn towards Florestan, and strives to overcome the impulse.]* My whole heart yearns towards him. *[To Florestan.]* Be composed, I beg you. Do not forget, whatever you may hear and see, that there is a Providence over all! Yes, yes, there is a Providence over all.
    [She leaves him, and goes towards the cistern

AUFTRITT III.—*Vorige,* PIZARRO, *in einem Mantel vermummt.*

SCENE III.—*The same—*PIZARRO, *disguised in a mantle.*

Piz. *[Zu Rokko.]* Ist Alles bereitet?	**Piz.** *[To Rocco.]* Is all ready?
Rok. Ja, die Cisterne braucht nur geöffnet zu werden.	**Roc.** Yes; nothing remains but to open the cistern
Piz. Gut!—der Bursche soll sich entfernen.	**Piz.** Then send away the lad.
Rok. *[zu Leonoren]* Geh, entferne dich!	**Roc.** Go; you may withdraw.
Leo. *[in grösster Verwirrung.]* Wer? Ich?—und Ihr?	**Leo.** *[Greatly perplexed.]* Who? I go? and you?

Rok. Muss ich nicht dem Gefangenen die Eisen abnehmen? Geh! geh!

[*Leonore entfernt sich in den Hintergrund und nähert sich
allmählig wieder im Schatten gegen Florestan, die
Augen immer auf die vermummte person richtend.*

Piz. [*bei Seite, einen Blick auf Rokko und Leonore werfend.*] Die muss ich mir heute noch Beide vom Halse
schaffen, damit Alles auf immer im Dunkeln bleibt.

Rok. [*zu Pizarro.*] Soll ich ihm die Ketten abnehmen?

Piz. [*Zieht einen Dolch hervor.*] Nein!

QUARTETTO.

Er sterbe! doch er soll erst wissen,
Wer ihm sein stolzes Herz zerfleischt.
Der Rache Dunkel sey zerrissen:
Sieh her! Du hast dich nicht getäuscht,
                    [*Er schlägt den Mantel auf.*
Pizarro, den du stürzen wolltest,—
Pizarro, den du fürchten solltest,
Steht nun als Rächer hier!

Flo. [*gefasst.*] Ein Mörder steht vor mir!

Piz. Noch einmal ruf' ich dir,
Was du gethan, zurück;
Nur noch ein Augenblick,
Und dieser Dolch—   [*Er will ihn durchbohren.*

Leo. [*stürzt mit einem durchdringenden Schrei hervor und
bedeckt Florestan mit ihrem Körper.*]
Zurück?

Flo.   O Gott!

Rok.   Was soll's?

Leo.   Durchbohren!
Musst du erst diese Brust.
Der Tod sey dir geschworen
Für deine Mörderlust.

Piz. [*schleudert sie fort.*] Wahnsinniger!

Rok. [*zu Leonoren*] Halt ein!

Piz. Er soll bestraft seyn.

Leo. [*noch einmal ihren Mann bedeckend.*]
Tödte erst sein Weib!

Piz. Sein Weib!

Rok.   Sein Weib!

Flo.   Mein Weib!

Leo. [*zu Florestan.*] Ja, sieh hier Leonoren.

Flo. Leonore!

Leo. [*zu den Andern.*] Ich bin sein Weib, geschworen
Hab' ich ihm Trost, Verderben dir!

Piz. Sein Weib! [*für sich.*] Welch unerhörter Muth!

Flo. [*zu Leonoren.*] Vor Freude starrt mein Blut!

Rok. Mir starrt vor Angst das Blut!

Leo. Ich trotze seiner Wuth!

Piz. Soll ich vor einem Weibe beben?
Nun opfr' ich beide meinem Grimm!
Getheilt hast du mit ihm das Leben,
So theile nun den Tod mit ihm.

[*Er will auf sie eindringen, Leonore zieht hastig eine
kleine Pistole aus der Brust und hällt sie Pizarro
vor.*

Leo. Noch einen Laut und du bist todt!
                    [*Man hört die Trompete auf dem Thurm.*

Piz. Ha! der Minister! Hell und Tod!

Rok. O, was ist das? gerechter Gott!

[*Pizarro steht betäubt, Rokko ebenso. Leonore hängt an
Florestans Halse. Man hört die Trompeten stärker.*

AUFTRITT IV.—*Vorige—*JAQUINO, *Offiziere und Soldaten erscheinen an der obersten Gitteröffnung der Treppe.*

Jaq. [*spricht während der angezeigten Musikpause*] Vater
Rokko! der Herr Minister kommt an! sein Gefolge ist
schon vor dem Schlossthore.

Roc. [*To Pizarro.*] Shall I remove the fetters from the
prisoner? [*To Leonora.*] Go! go!

[*Leonora withdraws to the background, and gradually
approaches Florestan in the shade, her eyes fixed on
the person in disguise.*

Piz. [*Aside, casting a look at Rocco and Leonora.*]
These two I must also get rid of to-day, that all may remain secure.

Roc. [*To Pizarro.*] Shall I take off his chains?

Piz. [*Drawing a dagger.*] No!

QUARTETT.

He shall die! his fate is seal'd,
But first he shall know by whom he falls;
Whose hand the mortal blow shall strike:
Yes, yes! the traitor all shall know:
                    [*Throwing open his mantle.*
Pizarro all thy projects has foreseen,—
Pizarro, whom thou would'st o'erthrow,
As avenger now stands before thee!

Flo. A murderer stands before me!

Piz. No more will I withhold my rage—
There is but an instant
Between thee and death, and
Thus I sate my fury—   [*He tries to stab him.*

Leo. [*Springing forward with a piercing shriek, and protecting Florestan with her body.*]
Back, tyrant!

Flo.   Oh, Heaven!

Roc.   What would'st thou?

Leo.   Would'st thou stab him!
Through this breast to his!
In vain shall be thy fury;—
With my body I'll protect him.

Piz. [*Thrusts her away.*] Madman!

Roc. [*To Leonora.*] Oh, desist!

Piz. He shall be punished.

Leo. [*Once more shielding her husband.*]
Kill first his wife!

Piz. His wife!

Roc.   His wife!

Flo.   My wife!

Leo. [*To Florestan.*] Yes, your own Leonora.

Flo. Leonora!

Leo. [*To the others.*] I am his wife, and have sworn
To save him and punish his oppressor.

Piz. His wife! [*Aside.*] What unheard of courage!

Flo. My heart now throbs with joy!

Roc. Terror my blood congeals!

Leo. His rage I defy!

Piz. With rage I am o'erpower'd!
Shall I before a woman tremble?
Thou also shalt fall before my rage!
Stand off, or thou shalt share his death.

[*Pizarro advances, raising the dagger. Leonora suddenly draws a small pistol from her bosom and presents it at him.*

Leo. Another word, and thou art dead!
                    [*The sound of a trumpet is heard from a tower.*

Piz. Ah! the Minister!—Hell and death!

Roc. What is that? Just Heaven!

[*Pizarro and Rocco stand confounded. Leonora hang·
on Florestan's neck.—The trumpet sounds louder.*

SCENE IV.—*The same—Enter* JACQUINO, *two Officers,
and Soldiers with torches.*

Jac. [*Speaks during a pause in the music.*] Rocco, the
minister is coming: He and his suite have already arrived
at the postern.

Rok. [*freudig und überrascht—für sich.*] Gelobt sey Gott ! [*zu Jaquino sehr laut.*] Wir kommen ! ja, wir kommen augenblicklich ! und diese Leute mit Fackeln sollen heruntersteigen und den Herrn Gouverneur hinauf begleiten.

[*Die Soldaten kommen bis an die Thüre herunter. Die Offiziere und Jaquino gehen oben ab.*

Piz. Verflucht sey diese Stunde !
Die Hölle spottet mein.
Verzweiflung wird im **Bunde**
Mit meiner Rache seyn.

Rok. O fürchterliche Stunde !
O Gott ! was wartet mein ?
Ich will nicht mehr im **Bunde**
Mit diesem Wüthrich seyn.

Leo. und *Flo.* { Es schlägt der Rache Stunde,
Du sollst
Ich soll } gerettet seyn.
Die Liebe wird im Bunde
Mit Muthe dich / mich befrei'n.

[*Pizarro stürzt fort, indem er Rokko einem Wink giebt, ihm zu folgen. Dieser benutzt den Augenblick, da Pizarro schon geht, fasst die Hände beider Gatten, drückt sie an seine Brust, deutet gegen Himmel und eilt nach. Die Soldaten leuchten Pizarro vor.*

AUFTRITT V.—LEONORE, FLORESTAN.

Flo. Treues Weib ! was hast du meinetwegen erdulet ?
Leo. Nichts, nichts ! mein Florestan !

Roc. [*Joyfully surprised—aside.*] Praised be God ! He's happily arrived ! [*Aloud.*] We come ! The soldiers shall ascend, and with lighted torches hence accompany the Governor.

[*The Soldiers come down to the door.—Exeunt Officers and Jacquino.*

Piz. No longer is there hope for me !
Hell mocks !
I must be firm, or fell despair
Will be my future lot.

Roc. Oh ! Heaven ! his great arrogance
Makes me tremble yet.
No longer shall I be
In league with this fell tyrant.

Leo. & *Flo.* { The moment of avenge
For us at length hath come.
The triumph of my / her constancy
In his / her love I now shall find.

[*Pizarro rushes away, giving Rocco a sign to follow him. The latter avails himself of the opportunity to grasp the hands of Leonora and Florestan, presses them to his bosom, points to Heaven, and then hastens after him.*

SCENE V.—LEONORA, FLORESTAN.

Flo. My ever-faithful Leonora ! for me how much hast thou suffered ?
Leo. Oh ! nothing, my own dear Florestan !

O NAMENLOSE FREUDE!—OH, JOY ! OH, RAPTURE PAST EXPRESSING. DUET
FLORESTAN and LEONORA.

Mann an mei-ner Brust! O na-men-lo-se Freu-de! Mein Mann an mei-ner
soul but lives in thee! The world is bright to me— My soul but lives in

ü-ber-gros-se Lust! An Le-o-no-rens Brust! So ü-ber-gros-se
soul but lives in thee! The world is bright to me— My soul but lives in

Brust!...... Mein Mann an mei-ner Brust! Mein Mann an mei-ner Brust!
thee!........ The world is bright to me— My soul but lives in thee!

Lust!..... So ü-ber-gros-se Lust! So ü-ber-gros-se Lust!
thee! The world is bright to me— My soul but lives in thee!

Leo. Du wieder nun in meinen Armen	*Leo.* Once again in these fond arms !
Flo. Gott ! wie gross ist dein Erbarmen	*Flo.* Heaven has kindly heard our prayer !
Beide. O Gott ! dir Dank ! für diese Lust !	*Both.* Oh, thus our thanks we raise !
Leo. Mein Mann an dieser Brust !	*Leo.* Life can boast no greater charms'
Flo. Mein Weib an meiner Brust !	*Flo.* Oh, now no more will we despair

AUFTRITT VI.—*Die Vorigen.*—ROKKO.

SCENE VI.—*The same.—Enter* ROCCO.

Rok. [*hereinstürzend.*] Gute Bothschaft! ihr armen Leidenden! Der Herr Minister hat eine Liste aller Gefangenen—alle sollen ihm vorgeführt werden. [*Zu Florestan.*] Ihr allein seyd nicht erwähnt ; euer Aufenthalt hier, ist eine Eigenmächtigkeit des Gouverneurs. Kommt, folget mir hinauf. [*Alle drei ab.*]

Roc. Good news ! my poor sufferers ! The Minister has a list of all of you, who are forthwith to appear before him. [*To Florestan.*] You are not named. Your imprisonment has evidently been unknown to the Minister, and is a stretch of arbitrary power, no doubt. Come, follow me all, follow me ! [*Exeunt.*]

AUFTRITT VII.—*Paradeplatz des Schlosses mit der Statue des Königs. Die Schlosswachen marschieren auf und bilden ein offenes Viereck. Dann erscheint der Minister,* DON FERNANDO, *von Pizarro und Offizieren begleitet, von der einen Seite. Volk strömt herbei. Von der andern Seite erscheinen, von* JAQUINO *und* MARZELLINEN *begleitet, die Staats-gefangenen. Sie werfen sich alle vor Don Fernando auf die Knie. Später dringt* ROKKO *mit* FLORESTAN *und* LEONOREN *sich durch das Volk und durch die Wachen.*

SCENE VII.—*Parade before the Castle. Enter the Guard, marching ; then the Minister,* DON FERNANDO, *accompanied on one side by* PIZARRO *and Officers. The People crowd around. On the other side appear the State Prisoners, accompanied by* JACQUINO *and* MARCELLINA.—*They all throw themselves on their knees before Don Fernando. Afterwards* ROCCO, *with* FLORESTAN, *press through the Guard and the People.*

FINALE.

CHOR.—*der Gefangenen und des Volks.*

Heil sey dem Tag ! Heil sey der Stunde ;
Da, lang ersehnt, doch unvereint,
Gerechtigkeit mit Huld im Bunde,
Vor unsers Grabes Thor erschient.

Fer. Des besten Königs Wink und Wille !
Führt mich zu Euch, ihr Armen her,
Das ich der Frevel Nacht enthülle,
Die All' umfangen schwarz und schwer.
Nicht länger knieet sclavisch nieder.
Tyrannenstrenge sey mir fern ;
Es sucht der Bruder seine Brüder,
Und kann er helfen, hilft er gern.

FINALE.

CHORUS—*of Prisoners and People.*

Thanks, thanks, and all hail !
To him who comes our chains to sunder
Justice comes, at length, to give us
Long-lost liberty !

Fer. Of a gracious King I am the Minister,
And of Justice the humble instrument :
He desires not to oppress,
But to check crimes by fitting punishment.
Though under his just anger fallen,
His beneficence you shall now experience ·
From chains and bolts he sets you free,
Once more you are at liberty.

AUFTRITT VIII.—*Die Vorigen.*—ROKKO LEONORE *und* FLORESTAN.

SCENE VIII.—*The same.*—ROCCO, LEONORA *and* FLORESTAN.

Rok. Wohlan ! so helfet, helft den Armen !	*Roc.* There, all will be well—help the poor captive '
Piz. Was seh ich ? ha !	*Piz.* What do I see ? Ha !
Rok. Bewegt es dich ?	*Roc.* Does it surprise thee ?

FIDELIO.

Piz.	Fort' fort !
Fer.	Nein, rede !
Rok.	All Erbarmen
	Vereine diesem Paare sich !
	[Florestan vorführend.
	Don Florestan !
Fer.	Der Todtgeglaubte ?
	Der Edle, der für Wahrheit stritt ?
Rok.	Und Qualen, ohne Zahl, erlitt.
Fer.	Mein Freund ! der Todtgeglaubte !
	Gefesselt, bleich, steht er vor mir.
Rok. *Leo.* }	Ja, Florestan ! Ihr seht ihn hier.
Rok.	Und Leonore ! *[Sie vorstellend.*
Fer.	*[noch mehr betroffen.]* Leonore ?
Rok.	Der Frauen Zierde führ' ich vor ;
	Sie kam hierher—
Piz.	Zwei Worte sagen—
Fer.	*[zu Pizarro..]* Kein Wort !
	[zu Rokko.] Sie kam ?——
Rok.	Dort an mein Thor,
	Und trat als Knecht in meine Dienste,
	Und that so brave, treue Dienste,
	Dass ich zum Eidam sie erkor !
Mar.	O weh mir ! was vernimmt mein Ohr ?
Rok.	Der Unmensch wollt in dieser Stunde
	An Florestan vollziehn den Mord.
Piz.	Vollziehn !—Mit ihm—
Rok.	*[auf sich und Leonoren deutend.]*
	Mit uns im Bunde !
	Nur Euer Kommen rief ihn fort.
Cho.	Bestrafet sey der Bösewicht,
	Der Unschuld unterdrückt :
	Gerechtigkeit hält zum Gericht
	Der Rache Schwerdt gezückt.
Flo.	*[zu Rocco.]* Du schlossest auf des Edlen Grab,
	Jetzt nimm ihm seine Ketten ab !
	Doch halt !—Euch, edle Frau, allein
	Euch ziemt es ganz ihn zu befrein.
	[Leonore nimmt die Schlüssel, lässt in grösster Bewegung Florestan die Ketten ab : er sinkt in Leonorens Arme.
Leo.	O Gott ! o welch ein Augenblick !
Flo.	O unaussprechlich süsses Glück !
Fer.	Gerecht, o Gott ! ist dein Gericht !
Rok. *Mar.* }	Du prüfest, du verlässt uns nicht
Cho.	Wer ein solches Weib errungen,
	Stimm in unsern Jubel ein !
	Nie wird es zu hoch besungen,
	Retterinn des Gatten seyn.
Flo.	Deine Treu erhielt mein Leben ;
	Tugend schreckt den Bösewicht.
Leo.	Liebe führte mein Bestreben,
	Wahre Liebe fürchtet nicht.
Cho.	Preist mit hoher Freude Gluth
	Leonorens edlen Muth.
Flo.	*[vortretend und auf Leonoren deutend.]*
	Wer ein solches Weib errungen,
	Stimm in unsern Jubel ein !
	Nie wird es zu hoch besungen,
	Retterinn des Gatten seyn.
Leo.	*[umarmt ihm.]* Liebend ist es mir gelungen,
	Dich aus Ketten zu befreien ;
	Liebend seh es hoch gesungen,
	Florestan ist wieder mein !
Rok. *und* *Cho.* {	Wer ein solches Weib errungen,
	Stimm in unsern Jubel ein !
	Nie wird es zu hoch besungen,
	Retterinn des Gatten seyn.

Piz.	Away ! away !
Fer.	No—speak !
Roc.	For mercy's sake, have pity on
	And re-unite this hapless pair !
	[Florestan adva...
	Don Florestan !
Fer.	He that was supposed to be dead ?
	Who so bravely fought for truth and right ?
Roc.	And who has suffered torments inconceivable
Fer.	My friend ! whom I thought dead !
	Yet standing thus exhausted and in chains !
Roc. *Leo.* }	Yes, it is Florestan whom you now behold !
Roc.	And Leonora ! *[Presenting he*
Fer.	*[Still more affected.]* Leonora !
Roc.	I present a woman, the pride and ornament
	Of her sex ; she came hither—
Piz.	*[Threateningly.]* Speak but two words——
Fer.	*[To Pizarro.]* Not a syllable.
	[To Rocco.] She came ?——
Roc.	Here, to my gate ;—
	She entered my service as a hireling lad,
	And served me so well and faithfully,
	That I chose the unknown for my son-in-law
Mar.	Oh, woe's me ! what do I hear ?
Roc.	The monster, within this very hour,
	Had planned to do a deed of murder on Florestan
Piz.	Murder ! on him !
Roc.	*[Pointing to himself and Leonora.]*
	Yes, my lord ! he sought to involve us in his crime
	But your arrival upset his plans.
Cho.	Punishment befall the wretch
	Who oppresses the innocent :
	Justice holds aloft, for punishment,
	The sword of Revenge.
Fer.	*[To Rocco.]* His threatened death has been averted !
	Now, take off his chains !—yet, stay !
	You, heroic woman ! you, alone, deserve
	The happiness completely to set him free !
	[Leonora takes the keys, and, in great agitation, unfastens the chains which bound Florestan : who rushes into Leonora's arms.
Leo.	Oh, what a moment !
Flo.	Oh, happiness inexpressible !
Fer.	O heaven ! how just are all thy judgments !
Roc. *Mar.* }	Thou triest—but dost not forsake.
Cho.	Whoever has possessed such a partner of his heart,
	Let him join in our jubilee !
	Never can the praise be too loudly sounded
	Of the wife that is the preserver of her husband !
Flo.	Thy fidelity has restored me to life !
	Thy virtues have unnerved the wicked !
Leo.	Love guided my endeavors,
	Such true love as never knows fear
Cho.	Celebrate, in joyous measure,
	Leonora's noble courage.
Flo.	*[Advancing, and pointing to Leonora.]*
	Whoever has possessed such a partner of his heart
	Let him join in our jubilee !
	Never can the praise be too loudly sounded,
	Of the wife that is the preserver of her husband !
Leo.	*[Embracing him.]* Having succeeded in delivering
	You from captivity !—Loving and beloved !
	Loudly let it be proclaimed !
	Florestan is again mine own !
Roc. *and* *Cho.* {	Whoever has possessed such a partner of his heart
	Let him join in our jubilee !
	Never can the praise be too loudly sounded
	Of the wife that is the preserver of her husband !

THE END

THE MAGIC FLUTE

(DIE ZAUBERFLÖTE)

by

W. A. MOZART

Introduction

In former times when the worship of Isis and Osiris prevailed in Egypt, there dwelt upon the banks of the Nile a man of grand and lofty nature, who united in himself the characters of an earthly prince and high priest of the gods. His name was Sarastro. His dwelling was a huge edifice, half palace, half temple.

Sarastro was the grand master of the Mysteries of Isis, and the great duty of his life was to encourage virtue, to aid all who sought true wisdom, to watch over and guard them during their periods of probation, and finally, to consecrate them as members of the holy fraternity of which he was the head.

In the same region of the world, in a castle built in the darkest and most gloomy style of Egyptian architecture, dwelt a mysterious being—the Queen of Night. She was of a haughty, proud and revengeful nature, loving darkness rather than light. Her dress was black as the thick darkness, but sparkling with bright stars. Three women, also dressed and veiled in black, were her familiar spirits and executed her commands. The widowed Queen had a single daughter, Pamina, a lovely and gentle being, whose spiritual tendencies were as virtuous as her person was charming. To give her virtues the opportunity of development, and to save her from temptation and sin, Sarastro had caused her to be taken from her mother and brought to his abode of wisdom and peace.

In the Queen's mind grief and revenge struggled for the mastery—but against the power of the great ruler and priest she was helpless. She sought in vain to regain her daughter, equally in vain to punish Sarastro.

It happened that while the Queen was in this state of mind, a young prince upon his travels, Tamino by name, became separated from his followers, and, while unarmed and defenceless, was attacked by a huge serpent near her castle; he could only fly and call for help, and at length, overcome by fatigue and terror, he swooned and fell. At this instant the three women, attendants of the Queen, flew from the cave and transfixed the monster with their silver javelins. After gazing with admiration on the sleeping youth they left him still in his swoon, from which he was awakened by a jolly, rollicking, prating, cowardly knave, by name Papageno, by occupation a bird-catcher, a huge eater and drinker, and admirer of pretty damsels, and now come, with cage on back, to strike bargains with the Queen's ladies. Placing his cage upon the ground in front of the palace, he announced his presence by repeated blasts of his Pan's pipes and a lively song: the Prince awoke, and, seeing the monster killed, addressed himself to Papageno with the inquiry whether it was to him he was indebted for his life. The bird-catcher trembled at the sight, until convinced that it was dead, when he at once claimed the credit of having slain it. The three women had drawn near unperceived, and overheard this falsehood, as well as others which he added to it. One of them suddenly stepped up to him, applied a padlock to his lips, reducing his entire vocabulary to "hm, hm, hm," and sent him about his business.

They then addressed themselves to the Prince, told him of the Queen, their mistress, and of the loss she had sustained. The Queen had determined to make Tamino the instrument by which she should regain Pamina, and be revenged upon Sarastro. In hope of awaking in him a passion for her daughter, she sent him by the women Pamina's miniature. It had the desired effect. His breast was agitated, as he looked at it, with feelings until then unknown—it kindled a passion as deep and strong as it was sudden.

The Queen suddenly made her appearance, addressed herself at once to Tamino, bade him not fear, and promised him, should he succeed in rescuing Pamina, to give her to him in marriage. The Prince gladly undertook the adventure, and the Queen then vanished. Poor Papageno now came with piteous gestures and sorrowful "hm, hm, hm," and besought Tamino to remove the padlock. But this was beyond his power. The women, however, thinking him sufficiently punished, relieved him, with an earnest caution to beware in future of lying.

To Tamino, now engaged in her service, they brought from their mistress an enchanted flute, in whose tones was hidden so magical a power as to protect its bearer in all dangers, to change the passions of men, make the sad joyous, and fill the envious and proud heart with friendship and love.

To Papageno, who was forced into the service of Tamino by command of the Queen, they gave a casket containing a set of musical bells, similar in power to the Magic Flute.

They then separate and the Prince takes his way towards Sarastro's Palace.

Pamina, meantime, might have been happy in the peaceful halls of the priest of Isis, but for the feelings natural to a daughter, and for the audacious passion of an ugly negro, Monostatos, the head of Sarastro's troop of black slaves, who took advantage of his position to treat her as a prisoner, and to force his disgusting attentions upon her. In the afternoon of that day upon which the Queen of Night had gained an ally in Prince Tamino, the negro succeeded in forcing Pamina into a lonely apartment in the castle, and threatened her with death unless she would consent to become his bride. The poor

girl fainted, and fell back upon the divan. At this moment, Papageno, who had been sent to seek Pamina, came stealthily into the apartment. The figure and face of the beautiful Pamina instantly caught his eye and filled him with admiration, to which his tongue, as usual, gave utterance. The negro started up affrighted. Papageno was no less frightened by the black face of Monostatos. Each took the other for the devil and fled in different directions. Papageno, however, soon conquered his fear, and returned to Pamina. He related to her all that had passed, and besought her to trust herself to him and escape. After some hesitation, Pamina acceded, and they left the castle together.

Tamino advanced directly towards the great gates of Sarastro's castle. Having reached the open space before them, he gazed upon the vastness and grandeur of the edifice with astonishment and wonder—nevertheless so strongly was he prejudiced by the Queen against Sarastro that he saw nothing in all this magnificence but the emblems of a tyrannical ruler. He advanced to the temple. Refused admittance at two of the gates, he turned to the third, from which a priest came forth and enlightened him as to the real character and intentions of Sarastro, upon which he disappeared through the same portal.

The Prince's bosom was torn with conflicting emotions. The desire for true wisdom, pity for the Queen, love for the original of the miniature, all agitated him, and, above all, the desire to know the real character of Sarastro. In his spirit all was darkness and gloom, and an indescribable longing for something, we knew not what, had seized him.
"When wilt thou pass, oh, everlasting night,
And these too weary eyes behold celestial light?"

To this cry of the Prince, a choir of invisible voices replied in mysterious tones: "Ere long, or never!"

Surprised, but rejoiced that his words, involuntarily spoken, had been heard and answered, he ventured to ask if Pamina still lived, and the same chorus replied, "Pamina still liveth!"

In a transport of joy he applied the flute to his lips, and was delighted by its magical effect. In a few moments his tones were answered by the Pan's pipe of Papageno in the distance. Tamino instantly knew the sound, and hurried away to find his servant. Deceived by the echoes, he took the wrong direction, and was hardly out of sight when Papageno and Pamina, who had succeeded in eluding their pursuers, appeared in front of the castle. Pamina in her anxiety and terror thoughtlessly called aloud for Tamino, Papageno hushed her at once, and applied himself to his Pan's pipe. The flute at once answered the tone, and in the next moment they would all have been together and might easily have escaped but for the unfortunate call of Pamina, which had betrayed them and brought at this instant the negro and his whole train of slaves upon them. Pamina at once lost all hope, and so for the moment did her companion; but it suddenly occurred to him that the three women had given him the casket of bells as a protection. He immediately opened it and began to play. The slaves were instantly enchanted, and could move their limbs only in accordance with the music, after which they departed. The way was now clear and the fugitives again set out upon the search for Tamino. It was too late.

From the opposite sides of the open space where they were now entered Sarastro with a host of followers, in splendor and majesty. Pamina threw herself at his feet, but he gently lifted her up. At this moment they were interrupted by the entrance of Monostatos and his slaves, bringing Tamino as a captive.

But now came one of those moments when a sudden feeling overpowers all considerations of time and place. Each lived but for the other—and in the very presence of Sarastro—

within reach of his hand, they rushed into each other's arms—their first, perhaps their final embrace.

Sarastro turned to two of the chief priests, and commanded them to conduct Tamino and Papageno to the temple of probation and purification, then giving his hand to Pamina, he led her, through the grand portal, once more into the palace.

We now proceed to the Court of Sarastro.

It was the custom at these solemn meetings, in the discussion of important questions, for the priests to make known their concurrence with the views of their chief by joining with him in a long blast upon the trumpet. So now, in reply to the question whether Tamino had thus far proved himself worthy to be admitted to the final trials of his courage, steadfastness, self-control, truth, and faith, all raised the trumpets to their lips, and gave their assent in loud and joyful tones. Sarastro then raised his hands to the gods, while the choir of priests bowed reverently, occasionally joining in the invocation, and solemnly prayed to Isis and Osiris to grant the spirit of virtue and wisdom to the candidates.

The high priests, obeying the orders of their master, came immediately to release the prisoners from their confinement. As the prince had borne his confinement with courage, he was now to be subjected to a new trial of his faith in Sarastro's wisdom and good will. The priests warned him and his servant to beware of the arts of women, and let what would happen, to answer them not; and with these warnings led them away to one of the beautiful gardens, where they left them. They were not long alone, for suddenly Tamino, looking up from the bank upon which he had thrown himself, saw the three women of the Queen of Night before him. They besought him to fly at once if he held his life dear; assured him that his death was already determined upon, and reminded him of his promises to their mistress, who, they informed him, had made her way into the castle in search of Pamina. Tamino heard them in silence. He answered them not, trusted them not.

Meantime, in another garden, which extended down to the bank of the river, Pamina, weary and exhausted, had thrown herself upon a seat and fallen asleep. Monostatos, with all evil passions raging in his bosom, entered, determined to steal a kiss from the sleeping girl. His design was frustrated by a peal of thunder—the Queen of Night was there. Here was the time of trial for Pamina. Her mother, unable to take her away from Sarastro, now only desired revenge upon him. Glowing with hatred and rage, she gave Pamina a dagger, and in an awful oath, swore by the gods that unless she plunged it into the heart of Sarastro, she should forever be cast out of the mother's heart. With this threat she vanished. Sarastro now approached, and taking Pamina again gently by the hand, comforted her with the assurance that the probation was over, and that the next day, did Tamino conquer, she should be made happy with him.

Another great test of Tamino's steadfastness and faith now came. Pamina appeared, seeking her lover. Obedient to his vow, he turned from her, and to all her expressions of love, to all her appeals made no reply, though he waved her off with feelings of agony no less heart-breaking than her own. Still he preserved his faith in Sarastro, and broke not his vow. As Pamina retired, the two high priests returned to lead the prince and his servant away. Tamino obeyed at once.

The priests with Sarastro again assembled in the dark temple. The chief ordered the prince and princess to be brought in. Pamina had lost her faith in Sarastro's promise. He bade the lovers take leave of each other, but comforted them with the assurance that Tamino would endure to the end, and that they would soon meet in joy. The cause of Tamino's apparent coldness at the interview in the garden was explained to Pamina; but her faith was shaken, and when her lover was again led from the assembly, her reason gave way.

But the crisis had passed. The sound of the flute in the distance, and the assurance that the coldness of Tamino was not real, that her love was returned in fullest measure, restored her to herself, and she besought to be brought at once to him to share his fate, whatever it might be. This was granted.

Tamino was now brought to the last test—that of purification by the elements. He was led to the gates of the burning lake, and boldly gave the command, "Open the terrible portals!" At this moment came Pamina. She unhesitatingly besought permission to join him. It was granted. So, leaning on his arm, they passed through the fiery billows—ascended the broad stairs into the temple, and knelt before the altar and Sarastro, amid acclamations of triumph.

The eventful night was now nearly over, but the Queen of Night still hoped to have her revenge. Her three women, accompanied by Monostatos, whom she had enflamed against Sarastro, sought stealthily to destroy him. But at this moment, at a sign from him, the wall, which alone divided him from his enemies, disappeared, and the bright rays of the glorious morning sun darted full upon them. Like obscene birds of night, they fled its rays forever, while Tamino and Pamina joined hands, and received the blessing of the Priest-Ruler, amid the joyous and triumphant chorus of priests and the grand assembly.

The Magic Flute

ACT I.	ERSTER AUFZUG.
(Rugged cliffs. To the left in the foreground a cave.)	(Rauhe Felsengegend. Links vorn ein Felsenlager. Rechts
(Tamino rushes in with a bow but no arrow.)	und links vom Darsteller.)
	(Tamino, mit einem Bogen aber ohne Pfeil, eilt herbei.)

Tamino.

Help! Oh, help! or else I am lost.

Of the cunning serpent a certain victim.

Merciful gods! it even now approaches.

(A large serpent follows Tamino.)

Oh, save, oh, protect me!

(He reaches the cave and sinks down exhausted and unconscious.)

(Tamino at the cave Three Ladies, carrying silver darts, enter.)

The Ladies.

Die, monster, by our hands.

(They pierce the serpent with their darts, and it lies motionless.)

Triumph! Triumph! it is accomplished.

'Tis a heroic deed! By the courage

Of our arm he is freed.

First Lady

(looking at Tamino.)

A noble youth, gentle and handsome!

Second Lady.

So handsome as I ne'er have seen!

Third Lady.

Yes, yes, handsome enough to be painted!

All three.

Could I my heart to love devote

'Twould be to this fair youth.

Let us to our princess hasten,

To her this news to impart.

Perhaps this young and handsome man

May bring her back her former calm.

First Lady.

Go then and tell the news

And I meanwhile will stay.

Second Lady.

No, no, go you yourself,

I will watch over him.

Tamino.

Zu Hilfe! zu Hilfe! Sonst bin ich verloren,

Der listigen Schlange zum Opfer erkoren!

Barmherzige Götter! Schon nahet sie sich!

(Eine grosse Schlange verfolgt Tamino.)

Ach, rettet mich! ach, schützet mich!

(Tamino auf dem Felsenlager Die drei Damen, mit silbernen Wurfspiessen, treten ein.)

Die drei Damen.

Stirb, Ungeheu'r, durch uns're Macht!

(Sie durchbohren mit ihren Wurfspiessen die Schlange, die regungslos liegen bleibt.)

Triumph! Triumph! Sie ist vollbracht,

Die Heldenthat! Er ist befreit

Durch unsers Armes Tapferkeit.

Erste Dame.

(Tamino betrachtend.)

Ein holder Jüngling, sanft und schön!

Zweite Dame.

So schön, als ich noch nie geseh'n!

Dritte Dame.

Ja, ja, gewiss zum Malen schön!

Alle drei.

Würd' ich mein Herz der Liebe weih'n,

So müsst es dieser Jüngling sein.

Lasst uns zu uns'rer Fürstin eilen,

Ihr diese Nachricht zu ertheilen.

Vielleicht, dass dieser schöne Mann

Die vor'ge Ruhe ihr geben kann.

Erste Dame.

So geht und sagt es ihr,

Ich bleib' indessen hier.

Zweite Dame.

Nein, nein, geht ihr nur hin,

Ich wache hier für ihn!

Third Lady.

No, no, that cannot be—
I will remain to guard him!

First Lady.

I meanwhile will stay.

Second Lady.

I will watch over him!

Third Lady.

I will remain to guard him!

First Lady.

I remain!

Second Lady.

I watch!

Third Lady.

I guard!

All three.

I! I! I!

All three   (each to herself.)

I should away? ha! ha! how good.
They'd gladly be with him alone.
No, no, that cannot be!
(One after the other, then all three together.)
What would I give
If I but with this youth might live!
That is, all by myself.
It cannot be, they do not go.
It's best then that I go myself.
Thou handsome and beloved youth,
Thou gentle one, farewell,
Until I see thee once again!

(Exeunt.)

(PAPAGENO in a dress of feathers, with a large bird cage on his back, which he raises high over his head, and which contains various birds, hastens in. In his hands he holds a fawn-flute.)

Dritte Dame.

Nein, nein, das kann nicht sein,
Ich schütze ihn allein.

Erste Dame.

Ich blieb indessen hier!

Zweite Dame.

Ich wache hier für ihn!

Dritte Dame.

Ich schütze ihn allein!

Erste Dame.

Ich bleibe!

Zweite Dame.

Ich wache!

Dritte Dame.

Ich schütze!

Alle drei.

Ich! ich! ich!

Alle drei   (jede für sich.)

Ich sollte fort? Ei, ei! Wie fein!
Sie wären gern bei ihm allein.
Nein, nein, das kann nicht sein.
(Eine nach der anderen und dann alle drei zugleich.)
Was wollte ich darum nicht geben,
Könnt' ich mit diesem Jüngling leben!
Hätt' ich ihn doch so ganz allein!
Doch keine geht, es kann nicht sein.
Am besten ist es nun, ich geh'.—
Du Jüngling, schön und liebevoll!
Du trauter Jüngling, lebe wohl,
Bis ich dich wieder seh'.

(Sie entfernen sich.)

(PAPAGENO in einem Federkleid, auf dem Rücken einen grossen Vogelbauer, der sich hoch über seinen Kopf erhebt und verschiedene Vögel enthält, eilt von links herbei. In den Händen hält er ein Faunenflötchen.)

DER VOGELFANGER BIN ICH JA—*A FOWLER BOLD IN ME YOU SEE*
Air (Papageno)

Der Vo-gel-fän-ger bin ich ja, stets lu-stig, hei-sa! hop-sa-sa! der
A fowl-er bold in me you see, A man of mirth and min-strel-sy; My

Vo-gel-fän-ger ist be-kannt bei alt und jung im gan-zen Land.
name is ev-er in de-mand With old and young thro'-out the land.

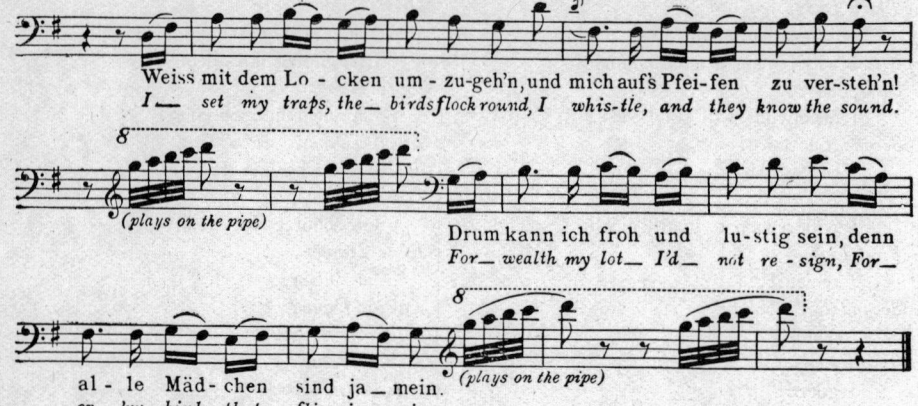

Weiss mit dem Lo - cken um - zu-geh'n, und mich auf's Pfei-fen zu ver-steh'n!
I— set my traps, the— birds flock round, I whis-tle, and they know the sound.

(plays on the pipe)

Drum kann ich froh und lu-stig sein, denn
For— wealth my lot— I'd— not re - sign, For—

al - le Mäd- chen sind ja_ mein.
ev - 'ry bird that flies is — mine. *(plays on the pipe)*

(whistles and takes down the bird cage.)

The fowler merry and gay am I,
Ever happy, heigh ho high!
The merry fowler too is known,
By young and old from zone to zone
A net for maidens I should like,
Would catch the pretty dears by dozens.
I'd shut them safely up at home
And never from me would they roam.
Then I would some sugar buy,
And to her who loved me, I
Gladly would the sugar give,
And if she kissed me tenderly,
Man and wife we then would be.
At my side she then would lie,
And I'd sing her a lullaby.
(He pipes and goes to the right exit.)

(Er pfeift und nimmt dann den Vogelbauer ab.)

Der Vogelfänger bin ich ja,
Stets lustig, heisa, hopsasa!
Der Vogelfänger ist bekannt
Bei Alt und Jung im ganzen Land,
Ein Netz für Mädchen möchte ich,
Ich fing sie dutzendweis für mich;
Dann sperrte ich sie bei mir ein,
Und alle Mädchen wären mein.
Wenn alle Mädchen wären mein,
Dann tauschte ich brav Zucker ein,
Die, welche mir am liebsten wär',
Der gäb' ich gleich den Zucker her.
Und küsste sie mich zärtlich dann,
Wär' sie mein Weib und ich ihr Mann,
Sie schlief an meiner Seite ein,
Ich wiegte wie ein Kind sie ein.
(Er pfeift und wendet sich dann zum Abgang nach rechts.)

(TAMINO and PAPAGENO.)

Tamino   (awakes.)
    Holla!
Papageno.
    What's that?
Tamino.
    Tell me, jolly friend, who you are.

Papageno.
    Who I am?
                (aside.)
    Foolish question.

(TAMINO, PAPAGENO.)

Tamino   (er erwacht.)
    He da!
Papageno.
    Was da?
Tamino.
    Sag' mir, du lustiger
    Freund, wer du bist?
Papageno.
    Wer ich bin?
                (für sich.)
    Dumme Frage!

(Aloud.)

A man like you.—And if I should ask who you are?

Tamino.

My father is a King who rules over many lands and peoples; therefore am I called Prince.

Papageno

(aside).

How he stares at me! I am beginning now to fear him. Do not approach, I tell you, and do not trust me, for I have gigantic strength.

Tamino.

Gigantic strength?

(He looks at the serpent.)

So you were my deliverer, who conquered this poisonous serpent?

Papageno.

Serpent?

(He looks around, and trembling, takes a few steps backward.)

Is it dead or alive?

Tamino.

How on earth have you conquered this monster? You are without weapons!

Papageno.

I need none! My hands serve me better than weapons.

Tamino.

Then you have strangled it?

Papageno.

Strangled!

(Aside.)

Never have I been so strong as to-day!

(The three LADIES appear, veiled, from the right; the FIRST LADY carries a vase of water, the SECOND a stone, the THIRD a padlock and a portrait for a medallion.)

The three Ladies

(they still keep at a distance, threaten and shout all together).

Papageno!

Papageno.

Aha! they call me!

(TO TAMINO.)

Look around, friend.

(Laut.)

Ein Mensch wie du.—Wenn ich dich nun fragte, wer du bist?

Tamino.

Mein Vater ist Fürst, der über viele Länder und Menschen herrscht; darum nennt man mich Prinz.

Papageno

(für sich).

Wie er mich so starr anblickt! Bald fang' ich an, mich vor ihm zu fürchten. Bleib zurück, sag' ich, und traue mir nicht, denn ich habe Riesenkraft.

Tamino.

Riesenkraft?

(Er sieht auf die Schlange.)

Also warst du wohl gar mein Erretter, der diese giftige Schlange bekämpfte?

Papageno.

Schlange?

(Er sieht sich um, weicht zitternd einige Schritte surück.)

Ist sie todt oder lebendig?

Tamino.

Aber um alles in der Welt, Freund, wie hast du dieses Ungeheuer bekämpft? Du bist ohne Waffen!

Papageno.

Brauch' keine! Bei mir ist ein starker Druck mit der Hand mehr als Waffen.

Tamino.

Du hast sie also erdrosselt?

Papageno.

Erdrosselt!

(Für sich.)

Bin in meinem Leben nicht so stark gewesen, als heute.

(Ersieht sich um, weicht zitternd einige Schritte zurück.)

(Die drei DAMEN erscheinen verschleiert von rechts; die erste DAME trägt ein Gefäss mit Wasser, die zweite DAME einen Stein, die dritte DAME ein Vorhängeschloss und ein Medaillonbildnis.)

Die drei Damen

(halten sich noch zurück, drohen und rufen zugleich).

Papageno!

Papageno.

Aha! Das geht mich an.

(Halblaut zu TAMINO.)

Sieh dich um, Freund!

Tamino (in a low tone).
Who are these ladies?

Papageno (in a low tone).
I really do not know who they are.

Tamino (in a low tone).
They are doubtless very beautiful.

Papageno
(in a low tone).
I do not think so. For were they beautiful they would not thus conceal their faces.

The three Ladies
(drawing nearer, and threatening).
Papageno!

Papageno
(in a low tone).
Be still! They chide me now. Here, my fair ones, here are my birds!
(The three LADIES stand between TAMINO and PAPAGENO.)

First Lady
(hands PAPAGENO the vase with water).
In return our princess sends to-day clear water instead of wine.

Second Lady
(steps into her place).
And she commanded me to give you this stone instead of cake.
(She gives him the stone.)

Third Lady
(steps into her place).
And instead of sweet figs I have the honor to put this golden padlock on your mouth.
(To TAMINO.)
'Twas we, dear youth, who freed you. Here, this picture our great princess sends to you. 'Tis the portrait of her daughter!
(She presents it.)
Farewell!

Second Lady.
Adieu, sir Papageno!
(The second and third take the bird-cage and go with it to the right.)

Tamino (halblaut).
Wer sind diese Damen?

Papageno
(ebenso).
Wer sie eigentlich sind, weiss ich selbst nicht.

Tamino (ebenso).
Sie sind vermuthlich sehr schön?

Papageno
(ebenso).
Ich denke nicht! Denn wenn sie schön wären, würden sie ihre Gesichter nicht bedecken.

Die drei Damen
(näher tretend, drohend).
Papageno!

Papageno
(halblaut).
Sei still! sie drohen mir schon. Hier, meine Schönen, übergeb' ich meine Vogel.
(Die drei DAMEN nehmen die Mitte zwischen TAMINO und PAPAGENO.)

Erste Dame
(reicht PAPAGENO das Gefäss mit Wasser).
Dafür schickt dir unsere Fürstin heute zum erstenmal statt Wein reines, helles Wasser.

Zweite Dame
(tritt an deren Stelle).
Und mir befahl sie, dass ich, statt Zuckerbrot, diesen Stein dir überbringen soll.
(Sie überreicht PAPAGENO den Stein.)

Dritte Dame
(an die Stelle der zweiten DAME tretend).
Und statt der süssen Feigen hab' ich die Ehre, dir dies goldene Schloss vor den Mund zu legen.
(Zu TAMINO.)
Wir waren's, Jüngling, die dich befreiten. Hier, dies Gemälde überschickt dir die grosse Fürstin, es ist das Bildnis ihrer Tochter!
(Sie überreicht es.)
Auf Wiedersehen!

Zweite Dame.
Adieu, Monsieur Papageno!
(Die zweite und dritte DAME fassen den Vogelbauer und gehen damit rechts ab.)

First Lady.

He did not drink that so quickly.

(She follows the two others, laughing.)

(PAPAGENO hastens away in dumb astonishment to the left.)

(TAMINO, immediately upon the receipt of the picture, gives his whole attention to it.)

Tamino.

Oh, beauteous form with semblance fair.
No mortal may with thee compare!
What rapture does the sight impart,
What mingled feelings fill my heart.
I know not how this state to call,
But with its fire it fills me all.
And is it love that in me wakes?
'Tis only love that this form takes!
O could I but her now behold,
Could she but now before me stand!
O I would then be pure and true,
What would I be? I her would woo,
Press her fair form to my warm heart
And she ne'er from me would depart!

(A short, loud clap of thunder.)
(It grows dark.)

Tamino.

Great gods, what is it?

The three Ladies.

Courage!

First Lady.

It announces the approach of our Queen.

(Thunder.)

The three Ladies.

She comes!

(Very loud thunder.)

CHANGE OF SCENE.

(The mountains open up. A starry heaven appears, in the middle of which stands the star-covered throne of the QUEEN OF THE NIGHT. Clear, bluish moonlight.)

Queen.

O tremble not, beloved son!
You're innocent, devout and wise.
A youth like you does sure know best
A mother's heart to put at rest.
For I am doomed to mourn and sorrow.
My daughter left me in dismay.
With her my happiness has vanished,

Erste Dame.

Fein nicht so hastig getrunken!

(Sie folgt lachend den beiden andern.)

(PAPAGENO eilt in stummer Verlegenheit nach links ab.)

(TAMINO hat gleich nach dem Empfang des Bildnisses seine Aufmerksamkeit nur diesem zugewendet.)

Tamino.

Dies Bildnis ist bezaubernd schön,
Wie noch kein Auge je gesehn!
Ich fühl' es, wie dies Götterbild
Mein Herz mit neuer Regung füllt.
Dies Etwas kann ich zwar nicht nennen.
Doch fühl' ich's hier wie Feuer brennen.
Soll die Empfindung Liebe sein?
Ja, ja! die Liebe ist's allein.—
O, wenn ich sie nur finden könnte!
O, wenn sie doch schon vor mir stände!
Ich würde—würde—warm und rein—
Was würde ich?—Ich würde sie voll Entzücken
An diesen heissen Busen drücken,
Und ewig wäre sie dann mein.

(Kurzer, starker Donner.)
(Es wird dunkel.)

Tamino.

Ihr Götter! Was ist das?

Die drei Damen.

Fasse dich!

Erste Dame.

Es verkündet die Ankunft unserer Königin.

(Donner.)

Die drei Damen.

Sie kommt!

(Sehr starker Donner.)

OFFENE VERWANDLUNG.

(Die Berge theilen sich, man erblickt einen Sternenhimmel und in dessen Mitte den mit Sternen gezierten Thron der KÖNIGIN DER NACHT. Helles, blaues Mondlicht.)

Königin.

O zitt're nicht, mein lieber Sohn!
Du bist unschuldig, weise, fromm;
Ein Jüngling, so wie du, vermag am besten,
Das tiefbetrübte Mutterherz zu trösten.
Zum Leiden bin ich auserkoren,
Denn meine Tochter fehlet mir;

A scoundrel bore my child away.
I still see her shiver,
Tremble and quiver,
I still hear her shrieking,
In vain for aid seeking.
I had to see her stolen from me,
"Oh, help!" was all the poor child said
Alas! in vain was all her pleading,
Too weak, O heaven, was my aid!

Durch sie ging all mein Glück verloren.
Ein Bösewicht entfloh mit ihr.
Noch seh' ich ihr Zittern
Mit bangem Erschüttern,
Ihr ängstliches Beben,
Ihr schüchternes Streben.
Ich musste sie mir rauben sehen,
Ach helft! war alles, was sie sprach;
Allein vergebens war ihr Flehen,
Denn meine Hilfe war zu schwach.

DU WIRST SIE ZU BEFREIEN—*THOU SHALT RESCUE MY CHILD* Air (Queen)

Allegro moderato

Du, du, du wirst sie zu be-frei-en ge— hen,
Thou, thou, thou shalt res-cue my child from thral dom,

du wirst der Toch-ter— Ret-ter sein, ja, du —wirst der
That no-ble task I— thee as-sign, yea, that— no-ble

Toch-ter Ret-ter— sein! Und werd' ich dich als— Sie-ger—
task— I— thee— as-sign! And when as vic-tor— i— can—

se-hen, so sei sie dann auf e—wig— dein, so sei sie
hail thee, Her plight-ed love be ev-er— thine, Her plight-ed

dann ___
love ___

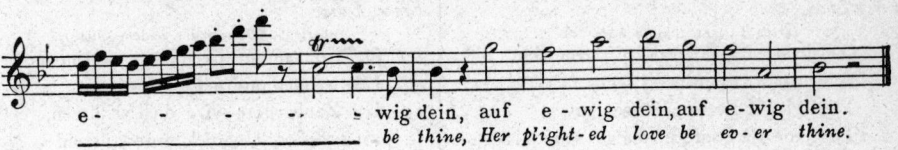

e - - - - wig dein, auf e - wig dein, auf e - wig dein.
be thine, Her plight-ed love be ev-er thine.

(She steps back.)	(Sie tritt zurück.)
(Very loud thunder.)	(Sehr starker Donner.)
(TAMINO stands in the foreground greatly moved.)	(TAMINO bleibt bewegt im Vordergrund stehen.)

Papageno

 (points sadly at the lock on his mouth).

 Hm, hm, hm, hm, hm, hm.

Tamino.

 He was guilty of a falsehood

 And as a penalty he's dumb.

Papageno.

 Hm! hm! hm! hm! hm! hm! hm!

Tamino.

 I can do nothing, except sympathize with you,

 As I am powerless to help.

Papageno.

 Hm! hm! hm! hm! hm! hm! hm!

 (The three LADIES appear from the right. The FIRST LADY carries a flute and chimes.)

 (The three LADIES step between TAMINO and PAPAGENO.)

The first Lady

   (to PAPAGENO).

 The Queen is merciful,

 (She takes the lock off from his mouth, and hands it to the SECOND LADY.)

 And remits your punishment through me.

Papageno.

 Now Papageno will chatter again.

Second Lady.

 Yes, chatter, but never lie again.

Papageno.

 I'll never lie again, no, never, never.

The three Ladies.

 Let this lock your warning be!

Papageno.

 This lock shall my warning be.

All.

 If every tongue, when falsehool speaking,

Papageno

 (zeigt traurig auf das Schloss an seinem Mund.)

 Hm! hm! hm! hm! hm! hm! hm! hm!

Tamino.

 Der Arme kann von Strafe sagen,

 Denn seine Sprache ist dahin.

Papageno.

 Hm! hm! hm! hm! hm! hm! hm! hm!

Tamino.

 Ich kann nichts thun, als dich beklagen,

 Weil ich zu schwach zu helfen bin.

Papageno.

 Hm! hm! hm! hm! hm! hm! hm! hm!

 (Die drei DAMEN erscheinen von rechts; die erste DAME trägt eine Flöte und ein Glockenspiel.)

 (Die drei DAMEN treten zwischen TAMINO und PAPAGENO.)

Erste Dame

   (zu PAPAGENO).

 Die Königin begnadet dich,

 (sie nimmt ihm das Schloss vom Mund und übergiebt es der zweiten Dame)

 Erlässt die Strafe dir durch mich.

Papageno.

 Nun plaudert Papageno wieder.

Zweite Dame.

 Ja, plaud're! Lüge nur nicht wieder.

Papageno.

 Ich lüge nimmermehr. Nein! Nein!

Die drei Damen.

 Dies Schloss soll deine Warnung sein!

Papageno.

 Dies Schloss soll meine Warnung sein!

Alle.

 Bekämen doch die Lügner alle

Could have a lock his lips to seal,
Instead of grief and scandal seeking,
We all would love and friendship feel.

First Lady
(gives TAMINO the golden flute).
O prince, take this rare gift from me,
Which our fair princess sends to thee!
This Magic Flute possesses power
To guide thee safe in danger's hour!
The three Ladies.
The power lies now in your hand
All human passions to command.
The sad will ever happy be,
The loveless ne'er from love be free.
All.
O such a flute is worth its weight in gold,
Bringing both love and happiness untold.

Papageno.
And now, ladies,
With your leave I'll go.
The three Ladies.
You can freely go,
But the princess fair commands you
With the prince to take your way
To the castle of Sarastro.
Papageno.
No, I thank for the honor,
But myself I've heard you say
That he is a very tiger!
And he would without delay,
Have me plucked and quickly roasted,
For his dogs a tasty prey.
The three Ladies.
Trust the Prince, for he'll protect you,
You'll his faithful servant be.
Papageno (aside).
The Prince may risk his royal being,
But I value mine more.
He may repent when all too late,
I'd rather now decline.
First Lady
(presents PAPAGENO with a casket containing chimes).
Pray, take this treasure, it is thine.

Ein solches Schloss vor ihren Mund:
Statt Hass, Verleumdung, schwarzer
  Galle,
Bestünde Lieb' und Bruderbund.
Erste Dame
(übergiebt TAMINO die goldene Flöte).
O Prinz, nimm dies Geschenk von mir!
Dies sendet uns're Fürstin dir.
Die Zauberflöte wird dich schützen,
Im grössten Unglück unterstützen.
Die drei Damen.
Hiermit kannst du allmächtig handeln,
Der Menschen Leidenschaft verwandeln.
Der Traurige wird freudig sein,
Den Hagestolz nimmt Liebe ein.
Alle.
O, so eine Flöte ist mehr als Gold und
  Kronen werth,
Denn durch sie wird Menschenglück und
  Zufriedenheit vermehrt.
Papageno.
Nun, ihr schönen Frauenzimmer,
Darf ich—so empfehl' ich mich.
Die drei Damen.
Dich empfehlen kannst du immer,
Doch bestimmt die Fürstin dich,
Mit dem Prinzen ohn' Verweilen
Nach Sarastros Burg zu eilen.
Papageno.
Nein, dafür bedank' ich mich!
Von Euch selber hörte ich,
Dass er wie ein Tigerthier!
Sicher liess ohn' alle Gnaden
Mich Sarastro rupfen, braten,
Setzte mich den Hunden für.
Die drei Damen.
Dich schützt der Prinz, trau' ihm allein!
Dafür sollst du sein Diener sein.
Papageno (für sich).
Dass doch der Prinz beim Teufel wäre!
Mein Leben ist mir lieb;
Am Ende schleicht bei meiner Ehre,
Er von mir wie ein Dieb.
Erste Dame
(übergiebt PAPAGENO ein Kästchen mit einem Glockenspiel).
Hier, nimm dies Kleinod, es ist dein.

Papageno.

Oh, oh, what can it be?

The three Ladies.

Within you can hear the bells ringing.

Papageno.

And will I, too, have power to play them?

The three Ladies.

Why certainly; of course you will.

The three Ladies.

Silver bells and flute of magic
To protect you are attuned,
Fare thee well, we must away,
Now we bid you both good day.

Papageno and Tamino.

Silver bells and flute of magic
To protect us are attuned.
Fare thee well, we must away,
Now we bid you all good day.

(The three LADIES go to the right.)
(TAMINO and PAPAGENO go at the same time to the left; coming back.)

Tamino.

Fair ladies, will you tell us, pray—

Papageno.

To this castle great the way?

Both.

How to find the way to this great castle?

The three Ladies.

Three handsome youths will fly before you,
And point you out the way;
Follow the counsel they may give,
Farewell, away, away!

Tamino and Papageno.

Three handsome youths will fly before us
And point us out the way.

All

Fare thee well, we must away,
Now we bid you both good day.

(The three LADIES go away to the right.)
TAMINO and PAPAGENO go at the same time to the left.)

Papageno.

Ei, ei! was mag darinnen sein?

Die drei Damen.

Darinnen hörst du Glöckchen tönen.

Papageno.

Werd' ich sie auch wohl spielen können?

Die drei Damen.

O ganz gewiss! ja, ja, gewiss!

Die drei Damen.

Silberglöckchen, Zauberflöten
Sind zu eurem Schutz vonnöten.
Lebet wohl! wir wollen gehn,
Lebet wohl; auf Wiedersehn.

Tamino und Papageno.

Silberglöckchen, Zauberflöten
Sind zu unserm Schutz vonnöten.
Lebet wohl! wir wollen gehn,
Lebet wohl! auf Wiedersehn.

(Die drei DAMEN wenden sich nach rechts.)
(TAMINO und PAPAGENO wenden sich gleichzeitig nach links; zurückkommend.)

Tamino.

Doch, schöne Damen, saget an:

Papageno.

Wie man die Burg wohl finden kann?

Beide

Wie man die Burg wohl finden kann?

Dei drei Damen

(ebenso).

Drei Knäbchen, jung, schön, hold und weise,
Umschweben euch auf eurer Reise;
Sie werden eure Führer sein,
Folgt ihrem Rathe ganz allein.

Tamino und Papageno.

Drei Knäbchen, jung, schön, hold und weise,
Umschweben uns auf unsrer Reise.

Alle.

So lebet wohl! wir wollen gehn,
Lebt wohl, lebt wohl! Auf Wiedersehn!

(Die drei DAMEN ab nach rechts.)
(TAMINO und PAPAGENO gleichzeitig ab nach links.)

CHANGE OF SCENE.

(Sumptuously furnished room of PAMINA in Sarastro's palace.)

(MONOSTATOS, PAMINA, Slaves enter.)

Monostatos
(patting PAMINA's hand).
Come in, little dove!

Pamina.

Oh, wretched martyrdom, direful pain!

Monostatos.
Your life is lost.

Pamina.

The pains of death I fear not,
But my poor mother dies of grief,
With no one to bring her relief!

Monostatos
(to the slaves who are waiting in the back).
Hola, slaves, let her straight be bound!
My hatred will be sated.

(Slaves rush up to bind PAMINA.)

Pamina.

Oh, let me, tyrant, rather die,
For nothing has your rage abated.

(She sinks down unconscious on a couch.)

Monostatos.

Away! Leave me alone with her!

(The slaves withdraw with the chains.)

(PAPAGENO appears in the middle door.)

(MONOSTATOS absorbed in watching PAMINA does not notice PAPAGENO's arrival.)

Papageno
(still in the door).

Where am I now? Where can I be?
Aha, I see some people,
I'll even venture in.

(He comes in and approaches the couch.)

A maiden greets my sight,
As snow so pure and white.

(MONOSTATOS turns around.)

(PAPAGENO is terrified by MONOSTATOS's gaze; the one is frightened by the other.)

Both.

That is the devil sure as fate,
Have mercy and commiserate!
Alas, alas, alas!

(They run away, looking back at each other cautiously over the shoulder. At the middle door they run into each other and rush with a cry through the middle door in different directions.)

VERWANDLUNG.

(Reich ausgestattetes Zimmer der PAMINA in SARASTRO's Palast. Mittelthür.)

(MONOSTATOS, PAMINA, Sklaven treten ein.)

Monostatos
(PAMINA an der Hand hereinschleudernd).
Du feines Täubchen, nur herein!

Pamina
(zu seiner Rechten).
O welche Marter! Welche Pein!

Monostatos
Verloren ist dein Leben.

Pamina.

Der Tod macht mich nicht beben,
Nur meine Mutter dauert mich;
Sie stirbt vor Gram ganz sicherlich.

Monostatos
(zu den im Hintergrund verweilenden Sklaven).
He, Sklaven! Legt ihr Fesseln an!
Mein Hass soll dich verderben.

(Sklaven eilen hinzu, um PAMINA zu fesseln.)

Pamina.

O lass mich lieber sterben,
Weil nichts, Barbar! dich rühren kann.

(Sie sinkt ohnmächtig rechts vorn auf eine Ottomane.)

Monostatos.

Nun fort! lasst mich bei ihr allein.

(Sklaven eilen mit den Fesseln durch die Mitte ab.)

(PAPAGENO erscheint in der Mittelthür.)

(MONOSTATOS im Anschauen PAMINA's versunken, bemerkt das Erscheinen PAPAGENO's nicht.)

Papageno
(noch in der Thür).

Wo bin ich wohl? Wo mag ich sein?
Aha, da find' ich Leute!
Gewagt, ich geh' herein.

(Er tritt ein und nähert sich der Ottomane rechts vorn.)

Schön Mädchen, jung und fein,
Viel weisser noch als Kreide!

(MONOSTATOS wendet sich.)

(PAPAGENO steht bei MONOSTATOS Anblick erstarrt; einer erschrickt über den andern.)

Beide.

Hu! Das ist—der Teu..fel si..cherlich!
Hab' Mitleid—und verschone mich!
Hu! hu! hu!

(Sie laufen, indem sie sich gegenseitig verstohlen über die Schulter zu beobachten trachten, nach der Mittelthür; dort stossen sie aufeinander und eilen mit einem Aufschrei durch die Mitte nach verschiedenen Seiten hin davon.)

Pamina

(alone, awakening, speaks as in a dream).

Mother! Mother! Mother!

(She recovers and looks around.)

What? Does my heart still beat? Does it awake to new tortures? O, 'tis so cruel, so cruel! 'Tis more bitter than death!

(PAPAGENO with careful steps comes in and watches her.)

Papageno.

Am I not a fool that I allowed myself to be frightened? There are black birds in this world then why not black people?

(He notices PAMINA.)

Ah, behold! here is the lovely maiden still!

(To PAMINA.)

O daughter of the Queen of night!

Pamina.

I am she.

Papageno.

I'll know that right away.

(He examines the portrait which the Prince received and which PAPAGENO now wears on a ribbon around his neck.)

Blue eyes (black)—very blue (black)—red lips—very red—blond (brown) hair—blond (brown) hair. Everything tallies.

Pamina.

Permit me—

(PAPAGENO shows her the portrait.)

Pamina.

Yes, it's I. How did it come into your hands?

Papageno.

I must relate it to you in very great detail. I came very early, as is my custom, to your mother's palace to deliver my birds, when I saw a man before me who is called Prince. This Prince so charmed your mother that she gave him your portrait, and ordered him to free you. His resolution was as hasty as his love for you.

Pamina

(allein, erwachend, spricht wie im Traum).

Mutter! Mutter! Mutter!

(Sie erholt sich, sieht sich um.)

Wie? Noch schlägt dieses Herz? Zu neuen Qualen erwacht? O, das ist hart, sehr hart—mir bitterer als der Tod!

(PAPAGENO mit vorsichtigen Schritten beobachtend durch die Mitte.)

(PAMINA. PAPAGENO zu ihrer Linken.)

Papageno.

Bin ich nicht ein Narr, dass ich mich schrecken liess? Es giebt ja schwarze Vögel in der Welt, warum denn nicht auch schwarze Menschen?

(Er erblickt PAMINA.)

Ach, sieh da! Hier ist das schöne Mädchen noch.

(Zu PAMINA.)

Du Tochter der nächtlichen Königin.

Pamina.

O, ich bin es.

Papageno.

Das will ich gleich erkennen.

(Er prüft das Porträt, welches der Prinz zuvor empfangen, und das PAPAGENO nun an einem Band am Hals trägt.)

Die Augen blau (schwarz)—richtig blau (schwarz)—die Lippen roth—richtig roth—blonde (braune) Haare—blonde (braune) Haare. Alles trifft ein.

Pamina.

Erlaube mir—

(PAPAGENO zeigt ihr das Porträt.)

Pamina.

Ja, ich bin's. Wie kam es in deine Hände?

Papageno.

Ich muss dir das umständlicher erzählen. Ich kam heute früh, wie gewöhnlich, zu deiner Mutter Palast meine Vögel abzugeben, dort sah ich einen Menschen vor mir, der sich Prinz nennen lässt. Dieser Prinz hat deine Mutter so eingenommen, dass sie ihm dein Bildnis schenkte und ihm befahl, dich zu befreien. Sein Entschluss war so schnell, als seine Liebe zu dir.

Pamina.

Love?

(Joyfully.)

Then he loves me? Tell it to me once again, for I rejoice at the sound of that word.

Papageno.

And I believe you (without swearing) for you are a maiden—Where did I leave off?

Pamina.

At the word love.

Papageno.

Yes, you are right, at the word love. (I call that having a fine memory!) Now we are here to hasten you to your mother's palace.

Pamina.

Well then, let us attempt it. And if he be a villain in Sarastro's employ?

(She looks attentively at him.)

Papageno.

I a villain? What are you thinking of? I am the best man on earth.

Pamina.

Dear friend, forgive me if I have offended you. You have a loving heart.

Papageno.

Ah, luckily I have a loving heart. But what is the good of it? I sometimes want to pluck out all my feathers when I remember that Papageno has no loving mate.

Pamina.

Poor man! So you have no wife?

Papageno.

Not even a fair maiden, the less a wife. And every one of us has his happy moments which he would like to spend in company.

Pamina.

Liebe?

(Freudig.)

Er liebt mich also? O sage mir das noch einmal, ich höre das Wort Liebe gar zu gern.

Papageno.

Das glaub' ich dir (ohne zu schwören), du bist ja ein Mädchen.—Wo blieb ich denn?

Pamina.

Bei der Liebe.

Papageno.

Richtig, bei der Liebe. (Das nenn' ich ein Gedächtnis haben.) Nun sind wir hier, in den Palast deiner Mutter zu eilen.

Pamina.

Wohl denn, es sei gewagt! Wenn dieser nun ein böser Geist von Sarastro's Gefolge wäre?

(Sie sieht ihn bedenklich an.)

Papageno.

Ich ein böser Geist? Wo denkst du hin. Ich bin der beste Geist von der Welt.

Pamina.

Freund, vergieb, vergieb, wenn ich dich beleidigte. Du hast ein gefühlvolles Herz.

Papageno.

Ach, freilich hab' ich ein gefühlvolles Herz. Aber was nützt mir das alles? Ich möchte mir oft alle meine Federn ausrupfen, wenn ich bedenke, dass Papageno noch keine Papageno hat.

Pamina.

Armer Mann! Du hast also noch kein Weib?

Papageno.

Noch nicht einmal ein Mädchen, veil weniger ein Weib! Und unsereiner hat doch auch bisweilen seine lustigen Stunden, wo man gern gesellschaftliche Unterhaltungen haben möchte.

Pamina.

    Patience, my friend; heaven will reward you. It will send you a companion before you know it.

Papageno.

    Would that it did it soon!

Pamina.

    Geduld, Freund! Der Himmel wird auch für dich sorgen; er wird dir eine Freundin schicken, ehe du dir's vermuthest.

Papageno.

    Wenn er sie nur bald schickte.

BEI MÄNNERN WELCHE LIEBE FÜHLEN—*THE MANLY HEART*

Duet (Pamina and Papageno)

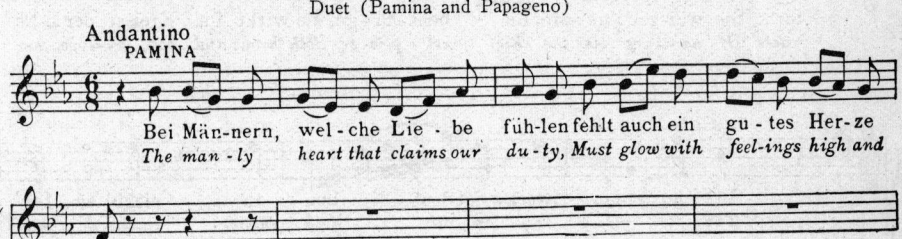

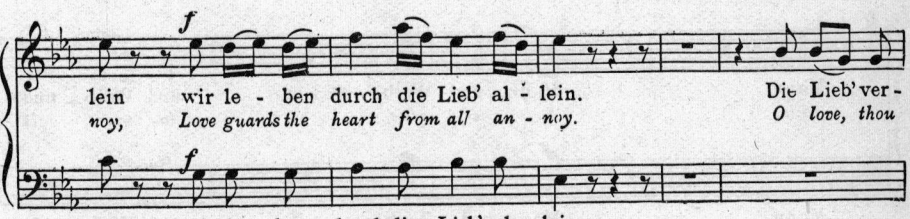

sü - sset je - de - Pla - ge, ihr o - pfert je - de - Kre - a -
art - of life - the flow - er, The world with - out - thee were - a -

PAPAGENO

tur. - Sie wür - zet un - sre Le - bens - ta - ge, sie wirkt im Krei - se der - Na -
wast? Of na - ture 'tis the chief est pow - er, Both throne and cot - by love - are

PAMINA

Ihr ho - her Zweck zeigt deut - lich an, nichts ed - ler
Thy glo - rious ray on all — doth shine, Burns in our

tur. Ihr ho - her Zweck zeigt deut - lich an, nichts ed - ler
graced. Thy glo - rious ray on all doth shine, Burns in our

sei als Weib — und Mann, nichts ed - ler — sei als — Weib und —
hearts with flame - di - vine, Burns in — our — hearts with flame di

sei als Weib und Mann, nichts ed - ler sei als Weib und
hearts with flame di - vine, Burns in our hearts with flame di

Mann. Mann — und Weib, und Weib — und
vine. Love — di - vine, to mor - tals

Mann, Mann und Weib, und Weib und
vine, Love di - vine, to mor - tals

Mann, Mann und Weib, und Weib und Mann rei-chen an die Gott-heit
giv'n, Love di-vine, to mor-tals giv'n, Fills our life with joys of

Mann, Mann und Weib, und Weib und Mann rei-chen an die Gott-heit
giv'n, Love di-vine, to mor-tals giv'n, Fills our life with joys of

an; Mann und Weib, und Weib und Mann rei-chen an die Gott-heit
heav'n; Love di-vine, to mor-tals giv'n, Fills our life with joys of

an; Mann und Weib, und Weib und Mann rei-chen an die Gott-heit
heav'n; Love di-vine, to mor-tals giv'n, Fills our life with joys of

an, die Gottheit an, die Gottheit an.
heav'n, with joys of heav'n, with joys of heav'n.

an, an, die Gott-heit an, an, die Gottheit an.
heav'n, yea, with joys of heav'n, yea, with joys of heav'n.

(Exeunt.)   (Beide durch die Mitten ab.)

CHANGE OF SCENE.

(Sacred grove in the middle of which are three temples.)

(The three youths with silver palm branches in their hands come out from the left accompanying TAMINO. His flute hangs at his side.)

The three Youths.

To the goal this path will lead,
But heroic you must be!
Therefore to our counsel heed
And you'll set the captive free.

VERWANDLUNG.

(Hain, in dessen Mitte drei Tempel.)

(Die drei KNABEN mit silbernen Palmzweigen in der Hand von links vorn kommend, geleiten TAMINO, der seine Flöte umgehängt trägt.)

Die drei Knaben.

Zum Ziele führt dich diese Bahn.
Doch musst du, Jüngling, männlich siegen.
Drum höre uns're Lehre an:
Sei standhaft, duldsam und verschwiegen.

Tamino.

Fair youths, an answer true I crave—
Think ye Pamina I can save?

The three Youths.

To make this known rests not with us,
Be steadfast, patient and discreet!
Think of our words and be a man,
And this will help you if aught can.
(They go out.)
(TAMINO alone, voices.)

Tamino.

The wisdom of these fair youths three,
May in my heart engraved be!
Where am I now? Where did I roam?
Is this perhaps of gods the home?
The portals and the gates impart,
It is the home of work and art,
Where industry full sway obtains,
Vice no more can hold the reins.
(He points to the right.)
I'll boldly enter the temple door,
My purpose is noble and good and pure.
Tremble, villain bold. Beware!
To save Pamina is my care!
(He approaches the temple door at the right.)

Voices
(chorus).
Back!

Tamino.

Back? Here must I try my luck.
(He goes to the temple door at the left.)

Voices.

Back!

Tamino.

Here too they call: back!
(He goes to the middle temple door.)
There I see another door,
Perhaps I'll find one entrance more.
(While he goes to the middle door it opens and a priest
with white hair and beard comes out.)

Priest.

Where are you going, daring youth?
What in this sanctuary do you seek?

Tamino.

The home of virtue and of love.

Tamino.

Ihr holden Kleinen, sagt mir an,
Ob ich Pamina retten kann?

Die drei Knaben.

Dies kund zu thun, steht uns nicht an;
Sei standhaft, duldsam und verschwiegen.
Bedenke dies; kurz, sei ein Mann,
Dann, Jüngling, wirst du männlich siegen.
(Sie gehen ab.)
(TAMINO allein. STIMMEN.)

Tamino.

Die Weisheitslehre dieser Knaben
Sei ewig mir ins Herz gegraben.
Wo bin ich nun? Was wird mit mir?
Ist dies der Sitz der Götter hier?
Es zeigen die Pforten, es zeigen die Säulen,
Dass Klugheit und Arbeit und Künste hier
    weilen;
Wo Thätigkeit thronet und Mässiggang
    weicht,
Erhält seine Herrschaft das Laster nicht
    leicht.
(Er zeigt nach rechts.)
Ich wage mich muthig zur Pforte hinein,
Die Absicht ist edel und lauter und rein.
Erzitt're, feiger Bösewicht!
Pamina retten ist mir Pflicht.
(Er nähert sich mit einigen Schritten der Tempelpforte
rechts.)

Stimmen
(Chor).
Zurück!

Tamino.

Zurück? So wag ich hier mein Glück!
(Er wendet sich nach der Tempelpforte links.)

Stimmen
(Chor).
Zurück!

Tamino.

Auch hier ruft man; zurück?
(Er wendet sich nach der Tempelpforte in der Mitte.)
Da sehe ich eine Thür,
Vielleicht find' ich den Eingang hier.
(Indem er sich der Mittelpforte nähert, öffnet sich diese
und ein PRIESTER in weissem Haar und Bart tritt heraus.)

Priester.

Wo willst du, kühner Fremdling hin?
Was sucht du hier im Heiligthum?

Tamino.

Der Lieb' und Tugend Eigenthum.

Priest.

Thy words are certainly high sounding,
But where do you expect to find these?
Love and courage do not guide you,
Death and vengeance dire inflame you.

Tamino.

Only for vengeance on the villain.

Priest.

You surely will not find him here.

Tamino.

Does Sarastro govern here?

Priest.

Yes, Sarastro governs here.

Tamino.

But in the Temple of Wisdom?

Priest.

Yes, in the Temple of Wisdom.

Tamino   (stepping to the left).

Then all is but hypocrisy.

Priest.

Wilt thou depart again, then?

Tamino.

Yes, I will gladly go from here,
And never again your temple see.

Priest.

Explain yourself to me: a mistake deludes
      you.

Tamino.

Sarastro governs here,
That is enough for me.

Priest.

If your life you prize,
Speak, and here remain!
Do you hate Sarastro?

Tamino.

I hate him, yes; and ever shall.

Priest.

And pray, what are your reasons?

Tamino.

He is a tyrant and a brute.

Priest.

Where is the proof of what you say?

Tamino.

By a luckless woman 'tis confessed,
Who by great sorrow is oppressed.

Priester.

Die Worte sind von hohem Sinn!
Allein wie willst du diese finden?
Dich leitet Lieb' und Tugend nicht,
Weil Tod und Rache dich entzünden.

Tamino.

Nur Rache für den Bösewicht.

Priester.

Den wirst du wohl bei uns nicht finden.

Tamino.

Sarastro herrscht in diesen Gründen?

Priester.

Ja, ja! Sarastro herrschet hier!

Tamino.

Doch in dem Weisheitstempel nicht?

Priester.

Er herrscht im Weisheitstempel hier.

Tamino   (mit einigen Schritten nach links).

So ist denn alles Heuchelei!

Priester.

Willst du schon wieder gehn?

Tamino.

Ja, ich will gehn, froh und frei,
Nie euren Tempel sehn.

Priester.

Erklär' dich näher mir,
Dich täuschet ein Betrug.

Tamino.

Sarastro wohnet hier,
Das ist mir schon genug.

Priester.

Wenn du dein Leben liebst,
So rede, bleibe da!
Sarastro hassest du?

Tamino.

Ich hass' ihn ewig! Ja!

Priester.

Nur gieb mir deine Gründe an.

Tamino.

Er ist ein Unmensch, ein Tyrann.

Priester.

Ist das, was du gesagt, erwiesen?

Tamino.

Durch ein unglücklich' Weib bewiesen,
Das Gram und Jammer niederdrückt.

Priest.

   'Tis then a woman who beguiled you?
   Women do little and talk much.
   Do you give heed to empty talk?
   But still Sarastro has explained
   The motives of his actions.

Tamino.

   His motives are, alas! too clear,
   Did not the robber without pity
   Tear Pamina from her mother's arms?

Priest.

   Yes, youth, all you say is true.

Tamino.

   Where is she whom he stole away?
   Perhaps by this time sacrificed?

Priest.

   To tell you this, dear friend,
   Is not yet permitted.

Tamino.

   Explain this riddle—do not deceive me.

Priest.

   My tongue is bound by oath and duty.

Tamino.

   When then will it be released?

Priest.

   As soon as friendship's hand shall lead you
   Into the sanctuary of immortal union.

(He turns around and goes out slowly through the middle door.)

       (TAMINO alone, voices.)

Tamino.

   Oh, endless night, how soon wilt thou have
     vanished?
   When will the daylight greet my sight?

Voices

     (chorus behind the middle door).
   Soon, youth, or never!

Tamino.

   Soon, say you, or never?
   Tell me, invisible ones,
   Does Pamina still live?

Voices.

   Pamina still lives!

Tamino

     (rejoicing).
   She lives? I thank you all for that.
   (He takes his flute in his hand.)

Priester.

   Ein Weib hat also dich berückt?
   Ein Weib thut wenig, plaudert viel.
   Du, Jüngling, glaubst dem Zungenspiel?
   O legte doch Sarastro klar
   Die Absicht seiner Handlung dar.

Tamino.

   Die Absicht ist nur allzuklar;
   Riss nicht der Räuber ohn' Erbarmen
   Pamina aus der Mutter Armen?

Priester.

   Ja, Jüngling! Was du sagst, ist wahr.

Tamino.

   Wo ist sie, die er uns geraubt?
   Man opferte vielleicht sie schon?

Priester.

   Dir dies zu sagen, theurer Sohn,
   Ist jetzt und mir noch nicht erlaubt.

Tamino.

   Erklär' dies Räthsel, täusch' mich nicht.

Priester.

   Die Zunge bindet Eid und Pflicht.

Tamino.

   Wann also wird die Decke Schwinden?

Priester.

   Sobald dich führt der Freundschaft Hand
   Ins Heiligthum zum ew'gen Band.

(Er wendet sich und geht langsam durch die Mittelpforte ab.)

       (TAMINO allein. STIMMEN.)

Tamino.

   O ewige Nacht! wann wirst du schwinden!
   Wann wird das Licht mein Auge finden?

Stimmen

     (Chor hinter der Mittelpforte).
   Bald, Jüngling, oder nie!

Tamino.

   Bald, sagt ihr, oder nie?
   Ihr Unsichtbaren, sagt mir,
   Lebt denn Pamina noch?

Stimmen

     (Chor).
   Pamina lebet noch!

Tamino

     (freudig).
   Sie lebt? Ich danke euch dafür.
   (Er nimmt seine Flöte zur Hand.)

Oh, if I only had the power,
Almighty ones, in praise of you,
My thanks with each tone to express,
To show the feelings in my heart!
(Points to his heart.)
(He plays on his flute. Instantly wild animals and birds of every kind appear. He stops and they flee.)

Wenn ich doch nur imstande wäre,
Allmächtige, zu euer Ehre,
Mit jedem Tone meinen Dank
Zu schildern, wie or hier
(aufs Herz zeigend)
Entsprang!
(Er spielt auf seiner Flöte.)
(Sogleich erscheinen wilde Thiere und Vögel aller Art. Er hört auf und sie fliehen.)

WIE STARK IST NICHT DEIN ZAUBERTON—*THY MAGIC TONES SHALL SPEAK FOR ME* Air (Tamino)

(He plays.)
Pamina! hear, oh hear me!
In vain!
(He plays.)
Where?
Oh, where can I find you?
(PAPAGENO answers with his fawn-flute.)

(Er spielt.)
Pamina! höre, höre mich!
Umsonst!
(Er spielt.)
Wo? Ach, wo find' ich dich?
(PAPAGENO antwortet von links hinten mit seinem Faunenflötchen.)

Tamino.

Ah, that is Papageno's tone!
(He plays.)
(PAPAGENO answers as before.)
Perhaps he has already seen Pamina,
Perhaps with him she comes to me,
Perhaps these tones will lead me to her.
(He goes out.)
(PAPAGENO and PAMINA appear when TAMINO has disappeared. They wear no chains.)

Pamina and Papageno.

Nimble feet and dauntless courage
May save us from the foe's dread rage.
Could we but Tamino find!
Now, they surely will surprise us.

Pamina
(takes a few steps back, calling).
Handsome youth!

Papageno.

Be still, I'll do it better.
(He whistles.)
(TAMINO answers with his flute from behind.)

Both.

Can there be a greater joy?
Friend Tamino hears us now.
(Pointing to the left.)
From here came the sweet tones.
O what joy when I shall find him!
Quick, quick, let us hasten to him!
(They run to the left. MONOSTATOS meets them.)

Monostatos
(mocking her.)
Quick, quick, let us hasten to him!
Ha, ha, I have caught you then?
Quickly, bind these daring ones!
Wait, I'll teach you manners!
You will ne'er again deceive me!
Hither, slaves, come here and bind them!
Take your ropes and bind them fast.
(Slaves come up with chains.)

Pamina and Papageno.

Ah, it is all over with us!

Papageno.

Who ventures much, much ofttimes wins.
Come, magic set of bells,
Let your soft tones fill the air
And resound in every ear!
(He plays.)

Tamino

Ha, das ist Papagenos Ton!
(Er spielt.)
(PAPAGENO antwortet wie vorher.)
Vielleicht sah er Pamina schon,
Vielleicht eilt sie mit ihm zu mir,
Vielleicht führt mich der Ton zu ihr.
(Er eilt nach links hinten ab.)
(PAPAGENO und PAMINA eilen, wenn TAMINO verschwunden ist, ohne Fesseln von links vorn herbei.)

Pamina und Papageno.

Schnelle Füsse, rascher Muth,
Schützt vor Feindes List und Wuth,
Fänden wir Tamino doch,
Sonst erwischen sie uns noch.

Pamina
(mit einigen Schritten nach hinten rufend.)
Holder Jüngling!

Papageno.

Stille, stille, ich kann's besser.
(Er pfeift.)
(TAMINO antwortet links hinten mit seiner Flöte.)

Beide.

Welche Freude ist wohl grösser?
Freund Tamino hört uns schon;
(nach links hinten zeigend.)
Hierher kam der Flötenton.
Welch ein Glück, wenn ich ihn finde,
Nur geschwinde! nur geschwinde!
(Sie wollen nach links hinten davon eilen.)
(MONOSTATOS tritt ihnen von dort her entgegen.)

Monostatos
(ihrer spottend.)
Nur geschwinde! nur geschwinde!
Ha, hab' ich euch noch erwischt?
Nur herbei mit Stahl und Eisen;
Wart, ich will euch Mores weisen.
Den Monostatos berücken!
(Nach links hinten rufend.)
Nur herbei mit Band und Stricken,
He, ihr Sklaven, kommt herbei!
(Sklaven kommen von links hinten mit Fesseln.)

Pamina, Papageno.

Ach, nun ist's mit uns vorbei!

Papageno.

Wer viel wagt, gewinnt oft viel,
Komm' du schönes Glockenspiel!
Lass' die Glöckchen klingen, klingen,
Dass die Ohren ihnen singen.
(Er spielt sein Glockenspiel.)

Monostatos and the Slaves
(they are subdued by the sound, sing and dance in time).

Its sound is so soothing, its sound is so
sweet,

Tralala, lalala, tralalalala!

Oh, never, oh, never did I its equal meet!

Tralalala, trala, lalala!
(They withdraw singing and dancing.)

Papageno and Pamina.

If but every one could own
Bells of such melodious tone,
All our enemies would flee
And we all would happy be.
Without them each one can live
In the greatest harmony.
Only friendship's harmony
Softens every malady.
And without its sympathy,
No happiness on earth can be.
(There is heard a loud march with trumpets and kettle-drums.)

Voices
(from without).

Long live Sarastro! Long live Sarastro!

Papageno
(with a few steps to the right).

What can this mean? I tremble, I shudder!

Pamina
(following him).

O friend, we are lost forever!
The great Sarastro is announced.

Papageno.

O were I but a little mouse,
In some dark corner I would hide.
And were I as a snail,
I'd creep into my little house,
My child, what words will now avail?

Pamina.

Let's speak the truth, at any cost.
(Enter SARASTRO and his suite. The priest goes through the middle door to the left, the soldiers and the people to the right; the women behind the chariot of SARASTRO at the right. The slaves at the right and left. SARASTRO is borne in on an elephant.)

Chorus.

Long live Sarastro, long live Sarastro!
'Tis he to whom we are all so devoted.
May he as a wise man enjoy life forever.
Our idol is he whom we worship and love!

Monostatos und die Sklaven
(davon besänftigt, singen und tanzen nach dem Takt).

Das klinget so herrlich, das klinget so schön!

Tralla lalala trallalalala!

Nie hab' ich so etwas gehört und gesehn!

Trallalala tralla lalala!
(Sie entfernen sich singend und tanzend nach links hinten.)

Papageno and Pamina.

Könnte jeder brave Mann
Solche Glöckchen finden,
Seine Feinde würden dann
Ohne Mühe schwinden,
Und er lebte ohne sie
In der besten Harmonie.
Nur der Freundschaft Harmonie
Mildert die Beschwerden;
Ohne diese Sympathie
Ist kein Glück auf Erden!
(Ein starker Marsch mit Trompeten und Pauken fällt ein.)

Stimmen
(Chor von aussen).

Es lebe Sarastro! Sarastro lebe!

Papageno
(mit einigen Schritten nach rechts).

Was soll das bedeuten? Ich zittre, ich bebe!

Pamina
(ihm folgend).

O Freund, nun ist's um uns gethan!
Dies kündigt den Sarastro an.

Papageno.

O wär' ich eine Maus,
Wie wollt ich mich verstecken!
Wär' ich so klein wie Schnecken,
So kröch ich in mein Haus.
Mein Kind, was werden wir nun sprechen?

Pamina.

Die Wahrheit, sei sie auch Verbrechen.
(SARASTRO und GEFOLGE treten ein. Die PRIESTER durch die Mittelpforte und von links ganz vorn; die Bewaffneten und das Volk von rechts; die Frauen hinter dem Wagen des SARASTRO von rechts; die Sklaven von rechts und links.)
(SARASTRO zuletzt von rechts auf einem Elefanten.)

Chor.

Es lebe Sarastro! Sarastro soll leben!
Er ist es, dem wir uns mit Freuden ergeben
Stets mög' er des Lebens als Weiser sich
freun,
Er ist unser Abgott, dem alle sich weihn

Pamina
(kneels).

O Lord, 'tis true that I am guilty,
That I from your power wished to flee.
The guilt rests not only on me—
The wicked Moor desired my love,
Therefore, O sire, I fled from thee.

Sarastro.

Arise, my love, and happy be,
For without further questioning thee,
I know the secret of thy heart.
For thou already lov'st another.
To love I never will compel thee,
And yet I cannot give you freedom.

Pamina.

My filial duty calls me,
For my mother—

Sarastro.

Is in my power.
Your happiness would all be ended
Were I to give you up to her.

Pamina.

The name of mother sounds so sweet,
'Tis she. . . .

Sarastro.

A haughty woman,
Only a man should guide your hearts.
Without him, woman is accustomed
To wend her way out of her sphere.
(MONOSTATOS and TAMINO come from the left.)

Monostatos.

Proud youth, come hither, here you see
Sarastro, our dear lord.

Pamina.

'Tis he!

Tamino.

'Tis she!

Pamina.

I scarcely can believe it.

Tamino.

'Tis she!

Pamina.

'Tis he!

Tamino.

'Tis no dream.
(They approach each other.)

Pamina
(kniet).

Herr, ich bin zwar Verbrecherin!
Ich wöllte deiner Macht entfliehn,
Allein die Schuld ist nicht an mir—
Der böse Mohr verlangte Liebe;
Darum, O Herr! entfloh ich dir.

Sarastro.

Steh' auf, erheitere dich, O Liebe!
Denn ohne erst in dich zu dringen,
Weiss ich von deinem Herzen mehr:
Du liebest einen andern sehr.
Zur Liebe will ich dich nicht zwingen,
Doch gib' ich dir die Freiheit nicht.

Pamina.

Mich rufet ja die Kindespflicht,
Denn meine Mutter--

Sarastro.

Steht in meiner Macht.
Du würdest um dein Glück gebracht,
Wenn ich dich ihren Händen liesse.

Pamina.

Mir klingt der Muttername süsse;
Sie ist es—

Sarastro.

Und ein stolzes Weib.
Ein Mann muss eure Herzen leiten,
Denn ohne ihn pflegt jedes Weib
Aus seinem Wirkungskreis zu schreiten
(MONOSTATOS mit TAMINO von links.)

Monostatos.

Nun, stolzer Jüngling, nur hierher,
Hier ist Sarastro, unser Herr.

Pamina.

Er ist's!

Tamino.

Sie ist's!

Pamina.

Ich glaub' es kaum!

Tamino.

Sie ist's!

Pamina.

Er ist's!

Tamino.

Es ist kein Traum!
(Sie nähern sich beiderseitig.

Pamina.

Oh, I would embrace him!

Tamino.

Oh, I would embrace her!

Both.

Even if it brought death upon me.
(They embrace.)

All.

What does that mean?

Monostatos.

What hardihood!
(He steps between PAMINA and TAMINO, and separates them.)

Stop it at once. You go too far!
(He kneels to SARASTRO.)

Thy slave is kneeling at thy feet,
Make the presumptuous youth do penance.
How impudent the bold youth is!
By the tricks of this rare bird
(Pointing at PAPAGENO.)

He sought to rob thee of Pamina.
But I alone 'twas who could track him.
You know me and my vigilance—

Sarastro
(beckons).

Deserves the laurel wreath.
Here! Give to this gentleman at once—

Monostatos.

Alone your favor makes me rich.

Sarastro.

But seventy-seven bastinado stripes.

Monostatos.

Ah, sir, I did not merit such reward!

Sarastro.

Preserve your thanks, 'tis but my duty.
(MONOSTATOS is led away by slaves.)

All.

Long live Sarastro, the sage divine!
He justly punishes and rewards.

Sarastro.

Lead these two strangers
To our temple of probation.
Cover their heads,
For they must first be purified.
(Two priests go out and come back with veils and cover the heads of TAMINO and PAPAGENO.)

Pamina.

Es schling' mein Arm sich um ihn her!

Tamino.

Es schling' mein Arm sich um sie her!

Beide.

Und wenn es auch mein Ende wär'!
(Sie umarmen sich.)

Alle.

Was soll das heissen?

Monostatos.

Welch' eine Dreistigkeit!
(Indem er zwischen PAMINA und TAMINO tritt und sie trennt.)

Gleich auseinander, das geht zu weit!
(Er kniet vor SARASTRO.)

Dein Sklave liegt zu deinen Füssen,
Lass den vermess'nen Frevler büssen!
Bedenk', wie frech der Knabe ist:
Durch dieses selt'nen Vogels List
(auf PAPAGENO zeigend)

Wollt' er Pamina dir entführen.
Allein ich wusst ihn auszuspüren!
Du kennst mich! Meine Wachsamkeit—

Sarastro
(winkt).

Verdient, dass man ihr Lorbeer streut.
He! Gebt dem Ehrenmann sogleich—

Monostatos.

Schon deine Gnade macht mich reich.

Sarastro.

Nur siebenundsiebzig Sohlenstreich'.

Monostatos.

Ach Herr, den Lohn verhofft' ich nicht!

Sarastro.

Nicht Dank', es ist ja meine Pflicht!
(MONOSTATOS wird von einigen Sklaven, die vortreten, nach rechts abgeführt.)

Alle.

Es lebe Sarastro, der göttliche Weise!
Er lohnet und strafet in ähnlichem Kreise.

Sarastro.

Führt diese beiden Fremdlinge
In unsere Prüfungstempel ein;
Bedecket ihre Häupter dann,
Sie müssen erst gereinigt sein.
(Zwei Priester gehen ab, kommen zurück mit Schleiern und bedecken damit die Häupter von TAMINO und PAPAGENO.)

Chorus.

When virtue joined to justice
Strews the path with fame,
Then earth a heaven is indeed,
And mortal men are like to gods!

(SARASTRO takes PAMINA'S hand and goes with her to the middle door.)

(TAMINO and PAPAGENO go out with the two priests. The priests, soldiers, women, populace, slaves turn toward the background.)

(Curtain.)

ACT II.

(A Subterranean Temple.)

(The priests come in from the right and left, walk to the front and meet in the center. They shake hands, cross themselves, pass each other, go to the right and left. SARASTRO appears and takes his place in the middle. In front of him the two SPEAKERS; to his right and left the priests.)

Sarastro

(after a pause).

You, in the Temple of Wisdom ordained servants of the great gods, Osiris and Isis! With a pure heart I declare to you that our meeting of to-day is the most important of our time. Tamino, the son of a king waits before the north door of our temple. To protect this virtuous youth, to extend a friendly greeting to him, is to-day one of our most urgent duties. If you hold him worthy then follow my example.

(SARASTRO and the priests blow once into the horns.)

Sarastro.

Moved by the unanimity of your hearts, Sarastro thanks you in the name of humanity. Let Tamino and his companion be led to the vestibule of our temple.

(To the SPEAKER who kneels before him.)

And you, friend, fulfill your holy office, and teach them to recognize the power of the gods.

(The priests form a semi-circle around SARASTRO.)

Schlusschor.

Wenn Tugend und Gerechtigkeit
Den grossen Pfad mit Ruhm bestreut,
Dann ist die Erd' ein Himmelreich,
Und Sterbliche den Göttern gleich.

Sarastro

(reicht PAMINA die Hand und geht mit ihr zur Mittelpforte).

(TAMINO, PAPAGENO wenden sich an der Hand der beider Priester nach rechts.)

(Die Priester, die Bewaffneten, die Frauen, das Volk, die Sklaven wenden sich dem Hintergrunde zu.)

(Der Vorhang fällt.)

ZWEITER AUFZUG.

(Unterirdischer Tempel.)

(Die PRIESTER treten von rechts und links ein, schreiten nach vorn, begegnen sich in der Mitte; reichen sich die Hand, kreuzen sich, gehen nach rechts und links. SARASTRO erscheint zuletzt und nimmt die Mitte; vor ihm die beiden SPRECHER, zu seiner Rechten und Linken die PRIESTER.)

Sarastro

(nach einer Pause).

Ihr, in dem Weisheitstempel eingeweihten Diener der grossen Götter Osiris und Isis! Mit reiner Seele erklär' ich euch, dass unsere heutige Versammlung eine der wichtigsten unserer Zeit ist. Tamino, ein Königssohn, wandelt an der nördlichen Pforte unseres Tempels. Diesen Tugendhaften zu bewachen, ihm freundschaftlich die Hand zu bieten sei heute eine unserer wichtigsten Pflichten. Haltet ihr ihn für würdig, so folgt meinem Beispiel.

(SARASTRO und die PRIESTER blasen dreimal in die Hörner.)

Sarastro.

Gerührt über die Einigkeit Eurer Herzen, dankt Sarastro euch im Namen der Menschheit. Man führe Tamino mit seinem Reisegefährten im Vorhof des Tempels ein.

(Zum SPRECHER, der vor ihm niederkniet.)

Und du, Freund, vollziehe dein heiliges Amt und lehre sie die Macht der Götter erkennen

(Die PRIESTER bilden um SARASTRO einen Halbkreis.)

O ISIS UND OSIRIS—*O ISIS AND OSIRIS* Air and Chorus (Sarastro and Priests)

(SARASTRO and the priests depart in solemn procession.) | (SARASTRO und die PRIESTER entfernen sich in feierlicher Weise.)

(Tamino, Speaker, Papageno, Second Priest.)

Speaker.

Stranger, what do you seek or ask from us?

Tamino.

Friendship and love.

Speaker.

And are you prepared e'en if it cost you your life?

Tamino.

I am.

Speaker.

Give me your hand!

(They shake hands.)

So!

Second Priest (to Papageno).

Will you, too, struggle for the love of wisdom?

Papageno.

Fighting is not my business. I am a son of nature, content with sleep, food, and drink, and were it only possible, I should like to find a pretty little wife.

Second Priest.

But you will ne'er obtain one, if you do not submit to our probation.

Papageno.

Of what does it consist?

Second Priest.

To follow all our laws, and not to shrink from death.

Papageno.

I'll remain single.

Second Priest.

But if Sarastro has reserved for you a pretty maid who in dress and color is just like you?

Papageno.

Just like me? Is she young?

Second Priest.

Young and beautiful.

Papageno.

And her name?

Tamino rechts vorn, Sprecher zu seiner Linken, Papageno links vorn. Zweiter Priester zu seiner Rechten.)

Sprecher.

Ihr Fremdlinge! was sucht oder fordert ihr von uns?

Tamino.

Freundschaft und Liebe.

Sprecher.

Bist du bereit, es mit deinem Leben zu erkämpfen?

Tamino.

Ja.

Sprecher.

Reiche mir deine Hand!

(Sie reichen sich die Hände.)

So!

Zweiter Priester (zu Papageno).

Willst auch du dir Weisheitsliebe erkämpfen?

Papageno.

Kämpfen ist meine Sache nicht. Ich bin so ein Naturmensch, der sich mit Schlaf, Speis' und Trank begnügt; und wenn es ja sein könnte, dass ich nur einmal ein schönes Weibchen fänge.

Zweiter Priester.

Die wirst du nie erhalten, wenn du dich nicht unseren Prüfungen unterziehst.

Papageno.

Worin besteht diese Prüfung?

Zweiter Priester.

Dich allen unseren Gesetzen zu unterwerfen, selbst den Tod nicht zu scheuen.

Papageno.

Ich bleibe ledig.

Zweiter Priester.

Wenn nun aber Sarastro dir ein Mädchen aufbewahrt hätte, das an Farbe und Kleidung dir ganz gleich wäre?

Papageno.

Mir gleich? Ist sie jung?

Zweiter Priester.

Jung und schön.

Papageno.

Und heisst?

Second Priest.

Papagena.

Papageno.

What?—Pa—?

Second Priest.

Papagena.

Papageno.

Papagena? I'd like to see her out of mere
curiosity.

Second Priest.

You can see her.

Papageno.

And when I shall have seen her, must I
die?

(SECOND PRIEST makes a sign of doubt.)

Papageno.

If so, then single I remain.

Second Priest.

You can see her, but till the appointed hour
you must not speak to her.

Speaker

(to TAMINO.)

And on you too, prince, the gods impose a
holy silence. You shall see Pamina, but
must not speak to her. The time of your
probation now commences.

Speaker and Priest.

Beware of woman's treachery,
'Tis the first duty to observe,
Many a wise man was ensnared.
He failed, and then was led astray.
He saw himself at last forsaken,
His faithfulness was met with scorn.
Alas, he wrung his hands in vain,
For his reward was death and pain.

(Both Priests leave. It grows dark.)

Papageno.

Here, let us have light! Light!

Tamino.

Come, hear it patiently, it is the will of
God!

(The three LADIES rush in with torches. It grows lighter.)

The three Ladies.

What? what? what?
You are in this place of terror?

Zweiter Priester.

Papagena.

Papageno.

Wie—Pa—?

Zweiter Priester.

Papagena.

Papageno.

Papagena? Die möchte ich aus blosser
Neugierde sehen.

Zweiter Priester.

Sehen kannst du sie!

Papageno.

Aber wenn ich sie gesehen habe, hernach
muss ich sterben?

(ZWEITER PRIESTER macht eine zweifelnde Bewegung.)

Papageno.

Ja?—Ich bleibe ledig.

Zweiter Priester.

Sehen kannst du sie, aber bis zur verlaufenen
Zeit kein Wort mit ihr sprechen.

Sprecher

(zu TAMINO.)

Auch dir, Prinz, legen die Götter ein heil-
sames Stillschweigen auf. Du wirst
Pamina sehen, aber nicht sie sprechen
dürfen; dies ist der Anfang eurer
Prüfungszeit.

Sprecher und Priester.

Bewahret euch vor Weibertücken:
Dies ist des Bundes erste Pflicht!
Manch' weiser Mann liess sich berücken,
Er fehlte und versah sich's nicht.
Verlassen sah er sich am Ende,
Vergolten seine Treu mit Hohn!
Vergebens rang er seine Hände,
Tod und Verzweiflung war sein Lohn.

(Beide PRIESTER ab nach rechts. Es wird dunkel.)

Papageno.

He! Lichter her! Lichter her!

Tamino.

Ertrag' es mit Geduld und denke, es ist der
Götter Wille.

(Die drei DAMEN eilen mit Fackeln von links herbei.)
(Es wird heller.)

Die drei Damen.

Wie? Wie? Wie?
Ihr an diesem Schreckensort?

Never! never! never!
Will you come out safe from here.
Tamino, you are sworn to death!
Papageno, you are lost!

Papageno.

No, no, no, that is too much!

Tamino.

Papageno, pray be still!
Do you want to break your oath
Never here to speak to women?

Papageno.

You hear, we both are lost!

Tamino.

Still! I tell you, pray be still!

Papageno.

All you say is "still, still, still"!

The three Ladies.

The Queen is very near you.
She stole secretly into the temple.

Papageno.

What? How? She is in the temple?

Tamino.

Silence, I tell you, silence!
Will you ever be so bold
And forget what you have sworn?

The three Ladies.

Tamino, listen! You are lost!
Think of the wretched Queen.
Much is whispered in these realms
Of the priests' false nature.

Tamino

(aside.)

A wise man heedeth not
What by the vulgar crowd is said.

The three Ladies.

They say who to their union swears
Is doomed for all his life!

Papageno.

One would not e'en expect it of the devil!
Tell me, Tamino, is it true?

Tamino.

But idle talk, that women have repeated
And that bigots have invented!

Papageno.

Still our Queen has said it too.

Nie, nie, nie,
Kommt ihr wieder glücklich fort!
Tamino, dir ist Tod geschworen!
Du, Papageno, bist verloren!

Papageno.

Nein, nein, nein! Das wär' zu viel.

Tamino.

Papageno, schweig still!
Willst du dein Gelübde brechen,
Nichts mit Weibern hier zu sprechen?

Papageno.

Du hörst ja, wir sind beide hin.

Tamino.

Stille, sag' ich! schweige still!

Papageno.

Immer still und immer still!

Die drei Damen.

Ganz nah' ist euch die Königin!
Sie drang im Tempel heimlich ein.

Papageno.

Wie? Was? Sie soll im Tempel sein?

Tamino.

Stille, sag' ich! schweige still!
Wirst du immer so vermessen
Deiner Eidespflicht vergessen?

Die drei Damen.

Tamino, hör'! Du bist verloren!
Gedenke an die Königin!
Man zischelt viel sich in die Ohren
Von dieser Priester falschem Sinn.

Tamino

(für sich.)

Ein Weiser prüft und achtet nicht,
Was der gemeine Pöbel spricht.

Die drei Damen.

Man sagt, wer ihrem Bunde schwört,
Der ist verwünscht mit Haut und Haar

Papageno.

Das wär' beim Teufel unerhört!
Sag' an, Tamino, ist das wahr?

Tamino.

Geschwätz, von Weibern nachgesagt,
Von Heuchlern aber ausgedacht.

Papageno.

Doch sagt es auch die Königin.

Tamino.

    She is a woman, has but woman's sense,
    Be silent, let my word suffice.
    Think of your duty and be prudent!

The three Ladies
              (to TAMINO).
    Why are you so shy with us?
    (TAMINO intimates to them that he must not speak.)

The three Ladies.
    And Papageno too is silent—speak!

Papageno
            (secretly to the LADIES).
    I'd like to, but—

Tamino.
    Be still!

Papageno
            (aside).
    You see I must not.

Tamino.
    Still!
    That you cannot leave off talking
    Is really a disgrace!

Papageno.
    That I cannot leave off talking
    Is really a disgrace!

The three Ladies.
    We must leave you now with shame,
    No one speaks with surety,
    He is a man with judgment sound,
    Who's not afraid to speak his mind.

Tamino, Papageno.
    They must leave us now with shame,
    No one speaks with surety;
    He is a man with judgment sound
    Who's not afraid to speak his mind.
    (The three LADIES are about to go.)

Chorus of Priests
            (from without).
    The sacred threshold is defiled!
    Away, away with women!
              (Thunder.)

The three Ladies
            (rush out in despair).
    O woe, O woe, O woe!

Papageno
            (falls down in fright).
    O woe, O woe, O woe!
    (The three YOUTHS come in. One carries the flute, the other the bells.)

Tamino.

    Sie ist ein Weib, hat Weibersinn,
    Sei still, mein Wort sei dir genug,
    Denk' deiner Pflicht und handle klug.

Die drei Damen
            (zu TAMINO.)
    Warum bist du mit uns so spröde?
    (TAMINO deutet bescheiden an, dass er nicht sprechen darf.)

Die drei Damen.
    Auch Papageno schweigt—so rede!

Papageno
            (heimlich zu den DAMEN.)
    Ich möchte gern—wohl—

Tamino.
    Still!

Papageno
            (heimlich.)
    Ihr seht, dass ich nicht soll.—

Tamino.
    Still!
    Dass du nicht kannst das Plaudern lassen,
    Ist wahrlich eine Schand für dich!

Papageno.
    Dass ich nicht kann das Plaudern lassen,
    Ist wahrlich eine Schand' für mich!

Die drei Damen.
    Wir müssen sie mit Scham verlassen,
    Es plaudert keiner sicherlich;
    Von festem Geiste ist ein Mann,
    Er denket, was er sprechen kann.

Tamino, Papageno.
    Sie müssen uns mit Scham verlassen,
    Es plaudert keiner sicherlich;
    Vom festen Geiste ist ein Mann,
    Er denket, was er sprechen kann.
    (Die drei DAMEN wollen sich nach links entfernen.)

Chor der Priester
            (von aussen.)
    Entweiht ist die heilige Schwelle!
    Hinab mit den Weibern zur Hölle!
             (Donner.)

Die drei Damen
            (stürzen entsetzt nach links hinaus.)
    O weh! o weh! o weh!

Papageno
            (fällt vor Schrecken zu Boden.)
    O weh! o weh! o weh!
    (Die drei KNABEN kommen von links; der eine trägt die Flöte, andere das Glockenspiel.)

The three Youths.

> A second time be you here welcome,
> Dear friends, in Sarastro's kingdom.
> He sends you what he's taken from you,
> Your mellow flute and bells.
> (A golden table covered with food and drink appears.)
>
> If you do not scorn our table,
> Drink and eat freely from it.
> When a third time we shall meet,
> You'll be with happiness rewarded.
> Tamino, courage, near is your goal,
> And, Papageno, you be still!
> (They present the flute to TAMINO, the bells to PAPAGENO; exit.)

Papageno.

> Tamino, shall we eat?
>   (TAMINO plays his flute.)

Papageno.

> You blow on your flute and I will eat.
>
>   (He goes to the table and eats.)
> Sir Sarastro has a fine kitchen! Now I shall
> see if his cellar is just as good.
>
>   (He fills his glass and drinks.)
> Ha, this is nectar!
>   (TAMINO stops playing his flute.)
>   (PAMINA rushes in from the left.)
> (TAMINO, PAMINA, PAPAGENO eating and drinking at the table in the middle.)

Pamina

>   (happily).
> Are you here? Good gods, I thank you!
> But you are sad. Won't you even say a
> word to your Pamina? Papageno, tell
> me what is the trouble with my friend.

Papageno

> (motions to her, with full mouth, to go away).
> Hm, hm, hm.

Pamina.

> What? you too? That is worse than death.
> Oh, I feel that all has vanished,
> The happiness of love has flown
> From my heart; forever banished
> Are the blissful hours I've known.
> These my tears Tamino see,
> Love, they flow alone for thee,

Die drei Knaben.

> Seid uns zum zweitenmal willkommen,
> Ihr Männer in Sarastros Reich.
> Er schickt, was man euch abgenommen,
> Die Flöte und die Glöckchen euch.
> (Ein goldener, mit Speisen und Getränken reich versehener Tisch kommt von rechts.)
>
> Wollt ihr die Speisen nicht verschmähen,
> So esset, trinket froh davon.
> Wenn wir zum drittenmal uns sehen,
> Ist Freude eures Muthes Lohn!
> Tamino, Muth! nah' ist das Ziel.
> Du, Papageno, schweige still!
> (Während des Terzetts überreichen sie TAMINO die Flöte, PAPAGENO das Glockenspiel und entfernen sich dann nach links.)

Papageno.

> Tamino! wollen wir nicht speisen?
>   (TAMINO bläst auf seiner Flöte.)

Papageno.

> Blase du nur fort auf deiner Flöte, ich will
> meine Brocken blasen.
>   (Er tritt hinter den Tisch und isst.)
> Herr Sarastro führt eine gute Küche. Nun,
> ich will sehen, ob auch der Keller so gut
> bestellt ist.
>   (Er schenkt sich ein und trinkt.)
> Ha, das ist Götterwein!
>   (TAMINO beendet sein Flötenspiel.)
>   (PAMINA eilt von links herbei.)
> (TAMINO rechts vorn. PAMINA zu seiner Linken. PAPAGENO essend und trinkend hinter dem Mitteltisch.)

Pamina

>   (freudig).
> Du hier? Gütige Götter! Dank euch!
> Aber du bist traurig? Sprichst nicht eine
> Silbe mit deiner Pamina? Papageno, sage
> du mir, was ist meinem Freund?

Papageno

> (winkt ihr mit gefülltem Mund, fortzugehen.)
> Hm, hm, hm!

Pamina.

> Wie? Auch du? O das ist mehr als Tod!
> Ach, ich fühl's, es ist verschwunden,
> Ewig hin der Liebe Glück!
> Nimmer kommt ihr, Wonnestunden,
> Meinem Herzen mehr zurück!
> Sieh' Tamino, diese Thränen,
> Fliessen, Trauter, dir allein.

If you do not feel love's longing,
Rest in death will be for me.
(She goes out sadly.)

Papageno
(eats hastily).
Is it not true, Tamino, that I too can be
silent if it's necessary?
(Drinks.)
Long live the cook and the butler!
(Three trumpet calls.)
(Exit TAMINO.)

Papageno.
You go first, and I will follow. Now I
can really begin to enjoy it. I should go
when my appetite is at its best? I'd like
to see anyone get me away.
(PAPAGENO, VOICES, SPEAKER.)

Papageno
(from without).
Tamino! Tamino!
(He looks about him.)
If I only knew where I am!

Voice
(calls to him).
Go back!
(Thunder clap. Fire darts out of the door.)

Papageno.
Merciful gods! Where shall I go?
If I only knew which way I came in!
(Goes to the door through which he came.)

Voice
(calls to him).
Back!
(Thunder and fire as above.)

Papageno.
Now I go neither forward nor backward,
(he weeps)
and must perhaps die of hunger in the
bargain! Serves me right! Why did I
come along?

Speaker.
Man, you deserve to wander forever in the
dark recesses of the earth!

Papageno.
Perhaps; still there are many like me on
this earth. Now I'd enjoy a glass of
wine better than anything!

Fühlst du nicht der Liebe Sehnen,
So wird Ruh' im Tode sein!
(Sie geht traurig ab nach links.)

Papageno
(isst hastig.)
Nicht wahr, Tamino, ich kann auch schwei-
gen, wenn's sein muss?
(Er trinkt.)
Der Herr Koch und der Herr Kellermeister
sollen leben!
(Dreimaliger Posaunenton.)
(TAMINO geht durch die Mitte ab.)

Papageno.
Geh' du nur vorous, ich komm' schon nach.
Jetzt will ich mir's erst recht wohl sein
lassen. Da ich in meinem besten Ap-
petit bin, soll ich gehen? Dass lass ich
wohl bleiben.
(PAPAGENO, Stimmen, SPRECHER.)

Papageno
(von aussen rechts.)
Tamino! Tamino!
(Er sucht von rechts herein).
Wenn ich nur wenigstens wüsste, wo ich
wäre?

Stimme
(ruft ihm entgegen.)
Zurück!
(Donnerschlag, Feuer schlägt zur Thür hinaus.)

Papageno.
Barmherzige Götter! Wo wend' ich mich
hin? Wenn ich nur wüsste, wo ich
hereinkam.
(Er kommt zur Thür rechts vorn, durch die er hereinkam.)

Stimme
(ruft ihm entgegen.)
Zurück!
(Donner und Feuer, wie oben.)

Papageno.
Nun kann ich weder zurück noch vorwärts,
(er weint)
muss vielleicht am Ende gar verhungern!
Schon recht! Warum bin ich mitgereist!

Sprecher.
Mensch, du hättest verdient, auf immer in
finsteren Klüften der Erde zu wandern.

Papageno.
Je nun, es giebt ja noch mehr Leute mein-
esgleichen. Mir wäre jetzt ein gutes
Glas Wein das grösste Vergnügen.

Speaker.

Have you no other wish at all?

Papageno.

So far none other.

Speaker.

You will be served some.
(Exit.)

(A large jug filled with wine comes up from the ground.)

Papageno.

Hurrah! There it comes!
(He drinks.)
Great!—Heavenly! Divine! My heart
feels quite strange; I'd like—I wish—
now, what then?
(Plays on the bells.)
For why fair maidens should like me
Does Papageno sigh.
O such a gentle turtle-dove
Is a blessing from on high!
Then never while eating nor drinking
Would I envy fair princes, I'm thinking.
Like wise man I'd find joy in life
If only I got me a wife!
For maiden fair, etc.
For my fair maidens should like me
Far less than others I can't see.
Help me in my misery.
Else for death I'll praying be!
For maiden fair, etc.
If no one grants her love to me,
By flames of love consumed I'll be!
Still if one kiss I should receive,
I would revive—this I believe!

(The old WOMAN dancing and leaning on her cane, comes
to the scene.)

Woman.

Here I am now, my fair angel!

Sprecher.

Sonst hast du keinen Wunsch in dieser
Welt?

Papageno.

Bis jetzt nicht.

Sprecher.

Man wird dich damit bedienen.
(Ab nach links.)

(Ein grosser mit Wein gefüllter Becher kommt aus der
Erde.)

Papageno.

Juhe! Da ist er schon!
(Er trinkt.)
Herrlich!—Himmlisch!—Göttlich!
Ha! Mir wird ganz wunderlich ums
Herz; ich möchte—ich wünschte—ja, was
denn?
(schlägt dazu das Glockenspiel.)
Ein Mädchen oder Weibchen
Wünscht Papageno sich.
O so ein sanftes Täubchen
Wär' Seligkeit für mich!
Dann schmeckte mir Trinken und Essen.
Dann könnt ich mit Fürsten mich messen.
Des Lebens als Weiser mich freu'n,
Und wie im Elysium sein.
Ein Mädchen oder Weibchen
Wünscht Papageno sich.
O, so ein sanftes Täubchen
Wär' Seligkeit für mich.
Ach, kann ich denn keiner von allen
Den reizenden Mädchen gefallen?
Helf' eine mir nur aus der Noth,
Sonst gräm' ich mich wahrlich zu Tod.
Ein Mädchen oder Weibchen
Wünscht Papageno sich.
O, so ein sanftes Täubchen
Wär' Seligkeit für mich.
Wird keine mir Liebe gewähren,
So muss mich die Flamme verzehren!
Doch küsst mich ein weiblicher Mund,
So bin ich schon wieder gesund!

(Das alte WEIB, tanzend und sich dabei auf einen Stock
stützend, kommt von rechts und tritt ihm zur Linken.)

Weib.

Da bin ich schon, mein Engel!

Papageno (turns around).

    Did you take pity on me?

Woman.

    Yes, my angel! Come, give me your hand
as a pledge of our union.

Papageno.

    Not quite so hasty, dear angel!

Woman.

    Papageno, I advise you, do not hesitate.
Your hand or you are here imprisoned
forever.

Papageno.

    Imprisoned?

Woman.

    Bread and water will be your daily meal.

Papageno.

    Bread and water? To renounce the world?
If that is so, I'd rather take an old one
than none at all. Here is my hand with
the assurance that I will always remain
true to you,

(aside)

    as long as I see no fairer one.

Woman.

    Do you swear that?

Papageno.

    Yes, I swear it to you.

(The WOMAN changes into a young woman, who is dressed
like PAPAGENO.)

Papageno.

    Pa-Pa Papagena!

(He tries to embrace her.)

(The SPEAKER comes in quickly between the two.)

Speaker (takes her quickly by the hand).

    Away with you, young woman, he is not yet
worthy of you!

(He takes her away.)

CHANGE OF SCENE.

(Garden with a lake in the background. To the right a
bench overhung with roses. Clear moonlight floods the
scene.)

(PAMINA sleeping on the bench under the roses. MONO-
STATOS in the back.)

Monostatos.

    Ah, here I find the timid maiden. The
flame which in me burns will consume
me.

(He looks around.)

Papageno (drecht sich un.)

    Du hast dich meiner erbarmt?

Weib.

    Ja, mein Engel! Komm, reich mir zum
Pfand unseres Bundes deine Hand.

Papageno.

    Nur nicht so hastig, lieber Engel!

Weib.

    Papageno, ich rathe dir, zaudre nicht.
Deine Hand, oder du bist auf immer hier
eingekerkert.

Papageno.

    Eingekerkert?

Weib.

    Wasser und Brod wird deine tägliche Kost
sein.

Papageno.

    Wasser trinken? Der Welt entsagen?
Nein, da will ich doch lieber eine Alte
nehmen, als gar keine. Nun, da hast du
meine Hand, mit der Versicherung, dass
ich dir immer getreu bleibe,

(für sich)

    solange ich keine Schönere sehe.

Weib.

    Das schwörst du?

Papageno.

    Ja, das schwör' ich dir!

(WEIB verwandelt sich in ein junges Weib, welches ebenso
gekleidet ist, wie PAPAGENO.)

Papageno.

    Pa—pa Papagena!

(Er will sie umarmen.)

(SPRECHER tritt rasch von links ein und zwischen beide.)

Sprecher (nimmt sie hastig bei der Hand.)

    Fort mit dir, junges Weib, er ist deiner
noch nicht würdig.

(Er drängt sie nach links ab.)

VERWANDLUNG.

(Garten mit einem See im Hintergrund. Rechts ein von
blühenden Rosen überhangener Sitz. Heller Mondschein
überfluthet die Gegend.)

(PAMINA schlafend auf dem Sitz unter den Rosen. MONO-
STATOS von links hinten.)

Monostatos.

    Ha! Da find' ich ja die spröde Schöne!
Das Feuer, das in mir glimmt, wird mich
noch verzehren.

(Er sieht sich um.)

If I only knew whether I am alone and no one listening. A little kiss, I should think would be excusable.	Wenn ich wüsste—dass ich so ganz allein und unbelauscht wäre! Ein Küsschen, dächte ich, liesse sich entschuldigen.
Love in every heart is reigning,	Alles fühlt der Liebe Freuden.
Bills and coos, caresses and embraces,	Schnäbelt, tändelt, herzt und küsst;
But my love she is disdaining	Und ich soll die Liebe meiden,
Just because my skin is brown.	Weil ein Schwarzer hässlich ist!
Have I not a heart within me?	Ist mir denn kein Herz gegeben?
Why should maidens at me frown?	Ich bin auch den Mädchen gut!
Without wife ever to dwell,	Immer ohne Weibchen leben,
Is worse than the fire of hell.	Wäre wahrlich Höllengluth!
Therefore will I while I live,	Drum so will ich, weil ich lebe,
Bill and kiss and tender be.	Schnäbeln, küssen, zärtlich sein!
Dear good moon, forgive, forgive,	Lieber guter Mond, vergebe,
A white maid has enticed me.	Eine Weisse nahm mich ein,
White is lovely, I must kiss.	Weiss ist schön! ich muss sie küssen;
Moon, oh hide thyself the while,	Mond, verstecke dich dazu!
And if it disturbs thy bliss,	Sollt' es dich zu sehr verdriessen,
Close thine eyes, and take it not amiss.	O so mach' die Augen zu!
(He creeps up slowly and softly to PAMINA.)	(Er schleicht langsam und leise zu PAMINA hin.)
(The QUEEN enters hastily.)	(Die KÖNIGIN eilt von rechts hinten herbei.)

Queen	*Königin*
(to MONOSTATOS).	(gebietend zu MONOSTATOS.)
Back!	Zurück!
Monostatos.	*Monostatos.*
Heavens!	O weh!
(PAMINA, the QUEEN, MONOSTATOS.)	(PAMINA rechts vorn schlafend, die KÖNIGIN mit drohender Geberde die Mitte nehmend. MONOSTATOS zu ihrer Linken.)

DER HÖLLE RACHE KOCHT IN MEINEM HERZEN—*THE PANGS OF HELL ARE RAGING* Air (Queen)

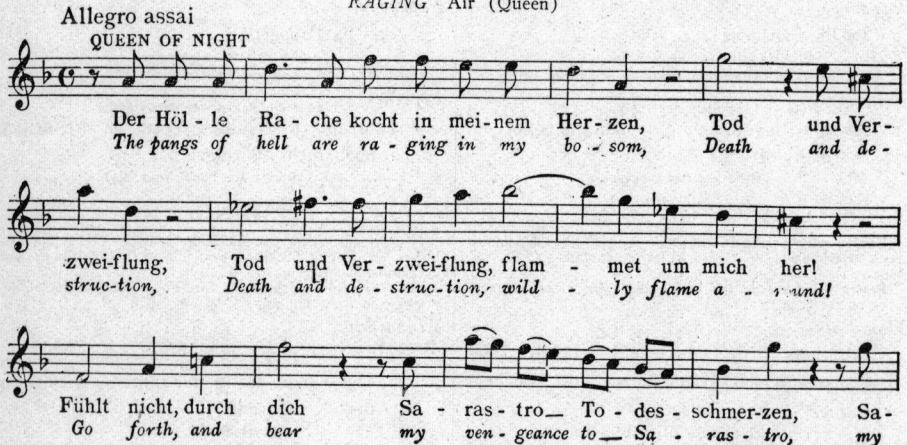

Der Höl-le Ra-che kocht in mei-nem Her-zen, Tod und Ver-
The pangs of hell are ra-ging in my bo-som, Death and de-

zwei-flung, Tod und Ver-zwei-flung, flam - met um mich her!
struc-tion, Death and de-struc-tion, wild - ly flame a - round!

Fühlt nicht, durch dich Sa - ras-tro To-des-schmer-zen, Sa-
Go forth, and bear my ven-geance to Sa - ras-tro, my

ras - tro__ To - des - schmer - zen,   so bist du mei - ne   Toch - ter nim - mer -
ven geance to__ Sa - ras' - tro,   Or as my daugh - ter   thou shalt be dis -

mehr,   so bist du mein',   mei - ne Toch - ter nim - mer - mehr, _____
own'd,   be thou dis - own'd,   as my daugh - ter be dis - own'd, _____

mei - ne Toch - ter nim - mer - mehr, _____
as my daugh - ter be dis - own'd, _____

so bist du mei - ne Toch - ter nim - mer - mehr
For ev - er as my daugh - ter be dis - own'd.

Rejected be forever and forlorn,	Verstossen sei auf ewig und verlassen,
To pieces all the ties of nature torn,	Zertrümmert alle Bande der Natur,
If through thee vile Sarastro dies not now,	Wenn nicht durch dich Sarastro wird erblassen!
Hear, gods of vengeance, hear a mother's vow!	Hört! Rachegötter! Hört der Mutter Schwur!

Pamina | *Pamina*
(arising). | (sich erhebend.)
Mother, mother, my mother! | Mutter! Mutter! Meine Mutter!
(She falls into her arms.) | (Sie fällt ihr in die Arme.)

Queen (draws out a dagger).

Do you see this steel? It is sharpened for Sarastro. You are to kill him and bring back to me the powerful zodiac.
(She forces the dagger on her.)

Pamina.

But, dearest mother!

Queen.

Not a word!
(Thunder. The QUEEN disappears.)

Pamina (with dagger in hand).

Murder must I? Gods! That I cannot. What shall I do?

Monostatos (takes away her dagger).

Trust in me.

Pamina (frightened).

Ha!

Monostatos.

Why do you tremble?
Is it because of my black skin or the intended murder?

Pamina (timidly).

Then you know?

Monostatos.

All. Only one way is left you now to save yourself and your mother.

Pamina.

Which is?

Monostatos.

To love me.

Pamina (trembling, aside).

Heavens!

Monostatos.

Now, maiden, yes or no!

Pamina (decidedly).

No!

Monostatos (in anger).

No? then die!

Sarastro
(comes between them, raises a threatening arm, and hurls
MONOSTATOS back).

Back!

Königin (zieht einen Dolch hervor.)

Siehst du hier diesen Stahl? Er ist für Sarastro geschliffen. Du wirst ihn tödten und den mächtigen Sonnenkreis mir überliefern.
(Sie dringt ihr den Dolch auf.)

Pamina.

Aber liebste Mutter!

Königin.

Kein Wort!
(Donner. Sie verschwindet.)

Pamina
(den Dolch in der Hand, mit einigen Schritten nach links.)

Morden soll ich? Götter! Das kann ich nicht. Was soll ich thun?

Monostatos (nimmt ihr den Dolch weg.)

Dich mir anvertrauen.

Pamina (erschrickt.)

Ha!

Monostatos.

Warum zitterst du? Vor meiner schwarzen Farbe oder vor dem ausgedachten Mord?

Pamina (schüchtern.)

Du weisst also?

Monostatos.

Alles! Du hast also nur einen Weg, dich und deine Mutter zu retten.

Pamina.

Der wäre?

Monostatos.

Mich zu lieben!

Pamina (zitternd, für sich.)

Götter!

Monostatos.

Nun, Mädchen, ja oder nein!

Pamina (entschlossen.)

Nein!

Monostatos (voll Zorn.)

Nein? So fahr' hin!

Sarastro
(tritt gebietend zwischen beide, erhebt drohend den Arm und schleudert MONOSTATOS zurück.)

Zurück!

Monostatos

(turning around like a flash and falling at SARASTRO's feet).

Sir, I am not guilty!

Sarastro.

I know that your soul is as black as your face. Go!

(Exit MONOSTATOS.)

Pamina.

Master, do not punish my mother!

Sarastro.

I know all. You shall see how I shall vengeance take upon your mother.

Monostatos

(sich blitzschnell um sich selbst drehend und vor SARASTRO auf die Knie fallend.)

Herr, ich bin unschuldig!

Sarastro.

Ich weiss, dass deine Seele eben so schwarz als dein Gesicht ist. Geh!

(Er eilt nach rechts hinten ab.)

Pamina.

Herr! Strafe meine Mutter nicht!

Sarastro.

Ich weiss alles. Du sollst sehen, wie ich mich an deiner Mutter räche.

IN DIESEN HEIL'GEN HALLEN—*WITHIN THIS HALLOWED DWELLING*—Air (Sarastro)

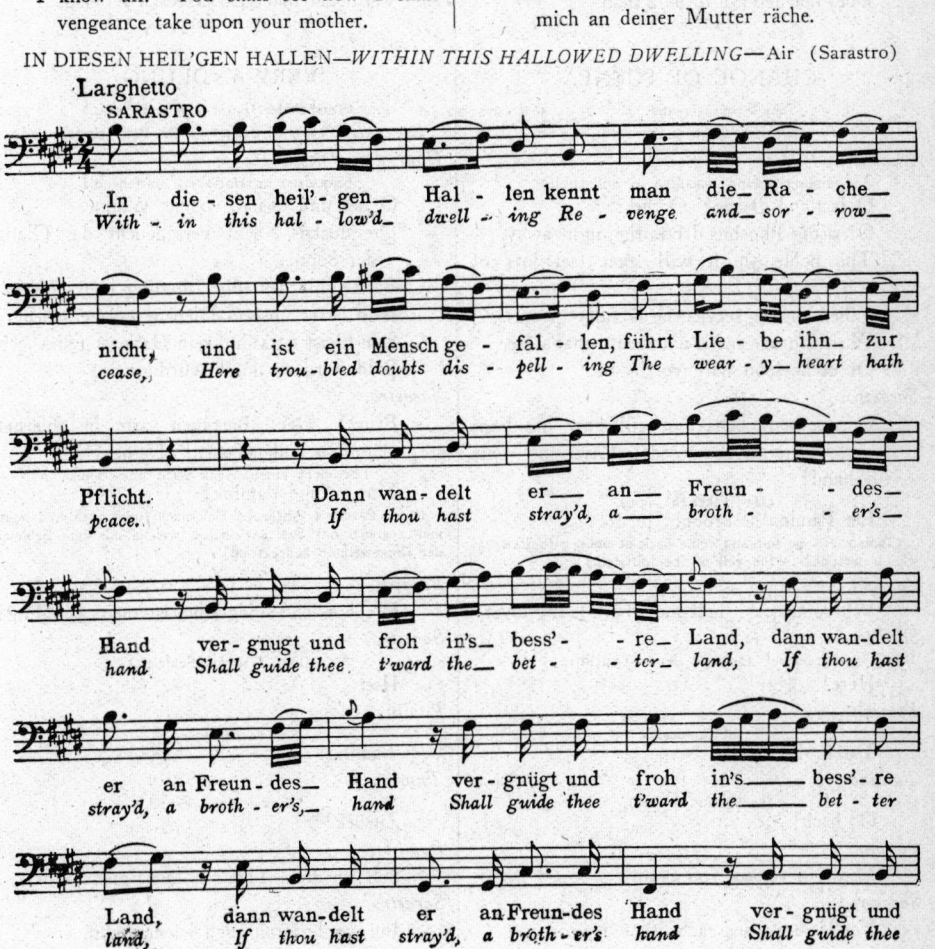

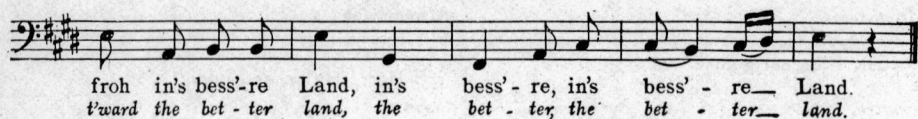

froh in's bess'-re Land, in's   bess'-re, in's   bess'-re_ Land.
t'ward the bet-ter land,   the   bet-ter, the'   bet-ter_ land.

Within these holy walls	In diesen heil'gen Mauern,
Where man loves brother man,	Wo Mensch den Menschen liebt,
There can no traitor lurk.	Kann kein Verräther lauern,
The enemy is forgiv'n.	Weil man dem Feind' vergiebt.
He whom this teaching does not gladden,	Wen solche Lehren nicht erfreun,
Does not deserve to be a man.	Verdienet nicht ein Mensch zu sein.
(Exit both.)	(Beide gehen nach links ab.)

CHANGE OF SCENE.

(Temple of Isis and Osiris.)

(SPEAKER, PRIESTS, SARASTRO.)

Chorus of Priests

(standing around SARASTRO in semi-circle).

O Isis and Osiris! O the ray
Of rising Phoebus drives the night away.
The noble youth will soon feel joys of
    heaven,
When to our service he is fully given.
With courage bold, and heart that's free,
Of us he soon will worthy be.

Sarastro.

Prince, your behaviour till now has been
    manly and composed. Give me your
    hand!

(He makes a sign.)

Let Pamina be brought in.

(Two priests go out and come back at once with PAMINA,
who is wrapped in the veil of the initiated.)

Pamina.

Where am I? Tell me where is my lover?

Sarastro

(removes the veil from TAMINO).

Here!

Pamina

(in rapture).

Tamino!

Tamino

(beckoning to her).

Go back!

Pamina.

May I never see you again?

Sarastro.

You'll surely see each other again.

VERWANDLUNG.

(Tempel der Götter Isis und Osiris.)

(SPRECHER, PRIESTER, SARASTRO, die Mitte einnehmend.)

Chor der Priester

(SARASTRO im Halbkreis umstehend.)

O Isis und Osiris, welche Wonne.
Die düstre Nacht verscheucht der Glanz
    der Sonne.
Bald fühlt der edle Jüngling neues Leben;
Bald ist er unserm Dienste ganz ergeben.
Sein Geist ist kühn, sein Herz ist rein,
Bald wird er unser würdig sein.

Sarastro.

Prinz! Dein Betragen war bis hierher
    männlich und gelassen. Deine Hand!

(Er giebt einen Wink nach links hin.)

Man bringe Pamina!

(Zwei PRIESTER entfernen sich nach links vorn und kommen sogleich mit PAMINA zurück, welche mit dem Schleier
der Eingeweihten bedeckt ist.)

Pamina.

Wo bin ich? Sagt, wo ist mein Jüngling?

Sarastro

(löst TAMINOS Schleier.)

Hier.

Pamina

(enzückt.)

Tamino!

Tamino

(sie von sich weisend.)

Zurück!

Pamina.

Soll ich dich, Theurer, nicht mehr sehn?

Sarastro.

Ihr werdet froh euch wieder sehn.

Pamina.

 Deadly dangers await you!

Tamino.

 May the gods protect me!

Pamina.

 Deadly dangers await you!

Sarastro.

 May the gods protect him!

Tamino.

 May the gods protect me!

Pamina.

 From death you cannot now escape,
 My saddened heart forebodes it!

Sarastro.

 May the will of the gods be done,
 And their desire be law for him.

Tamino.

 May the will of the gods be done,
  And their desire be law for me.

Pamina.

 O if you were to love like me,
 You surely would not be so calm!

Sarastro.

 Yes, he loves with equal passion,
 And ever will your lover be!

Tamino.

 Yes, I love with equal passion,
 And ever will your lover be!

Sarastro.

 The hour has come when you must part!

Tamino and Pamina.

 How bitter are the pains of parting!

Sarastro.

 The hour has come when you must part!

Tamino and Pamina.

 How bitter are the pains of parting!

Sarastro.

 Tamino must at once depart!

Tamino.

 Yes, I must at once depart!

Pamina.

 Tamino must at once depart!

Sarastro.

 He must depart!

Pamina.

 Dein warten tödliche Gefahren!

Tamino.

 Die Götter mögen mich bewahren!

Pamina.

 Dein warten tödliche Gefahren!

Sarastro.

 Die Götter mögen ihn bewahren!

Tamino.

 Die Götter mögen mich bewahren!

Pamina.

 Du wirst dem Tode nicht entgehen;
 Mir flüstert dieses Ahnung ein.

Sarastro.

 Der Götter Wille mag geschehen,
 Ihr Wink soll ihm Gesetze sein.

Tamino.

 Der Götter Wille mag geschehen,
 Ihr Wink soll mir Gesetze sein!

Pamina.

 O liebtest du, wie ich dich liebe,
 Du würdest nicht so ruhig sein.

Sarastro.

 Glaub' mir, er fühlet gleiche Triebe,
 Wird ewig dein Getreuer sein.

Tamino.

 Glaub' mir, ich fühle gleiche Triebe,
 Werd' ewig dein Getreuer sein!

Sarastro.

 Die Stunde schlägt, nun müsst ihr scheiden!

Tamino und Pamina.

 Wie bitter sind der Trennung Leiden!

Sarastro.

 Die Stunde schlägt, nun müsst ihr scheiden!

Tamino und Pamina.

 Wie bitter sind der Trennung Leiden!

Sarastro.

 Tamino muss nun wieder fort.

Tamino.

 Pamina, ich muss wirklich fort!

Pamina.

 Tamino muss nun wirklich fort!

Sarastro.

 Nun muss er fort!

Tamino.

I must depart!

Pamina.

He must depart!

Tamino.

Pamina, fare thee well!

Pamina.

Tamino, fare thee well!

Sarastro.

Now hasten away,
Your promise calls you!
The time has come! We'll meet again!

Tamino and Pamina.

O longed-for calm, return again.

(She is led away by two priests.)
(SARASTRO leaves with TAMINO; exit the priests.)

CHANGE OF SCENE.

(Small palm garden. Twilight. It grows gradually lighter.)
(The three YOUTHS come from the left.)

The three Youths.

The sun comes in the night to ban'sh,
And beams upon earth brilliantly.
All superstition must soon vanish,
The wise man goes to victory.
O heavenly quiet, now descend,
Return into the heart of man.
Then will the earth as a heaven be
And mortals like Divinity.

First Youth.

But see, Pamina's in despair.

Second and Third Youth.

Where is she?

First Youth.

She is out of her mind.

The three Youths.

She suffers pangs of disdained love,
Let us endeavor to console her,
Her fate indeed has greatly moved me,
Would that her lover here would be!
She comes, let us draw aside,
So that we better can observe her!

(They step to the back of the stage.)
(PAMINA rushes in half insane, with the dagger given her
by the QUEEN.)

Tamino.

Nun muss ich fort!

Pamina.

So musst du fort!

Tamino.

Pamina, lebe wohl!

Pamina.

Tamino, lebe wohl!

Sarastro.

Nun eile fort.
Dich ruft dein Wort.
Die Stunde schlägt, wir sehn uns wieder!

Tamino und Pamina.

Ach, goldne Ruhe, kehre wieder!

(Sie wird von zwei Priestern nach rechts vorn abgeführt.)
(SARASTRO entfernt sich mit TAMINO an der Hand und
allen PRIESTER nach links vorn.)

VERWANDLUNG.

(Kurzer Palmengarten. Halbdunkel. Es wird nach und
nach ganz hell.)
(Die drei KNABEN kommen von links.)

Die drei Knaben.

Bald prangt, den Morgen zu verkünden,
Die Sonn' auf gold'ner Bahn!
Bald soll der Aberglaube schwinden,
Bald siegt der weise Mann.
O holde Ruhe, steig' hernieder.
Kehr' in der Menschen Herzen wieder;
Dann wird die Erd' ein Himmelreich,
Und Sterbliche den Göttern gleich.

Erster Knabe.

Doch seht, Verzweiflung quält Paminen.

Zweiter und dritter Knabe.

Wo ist sie denn?

Erster Knabe.

Sie ist von Sinnen.

Die drei Knaben.

Sie quält verschmähter Liebe Leiden.
Lasst uns der Armen Trost bereiten!
Fürwahr, ihr Schicksal geht mir nah!
O wäre nur ihr Jüngling da!—
Sie kommt, lasst uns beiseite gehn,
Damit wir, was sie mache, sehn.

(Sie ziehen sich nach links hinten zurück.)
(PAMINA, halb wahnsinnig, mit dem Dolch, den sie von
der KÖNIGIN empfing, herbeistürzend.)

Pamina
   (to her dagger).
 In you my bridegroom now I see,
 Through you my grief will ended be!
The Youths
   (aside).
 Oh, woe! what said Pamina here!
 And see, she is to madness near!
Pamina.
 Patience, beloved, I am thine.
 Soon shall we now united be.
The Youths
   (draw nearer).
 Madness lurks in her poor brain,
 Suicide she contemplates.
   (To PAMINA)
 Gracious maiden, here behold us!
Pamina.
 Die I must, since the man
 Whom detest I never can
 His loved one has forsaken!
   (Raises the dagger.)
 This my mother gave to me.
The three Youths.
 Suicide by God is punished.
Pamina.
 Better by this steel to die,
 Than through grief and love to perish,
 Mother, alas, I suffer through thee,
 And your curse pursueth me!
The three Youths.
 Maiden, will you go with us?
Pamina.
 The measure of my grief is full,
 Faithless lover, fare thee well!
 See, Pamina dies through thee.
 May this dagger destroy me!
   (She tries to stab herself.)
The three Youths
  (come up and snatch the dagger from her).

 Hold, unhappy one, and hear.
 Were your lover this to see,
 He with sorrow would expire,
 For he loves but you alone.
Pamina
   (recovers herself).
 What? He, too, felt love?
 And concealed his feelings for me?

Pamina
   (zu dem Dolch.)
 Du also bist mein Bräutigam?
 Durch dich vollend' ich meinen Gram!
Die Knaben
   (beiseite.)
 Welch' dunkle Worte sprach sie da?
 Die Arme ist dem Wahnsinn nah'.
Pamina.
 Geduld, mein Trauter, ich bin dein,
 Bald werden wir vermählet sein.
Die Knaben
   (treten näher.)
 Wahsinn tobt ihr im Gehirne;
 Selbstmord steht ihr auf der Stirne.
   (Zu PAMINA.)
 Holdes Mädchen, sieh uns an!
Pamina.
 Sterben will ich, weil der Mann,
 Denn ich nimmermehr kann hassen,
 Seine Traute kann verlassen.
   (Den Dolch erhebend.)
 Dies gab meine Mutter mir.
Die Knaben.
 Selbstmord strafet Gott an dir.
Pamina.
 Lieber durch dies Eisen sterben,
 Als durch Liebesgram verderben.
 Mutter, durch dich leide ich,
 Und dein Fluch verfolget mich.
Die Knaben.
 Mädchen, willst du mit uns gehn?
Pamina.
 Ha, des Jammers Mass ist voll!
 Falscher Jüngling, lebe wohl!
 Sieh, Pamina stirbt durch dich:
 Dieses Eisen tödte mich.
   (Sie will sich erstechen.)
Die Knaben
(treten, zwei von rechts, einer von links, zu PAMINA vor
  und entreissen ihr den Dolch.)
 Ha, Unglückliche! halt ein!
 Sollte dies dein Jüngling sehen,
 Würde er vor Gram vergehen;
 Denn er liebet dich allein.
Pamina
   (erholt sich.)
 Was? Er fühlte Gegenliebe?
 Und verbarg mir seine Triebe,

Turned his countenance away.
Why did he not speak to me?

The three Youths.

This, alas, we must not tell,
But we will now show him to you.
And you will see with surprise,
That he gave his heart to you,
And for you his life he'd give!

Pamina.

Take me where I now can see him!

The three Youths.

Come to him, we now will lead you.

All Four.

Two hearts that with true love are burning
Can human weakness never part.
Vain are the efforts of the enemy,
For by the gods they will protected be!

(Exeunt.)

CHANGE OF SCENE.

(Wild mountain spot, with an iron middle gate. To the right and left, iron doors as entrances. In the background, on both sides of the middle door, small caves in the rocks. Within the one to the right, one sees through an iron gate, a roaring stream. In the one to the left, a brightly glowing fire. Twilight.)

(TAMINO with two priests. PAMINA's voice heard without.)

Men.

He who pursueth his path with dangers full
Becometh pure by fire, water, air and earth
If he can overcome the pangs of death,
From out of earth he rises unto heaven.
Thus purified he then will able be,
To devote himself to Isis' mystery.

Tamino.

I fear not death, for as a man
I'll follow ever virtue's path,
Open the gates of horror wide,
I'll gladly risk the dangerous tide!

Pamina

(from without).

Tamino, wait! for I must see you!

Wandte sein Gesicht von mir?
Warum sprach er nicht mit mir?

Die Knaben.

Dieses müssen wir verschweigen,
Doch, wir wollen dir ihn zeigen!
Und du wirst mit Staunen sehn,
Dass er dir sein Herz geweiht,
Und den Tod für dich nicht scheut.

Pamina.

Führt mich hin, ich möcht' ihn sehen.

Die Knaben.

Kommt, wir wollen zu ihm gehen.

Alle Vier.

Zwei Herzen, die von Liebe brennen,
Kann Menschenohnmacht niemals trennen
Verloren ist der Feinde Müh',
Die Götter selbst beschützen sie.

(Sie gehen nach rechts ab.)

VERWANDLUNG.

(Wilde Felsengegend mit einem eisernen Mittelthor. Rechts und links eiserne Thore als Eingänge. Im Hintergrund zu beiden Seiten des Mittelthores Felsenhöhlen; in der einen rechts sieht man durch ein eisernes Gitter eine brausende Wasserfluth, in der andern links eine hellflammende Feuergluth,—Es ist halbdunkel.)

(TAMINO mit zwei PRIESTERN von links. PAMINA's Stimme rechts draussen.)

Die zwei Geharnischten.

Der, welcher wandert diese Strasse voll
  Beschwerden.
Wird rein durch Feuer, Wasser, Luft und
  Erden;
Wenn er des Todes Schrecken überwinden
  kann,
Schwingt er sich aus der Erde himmelan
Erleuchtet wird er dann imstande sein,
Sich den Mysterien der Isis ganz zu weihn.

Tamino.

Mich schreckt kein Tod, als Mann zu han
  deln,
Den Weg der Tugend fortzuwandeln.
Schliesst mir die Schreckenspforten auf,
Ich wage froh den kühnen Lauf.

Pamina

(von rechts draussen.)

Tamino, halt! Ich muss dich sehen.

Tamino.

    What do I hear? Pamina's voice?

Men.

    Yes, yes, it is Pamina's voice.

Tamino.

    Now she can surely go with me,
    Nothing can us separate,
    Even if death should be our fate.

Men.

    Now she can surely go with you,
    Nothing can you separate,
    Even if death should be your fate.

Tamino.

    Is it permitted me to speak to her?

Men.

    It is permitted you to speak to her.
            (The two priests exit.)

Tamino.

    What happiness if we should meet again!

Men.

    What happiness if we should meet again!

Tamino and Men.

    Joyfully go hand in hand to the temple,
    A wife whom neither night nor death dismay
    Is worthy, and will be ordained.
          (Priests come back with PAMINA.)
             (Above. PAMINA.)

Pamina   (embracing TAMINO).

    Tamino mine! What happiness is this!

Tamino.

    Pamina mine! What happiness is this!
         (He points to both mountain caverns.)
    Here are the gates of horror,
    They threaten danger dire and death.

Pamina.

    I will always.
    Be your true companion.
    Myself I lead you,
    And love guides me on:
         (Takes him by the hand.)
    Love will deck thy thorny way,
    And the path with roses strew.
    Now your magic flute you'll play,
    It will protect us on our way.
    My father in a magic hour
    Fashioned it himself

Tamino.

    Was hör' ich? Paminens Stimme?

Die Geharnischten.

    Ja, ja, das ist Paminens Stimme.

Tamino.

    Wohl mir, nun kann sie mit mir gehn,
    Nun trennet uns kein Schicksal mehr,
    Wenn auch der Tod beschieden wär'!

Die Geharnischten.

    Wohl dir, nun kann sie mit dir gehn,
    Nun trennet euch kein Schicksal mehr,
    Wenn auch der Tod beschieden wär!

Tamino.

    Ist mir erlaubt, mit ihr zu sprechen?

Die Geharnischten.

    Dir sei erlaubt, mit ihr zu sprechen!
        (Die zwei PRIESTER gehen rechts ab.)

Tamino.

    Welch' Glück, wenn wir uns wiedersehn.

Die Geharnischten.

    Welch' Glück, wenn wir euch wiedersehn

Tamino und die Geharnischten.

    Froh Hand in Hand im Tempel gehn.
    Ein Weib, das Nacht und Tod nicht scheut.
    Ist würdig und wird eingeweiht.
    (Die beiden PRIESTER kommen mit PAMINA von rechts zurück.)
         (Die Vorigen, PAMINA.)

Pamina   (TAMINO unarmend).

    Tamino mein! o welch' ein Glück!

Tamino.

    Pamina mein! o welch' ein Glück!
        (Er zeigt nach den beiden Felsenhöhlen.)
    Hier sind die Schreckenspforten,
    Die Noth und Tod mir dräun.

Pamina.

    Ich werd' an allen Orten
    An deiner Seite sein.
    Ich selber führe dich,
    Die Liebe leite mich.
         (Sie nimmt ihn bei der Hand.)
    Sie mag den Weg mit Rosen streun,
    Weil Rosen stets bei Dornen sein.
    Spiel du die Zauberflöte an,
    Sie schütze uns auf unsrer Bahn.
    Es schnitt in einer Zauberstunde
    Mein Vater sie aus tiefstem Grunde

Out of a thousand-year old oak,
In thunder, lightning, storm and gale,
Now your magic flute you'll play,
It will protect us on our way.

Tamino, Pamina.

We wander by the flute's sweet might,
Merrily into death and night.

Men.

They wander by the flute's sweet might,
Merrily into death and night.

(TAMINO and PAMINA go toward the cavern of fire, through which they pass, PAMINA keeping her hand on TAMINO's shoulder, and TAMINO playing his flute. As soon as they emerge from the purgation by fire, they embrace.)

Both.

We wandered through the flames,
And bravely met the dangers.
            (To the flute.)
May your tones protect us in the flood of
            waters,
As they did when fire was near.

(TAMINO and PAMINA proceed into the cave of water. They soon come out of the purgation by water.)
(Above. SARASTRO, Priests high up in the temple.)

Tamino, Pamina.

Oh gods, what a glorious sight!
The joy of Isis is upon us!

Chorus of Priests.

Triumph, triumph, noble pair,
The danger you have overcome.
To Isis you we consecrate;
Walk now within the temple gate.

(TAMINO and PAMINA take their way to the temple.)

CHANGE OF SCENE.

(Small garden. To the right a tree with a dried up branch. It is daylight.)

(PAPAGENO, alone, with a rope around his waist.)

Papageno
            (calls on his pipe).

Papagena, Papagena, Papagena!
Little darling, little dove!
In vain I sigh, to me she's lost.
Oh, I am born to misery!
I talked, I know, and that was wrong.
And so they'll say it served me right.

Der tausendjähr'gen Eiche aus,
Bei Blitz und Donner, Sturm und Braus.
Nun komm' und spiel' die Flöte an,
Sie leite uns auf grauser Bahn.

Tamino, Pamina.

Wir wandeln durch des Tones Macht,
Froh durch des Todes düst're Nacht!

Die Geharnischten.

Ihr wandelt durch des Tones Macht,
Froh durch des Todes düst're Nacht.

(TAMINO und PAMINA wenden sich nach links zur Feuerhöhle, die sie durchwandern, indem PAMINA ihre Hand auf TAMINO's Schulter legt, wobei TAMINO seine Flöte bläst. Sobald sie aus der Feuerprobe heraus kommen, umarmen sie sich und bleiben in der Mitte.)

Beide.

Wir wandelten durch Feuergluthen,
Bekämpften muthig die Gefahr.
            (Zur Flöte.)
Dein Ton sei Schutz in Wasserfluthen,
So wie er es im Feuer war.

(TAMINO und PAMINA wenden sich nun ganz wie vorhin nach rechts zur Wasserhöhle. Sobald sie aus der Wasserprobe herauskommen:)
(Die Vorigen, SARASTRO, die PRIESTER hoch oben im Tempel.)

Tamino, Pamina.

Ihr Götter! Welch' ein Augenblick!
Gewähret ist uns Isis Glück.

Chor der Priester.

Triumph! Triumph! du edles Paar!
Besieget hast du die Gefahr,
Der Isis Weihe ist nun dein,
Kommt, tretet in den Tempel ein!

(TAMINO und PAMINA wenden sich nach hinten zum Tempel.)

VERWANDLUNG.

(Kurze Gartendekoration; rechts ein Baum mit einem verdorrten Ast.—Es ist hell.)

(PAPAGENO allein, mit einem Strick umgürtet.)

Papageno
            (ruft mit seinem Pfeifchen.)

Papagena! Papagena! Papagena!
Weibchen! Täubchen! Meine Schöne!
Vergebens! Ach, sie ist verloren!
Ich bin zum Unglück schon geboren.
Ich plauderte—und das war schlecht,
Darum geschieht es mir schon recht.

But since I tasted of that wine,
And since her eyes had first met mine,
A constant fire burns in my heart,
And I am tortured day and night!
Papagena, light of life,
Papagena, darling wife!
In vain for thee again I sigh,
So naught is left me but to die!
I'm tired of life, so from it part,
To quench the flame that fires my heart!
(He takes off the rope.)
I will single out this tree,
And from its high branches swing.
For since life has lost its worth,
I will say farewell to earth.
Since to me you are so cruel,
And refuse to grant my prayer,
All is over, I shall die,
Since there's none to mourn or sigh,
Still if only one there be,
Who would love or pity me,
Then I will not end my woe.
Only tell me, yes or no—
No one hears me, all is still.
(Looks around.)
Tell me, then, is it your will?
Papageno, swing on high,
And nobly like a hero die!
(He looks around.)
Now I'm waiting, let it be
While I'm counting, one, two, three!
(He whistles.)
One!
(He looks around and whistles.)
Two!
Two's already past!
(He whistles.)
Three!
(He looks around.)
Now away, and let it be!
There is nothing to keep me!
Good night, false world, farewell to thee!
(He tries to hang himself.)
(The three YOUTHS hurry in.)

The three Youths.

Stop, Papageno, and prudent be,
Man lives but once—be this enough for thee!

Seit ich gekostet diesen Wein.
Seit ich das schöne Weibchen sah,
So brennt's im Herzenskämmerlein,
So zwickt es hier, so zwickt es da.
Papagena! Herzenstäubchen!
Papagena! liebes Weibchen!
's ist umsonst! Es ist vergebens!
Müde bin ich meines Lebens!
Sterben macht der Lieb' ein End',
Wenn's im Herzen noch so brennt.
(Er nimmt den Strick von seiner Mitte.)
Diesen Baum da will ich zieren,
Mir an ihm den Hals zuschnüren,
Weil das Leben mir missfällt;
Gute Nacht, du falsche Welt.
Weil du böse an mir handelst,
Mir kein schönes Kind zubandelst:
So ist's aus, so sterbe ich,
Schöne Mädchen, denkt an mich.
Will sich eine um mich Armen,
Eh' ich hänge, noch erbarmen,
Wohl, so lass ich's diesmal sein!
Rufet nur, ja—oder nein.—
Keine hört mich, alles stille!
(Er sieht sich um.)
Also ist es euer Wille?
Papageno, frisch hinauf!
Ende dienen Lebenslauf.
(Er sieht sich um.)
Nun, ich warte noch, es sei,
Bis man zählet, eins, zwei, drei.
(Er pfeift.)
Eins!
(Er sieht sich um und pfeift.)
Zwei!
Zwei ist schon vorbei.
(Er pfeift.)
Drei!
(Er sieht sich um.)
Nun wohlan, es bleibt dabei!
Weil mich nichts zurücke hält!
Gute Nacht, du falsche Welt.
(Er will sich aufhängen.)
(Die drei KNABEN eilen von links herbei.)

Die drei Knaben.

Halt ein, o Papageno, und sei klug;
Man lebt nur einmal, dies sei dir genug.

Papageno.

 Your talk and joking's very fine,
 Still, if your hearts would burn like mine,
 You, too, would after fair maids run.

The three Youths.

 Then let your sweet bells ring,
 They will your maiden to you bring.

Papageno.

 Fool that I am, to forget the magic thing,
 Ring, bells, ring, ring, ring!
 My little wife I now would see.
    (Rings.)
 Ring, bells, ring, ring, ring!
 My little maiden to me bring!
 Ring, bells, ring, ring, ring!
 My little maiden to me bring!

 (At the sound the three YOUTHS go out and return with PAPAGENA.)

 Now, Papageno, look about you!
    (Exit the YOUTHS.)
 (PAPAGENO looks around—silly dumb show.)
 (PAPAGENO, PAPAGENA at his left.)

Papageno

    (dancing around her).
 Pa—Pa—Pa—Pa—Pa—Papagena!

Woman

    (dancing around him).
 Pa—-Pa—Pa—Pa—Pa—Papageno!

Both.

 Pa—Pa—Pa—Pa—Pa—Papageno!
 Papagena!

Papageno.

 Are you now all my own?

Woman.

 Now I am all your own.

Papageno.

 Well, then be my little love!

Woman.

 Well, then be my turtledove!

Both.

 What a joy we now shall feel,
 When the gods their gifts reveal,
 Little boys and girls galore,
 All we want and many more!

Papageno.

 First a little Papageno.

Woman.

 Then a little Papagena.

Papageno.

 Ihr habt gut reden, habt gut scherzen.
 Doch brennt es euch, wie mich im Herzen,
 Ihr würdet auch nach Mädchen gehn.

Die drei Knaben.

 So lasse deine Glöckchen klingen,
 Dies wird dein Mädchen zu dir bringen.

Papageno.

 Ich Narı vergass der Zauberdinge!
 Erklinge, Glockenspiel, erklinge!
 Ich muss mein liebes Mädchen sehn.
   (Er schlägt sein Glockenspiel.)
 Klinget, Glöckchen, klinget,
 Schafft mein Mädchen her!
 Klinget, Glöckchen, klinget,
 Bringt mein Weibchen her!

 (Die drei KNABEN eilen unter diesem Schlagen nach link ab und kehren sogleich mit PAPAGENA zurück.)

 Nun, Papageno, sieh' dich um!
   (Sie entfernen sich nach links.)
 (PAPAGENO sieht sich um, komisches Spiel.)
 (PAPAGENO, PAPAGENA zu seiner Linken.)

Papageno

    (sie umtanzend.)
 Pa—Pa—Pa—Pa—Pa—Papagena!

Weib

    (ihn umtanzend.)
 Pa—Pa—Pa—Pa—Pa—Papageno!

Beide.

 Pa—Pa—Pa—Pa—Pa—Papageno!
 Papagena!

Papageno.

 Bist du mir nun ganz gegeben?

Weib.

 Nun bin ich dir ganz gegeben

Papageno.

 Nun, so sei mein liebes Weibchen!

Weib.

 Nun, so sei mein Herzenstäubchen!

Beide.

 Welche Freude wird das sein!
 Wenn die Götter uns bedenken,
 Uns'rer Liebe Kinder schenken,
 So liebe kleine Kinderlein!

Papageno.

 Erst einen kleinen Papageno!

Weib.

 Dann eine kleine Papagena!

Papageno.

Then another Papageno.

Woman.

Then another Papagena.

Both.

Papagena! Papagena! Papagena!
It is the greatest pleasure,
When many, many, many, many
Pa—Pa—Pa—Pa—geno,
Pa—Pa—Pa—Pa—gena,
The blessing of fond parents are!
(Both go out arm in arm.)

CHANGE OF SCENE.

(Rugged cliffs. It is dark.)
(MONOSTATOS, the QUEEN with her three LADIES IN WAIT-
ING; they carry lighted torches.)

Monostatos (at the left of the QUEEN).

Now silence, silence, silence!
Soon we will enter the temple.

All the Ladies.

Now silence, silence, silence!
Soon we will enter the temple.

Monostatos.

But, princess, thou wilt keep thy word—
Thy child must be my wife.

Queen.

I keep my word, it is my will!

All the Ladies.

Her child must be his wife.
(Thunder, noise, rushing of water.)

Monostatos.

Be still! I hear a horrid noise,
Like thunder and like water-fall.

Queen and Ladies.

Yes, a horrible noise,
Like thunder and like water-fall.

Monostatos.

Now we are in the temple hall.

All.

There, we will surprise them,
Remove the hypocrites from the earth,
With sword and fire destroy them!

Ladies and Monostatos.

To you, Queen of the Night,
We'll bring our sacrifice.
(Thunder, lightning, storm.)

Papageno.

Dann wieder einen Papageno!

Weib.

Dann wieder eine Papagena!

Beide.

Papagena! Papagena! Papagena!
Es ist das höchste der Gefühle,
Wenn viele, viele, viele, viele
Pa—Pa—Pa—Pa—geno,
Pa—Pa—Pa—Pa—gena,
Der Segen froher Eltern sein.
(Beide eilen Arm in Arm nach links ab.)

VERWANDLUNG.

(Kurze Felsengegend. Es ist Nacht.)
(MONOSTATOS, Die KÖNIGIN mit ihren drei DAMEN von
rechts; sie tragen schwarze, brennende Fackeln in der Hand.)

Monostatos (der KÖNIGIN zur Linken.)

Nur stille! stille! stille! stille!
Bald dringen wir im Tempel ein.

Alle Damen (zuruckstehend.)

Nur stille! stille! stille! stille!
Bald dringen wir im Tempel ein.

Monostatos.

Doch Fürstin, halte Wort! Erfülle—
Dein Kind muss meine Gattin sein.

Königin.

Ich halte Wort; es ist mein Wille.

Alle Damen.

Ihr Kind soll deine Gattin sein.
(Man hört dumpfen Donner, Geräusch und Wasser.)

Monostatos.

Doch still! ich höre schrecklich Rauschen,
Wie Donnerton und Wasserfall.

Königin und Damen.

Ja, fürchterlich ist dieses Rauschen,
Wie fernen Donners Wiederhall.

Monostatos.

Nun sind sie in des Tempels Hallen.

Alle.

Dort wollen wir sie überfallen—
Die Frömmler tilgen von der Erd'
Mit Feuersgluth und mächt'gem Schwert

Die drei Damen und Monostatos.

Dir grosse Königin der Nacht,
Sei unsrer Rache Opfer gebracht.
(Sie versinken. Man hört starken Donner, Sturm.)

Monostatos, Queen, Ladies.

    Destroyed and demolished is our power,
    We all will be hurled into darkness.

        (They sink into the earth.)

CHANGE OF SCENE.

        (Temple of the Sun.)

(Priests and Priestesses, SARASTRO, elevated, TAMINO and PAMINA before him, both in priestly garb. Priests on both sides. The three YOUTHS hold flowers in their hands.)

Sarastro.

    The rays of the sun chase away the night,
    Destroy the sneaking power of the dis-
    sembler.

Chorus of Priests.

    Glory to the consecrated! You passed
      through darkness,
    May thanks to thee, Isis and Osiris, be
      given!
    May the strong conquer!
    And bring to wisdom and beauty
    The crown eternal!

          THE END.

Monostatos, Königin und die Damen.

    Zerschmettert, vernichtet ist unsere Macht,
    Wir alle gestürzet in ewige Nacht.

        (Exeunt.)

OFFENE VERWANDLUNG.

        (Sonnentempel.)

(PRIESTER und PRIESTERINNEN, SARASTRO steht erhöht. Vor ihm TAMINO und PAMINA, beide in priesterlicher Kleidung, DIE PRIESTER auf beider Seiten, die drei KNABEN halten Blumen.)

Sarastro.

    Die Strahlen der Sonne vertreiben die
      Nacht,
    Zernichten der Heuchler erschlichene
      Macht.

Chor der Priester.

    Heil sei euch Geweihten! Ihr dranget durch
      Nacht,
    Dank sei dir, Osiris und Isis, gebracht!
    Es siegte die Stärke und krönet zum Lohn—
    Die Schönheit und Weisheit mit ewiger
      Kron'!

          ENDE.

THE BARTERED BRIDE

(DIE VERKAUFTE BRAUT)

by

FRIEDRICH SMETANA

432

CHARACTERS

KRUSCHINA, a peasant . . . . . . *Baritone*
KATHINKA, his wife . . . . . . *Soprano*
MARIE, their daughter . . . . . . *Soprano*
MICHA, landed proprietor . . . . . . *Bass*
AGNES, his wife . . . . . . *Mezzo-Soprano*
WENZEL, their son . . . . . . *Tenor*

HANS, Micha's son by a former marriage . *Tenor*
KETSAL, matrimonial agent . . . . . *Bass*
SPRINGER, director of a troupe of itin-
erant actors . . . . *Bass*
ESMERALDA, dancer . . . . . . *Soprano*
MUFF, an Indian comedian . . . . . *Tenor*

VILLAGERS, ACTORS.
Place: A large village in Bohemia. Time: the present.

First performed in New York, in Bohemian, May 12, 1894.
First performed in New York, in German, at the Metropolitan Opera House.

PREFATORY NOTE

BEDRICH (or Friedrich) SMETANA, the greatest of Czech composers, was born in 1824. He was at first a pupil of Proksch at Prague, and subsequently studied with Liszt, under whom he became a skilled pianist. Although he lived for a while in Sweden as director of the Philharmonic Society at Gothenburg, the greater part of his life was spent in his native Bohemia, where he composed industriously and held the position of conductor at the Theater in Prague. Into his later life there entered an element of tragedy which places him in the not inconsiderable company of great composers who have been tried by the fierce fires of suffering. Deafness, which first showed itself in connection with an affection of the throat, gradually increased through seven years, and physicians were unable to stop the progress of his malady, which had a distressing accompaniment in the form of a perpetual buzzing and whistling noise in a high octave. He was obliged to exercise great care as conductor, as there were days when all voices and all octaves sounded confused and false. In 1874, after an opera performance which had given him great enjoyment, he improvised for an hour at the piano. The next day he was stone deaf, and remained so until his death. This put an end to his activities as conductor, but his powers in composition were not impaired, and the years of his deafness were marked by the production of great works. Finally, however, the perpetual nervous suffering affected his reason; he was not allowed to compose, and became the victim of strange hallucinations. At last the destruc-

tion of his mind became complete, and he died in an insane asylum at Prague (May 12, 1884) in utter darkness.

Although Smetana's work has been slower in becoming known outside of his own country than that of his compatriot Dvořák, his fame is based upon a more enduring achievement. Though he deliberately took his stand as an exponent of the art of his native country, he is a great deal more than this, for his work is marked by those universal qualities which make it the property of no particular place or race. Chiefly known hitherto in English-speaking countries by one or two of his great symphonic poems, and by the overture to his comic opera "The Bartered Bride," he composed during his connection with the theater several operas which attained great popularity in Bohemia. This popularity his now famous opera, "The Bartered Bride" is winning in other countries, and most deservedly, since it is one of the most beautiful of modern comic operas, and when presented by performers who understand the true comic traditions it must always impress itself upon the audience. Filled with lovely music, in which the national dance rhythms are refreshingly evident, vivid in orchestration and fluent in melody, it is from beginning to end quite original and characteristic. Thus far it is the only one of his operas which has crossed the borders of Bohemia, but it is in itself sufficient to assure Smetana's fame in the world's opera houses, and will probably suffice to obtain ultimately an introduction for others of his dramatic works. C. F. M.

3

ARGUMENT

Act I. — The scene is laid in a small village in Bohemia, at the season of the yearly church fair and festival. It is a time of rejoicing. The opera opens with a chorus, in the market-place before an inn, singing of love and marriage. Hans and Marie have fallen in love and the latter bewails the fact that her parents want to marry her to a man she does not care for. Hans consoles her, bidding her trust in him and that all will turn out well in the end.

At the sound of approaching footsteps, Hans goes away and Marie hides. Then appears Ketsal, a matrimonial agent, a feature at such festivals, who is negotiating with Krushina and Kathinka, Marie's father and mother, about a proposed marriage of Marie to Wenzel, son of Micha, who owns property in the same town. Marie knows nothing of this, nor of the man to whom she is to be betrothed. Ketsal, however, praises the young man so highly that the parents declare themselves agreeable to the match, particularly as Krushina is in debt to Micha. But Marie flatly refuses her consent to this arrangement in spite of the existence of a document in which her father, in view of the obligation, promises to give her in marriage to Micha's son. She loves Hans and will have no one else. Then Ketsal proposes that Krushina should go to Micha himself and have a talk, while he will try to arrange matters with Hans. The people then come out and gather in front of the inn to sing and dance.

Act II. — The act opens in a room in the interior of the inn. The young people are seated at tables singing the praises of beer, the great national drink. Hans then extols love above everything else, whereupon Ketsal puts money above all. Of course they disagree. The young people then dance and leave the inn.

Now Marie comes in and accidentally meets Wenzel, who stutters and is a simpleton. She induces him to give up all idea of marrying Marie, and to swear that he will not have her, nor even see her, because she will worry him to death; but she knows of another girl who is dying for love of him, and she pretends to be that girl. This is only to get rid of him, as he has never seen her, and of course does not know her. Meanwhile Ketsal meets Hans, and after trying various arguments resorts to money. He offers Hans one hundred, two hundred, and even three hundred florins. At last Hans yields, and promises to give up Marie, but with the express proviso that she will marry Micha's son and no other. He could safely enter into such agreement, because he himself is a son of Micha by a first wife. This is known to no one, not even Marie, since he had been away from home so long that Ketsal could not know him, and he had up to this time carefully avoided his parents. A contract is then drawn up and signed, to the disgust of the young people who knew of this love affair and who revile Hans.

Act III. — The scene is once more outside the inn. A traveling company of athletes and circus performers comes to the town. Wenzel admires one of the dancers, Esmeralda, and even makes love to her. While he is doing so the ring-master and manager is told that the man who did the part of the bear is dead drunk and cannot appear, thus threatening to spoil one of the most attractive features of the show. So he and Esmeralda use their wiles to induce Wenzel to impersonate the part, to which the latter ultimately consents. Just then his mother, Agnes, comes to lead him to Marie, and he refuses, saying that she will worry him to death.

Marie is then told of her lover's apparent faithlessness, and although she refuses to believe in his perfidy she is finally forced to acknowledge the documentary proof, the contract itself. She then meets Hans and upbraids him, whereupon he tries to explain, but she will not listen to him. So he banters her and Ketsal and gets them to call the parents and witness. As he expected, he was at once recognized by his parents, and dumbfounds Ketsal, who sees before him another son of Micha. He then gives the choice to Marie, who at last sees how matters stand, and joyfully throws herself into Hans's arms. Ketsal runs away in disgrace followed by the jeers of the people. Wenzel then appears in the disguise of a bear, and that and the fact of his being a simpleton decides Micha to acknowledge Hans as his son, and to give his blessing to the happy pair.

Thus the Bartered Bride receives the congratulations and good wishes of all concerned.

THE BARTERED BRIDE

ACT I.	ERSTER ACT.
(Main square in the village, with an inn at the side, at the time of the church fair in spring.)	(Der Hauptplatz des Dorfes mit Wirthshaus zur Zeit des Kirchweib festes im Frühling.)
SCENE I.	ERSTE SCENE.
MARIE and HANS. Chorus of Villagers.	Chor der Landleute. MARIE und HANS.

CHORUS OF VILLAGERS

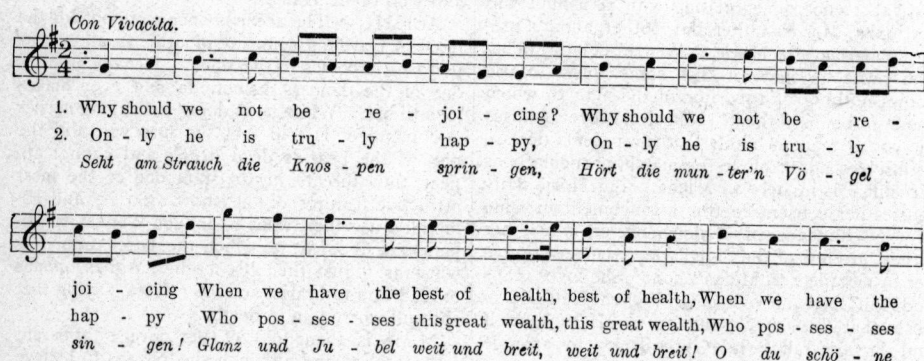

1. Why should we not be re - joi - cing? Why should we not be re -
2. On - ly he is tru - ly hap - py, On - ly he is tru - ly
Seht am Strauch die Knos - pen sprin - gen, Hört die mun - ter'n Vö - gel

joi - cing When we have the best of health, best of health, When we have the
hap - py Who pos - ses - ses this great wealth, this great wealth, Who pos - ses - ses
sin - gen! Glanz und Ju - bel weit und breit, weit und breit! O du schö - ne

best of health, best of health, When we have the best of health, best of health?
this great wealth, this great wealth, Who pos - ses - ses this great wealth, this great wealth.
Früh - lings - zeit, Früh - lings - zeit! O du schö - ne Früh - lings - zeit, Früh - lings - zeit!

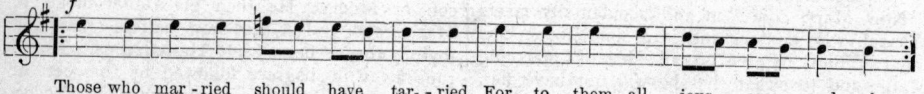

Those who mar - ried should have tar - -ried, For to them all joys are end - ed.
Je - der leicht ein Schät - zlein fin - det In der Ju - gend heis - sen Jah - ren,

Hus - band out to seek his pleas - ure, Wife at home, no mo - ment's lei - sure.
Doch be - vor man fest sich bin - det, Soll man kei - ne Vor - sicht spa - ren.

Chorus.   Woe's me!
              Woe's me!
   Pleasure at an end;
   Cares their bosom rend,
   Troubles and vexations.
   Why should we not be rejoicing
   When we have the best of health?
   Why should we not be rejoicing
   When we have the best of health?
   Only he is truly happy
   Who possesses this great wealth.
   Only he is truly happy
   Who possesses this great wealth.
Hans. Why are you so downcast
   And so sad, my darling?
Marie. Sad, sad is my fate!
   My dear mother told me
   That the man chosen to be my husband
   Is to meet me here to-day.
   O God! How will all this end?
Hans.   Listen!
   Have no fear, and trust to me;
   Then will all be well.   Only if your will
   Is strong and firm, to their wishes
   You'll not incline.   Then you'll be mine.
Chorus. Stop your sighing, stop complaining.
   Your true love will sure be gaining
   Its reward for e'er remaining.
   Why should we not be rejoicing
   If we have the best of health?
   Why should we not be rejoicing
   If we have the best of health?
   Only he is truly happy
   Who possesses this great wealth.
   Only he is truly happy
   Who possesses this great wealth.
   O come with us, dance and warble;
   Let not anger fill your bosom.
   Come then! To music lightly step.
        Sing and dance.
        (Exit Chorus.)

Chor.   Ehe,
            Wehe
   Sind gar nah' verwandt!
   Mög' uns Gott bewahern!
   Mancher hat's erfahren.
   Liebe lockt uns in die Falle,
   Das ist leider weltbekannt!
   Darum nehmt in Acht Euch Alle,
   Ihr Verliebten rings im Land!

Hans. Sprich, mein liebes Herz, warum
   Du so schweigsam bist und traurig!
Marie. Wie auch sollte ich's nicht sein!?
   Hat die Mutter doch gesagt,
   Dass er, der für mich Erwählte,
   Heute zu uns kommen würde!
   Weisst Du keine Hilfe?
Hans. Höre!
   Wenn der Freier Dir verhasst,
   Mög' er immer kommen nur.
   Bleibe standhaft! Glaube mir:
   Niemand zwingt ein starkes Herz!
Chor. Nur nicht klagen, nicht verzagen!
   Liebe lehrt uns Leid ertragen,
   Alles, Alles darf sie wagen!
   Seht am Strauch die Knospen springen,
   Hört die munter'n Vögel singen!
   Glanz und Jubel weit und breit!
   O, du schöne Frühlingszeit!
   Aber nehmt in Acht Euch Alle,
   Ihr Verliebten, rings im Land:
   Liebe lockt uns in die Falle,
   Das ist leider weltbekannt!
   Nun zum Tanze! Rührt die Glieder!
   Lustig geht es auf und nieder!
   Hei, da zeige Jedermann,
   Was er kann!
        (Chor ab.)

SCENE II.

Marie and Hans.

Marie. Then is it really all to happen? . . .
Unhappy me!

Hans. Why! my darling! What makes you so
very sad?
What has happened?

Marie. Do not be surprised!
To-day Micha and his son are to visit us
And ask for my hand.

Hans. And you!
What will be your answer?

Marie. What will be my answer?
How can you ask me such a question?
Can I belong to any one but you,
Hans, my darling? But my father is under
obligations.

Hans. That is really awful.

Marie. You seem timid, Hans! or even bashful,
As if you were afraid of something, or some-
body.
Swear to me, Hans, that you have no other
love,
Nor obligation, that binds you.
Believe me,
That more than once I had an idea
That you had another sweetheart.

Hans. No, never!

Marie. If I ever should find out
That such a thing is really so,
I would turn against you,
Hatred take the place of love's pure glow.
Tell me now, my dearest lover,
How came you to such a pass,
As to leave your home in anger,
And perhaps give up a lass?
Tell me now, as your past is shrouded in
deep mystery,
So that my father even noticed it, and spoke
of it.

ZWEITE SCENE.

Marie und Hans.

Marie. Zum Tanze rufen sie mich heut'
umsonst. . . .
O, mir ist weh' um's Herz!

Hans. Mein Liebchen, wie? Noch immer trübe
Augen?
Was kann es helfen?

Marie. Kaum zu denken wag' ich's!
Bald werden kommen sie zur Brautschau·
Micha,
Vater und Sohn, und um mich werben!

Hans. Nun gut. . .
Was willst Du thun?

Marie. Was soll ich thun? Ja, wollte
Gott, dass ich etwas wüsste! Eins nur weiss
ich,
Dass ich für alle Zeiten bin die Deine!
Wenn nur die Eltern mich nicht zwingen
werden!

Hans. Das wäre freilich traurig.

Marie. Doch Dich scheint
Es wenig zu bekümmern. . . Gar so ruhig,
Freund? . . .
Wenn Dir der widrige Fall gelegen käme? . . .
Ich bin verzweifelt, voller Angst und Sorgen,
Und Dich berührt dies Alles kaum! . . .
Ach, wenn
Mein treues Herz Du hintergingest, wenn
heimlich
Du eine Andere liebtest!?

Hans. O niemals!

Marie. Gern ja will ich Dir vertrauen,
Gläubig blicken auf zu Dir!
Ach, worauf noch könnt' ich bauen,
Wärst Du, Liebster, untreu mir!
Der von fern Du hergekommen,
Wer Du bist, ich weiss es nicht,
Habe Dich zum Schatz genommen
Auf Dein ehrliches Gesicht!
O sage, was Dich fort von Hause in
Die Fremde trieb? Von Deiner frühen
Jugend
Sprachst Du noch nie zu mir!

Hans. My! history is really a painful subject.
I am a son of parents comfortably well off.
But I lost my mother very early.
Unfortunately my father married a second time,
And my stepmother soon drove me out of the house.
I went out into the world,
And made my living among strangers.
Sweetest blessing is a mother,
A curse who takes her place!
With no feeling for another,
But only hatred in her face.

Marie. Sweetest blessing is a mother,
A curse who takes her place,
With no feeling for another
But only hatred in her face.

Hans. There may happen what will,
True and pure affection
Will resist all force
To bring about defection.

Hans. Nur ungern red' ich
Davon, es ist zu schmerzlich! . . . Wohl bin ich
Aus einem reichen Hause, doch es starb
Mir die geliebte Mutter. Bald darauf
Nahm sich der Vater eine zweite Frau.
Voll Falschheit hat sie mir des Vaters Herz
Entwendet, . . . aus dem Hause jagt' er mich!
Bei fremden Leuten dien' ich nun um's Brot.
Mit der Mutter sank zu Grabe
Meiner Jugend ganzes Glück,
Was ich früh verloren habe,
Bringt kein Sehnen mir zurück!

Marie. O Du guter, armer Knabe,
Wie beklag' ich Dein Geschick!
Doch getrost nur: freundlich labe
Dich ein warmer Liebesblick.

Hans. Nun wirst Du länger wohl nicht zweifeln!
Heimath
Und Vaterhaus ist Deine Liebe für
Den Frühverwaisten!

DUET

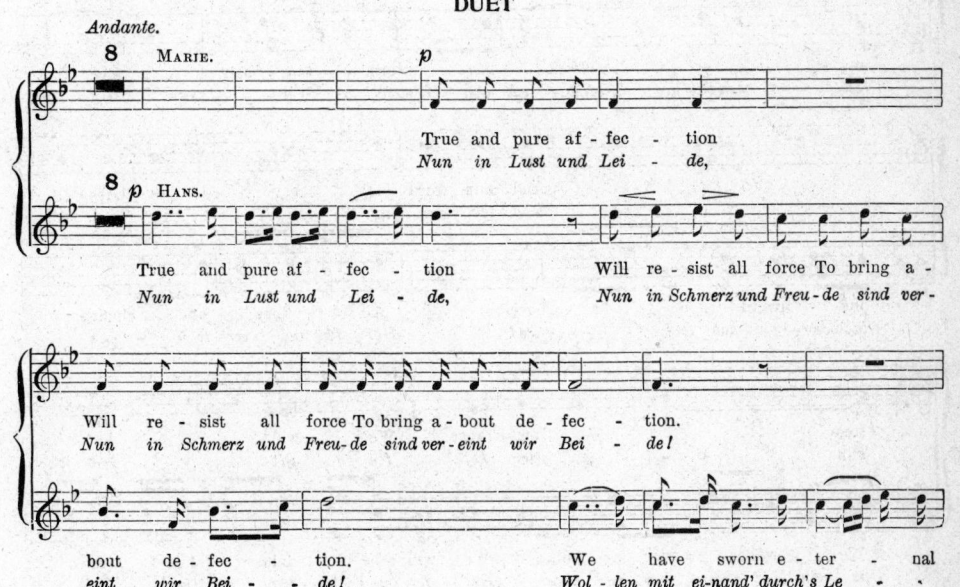

faith - ful for ev - - er, . . .   ev - er,
trau'n, uns ein Nest - chen bau'n . .   Bei - de

ev - - er,   Faith - ful for ev - er,
Nest - chen bau'n,   Sind ver- eint wir Bei - de,

Faith - ful for ev - er. We will be   ev - er
Bei - de wol - len wir ver- trau'n!   Bei - de,

Faith - ful for ev - er
nun in Lust und Lei - de

faith - ful, faith - ful, Faith - ful, we will be faith - ful for e'er.
Bei - de, bei - de, bei - de ver- trau'n, wol - len wir ver- trau'n,

Marie. Here they are! Father is coming with them.

They are looking for me.

Hans. They must not see me.

Farewell, my love'

Think often of me.

(HANS exit.)

(MARIE hides.)

Marie. Doch still! Man kommt! O, grosser Gott, der Vater!

Man sucht mich schon!

Hans. Dann ist's Zeit wohl, dass ich geh'!

Scheiden! Scheiden! Das thut weh.

Lebwohl, bis ich Dich wiederseh'!

(Ab.)

(MARIE verbirgt sich.)

SCENE III.

KRUSHINA, KATHINKA, and KETSAL.

Ketsal. Now I say, with great assurance,
 You gave your word and promise
 To uphold your pact and bargain,
 Then ev'rything is done.
 Only trust to my experience
 And my great wisdom.
 For many a doubtful case,
 Which to others was a problem,
 I brought to a happy close.
 And perhaps if your dear daughter
 Should refuse to marry,
 Then you'll see how I'll teach her to yield
 And to obey you. So trust to me.

Krushina. (to Kathinka).
 Well! what do you think, mother?
 I — I am satisfied.

Kathinka. This is so sudden, and too much for
 one day,
 For we must stop to consider, and ask the
 bride,
 If there is no impediment
 Or some other objection in the way.

Ketsal. What objection! What objection!
 Your decision and my craft
 Will overcome ev'ry obstacle.

Kathinka. It depends on who is the bridegroom.

Ketsal. Who the bridegroom?
 In vain is such a question.
 You can see that he is proper,
 If security go I.
 Tobias Micha you know surely.
 But perhaps not. Then I say,
 For his farm and buildings
 I'll give forty thousand cash.
 Now I say with great assurance,
 You gave your word and promise,
 To uphold your pact and bargain,
 Then ev'rything is done.

Kathinka. This is so sudden, and too much for
 one day.

Krushina (to himself).
 I — I am satisfied

DRITTE SCENE.

KRUSCHINA, KATHINKA und KEZAL.

Kezal. Alles ist so gut wie richtig,
 Und das Eine nur ist wichtig:
 Euer Wort gabt Ihr zum Pfande.
 Und somit ist Alles gut.
 Ja, was glücklich ist im Lande,
 Bracht' ich Alles unter'n Hut.
 Denn auf Scharfblick und Verstande
 Der Erfolg allein beruht.
 Kommt das Pärchen erst zusammen,
 Ei, so soll mich Gott verdammen,
 Stehen beide nicht in Flammen,
 Lodern beide nicht in Gluth!

Kruschina. (zu KATHINKA).
 Nun, so sag', was meinst Du, Alte?
 Steh' ich doch schon halb im Wort!

Kathinka. Eines ich mir vorbehalte:
 Soll es sein, dann nicht sofort!
 Ohne uns'rer Tochter Beirath
 Kommt zu Stande keine Heirath;
 Bin zu fragen gern erbötig,
 Ob sie schon entschlossen sei!

Kezal. Gar nicht nöthig, gar nicht nöthig!
 Euer Wort. . . es bleibt dabei.

Kathinka. Doch erst seh'n muss sie den Fre

Kezal. Auch noch sehen? Ei, zum Geier!
 Nichts da giebt es zu bekritteln!
 Würd' ich sonst wohl hier vermitteln?
 Bin ich denn zum Spasse da?
 Micha's lieber Sohn wird Allen,
 Gleich dem Vater, wohlgefallen!
 Nun, Ihr kennt ihn ja!
 Hochgeehrt!
 Sein Besitz ist unter Brüdern
 Volle dreissig Tausend werth.
 Alles ist so gut wie richtig,
 Und das Eine nur ist wichtig:
 Euer Wort gabt Ihr zum Pfande,
 Und somit ist Alles gut.

Kathinka. Doch man will erst wissen, was man
 thut.

Kruschina (für sich).
 Ihr zu widersprechen, fehlt der Muth.

Ketsal. Only trust to my experience
And my great wisdom, . . . happy close.
Krushina. Surely! I knew Tobias Micha when
he was a child.
He had two sons,
Hans by the first wife
And Wenzel by the second.
Of these, I know neither one nor the other.
Ketsal. That is true. Many years ago,
Before witnesses, you promised
To give your daughter
To his son for a wife.
Kathinka. But say! for which of the sons are you
speaking?

Ketsal. For which one? He has only one,
And his name is Wenzel.
The other one, by the first
Wife, is a tramp and good for
Nothing. Nobody knows where he is.
Krushina. Well, what kind of a fellow is this
Wenzel?
Why did you not bring him with you at
once?
Ketsal. He did not come now because he is bashful.
He is not flighty but thoroughly in earnest.
He is as gentle as gentlest lamb, though of
high condition.
Faults he has not any, neither vices.
Ev'ry mother would be proud to have a son
With such a lovely disposition.
He is neither tall nor little,
Nor's his health so very brittle.
Neither proud, nor very haughty,
Neither loud, nor rough, nor naughty,
Neither lavish, nor too stingy.
Well, in short, he is as normal
As a human being can be.
With a farm worth thirty thousand.
        Well then! Well then!
Who can ask for more!
He did not come now because he is bashful.
He is not flighty but thoroughly in earnest.
He is as gentle as gentlest lamb,
Though of high condition.

Kezal. Ja, was glücklich ist im Lande,
Bracht' ich Alles unter'n Hut.
Kruschina. Nun freilich! Den Tobias Micha
kannte
Als Kind ich schon, doch wenig habe ich
Erfahren noch von seinen beiden Söhnen,
Kaum, dass ich ihrer Namen mich erinn're

Kezal. Wie seltsam! Denn vor wenig Jahren habt
Ihr ihm versprochen Euer Töchterlein
Dem Sohn zur Frau zu geben!

Kathinka. Sagt doch, sagt:
Für welchen von den beiden denn bewerbt
Ihr Euch?
Kezal. Könnt Ihr noch fragen? Hat er ja
Nur Einen, der heisst Wenzel. Denn der
Sohn
Von seiner ersten Frau ist längst verschollen,
Ja, wie man glaubt, gestorben.
Kruschina. Und was ist
Mit unserm Wenzel? Wohl nicht ohne
Grund
Hält er sich fern, versteckt?
Kezal. Gekommen wär' er mit, wie gerne!
Doch zarte Rücksicht hält ihn ferne,
Er sieht auf Anstand, feinen Ton.
Ja, seine Tugenden und Sitten,
Sie machen überall ihn wohlgelitten,
Wohl jede Mutter wünscht sich solchen Sohn
's ist kein Schlemmer und kein Säufer,
Spätausgeher, Kneipenläufer,
Auch kein Prahler und kein Pracher,
Kartenspieler, Schuldenmacher,
Kein verweg'ner Messerträger,
Pascher, Schwärzer, wilder Jäger,
Auch kein Zänker
Und kein Stänker,
Läst'rer, Flucher,
Händelsucher!
Er ist wohlabgeschliffen,
Er ist leicht von Begriffen,
Nüchtern,
Schüchtern,
Fein im Ton . . .
Doch, das sagt' ich schon.

Krushina and Kathinka.
>Your description is sufficient,
>Your description is sufficient.
>We trust to your honesty.

Kruschina und Kathinka.
>Wär' er nur gleich mitgekommen!
>Staunend haben wir's vernommen,
>Und sind sehr erstaunt davon.

SCENE IV.

MARIE and the preceding.

Ketsal. Now we have her, now we have her.
>Seriously, we now can take her.

Marie. My dear father, my dear mother!
>Are you looking for me?

Ketsal. I just asked them if you love somebody,
>If you have not any swain
>Who to your love would attain.
>I can bring you a young man
>Who will be to your gain.

Marie. What! who will be to my gain?

Krushina. You will see him
>And can judge for yourself.

Kathinka   (whispers to MARIE).
>If you do not like him,
>Why, he can go by himself.

Marie. I shall see him,
>And can judge for myself.
>If I do not like him,
>Why, he can go by himself.

Kathinka. You will see him,
>And can judge for yourself.
>If you do not like him,
>Why, he can go by himself.

Krushina and Ketsal.
>You will see him,
>And can judge for yourself.
>If you do not like him,
>Why, he can go by himself.

Ketsal. Then let us at once
>The contract put together.
>Let Marie give her consent now,
>And all will be fixed forever.

Marie. That — that cannot be done as quickly as
>you think. No, really not,
>For there is a something which will prevent it.

VIERTE SCENE.

MARIE und die VORIGEN.

Kezal. Seht, da kommt sie sonder Ahnung!
>Zeit jetzt wär 'es zur Vermahnung!

Marie. Lieber Vater, liebe Mutter,
>Was wollt Ihr mir sagen?

Kezal. Darf ich, schönstes Kindchen,
>Dich wohl fragen:
>Hast Du nicht daran gedacht,
>Dass ich Dir was mitgebracht?
>Rathe schnell, wer rathen kann!
>Einen jungen Mann.

Marie. Was geht mich an
>Ein fremder Mann?

Kruschina. Sollst sein Weibchen sein,
>Liebes Töchterlein!

Kathinka   (leise zu MARIE).
>Willst Du aber ihn nicht haben.
>Nun, so sagst Du nein!

Marie. Ich sein Weibchen sein?
>Ei, was fällt Euch ein!?
>Er mag ruhig weiter traben
>Und wo anders frei'n!

Kathinka. Sollst sein Weibchen sein,
>Liebes Töchterlein!
>Willst Du aber ihn nicht haben,
>Nun, so sagst Du nein!

Kruschina und Kezal.
>Sollst sein Weibchen sein,
>Liebes Töchterlein!
>Diesem feinen jungen Knaben
>Deine Liebe weih'n!

Kezal. Nicht lange mehr sich zieren!
>Nur keine Zeit verlieren!
>Ein fröhlich Ja gesprochen,
>Und Hochzeit giebt es in vier Wochen!

Marie. Fein langsam! Denn es eilt nicht sehr
>Ein Umstand ist dagegen
>Gewichtig, voll und schwer.

Ketsal. Something this, something that,
No obstacle can ever stop me.
To whate'er I put my mind
A complete success will surely be.

Marie. I love another
More than a brother.

Ketsal. Give him up as you'll be no pair,
Let him seek his fortune elsewhere.

Marie. My word I gave him, and my troth.

Ketsal. Word and troth are of no value.

Marie. Our contract also has been signed.

Ketsal. We shall tear it into pieces.

Marie. Just you try, just you try.

Ketsal. Trust all to my ready wit.
All will be well if you have grit.
And my massive brain,
My mind, my mind,
Will soon conquer the whole world.
What no one can unravel
That my great mind can achieve.

Marie, Krushina, Kathinka.
What no one can unravel
That his great mind can achieve.

Marie. My Hans will never give me up,
I can stake my life on it.

Krushina (with forceful energy).
Give you up, or not give you up,
That is not the question.

(To KATHINKA to excuse himself.)

I put myself under obligation
To Tobias Micha before witnesses.

Kathinka. But pray, dear husband!
What obligation?

Ketsal (drawing out a paper).
Here it is! Black on white!
Signed by Micha, Krushina, and witnesses.

Marie. What does that amount to?

(Knocks the paper out of his hand.)

That is of no value.
Hans and I know nothing of it, and we
never can yield.

(Exit.)

Kezal. Umstand hin . . . Umstand her . . .
Was ist daran gelegen!
Nein, Hindernisse giebt's nicht mehr,
Wo meine Kräfte sich regen!

Marie. So muss ich bekennen?
Muss meinen Liebsten nennen?

Kezal. Pah! Von solchen Kindereien
Will ich Dich gar bald befreien!

Marie. Treue hab' ich ihm geschworen . . .

Kezal. Damit ist noch nichts verloren!

Marie. Der zur Gattin mich erkoren!

Kezal. Laufen lass den armen Thoren!

Marie. Ihm gehören Herz und Hand.

Kezal. Das war eitel Spiel und Tand!
Wozu hätte ich Verstand?
Dafür bin ich ja bekannt!
Und zum Ziele wird gelangen,
Wer die rechte Strasse fand.

Marie, Kruschina, Kathinka.
Ja, zum Ziele wird gelangen,
Wer die rechte Strasse fand.

Marie. Mit Hans bin ich vereinigt, denn wir haben
Uns ew'ge Treue heute noch gelobt!

Kruschina (mit gewaltsamer Energie).
Was? Ohne Vorspruch und Bewilligung?
Ich, als der Vater, sage: Nein!

(Zu KATHINKA, sich gleichsam entschuldigend.)

Ich steh'
Dem Micha doch im Wort, sie seinem Sohn
Zu geben.

Kathinka. O, wie ungeschickt von Dir,
Dass Du's versprochen hast!

Kezal (zieht ein Papier hervor).
Ja, schwarz auf weiss!
Hier steht es Alles deutlich, unterschrieben
Von den Parteien und den Zeugen auch.

Marie. Nur bin ich nicht dabei!

(Schlägt ihm das Papier aus der Hand.)

Und also gilt
Es nichts! Was ich gesagt, ist meine
Meinung
Und soll es bleiben!

(Ab.)

Ketsal. Oh, what a perverted world this is.

Krushina. Where did you leave Micha, and his son, that honored and respected bridegroom?

It would have been proper for him to speak to Marie.

Ketsal. Oh well! of course he is not accustomed to speak to women.

He is as bashful as a country maiden.

Krushina. Then the courting will be hard.

Ketsal. And, now, my dear sir, I think it best for you to go over

To the other inn, and meet Micha and his son as if by chance.

It will be noisy here;

They are going to dance.

Meanwhile, I'll look up Hans and convince him

That it's for his best.

(They go off in different directions.)

SCENE V.

(The villagers come in. The older ones seat themselves at the tables and drink. The younger ones prepare to dance.)

Chorus. Come, my darling!

Start the bounding

While the Polka

Still is sounding.

Hands entwining,

Eyes in trance,

Let the whole world

Join the dance.

Hear the basses

Set in motion,

All the band

In great commotion.

All the earth

Is moving fast.

Let us dance

While life does last.

END OF ACT I.

Kezal. Darauf war ich nicht gefasst!

Kruschina. Von Euch war es ein grosser Fehler,

Allein zu kommen! Warum habt Ihr uns

Den Wenzel nicht gleich mitgebracht? Er hätte

Bei seiner Braut sich vorgestellt zum Mind'sten.

Kezal. Ja freilich! Doch er war nicht zu bewegen.

Er ist verzagt und schüchtern, des Verkehres

Mit Weibern gänzlich ungewohnt.

Kruschina. Dann wird es schwerlich etwas werden.

Kezal. Hört,

Was ich Euch rathen will: Das Beste wäre,

Ihr sprächet Euch jetzt einmal gründlich aus.

Mit Vater Micha in dem Wirthshaus dort!

Man stört Euch nicht, denn Alles läuft zum Tanze.

Mit Hans will ich inzwischen reden, ich

Krieg' ihn herum!

(Sie gehen nach verschiedenen Seiten ab.)

FÜNFTE SCENE.

(Das Landvolk versammelt sich vor dem Wirthshause, die Aelteren setzen sich an die Tische und trinken; die Jüngeren bereiten sich zum Tanz vor.)

Chor. Durch die Reihen

Hinzufliegen!

Sich zu Zweien

Anzuschmiegen!

Herz am Herzen

Fühlt man schlagen.

Unter Scherzen.

Fortgetragen!

Frohe Weise,

Laut und leise

Sollst Du geben

Neues Leben!

Ging' es, wie es uns gefällt,

Tanze mit die ganze Welt!

Violin' und Clarinette

Jauchzen trillernd um die Wette

Selbst dem alten Rumpelbass

Macht das tolle Wesen Spass.

ENDE DES ERSTEN ACTES.

ACT II.

Interior of the inn.

SCENE I.

(HANS, with young villagers, sits at a table on the one side and KETSAL on the other side of the room. They drink beer.)

Chorus. Oh, beer a blessing really is unto all;
For troubles and worries it drives to the wall,
And gives us the strength to bear our fate.
Hurrah!
A man who does not drink is a solemn guest.
The world full of troubles is e'en at its best.
So let us partake and not come late.
Hurrah!

Hans
(gets up).
Well, boys, believe me, I say it from my heart,
That love really is above all wine and beer
The only thing that makes life worth living,
And makes us hopefully look to the future.

Chorus (*Tenors*).
Hans, you are in love, we see with half an eye.
Chorus (*Basses*)
(alluding to Ketsal).
Look, that one his finger may put in your pie!

Ketsal
(also stands up).
No, if it should be so, he thereby will be no loser.
Good advice and real sound money
Are the greatest powers in this world.
He who uses them with wisdom
Cannot, cannot ever go astray.
(Raises his glass.)
Here's to sound money.

Hans
(raises his glass).
Here's to love the best of all.

ZWEITER ACT.

Wirthsstube.

ERSTE SCENE.

(HANS, mit jungen Landleuten, sitzt am Tisch auf der einen, KEZAL auf der anderen Seite der Stube. Sie trinken Bier.)

Chor. Wie schäumst Du in den Gläsern, edler Gerstensaft!
An Dir trinkt sich ein Jeder Feuer und Kraft!
Dich preisen die Jungen und Alten.
Heissassa!
Wenn wir bei'm Biere sitzen, Mann gereiht an Mann,
Was geht uns das Andere weiter noch an?
In Gnaden wird uns Gott erhalten!
Heissassa!

Hans
(steht auf).
Ihr Freunde, wohl stimm' ich von Herzen mit ein,
Doch denk' ich dabei auch an das Liebchen mein.
Denn das allein ist Himmelslust auf Erden:
Zu lieben und geliebt zu werden!
Chor. (*Tenöre.*)
Aus Liebe verlierst Du den Kopf noch, Du Thor!
(*Basse.*)
(auf KEZAL anspielend).
Sieh' lieber beizeiten vor Dem da Dich vor!

Kezal
(steht ebenfalls auf).
Was hilft die Liebe Dem, der Hab' und Gut verlor'!?
Zuverlässig ist nur Eines,
Und das ist das baare Geld!
Armer Schlucker, hast Du keines
Dann verlacht Dich alle Welt!
(Erhebt das Glas.)
Hoch das baare Geld!

Hans
(erhebt das Glas).
Mein Mädchen ist's die mir gefällt!

(Girls enter one by one, and take part in the dance, after the drinking song.)

Chorus. Oh, beer a blessing really is unto us all;
   For troubles and worries it drives to the
      wall,
   And gives us strength to bear our fate.
      Hurrah!

(Dance Furiant, a Bohemian national dance. After the dance the girls drag the young men out of the room.)
                    (Exeunt.)

SCENE II.

Venzel
               (enters timidly)

   Mo-mother dear
      Said to me
   That she would like
      Soon to see
   Me get happ'ly
      Married.
   So long had
      I tarried
   That they all,
      Round about,
   Do think me
      A great big lout.

SCENE III.

MARIE and WENZEL.

(Both begin to laugh, when they catch sight of one another.)
                 (Recitative.)

Marie. Are you not the one chosen to become
      Marie Krushina's husband?
Wenzel
      (first afraid, then more trustingly).
      Ye-ye-yes, of course. But ho-how did you
         know it?
Marie. Why! Cannot every one see it?
      How dressed up you are!
      The whole town is talking about you
      And is sorry for you.

Wenzel
               (anxiously).
   So-so-sorry for me! and why?

(Mädchen treten nach und nach herein und betheiligen sich an dem Tanze nach dem Trinkliede.)

Chor. Wie schäumst Du in den Gläsern, edler
      Gerstensaft,
      An Dir trinkt sich ein Jeder Feuer und
         Kraft!
      Dich preisen die Jungen und Alten.
            Heissassa!
               (Tanz Furiant).

(Nach dem Tanze ziehen die Mädchen die jungen Leute aus der Wirthsstube. Alle ab.)

ZWEITE SCENE.

Wenzel
            (schüchtern eintretend).

   Theu' . . . theurer Sohn,
   Sprach Mütterlein,
   Zeit ist es schon
   Für Dich zu frei'n!
   Fa . . . fass' Dir Muth
   Und sei ein Mann:
   Was Jeder thut,
   Ist wohlgethan.
   Si . . . sicherlich,
   Kehrt' ich nach Haus,
   La . . . lachte mich.
   A . . . alles aus.

DRITTE SCENE.

MARIE und WENZEL.

(Beide lachen laut, wie sie sich erblicken.)
                (RECITATIV.)

Marie. Seid der Verlobte Ihr von Kruschina's
      Mariechen nicht?
Wenzel
      (erst erschreckt, dann zutraulicher).
      A . . . allerdings, mein schö . . .
      Schö . . . schönes Kind, der bin ich.
Marie.   Hab' ich's Euch
      Doch angesehen . . . Nein, wie hübsch
         Ihr seid!
      Die Mädchen alle hier im Dorfe schon
      Beklagen Euch.
Wenzel
               (ängstlich).
   Beklagen mich? Warum?

Marie. Because she will deceive you.
She loves another.

Wenzel

(stupidly).

Ho-how can she love another
If she's to have me?

Marie

(laughs).

Ha ha! You? Does she know you? Or you
her?

Wenzel. She-she does not. But she knows
That I am to be her hu-hu-husband.

Marie. Of course she does,
And that is why she enjoys the prospect
of teasing you, deceiving
You, and worrying you to death.

Wenzel

(horrified).

Wh-why, that's awful!
Bu-but my mo-mother told me
That I must marry,
So-so marry I must.

Marie. Of course! Why not? Such a fine fellow!

(Coquettishly.)

There are lots of fine girls here.
Pick one out yourself!

Wenzel

(relieved).

I will.

Marie. I know a charming maiden
Wants you with all her might.
With love her heart is laden,
Without you all is night.

Wenzel

(joyously).

Oh, oh, what ecstasy!
When such a girl really loves me.
Oh, oh, what ecstasy!
Bu-but, Marie! What will she say?

Marie. Euere Braut — ich sag's Euch — meint's
nicht ehrlich.
'nen Andern liebt sie!

Wenzel

(einfältig).

Ka . . . ka . . . kann sie lieben
Denn einen Anderen? Ich bin ja da!

Marie

(lacht).

Haha! Kennt sie Euch denn, und kennt
Ihr sie?

Wenzel. Ke . . . kennen? Nein. Do . . . doch
sie weiss, dass ich
Ihr Ga . . . Ga . . . Gatte werde!

Marie.   Mag wohl sein,
Und eben d'rum lacht sie Euch aus!
Sie wird
Euch schmäh'n, Euch hintergeh'n,
Euch quälen bis
Zu Tode.

Wenzel

(entsetzt).

Wa . . . was sagst Du da? Doch wenn
Die Mutter haben will, dass ich sie nehme!
Heirathen mu . . . mu . . . muss ich nun
einmal!

Marie. Ei, freilich, warum nicht? Das sollt Ihr
auch!

(Kokett.)

Es giebt ja hier noch and're Mädchen!
— Sucht
Euch eine aus!

Wenzel

(erleichtert).

Ich will's.

Marie. Ich weiss Euch einen lieben Schatz,
Den Mancher schon begehrt,
Ein schönes Mädchen, hier am Platz,
Die lange Euch verehrt.

Wenzel

(froh).

Wär's möglich wohl? Versteh' ich recht?
Ein schönes Kind ? Das wär' nicht
schlecht!
Jedoch Mariechen wird sich grämen.

Marie

(decidedly).

Naught! For surely
After marrying you
She'll run away.
Wenzel. Bu-but my mother!
She will raise a row.
Marie. As soon as she'll see the bride
A smile will light her brow.
Wenzel. Is she then so lovely?
Marie. Just the same as Marie.
Wenzel. A-and is she young, too?
Marie. Just the same as Marie.
Wenzel. A-a-and that one would really take me?
Marie. If you would not want her
Grief sure would make her rave, and water
be her grave.
Charcoal would end her days and she would
weep always, if she could not get you.

(She pretends to be crying.)

Wenzel

(touched).

Wh-why do you weep?
Marie. Oh, because you do not want her.
Wenzel

(undecided).

I, I do not dare.
My mother is there.

Marie

(reproachfully).

You only make excuses,
And she who loves you dearly
You let grieve so sorely.
Wenzel

(puzzled).

No, no, no. I do not.

(Timidly.)

If she is just like you, then,

(Decidedly.)

Her I'll love.
Marie

(coquettishly).

You would love me all your life?
Wenzel. My-my life.
Marie. Make me your own darling wife?

Marie

(immer überlegen und doppelsinnig).

Die wird sich schon den Andern nehmen.

Wenzel. Doch mein Mütterlein,
Das wird Zeter schrei'n.
Marie. Sie wird mit Eurer Wahl zufrieden sein.

Wenzel. Ist schön die Andre?
Marie. Gerade wie Mariechen.
Wenzel. Und jung an Jahren?
Marie. Gerade wie Mariechen.
Wenzel. Doch will sie mich denn auch zum Mann?
Marie. Wenn ohn' Euch sie nicht leben kann!
Verzichtet auf Marie,
Sonst geht zu Grunde sie,
Die Tag und Nacht
An Euch gedacht!

(Sie thut, als ob sie weine.)

Wenzel

(gerührt).

Wei . . . wei . . . weinen seh' ich Dich?
Marie. Ach, ihr Loos bekümmert mich!
Wenzel

(schwankend).

Ich darf es ja nicht,
Mich bindet die Pflicht!
Marie

(vorwurfsvoll).

So grausam fand ich Keinen!
Vor Gram um Euch zehrt sie sich auf,
Ihr aber lasst sie weinen.
Wenzel

(rathlos).

Wer sagt mir, was ich thu'?

(schüchtern.)

Ja, wäre sie wie Du,
Dann . . .

(entschlossen.)

nur immerzu
Marie

(kokettirend).

So wie ich? Wollt Ihr sie so?
Wenzel. Ja, Ja, gerade so.
Marie. Macht' Euch meine Liebe froh?

Wenzel. My-my wife.

Marie

(affectionately).

Then you I'll love with all my heart,
And from you never part.

(Determinedly.)

Put your hand in mine, here.
You must swear now.
You must swear you are in earnest and
  sincere,
To resign and give up Marie
From now, for evermore.
You must swear that.

Wenzel

(suspiciously).

Must I swear? That makes me sore.

Marie

(apparently grieved.)

Well, I see you are a fool.
You will only be her tool,
And she'll treat you awfully.
So for the worst prepare,
Unless you will now swear.

(Pretends to go away.)

Wenzel

(holds her back.)

Wa-wait. I'll swear.

Marie. " Marie solemnly I give up."

Wenzel. I-I-gi-give up.

Marie. Never hope to see her again.
Wenzel. S-s-see her again.
Marie. Never hope to hear of her, then.
Wenzel. He-he-hear of her, then.
  I'll give her up for evermore.
Marie. I know a charming maiden
Wants you with all her might.
With love her heart is laden,
Without you all is night.
Wenzel. O-oh, ecstasy and joy!
  You have fully conquered this boy!

(He tries to embrace her, but she dodges him, and laughing runs
away; he after her.)

Wenzel. Ja, sie macht mich froh.

Marie

(innig).

Dem halt' ich Treue bis an's Grab,
Den ich in's Herz geschlossen hab'!

(bestimmt.)

Was ich jetzt Euch sage, höret:
  Ihr beschwöret,
Dass Ihr fest entschlossen seid,
Von Marie Euch loszusagen,
  Jetzt und alle Zeit!

Wenzel

(misstrauisch).

Nu . . . nu . . . nur nicht schwören!
Da . . . das geht zu weit!

Marie

(scheinbar gekränkt).

Ihr wollt nicht? Gut, lasst es sein!
Eure Lieb' ist wahrlich klein.
Möget Ihr es nie bereuen,
An Marien's Seite Euch
Eures Lebens freuen!

(Thut, als wollte sie gehen.)

Wenzel

(sie zurückrufend).

Ha . . . ha . . . halt! Ich schwöre ja!

Marie

(den Schwur vorsprechend).

„Was geschieht und was geschah,"

Wenzel

(nachstammelnd).

Ge . . . geschieht und ge . . . geschah. .

Marie. „Niemals komm' ich mehr ihr nah,"
Wenzel. Me . . . mehr ihr na . . . na . . .nah . . .
Marie. „Und für mich ist sie nicht da! "
Wenzel. Sie . . . sie . . . sie nicht da . . . da . . .
  da.
Marie. Ich weiss Euch einen lieben Schatz,
Den Mancher schon begehrt,
Ein schönes Mädchen hier am Platz,
Die lange Euch verehrt!
Wenzel. Wär's möglich, und versteh' ich recht?
  Du ha . . . ha . . . hast mein Herz bekehrt.

(Er will sie umarmen; sie entzieht sich ihm und läuft lachend davon
WENZEL hinter ihr her.)

### SCENE IV.	### VIERTE SCENE.
<small>Hans and Ketsal.</small>	<small>Hans und Kezal.</small>

Ketsal

<small>(drags Hans in).</small>

Come, my friend, don't make a row!
Something good I'll tell you.

Hans.

<small>(struggling).</small>

Let me go, I'm busy now,
Else I'd not repel you.

Ketsal. Don't you know then who I am?

Hans. I have not that honor, sir!
Neither do you, who I am.

Ketsal. You are quick, and smart and bright;
They tell me you're a wonder.
But beyond this, you're beloved
By a maiden yonder.
Have you enough of money?

Hans. No, but many a happy pair
So got along, it seems.
Honest maidens, blithe and fair,
Love men and not their means.

Ketsal. Believe me, I have knowledge great
And tell you that to shun.
Without cash, marriage is only confusion.
Tell me now whence you come,
And perhaps something you'll hear
To your advantage.

Hans. From afar do I come,
From a distant country.
Where the Moldau rolls
Is my childhood's home.

Ketsal. Then at once to it return.
To love a stranger our
Maidens never learn.

Kezal

<small>(zieht Hans herein).</small>

Komm', mein Söhnchen, auf ein Wort
Will Dir was vertrauen!

Hans

<small>(sträubt sich).</small>

Lasst mich gehen, ich muss fort,
Auf die Felder schauen!

Kezal. Weisst Du denn nicht, wer ich bin?

Hans. Ja, man sagt' es mir vorhin;
Und wonach steht Euer Sinn?

Kezal. Bist gescheidt, flink und gewandt,
Magst zu Vielem taugen,
Einem Mädchen, wie bekannt,
Stachst Du in die Augen.
Hast Du auch Vermögen?

Hans. Meinetwegen Sorgen gar?
Steht in Gottes Segen
Doch ein jedes treue Paar!

Kezal. Thorheit! Das lieget auf der Hand:
Dass Dein Glück nicht von Bestand!
Ohne Geld ist alles Tand.
Drum ein Sümmchen sparen! . . .
Hab' es selbst erfahren
Einst in jungen Jahren.

<small>(Verlegenheitspause.)</small>

Eines noch
Sag' mir doch:
Gern hätt' ich vernommen,
Wo Du hergekommen?

Hans. Weit von hier
Wohnen wir.
Von der Moldau Wogen
Bin ich hergezogen.

Kezal. Dort sollst Du Dein Weibchen finden!
In der Fremde sich zu binden,
Thut nicht gut, das glaube mir!

Hans. All may think that way but one.
That one I have surely won.
She to me is all my life,
And her I'll make my wife.

Ketsal. Every one like you
Thinks his love is true;
In her naught but
Goodness he believes.
But how dreadful
When she him deceives!
Then he sighs and weeps,
And so quietly reaps
What he cannot cure.
Then he sighs and weeps,
And so quietly reaps
What he must endure.
But a man of sense
Will well prepare,
And before the time
All things weigh with care.
He will count
The profit
All the same.
And if none,
Why he will
Quit the game.

Hans

(impatiently).

What do you mean with all this?
I do not understand you.

Ketsal. That I know a better bride, for you, my
dear boy.

Hans. Was ich in der Fremde fand,
Bietet mir kein Heimathland.
Einen Engel nenn' ich mein,
Und der soll mein Weibchen sein!

Kezal. Wer in Lieb' entbrannt,
Hält aus Unverstand
Weiber für Engel,
Meint in Schwärmerei
Dass sein Mädchen sei.
Ganz ohne Mängel.
Ja, so manches Schätzchen
Ist ein Schmeichelkätzchen,
Das mit Sammetpfötchen Dich umspielt:
Aber, wie entsetzlich,
Wenn man später plötzlich
Ihre scharfen Tigerkrallen fühlt!
Einer sorgt und sinnt
Um ein schönes Kind,
Bis er sie gewinnt,
Und das Glück ist gross;
Leider hinterher
Seufzt er bang und schwer:
Du, mein Gott und Herr,
Wär' ich sie erst los!
Doch ein Praktikus
Stets sich wohl bewahrt;
Vielerlei Verdruss
Bleibt ihm dann erspart.
Nichts schlägt ihn darnieder,
Weil das Für und Wider
Er zuvor sich weislich überlegt.
Der kann heiter scherzen,
Der nicht blos im Herzen
Seinen Schatz, nein, auch im Beutel trägt.
Was ist Dir geblieben?
Freund, hab' Acht!
Froher Sinn und Lieben
Gute Nacht!

Hans

(unwirsch).

Bin ich dafür Dank Euch schuldig?
Treibt mit Andern Euren Spass!

Kezal. Freundchen, nur nicht ungeduldig,
Dir zu bieten hab' ich 'was.

She will al - so get a house from
Je - des hof - fen er sagt's of - fen

get a house from Pa, you bet, my hon - ey,
ich sag's of - fen wil - les ü - ber - stei - gen,

Pa, you bet, my hon - ey.
wil - les ü - ber - stei - gen.

She has two cows, And one calf to match them;
Häu - schen und Gar - ten Vieh al - ler Ar - ten!

Fowls by the doz - en, pigs you can't watch them; A great big farm and
Mil - chen - de Kü - he, loh - nen - der Mü - he Schwein - chen im Ko - ben

well filled bran new till, a well filled, well filled bran new till, A great big
hoch zu lo - ben, Hüh - ner, Tau - ben kaum zu glau - ben, Trö - ge, Wan - nen,

She has two
Häu - schen und

farm, a great big farm, And well filled, well filled bran new till. She has two cows, And
Krü - ge, Kan - nen, in der Tru - he Klei - der, Schu - he! Häu - schen und Gar - ten,

Ketsal. If you will stop this flirtation,
I shall moreover pay you something.
Will you? Here I give you my promise,
A hundred florins,
If you'll give up your love.

Hans. One hundred only?
That is little money for such an
Amount of love;
I cannot sell it so cheaply.

Ketsal

(eagerly).

I will give you twice as much.

Hans. Even that is too little.

Ketsal. Then, three hundred florins.
I do it only because I want the thing over
with.
But if you do not consent now,

(Threateningly.)

I will do my very, very best to have
You finally sent away from
Here in disgrace. And then
You will neither have the girl
Nor the three hundred florins.

Hans. Well, well! but who is going to give me the
promised sum?

Ketsal. I! I!

Hans

(surprised and distrustful).

You? Surely not for yourself?
I would not give her to you for a million!

Ketsal Don't be silly! I don't want her for my-
self. I have one of
My own, up to the neck. Don't
You know that I am arranging
This for the son of Tobias Micha?
As soon as the contract is
Signed, you will get your
Money, and then away with you!

Hans. Well, then, I consent.
Money is money!
Put down the cash, and all
Will be settled.

Kezal. Gieb doch die dumme Liebschaft auf! Es
soll
Dich nicht gereuen! . . . Willst Du? . . .
Ohne Faxen:
Ich lass' es hundert Gulden kosten mich.

Hans. Nur hundert Gulden? So viel also gälte
Ein solches Opfer Euch!? Nein, lieber
Herr,
Das nehm' ich nicht!

Kezal

(eifrig).

Mein'thalb' das Doppelte!

Hans. Was Euch nicht einfällt!

Kezal. Na, dreihundert Gulden!
Doch eilig zugegriffen, dass die Sache
Einmal zum Ende kommt! . . . Wie? Du
zögerst
Noch immer?

(Drohend.)

Hüte Dich! Ich habe hier
Sehr gute Freunde; sag' ich nur ein Wort,
Bringt man Dich weg von hier der Schub!
Sodann
Hast weder eine Braut Du, noch'nen
Kreuzer!

Hans. Und wer giebt die versproch'ne Summe
her?

Kezal. Ich! Ich!

Hans

(stellt sich erstaunt und ungläubig).

Ihr? Etwa für Euch selbst? Euch liess' ich
Das Mädchen nicht, um keine Million!

Kezal. Was für ein Einfall! Ich bin längst ver-
sehen,
Hab' an der Meinen auch genug schon! —
Weisst
Du nicht, dass ich vermitt'le für den Sohn
Tobias Micha's nur? Wir setzen auf
Ein kleines Schriftstück, Du bekommst
Dein Geld . . .
Dann aber, mach' Dich auf den Weg!

Hans. Nun, also,
Sei's d'rum! Es ist ein schönes Geld
Habt Ihr.
Gezahlt. dann ist in Ordnung Alles.

(Hesitatingly.)

Under one condition,
That nobody else will get
My Marie, but the son of
Tobias Micha! Otherwise,
This contract will be null and void.

Ketsal. Why, of course, most assuredly!
That nobody else gets her, or
Will be allowed to take her, but Micha's
son.

Hans. And I shall leave her to no
Other than Micha's son.
That must specially be stated
When you draw up the contract.

Ketsal. I shall write out the contract at once and
call the witnesses together.

Hans. Still another word.
It shall also be stated, that
As soon as Marie and Micha's son have
joined hands
In wedlock, then shall
The elder Micha cease from
Insisting on the payment of Krushina's debt.
It shall be regarded as wiped out.

Ketsal. Yes, I agree to that.

(Exit, contented.)

SCENE V.

Hans

(alone).

When you'll see who by the bargain has
profited,
You'll return quite discomforted.
Who could believe
That I'd sell
My darling Marie!
The angel of my life,
My crowning glory when
She'll be my wife.
Not for a thousand would I her exchange.

(Zögernd.)

Doch noch Eins beding' ich aus: Kein
Anderer
Darf sie bekommen, die Marie, als
Der Sohn Tobias Micha's! Andernfalls
Gilt der Vertrag für nichts!

Kezal. Ganz selbstverständlich!
Das will ja ich! Kein And'rer soll sie haben
Als Micha's Sohn.

Hans. Nur unter der Bedingung
Setz' ich den Namen hin; denn keinem
Andern
Tret' ich sie ab. So laut' es deutlich im
Vertrage!

Kezal. Gleich will ich schreiben den Vertrag und
auch
Die Zeugen schnell beschaffen!

Hans. Ferner bitt' ich,
Ausdrücklich sei vermerkt: sobald
Als meine früh're Braut und Micha's Sohn
Die Hände sich gereicht zum Ehebunde,
Darf Micha von Mariens Vater nicht
Des Geldes Rückbezahlung mehr verlangen.
Er trägt des Kaufes Preis allein!

Kezal.   Das ist
Sehr klug und wohlbemerkt.

(Er geht vergnügt ab.)

FÜNFTE SCENE.

Hans

(allein).

Armer Narr, Du glaubtest mich zu fangen?
Bist nun selber in das Netz gegangen!
Es muss gelingen!
Alles soll
Nach Wunsch und Willen gehen!
So feine Schlingen,
Kann Liebeslust nur drehen.
Schlau und toll,
Dir, Treue, Süsse,
Viel tausend Grüsse'

In the whole world
There's none like her, I know.
She loves but me, and I too love her so.

In wenig Stunden
Ist es gescheh'n,
Dass wir, verbunden,
Uns wiederseh'n!
Nach Wetterschlägen,
Nach Angst und Pein,
Nach Sturm und Regen
Lacht Sonnenschein,
Himmlischer Segen.
Bald bist Du mein!

SCENE VI

HANS, KETSAL, KRUSHINA and people.

Ketsal   (holding off the curious ones).

Not so wildly there
Without tension!
Follow the contract
With attention.

Chorus.   We'll follow that contract with attention.

Ketsal.   Bear in mind that this document
Is of the whole transaction a record true.
All therein let me now proclaim,

(Reads.)

" To my bride I give up all claim."

Chorus

(crowding in around him).

All therein let him now proclaim,
To his bride he gives up all claim.

Hans

(points to the paper and reads).

" But to none other than the honorable
and honored son of Sir Tobias Micha."

Ketsal.   Yes, son of Sir Tobias Micha.

Hans

(as above).

If indeed he truly loves,
And to her devotes his life,
And before the people swears
That he freely makes her his wife.

SECHSTE SCENE.

HANS, KEZAL, KRUSCHINA und VOLK.

Kezal

(die Neugierigen abwehrend).

Nicht zu hitzig! Ihr werdet hören
Alles, was wir abgemacht!
Den Verlauf der Sache nicht zu stören
Haltet Ruhe, gebet Acht!

Chor.   Ja, wir wollen's endlich hören!

Kezal.   Denkt daran: Ihr müsst beschwören
Ob es richtig zu Papier gebracht!
Was hier steht, lasst mich berichten:

(Liest.)

„Auf die Braut will ich verzichten" .

Chor.

(sich um KEZAL drängend).

Ja, so steht's! Was für Geschichten!?
Auf die Braut will er verzichten!?

Hans

(zeigt auf das Papier und liest).

„Doch zu Gunsten keines Andern,
Als des Sohns des hochverehrten,
Wackeren Tobias Micha! "

Kezal.   Ja, des Sohns Tobias Micha's.

Hans

(wie oben).

„Wenn er sie von Herzen liebt,
Wenn er treu sich ihr ergiebt,
Wenn vor Zeugen er beschwört,
Dass nur ihr sein Herz gehört."

Ketsal. Here it's written, as he said it.
  See, it's all here.

Chorus. We cannot grasp now what has happened.

Krushina

(to HANS).

I would never have believed
That you have such a noble heart,
And so quickly us relieved
Of great trouble, on your part.

Ketsal. This affair is almost ended,
  But with other matter blended.

(To KRUSHINA.)

You to him are under no great obligations.
I agreed to pay three hundred florins.
And for this price you here behold,
His Marie he has sold.

Chorus. What a shame. Oh, what a shame.
  To sell his bride, to sell his bride.

Krushina. What! Have you been guilty of such
  an act?
  Then I must say you are a rascal for a fact.

Ketsal. Punctum, satis. Let all things go on as
  in the pact.
  Now affix your names.

(To HANS.)

First of all you, Hans,
Then the witnesses.

Hans. Here 'tis written.

(Signs.)

Hans Ehrentraut.

Chorus. He has sold his bride,
  Oh, what a shame!

END OF ACT II.

Kezal. Ganz genau so steht's geschrieben,
  Ueberzeugt Euch, meine Lieben!

(Er lässt die Umstehenden in den Vertrag sehen.)

Chor. Nicht versteh'n wir, was geschehen!

Kruschina

(zu HANS).

Dankbar sollst Du stets mich sehen!
Gott sei Lob, wir sind so weit!
Weg ist jede Schwierigkeit.

Kezal. Ja, Gottlob, wir sind im Reinen!
  Etwas noch will wichtig scheinen!

(Zu KRUSCHINA.)

Braucht ihm weiter keinen Dank zu schul
  den,
Denn ich zahl' ihm baar dreihundert Gulden
Um diesen Preis, so steht's allhier,
Verkauft er die Marie!

Chor. Ha, wie schändlich, zu verschachern seine
  Braut!

Kruschina. Dass er auf das Geld nur schaut—
  Frei will ich es Euch gestehen, —
  Hätt'ich ihm nicht zugetraut!

Kezal. Punctum, satis. So geschehen
  Nach Gesetzeslaut.
  Unterschreibt nun!

(Zu Hans.)

Du zuerst.
Hier, mein Lieber! Dann die Zeugen!

Hans. Hier mein Nam':

(unterschreibt.)

Hans Ehrentraut.

Chor. Er verkaufte seine Braut!
  O Schande.

ENDE DES ZWEITEN ACTES.

ACT III.

(Stage setting the same as for Act I.)

SCENE I.

Wenzel

(alone. Very downhearted.)

It wo-won't go out of my head,
Tha-that I soon may be dead!
She wi-will worry me; I'll die;
The-then will bury me, oh, my!
She wi-will tease me, she says,
And de-deceive me, I guess.
It wo-won't go out of my head,
Tha-that I soon may be dead!

SCENE II.

Wenzel, Ringmaster and Esmeralda, Acrobats.

Ringmaster

(announces).

We hereby announce to the
Honored audience here assembled,
That we shall give them a performance
In the air and on the ground,
Never before witnessed by mortal eyes.
First of all we present

(Flare of trumpets.)

Senorita Esmeralda Salamanka,
The celebrated Spanish dancer,
Queen of the tight-rope,
Daughter of the air, who will
Perform numerous graceful,
Daring and hazardous feats.
Then will appear

(Flare of trumpets.)

A real Indian from the Fiji
Islands, especially brought over at an
enormous
Expense of money and trouble.

DRITTER ACT.

(Dekoration wie im ersten Act.)

ERSTE SCENE.

Wenzel

(allein. Sehr niedergeschlagen).

Wa . . . was ich mich betrübe!
Schwie . . . schwierig ist die Liebe!
Kä . . . Kämpfe mich bedrohen!
Mä . . . Mädchen ist entflohen!
Sche . . . Schelten wird die Mutter!
He . . . Herz ist weich wie Butter!
We . . . Wenzel, weh Dir, Armer!
Hi . . . hilf, Du, mein Erbarmer!

ZWEITE SCENE.

Wenzel, Springer und Esmeralda, Statisten.

Springer

(ruft aus).

Dem nie genug verehrten Publikum
Wird unterthänigst bekannt gemacht,
Dass heut' Nachmittag eine Vorstellung
Zwei- und vierbeiniger Celebritäten
Von seltener Niedagewesenheit
Schlag drei Uhr pünktlich vor sich gehen
wird,
Theils auf der Erde, theils auch in der Luft.
Besond're Zierden der Gesellschaft sind:

(Fanfare.)

Vorerst die wunderschöne Esmeralda,
Gebor'ne Spanierin aus Napagedos,
„Die Königin des Drathseils," „Tochter
der Luft" —
Springt auf Verlangen über ihren Schatten.

(Fanfare.)

Sodann der Indianerhäuptling Murru,
Gefangen auf der Insel Bummerang,
Die hunderttausend Meilen weit entfernt,
Waschecht und braun bei Sonnenschein
und Regen,

Although he must now
Content himself with ordinary
Fare, he is really a man-eating cannibal.
He will swallow wives — I mean
Knives and swords with great alacrity.
Then will appear the most wonderful
number of the whole programme.

(Flare of trumpets.)

A real American Grizzly Bear,
Whom I tamed myself.
After performing many astonishing
Feats, such as walking and hopping
On his hind legs and front paws,
He will dance a Ballet with
Esmeralda in the most approved
Graceful and artistic manner.
That you may not think that
I too highly praised this collection,
I will give you a small production.
But more hereafter.
And now! Let's begin.

(Dance and performance of acrobats, who then retire, and the people after them.)

Wenzel

(casting admiring glances at ESMERALDA).

Oh my, oh my! How lovely!
And that Spanish dancer, what beautiful
legs she has!

Esmeralda

(to WENZEL).

And is this fine gentleman coming to our
show?

Wenzel. Why, of course. I would love
To see you dance on the tight-rope.

Muff, the Indian

(rushes in excitedly).

Ringmaster! Ringmaster!
A great misfortune has happened.
Mike got drunk in the other
Inn, and there he lies under
The table, and I cannot
Induce him to play the bear,
Try as I may.

Von Haus aus Kannibal' und Menschen-
fresser. —
Er thut Euch nichts! — Jetzt frisst er nur
noch Hühner
Und Tauben — die man mitzubringen
hat! —
Mit Haut und Haar und schluckt nebstbei
auch Gabeln.

(Fanfare.)

Doch das Erstaunlichste von Allem kommt
Zuletzt, „Das Wunder der Dressur!" Ein
grosser
Lebend'ger Landbär aus Amerika,
Den ich mir selbst gezähmt. Mit Es-
meralda
Tanzt er ein Pas de deux wie im Ballet,
Geht auf den Zeh'n und hüpft auf einem
Bein.
Damit man sehe, dass ich nicht zuviel
Gesagt, so finde gleich die Probe statt.
Das Weit're folgt dann . . . He! Hollah.
Fangt an!

(Tanz und Production der Komödianten, die dann abziehen, das Volk hinter ihnen her.)

Wenzel

(der ESMERALDA mit Entzücken bewundert hat).

Ei, ei, ei, ei, wie rei . . . rei . . . reizend!
Was
Die Spa . . . pa . . . panierin für Füss-
chen hat!

Esmeralda

(zu WENZEL).

Kommt wohl der schöne Herr heut' Mittag
auch?

Wenzel. Versteht sich! Wenn Ihr auf dem Seile
tanzt,
So will ich kommen!

Muff, der Indianer

(kommt eilig und erschreckt).

Direktor! Herr Direktor!
Sagt' ich es doch: ein Unglück giebt's!
Der Michel
Hat sich betrunken, vollständig betrunken!
Im Wirthshaus liegt er unterm Tische da
Und rührt sich nicht! Und Keinen sonst,
der uns
Den Bären spielt, besitzen wir!

Ringmaster. The deuce! the deuce! It is our best number.

(Aside.)

If the bear cannot appear, we cannot perform
The celebrated ballet. No, no, no, that cannot be! That must not be!

(Aloud.)

We will have to look for somebody else —
Any old youngster out of the town.

Muff. He would give it away,
And the people would ridicule us.
Where could we find somebody?
He must be fully grown;
Otherwise the bear's skin will not fit him.
The people are coming in, and
We really have no time left to look around.

Ringmaster. What can we do, Esmeralda?

Wenzel

(who during all this time has been casting loving glances at Esmeralda).

What a fine girl she is!
Her I like! Well, well, if
She should become my wife,
The whole town would admire, and envy me.

Esmeralda

(encouraging him).

I like you very much, and would like to marry you.

Wenzel

(bashfully.)

Ma-marry me?

Muff

(who took WENZEL in with the eye of a connoisseur, to RINGMASTER.)

That one the bear's skin would fit like a glove,
As if expressly made for him.

Springer. Den Teufel!
's ist unsre beste Nummer!

(Für sich.)

Was zu thun?
Nein, ohne Bären geht's nun einmal nicht!
Sonst prügeln uns am End' die Bauern durch . . .
Mein Künstlerruf steht auf dem Spiel dabei.

(Laut.)

Lauf' nur und such' mir einen Andern.
Irgend
Ein Bursche find't sich schon.

Muff. Es ist vergebens,
Besehen hab' ich Alles. Keiner ist,
Der passte: Der zu dick und der zu dünn,
Einer zu gross, ein Anderer zu klein!
In's Fell will Niemand auch hinein, und Zeit
Ist weiter nicht mehr zu verlieren, sollen
Wir fertig sein!

Springer. Was meinst Du, Esmeralda?

Wenzel

(der die ganze Zeit über ESMERALDA mit verliebten Blicken betrachtet hat).

Das wär 'ein Mädchen, die . . . die mir gefällt,
So schön! We . . . wenn ich die zur Frau bekäme!
Beneiden sollte mich das ganze Dorf!

Esmeralda

(ihn ermuthigend).

Was seht Ihr mich so an? Gelt ja, Ihr habt
Noch eine Frage?

Wenzel

(verschämt).

Kö . . . kö . . . könntet Ihr
Mich lieben wohl?

Muff

(der den WENZEL mit Kennerblicken gemustert hat, zu SPRINGER).

Ei, seht mir doch: dem sässe
Das Bärenfell so trefflich, dass man schwört'
Es sei für ihn gemacht!

Ringmaster. Well, then, go and announce the performance!
This young man I will look after myself.

(Exit MUFF.)

(To WENZEL.)

Well, my dear sir! If you really love Esmeralda, then you
Can easily get her.
Become one of the members of my troupe,
And you shall yet dance to-day with Esmeralda.

Wenzel

(joyfully).

I da-dance?

(Sadly.)

I do not know how!

Esmeralda. My love will teach you how to do everything.

Wenzel

(happily).

Love! Well, that's worth hearing.

Ringmaster. You will always have a happy time with us.
Bright and lively,
Late and early,
Dancing, singing,
Joking, springing.
Here to-day and gone to-morrow.
Well, as you see, we are honored as actors,
Yes, the profession of actor is called the art of all arts;
Malum malorum, as they call it in Latin.
We know all the world is a stage;
And the people actors more or less.
Only their play is important and more serious,
But not as entertaining as ours,
Nor as gay.

Esmeralda. Well, then, my dear!
Come and join us.
My love shall be to you the sweetest of rewards.

Springer. So geh' und ruf' die
Vorstellung aus! Und Den da nehm' ich gleich
Hier in die Arbeit.

(Der Indianer ab.)

(Zu WENZEL.)

He, mein Theuerster!
Liebt Ihr sie, meine Esmeralda, dann
Den Segen geb' ich Euch! Ihr tretet gleich
Bei meiner Truppe ein; mit Esmeralda
Sollt Ihr noch heute tanzen!

Wenzel

(froh bestürzt).

Ta . . . ta . . . tanzen!?

(Traurig.)

Ach, tanzen ka . . . ka . . . kann ich nicht!

Esmeralda. Gar leicht
Lehrt Euch die Liebe, was Euch etwa fehlt.

Wenzel

(beglückt).

Die Liebe! Lasst doch hören!

Springer. Euch erwartet
Vergnügtes Leben: immer frisch und lustig!
Von früh bis Abends singen, scherzen, springen!
Heut' hier und morgen dort! Und angeseh'n
Sind allenthalben wir als Künstler! Ja,
Den Stand der Komödianten nennt man wohl
Den Stand der Stände auch, malum malorum,
So heisst es auf Lateinisch! Komödie wird
Gespielt allüberall, nicht im Theater nur,
Ja, manchmal besser noch und täuschender
Im Leben, aber nicht so heiter, harmlos,
Als wie bei uns.

Esmeralda. Wie? Ihr bedenkt Euch noch?
Fasst Euch ein Herz! Die Liebe reiche Euch
Den ersten Lorbeer!

Ringmaster.   What can happen to you?
     You are not bound as yet.
     Try it for once,
     You can now.

Esmeralda.   Yes, to-day you can try it.
     Come, my darling, only once!
     And then
     I shall be yours forever.

Wenzel.   What must I do?

Esmeralda.   Dance the ballet.

Wenzel.   Dance the ballet?
     What is that?

Esmeralda.   We are to dance together;
     You with me, and I with you.

Wenzel.   Bu-but my mother!

Esmeralda.   She will not know you.

Esmeralda and Ringmaster.
     A most charming creature
     We will make of you.
     It will be a feature
     Only known to few.
     We will put a lovely mask o'er face and nose,
     And the softest shoes upon your feet and toes.
     You will be a cherub
     Who will all entrance,
     And the people
     Will hasten to see you dance.
     A most charming creature
     We will make of you.
     It will be a feature
     Only known to few.

(ESMERALDA and RINGMASTER go because they see the people approaching. They motion to WENZEL to follow.)

Springer.   Was kann Euch geschehen?
     Ihr seid ja nicht gebunden!   Eine Probe ..
     Und heute nur!

Esmeralda.   Lasst Ihr umsonst mich bitten?
     Ach, mein Geliebter, thätet Ihr's, ja dann ...
     Wär' ich die Eure!

Wenzel

       (bekommt Lust).

     Wa . . . was soll ich machen?

Esmeralda.   Tanzen!

Wenzel.   Ta . . . tanzen, kann ich's denn?

Esmeralda.   Ich will's
     Euch zeigen: beide tanzen wir zusammen,

Wenzel.   Doch die Mu . . . Mutter!

Esmeralda.   Die erkennt Euch nicht.

Esmeralda und Springer.
     Alles geht am Schnürchen,
     Da man Dich nicht quält,
     Hab' ein hübsches Thierchen
     Für Dich ausgewählt.
     Prinz im Märchen,
     Braunes Bärchen
     Sollst Du sein!
     Das verstehst Du,
     Artig gehst Du,
     Schmuck und fein!
     Freundlich musst Du nicken,
     Denn Du bist in mich verliebt!
     Hold und zärtlich blicken . . .
     's wird ein Spass, wie's keinen giebt!
     Alles geht am Schnürchen,
     Da man Dich nicht quält,
     Hab' ein hübsches Thierchen
     Für Dich ausgewählt.

(ESMERALDA und SPRINGER ab [weil sie die neu Auftretenden von Weitem sehen]. Sie winken WENZEL nachzukommen.)

SCENE III.

WENZEL, then MICHA, AGNES and KETSAL.

Wenzel.

(sadly).

Oh, poor unfortunate me!
All the girls want to marry me, and then
kill me.

(He practices dancing.)

Agnes. O why are you so sad, my dear boy!
Brace up and be joyful!
You get married and all
Your troubles and sorrows will
Quickly be ended.

Wenzel. I-I am afraid.

Agnes. What are you afraid of, my darling?
Nothing bad can ever happen to you.
You will get a wife,
And that is the finest thing in the world.

Ketsal. Yes, just so! Wenzel will here sign the
contract.
And everything will be settled.

Wenzel. What-what kind of a contract is this?

Micha. That you promise to make Marie Krushina
your wife.

Wenzel. I-I do not want her!

Agnes, Micha and Ketsal.
What, really, not want her!
What can it be that makes him waver?
Speak, speak, Wenzel!
What nonsense were you led
To take into your head?

Wenzel. I'm-I'm afraid she'll tease me all my life,
And will deceive me, and worry me to death.

Agnes, Micha and Ketsal.
Oh, what a foolish notion!
Speak, where did you get it?

Wenzel. Someone told me and warned me to-day.

Agnes, Micha and Ketsal.
Who was that villainous person?

Wenzel. A beautiful girl.

DRITTE SCENE.

WENZEL. Gleich darauf MICHA, AGNES und KEZAL.

Wenzel. A . . . ach, wie wird es mir ergehen?
Alle
Die schönen Mädchen, sie entbe . . . be . . .
brennen
Für mich in Liebe.

(Er übt sich im Tanzen.)

Agnes. Endlich sieht man Dich!
Was treibst Du denn? Bist Du von Sinnen?
Komm'
Jetzt mit uns, damit wir zu dem niedlichsten
Bräutchen des Dorfs Dich führen!

Wenzel. Lasst mich gehen!

Agnes. Nimm doch Vernunft an! Vater und ich
wir haben
Geordnet Alles. Zeit wird es nun endlich,
Dir 'ne verständ'ge Frau zu geben!

Kezal. Wenzel
Wird das hier unterschreiben, abgethan
Ist dann die Sache.

Wenzel. Wo . . . wozu verpflichtet
Mich das Papier?

Micha. Dass Du Maria Kruschina
Zum Weibe nehmen wirst!

Wenzel. Nei . . . nein! Die will
Ich gar nicht haben.

Agnes, Micha und Kezal.
Ha, das trifft wie ein Donnerschlag!
Ich weiss nicht, trau' ich meinen Ohren?
So sage mir doch, Wenzel, sag',
Wo hast Du den Verstand verloren?

Wenzel. Das Schicksal kenn' ich, das mir droht:
Sie will mich quälen bis zum Tod!

Agnes, Micha und Kezal.
Woher stammt diese Kunde?
O sprich, aus wessen Munde?

Wenzel. Je . . . jemand, der sein Herz mir
bot . . .

Agnes, Micha und Kezal.
Der feindlich Deinem Bunde.

Wenzel. O nein, O nein!
Ein rei . . . rei . . . reizend Mägdelein.

agnes, Micha and Ketsal.
　　And what did she say to you?
Wenzel.　She said to me, she loves me so!
Agnes.　And do you know her?
Wenzel.　No, not I!
　　　　　　　(He runs away.)
Agnes, Micha and Ketsal.
　　This is a pesky matter.
　　Someone has spoken to him,
　　And turned his trusting mind.
　　I'll the culprit find.

SCENE IV.

MARIE, KRUSHINA, KATHINKA, and the foregoing, later WENZEL.

Marie
　　(rush's in, followed by KRUSHINA and KATHINKA).
　　No, no, no!
　　I cannot believe that!
　　It is a mere trick put up to deceive me.
　　My love can never be a rascal.

Krushina.　And still it is the truth.
Ketsal.　What, is she still in doubt?
Krushina.　Hans gave you up forsooth!
Ketsal.　Here it is in black and white!
　　　　　　　(Shows her the paper.)
　　For three hundred florins
　　Hans did sell to us his bride.
Marie.　Oh, what an awful blow this is!
　　　　　　　(Weeping.)
　　O men, ye are deceitful!
　　'Tis solemn word he gave to me,
　　That all the world he'd brave for me.

Krushina.　Take comfort, my dear child.
　　Though you on him relied,
　　You will now another find,
　　Who will be always kind.
Ketsal.　Now you will sign, my hearty!
　　　　　　(WENZEL appears in the background.)
　　And our Wenzel, where is he?
Kathinka.　Just see him on the common.
　　What is he staring at?

Agnes, Micha und Kezal.
　　Was machte Dir das Mädchen weis?
Wenzel.　Sie sagt' es mir, sie liebt mich heiss!
Agnes.　Und kennst Du sie?
Wenzel.　Ach nein!
　　　　　　　(Läuft davon.)
Agnes, Micha und Kezal.
　　Das sind verwünschte Dinge!
　　Man legt' ihm eine Schlinge!
　　Drum, wie ich zur Vernunft ihn bringe,
　　Soll meine Sorge sein.

VIERTE SCENE.

MARIE, KRUSCHINA, KATHINKA und die VORIGEN.　Später WENZEL

Marie
　　(stürzt herein, KRUSCHINA und KATHINKA hinter ihr her).
　　Nein, nein, nein!
　　Es ist erlogen!
　　Sie lästern, schreien,
　　Uns zu entzweien!
　　Sie lästern, schreien,
　　Mein Liebster habe mich betrogen.
Kruschina.　Die Arme zweifelt noch!
Kezal.　Komm' her und schaue doch.
Kruschina.　Er gab Dich schämlos preis.
Kezal.　Hier steht es schwarz auf weiss!
　　　　　　　(Zeigt das Papier.)
　　Ja, um dreihundert Gulden
　　Verkauft' er seine Braut.
Marie.　Wer hätte das ihm zugetraut!?
　　　　　　　(Weinend.)
　　Gott mög' es ihm verzeih'n!
　　Hab' ich verdient so tiefe Schmach?
　　Noch immer klingt es in mir nach:
　　„Ja, Dein bin ich allein!"
Kruschina.　Sei ruhig, armes Kind,
　　Vergiss den Sausewind!
　　Nimm einen Besser'n Dir,
　　Der rein und treu gesinnt!
Kezal.　Hier unterschreib' geschwind!
　　　　　　(WENZEL ist im Hintergrunde wieder sichtbar.)
　　Nun, Wenzel, schnell herbei!
Kathinka.　Mein Kind, Du musst Dich fassen,
　　Es sei nun, wie es sei!

Marie. I'll never sign this contract,
 For Wenzel I'll not take!
 I'd rather, rather live alone and all my
  friends forsake.
The Others. You cannot do that now!
 The moments hasten!
 You must decide.
Ketsal
  (catches sight of WENZEL and calls him).
 Hey, Wenzel, hey, Wenzel dear!
 Come and drop your bashfulness.
Wenzel
  (comes up angrily).
 Well, what is now the matter?
  (Notices MARIE, agreeably surprised.)
 She-she-she spoke to me this morning.

Kathinka, Agnes, Krushina, Micha, Ketsal.
 Was it really Marie then
 Who did scare him thus?
Wenzel. She told me that all apart,
 Me she loved with all her heart.
Kathinka, Agnes, Krushina, Micha, Ketsal.
 Well, this is the lady we picked to be your
  wife.
Wenzel. Yes, yes, her do I like.
Ketsal. Then let us not wait longer,
 For that won't make it stronger,
 But sign the contract now.
Marie. Leave me here a moment all alone to
 think.

Marie. Und hat er mich verlassen,
 Ich bleibe dennoch frei!
 Vertrauern will ich meine Zeit
 In stiller Einsamkeit!
Die Andern. Wohl in Vergessenheit
 Wird Dir entschwinden bald Dein Leid.

Kezal
  (erblickt WENZEL und ruft).
 He, Wenzel! He, mein Wenzelchen!
 Lass fahren Deine Blödigkeit!
Wenzel
  (kommt hervor, ärgerlich).
 Was giebt es denn schon wieder?
  (Erblickt Marie, freudig erstaunt.)
 Die-die-die sprach ich heute Morgen!
 Nu . . . nun ist nichts mehr zu besorgen,

Kathinka, Agnes, Kruschina, Micha, Kezal.
 Weiss ich doch nicht wo und wie?
 Sprach er wirklich mit Marie?
Wenzel. Ja, heut' Morgen in der Früh'!
 Ich gefiel' ihr, sagte sie.
Kathinka, Agnes, Kruschina, Micha, Kezal.
 Das ist ja das Bräutchen,
 Das Dir zugedacht!
Wenzel. Dann ist's abgemacht!
Kezal. Nicht lange mehr geplaudert,
 Gezweifelt und gezaudert,
 Jetzt sind am Ziele wir!
Marie. Ich bitte, nur ein Weilchen
 Lasst noch allein mich hier!

SEXTETTE

KATHINKA, KRUSHINA, AND KETSAL, *repeat* AGNES, MICHA, AND KETSAL, *then all together.*

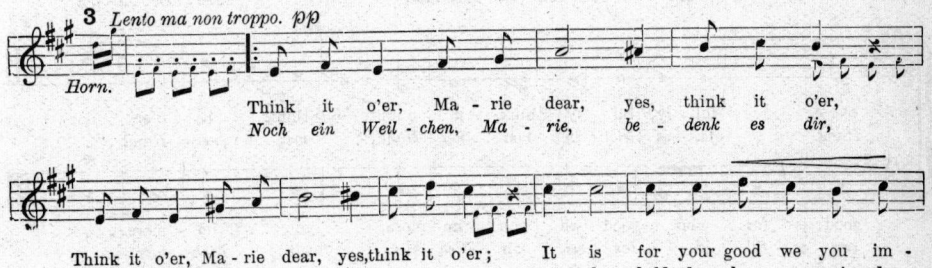

Think it o'er, Ma - rie dear, yes, think it o'er,
Noch ein Weil - chen, Ma - rie, be - denk es dir,

Think it o'er, Ma - rie dear, yes, think it o'er; It is for your good we you im -
Noch ein Weil - chen, Ma - rie, be - denk' es dir, A - ber bald dann kom - men wie - der

SCENE V.

Marie

(alone).

What shall I do?
Deserted now, and weighed down by my
  sorrow.
Still I cannot understand it.
His name is there most plainly.
How can he countermand it?
Perhaps, I doubt him vainly!
Would to God that out of all
This confusion no harm my love befall.

(Dreamily.)

My dream of love how fair it was,
So full of rapture and hope.
It shone so brightly in my heart
It seemed we would never part.
What happy life I pictured here
With Hans, to live together;
But love is killed, I greatly fear
It's killed by wintry weather.

(As if awakening.)

No, can there happen such deceit,
Can love live on unfulfilled?
The world would shed a tear, indeed,
O'er love that's so cruelly killed.
My dream of love how fair it was,
It shone so brightly in my heart;
It seemed we would never part.
My dream of love, how fair it was!

SCENE VI.

MARIE and HANS.

Hans

(rushes in joyfully).

How you I sought,
My darling Marie!
Star of my being!
O speak, do you still know of aught
That might prevent our marriage?

FÜNFTE SCENE.

Marie

(allein).

Endlich allein!
Allein mit mir, mit meinem Grame!
Noch immer kann ich es nicht glauben,
Steht auch dabei sein Name! . . .
Was hier noch leise für ihn spricht,
Ich darf es hören nicht.
War seine Liebe nur ein Wahn?
Wehe mir Armen!
Was hab' ich ihm gethan?

(Träumerisch.)

Wie fremd und todt ist Alles umher,
Und war so traut, voll Leben!
Die Welt hat keine Freuden mehr,
Ich muss mich d'rein ergeben.
O Lenz, Dein buntes Blumenkleid,
Wie welk ist es geworden!
Der böse Herbst kam vor der Zeit
Einhergeweht von Norden . . .

(Wie erwachend.)

Nein! Alles ist noch, wie es war
Und will nur anders scheinen,
Weil trübe ward mein Augenpaar
Vom Weinen.
Du Maienzeit, wie warst Du schön
Mit Deinen frischen Trieben!
Ade nun, helles Lustgetön!
Ade, Du junges Lieben!

SECHSTE SCENE.

MARIE und HANS.

Hans.

(stürmt fröhlich herein).

So find' ich Dich, Feinsliebchen, hier,
Mein Sehnen, mein Verlangen?
O sprich, erzähle, wie es Dir
Inzwischen ist ergangen!

Marie. Away! I am your star no more,
Our dream of love is o'er.
You stole my heart and lower'd yourself
By selling it for worthless pelf.
Speak, is it true, or is it not?
But yes or no, one word alone!

Hans
              (teasingly).

So simply—that cannot be done!
Marie. I want no explanations, now!
Speak, is it true as written?
Hans
              (the same).

Yes, then, yes, then, yes, then!
Marie. Now go away, and never more
Let me behold your features.
Hans
              (affectionately, playfully).

O let me all explain before
I go, you loveliest of creatures!
Marie. Our love is ended, bear in mind,
And I am going to marry Wenzel.

Hans
              (laughs).

Ha, ha, ha, that would truly be
A stupendous joke!

Marie
              (angrily).

What, is this all so very gay?
Hans
              (still laughing).

I want to tell you something.
Then listen, only let me say —
Marie. No, you can tell me nothing.

Hans. You are an awful stubborn case
For you'll not let me tell you.
How could I look into your face
If really I did sell you.
You are an awful stubborn case
For you'll not let me tell you.

Marie. Hinweg! Nicht bin ich mehr Dein Lieb,
Lass' Deinen schlechten Scherz!
Erst stahlst Du mir, ehrloser Dieb,
Und dann verkauftest Du mein Herz!
Sag', ist es Wahrheit oder nicht?
      Ein Wort allein:
      Ja oder nein!
Hans
              (übermüthig).

So einfach geht es schwerlich an.
Marie. Ich will nur Antwort, falscher Mann
Sag', war's Du so abscheulich?
Hans
              (wie vorher).

Nun ja doch, freilich, freilich
Marie. Von Reue zeigst Du keine Spur,
Genug hab' ich vernommen!
Hans
              (zärtlich, schalkhaft).

O Du Geliebte, lass' mich nur
Einmal zu Worte kommen !
Marie. Mit uns'rer Liebe
Ist's aus nun, merk Dir das!
Ich nehme mir den Wenzel!
Hans
              (lacht).

Ha, ha, ha, ha!
Das ist wahrhaftig
Ein höchst gelung'ner Spass!
Marie
              (zornig).

Ha, Spott ist meiner Liebe Lohn?
Hans
              (immer lachend).

Ich muss Dir was erzählen,
Zwar stimmt's nicht zu dem Trauerton.
Marie
              (unterbricht).

Ich lass' mich nimmer quälen.
Hans. Mein lieber Schatz, nun aufgepasst.
Ich geb' Dir was zu hören!
Nur gönne mir ein wenig Rast
Und wolle mich nicht stören!
Mein lieber Schatz, nun aufgepasst,
Ich geb' Dir was zu hören!

Marie. You are an awful wicked case,
The devil cannot beat you.
I'll never look into your face,
And never want to meet you,
You are an awful wicked case,
The devil cannot beat you.

Marie. Ein Märchen wohl, von Dir verfasst,
Um Dich herauszuschwören?
Ich weiss, was Du verbrochen hast,
Du wirst mich nicht bethören . . .
Ein Märchen wohl, von Dir verfasst,
Um Dich herauszuschwören?

SCENE VII.

KETSAL and the foregoing.

Ketsal. Here, Hans! You, I suppose, wait for
your money?
Well, have a little patience!
As soon as Marie signs the contract
You will get every penny.
Marie. Ha, how disgraceful!

Ketsal. Well, and you? Will you take for your
husband Micha's son?

Hans. Of course she will, I say!
That he will get her and nobody else, is
fixed by the contract,
And to that, I swear.
Ketsal. You're a good boy, with good under-
standing.

Marie. You're a villainous liar!
No, no, now surely not!
I will not take him
If I die on the spot for it.
Hans. What will you give if I induce her
That she will take Tobias Micha's son?

Marie. What! Hans, you want to induce
Me to do such a thing!
No, such a bold proceeding
The world never did see nor ever hear.

Hans. Have patience, and do not give up hope,
But trust to me as you did ne'er before.
You hardly know what happiness
For you there is in store.

SIEBENTE SCENE.

KEZAL und die VORIGEN.

Kezal. He, Hans? Du möchtest wohl Dein Geld
schon haben?
Warte nur noch ein Bischen hier!
Giebt die Marie mir ihre Unterschrift,
Erhälst Du, was Dir zukommt!
Marie.   Ha!
Der glatte Heuchler!
Kezal

(zu Marie).

Nun, und Du? Nimmst Du
Dafür zu Deinem Mann des Micha Sohn?
Hans. Ja, das verbürg' ich Euch! Sie wird ihn
nehmen.
Kein Anderer als er soll sie bekommen.
So ward es abgemacht!
Kezal

(scherzend).

Und so ist's recht.
Du Heirathsmittler!
Marie. Nichts da! Er lügt Euch an!
Nein, sag' ich, nein, nein! Nun und nim-
mermehr!
Und stürb' ich d'rum hier auf der Stelle!
Hans. Was wollt Ihr wetten, dass sie's dennoch
thut?
Wenn ich es will, so nimmt sie Micha's Sohn!
Marie. Wie? Hans? Und dazu wollest Du
Im Ernst mich bringen? Solch' ein Unge-
heuer
Hab's auf der Welt noch nie! Du Teufel,
Du!
Hans. Gesegnet, wer da liebt und auch vertraut!
Kein Zweifel trübt sein Glück.
Bald kehret Dir, verkaufte Braut,
Was Du verlorst, zurück!

He loves you more than anything
In this wide world of ours,
And Micha's son will brighten your life
With bliss and all its powers.

Marie. O heavens, O heavens, how these
Words are racking my poor heart!

Ketsal. I never heard a wiser word.

(Aside.)

He is indeed a glorious bird.

(Aloud.)

Now let us call the parents here
And witnesses together,
As nothing more will interfere
To end this joyous matter.

(Exit.)

Marie

(resigned).

Now I will call my parents here
And all my friends together,
As nothing more will interfere
To end this painful matter.

Hans. Yes, you may call the parents here
And witnesses together,
As nothing more will interfere
To end this lud'crous matter.

(To MARIE.)

What, do you still not understand?

Marie. Go! What do you want here?

Es liebt Dich jenes Micha Sohn
Wie keiner sonst auf Erden,
Für Deine Treue Dank und Lohn
Kann Dir von ihm nur werden!

Marie. Ein Schmeichler und ein Heuchler s
Macht hier sein Meisterstück!

Kezal. Das ist ein zweiter Salomo!

(Für sich.)

Oder ein Galgenstrick!
Jetzt rufen wir die Eltern her,
Dazu die andern Zeugen!
Nun kommt mir nichts mehr in die Quer
Der Himmel hängt voll Geigen.

(Geht ab.)

Marie

(ergeben).

Ich habe keine Wünsche mehr
Und will in's Joch mich beugen,
Mein Sinn ist trüb', mein Herz ist schwer
Was kann ich thun als schweigen?

Hans. Die Alten, ja, das freut mich sehr!
Willkommen sind die Zeugen,
Und käme gleich ein ganzes Heer,
Was mein ist, bleibt mein Eigen!

(Zu MARIE.)

Des Micha Sohn wird doch Dein Mann!

Marie. Nur fort! Ich schaue Dich nicht an!

SCENE VIII.

AGNES, KATHINKA, KRUSHINA, MICHA, KETSAL, Chorus and
the preceding.

Chorus. Have you decided and thought out with
care,—
Speak — what you shall do in this mixed
up affair?

Marie

(aside).

I'll have revenge, and I shall do,
What to prevent he is trying.
O sadly and mournfully
Me he'll be eyeing.

ACHTE SCENE.

AGNES, KATHINKA, KRUSCHINA, MICHA, KEZAL. CHOR und die
VORIGEN.

Chor. Kommen wir gerne, so kommen wir gleich
Aber Mariechen, weshalb so bleich?

Marie

(für sich).

So räch' ich mich für den Verrath!
Er soll mich nimmer äffen!
Um was er höhnisch erst mich bat,
Ich thu's, um ihn zu treffen!

(Aloud with exertion.)

I shall do all that you desire.

Chorus. Good luck, to you, Marie!
All discontent must emigrate.
The marriage feast we'll celebrate.

Hans

(stepping to the front).

The marriage feast we'll celebrate,
And all the world will think it great.

Agnes and Micha.
What do I see? Is this really Hans?

Hans. Yes, father! Many a long and weary day
From you I've been away.
I have no wish again to roam,
And so shall found my own sweet home.

Ketsal. What, is it truth or only fun?
That simple chap, old Micha's son,
The elder, is that truly so?
I thought he'd gone to fight the foe.

Hans. I am truly old Micha's son,
From foreign part; and not for fun
But no real earnest battles fought,

(Referring to AGNES and KETSAL.)

'Gainst adverse foes my fortune sought.

Agnes. And you have time enough on hand
To do it more! You understand?

Hans. I know, that goes without saying,
I am not a welcome guest.
But never mind we'll pass the rest,
Since to my love I have a claim,
I, Micha's son by blood and name.

Agnes. That is not fair, that's cheating quick!

Hans. Not cheating, but only a trick.
'Tis written here, 'tis written.
See, we are two, put it to her.
Let her say whom she'll prefer!

(To Marie.)

Whom do you want to marry?

Marie. Now, at last, I understand.

(Throws herself into HANS' arms.)

Thee, my darling Hans'
I'm thine. I'm thine!

(Laut, mit Anstrengung.)

Was Ihr gewollt, das thu' ich gern!

Chor. Das Brautpaar soll leben!
Mariechen kriegt nun einen Herrn!
Der Tag der Hochzeit ist nicht fern!

Hans

(vortretend).

Ja, lustig wird es werden da,
Denn solch' ein Paar noch Keiner sah!

Agnes und Micha.
Was seh' ich? Das ist ja der Hans!

Hans. Herr Vater und Frau Mutter auch.
Da bin ich wieder, heil und ganz!
Bin aus der Fremde heimgekehrt,
Zu gründen einen eig'nen Herd!

Kezal. Ei! Soll ich's glauben oder nicht,
Was dieser Flausenmacher spricht?
Er wäre, Micha, Euer Sohn?
Der ist ja wohl gestorben schon!

Hans. Erkannten mich die Eltern doch!
Und schätzt mich auch nicht jeder hoch.

(mit Beziehung auf KEZAL und die Stiefmutter.)

Das Beste ist: ich lebe noch!

Agnes. Hier bist Du nicht am rechten Ort
Mit Deinen alten Ränken!

Hans. Ich kann es mir wohl denken,
Gern schicktet Ihr mich wieder fort!
Doch wenn ich geh', dann nicht allein!
Mit Micha's Sohn die Liebste sein
Marie, die nun für ewig mein!

Agnes. Das gilt nicht, weil Betrug es ist!

Hans. Betrug nicht, nein, nur eine List;
Geschrieben ist geschrieben!
Ihr bleibt die Wahl: Den Wenzel oder mich!

(Zu MARIE.)

Triff die Entscheidung nun und sprich:
Wen von uns willst Du lieben?

Marie. Hab' ich doch läugst entschilden!

(Eilt HANS in die Arme.)

Ja, Dein bin ich, ja, Dein bin ich!

Ketsal. This fellow is a tricky scamp,
  He's beaten me all over.
  A great big blot upon my name,
  My reputation gone, my fame,
  How can I them e'er again recover?

Micha

   (sarcastically to KETSAL).

  Your wisdom has just left you,
  Truly and for a fact.

Agnes

   (the same).

  And may we mention, made you
  Do and perform a very stupid act.

Marie, Hans, Kathinka and Krushina.
  Your wisdom has just left you,
  Truly and for a fact.

Chorus. Ha, ha, ha, ha, a stupid act.

   (KETSAL runs away.)

LAST SCENE.

(A loud noise behind the scenes. Boys run across the stage. One boy cries: "Run for your life! The bear got loose." Another, " He's coming this way, run!")

   WENZEL and Foregoing.

Wenzel

   (disguised as a bear)

  Don't be afraid! I am not a wild bear! I
   am Wenzel!

Agnes

   (enraged).

  You donkey, what are you doing?
  Oh, what a disgrace! Get away from here,
   You ninny, and get out of that rank
   disguise.

   (She drags WENZEL away.)

Krushina. Now, my dear friend Micha, you
  Yourself must acknowledge that
  There can be no talk of Wenzel.
  Why, he hasn't his reason yet.

Kezal. Wer hätte das von ihm gedacht!
  Mir schwillt vor Zorn die Galle!
  Um Einfluss, um Gewicht und Macht
  Hat der Hallunke mich gebracht,
  Ich ging ihm in die Falle!

Micha

   (höhnisch zu KEZAL).

  Lasst Euch bewundern! Ja, das habt
  Ihr wirklich gut gemacht!

Agnes

   (ebenso).

  Der Wichtigthuer, hochbegabt!
  Nun wird er ausgelacht.

Marie, Hans, Kathinka, Kruschina.
  Lasst Euch bewundern! Ja, das habt
  Ihr wirklich gut gemacht!

Chor. Ha, ha, ha, ha! Er wird verlacht!

   (KEZAL läuft wüthend fort.)

LETZTE SCENE.

(Grosser Lärm hinter der Bühne. Knaben rennen über die Bühne. Ein Knabe schreit: „ Rettet Euch, der Bär ist los!" Ein Anderer· „ E. rennt geradenwegs hierher!")

   WENZEL und die VORIGEN.

Wenzel

   (als Bär verkleidet).

  Seid ohne Furcht! Ich bin kein Landbär,
   nur
  Der We . . . We . . . Wenzel!

Agnes

   (erbost).

  Du Gimpel, was hast Du gethan? O
   Schande!
  Schere, Du Narr, Dich weg von hier! Denn
   man
  Verlacht uns und verspottet uns!

   (Sie zieht WENZEL mit sich fort.)

Kruschina. Gevatter Micha werdet selbst begreifen
  Wohl, dass sein Kind man ihm verweigert
   Ja,
  Da ist der Hans mir lieber!

(Coaxingly.)

But bear in mind that Hans is, too,
Your son and you're his father.

Kathinka. You should be glad that your son
Has returned from a foreign land.
Receive him joyfully with love,
And extend to him your hand.

Micha. Well, well, so be it, so be it!
I'll give you now my blessing.

(He blesses the pair kneeling before him.)

All and Chorus.

Let us sing and shout and rattle,
For true love has won the battle.
We now wish with joy and pride
Happiness to the " Bartered Bride."

END OF THE OPERA.

(Begütigend.)

's ist Euer Blut
Ihr seid der Vater!

Kathinka. Ja, Gnade hat Euch Gott verlieh'n,
Dass Ihr ihn noch bekommen,
An Eurer Stelle hätt' ich ihn
Mit Freuden aufgenommen!

Micha. Nun meinetwegen, meinetwegen!
Da habt Ihr meinen Vatersegen!

(Er segnet das vor ihm niederknieende Paar.)

Alle und Chor.

So ist's recht, es freut uns Alle!
Stimmet ein mit Jubelschalle!
Und von Herzen tön' es laut:
Vivat die „verkaufte Braut "!

ENDE DER OPER.

HANSEL AND GRETEL

An Opera in Three Acts

by

Engelbert Humperdinck

Libretto by
Adelheid Wette

THE opera opens in a poor broom-maker's hut in a forest in the Harz mountains. Hansel and Gretel are alone, working and bemoaning the lack of food. Eventually they start playing and dancing about when suddenly their mother enters, tired and discouraged. She scolds them and sends them out to pick a basketful of wild strawberries for supper. Later, their father returns after a good day but when he learns that the children are out alone in the forest he is terribly fearful that the evil witch of the woods may have captured them.

In Act II we see the children in the woods. At first they gaily pick the berries. Then as it gets darker they get lost and frightened by fears of vague shapes and haunts. But a Sandman comes, they say their "fourteen angels" prayer and fall asleep. We see their dream of the fourteen angels guarding them.

At dawn (Act III) the children awake and sing. Suddenly they see an amazing cottage all made of cake and candy. It is the trap of the witch who lures little boys and girls. Once she catches them she bakes them into gingerbread, her favorite food. Hansel and Gretel start nibbling away at the wonderful house and the witch casts her spell over them. She cages Hansel but when she tries to shove Gretel into the oven, the two children shove the witch in, instead. Then all the gingerbread around the house is retransformed into boys and girls who thank Hansel and Gretel for their rescue. Father and mother come on the scene and all dance and sing a hymn of joy.

HÄNSEL UND GRETEL

ACT I	ERSTES BILD
AT HOME	*DAHEIM*

SCENE I	ERSTE SCENE

(A small and poorly furnished ...om. In the background a door; a small window near it, looking on to the forest. On the left a fireplace with chimney above it. On the walls are hanging brooms of various sizes. Hansel is sitting by the door, making brooms, and Gretel opposite him by the fireplace, knitting a stocking.)

(Dürftige Stube. Im Hintergrunde rechts eine niedrige Thür, in der Mitte ein kleines Fenster mit Aussicht in den Wald. Links ein Herd mit einem Rauchfang darüber. An der rechten Wand hängen Besen in verschiedenen Formen. Hänsel, an der Thüre mit Besenbinden, Gretel, am Herde Strumpfstricken beschäftigt, sitzen einander gegenüber.)

Gretel. Susy, little Susy, pray what is the news?
 The geese are running barefoot, because
 they've no shoes!
 The cobbler has leather, and plenty to spare,
 why can't he make the poor goose a new
 pair?

Hänsel. Then they'll have to go barefoot!
 Eia-popeia, pray what's to be done?
 Who'll give me milk and sugar, for bread
 I have none?
 I'll go back to bed and I'll lie there all day;
 where there's nought to eat, then there's
 nothing to pay!

Gretel. Then we'll have to go hungry!

Hänsel. If mother would only come home again!
 Yes, I am so hungry,
 I don't know what to do!
 For weeks I've eaten nought but bread—
 It's very hard, it is indeed!

Gretel. Hush, Hänsel, don't forget what father said,
 when mother, too, wished she were dead:
 "When past bearing is our grief,
 The Lord God, will send relief!"

Hänsel. Yes, yes, that sounds all very fine,
 but of course off maxims we cannot dine!
 O Gret, it would be such a treat
 if we had something nice to eat!
 Eggs and butter and suet paste,
 I've almost forgotten how they taste.
 O Gretel, I wish—

Gretel. Hush, don't give way to grumps;
 have patience awhile, no doleful dumps!
 This woeful face, whew! what a sight!
 Looks like a horrid old crosspatch fright!
 Crosspatch, away!
 Leave me, I pray!
 Just let me reach you,
 quickly I'll teach you
 how to make trouble,
 soon mount to double!
 Crosspatch, crosspatch,
 what is the use,
 growling and grumbling,
 full of abuse?
 Off with you, out with you,
 shame on you, goose!

Hänsel. Crosspatch, away!
 Hard lines, I say.

Gretel. Suse, liebe Suse,
 was raschelt im Stroh?
 Die Gänse gehn barfuss
 und haben kein' Schuh.
 Der Schuster hat's Leder,
 kein'n Leisten dazu.
 Drum kann er den Gänslein
 auch machen kein' Schuh.

Hänsel. Eia popeia,
 das ist eine Not!
 Wer schenkt mir einen Dreier
 zu Zucker und Brot?
 Verkauf ich mein Bettlein
 und leg mich auf's Stroh,
 sticht mich keine Feder
 und beisst mich kein Floh!
 Ach, käm doch die Mutter nun endlich nach
 Haus!

Gretel. Auch ich halt's kaum noch vor Hunger aus.

Hänsel. Seit Wochen nichts als trocken Brot;
 ist das ein Elend! Potz schwere Not!

Gretel. Still, Hänsel, denk daran, was Vater sagt,
 wenn Mutter manchmal so verzagt:
 Wenn die Not auf's höchste steigt,
 Gott der Herr die Hand euch reicht!"

Hansel. Jawohl, das klingt ganz schön und glatt,
 aber leider wird man davon nicht satt.
 Ach, Gretel, wie lang' ist's doch schon her,
 dass wir nichts Gutes geschmauset mehr!
 Eierfladen und Butterwecken—
 kaum weiss ich noch, wie die thun
 schmecken.
 Ach, Gretel, ich wollt' . . .

Gretel. Still, nicht verdriesslich sein:
 Gedulde dich fein, sieh freundlich drein!
 Dies lange Gesicht,—hu, welcher Graus!
 Siehst ja wie der leibhaftige Griesgram aus!
 Griesgram, hinaus!
 Fort aus dem Haus!
 Ich will dich lehren,
 Herz zu beschweren,
 Sorgen zu mehren,
 Freuden zu wehren:
 Griesgram, Griesgram, greulicher Wicht,
 griesiges, grämiges Galgengesicht,
 packe dich, trolle dich, schäbiger Wicht!

Hänsel. Griesgram, hinaus!
 Halt's nicht mehr aus!

Hänsel.	When I am hungry, surely I can say so, cannot allay so, can't chase away so!
Gretel.	If I am hungry, I'll never say so, will not give way so, chase it away so!
Gretel.	That's right. Now, if you leave off complaining, I'll tell you a most delightful secret!
Hansel.	O delightful! it must be something nice!
Gretel.	Well, listen, brotherkin—won't you be glad! Look here in the jug, here is fresh milk, 'twas given to-day by our neighbour, and mother, when she comes back home, will certainly make us a rice-blancmange.
Hänsel.	Rice-blancmange! When blancmange is anywhere near, then Hänsel, Hänsel, Hänsel, is there! How thick is the cream on the milk; let's taste it! O Gemini! wouldn't I like to drink it!
Gretel.	What, Hänsel, tasting? Aren't you ashamed? Out with your fingers quick, greedy boy! (Gives him a rap on the fingers.) Get back to your work again, be quick, that we may both have done in time! If mother comes and we haven't done right, then badly it will fare with us to-night!
Hänsel.	Work again? No, not for me! That's not my idea at all; it doesn't suit me! It's such a bore! Dancing is jollier far, I'm sure!
Gretel.	(Delighted.) Dancing, dancing! O yes, that's better far; and sing a song to keep us in time! One that our grandmother used to sing us: sing then, and dance in time to the singing! (Claps her hands.) Brother, come and dance with me, both my hands I offer thee; right foot first, left foot then, round about and back again!
Hänsel.	I would dance, but don't know how, when to jump, and when to bow; show me what I ought to do, so that I may dance like you.
Cretel.	With your foot you tap, tap, tap; with your hands you clap, clap, clap; right foot first, left foot then, round about and back again!
Hänsel.	With your hands you clap, clap, clap; with your foot you tap, tap, tap; right foot first, left foot then, round about and back again!

	Immer mich plagen, Hungertuch nagen, muss ja verzagen, mag's nicht ertragen!
	Griesgram, Griesgram, greulicher Wicht, griesiges, grämiges Galgengesicht, packe dich, trolle dich, schäbiger Wicht!
Gretel.	So recht! Und willst du nun nicht mehr klagen, so will ich dir auch ein Geheimnis sagen.
Hansel.	Ein Geheimnis? Wird wohl was Rechtes sein!
Gretel.	Ja, hör nur, Brüderchen! Darfst dich schon freun, Guck her in den Topf, Milch ist darin, die schenkte uns heute die Nachbarin. Mutter kocht uns, kommt sie nach Haus, gewiss einen leckeren Reisbrei daraus.
Hänsel.	Reisbrei, Reisbrei, herrlicher Brei! Giebt's Reisbrei, da ist Hänsel dabei! Wie dick ist der Rahm auf der Milch! Lass schmecken! Herrjemine, den möcht' ich ganz verschlecken! Wie, Hänsel, naschen? Schämst du dich nicht?
Gretel.	Fort mit den Fingern, du naschhafter Wicht! (Giebt ihm eins auf die Finger.) Und jetzt an die Arbeit zurück, geschwind, dass wir beizeiten fertig sind! Kommt Muter heim, und wir thaten nicht recht, Dann, weisst du, geht es den Faulpelzen schlecht.
Hänsel.	Arbeiten? Brr! Wo denkst du hin? Danach steht mir jetzt nicht der Sinn. Immer mich plagen, das fällt mir nicht ein, jetzt lass uns tanzen und fröhlich sein!
Gretel.	(Entzückt.) Tanzen? Das wär' auch mir eine Lust! Dazu ein Liedchen aus froher Brust, wie's uns die Muhme gelehrt zu singen: *Tanzliedchen* soll jetzt lustig erklingen! (Klatscht in die Hände.) Brüderchen, komm, tanz' mit mir, beide Händchen reich' ich Dir; einmal hin, einmal her, rund herum, es ist nicht schwer!
Hänsel.	Tanzen soll ich armer Wicht, Schwesterlein, und kann es nicht. Darum zeig' mir, wie es Brauch, dass ich tanzen lerne auch!
Gretel.	Mit den Füsschen tapp tapp tapp, mit den Händchen klapp klapp klapp, einmal hin, einmal her, rund herum, es ist nicht schwer.
Hänsel.	Mit den Füsschen tapp tapp tapp, mit den Händchen klapp klapp klapp, einmal hin, einmal her, rund herum, es ist nicht schwer.

Gretel.
That was very good indeed,
O, I'm sure you'll soon succeed!
Try again, and I can see
Hänsel soon will dance like me!
With your head you nick, nick, nick;
with your fingers you click, click, click;
   right foot first,
   left foot then,
round about and back again.

Hänsel.
With your head you nick, nick, nick;
with your fingers you click, click, click;
   right foot first,
   left foot then,
round about and back again!

Gretel.
Brother, watch what next I do,
you must do it with me too.
You to me your arm must proffer,
I shall not refuse your offer!
Come!
What I enjoy is dance and jollity,
love to have my fling;
in fact, I like frivolity,
and all that kind of thing.
Tralala, tralala, tralala!

Come and have a twirl, my dearest Hänsel,
come and have a turn with me, I pray;
come here to me, come here to me,
I'm sure you can't say nay!

Hänsel.
Go away from me, go away from me,
I'm much too proud for you:
with little girls I do not dance,
and so, my dear, adieu!

Gretel.
Go, stupid Hans, conceited Hans,
you'll see I'll make you dance!
Tralala, tralala, tralala!
Come and have a twirl, my dearest Hänsel,
come and have a turn with me, I pray!

Hänsel.
O Gretel dear, O sister dear,
your stocking has a hole!

Gretel.
O Hänsel dear, O brother dear,
d'you take me for a fool?
With naughty boys I do not dance,
and so, my dear, adieu!

Hänsel.
Now don't be cross.
you silly goose,
you'll see I make you dance!

Gretel.
   Tralala, tralala, tralala!
Come and have a twirl, my dearest Hänsel,
come and have a turn with me, I pray.
Sing lustily hurrah! hurrah!
while I dance with you;
and if the stockings are in holes,
why, mother'll knit some new!

Hänsel.
   Tralala, tralala, tralala!
Sing lustily hurrah! hurrah!
while I dance with you;
and if the shoes are all in holes,
why mother'll buy some new!
   Tralala, tralala, tralala!

Gretel.
Ei, das hast Du gut gemacht,
ei, das hätt' ich nicht gedacht!
Seht mir doch den Hänsel an,
wie der tanzen lernen kann!
Mit dem Köpfchen nick nick nick,
mit dem Fingerchen tick tick tick,
   einmal hin, einmal her,
   rund herum, es ist nicht schwer!

Hänsel.
Mit dem Köpfchen nick nick nick,
mit dem Fingerchen tick tick tick,
   einmal hin, einmal her,
   rund herum, es ist nicht schwer!

Gretel.
Hänsel, komm und gieb mal acht,
wie's die Gretel weiter macht!
Lass uns Arm in Arm verschränken,
unsre Schrittchen paarweis lenken!
Ich liebe Tanz und Fröhlichkeit
und bin nicht gern allein;
ich bin kein Freund von Traurigkeit,
und fröhlich will ich sein.
   Tralala, tralala, tralala la la,
   Dreh dich herum, mein lieber Hans!

Gretel.
Komm her zu mir, komm her zu mir,
zum Ringelreigentanz!

Hänsel.
Geh weg von mir, geh weg von mir,
ich bin der stolze Hans!
Mit kleinen Mädchen tanz ich nicht,
das ist mir viel zu dumm!

Gretel.
Geh, dummer Hans, geh, stolzer Hans,
ich krieg dich doch herum!
   Tralala, tralala, tralala la la,
   dreh dich herum, mein lieber Hans!

Hänsel.
Ach, Schwesterlein, ach, Gretelein,
Du hast im Strumpf ein Loch!

Gretel.
Ach Brüderlein, ach Hänselein,
Du willst mich hänseln noch!
Mit bösen Buben tanz ich nicht,
das ist mir viel zu dumm!

Hänsel.
Nicht böse sein, lieb Schwesterlein,
ich krieg Dich doch herum!
   Tralala, tralala, tralala, la la,
   Dreh dich doch herum, mein Gretelein!

Hänsel.
Tanz lustig, heissa, lustig tanz!
   Lass dich's nicht gereu'n;
und ist der Strumpf auch nicht
     mehr ganz,
   die Mutter strickt dir 'n neu'n!
   Dreh dich doch herum!
   Sei nicht so dumm!
   Tralala, tralala u. s. w.

Gretel.
Tanz lustig, heissa, lustig tanz!
   Lass dich's nicht gereu'n;
und ist der Schuh' auch nicht mehr
     ganz,
   der Schuster flickt dir 'n neu'n!
   Dreh dich doch herum!
   Sei nicht so dumm!
   Tralala, tralala u. s. w.

(They dance round each other as before. They then seize each other's hands and go round in a circle, quicker and quicker, until at last they lose their balance and tumble over one another on the floor. Suddenly the door opens, the mother appears and the children jump up.)

SCENE II

Mother. Hallo!

Hänsel and Gretel.
Heavens! Here's mother!

Mother. What is all this disturbance?

Cretel. 'Twas Hänsel, he wanted—

Hänsel 'Twas Gretel, she said I—

Mother. Silence, idle and ill-behaved children!
(The mother comes in, unstraps the basket, and puts it down.)
Call you it working, yodelling and singing?
As through 'twere fair time, hopping and
    springing!
And while your parents from early morning
till late at night are slaving and toiling!
Take that!
(Gives Hänsel a box on the ear.)
Now come, let's see what you've done.
Why, Gretel, your stocking not ready yet?
And you, you lazybones, have you nothing
    to show?
Pray how many brooms have you finished?
I'll fetch my stick, you useless children,
and make your idle fingers tingle!

(In her anger at the children she gives the milk-jug a push, and it smashes.)

Gracious! there's goes the jug all to pieces!
What now can I cook for supper?
(She looks at her skirt, down which the milk is streaming. Hänsel covertly titters.)

How, saucy, how dare you laugh?
(Going with a stick after Hänsel, who is running out of the open door.)

Wait, wait till the father comes home!
(She snatches a basket from the wall, and pushes it into Gretel's hands.)

Off, off, to the woods!
There seek for strawberries! Quick, away!
And if you don't bring the basket brimful,
I'll whip you so that you'll both run away!
(The children run off into the forest. She sits down exhausted by the table.)

Alas! there my poor jug lies all in pieces!
Yes, blind excitement only brings ruin.
O Heaven, send help to me!
Nought have I to give them—
        (Sobbing.)

No bread, not a crumb, for my starving
    children!

(Dann fassen sie sich bei den Haenden und drehen sich immer schneller im Kreise, bis sie schliesslich das Gleichgewicht verlieren und uebereinander auf den Boden hinpurzeln. In diesem Augenblicke geht die Thüre auf; die Mutter wird sichtbar, worauf die Kinder schnell vom Boden aufspringen.)

ZWEITE SCENE

Mutter. Holla!

Hänsel und Gretel.
Himmel, die Mutter!

Mutter. Was ist das für eine Geschichte?

Gretel. Der Hänsel . . .

Hänsel. Die Gretel . . .

Gretel. Er wollte . . .
Hänsel.
Ich sollte . . .

Mutter.
        (In Zorn ausbrechend.)
Wartet, ihr ungezogenen Wichte!
Nennt ihr das Arbeit? Johlen und singen?
Wie auf der Kirmes tanzen und springen?
Indes die Eltern vom frühen Morgen
bis spät in die Nacht sich mühen und
    sorgen?
Dass dich!
    (Giebt Hänseln einen Puff.)
Lasst seh'n, was habt ihr beschickt?
—Wie, Gretel, den Strumpf nicht fertig
    gestrickt?
—Und du?—Du, Schlingel! In all den
    Stunden
nicht mal die wenigen Besen gebunden?
Ihr unnützigen Kinder! Den Stock will ich
    holen,
den Faulpelz werd' ich euch beiden ver-
    sohlen!

(In ihrem Eifer hinter den Kindern her stösst sie den Milchtopf vom Tisch, dass er klirrend zu Boden fällt.)

Jesses! Nun auch den Topf noch
    zerbrochen!
    (Weinend.)
Was soll ich nun zum Abend kochen?
(Besieht ihren mit Milch begossenen Rock; Hänsel kichert verstohlen.)

Was, Bengel, du lachst mich noch aus?
(Mit dem Stock hinter Hans her, der zur offenen Thür hinausrennt.)

Wart, kommt nur der Vater nach Haus—
(Lays her head down on her arm and drops to sleep.)
(Reisst einen kleinen Korb von der Wand und drängt ihn Gretel in die Hand.)

Marsch, fort—in den Wald!
Dort sucht mir Erdbeeren!—Nun, wird es
    bald?

(Treibt auch Gretel zur Stube hinaus und droht mit dem Stocke den sich furchtsam umschauenden Kindern.)

Und bringt ihr den Korb nicht voll bis zum
    Rand,
so hau ich euch, dass ihr fliegt an die
    Wand!
(Setzt sich erschöpft an den Tisch.)

Da liegt nun der gute Topf in Scherben!
Ja, blinder Eifer bringt immer Verderben.—
Herrgott, wirf Geld herab! Nichts hab' ich
zu leben,

No crust in the cupboard, no milk in the
   pot—
(Resting her head on her hands.)
Weary am I, weary of living!
Father, send help to me!'

SCENE III

(A voice is heard in the distance.)
Tralala, tralala! little mother, here am I!
Tralala, tralala! bringing luck and jollity!
O, for you and me, poor mother,
every day is like the other;
with a big hole in the purse,
and in the stomach an even worse.
    Tralala, tralala!
Hunger is the poor man's curse!
    Tralala, tralala!
Hunger is the poor man's curse!
(The father appears at the window, and during the following
he comes into the room in a very happy mood, with a basket
on his back.)

'Tisn't much that we require;
just a little food and fire!
But alas! it's true enough,
life on some of us is rough!
Hunger is a customer tough!
Yes, the rich enjoys his dinner,
while the poor grows daily thinner!
Strives to eat, as well he may,
somewhat less than yesterday!
    Tralala, tralala!
hunger is the devil to pay!
    Tralala, tralala!
hunger is the devil to pay!
    (He puts down his basket.)
Yes, hunger's all very well to feel,
if you can get a good square meal;
but when there's nought, what can you do,
supposing the purse be empty too?
    Tralalala, tralalaia!
O for a drop of mountain dew!
    Tralalala, tralalala!
Mother, look what I have brought!
(Reels over to his sleeping wife and gives her a smacking
kiss.)

Mother.

(Rubbing her eyes.)
Oho!—
Who's sing-sing-singing
all around the house,
and tra-la-la-ing me
out of my sleep?

Father.

(Inarticulately.)
How now!—
The hungry beast
within my breast
called so for food
I could not rest!
Tralala, tralala!
Hunger is an urgent beast!
Tralala, tralala!
pinches, gnaws, and gives no rest!

Mother.

So, so!

kein Krümchen den Würmern zu essen zu
   geben;
kein Tröpfchen im Topfe, kein Krüstchen
   im Schrank,
schon lange nichts als Wasser zum Trank.
   (Stützt den Kopf mit der Hand.)
Müde bin ich—müde zum Sterben—
Herrgott, wirf Geld herab——
(Legt den Kopf auf den Arm und schläft ein.)

DRITTE SCENE

(Man hört eine Stimme von weitem:)
Ach, wir armen, armen Leute!
Alle Tage so wie heute:
In dem Beutel ein grosses Loch
und im Magen ein gröss'res noch—
    Rallalala, rallalala,
Hunger ist der beste Koch!
(Am Fenster wird der Kopf des Vaters sichtbar, der während des Folgenden in angeheitertem Zustande mit einem
Kober auf dem Rücken in die Stube tritt.)

Ja, ihr Reichen könnt euch laben!
Wir, die nichts zu essen haben,
nagen, ach, die ganze Woch',
sieben Tag an einem Knoch'!
    Rallalala, rallalala,
Hunger ist der beste Koch!
Ach, wir sind ja gern zufrieden,
 denn das Glück ist so verschieden,
aber, aber wahr ist's doch:
Armut ist ein schweres Joch!
    Rallalala, rallalala,
Hunger ist der beste Koch!
(Er setzt seinen Kober nieder und tritt an die Rampe.)
Ja ja, der Hunger kocht schon gut,
sofern er kommandieren thut.
Allein was nutzt der Kommandör,
fehlt euch im Topf die Zubehör?
    Rallalala, rallalala,
Kümmel ist mein Leiblikör!
    Rallalala, rallalala,
Mutter, schau, was ich bescheer!
(Giebt ihr einen derben Schmatz.)

Mutter.

(Sich die Augen reibend.)
Hoho!—
Wer spek—spektakelt
mir da im Haus
und rallakakelt
aus dem Schlaf mich heraus?

Vater.

(Lallend.)
Das tolle Tier,
im Magen hier,
das bellte so, das glaube mir!
Rallalala, rallalala,
Hunger ist ein tolles Tier.
Rallalala, rallalala,
beisst und kratzt, das glaube mir!

Mutter.

So, so!

And this wild beast,
you gave him a feast.
He's had his fill,
to say the least!

Father. Well, yes! H'm it was a lovely day,
don't you think so, dear wife?

Mother.
(Angrily.)
Have done! You have no troubles to bear,
'tis I must keep the house!

Father. Well, well,—then let us see, my dear,
what we have got to eat to-day.

Mother. Most simple is the bill of fare,
our supper's gone, I know not where!
Larder bare, cellar bare,
nothing, and plenty of it to spare!

Father. Tralalala, tralalala!
Cheer up, mother, for here am I,
bringing luck and jollity!
(He takes his basket and begins to display the contents.)
Look, mother, doesn't all this food please
you?

Mother. Man, man, what see I?
Ham and butter,
flour and sausage—
eggs, a dozen . . .
(Husband, and they cost a fortune!)
Turnips, onions, and—for me!
Nearly half a pound of tea!

Father. Tralala, tralala,
hip hurrah!
Won't we have a festive time!
Tralala, hip hurrah!
Won't we have a happy time!
Now listen how it all came to pass!
(Sits down. Meanwhile the mother packs away the things,
lights a fire, breaks eggs into a saucepan, etc.)
Yonder to the town I went,
there was to be a great event,
weddings, fairs, and preparation
for all kinds of jubilation!
Now's my chance to do some selling,
and for that you may be thankful!
He who wants a feast to keep,
he must scrub and brush and sweep.
So I brought my best goods out,
tramped with them from house to house:
"Buy besoms! good besoms!
Buy my brushes! sweep your carpets,
sweep your cobwebs!"
And so I drove a roaring trade,
and sold my brushes at the highest prices!
Now make haste with cup and platter,
bring the glasses, bring the kettle—
here's a health to the besom-maker!

Mother. Here's a health to the besom-maker!

Father. But stay, why, where are the children?
Hänsel, Gretel, what's gone with Hans?

Mother. Gone with Hans? O, who's to know?
But at least I do know this,
that the jug is smashed to bits.

Das tolle Tier,
es ist wohl! schier
stark angezecht—das glaube mir!

Vater. Nun ja, 's war heut ein heitrer Tag!
Fondst du nicht auch, lieb' Weib?

Mutter.
(Ärgerlich.)
Ach geh! Du weisst, nicht leiden mag
ich Wirtshaus-Zeitvertreib!

Vater. Auch gut! So sehen wir, wenn's beliebt,
was es für heut zu schmausen giebt.

Mutter. Höchst einfach ist das Speiseregister
der Abendschmaus—zum Henker ist er!
Teller leer,
Keller leer,
und im Beutel ist gar nichts mehr.

Vater. Rallalala, rallalala,
lustig, Mutter, bin auch noch da!
Rallalala, rallalala,
bringe Glück und Gloria!
(Nimmt den Kober und kramt aus.)
Schau, Mutter!
Wie gefällt Dir dies Futter?

Mutter. Mann, was seh' ich? Speck und Butter!
Mehl und Würste! . . . vierzehn Eier—
—Mann! Sie sind jetzunder teuer!—
Bohnen, Zwiebeln und—herrjeh!
Gar ein viertel Pfund Kaffee!

Vater.

Rallalala, hopsassa!
Heute woll'n wir lustig sein!
Ja, hör nur, Mütterchen, wie's geschah!

(Er setzt sich nieder, die Mutter kramt inzwischen die
Sachen ein, zuendet Feuer im Herd an, schlaegt Eier in eine
Pfanne u.s.w.)

Drüben hinterm Herrenwald
prächt'ge Feste giebt's da bald,
Kirmes, Hochzeit, Jubiläum,
Böllerknall und gross Tedeum.
Mein Geschäft kommt nun zur Blüte;
dessen froh sei Dein Gemüte!
Sieh! wer feines Fest will feiern,
der muss kehren, schrubben und scheuern.
Bot drum meine Waren aus,
zog damit von Haus zu Haus:
"Kauft Besen! Gute Feger!
Feine Bürsten! Spinnejäger!"
Sieh, da verkauft' ich massenweise
meine Waren zum höchsten Preise!—
Schnell nun her mit Topf und Pfanne,
her mit Kessel, Schüssel, Kanne!

Mutter. Vivat hoch die Besenbinder!

Vater. Doch halt—wo bleiben die Kinder?
Hänsel! Gretel!—Wo steckt der Hans?

Mutter. Wo er steckt? Ja, wüsste man's!
Nur das weiss ich klar wie Tag,
dass der Topf in Scherben lag!

Father.	What! the jug is smashed to bits?	*Vater.*	

Vater.

      (Zornig.)
Was? der neue Topf entzwei?

Mother.   And the cream all run away.

Mutter.   Und am Boden quoll der Brei!

Father.

   (Striking his fist on the table in a rage.)
    Hang it all! So those little scapegraces have
    been again in mischief!

Vater.

  (Mit der Faust auf den Tisch schlagend.)
    Donnerkeil! So haben die Rangen
    Unfug wieder angefangen?

Mother.   Been in mischief? I should think so!
    Nothing have they done but their mad
      pranking;
    as I came home I could hear them
    hopping and cutting the wildest capers,
    till I was so cross that I gave a push—
    and the jug of milk was spilt!

Mutter.   Unfug viel und Arbeit keine
    hatten sie getrieben alleine.
    Hörte schon draussen sie juchzen und
      johlen,
    hopsen und springen wie wilde Fohlen.
    wusste nicht, wie mir stand der Kopf.
    Und vor Zorn

Father.   And the jug of milk was spilt!
    Ha ha ha ha!
        (Both laughing.)
    Such anger, mother, don't take it ill,
    seems stupid to me, I must say!
    But where, where think you the children
      can be?

Vater.   —zerbrach der Topf.
    Hahahaha!
    (Beide lachen aus vollem Halse.)
    Na, Zornmütterchen, nimm mir's nicht
      krumm,
    solche Zorntöpfe find' ich recht dumm!
    Doch sag, wo mögen die Kinderchen sein?

Mother.

      (Snappishly and curtly.)
    For aught I know, at the Ilsenstein!

Mutter.

      (Schnippisch.)
    Meinethalben am *Ilsenstein!*

Father.

      (Horror-struck.)
    The Ilsenstein! Come, come, have a care!
    (Fetches a broom from the wall.)

Vater.

      (Erschrocken.)
    Am Ilsenstein?—Ei, juckt Dich das Fell?
    (Nimmt einen Besen von der Wand.)

Mother.   The broom, just put it away again!

Mutter.   Den Besen lass nur an seiner Stell.

Father.

  (Lets the broom fall and wrings his hands.)
    My children astray in the gloomy wood,
    all alone without moon or stars!
    Dost thou not know the awful magic place,
    the place where the evil one dwells?

Vater.

  (Lässt den Besen fallen und ringt die Hände.)
    Wenn sie sich verirrten im Walde dort,
    in der Nacht, ohne Stern und Mond!
    Kennst Du nicht den schauerlich düstern
      Ort?
    Weisst nicht, dass die *Böse* dort wohnt?

Mother.   The evil one! What mean'st thou?

Mutter.   Die Böse? Wen meinst Du?

Father.

    (With mysterious emphasis.)
    The gobbling ogress!
  (The mother draws back, the father takes up the broom
again.)

Vater.

   (Mit geheimnisvollem Nachdruck.)
    Die *Knusperhexe!*—

Mother.   The gobbling ogress!
    But—tell me, what help is the besom!

Mutter.

      (Fährt zusammen.)
    Die Knusperhexe!—
    Mein! Sag doch, was soll denn der Besen?

Father.   The besom, the besom, why what is it for?
    They ride on it, they ride on it, the witches!
    An old witch within that wood doth dwell
    and she's in league with the powers of hell.
    At midnight hour, when nobody knows,
    away to the witches' dance she goes.
      Up the chimney they fly,
      on a broomstick they hie—
        over hill and dale,
        o'er ravine and vale,
        through the midnight air
        they gallop full tear—

Vater.   Der Besen! Der Besen!
    Was macht man damit? Was macht man
      damit?
    Es reiten drauf, es reiten drauf die Hexen!
      Eine Hex' steinalt,
      haust tief im Wald,
    vom Teufel selber hat sie Gewalt!
      Um Mitternacht,
      wann niemand wacht,
    dann reitet sie aus zur Hexenjagd,
      Zum Schornstein hinaus
      auf dem Besen, o Graus!

on a broomstick, on a broomstick,
hop hop, hop hop, the witches!

Mother. O horror!
But the gobbling witch?

Father. And by day, they say, she stalks around,
with a crinching, crunching, munching
sound,
and children plump and tender to eat
she lures with magic gingerbread sweet.
On evil bent,
with fell intent,
she lures the children, poor little things,
in the oven red-hot
she pops all the lot;
she shuts the lid down
until they're done brown,
in the oven, in the oven,
the gingerbread children!

Mother. And the gingerbread children?

Father. Are served up for dinner!

Mother. For the ogress?

Father. For the ogress!

Mother. O horror!
Heav'n help us! the children!
O what shall we do?
(Runs out of the house)

Father. Hi, mother, mother, wait for me!
(Takes the whiskey bottle from the table and runs after her.)
We'll both go together the witch to seek!
(The curtain falls quickly.)

ACT II

IN THE FOREST

SCENE I

(The curtain rises. The middle of the forest. In the background is the Ilsenstein, thickly surrounded by fir-trees. On the right is a large fir-tree, under which Gretel is sitting on a mossy tree-trunk and making a garland of wild roses. By her side lies a nosegay of flowers. Amongst the bushes on the left is Hänsel, looking for strawberries. Sunset.)

Gretel.
(Humming quietly to herself.)
There stands a little man in the wood alone,
he wears a little mantle of velvet brown.
Say, who can the mankin be,
standing there beneath the tree,
with the little mantle of velvet brown?
His hair is all of gold, and his cheeks are
red,
he wears a little black cup upon his head
Say, who can the mankin be,
standing there so silently,
with the little black cap upo nhis head?
(She holds up the garland of roses, and looks it all round.)
with the little black cap upon his head?

Braus!
Über Berg und Kluft,
Über Thal und Gruft
durch Nebelduft
im Sturm durch die Luft:
Ja so reiten, ja so reiten,
juchheissa, die Hexen!

Mutter. Entsetzlich!

Vater. Ja, bei Tag, o Graus:
zum Hexenschmaus
ins Knisper-Knasper-Knusperhaus
die Kinderlein,
Armsünderlein,
mit Zauberkuchen lockt sie herein.
Doch übelgesinnt
ergreift sie geschwind
das arme Kuchen knuspernde Kind.
In den Ofen, hitzhell,
schiebt's die Hexe blitzschnell:
dann kommen zur Stell,
gebräunt das Fell,
aus dem Ofen, aus dem Ofen
die *Lebkuchenkinder!*

Mutter. Und die Lebkuchenkinder?

Vater. Die werden gefressen!

Mutter. Von der Hexe?

Vater. Von der Hexe.

(Händeringend.)
O Graus!
Hilf, Himmel! die Kinder! Ich halt's nicht
mehr aus!
(Rennt aus dem Hause.)

Vater.

(Nimmt die Kümmelflasche vom Tisch.)
He, Alte, so wart' doch! Nimm mich mit!
Wir wollen ja beide zum Hexenritt!
(Eilt ihr nach. Der Vorhang fällt schnell.)

ZWEITES BILD

IM WALDE

ERSTE SCENE

(Im Hintergrunde der Ilsenstein, von dichtem Tannengehölz umgeben. Rechts eine mächtige Tanne; darunter sitzt Gretel auf einer moosbedeckten Wurzel und windet einen Kranz von Hagebutten; neben ihr liegt ein Blumenstrauss. Links, abseits im Gebüsch, Hänsel, nach Erdbeeren suchend Abendrot.)

Gretel. Ein Männlein steht im Walde
ganz still und stumm;
es hat von lauter Purpur
ein Mäntlein um.
Sagt, wer mag das Männlein sein,
das da steht im Wald allein
mit dem purpurroten Mäntelein?
Das Männlein steht im Walde
auf einem Bein
und hat auf seinem Kopfe
schwarz Käpplein klein.
Sagt, wer mag das Männlein sein,
das da steht im Wald allein
mit dem kleinen schwarzen Käppelein?

Hänsel.
(Comes out, swinging his basket joyfully.)
> Hurrah! my strawberry basket is nearly
>   brimful!
> O won't the mother be pleased with Hänsel!

Gretel.   My garland is ready also!
> Look! I never made one so nice before!
(Tries to put the wreath on Hänsel's head.)

Hänsel.
(Drawing back roughly.)
> You won't catch a boy wearing that!
> It is only fit for a girl!
(Puts the wreath on her.)
> Ha, Gretel! "Fine feathers!"
> O the deuce!
> You shall be the queen of the wood!

Gretel.   If I am to be queen of the wood,
> then I must have the nosegay too!

Hänsel.   Queen of the wood, with sceptre and crown,
> I give you the strawberries,
> but don't eat them all!
(He gives the basket full of strawberries into her other hand, at the same time kneeling before her in homage. At this moment the cuckoo is heard.)

> Cuckoo, cuckoo, how d'you do?

Gretel.   Cuckoo, cuckoo, where are you?
(Takes a strawberry from the basket and pokes it into Hänsel's mouth; he sucks it up as though he were drinking an egg.)

Hänsel.
(Jumping up).
> Oho, I can do that just like you!
(Takes some strawberries and lets them fall into Gretel's mouth.)
> Let us do like the cuckoo too.
> who takes more than his lawful due!
(It begins to grow dark.)

Hänsel.
(Helping himself again).
> Cuckoo, cuckoo, how are you?

Gretel.   Cuckoo, where are you?

Hänsel.   In your neighbour's nest you go.
Gretel.
(Helping herself.)
> Cuckoo, cuckoo!

Hänsel.   Cuckoo, why do you do so?
(Pours a handful of strawberries into his mouth.)

Gretel.   And you are very greedy too!
> Tell me, cuckoo, why are you?

Hänsel.   Cuckoo, cuckoo!
(They get rude and begin to quarrel for the strawberries. Hänsel gains the victory, and puts the whole basket to his mouth until it is empty. During this time, it has grown dark.)

Gretel.
(Horrified, clasping her hands together.)
> Hänsel, what have you done?
> O Heaven! all the strawberries eaten.
> You glutton! Listen, you'll have a punish-
>   ment
> from the mother—this passes a joke!

Hänsel.
(Kommt hervor und schwenkt jubelnd sein Körbchen.)
> Juchhe!
> Mein Erbelkörbchen ist voll bis oben;
> wie wird die Mutter den Hänsel loben!

Gretel.   Mein Kränzel ist auch schon fertig, sieh!
> So schön wie heute ward's noch nie!
(Will den Kranz Hänsel auf den Kopf setzen.)

Hänsel.
(Barsch abwehrend.)
> Buben tragen doch so was nicht,
> 's passt nur für ein Mädchengesicht.
(Setzt ihr den Kranz auf.)
> Hei, Gretel, feins Mädel!
> Ei, der Daus,
> siehst ja wie die Waldkönigin aus!

Gretel,   Seh ich wie die Waldkönigin aus,
> so reich' mir auch den Blumenstrauss!

Hänsel.   Waldkönigin mit Scepter und Kron',
> da nimm auch die Erbeln, doch nasch' nicht
>   davon!
(Reicht ihr das Körbchen voll Erdbeeren und hockt, gleichsam huldigend, vor ihr nieder. In diesem Augenblick ertönt der Ruf eines Kuckucks.)

Hänsel.   Kuckuck! Eierschluck!
Gretel.
(Schalkhaft.)
> Kuckuck! Erbelschluck!
(Nimmt eine Beere aus dem Körbchen und hält sie Hänsel hin, der sie schlürft, als ob er ein Ei austränke.)

Hänsel.
(Springt auf.)
> Hoho! Das kann ich auch! Gieb nur acht!
(Nimmt einige Beeren und lässt sie Gretel in den Mund rollen.)
> Wir machen's, wie der Kuckuck schluckt,
> wenn er in fremde Nester guckt.
(Es beginnt zu dämmern.)

Hänsel.
(Greift wieder zu.)
> Kuckuck! Eierschluck!

Gretel.
(Ebenso.)
> Kuckuck! Erbelschluck!

Hänsel.   Setzest Deine Kinder aus!
> Kuckuck!
> Trinkst die fremden Eier aus!
> Gluckgluck!
(Lässt sich eine ganze Handvoll Erdbeeren in den Mund rollen.)

Gretel.   Sammelst Beeren schön zuhauf!
> Kuckuck!
> Schluckst sie, Schlauer, selber auf!

> Schluckschluck!
(Sie werden übermütiger und raufen sich schliesslich um die Beeren. Hänsel trägt den Sieg davon und setzt den Korb vollends an den Mund, bis er gänzlich leer geworden. Indessen hat die Dunkelheit immer mehr zugenommen.)

Gretel.
(Hänsel den Korb entreissend.)
> Hänsel, was hast Du gethan! O Himmel!
> Alle Erbeln gegessen, Du Lümmel!
> Wart' nur, das giebt ein Strafgericht,
> denn die Mutter, die spasst heute nicht!

Hänsel.

(Quietly.)

Now come, don't make such a fuss;
you, Gretel, you did the same thing yourself!

Gretel. Come, we'll hurry and seek for fresh ones!

Hänsel. What, here in the dark, under hedges and
bushes?
Why, naught can we see of fruit or leaves!
It's getting dark already here!

Gretel. O Hänsel! O Hänsel! O what shall we do?
What bad disobedient children we've been!
We ought to have thought and gone home
sooner!

(Cuckoo behind the scenes rather nearer than before.)

Hänsel. Hark, what a noise in the bushes!
Know you what the forest says?
"Children, children," it says,
"Are you not afraid?"

(Hänsel spies all around uneasily, at last he turns in despair
to Gretel.)

Gretel, I cannot find the way!

Gretel.

(Dismayed.)

O God! what say you?
Not know the way?

Hänsel.

(Pretending to be very brave).

Why, how ridiculous you are!
I am a boy, and know not fear!

Gretel. O Hänsel, some dreadful thing may come!

Hänsel. O Gretel, come, don't be afraid!

Gretel. What's glimmering there in the darkness?

Hänsel. That's only the birches in silver dress.

Gretel. But there, what's grinning so there at me?

Hänsel.

(Stammering.)

Th— that's only the stump of a willow-tree.

Gretel.

(Hastily.)

But what a dreadful form it takes,
and what a horrid face it makes!

Hänsel.

(Very loud.)

Come, I'll make faces, you fellow!
D'you hear?

Gretel.

(Terrified.)

There, see! a lantern,
it's coming this way!

Hänsel. Will-o'-the-wisp is hopping about—
Gretel, come, don't lose heart like this!
Wait, I'll give a good loud call!

(Goes back some steps to the back of the stage and calls
through his hands.)

Who's there?

Echo. You there!
There!

(The children cower together.)

Hänsel.

(Ruhig.)

Ei was, stell Dich doch nicht so an, ...
Du, Gretel, hast es ja selber gethan!

Gretel. Komm nur, wollen rasch neue suchen!

Hänsel. Im Dunkeln wohl gar, unter Hecken und
Buchen?
Man sieht ja nicht Blatt, nicht Beere mehr!
Es wird schon dunkel rings umher!

Gretel. Ach, Hänsel, Hänsel! Was fangen wir an?
Was haben wir thörichten Kinder gethan?
Wir durften hier gar nicht so lange säumen!

Hänsel. Horch, wie rauscht es in den Bäumen!—
Weisst Du, was der Wald jetzt spricht?
"Kindlein!" sagt er, "fürchtet ihr euch
nicht?"

(Späht unruhig umher.)

Gretel! Ich weiss den Weg nicht mehr!

Gretel.

(Bestürzt.)

O Gott! Was sagst Du? den Weg nicht
mehr?

Hänsel.

(Sich mutig stellend.)

Was bist Du doch für ein furchtsam Wicht!
Ich bin ein Bub', ich fürchte mich nicht!

Gretel. Ach, Hänsel! Gewiss geschieht uns ein
Leid!

Hänsel. Ach, Gretel, geh, sei doch gescheit!

Gretel. Was schimmert denn dort in der Dunkelheit?

Hänsel. Das sind die Birken im weissen Kleid.

Gretel. Und dort, was grinset daher vom Sumpf?

Hänsel.

(Stotternd.)

D— d— das ist ein glimmender Weiden-
stumpf!

Gretel. Was für ein wunderlich Gesicht
Macht er soeben—siehst Du's nicht?

Hänsel.

(Sehr laut.)

Ich mach' dir ne Nase, hörst du's, Wicht?

Gretel.

(Angstlich.)

Da, sieh', das Lichtchen—es kommt immer
näh'r!

Hänsel. Irrlichtchen hüpfet wohl hin und her!
Gretel, Du musst beherzter sein—
wart, ich will einmal tüchtig schrein!

(Ruft durch die hohlen Hände.)

Wer da?

Echo. Er da!

(Die Kinder schmiegen sich erschreckt aneinander.)

Gretel.	Is some one there?
Echo.	Where?
	Here!
Gretel.	Did you hear? a voice said, "Here!"
	Hänsel, surely some one's near.
	(Crying.)
	I'm frightened, I'm frightened,
	I wish I were home!
	I see the wood all filled with goblin forms!
Hänsel.	Gretelkin, stick to me close and tight,
	I'll shelter you, I'll shelter you!

(A thick mist rises and completely hides the background.)

Gretel.	I see some shadowy women coming!
	See, how they nod and beckon, beckon!
	They're coming, they're coming,
	they'll take us away!

(Crying out, rushes horror-struck under the tree and falls on her knees, hiding herself behind Hänsel.)

	Father! mother! Ah!

(At this moment the mist lifts on the left; a little grey man is seen with a little sack on his back.)

Hänsel.	See there, the mankin, sister dear!
	I wonder who the mankin is?

SCENE II

Sandman.

(The little man approaches the children with friendly gestures, and the children gradually calm down. He is strewing sand in the children's eyes.)

> I shut the children's peepers, sh!
> and guard the little sleepers, sh!
> for dearly do I love them, sh!
> and gladly watch above them, sh!
> And with my little bag of sand,
> By every child's bedside I stand;
> then little tired eyelids close,
> and little limbs have sweet repose.
> And if they're good and quickly go to sleep,
> then from the starry sphere above
> the angels come with peace and love,
> and send the children happy dreams,
> while watch they keep!
> Then slumber, children, slumber,
> for happy dreams are sent you
> through the hours you sleep.
> (Disappears. Darkness.)

Hänsel.	
	(Half asleep.)
	Sandman was there!
Gretel.	
	(Ditto.)
	Let us first say our evening prayer.

(They cower down and fold their hands.)

Both.	When at night I go to sleep,
	fourteen angels watch do keep:
	two my head are guarding,
	two my feet are guiding,
	two are on my right hand,
	two are on my left hand,
	two who warmly cover,
	two who o'er me hover,
	two to whom 'tis given
	to guide my steps to Heaven.

(They sink down on to the moss, and go to sleep with their arms twined round each other. Complete darkness.)

Gretel.	Ist jemand da?
Echo.	Ja!
	(Die Kinder schaudern zusammen.)
Gretel.	Hast du's gehört? 's rief leise: Ja!
	Hänsel, sicher ist jemand nah'!
	(Weinend:)
	Ich fürcht' mich, ich fürcht' mich!—O wär'
	ich zu Haus!
	Wie sieht der Wald so gespenstig aus!
Hänsel.	Gretelchen, drücke Dich fest an mich!
	Ich halte Dich, ich schütze Dich!

(Ein dichter Nebel steigt auf und verhüllt den Hintergrund gänzlich.)

Gretel.	Da, kommen weisse Nebelfrauen,
	sieh', wie sie winken und drohend schauen.
	Sie schweben heran!
	Sie fassen uns an!
	(Schreiend:)
	Vater! Mutter!

(Eilt entsetzt unter die Tanne und verbirgt sich, auf die Kniee stürzend, hinter Hänsel. In diesem Augenblicke zerreisst links der Nebel; ein kleines graues Männchen, mit einem Säckchen auf dem Rücken, wird sichtbar.)

Hänsel.	Sieh' dort das Männchen, Schwesterlein!
	Was mag das für ein Männchen sein?

ZWEITE SCENE

Sandmännchen.

(Nähert sich mit freundlichen Gebärden den Kindern die sich allmählich beruhigen, und wirft ihnen beim Singen Sand in die Augen.)

> Der kleine Sandmann bin ich—s-t!
> und gar nichts Arges sinn ich—s-t!
> Euch Kleinen lieb ich innig—s-t!
> bin euch gesinnt gar minnig—s-t!
> Aus diesem Sack zwei Körnelein
> euch Müden in die Äugelein;
> die fallen dann von selber zu,
> damit ihr schlaft in sanfter Ruh.
> Und seid ihr fein geschlafen ein,
> dann wachen auf die Sterne,
> und nieder steigen Engelein
> aus hoher Himmelsferne
> und bringen holde Träume.
> Drum träume, Kindchen, träume!
> (Verschwindet. Völlige Dunkelheit.)

Hänsel.	
	(Schlaftrunken.)
	Sandmann war da!
Gretel.	
	(Ebenso.)
	Lass uns den Abendsegen beten!

(Sie kauern nieder und falten die Hände.)

Beide.	Abends, will ich schlafen gehn,
	vierzehn Engel um mich stehn,
	zwei zu meinen Häupten,
	zwei zu meinen Füssen,
	zwei zu meiner Rechten,
	zwei zu meiner Linken,
	zweie, die mich decken,
	zweie, die mich wecken,
	zweie, die mich weisen
	zu Himmelsparadeisen.

(Sie sinken aufs Moos zurück und schlummern Arm in Arm verschlungen alsbald ein.)

SCENE III

(Here a bright light suddenly breaks through the mist which forthwith rolls itself together into the form of a staircase, vanishing in perspective, in the middle of the stage. Fourteen angels, in light floating garments, pass down the staircase, two and two, at intervals, while it is getting gradually lighter. The angels place themselves, according to the order mentioned in the evening hymn, around the sleeping children; the first couple at their heads, the second at their feet, the third on the right, the fourth on the left, the fifth and sixth couples distribute themselves amongst the other couples, so that the circle of the angels is completed. Lastly the seventh couple comes into the circle and takes its place as "guardian angels" on each side of the children. The remaining angels now join hands and dance a stately step around the group. The whole stage is filled with an intense light. Whilst the angels group themselves in a picturesque tableau, the curtain slowly falls.)

ACT III

THE WITCH'S HOUSE

SCENE I

(The curtain rises. Scene the same as the end of Act II. The background is still hidden in mist, which gradually rises during the following. The angels have vanished. Morning is breaking. The Dew Fairy steps forward and shakes dewdrops from a bluebell over the sleeping children.)

Dew Fairy.
I'm up with early dawning,
and know who loves the morning,
who'll rise fresh as a daisy,
who'll sink in slumber lazy!
Ding! dong! ding! dong!
And with the golden light of day
I chase the fading night away,
fresh dew around me shaking,
and hill and dale awaking.
Then up, with all your powers
enjoy the morning hours,
the scent of trees and flowers—
then up, ye sleepers, awaken!
The rosy dawn is smiling,
then up, ye sleepers, awake, awake!

(Hurries off singing. The children begin to stir. Gretel rubs her eyes, looks around her, and raises herself a little, whilst Hänsel turns over on the other side to go to sleep again.)

Gretel.
Where am I? Waking? Or do I dream?
How come I in the wood to lie?
High in the branches I hear a gentle twittering,
birds are beginning to sing so sweetly;
from early dawn they are all awake,
and warble thier morning hymn of praise.
Dear little singers, little singers, good morning!

(Turns to Hänsel.)

See there, the sleepy lazybones?
Wait now, I'll wake him!
Tirelireli, it's getting late!
Tirelireli, it's getting late!
The lark his flight is winging,
on high his matin singing,
Tirelireli! tirelireli!

Hänsel.

(Suddenly jumps up with a start.)

Kikeriki! it's early yet!
Kikeriki! it's' early yet!
Yes, the day is dawning;
awake, for it is morning!
Kikeriki! kikeriki!

DRITTE SCENE

(Vierzehn Engel, die kleinsten voran, die grössten zuletzt, schreiten paarweise, wahrend das Licht an Helligkeit zunimmt, in Zwischenräumen die Wolkentreppe hinab und stellen sich, der Reihenfolge des Abendsegens entsprechend, um die schlafenden Kinder auf, das erste Paar zu Häupten, das zweite zu Füssen, das dritte rechts, das vierte links; dann verteilen sich das fünfte und sechste Paar zwischen die übrigen Paare, so dass der Kreis der Engel vollständig geschlossen wird. Zuletzt tritt das siebente Paar in den Kreis und nimmt als „Schutzengel" zu beiden Seiten der Kinder Platz waehrend sie sich zu einem malerischen Schlussbilde ordnen, schliesst sich langsam der Vorhang.)

DRITTES BILD

DAS KNUSPERHÄUSCHEN

ERSTE SCENE

(Scene wie vorhin. Der Hintergrund noch von Nebel verhüllt, der sich während des Folgenden langsam verzieht. Die Engel sind verschwunden.)
(Früher Morgen. Taumännchen tritt auf und schüttelt aus einer Glockenblume Tautropfen auf die schlafenden Kinder.)

Taumännchen.
Der kleine Tau-Mann heiss' ich—kling!
Mit Mutter Sonne reis' ich—klang!
Von Ost bis Westen weiss ich—kling!
Wer faul ist und wer fleissig—klang!
Ich komm mit lichtem Sonnenschein
und strahl in eure Äugelein,
und weck mit kühlem Taue,
was schläft auf Flur und Aue.
Dann springet auf, wer fleissig
zur frühen Morgenstunde,
denn sie hat Gold im Munde.
Drum, Schläfer, auf, erwachet,
der lichte Tag schon lachet!
(Ab.)

(Öffnet die Augen, richtet sich halb auf und blickt verwundert um sich, während Hänsel sich auf die andere Seite legt, um weiter zu schlafen.)

Gretel.
Wo bin ich? Wach ich? Ist es ein Traum?
Hier lieg' ich unterm Tannenbaum.
Hoch in den Zweigen lispelt es leise,
Vöglein singen so süsse Weise.
Wohl früh schon waren sie aufgewacht
und haben ihr Morgenlied dargebracht.
Guten Morgen, liebe Vöglein, guten Morgen!

(Sie erblickt Hänsel.)

Sieh da, der faule Siebenschläfer!
Wart nur, Dich weck' ich!
Tirelireli,
's ist nicht mehr früh!
Die Lerche hat's gesungen
und hoch sich aufgeschwungen.
Tirelireli,

Hänsel.

(Aufspringend.)

Kikeriki!
's ist noch früh!
Ja, hab's wohl vernommen,
der Morgen ist gekommen,
Kikeriki!

> I feel so well, I know not why!
> I never slept so well, no, not I!

Gretel. But listen, Hans; here 'neath the tree
a wondrous dream was sent to me!

Hänsel. Really! I, too, had a dream!

Gretel. I fancied I heard a murmuring and rushing,
as though the angels in Heav'n were
singing;
rosy clouds above me were floating—
hovering and floating in the distance away,
Sudden—all around a light was streaming,
rays of glory from Heaven beaming,
and a golden ladder saw I descending,
angels adown it gliding,
such lovely angels with shining golden
wings.

Hänsel. Fourten angels there must have been!

Gretel.

(Astonished.)
And did you also behold all this?

Hänsel. Truly, 'twas wondrous fair!
And upward I saw them float.

(He turns towards the background; at this moment the last
remains of the mist clear away. In place of the firtrees is
seen the "Witch's house at the Ilsenstein," shining in the
rays of the rising sun. A little distance off, to the left, is an
oven; opposite this, on the right, a large cage, both joined to
the Witch's house by a fence of gingerbread figures.)

SCENE II

Gretel.

(Holds Hänsel back in astonishment.)
Stand still, be still!

Hänsel.

(Surprised.)
O Heaven, what wondrous place is this,
as ne'er in all my life have I seen!

Gretel.

(Gradually regains her self-possession.)
What odor delicious!
O say, do I dream?

Both. A cottage all made
of chocolate cream.
The roof is all covered
with Turkish delight
the windows with lustre
of sugar are white;
and on all the gables
the raisins invite,
and think! all around
is a gingerbread hedge!
O magic castle,
how nice you'd be to eat!
Where hides the princess
who enjoys so great a treat?
Ah, could she but visit
our little cottage bare,
she'd ask us to dinner,
her dainties to share!

> Mir ist so wohl, ich weiss nicht wie;
> so gut wie heute schlief ich nie.

Gretel. Doch höre nur! Hier unter dem Baum,
da hatt' ich einen wunderschönen Traum.

Hänsel. Richtig! Auch mir träumte so was!

Gretel. Mir träumt' ich hört' ein Rauschen und
Klingen,
wie Chöre der Engel ein himmlisches
Singen;
lichte Wölkchen im rosigen Schein
wallten und wogten ins Dunkel herein.
Siehe, hell ward's mit einem Male,
lichtdurchflossen vom Himmelsstrahle,
eine goldene Leiter sah ich sich neigen,
Englein zu mir herniedersteigen,
Engel mit goldenen Flügelein—

Hänsel. Vierzehn müssen's gewesen sein!

Gretel.

(Erstaunt.)
Hast Du denn alles das auch gesehn?

Hänsel. Freilich! 's war halt wunderschön—
Und dort hinaus sah ich sie gehn!

(Er wendet sich nach dem Hintergrunde. In diesem Augenblick zerreisst der letzte Nebelschleier. An Stelle des Tannenge-
hölzes erscheint glitzernd im Strahl der aufgehenden Sonne
das „Knusperhäuschen" am Ilsenstein. Links davon in einiger
Entfernung befindet sich ein Backofen, diesem rechts gegenüber ein grosser Käfig, beide mit dem Knusperhäuschen durch
einen Zaun von Kuchenmännern verbunden.)

ZWEITE SCENE

Gretel.

(Hält Hänsel betroffen zurück.)
Bleib stehn! Bleib stehn!

Hänsel. Himmel, welch Wunder ist hier geschehn!
Nein, so was hab ich mein Tag nicht
gesehn!

Gretel.

(Gewinnt allmählich die Fassung wieder.)
Wie duftet's von dorten,
O schau nur die Pracht!
Von Kuchen und Torten
Ein Häuslein gemacht!
Mit Fladen, mit Torten
ist's hoch überdacht!
Die Fenster wahrhaftig
wie Zucker so blank,
Rosinen gar saftig
den Giebel entlang!
Und—traun!
Rings zu schaun
gar ein Lebkuchen-Zaun!

Beide. O herrliches Schlösschen,
Wie bist du schmuck und fein
Ach wär' doch zu Hause
die Wald-Prinzessin fein
Sie lüde zum Schmause
bei Kuchen und Wein
zum herrlichen Schmause
sie lüde zur Klause
uns beide wohl ein!

Hänsel.
(After a while.)
No sound do I hear; no, nothing is stirring!
Come, let's go inside it!

Gretel.
(Pulling him back horrified.)
Are you senseless?
Hänsel, however can you make so bold?
Who knows who may live there,
in that lovely house?

Hänsel. O look, do look how the house seems to
smile!
(Enthusiastically.)
Ah, the angels did our footsteps beguile!

Cretel.
(Reflectively.)
The angels? Yes, it must be so!

Hänsel. Yes, Gretel, the angels are beck'ning us in!
Come, let's nibble a bit of the cottage.

Both. Come, let's nibble it,
like two mice persevering!
(They hop along, hand in hand, towards the back of the
stage; then stand still, and then steal along cautiously on
tiptoe to the house. After some hesitation Hänsel breaks off
a bit of cake from the right-hand corner.)

SCENE III

A Voice from the House.
Nibble, nibble, mousekin,
who's nibbling at my housekin?
who's nibbling at my housekin?

Hänsel.
(Hänsel starts, and in his fright lets the piece of cake fall.)

Gretel.
(Somewhat timidly.)
The wind—

Hänsel. The Wind!

Both. The heavenly wind!

Gretel.
(Picks up the piece of cake and tastes it.)
H'm!

Hänsel.
(Looking longingly at Gretel.)
D'you like it?

Gretel.
(Lets Hänsel bite it.)
Just taste and try it!

Hänsel.
(Lays his hand on his breast in rapture.)
Hi!

Gretel.
(Ditto.)
Hi!

Both. Hi, hi! O cake most delicious,
some more I must take!
It's really like Heaven
to eat such plum-cake!

Hänsel. O how good, how sweet, how tasty!

Hänsel.
(Nach einer Pause.)
Alles bleibt still. Nichts regt sich da
drinnen.
Komm lass uns hineingehn!

Gretel.
(Erschrocken ihn zurückhaltend.)
Bist du bei Sinnen?
Junge, wie magst du so dreist nur sein?
Wer weiss, wer da drin wohl im Häuschen
fein?

Hänsel.
O sieh nur, wie das Häuschen uns lacht!
(Begeistert.)
Die Englein haben's uns hergebracht!

Gretel.
(Sinnend.)
Die Englein?—Ei, so wird es wohl sein!

Hänsel. Ja, Gretel, sie laden freundlich uns ein!
Komm, wir knuspern ein wenig vom
Häuschen!

Beide. Ja, knuspern wir, wie zwei Nagemäuschen!
(Sie hüpfen Hand in Hand nach dem Hintergrunde, bleiben
wiederum stehen und schleichen dann vorsichtig auf den Fuss-
spitzen bis an das Häuschen heran. Nach einigem Zögern
bricht Hänsel an der rechten Kante ein Stückchen Kuchen
heraus.)

DRITTE SCENE

Stimme aus dem Häuschen.
Knusper, knusper Knäuschen,
wer knuspert mir am Häuschen?

Hänsel.
(Lässt erschrocken das Stück zu Boden fallen.)

Gretel.
(Zaghaft.)
Der Wind!

Hänsel. Der Wind!

Beide. Das himmlische Kind.

Gretel.
(Hebt das Stück wieder auf und versucht es.)
Hm!

Hänsel.
(Gretel begehrlich anschauend.)
Wie schmeckt das?

Gretel.
(Ihn beissen lassend.)
Da hast du auch was!

Hänsel.
(Legt entzückt die Hand auf die Brust.)
Hei!

Gretel.
(Ebenso.)
Hei!

Beide. O köstlicher Kuchen,
Wie schmeckst du nach mehr!
Mir ist ja, als wenn ich
im Himmel schon wär!

Hänsel. Hei, wie das schmeckt! 's ist gar zu lecker!

Gretel.   How tasty, how sweet!
         It's p'r'aps the house of a sweety-maker!

Hänsel.   Hi, sweety-maker! Have a care!
         A little mouse your sweeties would share!
         (He breaks a big piece of cake off the wall.)

A Voice from the House.
         Nibble, nibble, mousekin,
         who's nibbling at my housekin?

Hänsel and Gretel.
         The wind, the wind,
         the heavenly wind!

(The upper part of the house-door opens gently and the Witch's head is seen at it. The children at first do not see her, and go on feasting merrily.)

Gretel.   Wait, you gobbling mousekin,
         here comes the cat from the housekin!

Hänsel.   Eat what you please,
         and leave me in peace!

Gretel.
         (Snatches the piece from his hand.)
         Don't be unkind,
         Sir wind, Sir wind!

Hänsel.
             (Takes it back from her.)
         Heavenly wind,
         I take what I find!

Both.
                 (Laughing.)
         Ha, ha, ha!

The Witch. Hi, hi! hi, hi!

Hänsel.
             (Horror-struck.)
         Let go! Who are you?
         Let me go!

The Witch. Angels both!
         (And goosey-ganders!)
         You've come to visit me, that is sweet!
         You charming children, so nice to eat!

Hänsel.   Who are you, ugly one?

The Witch. Now, darling, don't give yourself airs!
         Dear heart, what makes you say such
             things?
         I am Rosina Dainty-mouth,
         and dearly love my fellow-men.
         I'm artless as a new born child!
         That's why the children to me are so dear,
         so dear, so dear, ah, so che-arming to eat!

Hänsel.
             (Turning roughly away.)
         Go, get you gone from my sight!
         I hate, I loathe you quite!

The Witch. Hi hi! hi hi!
         These dainty morsels I'm really gloating on,
         and you, my little maiden, I'm doting on!
         Come, little mousey,

Gretel.   Vielleicht gar wohnt hier ein Zucker-bäcker!

Hänsel.   He, Zuckerbäcker, nimm dich in acht,
         Ein Loch wird dir jetzt vom Mäuslein
             gemacht!
         (Bricht ein grosses Stück aus der Wand heraus.)

Stimme aus dem Häuschen.
         Knusper, knusper Knäuschen,
         wer knuspert mir am Häuschen?

Hänsel und Gretel.
         Der Wind, der Wind,
         das himmlische Kind!

(Der obere Teil der Hausthüre öffnet sich leise, und der Kopf der Knusperhexe wird sichtbar. Die Kinder bemerken sie nicht und schmausen lustig weiter.)

Gretel.   Wart, du näschiges Mäuschen,
         gleich kommt die Katz' aus dem Häuschen!

Hänsel.   Knuspre nur zu
         und lass mich in Ruh!

Gretel.
         (Entreisst ihm ein Stück Kuchen.)
         Nicht so geschwind,
         Herr Wind, Herr Wind!

Hänsel.
             (Nimmt es ihr wieder ab.)
         Himmlisches Kind,
         ich nehm, was ich find!

Hexe.
                 (Kichernd.)
         Hihi, hihi, hihihi!

Hänsel.
             (Entsetzt.)
         Lass los!—Wer bist du?

Hexe.
                 Engelchen!
         Und du, mein Zuckerbengelchen!
         Ihr kommt mich besuchen?—Das ist nett!
         Liebe Kinder!—So rund und fett!

Hänsel.   Wer bist du, Garstige?—Lass mich los!

Hexe.   Na, Herzchen, zier dich nicht erst gross!
         Wisst denn, dass euch vor mir nicht graul:
         Ich bin *Rosina Leckermaul,*
         höchst menschenfreundlich stets gesinnt,
         unschuldig wie ein kleines Kind.
         Drum hab ich die kleinen Kinder so lieb.
         So lieb—ach zum Aufessen lieb!

Hänsel.
             (Barsch abwehrend.)
         Geh!—bleib mir doch aus dem Gesicht!
         Hörst du? Ich mag dich nicht!

Hexe.   Hihihi!
         Was seid ihr für leckere Teufelsbrätchen.
         besonders du, mein herzig Mädchen!
                 (Lockend.)
         Kommt, kleine Mäuslein,

come into my housey!
Come with me, my precious,
I'll give you sweetmeats delicious!
Of chocolate, tarts, and marzipan
you shall both eat all you can,
and wedding-cake and strawberry ices,
blancmange, and everything else that nice is,
and raisins and almonds,
and peaches and citrons are waiting—
you'll both find it quite captivating,
yes, quite captivating!

Hänsel.   I won't come with you, hideous fright!
You are quite too friendly!

The Witch.   See, see, see how sly!
Dear children, you really may trust me in
    this,
and living with me will be perfect bliss!
Come, little mousey,
come into my housey!
Come with me, my precious,
I'll give you sweetmeats delicious!

Gretel.   But say, what will you with my brother do?

The Witch.   Well, well!
I'll feed and fatten him up well,
with every sort of dainty delicious,
to make him tender and tasty.
And if he's brave and patient too,
and docile and obedient like a lamb,
then, Hänsel, I'll whisper it you,
I have a great treat in store for you!

Hänsel.   Then speak out loud and whisper not.
What is the great treat in store for me?

The Witch.   Yes, my dear children, hearing and sight
in this great pleasure will disappear quite!

Hänsel.   Eh? both my hearing and seeing are good!
You'd better take care you do me no harm!
    (Resolutely.)
Gretel, trust not her flattering words,
come, sister, come, let's run away!

(He has in the meantime got out of the rope and runs with
Gretel to the foreground. Here they are stopped by the Witch,
who imperiously raises against them both a stick which hangs
at her girdle, with repeated gestures of spellbinding.)

The Witch. **Hold.**
    (The stage becomes gradually darker.)
Hocus pocus, witches' charm!
Move not, as you fear my arm!
Back or forward do not try,
fixed you are by the evil eye!
Head on shoulders fixed awry!
Hocus, pocus, now comes jocus,
children, watch the magic head,
eyes are staring, dull as lead!
Now, you atom, off to bed!

(Fresh gestures; then she leads Hänsel, who is gazing
fixedly at the illuminated head, into the stable, and shuts the
lattice door upon him.)

Hocus pocus, bonus jocus,
malus locus, hocus pocus,
bonus jocus, malus locus!

(The stage gradually becomes lighter, whilst the light of
the magic head diminishes.)

Now Gretel, be obedient and wise,
while Hänsel's growing fat and nice.

Hänsel.   Ich geh nicht mit dir, garstige Frau!—
Du bist gar zu freundlich.

Hexe.   Schau, schau, wie schlau,
Ihr Kinder, ich mein's doch so gut mit euch,
seid ja bei mir wie im Himmelreich!
Kommt, kleine Mäuslein!
kommt in mein Häuslein!
Sollt es gut bei mir haben,
will drinnen köstlich euch laben!

Gretel.   Was willst du meinem Bruder thun?

Hexe.   I nun, ich will ihn fuettern und nudeln
mit allerhand vortrefflichen Sachen
will ich ihn zart und wohlschmeckend
    machen
und ist er dann recht zahm und brav,
geduldig und fügsam wie ein Schaf,
dann—höre, Hänsel, ich sag dir's ins Ohr:
dir steht eine grosse Freude bevor!

Hänsel.   So sag's doch laut und nicht ins Ohr!
Welche Freude steht mir bevor?

Hexe.   Ja liebe Kinder, Hoeren und Sehen
wird euch bei diesem Vergnügen vergehn!

Hänsel.   Ei, meine Augen und Ohren sind gut,
haben wohl acht, was Schaden mir thut.
Gretel, trau nicht dem gleissenden Wort
    (Leise.)
Schwesterchen, komm, wir laufen fort!

(Er hat sich inzwischen von der Schlinae befreit und will
mit Gretel fortlaufen, sie werden aber von der Hexe zurück-
gehalten, die gebieterisch einen Stab gegen die beiden erhebt.)

Hexe.   **Halt!**
    (Die Bühne verfinstert sich.)
Hocus pocus, Hexenschuss!
Rühr dich, und dich deisst der Fluss!
Nicht mehr vorwärts, nicht zurück,
bann dich mit dem bösen Blick;
Kopf steh starr dir im Genick!
Hocus Pocus, nun kommt Jocus!
Kinder, schaut den Zauberknopf!
Äuglein, stehet still im Kopf!—
Nun zum Stall hinein, du Tropf!
Hocus pocus, bonus jocus,
Malus locus, hocus pocus!

(Leitet Hänsel zum Stalle und schliesst hinter ihm die
Gitterthüre.)

Hexe.

    (Vergnügt zu Gretel.)
Nun, Gretelchen, sei vernünftig und nett!
Der Hänsel wird nun balde fett.
Wir wollen ihn, so ist's am besten,
mit Mandeln und Rosinen mästen.

We'll fed him up, you'll see my reason,
and with sweet almonds and raisins season.
I'll go indoors, the things to prepare,
and you remain here where you are!

(She grins as she holds up her finger warningly, and goes into the house.)

Gretel.

(Stiff and motionless.)
O, what a horrid witch she is!

Hänsel.

Gretel, sh! don't speak so loud!
Be very sharp, watch well and see
whatever she may do to me!
Pretend to do all she commands—
O, there she's coming back, sh! hush!

(The Witch comes out, satisfies herself that Gretel is still standing motionless, and then spreads before Hänsel almonds and raisins from a basket.)

The Witch. Now, little man,
come prithee enjoy yourself!

(Sticking a raisin into Hänsel's mouth.)

Eat, minion, eat or die!
Here are cakes, O so nice!

(Turns to Gretel and disenchants her with a juniper-branch.)

Hocus pocus, elder-bush!
Rigid body loosen, hush!

(Gretel moves again.)

Now up and move again, bright and blithe-
some,
limbs are become again supple and lithe-
some.
Go, my poppet, go my pet,
you the table now shall set,
little knife, little fork, little dish, little
plate,
little serviette for my little mate!
Now get everything ready and nice,
or else I shall lock you up too in a trice!

(She threatens and titters. Gretel hurries off. The Witch, to Hänsel, who pretends to be asleep.)

The fool is slumb'ring, it does seem queer
how youth can sleep and have no fear!
Well, sleep away, you simple sheep,
soon you will sleep your last long sleep!
But first with Gretel I'll begin—
off you, dear maiden, I will dine;
you are so tender, plump, and good,
just the thing for witches' food!

(She opens the oven door and sniffs in it, her face lighted up by the deep red glare of the fire.)

The dough has risen, so we'll go on preparing.
Hark, how the sticks in the fire are
crackling!

(She pushes a couple more faggots under, the fire flames up and then dies down again. The Witch, rubbing her hands with glee.)

Yes, Gretel mine,
how well off you I'll dine!
See, see, O how sly!
When in the oven she's peeping,
quickly behind her I'm creeping!
One little push, bang
goes the door, clang!
Then soon will Gretel be
just done to a T!
and when from the oven I take her

Ich geh ins Haus und hol sie schnell—
Du rühre dich nicht von der Stell!

(Hinkt ins Haus.)

Gretel.

(Starr und unbeweglich.)
Hu—Wie mir vor der Hexe graut!

Hänsel.

Gretel! Pst! sprich nicht so laut!
Sei hübsch gescheit und gieb fein acht
auf jedes, was die Hexe macht.
Zum Schein thu alles, was sie will—
da kommt sie schon zurück—Pst! Still!

(Dem Hänsel aus einem Korbe Mandeln und Rosinen hin-streuend.)

Hexe.

Nun, Jüngelchen,
ergötze dein Züngelchen!
Friss, Vogel, oder stirb—
Kuchen-Heil dir erwirb!

(Wendet sich zu Gretel und entzaubert sie mit einem Wachholderbusch.)

Hocus pocus, Holderbusch!
Schwinde, Gliederstarre, husch!
Nun wieder kregel, süsses Kleinchen,
rühr mir geschwind die runden Beinchen!
Geh, Zuckerpüppchen, flink und frisch
und decke drinnen hübsch den Tisch!
Schüsselchen, Tellerchen, Messerchen,
Gäbelchen,
Serviettchen für mein Schnäbelchen;
und mach nur alles recht hurtig und fein,
sonst sperr ich auch dich in den Stall
hinein!

(Sie droht kichernd; Gretel eilt ins Haus.)

Hexe.

(Zu dem sich schlafend stellenden Hänsel.)

Der Lümmel schläft ja nun—sieh mal an,
wie doch die Jugend schlafen kann!
Na, schlaf nur brav, du gutes Schaf,
bald schläfst du deinen ewigen Schlaf.
Doch erst muss mir die Gretel dran;
mit dir, mein Liebchen, fang ich an,
bist so niedlich, zart und rund,
wie gemacht für Hexen-Mund!

(Sie öffnet die Backofenthür und riecht hinein.)

Der Teig ist gar, wir können voran machen.
Hei, wie im Ofen die Scheite krachen!
Ja, Gretelchen,
wirst bald ein Brätelchen!
Schau, schau,
wie ich schlau bin, so schlau!
Sollst gleich im Backofen hucken
und nach dem Lebkuchen gucken.
Und bist du dann drin—schwaps,
geht die Thür—klaps!
Dann ist fein Gretelchen
mein Brätelchen!

she'll look like a cake from the baker,
by magic fire red
changed into gingerbread!
See, see how sly!
Hi hi! hi hi!
(In her wild delight she seizes a broomstick and begins to ride upon it.)

So hop, hop, hop,
gallop, lop, lop!
My broomstick nag,
come do not lag!
(She rides excitedly round on the broomstick.)

At dawn of day
I ride away,
am here and there
and everywhere!
(She rides again; Gretel meanwhile is watching at the window.)

At midnight hour, when none can know,
to join the witches' dance I go!
And three and four
are witches' lore,
and five and six
are witches' tricks,
and nine is one,
and ten is none,
and seven is nil,
or what she will!
And thus they ride till dawn of day!
(Hopping madly along, she rides to the back of the stage and vanishes for a time behind the cottage. Here the Witch becomes visilble again; she comes to the foreground, where she suddenly pulls up and dismounts.)

Prr, broomstick, hi!
(She hobbles back to the stable and tickles Hänsel with a birch twig till he awakes.)

Up, awake, my mankin young;
come show to me your tongue!
(Hänsel puts his tongue out. The Witch smacks with her tongue.)

Dainty morsel! dainty morsel!
Little toothsome mankin come,
now let me see your thumb!
(Hänsel pokes out a small bone.)

Gemini! Oho!
O how scraggy, how lean!
Urchin, you're a scraggy one,
as bad as a skeleton!

(Calls.)

Maiden, Gretel!

(Gretel appears at the door.)

Bring some raisins and almonds sweet,
Hänsel wants some more to eat.

(Gretel runs into the house and returns immediately with a basket full of almonds and raisins.)

Gretel.   Here are the almonds.
(Whilst the Witch is feeding Hänsel, Gretel gets behind her and makes the gestures of disenchantment with the juniper-branch.)

Gretel.

(Softly.)

Hocus pocus, elder-bush,
Rigid body loosen, hush!

The Witch.

(Turning suddenly round.)

What were you saying, little goose?

Das Brätelchen soll sich verwandeln
in Kuchen mit Zucker und Mandeln!
Im Zauberofen mein
wirst du ein Lebkuchen fein!
Hurr, hopp, hopp, hopp!
Galopp, Galopp!
mein Besengaul,
hurr, hopp, nit faul!
Sowie ich's mag
am lichten Tag
spring kreuz und quer
um Häuschen her!
Bei dunkler Nacht,
wann niemand wacht,
zum Hexenschmaus
am Schornstein raus!
Aus fünf und sechs,
so sagt die Hex,
mach sieb und acht,
so ist's vollbracht;
und neun ist eins,
und zehn ist keins,
und viel ist nichts,
die Hexe spricht's.
So reitet sie
bis morgens früh—
Prr! Besen! hüh!
Auf, auf, mein Jüngelchen!
Zeig mir dein Züngelchen!
(Hänsel streckt die Zunge heraus.)

(Schnalzend.)

Schlicker, schlecker,
lecker, lecker!
Kleines leckres Schlingerchen,
Zeige mir dein Fingerchen!

(Hänsel streckt ein Stöckchen heraus.)

Jemine, je!
Wie ein Stöckchen, o weh!
Bübchen, deine Fingerchen
sind elende Dingerchen!

(Ruft.)

Mädel! Gretel!
(Gretel zeigt sich an der Thür.)
Bring Rosinen und Mandeln her;
Hänsel meint, es schmeckt nach "mehr!"

(Gretel springt in's Haus und kehrt alsbald mit einem Körbchen voll, Rosinen und Mandeln zurueck. Sie stellt sich, waehrend die Hexe den Haensel fuettert, hinter sie und macht mit dem Wachholder die Entzauberungsgebaerde.)

Gretel.

(Leise.)

Hocus pocus, Holderbusch!
Schwinde, Gliederstarre—husch!

Hexe.

(Sich rasch umwendend.)

Was sagtest du, mein Gänselchen!

Gretel.

(Confusedly.)
Only—much good may it do to Hans!

The Witch. Eh?

Gretel.

(Louder.)
Much good may it do to Hans!

The Witch. He he he, my little miss,
 I'll stop your mouth with this!
  (Sticks a raisin into Gretel's mouth.)
 Eat, minion, eat or die!
 Here are cakes, O so nice!
(She opens the oven door; the heat has apparently dimin-
ished. Meanwhile Hänsel makes violent signs to Gretel.)

Hänsel.

(Softly opening the stable door.)
Sister dear,
O beware!

The Witch.

(Looking greedily at Gretel.)
She makes my mouth water,
this pretty little daughter!
 Come, Gretel mine,
 sugar-maiden mine!
  (Gretel comes towards her.)
Peep in the oven, be steady,
see if the gingerbread's ready!
 Carefully look, pet,
 whether it's cooked yet,
 but if it wants more,
 shut quick the door!
  (Gretel hesitates.)

Hänsel.

(Slipping out of the stable.)
Sister dear,
have a care!

Gretel.

(Making herself out very awkward.)
I don't understand what I have to do!

The Witch. Just stand on tip-toe,
 head bending forward;
 try it, I pray,
 it's merely play!

Hänsel.

(Pulling Gretel back by her frock.)
Sister dear,
now take care!

Gretel.

(shyly.)
I'm such a goose, don't understand!
You'll have to show me
how to stand on tip-toe!

The Witch.

(Makes a movement of impatience.)
Do as I say,
it's' merely play!
(She begins creeping up to the oven, muttering all the
time, and just as she is bending over it, Hänsel and Gretel
give her a good push, which sends her toppling over into it,
upon which they quickly shut the door.)

Hänsel and Gretel.

(Mocking her.)
Then "One little push, bang
goes the door, clang!"
You, not Gretel, then will be
just done to a T!
(Hänsel and Gretel fall into ane another's arms.)

Gretel. Meint' nur: wohl bekomm's, mein Hän-
 selchen!

Hexe. Hihihi! Mein gutes Tröpfchen,
 da—steck dir was ins Kröpfchen!
 Friss, Vogel, und stirb—
 Kuchen-Heil dir erwirb!
(Sie öffnet die Backofenthür; Hänsel giebt Gretel lebhafte
Zeichen.)

Hänsel.

(Leise die Stallthür öffnend.)
Schwesterlein,
hüt dich fein!

Hexe.

(Gretel gierig betrachtend.)
Wie wässert mir das Mündchen
nach diesem süssen Kindchen!
 Komm, Gretelchen!
 Zuckermädelchen!
Sollst in den Backofen hucken
und nach den Lebkuchen gucken,
 sorgfältig schaun—ja,
 ob sie schon braun da,
 oder ob's zu früh—
 's ist kleine Müh!

Hänsel.

(Aus dem Stall schleichend.)
Schwesterlein,
hüt dich fein!

Gretel.

(Sich ungeschickt stellend.)
Ei, wie fang ich's an,
dass ich komme dran?

Hexe. Musst dich nur eben
 ein bisschen heben,
 Kopf vorgebeugt—
 's ist kinderleicht!

Hänsel. Schwesterlein,
 hüt dich fein!

Gretel.

(Schüchtern.)
Bin gar so dumm,
nimm mir's nicht krumm;
drum zeige mir eben,
wie soll ich mich heben?

Hexe.

(Macht eine ungeduldige Bewegung.)
Kopf vorgebeugt!
's ist kinderleicht!
(Sie schickt sich murrend an, in den Backofen zu kriechen:
indem sie sich mit halbem Leibe vorbeugt, geben ihr Haensel
und Gretel einen derben Stoss, so dass sie vollends hinein-
fliegt, und schlagen dann rasch die Tuere zu.)

Hänsel und Gretel.
 Und bist du dann drin—schwaps!
 Geht die Thür—klaps!
 Du bist dann statt Gretelchen ein
  Brätelchen!
(Hänsel und Gretel fallen sich jubelnd in die Arme, fassen
sich bei der Hand und tanzen.)

Both. Hurrah! now sing the witch is dead, really
dead!
No more to dread!
Hurrah! now sing the witch is still, deathly
still!
We can eat our fill!
Now all the spell is o'er,
really o'er!
We fear no more!
  They seize each other's hands.)
    Yes, let us happy be,
    dancing so merrily;
    now the old witch is gone,
    we'll have no end of fun!
    Hey! hurrah, hurrah!
    Hip hurrah! Hip hurrah!
    Hurrah!

Hänsel and Gretel.
  (Spoken.)
There, see those little children dear,
I wonder how they all came here!

(They take each other around the waist and waltz together,
first in the front of the stage, and then gradually in the direction of the Witch's house. When they get there Hänsel breaks
loose from Gretel and rushes into the house, shutting the door
after him. Then from the upper window he throws down
apples, pears, oranges, gilded nuts, and all kinds of sweetmeats
into Gretels oustretched apron. Meanwhile the oven begins
crackling loudly, and the flames burn high. Then there is a
loud crash, and the oven falls thundering into bits. Hänsel
and Gretel, who in their terror let their sweetmeats all fall
down, hurry towards the oven startled, and stand there
motionless. Their astonishment increases when they become
aware of a troop of children around them, whose disguise of
cakes has fallen from them.)

SCENE IV.

The Gingerbread Children.
(Motionless and with closed eyes, as the cake figures were
before.)
  We're saved, we're freed
  for evermore!

Gretel. Your eyes are shut—pray who are you?
You're sleeping, and yet you're singing too!

The Gingerbread Children.
  (Always very softly.)
  O touch us, we pray,
  that we may all awake!

Hänsel.
  (To Gretel embarrassed.)
  O touch them for me,
  I dare not try!

Gretel. Yes, let me stroke this innocent face!
(She caresses the nearest child, who opens its eyes and smiles.)

Other Gingerbread Children.
  O touch me too, O touch me too,
  that I also may awake!

(Gretel goes and caresses all the rest of the children, who
open their eyes and smile, without moving; meanwhile Hänsel
seizes the juniper-branch.)

Hänsel. Hocus pocus, elder-bush!
Rigid body loosen, hush!

Juchhei! Nun ist die Hexe tot,
  mausetot!
Nun ist geschwunden Angst und Not!
Juchhei! Nun ist die Hexe still,
  mäuschenstill,
Und Kuchen giebt's die Hüll und Füll!
Juchhei! Nun ist zu End der Graus,
  Hexengraus!
Und böser Zauberspuk ist aus!
  Drum lasst uns fröhlich sein,
  tanzen im Feuerschein,
  halten im Knusperhaus
  herrlichsten Freudenschmaus!
  Juchhei, juchhei!

(Sie umfassen sich und walzen mit einander, erst im Vorder
grund, dann allmaehlich in der Richtung auf das Knusperhaeuschen zu. Als sie beim Knusperhaeuschen angekommer,
sind, reisst sich Haensel von Gretel los, eilt in's Haeuschen,
indem er die Tuere hinter sich zuschlaegt, und wirft Gretel
durch das obere Luke Aepfel, Birnen, Apfelsinen, vergoldete
Nuesse und allerhand Zuckerwerk in die aufgehaltene Schuerze.
Mittlerweile faengt der Hexenofen gewaltig an zu knistern;
die Flamme Schlaegt hoch empor. Dann gibt's einen starken
Krach, und der Ofen stuerzt donnernd zusamnien.)

VIERTE SCENE

Gretel. Da, sieh nur die artigen Kinderlein,
wo mögen die hergekommen sein?

Die Kuchenkinder.
  (Ganz leise.)
  Erlöst—befreit
  für alle Zeit!

Gretel.
  Geschlossen sind ihre Äugelein;
  sie schlafen und singen doch so fein!

Kuchenkinder.
  (Leise.)
  O rühre mich an,
  dass ich erwachen kann!

Hänsel.
  (Verlegen.)
  Rühr du sie doch an—ich traue mir's nicht.

Gretel. Ja, streicheln will ich dies hübsches
  Gesicht!
(Sie streichelt das nächste Kind; dieses öffnet die Augen
und lächelt.)

Andre Kuehenkinder.
  O rühre auch mich—auch mich rühr' an,
  dass ich die Äuglein öffnen kann.

(Gretel geht streichelnd zu den übrigen Kindern, die lächelnd
die Augen öffnen, ohne sich zu rühren; endlich ergreift
Hänsel den Wachholder.)

Hänsel. Hocus pocus, Holderbusch!
Schwinde, Gliederstarre—husch!

Some of the Children.
(Jump up and hurry towards Hänsel and Gretel from all sides.)
We thank, we thank you both!

The Children.
The spell is broke and we are free,
we'll sing and we'll dance and we'll shout
for glee!
Come, children all, and form a ring,
join hands together while we sing.
Then sing and spring,
then dance and sing,
for cakes and all good things we bring.
Then sing and spring,
then dance and sing,
that through the wood
our song of praise may sound,
and echo repeat it all around!
We thank, we thank, we thank!

Hänsel.
The angels whispered in dreams to us in
silent night
what this happy, happy day has brought
tonight.
(Four Gingerbread Children at a time surround Hänsel and Gretel, and bow gracefully to them.)

Gretel.
Ye angels, who have watched o'er our steps
and led them right,
we thank for all our joy and wondrous
delight.

The Gingerbread Children.
(Who all press round Hänsel and Gretel to shake hands with them.)
We'll thank you both all our life!

Father.
(Behind the scene.)
Tralala, tralalala!
Were our children only here!
Tralala, tralalala!
(The Father appears in the background with the Mother, and stops when he sees the children.)
Ha! Why, they're really there!

LAST SCENE

Hänsel.
(Running towards them.)
Father! mother!

Gretel.
(The same.)
Father! mother!

Mother.
Children dear!

Father.
O welcome,
poor children innocent!
(Joyfully embracing. Meanwhile two of the boys have dragged the Witch, in the form of a big gingerbread cake, out of the ruins of the magic oven. At the sight of her they all burst into a shout of joy. The boys place the Witch in the middle of the stage.)

Father.
Children, see the wonder wrought,
how the Witch herself was caught unaware
in the snare
laid for you with cunning rare!

All the Rest.
See, O see the wonder wrought,
how the Witch herself was caught
unaware
in the snare
laid for us with cunning rare!
(The two boys drag the Witch in the cottage.)

Father.
Such is Heaven's chastisement;
evil works will have an end.
"When past bearing is our grief,
Then God, the Lord, will send us relief!"

All.
"When past bearing is our grief,
Then God, the Lord, will send relief!"

Die Kuchenkinder.
Habt Dank, habt Dank
euer Leben lang!
Juchhei!
Die Hexerei
ist nun vorbei;
nun singen und springen wir froh und frei!
Kommt, Kinderlein,
zum Ringelreihn,
reicht allzumal die Händchen fein!
Drum singt und springt,
drum tanzt und singt,
dass laut der Jubelruf durchdringt den
Wald,
und rings erschallt
von Lust der Wald.

Hänsel und Gretel.
Die Englein haben's im Traum gesagt in
stiller Nacht,
was nun so herrlich uns der Tag hat wahr
gemacht.
Ihr Englein, die uns so treu bewacht bei
Tag und Nacht,
habt Lob und Dank für all die Pracht, die
uns hier lacht.

Die Kuchenkinder.
Habt Dank, habt Dank
euer Leben lang!

LETZTE SCENE

(Aus dem Hintergrund ertönt die Stimme des Vaters.)

Vater.
Rallalala, rallalala,
wären doch unsre Kinder da!
Rallalala, rallalala.—
(Er erblickt Hänsel und Gretel.)
Juch—! Ei, da sind sie ja!

Hänsel und Gretel.
(Den Eltern entgegen eilend.)
Vater! Mutter!

Mutter.
Kinderchen!

Vater.
Da sind ja die armen Sünderchen!
(Frohe Umarmung; unterdes haben zwei Knaben die Hexe als grossen Lebkuchen aus den Trümmern des Zauberofens gezogen.)

Vater.
Kinder, schaut das Wunder an,
wie solch Hexlein hexen kann,
wie sie hart,
knusperhart
selber nun zum Kuchen ward!
Merkt des Himmels Strafgericht:
böse Werke dauern nicht!
Wenn die Not aufs höchste steigt,
Gott der Herr die Hand uns reicht!

Alle.
Wenn die Not aufs höchste steigt,
Gott der Herr die Hand uns reicht!
(Indem die Kinder einen lustigen Reigen um die Gruppe tanzen, fällt der Vorhang.)

THE END

So that I may dance like you.

Gretel. With your foot you tap tap tap,

With your hand you clap clap clap, Right foot first, Left foot then, Round about and

Hänsel. back a-gain! With your foot you tap tap tap, With your hand you clap clap clap,

Right foot first, Left foot then, Round and back a-gain!

Gretel. That was ve-ry good indeed,

Second Act.
In the forest.
Scene I.

gold, and his cheeks are red, He wears a lit-tle black cap up-on his

head, Say who can the mankin be, Standing there so si-lently, With the little

(She holds up the garland of roses and looks it all round)

black cap up-on his head?

With the little black cap up-on his head?

Abendsegen

aus Hänsel und Gretel.

„Abends, will ich schlafen gehn."

Evening-Prayer

from Hänsel and Gretel.

"When at night I go to sleep."

E. Humperdinck

VOLUME THREE

THE LIBRETTOS
OF THE
ITALIAN OPERAS

CONTENTS

Foreword v

Rigoletto. 1

Il Trovatore 49

La Traviata. 99

La Forza Del Destino. 151

Aïda 213

Lucia Di Lammermoor 253

La Gioconda. 295

Cavalleria Rusticana 337

I Pagliacci 363

Don Giovanni. 389

Barber of Seville 429

FOREWORD

The music is not everything in opera. Its full enjoyment can be achieved only with the knowledge of the words that are being sung—usually in a foreign language. In this volume, the librettos are presented in the original language with an English line by line translation. Thus, it is possible to follow the song and to understand the meaning of the foreign words.

It was in Italy that opera received its most enduring impetus. The Italian composers' "Musica Parlante" (Speaking Music) spread throughout the continent and made Italian opera supreme. And today undoubtedly more opera performances are given in Italian than in any other language.

But there is no one Italian composer who stands out as Wagner does among the Germans. Verdi, of course, is most important. He was prolific and his "Aïda" has the distinction of being first in number of performances by the Metropolitan. But only a few of his operas have retained their popularity.

The selection of the operas to be included in this volume was determined largely by importance and popularity as indicated by the number of performances at the Metropolitan Opera House from 1883 to 1938. The Puccini operas had to be omitted because of insurmountable copyright difficulties. Mozart's "Don Giovanni" may seem out of place among Italian operas. But since the libretto, by Lorenzo da Ponte, is in Italian and it is sung invariably in that language, it is included in this volume.

The record of performances of these operas at the Metropolitan Opera House, 1883-1938: Aïda, 284; I Pagliacci, 214; Cavalleria Rusticana, 187; La Traviata, 157; Rigoletto, 155; Il Trovatore, 127; Lucia di Lammermoor, 106; Barber of Seville, 96; La Gioconda, 94; Don Giovanni, 54; La Forza del Destino, 37.

VOLUME THREE

THE LIBRETTOS
OF THE
ITALIAN OPERAS

RIGOLETTO

by

GIUSEPPE VERDI

THE STORY OF "RIGOLETTO"

RIGOLETTO, a hunchback buffoon, or jester to the libertine Duke of Mantua, and willing pander to his licentious habits, has by his ribald and unfeeling jests, together with his villanous connivance at the Duke's open disdain for all considerations of honor, rendered himself highly objectionable to the courtiers, particularly the Counts of Ceprano and Monterone, whose wife and daughter respectively have become victims to the unbridled passions of the Duke. Monterone, in indignation at the dishonor to which he is subjected, seeks the Duke's presence and boldly denounces his conduct, and that of his vile abettor, Rigoletto, who is inwardly terror-stricken by his vehement maledictions.

Rigoletto has a young and beautiful daughter, whom he conceals from public observation with the most jealous care; so strictly has she been guarded that she has not been allowed to leave her home, except to attend her religious observances at church. She, however, has not escaped the notice of the Duke, who has repeatedly observed her at her devotions, and contrived to track her to her humble habitation, where, by bribing her servant, he gains access to her. Representing himself to be a poor student deeply impressed with her attractions, he succeeds in inspiring her with reciprocal sentiments, never dreaming that it is the daughter of his buffoon he is thus beguiling.

The fact of the existence of a young and lovely woman in the dwelling of Rigoletto becoming known to the courtiers, they form a plot to abduct her therefrom by force and deliver her to the Duke. At a late hour in the evening they assemble (masked) in the neighborhood of Rigoletto's dwelling, and, under pretence that they are going to carry off the wife of Ceprano, whose house adjoins Rigoletto's, they induce him to assist. He is accordingly masked and bandaged, and is made to hold the ladder by which some of the party ascend to the window of his house, which they enter, and tear away the bewildered Gilda, whose mouth they cover, to prevent her giving any alarm, and carry her off triumphantly to the Ducal Palace.

The outwitted jester, finding himself deserted, immediately suspects that all is not right, and tearing off the bandage, perceives the scarf of his daughter, which has been dropped in the flight; he is instantly struck with the conviction that he has been robbed of his beloved Gilda, his only treasure, and that the curse of Count Monterone has already begun to work.

The courtiers relate to the Duke as a good joke how they have carried off the jester's *mistress*, but he knows full well from their description that it is Gilda they have abducted, and the unfortunate girl soon becomes a prey to his insatiate passions.

Rigoletto hastens to the palace, and demands his daughter from the courtiers, who treat him with contempt and derision, baffling all his endeavors to obtain access to the Duke. He is presently joined by his daughter, who has at length freed herself from the vicious attentions of the Duke, and after mutual condolence they quit the place, cursing the scene of their disgrace. Resolving to be revenged on the author

4

of his daughter's and his own misery, Rigoletto hires a bravo named Sparafucile, for a stipulated sum, to assassinate the Duke, who is enticed by the blandishments of Maddelene, the sister of Sparafucile, to the bravo's house, a ruinous and lonely inn.

Gilda has been desired by her father to put on male attire and fly to Verona, but previous to starting, in order to extinguish the lingering affection which she still entertains for her unprincipled seducer, she is made an eye-witness, through crevices in the wall of the inn, of his inconstancy and perfidy. She overhears the sister of the bravo earnestly endeavoring to dissuade him from murdering the handsome guest; but he resolutely persists in his determination to fulfil his contract, unless some person should chance to come to the inn before midnight whom he might kill instead, and pass the body in a sack to Rigoletto as that of the murdered

Duke. Upon hearing this Gilda at once resolves to save the life of the undeserving object of her affections by sacrificing her own. She knocks at the door of the inn, is admitted, and instantly stabbed by the cold-blooded assassin. Shortly after, Rigoletto appears, pays the bravo, and receives from him the sack containing (as he supposes) the body of the Duke; he proceeds to throw it into the river which runs at the back of the inn, but before he has time to accomplish it, he is astounded by the voice of the living Duke, which he hears at a short distance; he instantly suspects foul play, tears open the sack, and is horrified to find, instead of the dead body of the hated Duke, the dying form of his beloved daughter, who almost immediately expires. Overwhelmed with terror and anguish at the fulfilment of the dreaded malediction, he falls senseless on the body of his unfortunate daughter.

RIGOLETTO

ACT I.

SCENE I—Magnificent salon in the Ducal Palace, with opening in the back scene, through which other salons are seen, the whole brilliantly lighted for a Fête, which is at its height. Nobles and ladies in magnificent costumes moving in all directions. Pages passing to and fro. Music heard in the distance, and occasional bursts of merriment.

(Enter the DUKE and BORSA, from the back.)

Duke.

Beautiful as youthful is my unknown charmer,
And to the end I will pursue the adventure.

Borsa.

The maiden, you mean, whom you see at the church?

Duke.

For three months past, on every Sunday.

Borsa.

Know you where she lives?

Duke.

In a remote part of the city,
Where a mysterious man visits her nightly.

Borsa.

And do you not know who he is?
Is he her lover?

Duke.

I do not know.

(A group of ladies and gentlemen cross the stage.)

Borsa.

What beauty!—Do you not admire it?

Duke.

Ceprano's wife surpasses the handsomest of them.

Borsa.

Mind the Count does not hear you, Duke.

(Softly.)

Duke.

What care I for him?

Borsa.

It may get talked about.

ATTO I.

SCENA I—Sala magnifica nel Palazzo Ducale, con porte nel fondo, che mettono ad altre sale, pure splendidamente illuminate; folla di cavalieri e dame in gran costume nel fondo delle sale; paggi che vanno e vengono. La festa è nel suo pieno. Musica interna da lontano e serosci di risa di tratto in tratto.

(Il DUCA e BORSA, che vengono da una porta del fondo.)

Duca.

Della mia bella incognita borghese,
Toccare il fin dell' avventura io voglio.

Borsa.

Di quella giovinche vedete al tempio?

Duca.

Da tre lune ogni festa.

Borsa.

La sua dimora?

Duca.

In un remoto calle;
Misterioso un uom v'entra ogni notte.

Borsa.

E sa colei chi sia
L'amante suo?

Duca.

Lo ignora.

(Un gruppo di dame e cavalieri attraversan la sala.)

Borsa.

Quante beltà!—Mirate.

Duca.

Le vince tutte di Cepran la sposa.

Borsa.

Non v'oda il Conte, o Duca—

(Piano.)

Duca.

A me che importa?

Borsa.

Dirlo ad altra ei potria—

Duke.

That would not much affect me.

Duca.

Nè sventura per me certo saria.

QUESTA O QUELLA——'MID THE FAIR THRONG   Air (Duke)

Ques-ta o quel-la__ per me pa-ri so-no A quan-t'al-tre d'in-
'Mid the fair throng that spar-kles a-round me, Not one__ o'er my

tor-no,__ d'in-tor-no mi ve-do, Del mio co-re
heart—no!__ not one o'er my heart holds sway; Though a sweet smile__

__l'im-pe-ro non ce-do__ Meg-lio ad u-na
__one mo-ment may charm me,__ A glance from some bright eye__

__che ad al-tra bel-tà. La co-sto-ro av-ve-nen-za e qual
its spell drives a-way. All a-like may at-tract, each in

do-no Di che il fa-to ne in-fio-ra la
turn__ may please; Now with one I may tri-fle and

vi-ta;__ S'og-gi ques-ta__ mi tor-na gra-di-ta, For-se un'
play,__ Then an-oth-er may sport with and tease—Yet all my

al-tra, for-se un' al-tra__ do-man lo sa-rà, un' al-
heart to en-slave their wiles dis-play,__ my heart to en-slave their wiles__

-tra, for-se un' al-tra__ do-man lo sa-rà.
dis-play, their wiles dis-play,__ their wiles__ dis-play.

As a dove flies, alarmed, to seek shelter,
  Pursued by some vulture, to bear it aloft
    in flight,
Thus do I fly from constancy's fetter:
  E'en women's spells I shun—all their ef-
    forts I slight.
A husband that's jealous I scorn and de-
    spise,
  And I laugh at and heed not a lover's
    sighs;
If a fair one take my heart by surprise,
  I heed not scornful tongues or prying
    eyes.

(Enter COUNT CEPRANO, watching his wife, who is seen
advancing from the distance, attended by a cavalier. Lords
and ladies promenading at back.)

Duke
(meeting the COUNTESS, and addressing her with gallantry).

  Are you already going, cruel one?

Countess.
  I must obey my husband:
  Ceprano desires me to leave.

Duke.
  The light of your face
  Sheds upon the court more lustre than the
    sun;
  For your smile all alike must sigh;
  For you love's flame doth all around con-
    sume;
  Enslaved, enchanted, for you my heart is
    breaking.
          (Kissing her hand with warmth.)

Countess.
  Be more circumspect.

Duke.
  No! (Giving her his arm, and leading her off.)
  (Enter RIGOLETTO, meeting the COUNT CEPRANO and nobles.)

Rigoletto.
  What troubles your thoughts,
  Signor Ceprano?
  (COUNT shows impatience, and goes off after the DUKE.)

Rigoletto   (to the Cavaliers).
  He is out of temper, I see.

Chorus.
  What sport!

Rigoletto.
  Indeed!

La costanza tiranna del core
  Detestiamo qual morbo crudele,
  Sol chi vuole si serbi fedele;
    Non v' ha amor, se non v' è libertà.
De' mariti il geloso furore,
  Degli amanti le smanie derido,
  Anco d'Argo i cent' occhi disfide
    Se mi punge una qualche beltà.

(Entra il CONTE DI CEPRANO, che segue da lungi la sua
sposa, seguita da altre cavaliere. Dame e signor. entrano du
varie parti.)

Duca
(alla SIGNORA DE CEPRANO, movendo ad incontrarla con
          molta galanterie).

  Partite? Crudele!

Conte.
  Seguire lo sposo.
  M' è forza a Ceprano.

Duca.
  Ma dee luminoso
  In Corte tal astro qual sole brillar.
  Per voi qui ciascuno dovrà palpitar.
  Per voi già possente la fiamma d'amore
  Inebria, conquide, distrugge il mio core.
          (Con enfasi baciandole la mano.)

Conte.
  Calmatevi—

Duca.
  No! (Ce da il braccio, ed esce con lei.)
  Entra e RIGOLETTO, che s'incontra nel SIGNOR DI CEPRANO,
poi cortigiani.)

Rigoletto.
  In testa che avete,
  Signor di Ceprano?
  (CEPRANO fa un gesto d'impazienza, e segue il DUCA.)

Rigoletto   (ai Cortigiani).
  Ei sbuffa, vedete?

Coro.
  Che festa!

Rigoletto.
  Oh sì—

Borsa.

The Duke is having his diversion.

Rigoletto.

Is it not always so? What is there new in
it?
Gambling and drinking, feasting and danc-
ing,
Fighting and banqueting, all come to him
alike.
Now 'gainst the Countess siege he is laying,
Her husband's jealousy wholly deriding.
(Exit.)
(Enter MARULLO.)

Marullo (eagerly).

Oh, such news! such news I have!

Chorus.

What has happened? Tell us!

Marullo.

You will be quite surprised.

Chorus.

Narrate it! narrate it!

Marullo.

Ah! ah! Rigoletto—

Chorus.

What of him?

Marullo.

A strange adventure.

Chorus.

Has he lost his hump? Is he no longer
deformed?

Marullo.

Stranger much than that! The idiot has
taken—

Chorus.

Taken what?

Marullo.

An inamorata!

Chorus.

An inamorata!—Incredible.

Marullo.

Into a Cupid the hunchback is transformed.

Chorus.

Oh, what a Cupid!—What a comical
Cupid!

(Enter the DUKE, followed by RIGOLETTO, and CEPRANO in
the background.)

Borsa.

Il Duca quì pur si diverte.

Rigoletto.

Così non è sempre? che nuove scoperte!
Il giuoco ed il vino, le feste, la danza,
Battaglie, conviti, ben tutto gli sta.
Or della Contessa l'assedio egli avanza,
E intanto il marito fremendo ne va.
(Esce.)

(Entra MARULLO.)

Marullo (premuroso).

Gran nuova! gran nuova!

Coro.

Che avvenne? parlate!

Marullo.

Stupir ne dovrete—

Coro.

Narrate, narrate—

Marullo.

Ah! ah!—Rigoletto—

Coro.

Ebben?

Marullo.

Caso enorme!—

Coro.

Perduto ha la gobba? non è più difforme!

Marullo.

Più strana è la cosa!—Il pazzo possiede—

Coro.

Infine?

Marullo.

Un' amante!

Coro.

Amante! Chi il crede?

Marullo.

Il gobbo in Cupido or s' è trasformato!—

Coro.

Quel mostro Cupido!—Cupido beato!—

(Entra il DUCA, seguito da RIGOLETTO, indi CEPRANO.)

Duke   (to RIGOLETTO).

What a troublesome fellow is that Ceprano!
But his wife—to my mind she's an angel!

Rigoletto.

Then carry her off.

Duke.

That is easily said—but how to do it?

Rigoletto.

Do it to-night.

Duke.

You do not consider the Count.

Rigoletto.

Can you not put him in prison?

Duke.

Ah! no.

Rigoletto.

Then why not banish him?

Duke.

Buffoon, I dare not.

Rigoletto.

His head, then.
                (Making signs of cutting it off.)

Ceprano   (coming forward).

(Black-hearted villain!)

Duke.

Is this the head you speak of?
(Placing his hand on the shoulder of the COUNT.)

Rigoletto   (laughing).

Of what value is such a head as that?

Ceprano.

Miscreant!
            (Furiously, and drawing his sword.)

Duke.

Forbear.   (To CEPRANO.)

Rigoletto.

He only makes me laugh.

Chorus.

He is frantic with rage.
                (Among themselves.)

Duke.

Buffoon, come hither.
                (To RIGOLETTO.)

You always carry your jokes too far;—
The anger you provoke may one day on
   your head alight.

Rigoletto.

Who can hurt me?—I have no fear.

Duca   (a RIGOLETTO).

Ah, quanto Ceprano, importuno niun v' è,
La cara sua posa è un angiol per me!

Rigoletto.

Rapitela.

Duca.

E detto; ma il farlo?

Rigoletto.

Stassera.

Duca.

Nè pensi tu al Conte?

Rigoletto.

Non c' è la prigione?

Duca.

Ah, no.

Rigoletto.

Ebben—s'esilia.

Duca.

Nemmeno, buffone.

Rigoletto.

Adunque la testa—
                (Indicando di farla tagliare.)

Ceprano.

(Oh, l'anima nera!)

Duca.

Che di' questa testa?—
            (Battendo colla mano una spalla al Conte.)

Rigoletto.

Che far di tal testa?—A cosa ella vale?

Ceprano.

Marrano.
            (Infuriato, battendo la spada.)

Duca.

Fermate—   (A CEPRANO.)

Rigoletto.

Da rider mi fa.

Coro.

In furia è montato!
                (Tra loro.)

Duca.

Buffone, vien quà.
                (A RIGOLETTO.)

Ah! sempre tu spingi lo scherzo all' estremo,
Quell' ira che sfida colpir ti potrà.

Rigoletto.

Che coglier mi puote? Di loro non temo;

The Duke's protégé no one dares to injure!

Ceprano   (aside to Courtiers).
   Vengeance on the buffoon!

Chorus.
   And who amongst us
   Has not some wrong to be avenged!

Ceprano.
   And they shall be avenged!

Chorus.
   But how?

Ceprano.
   To-morrow, let all who have the courage,
   By my side, and armed, appear.

Chorus.
   Be it so.

Ceprano.
   At night.

Chorus.
   Agreed.
     (Groups of Dancers appear.)
   All here is joyful—all here is festive;
    To pleasure all here invites;
   Oh, look around, and in all faces see
    The reign of voluptuous delights.

Count Monterone   (from without).
   I will speak to him.
     (Enter Count Monterone.)

Duke.
   No.

Monterone.
   But I will.

Chorus.
   Monterone!

Monterone
    (looking scornfully at the Duke).
   Yes, Monterone—against crimes like thine
   There is yet one to raise a voice.

Rigoletto
   (to the Duke, mimicking the voice of Monterone).
   I will speak to him.
     (With mock gravity.)
   Against us you have conspired, signor,
   And we, in our clemency, have pardoned
    you.
   'Tis madness in all seasons to come here,
   Wailing about the honor of your daughter.

Del Duca un protetto nessun toccherà.

Ceprano   (ai Cortigiani, a parte).
   Vendetta del pazzo—

Coro.
   Contr' esso un rancore
   Pei tristi suoi modi, di noi chi non ha?

Ceprano.
   Vendetta.

Coro.
   Ma come?

Ceprano.
   Domani, chi ha core,
   Sia in armi da me.

Tutti.
   Sì.

Ceprano.
   A notte.

Tutti.
   Sarà.
    (La folla de' danzatori invade la sala.)
   Tutto è gioja, tutto è festa,
    Tutto invitaci a goder!
   Oh, guardate, non par questa,
    Or la reggia del piacer!

Conte di Monterone   (dall intorno).
   Ch' io gli parli.
     (Entra il Conte di Monterone.)

Duca.
   No.

Monterone.
   Il voglio.

Tutti.
   Monterone!

Monterone
    (fissando il Duca con nobile orgoglio).
   Sì Monteron—la voce mia qual tuono
   Vi scuoterà dovunque—

Rigoletto
   (al Duca, contraffacondo la voce di Monterone).
   Ch' io gli parli.
     (Si avanza con ridicola gravità.)
   Voi congiuraste contro noi, signore,
   E noi, clementi in vero, perdonammo—
   Qual vi piglia or delirio—a tutte l'ore
   Di vostra figlia reclamar l'onore?

Monterone (looking scornfully at RIGOLETTO).

Despicable buffoon!—

(To DUKE.)

Ah! thus will I
Thy vile orgies ever disturb. In all places
Shall my weeping voice attend you,
While unavenged shall remain
The gross insult on my family inflicted.
And if to the hangman you consign me,
As a spirit will I again visit thee,
Till the vengeance of God and man o'er-
    whelm thee.

Duke.

No more of this—arrest him.

Rigoletto.

He is mad!

Chorus.

What ravings!

Monterone.

Oh! on both of ye be my malediction!

(To the DUKE and RIGOLETTO.)

Vile is he who hounds the dying lion,
But viler thou, O Duke, and thy serpent
    there,
Who the anguish of a parent can deride!
A parent's curse be on ye both!

Rigoletto.

(What do I hear? Oh, horror!)

(Greatly agitated.)

All   (except RIGOLETTO).

Audaciously thou hast this fête disturbed,
By an infernal spirit hither led.
Vain are thy words—deaf to them our ears.
Go, tremble, old man, at the sovereign anger
Thou hast provoked. No hope for thee re-
    mains;
Fatal will this day prove to thee.

MONTERONE is marched off between halberdiers—the others
follow the DUKE.

SCENE II—The extremity of a street that has no thor-
oughfare. On the left a house of retired appearance, within
a court-yard, from which there is a doorway into the
street. In the court-yard are seen a tall tree and a marble
seat. At the top of the wall, a terrace, supported by arches,
and reached by a flight of steps in front. On the right of
the passage is the highest wall of the garden, and the gable
end of the palace of CEPRANO. It is night.

(Enter RIGOLETTO, enveloped in a cloak, followed by SPAR-
AFUCILE, who has a long sword under his cloak.)

Rigoletto.

(How fearfully that man cursed me!)

Monterone (guardando RIGOLETTO con ira sprezzante).

Novello insulto!—

(Al DUCA.)

Ah, sì a turbare
Sarò vestr' orgie—verrò a gridare,
Fino a che vegga restarsi inulto
Di mia famiglia l'atroce insulto;
E se al carnefice pur mi darete
Spettro terribile mi rivedrete,
Portante in mano il teschio mio,
Vendetta chiedere al mondo e a Dio.

Duca.

Non più, arrestatelo.

Rigoletto.

E matto!

Coro.

Quai detti!

Monterone.

Oh, siate entrambi voi maledetti.

(Al DUCA e RIGOLETTO.)

Slanciare il cane al leon morente
E vile, o Duca—e tu serpente,

(A RIGOLETTO.)

Tu che d'un padre rida al dolore,
Sii maledetto!

Rigoletto.

(Che sento? orrore!)

(Colpito.)

Tutti   (meno RIGOLETTO).

Oh, tu che la festa audace hai turbito,
Da un genio d'inferno quì fosti guidato;
E vano ogni detto, di quà t'allontana—
Va, trema, o vegliardo, dell' ira sovrana—
Tu l' hai provocata, più spheme non v' è.
Un' ora fatale fu questa per te.

(MONTERONE parte fra due alabardieri; tutti gli altr
seguirono il DUCA in altra stanza.)

SCENA II—L'estremita più deserta d'una Via Cieca. A
sinistra, una casa di discreta apparenza, con una piccola
corte circondato da muro. Nella corte un grosso ed alto
albero ed un sedile di marmo; nel muro una porta che mette
ella strada; sopra il muro un terrazzo practicabile, sostenuto
da arcate. La porta del primo piano dà su detto terrazzo,
a cui si ascende per una scala di fronte. A destra, della
via è il muro altissimo del giardino, e un fiance del Palazzo
di CEPRANO. E notte.

(RIGOLETTO chiuso nel suo mantello. SPARAFUCILE lo
segue, portando sotto il mantello una lunga spada.)

Rigoletto.

(Quel vecchio maledivami!)

Sparafucile.
  Signor—
Rigoletto.
  Go: I have no need of you.
Sparafucile.
  Be that as it may, you have before you
  A man who knows how to use a sword.
Rigoletto.
  A robber?
Sparafucile.
  No— a man who, for a trifle,
  Will from a rival free you;—
  And have you not one?
Rigoletto.
  Who is he?
Sparafucile.
  Have you not a mistress here?
Rigoletto.
  (What do I hear?) What would it cost me
  To rid me of a signor?
Sparafucile.
  More than for a lesser man.
Rigoletto.
  When must it be paid?
Sparafucile.
  One-half beforehand,
  The other when the deed is done.
Rigoletto.
  (O demon!) And how can you
  Be sure of success?
Sparafucile.
  In the street sometimes they fall.
  At other times in my own house;—
  I waylay my man at night—
  A single blow, and he is dead.
Rigoletto.
  And how in your own house?
Sparafucile.
  All the easier—
  I have a sister there who helps.
  She dances in the streets—she is handsome—
  Those I want she decoys—and then—
Rigoletto.
  I comprehend

Sparafucile.
  Signor?
Rigoletto.
  Va non ho niente.
Sparafucile.
  Nè il chiesi—a voi presente
  Un uom di spada sta.
Rigoletto.
  Un ladro?
Sparafucile.
  Un uom che libera
  Per poco da un rivale,
  E voi ne avete—
Rigoletto.
  Quale?
Sparafucile.
  La vostra donna è là.
Rigoletto.
  (Che sento?) E quanto spendero
  Per un signor dovrei?
Sparafucile.
  Prezzo maggior vorrei—
Rigoletto.
  Com' usasi pagar?
Sparafucile.
  Una metà s'anticipa,
  Il resto si da poi—
Rigoletto.
  (Dimonio!) E come puoi
  Tanto securo oprar?
Sparafucile.
  Soglio in cittade uccidere,
  Oppure nel mio tetto.
  L'uomo di sera aspetto—
  Une stoccata, e muor.
Rigoletto.
  E come in casa?
Sparafucile.
  E facile—
  M'ainta mia sorella—
  Per lè vie danza—è bella—
  Chi voglio attira—e allor—
Rigoletto.
  Comprendo—

Sparafucile.

There is nothing to fear;
My trusty weapon never betrays me.
(Showing his sword.)
Can I serve you?

Rigoletto.

No; not at present.

Sparafucile.

The worse for you.

Rigoletto.

Your name?

Sparafucile.

Sparafucile is my name.

Rigoletto.

A foreigner?

Sparafucile.

From Burgundy.
(About to go.)

Rigoletto.

Where are you to be found?

Sparafucile.

Hereabouts, every night.

Rigoletto.

Go.   (Exit SPARAFUCILE.)
How like are we!—the tongue my weapon,
the dagger his!
To make others laugh is my vocation—his
to make them weep!
How that old man cursed me!
O man!—O human nature!
What scoundrels dost thou make of us!
O rage! To be deformed—the buffoon to
have no play!
Whether one will or not, to be obliged to
laugh!
Tears, the common solace of humanity,
Are to me prohibited!
Youthful, joyous, high-born, handsome,
An imperious master gives the word—
"Amuse me, buffoon,"—and I must obey.
Perdition! How do I not despise ye all,
Ye sycophants—ye hollow courtiers!
If I am deformed, 'tis ye have made me so;
But a changed man will I now become.

Sparafucile.

Senza strepito—
E questo il mio stromento.
(Mostra la spada.)
Vi serve?

Rigoletto.

No—al momento—

Sparafucile.

Peggio per voi—

Rigoletto.

Chi sa?

Sparafucile.

Sparafucile mi nomino—

Rigoletto.

Straniero?—

Sparafucile.

Borgognone—
(Per andarsene.)

Rigoletto.

E dove all' occasione?—

Sparafucile.

Qui sempre a sera.

Rigoletto.

Va.   (SPARAFUCILE parte.)
Pari siamo!—Io la lingua, egli ha il pug-
nale;
L'uomo son io che ride, ei quel che spegne!
Quel vecchio maledivami!
O uomini!—o natura!
Vil scellerato mi faceste voi!
Oh rabbia!—esser difforme!—esser buffone!
Non dover, non poter altro che ridere!
Il retaggio d'ogni uom m' è tolto—il pianto!
Questo padrone mio,
Giovin, giocondo, sì possente, bello
Sonnecchiando mi dice;
Fa ch'io rida, buffone.
Forzarmi deggio, e farlo! Oh, dannazione!
Odio a voi, cortigiani schernitori!
Quanta in mordervi ho gioia!
Se iniquo so, per cangion vostra e solo—
Ma il altr' uom qui mi cangio!
Quel vecchio malediami! Tal pensiero
Perchè conturba ognor la mente mia?

That old man cursed me! Why does that
  curse
Thus ever haunt my harassed mind?
What have I to fear? Ah, no, this is mere
  folly!
(Opens a door with a key, and enters the yard.)

(Enter GILDA, coming from the house, and throwing herself into her father's arms.)

Rigoletto.
  My daughter!

Gilda.
  My dear father!

Rigoletto.
  Only when near to thee
  Does my oppressed heart know joy.

Gilda.
  Oh, what affection!

Rigoletto.
  My only life art thou!
  What other earthly happiness have I?
                      (Sighing.)
Gilda.
  Why do you sigh? What ails you?
  Open your mind to your poor daughter.
  If any secret you have, to her confide it;
  And do about her family inform her.

Rigoletto.
  Thou hast not any.

Gilda.
  What is your real name?

Rigoletto.
  What matters it to thee?

Gilda.
  If you are not willing
  Of your family to speak—

Rigoletto.
  Do you ever go out?
                  (Interrupting her.)
Gilda.
  Only when I go to church.

Rigoletto.
  In that thou dost right.

Gilda.
  If of yourself you will not speak,
  At least tell me something of my mother.

Mi coglierà sventura? Ah no, è follia.
(Apre con chiave, ad entra nel cortile.)

(Entra GILDA, ch'esce dalla casa e segetta nelle sue braccia.

Rigoletto.
  Figlia!

Gilda.
  Mio padre!

Rigoletto.
  A te dapresso
  Trova sol gioia il core oppresso.

Gilda.
  Oh, quanto amore!

Rigoletto.
  Mia vita sei!
  Senza te in terra qual bene avrei?
                      (Sospira.)
Gilda.
  Voi sospirate!—che v'ange tanto?
  Lo dite a questa povera figlia—
  Se v' ha mistero—per lei sia franto—
  Ch'ella conosca la sua famiglia.

Rigoletto.
  Tu non ne hai—

Gilda.
  Qual nome avete?

Rigoletto.
  A te che importa?

Gilda.
  Se non volete
  Di voi parlarmi—

Rigoletto.
  Non uscir mai.
                  (Interrompendola.)
Gilda.
  Non vo che al tempio.

Rigoletto.
  Or ben tu fai.

Gilda.
  Se non di voi, almen chi sia.
  Fate ch'io sappia la madre mia.

DEH NON PARLARE — *SPEAK NOT OF ONE* Air (Rigoletto)

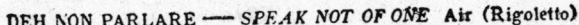

Deh non par-la-re al mi-se-ro   Del suo per-du-to be — ne;
Speak not of one, whose loss to thee,   All earth can boast could ne'er— re-store;

El - la sen - tia, quell' an - ge-lo,   Pie - tà — del - le — mie
Her an-gel form me-thinks I see,   Who loved me, though de-form'd and

pe - ne;   So-lo,   dif-for-me,   po-ve-ro,   Per com-pas-sion mi a -
poor. —   Pi-ty,   O Gil-da;   spare me!   Ask it, my child,   no

mò. Ah! mo - ri - a,   mo - ri - a,   le zol - le co-pra-no Lie-vi quel ca-po a-
more. Ah! she died; —   may earth   rest light-ly on — her; To me she's lost for-

ma-to;   So-la or tu re - sti,   So-la or tu res-ti al   mi - se - ro; —
cov - er.   Thou art my on - ly hope,   Thou art my on - ly hope, my child!

Di - o,   sii rin - gra - zia - to,   si rin - gra - zia-to.
Fa - ther of all! —   oh! bless her with Thy mer - cy   mild!

Gilda.

Alas! what anguish! such bitter grief
What language can express!
Father, dear father, calm yourself,
Or my heart will surely break.
To me your name pray tell;
The grief that saddens you impart.

Rigoletto.

'Twere useless myself to discover;
Suffice it that thy father I am.
Some in the world there are who fear me,
In others, perhaps, envy I excite;
But one there is who has cursed **me!**

Gilda.

Quanto dolor! che spremere
Sì amaro pianto può?
Padre, non più, calmatevi—
Mi lacera tal vista—
Il nome vostro ditemi,
Il duol che sì v'attrista—

Rigoletto.

A che nomarmi? è inutile!
Padre ti sono, e basti—
Me forse al mondo temono,
D' alcuno ho forse gli asti:
Altri mi maledicono—

Gilda.

　　Country, family, friends,
　　Possess you none of them?

Rigoletto.

　　Country, family, friends, say'st thou?
　　Thou art my country, family, and friends!
　　The whole universe thou art to me!
　　　　　　　　(Passionately.)

Gilda.

　　Ah! if happier I could render you,
　　What joy to my heart it would bring!
　　Three months full it is since hither I came,
　　And nothing yet have I of the city seen.
　　With your permission I should like to see it.

Rigoletto.

　　Never! never! Hast thou ever left the
　　house?

Gilda.

　　No.

Rigoletto.

　　That's well.

Gilda.

　　(What have I said?)

Rigoletto.

　　I'll take care thou shalt not!
　　(She might be followed—stolen from me!
　　To dishonor the daughter of a buffoon
　　Would here be laughed at. Horror!) Ho,
　　there!
　　　　　(Turning towards the house.)
　　　　(Enter GIOVANNA, from the house.)

Giovanna.

　　Signor?

Rigoletto.

　　Has any one seen me come hither?
　　Mind—speak the truth.

Giovanna.

　　Oh, no—no one.

Rigoletto.

　　That is well. The gate that to the bastion
　　leads—
　　Is that always closed?

Giovanna.

　　It is, and shall be.

Gilda.

　　Patria, parenti, amici,
　　Voi dunque non avete?

Rigoletto.

　　Patria! parenti! dici?
　　Culto, famiglia, patria,
　　Il mio universo è in te!
　　　　　　　　(Con effusione.)

Gilda.

　　Ah! se può lieto rendervi,
　　Gioia è la vita a me!
　　Già da tre lune son quì venuta,
　　Nè la cittade ho ancor veduta;
　　Se il concedete, farlo or potrei—

Rigoletto.

　　Mai! mai! uscita, dimmi, unqua sei?

Gilda.

　　No.

Rigoletto.

　　Guai!

Gilda.

　　(Che dissi?)

Rigoletto.

　　Ben te ne guarda!
　　Potrian seguirla, rapirla ancora!
　　Qui d'un buffone si disonora
　　La figlia, e ridesi—Orror! Olà?
　　　　　　　　(Verso la casa.)

　　　　(Entra GIOVANNA, dalla casa.)

Giovanna.

　　Signor?

Rigoletto.

　　Venendo, mi vide alcuno?
　　Bada, di' il vero—

Giovanna.

　　Ah, no, nessuno.

Rigoletto.

　　Sta ben—la porta che dà al bastione
　　E sempre chiusa?

Giovanna.

　　Lo fu e sarà.

VEGLIA O DONNA—— *SAFELY GUARD THIS TENDER BLOSSOM* Duet (Rigoletto and Gilda)

RIGOLETTO

Ve-glia, o don - na, ques-to fio - re, Che a te pu - ro con-fi-
Safe - ly guard this ten - der blos - som, Which to thee I am con-

da - i; Ve-gli at - ten - ta e non sia ma - i Che s'of-
fid - ing, In her guile - less heart and bos - om May no

fu - schi il suo can - dor. Tu dei ven - ti dal fu - ro - re Ch'al-tri
thought of ill be - tide; From the arts of vice pro - tect her, May its

fio - ri han-no pie - ga - to, Lo di - fen - di, e im-ma-co-
snares be laid in vain; Her fa - ther will from thee ex-

la - te Lo ri - do - na al ge - ni - tor, Quan-to af - fet - to! qua-li
pect her Pure re - stored to him a - gain. Ah! such fear for me re-

cu - re! Che te - me - te, pa - dre mi - o? Las - sù in
veal - ing, Fa - ther dear, why thus dis - play? One from

cie - lo, pres-so Di - o Ve-glia un an - giol pro - tet - tor. Da noi
whom there's no con - ceal - ing Guides me ev - er on my way. From on

sto - glie le sven - tu - re Di mia ma - dre il prie-go san - to Non fia
high my moth-er's spir - it Leads me on with ten-der care; While this

mai dis - vel - to o fran - to Ques-to a voi di - let - to fior.
heart bears life with - in it, 'Twill de - fy each art - ful snare.

(The Duke, in disguise, is seen to arrive in the street.)

Rigoletto.

There is some one outside.

(Rigoletto comes through the garden-gate, and looks about the street; while doing so, the Duke stealthily glides in, and hides himself behind a tree, throwing a purse to Gio-7anna.)

Gilda.

Oh, Heavens!
He is always suspicious.

Rigoletto (returning to Gilda.)

Does any one ever follow you to church?

Gilda.

No.

Duke.

(Rigoletto.)

Rigoletto.

Should any one knock,
On no account admit him.

Giovanna.

Not even the Duke?

Rigoletto.

Above all others keep him out.   Daughter, adieu!

Duke.

(His daughter!)

Gilda.

Adieu, dear father.

(They embrace, and Rigoletto departs, closing the door after him.)

Gilda (in the yard).

Giovanna, I am struck with remorse.

Giovanna.

What about, pray?

Gilda.

I did not tell him of the youth who follows me to church.

Giovanna.

Why should you tell him? Do you hate the youth,
And would you thus dismiss him?

Gilda.

No, no! his looks are pleasing to me.

Giovanna.

And he has the appearance of a wealthy signor.

Gilda.

Neither signor nor wealth do I wish to have;

(Entra il Duca, in costume borghese, della strada.)

Rigoletto.

Alcuno è fuori—

(Apre la porta della corte e, mentre esce a guardar sulla strada, il Duca guizza furtivo nella corte, e si nasconde dietro l'albero; gettando a Giovanna una borsa la fa tacere.)

Gilda.

Cielo!
Sempre novel sospetto—

Rigoletto (a Gilda, tornando).

Vi seguiva alla chiesa mai nessuno?

Gilda.

Mai.

Duca.

(Rigoletto.)

Rigoletto.

Se talor quì picchiano
Guardatevi d'aprire—

Giovanna.

Nemmeno al Duca?

Rigoletto.

Meno che a tutti a lui.   Mia figlia, addio.

Duca.

(Sua figlia!)

Gilda.

Addio, mio padre.

(S'abbraciano, e Rigoletto parte, chiudendosi dietro la porta.)

Gilda (nella corte).

Giovanna, ho dei rimorsi—

Giovanna.

E perchè mai?

Gilda.

Tacqui che un giovin ne sequiva al tempio.

Giovanna.

Perchè ciò dirgli?—l'odiate dunque
Cotesto giovin, voi?

Gilda.

No, no, chè troppo è bello, e spira amore—

Giovanna.

E magnanimo sembra e gran signore.

Gilda.

Signor nè principe—io lo vorrei:

The poorer he prove, the more shall I love
him.
Sleeping or waking, my thoughts are all of
him,
And my heart longs to tell him I lo—

Duke
(suddenly coming forward, motioning GIOVANNA to retire, and kneeling at the feet of GILDA).

I love thee!
The words repeat! Such delicious accents
Open to me a heaven of enjoyment.

Gilda.

Giovanna? Alas, no one answers me!
There's no one here! Oh, heavens, I'm
alone!

Duke.

No! I am here; and to thee I respond—
Against all the world I will protect thee!

Gilda.

Why thus address yourself to me?

Duke.

Whate'er your state, to me it matters not—
I love thee!

Gilda.

Oh, go away.

Duke.

Go away! No, not yet!
If love's fire within us both be lighted,
Inseparable we should henceforth be;
O maiden bright, thy lot with mine unite!

Sento che povero—più l'amerei.
Sognando o vigile— sempre lo chiamo,
E l'alma in estasi—gli dice t'a—

Duca
(esce improvviso, fa cenno a GIOVANNA d'andarsene, e in ginocchiandosi a' pied di GILDA termina la frase).

T'amo!
T'amo, ripetilo—si caro accento,
Un puro schiudimi—ciel di contento!

Gilda.

Giovanna? Ahi, misera! non v' è più alcuna
Che quì rispondami! Oh Dio! nessuno!

Duca.

Son io coll' anima—che ti rispondo—
Ah, que che s'amano—son tutto un mondo!

Gilda.

Chi mai, chi giungere—vi fece a me?

Duca.

S'angelo o demone—che importa a te?
Io t'amo—

Gilda.

Uscitene.

Duca.

Uscire! adesso!
Ora che accendene—un fuoco istesso!
Ah, inseparabile—d'amore, il dio
Stringeva, o vergine—tuo fato al mio!

E IL SOL DELL' ANIMA — *LOVE IS THE SUN* Air (Duke)

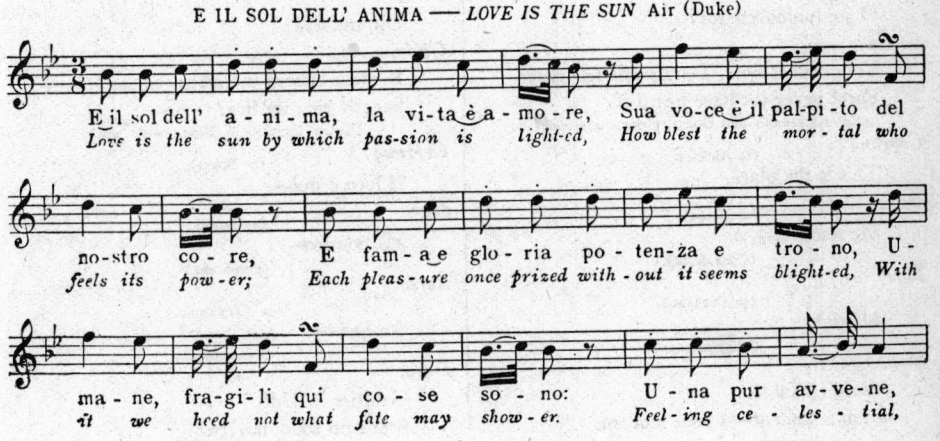

E il sol dell' a-ni-ma, la vi-ta è a-mo-re, Sua vo-ce è il pal-pi-to del
Love is the sun by which pas-sion is light-ed, How blest the mor-tal who

no-stro co-re, E fam-a e glo-ria po-ten-za e tro-no, U-
feels its pow-er; Each pleas-ure once prized with-out it seems blight-ed, With

ma-ne, fra-gi-li qui co-se so-no: U-na pur av-ve-ne,
it we heed not what fate may show-er. Feel-ing ce-les-tial,

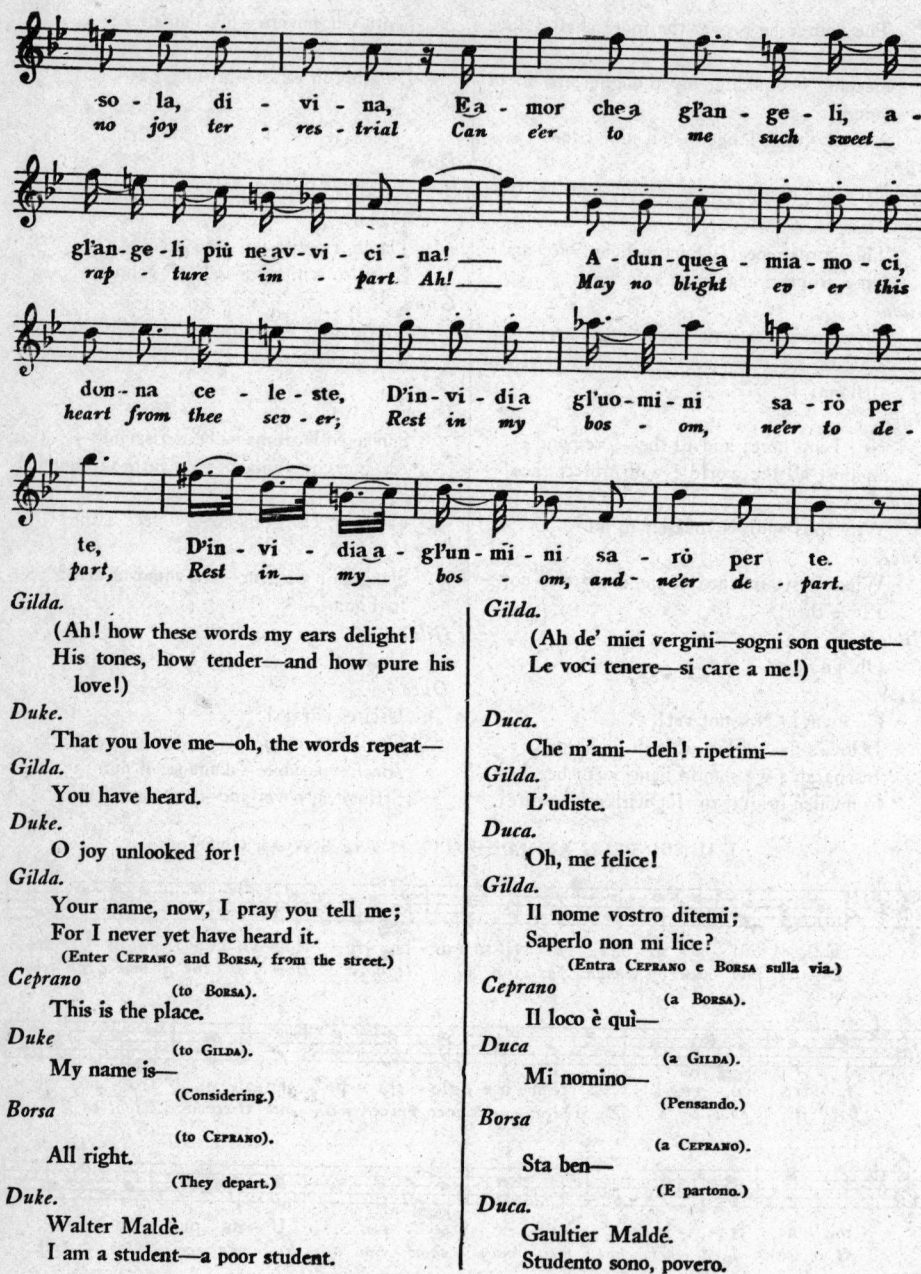

so - la, di - vi - na,　Ea - mor che a gl'an - ge - li, a-
no　joy　ter - res - trial　Can　e'er　to　me　such　sweet__

gl'an - ge - li più ne av - vi - ci - na! ___　A - dun - que a - mia - mo - ci,
rap - ture　im - part　Ah! ___　May　no　blight　ev - er　this

don - na ce - le - ste, D'in - vi - dia gl'uo - mi - ni　sa - rò per
heart from thee sev - er; Rest in my bos - om, ne'er to de-

te,　D'in - vi - dia a - gl'un - mi - ni sa - rò per te.
part,　Rest in__ my__ bos - om, and - ne'er de - part.

Gilda.	*Gilda.*
(Ah! how these words my ears delight! His tones, how tender—and how pure his love!)	(Ah de' miei vergini—sogni son queste— Le voci tenere—si care a me!)
Duke.	*Duca.*
That you love me—oh, the words repeat—	Che m'ami—deh! ripetimi—
Gilda.	*Gilda.*
You have heard.	L'udiste.
Duke.	*Duca.*
O joy unlooked for!	Oh, me felice!
Gilda.	*Gilda.*
Your name, now, I pray you tell me; For I never yet have heard it.	Il nome vostro ditemi; Saperlo non mi lice?
(Enter Ceprano and Borsa, from the street.)	(Entra Ceprano e Borsa sulla via.)
Ceprano (to Borsa).	*Ceprano* (a Borsa).
This is the place.	Il loco è quì—
Duke (to Gilda).	*Duca* (a Gilda).
My name is—	Mi nomino—
(Considering.)	(Pensando.)
Borsa (to Ceprano).	*Borsa* (a Ceprano).
All right.	Sta ben—
(They depart.)	(E partono.)
Duke.	*Duca.*
Walter Maldè. I am a student—a poor student.	Gaultier Maldé. Studento sono, povero.

Giovanna. (In alarm.)

I hear footsteps outside.

Gilda.

Perhaps it is my father.

Duke.

Ah! could I the traitor catch
Who thus presumes to interrupt
The joy I have in being with thee!

Gilda (to GIOVANNA).

(Quickly away!
To the bastion conduct him—go!)

Duke.

First say that you love me?

Gilda.

And you?

Duke.

With my whole heart I swear it.

Gilda.

No more, no more, at once depart.

Both.

Farewell, my hope, my soul, farewell;
For thee alone henceforth I'll live;
Farewell! Immutable as Fate
Shall be my love and truth to thee.

(Exit the DUKE, escorted by GIOVANNA, GILDA following his steps with her eyes.)

Gilda (alone).

Walter Maldè! What a romantic name!
Already is it on my heart engraven!

Giovanna. (Spaventata.)

Rumor di passi è furore.

Gilda.

Forse mio padre.

Duca.

Ah! cogliere
Potessi il traditore
Che sì mi sturba!

Gilda (a GIOVANNA).

(Adducilo
Di quà al bastione, ite!)

Duca.

Di m'amerai tu?

Gilda.

E voi?

Duca.

L'intera vita, poi.

Gilda.

Non più, non più, partite.

A 2.

Addio, speranza ed anima
Sol tu sari per me.
Addio, vivrà immutabile
L'affretto mio per te.

(Parte il DUCA scortato da GIOVANNA, GILDA resta fissando è partito.)

Gilda (sola).

Gualtier Maldè! nome di lui si amato.
Scolpiciti nel core innamorato!

CARO NOME CHE IL MIO COR — *DEAR NAME WITHIN THIS BREAST* Air (Gilda)

Ca-ro no-me che jl mio cor Fes-ti pri-mo pal-pi-
Dear name, with-in this breast, Thy mem-'ry will re-

tar, Le de-li-zie dell' a-mor Mi dèi sem-pre ram-men-
main; My love, for thee con-fess'd, No pow-er can re-

tar! Col pen-sier il mio de-sir A te sem-pre vo-le-
strain. Ah! yes, 'tis bliss to own The joy that fills my

ra, E fin l'ul - ti - mo   so - spir, Ca - ro no - me, tuo   sa -
heart; 'Twill beat   for   thee   a - lone;   Till   death 'twill ne'er de -

rà.   Col pen - sier il mio de - sir   A te sem - pre vo - le - rà.
part!   'Twill___ beat for thee a - lone; Ah! till death 'twill ne'er de - part!

                E fin l'ul - ti - mo   mi - o   so -
                'Twill   beat, 'twill beat   for   thee   a :

spir, Ca - ro   no -   - me, tuo sa - rà.
lone, Ah!___ till   death _____ 'twill ne'er de - part.

(She ascends the terrace, with a lantern in her hand.)	(San al terrazzo con una lanterna, che tono entra in casa.)
(Enter MARULLO, CEPRANO, and BORSA, accompanied by courtiers, in masks, and armed.)	(Entrano MARULLO, CEPRANO, e BORSA, cortigiani, armati e mascherati, dalla via.)
Borsa.	*Borsa.*
Look there!	E là.
(Pointing towards GILDA.)	(Indicanda GILDA.)
Ceprano.	*Ceprano.*
Ah! there she is—	Miratela—
Chorus.	*Coro.*
Oh! how beautiful she is!	Oh! quanto è bella!
Marullo.	*Marullo.*
A fairy or an angel!	Par fata od angiol!
Chorus.	*Coro.*
Can that the mistress be	L'amante è quella
Of Rigoletto?	Di Rigoletto?
(They all laugh.)	
(Enter RIGOLETTO, absorbed in thought.)	(Entra RIGOLETTO, concentrato.)
Rigoletto.	*Rigoletto.*
(Laughing! what can it mean?)	(Riedo! perche?)
Borsa.	*Borsa.*
Silence, to our work; we've no time for laughing.	Silenzio, all' opra, badate a me.
Rigoletto.	*Rigoletto.*
(Ah, how fiercely that old man cursed me!) Who is there?	(Ah da quel vecchio fui maledetto!) Chi è là?

Borsa (to his companions).
Be silent, 'tis Rigoletto.

Ceprano.
A double capture! We can also slay him.

Borsa.
No; to-morrow it will make more sport.

Marullo.
But now everything is ready.

Rigoletto.
(Who is speaking there?)

Marullo.
Is't you, Rigoletto—say.

Rigoletto (considerably agitated).
Who goes there?

Marullo.
You will not betray us—I am—

Rigoletto.
Who?

Marullo.
Marullo.

Rigoletto.
In the dead of night for good you are not
here.

Marullo.
'Tis a ridiculous frolic brings us here;
Ceprano's wife we mean to carry off.

Rigoletto.
(Once more do I breathe.) But how do you
enter?

Marullo (to CEPRANO).
Hand here the keys!
            (To RIGOLETTO.)
Doubt us not;
We are not to be foiled in a stratagem.
    (Handing him the keys taken from CEPRANO.)
Here are the keys.

Rigoletto (feeling the keys).
I feel that this is his crest.
(Ah! then all my terrors have been need-
less!)
        (He breathes more freely.)
Yonder is his palace—I will go with you.

Marullo.
We are all disguised.

Borsa (ai compagni).
Tacete, c' è Rigoletto.

Ceprano.
Vittoria doppia! L'uccideremo.

Borsa.
No: chè domani più rideremo.

Marullo.
Or tutto aggiusto.

Rigoletto.
(Chi parla quà?)

Marullo.
Ehi, Rigoletto?—di

Rigoletto (con voce terribile).
Chi va là?

Marullo.
Eh, non mangiarci—son—

Rigoletto.
Chi?

Marullo.
Marullo.

Rigoletto.
In tanto bugo lo squardo è nullo.

Marullo.
Quì ne condusse ridevol cosa;
Tòrre a Ceprano vogliam la sposa.

Rigoletto.
(Ohimè, respiro.)   Ma come entrare?

Marullo (a CEPRANO).
La vostra chiave?
            (A RIGOLETTO.)
Non dubitare;
Non de mancarci lo stratagemma.
    (Gli dà chiave avuta da CEPRANO.)
Ecco le chiavi.

Rigoletto (palpandole).
Sento il suo stemma.
(Ah, terror vano fu dunque il mio!)

        (Respirando.)
N' è là palazzo—con vio son io.

Marullo.
Siam mascherati.

Rigoletto.

Then so will I be;
Give me here a mask.

Marullo.

Well, here is one.
You shall hold the ladder.

(Puts a mask on the face of RIGOLETTO, fastens it by a handkerchief across his eyes, and places him at a ladder, against the terrace wall, to keep it steady.)

Rigoletto.

How very dark it has become!

Marullo.

The bandage renders him both blind and
deaf.
(To his companions.)

All.

Silence! silence! while vengeance we seek;
In his own trap now let him be caught;
The jester who constantly makes us his
sport,
Shall now, in his turn, our laughter provoke.
Hush! be quiet! his mistress we'll seize,
And, to-morrow, at court have our laugh.

(Some ascend to the terrace, force a window, by which they enter, and descend to the door, which they open to others, who enter and drag out GILDA. She has her mouth gagged with a handkerchief. While being dragged across the stage, a scarf falls from her.)

Gilda.

Help! help! Father, dear, help!

Chorus.

Victory!

Gilda.

Help! help!
(At a distance.)

Rigoletto.

Is it not yet done? What a capital joke!
(Putting his hands to his face.)
Why, my eyes are bandaged!

(He snatches off the bandage and mask, and, by the light of the lantern, recognizes the scarf, and sees the door open; he rushes in, and drags out GIOVANNA, greatly frightened; he fixes his eyes upon her in stupefaction, tears his hair in agony, and, after many ineffectual efforts to speak, exclaims:)

Ah! this is the Malediction!
(Swoons.)

END OF ACT I.

Rigoletto.

Ch' io pur mi mascheri;
A me una larva?

Marullo.

Sì pronta è già.
Terrai la scala.

(Gli mette una maschera, e nello stesso tempo lo benda col un fazzoletto, e lo pone a reggere una scala, che avranna appostata al terrazzo.)

Rigoletto.

Fitta è la tenebra!

Marullo.

La benda cieco e sordo il fa.
(A compagni.)

Tutti.

Zitti, zitti, moviamo a vendetta,
Ne sia còlto, or che meno l'aspetta.
Derisorë sì audace constante
A sua volta schernito sarà!
Cheti, cheti, rubiamgli l'amante,
E la Corte doman riderà.

(Alcuni salgono al terrazzo, rompon la porta del primo piano, scendono, aprono ad altri ch'entrano dalla strada, e riescono, trascinando GILDA, la quale avrà la bocca chiusa da un fazzoletto. Nel traversare la scena ella perde una sciarpa.)

Gilda.

Soccorso, padre mio——

Coro.

Vittoria!

Gilda.

Aita!
(Più lontano.)

Rigoletto.

Non han finito ancor! qual derisione!
(Si tocca gli occhi.)
Sono bendato!

(Si strappa impetuosamente la benda e la maschera, ed al chiarore d'una lanterna scordata riconosce la sciarpa; vede la porta aperta, entra, ne trae GIOVANNA spaventata; la fissa con istapore, si strappa i capelli senza poter gridare; finalmente, dopo molti sforzi, esclama:)

Ah!—la Maledizione!

FINE DELL' ATTO PRIMO

ACT II.

SCENE I—Salon in the DUKE's Palace. Large folding-doors in back-scene, and smaller ones on each side, above which hang portraits of the DUKE and the DUCHESS. A table covered with velvet, handsome chairs, and other appropriate furniture.

(Enter the DUKE, by centre doorway, much agitated.)

Duke.

She has been stolen from me!

But how, and by whom? Oh, heavens!

Thus to lose her at the very moment

When my passion most demanded her!

The door was wide open—the house deserted!

Whither can the dear angel have flown!

She who first within this wandering heart

The joys of a true love hath awakened—

She so pure that, by her modest bearing,

To truthfulness I feel me now inclined.

She has been stolen from me! But, to do it,

Who has dared! On him shall vengeance alight!

Grief for my beloved one vengeance demands!

ATTO II.

SCENA I—Salotto nel Palazzo DUCALE. Vi sono due porte laterali, una maggiore nel fondo che si chiude. A suoi lati pendono i ritrati, in tutta figura, a sinistra, d. DUCA, a destra della sua sposa. V' ha un seggiolone pre: una tavola coperta di velluto, ed altri mobili.

(Entra il DUCA, dal mezzo, agitato.)

Duca.

Ella mia fu rapita!

E quando, o ciel?—ne' brevi istanti, prima.

Che un mio presagio interno

Sull' orma corsa ancora mi spingesse!

Schiuso era l'uscio! la magion deserta!

E dove ora sarà quell' angiol caro!

Colei che potè prima in questo core

Destar la fiamma di costanti affetti?

Colei sì pura, al cui modesto accento

Quasi tratto a virtù talor mi credo!

Ella mi fu rapita!

E chi l'ardiva?—ma ne avrò vendetta:

Lo chiede il pianto della mia diletta.

PARMI VEDER LE LAGRIME — *DEAR MAID, EACH TEAR*   Air (Duke)

Par - mi ve - der le la - gri - me Scor - ren - ti da_ quel ci - glio,
Dear maid, each tear of thine that falls, Each sad sigh that bos - om heav - ing,

Quand - do fra il dub - bio e l'an - sia Del su - bi - to pe -
Pin - ing with - in some dark walls, Fills me_ with pain and

reg - lio, Dell' a - mor no - stro me - mo - re, Dell' a - mor no - stre
griev - ing. Ah! vain - ly didst thou cry to me, Ah!_ vain - ly didst thou.

me - mo - re, Il suo Gual - tier chia - mò. Ned ei pe - tea soc -
cry_ to me, "Help me, dear Wal - ter, help!" I then, a - las! was

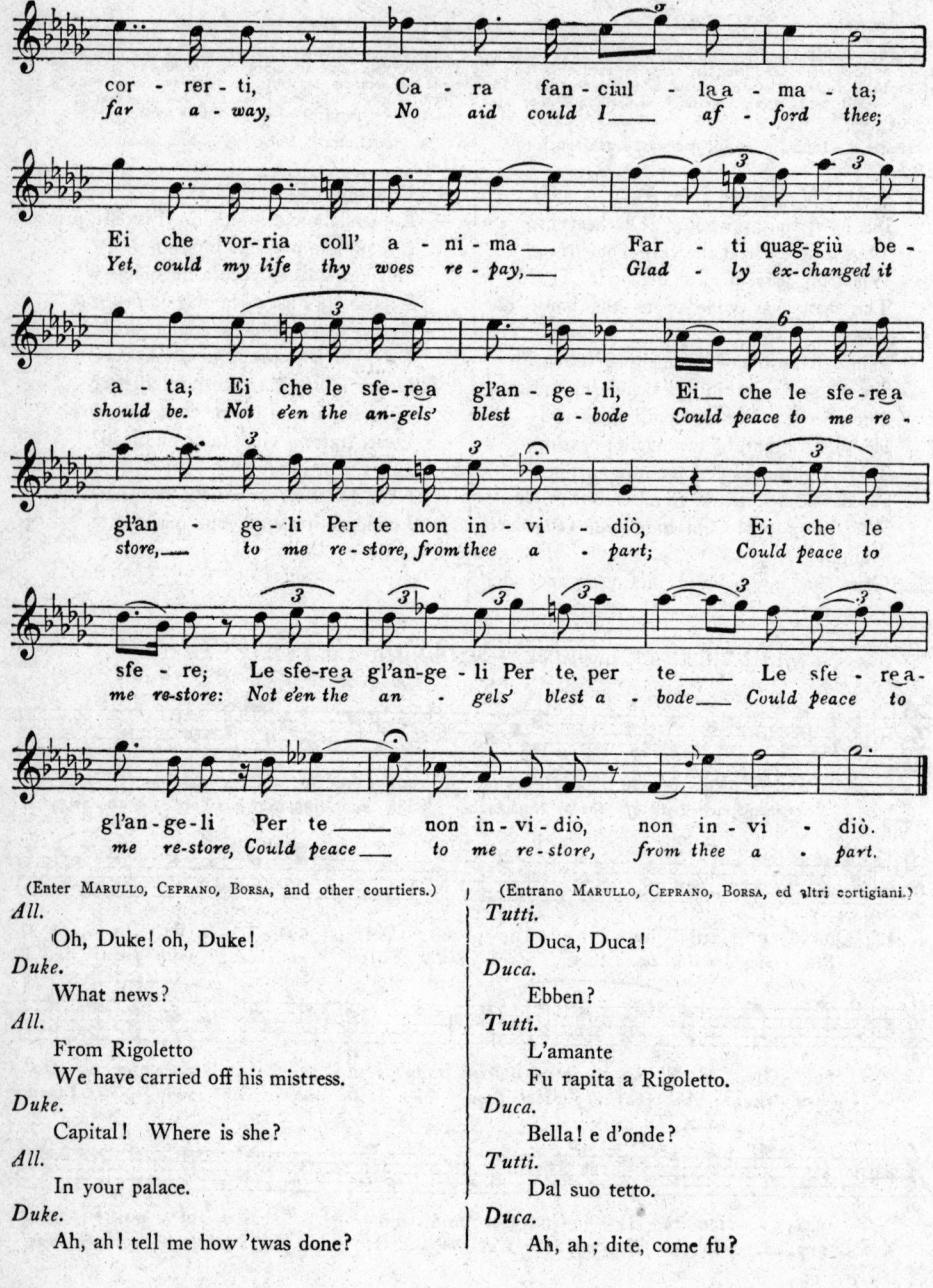

cor - rer - ti,   Ca - ra fan - ciul - laa a - ma - ta;
far   a - way,   No aid could I___ af - ford thee;

Ei che vor - ria coll' a - ni - ma___   Far - ti quag - giù be -
Yet, could my life thy woes re - pay,___   Glad - ly ex - changed it

a - ta; Ei che le sfe - rea gl'an - ge - li, Ei che le sfe - rea
should be. Not e'en the an - gels' blest a - bode Could peace to me re -

gl'an - ge - li Per te non in - vi - diò,   Ei che le
store,___ to me re - store, from thee a - part;   Could peace to

sfe - re; Le sfe - rea gl'an - ge - li Per te, per te___ Le sfe - rea
me re - store: Not e'en the an - gels' blest a - bode___ Could peace to

gl'an - ge - li Per te___ non in - vi - diò, non in - vi - diò.
me re - store, Could peace___ to me re - store, from thee a - part.

(Enter MARULLO, CEPRANO, BORSA, and other courtiers.)

All.

  Oh, Duke! oh, Duke!

Duke.

  What news?

All.

  From Rigoletto

  We have carried off his mistress.

Duke.

  Capital! Where is she?

All.

  In your palace.

Duke.

  Ah, ah! tell me how 'twas done?

(Entrano MARULLO, CEPRANO, BORSA, ed altri cortigiani.)

Tutti.

  Duca, Duca!

Duca.

  Ebben?

Tutti.

  L'amante

  Fu rapita a Rigoletto.

Duca.

  Bella! e d'onde?

Tutti.

  Dal suo tetto.

Duca.

  Ah, ah; dite, come fu?

SCORRENDO UNITI — *AS WE WITH GLEE* (Chorus)

Scor-ren-dou-ni-ti re-mo-ta
As we with glee on mis-chief bent last

vi-a Bre-v'o-ra do-po ca-du-toil
night roved, When hush'd in peace-ful sleep the world seem'd

dì,— Co-me pre-vi-sto ben s'e-ra in pri-a, Ra-ra bel-
bu-ried, The one we sought we met, a-lone, mis-trust-ing, Be-side the

tà ci si sco-pri, ci si sco-pri. E-ra l'a-
house in which we guess'd the bird was caged. The charm-ing

man-te di Ri-go-let-to Che, vis-ta ap-
fair was Ri-go-let-to's mis-tress; But she af-

pe-na, si di-le-guò.— Già di ra-pir-la s'a-vea il pro-
fright-ed to her home then ran;— The jest-er then ap-pear'd, with whom we

get-to, Quan-do il buf-fon ver noi spun-tò, ver noi spun-
sport-ed: "Give us thy aid, Ce-pra-no's wife to steal a-

tò; Che di Ce-pra-no noi la Con-tes-sa Ra-pir vo-
way!" The trap he fell in; oh, sport worth tell-ing! A ban-dage

les - si - mo, stol-to, cre - de; La sca - la quin - di all' uo - po
then we placed be - fore his eyes; A lad - der quick - ly placed to the

mes - sa, Ben - da - to_ei stes - so fer - ma te -
win - dow, We bade him stand by, and firm - ly

nè, La sca - la quin - di_ei stes - so_ei stes - so fer-ma, fer-ma te-nè.
hold. Ah, yes, he firm - ly held the lad - der; the lad - der firm-ly held.

All.	**Tutti.**
In haste we mounted, and searched the chambers,	Salimmo, e rapida la giovinetta,
And with the lady away we sped;	Ci venne, fatte quinci asportar.
But when he'd found out the trick we'd played him,	Quand' ei s'accorse della vendetta
He raved for vengeance upon our heads.	Restò scornato ad imprecar.
Duke.	**Duca.**
(What do I hear? Of my own charmer they are speaking!	(Che sento?—è dessa la mia diletta!
I have yet a chance of regaining her.)	Ah, tutto il cielo non mi rapì!)
But where is the poor creature to be found?	Ma dove or trovasi, la poveretta?
(To the Chorus.)	
All.	(Al Coro.)
	Tutti.
All proper care we have taken of her.	Fu da noi stessi addotta or qui.

POSSENTE AMOR — *TO HER I LOVE*   Air (Duke)

Pos - sen - te_a-mor mi chia - ma, Vo-lar io deg - gio a
To her I love with rap - ture, I must with speed flee a -

le - i; Il ser - to mio da - rei____ Per____ con-so - lar____ quel
way;____ All thought of her base cap - ture I'll gen - tly soothe a -

cor. Il ser - to mio da - rei _____ Per con - so - lar_ quel_
way; All thought of her base cap - ture I'll gen - tly soothe a -

cor. Ah! sap - pi al - fin chi l'a - ma Co - no - sca al - fin chi
way. From her my name and sta - tion I can - not now con -

so - no, Ap - pren - do ch'an - co in tro - no Ha deg - li schia - vi A -
ceal, _____ Yet, free from ob - ser - va - tion, I may my love re -

mor; Ap - - pren - do ch'an - co in tro - no, ch'an - co in
veal; I _____ may_____ my_____ love re - veal_____ I_____ may my

tro - no Ha deg - li schia - vi, Ha_ deg - li schia - vi A - mor.
love, yes, my love to her_ re - veal, My_ love to her may re - veal.

(What new thought now has seized him—
A sudden change has just come o'er him.)

Marullo.

Unlucky Rigoletto!—

Chorus.

Here he comes—be silent, all.

(Enter RIGOLETTO.)

All.

Good morning to you, Rigoletto.

Rigoletto.

(They are all of them in the plot.)

Ceprano.

What news do you bring,
Buffoon?

Rigoletto.

More than ever
Are you wearisome to me.

All.

Ah! ah! ah!

(O qual pensiero l'agita
Come congiò d' umor!)

Marullo.

Povero Rigoletto!—

Coro.

Ei vien—silenzio.

(Entra RIGOLETTO.)

Tutti.

Buon giorno, Rigoletto—

Rigoletto.

(Han tutti fatto il colpo!)

Ceprano.

Ch' hai di nuovo,
Buffon?

Rigoletto.

Che dell' usato
Più noioso voi siete

Tutti.

Ah! ah! ah!

Rigoletto.

(Whither can they have carried her?)
(Looking about anxiously.)

All.

(See how uneasy he appears!)

Rigoletto   (sardonically).

Happy I am
To see that no hurt you have taken
From the cold air of last night.

Marullo.

Last night, said you?

Rigoletto.

Yes—Ah! 'twas a capital trick.

Marullo.

I was asleep, all night.

Rigoletto.

Oh! you were asleep! then I have been
dreaming!

(He is about to go, when, seeing a handkerchief on the table, he anxiously examines the cipher on it.)

All.

(See how everything he scrutinizes!)

Rigoletto.

(It is not hers.)
(Throwing it down.)
Is the Duke still sleeping?

All.

Yes, he is still sleeping!
(Enter a Page of the DUCHESS.)

Page.

The Duchess desires to speak to her lord.

Ceprano.

He sleeps.

Page.

Was he not here but lately?

Borsa.

He has gone hunting.

Page.

Without his suite! without arms!

All.

Canst thou not understand,
That for a short time he cannot be seen?

Rigoletto
(who has been anxiously listening, suddenly rushes amongst them, and exclaims:)

Ah! she is here, then. She is with the Duke!

All.

Who?

Rigoletto.

(Dove l'avran nascosta?)
(Spiando inquieto dovunque.)

Tutti.

(Guardate com' è inquieto!)

Rigoletto.

Son felice
Che nulla a voi nuocesse
L'aria di questa notte.

Marullo.

Questa notte!

Rigoletto.

Sì—Ah! fu il bel colpo!

Marullo.

S' ho dormito sempre!

Rigoletto.

Ah! voi dormiste! avrò dunque sognato!

(S'allontana, e vendendo un fazzoletto sopra una tavola ne osserva inquieto la cifra.)

Tutti.

(Ve' come tutto osserva!)

Rigoletto.

(Non è il suo.)
(Gettandolo.)
Dorme il Duca tuttor?

Tutti.

Sì, dorme ancora.
(Entra un Paggio della DUCHESSA.)

Paggio.

Al suo sposo parlar vuol la Duchessa.

Ceprano.

Dorme.

Paggio.

Quì or or con voi non era?

Borsa.

E a caccia.

Paggio.

Senza paggi! senz' armi!

Tutti.

E non capisci
Che vedere per ora non può alcuno?

Rigoletto
(che a parte e stato attentissimo al dialogo, balzande provviso tra loro prorompe).

Ah, ell' è quì dunque! Ell' è col Duca!

Tutti.

Chi?

Rigoletto.

    The maiden whom last night
    From my house you forced away.

All.

    You must be mad.

Rigoletto.

    But I will have her back—she must be here.

All.

    If your mistress you have lost, elsewhere
    Seek for her.

Rigoletto.

    I will have back my daughter!

All.

    His daughter, says he?

Rigoletto.

    Yes, she is my daughter; you will not now
    O'er such a victory exult.
    She is here, I will have her, give her back
      to me!

(He rushes towards the door in the centre, but the courtiers bar his progress.)

    Minions, sycophants, panders, thieves,
    At what price have you my daughter sold?
    Your sordid souls no crime intimidates,
    But priceless is a daughter to her father.
    Restore her, or, though unarmed I am,
    Fearfully shall this hand assail ye;
    Naught on earth can a father dismay,
    When the honor of his child he doth defend!
    Assassins, open that door, and let me pass.

(He again attempts to pass the door, but is restrained by the courtiers; he struggles with them for a while and then sinks exhausted to the ground.)

    Ah! come ye thus all against me!
            (Weeping.)
    Well, see; I weep! Marullo—Signor,
    In heart and mien thou seemest gentle,—
    Tell me where they have my daughter hidden!
    Is she here? Tell me truly! Silent! Why?
    O, my lords, I pray you to have pity on me—
    To an old man give back his daughter!
    To restore her will you nothing cost,
    While to me my child is all the world.

(Enter GILDA, through the doorway on the left. She rushes into the arms of her father.)

Gilda.

    O, my father!

Rigoletto.

    Le giovin che stanotte
    A mio tetto rapisti—

Tutti.

    Tu deliri!

Rigoletto.

    Ma la saprò riprender—Ella è quì.

Tutti.

    Se l'amante perdesti, la ricerca
    Altrove.

Rigoletto.

    Io vo' mia figlia!

Tutti.

    La sua figlia!

Rigoletto.

    Sì, la mia figlia—D'unta tal vittoria—
    Che? adesso non ridete?
    Ella è là, la vogl' io, la renderete.

(Corre verso la porta di mezzo, ma i cortigiani gli attraversano il passaggio.)

    Cortigiani, vil razza dannata,
    Per qual prezzo vendeste il mio bene?
    A voi nulla per l'oro sconviene,
    Ma mia figlia è impagabil tesor.
    La rendete—o se pur disarmata
    Questa man per voi fora cruenta;
    Nulla in terra più l'uomo paventa,
    Se dei figli difende l'onor.
    Quella porta, assassina, m'aprite:

(Si getta ancor sulla porta che gli è nuovamente contesa dai gentiluomini; lotta alquanto, poi torna spossato sul davanti del teatro.)

    Ah! voi tutti a me contro venite!
            (Piange.)
    Ebben piango—Marullo—signore,
    Tu ch' hai l'alma gentil come il core,
    Dimmi or tu, dove l'hanno nascosta?
    E là? E vero? tu taci? perchè?
    Miei signori—Perdono, pietate;
    Al vegliardo la figlia ridate;
    Ridornarla a voi nulla ora costa,
    Tutto il mondo è tal figlia per me.

(Entra GILDA, ch'esce dalla stranza a sinistra, e si getta nelle paterne braccia.)

Gilda.

    Mio padre!

Rigoletto.

O God! my own Gilda!
Signors, in her you behold
My whole family. Have no further fear,
My angel child! It was a joke—was it not
so?   (To the courtiers.)
I wept, but now I laugh. Yet thou—why
    weepest thou?

Gilda.

For shame, father! I have been maltreated!

Rigoletto.

Heaven! what say'st thou?

Gilda

What I have to say no one else must hear.

Rigoletto

(turning towards the courtiers, imperatively).
Away, away! all of ye!
And if your Duke should hither dare approach,
Tell him not to enter—for I am here.
    (Falling into a chair.)

All.

(With children and madmen
It is sometimes well to simulate;
Therefore will we depart; but what he does
We will not fail unseen to watch.)
(Exeunt through doorway in front, closing it after them.

Rigoletto.

Now speak—we are alone.

Gilda.

(Heaven, now grant me courage!)
Whene'er to church I went,
There my prayers to say,
A youth of handsome mien
Before me always stood.
Although our lips were silent,
Our hearts discoursed through our eyes.
Stealthily, in night's darkness,
While alone, he came to me:
"A student poor am I,"
Plaintively he said to me;
And with ardent sighings
His love for me protested.
Then he left me; and my heart
To hope's bright visions opened,
When men ferocious and unlook'd-for
Tore me from our home away.

Rigoletto.

Dio! mia Gilda!
Signori, in essa è tutta
La mia famiglia. Non temer più nulla,
Angelo mio—fu scherzo non è vero?
    (Ai cortigiani.)
Io che pur piansi or rido—E tu a che piangi?

Gilda.

Ah! l'onta, padre mio!

Rigoletto.

Cielo! che dici?

Gilda.

Arrossir voglio innanzi a voi soltanto.

Rigoletto

(trivolto ai cortigiani, con imperioso modo.)
Ite di quà, voi tutti—
Se il Duca vostro d'appressarsi osasse,
Che non entri gli dite, e ch' io ci sono
    (Si abbandona sul seggiolone.)

Tutti.

(Co' fanciulli e coi dementi
Spesso giova il simular.
Partiam pur, ma quel ch' ei tenti
Non lasciamo d'osservar.)
    (Escon dal mezzo e chindon la porta.*

Rigoletto.

Parla—siam soli.

Gilda.

(Ciel, dammi corraggio!)
Tutte le feste al tempio
Mentre pregava Iddio,
Bello e fatale un giovane
S'offerse àl guardo mio—
Se i labbri nostri tacquero,
Dagli occhi il cor parlò.
Furtivo fra le tenebre
Sol iera a me giungeva;
Sono studente, povero,
Commosso mi diceva,
E con ardente palpito
Amor mi protestò.
Parti—i! mio core aprivasi
A speme più gradita,
Quando improvvisi apparvere
Color che m' han rapita.

And hither forcibly brought me,
To my ruin and dismay.

Rigoletto.

Stop—say no more, my angel—
(I know all! Avenging Heaven,
Upon my head falls the infamy
I have of thee invoked!) O God!
That she might be exalted,
How miserably have I fallen!
Ah! often near the altar
The scaffold should be reared;
But now all is out of order,
And e'en the altar desecrated.
Weep, my child, and let thy tears
Within thy father's bosom fall.

Gilda.

Father, like an angel you speak to me
These words of consolation.

Rigoletto.

What must be done I will quickly dispose of,
And then for ever will we quit this fatal place.

Gilda.

Yes!

Rigoletto.

How changed in one short day may be our destiny!

(Enter a Herald and the COUNT MONTERONE, who is marched across the back of the stage, between guards.)

Herald.

Make way; he is ordered to the prison of Castiglion.

(To the guards.)

Monterone.

Since in vain thou hast by me been cursed,
(Stopping before the portrait.)
The wrath of neither heaven nor earth can reach thee,
And happy wilt thou yet live, O Duke!
(Exit, between the guards.)

Rigoletto.

No, old man, not so—thou shalt be avenged!
Yes, vengeance, dire vengeance, awaits thee!
The one hope of my soul is thee to punish!
And the hour of retribution is nigh
That to thee shall prove fatal.

E a forza quì m'addussero
Nell' ansia più crudel.

Rigoletto.

Non dir; non più, mio angelo.
(T'intendo, avverso ciel!
Solo per me l'infamia
A te chiedeva, o Dio!
Ch' ella potesse ascendere
Quanto caduto er' io;
Ah! presso del patibolo
Bisogna ben l'altare!
Ma tutto ora scompare;
L'altar si roversciò!)
Piangi, fanciulla, e scorrere
Fa il pianto sul mio cor.

Gilda.

Padre, in voi parla un angelo
Per me consolator.

Rigoletto.

Compiuto pur quanto a fare mi resta,
Lasciare potremo quest' aura funesta.

Gilda.

Sì.

Rigoletto.

(E tutto un sol giorno cangiare potè!)

(Entra un Usciere ed il CONTE DI MONTERONE, che dalla destra attraversa il fondo della sala fra gli alabardieri.)

Usciere.

Schiudete—ire al carcere Castiglion dee.

(Alle guardie.)

Monterone.

Poichè fosti invano, da me maledetto,
(Fermandosi verso il ritratto.)
Nè un fulmine o un ferro colpiva il tuo petto,
Felice per anco, o Duca, vivrai—
(Esce fra le guardie dal mezzo.)

Rigoletto.

No, vecchio, t'inganni—un vindice avrai.
Sì, vendetta, tremenda vendetta
Di quest' anima è solo desio—
Di punirti giè—l'ora s'affretta,
Che fatale per te tuonerà.

Like thunder from the heavens hurled,
Shall fall the blow of the despised buffoon.

Gilda.

O father dear, what joy ferocious
I see your flashing eyes light up!
Ah! pardon him, as we ourselves
The pardon of heaven hope to gain.
(I dare not say how much I love him,
And pity him who none for me hath
shown!)

(*Exeunt, through centre door.*)

END OF THE SECOND ACT.

ACT III.

SCENE I—A desolate place on the banks of the Mincio.
On the right, with its front to the audience, a house, two
stories high, in a very dilapidated state, which is nevertheless used as an inn. The doors and walls are so full of
crevices, that whatever is going on within can be seen from
without. In front, the road and the river. In the distance,
the city of Mantua. It is night.

(GILDA and RIGOLETTO discovered, in apparent altercation,
SPARAFUCILE seen in the house, cleaning his belt, unconscious
of what is going on outside.)

Rigoletto.

Yet you love him?

Gilda.

I cannot help it.

Rigoletto.

Surely
This madness ere now you should have con-
    quered.

Gilda.

Yet I love him!

Rigoletto.

How weak is the heart of woman!
Her vile seducer she'd forgive—
But avenged thou shalt be, my Gilda.

Gilda.

Have pity on him, dear father!

Rigoletto.

If of his treachery I convince you,
Will you then from your heart discard him?

Gilda.

I do not know;—but he to me is true.

Rigoletto.

He!

Come fulmin scagliato da Dio
Il buffone colpirti saprà.

Gilda.

O, mio padre, qual gioja feroce,
Balenarvi negli occhi vegg' io!
Perdonate—a noi pure una voce
Di perdono dal cielo verrà.
(Mi tradiva, pur l'amo, gran Dio,
Per l'ingrato ti chiedo pietà!)

(*Escon dal mezzo.*)

FINE DELL' ATTO SECONDO.

ATTO III.

SCENA I—Deserta sponda del Mincio. A sinistra è una
casa in due piani, mezzo diroccata, la cui fronte, volta allo
spettatore, lascia vedere per una grande arcata l'interno
d'una rustica osteria; il muro poi n' è sì pien di fessure, che
dal di fuori si può facilmente scorgere quanto avviene nell'
interno. Al di là del fiume è Mantova. E notte.

(GILDA e RIGOLETTO inquieto, sono sulla strada. SPARAFU-
CILE nell' interno dell' osteria, seduto presso una tavola sta
ripulendo il suo cinturone, senza nulla intenders di quanto
accade al di fuori.)

Rigoletto.

E l'ami?

Gilda.

Sempre.

Rigoletto.

Pure
Tempo a guarirne t' ho lasciato.

Gilda.

Io l'amo.

Rigoletto.

Povero cor di donna! Ah, il vile infame!
Ma avrai vendetta, o Gilda—

Gilda.

Pietà, mio padre—

Rigoletto.

E se tu certa fossi
Ch' ei ti tradisse, l'ameresti ancora?

Gilda.

Nol so, ma pur m'adora.

Rigoletto.

Egli!

Gilda.	*Gilda.*
Yes.	Sì.
Rigoletto.	*Rigoletto.*
Well, then, this way come, and see.	Ebbene, osserva dunque.
(He conducts her to one of the crevices in the wall, and motions her to look through.)	(La conduce presso una delle fezzure del muro, ed ella vi guarda.)
Gilda.	*Gilda.*
A man, surely,	Un uomo
I see!	Vedo.
Rigoletto.	*Rigoletto.*
Wait a little longer.	Per poco attendi.
(Enter the DUKE, dressed as a private soldier, through a door on the left, opening into the ground-floor room.)	(Entra il DUCA, in assisa di semplice officiale di cavalleria nella sala terrena per un aporta a sinistra.)
Gilda.	*Gilda.*
Ah, my father!	Ah, padre mio!
(Surprised.)	(Trasalendo.)
Duke.	*Duca.*
Two things I want, and quickly.	Due cose, e tosto—
(To SPARAFUCILE.)	(A SPARAFUCILE.)
Sparafucile.	*Sparafucile.*
What are they?	Quali?
Duke.	*Duca.*
A room and some wine.	Una stanza e del vino—
Rigoletto.	*Rigoletto.*
(His usual custom, no doubt.)	(Son questi i suoi costumi!)
Sparafucile.	*Sparafucile.*
(Oh! the fine gentleman!)	(Oh, il bel zerbino!)
(Goes off into an adjoining room.)	(Parte nella vicina stanza.)

LA DONNA E MOBILE — *HOW FICKLE WOMEN ARE*   Air (Duke)

gne - ro   La_ don-na è - mo - bil   Qual piu-ma al ven - to,
o - cean.   Yet_ there's no feel - ing   Love's pleas-ure steal - ing,

Mu - ta d'ac - cen - to_   e_ di pen - sier,   Their
Like that of seal - ing Their lips_ with a kiss,

e_ di pen - sier!   e, _____   e_ di pen - sier!
lips_ with a kiss!   Their_____   lips with a_ kiss!

(Re-enter SPARAFUCILE, with a bottle of wine and two glasses, which he places on the table, and then twice strikes the ceiling with the hilt of his sword. At this signal, MADDELENE, a smiling lass, in Gipsy costume, descends by a ladder. The DUKE approaches to embrace her, but she repulses him. Meanwhile SPARAFUCILE goes out into the road, and says to RIGOLETTO:)	(Rientra SPARAFUCILE, con una bottiglia di vino e due bicchieri, che depone sulla tavola, quindi batte col pomo della sua lunga spada due colpi al soffito. A quel segnale, una ridente GIOVANE, in costume di Zingara, scenda a salti la scala. Il DUCA corre per abbracciarla, ma ella gli sfugge. Frattanto SPARAFUCILE, uscito sulla via, dice a parte a RIGOLETTO:)
Your man is there! Is he to live or die?	E là il vostr' uomo—viver dee o morire?
Rigoletto.	*Rigoletto.*
Wait awhile; and then my pleasure you shall learn.	Più tardi tornero l'opra a compire.
(SPARAFUCILE goes off between the house and the river, GILDA and RIGOLETTO remaining in the road.)	(SPARAFUCILE si allontana dietro la casa lungo il fiume GILDA e RIGOLETTO sulla via.)
Duke.	*Duca.*
One day, if I remember rightly,	Un dì, se ben rammentomi,
O beauty bright, I thee encountered,	O, bella, t'incontrai,
And ever since I've sought thee out,	Mi piacque di te chiedere,
Till here at last I've found thee;	E intesi che quì stai.
Ah! now believe me, while I swear,	Or sappi, che d'allora
That henceforth this heart will thee adore.	Sol te quest' alma adora.
Maddelene.	*Maddalena.*
Ah, ah! and since then twenty others	Ah, ah!—e vent' altre appresso
Are by you quite as much remembered,	Le scorda forse adesso?
(To give the gentleman his due, though,	(Ha un' aria il signorino
He has a cavalier-like bearing.)	Da vero libertino.)
Duke.	*Duca.*
Yes; a bad one I am!	Sì; un mostro son!
(Attempts to kiss her.)	(Per abbraciarla.)
Maddelene.	*Maddalena.*
Leave me alone,	Lasciatemi,
Stupid, do.	Stordito.
Luke.	*Duca.*
Eh! what a fuss!	Ih! che fracasso!

Maddelene.

Be quiet, will you?

Duke.

If you'll be gentle,
And not make so much resistance.
When the joys of love await us,
Virtue need not be so prudish.
(Taking her hand.)
How beautiful and white your hand is.

Maddelene.

You're pleased to joke me, signor.

Duke.

No, no.

Maddelene.

I know I'm ugly.

Duke.

Embrace me.

Maddelene.

Thou'rt drunk!

Duke.

With love of thee I may be.
(Laughing.)

Maddelene.

Signor, these words unmeaning
Why to me address?

Duke.

No, no—I will marry you.

Maddelene.

Your word of honor, then, give me.

Duke.

Most lovely of your sex art thou!
(Ironically.)

Rigoletto.

Well! have you now heard enough?
(To GILDA, who has seen and heard all that has passed.)

Gilda.

Oh! the wicked traitor!

Duke.

Ah! of Venus the fairest daughter,
The slave of your charms here behold;
One word from thy beautiful lips
My suffering alone can assuage;
Come, and my fond heart relieve
Of its anxious palpitations.

Maddelene.

Ah, ah! with all my heart I laugh
At stories which so little cost;

Maddalena.

Stia saggio.

Duca.

E tu sii docile,
Non farmi tanto chiasso.
Ogni saggezza chiudesi
Nel guadio e nell' amore.
(Le prende la mano.)
La bella mano candida!

Maddalena.

Scherzate voi, signore.

Duca.

No, no.

Maddalena.

Son brutta.

Duca.

Abbracciami.

Maddalena.

Ebro.

Duca.

D'amore ardente.
(Ridendo.)

Maddalena.

Signor, l'indifferente,
Vi piace canzonar?

Duca.

No, no—ti vo' sposar.

Maddalena.

Ne voglio la parola.

Duca.

Amabile figliuola!
(Ironico.)

Rigoletto.

Ebben?—ti basta ancor?
(A GILDA, che avrà tutto osservato ed inteso.)

Gilda.

Iniquo traditor!

Duca.

Bella figlia dell' amore,
Schiavo son de' vezzi tuoi;
Con un detto sol tu puoi
Le mie pene consolar.
Vieni, e senti del mio core
Il frequente palpitar.

Maddalena.

Ah! ah! rido bèn di core,
Chè tai baie costan poco;

Your jokes I prize, you may believe me,
At just as much as they are worth.
Accustomed am I, my gallant signor,
To badinage as good as this.

Gilda.

Ah! thus to me of love he spoke,
Thus the wretch hath me betrayed;
Unhappy me!—forlorn, deserted,
With anguish how my heart doth ache!
Oh! what a weak credulity
In such a libertine to trust!

Rigoletto.

Be silent;—now to grieve is useless;
That he deceived thee thus thou see'st;
Be silent, and on me depend
Vengeance eternal to insure;
Prompt as dreadful shall it be—
Like thunder on his head 'twill fall!
Hear me;—at once to the house return,
What gold you may require there obtain;
A horse provide, and the apparel of a youth;
Then to Verona hasten,
Where to-morrow I will join thee.

Gilda.

Come now with me.

Rigoletto.

Impossible.

Gilda.

I tremble.

Rigoletto.

Go.

(Exit Gilda.)

(Rigoletto goes behind the house, and returns in conversation with Sparafucile. During the scene between them the Duke and Maddeline remain seated in the inn, talking, laughing, and drinking.)

Rigoletto.

Twenty crown-pieces, say you?—Here are ten;
When the deed is done, ten more you shall have.
Is he still here?

Sparafucile.

Yes.

Rigoletto.

At the hour of midnight.
I shall return.

Quanto valga il vostro giuoco,
Mel credete, so apprezzar.
Sono avvezza, bel signore,
Ad un simile schervar.

Gilda.

Ah! così parlar d'amore
A me pur l'infame ho udito!
Infelice cor tradito,
Per angoscia non scoppiar.
Perchè o credulo mio core,
Un tal uom dovevi amar!

Rigoletto.

Taci, il piangere non vale;
(A Gilda.)
Ch' ei mentiva or sei secura—
Taci, e mia sarà la cura
La vendetta, d'affrettar.
Pronta fia, sarà fatale;
Io saprollo fulminar.
M'odi, ritorna a casa—
Oro prendi, un destriero,
Una veste viril che t'apprestai,
E per Verona parti—
Sarrovvi io pur domani—

Gilda.

Or venite.

Rigoletto.

Impossibil.

Gilda.

Tremo.

Rigoletto.

Va.

(Gilda parte.)

(Rigoletto va dietro la casa, e ritorna parlando con Sparafucile e contandogli della monete. Durante questa scena e la sequente il Duca e Maddalena stanno fra loro parlando, ridendo, bevendo.)

Rigoletto.

Venti scudi hai tu detto? Eccone dieci;
E dopo l'opera il resto.
Ei quì rimane?

Sparafucile.

Sì.

Rigoletto.

Alla mezzanotte
Ritornerò.

Sparafucile.

You need not hurry.

Alone into the river I can cast him.

Rigoletto.

No, no,—I wish to throw him in myself.

Sparafucile.

Well, so let it be.   But what is his name?

Rigoletto.

Perhaps of both you'd like to know the
names?

His name is *Crime,* and mine is *Punishment.*

(Exit—the darkness increases, distant thunder heard.)

Sparafucile.

A storm in the distance is arising;

Darker the night is becoming.

Duke.

Maddelene!
                    (Attempting to take hold of her.)

Maddelene.

Desist—my brother comes.
                    (Repelling him.)

Duke.

Well, what matters his coming?
                    (Thunder.)

Maddelene.

It thunders.
                    (Enter SPARAFUCILE.)

Sparafucile.

And rain is coming.

Duke.

So much the better;

I will lodge here—in the stable you may
sleep—

Or in the regions below—or where you
please.

Sparafucile.

Thank you.

Maddelene.   (Aside to the DUKE.)

(Ah, no—depart.)

Duke   (to MADDELENE).

In such weather as this?

Sparafucile   (to MADDELENE).

Twenty crowns of gold, remember.

Signor,

To offer you my room I shall be happy:

At once I'll show you to it, if you please.

(He takes a light, and goes toward the staircase.)

Sparafucile.

Non cale,

A gettarlo nel fiume basto io solo.

Rigoletto.

No, no,—il vo' far io stesso.

Sparafucile.

Sia—il suo nome?

Rigoletto.

Vuoi saper anco il mio?

Egli è *Delitto, Punizion* son io.

(Parte—Il cielo ci oscura e tuona.)

Sparafucile.

La tempesta è vicinia.

Più scura fia la notte.

Duca.

Maddalena!
                    (Per prenderla.)

Maddalena.

Aspettate—mio fratello viene.
                    (Sfuggendogli.)

Duca.

Che importa?
                    (S' ode il tuona.)

Maddalena.

Tuona.
                    (Entra SPARAFUCILE.)

Sparafucile

E pioverà tra poco.

Duca.

Tanto meglio.

Io qui mi tratterrò—tu dormirai

In scuderia—all' inferno—ove vorra

Sparafucile.

Grazie.

Maddalena.   (Piano al DUCA.)

(Ah, no—partite.)

Duca   (a MADDALENA).

(Con tal tempo?)

Sparafucile   (piano a MADDALENA).

Son venti scudi d'ore.

Ben felice.   (Al DUCA.)

D' offrivi la mia stanza—se a voi piace

Tosto a vederla andiamo.

(Prende una lume e s' avvia per la scaia.)

Duke.

With all my heart—be quick, let me see it.
(Whispers to MADDELENE, and follows SPARAFUCILE.)

Maddelene.

(Poor young man! so much, too, the gentleman!

O God!—what a fearful night is coming!)
(Thunder.)

Duke
(observing that the window has no shutters).

If here you sleep, plenty of air you get.
Well, good night!

Sparafucile.

May God protect you, signor.

Duke.

Quickly I shall be asleep, so weary am I.
(He lays down his hat and sword, throws himself on the bed, and in a short time falls asleep. MADDELENE, below, stands by the table. SPARAFUCILE finishes the contents of the bottle left by the DUKE. Both remain silent for awhile, and apparently in deep thought.)

Maddelene.

What pleasing manners the young man has!

Sparafucile.

Oh, truly; but twenty crowns I'm to have.

Maddelene.

Only twenty! too little! much more he's worth!

Sparafucile.

Go—and, if he sleeps, his sword bring hither.

Maddelene
(ascending, and contemplating him while sleeping).

It is a sin to kill so nice a youth!
(She takes up the DUKE's sword, and begins to descend.)
(Enter GILDA, approaching by the passage, in the attire of a youth, with whip and spurs; she advances slowly towards the house; SPARAFUCILE continues drinking. It lightens and thunders.)

Gilda.

Ah! my reason seems quite to desert me!
Love overcomes me! O father, pardon!
(Thunder.)
What a night of horrors! How will it end?

Maddelene.

Brother!
(Having descended, she deposits the DUKE's sword on the table.)

Gilda.

Who speaks?
(Looking through the crevices.)

Duca.

Ebben sono con te—presto, vediamo.
(Dice una parola all' orecchio di MADDALENA e segue SPARAFUCILE.)

Maddalena.

(Povero giovin!—grazioso tanto!
Dio!—qual mai notte è questa!)
(Tuona.)

Duca
(vedendone il balcone senza imposte).

Si dorme all' aria aperta? bene, bene—
Buona notte.

Sparafucile.

Signor, vi guardi Iddio.

Duca.

Breve sonno dormiam—stanco son io.
(Depone il capello, la spada, e si stende, sul letto, dove in breve addormentasi. MADDALENA frattanto siede presso la tavola. SPARAFUCILE beve dalla bottiglia lasciata dal DUCA—Rimangono ambidue taciturni per qualche istante, e preoccupati da gravi pensieri.)

Maddalena.

E amabile invero cotal giovinotto.

Sparafucile.

Oh sì—venti scudi ne dà di prodotto.

Maddalena.

Sol venti!—son pochi—valeva di più.

Sparafucile.

La spada, s' ei dorme, va, portami giù.

Maddalena
(sale, e contemplando il dormente).

Peccato! è pur bello!
(Prende la spada del DUCA, e scende.)
(Entra GILDA, che comparisce nel fondo della via in costume virile, con stivali e speroni, e lentamente si avanza verso l' osteria, mentre SPARAFUCILE continua a beve. Spess lampi e tuoni.)

Gilda.

Ah, più non ragiono!
Amor mi trascina!—mio padre, perdono!
(Tuona.)
Qual notte d' orrore! Gran Dio, che accadrà.

Maddalena.

Fratello!
(Sara discesa, ed avrà posata la spada del DUCA sulla tavola.)

Gilda.

Chi parla?
(Osserva pella fessura.)

Sparafucile.

To the devil be gone!
    (Seeking something in a cupboard.)

Maddelene.

Handsome as an Apollo is this youth—
I love him—he loves me—so slay him not.

Gilda.

Oh, heavens! (Listening.)

Sparafucile.

Mend the holes in that sack.

Maddelene.

Why?

Sparafucile.

Thy beautiful Apollo I must kill,
And into the river cast.

Gilda.

O hellhound!

Maddelene.

The promised money you may yet obtain
And spare his life.

Sparafucile.

I think that difficult.

Maddelene.

Listen, and hear how easy my project.
Ten crowns already from the hunchback
Thou hast received. In a little time
Hither with the other ten he will come;
Kill him, and then the twenty thou wilt
have.

Sparafucile.

Kill the hunchback! What dost thou suggest?
For a thief, or a swindler, do you take me?
Did I ever a client betray? No!
The man who pays me faithful ever finds
me!

Gilda.

What do I hear? My father!

Maddelene.

Ah, mercy on him!

Sparafucile.

He must die!

Maddelene.

I'll give him a hint to fly.
    (About to go.)

Sparafucile.

Al diavol ten va.
    (Frugando in un credenzone.)

Maddalena.

Somiglia un Apollo quel giovine—io l'amo—
Ei m'ama—riposi—nè più l'uccidiamo.

Gilda.

Oh, cielo! (Ascoltando.)

Sparafucile.

Rattoppa puel sacco—

Maddalena.

Perche?

Sparafucile.

Entr' esso il tuo Apollo, sgozzato da me,
Gettar dovro al fiume.

Gilda.

L'inferno qui vedo!

Maddalena.

Eppure il danaro salvarti scommetto,
Serbandolo in vita.

Sparafucile.

Difficile il credo.

Maddalena.

M'ascolta—anzi facil ti svelo un progetto
De' scudi, già dieci dal gobbo ne avesti;
Venire cogli altri più tardi il vedrai—
Uccidilo, e venti allora ne avrai,
Così tutto il prezzo goder si potrà.

Sparafucile.

Uccider quel gobbo!—che diavol dicesti!
Un ladro son forse? Son forse un bandito!
Qual altro cliente da me fu tradito?
Mi paga quest' uomo—fedele m' avrà.

Gilda.

Che sento! mio padre!

Maddalena.

Ah, grazia per esso.

Sparafucile.

E d'uopo ch' ei muoia—

Maddalena.

Fuggire il fo adesso.
    (Va per saiire.)

Gilda.

   O kind-hearted woman!

Sparafucile.

   The reward we shall lose.

Maddelene.

   That's true.

Sparafucile.

   Let me do it.

Maddelene.

   He must be saved.

Sparafucile.

   Should any other before midnight arrive,
   Him I will slay instead of him now here.

Maddelene.

   The night is dark, through the sky the
      thunder roars,
   No one at such a time this place will pass.

Gilda.

   Oh, what a temptation—for th' ingrate to
      die!
   And for thee, father! O heaven, guide me!
      (The clock strikes the half-hour.)

Sparafucile.

   There is still half an hour.

Maddelene.

   Brother, wait.   (Weeping.)

Gilda.

   What! that woman weep, and I not help
      him!
   Ah! although to my love truthless he be,
   My life for his shall be the sacrifice!
      (Knocks at the door.)

Maddelene.

   Who knocks?

Sparafucile.

   'Tis the wind.

Maddelene.

   Some one knocks, I'm sure.

Sparafucile.

   It is strange.

Maddelene.

   Who's there?

Gilda.

   Have pity on a stranger;
   A lodging grant him for this bitter night.

Gilda.

   Oh, buona figliuola!

Sparafucile.

   Gli scudi perdiamo.

Maddalena.

   E ver!

Sparafucile.

   Lascia fare—

Maddalena.

   Salvarlo dobbiamo.

Sparafucile.

   Se pria ch' abbia il mezzo la notte toccat
   Alcuno qui giunga, per esso morrà.

Maddalena.

   E buia la notte, il ciel troppo irato,
   Nessuno a quest' ora di qui passerà.

Gilda.

   Oh, qual tantazione! morir per l'ingrato
   Morire! e mio padre! Oh, cielo pietà!

      (Battono le undici e mezzo.)

Sparafucile.

   Ancor c' è mezz' ora.

Maddalena.

   Attendi, fratello.   (Piangendo.)

Gilda.

   Che! piange tal donna! Nè a lui darò ait
   Ah, s' egli al mio amore divenne rubell
   Io vo' per la sua gettar la mia vita.
      (Picchia alla porta.)

Maddalena.

   Si picchia?

Sparafucile.

   Fu il vento—

Maddalena.

   Si picchia, ti dico.

Sparafucile.

   E strano!

Maddalena.

   Chi è?

Gilda.

   Pietà d'un mendico;
   Asil per la notte a lui concedete.

Maddelene.

  A long night 'twill be for him!

Sparafucile.

  Wait awhile.

  (He searches the cupboard for something.)

Gilda.

  Ah! so near to death, and yet so young!

  Oh! for these wretches God's pardon I ask;

  Forgive, O father, thine unhappy child!

  And happy live the man I die to save!

Maddelene.

  Now hasten, quick, the fatal deed enact;

  To save one life another I yield up.

Sparafucile.

  Well, I am ready the issue to abide,

  I care not so that the reward I get.

  (He goes behind the doorway with a dagger. MADDELENE
  opens the door, and then runs forward, to close that in
  front. GILDA enters and SPARAFUCILE closes the door. All
  the rest is buried in silence and darkness.)

  (Enter RIGOLETTO, enveloped in a cloak; he advances from
  the road to the front of the scene. The violence of the
  storm has abated, the lightning and thunder still continuing
  occasionally.)

Rigoletto.

  At last the hour of my revenge is nigh;

  Full thirty days and nights for this I've
    waited,

  My soul with tears of blood consuming,

  Under the guise of a buffoon. That door

  (Examining the house.)

  Is shut! 'Tis not yet the hour—I must
    wait.

  What a night of foul mystery is this!

  The heavens in a tempest,

  On the earth a homicide!

  Oh, how truly great do I now feel!

  'Tis midnight!

  (The clock strikes twelve.)

  (Enter SPARAFUCILE, from the house.)

Sparafucile.

  Who is there?

Rigoletto.

  It is I.

  (About to enter.)

Sparafucile.

  Wait where you are.

  (Re-enters the house, and returns, dragging a sack.)

  Your man is here disposed of.

Rigoletto.

  O joy—a light!

Maddalena.

  Fia lunga tal notte!

Sparafucile.

  Alquanto attendete.

  (Va a cercare nel credenzone.)

Gilda.

  Ah, presso alla morte, sì giovane, sono!

  Oh cielo, pegli empi ti chiedo perdono.

  Perdona tu, o padre, a questa infelice!

  Sia l' uomo felice—ch' or vado a salvar.

Maddalena.

  Su, spicciati, presto, fa l'opra compita;

  Anelo una vita—con altra salvar.

Sparafucile.

  Ebbene—son pronto, quell' uscio dischiudi;

  Piucch' altro li scudi—mi preme salvar.

  (Va a postarsi con un pugnale dietro la porta. MADDALENA
  apre, poi corre a chiudere la grande arcata di fronte. Mentre
  entra GILDA, dietro a cui SPARAFUCILE chiude la porta, e
  tutto resta sepolto nel silenzio e nel buoi.)

  (Entra RIGOLETTO, solo, si avanza dal fondo della scena
  chiuso nel suo mantello. La violenza del temporale e dimi-
  nuita, nè più si vede e sente che qualche lampo e tuono.)

Rigoletto.

  Della vendetta olfin giunge l'istante!

  Da trenta di l'aspetto

  Di vivo sangue a lagrime piangendo

  Sotto la larva del buffon—Quest' uscio!

  (Esaminando la casa.)

  E chiuso! Ah, non è tempo ancor! S'at
    tenda.

  Qual notte di mistero!

  Una tempesto in cielo!

  In terra un omicidio!

  Oh, come invero qui grande mi sento!

  Mezza notte!

  (Suona mezza notte.)

  (Entra SPARAFUCILE, dalla casa.)

Sparafucile.

  Chi è là?

Rigoletto.

  Son io.

  (Per entrare.)

Sparafucile.

  Sostate.

  (Rientra, e torna, trascinando un sacco.)

  E qui spento il vostr' uomo—

Rigoletto.

  Oh, gioja! un lume!

Sparafucile.

A light? No—first the money.
(RIGOLETTO hands him a purse.)

Sparafucile.

Let us into the river cast him.

Rigoletto.

No! alone I'll do it.

Sparafucile.

As you please; but this place is not the best;

Higher up, the stream is deeper. Be quick,

That no one may observe you. Good night.
(He re-enters the house.)

Rigoletto.

Here he is!—dead. I should like to see him!

But what matters? 'Tis done! Here are his spurs.

Now will the world again look well with me!

Here is the buffoon, and here his master!

At my feet he lies. It is he! It is he!

Now hath my grief its just revenge attained!

In the sea shall be his sepulchre,

This sack his winding-sheet!

(He tries to drag the sack towards the river, when he is surprised at hearing the voice of the DUKE, who passes along the background.)

What voice is that! Or is it an illusion?

No! no! it is he! it is he himself!
(Greatly alarmed.)

The Malediction! Oh, there! demon of hell!
(Nearing the house with the sack.)

But who, instead of him, can be in the sack!
(Tearing open the sack.)

I tremble. It is a human body!
(Lightning.)

My daughter! O God, my daughter!

Ah, no! it is impossible;

Towards Verona she journeyeth;

A dreadful vision this must be.
(Kneeling down.)

O my Gilda! Tell me who this has done?

The assassin to me reveal! Ho! who's here?
(Knocking violently at the door.)

No one! Oh, my daughter!

Sparafucile.

Un lume? No, il danaro.
(RIGOLETTO gli dà una borsa.)

Sparafucile.

Lesti all' onda il gettiam—

Rigoletto.

No—basto io solo.

Sparafucile.

Come pi piace—Qui men atto è il sito--

Più avanti è più profondo il gorgo—Prestu

Che alcun non vi sorprenda—Buono notte.
(Rientra in casa.)

Rigoletto.

Egli è là! morto! O sì—vorrei vederlo!

Ma che importa! è ben desso! Ecco i suo sproni!

Ora mi guardo, o mondo—

Quest' è un buffone, ed un potente è questo!

Ei sta sotto a' miei piedi. E desso! E desso!

E giunta alfin la tua vendetta, o duolo!

Sia l'onda a lui sepolcro,

Un sacco il suo lenzuolo!

(Fa per trascinare il sacco verso la sponda, quandu è sorpreso dalla lontana voce del DUCA, che nel fondo attraversa la scena.)

Qual voce! illusion notturna è questa!

No! no! egli è desso! è desso!

Maledizione! Olà—dimon bandito?
(Trasalendo verso la casa.)

Chi è mai, chi è qui in sua voce;
(Taglio il sacco.)

Io tremo—E umano corpo!
(Lampeggia.)

Mia figlia! Dio! mia figlia!

Ah no—è impossibil! per Verona è in via!

Fu visïon! E dessa!
(Inginocchiandosi.)

Oh, mia Gilda! fanciulla a me rispondi!

L' assassino mi svela—Olà? Nessuno!
(Picchia disperatamente alla casa.)

Nessun! mia figlia—

Gilda.

    Who calls on me?

Rigoletto.

    She speaks! she moves! she lives! Oh, heaven!

    Ah! my only worldly solace,

    Look on me; dost thou not know me?

Gilda.

    Father!

Rigoletto.

    Unveil this mystery! Art thou wounded?

Gilda.

    The sword pierced me here.

              (Points to her breast.)

Rigoletto.

    Who was it stabbed you?

Gilda.

    I have deceived you! I am guilty!

    Too much I loved him—now I die for him!

Rigoletto.

    (O awful fate, by my hand hath she fallen,

    Of my righteous vengeance the sole victim.)

    Angel dear, look on me, to me listen;

    Speak, oh, speak to me, my darling daughter!

Gilda.

    More I cannot say; pardon me and him!

    O my father, bless your dying daughter.

Gilda.

    Chi mi chiama?

Rigoletto.

    Ella parla! si move! è viva! oh Dio!

    Ah! mio ben solo in terra;

    Mi guarda—mi conosci—

Gilda.

    Ah, padre mio—

Rigoletto.

    Qual mistero! che fu! sei tu ferita?

Gilda.

    L'acciar qui mi piagò—

              (Indicando il core.)

Rigoletto.

    Chi t' ha colpita?

Gilda.

    V' ho ingannata—colpevole fui;

    L'amai troppo—ora muoio per lui!

Rigoletto.

    (Dio tremendo! ella stesso fu côlta

    Dallo stral di mia giusta vendetta!)

    Angiol caro; mi guarda, m'ascolta.

    Parla; parlami, figlia diletta!

Gilda.

    Ah! ch'io tacchia! a me—a lui perdonate;

    Benedite alla figlia, o mio padre.

LASSU IN CIELO — *IN HEAV'N ABOVE* Duet (Rigoletto and Gilda)

GILDA

Las - sù in cie - lo, vi - ci - na al - la ma - dre, In e - ter - no per voi pre - ghe - rò. Non mo - rir, mio te - so - ro pie -
In heav'n a - bove, at the side of my moth - er, There shall my pray'rs be up - lift - ed for thee! Ah! leave me not here a - lone, my on - ly

RIGOLETTO

ta - te, Mi a co - lom - ba, la - sciar - mi non
treas - ure, Part - ed from thee, ten - der dove, all dark will

GILDA

RIG.

Las - sù in cie - lo, vi - ci - na al - la
In heav'n a - bove at the side of my

dêi, no la - sciar - mi non dêi
be. all dark. all dark will be!

ma - dre   In e - ter - no per voi pre - ghe -
moth - er,   *There shall my pray'rs be up - lift - ed for*

Oh mia fi - glia!
Oh, stay, dear child!

rò,   Pre - ghe - rò,   Per voi pre - ghe -
thee!   *There I will pray,*   *I will pray for*

No, la - sciar - mi non dêi   non mo - rir
Ah, no, thou must not die!   *leave me not!*

rò
thee.

Se t'in - vo - li - qui sol qui sol — ri - mar - rei, Non mo - ri - re o qui te - co — mor -
Ah! do not leave me here a - lone, — my — child. Part - ed from thee, my child, all dark — will

Non più A lui per-do-na-te, mio pa-dre, Ad-
And when I'm gone, give him par-don, my fa-ther! Then

ró! O mia fi-glia! o mia Gil-da! no, la-sciar-mi non
bel Oh! stay, my child! Oh! my Gil-da! Leave me not here a-

di—o! las-sù in ciel, las-sù in
fare—well! In heav'n a-bove, In heav'n a-

dêi, non mo,-rir,
lonel do not die!

ciel Pre-ghe-rò, per voi, pre-ghe-
bove, There shall my pray'rs be raised for

No, la-sciar-mi non dêi, non mo-rir,
Leave me' not here a-lone! do not die!

RIG.
Gil-da! mia Gil-da! È mor-ta! Ah! la ma-le-di-zio—ne!
Gil-da! my Gil-da! All's dark, now! Ah! yes, his curse is on—me!

(Falling and tearing his hair over the corpse of his
daughter.) | (Strappendosi e capelli, cade sul cadavere della figlia.)

END OF THE OPERA.

IL TROVATORE
(The Troubadour)

by

GIUSEPPE VERDI

THE STORY OF "IL TROVATORE"

THE old Count di Luna, now deceased, had two sons, not much apart in age. One night, while they were both yet in their infancy and under the care of a nurse, an old gipsy-woman — a tribe which, at that dark age, was universally believed to be closely allied to evil spirits, and possessing great magic powers — was discovered by the servants near the cradle of the youngest of the two children, to whose chamber she had stealthily gained access, while the nurse was asleep. The gipsy was quickly and violently expelled from the castle, but from that day the child's health began to fail. No remedies proving of avail, the old gipsy was suspected of having bewitched the child. Search was instituted, the woman taken prisoner, and, agreeably to the barbarous modes of punishment of the times, burned alive. A daughter of the gipsy, with her child in her arms, witnessed the execution. To her the unhappy victim of superstition bequeathed the task of vengeance. During the night following the young gipsy managed to steal the youngest child of the Count from the castle. She hurried with it to the stake, where the flames were still raging over the remains of her ill-fated mother. Arrived there, and almost out of her senses by the vivid recollection of the horrible scene she had just witnessed, she, by a fatal mistake, hurled her own child into the flames instead of the young Count. She discovered her error too late. But still she was not to be baffled in her dark designs. She fled, taking the child with her, joined her tribe, and brought him up — Manrico, the Troubadour — as her own son, trusting the secret of his parentage to no one, and waiting for a favorable moment to make him the tool of her vengeance against his own kindred.

In the meanwhile the old Count died, leaving the oldest son sole heir of his title and possessions, but doubting, up to his last moment, the death of his last born, although a heap of infant's bones, found among the ashes around the stake, seemed to be proof conclusive.

After this preliminary knowledge we now come to the actual business of the piece.

Manrico, grown up a valiant and daring knight, well skilled in arms, and of high mind and bearing, entered the contest at a tourney disguised, won all the honors, and was crowned victor by the hands of the Duchess Leonora, lady attendant on the Queen. From this moment dated a passionate love, shared by both. The Troubadour made his feelings known by nightly serenades performed below the window of the Duchess.

Unhappily, the Count di Luna (brother to Manrico, although this was unknown to both of them) was also smitten with a deep passion for the Duchess. One night, while the Count was lingering in the gardens attached to the Royal palaces, he suddenly heard the voice of the Troubadour in a thicket close by. Presently a door in the palace buildings opened, the Duchess stole out, and mistaking the Count for his sweet-voiced rival, she hastened towards him. Manrico stepping out from the foliage, she saw her mistake and sought his protection. Hard words passed between the two rivals. The Troubadour unmasked himself, revealing to his antagonist the features of one whose life had been forfeited to the laws by some act of violence against the existing government. The two knights retired with drawn swords to a more secluded spot, leaving the Duchess insensible on the ground.

The duel — this we learn from a conversation between Azucena and her supposed son, at the beginning of the second act — quickly terminated in favor of the Troubadour. The latter had already lifted his sword, to pierce the heart of his adversary, when he felt the influence of some secret power suspending the intended motion. A voice from heaven seemed to say to him, "Spare thy foe." Manrico, obeying reluctantly, retired. Joining the army, opposing his country's forces, he was left for dead on the battle-field of Pelilla. His mother sought him out by night, intending to give him fit burial. She discovered that life was not yet extinct, and had him removed to one of the mountain resorts of her tribe, and there restored him to health. Thus we find him at the beginning of Act Second, yet feeble and suffering.

His Prince, having heard of Manrico's being still alive, despatched a messenger to his retreat, bidding him to repair to the fortress of Castellar and to defend it against the forces of the Count di Luna. At the same time he communicated to him that the Duchess Leonora, believing in the current reports of his death, was about to take the veil that very evening, at a convent in the neighborhood of Castellar. Upon receipt of this message Manrico at once departed, and arrived at the convent just in time to rescue Leonora, who was about to be carried off forcibly by the Count di Luna and his followers. The Troubadour conducted the Duchess to Castellar, which place was immediately enclosed and besieged by the Count di Luna's troops.

Azucena, following Manrico (to whom she had become unconsciously attached) to Castellar, had ventured too far in the lines of the enemy, was taken prisoner and led before the Count,

charged with being a spy. Here it happened that an old servant of the house of Luna, Ferrando, recognized her features. The gipsy, frightened and confounded by this unexpected discovery, called for her son Manrico to protect her. This only added to the Count's wrath, who gave orders to have her burned immediately in face of the castle.

The Troubadour, in the meanwhile, was making preparations to celebrate his union with Leonora on the morrow, when he was informed by the sentinels that a gipsy woman was about to be burned alive in front of the enemy's camp. Quickly recognizing the form of his mother, he gathered a squad of his troops around him and sallied out to rescue his ill-fated mother. But fortune was against him; his forces were repulsed and himself taken.

The Count di Luna, after storming the fortress of Castellar on the day following — but without finding a trace of Leonora — took his prisoners to the capital of the province. Here, on the eve before the day fixed for the execution of son and mother, Leonora suddenly appeared before the Count, offering him her hand in exchange for the life of Manrico. The Count consents, and Leonora is admitted into the dungeon, to restore Manrico to liberty. Before she enters, however, she takes poison, which she carried concealed in a ring on her finger. Manrico refuses to accept of his liberty, accusing the Duchess of basely betraying his affections. During this delay the poison begins to take its effect. Manrico discovers the extent of her sacrifice too late. The Count enters, understands at a glance what has happened, and orders Manrico to be beheaded immediately. While his order is being obeyed, he rouses the gipsy from the stupor in which she has been lying, motionless, in a corner of the dungeon. He drags her to the window, showing her the execution of her supposed son. Then the gipsy triumphantly divulges her secret. "Manrico is thy brother!" exclaims she to the horror-stricken Count, and with a "Mother! thou art avenged," she falls lifeless.

IL TROVATORE

(THE TROUBADOUR)

### ACT I.	### ATTO I.
#### THE DUEL.	#### IL DUELLO.

SCENE I—Vestibule in the palace of Aliaferia, with side door conducting to the apartments of COUNT DI LUNA. FERRANDO and servants of the COUNT reclining near the door. Armed men are seen walking in the background.

Ferrando
> (to the servants, who are falling asleep).

Arouse ye! arouse ye! The Count's approach
Must find us watchful:
Ye know 'tis his wont
Under the casement of his beloved one
To pass whole nights unsleeping.

Servants.

'Tis the venom of jealous doubt
That has entered his bosom.

Ferrando.

This minstrel knight, who in the garden
Sings with his lute at midnight,
Seems a rival not idly dreaded.

Servants.

Pray dispel from our eyelids
The sleep that on us falls,
By now relating the truthful tale
Of Garzia, late brother to Count Luna.

Ferrando.

Be it so;
Come close around me here.
> (The servants cluster around him.)

Soldiers.

We're ready.

Servants.

We hear thee.
> (All surround FERRANDO.)

Ferrando.

With two sons, heirs of fortune and affection,

SCENA I—Atrio nel palazzo dell' Aliaferia; porta da un lato, che mette agli appartamenti del CONTE DI LUNA. FERRANDO, e molti famigliari del CONTE, che giacciono presso la porta, alcuni uomini d'arme che passeggiano in fondo.

Ferrando
> (parla ai famigliari).

All' erta, all' erta! Il Conte
N' è d'uopo attender vigilando; ed egli
Talor, presso i veroni
Della sua cara, intere
Passa le notti.

Famigliari.

Gelosia le fiere
Serpi gli avventa in petto!

Ferrando.

Nel Trovator, che dai giardini muove
Notturno il canto, d'un rivale a dritto
Ei teme.

Famigliari.

Dalle gravi
Palpêbre il sonno a discacciar, la vera
Storia ci narra di Garzia, germano
Al nostro Conte.

Ferrando.

La dirò: venite
Intorno a me.
> (Famigliari eseguiscono accostandosi pur essi.)

Arme.

Noi pure—

Famigliari.

Udite, udite.
> (Tutti accerchiano FERRANDO.)

Ferrando.

Di due figli vivea, padre beato,
Il buon Conte di Luna

Lived the Count in enjoyment;
Watching the younger for his safe protection
The good nurse found employment.
One morning, as the dawn's first rays were shining,
From her pillow she rose,—
Who was found, think ye, near the child reclining?

Chorus.
Who? Pray tell us! speak, disclose!

Fida nutrice del secondo nato
  Dormia presso la cuna
Sul romper dell' aurora un bel mattino
  Ella dischiude i rai,
E chi trova d'accanto a quel bambino?

Coro.
Chi?—Favèlla—chi mai?

ABBIETTA ZINGARA — *SAT THERE A GIPSY HAG* Ballad (Ferrando)

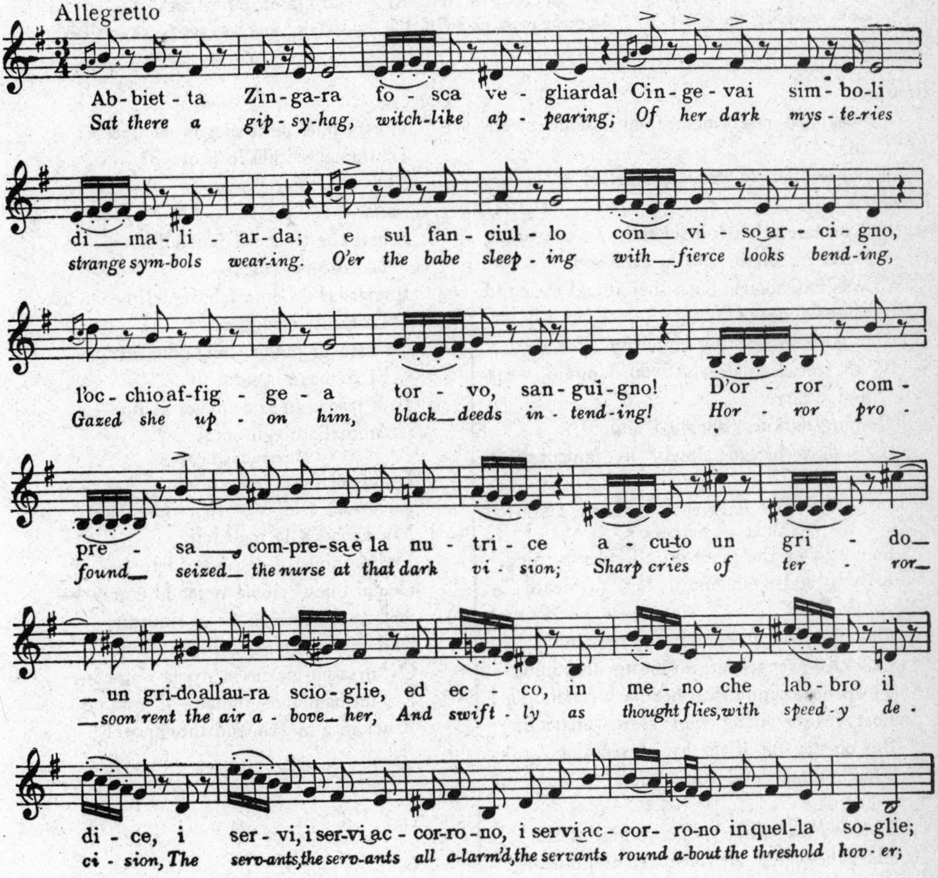

Allegretto

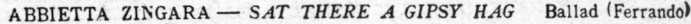

Ab-biet-ta Zin-ga-ra fo-sca ve-gliarda! Cin-ge-vai sim-bo-li
Sat there a gip-sy-hag, witch-like ap-pearing; Of her dark mys-te-ries

di-ma-li-ar-da; e sul fan-ciul-lo con vi-so ar-ci-gno,
strange sym-bols wear-ing. O'er the babe sleep-ing with fierce looks bend-ing,

l'oc-chio af-fig-ge-a tor-vo, san-gui-gno! D'or-ror com-
Gazed she up-on him, black deeds in-tend-ing! Hor-ror pro-

pre-sa com-pre-sa è la nu-tri-ce a-cu-to un gri-do,
found seized the nurse at that dark vi-sion; Sharp cries of ter-ror

un gri-do all'au-ra scio-glie, ed ec-co, in me-no che lab-bro il
soon rent the air a-bove her, And swift-ly as thought flies, with speed-y de-

di-ce, i ser-vi, i ser-vi ac-cor-ro-no, i ser-vi ac-cor-ro-no in quel-la so-glie;
ci-sion, The ser-vants, the ser-vants all a-larm'd, the ser-vants round a-bout the threshold hov-er;

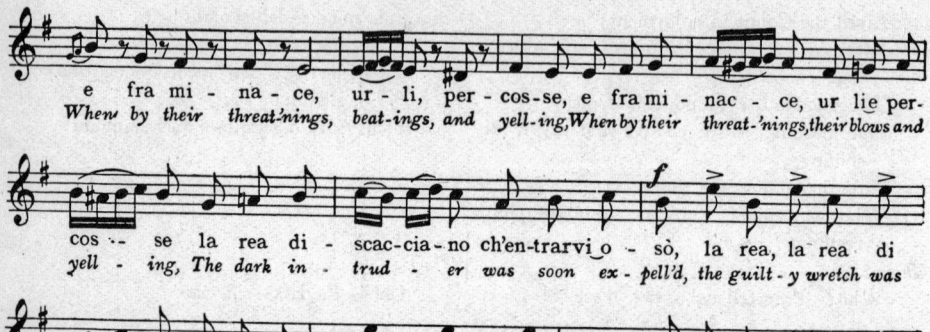

e fra mi — na — ce, ur - li, per - cos-se, e fra mi - nac — ce, ur lie per-
When by their threat-'nings, beat-ings, and yell-ing, When by their threat-'nings, their blows and

cos -— se la rea di — scac-cia-no ch'en-trarvi o - sò, la rea, la rea di
yell — ing, The dark in — trud — er was soon ex - pell'd, the guilt - y wretch was

scac-cia-no ch'en-trar-vio - sò, la rea, la rea, di — scac-cia-no ch'en-trarvi o - sò.
soon ex-pell'd, the guilt - y hag was soon ex-pell'd, the guilt-y, hag was soon ex - pell'd.

Chorus.

    'Twas just resentment their bosoms swelling;

For her offences was she expelled.

Ferrando.

    She declared that to read the stars prevailing
        At his birth, was her mission.
'Twas falsehood! Soon they found the child was failing,
        And in wasting condition;
With features pale and wan, languid, weak and weary.
Coming darkness appalled him,
The days passed slowly in lamentations dreary;
        The hag's dark spell enthralled him!
          (All appear horrified.)
Sought they the gipsy on all sides turning,
Seized, and condemned her to death by burning.
One child, accursed, left she remaining,
Quick to avenge her, no means disdaining.
Thus she accomplished her dark retribution!
Lost was the young child; search unavailing;
But on the site of the hag's execution
They found, 'mid the embers (a scene of horror
Their eyes assailing), of a young infant,
Alas! the bones half consumed and burning.

Coro.

    Giusto quei petti sdegno commosse;
    L'infame vecchia lo provocò!

rando.

    Asserì che tirar del fanciullino
        L'oroscopo volea—
Bugiarda!—Lenta febbre del meschino
        La salute struggea!
Coverto di pallor, languido, affranto
        Ei tremava la sera,
Il dì traeva in lamentevol pianto—
        Ammaliato egli era!
          (Il coro inorridisce.)
La fattuchiera perseguitata
Fù presa, e al rogo fù condannata;
Ma rimanea la maledetta
Figlia, ministra di ria vendetta!—
Compì quest' empia nefando eccesso!—
Sparve il bambino—e si rinvenne
Mal spenta brage, nel sito stesso
Ov' arsa un giorno la strega venne!—
E d'un bambino—ohimè!—l' ossame
Bruciato a mezzo, fumante ancor!

Chorus.
Ah! fiend inhuman! such deeds revolting
My soul with horror and hatred fill!

Some of Chorus.
The father?

Ferrando.
Few his days, and filled with sorrow;
Yet a secret presentiment at heart made
   him still hopeful;
It told him his son was living;
And on his dying bed he claimed of the
   Count, our master,
His solemn promise, a careful search to in-
   stigate.
Ah! how vainly!

Chorus of Soldiers.
But what of her?
No tidings as yet you've heard?

Ferrando.
No word hath reached us! Oh, heaven grant
That haply we may meet one day!

Chorus of Servants.
And were it so, would'st thou know her?

Ferrando.
Yes, by counting the years
That have vanished, I should know her.

Chorus of Soldiers.
Be that
The moment, down near her mother
In perdition to send her!

Ferrando.
To perdition? 'Tis believed, that on this
   earth
She's doomed to wander—she, the soul-ac-
   cursed, the witch infernal,
And when the skies are darkened,
In forms oft-changing have some beheld her.

Chorus.
'Tis true!

Some of Chorus.
They say some have seen her o'er housetops
   careering!

Coro.
Oh, scellerata!—oh, donna infame!
Del par m'investe odio ed orror.

Alcuni.
E il padre?

Ferrando.
Brevi e tristi giorni visse;
Pure ignoto del cor presentimento
Gli diceva, che spento
Non era il figlio; ed a morir vicino
Bramò che il signor nostro a lui giurasse
Di non cessar le indagini—ah!—fur vane!

Arme.
E di colei non s'ebbe
Contezza mai?

Ferrando.
Nulla contezza—Oh! dato
Mi fosse rintracciarla
Un dì!

Famigliari.
Ma ravvisarla potresti?

Ferrando.
Calcolando
Gli anni trascorsi—lo potrei.

Arme.
Sarebbe
Tempo presso la madre
All' inferno spedirla.

Ferrando.
All' inferno?—E credenza, che dimori
Ancor nel mondo l'anima perduta
Dell' empia strega, e quando il cielo è nero
In varie forme altrui si mostri.

Coro.
E vero!

Alcuni.
Sull' orlo dei tetti alcun l' ha veduta!

Others.

Transformed to a bird, or a vampire appearing!

Still Others.

Sometimes like a raven, or owl, shrilly crying,

From daylight and thunder she's seen madly flying!

Ferrando.

The Count's faithful servant, the old witch assaulting,

Soon died in an access of terror revolting!

(All manifest great terror.)

She came to his chamber, an owl's form assuming,

The silence disturbing, the darkness illuming;

She gazed on him fiercely with eyes brightly flaming;

With loud cries of anguish the still air was rent!

That moment the bell struck, midnight proclaiming.

(A bell suddenly strikes the hour of midnight.)

Chorus.

Ah! maledictions fall on the witch of infernal descent!

(The servants hasten towards the door. The soldiers retire in the background.)

SCENE II—Gardens of the Palace; on one side a flight of marble steps, leading to the apartments. Thick clouds conceal the moon.

(Enter LEONORA and INEZ.)

Inez.

What still detains thee? late 'tis growing;

Come then; already her Highness has called thee;

Did'st hear her?

Leonora.

Another night goes by,

Yet him I behold not!

Inez.

Peril tends the flame

That thou dost nourish.

Oh, tell me, prithee, how the spark

First was kindled in thy bosom?

Altri.

In upupa o strige talora si muta!

Altri.

In corvo tal' altra; più spesso in civetta,

Sull' alba fuggente al par di saetta!

Ferrando.

Morì di paura un servo del conte,

Che avea della zingara percossa la fronte!

(Tutti si pingono, di superstizzoso terrore.)

Apparve a costui d' un gufo in sembianza

Nell' alta quiete di tacita stanza!—

Con occhi lucenti guardava—guardava,

Il cielo attristando con urlo feral!

Allor mezzanotte appunto suonava—

(Suona mezzanotte.)

Tutti.

Ah! sia maledetta la strega infernal!

(Con subito soprasalto.)

(Odonzi alcuni tocchi di tamburo. Gli uomini d'arme accorrono in fondo; i famigliari traggonsi verso la porta.)

SCENA II—Giardini del palazzo; sulla destra narmori scalinata che mette negli appartamenti. La notte è inoltrata ed dense nubi cuoprono la luna.

(Entra LEONORA ed INEZ.)

Ines.

Che più t'arresti?—l'ora è tarda; vieni,

Di te la regal donna

Chiese, l'udisti.

Leonora.

Un' altra notte ancora

Senza vederlo!

Ines.

Perigliosa fiamma

Tu nutri!—Oh, come, dove

La primieri favilla

In te s'apprese?

Leonora.

At the Tournay. He entered;
Dark were his vestments and his crest;
His shield and banner no devices bearing;
An unknown Knight he came,
And in the lists bore away all the honors;
  mine was the hand
That crowned his brow as victor. Soon, a
  civil war outbreaking,
He disappeared. Ah! like a golden vision
Fled his dear image! One other moment,
Long after this,—but then—

Inez.

What chanced then?

Leonora.

Now hear!

Leonora.

Ne' tornei. V'apparvo
Bruno le vesti ed il cimier, lo scudo
Bruno e di stemma ignudo,
Sconosciuto guerrier, che dell' agone
Gli onori ottene—Al vincitor sul crine
Il serto io posi—Civil guerra intanto
Arse—nol vidi piú!—come d'aurato
Sogno fuggente imago!—ed era volta
Lunga stagion—ma poi—

Ines.

Che avvenne?

Leonora.

Ascolta!

TACEA LA NOTTE PLACIDA — *THE NIGHT, CALMLY AND PEACEFULLY*   Air (Leonora)

Words, like the prayers, a humble heart
Outpours to heaven when lonely,
In which one well-known name was oft
Repeated; 'twas mine, mine only!
Reaching in haste the balcony,
I saw him standing before me!
Joy, such as only angels know,
With glowing thrill came o'er me!
To heart, and eyes, with rapture filled,
The earth like heaven appeared.

Inez.

What thou relatest sadly disturbs me,
Filling my bosom with terror.

Leonora.

'Tis idle!

Inez.

Doubtings and dark forebodings arise within
me,
Concerning this Knight's strange movements!
Try to forget him!

Leonora.

What saidst thou! No more, then!

Inez.

Heed friendly counsel; heed it,
I pray; heed it!

Leonora.

To forget him! Ah, thou art speaking
words
Which the soul can ne'er comprehend.

Versi di prece, ed umile,
Qual d'uom che prega Iddio;
In quella ripeteasi
Un nome—il nome mio!
Corsi al veron sollecita—
Egli era, egli era desso!—
Gioja provai che agli angeli
Solo è provar concesso!—
Al core, al guardo estatico
La terra un ciel sembrò!

Ines.

Quanto narrasti di turbamento
M' ha piena l'anima!—Io tremo—

Leonora.

Invano!

Ines.

Dubbio, ma tristo presentimento
In me risveglia quest' uomo arcano!
Tenta obliarlo—

Leonora.

Che dici!—Oh, basti!

Ines.

Cedi al consiglio dell' amistà--
Cedi—

Leonora.

Obliarlo!—Ah! tu parlasti
Detto, che intendere l'alma non sà.

DI TALE AMOR—*OF LOVE LIKE THIS, HOW VAINLY*. Air (Leonora)

Di ta - lea-mor che dir - - si Mal può dal-la pa-ro-
Of love like this, how vain - - ly Do words at-tempt ex - pres -

la, D'a-mor, che intendo io so - - la Il cor,___ il_
*sion; A love, at whose con - fes - - sion The heart,___ the_*

cor,____ il_ cor si-ne-bri-ò. Il mio des-ti-no com-pir-
heart,____ the_ heart with rap-ture glows. My fate would not com-piet-ed

si, non puo che a lui d'ap-pres-____-so, S'io non vi-vrò per es-___-
be, If he were not be-side____ me; Were life with him de-nied____

so, Per es-so, per es-so, per es-so,_mo-ri-ròl S'i-o non vi-vrò per
me, Then wel-come, then wel-come, then wel-come death's re-pose. Yes, were life with him de-

es-so, per es-so io mo-ri-rò, Ah! sì per es-so,_ mo-ri-
nied_me, I'd wel-come death's re-pose, ah! yes, for him, in_ death re-

ròl_ per_ es-so mo-ri-rò, mo-____-ri-ròl
pose, in_death would I re-pose, I'd_____ re-pose.

Inez (aside).	Ines (da se).
No cause for sad repentance	Non debba mai pentirsi
May coming time disclose!	Chi tanto un giorno amo!
(They ascend to the apartments.)	*(Ascendono agli appartamenti.)*
Count. *(Enter the COUNT.)*	**Conte.** *(Entra il CONTE.)*
Night reigns in silence! Her Highness, no doubt,	Tace la notte! Immersa
Is now immersed in peaceful slumber;	Nel sonno è, certo, la regal signora;
Not yet sleeps her companion—Oh! Leonora,	Ma veglia la sua dama—Oh! Leonora,
Thou art still wakeful; the tremulous light	Tu desta sei; mel dice
Now shining from thy casement tells me	Da quel verone tremolante un raggio
Of thy nocturnal vigils—	Della notturna lampa—
Ah! how this amorous passion	Ah!—l'amorosa vampa
Thrills each nerve within me!—I must now behold thee,	M'arde ogni fibra!—Ch'io ti vegga è d'uopo, Che tu m'intenda—Vengo—A noi supremo
And thou shalt hear me! Loved one! To us belongs	E tal momento—
This blissful moment—	*(Cieco d'amore avviasi alla gradinata; odonsi gli accordi d'un liuto; egli si arresta.)*
(Blinded by passion, he approaches the steps, but suddenly pauses, on hearing the sound of a lute.)	Il Trovator!—Io fremo,
The Troubadour! I tremble!	

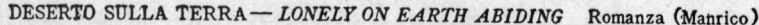

DESERTO SULLA TERRA— *LONELY ON EARTH ABIDING*   Romanza (Manrico)

De - ser - to sul - la ter - ra, col rio de -
Lone - ly on earth a - bid - ing, War - ring 'gainst

sti - no in guer - ra, è so - la spe-me un cor, è so - la spe-me un
fate's cru-el chid - ing, Hope doth one heart im - plore, Hope doth one heart im -

cor, è so - la spe-me un cor, un cor al Tro - va - tor!
plore, Hope doth one heart im - plore, To love the Trou - ba - dour!

Count.	**Conte.**
Oh, accents! I shudder!	Oh, detti! Io fremo!
Manrico.	**Manrico.**
But that fond treasure gaining,	Ma s'ei quel cor possiede,
Its faith and love obtaining,	Bello di casta fede,
High o'er all kings would soar,	E d'ogni re maggior
The happy Troubadour!	Il Trovator!
Count.	**Conte.**
Oh, accents! Oh, jealous anger!	Oh detti, oh gelosia!—
'Tis no error—she approaches!	Non m'inganno—Ella scende;
(Wraps himself in his mantle.)	(Si avvolge nel suo mantello.)
(Enter LEONORA.)	(Entra LEONORA.)
Leonora	**Leonora**
(hastening towards the COUNT).	(correndo verso il CONTE).
Oh, my beloved!	Anima mia!
Count.	**Conte.**
What now?	(Che far!)
Leonora.	**Leonora.**
More late than usual	Più dell' usato
Is thy coming; each moment have I counted	E tarda l'ora; io ne contai gl'istanti
With heart and pulses beating!—At length	Coi palpiti del core!—Alfin ti guida
'Tis love filled with pity that brings thee	Pietoso amor tra queste braccia—
to these loving arms.	
Voice of the Troubadour.	**Le Voce del Trovatore.**
Deceiver!	Infida.
(The moon emerging from the clouds reveals the figure of a masked cavalier.)	(La luna mostrasi dai nugoli, e lascia scorgere una persona di cui la visiera nasconde il volto.)
(Enter MANRICO.)	(Entra MANRICO.)
Leonora	**Leonora.**
(recognizing each and falling at the feet of MANRICO).	(Riconoscendo entrandi, e gettandosi ai piedi di MANRICO.)
That voice!—Ah, darkness and unrest	Qual voce!—Ah, dalle tenebre

My eager steps misguided!
'Twas thee, I thought, my words addressed!
In thee, not him, confided.
To thee my soul expandeth!
No other bliss demandeth!
I love thee, ah, believe me,
With lasting, boundless love!

Count.
And dar'st thou?

Manrico
    (raising LEONORA).
Enough, forgive me!

Count.
With rage my heart doth move!
If thou'rt not base, reveal thyself!

Leonora.
Alas!

Count.
Thy name declaring—

Leonora.
Oh, speak, I pray!
   (Aside to MANRICO).

Manrico.
Behold me, then,
Manrico!

Count.
Thou?—wherefore?
Rash traitor! bold and daring!
Urgel's accomplice, the laws have condemned
 thee.
And dar'st thou thus return
Within these royal portals?

Manrico.
What stays thee? Go call the guards, to
 aid thee;
Seize me, thy rival,
And to the headsman's gleaming axe
Consign me.

Count.
Thy fatal hour,
Perchance, already is at hand!
Oh, insensate! Come then—

Leonora.
Stay thee!

Tratta in errore io fui!
A te credei rivolgere
L'accento, e non a lui—
A te, che l'alma mia
Sol chiede, sol desia—
Io t'amo, il giuro, io t'amo
D' immenso eterno amor!

Conte.
Ed osi?—

Manrico
    (sollevandola).
(Ah, più non bramo!)

Conte.
Avvampo di furor!
Se un vil non sei, discovriti.

Leonora.
(Ohimè!)

Conte.
Palesa il nome—

Leonora.
Deh, per pietà!—
   (Sommessamente a MANRICO.)

Manrico.
Ravvisami,
Manrico io son.

Conte.
Tu!—Come!
Insano, temerario!
D'Urgel seguace, a morte
Proscritto, ardisci volgerti
A queste regie porte?—

Manrico.
Che tardi?—or via le guardie
Appella, ed il rivale
Al ferro del carnefice
Consegna.

Conte.
Il tuo fatale
Istante assai più prossimo
E, dissennato!—Vieni—

Leonora.
Conte!—

Count.

    To my rage thou'rt victim doomed,
    And fate wills I must slay thee.

Leonora.

    One moment stay thee!

Count.

    Follow me.

Manrico.

    Lead on!

Leonora.

    (What must I do?—
    A single cry from me
    May cause his ruin!)   Hear me.

Count.

    No!
    Fires of jealous, despised affection
    In my heart are fiercely raging!
    Wretch! thy blood for this foul defection
    Soon shall flow, its pains assuaging!
              (To LEONORA.)
    Thou hast dared me, thy passion revealing!
    He thou lovest in death shall lie,
    Thy fond words his fate now sealing,
    By this hand he's doomed to die!

Leonora.

    One short moment thy fury restraining,
    Let thine anger give way to reason;
    I, alone, thy base passion disdaining,
    Roused thy hateful charge of treason!
    Let thy vengeance on me then descending,
    Who have scorned thee, and still can defy,—
    Strike thy dagger in this heart offending,
    From thy love that dared to fly.

Manrico.

    Vainly anger his proud heart is moving,
    He shall soon fall by death inglorious;
    Haply he who inspires thee with loving
    Is by thy love made ever victorious.
            (To the COUNT.)
    Thy dark fate is already decided,
    Doomed to perish, thy last hour is nigh!
    Heart and life to my hand are confided,
    Heaven condemns thee, and thou shalt die!

(The two rivals retire with drawn swords. LEONORA falls senseless.)

END OF FIRST ACT.

Conte.

    Al mio sdegno vittima
    E forza ch' io ti sveni—

Leonora.

    Oh ciel!—t'arresta—

Conte.

    Seguimi—

Manrico.

    Andiam—

Leonora.

    Che mai farò?—
    Un sol mio grido perdere
    Lo puote!)—M'odi—

Conte.

    No.
    Di geloso amor sprezzato
    Arde in me tremendo foco!
    Il tuo sangue, o sciagurato,
    Ad estinguerlo fia poco!
             (A LEONORA.)
    Dirgli, o folle—io t'amo—ardisti—
    Ei più vivere non può—
    Un accento proferisti,
    Che a morir lo condannò!

Leonora.

    Un istante almen dia loco
    Il tuo sdegno alla ragione—
    Io, sol io di tanto foco
    Son, pur troppo, la cagione!
    Piombi, ah! piombi il tuo **furore**
    Sulla rea che t'oltraggiò—
    Vibra il ferro in questo core,
    Che te amar non vuol, non può.

Manrico.

    Del superbo vana è l'ira;
    Ei cadrà da me trafitto.
    Il mortal che amor t'inspira,
    Dall' amor fu reso invitto.
    La tua sorte è già compita—
             (Al CONTE.)
    L'ora omai per te suonò!
    Il tuo core e la tua vita
    Il destino a me serbò!

(I due rivali si allontanano con le spade **sguainate**; LEONORA cade priva di sentimento.)

FINE DELL' ATTO PRIMO.

ACT II.

THE GIPSY.

SCENE I—A ruined house at the foot of a mountain in Biscay; the interior is partly exposed to view; within, a great fire is lighted. Day begins to dawn.

(AZUCENA is seated near the fire. MANRICO, enveloped in his mantle, is lying upon a mattress; his helmet is at his feet; in his hand he holds a sword, which he regards fixedly. A band of gipsies are sitting in scattered groups around them.)

Gipsies.

See, how the shadows of night are flying!
Morn breaketh, heaven's glorious arch unveiling;
Like a young widow, who, weary of sighing,
Lays by her garments of sorrow and wailing.
Rouse up to labor! Take each his hammer!
Who makes the gipsy's a life with pleasure laden?
The gipsy maiden.

(They take up the implements of labor, and strike with their hammers upon anvils, in regular measure.)

Men

(resting awhile from their labor, they address the women).

Fill me a bumper; both arm and hand
New strength and courage draw from flowing beakers.

(The women pour out wine for them in rustic cups.)

All.

See how the sunlight, radiantly glowing,
Borrows new beams from our wine-cups o'erflowing!
Resume our labor! Take each his hammer!
Who makes the gipsy's a life with pleasure laden?
The gipsy maiden!

Azucena

(as she begins to sing, the gipsies gather about her).

ATTO II.

LA GITANA.

SCENA I—Un diruto abituro sulle falde d'un Monte della Biscaglia—nel fondo, quasi tutto aperto, arde un gran fuoco. I primi albori.

(AZUCENA siede presso il fuoco—MANRICO, le sta disteso accanio sopra una coltrice, ed avviluppato nel suo mantello; ha l'elmo ai piedi, e fra le mani la spada, su cui figge immobilmente lo sguardo—Una banda di Zingari è sparso all'intorno.)

Zingari.

Vedi! le fosche notturne spoglie
De' cieli sveste l'immensa volta;
Sembra una vedova che alfin si toglie
I bruni panni ond' era involta.
All' opra, all' opra. Dagli, martella.
Chi del gitano i giorni abbella?
La zingarella.

(Danno di piglio ai loro ferri di mestiere—al misurato tempestar dei martelli cadenti sulle incudini, ou uomini, ou donne, e tutti in un tempo in fine intuonano la cantilena seguente.)

Uomini

(alle donne, sostando un poco dal lavoro).

Versami un tratto: lena e coraggio
Il corpo e l'anima traggon dal bere.

(Le donne mescono ad essi in rozze coppe.)

Tutti.

Oh, guarda, guarda! del sole un raggio
Brilla più vivido nel {tuo / mio} bicchiere—
All' opra, all' opra—Dagli, martella—
Quale a {voi / noi} splende propizia stella?—
La zingarella.

Azucena

(canta: gli zingari le si fanno allato).

STRIDE LA VAMPA — *UPWARD THE FLAMES ROLL*   Air (Azucena)

Stri - de la vam- - pa! La___ fol-la in-do - mi-ta Cor -
Up - ward the flames___ roll; crowds___ press-ing fierce - ly on, Rush

re a quel fuo - - co - Lie - - ta in sem bian - - za: Ur -
to the burn - - ing with_ - seem-ing glad - - ness; Loud

- li - di - gio - ja - D'in - tor - no ec-cheg-gia-no — Cin - ta - di _
_ cries of _ plea - sure from _ all sides re-ech - o -ing! By _ guards sur -

sgher - ri - Don - na s'a - van - za! Si - nis - tra splen -
round- ed— forth _ comes a _ wo - man! While, o'er them shin - -

de Sui _ vol-ti or - ri - bi - le, La te - tra fiam - ma - che
ing, with _ wild, un - earth - ly glare, Dark wreaths of flame curl _ as-

s'al - za, Che s'al - za al ciel! _ che _ s'al-za al ciel!
cend-ing, as - cend-ing to heav'n, _ roll _ up to heav'n!

Upward the flames roll! on comes the victim still;	Stride la vampa!—giunge la vittima
Robed in dark garments, ungirt, unsandalled,	Nero-vestita—discinta e scalza!
Fierce cries of vengeance from that dark crowd arise;	Grido feroce—di morte levasi;
Echo repeats them from mountain to mountain.	L'eco il repete—di balza in balza!
O'er them reflecting, with wild, unearthly glare,	Sinistra splende—su' volti orribili
Dark wreaths of flame curl, ascending to heaven.	La tetra fiamma che s' alza al ciel!

Gipsies.

Thine is a mournful song!

Azucena.

Yes, sad indeed,

As is the mournful story,

From which it draws its dreary burthen.

(Turns her face to MANRICO and murmurs)

Avenge thou me!

Zingari.

Mesta è la tua canzon!

Azucena.

Del pari mesta

Che la storia funesta

Da cui tragge argomento!

(Rivolge il capo dalla parte di MANRICO, e mormora cupamente)

Mi vendica—mi vendica!

Manrico.

(Again those mysterious words!)

Elderly Gipsy.

Companions, day advances;

'Tis time to seek for food; let us descend

To the towns that lie beneath us.

Manrico.

Come on, then!

(Putting away their tools.)

Women.

Come on, then!

(Commence descending promiscuously; their song is heard growing fainter in the distance.)

Gipsies.

Who makes the gipsy's a life with pleasure laden?

The gipsy maiden!

Manrico

(rising).

All have left us; ah, now relate

That dark mournful story!

Azucena.

Thou dost not know it as yet?

Thou wert but still young, when,

Spurred on by ambition, far away

Thou didst wander!—My mother's final doom

This tale relateth. She was charged

With fearful crimes by a haughty noble,

Whose failing infant she was accused of charming!

Doomed to the stake, she perished

Where this fire is burning!

Manrico.

Ah, fate unhappy!

(Drawing back with horror from the fire).

Azucena.

In fetters, they led her onward to meet her dark fate impending;

With babe in hand, I followed sadly, with tears descending.

In vain tried I to approach her, through crowds that round her were pressing;

In vain did she attempt to stay, to leave with me her blessing.

Goaded by spears and lances, with oaths and jeers assaulted,

Manrico.

(L'arcana parola ognor!)

Vecchio Zingara.

Compagni, avanza il giorno;

A procacciarci un pan, sù, sù!—scendiamo

Per le propinque ville.

Uomini.

Andiamo.

(Ripongona sollecitamente nei sacchi i loro arnesi.)

Donne.

Andiamo.

(Tutti scendono alla rinfusa giù per la china; tratto tratto e sempre a maggior distanza, odesi il loro canto.)

Zingari.

Chi del gitano i giorni abbella?

La zingarella!

Manrico

(sorgendo).

Soli or siamo; deh narra

Quella storia funesta.

Azucena.

E tu la ignori,

Tu pur!—Ma giovinetto i passi tuoi

D'ambizïon lo sprone

Lungi traca!—Dell' ava il fine acerbo

E quella storia—La incolpò superbo

Conte di malefizio, onde apparia

Côlto un bambin suo figlio—Essa bruciata

Fù dov' arde or quel foco!

Manrico.

Ahi! sciagurata!

(Rifuggendo con raccapriccio dalla fiamma.)

Azucena.

Condotta ell' era in ceppi al suo destin tremendo

Col figlio—teco in braccio io la seguia piangendo:

Infino ad essa un varco tentai, ma invano, aprirmi—

Invan tentò la misera fermarsi, e benedirmi

Che, fra bestemmie oscene, pungendola coi ferri

Al rogo la cacciavano gli scellerati sgherri!

The guards pursued her ruthlessly, 'till at
the stake they halted.
At length, with broken accents, "Avenge
thou me," she cried!
Those dying words will ever within my
heart abide.

Manrico.
Didst thou avenge her?

Azucena.
The Count's young child, ere the day was
ended,
I stole and brought him hither; the flames
still to heaven ascended!

Manrico.
The flames?—Oh, heav'n—thou couldst
not—

Azucena.
Sadly the child began weeping;
Rent was my heart with his sorrow, o'er
me pity was creeping,
When quickly, my mind disordered, saw
what like dreams came o'er me.
Deadly shapes and phantoms brought the
dark scene before me;
The guardsmen, this place of torture, the
mother pale, confounded,
Barefoot, ungirdled, the outcry of anguish,
That cry within me resounded: "Avenge
thou me!"
All heedless, my hand extended held fast the
victim pale;
The flames rolled expectant; in I hurled
him!
Calmed was the fatal madness, fled was the
horrid vision;
The fire still glowed in silence, gorged with
its foul commission!
Gazing around in sadness, I saw the infant
cherished
Of that vile Count approaching!

Manrico.
Ah, what say'st thou?

Azucena.
My child had perished,
My child through me had perished!

Allor, con tronce accento, mi vendica! es-
clamò—
Quel detto un eco eterno in questo cor
lasciò.

Manrico.
La vendicasti?

Azucena.
Il figlio giunsi a rapir del Conte;
Lo trascinai qui meco—le fiamme ardean
già pronte.

Manrico.
Le fiamme?—oh ciel!—tu forse?—

Azucena.
Ei distruggeasi in pianto—
Io mi sentiva il cor dilaniato, infranto!—
Quand'ecco agli egri spirti, come in un sogno,
apparva,
La vision ferale di spaventose larve!—
Gli sgnerri ed il supplizio!—la madre
smorta in volto—
Scalza, discinta!—il grido, il noto grido as-
colto—
Mi vendica!—La mano convulsa tendo
stringo
La vittima—nel foco la traggo, la sos
pingo!—
Cessa il fatal delirio—
L'orrida scena fugge—
La fiamma sol divampa,
E la sua preda strugge!
Pur volgo intorno il guardo,
E innanzi a me vegg' io
Dell' empio Conte il figlio!—

Manrico.
Ah! come?

Azucena.
Il figlio mio,
Mio figlio avea bruciato!

Manrico.

   Horrid crime!

Azucena.

   Once more my thin locks with horror rise
     up, unsoothed by time!

(AZUCENA falls fainting on her seat; MANRICO is struck dumb with surprise and horror.)

Manrico.

   I'm not thy son, then? tell me, who am I,
     I pray thee?

Azucena

   (hastily, as if to repair an involuntary admission).

   Mine art thou ever.

Manrico.

   Thy words denied it.

Azucena.

   It may be; what wouldst thou?
   When wandering thoughts such terrible
     scenes encounter!
   The mind, disordered, heeds not all the fol-
     lies
   Unguarded lips may utter. Mother tender
     and true,
   Hast thou not found me ever?

Manrico.

   Can I disown it?

Azucena.

   To me thy life's protection
   Thou owest. At midnight, on the field of
     battle
   At Petilla, where reports declared thou hadst
     fallen,
   Did I not come to give thee fit burial?
   In thy breast, my cares revived the vital
     spark,
   But there the affection fond, maternal,
     stayed not.
   How many hours did I tend thee, healing
     thy wounds
   So ghastly and numerous?

Manrico   (with noble pride).

   Wounds obtained on that dark morning;
   My breast alone received them! 'Mid all
     the thousands that disbanded,
   I alone faced the foe, still firm, unyielding.
   The vile de Luna then

Manrico.

   Che dici quale orror!

Azucena.

   Sul capo mio le chiome sento drizzarsi ancor!

(AZUCENA ricade trambasciata sul proprio seggio: MAN-RICO ammutisce, colpito d'orrore e di sorpresa—Momenti di silenzio.)

Manrico.

   Non son tuo figlio?—E chi son io, chi dun-
     que?

Azucena

   (con sollecitudine di chi cerca emendare involontario fallo).

   Tu sei mio figlio!

Manrico.

   Eppur dicesti—

Azucena.

   Ah!—forse—
   Che vuoi!—Quando al pensier s'affaccia il
     truce
   Caso, lo spirto intenebrato pone
   Stolto parole sul mio labbro—Madre,
   Tenera madre non m'avesti ognora?

Manrico.

   Potrei negarlo?—

Azucena.

   A me, se vivi ancora,
   Nol dèi? Notturna, nei pugnati campi
   Di Petilla, ove spento
   Fama ti disse, a darti
   Sepoltura non mossi? La fuggente
   Aura vital non iscovri, nel seno
   Non l'arrestò materno affetto?—E quanta
   Cure non spesi a risanar le tante ferite!

Manrico   (con nobile orgoglio).

   Che portai quel dì fatale—
   Ma tutte qui, nel petto?—Io sol, fra mille
   Già sbandati, al nemico
   Volgendo ancor la faccia!—Il rio de Luna,
   Sù me piombò col suo drappello; io caddi,

Charged me with his troops o'erwhelming;
I faltered and fell,
Yet brave and unconquered!

Azucena.

Such were the thanks
Which the villain did repay thee,
For sparing his base life in that combat at
night!
What then did blind thee?
Was it a strange compassion?

Manrico.

Oh, mother! I cannot tell thee! I know
not!

Però da forte io caddi!

Azucena.

Ecco mercede
Ai giorni, che l'infame
Nel singolar certame
Ebbe salvi da te?—qual t'acciecava
Strana pietà per esso?

Manrico.

Oh madre!—non saprei dirlo a me stesso!

MAL REGGENDO — *ILL SUSTAINING* Air (Manrico)

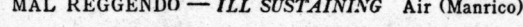

Mal reg-gen-do all' a-spro as-sal-to   Ei già toc-co il
Ill sus-tain-ing the fu-rious en-coun-ter,   At my mer-cy he

suo-lo a-ve-a: Ba-le-na-va il col-po in al-to
fell un-de-fend-ed: Bright-ly gleam-ing, my sword was up-lift-ed

agitato e cupo

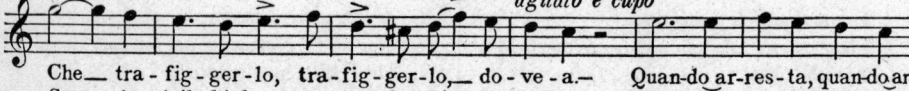

Che tra-fig-ger-lo, tra-fig-ger-lo, do-ve-a.— Quan-do ar-res-ta, quan-do ar-
Soon to strike his heart, to pierce his heart in-tend-ed. When some se-cret pow'r, some

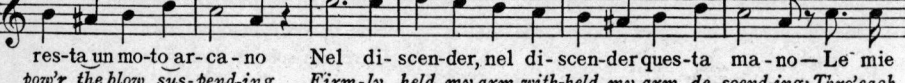

res-ta un mo-to ar-ca-no Nel di-scen-der, nel di-scen-der ques-ta ma-no— Le mie
pow'r the blow sus-pend-ing, Firm-ly held my arm, with-held my arm de-scend-ing; Thro' each

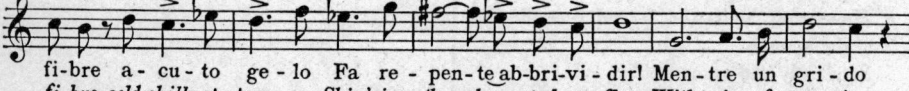

fi-bre a-cu-to ge-lo Fa re-pen-te ab-bri-vi-dir! Men-tre un gri-do
fi-bre cold chills op-press me, Shiv'-rings through my pul-ses flow: With cries of warn-ing,

cresc.   *ff*   *pp*

vien dal cie-lo, Men-tre un gri-do viem dal cie-lo, Che mi di-ce: non fe-rir.
Heav'n ad-dress'd me, with a loud commanding cry, Heav'n thus ad-dress'd me, "Spare thy foe."

Azucena.

But within that soul ungrateful
Not one word from heaven hath resounded!
Oh! if with that villain hateful
Thou in fight shouldst be confounded,
Haste to accomplish (Heaven doth will it)
What I command thee, hear and fulfil it!
To the handle send this weapon
Through the monster's cruel heart.
(The prolonged note of a horn is heard.)

Manrico.

Ruiz sends hither th' accustomed courier,
Haply—
(Sounds his horn in reply.)

Azucena.

Avenge thou me!
(Remains in thought and seemingly unconscious of what is passing.)
(Enter a Messenger.)

Manrico
(to the Messenger).

Approach this way. Proceed
And tell me what news thou bringest.

Messenger.

The scroll I bring here will tell thee all.
(Presenting a letter.)

Manrico
(reads).

"Within our power is Castellor;
By the order of our prince thou must watch o'er
And defend it. Wherever this may reach thee,
Come in haste. Kept in error still by thy reported death,
This very evening Leonora will assume the nun's dark veil within the neighboring convent."
Just heaven, forbid it!
(With exclamations of sorrow.)

Azucena
(starting).

What dost thou?

Manrico
(to the Messenger).

Hence quickly down to the valley
Without delay, a steed provide me.

Messenger.

Be it so.

Azucena.

Ma nell' alma dell' ingrato
Non parlò del cielo il detto!
Oh! se ancor ti spinge il fato
A pugnar col maledetto,
Compi, o figlio, qual d'un Dio,
Compi allora il cenno mio:
Sino all' elsa questa lama
Vibra, immergi all' empio in cor.
(Odesi un prolungato suono di corno.)

Manrico.

L'usato messo Ruiz invia!—
Forse—
(Dà fiato anch' esso al corno che tiene ad armacello.)

Azucena.

Mi vendica!
(Resta concentrata, quasi inconsapevole di ciò che succede.
(Entra il Messo.)

Manrico
(al Messo).

Inoltra il piè.
Guerresco evento, dimmi, seguia?

Messo.

Risponda il foglio che reco a te.
(Porgendo il foglio, che MANRICO legge.)

Manrico.

"In nostra possa è Castellor; ne dêi,
Tu, per cenno del prence,
Vigilar le difese. Ove ti è dato,
Affrettati a venir. Giunta la sera
Tratta in inganno di tua morte al grido
Nel vicin claustro della croce il velo
Cingerà Leonora." Oh, giusto cielo!
(Con dolorosa esclamazione.)

Azucena
(scuotendosi).

(Che fia!)

Manrico
(al Messo).

Veloce scendi la balza,
E d'un cavallo a me provvedi—

Messo.

Corro—

Azucena (interposing).

Manrico!

Manrico.

The time flies swiftly.   Haste thee, and yonder
My coming awaits thee.

(The MESSENGER departs hastily.)

Azucena.

What hopest thou? what wouldst thou?

Manrico.

(Lose her thus!   Oh, torment!
Thus lose that angel!)

Azucena.

(His brain is turned!)

Manrico.

Farewell now.

(Replacing his helmet upon his head, and wrapping his cloak around him.)

Azucena.

No! stay thee! hear me!

Manrico.

Release me!
But a moment lost may wither
All the hopes that now sustain me;
Earth and heaven, combined together,
Would be powerless to restrain me!

Azucena.

Insensate!

Manrico.

Ah, release me, O mother, I pray thee!
Woe betide if here I stay me!
Thou wilt see thy son, extended
At thy feet, with grief expire.

Azucena.

No, I'll ne'er permit thy going.
In thy veins my blood is flowing;
Every crimson drop thou losest
From thy mother's heart doth flow.

(MANRICO departs, AZUCENA striving in vain to detain him.)

SCENE II—Cloister of a Convent in the vicinity of Castellor.   Night.

(The COUNT, FERRANDO and followers advance cautiously, enveloped in their cloaks.)

Count.

All is deserted; through the air comes yet
No sound of th' accustomed chanting.
I come in time then.

Azucena (frapponendosi).

Manrico!—

Manrico.

Il tempo incalza—
Vola; m'aspetta dell cole a' piedi.

(Il Messo parte, affrettatamente.)

Azucena.

E speri, e vuoi?

Manrico.

(Perderla?—Oh, ambascia!—
Perder quell' angelo?—)

Azucena.

(E fuor di sè!)

Manrico.

Addio—

(Postosi l'elmo sul capo, ed afferrando il mantello.)

Azucena.

No—forma—odi—

Manrico.

Mi lascia—
Un momento può involarmi
Il mio ben, la mia speranza!
No, che basti ad arrestarmi
Terra e ciel non ha possanza.

Azucena.

Demente!

Manrico.

Ah! mi sgombra, o madre, i passi—
Guai per te, s'io qui restassi:
Tu vedresti a' piedi tuoi
Spento il figlio di dolor!

Azucena.

No soffrirlo non poss' io.
Il tuo sangue è sangue mio!
Ogni stilla che ne versi
Tu la spremi dal mio cor!

(Si allontana, indarno trattenuto da AZUCENA.)

SCENA II—Chiostro d'un cenobio, in vicinanza di Castellor.   E notte.

(Il CONTE, FERRANDO, ed alcuni sequaci, ed avviluppati nei loro mantelli, inoltrandesi cautamente.)

Conte.

Tutto è deserto; nè per l'aura ancora
Suona l'usato carme—
In tempo io giungo!

Ferrando.

A daring labor here, my lord,
Awaits thee.

Count.

'Tis daring; and such alone as burning pas-
sion
And wounded pride from me should demand.
My rival dead—each hindrance opposed to
my wishes
Seemed fallen and vanquished;
Till lately she discovered one still more po-
tent,
The altar. Ah, no! For none else is
Leonora!
She is mine, mine only!

Ferrando.

Ardita opra, o signore,
Imprendi.

Conte.

Ardita, e quel furente amore
Ed irritato orgoglio
Chissero a me. Spento il rival, caduto
Ogni ostacol sembrava a' miei desiri;
Novello e più possente ella ne appresta—
L'altare!—Ah no, non fia
D'altri Leonora!—Leonora è mia!

IL BALEN DEL SUO — OF HER SMILE THE RADIANT   Air (Count)

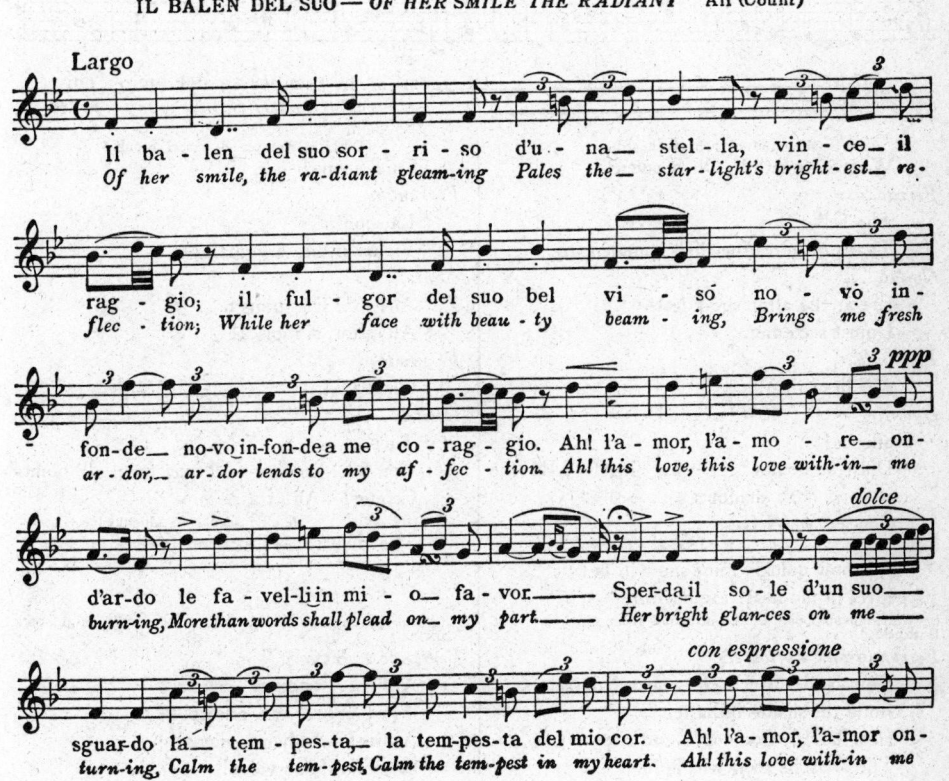

Il ba-len del suo sor-ri-so d'u-na stel-la, vin-ce il
Of her smile, the ra-diant gleam-ing Pales the star-light's bright-est re-

rag-gio; il ful-gor del suo bel vi-so no-vo in-
flec-tion; While her face with beau-ty beam-ing, Brings me fresh

fon-de no-vo in-fon-de a me co-rag-gio. Ah! l'a-mor, l'a-mo-re on-
ar-dor, ar-dor lends to my af-fec-tion. Ah! this love, this love with-in me

d'ar-do le fa-vel-li in mi-o fa-vor. Sper-da il so-le d'un suo
burning, More than words shall plead on my part. Her bright glan-ces on me

sguar-do la tem-pes-ta, la tem-pes-ta del mio cor. Ah! l'a-mor, l'a-mor on-
turn-ing, Calm the tem-pest, Calm the tem-pest in my heart. Ah! this love with-in me

d'ar-de le fa-vel-li in mio fa-vo-re, sper-da il so-le d'un suo
burn-ing, More than words shall win me fa-vor, Her bright glan-ces on me

sguar-do la— tem-pe-sta del— mio cor. Ah! l'a-mor, l'a-mor on-
turn-ing calm the tem-pest in— my heart. Ah! this love with-in me

d'ar-do le fa-vel-li in mio fa-vore, sper-da il so-le d'un suo sguar-do ia tem-pe-sta,
burn-ing More than words shall win me fa-vor, Her bright glan-ces on me turn-ing, Calm the tem-pest,

Ah!_____ si. la tem-pes-ta del mio cor.
Ah!_____ calm the tem-pest in my heart.

(A sound of bells is heard.)	(Odesi il rintocco de' sacri bronzi.)
What soundeth? Oh, heaven!	Qual suono!—oh, ciel!—
Ferrando.	*Ferrando.*
The bell	La squilla
That proclaims the rite's commencing.	Vicino il rito annunzia!—
Count.	*Conte.*
Ere at the altar she kneels	Ah! pria che giunga,
I must seize her.	All' altar, si rapisca!
Ferrando.	*Ferrando.*
Ah! heed thee!	Oh, bada!
Count.	*Conte.*
Silence!	Taci!
Didst hear not? Depart then! 'Mid the trees' dark shadows	Non odo—andate—Di quei faggi all' ombra Celatevi—Ah! fra poco.
Conceal yourselves.	
(Ferrando and followers retire.)	(Ferrando e gli altri seguaci si allontanano.)
Ah! how quickly mine she will be!	Mia diverrà!—Tutto m' investe un foco!
Fires in my heart are burning!	
(Watching anxiously in the direction from which Leonora is expected.)	(Ansioso, guardingo osserva dalla porte onde deve giunger Leonora.)
Ferrando and Followers.	*Ferrando e Seguaci.*
How bold! Let's go—conceal ourselves	Ardire!—Andiam—celiamoci
Amid the shades in haste.	Tra l'ombre—nel mister!—
How bold! Come on—and silence keep,	Ardire!—Andiam—silenzio!—
The prize he soon will hold.	Si comia il suo voler!

PER ME ORA FATALE — OH, FATAL HOUR   Air (Count)

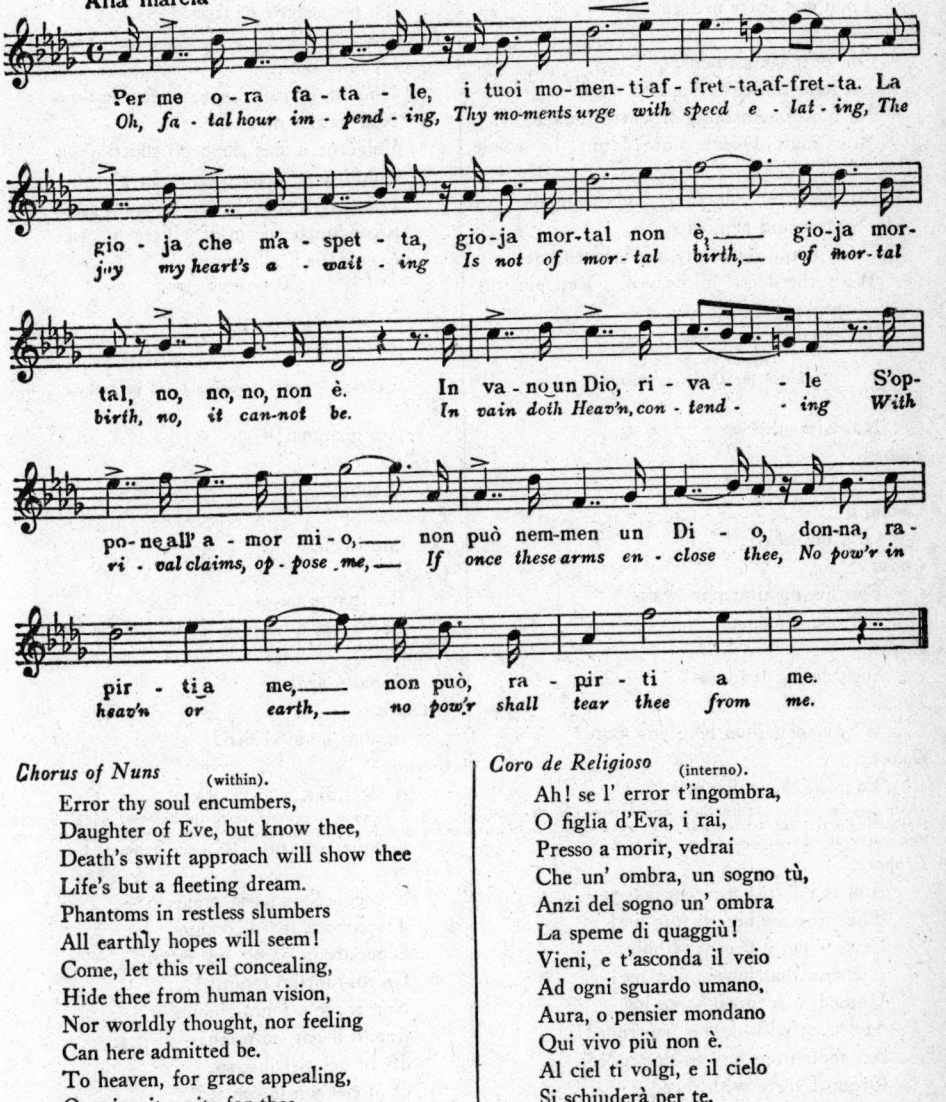

Alla marcia

Per me o - ra fa - ta - le, i tuoi mo - men - ti af - fret - ta, af - fret - ta. La
Oh, fa - tal hour im - pend - ing, Thy mo - ments urge with speed e - lat - ing, The

gio - ja che m'a - spet - ta, gio - ja mor - tal non è,___ gio - ja mor -
joy my heart's a - wait - ing Is not of mor - tal birth,___ of mor - tal

tal, no, no, no, non è.   In va - no un Dio, ri - va - - le S'op-
birth, no, it can - not be.   In vain doth Heav'n, con - tend - - ing With

po - ne all' a - mor mi - o,___ non può nem - men un Di - o, don - na, ra -
ri - val claims, op - pose me,___ If once these arms en - close thee, No pow'r in

pir - ti a me,___ non può, ra - pir - ti a me.
heav'n or earth,___ no pow'r shall tear thee from me.

Chorus of Nuns (within).

Error thy soul encumbers,
Daughter of Eve, but know thee,
Death's swift approach will show thee
Life's but a fleeting dream.
Phantoms in restless slumbers
All earthly hopes will seem!
Come, let this veil concealing,
Hide thee from human vision,
Nor worldly thought, nor feeling
Can here admitted be.
To heaven, for grace appealing,
Opening it waits for thee.

(Enter LEONORA with INEZ and female followers.)

Leonora.

Why art thou weeping?

Coro de Religioso (interno).

Ah! se l' error t'ingombra,
O figlia d'Eva, i rai,
Presso a morir, vedrai
Che un' ombra, un sogno tù,
Anzi del sogno un' ombra
La speme di quaggiù!
Vieni, e t'asconda il veio
Ad ogni sguardo umano,
Aura, o pensier mondano
Qui vivo più non è.
Al ciel ti volgi, e il cielo
Si schiuderà per te.

(Entra LEONORA con INEZ, e seguiti.)

Leonora.

Perchè piangete?

Inez.

Ah! truly
Thou wilt leave us forever!

Leonora.

Oh, dear companions,
No fond smile, no hope to cheer me,
No flower remaining on earth for me!
Now must I turn unto Him, the whole support
Of those in affliction, and after days of prayer and penitence,
I may haply rejoin my lost beloved one
With the blest in heaven. Restrain thy weeping;
To the altar now lead me.

> (About to proceed.)
> (Enter the COUNT, suddenly.)

Count.

No, withhold!

Ladies.

The Count here!

Leonora.

Gracious heaven!

Count.

For thee no altar now waits
But one hymenial.

Ladies.

Such daring boldness!

Leonora.

Why comest thou here, insensate?

Count.

To make thee mine now!

> (On saying so, he approaches, and seizes LEONORA—but MANRICO appears, like a phantom, and places himself between them—general consternation.)

Leonora.

And can I still my eyes believe
That see thee here before me!
Or is it but a dream of bliss,
A charm that hovers o'er me!
Unused to such excessive joy
My heart with doubts contended!
Art thou from heaven descended,
Or am I there with thee?

Count.

Do souls departed thus return
From death's domains eternal?

Ines.

Ah!—dunque
Tu per sempre ne lasci!

Leonora.

O dolci amici
Un riso, una speranza, un fior la terra
Non ha per me! Degg' io
Volgermi a quei che degli afflitti è solo
Conforto, e dopo i penitenti giorni,
Púò fra gli eletti al mio perduto bene
Ricongìungermi un di. Tergete i rai,
E guidatemi all' ara.

> (Incamminandosi.)

> (Entra il CONTE, irrompendo ad un tratte.)

Conte.

No, giammai!—

Donne.

Il conte!

Leonora.

Giusto ciel!

Conte.

Per te non havvi
Che l' ara d' imeneo—

Donne.

Cotanto ardia!—

Leonora.

Insano! e qui venisti?

Conte.

A farti mia.

> (E si dicendo, scagliasci verso de LEONORA onde impadronirsi di lei; ma fra esso e la preda trovasi, qual fantasma surle di sotterra, MANRICO. Un grido universal irrompe.)

Leonora.

E deggio?—e posso crederlo?—
Ti veggo a me d'accanto!
E questo un sogno, un' estasi,
Un sovrumano incanto!
Non regge a tanto giubilo
Rapito il cor, sorpreso!—
Sei tu dal ciel disceso,
O in ciel son io con te?

Conte.

Dunque gli estinti lasciano
Di morte il regno eterno!

Thus to condemn me, doth hell indeed
Renounce its prey infernal!
But if as yet thy fatal thread
Of time remains unmeasured,
If life by thee is treasured,
Then fly from her and me.

Manrico.

Heaven's blest abode, nor regions infernal
Have yet possessed me.
True, base assassins mortal blows may deal,
Thy deeds impressed me.
O'erwhelming power that naught can stay
Have ocean's waves unbounded!
He, who thy guilt confounded!
His arm has aided me.

Ladies.

In heaven thy faith reposing,
                    (To LEONORA.)
Thence comes this aid to thee.

Ferrando and Followers.

'Tis fate thou'rt now opposing,
From harm it holds him free.
                    (Enter RUIZ and Soldiers.)

Ruiz and Followers.

Long live Urgal!

Manrico.

My brave-hearted soldiers!

Ruiz.

Come then.

Manrico
                    (To LEONORA).
Lady, I wait thee.

Count.

Wouldst thou rob me of her?
                    (Opposing him.)

Leonora.

Oh!

Manrico
                    (to the COUNT).
Withhold there!

Count.

Wouldst thou deprive me of her?
No!
                    (Drawing his sword.)

Ruiz and Soldiers.

He rayeth!
                    (Surrounding the COUNT.)

A danno mio rinunzia
Le prede sue l' inferno!—
Ma se non mai si fransero
De' giorni tuoi gli stami,
Se vivi e viver brami,
Fuggi da lei, da me.

Manrico.

Nè m' ebbe il ciel, nè l' orrido
Varco infernal sentiero—
Infami sgherri vibrano
Colpi mortali, è vero!
Potenza irrestibile
Hanno de fiumi l' onde!—
Ma gli empj un Dio confonde!—
Quel Dio soccorse a me!

Donne.

Il cielo in cui fidasti,
                    (A LEONORA.)
Pietade avea di te.

Ferrando e Seguaci.

Tu col destin contrasti;
                    (Al CONTE.)
Suo difensore egli è.
                    (Entra RUIZ, seguìto da lunga tratta d' armati.)

Ruiz.

Urgel viva!

Manrico.

Miei prodi guerrieri!—

Ruiz.

Vieni.

Manrico
                    (A LEONORA.)
Donna, mi segui.

Conte.

E tu speri?
                    (Opponendosi.)

Leonora.

Oh!

Manrico
                    (Al CONTE.)
T'arretra.

Conte.

Involarmi costei!
No!
                    (Sguainando la spada.)

Ruiz e Armati.

Vaneggi!
                    (Accerchiando il CONTE.)

Ferrando and Followers.

 What wouldst thou, my lord?

 (The Count is disarmed by the soldiers of Ruiz.)

Count.

 All my reason in fury is lost!

  (with gestures and accents of fury.)

Leonora.

 (He affrights me!)

Count.

 Furies dwell in my heart!

Ruiz and Soldiers.

 Come then, a future of smiles waits for thee.

  (To Manrico.)

Ferrando and Followers.

 Yield thee, since yielding no baseness implies.

 (Exit Manrico, leading Leonora—the Count is driven back, the ladies retreat to the Convent, as the curtain falls.)

END OF THE SECOND ACT.

Ferrando e Seguaci.

 Che tenti, signor!

 (Il Conte è disarmato ca quei di Ruiz.)

Conte.

 Di ragione ogni lumi perdei!

  (Con gesti ed accenti di maniaco furore.)

Leonora.

 (M'atterrisce.)

Conte.

 Ho lo furie nel cor!

Ruiz e Armati.

 Vieni; è lieta la sorte per te.

  (A Manrico.)

Ferrando e Seguaci.

 Cedi; or ceder viltade non è!

 (Manrico tragge seco Leonora—il Conte è respinto, le donne rifuggono al cenobio—scende subito la tela.)

FINE DELL' ATTO SECONDO.

ACT III.

THE GIPSY'S SON.

Scene I—A camp. On the right, the tent of the Count di Luna, on which is displayed a banner, indicative of his supremacy. The fortress of Castellor seen in the distance. The scene full of Soldiers, some playing, some polishing their accoutrements, some walking in apparent conversation, while others are on duty as Sentinels.

 (Enter Ferrando, from the tent of the Count.)

Some of the Soldiers.

 Now with dice, may fortune speed us;
 Other games will shortly need us!
 From our swords this blood we burnish,
 Coming deeds fresh stains will furnish.

 (Sounds of warlike instruments are heard; all start and turn towards the sounds.)

Some Soldiers.

 Lo! they come for succor praying!

 (A strong band of soldiers crosses the camp.)

Other Soldiers.

 Still, they make a brave display!

All.

 Let us, without more delaying
 Castellor attack to-day.

Ferrando.

 Yes, brave companions; at dawn, to-morrow,

ATTO III.

IL FIGLIO DELLA ZINGARA.

Scena I—Accampamento—A destra, il padiglione dei Conte di Luna, su cui sventola la bandiera in segno di supremo comando—da lungi Torreggia Castellor.—Scolte di uomini d'arme da per tutto; altri giocano, altri forbiscono le armi, altri passeggiano.

 (Entra Ferrando, dal padiglione del Conte.)

Alcuni Uomini d'Arme.

 Or co' dadi, ma fra poco
 Giocherem ben altro gioco!
 Questo acciar, dal sangue or terso,
 Fia di sangue in breve asperso!

 (Odonsi strumenti guerrieri; tutti si volgono là dove avanza il suono.)

Alcuni.

 Il soccorso dimandato!

 (Un grosso drappello di balestrieri, in completa armatura, traversa il campo.)

Altri.

 Han l'aspetto del valor!

Tutti.

 Più l'assalto ritardato
 Or non fia di Castellor.

Ferrando.

 Sì prodi amici; al dì novello, è mente

Our leader has now resolved
On storming the fortress on all sides.
Within its walls a booty immense
We're sure to find; 'tis more than hopeful;
If conquered 'tis ours then.

Some of the Soldiers.

Pleasure there invites us.

Ferrando and Chorus.

Now let the trumpet in war tones resound-
ing,
Call to arms; with courage bold, we'll march
undaunted.
Haply, to-morrow, our proud foes confound-
ing,
On those walls shall our banners be planted.
Ne'er more brilliant were prospects victor-
ious
Than the hopes which our hearts now elate.
Thence, we'll gather renown, bright and
glorious;
Pleasure, honor and profit there await us,
Honor and booty for us there await.

(Enter the COUNT, from the tent; turns with lowering
gaze towards Castellor.)

Count.

Within my rival's arms! How this reflec-
tion,
Like a taunting demon, follows me
Wherever I wander. Within my rival's
arms! To-morrow
Ere the day dawns, I'll hasten to sunder
them forever!
Oh! Leonora!

(A tumult is heard.)
(Enter FERRANDO.)

Count.

What now?

Ferrando.

Around the camp
Was seen a gipsy-woman, loitering:
Surprised by the sentinels on duty
To escape she attempted. With reason
They suspected her of spying out our move-
ments,
And pursued.

Count.

Was she taken?

Del capitan la rôcca
Investir da ogni parte.
Colà pingue bottino
Certezza è rinvenir, più che speranza.
Si vinca, è nostro.

Uomini d'Arme.

Tu c'inviti a danza!

Ferrando con Coro.

Squilli, eccheggi la tromba guerriera
Chiami all' armi, alla pugna, all' assalto;
Fia domani la nostra bandiera
Di quei merli piantata sull' alto.
No, giammai non sorrise vittoria
Di più liete speranze finor!
Ivi l'util ci aspetta e la gloria;
Ivi opimi la preda e l'onore!
Ivi opimi la preda e l'onor!

(Entra il CONTE, uscito dalla tenda, volge uno sguardo
bieco a CASTELLOR.)

Conte.

In braccio al mio rival!—Questo pensiero
Come persecutor dernone ovunque
M'insegue! In braccio al mio rival!—Ma
corro
Surta appena l'aurora,
Io corro a separavi—Oh, Leonora!

(Odesi tumulti.)

(Entra FERRANDO.)

Conte.

Che fu?

Ferrando.

D'appresso il campo
S'aggirava una zingara; sorpresa
Da' nostri esploratori,
Si volse in fuga; essi, a ragion temendo
Una spia nella trista,
L'inseguir—

Conte.

Fu raggiunta?

Ferrando.

They seized her.

Count.

Hast seen her yet?

Ferrando.

No; the conductor
Of the escort hath so
Informed me.

Count.

Here she comes.

(AZUCENA, with her hands bound together, is dragged in by the Sentinels.)

Soldiers.

Come on, thou sorceress, come forward!

Azucena.

Oh, help me! Pray release me! Ah, maddened wretches,
Of what accuse me?

Count.

Come hither.

(AZUCENA is led before the COUNT.)

To me reply now, and tremble if thou liest.

Azucena.

Ask, then.

Count.

Whither bound?

Azucena.

I know not.

Count.

How?

Azucena.

'Tis a custom of the gipsies
Without purpose to wander
Wherever fancy leads them,
Their only shelter heaven,
The wide world their country.

Count.

Whence comest thou?

Azucena.

From Biscalia, where, till of late,
Was my sole abode, amid its wild, barren
mountains.

Count.

(From Biscalia!)

Ferrando.

E presa.

Conte.

Vista l' hai tu?

Ferrando.

No; della scorta
Il condottier m'apprese
L'evento.

(Tumulto più vicino.)

Conte.

Eccola.

(Entra AZUCENA, con le mani avvinte, è trascinata dagli Esploratori—un codazzo d'altri soldati.)

Esploratori.

Innanzi, o strega, innanzi.

Azucena.

Aìta!—Mi lasciate—Oh! furibondi,
Che mal fec' io?

Conte.

S'appressi.

(AZUCENA è tratta innanzi il CONTE.)

A me rispondi.
E trema dal mentir!

Azucena.

Chiedi.

Conte.

Ove vai?

Azucena.

Nol so.

Conte.

Che?

Azucena.

D'una zingara è costume
Muover senza disegno
Il passo vagabondo,
Ed è suo tetto il ciel, sua patria il mondo

Conte.

E vieni?

Azucena.

Da Biscaglia, ove finora
La sterili montagne ebbi ricetto.

Conte.

(Da Biscaglia!)

Ferrando.
(What heard I? oh, dark suspicion.)

Ferrando.
(Che intesi!—Oh, qual sospetto!)

GIORNI POVERI— *I WAS POOR, YET UNCOMPLAINING* (Azucena)

Con espressione

Gior-ni po-ve-ri vi-ve-a, pur con-ten-ta del mio
I was poor, yet un-com-plain-ing, Lived con-tent-ed, grate-ful

sta-to; so-la spe-me un fi-glio a-ve-a, Mi la-sciò! m'ob-
heart-ed. With one son, sole hope re-main-ing, But, a-las! from

bli-a l'in-gra-to. Io de-ser-ta, va-do er-ran-do di quel
me he hath part-ed. Now I wan-der sad and lone-ly Through the

fi-glio ri-cer-can-do, di quel fi-glio che al mio co-
world, seek-ing him on-ly; All my heart's trou-bled e-mo-

re pe-ne or-ri-bi-li-co-stò!— Qual per es-so pro-vo a-mo-re,
tion For his loss, no words can show!— Ah! for him my warm de-vo-tion,

qual per es-so pro-vo a-mo-re ma-dre in ter-ra non-pro-vò.
Ah! for him, my warm de-vo-tion, No earth-ly moth-er else— can know.

Ferrando.
Ah! those features!

Count.
Say, long time
Didst thou abide among those mountains?

Azucena.
Long time, yes.

Ferrando.
(Il suo volto.)

Conte.
Di' traesti
Lunga etade fra quei monti!

Azucena.
Lunga, sì.

Count.

Dost thou remember
A child, son of a noble,
Who was stolen from his castle
Many years since and carried thither?

Azucena.

And thou, tell me—art?

Count.

A brother
Of the lost one.

Azucena.

Ah!

Ferrando.

Yes!
(Noting the ill-concealed terror of AZUCENA.)

Count.

Hast heard what there befell him?

Azucena.

I?—No!—Oh! grant
That I may now my search continue.

Ferrando.

Stay, impostor!

Azucena.

(Alas!)

Ferrando.

Thou seest here
The guilty wretch who that dark crime
Committed!

Count.

Continue!

Ferrando.

Behold her.

Azucena.

Silence!
(Softly to FERRANDO.)
Ferrando.

'Tis she, who stole the child, and burned
him!

Count.

Ah! guilty one!

Chorus.

'Tis the same one!

Azucena.

He speaks falsehood.

Conte.

Rammenteresti
Un fanciul, prole di conti,
Involato al suo castello,
Son tre lustri, e tratto quivi?

Azucena.

E tu, parla—sei?

Conte.

Fratello
Del rapito.

Azucena.

(Ah!)

Ferrando.

(Sì!)
(Notando il mal nascoto terrore di AZUCENA.)

Conte.

Ne udivi
Mai novella?

Azucena.

Io?—No!—Concedi
Che del figlio l'orme io scopra.

Ferrando.

Resta, iniqua—

Azucena.

(Ohimè!)

Ferrando.

Tu vedi
Chi l'infame, orribil opra
Commettea!

Conte.

Finisci.

Ferrando.

E dessa!

Azucena.

(Taci.)
(Piano a FERRANDO.)
Ferrando.

E dessa, che il bambino arse!

Conte.

Ah, perfida!

Coro.

Ella stessa!

Azucena.

Ei mentisce.

Count.
Thou canst not fly
Thy fate impending.

Azucena.
Ah!

Count.
Those bonds
Draw still more closely.
(The soldiers obey.)

Azucena.
Oh! heaven! Oh! heaven!

Chorus.
Vent thy rage!

Azucena.
And comest thou not,
My son, Manrico, to release me?
Thy unhappy mother now
To aid and succor?

Count.
Thou the mother of Manrico?

Ferrando.
Tremble!

Count.
Oh! fate! thus in my power!

Azucena.
Ah! loose awhile, ye monsters vile,
These bonds that now confine me.
Such fierce and cruel torments
To lingering death consign me!
Descendant of a wicked sire,
Than he more guilty, tremble!
For God protects the weak,
And he will punish thee!

Count.
Thy son, oh, wretched Zingara,
Is he that base betrayer?
And can I, thee condemning,
Strike, too, the traitor's heart?
The joy my soul o'erflowing,
Words lack the power of showing!
To my arm, for vengeance, a brother's ashes
call!
Avenged in full shall they be!

Ferrando and Chorus.
Base wretch, the fatal pile prepared,

Conte.
Al tuo destino.
Or non fuggì.

Azucena.
Deh!

Conte.
Quei nodi
Più stringete
(I soldati esequiscono.)

Azucena.
Oh, Dio! Oh, Dio!

Coro.
Uria pure.

Azucena.
E tu non m'odi,
Oh, Manrico,—oh, figlio mio?
Non soccorri all' infelice
Madre tua!

Conte.
Di Manrico genitrice!

Ferrando.
Trema!

Conte.
Oh, sorte! in mio poter!

Azucena.
Deh, ralentate, o barbari,
Le acerbe mie ritorte—
Questo crudel supplizio
E prolungata morte!
D' iniquo genitore
Empio figliuol peggiore,
Trema—V' è Dio pe' miseri,
E Dio ti punirà!

Conte.
Tua prole, o turpe zingara,
Colui, quel seduttore!
Portò col tuo supplizio
Ferirlo in mezzo al core!
Gioja m'inonda il petto,
Ciu non esprimo il detto!
Meco il fraterno cenore
Piena vendetta avra!

Ferrando e Coro.
Infame, pira sorgere;

Ah! yes, thou soon shalt see
Bright flames the heavens illuming!
Not this alone awaits thee,
These earthly fires consuming!
Condemned to flames infernal
There shall thy wicked spirit dwell!

(AZUCENA is dragged away by the soldiers, by command of the COUNT. He enters the tent, followed by FERRANDO.)

SCENE II—Hall adjoining the Chapel of Castellor; a balcony in the background.

(MANRICO, LEONORA, RUIZ.)

Leonora.

Ah! what clamor of arms
Is that which reached me?

Manrico.

Great is the danger;
Vain are all my attempts to hide it!
At early dawn to-morrow
The foe will assail us.

Leonora.

Alas! what sayst thou?

Manrico.

Be assured that our swords will be victorious!
We can equal them
In arms, boldness, and courage.
Depart.
(To RUIZ.)
The preparations for the strife
In my absence, thou wilt accomplish.
Let nought be wanting.
(Exit RUIZ.)

Leonora.

What a sombre splendor
Is o'er our bridal shining!

Manrico.

All this mournful foreboding
Pray banish, dearest!

Leonora.

And can I?

Manrico.

'Tis love, sublime emotion, at such a moment
Bids thy heart still be hopeful.
Ah! love; how blest our life will be

Empia, vedrai tra poco—
Nè solo tuo supplizio
Sarà l'orrendo foco!
Le vampe dell' inferno
A te fian rogo eterno;
Ivi penare ed ardere
L'anima tua dovrà!

(Al cenno del CONTE, i soldati traggono seco loco AZUCENA. Egli entra nella sua tenda, seguito da FERRANDO.)

SCENA II—Sala adjacente alla Cappella in Castellor, con verone in fondo.

(MANRICO, LEONORA, e RUIZ.)

Leonora.

Quale d'armi fragore
Foc' anzi intesi?

Manrico.

Alto è il periglio!—Vano
Dissimularlo fora!
Alla novella aurora
Assaliti saremo!

Leonora.

Ahimè!—che dici!

Manrico.

Ma de' nostri nemici
Avrem vittoria.—Pari
Abbiamo al loro ardir, brando e coraggio.
Tu va.
(a RUIZ).
Le belliche opre,
Nell' assenza mia breve, a te commetto.
Che nulla manchi!
(RUIZ parte.)

Leonora.

Di qual tetra luce
Il nostro imen risplende!

Manrico.

Il presagio funesto,
Deh, sperdi, o cara!

Leonora.

E il posso?

Manrico.

Amor—sublime amore,
In tal istante ti favella al core.
Ah! sì, ben mio, coll' essere
Io tuo, tu mia consorte,

Our fond desires attaining,
My soul shall win fresh ardor,
My arm new courage gaining.
But, if, upon the fatal page
Of destiny impending,
I'm doomed among the slain to fall,
'Gainst hostile arms contending,
In life's last hour, with fainting breath,
My thoughts will turn to thee.
Preceding thee to heaven, will death
Alone appear to me.
(Tones of organ heard from the neighboring chapel.)

Leonora.

The mystic tide of harmony
Within our hearts doth flow!
The church unfolds the raptures
From holy love that grow!
(While they are about to enter the chapel, RUIZ enters hurriedly.)

Ruiz.

Manrico!

Manrico.

How?

Ruiz.

The Zingara,
Yonder, in chains, behold her!

Manrico.

Oh, heaven!

Ruiz.

Led on by cruel men,
They near the stake already.

Manrico.

Oh, heavens! my limbs are failing me;
Shadows my eyes are veiling!
(Approaching the balcony.)

Leonora.

Thou tremblest!

Manrico.

With reason. Know the cause:
I am—

Leonora.

Thou'rt what?

Manrico.

Her offspring.
Ah! monsters! this dark revolting scene
Almost of my breath deprives me!

Avrò più l' alma intrepida,
Il braccio avrò più forte.
Ma pur, se nella pagina
De' miei destini è scritto,
Ch' io resti fra le vittime,
Dal ferro ostil trafitto,
Fra quegli estremi aneliti,
A te il pensier verrà, verrà,
E solo in ciel precederti
La morte a me parrà!

(Odesi il suono dell' organo dalla vicina cappella.)

Leonora.

L'onda de suoni mistici
Pura discende al cor!
Vieni; ci schiude il tempio
Gioje di casto amor!

(Mentre s' avviano giubilanti al tempio, RUIZ soppragiunge frettoloso.)

Ruiz.

Manrico!

Manrico.

Che?

Ruiz.

La zingara,
Vieni, tra ceppi mira!

Manrico.

Oh, Dio!

Ruiz.

Per man de' barbari
Accesa è girà la pira.

Manrico.

Oh, ciel! mie membra oscillano—
Nube me copre il ciglio!
(Accostandosi al verone.)

Leonora.

Tu fremi.

Manrico.

E il deggio! Sappilo,
Io son—

Leonora.

Che mai?

Manrico.

Suo figlio!
Ah, vili! Il rio spettacolo
Quasi il respir m'invola!

Collect our forces without the least delay.
Ruiz—go—speed thee, quickly!
(Ruiz departs hastily.)

Raduna i nostri—affrettati.
Ruiz—va—torna—vola!
(Ruiz parte.)

DI QUELLA PIRA — *OF THAT DARK SCAFFOLD*   Air. (Manrico)

Di quel-la pi - ra l'or-ren-do fo - co Tu-te le fi - bre
Of that dark scaf - fold, those flames as - cend - ing Thrill thro' each fi - bre

m'ar-se av-vam-po! Em - pi, spe-gne-te - la, o ch'io fra po - co Col san-gue
with mad-d'ning glow! Quench them, ye mon-sters vile or, still of - fend - ing, To stay their

vos - tro la spe - gne - rò. E - ra già fi - glio pri - ma d'a -
fu - ry, your blood shall flow! I was her off - spring, ere love I

mar - ti, Non puo fre - nar - mi il tuo mar - tir!__ Ma-dre in - fe -
gave__ thee, In vain to hold__ me, thy griefs would try.__ Moth - er un -

li - ce, cor-ro a sal - var - ti, O te-co al - me - no cor-ro a mo-rir!
hap - py! I fly to save thee, Or, all else fail - ing, with thee to die.

Leonora.
Such heavy sorrows my heart o'erpowering.
Oh! better far would it be to die!
(Re-enter Ruiz, with Soldiers.)

Ruiz.
Arouse ye to arms now!
The foe we will defy!
(Manrico rushes out, followed by Ruiz and Soldiers. From within a noise of arms and warlike instruments is heard.)

END OF THE THIRD ACT.

Leonora.
Non reggo a colpi tanto funesti.
Oh, quanto meglio saria morir!
(Entra Ruiz, torna armati.)

Ruiz.
All' armi, all' armi! eccone presti
A pugnar teco, teco a morir.
(Manrico parte frettoloso seguito da Ruiz, e dagli armati, mentre odesi dall' interno fragor d'armi e di bellici strumenti.)

FINE DELL' ATTO TERZO.

ACT IV.

THE PUNISHMENT.

SCENE I—A wing of the palace of Aliaferia; in the angle, a tower with window secured by iron bars. Night; dark and clouded.

(Enter Leonora and Ruiz, enveloped in cloaks.)

Ruiz (in an undertone).

Here stay we;
Yonder's the tower where are confined the
  prisoners for state offences;
Hither they brought him whom we are seeking.

Leonora.

Go thou:
Leave me here; be not anxious for my safety;
Perchance I yet may save him.

(Ruiz retires.)

Afraid for me? Secure
And ready are my defences!

(She gazes upon a jewel which she wears on her right hand.)

In this dark hour of midnight
I hover round thee near approaching.
Unknown to thee, love! Ye moaning breezes
  around me playing.
In pity aid me, my sighs to him conveying!

ATTO IV.

IL SUPPLIZIO.

SCENA I—Un' ala del palazzo dell' Aliaferia—all' angolo una torre, con finestre assicurate da spranghe di ferro. Notte oscurissima.

(Si avanzano due personne ammentellate; sono Ruiz e Leonora.)

Ruiz (sommessamente).

Siam giunti:
Ecco la torre, ove di stato
Gemono i prigionieri.—Ah! l'infelice
Ivi fu tratto!

Leonora.

Vanne.
Lasciami, nè timor di me te prenda—
Salvarlo io potrò, forse.

(Ruiz si allontana.)

Timor di me?—Sicura,
Presta è la mia difesa!

(I suoi occhi figgonsi ad una gemma che le fregia la maz destra.)

In questa oscura
Notte ravvolta, presso a te son io,
E tu nol sai! Gemente
Aura, che intorno spiri,
Deh, pietosa gli arreca i miei sospiri.

D'AMOR SULL' ALI ROSEE — *ON ROSY WINGS OF LOVE*   Air. (Leonora)

de-sta al-le me - mo - rie, Ai so-gni, ai so-gni dell' a - mor,___
call to his fond re - mem - brance Sweet vi - sions, sweet vi-sions of our___ love;___

dolce

Ma, deh! non dir-gli im-prov-vi-do le pe - ne, le pe-ne, le pe - ne del mio cor.
But, let no ac - cent re - veal to him The sor - rows, the sor-rows, the griefs my heart doth prove.

con forza   *dolce*   *tr*

Deh! non dir - gli im-prov-vi-do le pe - - - ne del mio cor, le pe -
Let no ac - cent re - veal to him the tri - - als I now prove, the sor -

ne, le pe - - - - - - ne del cor.
rows, the sor - - - - - - rows I prove.

Chorus (The passing bell.) (within).	Voci (Suona la campana dei morti.) (interne).
Have compassion upon a soul departing For that abode, from whence there's no re- turning; Thy forgiveness, oh! power divine, impart- ing, Let him not be a prey to endless burning.	Miserere d'un' alma già vicina Alla partenza che non ha ritorno; Miserere di lei, bontà divina, Preda non sia dell' infernal soggiorno.
Leonora. That solemn petition, so sadly ascending, With terror and mystery the air seems to fill! 'Gainst fatal foreboding my heart is con- tending, My breath is suspended, my pulses are still.	*Leonora.* Quel suon, quelle preci solemni, funeste, Empiron quest' aere di cupo terrore! Contende l'ambascia, che tutta m'investe Al labbro il respiro. i palpiti al core!

AH, CHE LA MORTE — *AH, HOW DEATH*   Air (Manrico)

Ah!___ che la mor-te o-gno - ra   È___ tar-da nel ve-nir A chi de-
Ah!___ how death still de - lay - eth,   Lin - gers, or seems to fly From him, who

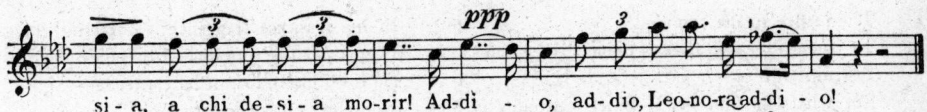

si - a, a chi de-si-a mo-rir! Ad-dì - o, ad-dio, Leo-no-ra ad-di - o!
long-eth, from him who long-eth to die! Fare-well,— love, fare-well, Leo-no-ra, fare-well!

Leonora.

Oh, heaven! faintness o'erpowers me!

Chorus

(within).

Have compassion upon a soul departing
For that abode, from whence there's no re-
turning;
Thy forgiveness, oh! power divine, impart-
ing,
Let him not fall a prey to endless burning.

Leonora.

O'er yonder dark tower, ah, death waits the
morrow
With wings pale and shadowy his watch
seems to hold.
Ah! ne'er will they open those portals of sorrow
'Till after the victim is lifeless and cold.

Manrico

(in the tower).

Now with my life fulfilling
Love's fervent vows to thee!
Do not forget; let me remembered be.
Farewell, my love, farewell, Leonora!

Leonora.

And can I ever forget thee!
Thou shalt see that more enduring
Love, than mine, ne'er had existence,
Triumph over fate securing,
Death shall yield to its resistance.
At the price of mine, now blighted,
Thy dear life will I defend,
Or again with thee united,
To the tomb will I descend!

(Enter the Count and his followers. Leonora stands aside.)

Count.

You hear me? Give the son to the axe
At daybreak; lead to the stake the mother.

(The followers enter the tower.)

Perhaps, thus acting, I abuse the power

Leonora.

Oh, ciel!—sento mancarmi!

Voci

(internè).

Miserere d'un' alma già vicina
Alla partenza che non ha ritorno!
Miserere di lei, bontà divina,
Preda non sia dell' infernal soggiorno!

Leonora.

Sull' orrida torre, ah! par che la morte
Con ali di tenebre librando si và!
Ahi! forse dischiuse gli fian queste port'
Sol quando cadavere già freddo ei sarà!

(Rimane assorta, dopo qualche momento scuotesi, ed procinto di partire, allorchè vienne dalla torre un gemito e quindi un mestó suono; elle si ferma.)

Manrico.

(Dalla torre.)

Sconto col sangue mio
L'amor che posi in te!
Non ti scordar di me!
Leonora, Addio!

Leonora.

Di te, di te scordar me!

(S'apre una porta.)

Tu vedrai che amore in terra
Mai del mio non fù più forte:
Vinse il fato in aspra guerra,
Vincerà la stessa morte.
O col prezzo di mia vita
La tua vita salverò,
O con te per sempre unita
Nella tomba scenderò.

(Entra il Conte, ed alcuni seguaci. Leonora si pene in disparte.)

Conte.

Udiste? Come albeggi,
La scure al figlio, ed alla madre il rogo.

(Entrano i seguaci per un piccolo uscio nella torre.)

Abuso io forse quel poter che pieno

The prince to me confided.	In me trasmise li prence! A tal mi tragg
To such excesses that woman's love con-strains me!	Donna per me funesta!—Ov' ella è mai?
But where to find her? Since Castellor is ours	Ripresso Castellor, di lei contezza
Of her no tidings have reached me;	Non ebbi, e furo indarno
All my researches on every side are fruit-less!	Tante ricerche e tante!
Ah! cruel love, where art thou?	Oh!—dove sei crudele?

Leonora   (advancing).
Standing before thee!
Count.
    Those accents! Lady! thus near me?
Leonora.
    Thou see'st me.
Count.
    What brought thee hither?
Leonora.
    Already his last hour approaches
    And thou dost ask me?
Count.
    Thou still wouldst dare me?
Leonora.
    Ah, yes! for him
    I would ask of thee compassion.
Count.
    How? art thou raving?
    Mercy to him, my rival, show?
Leonora.
    May heaven with mercy inspire thee!
Count.
    My whole desire is for vengeance. Go!
(LEONORA throws herself despairingly at his feet.)

Leonora   (avanzandosi).
A te dinante.
Conte.
    Qual voce!—Come!—tu, donna?
Leonora.
    Il vedi.
Conte.
    A che venisti?
Leonora.
    Egli è gia presso
    All' ora estrema, e tu lo chiedi?
Conte.
    Osar potresti?
Leonora.
    Ah, si, per esso
    Pietà domando—
Conte.
    Che! tu deliri!
    Io del rivale sentir pietà?
Leonora.
    Clemente il Nume a te l'inspiri—
Conte.
    E sol vendetta mio nume. Va!
(LEONORA si getta disperata ai suoi piedi.)

MIRA DI ACERBE — *WITNESS THE TEARS OF AGONY*   Air (Leonora)

Mi - ra, dia-cer-be la-gri-me Spar-goal tuo pie-deun ri - o.
Wit-ness the tears of ag - o - ny Here, at thy feet, now rain-ing

Non bas-tail pian-to? sve-na-mi, Ti be - vi il san-gue mi - o!
If these suf-fice not, tor - ture me, My life's crim-son cur-rent drain-ing!

Sve - na - mi, sve - na - mi; Ti be - vi il san - gue mi - o
Tor - ture me, tor - ture me, My life's crim - son cur - rent drain - ing!

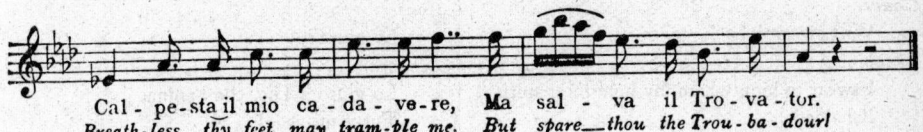

Cal - pe - sta il mio ca - da - ve - re, Ma sal - va il Tro - va - tor.
Breath - less, thy feet may tram - ple me, But spare thou the Trou - ba - dour!

Count.
Ah! rather would I speedily
Add to his fate impending
Thousands of bitter cruelties,
Torments and death unending;
The more thy love to his replies
My rage inflames the more.
(About to go.)

Leonora.
Hear me!
(Clinging to him.)

Count.
What more now?

Leonora.
Mercy!

Count.
Price is there none, which offered,
Could obtain it. Leave me now!

Leonora.
One yet there is, one only,
And that price I offer.

Count.
Offer, what?
Explain then! speak!

Leonora.
Myself, then!
(Extending her right hand to the COUNT, with anguish.)

Count.
Heaven! what dost tell me?

Leonora.
That I will perform
What here I promise.

Count.
Am I not dreaming?

Conte.
Ah! dell' indegno rendere
Vorrei peggior la sorte—
Fra mille atroci spasimi
Centuplicar sua morte—
Più l'ami, e più terribile
Divampa il mio furor!
(Vuol partire.)

Leonora.
Conte!
(Si aviticchia ed esso.)

Conte.
Nè cessi.

Leonora.
Grazia!

Conte.
Prezzo non avvi alcuno
Ad ottenerla—scostati!

Leonora.
Uno ve n' ha—sol uno,
Ed io ta l'offro.

Conte.
Spiegati,
Qual prezzo, di'?

Leonora.
Me stessa!
(Stendendogli la sua destra con dolore.)

Conte.
Ciel! tu dicesti?

Leonora.
E compiere
Saprò la mia promessa.

Conte.
E sogno il mio?

Leonora.

    Unclose for me
    The gates of yonder prison;
    Escaping, let the prisoner but hear me—
    Then I'll be thine.

Count.

    Wilt swear it?

Leonora.

    I swear to him, whom my innermost spirit
    Beholdeth!

Count.

    What ho!

(A jailer appears, in whose ear the COUNT whispers. While the COUNT is speaking to him, LEONORA sucks the poison concealed in the ring.)

Leonora.

    (A cold and lifeless bride
    Thou wilt have in me!)

Count
           (turning to LEONORA).
    My foe shall live!

Leonora
      (aside, her eyes filled with tears of joy).
    Shall live! Oh heaven! this boundless joy
    Too great is for words' expression;
    But from my throbbing, panting heart
    Flow thanks in grateful confession!
    Unmoved, my fate I now await;
    Rapture, thus life completing,
    With dying breath repeating
    Thou'rt saved from death through me!

Count.

    What words are those? oh! turn once more
    To me thy thoughts confiding.
    Ah! like a rapturous vision
    Seemeth thy kind decision.
    Thou wilt be mine! again declare,
    My heart of doubts relieving,
    Scarce in its bliss believing,
    Though promised still by thee!

Leonora.

    Now come—

Count.

    Remember! Thou hast sworn!

Leonora.

    My oath is sacred still.

        (They enter the tower.)

Leonora.

    Dischiudimi
    La via tra quelle mura;
    Ch' ei m' oda—che la vittima
    Fugga, e son tua.

Conte.

    Lo giura?

Leonora.

    Lo giuro a Dio, che l'anima
    Tutta mi vede!

Conte.

    Ola!

(Correndo al uscio della torre. Si presenta un custode— mentre il CONTE gli parla all' orecchio, LEONORA sugge il veleno chiuso nell' anello.)

Leonora.

    (M'avrai, ma fredda, esanime
    Spoglia.)

Conte
           (a LEONORA tornado).
    Colui vivrà.

Leonora
    (Da sè, alzando gli occhi, cui fan velo lagrime di letizia.)
    (Vivrà! Contende il giubilo
    I detti a me, Signore!)
    Ma coi frequenti palpiti
    Mercè ti rende il core!
    Ora il mio fine impavida,
    Piene di gioja attendo—
    Dirgli potrò, morendo;
    Salvo tu sei per me!

Conte.

    Fra te che parli?—Ah! volgimi.
    Volgimi il detto ancora,
    O mi parrà delirio
    Quan ascoltai finora—
    Tu mia! tu mia! ripetilo,
    Il dubbio cor serena—
    Ah! ch'io lo credo appena
    Udendolo da te!

Leonora.

    Andiam.

Conte.

    Giurasti—pensaci!

Leonora.

    E sacra la mia fè!

        (Entrano nella torre.)

SCENE II—A gloomy dungeon.

(AZUCENA lying upon an old mattress, MANRICO seated near her.)

Manrico.

Mother, thou sleepest not?

Azucena.

I have sought for slumber,
But, ah! it flies from my weary eyelids!—
I'll pray.

Manrico.

'Tis the air, cold and damp,
Perchance, with chills disturbs thee?

Azucena.

No; but from this tomb
Of the living would I escape forever,
Where confinement o'erpowers and suffo-
cates me.

Manrico.

Escape!   (Wringing his hands.)

Azucena.

Do not distress thee;
(Rising.)
These cruel tyrants cannot long oppress me.

Manrico.

Ah, wherefore?

Azucena.

Look ye! and behold already upon my brow
The finger of death has left its impress!

Manrico.

Ah!

Azucena.

They will find here
But a lifeless form, silent, cold and dead!
Merely a skeleton!

Manrico.

Cease ye!

Azucena.

Dost hear not?—coming footsteps—
Ah! the jailors approach, who to the stake
will drag me!
Defend, and save thy mother!

Manrico.

There's no one,
Resume thy courage.   There's no one here
approaching.

SCENA II—Orrido carcere.

(AZUCENA giacente sopra una specie di rozza coltre, MAN-RICO seduto a lei d'appresso.)

Manrico.

Madre, non dormi!

Azucena.

L'invocai più volte,
Ma fugge il sonno a queste luci, prego.

Manrico.

L'aura fredda è molesta
Alle tue membre forse?

Azucena.

No; da questa
Tomba di vivi sol fuggir vorrei,
Perchè sento il respiro soffocarmi!

Manrico.

Fuggir!   (Torcendosi le mani.)

Azucena.

Non attristarti;
(Sorgendo.)
Far di me strazio non potranno i crudi!

Manrico.

Ah! come?

Azucena.

Vedi? le sue forsche, impronte
M' ha già stampate in fronte
Il dito della morte!

Manrico.

Ahi!

Azucena.

Troveranno
Un cadavere muto, gelido!—anzı
Uno scheletro!

Manrico.

Cessa!

Azucena.

Non odi?—gente appressa!
I carnefici son—vogliono al rogo
Trarmi!—Difendi la tua madre!

Manrico.

Alcuno,
Ti rassicura, qui non volge.

Azucena.

    The scaffold!

    That word of terror!

Manrico.

    Oh! mother! oh! mother!

Azucena.

    One morning

    Fierce crowds assembled, seized my mother
      and led her

    To torture! Mark how the abhorrent
      flames curl!

    Round her they madly cling! her hair con-
      suming

    Now streams upward to heaven!

    Observe the glaring eyeballs

    From their orbits protruding! Ah! who has
      brought me

    To behold this dread vision?
      (Falls convulsed in the arms of Manrico.)

Manrico.

    If filial love and words of affection

    Have power to move thy feelings maternal,

    Strive to banish these terrors,

    And seek in slumbers forgetful, both rest
      and composure.
      (Conducts her to the mattress.)

Azucena.

    Il rogo!

    Parola orrenda!

Manrico.

    Oh, madre!—oh, madre!

Azucena.

    Turba feroce l'ava tua condusse

    Al rogo—mira la terribil vampa!

    Ella n' è tocca già!—già l'arso crine

    Al ciel manda faville!—

    Osserva le pupille

    Fuor dell' orbita lor!—Ahi!—chi mi toglie

    A spettacol sì stroce!

    (Cadendo tutta convulsa tra le braccia di Manrico.)

Manrico.

    Se m'ami ancor, se voce

    Di figlio ha possa di una madre in core,

    Ai terrori dell' alma

    Obli cerca nel sonno, e posa e calma.
      (La conduce presso la coltre.)

SI, LA STANCHEZZA — YES, HEAVY WOES Duet. (Manrico and Azucena)

AZU.

Men tri-sti im-ma-gi-ni al tuo cor.
Send thee bright vi-sions, sooth-ing thy paint

Ai no-stri mon-ti
Back to our moun-tains,

ri-tor-ne-re-mo, L'an-ti-ca pa-ce i-vi go-dre-mo! Tu can-te-
our steps re-tra-cing, There, peace and qui-et once more em-bra-cing, Songs thou wilt

ra-i, sul tuo li-u-to, In son-no pla-ci-do io dor-mi-rò.
sing me with lute at tend-ing, Sweet dreams shall vis-it our sleep as of yore.

MAN.

Ri-po-sa o ma-dre; io pro-no e mu-to La men-te al cie-lo ri-vol-ge-
Re-pose, O moth-er; si-lent-ly bend-ing O'er thee, my spir-it heav'n-ward shall

AZU.

Tu can-te-ra-i sul tu-o li-u-to In son-no
Loved songs thou'lt sing me thy soft lute aid lend-ing. Sweet dreams shall

MAN.

rò.
soar.

La men-te al
My soul, with de-

pla-ci-do io dor-mi-rò, tu can-te-ra-i, sul tu-o li-
vis-it our sleep as of yore: Loved songs thou'lt sing me, thy soft lute aid

cie-lo ri-vol-ge-rò,
vo-tion heav'n-ward shall soar.

u - to, In son - no pla - ci - do io dor - mi - rò, Io
lend - ing, Sweet dreams shall vis - it our sleep as of yore. Sweet

La men - te al cie - lo___ ri - vol - ge - rò.
My soul, with de - vo - tion,___ heav'n - ward shall soar.

dor - mi - rò, Io dor - mi - rò, Io dor - mi - rò,
dreams of yore, Sweet dreams of yore, Sweet dreams of yore,

Ri - po - sa, o ma - dre, ri - po - sa, o
Re - pose thee, O moth - er, re - pose___ thee, O

Io dor - mi - ro, Io dor - mi - ro, Io dor - mi - ro.
Sweet dreams of yore, Sweet dreams of yore, Sweet dreams of yore.___

ma - dre la men - te al ciel ri - vol - ge - rò.___
moth - er, my wear - y soul heav'n - ward shall soar.___

(AZUCENA yields herself to sleep; MANRICO remains kneeling beside her.)	(AZUCENA si addormenta; MANRICO resta genuflesso accanto a lei.)
SCENE III—The door opens; enter LEONORA.	SCENA III—Si apre la porta, entra LEONORA.
Manrico.	*Manrico.*
How! In this darkness do I deceive me?	Che!—non m'inganno! quel fioco lume!
Leonora.	*Leonora.*
'Tis I, Manrico!	Son io, Manrico—
Manrico.	*Manrico.*
Oh! my Lenora!	Oh, mia Leonora!
Oh, heaven, dost grant me in thy compassion	Ah, mi concedi, pietoso Nume,
Rapture so boundless ere to death they lead me?	Gioja si grande, anzi ch'io morra?

Leonora.

Thou shalt not die, love! I come to save thee.

Manrico.

Truly! to save me? What meanest thou?

Leonora.

Farewell, love!
Let nought delay thee, depart now, quickly!

Manrico.

Thou comest not with me?

Leonora.

I must remain here!

Manrico.

Remain!

Leonora.

Ah, fly thee!

Manrico.

No.

Leonora.

Woe awaits thee!
(Endeavoring to force him towards the door.)

Manrico.

No!

Leonora.

Life's before thee!

Manrico.

Ah! no, I scorn it!
But, lady, bend thy gaze upon me!
Whence comes this power? what price has
    bought it?
Thou wilt not speak? oh, dark suspicion!
'Twas from my rival thou purchased thy
    mission!
Ah! thou hast sold him thy heart's affection!
Bartered a love, once devoted to me!

Leonora.

Oh, how thine anger doth blind thy vis-
    ion!
Oh, how unjust is thy cruel suspicion!
Obey, and fly thee, not heaven's protection,
If thou dost linger, can succor thee!

Azucena
                (sleeping).

Back to our mountains, our steps retracing.
There peace and quiet once more embracing.

Leonora.

Tu non morrai—vengo a salvarti.

Manrico.

Come!—a salvarmi?—Fia vero!

Leonora.

Addio!
Tronca ogni indulgio!—t'affretta!—parti!
                (Accennandogli la porta.)

Manrico.

E tu non vieni?

Leonora.

Restar degg' io!

Manrico.

Restar!

Leonora.

Deh! fuggi!

Manrico.

No.

Leonora.

Guai se tardi!
                (Cercando di trarlo verso l'uscio.)

Manrico.

No!

Leonora.

La tua vita!

Manrico.

Io la dispresso—
Pur—figgi, o donna, in me gli sguardi!—
Da chi l'avesti?—ed a qual prezzo?—
Parlar non vuoi?—Balen tremendo!—
Dal mio rivale!—intendo—intendo!—
Ha quest' infame l'amor venduto—
Venduto un core che mio giurò!

Lernora.

Ahi, come l'ira ti rende cieco!—
Ahi, quanto ingiusto, crudel sei meco!—
T' arrendi—fuggi, o sei perduto!—
O, il ciel nemmen salvar ti può!

Azucena
                (Dormendo.)

Ai nostri monti ritorneremo—
L'antica pace—ivi godremo!

Songs thou wilt sing me with lute attending,
Sweet dreams shall visit our sleep as of yore.

Manrico.

Begone now!

Leonora

(casting herself down at the feet of MANRICO).

Oh! repulse me not!
See'st thou? I languish,
Oppressed and fainting.

Manrico.

Go! I hate thee now;
May curses blight thee!

Leonora.

Ah! cease reviling;
Curse me no more, but raise thy thoughts
To heaven in prayers for me
At this dark moment!

Manrico.

A chill through my bosom is swiftly coursing.

Leonora.

Manrico!

(Falls on her face.)

Manrico

(hastening to lift her up).

Lady! what mean you?
Tell me!

Leonora.

Death's cold hand is on me!

Manrico.

What, dying?

Leonora.

Ah! far more rapidly
The poison sped its mission
Than I intended!

Manrico.

Oh! mortal blow!

Leonora.

Feel now, my hand is freezing—
But here, within me, dread fires are burning!

(Placing her hand on her breast.)

Manrico.

Oh, heaven, what didst thou?

Leonora.

Sooner than live, another's bride,
Near thee, I preferred to die!

Tu canterai—sul tuo lïuto—
In sonno placido—io dormirò—

Manrico.

Ti scosta.

Leonora

(è caduta ai piedi di MANRICO).

Non respingermi—
Vedi?—Languente, oppressa,
Io manco—

Manrico.

Va—ti abbomino—
Ti maledico—

Leonora.

Ah, cessa!—
Non d'imprecar, di volgere
Per me la prece a Dio
E questa l'ora!

Manrico.

Un brivido corse nel petto mio!

Leonora.

Manrico!—

(Cade boccone.)

Manrico

(accorrendo a sollevarla).

Donna, svelami—
Narra—

Leonora.

Ho la morte in seno.

Manrico.

La morte!—

Leonora.

Ah, fu più rapida
La forza del veleno
Ch'io non pensava!—

Manrico.

Oh, fulmine!

Leonora.

Senti!—la mano è gelo—
Ma quì foco orribile
Arde—

(Toccandosi il vetto.)

Manrico.

Che festi—oh, cielo!

Leonora.

Prima che d'altri vivere,—
Io volli tua morir!—

Manrico.

    Insensate! and I this angel's love
    With curses dared repay!

Leonora.

    I strive no longer!

Manrico.

    Ah! hapless one!
       (The Count enters, but stops on the threshold.)

Leonora.

    Behold the moment! I'm dying, Manrico!
    Now, heavenly Father, pardon me, I implore
      Thee!

Count.

    (Ah! she deceived me purposely,
    That for him she might die!)
    The block awaits him!
      (To the soldiers, pointing out MANRICO.)

Manrico.

    Mother! farewell forever!
      (Goes out with the soldiers.)

Azucena

      (awakening).
    Manrico! my son, where art thou?

Count.

    To death delivered!

Azucena.

    Ah, stay thee! hear me—
      (The Count drags AZUCENA to the window.)

Count.

    Look ye!

Azucena.

    Heaven!

Count.

    'Tis over!

Azucena.

    The victim was thy brother!

Count.

    He! horrid fate!

Azucena.

    Thou art avenged, O mother!
      (Falls near the window.)

Count

      (with horror).
    And I still live!

Manrico.

    Insano!—Ed io quest' angelo
    Osava malodir!

Leonora.

    Più non—resisto!—

Manrico.

    Ahi, misera!—
      (Entra il CONTE, arrestandosi sulla seglia.)

Leonora.

    Ecco l'instante—io moro—
    Manrico!—Or la tua grazia,
    Padre del cielo, imploro!

Conte.

    (Ah! volle me deludere
    E per costui morir!)
    Sia tratto al ceppo!
      (Indicando agli armati MANRICO.)

Manrico.

    Madre!—Oh, madre, addio!
      (Parte, tra gli armati.)

Azucena

      (Destandosi.)
    Manrico!—Ov' è mio figlio?

Conte.

    A morte ei corre!—

Azucena.

    Ah ferma!—m'odi—
      (Franscinando AZUCENA presso la finestra.)

Conte

    Vedi!

Azucena.

    Cielo!

Conte.

    E spento!

Azucena.

    Egli era tuo fratello!—

Conte.

    Ei!—quale orror!

Azucena.

    Sei vendicata, O madre!
      (Cade a piè della finestra.)

Conte.

    E vivo ancor!
      (Inorridito.)

END OF THE OPERA.

LA TRAVIATA

by

GIUSEPPE VERDI

LIBRETTO ADAPTED FROM "LA DAME AUX CAMELIAS"
BY ALEXANDRE DUMAS FILS

THE STORY OF "LA TRAVIATA"

THE first act commences with a gay party in the house of Violetta (the heroine), a young and beautiful creature, thrown by circumstances, and the loss of her parents in childhood, into a course of voluptuous living. She is surrounded by a circle of gay and thoughtless beings iike herself, who devote their lives to pleasure. Amongst the throng who crowd to her shrine is Alfred Germont, a young man, who becomes seriously enamored with Violetta. Touched by the sincerity of his passion, she yields to its influence, a new and pure love springs up in her heart, and for the first time she becomes conscious of the misery of her position, and the hollowness of the pleasures in which she has basked. In the second act, we discover her living in seclusion with her lover, in a country-house near Paris, three months after the events narrated in the preceding act. Alfred accidentally discovers that Violetta has been secretly selling her houses and property in Paris, in order to maintain this establishment; and, revolting at the idea of being a dependent on her bounty, he leaves hurriedly for Paris, to redeem his honor from this disgrace. During his absence, his father, who has discovered his retreat, arrives, and, representing to Violetta that his son's connection with her is not only lowering him in the opinion of the world, but will be ruinous to his family, inasmuch as his sister was betrothed to a wealthy noble, who had, however, declared his intention of renouncing her, unless Alfred would give up Violetta, the generous girl resolves to sacrifice her affections and happiness for her lover's sake, and returns alone to Paris, whither Alfred, overwhelmed with despair when he discovers her flight, follows her. We are then transported to a saloon in the hotel of Flora, one of Violetta's former friends, during a festival given by the fair mistress of the mansion. There Alfred again meets Violetta, now under the protection of the Baron Dauphol, and being unaware of the generous motive which made her desert him, he overwhelms her with reproaches, and flings a purse containing money at her feet, in the presence of the company. Degraded and heartbroken, the unfortunate Violetta returns home to die; and in the last act we find the sad romance of her life drawing to its close. Alfred, too late, learns the truth, and discovers the sacrifice she has made to secure his happiness. Penetrated with grief and shame, he hastens, with his father, to comfort and console her, and to offer her his hand and name in reparation of the wrong he has done her, — but too late. The fragile flower, broken on its stem. can never more raise its beauteous head. One gleam of happiness, the purest and brightest that she has known, arising from her lover's assurance of his truth, and his desire to restore her reputation, gilds the closing moments of her life, and in a transport of joy her soul suddenly quits its fragile tenement of clay,

LA TRAVIATA

ACT I.

SCENE I—A salon in the house of VIOLETTA; in the back scene is a door, which opens into another salon; there are also side doors; on the left is a fireplace, over which is a mirror. In the centre of the apartment is a dining-table, elegantly laid.

(VIOLETTA, seated on a couch, is conversing with the DOCTOR and some friends, whilst others are receiving the guests who arrive, among whom are the BARON, and FLORA on the arm of the MARQUIS.)

Chorus 1.

Past already's the hour of appointment—
You are tardy.

Chorus 2.

We played deep at Flora's,
And while playing the hours flew away.

Violetta.

Flora, and kind friends, the night is before us.
Other pleasures we here will display.
(Goes to meet them.)
'Mid the wine-cups the hours pass more gaily.

Flora. }
Marquis. } Can you there find enjoyment?

Violetta.

I strive to;
Yes, to pleasure I yield, and endeavor
With such remedies illness to stay.

All.

Yes! enjoyment will lengthen our days.

SCENE II—The same. GASTON and ALFRED enter. Servants are busy about the table.

Gaston.

In Alfred Germont, fairest lady,
Another behold, who esteems you;
There are few friends like him; he's a treasure.

Violetta.

Thanks, dear Viscount, for so great a pleasure.
(She gives her hand to ALFRED, who kisses it.)

ATTO I.

SCENA I—Salotto in casa di VIOLETTA; nel fondo è la porta che mette ad altra sala; ve ne sono altre due laterali; a sinistra un caminetto con sopra uno specchio. Nel mezzo è una tavola riccamente imbandita.

(VIOLETTA seduta sur un divano sta discorrendo col DOTTORE, e con alcuni amici, mentre altri vanno ad incontrare quelli che sopraggiungono, tra' quali sono il BARONE e FLORA al braccio del MARCHESE.)

Coro 1.

Dell' invito trascorsa è già l' ora—
Voi tardaste.

Coro 2.

Giocammo da Flora,
E giocando quell' ore volâr.

Violetta.

Flora, amici, la notte chè resta
D'altre gioie quì fate brilla—
(Andando ore incontre.)
Fra le tazze è più viva la festa.

Flora. }
Marchese. } E goder voi potrete?

Violetta.

Lo voglio;
Alla danza m'affido, ed io soglio
Con tal farmaco i mali sopir

Tutti.

Sì, la vita s'addoppia al gioir.

SCENA II—Detti, il Visconte GASTONE DI LETORIÈRES, ALFREDO GERMONT; servi affaccendati interno all mensa.

Gastone.

In Alfredo Germont, o signora,
Ecco un altro che molto vi onora;
Pochi amici a lui simili sono.

Violetta.

Mio Visconte, mercè di tal dono.
(Dà la mano ad ALFREDO, che gliela bacia.)

Marquis.

Dear Alfred!

Alfred.

Kind Marquis!

(They shake hands.)

Gaston

(to ALFRED).

I told you

That combined here are friendship and pleasure.

(During this dialogue the servants have placed the viands upon the table.)

Violetta.

All is ready?

(A servant bows assent.)

My dear friends, be seated;

'Tis at the banquet that each heart unfolds.

Chorus.

Thou hast wisely the maxim repeated,

Cure for trouble the wine-cup still holds.

(They seat themselves, VIOLETTA between ALFRED and GASTON, and opposite to them FLORA, the MARQUIS, and the BARON; the rest take their seats promiscuously; there is a momentary silence, during which the dishes are passed round, and VIOLETTA and GASTON converse in an undertone.)

Gaston

(to VIOLETTA).

Thou'rt the sole thought of Alfred.

Violetta.

Art jesting?

Gaston.

Thou wert ill, and each day in distress

He came to ask thy condition.

Violetta.

Be silent;

No, I am naught to him.

Gaston.

I deceive not.

Violetta

(to ALFRED).

Is it true then? Can it be? Ah, I know not.

Alfred

(sighing).

Yes, it is true.

Violetta

(to ALFRED).

Grateful thanks, then, I give you.

(To the BARON.)

You, dear Baron, were not so enamored.

Baron.

But 'tis only a year I have known you.

Marchese.

Caro Alfredo!

Alfredo.

Marchese!

(Si stringono la mano.)

Gastone

(ad ALFREDO).

T' ho detto

L' amistà quì s' intreccia al diletto.

(I servi frattanto avranno imbandite le vivande.)

Violetta.

Pronto è il tutto?

(Un servo accenna che sì.)

Miei cari, sedetè;

E al convito che s' apre ogni cor.

Tutti.

Ben diceste—le cure segrete

Fuga sempre l'amico licor.

(Siedono in modo che VIOLETTA resti tra ALFREDO e GASTONE; di fronte vi sarà FLORA, il MARCHESE ed il BARONE; gli altri siedono a piacere. Vi ha un momento di silenzio; frattanto passano i piatti, e VIOLETTA e GASTONE parlano sotto voce tra loro.)

Gastone.

Sempre Alfredo a voi pensa.

Violetta.

Scherzate?

Gastone.

Egra foste, e ogni dì con affanno

Quì volò, di voi chiese.

Violetta.

Cessate.

Nulla son io per lui.

Gastone.

Non v' inganno.

Violetta

(ad ALFREDO).

Vero è dunque?—Onde ciò? Nol comprendo.

Alfredo

(sospirande).

Sì, egli è ver.

Violetta.

Le mie grazie vi rendo.

(Al BARONE.)

Voi, barone, non feste altrettanto.

Barone.

Vi conosco da un anno soltanto.

Violetta.
And Alfred a few minutes only.

Flora
(softly to the BARON).
'Twould be better if you had not spoken.

Baron
(softly to FLORA).
For this youth I've no liking.

Flora.
But why?
As for me, now, he pleases me well.

Gaston
(to ALFRED).
Thou art silent; hast nothing to offer?

Marquis.
Madame alone has the power to arouse him.

Violetta
(fills the glass of ALFRED).
I will fill, then, like Hebe!

Alfred.
And, like her,
I proclaim thee immortal.

All.
We pledge thee!

Gaston
(to the BARON).
Can you not, in this moment of pleasure,
Give a toast, or a gay tuneful measure?
(The BARON declines.)
(To ALFRED.)
Then wilt thou—

All.
Yes, yes, a drinking song.

Alfred.
I've no inspiration.

Gaston.
Art thou not then a singer?

Alfred
(to VIOLETTA).
Will it please you?

Violetta.
Yes.

Alfred
(rising).
Yes? Then I yield.

Marquis.
Pay attention!

Violetta.
Ed ei solo da qualche minuto.

Flora
(piano al BARONE).
Meglio fora, se aveste taciuto.

Barone
(piano a FLORA).
M'è increscioso quel giovin.

Flora.
Perchè?
A me invece simpatico egli è.

Gastone
(ad ALFREDO).
E tu dunque non apri più bocca?

Marchese
(a VIOLETTA).
E a madama che scuoterlo tocca.

Violetta
(mesce ad ALFREDO).
Saro l'Ebe che versa.

Alfredo.
E ch' io bramo
Immortal come quella.
(Con galanteria.)

Tutti.
Beviamo.

Gastone.
O Barone, nè un verso, nè un viva
Troverete in quest' ora giuliva?
(BARONE accenna di nò.)
(Ad ALFREDO.)
Dunque a te.

Tutti.
Sì, sì, un brindisi.

Alfredo.
L'estro non m'arride.

Gastone.
E non se' tu maestro?

Alfredc
(a VIOLETTA).
Vi fia grato?

Violetta.
Sì.

Alfredo
(si alza).
Sì?—L'ho in cor.

Marchese.
Dunque attenti.

All.

Yes, attention we'll pay!

Tutti.

Sì, attenti al cantor.

LIBIAMO NE' LIETI — *A BUMPER WE'LL DRAIN* (Alfred)

Li - bia - mo, li - bia - mo ne' lie - ti ca - li - ci che la__ bel -
A bump - er we'll drain from the wine-cup flow - ing, That fresh charms to__

lez - za in - fio - ra, e la____ fug - ge-vol, fug - gè - vol o -
beau - ty is lend - ing, O'er fleet - ing mo-ments, so quick - ly end -

- ra s'in - e - brii a vo - lut - tà. Li - biam ne' dol - ci____
ing, Gay pleas-ure a - bone should__ reign. We'll drink the thrill-ing__

fre - mi - ti che su - sci - ta l'a - mo - re, poi - chè quel l'oc-chio al
ec - sta - sies, That love ex - cites with in us, When her bright eye doth__

co - re on - ni - po - ten - te____ và____ Li - bia - mo, a - mo - re a -
win us, And ev - 'ry heart re - tain__ A bump - er to love, mid the

mor fra i ca - li - ci più cal - di - ba - ci a - vrà.
wine - cups flow - ing, Fresh warmth will our__ pleas - ures re - gain.

Ah! to love, 'mid wine-cups flowing
New delight our joys will gain.

Violetta.

Surrounded by you, I shall learn to lighten
The footsteps of time with gladness;
All of this world is but folly and madness
That is not pleasure gay.
Enjoy the hour, for rapid
The joys of life are flying—

Libiamo; amor fra i calici
Più caldi baci avrà.

Violetta (s' alza).

Tra voi, saprò dividere
Il tempo mio giocondo;
Tutto è follia nel monde
Ciò che non è piacer.
Godiam; fugace e rapido
E il gaudio dell' amore;

Like summer flow'rets dying—
Improve them while we may!
Enjoy! the present with fervor invites us,
Its flattering call obey.

All.

Enjoy then the wine-cup with songs of pleasure
That make night so cheerful and smiling,
In this charming paradise, beguiling,
That scarcely we heed the day.

Violetta
                    (to ALFRED).
The sum of life is pleasure.

Alfred
                    (to VIOLETTA).
While still unloved, unloving?

Violetta
                    (to ALFRED).
Experience ne'er has taught me.

Alfred
                    (to VIOLETTA).
And thus my fate must be.
                (Music is heard in another room.)

All.

What's this?

Violetta.

Will you not join the gay group of dancers?

All.

Oh! a happy thought! We'll gladly join them.

Violetta.

Then let us enter!
(Approaching the door, VIOLETTA, seized with a sudden faintness, cries out:)

Alas!

All.

What ails thee?

Violetta.

Nothing, nothing.

All.

Why do you pause then?

Violetta.

Let's go now.
(Takes a few steps, but is obliged to re-seat herself.)

Oh, Heaven!

All.

Again still!

E un fior che nasce e muore
Nè più si può goder.
Godiam—c'invita un fervido
Accento lusinghier.

Tutti.

Godiam—la tazza e il cantico
Le notti abbella e il riso;
In questo paradiso,
Ne scuopra il nuovo dì.

Violetta
                    (ad ALFREDO).
La vita è nel tripudio.

Alfredo
                    (a VIOLETTA).
Quando non s'ami ancora.

Violetta
                    (ad ALFREDO).
No! dite a chi l'ignora.

Alfredo
                    (a VIOLETTA).
E il mio destin così.
                (S' ode musica dall' altra sala.)

Tutti.

Che è cio.

Violetta.

Non gradireste ora le danze?

Tutti.

Oh, il gentile pensier!—Tutti accetiamo.

Violetta.

Usciamo dunque?
(S' avviano alla porta di mezzo, ma VIOLETTA e colta d subito pallore.)

Ohimè!

Tutti.

Che avete?

Violetta.

Nulla, nulla.

Tutti.

Che mai v'arresta?

Violetta.

Usciamo.
(Fà qualche passo, ma è obbligata a nuovamente ferman e sedere.)

Oh Dio!

Tutti.

Ancora!

Alfred.

　　Ah! you suffer—

All.

　　Oh, Heaven! what means this?

Violetta.

　　A sudden tremor seized me.　Now—there,
　　　pray enter.
　　　　　　(Pointing to the other room.)
　　I will rejoin you ere long.

All.

　　As you desire, then.
　　　(All pass into the other room, except ALFRED.)

SCENE III—VIOLETTA, ALFRED, afterward GASTON.

Violetta

　　　　(rises and regards herself in a mirror).
　　Ah me! how pale!
　　　　　(Turning, she perceives ALFRED.)
　　You here?

Alfred.

　　Are you relieved from recent distress?

Violetta.

　　I'm better!

Alfred.

　　Ah, these gay revels soon will destroy thee.
　　Great care is needful—on this depends your
　　　being.

Violetta.

　　Canst thou then aid me?

Alfred.

　　Oh! wert thou mine now, with vigilance
　　　untiring
　　I'd guard thee with tenderest care.

Violetta.

　　What say'st thou?
　　Some one, perchance, then, cares for me?

Alfred

　　　　　(confusedly).
　　No one in all the world doth love you.

Violetta.

　　No one?

Alfred.

　　I, only, love you.

Violetta.

　　Ah! truly!
　　　　　(Laughing.)
　　Your great devotion I had quite forgotten.

Alfredo.

　　Voi soffrite.

Tutti.

　　Oh ciel!—ch'è questo?

Violetta.

　　E un tremito che provo—or là passate,
　　　　　(Indicando l' altra stanza.)
　　Tra poco anch' io sarò.

Tutti.

　　Come bramate.
　　　(Tutti passano all' altra sala, meno ALFREDO, che resta
indietro.)

SCENA III—VIOLETTA, ALFREDO, e GASTONE, a tempo.

Violetta

　　　　　(si guarda nello specchio).
　　Oh, qual pallor!
　　Voi qui!
　　　　　(Volgendosi s' accorge d' ALFREDO.)

Alfredo.

　　Cessata è l'ansia, che vi turbò?

Violetta.

　　Sto meglio.

Alfredo.

　　Ah, in cotal guisa v'ucciderete!
　　Aver v'è d'uopo cura dell' esser vostro.

Violetta.

　　E lo potrei?

Alfredo.

　　Se mia foste, custode io veglierei
　　Pe' vostri soavi dì.

Violetta.

　　Che dite?
　　Ha forse alcuno cura di me?

Alfredo.

　　Perchè nessuno al mondo v'ama.

Violetta.

　　Nessun?

Alfredo.

　　Tranne sol io.

Violetta.

　　Gli è vero!
　　　　　(Ridende.)
　　Si grande amor dimenticato avea.

Alfred.

Dost mock me? Have you a heart then?

Violetta.

A heart? Yes—haply—but why do you thus question?

Alfred.

Ah, if you had one you would not thus trifle with me.

Violetta.

Are you then truthful?

Alfred.

You, I deceive not.

Violetta.

'Tis long, that you have thus loved me?

Alfred.

Ah, yes; a year now.

Alfredo.

Ridete!—e in voi v' ha un core?

Violetta.

Un cor? Sì, forse—e a che lo richiedete?

Alfredo.

Oh, se ciò fosse, non potreste allora celiar.

Violetta.

Dite davvero?

Alfredo.

Io non v'inganno.

Violetta.

Di molto è che mi amate?

Alfredo.

Ah sì, da un anno.

UN DI FELICE——*ONE DAY, A RAPTURE*   (Alfred)

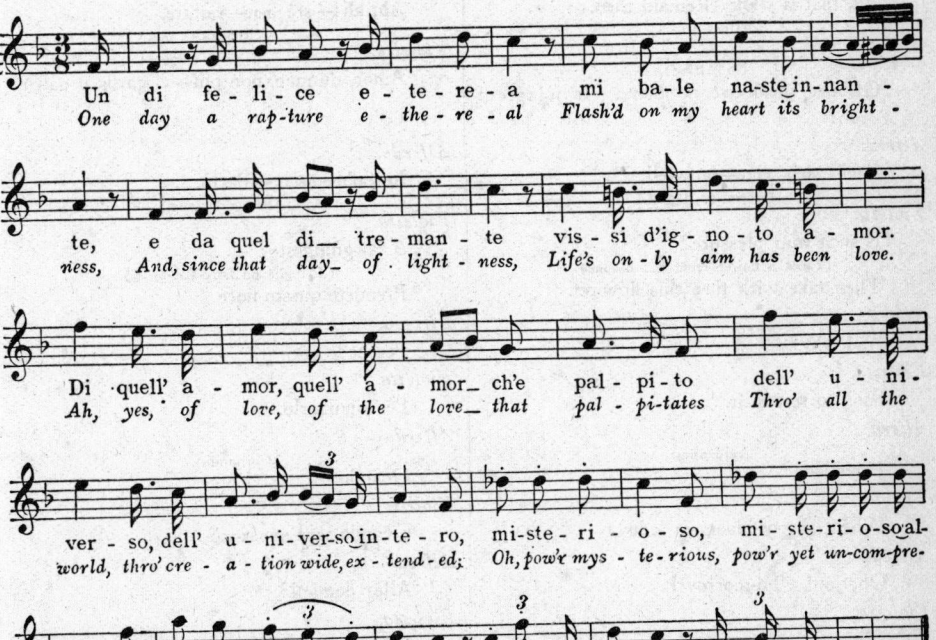

Violetta.

If this be true, ah! fly from me.
Friendship alone I offer,
I neither know nor suffer
A feeling of such devotion.
I am sincere and frank with thee;
Look for one warmer, kinder;
'Twill not be hard to find her,
Then think no more of me.

Alfred.

Oh love, sublime, yet mysterious,
Power ne'er yet comprehended,
Torments and raptures of love!

Gaston
　　　　(appearing at the door).
How now? What here employs you?

Violetta.

Trifles and folly.

Gaston.

Ah, that is well. Remain then.
　　　　(Goes back.)

Violetta
　　　　(to Alfred).
Of love speak we no more. Is it agreed
on?

Alfred.

I will obey you—farewell.
　　　　(About to depart.)

Violetta.

Is such your pleasure?
　　　　(Takes a flower from her bosom.)
Then take with thee this flow'ret.

Alfred.

And why?

Violetta.

Soon to return it.

Alfred
　　　　(returning).
How soon?

Violetta.

When its gay bloom is faded.

Alfred.

Oh, joy! To-morrow!

Violetta.

'Tis well—to-morrow!

Alfred.

I am at last so happy!
　　　　(Seizes the flower with transport.)

Violetta.

Ah, se ciò è ver, fuggitemi—
Pura amistade io v'offro;
Amar non sò, nè soffro
Di cosi eroico ardor.
Io sono franca, ingenua;
Altra cercar devoto—
Non arduo troverete
Dimentecarmi allor.

Alfredo.

Oh amore misterioso,
Misterioso altero,
Croce e delizia al cor.

Gastone
　　　　(presentandosi sulla porta di mezzo).
Ebben?—che diavol fate?

Violetta.

Si folleggiava.

Gastone.

Ah, ah!—stà ben—restate.
　　　　(Rientra.)

Violetta.

Amor, dunque, non più—vi garba il patto

Alfredo.

Io v'obbedisco.—Partò.
　　　　(Par andarsene.)

Violetta.

A tal giungeste?
　　　　(Si toglie un fiore dal seno.)
Prendete questo fiore.

Alfredo.

Perche?

Violetta.

Per riportarlo.

Alfredo
　　　　(tornando).
Quando?

Violetta.

Quando sarà appassito.

Alfredo.

Allor domani?

Violetta.

Ebbene domani.

Alfredo.

Io son felice!
　　　　(Prende con trasporto il fiore.)

Violetta.

You still declare you love me?

Alfred.

How much I love thee!

Violetta. (Going.)

You go then.

Alfred.

Yes, love! (Returns and kisses her hand.)

Violetta.

To-morrow—

Alfred.

More I will ask not.
(Exit.)

SCENE IV—VIOLETTA, and all the others, returning from the dancing-room.

All.

In the east the dawn is breaking,
And perforce we must depart,
Gentle lady, leave now taking,
Thanks we give thee from each heart.
Full the city is of pleasure,
Brief the time for love and joy,
To repose give needful measure,
Lest enjoyment we destroy!
(Exeunt.)

SCENE V—VIOLETTA, alone

How wondrous! how wondrous! those accents
Upon my heart are graven!
Will it misfortune bring me, a love in earnest?
What shall be thy resolve, my troubled spirit?
No living man hath yet enflamed thee!
Oh, rapture that I have known not, to be loved and loving.
Can my heart still disdain it
For follies dry and heartless, which now enchain me?

Violetta.

D' amarmi dite ancora?

Alfredo.

Oh, quanto v'amo!

Violetta. (Per partire.)

Partite?

Alfredo.

Parto. (Torna a lei, e le bacia la mano.)

Violetta.

Addio.

Alfredo.

Di più non bramo.
(Esce.)

SCENA IV—VIOLETTA e tutti gli altri che tornano dall sala della danza.

Tutti.

Si ridesta in ciel l' aurora,
E n' è forza ripartire;
Mercè a voi, gentil signora,
(a VIOLETTA).
Di sì splendido gioir
La città di feste è piena,
Volge il tempo del piacer;
Nel riposo omai la lena
Si ritempri per goder.
(Partono dalla destra.)

SCENA V—VIOLETTA sola.

E strano!—è strano!—In core
Scolpiti ho quegli accenti!
Saria per mia sventura un serio amore?
Che risolvi, o turbata anima mia?
Null' uomo ancora t' accendeva.—Oh, gioia
Ch'io non conobbi, esser amata amando!
E sdegnarla poss' io
Per l' aride follie del viver mio?

AH, FORS' È LUI — *'TWAS HE, PERCHANCE* (Violetta)

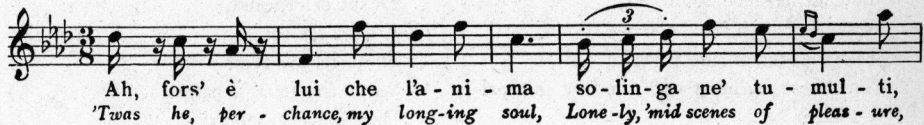

Ah, fors' è lui che l'a-ni-ma so-lin-ga ne' tu-mul-ti,
'Twas he, per-chance, my long-ing soul, Lone-ly, 'mid scenes of pleas-ure,

so - lin - ga ne' tu - mul - ti, go - dea so - ven - te pin - ge - re
lone - ly, 'mid scenes of pleas - ure, Oft loved to paint in col - ors bright,

de' suoi co - lo - ri oc - cul - ti, de' suoi co - lo - ri oc - cul - ti! Lui che, mo - des - to e
In its own gold and a - zure, In its own gold and a - zure. He, who with mod - est

vi - gi - le, all' e - gre sog - lie a - sce - se, e nuo - va feb - bre ac - ce - se
vi - gi - lance, To my sick room re - turn-ing, Kin-dled new flames, still burn-ing,

des - tan - do - mi all' a - mor! A quell a - mor, quell' a - mor che è pal - pi - to dell' u - ni -
Des-tined my heart to love! Yes! this is love, 'tis the love that pal - pi-tates Through all the

ver - so, dell' u - ni - ver - so in - te - ro, mi - ste - ri - o - so, mi - ste - ri - o-so al-
world, through cre - a - tion wide-ly ex - tend - ed, Oh, pow'r mys - te - rious, Pow'r ne'er yet com-pre-

te - ro, cro - ce, cro - ce e de - li - zia, cro - ce e de - li - zia, de - li - zia al cor.
hend - ed, Tor - ment, tor - ment and rap - ture, tor - ment and rap - ture each do we prove.

To my young heart, all guileless then,	A me, fanciulla, un candido
Filled with intrepid yearning,	E trepido desire
This dream was imaged, fair, serene,	Quest' effigiò, dolcissimo
Bright o'er my pathway burning.	Signor dell' avvenire,
When like a star from heaven,	Quando ne' cieli il raggio
Radiant he stood before me,	Di sua beltà vedea,
Visions of hope came o'er me.	E tutta me pascea
Like the fond dreams I wove.	Di quel soave error
Then beat my heart with the love that pal-pitates	Sentia che amore è palpito
	Dell' universo intero,

Through all the world, thro' creation wide extended.

Oh! pow'r mysterious, pow'r ne'er yet comprehended.

Torment and rapture, each do we prove.

(Remains for an instant buried in thought, then says:)

What folly! All this is vain delirium!

Child of misfortune, lonely,

By all abandoned, in this gay crowded desert,

This vortex of pleasure they call Paris,

What hope remains? what must I do, then?

Surrender to pleasure's maddening whirl again?

Misterioso, altero,

Pena e delizia al cor.

(Resta concentrata un istante poi dice.)

Follie!—follie!—delirio vano è questo!

In quai sogni mi perdo!

Povera donna, sola,

Abbandonata in questo popoloso deserto,

Che appellano Parigi,

Che spero or più?—Che far degg' io?— gioire.

Di voluttà nei vortici finire.

SEMPRE LIBERA — *EVER FREE, SHALL I STILL WANDER* (Violetta)

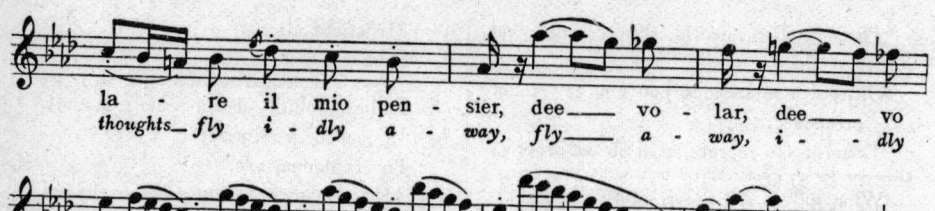

la — re il mio pen - sier, dee___ vo - lar, dee___ vo
thoughts__ fly i - dly a - way, fly___ a - way, i - dly

lar ————————————————————————— il pen - sier.
fly, ————————————————————————— fly a - way.

<table>
<tr><td>(Exit on the left.)
END OF THE FIRST ACT.</td><td>(Parte, a sinistra.)
FINE DELL' ATTO PRIMO.</td></tr>
</table>

ACT II.	ATTO II.
SCENE I—A country house near Paris. A salon on the ground floor. At the back, facing the audience, a fireplace, over which is a looking-glass. A clock hangs between two glass doors, which are closed. There are also two side doors, seats, tables, and writing materials.	SCENA I—Casa di Campagna presso Parigi. Salotto terreno. Nel fondo, in faccia agli Spettatori, è un camino sopra il quale uno specchio ed un orologio, fra due porte chiuse da cristalli, che mettono ad un giardino. Al primpanno due altre porte, una di fronte all' altra. Sedie, tavolini, qualche libro, l'occorrente per scrivere.
(ALFRED enters, in sporting costume.)	(ALFREDO entra, in costume da caccia.)
Alfred.	*Alfredo.*
Out from her presence, for me there's no enjoyment.	Lunge da lei per me non v' ha dilette!
(Puts down his gun.)	(Depone il fucile.)
Three months have flown already	Volaron già tre lune
Since my beloved Violetta	Dacchè la mia Violetta
So kindly left for me her riches, admirers,	Agi per me lascio, dovizie, onori.
And all the haunts of pleasure,	E le pompose feste,
Where she had been accustomed	Ove agli omaggi avvezza,
To homage from all hearts, for charms transcendent.	Vedea schiavo ciascun di sua bellezza—
Yet now contented in this retreat, so quiet,	E dal suffio d'amor rigenerato
She forgets all for me. Here, near my loved one,	Solo esiste per me—qui presso a lei
New life springs within me;	Io rinascer mi sento,
From the trials of love restored and strengthened,	E dal suffio d' amor rigenerato
Ah! in my present rapture past sorrows are forgotten.	Scordo ne' gaudj suoi tutto il passato.

DI MIEI BOLLENTI SPIRITI — *ALL MY IMPULSIVE ECSTASIES* (Alfred)

De miei bol - len - ti spi - ri - ti il gio - va - ni le ar - do - re, el - la tem - prò col
All my im - pul - sive ec - sta - sies, Sprung from a youth - ful ar - dor, She hath sub - dued with

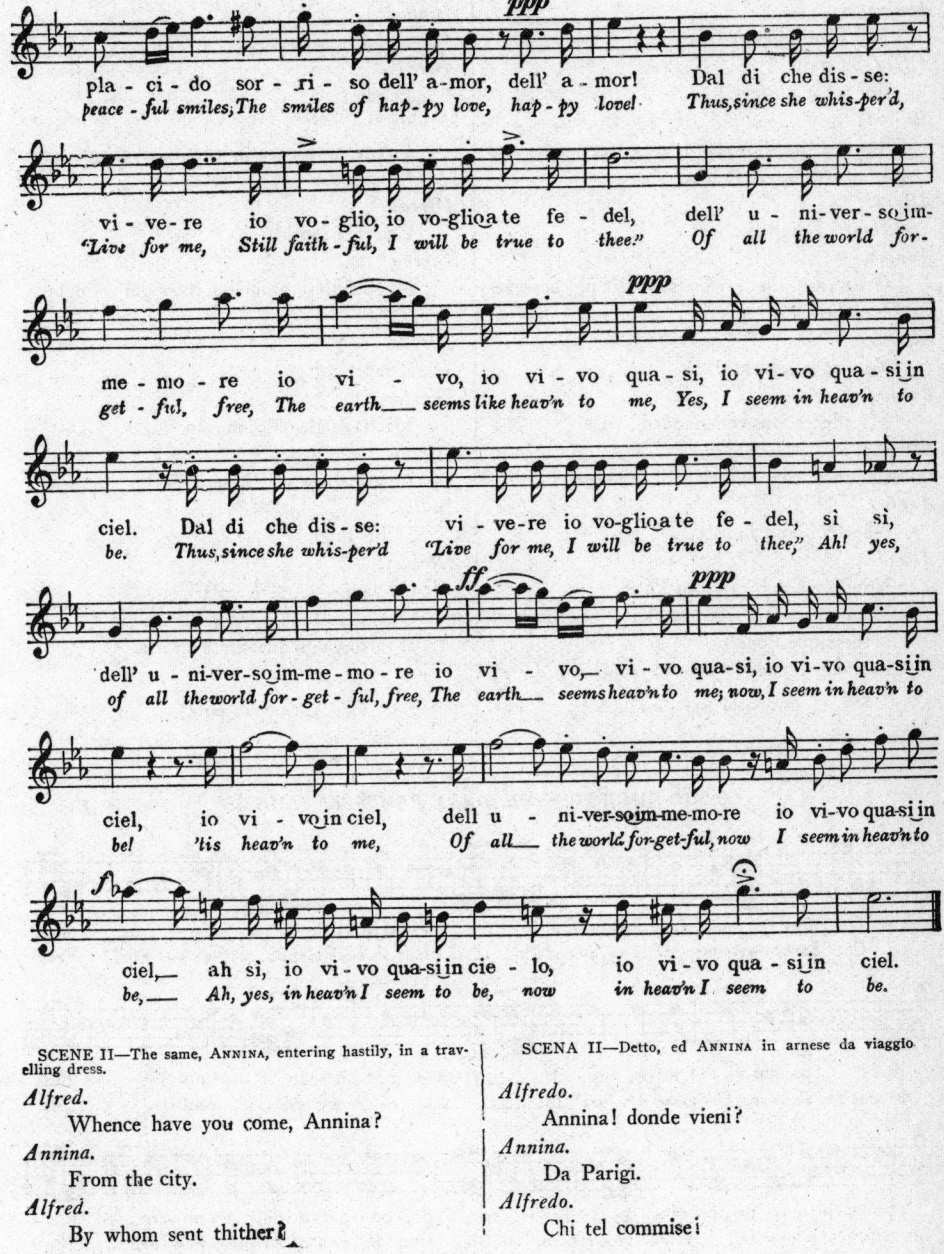

pla - ci - do sor - ri - so dell' a - mor, dell' a - mor! Dal di che dis - se:
peace - ful smiles; The smiles of hap - py love, hap - py love! Thus, since she whis - per'd,

vi - ve - re io vo - glio, io vo - glio a te fe - del, dell' u - ni - ver - so im -
"Live for me, Still faith - ful, I will be true to thee." Of all the world for -

me - mo - re io vi - vo, io vi - vo qua - si, io vi - vo qua - si in
get - ful, free, The earth seems like heav'n to me, Yes, I seem in heav'n to

ciel. Dal di che dis - se: vi - ve - re io vo - glio a te fe - del, sì sì,
be. Thus, since she whis - per'd "Live for me, I will be true to thee," Ah! yes,

dell' u - ni - ver - so im - me - mo - re io vi - vo, vi - vo qua - si, io vi - vo qua - si in
of all the world for - get - ful, free, The earth seems heav'n to me; now, I seem in heav'n to

ciel, io vi - vo in ciel, dell u - ni - ver - so im - me - mo - re io vi - vo qua - si in
bel 'tis heav'n to me, Of all the world for - get - ful, now I seem in heav'n to

ciel, ah sì, io vi - vo qua - si in cie - lo, io vi - vo qua - si in ciel.
be, Ah, yes, in heav'n I seem to be, now in heav'n I seem to be.

SCENE II—The same, ANNINA, entering hastily, in a travelling dress.

Alfred.

Whence have you come, Annina?

Annina.

From the city.

Alfred.

By whom sent thither?

SCENA II—Detto, ed ANNINA in arnese da viaggio

Alfredo.

Annina! donde vieni?

Annina.

Da Parigi.

Alfredo.

Chi tel commise?

Annina.

　My kind mistress sent me.

Alfred.

　For what purpose?

Annina.

　To sell her jewels, horses, carriages, and all that's left to her.

Alfred.

　Heard I rightly?

Annina.

　Great are the expenses of living here secluded.

Alfred.

　You ne'er told me!

Annina.

　My silence was commanded.

Alfred.

　Commanded!　Much still is needed?

Annina.

　One thousand louis'!

Alfred.

　Now leave me.　I go to Paris.

　Mind that your mistress knows nothing of these questions.

　Ere long I shall be able to repair all.　Go— go!　(ANNINA goes out.)

SCENE III—ALFRED, alone.

Annina.

　Fu la mia signora.

Alfredo.

　Perchè?

Annina.

　Per alienar cavalli, cocchi, e quanto ancor possiede.

Alfredo.

　Che mai sento!

Annina.

　Lo spendio è grande a viver quì solinghi.

Alfredo.

　E tacevi?

Annina.

　Mi fu il silenzio imposto.

Alfredo.

　Imposto!—e v'al bisogna?—

Annina.

　Mille luigi.

Alfredo.

　Or vanne—Andrò a Parigi—

　Questo colluquio ignori la signora—

　Il tutto valgo a riparere ancora.

(ANNINA parte.)

SCENA III—ALFREDO, solo.

O MIO RIMORSO! — *OH! DARK REMORSE!* (Alfred)

O— mio ri-mor-so! oh in-fa-mia! io___ vis-si in ta-le er - ro - re! ma il
Oh, dark re-morse! oh! in-fa-my! To___ live in such blind___ er - ror! From.

tur - pe son-no a fran-ge - re il___ ver mi ba - le - no! Per
dreams so base, I wake at last To___ truth, all now re - veal'd! One

po - co in se - no ac-que - ta - ti, o - gri-do, o gri-do dell' o' - no - re___ m'a-
mo-ment more thy voice re - strain, Oh, cry, oh, cry of in-jured hon - or! For

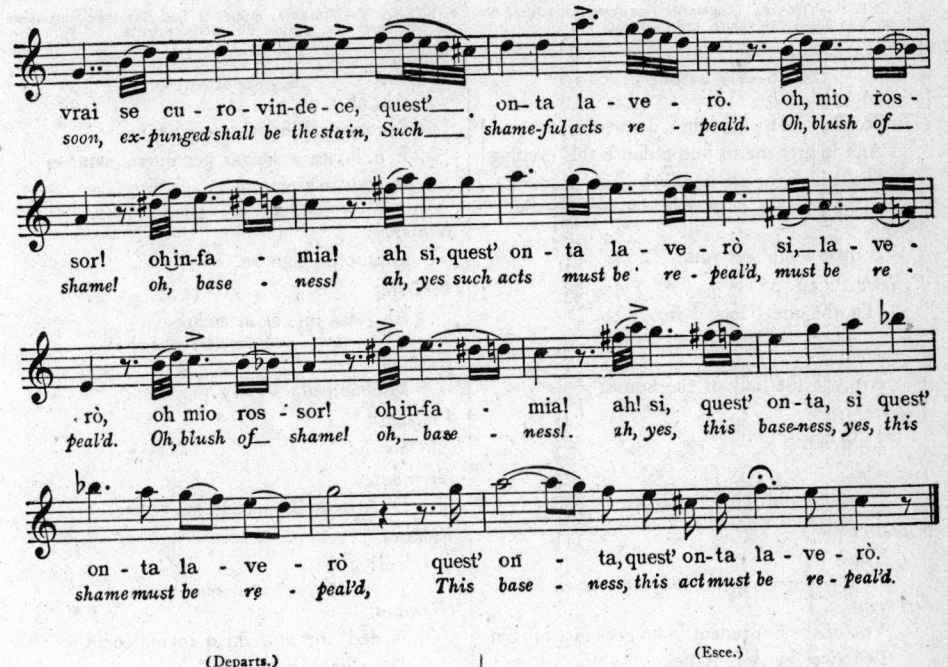

vrai se cu - ro - vin-de - ce, quest'___ . on-ta la - ve - rò. oh, mio ros -
soon, ex-punged shall be the stain, Such___ shame-ful acts re - peal'd. Oh, blush of___

sor! oh in-fa - mia! ah sì, quest' on-ta la - ve - rò si,___ la - ve -
shame! oh, base - ness! ah, yes such acts must be re - peal'd, must be re -

- rò, oh mio ros - sor! oh in-fa - mia! ah! si, quest' on-ta, sì quest'
peal'd. Oh, blush of___ shame! oh,___ base - ness! ah, yes, this base-ness, yes, this

on-ta la - ve - rò quest' on - ta, quest' on-ta la - ve - rò.
shame must be re - peal'd, This base - ness, this act must be re - peal'd.

(Departs.)	(Esce.)
SCENE IV—Violetta enters with papers in her hand; Annina, Joseph.	SCENA IV—Violetta, ch'entra con alcune carte, parlando, con Annina, poi Giuseppe a tempo.
Violetta (to Annina).	*Violetta.*
Alfred?	Alfredo!
Annina.	*Annina.*
He has gone to Paris, madame.	Per Parigi or or partiva.
Violetta.	*Violetta.*
When to return?	E tornerà?
Annina	*Annina.*
Before the day is ended, He bade me tell you.	Pria che tramonti il giorno—dirvel m'im-pose.
Violetta.	*Violetta.*
'Tis strange, this!	E strano!
Joseph (presents a letter).	*Giuseppe* (le presenta una lettera).
For you.	Per voi.
Violetta.	*Violetta* (la prende).
'Tis well. A business agent shortly will arrive here; At once admit him.	Sta bene. In breve Giungerà un uom d' affari—entri all' istante.
(Exeunt Annina and Joseph.)	(Annina e Giuseppe escono.)

SCENE V—Violetta, afterwards Germont, introduced by Joseph, who places two chairs, and goes out.

Violetta
(reading the letter).

Ah! ah!
So Flora hath my home discovered,
And invites me to join a dance this evening!
She'll look for me in vain!
(Throws the letter on a table and seats herself.)

Joseph.

A man would see you.

Violetta.

'Tis the one I look'd for.
(Bids Joseph show him in.)

Germont.

Are you the lady of the house?

Violetta.

I am, sir.

Germont.

In me behold Alfred's father.

Violetta.

You?
(With surprise, invites him to be seated.)

Germont.

Yes, of the imprudent, who goes fast to ruin,
Led away by your follies.

Violetta
(rising, resentfully).

Stay, sir, I am a lady in my own dwelling,
And perforce I must leave you, for your
    sake more than mine.
(About to retire.)

Germont.

(What manners!) But then—

Violetta.

You have been led in error.
(Returns to her seat.)

Germont.

He will spend all his fortune upon you.

Violetta.

He has not yet offered. I should refuse.

Germont.

How then such grandeur?
(Looking around.)

Violetta
(gives him a paper).

This deed is to all else a mystery—to you
    'twill not be.

SCENA V—Violetta, quindi il Sig. Germont, introdotto da Giuseppe, che, avanza due siede, e parte.

Violetta
(leggendo la lettera).

Ah, ah,
Scuopriva Flora il mio ritiro!—
E m'invita a danzar per questa sera!—
In van m'aspetterà.
(Getta il foglio sul tavolino e siede.)

Giuseppe.

Giunse un signore.

Violetta.

Ah! sarà lui che attendo.
(Accenna a Giuseppe d'introd.)

Germont.

Madamigella Valery?

Violetta.

Son io.

Germont.

D' Alfredo il padre in me vedete.

Violetta.

Voi!
(Sorpresa gli accenna di sedere.)

Germont.

Sì, dell' incanto, che a rovina corre,
Ammaliato da voi.
(Sedendo.)

Violetta
(alzandosi risentita).

Donna son io, signore, ed in mia casa;
Ch'io vi lasci assentite,
Più per voi, che per me.
(Per uscire.)

Germont.

(Quai modi!) Pure—

Violetta.

Tratto in error voi foste.
(Torna a sedere.)

Germont.

De' suoi beni donovuol farvi.

Violetta.

Non l' oso finora.—Rifiuterei.

Germont.

Pur tanto lusso—

Violetta
(gli da le carte).

A tutti è mistero quest' atto.—A voi no) sia

Germont   (reads the paper).

Heav'n, what a statement!
Have you then determined all your wealth
   to dispose of?
But, your past life, ah, why must that accuse
   you?

ıoletta.

It does so no longer; Alfred I love now, and
   Heav'n
Has cancell'd all the past with my repent
   ance.

Germont.

Ah, you have noble feelings.

Violetta.

Like sweet music my ear receives your accents.

Germont   (rising).

And of such feelings a sacrifice I ask now.

Violetta   (rising).

Ah, no, pray do not!
A dreadful thing thou wouldst require, I'm
   certain.
I foresaw it, with terror; ah, I was far too
   happy!

Germont.

A father's honor requires it,
And the future of his two dear children
   claims it.

Violetta.

Of two children?

Germont.

Yes.

Germont   (dopo averle scorse coll' occhio).

D'ogni avere pensate dispogliarvi!—
Ah, il passato perchè, perchè v'accusa!

Violetta.

Più non esiste—or amo Alfredo, e Dio
Lo cancellò col pentimento mio.

Germont.

Nobile sensi invero!

Violetta.

Oh, come dolce mi suona il vostra accento!

Germont.

Ed a tai sensi un sacrifizio chieggo.

Violetta   (alzandosi).

Ah, no, tacete—
Terribil cosa chiedereste certo—
Il predevi, v'attesi, era felice troppo.

Germont.

D'Alfredo il padre la sorte,
L'avvenir domanda or qui de' suoi due figli.

Violetta.

Di due figli?

Germont.

Sì.

PURA SICCOME UN ANGELO — *PURE AS AN ANGEL* (Germont)

Allegro moderato

Pu - ra sic - co - me un an - ge - lo   Id - dio mi diè u - na   fi - glia,
Pure as an an - gel from a - bove, *Kind heav'n a daugh - ter gave me,*

se Al - fre - do nie - ga   rie - de - re in   se - no al - la fa - mi - glia,
If now Al - fre - do   to   our love Will not re - turn and save me,

l'a - ma-to e a-man -te   gio - vi - ne,   cui spo-sa an-dar do -
He, the be - lov'd and   lov - ing youth,   Who soon should wed   my

ve - - a,   or si ri - cu-sa al   vin - co - lo__   che__
daugh - - ter,   Must then with-draw his   plight - ed troth,   With__

lie - ti, lie-ti ne ren - de - va.   Deh non mu - ta - te in tri - bo-li
all   the joy, the joy it   brought her.   Then do not change love's ro - ses fair

le ro - se dell' a - mor, ah, non mu - ta - te in tri - bo-li le ro-se dell' a -
To thorns of grief and   pain, Ah, do not change love's ro - ses fair To thorns of grief and

mor   a' prie - ghi miei re - sis - te - re no, no, non vo-glia il vos-tro cor, no,   no.
pain, Your gen-'rous heart, to   my fond pray'r, no, no, Will not op-posed re-main, no,   no.

Violetta.

Ah! I see now, that I must for a season
Be from Alfred parted. 'Twill be painful,
Dreary for me, yet—

Germont.

That will not suffice me!

Violetta.

Heav'ns! What more dost seek for?
Enough I've offered!

Germont.

No, not quite yet.

Violetta.

You wish that I forever should renounce him?

Germont.

It must be.

Violetta.

Ah, no! I cannot—never!
Ah! thou know'st not what affection
Burns within me, ardent, living!

Violetta.

Ah, comprendo—dovrò per alcun tempo
Da Alfredo allontanarmi—doloroso
Fora per me—pur—

Germont.

Non è ciò che chiedo.

Violetta.

Cielo!—che più cercate?—offersi assai!

Germont.

Pur non basta.

Violetta.

Volete che per sempre a lui renunzi?

Germont.

E d'uopo.

Violetta.

Ah, no—giam no, mai!
Non sapete quale affetto
Vivo, immensò in' arda il petto?

Not one kind friend or connexion
Can I number, still surviving?
But Alfred has declared it,
All in him my heart should find!
Ah! thou know'st not what dark sorrow
Mocked my being with its shadow?
All is over—how sad the morrow,
Parted thus from dear Alfred!
Ah! the trial is too cruel;
It were better far to die.

Germont.

The sacrifice is heavy;
But hear me with tranquillity.
Lovely thou art still, and youthful, too.
Hereafter—

Violetta.

No more persuade me. I know all,
But it cannot be. Him only I love and
live for!

Germont.

So be it. But the men are oft unfaithful
still—

Violetta (astounded).
Great Heaven!

Germont.

Some day, when love hath colder grown,
And time's broad gulf yawns wider;
When all the joys of life have flown,
What then will be? Consider!
No healing balm shall soothe your rest,
No warm and deep affection,
Since Heav'n your ties will ne'er have blest
With holy benediction.

Violetta.

'Tis all true!

Germont.

Then haste to dissipate the spell
Of this bright dream, controlling;
Be to my home and loved ones
Our angel, good, consoling.
Violetta, oh, consider well
While yet there may be time.
'Tis Heav'n itself that bids me speak,
'Tis Heav'n inspiring
These words in faith sublime.

Che nè amici, nè parenti
Io non conto tra' viventi?
E che Alfredo m' ha giurato
Che in lui tutto io troverò?
Non sapete che colpita
D'atro murbo è la mia vita?
Che già presso il fin ne vedo?
Ch'io mi separi da Alfredo!
Ah, il supplizio è si spietato,
Che morir preferiro.

Germont.

E grave il sacrifizio,
Ma pur, tranquilla udite.
Bella voi siete e giovane—
Col tempo—

Violetta.

Ah, più non dite—v'intendo—
M' è impossibile—Lui solo amar vogl'io.

Germont.

Sia pure—ma volubile sovente è l'uom.

Violetta (colpita).
Gran Dio!

Germont.

Un di, quando le veneri
Il tempo avrà fugate,
Fia presto il tedio a sorgere—
Che sarà allor!—pensate—
Per voi non avran balsamo
I più soavi affetti!
Da un genitor non furono
Tai nodi benedetti.

Violetta.

E vero!

Germont.

Ah, dunque, sperdasi
Tal sogno seduttore—
Siate di mia famiglia
L'angiol consolatore—
Violetta, deh pensateci,
Ne siete in tempo ancor.
E Dio che inspira, o giovane,
Tai detti a un genitor.

Violetta.

Thus, to the wretched, who falls, frail and erring,

When once again she would rise, hope is silent.

Though Heaven's indulgent, its pardon conferring,

Man unforgiving to her will be.

Say to this child of thine, young, pure and lovely,

Thou hast a victim found, whose life of sadness

Had but one single ray of rapture and gladness

Which she will yield to her, then gladly die.

Germont.

Weep on, thou hapless one,

Weep on; I witness thy trial

In what I ask of thy selfdenial.

Bear up, thou noble heart, triumph is nigh.

Violetta.

Now command me.

Germont.

Tell him that thou lovest him not.

Violetta.

He'll not believe.

Germont.

Then leave him.

Violetta.

He'll follow.

Germont.

Well, then—

Violetta.

Embrace me as thy daughter, then will my heart be strong.
        (They embrace.)

Ere long, restored you'll find him; but sad beyond all telling.

Then, to console him, from the arbor approach him.
    (Points to the garden and sits down to write.)

Germont.

What art thinking?

Violetta.

Così alla misera, ch' è un dì caduta,

Di più risorgere speranza è muta!

Se pur benefico le indulga Iddio

L'uomo implacabile per lei sarà.

Dite alla giovine sì bella e pura.

Ch'avvi una vittima, della sventure

Cui resta un unico raggio di bene

Che a lei il sagrifica e che morrà.

Germont.

Piangi, piangi, o misera,

Supremo il veggo è il sagrifizio

Ch'orati chieggo.

Sento nell' anima già le tue pene

Coraggio, è il nobile cor vincerà.

Violetta.

Imponete.

Germont.

Non amarlo ditegli.

Violetta.

Nol crederà.

Germont.

Partite.

Violetta.

Seguirammi.

Germont.

Allor.

Violetta.

Qual figlia m'abbraciate—forte così sarò.
        (S'abbracciano.)

Tra breve ei vi fia reso, ma afflitto oltare ogni dire;

A suo conforto di colà volerete.
    (Indicandogli il giardino, va ver iscrivere.)

Germont.

O che pensate!

Violetta.

If you my thoughts could know, you would then oppose me.

Germont.

Generous-hearted! How can I e'er repay thee?

Violetta.

I shall die! let not my memory
By him be execrated,
But let my woes and trials dark
To him be all related.
This sacrifice o'erwhelming
I make of love to duty,
Will be the end of all my woe,
The last sigh of my heart.

Germont.

No, noble heart, thou still shalt live!
A bright fate shall redress thee;
These tears announce the happy day
That Heav'n will send to bless thee.
This sacrifice unbounded
You make of love to duty,
So noble is, 'twill soon a glow
Of pride to you impart.

Violetta.

Some one comes, retire now.

Germont.

Oh, how my heart is grateful!

Violetta.

We meet no more forever!
(They embrace.)

Both.

May you be happy—Heav'n bless thee!
(GERMONT goes out by the garden door.)

SCENE VI—VIOLETTA, then ANNINA, then ALFRED.

Violetta.

Oh, grant me strength, kind Heaven!
(Sits down, writes, and then rings the bell.)

Annina.

Do you require me?

Violetta.

Yes; take and deliver thou this letter.

Annina
(looks at the direction with surprise).
Oh!

Violetta.

Sapendo, v' opporreste al pensier mio

Germont.

Generosa!—e per voi che far poss' io?

Violetta
(tornando a lui).
Morrò—la mia memoria;
Non fia ch' ei maledica,
Se le mie pene orribili
Vi sia chi almen gli dica.
Conosca il sacrifizio
Ch' io consumai d'amor.
Che sarà suo fin l'ultimo
Sospiro del mio cor.

Germont.

No, generosa, vivere,
E lieto voi dovrete,
Mercè di queste lagrime
Dal cielo un giorno avrete,
Premiato il sacrifizio
Sarà del vostro cor.
D'un' opra cosi nobile
Andrete fiera allor.

Violetta.

Quì giunge alcun; partite!

Germont.

Ah, grato v' è il cor mio!

Violetta.

Non ci vedrem più, forse.
(S'abbracciano.)

A due.

Felice siate—Addio!
(GERMONT esce la porta del giardino.)

SCENA VI—VIOLETTA, poi ANNINA, quindi ALFREDO

Violetta.

Dammi tu forza, o cielo!
(Siede, scrive, poi suona il campanello.)

Annina.

Mi chiedeste?

Violetta.

Sì, reca tu stessa questa foglio.

Annina
(ne guarda la direzione, a se na mestra sorpresa)
Oh!

Violetta.

    Be silent; go directly.

                (Exit Annina.)

    I must write to him now. What shall I say?

    Where shall I find the courage?

          (Writes, then seals the letter.)

Alfred   (coming in).

    What now?

Violetta   (conceals the letter).

    Nothing.

Alfred.

    Wert writing?

Violetta.

    Yes—no—

Alfred.

    What strange confusion! To whom wert writing?

Violetta.

    To thee.

Alfred.

    Give me the letter.

Violetta.

    No—directly.

Alfred.

    Forgive me; my thoughts are quite disturbed.

Violetta   (rising).

    By what?

Alfred.

    News from my father.

Violetta.

    Hast seen him?

Alfred.

    Ah no! but he hath sent a cruel letter! I soon expect him. At a glance he will love thee.

Violetta   (with agitation).

    Let him not here surprise me.

    Allow me to retire now, thou wilt calm him;

    Then at his feet—I'll humbly fall—

         (Scarcely restraining her tears.)

    He cannot will that we should part—we shall be happy—

    Because thou lov'st me, Alfred—is it not so?

Violetta.

    Silenzio—va all'istante.

             (Annina parte.)

    Ed or si scriva a lui—che gli dire?

    Chi men darà il coraggio?

         (Scrive e poi suggella.)

Alfredo.

    Che fai?

Violetta   (nascendendo la lettera).

    Nulla.

Alfredo.

    Scrivevi?

Violetta.

    No—sì—   (Confusa.)

Alfredo.

    Qual turbamento?—a chi scrivevi?

Violetta.

    A te.

Alfredo.

    Dammi quel foglio.

Violetta.

    No, per ora.

Alfredo.

    Mi perdona—son io preoccupato.

Violetta   (alzandosi).

    Che fu?

Alfredo.

    Giunse mio padre.

Violetta.

    Lo vedesti?

Alfredo.

    Ah, no; un severo scritto mi lasciava—

    Ma verrà—t'amerà solo in vederti.

Violetta   (molte agitata).

    Ch'io quì non mi sorprenda—

    Lascia che m'allontani—tu lo calma—

    Ai piedi suoi mi getterò—divisi

         (Mal frenande il piante.)

    Ei più non è vorrà—sarem felici—

    Perchè tu m'ami, Alfredo, non è vero?

Alfred.

　Oh, dearly!　Why dost weep thus?

Violetta.

　My heart, o'ercharged, had need of weep-
　　ing—I now am tranquil,
　Thou seest it?—Smiling on thee!
　　　　　(With great effort.)
　I'll be there—'mid the flow'rs, ever near
　　thee,—
　Love me, Alfred, love me as I now love
　　thee.
　Farewell, love!
　　　　　(Runs to the garden.)

SCENE VII—ALFRED, then JOSEPH, then a MESSENGER.

Alfred.

　Ah, that fond heart lives only in my de-
　　votion!
(Sits down and opens a book, reads a little, then rises,
and looks at the clock, which is upon the chimneypiece.)
　'Tis late now! to-day it's doubtful
　If I shall see my father.

Joseph
　　　　　(enters hurriedly).
　Sir, my lady has departed,
　In a carriage that awaited,
　And is already upon the road to Paris.
　Annina, too, disappeared some time before
　　her.

Alfred.

　I know—be quiet.

Joseph.

　(What does this mean?)
　　　　　(Retires.)

Alfred.

　She goes, perhaps, to hasten
　The sale of all her property.
　Annina will stay all that.
(His father is seen in the distance, crossing the garden.)
　Some one is in the garden!
　Who's there?
　　　　　(Going out.)

Messenger
　　　　　(at the door).
　You, sir, are Germont?

Alfred.

　I am, sir.

Alfredo.

　Oh, quanto!—perchè piangi?

Violetta.

　Di lagrime avea duopo—or son tranquilla—
　Lo vedi?—ti sorrido—
　　　　　(Forzandosi.)
　Sarò là, tra quei fior, presso a te sempre—
　Amami, Alfredo, quant' io t'amo.—Addio.
　　　　　(Corre in giardino.)

SCENA VII—ALFREDO, poi GIUSEPPE, indi un COMMIS
SIONARO, a tempo.

Alfredo.

　Ah, vive sol quel core all' amor mio!
(Siede, prende a caso un libro, legge alquanto, quand
s'alza, guarda l'ora sull' orologio sovrapposto al camino.)
　E tardi; ed oggi forse.
　Più non verrà mio padre.

Giuseppe
　　　　　(entrando frettoloso).
　La signora è partita—
　L' attendeva un calesse, e sulla via
　Già corre di Parigi.—Annina pure
　Prima di lei spariva.

Alfredo.

　Il sò, ti calma.

Giuseppe
　　　　　(da se).
　Che vuol dir ciò!
　　　　　(Esce.)

Alfredo.

　Va forse d' ogni avere
　Ad affrettar la perdita—
　Ma Annina la impedirà.
(Si vede il Padre attraversare in lontane il giardino.)
　Qualcuno è nel giardino!
　Chi è là?
　　　　　(Per uscire.)

Commissionaro
　　　　　(alla porta).
　Il Signor Germont?

Alfredo.

　Son io.

Messenger.

Sir, a lady in a coach, gave me,
Not far from this place, a note, to you di-
rected.
(Gives a letter to Alfred, is paid and departs.)

SCENE VIII—Alfred, then Germont, from the garden.

Alfred.

From Violetta! ah, why am I thus moved?
To rejoin her, perhaps she now invites me.
I tremble.

Oh, Heav'n! send courage!
(Opens and reads.)
"Alfred, at the moment this note shall reach
you"—
Ah!
(He utters a cry like one struck by a thunderbolt, and in
turning finds himself in the presence of his father, into
whose arms he throws himself, exclaiming:)

Oh, my father!

Germont.

My dear son!
How thou dost suffer! restrain thy weeping,
Return and be the glory, the pride of thy
father.
(ALFRED despairingly sits at a table, with his face concealed
in his hands.)

Commissionaro.

Una dama, da un cocchio, per voi,
Di quà non lunge mi diede questo scritto.
(Da una lettera ad ALFREDO, ne riceve qualche moneta, e
parte.)

SCENA VIII—Alfredo, poi Germont, ch'entra dal giardino

Alfredo.

Di Violetta!—Perchè son io commosso?—
A raggiungerla forse ella m' invita—
Io tremo!—Oh ciel!—Coraggio!
(Apre e legge.)
"Alfredo, al giungervi di questo foglio"—
(Come fulminato, grida.)
(Volgendosi, si trava a fronte del padre, nelle cui braccia
si abbandona, esclamando:)

Ah!—Padre mio!

Germont.

Mio figlio!
Oh, quanto soffri—tergi, ah, tergi il pianto—
Ritorna di tuo padre orgoglio e vanto.
(ALFREDO disperato siede presso il tavolino col volte tra
le mani.)

DI PROVENZA IL MAR — *FROM FAIR PROVENCE'S SOIL AND SEA* (Germont)

Di Pro-ven-za il mar il suol chi dal cor-ti can-cel-lò? chi dal
From fair Pro-vence soil and sea, Who hath won thy heart a-way, Who hath

cor-ti can-cel-lò? di Pro-ven-za il mar il suol? al na-tio ful-gen-te sol qual de-
won thy heart a-way, From fair Pro-vence soil and sea? From thy na-tive sunny clime, What strange

sti-no ti fu-rò? qual de-sti-no ti fu-rò? al na-tio ful-gen-te sol? Oh, ram-
fate caused thee to stray, What strange fate caused thee to stray From thy na-tive sun-ny clime? Oh, re-

men -ta pur nelduol ch'i - vi gio-ja a te bril-lò, e che pa - ce co - la sol su te
mem-ber in thy woe All the joy that waits for thee, All the peace thy heart would know, On-ly

splen-de-re an-cor può, e che pa-ce co - la sol su te splen-de-re an-cor può.
there still found may be. All the peace thy heart would know, On-ly there, still found may be.

Dio mi gui - dò!_____ Dio mi gui - dò! Dio mi gui - dò!
Heav'n guid - ed me!_____ Heav'n guid - ed me! Heav'n guid-ed me!

Ah! thy father old and worn,
  What he felt, thou ne'er canst know.
In thine absence, so forlorn
  Seemed his home, with grief and woe.
But I find thee now again,
  If my hope doth not mislead,
If yet honor doth remain
  With its voice not mute or dead,
Heav'n sends me aid!
Wilt not answer a father's affection?
          (Embracing him.)

Alfred.
  Countless furies within my heart are rag-
    ing!
  Go and leave me—
          (Repulses his father.)
Germont.
  How, leave thee?
Alfred.
  (Oh, for vengeance!)
Germont.
  Do not linger, let's go now, oh, haste thee!
Alfred.
  (It was Dauphol!)
Germont.
  Dost thou not hear?
Alfred.
  No!

Oh! il tuo vecchio genitor
  Tu non sai quanto soffri—
Te lontano, di squallor
  Il suo tetto si copri—
Ma se alfin ti trovo ancor
  Se in me speme non falli.
Se la voce dell' onor
  In te appien non ammuti—
Dio m'esaudi!
Nè rispondi d'un padre all'affeto.
          (Abbracciando.)

Alfredo.
  Mille furie divorammi il petto—
  Mi lasciate—
          (Respingendolo.)
Germont.
  Lasciarti!
Alfredo
  (Oh, vendetta!)
          (risoluto).
Germont.
  Non più indugi; partiamo—t'affretta.
Alfredo.
  (Ah, fu Douphol!)
Germont.
  M'ascolti tu?
Alfredo.
  No!

Germont.

All in vain then my search will have been?
No, no, I will not chide thee now,
But hide the past forever;
The love that guides me ever
Full pardon will bestow.
Then come and drown thy cares in joy
With me again returning;
For thee loved ones are yearning;
Such hopes thou'lt not destroy!
Fond hearts at home are burning
Their soothing care to show.

Alfred

(Arousing himself; sees upon the table the letter of FLORA,
glances at its contents, and exclaims:)

Ah! She's at the fête, then!
Thither will I fly, and seek revenge.

Germont.

What say'st thou? ah, stay thee!

(ALFRED departs precipitately, followed by his father.)

SCENE IX—A salon in FLORA's palace, richly furnished
and lighted up. A door in the back scene, and two lateral
ones. On the right, a little forward, a table, on which
are cards and other implements of play. On the left a small
table, with flowers and refreshments; chairs and a settee.

(FLORA, the MARQUIS, the DOCTOR, and other guests, enter
from the left, and converse amongst themselves.)

Flora.

There'll be fun here to-night with maskers
    merry;
The Count will be their leader;
Violetta and Alfred both will be here.

Marquis.

Have you not heard the news then?
Germont and Violetta are divided.

Flora.
Doctor. } Is that true?

Marquis.

Yes, and she will come with the Baron.

Doctor.

I saw them yesterday, appearing quite happy.

(A noise is heard on the right.)

Flora.

Be silent—you hear them?

All.

Yes, our friends are coming.

Germont.

Dunque invano trovoato t'avrò!
No, non udrai rimproveri;
Copriam d'oblio il passato;
L'amor che m'ha guidato
Sa tutto perdonar.
Vieni, i tuoi cari in giubilo
Con me rivedi ancora;
A chi penò finora
Tal gioja non niegar
Un'padre ed una suora
T'affretta a consolar.

Alfredo

(Scuotendosi, getta a caso gli occhi sulla tavola, a vede
la lettera di FLORA, la scorre ed esclama:)

Ah!—ell' è alla festa!—volisi
L' offesa a vendicar.

Germont.

Che dice? ah ferma!

(Fugge precipitoso seguito dal padre.)

SCENA IX—Galleria nel palazzo di FLORA, riccamente
addobata ed illuminata. Una porta nel fondo e due laterali.
A destra piu avanti un tavoliere con quanto occorre pel
giuoco; a sinistra, ricco tavolino con fiori e rinfreschi, varie
sedis e un divano.

(FLORA, il MARCHESE, il DOTTORE, ed altri invitati entrano
dalla sinistra, discorrendo tra loro.)

Flora.

Avrem lieta di maschere la notte;
N' è duce il viscontino—
Violetta ed Alfredo anco invitai.

Marchese.

La novita ignorate?
Violetta e Germont son disgiunti.

Dottore.
Flora. } Fia vero.

Marchese.

Ella verrà qui col barone.

Dottore.

Li vidi jeri ancor—parean felici.

(S' ode rumore a destra.)

Flora.

Silenzio—Udite?

Tutti

(vanno verso la destra).

Giungono gli amici.

SCENE X—The same, and a number of ladies masked as GIPSIES, some of whom hold a staff in the hand, some have tambourines, with which to beat time.

SCENA X—Detti, e molte Signore mascherate da ZINGARE, che entrano dalla destra.

NOI SIAMO ŻINGARELLE — *WE'RE GIPSIES GAY AND YOUTHFUL* (Chorus)

Allegro moderato

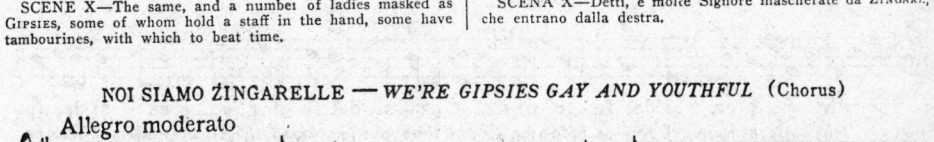

Noi sia - mo zin - ga - rel - le ve - nu - te da lon - ta - no: d'o-
We're gip - sies gay and youth - ful, From dis - tant shores ar - riv - ing: With

gnu - no sul - la ma - no leg - gia - mo l'av - ve - nir, Se—
skil - ful art con - triv - ing The fu - ture to fore - tell, We—

con - sul - tiam le stel - le, con - sul - tiam le stel - le null' av - vi - a noi d'os - cu - ro no, null'
read the plan - ets truth - ful, read the plan - ets truthful, Their se - crets dark un - fold - ing, all their

av - vi - a noi d'os - cu - ro, e i ca - si del fu - tu - ro pos - sia - mo al - trui pre-
se - crets dark un - fold, The realms of fate be - hold - ing, We can your for - tunes

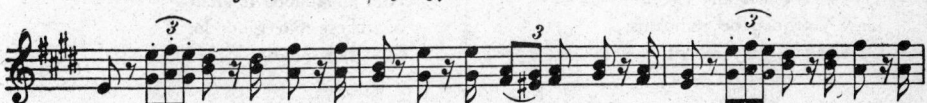

dir. Se - con - sul - tiam le stel - le null' av - vi - a noi d'os - cur, e i ca - si del fu-
tell. We— read the plan - ets truth - ful, Their se - crets dark un - fold, The realms of fate. be-

tu - ro pos - sia - mo al - trui pre - dir, e i ca - si del fu - tu - ro, e i ca - si del fu-
hold - ing, We can your for - tunes tell, The realms of fate be - hold - ing, We can thus your fortunes

tur e - i ca - si del fu - tu - ro pos - sia - mo al - trui, pos - sia - mo al - trui pre-
tell, All the realms of fate be - hold - ing, we thus can tell, For-tunes we thus can

dir e — i ca - si del fu - tu ro, e — i ca - si del fu - tur, e — i ca - si del fu-
tell, All the realms of fate be-hold-ing, We can thus your for-tunes tell, All the realms of fate be-

tu - ro — pos - sia - mo al - trui, pos-sia-mo al-trui pre - dir.
hold - ing, We thus can tell, for-tunes we thus can tell.

First Gipsy	**1. Zingara**
(examining the hand of FLORA).	(prendono la mano a FLORA, e la osservano).
Let's see now. You, fair lady,	Vediamo?—Voi, signora,
Have rivals gay and sprightly.	Rivali alquante avete.
Second Gipsy	**2. Zingara**
(examining the hand of the MARQUIS).	(fanno lo stesso al MARCHESE).
And you, if we read rightly,	Marchese, voi non siete
Are not the type of truth.	Model di fedeltà.
Flora (to the MARQUIS).	**Flora** (al MARCHESE).
You play me false already?	Fate il galante ancora?
I'll take good care to pay you.	Ben vo' me la paghiate.
Marquis (to FLORA).	**Marchese** (a FLORA).
Ah, what the deuce thus say you?	Che diacin vi pensate?
The charge is base untruth.	L' accusa è falsità.
Flora.	**Flora.**
The fox, howe'er disguising,	La volpe lascia il pelo,
Will yet be low and VICIOUS ;	Non abbandona il vizio—
Gay Marquis, be judicious,	Marchese mio, giudizio,
Or else you may repent.	O vi faro pentir.
All.	**Tutti.**
Let now a veil oblivious	Su via, si stenda un velo
Be o'er the past extended ;	Sui fatti del passato ;
What's done may not be mended,	Già quel ch' è stato è stato,
But future wrongs prevent.	Badiano al l'avvenir.
(FLORA and the MARQUIS shake hands.)	(FLORA ed il MARCHESE si stringono la mano.)

SCENE XI—The same; GASTON and others, masked as Spanish Mattadores, and others as Piccadores, who enter in a lively manner from the right.

SCENA XI—Detti, GASTONE ed altri mascherati di Mattadori e Piccadori spagnuoli, ch'entrano vivacemente dalla destra.

Gaston and Tenors.	**Gastone e Mattadori.**
We are Mattadores from Madrid, so famous;	Di Madride noi siam mattadori,
Bold and valiant in Bull-fights all name us;	Siamo i prodi del circo de' tori;
Just arrived here, to join with discretion	Testè giunti a godere del chiasso
In the fun of the "Fat ox" procession.	Che a Parigi si fa pel Bue grasso;
If a tale may command your attention,	E una storia se udire vorrete,
You will find us gallants of pretention.	Qualti amanti noi siamo, saprete.

All the Others.
    Yes, yes, bravi! go on now relating.
    With much pleasure we'll listen.
Gaston .and Chorus.
    Hear then.

Gli Altri.
    Sì, sì, bravi; narrate, narrate;
    Con piacere l'udremo.
Gastone e Mattadori.
    Ascoltate.

E PIQUILLO UN BEL GAGLIARDO — *YOUNG PIQUILLO* (Gaston and Chorus)

E__ Pi-quil-lo un bel ga-gliar-do bi-sca-gli-no mat-ta-dor,
Young Pi-quil-lo, gay__ and dar-ing, Was__ a val-iant mat-ta-dor,

for-te il brac-cio, fie-ro il guar-do, del-le gio-stre e-gli è sig-nor.
Strong his arm was, proud his bear-ing, In__ all sports, the prize he bore.

D'An-da-lu-sia gio-vi-net-ta fol-le-men-te in-na-mo-rò;
One__ of Spain's fair maids en-chant-ing, With this youth fell mad-ly in love:

ma-la bel-la ri-tro-set-ta co-si al gio-va-ne__ par-lò:
But__ the maid, ere fa-vors grant-ing, Bade_ him thus his val-or prove—

Cin-que to-ri in un sol gior-no vo' ve-der-ti ad at-ter-rar,
"Five stout bulls, in one brief morn-ing I would see__ thee meet and slay;

e se vin-ci, al tuo ri-tor-no ma-no e cor-ti vo'__ do-nar.
If suc-cess-ful, here re-turn-ing, Hand and heart shall thee re-pay."

Si__ gli dis-se e il mat-ta-do-ro al-le gio-stre mos-se il piè;
Then the mat-ta-dor as-sent-ed, To__ the tri-al led the way;

cin - que to - ri vin - ci - to - re   sull' a - re - na e - gli sten - dè,
Five fierce bulls, in turn pre - sent - ed,   His strong arm did van-quish that day,

cin - que to - ri vin - ci - to - re   sull' a - re - na e - gli sten - dè.
Five fierce bulls, in turn pre-sent -ed,   His strong arm did van-quish that day.

Flora and Others.	*Gli Altri.*
Bravely he with courage daring	Bravo invero il mattadore
Did his gallantry display!	Ben gagliardo si mostrò,
While his love, with strength unsparing,	Se alla giovine l' amore
He declared in such gallant way.	In tal guisa egli provò.
Gaston and Chorus.	*Gastone e Mattadori.*
Then, 'mid plaudits loud, returning	Poi, tra plausi, ritornato
To the maid, with winning grace,	Alla bella del suo cor,
Took the prize with blushes burning,	Colse il premio desïato
Held her fast in love's embrace.	Dal a fede, dall' amor.
Others of the Chorus.	*Gli Altri.*
Proofs we Mattadores thus render,	Con tai prove i Mattadori
How we can vanquish all the fair!	San le amanti conquistar!
Gaston.	*Gastone e Mattadori.*
Here, the hearts are far more tender,	Ma diù sen più miti i cori;
We content with trifling are.	A noi basta folleggiar.
All.	*Tutti.*
Yes, let's try now to discover	Sì, sì allegri—Or pria tentiamo
All the various moods of fate;	Della sorte il vario umor.
The arena we uncover,	La palestra dischiudiamo
And for all bold players wait!	Agli audaci giuocator.
(The men take off their masks—some walk about, while others commence playing.)	(Gli uomini si tolgono la maschera, chi passeggia e chi s accinge a giuocare.)
SCENE XII—The same, and ALFRED; then VIOLETTA with the BARON; afterwards, a servant.	SCENA XII—Detti, ed ALFREDO, quindi VIOLETTA co BARONE; un Servo a tempo.
All.	*Tutti.*
Alfred!—you!	Alfredo!—Voi!
Alfred.	*Alfredo.*
Yes, my kind friends.	Sì, amici.
Flora.	*Flora.*
Violetta?	Violetta?
Alfred.	*Alfredo.*
I don't know.	Non ne so.
All.	*Tutti.*
What cool indifference! Bravo! We'll now commence to play.	Ben disinvolto!—Bravo!—Or via, giuocar Si può.
(GASTON shuffles the cards, ALFRED and others put up their stakes. VIOLETTA enters, leaning on the arm of the BARON.)	(GASTONE si pone a tagliare: ALFREDO ed altri puntano, VIOLETTA entra al braccia del BARONE.)

Flora
(going to meet them).

Here comes the guest most welcome.

Violetta.

To your kind wish I yielded.

Flora.

Thanks to you, also, Baron, for your polite
acceptance.

Baron
(softly to VIOLETTA).

Germont is here! do you see him?

Violetta.

(Heav'n! 'tis he, truly!)   I see him.

Baron.

Let not one word escape you, addressed to
this Alfred!

Violetta.

(Why, ah, why came I hither? In mercy,
Heaven, thy pity send to me!)

Flora.

Sit here beside me. Tell me now, what
new and strange is passing.

(To VIOLETTA, making her sit beside her on the settee. The
DOCTOR approaches them while they are conversing in an undertone. The MARQUIS converses with the BARON. GASTON
continues to play. ALFRED and others stake, and the rest
walk about.)

Alfred.

A four-spot!

Gaston.

Ah! thou hast won it.

Alfred.

Unfortunate in loving, makes fortunate in
gaming—
(Stakes again and wins.)

All.

Still he remains the victor.

Alfred.

O I shall gain this evening, and with my
golden winnings,

To the green fields returning, I shall again
be happy.

Flora.

Singly?

Alfred.

No, no. With some one like her who once
was with me, but fled and left me!

Flora.
(andandole incontro).

Qui desïata giungi.

Violetta.

Cessi al cortese invito.

Flora.

Grata vi son, Barone, d' averlo pur gradito.

Barone
(piano a VIOLETTA).

Germont è qui! il vedete?

Violetta.

Cielo!—egli è vero!
(Da sè.)

Il vedo.

Barone.
(piano a VIOLETTA).

Da voi non un sol detto si volga a questo
Alfredo.

Violetta
(da sè).

Ah, perchè venni incauta! Pieta di me, gran
Dio!

Flora.

Meco t' assidi; narrami—quai novità vegg'
io?

(A VIOLETTA, facendola sedere presso dis è sul divano. Il
DOTTORE si avvicina ad esse, che commessamente conversano.
Il MARCHESE si trattiene a parte col BARONE; GASTONE taglia;
ALFREDO ed altri puntano altri passegiano.)

Alfredo.

Un quattro!

Gastone.

Ancora hai vinto!

Alfredo.

Sfortuna nell' amore vale fortuna al giuco.
(Punta e vince.)

Tutti.

E sempre vincitore!

Alfredo.

Oh, vincerò stassera; e l' oro guadagnato
Poscia a goder fra' campi ritornerò beato.

Flora.

Solo?

Alfredo.

No, no, con tale, che vi fu meco ancor,
Poi mi sfuggia.

Violetta.

(Oh, Heaven!)

Gaston
(to ALFRED, pointing to VIOLETTA)
Some pity show.

Baron
(with ill-restrained anger).
Beware!

Violetta
(softly to the BARON).
Be calm, or I must leave you.

Alfred
(carelessly).
Did you address me, Baron?

Baron
(ironically).
You are in such good fortune
I fain would try against you.

Alfred.
Yes? I accept your challenge.

Violetta.
(Who'll aid me? Death seems approaching.
O Heaven, look down and pity me!)

Baron
(staking).
Here at the right one hundred.

Alfred
(staking).
I, at the left one hundred.

Gaston
(dealing off).
An ace there, a knave, too; thou'st won it!
(To ALFRED.)

Baron.
Wilt double?

Alfred.
A double be it.

Gaston
(dealing off).
A four-spot—a seven.

Alfred.
Then I'm again victorious.

All.
Bravely indeed! good fortune seems partial to Alfred!

Violetta
(da sè).
Mio Dio!

Gastone
(ad ALFREDO indic. VIOLETTA).
Pietà di lei.

Barone
(ad ALFREDO, con mal frenata ira).
Signor!

Violetta
(piano al BARONE).
Frenatevi, o vi lascio.

Alfredo
(disinvolto).
Barone, m' appellaste?

Barone
(ironico).
Siete in sì gran fortuna,
Che al gioco mi tentaste.

Alfredo.
Sì!—la disfida accetto.

Violetta
(da sè).
Che fia?—morir mi sento!
Pietà, gran Dio, di me!

Barone
(punta).
Centro luigi a destra.

Alfredo
(punta)
Ed alla manca cento.

Gastone
(ad ALFREDO).
Un asso—un faute—hai vinto!

Barone.
Il doppio?

Alfredo.
Il doppio sia.

Gastone
(tagliando).
Un quattro, un sette—

Tutti.
Ancora!

Alfredo.
Pur la vittoria è mia!

Coro.
Bravo davver!—la sorte è tutta per Alfredo!

Flora.

Ah! for the rustic dwelling the Baron pays
expenses.

Alfred
(to the BARON).

Now we'll go on!

Servant
(entering).

The banquet is ready!

Flora.

Let's go then.

All
(starting).

Let's go, then.

Alfred
(to the BARON).

Shall we our game continue?

Baron.

At present, no, we cannot;
Ere long, my losses I'll regain.

Alfred.

At any game that suits you.

Baron.

Our friends we'll follow. After—

Alfred.

Whene'er you call, you'll find me.

(All retire through a door in the centre—the stage left
empty for a moment.)

SCENE XIII—VIOLETTA returns, breathless, followed by
ALFRED.

Violetta.

I have asked him to come hither.
Will he do so? And will he hear me?
Yes, he will, for bitter hate
Controls him more than my sad accents.

Alfred.

Didst thou call me? What dost wish for?

Violetta.

Quickly leave this place, I pray you;
Danger o'er you is suspended.

Alfred.

Ah! you're clearly comprehended.
E'en so base you then believe me?

Violetta.

Ah no, no, never!

Alfred.

But what then fear you?

Flora.

Del villeggia la spesa farà il Baron, già il
vedo.

Alfredo
(al BARONE).

Seguite pur!

Serve.

La cena è pronta.

Flora.

Andiamo.

Coro
(avriandosi).

Andiamo.

Alfredo
(tra loro a parte).

Se continuar v' aggrada—

Barone.

Per ora nol possiamo.
Più tardi la rivincita.

Alfredo.

Al gioco che vorrete.

Barone.

Seguiam gli amici; poscia—

Alfredo.

Sarò qual mi vorrete.

(Tutti entrano nella porta di mezze: la scena rimane un
istante vuota.)

SCENA XIII—VIOLETTA, che ritorna affannata, indi ALFREDO.

Violetta.

Invitato a qui seguirmi,
Verrà desso?—vorrà udirmi?
El verrà—chè l' odio atroce
Puote in lui più di mia voce.

Alfredo.

Mi chiamaste?—Che bramate?

Violetta.

Questi luoghi abbandonate—
Un periglio vi sovrasta.

Alfredo.

Ah, comprendo!—Basta, basta—
E si vile mi credete?

Violetta.

Ah, no, mai.

Alfredo.

Ma che temete?

Violetta.

    Ah, I fear the Baron's fury.

Alfred.

    An affair of death's between us;
    Should this hand in death extend him,
    One sole blow would then deprive thee
    Both of lover and protector;
    Would such losses sorrow give thee?

Violetta.

    But if he should prove the victor!
    There behold the sole misfortune,
    That, I fear, would prove me fatal.

Alfred.

    Pray, what care you for my safety?

Violetta.

    Hence, depart now, this present instant!

Alfred.

    I will go, but swear this moment,
    Thou wilt follow now and ever,
    Where I wander.

Violetta.

    Ah, no; never.

Alfred.

    No! and never!

Violetta.

    Go, thou, unhappy! and forget me.
    Thus degraded, go and leave me!
    At this moment, to escape thee
    I a sacred oath have taken!

Alfred.

    To whom? tell me! who could claim it?

Violetta.

    One who had the right to name it.

Alfred.

    'Twas Dauphol?

Violetta

                (with great effort).
    Yes.

Alfred.

    Then thou lov'st him?

Violetta.

    Ah, well, I love him.

Alfred

(Runs furiously, throws open the doors and cries out:)
    Come hither all!

Violetta.

    Tremo sempre del Barone.

Alfredo.

    E tra noi mortal quistione—
    S' ei cadrà per mano mia
    Un sol colpo vi torria
    Coll' amante il protettore—
    V'atterrisce tal sciagura?

Violetta.

    Ma s' ei fosse l' uccisore!—
    Ecco l' unica sventura—
    Ch' io pavento a me fatale!

Alfredo.

    La mia morte!—Che ven cale?

Violetta.

    Deh, partite, e sull' istante.

Alfredo.

    Partiro, ma giura innante
    Che dovunque seguirai
    I miei passi.

Violetta.

    Ah no, giammai.

Alfredo.

    No!—giammai!

Violetta.

    Va, sciagurato,
    Scorda un nome ch' è infamato—
    Va—mi lascia sul momento—
    Di fuggirti un giuramento
    Sacro io feci.

Alfredo.

    E chi potea?

Violetta.

    Chi diritto pien ne avea.

Alfredo.

    Fu Douphol?

Violetta

              (con supremo sforzo).
    Sì.

Alfredo.

    Dunque l'ami?

Violetta.

    Ebben—l'amo.

Alfredo

(corre furente sulla porta, e grida:)
    Or tutti a me.

SCENE XIV—The same, and all the others, who enter in confusion.

All.

Did you call us? Now what would you?

Alfred
(pointing to VIOLETTA, who leans fainting against the table).

Know ye all this woman present?

All.

Who? Violetta?

Alfred.

Know ye, too, her base misconduct?

Violetta.

Ah! spare me!

All.

No!

Alfred.

All she possessed, this woman here
Hath for my love expended.
I blindly, basely, wretchedly,
This to accept, condescended.
But there is time to purge me yet
From stains that shame, confound me.
Bear witness all around me
That here I pay the debt.

(In a violent rage he throws a purse at VIOLETTA's feet—she faints in the arms of FLORA and the DOCTOR. At this moment Alfred's father enters.)

SCENE XV—The same, and GERMONT, the elder, who has entered at the last words.

All.

Oh, to what baseness thy passions have
    moved thee.
To wound thus fatally one who has loved
    thee!
Shameless traducer of woman-defenceless,
Depart hence, speedily, scorned and de-
    spised!

Germont.

Of scorn most worthy himself doth render
Who wounds in anger a woman tender!
My son, where is he? No more I see him;
In thee, Alfred, I seek him, but in vain.

Alfred
(aside).

Ah! yes, 'twas shameful! a deed, abhorrent,
A jealous fury—love's maddening torrent

SCENA XIV—Detti, e TUTTI i precedenti, che confusamente ritornano.

Tutti.

Ne appellaste?—Che volete?

Alfredo
(additando VIOLETTA che abbattuta, si appeggia al tavolino).

Questa donna conoscete?

Tutti.

Chi? Violetta?

Alfredo.

Che facesse
Non sepete?

Violetta.

Ah, taci.

Tutti.

No.

Alfredo.

Ogni suo aver tal femina
Per amor mio sperdea.
Io cieco, vile, misero,
Tutto accettar potea,
Ma, è tempo ancora! tergermi,
Da tanta macchia bramo
Qui testimon vi chiamo,
Che quì pagato io l'ho!

(ALFREDO getta con furente sprezzo il ritratto di VIOLETTA ai piedi di lei, ed essa sviene tra le braccia di FLORA e del DOTTORE. In tal momento entra il Padre.)

SCENA XV—Detti, ed il Signor GERMONT, ch' entra all' ultime parole.

Tutti.

Oh, infamia orribile tu commettesti!—
Un cor sensibile così uccidesti!—
Di donne ignobile insultatore,
Di qua allontanati, ne desti orror.

Germont.

Di sprezzo degno sè stesso rende
Chi pur nell' ira la donna offende.
Dov' è mio figlio?— Più non lo vedo.
In te più Alfredo—trovar non so.

Alfredo
(da se).

Ah, sì!—che feci!—ne sento orrore!
Gelosa smania, deluso amore

Oppressed my senses, destroyed my reason;
From her, no pardon shall I obtain!
To fly and leave her, strength was denied
    me,
My angry passions did hither guide me.
But now that fury is all expended,
Remorse and horror to me remain.

Germont
         (aside).
I 'mid them only know what bright virtues
Dwell in that sad heart so torn and bleed-
    ing.
I know she loves him, all else unheeding;
Yet must, tho' cruel, silent remain.

Gaston. ⎱Oh! thou dost suffer! but cheer thy
Flora. ⎰ heart,
Here in thy trials we all take part.
Kind friends surround thee, care o'er thee
    keeping,
Cease then thy weeping, thy tears restrain.

Baron.
This shameful insult against this lady
Offends all present; behold me ready
To punish outrage! Here now declaring
Such pride o'erbearing I will restrain.

Violetta
        (reviving).
Ah, loved Alfred, this heart's devotion
Thou canst not fathom yet—its fond emo-
    tion!
Thou'rt still unknowing that at the meas-
    ure
Of this displeasure. 'tis proved again.
But when, hereafter, the truth comes o'er
    thee,
And my affection shall rise before thee,
May Heav'n in pity then spare thee re-
    morse.
Ah, tho' dead, still loving, ever will I re-
    main!

(Germont takes his son with him; the Baron follows;
Violetta is taken into an adjoining room by the Doctor
and Flora, and the rest disperse.

END OF THE SECOND ACT.

Mi strazian l'alma—più non ragiono-
Da lei perdono—più non avro.
Volea fuggirla—non ho potuto!—
Dall' ira spinto, son qui venuto!—
Or che lo sdegno ho disfogato.
Me sciagurato!—rimorso io n' ho.

Germont
        ⸜da se).
Io sol fra tutti so qual virtude
Di quella misera il sen racchiude—
Io so che l'ama, che gli è fedele;
Eppur, crudele, tacer dovrò!

Gastone. ⎱Oh quanto peni! ma pur fi cor
Flora. ⎰Quì soffre ognuno del tuo dolor;
Fracari amici quì sei soltanto,
Rascinga il pianto che t' inondò.

Barone.
A questa donna l' atroce insulto
Qui tutti offese ma non inulto
Fia tanto oltraggio! Provar vi voglio
Che il vostro orgoglio fiaccar saprò!

Violetta
        (riavendosi).
Alfredo, Alfredo, di questo core
Non puoi comprendere tutto l'amore;
Tu non conosci che fino a prezzo
Del tuo disprezzo—provato io l' ho!
Ma verrà giorno, in che il saprai—
Com' io t'amassi confesserai—
Dio dai rimorsi ti salvi allora
Io penta ancora—pur t'amero.

(Germont trae seco il figlio; il Barone lo segue. Violetta
è condotta in altra stanza dal Dottore e da Flora; gli
altri si disperdano.)

FINE DELL' ATTO SECONDO.

ACT III.

SCENE 1—Violetta's bed-room. At the back a bed, with the curtains partly drawn. A window shut by inside shutters. Near the bed a table with a bottle of water, a crystal cup, and different kinds of medicine on it. In the middle of the room a toilet-table and settee; a little apart from which is another piece of furniture, upon which a night-lamp is burning. Chairs and other articles of furniture. On the left a fireplace with a fire in it.

(VIOLETTA discovered sleeping on the bed—ANNINA, seated near the fireplace, has fallen asleep.)

Violetta (awaking).

Annina!

Annina (waking up, confusedly).

Did you call me?

Violetta.

Poor creature, were you sleeping?

Annina.

Yes, but forgive me.

Violetta.

Bring me here some water.

(ANNINA does so.)

Look out now—is it yet daylight?

Annina.

It is seven.

Violetta.

To a little light give access.

(ANNINA opens the blinds, and looks into the street.)

Annina.

Doctor Grenvil has come—

Violetta.

A friend most faithful!

I wish to rise, assist me!

(She rises, but falls again—then, supported by ANNINA, she walks slowly towards the settee, and the DOCTOR enters in time to assist her to sit upon it—ANNINA places cushions about her.

SCENE II—The same, and the DOCTOR

Violetta.

How kind in you thinking of me thus early.

Doctor (feeling her pulse).

Yes, are you somewhat better?

Violetta.

With pain I suffer; but my mind is tranquil. A priest came here last evening and brought me comfort. Ah! religion is a solace to us in affliction.

Doctor.

Last night, how were you?

ATTO III.

SCENA I—Camera da letto di VIOLETTA. Nel fondo e un letto con cortine mezzo tirate; una finestra chiusa da imposte interne; presso il letto uno sgabello su cui una bottiglia d'acqua, una tazza di cristallo, diverse medicine. A metà della scena una toilette, vicino un canapè; più distante un altro mobile, su cui arde un lume da notte, varie sedie ed altri mobili. La porta è a sinistra; di fronte v' è un caminnetto con fuoco acceso.

(VIOLETTA dorme sul letto—ANNINA, seduta presso il caminetto, è pure addormita.)

Violetta (destandosi).

Annina!

Annina (svegliandosi confusa).

Comandate?

Violetta.

Dormivi, poveretta?

Annina.

Sì, perdonate.

Violetta.

Dammi d' acqua un sorso.

(ANNINA esequisce.)

Osserva, è pieno il giorno?

Annina.

Son sett' ore.

Violetta.

Dà accesso a un pò di luce.

(Apre le imposte, e guarda nella via.)

Annina.

Il Signor Grenvil!

Violetta.

Oh, il vero amico!—

Alzar mi vo'—m'aita.

(Si alza e ricade; poi sostenuta da ANNINA va lentamente verso il canapè, ed il DOTTORE entra in tempo per assisterla ad adagiarvisi—ANNINA vi aggiunge dei cuscini.)

SCENA II—Dette, ed il DOTTORE.

Violetta.

Quanta bontà!—Pensaste a me per tempo!

Dottore (le tocca il polso).

Or come vi sentite?

Violetta.

Soffre il mio corpo, ma tranquilla ho l'alma. Mi confertò ier sera un pio ministro. Religione è sollievo a' sofferenti.

Dottore.

E questa notte?

Violetta.

Calmly I slept till morning.

Doctor.

Then keep your courage.

Convalescence, haply, is not far distant.

Violetta.

Oh! that's a kind deception

Allowed to all physicians.

Doctor
(pressing her hand).

Farewell now. I'll return soon.

Violetta.

Be not forgetful.

Annina
(in a low tone, whilst following the Doctor).

Is her case more hopeful?

Doctor.

But few brief hours of life are to her remaining.
(Departs.)

SCENE III—Violetta and Annina

Annina.

Now cheer thy heart.

Violetta.

Is this a festal morning?

Annina.

Paris gives up to folly—'tis carnival day.

Violetta.

Ah, 'mid this gay rejoicing, Heav'n alone
doth know

How the poor are suffering! What amount
Is there in that casket?

Annina
(opens and counts).

Just twenty louis'.

Violetta.

Take from it ten, and give them to the
needy.

Annina.

Little you'll have remaining.

Violetta.

Oh, 'twill for me be plenty!
(Sighing.)

You can bring then my letters here.

Annina.

But you?

Violetta.

Ebbi tranquillo il sonno.

Dottore.

Coraggio adunque—la convalescenza
Non è lontana.

Violetta.

Oh, la bugia pietosa
A' medici è concessa.

Dottore
(stringendole la mano).

Addio—a più tardi.

Violetta.

Non mi scordate.

Annina
(piano al Dottore, accompagnandolo).

Come va, Signore?

Dottore.

La tisi non le accorda che poch' ore.
(Piano, e parte.)

SCENA III—Violetta ed Annina.

Annina.

Or fate cor.

Violetta.

Giorno di festa è questo?

Annina.

Tutta Parigi impazza—è carnevale.

Violetta.

Oh, nel comun tripudio, sallo il cielo
Quanti infelici gemon!—Quale somma
V' ha in quello stipo?
(Indicandolo.)

Annina
(l'apre e conta).

Venti luigi.

Violetta.

Dieci ne reca ai poveri tu stessa.

Annina.

Poco rimanvi allora.

Violetta.

Oh, mi sarà bastante!—
(Sospirando.)

Cerca poscia mie lettere.

Annina.

Ma voi?

Violetta.

Naught will occur. You need not long be absent.

(Exit ANNINA.)

SCENE IV—VIOLETTA takes a letter from her bosom and reads:

"Thou hast kept thy promise. The duel took place. The Baron was wounded, but is improving. Alfred is in foreign countries. Your sacrifice has been revealed to him by me. He will return to you for pardon. I too will return. Haste to recover, thou deservest a bright future.

"GEORGIO GERMONT."

Violetta.

'Tis too late!

Still watching and waiting, but to me they come not!

(Looking in the mirror.)

Oh, how I'm changed and faded!

But the Doctor doth exhort me to be hopeful;

Ah! thus afflicted, all hope is dead within me!

Violetta.

Nulla occorrà, sollecita, se puoi.

(ANNINA esce.)

SCENA IV—VIOLETTA, che trae dal seno una lettera, e legge

"Teneste la promessa—La disfida ebbe luogo; il Barone fu ferito, però migliora Alfredo è in stranio suolo; il vostro sacrifizio io stesso gli ho svelato. Egli a voi tornerà pel suo perdono; io pur verrò— Curatevi—mertaste un avvenir migliore.

"GIORGIO GERMONT."

Violetta.

E tardi!—

(Desolata.)

Attendo, attendo—Nè a me giungon mai?

(Si guarda nello specchio.)

Oh, come son mutata!—

Ma il Dottore a sperar pure m' esorta!—

Ah, con tal morbo ogni speranza è morta.

ADDIO DEL PASSATO — *FAREWELL TO THE BRIGHT VISIONS* (Violetta)

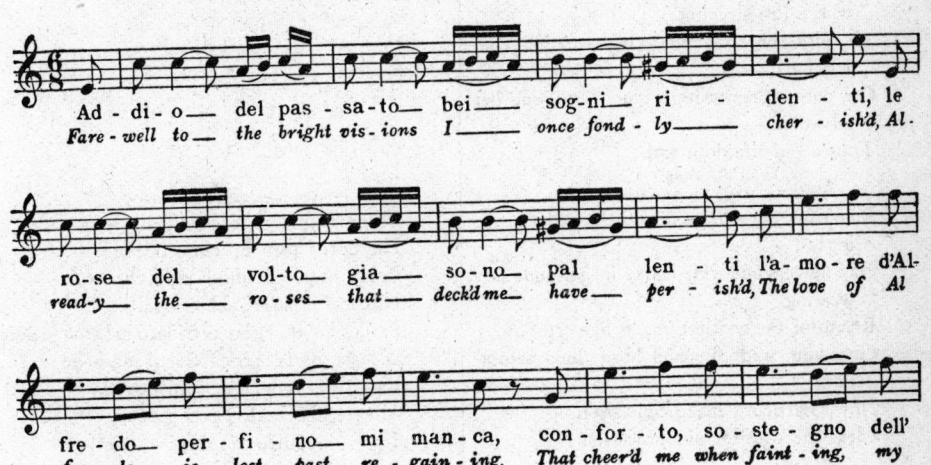

Ad - di - o— del pas - sa - to— bei— sog - ni ri - den - ti, le
Fare - well to— the bright vis - ions I— once fond - ly— cher - ish'd, Al -

ro - se del— vol - to gia - so - no— pal len - ti l'a - mo - re d'Al
read - y the— ro - ses that— deck'd me have— per - ish'd, The love of Al

fre - do— per - fi - no— mi man - ca, con - for - to, so - ste - gno dell'
fre - do— is lost, past— re - gain - ing, That cheer'd me when faint - ing, my

a - ni - ma stan-ca,   con - for-to,   so -
spir-it sus-tain-ing,   *sole com-fort,*   *sup -*

ste-gno ah! del-la tra - via-ta sor - ri - di al de - si - o, a
port, ah! Pi - ty the stray one, and send her con-so - la - tion, Oh,

le - i deh per - do - na tu ac - co - gli-la o Di-o!   ah! tut - to -
par - don her trans-gress-ions, and grant her sal - va-tion.   *Ah! thus all*

tut-to fi - ni, or tut - to, tut - to fi - ni.
of life doth end, Ah! thus all of life doth end.

The sorrows and enjoyments of life will soon be over,	Le gioie, i dolori fra poco avran fine;
The dark tomb in oblivion this mortal form will cover!	La tomba al mortali di tutto è confine!—
No flowers for my grave, no kind friends o'er me weeping.	Non lagrima o fiore avrà la mia fossa,
No cross, with my name, mark the spot where I'm sleeping.	Non croce, col nome, che copra quest' ossa!—
Ah, pity the stray one, and send her consolation!	Ah, della traviata sorridi al desio,
Oh, pardon her transgressions, and send her salvation.	A lei, deh perdona, tu accoglila, o Dio!
Thus all of life doth end.	Or tutto finì.
(Sits down.)	(Siede.)

BACCHANALIAN CHORUS (outside).   CORO BACCANTE (esterno).

Room for the prize-ox, with honors appearing!	Largo al quadrupede sir della festa
Gay flowers and vine-leaves in garlands he's wearing.	Dio fiori e pampini cinto la testa—
Room for the gentlest one of like creation,	Largo al più docile d' ogni cornuto.
Give him, with fife and horn, loud salutation.	Di corni e pifferi abbia il saluto.
Now, Parisians, make concession.	Parigini, date passo al trionfo del Bue grasso
Clear the way for our procession.	L' Asia, nè L' Africa vide il più bello,
	Vanto ed orgoglio d' ogni macello—
	Allegre maschere, pazzi garzoni,
	Tutti plauditelo con canti e suoni!—
	Parigini, etc.—

Asia or Afric ne'er saw one to beat him!

He is the proud boast of all those who meet
him.

Maskers and merry boys with fun o'erflowing,

Songs in his honor raise, plaudits bestowing.

Now, Parisians, etc.

SCENE V—Violetta, and Annina, returning hastily.

Annina   (hesitating).

My lady—

Violetta.

What has happened?

Annina.

This morning—'tis true then? You are
really better?

Violetta.

Yes; but why?

Annina.

Will you promise to be tranquil?

Violetta.

Yes, what wouldst tell me?

Annina.

I would now prepare you
For a pleasure unexpected.

Violetta.

For a pleasure, thou sayest?

Annina.

Yes, gentle mistress.

Violetta.

Alfred! Ah, thou hast seen him?
He comes! oh, haste thee!

(Annina makes signs with her hand in the affirmative, and
goes to open the door.)

SCENE VI—Violetta, Alfred, and Annina.

Violetta.

Alfred! (Going towards the door.)

Alfred.

(Alfred enters, pale with emotion, and they throw themselves into each others' arms, exclaiming:)

Violetta.

Beloved Alfred!

Alfred.

My own Violetta!
Ah! I am guilty! I know all, dearest.

Violetta.

I only know, love, that thou art near me!

SCENA V—Detta, ed Annina, che torna frettolosa.

Annina   (esitando).

Signora—

Violetta.

Che t' accadde?

Annina.

Quest oggi, è vero? vi sentite meglio?

Violetta.

Sì; perchè?

Annina.

D' esser calma promettete?

Violetta.

Si; che vuoi dirmi?

Annina.

Prevenir vi volli—
Una gioia improvvisa.

Violetta.

Una gioia!—dicesti?

Annina.

Si, o Signora.

Violetta.

Alfredo!—Ah, tu il vedesti!
Ei vien! l' affretta.

(Annina afferma col capo, e va ad aprire la porta.)

SCENA VI—Violetta, Alfredo ed Annina.

Violetta.

Alfredo?— (Andando verso l' uscio.)

Alfredo

(comparisce, pallido pella commozione, ed ambidue gettandosi le braccia al collo, esclamano:)

Violetta.

Amato Alfredo!

Alfredo.

Mia Violetta!—
Colpevol sono—so tutto, o cara—

Violetta.

Io so che alfine reso mi sei.

Alfred.

This throbbing heart will show how I still love thee.

I could no more exist, if from thee parted.

Violetta.

If thou hast found me yet with the living,

Believe that grief and woe no more can kill.

Alfred.

Forget the sorrow in love forgiving,

Both sire and son thou'lt pardon still.

Violetta.

Ask me for pardon? 'Tis I am guilty,

Thus rendered by my loving heart.

Both.

No earthly power, nor friend, beloved,

Shall tear us hence apart.

Alfredo.

Da questo palpito, s' io t'ami, impara—

Senza te esistere più non potrei.

Violetta.

Ah, s'anco in vita m' hai ritrovata,

Credi, che uccidere non può il dolor.

Alfredo.

Scorda l'affanno, donna adorata.

A me perdona e al genitor.

Violetta.

Ch' io ti perdoni?—La rea son io;

Ma solo amore tal mi rendè.

Alfredo e Violetta.

Null' uomo o demone, angelo mio.

Mai più staccarti portà da me.

PARIGI, O CARA — *GAY PARIS, DEAREST* (Duet, Alfred and Violetta)

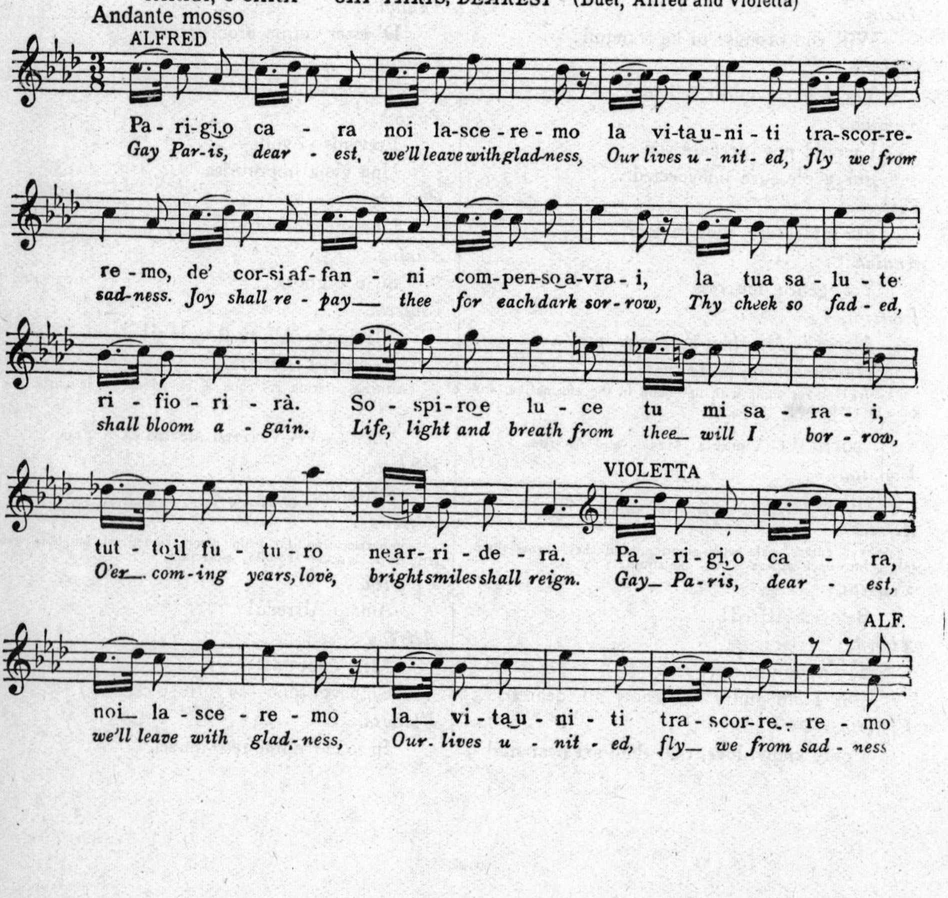

Andante mosso

vra - i, la mia sa - lu - te, la mia sa - lu - te ri - fio - ri - rà, ri - fio - ri -.
pay thee, My cheek so fad - ed, My cheek so fad - ed, shall bloom a - gain, shall bloom a -

ah! si la tua sa - lu - te, la tua sa - lu - te ri - fio - ri - rà.
Ah! yes, thy cheek so fad - ed, thy cheek so fad - ed, shall bloom a - gain.

rà.
gain.

De' cor - si af - fan - ni com - pen - so a -
Joy shall re - pay thee for ev - 'ry

Pa - ri - gio ca - ra, noi la - sce - re - mo, si, noi
Gay Par - is, dear - est, we'll leave with glad - ness, Yes, we'll

vra - i, tut - to il cre - a - to ne ar - ri - de - rà.
sor - row, O'er com - ing years, love, bright smiles shall reign.

la - sce - re - mo, la vi - ta u - ni - ti
leave with glad - ness, Our lives u - nit - ed,

De cor - si af - fan - ni com - pen - so a - vra - i tut - to il fu -
Joy shall re - pay thee for ev - 'ry sor - row, O'er com - ing

tra - scor - re - re - mo, noi tra - scor - re -
fly we from sad - ness, we will fly from

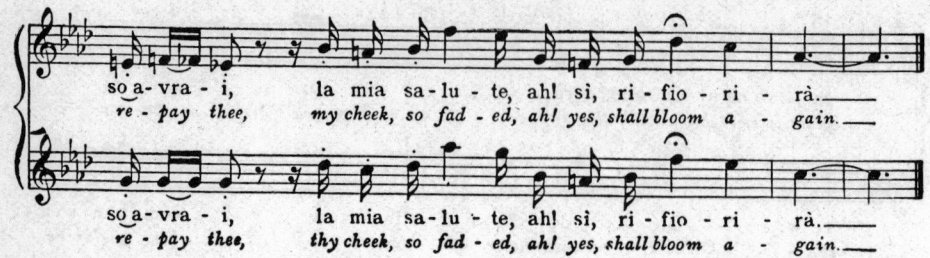

so a - vra - i,   la mia sa - lu - te, ah! sì, ri - fio - ri - rà.___
re - pay thee,   my cheek, so fad - ed, ah! yes, shall bloom a - gain.___

so a - vra - i,   la mia sa - lu - te, ah! sì, ri - fio - ri - rà.___
re - pay thee,   thy cheek, so fad - ed, ah! yes, shall bloom a - gain.___

Violetta.

Ah, no more! to church let us be going,
Our thanks to render with hearts o'erflow-
     ing.
                         (Staggers.)

Alfred.

Thou'rt growing pale!

Violetta.

'Tis nothing, mark me; unlooked for pleas-
     ure can never enter
Without disturbing a heart o'erburdened.
(She sinks on a chair fainting, and her head falls back-
wards.)

Alfred.

Great Heaven!—Violetta!
            (Alarmed, and supporting her.)

Violetta.

'Tis but the weakness
From recent illness. Now, love, I'm
     stronger—
See'st thou? and smiling—
                    (With effort.)

Alfred.

(Ah! cruel fortune!)

Violetta.

'Twas nothing! Annina, a shawl bring
     hither.

Alfred.

What now, love? but wait then—

Violetta.

No! I will go now.
(ANNINA presents the shawl, which she makes an effort to
put on, but finds she is too weak, and exclaims:)

Great Heav'n, I cannot.
(She throws away the shawl vexedly, and sinks again on
the chair.)

Alfred.

Heavens, what is it!
Go, call the Doctor.
              (To ANNINA.)

Violetta.

Ah, non più—a un tempio—Alfredo, andi-
     amo,
Del tuo ritorno grazie rendiamo.
                    (Vacilla.)

Alfredo.

Tu impallidisci!

Violetta.

E nulla, sai? Gioja improvvisa non entra
     mai,
Senza turbarlo, in mesto core.
(S' abbandona, come sfinita, sopra una sedia, col capo
pendente all' indietro.)

Alfredo.

Gran Dio!—Violetta!
            (Spaventato, sorreggendola.)

Violetta.

E il mio malore.
Fe debolezza—ora son forte—
Vedi?—sorrido.
                    (Sforzandosi.)

Alfredo.

(Ahi, cruda sorte!)

Violetta.

Fu nulla—Annina, dammi a vestire.

Alfredo.

Adesso!—Attendi.

Violetta.

No—voglio uscire.
(ANNINA le presenta una vesta ch'ella fa per indossare,
impeditane dalla debolezza, exclama:)

Gran Dio!—non posso!
(Getta con dispetto la veste, e ricade sulla sedia.)

Alfredo.

Cielo, che vedo!
Va pel Dottore.
              (Ad ANNINA.)

Violetta.

Ah, tell him—say that Alfred is now beside
  me.
Return'd and faithful to my affection—
Tell him I wish still to live.
    (ANNINA returns.)
        (To ALFRED.)
But though returned, love, thou hast not
  saved me,
No earthly power from the tomb can shield
  me.

SCENE VII—VIOLETTA and ALFRED.

Violetta.

Ah, cruel fate to die so young,
Tho' much I've borne of sorrow.
To die when hopes, to which I clung,
Reveal a brighter morrow!
Ah! then 'twas naught but madness.
The love to which I yielded!
In vain my heart was shielded,
Armed with faith, all, all in vain.

Alfred.

Oh, dearer far than breath or life,
Beloved one, fondly treasured!
My burning tears, in this dark hour,
With thine shall flow, unmeasured.
But, ah! far more than e'er before
I need thy fond devotion;
Yield not to sad emotion
While hope doth still remain!
    (VIOLETTA throws herself upon the lounge.)

SCENE THE LAST—The same, GERMONT, and the DOCTOR.

Germont
        (entering)
  Ah! Violetta—
Violetta.
  You, my friend?
Alfred.
  My father—
Violetta.
  Thou'st not forgot me?

Violetta.

Digli che Alfredo
E ritornato all' amor mio—
Digli che vivere ancor vogl' io.
    (ANNINA parte.)
    (Ad ALFREDO.)
Ma se tornando non m'hai salvato.
A niuno in terra salvarmi è dato.

SCENA VII—VIOLETTA ed ALFREDO.

Violetta.

Gran Dio! morir sì giovane,
Io, che penato ho tanto!
Morir si presso a tergere
Il mio si lungo pianto!
Ah, dunque fu delirio
La credula speranza;
Invano di costanza
Armato avrò il mio cor!
Alfredo—oh, il crudo termine
Serbato al nostro amor!

Alfredo.

Oh, mio sospiro,—oh, palpito
Diletto del cor mio!
Le mie colle tue lagrime
Confondere degg' io—
Or più che mai nostr' anime
Han duopo di costanza—
Ah, tutto alla speranza
Non chiudere il tuo cor!
Violetta mia, deh calmati.
M' uccide il tuo dolor.
    (VIOLETTA s'abbandona sul canapè.)

SCENA ULTIMA—Detti, GERMONT, ed il DOTTORE

Germont
        (entrando).
  Ah, Violetta!
Violetta.
  Voi, signor!
Alfredo.
  Mio padre!
Violetta.
  Non mi scordaste?

Germont.

　　I redeem my promise—
　　And come, thou noble-hearted,
　　As my daughter to embrace thee.

Violetta.

　　Alas, too late thou comest!
　　Yet, in truth, I am grateful.
　　　　　　(They embrace.)
　　You see me, Grenvil? dying in the embrace
　　Of those I love most dearly!

Germont.

　　Ah, what say'st thou?
　　　　　　(Looking at her, aside.)
　　Oh, Heaven! 'tis true.

Alfred.

　　Oh, father, dost thou see her?

Germont.

　　Withhold! no more thus rend me;
　　For dark remorse devours my heart already!
　　Like the pealing of thunder each word con-
　　　　founds me—
　　Ah! incautious old father!
　　The wrong accomplished, now stands be-
　　　　fore me!

Violetta

(having opened a drawer over her toilet-table, she takes out
　　a medallion, and says:)

　　Approach more nearly, beloved Alfred, and
　　　　hear me;
　　Take this, a fair resemblance still
　　Of me in days of gladness;
　　A thought 'twill bring in sadness
　　Of her who loved thee well.

Alfred.

　　Oh, say not so, thou wilt not die,
　　But live, with love to bless me!
　　With such a dread bereavement
　　Kind Heav'n will not distress me.

Germont.

　　Oh, noble victim! noble sacrifice
　　To generous devotion!
　　Forgive me all the anguish
　　Thy heart has borne through me.

Violetta.

　　Should some young maiden, pure and fair,
　　Fresh as a flower, just blowing,

Germont.

　　La promessa adempio—
　　A stringervi qual figlia vengo al seno,
　　O generosa.

Violetta.

　　Ohimé! tardi giungeste!
　　Pure, grata ven sono—
　　　　　　(La abbraccia.)
　　Grenvil, vedete?—Tra le braccia io spiro
　　Di quanti ho cari al mondo.

Germont.

　　Che mai dite!
　　　　　　(Da se.)
　　Oh cielo!—è ver!
　　　　　　(La osserva.)

Alfredo.

　　La vedi, padre mio?

Germont.

　　Di più, non lacerarmi—
　　Troppo rimorso l'alma mi divora—
　　Quasi fulmin mi atterra ogni suo detto—
　　Oh, malcauto vegliardo!
　　Ah, tutto il mal che feci ora sol vedo!

Violetta

(frattanto avrà aperto a stento un ripostiglio della toilet
　　e toltone un medaglione, dici:)

　　Prendi, quest è l' immagine
　　De' miei passati giorni.
　　A rammentar ti torni
　　Colei che sì t'amo.

Alfredo.

　　No, non morrai, non dirmelo.
　　Dêi vivere, amor mio—
　　A strazio cosi orribile
　　Qui non mi trasse Iddio.

Germont.

　　Cara, sublime vittima
　　D'un generoso amore
　　Perdonami lo strazio.
　　Recato al tuo bel core.

Violetta.

　　Se una pudica vergine
　　Degli anni suoi nel fiore

Love thee with heart o'erflowing,
Make her, I wish it, thy bride;
Show her this pictured likeness,
Say, 'tis a gift from me,
Who, now in heav'n, 'mid angels bright,
Prayeth for her, for thee.

Germont. ⎫ While yet these eyes have tears to
Doctor.   ⎬   flow,
Annina.   ⎭ I shall still weep, still weep for
              thee.

Go, join the blessed spirits now:
God calls thee heavenward, his own to be.

Violetta   (reviving).
'Tis wondrous!

All.
What?

Violetta
                (speaking).
They all have ceased.
The paroxysms that distressed me.
Fresh life awakens within me, giving me
A vigor new and rare!
I am to life restored now!
Oh, rapture!
                (She falls upon the sofa.)

All.
Oh, heaven! Dead!

Alfred.
Violetta!

All.
May Heav'n her soul receive!

Doctor
                (examining the pulse).
'Tis over!

All.
Oh, grief and woe!

A te donasse il core—
Sposa ti sia—lo vo'
Le porgi questa effigie,
Dille che dono all' è
Di chi, nel ciel tra gli angeli
Prega per lei, per te.

Germont. ⎫ Finchè avrà il ciglio lagrime
Dottore. ⎬ Io piangerò per te.
Annina.   ⎭ Vola a' beati spiriti;
              Iddio ti chiama a sè.

Violetta   (alzandosi riammata).
E strano!

Tutti.
Che!

Violetta.
Cessarono
Gli spasmi del dolore.
In me rinasce, m'anima
Insolito vigore!
Ah!—io ritorno a vivere!
                (Trasalendo.)
Oh, gio—ia!
                (Ricade sul canapè.)

Tutti.
Oh, cielo!—muori!

Alfredo.
Violetta!

Tutti.
Oh, Dio!—soccorrasi.

Dottore
                (dapo averle toccato il polso).
E spenta!

Alfredo e Tutti.
Oh, ⎧ rio ⎫ dolor!
    ⎩ mio ⎭

LA FORZA DEL DESTINO
(The Force of Destiny)

by

GIUSEPPE VERDI

ARGUMENT.

DONNA LEONORA has a lover, in the person of *Don Alvaro*, with whom she is on the point of eloping from the house of her father, the *Marquis of Calatrava*, when the latter enters; a scene ensues, and the *Marquis* is slain by the accidental discharge of *Don Alvaro's* pistol.

Leonora, after the death of her father, believing that *Alvaro* has deserted her, flies, and, disguised in male attire, becomes a recluse, living in a cavern, the privacy of which is secured to her by *Father Guardiano*, the superior of a religious community. Her brother, *Don Carlos di Vargas*, becomes imbued with the belief that it is his paramount duty to hunt the world through until he finds *Leonora* and her lover, and by their deaths to avenge his father's and the dishonor brought on the name he bears.

Don Carlos and *Don Alvaro*, under assumed names, and unknown to each other, being in the camp of the Italian and Spanish armies, *Alvaro* is the means of saving the life of *Don Carlos* from assassins, and they vow lasting friendship. Soon after this *Alvaro* is wounded in battle, it is supposed mortally. *Don Carlos* finds in the wounded man's possession a portrait of *Leonora*, which confirms him in his suspicion that his new friend is none other than *Alvaro*.

Alvaro, under the name of Father Raffaello, becomes a friar in a religious establishment situated in the immediate vicinity of the cavern in which *Leonora* is secluded. *Don Carlos* agains finds and compels him to fight; *Carlos* falls—this time mortally wounded. *Leonora* enters from her cavern, and the three recognize each other. *Don Carlos* calls upon his sister to embrace him ere he dies, seizes the opportunity to stab her, and then expires. *Leonora* implores the forgiveness of Heaven for *Alvaro*, who, humbled in heart by her earnest accents, throws himself penitent at her feet, and the curtain falls at the death of *Leonora*.

CHARACTERS.

IL MARCHESE DI CALATRAVA.

DONNA LEONORA,
DON CARLO DI VARGAS, } *his Children.*

DON ALVARO, *Donna Leonora's Lover.*

PREZIOSILLA, *a Young Gipsy.*

PADRE GUARDIANO,
FRA MELITONE, } *Franciscan Friars.*

CURRA, *Waiting-Woman to Leonora.*

MASTRO TRABUCO, *A Muleteer, afterwards a Pedlar.*

Alcade, a Magistrate.

A Spanish Military Surgeon.

Muleteers, Spanish and Italian Peasants, Spanish and Italian Soldiers, Franciscan Friars, Beggars, Vivandiers, Tumblers, Host, Hostess, Servants, Pedlars, Trumpeters, etc.

Scene, —SPAIN and ITALY. Time — End of the 18th Century.

LA FORZA DEL DESTINO

[THE FORCE OF DESTINY]

ATTO I

SCENA I—Siviglia.—Una sala, tappezzata di damasco, con ritratti di famiglia, ed arme gentilizie, addobbata nello stile del secolo 18.0 pero in cattivo stato. Di fronte due finestre; quella a sinistra chiusa, l'altra a destra aperta e praticable, dalla quale si vede un cielo purissimo, illuminato dalla Luna, e cime d'alberi. Tra le finestre e un grande armadio chiuso, contenente vesti, biancherie, ecc. Ognuna delle pareti laterali ha due porte. La prima a destra della spettatore e la comune; la seconda mette alla stanza di CURRA. A sinistra in fondo e l' appartamento del MARCHESE; piu presso al proscenio quello di LEONORA. A mezza scena, alquanto a sinistra, e un tavolino coperto da tappeto di damasco, e sopra il medesimo una chitarra. vasi di fiori, due candelabri d' argento accesi con paralumi, sola luce che schiarira la sala. Un seggiolone presso il tavolino; un mobile con sopra un oriuolo fra le due porte a destra; altro mobile sopra il quale e il ritratto, tutta figura, del MARCHESE, appoggiato alla parete sinistra. La sala sara parapettata.

Il MARCHESE DI CALATRAVA, con lume in mano, sta congedandosi da DONNA LEONORA preoccupata. CURRA viene dalla sinistra.

Marchese.
> (Abbracciandola con affetto.)

Buona notte, mia figlia ! Addio, diletta !
Aperto ancora è quel verone !
> (Va a chiuderlo.)

Leonora.
(Oh angoscia !)

Marchese.
Nulla dice il tuo amor ? Perchè si trista ?
> (Tornando a lei.)

Leonora.
Padre—Signor—

Marchese.
La pura aura de' campi
Calma al tuo cor donova ;
Fuggisti lo straniero di te indegno
A me lascia la cura
Dell' avvenir. Nel padre tuo confida,
Che t' ama tanto.

Leonora.
Ah, padre !

ACT I

SCENE I.—Seville.—A room, hung with damask, family portraits, and arms of nobility, furnished in the style of the 18th century, all, however, in a shabby condition. Two windows face the audience; that on the left is closed, that on the right open and practicable, from which is seen a clear sky, and the tops of trees, with a bright moonlight? Between the windows a large wardrobe, containing clothes, etc. Each side has two doors. The first to the right of the spectator is the common door; the second leads to CURRA'S room. On the left side farthest off, is the apartment of the MARQUIS; that nearest the proscenium leads to LEONORA'S room. Halfway, a little to the left, is a table with a damask cover, and on it a guitar, vases of flowers, and two lighted silver candlesticks with shades, the only light in the room. A large chair near the table; a piece of furniture with a clock on it between the two doors on the right; other furniture on the left, above which, hung against the wall, is the full-length portrait of the MARQUIS. The room is entirely enclosed.

MARQUIS OF CALATRAVA, with a light in his hand is taking leave of DONNA LEONORA, who is thoughtful. CURRA comes from the left.

Marchese.
> (Embracing her affectionately.)

Good night, my child ! Adieu, my dear one!
That balcony-window still open ?
> (Goes and shuts it.)

Leonora.
(Oh, anguish !)

Marchese.
Not a word of love ? Why so sad ?
> (Turning to her.)

Leonora.
Father—sir—

Marchese.
The pure air of the fields
Has brought peace to thy heart,
Thou hast left a stranger unworthy of thee,
And to me leave the care
Of thy future. In thy father confide,
Who so dearly loves thee.

Leonora.
Ah, my father !

Marchese.

    Ebben, che t' ange ?
      Non pianger, io t'adoro !

Leonora.

    (Oh, mio rimorso !)

Marchese.

    Ti lascio.

Leonora

    (Gettandosi con effusione tra le braccia del padre.)

    Ah, padre mio !

Marchese.

    Ti benedica il cielo ! Addio !

Leonora.

    Addio !

(Il MARCHESE bacia, riprende il lume, e va nelle sue stanze.)

SCENA II.—CURRA segue il MARCHESE, chiude la porta ond' e uscito, e riviene a LEONORA abbandonatasi sul seggiolone piangente)

Curra.

    Temea restasse qui fino a domani !
    Si riapra il veron.
            (Eseguisce.)
    Tutto s'appronti. E andiamo.

Toglie dall' armadio un sacco da notte in cui ripone biancherie e vesti.)

Leonora.

    E si amoroso padre avverso
    Fia tanto a' voti miei ?
    No, no, decidermi non so.

Curra

          (Affaccendata.)
    Che dite ?

Leonora.

    Quegli accenti nel cor come pugnalia
    Scendevanmi. Se ancor restava, appreso
    Il ver gli avrei.

Curra

          (Smette il lavoro.)
    Domani allor nel sangue
    Suo saria don Alvaro,
    Od a Siviglia prigioniero, e forse
    Al patibol poi—

Leonora.

    Taci !

Marchese.

    What disturbs thee ?
    Do not weep—I love thee dearly.

Leonora.

    (Oh, what remorse !)

Marchese.

    I leave thee.

Leonora

    (Throwing herself with transport into his arms.)

    Ah, dearest father !

Marchese.

    Heaven bless thee ! Adieu !

Leonora.

    Adieu !

(The MARQUIS kisses her, takes up a light, and goes to his room.)

SCENE II.—CURRA follows the MARQUIS, closes the door, at which he went out, and returns to LEONORA, who has thrown herself in the chair.

Curra.

    I thought he would stay till daylight !
    Let us re-open the balcony.
            (Opens it.)
    Prepare everything and let us go.

(Takes travelling bag from the wardrobe, and fills it with linen and clothes.)

Leonora.

    Can so fond a father
    Oppose my dearest wishes ?
    No, no, I cannot leave.

Curra

          (Very busy.)
    What do you say ?

Leonora.

    His loving tones struck like a dagger
    To my soul. Had he remained,
    The truth I should have spoken.

Curra

          (Leaving off work.)
    Then to-morrow
    Don Alvaro would lie weltering in his
      blood,
    Or be a prisoner in Seville,
    And perhaps on the scaffold—

Leonora.

    Be silent !

Curra.

E tutto puesto
Perch' egli volle amar chi non l' amava.

Leonora.

Io non amarlo ! Tu ben sai s'io l'ami !
Patria, famiglia, padre,
Per lui non abbandono !
Ahi troppo !—troppo sventurata sono !
Me pellegrina ed orfana
Lungi dal natio nido,
Un fato inesorabile
Trascina a stranio lido,
Colmo di triste immagini,
Da' suoi rimorsi affranto
E il cor di questa misera
Dannato a eterno pianto.
Ti lascio, ahimè, con lacrime,
Dolce mia terra !—Addio !
Ahimè, non avrà termine
Si gran dolore !—Addio !

Curra.

M' aiuti, signorina—
Più presto andrem.

Leonora.

S' ei non giungesse ?
(Guarda l' orologio.)
E tardi.
Mezzanotte è suonata !
(Contenta.)
Ah no, più non verrà !

Curra.

Quale romore !
Calpestio di cavelli !

Leonora
(Corre al verone.)
E desso !

Curra.

Era impossibil
Ch' ei non venisse !

Leonora.

Ciel !

Curra.

Bando al timore.

Curra.

And all because he loves one
Who does not return his love.

Leonora.

Does not return it ?
Well thou knowest I love him !
Country, family, father, for him do I not
  leave ?
Ah me !—I am indeed unhappy !
A friendless wanderer,
Far from my native land !
An inexorable fate
Drags me to a foreign country,
Overwhelmed in dire woe,
Crushed with deep remorse,
My miserable spirit
Is condemned to constant grief.
With tears, alas ! I leave thee,
My own sweet native land.—Adieu !
Never, never will end
This bitter woe !—Adieu !

Curra.

Help me, signora—
We shall the sooner be ready.

Leonora.

If he should not come?
(Looks at the clock.)
It is late—
Midnight has struck !
(Contentedly.)
Ah no, he will not come.

Curra.

What noise is that ?
It is the tread of horses !

Leonora
(Running to balcony.)
It is he !

Curra.

It was impossible
That he should fail to come.

Leonora.

Heavens !

Curra.

Away with fear.

SCENA III.   Detti.—DON ALVARO senza mantello, con giusta-cuore a maniche larghe, e sopra una giubbetta da Majo, rete sul capo, stivali, speroni, entra dal verone e si getta tra le braccia di LEONORA.

Alvaro.

    Ah, per sempre, o mio bell' angelo,
    Ne congiunse il cielo adesso
    L'universo in questo amplesso
    Con me veggo giubilar.

Leonora.

    Don Alvaro !

Alvaro.

    Ciel, che t' agita ?

Leonora.

    Presso è il giorno.

Alvaro.

    Da lung' ora
    Mille inciampi tua dimora
    M'han vietato penetrar;
    Ma d' amor si puro e santo
    Nulla opporsi può all' incanto,
    E Dio stesso il nostro palpito
    In letizia tramutò.

         (A CURRA.)

    Quelle vesti dal verone
    Getta.

Leonora

         (A CURRA.)

    Arresta.

Alvaro

         (A CURRA.)

    No, no !

         (A LEONORA.)

    Seguimi;
    Lascia omai la tua prigiane.

Leonora.

    Ciel ! risolvermi non so !

Alvaro.

    Pronti destrieri di già ne attendono;
    Un sacerdote ne aspetta all' ara !
    Vieni, d'amore in sen ripara
    Che Dio dal cielo benedirà!
    E quando il sole, nume dell' India,
    Di mia regale stirpe signore,
    Il mondo innondi del suo splendore,
    Sposi, oh diletta, ne troverà.

SCENE III.—The same,—DON ALVARO, without a cloak, wear-ing a tight vest, with large sleeves and a slashed doublet, a net on his head, boots and spurs, he enters throught the balcony, and throws himself into LEONORA'S arms.

Alvaro.

    Ah, for ever, my lovely angel,
    Heaven now unites us !
    All the universe is glad
    With me, in this embrace.

Leonora.

    Don Alvaro !

Alvaro.

    Oh Heaven, why thus agitated ?

Leonora.

    The dawn is nigh.

Alvaro.

    For a long time
    Many obstacles kept me
    From reaching thy dwelling;
    But nought can stay the power
    Of a love so pure and holy,
    And Heaven itself our fears
    Changes to contentment.

         (To CURRA.)

    Those vestments
    Throw from the balcony.

Leonora

         (To CURRA.)

    Stay.

Alvaro

         (To CURRA.)

    No, no !

         (To LEONORA.)

    Follow me.
    Leave thy prison now for ever.

Leonora.

    Oh Heaven ! I cannot decide !

Alvaro.

    Swift steeds are waiting,
    A priest at the altar attends !
    Come, shelter find in the love
    Which Heaven will richly bless.
    And when the sun, the god of India,
    Sire of my royal race
    Shall flood the earth with splendor,
    Oh, beloved ! it will find us united.

Leonora.

E tarda l' ora.

Alvaro
(A CURRA.)
Su via t' affretta !

Leonora.

Ancor sospendi !

Alvaro.
Eleonora !

Leonora.
Diman.

Alvaro.
Che parli ?

Leonora.
Ten prego aspetta !

Alvaro
(Assai turbato.)
Diman.

Leonora.
Domani si partirà.
Anco una volta il padre, veder desio;
E tu contento, gli è ver, ne sei?

Sì perchè m'ami—
(Si confonde.)
Nè opporti dèi—
Oh anch' io, tu il sai— t' amo io tanto !
Ne son felice ! oh cielo, quanto !
Gonfio di gioia ho il cor ! Restiamo !

Sì, Don Alvaro, io t'amo, io t' amo !
(Piange.)

Alvaro.
Gonfio hai di gioia il core—e lagrimi!

Come un sepolcro tua mano è gelida !
Tutto comprendo—tutto, signora.

Leonora.
Alvaro !—Alvaro !

Alvaro
Eleonora !
(Lunga pausa.)
Saprò soffrire io solo. Tolga Iddio
Che i passi miei per debolezza segua—

Leonora.
The hour is late.

Alvaro
(To CURRA.)
Away—make haste !

Leonora
(To CURRA.)
Wait awhile !

Alvaro.
Eleonora !

Leonora.
To-morrow.

Alvaro.
What sayest thou ?

Leonora.
I pray thee, wait !

Alvaro
(Much disturbed.)
To-morrow.

Leonora.
To-morrow we will go
Once more my father
I desire to see !
Thou art willing—is it not so ?
Yes, for thou lovest me, and wilt not refuse.
I too, thou knowest, love thee !
(Confusedly.)
Am I not happy ? O heaven !
How my heart swells with joy !—Let us wait !
Yes, Alvaro, I love thee ! I love thee !
(Weeps.)

Alvaro.
Thy heart swells with joy—then why these tears ?
Thy hand is cold as death !
I understand all, signora—all !

Leonora.
Alvaro !—Alvaro !

Alvaro.
Eleonora !
(A long pause.)
I can suffer alone. Heaven forbid
That weakly thou shouldst follow me—

Sciolgo i tuoi giuri. Le nuziali tede
Sarebbero per noi segnal di morte,
Se tu, com' io non m' ami—se pentita—
Leonora.
    Son tua, son tua col core e colla vita !

I absolve thy vows. The nuptial tie
Would be for us the stroke of death,
If thou lovest not as I do—if, repenting—
Leonora.
    I am thine ! thine with heart and soul !

AH! SEGUIRTI FINO — *AH! I'LL FOLLOW* Air (Leonora)

Ah! se - guir - ti fi - no a - gl'ul - ti - mi Con - fi - ni del - la
Ah! I'll fol - low ev - er in thy path To earth's far con - fines

ter - ra; Con te sfi - dar im - pa - vi - da Di rio des - tin la
wing - ing, And bold - ly with thee I de - fy The ter - rors war is

guer - ra; Mi fia pe - ren - ne gau - di - o D'e - te - rea vo - lut - ta. Ti
bring - ing, I'll share all dan-gers by thy side, With love and joy e - late, I'll

se - guo, an-diam di - vi - der-ci, Il fa - to, no, no, non po - tra.
fol - low thee what - e'er may be - tide, We win a hap-py fate.

Alvaro.

Sospiro, luce ed anima
Di questo cor che t' ama ;
Finchè mi batta un palpito,
Far paga ogni tua brama
Il solo ed immutabile
Desio per me sarà.
Mi segui ! Andiam, dividerci
Il mondo non potrà.

Alvaro.

Hope, light and life
Of the heart that adores thee !
Till my pulses beat no more
My sole desire will be
To meet thy every wish,
To cherish thee for aye.
Follow me—let us go !
The world has no power to part us.

(S' avvicinano al verone, quando ad un tratto si sente a sinistra un aprire e chiudere di porte.)

(They approach the balcony when of a sudden is heard the opening and shutting of a door.)

Leonora.
    Quale rumor !

Leonora.
    What is that noise ?

Curra
        (Ascoltando.)
Ascendono le scale !

Curra
            (Listening.)
    Some one is coming up stairs !

Alvaro.
Presto, partiamo !

Leonora.
E tardi.

Alvaro.
Allor di calma
E duopo.

Curra.
Vergin santa !

Leonora
(A ALVARO.)
Colà t' ascondi !

Alvaro.
No. Degg' io difenderti.
(Traendo una pistola.)

Leonora.
Ripon quell' arma—contro al genitore
Vorresti ?

Alvaro.
No, contro me stesso.
(Ripone la pistola.)

Leonora.
Orrore !

SCENA IV.—Dopo vari colpi apresi con istrepito la porta del fondo a sinistra, ed il MARCHESE DI CALATRAVA entra infuriato brandendo una spada e seguito da due servi con lume.

Marchese.
Vil seduttor !—infame figlia !

Leonora
(Correndo a' suoi piedi.)
No, padre mio !

Marchese.
Più non lo sono.
(La respinge.)

Alvaro
(Al MARCHESE.)
Il solo colpevole son io
Ferite vendicatevi !
(Presentandogli il petto.)

Marchese
(Al ALVARO)
No la condotta vostra
Da troppo abbietta origine uscito vi dimostra.

Alvaro.
Quick ! Let us go !

Leonora.
Too late !

Alvaro.
Well, then,
We must be calm and firm.

Curra.
Holy Virgin !

Leonora
(To ALVARO.)
Conceal thyself there !

Alvaro.
No. I must defend thee.
(Drawing out a pistol.)

Leonora.
Put back that weapon—
Wouldst use it 'gainst my father ?

Alvaro.
No, against myself.
(Replaces the pistol.)

Leonora.
Horrible !

SCENE IV.—After repeated blows the door at the back, on the left, is burst open, and the MARQUIS OF CALATRAVA enters, enraged, sword in hand, and followed by two servants with lights.

Marchese.
Vile seducer !—shameless daughter !

Leonora
(Rushing to his feet.)
No, father, no.

Marchese.
I am no longer thy father.
(Repulsing her.)

Alvaro
(To the MARQUIS.)
I alone am guilty.
Strike !—avenge thyself !
(Presenting himself.)

Marchese
(To ALVARO.)
No, thy conduct
Shows thee of origin too low.

Alvaro.

Signor Marchese !

        (Risentito.)

Marchese

        (A LEONORA.)

Scostati—

        (Ai Servia.)

S' arresti l' empio !

Alvaro

    (Cavando nuovamente la pistola)

Guai
Se alcun di voi si move.

    (Ai Servi, che retrocedono.)

Leonora

      (Currendo a lui.)

Alvaro, oh ciel, che fai !

Alvaro

      (Al MARCHESE.)

Cedo a voi sol—ferite !

Marchese.

Morir per mano mia !
Per mano del cranefice tal vita estinta fia.

Alvaro.

Signor di Calatrava,
Pura siccome gli angeli è vostra figlia—
Il giuro—reo son io solo. Il dubbio
Che l' ardir mio qui desta, si tolga colla
    vita.
Eccomi inerme.

(Getta la pistola, che percuote al suolo, scarica il colpo, e
ferisce mortalmente il MARCHESE.)

Marchese.

Io muoio !

Alvaro

      (Disperato.)

Arma funesta !

Leonora

    (Correndo a' piedi del padre.)

Aita !

Marchese

    (A LEONORA)

Lungi da me—
Contamina tua vista la mia morte !

Leonora.

Padre !

Alvaro.

Marquis !

      (Excitedly.)

Marchese

      (To LEONORA.)

Stand aside—

    (To the Servants.)

Seize the wretch !

Alvaro

  (Again taking out his pistol.)

Approach me, if you dare !

  (To the Servants, who retire.)

Leonora

    (Running to him.)

Alvaro, what madness is this ?

Alvaro

    (To the MARQUIS.)

To thee alone I yield—strike !

Marchese.

Not by my hand you die ;
So base a life belongs only to the execu-
    tioner.

Alvaro.

Signor de Calatrava, your child
Is innocent as an angel ;
I alone am guilty.
Let the doubt which my rashness has raised
Be dispelled with my life. Behold me
    unarmed.

(Throws away the pistol, which in falling, goes off, and kills
the MARQUIS.)

Marchese.

I am dying !

Alvaro

    (In despair.)

Ill-fated weapon !

Leonora

    (Rushing to her father.)

Help !

Marchese

    (To LEONORA.)

Begone—
Thy presence disgraces me in death!

Leonora.

Father !

Marchese.

    Ti maledico !

        (Cade tra le braccia dei Servi.)

Leonora.

    Cielo pietade !

Alvaro.

    Oh sorte !

(I Servi portano il MARCHESE alle sue stanze, mentre DON ALVARO trae seco verso il verone la sventurata LEONORA. Cade la tela.)

FINE DELL' ATTO PRIMO:

Marchese.

    My curse upon thee !

        (Falls into the Servants' arms.)

Leonora.

    Have mercy, kind Heaven !

Alvaro.

    O cruel fate !

(The Servants bear the MARQUIS to his apartments, whilst DON ALVARO drags the unhappy LEONORA towards the balcony. The Curtain falls.)

END OF THE FIRST ACT

ATTO II.

SCENA I. Villaggio d' Hornachuelos e vicinanze.—Grande cucina d'una Osteria a pian terreno. A sinistra, e la porta d' ingresso che da sulla via; di fronte una finestra ed un credenzone con piatti, ecc. A destra, in fonda un gran focolare ardente con varie pentole; piu vicino alle bocca-scena breve scaletta che mette ad una stanza, la cui porta e praticabile. Da un lato gran tavola apparecchiata con sopra una lucerna accesa. L' Oste e l' Ostessa che non parlano, sono affaccendati ad ammanir la cena. L' ALCADE e seduto presso al foco; uno STUDENTE presso la tavola. Alquanti MULATTIERI, fra quali MASTRO TRABUCO, ch' e al dinanzi sopra un suo basto. Due CONTADINI. due CONTADINE, la SERVA, ed un MULATTIERE. ballano la SEGUIDILLA. Sopra altra tavola, vino, bicchieri fiaschi, una bottiglia d'acquavite.

L'ALCADE, uno STUDENTE, MASTRO TRABUCO, MULATTIERI, PAESANI FAMIGLI, PAESANE ecc. A tempo LEONORA in vesti virile.

Coro.
    Hola, hola, hola !
    Ben giungi, o mulattier,
    La notte a riposar.
    Hola, hola, hola !
      Qui devi col bicchier
      Le forze ritemprar !

(L' Ostessa mette sulla tavola una grande suppiera.)

Alcade.
    La cena è pronta.
        (Sedendosi alla mensa.)

Tutti
      (Prenendo posto presso la tavolo.)
    A cena, a cena !

Studente
      (Frattanto sul d' avanti dice.)
    (Ricerco invan la suora e il eduttore.)
     Perfidi !

Coro
      (All' ALCADE.)
    Voi la mensa benedite ?

Alcade.
    Può farlo il Licenziato.

Studente.
    Di buon grado. Benedetto
    E il pane che il Padre del ciel ci manda.

Tutti
      (Sedendo.)
    Cosi sia.

ACT II.

SCENE I. The Village of Hornachuelos and neighborhood. A large kitchen on the ground-floor of an Inn. On the left, the entrance-door leading to the road, facing the audience; a window, and a large dresser, with plates, etc. On the right, at the back, a large fireplace, with cauldrons, etc., nearer the proscenium, a short staircase, leading to a room which has a practicable door. On one side a large table, laid out, and on it a lighted lamp. The Host and Hostess, who do not speak, are busy preparing the supper. The ALCADE is seated near the fire; a STUDENT s seated near the table. Some MULETEERS, amongst others MASTER TRABUCO, who is in front, leaning on his pack saddle. Two male and two female PEASANTS, the female SERVANT and a MULETEER dance the Seguidilla. Upon another table, wine, glasses, flasks, and a bottle of brandy.

The ALCADE, a STUDENT, MASTER TRABUCO, MULETEERS, PEASANTS ATTENDANTS, FEMALE PEASANTS, etc. Later LEONORA, in male attire.

Chorus.
    Hurrah, hurrah, hurrah !
    Now welcome, O muleteer,
    Who comes to pass the night ;
    Hurrah, hurrah, hurrah !
    Here is the brimming cup,
    Thy strength thou canst restore.

(The Hostess places a large soup-tureen on the table.)

Alcade.
    The supper is ready.
        (Seating himself at table.)

All
      (Taking their places at table.)
    To supper, to supper !

Student
      (In the foreground.)
    In vain my sister and her betrayer I seek !
    The ingrates !

Chorus
      (To the ALCADE.)
    Will you not ask a blessing ?

Alcade.
    The Licentiate can do it.

Student.
    With all my heart. Blessed be
    The bread that Heaven sends us from
      above.

All
      (Seated.)
    Amen.

Leonora

(Presentandosi alla potra della stanza a destra, che terra socchiusa

(Che vedo !—mio fratello !)

(Si ritira.)

(L' Ostessa avra gia distribuito il riso e siede cogli altri. In-
seguito e servito altro piatto. TRABUCO e in disparte, sempre appoggiato al suo basto.

Alcade

(Assaggiando.)

Buono.

Studente

(Mangiando.)

Eccellente !

Mulattieri.

Par che dica mangiami.

Studente

(All' Ostessa.)

Tu das epulis accumbere divum.

Alcade.

Non sa Latino ma cucina bene.

Studente.

Viva l'Otessa !

Tutti.

Evviva !

Studente.

Non vien Mastro
Trabuco ?

Trabuco.

E Venerdi.

Studente.

Digiuna ?

Trabuco.

Appunto.

Studente.

E quella personcina con lei guinta?

SCENA II.   Detti, e PREZIOSILLA, ch' entra saltellando.

Preziosilla.

Viva la guerra !

Leonora

(Appearing at the door of the room on the right, which she
keeps half closed.)

What do I see !—my brother !

(She retires.)

(The Hostess has already distributed the rice, and sits down with
the others. Other dishes are served up. TRABUCO on one side
leans on his pack-saddle.)

Alcade

(Tasting.)

Capital !

Student

(Eating.)

Excellent !

Muleteer.

It seems to say, 'Come, eat me.'

Student

(To the Hostess.)

Tu das epulis accumbere divum.

Alcade.

She does not know Latin, but she cooks
well.

Student.

Long live the Hostess !

All.

Hurrah !

Student.

Does not Master Trabuco
Come to supper ?

Trabuco.

It is Friday.

Student.

Oh, you are fasting ?

Trabuco.

Just so.

Student.

And the little person who came with you

SCENE II.   The same, enter PREZIOSILLA, dancing.

Preziosilla.

Success to war !

Tutti.

Preziosilla !—**Brava !**
Brava !

Studente.

Qui, presso a me.

Tutti.

Tu la ventura.
Dirne potrai.

Preziosilla.

Chi brama far fortuna ?

Tutti.

Tutti il vogliam.

Preziosilla.

Correte allor soldati.
In Italia, dov' è rotta **la guerra**
Contro al Tedesco.

Tutti.

Morte
Ai Tedeschi !

Preziosilla.

Flagel d' Italia eterno
E de' figluoli suoi.

Tutti.

Tutti v' andremo.

Preziosilla.

Ed io saro con voi.

All.

Preziosilla !—Bravo !
Bravo !

Student.

Here, sit by me.

All.

You will be able
To tell us our fortunes.

Preziosilla.

Who wishes to make his fortune ?

All.

Everyone wishes it.

Preziosilla.

Haste, then, to Italy, as soldiers,
Where war has broken out
Against the Germans.

All.

Death
To the Germans !

Preziosilla.

Of Italy and her sons
They are the eternal scourge.

All.

We will all go.

Preziosilla.

And I shall be with you.

AL SUON DEL TAMBURO —*THE DRUM GAILY BEATING* (Preziosilla and Chorus)

Al suon del tam - bu - ro, Al brio del cor - sie - ro, Al nu - go-lo az -
The drum gai - ly beat - ing The hors - es swift fleet - ing, And vol - leys re -

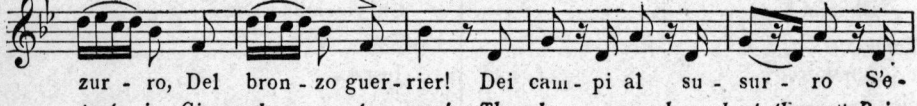

zur - ro, Del bron - zo guer - rier! Dei cam - pi al su - sur - ro S'e -
peat - ing Give glo - ry to war! The bu - sy sounds a - bout the camp Drive

sal - ta il pen-sier! E bel - la la guer - ra, E bel - la la
anx-ious thought a - far! In bat - tle is glo - ry, In bat - tle is

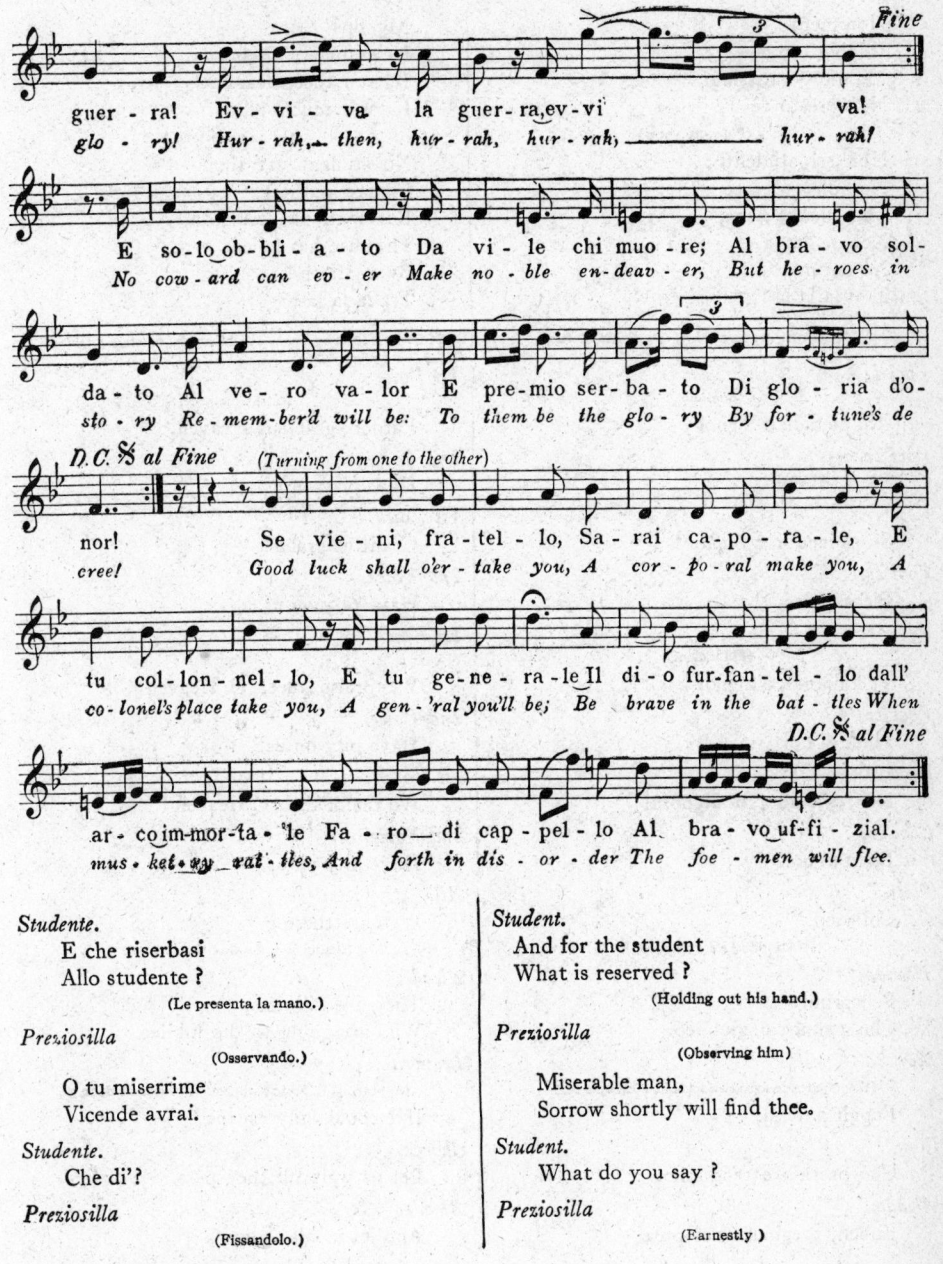

guer - ra! Ev-vi - va la guer-ra,ev-vi va!
glo - ry! Hur-rah, then, hur-rah, hur-rah,____ hur-rah!

E so-lo_ob-bli - a - to Da vi-le chi muo-re; Al bra-vo sol-
No cow-ard can ev-er Make no-ble en-deav-er, But he-roes in

da-to Al ve-ro va-lor E pre-mio ser-ba-to Di glo-ria d'o-
sto-ry Re-mem-ber'd will be: To them be the glo-ry By for-tune's de

D.C. ℀ al Fine (Turning from one to the other)

nor! Se vie-ni, fra-tel - lo, Sa-rai ca-po-ra-le, E
cree! Good luck shall o'er-take you, A cor-po-ral make you, A

tu col-lon-nel - lo, E tu ge-ne-ra-le Il di-o fur-fan-tel-lo dall'
co-lonel's place take you, A gen-'ral you'll be; Be brave in the bat-tles When

D.C. ℀ al Fine

ar - co im-mor-ta - 'le Fa - ro di cap-pel-lo Al bra-vo uf-fi - zial.
mus-ket-ry rat-tles, And forth in dis-or-der The foe-men will flee.

Studente.	*Student.*
E che riserbasi	And for the student
Allo studente ?	What is reserved ?
(Le presenta la mano.)	(Holding out his hand.)
Preziosilla	*Preziosilla*
(Osservando.)	(Observing him)
O tu miserrime	Miserable man,
Vicende avrai.	Sorrow shortly will find thee.
Studente.	*Student.*
Che di'?	What do you say ?
Preziosilla	*Preziosilla*
(Fissandolo.)	(Earnestly)

Non mente
Il labbro mai—
Ma a te—carissimo,
Non presto fè

(Pol sotto voce.)

Non sei studenti ;
Non dirò niente,
Ma, gnaffe, a me,
Non se la fa,—
No per mia fè.
Tral la la là !

My lips
Ne'er utter falsehoods,
But on thee, dear sir,
I don't much rely.

(In an undertone.)

No student art thou.
I'll say nothing,
But with me, forsooth,
The ruse has failed,
By my faith !
Tra la la la !

SCENA III. Detti, e PELLEGRINI, che passao da furol.

SCENE III. The same, and PILGRIMS, passing outsid

Voci 1e.

(Lontane.)

Ah, pietade o Signor !

1st Voice

(In the distance.)

Pardon, gracious Heaven.

Voci 2e.

Pieta di noi.

2nd Voice.

Have pity on us.

Voci 1e.

Sii clemente, o Signor !

1st Voice.

Grant us grace !

Voci 2e.

Pietà di noi.

2nd Voice.

Have pity on us.

Voci 1e.

(Piu vicine.)

Te lodiamo, o Signor !

1st Voice

(Nearer.)

We praise thee, O Heaven !

Voci 2e.

Pietà di noi.

2nd Voice.

Have pity on us.

Voci 1e.

Deh, pietade, o Signorà!

1st Voice.

We thank thee, O Heaven !

Voci 2e.

Pietà di noi.

2nd Voice.

Have pity on us.

Tutti.

Chi sono ?

(Alzandosi e scoprendosi.)

All.

Who are these ?

(Rising and showing themselves.)

Alcade.

Pellegrini,
Che vanno al giubileo.

Alcade.

They are Pilgrims,
Who are going to the jubilee.

Leonora

(Ricomparendo agitatissima sulla stessa porta.)

Fuggir potessi.

Leonora

(Appearing, in great agitation, at the same door.)

If I could only escape !

Coro.

Che passino attendiamo.

Chorus.

Let us wait till they pass.

Alcade.

Ebben, preghiam noi pure.

Alcade.

And let us also pray.

Coro.

Si preghiamo.

Tutti

(Lasciando ia mensa s' inginocchiano.)

Suo noi concordi e supplici,
Stendi la man, Signore ;
Dall' infernal malore
Ne salvi tua pietà.

Leonora.

(Ah, da un fratello salvami
Che anela il sangue mio ;
Se tu nol vuoi, gran Dio,
Nessun mi salverà !)

(Rientra nella stanza chiudendone la porta. Tutti riprendono
i loro posti. Si passano un fiasco.)

Studente.

Viva la buona compagnia !

Tutti.

Viva !

Studente.

Salute qui, l' eterna gloria poi !

(Alzando il bicchiere)

Tutti.

Cosi sia.

(Fanno altrettanto.)

Studente.

Già cogli angioli, Trabuco ?

Trabuco.

E che ?—con questo inferno ?

Studente.

E quella personcina con lei giunta,
Venne pel giubileo ?

Trabuco.

Nol so.

Studente.

Per altro.
E gallo, oppur gallina ?

Trabuco.

De' forastier non bado che al danaro.

Siudente.

Molto prudente !

(Poi all' ALCADE.)

Chorus.

Yes, let us pray.

All

(Leaving the table and kneeling down.)

O'er us, imploring Thee,
Extend Thy hand, O Lord,
From the power of ill
Let Thy mercy save us.
And mercy protect us.

Leonora.

Ah, from a brother save me,
Who thirsts for my blood ;
Thy hand alone, O Lord,
Can save me from his wrath.

(Re-enters the room and shuts the door. A'l reseat themselve
and pass the bottle.

Student.

Long live this goodly company.

All.

Hurrah !

Student.

Health here, and happiness hereafter !

(Raises the goblet.)

All.

So be it.

(They do the same.)

Student.

Already dreaming, Trabuco ?

Trabuco.

What ? in this uproar ?

Student.

And the little person who came with you
Does she go to the Jubilee ?

Trabuco.

I do not know.

Student.

By the by,
Is it man or woman ?

Trabuco.

With strangers, I only think of the money

Student.

Most prudent !

(To the ALCADE.)

Ed ella
Che giungere la vide— perchè a cena.
Non vien ?

Alcade.
L'ignoro.

Studente.
Dissero chiedesse
Acqua ed aceto.—Ah ah !—per rinfrescarsi.

Alcade.
Sara.

Studente.
E ver ch' è gentile, e senza barba ?

Alcade.
Non so nulla.

Studente.
(Parlar non vuol !) Ancora
                    (To TRABUCO.)
A lei.
Stava sul mulo,
Seduta o a cavalcioni ?

Trabuco
                    (Impazientato.)
Che noia !

Studente.
Onde veniva ?

Trabuco.
So che andrè, presto o tardi, in Paradiso.

Studente.
Perchè ?

Trabuco
                    (Alzandosi.)
Ella il purgatorio.
Mi fa soffrir.

Studente.
Or dove va ?

Trabuco.
In istalla,
Dormir colle mie mule,
Che non san di Latino,
Nè sono Baccellieri.
          (Prende il suo basto e parte.)

And you,
Who saw her arrive, say
Why she comes not to supper ?

Alcade.
I cannot tell.

Student.
They say she asked—ha ha !—
For vinegar and water, as refreshment.

Alcade.
May be.

Student.
Is it true that she is pretty, and has no
beard ?

Alcade.
I really do not know.

Student.
(He will not speak.)
                    (To TRABUCO.)
Once more,
Was she seated on the mule,
Or rode astride ?

Trabuco
                    (Impatiently.)
What vexation !

Student.
Whence came she ?

Trabuco.
I know I shall go, sooner or later, to
Paradise.

Student.
Why ?

Trabuco
                    (Rising.)
Because you make me
Suffer purgatory here.

Student.
Where are you going now ?

Trabuco.
To the stable,
To sleep with my mules,
Who don't know Latin,
And are not Bachelors of Arts.
          (Takes his pack-saddle and goes.)

SCENA IV. I Suddettie meno MASTRO TRABUCO.

Tutti.
 Ah ah ! è fuggito !
Studente.
 Poich' è imberbe l'incognito facciamgli
 Col nero du baffetti,
 Doman ne rideremo.
Alcuni.
 Bravo ! bravo !
Alcade.
 Protegger debbo il viaggiator; m' oppongo.
 Meglio farebbe dirne

 D' onde venga, ove vade, e chi ella sia ?

Studente.
 Lo vuol saper ?—Ecco l'istoria mia.

SCENE IV. The same, except TRABUCO.

All.
 Ha ha ! he is off !
Student.
 As the unknown is a stripling,
 Let us paint on him a pair of moustaches,—
 That will make us all laugh to-morrow.
Some of them.
 Bravo ! Bravo !
Alcade.
 I am bound to protect travellers,
 And therefore object.—You had better
  tell us
 Whence you come, where going, and who
  you are.
Student.
 You wish to know ?—This is my tale.

SON PEREDA — *I'M PEREDA* Air (Student)

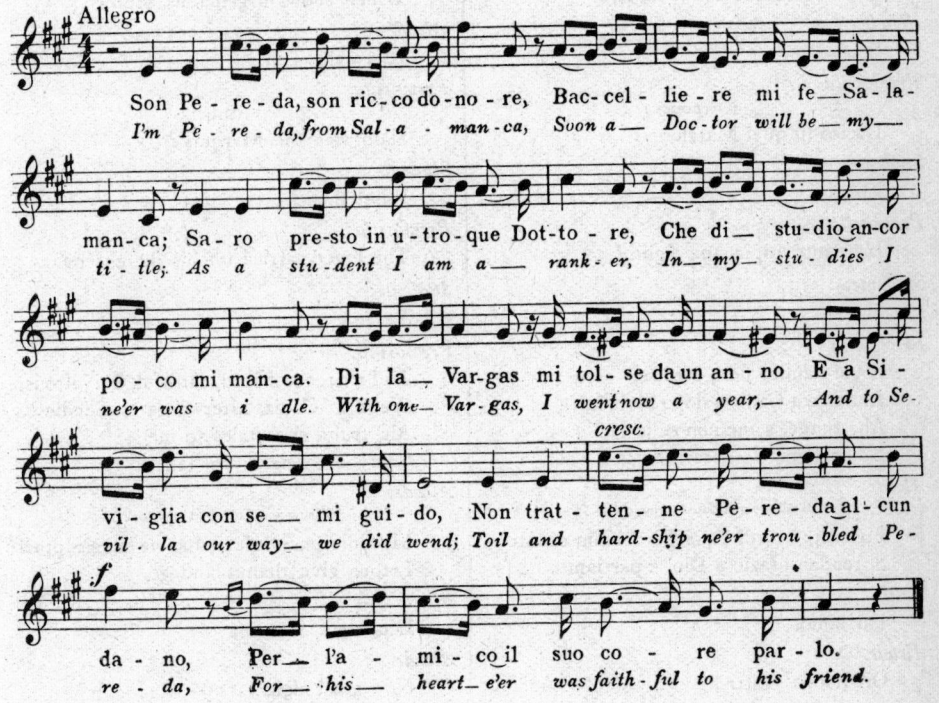

Della suora, un amante straniero,
Colà il padre gli avea trucidato,
Onde il figlio, da pro' cavaliero,
La vendetta ne aveva giurato.
Gl' inseguimmo di Cadice in riva,
Nè la coppia fatal si trovò.
Per l' amico Pereda soffriva,
Chè l suo core per esso parlò.
Là e dovunque narrar che del pari
La sedotta col vecchio peria,

Chè a una zuffa di servi e sicari,
Solo il vil seduttore sfuggia,
Io da Vargas allor mi staccava ;
Ei seguir l' assassino giurò.
Verso America il mare solcava,
E Pereda a' suoi studi torno.

Coro.
Truce storia Pereda narrava,
Generoso il suo cor si mostrò.

Alcade.
Sta bene.

Preziosilla
(Con finezza.)
Ucciso fu quel Marchese ?

Studente.
Ebben ?

Preziosilla.
L'amante rapia sua figlia ?

Studente.
Si.

Preziosilla.
E voi l'amico fido, cortese,
Andaste a Cadice, dopo Siviglia ?
Ah, gnaffe, a me non se la fa,
No, per mia fè—tra la la là !

Alcade
(S' alza, e guardato l' oriuolo dice.)
Figliuoli, è tardi ; poichè abbiam cenato
Si rendan grazie a Dio, e partiam

Tutti.
Partiamo.

Alcade.
Or buona notte !

A stranger, the lover of his sister,
Had there his father slain,
Wherefore his son, as true knight
Had sworn to be avenged.
We followed to the shores of Cadiz.
But ne'er o'ertook the guilty pair.
Pereda felt for his friend's distress,
Whom he most truly loved.
Here it is needful to inform you;
That the seduced one perished with her
    sire:
In a struggle 'twixt servants and assassins
The vile seducer fled alone.
From Vargas then I parted ;
For he swore to follow the assassin:
He crosses the ocean to America,
And Pereda to his studies returns.

Chorus.
A dismal story Pereda has related,
Which shows a generous soul.

Alcade.
It is well.

Preziosilla
(Slyly.)
Slain was the Marquis ?

Studente.
What then ?

Preziosilla.
The lover carried off his daughter ?

Studente.
Yes.

Preziosilla.
And you, the friend, faithful, chivalrous,
Went to Cadiz, afterwards to Seville ?
Ah, truly, such tales to me
Carry no weight, tra la !

Alcade
(Rising and looking at the clock.)
My children, it is late, and we have supped:
Let us give thanks and go.

All.
Let us go.

Alcade.
Now good night !

Coro.

Buona notte!

Tutti.

Andiamo.

(Partono.)

SCENA V. Una piccola spianata sul declivio di scoscesa Montagna. A sinistra precipizii e rupi; di fronte la facciata della chiesa della Madonna delgi Angeli, di povera ed umile architettura, a destra la porta del Convento, in mezzo alla quale una fine strella, da un lato la corda del companello. Sopra vi e una piccola tettoia sporgente. Al di la della chiesa alti monti col villaggio d' Hornachueios. La porta della chiesa e chiusa, ma larga, sopra dessa una finestra semicircolare lasciera vedere la luce interna. A mezza scene, un po' a sinistra, sopra quattro gradini s' erge una rozza croce ei pietra, corrosa dal tempo. La scena sara illuminata da luna chiarissima.

DONNA LEONORA giunge, ascendendo dalla destra, stanca, vestita da uomo, con pastrano a larghe maniche, largo capello e stivali.

Leonora.

Son giunta—grazie, o Dio!
Estremo asil quest' è per me—son giunta!
Io tremo! La mia orrenda storia è nota
In quell' albergo—e mio fratel narrolla!
Se Scoperta m'avesse! Cielo! Ei disse
Naviga verso occaso Don Alvaro!
Nè morto cadde quella notte in cui
Io, io del sangue di mio padre intrisa,
L' ho seguito, e il perdei! ed or mi lascia,
Mi fugge! ohimè, non reggo a tanta ambascia!

(Cade inginocchio.)

Chorus.

Good night!

All.

Let us go.

(They depart.)

SCENE V. A small level space, on the side of a steep Mountain. On the left, precipices and rocks; facing the audience, the facade of the Church of the "Madonna degli Angeli," of simple architecture: on the right, the door of the Convent in the middle of which is a small window, on one side the cord of the bell, above which is a small projecting roof. On the other side of the church are high mountains, and the village of Hornachuelos. The door of the church is closed, but spacious; above it a semicircular window shows the light within. Half way down the stage, a little to the left, on four steps, is a rough stone cross, corroded by time. There is a bright moonlight over the whole scene.

DONNA LEONORA arrives, in male attire, ascending from the right, wearing a cloak with large sleeves, a large hat, and boots

Leonora.

I have arrived—thank Heaven!
This is my last refuge—I am here!
I tremble! My dreadful story is known:
In that inn my brother did recount it.
Oh Heavens! had he discovered me!
He said Don Alvaro was sailing westward,
And fell not on that fearful night
When, steeped in my father's blood,
I followed and lost him! Now he leaves me—
Flies from me!—Ah me, I cannot bear it!

(Falls on her knees.)

MADRE, MADRE — *O HOLY MOTHER* (Leonora and Chorus)

Allegro moderato

Ma-dre, Madre, pie-to-sa Ver-gi-ne, Per-do-na al mio pec-ca-to, M'a-i ta quell'in-gra-to Dal co-re a can-cel-lar. In que-ste so-li-tu-di-ni F-spi-e-ro, e-spi-e-ro l'er-

Mo-ther, O, Ho-ly Mo-ther, hear my pray'r; For-give my sin ap-pal-ling, Then from this love en-thral-ling May my poor soul be freed, Re-pen-tant here in so-li-tude I'll make a-mends, I'll make a-mends com-

ro - re. Pie - ta di me, pie - ta, Si - gnor, pie - ta di me, pie - ta, Si -
plete - ly, In mer - cy hear, in mer - cy hear, in mer - cy hear my fer - vent

gno - re, Deh! non m'ab-ban-do-nar, pie - ta, Pie - ta di me, Si -
plead - ing! For - sake me not, for - sake me not, for - sake me not, O

LEONORA
gno - re! Deh! non m'ab-ban-do-nar, ah!——— Pie - ta, pie - ta, di me, Si
Heav - en! For - sake me not, O Heav - en, Ah,——— for - sake me not, for - sake me

CHORUS (Within)
Ve -

gnor!   Ah! que su - bli - mi can - ti - ci,
not!   Ah! how sub - lime the an - them sounds,

ni - te, a - do - re - mus et pro - ce - da - mus   an - - te

Dell' or - ga - no i con - cen - ti, Che co - me in - cen - so as -
With sol - emn or - gan blend - ing, It floats like in - cense

De - - - - - - - - -

cen - do - no A Dio sui fir - ma - men - ti, In - spi - ra - no, in -
on the air, To heav - en's gate as - cend - ing, Un - to my soul, un -

um,   plo - re - mus, plo - re - mus

spi-ra-no a quest'al - ma Fe - de, Con - for-to e cal - ma!
to my soul 'tis bring - ing Calm - ness, and faith un - sha - ken.

co - ram Do-mi-no co-rum, Do-mi-no qui fe - cit nos.

Al santo asilo accorrasi.	Let me to the sacred asylum haste.
(S' avvia.)	(Going.)
E l'oserò a quest' ora ?	But dare I, at this hour ?
(Arrestandosi.)	(Stopping.)
Ma si potria sorprendermi !	Yet I may be o'ertaken !
Oh, misera Leonora,	Oh, wretched Leonora,
Tremi ?—il pio frate accoglierti	Dost fear ?—the holy friar
No, non ricuserà.	To receive thee will not refuse.
Non mi lasciar, soccorrimi,	Have mercy, Heaven, mercy !
Pietà, Signor, pietà.	Aid me, desert me not !
(Va a suonare il campanello del Convento.)	(Rings the convent-bell.)

SCENA VI. Si apre la finestrella della porta, e n'esce la luce d' una lanterna. Che riverbera sul volto di DONNA LEONORA, la quale si arresta spaventata. FRA MELITONE parla sempre all' interno.

SCENE VI. The little window in the door opens, through which is seen a light, which is reflected in DONNA LEONORA'S face, who starts back alarmed. BROTHER MELITONE speaks from within.

Melitone.
  Chi siete ?

Leonora.
  Chiedo il Superiore,

Melitone.
  S' apre
  Alle cinque la chiesa,
  Se al giubileo venite.

Leonora.
  Il Superiore—
  Per carità !

Melitone.
  Che carità a quest' ora !

Leonora.
  Mi manda il Padre Cleto.

Melitone.
  Quel sant' uomo ? Il motivo ?

Leonora.
  Urgente.

Melitone.
  Who is it ?

Leonora.
  I seek the Superior.

Melitone.
  At five o'clock
  The church will open,
  If to the jubilee you come.

Leonora.
  The Superior—
  For charity's sake !

Melitone.
  Charity at this hour !

Leonora.
  I am sent by Father Cleto.

Melitone.
  By that holy man ? The reason ?

Leonora.
  Most urgent.

Melitone.
    Perchè mai ?

Leonora.
    Un infelice !

Melitone.
    Brutta solfa—però v' apro ond' entriate.

Leonora.
    Nol posso.

Melitone.
    No ?   Scomunicicato siete ?
    Chè strano fia aspettar a ciel sereno.
    V' annuncio—e se non torno,
    Buona notte.
                    (Chiude la finestrella.)

    SCENA VII.   DONNA LEONORA, sola.

Leonora.
    Ma s' ei mi respingesse !
    Fama pietoso il dice,
    Ei mi proteggerà;—Vergin, m'assisti !

    SCENA VIII.   DONNA LONORA, il PADRE GUARDIANO. fra
                    MELITONE.

Guardiano.
    Chi mi cerca ?

Leonora.
    Son io.

Guardiano.
    Dite.

Leonora.
    Un segreto—

Guardiano.
    Andate Melitone.

Melitone
                    (Partendo.)
    (Sempre   segreti !
    E questi santi soi han da saperli !
    Noi siamo tanti cavoli.)

Guardiano.
    Gratello
    Mormorate ?

Melitone.
    Oibò, dico ch' è pesante
    La porte, e fa romore.

Guardiano.
    Obbedite.

Melitone.
    Why so ?

Leonora.
    An unfortunate creature !

Melitone.
    A likely tale—however, I will let you in.

Leonora.
    I cannot enter.

Melitone.
    No ?   Are you excommunicated ?
    'Tis strange you should prefer the open air,
    I will announce you—and if I don't return,
    Good night.
                    (Shuts the window)

    SCENE VII.   DONNA LEONORA, alone.

Leonora.
    But if he should repulse me ?
    He is reputed merciful.
    He will protect me ;—Holy Virgin, aid me !

    SCENE VIII.   DONNA LEONORA, the FATHER GUARDIANO,
                    BROTHER MELITONE.

Guardiano.
    Who asks for me ?

Leonora.
    'Tis I.

Guardiano.
    Speak on.

Leonora.
    A secret—

Guardiano.
    Go, Melitone.

Melitone
                    (Going.)
    (Always secrets !
    And these saints only know them !
    We are nobodies !)

Guardiano.
    Brother,
    Are you grumbling ?

Melitone.
    Oh no, I said the door
    Was heavy, and creaked,

Guardiano.
    Obey.

Melitone.
(Che tuon da Superiore !)

(Rientra in Convento socchiudendone la porta.)

SCENA IX. DONNA LEONORA e il PADRE GUARDIANO.

Guardiano.
Or siam soli.

Leonora.
Una donna son io.

Guardiano.
Una donna a quest' ora !—gran Dio !

Leonora.
Infelice, dulusa, rejetta,
Dalla terra, e dal ciel maledetta,
Che nel pianto prostratavi al piede,
Di sottrarla all' inferno vi chiede.

Guardiano.
Come un povero frate lo può ?

Leonora.
Padre Cleto un suo foglio v'inviò ?

Guardiano.
Ei vi manda ?

Leonora.
Sì.

Guardiano
(Sorpreso.)
Dunque voi siete
Leonora di Varges ?

Leonora.
Fremete !

Guardiano.
No: venite fidente alla croce,
Là del Cielo v' inspiri la voce.

Leonora
(S' inginocchia presso la croce, la bacia, quindi torna meno agitata
al PADRE GUARDIANO.)
Ah, tranquilla l' alma sento
Dacchè premo questa terra ;
De' fantasmi lo spavento
Più non provo farmi guerra ;
Più non sorge sanguinante
Di mio padre l' ombra innante,
Nè terribile l' ascolto
La sua figlia maledir.

Melitone.
(Quite the voice of the Superior !)

(Re-enters the Convent, half-closing the door.)

SCENE IX. DONNA LEONORA and the FATHER GUARDIANO.

Guardiano.
Now, we are alone.

Leonora.
I am a woman.

Guardiano.
A woman at this hour !—good heavens !

Leonora.
Unhappy, deluded, rejected
On earth, and cursed by Heaven !
Who, prostrate at your feet, with tears
Implores you to save her from destruction

Guardiano.
How can a poor friar do so ?

Leonora.
Father Cleto sent you a letter ?

Guardiano.
He sent you ?

Leonora.
Yes.

Guardiano
(Surprised.)
Then you must be
Leonora di Vargas ?

Leonora.
You shudder !

Guardiano.
No: in confidence approach the cross,
There may Heaven inspire you.

Leonora
(Kneeling close to the cross, kisses it, then turning with less
agitation to FATHER GUARDIANO.)
Ah, my soul is calm
Now I tread this soil;
The dread forebodings
I no longer feel within me ;
Nor does there rise before me
The bleeding shade of my sire;
I do not hear with horror
His curses on his child.

Guardiano.

Sempre indarno qui rivolto
Fu di Satana l' ardir.

Leonora.

Perciò tomba qui desio,
Fa le rupi ov' altra visse.

Guardiano.

Che !—sapete —

Leonora.

Cleto il disse.

Guardiano.

E volete—

Leonora.

Darmi a Dio !

Guardiano.

Guai per chi si lascia illudere
Dal delirio d'un momento !
Più fatal per voi, si giovane,
Sorgerebbe il pentimento.
Nel futuro chi può leggere,
Chi immutabil farvi il cor.
E l' amante ?

Leonora.

Involontario
Di mio padre è l' uccisor.

Guardiano.

Il fratello ?

Leonora.

La mia morte
Di sua mano egli giurò.

Guardiano.

Meglio a voi la sante porte.
Schiuda un chiostro.

Leonora.

Un chiostro ? No.
Se voi scacciate questa pentita,
Andrò per balze gridando aita.
Ricovro ai monti ciba, alle selve,
E fin le belve ne avran pietà.
Qui, qui del ciela udii la voce:
Salvati all' ombra di questa croce—
Voi mi scacciate ?   E questo il porto;
Chi tal conforto mi toglierà ?

(Corre ad abbracciar la croce.)

Guardiano.

Never has Satan dared
These precincts to approach,

Leonora.

Therefore a tomb I seek
Among the rocks where one other lived.

Guardiano.

What !—do you know—

Leonora.

Cleto mentioned it,

Guardiano.

And you wish—

Leonora.

To devote myself to Heaven !

Guardiano.

Woe unto those who delude themselves
In the wild frenzy of a moment !
More wretched for you, so young,
Would repentance hereafter become.
Who can read the future,
Or make the heart steadfast ?
And thy lover ?

Leonora.

He by mischance
My father killed.

Guardiano.

Thy brother ?

Leonora.

My death he has sworn
By his own hand.

Guardiano.

For you 'twere best to seek
A cloister's holy shelter.

Leonora.

A cloister ? No.
If you reject the penitent,
Aid will I shrieking ask the rocks,
Shelter the mountains, food the woods ;
The savage beasts at least will pity me.
Here, where heaven's voice is heard
Salvation in the shadow of the Cross I seek.
You cast me out ? This is the haven
Of solace—you will tear me from it ?

(Runs and clings to the cross.)

Guardiano.

(A te sia gloria, o Dio clemente,
Padre dei miseri onnipossente,
A qui sgabello sono le sfere !
Il tuo volere—si compirà !)
E fermo il voto ?

Leonora.

E fermo,

Guardiano.

V' accolga dunque Iddio !

Leonora.

Bontà divina ?

Guardiano.

Sol io saprò chi siate.
Tra le rupi è uno speco ; ivi starete.
Presso una fonte, al settimo, di scarso
Cibo porrovvi io stesso.

Leonora.

V' andiamo.

Guardiano
(Versa la porta.)

Melitone !
(A MELITONE chi comparisce.)

Tutti i fratelli con ardenti ceri,
Dov' è l' ara maggiore,
Nel tempio si raccolgan del Signore.
(MELITONE rientra.)

Guardiano.

(Thine be the glory, O merciful Heaven !
Father of sinners, omnipotent,
Who o'er all worlds reigns,
Let Thy will be accomplished.)
Thou art resolved ?

Leonora.

I am.

Guardiano.

Heaven accept thee !

Leonora.

Oh, clemency divine !

Guardiano.

I alone shall know who thoù art.
Among the rocks is a cave, thy future abode:
Beside a spring, every seven days,
Thy scanty food I myself will bring.

Leonora.

Let us go.

Guardiano
(Turning to the door.)

Melitone !
(To MELITONE who enters.)

Let all the brothers, with lighted torches,
Before the high altar assemble,
In the temple of our Lord.
(MELITONE withdraws.)

SULL' ALBA IL PIEDE — *TO SEEK THE LONELY HERMITAGE* Duet. (Guardiano and Leonora)

GUARDIANO

Allegro moderato

Sull' al-ba il pie-de all' e - re - mo So - lin - ga _ vol - ge - re - te, Ma
To seek the low - ly her-mit-age At dawn you _ must be stir - ring But

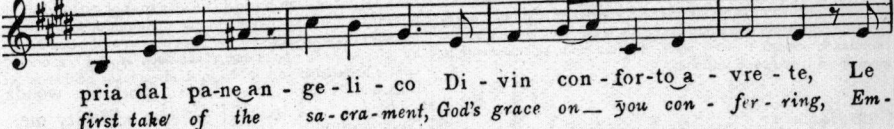

pria dal pa-ne an - ge-li - co Di - vin con-for-to a - vre - te, Le
first take of the sa - cra - ment, God's grace on _ you con - fer - ring, Em-

san-te la-ne a cin ge - re I - te, sia fer-mo il cor. Sul nuo-vo cal-le a
brace the cross with sim-ple faith To set your mind at rest, And Heav'n will not de -

LEONORA

Tua gra - zia, o Di - o, Sor-
My pray'rs and thanks - giv - ing To

reg-ger-vi___ V'as-sis-te-ra il Si - gnor.
ny you aid,___ You will be rich-ly___ blest.

[Enters the Convent, but returns immedi- ately with the dress of the Franciscan or- der, and gives it to Leonora.

LEONORA

ri - de al-la___ re - jet - ta! Oh, gau - dio in - so - li - to! Io
Thee on high are___ wing-ing, And hap - pi-ness un - mer - it - ed Thy

son,___ Io son ri - be - ne - det - ta! Gia sen-to in me ri - na-sce - re A
peace. to my poor heart is bring-ing, New hope once more with - in I feel, New

nuo-va vi-ta il cor; Plau - di - te, o co-ri an-ge - li - ci, Mi per-do-no___ il Si-
cour-age in my breast; Me - thinks an-gel - ic songs I hear And par - don makes me___

gnor, Mi per-do - no il Si - gnor_____ Mi per-do-no il Si - gnor.
blest, And par-don, par-don makes me blest,_____ Thy par-don makes me blest.

SCENA X. La gran porta della Chiesa si apre. Di fronte vedesi l' altar maggiore, illuminato. L' organo suona. Dai lati del coro procedono due lunghe file di FRATI, con cerei ardenti. Piu tardi il PADRE GUARDIANO precede LEONORA in abito da FRATE. Egli la conduce fuor della chiesa, FRATI che gli si schierano intorno. LEONORA si prostra innanzi a lui, che stendendo solennemente le mani spora il suo capo intuona.

SCENE X. The great door of the Church opens. In front is seen the high altar, illuminated. The organ is sounded. From the sides of the choir proceed two long rows of FRIARS, with lighted tapers. A little later, the FATHER GUARDIANO, followed by LEO- NORA, in the FRIAR'S dress. He leads her out of the church, followed by the FRIARS, who range themselves around. LEONORA pro- strates herself before him. he solemnly spreads his hands over her head, and chants.

Guardiano.

Il santo nome di Dio Signore
Sia benedetto.

Tutti.

Sia benedetto.

Guardiano.

The holy name of the Lórd
Be blessed.

All.

Be blessed.

Guardiano.

Un' alma a piangere viene l' errore,
I queste balze chiede ricetto.
Il santo speco noi la schiudiamo—
V' è noto il loco ?

Tutti.

Lo conosciamo.

Guardiano.

A quell' asilo sacro inviolato
Nessun si appressi.

Tutti.

Obbediremo.

Guardiano.

Il cinto umile non sia varcato.
Che nel divide.

Tutti.

Nol varcheremo.

Guardiano.

A chi il divieto frangere osasse,
O di quest' anima scoprir tentasse
Nome o mistero, maledizione !

Tutti.

Maledizione ! maledizione !
Il cielo fulmini incenercisa
L' empio mortale se tanto ardisca ;
Su lui scatenisi ogni elemento,
L' immonda cenere ne sperda il vento.

Guardiano   (A LEONORA.)

Alzatevi, e partite.
Alcun vivente più non vedrete.
Dello speco il bronzo
Ne avverta se periglio vi sovrasti,
O per voi giunto s'a l' estremo giorno—
A confortarvi l' alma
Volerem, pria ch' a Dio faccia ritorno.
La Vergine degli angeli
Vo copra del suo manto,
E voi protegga vigile
Di Dio l' angelo santo.

Tutti.

La Vergine, ec.

(LEONORA bacia la mano del PADRE GUARDIANO s' avvia all'
eremo sola. Il GUARDIANO stendendo le braccia verso di lei, la
benedice. Cade la tela.)

FINE DELLA' ATTO SECONDO.

Guardiano.

A penitent soul, to atone for errors,
Demands a shelter in these rocks.
The holy cave we will open—
Do you know the place ?

All.

We know the place.

Guardiano.

The sacred holy asylum
Let none approach.

All.

We will obey.

Guardiano.

The low boundary enclosing it
Let none pass.

All.

We will not.

Guardiano.

To him who dares this rule to break,
Or of this poor soul seeks to discover
The name or story, malediction !

All.

Malediction ! malediction !
May the thunderbolt reduce to ashes
The impious mortal who dares attempt it ;
May all the elements be loosed upon him,
And his impure ashes be scattered by the
        wind.

Guardiano   (TO LEONORA.)

Rise and depart. No living soul
Will see you more. The bell in the cave
Will give us notice if you are in danger :
If your last hour be at hand,
We will haste to bring absolution
Ere thy soul to God returns.
The Virgin of the heavenly host
Cover you with her holy mantle,
And the holy angels of God
Be to you watchful guardians.

All.

The Virgin, etc.

(LEONORA kisses the hand of FATHER GUARDIANO, and sets out
alone for the hermitage. GUARDIANO, extending his arms towards
her, blesses her. The curtain falls.)

END OF THE SECOND ACT.

ATTO III	ACT III
In Italia. presso Velletri.	In Italy, near Villeteri.

SCENA I. Bosco. Notte oscurissima. DON ALVARO in uniforme di Capitano Spagnuolo de' Granatieri del Re, si avanza lentamente dal fondo. Si sentono voci interno a destra.

1a Voce.
    Attenti, gioco.—Un asso a destra.

2a Voce.
    Ho vinto.

1a Voce.
    Un tre alla destra—cinque a manca.

2a Voce.
    Perdo !

Alvaro
      (Che si sara innoltrato.)

La vita e inferno all infelice invano
Morte desio !—Siviglia !—Leonora !
Oh, rimembranze !—Oh notte !
Ch' ogni mio ben rapisti !
Sarò infelice eternamente è scritto.

Della natal sua terra il padre volle
Spezzar l' estranio giogo, el coll', unirsi ;
All' ultima degli Incas la corona
Cingerne confidò—fallì l' impresa,
In un carcere nacqui.; m' educava
Il deserto ; sol vivo per chè ignota
E mia regale stirpe. I miei parenti
Sognaro un trono e, li destò la scure !

Oh, quando fine avran le mie sventure ?

SCENE I. A wood. A dark night. DON ALVARO, in the uniform of a Captain of Royal Spanish Grenadiers, advances slowly from the back. Voices are heard on the right, from within.

1st Voice.
    Attention, I play. An ace to the right.

2nd Voice.
    I have won.

1st Voice.
    A three to the right—five to the left.

2nd Voice.
    I have lost.

Alvaro
      (Who has come forward.)

Life has no charms for unhappy souls.
In vain I seek to die !—Seville !—Leonora !
Oh, sad memories !—Fatal night,
Which of every good deprived me !
It is decreed that I shall ever be unfortunate.

My father sought to free his native land
From foreign rule ;
United to the last of the Incas,
He hoped to obtain the crown.
He failed—and in prison I was born,
In the desert reared, and only live because
My royal birth is unknown. My parents
Dreamt of thrones, and suffered by the scaffold.

Ah, when will my sorrows end ?

OH, TU CHE IN SENO —— *O SAINTED SOUL* Air. Alvaro

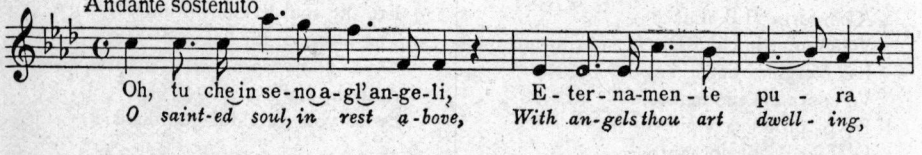

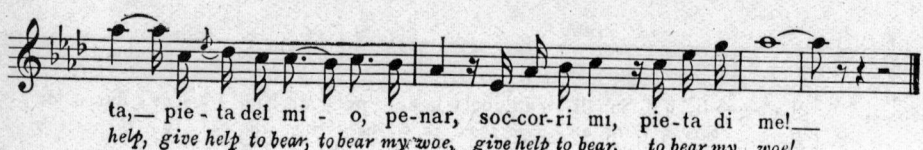

ta,— pie - ta del mi - o, pe-nar, soc-cor-ri mi, pie-ta di me!__
help, give help to bear, to bear my woe, give help to bear, to bear my woe!__

Voce
   (Dall' interno a destra.)
	Voice
	   (From within.)

Al tradimento !	Treachery !
Voci.	*Voices.*
Muoia !	Down with him !
Alvaro.	*Alvaro.*
Quali grida ?	What cries are these ?
Voce.	*A Voice.*
Aita !	Help !
Alvaro.	*Alvaro.*
Si soccorra !	To your aid !

(Accorre al luogo onde si udivano le grida. Si sente un picchiare di spade. Alcuni Ufficiali attraversano la scena, fuggendo in disordine da destra a sinistra.)	(Runs to the place from whence the sounds proceed. A clashing of swords is heard. Some Officers cross the stage in disorder flying right and left.
SCENA II. DON ALVARO ritorna con DON CARLO.	SCENE II. DON ALVARO returns with DON CARLOS.
Alvaro.	*Alvaro.*
Fuggir ! Ferito siete ?	They are fled ! Are you wounded ?
Carlo.	*Carlos.*
No, vi debbo La vita.	No : but I owe to you my life.
Alvaro.	*Alvaro.*
Chi erano ?	Who are they ?
Carlo.	*Carlos.*
Assassini.	Assassins.
Alvaro.	*Alvaro.*
Presso ! Alcampo così ?	What so near the camp ?
Carlo.	*Carlos.*
Franco Dirè : fu alterco al gioco.	Frankly, it was a gambling quarrel.
Alvaro.	*Alvaro.*
Comprendo, colà, a destra ?	I understand ; there on the right ?
Carlo.	*Carlos.*
Si.	Yes.
Alvaro.	*Alvaro.*

Ma come,
  Si nobile d' aspetto, a quella bisca
  Scendeste ?
	But, how, seeming so noble,
	  Descend to such low company ?

Carlo.

Nuovo sono.
Del general con ordini sol jeri
Giunsi ; senza voi morto
Sarei. Or dite a chi miei giorni debbo ?

Alvaro.

Al caso.

Carlo.

Pria il mio nome
Dirò—(non sappia il vero)—
Don Felice de Bornos, ajutante
Del Duce.

Alvaro.

Io Capitan de' Granatieri
Don Federico Herreros !

Carlo.

La gloria dell' esercito !

Alvaro.

Signore—

Carlo.

Io l' amistà ne ambia, la chiedo, e spero.

Alvaro.

Io pure della vostra sarò fiero.

(Si stringono le destre.)

Voci

(Interne, a sinistra, e squillo di trombe.)

All' armi !

A 2.

Andiamo—all' armi !

Carlo.

Ah più gradito questo suono or parmi !
Con voi scendere al campo d' onore,
Emularne l' esempio potrò.

Alvaro.

Testimone del vostro valore,
Ammirarne le prove saprò.

SCENA III. E il Mattino. Salotto nell' abitazione d' un ufficiale superiore dell' esercito Spagnuolo in Italia non lungi da Velletri. Nel fondo sonvi due porte, quella a sinistra mette ad una stanza da letto, l' altra e la comune. A sinistra presso il proscenio a una finestra. Si sente il romore della vicina battaglia.

Un Chirurgo Militare, ed alcuni Soldati, ordinanze dalla comune ʼorrono alla finestra.

Soldati.

Arde la mischia !

Carlos.

I am a stranger, with orders from the general.
I yesterday arrived, and but for you I had
died.
Say, to whom do I owe my life ?

Alvaro.

To chance.

Carlos.

I will first tell my name—
(Not my true one)—
Don Felice de Bornos,
Adjutant to the Duke.

Alvaro.

I Captain of the Grenadiers,
Don Federico Herreros !

Carlos.

The pride of the army !

Alvaro.

Signor—

Carlos.

I desire and would obtain your friendship.

Alvaro.

I shall be proud to have yours.

(They shake hands.)

Voices

(Within, to the left, with sound of a trumpet.)

To arms !

Together.

Let us go—to arms !

Carlos.

Ah, that sound is more agreeable now !
With you I will go to the field of honor,
And seek to emulate your bright example.

Alvaro.

Witness of your valor,
In future I shall know how to admire it.

SCENE III. Morning. A small room in the house of a superior officer in the Spanish army, in Italy, not far from Velletri. At the back are two doors, one on the left leads to a bedroom, the other is the common door. On the left, near the proscenium, is a window. The noise is heard of the neighboring battle.

A Military Surgeon, and some common Soldiers, run to the window.

Soldiers.

The battle rages !

Chirurgo
(Guardando con cannocchiale.)

Prodi i granatiere !

Soldati.

Li guida Herreros.

Chirurgo
(Guardando con cannocchiale.)

Ciel ! ferito o spento
Ei cadde ! Piegano i suoi ! l'Ajutante
Li raccozza alla carica li guida !
Già fuggono i Tedeschi ! I nostril han vinto
Portan qui il Capitano.

Soldati.

Ferito !
(Corrono ad incontrarlo.)

Voci
(Fuori.)

A Spagna gloria !

Altre.

Viva l' Italia !

Tutti.

E nostra la vittoria !

SCENA IV   DON ALVARO, ferito e svenuto e portato in una lettiga da quattro Granatieri. Da un lato e il Chirurgo, dall' altro DON CARLO, coperto di polvere ed assai afflitto. Un Soldato depone una valigia sopra un tavolino. La lettiga e collocata quasi nel mezzo della scena.

Carlo.

Piano—qui posi—approntisi il mio letto.

Chirurgo.

Silenzio.

Carlo.

V' ha periglio ?

Chirurgo.

La palla che ha nel petto mi spaventa.

Carlo.

Deh, il salvate.

Alvaro
(Rinviene.)

Ove son ?

Cerlo.

Presso l' amico.

Alvaro.

Lasciatemi morire.

Surgeon
(Looking through a telescope.)

Brave grenadiers !

Soldier.

Herreros leads them.

Surgeon
(Looking through a telescope.)

Heavens ! he falls
Wounded or dead ! His men give way !
The Adjutant rallies and leads them to
   the charge !
The Germans fly ! Our troops conquer !
They bring hither the Captain.

Soldier.

Wounded !
(They run to meet him.)

Voices
(Without.)

Glory to Spain !

Others.

Long live Italy !

All.

Ours is the victory !

SCENE IV.   DON ALVARO, wounded and insensible, is borne in on a litter by four Grenadiers. On one side the Surgeon, on the other DON CARLOS, covered with dust and sorrowful. A Soldier places a traveling-bag on a small table. The litter is placed nearly in the middle of the scene.

Carlos.

Gently—lay him here—get ready my bed.

Surgeon.

Silence !

Carlos.

Is there danger ?

Surgeon.

The bullet in his chest alarms me.

Carlos.

Ah, try to save him !

Alvaro
(Recovering his senses.)

Where am I ?

Carlos.

With your friend.

Alvaro.

Leave me to die.

Carlo.
Vi salveran le nostra cure premio
L' ordine vè sarà di Calatrava.

Carlos.
Our cares will save you.
The Order of Calatrava will be conferred
upon you.

Alvaro
(Trasalendo.)
Di Calatrava ! No—mai !

Alvaro
(Shuddering.)
Of Calatrava ! No—never !

Chirurgo.
Siate calmo.

Surgeon.
Be calm.

Carlo.
(Ch, ! inorridi di Calatrava al nome !)

Carlos.
(He shuddered at the name of Calatrava !)

Alvaro.
Amico—

Alvaro.
My friend—

Chirurgo.
Se parlate—

Surgeon.
If you speak—

Alvaro.
Un detto sol.

Alvaro.
Only one word.

Carlo
(Al Chirurgo.)
Ven prefo ne, lasciate.
(Chirurgo si ritrae al fonde.)

Carlos
(To the Surgeon.)
Leave us, I pray you.
(The Surgeon retires to the back.)

SOLENNE IN QUEST' ORA — *IN THIS SOLEMN HOUR*—Duet (Don Alvaro and Don Carlo)

me - co mor - rà. S'ab - bru - ci me spen-to. Lo giu - ro, sa -
die with my death. To burn it I pray thee. On hon - or I

Andante
ALVARO
Or muo - jo tran - quil - lo Vi strin - go al cor
I die__ now con - tent - ed, As to my heart__ I

CARLO
rà.
swear.

mi - o, al co -
hold thee, I hold_____

A - mi - co fi - da - te, fi - da - te nel cie - lo, fi - da - te nel
My friend, put thy faith now in Heav - en, thy faith now in Heav - en a

re,____ or muo - jo tran - quil - lo vi strin-go al cor mi -
thee,____ Con - tent - ed I die__ as I hold thee up - on my

ciel;____ a - mi - co, fi - da - te nel cie - lo, fi - da -
bove,____ in Heav - en a - bove,__ put thy faith now in Heav -

o, or muo - jo tran - quil - lo, vi strin - go al cor
heart. I die__ now con - tent - ed, as to my heart__ I

te.
en.

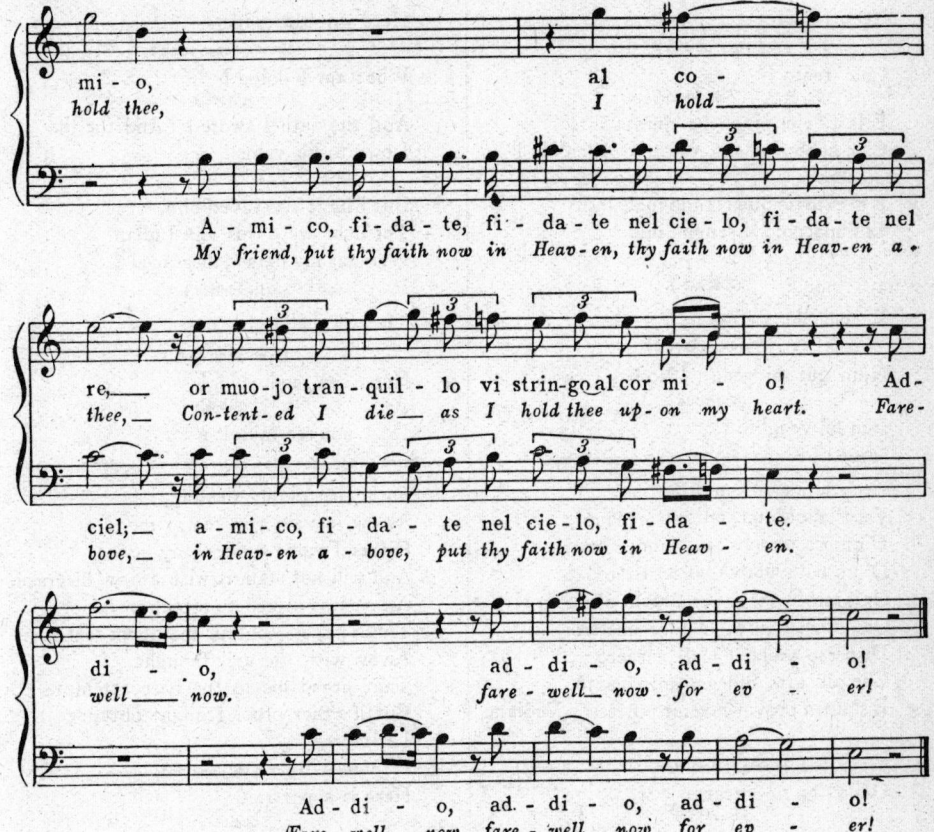

mi - o,
hold thee,
al co -
I hold

A - mi - co, fi - da - te, fi - da - te nel cie - lo, fi - da - te nel
My friend, put thy faith now in Heav-en, thy faith now in Heav-en a -

re, or muo-jo tran-quil - lo vi strin-go al cor mi - o! Ad -
thee,— Con-tent-ed I die— as I hold thee up-on my heart. Fare-

ciel;— a - mi - co, fi - da - te nel cie - lo, fi - da - te.
bove,— in Heav-en a - bove, put thy faith now in Heav - en.

di - o.
well — now.
ad - di - o, ad - di - o!
fare - well — now for ev - er!

Ad - di - o, ad - di - o, ad - di - o!
[Fare - well now, fare - well now for ev - er!

(Il Chirurgo e le Ordinanze trasportano il ferito nella stanza da letto.)

S ENA V. DON CARLOS, poi il Chirurgo.

Carlo.

Morir ! Tremenda cosa !
Sì intrepido, sì prode,
Ei pur morrà ! Uom singolar costui !
Tremò di Calatrava !
Al nome ! A lui palese
N' è forse il disonor ? Cielo ! qual lampo !
S' ei fosse il seduttore ?
Desso in mia mano, e vive !
Se m' ingannassi ? Questa chiave il dica.

(Apre convulso la valigia, e ne trae un plicco suggellato.)

(The Surgeon and Soldiers carry the wounded man into the bed-room)

SCENE V. DON CARLOS, afterwards the Surgeon.

Carlos.

Die ! How terrible !
So fearless, so brave.
Yet he must die ! What a strange man !
He shuddered at the name of Calatrava !
Does he know it has been disgraced ?
Heavens ! a thought strikes me !
What if he were the vile seducer ?
In my hands, and yet alive !
But if I should mistake ? This key will tell.

(He hastily opens the bag, and draws out a sealed packet.)

Ecco i fogli.
(Fa per aprirlo.)

Che tento ?
(S' arresta.)

E la fè che giurai ? e questa vìta
Che debbo al suo valor ? Anch' io l' ho
  salvo !
E s' ei fosse quell' Indo maledetto
Che macchiò il sangue mio ?

(Risoluto.)

Il suggello si franga.
(Sta per eseguire.)

Niun qui mi vede ; No !
(S' arresta.)

Ben mi vegg' io ?

(Getta il plicco, e se ne allontana con raccapriccio.)

Urna fatale del mio destino,
Va, t' allontana, mi tenti insano ;
L' onor a tergere qui venni, e insano
D' un onta nuova nol brutterò.
Un giuro è sacro per l' uom d' onore ;
Que' fogli chiudano il lor mistero—
Disperso vada il mal pensiero ;
Che all' atto indegno mi concitò.
E s' altra provar invenir potessi ? Vediam.

(Torna a frugare nella valigia e vi trova un astuccio.)

Qui v' ha un ritratto.
(Lo esamina.)

Suggel non v' e'—nulla ei ne disse—nulla—
Promisi—s' apra dunque.
(Eseguisce.)

Ciel ! Leonora !
(Con estaltazione.)

Don Alvaro e' il ferito !
Ora egli viva—
Edi mai man poi mueoia.

Chirurgo
(Si presenta lieto sulla porta della stanza.)

Lieta novella è salvo.
(Rientra.)

Carlo.

Oh gioia ! oh gioia !

Here are the papers.
(About to open them.)

What am I doing ?
(Stops.)

And the oath I swore ?   And the life
I owe to his valor ?

But I have also saved him.
Yet if he were this vile Indian
Who has my named disgraced ?
(Resolutely.)

The seal shall be broken.
(Is about to do it.)

None see me ! No. !
(Stops.)

Do I not see myself ?

(Throws away the packet, and turns from it with horror.)

Fatal urn of my destiny,
Away, in vain you tempt me ;
Hither I came to clear my honor,
And will not stain it with a new disgrace.
An oath is sacred to a man of honor ;
Those papers contain their own secret—
Away with the evil thought
That urged me to the base attempt.
But if other proof I might obtain ;
Let me see.

(Looks into the bag, and finds a case.)

Here is a portrait.
(Examines it.)

Here is no seal—he spoke not of it—
Nothing did I promise.
(Opens it.)

Heavens ! Leonora !
(Excitedly.)

The wounded man is then Alvaro !
Let him live—then, later die by my hands !

Surgeon
(Appearing at the door of the room.)

Here is the ball: he is saved !
(Retires.)

Carlos.

Oh, happiness ! oh, joy !

AH! EGLI E SALVO — *OH, WHAT A JOY* Air. (Don Carlos)

Ah! e-glie sal - vo! oh gio-ja im-men-sa Che m'in - non - di il
Oh, what a joy____ my heart is know-ing That ere long____ my

cor,____ ti sen-to! Po-tro al fi - ne il tra - di-men-to Sull' in-
sword____ shall find him! Soon his blood____ for ven-geance flow-ing, Shall re-

fa - me ven-di - car.   Le - o - no-ra, ove t'a - scon-di? Di': se-
pay____ me for the wrong.   Where, Leo - no - ra, art thou hid - ing? If with

gui-sti tra le squa-dre. Chi del san-gue di tuo pa-dre, Chi del
that vile man thou'rt bid - ing, Who did slay thy a - ged fa - ther, Who did

san-gue di tuo pa-dre. Ti fe il vol-to ros - seg - giar.
slay thy a - ged fa - ther, None can see thee with - out scorn.

Ah, felice appien sarei	Ah, I should be truly happy
Se potesse il brando mio,	If with my own sword,
Amendue d' averno al Dio,	And with the selfsame blow
D' un sol colpo consacrar.	I might send both to realms below.
(Parte rapidamente.)	(Exit.)

SCE A VI. Accampamento Militare presso elletri. Sul davanti a sinistra e una bottega da rigattiere; a destra altra ove si vendono cibi, bevande, frutta. All' ingiro tende militari, baracche di rivenduglioli, ecc. E notte, la scena e deserta. Una Patt glia entra cautamente in scena, esplorando i campo.

SCENE VI. Millitary Encampment, near Velletri. In front is a sutler's booth. To the right, others with food, fruits, bottles. Around are soldiers' tents, huxter's stalls etc. Night. he scene is vacant. The watch-guard enter cautiously, and search the camp

Coro.	**Chorus.**
Compagni, sostiamo,	Comrades, halt !
Il campo esploriamo ;	The camp explore.
Non s' ode rumore,	No sound is heard,
Non brilla un chiarore ;	No light is seen,
In sonno profondo	In sleep profound
Sepolto ognun sta.	Now all repose.
Compagni, inoltriamo.	Comrades, forward !
(Allontonandosi a poco a poco.)	(Go off gradually.)

Fra poco la sveglia
Suonare s' udra.

SCENA VII. Spunta l' alba lentamente. Entra DON ALVARO pensoso.

Alvaro.

Nè gustare m' è dato
Un'.ora di quiete ; affranta è l' alma
Dalla lotta crudel.
Pace ed oblio indarno io chieggo al Cielo.

SCENA VIII. Detto e DON CARLO.

Carlo.

Capitan.

Alvaro.

Chi mi chiama ?

(Avvicinandosi e riconoscendo CARLO gli dice con affetto.)

Voi che sì larghe cure
Mi prodigaste ?

Carlo.

La ferita vostra
Sanata è appieno ?

Alvaro.

Sì.

Carlo.

Forte ?

Alvaro.

Qual prima.

Carlo.

Sosterreste un duello ?

Alvaro.

E con chi mai ?

Carlo.

Nemici non avete ?

Alvaro.

Tutti ne abbian—ma a stento
Comprendo—

Carlo.

No ?—Messaggio non v'inviava
Don Alvaro l' Indiano ?

Alvaro.

Oh tradimento !
Sleale ? il segreto fu dunque violato ?

Ere long the morning call
Will rouse them.

SCENE VII. The day slowly dawns. Enter DON ALVARO, in deep thought.

Alvaro.

Not one hour of rest
Can I enjoy. Tortured is my soul
With the cruel struggle.
Peace and oblivion I ask of Heaven in vain.

SCENE VIII. Enter DON CARLOS.

Carlos.

Captain.

Alvaro.

Who calls me?

(Advancing recognizes CARLOS with gladness.)

Is it you who such great care
Upon me lavished ?

Carlos.

Has your wound
Healed completely ?

Alvaro.

Yes.

Carlos.

Strong ?

Alvaro.

As ever.

Carlos.

Could you fight a duel ?

Alvaro.

And with whom ?

Carlos.

Have you no enemy ?

Alvaro.

All have some—but I hardly
Understand—

Carlos.

No ?—Don Alvaro the Indian,
Did he not send you a message?

Alvaro.

Oh, treachery ! disloyal man?
The secret has been there disclosed ?

Carlo
    Fu illeso quel piego, l' effigie ha parlato ;

    Don Carlo di Vargas, tremate, io sono.

Alvaro.
    D' ardite, minaccie non m' agito al suono.

Carlo.
    Usciamo, all' istante un di noi dee morire.

Alvaro.
    La morte disprezzo, ma duolmi inveire

    Contr' uom che per primo amistade m' offria.

Carlo.
    No, no profanato tal nome non sia.

Alvaro.
    Non io, fu il destino, che il padre v' ha
        ucciso ;
    Non io che sedussi quell' angiol d' amore—
    Ne guardano entrambi, e dal paradiso
    Ch' io sono innocente vi dicono al core—

Carlo.
    Adunque colei ?

Alvaro.
    La notte fatale
    Io caddi per doppia ferita mortale ;
    Guaritone, un anno in traccia ne andai—
    Ahimè, ch' era spenta Leonora trovai.

Carlo.
    Menzogna, menzogna !
    La suora—ospitavala antica parente ;
    Vi giunsi, ma tardi—

Alvaro
          (Con ansia.)
    Ed ella—

Carlo.
    E fuggente.

Alvaro
          (Trasalendo.)
    E vive ! o amico, il fremito
    Ch' ogni mia fibra scuote,
    Vi dica che quest' anima
    Infame esser non puote—
    Vive ! gran Dio, quell' angelo !

Carlos.
    Unopened was the packet, but the por-
        trait spoke ;
    Tremble, for I am Don Calros di Vargas.

Alvaro.
    Threats disturb me not.

Carlos.
    Come, on the instant one of us must die !

Alvaro.
    Death I despise, but it grieves me to
        injure
    Him who first offered me friendship.

Carlos.
    Profane not the word.

Alvaro.
    Not I, but fate, your father slew ;

    I ne'er seduced that lovely angel ;
    Both look on us, and from heaven
    Tell your heart I am innocent.

Carlos.
    And she ?

Alvaro.
    That fatal night I fell,
    Through many mortal wounds ;
    Then, cured, I sought her for a year.
    And found Leonora dead.

Carlos.
    False, false !
    My sister found refuge with a relative ;
    I arrived too late.

Alvaro
          (With anxiety.)
    And she ?

Carlos.
    Has fled.

Alvaro
          (Joyously.)
    She lives ! Ah, my friend.
    The trembling which my frame pervades
    Will tell you that my soul
    Cannot be so debased.
    She lives ! thank God !

Carlo.

  Ma in breve morirà.

Alvaro.

  No, d' un imene il vincolo
  Stringa fra noi la speme ;
  E s'ella vive, insieme
  Cerchiamo ove fuggì.
  Giuro che illustre origine
  Eguale a voi mi rende,
  E che il mio stemma splende
  Come rifulge il dì.

Carlo.

  Stolto ! fra noi dischiudesi
  Insanguinato avello ;
  Come chiamar fratello
  Chi tutto mi rapì ?
  D' eccelsa o vile origine,
  E duopo ch' io vio spegna,
  E dopo voi l' indegna
  Che il sangue suo tradì.

Alvaro.

  Che dite ?

Carlo.

  Ella morrà.

Alvaro.

  Tacete !

Carlo.

  Il giuoro
  A Dio ; cadrà l' infame.

Alvaro.

  Voi pria cadretc nel fatal certame.

Carlo.

  Morte ! ov 'io non cada esangue
  Leonora giungerò.
  Tinto àncor del vostro sangue
  Questo acciar le immergerò.

Alvaro.

  Morte, sì !—col drando mio.
  Un sicario ucciderò ;
  Il pensier volgete a Dio,
  L' ora vostra alfin suonò.

  (Sguainano le spade e si battono furiosamente.)

Carlos.

  But she will shortly die.

Alvaro.

  No, by the fond nuptial tie
  Soon may we be united ;
  If yet she lives, together
  Let us seek her abode.
  I swear that rank as noble
  Even as thine, I own,
  And that my birth is pure,
  Unstained, as light of day.

Carlos.

  Madman ! rising between us
  A river of blood is flowing ;
  How can I call him brother,
  Who did my hopes efface ?
  Whate'er may be thy origin,
  I live but to destroy thee ;
  Then too shall die the unworthy one
  Who did her race betray.

Alvaro.

  What sayest thou ?

Carlos.

  She shall die !

Alvaro.

  Hold !

Carlos.

  I swear to heaven
  The infamous wretch shall die !

Alvaro.

  Thou shalt first die thyself in mortal combat.

Carlos.

  But ere I fall, Leonora shall perish!
  This sword, with your blood dyed red
  Will I plunge into her heart.

Alvaro.

  Die thou ! with my steel
  Will I slay the assassin ;
  Turn your thoughts to heaven,
  For your last hour is nigh.

  (They draw swords and fight furiously.)

SCENA IX. Accore la Pattuglia del campo per separati.)

Coro.

Fermi, arrestate !

Carlo

(Furente.)

No. La sua vita.

Coro.

Lunge di qua si tragga.

Alvaro.

(Forse—del ciel l' aita a me soccorre.)

Carlo.

Colui morrà !

Coro

(A CARLO che cerca svincolarsi.)

Vieni

Carlo.

Carnefice del padre mio !

(A DON ALVARO viene trascinato altrove dalla pattuglia.)

Alvaro.

Or che mi resta ! Pietoso Iddio

Tu inspira, illumina il mio pensier.

(Gettando la spada.)

Al chiostro, all' eremo, ai santi altari

L'obblio, la pace chiegga il guerrier.

(Esce.)

SCENA X. Spunta il sole.—il rullo dei tamburi e lo squillo delle trombe danno il segnale della sveglia. La scena va animandosi a poco a poco. Soldati Spagnuoli ed Italiani di tutte le armi sortono dalle tende ripulendo schioppi, spade, uniformi, ecc., ecc. Ragazzi militari giuocano ai dadi sui tamburi. Vivandiere che vendono liquori, frutta, pane, ecc., PREZIOSILLA dall' alto d' una baracca predice la buona ventura. Scena animatissima.

Coro.

Lorchè pifferi e tamburi

Par che assordino la terra,

Siam felici, ch' è la guerra

Gioja e vita al militar.

Vita gaia, avventurosa,

Cui non cal doman nè jeri,

Ch' ama tutti i suoi pensieri

Sol nell' oggi concentrar.

Preziosilla

(Alle Donne.)

Venìte all' indovina.

Ch' è giunta di lontano,

E puote a voi l' arcano,

SCENE IX. The Sentries of the Camp run to part them

Chorus.

Hold ! stay !

Carlos

(Raging.)

No : his life !

Chorus.

Drag him hence !

Alvaro.

(Heaven has sent me aid.)

Carlos.

He shall die.

Chorus

(To DON CARLOS, who tries to fight him.)

Come away.

Carlos.

Murderer of my father !

(To DON ALVARO, as he is dragged off by the Sentries.)

Alvaro.

What now remains for me ? Merciful Heaven,

A thought from above inspires me.

(Throws down the swor.d)

To the cloister I go and at the holy altar,

Peace and oblivion will the warrior seek.

(Exit.)

SCENE X. Sunrise. The roll of drums and call of trumpets give the signal for waking. The scene gradually becomes full of life. Spanish and Italian soldiers emerge from their tents, cleaning muskets, swords, uniforms, etc. etc. Young recruits play at dice on the drum heads. Vivandiers sell liquors, fruit, bread, etc. PREZIOSILLA, mounted on a stand, tells fortunes. Great animation

Chorus.

When fife and drums

Deafen the world,

We rejoice, for war to the soldier

Is life and full delight.

A life of joy and adventure

To him who cares naught for the morrow;

Who loves in his thoughts to dwell

On the bright hopes of to-day.

Preziosilla

(To the Women.)

Come to the fortune-teller,

Who has come from distant parts ;

She to you can reveal

Futuro   decifrar.

(Ai Soldati.)

Corrette a lei d' intorno,
La mano le porgete.
Le amanti apprenderete
Se fide vi restar.

Coro.

Corriamo all' indovina
La mano le porgiamo,
Le belle udir possiamo
Se fide vi restar.

Preziosilla.

Chi vuole il paradiso
Si accendo di valore,
E il barbaro invasore
S' accenga a debellar.
Avanti, avanti, avanti.
Predirvi sentirete
Qual premio coglierete
Dal vostro battagliar.

(Molti la circondano.)

Coro.

Avanti, ec.

Soldati.

Qua, vivandiere, un sorso.

(La Vivandiere versano loro.)

Uno.

Alla salute nostra !

Tutti

(Bevendo.)

Viva !

Altro.

A' Spagna ! ed all' Italia unite !

Tutti.

Evviva !

Preziosilla.

Al nostro eroe, Don Federico Herreros.

Tutti.

Viva ! Viva !

Uno.

Ed al suo degno amico
Don Felice de Bornos.

Tutti.

Viva ! viva !

What the future will bring.

(To the Soldiers.)

Come around her,
And hold out your hands ;
So all you can learn
If your maidens be true.

Chorus.

Let us haste to the teller of fortunes,
And show her our hands,
Thus we all can learn
If our fair ones are true.

Preziosilla.

He who longs for Paradise
Must show himself brave,
Prepare to subdue
The savage horde of invaders,
Come on, come on, come on,
And you shall hear foretold
What the prize you shall win
In the war that you wage.

(Many surround her.)

Chorus.

Come on, etc.

Soldiers.

Here, vivandiers, give us to drink.

(The vivandiers give them drink.)

A Soldier.

To our own health we drink !

All

(Drinking.)

Hurrah !

Another.

To Spain and Italy united !

All.

Hurrah !

Preziosilla.

To our hero, Don Federico Herreros !

All.

Hurrah ! hurrah !

A Soldier.

And to his noble friend,
Don Felice de Bornos !

All.

Hurrah ! Hurrah !

SCENA XI L' attenzione e attirata da TRABUCO. rivendugliolo, che dalla bottega a sinistra viene con una cassetta al colla portante vari oggetti di meschino valore?.

Trabuco.

A buon mercato chi vuol comprare ?
Forbici, spille, sapon perfetto !
(Lo attorniano.)
Io vendo e compero qualunque oggetto,
Concludo a pronti qualunque affare.

Soldato 1.

Ho qui un monile, quanto mi dai ?
(Lo mostra.)

Soldato 2.

Ve' una collana ? Se vuoi la vendo.
(Lo mostra.)

Soldato 3.

Questi orecchini li pagherai ?
(Lo mostra.)

Coro.

Vogliamo vendere ?
(Mostrando orologi, anelli, ecc.)

Trabuco.

Ma quanto vedo
Tutto è robaccia, brutta robaccia !

Coro.

Tale, o furfante, è la tua faccia.

Trabuco.

Pure aggiustiamoci ; per ogni pezzo
Do trenta soldi.

Tutti
(Tumultuando.)
Da ladro è il prezzo.

Trabuco.

Ih ! quanta furia ! c' intenderemo,
Qualch' altro soldo v' aggiungeremo—
Date qua, subito !

Coro.

Purchè all' istante
Venga il danaro bello e sonante.

Trabuco.

Prima la merce—qua—colle buone.

Soldati.

A te.
(Dandogli gli affetti.)

Altri.

A te.
(Dandogli gli affetti.)

SCENE XI. TRABUCO, the Pedlar, attracts their attention, who, from the shop on the left, comes with a box at his waist, carrying various objects of small value.

Trabuco.

Who will buy at a bargain?
Scissors, pins, scented soap !
(They surround him.)
I buy and sell all sorts of things
And quickly conclude my bargains.

1st Soldier.

Here is a necklace—what will you give ?
(Showing it.)

2nd Soldier.

Here is another—I will sell it.
(Showing it.)

3rd Soldier.

Wilt pay the price of these earrings ?
(Showing them.)

Chorus.

We'll sell ?
(Showing watches, rings, etc.)

Trabuco.

But what you show me
Is all rubbish, mere rubbish !

Chorus.

Just like yourself, you rogue !

Trabuco.

However, we may agree: for each article
I will give thirty soldi.

All
(Enraged.)
'Tis the price of a thief !

Trabuco.

Eh ! what a fuss ! we shall agree,—
Another soldo we will add:
Give them here—quick.!

Chorus.

Provided on the instant
We see the money sound and shining.

Trabuco.

The merchandise first—here—fair play

Soldiers.

There's for thee.
(Giving the things.)

Others.

For thee.
(Giving things.)

Altri.

A te.

(Dandogli gli affetti.)

Trabuco

(Ritira le robe e paga.)

A voi, a voi, benone !

Coro.

Al diavol vattene !

(Cacciandolo.)

Trabuco

(Da se contento.)

(Che buon affare !)

A buon mercato chi vuol comprare ?

(Avviandosi ad altro lato del compo.)

SCENA XII. Detti, e Contadini questuanti, con Ragazzi a mano

Contadini.

Pane, pan per caritò!
Tetti e campi devastati
N' ha la guerra, ed affamati,
Cerchiam pane per pietà.

SCENA XIII. Detti, ed alcuni RECLUTE, piangenti, che giungono scortate.

Reclute.

Povere madri deserte nel pianto !

Per dura forza dovemmo lasciar.
Della beltà n' han rapiti all' incanto,
A' nostre case vogliamo tornar.

Vivandiere

(Accostandosi gaiamente alle RECLUTE. e offerendo loro da bere.)

Non piangete, giovanotti,
Per le madri e per la belle ;
V' ameremo quai sorelle,
Vi sapremo confortar.
Certo il diavolo non siamo ;
Quelle lacrime tergette.
Al passato, ben vedete,
Ora è inutile pensar.

Preziosilla

(Entrando fra le RECLUTE. ne prende alcune pel braccio, e dice loro burlescamente.)

Che vergogna !—Su coraggio !
Bei figliuoli, siete pazzi ?
Sè piangete quai ragazzi,
Vi farete corbellar.

Others.

For thee.

(Giving things.)

Trabuco

(Taking the things and paying.)

To you, to you, very good !

Chorus.

Go to the devil !

(They drive him away.)

Trabuco

(Highly pleased.)

(What good luck !)

Who will buy everything cheap ?

(Goes to the other side of the camp.)

SCENE XII. The same, and PEASANTS begging and leading Children

Peasants.

Bread, for charity's sake !
The war has destroyed
Our homes and our fields ;
Starving we ask for bread !

SCENE XIII. The same, and some RECRUITS, weeping, with an escort.

Recruits.

Our poor mothers are deserted in their grief !

By force we were made to leave,
And from our lovers' arms torn away.
To our homes we wish to return.

Vivandiers

(Approaching gaily the RECRUITS, and offering them drink.)

Do not repine, O young men,
For your mothers and your lovers ;
Like sisters we will love you,
And seek to console you.
Truly fiends we are not,
Then dry your tears
And cease to think
Upon the happy past.

Preziosilla

(Mixing with the RECRUITS, takes some of them by the arm, and says, jeeringly.)

Shame on you !—Show more courage !
Great babies, are you mad ?
If you wail like little children
You will be jeered and hooted.

Un' occhiata a voi d' intorno,
E scommetto che indovino ;
Ci sarà più d' un visino,
Che sapravvi consolar.

Tutti.

Nella guerra è la follia
Che dee il campo rallegrar.
Viva ! viva la pazzia,
Che qui sola ha da regnar !

(Le Vivandiere prendono francamente le RECLUTE pel braccio,
o s' incominica vivacissima danza generale. Ben presto la confusione e lo schiamazzo giungono al como.)

SCENA XIV. Detti e Fra MELITONE, che preso nel vortice
della danza, e per un momento costretto a ballare colle Vivandiere.
Finalmente, riuscito a fermarsi, esclama:

Melitone.

Toh, toh ! poffare il mondo ! oh che tem-
pone !
Corre ben l'aventura !—Anch' io ci sono !
Venni di Spagna a medicar ferite,
Ed alme a medicar. Che vedo ! è questo
Un campo di Christiani, o siete Turchi ?
Dove s' è visto berteggiar la santa
Domenica cosi ? Ben più faccenda

Le *bottiglie* vi dan che le *battaglie* !
E invece di vestir *cenere* e *sacco*
Qui si tresca con *Venere*, con *Bacco* ?
Il mondo è fatto una casa di pianto ;
Ogni convento, o qual profanazione !
Or è *covo del vento* ! I *Santuari*
Spelonche diventàr di sanguinari
E perfino i *tabernacoli di Cristo*
Fatti son *ricettacoli del tristo*.
Tutto è soqquadro.
E la ragion ? pe' vostri
Peccati

Soldati.

Ah, frate ! frate !

Melitone.

Voi le feste
Calpestate, rubate, bestemmiate—

Soldati Italiano.

Togone infame !

Soldato Spag.

Segui pur, padruccio,

Cast your eyes around,
And I'll wager you can find
More than one face here
To console your vain regrets.

All.

In war it is folly only
That makes the camp resound.
Hurrah ! long life to folly.
That alone has a right to reign !

(The Vivandiers boldly sieze the RECRUITS by the arm, and commence a dance all around. Soon the noise and confusion reach
its height.)

SCENE XIV. The same, and BROTHER MELITONE, who,
seized in the whirl of the dance, is obliged to dance with the
Vivandiers. At last, managing to release himself, he exclaims:

Melitone.

Oh, oh ! good heaven ! what a wild life !
Adventures are coming fast !—I am in
for it !
I came from Spain wounds to heal,
And souls to cure. What do I see ?
Is this a camp of Christians or of Turks ?
Where do people make such a mockery
Of the holy Sabbath ? You have more
to do
With bottles than with battles !
And instead of putting on sackcloth and
ashes,
You play tricks with Venus and Bacchus.
The world is made a place of tears ;
Every convent—oh, what profanation—
Is open to the winds. The sanctuaries
Are become dens of murderers !
And, to crown all, the most sainted shrines
Made refugees for rascals.
All is upset ; and wherefore ?
Through your sins.

Soldiers.

Ah, friar ! friar !

Melitone.

You despise the feasts of the Church,
You rob, you swear—

Italian Soldier.

Infernal friar !

Spanish Soldier.

Go on, old fellow.

Melitone.

  E membra e capi siete d' una stampa ;
  Tutti eretici.

Italiano.

  Or or l' aggiustiam noi.

Melitone.

  Tutti, tutti, cloaca di peccati,
  E finchè il mondo puzzi di tal *pece*
  Non isperi mai la terra alcuna *pace*.

Italiano.

  Dàlle, dàlli !
        (Serrandolo intorno)

Spagno
        (Difendendolo.)

  Scappa ! scappa !

Italiano.

  Dàlli, dàlli sulla cappa !

(Cercano picchiarlo, ma egli se la svigna, declamando sempre.)

Preziosilla

  (Ai Soldati che lo inseguono uscendo di scena.)

  Lasciatelo, ch' ei vada.

  Far guerra ad un cappuccio!—bella impresa !

  Non m' odon?—sia il tamburo sua difesa.

(Prende a caso un tamburo, e imitata da qualche Tamburino, lo suona. I Soldati accorrono tosto a circondarla seguiti da tutta la turba.)

Melitone.

  And chiefs and soldiers all of a stamp,
  All heretics.

Italian.

  We will soon settle you.

Melitone.

  All, all, sinks of iniquity ;
  And until the world is smothered with tar,
  The earth cannot hope for peace.

Italian.

  Give it him!
        (Crowding round him)

Spanish
        (Defending him)

  Escape ! be off !

Italian.

  Give it him—knock him on the head !

(They try to beat him, but he avoids them, continuing to exclaim.)

Preziosilla.

  (To the Soldiers, who follow him off the stage.)

  Let him alone, let him go.

  Make war upon a friar !—a fine affair !

  They hear me not—the drum shall defend him.

(Takes up a drum, and, imitated by a little Drummer, sounds it.) The Soldiers immediately surround her, followed by the whole throng.)

RATAPLAN, DELLA GLORIA — *RATAPLAN, SONGS OF GLORY* (Preziosilla and Chorus)

Ra - ta - plan, ra - ta-plan, del - la glo - ria Nel sol - da - to ri -
Ra - ta - plan, ra - ta-plan, songs of glo - ry Make the sol-dier's heart

tem - pra l'ar - dor; Ra - ta - plan, ra - ta-plan, di vit - to - ria Que-sto
thrill with de - light; Ra - ta - plan, ra - ta-plan, in sto - ry All their

suo - no e se - gnal pre-cur - sor! Ra - ta - plan, ra - ta - plan, ra - ta-
val - or - ous deeds we re - cite. Ra - ta - plan, ra - ta - plan, ra - ta -

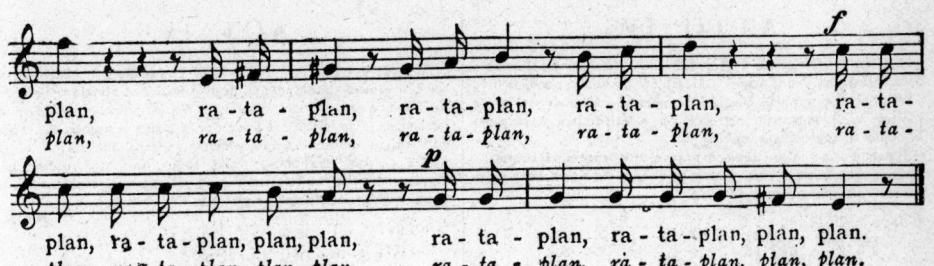

plan,   ra - ta - plan,   ra - ta - plan,   ra - ta - plan,   ra - ta -
plan,   ra - ta - plan,   ra - ta - plan,   ra - ta - plan,   ra - ta -

plan, ra - ta - plan, plan, plan,   ra - ta - plan,   ra - ta - plan, plan, plan.
plan, ra - ta - plan, plan, plan,   ra - ta - plan,   ra - ta - plan, plan, plan.

Rataplan, si raccolgon le schiere,
Rataplan, son guidate a pugnar.
Rataplan, rataplan, le bandiere
Del nemico si veggon piegar !
Rataplan, pim, pum, pam, inseguite
Chi le terga, fuggendo, voltò.
Rataplan, le gloriose ferite
Col trionfo il destin coronò.
Rataplan, della patria la gloria,
Più rifulge de' fili al valor !
Rataplan, rataplan, la vittoria
Al guerriero conquista ogni cor.

FINE DELL' ATTO TERZO.

Rataplan, the troops assemble,
Rataplan, are led to the fight,
Rataplan, rataplan, the banners
Of the enemy give way before us.
Rataplan, pim, pum, pam, pursue
The coward who flees from the foe.
Rataplan, the wounds of the brave
Are with triumph crowned by fate.
Rataplan, the glory of the country
Shines forth in the valor of her sons !
Rataplan, rataplan, victory
Has won each warrior's heart.

END OF THE THIRD ACT.

ATTO IV

SCENA I. Vicinanze d' Hornachuelos. Interno del Convento della Madonna degli Angeli. Meschino porticato circonda una Corticella con aranci, oleandri, gelsomini. Alla sinistra dello spettatore, e la porta che mette alla via; a destra altra porta, sopra la quale si legge 'Clausura.'

Il PADRE GUARDIANO passeggia gravemente leggendo il breviario. Dalla sinistra entrano molt Pezzenti, d' ogni eta e sesso, con rozze scodelle, alla mano pignatte o piatti.

Coro.

> Fate la carità,
> E un' ora che aspettiamo !
> Andarcene dobbiamo;
> Fate la carità.

SCENA II. Detti e FRA MELITONE, che viene dalla destra, caperto il ventre d' ampio grembiale bianco ed ajutato da altro Laico, porta una grande caldaja a due manichi, che depongono nel centro; il Laico riparte.

Melitone.

> Che ! siete all' osteria ! Quieti.

(Incomincia a distribuire col ramaiuolo la ministra.)

Donne
(Spingendosi fra loro.)

> Qui, presto a me.

Vecchi.

> Quante porzioni a loro.

Altri.

> Tutti vorrian per sè.

Tutti.

> N' ebbe già tre Maria.

Una
(A MELITONE.)

> Quattro a me.

Tutti.

> Quattro a lei !

Detti.

> Sì, perchè ho sei figliuolì.

Melitone.

> Perchè ne avete sei ?

Detta.

> Perchè li mandò Iddio.

Melitone.

> Sì, sì, Dio—non li avreste
> Se al par di me voi pure la schiena per-
> coteste
> Con aspra disciplina, e più le notti intere
> Passaste recitando rosari e miserere.

ACT IV

SCENE I. The neighborhood of Hornachuelos. Interior of the Convent of the 'Madonna degli Angeli.' A simple Colonnade surrounds a small Court, filled with orange trees, oleanders, and jessamines. On left of the spectator, a door opening on the road; on the right another door, on which is written 'Clausura.'

The FATHER GUARDIANO walks about, seriously reading his breviary. From the left enter many Beggars, of each sex, with rough porringers, pipklns, or plates in their hands.

Chorus.

> Alms we beg of you.
> An hour we have waited,
> And soon we must go.
> Alms ! Alms !

SCENE II. The above and BROTHER MELITONE, who comes from the right, with a large white apron in front, and, aided by another Lay-brother, carries a great cauldron with two handles, which they place in the middle; the Lay-brother goes away.

Melitone.

> What ! do you take this for an inn ? Be
> silent.

(Begins to distribute the minestra with a ladle.)

Women
(Pushing forward.)

> Quick, give me some.

Old Men.

> What a quantity for them.

Others.

> Each wants for it himself.

All.

> Maria has already had three.

A Woman
(To MELITONE.)

> Four for me.

All.

> Four for her !

Woman.

> Yes, for I have six children.

Melitone.

> Why have you six ?

Woman.

> Because Heaven sent them to me.

Melitone.

> Ay, ay, Heaven—you would not have
> them
> If, like me, you scourged your back
> With a sharp scourge, and spent the night
> In reciting rosaries and misereres.

Guardiano.
Fratel—

Melitone.
Ma tai pezzenti son di fecondità.
Davvero spaventosa.

Guardiano.
Abbiate carità.

Vecchi.
Un po' di quel fondaccio ancora ne donate.

Melitone,
Il ben di Dio, bricconi, fondaccio voi chiamate ?

Alcuni.
A me padre !
        (Presentando le scodelle.)

Altri.
A me.
        (Presentando le scodelle.)

Melitone.
Oh andatene in malora,
O il ramajuol sul capo v' aggiusto bene or ora !
Io perdo la pazienza !

Guardiano.
Oh, carità, fratello !

Donne.
Più carità ne usava il padre Raffaello.

Melitone.
Sì, sì ma in otto giorni, avutone abbastanza.
Di poveri e ministra, restò nella sua stanza.
E scaricò la soma sul dosso a Melitone,
E poi con tal canaglia usar dovrò le buone ?

Guardiano.
Soffrono tanto i poveri : la carità è un dovere.

Melitone.
Carità con costoro che il fanno per mestiere ?
Che un campanile abbattere co' pugni sarien buoni,
Che dicono fondaccio il ben di Dio?
Bricconi!

Alcuni.
Oh, il padre Raffaele—

Guardiano.
Brother—

Melitone.
But these beggars are prolific
To such a wonderful degree.

Guardiano.
Be merciful.

Old Men.
Give us a little more of these dregs.

Melitone.
A godsend, you rogues, and you call it dregs !

Some.
To me, Father !
        (Presenting their porringers.)

Others.
To me?
        (Presenting theirs.)

Melitone.
Go to Jericho,
Or I will lay the ladle about your heads !

I lose all patience !

Guardiano.
Be merciful, brother !

Women.
Father Raffaello was more kind.

Melitone.
True, true, but after a week of soup and beggars
He had enough and took to his bed.
He left his burden on the back of Melitone.
And how can I be gentle with such rabble ?

Guardiano.
They suffer much : charity toward them is a duty.

Melitone.
Charity to those who make it their trade ?
Who could fell a steeple with their fists ?

Who call this godsend dregs ? The rogues !

Some.
Oh, Father Raffaello—

Altri.

Era un angelo.

Altri.

Un santo !

Tutti.

Se il padre Raffaele—

Melitone.

Non m'annojate tanto !

(Distribuisce in fretta il residuo, dicendo—

Il resto, a voi, prendetevi,
Non voglio più parole !

(Fa rotolare la caldaia con un calcio.)

Fuori di qua, lasciatemi,
Sì fuori, al sole, al sole :
Pezzenti più di Lazzaro,
Sacchi di pravità,
Via, via, bricconi, al diavolo !
Toglietevi di qua !

(Indispettito le scaccia, confusamente, percuotendoli col grembiale che si sara tolto, e chiude la porta, restandone assai adirato e stanco.)

SCENA III.   Il PADRE GUARDAINO e MELITONE.

Melitone

(Asciugandosi il sudore con un fazzoletto bianco che avara cavato da una manica.)

Auf ! pazienza non v'ha che basti !

Guardiano.

Troppa
Dal Signor non ne aveste :
Facendo carità un dover s' adempie
Da render fiero un angiol.

Melitone

(Prendendo tabacco.)

Che al mio posto
In tre dì finerebbe
Col ministrar de' schiaffi.

Guardiano.

Tacete ; umil sia Meliton, nè soffra
Se veda preferirsi Raffaele.

Melitone.

Io? no—amico gli son, ma ha certi gesti.
Parla da sè—ha cert' occhi.

Others.

Was an angel !

Others.

A saint !

All.

Yes, Father Raffaello—

Melitone.

Don't bother me so !

(Hastily distributing what remains, saying—)

Take what is left.

(Makes the cauldron roll over with a kick.)

I will have no more words—go ?
Out of here—leave me !
Yes, go and warm yourselves in the sun
Beggars greater than Lazarus.
Bags of depravity,
Go, rascals, go to the devil !
Be off from here !

(He angrily drives them out, striking them with the apron he has taken off, and shuts the door, remaining very angry and tired.)

SCENE III.   FATHER GUARDIANO and MELITONE.

Melitone

(Wiping off the perspiration with a white handkerchief, which he takes from his sleeve.)

Ouf !   I have no more patience !

Guardiano.

Truly Heaven has not
Blessed you with over much ;
Giving charity is fulfilling a duty
Which might rejoice an angel.

Melitone

(Taking snuff.)

Who would be done for in my place
In three days.

Guardiano.

Silence : be humble, Melitone, not be
vexed.
Though Raffaello be preferred.

Melitone.

I? no—I am his friend : but he has such
ways.
He talks to himself—has such looks.

Guardiano.
  Son le preci,
  Il digiun.

Melitone.
  Jer nell' orto lavorava
  Cotanto stralunato, che scherzando,

  Dissi : Padre, un mulatto
  Parmi—Guardommi bieco,
  Strinse le pugna, e—

Guardiano.
  Ebbene ?

Melitone.
  Quando cadde
  Sul campanil la fulgore, ed usciva
  Fra la tempesta gli gridai : Mi sembra
  Indo selvaggio un urlo
  Cacciò che mi gelava.

Guardiano.
  Che v' ha a ridir ?

Melitone.
  Nulla, ma il guardo e penso
  Che il demonio, narraste,
  Qui stette un tempo in abito da frate,
  Gli fosse il padre Raffael parente ?

Guardiano.
  Giudizzii temerarii.   Il ver narrai ;
  Ma n' ebbe il superior revilazione
  Allora.   Io, no.

Melitone.
  Ciò è vero !
  Ma strano è molto il padre !   La ragione ?

Guardiano.
  Del mondo i disinganni,
  L' assidua penitenza.
  Le veglie, l' astinenza
  Quell' anima turbar.

Melitone.
  Saranno i disinganni
  Adunque e l'astinenza.
  L' assidua penitenza,
  Che il capo gli guastar !

    (Si suona con forza il campanello alla porta.)

Guardiano.
  It is through his praying
  And fasting.

Melitone.
  Yesterday, as he worked in the orchard.
  His eyes seemed so starting out, that
    jestingly
  I said, 'Father, you look like a mulatto !'
  He turned an angry glance on me,
  Clenched his fist, and—

Guardiano.
  What then ?

Melitone.
  When the lightning struck the steeple,
  As he went out into the storm, I cried,
  'You look to me like a wild Indian !'
  Whereupon he uttered a howl
  That froze my blood.

Guardiano.
  What followed ?

Melitone.
  Nothing ; but I looked at him, and thought
  That the demon you told us of,
  Who once lived here in a friar's dress,
  Might be a relative of Father Raffaello.

Guardiano.
  A rash judgment.   I told the tale ;
  But to the superior 'twas revealed,
  And not to me.

Melitone.
  That is true ;
  But the father is most strange !   What is
    the cause ?

Guardiano.
  Finding out the deceit of the world,
  Constantly performing penance,
  Vigils and abstinence,
  Have disturbed his mind.

Melitone.
  Discovering the world's deceit,
  The various abstinences,
  And the frequent penances,
  Have upset his brain !

    (The bell at the door is rung violently.)

Guardiano.

   Giunge qualcuno—aprite.

       (Parte.)

SCENA IV.   FRA MELITONE e DON CARLO, che avviluppato in un grande mantello, entra francamente.

Carlo

           (Alteramente.)

   Siete voi il portiere ?

Melitone.

   (E goffo ben costui !)
   S' ora v' apersi, parmi.

Carlo.

   Il padre Raffaele ?

Melitone.

   (Un altro !) Due ne abbiamo ;
   L' un di Porcuna, grasso,
   Sordo come una talpa, l' altro scarno,
   Bruno, occhi (ciel quali occhi !) voi chiedete ?

Carlo.

   Quell dell' inferno.

Melitone.

   (E desso !)   E chi gli annuncio ?

Carlo.

   Un cavalier.

Melitone.

   (Qual boria ! è un mal arnese.)

       (Parte.)

SCENA V.   DON CARLOS, poi DON ALVARO in abito da frate.

Carlo.

   Invano Alvaro ti celasti al mondo

   E d'ipocrita veste
   Scudo fecesti alla viltà.   Del chiostro

   Ove t' ascondi m' additàr la via
   L'odio e la sete di vendetta ; alcuno
   Qui non sarà che ne divida ;
   Solo il tuo sangue può lavar l' oltraggio
   Che macchiò l' onor mio ;
   E tutto il verserò, lo giuro a Dio.

Guardiano.

   Someone has arrived—open.

       (Exit.)

SCENE IV.—FATHER MELITONE, and DON CARLOS, who enter boldly, wrapped in a great cloak.

Carlos

          (Haughtily.)

   Are you the porter ?

Melitone.

   (The man must be a fool !)
   It appears to me I just let you in.

Carlos.

   Father Raffaello ?

Melitone.

   (Another !)   We have two of them ;
   One from Porcuna, fat,
   Deaf as a post ; the other lean, dark eyes,
   (Heavens, what eyes !)   Which do you want ?

Carlos.

   The fiend.

Melitone.

   ('Tis he !)   And whom shall I announce ?

Carlos.

   A cavalier.

Melitone.

   (What arrogance ! an ill-bred fellow.)

       (Exit.)

SCENE V.   DON CARLOS, after him DON ALVARO, in a monk's habit.

Carlos.

   In vain, Alvaro, from the world thou hidest,

   And with hypocrite's garb
   Wouldst shield thy villainy.   To the cloister
   Which concealed thee, hate
   And vengeance pointed out the way.
   None here shall hold me from thee ;
   Thy blood alone can cleanse the stain
   From my outraged honour :
   And before heaven I swear to shed it !

Alvaro.
  Fratello—

Carlo.
  Riconoscimi.

Alvaro.
  Don Carlo ! Voi vivente !

Carlo.
  Da un lustro ne vo' in traccia,
  Ti trovo finalmente :
  Col sangue sol cancellasi
  L' infamia ed il delitto.
  Ch' io ti punisca è scritto
  Sul libro del destin.
  Tu prode fosti, or monaco,
  Un' arma qui non hai ;
  Deggio il tuo sangue spargere,
  Scegli, due ne portai.

Alvaro.
  Vissi nel mondo—intendo ;
  Or queste vesti l' eremo,
  Dicon che i falli ammendo,
  Ah ! cessi il sangue alfin !
  Lasciateme.

Carlo.
  Difendere
  Quel sajo, nè il deserto.
  Codardo, non ti possono.

Alvaro
        (Trasalendo.)
  Codardo ! tale asserto—
        (Poi frenandosi.)
  (Ah no !—assistima, Signore !)
        (A DON CARLO.)
  La minaccie, i fieri accenti,
  Portin seco in preda i venti;
  Perdonatemi, pietà.
  A che offendere cotanto
  Chi fu solo sventurato !
  Deh chiniam la fronte al fato. :
  O fratel, pietà, pietà !

Carlo.
  Tu contamini tal nome.
  Una suora mi lasciasti
  Chi tradita abbandonasti
  All' infamia, al disonor.

Alvaro.
  Brother—

Carlos.
  Behold and know me.

Alvaro.
  Don Carlos ! Alive !

Carlos.
  For five years I have been on thy track,
  At length I find thee :
  With blood alone can thy imfamy
  And misdeeds be blotted out.
  'Tis written in the book of fate
  That I shall punish thee.
  Thou wert then valiant, now a monk ;
  Thou hast no weapon here ;
  As I must shed thy blood,
  Two have I brought : choose.

Alvaro.
  In the world I have lived—I understand ;
  The garments I wear, this desert place,
  Proclaim my errors reformed,
  Ah ! at least cease this strife ;—
  Leave me.

Carlos.
  Coward,
  Neither the cassock, or the desert,
  Can protect thee !

Alvaro
        (Shrinking.)
  Coward ! that assertion—
        (Restraining himself.)
  (Ah no !—help me, Heaven !)
        (To DON CARLOS.)
  Threats, fierce and angry tones
  Are cast to the winds ;
  Pardon and pity me.
  Wherefore goad so far
  Him who was only unfortunate ?
  Let us yield to fate :
  Brother, mercy, mercy !

Carlos.
  Thou dost contaminate the name.
  Thou hast left me a sister
  Whom thou didst betray, and then abandon
  To infamy and dishonour !

Alvaro.

No, non fu disonorata,
Ve lo giura un sacerdote !
Sulla terra l'.ho adorata
Come in cielo amar si puote.
L'amo ancora, e s' ella m' ama
Più non brama questo cor.

Carlo.

Non si placa il mio furore
Per mendace e vile accento ;
L' arme impugna, ed al cimento
Scendi meco, o traditor.

Alvaro.

Se i rimorsi, il pianto omni.
Non vi parlano per me,
Qual nessun mi vide mai,
Io mi prostoro al vostro piè !
        (Eseguisce.)

Carlo.

Ah, la macchia del tuo stemma
Or provasti con quest' atto !

Alvaro
      (Balzando in piedi furente.)

Desso splende piucchè gemma.

Carlo.

Sangue il tinge di mulatto.

Alvaro
      (Non potendo piu frenarsi.)

Per la gola voi mentite !
A me un brando .
      (Glielo strappa di mano.)

Un brando—uscite !

Carlo
      (Avviandosi.)

Finalmente !

Alvaro
      (Ricomponendosi.)

No; l' inferno
Non trionfi. Va—riparti.
      (Getta la spada.)

Carlo.

Ti fai dunque di me scherno ?
S' ora meco misurarti,
O vigliacco, non hai core,
Ti consacro al disonore !
      (Gli da uno schiaffo.)

Alvaro.

No, she was not dishonoured,
It is a priest who swears it !
On earth I have adored her.
As only in Heaven they can love.
I love her still, and if she love me,
My heart has no other wish.

Carlos.

My rage will not be quelled
By base and lying words ;
Take the weapon, and to the combat
I challenge thee, O villain.

Alvaro.

If my remorse and tears
Speak not to you in my favour,
I will do what none have ever seen—
Prostrate myself at your feet !
        (Kneels.)

Carlos.

Ah, the baseness of thy birth
Thou hast now proved by this act !

Alvaro
      (Rising up furiously.)

That is more than jewels resplendent.

Carlos.

It is tinged with the blood of the mulatto

Alvaro
      (No longer able to restrain himself.)

I cast the lie in your teeth !
Give me a sword !
      (Snatches one from his hand.)

A weapon—lead on !

Carlos
      (Moving on.)

Al last !

Alvaro
      (Recovering himself.)

No ; the fiend shall not
Prevail. Go—away !
      (Throws away the sword.)

Carlos.

What, dost thou make a jest of me ?
If to measure weapons with me
Thou hast not courage, coward,
Thus I disgrace thee !
      (Gives him a blow.)

Alvaro

(Furente.)

Ah, seguasti la tua sorte !
Morte a entrambi !

(Raccogliendo la spada.)

Carlo.

A entrambi morte !

A 2.

Paga l' ira alfin sarà.
Te l' inferno ingoierà !

(Escono currendo dalla sinistra.)

SCENA VI. Valle tra rupi inaccessibili, attraversata da un ruscello. Nel fondo, a sinistra dello spetattore, e una Grotta con porta practicabile, e sopra una campana che si potra suonare dall' interno. E il tramonto. La scena si oscura lentamente; la luna apparisce splendidissima.

DONNA LEONORA pallida, sfigurata, esce dalla grotta agitatissima

Leonora.

Pace, pace, mio Dio ! cruda sventura
M' astringe, ahimè, a languir ;

Come il dì primo da tant' anni dura
Profondo il mio soffrir.
L'amai, gli è ver ! ma di beltà e valore
Cotando Iddio l' ornò.
Che l' amo ancor, nè togliermi dal core
L' imagine saprò.
Fatalità ! fatalità !—un delitto
Disgiunti n' ha quaggiù !
Alvaro, io t' amo, e su mel cielo è scritto ;

Non ti vedrò mai più !
Oh, Dio, Dio fa ch' io muoja ; chè la calma
Può darmi morte sol.
Invan la pace qui sperò quest' alma
In preda a lungo duol.

(Va ad un sasso, ove sono alcune provigione deposte da lPADRE GUARDIANO.)

Misero pane, a prolungarmi vieni
La sconsolata vita—ma chi giunge ?
Profanare che ardisce il sacro loco ?
Maledizione ! maledizione !

(Torna rapidamente alla Grotta, e vi si rinchiude)

SCENA VII. Si ode dentro la scena un cozzar di spade.

Carlo

(Dal' interno.)

Io muojo !—Confession !—

Alvaro

(Furiously.)

Thy death warrant is sealed !
Death to both !

(Picks up the sword.)

Carlos.

Death to both !

Both.

Wrong shall at last be avenged,
And hell shall receive thee !

(They rush out towards the left.)

SCENE VI. A valley amongst inaccessible rocks, traversed by a stream. At the back, on the left of the spectator, is a Grotto with a practicable door, and above it a bell, which can be sounded from within. The sun has set. The scene darkens gradually; The moon rises brightiy.

DONNA LEONORA, pale, wan, enters agitated from the grotto.

Leonora.

Peace, grant me peace, O Lord ;
By dire misfortune I'm condemned to
languish ;

As on the first day, during so many years,
Profound has been my grief.
I loved him ! with beauty and courage
Heaven had so endowed him.
I love him still, nor can I from my heart
Banish his image.
O cruel fate !—a crime
Has parted us forever here below !
Alvaro, I love thee, and in heaven 'tis
decreed
That I shall never see thee more !
O Lord, suffer me to die, for peace
To my soul comes only in death.
Here in vain I hope for peace,
A prey to lingering woe.

(She goes to a stone, on which are some provisions, placed there by FATHER GUARDIANO.)

Miserable food, thou comest to prolong
A wretched life—but who approaches ?
Who dares profane this sacred spot ?
Malediction ! malediction !

(Returns quickly to the Grotto and shuts herself in.)

SCENE VII. A clashing of swords is heard close at hand.

Carlos

(Without.)

I am slain !—Absolution !

L'alma salvate.

(ALVARO entra in scena colla spada sguainata.)

E questo ancor sangue d'un Vargas.

Carlo

(Sempre dall' interno.)

Padre.   Confession.

Alvaro

(Getta la spada.)

Maledetto io son ; ma è presso
Un eremita.

(Corre alla grotta e batte alla porto.)

A confortar correte
Un uom che muor.

Leonora

(Dall' interno)

Nol posso.

Alvaro.

Fratello ! in nome del Signor.

Leonora.

Nol posso.

Alvaro

(Batte con piu forza.)

E d' uopo.

Leonora

(Dall' interno suonando la campana.)

Ajuto !   Ajuto !

Alvaro.

Deh venite.

SCENA VIII.   Detto e LEONORA che si presenta sulla porta.

Leonora.

Temerarii, del ciel l' ira fuggite !

Alvaro.

Una donna ! qual voce—ah no—uno
spettro.

Leonora

(Riconoscendo DON ALVARO.)

Che miro ?

Alvaro.

Tu—Leonora !

Leonora.

Egli è ben desso.

(Avvicinandosi ad ALVARO.)

Io ti riveggo ancora.

Save my soul.

(ALVARO enters, with unsheathed sword.)

Again is the blood of Vargas shed.

Carlos

(Still without.)

A priest—absolution.

Alvaro

(Throwing down the sword.)

I am accursed :
But here dwells a hermit.

(Runs to cave, and beats at the door.)

Hasten to aid.
A dying man.

Leonora

(From the cave.)

I cannot.

Alvaro.

Brother, in the name of heaven !

Leonora.

I cannot come.

Alvaro

(Beating furiously.)

His last moments are near.

Leonora

(Ringing the bell in the cave.)

Help ! help !

Alvaro.

Come quickly !

SCENE VIII.   LEONORA appears at the door of the cave.

Leonora.

Rash one, fly from the wrath of heaven !

Alvaro.

A woman ! that voice ! ah, no—'tis a
vision !

Leonora

(Recognizing DON ALVARO.)

What do I see !

Alvaro.

Leonora !

Leonora.

'Tis he.

(Advancing to ALVARO)

Again I see thee !

Alvaro.

Lungi—lungi da me— queste mie mani
Grondano sangue. Indietro !

Leonora.

Che mai parli ?

Alvaro

(Accennando.)

Là giace spento un uom.

Leonora.

Tu l'uccidesti ?

Alvaro.

Tutto tentai per evitar la pugna.
Chiusi i meie dì nel chiostro.

Ei mi raggiunse—m' insultò—l'uccisi.

Leonora.

Ed era ?

Alvaro.

Tuo fratello !

Leonora.

Gran Dio ?

(Corre ansante verso il bosco.)

Alvaro.

Destino avverso
Come a scherno mi prendi !
Vive Leonora e ritrovarla deggio
Or che versai di suo fratello il sangue !

Leonora

(Dall' interno, mette un grido.)

Ah !

Alvaro.

Qual grido !—che avvenne ?

SCENA IX. LEONORA ferita entra sostenuta dal GUARDIANO
e detto.

Alvaro.

Ella—ferita !

Leonora

(Morente.)

Nell' ora estrema perdonar non seppe.
E l'onta vendicò nel sangue mio.

Alvaro.

E tu paga non eri
O vendetta di Dio !—Maledizione !

Alvaro.

Away, away from me, my hands
Are stained with blood.   Look yonder.

Leonora.

What meanest thou ?

Alvaro

(Pointing.)

See, there lies a dying man.

Leonora.

Thou has killed him ?

Alvaro.

Vainly I tried to evade this fray.
Within the cloister's shelter passed my
life !
He sought me out there—insulted me,—
I slew him.

Leonora.

And he was ?

Alvaro.

Thy brother !

Leonora.

Great heaven !

(Runs breathlessly towards the wood.)

Alvaro.

Relentless destiny
Thus mocks me ever !
Leonora lives, and I meet her
With her brother's blood upon me.

Leonora

(Shrieks without.)

Ah !

Alvaro.

That cry ! what has happened.

SCENE IX. LEONORA enters, wounded, supported by GUARD-
IANO.

Alvaro.

'Tis she—wounded !

Leonora

(Dying)

In his last hour he pardoned not ;
And with my blood revenged his shame.

Alvaro.

And thou art thus repaid,
Oh, vengeance of heaven ! malediction !

Guardiano

(Solenne.)

Non imprecare ; umiliati
A lui ch'è giusto e santo—
Che adduce a eterni gaudii
Per una via di pianto.
D'ira e furor sacrilego.
Non profferir parola,
Mentre quest' angiol vola
Al trono del Signor.

Leonora

(Con voce morente.)

Si, piangi— e prega.

Alvaro.

Un reprobe, un maledetto io sono.
Flutto di sangue inalzasi.
Fra noi.

Leonora.

Di Dio il perdono io ti prometto.

Guardiano.

Prostrati !

Leonora.

Alvaro.

Alvaro.

A quell' accento
Più non poss' io resistere.

(Gettandosi ai piedi di LEONORA.)

Leonora, io son redento,
Dal ciel son perdonato !

Leonora e Guardiano.

Sia lode a te Signor.

Leonora.

(Ad ALVARO.)

Lieta or poss' io precederti.
Alla promessa terra.
Là cesserà guerra.
Santo l'amor sarà.

Alvaro.

Tu mi condanni a vivere,
E mi abbandoni intanto !
Il reo, il reo soltanto.
Dunque impunito andrà !

Guardiano

(Solemnly.)

Curse thou not. Humble thyself
Before Him who is just and holy ;
Who by a path of tears
To eternal joys conducts thee.
Pour not forth words.
Of ire and sacrilegious fury.
While this angel ascends
To the heavenly throne.

Leonora

(With dying accents.)

Yes,—weep and pray.

Alvaro.

Reprobate, accursed am I.
Barriers of blood between us
Have arisen.

Leonora.

Heaven grants me power to pardon thee.

Guardiano.

Kneel.

Leonora.

Alvaro—

Alvaro.

Those loved tones
No more can I resist.

(Throwing himself at LEONORA'S feet.)

Leonora, I am saved,
Heaven has forgiven my sins.

Leonora & Guardiano.

Power eternal, praise be to Thy name !

Leonora

(To ALVARO.)

Gladly now can I precede thee
To the promised land ;
There strife shall cease.
And holy love shall reign.

Alvaro.

Thou condemnest me to live
While thus forsaking me ;
I, the guilty one,
Alone go unpunished.

Guardiano.
Santa del suo màrtirio
Ella al Signore ascenda.
E il suo morir ti apprenda
La fede e la pieta !

Leonora.
O Ciel ti attendo, addio !
Io ti precedo Alvaro.

Alvaro.
Morta !

Guardiano.
Salita a Dio.
(Cala lentamente la tela.)

FINE DELL' OPERA.

Guardiano.
Holy in her martyrdom,
She now departs to heaven ;
And piety and faith
Her death will teach thee.

Leonora.
Oh, heaven, I await thee ; farewell,
I do but precede thee, Alvaro.

Alvaro.
Dead !

Guardiano.
Ascended to heaven !
(Curtain slowly falls.)

END OF THE OPERA.

AÏDA

by

GIUSEPPE VERDI

LIBRETTO BY ANTONIO GHISLANZONI

THE STORY OF THE ACTION

Aïda, daughter of Amonasro, King of Ethiopia, has been led into captivity by the Egyptians. While in bondage she conceives a tender passion for Radames, a young Egyptian warrior, who warmly responds to her affection. The opening incidents of the opera disclose these facts, and set forth, besides, the choice of Radames as leader of an expedition against the invading forces of Ethiopia, and the love, still unrevealed, of Amneris, daughter of Egypt's sovereign, for the fortune-favored chieftain. Amneris suspects the existence of a rival, but does not learn the truth until Radames returns victorious. The second act commences with a scene between the Princess and the slave. Amneris wrests from Aïda the secret she longs and yet dreads to fathom, and dire hate at once possesses her. Radames comes back, laden with spoils. Among his prisoners—his rank being unknown to his captors—is Amonasro, father of Aïda. Radames asks of his sovereign that the captives be freed. The King consents to releasing all of them except Aïda and Amonasro. The monarch then bestows upon the unwilling Radames the hand of Amneris, and amid songs of jubilation the act terminates. In the third act the marriage of Amneris and Radames is on the eve of celebration. Radames, however, is devotedly attached to Aïda, and the maiden, urged thereunto by Amonasro, seeks to persuade the soldier to flee to Ethiopia and turn his sword against his native land. Without resolving upon the act of treachery, Radames lends an ear to her supplications. The party is about to take to flight, when the High Priest, Ramphis, and Amneris, both of whom have overheard the lovers, appear. Aïda and Amonasro, on the advice of Radames, escape. Radames remains to await his fate. This is speedily decided. Radames, in act the fourth, is tried on a charge of treason. Amneris, repentant, vainly endeavors to save his life,—for the lover of Aïda scorns to renounce her,—and he is deaf to the entreaties of the daughter of the King, whose jealousy, as Amneris herself is aware, has brought about his downfall. The dénouement is not long delayed. The final picture shows the interior of the Temple of Vulcan. Above is the hall of worship; below, the vault in which Radames, doomed to die, is interred alive by the priests. As the stone is sealed over his head, Aïda, who has awaited Radames in the tomb, rises before him. The lovers are locked in a last embrace as Amneris, heart-broken, kneels in prayer on the marble which parts from the living the couple now united in death.

AÏDA

ACT I.

SCENE I.—Hall in the Palace of the King at Memphis; to the right and left a colonnade with statues and flowering shrubs; at the back a grand gate, from which may be seen the temples and palaces of Memphis and the Pyramids.

(RADAMES and RAMPHIS.)

Ramphis.

Yes, a report runs that the Ethiopian dares
Again defy us, and the Valley of the Nile
And Thebes to threaten.—A messenger
  shortly
Will bring the truth.

Radames.

The sacred Isis
Didst thou consult?

Ramphis.

She has named
Of the Egyptian phalanxes
The supreme leader.

Radames.

Oh! happy man!

Ramphis

(with meaning, gazing at RADAMES).

Young and brave is he. Now to the king
I convey the decrees of the goddess.
(Exit.)

Radames

(alone).

If that warrior I were! If my dream
Should be verified! An army of brave men
Led by me—victory—the applause
Of all Memphis! And to thee, my sweet
  Aïda,
To return, crowned with laurels!
To say to thee,—for thee I have fought, and
  for thee conquered!

ATTO I.

SCENA I.—Sala nel Palazza del Re a Menfi. A destra e a sinistra una colonnata con statue e arbusti in flori—Grande porta nel fondo, de cui appariccone i tempii, i palazzi d Menfi e le Piramidi.

(RADAMES e RAMFIS.)

Ramfis.

Sì: corre voce che l'Etiope ardisca
Sfidarci ancora, e del Nilo la valle
E Tebe minacciar—Fra breve un messo
Recherà il ver.

Radames.

La sacra
Iside consultasti?

Ramfis.

Ella ha nomato
Delle Egizie falangi
El condottier supremo.

Radames.

Oh lui felice!

Ramfis

(con intenzione, fissando RADAMES).

Giovine e prode è desso—Ora, del Nume
Reco i decreti al Re.
(Esce.)

Radames

(solo).

Se quel guerrier
Io fossi! se il mio sogno
Si avverasse!... Un esercito di prodi
Da me guidato... e la vittoria... e il plauso
Di Menfi tutta!—E a te, mia dolce Aïda,
Tornar di lauri cinto...
Dirti: per te ho pugnato e per te ho vinto!

CELESTE AÏDA—*RADIANT AÏDA*   Air (Radames)

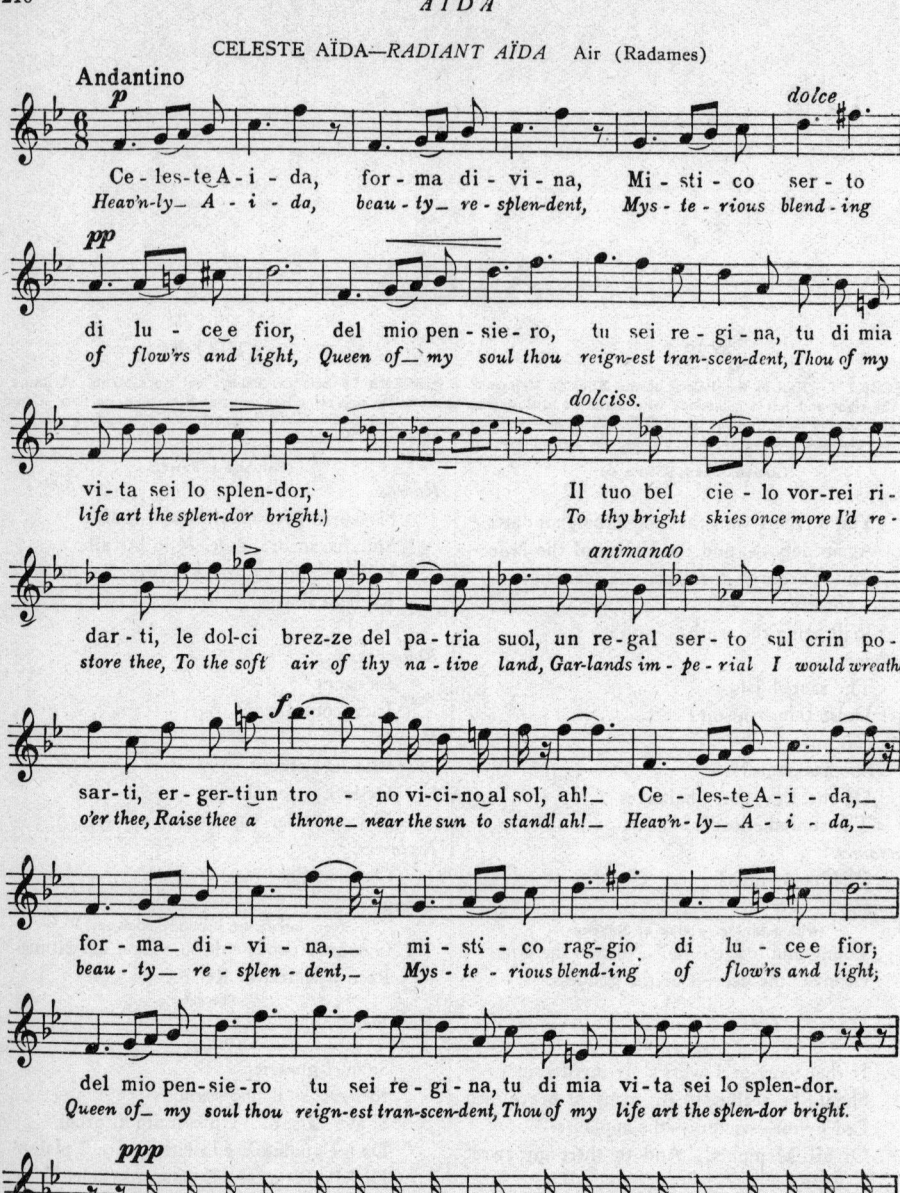

Ce - les-te A - i - da,   for - ma di - vi - na,   Mi - sti - co ser - to
Heav'n-ly A - i - da,   beau - ty   re - splen-dent,   Mys - te - rious blend - ing

di lu - ce e fior,   del mio pen - sie - ro,   tu sei re - gi - na, tu di mia
of flow'rs and light,   Queen of my   soul thou   reign-est tran-scen-dent, Thou of my

vi - ta sei lo splen-dor,   Il tuo bel   cie - lo vor-rei ri -
life art the splen-dor bright.)   To thy bright   skies once more I'd re -

dar - ti, le dol - ci brez - ze del pa - tria suol, un re - gal ser - to   sul crin po -
store thee, To the soft   air of thy na - tive   land, Gar-lands im - pe - rial   I would wreathe

sar - ti, er - ger-ti un tro - no vi-ci-no al sol, ah!   Ce - les-te A - i - da,—
o'er thee, Raise thee a   throne near the sun to stand! ah!   Heav'n-ly A - i - da,—

for - ma   di - vi - na,—   mi - sti - co rag - gio   di   lu - ce e fior;
beau - ty   re - splen - dent,—   Mys - te - rious blend-ing   of   flow'rs and light;

del mio pen - sie - ro   tu sei re - gi - na, tu di mia vi - ta sei lo splen-dor.
Queen of my   soul thou   reign-est tran-scen-dent, Thou of my   life art the splen-dor bright.

Il tuo bel cie - lo vor-rei ri - dar - ti; le dol - ci brez - ze del pa-tria
To thy bright skies once more I'd re - store thee, To the soft air of thy na-tive

suol; un re - gal ser - to sul crin po - sar - ti, er - ger - ti un tro - no vi - ci - no al
land, Gar-lands im - pe - rial I would wreathe o'er thee, Raise thee a throne e - ter - nal to

sol, un tro - no vi - ci - no al sol, un tro - no vi - ci - no al sol. ___
stand, A throne near the sun to stand, A throne near the sun to stand ___

Amneris. (Enter AMNERIS.)	**Amneris.** (AMNERIS e detto.)
What unwonted fire in thy glance!	Quale insolita givia
With what noble pride glows thy face.	Nel tuo sguardo! Di quale
Worthy of envy—oh, how much—	Nobil fierezza ti balena il volto!
Would be the woman whose beloved aspect	Degna di invidia oh! quanto
Should awaken in thee this light of joy!	Saria la donna il cui bramato aspetto
	Tanta luce di gaudio in te destasse!
Radames.	**Radames.**
With an adventurous dream	D'un sogno avventuroso
My heart was blessed. To-day the goddess	Si beava il mio cuore—Oggi, la diva
Declared the name of the warrior who to the field	Profferse il nome del guerrier che al campo
	Le schiere Egizie condurrà... S'io fossi
The Egyptian troops shall lead. If I were	A tale onor prescelto...
To such honor destined!	
Amneris.	**Amneris.**
Has not another dream	Nè un altro sogno mai
More gentle, more sweet,	Più gentil... più soave...
Spoken to thy heart? Hast thou not in Memphis	Al cuore ti parlò?... Non hai tu in Menfi
Desires—hopes?	Desiderii... speranze?
Radames.	**Radames.**
I! (What a question!	Io!... (quale inchiesta!)
Perhaps—the hidden love	Forse... l'arcano amore
Which burns my heart she has discovered—	Scoprì che m' arde in core...
The name of her slave	Della sua schiava il nome
She reads in my thoughts!)	Mi lesse nel pensier!)
Amneris.	**Amneris.**
(Oh! woe if another love	(Oh! guai se un altro amore
Should burn in his heart;	Ardesse a lui nel core!...
Woe, if my search should penetrate	Guai se il mio sguardo penetra
This fatal mystery!)	Questo fatal mister!)
(Enter AÏDA.)	(AÏDA e detto.)
Radames (seeing AÏDA).	**Radames** (vedendo AÏDA).
She!	Dessa!

Amneris.

    (He is moved! And what
A glance he turns to her!
Aïda!—My rival—
Perhaps is she?)
     (After a short silence turning to AÏDA.)

Amneris.

    (Ei si turba... e quale
Sguardo rivolse a lei!
Aïda!... a me rivale...
Forse saria costei?)
     (Dopo breve silenzio volgendois ad AÏDA.)

VIENI, O DILETTA—*COME, DEAREST FRIEND* Trio (Amneris, Aïda and Radames)

Andante mosso   AMNERIS

Vie _ ni o di - let - ta ap-pres-sa-ti   schia - va non sei ne an-
Come, dear-est friend, come near to me,   *Slave _ I no long-er*

cel - la,   Qui _ do-ve in dol - ce   fa - sci-no   Io ti chia-mai so -
name _ thee;   *Here _ in af-fec-tion's ten- der bonds,*   *My sis-ter I pro-*

rel - la   Pian - gi?   del-le tue   la - cri-me sve - la il se -
claim thee,   *Weep'st thou?*   *Why are these   tears flow-ing, tell   me thy*

AÏDA *Più mosso*

gre - to, _ sve-la il se - gre-to a me. Ohi-mè!   di guer-ra fre - me-re   l'a-
se - cret, _ thy se-cret tell to me. A-las!   the din of strife re-sounds,   The

tro - ce gri-do io sen - to   Per l'in-fe-li - ce pa-tri-a,   per me,   per voi pa-
war-like hosts as - sem-ble,   For my un-hap-py na-tive land,   For me,   for thee, I

AMN

ven - to.   Fa-vel-li il ver?   nè s'a-gi-ta   più gra-ve cu-ra in te?
trem - ble.   *Dost tru-ly speak?*   *no grav-er care dis-turbs thy gen-tle heart?*

Allegro   RADAMES

Tre-ma,   o re - a schia-va,   Nel vel-
Trem-ble,   *O slave dis-sem-bling!*   *Up - on _*

ra- to a-mor è___ pian-to di___ sven-tu- ra - - - to a-mor.
hap- py smart, Are flow-ing from love's un- hap - - - py smart!

(Enter the KING, preceded by his Guards and followed by RAMPHIS, his Ministers, Priests, Captains, etc., etc. An Officer of the Palace, and afterwards a Messenger.)

King.

Great cause summons you,
O faithful Egyptians, around your king.
From the confines of Ethiopia a Messenger
Just now arrived—grave news he brings.
Be pleased to hear him.

(To an Officer.)

Let the messenger come forward.

Messenger.

The sacred soil of Egypt is invaded
By the barbarous Ethiopians! Our fields
Are devastated! The crops burned!
And emboldened by the easy victory, the depredators
Already march on Thebes.

All.

They dare so much!

Messenger.

A warrior indomitable and fierce
Conducts them—Amonasro.

All.

The King!

Aïda.

(My father!)

Messenger.

Already Thebes is in arms, and from the hundred gates
Breaks forth upon the invading barbarian,
Carrying war and death.

King.

Yes, be war and death our cry!

All.

War! War!

King.

Tremendous! inexorable!

(Addressing RADAMES.)

Of our unconquered legions
Venerated Isis

(Il Re, preceduto dalle sue guardie e seguito da RAMFIS, da Ministri, Sacerdoti, Capitani, ecc., ecc. Un Uffiziale di Palazzo, indi un Messaggiero.)

Il Re.

Alta cagion vi aduna,
O fidi Egizii, al vostro Re d'intorno.
Dal confin d'Etiópia un Messaggiero
Dianzi giungea—gravi novelle ei reca...
Vi piaccia udirlo...

(Ad un Ufficiale.)

Il Messaggier si avanzi!

Messaggiero.

Il sacro suolo dell' Egitto è invaso
Dai barbari Etiope—i nostri campi
Fur devastati... arse le messi... e baldi
Della facil vittoria, i predatori
Già marciano su Tebe...

Tutti.

Ed osan tanto!

Messaggiero.

Un guerriero indomabile, feroce,
Li conduce—Amonasro.

Tutti.

Il Re!

Aïda.

(Mio padre!)

Messaggiero.

Già Tebe è in armi e dalle cento porte
Sul barbaro invasore
Proromperà, guerra recando e morte.

Il Re.

Si: guerra e morte il nostro grido sia.

Tutti.

Guerra! guerra!

Il Re.

Tramenda, inesorata...

(Accostandosi a RADAMES.)

Iside venerata
Di nostre schiere invitte

Has already designated the supreme leader—
   Radames.

All.

   Radames!

Radames.

   Thanks be to the gods!
   My prayers are answered.

Amneris:

   (He leader!)

Aïda.

   (I tremble!)

King.

   Now move, O warrior,
   To the temple of Vulcan. Gird thee
   With the sacred arms, and fly to victory.
   Up! To the sacred bank of the Nile
   Hasten, Egyptian heroes;
   From every heart let burst the cry,
   War and death to the foreigner!

Ramphis and Priests.

   Glory to the gods! Remember all
   That they rule events;
   That in the power of the gods alone
   Lies the fate of warriors.

Ministers and Captains.

   Up! Of the Nile's sacred shore
   Be our breasts the barrier;
   Let but one cry resound:
   War and death to the foreigner!

Radames.

   Holy rage of glory
   Fills all my soul.
   Up! Let us rush to victory:
   War and death to the foreigner!

Amneris
   (bringing a banner and consigning it to RADAMES).
   From my hand receive, O leader,
   The glorious standard.
   Be it thy guide, be it thy light,
   On the path of glory.

Aïda.

   (For whom do I weep? For whom pray?
   What power binds me to him!
   I must love him! And this man
   Is an enemy—an alien!)

Già designava il condottier supremo:
   Radames.

Tutti.

   Radames.

Radames.

   Sien grazie ai Numi!
   I miei voti fur paghi.

Amneris.

   (Ei duce!)

Aïda.

   (Io tremo!)

Il Re.

   Or, di Vulcano al tempio
   Muovi, o guerrier—Le sacre
   Armi ti cingi e alla vittoria vola.
   Su! del Nilo al sacro lido
   Accorrete, Egizii eroi;
   Da ogni cor prorompa il grido.
   Guerra e morte allo stranier!

Ramfis e Sacerdoti.

   Gloria ai Numi! ognun rammenti
   Ch'essi reggono gli eventi—
   Che in poter d'e Numi solo
   Stan le sorti guerrier.

Ministri e Capitani.

   Su! del Nilo al sacro lido
   Sien barriera i nostri petti;
   Non echeggi che un sol grido:
   Guerra e morte allo stranier!

Radames.

   Sacro fremito di gloria
   Tutta l'anima mi investe—
   Su! corriamo alla vittoria!
   Guerra e morte allo stranier!

Amneris
   (recando una bandiera e consegnandota a RADAMES).
   Di mia man ricevi, o duce,
   Il vessillo glorioso;
   Ti sia guida, ti sia luce
   Della gloria sul sentier.

Aïda.

   (Per chi piango? per chi prego?...
   Qual poter m'avvince a lui!
   Deggio amarlo... ed è costui
   Un nemico... uno stranier!)

Ill.

War! War! Extermination to the invader!
Go, Radames, return conqueror!

(Exeunt all but AïDA.)

Aida.

Return victorious! And from thy lips
Went forth the impious word! Conqueror
Of my father—of him who takes arms
For me—to give me again
A country, a kingdom; and the illustrious
    name
Which here I am forced to conceal! Con-
    queror
Of my brothers, with whose dear blood
I see him stained, triumphant in the ap-
    plause
Of the Egyptian hosts; and behind the
    chariot
A king!—my father—bound with chains!
The insane word
Forget, O gods!
Return the daughter
To the bosom of her father;
Destroy the squadrons
Of our oppressors!
Unhappy one! What did I say?—And my
    love
Can I ever forget,
This fervid love which oppresses and en-
    slaves,
As the sun's ray which now blesses me?
Shall I call death
On Radames?—On him whom I love so
    much?
Ah! Never on earth was heart torn
By more cruel agonies.
The sacred names of father, of lover,
I can neither utter, nor remember—
For the one—for the other—confused—
    trembling—
I would weep—I would pray;
But my prayer changes to blasphemy.
My tears are a crime—my sighs a wrong—
In dense night the mind is lost—
And in the cruel anguish I would die.

Tutti.

Guerra! guerra! sterminio all' invasor!
Va, Radames, ritorna vincitor!

(Escono tutti meno AïDA.)

Aida.

Ritorna vincitor!... E dal mio labbro
Uscì liempi parola!—Vincitore
Del padre mio... di lui che impugna l'armi
Per me... per ridonarmi
Una patria, una reggia! e il nome illustre
Che qui celar mie è forza—Vircitore
De' miei fratelli... ond' io lol vegga, tinto
Del sangue amato, trionfar nel plauso
Dell' Egizie coorti!... E dietro il carro,
Un Re... mio padre... di catene avvinto!...

L'insana parola,
O Numi, sperdete!
Al seno d'un padre
La figlia rendete;
Struggete le squadre
Dei nostri oppressor!
Sventurata! che dissi?... e l'amor mio?..
Dunque scordar poss' io
Questo fervido amor che oppressa e schiava
Come raggio di sol qui mi beava?
Imprecherò la morte
A Radames... a lui che amo pur tanto!
Ah! non fu in terra mai
Da più crudeli angoscie un core affranto.
I sacri nomi di padre... di amante
Nè profferir poss' Io, nè ricordar...
Per l'un... per l'altro... confusa... tremante...
Io piangere vorrei... vorrei pregar.
Ma la mia prece inbestemmia si muta...
Delitto è il pianto a me... colna il sospir...
In notte cupa la mente è perduta...
E nell' ansia crudel vorrei morir.

NUMI, PIETÀ!—*PITY, KIND HEAVEN* Air (Aïda)

Cantabile

Nu - mi, pie - tà— Del mio sof - frir! Spe - me__ non v'ha pel mio do -
Pi - ty, kind Heav'n, To Thee I fly; Hope there is none in this my

lor. A - mor fa - tal, Tre - men-do a - mor Spez - za__ mi il
woe. Oh! fa - tal love, Thy pow'r I know, Break thou, my

poco string.

cor,___ fam - mi mo - rir! Nu - mi,__ pie - tà del mio__ sof -
heart,___ cause me to die. Pi - ty,__ kind Heav'n, Thy pow'r I

frir, Ah!__ pie - tà, Nu - mi, pie - tà,__ del mio__ sof - frir,__ Nu - mi, pie -
know. Oh,__ kind Heav'n, pi - ty my woe, Thy mer - cy show,__ pi - ty, kind

pp

tà del mio__ sof - frir, pie - tà, pie - tà, del mio sof - frir
Heav'n, re - lieve__ my__ woe: re - lieve my woe, re - lieve my woe.

SCENE II.—Interior of the Temple of Vulcan at Memphis. A mysterious light descends from above; a long row of columns one behind another is lost in the darkness; Statues of various deities; in the middle of the scene, above a platform covered with carpet, rises the altar, surmounted by sacred emblems; from golden tripods rises the smoke of incense.

PRIESTS and PRIESTESSES—RAMPHIS at the foot of the altar, afterwards RADAMES—The song of the PRIESTESSES accompanied by harps, is heard from the interior.

Priestesses   (in the interior).

Infinite Phthah, of the world
Animating spirit,
We invoke thee!

Infinite Phthah, of the world
The fructifying spirit,
We invoke thee!

SCENA II.—Interno del Tempio di Vulcano a Menfi. Una luce misteriosa scende dal' alto.—Uno lunga fila di colonne l'una all' altra addossate, si perde fra le tenebre. Statue di varie Divinità. Nel mezzo della scena, sovra un palco coperto da tappeti, sorge l'altare sormontato da emblemi sacri. Dai tripedi d'oro si innalza il fumo degli incensi.

SACERDOTI e SACERDOTESSE—RAMFIS ai piedi dell' altare—A suo tempo, RADAMES—Si sente dall' interno il canto delle SACERDOTESSE accompagnato dalle arpe.

Sacerdotesse   (nell' interno).

Immenso Fthà, del mondo
Spirito animator,
Noi ti invochiamo!

Immenso Fthà, del mondo
Spirito fecondator,
Noi ti invochiamo!

Fire uncreate, eternal,
Whence the sun has light,
We invoke thee!

Priests.

Thou who from nothing hast made
The waters, the earth and the heavens,
We invoke thee!

God, who of thy spirit
Art son and father,
We invoke thee!

Life of the Universe
Gift of eternal love,
We invoke thee.

(Enter RADAMES, introduced unarmed—While he goes to the altar the PRIESTESSES execute the sacred dance—On the head of RADAMES is placed a silver veil.)

Ramphis.

Mortal, beloved of the gods, to thee
Is confided the fate of Egypt. Let the holy sword
Tempered by the gods, in thy hand become
To the enemy, terror—a thunderbolt—death.

(Turning himself to the gods.)

God, guardian and avenger
Of this sacred land,
Spread thy hand
Over the Egyptian soil.

Radames.

God, who art leader and arbiter
Of every human war,
Protect thou and defend
The sacred soil of Egypt.

(While RADAMES is being invested with the consecrated armor, the PRIESTS and PRIESTESSES resume the religious hymn and mystic dance.)

END OF THE FIRST ACT.

Fuoco increato, eterno,
Onde ebbe luce il sol,
Noi ti invochiamo!

Sacerdoti.

Tu che dal nulla hai tratto
L'onde, la terra e il ciel,
Noi ti invochiamo!

Nume che del tuo spirito
Sei figlio e genitor,
Noi ti invochiamo!

Vita dell' Universo,
Mito di eterno amor,
Noi ti invochiamo!

(RADAMES viene introdotto senz' armi—Montre va all' altare, le SACERDOTESSE eseguiscono la danza sacra—Sul capo di RADAMES vien steso un velo d'argento.)

Ramfis.

Mortal, diletto ai Numi—A te fidate
Son d'Egitto le sorti,—Il sacro brando
Dal Dio temprato, per tua man diventi
Ai nemici terror, folgore, morte.

(Volgendozi al Nume.)

Nume, custode e vindice
Di questa sacra terra,
La mano tua distendi
Sovra l'Egizio suol.

Radames.

Nume, che duce ed arbitro
Sei d'ogni umana guerra,
Proteggi tu, difendi
D'Egitto il sacro suol!

(Mentre RADAMES viene investito delle armi sacre, le SACERDOTESSE e SACERDOTI riprendono l'inno religioso e la mistica danza.)

FINE DELL' ATTO PRIMO.

ACT II.

SCENE I.

A Hall in the Apartments of AMNERIS.

AMNERIS surrounded by female SLAVES, who are adorning her for the triumphal festival. From tripods arise aromatic perfumes. Moorish Slave Boys dancing and agitating feather fans.

Slave Girls.

Thou who amidst hymns and plaudits
Raisest thy flight to glory
Terrible even as a god!
Effulgent as the sun,
Come, on thy tresses rain
Laurels and flowers interwoven;
Let sound the songs of glory
With the songs of love.

Amneris.

(Come, my love, intoxicate me;
Make my heart blessed!)

Slave Girls.

Now where are the barbarian
Hordes of the foreigner?
Like a mist they scatter
At the breath of the warrior.
Come: gather the reward
Of glory, O conqueror;
Victory smiled upon thee—
Love shall smile upon thee.

Amneris.

(Come, my love, revive me
Again with thy dear voice!)
Silence! Aïda approaches us;
Daughter of the vanquished, her grief to me
is sacred.

(At a sign from AMNERIS all withdraw to a distance.)

In seeing her again, the fearful doubt
Awakens itself within me.
Let the fatal mystery be at last rent.

(Enter AÏDA.)

Amneris

(to AÏDA, with feigned affection).

The fate of arms was deadly to thy people,
Poor Aïda. The grief
Which weighs down thy heart I share with
thee.
I am thy friend:
Thou shalt have all from me—thou shalt live
happy.

ATTO II.

SCENA I.

Una Sala nell' Appartmento di AMNERIS.

AMNERIS circondata dalle SCHIAVE che li abbigliano per la festa trionfale. Dai tripodi si eleva il profumo degli aromi. Giovani schiavi mori denzando agitano i ventagli di piume.

Schiave.

Chi mai fra gli inni e i plausi
Erge alla gloria il vol,
Al par di un Dio terribile,
Fulgente al par del sol?
Vieni; sul crin ti piovano
Conteste ai lauri i fior;
Suonin di gloria i cantici
Coi cantici d'amor

Amneris.

(Vieni, amor mio, mi inebria...
Fammi beato il cor!)

Schiave.

Or, dove son le barbare
Orde dello stranier?
Siccome nebbia sparvero
Al soffio del guerrier.
Vieni: di gloria il premio
Raccogli, o vincitor;
T'arrise la vittoria,
T'arriderà l'amor.

Amneris.

(Vieni, amor mio, ravvivami
D'un caro accento ancor!)
Silenzio! Aïda verso noi si avanza...
Figlia dei vinti, il suo dolor mi è sacro.

(Ad un cenno di AMNERIS tutti allontanano.)

Nel rivederla, il dubbio
Atroce in me si desta...
Il mistero fatal si squarci alfine!

(AMNERIS ed AÏDA.)

Amneris

(ad AÏDA con simulata amorevolezza).

Fu la sorte dell' armi a' tuoi funesta,
Povera Aïda!—Il lutto
Che ti pesa sul cor teco divido.
Io son l'amica tua...
Tutto da me tu avrai—vivrai felice!

Aïda.

Can I be happy,
Far from my native land; here where un-
known
To me is the fate of father and brothers?

Amneris.

Deeply do I pity thee! Nevertheless they
have an end,
The ills of this world. Time will heal
The anguish of thy heart.
And more than time—a powerful god—love.

Aïda.

Felice esser poss' io
Lungi dal suol natio... qui dove ignota
M'è la sorte del padre e dei fratelli?

Amneris.

Ben ti compiango; pure hanno un confine
I mali di quaggiù... Sanerà il tempo
Le angosce del tuo core...
E più che il tempo, un Dio possente...
Amore.

AMORE, AMORE!—*O LOVE IMMORTAL!* Duet (Aïda and Amneris)

ri - so mi — schiu-de_il ciel,_____ Ne' tuoi do - lo - ri la vi - ta_io
rap - ture thy — smiles dis - close,_____ As in thy tri - als new life I

D'in - ter - ro - gar - la qua-si_hò sgo-men - to,
Her will I ques - tion — feign - ing com - mo - tion,

sen - to un tuo sor - ri - so mi schiu-de_il ciel.
bor - row, A heav'n of rap-ture thy smiles dis - close.

Di - vi - do l'an - sie del su - - o ter - ror.
As if her trou - ble to share_____ or re - move.

AMNERIS

Eb - ben qual nuo - vo fer - mi - to t'as - sai, gen - til A - ï - da?
What new a - larm dis - turbs thee now, my gen - tle friend, A - ï - da?

I tuoi se - gre - ti sve - la - mi, al - l'a - mor mi - o, al - l'a-mor mio t'af -
Thy se - cret thoughts un - veil to me, trust my — af - fec - tion, to my fond love con -

fi - da, Trai for - ti che pu - gna - ro - no del - la tua pa-tria_a dan - ne, quel -
fide thee! A - mong the braves who fought so well, lost in their coun - try's ser - vice, Has

AIDA

cu - no un dol - ce_af - fan - no for - se a te_in cor de - stò? Che
some one a ten - der sor - row hap - ly wak - en'd in your heart? What

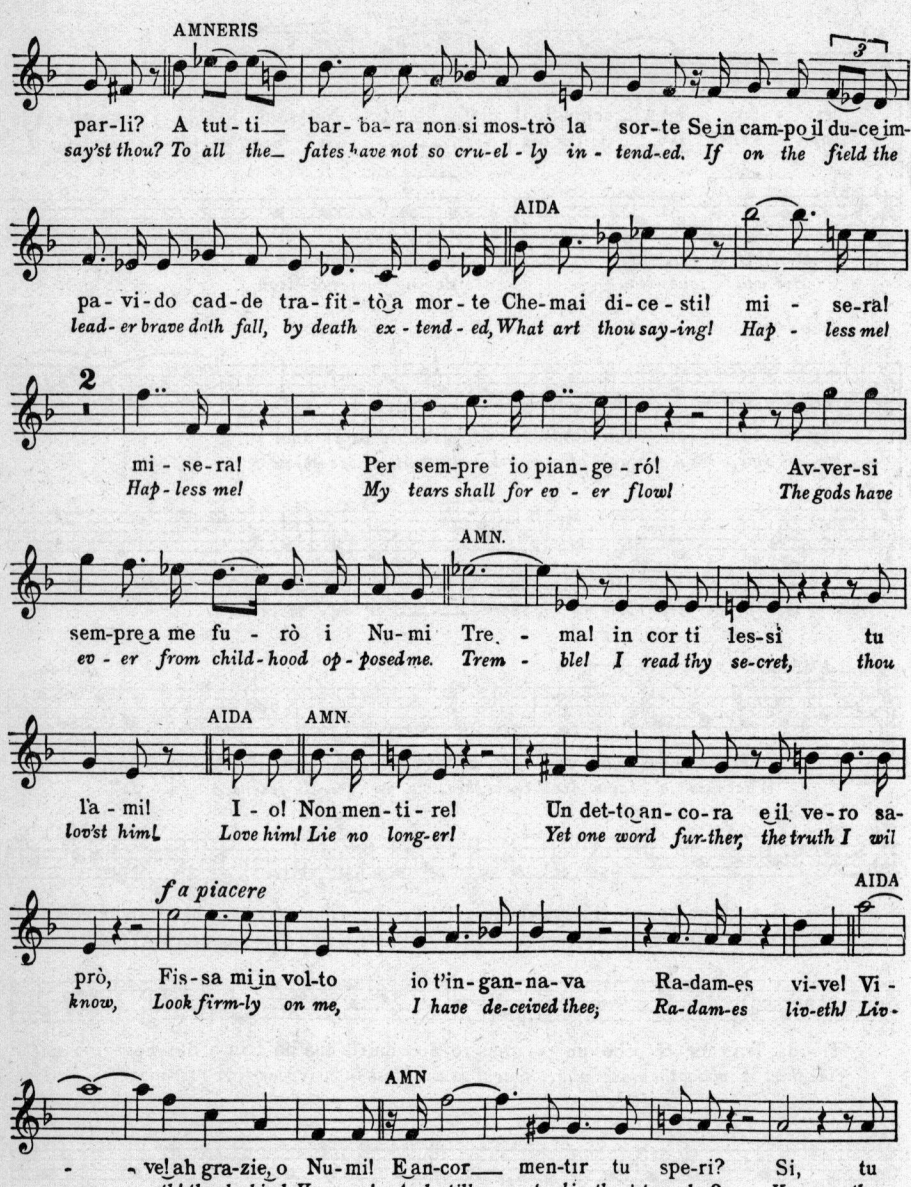

AMNERIS

par-li? A tut-ti bar-ba-ra non si mos-trò la sor-te Se in cam-po il du-ce im-
say'st thou? To all the_ fates have not so cru-el-ly in-tend-ed. If on the field the

AIDA

pa-vi-do cad-de tra-fit-tò a mor-te Che mai di-ce-sti! mi-se-ra!
lead-er brave doth fall, by death ex-tend-ed, What art thou say-ing! Hap-less me!

2

mi-se-ra! Per sem-pre io pian-ge-ró! Av-ver-si
Hap-less me! My tears shall for ev-er flow! The gods have

AMN.

sem-pre a me fu-rò i Nu-mi Tre-ma! in cor ti les-sì tu
ev-er from child-hood op-posed me. Trem-ble! I read thy se-cret, thou

AIDA   AMN.

l'a-mi! I - o! Non men-ti-re! Un det-to an-co-ra e il ve-ro sa-
lov'st him! Love him! Lie no long-er! Yet one word fur-ther, the truth I wil

f a piacere   **AIDA**

prò, Fis-sa mi in vol-to io t'in-gan-na-va Ra-dam-es vi-ve! Vi-
know, Look firm-ly on me, I have de-ceived thee; Ra-dam-es liv-eth! Liv-

AMN.

- ve! ah gra-zie, o Nu-mi! E an-cor___ men-tir tu spe-ri? Si, tu
- eth! thanks, kind Heav-en! And still___ to lie thou'rt read-y? Yes, thou

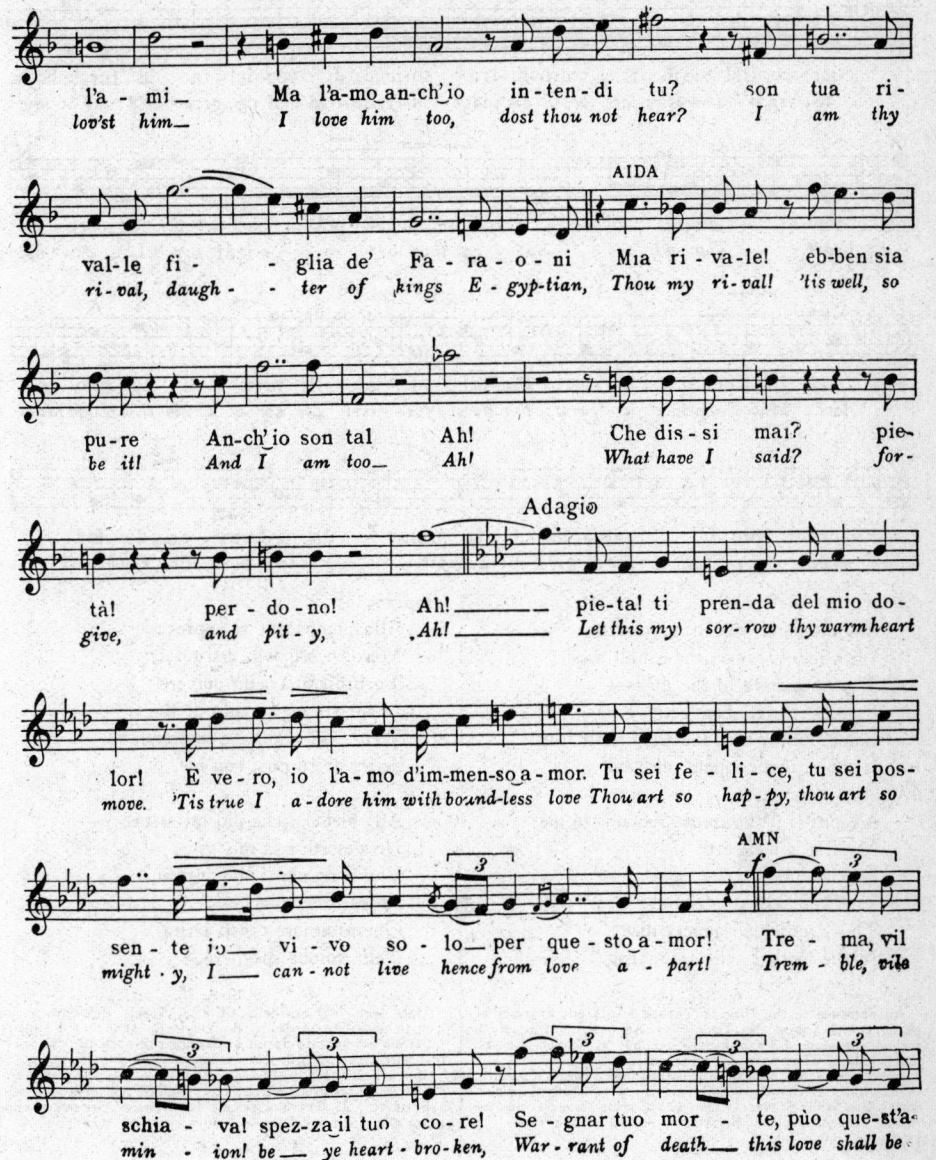

l'a - mi_ Ma l'a-mo an-ch'io in-ten-di tu? son tua ri-
lov'st him_ I love him too, dost thou not hear? I am thy

AIDA

val-le fi - - glia de' Fa-ra-o-ni Mia ri-va-le! eb-ben sia
ri-val, daugh- - ter of kings E-gyp-tian, Thou my ri-val! 'tis well, so

pu-re An-ch'io son tal Ah! Che dis-si mai? pie-
be it! And I am too_ Ah! What have I said? for-

Adagio

tà! per - do - no! Ah!_____ pie-ta! ti pren-da del mio do-
give, and pit-y, Ah!_____ Let this my) sor-row thy warm heart

lor! È ve - ro, io l'a-mo d'im-men-so a-mor. Tu sei fe - li-ce, tu sei pos-
move. 'Tis true I a-dore him with bound-less love Thou art so hap-py, thou art so

AMN

sen-te io vi-vo so-lo per que-sto a-mor! Tre-ma, vil
might-y, I_ can-not live hence from love a-part! Trem-ble, vile

schia - va! spez-za il tuo co-re! Se-gnar tuo mor - te, può que-st'a-
min - ion! be_ ye heart-bro-ken, War-rant of death_ this love shall be

mo - re, Del tuo des-ti - no ar-bi-tra so-no,d'o-dioe ven-det - ta le fur-ie hò in
to - ken,What may thy fate be, I am judge on-ly, Ha-tred and ven-geance hold sway in my

AIDA

cor.   Tu sei fe - li - ce, tu sei pos - sen - te, io — vi - vo
heart.   *Thou art so hap - py, thou art so might - y, I — can - not*

so - lo — per quest'a - mor! Pie-tà! pie-tà! ti pren - da del mio do -
live hence from love a - part! For-give! for-give! Let sor - - row thy warm heart

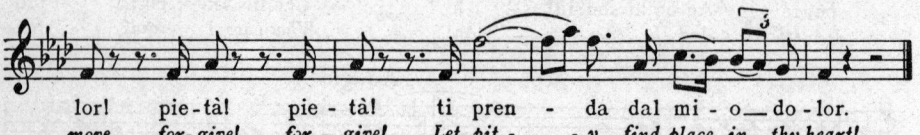

lor!   pie-tà!   pie-tà!   ti pren - da dal mi - o do - lor.
move,   for-give!   for - give!   Let pit - - y find place in — thy heart!

Amneris.

Ah, the pomp which approaches,
With me, O slave, thou shalt assist;
Thou prostrate in the dust—
I on the throne beside the King;
Come, follow me, and thou shalt learn
If thou canst contend with me.

Aïda.

Ah, pity! What more remains to me?
My life is a desert;
Live and reign, thy rage
I will quickly appease.
This love which angers thee
In the tomb I will extinguish.

Amneris.

Alla pompa che si appresta,
Meco, o schiava, assisterai;
Tu prostrata nella polvere,
Io sul trono, accanto al Re.
Vien... mi segui... e apprenderai
Se lottar tu puoi con me.

Aïda.

Ah! pietà!... che più mi resta?
Un deserto è la mia vita:
Vivi e regna, il tuo furore
Io tra breve placherò.
Questo amore che ti irrita
Nella tomba spegnerò.

SCENE II.

An entrance to the City of Thebes. In front a group of palms; to the right the Temple of Ammon; to the left a throne surmounted by a purple canopy; at the back a triumphal gate. The scene is crowded with people.
Enter the KING, followed by Ministers, Priests, Captains, Fan-Bearers, Ensign-Bearers, etc., etc. Afterwards AMNERIS, with AÏDA and SLAVES. The KING seats himself on the throne; AMNERIS places herself to the left of the KING.

People.

Glory to Egypt, and to Isis,
Who the sacred soil protects;

SCENA II.

Uno degli ingressi della Città di Tebe. Sul davanti un gruppo di palme; a destra il Tempio di Ammone; a sinistra un trono sormontato da un baldacchino di porpora; nel fondo una porta trionfale; la scena è ingombra di popolo.
Entra il RE, seguito dai Ministri, Sacerdoti, Capitani, Flabelliferi, Porta-Insegne, ecc., ecc. Quindi AMNERIS con AÏDA e SCHIAVE. Il RE va a sedere sul trono. AMNERIS prende posto alla sinistra del RE.

Popolo.

Gloria all Egitto e ad Iside
Che il sacro suol protegge;

To the king who rules the Delta
Festal hymns let us raise.
Come, O champion warrior,
Come to rejoice with us;
In the path of the heroes,
Laurels and flowers let us strew.

Women.

Weave the lotus with the laurel
On the hair of the conqueror
A sweet shower of the flowers,
Spread on their arms a veil.
Let us dance, daughters of Egypt,
The mystic dances,
As around the sun
Dance the stars of heaven!

Priests.

To the supreme arbiters of victory
Raise your eyes;
Render thanks to the gods
On the happy day.
Thus for us with glory
May the future be marked,
Nor may that fate seize us
That struck the barbarians.

(The Egyptian troops, preceded by trumpets, defile before the KING—the chariots of war follow—the ensigns—the sacred vases and statues of the gods—troops of Dancing GIRLS who carry the treasures of the defeated—and lastly RADAMES, under a canopy borne by twelve Officers.)

King

(who descends from the throne to embrace RADAMES).

Saviour of thy country, I salute thee.

Come, and let my daughter with her own
hand
Place upon you the triumphal crown.

(RADAMES bows before AMNERIS, who places the crown upon him.)

King

(to RADAMES).

Now ask of me
What thou most wishest. Nothing denied
to thee
On such a day shall be—I swear it
By my crown, by the sacred gods.

Radames.

Deign first to let the prisoners
Be drawn up before thee.

(Enter between the Guards the Ethiopian prisoners, AMONASRO last, dressed as an Officer.)

Al Re che il Delta ragge
Inni festosi alziam!
Vieni, o guerriero vindice,
Vieni a gioir con noi;
Sul passo degli eroi
I lauri e i fior versiam!

Donne.

S'intrecci il loto al lauro
Sul crin dei vincitori;
Nembo gentil di fiori
Stenda sull' armi un vel.
Danziam, fanciulle Egizie,
Le mistiche carole,
Come d'intorno al sole
Donzano gli astri in ciel!

Sacerdoti.

Della vittoria agli arbitri
Supremi il guarde ergete;
Grazie agli Dei rendete
Nel forsunato di.
Così per noi di gloria
Sia l'avvenir segnato,
Nè mai ci colga il fato
Che i barbari colpi.

(Le truppe Egizie precedute dalle fanfare sfilano dinanze al RE—Seguono i carri di guerra, le insegne i vasi sacri, le statue degli Dei—Un drapello di danzatrici che recano i tesori dei vinti—Da ultimo, RADAMES, sotto un baldacchino portato da dodici Ufficiali.)

Il Re

(che scende dal trono per abbracciare RADAMES).

Salvator della patria, io ti saluto.

Vieni, e mia figlia di sua man ti porga
Il serto trionfale.

(RADAMES si inchina davanti AMNERIS che gli porge la corona.)

Il Re

(a RADAMES).

Ora, a me chiedi
Quanto più brami. Nulla a te negato
Sarà in tal dì—lo giuro
Per la corono mia, pei sacri Numi.

Radames.

Concedi in pria che innanzi a te sien tratti
I prigionier...

Entrano fra le guardie i prigionieri Etiopi, ultimo, AMONASRO, vestito da Uffiziale.)

Aïda.

What do I see? He!—my father!

All.

Her father!

Amneris.

In our power!

Aïda

(embracing her father)

Thou prisoner!

Amonasro

(softly to AÏDA)

Betray me not!

King

(to AMONASRO).

Draw thou near—
Then—thou art?

Amonasro.

Her father.—I also fought—
Was conquered, and death I sought in vain.
(Pointing to the uniform in which he is dressed.)
This livery that I wear may tell you
That I have defended my king and my country.
Fate was hostile to our arms;
Vain was the courage of the brave.
At my feet in the dust extended
Lay the king, transfixed by many wounds;
If the love of country is a crime
We are all criminals—all ready to die!
(Turning to the KING with a supplicating motion.)
But thou, O king, thou puissant lord,
Be merciful to those men.
To-day we are stricken by Fate,
To-morrow Fate may smite you.

Aïda, Prisoners and Female Slaves.

Yes; by the gods we are stricken;
Thy pity, thy mercy we implore;
Ah! May you never have to suffer
What is now given to us to suffer.

Ramphis and Priests.

Destroy, O king, these savage hordes,
Close your heart to their perfidious voices,
By the gods they were doomed to death,
Let the will of the gods be accomplished.

People.

Priests, your anger soften,

Aïda.

Che veggo?... Egli!... mia padre!

Tutti.

Suo padre!

Amneris.

In poter nostro!...

Aïda

(abbracciando il padre).

Tu! Prigionier!

Amneris

(piano ad AÏDA).

Non mi tradir!

Il Re

(ad AMONASRO).

Ti appressa...
Dunque... tu sei?...

Amonasro.

Suo padre—Anch' io pugnai...
Vinti noi fummo e morte invancercai.
(Accennando alla divisa che lo veste.)
Questa assisa ch'io vesto vi dica
Che il mio Re, la mia patria ho difeso:
Fu la sorte a nostr' armi nemica...
Tornò vano dei forti l'ardir.
Al mio piè nella polve disteso
Giacque il Re da più colpi traffito;
Se l'amor della patria è delitto
Siam rei tutti, siam pronti a morir!
(Volgendosi al RE con accento supplichevole.)
Ma tu, o Re, tu signore possente,
A costoro ti volgi clemente...
Oggi noi siam percossi dal fato
Doman voi potria il fato colpir.

Aïda, Prigionieri e Schiava.

Sî: dal Numi percossi non siamo;
Tua pietà, tua clemenza imploriamo;
Ah! giammai di soffrir vi sia dato
Ciò che in oggi n'è dato soffrir!

Ramfis e Sacerdoti.

Struggi, o Re, queste ciurme feroci,
Chiudi il core alle perfide voci,
Fur dai Numi votati alla morte,
Si compisca dei Numi il voler!

Popolo.

Sacerdoti, gli sdegni placate,

The humble prayer of the conquered hear,
And thou, O king, powerful and strong,
Open thy thoughts to mercy.

Radames
(fixing his eyes on AÏDA).

(The sorrow which speaks in that face
Renders it more beautiful to my sight;
Every drop of the beloved tears
Reanimates love in my breast.)

Amneris.

(What glances on her he turns!
With what flame their faces flash!
To such a fate as this am I destined?
Revenge groans in my heart.)

King.

Now that events smile favor upon us,
To these people let us show ourselves merciful;
Pity ascends grateful to the gods,
And confirms the power of princes.

Radames
(to the KING).

O King! by the sacred gods,
By the splendor of thy crown,
Thou sworest to fulfill my vow?

King.

I swore.

Radames.

Well; of thee for the Ethiopian prisoners,
Life I demand and liberty.

Amneris.

(For all!)

Priests.

Death to the enemies of the country!

People.

Grace
For the unhappy.

Ramphis.

Listen, O King,
(To RADAMES.)

Even thou,
Young hero, listen to wise counsel:
They are enemies and they are warriors—
They have revenge in their hearts.
Emboldened by thy pardon
They will run to arms again.

L'umil prece dei vinti ascoltate;
E tu, o Re, tu possente, tu forte,
A clemenza dischiudi il pensier.

Radames
(fissando AÏDA).

(Il dolor che in quel volte favella
Al mio sguardo la rende più bella;
Ogni stilla del pianto adorato
Nel mio petto ravviva l'amor.)

Amneris.

(Quali sguardi sovr' essa ha rivolti!
Di qual fiamma balenano i volti!
E a tal sorte serbata son io?...
La vendetta mi rugge nel cor.)

Il Re.

Or che fausti ne arridon gli eventi
A costoro mostriamci clementi:
La pietà sale ai Numi gradita
E rafferma dei Prenci il poter.

Radames
(al RE).

O Re: pei sacri Numi,
Per lo splendore della tua corona.
Compier giurasti il voto mio...

Il Re.

Giurai.

Radames.

Ebbene: a te pei prigionieri Etiopi
Vita domando e libertà.

Amneris.

(Per tutti!)

Sacerdoti.

Morte ai nemici della patria!

Popolo.

Grazie
Per gli infelici!

Ramfis.

Ascolta, o Re—
(A RADAMES.)

Tu pure
Giovine eroe, saggio consiglio ascolta:
Son nemici e prodi sono...
La vendetta hanno nel cor,
Fatti audaci dal perdono
Correranno all' armi ancor!

Radames.

Amonasro, the warrior king slain,
No hope remains to the vanquished.

Ramphis.

At least
As an earnest of peace and security, among us
With her father let Aïda remain.
Let the rest be free.

King.

To thy counsel I yield.
Of security and peace a better pledge
I will now give: Radames, the country
Owes all to thee. The hand of Amneris
Be thy reward. Over Egypt one day
With her shalt thou reign.

Amneris.

(Now let the slave come—
Let her come to take my love from me—if
she dares!)

King.

Glory to Egypt and to Isis,
Who the sacred soil defends,
Weave the lotus with the laurel
On the hair of the victors.

Priests.

Hymns let us raise to Isis,
Who the sacred soil defends;
Let us pray that the Fates may ever smile
Propitious on our country.

Aïda.

(What hope more remains to me?
To him glory and the throne.
To me, oblivion—the tears
Of hopeless love.)

Prisoners.

Glory to the merciful Egyptian
Who has unloosed our fetters,
Who restores us to the free
Paths of our native land!

Radames.

(The Thunder of the adverse gods
On my head descends—
Ah! no, the throne of Egypt
Is not worth the heart of Aïda.

Radames.

Spento Amonasro il re guerrier, non resta
Speranza ai vinti.

Ramfis.

Almeno,
Arra di pace e securtà fra noi
Resti col padre Aïda...
Gli altri sien sciolti...

Il Re.

Al tuo consiglio io cedo.
Di securità, di pace un miglior pegno
Or io vuo' darvi—Radames, la patria
Tutto a te deve—D'Amneris la mano
Premio ti sia. Sovra l'Egitto un giorno
Con essa regnerai...

Amneris.

(Venga or la schiava,
Venga a rapirmi l'amor mio... se l'osa!)

Il Re.

Gloria all' Egitto e ad Iside
Che il sacro suol difende,
S'intrecci il loto al lauro
Sul crin del vincitor!

Sacerdoti.

Inni leviamo ad Iside
Che il sacro suol difende;
Preghiam che i fati arridano
Fausti alla patria ognor.

Aïda.

(Qual speme omai più restami?
A lui la gloria e il trono...
A me l'oblio... le lacrime
Di disperato amor.)

Prigionieri

Gloria al clemente Egizio
Che i nostri ceppi ha sciolto,
Che ci ridona ai liberi
Solchi del patrio suol!

Radames.

(D'avverso Nume il folgore
Sul capo mio discende...
Ah no! d'Egitto il soglio
Non val d'Aïda il cor.)

Amneris.

(By the unexpected joy
I am intoxicated;
All in one day are fulfilled
The dreams of my heart.)

Amonasro   (to AÏDA).

Take heart, for thy country
Expects happy events;
For us the dawn of vengeance
Is already near.

People.

Glory to Egypt and to Isis,
Who the sacred soil defends.
Weave the lotus with the laurel
On the hair of the victors!

END OF THE SECOND ACT.

Amneris.

(Dall' inatteso giubilo
Inebbriata io sono:
Tutti in un dì si compiono
I sogni del mio cor.)

Amonasro   (ad AÏDA).

Fa cor: della tua patria
I lieti eventi aspetta;
Per noi della vendetta
Già prossimo è l'albor.

Popolo.

Gloria all' Egitto e ad Iside
Che il sacro suol difende!
S'intrecci il loto al lauro
Sul crin del vincitor!

FINE DELL' ATTO SECONDO.

ACT III.

SCENE.—The Banks of the Nile. Rocks of granite, among which grow palm trees; on the top of the rocks the Temple of Isis, half concealed among the foliage; it is starlight and bright moonlight.

Chorus   (in the temple).

O Thou who art of Osiris,
Mother immortal and spouse,
Goddess who awakenest the beatings
In the heart of human creatures,
Come piteous to our help,
Mother of eternal love.

(From a boat, which approaches the shore, descend AMNERIS, RAMPHIS, some Women closely veiled, and Guards.)

Ramphis   (to AMNERIS).

Come to the Temple of Isis.
On the eve of thy nuptials implore
The favor of the goddess. Isis rules
The heart of mortals; every mystery
Of mankind to her is known.

Amneris.

Yes: I will pray that Radames may give me
His whole heart, as mine to him
Is consecrated forever.

Ramphis.

Let us enter.
Thou shalt pray till dawn. I shall be with thee.

(All enter the temple. The Chorus repeat the sacred song.)

ATTO III.

SCENA.—Le Rive del Nilo. Roccie di granito fra cui crescono dei palmizii. Sul vertice delle roccie il Tempio d'Iside per metà nascosto tra le fronde. E notte stellata Splendore di luna.

Coro   (nel tempio).

O tu che sei d'Osiride
Madre immortale e sposa,
Diva che i casti palpiti
Desti agli amani in cor;
Soccorri a noi pietosa,
Madre d'eterno amor.

(Da una barca che approda alla riva, discendono AMNERIS, RAMFIS, alcune donne coperte da fitto velo e Guardie.)

Ramfis   (ad AMNERIS).

Vieni d'Iside al Tempio—alla vigilia
Della tue nozze, implora
Della Diva il favore—Iside legge
Dei mortali nel cuore—ogni mistero
Degli umani è a lei noto.

Amneris.

Sì: pregherò che Radames mi doni
Tutto il suo cor, come il mio core a lui
Sacro è per sempre.

Ramfis.

Pregherai fino all' alba—io sarò teco.

(Tutti entrano nel tempio. Il Coro ripete il canto sacro.)

Aïda

(entering cautiously, covered with a veil).

Here Radames will come. What would he say to me?

I tremble—ah, if thou comest

To give me, O cruel one, the last farewell,

The deep water of the Nile

Shall give me a tomb—and peace perhaps—and oblivion.

Aïda

(entra cautamente coperta da un velo).

Qui Radamès verrà... Che vorrà dirmi?

Io tremo... Ah! se tu vieni

A recarmi, o crudel, l'ultimo addio,

Del Nilo i cupi vortici

Mi daran tomba... e pace forse... e oblio.

OH! CIELI AZZURI—*O SKIES OF TENDER BLUE* Air (Aïda)

Aïda.   (Enter Amonasro.)

Heaven! My father!

Amonasro.

Grave occasion
Leads me to thee, Aïda. Nothing escapes
My sight; thou art destroying thyself with
  love
For Radames. He loves thee, and here thou
  awaitest him,
The daughter of the Pharaohs is thy rival—
An infamous race, abhorred and fatal to us.

Aïda.

And I am in her power!—I, the daughter
Of Amonasro.

Amonasro.

In her power! No! If thou wishest,
This powerful rival thou shalt defeat,
And country, and throne, and love all shall
  be thine.
Thou shalt see again the balmy forests,
The fresh valleys, our temples of gold!

Aïda.   (with transport).

I shall see again the balmy forests,
Our valleys, our temples of gold!

Amonasro.

Happy bride of him whom thou lovest so
  much,
Great jubilee thence shall be thine.

Aïda.   (with transport).

One day only of such sweet enchantment,
One hour of such joy—and then to die!

Amonasro.

Nevertheless thou rememberest that the
  merciless Egyptian
Profaned our houses, temples, and altars;
He drew in fetters the ravished virgins—
Mothers, old men and children he has slain.

Aïda.

Ah! well I remember those unhappy days.
I remember the grief that my heart suffered.
Ah! make return to us, O gods,
The longed-for dawn of peaceful days.

Amonasro.

Delay not. In arms now are roused
Our people—everything is ready—

Aïda.   (Amonasro e Aïda.)

Cielo! mio padre!

Amonasro.

A te grave cagione
Mi adduce, Aïda. Nulla sfugge al mio
Sguardo—D'amor ti struggi
Per Radames... ei t'ama... e qui lo attendi,
Dei Faraon la figlia è tua rivale...
Razza infame, aborrita e a noi fatale!

Aïda.

E in suo potere io sto!... Io d'Amonasro
Figlia!...

Amonasro.

In poter di lei!... No!... se lo brami
La possente rival tu vincerai,
E patria, e trono, e amor, tutto avrai.
Rivedrai le foreste imbalsamate,
Le fresche valli, i nostri templi d'ôr...

Aïda.   (con trasporto).

Rivedrò le foreste imbalsamate...
Le nostre valli... i nostri tempii d'ôr!

Amonasro.

Sposa felice a lui che amasti tanto,
Tripudii immensi ivi potrai gioir...

Aïda.   (con trasporto)

Un'giorno solo di sì dolce incanto.
Un'ora di tal gaudio. . e poi morir!

Amonasro.

Pur rammenti che a noi l'Egizio immite,
Le case, i tempii e l'are profanò. .
Trasse in ceppi le vergini rapite. .
Madri, vecchi e fanciulli ei trucidè.

Aïda.

Ah! ben rammento quegli infausti giorni
Rammento i lutti che il mio cor soffrì. .
Deh! fate o Numi che per noi ritorni
L'alba invocata dei sereni dì.

Amonasro.

Non fia che tardi—In armi ora si desta
Il popol nostro—tutto e pronto già. .

Victory we shall have. It only remains for
me to know
What path the enemy will follow.

Aïda.

Who will be able to discover it? Who?

Amonasro.

Thyself!

Aïda.

I?

Amonasro.

Radames will come here soon—he loves
thee—
He leads the Egyptians. Dost thou understand?

Aïda.

Horror!
What dost thou counsel me? No, no! Never!

Amonasro (with savage fury).

Up, then! Rise,
Egyptian legions!
With fire destroy
Our cities—
Spread terror,
Carnage and death.
To your fury
There is no longer check.

Aïda.

Ah, father!

Amonasro (repulsing her).

My daughter
Dost thou call thyself?

Aïda (terrified and beseeching).

Pity!

Amonasro.

Rivers of blood pour
On the cities of the vanquished—
Seest thou?—From the black gulfs
The dead are raised—
To thee they point and cry:
"For thee the country dies."

Aïda.

Pity!

Amonasro.

A horrible ghost
Among the shadows to us approaches—

Vittoria avrem.. Solo a saper mi resta
Qual sentier il nemico seguirà..

Aïda.

Chi scoprirlo potria? chi mai?

Amonasro.

Tu stessa!

Aïda.

Io!..

Amonasro.

Radamès so che qui attendi.. Ei t'ama..
Ei conduce gli Egizii.. Intendi?

Aïda.

Orrore!
Che mi consigli tu? No, no, giammai!

Amonasro (con impeto selvaggio).

Su, dunque! sorgete
Egizie coorti!
Col fuoco struggete
Le nostre città..
Spargete il terrore,
Le stragi' le morti..
Al vostro furore
Più freno non v'ha.

Aïda.

Ah padre!

Amonasro (respingendola).

Mia figlia
Ti chiami!..

Aïda (atterrita e supplichevole).

Pietà!

Amonasro.

Flutti di sangue scorrono
Sulle città dei vinti..
Vedi?..dai negri vortici
Si levano gli estinti..
Ti additan essi e gridano:
"Per te la patria muor."

Aïda.

Pietà!..

Amonastro.

Una larva orribile
Fra l'ombre a moi s'affaccia..

Tremble! the fleshless arms
Over thy head it raised—
It is thy mother—recognize her—
She curses thee.

Aïda   (in the greatest terror).

Ah, no!
Father.

Amonasro   (repulsing her).

Go, unworthy one! Thou'rt not my offspring—
Thou art the slave of the Pharaohs!

Aïda.

Father, their slave I am not—
Reproach me not—curse me not;
Thy daughter again thou canst call me—
Of my country I will be worthy.

Amonasro.

Think that a people conquered, torn to
pieces,
Through thee alone can arise—

Aïda.

O my country, O my country—how much
thou costest me!

Amonasro.

Courage! he comes—there I shall hear all.
(Conceals himself among the palm trees.)
(Enter RADAMES.)

Radames.

I see thee again, my sweet Aïda.

Aïda.

Stop! begone. What, hopest thou still?

Radames.

Love guided me to thee.

Aïda.

The rites of another love await thee,
Spouse of Amneris.

Radames.

What sayest thou?
Thee alone, Aïda, must I love.
Hear me, gods!—Thou shalt be mine!

Aïda.

Stain not thyself with perjury.
Valiant I loved thee; foresworn I should not
love thee.

Radames.

Doubtest thou my love, Aïda?

Trema! le scarne braccia
Sul capo tuo levò..
Tua madre ell'è..ravvisala..
Ti maledice..

Aïda   (nel massimo terrore).

Ah, no!..
Padre.

Amonasro   (respingendola).

Va, indegna! non sei mia figlia!
Dei Faraoni tu sei la schiava.

Aïda.

Padre, a costoro schiava io non sono..
Non maledirmi.. non imprecarmi..
Tua figlia ancora potrai chiamarmi..
Della mia patria degna sarò.

Amonasro.

Pensa che un popolo, vinto, straziato
Per te soltanto risorger può..

Aïda.

O patria! o patria.. quanto mi costi!

Amonasro.

Corraggio! ei giunge.. là tutto udrò..
(Si nasconde fra i palmizii.)
(RADAMES e AÏDA.)

Radames.

Pur ti riveggo, mia dolce Aïda...

Aïda.

Ti arresta, vanne... che speri ancor?

Radames.

A te dappresso l'amor mi guida.

Aïda.

Te i riti attendono d'un altro amor.
D'Amneris sposo...

Radames.

Che parli mai?
Te sola, Aïda, te deggio amar.
Gli Dei mi ascoltano... tu mia saréi...

Aïda.

D'uno spergiuro non ti machiar?
Prode t'amai, non t'amerei spergiuro.

Radames.

Dell' amor mio dubiti, Aïda?

Aïda.

And how
Hopest thou to free thyself from the love of
  Amneris,
From the King's will, from the vows of thy
  people,
From the wrath of the priests?

Radames.

Hear me, Aïda.
To the fierce pant of a new war
The land of Ethiopia has re-awakened—
Thy people already invade our country.
I shall be leader of the Egyptians.
Amid the fame, the applause of victory,
I prostrate myself before the King, I unveil
  to him my heart.
Thou shalt be the reward of my glory,
We shall live blessed by eternal love.

Aïda.

Nor fearest thou Amneris and
Her vindictive fury? Her revenge,
Like a dreadful thunderbolt,
Will fall on me, on my father, on all.

Radames.

I protect thee.

Aïda.

In vain! Thou couldst not—
Still—if thou lovest me—again a way
Of escape opens to us.

Radames.

Which?

Aïda.

To fly!

Radames.

To fly!

Aïda.

E come
Speri sottrarti d'Amneris ai vezzi,
Del Re al voler, del tuo popolo ai voti,
Dei sacerdoti all' ira?

Radames.

Odimi, Aïda.
Nel fiero anelito di nuova guerra
Il suolo Etiope si ridestò...
I tuoi già invadono la nostra terra,
Io degli Egizii duce sarò.
Fra il suon, fra i plausi della vittoria,
Al re mi prostro, gli svelo il cor...
Sarai tu il serto della mia gloria,
Vivrem beati d'eterno amor.

Aïda.

Nè d'Amneris paventi
Il vindice furor? la sua vendetta,
Come folgor tremenda
Cadrà su me, sul padre mio, su tutti.

Radames.

Io vi difendo.

Aïda.

Invan tu nol potresti..
Pur... se tu m'ami... ancor s'apre una vìa
Di scampo a noi...

Radames.

Quale?

Aïda.

Fuggire...

Radames.

Fuggire!

FUGGIAM GLI ARDORI—*AH! FLY WITH ME* Duet (Aïda and Radames)

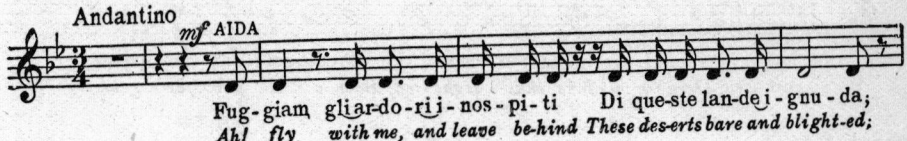

U - na no-vel - la pa - tri - a, al no-stroa-mor si schiu - de.
Some coun-try,new and fresh to find, Where we may love u - nit - ed.

Là - tra fo-re-ste ver-gi-ni, Di fio-ri pro - fu - ma - te, in
There 'mid the vir - gin for - est groves, By fair and sweet flow'rs scent - ed, In

e - sta - si be - a - te la ter-ra scor-de-rem, in e - sta-si,_
qui-et joy con - tent-ed, The world will we for - get, in qui - et joy,_

_ in e - - sta - si la_ ter - . - ra_ scor-de-
_ in qui - - et_ joy, The_ world_ will_ we for-

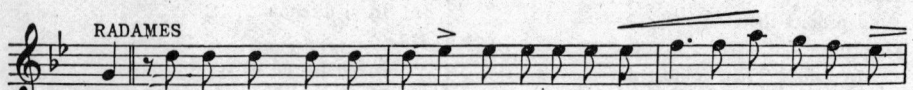

RADAMES

rem, So-vrau-na ter-ra e-stra-nia te - cò fug-gir do-vrei! ab-ban-do-nar la
get, To some strange land far dis-tant Must I then with you fly! Our home and coun-try

pa-tria là - re de' no-stri Dei! il suol dov' io rac-col-si di glo-ria i pri-mi al-
leav-ing, Our gods and al-tars high! The soil where first I gath-er'd The bays that deeds re-

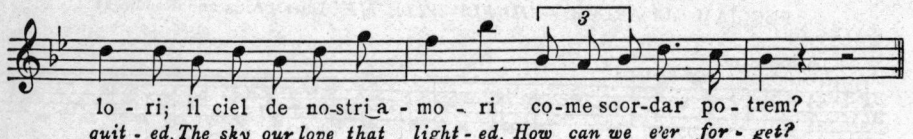

lo - ri; il ciel de no-stri a-mo - ri co-me scor-dar po-trem?
quit-ed, The sky our love that light-ed, How can we e'er for-get?

AIDA

Là - tra for - es - ti ver - gi - ni, di fio - ri pro - fu - ma - te, in
There 'neath the vir-gin for - est groves; By fair and sweet flow'rs scent - ed, In

e - sta - si be - a - te la ter - ra scor - de - rem, in e -
qui - et joy con - tent - ed The world will we for - get, In qui -

- sta - si, — in è - sta - si la ter - - ra scor - de -
- et joy, — in qui - - et joy The — world _____ will we for -

RADAMES   AIDA

rem. Il ciel di nos - tri a - mo - ri co - me scor - dar po - trem? Sot-to il mio ciel, più
get, The sky our love that - light - ed. How can we e'er for - get? Be-neath my sky more

li - be - re là - mor ne fia con - ces - so, i - vi nel tem - pio i
light and free Love's gen - 'rous aid con - fid - ing; In tem - ples there a -

stes - so gli stes - si Nu - mi a - vrem, i - vi nel tem - pio i
bid - ing, Gods like your own we'll find, In tem - ples there a -

stes - so gli stes - si Nu - mi a - vrem; I - vi nel tem - pio i
bid - ing, The self - same gods we'll find, In tem - ples there a -

stes - so gli stes - si Nu - mi a - vrem; fug - giam, fug - giam! _____
bid - ing the self - same gods we'll find, then fly! ah! fly! _____

Radames   (hesitating).
    Aïda!
Aida.
    Thou lovest me not—go!
Radames.
    I love thee not?
    Never mortal, nor god,
    Burnt with love so powerful as mine!
Aida.
    Go, go! Amneris awaits thee
    At the altar.
Radames.
    No, never!
Aida.
    Never, saidst thou?
    Then falls the axe
    On me, on my father.
Radames.
    Ah, no, let us fly!
                    (With impassioned resolution.)
    Yes; let us fly from these walls,
    To the desert let us fly together;
    Here misfortune reigns alone.
    There opens to us a heaven of love.
    The boundless deserts
    Shall be our nuptial couch,
    On us the stars will shine
    With a more limpid effulgence.
Aida.
    In the happy land
    Of my fathers heaven awaits us;
    There the air is perfumed,
    There the ground is fragrant with flowers.
    Fresh valleys and green fields
    Shall be our nuptial couch,
    On us the stars will shine
    With a more limpid effulgence.
Aida and Radames.
    Come with me—together let us fly
    This land of grief.
    Come with me—I love thee, I love thee!
    Love shall be our leader.
Aida   (They go rapidly aside.)
                (stopping suddenly).
    But tell me by what road
    Shall we avoid the armed hosts?

Radames   (esitante).
    Aïda!
Aïda.
    Tu non m'ami... Va!—
Radames.
    Non t'amo!
    Mortal giammi nè Dio
    Arse d'amore al par del mio possente.
Aida.
    Va... va... ti attende all' ara
    Amneris...
Radames.
    No!... giammai!...
Aïda.
    Giammai, dicesti?
    Allor piombi la scure
    Su me, sul padre mio...
Radames.
    Ah no! fuggiamo!
                    (Con appassionata risoluzione.)
    Sì: fuggiamo da queste mura,
    Al deserto insiem fuggiamo;
    Qui sol regna la sventura,
    Là si schiude un ciel d'amor.
    I deserti interminati
    A noi talamo saranno,
    Su noi gli astri brilleranno.
    Di più limpido fulgor.
Aïda.
    Nella terra avventurata
    De' miei padri, il ciel ne attende;
    Ivi l'aura è imbalsamata,
    Ivi il suolo è aromi e fior.
    Fresche valli e verdi prati
    A noi talamo saranno,
    Su noi gli astri brilleranno.
    Di più limpido fulgor.
Aïda e Radames.
    Vieni meco—insiem fuggiamo
    Questa terra di dolor—
    Vieni meco—io t'amo, io t'amo!
    A noi duce fia l'amor!
Aïda   (Si allontanano rapidamente.)
                (arrestandosi all' improvviso).
    Ma, dimmi; per qual via
    Eviterem le schiere
    Degli armati?

Radames.

The path chosen by our troops
To fall on the enemy will be deserted
Until to-morrow.

Aïda.

And that path?

Radames.

The Pass
Of Napata.

(Enter AMONASRO.)

Amonasro.

The Pass of Napata!
There shall be my people.

Radames.

Oh! who hears us?

Amonasro.

The father of Aïda and King of the Ethiopians.

Radames

(greatly agitated).

Thou, Amonasro! Thou, the King! Gods,
what said I?
No! It is not true!—I dream—this is di-
lirium.

Aïda.

Ah, no! calm thyself—listen to me,
Trust thyself in my love.

Amonasro.

Aïda's love shall raise thee
To a throne.

Radames.

For thee to betray my country!
I am dishonored.

Amonasro.

No; Thou art not guilty—
It was the will of fate.
Come; beyond the Nile await us
The brave men devoted to us;
There the vows of thy heart
Shall be crowned with love.

(Enter AMNERIS from the Temple, then RAMPHIS, PRIESTS
and GUARDS.)

Amneris.

Traitor!

Aïda.

My rival!

Radames.

Il sentier scelto dai nostri
A piombar sul nemico fia deserto
Fino a domani...

Aïda.

E quel sentier?...

Radames.

Le gole
Di Nàpata?

(AMONASRO e AÏDA e RADAMES.)

Amonasro.

Di Nàpata le gole!
Ivi saranno i miei...

Radames.

Oh! chi ci ascolta?

Amonasro.

D'Aida il padre e degli Etiopi il Re.

Radames

(agitatissimo).

Tu! Amonasro!... Tu il Re?
Numi! che dissi?
No!..non è ver!..sogno... delirio è questo..

Aïda.

Ah, no! ti calma. .ascoltami,
All' amor mio t'affida.

Amonasro.

A te l'amor d'Aïda
Un soglio innalzerà!

Radames.

Per te tradii la patria!
Io son disonorato..

Amonasro.

No: tu non sei colpevole—
Era voler del fato.
Vieni: oltra il Nil ne attendono
I prodi a noi devoti,
Là del tuo core i voti
Coronerà l'amor.

(AMNERIS, dal tempio, indi RAMFIS, SACERDOTI, GUARDIE e
detti.)

Amneris.

Traditor!

Aïda.

La mia rivale!..

Amonasro
>   (rushing upon AMNERIS with a dagger).

Comest thou to destroy my work?
Die!

Radames   (interposing himself).

Stop, madman!

Amonasro.

Oh, fury!

Ramphis.

Guards, hither!

Radames   (to AÏDA and AMONASRO).

Haste!—fly!

Amonasro   (drawing AÏDA away).

Come, O daughter!

Ramphis   (to the GUARDS).

Follow them!

Radames   (to RAMPHIS).

Priest, I remain with thee.

END OF THE THIRD ACT.

Amonasro
>   (avventandosi ad AMNERIS con un pugnale).

Vieni a strugger l'opre mia!
Muori!

Radames   (frapponendosi).

Arresta, insano!..

Amonasro.

Oh rabbia!

Ramfis.

Guardie, olà.

Radames   (ad AÏDA e AMONASRO)

Presto! fuggite!..

Amonasro   (transciando AÏDA).

Vieni, o figlia!..

Ramfis   (alle GUARDIE).

Li inseguite!

Radames   (a RAMFIS).

Sacerdote, io resto a te.

FINE DELL' ATTO TERZO.

ACT IV.
SCENE I.

Hall in the King's Palace; to the left a grand gate, which opens on the subterranean hall of judgment; passage to the right which leads to the prison of RADAMES.

Amneris
>   (in a sad attitude before the gate of the hall).

My abhorred rival escapes me—
Radames awaits from the priests
The punishment of a traitor. Traitor
He is not, though he revealed
The high secret of war. He wished to fly—
To fly with her—traitors all!
To death, to death! Oh, what did I say? I
>   love him—
I love him always—desperate, mad
Is this love which destroys my life.
Oh! if he could love me!
I would save him—and how?
Let me try. Guards: Radames comes.
>   (Enter RADAMES, guarded.)

Amneris.

Already the priests assemble.
Arbiters of thy fate;
Of the horrible crime however

ATTO IV.
SCENA I

Sala nel Palazzo del Re. Alla sinistra, una gran porta che mette alla sala sotterranea della sentenze.—Andito r destra che conduce alla prigione di RADAMES.

Amneris
>   (mestamente atteggiata davanti la porta del sotteraneo).

L'abborrita rivale a me sfuggia..
Dai sacerdoti Radamès attende
Dei traditor la pena,—Traditore
Egli non è..Pur rivelò di guerra
L'alto segreto..egli fuggir volea..
Con lei fuggire.. Traditori tutti!
A morte! A morte!..Oh! che mai parlo?
>   Io l'amo,
Io l'amo sempre..Disperato, insano
E quest' amor che la mia vita strugge.
Oh! s'ei potesse amarmi!..
Vorrei salvarlo.. E come?
Si tenti!.. Guardie: Radamès qui venga.
>   (RADAMES condotto dalle guardie, e AMNERIS.)

Amneris.

Già i sacerdoti adunansi
Arbitri del tuo fato;
Pur della accusa orribile

Still it is given thee to exculpate thyself.
Exculpate thyself, and grace for thee
I will beg from the throne;
And a messenger of pardon—
Of life, to thee I will be.

Radames.
Of my exculpation the judges
Will never hear the sound.
Before gods and men
Neither vile nor guilty do I feel.
My incautious lips
Uttered the fatal secret, it is true,
But pure my thought
And my honor remained.

Amneris.
Then save and exculpate thyself.

Radames.
No.

Amneris.
Thou wilt die.

Radames.
Life
I abhor; the font
Of every joy dried up,
Every hope vanished,
I wish only to die.

Amneris.
To die!. Ah; thou shouldst live!
Yes, for my love thou shalt live;
For thee I have undergone
The dreadful anguish of death.
I loved thee—I suffered so much—
I watched through the nights in tears.
Country and throne and life—
All I would give for thee.

Radames.
For her I too betrayed
The country and my honor.

Amneris.
Of her no more——

Radames.
Infamy
Awaits me, and thou wishest that I live?
Utterly wretched thou madest me;
Aïda thou hast taken from me;

Scolparti ancor ti è dato:
Ti scolpa, e la tua grazia
Io pregherò dal trono,
E nunzia di perdono,
Di vita, a te sarò.

Radames.
Di mie discolpe i giudici
Mai non udran l'accento;
Dinanzi ai Numi e agli uomini
Nè vil, nè reo mi sento.
Profferse il labbro incauto
Fatal segreto, è vero,
Ma puro il mio pensiero
E 'l onore mio restò.

Amneris.
Salvati dunque e scolpati.

Radames.
No.

Amneris.
Tu morrai. .

Radames.
La vita
Abhorro; d'ogni gaudio
La fonte inaridita,
Svanita ogni speranza,
Sol bramo di morir.

Amneris.
Morire!..ah!..tu dei vivere!..
Si, all' amor mio vivrai;
Per te le angoscie orribili
Di morte io già provai;
T'amai. .soffersi tanto. .
Vegliai le notti in pianto. .
E patria, e trono, e vita
Tutto darei per te.

Radames.
Per essa anch' io la patria
E l'onor mio tradiva...

Amneris.
Di lei non più!...

Radames.
L'infamia
Mi attende e vuoi che io viva?..
Misero appien mi festi,
Aïda a me togliesti,

Killed her perhaps! And for gift
Thou offerest life to me?

Amneris.

I—the cause of her death?
No! Aïda lives!

Radames.

Lives?

Amneris.

In the desperate struggle
Of the fugitive hordes
Fell her father alone——

Radames.

And she?——

Amneris.

She disappeared, nor more news
Had we.

Radames.

May the gods lead her
Safe to her native walls,
And let her not know the unhappy fate
Of him who will die for her.

Amneris.

Now, if I save thee, swear to me
That thou wilt not see her more.

Radames.

I cannot do it!

Amneris.

Renounce her
Forever, and thou shalt live!

Radames.

I cannot do it!

Amneris.

Yet, once more;
Renounce her!

Radames.

It is in vain!

Amneris.

Wouldst thou die, then, madman?

Radames.

I am ready to die.

Amneris.

Who saves thee, O wretch,
From the fate that awaits thee?
To fury hast thou changed
A love that had no equal.

Spenta l' hai forse... e in dono
Offri la vita a me?

Amneris.

Io...di sua morte origine!
No!... vive Aïda...

Radames.

Vive!

Amneris.

Nei disperati aneliti
Dell' orde fuggitive
Sol cadde il padre..

Radames.

Ed ella?

Amneris.

Sparve, nè più novella
S'ebbe...

Radames.

Gli Dei l'adducano
Salve alle patrie mura,
E ignori la sventura
Di chi per lei morrà!

Amneris.

Or, s'io ti salvo, giurami
Che più non la vedrai...

Radames.

Nol posso!

Amneris.

A lei rinunzia
Per sempre...e tu vivraI...

Radames.

Nol posso!

Amneris.

Anco una volta
A lei rinunzia..

Radames.

E vano..

Amneris.

Morir vuoi dunque, insano?

Radames.

Pronto a morir son già.

Amneris.

Chi ti salva, o sciagurato,
Dalla sorte che ti aspetta?
In furore hai tu cangiato
Un amor ch' equel non ha

Revenge for my tears
Heaven will now consummate.

Radames.

Death is a supreme blessing,
If for her it is given me to die;
In undergoing the last extremity
My heart will feel great joy.
Human anger I fear no more,
I fear only thy pity.

(Exit RADAMES, surrounded by Guards.)

Amneris (falls desolate on a seat).

Ah me! I feel myself dying. Oh! who will
save him?
And in their power
I myself threw him. Now I curse thee,
Atrocious jealousy, who didst cause his death
And the eternal grief of my heart!

(Turns and sees the PRIESTS, who cross the stage to enter the subterranean hall.)

What do I see? Behold the fatal,
The merciless ministers of death!
Oh, that I might not see those white ghosts!

(Covers her face in her hands.)

Priests (in the subterranean hall).

Spirit of the gods descend upon us!
Awaken us to the ray of thy eternal light:
By our lips make thy justice known.

Amneris.

Gods, pity my torn heart.
He is innocent; save him, O gods!
Desperate, tremendous is my sorrow!

(RADAMES, between Guards, crosses the stage and descends to the subterranean hall—AMNERIS on seeing him utters a cry.)

Ramphis (in the subterranean hall).

Radames, Radames: thou didst reveal
The country's secrets to the foreigner.

Priests.

Defend thyself!

Ramphis.

He is silent.

All.

Traitor!

Ramphis.

Radames, Radames: thou didst desert
From the camp the day preceding the battle.

De'miei pianti la vendetta
Ora il cielo compirà.

Radames.

E la morte un ben supremo
Se per lei morir m' è dato:
Nel subir l'estremo fato
Gaudii immensi il core avrà;
L'ira umana io più non temo,
Temo sol la tua pietà.

(RADAMES parte circondato dalle Guardie.)

Amneris (cade desolata su un sedile).

Ohimè!..Morir mi sento.. Oh! chi lo
salva?
E in poter di costoro
Io stessa lo gettai!...Ora, a te impreco
Atroce gelosia, che la sua morte
E il lutto eterno del mio cor segnasti!

(Si volge e vede i SACERDOTI che attraversano la scena per entrare nel sotterraneo.)

Che veggo! Ecco i fatali
Gli inesorati ministri di morte...
Oh! ch' io non veggo quelle bianche larve!

(Si copre il volto colle mani.)

Sacerdoti (nel sotterraneo).

Spirito de l'Nume sovra noi discendi!
Ne avviva al raggio dell' eterna luce;
Pel labbro nostro tua giustizia apprendi.

Amneris.

Numi, pietà del mio straziato core...
Egli è innocente, lo salvate, o Numi!
Disperato, tremendo è il mio dolore!

(RADAMES, fra le Guardie, attraversa la scena e scende nel sotterraneo—AMNERIS al vederlo, mette un grido.)

Ramfis (nel sotterraneo).

Radamès—Radamès: tu rivelasti
Della patria i segretti allo straniero...

Sacerdoti.

Discólpati!

Ramfis.

Egli tace..

Tutti.

Traditor!

Ramfis.

Radamès, Radamès: tu disertasti
Dal campo il dì che precedea la pugna.

Priests.

Defend thyself!

Ramphis.

He is silent.

All.

Traitor!

Ramphis.

Radames, Radames: thou brokest thy faith,
Foresworn to thy country, king and honor.

Priests.

Defend thyself!

Ramphis.

He is silent.

All.

Traitor!
Radames thy fate is decided:
Thou shalt die the death of the infamous.
Under the altar of the angered god
To thee alive be opened the tomb.

Amneris.

To him alive—the tomb! Oh the infamous
    wretches!
Never satisfied with blood:
And then call themselves ministers of
    heaven!
(Attacking the PRIESTS, who issue from the subterranean
hall.)
Priests, you have done a wicked deed—
Infamous tigers! thirsting for blood;
You outrage earth and gods.
You punish him who has done no wrong.

Priests.

He is a traitor! he shall die.

Amneris

(to RAMPHIS).
Priest, this man whom thou slayest—
Thou knowest it—was loved by me.
The curse of a broken heart,
With his blood, will recoil on thee!

Priests.

He is a traitor! He shall die!
(They withdraw slowly.)

Amneris.

Impious band—anathema! On you
The vengeance of heaven will fall!
(Exit in despair.)

Sacerdoti.

Discólpati!

Ramfis.

Egli tace..

Tutti.

Traditor!

Ramfis.

Radamès, Radamès: tua fè violasti,
Alla patria spergiuro, al Re, all' onor.

Sacerdoti.

Discólpati!

Ramfis.

Egli tace..

Tutti.

Traditor!
Radamès è deciso il tuo fato;
Degli infami la morte tu avrai;
Sotto l'ara del Nume sdegnato
A te vivo fia schiuso l'avel.

Amneris.

A lui vivo..la tomba..Oh! gli infami!
Nè di sangue son paghi giammai..
E si chiaman ministri del ciel!
(Investendo i SACERDOTI che escono die sotterraneo.)
Sacerdoti: compiste un delitto..
Tigri infami di sangue assetate..
Voi le terra ed i Numi eltraggiate..
Voi punite chi colpa non ha.

Sacerdoti.

E traditor! morrà.

Amneris

(a RAMFIS).
Sacerdote! quest' uomo che uccidi,
Tu io sai.. da me un giorno fu amato..
L'anatéma d'un core straziato
Col suo sangue su te ricardrà!

Sacerdoti.

E traditor! morrà.
(Si allontanano lentamente.)

Amneris.

Empia razza! anatéma! su voi!
La vendetta del ciel scenderà!
(Esce disperata.)

SCENE II.

The Scene is divided into two floors. The upper floor represents the Interior of the Temple of Vulcan, resplendent with light and gold; the lower floor a subterranean hall; long rows of arcades which are lost in the darkness; colossal statue of Osiris, with the hands crossed, sustains the pilasters of the vault.

RADAMES is in the subterranean hall, on the steps of the staircase by which he has descended; above, two PRIESTS, engaged in closing the stone over the subterranean entrance.

Radames.

    The fatal stone is closed above me—
    Behold my tomb. The light of day
    I shall see no more. I shall no more see
      Aïda.
    Aïda, where art thou? May thou at least
    Live happy, and my dreadful fate
    Never know. What a groan! A ghost!
    A vision—No, it is a human shape—
    Heavens! Aïda!

Aïda.

    It is I.

Radames.

    Thou—in this tomb?

Aïda.

    My heart, prophetic of thy sentence,
    Into this tomb which opened itself for thee
    I furtive made my way.
    And here afar from every human glance
    In thy arms I wished to die.

Radames.

    To die! So pure and beautiful!
    To die for love of me;
    In the flower of thy youth
    To fly from life!
    Heaven created thee for love,
    And I kill thee by having loved thee!
    No, thou shalt not die!
    Too much I loved thee—
    Too beautiful art thou.

Aïda
            (raving).

    Seest thou the angel of death
    Radiant to us approaches?
    He takes us to eternal joys
    Under his golden pinions.
    Above us heaven has already opened;
    There every grief ceases;

SCENA II.

La Scena è divisa in due piani. Il piano superiore rappresenta l'interno del Tempio di Vulcano splendente d'oro e di luce; il piano inferiore un sotterraneo. Lunghe file d'arcate si perdono nell' oscurità. Statue colossali d'Osiride colle mani incrociate sostengono i pilastri della volta.

RADAMES è nel sotterraneo sui gradini della scala per cui è disceso—Al di sopra, due SACERDOTI intenti a chiudere la pietra del sotterraneo.

Radames.

    La fatal pietra sovra me si chiuse..
    Ecco la tomba mia.—Del dì la luce
    Più non vedrò..Non rivedò più Aïda...
    —Aïda, ove sei tu? Possa tu almeno
    Viver felice e la mia sorte orrenda
    Sempre ignorar!—Qual gemito!—Una
      larva..
    Una vision..No; forma umana è questa..
    Cielo!..Aïda!

Aïda.

    Son io..

Radames.

    Tu.. in questa tomba!

Aïda.

    Presago il core della tua condanna,
    In questa tomba che per te si apriva
    Io penetrai furtiva..
    E qui lontana da ogni umano sguardo
    Nelle tue braccia desiair morire.

Radames.

    Morir! si pura e bella!
    Morir per me d'amore..
    Degli anni tuoi nel fiore
    Fuggir la vita!
    T'aveva il cielo per l'amor creata,
    Ed io t'uccido per averti amata!
    No, non morrai!
    Troppo io t'amai!..
    Troppo sei bella!..

Aïda
            (vaneggiando).

    Vedi?..di morte l'angelo
    Radiante a noi si appressa..
    Ne adduce a eterni gaudii
    Sovra i suoi vanni d'ôr.
    Su noi già il ciel dischiudersi..
    Ivi ogni affanno cessa..

There begins the ecstasy
Of an immortal love.
(Songs and dances of the PRIESTESSES in the Temple.)

Aïda.

Sad song!

Radames.

The jubilee
Of the priests!

Aïda.

Our hymn of death . . . .

Radames
(trying to move the stone of the vault).
My strong arms
Cannot move thee, O fatal stone!

Aïda.

It is vain—all is over
For us on earth.

Radames
(with desperate resignation).
It is true—it is true!
(Goes to AÏDA and supports her.)

Aïda and Radames.

O earth, farewell! Farewell, vale of
tears—
Dream of joy which vanished in grief.
Heaven opens itself to us, and the wander-
ing souls
Fly to the rays of eternal day.
(AÏDA falls gently into the arms of RADAMES.)
(AMNERIS in mourning robes appears in the temple, and
goes to prostrate herself on the stone which closes the vault.)

Amneris.

Peace I pray for thee, O adored corse;
Isis appeased, may she unclose heaven to
thee!

Ivi comincia l'estasi
D'un immortale amor.
(Canti e danze della SACERDOTESSE nel Tempio.)

Aïda.

Triste canto!..

Radames.

Il tripudio
Dei Sacerdoti..

Aïda.

Il nostro inno di morte..

Radames
(cercando di smuovere la pietra del sotteraneo).
Nè le mie forti braccia
Smuovere ti potranno o fatal pietra!

Aïda.

Invan!..tutto è finito
Sulla terra per noi..

Radames
(con desolata rassegnazione).
E vero! è vero!
(Si avvicina ad AÏDA e la sorrege.)

Aïda e Radames.

O terra, addio; addio valle di pianti..
Sogno di gaudio che in dolor svani..
A noi si schiude il cielo, e l'alme erranti
Volano al raggio dell' eterno di.
(AÏDA cade dolcemente fra le braccia di RADAMES.)
(AMNERIS in abito di lutto apparisce nel Tempio e va a
prostrarsi sulla pietra che chiude il sotterraneo.)

Amneris.

Pace t'imploro—salma adorata..
Isi placata—ti schiuda il ciel!

THE END.

LUCIA DI LAMMERMOOR

by

GAETANO DONIZETTI

THE STORY OF
"LUCIA DI LAMMERMOOR"

LORD HENRY ASHTON, of Lammermoor, brother of Lucy, in order to retrieve his fallen fortunes, and extricate himself from a perilous position in which his participation in political movements, directed against the reigning dynasty, has placed him, arranged a marriage between his sister and Lord Arthur Bucklaw.

He (Lord Henry) is at this time ignorant of an attachment which exists between his sister Lucy and Sir Edgar Ravenswood, whose family has long been in a state of deadly enmity with his own.

Sir Edgar, absent on an embassy to France to look to the interests of his native country, Scotland, despatches many letters to his beloved Lucy. These letters are intercepted, and a forged paper tending to show the infidelity of Sir Edgar, is shown to the bewildered maiden.

Maddened by disappointed love, and urged by the necessities of her brother, Lucy unwillingly consents to become the bride of Lord Arthur Bucklaw, who is already at the gates of the castle, invited by Lord Ashton, who never doubts of his success in bending her to his schemes. When Lucy had signed the marriage contract, Edgar of Ravenswood suddenly appeared among the assemblage. Having just returned from France, he had come to claim the hand of Lucy. He was too late. Henry and his partisans repulsed the intruder with bitter words; swords were drawn, and but for the timely interference of the old Chaplain of the house of Ashton blood would have been spilt. Edgar yielded reluctantly to the entreaties of the Chaplain to quit the scene, but not before he had hurled the fiercest curses upon the hated house of Lammermoor. At night he was sought out in his retreat by the infuriated Henry, and the foes agreed upon a meeting on the ensuing morning, when Edgar, weary of life, would have thrown himself on his adversary's weapon, the last of a doomed race.

But Fate had willed it otherwise. The burden of woe heaped upon Lucy was too much for the mind of the unfortunate maiden. She had heard Edgar's reproaches with stupor, and remained absent-minded during the remainder of the ceremonies. At night, after the newly married pair had retired, and the inhabitants of the Castle were noisy with revels and mirth, groans were heard from the nuptial chamber, like those of a dying man. The Chaplain immediately burst the door open. On entering the room, Lord Bucklaw is discovered bleeding to death, while Lucy, in a fit of insanity, brandishes the sword of her victim, reeking with his blood. Her senses return, but she sinks under the horror of her situation, and dies the victim of disappointed love.

Edgar was meanwhile waiting for his enemy in the churchyard of Ravenswood; but Ashton came not. Struck with remorse at the scene of misery which his selfishness had wrought, he had fled. But Edgar's solitude was interrupted by a train of mourners coming from the Castle. They reported Lucy dying, and while they yet stayed, her decease was announced by the funeral-bell from the Castle. Edgar, upon hearing this, plunged his dagger into his breast, and sank down lifeless among the tombstones of his ancestors.

LUCIA DI LAMMERMOOR

ACT I.

SCENE I—A Vestibule. NORMAN and Chorus.

Norman and Chorus.

Search ye well through the neighboring val-
ley,
Through the ruins of yon gloomy tower.
This dark mystery that round us doth lower,
It concerneth our honor to clear.
As the lightning the stormcloud uprendeth,
So asunder this veil we will tear.
(Exeunt Chorus.)

SCENE II—Enter HENRY and RAYMOND.

Norman.

Thou seemest troubled?

Henry.

And 'tis with reason;
Thou knowest that of my destiny
Darkly the star declineth;
This hated Edgar, to my race
Bearing enmity deep and deadly,
From his rockbound tower laughing
To scorn my vows of vengeance, doth brave
me!
One hand alone can prop my falling fortune!
There is but one thing now can save me. Yet
Lucy
To Arthur still her hand refuseth! Ah!
sister
She is no longer.

Raymond.

A sorrowing
Maiden, who mourns o'er the tomb of a
parent,
A dear loved mother, say how canst thou
suppose
She'll yet think of marriage? Ah, respect
that heart
Which, enslaved of grief, dreams not of love.

ATTO I.

SCENA I—Vestibulo. NORMANDO e Coro.

Normando e Coro.

Percorrete ⎱
Percorriamo ⎰ le spiagge vicine—
Della torre le vaste rovine.
Cada il vel di sì turpe mistero;
Lo domanda, lo impone l'onor!
Fia che splenda il terribile vero,
Come lampo fra nubi d'orror!

SCENA II—ENRICO, RAIMONDO.

Normando.

Tu sei turbato?

Enrico.

E n'ho ben d'onde.
Il sai, del mio destin
Si ottenebrò la stella; intanto Edgardo,
Quel mortale nemico
Di mia prosapia, dalle sue rovine
Erge la fronte baldanzosa, e ride.
Sola una mano raffermar mi puote
Nel vacillante mio poter: Lucia
Osa respinger quella mano! Ah! suora
Non m'è colei!

Raimondo.

Dolente
Vergin, che geme sull' urna recente
Di cara madre, al talamo potria
Volger io sguardo? Ah! rispettiam quel core
Che, traffitto dal duol, schivo è d'amore.

Norman.
> Dreams not of love?
> Thou'rt fearfully mistaken.

Henry.
> What sayest thou?

Raymond.
> (I tremble.)

Norman.
> But hearken. Lucy some few weeks since
> Was walking home alone thro' the park.
> As near her mother's tomb she was passing,
> Furious a bull pursued her;
> Death at that time seemed certain,
> When thro' the still air came the short,
>   sharp ring
> Of a rifle; the ball sped truly;
> The bull fell lifeless.

Henry.
> And who was he that saved her?

Norman.
> One who in mystery still himself enshroud-
>   eth.

Henry.
> And think'st thou Lucy—

Norman.
> She loves him!

Henry.
> Then they have met since?

Norman.
> Each morning.

Henry.
> Say where?

Norman.
> By yonder fountain.

Henry.
> I tremble;
> Dost know the vile seducer's name?

Norman.
> Shrewdly
> I have suspicions—

Henry.
> Proceed! speak!

Norman.
> That 'tis an enemy!

Normando.
> Schivo d' amor! Lucia
> D' amore avvampa!

Enrico.
> Che favelli?

Raimondo.
> (Oh, detto!)

Normando.
> M'ascolta. Ella sen gia colà
> Del parco nel solingo vial
> Dove la madre giace sepolta—
> Impetuoso toro
> Ecco su lor s'avventa—
> Quando per l'aria sibilar si sente
> Un colpo, e al suol repente
> Cade la belva—

Enrico.
> E chi vibrò quel colpo?

Normando.
> Tal—che il suo nome ricopri d'un velo.

Enrico.
> Lucia, forse—

Normando.
> L' amò!

Enrico.
> Dunque il rivide?

Normando.
> Ogni alba!

Enrico.
> E dove?

Normando.
> In quel viale.

Enrico.
> Io fremo!
> Nè tu scopristi il seduttor?

ormando.
> Sospetto
> Io n'ho soltanto—

Enrico.
> Ah, parla!

Normando.
> E tuo nemico!

Raymond.	Raimondo.
(Oh, heaven!)	(Oh, Ciel!)
Norman.	Normando.
One thou detestest!	Tu lo detesti!
Henry.	Enrico.
Say whom thou meanest. Is't Edgar?	Esser potrebbe—Edgardo?
Norman.	Normando.
Ah! thou hast named him!	Ah, lo dicesti!

CRUDA, FUNESTA — *EACH NERVE WITH FURY* (Enrico)

Larghetto

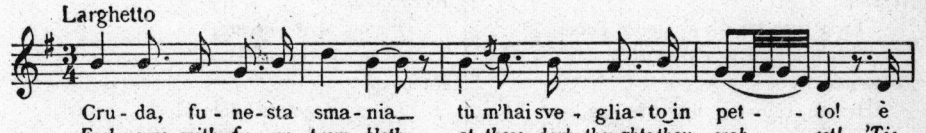

Cru - da, fu - ne - sta sma - nia tu m'hai sve - glia-to in pet - to! è
Each nerve with fu - ry trem - bleth at these dark thoughts thou wak - est! 'Tis

trop-po, è trop-poor-ri - bi-le, que-sto fa-tal sos-pet - to! Mi fa ge-la-re e
too fright-full 'tis too hor - ri-ble! Say but that thou mis - tak - est! My blood con-geal'd with

fre - me - re! sol - le-va in fron-te il crin, ah! mi fa ge-la-re e
rage doth freeze, And stag-nant stands each vein, ah! My ve-ry blood con-

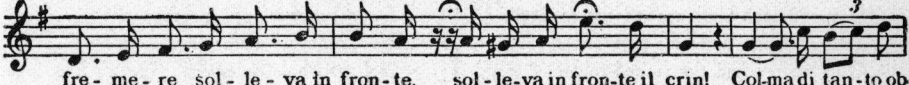

fre - me - re sol - le-va in fron-te, sol-le-va in fron-te il crin! Col-ma di tan-to ob
geal'd with rage doth freeze, and' stag-nant, and stag-nant stands each vein! Broth-er's coun-sel

bro-brio chi suo-ra a me nas-ce - a! Ah! pria che d'a-mor si per-fi-do
slight-ed, A sis-ter's hon-or blight-ed! Ah! thy black and match-less per-fi-dy

a me sve-lar-ti re - a se ti col-pis-se un ful-mi-ne, se ti col-pis-se un
full soon shall be re - quit - ed, On his head fall heav'n's thun-der-bolt, On his head fall heav'n's

ful - mi - ne, fo - ra men ri - o fo - ra men - ri - o do - lor ah,___
thun - der - bolt, Who thus our lin - eage, who thus our lin - eage would stain,___

_ fo - ra men - ri - o fo - ra men - ri - o fo - ra men ri - o do - lor.
Ah, who__ thus our lin - eage, who thus our lin - eage, Thus__ our lin - eage would stain.

Norman.	**Normando.**
'Twas cure for thy wounded honor	Pietoso al tuo decoro,
That made me give thee pain!	Io fu con te crudel!
Raymond.	**Raimondo.**
Heaven, calm his angry feeling,	La tua clemenza imploro!
This fury now restrain!	Tu lo smentisci, o Ciel!
SCENE III—Chorus of Hunters, and the above	SCENA III—Coro di Cacciatori, e detti.
Chorus.	**Coro**
	(entrandi).
Thy suspicions are now confirmed.	Il tuo dubbio è omai certezza.
Norman.	**Normando.**
Dost thou hear?	Odi tu?
Henry.	**Enrico.**
Proceed ye!	Narrate!
Raymond.	**Raimondo.**
Oh, dark hour!	(Oh, giorno!)
Chorus.	**Coro.**
Long we wandered o'er the mountain,	Como venti da stanchezza
Searched each cleft around the fountain,	Dupo lungo errare intorno,
Dale and hill, and vale and bower,	Noi posammo della torre
'Till we reached the ruined tower.	Nel vesti bole cadente.
There we saw a man who silently strode	Ecco tosto lo trascorre
From out the portal; mounting	In silenzio un uom palente
Straight his steed, he rapidly rode	Come appresso ei n'è venuto,
Down yonder valley, at a bound	Ravvisiam lo scono sciuto,
The torrent clearing.	Ei su rapido destriero
Then like lightning disappearing.	S'involò dal nostro guardo.
From a falconer passing near us	Qual s'appella un falconiero
We the intruder's name demanded.	Ne apprendeva qual s'appella.
Henry.	**Enrico.**
Who was it?	E quale?
Chorus.	**Coro.**
'Twas Edgar.	Edgardo!

Henry.	Enrico.
Edgar? Ah, vengeance! What deadly fury fires me.	Egli? Oh rabbia che m'accendi!
Thus to brave me doth he dare!	Contenerti un cor non può!
Raymond.	*Raimondo.*
Ah, not believe it yet—	Ah no, non credere! no, no—
Suspend your anger—Lucy—	Deh sospendi—Ma—
Henry.	*Enrico.*
No, no!	No, no!
Raymond.	*Raimondo.*
Hear me!	M'odi!
Henry.	*Enrico.*
I'll hear no more!	Udir non vuò.

LA PIETADE — *FROM MY BOSOM*   (Enrico and Chorus)

La pie - ta - de in suo_ fa - vo - re mi ti sen - si in-van mi
From my bos - om all fear_ I - ban - ish, From my breast now mer - cy doth

det - - ta Se mi par - li di_ ven - det - - ta so - lo in
an - ish, For the wrongs_ this man hath wrought me, Nought but

ten - der - ti_ po - trò! Scia - gu - ra - ti! il mi - o fu -
his blood can_ re - pay! Ev - 'ry pulse_ for re - venge_ wild - ly

ro - - re già su voi tre - men - do rug - ge, l'em-pia fiam - ma che vi
bound - ing, Ev - 'ry nerve is_ strung to_ mad - ness, And de - spair,_ with dead - ly

strug - ge io_ col - san - gue spe - gne - ro, io_ col san - gue, io_ col san -
fu - ry, Now to ven - geance points the way, now to ven - geance, _now to_ ven -

gue l'em - pia fiam - ma che_ vi strug - ge_ spe - gne - rò, spe - gne -
geance, now to ven - geance, now_ to ven - geance points the way, vengeance points the.

 rò,   col san- gue spe-gne-rò, l'em-pia fiam - ma chei vi strug-
way,   to ven-geance points the way. Nought, nought but blood my hate can al -

ge,   l'em-pia fiam-ma che vi strug-ge io col san-gue spe- gne- rò, si,
lay,   And de - spair with dead-ly fu - ry un - to ven-geance points the way, Yes,

spe - gne - rò, si, si, col   san- gue   spe- gne - rò, si, spe-gne - rò, si,
points the   way, Yes, yes, to ven-geance points the way, De - spair to   ven-geance

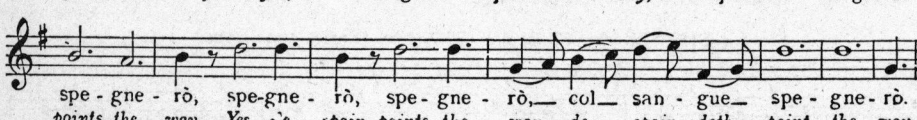

spe - gne - rò,   spe-gne - rò,   spe- gne - rò, col   san - gue spe - gne - rò.
points the   way, Yes, de-spair points the   way, de - spair doth point the way.

Norman and Chorus.	Normando e Coro.
He thy foe can ne'er escape thee,	Quell' indegno al nuovo albore
Let that thought thy rage allay.	L'ira tua fuggir non può.
(O'er thy house dark clouds do lower	(Ahi! qual nube di terrore
On this inauspicious day.)	Questa casa circondò!)
(Exeunt.)	(Partone.)
SCENE IV—A park. Enter LUCY and ALICE.	SCENA IV—Parco. LUCIA ed ALISA.
Lucy.	Lucia.
Still, still he comes not!	Ancor non giunse!
Alice.	Alisa.
Thou darest much in hither venturing;	Incauta a che mi traggi?
Think, should thy brother suspect, or aught	Avventurarti or che il fratel qui venne
discover,	E folle ardir!
Dark were thy doom.	
Lucy.	Lucia.
'Tis too true! Ah, Edgar knoweth not	Ben parli. Edgardo sappia
What fearful perils, what dangers circle	Qual ne circonda orribile periglio!
round me!	
Alice.	Alisa.
Why turn'st thou toward yon fountain	Perchè d' intorno il ciglio
That glance of terror!	Volgi alterrita?
Lucy.	Lucia.
Yonder fountain! ah! Alice,	Quella fonte, ah!
Whenever I behold it	Mai senza temar non veggo.
Dark fears oppress me! A Ravenswood here	Ah tu lo sai; un Ravenswood ardende
By jealousy with mad fury inspired,	Di geloso furor, l'amata donna

LUCIA DI LAMMERMOOR

His dear loved lady most foully murdered,
And she unhappy in those dark waters
Was cast, and there did find a sepulchre.
Her shade hath once appeared to me.

Alice.

What say'st thou?

Lucy.

Dear Alice, ah, listen.

Colà trafisse; e l' infelice cadde
Nell' onda ed ivi rimanca sepolta.
M'apparve l'ombra sua.

Alisa.

Che dici?

Lucia.

Ascolta.

REGNAVA NEL SILENZIO — *SILENCE O'ER ALL*   (Lucia)

Reg-na-va nel si-len-zio al-ta la not-te bru-na,
Si-lence o'er all was reign-ing, Dark was the night and low-'ring,

col-pia la fon-te un pal-li-do rag-gio di te-tra Lu-na,
And o'er yon foun-tain her pal-lid ray Yon-der pale moon was pour-ing,

quan-do un som-mes-so ge-mi-to fra l'au-re u-dir si fè, ed
Faint-ly a sharp but sti-fled sigh Fell on my star-tled ear, And

ec-co, ec-co su quel mar-gi-ne l'om-bra mo-strar-si, l'om-bra mo-strar-si a
straight-way up-on that same foun-tain's brink, The spec-tre did ap-pear, spec-tre did ap-

me, ah! qual di chi par-la muo-ver-si il lab-bro su-o ve-
pear, ah! Fast fixed it kept its blood-less lip, No fur-ther sound e-

de-a, e con la ma-no e-sa-ni-me chia-mar-mi a se pa-
mit-ting, But slow on high its phan-tom hand, Threat-'ning it did up-

re-a; stet-te un mo-men-to im-mo-bi-le, poi rat-ta di le-
rear, Stood for a mo-ment im-mov-a-ble, Then van-ish'd from my

gnò_____ e l'on-da pria si lim-pi - da di_____ san-gue ros- seg -
view,_____ While that pure and lim-pid_____ stream to_____ blood had____changed its

giò, si, pria si, lim-pi - da di_ san-gue ros- seg- gio, si, pria si,
hue, While that pure lim-pid stream to_ blood had changed its hue, While that pure

lim-pi - da, ah, _____ di ros - seg - gio.
lim-pid stream, ah, _____ had changed its hue.

Oh, what horrid presage	Ah, il pressagio orenda
Is this? I ought to banish	E questa cancellar,
From my heart the fatal,	Dovrei dal petto
Loved object, but I cannot,	Il fatale amato oggnetto ma nol posso,
No, I cannot; it is my life,	Egli è una luce e conforto al mio penar.
And comfort to my suffering.	

QUANDO RAPITA — *THEN SWIFT AS THOUGHT*   (Lucia)

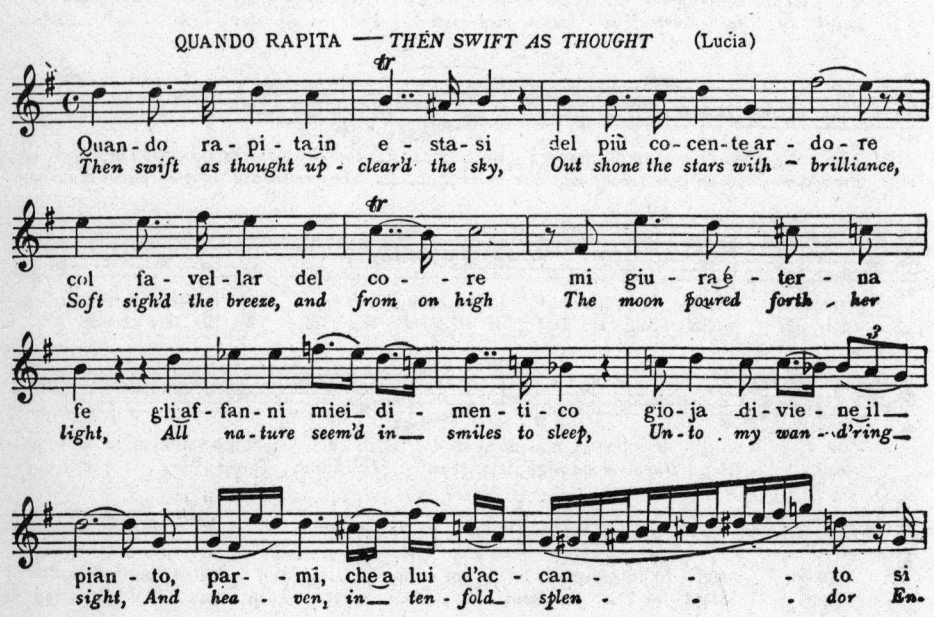

Quan- do ra - pi - ta in e - sta - si del più co-cen-te ar- do - re
Then swift as thought up - clear'd the sky,   Out shone the stars with ~ brilliance,

col fa - vel- lar del co - re mi giu-ra é-ter - na
Soft sigh'd the breeze, and from on high   The moon poured forth, her

fe gli af - fan - ni miei di - men - ti - co gio - ja di - vie - ne il_
*light, All na- ture seem'd in_ smiles to sleep, Un- to my wan- d'ring_*

pian- to, par - mì, che a lui d'ac - can - - - to, si
sight, And hea- ven, in_ ten- fold_ splen - - - dor En-

schiu- da il ciel per - me _____ si ____ in ____
robed __ then the wan-ing night, _____ in ____

schiu- da il ciel per - me ____ si ____ in ____
splen - dor en - robed the night, _____ in ____

schiu- da il ciel ____ per me a lui d'ac - - can- to si
splen - dor en - robed ____ the night, En-robed then ____ the night, Heav'n

schiu- da ____ il ciel ____ per - me ah!
robed then ____ the wan - ing ____ night, ah! ____

____ si ____ schiu- da il ciel, il ciel per me, si, si, a
in ____ ten - fold splen - dor robed the night, Ah, yes, in

lui d'ac - can - - to par - che si schiu- da il ciel ____ per - me.
splen - dor robed the night, Heav'n in splen - dor __ robed __ the __ night.

Alice.	Alisa.
At length he comes! Concealed behind the foliage	Egli s'avanza! La vicina soglia
A careful watch I'll keep.	Io cauta veglierò.
(Exit ALICE.)	
SCENE V—EDGAR and LUCY.	SCENA V—EDGARDO e LUCIA.
Edgar.	Edgardo.
My Lucy, your pardon	Lucia perdona
That past the hour appointed	Se ad ora inusitata
I've delayed thus our meeting.	Io vederti chiedea—
Most powerful reasons from thee detained me!	Ragion possente a ciò mi trasse.
On the coming morn, love,	Pria che in Ciel biancheggi
Ere breaks the dawn, from my home and country	L'alba novella, delle patrie sponde
I must depart.	Lung͟ garò.

Lucy.

What say'st thou?

Edgar.

To France I bend my steps, love!
Business of moment calls me thus early from
  thee.
'Tis Scotland needs my service!

Lucy.

And unto misery
Thou thus abandonest me!

Edgar.

Yet ere I leave thee
I'll seek thy brother; to him in truth and
  friendship
This hand I'll tender, and as a pledge of
  peace
'Twixt our houses I'll ask of him thine!

Lucy.

What hear I?
Ah, no, I pray thee—In secrecy and silence
Still let our loves concealed be!

Edgar.

I comprehend thee. Thy fell brother,
My dark, relentless foe, for blood
Still yearneth, nor vengeance will forego.
  He killed my father,
He hath ta'en away my heritage! What
  more?
What seeks he more? That heart
Ferocious, what would it?
My entire utter ruin? He'd take my life!
Yes, he hates me!

Lucy.

Ah, no!

Edgar.

Abhors me!

Lucy.

Calm, oh, calm this fearful passion!

Edgar.

Deadly fury my heart inflameth!
Hear me!

Lucy.

My Edgar!

Edgar.

Hear me, and tremble!

Lucia.

Che dici?

Edgardo.

Pe' Franchi lidi amici
Sciolgo le vele—ivi trattar m'è dato
Le sorti della Scozia.

Lucia.

E me nel pianto
Abbandoni così?

Edgardo.

Pria di lasciarti
Ashton mi vegga—stenderò placato
A lui la destra, e la tua destra, pegno
Fra noi di pace, chiederò.

Lucia.

Che ascolto?
Ah, no! Rimanga nel silenzio avvolte
Per or l'arcano affetto.

Edgardo.

Intendo. Di mia stirpe
Il reo persecutore
Ancor pago non è. Mi tolse il padre,
Il mio retaggio avito—nè basta?
Che brama ancor?
Quel cor feroce e rio?
La mia perdita intera? il sangue mio
Ei m'odia!

Lucia.

Ah, no!

Edgardo.

M'abborre!

Lucia.

Calma! Oh, Ciel, quell' ira estrema!

Edgardo.

Fiamma ardente in sen mi corre!
M'odi.

Lucia.

Edgardo!

Edgardo.

M'odi, e trema!

By this lone tomb, o'er the cold grave
Where my father's bones lie moulding,
With thy kindred eternal warfare
To the death I swore to wage.
Ah! when I saw thee my heart relented
Of my dark vow I half repented;
But my oath remains unbroken,
Still I've power to redeem my gage.

Lucy.

Ah! pray calm thee, ah, restrain thee;
Think what misery will soon enthral me;
I can scarce from fear sustain me;
Would'st thou have me die with terror?
Yield thee, yield thee to the dictates of af-
fection.
'Tis a nobler, purer passion,
Let that thought thy wrath assuage!

Edgar.

Here, then! here in the eye of heaven
Swear, thy true faith to me now is given;
Him above, who sees and hears us,
Witness these mutual vows of love!
Thy fate forever to mine united!
Thou art mine, love!

Lucy.

Yes, I am thine, love.
Thou who see'st us, Thou who hearest us,
Witness these our vows of love!
Power eternal, oh, grant Thy blessing,
Look down kindly from above.

Edgar.
Now at length we must part, love!

Lucy.
Heavy falleth that word on my heart, love,
Thou with thee this heart wilt bear—

Edgar.
Mine with thee will stay forever!

Lucy.
Ah! thou wilt not fail to write me?
Each dear letter thou dost send me,
Each fond word thou dost indite me,
Many a lonely hour will cheer.

Edgar.
A cherished memory of thee,
Dearest, shall ever treasured be!

Sulla tomba che rinserra
Il tradito genitore,
Al tuo sangue eterna guerra
Io giurai nel mio furore!
Ma ti vidi, in cor mi nacque
Altro affetto, e l'ira tacque.
Pur quel voto non è infranto—
Io potrei compirlo ancor!

Lucia.

Deh, ti placa! deh, ti frena!
Può tradirne un solo accento!
Non ti basti la mia pena?
Vuoi ch'io mora di spavento?
Ceda, ceda ogn' altro affetto,
Solo amor t'infiammi il petto!
Ah, il più nobile, il più santo
De tuoi voti è un puro amor!

Edgardo.
Quì, di sposa eterna fede
Quì mi giura, al Cielo innante!
Dio ci ascolta, Dio ci vede!
Tempio ed ara è un core amante.
Al tuo fato unisco il mio:
Son tuo sposo!

Lucia.
E tua son io!
A' miei voti amore invoco!
A' miei voti invoco il Ciel!
Ah soltanto il nostro foco
Spegnerà di morte il gel.

Edgardo.
Separarci omai conviene.

Lucia.
Oh, parola a me funesta!
Il mio cor con te ne viene!

Edgardo.
Il mio cor con te quì resta!

Lucia.
Ah, talor del tuo pensiero
Venga un foglio messaggiero
E la vita fuggitiva
Di speranza nudrirò!

Edgardo.
Io di te memoria viva
Sempre, o cara, serberò!

VERRANNO LA SULL' AURE —*MY SIGHS SHALL ON THE BALMY* Duet (Lucia and Edgardo)

Moderato legato

LUCIA

Ver - ran - no là sull' au - re i miei sos - pi - ri ar - den - ti, u -
My sighs shall on the balm-y breeze That hith-er wafts thee, be borne, love; Each

drai nel mar che mor-mo - ra___ l'e-co de' miei la - men - ti, pen -
mur-m'ring wave shall e -cho make___ how I thy absence do mourn,__ love!___ Ah!

san - do ch'io di ge - mi - ti mi pas-co e di do - lor,___ spar-gi un a -
think of me when far__ a - way, with nought my heart to cheer;__ I shall be -

ma - ra la - gri - ma su' ques-to peg-no al - lor, ah!___ su___ ques-to .
dew each thought of thee with ma-ny a bit -ter tear! Ah!___ with___ ma -ny a

peg-no al - lor, ah,___ sù___ ques-to peg-no al - lor,___ ah!___ su quel__
bit - ter tear' Ah!___ with___ ma-ny a bit - ter tear!___ Ah!___ ma -ny a..

EDGARDO tear.

peg-no al-Ver-ran-no a te sull' au - re i miei sos - pi-ri ar-den -
bit - ter The balm - y breeze that bears thy sigh, will waft one back from me,__

ti; u - drai nel mar che mor-mo - ra___ l'e-co de miei la - men - ti: pen -
love; The mur-m'ring waves re - e-choing still__ I'm ev - er constant to thee, love, Ah!

san - do ch'io di ge - mi - ti mi pas-co e di do - lor,___ spar-gi un a -
think of me when far__ a - way with nought my heart to cheer;__ I shall be -

ma - ra la - gri - ma su ques-to peg-no al-lor, ah!___ su___ ques-to peg-no al -
dew each thought of thee with ma-ny a bit -ter tear! Ah!___ with___ ma-ny a bit -ter

ah!___ si,___ su quel peg-no al-lor, Ed - gar - do.
Ah!___ with___ ma-ny a bit - ter tear,___ Ed - gar.

lor, ah!___ sú___ ques-to peg-no al-lor,___ ah,___ su quel peg-no al-lor.
tear, Ah!___ with___ ma-ny a bit - ter tear!___ Ah!___ ma-ny a bit - ter tear.

Il tuo scrit-to sem-pre vi-va   la me-mo-ria in me ter - rà!
Ah! thou wilt not fail to write me,   ma-ny a lone-ly hour 'twill cheer;

Ah!   si!   si, si, Lu - ci-a, si,
Fear   not!   Have no fear, thou shalt

ah!_____ ver - ran-no a te sull' au - re i tuoi sos-
Ah!_____ my sighs shall on the balm-y breeze that hith - er

si!   ah!_____ ver - ran-no a te sull' au - re i miei sos-
hear!   Ah!_____ my sighs shall on the balm-y breeze that hith - er

pi - ri ar-den - ti, u - dro nel mar che mor-mo - ra___ l'e-co de tuoi la-
wafts thee be borne, love; Each mur-m'ring wave shall e - cho make how I thy ab-sence do

pi - ri ar-den - ti, u - drai nel mar che mor-mo - ra___ l'e-co de miei la-
wafts thee be borne, love; Each mur-m'ring wave shall e - cho make how I thy ab-sence do

men - ti pen - san - do che di ge - mi - ti mi pas - coe di do-
mourn,— love! Ah! think of me when far - a - way, with nought my heart to

men - ti!
mourn, love!

lor___ spar - gi su ques - to pe - gno al -
cheer;— Ah! dear love! with ma - ny a bit - ter

spar - gi un a - ma - ra la - gri - ma su ques - to pe - gno al -
I shall be - dew each thought of thee with ma - ny a bit - ter

lor, ah!___ su___ ques - to pe - gno al - lor, ah!___ su___ ques -
tear, Ah!___ with___ ma - ny a bit - ter tear, ah!___ with___ ma - ny a

lor, ah!___ su___ ques - to pe - gno al - lor, ah!___ su___ ques -
tear, Ah!___ with___ ma - ny a bit - ter tear, ah,___ with___ ma - ny a

to pe - gno al - lor,___ ah!___ ques - to pe - - gno al - lor.
bit - ter tear, ah,___ ah,___ ma - ny a bit - - ter tear!

to pe - gno al - lor,___ ah!___ ques - to pe - - gno al - lor.
bit - ter tear, ah,___ ah,___ ma - ny a bit - - ter tear!

END OF THE FIRST ACT.

ACT II.

SCENE I—An Apartment. HENRY and NORMAN.

Norman.

Thy sister will shortly now be here.

Henry.

I tremble
To meet her. The nuptial guests are fast as-
sembling!
Within the castle my noble friends and kins-
men
Wait now to greet the bridegroom: for
Arthur only
We tarry! Should she still pertinaciously
persist
In opposing—

Norman.

Have no fear! The long absence
Of him she mourneth, the letters
We've intercepted, and the false news thou'lt
tell her,
Will quench all hope that yet may linger.
Believing Edgar faithless, from her bosom
love will vanish!

Henry.

See, she approaches! Thou hast that forged
letter,
Give it me—Now haste thee to the northern
entrance,
There keep watch, and wait
The approach of Arthur, and with all speed,
on his arrival
Conduct him hither!

(Exit NORMAN.)

SCENE II—HENRY and LUCY.

Henry.

Draw nearer, my Lucy,
On this fair morn accept a brother's greeting!
May this glad day, sacred to love and
Hymen,
Auspicious prove to thee. Thou hearest me?
Thou'rt silent!

ATTO II.

SCENA I—Sala. ENRICO e NORMANDO.

Normando.

Lucia fra poco a te verrà.

Enrico.

Tremante
L'aspetto. A festeggiar le nozze illustri
Già nel castello i nobili congiunti
Di mia famiglia accolsi; in breve Arturo
Quì volge; e s'ella pertinace osasse
    D'opporsi—

Normando.

Non temer; la lunga assenza
Del tuo nemico—i fogli
Da noi rapiti e la bugiarda nuova
Ch'egli s'accese di altra fiamma—in core
Di Lucia spegneranno il cieco amore.

Enrico.

Ella s'avanza! Il simulato foglio
Porgimi; ed esci sulla via che tragge
Alla città regina
Di Scozia; e quì fra plausi e liete grida
Conduci Arturo.

(Parte NORMANDO.)

SCENA II—ENRICO e LUCIA.

Enrico.

Appressati, Lucia.
Sperai più lieta in questo dì vederti,
In questo dì, che d'imeneo le faci
Si accendono per te. Mi guardi e taci?

IL PALLOR FUNESTO — *SEE THESE CHEEKS* (Lucia)

Il pal - lor fun-es-to or-ren - do che ri - co-pre il vol - to
See these cheeks so pale and hag-gard, See these fea-tures so worn with

mi - o ti rim-pro - ve-ro ta-cen - do il mio
sad - ness! Do not they be-tray too plain - ly all my

stra-zio il mio do-lo - re per-do - na-re ti pos-sa un
an-guish, All my de - spair,— too? Par - don— may'st thou from Heav'n not—

Di-o l'i-nu-ma-no tu-o ri-gor, per-do-nar-ti pos-sa un Di-o, ah,— l'i-nu-
vain-ly ask for this thy in-hu-man con-straint, Par-don may'st thou ask from Heav'n for— thy in-

ma - no— tuo ri - gor,
hu - man, cruel con - straint,

l'i-nu - ma - no— tuo ri -
this thy harsh and— cruel con -

gor, il— tuo ri - gor, il— tuo ri - gor e il mi-o do - - - lor.
straint, This harsh, in - hu - man, cruel con - straint, cru-el con - - straint

Henry.	Enrico.
Cease this wild recrimination,	A ragion mi fe' spietato,
Both to thee and me degrading.	Quel che t'arse indegno affetto;—
Of the past be thou but silent!	Ma si taccia del passato—
I thy brother will no further make complaint!	Tuo fratello io sono ancor;
	Spenta è l'ira nel mio petto—

Flown has my anger! Banish thy dejection,
Buried be all that thine honor could taint.
A noble husband—

Lucy.

Cease to urge me!
To another true faith I have sworn!

Henry.

To another!

Lucy.

My brother!

Henry.

'Tis well!
By this letter thou may'st see
How he keeps his faith with thee!
Read it! (Hands her a letter.)

Lucy.

How beats my fluttering heart!

Henry.

Thou dost falter—

Lucy.

Ah! great Heaven!
(Reads.)
Break, poor heart!

Spegni tu l'insano amor.
Nobil sposo—

Lucia.

Cessa! ah, cessa!
Ad altr' uom giurai la fè.

Enrico.

Nol potevi.

Lucia.

Enrico!

Enrico.

Basti!
Questo foglio appien ti dice,
Qual crudel, qual empio amasti
Leggi!

Lucia.

Il core mi balzò!

Enrico.

Tu vacilli!

Lucia.

Me infelice!
(Legge.)
Ahi! la folgore piombò!

SOFFRIVA NEL PIANTO — *MY SUFF'RINGS* (Lucia and Enrico)

Sof-fri-va nel pian-to, lan-gui-a nel do-lo-re, la
My suf-frings and sor-rows I've borne with-out re-pin-ing, I

spe-me la vi-ta ri-po-si in un cor l'istan-te di
hoped that the mor-row some com-fort might dawn! All's lost now, for-

mor-te e giun-to per me quel co-re in-fe-
sa ken, de-sert-ed, for-lorn, My last hope de-

de-le ad al-tra ad al-tra si die! Un fol-le t'ac-
part-ed, my true love, my love turn'd to scorn. Thy name thou dis-

se - se un per-fi - do co - re tra-dis-ti il tuo san - gue per vil se-dut -
gra-cest, Thy blood thou de - ba - sest, Thy love he dis - dain - eth, Thy-self hè de-

to - re ma de-gna del -cie - lo nea-ves-ti mer - ce - de quel co-re in-fe-
fam - eth, The judgment of Heav - en at length o - ver - takes thee, Thy ra - ce's dark

LUCIA

Ohi - me! l'i-stan-te tre - men-do e giun-to per
Ah me, my suff-'rings and sor - rows I bore un - re

de - le ad al-tra si die un fol-le t'ac - ce se un per-fi-do a
foe - man doth treat thee with scorn, Thy name thou dis - gra - cest, Thy blood thou de -

me, si quel co - re in-fe - de - le ad al - tra si
pin - ing, I hoped that to - mor - row some com - fort might

mo - re tra - dis-ti il tuo san - gue per vil se-dut-
bas - est, Thy love he dis - dain - eth, thy - self he de -

die - do, quel so - re in-fe - de - le ad al-tra si diè quel co -
dawn_____ All's lost_ now! for - sak - en, de-sert-ed, for-lorn! My last

to - re, ma de - gna del cie - lo nea-ves-ti mer-ce quel co -
fam - eth, Thy ra - ce's dark foe - man doth treat thee with scorn, Thy ra -

(Noise heard without.)

(Gridi al di fuori.)

Lucy.

What hear I?

Henry.

Those sounds of gladness
Tell the arrival—

Lucy.

Of whom?

Henry.

Thy destined husband.

Lucy.

Through every vein
My blood doth seem congealing.
I tremble!

Lucia.

Che fia?

Enrico.

Suonar di giubilio
Odi la riva?

Lucia.

Ebbene?

Enrico.

Giunge il tuo sposo!

Lucia.

Un brivido
Mi corse per le vene!
Tremo!

Henry.
The marriage rites await thee now!
Lucy.
The dark grave be my refuge rather!
Henry.
Oh, fatal hour of dark despair!
Hear me. The late rebellion
I was one who secretly abetted;
To Arthur, for my present safety
I'm alone indebted!
He from a foul, a traitor's doom,
Alone hath power to save me.
Lucy.
And I then?
Henry.
Thou must
Wed him.
Lucy.
My brother!
Henry.
Come to the altar.
Lucy.
I love another.
Henry.
Still dost thou falter?
Lucy.
But—
Henry.
To the altar!
Lucy.
Oh, heaven!
Henry.
I'm thy guardian, darest thou brave me?
I'm thy brother—wilt thou save me?
From the hands of thee, my sister,
Must I meet a traitor's doom?

See the axe, by one thread hanging;
Hark; the deep-toned deathbell clanging.
Hath affection lost all power?
Wilt consign me unto the tomb?
Lucy.
I'm thy sister, dost thou love me!
I am dying, will that move thee!
From the hands of thee, my brother,
Must I meet now this dreadful doom!

Enrico.
A te appresta il talamo.
Lucia.
La tomba a me s'appresta!
Enrico.
Ora fatale è questa!
Spento è Guglielmo ascendere
Vedremo il tron Maria.
Prostrata è nella polvere
La parte ch'io seguia;
Dal precipizio solo
Arturo può salvarmi sol egli.
Lucia.
Ed Io—
Enrico.
Salvarmi
Devi—
Lucia.
Enrico!
Enrico.
Vieni allo sposo.
Enrico.
Ad altri giurai.
Enrico.
Devi salvarmi?
Lucia.
Ma—
Enrico.
Il devi!
Lucia.
Oh, Ciel!
Enrico.
Se tradirmi tu potrai,
La mia sorte è già compita
Tu m' involi onore e vita:
Tu la scure appresti a me!

Ne' tuoi sogni mi vedrai
Ombra irata e minacciosa.
Quella scure sanguinosa
Starà sempre innanzi a te.
Lucia.
Tu, che vedi il pianto mio,—
Tu, che leggi in questo core,—
Se respinto il mie dolore,
Come in terra, in Ciel non è!

Hopeless misery all surrounding,
E'en while the marriage bell is sounding;
Fear and hate will be my dower;
Better had I wed the tomb.

(Exeunt.)

SCENE III—Corridor. LUCY and RAYMOND.

Lucy.

Thy news?

Raymond.

Hope hath departed,
Even the last faint ray hath fled!
Believing as thou suspectest,
That perchance thy brother,
His ends to answer, thy notes had intercepted,
And bared all correspondence
Between thee and young Edgar,
I took thy letter! To France I sent it,
By secure conveyance. He did receive it
Five weeks since! Still is he silent!
'Tis too certain that he to thee hath proved
unfaithful.

Lucy.

What dost thou counsel?

Raymond.

To submit to thy destiny.

Lucy.

The oath I pledged him?

Raymond.

Thou talkest wildly—
The holy nuptial vow
Through the priest can alone be sworn, at
the altar,
Nor heaven nor man holds aught else binding.

Lucy.

Ah, cease, pray; tho' my mind thou convincest,
Still deaf to reason's voice my heart resisteth!

Raymond.

Be firm and conquer!

Lucy.

What utter misery awaits me!

Tu mi togli, eterno Iddio!
Questa vita disperata!
Io son tanta sventurata,
Che la morte è un ben per me!

(Partone.)

SCENA III—LUCIA e RAIMONDO.

Lucia.

Ebben?

Raimondo

Di tua speranza
L'ultimo raggio tramontò.
Credei al tuo sospetto
Che il fratel chiudesse
Tutte le strade, onde sul Franco suolo,
All uom che amar giurasti
Non guingesser tue nuove;
Io stesso un foglio date vergato,
Per secura mano; recarglifeci
In vano! Tace mai sempre—
Quel silenzio assai d'infidelta ti parlà!

Lucia.

E me consigli?

Raimondo.

Di piegarti al destino.

Lucia.

E il giuramento?

Raimondo.

Tu pur veneggi!
I nuziati voti
Che il ministro di Dio non bene,
Nè il ciel nè il mondo riconosce.

Lucia.

Ah! cede persuasa la mente,
Ma sordo alla ragion resisto il core.

Raimondo.

Vincerlo è forza.

Lucia.

Oh sventurato amore!

Raymond.

Ah, to thy destiny calmly resign thee!
Horrors greater far will else befall thee;
To the voice of affection incline thee!
From her grave thy mother doth call thee.
From this peril save thy brother!
'Tis a parent doth implore.
See yon angry shade uprise before thee,
Mark yon blood-stained scaffold drenched
   with gore.

Lucy.

Cease—

Raymond.

Save him!

Lucy.

Thou hast conquered!
I will act as thou requirest.

Raymond.

O what rapture! In me confide thee.
Every cloud now disappeareth!
This thy heroic sacrifice,
Laid on the shrine of duty,
Shall be by holy angels
Recorded in heaven above.
Tho' man may not regard it,
Tho' earth may not reward it,
Thy Maker who ruleth thy destiny
Doth mark this deed of love.

Lucy.

Guide thou me, support me,
Thou hast conquered, I confide in thee!

Raimondo.

Ah, cedi, o più sciagure
Ti sovra stanti infelice,
Per te venere mie cure
Per l'estinta genitrice,
Il periglio d' un fratello
Deh ti muova e cangi il cor!
O la madre nell' avello
Fremerà per te d'orror.

Lucia.

Taci—

Raimondo.

Cedi—

Lucia.

Ah, vincerti.
Non son tanto suatuarata.

Raimondo

Oh! qual giosa; in me tu desti!
Oh qual nube hai dissipata!
Al ben de' tuoi vittima
Offri, Lucia, te stessa,
E tanto sagrifizio
Scritto nel ceil sarà.
Se la pietà degli uomini
A te non fia concessa,
V' è un Dio, che tergere
Il pianto tuo saprà.

Lucia.

Guidami tu, tu reggime
Son fuori, di me stessa!

SCENE IV—Henry, Arthur, Norman; Knights and Ladies related to Ashton; Pages, Squires; Inhabitants of Lammermoor, and Domestics.

SCENA IV—Enrico, Arturo, Normando; Cavalieri e Dame congiunti di Ashton; Paggi, Armigeri; Abitanti di Lammermoor, e Domestici.

PER TE IMMENSO — *HOPE BRIGHTLY* (Chorus)

Per te d'im-men-so giu-bi-lo   tut-to s'av-vi-va in-tor-no, · per te veg-giam ri-
Hope bright-ly beams be-fore thee now,   *Ah, day of joy and glad-ness, Heav'n sheds its sun-light*

na-sce-ra   del-la spe-ran-za il   gior-no,   qui l'a-mis-tà ti
o'er thee now,   *No more of grief or*   *sad-ness.*   *Dark tho' the clouds did*

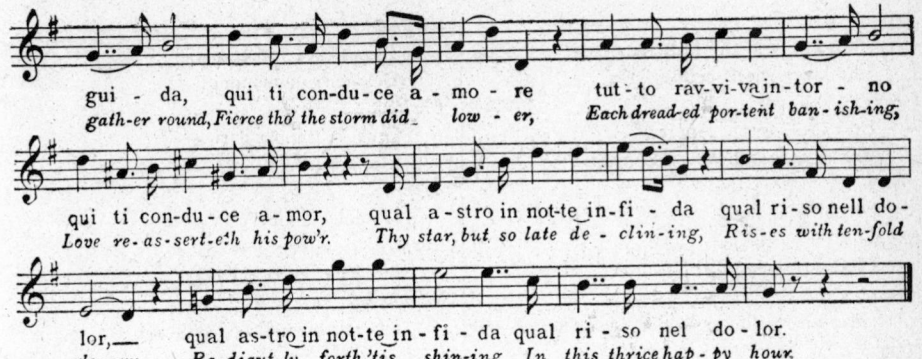

gui - da, qui ti con-du-ce a - mo - re tut - to rav-vi-va in tor - no
gath-er round, Fierce tho' the storm did_ low - er, *Each dread-ed por-tent ban-ish-ing,*

qui ti con-du-ce a-mor, qual a-stro in not-te in-fi - da qual ri-so nell do-
Love re-as-sert-eth his pow'r. *Thy star, but so late de - clin-ing,* *Ris-es with ten-fold*

lor,— qual as-tro in not-te in-fi - da qual ri - so nel do-lor.
glo - ry, *Ra-diant-ly forth 'tis shin-ing In this thrice hap-py hour.*

Arthur.	Arturo.
My friend, I joy to meet thee;	Per poco fra le tenebre
As brother here I greet thee!	Sparsi la vostra stella,
Ever may this our union	Io la farò risorgere
In friendship's bonds combining,	Più fulgida e più bella,
In friendship's bonds entwining,	La man mi porgi Enrico,
Prove prosperous unto thee;	Ti stringi a questo cor,
This hand I give thee, shall henceforth thy	A te ne vengo amico, fratello, e defensor
defender be!	Dov' è Lucia?
But where is Lucy?	
Henry.	Enrico.
Shortly now will she be here.	Qui guingere or la vedrem.
If she in tears perchance appeareth,	Se in lei soverchia è la mestizia,
This her demeanor I pray you pardon;	Ma ravigliarti non dei
Her mother's death she mourns,	Dal duolo oppressa e vinta
By grief her heart is torn.	Piange la madre estinta.
Arthur.	Arturo.
'Tis well. One thing tell me.	M'è noto. Orsolvo un dubbio
Fame says that young Edgar	Famo suonò, ch' Edgardo
Some months since, with mad presumption's	Sovr' essa temerario
boldness,	Alzare osò lo sguardo.
Of you did ask her hand—	
Henry.	Enrico.
'Tis true he had that boldness, but—	E vero, quel folle ardia, ma—
Chorus.	Coro.
See, Lucy comes!	S' avvanza a te Lucia!
Henry. (Enter Lucy.)	Enrico. (Entra Lucia.)
Still for our mother weeping?	Piange la madre estinta.
There stands thy husband—(Ungrateful!	Ecco il tuo sposo. (Incauta!
Would'st be my ruin?)	Perdermi vuoi!)
Lucy.	Lucia.
Great Heaven!	Gran Dio!

Arthur.

Thus lowly at thy feet, fair maid,
Thy lover kneels before thee.

Henry.

Dost hear, girl? Approach,
And sign thy dower. We wait thee.

Arthur.

Oh, blissful hour!

Lucy.

(I go to the sacrifice!)

Raymond.

(Heaven shield her in this trying hour.)

Henry.

(Thou know'st my power.)—Sign it!

Lucy.

Ah, misery! (She signs.)
'Tis done! I've writ I have signed it.

Henry.

(I breathe again!)

Lucy.

(My blood seems turned to ice.
All is over!)

Chorus.

What means this?
Who cometh?

SCENE V—Edgar and the above.

Edgar.

'Tis Edgar!

Lucy.

Edgar!
Oh, hide me, earth!

Chorus.

Fearful hour!

Arturo.

Ti piaccia i voti accogliere
Del tenero amor mio!

Enrico.

Omai si compia il rito—
T'appressa!

Arturo.

Oh dolce invito!

Lucia.

(Io vado al sacrifizio!)

Raimondo.

(Reggi, buon Dio, l'afflitta!)

Enrico.

Non esitar!

Lucia.

(Me misera!
La mia condanna ho scritta!)

Enrico.

(Respiro!)

Lucia.

(Io gelo ed ardo!
Io manco!)

Tutti.

Qual fragor!
Chi giunge?

SCENA V—Edgardo, Lucia, servi e detti.

Edgardo.

Edgardo!

Lucia.

Edgardo!
Oh, fulmine!

Gli Altri.

Oh, terror!

CHI MI FRENA —— *WHAT RESTRAINS ME* (Edgardo and Enrico)

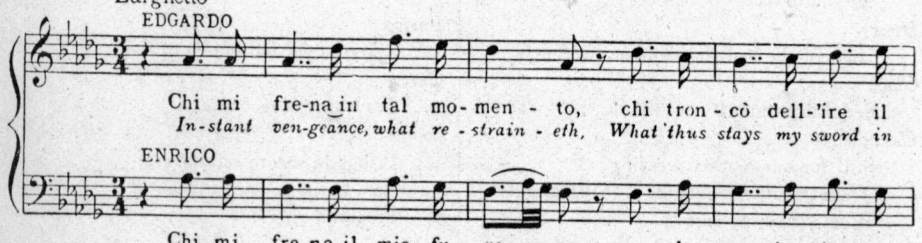

cor - so? il suo duo - lo il suo spa - ven - to son la
scab - bard? Is't af - fec - tion that still re - main - eth . And each

cor - so? del - la mi - se - ra in fa - vo - re nel mio
scab - bard? Is't af - fec - tion still re - main - eth And each

pro - va, son la pro - va d'un ri - mor - so! ma qual ro - sa i - na ri -
an - gry thought, each an - gry thought en - chain - eth. Of thine own___ blood thou'rt be -

pet - to un gri - do cor - se! è mio san - gue! l'ho tra -
an - gry, dark thought en - chain - eth. Of mine own___ blood I'm be -

di - ta, el - la sta___ fra mor - te e vi - ta! io son vin - to son com -
tray - er! Now, 'twixt life___ and death she stand - eth! Ah! de - spair, my heart doth

di - ta, el - la sta___ fra mor - te e vi - ta! ah! che spe - gne - re non
tray - er! Now, 'twixt life___ and death she stand - eth! Ah! de - spair her heart doth

mos - so! t'a - mo, in - gra - ta, t'a - mo, t'a - mo in - gra - ta, t'a - mo an - cor!
with - er, Yet, un - grate - ful one, I love thee, yes, I love thee still!___

pos - so i ri - mor - si del mio co - re, del mio cor!___
with - er, And re - morse my breast doth fill, my breast doth fill!___

Lucy. | Lucia.
(I had hoped that death had found me, | (Io sperai che e me la vita
And in his drear fetters bound me, | Tronca avesse il mio spavento;

But he comes not to relieve me!
Ah! of life will none bereave me?
Still in dark despair I languish,
Nought to hope but ceaseless anguish;
Even tears mine eyes abandon,
My cup of woe to fill.)

Raymond.

(Time, thou hast wrought thy worst, terrible moment,
No longer sense hath mastery over words;
Dense and impervious clouds of fear are seen,
As threatening e'en the brilliance of the sun.
Ah! like a rose that withers on the stem,
She now is hovering 'twixt death and life!
He who for her by pity is not moved,
Has of a tiger in his breast the heart.)

Henry, Arthur, Norman and Chorus.

Hence, thou traitor, hence betake thee.
Ere our rage o'erwhelm thee.

Edgar.

Dare advance one single step,
And other blood with mine shall flow!

Raymond.

Stay, ye rash, ye impious men,
Your sinful purposes forego.
Heaven's servant now here stand I!
In your Maker's name, command I.
Sheathe your weapons! Know that the murderer
He abhorreth! What saith His word?
"He that wieldeth the sword in anger
By the sword shall be laid low."

Henry.

Vile intruder, say what within these walls
Thou seekest?

Edgar.

Hither came I
For my bride. Thy sister
Unto me her faith hath sworn!

Raymond.

Thou must all hope of her relinquish;
She's another's!

Edgar.

Another's? no!

Ma la morte non m' aita—
Vivo ancor per mio tormento!
Da' miei lumi cadde il velo—
Mi tradì la terra e il Cielo!
Vorrei pianger, ma non posso:
Ah! mi manca il pianto ancor!)

Raimondo.

(Qual terrible momento!
Più formar non so parole;
Densa nube di spavento
Par che copra i rai del sole.
Come rosa inaridita
Ella sta fra morte e vita!
Chi per lei non è commosso
Ha di tigre in petto il cor.)

Enrico, Arturo, Normando e Cavalieri.

T' allontana! sciagurato,
O il tuo sangue fia versato.

Edgardo.

Morirò; ma insiem col mio
Altro sangue scorrerà.

Raimondo.

Rispettate in me di Dio
La tremenda maestà!
In suo nome io vel comando,
Deponete l'ira e il brando.
Pace, pace;—egli abborrisce
L'omicida, e scritto sta—
Chi di ferro altrui ferisce,
Pur di ferro perirà.

Enrico.

Ravenswood in queste porte
Chi ti guida?

Edgardo.

La mia sorte!
Il mio dritto; sì, Lucia
La sua fede a me giurò!

Raimondo.

Questo amor per sempre obblia
Alla è d'altri.

Edgardo.

D'altri! ah, no!

Raymond.
Read!

Edgar   (to Lucy).
Tremblest? Art confounded?
Didst thou write this? I wait thy answer!
Didst thou write this?

Lucy.
Yes.

Edgar.
Beholdest thou
This token? Perfidious heart!
I return it.

Lucy.
Ah, no—

Edgar.
Receive it—
Thou fallen traitress to heaven, to Love,
Accursed forever be the day on which I saw
        thee!
Blotted from time be that dark hour when
        first I met thee!
For thy shameless, base desertion,
Pardon vainly thou'lt ask above.
Despair and anguish grant thy heart
May desolation!

Henry and Chorus.
No further dare.
Hence away, ere our fury o'erwhelm thee;
Hence away, if thy life thou regardest.
But a moment the blow is suspended;
Tempt us no longer, we bid thee beware!

Edgar.
Strike, the frail strings of life now dividing,
At her nuptials my pale corpse presiding.
Drain my heart's blood at thy wedding ban-
        quet.
Strike! why pause ye? I'm ready; prepare.

Lucy.
Heaven, in mercy, oh save him, protect him,
And through this fearful danger direct him!
By the woe thou hast now heaped upon me,
I do implore for him thy kindly care.
Since to me thou hast doomed a life of
        misery,
Ah, refuse not my last, my dying prayer.

Raimondo.
Mira!

Edgardo.
Tremi, ti confondi!
Son tue ciffre? A me rispondi!
Son tue ciffre?

Lucia.
Sì!

Edgardo.
Riprendi
Il tuo pegno, infido cor!
Il mio dammi.

Lucia.
Almen—

Edgardo.
Lo rendi!
Hai tradito il Cielo e amor!
Maledetto sia l'istante
Che di te mi resi amante!
Stirpe iniqua, abbominata—
Io dovea da te fuggir!
Ah, di Dio la mano irata
Ti desperda!

Tutti
Insano ardir!
Esci, fuggi il furor che m' accende.
Solo un punto i suoi colpi sospende,
Ma fra poco più atroce più fiero,
Sul tuo capo abborrito cadrà!

Edgardo.
Trucidatemi! e pronubo al rito
Sia lo scempio d'un core tradito!
Del mio sangue bagnata la soglia,
Dolce vista per l'empia sarà:
Calpestando l'e sangue mia spoglia
All' altare più lieta ne andrà.

Lucia.
Dio, lo salva! in sì fiero momento
D' una misera ascolta l' accento.
E la prece d' immenso dolore
Che più in terra speranza non ha:
E l'estrema domanda del core,
Che sul labbro spirando mi sta!

Raymond, Alice and Ladies.

    Unhappy man, fly hence—let prudence haste
      thee;
    Thy life, the claims of station, rank, respect.
    Live! it may be thy grief may find an end;
    All woes must end by never-ending pity,
    How often is it to a single torture
    A thousand joys have in their turn succeeded!

             END OF ACT II.

ACT III.

    SCENE I—A Room in the Tower of Wolf's Crag.

Edgar.

    Darkly the night is lowering,
    Even as is my destiny. Yes! roll on, thou
      thunders!
    Flash, ye fierce forked lightning; convulsion,
    Shake the vast womb of nature, the world
      o'erwhelming!
    Ah! Is't deception? On the hard earth
      beating
    A horse's hoof I hear! It stops—
    Who is it that thro' the tempest
    With fierce and threatening gesture
    Comes at this hour to meet me!

          SCENE II—Enter HENRY.

Henry.

    'Tis I.

Edgar.

    Ha! what boldness! Ashton!

Henry.

    Yes.

Edgar.

    Within these drear walls
    Darest thou thus at this hour present thee?

Henry.

    Doth my presence not content thee?
    I do but return thy visit!

Edgar.

    See my father's shade uprising,
    For his wrongs revenge demanding!
    Death is in the air thou breathest;

Raimondo, Alisia e Dame.

    Infelice, t'invola—t'affretta:
    I tuoi giorni, il suo stato rispetta.
    Vivi! e forse il tuo duolo fia spento:
    Tutto è lieve all' eterna pietà.
    Quante volte ad un solo tormento
    Mille gioje succeder non fa!

             FINE DELL' ATTO II.

ATTO III.

    SCENA I—Sala terreno nella terre di Volfureng.

Edgardo.

    Orrida è questa notte
    Come il destino mio! Sì, tuona, o cielo—
    Imperversate, o turbini—sconvolto
    Sia l'ardin di natura, e pera il mondo—
    Io non m' inganno! scalpitar d' appresse
    Odo un destrier—s' arresta—
    Chi mai della tempesta
    Fra le minaccie e l'ire,
    Chi puote a me venire?

          SCENA II—Entra ENRICO.

Enrico.

    Io.

Edgardo.

    Quale ardire!—Ashton!

Enrico.

    Sì.

Edgardo.

    Fra queste mura
    Osi offrirti al mio cospetto?

Enrico.

    Io vi sto per tua sciagura.
    Non venisti nel mio tetto!

Edgardo.

    Quì del padre ancor s' aggira
    L'ombra inulta—e par che frema!
    Morte ogn' aura a te quì spira!

E'en the earth shaketh, trembleth, where
    thou'rt standing,
When thou didst cross the threshold
Did thy heart not quake with fear,
As a living man descending
To thy tomb with no help near?

Henry.
    Even now the bridal chamber
    Opens for the blooming bride!

Edgar.
    Ah, infuriating thought this!
    Oh, what torments! what torture!

Henry.
    But hearken. Tho' the sounds of mirth and
        gladness
    Echoed far and wide around me,
    Stronger far than ties of pleasure
    Are the bonds in which hate for thee hath
        bound me,
    Friends, relations, guests forsaking,
    Flew I straight to meet thee here,
    While the mad and furious tempest
    Shouted vengeance in my ear.

Edgar.
    What here hath brought thee?

Henry.
    Thou now shalt hear.
    Think of the wrongs thou hast done me,
    And dare not to falter or shun me;
    Words were too poor to express them—
    This arm alone can redress them!
    I give thee defiance to death—
    Nought else can wipe away the stain.

Edgar.
    By my dead father's ashes,
    Thy heart's blood I will drain!

Henry.
    Thou!

Edgar.
    When meet we?

Henry.
    At earliest dawning of the next approach-
      ing day.

Edgar.
    Where?

Il terren per te quì trema!—
Nel varcar la soglia orrenda
Ben dovesti palpitar,
Come un uom che vivo scenda
La sua tomba ad albergar!

Enrico.
    Fu condutta al sacra rito,
    Quindi al talamo Lucia.

Edgardo.
    (Ei più squarcia il cor ferito!
    Oh tormento!—oh gelosia!)

Enrico.
    Ascolta. Di letizia il mio soggiorno,
    E di plausi rimbombava;
    Ma più forte al cor d'intorno
    La vendetta a me parlava!
    Quì mi trassi—in mezzo ai venti
    Le sua voce udia tuttor,
    E il furor degli elementi
    Rispondeva al mio furor.

Edgardo.
    Da me che brami?

Enrico.
    Ascoltami:
    Onde punir l'offessa,
    De' miei la spada vindice
    Pende su te sospesa—
    Onde punir l'offessa,
    Ch'altri to spenga? Ah! mai—
    Chi dee svenarti il sai!

Edgardo.
    So che al paterno cenere
    Giurai strapparti il core.

Enrico.
    Tu!

Edgardo.
    Quando?

Enrico.
    Al primo sorgere del mattutino albore.

Edgardo.
    Ove?

Henry.
  By the icy tombs
  Of Ravenswood.
	Enrico.
	  Fra l' urne gelide
	  De Ravenswood.

Edgar.
  Agreed.
	Edgardo.
	  Verrò.

Henry.
  There shalt thou join thy ancestors.
	Enrico.
	  Ivi a restar preparati.

Edgar.
  There too thyself shalt fall.
	Edgardo.
	  Ivi t'ucciderò.

O SOLE PIÙ RATTO — *OH, HASTE, CRIMSON MORNING* (Edgardo and Enrico)

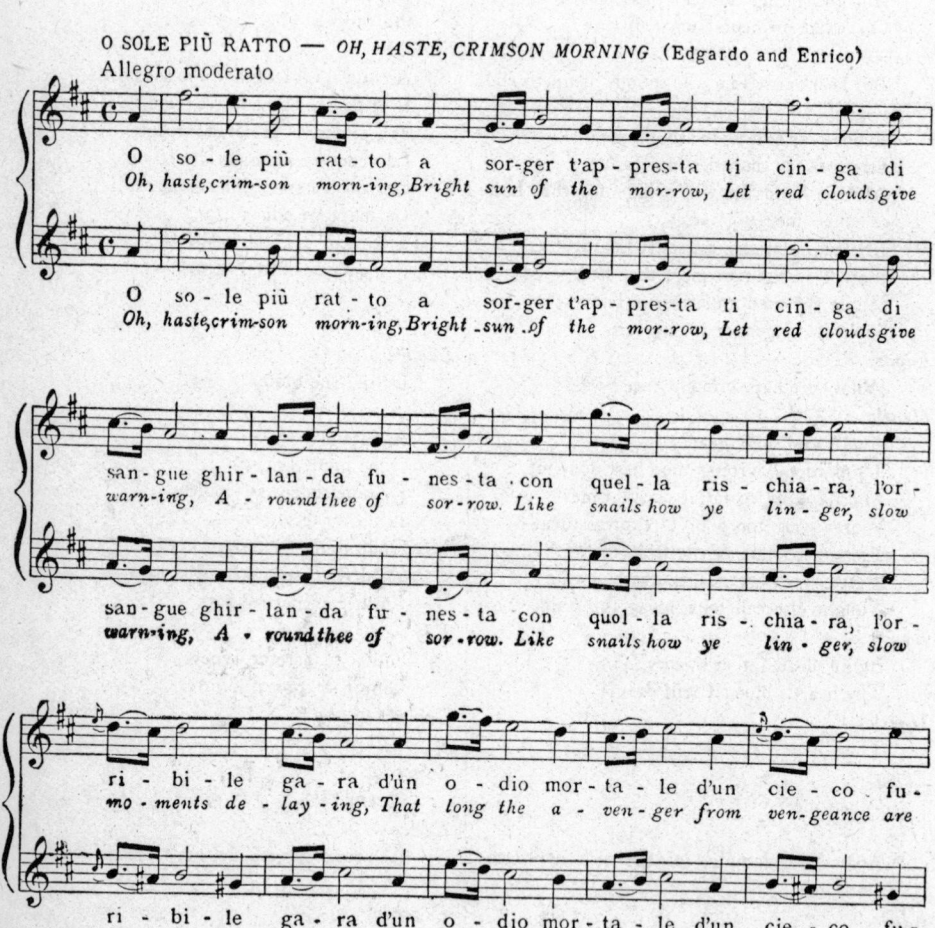

ro - re, O so - le più rat - to ri - sor-giè ris - chia-ra d'un o - dio mor-
stay - ing, Oh, haste, crim-son morn-ing, Bright sun of the mor-row, Let the red—

ro - re, O so - le più rat - to ri - sor-giè ris - chia-ra   d'un
stay - ing, Oh, haste, crim-son morn-ing, Bright sun of the mor-row,   Let

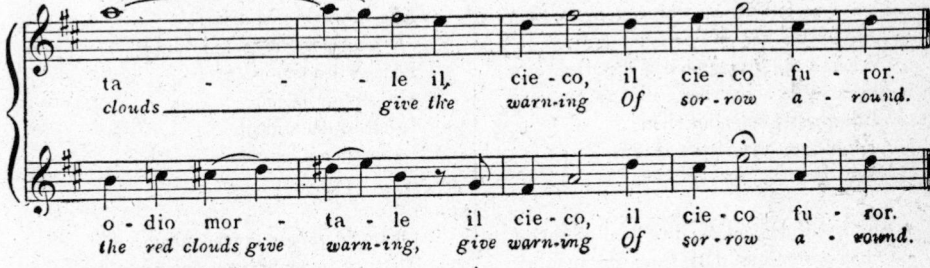

ta - - - le il, cie - co, il cie - co fu - ror.
clouds_____ give the warn-ing Of sor-row a - round.

o - dio mor - ta - le il cie - co, il cie - co fu - ror.
the red clouds give warn-ing, give warn-ing Of sor-row a - round.

SCENE III—Hall in HENRY's Castle. Peasants and Domestics of the Castle.

Chorus.

 Ah, happy, happy day,
 Swell high the choral lay
 Through all Scotland,
 To all her shores
 Tell the wretches,
 Our enemies,
 That more terrible,
 As more happy,
 The presence renders us
 Of our great joy.
 Ah! e'en the stars themselves
 Smile happily down on us.

SCENE IV—RAYMOND, NORMAN, and the above.

Raymond.

 Cease, ah, cease these sounds of gladness!

Chorus.

 Thou dost seem aghast with fear!
 What has chanced?

Raymond.

 Horrible event!

Chorus.

 Thou freezest our souls with terror.

SCENA III—Sala.

Coro.

 D'immenzo giubilo
 S'innalzi un grido
 Corra di Scozia
 Per ogni lido,
 E avverta i perfidi
 Nostri nemici, ,
 Che più terribili,
 Che più felici
 Ne rende l'aura
 D'alto favor;
 Ch' a noi sorridono
 Le stelle ancor.

SCENA IV—RAIMONDO, NORMANDO, e detti.

Raimondo.

 Cessi, ah cessi quel contento!

Coro.

 Sei cosparso di pallore!
 Ciel, che rechi?

Raimondo.

 Un fiero evento!

Coro.

 Tu ne agghiacci di terrore!

Raymond.

    To their chamber the bride and bridegroom
    Scarce a moment had departed,
    When a shriek came, a cry of anguish!
    As a man in death throes did languish.
    Straight I forced the door; trembling entered;
    Moment terrible! sight of horror!
    There poor Arthur, upon the floor, lay
    Pale and deathlike, besmeared with blood,
    While Lucy, brandishing a sword,
    Like some fell demon, threatening stood!
    Then on me her eyes fast fixing,
    "Where's the bridegroom?" she cried.
    And a smile across her pallid face
    With ghastly splendor shone.
    Ah, unhappy maid! thy reason
    From thee had forever flown!

Chorus.

    Ah, dreadful moment, dire deed of horror;
    Omen portentous, dark fears confound us.
    Night, thy dark mantle throw close around us;
    Cover this deed with thy densest veil.
    Ah, let not the hand that this did compass
    Upon her kindred thy wrath entail.

Raymond.

    Ah! she comes!

SCENE V—Lucy, Alice, and the above.

Lucy.

    How sweetly, gently
    Steals thy voice on mine ear. Ah, those dear accents
    Once more, once more I hear.
    My Edgar, at length I'm safe with thee,
    To thee I've flown from all thine enemies.
    —What coldness
    Shoots like ice through my veins! Each fibre trembleth;
    My foot doth fail! Here, at the fountain,
    Once more I'm at thy side, love. Oh, Heaven, see'st thou
    Yon dark, fearful phantom! Ah! it would part us!—

Raimondo.

    Dalle stanze ove Lucia
    Trassi già col suo consorte,
    Un lamento, un grido uscìa,
    Come d'uom vicino a morte.
    Corsi ratto in quelle mura:
    Ahi! terribile sciagura!
    Steso Arturo al suol giaceva
    Muto, freddo, insanguinato;
    E Lucia l'acciar stringeva—
    Che fu già dei trucidato.
    Ella in me le luci affisse:
    "Il mio sposo ov' è?" mi disse;
    E nel volto suo pallente
    Un sorriso balenò.
    Infelice! della mente
    La virtude a lei mancò!

Tutti

    Oh! qual funesto avvenimento!
    Tutti ne ingombra cupo spavento!
    Notte, ricopri la ria sventura
    Col tenebroso tuo denso vel!
    Ah, quella destra di sangue impura
    L'ira non chiami su noi del Ciel!

Raimondo.

    Eccolà!

SCENA V—Lucia, Alisa, e detti.

Lucia.

    Il dolce suono
    Mi colpì di sua voce. Ah! quella voce
    M' è quì nel cor discesa!
    Edgardo, io ti son resa—
    Fuggita lo son da' tuoi nemici. Un gelo
    Mi serpeggia nel sen—trema ogni fibbra
    Vacilla il piè, presso la fonte meco
    T'assidi alquanto. Ahimè! sorge il tremendo
    Fantasma e ne separa!
    Un serto io voglio. Un armonia celeste
    Di, non ascolti? Ah! l'inno
    Suona di nozze. Il rito
    Per noi s'appressa! oh! me felice!
    Oh! gioia che si sente e non si dice!

Hark, thro' the dark air heavenly harmony
swelleth!
Say! dost thou hear it? Ah, 'tis the hymn
Of our nuptials! They wait us
At the altar; oh, I am happy.
The joy that fills my bosom words cannot
tell thee.
They light the incense! See now
The sacred tapers brightly are burning;
The priest approaches. Place thy hand
In mine now! oh, blissful moment,
At length thou'rt mine, love, and I am
thine;
What rapture boundless for me is now pre-
paring!
Each pleasure doubly sharing.
Yes! doubly enjoying, if 'tis shared with
thee,
Thanks, bounteous Heaven!
Thou hast given new life to me!

Raymond.
　Here comes her brother!

SCENE VI—Henry and the above.

Henry.
　Answer me,
　Can this dark deed be real?
Raymond.
　But too surely.
Henry.
　Abandoned one,
　Thy punishment condign shall be!
All.
　Stay thee, oh, heaven!
Raymond.
　Seest thou not
　Her fearful state?
Lucy.
　What say'st thou?
Henry.
　What death-like paleness!
Lucy.
　Ah, what misery!
Raymond.
　Her reason has for ever fled from her!

Ardon gl'incensi—splendono
Le sacre facì intorno!—
Ecco il ministro! Porgini
La destra—oh! lièto giorno!
Alfin son tua, alfin sei mio,
A me ti dona un Dio
Ogni piacer più grato
Sì ogni piacere mi fia conte diviso.
Del ciel demente un riso
La vita a noi sarà.

Raimondo.
　S' avanza Enrico!

SCENA VI—Enrico, e detti.

Enrico.
　Ditemi,
　Vera è l'atroce scena?
Raimondo.
　Vera, pur troppo!
Enrico.
　Ah! perfida!
　Ne avrai condegna pena—
Alisa, Raimondo e Coro.
　T'arresta! oh, Ciel!
Raimondo.
　Non vedi
　Lo stato suo?
Lucia.
　Che chiedi?
Enrico.
　O qual pallor!
Lucia.
　Me misera!
Raimondo.
　Ha la ragion smarrita!

Henry.
    Great Heaven!—

Raymond.
    Tremble, heartless man,
    Thou should'st, for her life.

Lucy.
    Frown not so harshly on me,
    Although 'tis true I signed it;
    Ah, look not, love, so fearfully,
    Break not the ring I gave thee;
    And do not curse me; I was the victim
    Of a cruel brother.
    I love but thee, my Edgar!
    Whom did'st thou name? was't Arthur?
    Ah! fly me not; have mercy, pray!

Enrico.
    Gran Dio!—

Raimondo.
    Tremare, o barbaro!
    Tu dei per la sua vita.

Lucia.
    Non mi guardar sì fiero;
    Segnai quel foglio è vero;
    Nell' ira sua terribile
    Calpesta, oh Dio! l'anello—
    Mi maledice! Ah! vittima
    Fui d'un crudel fratello!
    Ma ognor t'amai—lo giuro.
    Chi mi nomasti—Arturo?
    Ah, non fuggir! perdone!

SPARGI D' AMARO PIANTO — *SHED THOU ONE TEAR* (Lucia)

per———— me,———— per———— me.
no—— joy———— to—— me

Henry.
> (Bitter remorse and misery
> Ever my lot will be.)
> With care remove her! Alice, kinsmen and
> friends,
> I pray you with gentlest kindness treat her;
> Remorse is henceforth my earthly portion!

Raymond.
> Man of blood, in this thy work now exult
> thee!

Norman.
> What meanest thou?

Raymond.
> Thou broughtest the brand that this dire
> flame engendered,
> 'Twas thy fell hand that fired it!
> Each spark that kindled, thou didst fan to a
> blaze.

Norman.
> But I believed not—

Raymond.
> Thou of this crime art author. Traitor!
> E'en now
> His blood cries for vengeance! At heaven's
> bar
> It doth accuse thee and there the hand su-
> preme
> Thine awful sentence signeth! Depart hence
> and tremble.

(Exeunt.)

SCENE VII—Exterior part of the Castle. Night.

Edgar.
> Tombs of my far-famed ancestors, open wide
> your portal,
> And the last fated scion
> Of your doomed race receive ye!
> My hate has vanished! Past is resentment.
> On his vengeful blade now

Enrico.
> (Giorni d'amaro pianto
> Serba il rimorso a me.)
> Si tragga altrove! Alisa, pietoso amico,
> Deh! voi la misera vegliate
> Io più me stesso in me non trovo!

Raimondo.
> Delator! gioisci dell' opra tuo!

Normando.
> Che parli?

Raimondo.
> Si, dell' incendio che divampa e strugge
> Questa casa infelice,
> Hai tu destata la primiera favilla.

Normando.
> Io non credei—

Raimondo.
> Tu del versato sangue, impio! tu sei
> La ria cagion!—Quel sangue
> Al ciel t'accusa, e già la man suprema
> Segna la tua sentenza—or vanne, e trema.

(Parte.)

SCENA VII—Parte esterna del Castello. Notte.

Edgardo.
> Tombe degli avi miei, l'ultimo avanzo
> D'una stirpe infelice,
> Deh! raccogliete voi!
> Cessò dell' ira il breve foco—
> Sul nemico acciaro
> Abbandonar mi vo'. Per me la vita

How gladly would I fall. This life of misery,
I cannot bear it! The vast universe
Is but one desert, unless with her I share it!
The sounds of mirth and feasting
Echo around me. Ah, swiftly
Flies the night mid their revelry. Ungrateful woman,
While here I struggle, desperate in mine anguish.
With mockery thou deridest me!
Thou most false, thou most shameless!
Thy heart with rapture boundeth,
While death me surroundeth.

E orrendo peso—l' universo intero
E un deserto per me senza Lucia!
Di faci tutta via
Splende il castello! Ah! scarsa
Fu la notte al tripudio! Ingrata donna!
Mentr' io mi struggo in disperato pianto,
Tu ridi,—esulti accanto
Al felice consorte!
Tu delle gioje in seno,
Io—della morte!

FRA POCO A ME — *WILD FLOWERS SOON* (Edgardo)

Fra po-co a me ri - co-ve - ro da - rà ne-glet-to a vel - lo,—
The wild flow'rs soon will shed their bloom A - round my sad and lone-ly tomb,

u - na pie-to - sa la-gri-ma non scen-de - rà su quel - lo, ah!
No kind-ly tear shall bless the spot Where blight-ed love's for - got - ten Ah!

fin de-gli e-stin-ti, ahi mi - se-ro! man-ca il con-for-to a me. Tu
my wear - y wound-ed soul to heav'n Shall wing its rap - id flight Oh!

pur, tu pur di - men-ti-ca quel mar-mo dis-preg-gia - to:
Lu - cy, should you with your spouse Roam near the tomb you've here — made,

mai non pas-sar-vi o bar-ba-ra, del — tuo con-sor-te a la-to, ah! ris-
In si-lence pass, a word of love Would — rouse my sleep-ing shade: Oh! re-

pet-ta al-men le ce - ne-ri di chi mo-ria per te, ri-spet-ta al-men le
spect at least, thou faith-less girl, The dust of him who died for thee, Re - spect at

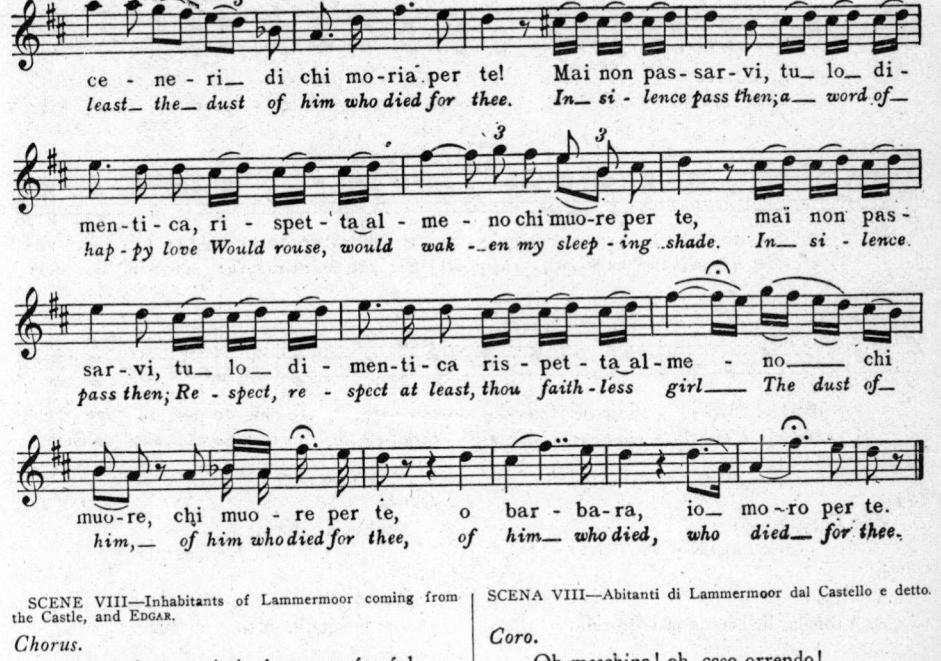

ce - ne - ri di chi mo - ria per te! Mai non pas - sar - vi, tu lo di -
least the dust of him who died for thee. In si - lence pass then; a word of

men - ti - ca, ri - spet - ta al - me - no chi muo - re per te, mai non pas -
hap - py love Would rouse, would wak - en my sleep - ing shade. In si - lence.

sar - vi, tu lo di - men - ti - ca ris - pet - ta al - me - no chi
pass then; Re - spect, re - spect at least, thou faith - less girl The dust of

muo - re, chi muo - re per te, o bar - ba - ra, io mo - ro per te.
him, of him who died for thee, of him who died, who died for thee.

SCENE VIII—Inhabitants of Lammermoor coming from the Castle, and EDGAR.

Chorus.

Poor forlorn one! oh, fate most fearful,
Hope of life at length hath vanished,
Ere on this dark night of sorrow
Morning dawns she'll be no more.

Edgar.

Gracious heaven! say, what mean ye?
What doth mean this wailing cry?

Chorus.

'Tis for Lucy.

Edgar.

Say ye for Lucy?

Chorus.

She, alas, is surely dying.

SCENA VIII—Abitanti di Lammermoor dal Castello e detto.

Coro.

Oh meschina! oh, caso orrendo!
Più sperar non giova omai.
Questo dì che sta sorgendo,
Tramontar tu non vedrai!

Edgardo.

Giusto Cielo! ah, rispondete!
Di chi mai, di chi piangete?

Coro.

Di Lucia!

Edgardo.

Lucia diceste?

Coro.

Sì; la misera sen muore.

FUR LE NOZZE — *THIS UNHAPPY, FATAL MARRIAGE* (Chorus)

Fur le noz - ze a lei fu - nes - te di ra - gion la tras - se a - mo - re s'av - vi -
This un - hap - py, fa - tal mar - riage Hath of rea - son quite de - prived her, All for

ci - na all'ore es - tre - me   e te chie-de per te   ge - me. Ques-to
lorn and bro - ken - heart-ed, Life hath from her nigh de - part - ed; Death his

di, ques-to sol che-stà sor - gen-do tra-mon-tar, tra-mon-tar più non ve-
vic-tim, his vic-tim sure-ly claim-eth; Ere the morn-ing, the morn-ing sun doth

dra! di ra - gion le tras-se a - mo - re, e te chie-de per te ge-me.
rise. E'en while mad-ness sense en - thrall-eth, Still on thee for aid she call-eth.

Edgar.	*Edgardo.*
Ah! Lucy, Lucy!	Ah Lucia! Lucia!
(A bell sounds without.)	
Chorus.	*Coro.*
That sad	Rimbomba
And solemn bell her end doth tell.	Già la squilla in suon di morte!
Edgar.	*Edgardo.*
It rings both hers and my knell!	Ahi! quel suono al cor mi piomba!
Yes, my fate is now decided!	E decisa la mia sorte:
In death we will not be divided.	Rivederla ancor vogl' io;
Soon I'll join thee, dearest Lucy!	Rivederla, e poscia—
Chorus.	*Coro.*
Oh, heaven! Whither goest thou?	Oh Dio!
O calm thee, nought can now the past recall.	Qual trasporto sconsigliato!
	Ah, desisti! ah, riedi in te!
SCENE THE LAST—Raymond and the above.	SCENA ULTIMA—Raimondo, e detti.
Raymond.	*Raimondo.*
Stay, rash man, what seekest thou further?	Ove corri, sventurato?
She's forever lost to thee.	Ella in terra più non è.
Edgar.	*Edgardo.*
My Lucy.	Lucia!
Raymond.	*Raimondo.*
All is over.	Sventurata.
Edgar.	*Edgardo.*
Forever lost to me!	In terra più non è.
She hath departed—	Ella dunque—

Raymond. | Raimondo.
To heaven! | E in cielo.

TU CHE A DIO — *THO'·FROM EARTH THOU'ST FLOWN* (Edgardo)

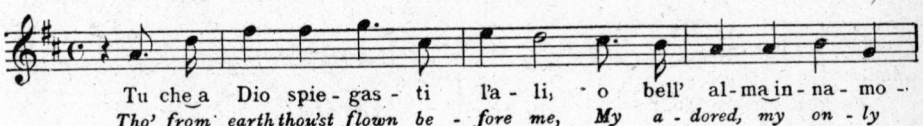

Tu che a Dio spie - gas - ti l'a - li, o bell' al - ma in - na - mo -
Tho' from earth thou'st flown be - fore me, My a - dored, my on - ly

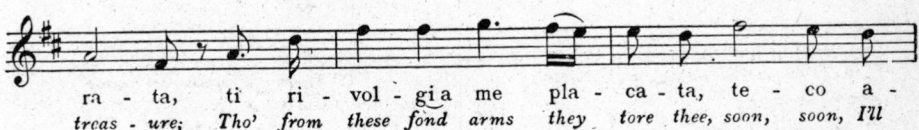

ra - ta, ti ri - vol - gia me pla - ca - ta, te - co a -
treas - ure; Tho' from these fond arms they tore thee, soon, soon, I'll

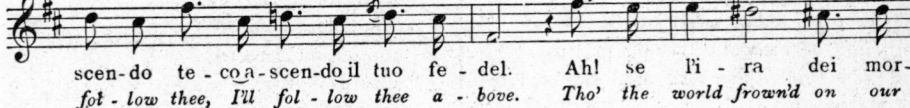

scen - do te - co a - scen - do il tuo fe - del. Ah! se l'i - ra dei mor -
fol - low thee, I'll fol - low thee a - bove. Tho' the world frown'd on our

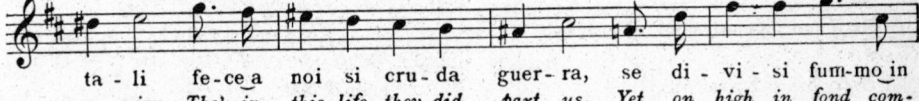

ta - li fe - ce a noi si cru - da guer - ra, se di - vi - si fum - mo in
u - nion, Tho' in this life they did part us, Yet on high in fond com -

ter - ra, ne con - giun - ga il nu - me in ciel, o bell' al - ma in na - mo -
mun - ion, shall our hearts be tuned to love. Tho' from these fond arms they

ra - ta, bell al - ma in - na - mo - ra - ta, ne con - giun - ga il nu - me in
tore thee, from these fond arms they tore thee, soon I'll fol - low thee a -

ciel, o bell' al - ma in - na - mo - ra - ta bell' al - ma in - na - mo -
bove. Tho' from these fond arms they tore thee, tho' from these arms they

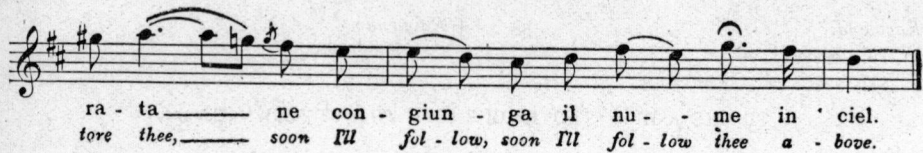

ra - ta____ ne con - giun - ga il nu - - me in ' ciel.
tore thee,____ soon I'll fol - low, soon I'll fol - low thee a - bove.

Soon I'll join thee.	Io ti seguo!
Chorus.	*Coro.*
Ah, what wouldst thou?	Ah, che fai?
Edgar.	*Edgardo.*
Die with her!	Morir voglio.
Chorus.	*Coro.*
Forbear! or heaven forever is lost to thee!	Ritorna in te.
(EDGAR plunges his poignard in his breast.)	(S' immerge il pugnale nel cuore.)
Raymond.	*Raimondo e Coro.*
What hath he done?	Che facesti?
Edgar.	*Edgardo.*
Die avenged then, O adored one;	A te vengo a bell' alma—
Soon I'll follow thee above—	Ti rivolgi al tuo fedel;
Tho' in this world they did part us—	Ah, se l'ira demorteli
Tho' from these fond arms they did tear thee,	Fe cruda guerra—
Yet—we part not—above!	Ne congiunga il nume in ciel.
Raymond.	
Rash and impious, think of heaven!	*Raimondo.*
Chorus.	Sciagurato, pensa al ciel!
Every breast horror fills,	*Coro.*
Horror dire. Ah, may kind heaven	Quale orror!
Pardon grant him from above.	Ahi tremendo! ahi crudo fato!
(Raising his hands to heaven, EDGAR expires.)	Dio, perdona un tanto error!
	(Alzando le mani al cielo EDGARDO spira.)

THE END.

LA GIOCONDA

by

AMILCARE PONCHIELLI

DRAMATIS PERSONÆ.

LA GIOCONDA, *a ballad-singer.*
      Mme. Christine Nilsson.
LA CIECA, *her blind mother.* Mme. Scalchi.
LAURA, *wife of* ALVISE.   Mme. Fursch-Madi.
BARNABA, *a spy of the Inquisition.* Signor Del Puente.
ALVISE BADOÈRO, *one of the heads of the State In-*
  quisition.   Signor Novara.

ZUÀNE, *a boatman.*   Signor Augier
ISÈPO, *a public letter-writer.* Signor Grazzi
ENZO, *a Genoese noble.*   Signor Stagno
A PILOT.   Signor Barberis
Monks, Senators, Sailors, Shipwrights Ladies, Gentlemen
  Populace, Masquers, etc.

The action takes place in Venice in the 17th Century.

First produced in America at the Metropolitan Opera House, New York, Dec. 20, 1883, under the direction of Signor Vianesi.

ARGUMENT.

Act. I. The place and time are Venice in the seventeenth century. Act I. opens with a festal chorus of the people — monks, sailors, masquers, etc., gathered in the courtyard of the ducal palace. *Barnaba*, a spy of the Council of Ten, comments on their gayety, and begins his plans to capture the affections of *Gioconda*, a ballad-singer, with whom he is deeply in love. *Gioconda* enters leading and comforting her blind mother, *Cieca*. The former is in love with *Enzo*, a Genoese noble. originally the betrothed of *Laura*, who is now the wife of *Alvise*, chief of the Council of Ten. *Gioconda* repulses *Barnaba's* advances, and the latter determines to get the girl's mother in his power to further his designs. When the people return from the regatta, *Barnaba* persuades the defeated boatman *Zuàne* that *Cieca* has caused his disappointment by witchcraft, and the fate of the old woman hangs in the balance, when *Enzo* enters and saves her life. *Alvise* and *Laura* appear upon the scene, and the latter secures the pardon of *Cieca*, who gives her deliverer a rosary. *Laura* and *Enzo* recognize each other, and when *Barnaba*, bent upon getting *Enzo* out of the way so that he may have *Gioconda* to himself, tells him that *Laura* will be on his ship at nightfall, the rapture of the lover is boundless. *Barnaba's* real designs are not suspected. He then warns *Alvise* that his wife is about to elope with *Enzo*, and *Gioconda*, learning this, laments the perfidy of *Enzo*, while the monks and people are singing the vesper hymn.

Act II. takes place on board *Enzo's* vessel, and on the bank of the Fusina Lagoon. The sailors are carousing. *Barnaba* arrives with *Isèpo*, both disguised as fishermen, and the spy despatches *Isèpo* to summon three war galleys. He then departs; *Enzo* comes on deck, and sends the crew below leaving him on deck, waiting for *Laura*, who presently arrives. The reunited lovers determine to set sail during the night; *Enzo* goes below to complete his preparations, and *Laura* prays to the Virgin for aid. *Gioconda* rushes upon her and is about to slay her, but on *Laura* lifting up the rosary remembers it was the grateful gift of *La Cieca;* gives her own mask to *Laura*, calls up two boatmen and sends *Laura* away in safety before the arrival of *Alvise* and *Barnaba*. The Venetian galleys bear down on the "Hecate," which is set on fire by *Enzo* as the curtain falls.

Act III. opens on the following night, in *Alvise's* residence. He has resolved to poison *Laura* and when she comes, at his summons, he tells her that she must drink the phial of poison he places on the table, before the last note shall be sung of a Serenata which is being chanted by some passing gondoliers. He no sooner quits the room than *Gioconda* enters. She brings a flask containing a powerful narcotic; makes *Laura* drink it; pours into the empty flask the poison contained in the phial, and departs to mingle with the masquers. *Alvise* enters; finds the phial empty, and believes his revenge complete. The scene changes to a grand fête, in which the ballet of "The Hours" is introduced. *Barnaba* drags in *La Cieca*, whom he has found in one of the reserved apartments. She declares that she was "praying for her, just dead," and the guests are dismayed. *Alvise* asks who has the right to be gloomy when *Alvise Badoèro* is gay? *Enzo*, who has learned from *Barnaba* that it is *Laura* who lies dead, rushes forward, throws off his mask, denounces *Alvise*, and is seized by the guards. *Gioconda* promises *Barnaba* to become his if he will obtain *Enzo's* liberty, and he accepts this compact. The grand finale is brought to a close by *Alvise* opening the curtain of the funeral chamber, and showing *Laura*, extended on her bier. He proudly avows that he has taken her life, to avenge his outraged honor, and the curtain falls on a scene of fearful interest.

In Act IV. the sleeping *Laura* is brought to the dwelling of *Gioconda*, who meditates suicide then is tempted to destroy her rival. While she is hesitating, *Enzo* arrives, grateful to her for obtaining his freedom, but resolved to end his life. *Laura* — waking from her trance — calls out "Enzo!" and presently comes from behind the screen which had concealed her. The two lovers offer grateful thanks to their deliverer, and escape in a boat provided by her. Left alone, she remembers her compact with *Barnaba*, and resolves to fly. She prays to the Virgin for deliverance "from the foul demon," and her prayer is overheard, through the half-open door, by *Barnaba*, who confronts her as she is about to come forth. Summoning all her courage, she tells him gayly that she means to keep her word, but must put on her gayest ornaments, to do him honor, and while — to his delight — adorning herself with trinkets, contrives to seize a dagger, with which she stabs herself to the heart saying, "I have sworn to be thine. Take me. I am thine!"

LA GIOCONDA.

ATTO I.

LA BOCCA DEI LEONI.

Il cortile del Palazzo Ducale parato a festa. Nel fondo la SCALA DEI GIGANTI *e il* PORTICO DELLA CARTA *colla porta che adduce nell' interno della chiesa di S. Marco. A sinistra lo scrittoio d' uno scrivano pubblico. Sopra una parete del cortile si vedrà una fra le storiche bocche dei leoni colla seguente scritta incisa sul marmo a caratteri neri:*

DENONTIE SECRETE PER VIA
D' INQVISITIONE CONTRA CADA
VNA PERSONA CON L' IMPVNITÁ
SEGRETEZA ET BENEFITTI
GIVSTO ALLE LEGI.

È uno splendido meriggio di primavera. La scena è ingombra di popolo festante. BARNABOTTI, ARSENALOTTI, MARINAI, *maschere d' ogni sorta,* ARLECHINI, PANTALONI, BAUTTE, *e in mezzo a questa turba vivace alcuni* DALMATI *ed alcuni* MORI. BARNABA *addossato ad una colonna, sta osservando il popolo; ha una piccola chitarra ad armacollo.*

SCENA I.

Marinai, Popolo e BARNABA.

Coro di Marinai e Popolo.
Feste e pane! la Repubblica
Domerà le schiatte umane
Finche avran le ciurme e i popoli
Feste e pane.
L'allegria disarma i fulmini
Ed infrange le ritorte.
Noi cantiam! chi canta è libero,
Noi ridiam! chi ride è forte.
Quel sereno Iddio lo vuol
Che allegrò questa laguna
Coll' argento della luna
E la porpora del sol.
   [campane a distesa, squilli di trombe.
Feste e pane! a gioia suonano
Di San Marco le campane.
Viva il Doge e la Repubblica!
Feste e pane!

BAR. (*si muove dal posto. Dominando il frastuono festosamente*).
Comparì! già le trombe
V' annuncian la regata.
Marinai (*correndo a sinistra*). Alla regata!
Popolo. Alla regata!
  [gridando e saltando, il popolo esce dal cortile. Il tumulto s' allontana.

ACT I.

THE LION'S MOUTH.

Scene.— The Grand Courtyard of the Ducal Palace, decorated for festivities. At back, the Giant's Staircase and the Portico della Carta, with doorway leading to the interior of the Church of St. Mark. On the left, the writing-table of a public letter-writer. On one side of the court-yard is seen one of the historical Lion's Mouths, with the following inscription cut in black letters into the wall:

FOR SECRET DENUNCIATIONS
TO THE INQUISITION
AGAINST ANY PERSON,
WITH IMPUNITY, SECRECY, AND
BENEFIT TO THE STATE.

It is a splendid afternoon in spring. The stage is filled with holiday folks, Monks, Sailors, Shipwrights, Masquers, etc., and amidst the busy crowd are seen some Dalmatians and Moors. BARNABA, *leaning his back against a column, is watching the people. He has a small guitar, slung around his neck.*

SCENE I.

BARNABA, *Sailors, and People.*

Opening Chorus.
Sports and feasting! Feasting and sports !
   Our Republic wise,
That rules the world from farthest East to
   West,
Provides us — galley-slaves and populace —
      Sports and feasts.
Joy disarms the angry thunderbolt,
And breaks the fetters forged by sinners!
Let us sing ! for free are they who sing:
Let us laugh ! for they who laugh are winners!
Calmly, brightly, the heavens are shining
Pouring joy o'er yon lagoon!
While rays, sent from the rising moon,
Blend with the sunset glow declining.
  [pealing of bells in the distance, sound of trumpets
But hark! the joyous bells of St. Mark are
   loudly pealing!
Cheers for our Republic and our Doge !
BAR. (*coming forward*).
The Regatta now commences! The trumpets loud are pealing!

People. To the Regatta let us hasten.   [*exeunt*

SCENA II.

BARNABA (*solo*).

BAR. (*accennando gli spiragli delle prigioni sot-*
terranee).
E danzan su lor tombe !
E la morte li guata !   [*cupamente.*
E mentre s' erge il ceppo o la cuccagna,
Fra due colonne tesse la sua ragna,
Barnaba, il cantastorie ; e le sue file
       [*Guarda e tocca la sua chitarra.*
Sono le corde di questo apparecchio.
Con lavorio sottile
E di mano e d' orecchio
Colgo i tanfani al volo
Per conto dello Stato.   E mai non falla
L' udito mio.   Coglier potessi solo
Per le mie brame e tosto
Una certa vaghissima farfalla !

SCENA III.

LA GIOCONDA *colla* CIECA *entrando da destra, e detto.
La vecchia ha il volto coperto fin sotto gliocchi da un
povero vendado.*

GIO. (*conducendo per mano la madre e avviandosi alla
chiesa lentamente*) Madre adorata, vieni.
BAR. (*scorge la* GIO. *e si ritrae accanto alla colonna.*)
         (Eccola ! al posto.)
CIECA. Figlia, che reggi il tremulo
Piè che all' avel già piega,
Beata è questa tenebra
Che alla tua man mi lega.
Tu canti agli uomini
Le tue canzoni,
Io canto agli angeli
Le mie orazioni
Benedicendo
L' ora e il destin,
E sorridendo
Sul mio cammin.
" Io per la tua bell' anima
" Prego chinata al suol,
" E tu per me coi vividi
" Sguardi contempli il sol.
GIO. Vien ! per securo tramite
Da me tu sei guidata.
Vien ! ricomincia il placido
Corso la tua giornata.
Tu canti agli angeli
Le tue orazioni,
Io canto agli uomini
Le mie canzoni,
Benedicendo
L' ora e il destin,
E sorridendo
Sul mio cammin.
" Ed io pel tuo dimane
" A te guadagno il pane ;
" Tu col pregar fedel
" A me guadagni il ciel.

SCENE II.

BARNABA (*alone*)

BAR. (*moodily, pointing to the gratings of the
subterranean prisons*).
Above their graves they 're dancing !
Death upon them is stealing !
And while the reckless victims seek their
    pleasure,
Here will I weave my nets for them at
    leisure.
Stories, and songs, and legends, are attrac-
    tions
Whose power no mortal e'er thinks of
    denying !
I watch the listening gadflies, — note all
    their actions,
And catch them while they 're flying.
Woe to them thereafter ! — My ear, unfailing, has
worked their ruin ! Ah ! how I am longing
to make my captive, at once and securely,
the wayward Gioconda.

SCENE III.

Enter LA GIOCONDA, *with* LA CIECA.

GIO. (*leading her mother by the hand, and ad-
vancing slowly toward the church*).
This way, dear mother !
BAR. (*aside*). She is here !
GIO. (*to* CIECA). This way.
BAR. (*aside*). I 'll hide me !
        [*Hides behind a column*
CIECA. Daughter, in thee my faltering steps
Find guidance and protection ;
I gratefully bless my loss of sight,
That heightens thy affection !
While thou into mankind thy songs art
    singing,
To Heav'n my ceaseless pray'rs their flight
    are winging,
For thee I pray, and render thanks to Fate
That left me sightless, — but not desolate.

GIO. Place thy dear hand once more in mine,
Thy steps I 'm safely guiding ;
Here recommence thy daily life,
In calm contentment gliding.

BAR. (*in disparte*). (Sovr' essa stendere
La man grifagna!
Amarla e coglierla
Nella mia ragna!
Terribil estasi
Dell' alma mia!
Sta in guardia! l' agile
Farfalla spia!)

GIO. L' ora non giunse ancor del vespro sante!
Qui ti riposa appiè del tempio ; intanto
Io vado a rintracciar l' angelo mio.

BAR. (Derisìon!)

GIO. Torno con Enzo.

CIECA. Iddio
Ti benedica. Taciturna ed erma.

GIO. Pace qui spira.

CIECA (*estrae da tasca un rosario*). Addio figliuola.

BAR. (*sbucando e sbarrando la via a* GIO., *che
fa per escire da destra*). Ferma.

GIO. Che ?

BAR. Un uom che t' ama, e che la via ti sbarra.

GIO. Al diavol vanne colla tua chitarra !
[*Vivacemente.*
Già l' altra volta tel dissi : funesta
M' è la tua faccia da mistero.
[*Per andarsene.*

BAR. (*trattenendola e ironicamente*). Resta.
Enzo attender potrà.

GIO. Va, ti disprezzo.

BAR. (*incalzando*). Ancor m' ascolterai.

GIO. Mi fai ribrezzo !

BAR. Resta . . t' adoro, o vaga creatura.

GIO. Vanne !

BAR. Non fuggirai ! [*Slandiandosi su
essa.*

GIO. Mi fai paura !
Ah ! [*Fugge.*

CIECA (*alzandosi spaventata*).
Qual grido ! mia figlia ! Aita ! aita !
La voce sua !

BAR. (La farfalla è sparita. . .)

CIECA (*brancolando*).
Figliuola ! o raggio della mia pupilla,
Dove sei ? dove sei ?

BAR (*ridendo*). La Cieca strilla ;
Lasciamola strillar.)

CIECA (*lentamente e protendendo le palme ritorna
a sedersi sui gradini*). Tenèbre orrende!

BAR. (*osservandola pensieroso*).
(Pur quella larva che la man protende,
Potrebbe agevolar la meta mia . .
Se la madre è in mia man . .

CIECA (*rigirando con fervore le Ave Marie del
suo rosario*). Ave Maria.

BAR. (*sempre meditando*).
Tengo il cor della figlia incatenato . .

CIECA. Ave Maria . .

BAR. . . con laccio inesorato.
L' angiol m' aiuti dell' amor materno,
E la Gioconda è mia ! Giuro all' Averno!)

BAR. (*aside*). With fiercest joy my soul would
be enraptured
If in my net she were securely captured!
The wildest ecstasies within me waken!
Beware thee, moth, if in my net thou 't
taken!

GIO. Erelong the vesper chimes will loud be
ringing;
Here rest thee near the sacred shrine,
while — singing —
I seek him I love tenderly and truly.

BAR. (Silly fool!)

GIO. I 'll return with Enzo.

CIECA. Heaven duly
Will bless thy footsteps! Adieu, my
daughter! [*Takes rosary from her pocket*

BAR. (*quitting his hiding place and stopping*
GIO.). Stay thee!

GIO. How?

BAR. A man who loves thee, and bars thy
onward progress.

GIO. Go thou to the devil, thou and thy guitar
too!
Stand thou aside from my pathway! Away
I love not faces full of myst'ry.
Stay!

BAR. Enzo yonder can wait.

GIO. Go! go! I despise thee.

BAR. Once more ; — say, wilt thou listen?

GIO. (*trying to pass* BAR.). At thee I shudder!

BAR. Stay, I adore thee, angelic creature!

GIO. Quit me.

BAR. Ah no, thou shalt not fly me!

GIO. I hate and fear thee.
Ah! [*Escapes from the grasp of* BAR.

CIECA. My daughter in danger. Help! No one
hears me!
It was her voice.

BAR. So the moth has escaped me!

CIECA. My daughter, sole ray o'er my existence
beaming,
Where art thou? Where art thou?

BAR. La Cieca is screaming
Well let her scream her best!

CIECA. O darkness fearful!

BAR. Yet may this spectral creature, weak and
tearful,
Aid me to conquer thee, *Gioconda mia!*
(CIECA *has seated herself again by the church door.*)
Once the mother is mine —

CIECA. (*praying*). Ave Maria!

BAR. Then the daughter to foil me in vain will
endeavor.

CIECA. Ave Maria!

BAR. She 's fettered fast forever!
Thanks to thine aid, angel of love maternal,
She shall be mine ; I swear it, powers in-
fernal!

SCENA IV.

Barnaba, La Cieca, Isepo, Zuane, Coro. Indi sei
sgherri. La Gioconda, Enzo, più tardi Laura, Alvise. Il Popolo porta in trionfo il Vincitore della
Regata, il quale tien alto il pallio verde (la bandiera
del premio). Donne, Marinai, Fanciulli con fiori e
ghirlande, Zuane triste in disparte.

Arsenalotti (ai vincitore). Polso di cerro!
Barnabotti (idem). Occhio di lince!
Arsenalotti. Remo di ferro!
Donne. Gagliardo cor!
Tutti. Gloria a chi vince
    Il pallio verde!
Donne (guardando Zua.). Beffe a chi perde!
Tutti.   Lieta brigata,
    Per lieto calle
    Portiamo a spalle
    Il vincitor
    Della regeta,
    Fra canti e fior.
    Gli sguardi avvince,
    I flutti ei sperde!
    Gloria a chi vince!
    Beffe a chi perde!
[Quasi tutti affluiscono verso la Scala dei Giganti,
ove depongono il vincitore.
Bar. (che già da qualche tempo avrà osservato
  Zua. lo arresta).
  (Questi è l' uomo ch' io cerco. Non m'
   inganno)
  Patron Zuàne, hai faccia da malanno.
  Si direbbe davver che alla regata
  Non hai fatto bandiera.
Zua. T' inforchi Satanasso!
Bar.   E se la vera
  Cagione io ti dicessi del tuo danno?

Zua. Lo so, la prora ho greve ed arrembata.
Bar. Baje!
Zua. E che dunque?
Bar. (con mistero). T' avvicina. — O lasso!
  (sottovoce) Hai la barca stregata,
Zua. (inorridito). Vergine santa!
Bar.   Una malìa bieca
Sta sul tuo cap. Osserva quella cieca . .
Coro (Accanto alla Scala dei Giganti.)
Arsenalotti. Dadi e bambàra!
  Cuccagne e corse!
Barnabotti. Giuochiamo a zara
  Le nostre borse!
Tutti. Tentiam la mobile
  Fortuna a gara.
  Ginochiamo a zara.
[alcuni estraggono dei dadi, molti si siedono sui gradini,
e intavolano un giucco di zara.
Bar. (continuando e sempre facendo fissare
  Cieca a Zua.). (La vidi stamani gittar
  sul tuo legno
  Un segno maliardo, un magico segno.
Zua. Orror!
Bar. La tua barca sarà la tua bara.
  Sta in guardia, fratello!)
Arsenalotti. Sei!
Barnabotti. . Cinque!
Arsenalotti.   Tre!
Tutti.   Zara!
Cieca (pregando). Turris eburnea...
  Mistica rosa ...

SCENE IV.

Enter Isepo, Zuane, La Gioconda, and Enzo, after
wards Laura and Alvise. Chorus People, etc. bring
ing in triumph the victor in the regatta.

Chorus. Hail to the victor!
  Wrists that are oaken! Eyes of lynx!
  Sinews of iron ! the victor hail !
  Hail to the winner of the green banner !
  Laugh at the losers ! Why did they fail,
  Merry, light-hearted, onward we go,
  With songs and with flowers our path to
   cheer;
  Bearing the victor in the regatta
  High on our shoulders — see him here !
[They carry the victor to the foot of the Giant's
Staircase.
  All eyes beheld him the waves dispersing;
  Hail to the winner of the green banner !
  Laugh at the losers ! Why did they fail ?
Bar. (who has been observing Zua.).
  'T is he whom I was seeking. I'm ne'er
   mistaken.
  How now, Zuane? by fortune you 're for-
   saken.
  If 't is true, as I 'm told, that in the race
  You never once were seen leading ?
Zua. May Satan send you torments !
Bar.   Suppose the case
  That I explained what cause has hindered
   your succeeding ?
Zua. I know; my boat was sadly overweighted.
Bar. Nonsense.
Zua.   What mean you ?
Bar.   Draw nearer. 'T was fated.
  'T was the spell of a sorceress. Wherever
   you wander,
  Witchcraft enfolds you. Observe the blind
   woman yonder.
Chorus. Dice and Bambara!
   Races and frisking !
   We 'll play at Zara,
   Our purses risking.

Bar. (to Zua.).
  I saw her this morning throw over your
   line
  Some foul spell of her witchcraft — a mag-
   ical sign.
Zua. Alas!
Bar. (to Zua.).
  Lest thy barque be thy bier — through lo
   cara,
  Be watchful, Zuane. [points to Cieca.
Chorus. Six! Five! Three! — Zara!

BAR. (a ZUÀ.). La vidi tre volte scagliar su tuoi remi
Parole tremende —lugùbri anatèmi.

ZUÀ. e ISÀ. (ISÀ. *sarà mosso verso* BAR. *e ascoll' a curioso*). Gran Dio!
BAR. La tua barca sarà la tua bara.
Sta in guardia, fratello...
Arsenalotti. Sette!
Barnabotti. Otto!
Arsenalotti. Tre!
Tutti. Zara.
CIECA (*come sopra*). *Turris Davidica..*
Mater gloriosa..

BAR. (*come sopra*).
Suo covo è un tugurio—laggiù alla Giudeca,
Tien sempre quell' orrido zendado, ed è cieca..
Ha vuote le occhiaie—ma pure (e chi il crede?!)
La Cieca ci guarda—la Cieca ci vede!
4 *Marinai* (*che si saranno aggiunti al gruppo*). Ci vede!
ISÀ. Oh spavento!
3 *Arsenalotti* (*aggiunto anch' essi al gruppo*). Che avvenne?
ZUÀ. Oh maliarda!
3 *Barnabotti.* Che avvenne? che mormori?..
BAR., ZUÀ., ISÀ. La Cieca ci guarda!
[*il gruppo si fa sempre più numeroso.*
Coro. Addosso! accoppiamola!
ISÀ. Coraggio..
ZUÀ (*per avventarsi alla* CIECA, *poi retrocede*) Ho paura.
BAR. Badate, può cogliervi la sua jettatura.
Coro. Al rogo l' eretica!
ZUÀ. Davver, più l'addocchio, Più i rai le balenano,
BAR. (*ridendo*). La Cieca ha il mal occhio.
Coro. Ah! ah! qual facezia!
ZUÀ. (*ad* ISÀ. *che si sarà avvicinato pianamente alla* CIECA, *che gira sempre il rosario?*) Che brontola?
ISÀ. Prega.
(a. *parte del Coro.* Addosso alla strega!
2 a. *parte* (*si scagliano sulla* CIECA). Addosso alla strega!
BAR. (Già l' aure s' annuvolano,
Già i nembi s' accumulano.
Ah! ah! greggie umana!
Scagliato ho il mio ciottolo,
Or faggo la frana!)
CIECA (*afferrata dal popolo e trascinata in mezzo ai palce*). Aiuto!
Coro. Mandràgora!
CIECA. Ah! chi mi trascina!
Son Cieca!
Donne. Vediamola salir la berlina!
Uomini. Ai piombi!
CIECA. Soccorso! soccorso!
Donne. Ai marrani!
Uomini. Ai pozzi!
Donne. Fra Todero e Marco!

BAR. (*to* ZUÀ.). I heard her three times curse thy oars and thy rudder,
In accents infernal, that made my soul shudder
ZUÀ. Great Heaven.
BAR. Lest thy barque be thy bier, through la cara,
Be watchful, Zuàne!
Chorus. Seven! Eight! Six! — Zara.

BAR. (*to* ZUÀ. *and* ISÀ.).
Her den is a cabin, hard by the Giudeca;
And there with the demons, her companions, dwells la Cieca.
Her eye-sockets are empty, yet that will not free you.
La Cieca is watchful, la Cieca can see you
Sailors. (*who have drawn nigh*). Can see us!
ISÀ. Hateful monster!
Laborers. What has happened?
ZUÀ. Heaven free us!
4 *Monks.* What has happened? What mean these cries?
BAR., ZUÀ. *and* ISÀ. La Cieca can see us!
Chorus. Upon her! Let us bind her fast!
ZUÀ. (*venturing toward* CIECA).
Now, courage! Ah! I fear her!
BAR. Be careful! Lest she bewitch ye, if ye ge near her.
Chorus. We 'll burn the old heretic!
ZUÀ. The more I look at her More spiteful her glances seem!
BAR. (*mockingly*). The evil-eyed Cieca!
Chorus. The evil-eyed Cieca? — ha, ha! A blind woman's glances? — ha, ha!
BAR. (*aside*). (Already the clouds gather fast.)
ZUÀ. (*to* ISÀ.). What 's she about?
ISÀ. Praying.
ZUÀ. *and Chorus.* Her pray'rs she 's backward saying.

CIECA. (*seized by the populace, and dragged into the middle of the stage*).
O, help me! I'm sightless! Have mercy! Help!
BARN. (*aside*). (The ball I 've sent rolling, now on let it wander.)
(*To the Guards.*)
Friends, there lodge her in prison.

BAR. (*ad una pattuglia di sgherri in disparte*).
                    Sgherrani,
  Sia tratta nel carcere.
Uomini.   Al rogo !
Donne.   Alla pira '
Tutti (*sghignazzando*). Ah ! ah !
CIECA.   Santa Vergine !
Donne.   Martira !
Tutti.   Martira !
BAR. (Ho in man la mia vittima, ho in man due
    destini.)
Tutti. A morte la strega !
GIO. (*rientrando e slanciandosi*). Mia madre !
ENZO. (*vestito da marinaio dalmato, rompendo la calca
    con uno scoppio d' ira*). Assassini !
  Assassini ! quel crin venerando
  Rispettate ! o ch' io snudo il mio brando.
  Contro un' egra rejetta dal sole
  Generosa è la vostra tenzon !
  Vituperio ! è cresciuta una prole
  Di codardi all' alato leon !

Coro. Iddio vuol ciò che il popolo vuole;
  No, la strega non merta perdon.
CIECA. Ah ! su me si scatena l' averno !
GIO. Niun mi tolga all' amplesso materno !
CIECA. Figlia. .

Coro. A morte !
ENZO. (*con impeto far per togliere i ceppi alla* CIECA, *ma
    è impedito dal popolo*). Quel ceppo la
    strazia.
    Sciolta sia.
Coro.   La vogliam giudicare.
    Spenta sia !
ENZO. (*correndo all' ingresso della riva furiosamente ed
    esce*). Su, fratelli del mare !
    Alla lotta !
Coro.   Al patibolo !
  [*Intanto sull' alto della scata saranno apparsi* ALV. *e*
    LAU., *che avranno assistito al tumulto.*
LAU. (*dall' alto della scala, scendendo. Il lembo della
    sua vesta sarà sostenuto da due paggi. Ha una
    maschera di velluto nero sul volto.*)

(*Aside*). Ha, ha! the fools yonder!
Chorus. The pillory steps she will soon be as
    cending!
    To the Piombi! the Pozzi! The sorceress
    shall suffer! [*Enter* GIO. *with* ENZO
CIECA. Mercy! I'm sightless! Help!
Chorus. We'll destroy her, we'll burn her!

GIO. (*rushes toward* LA CIECA). My mother!
ENZO.   Base assassins!
    Base assassins! these locks, gray and scat
    tered,
    Harm no longer! My sword shall protect
    them!
    'Gainst a woman, old, feeble, and sightless
    It is noble and safe to contend!
    Ye are monsters! Descendants or heroes
    All are cowards, yon wing'd lion disgracing.
Chorus. No! Heav'n wills what the populace wills!
    The sorceress' life now must end.
ENZO. Let me free her! these fetters will kill her
GIO. Mother, darling!
ENZO.   Quick release her, base assassins!
    Quick release her.
Chorus.   We will bring her to trial.
ENZO (*calling out at the back of the stage*).
    Rise, comrades, rise, for mercy meets de
    nial.
    Now for fighting, for fighting!
CIECA. On me hell's fury is lighting.
Chorus. Burn her! destroy her !
  [LAU. *and* ALV. *are seen at the head of the staircase,
    about to descend.* LAU. *wearing a black mask de
    scends the staircase, while* LA CIECA *is struggling
    with her persecuters.*
Chorus. Destroy her !
LAU. Mercy !

SCENA V.

LA CIECA, GIOCONDA, ALVISE, LAURA, BARNABA, *Coro, poi* ENZO.

ALV. (*alteramente e con gravità*).
Ribellion! che? la plebe or qui si arroga
Fra le ducali mure
I dritti della toga
E della scure
[*Movimento di rispetto nella folla.*
Parla, o captiva!
Perchè stai china là fra quelle squadre?

Coro. È una strega!

GIO. E mia madre!

LAU. (*la* CIECA *alza ta testa*).
È Cieca! o mio signor! fa ch' essa viva!

ALV. (*freddamente a* BAR.). Barnaba! è rea
costei?

BAR. (*assai sottovoce all' orecchio d'* ALV.). Di malefizio.

GIO. (*a* BAR.). T' ho udito! . . menti!

ALV. Sia tratta in giudizio.

GIO. (*gettasi ai piedi di* ALV.).
Pietà . . ch' io parli attendete ora infrango
Il gel che m' impietrava . . e sgorga l' onda
Del cor . . Costei della mia infanzia bionda
L' angelo fu . . Sempre ho sorriso . . or
piango.
Mi chiaman . . *la Gioconda.*
Viviam cantando ed io
Canto a chi vuol le mie liete canzoni,
Ed essa santa a Dio
Le sue sante orazioni. . .

ENZO (*che sarà ritornato da qualche tempo seguito dai marinai dalmati*). Salviamo l' innocente.

LAU. (*scorgendo* ENZO). Qual volto!

GIO. (*alzandosi e trattenendo* ENZO).
Ah! no! ti ferma! Quel possente
La salverà!

BAR. (*osservando* LAU., *poi* ENZO).
(Come lo guarda fiso!)

LAU. (*ad* ALV. *in disparte*).
(" Concedi, o mio signor, se non ti duole,
" Ch' io mi levi la maschera dal viso.

ALV. " No, madonna, nemmen l' occhio del sole
" Non dee mirarti.")

GIO. (*ad* ALV.). Dalle tue parole
La vita attendo.

BAR. (*ad* ALV. *sottovoce*). È una strega, il nefario
Suo silenzio tel dica.

LAU. Essa ha un rosario!
No, l' inferno non è con quella pia.

ENZO. (Qual voce!)

BAR. Muoia!

LAU. (*ad* ALV. *supplichevole*). La salva!

ALV. E salva sia.

BAR. (Furore!!)

GIO. Gioia!!

CIECA (*liberata da* LAU. *che l' allontana dagli Sgherri*)

SCENE V.

LA CIECA, GIOCONDA, ALVISE, LAURA, BARNABA, *and Chorus, afterward* ENZO.

ALV. (*imperiously*). Rebellion? What? the populace can venture here, near our Ducal
Palace — to claim to act as judges? — and
as executioners? (*To* CIECA.) Answer me,
captive. Why art thou kneeling to yonder
people?

Chorus. She 's a sorceress.

LAU. (*toward whom* LA CIECA *has turned her face*).
She 's sightless, see, signor! save her from
outrage!

ALV. (*aside to* BAR.). Barnaba, has she been
guilty?

BAR. (*aside to* ALV.). Guilty of witchcraft.

GIO. (*to* BAR.). I heard thee! Thou liest!

ALV. To trial conduct her.

GIO. (*kneeling to* ALV.).
Mercy! ah, hear me one moment! I break
The ice that in fetters my soul was keeping!
She of my life has been the angel bright;
I once was ever smiling, now I 'm weeping.
" La Gioconda " they call me.
We are always singing; to all comers
I sing my gay songs till day 's ending;
While gentle strains of pious rapture
Are from her pure lips ascending.

ENZO (*to his Sailors*).
We will save the innocent victim.

LAU. (*observing him*). (Those features?)

GIO. (*to* ENZO). Ah, no! have patience! The
Duke will protect La Cieca.

BAR. (*aside, watching* ENZO *and* LAU.).
(His gaze is fixed upon her.)

GIO. (*to* ALV.).
Thou alone hast power to save my mother.

BAR. She is a sorceress! her guilty silence betrays her.

LAU. She bears a rosary. Satan has naught to
do with this pious woman.

ENZO (*observing* LAU.). (Those accents!)

BAR. Burn her!

LAU. (*to* ALV.). O save her!

ALV. She is saved, and pardoned!

GIO. Ah, joy!

BAR. (They foil me!)

GIO. What rapture!

CIECA (*to* LAU.).

CIECA'S SONG.

English verses by L. M. Underwood.

ALV. (ο BAR.   *damente mentre canta la* CIECA).
(Barnaba!)
BAR.   Mio padron.
ALV.   Facesti buona caccia
Quest' oggi?
BAR.   Sulla traccia
Cammino d' un leon.
LAU. *ed* ENZO.   Ascolti il dette pio
L' onnipossente Iddio!
GIO.   O madre mia, ti guarda
Un angelo fedel.
Coro.   Protegge la vegliarda
Visibilmente il ciel!

[LAU. *s' avvicina alla* CIECA *e prende il rosario, la*
CIECA *stende le mani come per benedirla,* LAU. *fa
per i·ginocchiarsi,* ALV. *vede e afferra il braccio di*
LAU. *sforzandola a rialzarsi.*

ALV. (*a* LAU.).   Che fai? vaneggi?
                [*Gettando una borsa a* GIO.
Bella cantatrice,
Quest' oro a te.
GIO. (*raccoglie e s' inchina*).   Sia grazia a voi,
Mesere. (*a* LAU.) Acciò ch' io l' abbia
nelle mie preghiere.   Dimmi il tuo nome,
o ignota salvatrice.

LAU. (*guardando* ENZO).   Laura.
ENZO (*colpito*).   (È dessa!)
ALV. (*a* LAU. *assorta*).   Ti scuoti! al tempio an-
diamo!
GIO.   Madre! — Enzo adorato! Ah! come t' amo!

[*Tutti si dirigono al tempio.* ALV. *e* LAU. *primi, i due
paggi dopo, indi tutto il Coro, e* GIO. *fra la madre ed*
ENZO. *Giunto alla porta della chiesa,* ENZO *s'
arresta, e rimane indietro assorto profondamente ne'
suoi pensieri.* BAR. *lo sta fissando.* La scena si
vuota.

SCENA VI.

ENZO *e* BARNABA.

BAR. (*avvicinandosi ad* ENZO).
Enzo Grimaldo, Principe di Santafior, che
pensi?
ENZO.   (Scoperton son.)
BAR.   Qual magico stupor t' invade i sensi?
Pensi a Madonna Laura d' Alvise Badoèro.

ENZO. (*scosso*).   Chi sei?
BAR.   So tutto: e penetro in fondo al tuo pensiero.
Avesti culla in Genova. .

ENZO   Prence non son, sui flutti
Guido un vascel, son dalmato: Enzo Gior-
dan. .
BAR.   Per tutti
Ma non per me.   Venezia t' ha proscritto,
ma un forte
Disio qui ancor ti trasse ad affrontar la
morte.
Amasti un dì una vergine — là, sul tuo mar
beato,
A estranio imene vittima — la condannava
il fato.

GIO.   Ah, mother, 't was an angel, sent down from
yonder heaven!
LAU. *and* ENZO.   The pious pray'rs she utters
may they be heard in heaven!
Chorus.   'T is evident unto her celestial aid is
given.
ALV. (*to* BAR.).   Barnaba!
BAR.   Signor!
ALV.   Say, have you had good hunting to-day?
BAR.   I 'm in chase of a lion, gone astray.

[LAU. *approaches* LA CIECA, *and takes the rosary.* LA
CIECA *extends her hands as if to bless* LAU., *who
kneels before her.* ALV. *abruptly seizes the arm
of* LAU., *and compels her to rise.*

ALV. (*to* LAU.).   What now?   'T is folly.
(*To* GIO.)   Pretty singing maiden
This gold is thine. [*Giving purse to* GIO.
GIO.   Thanks, signor !
(*To* LAU.)   That I may never in my prayers for-
get it,
Tell me thy name, unknown, generous
benefactress.
LAU. (*looking at* ENZO).   Laura.
ENZO. (*aside*).   'T is she!
ALV. (*to* LAU.).   Arouse thee.   To church let us
hasten.
GIO.   Beloved mother! Enzo, how I love thee!

[*Exeunt all into the church, except* ENZO, *who stands ab·
sorbed in thought, and* BAR., *who watches him intently*

SCENE VI.

ENZO *and* BARNABA.

BAR. (*approaching* ENZO).   Enzo Grimaldo,
Prince of Santa Fior, thou art pensive.
ENZO (*aside*).   (I am discovered.)
BAR.   What magic stupor steals away thy senses?
'T is of the Lady Laura, Alvise's wife
thou 'rt thinking.
ENZO.   Who art thou?
BAR.   I know all; can penetrate
Thy thoughts, however secret.   Thy birth-
place was Genoa!
ENZO.   Prince I am not, but sailor.   Yonder's
my ship.
I am Dalmatian, Enzo Giordan.
BAR.   For others,
But not for me.   Proscribed thou wert by
Venice,   [pulse,
Yet hither thou art led, by chainless im-
Thy life to peril.   Thou didst love a maiden
Yonder, in thine own Genoa, but she
Another's bride became.   Fate to ye both
was cruel.

ENZO. Giurai fede a Gioconda.

BAR. (*sorridendo*).   La cantatrice errante
Ami come sorella, e Laura come amante.
Già disperavi in terra di riveder quel volto,
E l' amor di Gioconda hai per pietà raccolto,
Ed or, sotto la maschera l' angelo tuo t' apparve.
Ti riconobbe. .

ENZO.   (Oh giubilo!)

BAR.   L' amor passa le larve.
Sulla sua sposa vigila con cuor geloso, il tetro
Inquisitor, nell' aurea prigione io sol penètro,
E spesso fra le lagrime io la sorpresi, e muto
Lo sguardo suo mestissimo al ciel chiedeva aiuto.
Badoër questa notte — veglia al dogale ostello
Col Gran Consiglio, Laura sarà sul tuo vascello.

ENZO. Diodi pietà!

BAR.   'Le angosce dell' amor tuo soccorro.

ENZO. ¿O grido di quest' anima, scoppia dal gonfio core!
Ho ritrovato l' angelo del mio celeste amore.)
Ma alfin ch' sei? mio lugubre benefattor?

BAR.   T' abborro.
[*Apre il suo mantello e la giubba e mostra sul giustacuore queste lettere in argento "C. X."*
Sono il possente démone del *Consiglio dei Dieci*.
Leggi.

ENZO. Infamia!

BAR.   Al supplizio trarti potea, nol feci.
Gioconda amo, essa m' odia. . giurai schiantarle il cor.
Enzo morto era poco — ti volli traditor.

ENZO. "O sàtana furente, lordo di sangue e fiel.
" Coll' ira tua demente tu m' hai scagliato in ciel.
(Gran Dio! la togli all' orrida condanna di dolor,
L' idolatrata Laura a me ridona ancor.)

BAR. Va: corri al tuo desio: spiega le vele in mar,
Tutto il trionfo mio negli occhi tuoi m' appar.
Ebbene?

ENZO.   A notte bruna sul brigantino aspetto Laura.

BAR. (*inchinandosi e sogghignando*). Buona fortuna!

ENZO (*sul limitare della scena*). E tu sia maledetto!
[*Esce.*

ENZO. I have pledged my faith to Gioconda

BAR. Poor wand'ring ballad-singer!
Her thou dost love as sister, but Laura as thy mistress.
Thou hadst all hope abandoned, dreamed not to see her features,
But here, under her velvet mask, thy beauteous angel saw thee,
And recognized thee.

ENZO.   O happiness!

BAR.   Love sees through disguises
All this night will her husband stay at the Doge's palace,
With the Great Council. Laura shall be on board thy vessel.

ENZO. Powers divine!

BAR.   Love's sweetest consolations await thee.

ENZO. Ah, with what joy my heart is filled,
Fortune at last is kind!
Soon shall I clasp the angel-form
In this fond heart enshrined.
But who art thou, O gloomy messenger of joy?

BAR. I hate thee! I am the demon-in-chief
Of the Council of Ten. Read this Beware thee!
[*Opens his dress, and shows the letters " C.X." (Council of Ten) embroidered in silver on his vest.*

ENZO. Oh horror!   [spare thee.

BAR. To thy doom at once I could bring thee. I
Gioconda loves thee, hates me fiercely;
I have sworn to crush her heart.
Enzo's death would serve me little;
She must learn how false thou art.

ENZO (*aside*). Kind heaven, to her thy mercy show,
Save her from grief and pain;
But ah, sweet Laura, my adored,
Bring to my arms again!

BAR. (*to* ENZO). Go! not a moment lose,
Spread thy white sails to the skies,
I can my triumph read
In each glad glance of thine eyes.
Well?

ENZO. When the dark night falls, on board my ship I shall wait my Laura.

BAR. (*sneeringly*). Good luck attend you!

NZO. And thou — be thou accursed! [*Exit

SCENA VII.

Barnaba, poscia Isèpo, *indi per un instante* La Gioconda *e* La Cieca.

Bar. Maledici? sta ben . . l' amor t' accieca.
Compiam l' opra bieca,
L' idolo di Gioconda sia distrutto . .
S' annienti tutto.
[*Va nel fondo, apre una porta accanto le prigioni.*
Isèpo!
Isèpo (*escendo*). Padron Barnaba . .
Bar. Scrivano,
L' anima m' hai venduto e la contenna
Fin che tu vivi; [*lo conduce al banco.*
In son la mano
E tu la penna.
Scrivi. [*dettando.*
AL CAPO OCCULTO DELL' INQUISIZIONE.
[*Isèpo scriv. Intanto alla porta del tempio appariscono* Gioconda *e* La Cieca.
Gio. (Ti nascondi, c'è Barnaba.)
[*Alla madre ritraendola e sta spiando nascosta dal pilastro.*
Bar. LA TUA SPOSA CON ENZO IL MARINAR.
Gio. (Oh ciel!)
STA NOTTE IN MAR
TI FUGGIRÀ SUL BRIGANTINO DALMATO.
Gio. Ah! [*Disperatamente e scompare in chiesa.*
Bar. Più sotto: LA BOCCA DEL LEONE.
Qua, porgi, taci, vanne.
[*Prende il foglio,* Isèpo *esce.*

SCENE VII.

Barnaba, Isèpo, La Gioconda, *and* La Cieca.

Bar. Accursed? We shall see. 'T is love that
blinds thee.
Should my dark plots be successful,
This idol of Gioconda's will be shattered,
And dashed to pieces. Isèpo!
[*Calling at a door near the prison. Enter* Isè.
Isè. Padron Barnaba!
Bar. Now, penman, long since thy soul to me
thou didst sell;
Thy skin also, to save thy life.
I am the hand, and thou art the pen.
Write! [*Enter* Gio. *and* Cieca *from the
church.*
Bar. (*to* Isè.).
"Unto the secret chief of the inquisition—
Gio. (*to* Cieca). Quick conceal thee. 'T is Barnaba.
[*They hide behind a column.* Gio. *listens*
Bar. "Thy wife will with Enzo, the young
sailor,
This night elope; will sail away from thee
On board his vessel."
Gio. Ah! [*Exeunt* Gio. *and* Cieca *into the churc.*
Bar. Now, lower down,
"The Mouth of the Lion." Give it me
Silence! Go! [*Exit* Isè.

SCENA VIII.

Barnaba *solo.*

Bar. (*col piego in mano contemplando la scena*).
O monumento!
Regia e bolgia dogale! Atro portento!
Gloria di questa e delle età future;
Ergi fra due torture
Il porfido cruento.
Tua base i pozzi, tuo fastigio i piombi!
Sulla tua fronte il volo dei palombi,
I marmi e l'ôr.
Gioia tu alterni e orror con vece occulta,
Quivi un popolo esulta,
Quivi un popolo muor.
Là il Doge, un muto scheletro
Coll' acidaro in testa,
Sovr' esso il Gran Consiglio,
La Signoria funesta;
Sovra la Signoria
Più possente di tutti, un re; la spia.
O monumento! Apri le tue latèbre,
[*Vicino alla bocca del leone.*
Spalanca la tua fauce di lenèbre,
S' anco il sangue giungesse a soffocarla!
Io son l' orecchio e tu la bocca: Parla!
[*Getta il piego nella bocca del leone ed esce.*

SCENE VIII.

Barnaba, *alone.*

Bar. (*contemplating the palace*).
O mighty monument, palace and den of the
Doges!
Gloomy and wondrous, glory of this age,
And of the ages yet unborn,
Between twin tortures glistens
Thy porphyry ensanguined!
Below are the Pozzi, 'neath thy roof the
Piombi;
Thy front is gay, with its fearless flocks of
pigeons,
Its marble and gold.
Joy thou dost alternate with woe, in work-
ings secret.
Here is a nation exulting; there a nation
dies.
There the Doge, an ancient skeleton,
Sits in state, in his headdress quaint;
Above him, the Great Council — sinister
oligarchy!
Over the oligarchs, far more powerful than
they,
A King — the Spy!
O mighty monument, open thy jaws capacious!
Spread wide thy throat, that waits in sullen
darkness,
Until blood, poured in torrents, shall choke
it forever!
I am the ear, and thou the mouth-piece.
Speak!
[*Throws the letter into the Lion's Mouth, and exit*

SCENA IX.

*Entra nei cortile una Mascherata; la segue il popolo can-
tando e danzando. Poscia un Barnabotto, GIOCONDA e
LA CIECA.*

Coreo e Danza.   Viva il Doge e la Repubblica!
   La baldoria e el carnevale!
   Baccanale! Baccanale!!
   Gaia turba popolana
   Su! correte al torneamento!
   Su! danzate la *furlana!*
   Chiome al sol! zendadi al vento !
   Fate un chiasso da demóni
   Colle palme e coi talloni !
   Tuoni il portico ducale
   Sovra il pazzo baccanale !
         [si odono alcuni tocchi di campana.
Voci interne (dalla chiesa). Angelus Domini. . .
                    [cessa la danza.
*Un Barnabotto (schiudendo la tenda che copre la porta
della basilica).* Tramonta il soi.

    Udite il canto
    Del vespro santo
    Prostrati al suol.
    [tutti si prostrano rivolti verso il fondo.

LA GIOCONDA e LA CIECA *attraversano la folla inginocchiata mentre dura l'orazione.*

GIO. *(con passo vacillante, lentissimo, appoggiandosi
alla* CIECA).
   Tradita?..Ahimè!..soccombo   il fianco
   mio
   Vacilla .. o madre .. mi soreggi.   O Dio!
   Cuore! dono funesto!
   Retaggio di dolor!
   Il mio destino è questo!
   O Morte o Amor!

CIECA. Dimmi dov' è il tuo cor! la man vi guida..
   Ch' io lo posi sul mio!
   Vieni e facciamo un sol di due dolor!
GIO. *(prendendo la mano della* CIECA *e por-
tandosela al cuore).* Ah sì! la mano tua
   sovra il mio cor!
   Senti e comprendi, o madre, il mio dolor!
       [si slancia fra le braccia della CIECA.
Voci interne. Angelus Domini . .
La Folla (inginocchiata). Glor a al Signor
   E pace agli uomini!   *[cala lentamente la tela.*

FINE DELL' ATTO I.

SCENE IX.

Enter Masquers and Populace, dancing and singing

Chorus. Carnival ! Baccanal !
   Day's last beams are o'er as glancing,
   Let us pass our time in dancing
     La Furlana!

BALLET.

Chorus (inside the church). Angele Dei.
Chorus (on the stage). Glory to God!

*A Monk (to the people, drawing aside the curtain from
before the door of the church).*
   The sun sinks low, the vesper hymn is
   pealing;
   Now listen to the holy strain, devoutly
   kneeling.
Chorus. Angele Dei, qui custos es mei,
   Me, tibi commissum, nocte illumina,
   Rege, custodi et rege,
   Rege et guberna, custodi,
   Angele Dei, qui custos es mei.
[While the vesper prayer is being sung, enter GIO. *and*
LA CIECA *from the church.* GIO. *is supported*
by LA CIECA.

GIO. Forsaken! Betrayed! All is over! In
   every limb
   I am trembling. Thou must support me
   dear mother.
   O heart, gone is thy gladness!
   Thy heritage is sadness!
   My doom was framed by pow'rs above:
   To die! to die, if robbed of love!
   Upon my heart, dear mother,
   Place thy hand, and thou 'lt know,
   The while it throbs so wildly,
   How great, alas, my woe!

CIECA. Ah, come, my child, my darling,
   Hand in hand let us go,
   One grief of two griefs making,
   Sharing each other's woe!

Chorus. Angele Dei, qui custos es mei. etc.

END OF ACT I.

ATTO II.

IL ROSARIO.

Notte. Un brigantino visto di fianco. Sul davanti una riva deserta d' isola disabitata nelle acque di Fusina. Nell' estremo fondo il cielo in qualche parte stellato, e la laguna; a destra la luna tramonta dietro una nube. Sul davanti un altarino della Vergine con una lampada rossa accesa. "HECATE," il nome del brigantino, sta scritto a prua. Alcune lanterne sul ponte.

All' alzarsi della tela alcuni Marinai sono seduti sulla tolda, altri in piedi aggruppati; tutti hanno un portavoce in mano; molti Mozzi sono arrampicati, o seduti, o sospesi alle sartie degli alberi e stanno cantando una marinaresca.

SCENA I.

MARINARESCA.

Primi Marinai (a destra sul ponte cantando attraverso il portavoce).

> Ha! He! Ha! He!
> Fissa il timone!

Secondi Marinai (a sinistra col portavoce).
> Fissa!
> Ha! He! Ha! He!
> Issa artimone!

Primi Marinai. Issa!
> La ciurma ov' è?

Primi e Secondi Marinai.
> Ha! He! Ha! He!

Mozzi (ragazzi sulle antenne).
> Siam qui sui culmini,
> Siam sulla borda,
> Siam sulle tremule
> Scale di corde.
> Guardate gli agili
> Mozzi saltar;
> Noi gli scoiattoli
> Siamo del mar.

Marinai (sotto la tolda, nel cassero).
> Siam nel fondo più profondo
> Della nave, della cala,
> Dove il vento furibondo
> Spreca i fischi e infrange l' ala
> Siam nel fondo più profondo
> Della nave, della cala.

Primi Marinai (sul ponte).
> Ha! Ho! Ha! Ho!
> Vele a babordo!

Secondi Marinai. Issa!
> Ha! Ho! Ha! Ho!
> Remi a tribordo!

Primi Marinai. Issa!
> Il ciel tuonò!
> Ha! Ho! Ha! Ho!

Mozzi (sulle antenne).
> In mezzo ai fulmini
> Delle tempesta,
> Noi tra le nuvole

ACT II.

THE ROSARY.

Night. A brigantine, showing its starboard side. In front, the deserted bank of an uninhabited island in the Fusina Lagoon. In the farthest distance, the sky and the lagoon. A few stars visible. On the right, a cloud, above which the moon is rising. In front, a small altar of the Virgin, lighted by a red lamp. The name of the brigantine — "Hecate" — painted on the prow. Lanterns on deck.

At the rising of the curtain Sailors are discovered some seated on the deck, others standing in groups each with a speaking-trumpet. Several Midshipmen are seen; some clinging to the shrouds, some seated. Remaining thus grouped, they sing a Marinaresca.

SCENE I.

Sailors (on deck, singing through speaking-trumpets.

> Ho, he! ho, he!
> Look to the rudder!
> Ho, he! ho, he!

1st Sailor. Look well!

2d Sailor. Look well!
> Ho, he! ho, he!
> Up with the mainsail!
> Up with it!
> Where are the rowers?

1st Sailor. Ay! where?

All. Ho, he! ho, he!
> Rowers, reply!

Basses (under the deck in the hold).
> Here are we, in depths profoundest
> Of the vessel; in the hold,
> While angry winds, in fury howling
> Shriek, while rending sails to tatters
> Here are we. in depths profoundest.

Tuffiam la testa.
Come sugli alberi
D' una foresta,
Oslam le pendule
Sartie scalar.
Noi gli scoiattoli
Siaom del mar.

Marinai (sotto il ponte).
Sotto prora, sotto poppa
È una placida dimora,
Qui vuotiam l' ardente coppa
Del liquor che inganna l' ora.
Sotto poppa, sotto prora.

Mozzi (sulle antenne).
Il mar mugghiante,
Il ciel furente,
Greco a Levante,
Bora a Ponente,
Scioni e turbini
Sappiam sfidar.
Noi gli scoiattoli
Siamo del mar!

Una Voce Sola (di dentro).
Bar.   Pescator, affonda l' esca,
E sia l' onda a te fedel,
Lieta sera e buona pesca
Ti promette il mare e il ciel.

Midshipmen and Boys.
We're here; some perched aloft, some on the
gunwale,
Some to the tremulous rope-ladders clinging
See how the nimble midshipmen can climb!
Behold in us the squirrels of the sea!

1st Midshipman.   Ho, he! ho, he!

BAR. *(from behind).*
Fisher-boy, thy bait now lower:
May the waves prove true to thee!
                    [He enters
Now good night! May luck attend thee!

SCENA II.

Coro, BARNABA, ISÈPO.

BARNABA *è vestito da pescatore con una rete in mano.*

Il Pilota.   Chi va là?

BAR.   La canzon ve lo dicea:
Un pescator che attende la marea.
Ho la barca laggiù nell' acqua bassa.
E tèmpora domani, e si digiuna,
(Per mia fortuna)
La mensa magra il pescatore ingrassa.

Marinai (ridendo). Ha! Ha!

BAR. *(ad Isè.).* (Siam salvi! Han riso. Sono
ottanta
Fra marinari e mozzi. Han tre decine
Di remi e nulla più; due colubrine
Di piccolo calibro. Or va, con quanta
Lena ti resta, e disponi le scolte
Colà dove le macchie son più folte.
Io qui rimango a far l' ufficio mio.
Vanne con Dio.)   *[Isè esce.*

SCENE II.

Chorus, BARNABA, ISÈPO.

A Pilot. Who goes there?

BAR. My song itself will tell you.
I am a fisher; for the tide I am waiting,
And my boat waits for me
In yon deep waters.
To-morrow is a fast day. When people fast
They bring me good fortune:
And but for fast days, fishermen ne'er would
fatten.

Sailors (laughing). Ha! Ha!

BAR. *(to Isè.).* We are safe now! They 're laugh
ing. They, in all,
Number eighty, men and boys. They have
three ranks
Of ten oars each, and no more; only two cul-
verins,
Both of small calibre. Now go, with all
The breath that is left thee, and place out
the scouts
Down yonder, where the bushes are thickest.
I here remain, till the moment comes for
action.
Heaven go with thee.   *[Exit Isè.*

"FISHER-BOYS, YOUR BOATS MAKE READY."

English adaptation by THEO. T. BARKER.

BARNABA.

f con brio.

Ah!.............. Fish - er - boys, your boats make rea - dy, True to
Ah!.............. Pes - ca - tor, af - fon - da l'e - sca, a te

you will o - cean be,...... Pleasant night and for - tune stea - dy, Prom - ise
l'on - da.... sia fe - del,...... Lie - ta se - ra e buo - na pes - ca Ti pro -

both the sky and sea. Off, your tran - quil songs up - lift - ing, O'er the
met - te il ma-re, il ciel. Va, tran - quil - la.... can - ti - le - na, Per l'az -

broad and a - zure tide,.............. Ah! some sweet
sur - ra im - men - si - tà;.............. Ah! u - na

Chorus of Sailors.

Sy - ren, while you're drift - ing In your nets will coy - ly hide. Some sweet
plà - ci - da si - re - na nel - la re - te.... cas-che - ra. U - na

(aside.)

Sy - ren, while we're drift - ing, In our nets will coy - ly hide.
pla - ci - da si - re - na nel - la re - te casche - rà

BARNABY. Watch, with the thunders send your lightnings
Spia coi ful - mi - ne - i tuoi sguardi ac

flash - ing, And count your dead up - on the dark strand dash -
cor - ti, E fra le te - ne - bre conta i tuoi mor -

poco rall.

ing, Yes, on this island bleak, brown and de - sert - ed, Should rise your fortune, thro' plans well con -
ti, Si, da ques-t'i-so - la de - ser-ta e bru - na or de - ve sor-ge - re la tua for -

a tempo

cer - ted, Be watch - - ful! And ris - ing mis - trust drive a -
tu - na, Sta in guar - - dia! E il ra - pi - do so-spet - to

rail.

way. While laugh - ing, And vig - il - ant, And sing - ing, And
svia, E ri - di, E vi - gi - la, E can - ta, E

watch - ing, And sing - ing, And watch - ing — laugh - ing! sing - ing....
spi - a, E can - ta, E spi - a - ri di! can - ta!...

Ah! fair as shines the star of ev'ning—In a heaven of...... sweet de-
Ah! brilla Ve-ne-re se-re-na In un ciel di...... ve-lut-

light. So a bril-liant Sy-ren stray-ing, To your nets will drift to-
tà; U-na ful-gi-da si-re-na nel-la re-te ca-sche-

night,To your nets,to your nets,to your nets,Will a Sy-ren drift to-night.Will a Sy-ren, drift to-
rà, cascherà, casche-rà, caschera, nel-la Re-te ca-sche-rà, la si-re-na nel-la

night, Yes, in your nets, will a Sy-ren...... drift to-night, will take shel-ter to-
re-te ca-sche-rà, nel-la re-te...... ca-sche-rà, ca-sche-rà, ca-sche

(BARNABA goes out as
ENZO enters.)

night. Yes, will take shel-ter to-night, yes to-night.
rà, Sì ca-sche-rà, ca-sche-rà, ca-sche-rà.

SCENA III.	SCENE III.
ENZO. *Marinai e Mozzi, il Nostromo, il Maestro delle vele, il Pilota.*	*Enter* ENZO, *Sailors,* Midshipmen, the Nostromo, the Master of the Sails.

ENZO (*esce da sotto coperta con una lanterna in mane avanzandosi gaiamente, alla ciurma*).

    Sia gloria ai canti
    Dei naviganti!
    Questa notte si salpa!

Marinai.   Evviva il nostro
    Principe e capitan!

ENZO (*esplorando il cielo*). Soffia grecale,
Vento buono per noi. . nella carena   [*al Nos.*
Tu, Nostromo, raccogli la gomena.
Tu, Maestro delle vele, affiggi al rostro
Del brigantino il dalmato segnale
che ci protesse in molte aspre fortune,
E al maggior pino inalbera il fanale.
          [*ai Mozzi.*
Voi siate pronti a distaccar la fune
D' amarra a un cenno mio. "Quest' erme dune
"Più non vedremo all' ora mattutina.
"Nocchier, l' abbrivio è verso Palestrina."

[*Alcuni uomini della ciurma eseguiscono gli ordini di* ENZO; *mentre gli altri ricantano la* MARINARESCA.

ENZO (*a tutti*). Ed or scendete a riposarvi. Io vigilo
Solo sul ponte le inimiche flotte.
          [*Guarda le stelle.*
È tardi.

Ciurma.   Buona guardia.

ENZO.   Buona notte.
    [*La ciurma scende sotto il ponte.*

ENZO *enters from below deck with a lantern in his hand, advancing gayly.*

ENZO. Long live the songs
    Of the sons of the sea!
    We to-night will weigh anchor.

Chorus (*surrounding him*).
    Long live our noble Prince!
    Long live our captain.

ENZO (*observing the sky*). Northeast the wind is.
  'T is a good wind for us. Down in the hold
          [*to the Nostromo*
Do thou, Nostromo, securely stow the cable.
Thou, master of the sails, upon the prow
Of our ship see hoisted the Dalmatian flag.
There it has floated through many sharp ordeals!
And on the mainmast at once hang out the lantern.   [*to the Midshipmen.*
And you, be ready to let go the mooring cable
At my first signal.

[*Some of the crew execute* ENZO'S *orders, while the others repeat the Marinaresca.*

Chorus. Ho, he! ho, he!

1st Sailors. Out with the oars!

2d Sailors. Hoist now.
    Oars to the starboard!
    The thunder roars.

Boys. Amid the lightning-flashes of the tempest,
    Unto the clouds we turn our brows un daunted;
    We dare the quiv'ring shrouds to climb.
    Behold in us the squirrels of the sea'

ENZO. Now go below; betake ye to slumber,
    While I alone upon deck
    Watch the enemy's vessels.
    'T is late now. Good night to all!

Chorus. Heav'n watch o'er thee!
          [*The crew go below deck*

SCENA IV.

SCENE IV.

English adaptation by THEO. T. BARKER.

sweetest boon of life and love, Come, oh! dear - est, here I wait thee, with a pulse that scarce doth
del - la vi - ta e dell' a - mor, vie - ni, o don - na, qui t'at - ten - do, coll' a - ne - li - to del

move, Come, O darl - ing, and take my kiss - es, Come love, Come love, Come, O my
cor, vie - ni, o don - na, ah vie - ni al ba - cio, vie - ni, vie - ni, vie - ni al

darl - ing, take my kiss - es, the sweet - est boon of life and love, ah! ....
ba - cio del - la vi - ta e dell' a - mo - re, dell' a - mor, ah! ....

come! ah! come! ....
vien! ah! vien! ....

Ah! chi è la? non è uno spetro
Del pensier! quella è una barca.
Odo già de' remi il metro,
Verso me volando varca ...
La voce di Bar. (dietro il brigantino).
    Capitan.. a bordo!
Enzo (sclamando verso la direzione della voce di
    Bar.).
                    Avanti!!
(Dio! sostieni ancor la piena
Della gioia!) O naviganti,
Costeggiate la carena!
    [prende una fune e la getta al di là della sponda.
Qua la fune ... aggrappa ... annoda
Le tue mani .. un passo ancor ...
Non cadere! approda! approda! ...

[gazing at the sea.
But who comes? 'T is not a phantom
Of my brain? A boat approaches!
I already hear the rowers;
They towards me are swiftly steering.
Bar. (from behind). Signor Captain, on board
    there?
Enzo. Come this way.
(*Aside.*) (Heaven aid me to bear the fulness
Of this rapture!) Now then, boatmen,
Keep on this side of the vessel.
    [throws a rope over the side
There! the guide rope hold tightly.
Now tie it, keep from falling. **Mount**
quickly!

SCENA V.

ENZO, LAURA.

Lau. (nelle braccia di Enzo). Enzo!
Enzo. Laura! Amore! Amor!
La voce di Bar. (sinistramente, allontanandosi).
    Buona fortuna!
Lau.   Oh! la sinistra voce!
    Fuggiam! fuggiam!
Enzo.   S' ei fu che ti salvò! ...
Lau. Pur sorridea d'un infernal sorriso! ...

SCENE V.

Enter LAURA.

Enzo. Laura! Laura! dearest, I am thine!
Lau. Enzo, my Enzo! Ah, dearest, I am thine!
Bar. (departing). Good luck attend ye!
Lau. Ah! at that voice I shudder!
Enzo. It is by him thou 'rt saved.
Lau. Yet, when he smiles, his smile appears in-
fernal.

Enzo. E l' uomo che ci aperse il paradiso!
Deh! non turbare — con ree paure
Di questo istante — le ebbrezze pure;
D' amor soltanto — con me ragiona,
E il cielo, o cara — che schiudi a me!

Lau. Ah! del tuo bacio — nel dolce incanto
Celeste gioia — diventa il pianto,
A umano strazio — Dio non perdona,
Se perdonato — amor non è!

Enzo. Ma dimmi come, — angelo mio,
Mi ravvisasti?
Lau. — Nel marinar
Enzo conobbi. —
Enzo. Al pari anch' io
Te al primo suono — della parola . . .
Lau. Enzo adorato! — ma il tempo vola.
All' erta! all' erta! —
Enzo. Deh! non tremar!
Siamo in un' isola — tutta deserta,
Tra mare e cielo — tra cielo e mar!
Vedrem pur ora tramontar la luna . . .
Quando sarà corcata, all' aura bruna
Noi salperem; cogli occhi al firmamento,
Coi baci in fronte e colle vele al vento!

[La luna bassa si svolve dalle nuvole, il suo disco s'
asconderà dietro il vascello.

§ 2. Laggiù nelle nebbie remote,
Laggiù nelle tenebre ignote,
Sta il segno del nostro cammin.
Nell' onde, nell' ombre, nei venti,
Fidenti, ridenti, fuggenti,
Gittiamo la vitae il destin.
La luna discende, discende
Ricinta di roride bende,
Siccome una sposa all' altar.
E asconde — la spenta — parvenza
Nell' onde; — con lenta — cadenza,
La luna è discesa nel mar!

Enzo (staccandosi). E il tuo nocchiere
Or la fuga t' appresta — O amata donna,
Tu qui resta. [scende sotto il ponte.

SCENA VI.

Laura sola, poi Gioconda.

Lau. Ho il cuor pieno di preghiere.
Quel lume! Ah! una Madonna!
[Davanti all' immagine della Madonna orando con pas-
sione; mentre ch' essa prega, Gio. mascherata escirà
da un nascondiglio sotto prora, e s' avanzerà lenta.
Stella del marinar! Vergine Santa,
Tu mi difendi in quest' ora suprema,
Tu vedi quanta passione e quanta
Fede mi trasse a tale audacia estrema!
Sotto il tuo velo che i prostrati ammanta
Ricovera costei che prega e trema,
Scenda per questa fervida orazion
Sul capo mio, Madonna del perdon.
Una benedizion.

Enzo. 'T is he who for us opens Paradise.
Ah! cloud not, dearest, with fears and
doubtings
The pure enjoyment of these blessed mo
ments.
Of love, love only, let our discourse be!
Love is the heaven unveil'd to-night.

Lau. Ah, love, thy kisses, with sweet enchant
ment,
Change ev'ry sorrow to rapture celestial.
No human frailty will heaven pardon.
If 't will not pardon love's delight.

Enzo. But tell me how, my angel,
Thou didst recognize me?
Lau. The sailor's dress hid not my Enzo.

Enzo. 'T was thus with me, love. Soon as thy voice
Bless'd the air with its music.
Lau. Enzo, beloved!
(Starting.) But time is flying — be watchful!
Enzo. Fear not, my love!
This is an island wholly deserted,
'Mid sky and ocean, ocean and sky.
We soon shall see yonder the moon de
scending,
And when she sinks to slumber, favor'd by
darkness,
We will set sail, with kisses on our fore
heads,
And fav'ring winds our sails filling.

Ensemble.

Down yonder, amid the dim far-off mists,
Down yonder, amid the dark, unknown
clouds,
Our goal will, erelong, be espied.
To the billows, the shadows, the breezes.
Both faithful, and smiling, and flying,
Our lives and our fate we confide.
The moon is descending, descending,
Surrounded and veiled by the night dews
Like bride for the altar attired;
And, hiding her fast fading lustre,
Sinks under the waves in slow cadence;
The moon 'neath the sea has retired.
Enzo. It is thy pilot.
For flight now prepare thee. O my beloved
Rest here awhile. [descends below deck

SCENE VI.

Laura, alone; then Gioconda.

Lau. My heart is full of happy tears.
[Throws herself at the foot of the altar, and prays ear-
nestly. While she is praying, Gio., masked, comes
from her hiding-place, under the prow of the ship, and
advances slowly toward Lau.
Star of the mariner, Virgin most holy!
Be my defender in this hour of trial!
Thou seest by how much ardor, by how
much faith,
I am led to adventure this audacious step!
Under thy mantle, kneeling sinners shel
t'ring,
Find refuge for one who is praying and trem
bling.
Send down, in answer to my fervent prayer
Upon my head, O Virgin, full of mercy,
A blessing from on high'

SCENA VII.   SCENE VII.

GIOCONDA and LAURA.

English adaptation by THEO. T. BARKER.

GIOCONDA.

Curs - es at - tend you,
Fun a - na - tè - ma!
Who am I, ask you? I'm your
Chi son tu chia - mi? So - no

LAURA.   (with a cry of terror.)

Ah!
Ah!
Who are you?
chi sei?

prestissimo.

shadow in at - tend-ance! All the world thro' My name is Vengeance. And I love the man you love, too.
un' om-bra che t'a - spet - ta! Il mio no-me è la Vendet - ta. A - mo l'uo-mo che tu a - mi.

Heaven!
Ciel!

(with suppressed anger, pointing at the prow.)   cres.

There, his time and chance he's bid-ing, Like a beast of prey in hiding, Ah! with
Là at - te - sie il tem - po col - si co - me bel - va nel - la ta - na, ah! la

a piacere poco.   ten.   ff   *a tempo.*

force past hu - man show - ing, Fu - ry in my heart is glow - ing! Would you
for - za so - vru - ma - na del fu - ror m'invade i poi - si! Vuoi fug-

fly? Is't love de - lays you! Would you fly from here, hap - py riv - al? Well, the
gir? D'amor ti struggi? Vuoi fug - gi - re? l'te - ta ri - va - le? Sì, l'an

ff

sails and rud - der still your pleas - ure wait, 'Tis well, 'tis well, go, go! Naugh'
ten - na e il go - ve - na - le pron - ti son, sta ben, sta ben, va, va, Va

GIO. Il mio braccio t' afferra!
Vien ch' io ti scorga in viso! a terra a
terra!
Presso a quel lume .. o i lagrimosi rai ..
Or più scampo non hai!
Questo pugnale ..
Ma no .. tu avrai per sorte
Un fulmin più fatale ..
In quella barca bruna ..

LAU. O ciel!
GIO. Là è il tuo consorte!

LAU. Perduta io son!
GIO. La morte
Voga sulla laguna.
Ecco! oramai nè un nume, nè un santuario
Salvar ti può.
LAU. (alzando il rosario). M' aita!

GIO. Ah! quel rosario!
Esso è per te benedizione e schermo.
[la trascina verso la riva.

LAU. Che fai?
GIO. Ti salvo! Olà, il mio palischermo!
[appariscono due Marinai con una barca.
Fuggi! .. a te .. questa maschera ti ascoda!
[stacca la maschera e la pone sul volto a LAU.
LAU. Ma mi dirai chi sei?
GIO. Son la Gioconda!
[GIO. spinge quasi a forza LAU. nella barca che si
allontana rapidamente. GIO. scomparisce un istante
dietro al brigantino, come per assicurarsi della fuga
di LAU.

BAR. (dalla riva, osservando i movimenti della barca che
porta LAU. e scorgendo in distanza la gondola
D' ALVISE).
Maledizione! Ha preso il vol! Padron!
Nel canal morto .. là .. forza di remi!
[scomparisce.
GIO. È salva! O madre mia, quanto mi costi! ..

GIO. In my grasp now I hold thee!
Come, let me see thy features! Kneel down!
No escape for thee now!
Soon shall this poniard —
[about to strike, stops suddenly
But no! for thee approaches
A punishment more fatal!
[holding her tightly with one hand, and with the other
pointing to the sea, on which a boat is seen approach-
ing.
There! look there!
LAU. Heaven!
GIO. There in yonder boat,
There is thy husband!
LAU. Heaven! I am lost.
GIO. My curse is now accomplished.
No one on earth, nor even in Heaven,
Can save thee now.

LAU. (lifting up the Rosary).
Virgin, oh aid me! grant thine aid!
GIO. (struck at recognition of the Rosary).
What! 't is the Rosary!
[takes off her mask, and places it over the face of
LAU.
LAU. What dost thou?
GIO. I save thee! Ho there! my boat bring
quickly!
[a boat arrives with two Sailors
LAU. But tell me first, who art thou?
GIO. I am La Gioconda.
[hurries to the boat. Exeunt behind vessel

Enter BARNABA.

BAR. (looking on all sides). May they be curst!
They have taken flight. Signor!
[makes signs to ALV., who is seen in his boat at back
of stage.
By the canal, out there — (pointing) there!
Urge on the rowers, urge them! [Exit
GIO. (entering again).
I 've sav'd her. Alas, dear mother,
How much thou dost cost me!

SCENA VIII.

GIOCONDA, ENZO.

ENZO (scendendo dal ponte). Laura, Laura! ove sei?

GIO. (avanzandosi verso ENZO fieramente).
Laura è scomparsa!
ENZO. Gioconda! o ciel! che avvenne?
GIO. Invano a' rei
Baci sognati il tuo sospir la chiama ...
ENZO. Menti, menti, o crudel!
GIO. No! più non t' ama!
[trascinandolo verso la riva.
Vedi là, nel canal morto,
Un navil che forza il corso?
Essa fugge! il suo rimorso
Fu più forte dell' amor!
Questo lido è a lei funesto,
Chè la morte intorno sta ..
Essa fugge ed io qui resto! ..
Chi di noi più amato avrà?
ENZO. Taci! ahimè! da che t' ho scôrto,
Sospettai nefando agguato,
Non mi dir d' avermi amato.

SCENE VIII.

GIOCONDA, ENZO.

ENZO (entering from below deck).
Laura, Laura! where art thou?
GIO. (advancing haughtily toward ENZO).
Laura has vanish'd.
ENZO. Gioconda! oh heaven! what has happened
GIO. In vain, to taste dreamy soft guilty kisses
Thy sighs may seek to recall her.
ENZO. Falsehood! cruel! 't is false!
GIO. No more she loves thee!
See out there, in yonder channel,
Fast a boat its way is making.
She flies from thee: the pangs of conscience
Were far stronger than her love.
From these shores, to her ill-omened,
Where pale death reigns all around,
She is flying; I am here remaining;
Which of us shows truest love?

ENZO. Silence! alas! since first I met thee,
I have evil plots suspected.
Tell me not that thou hast loved me!

Odio sol tu porti in cor!
Ma al suo barbaro consorte
L' angiol mio saprò strappar! . .
Là è la vita!   [*slanciandosi verso la riva.*
Gio.   Là è la morte!
Enzo.   Che di' tu?

Gio.   Riguarda al mar!
Tu sei tradito! Un infame, un crudele
Al Gran Consiglio il tuo nome svelò
Rompi gli indugi, — fa forza di vele,
Il cielo ancora salvare ti può!
Enzo.   Taci! è un insulto dei vili il consiglio,
Dove è la morte, là impavido io sto!
Noto m' è il rombo del fiero naviglio,
Fuga od arresa che sieno non so!
[*si ode un colpo di cannone. Alcuni Marinai dell'*
Hecate *sbucano dal ponte altri irrompono dalla scena*
alcuni con fiaccole in mano.]
Marinai.   Le galèe! le galèe! Salvi chi può!
Enzo (*strappando la fiaccola ad uno dei Marinai*).
Sin ch' io sia vivo, no!
Al nemico darem cenere e brage!
Incendio!   [*dà fuoco all'* Hecate. *La nave*
arde.
Tutti.   Incendio! guerra! morte! strage!
Fuggiam! fuggiam! più speranza non v' ha!
Enzo (*dalla tolda slanciandosi in mare*).
O Laura, addio!
Gio. (*dalla riva*).
E sempre Laura! oh almeno con te morir
poss' io!
[*La nave si sprofonda. Cade la tela.*

FINE DELL' ATTO II.

Hate alone thy heart doth nourish.
But from thy detested consort,
Dearest love, I 'll bear thee away!
Life is yonder.   [*rushing toward the water*
Gio.   Death is yonder!
Enzo.   What say'st thou?
Gio.   Look out to sea.
Sailors (*entering*). See the galleys! your safety
seek!
Gio. (*to* Enzo).
Thou art betrayed by a wretch vile and cruel
To the Council thy name was revealed.
Delay not a moment, hoist every sail,
And heav'n may yet spare thy life.
Enzo.   Silence! 't is an insult to give such vile
counsels;
Where death is nearest I fearless will stand
Well do I know how to steer a tight vessel.
Flight and surrender I ne'er understand.
         [*enter Sailors in confusion*
Sailors.   No hope is left us. Ah, fly!
Enzo (*taking a lighted torch from a Sailor*).
While I 'm living, no!
To the enemy we 'll give ashes and embers!
        [*sets fire to ship, flames break ou...*
We 'll burn her!
Sailors.   We 'll burn her! Fight them! kill them
Enzo.   Adieu, my Laura.
Gio. (*aside*). 'T is ever Laura! Yet I, at least, may
die with thee!

         [*The burning vessel sinks*

END OF ACT II.

ATTO III.

CÀ D'ORO.

*Una camera nella CÀ D'ORO. Sera; lampada accesa.
Da un lato un' armatura antica.*

SCENA I.

ALVISE entrando in preda a violenta agitazione.

ALV. Sì! morir ella de'! Sul nome mio
Scritta l' infamia impunemente avrà?
Chi un Badoèr tradì
Non può sperar pietà!..
Se ier non la ghermì
Nell' isola fatal questa mia mano,
L'espïazion non fia tremenda meno!
Ieri un pugnal le avria squarciato il seno,
Oggi.. un ferro non è.. sarà un veleno!

[*accennando alle sale contigue*

Là turbini e farnetichi
La gaia baraonda,
Dell' agonia col gemito
Qui l' orgia si confonda!
Ombre di mia prosapia
Non arrossite ancor!
Tutto la morte vendica,
Anche il tradito amor!
Là del patrizio veneto
Si compia il largo invito,
Quivi il feral marito
Provveda al proprio onor!
Fremete, o danze, o cantici!
È una infedel che muor!

SCENA II.

LAURA, ALVISE.

LAU. (*entra in ricca veste da ballo, con perle e gemme;
ad* ALV.).
Qui chiamata m' avete?
ALV. (*con affettata cortesia*). Pur che vi piaccia...

LAU. Mio signor...
ALV. Sedete!

[*siedono ai due lati di un ampio tavolo.*

Bella così, madonna, — io non v' ho mai veduta;
Pur il sorriso è languido; — perchè ristarvi
muta?
Dite: un gentil mistero — v' è grave a me
svelar,
O un qualche velo nero — dovrò da me strappar?
LAU. Dal vostro accento insolito — cruda ironia
traspira,
Il labro a grazia atteggiasi — e fuor ne scopia
l'ira..
Mio nobile consorte, — non vi comprendo ancora!

ACT III

THE HOUSE OF GOLD.

*A Chamber in the House of Gold. Night; a lamp
lighted. On one side of the stage, a suit of ancient
armor.*

SCENE I.

ALVISE.

ALV. (*in violent agitation*).
Yes, to die is her doom! My name in
honor,
Shall not with impunity be disgraced.
From Badoers, when betrayed,
Pity 't were vain to hope.
Though yesterday upon the fatal isle
She 'scaped this vengeful hand,
She shall not escape a fearful expiation.
Last night a sharp poniard should have
pierced her bosom;
This night no poniard I 'll use; she dies by
poison! [*pointing to the adjoining room*
While there the dancers sing and laugh,
In giddy movements flying,
Their mirthful tones shall blend with
groans,
Breath'd by a sinner dying.
Shades of my honor'd forefathers!
Soon shall your blushes disappear;
Soon shall a deadly vengeance prove
Honor to me is dear.
While dance the giddy crowd,
In mirthful movements flying,
Here shall be heard the bitter groans
The sinner breathes in dying.
Yonder, the nobles of the nation
Are gathered at my invitation;
Here, an insulted husband
For signal vengeance cries!
Exult, in dances and in songs,
While here a faithless one dies!

SCENE II.

LAURA, ALVISE.

Enter LAURA, *in a rich ball dress.*

LAU. You have summon'd me hither?
ALV. (*with an affectation of courtesy*).
Hoping to please you.
LAU. My lord— [*slowly seating herself*
ALV. Be seated.

[*they sit at opposite sides of large table*

Lovely as this, signora, I never yet have
seen you;
Yet faint and languid your smiles appear
Why thus do you sit speechless?
Tell me, is some gentle secret
About to be revealed?
Or will some veil of blackest dye
From sin at once be torn?
LAU. Throughout these accents unusual
Irony still is breathing;
Your lips may kindness simulate,
Yet they are white with anger.
My noble lord and consort,
I do not understand you.

ALV (*concitato*). Pur d'abbassar la maschera, — madonna, è giunta l'ora.
[alzandosi con violenza.
Giunta è l'ora! — ad altr' uomo rivolto,
Donna impura, è il tuo primo sospir...
LAU. Ad altr' uomo? Che dite? Che ascolto!
[fra sè.
(Cielo! orrendo m' imponi martir.)
ALV. Ieri quasi t' ho côlta in peccato,
Pur potesti salvarti e fuggir...
Col mio guanto t' ho oggi afferrato,
Più non fuggi, — ti è d' uopo morir!
[la atterra violentemente. LAU. getta un grido.

LAU. (*a piedi di* ALV.).
Morir! è troppo orribile!
Aver davanti il ciel...
E scender nelle tenebre
D' un desolato avel!
Senti! di sangue tiepido
In sen mi scorre un rivo...
Perchè, se piango e vivo,
Dirmi : tu dêi morir?
La morte è pena infame
Anche a più gran fallir!
ALV. Invan tu piangi — invan tu speri,
Dio non ti può esaudir!
In lui raccogli — i tuoi pensieri;
Preparati a morir!
E già che ai nuovi imeni
L' anima tua sospira,
Indocil spossa, ten vieni
E mira!

LAU.   Ahimè!
Ove m' adduci?
ALV. (*con forza sollevando la drapperia della camera attigua e indicando un catafalco. Si vedrà il riverbero dei ceri*). Vieni!
LAU. (*inorridita*).   Ah! orribil cosa!
Serenata interna (sulla laguna).
Ten va serenata,
Per l' aura serena,
Ten va, cantilena,
Per l' onda incantata.

Entra GIOCONDA *e s' appiatta in fondo. La serenata cessa per un momento.*
ALV. (*estraendo una fiala*).
Prendi questo velen; e gia che *Serenata interna.*
forte
Tanto mi sembri ne' tuoi detti   —
audaci,   *La gaia canzon*
Con quelle labbra che succhi-
aro i baci,   *Fa l' eco languir,*
Suggi la morte.
"La tua condanna confido a te   *E l' ilare suon*
stessa;
"Non far che mal securo
"Voler t' arresti la mano per- *Si muta in sospir.*
plessa,
"Non far che il mio pugnale ti *Con vago miraggio*
percota
"E insozzi i lari del tuo san- *Riflette la luna*
gue impuro.
Scampo non hai,   [vrai.
Odi questa canzon? Morir do-   *L' argenteo sue raggie*
Pria ch' essa giunga all' ultima sua
ata.   *[esce. Sull' ampia laguna*

ALV. (*with sudden violence*).
Well, then, to tear away the mask,
The hour has come, signora;
This is the moment. To another was given
Shameless woman, thy first loving sigh!
LAU. To another? What mean you?

ALV. Yes, vilest of women.
I last night had nigh caught thee when
sinning,
But from me thou wert able to fly!
In my grasp I to-day have enchained thee,
Ne'er to fly me; for now thou must die.
[throws her down violently
LAU. To die! alas, 'tis a fate too horrible!
To quit a smiling sky,
And, 'mid the deepest, darkest gloom,
In desolation die!
Lo! here, my life-blood's rapid stream
Its onward course is keeping;
Yet life for me means weeping!
Why say'st thou I must die?
Death is the shameful punishment
For crimes of deepest dye!

ALV. In vain thou weepest, in vain thou hopest,
Heav'n will not heed thy pray'r.
To yonder heav'n thy thoughts directing,
For death at once prepare.
And now that for fresh nuptials
Fondly thy soul is sighing,
Unfaithful consort, come hither;
Admire this!
[drags her towards the curtained doo
LAU. (*terrified*). Where wouldst thou lead me?

ALV. (*violently uplifting the draperies of the adjoining chamber, and pointing to a funereal bier*).
Nearer! 'T is thy bridal bed.
LAU. (*horrified*). Ah!
Serenade behind (far off on the Lagoon).
Enter GIOCONDA, *who conceals herself.*
Chorus. Our gay songs are ending;
The soft echoes die,
And blithe, careless laughter
Is chang'd to a sigh.

ALV. (*producing a flask*).   Chorus
This poison thou must take.
Thou hast dar'd   Our gay songs are
To utter words that seem to   ending,
me audacious,   The soft echoes die,
Now let the lips that spoke   And blithe, careless
them, that drank kisses,   laughter
Drink in thy death. No hope   Is chang'd to a sigh.
is left thee.   The wavelets and
Dost thou hear yonder song?   moonbeams
Thy life must cease   Together are blending,
Ere of that song the last note has The bright rays of sil-
sounded!   ver
              [exit ALV.   On ocean descending

SCENA III.

LAURA e GIOCONDA.

GIO. (accorrendo verso LAU., afferra il veleno che LAU. ha tra le mani e le porge un' ampolla).
A me quel filtro! a te codesto! bevi!

LAU. Gioconda, qui?
GIO. Previdi la tua sorte,
Per salvarti mi armai, ti rassicura.
Quel narcotico è tal, che della morte
Finge il letargo... Angosciosi, brevi
Sono gl' istanti... bevi... ame la cura
Lascia dell' opra. — Or via!!

LAU. Mi fai paura!
GIO. S' ei qui torna t' uccide.

LAU. Atra agonia!
GIO. Prega per te quaggiù la madre mia,
Nell' oratorio, i miei fidi cantori
Son presso.. ascolta.

LAU. Orror!
Già la canzone muor!

GIO. Con essa muori!
La condanna t' è nota:
Pria ch' essa giunga all' ultima sua nota...

LAU. Porgi! ho bevuto.
[prende la fiala dalle mani di GIO. poi scompare dietro le cortine della camera mortuaria.

GIO. La fiala a me! oh gran Dio!
[travasa il veleno d' ALV. nella fiala del sonnifero e lascia l' ampolla del veleno vuota sul travolo. Esce precipitosa.

SCENE III.

LAURA and GIOCONDA.

Enter GIOCONDA, who runs to LAURA, from whose hand she takes the poison, and gives her a phial.
GIO. Give me that phial, and take this quickly! Drink it.
LAU. Gioconda here?
GIO. Thy cruel doom foreseeing,
I came hither to save thee.
All fear now banish.
This narcotic is such, that in a trance
Like death it will plunge thee. Drink it, drink it!
Full of anguish, yet brief
Are the moments now left thee.
LAU. Of thee I am fearful.
GIO. He who returns here will kill thee.
LAU. O dark despair!
GIO. For thy safety my mother in yon oratory
Is praying, and some stanch friends are nigh.
Their singing thou hearest.
LAU. Alas! slowly the song dies out.
GIO. Drink, then. With it, thy life was to cease!
This was the sentence:
"Ere of that song the last note has sounded."
LAU. Give me.
[drinks the narcotic.
I have drained it.
[rushes behind the curtains of the funereal chamber.
GIO. Give me the flask.
[pours the poison into the flask which had contained the narcotic, and leaves the empty flask on the table.
Great heaven!
[exit precipitately.

E in quel sì sublime
Riverbere pio,
Patetica rima
Creata da Dio.
—
Ten va, cantilena,
Per l' aura serena,
Ten va, serenata,
Per l' onda incantata.
Udite le blande
Canzoni vagar.
Il remo ci scande
Gli accordi sul mar.
Ten va, serenata,
Sull' onda incantata.
—
Il canto è la vita,
Di sogni si pasce,
Ai sogni c' invita,
Dai sogni rinasce,
D' un' anima ignota
È l' eco fedel;
L' estrema sua nota
Si perde nel ciel.

Sublime is the message
By nature new given,
In tenderest cadence,
Created in Heaven!
—
Our gay songs are ending,
The soft echoes die,
And blithe, careless laughter
Is chang'd to a sigh.
We listen to songs
Full of innocent glee,
Our oars keeping time
As we float o'er the sea.
Float on, serenade!
Heaven soft air is granting;
In harmony float
O'er the waters so chanting.
—
We listen to songs
Full of innocent glee,
Our oars keeping time
As we float o'er the sea.
From some unknown soul
Comes Echo's reply;
The last note, ascending,
Is lost in the sky!

SCENA IV.

ALVISE solo, mentre la cadenza della serenata è alle ultime sue note. Osserva l' ampolla vuota sui tavolo.

ALV. Tutto è compiuto!
Vuoto è il cristal.
[entra nella cella funeraria, vi rimane un momen te e torna in scena.
Vola su lei la morte.
La morte è il nulla e vecchia fola è il ciel!
[esce lentamente.

SCENE IV.

Enter ALVISE; he observes the flask empty on the table.

ALV. All now is over!
Empty is the flask.
[enters the funereal chamber for a moment, then re-enters.
Death has forever claim'd her!
[exit

LA GIOCONDA.

<table>
<tr><td>

SCENA V.

GIOCONDA sola.

Gia. *(ricomparisce dal lato opposto a quello donde è uscito*
ALV. Si guarda interno, solleva la cortina
della cella, poi, vistasi sola, esclama:
O madre mia, nell' isola fatale
Frenai per te la sanguinaria brama
Di rejetta rival. Or più tremendo
E il sacrifizio mio . . .
Io la salvo per lui, per lui che l' ama!
[esce precipitosamente.

</td><td>

SCENE V.

Re-enter GIOCONDA from her hiding-place.

GIO. O dearest mother, on yonder fatal island,
For thy dear sake, I check'd the burning
frenzy
Of a passion disdain'd. Now, more tremen
dous
The sacrifice I 'm making!
I save her; but for his sake, who loves her.
[exit precipitately

</td></tr>
<tr><td>

SCENA VI.

Sontuosissima sala attigua alla cella funeraria, splendi-
damente parata a festa. Ampio portone nel fondo a
sinistra, un consimile a destra, ma queste tutte chiuse
da una drapperia. Una terza porta nella parete a
sinistra.

Entrano Cavalieri, Dame, Maschere. ALVISE moverà loro
incontro ricevendo e complimentando chi entra Il
Paggio gli sta accanto. GIOCONDA.

ALV. Benvenuti messeri! Andrea Sagredo!
Erizzo, Lordan! Venier! Chi vedo?
Isèpo Barbarigo, a noi tornato
Dalla pallida China! e il ben amato
Cugino mio Partecipazio! O quanti
Bei cavalieri! . . . Belle dame! Avanti,
Avanti! e voi, vispi cantori e maschere,
Presto sciogliete le carole e i canti.

</td><td>

SCENE VI.

A magnificent hall, adjoining the funereal chamber, and
splendidly adorned for a festivity. At back, wide
entrance door. A similar door, completely closed by
curtains. A third door, opening from the side.

Enter Cavaliers, Ladies and Masquers. ALVISE ad-
vances to meet them, and exchanges compliments with all
who arrive. A Page stands behind him. GIOCONDA
enters unobserved.

ALV. *(receiving the Guests).*
Worthy friends, you are welcome! Andrea
Sagredo!
Erizzo, Loredan, Venier! Whom see I?
Isèpo Barbarigo, to us returning
From pale, far-distant China?
And here my much lov'd cousin comes,
Partecipazio!
Of splendid knights what a concourse!
Pass onward, charming ladies, pass onward,
Ye signors, too, are welcome, and ye, cava-
liers,
And ye, merry young singers, and masquers
too.
Brighten the revelry with songs and dances!

</td></tr>
<tr><td>

Coro. S' inneggi alla *Cà d' Oro*
Che intreccia in rami d' òr
Della virtù l' alloro
Col mirto dell' amor.
ALV. Grazie vi rendo per le vostre laudi,
Cortesi amici. A più leggiadri gaudi
Ora v' invito. Ecco una mascherata
Di vaghe danzatrici. — Ognuna è ornata
Di bellezza e fulgore
E tutte in cerchio rappresentan l' ore.
Incomincia la danza.

</td><td>

Chorus. We sing in praise of the House of Gold,
Where twine, in golden chaplets,
With virtue's laurel leaves,
The myrtles of true love.
ALV. Thanks let me offer ye for these kind praises,
These accents courteous. And now, to
gayer spectacles
Let me invite ye. Hither come the mas-
queraders,
A troop of lovely dancers. Each one is
glowing
With beauty and ardor. In graceful move
ments
The Hours representing;
And their dance now commences.

</td></tr>
<tr><td>

DANZA DELLE ORE.

Le Ore del Mattino — del Giorno — della Sera — della
Notte.

</td><td>

DANCE OF THE HOURS.

The Hours of the Daybreak. — The Hours of the Day.
The Hours of the Evening. — The Hours of the
Night.

</td></tr>
</table>

SCENA VII.

i precedenti, BARNABA, LA CIECA, ENZO.

BAR. (*trascinando* LA CIECA *che invano cerca svin-
  colarsi dalle sue strette*). Vieni!
CIECA. Lasciami! Ahimè!
Coro e ALV. La Cieca!
GIO. (*accorrendo*). O madre!
ALV. (*alla* CIECA). Qui che fai tu?
BAR. Nelle vietate stanze
  Io la sorpresi al maleficio intenta!

CIECA. Pregavo per chi muor!
Coro. Per chi muor? che di' tu?
[*si odono i lenti rintocchi della campana degli agoniz-
  zanti.*
  Qual suon funèbre!
ENZO (*a* BAR.). Un' agonìa! per chi?

BAR. (*sottovoce ad* ENZO). Per Laura!
ENZO. Orror!
  Che più mi resta se quell' angiol muor?
ALV (*avanzandosi tra la folla atterrita e confusa*).
  E che? la gioia sparve!
  Se gaio è Badoèro,
  Chi ha fra gli ospiti suoi dritto al dolor?

ENZO. Io l' ho più ch' altri.
ALV. Tu? ma tu chi sei?
ENZO (*gettando la maschera*).
  Il tuo proscritto io sono, Enzo Grimaldo,
  Prence di Santafior! Patria ed amore
  Tu m' hai rubato un di . . .
  Or compi il tuo delitto!
Tutti. Audacia!
CIECA e GIO. Orror!

ALV. Sul capo tuo rispondi,
  Barnaba, del codardo insultator!

Coro. D' un vampiro fatal — l' ala fredda passò
  E in teda funeral — ogni face mutò.
  Un sinistro baglior — le fronti illuminò,
  Più la gioia regnar — nella festa non può!

ENZO (*fra sè*).
  (O mia stella d' amor, — o mio Nume fedel,
  Se rapita a me sei, — ti raggiungo nel ciel!)

GIO. (*fra sè*). (Oh tortura crudel! — inaudito martir!
  Quanto ei l' ama! è per lei — qui venuto a
  morir!)
CIECA (*a* BAR.). O fatal delator, —'se trafitte
  alcun fu,
  Riconosco la man, — l' assassino sei tu!

BAR. (*alla* CIECA).
  Giuro al cielo, se ier — quella rea ti salvò,
  La vendetta oggimai — più sfuggirmi non
  può!

ENZO (*fra sè*). (Già ti vedo immota e smorta
  Tutta avvolta in bianco vel,
  Tu se morta, tu sei morta,
  Angiol mio dolce e fedel!
  Su di me piombi la scure,
  S' apra il baratro fatal,
  E mi guidin le torture
  All' imene celestial.)

SCENE VII

Enter BARNABA, ENZO, *and* LA CIECA.

BAR. (*dragging in* CIECA). Come on!
CIECA. Let me go! Ah me!
Chorus. La Cieca!
GIO. (*running*). My mother!
ALV. (*to* CIECA). What dost thou here?
BAR. In the forbidden chambers
  I just now caught her, intent upon some
  malice.
CIECA. For her, just dead, I prayed.
[*the passing bell for the dying and dead is heard slowly
  tolling.*
Chorus. Her, just dead! What say'st thou?
  Ah! That sound funereal!
ENZO (*in an undertone to* BAR.).
  The knell of death! For whom?
BAR. (*aside to* ENZO). For Laura.
ENZO. For Laura? O Heaven
  What now remains for me, if she be dead?
ALV. (*with sudden animation*).
  What now? Joy is immortal!
  If gay is Badoèro,
  Who, amongst all his guests, has the right to
  be gloomy?
ENZO (*advancing*). I, of all others!
ALV. Thou! But who art thou?
ENZO (*unmasking*).
  By thee proscribed; Enzo Grimaldo,
  Prince of Santafior. My country, my be
  loved,
  Were stolen from me by thee.
  Of crime thou may'st now fill up the measure
ALV. Audacious!
Chorus. Audacious! He dies!
ALV. Barnaba, thy head for him shall answer,
  Should the vile insulter escape.
Chorus. As if over our brows a vampire's wing
  had passed,
  A shudder takes the place of the smiles that
  each wore;
  With a sinister gleam our foreheads are
  illum'd,
  And gay, light-hearted joy at the feast reigns
  no more.

ENZO (*aside*).
  O bright star of my soul, ever constant and
  sweet,
  Though from me thou art torn, we in Heaven
  shall meet!

GIO. (*aside*).
  Cruel tortures are mine, evil fated am I!
  True love's martyr is he; he for her came to
  die!
CIECA (*to* BAR.).
  O vile, hated spy! I too well know thee, now!
  If a death wound was given, the assassin —
  't was thou!

BAR. (*to* CIECA).
  Ah, hear me swear! If last night thou wert
  sav'd,
  I 'll to-day be reveng'd, too long I 've been
  brav'd!
ENZO (*aside*). I behold thee motionless, pallid,
  Shrouded in thy snowy veil!
  Thou art dead, love! thou art dead, love!
  Ah! my darling, hopeless I wail
  The sharp axe for me is waiting,
  Opens wide a dark abyss;
  But to thee shall torture guide me,
  Soon we 'll share celestial bliss!

GIO. (Scorre il pianto a stilla a stilla
Nel silenzio del dolor.
Piangi, o turgida pupilla,
Mentre sanguina il mio cor.)

BAR. (a GIO.).
Cedi alfin, della mia mano
Vedi qui l' opra fatal.
Mi paventa! un genio arcano
Mi trascina verso il mal.

GIO. (sottovoce, a BAR.).
Se lo salvi e adduci al lido,
Laggiù presso all Redentor,
Il mio corpo t' abbandono,
O terribile cantor.

BAR. (come sopra, a GIO.).
Disperato è questo dono,
Pur lo accetta il tuo cantor.
Al destin spietato irrido,
Pur d' averti sul mio cor.

CIECA (a GIO.).
Le tue lagrime, o Gioconda,
Che non versi sul mio cor?
Un amor non ti circonda
Che sia pari a questo amor!

ALV. (cupamente guardando ENZO).
Nel fulgor di questa festa
Mal venisti, o cavalier,
Par che sia per te funesta
L' allegria dei Badoèr!
Ma già appresto a' tuoi sgomenti
Nuova scena di terror!
Tu saprai, se invan si attenti
Del mio nome al puro onor!

Coro. Tristi eventi! Audacie orrende!
Spaventevole festin!
Come rapida discende
La valanga del destin!

ALV. (avanzandosi in mezzo della scena, con atto di suprema dignità).
Or tutti a me! La donna che fu mia
L' estremo oltraggio al nome mio recò!
[Va verso la cella funeraria ed alza le cortine. LAU. apparisce vestita di bianco stesa sul sue letto di morte. La cella è rischiarata da molti doppieri.
Miratela! Son io che spenta l' ho!
ENZO (si slancia brandendo il pugnale ma è trattenuto dalle guardie). Carnefice!
GIO., CIECA. Sventura!
Coro. Orror! orror!
[GIO. corre verso ENZO che viene trascinato dalle guardie. BAR. afferra per la mano CIECA e, giovandosi della confusione la spinge entro una porta segreta. ALV. resta immobile presso la cella funeraria, additando il cadavere di LAU. Gli invitati si atteggiano ad espressioni di raccapriccio, di sdegne e di pietà. Quadro. Cala la tela.

GIO. Sadly fall the tear-drops,
In the silence of despair;
Break, oh heart! sad eyes, rain torrents
Fate, thy sharpest doom prepare!

BAR. (aside to GIO.).
Yield thee, yield thee! all around thee
See what pow'r I have for ill!
Well may'st thou fear me; pow'rs infernal
To ill deeds attract me still!

GIO. (aside to BAR.).
Do thou save him, bring him safe out there
Close by the Redentor, and then
Myself I will surrender
To thee, fearfullest of men.

BAR. (to GIO.).
Though despair may prompt thy offer,
I accept it for my part,
And the bitterest fate will welcome,
Once to press thee to this heart.

CIECA. Thou art weeping, O Gioconda,
Let me fold thee to my breast.
Never love, like love maternal,
Can encounter ev'ry test.

ALV. 'Mid the splendor this fête surrounding,
Thou art unwelcome, cavalier;
But, erelong, new scenes of horror
Shall from thee attention claim.
Thou shalt soon see if I am watchful
Of the honor of my name.

Chorus. Mournful feasting, fearful horrors
Mournful feast, soon desolate!
Ah! how rapidly descending,
Falls the avalanche of fate!

ALV. (proudly glancing around).
Now, all draw nigh! A woman, once my
wife,
The foulest outrage brought upon my name.
[Opens the curtain of the funereal chamber, and points to LAU. extended on her bier.
Behold her now! 'T was I who took her life!
ENZO (brandishing a poniard, rushes on ALV., but is seized by the Guards).
Base murderer!
Chorus. Horror! despair! woe!

ATTO IV.

Il Canal Orfano.

L' atrio di un palazzo diroccato nell' isola della GIUDECCA. — Nell' angolo di destra un para-vento disteso, dietro il quale sta un letto. — Un gran portone di riva nel fondo da cui si vedrà la laguna e la piazzetta di San Marco illuminata a festa. — Una immagine della Madonna ed una croce appesa al muro. — Un tavolo, un canapè, sul tavolo una lucerna ed una lanterna accese, un' ampolla di veleno, un pugnale. — Sul canapè varii adornamenti scenici di GIOCONDA. A destra della scena una lunga e buia calle.

SCENA I.

GIOCONDA *sola, cupamente assorta ne' suoi pen-sieri.*

(Intanto dal fondo della calle si avanzano due uomini che portano in braccio LAURA avvolta in un mantello nero. Battono all' uscio. GIOCONDA si scuote e va ad aprire. Entrano.)

GIO. Nessun v' ha visto?
Primo Cantore. Nessuno.
GIO. Sul letto
    La deponete.
    [GIO. *va al paravento.* LAU. *deposta sul letto.*
Cantore. "Ad un' occulta riva
    "Sbarcati siam per evitar gl' incontri.
GIO. "Sta ben. E quando fu sepolta?
Cantore. "A vespro.
GIO. "E quanto tempo giacque?
Cantore. "In circa un' ora.
GIO. "Era vasto l' avel?
Cantore. "Vasto.
GIO. I compagni
    Verranno questa notte?
Cantore. Si.
GIO. Ecco l' oro
    Che vi promisi.
Cantore. Nol vogliam . . . gli amici
    Prestan opra da amici.
GIO. *(mutando accento e supplicando).* O
    pietosi.
    Per quell' amor che v' ha creati, un' altra
    Grazia vi chiedo. Nella scorso notte
    Mi scompariva la mia cieca madre,
    Già disperata la cercai ma invano.
    Deh! scorrete le vie, le piazze e l' orme
    Della mia vecchierella Iddio v' insegni.
    Doman, se la trovate, a Canareggio
    V' aspetterò, Quest' antro di Giudecca
    Fra brev'ora abbandono.

ACT IV.

The Orfano Canal.

SCENE. — *The vestibule of a palace in ruins, on the island of Giudeca. In the right-hand corner an opened screen, behind which is a bed. Large porch at back, through which are seen the Lagoon, and the square of St. Mark, brilliantly illuminated. A picture of the Virgin, and a crucifix, hang against the wall. Table and couch; on the table a lamp and a lighted lantern, a flask of poison, and a dagger; on the couch various scenic orna-ments belonging to GIOCONDA. On the right of the scene, a long, dimly lighted street.*

SCENE I.

GIOCONDO, *sola, gloomily buried in thought.*

From the end of the street two men advance, carrying in their arms LAURA, who is en-veloped in a black cloak. The two Cantori (street singers) knock at the door, which is opened by GIOCONDA.

GIO. No one has seen you?
1st Cant. No one.
GIO. Upon yonder bed
    Now place her.
    [*the Cantori carry* LAU. *behind the screen.*
    Our companions?
    Will they to-night be ready?
Cant. Yes.
GIO. Here 's the gold
    That to you I promised.
Cant. Take it back; true friends
    Willingly help one another.

GIO. O have pity! By the love of those who
    bore ye,
    For further aid I implore ye. During
    yesternight
    From my blind mother I was separated
    Since then despairingly have sought her
    but vainly.
    Ah, then, search ev'ry highway and
    piazza!
    To the traces of my blind angel mother
    Kind heaven will guide ye.
    To-morrow, if ye find her, at Cana
    reggio
    I shall be found. This den, this foul
    Giudeca,
    I erelong shall abandon.

Cantori.   A noi t' affida.
[GIO. *stringe ad essi la mano; escono da*
dove sono entrati.

SCENA II.

GIOCONDA *sola presso il tavolo guarda il pug-*
nale, la tocca, poi prende l' ampolla del veleno.

GIO.   Suicidio ! . . . in questi
             Fieri momenti
             Tu sol mi resti,
             Tu sol mi tenti.
             Ultima voce
             Del mio destin,
             Ultima croce
             Del mio cammin.
             E un dì leggiadre
             Volavan l' ore ;
             Smarrii la madre,
             Perdei l' amore,
             Vinsi l' infausta
             Gelosa febre !
             Or piombo essausta
             Fra le tenebre ! . . .
             Tocco alla mèta . . .
             Domando al ciel
             Di dormir queta
             Dentro l' avel.
                  [*guardando ancora l' ampolla.*
Ecco, il velen di Laura, a un' altra vittima
Era serbato ! io lo berrò ! — Quand' esso
Questa notte qui giunga, io non vedrò
Il loro immenso amplesso ;
Ma chi provvede alla lor fuga ? ah ! no !
                  [*getta il veleno sul tavolo.*
No, tentator, lungi da me ! conforta,
Anima mia, le tue divine posse !
Laura è là . . . là sul letto . . . viva . . .
     morta . . .
Nol so . . . se spenta fosse ! ! !
Io salvarla volea, mio Dio lo sai !
Pur, s' ella è spenta !? . . . un indistinto
     raggio
Mi balena nel cor . . . vediam . . . co-
     raggio.
prende la lanterna, fa per avviarsi al letto e
poi si pente.
No . . . no . . . giammai, giammai !
No, non mi sfugga questo dubbio arcano !

Cant.   On us rely.
[GIO. *clasps the hands of the Cantori, who*
depart through the porch by which they had
entered.

SCENE II.

GIOCONDA *sola.   She approaches the table, and*
looks fixedly at the dagger, which she exam-
ines, and then takes up the flask of poison.

GIO.   Yes, suicide ! the sole
             Resource now left me !
             Stern fate forever
             Of hope has bereft me.
             I the last accents
             Of destiny hear,
             Bear my last cross ;
             Know the end draweth near
             Bright is the day,
             The hours gayly flying !
             Lost is my mother ;
             Love lies a-dying.
             Conquer'd by jealousy's
             Terrible fever,
             I sink exhausted ;
             Sink down forever !
             Nigh draws the end now !
             If Heav'n prove kind,
             Erelong in the grave
             Repose I may find.
[*again contemplating the flask of poison.*
The poison, meant for Laura, to another
     victim
Soon will be fatal.   Let me drink it !
     When *he*
Shall to-night hither come, I shall not see
How fervent their embraces.
But who for their escape will answer ?
     Ah, no !
     [*throwing the poison on the table.*
Tempter, away ! out of my sight !
     Take comfort,
O my soul, in thy divine endurance !
     [*with ferocious joy.*
Laura is there ! yonder lying : dead ?
     — or living ?
None knows.   She 's in my power —
I to save her endeavor'd, great Heav'n,
     thou knowest !
Still, were she dead ?   An indistinct
     suggestion,
Like a lightning-flash comes.   Let 's
     see !   Now, courage !
[*takes up the lantern, and is about to ap-*
proach the bed, but stops.
Ah, no ! no, never !   No, never !
And yet — and yet the gloomy doubt
     still haunts me

Ma s' ella vive? ebben. . . Laura è in mia
 mano.   [biecamente.
Siam soli — E notte — Nè persona alcuna
Saper potria . . . profonda è la laguna . . .

Una voce lontana sull' acqua.
 Ehi! dalla gondola,
 Che nuove porti?

*Altra voce piu lontana.   Nel Canal Orfano Ci-
 son de' morti.*

Gio.   Orrore! orrore!! orrore!!!
 Sinistre voce! illuminata a festa
 Splende Venezia nel lontano . . . in core
 Già si ridesta
 La mia tempesta
 Immane! furibonda!
 O amore! amore!!
 Enzo! pietà! . . .
 [al culmine della disperazione si getta accanto
 a tavolo.

SCENA III.

*Intanto si vedrà Enzo venir dalla calle, trova
 la porta socchiusa, entra.*

Enzo.   Gioconda!
Gio.   Enzo! . . . sei tu!
Enzo (*cupamente*).   Dal carcere
 M' hai tratto; e i miei legami
 Sciogliesti, e armato e libero
 Qui son. Da me che brami?

Gio. (*con accento d' esaltazione straziante*).
 Da te che bramo? ahi! misera!
 Ridarti il sol, la vita!
 La libertà infinita!
 La gioia e l' avvenir!
 L' estatico sorriso,
 L' estatico sospir!
 L' amor . . . il paradiso!
 (Gran Dio! fammi morir!)
 o. Donna! col tuo delirio
 Tu irridi a un moribondo,
 Per me non ha più balsami
 L' amor, nè raggi il mondo.
 Addio . . .
Gio.   Che fai?
Enzo.   Non chiedere.
Gio. (*afferrandolo*). Resta . . . M' ascolta.
Enzo (*svincolandosi*).   Cessa.
Gio.   Tu vuoi morir per essa!
Enzo.   Sì, sul suo santo avel
 Baciare anco una volta
 La povera sepolta

But — were she living? Well, then,
 we are alone —
Without witness; 't is night, and no
 human being
Could know when 't was over. And
 deep is yon Lagoon.

A voice (in the distance).
 Ho! gondolier! hast thou any fresh
 tidings?

Other voice in the distance.
 In the Orfano Canal there are corpses.

Gio.   Ah me! ah me! oh horror!
 O sinister voices! Illuminated brightly,
 Resplendent Venice shines, out yonder!
 My heart
 Is thus illumined
 By flames of vengeance,
 Relentless, unforgiving.
 O Love! O Love!
 Enzo, have pity! Have pity, love, on
 me!
 [in despair throws herself down, weeping and
 exhausted, near the table.

SCENE III.

Enter Enzo.

Enzo. Gioconda!
Gio.   Enzo! — 't is thou!
Enzo.   From prison
 Thou hast freed me: by thee my chains
 Have been unfastened, and armed and
 free
 Behold me here. Of me what wouldst
 thou?

Gio. (*in accents of passionate exaltation*).
 Of thee what would I? Alas!
 With smiles thy life is surrounded,
 Thy liberty unbounded,
 Bright joys in thy pathway lie.
 The smiles that speak love's yearning,
 The sighs of rapture burning,
 This earth to Eden turning!
(*Aside.*)   Great Heaven, now let me die!
Enzo. Woman, thy frenzied passion calm;
 My days will soon be over:
 New life, new love, no balm can bring
 A broken-hearted lover.
 Adieu now!
Gio.   What dost thou?
Enzo.   Seek not to know.
Gio.   Stay here, and listen?
Enzo.   Cease!
Gio.   Thou wilt then die for Laura?
Enzo.   Yes, unto Laura's tomb I go,
 Once more to kiss, while dying,
 My lost love, lifeless lying.

Gio. (con possente ironia).   Ebben, corri al
    tuo voto,
Eroe mesto e fedel !
L' avel di Laura è vuoto ;
Io l' hò rapita !
Enzo.   O ciel !   [con un grido.
No, menti, menti. . .
Gio. (accennando alla croce appesa al muro).
                 Giuro,
Giuro su quella croce.
Enzo. No : la bestemmia atroce
Tergi dal labbro impuro !
Di' che hai mentito !
Gio. (con fierezza, poi supplichevole). Il vero
Dissi ! il furor . . . deh ! frena !
Enzo. O furibonda jena
Che frughi il cimitero !
O maledetta Eumènide,
Gelosa della morte,
Dimmi ove celi l' angelo
Mio dalle guance smorte.
Parla ! o in quest' ora lùgubre
Convien che qui tu muoia. . .
Vedi ! già brilla il fulmine
Del mio pugnal. . .
    [sguainando il suo pugnale e afferrando
Gio.

Gio.   (Oh gioia !
M' uccide !)
Enzo   Il tuo mister saprò.
Parla. . .

Gio.   No.
Enzo.   Parla.
Gio.   No.
Enzo. Ebben. . . infame. . . muori !
             [per ferirla.

Gio. (mockingly).
'T is well ; fulfil thy purpose,
O faithful hero, but know,
The tomb of Laura is vacant.
Enzo. Heaven !
Gio.   I have remov'd her.
Enzo. No ! Falsehood ! falsehood !
Gio. (pointing to the crucifix on the wall). I
    swear it !
Swear it by yon Redeemer.
Enzo. No ! thou art a blasphemer ;
Yon crucifix profaning.
No ! thou art perjur'd !
Gio.   No !
No ! the truth I have sworn.
Enzo. O furious hyena,
The sepulchre despoiling !
O worse than the Eumenides !
For thou of the dead art jealous.
Say, where hast thou my angel con
    cealed ?
Where doth she lie with cheeks cold
    and faded ?
Answer ! or in this fatal hour
Thy life shall pay the forfeit !
See with gleam-like lightning flash
Shines my keen poniard !
    [drawing his dagger and grasping Gio.

Gio. (aside).   (O joy,
He will kill me !)
Enzo. Thy mystery unfold !
Gio.   No !
Enzo. Answer !
Gio.   No !
Enzo.   Answer !
Gio.   No !
Enzo. Then thou thy life shall forfeit.
             [about to stab her

SCENA IV.

Laura, Gioconda, Enzo.

Lau. (dall' alcova).   Enzo !
Enzo.   Chi è là !
Gio. (atterrita).   Mio Dio !
Lau. (comparendo).   Enzo ! amor mio !
Ah ! il cor mi si ravviva . . .
Respiro all' aura . . .
    [Enzo, immobile, trasognato.
Enzo, vieni . . . sei tu, vieni . . . son
    viva !
Enzo (slanciandosi, abbracciando Lau.).
Laura ! ciel ! non deliro ! Ah ! Laura !
Laura !
Gio. (avviluppandosi la testa nel suo manto).
    (Nascondili, o tenèbra !)

SCENE IV.

Laura, Gioconda, Enzo.

Lau. (from the alcove).   Enzo !
Enzo.   Who 's there ?
Gio.   (Great Heaven !
    Enter Laura.
Lau. Enzo ! my beloved !
My strength is fast reviving —
I breathe the pure balmy air —
Enzo. I 'm not dreaming ?
Lau. Enzo !   Come, love ! I 'm living !
Enzo. I 'm not dreaming ! — Heaven ! — Liv
    ing !
    [he rushes forward and embraces Lau
Gio. (covering her face with her mantle).
    (Let darkness hide them from me.)

Lau. (*guardando verso* Gio.). Ahimè! quell' ombra
È Alvise . . . fuggi . . .

Enzo. No, il terror disgombra.

Lau. (*avvicinandosi riconosce* Gio. *che si sarà scoperta*).
Sei tu? costei salvò la vita a me.

Enzo. Fanciulla santa!
Ch' io mi ti prostri ai piè!
[Lau. ed Enzo *cadono in ginocchio davanti a* Gio. — *Quadro.*

Voci lontane. Ten va, serenata,
Per l' aura serena,
Ten va cantilena,
Per l' onda incantata.
Udite le blande
Canzoni vagar,
Il remo ci scande
Gli accordi sul mar.
Il canto è la vita,
Di sogni si pasce,
Ai sogni c' invita,
Nei sogni rinasce,
D' un' anima ignota
È l' eco fedel,
L' estrema sua nota
Si perde nel ciel.

Gio. (*con calma dolcissima*).
Questa canzone ti rammenti o Laura?
È la canzone della tua fortuna.
Essa viene, vêr noi. Attenti udite,
Fratelli miei, quei rematori in salvo
V' addurran questa notte. Per la fuga
Tutto provvidi cautamente. "Alzate
"Le vostre fronti, ch' io veda il sorriso
"Ch' io vi creai. No, d' attristar Gio-
"conda
"Più non temete. . . amatevi. . .
"Ho il cuore rassegnato.
"Nessuno è qui colpevole,
"So che l' amore è un fato!

Enzo e Lau. (*al colmo della commozione*).
Oh! benedetta!

Gio. (*sempre con maggior fretta*).
Basta! il tempo fugge!
La barca s' avvicina. . . i miei compagni
Vi condurran prima dell' alba al lido
Dei Tre Porti. . . "ed appena giunti a terra
"Domanderete due corsieri e lesti."
Verso Aquileja drizzerete il volo,
E di là poco lunge il sol d' Illiria
Vi splenderà liberamente in viso.
"Tu per lenir il trepido viaggio [a Lau.
"Gli narrerai la tua ventura. Addio. .
Ecco la barca. . . il mio mantel t' asconda.

Lau. (*looking toward* Gio.). Ah, me! your shadow in mantle shrouded! Alvise! Fly!

Enzo. Dearest, have no fear!

Lau. (*approaching and recognizing* Gio., *who has uncovered her face*).
'T is thou! 'T is she by whose aid my life was sav'd.

Enzo (*to* Gio.). Angelic maiden,
Ah, let me kiss thy feet!

Chorus (*at a great distance off*).
Float on, serenade!
Heaven soft airs is granting;
Float on, serenade,
O'er the waters enchanting!
We listen to songs
Full of innocent glee;
Our oars keeping time
As we float o'er the sea.
A song is Existence,
On dreams it has flourished.
To dream we 're invited,
By dreams we are nourished.
From some unknown soul,
Comes echo's reply;
The last note, ascending,
Is lost in the sky.

Gio. Dost thou remember yonder song, O Laura?
It is the song with which was linked thy fortunes.
'T is for us it is sung. Attentively listen!
Dearest companions, yon rowers shall in safety
Place ye both, ere morning dawns. For your flight
All is provided, with due caution.
The barque is fast approaching: my companions
Will arrive, just before daybreak, abreast
Of the Three Gates: swiftly
Towards Aquileja then your flight directing,
You from thence (not far off) will see Illyria
Smiling a welcome to the wand'ring lovers.
Here are the boatmen. (*To* Lau.) My cloak will serve to hide thee.

[*Si vede la barca dei cantori che s' arresta alla riva. GIO. si toglie il mantello di dosso e copre* LAU.; *poi scorge al collo di* LAU. *il rosario.*

Che vedo là ! Il rosario ! oh sommo Dio !
Così dicea la profezia profonda :
A te questo rosario
Che le preghiere aduna,
Io te lo porgo, accettalo,
Ti porterà fortuna . . .
E così sia ! quest' ultimo
Bacio che il pianto innonda
V' abbiate in fronte, è il povero
Bacio del labbro mio.
Talor nei vostri mèmori
pensieri alla Gioconda
Date un ricordo. **Amatevi . . .**
Lieti vivete . . . Addio !

ENZO e LAU.   Sulle tue mani l' anima
Tutta stempriamo in pianto.
No, mai su queste lagrime
Non scenderà l' oblio.
Ricorderem la vittima
Del sacrificio santo.
Ti benedican gli angeli.
Addio . . . Gioconda — Addio.
[*Sull' ultimo verso* LAU. *ed* ENZO *avranno già un piede sulla barca.—Quadro.—Partono. — Pausa.*

SCENA V.

GIOCONDA *sola, poi* BARNABA *nella calle.*

GIO. (*afferra l' ampolla del veleno*).
Ora posso morir. Tutto è compiuto.
Ah no ! mia madre ! aiuto !
Aiuto, o santa Vergine !
Troppi dolori sovra un solo cuore !
Vo' ricercar mia madre ! . . . Oh ! mio
terrore !
[*còlta da un pensiero improvviso.*
Il patto or mi rammento ! Ah ! la paura
Di Barnaba m' agghiaccia !
Qui riveder l' orribile sua faccia !
[*corre all' immagine della Madonna e si prostra.*
Vergine Santa, allontana il Demonio ! !
BAR. (*viene dalla calle, si ferma alla porta socchiusa e sta spiando*).
Il ciel s' oscura.   [*scompare la luna.*
' ed essa non sa qual testimonio.
la guarda.

[*The barque of the* Cantori *arrives, and stops at the bank.* GIO. *takes off her mantle, which she places on* LAU., *then sees the rosary on* LAU.'s *breast.*

What do I see ? 'T is the rosary
Eternal Heaven !
Thus did my mother speak in tones
prophetic :
" *This rosary I offer,*
No richer prize possessing ;
Deign to accept the humble gift !
'T will bring to thee a blessing."
It brings thee blessing ; this last gentle
kiss,
By my tears inundated,
I place on thy forehead ; the last kiss
That my lips will proffer.
Recall sometimes to memory
Kind thoughts of La Gioconda ill-fated !
Keep me in memory, and love each
other :
May ye both be happy !   Farewell !

ENZO *and* LAU.
Upon thy hands thy generous tears
Of sympathy are falling.
These mournful parting tears of thine
Shall be forgotten never.
Thy memory we 'll cherish aye,
Thy sacrifice recalling ;
May angels bring thee bliss divine.
Adieu, Gioconda, adieu !
[*Exeunt* LAU. *and* ENZO.

SCENE V.

GIOCONDA, *alone, then* BARNABA.

GIO. (*clutching the flask of poison*).
Now I can die. All is over.
Ah, no ! — my mother ! O aid me,
Aid me, O Holy Virgin !
Too heavy is for one sad heart this
anguish ;
I go to seek my mother. Oh, woe is me !
That compact I remember. Ah me !
the terror
[*struck with a sudden thought*
Of Barnaba o'erwhelms me :
Here to behold again those hellish fea-
tures

Gio.   Vergine Santa, allontana il Demonio..
       Ebben, perchè son così affranta e tarda,
       La fuga è il mio riscatto !
Bar.   (Ah ! vuol fuggir . . .)
       [mentre Gio. fa per fuggire s' incontra con
       Bar. che spalanca l' uscio ed entra.

SCENA ULTIMA.

GIOCONDA e BARNABA.

Bar.   (terribilmente).   Così mantieni il patto ?
Gio.   (prima atterrita, poi con coraggio supremo
       sino alla fine).

       Sì, il patto mantengo — lo abbiamo
       giurato,
       Gioconda none deve — quel giuro tradir.
       Che Iddio mi perdoni — l' immenso
       peccato
              Che sto per compir !
Bar.   (fra sè).

       Ebbrezza? delirio ! — Mio sogno su-
       premo !
       Ti colgo e repente — quest' arido cuor
       S' innonda di gioia ! — già palpito e
       tremo
              Ai rai dell' amor !
Gio.   (a Bar. che fa per avvicinarsi).
       Raffrena il selvaggio — delirio ! t' arresta.
       Vo' farmi più gaia, — più fulgida ancor.
       Per te voglio ornare — le bionda mia
       testa
              Di porpora e d' ôr !
              [va ad ornarsi.
       Con tutti gli orpelli — sacrati alla scena
       Dei pazzi teatri — coperta già son.
       Ascolta di questa — sapiente sirena
              L' ardente canzon.
       T' arresta, che temi ? — mantengo il
       mio detto,
       Non mento, non fuggo, — tradirti non
       vo'.
       Volesti il mio corpo, — dimon maledetto?
              E il corpo ti do !

si trafigge nel cuore col pugnale che avrà
raccolto furtivamente nelle resti adornan-
dosi e piomba a terra come fulmine -

[flies to the image of the Virgin and kneels before it.
O Holy Virgin ! keep away the foul demon

SCENE THE LAST

Enter Barnaba.   He comes down the street, and
       stops at the half-opened door.
Bar.   (watching Gio.).   The sky is cloudy.
              [the moon disappears.
       Praying ! but she little knows what wit-
       ness here unto her pray'rs is list'ning.
Gio.   .O Holy Virgin, keep away the foul
       demon !
       And now, why am I thus exhausted. 'T is
       late.
Bar.   (aside).   (Ah ! she would fly !)
Gio   In flight is my only safety
       [Gio., when about to fly, meets Bar. who
       throws the door wide open, and enters
Bar.   (in terrible tones)   Thy compact thus
       thou keepest?
Gio.   (at first terrified, recovers her courage
       and retains it to the end).

       Yes, I keep to my compact : we both
       swore to keep it,
       And ne'er will Gioconda be false to her
       oath.
       May Heaven in mercy withhold condem-
       nation,
              And pardon us both !
Bar.   O rapture ecstatic !   O dream of
       Elysium !
       Thou 'rt mine now ! and swift, from
       this desolate heart,
       Expell'd by love's rays, sombre shadows
       depart.
Gio.   (to Bar., who is approaching her).
       Restrain awhile thy ardent passion !
       Thou soon shalt in splendor Gioconda
       behold ;
       For thee, I am braiding my clustering
       tresses
              With purple and gold.
              [begins to adorn herself
       With glittering jewels, the gay jewels
       worn nightly
       By madcaps theatrical, cover'd I 'll be
       Now list to the song that this ardent
       young siren
              Will sing unto thee !
       i keep to my compact ; no false oath
       was mine ;
       Thou claimest Gioconda ?   Now, demon
       accursed,
              Gioconda is thine.

BAR.   Ah! ferma! irrisïon... ebben... or tu
       ... M' odi ... e muori dannata:

[curvandosi sul cadavere di GIO. *e gridandogli
al l' orecchio con voce furibonda.*

     Ier tua madre m' ha offeso!   Io l' ho
     affogata!

         Non ode più!!

*[esce precipitosamente e scompare nelle tene-
bre della calle.*

                  [Cade la tela.

FINE DELL' OPERA.

*[stabs herself to the heart with the dagger
that she had furtively secreted while
adorning herself, and falls dead, as if
lightning-struck.*

BAR.   Ah, stay thee!   'T is a jest!   Well,
     then, thou shalt hear this,
     And die ever damned!

[bending over the corpse of GIO., *and screaming furiously into her ear.*

     Last night thy mother did offend me:
     I have strangled her!
     She hears me not!

*[with a cry of half-choked rage, rushes down
the street.   [Curtain*

END OF THE OPERA.

CAVALLERIA RUSTICANA
(Rustic Chivalry)

by

PIETRO MASCAGNI

RUSTIC CHIVALRY.

TURIDDU. (Behind the scenes.)

affrett.

O Lo - la, fair as flow'rs in beau - ty smil - ing, . . Love from thy soul - lit
O Lo - la, bian - ca co - me fior di spi - no, . . quan - do t'af - fac - ci

a tempo. *mf*

eyes Soft - ly is glow - ing; . . He who would kiss thy lips, red and be -
te s'affac - cia il so - le; . . Chi t'ha ba - cia - to il lab - bro por - po

rit. *a tempo.*

guil - ing . . Bliss - ful and fa-vor'd were he, Such heav-en know - ing! . .
ri - no . . Gra - zia più bel - la a Di - o chie-dernon vô - le . .

affrett. *a tempo.* *mf poco rit*

Tho' thy thresh-old blood, crim - son, is stain - ing, . . Car - ing for naught, I
C'è scrit - to san - gue so - pra la tua por - ta; . . Ma di re - star - ci a

stentando.

seek thee, scorning to hide me; . . What tho' I for - feit life, thy pres - ence
me non me n'in - por - ta; . . Se per te mo - jo e va - do in pa - ra

portando.

gain - ing? What were the joy of heav'n, wert thou de - nied me!
di - so, Non c'en - tro se . . non ve - do il tuo bel vi so,

(3)

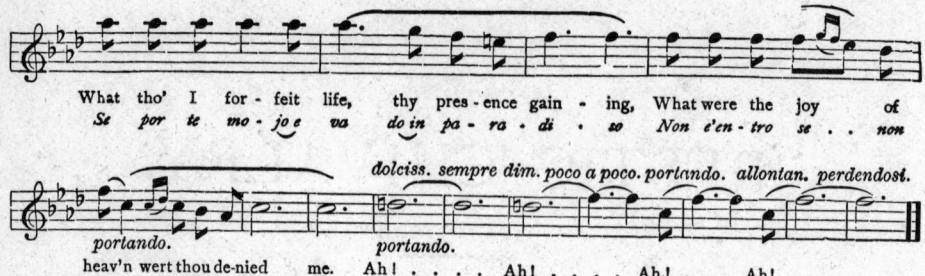

What tho' I for-feit life,   thy pres-ence gain - ing,   What were the   joy   of
Se   por   te   mo - jo e   va   do in pa - ra - di - so   Non c'en - tro   se . . non

portando.   *portando.*
heav'n wert thou de-nied   me.   Ah! . . . .   Ah! . . . .   Ah! . . . Ah! . . . .
ve - do   il tuo bel vi - so.   Ah! . . . .   Ah! . . . .   Ah! . . . Ah! . . . .

(Curtain rises.)

## Scene I.	## Scena I.
A public place or square in a Sicilian village. At right, in background, a church. At left, the inn and dwelling of Mamma Lucia. Time, Easter morning. (Peasants, countrymen, country-women, and children, cross the stage.) (The church doors open and the throng enters.) (The movement continues until the following:)	La scena rappresenta una piazza in un paese della Sicilia. Nel fondo, a destra, Chiesa con porta practicabile. A sinistral'o steria e la casa di Mamma Lucia. E il giorno Pasqua.

INTRODUCTORY CHORUS.

Chorus of women.

(Behind scenes.)

Ah! Ah!

Chorus of men.

(Behind scenes.)

Ah! Ah!

Chorus of women.

(Behind scenes.)

Sweet is the air with the blossoms of oranges;
  Sings now the lark from the myrtles in
    flow'r;
Murmurs of tender song tell of a joyful world,
  And of thankful hearts.   Ah! gladsome
    hour!

(The women enter.)

Chorus of men.

(Behind scenes.)

Your spinning wheels now busily are humming,
O'er fields of golden corn the sound is coming;
We linger where the leafy shade is restful;
Of you we think, and every heart is zestful.
Oh lovely women!   Allured by you and
    enraptured,
Like the bird by the lure held, now are we
    captured!

(The men enter.)

CORO D'INTRODUCIONE.

(Campane interne dalla Chiesa. Si alza la tela. Lascena sul principio è vuota. Albeggia. Paesani, contadini e ragazzi traversano la scena. Si apre la chiesa e la folla vi entra. Il movimento del popolo continua fino al Coro punto in cui rimane la scena vuota.)

Coro.

(Donne di dentro,)

Ah!

(Uomini di dentro.)

Ah!

(Donne di dentro.)

Gli aranci olezzano sui verdi margini,
Cantan le allodole tra i mirti in fior;
Tempo è si mormori da ognuno il tene ro canto
              che i palpiti —
Raddoppia al cor.

(Le donne entrano in iscena.)

(Uomini di dentro.)

Coro.   In mezzo al campo tra le spiche d'oro
Giunge il rumore delle vostre spole,
Noi stanchi riposando dal lavoro
A voi pensiamo, o belle occhidisole.
O belle occhidisole, a voi corriamo,
Come vola l'augelo — al suo richiamo.

(Gli uomini entrano in iscena.)

Women.
Work in the field now is ended; —
    The Holy Mother mild
    In ecstasy fondles the Child.

All.
        (Withdrawing from stage.)
Murmurs of tender song tell of a joyful world,
And of thankful hearts.
Ah ! gladsome hour !

(Enter, Santuzza, approaching Lucia's dwelling.)

Scene II.

(Santuzza, Lucia, Alfio, and chorus.)

Santuzza.   Tell me, mother Lucia —

Lucia.
        (Coming from house.)
It is thou?   What wilt thou?

Sant.   Where is Turiddu?

Lucia.   For him you ask?   For him, my son
    Turiddu !

Sant.   Only for him I ask you.   Pardon, but
    answer !   Where is Turiddu?

Lucia.   Ask me not !   I know not; I want no
    trouble.

Sant.   Mamma Lucia, with weeping do I pray
    you !
Even as spake the Saviour to the Magdalen,
Say, in pity say, where is Turiddu !

Lucia.   He 's gone to bring some wine from
    Francofonte.

Sant.   No !   Last night some within the village
    saw him.

Lucia.   What says't thou?   Who told it?
    Nay, he hath not yet returned.
    Enter !

Sant.   I may not step across your threshold,
    I cannot pass it, I, most unhappy out-
    cast !
    Excommunicated !

Lucia.   What of my son?   What hast thou to
    tell me?

Sant.   Ah ! the torture, the heart-pain.

[Cracking of whips and jingling of bells behind scenes.)
    (Chorus enters, followed soon by Alfio.)

Donne.   Cessin le rustiche opre :   [tor;
    La Virgine serena allietasi del Salva-
    Tempo è si mormori da ognuno il
        tenero canto che i palpiti —
    Raddoppia al cor.

Uomini.
        (Allontanandosi.)
    In mezzo al campo, etc.

Donne.
        (Allontanandosi.)
    Gli aranci olezzano, etc.

Scena II.

Sortita di Alfio.

Santuzza.
    (Entra e si dirige alla casa di Lucia.)
    Dite, Mamma Lucia —

Lucia.
        (Sortendo.)
    Sei tu? che vuoi?

Santuzza.   Turiddu ov'è?

Lucia.   Fin qui vieni a cercare il figlio mio?

Santuzza.   Voglio saper soltanto,
    Perdonatemi voi, dove trovarlo.

Lucia.   Non lo so, non lo so, non voglio
    brighe !

Santuzza.   Mamma Lucia, vi supplico pian-
    gendo,
    Fate come il Signore a Maddalena,
    Ditemi per pietà, dov' è Turiddu.

Lucia.   E andato per il vino a Francofonte.

Santuzza.   No !   l'hanvisto in paese ad alta
    notte.

Lucia.   Che dici? che dici? se non è tornato
    casa !   Entra !

Santuzza.   Non posso entrare in casa vostra.
    Sono scomunicata !

Lucia.   E che ne sai del mio figliuolo?

Santuzza.   Quale spina ho in core !

(Dall' interno schiocchi di frusta e tintinnio di sonagli
    Entrano in iscena i coristi indi Alfio.)

Snap, now, the lash goes,
schioc-chi la fru-sta,

is a jol-lier man?   Where is a jol-lier man, a jol-lier
dar - di quà e di là,   an - dar di quà e di là, di quà e di

I come! I'm the mer-ry car-rier! I'm the mer-ry car-rier, Who hath call-ing
Son quà! Oh che bel me - stie - re fa - re il car - ret - tie - re, oh che bel me-

man? . . .
là, ...

mer-rier than the life, the life of car - rier, than the life, this life of mine, A
stier, an - dar di quà, an - dar di là, an - dar di quà, an - dar di là!

hap-pier man than I? . . . Where is a jol - lier man, where is a jol - lier man? 'Tis
Pasqua ed io son quà, . . an - dar di quà e di là, an - dar di quà e di là, E

Eas - ter, home come I, ... come I! . . . .
Pas - qua ed io son qua, . . . sou qua! . . . .

(Chorus withdraws into the church; others separate in various directions.)

(Il Coro esce, alcuni entrano in chiesa, altri prendoni direzioni diverse.)

SCENE III.

SCENE AND PRAYER.

Lucia. Blest are you, friendly Alfio!
        So favored, ever thus to be gay!

Alfio. Mamma Lucia, have you that rare old wine,
        The same as ever?

SCENA III.

Lucia. Beato voi, compar Alfio,
        Che siete sempre allegro così!

Alfio.

(Spigliato.)
Mamma Lucia,
N'avete ancora di quel vecchio vino?

Lucia. Not now; Turiddu has gone to buy a plenty.

Alfio. No; he is here! I saw him here this morning;
He lingered near my cottage.

Lucia.
(Surprised.)
What now!

Santuzza.
(Rapidly, to Lucia.)
Be silent!

Alfio. I will not tarry,
You will to church devotedly?
(Exit.)

Chorus.
(In church.)
Queen of the Heavens, sorrow flieth!

People.
(External chorus.)
Hallelujah!

Chorus.
(In church.)
Thy holy Son lives, nor dieth!

People. Hallelujah!

Chorus.
(within.)
From the dead He now hath risen,
Truly hath He risen.

People. Hallelujah.

Chorus.
(External. Grouping in devotional attitudes.)
We will sing of the Lord now victorious!
All the terrors of death were in vain!
Let us sing of the Christ ever glorious;
He is risen, in glory to reign!

Santuzza. We will sing of the Lord now victorious;
We will sing of the Christ ever glorious;
Pow'r of death was in vain.
Unto heaven the Lord now riseth,
Now riseth in glory to reign.

Lucia. Non so; Turiddu è andato a prov vederne.

Alfio. Se è sempre qui!
L'ho visto stamattina vicino a casa mia

Lucia.
(Sorpresa.)
Come?

Santuzza.
(A Lucia rapidamente.)
Tacete.

Alfio. Io me ne vado, ite voi altre in chiesa
(Esce.)

Coro.
(Interno.)
Regina Cœli, lætare—

Alleluja!

Quia, quem meruisti potare—

Alleluja!

Resusrexit sicut dixit—

Alleluja!

Coro.
(Esterno.)

(Uomini e donne entrano e si schierano innanzi alla Chiesa in atteggiamento devoto.)

Inneggiamo, il Signor non è morto!
Ei fulgente ha dischiuso l'avel,
Inneggiamo al Signore risorto
Oggi asceso alla gloria del ciel!

Chorus. We will sing, of the Lord now victorious!
    All the terrors of death were in vain!
    Let us sing of the Christ ever glorious;
    He is risen, in glory to reign.
    Praise the Lord.

(All enter the church, except Santuzza and Lucia.)

Scene IV.

ROMANZA.

Lucia.
(To Santuzza.)
And why with signals would you gain my silence?

Santuzza. Now shall you know, kind mother :
Ere he went forth as a soldier,
Turiddu pledged his love to Lola,
    All his faithfulness renewing
But; ah! homeward returning,
Married he found his Lola!
And, her falsity shaming —
    All the old love subduing —
    Loved *me!*
And I loved *him!*
With jealousy, hatefully, and with madness,
    Scorning wifely duty, envious of my gladness,
    Lola, in malice shameful, regains Turiddu!
Fate disgraceful o'ertakes me,
My own Turiddu forsakes me!
Lola and he in joy remain,
Having each other's love again!
Ah me! alone I weep, I weep!

Lucia. Grief is upon us!
    Such dire and woeful tidings to hear this holy morning.

Santuzza. I am accursed! I am accursed!
    Good mother, go pray for me unto the Saviour!
Thou 'lt beseech Him for me!
I 'll seek Turiddu, and pray to him
That he again may love me!

Lucia. Holy Mary be with thee — the blessed Mary!

(Lucia enters the church)

Inneggiamo, il Signor non è morto!
Ei fulgente ha dischiuso l'avel,
Inneggiamo al Signore risorto
Oggi asceso alla gloria del ciel!

(Tutti entrano in chiesa tranne Santuzza e Lucia.)

Scena IV.

Lucia. Perchè m'hai fatto segno di tacere?

Santuzza. Voi lo sapete, o mamma, prima d'andar soldato
Turiddu aveva a Lola eterna fè giurato.
Tornò, la seppe sposa; e con un nuovo amore
Volle spegner la fiamma che gli bruciava il core
M'amò, l'amai, l'amai, ah!
Quell' invida d'ogni delizia mia,
Del suo sposo dimentica, arse di gelosia.
Me l'ha rapito. Priva dell' onor mio,
Dell' onor mio rimango :
Lola e Turiddu s'amano, io piango!

Lucia. Miseri noi, che cosa vieni a dirmi
In questo santo giorno?

Santuzza. Io son dannata.
Andate, o mamma, ad implorare Iddio,
E pregate per me. Verrà Turiddu,
Vo' supplicarlo un' altra voltra ancora!

Lucia. Ajutatela voi, Santa Maria!

(Lucia entra in chiesa.)

Scene V.

Duet. Santuzza and Turiddu.

Turiddu.

(Entering.)

Thou here, Santuzza!

Santuzza. Here I await thee.

Turiddu. Attending not the service of Easter?

Santuzza. Not now! Thee would I speak with.

Turiddu. I seek my mother.

Santuzza. Thee would I speak with!

Turiddu. Not here, not here!

Santuzza. From whence dost thou come?

Turiddu. Why dost thou ask me? —
From Francofonte.

Santuzza. Ah, that is false!

Turiddu. Santuzza, believe me!

Santuzza. No! thou art lying!
Over yon path I beheld thee approach:
And thou wert seen to-day returning homeward
From the dwelling of Lola!

Turiddu. Ah! thou wert spying!

Santuzza. No, I do swear it!
Her husband, Alfio, saw thee
Here within the town, and told it me!

Turiddu. So thou rewardest the love I gave thee,
What though he slay me!

Santuzza. Ah! Tell me not of murder!

Turiddu. Leave me, I tell thee! leave me!
The rage within me burning —
My righteous wrath, thou cast not assuage!

Scena V.

Turiddu.

(Entrando.)

Tu qui Santuzza?

Santuzza. Qui t'aspettavo

Turiddu. È Pasqua in chiesa non vai?

Santuzza. Non vo. Debbo parlarti.

Turiddu. Mamma cercavo.

Santuzza. Debbo parlarti.

Turiddu. Qui no! qui no!

Santuzza.

(Parlato.)

Dove sei stato?

Turiddu.

(Parlato.)

Che vuoi tu dire? A Francofonte.

Santuzza. No, non è ver.

Turiddu. Santuzza credimi.

Santuzza. No, non mentire
Ti vidi volgere giù dal sentir.
E stamattina all' alba t'hanno
Scorto presso l'uscio di Lola.

Turiddu. Ah! mi hai spiato!

Santuzza. No! te lo giuro, a noi l'ha raccontato
Campar Alfio il marito poco fa.

Turiddu. Cosi ricambi l'amor che ti porto?
Vuoi che m'uccida?

Santuzza. Oh! questo non lo dire.

Turiddu. Lasciami dunque, lasciami invan
tenti sopire
Il giusto sdegno colla tua pietà.

Santuzza.   Then, thou dost love her!
         More fair than I is Lola!
         False friend! Oh, curses on her!

Turidda.   Santuzza!

Santuzza.   She — vilest woman, steals the
love that should be mine!

Turiddu.   Heed thou!
         I am no slave to thy envy
         Scornfully showing, jealously
showing

Santuzza.   Insult and punishment I am unheeding!
         Yet do I love thee,
         Even though anguish my heart is
rending,
         E'en though in sorrow my life is
ending.

SCENE VI.

LOLA'S DITTY.

Lola.
         (Behind scenes.)
Bright flower, so radiant!
Angelic thousands stand arrayed in
heaven,
Yet none so fair as thou hath yet
been given!
         (Enters. Pauses suddenly.)
Oh! Turiddu, hast thou seen Alfio?

Turiddu.   I came but this moment: I have
not.

Lola.   Then at the forge perchance he
awaiteth.
         Here I must not linger.
            And thou?
         Is 't here in public thou art praying?

Turiddu.
         (Confusedly.)
Santuzza here was telling —

Santuzza.
I was saying this is Easter!
         (Meaningly.)
And the Lord all things beholdeth!

Lola.
         (To Santuzza.)
Thou wilt not go to the service?

Santuzza.   Tu l'ami dunque?

Turiddu.   No!

Santuzza.   Assai più bella è Lola!

Turiddu.   Taci, non l'amo.

Santuzza.   L'ami, l'ami, Oh! maledetto!

Turiddu.   Santuzza!

Santuzza.   Quella cattiva femmina ti tolse a
me!

Turiddu.   Bada, Santuzza, schiavo non sono
Di questa vanatua gelosia.

Santuzza.
         (Con angoscia.)
Battimi, insultami, t'amo e perdono
Ma è troppo forte l'angoscia mia.
         (Troncando nel sentire avvicinarsi Lola.)

SCENA VI.

Lola.
         (Dentra alla scena.)
Fior di giaggiolo
         Gli angeli belli stano
A mille in cielo
         Ma belli come lui
         Ce n'è uno solo.
         (Entra in iscena e s'interrompe.)
Oh! Turiddu, è passato Alfio?

Turiddu.   Son giunto ora in piazza non so.

Lola.   Forse è rimasto dal maniscalco ma non
                può tardare!
         E voi sentite le funzioni in piazza?

Turiddu.
         (Confuso affret.)
Santuzza mi narrava -

Santuzza.   Gli dicevo che oggi è Pasqua
E il Signor vede ogni cosa.

Lola.   Non venite alla messa?

Santuzza.

No, no! None shall attend but those
Who know they are not guilty!

Lola.

(Vehemently.)

In the grace of the Saviour
I bow before thee!

Santuzza.

(Bitterly.)

O, well thou speakest! —
Lola!

Turiddu.

(Embarrassed.)
(To Lola.)

Away then! Come, Lola;
Here there is naught to hold us.

Lola.

(Ironically.)

Oh, stay thou with *her!*

Santuzza.

(To Turiddu.)

Yes, stay thou!

(Firmly.)

I have something yet to tell thee :

Lola.

(Mockingly.)

May the Saviour assist thee!

(Going.)

So, I will leave thee.

(Enters the church.)

SCENE VII.

CONTINUATION OF THE DUET.

Turiddu.

(To Sant.)

Ah! how foolish! naught availing!

Santuzza.

(Coldly.)

I have spoken; 't is well — 't is the truth.

Santuzza.

(Subito.)

Io no, ci deve andar chi sa

(Con intensione.)

Di non aver peccato!

Lola.

(Con forza.)

Io ringrazio il Signore, e bacio in terra!

Santuzza.

(Esprimendosi.)

Oh! fate bene, fate bene,

(Con amarezza.)

Lola!

Turiddu.

(A Lola.)
(Impacciato.)

Andiamo, andiamo, Oni non abbiam
che fare.

Lola.

(A Turiddu.)

Oh!

(Con ironia.)

Rimanete.

Santuzza.

(A Turiddu con fermezza.)

Si, resta, resta,
Ho da parlarti ancora.

Lola.

(Sempre ironica.)

E v'assista il Signore,

(Con caricatura.)

Io me ne vado.

(Entra in chiesa.)

SCENA VII.

Turiddu.

(Con ironia.)

Ah! lo vedi, che hai tu detto!

Santuzza.

(Fredda.)

L'hai voluto e ben ti sta!

RUSTIC CHIVALRY.

Turiddu.

(Threateningly.)

Ah! by heaven!

Santuzza. My heart is breaking!

Turiddu.

(Approaching her.)

No!

Santuzza.

(Warding him away.)

Turiddu, ah! hear me!

Turiddu.

Go!

(Turns from her.)

Turiddu.

(S'avventa.)

Ah! per Dio!

Santuzza. Squarciami il petto.

Turiddu.

(S'avvia.)

No!

Santuzza.

(Trattenendolo.)

Turiddu, ascolta!

Turiddu. Va!

Santuzza.	Santuzza.
(Threateningly.)	*(Minacciosa.)*
False! false!	Bada!
Turiddu.	**Turiddu.**
(With increased rage.)	*(Con moltissíma forza.)*
Thus I reward thee in my anger.	Dell' ira tua non mi curo!
(Throws her aown, and hastens into the church.)	*(La getta a terra e fugge in chiesa.)*
Santuzza.	Santuzza.
(In the height of fury.)	*(Nel colmo dell' ira.)*
Accurs'd! accurs'd at Easter, thou false one.	A te la mala Pasqua, spergiuro!
(Falls, despairingly.)	*(Cade affranta ed angosciata.)*

SCENE VIII.

DUET, SANTUZZA AND ALFIO.

(Enter, Alfio.)

Santuzza.

(Calming herself.)

Oh! doth the Saviour send thee,
neighbor Alfio?

Alfio. At what point is the service?

Santuzza. 'T is now at closing.
But I tell thee Lola has gone with
Turiddu!

Alfio.

(Surprised.)

What are you saying?

Santuzza. While thou dost labor to earn an
honest living,
Lola unfaithfully her love is
giving.

Alfio. Ah! in the name of heaven, Santuzza,
what sayest thou?

Santuzza. The truth!
Turiddu forsakes me — and he
hath betrayed me!
'T was your wife who enticed him
away from me!

Alfio.

(Threateningly.)

And if thou art lying
I'll have thy heart's blood!

Santuzza. Lies, as yet, my lips have never
uttered.
Prone to be truthful am I.

Alfio.

(After a pause.)

Santuzza, I am thankful that you have
spoken.

Santuzza. But ah! what shame!
And I have told it thee!

Alfio.

(Suddenly, in fury.)

T'is they who are shameful!
Revenge I'll have upon them!
This day and hour my wrath
Shall fall upon them!

SCENA VIII.

(Sorte Alfio e s'incontra con Santuzza.)

Santuzza.

(Ad Alfio rianimandosi.)

Oh! Il Signore vi manda, compar
Alfio.

Alfio.

(Tranquillo.)

A che punto è la messa?

Santuzza.

È tardi ormai, ma per voi

(Con intenzione.)

Lola è andata con Turiddu!

Alfio.

(Sorpreso.)

Che avete detto?

Santuzza. Che mentre correte
All' acqua e al vento a guadagnarvi
il pane,
Lola v'adorna il tetto in malo
modo!

Alfio. Ah! nel nome di Dio, Santa che dite?

Santuzza. Il ver. Turiddu mi tolse, mi tolse
l'onore,
E vostra moglie lui rapiva a me!

Alfio.

(Minaccioso.)

Se voi mentite, vo' schiantarvi il core.

Santuzza. Uso a mentire il labbro mio, il
labbro mio non è!
Per la vergogna mia, pel mio dolore
La trista verità — vi dissi, ahimè!

Alfio.

(Dopo un poco di pausa.)

Comare Santa, allor grato vi sono.

Santuzza. Infame io son che vi partai così!

Alfio. Infami loro, ad essi non perdono
Vendetta avrò pria che tra monti il dì!
Io sangue vo glio, all'ira m'abbandono,
In odio tutto l'amor mio finì!

(Escono.)

INTERMEZZO.

Scene IX.

Chorus and Brindisi.

(The people enter from the church. Lucia crosses and enters the inn.)

Chorus of men.

(sotto voce.)

Now homeward, now homeward ye neighbors,
Good cheer is awaiting there;
And wives our joy will share,
Now Easter day shall be for all a time of rest,
Without sorrow or care.

Chorus of women.

(Lola and Turiddu come from the church.)

Turiddu. My pretty Lola! Have you not a greeting,
When honest people we are meeting?

Lola. I must leave thee.
I must go and welcome Alfio!

Turiddu. Here he will seek thee.
Do not hasten!

(To the people.)

Meanwhile, good friends, come hither.

(All come forward.)

We'll try the merry wine!

(All take cups from the bar of the inn.)

Scena IX.

(Tutti escono di chiesa. Lucia attraversa la scena de entra in casa. A gruppi soto voce fra loro.)

Coro.

(Uomini.)

A casa, a casa, amici, ove ci aspettano
Le nostre donne, andiam,
Or che letizia rasserena gli animi.

Coro.

(Donne.)

A casa, a casa, amiche, ecc.

[Lola e Turiddu escono dalla chiesa.]

Turiddu. Comare Lola, ve ne andante via
Senza nemmeno salutare?

Lola. Vado a casa; Non ho visto compar Alfio!

Turiddu. Non ci pensate, verrà in piazza.

(Rivolgendosi al Coro che s'avvia.)

Intanto, amici, qua,
Beviamone un bicchiere.

(Tutti si avvicinano alla tavola dell' osteria e prendono in mano i bicchieri.)

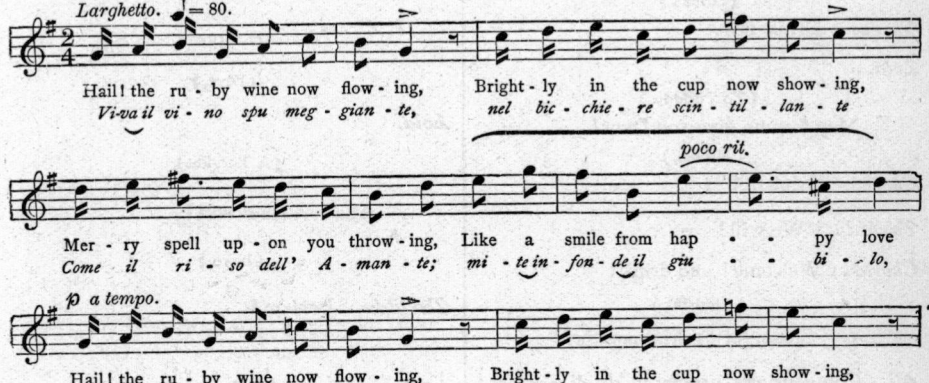

TURIDDU.
Larghetto. ♩ = 80.

Hail! the ru - by wine now flow - ing,
Vi-va il vi - no spu meg - gian - te,
Bright - ly in the cup now show - ing,
nel bic - chie - re scin - til - lan - te

poco rit.

Mer - ry spell up - on you throw - ing,
Come il ri - so dell' A - man - te;
Like a smile from hap - - py love
mi - te in - fon - de il giu - - bi - - lo,

p a tempo.

Hail! the ru - by wine now flow - ing,
vi - va il vi - no spu - meg - gian - te,
Bright - ly in the cup now show - ing,
nel bic - chie - re - scin - til - lan - te

Mer-ry spell around you throw-ing, Like the smile of hap—py love! Hail! ah,
come il ri-so dell'a-man-te, mi-te in-fon-de il giu—bi-lo! Vi-va il

wine so rich-ly gleam-ing! In thy crim-son joy is beam-ing! All thy
vi-no ch'è sin-ce-ro che ci al-lie-ta o-gni pen-sie-ro, e che af

com-fort lend us, With thy cheer at-tend us—Hope and love! . . . Hail! ah,
fo-ga l'u-mor ne-ro nell' eb-brez-za ten-e-ra. . . . Vi-va il

wine so rich-ly gleam-ing! In thy crim-son joy is beam-ing! All thy
vi-no ch'è sin-ce-ro che ci al-lie-ta o-gni pen-sie-ro, e che af-

com-fort lend us, With thy cheer at-tend us—Hope and love!
fo-ga l'u-mor ne-ro nell' eb-brez-za te-ne-ra.

Chorus. Welcome!	*Coro.* Viva, beviam! Rinnovisi la giostra!
Turiddu.	
(To Lola.)	*Turiddu.*
To those who love you!	(A Lola.)
(Drinks.)	Ai vostri amori!
Chorus. Drink it!	(Beve.)
Lola.	*Lola.*
(To Turiddu.)	(A Turiddu.)
May fortune give you favor!	Alla fortuna vostra!
(Drinks.)	(Beve.)
Chorus. Drink it!	
Turiddu. We will!	
Chorus. Welcome! and drink!	*Turiddu.* Beviam!
(All drink.)	
Come, let us drink another!	
All. Come, drink; yes, let us drink another!	*Lola, Turiddu e Coro.*
Hail! the ruby wine now flowing, etc.	Beviam, beviam! rinnovisi la giostra!

FINALE.

Alfio. Unto all of you, greeting!

Chorus. Neighbor Alfio, greeting!

Turiddu.

(To Alfio.)

Hearty welcome!
Now join with us in revel.

(Fills a glass for him.)

Look you! drink you this measure!

Alfio. Thank you! but I must refuse the offer!
A cup of deadly poison perhaps you proffer!

Turiddu. Then suit your pleasure!
(Throws away the wine.)

Lola. Ah me! what now befalls!

(Some of the women consult together, and then approach Lola, saying:)

Neighbor Lola, come, haste away from here!

(Exit, all the women, with LOLA.)

Turiddu.

(To Alfio.)

Perhaps you have something to tell me!

Alfio. I? nothing!

Turiddu. Then hear me!
You will find me at your service!

Alfio. This moment?

Turiddu. This moment!

(They embrace, Turiddu bites Alfio's ear, viciously.)

Alfio. Neighbor Turiddu, you give a ready challenge!
And I accept it! you understand me!

Turiddu. Neighbor Alfio!
I own thou shouldst have vengeance,
And I admit, in the name that is holy,
That I should be dealt with as a dog, by thee!
But, shouldst thou kill me — if I perish

FINALE.

(Entra Alfio.)

Alfio. A voi tutti salute.

Coro. Compar Alfio, salute.

Turiddu. Benvenuto! con noi dovete bere,

(Empie un bicchiere.)

Ecco pieno e il bicchiere.

(Troncando.)

Alfio. Grazie, ma il vostro vino io non l'accetto,
Diverrebbe veleno entro il mio petto!

Turiddu.

(Parlato.)

A piacer vostro.

(Getto il vino.)

Lola. Ahimè che mai sarà?

(Alcune donne nel Coro si consigliano fra loro poi si avvicinano a Lola dicendole sotto voce.)

Coro. Comare Lola, andiamo via di qua.

(Tutte le donne escono conducendo Lola.)

Turiddu. Avete altro a dirmi?

Alfio. Io nulla.

Turiddu. Allota sono agli ordini vostri —

Alfio. Or ora?

Turiddu. Or ora!

(Si abbracciano. Turiddu morde l'orecchio destro d Alfio.)

Alfio. Compar Turiddu, a vete morso, a buono

(Con intenzione.)

Cintenderemo bene a quel che pare!

Turiddu. Compar Alfio.
Lo so che il torto è mio;
E ve lo giuro nel nome di Dio
Che al par d'un cane mi farè
sgozzar —
Ma s'io non vivo,

(Dolorosamente.)

By thine arm — yes, if I perish, —
Unhappy Santa, she whom I have cherished —
    Lone, unhappy Santa, my dagger
Will embed within thy heart!

Alfio.   Good neighbor, act upon it as may suit you!
    You will find me yonder in the orchard.

         (*Exit.*)

Turiddu.

         (*Calling.*)

My mother!

         (Enter LUCIA.)

Mother! the wine-cup too freely passes!
Exciting, crazing!
Too many cups I have been drinking!
—— I must leave you, good mother!

But first let me ask for a kindly blessing,
As on that day when I became a soldier.
And, mother, hear me — and heed it:
If I return not, thou unto my Santa
Must be a kindly mother!
Santa, whom I promised I would lead
to the altar!
—If I return —

Lucia.   Why say you this to me?
What is it? tell me!

Turiddu.   Ha—nothing!
'T is wine — that I have drunk so freely.
—For me oh! pray to heaven,
    That I may be forgiven!
One kiss, one kiss, my mother!
And yet — and yet another!
Farewell!

         (Rushes off, desperately.)

Lucia.   Turiddu! Ah!

        (Retires to back of stage, crying.)
        (Enter, Santuzza.)

    Santuzza!

Santuzza.   Ah! good mother!

    (Throws her arms around Lucia's neck.)

    (People crowd upon the stage.)

    (Excitement and agitation.)

(Enter a woman in the distance crying, "Neighbor Turiddi is murdered.")

Resta abbandonata povera Santa!
Lei che mi s'è data!

        (Con impeto.)

Vi saprò in core il ferro mio pian-
                tar!

Alfio.

        (Freddamente.)

Compare fate come più vi piace,
Io v'aspetto qui fuori dietro l'orto.

        Esce.

Turiddu.

        (Chiamando.)

Mamma —

        (Entra Lucia.)

Mamma — quel vino è generoso,
E certo oggi troppi bicchieri
Ne ho traccannati —
Vado fuori all' aperto —
Ma prima voglio che mi benedite—
Come quel giorno che partii sol-
               dato:
E poi mamma,
Sentite, s'io non tornassi —
Voi dovrete fare da madre a Santa,
Ch'io le avea giurato di condurla
               all' altare.

Lucia.   Perchè parli così, figliolo mio?

Turiddu.

        (Con disinvoltura.)

Oh! nulla, è il vino che m'ha sug-
               gerito!
M'ha suggerito il vino —
Perme pregate Iddio,
Un bacio mamma! un altro bacio
Addio!

        (Fugge disperatamente.)

Lucia.   Turiddu! che vuoi dire!

    (Va in fondo alla scena a disperatamente chiama.)

     Turiddu! Turiddu! ah!

        (Entra Santuzza.)

    Santuzza.

Santuzza.   Oh! madre mia!

    (Le getta le braccia al collo. La scena si popolo. L'agi-
tazione si scorge sul volto di tutti. Che scambievolmente
s'interrogano con terrore. Si ode un mormorio confuso
da lontano. Una donna sola, assai lontano, gridando.)

     Hanno ammazzato compare Tu-
               riddu!

Several women hastily enter, terrified. One of them shrieks —	(Si sentono delle voci confuse piu vicine. Alcune donne entrano atterite correndo, ed una di esse grida disperatamente.)

"Neighbor Turiddu is murdered."

Hanno ammazzato compare Turriddu !

(All rush upon the stage.)

(Tutti si precipitano sulla scena.)

Santuzza, Lucia e Coro.

(Gridando.)

All. Ah !

Ah !

(Santuzza falls ; swooning. Lucia faints, and is supported by some of the women.)

(Santuzza cade priva di sensi, Lucia sviene ed è sorretta dalle donne del Coro. Tutti restano atterriti.)

THE CURTAIN FALLS RAPIDLY.

CALA RAPIDAMENTE LA TELA.

I PAGLIACCI

(Punchinello)

by

RUGGIERO LEONCAVALLO

PREFATORY NOTE.

RUGGIERO LEONCAVALLO, who wrote both the book and music of *Pagliacci*, belongs to the feverish neo-Italian school of composers for the theatre, whose other leading lights are his contemporaries, Puccini, Mascagni, and Giordano. *Pagliacci* was written at about the same time as Mascagni's *Cavalleria Rusticana*, and was likewise submitted to the prize competition of the publisher Sonzogno, in which Mascagni's opera was the successful work; but there is a credible story that *Pagliacci* would have received the award, but for the fact of its being in two acts instead of one, which placed it outside the conditions. The astute publisher, however, secured and issued both operas; and *Pagliacci* made a sensation only second to that of the triumphant *Cavalleria*. It was first produced, May 21, 1892, at the Dal Verme Theatre, Milan, with the following cast:

CANIO	GIRAUD.
TONIO	MAUREL.
SILVIO	ANCONA.
BEPPE	DODDI.
NEDDA	MME. STEHLE.

It soon made its way into the leading Italian and German theatres, scored a season's success in London, and was heard the following year in New York. Now the work holds a permanent place in the repertory of the great opera-houses.

Leoncavallo asserts that the tragedy on which he founded his libretto actually took place in the mountains of Calabria at a given date; but the idea is not a new one in stage-literature, having been previously used in somewhat similar form by both Spanish and French dramatists. The nearest approach to the opera is found in "La Femme du Tabarin," a tragi-parade by Catulle Mendès, which was performed, in 1887, at the *Theatre Libre* in Paris.[1] In fact, Mendès attempted to enjoin the performance of *Pagliacci* at Brussels, on the ground that Leoncavallo had stolen his plot; but the latter was able to demonstrate that the same story had been used long before.

In his treatment of the tragedy, Leoncavallo has made both text and music poignantly effective. The one purpose of the music is to vivify the dramatic significance of the text in every detail; the raw passions and brute impulses of a crude people are dealt with swiftly and directly, and the ironic contrasts which the action invites are seized and brought surely home to the spectator.

THE ARGUMENT.

THE scene of the story is laid in Calabria at the time of the Feast of the Virgin di Mezzagosto. During the prelude Tonio comes forward, as in the Prologue of ancient Greek tragedy, and explains that the subject of the play is taken from real life, and that the composer has devoted himself to expressing the sentiment, good or bad, but always human, of the characters he introduces, without commenting on their social condition. He then makes a sign for the curtain to rise.

The first act shows the meeting of two roads at the entrance of a village; at the right a travelling theatre. Villagers greet the arrival of a troupe of strolling players. Canio, the *Punchinello*, and chief of the little troupe, invites the crowd to attend the performance at seven o'clock, and then goes off with Beppe (the *Harlequin*) and several peasants to drink at the tavern. Tonio the *Clown* remains behind to care for the donkey, but takes advantage of Canio's absence to declare his love to Nedda, who is the *Columbine* of the troupe, and also Canio's wife. Upon being pressed for a kiss, she strikes Tonio with a whip, and he goes off vowing to be revenged. Then Silvio, a rich young villager, joins Nedda and tries to induce her to leave her husband, and the forlorn life of a stroller, which she loathes, to run away with him. Tonio espies

[1] The play has had at least one performance in New York, in which George Fawcett played the part of Tabarin.

the lovers, and runs to fetch Canio the husband. They return in time to hear Nedda's parting words to Silvio in which she appoints to meet him at night. Canio breaks from the restraining hands of Tonio to attack Silvio, but the latter succeeds in escaping over the wall without being recognized. Canio, baffled and jealous, orders Nedda to tell the name of her lover; but she refuses, and Canio is about to stab her, when Beppe interferes, persuades Nedda to go to the theatre to dress for her part, and induces Canio to be calm and prepare for the performance. The act closes with a cry of despair from Canio, who is obliged to act a comedy with death in his very soul.

In the second act the peasants arrive to witness the performance. By chance this proves to be a burlesque of all that has taken place in the first act. Tonio, who plays the part of the idiot servant, makes a declaration of love to *Columbine* (Nedda), which she receives with scorn. *Harle-quin* (Beppe), in love with *Columbine*, then appears, but after a short interview is nearly surprised by the *Pagliaccio* (Canio), who arrives just as *Columbine* is helping *Harlequin* to run away, and hears her repeat to him the very words which she had used to Silvio when she bade him meet her after the play that night. At this Canio loses his head, forgets his part, and furiously demands the name of her lover. Nedda laughs in order to put the public off the scent, and they, failing to grasp the truth, are much amused. Suddenly, however, Canio, beside himself with rage and jealousy, seizes the knife on the table and stabs Nedda to the heart, declaring that she will reveal the name of her lover with her last despairing cry. She calls to Silvio for help, and he attempts to reach her, but is attacked by Canio, who slays him also. The peasants disarm Canio, who says, stupefied, " The comedy is finished."

CHARACTERS.

NEDDA (in the play, Columbine), a strolling player, wife of Canio . . *Soprano.*

CANIO (in the play, Punchinello), master of the troupe . . . . . *Tenor.*

TONIO, the clown, (in the play, Taddeo), *Baritone.*

BEPPE (in the play, Harlequin) . . *Tenor.*

SILVIO, villager . . . . *Baritone.*

Villagers.

The scene is laid in Calabria, near Montalto, on the Feast of the Assumption.

Period between 1865 and 1870.

PERSONAGGI.

NEDDA (nella commedia Colombina), attrice da fiera, moglie di . . *Soprano.*

CANIO (nella commedia Pagliaccio), capo della compagnia . . . *Tenore.*

TONIO, lo scemo (nella commedia Taddeo) commediante . . *Baritono*

PEPPE (nella commedia Arlecchino), commediante . . . . . . *Tenore.*

SILVIO, campagnuolo . . . . . . *Baritono*

Contadini e Contadine.

La Scena si passa in Calabria presso Montalto, il giorno della festa di Mezzagosto.

Epoca presente, fra il 1865 e il 1870.

PAGLIACCI.

PROLOGUE.

Tonio, dressed as Taddeo of the Comedy, comes in front of the curtain.

Tonio. A word — allow me! (*bowing*) sweet
    ladies and gentlemen,
I pray you, hear, why alone I appear,
I am the Prologue!
Our author loves the custom of a prologue
    to his story,
And as he would revive for you the ancient
    glory,
He sends me before you to speak the pro-
    logue!
But not to prate, as once of old,
That the tears of the actor are false, unreal,
That his sighs and cries, and the pain that
    is told,
— He has no heart to feel!
No! No! Our author to-night a chapter will
    borrow
From life with its laughter and sorrow.
Is not the actor a man with a heart like you?
So 'tis for men that our author has written,
And the story he tells you is — true!

A song of tender memories deep in his lis-
    tening heart
One day was ringing; with trembling heart,
    he wrote it,
And marked the time with sighs and
    tears. . . . Come then,
Here on the stage you shall behold us, in
    human fashion,
And see the sad fruits of love and passion!
Hearts that weep and languish, cries of rage
    and anguish,
And bitter laughter. . . . Ah, think then
    — sweet people,
When ye look on us, clad in our motley and
    tinsel,
Ours are human hearts, beating with passion,
We all are men like you, for gladness or
    sorrow.
'Tis the same broad Heav'n above us,
The same wide lonely world before us!

Will ye hear then the story, how it unfolds
    itself, surely and certain?
Come then! ring up the curtain!

(Exit. The curtain rises.)

PROLOGO.

Tonio, in costume da Taddeo come nella commedia, passando a traverso al telone.

Tonio. Si può? . . . (*poi salutando*) Signore!
Signori! . . . Scusatemi se solo mi presento. —
Io sono il Prologo. Poichè in iscena ancor le
antiche maschere mette l' autore, in parte ei
vuol riprendere le vecchie usanze, e a voi di
nuovo inviami. Ma non per dirvi come pria:
" Le lagrime che noi versiam son false: Degli
spasimi e dei nostri martir non allarmatevi!"
No: L'autore ha cercato invece pingervi uno
squarcio di vita. Egli ha per massima sol che
l' artista è un uomo e che per gli uomini scri-
vere ei deve. — Ed al vero ispiravasi.

Un nido di memorie in fondo a l' anima cantava
un giorno, ed ei con vere lacrime sorisse, e i
singhiozzi il tempo gli battevano! Dunque,
vedrete amar sì come s' amano gli esseri umani;
vedrete de l' odio i tristi frutti. Del dolor gli
spasimi, urli di rabbia, udrete, e risa ciniche!

E voi, pruttosto che le nostre povere gabbane d'
istrioni, le nostr' anime considerate, poichè noi
siam uomini di carne e d' ossa, e che di quest'
orfano mondo all pari di voi spiriamo l' aere!

Il concetto vi dissi. — Or ascoltate com' egli è
svolto. (*Gridando verso la scena.*) Andiamo.
Incominciate!

(Rientra e la tela si teva.)

ACT I.

SCENE I.

SCENE: The entrance of a village,—where two roads meet. On right, a travelling theatre. As the curtain rises, sounds of a trumpet out of tune and a drum are heard. Laughing, shouting, whistling voices approaching. Enter Villagers in holiday attire. TONIO looks up road on left. Then, worried by the crowd which stares at him, lies down in front of the theatre.

Time 3 o'clock.—Bright sunlight.

Men and Women

(entering one by one).

This way they come
With pipe and drum,
This way they come,
This way they come.
Here's a pretty Columbine
And Punchinello,
A merry fellow.
With laugh and jest
They come, they come.
Look how sedately
He smiles and passes,
Beating his drum
With a nod to the lasses.

Boys

(behind).

Hi there! Harlequin!
Whip up your donkey!

Canio

(behind).

Go to the devil!

Beppe

(behind).

Take that, you monkey!

(Crowd of boys run on from left.)

Keep back! They're coming now,
The wagon's coming!
Oh what an awful row!
Oh what a drumming!

(Enter BEPPE, dressed as harlequin leading donkey, which draws a gaily painted cart, in which NEDDA is lying. Behind her, the drum, and CANIO dressed as Punchinello in back of cart, trumpet in his right hand, drumsticks in left. The villagers surround the cart.)

Villagers. Hail, Punchinello!
Long live the merry king,
Who keeps us mellow!
He is the blithest fellow!
Long life to him we sing,
Hail, Punchinello!

ATTO PRIMO.

SCENA I.

La scena rappresenta un bivio di strada in compagna, al l' entrata di un villaggio. La destra occupata obliquamente da un teatro di fiera. All' alzarsi della tela si sen ono squilli di tromba stonata alternantisi con dei colpi di cassa, ed insieme risa e, grida allegre, fischi di monelli e vociare che vanno appressandosi. — Attirati dal suono e dal frastuono i contadini di ambo i sessi, in abito da fes a, accorrono a frotte dal viale, mentre TONIO il gobbo, va a guardare verso la strada a sinistra, poi, annojato dalla folla che arriva, si sdraia, ainanzi al teatro. Son tre ore dopo mezzogiorno; il sole di agosto splende cocente.

Coro di Contadini, NEDDA, CANIO, TONIO, e PEPPE.

Coro di uomini e donne

(arrivando a poco a poco).

— Son quà!
— Ritornano...
— Pagliaccio è là.
— Tutti lo seguono
grandi e ragazzi
e ognuno applaude
ai motti, ai lazzi.
— Ed egli serio
saluta e passa
e torna a battere
su la gran cassa.
— In aria gittano
i lor cappelli,
fra strida e sibili,
tutti i monelli.

Ragazzi

(di dentro).

Ehi, sferza l' asino, bravo Arlecchino!

Canio

(di dentro).

Itene al diavolo!

Peppe

(di dentro).

To, birichino!

(Un gruppo di monelli entra, correndo, in scena dalla sinistra.)

— Indietro, arrivano...
— Ecco il carretto...
— Che diavolerio
Dio benedetto!

(Arriva una pittoresca carretta dipinta a varî colori e tirata da un asino che PEPPE, in abito da Arlechino, guida a mano camminando mentre collo scudiscio allontana i ragazzi. Sulla carretta sul davanti e sdrajata NEDDA in un costume tra la zingara e l' acrobata. Dietro ad essaiè piazzata la gran cassa. Sul di dietro della carretta è CANIO in piedi, in costume di Pagliaccio, tenendo nella destra una tromba e nella sinistra la mazza della gran cassa. — I contadini e le contadine attor niano festosamente la carretta.)

Tutti. Evviva! il principe
se' dei pagliacci
Tu i guai discacci
co 'l lieto umor.
Evviva!

Canio. Thank you!	*Canio.* Grazie ...
Villagers. Bravo!	*Coro.* Bravo!
Canio. Allow me.	*Canio.* Vorrei ...
Villagers. Now then begin the play!	*Coro.* E lo spettacolo?

Canio
(beating drum)
Gentlemen all.
(Drowning the voices of the crowd.)

Canio
(picchiando forte e ripetutamente sulla cassa per dominar le voci,
Signori miei!

Villagers
(stopping their ears).
You deafen us. Do stop, I say!

Tutti
(scostandosi e turandosi le orecchie).
Uh! ci assorda! ... finiscila.

Canio
(politely).
A word, a word, I pray!
(Taking off his cap and bowing.)

Canio
(affettando cortesia e togliendosi il berretto con un gesto comico).
Mi accordan di parlar?

Villagers.
Hush! Hush! be quiet, pray,
Begin and say your say!

La Folla
, (ridendo).
Oh! con lui si dee cedere.
tacere ed ascoltar.

Canio. This evening at seven of the clock I
invite you
To see our performance, I know 'twill
delight you.
We'll show you the troubles of poor
Punchinello
And the vengeance he wreaked on a
treacherous fellow;
And Tony the clown with his big cor-
poration,
And strange combination of love and of
hate.
O come then, and honor us,
You'll all be delighted,
At seven you're invited,
At seven you're invited!

Canio. Un grande spettacolo
a ventitrè ore
prepara il vostr' umile
e buon servitore. (*Riverenza.*)
Vedrete le smanie
del bravo Pagliaccio;
e come ei si vendica
e tende un bel laccio.
Vedrete di Tonio
tremar la carcassa,
e quale matassa
d' intrighi ordirà.
Venite, onorateci
Signori e Signore.
A ventitrè ore!
A ventitrè ore!

Villagers. With pleasure, with pleasure!
We all are delighted.
At seven we're invited!
At seven we're invited!

La Folla. Verremo, e tu serbaci
il tuo buon umore.
A ventitrè ore!
A ventitrè ore!

(Tonio advances to help Nedda down from the cart, but Canio, who has already alighted, boxes his ears.)

(Tonio si avanza per ajutar Nedda a discendere dal carretto, ma Canio, che è già saltato giù, gl' dà un ceffone dicendo.)

Canio. Get away!
(Takes Nedda by the arms and lifts her down.)

Canio. Via da lì.
(Poi prende fra le braccia Nedda e la depone a terra.)

Women
(laughing at Tonio).
How d'you like it, pretty lover!

Le Donne
(ridendo, a Tonio).
Prendi questo, bel galante!

Boys
(whistling).
How d'you like it?

I Ragazzi
(fischiando).
Con salute!

(Tonio shakes his fists at the boys, who run away, and goes off, grumbling, right of theatre.)

(Tonio mostra il pugno ai monelli che scappano, poi si allontana bron olando e scompare sotto la tenda a destra del teatro.)

Tonio
(aside).

Oh, he shall pay me, you'll discover!
(Beppe leads off donkey and cart behind theatre.)

Villager
(to Canio).

Say! wilt drink with me a measure?
They sell good liquor at the tavern yonder.

Canio. With pleasure!

(Beppe reappears, and throws down his whip in front of theatre.)

Beppe. I say! Wait, you two!
I'll come with you!
(Enters theatre to change his dress.)

Canio
(calling towards theatre).

Hi! Tonio, art thou coming?

Tonio
(behind).

I've got to clean the donkey.
I'll soon be after you.

Villager
(laughing to Canio).

Take care, my master. He waits till you're
departed, to go a-courting Nedda!

Canio
(smiling and frowning).

You think so?

Canio
(half in earnest, half ironically).

Such a game, believe me, friends, is hardly
worth the playing.
Let Tonio ponder what I am saying.
For the Stage and Life are different, you'll
discover;
For if up there
(pointing to the theatre)
I caught her — my lady, with a lover,
I'd preach a little sermon, and get into a
passion,
Then calmly I would seat me there,
And let her lover beat me there,
While the people would applaud me in the
usual silly fashion!
But if Nedda — in earnest should deceive
me,
The ending would be different, believe me.
Mark the words that I am saying,
Such a game, believe me, friends, is hardly
worth the playing!

Tonio
(a parte).

La pagherai!... brigante.
(Intanto Peppe conduce l' asino col carretto dietro al teatro.)

Un Contadino
(a Canio).

Di', con noi vuo' tu bevere
un buon bicchiere sulla crocevia?

Canio. Con piacere.

Peppe
(ricompare di dietro al teatro; gitta la frusta, che ha ancora in
mano, dinanzi alla scena e dice).

Aspettatemi...
Anch' io ci sto!
(Poi entra dall' altro lato del teatro per cambiar costume.)

Canio
(gridando verso il fondo).

Di Tonio, vieni via?

Tonio
(di dentro).

Io netto il somarello.
Precedetemi.

Un Contadino
(ridendo).

Bada, Pagliaccio, ei solo vuol restare
per far la corte a Nedda.

Canio
(ghignando, ma con cipiglio).

Eh! Eh! vi pare?

Canio
(tra il serio e l' ironico).

Un tal gioco, credetemi, è meglio non gio-
carlo.
con me, miei cari; e a Tonio... e un poco
a tutti or parlo.
Il teatro e la vita non son la stessa cosa;
e se lassù Pagliaccio sorprende la sua sposa
col bel galante in camera, fa un comico
sermone,
poi si calma od arrendesi ai colpi di bastone!...
Ed il pubblico applaude, ridendo allegramente.
Ma se Nedda sul serio sorprendessi...
altramente
finirebbe la storia, com' è ver che vi parlo...
Un tal gioco, credetemi, è meglio non gio-
carlo.

Nedda
(aside).
What can he mean?

Villagers. But surely you cannot suspect her?

Canio
(slightly moved).
No, no, of course not.   That could not be.
I love her and respect her!

(Kisses NEDDA on her forehead.)

(Bagpipes heard from within.   The villagers ran to the left and look off.)

Boys. Hark! hark the bagpipes! The pipers
are coming!

Men. See where the people churchward are
going!

Old People. Hark to the bagpipes so merrily
blowing!
Gaily the couples to vespers are going!

Women Come away!
The gray twilight falleth,
The Angelus calleth!

Canio. Yes, but remember, pray,
At seven you're invited!

(Enter bagpipe Players from left, in holiday attire.   A troop of villagers follows. Villagers on stage greet them. All disperse in couples, and at close of chorus go off singing, down road behind theatre.)

Chorus. Ding, dong! the shadows fall,
Then come, one and all!
To the church come away
Ding, dong! we roam along,
In love's dream so fair.
But mothers have watchful eyes,
Beware! oh beware!
Soon in the twilight
Love will be told;
But the old folks are watching,
Be not too bold!
Ding, dong! all above,
All around, is bright with love.
Ding, dong! the shadows fall,
Come one and all!

(During the above, CANIO goes into theatre, and after taking off his Punchinello's dress, returns, nods good-bye to NEDDA with a smile, and goes off with BEPPE and several villagers, left. NEDDA remains.)

Nedda
(a parte).
Confusa io son!...

Alcuni Contadini.   Sul serio pigli dunque la cosa!

Canio
(un po' commosso).
Io?... Vi pare!... Scusatemi...
Adoro la mia sposa!

(CANIO va a baciar NEDDA in fronte.   Un suono di cornamusa si fa sentire all' interno; tutti si precipitano verso la sinistra, guardando fra le quinte.)

I Monelli
(gridando).
I zampognari!... I zampognari!...

Gli Uomini. Verso la chiesa vanno i compari

(Le campane suonano a vespero da lontano.)

I Vecchi. Essi accompagnano la comitiva
che a coppie al vespero sen va giuliva.

Le Donne. Andiam. — La campana
ci appella al signore.

Canio. Ma poi.. ricordatevi,
A ventitrè ore.

(I zampognari arrivano dalla sinistra in abito da festa con nastri dai colori vivaci e fiori ai cappelli acuminati. Li seguono una frotta di contadini e contadine anch' essi parati a festa. Il coro, che è sulla scena, scambia con questi saluti e sorrisi, poi tutti si dispongono a coppie ed a gruppi, si uniscono alla comitiva e si allontanano, cantando, pel viale del fondo, dietro al teatro.)

Coro Generale. Din, don,— suona vespero,
ragazze e garzon,
a coppie affrettiamoci,
al tempio — din, don!
Il sol diggia i culmini,
Din, don, vuol baciar;
Le mamme ci adocchiano,
attenti, compar.
Din, don. — Tutto irradiasi
di luce, d'amor;
Ma i vecchi sorvegliano,
gli arditi amador.
Din, don — suona vespero,
ragazze e garzon.
Le squille ci appellano
al tempio — din, don!

(Durante il coro, CANIO entra dietro al teatro e va a lasciar la sua giubba da Pagliaccio, poi ritorna, e dopo aver fatto, sorridendo, un cenno d' addio a NEDDA, parte con PEPPE e cinque o sei contadini per la sinistra. — NEDDA resta sola.)

SCENE II.

NEDDA, alone, then TONIO.

Nedda

(musing).

How fierce he looked and watched me!
I hung my head, fearing lest he should
  discover
My secret thoughts of my lover.
Heav'ns! if he should suspect me,
With all his brutal ways! No matter! I fear
  not,
These are but empty dreams and idle fancies.
Shine, oh thou glorious sun, upon me!
Every pulse is throbbing, glowing,
Like the tide, my passion flowing,
Oh my heart, my restless heart, where art
  thou going?

(Looking to the sky.)

Ah, ye beautiful song-birds! I hear your
  pinions.
What seek ye? Whither going? Who knows?
My mother knew the meaning of your sweet
  voices,
And the song she sang me in happy child-
  hood
Comes back for ever! High! high aloft they
  fly,
Through Heaven's blue ether launched in
  their flight,
Like arrows of light, in the sky,
The storm clouds and the tempest and the
  sunlight defying,
For ever flying, — through the boundless
  sky!
Afar, ever they journey! on, upward for
  ever!
On! wearying never, their fetterless wings
  unfold.
They have their visions, their tender, beauti-
  ful visions,
They soar for ever through clouds of gold.
What though the wind howls, and night is
  dark above them,
Spreading their pinions by planet and star,
No night dismays them, no storm delays
  them,
They soar for ever o'er sea and scar.
Far! oh so far they fly on wings untiring,
Seeking sweet regions they may never know,
For what can bar their dreams and their
  desiring?
'Tis fate that leads them; — still on they go!

SCENA II.

NEDDA sola, poi TONIO

Nedda

(pensierosa).

Qual fiamma avea nel guardo!
Gii occhi abbassai per tema ch' ei leggesse
il mio pensier segreto.
Oh! s'ei mi sorprendesse ...
brutale come egli è ... Ma basti, orvia.
Son questi sogni paurosi e fole!
      O che bel sole
di mezz' agosto! Io son piena di vita, e
  tutta illanguidita
per arcano desio, non so che bramo!

(Guardando in cielo.)

Oh! che volo d' augelli, e quante strida! ...
Che chiedon? dove van? chissà .. La
  mamma
mia, che la buona ventura ann o nciava,
comprendeva il lor canto e a me bambina
  così cantava:
Hui! stridono lassù, liberamente
lanciati a vol come frecce, gli augel.
Disfidano le nubi e 'l sol cocente,
e vanno, e vanno per le vie del ciel.
Lasciateli vagar per l' atmosfera
questi assetati d' azzurro e splendor:
seguono anch' essi un sogno, una chimera,
e vanno, e vanno fra le nubi d'or.
Che incalzi il vento e latri la tempesta,
con l' ali aperte san tutto sfidar;
la pioggia, i lampi, nulla mai li arresta,
e vanno, e vanno, sugli abissi e i mar.
Vanno laggiù verso un paese strano,
che sognan forse e che cercano invan.
Ma i boëmi del ciel seguon l'arcano
poter che li sospinge ... e vanno .. e van!

Nedda

(crossly).

What! thou? I thought that thou wast gone
    to market!

Tonio

(coming forward).

The fault lies in thy singing.

(Caressingly.)

The song bewitched me,
And I could not leave thee.

Nedda

(laughing scornfully).

Ha! ha! How very poetical.

Tonio. Do not laugh, Nedda.

Nedda. Go to the tavern!

Tonio. I know that you hate me and laugh in
    derision,
For what is the Clown? he plays but a part.
Yet he has his dream, and his hope and his
    vision,
        The Clown has a heart.
And ah when you pass me, uncaring, un-
    seeing,
You know not my sorrow, so cruel and
    sweet.
I give you my spirit, my life, and my being,
    I die at your feet.

(Approaching her.)

Ah, hear me then, hear me then,
    Let me tell thee—

Nedda

(interrupting and scoffing at him).

    — You love me.
'Tis time enough to tell me this evening,
To-night when you're playing the fool,
With sighs and grimaces.
Why not postpone the confession till then?

Tonio

(passionately).

No, 'tis now I will tell it thee,
And thou shalt hear me now.
I love thee, worship and long for thee.
To make thee mine for ever.

(Tonio durante la canzone sarà uscito di dietro al teatro e sarà ito
ad appoggiarsi all' albero, ascoltando beato. — Nedda, finito il canto.
fa per rientrare e lo scorge.)

Nedda

(bruscamente contrariata).

Sei là? credea che te ne fossi andato.

Tonio

(ridiscendendo, con dolcezza).

E colpa del tuo canto.   Affascinato
io mi beava!

Nedda

(ridendo con scherno).

Oh! quanta poesia!...

Tonio.   Non rider, Nedda...

Nedda.   Va, va all' osteria.

Tonio.   So ben che difforme, contorto son io;
che desto soltanto lo scherno o l' orror.
Eppure ha 'l pensiero un sogno, un desìo,
    e un palpito il cor!
Allor che sdegnosa mi passi d' accanto
non sai tu che pianto mi spreme il dolor,
perchè, mio maigrado, subito ho l' incanto
    m' ha vinto l' amor!

(Appressandosi.)

Oh! lasciami, lasciami
or dirti...

Nedda

(interrompendolo e beffeggiandolo).

che m'ami?
Hai tempo a ridirmelo
stasera, se il brami,
facendo le smorfie
colà, sulla scena.
Intanto risparmiati
per ora la pena.

Tonio

(delirante con impeto).

No, è qui che voglio dirtelo,
e tu m' ascolterai.
che t' amo ti desidero,
e che tu mia sarai!

Nedda
(with studied insolence)

Tell me, thou silly varlet,
Do thy shoulders itch for a drubbing?
Or do thy ears want a rubbing?
How shall I teach thee
To cool thy love?

Tonio. You mock me? Too long I've borne it.
By the cross of the Saviour, I'll make thee pay,
I've sworn it!

Nedda. You threaten?
Must I then call Canio to thee?

Tonio
(moving towards her).

But not before I kiss thee!

Nedda
(drawing back).

Hands off!

Tonio
(advancing and putting out his arms to embrace her).

No! No! thou shalt be mine.

(NEDDA goes up stage backwards, sees whip left by BEPPE, takes it up and strikes TONIO in the face.)

Nedda. Unhand me, wretch!

Tonio
(screaming and drawing back).

By the Holy Virgin of the Assumption, Nedda,
I swear it, I'll be revenged upon thee.

(Exit left, with threatening gestures.)

Nedda. Viper, begone! Thou hast revealed thy nature.
Tonio—the Fool! Thou hast a heart as foul
And ugly as thy body, ay! fouler still!

SCENE III.

SILVIO, NEDDA ; then TONIO.

SILVIO leans half over wall, right, and calls in a low voice.

Silvio. Nedda!

Nedda
(hurrying towards him`.

Silvio! at this hour. What madness!

Nedda
(seria ed insolente).

Eh! dite, mastro Tonio!
La schiena oggi vi prude, o una tirata
d' orecchi è necessaria
al vostro ardor?

Tonio. Ti beffi? sciagurata!
Per la croce di Dio, bada che puoi
pagarla cara!...

Nedda. Tu minacci?... Vuoi
che vada a chiamar Canio?

Tonio
(movendo verso di lei).

Non prima chio ti baci

Nedda
(retrocedendo).

Bada!

Tonio
(s' avanza ancora aprendo le braccia per ghermirla).

Oh, tosto sarai mia!...

Nedda
(sale retrocedendo verso il teatrino, vede la frusta lasciata da PEPPE, l' afferra e dà un colpo faccia a TONIO, dicendo).

Miserabile!...

Tonio
(dà un urlo e retrocede).

Ah! Per la vergin pia di mezz' agosto
Nedda, lo giuro... me la pagherai!...

(Esce minacciando dalla sinistra.)

Nedda
(immobile guardandolo allontanarsi).

Aspide! va. — Ti sei svelato ormai
Tonio lo scemo! — Hai l' animo
Siccome il corpo tuo difforme... lurido!..

SCENA III.

SILVIO, NEDDA, e poi TONIO.

Silvio
(sporgendo la metà dei corpo arrampicandosi dal muretto a destra, e chiama a bassa voce).

Nedda!

Nedda
(affrettandosi verso di lui).

Silvio! a quest' ora... che imprudenza.

Silvio
(jumping over and coming towards her).

Bah! Bah! No danger, dear, I'm thinking.
Canio I left at yonder tavern drinking.
By the pathway that we love, through the
bushes, I came hither.

Nedda. A moment sooner and Tonio would
have caught thee.

Silvio
(laughing).

Ha! ha! The fool!

Nedda. The fool is to be feared. He loves me,
Just now he told me.
With burning words and brutal fire,
He tried to kiss me in his mad desire.

Silvio. By Heaven!

Nedda. Nay, be not anxious! For such a
passion,
A whip's the fashion.
(Pointing to BEPPE's whip.)

Silvio. Why wilt thou live, then, for ever like
this, Nedda?
My fate is in thy hands.
Nedda, pity my sorrow.
To-night the fair is o'er,
Thou wilt be gone to-morrow.
Ah, what of me, when thou art departed?
How shall I live apart from thee
And broken-hearted?

Nedda
(deeply moved).

Silvio!

Silvio. Nedda, hear, I implore thee!
If for thy husband no passion inspires thee,
If all this roving life sickens and tires thee,
If this great love of thine is not empty de-
light,
Fly with me, fly with me, dearest, to-night!

Nedda. Ah, tempt me not! Has not life enough
of sadness?
Silvio, tempt me no more. 'Tis folly, 'tis
madness!
Have I not given thee my heart? Thou
hast my love for aye.
Then say good-bye and part. Thou wilt
not then betray.
Ah, tempt me not, for pity's sake, my heart
will break!

Silvio
(saltando allegramente e venendo verso di lei).

Ah bah! sapea che non
rischiavo nulla.
Canio e Peppe da lunge a la taverna
ho scorto con gli amici!... Ma prudente
per la macchia a me nota qui ne venni.

Nedda. E ancora un poco in Tonio t' imbattevi.

Silvio
(ridendo).

Oh! Tonio il gobbo!

Nedda. Il gobbo è da temersi.
M' ama...Ora qui mel! disse...e nel bestiale
delirio suo, baci chiedendo, ardiva
correr su me...

Silvio. Per Dio!

Nedda. Ma con la frusta
del cane immondo la foga calmai.

Silvio. E fra quest' ansie in eterno vivrai?
Decidi il mio destin,
Nedda, Nedda rimani!
Tu il sai; la festa ha fin
e parte ognun dimani.
E quando tu di qui sarai partita
che addiverrà di me... de la mia vita?...

Nedda
(commossa).

Silvio!

Silvio. Nedda, rispondimi.
Se è ver che Canio non amasti mai,
se è vero che t' è in odio
il ramingare e il mestier che tu fai,
se l'immenso amor tuo fola non è
questa notte partiam!... fuggi con me.

Nedda. Non mi tentar!... Vuoi tu — perder la
vita mia?
Taci Silvio, non più... — E deliro... è
follìa!...
Io mi confido a te — a te cui diedi il cor
Non abusar di me — de 'l mio febbrile
amor!...
Non mi tentar!... E poi... — Chissà!
meglio è partir

Who knows, dear heart, 'tis best to part!
Tears are vain, all is vain ; we must not meet
    again.
And yet remembering all our love, since first
    I met thee,
I shall dream of thee, live for thee, never
    forget thee.

        (Tonio appears at back, left.)

Silvio. No ! you do not love me !

Tonio
        (aside, watching).

I've caught thee, thou baggage !

    (Runs down pathway, with threatening gestures.)

Nedda. I love thee, love thee !

Silvio. And yet you leave me to-morrow.

      (Lovingly, trying to move her.)

Why hast thou taught me Love's magic
    story,
  If thou wilt leave me, hopeless, alone?
Why press to mine thy lips in their glory,
  Why fold thy heart unto mine own ?
If thou forgettest all our caresses,
  I still remember that dream divine,
I want thy heart, thy passionate kisses,
  I want thy spirit to melt in mine !

Nedda
      (overcome and yielding).

Can I forget, as I see thee before me,
The spell of love thy heart has woven o'er
    me ?
By the words thou hast spoken, the ties that
    have bound me,
All I want is thy love, folded around me.
Ah, do not leave me ! wherefore must we
    sever ?
Thou hast my heart, and I am thine for-
    ever !

Silvio
      (clasping her in his arms).

Wilt come ?

Nedda. Yes ! Kiss me, love !

Silvio. Forget the past, think not of to-morrow !

Nedda. Look in mine eyes, and kiss away my
sorrow.

Silvio. In thy dear eyes, I kiss away my sorrow.

Sta il destin contro noi. — E vano il nostro
    dir.
Eppure da 'l mio cor — strapparti non poss'
    io,
Vivrò sol de l' amor — ch' hai destato al cor
    mio.

        (Tonio appare dal fondo a sinistra.)

Silvio. No, più non m' ami !

Tonio
        (scorgendoli, a parte).

T' ho colta, sgualdrina !

    (Fugge dal sentiero minacciando.)

Nedda. Sì, t' amo ! t' amo !

Silvio. E parti domattina ? . . .

    (Amorosamente, cercando ammaliarla.)

E allor perchè, di', tu m' hai stregato
se vuoi lasciarmi senza pietà ?
Quel bacio tuo perchè me l' hai dato
fra spasimi ardenti di voluttà ?
Se tu scordasti l' ore fugaci
io non lo posso, e voglio ancor
que' spasmi ardenti, que' caldi baci
che tanta febbre m' han messo in cor !

Nedda
      (vinta e smarrita).

Nulla scordai — m' ha sconvolta e turbata
questo amor che ne 'l guardo ti sfavilla.
Viver voglio a te avvinta, affascinata
una vita d' amor calma e tranquilla.
A te mi dono; su me solo impera.
Ed io ti prendo e m' abbandono intera.

Silvio
      (stringendola fra le braccia).

Verrai ? . . .

Nedda. Sì — Baciami ! . . .

Silvio. Tutto scordiamo. . .

Nedda. Negli occhi guardami !

Silvio. Sì, ti guardo e ti bacio, t' amo . . t' amo !

SCENE IV.

The same. CANIO, and then BEPPE.

As NEDDA and SILVIO go off towards the wall, talking, CANIO and TONIO come stealthily by the short path.

Tonio
(holding CANIO back).

Tread lightly, lightly, and you will catch them so!

(CANIO advances cautiously, still held back by TONIO; they cannot see SILVIO getting over the wall.)

Silvio
(half over the wall).

At midnight, dearest, I wait thee below!
Come to me, love, when the starbeams shine.

(SILVIO disappears, and CANIO approaches the corner of the theatre.)

Nedda. To-night, love, and for-ever I am thine!

Canio
(who overhears).

Ha!

Nedda.
(turns round, frightened, and calls towards the wall).

Fly, love!

(CANIO with one bound reaches the wall; NEDDA places herself in front of him. After a short struggle he pushes her into a corner, gets over the wall and disappears. TONIO remains on left, watching NEDDA, who, as if pinned to the wall, tries to hear whether they are fighting.)

Nedda. Ah, Heav'n, preserve him now!

Tonio
(laughing ironically).

Ha! ha!

Canio
(outside).

Coward! where art thou?

Nedda
(turning at TONIO's laugh, looking with disgust at him).
Well done, well done, then, Tonio.

Tonio. Yes — yes, I did it.

Nedda. Just like you, you coward!

Tonio. But next time, I expect to do better!

Nedda. You make me hate and loathe you.

Tonio. Love me, or hate me! 'Tis naught to me.

SCENA IV.

I precedenti, CANIO e poi PEPPE.

Mentre SILVIO e NEDDA s' avviano parlando verso il muricciuolo, arrivano, camminando furtivamente dalla scorciatoia, CANIO e TONIO.

Tonio
(ritenendo CANIO).

Cammina adagio e li sorprenderai.

(CANIO s' avanza cautamente sempre ritenuto da TONIO, non potendo vedere, dal punto ove si trova, SILVIO che scavalca il muricciuolo.)

Silvio
(che ha già la metà del corpo dall' altro lato ritenendosi al muro)

Ad alta notte laggiù mi terrò.
Cauta discendi e mi ritroverai.

(SILVIO scompare e CANIO si appressa all' angolo del teatro.)

Nedda
(a SILVIO che sarà scomparso di sotto).

A stanotte — e per sempre tua sarò!

Canio
(che dal punto ove si trova ode queste parole, dà un urlo).

Oh!...

Nedda
(si volge spaventata e grida verso il muro).

Fuggi!

(D' un balzo CANIO arriva anch' esso al muro; NEDDA gli si para dinante ma dopo breve lotta egli la spinge da un canto, scavalca il muro e scompare. — TONIO resta a sinistra guardando NEDDA che come inchiodata presso il muro cerca sentire se si ode rumore di lotta mormorando.)

Nedda. Aitalo... Signor!...

Tonio
(ridendo cinicamente).

Ah!... ah!

La Voce di Canio
(di dentro).

Vile! t' ascondi!

Nedda
(al riso di TONIO si è voltata e dice con disprezzo fissandolo).
Bravo! Bravo il mio Tonio!

Tonio. Fo quel che posso!

Nedda. E quello che pensavo!

Tonio. Ma di far assai meglio non dispero.

Nedda. Mi fai schifo e ribrezzo.

Tonio. Oh, non sai come lieto ne sono!

(CANIO re-enters, over the wall, pale, and wiping the perspiration from his forehead.)

Canio. So again, she's fooled me. Baffled again!
He knows the path too well.
But no matter. This moment you shall tell me
Your lover's name.

Nedda   (turning in confusion).
Who?

Canio.
          (furiously).
You, by Heav'n eternal!
And if here now this moment, I have not cut your throat,
          (drawing dagger from his belt)
'Tis because before I kill thee, and thy blood stains my dagger,
Thou shameless woman, thou shalt tell me
Who is thy lover. Tell me!

Nedda. Vain are thy insults. My lips are sealed for ever.

Canio
          (shouting).
His name, I tell thee. This moment, thou shalt tell me.

Nedda. No! No! Never will I tell thee.

Canio
          (rushing on her furiously with dagger raised).
By Heav'n, I'll kill thee.

(BEPPE, entering left, hearing NEDDA's answer, snatches dagger from CANIO and throws it away among the trees.)

Beppe. Ah, stay, good master, for the love of Heav'n!
The people! see! they're coming.
Look, where they come from church, to see the play.
Come away. Be calm, I pray.

Canio.
          (struggling).
Leave me. I tell thee. His name, then, his name!

Beppe. Tonio, come here and hold him.
The people come this way. Don't let them see you.

(TONIO takes CANIO by the hand, while BEPPE turns to NEDDA.)

(CANIO intanto scavalca di nuovo il muro e ritorna in iscena pallido, asciugando il sudore con un fazzoletto di colore oscuro.)

Canio
          (con rabbia concentrata).
Derisione e scherno!
Nulla! Ei ben lo conosce quel sentiero
Fa lo stesso; poichè del drudo il nome
or mi dirai.

Nedda   (volgendosi turbata).
Chi?

Canio
          (furente).
Tu, pel padre eterno! . . .

          (Cavando dalla cinta lo stiletto.)
E se in questo momento quì scannata
non t' ho già, gli è perchè pria di lordarla
nel tuo fetido sangue, o svergognata,
codesta lama, io vo' il suo nome. — Parla.

Nedda. Vano è l' insulto. — E muto il labbro mio.

Canio
          (urlando).
Il nome, il nome, non tardare o donna!

Nedda. No, nol dirò giammai . . .

Canio
          (slanciandosi furente col pugnale alzato).
Per la madonna! . . .

(PEPPE, che sarà entrato dalla sinistra, sulla risposta di NEDDA corre a CANIO e gli strappa il pugnale che gitta via tra gli alberi.)

Peppe. Padron! che fate! . . . Per l' amor di Dio . . .
La gente esce di chiesa e a lo spettacolo
qui muovo . . . andiamo Canio, via, cal matevi!

Canio
          (dibattendosi).
Lasciami Peppe — Il nome, il nome.

Peppe. Tonio
vieni a tenerlo. Andiamo arriva il pubblico.

(TONIO prende CANIO per la mano mentre PEPPE si volge a NEDDA.)

And Nedda, you go hence, I say.
Go hence and dress yourself. You know
well, Canio
Is hasty but tender.

(Pushes NEDDA under the curtain and exit with her.)

Canio

(holding his head in both hands).

'Tis shameful, shameful!

Tonio.

(in a low voice to CANIO, pushing him towards front of stage).

Ah! calm thyself, my master. 'Tis best to
make believe!
The gallant will return. I am convinced
of it.
Trust me to watch her. Now it is time the
play began.

(CANIO makes a fierce gesture, but TONIO, pushing him by the elbow, comes forward slowly.)

Who knows? Haply the lover will be here
to-night,
And will betray it. Come, then, we must
dissemble,
If we would win.

Beppe

(entering, to CANIO).

Come, come, go dress yourself, I pray you.

(To TONIO.)

And you play up your drum there, Tonio!

(TONIO goes behind, BEPPE re-enters theatre. CANIO, worn out with emotion, walks slowly towards the curtain.)

Canio. To act, with my heart maddened with
sorrow.
I know not what I'm saying or what I'm
doing.
Yet I must face it. Courage, my heart!
Thou art not a man; thou'rt but a jester!
On with the motley, the paint and the
powder,
The people pay thee, and want their laugh,
you know.
If Harlequin thy Columbine has stolen,
Laugh, Punchinello! The world will cry
"Bravo!"
Go hide with laughter thy tears and thy
sorrow,
Sing and be merry, playing thy part,
Laugh, Punchinello, for the love that is
ended,
Laugh for the sorrow that is eating thy heart.

(Passes under the curtain of the stage theatre, while the curtain slowly falls.)

(End of the first act.)

Vi spiegherete. — E voi di lì tiratevi.
Andatevi a vestir, — Sapete, Canio,
è violento, ma buono ...

(Spinge NEDDA sotto la tenda e scompare con essa.)

Canio

(stringendo il capo fra le mani).

Infamia! infamia!

Tonio

(piano a CANIO, spingendolo sul davanti della scena).

Calmatevi padrone. — E meglio fingere;
il ganzo tornerà. — Di me fidatevi.

(CANIO ha un gesto disperato, ma TONIO spingendolo col gomito prosegue piano.)

Io la sorveglio — Ora facciam la recita.
Chissà ch' egli non venga a lo spettacolo
e si tradisca! Or via. — Bisogna fingere
per riuscir ...

Peppe

(uscendo dalle scene).

Andiamo, via, vestitevi
padrone. — E tu batti la cassa, Tonio.

(TONIO va di dietro al e teatro PEPPE anch esso ritorna all' interno, mentre CANIO accasciato si avvia lentamente verso la cortina.)

Canio. Recitar! ... mentre preso dal delirio
non so più quel che dico e quel che faccio!
Eppur ... è d' uopo ... sforzati!
Bah, se' tu forse un uom? Tu se' Pag-
liaccio!
Vesti la giubba e la faccia infarina.
La gente paga e rider vuole quà.
E se Arlecchin t' invola Colombina,
ridi, Pagliaccio ... e ognuno applaudirà!
Tramuta in lazzi lo spasmo ed il pianto;
in una smorfia il singhiozzo e 'l dolor ...
Ridi Pagliaccio, sul tuo amore infranto!
Ridi del duol che t' avvelena il cor!

(Entra commosso sotto la tenda, mentre la tela cade lentamente.)

(Fine del' atto primo.)

ACT II.

Scene as in Act I.

SCENE I.

TONIO appears with big drum and takes up his position at the left angle of the theatre. People come from different directions for the performance. BEPPE places benches for the women.

Women

(arriving).

Quickly, sweet gossips come,
  The show's beginning,
Hark, how they beat the drum,
  Oh, what a dinning!
Come, quickly, come, I say,
  Let's get good places.

Tonio

(beating drum).

Walk up and see the play,
  All take your places.

Men.   Look how they rush and run,
  Ribbons and laces,
Come here and see the fun,
  My pretty faces!
Oh, what a crush and rush,
  Just for first places!

(SILVIO comes from back, and takes his place in front, left, nodding to his friends.)

Tonio.   Walk up, walk up, I say,
  All take your places!

Women

(sitting down, pushing each other).

Why are you pushing, you?
  I'm nearly baking;
Help, Beppe, help us, do!
  Our places taking.

(NEDDA enters dressed as Columbine, holding plate to receive money. BEPPE tries to settle the women. TONIO re-enters theatre, carrying away the drum.)

Som of the Crowd

(to BEPPE).

Now, then, begin the play,
  Have done your prating!
Why keep us waiting?
  We all are here!

Beppe.   Keep back, keep back, I say!
  First you must pay, please,
This way, this way, please!

ATTO SECONDO.

La stessa scena dell' atto primo.

SCENA PRIMA.

TONIO compare dall' altro lato del teatro colla gran cassa e ra a piazzarsi sull' angolo sinistro del proscenio del teatrino. Intanto la gente arriva da tutte le parti per lo spettacolo e BEPPE viene a metters nei banchi per le donne.

DONNE, UOMINI, TONIO, NEDDA, SILVIO, PEPPE, CANIO e CORO.

Donne

(arrivando).

Presto, affrettiamoci
svelto, compare,
chè lo spettacolo
dee cominciare.
Cerchiam di metterci
ben sul davanti.

Tonio

(picchiando la cassa).

Si dà principio;
avanti! avanti!

Uomini.   Veh, come corrono
le bricconcelle!
Accomodatevi
comari belle.
O Dio, che correre
per giunger tosto!

(SILVIO arriva dal fondo e va a pigliar posto sul davanti a sinistra salutando gli amici.)

Tonio.   Si dà principio
pigliate posto!

Le Donne

(cervando sedersi, spingendosi).

— Ma non pigiatevi,
fa caldo tanto!
— Su; Peppe ajutaci.
V' è posto accanto!

(NEDDA esce vestita da COLOMBINA col piatto per incassare i posti. — PEPPE cerca di mettere a posto le donne. — TONIO rientra nel teatro portando via la gran cassa.)

Una Parte del Coro (a *Peppe*).   Suvvia, spiccia-
tevi
incominciate.
Perchè tardate?
Siam tutti là.

Peppe.   Che furia, diavolo!
Prima pagate.
Nedda, incassate.

All

(trying to pay at once).

This way !
This way !

Others.   See how they fight their way
To get between us !
You, there ! sit down, I say,
Take care, take care !

Silvio

(in a low voice to NEDDA as he pays for his seat).

Nedda !

Nedda.   Be careful,
He has not seen us !

Silvio.   To-night, remember, love !
I shall be there !

(NEDDA, leaving SILVIO, takes money for more seats, and then re-enters theatre with BEPPE.)

Full Chorus.   Now, then, begin the play,
Have done your prating !
Why keep us waiting ?
Begin, I say !
Time to begin ! —
Let's make a din !
It's seven o'clock, that's certain !
Ring up the curtain !
Time to begin !   We all are in.

(Bell rung loudly.)

Ring up the curtain.
Silence, you there !
Begin !   Begin !

(Some of the women sit on benches placed obliquely towards the stage of theatre, others stand with the men on rising ground under tree. Others at wing, left. SILVIO among them.)

SCENE II.

The Play.

NEDDA (Columbine), BEPPE (Harlequin), CANIO (Punchinello), TONIO (Taddeo), and SILVIO.

Curtain of the theatre rises.   SCENE: a small room with two side doors, practicable window at back.   NEDDA as Columbine is walking about anxiously.

Columbine.   My husband Punchinello
Comes not till morning ; empty lies the
street !
Taddeo's at the market — lazy fellow !
All is safe and sweet !

(A guitar is heard off.   COLUMBINE runs to window, with signs of love and impatience.)

Tutti

(volendo pagare nello stesso tempo).

Di qua — di qua !

Un' altra Parte del Coro.   Veh, si accapigliano !..
chiamano ajuto ! . . .
Ma via, sedetevi
senza gridar.

Silvio

(piano a NEDDA, pagando il posto).

Nedda !

Nedda.   Sii cauto !
Non t' ha veduto.

Silvio.   Verrò ad attenderti.
Non obliar ! . . .

(NEDDA dopo aver lasciato SILVIO riceve ancora il prezzo delle sedie da altri, e poi rientra anch' essa nel teatro con PEPPE.)

Coro Generale.   Questa commedia
incominciate.
Perchè tardate ?
Perchè indugiar ?
Facciamo strepito,
facciam rumore,
ventitrè ore
suonaron già.
Allo spettacolo
ognuno anela ! . . .

(Si ode una lunga e forte scampanellata.)

S' alza la tela !
Silenzio. — Olà.

(Le donne sono parte sedute sui banchi, situati obliquamente, volgendo la faccia alla scena del teatrino ; parte in piedi formano gruppo cogli uomini sui rialzo di terra ov' è il grosso albero.   Altri uomini in piedi lungo le prime quinte a sinistra. SILVIO è innanzi ad essi.)

SCENA II.

Commedia.

NEDDA (Colombina), PEPPE (Arlecchino), CANIO (PAGLIACCIO). TONIO (Taddeo), e SILVIO.

La tela del teatrino si alza. — La scena, mal dipinta, rappresenta una stanzetta con due porte laterali ed una finestra praticabile in fondo. Un tavolo e due sedie rozze di paglia son sulla destra del teatrino. — NEDDA in costume da COLOMBINA passeggia ansiosa.

Colombina.   Pagliaccio, mio marito,
a tar la notte sol ritornerà.
E quello scimunito
di Taddeo perchè ancora non è quà !

(Si ode un pizzicar di chitarra all' interno ; COLOMBINA corre alla finestra e dà segni d' amorosa impazienza.)

Harlequin

(behind the scene).

O Columbine, unbar to me
Thy lattice high.
I watch and sigh,
Longing to hear thee,
And be near thee, as the hours go by.
Ah, show thy little face to me.
So dear thou art,
Thou hast my heart.
Ah, do not vex me,
Tease and perplex me ! how can I live
Without thy loving heart?
O Columbine, then list to me,
Thy door unbar,
Come down, my star !
Come down, and love me,
See, where alone I sigh !
For if thou lov'st me not,
Then let me die !

Columbine

(returning anxiously to front).

Ah, yes ! 'tis now love's hour entrancing !
The moment's advancing !
And Harlequin is waiting there !

(Seats herself, with troubled looks, with her back to door on
right, through which TONIO, dressed as TADDEO, enters with basket on
left arm. He stops, and gazes at NEDDA with exaggerated expression
of love.)

Taddeo.   Behold her !

(Suddenly raising his hands and the basket to ceiling.)

Ah ! how surpassing fair !

(The audience laugh.)

Ah ! just to tell her, rebellious maiden,
Just to tell her the love with which I'm
laden !
All safe and clear, now !
No husband near, now !
Why should I fear, now !
There's no one to suspect me.
Come, Love !   Direct me !

(Loud and exaggerated sigh.   The audience laugh.)

Columbine

(turning).

Well, fool ?   Is't thou ?

Taddeo

(without moving).

Yes, 'tis I.

Columbine.   Hast thou seen Punchinello ?

La Voce di Arlecchino

(PEPPE, di dentro).

O Colombina, il tenero
fido Arlecchin
è a te vicin !
Ver te chiamando,
e sospirando — aspetta il poverin ! . .
La tua faccetta mostrami,
ch' io vo' baciar
senza tardar
la tua boccuccia.
Amor mi cruccia — e mi sta a tormentar !
O Colombina schiudimi
il finestrin,
che a te vicin
ver te chiamando
e sospirando — è il povero Arlecchin !

Colombina

(ritornando ansiosa sul davanti).

Di fare il segno convenuto appressa
l' istante, ed Arlecchino aspetta ! . . .

(Siede ansiosa volgendo le spalle alla porta di destra.   Questa si
apre e TONIO entra sotto le spoglie del servo TADDEO, con un paniere
infilato al braccio sinistro.   Egli si arresta a contemplare NEDDA con
aria esageratamente tragica, dicendo.)

Taddeo.   E dessa !

(Poi levando bruscamente al cielo le mani ed il paniere.)

Dei, com' è bella !

(Il pubblico sul teatro ride.)

Se a la rubella
io disvelassi
l' amor mio che commuove sino i sassi !
Lungi è lo sposo.
Perchè non oso ?
Soli noi stamo
e senza alcun sospetto !   Ors . Proviam
(Sospiro lungo, esagerato.)
Oh ! . . .
(Il pubblico ride.)

Colombina

(volgendosi).

Sei tu, bestia ?

Taddeo

(immobile).

Quell' io sono, sì !

Colombina.   E Pagliaccio è partito ?

Taddeo
(as before).
He went just now.

Columbine.   Come, then, what were you sent for?
Where is the fowl you went for?

Taddeo
(throwing himself on his knees before COLUMBINE and offering basket
as he approaches).
Low at thy feet it is lying,
See us both.
(Pointing to fowl in basket.)
Ah! I implore thee,
Luckless couple here before thee,
O Columbine — be mine, be mine!
Hear, O maiden tender!
From the day —
(COLUMBINE opens window and makes signal.)

Columbine
(turning to TADDEO).
How much, I say?
(Snatching basket.)
Your reck'ning render!

Taddeo.   (Just one and threepence!) —
Hear me say
How I love thee and adore thee!

Columbine
(near to table).
Get away, get away!

(HARLEQUIN enters by window, places bottle which he is carrying
under his arm on floor, and goes towards TADDEO, who pretends not
to see him.)

Taddeo
(to COLUMBINE pointedly).
Pure!   Yes, I know thou art,
Pure as the snowflake falling.
Why wilt thou close thy heart
Unto my calling?
Must I leave thee and forsake thee?

Harlequin
(taking him by the ear and kicking him up).
Yes, or I'll make thee!
(The audience laugh.)

Taddeo
(retiring comically to door, right; to HARLEQUIN).
Heav'ns!   You love her!
Then I must hand her over!
(Raising his hands.)
Bless you, my children!
(Retiring to door.)
Yonder I will watch o'er you!
(The audience laugh and applaud.)

Taddeo
(come sopra).
Egl partì!

Colombina.   Che fai così impalato?
Il pollo hai tu comprato?

Taddeo.   Eccolo, vergin divina!
(Precipitandosi in ginocchio, offrendo colle due mani il paniere a
COLOMBINA che si appressa.)

Ed anzi eccoci entrambi ai piedi tuoi.
Poichè l' ora è suonata, o Colombina,
di svelarti il mio cor.   Di', udirmi vuoi?
Dal dì . . .

(COLOMBINA va alla finestra la schiude e fa un segno; poi va verso
TADDEO.)

Colombina
(strappandogli il paniere).
Quanto spendesti dal trattore?

Taddeo.   Una e cinquanta.   Da quel dì il mio
core . . .

Colombina
(presso alla tavola).
Non seccarmi Taddeo!

ARLECCHINO scavalca la finestra, depone a terra una bottiglia che ha
(sotto il braccio, e poi va verso TADDEO mentre questi finge non vederlo.

Taddeo
(a COLOMBINA, con intenzione).
So che sei pura
E casta al par di neve!   E ben che dura
Ti mostri, ad obliarti non riesco!

Arlecchino
(lo piglia per l' orecchio dandogli un calcio e lo obbliga a levarsi.
Va a pigliar fresco! . . .
(Il pubblico ride.)

Taddeo
(retrocedendo comicamente verso la porta a destra).
Numi! s' aman! m' arrendo ai detti tuoi.

(Ad ARLECCHINO.)
Vi benedico! . . . là . . . veglio su voi!

(TADDEO esce.   Il pubblico ride ed applaude.)

Columbine.   Dear Harlequin!

Harlequin
(in exaggerated style).

  Sweet Columbine!   Ah, how we've prayed, dear,
  And Love has heard our prayer.

Columbine
(pointing to the table on which she has placed the fowl, knives, and forks, etc.).

  The supper's laid, dear !
  See here, see here, my dearest dear,
  The supper that I've bought you !

Harlequin
(pointing to the wine which he places on the table).

  See here, my love, my dainty dove,
  The splendid wine I've brought you!

Both
(sitting down opposite each other).

  For love is very fond of wine,
  And partial to the kitchen.

Harlequin.   My greedy little Columbine !

Columbine.   My toper most bewitchin' !

Harlequin
(taking a phial from his breast).

  Take then this little philtre fine,
  Give it to thy husband,
  Pour it in his wine,
  And then let's fly, my dear !

Columbine.   Yes — give it me !

Taddeo
(entering by door, on right, crosses stage, trembling in exaggerated style).

  Beware !   Thy husband is here !
  For weapons seeking, with anger stamping,
  All's discovered !   I'd better be decamping.

(Exit hurriedly through door, left.   The audience laugh.)

Columbine
(to HARLEQUIN).

  Fly, then.

Harlequin
(getting through window).

  Pour the philtre in his wine, love !

(Disappears.)

(CANIO, dressed as PUNCHINELLO, appears at door, right.)

Columbine.   To-night and for ever, I am thine, love !

Colombina.   Arlecchin !

Arlecchino
(con affetto esagerato).

  Colombina !   Alfin s' arrenda
  Ai nostri prieghi amor !

Colombina.   Facciam merenda !

(COLOMBINA prende dal tiretto due posate e due coltelli ARLECCHINO va a prender labottiglia, poi entrambi sieaono a tavola uno in faccia all altro.)

Colombina.   Guarda, mio ben, che splendida
  cenetta preparai !

Arlecchino.   Guarda, amor mio, che nettare
  divino t' apportai !

(A due.)

  L' amor ama gli effluvii
  del vin, de la cucina !

Arlecchino.   Mia ghiotta Colombina

Colombina.   Amabile beon !

Arlecchino
(prendendo un' ampolletta che ha nella tunica).

  Prendi questo narcotico,
  dallo a Pagliaccio pria che s' addormenti,
  e poi fuggiamo insiem.

Colombina.   Sì, porgi.

Taddeo
(spalanca la porta a destra e traversa la scena tremando esagerata-mente).

  Attenti ! . . .
  Pagliaccio è là tutto stravolto . . . ed armi
  cerca !   Ei sa tutto.   Io corro a barricarmi !

(Entra precipitoso a sinistra e chiude la porta.   Il pubblico ride.)

Colombina
(ad ARLECCHINO).

  Via !

Arlecchino
(scavalcando la finestra).

  Versa il filtro ne la tazza sua.

(Scompare.)

(CANIO in costume da PAGLIACCIO, compare sulla porta a destra.)

Colombina
(alla finestra).

  A stanotte. — E per sempre sarò tua !

Canio

(with his hand to his heart, aside).

God I am I dreaming? What she said this
  morning I
Courage I

(Advancing for his part.)

Some one was with you here I

Nedda. What nonsense I You've been drinking.

Canio

(looking at her).

Been drinking I . . . I think so I

Nedda

(resuming the play).

You're back too early.

Sanio

(pointedly).

Too early I Thou fearest I
Art sorry, my sweetest, my dearest?

(Resuming the play.)

Ah, nay, thou wast not lonely.

(Pointing to the table.)

Who has been with thee here?

Nedda. The Fool Taddeo — only I
In fact, he's in the cupboard hiding I

(Pointing to door, left.)

Come out I . . . explain I

Tonio

(from within).

Believe me, sir, thy wife is true. She'd
  never grieve thee I

(Pretending to be afraid, pointedly.)

Those pious lips of hers would ne'er deceive thee.

(The audience laugh.)

Canio. Do not trifle, false woman,
Dost thou forget that I am also human?
Tell me his name I

Nedda. Whose name?

Canio. Tell me, then, by God who made me,
Within whose shameless arms thou hast
  betrayed me ?

Canio

(porta la mano al cuore e mormora a parte).

Nome di Dio I . . . quelle stesse parole I .

(Avanzandosi per dir la sua parte.)

coraggio I

(Forte.)

Un uomo era con te.

Nedda. Che fole I
Ser briaco ?

Canio

(fissandola).

Briaco I sì . . da un' ora I . . .

Nedda

(riprendendo la commedia).

Tornasti presto.

Canio

(con intenzione).

Ma in tempo I
T' accora dolce sposina.

(Riprende la commedia.)

Ah I sola ti credea

(mostrando la tavola)

e due posti son là.

Nedda. Con me sedea
Taddeo che là si chiuse per paura.

(Verso la porta a sinistra.)

Orsù, parla I . . .

Tonio

(di dentro fingendo tremare ma con intenzione).

Credetela. Essa è pura I . . .
E abborre dal mentir quel labbro pio I

(Il pubblico ride forte.)

Canio

(rabbioso al pubblico).

Per la morte I

(Poi a NEDDA sordamente.)

Smettiamo. Ho Dritto anch' io
d' agir come ogni altr' uomo. Il nome suo.

Nedda

(fredda e sorridente).

Di chi ?

Canio. Vo' il nome de i' amante tuo,
del drudo infame a cui ti desti in braccio
O turpe donna I

Nedda
(continuing the play).

Punchinello! Punchinello!

Canio. No! Punchinello no more! I am a man again,
With aching heart and anguish deep and human,
Calling for blood to wash away the stain,
Thy foul dishonor, thou shameless woman!
No! Punchinello no more! Fool that I sheltered thee!
And made thee mine by every tender token!
Of the love that I gave thee, what is there left to me?
What have I now, but a heart that is broken?

(Falls on chair, overcome.)

Women
(aside to each other).

Sweet gossip, ah, it makes me weep,
So true it all is seeming.

Men. Silence, down there. Quiet keep.

Silvio
(aside).

Ah, can it be I'm dreaming?

Canio
(recovering himself, and becoming gradually more excited).

I hoped in my passion so blindly confiding,
If not for love, for pity sweet.
I loved thee more than God in heav'n abiding,
All my life and my being I laid at thy faithless feet!
I dreamt thou wast true! I would I ne'er had met thee!
I thought of thee pure and stainless as the morn.
Thou hast broken my heart, I live but to forget thee.
Thou hadst my love, but now thou hast my hate and scorn!

Audience
(with enthusiasm).

Bravo!

Nedda
(coldly, and in earnest).

Well, then, if thou deem'st me so unworthy,
Come, let me go and leave thee.

Nedda
(sempre recitando la commedia).

Pagliaccio! Pagliaccio!

Canio. No, Pagliaccio non son; se il viso è pallido
è di vergogna, e smania di vendetta!
L' uom riprende i suoi dritti, e il cor che sanguina
vuol sangue a lavar l' onta, o maledetta! ...
No, Pagliaccio non son! ... Son quei che stolido
ti raccolse orfanella in su la via
quasi morta di fame, e un nome offriati
ed un amor ch' era febbre e follìa! ...

(Cade come affranto sulla seggiola.)

Gruppi di Donne a Parte. Comare, mi fa piangere!
— Par vera questa scena!

Un Gruppo di Uomini. Zitte laggiù. — Che diamine!

Silvio
(a parte).

Io mi ritengo appena!

Canio
(riprendendosi ed animandosi a poco a poco).

Sperai, tanto il delirio accecato m' aveva,
se non amor, pietà ... mercè!
Ed ogni sacrifizio
al cor, lieto, imponeva,
e fidente credeva,
più che in Dio stesso, in te!
Ma il vizio alberga sol ne l' alma tua negletta;
tu viscere non hai ... sol legge è 'l senso a te ...
Va, non merti il mio duol, o meretrice abbietta,
vo' ne lo sprezzo mio schiacciarti sotto i piè! ...

La Folla
(entusiasta).

Bravo! ...

Nedda
(fredda, ma seria).

Ebben se mi giudichi
Di te indegna, mi scaccia in questo istante.

Canio

(laughing).

No doubt! no doubt! and set thee free,
And let thy lover's arms receive thee!
No! Thou shalt remain, I swear it.
I want thy lover's name — Come, then — declare it!

Nedda

(trying to resume the play, with forced smile).

I never knew, my dear, that you
Were such a tragic fellow!
You here will see no tragedy,
My dearest Punchinello!
The man who's been to sup with me,
And caused you all this bother,
Was only Harlequin, you see,
Poor Harlequin, no other!

(Stops laughing, seeing CANIO's attitude.)

Canio

(in fury).

Ah! dost thou mock me? My rage thou
still defiest.
Say who's thy lover — this moment — or
thou diest!

Nedda. No! By my mother's soul, unworthy
though thou call me,
I will not tell thee, whatever fate befall me!

Voices in the Crowd. Are they in earnest?
What are they doing?

(BEPPE tries to pass through door on left; TONIO detains him.)

Beppe. Let us be going, Tonio!

Tonio. Silence, fool!

Beppe. I am afraid!

Silvio

(aside).

Oh, the play is a strange one,
I can bear it no more!

Nedda. For thine anger, I care not. Love is a
weapon stronger!
Thus I defy thee! I fear thee no longer!

Canio

(yelling, rakes knife from table).

His name! His name!

Canio

(sogghignando).

Ah! ah! di meglio chiedere
Non dèi che correr testo al caro amante.
Sei furba! — No, per Dio, tu resterai
E 'l nome del tuo ganzo mi dirai.

Nedda

(cercando riprendere la commedia sorridendo forzatamente).

Suvvia, così terribile
davver non ti credeo!
Qui nulla v' ha di tragico.

(Verso la porta a sinistra.)

Vieni a dirgli, o Taddeo,
che l' uom seduto or dianzi a me vicino
era . . . il pauroso ed innocuo Arlecchino!

(Risa tosta represse dall' attitudine di CANIO.)

Canio

(terribile).

Ah! tu mi sfidi! E ancor non l' hai capita
Ch' io non ti cedo? Il nome, o la tua vita!

(Assieme.)

Nedda

(prorompendo).

No, per mia madre! Indegna esser poss' io,
quello che vuoi, ma vil non son, per Dio!
Di quel tuo sdegno è l' amor mio più
forte . . .
Non parlerò. No . . . A costo de la
morte! . . .

Voci tra la Folla. Fanno davvero? Sembrami
seria la cosa e scura!

(PEPPE vuol uscire dalla porta a sinistra, ma TONIO lo ritiene.)

Peppe. Bisogna uscire, Tonio.

Tonio. Taci sciocco! . . .

Peppe. Ho paura! . . .

Silvio

(a parte).

Oh la strana commedia!
Io non resisto più! . . .

Canio

(urlando dà di piglio a un coltello sul tavolo).

Il nome! Il nome!

Nedda
(defiantly).
No!

Silvio
(drawing his dagger).
What in the devil's name!... He's in earnest!

(The women draw back frightened, overturning the benches, preventing the men from getting to the front. SILVIO struggles to get clear. Meantime CANIO has seized NEDDA, and stabbed her from behind, as she tries to escape to the audience.)

Canio. Take that, and that!
In thy last dying agony thou'lt tell!

Voices in Audience. Stop him!

Nedda. Ah! Help me, Silvio!
(Dies.)

Silvio
(nearly reaching her).
Nedda!

(At the voice of SILVIO, CANIO turns savagely, leaps at him, and stabs him.)

Canio. So! 'Tis you, then? 'Tis well!
(SILVIO falls dead.)

Men. Help! help! arrest him!

Women
(screaming).
Father of pity!

(Several of the audience throw themselves on CANIO to disarm and arrest him; he stands stupefied and drops the knife.)

Canio. The comedy is ended.

CURTAIN.

Nedda
(sfidandolo).
No!

Silvio
(snudando il pugnale).
Santo diavolo!...
Fa davvero...

(Le donne che indietreggiano spaventate, rovesciano i banchi ed impediscono agli uomini di avanzare, ciò che obbliga SILVIO a lottare per arrivare alla scena. Intanto CANIO al parossismo della collera, ha afferrata NEDDA in un attimo e la colpisce per di dietro mentre essa cerca di correre verso il pubblico.)

Canio (a *Nedda*). Di morte negli spasimi
Lo dirai!

La Folla e Peppe
(che cerca svincolarsi da TONIO).
Ferma!

Canio. A te!

Nedda
(cadendo agonizzando).
Soccorso... Silvio!

Silvio
(che e quasi arrivato alla scena).
Nedda!

(Alla voce di SILVIO, CANIO si volge come una belva, balza presso di tui è in un attimo lo ferisce, dicendo.)

Canio. Ah! sei tu? Ben venga!
(SILVIO cade come fulminato.)

Gli Uomini del Coro. Arresta aita!

Le Donne
(urlando).
Gesummaria!...

(Mentre parecchi si precipitano verso CANIO per disarmarlo ed arrestarlo, egli, immobile, istupidito lascia cadere il coltello dicendo.)

Canio. La commedia è finita!...

(La tela cade.)
FINE.

DON GIOVANNI
(Don Juan)

by

WOLFGANG AMADEUS MOZART

LIBRETTO BY LORENZO DA PONTE

THE STORY OF "DON GIOVANNI"

DON GIOVANNI, a young Spanish nobleman, at a late hour of the day, under cover of darkness, entered the apartments of Donna Anna, who had not yet retired for the night, but sat musing on the divan. Donna Anna, supposing the intruder to be her betrothed, Don Ottavio, did not, at first, repulse this advance; when discovering her mistake, however, she cried for help. Don Giovanni ran out into the street, closely followed by Donna Anna, who held on to his mantle, repeating her cries, and trying to get a look at the features of the stranger, which Giovanni concealed with his mantle. Donna Anna's aged father, Don Pedro, the Commandant, at this juncture made his appearance from one of the side doors of the palace, carrying a sword in one hand and a lighted candle in the other. Donna Anna ran back, to call out others to assist her father. Don Giovanni, after striking the candle from the hand of the Commandant, was attacked by the latter, and, after only parrying his assailant's passes for a while, he, at last, getting exasperated, dealt him a death blow. Calling, then, his servant Leporello, who had been watching the above proceedings from a distance, both made off in haste. Donna Anna, returning with Ottavio and servants with torches, found the corpse of her father on the ground, and the murderer flown. To discover the perpetrator of this bloody deed and punish him, she declares shall henceforth be the object of her life. Ottavio vows his cooperation.

Happening to be outside of the walls of Seville, on the ensuing morning, Don Giovanni and Leporello fall in with Donna Elvira, a young lady from the city of Burgos, in pursuit of Giovanni, who had gained her affections and then left her. Giovanni, in order to escape from this unpleasant encounter, referred her to Leporello for the reasons which prompted his actions, and, while her attention was thus engaged by the valet for a few moments, the master slipped off. Leporello made merry with the grief of poor Elvira; he showed her a long catalog of the victims of the gay lord, and assuring her that she is neither the first of them, nor will be the last, he too departed.

A few days afterwards a rural wedding was celebrated in a village near Giovanni's country seat. While the peasants were in the midst of the festivities, the Don and his *valet-de-chambre* made their appearance among them. The pretty bride, Zerlina, struck the eye of the libertine, and led by her coquettishness of manner to consider her an easy conquest, he forthwith invited the whole party into his palace, whither they proceeded, led by Leporello, who had some trouble to allay the jealous fears of the bridegroom, Masetto, who saw his affianced detained by the handsome cavalier. Giovanni had nearly succeeded in fascinating the young peasant girl when Donna Elvira came in, aroused her suspicions, and conducted her from his presence. Scarcely had they left him when from the other side Donna Anna entered, accompanied by Don Ottavio. They asked for his assistance in discovering the murderer of the Commandant, which Giovanni readily promised, at the same time extending an invitation to join in the festivities, which were about to begin in the palace in honor of the peasant couple. While he was gallantly conversing with Donna Anna, Elvira returned, and seeing in her a new victim, began to denounce her former paramour vehemently. Giovanni gave his friends to understand that the fair stranger was out of her mind, but the others, struck by the earnestness of Elvira and the good sense of her speech, distrusted his assurances. Elvira left, overcome by her emotions; Giovanni, under the pretext of following her, and seeing to her safety, also quitted the scene. Just then Donna Anna, by something in the manner and speech of Giovanni, recognized in him the midnight assassin, under whose sword her father had fallen. She immediately communicated her discovery to her lover, and they resolved to visit the house of Giovanni, masked, in accordance with the custom of the country.

The gay festival in the palace had been interrupted by the entrance of Zerlina, led by Elvira, the latter denouncing the master of the mansion in the hardest terms, and creating thereby not a little disturbance. At length the wily Leporello succeeded in locking Elvira out into the street, and then hastened to inform his patron of the state of matters. Zerlina had made peace with Masetto, who, however, harbored still many misgivings as to the real condition of the heart of his affianced, and consequently exercised a close watch over her. They repaired to the ball room, which had a most brilliant look. Among the throng were to be noticed Anna, Elvira, and Ottavio, all in dominoes, and wearing masks. Everything went on harmoniously, until Giovanni, while unobserved by the jealous Masetto, led his unsuspecting victim, Zerlina, into an adjoining apartment, whence presently piercing shrieks were heard. Upon bursting the door open, Zerlina, pale and frightened, hurried out into the arms of Masetto. After her appeared Don Giovanni, sword in hand, and dragging Leporello with him. He tried to pass off Leporello as the real criminal, but when Donna Anna, Elvira, and Ottavio dropped their masks and confronted him, he made no stand on this pretext, but taking to the sword and making a resolute attack upon the exasperated crowd, he escaped into the garden.

Scarcely out of this predicament, Don Giovanni was again enamored. This time it was the chambermaid of Donna Elvira who had excited his passions. He considered that fine clothes would hardly secure him a good reception with the fair one; accordingly he changed mantle and cap with Leporello, when, at nightfall, both reconnoitered about Elvira's residence. Elvira just then sat down at the window, which Don Giovanni no sooner discovered, than, pushing Leporello towards the window, and himself crouching behind him, he commenced to implore Elvira's forgiveness, and asked her to come down into his loving embrace. Elvira consented, and Giovanni left his servant to act in his place, observing from a short distance how Leporello carried out the joke. The couple got along swimmingly, until Giovanni, assuming a rough voice and heavy gait, frightened them away. When thus the coast was cleared, he took his guitar and serenaded the object of his passion. But hardly had he concluded the second stanza of his song, when he heard footsteps approaching. Hearing Masetto call out to some others with him, Don Giovanni was put on his guard, and when discovered by the other party passed himself off for Leporello. He managed to send all of Masetto's comrades off, making them believe that they are put upon the track of Don Giovanni, to whom they were hired to administer a good thrashing. The simple-minded Masetto confidentially communicated to the disguised Giovanni that he

was going to kill him, and handed him over his weapons to examine. Giovanni, once in possession of these, gave the simpleton a good cudgeling and left him on the ground, crying lustily. It was not long before Zerlina came, attracted to the spot by his voice, and led him away.

Elvira and Leporello, in their precipitate flight, had accidentally got into a court-yard, upon which a side wing of Donna Anna's palace opened. Leporello, now feeling uncomfortable, tried to get away from his fair companion. Anna and Ottavio entered, scaring the fugitives to remote corners of the square. Leporello slowly wends his way to the middle door; but when he was about to make his escape, it was opened from the outside, and admitted the enraged Masetto, armed with a heavy stick, followed by peasants. He seized the unfortunate Leporello (still disguised in his master's clothes) and led him before Donna Anna. Pressed closely, and fairly aroused to a fear for his ultimate personal safety, Leporello discovered himself, and, amid the confusion which followed this unexpected *denouement*, succeeded in giving the company the slip.

After a hot flight, climbing over walls and fences, Leporello suddenly found himself in the presence of his master, who had just come down from the wall opposite, and there terminated a flight similar to Leporello's. They were before the Cathedral of Seville. The full moon shone bright upon the marble statue of the Commandant, in the middle of the vast and desolate square. Giovanni, observing that the sight of the statue excited fear in Leporello, bade him go and read the inscription. Leporello, after much coaxing and threatening, read as follows:—

"I here await that vengeance decreed by Heaven Unto the wretch who slew me."

Of course this only tended to increase Leporello's fright. Moreover he had seen the eyes of the statue glare at his master. Giovanni, who was highly amused at the fears of his servant, now ordered him to go and invite the statue to supper. Leporello did as he was bidden, and the statue nodded his head in token of assent. Don Giovanni's curiosity was now awakened by what his valet claimed to have seen. He stepped up to the statue himself, repeated the invitation, and received a loud "Yes" for an answer.

On the following evening, when Giovanni sat down at table, he had already forgotten that he was to have a guest for supper. While he was enjoying a bountiful repast, Donna Elvira made her appearance, venturing a last effort to bring the sinner to repentance. But Giovanni treated her with the most cruel indifference, mocked her earnest appeals, invited her to a seat at the table, and thus fairly drove her out of the room. Presently she returned, uttering a piercing shriek, rushed across the apartment and fled by another door. Giovanni bade his valet to see what the matter was. Leporello went out, but returned immediately, thoroughly frightened, and unable to tell what he had seen. Giovanni, seizing his sword, and taking a candle from the table, now went out to see for himself. On the corridor he encountered the statue of the Commandant, walking towards the supper room. He backed before it and regained the room; the statue following. Giovanni ordered Leporello to fetch another supper, but the statue stopped him, saying that he could not partake of food for mortals, and in his turn invited his host to sup with him. Giovanni accepted the invitation, and gave his hand to the spectre as earnest. But once in his grasp, the statue never released his hold of him. Three times it asked of Giovanni to repent; three times the latter refused. "Down to thy doom then pass!" were the last words of the statue. It sank, and from the abyss emerged a herd of demons, who seized Giovanni and hurled him down into the fiery gulf.

DRAMATIS PERSONÆ

DON PEDRO, THE COMMANDANT	BASS
DONNA ANNA, HIS DAUGHTER	SOPRANO
DON OTTAVIO, BETROTHED TO DONNA ANNA	TENOR
DON GIOVANNI, A YOUNG NOBLEMAN	BARITONE
LEPORELLO, HIS VALET-DE-CHAMBRE	BASS
DONNA ELVIRA, A YOUNG LADY FROM THE CITY OF BURGOS	SOPRANO
ZERLINA, A PEASANT GIRL	SOPRANO
MASETTO, BETROTHED TO ZERLINA	TENOR

PEASANTS, MASKS, MUSICIANS, ETC.

THE SCENE IS LAID IN AND ABOUT THE SPANISH CITY OF SEVILLE

THE LIBRETTO IS BY LORENZO DA PONTE. THE OPERA WAS COMPOSED AND PERFORMED FOR THE FIRST TIME (IN PRAGUE) IN THE YEAR 1787

DON GIOVANNI.

(DON JUAN.)

ACT I.

SCENE I.—*The stage represents an angle in the court-yard of the Palace of the Commandant at Seville: on the right hand stands a wing of the Palace, a window of which is seen with the jalousie partly open, and a door below it gives entrance into the court. In the middle distance stands the entrance—a handsome arch with pierced bronze gates, a dwarf wall extending from it on either side, surmounted by a richly ornamented iron railing; on the left hand tall trees are seen; beyond the railing are perceived the city of Seville, a bend of the Guadalquivir, the fortifications, the convent of San Francisco, and rising above all, the lofty steeple of the Cathedral. It is night; the whole scene is illuminated by the moon, which is, however, from time to time dimmed by heavy scudding clouds; an universal stillness reigns, and the numerous lights of the distant town are calmly reflected in the river; all betokens the deepest and most solemn hour of the night.*

At the rising of the curtain, Leporello is discovered half asleep on a stone settle near the door on the right hand; his cloak is thrown over a pocket lantern standing beside him, so as to conceal it; he rouses himself, yawns, and comes forward, lantern in hand, his whole demeanor expressing lassitude and fatigue.

LEPORELLO, solus.

NOTTE E GIORNO FATICAR—NIGHT OR DAY. LEPORELLO.

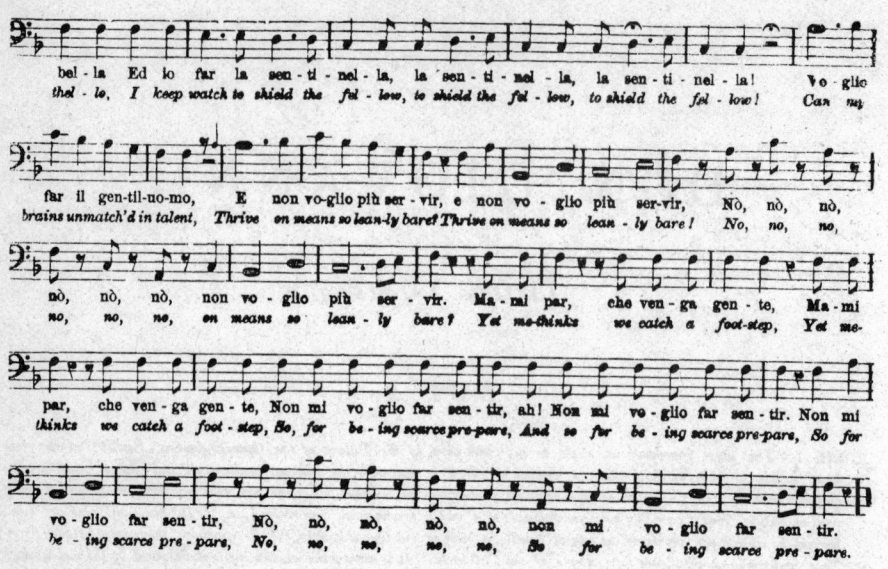

bel - la Ed io far la sen-ti-nel-la, la sen-ti-nel-la, la sen-ti-nel-la!   Vo-glio
thel - lo,   I keep watch to shield the fel - low, to shield the fel - low, to shield the fel-low!   Can my

far il gen-til-uo-mo, E non vo-glio più ser - vir, e non vo - glio più   ser-vir,   Nò, nò, nò,
brains unmatch'd in talent, Thrive on means so lean-ly bare? Thrive on means so   lean - ly bare!   No, no, no,

nò,   nò,   nò,   non vo - glio più ser - vir. Ma - mi par,   che ven - ga gen - te,   Ma - mi
no,   no,   no,   on means so   lean - ly bare?   Yet me-thinks   we catch a   foot-step,   Yet me-

par,   che ven - ga gen - te, Non mi vo - glio far sen - tir, ah! Non mi vo - glio far sen - tir. Non mi
thinks   we catch a foot - step, So, for   be - ing scarce pre-pare, And so for be - ing scarce pre-pare, So for

vo - glio far sen - tir, Nò, nò, nò, nò, nò, nò, non mi vo - glio far sen - tir.
be - ing scarce pre - pare, No, no, no, no, no, So for be - ing scarce pre - pare.

[The noise of approaching steps is heard. Don Juan rushes from the Palace sword in hand; he has endeavored to conceal his features by a large slouch hat, and his person by a great cloak; Donna Anna, in her robe-de-nuit, her hair all dishevelled, pursues him and tries to tear off his disguise. Don Juan, in preventing this, struggles with her. Leporello pockets his lantern and withdraws quickly to the back as they approach.]

SCENA II.—Donna Anna; Don Giovanni; e detto.	**SCENE II.—The same; Donna Anna; Don Juan.**

Anna. Non sperar, se non m' uccidi,   *Anna.* [*Clinging frantically to Don Juan.*]
    Ch' io ti lascio fuggir mai.   Villain, yield thy double seeming!
                          On thy craven flight I press.
Gio. Donna folle, indarno gridi;   *Juan.* [*Repulsing her.*] Senseless folly! idle dreaming!
    Chi son io tu non saprai.   Who I am, to hope to guess.
Lep. Che tumulto, oh ciel! che gridi!   *Lep.* (What an uproar! ye gods, what screaming!—
    Il padron in nuovi guai!   [*Aside.*] Master's in another mess.)
Anna. Genti! servi! traditore!   *Anna.* [*Calling aloud.*]
                         Help! assistance! seize the stranger!
Gio. Taci, e trema al mio furore.   *Juan.* Heav'ns, be still! or dread mine anger.
Anna. Scollorato!   *Anna.* [*Desperate.*] Vilest monster!
Gio. Sconsigliata!   *Juan.* [*Fingering his sword.*] Hold, Señora!
    Questa furia disperata   At this bedlamite behavior
    Mi vuol far precipitar.   I shall surely go too far.
Anna. Come furia disperata   *Anna.* As a fury will I rave here,
    Ti saprò perseguitar.   Of escape the firmest bar.
Lep. Sta a veder ch' il malandrino   *Lep.* [*Aside.*] (This particular manœuvre
    Mi farà precipitar.   Runs a little over par.)

[Hearing Donna Anna's cries, her father, the Commandant, comes to her assistance; he rushes in in his night robe, with drawn sword and a lamp which he has snatched from a table. Donna Anna escapes hastily back into the Palace.]

SCENA III.—Don Giovanni; Leporello; The Com- mandant.	**SCENE III.—Don Juan; Leporello; The Command- ant.**

Com. Lasciala, indegno,   *Com.* [*Advancing to Don Juan.*]
    Battiti meco   Wretch worse than vicious
                         Draw, and defend thee!

Gio. Va, non mi degno di pugnar teco.	*Juan.* [*With nonchalance, striking the lamp from the Commandant's hand with his sword, so that they are in darkness.*] Steel were too precious— Words would offend thee—
Com. Così pretendi da me fuggir?	*Com.* Ye shuffle sadly; My sword's from sheath!
Lep. Potessi almeno di quà partir.	*Lep.* [*Aside.*] (I'd stand excus'd here, In very faith.)
Gio. Misero! attendi, se vuoi morir, si battono.	*Juan.* [*On his defence.*] Fool! learn how madly You rush on death.

[*They cross swords: the Commandant, tremulous and hasty, makes several desperate passes at Don Juan, which the latter coolly parries: at last, watching his opportunity, Don Juan makes one home thrust, and wounds the Commandant mortally. Leporello, all the while, keeping out of the way at the back.*]

Com. Ah soccorso! son tradito. L' assassino m' ha ferito, e dal seno palpitante sento l' anima partir.	*Com.* [*His accents choked by approaching death.*] Lost were succor; vain, assistance, Soldier still,—I yield existence :— Yet—if sav'd—a daughter's honor, Life—its price—proves none too dear. [*He falls and dies.*]
Gio. Ah già cade lo sciagurato, affannoso e agonizzante, Già dal seno palpitante veggio l' anima partir.	*Juan.* Ah, the weakling dotard falleth, And a brawl ill-sought, ignoble, Bids yon haughty hasty noble Basely end a brave career. [*As he coolly wipes his sword, and returns it to the sheath.*]
Lep. (Qual misfatto! qual eccesso! Entro il sen dallo spavento palpitar il cor mi sento, io non so che far, che dir.)	*Lep.* [*Aside.*] (This completes him; what excesses! With such dying in real earnest, My poor brain, so swift thou turnest, I am twice as dead, I fear.)

SCENA IV.—Don Giovanni; Leporello.	SCENE IV.—Don Juan; Leporello.
Gio. [*Sotto voce.*] Leporello, ove sei?	*Juan.* [*In a semi-whisper.*] Leporello, where are ye?
Lep. Son quì per mia disgrazia, e voi?	*Lep.* [*From the back, in the same tone.*] Still here, to my great scandal; and you, Sir?
Gio. Son quì.	*Juan.* Here, too.
Lep. Chi è morto? voi, o il vecchio?	*Lep.* Who's dead there, you—or th' old man?
Gio. Che domanda da bestia! il vecchio.	*Juan.* [*Laughing.*] O ye saints, what a question!—the old man.
Lep. Bravo! Due imprese leggiadre, Sforzar la figlia, ed ammazzar il padre.	*Lep.* [*Rubbing his hands.*] Bravo! just two birds of a feather: To force the daughter; next, to kill the father.
Gio. L' ha voluto suo danno.	*Juan.* Was the deed not his seeking?
Lep. Ma Don Anna cos' ha voluto?	*Lep.* Donna Anna, she also sought it?
Gio. Taci. Non mi seccar vien meco, se non vuoi. Qualche cosa ancor tu.	*Juan.* [*Haughtily, and wrapping his mantle around him.*] Silence; annoy me not! And follow—[*raising his hand, as if about to strike Leporello*]—unless you seek a sound drubbing too.
Lep. Non vo' nulla, Signor, non parlo più. [*Partono.*	*Lep.* [*Crouching to avoid the blow, and picking up his cloak and lantern.*] My remarks on each point need thence be few. [*Don Juan and Leporello make their escape by the trees on the left.*]

SCENA V.—*Entra* Donna Anna, Don Ottavio, *servi con fiaccolle*	SCENE V.—Donna Anna; Don Octavio; *Attendants bearing torches.*
Anna. Ah del padre in periglio In soccorso voliam!	*Anna.* [*Heard within, as she is entering hastily and in alarm, followed by Don Octavio with his sword drawn, and escorted by Attendants bearing torches.*] Ah! my father endanger'd; to his help! to his aid!
Otta. Tutto il mio sangue verserò, se bisogno: Ma dov' è il scelerato?	*Oct.* [*With warmth.*] Freely this life-blood forth shall flow is service, an ye show me the villain!
Anna. In questo loco. Ma qual mai s' offre, Oh Dei, spettacolo funesto agli occhi miei! Padre mio! mio caro padre!	*Anna.* As they enter.] Yet one step further—[*she perceives the dead body of the Commandant extended upon the ground and bleeding; his sword lying by his side.*] But what horror, O God, now bursts upon my vision, A ghastly presence! [*Falling in frantic grief upon the corse.*] My father! father dearest! thou, mine own father!

Mtta. Signore!

Anna. Ah! l' assassino mel trucidò,
Quel sangue, quella piaga—
Quel volto tinto e coperto del color di morte,
Ei non respira più—
Fredde le membra,
Padre mio! caro padre!
Padre amato! io manco—
Io moro.

Otta. Ah soccorrete, amici, il mio tesoro.
Cercatemi, recatemi qualche odor,
Qualche spirto, ah non tardate!

Oct. [*Stooping, feeling, and addressing the body to see if any life be still left in it.*] Don Pedro—
Anna. [*Weeping.*]
Too well the monster hath done his work!
This wound here—this damp pallor—these cold cheeks
Foully incarnadine with once their beauty!
[*Musingly.*] Yet Angels kiss'd his soul forth from its dwelling.   [*Unable to control herself*
O my father! dearest father! more than existence!
I falter—I follow—   [*Falls fainting upon the body*
Oct. [*To the Attendants, as he stoops to raise her.*]
Friends, an immediate succor for this my treasure!
Procure me now, obtain me now, cooling scent,
Purest balsam, with speed of lightning.

[*Two of the Attendants depart at his order. To Donna Anna, as he tenderly lifts her, and parts the hair from her forehead.*]

Donn' Anna! sposa! amica!
Il duolo estremo la meschinella uccide.

Mine Anna!—darling!—beloved.
                    [*The Servants re-enter*
This deep extremest grief cannot prove but fatal.
[*As he applies the restoratives with which the Servants return*
Anna. [*Faintly.*] Ah!
Oct. She reviveth! [*To the Attendants.*] Help us with fresh assistance.
                    [*They hand him other restoratives.*]

Anna. Ahi!
Otta. Già riviene. Datele nuovi ajuti.

Anna. [*Recovering, as he applies them.*] Father! father!

Anna. Padre mio!
Otta. Celate, allontanate agli occhi
Suoi quell' oggetto d' orrore!

Oct. [*To the Attendants, pointing to the body.*]
Be speedy, to remove
That thing of terror from her sight far apart now.

[*The Attendants bear off the body. To Anna, whom he has lifted from the ground, and who reclines back in his embrace.*]

Anima mia, consolati, fa core.

Hope of my being; console thyself, take heart now!

SCENA VI.—Donna Anna; Don Ottavia.

Anna. Fuggi, crudele, fuggi;
Lascia che mora anch' io,
Ora ch' è morto, oh Dio!
Chi a me la vita diè.

Otta. Senti cor mio, deh senti!
Guardami un solo istante!
Ti parla il caro amante,
Che vive sol per te.

Anna. Tu sei—perdon—mio bene—
L'affanno mio—le pene—
Ah! il padre mio dov'è?

Otta. Il padre! lascia, o cara
La rimembranza amara;
Hai sposo e padre in me.

Anna. Ah! vendicar, s' il puoi
Giura quel sangue ognor.

Otta. Lo giuro agli occhi tuoi
Lo giuro al nostro amor.

Anna and *Otta.* Che giuramento oh Dei!
Che barbaro momento! Tra cento affetti e cento
Vammi ondeggiando il cor.
                    [*Partono.*

SCENE VI.—Donna Anna; Don Octavio.

Anna. [*Aroused to the misery of her bereavement, breaks wildly from Don Octavio.*]
Fly me, unkind one, fly me!
Hence! since for death I hunger;
Life becomes loathsome, longer,
Now more than life is ta'en.

Oct. [*Tenderly.*]
Hear, then; and turn upon me
Thy lucid eye's reflection:
This heart's divine affection
That life can give again.

Anna. [*Coming to herself more.*]
By thought thro' grief distracted
Wert thou one moment neglected.
My father still is slain.   [*Relapsing*

Oct. Lull, dearest, thine emotion;
And in my deep devotion
As husband, a father retain.

Anna. [*Impressively.*] Up! this ill deed's requiting
Swear by the stars above!

Oct. [*Solemnly.*] I swear it by our plighting,
I swear it by our love!

Anna and *Oct.* [*Raising their eyes.*]
Record the oath, O Heaven!
May righteous Justice, gracing
The cause we are embracing,
Soon its achievement prove!
                    [*Donna Anna is led off by Don Octavio*

The scene changes. The stage represents a rather desolate spot without the walls of Seville; an entrance road to the city leads down a mountain; on one side, the court-yard of an Inn. It is daylight.]

SCENA VII.—*Strada.*—*Entra* Don Giovanni, Lepo-
RELLO.

Gio. Orsù spicciati presto, cosa vuoi?

Lep. L' affar di cui si tratta
E importante.
Gio. Lo credo, e importantissimo.
Meglio ancora. Finiscila.
Lep. Ma giurate di non andar in collera.
Gio. Lo giuro sul mio onore,
Purchè non parli del commendatore.
Lep. Siamo soli?
Gio. Lo vedo.
Lep. Nessun ci sente?
Gio. Via?
Lep. Vi posso dire tutto liberamente?
Gio. Tutto sì.
Lep. Dunque quand' è così.
Caro signor padrone, la vita che menate è da bric-
cone.
Gio. Temerario, in tal guisa!

Lep. E il giuramento?

Gio. Zitto! non si parli
Di giuramento; taci, o ch' io.
Lep. Non parlo più, non fiato, padron mio.

Gio. Così saremo amici. Or odi un poco
Sai tu perchè son quì?
Lep. Non ne so nulla.
Ma essendo l' alba chiara,
Non sarebbe qualche nuova conquista?
Io lo devo saper per porla in lista.
Gio. Va là che sei l' grand' uom; sappi ch' io sono
Innamorato d'una bella dama, e son certo che
m'ama;
La vidi, le parli i meco al casino
Questa notte verrà—zitto mi pare
Sentir odor di femina.

Lep. Cospetto! Che odorato perfetto.

Gio. All' aria mi par bella.

Lep. E che occhia, dico!
Gio. Ritiriamoci un poco, e scopriamo terren.

Lep. Già presa foco.

[*Partono.*]

SCENA VIII.—*Entra* Donna Elvira Don Giovanni
e Leporello, *in disparte*

El. Ah chi mi dice mai
Quel barbaro dov' è?
Che per mio scorno amai,
Che mi manco di fè?
Ah se ritrovo l' empio,
E a me non torna ancor,

Juan. [*As he enters, adjusting his dress; to Leporello, who
follows.*] Well, well, now to the point, man;—what, your
matter?
Lep. Far too important, master, to be sloven'd.

Juan. [*Ironically.*] Most doubtless, as much as usual:—
to the best part, come finish it.
Lep. First swear you will not fly out in a passion.
Juan. I swear it on mine honor; so be't, ye say not
aught of yon Commander.
Lep. [*Mysteriously, looking round.*] Are we soli?
Juan. I hope so.
Lep. [*Whispering.*] With not a fly near?
Juan. [*Staring at him.*] Well!—
Lep. And I can speak my mind out excellent freely?
Juan. Yes—
Lep. [*Pompously.*] Courage, then, for here goes—
Master mine, imp of evil,
The life ye lead will take ye straight to the devil!
Juan. [*Angrily, laying his hand to his sword.*] Forward
rascal! this shall punish—
Lep. [*Making a movement back, and putting up his hand.*]
Your oath, Don Juan!—
Juan. Oaths are merely made for convenience; silence,
or I—
Lep. [*Making an obeisance.*] I will not dare to even
breathe, Sir Patron.
Juan. So do, and we are friends still; your ear one moment! know you my purpose here?
Lep. I ne'er know *nothing*; but since the day commences,
we conjecture *you* commence some new conquest; this I
ought now to know, who keep the record. [*Significantly tapping his jacket pocket.*]
Juan. See shells, and thou'lt guess eggs, wondrous di-
viner! I am enamor'd of a glorious beauty, and am certain she loves me: have seen her, have convers'd, and at
the Casino sure shall meet her to-night. [*He stops short, and
snuffs the air for a moment or two.*] Gently! the zephyr wafts
me an odor feminine—

Lep. [*Aside, astonished.*] (By Janus, his olfactories per-
fect!—)
Juan. [*Looking to one side; his tone heightened.*] Her *taille*
proclaims her lovely.
Lep. [*Aside.*] (And what an eye to match them!)
Juan. [*Pulling Leporello aside.*]
Let us watch the young lady
Just in hearing and sight.
Lep. [*Aside, as he conceals himself with Don Juan behind
a bush.*] (On fire already!)

Elv. [*Entering in a travelling equipment.*]
Mem'ried, his passion lingers
With still delusive sway,
Tho' Truth's relentless fingers
Long dash'd the dream away.
Wild in despairing anger,
I seek the wretch; to prove

Vò farne orrendo scempio,
Gli vò cavar il cor.
Gio. A *Lep.*] Udisti? Qualche bella
Dal vago abbandonata.
Poverina! poverina!
Cerchiam di consolar
Il suo tormento.
Lep. Così ne consola
Mille e ottocento.
Gio. Signorina! signorina!
Elv. Chi è là?
Gio. Stella! che vedo!
Lep. Oh bella! Donna Elvira
Elv. Don Giovanni!
Sei qui! mostro, fellon, nido d' inganni?
Lep. Che titoli cruscanti! manco male,
Che lo conosce bene.
Gio. Via, cara Donna Elvira,
Calmate quella collera;—
Sentite—lasciate mi parlar.
Elv. Cosa puoi dire dopo azion sì nera? In casa mia
entri furtivamente, a forza d' arte, di giuramenti, e
di lusinghe, arrivi a sedurre il cor mio; m' innamori,
o crudele! mi dichiari tua sposa, e poi, mancando della
terra e del ciel al santo dritto con enorme delitto dopo
trè di Burgos d' allontani, m' abbandoni, mi fuggi, e
lasci in preda al rimorso ed al pianto per pena for se
che t' amai cotanto.

Lep. (Pare un libro stampato!)
Gio. Oh, in quanto a questo ebbi le mie ragioni! [*A Lep.*]
E vero?
Lep. E vero, e che ragioni forti.
Elv. E quali sono, se non la tua perfidia, la leggerezza
tua: ma il giusto cielo volle ch' io ti trovassi prefar le
sue, le mie vendette.
Gio. Eh via, siate più ragionevole. Mi pone a cimento
costei. Se non credete al labbro mio, credete aqueste
galantuomo.

Lep. Salvo il vero.
Gio. Via dille un poco.
Lep. [*Piano.*] E cosa devo dirle?
Gio. [*Forte partendo.*] Sì sì, dille pur tutte.

SCENA IX.—DONNA ELVIRA; LEPORELLO

Elv. [*A Lep.*] Ebben, fa presto.
Lep. Madame—veramente, in questo mondo
Concio, sia cosa quando—fosse—che—
Il quadro non è tondo—
Elv. Sciagurata!
Così del mio dolor gioco ti prendi?
[*Versa Don G. che non crede partito.*
Ah voi—stelle! l' iniquo
Fuggì! misera me! dove? in qual parte?
Lep. Eh, lasciate che vada; egli non merta ch' a lui voi
più pensate.
Elv. Il scelerato m' inganno, mi tradì—
Lep. Eh consolatevi! non siete voi, non foste, e non sarete
nè la prima, nè l' ultima; guardate questo non picciol
libro; è tutto pieno dei nomi di sue belle; ogni villa,
ogni borgo ogni paese, è testimon di sue donne che
imprese.
Madamina! il catalogo è questo
Delle belle ch' amò il padron mio
Un catalogo egli è ch' ho fatt' io,
Osservate, leggete con me,

How woman can avenge her,
When stung by outrag'd love.
Juan. [*Aside to Leporello.*] (You hear that? 'tis a damsel
Abandon'd by her lover.
Poor young creature! poor young creature!
To quickly then console
A heart so sunder'd!)
Lep. (He hath "consol'd" thus
Fully eighteen hundred.)
Juan. Fair Señora!
Elv. That voice!
Juan. Gracious, whom see I?
Lep. (Delicious; 'tis Elvira!)
Elv. So, Don Juan, thou'rt here, monster of vice prince
of deceivers!
Lep. (Compliments with a vengeance! 'faith the girl hath
some little knowledge of him.)
Juan. I prithee, dear Elvira, to be, at least, more mod
erate;—just listen—and suffer me to speak—
Elv. Lips of an angel could not clear thy baseness
Within my dwelling entering as a stranger, perforce of
cos'nings of honied falsehood, and of passion, ye triumph'd
in seducing my affections, till, enamor'd to madness, ye de
clared ye mine husband; and then a recreant to the sacred
est ties of earth or heaven, an enormous delinquent, now
for three days from Burgos hast been absent, hast abandon
ed, has fled me, *me* left a prey to remorse and weary weep
ings, mine ineffectual penalty for folly.
Lep. (She hath learnt it by heart, pat!)
Juan. For all you touch on, I had my own good reasons.
[*To Leporello.*] Is't not so?
Lep. Aye, aye, Sir; reasons most truly cogent.
Elv. What other reasons, except that ye *must* gratify an
inborn lust for evil: but Heaven shares mine anger, and
bids Elvira become its instrument of vengeance.
Juan. If so, be but a little sensible. [*Aside.*] (She'll
worry the soul from my skin.) [*To Elvira.*] Since *my* tale
cannot gain you credence, pray credit this good, honest fel-
low. [*Pointing out Leporello.*]
Lep. ("Good!"—at lying.)
Juan. [*To Leporello.*] Explain the matter—
Lep. (Explain *what* explanation?)
Juan. Yes, yes: tell the whole truth. [*He pushes Leporello up to Donna Elvira; and so, attracting her attention, u
slips away.*]

SCENE IX.—DONNA ELVIRA; LEPORELLO.

Elv. Proceed, I prithee.
Lep. Fair lady, in old Euclid exists an axiom—which
goes-about-for-to-have-used-to was; a square is not a circle—
Elv. Senseless ribald! to make a jest of grief; mocking
my sorrows: [*turning, as if toward Don Juan, whom she still
believes near her,*] and you—[*not seeing him*]—heavens! the
cruel wretch hath fled; woe is my lot! whither? in what
direction?
Lep. Eh, just suffer him! "gang his gate," he is worth
less; thought were wasted upon such—
Elv. But then the villain hath deceiv'd, hath betray'd—
Lep. Madam, console thyself; you will not be, nor are
not, nor further have been, either the first one, or last of
'em. [*Taking a book from his pocket.*] Look, here's a not
unextensive volume, and cramm'd chuck full of the names
of even his mistress;
Ev'ry country, ev'ry township, fully confesses
Those of the sex whom to his ranks he presses.
Gentle lady, this my catalogue numbers
All whose charms lent my master beguiling:

In Italia, sei cento e quaran'a,
In Almagna, duecento trent' una ;
Cento in Francia, in Turchia novant' una ;
Ma in Ispagna son già mille e tre !
V' han fra queste, contadine,
Cameriere, cittadine
V' han contesse, Baronesse,
Marchesane, principesse
E v' han donne d' ogni grado,
D' ogni forma, d' ogni età.
Nelle bionda, egli ha l usanza
Di lodar la gentilezza,
Nella bruna la costanza,
Nella bianca la dolcezza ;
Vuol d' inverno la grassotta,
Vuol d' estate la magrotta ;
E la grande, maestosa,
La piccina, ognor vezzosa ;
Delle vecchie fa conquista
Per piacer di porle in lista :
Sua passion predominante
E la giovin princi piante ;
Non si picca, se sia ricca,
Se sia brutta, se sia bella !
Purchè porti la gonnella,
Voi sapete quel che fa.

[*Parte.*

'Tis a document of my compiling,
An it please ye, peruse it with me.
In Italia,—six hundred and forty ;
Then in Germany,—ten score and twenty
As for France,—double fifty seem plenty ;
Whiles in old Spain here,—we count *thousands three*
Some, you see, are country damsels,
Waiting-maids, and city ma'amselles,
Countess'—duchess'—baron-esses,
Viscount'—ev'ry kind of 'esses.
Womenfolk of all conditions,
Ev'ry form, and ev'ry state !
First, the fair one's unthinking blindness
He would dazzle with honied speeches ;
Toward the dark-ey'd all pure kindness,
With the blue-ey'd, he beseeches ;
Winter, he prefers the fatter,
Summer, thin girls suit him better ;
Toward the tallest, bold and haughty,
With the little, he's sly and naughty ;
Old maids' fancies he makes mistier,
Just to swell this scanty list here ;
But he chiefly loves the gender
Budding, young, and ripely tender ;
Rich, or poor, or fair, or hideous,
He, nor dainty nor invidious,
Is with woman most insidious :
You the sequel can relate.

[*He presses the book to his lips with a significant gesture then, pocketing the list, runs off.*

SCENA X.—DONNA ELVIRA, *sola.*

Elv. In questa forma dunque mi tradì il scelerato ! è questo il premio che quel barbaro rende all' amor mio ! ah, vendicar volg' io l' ingannato mio cor ; pria ch' ei mi fugga, si ricorra—si vada—io sento in petto sol vendetta parlar, rabbia, e dispetto.

[*Parte.*

SCENE X.—DONNA ELVIRA, *sola.*

Elv. And after such vile fashion hath the libertine us'd me ! with such a guerdon, doth this barbarian recompense my passion ! Gods, I will have rich justice ; he who stabs at my heart, pays for the mischief ! [*Exit*

The scene changes. The stage represents a beautiful rural prospect among the mountains surrounding Seville ; to the right is seen, amidst its rich gardens, the Palace of Don Giovanni, backed by woods of dark trees ; the Guadalquivir is perceived winding through a valley in the distance.

Zerlina and Masetto, attended by a troop of male and female Peasants, enter, all merrily dancing and singing, they bea[r] wreaths and baskets of flowers, and in their dancing form pretty and appropriate figures and groupings.

SCENA XI.—*Il Contado, con veduta del Palazzo di Don Giovanni.*

ZERLINA ; MASETTO ; *Contadini e Contadine.*

SCENE XI.—ZERLINA ; MASETTO ; *Chorus of Peasants.*

GIOVINETTE, QUE FATTE—PRETTY MAIDENS. CHORUS.

Mas. Giovinetti leggieri di testa,
　　　Non andate girando di quà
　　　Poco dura dei matti la festa,
　　　Ma per me cominciato non ha!
　　　　　Lera, lera la!
　　　Che piacer, che piacer, che sarà!
　　　　　Lera la, lera la!
Coro. Che piacer! La, la, lera!
Zer. } Vieni, vieni, carino carina godiamo,
M 18 }
　　　E cantiamo, e balliamo, e suoniamo!
　　　Che piacer, che piacer, che sarà!
Coro. Che piacer! La, la, lera!

SCENA XII.—*Entra* DON GIOVANNI *e* LEPORELLO.

Gio. (Manco male è partita ;) ah guarda, guarda ch'è bella
　　　gioventù ! che belle donne!
Lep. (Tra tanete per mia fè, vi sarà qualche cosa anchè
　　　per me.)
Gio. Cari amici, buon giorno ! seguitate a star' allegramente ; seguitate a suonar, o buona gente. C' è qualche sposalizio ?
Zer. Sì signore, e la sposa son io.
Gio. Mene consolo. Lo sposo ?
Mas. Io, per servirla.
Gio. Oh bravo ? per servirmi. Questo è vero parlar di
　　　galantuomo.
Lep. (Basta, che sia marito.)
Zer. Oh, il mio Masetto è un uom d' ottimo core.
Gio. Oh anch' io, vedete ! Voglio che siamo amici ; il
　　　vostro nome ?
Zer. Zerlina.
Gio. E il tuo ?
Mas. Masetto.
Gio. Oh, caro il mio Masetto! Cara la mia Zerlina, v'
　　　esibisco la mia protezione. Leporello!—Cosa fai lì,
　　　birbone ?
Lep. Anch' io, caro padrone, esibisco la mia protezione.

Gio. Presto va non costor; nel mio palazzo conducili sul
　　　fatto ; ordina ch' abbiano cioccolatte, caffè, vini, presciutti ; cerca, divertir tutti ; mostra loro il giardino la
　　　galeria, le camere ; (in effetto fa che resti contento il
　　　mio Masetto. Hai capito ?)

Lep. (Ho capito ;) andiam.

Mas. Signore !
Gio. Cosa c' è ?
Mas. La Zerlina senza me non può star.
Lep. In vostro loco ci sarà sua eccellenza, e saprà bene
　　　fare le vostro parti.
Gio. Oh, la Zerlina è in man d' un cavalier ; va pur ; fra
　　　poco ella meco verrà.
Zer. Và, non temere ; nelle mani son io d' un cavaliere.

Mas. E per ouesto ?
Lep. E per questo non c' è da dubitar.
Mas. Ed io, cospetto !
Gio. Olà ! Finiam le dispute ; se subito senz' altro rep
　　　car, non te ne vai, Masetto, guarda ben, ti penirai.

Mas. Hò capito, Signor, si !
　　　Chino il capo, e mene vò,
　　　Giacchè piace a voi così,
　　　Altre repiiche non fò.
　　　"Cavalier," voi siete già
　　　Dubitar non posso affè :

Mas. Gentle lads, flying hither and thither,
　　　Like a shuttle despatch'd thro' a loom,
　　Just behold me, and ponder it, whether
　　　Any joy near my pleasure can come.
　　　What a sunshine doth all now assume !
Cho. 　　La la la ! Lala la !
　　　What a sunshine doth all now assume !
　　　　　La la la, lera !
Zer. & } Then, my love, with our dancing and singing,
Mas. } Let the wide-spreading echo be ringing,
　　　An eternal adieu to all gloom !
Cho. 　　An eternal adieu to all gloom !
　　　　La la, la lera, la la la, la lera !

SCENE XII.—*The same;* DON JUAN; LEPORELLO.

Juan. So the pest has departed. O, look here ! look here
　　　what appetizing youth ! what lovely women !
Lep. (Egad, amongst so many, I hope to pick pickings
　　　for myself.)
Juan. Dearest friends, a good morning ! nay, stand not
　　　check'd thus of your joyful purpose ; pray continue
　　　the dance, my worthy people : surely this is a wedding ?
Zer. Truly Señor, and the bride is before you.
Juan. Gladly I learn it—thy bridegroom ?
Mas. Here, at your service.
Juan. O bravo ! "at my service," that bespeaks ye in truth
　　　a gallant fellow.
Lep. (Husbands that serve *him*, are so.)
Zer. Sir, my Masetto's a lad of ev'ry goodness.
Juan. That am I also ; let us be friends *instanter :* your
　　　name, my darling ?
Zer. Zerlina.
Juan. And thine, friend ?
Mas. Masetto.
Juan. My very dear Masetto, dearest mine own Zerlina, let
　　　this give an earnest of my protection. Leporello ! what
　　　art thou after, varlet ?
Lep. What after ! my good master : giving earnest of my
　　　protection, truly.
Juan. Pray postpone your intent : conduct these gentlefolk
　　　straightway to my palace ; order them chocolate, give
　　　them coffee, with wine, cake, and preserves too ; mind,
　　　amuse the whole bevy ; show them right round the garden, explain the pictures, the galleries ; (yet, in fact,
　　　make chief endeavor to occupy Masetto ; do you take,
　　　man ?

Lep. (Like a leech.) [*To the Peasants, placing himself between Masetto and Zerlina, and pushing the former before
　　　him.*] Away !
Mas. [*To Don Juan.*] But, Señor ?
Juan. What wouldst say ?
Mas. That Zerlina cannot stop here without me.
Lep. Good fellow, you must yield in place to his lordship,
　　　who doubtless knoweth well how to act in *your* part.
Juan. O, your Zerlina stays with a cavalier ; proceed, you
　　　shortly will see her again.
Zer. Go, dreading nothing ; in a gentleman's hands I fear
　　　no evil.
Mas. For which reason ?
Zer. For which reason I will not suffer doubt.
Mas. Nor I, by Pluto !—
Juan. What ho ! cut short this quarrelling ! Suppressing
　　　further syllables, if ye do not absent it, (*pointing to his
　　　sword,*) Masetto, have a care ; ye may repent it !
Mas. O, I take you ; Señor, see,
　　　Making reverence, I go ;
　　　My removal hath a plea,
　　　Guessing which, I am not slow ;
　　　"Cavalier" you well are nam'd,
　　　Could a doubt one moment be ?

Me lo dice la b :nth
Che volete aver per me
[A Zer.] (Bricconaccia, malandrina,
Fosti ognor la mia ruina.)
[A Lep.] Vengo, vengo! [A Zer!] resta, resta
E' una cosa molta onesta,
Faccia il nostr' Cavaliere,
Cavaliere ancora te.

[Parte con Leporello.

Since the title is proclaim'd
In this good design'd for me.
(Ugh, you hussey! born to ruin
Viper! bred to breed undoing.)
[To Lep.] Coming, coming! [To Zerlina.] Stay behind me
Artful slut, you cannot blind me;
Stay, and let your "cavalier" there
Have a leer again at thee!
[Pushed off unwillingly by Leporello, Masetto follows the
Peasants, who depart as Don Juan has directed.]

SCENA XIII.—Zerlina, Giovanni.

Gio. Alfin siam liberati, Zerlinetta gentil, da qual scioc-
cone. Che ne dite, mio ben, so far pulito?

Zer. Signore, è mio marito.
Gio. Chi? colui? vi par ch' un' onest' uomo, un nobil
cavalier, qual io mi vanto, possa soffrir che qual viserto
d' oro, quel viso inzuccherato da un bifolcaccio vil sia
strapazzato?

Zer. Ma, signore, io gli diedi parola di sposarlo.

Gio. Tal parola non vale un zero · voi non siete fatta per
esser paesana; un' altro sorte vi procuran quegli occhi
briconelli. Quei labretti si belli quelle ditaccia can-
dide, e odorose; parmi toccar giuncata, e fiutar rose.

Zer. Ah non vorrei!
Gio. Che non vorreste?
Zer. Alfine ingannata restar; io so che rado colle donne
voi altri cavalieri siete onesti e sinceri.

Gio. E un' impostura della gente plebea. La nobiltà ha
dipinta negli occhi l' onestà. Orsù non perdiam tempo; in quest' instante io voglio sposar.

Zer. Voi?
Gio. Certo: io. Qual casinetto e mio; soli saremo e la,
giojello mio, ci sposeremo.

SCENE XIII.—Zerlina, Don Juan.

Juan. Now are we liberated, Zerlinetta my love, from that
great baby; and is mine not, in truth, first-rate contrivance?

Zer. Señor he's my affianc'd.
Juan. He? your spouse? think you an honest gentle, a
noble cavalier, (the which I hold me,) ever can suffer
such enchanting beauty, such ravishing demeanors, to
waste their sweetness on a clownish clod-pole?

Zer. Soft! fair master; I have given my promise to espouse him.

Juan. Such promise is written on water; thou wert
not created merely to live a peasant; far other be
it! O those glances that glow in light like lode-stars,
O those lips of a Hebe, that voice whose whisper
breathes more music than a nightingale's soul, must
win thee a daintier fortune.

Zer. Ah, but I dare not—
Juan. You dare not, what, child?—
Zer. Be flatter'd,—then deceiv'd and betray'd · we know
you gentlefolk are strangely dishonest with us women
in the fashions of virtue.

Juan. That vulgar notion is too ultra-plebeian; for learn
that honesty e'er was co-nate with noble birth; the
hour is most propitious,—this very moment will I
make thee my wife.

Zer. [Astonished.] You?
Juan. Of a surety: Yonder secluded villa, snugly shall house
And there, joy of my being, will I espouse thee! [thee.

LA CI DAREM—NAY, BID ME NOT. DUET.

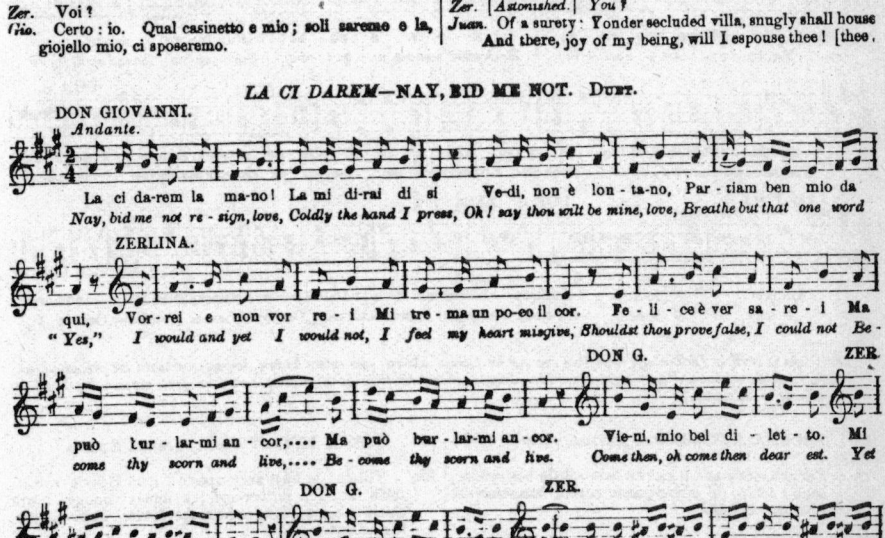

DON GIOVANNI.
Andante.

La ci da-rem la ma-no! La mi di-rai di sì Ve-di, non è lon-ta-no, Par-tiam ben mio da
Nay, bid me not re-sign, love, Coldly the hand I press, Oh! say thou wilt be mine, love, Breathe but that one word

ZERLINA.

qui, Vor-rei e non vor re-i Mi tre-ma un po-co il cor. Fe-li-ce è ver sa-re-i Ma
"Yes," I would and yet I would not, I feel my heart misgive, Shouldst thou prove false, I could not Be-

DON G.   ZER.

può tur-lar-mi an-cor,..... Ma può bur-lar-mi an-cor. Vie-ni, mio bel di-let-to. Mi
come thy scorn and live,..... Be-come thy scorn and live. Come then, oh come then dear-est. Yet

DON G.   ZER.

fa pie-tà Ma-set-to. Io cangie-rò tua sor-te. Pre-sto non son più for-te, non son più
should thy fondness al-ter, Nay, love, in vain thou fearest. Still, still this heart will fal-ter this heart will

for - te, non son più   for - te. Vie-ni vie - ni! La ci da-rem la ma-no. Vor-rei e non vor-rei - i.
fal - ter, this heart will fal-ter. Come then, come then! Nay, bid me not resign, love. I would, and yet I would not

La mi di rai di - sì. Mi trema un po-co il cor. Partiam ben mio, da qui. Ma.... può bur-lar - mi an
Oh say thou wilt be mine. I feel my heart mis-give. Nay, love, in vain thou fear'st. I.... feel my heart   mis

cor,   Mi fa   pie - ta Ma - set - to,   Pre - sto non son più
give.   Yet   should thy fond - ness al - tar, Still,... still this heart will

Vie - ni mio bel di - let - te,   Io cangie - rò tua sor - te.
Come then, oh come then dear - est,   Nay, love in vain thou fear-est.

for - te non son più for - te non son più for - te. An - diam, an - diam. An - diam.
fal - ter, this heart will fal - ter, this heart will fal - ter. Oh come, then come. I come.

Andim, andiam mio be - ne, A ri-sto-rar le pe - ne D'un in-no - cen-te a-mor.
Yes, hand and heart u-nit-ing, Each other's cause re-quit-ing, Our joy no bound shall know

Andiam andiam mio be - ne A ri-sto-rar le pe-ne D'un in-no-cen-te amor. Andiam.
Yes, hand and heart u-nit-ing, Each other's vows requit-ing, Our joy no bounds shall know. Oh come.

Andiam,   Andiam,   Andiam. Andiam mio be-ne andiam Le pene a ristorar D'un in-no-cen-te amo'
I come,   I come.   Oh come. Our joy no bounds shall know, Our joy no bounds shall know, Our joy, &c.

|*Don Juan is leading Zerlina off, when they are met by Donna Elvira, who enters hastily, having overheard the preceding, and indignantly snatches the Peasant-girl from Don Juan's grasp; he falls back angrily and annoyed, placing his hand instinctively to his sword.]*

SCENA XIV.—Donna Elvira, e detto.	SCENE XIV.—The same; Donna Elvira.
Elv. Fermati, scelerato, il ciel mi fede udir le tue perfidie; io sono a tempo di salvar questa misera, innocente dal tuo barbaro artiglio.	*Elv.* Villain! to what art purpos'd? kind Heav'n reveal thine hest for further evil; a timely coming, I will shield this pure dovelet from the fowler, from his barbarous snarings.
Zer. Meschina! cosa sento!	*Zer.* Ah, woe is me! what hear I?
Gio. (Amor, consiglio.) Idol mio, non v'adete ch' io voglio divertirmi?	*Juan.* (Now Cupid, counsel!) [*To Elvira.*] My dear creature, observe then, I merely wish to amuse me.

Elv. Divertirti, è vero, divertirti? io so crudele, come tu diverti

Zer. Ma, signor cavaliere, è ver quel ch' ella dice?

Gio. La provera infelice è di me innamorata e per pietà deggio fingere amore, ch' io son per mia disgrazia uom di buon core. [*Don G. parte.*

Elv. Ah, fuggi il traditor.
Non le lascia più dir;
Il labbro è mentitor,
Fallace il ciglio.
Da miei tormenti impara,
A creder a quel cor,
E nasca il tuo timor
Dal mio periglio!
[*Partono.*

SCENA XV.—*Entra* Don Giovanni, Don Ottavio *e* Donna Anna.

Gio. Mi par ch' oggi il demonio si diverta, d' opporsi a miei piace voli progressi, vanno mal tutti quanti.

Otta. Ah! ch' ora, idolo mio, son vani i pianti. Di vendetta si parli. Oh! Don Giovanni!

Gio. (Mancava questo intoppo.)

Anna. Amico, a tempo vi ritroviam; avete core, avete anima generosa?

Gio. (Sta a vedere, ch' il diavolo gli ha detto qualche cosa?) Che domanda! perchè?

Anna. Bisogno abbiamo della vostra amicizia.

Gio. (Mi torna il fiato in corpo,) Comandate? congiunti, i parenti, questa man, questo ferro, i beni, il sangue spenderò per servirvi. Ma voi, bella Donn' Anna, perchè così piangete? Il crudele che fù? che cosa la calma turbar del viver vostrò?

SCENA XVI.—*Entra* Donna Elvira

Elv. [*A Giov.*] Ah ti ritrove ancor, perfido mostro!
[*A Donna Anna.*] Non ti fidar, o misera,
Di quel ribaldo cor!
Me gia tradi quel barbaro,
Te vuol tradir ancor.

Otta e Anna. Cieli! che aspetto nobile!
Che dolce maesta!
Il suo dolor, le lagrime
M' empiono di pietà.

Gio. La povera ragazza
E pazza, amici miei;
Lasciatemi con lei,
Forse si calmera.

Elv. Ah non credete al perfido!

Gio. E pazza, non badate!

Elv. Restate, oh Dei! restate.

Anna e Otta. A chi si crederà!

Gio. *Anna e Otta.* Certo moto d' ignote tormento
Dentro l' alma girare mi sento,
Che mi dice per quella infelice
Cento cose ch' intender non sà.

Gio. (Certo moto d' ignoto tormento
D' entro l' alma girare mi sento,
Che mi dice per quella infelice
Cento cose che intender non sa.)

Elv. Sdegno, rabbia, dispetto, pavento,
Dentro l' alma giraremi sento,
Ch' mi dice di quel traditore
Cento cose che intender non sa.

Otta. Io di quà non vado via,
Se non so son com' è l' affar

Elv. "To amuse" ye, an't please you! "to amuse" ye! too clear acquaintance bear I, of thine amusements.

Zer. But Señor Cavalier now, haply her words are truth some?

Juan. Really she's mad about me, the unfortunate female;
From sheerest pity, I bend to her blindness,
My heart's chief failing, being too much of kindness
[*Exit*

Elv. A lie is on his lip,
Deceit behind his smile;
Their poison do not sip,
Else woe is ensuing.
His crimes are vast as ocean;
The trust I bade to sleep
Upon their treach'rous deep,
Did wake to ruin.
[*Donna Elvira retreats, leading Zerlina.*

SCENE XV.—Don Juan; *then* Donna Anna *and* Don Octavio.

Juan. Beelzebub's self hath made my plans his foot-ball;
I will that things should take a fixed progression, and they fly *vice versa.*

Oct. Ah, fain would I assure thee how vain are weepings; let all speech be of vengeance: welcome, Don Juan!

Juan. (This new hindrance gives the finish.)

Anna. Don Juan, most opportunely we meet; and have ye courage? and hast a generous noble spirit?

Juan. (Hath the foul fiend then set her scent right on that ugly mischief?) Strange your questions! and why?

Anna. We much have need, Sir, of your kindly assistance.

Juan. (Ouf! I take breath more freely!) Speak the mandate, mine adherents, my relations, this my hand, this my weapon, my poor wealth, life, and existence, stand at your service. Alas, loveliest Anna, why thus the child of sorrow? hath thy peace been assailed?
What vile occurrence hath basely ventur'd *this* deed?—

SCENE XVI.—*The scene;* Donna Elvira.

Elv. [*To Don Juan.*] Thee do I find again? monster of misdeed!
[*To Donna Anna.*] Rather repose thy faith on air
Than in that viper-tongue;
Lest it destroy thine own pure heart,
Even as mine it stung.

Anna & Oct. Surely; there, pure nobility
Maintains undoubted sway:
This mien of woe, this mournful plaint,
Much in her favor say.

Juan. A poor demented lady,
A source of frequent sadness;
If left to me, her madness
Haply I calm away.

Elv. Ah, credit not the foe to Truth.

Juan. Pray go; she's quite insane now.

Elv. Remain! O God, remain now!

Anna & Oct. (Each point a devious way;
An unutter'd expression of feeling
Is a watchful suspicion concealing
In my breast, where, for eloquent sorrow,
Thousand *thousand* kind sympathies lay.)

Juan. (An unutter'd expression of feeling
Is a watchful suspicion concealing,
Lest this woman run rampant in sorrow,
Half a hint at the real truth essay.)

Elv. Anger, fury, distractions, despairing
Ev'ry chord thro' my being are tearing:
Language lingers for passion and power
True in color the villain to lay.

Oct. I would scan the matter clearly
Ere from this affair we part.

Anna. Non ha l' aria di pazzia	*Anna.* She hath spoken sure, sincerely;
Il suo tratto, il suo parlar.	Sane her mind, tho' bruis'd the heart.
Gio. (Se men vado, si potrai,	*Juan.* (To conceal things, very nearly
Qualche cosa sospettar.)	Conquers my consummate art.)
Flv. Da quel ceffo si dovria	*Elv.* O, observe that glance! how really
La ner' alma giudicar.	It depicts his cold dark heart.
Otta. Dunque quella? [*A Don Giovanni.*	*Oct.* These, are fancies?—
Gio. E pazzarella.	*Juan.* She's lost her senses.
Anna. Dunque quegli? [*A Donna Elvira.*	*Anna.* So, Don Juan?—
Elv. E un traditore.	*Elv.* Would now deceive him
Gio. Infelice!	*Juan.* Poor lost creature!
Elv. Mentitore!	*Elv.* Ne'er believe him!
Anna e Otta. (Incomincio a dubitar.)	*Anna & Oct.* (Doubts, our various judgment part
Gio. Zitto, zitto? che la gente	*Juan.* Gently, gently, this mad gabble
Si raduna à noi d' intorno;	May excite a crowd's attention;
Siate un poco piu prudente	Somewhat roughly, too, your rabble
Vi farete criticar.	Exercise the critic art.
Elv. Non sperarlo, o scelerato!	*Elv.* That my weakling voice were thunder!
Ho perduta la prudenza,	That my throat were throat of iron!
Le tue colpe ed il mio stato	I, to Earth all mute with wonder
Voglio a tutti palesar.	Would thy myriad crimes impart.
Otta e Anna. Quegli accenti sì sommessi,	*Anna & Oct.* (These her accents, so impressive,
Quel cangiar sì di colore,	His attempt to treat them coolly,
Sono indizj troppo espressi	Are an index too expressive
Che mi fan determinar.	Of the shoals that throng the chart.)
[*Elvira parte.*	[*Donna Elvira quits the scene*

SCENA XVII.—DONNA ANNA; DON OTTAVIO; DON GIOVANNI.

SCENE XVII.—DONNA ANNA, DON OCTAVIO; DON JUAN.

Gio. Povera sventurata! i passi suoi voglio seguir; non voglio che faccia un precipizio; perdonate, bellissima Donn' Anna: se servirvi poss' io, in mia casa v' aspetto. Amici, addio.
[*Parte.*

Juan. [*To them.*] Wretched afflicted woman! with ev'ry haste I follow her steps; I would not she did herself some rashness: an my poor service suit ye, Donna Anna, of its aid freely borrow. 'Neath my roof I expect ye, 'till when friends, good morrow!
[*He runs off unconcernedly towards his Palace*

SCENA XVIII.—DONNA ANNA, DON OTTAVIO.

SCENE XVIII.—DONNA ANNA; DON OCTA

Anna. Don Ottavio, son morta!	*Anna.* Don Octavio, I perish!
Otta. Cos' è stato?	*Oct.* What hath happen'd?
Anna. Per pietà soccorretemi!	*Anna.* 'Tend me help, give me ev'ry aid!
Otta. Mio ben, fate coraggio.	*Oct.* Take courage, courage, fair mourner.
Anna. Oh Dei! quegli è il carnefice	*Anna.* O Heavens! O Heavens! that is the murderer
Del padre mio.	Who slew my father.
Otta. Che dite?	*Oct.* How say you?
Anna. Non dubitate più;	*Anna.* Without a shade of doubt:
Gli ultimi accenti che l' empio proferì,	Every accent his glozing lies gave birth,
Tutta la voce richiamar nel cor mio	Ev'ry demeanor doth proclaim him the wretch
Di quell' indegno che nel mio appartamento—	Who dar'd to violate my secluded chamber—
Otta. Oh, Ciel! possibile, che sotto	*Oct.* O God! could he beneath the sacred cloak of early
Il sacro manto d' amicizia—	friendship? [attempting
Ma come fu?—Narratemi lo strano avvenimento.	The sequel, pray; give me acquaintance of this dark
Anna. Era già alquanto avanzata la notte	*Anna.* Slumber and midnight held the rein of all Nature,
Quando, nelle mie stanze, (ove soletta	When, within mine apartment (where passing lonely
Mi trovai per sventura,) entrar io vidi	I sate buried in dreamings) behold there enter'd
In un mantello avvolto un uom,	Envelop'd in a mantle, a man,
Ch' al primo istante avea preso per voi:	Whom for the moment I did think to be thee, love
Ma riconobbi poi ch' un inganno era il mio.	That too delicious hope was destroyed in its budding.
Otta. Stelle! seguite.	*Oct.* Heavens! continue—
Anna. Tacito a me s' appressa,	*Anna.* Tacitly drew he near me
E m. vuol abbracciar; sciogliermi cerco,	With intent to embrace, back I repuls'd him;
E più mi stringe, io grido! non viene alcun;	He presses o me, I shriek aloud; none aid is nigh—
Con una mano cerca d' impedir la voce,	Now with one impious hand quite enhindering utterance
E coll' altra m' afferra stretta così,	He constrain'd with its fellow, so tight his grasp
Che già mi credo vinta.	I fear'd me all o'erpower'd—
Otta. Perfido! e alfin?	*Oct.* Terrible! and then?—
Anna. Alfine il duol, l' orrore	*Anna.* Grief, shame, and dread, worst horror [Samson
Dell' infame attentato accrebbe sì la lena mia,	Of the villainous purpose did nerve my frame into a
Che a forza di svincolarmi, torcermi,	Perforce of the subtlest writhings, tortuous and elusive
E piegarmi, da lui mi sciolsi.	From him I broke loose.

Ohimè ! respiro.	**Oct.** This heart again beats.
An. Allora rinforzo i stridi miei,	**Anna.** And then were my shrieks for help redoubled—
Chiamo soccorso ; fugge il fellon,	Dreading their upshot, he sought escape ;
Arditamente il seguo fin nella strada per fermarlo,	With lightning-speed I follow down the court-yard
E sono assalatrice d' assalita ;	to prevent him :
Il padre v' accorre, vuol conoscerlo, e l' indegno,	Becoming of mine assailant the assailer !
Cae del povero vecchio era più forte,	My father would rescue, straight doth challenge him ,
Compie il misfatta suo col dargli morte !	and the felon
	Overcoming those grey hairs 'neath our own portal,
Or sai chi l' onore	Fulfill'd his lust for evil, with blow too mortal !
Rapir' a me volse,	Now know the betrayer
Chi l h il traditore,	Who aim'd at mine honor,
Ch' il padre mi tolse.	Now learn who was slayer
Vendetta ti chieggio,	Of this life's dear donor !
La chiede il tuo cor,	To Vengeance I call thee,
Rammenta la piaga,	Need Love call for more ?
Del misero seno ;	Remember, o'er sorrow
Rimira di sangue	In mis'ry I've ponder'd ;
Coperto il terreno,	Bethink thee with anguish
Se l' ira in te langue	Whose blood hath been squander'd ;
D' un giusto furor. [*Parte.*	Nor tarry, nor languish
	Till Justice shall soar ! [*Exit.*

SCENA XIX.—Don Ottavio, *solo*.   **SCENE XIX.—Don Octavio, *solus*.**

Otta Come mai creder deggio	**Oct.** How can credence accept it ? than the blackest de-
Di nero delitto	linquent yon cavalier were viler : so be the truth dis-
Capace un cavaliere !	cover'd, not a means shall be lacking ; within this
Ah di scoprire il vero	bosom
Ogni mezzo si cerchi, io sento in petto	Both Affection and my Friendship are the heralds to
E di sposo, e d' amico	action,
Il dover che mi parla,	He who achiev'd this guilt,—yieldeth satisfaction !
Disingannarla voglio, o vendicarla.	

DALLA SUA PACE—ON HER APPEASING. Don Ottavio.

Quel che le in-cre - sce, mor - te mi dà,   mor - te,   mor - te mi da, Dal-la sua pa-ce   la mia di -
There her last grievings mor - tal - ly wound,   Griev - ings   mor - tal - ly wound. On her appeasing, all peace de

pen - de,   Quel ch' a lei pia - ce   vi - ta mi ren de   Quel che le in-cre - sce   mor - te mi
pendeth,   To that sweet pleasing   all ef-fort tend - eth, Here her last griev - ings   mor - tal - ly

dà,   mor - te, mor-te mi dà,   mor - te mi dà, quel che le in-cre - sce mor - te mi da.
wound,   Griev - ings mor - tal - ly wound,   mor - tal - ly wound, Here, her last griev - ings mor - tal - ly wound.

SCENA XX.—*Entra* LEPORELLO *e* DON GIOVANNI.

Lep.   Io deggio ad ogni patto per sempre abbandonar questo belmatto. Eccolo qui; guardate con qual indifferenzza se ne viene.

Gio.   Leporellino mio, va tutto bene ?

Lep.   Don Giovannino mio, va tutto male.

Gio.   Come, va tutto male ?

Lep.   Vado a casa, come voi m' ordinaste, con tutta quella gente.

Gio.   Bravo !

Lep.   A forza di chiacchere, di vezzi, e di bugie, ch' ho imparato sì bene a star con voi, cero d' intrattenerli.

Gio.   Bravo !

Lep.   Dico mille cose a Masetto per placarlo, per trargli dal pensier la gelosia.

Gio.   Ma bravo, in fede mia !

Lep.   Faccio che bevano e gli uomini e le donne : son già mezzo ubbriacchi ; altri canta, altri scherza, altra seguita a ber ; in sul più bello chi credete che capiti ?

Gio.   Zerlina.

Lep.   Bravo ! e con lei chi venne ?

Gio.   Donna Elvira.

Lep.   Bravo ! e disse di voi—

Gio.   Tutto quel mal ch' in bocca le venia.

Lep.   Ma bravo in fede mia.

Gio.   E tu, cosa facesti ?

Lep.   Tacqui.

Gio.   Ed ella ?

Lep.   Segui a gridar.

Gio.   E tu ?

Lep.   Quando mi parve che già fosse sfogata, dolcemente fuor dell' orto la trassi, e con bell' arte chiusa la porta a chiave io me n' andai, e sulla vio soletta io la lasciai.

Gio.   Bravo, bravo, arcibravo ! l' affar non può andar meglio, incominciasti, io saprò terminar ; troppo mi premono queste coutadinotte ; le voglio divertir finchè vien notte

SCENE XX.—LEPORELLO ; *then* DON JUAN.

Lep.   Now comes the tug of battle, for I must close accounts with this fine madman ! ah, here he is ; only just mark his cucumber-indiff'rence.

Juan.   Good little Leporello ; hath all gone rightly ?

Lep.   Good little Juanetto ; the rather—wrongly !

Juan.   What do you mean by " wrongly ?"

Lep.   All those people I conducted straightway up to your saintship's palace—

Juan.   Bravo !

Lep.   Perforce of much chattering, caressing, and such humbug, which I learnt, by the bye, in your sweet service, sought I to entertain them—

Juan.   Bravo ! on my very conscience.

Lep.   I then fudge up all I could think of to Masetto, to scour his cranium of that jealous nonsense.—

Juan.   Bravo ! on my very conscience.

Lep.   Then do I set about a-feasting men and women, 'till the best half are tipsy : some are jesting, some singing, some continue to drink ;—when, just guess ; who comes tumbling in ?

Juan.   Zerlina !

Lep.   Bravo ! and now, who came with her ?

Juan.   Why, Elvira !

Lep.   Bravo ! and expressing toward you—

Juan.   Ev'ry foul epithet her mouth could muster !

Lep.   [*Rubbing his hands.*] Bravo too ! upon my very conscience.

Juan.   And what were you amidst all ?—

Lep.   Mum, Sir.

Juan.   The lady ?—

Lep.   Kick'd up a row.

Juan.   And then ?—

Lep.   When it appear'd she'd fixa'd the whole of her rage off, I did lead her passing gently, forth from the garden, and having oos'd her gradually quite through the wicket, double-lock'd it : and she did find her shut out on the roadway.

Juan.   Bravo ! bravo ! extra bravo ! th' affair could not go better ; your good beginning, I now know how to end With these young country-girls, fain would I pass some slight time,

Amuse them therefore well, until the nigh' time

FIN CH' HAN DAL VINO—WINE, FLOW A FOUNTAIN! Don Juan.

Fin ch'han dal vi - no, Cal-da la tes-ta, U-na gran fes-ta Fa pre-pa-rar, Se trovi in piazza;
Wine, flow a foun-tain! Eve-ry ves-tal, Bid to the fes-tal, Quickly re-pair, Home, by the ci-ty,

Qual-che ra-gaz za, Te-co ancor quel-la Cer-ca me-nar, Teco an-cor quel-la Cer-ca me
All that are pret-ty, Take them beneath Thine ex-cel-lent care, Take them beneath Thine ex-cel-lent

nar; cer-ca me-nar, cer-ca me-nar. Sen-z'al-cun or-di-ne, La danza si-a, Ch'il min-u-et-to,
care, ex-cel-lent care, ex-cel-lent care, Then, set them tripping it, Wilful or willing; Those min-u-etting,

Chi la fo-li-a— Chi l'A-le-ma-na; Fa-rai bal-lar; Ch'il mi-nu-et-to Fa-rai bal-lar, Chi
Those segui-dilling, Some a Bo-le-ro On-ly may care. These se-gue-dill-ing On-ly may care, Some

la fol-li-a Fa-rai bal-lar; Chi l'A-le-ma-na, Fa-rai bal-lar; Ed io frattan-to, Dall' al-tro
a bo-le-ro On-ly may care, Some a bo-le-ro On-ly may care; I shall en-joy in Si-ly de

can-to, Con ques-ta e quel-la, Vo'amo-reg-giar, Vo'amo-reg-giar, Vo' amo-reg-giar...............
coy-ing One or a-noth-er, Love to de-clare, Love to de-clare, Love to de-clare............

Ah la mia li-sta, Do-man mat-ti-na, D'u-na de-ci-na de-vi aumen-tar.
My list a-dorn-ing, Long ere the morn-ing, Ful-ly with twen-ty Names of the fair.

[The scene changes. The stage represents the garden of Don Juan's Palace: on one side is a wing of that building, the open windows and colonades of which show, during the progress of the scene, the illuminations preparing within for the ball: a window has a balcony which projects; thick rose-bushes are scattered about: the valley of the Guadalquivir is seen in the distance. It is evening, and the new moon's crescent just peeps over the distant Sierra Nevada.
Zerlina enters following Masetto, who appears cross and out of humor with her.]

SCENA XXI.—Zerlina, Masetto.

Zer. Masetto! senti un pò; Masetto, dico.

Mas. Non mi toccar

Zer. Perchè?

Mas. Perchè mi chiedi? Perfida! il tutto sopportar dovrei d' una mano infedele?

Zer. Ah no! taci, crudele, io non merto Da te tal trattamento.

Mas. Come! ed hai l' ardimento di scusarti? star sola con un uom, abbandonarmi il dì delle mie nozze, porre in fronte a un villano d' onore questa marca d' infamia! ah se non fosse, se non fosse lo scandalo, vorrei—

Ma se colpa io non ho, ma se da lui ingannata rimasi: e poi che temi? tranquillati, mia vita, non mi toccò la punta delle dita. Non me lo credi ingrato? Vien mi, sfogati, ammazzami, fa tutto di me quel che ti piace; ma poi, Masetto poi, ma poi fa pace

SCENE XXI.—Zerlina; Masetto.

Zer. Masetto! list awhile; Masetto dearest—

Mas. Go, go away!

Zer. And why?

Mas. And why dost ask me? traitoress! to what conditions of distraction hath thy faithlessness brought me!

Zer. No, no; silence, unkind one; do I merit from thee so harsh a treatment?

Mas. How now? and have ye the face to dream excuses? to stay here with a man—and thus abandon me the day of our nuptials—and to chequer a peasant's rough honor with this mark of ill-favor! Ah, if it were not —if . were not too scandalous—I fain would—

Zer. If the fault be no more, if so his brilliancy dazzled one moment, what further fear, love? be tranquil, mine existence: for in his speech there nothing lay to harm me. [*Masetto turns away.*] Ah, give me credit, ungrateful! [*Putting her arms around his neck.*] Come here beat me, love; destroy me, love;
E'en do to me as it best may please thee;
Do all, Masetto dearest, so it appease thee

BATTI, BATTI.—CHIDE ME, CHIDE ME. ZERLINA.

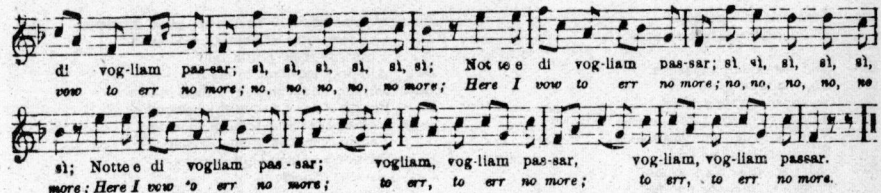

d! vog-liam pas-sar; sì, sì, sì, sì, sì, sì; Not-te e di vog-liam pas-sar; sì, sì, sì, sì, sì,
vow to err no more; no, no, no, no, no more; Here I vow to err no more; no, no, no, no, no

sì; Notte e di vogliam pas-sar; vogliam, vog-liam pas-sar, vog-liam, vog-liam passar.
more; Here I vow 'o err no more; to err, to err no more; to err, to err no more.

SCENA XXII.—Zerlina, Masetto, Don Giovanni.	SCENE XXII.—The same; Don Juan, within.
Mas. Guarda un pò, come seppe questa strega sedurmi! Siamo pure i deboli di testa.	*Mas.* Look you now, how this gipsy hath the clue to seduce me! O, a man is the weakest thing in Nature.
Gio. Sia preparato tutto a una gran festa. [*E dentro.*	*Juan.* [*Within.*] Cause that the entertainment be truly splendid.
Zer. Ah! Masetto! odi la voce del monzù cavaliero!	*Zer.* Ah Masetto, Masetto, hark to the accents of Monsieur your late rival!
Mas. Ebben, che c' è!	*Mas.* What's that to me?
Zer. Verrà.	*Zer.* He comes.
Mas. Lascia che venga.	*Mas.* Let him! and welcome.
Zer. Ah! se vi fosse un buco da fuggir—	*Zer.* Were there a nut-shell within which I could creep!
Mas. Di cosa temi? perchè diventi palìda! ah capisco, capisco, bricconcella; hai timor, ch' io comprenda com' è tra voi passata la faccenda. Presto! presto! pria ch' ei venga por mi vo da qualche lato: c' è una nicchia, qui celato cheto cheto mi vò star.	*Mas.* And why thus fearful? why quits the rose thy pallid cheek? so; I spy it! I spy the truth, sly hussey! Wouldst deceive me, and mean you I should not see the what hath pass'd between you! Presto, presto, ere he enter; Since a shade or so suspicious, To a niche here quite propitious, Coyly, coyly I repair.
Zer. Senti, senti! dove vai? non t' asconder, o Masetto, se ti trova, poveretto, tu non sai quel che può far.	*Zer.* But a whisper! why for hiding? Do not leave me, O Masetto; If he seek well where you get to, For a sequel too, prepare.
Mas. Faccia, dica quel che vuole.	*Mas.* Let him do or say his willing.
Zer. Ah! non giovan le parole.	*Zer.* My worst fear will gain fulfilling—
Mas. Parla forte, e qui t' arresta.	*Mas.* Speak aloud; I fain would test thee.
Zer. Che capriccio ha nella testa?	*Zer.* What caprice hath so possess'd thee?
Mas. Caprio se m' è fedele, e in qual modo andò l' affar.	*Mas.* (Now to know, if she be faithful, And the truth of this affair.) [*He conceals himself in a niche of the pavilion*
Zer. Quell' ingrato, quel crudele oggi vuol precipitar.	*Zer.* (Yon my lover, over wrathful, Just to-day should act with care.)

[*At this moment Don Juan enters, attired for the ball he is about to give; followed by a crowd of Peasants gaily dressed with masks and dominoes, and escorted by Attendants; lights begin to appear in the Palace. Zerlina steps out of his right behind a rose-bush.*]

SCENA XXIII.—Entra Don Giovanni e Contadine.	SCENE XXIII.—The same; Don Juan; Chorus of Peasants.
Gio. Su svegliatevi da bravi Su coraggio, o buonà gente Vogliam star allegramente, Vogliam ridere e scherzar. Alla stanza della danza Conducete tutti quanti: Ed a tutti in abbondanza Gran rinfreschi fate dar. [*Partono Contadine.*	*Juan.* [*To the Peasants and the Maskers, whom he motions towards the ball-room.*] Ye have hence but dream'd of Pleasure; Hail the night of joy before us With a shout in whirlwind-chorus Rousing earth, and rending air! All shall dance who swell the palace, Liber bleed to fill the chalice, Plenty's self shall welcome plenty, Rich refreshment then to share! [*Peasants and Maskers depart*

SCENA XXIV.—Zerlina; Don Giovanni Masetto	SCENE XXIV.—Zerlina; Don Juan; Masetto, as first concealed.
Zer. Tra quest' alboricelata, Si può far che non mi veda.	*Zer.* [*Running from beside the rose-bush, and endeavoring, unseen by Don Juan, to conceal herself behind the tall trees on the right.*] Friendly grove, thy shady distance May protect the timid maiden.

Gio. Zerlinetta mia garbata,
     T' ho già visto, non scappa.

Zer. Ah! lasciatemi andar via.
Gio. No, no, resta gioja mia!
Zer. Se pietade avete in core.
Gio. Sì, ben mio, son tutto amore.
     Vieni un poco—in questo loco,
     Fortunata io ti vò far.
Zer. (Ah! sei vele il sposo mio,
     So ben io quel che può far.)

[As Don Juan is pressing her toward the pavilion, Masetto confronts him; Don Juan falls back; Zerlina slips away from him.]

Gio. Masetto!
Mas. Sì, Masetto.
Gio. E chiuso e perchè?
     La bella tua Zerlina—
     Non può la poverina
     Piu star senza di te.
Mas. Capisco, sì Signore.
Gio. Adesso fate core; o suonatori udite.
     Venite omai con me.

Zer. e Mas. Sì, sì, facciamo core
     Ed a ballar cogli altri
     Andiamo tutti tre.   [Partono.

Juan. [Perceiving her.] Zerlinetta, mine existence
     ning after her, and catching her.]
     I can spy thee, gentle fair!
Zer. Ah, pray leave me to my duty—
Juan. No, no, stay; thou joy! thou beauty!
Zer. Bear'st a heart within thy bosom?
Juan. One all sunshine, thou its blossom!
     Let that heart in yonder bower
     Passion's golden light declare.
Zer. [Aside to Masetto.]
     (See me now, though weak, unwilling;
     So, my love, quell thy despair.)

Juan. Masetto?
Mas.   Aye, Masetto!
Juan.   Secluded why dost stay?
     Thine angel-bride Zerlina
     Will not so much demean her
     As dance, her spouse away.
Mas. I credit, Señor, truly.
Juan. Be wise, nor thus unruly;
     But hear that noble music,
     It calls, and all obey!
Zer. & Mas. See, see; we take it coolly,
     To trip it with our comrades
     We gladly will essay.   [Exeunt.

[Don Juan gives both an arm, and gallantly leads them unto his Palace. Donna Anna and Donna Elvira then enter the garden, escorted by Don Octavio; all three are disguised in black dominoes, and wear half-masks to conceal their features. the night darkens deeper and deeper.]

SCENA XXV.—*Entra* DONNA ANNA, DONNA ELVIRA *e* DON OTTAVIO.

Elv. Bisogna aver coraggio,
     O cari amici miei,
     E i suoi misfatti rei
     Scoprir potremo.
Otta. L' amica dice bene;
     Coraggio aver conviene.
     [A Donna Anna.] Discaccia, a vita mia,
     L' affanno ed il timor.
Anna. Il passo è periglioso,
     Può nascer qualche imbroglio;
     Temo pel caro sposo,
     E per noi temo ancor.

SCENE XXV.—DONNA ANNA; DONNA ELVIRA DON OCTAVIO.

Elv. Let one united purpose
     Thus nerve us to expose him,
     Lay bare his guilt, disclose him
     The angry world before.
Oct. [To Elvira.] A column'd strength is rising
     From such sweet sage advising,
     [To Anna.] Take heart! thy lover knoweth
     T' avenge, as to adore
Anna. The step is one of danger,
     For who may tell its issue?
     [To Octavio.] Tho' trembling for this fair stranger,
     I fear for thee still more.

[The music within the Palace is again heard: they turn to and fro in the garden; the window opens, and Leporello appears in the balcony with Don Juan.]

SCENA XXVI.—*Entra* DON GIOVANNI *e* LEPORELLO

Lep. [Dalla finestra.] Signor guardate un poco
     Che maschere galanti.
Gio. Falle passar avanti,
     Di che ci fanno onor.

Anna, Elv. e Otta. Al volto, ed alla voce,
     Si scopre il traditore.
Lep. Zi! zi! signore maschere!

Anna e Elv. Via rispondete.

Otta. Cosa chiedete?
Lep. Al ballo, se vi piace,
     V' invita il mio signor.

SCENE XXVI.—*The same;* LEPORELLO *and* DON JUAN *at the window.*

Lep. Master, I pray observe now
     Yon gentle-folk retreating.
Juan. Bid them a hearty greeting
     Unto our humble door.
     [Don Juan retires from the window.
Anna, Elv. & Oct. The voice and mien proclaim him
     That traitor we would punish.
Lep. [From the window, calling to them.]
     Ps! ps! my dainty masks below—
Anna, Elv. & Oct. [To Leporello.] Of what desirous?
Lep. Ps! ps!
Oct. Do you require us?
Lep. To grace a ball we hold here.
     So, pleasing our Señor

Don. Grazie, di tanto onore.
Andiam, compagne belle.

Lep. (L' amico anche su quella
Prova farà d' amor.)

Oct. Thanks for the noble honor;
   [*To Anna and Elvira.*] Then come, my fair companions.

Lep. [*Aside.*] ('Tis plain, its noble donor
   Looks to obtain two more.)

[*He retires and closes the window; Donna Anna, Donna Elvira an. Don Octavio advance forward, and remove their masks.*]

PROTEGGA IL GIUSTO CIELO—OH, GUARD ALL BOUNTEOUS HEAV'N. Trio.

The scene changes. The stage represents a magnificent suite of apartments in the Palace of Don Juan : beyond a saloon in the foreground, two more are observed leading one into the other ; in each is a raised Orchestra, containing a band of Musicians : in the principal saloon in front, side galleries are seen, illuminated with candelabra and lustres, and decorated with statuary ; to the right is the door of a cabinet ; beyond the farthest saloon is seen an open terrace, giving admission to or from the garden, amidst the distant trees of which colored lamps and illuminations may be perceived.

The stage is thronged with maskers, who pass to and fro through the various apartments ; numerous servants hand about refreshments ; Don Juan enters, leading Zerlina and Masetto, Leporello following ; the whole scene is brilliantly illuminated and is altogether one of the greatest festivity ; a dance has just concluded.

SCENA XXVII.—Entra ZERLINA, DON GIOVANNI, LE-	SCENE XXVII.—ZERLINA, DON JUAN, MASETTO, LE-
PORELLO, MASETTO, Contadini, Contadine, Servi, con	PORELLO ; Chorus of Peasants, Musicians, and Attend-
rinfreschi, Suonatori.	ants.
Gio. Riposate, vezzose ragazze.	Juan. Pause a moment, from joy too exciting—
Lep. Rinfrescatovi, vei giovinetti.	Lep. And partake of our luscious abundance ;
Gio. + Lep. Tornerete a far presto le pazze,	Juan. & Lep. Ere the many quadrille be inviting
Tornerete a scherzar, e ballar.	In a new glow of pleasure to share.

Otta. Ehi caffè!

Juan. [*Leading Zerlina to one of the tables.*]
Hey! some coffee!

Lep. Cioccolatte!

Lep. [*Leading some couples also.*] Hand the chocolate!

Mas. [*A Zer.*] Ah! Zerlina, giudizio!

Mas. (Pray Zerlina be careful!)

Gio. Sorbetti!
Lep. Confetti!

Juan. The spices!
Lep. Some ices!

Mas. e Zer. Troppo dolce comincia la scena
In amaro potria terminar.

Zer. & Mas. (Not unoften, a sunshine as brilliant
Will a showery future declare.)

Gio. Sei pur vaga, brillante, Zerlina.

Juan. Thy pure glances are music Zerlina!

Zer. Sua bontà.

Zer. Nay, my lord!

Mas La briccona fa festa.

Mas. Why, the girl is coquetting!

Lep. Sei pur cara, Giannotta, Sandrina

Lep. [*To one of the Peasant-girls, imitating his master.*]
Thy sour answers are physic, Sandrina!

Mas. Tocca pur, che ti cada la testa.
La briccona mi fa disperar.

Mas. His impertinence she is abetting,
I am smothered in rage and despair!

Zer. Quel Masetto mi par stralunato,
Brutto, brutto si fa quest' affar.

Zer. (Poor Masetto appears in a passion,
This is truly an awkward affair.)

Gio. e Lep. Quel Masetto mi par stralunato,
Quì bisogna cervello adoprar.

Juan & Lep. (You Masetto must bend to the fashion;
Now for action our talents prepare!)

SCENA XXVIII.—*Entra* DONNA ANNA, DONNA ELVIRA
e DON OTTAVIO.

SCENE XXVIII.—*The same;* DONNA ANNA, DONNA
ELVIRA, DON OCTAVIO.

Lep. Venite pur avanti
Vezzose mascherette!

Lep. Amid the throng advancing
Each gentle mask is welcome!

Gio. E aperto a tutti quanti,
"Viva la Libertà."

Juan. All Seville, join our dancing!
Pleasure, allow no bar!

Anna., Elv. e Otta. Siam grati a tanti segni
Di generosità.

Anna, Elv. & Oct. We grateful, thank your kindness
In truth without a par!

Anna, Elv., Otta, Gio. & Lep Viva la libertà!

Anna, Elv., Oct., Juan & Lep. Pleasure, allow no bar!

Gio. Ricominciate il suono.
[*A Lep.*] Tu accoppia i ballerini.

Juan. Strike up a stirring music!
Find ev'ry girl a partner.

[*The orchestra in the foremost saloon commences a menuet; Leporello forms the dance, in which several couples join.*]

Meco tu dei ballare,
Zerlina, vien pur quà.

Really, a dainty dancer,
Zerlina love, you are. [*They dance*

Lep. Da bravi via ballate.

Lep. Right *bravi!* swell the gambol.

Elv Quell' è la contadina.

Elv. That is the peasant-maiden.

Anna. Io moro!

Anna. I perish!

Otta. Simulate.

Oct. Still dissemble.

Gio. e Lep. Va bene, in verità!

Juan. Lep. (Our course receives no jar.)

Gio. [*A Lep.*] A bada tien Masetto.

Juan. [*To Leporello.*] Just occupy Masetto.

[*The orchestra in the next saloon strikes up another dance, (a gavotte,) in which other couples join; Leporello advances to Masetto.*]

Lep. Non balli poveretto?
Vien quà, Masetto caro,
Facciam quel ch' altri fa.

Lep. [*To Mas.*] Why not dance? where wouldst get to?
Come here, Masetto dearest,
You from the mark fly far.

Gio. Il tuo compagno io sono,
Zerlina, vien pur quà.

Juan. Unto such deep affection,
Zerlina, place no bar!

Mas. No, no, ballar non voglio.

Mas. No, no! I want no *dancing.*

Lep. Eh balla, amico mio!
Facciam quel ch' altri fa.

Lep. Jump high my friend; what aileth
You from the mark fly far!

Mas. No.

Mas. No.

Lep. Sì, caro Masetto.

Lep. Aye, dear Masetto.

Mas. Ballare no, non voglio.

Mas. No, I want no dancing.

Anna Resister non poss' io.

Anna. Resistance nearly faileth!

Otta. e Elv. Fingete, per pietà.

Elv. & Oct. Discov'ry all would mar.

[*A third dance (a waltz) commences in the farthest saloon.*]

Gio. e Zer. Vieni con me, mia vita.

Juan. [*Dancing to the gavotte, having led Zerlina to the door of
the cabinet on the right, forces her to enter it.*]
Passion and love nigh slay me!

Mas. [*A Lep.*] Lasciami, ah no! Zerlina.

Mas. [*Breaking loose from Leporello.*] Let me be!
Ah no!—Zerlina!

Gio. Vieni, vieni.

Juan. Zerlina! come then!

Zer. Oh numi! son tradita!

Zer. O monster! wilt betray me?

[*Juan and Zerlina disappear through the door of the side chamber.*]

Lep. Qui nasce una ruina.   [*Si nasconde.*]

Lep. (The devil! hath he seen her?)
  [*Masetto runs about amongst the groups of dancers, half distracted, Leporello is entering the cabinet to warn Don Juan.*

Anna., Elv. e Otta. L' iniquo da se scosse
  Nel laccio se ne va.

Anna, Elv. & Oct. Iniquity fulfilling,
  Now falls his evil star!

Zer. Gente! ajuto, gente!   [*Di dentro.*]

Zer. [*Within the cabinet.*] Help! give aid! give aid! assistance!

Anna. Elv. e Otta. Soccoriamo l' innocente!

Anna, Elv. & Oct. Rescue more than her existence!
  [*They all move from side to side, uncertain which way to go*

Mas. Ah Zerlina!

Mas. Ah, Zerlina!

Zer. [*Di dentro.*] Scellerato

Zer. [*In the cabinet.*] Hideous villain!

Anna. e Otta. Ora grida da quel lato.
  Ah gittiamo giù la porta

Anna, Elv. & Oct. [*Running to the door of the cabinet.*]
  Ha; her cry is through me thrilling!
  Break the lock! or force the portal!
  [*They dash in the door; Zerlina rushes from th*

Zer. [*Tornando.*] Soccorretemi! son morta.

Zer. O his guilt fulfill'd, 'twere mortal!

Gli Altri Siamo qui per tua difesa.

Anna, Elv., Oct. & Mas. [*To Zerlina.*] Our protections shall
  defend ye.

[*Don Juan follows Zerlina from the cabinet; in coming thence he encounters Leporello running in to warn him; he re-enters
the ball-room, his drawn sword in his hand, pale, and dragging in Leporello, half dead with fright and astonishment.*]

Gio. [*Tornando e verso Lep.*] Ecco il birbo! che t' ha off-
  ossa! ma da me la pena avrà. Mori, iniquo!

Juan. See! what scoundrel sought t' offend ye;
  Wrath condign thus cuts him down!
  [*Passing with his sword at Leporello*
  Die, base varlet!

Lep. An cosa fate!

Lep. [*On his knees.*] Ah, gracious goodness!

Gio. Mori, dico.

Juan. Die, I tell thee!

Otta., Anna e Elv. Nol sperate, nol sperate.
  L' empio crede con tal frode.
  Di nasconder l' empietà.

Oct., with Anna & Elv. [*To Don Juan.*]
  This pretence were too fallacious:
  View the pit that thou hast digged!
  Let the mask aside be thrown!
  [*They take off their masks*

Gio. Donna Elvira!

Juan. How! Elvira!

Elv. Sì, malvaggio.

Elv.   Aye, thou Satan!

Gio. Don Ottavio!

Juan. Don Octavio!

Otta. Sì, signore!

Oct.   Base betrayer!

Gio. Ah, credete!

Juan. Give some credence—

Anna.   Midnight slayer!

Anna, Elv., Otta., Zer. e Mas. Traditore! traditore!
  Tutto, tutto già si sa;
  Trema, scelerato!
  Sapra tosto il mondo intero
  Il misfatto orrendo e nero,
  La tua fiera crudeltà.

Anna, Elv., Zer., Oct. & Mas. [*To Don Juan.*]
  All thy *thousand* crimes are known!
  [*All advance, hemming in Don Juan and Leporello*
  Tremble, tremble! more than tremble!
  Farthest Universe shall learn thee,
  Hell, alike as Heaven, spurn thee,
  Nature, thee her curse, disown!

  Odi il tuon della vendetta,
  Che ti fischia intorno interno,
  Sul tuo capo in questo giorno
  il suo fulmine cadrà.

  [*Thunder is heard, and a storm seen in the distance*
  Hear our all-appalling vengeance
  Tear Creation's vault asunder,
  'Till its wrath, a mightier thunder,
  Hurl annihilation down!

Gio. e Lep. E confusa la mia testa,
  Non so più quel ch' io mi faccia;
  E un' orribile tempesta
  Minacciando oh mi va.

Juan, (*his sword in hand,*) *& Lep.*
  In confusion, do my senses
  Little know what point to weather;
  I perceive the storm to gather
  With a too portentous frown.

  Ma non manca in mi coraggio,
  Non mi perdo, o mi confondo;
  Se cadesse ancora il mondo,
  Nulla mai temer mi fa.

  These positions give me/him courage;
  Earth might lose her path in error
  Ere my/his heart could dream of terror
  Or the slightest tremor own!

[*Striking right and left with his weapon, Don Juan makes his way through the crowds that menace him, and escapes with
Leporello into the garden at the back, as the curtain falls.*

END OF THE FIRST ACT.

ACT II

The stage represents an open plaza in the city of Seville; to the left is a large mansion with projecting windows and balconies, in which Donna Elvira has taken up her residence.

It is evening; the moon is just perceived above the house-tops. Don Juan enters, with a mantle thrown over his shoulders, and carrying a mandoline; he is followed by Leporello.

SCENA I.—*Entra* Don Giovanni *e* Leporello.

Gio. Eh via, buffone, non mi seccar.

Lep. No no, padrone, non vò restar.

Gio. Sentimi, amico—

Lep. Vò andar, vi dico.

Gio. Ma che ti ho fatte,
Che vuoi lasciarmi !

Lep. Oh niente affatto !
Quasi ammazzarmi.

Gio. Va, che sei matto,
Fu per burlar.

Lep. Ed io non burlo
Ma voglio andar !

Gio. Leporello.

Lep. Signore.

Gio. Vien qui, facciamo pace. Prendi.

Lep. Cosa ?

Gio. Quattro doppie.

Lep. Oh sentite! per questa volta ancora la cerimonia accetto ; ma non vi ci avvezzaste, non credeste di sedurre i miei pari, come le donne, a forza di denari

Gio. Non parliam più di ciò; ti basta l' animo di far quel ch' io ti dico ?

Lep. Purchè lasciam le donne.

Gio. Lasciar le donne ! Pazzo! lasciar le donne ! Sai ch' esse per me son necessarie più del pan che mangio, più dell' aria che spiro ?

Lep. E avete core d' ingannarle poi tutte ?

Gio. E tutto amore. Chi a una sola è fedele, verso l' altra è crudele; io, ch' in me sento sì esteso sentimento, vo bene a tutte quante ; le donne poi che calcolar non sanno, il mio buon natural chiamano inganno.

Lep. Non ho veduto mai naturale più vasto, e più benigno. Orsù cosa vorreste ?

Gio. Odi ; vedesta tu la cameriera di donna Elvira ?

Lep. Io no.

Gio. Non hai veduto qualche cosa di bello, caro il mio Leporello ; ora io con lei vò tentar la mia sorte, ed ho pensato, giacchè siam verso sera, per aguzzarle meglio l' appetito, di presentarmi a lei col tuo vestito.

Lep. E perchè non potreste presentarvi col vostro ?

Gio. Han poco credito con gente di tal rango gli abiti signorili. Sbrigati, via

Lep. Signor—per più ragioni—

Gio. Finiscila, non soffro opposizioni.

SCENE I.—Don Juan, Leporello.

Juan. How now, Sir Stupid !
Tease me no more.

Lep. No, no, Don Cupid ;
Our union is o'er !

Juan. Friend, state your grievance—

Lep. I, Sir, would leave hence.

Juan. Cause for this loathing
Pray you to tell me ?

Lep. O, a mere nothing—
You sought to kill me !

Juan. Why, this is folly,
'Twas but a joke.

Lep. For which, I duly
Throw off the yoke.

Juan. Leporello !

Lep. Don Juan !

Juan. [*Taking a purse from his pocket.*] Here's that will make us friends yet, catch them.

Lep. What, Sir ?

Juan. Fifteen ducats !

Lep. [*Slipping the purse into his pouch.*] Oh,—now hear me, for this last once will I excuse such untoward joking: but make it not your practice, nor affect to gull a man of my firmness, as ye trap lasses, perforce of petty pelf. Sir.

Juan. On to something less trite : and have ye courage, friend, to do my present pleasure ?

Lep. If you forsake the women.

Juan. "Forsake the women !" jackass ! "forsake the women !" to me they are necessary far more than the bread that feeds me, than the air I am breathing.

Lep. And have you stomach to deceive the whole sex, then ?

Juan. 'Tis all for love, child ! he that's faithful to one girl, is unkind to the others ; I own a heart so philanthropic, it loves the wholesale bevey ; and women, whose calculating powers grasp not this *vast* idea, call it "deceiving."

Lep. My puny comprehensions cannot grapple with feelings of such extent, Sir ! pray you, explain your purpose.

Juan. Hear me ; hast ever seen the fair Elvira's enchanting servant ?

Lep. Not I.

Juan. Then thy twin optics never scann'd what is lovely, untutor'd Leporello: with this same damsel will I hazard my venture ; and it has struck me, since day droops down toward evening, to lend the jest a happier complexion, I'll introduce myself in these thy garments.

Lep. Surely are not your own, Sir, more at home in these matters ?

Juan. Too little credit, man, greets a genteel exterior from people in her station :
Whip them off quickly !

Lep. Señor—but my position—

Juan. Have done at once, I brook no opposition!

[Leporello unbuttons his mantle and takes off his hat, Don Juan does the same ; they exchange ; while Leporello is in the act of assisting his master to put on the other cloak, a jalousie in an upper story of a mansion on the left is thrown open, and Donna Elvira appears at the window ; taking her seat there, she leans her head upon her hand, and looks out pensively into the twilight, without perceiving Don Juan and Leporello in the street below.]

SCENA II.—Donna Elvira, e detto.

Elv. Ah taci, ingiusto core,
Non palpitarmi in seno !
E un empio, è un traditore,
E colpa aver pietà.
Lep. [A Don Gio.] Z... donna Elvira,
Signor, ia voce io ... to.
Gio. Cogliere io vò il momento,
Tu fermati un pò là—

[He pushes the disguised Leper (Don Juan's) voice, take Lep

Elvira, idolo mio !
Elv. Non è costui l' ingrato ?
Gio. Sì, vita mia, son io,
E chieggo carità.
Elv. (Numi ! Che strano affetto
Mi si risveglia in petto.)
Lep. State a veder la pazza,
Ch' ancor gli crederà.
Gio. Discendi, o gioja bella,
Vedrai che tu sei quella,
Che adora l' alma mia,
Pentito io sono già !
Elv. No, non ti credo, o barbaro.
Gio. Ah ! credimi, o m' uccido.
Lep. Se seguitate, io rido.
Gio. Idolo mio vien quà !
Elv. Dei, che cimento è questo ?
Non so s' io vado o resto—
Ah proteggete voi
La mia credulità !
Gio. Spero che cada presto ;
Che bel colpetto è questo !
Più fertile talento
Del mio no non si da.
Lep. Già quel mendace labbro
Torna a sedur costei ;
Deh proteggete, o Dei,
La sua credulità.

[Elvira parte.

SCENA III.—Don Juan, Leporello.

Gio. Amico, che ti par ?
Lep. Mi par ch' abbiate un' anima di bronzo.

Gio. Va là, che sè il gran gonzo. Ascolta bene—quando costei ,ui viene, tu corri ad abbracciarla, falle quattro Carezze, finge la voce mia ; poi con bell' arte cerca teco condurla in altra parte.

Lep. Ma signore.
Gio. Non più repliche.
Lep. E se poi mi conosce ?
Gio. Non ti conoscerà se tu non vuoi Zitto, ell' apre ; ehi, giudisio.

'He runs off to the side, leaving Leporello alone ; Donna Elvira enters from the house ; she advances to meet Leporello. Don Juan watches their movements from the side.]

SCENA IV.—Donna Elvira, e detto.

Elv. Eccomi a voi.
Gio. (Veggiamo che farà.)
Lep. (Che bell' imbroglio !)
Elv. Dunque creder potrò, ch' i pianti miei abbian Vinto quel cor ? dunque pentito l' amato Don Giovanni al suo dovere, e all' amor mio ritorna !

SCENE II.—The same ; Donna Elvira

Elv. [At the window.] Ah, lull thy rebel yearning
Fond heart, far too confiding ;—
The traitor but merits spurning,
'Twere more than crime to grieve.
Lep. Softly, I hear Elvira,
If sound be no false prophet.
Juan. Haply this turn may profit
Our purpose to achieve.

ward under the window, and crouches behind him, to make Elvira, when she hears it, to be the former.]

Elvira, thou mine idol !
Elv. Is this not the deceiver !
Juan. Aye ; grant a kindlier title
To one who would retrieve.
Elv. (Long dead within my bosom
Hope bids her bud re-blossom.)
Lep. (Now, ten to one, this ninny
Will actually believe.)
Juan. Descend, my joy ! my beauty !
A truant lost to duty,
Adoring still his treasure,
As penitent here receive.
Elv. No ; all is false, barbarian ;
Juan. First, credit me ; slay me, after.
Lep. (I die of smother'd laughter.)
Juan. Yon cruel casement leave.
Elv. (O, 'twere too keen a trial
Giving his pray'r denial ;
Forbid it, guardian angels,
That he this time deceive !)
Juan. (If she but yield, 'tis glorious,
Wit, be thou then victorious ;
For more consummate movement
I never did conceive.
Lep. (Jove ! this amount of lying
Fram'd in with vile pretences,
Slips through her foolish senses
Like water through a sieve.)

[Donna Elvira leaves the window above.

SCENE III.—Don Juan, Leporello.

Juan. Well, your opinion, friend.
Lep. That you're a substance of adamant and bronze. Sir !

Juan. Tut, tut, you gaby-gapeface ! now pay attention ; when the young lady comes out, run and embrace her quickly, give her twenty caresses, imitate all my manner ; and then, with dexterous seeming, try to conduct her to a distance.

Lep. Nay—good master—
Juan. Dare ye contradict !—
Lep. But suppose she should know me ?
Juan. That will she surely not, if you so will it. [He turns.] Gently ; she's coming : now, be careful !

SCENE IV.—Donna Elvira ; Leporello ; Don Juan, at the back.

Elv. [To Leporello.) Love, I am with you.
Juan. (Let us see what he'll do.)
Lep. (Here's a pickle !)
Elv. I at last may believe my frequent weepings quite have melted thy heart ? deeply repentant, doth now Don Juan unto his duty, and my pure faith return him '

Si, carinà !

Elv	Crudele ! se sapeste quante lagrime, e quanti sospir! oi mi costate.	*Lep.*	[*Putting his arm around Elvira's waist, and concealing his face with the cloak, while he endeavors to imitate Don Juan's voice.*] Yes, my duckey !
Lep.	Io, vita mia !	*Elv.*	Unkind one, if you knew how many heart-breakings and how many sighings ye have cost me !
Elv.	Voi.	*Lep.*	I; precious pet-lamb !
Lep.	Poverina ! quante mi dispiace !	*Elv.*	You, love.
Elv.	Mi fuggiste più ?	*Lep.*	Pretty poppet ! I am very sorry.
Lep.	No, muso bello.	*Elv.*	Wilt leave me e'er again ?
Elv.	Sarete sempre mio ?	*Lep.*	No ; ducksey-darling !
Lep.	Sempre.	*Elv.*	And thou art mine for ever ?
Elv.	Carissimo !	*Lep.*	Ever !
Lep.	Carissima ! (La burla mi dà gusto.)	*Elv.*	Caress me then !
		Lep.	Caress me too ! [*Aside.*] (This is becoming pleasant.)
Elv.	Mio tesoro !	*Elv.*	All my treasure !
Lep.	Mia venere !	*Lep.*	My precious one !
Elv.	Son per voi tutto foco.	*Elv.*	I am fir'd with affection !
Lep.	Io tutto cenere.	*Lep.*	I am burnt up with it.
Gio.	Il birbo si riscalda.	*Juan.*	(He warms him toward the business.)
Elv.	E non m' ingannerete ?	*Elv.*	You no more will deceive me ?
Lep.	Nò, sicuro.	*Lep.*	O, indeed no !
Elv.	Giuratelo.	*Elv.*	Dost promise me ?
Lep.	Lo giuro a questa mano, che bacio con trasporto, E a quei bei lumi—	*Lep.*	I swear it by this fair hand the which I kiss with transport : by those twin lode-stars—
Gio.	Ih, eh, ah, ih, sei morto.	*Juan.*	[*Calling out in a rough voice.*] Ih, eh, ah, ih, ye're both dead !
Elv.	Oh Numi ! *fuggone.*	*Elv. & Lep.*	[*Alarmed.*] O heaven !

[*Leporello throws his cloak around Elvira ; they both run away for fear. Don Juan leaves his place of concealment.*]

SCENA V.—Don Juan, *solus*		SCENE V.—Don Juan, *solus.*	
Gio.	Ih, eh, ah, ih ! par che la sorte mi secondi, veggiamo ; le finestre son queste ; ora cantiamo.	*Juan.*	[*Running toward the side by which they have fled, and still calling out.*] Ih, eh, ih, eh, ah, ih ! [*He turns back, and fetches his mandoline.*] Her luckiest chances that jade fortune is ringing; So so, this is the window, now for our singing.

DEH VIENI ALLA FINESTRA—OPE, OPE THY CASEMENT. Don Juan.

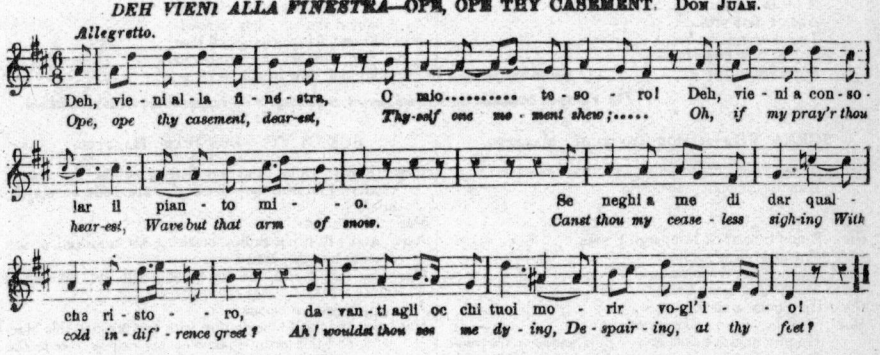

Deh, vie—ni al la fi—nè—stra, O mio...... te—so—ro ! Deh, vie—ni a con—so—
Ope, ope thy casement, dear-est, Thy-self one mo—ment shew;...... Oh, if my pray'r thou

lar il pian—to mi—o. Se neghi a me di dar qual—
hear-est, Wave but that arm of snow. Canst thou my cease—less sigh-ing With

che ri—sto—ro, da—van—ti agli oc chi tuoi mo—rir vogl'i—o!
cold in—dif'—rence greet ? Ah ! wouldst thou see me dy—ing, De—spair—ing, at thy feet ?

Tu ch' hai la bocca dolce più ch' del miele,
Tu ch' il zucchero porti in mezzo al core,
Non esser, gioja mio, con me crudele,
Lasciati almen veder, mio bell' amore.
Vè gente alla finestra.
Forse è dessa. Ps, ps !

Thy lip outvies Hymettian-honied bowers ;
Virtue worthy an angel, thy heart doth cherish;
Thy sigh were balm amid a heav'n of flowers ;
O, for one kiss, one word, this soul would perish !
[*He approaches nearer the house*] Some one is at the window
[*It's her perhaps ? ps, ps !* [*He is interrupted by Masetto, who enters, accompanied by several Villagers, all armed with muskets. Masetto also carries a pistol in his belt.*]

SCENA VI.—Don Giovanni ; Masetto, con seguito di Contadini armati.	**SCENE VI.**—The same ; Masetto ; some Villagers

Mas. Non ci stanchiamo ;—il cor mi dice
    Che trovarlo dobbiamo.
Gio. [*Aparte.*] Qualcuno parla,
Mas. Fermatevi—mi pare
    Ch' alcuno quì si muova.
Gio. [*Aparte.*] Se non fallo, è Masetto.
Mas. Chi va là ? Non risponde ?
    Animo, schioppo al muso :
    Chi va là ?
Gio. [*Aparte.*] Non è solo ;
    Ci vuol giudizio. [*Forte.*] Amici,
    Non mi voglio scoprir. Sei tu, Masetto ?
Mas. Appunto quello ; e tu ?
Gio. Non mi conosci ? Il servo
    Son io di Don Giovanni—
Mas.   Leporello !
    Servo di quell' indegno cavaliere ?
Gio. Certo, di quel briccone.
Mas. Di quell' uom senz' onore, ah dimmi un poco,
    Dove possiam trovarlo :
    Lo cerco con costor per trucidarlo.
Gio. [*Aparte.*] Bagatelle ! [*Forte.*] Bravissimo Masetto,
    Anch' io con voi m' unisco
    Per fargliela a quel birbo di padrone ;
    Ma udite un pò qual è la mia intenzione :
    Metà di voi quà vadano
    E gli altri vadanti ;
    E pian' pianin' lo cerchine,
    Lontan non sia di qua.
    Se un uom' e una ragassa
    Passeggian par la piazza,
    Se sotto a una finistra
    Fare all' amor sentite
    Ferite, pur ferite,
    Il mio patron sarà !
    In testo egli ha un cappello
    Con canai pennachini
    Addosso un gran mantello,
    E spada al fianco egli hà !
    Andate, fate presto !
    Tu sol verrai con me,
    Noi far dobbiamo il resto
    E già vedrai cos' è.   [*I Contadini partono.*

Mas. Come on, my hearties ; I feel assured we must fall in with his track.
Juan. (A man's voice spake then ?)
Mas. But stop a bit ; I'm certain that something passes yonder.
Juan. (Surely that is Masetto !)
Mas. Who goes there ? [*A pause.*] Give an answer, or we present and fire, lad ! who goes there ?
Juan. (He has friends, too ; this calls for prudence.) [*Assuming Leporello's voice.*] My masters, don't ye know an old chum ! Is that Masetto ?
Mas. A piece of him, Sir ;—and you ?
Juan. Again that question ? the servant unto my lord Don Juan.
Mas. Leporello ! servant of that dishonorable scoundrel !
Juan. Certes ; of that same "scoundrel."
Mas. Lost to shame, feeling, and honor : ah, give acquaintance where we may hope to find him ; we're seeking through the town intent to kill him.
Juan. (Very pretty.) Bravissimo, Masetto !
    Now list me in your reg'ment, I share a like dislike
    and wise intention,
    And here dispense the fruit of my invention.
    Do you pursue the right-hand path,
    You by the left repair ;
    And then advancing cautiously,
    You'll find your man, somewhere.
    Should ye spy cloak and hat, Sirs,
    Or in the streets, or piazzas,
    And aught of love proceeding
    'Twixt two close-muffled figures,—
    Present, and pull your triggers,
    My darling master's there !
    New doeskin upper-leathers,
    Toledo, a scarlet mantle,
    And sundry borrow'd feathers
    This dainty bird doth bear.
    About the job : hey, presto !
    Friend I take charge of thee ;
    And, prophet-like, profess to
    Foretell how it will be.

[*The Villagers attendant on Masetto depart, according to the supposed Leporello's directions.*

SCENA VII.—Il Don Giovanni ; Masetto.	**SCENE VII.**—Don Juan : Masetto.

Gio. (Zitte ! lascia ch' io senta. Ottimamente !)
    Dunque dobbiamo ucciderlo ?
Mas.   Sicuro.
Gio. E non ti basteria rompergli l' ossa,
    Fracassargli le spalle ?
Mas. No, no ! voglio ammazzarlo !
    Vo farlo in cento brani.
Gio. Hai buone arme ?
Mas.   Cospetto !
    Ho pria questo moschetto ;   *Dandole a Giovanni.*
    E poi questa pistola. |*Dandola.*
Gio. E poi ?
Mas. Non basta ?
Gio. En, basta certo. Or prendi
    Questa per la pistola,   [*Battendole.*
    Questa per il moschetto.

Mas. Ahi ! ahi ! La testa mia—
Gio. Taci, o t' uccido.   [*Battendolo ancora.*
    Questa per l' ammazzarlo,

Juan. (Softly, whiles that we listen ; so far the coast's clear.) [*To Masetto.*] Then you are bent on slaying him ?
Mas. Most surely.
Juan. And will it not suffice, breaking his numskull, or displacing his ribs, man ?
Mas. No, no ; I will his life-blood ; I'll cut him up to mince-meat !
Juan. Hast good weapons ?
Mas. Just hav'nt I ! beginning with this musket, this bludgeon, and this pistol—[*handing the articles over to Don Juan.*]
Juan. [*Holding out his hand for more.*] Go on, friend—
Mas. Too few then ?
Juan. Nay ; pretty tidy ! we'll prove them. [*He gives Masetto a violent blow from behind with the bludgeon. Masetto falls to the ground, uttering loud cries.*] That, for your cur-ship's pistol—[*another blow*]—that, for your cur-ship's musket—
Mas. Ah ! eh ! ih ! murder ! murder !
Juan. Hush, or I'll kill ye ! [*Gives him another and another blow.*]

Questa per farlo in brani ;—
Villano, mascalzon, ceffo da cani !　　　[*Parte.*

This, for your promis'd beating ; this for your prom
ised killing ;
Mean coward ! poltroon knave ! dog of a villain !

Administering one or two final blows, and catching up his mandoline, Don Juan steals off. Masetto lays half-dead with the beating and fright upon the ground. Zerlina, hearing his cries, comes to his assistance from the house ; she bears a cloak over her arm, and a small street-lantern in her hand.

SCENA VIII.—Masetto ; indi Zerlina.

Mas. [*Gridando forte.*] Ahi ! ahi ! La testa mia !
Ahi, ahi, le spalle ! E il petto !
Zer. Mi parvo di sentire la voce di Masetto.
Mas. Oh, Dio ! Zerlina ! Zerlina mia, soccorso !
Zer. Cos' è stato ?
Mas. L' iniquo, il scellerato mi ruppe l' ossa, e i nervi.

Zer. O poveretta me ! chi ?
Mas.　　　　　Leporello,
O qualche diavol che somiglia à lui.
Zer. Crudel ! non tel diss' io,
Che con questa tua pazza gelosia
Ti ridurresti a qualche brutto passo ?
Dove ti duole ?
Mas.　　　　Qui.
Zer. E poi ?
Mas.　　　Qui, e ancora qui.

Zer. E poi non ti duol altro ?
Mas. Duolmi un poco
Questo piè, questo braccio, e questa mano
Zer. Via, via, non è gran mal, s' il resto è sano.
Vien tene meco a casa.
Purchè tu mi prometta
D' essere men geloso,
Io, io ti guarirò, caro il mio sposo.

SCENE VIII.—Masetto ; Zerlina.

Mas. Ah ! ih ! I'm mash'd to jelly ; ih ! ah ! my back
bone ! my breast-bone !—
Zer. It would seem that I heard the voice of my Masetto
Mas. O heav'n, Zerlina—Zerlina dearest, give aid here !
Zer. What has happen'd ?
Mas. The monster has surely broken,—aye, every bone
about me.

Zer. O, my darling pet ! who ?
Mas. Leporello ! or some infernal fiend exactly like him.

Zer. The brute !—have I not told thee, giving way to thy
stupid jealous fancies would bring upon thee the very
worst mischances ? where has he hurt you ?

Mas. [*Pointing to his head.*] Here—
Zer. Where else, dear ?
Mas. [*Pointing to his back and shoulders.*] Here—and also
here—
Zer. Do you not suffer elsewhere ?
Mas. There's a pain in this my foot, in my elbow, and in
my hand too—
Zer. Come, come ; it is not much ; the rest is unhurt
back with me home to supper,
If you will truly promise next time to be less jealous
I have a care, thou most foolish of fellows.

VEDRAI CARINO—LIST, AND I'LL FIND, LOVE. Solo. Zerlina.

Andante.

Ve - drai ca - ri - no, Se sei buo - ni - no, Che bel ri - me - dio,— Ti vog-lio dar.
List, and I'll find, love, If you are kind, love, Balm for your mind, love,—Patient but be.

E na - tu - ra - le, Non da dis - gus - to, E lo spe - zia - le, Non lo sa far, nò
This balm so pure, love, Sim-ple and sure, love, Sweet to en-dure, love, None know but me,

Non lo sa far, nò Non lo sa far........ E un cer - to bal - samo, Che por - to a - dos - so,
None know but me, None know but me........ Thrilling and heal - ing, O - ver thee steal - ing,

Da - re tel pos - so, S' il vuoi pro - var. Sa - per vor - res - ti ? Do - ve mi stà, dove
Ex - qui - site feel - ing, Meant but for thee. Ex - qui-site feel - ing. Ex-qui - site feel - ing

do ve, do - ve mi stà ?... Sen - ti - lo bat - te - re Toc ca - mi qui, Sen - ti - lo
Meant but for thee ... To thy en - treat - ing, I'll yield it, dear ! Feel how ti

bat-te-re, Sen-ti-lo bat-te-re;   Toc-ca-mi quà,   Sen-ti-lo bat-te-re, Sen-ti-lo
beat - ing, beat-ing just here,......   *beating just here; Feel how 'tis beat - ing, Feel how 'tis*

bat-te-re, Sen-ti-lo bat-te-re, Toc-ca-mi quà. quà, quà!   Sen-ti-lo bat-te-re,
beat - ing, Feel how 'tis beat - ing, beating just here, here, here!   Feel how 'tis beat-ing, Feel

Toc-ca-mi quà, quà,   Toc-ca-mi quà, quà!   Toc-ca-mi quà, quà,   Toc-ca-mi quà!
how 'tis beating,   beat-ing just here!   Feel how 'tis beat - ing,   beat ing just here!

[*Placing the cloak round Masetto's shoulders, taking his arm, and gently showing him the way with her lantern, she leads him from the scene.*]

The scene changes.   The stage represents a retired court-yard in the Palace of the Commandant, now that of Donna Anna Donna Elvira and Leporello enter by one of the doors in the wall; the latter is still disguised in Don Juan's dress.

SCENA IX.—*Cortile Interno. Entra* LEPORELLO *e* DONNA ELVIRA.	SCENE IX.—DONNA ELVIRA; LEPORELLO.
Lep. Di molte faci il lume s' avvicina o mio bon! stiamo qui un poco, finchè da noi si scosta.	*Lep.* [*Still imitating his master's voice.*] Surely advancing torches track our path, O my love ? then stand aside here, lest that they should perceive us.
Elv. Ma che temi, adorato mio sposo ?	*Elv.* Why this tremor ? do you fear aught, ador'd one ?
Lep. Nulla, certi riguardi. Io vò veder, S' il lume è già lontano. (Ah come da costei Liberarmi?) Rimanti, anima bella.	*Lep.* Nothing, nothing—tho' somewhat cautious—I wish to see if now the lights are far off. (From this appendage *how* to relieve me !) Remain here, my existence !—
Elv. Ah non lasciarmi ! Sola, sola in bujo loco, Palpitar il cor mi sento, E m' assale un tal spavento, Che mi sembra di morir.	*Elv.* [*In a piteous tone.*] Ah, do not leave me ! In the solemn hush of darkness Wilt forsake and leave me lonely; Spurn'd in loving, the bosom only Knows a woe no pow'r can cheer.
Lep. Piu che cerco men ritrovo Questa porta sciagurata; Piano piano l' ho trovata, Ecco il tempo di fuggir.	*Lep.* More I seek it, more it fails me Where the deuce the door is lying ; Soft, I have it ! now for flying, Coast and conscience both are clear.

[*In endeavoring to find the door by which he entered with Elvira, he takes the other, and is just about to use it, when it is opened from the other side, and Donna Anna with Don Octavio, escorted by Attendants bearing torches, enter from it. Leporello slips aside unseen by them, and at their approach both he and Donna Elvira conceal themselves in different angles of the court-yard. Don Octavio advances, leading Donna Anna, and endeavoring to comfort her.*]

SCENA X.—*Entra* DON OTTAVIO *e* DONNA ANNA.	SCENE X.—*The same;* DONNA ANNA; DON OCTAVIO; *Attendants.*
Otta. Tergi il ciglio, o vita mia, E dà calma al tuo dolore, L' ombra omai del genitore Pena avrà de tuoi martir.	*Oct.* Let the beam of consolation Pour its balm on those that suffer ; Hence, toward the honor'd manes, offer Hallow'd love,—not tribute tear.
Anna. Lascia almen alla mia pena, Questo piccolo ristoro. Sol la morte, o mio tesoro, Il mio pianto può finir.	*Anna.* Grief like mine alone hath comfort In the soothing calm of weeping, Till the tomb's unsorrow'd sleeping Bring the peace denied us here.
Elv. Ah ! dov' è, lo sposo mio.	*Elv.* Thinks the wretch again to slight me ?
Lep. Se mi trova, son perduto !	*Lep.* (Should they find me, I am done for.)
Elv. Una porta la vegg' io, Cheto che to io vò partir.	*Elv. & Lep.* [*Aside, unseen by each other, trying to reach the same door.*] (Yonder portal doth invite me Gently now to disappear.)

They both meet at the door, which is opened at the same instant from the other side by Masetto and Zerlina, escorted by Peasants with clubs and torches; Masetto bears a thick stick in his hands—perceiving Don Juan as he supposes, he drags forward the disguised Leporello to the front; the latter all the while manages to conceal his face.

SCENA XI.—*Entra* Zerlina *e* Masetto.

SCENE XI.—*The same*; Masetto; Zerlina; *other* Attendants.

Zer e Mas. Ferma briccone, Dove ten vai?	*Mas.* [*Dragging Leporello forward.*] Luck ne'er was greater, He cannot 'scape us.
Anna e Otta. Ecco il fellone. Come era qua ?	*Anna & Oct.* How came the traitor Here in this place ?
A 4. Ah! mora il perfido Che m' ha tradito !	*Anna, Oct., Mas. & Zer.* Villain! thy perfidies Henceforth are over.
Elv. E mio marito, Pietà! pietà !	*Elv.* He is my lover, Ah, shew him grace !
Tutta. E Donna Elvira Quella ch' io vedo ! Appena io credo ; No, morirà.	*Anna, Oct., Mas & Zer.* The fair Elvira Such intercedence Barely gains credence ! No, no ; he dies !
Lep. Perdon, perdone, Signori miei, Quello io non sono, Sbaglia costei ; Viver lasciatemi Per carità.	*Lep.* O Sirs, forgive me For all this bother, Since I'm myself, Sirs, And not another ; [*Taking off his hat and shewing* Spare me my little life [*himself* To grow more wise.
Tutti. E Leporello ! Che inganno è questo ! Stupido resto Che mai sarà !	*The others.* Heav'n ! Leporello ! Most strange of fancies ! Scarcely our senses Believe our eyes.
Lep. Mille torbidi pensieri Mi s' aggiran per la testa ; Se mi salvo in tal tempesta, E un prodigio in verità.	*Lep.* Million turbulent vagaries In mine addled brain do gather ; To avoid the coming weather Were prodigious, in very truth.
Tutti. Mille torbidi pensieri Mi s' aggiran per la testa ; Che giornata, o stelle, è questa ! Che impensata novità !	*Anna, Elv., Oct. & Mas.* Million turbulent distractions In my brain arise and gather; Who could count on, or credit either, This dénouement so uncouth !

[*Donna Anna parte.*

[*Donna Anna leaves the scene, escorted by her Attendants*

SCENA XII.—Zerlina, Elvira, Ottavio, Masetto, Leporello.

SCENE XII.—Zerlina, Elvira, Octavio, Masetto, Leporello.

Zer. Dunque quello sei tu che il mio Masetto poco fà, crudelmente mal tratastì !	*Zer.* [*To Leporello.*] It was then at thy hands that my Masetto did receive such a scandalous mal-treatment.
Elv. [*A Lep.*] Dunque tu m' ingannasti, o scellerato, spacciandoti con me da Don Giovanni !	*Elv.* [*To Leporello.*] Then 'twas thy senseless jesting, heartless ribald, assumed the port and 'havior of Don Juan !
Otta. [*A Lep.*] Dunque tu in questi panni venisti quà per qualche tradimento !	*Oct.* [*To Leporello.*] And in this sacred Palace is not thy presence fraught with purpos'd mischief ?
Elv. A me tocca punirti.	*Elv.* With me rests thy chastisement.
Zer. Alzi a me.	*Oct.* Or with me.
Otta. No, no, a me.	*Oct.* Nay, nay ; with me.
Mas. Accopatelo meco tutti tre.	*Mas.* Lend a hand to his thrashing all ye three.
Lep. Ah, pieta ! Signori miei ! Pieta, pieta di me ! Do ragione a voi, a lei, Ma il delitto mio non è. Il padron con prepotenza L' innocenza mi rubò. Donna Elvira ! compatite ! Voi capite come andò ! Di Masetto non sò nulla Vel dirà questa fanciulla ! E' un oretta circa in circa, Che con lei girando vò. [*A Oct.*] A voi, Signore ! non dico niente ; Certo timore, certo accidente, Di fuori chiaro, di dentro oscuro, Non c' è riparo la porta, il muro, Vò da quel latto, poi qui celato ; L' affar si sà. Ma s' io saperò, fuggia per qua.	*Lep.* Tongue or blows I merit neither ; In grace to me incline ; With due def'rence to each and either, Learn how the real fault was not mine. Our gay Don a clean deception On mine innocence did throw. Fair Elvira, bear me witness ; How the matter went, you know. You, Masetto, mis-state sadly, And o'ershoot the mark most madly ; Some wild phrensy circumcurrent Through each brain begins to flow. Now, gentle Señor, I crave your pardon, But sorely frighten'd I 'spied the garden, Without, 'twas lamplight—within, obscure, Sir, That door stood open, inviting and sure, Sir— Whiles lurking cosey Came this *expose :* The rest is clear, O, quite clear ! Would I had known it, and slipp'd off here ! *Edging himself gradually up to the door, he takes to his heels and makes off.*

[*Leporello parte.*

SCENA XIII.—ZERLINA, ELVIRO OTTAVIO, MASETTO. | SCENE XIII.—ZERLINA, ELVIRA, OCTAVIO MASETTO

Elv.	Ferma, perfido, ferma !
Mas.	Il birbo ha l' ali si piedi.
Zer.	Con qual arte
	Si sottrasse l' iniquo !
Ott.	Amici miei
	Dopo eccessi sì enormi,
	Dubitar non possiam, che Don Giovanni
	Non sia l' empio uccisore
	Del padre di Donn' Anna. In questa casa
	Per poche ore fermatevi : un ricorso
	Vò far a chi si deve ; e in pochi istanti
	Vendicarvi prometto :
	Così vuole dover, pietade, affetto.

Elv.	Stay thee ! wicked one, stay thee !—
Mas.	His pace would baffle lightning—
Zer.	And how neatly he escaped further question—
Oct.	I claim your audience ; after crime so enormous there is no shade of doubt but that Don Juan was the midnight assassin of Anna's aged father : repair awhile within this Palace to comfort her—I will seek out the ministers of Justice, And work my Vengeance 'neath that mighty protection 'Tis the duty of Love ! the proof of Affection !

IL MIO TESORO—FLY THEN, MY LOVE. OCTAVIO.

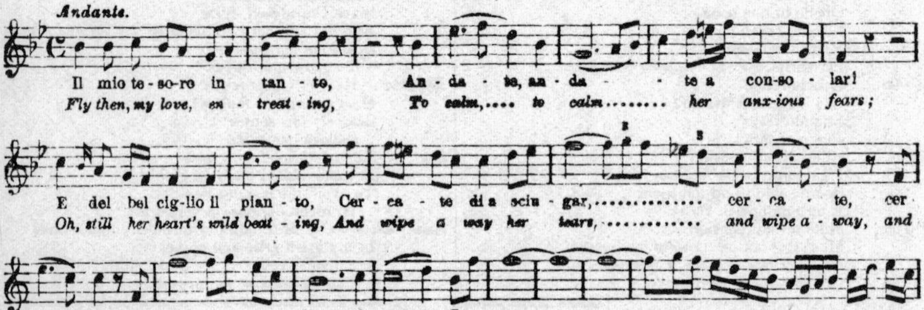

Andante.

Il mio te-so-ro in tan-to, An-da-te, an-da-te a con-so-lar!
Fly then, my love, en-treat-ing, To calm,.... to calm........ her anx-ious fears ;

E del bel cig-lio il pian-to, Cer-ca-te di a sciu-gar,.............. cer-ca-te, cer
Oh, still her heart's wild beat-ing, And wipe a way her tears,.............. and wipe a-way, and

ca-te, cer-ca-te di a-sciu-gar, Cer-ca-............-te
wipe away, and wipe.... a way her tears, And wipe.................. a

Fine.

di a-sciu-gar. Di-te le che i suoi tor-ti A ven-di-car io va-do ; A ven-di-car io
way her tears. Tell her I'll vengeance take On him who slew her sire, On him who slew her

va-do. Che sol di stra-gi e mor-ti Nun-zio vogl' io tor-nar, Nun zio vogl' io tor-
sire ; This arm his grave shall make, Or I'll by his ex-pire, Or I'll by his ex-

nar— Si, Nunzio vogl' io tor nar......................
pire— Yes, Or I'll by his ex-pire......................

D.C.

[Exeunt Don Octavio, Zerlina, Donna Elvira and Masetto

The scene changes. The stage represents an open square or plaza before the Cathedral of Seville, in the centre of which stands an equestrian Statue of marble to the memory of Don Pedro, the Commandant : on the pedestal of this Statue the following inscription is carved :

"I HERE AWAIT THE VENGEANCE DECREED BY HEAVEN UNTO THE WRETCH WHO SLEW ME."

It is about two in the morning

SCENA XIV.—Don Giovanni, salendo il muro; indi Leporello.

Gio. Ah! al! ah! questa è buona!
Or lasciala cercar. Che bella notte!
E piu chiara del giorno; sembra fatta
Per gir a zonzo, a caccia di ragazze.
Vediam s' è tardi? Ah, no!
Ancor non son le due di notte. Avrei
Voglia un pò di saper com' è finito
L' affar tra Leporello e Donna Elvira;
S' egli ha avuto giudizio.

Lep. [Senz' alito, dietro il muro.]
Alfin vuole ch' io faccia un precipizio!

Gio. E desso! Oh, Leporello!
Lep. Chi mi chiama?
Gio. Non conosci il padrone?
Lep. Cosi nol conoscessi!
Gio. Come? birbo!
Lep. Ah, siete voi? Scusate!
Gio. Cos' è stato?
Lep. Per cagion vostra io fui quasi accoppato.
Gio. Ebben, non era questo
Un onore per te?
Lep. Signor, vel dono!
Gio. Via, via, vien quà:
Che belle cose ti deggio dir!
Lep. Ma cosa fate quì?
Gio. Vien dentro, e lo saprai
Diverse istorielle,
Che accadute mi son, dacchè partisti,
Ti dirò un' altra volta; or la più bella
Ti vò solo narrar.
Lep. Donnesca, al certo.
Gio. C' è dubbio! Una fanciulla,
Bella, giovin, galante,
Per la strada incontrai; le vado appresso,
La prendo pe. la man—fuggir mi vuole;
Dico poche parole, ella mi piglia
Sai per chi?
Lep. Non lo sò.
Gio. Per Leporello!
Lep. Per me?
Gio. Per te!
Lep. Va bene!
Gio. Por la mano
Essa allora mi prende.
Lep. Ancora meglio!
Gio. M' accarezza, m' abbraccia—
" Caro il mio Leporello!
Leporello, mio caro!" Allor m' accorsi
Ch' era qualche tua bella.
Lep. [Aparte.] Oh, maledetto!
Gio. Dell' inganno approfitto: non sò come
Mi riconosce, grida, sento gente,—
A fuggire mi metto; e pronto pronto
Per quel muretto in questo loco io monte.
Lep. E mi dite la cosa
Con tal indifferenza—
Gio. Perchè no?
Lep. Ma se fosse costei stata mia moglie?
Gio. [Ridendo molto forte.] Meglio ancora!
[Parla la Statua.
Com. Di rider finirai
Pria dell' Aurora!
Gio. Chi ha parlato?
ep. Ah! qualch' anima sarà dell' altro mondo,
Che vi conosce a fondo.
Gio. Taci, sciocco! Chi va là?
Com. Ribaldo, audace!
Lascia ai morti la pace.

SCENE XIV.—Don Juan; afterwards Leporello.

Juan. [As he enters hastily.] Ha, ha, ha, ha! this is good
fun, now let her search away: [looking around him,] a
lovely night this, almost clearer than day-light; lady
moon gives her charter, too, toward the chasing pretty
damsels: what hour now? oh, barely turn'd of two in
the morning; 'twould like me to be well acquainted
how the matter ended 'twixt Leporello and Elvira
heaven grant he was prudent.

Lep. [Scrambling over the wall of the terrace, and sitting on it.
He'll ne'er pause, till I'm taken in and done for

Juan. Behold him: well, Leporello?
Lep. Who has call'd me?
Juan. Know ye not your liege lord?
Lep. O, would I ne'er had known him!
Juan. How so? villain!
Lep. Ah, is that you? your pardon.—
Juan. What has happen'd?
Lep. On your account have I nearly been murdered.
Juan. On my account, so please you; 'twere an honor for
thee.
Lep. Which I—relinquish.
Juan. Whu! whu! and list, my bird; a pretty story I have
to tell.
Lep. What art thou doing here?
Juan. Come down, and read that riddle. [Leporello jumps
down from off the wall, and advances.] Some ten or
twelve adventures have accrued to my share since last
we parted: I postpone them at present, keeping the
best for thine immediate ear.
Lep. A girl's at bottom.
Juan. I think so. [They re-exchange dresses during this narra-
tion.] Round by the Prado I encounter'd a dainty
blushing young damsel; I straight approach her—I
touch her dimpled hand; she would escape me but, a
word in due season bids her to take me—guess, for
whom?
Lep. I cannot.
Juan. For Leporello.
Lep. For me?
Juan. For thee.
Lep. So far,—good.
Juan. In her turn, by the hand, she too caught me—
Lep. And so far,—better.
Juan. She caresses—embraces—" darling little Leporello!"
—" Leporello, my darling!"—and then it struck me
she might just be your mistress.
Lep. O malediction!
Juan. I made hay while the sun shone: she soon found her
intense mistake, and scream'd out: steps draw near
us; I put wings to my trotters, and deftly I vault yon
wall to light here like a feather.
Lep. You can stand here, and tell me all this with brazen
coldness?
Juan. And why not?
Lep. But then what wouldst have done, were she my wife,
Sir?
Juan. So come o'er her.

The Statue of the Commandant.
With laughter chang'd to woe, greet you Aurora!
Juan. Who now spoke there?
Lep. [Trembling.] Ah, some spirit from the other world
who knows you, wishing more close acquaintance
Juan. Silence, blockhead! Who spoke there?
The Statue. Stay, ribald, this violence:
Leave to the dead their silence!

Lep. Ve l' ho detto !	*Lep.* As I told you.
Gio. Sarà qualcun di fuori, che si buria di noi	*Juan.* It must be some one o'er the wall then playing a
[*Con indifferenza e sprezzo.*	joke there. [*He approaches the Statue, and remarks it for*
Ehi! del Commendatore [*sion.*	*the first time.*] Eh! that Commandant's money here
Non è questa la statua ? Leggi un poc' quell' iscri-	has raised him a statue : read you yon inscription aloud.
Lep. Scusate : non ho imparato a leggere	*Lep.* Excuse me, I've heard it rated very bad to try and
A raggi della luna.	read by moonlight.—
Gio. Leggi, dico !	*Juan.* Read ! I tell you.
Lep. *Legge.*]	*Lep.* "I here—a-wait—that—vengeance, decreed—by—
" Dell' empio, che mi trasse al passo estremo.	Heav-en—
" Qui attendo la vendetta."	"Unto—the—wretch—who slew me."
Udiste ? io tremo !	You hear that ? I tremble !
Gio. O, vecchio buffonissimo !	*Juan.* Exquisite pithy epitaph ! tell him this very ev'ning I
Digli che questa sera l' attendo a cenar meco.	ask him home to supper.
Lep. Che pazzia ! Vi far ! Oh, Dei ! mirate	*Lep.* Gracious pow'rs ! are you mad ? O heav'n, observe,
Che terribili occhiate	Sir, what a terrible light his eyes assume ! he liveth !
Egli ci da ! Par vivo—par che senta—	he is breathing ! ye gods, he wants to speak !
E che voglia parlar.	
Gio. Orsù va là,	*Juan.* About the work !
O qui t' ammazzo ! E poi ti seppelisco !	Or I will slaughter, and 'neath this turf will lay thee.
Lep. Piano, piano, signore—	*Lep.* Piano, piano ! Señor, now I obey thee.
Ora ubbidisco.	[*Advancing and bowing to the Statue with great civility*
O, statua gentilissima	So please your marble mightiness,
Del gran Commendatore—	Most statuesque Commander—
Padron, mi trema il core ;	Lord, Sir! my senses wander,
Non posso terminar.	I cannot get it out.
Gio. Finiscila, o nel petto	*Juan.* Come, finish it ; or this weapon
Ti metto questo acciar.	Shall somewhat clear your throat.
[*Aparte.*] Che gusto, che spassetto !	(He flutters like a capon,
Lo voglio far tremar.	All flounder, quake, and flout.)
Lep. [*Aparte.*] Che impiccio ! che capriccio !	*Lep.* (To such insane caprices
Io sentomi gelar !	My fears refuse a vote.)
O, statua gentilissima,	[*Approaching the Statue again*
Benchè di marmo siate—	Most petrified of gentlemen,
Ah, padron mio ! mirate	Most polish'd marble statue—
Che seguita a guardar.	Ah, he is gazing right at you,
	Gods, how he glares about !
Gio. Mori, mori !	*Juan.* Die, Sir.
Lep. No, attendete ! [*Alla Statua.*	*Lep.* Not just at present.
Signore, il padron mio—	[*Advancing again to the Statue*
Badate ben, non io—	My lord so bold and high now
Vorria con voi cenar,	Invites you—mark ! not I, now,
Ah ! ah ! che sens è questa !	To join a drinking-bout.
Oh, Ciel !	[*The Statue bows in acquiescence ; Leporello falls on his knees.*
Chinò la testa !	Ah, ah ! I sink with dread, Sir,
	I swear he bow'd his head, Sir.
Gio. Va là che sei un buffone—	*Juan.* [*Laughing.*] All hope of cure you past are.
Lep. Guardate ancor, padrone.	*Lep.* Ah, look there, dear good master !
Gio. E che deggio guardar !	*Juan.* Ah, look at *what*, you lout ?
Lep. Colla marmorea testa	*Lep.* He made his marble helmet
Ei fa così così	To nod this way ! this way ! [*Imitating the Statue*
Gio. Parlate, se potete,	*Juan.* [*Advancing himself to the Statue.*
Verrete a cena ?	If an answer ;
	W.. per ?
Con. Si !	*The Statue.* Yea !
Lep. Mover mi posso appena !	*Lep.* Movement denied me ;
Mi manca, oh Dei, la lena !	That Earth ope, and hide me !
Per carità partiamo :	For mercy's , do quit, Sir,
Andiamo via di quà !	This most unpleasant place.
Gio. Bizzarra è inver la scena !	*Juan.* Bizarre ! though justly proper !
Verrà il buon vecchio a cena :	The old boy comes to supper ;
A preparala andiamo,	Away, bestir your wit, Sir,
Partiamo via di quà. [*Partono.*	To spread the board apace. [*Exeunt.*

The scene changes. The stage represents a vestibule in Donna Anna's Palace leading to her more private apartments, which are seen in the background.

Don Octavio enters, tenderly leading Donna Anna, whose whole demeanor still indicates that she is plunged in the deepest grief

SCENA XV.—*Camera.*—DONNA ANNA, DON OTTAVIO.	SCENE XV.—DONNA ANNA, DON OCTAVIO.
Ott. Calmatevi, idol mio, di quel ribaldo	*Oct.* Calm thee, mine own existence : thou soon shalt see
Vedrem puniti in breve i gravi eccessi,	this arch-ribald suffer for his vile excesses 'neath a
Vendicati sarem	mighty revenge.

Anna. Ma il padre, oh Dio!
Otta. Convien chinar il ciglio
Al volere del Ciel. Respira, o cara,
Di tua perdita amara
Fia domani, se vuoi, dolce compenso
Questo cor, questa mano, ch' il mio tenero amor!
Anna. Oh, Dei! che dite, in si tristi momenti
Otta. E che vorresti con indugi novelli
Accrescer le mie pene? Crudel!
Anna. Crudele! ah, no!
Mio ben, troppo mi spiace
Allontanarti un ben che lungamente
La nostr' alma desia;
Ma il mondo? oh Dio!
Non sedur la mia costanza
Del sensibil mio core;
Abbastanza per te mi parla amore.
Non rai dir, bell' idol mio,
Che son io crudel con te;
Tu ben sai quant' io t' amai,
Tu conosci la mia fè.
Calma, calma il tuo tormento!
Se di duol non vuoi ch' io mora,
Forse un giorno il Cielo ancora
Sentirà pietà di me.
[Parte.

Anna. Will't give back—my father?
Oct. We bow in mute submission to Heaven's decree
look up then, beloved; why, thy bitterest anguish on
the morrow might melt, kiss'd into gladness—for this
heart—this affection—this my tenderest love—

Anna. O God! such accents in these moments of sorrow!—
Oct. And why with this prolonged unneeded delaying in
crease my faithful yearning? unkind!
Anna. "Unkind" love? ah no, Octavio.
Poorly it likes me thus to defer a bliss
So long, so justly, so supremely our object:
The world though—O heaven!— [bleedeth
Still to try thy constant patience this my heart truly
For Love, all in thy cause fervently pleadeth.
Never say
That cold displeasure's
Joyless measures
Can chill my breath;
Poesy's power
In Phœbus bower,
Could not picture half my faith.
Calm, ah calm thy gentler sorrow,
If you grieve, my woes are double;
Haply these brief hours of trouble
Gem with smiles our future path. [Exit.

SCENA XVI.—Don Ottavio.

Otta. Ah! si segua il suo passo;
Io vò con lei dividere i martiri:
Saran meco men gravi i suoi sospiri.
[Parte.

SCENE XVI.—Don Octavio, solus.

Oct. [Looking after her.] Yes, I follow her footsteps
Participation can dull the edge of Sorrow,
And from Friendship, e'en Woe a sunbeam may
borrow. [Departs

The scene changes. The stage represents a grand banqueting-hall in the Palace of Don Juan: towards one side of which, a magnificent table is spread with a sumptuous repast. Don Juan is discovered seated at the table. Leporello stands at the beaufet, napkin in hand, wiping silver plates, &c., and directing the various servants in attendance on Don Juan. The gallery above is filled with musicians.

SCENA XVII.—Don Giovanni, Leporello.

Gio. Già la mensa è preparata—
Voi suonate, amici cari,
Già che spendo i miei danari,
Io mi voglio divertir
Leporello, presto in tavola
Lep. Son prontissimo a servir
Bravi! "Cosa Rara"
Gio. Che ti par del bel concerto?
Lep. E conforme al vostro merto.
Gio. Ah che piatto saporito!
Lep. Ah che barbaro appetito!
Che bocconi da gigante,
Mi par proprio di svenir
Gio. Nel veder i miei bocconi
Gli par proprio di svenir
Piatto!
Lep. Servo.
Gio. Versa il vino.

Lep. "Fra i due Litiganti"
Gio. Eccellente marsimino!
Lep. [Aparte.] Queste pezzo di fagiano,
Piano piano vo inghiottir

Gio. Sta mangiando quel marrano!
Fingerò di non capir

Gio. Silenzio ancora la musica.]
Questa poi la conosco par troppo

SCENE XVII.—Don Juan, Leporello, Ladies, Attendants, Servants, Musicians.

Juan. Richest dainties rise before me,
Play your best, to crown the pleasure;
Let expense be free from measure!
Let me boast right royal cheer!
Leporello, now the second course.
Lep. Sir, your most obedient, here.
[The Musicians strike up an air from Martini's "La Cosa Rara."] Bravi! bravi!—"Cosa Rara."
Juan. Is it not an air of spirit?
Lep. Aye,—and suited to your merit.
Juan. Why, this cream would honor "Gunter."
Lep. (He is hungry as a hunter,
And he eats just like a giant;
I may look and—long, I fear.)
Juan. (Did his mouth feed as his eyes do,
He would swallow all, I fear.)
Plates, here!
Lep. Serv'd, Sir.
Juan. Pour some sherry
[Leporello fills his master's glass; the Musicians have now changed to another air
Lep. From "I Due Litiganti."
Juan. 'Faith, that bottle makes us merry.
Lep. [Helping himself to the maccaroni, and eating as fast as he can.] (This small dish of maccaroni
Quickly, quickly let me clear.)
Juan. (What's that scamp at? eating, only;
Not to know it I'll appear.) [The Musicians play "Non più Andrai," from "Le Nozze di Figaro.
Lep. "Non più Andrai," from "Le Nozze," by Mozart

Gio.	Leporello!
Lep.	Padron mio!
Gio.	Parla schietto, mascalzone—
Lep.	Non mi lascia una flussione
	Le parole proferir.
Gio.	Mentre io mangio, fischia un poco.
Lep.	Non so far.
Gio.	Cos' è?
Lep.	Scusate!
	Si eccellente è il vostro cuoco,
	Che lo volli anch' io provar—
Gio.	Si eccellente è il cuoco mio,
	Che lo volle anch' ei provar.

Juan. Leporello!
Lep.   Your commands, Sir?
Juan. Speak more plainly, clear your throat. Sir!
Lep. I can boast no plainer note, Sir,
     Sore throat makes mine accent queer.
Juan. Nay; then whistle—this a joke is.
Lep. Don't know how—
Juan. And why?
Lep.   Excuse me;
     Such a paragon your cook is,
     I can swear he hath no peer.
Juan. "Such a paragon my cook is,
     How could he resist the cheer ·

SCENA XVIII.—Donna Elvira ; e detti.

SCENE XVIII.—The same ; Donna Elvira

Elv. [*A Don Giovanni.*] L' ultima prova dell' amor mio
     Ancor vogl' io fare con te :   [*S' inginocchia.*
     Più non rammento gl' inganni tuoi,
     Pietate io sento—
Gio. } [*Aparte.*]
Lep. } Cos' è? cos' è?
Elv. Da te non chiede quest' alma oppressa
     Eella sua fede qualche mercè.
Gio. Mi maraviglio ! Cosa volete?
     Se non sorgete—non resto in più.
Elv. Ah, non deridere gli affanni miei !
Lep. Quasi da piangere mi fa costei !
Gio. Io tederidere ! Cielo ! perchè ?
     Che vuoi, mio bene ?
Elv. Che vita cangi !
Gio.   Brava !
Elv. Cor perfido !
Gio. Lascia ch' io mangi ; a se ti piace,
     Mangia con me.
Elv. Mimanti, barbaro, nel lezzo immondo,
     Esempio orribile d' iniquità.
Lep. [*Aparte.*] Se non si muove al suo dolore,
     Di sasso ha il core—o cor non ha.
Gio. Vivan le femmine ! Viva il buon vino !
     Sostegno e gloria d' umanità.

Elv. All mine affection yearns to retrieve thee ;
     Love can reprieve thee ere Error slav.
     Mem'ry doth banish all thine offences ,
     'Neath Mercy, they vanish—
Juan. & Lep. What does she say ?
Elv. I will not hurt you clam'ring for justice ;
     Learn but one virtue ! Mend, while you may
Juan. Dear ! how surprising ! what more your will, her
     If you still kneel, then, I, too, essay,
Elv. Ah, do not ridicule such deep afflictions !
Lep. ('Gad, she is stirring up my sad reflections)—
Juan. I, lady—"ridicule ?" And in what way ?
     Come, love, what would you ?—
Elv. Teach thee repentance !
*Juan. Brava !
Elv.   Base, cruel wretch !
Juan. Sharp though that sentence, I can excuse it ;
     Sup with us, pray !
Elv. Monster ! I leave thee, then, slave to thy passions
     Sunken in brutal lust, hated by all !
Lep. (It is a stone heart takes it thus coolly ;
     Or, to speak truly, no heart at all !)
Juan. Long live the pretty girls ! long live the wine-cup !
     They are the glory of Earth's merry ball !

[*Donna Elvira rushes off by one of the extremes on the left ; but presently returns, uttering a piercing shriek.*]

Elv. [*Partendo.*] Ah !   [*Parte.*
Gio. Che grido è questo mai ?
     Va a veder che cos' è stato.

Elv. [*Re-entering.*] Ah !   [*Escapes by another door*
Juan. & Lep. [*To each other.*] And why that shriek of terror
Juan. [*To Leporello.*] Run and see what is the matter

SCENA XIX.—Don Giovanni, Leporello.

SCENE XIX.—Don Juan, Leporello.

Lep. Ah !   [*Sorte Leporello, e ritorna spaventato.*
Gio. Che grido indiavolato ?
     Leporello, che cos' è ?
Lep. Ah, signor, per carità,
     Non andate fuor di qua !
     L' uom di sasso, l' uomo bianco—
     Ah, padrone, io gelo, io manco !
     Se vedeste che figura,
     Se sentiste come fa—
     Ta, ta, ta, ta !
Gio. Non capisto niente affatto
     Tu sei matto in verità.

Lep. [*Goes out and returns presently, dropping his light*
     Ah !
Juan. Explain this dev'lish clatter !
     Leporello, what is up ?
Lep. Ah, Señor !—I—must—im-plore
     Do—not—venture—past—the—door !
     Sir,—the—Sta-tue !—that—huge white man,
     O dear master,—I'm dying—with fright, man
     If—you—could—but see—his—figure !
     Or—could—hear—his—step—a-far !
     Ta ! ta ! ta ! ta !
Juan. I can make nor head nor tail on't ;
     You're gone mad, and very far !

       [*A loud knocking is heard*

Lep. Ah sentite !
Gio.   Qualcun batte.
     Apri !
       Io tremo !
         Apri, dico !

           Ah ! ah !

Lep. Listen, listen !
Juan.   Who is knocking !
     Open !   [*Drawing his sword*
Lep. [*Falling on his knees.*] I—can—not !
Juan. [*Menacing Leporello with the sword.*]
     Open, quickly !
Lep. [*Shrieking.*] Ah !

no. **Matto!**	*Juan.* [*Snatching a candle from the table.*]
Per togliermi d' intrico	Idiot! ye tie the knot up faster,
Ad aprir io stesso andrò! [*Parte.*	I to gain the clue, must go. [*H goes ca.*
lep. Non vò più veder l' amico,	*Lep.* Now adieu to thee, poor master,
Pian pianin m' asconderò.	It were best be scarce, I trow.
[*Si nasconde sotto la Tavola.*	

Leporello hides himself under the table; the lights go out. Don Juan re-enters, candle and drawn sword in hand, backing before the Statue of the Commandant, which enters on foot, and advances one step into the apartment, remaining rigid and firm.

SCENA XX.—*Il Commendatore. E detti.* | **SCENE XX.**—DON JUAN; THE STATUE OF THE COMMANDANT; LEPORELLO, *under the table.*

Com. Don Giovanni, a cenar teco / M' invitasti—è son venuto!
Gio. Non l' avrei giammai creduto; / Ma farò quel che potró. / Leporello, un' altra cena / Fa che subito si porti.
Lep. Ah, padron, siam tutti morti!
Gio. Vanne, dico!
Com. Ferma un pò! / Non si pasce di cibo mortale / Chi si pasce di cibo celeste: / Altre cure più gravi di queste— / Altra brama quaggiù mi guido!
Lep. La terzana d' avere mi sembra, / E le membra fermar più non so!
Gio. Parla dunque—che chiedi? che vuoi!
Com. Parlo, ascolt! più tempo non ho!
Gio. Parla, parla! ascoltandoti sto.
Com. Tu m' invitasti a cena, / Il tuo dover or sai! / Rispondimi: verrai / Tu a cenar meco?
Lep. Oibò! oibò! tempo non hà—scusate.
Gio. A torto di viltate / Tacciato mai sarò.
Com. Risolvi!
Gio. Ho già risolto.
Com. Verrai?
Lep. Dite di no!
Gio. Ho fermo il core in petto; / Non hò timor: verrò!
Com. Dammi la mano in pegno!
Gio. Eccola.

Statue. So, Don Juan, thou didst invite me / To thy banquet,—lo, I am present!
Juan. Though unlook'd for, this is pleasant, / I will strive my best to do. [*Calling to Leporello, under the table.* / Leporello, clear the table, / And another supper run for—
Lep. Ah, Señor, we all are done for
Juan. Run, I tell thee—
Statue. Hold! do not go / He may never taste food that is mortal / Who is fed on the manna of Heaven; / Graver cares to these moments are given, / Other purpose I come here to show.
Lep. (O, the cold of an Arctic December / Shivers through me with terrible throe.)
Juan. Speak out bravely: your purpose? what want you?
Statue. Listen; for Time's precious seconds, fast flow.
Juan. Speak, then, speak: I am longing to know.
Statue. Thou bad'st me to thy supper; / Host of mine would I turn: / And wilt thou too, in thy turn / Come to my banquet—
Lep. [*To the Statue.*] Hallo! He is engag'd, excuse him
Juan. Thy guest, none can accuse him / As one whom fear could cow.
Statue. The answer?
Juan. My mind is made up.
Statue. Wilt come, then?
Lep. Please tell him "no!"
Juan. With firmer heart than iron, / If so you will,—be't so!
Statue. Pledge me thy hand as earnest.
Juan. Take it, then.

The moment the marble fingers of the Statue close upon his hand, a shuddering seizes Don Juan's whole frame, and a wild terror seems to possess him

Ohimè. / Che gelo è quest mai!
Com. Pentiti, cangia vita, / E l' ultimo momento!
Gio. No, no—ch' io non mi pento; / Vanne lontan da me!
Com. Pentiti! scelerato!
Gio. No, vecchio infatuato
Com. Pentiti!
Gio. Nò.
Com. & Lep. Sì!
Gio. Nò!
Com. Ah tempo più non v' è! [*Parte.*

Alas! / Mine hour of death is nigh.
Statue. Turn thee, repent thy vices / Ere Heav'n award the sentence.
Juan. [*Still in the Statue's grasp.*] / No, no; I scorn repentance! / Hence, dotard! end this farce!
Statue. Turn thee, insensate rev'ller!
Juan. Away, thou babbling driv'ller!
Statue. Yet repent!
Juan. No!
Statue. & Lep. Yes!
Juan. No!
Statue. [*Letting Don Juan's hand drop.*] / Down to thy doom then pass!

The Statue sinks; flames rise on all sides; and from the abyss that has engulfed the Statue, Demons rush forth and seize Don Juan.

SCENA XXI.—Don Giovanni, Leporello, *Chorus of Demons.*

Gio.
Da qual tremore insolito
  Sento assalir gli spiriti!
  Dond' escono quei vortici
Di foco pien d' orror?
Chi l' anima mi lacera,—
Chi m' agita le viscere!
Che strazio ohimè! che smania!
Che inferno! che terror!

Lep.
Che ceffo disperato!
Che gesti di dannato!
Che gridi! che lamenti
Come mi fa terror!

Coro.
Tutto a tue colpe è poco,
Vieni, v' è un mal peggior!

SCENE XXI.—Don Juan, Leporello, *Chorus of Demons.*

Juan.
Hideous fears are seizing me,
  Hell and its horrors rise around,
  The Awful Summons thundereth
Thro' Fire's eternal roar!
Each Sense that slav'd me withereth,
The heart they slew is slain at last,
The soul they burnt shall burn still
When Time itself is o'er!

Lep.
He shews the fate that waiteth
The doom'd and damn'd ungodly.
What shrieks! what cries of terror!
I dare to look no more!

Cho. of Demons. These pangs but ill requite thee,
Down! there are worse in store!

[*The Demons overcome Don Juan, and sink with him into the abyss*

SCENA XXII e Ultima.—Donna Anna, Zerlina, Donna Elvira, Don Ottavio, Masetto, Leporello.

Tutti.
{ Ah! dov' è il perfido!
{ Dov' è l' indegno!
  Tutto, il mio sdegno sfogar io vò.
Anna.
Solo mirandolo stretto in catene
  Alle mie pene calma darò.
Lep.
Più non sperate di ritrovarlo,
  Più non cercate lontano andò.
Tutti. Cos' è? favella—
Lep. Venne un colosso—ma se non posso—
Tutti. Via, presto sbrigati!
Lep.
Tra fume e foco, badate un poco,
  L' uomo di sasso fermate il passo—
  Giusto la sotto diede il gran botto—
  Giusto là il diavolo sel tranguigò
Tutto. Stelle! che sento!
Lep. Vero è l' evento.
Tutti. Ah! certo è l'ombra che l'incontra.
Otta.
Or che tutti, o mio tesoro!
  Vendicati siam dal cielo,
  Porgi, porgi a me un ristoro
Non mi fà languire ancor.

Anna.
Lascia, o caro, un anno ancora
  Allo sfogo del mio cor,
  Al desio di chi t' adora
Ceder deve un fido amor
Zer. e Mas. Noi { Masetto
              { Zerlina } a casa andiamo,
A cenar in compagnia.
Lep.
Ed io vado all' osteria
A trovar padron miglior.
Tutti.
Resti dunque quel birbon
  Con Proserpina e Pluton!
  E noi tutti, o buona gente
  Ripetiam allegramente
  L' antichissima canzon:
  Questo è il fin, di chi fà mal,
  E dì perfidi la morte.
  Alla vita è sempre egual.

SCENE XXII and Last.—Donna Anna, Zerlina, Donna Elvira, Don Octavio, Masetto, Leporello, *Attendants, Officers of Justice.*

Anna, Zer., Elv., Oct. & Mas.
  Where lurks the murderer? where hides the traitor
  Justice, ne'er greater, poiseth her blow.
Anna.
Viewing him bound in chains henceforth to languish
  Would o'er mine anguish calm gently throw.
Lep.
Gentlefolk, hope not ever to find him;
  Search not or grope not, he's off, I trow.
The Rest. And how befell it?
Lep. Came a colossus—Sirs—I can't tell it—
The Rest. Quickly! explain yourself!—
Lep.
Lightnings and thunder rent Earth asunder,—
  Gazing hard at you enter'd the Statue—
  Here, too, his foot was; here, his huge boot was
  Just there, the Devil did down with him go!
The Rest. Heav'n! speak you truly?
Lep. All is told fully
The Rest Aye; sure the Statue fulfill'd its vow!
Oct. [*To Donna Anna.*]
Since thy sorrows, mine angel-treasure,
  Are aveng'd by mightier Powers:
  Bid my hopes, wing'd with vision'd pleasure
  Reach the home whereto they soar.
Anna.
Let these pass, love, one twelvemonth o'er her
  That all tears may quit the shore,
  Ere the faithful true adorer
  Reap the rich reward in store.
Zer. & Mas. Come, my sweet, the priest tomorrow
Ushers in domestic blessing.
Lep.
Let me look to   possessing
Better master   'fore.
Zer., Mas. & Lep. Stay,   cause of all our wrong
  With old Pluto's crew along!
  Since our ev'ry heart rejoices,
  Let us gladly blend our voices
  In an old time-honor'd song.
All.
"Such his end—who doeth ill!
  To a like account, the wicked
  Ever did come—ever will!"

THE END

THE BARBER OF SEVILLE
(IL BARBIERE DI SIVIGLIA)

by

GIOACCHINO ROSSINI

THE STORY OF
"THE BARBER OF SEVILLE"

THE Count Almaviva, desperately in love with Rosina, the ward of Doctor Bartolo after serenading his mistress, encounters Figaro, the Barber and factotum of the town, a meddling busy-body; to him the Count confesses his love, and they mutually plot for the purpose of bringing about the introduction of Almaviva to the maiden.

Rosina is strictly watched by her guardian, Doctor Bartolo, who cherishes a desire of wedding his ward himself; in this design he is assisted by Basilio, a music-master. Rosina returns the affection of the Count, to whom, in spite of the watchfulness of her guardian, she contrives to convey a letter, declaring her passion, and her intention to break through her trammels, and at the same time requesting his name.

To obtain an interview with his mistress the Count disguises himself as a drunken soldier, and forces his way into Bartolo's house. Rosina has already been told by Figaro that the name of the Count is Signor Lindor. The disguise of Almaviva is discovered by the guardian, the pretended soldier is placed under arrest, and the first act concludes.

In the second act the Count again enters Bartolo's house, disguised as a music-teacher, pretending that he has been sent by Basilio to give a lesson in music, on account of the ill-ness of the latter. To obtain the confidence of Bartolo, he produces Rosina's letter to himself, and offers to persuade Rosina that the letter has been given to him by a mistress of the Count, and thus to break off the connection between the two. He obtains the desired interview, which proceeds satisfactorily, and Figaro manages to obtain the keys of the balcony, while at the same time an escape is determined on at midnight, and a private marriage arranged. In the meantime, Basilio himself makes his appearance, the lovers are disconcerted, and the Count makes his escape.

Bartolo, who possesses the letter of Rosina written to the Count, succeeds, by producing it, in exciting the jealousy of his ward, who, while under the influence of this feeling, discloses the plan of escape which had been arranged, and agrees to marry her guardian. At the appointed time Figaro and the Count make their appearance, and after some confusion the lovers are reconciled. A notary, procured by Bartolo, celebrates the marriage of the enamored pair. Immediately afterwards the guardian enters, accompanied by the officers of justice, into whose hands he is about to consign Figaro and the Count, when mutual explanations take place, and all parties are reconciled.

This opera was first produced at the Teatro Argentina, in Rome, at the Carnival in 1816.

IL BARBIERE DI SIVIGLIA
(THE BARBER OF SEVILLE)

ACT I.	ATTO I.
SCENE I.—A Street in Seville.—Dawn of Morning.	SCENA PRIMA.—Il momento dell'azione è sul termine della Notte.—La Scena rappresenta una Strada in Siviglia.
Fiorello, with a lantern in his hand, introducing various Musicians; the Count Almaviva, wrapped up in a mantle.	Fiorello, con lanterna nelle mani, introducendo vari Suonatori; indi il Conte Almaviva avvolto in un mantello.

Fiorello. Piano, pianissimo, in tender sound,
Let love's light airs now float
around.

Chorus. Piano, pianissimo,
Love's music sound.

Fiorello. All wrapped in silence, no soul is
near;
No wandering footstep falls on the
ear.

Count. Fiorello—ho!
(In a low voice.)

Fiorello. Sir, I am here.

Count. Well; and our friends?

Fiorello. They are all ready.

Count. All's well;
Keep silence.

Fiorello. Softly, softly!
Utter not a word.
Oh, moment full of rapture!
Oh, bliss almost divine!
Such beauty well may capture
A heart already thine.
Ho, Fiorello!
(They tune their instruments, and the Count sings, accompanied by them.)

Fiorello. Sir?

Count. Say, have you seen her?

Fiorello. No, sir.

Count. Ah, how vain is every hope!

Fiorello. Behold, sir, the dawn advances.

Count. Ah, what am I to think—what
shall I do?
All is vain. Well, my friends?

Chorus. Sir?
(Softly.)

Count. Retire, retire;
I have no longer need
Of your songs or your music.
(He gives a purse to Fiorello, who distributes money to all.)

Fiorello. Piano, pianissimo, senza parlar
Tutti con me venite quà.

Coro. Piano, pianissimo, eccoci quà
Piano, venite quà.

Fiorello. Tutto è silenzio, nessun qui c'è;
Che i nostri canti possa turbar.

Conte. Fiorello—olà!
(Sotto voce.)

Fiorello. Signor, son quà.

Conte. Ebben; gl'amici?

Fiorello. Son pronti già.

Conte. Bravi, bravissimi;
Fate silenzio.

Fiorello. Piano, pianissimo!
Senza parlar.
O, istante d'amor!
Felice momento!
O, dolce contento
Ch'eguale non ha.
Ei, Fiorello!
(Accordano gl'istrumenti, e il Conte canta accompagnato da essi.)

Fiorello. Mio signore?

Conte. Dì, la vedi?

Fiorello. Signor, nò.

Conte. Ah, che è vana ogni speranza!

Fiorello. Signor Conte, il giorno avanza.

Conte. Ah, che penso—che farò?
Tutto è vano. Buona gente?

Coro. Mio signore?
(Sotto voce.)

Conte. Avanti, avanti;
Più di suoni più di canti
Io bisogno ormai non ho.
(Dà una borsa a Fiorello, il quale distribuisce devari a tutti.)

ECCO RIDENTE IL CIELO—LO! SMILING IN THE ORIENT SKY

Ec - co ri - den - te il cie - - lo, Spun - ta la bel - la au -
Lo! smil - ing in the o - ri - ent sky, Morn in her beau - ty

ro - ra, E tu non sor - gi an - co - ra E -
breck - ing, Canst thou, my love, in - ac - tive lie My

puoi dor - mir co - si? Ah! Sòr - gi mia dol - ce spe - me,
life, art thou not wak - ing? A - rise, my heart's own treas - ure,

Vie - ni bell' I - dol mi - o, Ren - di men cru - do, oh Di - o! Lo
All that my soul holds dear; Oh! turn my grief to pleas - ure! A -

stral, lo stral che mi fe - rì; lo stral che mi, fe -
wake, my love, my love, ap - pear; a - wake, my love, ap -

rì. Oh, sor - te! gia veg - go? Quei
pear. Oh, joy! and do I see thee? My

ca - ro sem - bi - an - te; Quest' a - ni - ma a -
doubts all dis - ap - pear; Those eyes are heav - en

man - te ot - ten - ne pie - ta?
to me! What have I now to fear?

Fiorello. Good night to all;
I have nothing farther for you
to do.

(The Musicians surround the Count, thanking him and kissing his hand. Annoyed by the noise they make, he tries to drive them away. Fiorello does the same.

Chorus. Many thanks, sir, for this favor;
Better master, nor a braver,
Ever did we sing a stave for.
Pray, good sir, command our
throats!
We will ever sing and pray for
One who gives us gold for notes!

Count. Silence! silence! cease your
bawling,
Nor like cats with caterwauling
Wake the neighbors—stop your
squalling,
Rascals, or I'll dust your coats!
If this noise you still keep making,
All the neighbors you'll be waking.

Fiorello. Silence! silence! what an uproar!
For these favors—for such honor!
(Mocking them.)
Rascals, hence, away—
Scoundrels, quit the spot!
Eh, what a devilish uproar!
Are ye mad, or not?
(Exit Chorus.)

Count. The indiscreet rabble! They had
nearly,
With their importunate clamors,
Awakened the whole neighborhood.
At last they're gone! But she
appears not.
(Looking towards the balcony.)
It is in vain to hope; yet here will I
(He paces pensively up and down.)
Wait till I behold her. Every
morning
Does she come into this balcony
To breathe the fresh air at early
dawn.
Here will I wait.—Ho, Fiorello!
Do you also retire.

Fiorello. I go. Yonder
I will await your commands.
(He withdraws.)

SCENE II.—Figaro, with his Guitar round his neck, and the preceding.

Fiorello. Buona notte a tutti quanti;
Più di voi che far non so.

(Gli Suonatori circondano il Conte, ringraziandolo, e baciandogli la mano. Egli, indispettito per lo strepito che fanno li và cacciando. Lo stesso fa anche Fiorello.)

Coro. Mille grazie, mio Signore;
Del favore, dell'onore,
Ah! di tanta cortesìa.
Obbligati in verità!
O che incontro fortunato
È un signor di qualità!

Conte. Basta! basta! non parlate,
Ma non serve, non gridate,
Maledetti, andate via,
Ah, canaglia, via di quà!
Tutto quanto il vicinato
Questo chiasso sveglierà.

Fiorello. Zitti! zitti! che rumore!
Ma che onore—che favore!
(Con ironia.)
Maledetti, andate via—
Ah, canaglia, via di quà!
Veh, che chiasso indiavolato!
Ah, che rabbia che mi fa?
(Il Coro parte.)

Conte. Gente indiscreta! Ah quasi,
Con quel chiasso importuno,
Tutto quanto il quartier han risvegliato.
Alfin sono partiti! E non si vede.
(Guardando verso la Ringhiera.)
È inutile sperar; eppur quì voglio
(Passeggia riflettendo.)
Aspettar di vederla. Ogni mattina
Ella su quel balcone
A prender fresco viene in sull'
Aurora.
Proviamo.—Olà, tu ancora
Ritirati, Fiorello!

Fiorello. Vado. Là in fondo
Attenderò suoi ordini.
(Si ritira.)

SCENA II.—Figaro, con Chitarra appesa al collo, e detti.

LARGO AL FACTOTUM DELLA CITTA—*ROOM FOR THE CITY'S FACTOTUM*

FIGARO

Lar - go al fac - to — tum del-la cit - tà   lar - go,.   La, la,
Room — for the   cit -   y's — fac - to - tum, here,   La, la,

la, la, la, la, la, la, la, la. Pres-to a bot-te - ga che l'al-ba è già pres-
la, la, la, la, la, la, la, la. *I__must be off to my shop, for the dawn is*

to, la, la, la, la, la, la, la, la, la, la. Ah, che bel vi - ve-re,
near, *la, la, la, la, la, la, la, la, la, la.* *What a__ mer-ry life,*

che bel_pià-ce-re, che bel pia-ce-re, Per un bar - bie - re, di qua-li-
what pleas-ure gay,__ *what pleas-ure gay,_* *A-waits a bar - ber of qua-li-*

tà, di qua-li - tà. Ah,__ bra-vo, Fi - ga - ro; bra-vo, bra-
ty, *of qua-li - ty.* *Ah,__ bra - vo,* *Fi - ga - ro; bra-vo, bra-*

vis-si-mo bra - vo. La, la, la, la, la, la, la, la, la, la;
vis - si-mo bra - vo. *La, la, la, la, la, la, la, la, la, la;*

For - tu - na-tis-si-mo, per ve-ri - tà, bra - vo, la, la, la, la, la, la, la, la,
Of__men, the hap-pi-est, sure, art__ thou, bra - vo. *la, la, la, la, la, la, la, la,*

là, la; for - tu - na-tis - si - mo, per ve-ri - tà, for - tu - na-tis -si-mo
la, la; *Of__men, the hap-pi - est, sure, art__ thou,* *Of__ men, the hap-pi - est,*

per ve-ri - tà, la, la, la, la, la, la, la, la, la, la, la, la, la, la, la, la, la, la, la.
sure, art__ thou, la, la, la, la, la, la, la, la, la, la, la, la, la, la, la, la, la, la, la, la.

Figaro.　La ran la lera,	Figaro.　La ran la lera,
La ran la la!	La ran la la!
Ready to do everything	Pronto a far tutto
Both by night and by day—	La notte e il giorno—

Perpetually in bustle
And in motion.
What happier lot,
What nobler life
For a barber,
Than my own!
La ran la lera,
La ran la la!
Razors and combs,
Lancets and scissors—
Everything is
Ready at command!
Then there are the snug
Perquisites of business
With gay damsels,
With cavaliers.
La ran la lera,
La ran la la!
All call for me,
All want me—
Dames, maidens,
Old and young:
My peruke! cries one;
Quick, my beard! another;
Here, bleed me! a third:
Figaro! Figaro!
I am here, I am here.
Figaro up, Figaro down!
Figaro here, Figaro there!
I am activity itself—
I'm quick as lightning—
I'm the factotum
Of the city.
Ah, bravo, Figaro!
Bravo, bravissimo!
Most fortunate of men
In every truth.
La ran la lera,
La ran la la!
Ah! ah! what a happy life!
But little fatigue, and abundant
amusement;
Always with some doubloons in
my pocket,
The noble fruit of my reputation.
So it is: without Figaro
There's not a girl in Seville will
marry;
To me the little widows
Have recourse for a husband: I,
under excuse
Of my comb by day,
And under favor of my guitar by
night,
Endeavor—though I don't do it for
the sake of saying so—

Sempre d'intorno
In giro stà.
Miglior cuccagna,
Per un barbiere
Vita più nobile,
Nò non si dà.
La ran la lera,
La ran la la!
Rasori, e pettini,
Lancette, e forbici—
Al mio comando
Tutto quì stà!
Vi è la risorsa
Poi del mestiere
Colla donnetta,
Col cavaliere.
La ran la lera,
La ran la la!
Tutti mi chiedono,
Tutti mi vogliono—
Donne, ragazze,
Vecchi, fanciulle:
Quà la parucca!
Presto la barba!
Quà la sanguigna:
Figaro! Figaro!
Son quà, son quà.
Figaro sù, Figaro giù!
Figaro quà, Figaro la!
Pronto prontissimo—
Son come un fulmine—
Sono il factotum
Della città.
Ah, bravo, Figaro!
Bravo, bravissimo!
Fortunatissimo
Per verità.
La ran la lera,
La ran la la!
Ah! ah! che bella vita!
Faticar poco, e divertirsi assai;

È in tasca sempre aver qualche
doblone,
Gran frutto della mia reputazione.
Ecco quà: senza Figaro
Non si accasa in Siviglia una
ragazza;
A me la vedovella
Ricorre per marito: io, colla scusa

Del pettine di giorno,

Della chitarra col favor la notte,

A tutti onestamente—

	To please all in an honest way.
	Oh, what a life, what a life! Oh,
	what business!
	Now, away to the shop—
Count.	(It is he, or I am much deceived.)
Figaro.	(Who may this be?)
Count.	It is no less than himself.
	Figaro!
Figaro.	Good master!
	Oh, whom do I see?—your
	Excellency—
Count.	Hush! hush! be prudent;
	I am not known here,
	Nor do I wish to be—for this
	I have the best of reasons.
Figaro.	I understand, I understand—
	I'll not interrupt you.
Count.	Stop!
Figaro.	For what purpose?
Count.	No, I tell you—stop here:
	I will explain myself. On the Prado
	I beheld a flower of beauty—a
	maiden,
	The daughter of a certain silly old
	physician, who
	Within these few days has estab-
	lished himself here.
	Enamored of this damsel, I have
	left
	My country and relatives; and here
	I am come,
	Under the name of Lindor;
	And, night and day,
	I watch and wander near this
	balcony.
Figaro.	Near this balcony?—a physician?
	Zounds!
	You are very fortunate:
	And must make hay while the
	sun shines.
Count.	Explain!
Figaro.	Certainly.—In this house
	I am a barber, perruquier,
	surgeon,
	Botanist, apothecary, veterinary—
	The major-domo of the house.
Count.	Oh, how fortunate!
Figaro.	But this is not all: the girl is not
	The daughter of the physician—
	she is only his ward.
Count.	Oh, what a consolation!

	Non fo per dir—m'adatto a far
	piacere,
	Oh, che vita, che vita! oh, che
	mestiere!
	Orsù, presto a bottega—
Conte.	(È desso, o pur m'inganno.)
Figaro.	(Chi sarà mai costui?)
Conte.	Oh, è lui senz' altro.
	Figaro!
Figaro.	Mio padrone!
	Oh, chi veggo?—Eccellenza—
Conte.	Zitto! zittò prudenza:
	Quì non son conosciuto,
	Nè vò farmi conoscere—per questo
	Ho le mie gran ragioni.
Figaro.	Intendo, intendo—
	La lascio in libertà.
Conte.	No!
Figaro.	Che serve?
Conte.	No, dico—resta quà:
	Ora mi spiego. Al Prado
	Vidi un fior di bellezza—una
	fanciulla,
	Figlia di un certo medico barbogio,
	Che quà da pochi dì s'è stabilito.
	Io di questa invaghito
	Lasciai patria e parenti; e quà
	men venni,
	Col nome di Lindoro;
	E quà, la notte e il giorno,
	Passo girando a quei balconi
	intorno.
Figaro.	A quei balconi?—un medico? Oh,
	cospetto!
	Siete ben fortunato:
	Sui maccheroni il cacio v'è
	cascato.
Conte.	Come!
Figaro.	Certo.—Là dentro
	Io son barbiere, parucchier,
	chirurgo,
	Botanico, spezial, veterinario—
	Il faccendier di casa.
Conte.	Ah, bella sorte!
Figaro.	Non basta: la ragazza
	Figlia non è del medico—è soltanto
	La sua pupilla.
Conte.	Ah, che consolazione!

Figaro.	How so? but hush!
Count.	What is it?
Figaro.	See, the balcony opens.
	They retire under the Portico.)

SCENE III.—Rosina; afterwards Bartolo, on the Balcony; and the preceding, in the Street.

Rosina.	Is he not come yet? Perhaps—
Count.	Oh, my life! my angel! my treasure! At length do I behold you—at length—
Rosina.	(Oh, how provoking! I wished to give him this note.)
Bartolo.	Well, daughter, It is fine weather. Pray, what letter is that?
Rosina.	Nothing, sir: only the words Of an air in the "Useless Precaution."
Count.	Well and good!—of the "Useless Precaution!"
Rosina.	Unfortunate that I am! I have let drop the air. Make haste and pick it up.
Bartolo.	I go, I go. (He goes down.)
Rosina.	Hist! hist!—
Count.	I understand—
Rosina.	Make haste!
Count.	Never fear.
Bartolo.	Here I am. What is it? (Coming into the Street.)
Rosina.	Oh, the wind Has carried it away— Look again.
Bartolo.	I can't see it;—where, young lady? I'll search no more. (Zounds! She may have tricked me!) In! into the house! Come, come! Do you mind what I say? Quick, into the house!
Rosina.	Well, I am going;—what a fury!
Bartolo.	I will surely have that balcony walled up. In, I say!
Rosina.	Oh, what a scolding life I lead! (Entering.)

Figaro.	Perciò? zitto!
Conte.	Cos'è?
Figaro.	S'apre il balcone!
	(Si ritirano sotto il Portico.)

SCENA III.—Rosina; e poi Bartolo, sul Balcone; e detti in Strada.

Rosina.	Non è venuto ancora?—forse—
Conte.	Oh, mia vita! mio nume! mio tesoro! Vi veggo al fine—al fine—
Rosina.	(Ah, che vergogna! Vorrei dargli il biglietto.)
Bartolo.	Ebben, ragazza, Il tempo è buono. Cos'è questa carta?
Rosina.	Nulla, signore: sono le parole Dell'aria dell' "Inutil Precauzione."
Conte.	Ma brava!—dell' "Inutil Precauzione!"
Rosina.	Ah me meschina! l'aria mi è caduta: Raccoglietela presto.
Bartolo.	Vado, vado. (Scende.)
Rosina.	Pst! pst!—
Conte.	Ho inteso—
Rosina.	Presto!
Conte.	Non temete.
Bartolo.	Son quà. Dov'è? (Uscendo in Strada.)
Rosina.	Ah, il vento Se l'ha portato via— Guardate.
Bartolo.	Io non la veggo;—ehi, signorina? Io non vorrei. (Cospetto! Costei m'avesse preso!) In casa! in casa! Animo, sù! A chi dico? In casa, presto!
Rosina.	Vado, vado;—che furia!
Bartolo.	Quel balcone lo voglio far murare. Dentro, dico!
Rosina.	A che vita da crepare! (Entrando.)

Count.	Poor unhappy maid! Her wretched situation Still more interests me in her behalf.		*Conte.*	Povera disgraziata! Il suo stato infelice Sempre più m'interessa.
Figaro.	Come, come— Let us see what she has written.		*Figaro.*	Presto, presto— Vediamo cosa scrive.
Count.	Well, read.		*Conte.*	Appunto, leggi.
Figaro.	"Your assiduous attentions have excited my curiosity. My guardian is shortly going out: as soon as you perceive him quit the house, devise some ingenious method of acquainting me with your name, circumstances, and intentions. I can never appear at the balcony with- out being haunted by the insepar- able attendance of my tyrant. Be, therefore, assured, that entirely disposed to break her chains, is the unhappy—Rosina."		*Figaro.*	"Le vostre assidue premure hanno eccitato la mia curiosità. Il mio tutore è per uscir di casa: appena si sarà allontanato, procurate con qualche mezzo ingegnoso di indi- carmi il vostro nome, il vostro stato, e le vostre intenzioni. Io non posso giammai comparire al balcone senza l'indivisible com- pagnia del mio tiranno. Siate però certo che tutto à disposto a fare per rompere le sue catene, la sven- turata Rosina."

Count.	Yes, yes, she shall break them;—
	    but tell me,
	What kind of fellow is this guardi-
	    an of her's?
			Conte.	Sì, sì le romperò;—su, dimmi un
				    poco
				Che razza d'uomo è questo suo
				    tutore?

Figaro.	Oh, a very demon! All avarice and suspicion, a terrible blusterer, But have a care, have a care!		*Figaro.*	Un vecchio indemoniato! Avaro, sospettoso, brontolone; Ajuto, ajuto!
Count.	Oh what?		*Conte.*	Che?
Figaro.	The door opens.		*Figaro.*	S'apre la porta.

Bartolo.	So; I shall return in a few minutes.
	(Coming out of the door, and speaking towards the side.)
	Don't let any one in. If Don
	    Basilio
	Should come to inquire for me,
	    let him wait.
	(He shuts the door cautiously.)
	I wish to hurry on my marriage
	    with her.
	Yes, this very day I am going to
	    conclude the affair.
	(Exit.)
			Bartolo.	Ehi; fra momenti io torno.
				(Uscendo dalla porta, e parlando verso le quinte.)
				Non aprite a nessun. Se Don
				    Basilio
				Venisse a ricercarmi, che m'aspetti.
				(Chiude la porta di casa.)
				Le mie nozze con lei voglio
				    affrettare.
				Sì, dentr'oggi finir vò quest'affare.
				(Parte.)

Count.	This very day conclude his mar-
	    riage with Rosina?
	Oh, the foolish old dotard!
	But tell me, who is this Don
	    Basilio?
			Conte.	Dentr'oggi le sue nozze con
				    Rosina.
				Ah vecchio rimbambito!
				Ma dimmi or tu, chi è questo Don
				    Basilio?

Figaro.	A famous intriguing match-
	    maker—
	A hypocrite, a desperate fellow,
	With never a farthing in his pocket.
	He has lately turned music-master.
	And teaches this girl.
			Figaro.	È un solenne imbroglion di
				    matrimonj—
				Un collo torto, un vero disperato.
				Sempre senza un quattrino.
				Già è maestro di musica,
				Insegna alla ragazza.

Count.	Well and good! It is right to know all these things; And you shall be well rewarded for your trouble.	*Conte.*	Bene, bene! Tutto giova saper; di tue fatiche Largo compenso avrai.
Figaro.	Indeed!	*Figaro.*	Davver!
Count.	On my word.	*Conte.*	Parola.
Figaro.	Then, shall I touch the gold handsomely?	*Figaro.*	Dunque oro a discrezione?
Count.	To your heart's content. Come, be active.	*Conte.*	Oro a bizzeffe. Animo, via.
Figaro.	I'm all readiness. You cannot imagine What a prodigious effect the idea of a Reward has produced on me; and what sympathy I feel in the success of Signor Lindor.	*Figaro.*	Son pronto. Ah, non sapete I simpatici effetti prodigiosi; Che ad appagare il mio Signore Lindoro Produce in me la dolce idea dell' oro.

ALL' IDEA—*MIGHTY JOVE* (Duet)

dea_ di quel me-tal - lo un_ vul - ca - no, La_mia men - te   già_ come,_____   give_ to me_gold's daz - zling pow - er, Ev - 'ry maid would make me

min - - cia a di - ven - tar, a di - ven - tar, a di - ven-
bless'd,_____   would make me_bless'd, would make me bless'd, would make me

tar, Un vul - ca - no in - com - in - cia_a di - ven - tar.
bless'd,. Ev - 'ry__ maid__ would__ make__ me__ bless'd.

COUNT

Su ve - dia - mo, su ve - diam di quel mè - tal - lo,
Hold thy pom-pous, hold thy pom-pous sil - ly rail - ing,

Qual che ef - fet - to, qual che ef-fet - to sor - pren - den - te: Del vul-
Gold but wins,_ gold but wins the mean - er part:_ True love's

can,_   del vul - can del - la tua men - te,   Qual - che
song is more pre - vail - ing, more pre - vail - ing, Dear - est,

mos-tro,qual-che mos-tro, sin - go - lar, sì,. Del vul - can del - la_ tua_
give me,dear-est, give me heart for heart; Ah, true love's song_ is_ more_ pre-

men - te,_ Qual - che_ mo - - - stro,_ sin - go -
vail - ing,_ Dear - est,_ give_ me,_ dear - est,_ give me__

lar, sì, sì, Del vul-can— del-la— tua— men-te,— Qual-che—
heart for heart, True love's song— is— more— pre - vail - ing— Dear - est,—

mo - - - stro— sin - go - lar, sì, sin - go -
give— me,— dear - est,— give me— heart for heart, oh,

lar, sì, sin - go - lar; Qual-che— mo - stro sin - go - lar.
give me heart for heart; Dear - est,— give— me— heart— for— heart.

Figaro.	You must disguise yourself— For example, as a soldier.
Count.	As a soldier?
Figaro.	Even so, sir.
Count.	As a soldier!—and for what purpose?
Figaro.	To-day a regiment is expected here.
Count.	Yes; the Colonel is a friend of mine.
Figaro.	Excellent!
Count.	Why so?
Figaro.	Zounds! By means of a billet, yonder door Will soon open to you. What say you to this, my good sir? The invention is not amiss.
Count.	What an original genius. Excellent! excellent in truth!
Figaro.	What a capacious head is mine! Excellent! excellent in truth! Softly, softly—another thought. See the power of your gold! Drunk!—yes, my good sir, You must pretend to be drunk.
Count.	Drunk?
Figaro.	Even so, sir?
Count.	Drunk!—but for what purpose?
Figaro.	Because the guardian, believe me— The guardian would less distrust (Imitating the movements of a drunken man.) A man not quite himself But overcome with wine.

Conte.	Da soldato?
Figaro.	Sì, signore.
Conte.	Da soldato!—e che si fà?
Figaro.	Oggi arriva un reggimento.
Conte.	Sì, m'e amico il Colonello.
Figaro.	Va benon!
Conte.	Ma, e poi?
Figaro.	Cospetto! Dell' alloggio col biglietto, Quella porta si aprirà. Che ne dite, mio signore? L'invenzione è naturale.
Conte.	Oh, che testa universale! Bravo! bravo in verità!
Figaro.	Oh, che testa universale! Bella—bella in verità! Piano, piano—un altra idea. Veda l'oro cosa fà! Ubriaco!—sì ubriaco, Mio signor, si fingerà.
Conte.	Ubriaco?
Figaro.	Sì, signore.
Conte.	Ubriaco!—ma perchè?
Figaro.	Perchè d'un che poco è in se— Che dal vino casca già (Imitando i moti di Ubriaco.) Il tutor credete a me, Il tutor si fiderà.

Both.	This is excellent, by my faith. Bravo! bravo! excellent truly!		*Assieme.*	Questa è bella per mia fè. Bravo! bravo! in verità!
Count.	Well, then?		*Conte.*	Dunque?
Figaro.	To business.		*Figaro.*	All' opra.
Count.	Let us to it.		*Conte.*	Andiam.
Figaro.	With spirit.		*Figaro.*	Da bravo.
Count.	I go.—Oh, I had forgotten the important part of the business: Tell me, where is your shop? That I may not miss finding you.		*Conte.*	Vado.—Oh, il meglio mi scordavo: Dimmi un po, la tua bottega? Per trovarti dove stà.
Figaro.	My shop?—you cannot mistake it. Look yonder, there it is: (Pointing to the side.) Number fifteen, on the left hand, With four steps, a white front— there, Five wigs in the window; On a placard, "Pomade Divine;" A show-glass, too, of the latest fashion, And my sign is a lantern. There, without fail, you will find me.		*Figaro.*	La bottega?—non si sbaglia. Guardi bene, eccola là. (Additando fra le quinte.) Numero quindici, a mano manca, bianca— Quattro grandini, facciata bianca Cinque parrucche nella vetrina; Sopra un cartello, "Pommata Fina;" Mostra in azzurro alla moderna; V'è per insegna una lanterna. Là senza fallo mi troverà.
Count.	Do you be upon the alert.		*Conte.*	Ho ben capito.
Figaro.	Leave the rest to me.		*Figaro.*	Or, vado presto.
Count.	I perfectly understand.		*Conte.*	Tu guarda bene.
Figaro.	Haste, no delay!		*Figaro.*	Io penso al resto.
Count.	I repose in you.		*Conte.*	Di te mi fido.
Figaro.	I shall wait for you yonder.		*Figaro.*	Cola l'attendo.
Count.	My dear Figaro!		*Conte.*	Mio caro Figaro!
Figaro.	I understand, I understand.		*Figaro.*	Intendo, intendo.
Count.	I will bring with me—		*Conte.*	Porterò meco—
Figaro.	A purse well filled?		*Figaro.*	La borsa piena?
Count.	Yes, to your heart's content.		*Conte.*	Sì quel che vuoi.
Figaro.	And as for the rest— Oh, doubt not of our complete success.		*Figaro.*	Ma il resto poi— Oh, non si dubiti che bene andrà.

(Figaro enters the House.—Exit the Count.)

SCENE IV.—A Chamber in Don Bartolo's House.
(Rosina, with a letter in her hand.)

(Figaro entra in Casa.—Il Conte parte.)

SCENA IV.—Camera nella Casa di Don Bartolo.
(Rosina, con lettera in mano.)

Rosina.	A little voice I heard just now: Oh, it has thrilled my very heart! I feel that I am wounded sore; And Lindor 'twas who hurled the dart. Yes, Lindor, dearest, shall be mine! I've sworn it, and we'll never part. My guardian sure will ne'er consent; But I must sharpen all my wit:		*Rosina.*	Una voce poco fà: Quì nel cor mi risuonò! Il mio cor ferito è già; E Lindor fu che il piagò. Sì, Lindoro mio sarà! Lo giurai, la vincerò. Il tutor ricuserà; Io l'ingegno aguzzerò:

AH, CHE D'AMORE—*WHEN SONG IS FLOWING* (Duet)

La fiam - ma sen -
When love is glow;

gen - to, Già vie - ne l'o - ro, Vie - ne l'ar - gen - to; Già vie - ne
stream - ing, O'er mi - sers dream - ing, Then, then, are mine; As guin - eas

to, Nun - zia di giù - bi -
ing, O'er fan - cy throw.

lo - ro Già vie - ne l'o - ro, ec - co - lo; Ec - co - lo già vien' l'ar -
stream-ing, Then, then, are mine, then are mine; Thoughts bright and

lo E di con - ten -
ing Her light, her light di -

gen - to, Già' vien' l'ar - gen - to, ec - co - lo; Ec - co - lo in tas - ca
beam-ing, As guin-eas stream-ing, then are mine; O'er mi - sers

to! Ec - co pro - pi -
vine' O'er maid - ens dream -

scen - de, Ec - co - lo quà;
stream-ing, Then, then, are mine;

zia, Che in sen mi scen - de
ing, Then, then, are mine.

D'ar - dor in' - so - li - to, Que - st'al - ma ac - cen - de.
O'er mi - sers dream - ing, Then, then are mine

Content at last, he will relent,
    And we, oh, joy! be wedded yet,
Yes, Lindor I have sworn to love!
    And, loving, we'll our cares
        forget.
Yes, yes, he shall triumph. Could
    I but
Send him this letter!—but how?
There is no one here I can trust:
My guardian has a hundred eyes.
    —Well, well,
At least I will seal it.
From my window I beheld him
    conversing
For more than an hour with Figaro
    the barber;—

Alla fin s'acchetterà,
    E contenta io resterò,
Sì, Lindoro mio sarà!
    Lo giurai—la vincerò.
Sì, sì, la vincerò. Potessi almeno
Mandargli questa lettera!—ma
    come?
Di nessun quì mi fido:
Il tutor ha cent'occhi.—Basta,
    basta,
Sigilliamo intanto.
Con Figaro il barbiere dalla
    finestra
Discorrer l'ho veduto più d'un
    ora;—

IO SONO DOCILE—*WITH MILD AND DOCILE AIR*

ce - de - re, fa - rò gio - car,___ fa - rò___ gio - car, E cen-to
way - ward tricks, and sub-tle wiles,_____ I'd___ play, Ere they my

trap-po - le, Pri-ma di - ce - de - re, fa - rò gio - car,___ fa - rò___ gio -
will should guide, Ere they my will should guide, Ere they my will_____ should___

car; E___ cen-to___ trap-po - le, Pri-ma di - ce - de - re, E cen-to
guide; A___ thou-sand, thou-sand tricks, And sub - tle___ wiles I'd play, Ere they my

trap-po - - le fa - rò, fa - rò gio - - car.
will, my_____ will should___ guide, my_____ will should___ guide.

Figaro is an honest fellow,	Figaro è un galantuomo,
A good-hearted lad:	Un giovin di buon cuore:
Who knows but he may favor our love?	Chi sà ch'ei non protegga il nostro amore?

SCENE V.—Rosina and Figaro.		SCENA V.—Rosina e Figaro.	
Figaro.	Oh, good day! Signorina.	*Figaro.*	Oh, buon dì! Signorina.
Rosina.	Good day! Signor Figaro.	*Rosina.*	Buon giorno! Signor Figaro.
Figaro.	Well, what are you doing?	*Figaro.*	Ebbene, che si fa?
Rosina.	I am dying with ennui.	*Rosina.*	Si muor di noja.
Figaro.	Oh, the deuce! impossible! For one so handsome, so full of spirit.	*Figaro.*	Oh, diavolo! possibile! Una ragazza bella e spiritosa.
Rosina.	You make me smile, Figaro: Of what use is my spirit, What avails my beauty, If forever shut up between four walls, Which appear as dreary as a sepulchre?	*Rosina.*	Ah, ah, mi fate ridere Che mi serve lo spirito,— Che giova la bellezza, Se chiusa io sempre sto fra quattro mura, Che mi par d'esser proprio in sepoltura?
Figaro.	A sepulchre! good Heavens! (Taking her aside.) I wish to know—	*Figaro.*	In sepoltura! oibò! (Chaimandola a parte.) Sentite, io voglio—
Rosina.	See! see! my guardian!	*Rosina.*	Ecco il tutor!
Figaro.	Indeed!	*Figaro.*	Davvero!
Rosina.	Certainly, certainly! it is his voice!	*Rosina.*	Certo, certo! la sua voce!

Figaro.	Adieu! adieu! in a few moments (Exit.) I will see you again—I have some- thing to tell you.		*Figaro.*	alva! salva! fra poco (Parte.) Ci rivedremo—ho a dirvi qualche cosa.
Rosina.	And so have I, Signor Figaro.		*Rosina.*	E ancor io, Signor Figaro.
Figaro.	Adieu, fair lady!		*Figaro.*	Bravissima, vado!
Rosina.	A civil fellow this. (Exit.)		*Rosina.*	Quanto è garbato. (Parte.)

SCENE VI.—Bartolo and Don Basilio.   SCENA VI.—Bartolo e Don Basilio.

Bartolo.	Don Basilio, You come just in time. I wish Within to-morrow, either by force or love, To espouse my Rosina.—Do you understand?		*Bartolo.*	Don Basilio, Venite a tempo. Oh io voglio Per forza, oh per amor, dentro domani Sposar la mia Rosina.—Avete inteso?
Basilio.	Ah! you speak wisely; And I was just coming myself to advise with you. (Taking him aside.) But be secret!—The Count Almaviva Is arrived.		*Basilio.*	Eh, voi dite benissimo; E appunto io qui veniva ad avvisarvi. (Chiamandola a parte.) Ma segretezza!—è giunto Il Conte d'Almaviva.
Bartolo.	What! the unknown lover Of Rosina?		*Bartolo.*	Chi! l'incognito amante Della Rosina?
Basilio.	The very same.		*Basilio.*	Appunto quello.
Bartolo.	Oh, the devil Something must be done here.		*Bartolo.*	Oh, diavolo! Ah qui ci vuol riparo.
Basilio.	Certainly; but, between ourselves—		*Basilio.*	Certo; ma, alla sordina—
Bartolo.	That is to say—		*Bartolo.*	Sarebbe a dir—
Basilio.	We must boldly Begin by inventing Some plausible story, that may Disgrace him in the eyes of the public.		*Basilio.*	Così con buona grazia Bisogna principiare A inventar qualche favola Che al pubblico lo metta in mala vista.
Bartolo.	And would you? But a calumny—		*Bartolo.*	E vorreste?—Ma una calunnia—
Basilio.	Oh, then, You don't know what a calumny is?		*Basilio.*	Ah, dunque, La calunnia cos'è voi non sapete?
Bartolo.	No, indeed.		*Bartolo.*	No, davvero.
Basilio.	No?—Then hear, and be silent. Oh! calumny is like the sigh Of gentlest zephyrs breathing by; How softly sweet, along the ground, Its first shirll voice is heard around: So soft, that, sighing 'mid the bowers, It scarcely fans the drooping flowers. Thus will the voice of calumny,		*Basilio.*	No?—Uditemi, e tacete. La calunnia è un venticello Un'auretta assai gentile; Che insensibile, sottile, Leggermente, dolcemente Incomincia a susurrar Piano piano, terra terra, Sotto voce sibillando,

More subtle than the plaintive sigh,
In many a serpent-wreathing, find
Its secret passage to the mind,—
The heart's most inmost feelings
   gain,
Bedim the sense, and fire the brain.

Then passing on from tongue to
   tongue,
It gains new strength, it sweeps
   along
In giddier whirl from place to
   place,
And gains fresh vigor in its race;
Till, like the sounds of tempests
   deep,
That through the woods in mur-
   murs sweep
And howl amid their caverns
   drear,
It shakes the trembling soul with
   fear.
At length the fury of the storm
Assumes its wildest, fiercest form,—
In one loud crash of thunder roars,
And, like an earthquake, rocks the
   shores.
While all the frowning vault of
   heaven,
With many a fiery bolt is riven.
Thus calumny, a simple breath,
Engenders rain, wreck, and death;
And sinks the wretched man
   forlorn,
Beneath the lash of slander torn,
The victim of the public scorn.

(Exeunt.)

Và scorrendo, và ronzando
Nelle orecchie della gente,—
S'introduce destramente,
E le teste ed i cervelli,
Fà stordire, e fa gonfiar.

Dalla bocca fuori uscendo,

Lo schiamazzo và crescendo;

Prende forza a poco a poco,

Scorre già di loco in loco,
Sembra il tuono, la tempesta,

Che nel sen della foresta,

Va fischiando, brontolando,

E ti fa d'orror gelar.

Alla fin trabocca, e scoppia,
Si propaga, e si raddoppia,
E produce un esplosione
Come un colpo di cannone.

Un tremoto, un temporale,

Un tremoto generale,
Che fa l'aria rimbombar.
E il meschino, calunniato,
Avvilito, calpestato,

Sotto il pubblico flagello,
Per gran sorte và a crepar.

(Partono.)

SCENE VII.—Figaro, coming forth with precaution; then Rosina.

SCENA VII.—Figaro. uscendo con precauzione; indi Rosina.

Figaro. Bravo! all goes on well!
I have overheard everything.
So, so, good Mr. Doctor!
Your spouse!—a good joke. The
   grapes are sour.
While they remain shut up yonder,
I will endeavor to speak to the girl;
But here she is, *à propos.*

Rosina. Well, Signor Figaro?

Figaro. I have great things to tell you,
Signorina.

Rosina. Indeed!

Figaro. We shall eat weding-cake shortly.

Rosina. What do you mean?

Figaro. Ma bravi! ma benone!
Ho inteso tutto. Evviva il buon
   dottore!
Povero babbuino!
Tua sposa!—eh via. Pulisciti il
   bocchino
Or che stanno là chiusi,
Procuriam di parlare alla ragazza;
Eccola appunto.

Rosina. Ebbene, Signor Figaro?

Figaro. Gran cose Sigorina

Rosina. Sì, davver!

Figaro. Mangerem dei confetti.

Rosina. Come sarebbe a dir?

Figaro.	I mean
	That this fine guardian of yours
	    has settled
	That to-morrow he is to be your
	    husband.
			Figaro.	Sarebbe a dire
				Che il vostro bel tutore ha stabilito
				Esser dentro doman vostro marito.

Rosina.	Oh, pooh!		*Rosina.*	Eh, via!
Figaro.	Yes, I swear it: Even now he is closeted With your music-master, Drawing up the contract.		*Figaro.*	Oh, ve lo giuro; A stendere il contratto Col maestro di musica, Là dentro si è serrato.

Rosina.	Indeed! In truth he is much
	    mistaken!
	Poor fellow! he shall find with
	    whom he has to do.
	But tell me, Mr. Figaro,
	Just now, below my window,
	You were speaking to a gentle-
	    man—
			Rosina.	Sì! L'ha sbagliata affè!
				Povero sciocco! l'avrà da far con
				    me.
				Ma dite, Signor Figaro,
				Voi poco fa sotto le mie finestre,
				Parlavate a un signore—

Figaro.	Oh, a cousin of mine—
	An excellent young man, with a
	    good head,
	And the best of hearts; he is come
	    here
	To finish his studies, and to try,
	    poor fellow,
	To make his fortune.
			Figaro.	Ah! un mio cugino—
				E' un bravo giovinotto; buona
				    testa,
				Ottimo cuor! quì venne
				I suoi studj a compire, e il
				    poverino,
				Cerca di far fortuna.

Rosina.	His fortune?—Oh, he will make it.		*Rosina.*	Fortuna?—eh, la farà.
Figaro.	Aha, I doubt it much; in con- fidence, I tell you he has one great failing.		*Figaro.*	Oh, ne dubito assai; in confidenza, Ha un gran difetto addosso.
Rosina.	A great failing, said you?		*Rosina.*	Un gran difetto?
Figaro.	Yes, a great one; He is dying in love.		*Figaro.*	Ah, grande; E'innamorato morto.
Rosina.	Ah, indeed? Do you know that this young man Interests me extremely.		*Rosina.*	Sì, davvero? Quel giovine, vedete M'interessa moltissimo.
Figaro.	Good Lord!		*Figaro.*	Per Bacco!
Rosina.	Don't you believe it?		*Rosina.*	Non ci credete?
Figaro.	Oh, certainly.		*Figaro.*	Oh sì.
Rosina.	But tell me, does this fair one Live far from this place?		*Rosina.*	Ma la sua bella Dite, abita lontano?
Figaro.	Oh no!—that is— But two paces from hence—		*Figaro.*	Oh nò!—cioè— Quì a due passi—
Rosina.	Is she handsome?		*Rosina.*	Ma è bella?

Figaro.	Oh, very much so—behold her
	    portrait,
	Which I give you in two words:
	A handsome, graceful figure,
	Jetty locks, a rosy cheek,
	An eye that speaks, a hand whose
	    touch thrills one.
			Figaro.	Oh, bella assai—eccovi il suo
				    ritratto,
				Che vi fo in due parole:
				Svelta, gentil, vezzosa,
				Capelli neri, guancia porporina,
				Occhio che parla, mano che
				    innamora.

Rosina.	And her name?		*Rosina.*	E il nome?
Figaro.	Ah, her name too? Her name?—Ah, what a sweet name!— She's called—		*Figaro.*	Ah, il nome ancora? Il nome?—Ah, che bel nome!— Si chiama—
Rosina.	Well, what is she called?		*Rosina.*	Ebben? si chiama?
Figaro.	Sweet creature! She's called Ro-ro-ro-si-na— Rosina.		*Figaro.*	Poverina! Si chiama Ro-ro-ro-si-na—Rosina.

DUNQUE IO SON—*WHAT AM I, OR DOST THOU MOCK ME?*

Di Lin-do-ro il va-go og-get-to; Sie-te voi, bel-la Ro-si-na, sie-te
Yes, Lin-do-ro loves you, la-dy; Oft he sighs for his Ro-si-na, soft-ly

vo - i, sie - te vo - i, bel - là Ro - si - na—(Oh che vol -
sigh - ing, soft - ly sigh - ing for his Ro - si - na—(As a fox

pe so - praf - fi - na, ah! che vol - pe___ so - praf -
she cun - ning seems, ah! as a fox___ she___ cun - ning

fi - na___Mà___ l'a - vrà___ da___ far___ con___ me;) Si,___ mà___ l'a -
seems,__Ah!___by___ my___ faith,—she___ sees___ through all;) Yes,___by___ my___

vrà___ da___ far___ con___ me, Mà l'a - vrà___ da___ far___ con___ me.
faith__ she___ sees___ through_ all, By my___ faith___ she___ sees___ through all!

Rosina. Still one word, Sir, to my Lindor. How shall I contrive to speak.	*Rosina.* Senti, senti, ma a Lindoro, Per parlar come si fà.
Figaro. Patience, patience, and your lover Soon your presence here will seek.	*Figaro.* Zitto, zitto, quì Lindoro Per parlarvi or sarà.
Rosina. Will seek me here? Oh, joy supreme! Let him but with prduence come; I die to know how he will scheme! Where can he linger? why not come?	*Rosina.* Per parlarmi? bravo! bravo! Vengo pur, ma con prudenza; Io già moro d' impazienza! Ah che tarda? cosa fa?
Figaro. Poor man, he but awaits some sign Of your affection and assent: A little note, a single line, And he himself will soon present. To this, what say you?	*Figaro.* Egli attende qualche segno Poverin del vostro affetto Sol due righe di biglietto, Gli mandate, e quì verrà. Che ne dite?
Rosina. I do not know.	*Rosina.* Non saprei.
Figaro. Take courage, pray you.	*Figaro.* Su coraggio!
Rosina. I could not so—	*Rosina.* Non vorrei—
Figaro. A few lines merely.	*Figaro.* Sol due righe.
Rosina. I blush to write.	*Rosina.* Mi vergogno.
Figaro. At what?—why really—may I indite? Haste, haste, your lover quick invite. (Going to the desk.)	*Figaro.* Ma di che?—di che?—si sa? Presto, presto, quà un biglietto. (Andando allo scrittojo.)
Rosina. A letter! Oh, here it is. (Calling him; she takes a note from her bosom, which she gives him.)	*Rosina.* Un biglietto! eccolo quà. (Richiamandolo; cava dal seno il biglietto, e glie lo da.)

Figaro.	Already written!—What a fool
	(Astonished.)
	Was I to thing to be her master!
	Much fitter that she me should
	school:
	Her wits, than mine, can flow
	much faster.
	Oh, woman, woman! who can find,
	Or fathom, all that's in thy mind?
Rosina.	Upon my young desires,
	See love propitious shine;
	'Tis he, with his soft fires,
	Must ease a heart like mine.
	(Exit Figaro.)

SCENE VIII.—Rosina, then Bartolo.

Rosina.	Now I feel relieved.
	This Figaro is a kind creature!
Bartolo.	With fair words,
	May I know from my Rosina what
	this
	Fellow came to do here this
	morning?
Rosina.	Who? Figaro?—Oh, I know not.
Bartolo.	Didn't he speak to you?
Rosina.	Yes, he spoke to me.
Bartolo.	What said he?
Rosina.	Oh, he told me a hundred trifles:
	Of the fashions of France,—
	Of the ill health of the child,
	Marcellina.
Bartolo.	Indeed! now I would venture to
	wager
	That he brought an answer to your
	note.
Rosina.	What note?
Bartolo.	Oh, come, come! that air
	From the drama of the "Useless
	Precaution,"
	Which you dropped this morning
	from the balcony.
	You blush—(I have guessed it!)
	How came that finger
	To be so marked with ink?
Rosina.	With ink!—Oh, nothing:
	I had hurt myself,
	And used this ink by way of a cure.
Bartolo.	(The devil!) But these sheets of
	paper?
	There are now but five—there
	were six.

Figaro.	Già era scritto!—oh ve' che bestia!
	(Attonito.)
	E il maestro io faccio a lei!
	Ah, che in cattedra costei
	Di malizia può dettar.
	Donne, donne! eterni dei,
	Chi vi arriva a indovinar?
Rosina.	Fortunati affetti miei,
	Io comincio a respirar;
	Ah tu solo, amor tu sei,
	Che mi devi consolar.
	(Figaro parte.)

SCENA VIII.—Rosina, indi Bartolo.

Rosina.	Ora mi sento meglio.
	Questo Figaro è un bravo
	giovinotto!
Bartolo.	In somma, colle buone,
	Potrei sapere dalla mia Rosina
	Che venne a far colui questa
	mattina?
Rosina.	Figaro?—Non so nulla.
Bartolo.	Ti parlò?
Rosina.	Mi parlò.
Bartolo.	Che ti diceva?
Rosina.	Oh, mi parlò di certe bagatelle:
	Del figurin di Francia,—
	Del mal della sua figlia, Marcel-
	lina.
Bartolo.	Davvero! ed io scometto
	Che portò la risposta al tuo
	biglietto.
Rosina.	Qual biglietto?
Bartolo.	Che serve! quell'arietta.
	Del dramma del' "Inutil Pre-
	cauzione,"
	Che ti cadde staman giù dal
	balcone.
	Vi fate rossa—(l'avrei indovi-
	nato!)
	Che vuol dir questo dito
	Così sporco d'inchiostro?
Rosina.	Sporco!—Oh, nulla:
	Io me l'avea scottato,
	E con l'inchiostro or l'ho medicato.
Bartolo.	(Diavolo!) E questi fogli?
	Or son cinque—eran sei.

Rosina.	Those sheets? Oh, true: I made use of one of them To send some sweetmeats to Marcellina.
Bartolo.	Most excellent! And the pen— For what purpose has that been cut?
Rosina.	(Confound him!) That pen? To design a flower on my tambour.
Bartolo.	A flower?
Rosina.	A flower.
Bartolo.	A flower! Ah, you cunning minx!
Rosina.	It's true.
Bartolo.	Silence!
Rosina.	Believe me.
Bartolo.	Enough of this.
Rosina.	Sir—
Bartolo.	No more—be silent. To a doctor of my rank, These excuses, Signorina, I advise another time That you better should invent. The sweetmeats for the girl! The embroidery on the tambour! Out of my sight! begone! And is it thus my more than daughter Dares to trifle with me? Why is the paper missing? That I would wish to know. Useless, ma'am, are all your airs— Be still, nor interrupt me so. Another time, sweet Signorina, When the doctor quits his house, He will carefully provide For the keeping you inside. Useless now are your grimaces, No one heeds your affectation! A vow I make that no one now Shall come within my habitation. And poor innocent Rosina, Disappointed, then may pout: In her room shall she be locked, Till I choose to let her out. (Exeunt.)

SCENE IX.—Bertha, alone.

Bertha.	Methought just now
	I heard a noise within this
	    chamber,
	It perhaps was the guardian with
	    his ward;

Rosina.	Quei fogli? E vero: D' uno mi son servito A mandar de' confetti a Marcel- lina.
Bartolo.	Bravissima! E la penna— Perchè fu temperata?
Rosina.	(Maledetto!) La penna? Per disegnare un fiore sul tamburo.
Bartolo.	Un fiore?
Rosina.	Un fiore.
Bartolo.	Un fiore! Ah, fraschetta!
Rosina.	Davver.
Bartolo.	Zitto!
Rosina.	Credete.
Bartolo.	Basta così
Rosina.	Signor—
Bartolo.	Non più—tacete. A un dottor della mia sorte, Queste scuse, Signorina, Vi consiglio mia carina Un pò meglio a impostar. I confetti alla ragazza! Il ricamo sul tamburo! Vi scostate, e via! Ci vuol altra figlia mia Per potermi corbellar? Perchè manca là quel foglio? Vo' saper cotesto imbroglio. Sono inutili le smorfie— Ferma là, non mi toccate. Signorina, un altra volta Quando Bartolo andrà fuori, La consegna ai servitori A suo modo dar saprà. Ah, non servono le smorfie, Faccia pur la gatta morta! Cospetton per quella porta Nemmen l'aria entrar potrà E Rosina, innocentina, Sconsolata, disperata: In sua camera serrata, Fin ch'io voglio star dovrà. (Partono.)

SCENA IX.—Berta, sola.

Berta.	Finora in questa camera Mi parve di sentir un mormorìo; Sarà stato il tutor colla pupilla;

He has never an hour's peace.
  These girls
Will not hear;—some one knocks.
  (A knocking is heard.)

Non ha un'ora di ben. Queste
  ragazze
No la voglion capir;—battono.
  (Si ode picchiare.)

Count. Open the door!
   (Within.)

Conte. Aprite!
   (Di dentro.)

Bertha. Poor girl! she will be driven to
  some rash act,
  If she be longer confined in this
  sepulchral place.
  (Bertha opens the door, and exits.)

Berta. Alla fine farà qualche stortura?
  O anderà dalla noja in sepoltura.
  (Apre e parte.)

SCENE X.—The Count, disguised as a Soldier, and pretending to be drunk; then Bartolo.

SCENA X.—Il Conte travestito da Soldato contrafucando i moti d'ubriaco; indi Bartolo.

Count. Hallo! house here!—Hey! good
  people!
  Hallo! house here!—Faith, you'll
  sleep ill.

Conte. Ehi di casa!—buona gente!
  Ehi di casa!—niun mi sente!

Bartolo. Who can this be?—Ugly fellow!
  Drunken rascal, thus to bellow!

Bartolo. Chi è costui?—Che brutta faccia!
  E ubriaco, chi sarà!

Count. Hallo! house there!—All are still
  here!

Conte. Ehi di casa!—maledetti!

Bartolo. Signor Whiskers, what's your will
  here?

Bartolo. Cosa vuol, Signor Soldato?

Count. Hey! oh, oh!—Pray, how d'ye do,
  sir?
  (Seeing him, he searches in his pocket.)

Conte. Ah! sì, sì!—Ben obbligato?
  (Vedendolo, cerca in tasca.)

Bartolo. Stupid puppy!—Who are you sir?

Bartolo. Quì costui!—che mai vorrà?

Count. Are not you, sir—but steady—
  order!
  Doctor Balordo?

Conte. Siete voi—aspetta un poco!
  Siete voi—Dottor Balordo?

Bartolo. What, Balordo?

Bartolo. Che Balordo?

Count. Ah, ah! Bertoldo—
   (Reading.)

Conte. Ah, ah! Bertoldo—
   (Leggendo.)

Bartolo. Pooh! pooh! Bertoldo!
  No such person.—Hear me,
  fool, do!
  Doctor Bartolo!

Bartolo. Che Bertoldo.
  Eh, andate al diavolo!
  Dottor Bartolo!

Count. Ah, bravissimo!
  Doctor Barbaro; well and good;
  The difference, after all, is but
  trifling.
  (She appears not! what impatience
  I feel!
  How long she delays!—where can
  she be?)

Conte. Ah, bravissimo!
  Dottor Barbaro; benissimo;
  Già c'è poca differenza.
  (Non si vede! che impazienza!
  Quanto tarda!—dove stà?)

Bartolo. I am already out of all patience.
  Prudence is necessary here.

Bartolo. Io già perdo la pazienza.
  Quì prudenza ci vorrà.

Count. You, then—are a doctor?

Conte. Dunque voi—siete Dottore?

Bartolo. I am a doctor—yes, sir.

Bartolo. Son Dottore—sì, Signore.

Count.	Ah, how fortunate! let me embrace— Here, fellow collegian.
Bartolo.	Stand off.
Count.	Here! (Embracing him by force.) I also am a doctor of full degree, And marshal of the regiment: Here on the billet for my lodgings. (Presenting a billet.) Look, here it is.
Bartolo.	(With rage and vexation I'm ready to burst in good earnest; Ah, let me be cautious Not to commit some rash act!) (Reads the billet.)
Count.	(Ah, would my heart's dear idol come— Sole object of my love, appear; Haste, oh, haste; thy fond adorer, Full of love, awaits thee here.)

SCENE XI.—Rosina, and the preceding.

Rosina.	Methought I overheard e'en now, A most unusual clamor here. A soldier!—and my guardian!— What can they be doing here? (She advances softly.)
Count.	It is Rosina!—I now am content.
Rosina.	He looks at me, he approaches me!
Count.	I am Lindor. (Softly, to Rosina.)
Rosina.	Heavens! what do I hear? Prudence, for mercy's sake!
Bartolo.	The Signorina here? Quick, quick, your exit make. (Pushing Rosina.)
Rosina.	I am going; don't hallo so.
Bartolo.	Quick, quick, away, I tell you.
Count.	Well, sweetheart, and I'll follow you.
Bartolo.	Follow! where, sir?
Count.	To my quarters: oh, this is excellent!
Bartolo.	To your quarters? a pretty joke!
Count.	Dearest!
Rosina.	Help!
Bartolo.	Hold! zounds!
Count.	Quick, let drop your handkerchief; Quick, for goodness' sake! (To Rosina, showing her a note by stealth.)

Conte.	Ah, benissimo! un'abbraccio— Quà collega.
Bartolo.	Indietro.
Conte.	Quà! (Lo abbraccia per forza.) Sono anch' io Dottor perfetto, Marescalco al reggimento: Dell' alloggio sul biglietto. (Presentando il biglietto.) Osservate, eccolo quà.
Bartolo.	(Dalla rabbia—dal dispetto Io già crepo in verità; Ah ch'io fo se mi ci metto Qualche gran bestialità!) (Legge il biglietto.)
Conte.	(Ah, venisse il caro oggetto— Della mia felicità; Vieni, vieni; il tuo diletto, Pien d'amor, t'attende quà.)

SCENA XI.—Rosina, e detti.

Rosina.	D'ascoltar quà m'è sembrato, Un'insolito rumore. Un soldato!—ed il tutore!— Cosa mai faranno quà? (Si avanza piano piano.)
Conte.	E' Rosina! Or son contento.
Rosina.	Ei mi guarda, e s'avvicina!
Conte.	Son Lindoro. (Piano, a Rosina.)
Rosina.	Oh, ciel che sento? Ah, giudizio, per pietà!
Bartolo.	Signorina che cercate? Presto, presto, andate via. (Vedendo Rosina.)
Rosina.	Vado, vado, non gridate.
Bartolo.	Presto, presto, via di quà.
Conte.	Ehi ragazza vengo anch'io.
Bartolo.	Dove, dove, Signor mio?
Conte.	In caserma: oh, questa è bella!
Bartolo.	In caserma? bagatella!
Conte.	Cara!
Rosina.	Ajuto!
Bartolo.	Olà! cospetto!
Conte.	Via, gettate il fazzoletto; Fate presto per pietà! (A Rosina mostrandola furtivamente un biglietto.)

Rosina. Ah, he's looking!
        (To the Count.)
How unlucky!
Ah, discretion, for goodness' sake!
        (Eyeing Bartolo.)

Bartolo. A curse on this drunken fellow!
I am ready to burst with vexation

Count. Then I go—

Bartolo. Oh no; stop, sir!
        (Retaining him.)
You can have no lodging here.

Count. How say you?

Bartolo. Oh, it is in vain to remonstrate;
I am exempt from lodging troops.

Count. How are you exempt?
        (In a rage.)

Bartolo. Oh, my good sir,
A moment, and I will show you.
        (Goes to his desk.)

Count. Ah, if I cannot here remain,
Quick, take it—
(Making signs to her to take the note.)

Rosina. He looks at me again.

Rosina and Count. Oh, this heart is filled
      with pain!
Myself no more can I contain.

Bartolo. At present I have searched in vain,
But soon I hope to find it.
        (Searching in the desk.)
Oh, here it is.
        (Reads.)
"By these presents,
(He comes forward with a parchment.)
The Doctor Bartolo, etc., etc.
We exempt"—

Count. Oh, go to the devil!
(With a dash of his hand he sends the parchment into
      the air.)

Bartolo. My dear sir, what would you?

Count. Silence, Mr. Doctor Lomaro!
My lodging is fixed here,
And here will I remain.

Bartolo. Will remain!

Count. Yes, will remain.

Bartolo. My good sir, I have something else
to do:
I beg you will begone, or a cudgel
Shall dislodge you.
        (Threatening him.)

Count. Then you—you wish to fight with
me?

Rosina. Ah, ci guarda!
        (Al Conte.)
Maledetto!
Ah, giudizio, per pietà.
        (Guardando Bartolo.)

Bartolo. Ubriaco maledetto!
Ah costui crepar mi fa.

Conte. Dunque vado—

Bartolo. O no; Signore!
        (Trattenendolo.)
Quì d'alloggio star non può.

Conte. Come, come?

Bartolo. Eh, non v'è replica;
Ho il brevetto d'esenzione.

Conte. Che brevetto?
        (Adirato.)

Bartolo. Oh mio padrone,
Un momento, e il mostrerò.
        (Và allo scrittojo.)

Conte. Ah, se qui restar non posso,
Deh, prendete—
(Accennandolo di prendere un biglietto.)

Rosina. Ahimè! ci guarda.

Rosina e Conte. Cento smanie io sento
      addosso!
Ah, più reggere non so.

Bartolo. Ah trovarlo ancor non posso,
Mà sì, sì, lo troverò.
        (Cercando nello scrittojo.)
Ecco quì.
        (Legge.)
"Colla presente,
(Venendo avanti con una pergamena.)
Il Dottor Bartolo, *et cetera.*
Essentiamo"—

Conte. Eh, andate al diavolo!
(Con un rovescio di mano manda in aria la pergamena.

Bartolo. Cosa fa, Signor mio caro?

Conte. Zitto là, Dottor Lomaro!
Il mio alloggio è quì fissato,
E in alloggio quì vo star.

Bartolo. Vuol restar!

Conte. Restar, sicuro.

Bartolo. Ah, son stufo, mio padrone:
Presto fuori, o un buon bastone
Lo farà di quà sloggiar.

        (Minacciandolo.)

Conte. Dunque lei—lei vuol battaglia?

Well, you shall have your way.
(Drawing back.)
A battle is a fine thing, truly!
(Laughing.)
A specimen I'll show you duly.
(Advances, pretending to fight.)
This is the trench, observe,
And you are the enemy.
(Makes a pass at him.)
Now, mark! (Drop your hand-
kerchief.)
(Aside, to Rosina.)
Our friends are stationed here—
Now mark!

(He seizes the moment when Bartolo is less attentive. and
lets fall the note; Rosina drops her handkerchief
upon it.)

Bartolo. Hold! hold!

Count. What is it?—ah!

Bartolo. Let me see it.

Count. Prescriptions only are for you;
But letters go where they are due.
I ask your pardon.

(He bows to Rosina, and gives her the note and the
handkerchief.)

Rosina. Charming, charming, how
delightful!

Bartolo. Charming, truly!
Oh, 'tis frightful.

Count. Some little girlish love affair.
(Drawing him aside; meanwhile, Rosina changes the letter.)

Rosina. Could I but change the letter there!

Bartolo. I wish to see it.

Rosina. 'This naught to see.

Bartolo. Quick, give the paper—give it me.
(Enter Basilio on one side; Bertha on the other.)

Basilio. Look here!—what do I see?

Bertha. The barber! Eh, what stir is here!

Bartolo. Give here the paper, impertinence!
(To Rosina.)
Do you mind what I say—quick!

Rosina. The paper, sir, you wish to have,
Which slipped by chance from out
my hand,
Is but a list of linen.

Bartolo. Quick, give it here, hussy!
(He seizes it violently.)
What do I see?—I am mistaken!
This list I'd for a letter taken.
Oh, what a fool, indeed, am I!
Oh, what immense stupidity!

Ben, battaglia le vuò dar.
(Tirandosi indietro.)
Bella cosa una battaglia!
(Ridendo.)
Ve la voglio or quì mostrar.
(Avvicinandosi, amichevolmente a Bartolo.)
Osservate! questo è il fosso,
L'inimico voi sarete.
(Gli da una spinta.)
Attenzion! (Giù fazzoletto.)

(Piano, a Rosina.)
E gli amici stan di quà—
Attenzione!

(Cogli il momento in cui Bartolo l'osserva meno attenta-
mente, e lascia il biglietto, e Rosina vi fa cadere sopra
il fazzoletto.)

Bartolo. Ferma! ferma!

Conte. Che cos' è?—ah!

Bartolo. Vo' vedere.

Conte. Sì, se fosse una ricetta;
Mi dovete perdonar.

(Fa una riverenza a Rosina, e le da il biglietto, e il
fazzoletto.)

Rosina. Grazie, grazie!

Bartolo. Grazie, come!
Vo saper cotesto imbroglio!

Conte. Qualche intrigo di fanciulla.
(Tirandolo a parte; intanto, Rosina cambia la lettera.)

Rosina. Ah, cambiar potessi il foglio!

Bartolo. Vuò veder.

Rosina. Ma non è nulla.

Bartolo. Quì quel foglio, presto quà!
(Escono da una parte Basilio; e dall'altra, Berta.)

Basilio. Ecco quà!—oh, cosa vedo?

Berta. Il barbiere! Oh, quanta gente!

Bartolo. Quà quel foglio, impertinente!
(A Rosina.)
A chi dico?—presto quà!

Rosina. Ma quel foglio che chiedete,
Per azzardo m'è cascato,
E la lista del bucato.

Bartolo. Ah, fraschetta presto quà!
(Lo strappa con violenza a legge.)
Ah, che vedo?—ho preso sbaglio!
E la lista, son di stucco!
Ah, son proprio un mamalucco!
Ah, che gran bestialita!

Rosina and Count. Bravo! bravo! the old
  fool
  In his own snare at last is caught.

Basilio and Bertha. What it means I cannot
  tell:
  Confusion here some work has
  wrought.

Rosina. 'Tis ever thus you rate and school
  (Weeping.)
  me,
  And with rod of iron rule me;
  But I no more this life will lead—
  I'll from such tyranny be freed.

Bartolo. Ah, Rosina! poor young lady!

Count. Leave her, sir! What have you
  done?
  (Threatening him, and pushing him away by the arm.)

Bartolo. Holloa! help, there!

Rosina. Nay, be quiet.

Count. Unhand me, sir!

All. What's all this riot?

SCENE XII.—Enter Figaro, with a basin under his arm
  and the preceding.

Figaro. Holloa here!
  What has happened?—my good
  people,
  What clamor's this? Great gods!
  This tumult has together drawn
  Into the street one-half the city.
  (Softly to the Count.)
  (Prudence, sir, in pity!)

Bartolo. This is a rogue!
  (Pointing to the Count.)

Count. This is a knave!

Bartolo. Ah, the scoundrel!

Count. Ah, the rascal!
  (Threatening him with his sword.)

Figaro. Mr. Soldier, have a care,
  (Raising his basin and threatening the Count.)
  Or this basin soon shall teach you
  Of your manners to beware.

Count. You ugly savage—
  (To Bartolo.)

Bartolo. You low-born scoundrel—

All. Peace, Doctor—

Bartolo. I'll not hold my peace—

All. Hold, sir!
  (To the Count.)

Count. I am determined to kill him.

Rosina e Conte. Bravo! bravo! il mamalucco
  Che nel sacco entrato e già.

Basilio e Berta. Non capisco, son di stucco:
  Qualche imbroglio qui ci stà.

Rosina. Ecco quà sempre un istoria,
  (Piangendo.)
  Sempre oppressa, e maltrattata;
  Ah, che vita disperata—
  Non la so più sopportar.

Bartolo. Ah, Rosina! poverina!

Conte. Via quà tu! Cosa l'hai fatto?
  (Minacciando, e afferrandolo per un braccio.)

Bartolo. Gente, ajuto! soccorretemi!

Rosina. Ma chetatevi.

Conte. Lasciatemi!

Tutti. Gente, ajuto per pietà!

SCENA XII.—Figaro, entrando con bacile sotto il brac
  cio; e detti.

Figaro. Alto là! Alto là!
  Che cosa accadde?—Signori miei.
  Che chiasso è questo? Eterni Dei!
  Già sulla piazza a questo strepito
  S'e radunata mezza città.
  (Piano, al Conte.)
  (Signor, prudenza, per carità!)

Bartolo. Questo è un birbante!
  (Additando il Conte.)

Conte. Questo è un briccone!

Bartolo. Ah disgraziato!—

Conte. Ah maledetto!—
  (Minacciandolo con la sciabola.)

Figaro. Signor Soldato, porti respetto,
  (Alzando il bacile, e minacciando il Conte.)
  O questo fusto, corpo del diavolo,
  Or le creanze le insegnera.

Conte. Brutto scimiotto—
  (Al Bartolo.)

Bartolo. Birbo malnato—

Tutti. Zitto, Dottore—

Bartolo. Voglio gridare—

Tutti. Fermo, signore!
  (Al Conte.)

Conte. Voglio ammazzarlo.

All.	Silence, silence! For goodness' sake! (A knocking at the street door.) Silence! Who is it knocks? Who can it be?	*Tutti.*	Fate silenzio! Per carità! (Si ode bussare con violenza alla porta di strada.) Zitti, che battono? Chi mai sarà?
Bartolo.	Who is it?	*Bartolo.*	Chi è?
Chorus.	Open, and you soon shall see. (Within.)	*Coro.*	La forza. Aprite quà! (Di dentro.)
All.	The police!—Oh, the devil!—	*Tutti.*	La forza!—Oh diavolo!
Figaro.	You have done it now! (To the Count, Rosina, and Bartolo.)	*Figaro.*	L' avete fatta! (Al Conte, Rosina, e Bartolo.)
Count.	Fear not.	*Conte.*	Niente paura.
Bartolo.	Let them come in.	*Bartolo.*	Vengan pur quà.
All.	I wonder How the deuce This adventure will terminate!	*Tutti.*	Questa avventura Ah, come diavolo Mai finirà!

SCENE THE LAST.—An Officer, with Soldiers; and the preceding.

SCENA ULTIMA.—Un Uffiziale; con Soldati; e detti.

Officer.	Hold, here! Let no one stir. Good Sirs, what is the matter? What's the cause of this disturbance? What's the reason of this clatter?	*Uffiziale.*	Fermi tutti! Niun si muova. Miei Signori che si fa? Questo chiasso donde è nato? La cagione presto quà.
Count.	The reason—	*Conte.*	La cagione—
Bartolo.	It is not true.	*Bartolo.*	Non è vero.
Count.	Yes, sir.	*Conte.*	Si, Signore.
Bartolo.	No, sir.	*Bartolo.*	Signor nò.
Count.	He is a rascal.	*Conte.*	E un birbante.
Bartolo.	He is an impostor.	*Bartolo.*	E un impostore.
Officer.	One at a time.	*Uffiziale.*	Un per volta.
Bartolo.	But I will speak! Sir, this soldier has abused me, Like a very dog has used me.	*Bartolo.*	Io parlerò! Questo soldato, M' ha maltrattato.
Rosina.	Pray, sir, pity the poor fellow, Wine has made him rather mellow.	*Rosina.*	Il poverino, Cotto è dal vino.
Bartolo.	Pity! he his sabre drew! The villain spoke of murder, too.	*Bartolo.*	Cava la sciabola! Parla d'uccidere.
Figaro.	Sir, I came to hear the clatter, But know nothing of the matter.	*Figaro.*	Io son venuto Quì per dividere.
Officer.	Silence! silence! Hark ye, fellow, (To the Count.) You're our prisoner,— Quick, away! (The Soldiers are about to surround him.)	*Uffiziale.*	Fate silenzio! Che intesi già, (Al Conte.) Siete in arresto,— Fuori di quà! (I Soldati si muovano per circondarlo.)
Count.	I your prisoner? hold awhile— Now what is't you please to say?	*Conte.*	Io in arresto?— Io, fermi, ola?

(Repulsing the Soldiers with an air of authority. he calls the Officer towards him, privately shows him the order of the Grandees of Spain, which he has under his uniform, and whispers to him his name. The Officer surprised, makes a sign to the Soldiers, who retire, and he does the same. All remain astonished.)

(Con gesto autorevole trattiene i Soldati; chiama a se l'Uffiziale, gli mostra segretamente l'ordine di Grande di Spagna, che ha sotto l'uniforme, e gli dice all' orecchio suo nome. L'Uffiziale sorpreso, fa cenna ai Soldati che si ritirino, e anch'egli fa lo stesso. Tutti restono attoniti.)

FREDDO ED IMMOBILE—*COLD AND IMMOVABLE* (Trio)

ROSINA

Fred-da ed im-mo-bi - le Co-me u - na sta - tua, Fia-to non
Cold and im-mo-va - ble as___ sculp-tured fear,___ All pow'r has

e - sta - mi Da re-spi - - rar; Fia-to non
left___ me to see or___ hear; All pow'r has

COUNT

Fred - da ed im-
Cold and im-

re - sta - mi Da re-spi - rar, Fia - to non
left___ me to___ see or hear, All pow'r has

mo - bi - le Co-me u - na sta - tua, Fia-to non
mo - va - ble as___ sculp-tured fear,___ All pow'r has

re - sta - mi Da re - spi - rar; Fia - to non
left___ me to see or hear; All pow'r has

re - sta - gli Da re-spi - - rar, Fia - to non
left___ him to see or___ hear, All pow'r has

BARTOLO

Fred-da ed im-
Cold and im-

Figaro.	To see the doctor's Frantic fear, I'm laughing so, I scarce can hear.	Figaro.	Guarda Don Bartolo Sembra una statua, Ah, che dal ridere Sto per crepar.
Bartolo.	But, sir— (To the Officer.)	Bartolo.	Ma, Signore— (All' Uffiziale.)
Chorus.	Silence!	Coro.	Zitto tu!
Bartolo.	For a doctor—	Bartolo.	Ma un dottore—
Chorus.	I have done!	Còro.	Oh non più.
Bartolo.	But if she—	Bartolo.	Ma se lei—
Chorus.	Hold your tongue.	Coro.	Non parlar.
Bartolo.	She wished—	Bartolo.	La vorrai—
Chorus.	How you bawl.	Coro.	Non gridar.
All Three.	But if we—	A 3.	Ma se noi—
Chorus.	Silence, all.	Coro.	Zitti voi.
All Three.	But if—	A 3.	Ma se poi—

Chorus.	We'll think of it.	Coro.	Pensiam noi.
	Let every one the house now quit.		Vada ognun pe' fatti suoi.
	Let altercation cease.		Si finisca d' altercar.

MI PAR D'ESSER—*WHAT CONFUSION*

BARTOLO AND CHORUS

Chorus.	Like hammers on the anvil ringing,	Coro.	Alternando questo e quello,
	Till, echoing with the horrid sound,		Pesantissimo martello,
	The walls and vaulted roofs rebound.		Fà con barbara armonìa
	Thus does your outrage stun the brain,		Muri e volte rimbombar.
	That seeks for quiet here in vain,		E il cervello poverello.

Where furious tongues the sense
   confound,
Till reason's in the clamor
   drowned,
And madness seems to rage
   around!

END OF ACT I.

Già stordito, sbalordito,

Non ragiona, si confonde,

Si riduce ad impazzar!

FINE DELL' ATTO PRIMO.

ACT II.

SCENE I.—A Room in Bartolo's Home.

Bartolo. Do but see my ill-fortune! That
      (Alone.)
   soldier,
As far as I can learn,
Is known by no one in the regi-
   ment.
I doubt—zounds!
Doubt, did I say?—I would ven-
   ture to wager
That this fellow was sent here
By the Count Almaviva,
To sound the heart of Rosina.
Not even in one's own house
Can one be secure! but I—
      (A knocking is heard.)
Who knocks?
Holloa! who's there? they knock
   again,
Don't you hear?
I am in my own house, why should
   I be afraid?
Open the door.
      (Speaking to the side.)

SCENE II.—The Count, dressed as a Music-master, and
   the preceding.

Count. May heaven send you peace and
   joy!

Bartolo. A thousand thanks! no more, good
   sir.

Count. Joy and peace for thousands of
   years!

Bartolo. In truth I'm very much obliged.
   (That face is not unknown to me,
   I don't recollect—I can't
      remember—
   But that countenance—that dress—
   I can't devise who it can be.)

Count. (Ah, if before I was unsuccessful
   In deceiving this simpleton.
   My new metamorphosis
   May prove more propitious to me.)
   Joy and peace; peace and joy.

ATTO II.

SCENA I.—Camera in Casa di Bartolo.

Bartolo. Ma vedi il mio destino! Quel
      (Solo.)
   soldato
Per quanto abbia cercato,
Niun lo conosce in tutto il reg-
   gimento.
Io dubito—oh cospetto!
Che dubitar?—scommetto
Che dal Conte Almaviva,
E stato quà spedito quel Signore,
Ad esplorar della Rosina il core.
Nemmeno in casa propria
Sicura si può star! ma io—
      (Battone.)
Chi batte?
Ehi! chì è di la? battono,
Non sentite?
In casa io son, non ho timore?
Aprite.
      (Verso le quinte.)

SCENA II.—Il Conte, travestito da Maestro di Musica;
   e detto.

Conte. Pace e gioja il ciel vi dia!

Bartolo. Mille grazie! non s'incommoda.

Conte. Gioja e pace per mille anni!

Bartolo. Obbligato in verità.
   (Questo volto non m' è ignoto;
   Non ravviso—non ricordo—
   Ma quel volto—ma quell' abito—
   Non capisco chi sara.)

Conte. (Ah, se un colpo è andato a vuoto
   A gabbar questo balordo,
   La mia nuova metamorfosi
   Più propizia a me sarà.)
   Gioja, e pace; pace e gioja.

Bartolo. Enough—(Heavens! what an annoyance!)

Count. Joy and peace from my very heart.

Bartolo. Enough, enough! for mercy's sake.
(What a wretched fate is mine:
Every knave conspires against me!
What a cruel destiny.)

Count. (The old fellow knows me not:
How fortunate for me!
A few short moments, my love,
And we shall speak wthout restraint.)

Bartolo. In a word, sir,
Who are you? may I know?

Count. Don Alonzo,
Professor of music, and pupil
Of Don Basilio.

Bartolo. Well?

Count. Don Basilio,
Poor man, is taken ill; and in his stead—

Bartolo. Taken ill, say you?—I'll run and see him.
(About to depart.)

Count. Gently, gently,
(Detaining him.)
His illness is not so serious.

Bartolo. (I do distrust this fellow.) Come, let us go.

Count. But, sir!

Bartolo. Well, what?

Count. I wished to say—
(Taking him aside, and in a whisper.)

Bartolo. Well, speak out.

Count. But—

Bartolo. Speak out, I say!

Count. Well, as you wish:
(Raising his voice.)
Then you shall know who Don Alonzo is.
I came from the Count Almaviva—
(Going.)

Bartolo. Softly, softly—
(Gently restraining him.)
Speak, speak, I can hear you.

Count. The Count—
(Raising his voice.)

Bartolo. Softly, for goodness' sake.

Bartolo. Ho capito—(oh ciel che noja!)

Conte. Gioja e pace, ben di cuore.

Bartolo. Basta, basta! per pietà.
(Ma che perfido destino:
Tutti quanti a me davanti!
Che crudel fatalità.)

Conte. (Il vecchion non mi conosce:
Oh mia sorte fortunata!
Ah! mio ben, fra pochi instanti,
Parlerem con libertà.)

Bartolo. In somma, mio Signore,
Chi è lei, si può sapere?

Conte. Don Alonzo,
Professore di Musica, ed allievo
Di Don Basilio.

Bartolo. Ebbene?

Conte. Don Basilio,
Sta male il poverino, ed in sua vece—

Bartolo. Sta mal?—Corro a vederlo.
(In atto di partire.)

Conte. Piano, piano.
(Trattenendolo.)
Non è un mal così grave.

Bartolo. (Di costui non mi fido.) Andiamo, andiamo.

Conte. Ma, Signore!

Bartolo. Che c'è?

Conte. Voleva dirvi.
(Tirandolo a parte, e sotto voce.)

Bartolo. Parlate forte.

Conte. Ma—

Bartolo. Forte, vi dico.

Conte. Ebben, come volete.
(Alzando la voce.)
Ma chi sia Don Alonzo apprenderete.
Vo dal Conte Almaviva—
(In atto di partire.)

Bartolo. Piano, piano—
(Trattenendolo con dolcezza.)
Dite, dite, v'ascolto.

Conte. Il Conte—
(A voce alta.)

Bartolo. Piano, per carità.

Count.	This morning he came by chance To the same inn! and by accident I took up this note, which I found Directed to him by your ward.
Bartolo.	What do I see? It is indeed her writing!
Count.	Don Basilio being engaged with the lawyer, Knows nothing of this letter, and I, being sent To give lessons to your ward, in his stead, Wished to make a merit of the thing with you; Because, by means of this letter I might—
Bartolo.	You might what?
Count.	I will tell you, If I could but speak a few words with her, I think, with deference be it said, that I could Make her believe that it was given to me by a mistress of the Count's: A tolerable good proof to Rosina, That she is only made a fool of by the Count, And therefore—
Bartolo.	Softly, softly;—a calumny this! Oh, I see very well that you are A scholar worthy of Don Basilio! I shall know how to reward (Embraces him and puts the note in his pocket.) So happy a suggestion; I will go and call the girl. And as you interest yourself so much about me, I recommend myself to your good offices. (He goes into Rosina's apartment.)
Count.	Ne'er doubt me. This affair of the note Slipped from my tongue against my will. But what was I to do? Without some strategem I should have gone away like a simpleton I must now acquaint her With my plan: if she consent, I shall be completely happy. She comes! How my heart beats in my bosom!

Conte.	Stamane, (Calmandosi.) Nella stesa locanda Era meco d'alloggio, ed in mie mani Per caso capitò questo biglietto Dalla vostra pupilla a lui diretto.
Bartolo.	Che vedo? È sua scrittura!
Conte.	Don Basilio occupato col curiale, Nulla sà di quel foglio, ed io per lui Venendo a dar lezione alla ragazza, Volea farmene un merito con voi; Perchè, con quel biglietto, si potrebbe—
Bartolo.	Che cosa?
Conte.	Vi dirò, S' io potessi parlare alla ragazza, Io creder, verbigrazia le farei Che me lo diè del Conte un' altra amante: Prova significante, Che il Conte di Rosina si fa gioco, E perciò—
Bartolo.	Piano un poco;—una calunnia! Or sì vi riconosco Bravo e degno scolar di Don Basilio! Io saprò come merita (La abbraccia e mette in tasca il biglietto.) Ricompensar sì bel suggerimento; Vò a chiamar la ragazza. Poichè tanto per me v'interessate, Mi raccommando a voi. (Entra nella camera di Rosina.)
Conte.	Non dubitate L'affare del biglietto Dalla bocca mi è uscito non volendo. Ma come far? Senza di un tal ripiego Mi toccava andar via come un bagiano, Il mio disegno a lei Ora paleserò: s'ella consente, Io son felice appieno. Eccola! Ah, il cor sento balzarmi in seno!

SCENE III.—Bartolo, bringing in Rosina; and the preceding then Figaro.

Bartolo.	Come, Signorina; Don Alonzo, Whom you see here, will give you your lesson.
Rosina.	Ah!
	(Starting.)
Bartolo.	What's the matter?
Rosina.	It is a cramp in my foot.
Count.	Oh, nothing at all. Seat yourself by my side, fair lady; And, if not disagreeable, I will give you A little lesson in place of Don Basilio.
Rosina.	Oh, sir! with the greatest pleasure.
Count.	What will you sing?
Rosina.	Whatever you please.
Bartolo.	Well, let us hear, then.
Rosina.	Here it is.
Count.	Now let us begin with spirit.
	(Rosina sings an Air. chosen, ad libitum, for the occasion.)
Count.	Bravissimo! a fine voice, truly!
Rosina.	A thousand thanks!
Bartolo.	Yes, truly, a fine voice; But, then, good Lord! that air is very tiresome. In my time music was another thing: Oh! when, for instance, Cafariello sung that wondrous air— "La, la, la!" List, Don Alonzo, I will give it you. With that bewitching mien, ah! Oh, come to me, Rosina! And on my arm, oh, lean, ah! There let me chant my lay; Or, if you more incline, ah! To dancing, so divine, ah! Then thus in grace we'll twine, ah! With minuetto sway.
	(To Figaro. who enters, mimicking him.)
	Bravo! Mr. Barber.
Figaro.	Oh! no harm, sir; Excuse my folly.
Bartolo.	Well, rogue, And what are you come here for?
Figaro.	Here for! Why, I am come to shave you— this is your day.

SCENA III.—Bartolo, conducendo Rosina; e detti; indi Figaro.

Bartolo.	Venite, Signorina: Don Alonzo, Che quì vedete, or vi darà lezione.
Rosina.	Ah!
Bartolo.	Cos'è stato?
Rosina.	È un granchio al piede.
Conte.	Oh, nulla. Sedete a me vicin, bella fanciulla; Se non vi spiace, un poco di lezione Di Don Basilio invece io vi darò.
Rosina.	Oh! col più gran piacer la prenderò.
Conte.	Che vuol cantare?
Rosina.	Quel che lei aggrada.
Bartolo.	Or ben, dunque sentiamo.
Rosina.	Eccola quì.
Conte.	Da brava incominciamo.
	(Rosina canta qualche Aria, scelta, ad libitum, per 1 occasione.)
Conte.	Bela voce! bravissima!
Rosina.	Oh, mille grazie!
Bartolo.	Certo, bella voce; Ma quest' aria, cospetto! è assai nojosa. La musica a miei tempi era altra cosa: Oh! quando, per esempio, cantava Cafariello Quel' aria portentosa—"Là, là, là!" Sentite, Don Alonzo, eccola quà. Quando mi sei vicina, Amabile Rosina, L' aria dicèa Giannina, Ma io dico Rosina; Il cor mi balza in petto, Mi balla il minuetto.
	(A Figaro, che entra contra fiecondolo.)
	Bravo! Signore Barbiere!
Figaro.	Eh niente affatto. Scusi sue debolezze.
Bartolo.	Ebben, gridone, Che vieni a far?
Figaro.	O bella! Vengo a farvi la barba—oggi vi tocca.

Bartolo. Oh, not to-day—I don't wish it.

Figaro. Not to-day? but
To-morrow I can't come.

Bartolo. And why not?

Figaro. Because I am otherwise engaged.
And then—and then—what matters
it?
I cannot come to-morrow.

Bartolo. Come, less chattering;
I'll not be shaved to-day.

Figaro. What? Do you treat me
As you would some country
barber?
E'en find some other person;—I
am off.

Bartolo. Well, what signifies it?—this is his
way—
What a whimsical dog!
Quick! into my room, and bring
the cloth.
No; I'll go myself.

Figaro. (Oh, if he would but hand me
That bunch of keys, all would be
right.)
Tell me, is not the key
(To Rosina.)
Which opens that lattice among
them?

Rosina. Yes; and it is the newest.

Bartolo. (Oh, I'm mighty wise
To leave that devil of a barber
here!)
Here, go yourself:
(Giving the keys to Figaro.)
Pass yonder corridor, and on the
shelf
You will find everything.
Have a care, but touch nothing.

Figaro. Eh, I am no fool.
O be joyful! I'll be back in an
instant.
(The trick is done!)
(He goes in.)

Bartolo. That's the rascal, sir, who brought
(To the Count.)
The Count's letter to Rosina.

Count. He seems a very adept in intrigue.

Bartolo. Ah, he'll not trick me—
(A noise within, as of some earthen vessels breaking.)
Oh, I'm undone.

Rosina. What noise was that?

Bartolo. Oggi non voglio.

Figaro. Oggi non vuol? domani
Non potrò io.

Bartolo Perchè?

Figaro. Perchè ho da fare.
E poi—e poi—che serve?
Doman non posso.

Bartolo. Orsù, meno parole:
Oggi non vo' far barba.

Figaro. Ma? che mi avete preso
Per un qualche barbier da contadino?
Chiamate pur un altro;—io me
ne vado.

Bartolo. Che serve?—a modo suo—
(Vedi che fantasía!)
Và in camera a pigliar la bian-
cheria.
No; vado io stesso.

Figaro. (Ah, se mi dava in mano
Il mazzo delle chiavi, ero a
cavallo.)
Dite, non è fra quelle
(A Rosina.)
La chiave, che apre quella gelosía?

Rosina. Sì certo; è la più nuova.

Bartolo. (Ah son per buono
A lasciar quì quel diavolo di
barbiere!)
Animo, va tu stesso:
(Dando le chiavi a Figaro.)
Passato il corridor, sopra l'
armario
Il tutto troverai.
Bada non toccar nulla.

Figaro. Ah, non son matto.
(Allegri!) Vado e torno.
(Il colpo è fatto!)
(Entra.)

Bartolo. E quel briccon, che al Conte
(Al Conte.)
Ha portato il biglietto di Rosina.

Conte. Mi sembra un imbroglion di prima
sfera.

Bartolo. Eh, a me non me la ficca—
(Si sente di dentro rumore come di vasellonne che si
spezza.)
Ah, disgraziato me.

Rosina. Ah, che rumore?

Bartolo. Oh, the rascal! I felt my heart mis-
give me.
(Goes in.)
He has broken everything,
Six plates, eight basins, one tureen.

Figaro. A might matter, truly! had I not hit
Upon the key by good fortune,
(Showing the Count the key of the veranda.)
In that same cursed
Corridor, I should have broken
My head against the wall.
He keeps every room so dark; and
then—

Bartolo. No more of this!

Figaro. Come, then. (Be prudent.)
(To the Count and Rosina.)

Bartolo. Proceed to business.
(He seats himself to be shaved; at this moment enter
Basilio.)

SCENE IV.—Don Basilio, and the preceding.

Rosina. (Don Basilio!)

Count. (What do I see?)

Figaro. (What an unfortunate encounter!)

Bartolo. How is this?

Basilio. Good day to you all.

Bartolo. (What an unexpected visit!)

Figaro and Count. (Some courage here is
necessary.)

Rosina. (Alas! what will become of us!)

Bartolo. Basilio, how do you find yourself?

Basilio. Find myself!

Figaro. Who is to wait here?
(Interrupting him.)
That blessed beard of yours!
Shall I operate on it or no?

Bartolo. I'l be with you directly.
(To Figaro.)
And the lawyer—
(To Basilio.)

Basilio. The lawyer!—

Count. I have already told him
That everything is arranged;
Is it not true?

Bartolo. Yes; I know it all.

Basilio. But, Don Bartolo, explain to me—

Count. Doctor, a word with you—
(Interrupting him.)

Bartolo. Ah, che briccon! me lo diceva il
core.
(Entra.)
Tutto mi ha rotto, tutto;
Sei piatti, otto bicchieri, una
terrina.

Figaro. Vedete che gran cosa! ad una
chiave
Se mai non m'attaccava per
fortuna.
(Mostrando al Conte la chiave della golosia.)
Per qual maledettissimo
Corridor, così oscúro,
Spezzato mi sarei la testa al muro.
Tiene ogni stanza al bujo; e poi—
e poi—

Bartolo. Oh, non più.

Figaro. Dunque, andiam. (Giudizio.)
(Al Conte, e Rosina.)

Bartolo. A noi.
(Si siede a farsi radere.—Entra Basilio.)

SCENA IV.—Don Basilio, e detti.

Rosina. (Don Basilio!)

Conte. (Cosa veggo?)

Figaro. (Quale intoppo!)

Bartolo. Come quà?

Basilio. Servitor di tutti quanti.

Bartolo. (Che vuol dir tal novità!)

Figaro e Conte. (Quì franchezza ci vorrà.)

Rosina. (Ah, di noi che mai sarà!)

Bartolo. Don Basilio, come state?

Basilio. Come sto!

Figaro. Or che s'aspetta?
(Interrompendolo.)
Questa barba benedetta!
La facciamo sì, o nò?

Bartolo. Ora vengo.
(A Figaro.)
E là il curiale—
(A Basilio.)

Basilio. Il curiale!—

Conte. Io gli ho narrato
Che già tutto è combinato;
Non è ver?

Bartolo. Sì; tutto io sò.

Basilio. Ma, Don Bartolo spiegatemi—

Conte. (Ehi, dottore, una parola—)
(Interrompendolo.)

Don Basilio, I shall be with you
immediately.
(To Bartolo.)
Listen to me a moment.
(To Figaro.)
(Try and get him off,
Else I fear he will discover us.)
(Softly, to Bartolo.)
(Of the affair, sir, of the letter,
Recollect, he knows nothing.)

Bartolo. With this fever, Don Basilio,
Who taught you to walk abroad?
(Figaro, listening with attention, prepares to second the
Count.)

Basilio. With a fever!
(Astonished.)

Figaro. Why, what think you?
You are as yellow as a corpse.

Basilio. As a corpse, say what?

Figaro. Heavens, man!
(Feeling his pulse.)
Zounds, what a galloping pulse!
It's certainly the scarlet fever.

Figaro and Count. Go home, take medicine.
(The Count secretly gives a purse to Basilio.)

Figaro. Quick, quick, home to bed—

Count. I am quite alarmed for you—

Bartolo and Rosina. He says well; go home
to bed—

All. Quick, retire, and rest yourself.

Basilio. (A purse!—Go to bed!—
They all seem of the same mind.)

All. Quick, home to bed.

Basilio. Eh, I'm not deaf;
Pray cease your entreaties.

Figaro. What a color—eh!

Count. Oh! what a rueful visage!

Bartolo. Rueful visage!

Figaro and Count. Rueful, truly.

Basilio. Well, I'm going.

All. Go, go!

Don Basilio, son da voi.
(A Bartolo.)
Ascoltate un poco quà.
(A Figaro.)
(Fate un pò ch'ie vada via,
Ch'ei ci scopra ho gran timore.)
(Piano, a Bartolo.)
(Della lettera, Signore,
Ei l'affare ancor non sà.)

Bartolo. Colla febbre, Don Basilio,
Chi v'insegna a passeggiare?
(Figaro, ascoltando con attenzione, si prepara a secondare
il Conte.)

Basilio. Colla febbre!
(Attonito.)

Figaro. E chi vi pare?
Siete giallo come un morto.

Basilio. Come un morto?

Figaro. Bagatella!
(Tastandogli il polso.)
Cospetton che tremarella!
Questa è febbre scarlatina.

Figaro e Conte. Via, prendete medicina.
(Il Conte da a Basilio una borsa di soppiatto.)

Figaro. Presto, presto andate a letto—

Conte. Voi paura in ver mi fate—

Bartolo e Rosina. Dice bene, andate a
letto—

Tutti. Presto andate a riposar.

Basilio. (Una borsa!—Andate a letto!—
Ma che tutti sian d'accordo.)

Tutti. Presto a letto.

Basilio. Eh, non son sordo,
Non mi faccio più pregar.

Figaro. Che color—eh!

Conte. Che brutta cera!

Bartolo. Brutta cera!

Figaro e Conte. Oh, brutta assai.

Basilio. Dunque vado.

Tutti. Andate, andate.

BUONA SERA—*FARE YOU WELL, THEN* (Duet)

Rosina. (Plague upon you, can't you stir, ah!)
Quick, begone, and nurse yourself.

Basilio. Oh, good night, I quite agree—
Much obliged I really am.
(Guardy's in the trap I see!)
Cease your noise, I go, good man.
(*Exit.*)

Bartolo. I am here.
(*Bartolo seats himself, and Figaro prepares to shave him, during the operation he conceals the two lovers.*)
Now, work away.

Count. Rosina, now attend to me.

Rosina. I'm all attention, sir.
(*They sit down. pretending to be at their musical studies.*)

Count. At midnight precisely,
(*Cautiously, to Rosina.*)
We'll wait for you here;
For since we've the keys
We have nothing to fear.

Figaro. Ahi! ahi!
(*Calling off Bartolo's attention.*)

Bartolo. What's the matter?

Figaro. Something flew in my eye,
Look, but don't touch it:
Blow, for pity's sake.

Rosina. At midnight, precisely,
My love, I'll await thee;
Oh! fleet be the moments
That to thee shall unite me.

Bartolo. Nay, let me look!

Figaro. Well, look; who hinders you?

Rosina and Count. Do, re, mi, fa, sol, la.

Count. But now I tell you,
(*Bartolo rises, and draws near the lovers.*)
That I showed your letter,
In order that I might disguise
Myself much better.

Bartolo. Oh, excellent, forsooth!
Excelent, in very truth!
Rascals! scoundrels!
I see you've all
Conspired this day
To haste my fall.
Avaunt!
Or I shall slay you all!
With rage I'm nearly
Like to die.

Count, Rosina and Figaro. Your friend is delirious:
His head is oppressed.
Be silent, good doctor,

Rosina. (Maledetto seccatore!)
Presto, andate via di quà.

Basilio. Buona sera—ben di cuore—
Obligato—in verità.
(An, che in sacco va il tutore!)
Non gridate, intesi già.
(*Parte.*)

Bartolo. Son quà.
(*Bartolo siede, e Figaro disponesi a fargli la barba; durante l'operazione va coprendo i due amanti.*)
Stringi bravissimo.

Conte. Rosina, deh ascoltatemi.

Rosina. V'ascolto, eccomi quà.
(*Siedono fingendo studiar la musica.*)

Conte. (A mezza notte in punto,
(*A Rosina con cautela.*)
A prendervi quì siamo;
Or che la chiave abbiamo.
Non v'e da dubitar.)

Figaro. Ahi! ahi!
(*Distrando Bartolo.*)

Bartolo. Che cosa è stato?

Figaro. Un non sò che nell' occhio!
Guardate, non toccate—
Soffiate per pietà.

Rosina. A mezza notte in punto,
Anima mia, t'aspetto;
Io già l'istante affretto,
Che teco m' unirà.

Bartolo. Ma lasciami vedere!

Figaro. Vedete, chi vi tiene?

Rosina e Conte. Do, re, mi, fa, sol, la.

Conte. Ora avveritirvi voglio,
(*Bartolo si alza. e si avvicina agli amanti.*)
Cara che il vostro foglio,
Perchè non fosse inutile
Il mio travestimento.

Bartolo. Ma bravi, ma bravissimi!
Ma bravi, in verità!
Bricconi! birbanti!
Ah, voi tutti quanti
Avete giurato
Di farmi crepar.
Uscite furfanti!
Vi voglio accoppar!
Di rabbia, di sdegno
Mi sento crepar.

Conte, Rosina e Figaro. L' amico delira;
La testa gli gira.
Dottore, tacete,

'Tis only a jest.
Peace, peace, let's away;
   We've been overheard.
This clamor is useless—
   He'll not hear a word.
     (Exeunt.)

SCENE V.—Bertha, alone.

There is nothing but noise and
   clamor in this house;
Nothing but disputing, weeping,
   and threatening.
There's not an hour's peace
With this avaricious old wrangler.
Oh, what a house! what a house of
   confusion!
The fond old dotard seks a wife,
   The merest girls for husbands
     pine
The one a fool, the other mad—
   In jacket straight I'd all confine.
What con this love be
   That drives the folks mad?
Some all happiness seem,
   While other are sad.
'Tis something that teases,
   That plagues and inspires;
Even I am its prey,
   And am scorched by Love's fires.
But because I am old,
   I by all am passed by;—
Ah, with rage I expire!
   With vexation I die!
     (Exit.)

SCENE VI.—Don Bartolo, introducing Don Basilio.

Bartolo. Then you don't know
   Don Alonzo at all?

Basilio. Not at all.

Bartolo. Ah, surely
   He was sent by the Count! Some
     great scheme
   Is, no doubt, in agitation.

Basilio. I tell you
   That this friend
   Was no other than the Count
     himself.

Bartolo. The Count himself?

Basilio. The Count!
   (This purse clearly bespeaks it.)

Bartolo. Let him be what he may—to the
     notary
   I will hasten this moment,
   And settle the marriage contract.

Vi fate burlar.
Tacete, partiamo;
   Non serve a gridar.
Intesi ci siamo—
   Non v'è a replicar.
     (Partono.)

SCENA V.—Berta, sola.

Sempre gridi e tumulti in questa
   casa;
Si litiga, si piange, si minaccia.
Non v'e un'ora di pace
Con questo vecchio avaro e bron-
   tolone.
Oh, che casa! oh, che casa di
   confusione!
Il vecchietto cerca moglie,
   Vuol marito la ragazza:
   Quello freme questa è pazza—
Tutti e due son da legar.
Ma che cosa è questo amore
   Che fà tutti delirar?
   Egli è un male, universale,
Una smania, un pizzicore,
   Un solletico, un tormento;
   Poverina! anch'io lo sento,
Nè so come remediar.
Ah, vecchiaia maledetta!
Son da tutti disprezzata,
E arrabiata—disperata,
   Mi convien così crepar!
     (Parte.)

SCENA VI.—Don Bartolo, introducendo Don Basilio.

Bartolo. Dunque voi Don Alonzo
   Non conoscete affatto?

Basilio. Affatto.

Bartolo. Ah, certo
   Il Conte lo mandò. Qualche gran
     trama
   Quì si prepara.

Basilio. Io dico
   Che quel garbato amico,
   Era il Conte in persona.

Bartolo. Il Conte?

Basilio. Il Conte!
   (La borsa parla chiaro.)

Bartolo. Sia che si vuole—amico, al notaro
   Vo' in questo punto andare, in
     questa sera
   Stipular di mie nozze io vo' il
     contratto.

Basilio. To the notary! are you mad?
It rains in torrents; and, besides,
This evening the notary is to· be
    with Figaro: the barber
Gives his niece in marriage.

Bartolo. His niece?
What niece?—The barber
Has no nieces. Ah, there must be
    some plot here.
This very night the scoundrels will
Lie in wait to betray me. Haste,
    and call
The notary, instantly;
Here is the key of the door—go,
Make haste, for goodness' sake.
    (Gives him a key.)

Basilio. Don't be alarmed; in two minutes
    I will be here again.
    (Exit.)

SCENE VII.—Bartolo, then Rosina.

Bartolo. Either by force, or love,
Rosina shall yield, I am deter-
    mined!—
I have another thought. The note,
(Takes from his pocket the note given him by the Count.)
Which the girl wrote to Almaviva,
May serve—Oh, what a masterly
    thought!
That rascal, Don Alonzo,
Has undesignedly put weapons into
    my hands.
Eh, Rosina! Rosina!
(Rosina comes from her room without speaking.)
Come here, come here;
I have some news from your lover
    to give you.
Poor unhappy girl! in truth,
You have placed your affections on
    a noble object!
Know that, in the arms of another,
He makes a joke of your affections;
Behold the proof.
    (He gives her a note.)

Rosina. Oh, heaven! my note!

Bartolo. Don Alonzo and the barber
Are conspiring against you: do not
    trust them.
They wish to give you up
Into the arms of Count Almaviva—

Rosina. (Into the arms of another!
What do I hear?—Oh, Lindor!—
    Oh, betrayer!
Ah, yes!—vengeance—I will teach
    the wretch,

Basilio. Il notar! siete matto?
Piove a torrenti; e poi,
Questa sera il notaro
È impegnato con Figaro: il
    barbiere
Marita una nipote.

Bartolo. Una nipote!
Che nipote?—Il barbiere
Non ha nipoti. Ah, quì v'è qualche
    imbroglio,
Questa notte i bricconi
Me la voglion far. Presto, il
    notaro
Quà venga sull' istante;
Ecco la chiave del portone—
    andate,
Presto, per carità.
    (Gli dà una chiave.)

Basilio. Non temete; in due salti io torno
    quà.
    (Parte.)

SCENA VII.—Bartolo, indi Rosina.

Bartolo. Per forza, o per amore,
Rosina avrà da cedere, cospetto!—
Mi viene un altra idea. Questo
    biglietto,
(Cava dalla tasca il biglietto datogli dal Conte.)
Che scrisse la ragazza al Conte
    Almaviva,
Potria servir—Che colpo da
    maestro!
Don Alonzo, il briccone,
Senza volerlo mi diè l' armi in
    mano.
Ehi, Rosina! Rosina!
(Rosina dalla sue camere esce senza parlare.)
Avanti, avanti;
Del vostro amante io vi vo' dar la
    novella.
Povera sciagurata in verità,
Collocaste assai bene il vostro
    affetto!
Del vostro amor, sappiate,
Ch'ei si fa gioco in sen d'un altro
    amante;
Ecco la prova.
    (Le dà il biglietto.)

Rosina. Oh cielo! il mio biglietto!

Bartolo. Don Alonzo, e il barbiere
Congiuran contro voi; non vi
    fidate.
In potere del Conte d' Almaviva
Vi vogliono condurre—

Rosina. (In braccio a un'altro!—
Che mai sento?—Ah Lindoro!—
Ah traditore!

Who Rosina is.)
Tell me, sir, do you
Wish to marry me?

Bartolo.   I do.

Rosina.   Well, let it be done!
I am content—let it be instantly.
     Listen:
At midnight the wretch will be
     here,
With Figaro, the barber;—and it
     was settled,
That I should fly and espouse him.

Bartolo.   Oh, wretches!
I hasten to bar the door.

Rosina.   Oh, my dear sir!
They are to enter by the window:
     they have the key.

Bartolo.   I will not stir from this spot!
But supose they should be armed?
     My dear child,
Since you are now so awake to
     your situation,
Let us act thus. Shut yourself up
     in your room,
While I go and see for assistance.
I will declare they are two thieves,
     and as such,
By Bacchus! we shall see what the
     consequence will be!
Child, shut yourself up imme-
     diately: I go.
     (Exit.)

Rosina.   How cruel! how cruel is my fate!
     (Exit.)

(A storm. The veranda is seen to open, and one after
the other, Figaro and the Count enter, wrapped up
in mantles.)

SCENE VIII.—The Count, Figaro, then Rosina.

Figaro.   At last, here we are.

Count.   Figaro, your hand. By the powers!
What a tempestuous night!

Figaro.   Truly, a lover's night!
     (Figaro lights the candles, and looks around.)

Count.   Eh, show a light.
Where can Rosina be?

Figaro.   We soon shall see—
There she is.

Count.   Ah! treasure of my soul—
     (With transport.)

Rosina.   Stand off,
     (Repulsing him.)

Ah sì!—vendetta! e vegga
Quell'empio chi è Rosina.)
Signore, sposarmi,
Voi bramavate?

Bartolo.   E il voglio.

Rosina.   Ebben, si faccia!
Io son contenta—ma all'istante.
     Udite:
A mezza notte quì barbier;—con
     lui fuggire,
Per sposarlo io voleva.

Bartolo.   Ah, scellerati!
Corro a sbarrar la porta.

Rosina.   Ah, mio Signore!
Entran par la finestra: hanno la
     chiave.

Bartolo.   Non mi muovo di quì!
Ma—e se fossero armati?—Figlia
     mia,
Poichè ti sei si bene illuminata,
Facciam così. Ti chiudi a chiave
     in camera,
Io vo a chiamar la forza.
Dirò che son due ladri, e come tali,
Corpo di Bacco! l' avremo da
     vedere!
Figlia, chiuditi presto: io vado via.
     (Parte.)

Rosina.   Quanto, quanto è crudel la sorte
     mia!
     (Parte.)

(Un temporale. Si vede aprire la gelosia, ed entrare un
dopo l'altro Figaro, ed il Conte avvolti in mantelli.)

SCENA VIII.—Il Conte, Figaro, indi Rosina.

Figaro.   Al fine eccoci quà.

Conte.   Figaro, dammi man. Poter del
     mondo!
Che tempo indiavolato!

Figaro.   Tempo da innamorati!
     (Figaro accendde i lumi spiando.)

Conte.   Ehi, fammi lume.
Dove sarà Rosina?

Figaro.   Ora vedremo—
Eccola appunto.

Conte.   Ah mio tesoro—
     (Con trasporto.)

Rosina.   Indietro,
     (Respingendolo.)

	Wretch that thou art! I am come here To repair the fault of my Too foolish credulity; to show thee What I am, and what a mistress Thou hast lost, unworthy and thoughtless man.		Anima scellerata! Io quì di mia Stolta credulità venni soltanto A riparar lo scorno; a dimostrarti Qual io sono, e quale amante Perdesti, anima indegna, e sconoscento!
Count.	I am petrified!	*Conte.*	Io son di sasso!
Figaro.	I know not what this can mean.	*Figaro.*	Io non capisco niente.
Count.	But, for mercy's sake!—	*Conte.*	Ma per pietà!—
Rosina.	Peace! You have pretended love, In order to sacrifice me to the wishes Of the vile Count Almaviva—	*Rosina.*	Taci! Fingesti amore, Sol per sagrificarmi A quel tuo vil Conte Almaviva—
Count.	To the Count?— Ah, you are deceived. Happy that I am! Then you return with truth The affections of Lindor!— answer—	*Conte.*	Al Conte?— Ah, sei delusa. Ah me felice! adunque! Tu di verace amore. Ami Lindor!—rispondi—
Rosina.	Ah, yes! I loved him but too well!	*Rosina.*	Ah, sì! t'amai pur troppo!
Count.	This, then, is the moment At which to reveal myself. My sweetest life, *(He kneels, throwing aside his mantle.)* Behold one who so long Has followed thy steps; who sighs for thee: Who hopes to possess thee. See, treasure of my kind I am Almaviva: I am not Lindor.	*Conte.*	Ah, non è tempo Di più celarsi. Anima mia! ravvisa, *(S'inginocchia, gettando il mantello.)* Colui che sì gran tempo: Seguì tue traccie; e che per te sospira: Che suo ti vuol. Mirami, o mio tesoro! Almaviva son io: non son Lindoro.
Rosina.	What unexpected bliss, What peace without alloy! Oh, heavens! 'tis he indeed, I'm almost mad with joy!	*Rosina.*	Ah, qual colpo inaspettato, Egli stesso! oh ciel! che sento! Di sorpresa, di contento, Son vicina a delirar!
Count.	My triumph is complete No more shall doubt annoy! This moment all repays, I'm almost mad with joy!	*Conte.*	Qual trionfo inaspettato! Me felice! oh bel momento! Ah, d'amore, di contento, Son vicino a delirar!
Figaro.	One moment all was grief! The next they kiss and toy; But thanks to my designs, Their hearts are filled with joy!	*Figaro.*	Son rimasti senza fiato! Ora muojon dal contento; Guarda, guarda il mio talento, Che bel colpo seppe far!
Rosina.	Dear sir—but you—but I.	*Rosina.*	Mio Signore—ma voi—ma io—
Count.	Nay, never fear, my love! The blessed name of wife Awaits thee from above.	*Conte.*	Ah, non più, non più, ben mio! Il bel nome di mia sposa Idol mio! t'attende già.
Rosina.	The blessed name of wife! What joy it gives my heart.	*Rosina.*	Il bel nome di tua sposa; Ah, qual gioja al cor mi dà.
Rosina and Count.	Oh, happy bond of love, We'll never, never part!	*Rosina e Conte.*	Dolce nodo avventurato, Che fai paghi i miei desiri!

	The fates propitious proved,
	And gave us heart for heart.
Figaro.	Quick, let us hence: have done
	with sighs,
	All difficulty's passed;
	But often, acts too long delayed,
	To nothing come at last.
Rosina and Count.	Oh, happy bond of love!
	We'll never, never part!
	The fates propitious proved,
	And gave us heart for heart.
	(Figaro runs to the balcony.)
Figaro.	Ah, zounds! what do I see?
	At the door—a lantern—
	Two persons—what is to be done?

	Alla fin de' miei martiri,
	Tu sentisti Amor, pietà.
Figaro.	Presto, andiamo: vi sbrigate,
	Via, lasciate quei sospiri;
	Se si tarda, i miei raggiri,
	Fanno fiasco in verità.
Rosina e Conte.	Dolce nodo avventurato!
	Che fai paghi i miei desiri;
	Alla fin de' miei martiri,
	Tu sentisti, Amor, pietà.
	(Figaro va al balcone.)
Figaro.	Ah, cospetto! che ho veduto?
	Alla porta—una lanterna—
	Due persone—che si fa?

ZITTI, ZITTI, PIANO, PIANO—*STEP AS SOFT AS ZEPHYRS DYING* (Trio)

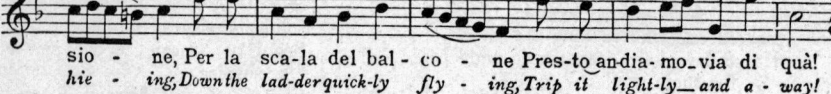

Count.   What has happened?
       (About to depart.)

Figaro.   The ladder—

Count.   Well—

Figaro.   The ladder is gone.

Count.   What say you?

Figaro.   Who could have taken it away?

Count.   What a cruel obstacle!

Rosina.   Unhappy that I am!

Figaro.   Ah, hush! somebody is coming,
           and here we are.
           What is to be done?

Count.   Courage, my dear Rosina.
       (Wraps himself in his mantle.)

Figaro.   Here they are.
       (They retire to the side.)

Conte.   Che avvenne mai?
       (Vanno per partire.)

Figaro.   La scala—

Conte.   Ebben—

Figaro.   La scala non v'è più.

       Che dici?

       Chi mai l'avrà levata?

       Quale inciampo crudel!

       Me sventurata!

Figaro.   Ah, zitti! sento gente, (ora ci
           siamo.)
        Signor mio, che si fa?

Conte.   Mia Rosina, coraggio.
       (Si ravvoglie nel mantello.)

Figaro.   Eccoli quà.
       (Si ritirano verso le quinte.)

SCENE IX.—Don Basilio with a lantern, introducing a Notary with a paper in his hand.)

Basilio. Come in, Don Bartolo.

Figaro. Don Basilio!
(Calling to the opposite side, beckoning to the Count.)

Count. And that other?

Figaro. Oh, oh, our notary. Delightful!
Leave the affair to me. Mr. Notary.
(Basilio and the Notary turn round, and remain surprised. The Notary approaches Figaro.)
This evening
You were to settle in my house,
The marriage contract between
The Count Almaviva and my niece
Here are the parties! Have you indorsed
The papers? Oh, very well!
(The Notary takes out a paper.)

Basilio. But softly;
Where is Don Bartolo?

Count. Here, Don Basilio,
(Calling Basilio aside, and taking a ring from his finger, beckons him to be silent.)
This ring is for you.

Basilio. But I—

Count. You
(Taking out a pistol.)
Will have two balls in your head
If you offer any opposition.

Basilio. O Lord! I take the ring.
Who signs?

Rosina and Count. Here we are.
(They sign.)

Count. Figaro and Don Basilio
Are witnesses;—this is my wife.

Figaro and Basilio. Viva!

Count. How am I blessed!

Rosina. Oh, long-sighed-for happiness!

All. Viva!
(While the Count is kissing the hand of Rosina, and Figaro is embracing Basilio, enter Bartolo in haste.)

SCENE THE LAST.—Don Bartolo; an Alcalde, Alguazils, Soldiers; and the preceding.

Bartolo. Hold, all of you. There they are.
(Pointing out Figaro and the Count to the Alcalde, and rushing towards Figaro.)

Figaro. Softly, sir, softly.

Bartolo. Sir, they are thieves;
Arrest them, arrest them.

SCENA IX.—Don Basilio con lanterna, introducendo un Notajo con carta in mano.

Basilio. Entrate quì Don Bartolo.

Figaro. Don Basilio!
(Chiamando dalla quinta apposta, accennando al Conte.)

Conte. E quell'altro?

Figaro. Ve', ve', nostro notajo. Allegramente!
Lasciate fare a me. Signor Notajo.
(Basilio e il Notajo si rivolgono, e restano sorpresi. Il Notajo si avvicina a Figaro.)
Dovevate in mia casa
Stipular questa sera
Un contratto di nozze
Fra il Conte d' Almaviva e mia nipote
Gli sposi, eccoli quà! Avete indosso
La scrittura? Benissimo!
(Il Notajo cava una scrittura.)

Basilio. Ma, piano;
Don Bartolo dov'è?

Conte. Ehi, Don Basilio,
(Chiamande a parte Basilio e cavandosi un'anello dal dito, e gli addita di tacere.)
Quest'anello è per voi.

Basilio. Ma io—

Conte. Per voi
Vi sono ancor due palle nel cervello
(Cavando una pistola.)
Se v'opponete.

Basilio. Oibò prendo l'anello.
Chi firma?

Rosina e Conte. Eccoci quà.
(Sottescrivono.)

Conte. Son testimonj
Figaro e Don Basilio;—essa è mia sposa.

Figaro e Basilio. Evviva!

Conte. Oh mio contento!

Rosina. Oh, sospirata mia felicità!

Tutti. Evviva!
(Nell' atto che il Conte bacia la mano a Rosina, e Figaro abbraccia Basilio, entra Bartolo come appresso.)

SCENA ULTIMA.—Don Bartolo, un Alcalde, Alguazils, Soldati, e detti.

Bartolo. Fermi tutti. Eccoli quà.
(Additando Figaro e il Conte all' Alcade, e slanciandosi contro Figaro.)

Figaro. Colle buone, Signor.

Bartolo. Signor, son ladri;
Arrestate, arrestate!

Officer.	Sir, your name. (To the Count.)		*Uffiziale.*	Signore, (Al Conte.) il suo nome.
Count.	My name? It is that of a man of honor; I am husband to this lady—		*Conte.*	Il mio nome? Egli è quel d'un nom d'onore; Lo sposo io son di questa—
Bartolo.	Eh! go to the devil! Rosina is to be mine;—is it not true?		*Bartolo.*	Eh, andate al diavolo! Rosina esser dève mia sposa, non e vero?
Rosina.	How! yours! No; not even in thought.		*Rosina.*	Come debbo esser sua? Oh nemmen per pensiero.
Bartolo.	How now, hussy! Ah, I am betrayed! Arrest him, I tell you: He is a thief! (Pointing to the Count.)		*Bartolo.*	Come, come, fraschetta! ah, son tradito. Arrestate, vi dico: E un ladro!
Figaro.	I shall be the death of him.		*Figaro.*	Or, or l'accoppo.
Bartolo.	He is a rogue—a scoundrel!		*Bartolo.*	E un birbante, è un briccone.
Officer.	Sir? (To the Count.)		*Uffiziale.*	Signore? (Al Conte.)
Count.	Stand off!		*Conte.*	Indietro!
Officer.	Your name—		*Uffiziale.*	Il nome—
Count.	Stand off, I say; stand off.		*Conte.*	Indietro, dico; indietro!
Officer.	Eh, my good sir, lower that tone;— Who are you?		*Uffiziale.*	Ehi, mio Signor, abbassi quel tuono;— E chi è lei?
Count.	I am the Count Almaviva! (Discovering himself.)		*Conte.*	D' Almaviva il Conte io sono. (Scoprendosi.)
Bartolo.	The fact is, I bear all the blame.		*Bartolo.*	Insomma, io ho tutti i torti.
Figaro.	Ay, and justly, too.		*Figaro.*	Pur troppo è così.
Bartolo.	But you, you rascal— Even you to betray me, and turn witness!		*Bartolo.*	Ma tu briccone— Tu pur tradirmi, e far da testimonio!
Basilio.	Ah, Doctor, The Count has certain persuasives And certain arguments in his pocket, Which there is no withstanding.		*Basilio.*	Ah Dottore Bartolo mio, Quei Signor Conte certe ragioni Ha in tasca; certi argomenti A cui non si risponde.
Bartolo.	Ay, ay! I understand you.		*Bartolo.*	Sì, sì, ho capito tutto.
Count.	Well, Doctor?		*Conte.*	Ebben, Dottore?
Bartolo.	Well, well, what matters it? what's done is done. Go; and may Heaven bless you!		*Bartolo.*	Sì, sì, che serve? quel ch'è fatto è fatto. Andate pur; che il Ciel vi benedica!
Figaro.	Bravo, bravo, Doctor! Let me embrace you.		*Figaro.*	Bravo, bravo, un'abbraccio! Venite quà, Dottore.
Rosina.	Oh, how happy we are!		*Rosina.*	Ah, noi felici!

Count.	Oh, propitious love!	*Conte.*	Oh, fortunato amore!
Figaro.	Young Love, triumphant smiling, All harsher thoughts exiling, All quarrels reconciling. Now waves his torch on high!	*Figaro.*	Di si felice innesto, Serbiam memoria eterna, Io smorzo la lanterna, Quì più non ho che far!
Bartolo.	Young Love, our hearts beguiling, Bids care and sorrow fly.	*Bartolo.*	Amore e fede eterna, Si vegga in voi regnar.
Rosina.	May all our lot now viewing, Find every hour renewing The joys of youth's first wooing, And happy prove as I.	*Rosina.*	Costò sospiri e pene, Un sì felice istante Alfin quest'alma amante, Comincia a respirar!
Count.	The humble Lindor wooed thee, And kind was thy reply; A brighter fate pursued thee— No more, then, heave a sigh.	*Conte.*	Dell' umile Lindoro, La fiamma a te fu accetta Più bel destin t'aspetta, Sù, vieni a giubilar.
Chorus.	May love, our hearts beguiling, Bid care and sorrow fly!	*Coro.*	Amore e fede eterna, Si vegga in voi regnar!

END OF THE OPERA.

NOTES